SCOREBUILDERS / PTEXAM: TH

PTEXAM

THE COMPLETE STUDY GUIDE

SCOREBUILDERS

ISBN 978-1-890989-44-6

For additional information on our review texts, review courses,
and web-based testing programs for physical therapists
and physical therapist assistants, please contact **Scorebuilders**.

SCOREBUILDERS

175 Innovation Way
Scarborough, Maine 04074

Phone: (207) 885-0304
Fax: (207) 883-8377

www.scorebuilders.com

Legal Notice

Scorebuilders strives to ensure that the information presented in ***PTEXAM: The Complete Study Guide*** is both accurate and relevant to the National Physical Therapy Examination (NPTE-PT). **Scorebuilders** assumes no responsibility for the accuracy or reliability of the information within the review book. Under no circumstance will **Scorebuilders** be liable for incidental or consequential damage arising from the use of our licensing products. Candidate performance on the sample examinations should be used only as a method to assess strengths and weaknesses and should not be utilized as a predictor of actual examination performance. Any similarity in the questions contained within the sample examinations and the questions on any version of the NPTE-PT is purely coincidental.

PTEXAM
THE COMPLETE STUDY GUIDE
SCOTT M. GILES

SCOREBUILDERS

Acknowledgments

Dedication

The new edition of ***PTEXAM: The Complete Study Guide*** and every future edition is dedicated to Gwenn Hoyt. Thanks for your years of support, love, and expertise. You are greatly missed for so many reasons.

Special Thanks

Therese Giles, Scorebuilders, Scarborough, Maine
I would like to thank my wife, Traci, for her substantial contributions to all areas of the project. You are a great teammate and, of course, my best friend.

Shawn Paquette, Scorebuilders, Scarborough, Maine
I would like to thank Shawn for his involvement in each of the many phases of this project. Your expanding role in content creation has been an incredible asset for our company.

Thank You

Thanks to the many individuals that served as reviewers throughout the project.

Lucian Burg, LU Design Studios, Portland, Maine
I would like to thank Lucian for his technical and artistic expertise throughout the creation of the new edition.

Kimberly Rose, Scorebuilders, Scarborough, Maine
I would like to thank Kim for her many contributions throughout virtually all aspects of this project.

Kevin Chugh, Main Street Computing, East Aurora, New York
I would like to thank Kevin as well as the entire Main Street Computing team for their technical expertise and making Insight come to life.

Author's Note

Scott M. Giles PT, DPT, MBA

President, Scorebuilders
Scarborough, Maine

Congratulations on your decision to purchase ***PTEXAM: The Complete Study Guide***. We have been assisting physical therapists and physical therapist assistants with their preparation for the licensing examination for over three decades. We take great pride in what we do and believe this edition of ***PTEXAM: The Complete Study Guide*** demonstrates our commitment to excellence. Leave no stone unturned in your preparation for this important examination and strive to make your examination score reflect your abilities as a physical therapist. Candidates that have a firm grasp of didactic information combined with a meaningful study plan emphasizing applied knowledge are often richly rewarded on this challenging examination. We are confident that our text will be a valuable component of your comprehensive study program. Although undoubtedly there will be many magical moments in your life, you will never forget the moment when you become licensed as a physical therapist. Best of luck on the examination and in your future career endeavors!

Contributors

This project could not have been completed without the willingness of these contributors to share their clinical expertise. We are indebted to each of you for your individual contributions that have significantly enhanced this edition of ***PTEXAM: The Complete Study Guide***. Thanks for your dedication and desire to assist students with their preparation for this critically important examination.

Therese Giles PT, MS

Shawn Paquette PT, DPT

Michael Fillyaw PT, MS

Daniel Lee PT, DPT, GCS

Holly Daniel PT, MSc

Danielle Cowan PT, DPT, CLT-LANA

Ryan Bailey PT, DPT

Introduction

PTEXAM: The Complete Study Guide is the most comprehensive resource available for the National Physical Therapy Examination and sets a new standard for review book excellence. The resource provides candidates with a number of powerful study tools each designed to prepare candidates for the breadth and depth associated with the current NPTE-PT. A brief description of each unit in the study guide is listed below.

Unit 1–Introduction to the National Physical Therapy Examination (NPTE-PT)

The unit provides candidates with information on the purpose, development, scoring, and administration of the NPTE-PT. Candidates are introduced to a systematic approach to answering multiple-choice questions and are exposed to recent developments in item construction. The unit also provides a detailed analysis of each of the system and content outline areas of the NPTE-PT. By exploring the categories and subcategories of each of these areas, candidates gain a better understanding of the breadth and depth of the current examination and as a result spend less time covering topics that are not clinically relevant. This unit offers a variety of study concepts that candidates can utilize to increase the effectiveness of study sessions.

Unit 2–Academic Review

The unit provides candidates with an efficient method to review didactic information from a physical therapy curriculum. The academic review consists of eight distinct chapters of academic information. The first six chapters consist of academic content in specific system areas (e.g., musculoskeletal) and non-system areas (e.g., equipment, devices, and technologies). Each chapter in the unit includes a description of the physical therapy management of commonly encountered medical diagnoses on the NPTE-PT. The academic review avoids attempting to cover every aspect of a physical therapist's academic training and instead focuses on the most essential information necessary to maximize examination performance. Since the examination is designed to assess entry-level practice, it is likely that candidates will encounter the information presented in the academic review frequently on the actual examination. Mastery of this information can significantly increase candidates' scores on the NPTE-PT.

Unit 3–Examinations

The unit includes an answer key for the three, 200 question sample examinations located on our eLearning site **INSIGHT**. Candidates have the option of selecting a full-length examination or creating custom examinations. The examinations were developed based on selected specifications from the current content outline and are designed to expose candidates to the nuances of computer-based testing. Candidates are able to generate a detailed performance analysis summary that identifies current strengths and weaknesses according to system and content outline areas. An answer key includes an explanation specifying why the correct answer is correct and an explanation specifying why each incorrect answer is incorrect. New video explanations provide candidates with the opportunity to watch videos that compare and contrast good, better, and best options for selected examination questions. The answer key also includes a cited resource with page number, an academic focus area, and the assigned system and content outline areas. The examinations provide candidates with the opportunity to refine test taking skills and assess current preparedness for the examination.

*Additional resources to assist candidates with their preparation for the NPTE-PT are located at the conclusion of the study guide.

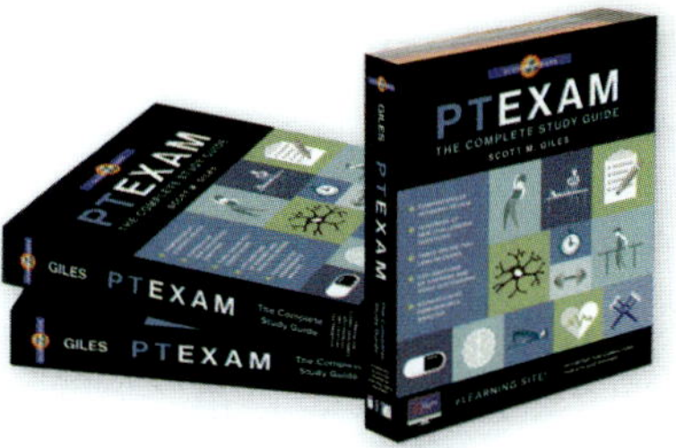

PTEXAM: The Complete Study Guide

The Gold Standard

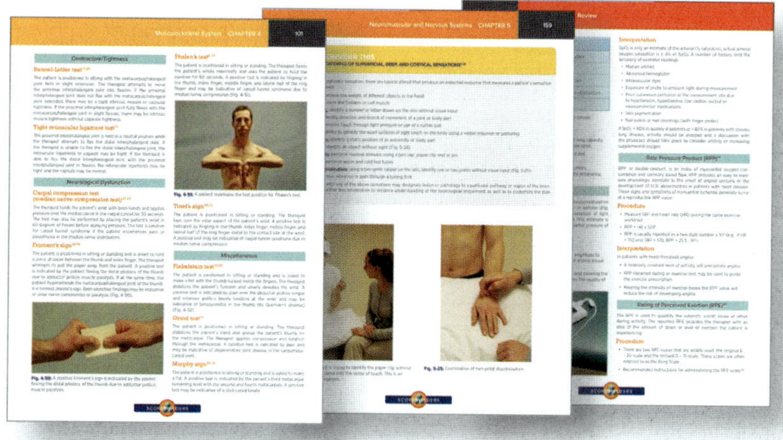

Content is King

The new edition of ***PTEXAM: The Complete Study Guide*** is the most comprehensive resource available for the NPTE-PT. The material represents both completely new content and significant expansions of existing content. Our academic review section is unparalleled in its breadth and depth and sets a new standard for review book excellence.

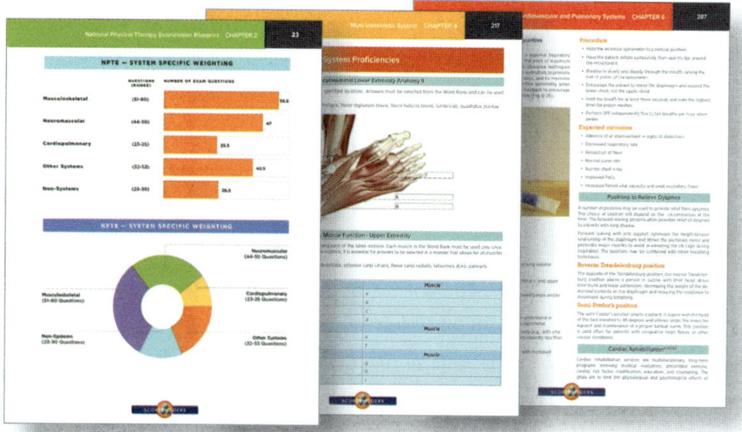

Design, Design, Design

Scorebuilders' products are known for their creative design and innovative features. The new edition of ***PTEXAM: The Complete Study Guide*** simply makes a very good thing even better. Break free from traditional encyclopedic resources and feel the power of well conceived design.

A Technology Monster

Scorebuilders has made a massive investment in technology and uses this competitive advantage to provide you with the most realistic testing experience possible. Our eLearning platform **Insight** will amaze you in its level of sophistication. Continuous innovation and commitment to technology widens the gap between **Scorebuilders** and all other licensing companies.

Test Drive the NPTE-PT

Our sample examination questions are thought provoking, challenging questions designed to be consistent with the specifications and rigor of the NPTE-PT blueprint. Scorebuilders' questions are consistently reported to be the most realistic questions available for the NPTE-PT. Use the detailed explanation of answers and videos to refine decision making skills.

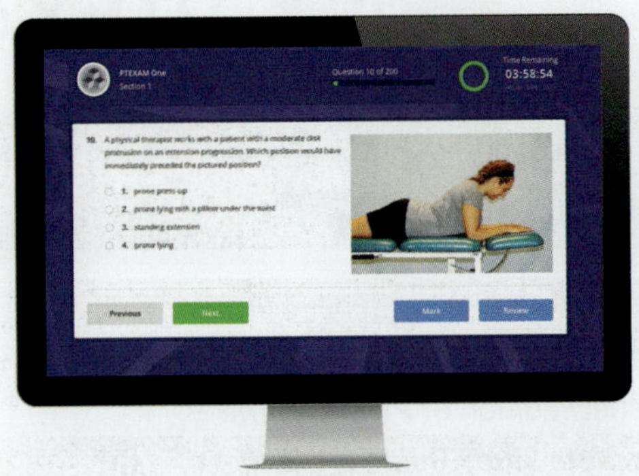

314 Unit 2 | Academic Review
SILVER
Hypertension

New Clinical Application Templates

Pathology has always been a substantive topic on the NPTE-PT and the new FSBPT blueprint makes it clear that this fact is not changing. The resource includes Gold, Silver, and Bronze Clinical Application Templates (CATs) which guide candidates through the patient/client management of commonly encountered medical conditions.

What's New!

Edition Guarantee!

We have always believed that sleep is overrated! As soon as we release a new edition of ***PTEXAM: The Complete Study Guide*** we immediately get to work on creating the next edition. Our eLearning site **Insight** includes an Edition Guarantee which delivers updates three times a year to existing users of the current edition.

Basecamp - Start Climbing!

Basecamp provides students with an incredibly efficient method to review academic content within ***PTEXAM: The Complete Study Guide***. The content is organized in five distinct Mountains and 140 Trails. Each trail has dedicated assignments, videos, and exams. Our **Arena App** allows **Basecamp** users to access 6,000 content-based questions within our competitive games - **King of the Mountain** and **Climb**. A $25 off coupon for **Basecamp** is included within **Insight**. Purchase **Basecamp** today and start climbing!

Table of Contents

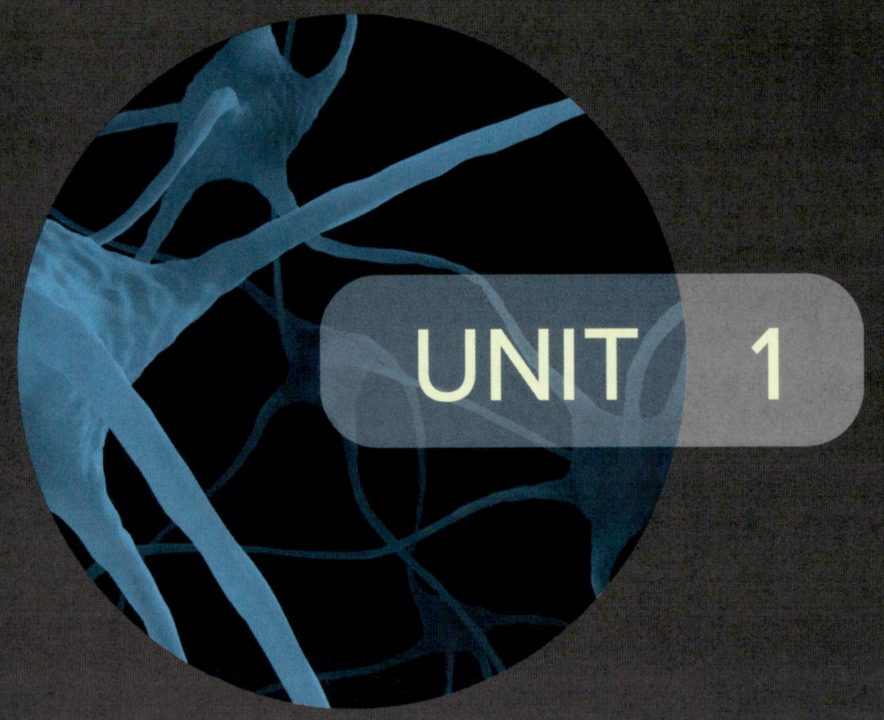

The National Physical Therapy Examination-PT

The National Physical Therapy Examination

The National Physical Therapy Examination (NPTE-PT) is a 250 question, five hour exam that is the final step required for physical therapists to become licensed practitioners. This unit addresses the application process and the essential information necessary to schedule and take the NPTE-PT. Candidates are introduced to an approach to answering multiple-choice questions and provided with examples of traditional examination questions and graphically enhanced questions.

A detailed analysis of the **NPTE-PT Blueprint** provides candidates with a thorough understanding of the relative system and content outline weighting of the examination. This information can assist students to establish a comprehensive study plan consistent with the structure of the NPTE-PT. Candidates can identify appropriate remedial activities by assessing sample examination performance in specific system and content outline areas.

Study concepts remind candidates that preparing for the NPTE-PT requires more than simply reviewing academic content and taking sample examinations. Each of the presented study concepts looks at a unique element of the study process such as learning style, automaticity, and time management. Use of this information allows candidates to establish a personalized study plan based on their unique learning needs.

Ready, Set, **GO!**

1

National Physical Therapy Examination-PT Basics

Scott Giles

CHAPTER 1
National Physical Therapy Examination-PT Basics

The National Physical Therapy Examination (NPTE-PT) is a 250 question (200 scored, 50 pre-test), multiple-choice examination designed to determine if candidates possess the minimal competency necessary to practice as physical therapists.

The examination is created under the auspices of the Federation of State Boards of Physical Therapy (FSBPT). According to the *National Physical Therapy Examination Candidate Handbook*, the examination program serves two main purposes:

1. To help ensure that only those individuals who have the requisite knowledge of physical therapy are licensed in the physical therapy field.
2. To help regulatory authorities evaluate candidates and provide standards that are comparable from jurisdiction to jurisdiction.

There are two primary methods to obtain a license to practice as a physical therapist in the United States. They are termed examination and endorsement. Licensure by examination is obtained after a candidate meets or exceeds the minimum scoring requirement on the NPTE-PT and has satisfied all other state requirements. This form of obtaining licensure is the traditional method for candidates seeking initial licensure.

Licensure by endorsement makes it possible for candidates who have already been licensed in a state by virtue of an examination to potentially gain licensure in another state without retaking the examination. Examination scores can be transferred to any physical therapy state licensing agency via the Federation of State Boards of Physical Therapy Score Transfer Service. The web site address for the Federation of State Boards of Physical Therapy is available in the Appendix.

Although the NPTE-PT is 250 questions, 50 of the questions serve only as pre-test items and are not officially scored. The pre-test items allow new examination questions to be evaluated throughout the year and eliminate lengthy delays in score reporting when new examinations are introduced. Candidates are unable to differentiate between pre-test and scored items on the examination.

The 250 questions are administered to candidates in five sections consisting of 50 questions each. Each section contains scored items and pre-test items, although the number of pre-test and scored items in each section may vary slightly. Candidates have five hours to complete the five sections at their own pace. Since the sections are not timed individually, it is important for candidates to effectively manage their allotted time as they progress through each of the five sections. Candidates have the opportunity to take one scheduled break at the conclusion of section two, immediately prior to beginning section three. Additional unscheduled breaks can be taken at the conclusion of a given section, however, the elapsed time will not stop. If a candidate does not want to take the break or prefers a shorter break, they can end the break by following the directions displayed on the computer screen. Candidates can leave the examination only when either a scheduled or unscheduled break message is displayed on the computer screen. Leaving the testing room while not on a designated break will result in an examination irregularity being reported to the FSBPT.

Candidates are unable to return to previously completed sections once a new section is initiated. The academic content is randomized within each section and scoring is based only on the number of questions a candidate answers correctly out of the 200 scored items. As a result, each of the examinations in ***PTEXAM: The Complete Study Guide*** consists of only 200 questions (four sections, each consisting of 50 questions). Candidates will have four hours to complete each of the 200 question sample examinations.

The FSBPT publishes a content outline which describes the specific categories and subcategories of the examination. The categories and subcategories are based on the tasks and roles that comprise the practice of physical therapy. Once established, the content outline remains active for a period of approximately five years. The most recent version was implemented in January of 2018. The five main categories of the examination are listed here, although the entire content outline will be discussed in detail in Chapter 2.

Candidates should attempt to integrate this information in conjunction with the performance analysis summary to accurately identify current strengths and weaknesses and develop appropriate remedial strategies. The computer-based examinations include a number of helpful tools to assist candidates to integrate this information. Candidates should avoid becoming overly excited or depressed based on the results of a given sample examination and use the number of questions answered correctly only as a general indicator of their current level of preparedness. Studying for the examination is much closer to running a marathon than running a sprint. By engaging in meaningful self-assessment activities, candidates can gather valuable information to improve future examination performance.

Examination Content Outline

Physical Therapy Examination

Foundations for Evaluation, Differential Diagnosis, & Prognosis

Interventions

Equipment, Devices, and Technologies; Therapeutic Modalities

Safety and Protection; Professional Responsibilities; Research and Evidence-Based Practice

According to the FSBPT, the involvement of a large representative group of practicing physical therapists and other professionals at each stage of examination development ensures that the examinations are relevant to the practice of physical therapy. Individual physical therapists are responsible for writing examination questions. The physical therapists involved are required to attend item-writing workshops that are taught by experienced testing professionals. Questions, once completed, are analyzed independently to make sure they are reflective of the current examination content outline. Examination questions tend to focus on decision making and not purely rote memorization of fact. Successful candidates on the examination must demonstrate the ability to apply knowledge in a safe and effective manner.

Examination Scoring

The questions on the examination are multiple-choice with four possible answers to each question. Each option is listed as 1, 2, 3, 4. Options such as "none of the above," "all of the above," and "1 and 2 only" are not included on the examination. Candidates are asked to identify the best answer to each of the questions. Each question has only one best answer while the other possible answers serve as distracters. A candidate's score is determined based on the number of scored questions answered correctly. Since there is no penalty for questions answered incorrectly it is imperative that candidates answer all of the available questions. A candidate's cumulative score is termed the total raw score. The maximum total raw score for the NPTE-PT is 200.

Criterion-referenced scoring is used to determine passing scores on the NPTE-PT. Passing scores are based on the judgment of selected experts on the minimum number of questions that should be answered correctly by a minimally qualified candidate. Criterion-referenced passing scores are determined independently of candidate performance and are designed to reflect the difficulty level of each examination. For example, if a given examination was judged to be particularly difficult, the criterion-referenced passing score would be lower than the criterion-referenced passing score for another examination that was judged to be less difficult. All state licensing agencies have adopted the FSBPT criterion-referenced passing score and therefore do not individually determine passing scores at the state level. As a result, a passing score for a given examination will always be the same in all jurisdictions.

Since the minimum passing score varies based on the difficulty level of each examination, it is impossible to determine an automatic passing score. If the criterion-referenced passing score was established as 142 for a given examination, a total raw score of greater than or equal to 142 would be considered a passing score, while a total raw score of less than 142 would be considered a failing score. Within a given examination cycle, criterion-referenced passing scores usually fluctuate within a very small range, perhaps by as few as one or two questions.

An individual examination score is often reported to candidates in the form of a scaled score. Scaled scores range from 200 - 800 with the minimum passing score always being equal to a scaled score of 600. Scaled scores are necessary as a method of equating examinations with different criterion-referenced passing scores. A few state licensing agencies use a slightly different scaled score system where the minimum passing score is equivalent to a scaled score of 75.

Applying for the Examination

The application process officially starts when a candidate's academic program initiates their FSBPT profile. This action results in each candidate receiving an email with specific login information. At this point a candidate can formally complete their FSBPT profile. In addition to registering through the FSBPT, candidates must be approved through the state licensing agency where they intend to practice as a physical therapist. The address, phone number, and web site for each agency is available at the FSBPT web site, www.fsbpt.org. Candidates are not permitted to apply for the examination in more than one jurisdiction at a time. All state licensing agencies offer online registration for the examination through the FSBPT.

Each state licensing agency can establish its own criteria to be eligible to sit for the NPTE-PT. The FSBPT has created a customized journey map located on their web site which assists candidates to navigate through the unique requirements of each state licensing agency. These items often include a photograph, a notarized birth certificate, an official transcript from an accredited school, professional reference letters, and a check or money order for the required application, examination, and licensing fees. After the necessary application forms have been completed, the information is returned along with any necessary fees to the state licensing agency or an identified intermediary. Candidates should recognize that even a small departure from the established eligibility criteria can lead to a significant delay in processing a candidate's application. To avoid such delays, it is prudent to read the application carefully and to inquire as to the status of the application approximately two weeks after the completed application has been submitted.

Foreign trained therapists are often subjected to a myriad of requirements before they are eligible to become licensed in the United States. Since the requirements vary significantly by state, it is recommended that candidates contact the state licensing agency within the state they intend to practice. The state licensing agency can provide detailed information on their individual requirements.

2022 Dates and Deadlines

Test Date	Registration and Payment Deadline	Jurisdiction Approval Deadline	Seat Reservation Deadline	Scores Reported to Jurisdictions
January 26	December 22*	January 4	January 12	February 2
April 27	March 23	March 30	April 13	May 4
July 27/28	June 22	June 29	July 13	August 4
October 26	September 21	September 28	October 12	November 2

*indicates 2021 date

2023 Dates and Deadlines

Test Date	Registration and Payment Deadline	Jurisdiction Approval Deadline	Seat Reservation Deadline	Scores Reported to Jurisdictions
January 25	December 21*	December 28*	January 11	February 1
April 26	March 29	March 29	April 12	May 3
July 25/26	June 21	June 28	July 12	August 2
October 25	September 20	September 27	October 11	November 1

*indicates 2022 date

There are two general requirements for foreign trained therapists that seem to be consistent in all states:

- Applicants are required to submit their educational credentials for evaluation of their equivalence to the United States trained applicant.
- Applicants must meet or exceed the minimum scoring requirement on the NPTE-PT.

Other state requirements can include, but are not limited to, the following:

- Demonstrate proficiency in written and spoken English
- Submit letters of reference
- Obtain a valid visa and resident alien card
- Complete an internship or period of supervised practice
- Appear for an interview
- Attain the United States equivalent of a grade of "C" or higher in all professional coursework

Some states offer candidates with verifiable employment the opportunity to practice prior to being licensed by issuing a temporary license. Typically, candidates are required to have a completed application on file and have met all other qualifications for licensure before being considered for the temporary license. In most states temporary licenses are revoked if a candidate receives notification that they were unsuccessful on the NPTE-PT.

In addition to the NPTE-PT, a significant number of states require candidates to successfully complete a jurisprudence examination. This type of examination is based on the state rules and regulations governing physical therapy practice. The examination can include multiple-choice items, short-answer questions or fill in the blanks. States can administer the examination using computer-based testing or even as a take-home examination.

The NPTE-PT officially moved from continuous testing to fixed-date testing on July 1, 2011. The change was necessitated by the need to substantially reduce or eliminate candidates' ability to gain a score advantage by having advance access to NPTE-PT questions. The move to fixed-date testing has resulted in the establishment of a number of important dates and deadlines that are critical for all candidates. Candidates taking the NPTE-PT in 2022 or 2023 must register for one of the four established testing dates.

Candidates are encouraged to visit the FSBPT web site frequently since established dates and/or registration deadlines are subject to change. A dedicated fixed-date testing page has been integrated into the FSBPT web site.

Examination Administration

The examination is offered on computer at over 300 Prometric Testing Centers within the United States. Candidates are encouraged to make an appointment at a Prometric Testing Center as soon as they receive notification from the FSBPT that they are eligible. The move to fixed-date testing has created shortages at selected Prometric Testing Centers on specific fixed dates. As a result, the FSBPT recommends that candidates wait to make travel arrangements until after they have secured a scheduled test date and location.

Many Prometric Testing Centers will offer both a morning and afternoon appointment. When possible, candidates should schedule their examination at a time consistent with their optimal level of functioning. For example, if a candidate tends to be a "morning person," it would be prudent to schedule the examination in the morning. Candidates with significant anxiety may also want a morning appointment in order to avoid worrying about the examination throughout the day. If candidates are not familiar with the exact location of the examination site, it may be desirable to travel to the site before the actual examination date. The trip will provide candidates with an accurate idea of the time necessary to travel to the site and avoid the possibility of getting lost and subsequently being late for the examination.

Within each Prometric Testing Center, candidates can concentrate on the examination without environmental distracters. Private, modular booths provide adequate work space with proper lighting and ventilation. All Prometric Testing Centers are fully accessible and in compliance with the Americans with Disabilities Act. Candidates requesting accommodation for a documented disability must do so through the state licensing agency. Candidates are not limited to the testing centers within the state they are applying for licensure. For example, a candidate that has recently graduated from a physical therapy program in Maine could apply for licensure in California and take the required examination while still residing in Maine.

Candidates must arrive 30 minutes prior to their scheduled appointment with two forms of acceptable identification which include a government issued photo ID and another piece of identification preprinted with a name and a signature. The first and last names on both forms of ID must match the name on the Authorization to Test letter issued by the FSBPT. Candidates are photographed and a digital image of their fingerprint is taken prior to beginning the examination. Candidates cannot bring any electronic devices (e.g., watches, cell phones) or food and drink into the testing area. A locker will be provided to store personal items. Candidates can request headphones if they want to minimize background noise.

It is important to note that computer skills are not necessary with computer-based testing. Prior to beginning the examination, candidates utilize a tutorial that explains topics such as selecting answers and navigating within the examination. Time spent on the computer tutorial does not count toward the allotted time for the actual examination. The tutorial typically takes candidates less than ten minutes and if necessary, candidates can go through the tutorial a second time.

Candidates have the option of entering their answers using a computer keyboard or mouse. Candidates can go back to previously answered or unanswered questions and make any desired changes within a given section of 50 questions. Once a candidate submits a given section, they are unable to return to the questions within the section. Paper and pencil are not permitted in the Prometric Testing Centers, however, candidates are given an erasable note board or an electronic writing board to utilize during the examination.

The FSBPT is responsible for scoring the examination and reporting results to the individual state licensing agencies. According to the FSBPT, score will be reported approximately one week after the test date. This time allows the FSBPT to receive, process, and deliver to jurisdictions several thousand exam score files. The FSBPT reports scores to the candidate and the associated state licensing agency. Candidates receive a free online score report from the FSBPT approximately 10 business days after the examination. The score report offers more detailed information on a candidate's performance in specific content areas.

If a candidate successfully completes the examination, in most cases they have fulfilled the final requirement for licensure. Conversely, if a candidate is unsuccessful on the examination, they are required to reapply to the state licensing agency. With computer-based testing there is no mandatory waiting period before retaking the examination, however, candidates will need to wait until the next fixed date. Some states limit the number of times a candidate can take the examination as well as mandate remedial coursework. In all states, candidates are prohibited from taking the examination more than three times in a 12 month period. The FSBPT has established a six-time lifetime limit on NPTE-PT attempts.

Candidates that were unsuccessful on the NPTE-PT can receive a performance feedback report from the FSBPT. The feedback report compares individual examination performance using the content outline and system specific categories with the performance of other candidates exposed to the same examination. Additional information on feedback is available through the FSBPT.

Test Taking Skills

Test taking skills are specific skills that allow individuals to utilize the characteristics and format of a selected examination in order to maximize their performance. These skills can be valuable when taking an examination such as the NPTE-PT. Despite the importance of this topic, very little, if any, academic time is set aside to address test taking skills. The good news is that test taking skills can be learned and that through dedication, desire, and determination, these skills can serve to improve examination performance.

The NPTE-PT consists of multiple-choice questions with four potentially correct answers to each question. Candidates are instructed to select the "best answer" to complete each question. Before exploring selected test taking strategies, we need to identify the various components of a multiple-choice question. Multiple-choice questions can be dissected into specific identifiable components:

Item

An item refers to an individual multiple-choice question and the corresponding potential answers. The NPTE-PT contains 200 scored items and 50 pre-test items. Each item consists of a stem and four options. Items may vary in content and length, but should utilize a consistent format.

Stem

The stem refers to the statement that asks the question. Typically, the stem conveys to the reader the necessary information needed to respond correctly to the question. In addition to the necessary information, extraneous information may be included in the stem. This information, when not recognized by the candidate as unnecessary, often can serve as a significant distracter.

The stem commonly takes on the form of a complete sentence or an incomplete sentence. The stem can be expressed in a positive or negative form. A positive form requires a candidate to identify correct information, while a negative form requires a candidate to identify incorrect information. It is important to scrutinize each stem, since a single key word such as "NOT," "EXCEPT" or "LEAST" can turn a positive stem into a negative stem. Failure to identify this can lead to the identification of an incorrect answer.

Options

The options refer to the potential answers to the question asked. One option in each item will be the "best answer," while the others are considered distracters. Options can take on a variety of forms, including a single word, a group of words, an incomplete sentence, a complete sentence or a group of sentences. The method for analyzing each option does not change, regardless of form.

Approach for Answering Multiple-Choice Questions

On the NPTE-PT there are 250 items (200 scored, 50 pre-test) that candidates must answer within a five hour time period. Due to the length of the examination and the time constraints associated with it, candidates need to approach the examination in a systematic and organized fashion. Loss of control during the examination will yield poor results that are not reflective of a candidate's actual knowledge. To assist candidates to minimize the impact of this potential pitfall, we will introduce a systematic approach to utilize when answering sample examination items.

The following six-step approach is recommended as a method for answering examination items:

1. Read the stem carefully to become familiar with the item and to determine the command words that indicate the desired action.
2. Read the stem again and identify relevant words or groups of words based on the identified command words.
3. Attempt to generate an answer to the stem.
4. Examine each option completely before moving to the next option.
5. Attempt to identify the best option.
6. Utilize deductive reasoning strategies.

The six-step approach begins with a candidate reading the stem. Candidates should read the stem initially to become familiar with the item and to determine the command words that indicate the desired action. Once this has been determined, candidates can reread the stem and attempt to extract the necessary components including relevant words or groups of words.

Perhaps the most important step in the six-step approach is to have candidates attempt to generate an answer to each question based on the identified command words. This is the only opportunity a candidate will have to objectively evaluate the question prior to exposing each of the options. Once a candidate exposes the options, they are no longer able to examine the question in a fully objective manner and instead become more likely to have their interpretation of the question influenced by a presented option. If for some reason a candidate is unable to generate a specific answer, they should attempt to think about the general topic and recall related information. Once a possible answer is generated, candidates should then begin to examine each option one at a time. It is important to read the entire option, since one word can often make a potentially correct answer incorrect. If the generated answer is consistent with one of the available options, the candidate should give the option strong consideration, however, since more than one option can be correct, it is imperative to analyze each presented option.

If candidates finish analyzing an item and are still unable to select one of the available options they should consider using a deductive reasoning strategy. Deductive reasoning strategies allow candidates to improve examination scores without direct knowledge of subject matter. This type of strategy should be applied only when candidates are unable to identify the correct response using academic knowledge. Deductive reasoning strategies often allow candidates to eliminate one or more of the potential answers. Elimination of any option significantly increases the probability of identifying the correct answer. On the NPTE-PT, eliminating one option increases the chance of selecting a correct answer from 25% to 33%. Eliminating two options increases the chance of selecting a correct answer to 50%. On the surface, this may not seem terribly significant, however, on an examination such as the NPTE-PT, this can often be the difference between a passing and a failing score. Selected deductive reasoning strategies that can be used effectively on the NPTE-PT are presented.

Absurd options

Many times a multiple-choice item will include an option that is not consistent with what the stem is asking or with the other options. In many cases, this option can be eliminated. Rapid elimination of specific options will allow candidates to spend additional time analyzing other more viable options.

Similar options

When two or more options have a similar meaning or express the same fact, they often imply each other's incorrectness. For this reason, candidates can often eliminate both options.

Obtainable information

There is a great deal of factual material that candidates must sift through when taking the NPTE-PT. In some instances, the material can provide candidates with valuable information that can assist them when answering other examination questions.

Degree of qualification

Particularly in the sciences, there seems to be many exceptions to general rules. Therefore, specific wording such as "always" or "never" often overqualify an option.

Activity One

In this activity, three sample questions are presented. Candidates should attempt to identify the best answer to each question by utilizing the six-step approach.

An analysis section immediately follows each of the three sample questions. The analysis section begins by showing the sample question with key terms underlined and command words in bold type. A brief narrative follows, which describes how the six-step approach can be applied to the sample question.

An answer key located at the conclusion of the exercise indicates the best answer and an explanation for each question.

Sample Question One

A physical therapist instructs a patient with a Foley catheter in ambulation activities. During ambulation, the therapist should position the collection bag:

1. above the level of the patient's bladder
2. below the level of the patient's bladder
3. above the level of the patient's heart
4. below the level of the patient's heart

Analysis

A physical therapist instructs a patient with a Foley catheter in ambulation activities. During ambulation, the therapist should **position** the collection bag:

1. above the level of the patient's bladder
2. below the level of the patient's bladder
3. above the level of the patient's heart
4. below the level of the patient's heart

A candidate should attempt to generate an answer to the question after reading the stem and identifying the pertinent information and command words. The candidate should then begin to reveal each of the available options one at a time. If a generated answer is consistent with one of the available options, there is a high probability that the answer is correct.

If a candidate was not able to generate an answer, they should expose the first option and give it careful consideration before moving on to the next option. They should progress through the remaining options in a similar manner. Candidates should remember it is possible to have more than one option that satisfactorily answers the question. It is then the candidate's responsibility to select the best answer from the viable options.

Sample Question Two

A group of physical therapists attempts to determine the relationship between two variables on an examination form. Which of the following correlation coefficients would indicate the strongest relationship?

1. +.86
2. +.45
3. -.34
4. -.89

Analysis

A group of physical therapists attempts to determine the relationship between two variables on an examination form. Which of the following correlation coefficients would indicate the **strongest relationship**?

1. +.86
2. +.45
3. -.34
4. -.89

After reading the stem and identifying the pertinent information and command words, a candidate should recognize that it is virtually impossible to generate an answer prior to viewing the available options. A candidate should, however, begin to think about correlation coefficients and determining the strength of the relationship between variables. The candidate should then expose each of the available options and attempt to identify the correct response.

Although the six-step approach does not directly supply a candidate with the correct response, by carefully reading the stem, a candidate can avoid an unnecessary mistake. In this item, the stem asks the candidate to identify the correlation coefficient that indicates the strongest relationship between the two variables. If a candidate does not read the question carefully, they may make an assumption that the stem is asking for the strongest positive relationship and subsequently answer the question incorrectly.

It is important that a candidate answer each item based only on the given information. By making even small assumptions or by not reading each item carefully, a candidate can make careless mistakes.

Sample Question Three

A physical therapist completes an isokinetic examination on an 18-year-old male rehabilitating from a medial meniscectomy. The therapist notes that the patient generates 140 ft/lbs of force using the uninvolved quadriceps at 60 degrees per second. Assuming a normal ratio of hamstrings to quadriceps strength, which of the following would be an acceptable hamstrings value at 60 degrees per second?

1. 64 ft/lbs
2. 84 ft/lbs
3. 114 ft/lbs
4. 116 ft/lbs

Analysis

A physical therapist completes an isokinetic examination on an 18-year-old male rehabilitating from a medial meniscectomy. The therapist notes that the patient generates 140 ft/lbs of force using the uninvolved quadriceps at 60 degrees per second. Assuming a normal ratio of hamstrings to quadriceps strength, which of the following would be **an acceptable hamstrings** value at 60 degrees per second?

1. 64 ft/lbs
2. 84 ft/lbs
3. 114 ft/lbs
4. 116 ft/lbs

For the purpose of discussion, let's assume a candidate has no idea of the normal ratio of quadriceps/hamstrings strength at 60 degrees per second. Lack of specific academic knowledge will result in a candidate not being able to identify the correct answer using the first five steps of the six-step approach. However, by utilizing deductive reasoning strategies, a candidate can significantly increase their chances of identifying the best answer without applying direct academic knowledge.

In this item, the stem asks a candidate to identify a value that would be representative of a normal quadriceps/hamstrings ratio at 60 degrees per second. As with many measurements in physical therapy, precise normal values are difficult to ascertain, and therefore often are expressed in ranges. Since options 3 and 4 are so close in value, they likely imply each other's incorrectness and can therefore be eliminated. Although in this example deductive reasoning strategies were not able to identify the correct answer, they were able to eliminate two of the four possible options. By eliminating two options, a candidate now has a 50% chance of identifying the best answer, even without utilizing any direct academic or clinical knowledge.

Activity One – Answer Key

1. Correct Answer: 2

The effect of gravity necessitates the collection bag being below the level of the patient's bladder.

2. Correct Answer: 4

Correlation coefficients range from +1.00 to -1.00. Since the question does not ask for a positive or negative correlation, the strongest relationship is indicated by -.89.

3. Correct Answer: 2

A gross estimate of quadriceps:hamstrings ratio is 3:2. Option 2, 84 ft/lbs is therefore the most consistent with the expressed ratio.

Alternate Examination Items

The NPTE-PT will include a number of graphically enhanced items. Although representing a relatively small percentage of the total examination, candidates need to be comfortable answering this type of item.

Graphically Enhanced Items

Graphically enhanced items consist of figures, diagrams, pictures or other static images that are combined with traditional text in an examination item.

Activity Two

Two graphically enhanced items are presented. Candidates should attempt to identify the best answer to each question. An answer key located at the conclusion of the exercise indicates the best answer and an explanation for each question.

The following image should be used to answer question 1:

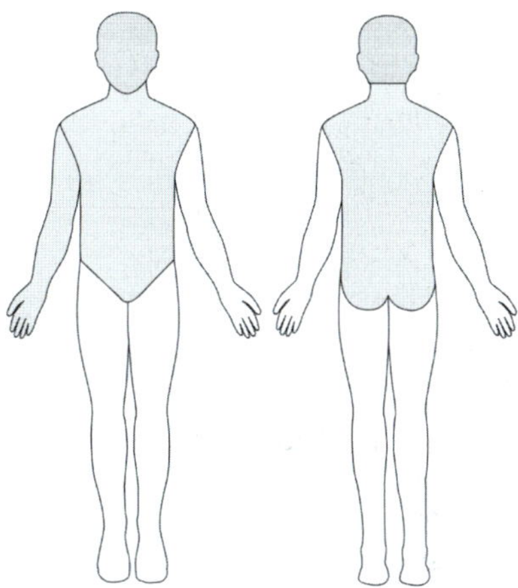

1. A 32-year-old male sustained extensive burns in a house fire. The shaded portion of the body diagrams represents the areas affected by the burns. Using the rule of nines, what percentage of the patient's body was involved?

   1. 40.5%
   2. 44.0%
   3. 49.5%
   4. 54.5%

The following image should be used to answer question 2:

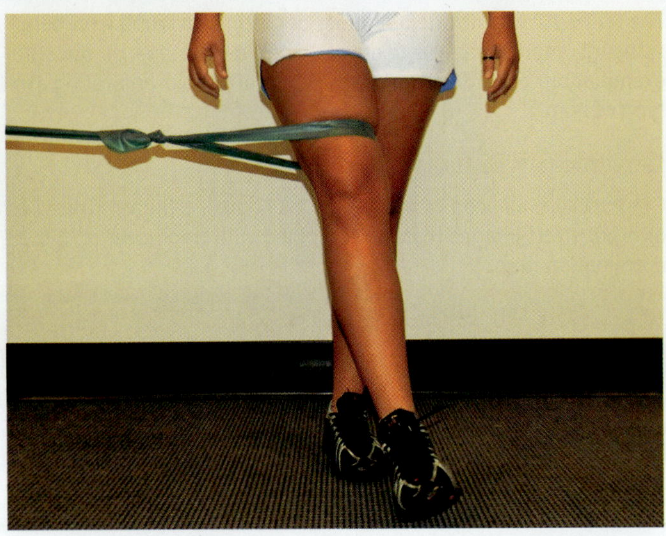

2. A physical therapist instructs a patient to complete an exercise activity using a piece of elastic band as pictured. The patient is a 14-year-old female rehabilitating from a lower extremity injury sustained in a soccer contest. The therapist's primary objective for the activity is to:

   1. strengthen the right hip abductor muscles
   2. strengthen the right hip adductor muscles
   3. stretch the right hip abductor muscles
   4. stretch the right hip adductor muscles

Activity Two – Answer Key

1. Correct Answer: 3

The percentage of the body surface burned in an adult can be calculated using the rule of nines: anterior thorax (18%) + posterior thorax (18%) + head (9%) + anterior arm (4.5%) = 49.5%.

2. Correct Answer: 2

Successful completion of the activity requires the adductor muscles to exert a force greater than the tension supplied by the elastic band while moving into hip adduction. Muscles acting to adduct the hip include the adductor longus, adductor brevis, adductor magnus, and gracilis.

Time Constraints

Like many objective examinations, candidates have a specific allotted time to complete the NPTE-PT. For physical therapists, the available time is five hours. Since the examination consists of 250 questions, candidates will have 72 seconds available to answer each question. This number, although correct when viewing the examination as a whole, can be misleading. There will be many questions that a candidate will be able to answer in much less than 72 seconds, whereas other questions will take somewhat longer. The key to success lies in progressing through the examination in a consistent and predictable manner.

Although 72 seconds per question does not seem like a great deal of time, the majority of candidates will have ample time to complete the examination. Despite this fact, it is important to pay attention to the elapsed time during the examination. It also is important to know your test taking history. Are you typically one of the first, one of the last, or somewhere in the middle of individuals completing an examination? This information is important as you plan your test taking strategy. In order to make sure your pace is appropriate during practice sessions and during the actual examination, it is important to formally check on the elapsed time, at a very minimum, when completing each section of 50 questions. This action will allow candidates to assess their progress and modify their pace, if necessary.

Preparing for the Examination

The simple thought of preparing for a comprehensive examination such as the NPTE-PT can be overwhelming. Many candidates ask themselves how it is possible to prepare adequately for an examination that encompasses up to three years of professional coursework. To further complicate matters, the majority of candidates take the NPTE-PT shortly after graduation. This can be a very anxious and unsettled time. Candidates often are actively seeking employment or are attempting to adjust to a new job. As a result, it is critical that candidates outline a well conceived and deliberate study plan for the examination.

One of the largest advantages of taking an examination such as the NPTE-PT is that it does not require candidates to demonstrate mastery of new material. On the surface, this may not seem like a significant advantage, but since candidates are, in effect, only reviewing or relearning previously presented information, their level of attainment should be significantly greater. Many candidates fail to utilize this advantage. Candidates who attempt to learn large quantities of new information, instead of focusing on understanding and applying basic concepts, often do themselves a tremendous disservice. It is true that there undoubtedly will be questions that contain information that was not part of a selected curriculum, but to attempt to study this new information in any significant detail would be a large mistake for most candidates. Instead, candidates should focus on reviewing or relearning basic concepts that are an integral component of all accredited physical therapy programs. It is this type of information that will make up the vast majority of the examination. Individuals who take this commonsense approach optimize their chances of success.

Although students typically exhibit mastery of selected material during a scheduled examination, they do not always retain the information for later use. Often times, simply reviewing information is enough for candidates to relearn the material, however, in some cases, a more in-depth approach is necessary. It is recommended that candidates pay particular attention to their practice-oriented professional coursework. Practice-oriented professional coursework includes, but is not limited to, study of the musculoskeletal, neuromuscular, and cardiopulmonary systems. The content outline from the FSBPT clearly demonstrates the need for candidates to also review "other systems" (i.e., integumentary, metabolic and endocrine, gastrointestinal, genitourinary, lymphatic, multi-system). In addition, candidates usually have coursework in patient care skills, physical agents, administration, ethics, research, and education. Each of these topics are important components of the content outline for the NPTE-PT, although the weighting of each item differs significantly. **Chapter 2** will offer specific information on the relative weighting of each area according to systems and non-systems categories.

Special attention must be taken not to become bogged down in one specific area for any significant amount of time. General concepts that are understood should be scanned quickly, while other concepts that are more difficult for a candidate should be read carefully. Concepts that remain unclear after being reviewed should be written down for future study sessions.

Other foundational coursework encountered earlier in the professional curriculum can be consulted as needed during various study sessions. This type of coursework often includes, but is not limited to anatomy and physiology, neuroanatomy, exercise physiology, and kinesiology. It is important to limit the amount of time spent reviewing this type of foundational coursework. Candidates often can make better use of their allotted time by reviewing coursework encountered later in the curriculum that may be more practice-oriented. By reviewing practice-oriented information, candidates not only keep their studying consistent with the format of the examination, but also at the same time indirectly review much of the information presented in the foundational coursework.

Before beginning to study, develop specific goals for each study session. Ideally, these goals should be established on a weekly basis. Establishing goals will ensure that candidates cover the desired material and will serve as a mechanism to keep them on schedule with their study plan. Candidates should be realistic with the goals they establish and should not attempt to cover more material than is possible in a particular study session.

2 National Physical Therapy Examination-PT Blueprint

Scott Giles

CHAPTER 2
National Physical Therapy Examination-PT Blueprint

Perhaps the most valuable piece of information a candidate can utilize when preparing for the NPTE-PT is the NPTE-PT Blueprint. The blueprint provides a detailed analysis of each of the content areas of the NPTE-PT. A thorough understanding of the content outline and system specific weighting will streamline a candidate's preparation. Less time will be spent covering topics that are not clinically relevant to the actual examination and as a result, more time will be available for reviewing and relearning.

This chapter will explore the examination in detail according to the content outline and system specific areas. Each of the sample examinations in ***PTEXAM: The Complete Study Guide*** offers candidates the opportunity to view their performance according to five system and five content outline categories. Candidates must be familiar with the content contained in each system and content outline category and use this information to develop remedial plans to improve performance on sample examinations. We will begin with an exploration of the NPTE-PT Content Outline. All examination information is publicly available from the Federation of State Boards of Physical Therapy.

Content Outline Summary

Content	Questions (Range)	Midpoint (Questions)	Midpoint (Percentage)
Physical Therapy Examination	44–57	50.5	25.25%
Foundations for Evaluation, Differential Diagnosis, and Prognosis	58–74	66	33%
Interventions	48–60	54	27%
Equipment, Devices, and Technologies; Therapeutic Modalities	11–14	12.5	6.25%
Safety and Protection; Professional Responsibilities; Research	12–16	14	7%

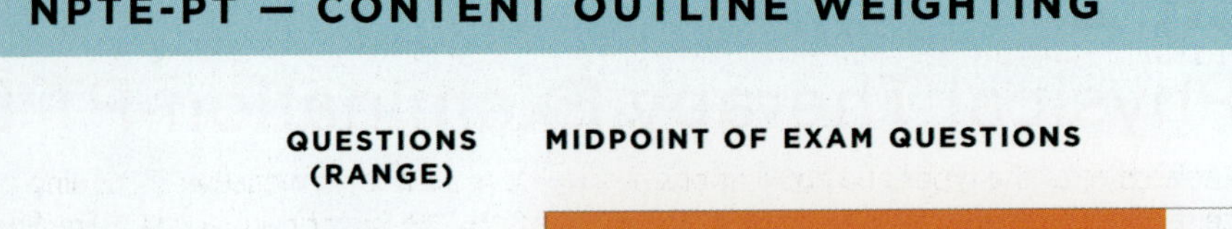
NPTE-PT — CONTENT OUTLINE WEIGHTING

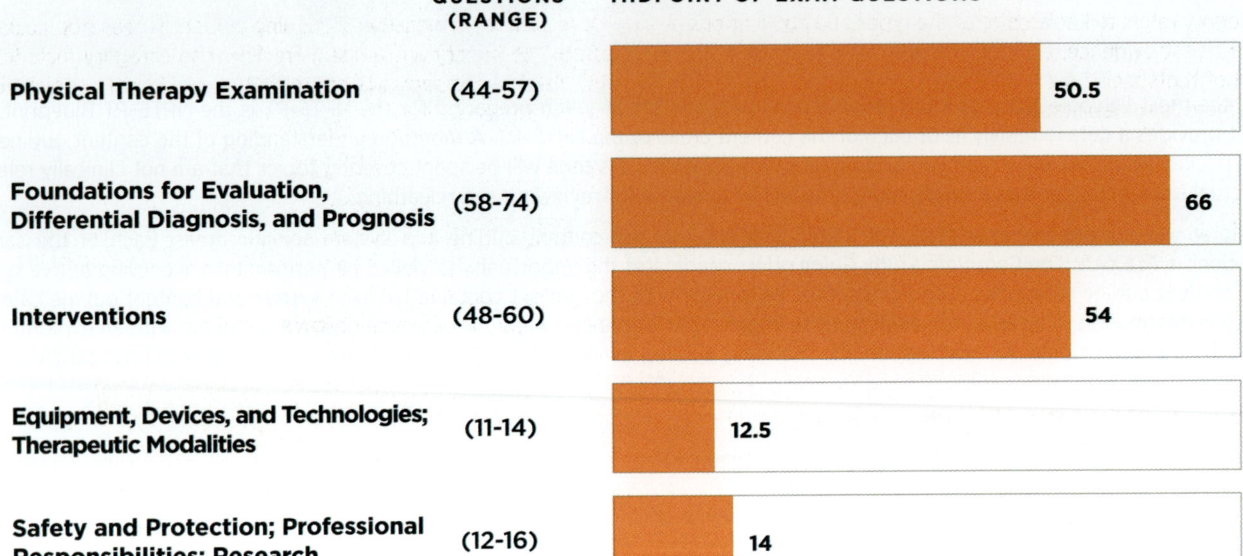
QUESTIONS (RANGE)
MIDPOINT OF EXAM QUESTIONS
Physical Therapy Examination
(44-57)
50.5
Foundations for Evaluation, Differential Diagnosis, and Prognosis
(58-74)
66
Interventions
(48-60)
54
Equipment, Devices, and Technologies; Therapeutic Modalities
(11-14)
12.5
Safety and Protection; Professional Responsibilities; Research
(12-16)
14

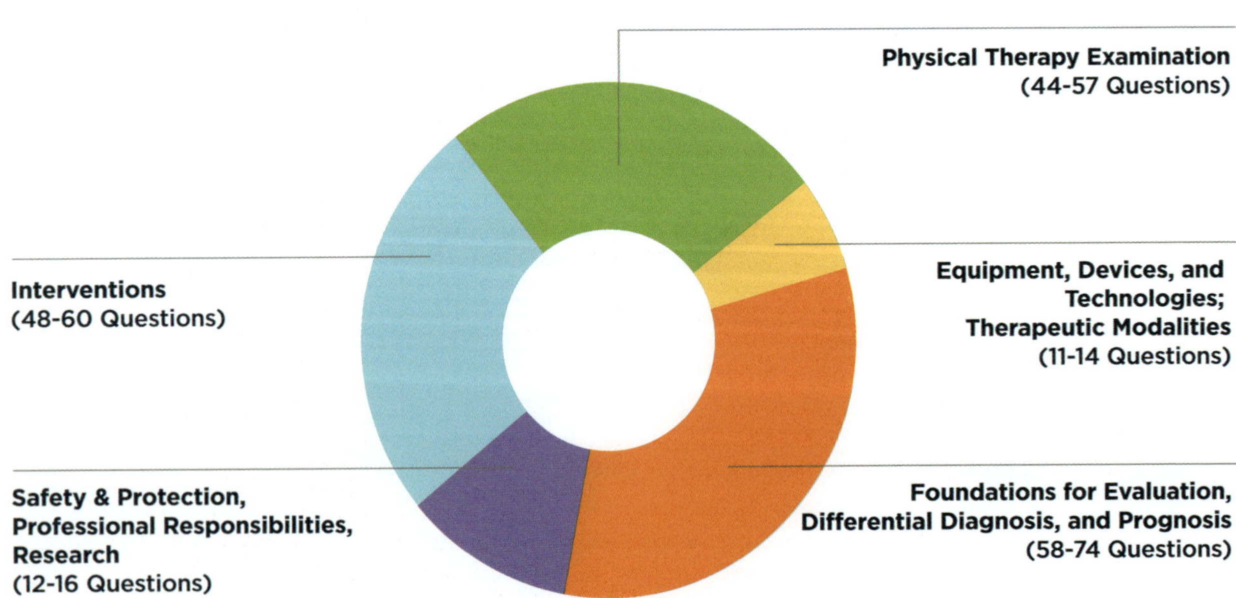
NPTE-PT — CONTENT OUTLINE WEIGHTING
Physical Therapy Examination (44-57 Questions)
Interventions (48-60 Questions)
Equipment, Devices, and Technologies; Therapeutic Modalities (11-14 Questions)
Safety & Protection, Professional Responsibilities, Research (12-16 Questions)
Foundations for Evaluation, Differential Diagnosis, and Prognosis (58-74 Questions)

SCOREBUILDERS

Physical Therapy Examination

Midrange: 50.5 Questions (25.25%)

This category refers to knowledge of the types and applications of specific system tests/measures, including outcome measures, according to current best evidence, and their relevance to information collected from the history and systems review. The category includes the reaction of the specific system to tests/measures. Information covered in these areas supports appropriate and effective patient/client management for rehabilitation, health promotion, and performance across the lifespan.

PHYSICAL THERAPY EXAMINATION

	QUESTIONS (RANGE)	MIDPOINT OF EXAM QUESTIONS
Musculoskeletal System	(18-21)	19.5
Neuromuscular and Nervous Systems	(15-17)	16
Cardiovascular and Pulmonary Systems	(7-9)	8
Other Systems	(4-10)	7

Foundations for Evaluation, Differential Diagnosis, and Prognosis

Midrange: 66 Questions (33%)

This category refers to the interpretation of knowledge about diseases/conditions impacting a specific system, according to current best evidence, in order to ensure appropriate and effective patient/client treatment and management decisions for rehabilitation, health promotion, and performance across the lifespan.

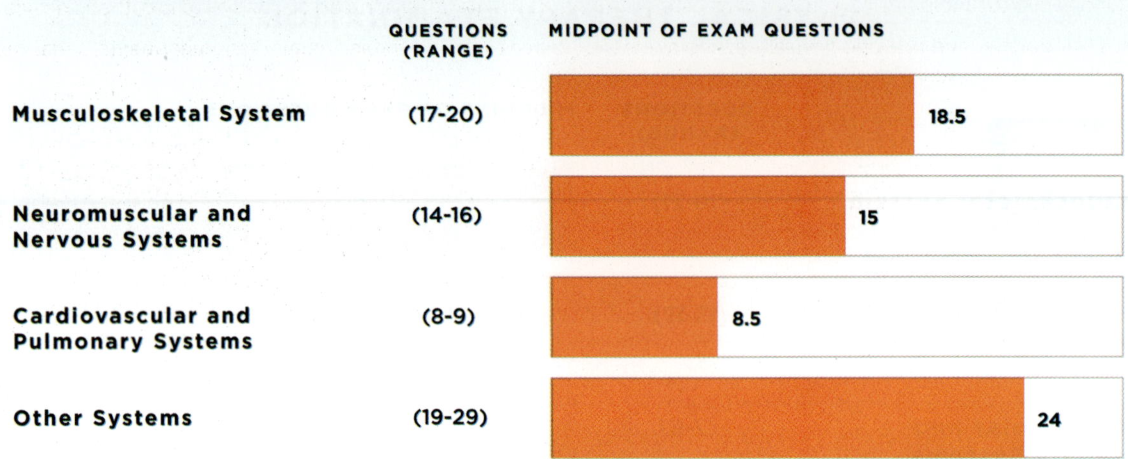

Interventions

Midrange: 54 Questions (27%)

This category refers to specific system interventions (including types, applications, responses, and potential complications), according to current best evidence, as well as the impact on the specific system of interventions performed on other systems in order to support patient/client management for rehabilitation, health promotion, and performance across the lifespan.

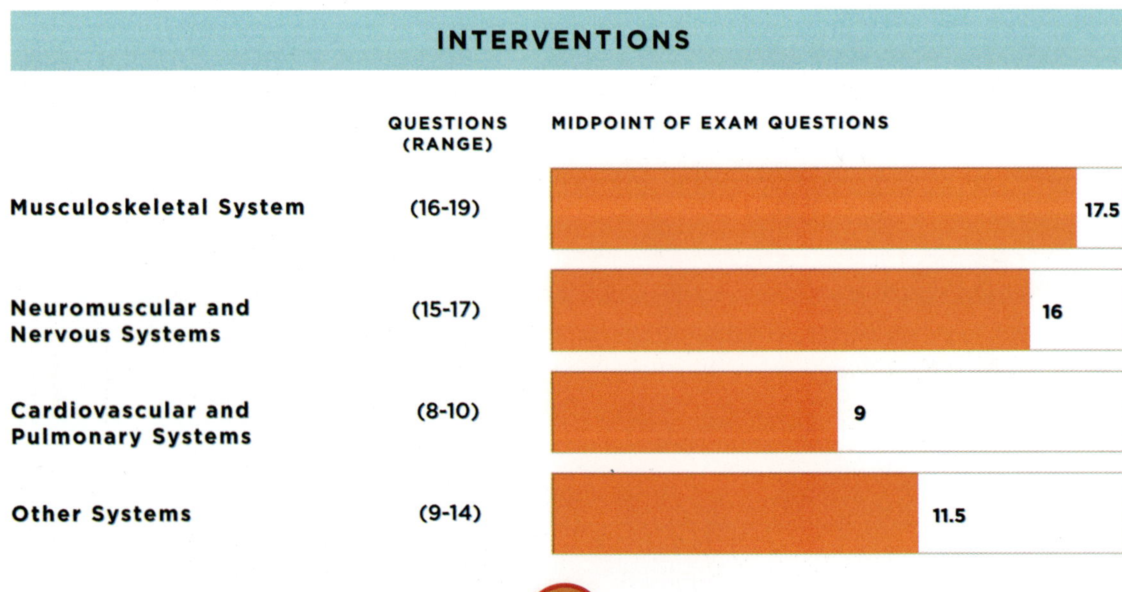

Equipment, Devices, and Technologies

Midrange: 5.5 Questions (2.75%)

This category refers to the different types of equipment, devices and technologies, use requirements, and/or contextual determinants, as well as any other influencing factors involved in the selection and application of equipment, devices, and technologies including consideration of current best evidence, in order to support appropriate and effective patient/client management for rehabilitation, health promotion, and performance across the lifespan.

- Assistive and adaptive devices/technologies (e.g., walkers, wheelchairs, adaptive seating systems and positioning devices, mechanical lifts)
- Prosthetic devices/technologies (e.g., lower extremity and upper extremity, microprocessor-controlled prosthetic devices)
- Protective, supportive, and orthotic devices/technologies (e.g., braces, helmets, taping, compression garments, serial casts, shoe inserts, splints, robotic exoskeleton)

Therapeutic Modalities

Midrange: 7 Questions (3.5%)

This category refers to the underlying principles for the use of therapeutic modalities as well as the justification for the selection and use of various types of therapeutic modalities, including consideration of current best evidence, in order to support appropriate and effective patient/client management for rehabilitation, health promotion, and performance across the lifespan.

- Thermal modalities
- Iontophoresis
- Electrotherapy modalities (e.g., neuromuscular electrical stimulation (NMES), transcutaneous electrical nerve stimulation (TENS), functional electrical stimulation (FES), interferential therapy, high-voltage pulsed current)
- Phonophoresis
- Ultrasound modalities
- Mechanical modalities (e.g., mechanical motion devices, traction devices)
- Biofeedback
- Intermittent compression

EQUIPMENT, DEVICES, AND TECHNOLOGIES; THERAPEUTIC MODALITIES

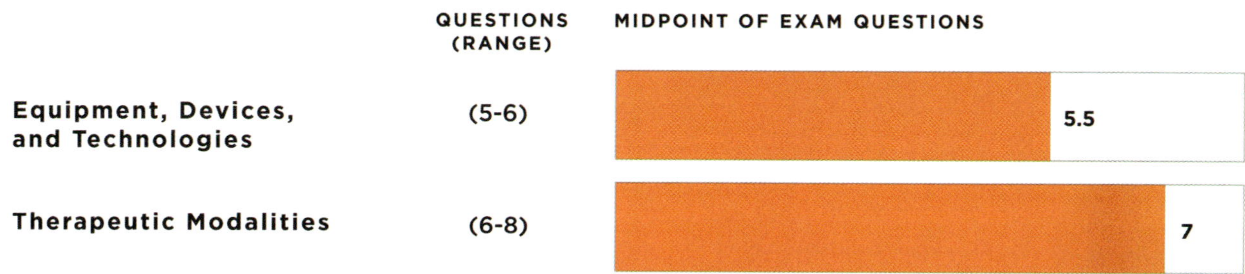

Safety and Protection

Midrange: 5.5 Questions (2.75%)

This category refers to the critical issues involved in patient/client safety and protection and the responsibilities of health-care providers to ensure that patient/client management and health-care decisions take place in a secure environment.

- Factors influencing safety and injury prevention (e.g., safe patient handling, fall prevention, equipment maintenance, environmental safety)
- Function, implications, and related precautions of intravenous lines, tubes, catheters, monitoring devices, and mechanical ventilators/oxygen delivery devices
- Emergency preparedness (e.g., CPR, first aid, disaster response)
- Infection control procedures (e.g., standard/universal precautions, isolation techniques, sterile technique)
- Signs/symptoms of physical, sexual, and psychological abuse and neglect

Professional Responsibilities

Midrange: 4.5 Questions (2.25%)

This category refers to the responsibilities of health-care providers to ensure that patient/client management and health-care decisions take place in a trustworthy environment.

- Standards of documentation
- Patient/client rights (e.g., ADA, IDEA, HIPAA, patient bill of rights)
- Human resource legal issues (e.g., OSHA, sexual harassment)
- Roles and responsibilities of the physical therapist, physical therapist assistant, other healthcare professionals, and support staff
- Standards of professional ethics
- Standards of billing, coding, and reimbursement
- Obligations for reporting illegal, unethical, or unprofessional behaviors (e.g., fraud, abuse, neglect)
- State and federal laws, rules, regulations, and industry standards set by state and accrediting bodies (e.g., state licensing entities, Joint Commission, CARF, CMS)
- Risk management and quality assurance (e.g., policies and procedures, incident reports, peer chart review)
- Cultural factors and/or characteristics that affect patient/client management (e.g., language differences, disability, ethnicity, customs, demographics, religion)
- Socioeconomic factors that affect patient/client management
- Health information technology (e.g., electronic medical records, telemedicine)

Research and Evidence-Based Practice

Midrange: 4 Questions (2%)

This category refers to the application of measurement principles and research methods to make reasoned and appropriate assessment and to the interpretation of information sources and practice research to support patient/client management decisions fundamental to evidence-based practice.

- Research methodology and interpretation (e.g., qualitative, quantitative, levels of evidence)
- Data collection techniques (e.g., surveys, direct observation)
- Measurement science (e.g., reliability, validity)
- Techniques for accessing evidence (e.g., peer-reviewed publications, scientific proceedings, guidelines, clinical prediction rules)
- Statistics (e.g., t-test, chi-square, correlation coefficient, ANOVA, likelihood ratio, effect size, confidence intervals)

SAFETY AND PROTECTION; PROFESSIONAL RESPONSIBILITIES, RESEARCH

	QUESTIONS (RANGE)	MIDPOINT OF EXAM QUESTIONS
Safety and Protection	(5-6)	5.5
Professional Responsibilities	(4-5)	4.5
Research and Evidence-Based Practice	(3-5)	4

System Summary

Systems	Questions (Range)	Midpoint (Questions)	Midpoint (Percentage)
Musculoskeletal System	51-60	55.5	27.75%
Neuromuscular and Nervous Systems	44-50	47	23.5%
Cardiovascular and Pulmonary Systems	23-28	25.5	12.75%
Other Systems			
Integumentary System	9-12	10.5	5.25%
Metabolic and Endocrine Systems	5-7	6	3%
Gastrointestinal System	3-7	5	2.5%
Genitourinary System	4-7	5.5	2.75%
Lymphatic System	3-8	5.5	2.75%
System Interactions	8-12	10	5%
Non-Systems	**Questions (Range)**	**Midpoint (Questions)**	**Midpoint (Percentage)**
Equipment, Devices, and Technologies; Therapeutic Modalities			
Equipment, Devices, and Technologies	5-6	5.5	2.75%
Therapeutic Modalities	6-8	7	3.5%
Safety and Protection; Professional Responsibilities; Research			
Safety and Protection	5-6	5.5	2.75%
Professional Responsibilities	4-5	4.5	2.25%
Research and Evidence-Based Practice	3-5	4	2%

NPTE-PT — SYSTEM WEIGHTING

	QUESTIONS (RANGE)	MIDPOINT OF EXAM QUESTIONS
Musculoskeletal System	(51-60)	55.5
Neuromuscular and Nervous Systems	(44-50)	47
Cardiovascular and Pulmonary Systems	(23-28)	25.5
Other Systems	(32-53)	42.5
Non-Systems	(23-30)	26.5

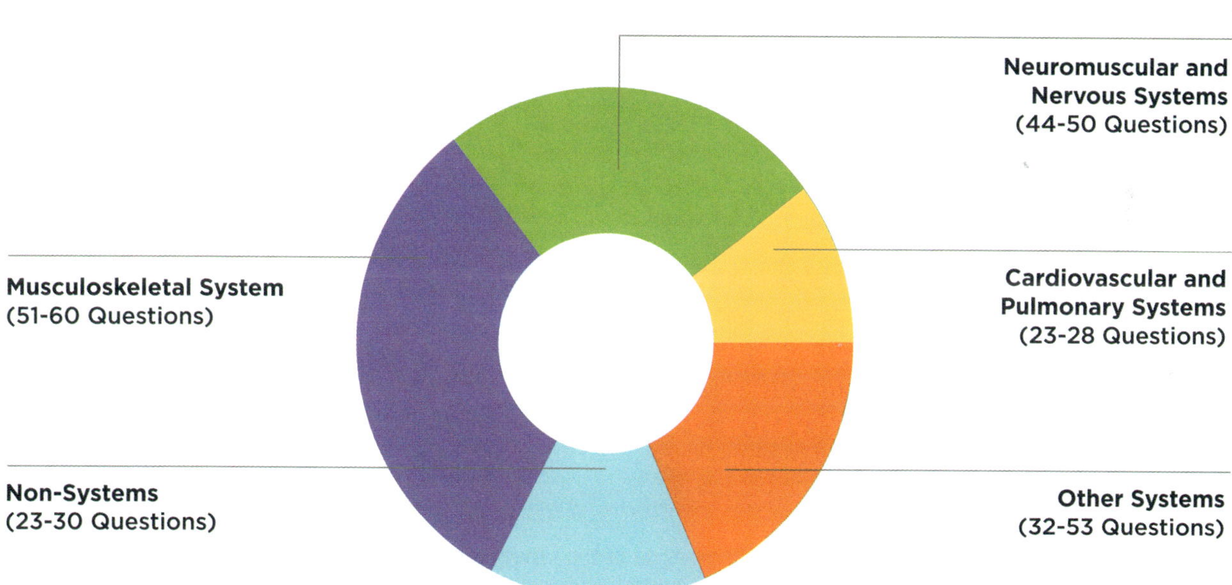

Musculoskeletal System

Midrange: 55.5 Questions (27.75%)

Physical Therapy Examination: This category refers to knowledge of the types and applications of musculoskeletal system tests/measures, including outcome measures, according to current best evidence, and their relevance to information collected from the history and systems review. The category includes the reaction of the musculoskeletal system to tests/measures and the mechanics of body movement as related to the musculoskeletal system. Information covered in these areas supports appropriate and effective patient/client management for rehabilitation, health promotion, and performance across the lifespan.

- Musculoskeletal system tests/measures, including outcome measures, and their applications according to current best evidence
- Anatomy and physiology of the musculoskeletal system as related to tests/measures
- Movement analysis as related to the musculoskeletal system
- Joint biomechanics and their applications

Foundations for Evaluation, Differential Diagnosis, and Prognosis: This category refers to the interpretation of knowledge about diseases/conditions of the musculoskeletal system, according to current best evidence, in order to support appropriate and effective patient/client management for rehabilitation, health promotion, and performance across the lifespan.

- Musculoskeletal system diseases/conditions and their pathophysiology to establish and carry out a plan of care, including prognosis
- Nonpharmacological medical management of the musculoskeletal system (e.g., diagnostic imaging, laboratory test values, other medical tests, surgical procedures)
- Pharmacological management of the musculoskeletal system
- Differential diagnoses related to diseases/conditions of the musculoskeletal system
- Connective tissue diseases/conditions and their pathophysiology to establish and carry out a plan of care, including prognosis
- Differential diagnoses related to diseases/conditions of the connective tissue

Interventions: This category refers to musculoskeletal system interventions (including types, applications, responses, and potential complications), according to current best evidence, as well as the impact on the musculoskeletal system of interventions performed on other systems in order to support appropriate and effective patient/client management for rehabilitation, health promotion, and performance across the lifespan.

- Musculoskeletal system physical therapy interventions and their applications for rehabilitation, health promotion, and performance according to current best evidence
- Anatomy and physiology of the musculoskeletal system as related to physical therapy interventions, daily activities, and environmental factors
- Adverse effects or complications on the musculoskeletal system from physical therapy interventions
- Adverse effects or complications on the musculoskeletal system from physical therapy interventions used on other systems

Neuromuscular and Nervous Systems

Midrange: 47 Questions (23.5%)

Physical Therapy Examination: This category refers to knowledge of the types and applications of neuromuscular and nervous systems tests/measures, including outcome measures, according to current best evidence, and their relevance to information collected from the history and systems review. The category includes the reaction of the neuromuscular and nervous systems to tests/measures and the mechanics of body movement as related to the neuromuscular and nervous systems. Information covered in these areas supports appropriate and effective patient/client management for rehabilitation, health promotion, and performance across the lifespan.

- Neuromuscular and nervous systems tests/measures, including outcome measures, and their applications according to current best evidence
- Anatomy and physiology of the neuromuscular and nervous systems as related to tests/measures
- Movement analysis as related to the neuromuscular and nervous systems

Foundations for Evaluation, Differential Diagnosis, and Prognosis: This category refers to the interpretation of knowledge about diseases/conditions of the neuromuscular and nervous systems, according to current best evidence, in order to support appropriate and effective patient/client management for rehabilitation, health promotion, and performance across the lifespan.

- Neuromuscular and nervous systems (CNS, PNS, ANS) diseases/conditions and their pathophysiology to establish and carry out a plan of care, including prognosis
- Nonpharmacological medical management of the neuromuscular and nervous systems (e.g., diagnostic imaging, laboratory test values, other medical tests, surgical procedures)
- Pharmacological management of the neuromuscular and nervous systems
- Differential diagnoses related to diseases/conditions of the neuromuscular and nervous systems (CNS, PNS, ANS)

Interventions: This category refers to neuromuscular/nervous systems interventions (including types, applications, responses, and potential complications), according to current best evidence, as well as the impact on the neuromuscular and nervous systems of interventions performed on other systems in order to support appropriate and effective patient/client management for rehabilitation, health promotion, and performance across the lifespan.

- Neuromuscular and nervous systems physical therapy interventions and their applications for rehabilitation, health promotion, and performance according to current best evidence
- Anatomy and physiology of the neuromuscular and nervous systems as related to physical therapy interventions, daily activities, and environmental factors
- Adverse effects or complications on the neuromuscular and nervous systems from physical therapy interventions
- Adverse effects or complications on the neuromuscular and nervous systems from physical therapy interventions used on other systems
- Motor control as related to neuromuscular and nervous systems physical therapy interventions
- Motor learning as related to neuromuscular and nervous systems physical therapy interventions

Cardiovascular and Pulmonary Systems

Midrange: 25.5 Questions (12.75%)

Physical Therapy Examination: This category refers to knowledge of the types and applications of cardiovascular and pulmonary systems tests/measures, including outcome measures, according to current best evidence, and their relevance to information collected from the history and systems review. The category includes the reaction of cardiovascular and pulmonary systems to tests/measures and the mechanics of body movement as related to the cardiovascular and pulmonary systems. Information covered in these areas supports appropriate and effective patient/client management for rehabilitation, health promotion, and performance across the lifespan.

- Cardiovascular and pulmonary tests/measures, including outcome measures, and their applications according to current best evidence
- Anatomy and physiology of the cardiovascular and pulmonary systems as related to tests/measures
- Movement analysis as related to the cardiovascular and pulmonary systems (e.g., rib cage excursion, breathing pattern)

Foundations for Evaluation, Differential Diagnosis, and Prognosis: This category refers to the interpretation of knowledge about diseases/conditions of the cardiovascular and pulmonary systems according to current best evidence, in order to support appropriate and effective patient/client management for rehabilitation, health promotion, and performance across the lifespan.

- Cardiovascular and pulmonary systems diseases/conditions and their pathophysiology to establish and carry out a plan of care, including prognosis
- Nonpharmacological medical management of the cardiovascular and pulmonary systems (e.g., diagnostic imaging, laboratory test values, other medical tests, surgical procedures)
- Pharmacological management of the cardiovascular and pulmonary systems
- Differential diagnoses related to diseases/conditions of the cardiovascular and pulmonary systems

Interventions: This category refers to cardiovascular and pulmonary systems interventions (including types, applications, responses, and potential complications) according to current best evidence, as well as the impact on the cardiovascular and pulmonary systems of interventions performed on other systems in order to support appropriate and effective patient/client management for rehabilitation, health promotion, and performance across the lifespan.

- Cardiovascular and pulmonary systems physical therapy interventions and their applications for rehabilitation, health promotion, and performance according to current best evidence
- Anatomy and physiology of the cardiovascular and pulmonary systems as related to physical therapy interventions, daily activities, and environmental factors
- Adverse effects or complications on the cardiovascular and pulmonary systems from physical therapy interventions
- Adverse effects or complications on the cardiovascular and pulmonary systems from physical therapy interventions used on other systems

Other Systems (overview)

Midrange: 42.5 Questions (21.25%)

The Other Systems category includes the Integumentary System, Metabolic and Endocrine Systems, Gastrointestinal System, Genitourinary System, Lymphatic System, and System Interactions.

OTHER SYSTEMS

	QUESTIONS (RANGE)	MIDPOINT OF EXAM QUESTIONS
Integumentary System	(9-12)	10.5
Metabolic and Endocrine Systems	(5-7)	6
Gastrointestinal System	(3-7)	5
Genitourinary System	(4-7)	5.5
Lymphatic System	(3-8)	5.5
System Interactions	(8-12)	10

Integumentary System

Midrange: 10.5 Questions (5.25%)

Physical Therapy Examination: This category refers to knowledge of the types and applications of integumentary system tests/measures, including outcome measures, according to current best evidence, and their relevance to information collected from the history and systems review. The category includes the reaction of the integumentary system to tests/measures and the mechanics of body movement as related to the integumentary system. Information covered in these areas supports appropriate and effective patient/client management for rehabilitation, health promotion, and performance across the lifespan.

- Integumentary system tests/measures, including outcome measures, and their applications according to current best evidence
- Anatomy and physiology of the integumentary system as related to tests/measures
- Movement analysis as related to the integumentary system (e.g., friction, shear, pressure, and scar mobility)

Foundations for Evaluation, Differential Diagnosis, and Prognosis: This category refers to the interpretation of knowledge about diseases/conditions of the integumentary system, according to current best evidence, in order to support appropriate and effective patient/client management for rehabilitation, health promotion, and performance across the lifespan.

- Integumentary system diseases/conditions and their pathophysiology to establish and carry out a plan of care, including prognosis
- Nonpharmacological medical management of the integumentary system (e.g., diagnostic imaging, laboratory test values, other medical tests, surgical procedures)
- Pharmacological management of the integumentary system
- Differential diagnoses related to diseases/conditions of the integumentary system

Interventions: This category refers to integumentary system interventions (including types, applications, responses, and potential complications), according to current best evidence, as well as the impact on the integumentary system of interventions performed on other systems in order to support appropriate and effective patient/client management for rehabilitation, health promotion, and performance across the lifespan.

- Integumentary system physical therapy interventions and their applications for rehabilitation, health promotion, and performance according to current best evidence
- Anatomy and physiology of the integumentary system as related to physical therapy interventions, daily activities, and environmental factors
- Adverse effects or complications on the integumentary system from physical therapy and medical/surgical interventions
- Adverse effects or complications on the integumentary system from physical therapy interventions used on other systems

Metabolic and Endocrine Systems

Midrange: 6 Questions (3%)

Foundations for Evaluation, Differential Diagnosis, and Prognosis: This category refers to the interpretation of knowledge about diseases/conditions of the metabolic and endocrine systems according to current best evidence, in order to support appropriate and effective patient/client management for rehabilitation, health promotion, and performance across the lifespan.

- Metabolic and endocrine systems diseases/conditions and their pathophysiology to establish and carry out a plan of care, including prognosis
- Nonpharmacological medical management of the metabolic and endocrine systems (e.g., diagnostic imaging, laboratory test values, other medical tests, surgical procedures)
- Pharmacological management of the metabolic and endocrine systems
- Differential diagnoses related to diseases/conditions of the metabolic and endocrine systems

Interventions: This category refers to metabolic and endocrine systems interventions (including types, applications, responses, and potential complications), according to current best evidence, as well as the impact on the metabolic and endocrine systems of interventions performed on other systems in order to support appropriate and effective patient/client management for rehabilitation, health promotion, and performance across the lifespan.

- Metabolic and endocrine systems physical therapy interventions and their applications for rehabilitation, health promotion, and performance according to current best evidence
- Anatomy and physiology of the metabolic and endocrine systems as related to physical therapy interventions, daily activities, and environmental factors
- Adverse effects or complications on the metabolic and endocrine systems from physical therapy interventions
- Adverse effects or complications on the metabolic and endocrine systems from physical therapy interventions used on other systems

Gastrointestinal System

Midrange: 5 Questions (2.5%)

Physical Therapy Examination: This category refers to knowledge of the types and applications of gastrointestinal system tests/measures, including outcome measures, according to current best evidence, and their relevance to information collected from the history and systems review. The category includes the reaction of the gastrointestinal system to tests/measures and the mechanics of body movement as related to the gastrointestinal system. Information covered in these areas supports appropriate and effective patient/client management for rehabilitation, health promotion, and performance across the lifespan.

- Gastrointestinal system tests/measures, including outcome measures, and their applications according to current best evidence (e.g., bowel dysfunction impact questionnaires, Murphy test, Rovsing test, McBurney's point sign)
- Anatomy and physiology of the gastrointestinal system as related to tests/measures
- Movement analysis as related to the gastrointestinal system (e.g., obturator, psoas, positioning for bowel movement)

Foundations for Evaluation, Differential Diagnosis, and Prognosis: This category refers to the interpretation of knowledge about diseases/conditions of the gastrointestinal system according to current best evidence, in order to support appropriate and effective patient/client management for rehabilitation, health promotion, and performance across the lifespan.

- Gastrointestinal system diseases/conditions and their pathophysiology to establish and carry out a plan of care, including prognosis
- Nonpharmacological medical management of the gastrointestinal system (e.g., diagnostic imaging, laboratory test values, other medical tests, surgical procedures)
- Pharmacological management of the gastrointestinal system
- Differential diagnoses related to diseases/conditions of the gastrointestinal system

Interventions: This category refers to gastrointestinal system interventions (including types, applications, responses, and potential complications), according to current best evidence, as well as the impact on the gastrointestinal system of interventions performed on other systems in order to support appropriate and effective patient/client management for rehabilitation, health promotion, and performance across the lifespan.

- Gastrointestinal system physical therapy interventions and their applications for rehabilitation, health promotion, and performance according to current best evidence (e.g., positioning for reflux prevention, bowel programs)
- Anatomy and physiology of the gastrointestinal system as related to physical therapy interventions, daily activities, and environmental factors
- Adverse effects or complications on the gastrointestinal system from physical therapy interventions
- Adverse effects or complications on the gastrointestinal system from physical therapy interventions used on other systems

Genitourinary System

Midrange: 5.5 Questions (2.75%)

Physical Therapy Examination: This category refers to knowledge of the types and applications of genitourinary system tests/measures, including outcome measures, according to current best evidence, and their relevance to information collected from the history and systems review. The category includes the reaction of the genitourinary system to tests/measures and the mechanics of body movement as related to the genitourinary system. Information covered in these areas supports appropriate and effective patient/client management for rehabilitation, health promotion, and performance across the lifespan.

- Genitourinary system tests/measures, including outcome measures, and their applications according to current best evidence
- Anatomy and physiology of the genitourinary system as related to tests/measures

Foundations for Evaluation, Differential Diagnosis, and Prognosis: This category refers to the interpretation of knowledge about diseases/conditions of the genitourinary system, according to current best evidence, in order to ensure appropriate and effective patient/client management for rehabilitation, health promotion, and performance across the lifespan.

- Genitourinary system diseases/conditions and their pathophysiology to establish and carry out a plan of care, including prognosis
- Nonpharmacological medical management of the genitourinary system (e.g., diagnostic imaging, laboratory test values, other medical tests, surgical procedures)
- Pharmacological management of the genitourinary system
- Differential diagnoses related to diseases/conditions of the genitourinary system

Interventions: This category refers to genitourinary system interventions (including types, applications, responses, and potential complications), according to current best evidence, as well as the impact on the genitourinary system of interventions performed on other systems in order to support appropriate and effective patient/client management for rehabilitation, health promotion, and performance across the lifespan.

- Genitourinary system physical therapy interventions and their applications for rehabilitation, health promotion, and performance according to current best evidence (e.g., bladder programs, biofeedback, pelvic floor retraining)
- Anatomy and physiology of the genitourinary system as related to physical therapy interventions, daily activities, and environmental factors
- Adverse effects or complications on the genitourinary system from physical therapy interventions
- Adverse effects or complications on the genitourinary system from physical therapy interventions used on other systems

Lymphatic System

Midrange: 5.5 Questions (2.75%)

Physical Therapy Examination: This category refers to knowledge of the types and applications of lymphatic system tests/measures, including outcome measures, according to current best evidence, and their relevance to information collected from the history and systems review. The category includes the reaction of the lymphatic system to tests/measures and the mechanics of body movement as related to the lymphatic system. Information covered in these areas supports appropriate and effective patient/client management for rehabilitation, health promotion, and performance across the lifespan.

- Lymphatic system tests/measures, including outcome measures, and their applications according to current best evidence
- Anatomy and physiology of the lymphatic system as related to tests/measures
- Movement analysis as related to the lymphatic system (e.g., posture, compensatory movement, extremity range of motion)

Foundations for Evaluation, Differential Diagnosis, and Prognosis: This category refers to the interpretation of knowledge about diseases/conditions of the lymphatic system according to current best evidence, in order to support appropriate and effective patient/client management for rehabilitation, health promotion, and performance across the lifespan.

- Lymphatic system diseases/conditions and their pathophysiology to establish and carry out a plan of care, including prognosis
- Nonpharmacological medical management of the lymphatic system (e.g., diagnostic imaging, laboratory test values, other medical tests, surgical procedures)
- Differential diagnoses related to diseases/conditions of the lymphatic system

Interventions: This category refers to lymphatic system interventions (including types, applications, responses, and potential complications), according to current best evidence, as well as the impact on the lymphatic system of interventions performed on other systems in order to support appropriate and effective patient/client management for rehabilitation, health promotion, and performance across the lifespan.

- Lymphatic system physical therapy interventions and their applications for rehabilitation, health promotion, and performance according to current best evidence
- Anatomy and physiology of the lymphatic system as related to interventions, daily activities, and environmental factors
- Adverse effects or complications on the lymphatic system from physical therapy interventions
- Adverse effects or complications on the lymphatic system from physical therapy interventions used on other systems

System Interactions

Midrange: 10 Questions (5%)

Foundations for Evaluation, Differential Diagnosis, and Prognosis: This category refers to the interpretation of knowledge about diseases/conditions involving system interactions according to current best evidence, in order to support appropriate and effective patient/client management for rehabilitation, health promotion, and performance across the lifespan.

- Diseases/conditions where the primary impact is on more than one system (e.g., cancer, multitrauma, sarcoidosis, autoimmune disorders, pregnancy) to establish and carry out a plan of care, including prognosis
- Nonpharmacological medical management of multiple systems (e.g., diagnostic imaging, other medical tests, surgical procedures)
- Pharmacological management of multiple systems, including polypharmacy
- Differential diagnoses related to diseases/conditions where the primary impact is on more than one system
- Impact of comorbidities/coexisting conditions on patient/client management (e.g., diabetes and hypertension; obesity and arthritis; dementia and hip fracture)
- Psychological and psychiatric conditions that impact patient/client management (e.g., grief, depression, schizophrenia)
- Dimensions of pain that impact patient/client management (e.g., psychological, social, physiological, neurological, mechanical)

Non-Systems

Equipment, Devices, and Technologies

Midrange: 5.5 Questions (2.75%)

This category refers to the different types of equipment, devices and technologies, use requirements, and/or contextual determinants, as well as any other influencing factors involved in the selection and application of equipment, devices, and technologies including consideration of current best evidence, in order to support appropriate and effective patient/client management for rehabilitation, health promotion, and performance across the lifespan.

- Assistive and adaptive devices/technologies (e.g., walkers, wheelchairs, adaptive seating systems and positioning devices, mechanical lifts)
- Prosthetic devices/technologies (e.g., lower extremity and upper extremity, microprocessor-controlled prosthetic devices)
- Protective, supportive, and orthotic devices/technologies (e.g., braces, helmets, taping, compression garments, serial casts, shoe inserts, splints, robotic exoskeleton)

Therapeutic Modalities

Midrange: 7 Questions (3.5%)

This category refers to the underlying principles for the use of therapeutic modalities as well as the justification for the selection and use of various types of therapeutic modalities, including consideration of current best evidence, in order to support appropriate and effective patient/client management for rehabilitation, health promotion, and performance across the lifespan.

- Thermal modalities
- Iontophoresis
- Electrotherapy modalities (e.g., neuromuscular electrical stimulation (NMES), transcutaneous electrical nerve stimulation (TENS), functional electrical stimulation (FES), interferential therapy, high-voltage pulsed current)
- Phonophoresis
- Ultrasound modalities
- Mechanical modalities (e.g., mechanical motion devices, traction devices)
- Biofeedback
- Intermittent compression

Safety and Protection

Midrange: 5.5 Questions (2.75%)

This category refers to the critical issues involved in patient/client safety and protection and the responsibilities of health-care providers to ensure that patient/client management and health-care decisions take place in a secure environment.

- Factors influencing safety and injury prevention (e.g., safe patient handling, fall prevention, equipment maintenance, environmental safety)
- Function, implications, and precautions related to intravenous lines, tubes, catheters, monitoring devices, and mechanical ventilators/oxygen delivery devices
- Emergency preparedness (e.g., CPR, first aid, disaster response)
- Infection control procedures (e.g., standard/universal precautions, isolation techniques, sterile technique)
- Signs/symptoms of physical, sexual, and psychological abuse and neglect

Professional Responsibilities

Midrange: 4.5 Questions (2.25%)

This category refers to the responsibilities of health-care providers to ensure that patient/client management and health-care decisions take place in a trustworthy environment.

- Standards of documentation
- Patient/client rights (e.g., ADA, IDEA, HIPAA, patient bill of rights)
- Human resource legal issues (e.g., OSHA, sexual harassment)
- Roles and responsibilities of the physical therapist, physical therapist assistant, other healthcare professionals, and support staff
- Standards of professional ethics
- Standards of billing, coding, and reimbursement
- Obligations for reporting illegal, unethical, or unprofessional behaviors (e.g., fraud, abuse, neglect)
- State and federal laws, rules, regulations, and industry standards set by state and accrediting bodies (e.g., state licensing entities, Joint Commission, CARF, CMS)
- Risk management and quality assurance (e.g., policies and procedures, incident reports, peer chart review)
- Cultural factors and/or characteristics that affect patient/client management (e.g., language differences, disability, ethnicity, customs, demographics, religion)
- Socioeconomic factors that affect patient/client management
- Health information technology (e.g., electronic medical records, telemedicine)

Research and Evidence-Based Practice

Midrange: 4 Questions (2%)

This category refers to the application of measurement principles and research methods to make reasoned and appropriate assessment and to the interpretation of information sources and practice research to support patient/client management decisions fundamental to evidence-based practice.

- Research methodology and interpretation (e.g., qualitative, quantitative, levels of evidence)
- Data collection techniques (e.g., surveys, direct observation)
- Measurement science (e.g., reliability, validity)
- Techniques for assessing evidence (e.g., peer-reviewed publications, scientific proceedings, guidelines, clinical prediction rules)
- Statistics (e.g., t-test, chi-square, correlation coefficient, ANOVA, likelihood ratio, effect size, confidence intervals)

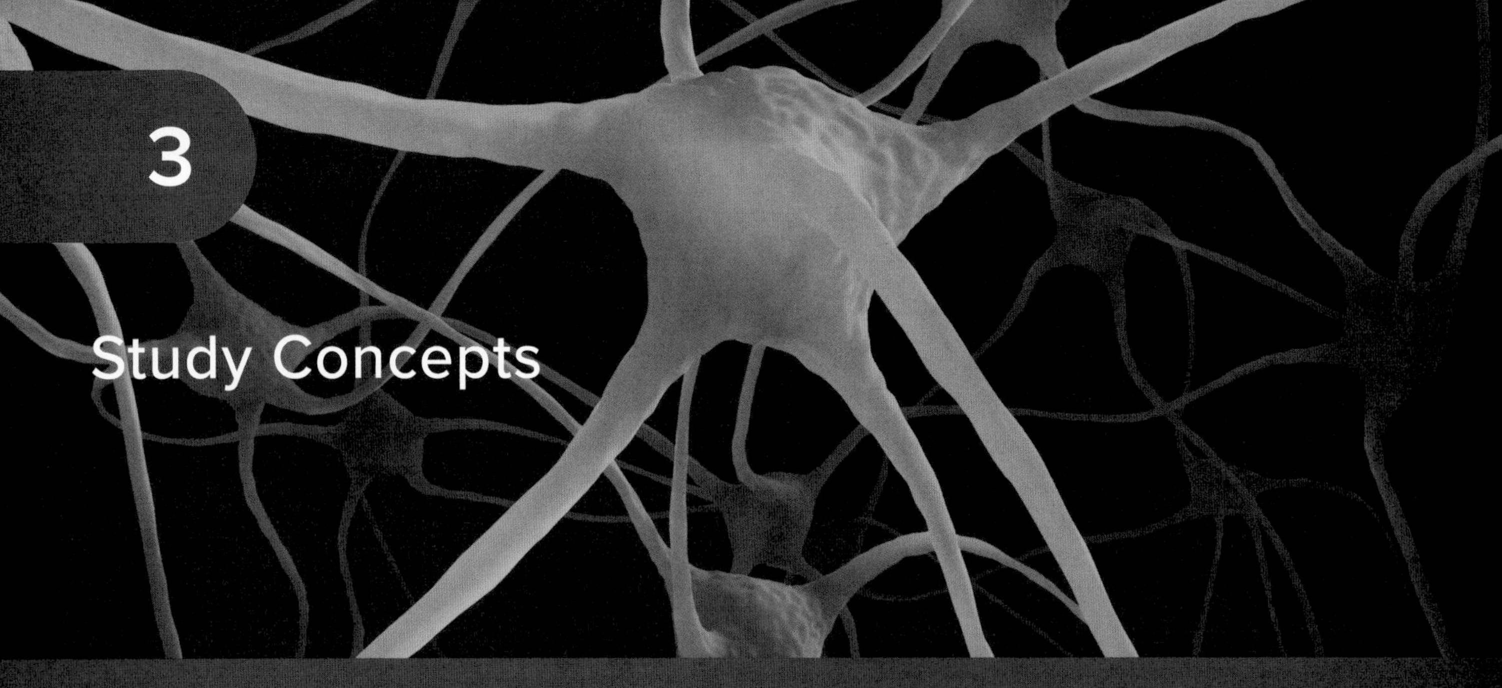

3

Study Concepts

Scott Giles

CHAPTER 3
Study Concepts

The inclusion of Study Concepts in ***PTEXAM: The Complete Study Guide*** serves to remind candidates that preparing for the NPTE-PT requires more than simply reviewing academic content and taking sample examinations.

Each of the presented Study Concepts provides candidates with an idea or concept to potentially integrate into their comprehensive study plan. For example, perhaps a candidate has a strong learning style preference where they tend to favor active learning over passive learning. To date, their study plan has consisted of purely passive activities such as reading the academic review section of a review book and reviewing class notes. Not surprisingly, the candidate has experienced a great deal of difficulty moving through the academic review and class notes and has serious doubts about how much of the material they have retained. In addition, the candidate finds they are unable to concentrate after approximately 90 minutes of studying and typically discontinues the study session at this point.

The presented Study Concept entitled "Learning Styles" offers a number of practical suggestions to assist candidates to identify their own unique learning style and to design study sessions to incorporate these preferences. Study plans that are designed to address decided learning preferences yield a much greater return on investment than generic study plans.

As a second example, consider the Study Concept entitled "Golden Rules." This item explores whether it is possible to develop specific rules that allow candidates to differentiate between two or more plausible options on multiple-choice questions used on the NPTE-PT. A potential rule would be something like the following: "When choosing between a number of acceptable interventions, always select the most conservative option in an effort to minimize any potential safety risk to the patient."

Potential rules like this are very tempting since they provide candidates with a means to make questions more objective and therefore less amorphous. The problem, however, is that the NPTE-PT is designed to assess a candidate's ability to make clinical decisions rather than to rely on memorization or simply apply a set of standardized rules. The Study Concept presents a variety of potential rules and walks candidates through a number of clinical scenarios demonstrating why rules are better used as only loose guidelines to consider when answering multiple-choice questions.

Study Concepts	
Study Concept 1	Learning Styles
Study Concept 2	Time Management
Study Concept 3	Levels of Knowledge and Understanding
Study Concept 4	Golden Rules
Study Concept 5	Automaticity
Study Concept 6	Truths and Myths
Study Concept 7	Blood Pressure
Study Concept 8	Lines, Tubes, and Equipment
Study Concept 9	Emergent Conditions
Study Concept 10	Assessment

In truth, many questions on the examination require candidates to make unique judgments based on the exact circumstances presented in the two to four sentences that make up the question stem. Candidates who develop the flexibility to apply clinical information in a wide variety of scenarios are well poised to be successful on the NPTE-PT.

Enjoy each of the presented Study Concepts and use the notes section to make observations of your present performance related to each of these unique topics.

Study Concept 1: Learning Styles

Studying for a comprehensive examination such as the NPTE-PT can be a significant challenge for any candidate. Given the volume of information required to be reviewed or relearned, it is critical for candidates to be as efficient as possible as they move through their established study plan. In order to maximize the efficiency of established study sessions, candidates should consider their preferred learning channels.

Perhaps the most critical question to answer relates to your preferred learning style for input and processing. Is your preferred learning style for input and processing more active or passive? Here is a brief description of each style that may assist you to label your individual preference.

ACTIVE LEARNING STYLE – when exposed to new material, a learner who likes to hear it, see it, say it, question it, interact with it, and then keep on doing this. Learners with this style tend to be multisensoral (visual, auditory, tactile/kinesthetic).

PASSIVE LEARNING STYLE – when exposed to new material, a learner who likes to hear it or read it and then keep on doing this. Learners with this style tend to determine the relationship to known material after input and before processing.

It is important to recognize that one learning style is not better than another, but each learning style can come with particular strengths and weaknesses. For example, a candidate who is active for both input and processing may be able to focus intently on the application and utility of ideas, however, may consider details boring and have a short attention span. Conversely, a candidate who is passive for both input and processing may be effective at sequential thinking and focusing on details, but may miss the "big picture."

Please recognize that an individual's learning style varies depending on the situation, however, it is equally important to recognize that most candidates have decided learning style preferences that when harnessed can result in greater efficiency of study sessions.

General Recommendations for Specific Learning Styles

Active learning style

Study sessions should consist of 60-90 minute sessions of interactive study. Study sessions should take place as frequently as possible. Group studying is recommended since multisensory stimulation is difficult to achieve alone. Learning tools should include items such as discussions, simulations, hands-on practice, and role playing.

Passive learning style

Study sessions should be two to three hours in length and focus on large pieces of material. Study sessions should take place three to five times per week. Group studying is recommended periodically with members who are application driven. Learning tools should include items such as lectures, briefings, observations, handouts, texts, and notes.

Awareness of one's learning style will not make an unqualified candidate qualified, however, it can significantly increase the rate of new learning, reviewing, and relearning. A well conceived study plan combined with an awareness of learning style is a powerful one-two combination that can pay significant dividends for candidates on the NPTE-PT.

Study Concept 2: Time Management

Physical therapy students by definition tend to have strong time management skills, however, these skills are severely tested when preparing for the NPTE-PT. The majority of students take the NPTE-PT shortly after graduation, which can be a very anxious and unsettled time. Candidates are often actively seeking employment or are attempting to adjust to a new job. They may have relocated to a different residence or perhaps moved to another part of the country.

The thought of preparing for an examination that represents a minimum of three years of graduate study makes it critical that available study time is spent in areas that will yield the highest return on investment. To illustrate this point, consider the relative systems weighting of the current examination.

System	Midpoint (percentage)
Musculoskeletal System	27.75%
Neuromuscular and Nervous Systems	23.5%
Cardiovascular and Pulmonary Systems	12.75%
Other Systems	21.25%
Non-Systems	13.25%

For example, on a typical examination a candidate will have between 51 and 60 Musculoskeletal system questions and between 23 and 28 Cardiovascular and Pulmonary systems questions. Given the relative weighting of these areas, a typical candidate should spend almost twice as much time studying musculoskeletal content than Cardiovascular and Pulmonary systems content. The actual percentage of time spent in each area may vary from candidate to candidate, but the relative weighting of the system on the examination should always remain an important variable to consider when determining the necessary breadth and depth in each area. Fortunately, there are a number of specific strategies candidates can utilize to ensure that they make meaningful progress in their study sessions.

Strategy: Master Study Schedule

Develop a master schedule for studying which emphasizes the relative weighting of the Systems and Non-Systems areas on the NPTE-PT.

Step One – Create a monthly calendar that identifies specific study days and the anticipated duration of each session.

Step Two – Allocate more frequent study sessions and therefore additional study time to systems that are more heavily weighted on the NPTE-PT.

Step Three – Integrate weekly activities that are designed to maintain a balance in life. These areas may address emotional, intellectual, physical, and social needs.

Step Four – Reassess your progress on a weekly basis and make any necessary changes to the master schedule.

PTEXAM: The Complete Study Guide offers a great deal of additional information on the NPTE-PT Blueprint. The blueprint specifies the relative weighting of the Systems and Non-Systems areas and introduces the Content Outline.

NOTES

Study Concept 3: Levels of Knowledge and Understanding

The NPTE-PT has evolved into an examination that requires candidates to demonstrate their ability to make clinical decisions rather than purely recall factual information. Candidates need to demonstrate solid didactic knowledge of entry-level physical therapy concepts, however, they also need to be able to apply the information in diverse clinical scenarios usually presented in multiple-choice questions of two to four sentences. Candidates who can effectively integrate physical therapy concepts into the various presented scenarios and make informed clinical decisions tend to perform strongly on the examination, while candidates who struggle with this skill tend to perform poorly.

When reviewing academic content, it is important that candidates familiarize themselves with the content at multiple levels of breadth and depth. The following table depicts a hierarchy of knowledge and understanding.

Typically, within a physical therapy academic program, students acquire the information in a hierarchical progression beginning with the lower cognitive levels (i.e., vocabulary level, literal level) and progress over time to higher cognitive levels (i.e., interpretive level, applied level). As candidates begin to prepare for the NPTE-PT, it is likely that the majority of candidates are comfortable at the vocabulary and literal level, however, there is far greater variability in comfort level at the interpretive and applied levels. Varying levels of comfort may result from exposure or lack thereof to specific subject matter on clinical education experiences or opportunities to develop competence with applied learning activities in the classroom. Regardless of where a candidate is on this spectrum, it is critical that candidates constantly challenge themselves to explore higher level cognitive knowledge as they progress through their academic review.

The presented hierarchy of knowledge and understanding can also be useful for candidates when answering multiple-choice questions. After reading the stem of a given examination question, it may be beneficial for candidates to ask themselves what the question is specifically asking. In this manner, candidates can ensure that their interpretation of the question is consistent with the intended meaning of each question. Failure to interpret the specific meaning of a question often results in a candidate selecting an incorrect response to a multiple-choice item. Test taking mistakes can be extremely harmful on the examination since once this occurs a candidate's examination score is no longer consistent with their true ability. As a candidate's score moves further away from their true ability there is a greater risk of failing the examination.

Applied Level: (How)
Process Analysis, Process Synthesis, Evaluation

Interpretive Level: (Why, When, Which)
Composition, Classification, Example of Purpose

Literal Level: (What, Where)
Characteristics, Background, Location, Function

Vocabulary Level: (Who, What, When)
Names, Definitions

NOTES

Study Concept 4: Golden Rules

We have all used certain rules to help us move through our education such as "I before E, except after C." When preparing for the NPTE-PT, candidates often look for similar rules that can assist them to make important distinctions between two or more plausible options to a given question. Unfortunately, these types of rules do not exist on the NPTE-PT since every question relies on the nuances of a particular scenario that is typically conveyed in two to four sentences. Perhaps this is best demonstrated by stating a possible rule and then providing several examples to explore the rule in more detail.

Hypothetical Golden Rule Number One: When confronted with a situation where patient safety is potentially compromised, always contact the referring physician.

RULE BUSTER: Candidates must be vigilant to identify and act on any potential threat to patient safety, but this does not mean that it is always necessary to contact the referring physician. In some cases, it would be appropriate for a physical therapist to minimize the threat to safety themselves. For example, consider the situation where a patient has a sudden and dramatic drop in their systolic blood pressure while working on vertical positioning. In this case, it may only be necessary for the physical therapist to lower the patient toward the horizontal; in other cases contact with the physician would undoubtedly be necessary.

NEW RULE: It depends.

Hypothetical Golden Rule Number Two: When choosing between a number of acceptable interventions, always select the most conservative option in an effort to minimize any potential safety risk to the patient.

RULE BUSTER: Patient safety is a critical component on the NPTE-PT, but in many cases, it is equally important to weigh the relative benefit of a selected option to achieving a desired patient outcome. How aggressive a therapist should be in a particular situation can only be determined after carefully weighing the relative risk versus the relative reward of each option. It is also important to recognize that all interventions have some degree of risk. If each of the available options to a given question offered no tangible difference in patient outcome, but were considered to be very different in terms of the relative degree of risk, it would then be sensible to select the safest or most conservative option.

NEW RULE: It depends.

Hypothetical Golden Rule Number Three: Physical therapist assistants should always contact the supervising physical therapist prior to changing any aspect of a patient's therapy session.

RULE BUSTER: Physical therapist assistants are licensed personnel in the vast majority of states and tend to have a fairly standardized list of acceptable work activities. Communication between a physical therapist and physical therapist assistant is strongly encouraged, however, in some instances, it may not always be necessary. For example, what about the case where a physical therapist assistant wants to change the sequence of resistive exercises or needs to increase or decrease a weight on an existing progressive resistive exercise? In this case, formal communication with the physical therapist would typically not be necessary since physical therapist assistants are able to engage in ongoing assessment. In other instances, formal communication would be necessary. For example, a physical therapist assistant may want to introduce a new intervention that falls outside the current established plan of care or perhaps identifies several findings that indicate a relevant change in a patient's medical status.

NEW RULE: It depends.

As you can see, the only safe rule to rely on is "it depends." Stated differently, the answer to a given question is always dependent on the specific terms and conditions presented in each clinical scenario. Candidates should attempt to inform future clinical decision making based on their experiences with previous sample examination items, but should avoid becoming inflexible or attempting to develop general rules that apply to all situations.

NOTES

Study Concept 5: Automaticity

On occasion, candidates attempt to complete an academic review by simply taking sample examinations and then reviewing and memorizing the correct answers. This strategy, although potentially helpful, is at best a scattered approach since the scope of the review is dependent solely on the questions asked.

For example, a given series of sample examinations may have a total of eight questions on ultrasound, but it is possible that the questions do not address necessary subject matter such as ultrasound using the underwater technique or explore important concepts such as beam nonuniformity ratio or effective radiating area. This example emphasizes the need for a thorough academic review which allows candidates access to the vast majority of didactic content potentially encountered on the NPTE-PT.

Consider another example dealing with accessibility standards such as a ramp. Most candidates would quickly recall that the ratio of rise:run is 1:12 or stated differently, each inch of rise requires a minimum of 12 inches of run. Although candidates are likely to be familiar with this concept, they may not be prepared to handle each of the various ways this concept could be tested on the NPTE-PT.

An examination item could require a candidate to:

- Determine the minimum length of a ramp after being given a specific height in inches or feet
- Determine the minimum height of a ramp after being given a specific length in inches or feet
- Determine if a ramp violates the minimum ADA requirements given a height and length in inches or feet
- Determine a given maximum percentage grade for a ramp (using rise:run formula)
- Determine if a ramp violates the maximum percentage grade given a height and length in inches or feet
- Determine the minimum length of a ramp in inches or feet given the need to safely traverse a height the equivalent of a given number of standard size steps

The examples illustrate both the need to be familiar with specific didactic content and the need to apply the information in different scenarios. In truth, each of the listed examination items related to ramps relies on the same basic formula (i.e., rise:run), but a candidate's ability to answer the question correctly will depend on their ability to recognize this and in some cases, utilize related information (i.e., the relationship of percentage grade to rise:run and the size of a standard step).

Candidates who have this skill are demonstrating automaticity. Automaticity is a test taking term that describes the ability to quickly recall relevant facts, procedures, and routines and apply this information within the context of a clinically-oriented multiple-choice question. As candidates become increasingly comfortable with the academic knowledge and the ability to apply the information via multiple-choice questions, they tend to score higher on sample examinations.

When reviewing completed sample examination items, candidates greatly benefit from considering other possible scenarios related to the same subject matter or topic being tested. In many cases, the incorrect options for a question are often correct for a variation of the question. For example, a question may ask specifically about the testing procedure for a given cranial nerve. In this case, a candidate may identify option 1 as being correct, but upon reviewing the question later may recognize that options 2, 3, and 4 are also correct for different cranial nerves. Given that there are literally thousands of potential questions that could be asked on the NPTE-PT, candidates who possess greater flexibility with particular subject matter have a greater probability of answering the item correctly.

NOTES

Study Concept 6: Truths and Myths

There are a variety of popular myths that exist in regard to the NPTE-PT. Most of the myths are simply misinformation that becomes perpetuated over time. The following section addresses some of the more common myths about the current examination and then sets the record straight.

TRUTHS AND MYTHS NUMBER ONE: The NPTE-PT has several different forms (i.e., versions), each which has a particular emphasis in terms of systems weighting. For example, a given form may emphasize the musculoskeletal system while another may emphasize the neuromuscular and nervous systems.

ANSWER: False

EXPLANATION: Each form of the NPTE-PT is designed based on the same blueprint. The blueprint provides a targeted number of items in each system and content outline area, however, slight variation is permitted in each area within a specified range. The Federation of State Boards of Physical Therapy publicly disseminates the blueprint that provides detailed information on the current examination.

TRUTHS AND MYTHS NUMBER TWO: When studying for the examination, it is critical to be familiar with multiple academic resources for a selected topic since a given question could require knowledge from a specific resource.

ANSWER: False

EXPLANATION: An examination question would not require a candidate to differentiate between multiple academic sources. For example, different academic resources sometimes have subtle differences in select subject matter such as dermatomes or temperature ranges for physical agents. Instead of focusing on this level of detail, a candidate should become comfortable with a given source and have confidence that if this information is encountered on the examination, their answer will be correct.

TRUTHS AND MYTHS NUMBER THREE: The 50 questions on the NPTE-PT that are considered pre-test items are clearly identifiable from scored items on the examination.

ANSWER: False

EXPLANATION: The 50 pre-test items are intermingled with 200 scored items to make up the 250 question NPTE-PT. The pre-test items are not distinguishable from scored items and exist in each of the five sections of the examination.

TRUTHS AND MYTHS NUMBER FOUR: Candidates have exactly one hour to complete each of the five sections of the NPTE-PT.

ANSWER: False

EXPLANATION: Candidates have a total of five sections, each with 50 questions, to complete on the NPTE-PT, however, they are not timed independently. The examination clock will begin at five hours and count down from this value regardless of the rate at which each of the sections is completed. The examination will conclude when the candidate submits their final section or when the five hours have elapsed.

TRUTHS AND MYTHS NUMBER FIVE: A score of 75% correct or 150 of 200 scored items is necessary to pass the NPTE-PT in most states.

ANSWER: False

EXPLANATION: Each form of the examination has an individual criterion-referenced passing score. The passing score may differ by a relatively small amount from form to form. If a particular form was determined to be slightly more difficult than another form, the more difficult form would have a slightly lower criterion-referenced passing score. Individual states do not have the ability to determine passing scores in their respective jurisdictions and instead rely on the established national criterion-referenced passing scores. Recently, criterion-referenced passing scores have been below 150 or 75% of the questions answered correctly.

TRUTHS AND MYTHS NUMBER SIX: Scores on subsequent attempts of sample examinations are good indicators of success on the NPTE-PT.

ANSWER: False

EXPLANATION: Scores on subsequent attempts of a given sample examination are usually better indicators of memory and less accurate as predictors of future performance. Candidates should always review correct and incorrect answers from a given sample examination, however, they should resist the urge to retake the same examination for the purpose of assessing performance.

Study Concept 7: Blood Pressure

Vital signs serve as an important screening tool for physical therapists and should be formally measured for all examinations and then periodically thereafter based on the particular medical diagnosis and specific physical therapy interventions. Given the obvious safety implications associated with measuring and interpreting the results of vital signs, it is critical that candidates have in-depth knowledge of this particular content. This section will present a variety of detailed information related to blood pressure.

- Systolic pressure measures the force exerted against the arteries during the ejection cycle, while diastolic pressure measures the force exerted against the arteries during rest.
- Blood pressure is directly related to cardiac output and peripheral vascular resistance and therefore is an effective non-invasive performance measure of the pumping mechanism of the heart.
- Systolic pressure increases with exertion in a linear progression, often at a rate of 8-12 mm Hg per metabolic equivalent, however, with sustained activity, no further increases typically occur. If systolic pressure does not rise with increasing workload, it may indicate that the functional reserve capacity of the heart has been exceeded.
- Diastolic pressure may increase or decrease a maximum of 10 mm Hg due to adaptive dilation of peripheral vasculature. In a typical clinical setting, the exercise session should be terminated if the systolic pressure exceeds 210 mm Hg or if the diastolic pressure exceeds 110 mm Hg.
- Pulse pressure, which is the difference between systolic and diastolic pressure, generally increases in direct proportion to the intensity of exercise since systolic pressure increases with exercise and diastolic pressure tends to stay the same. In a healthy adult it is common to see a 40-50 mm Hg change in systolic pressure with intense exercise. Excessive pulse pressure may be indicative of stiffening of the aorta secondary to atherosclerosis.
- Normally, systolic blood pressure in the legs is 10-20% higher than the pressure in the arms (brachial artery). This is why in some cases an ankle-brachial index value of greater than 1.0 is still considered to be normal. Blood pressure readings that are lower in the legs as compared to the arms are abnormal and may be indicative of peripheral vascular disease.
- Blood pressure increases during dynamic resistance exercise, such as free weights, machines or isokinetics, and continues to increase as an exercise set progresses. Blood pressure response is higher during weight training that incorporates a concentric and eccentric phase compared to isokinetic exercise. Blood pressure tends to be higher during the concentric phase of the repetition or when the Valsalva maneuver is used.
- With advancing age, the same amount of blood fills the ventricles, but the pumping mechanism is less effective. As a result, the body compensates by increasing blood pressure in an attempt to maintain homeostasis.
- During exercise testing, a systolic blood pressure that fails to increase or decrease with increasing workloads may signal a plateau or decrease in cardiac output.
- Systolic blood pressure normally decreases promptly with the cessation of exercise. As a general guideline, the three-minute post exercise systolic blood pressure should be less than 90% of the systolic blood pressure at peak exercise.

NOTES

Study Concept 8: Lines, Tubes, and Equipment

The NPTE-PT is designed to protect consumers from unqualified practitioners. Given the purpose of the examination, it is inevitable that candidates will encounter a variety of questions that deal with patients with a significantly compromised medical status.

This section presents information on various types of lines, tubes, and equipment. The purpose is to remind physical therapists of some of the more critical elements to consider when treating patients using these devices. Please remember that this is not an all-inclusive list and additional detail will be provided on the vast majority of items throughout **PTEXAM: The Complete Study Guide.**

Lines

Arterial Lines (A Line)

- Avoid applying a blood pressure cuff above the infusion site
- Grasp the IV line support pole so the infusion site is at heart level
- Avoid activities that require the infusion site to be above the level of the heart for a prolonged period
- Exercise is possible with the line, but avoid disturbing the apparatus

Swan-Ganz Catheters (Pulmonary Artery Catheters), Central Venous Pressure Catheters, Indwelling Right Atrial Catheters

- Exercise is possible with the line, but mobility may need to be restricted near the catheter insertion

Total Parenteral Nutrition, Hyperalimentation Devices (Intravenous Feeding)

- Alarm sound indicates the fluid source is empty or the system has become unbalanced
- Disruption or disconnection may result in an air embolus
- Shoulder motion on the side of the infusion site may be restricted primarily in flexion and abduction
- Exercise is possible with the line, but mobility may need to be restricted near the catheter insertion

Intracranial Monitoring

- Isometric exercise and the Valsalva maneuver should be avoided since these activities increase intracranial pressure
- Avoid neck flexion, hip flexion greater than 90 degrees, and lying down in a prone position
- Venous drainage is maximal with the head of the bed elevated 30 degrees
- Momentary elevation of intracranial pressure is normal, but sustained increases are not and therefore should be reported

Tubes

Nasogastric Tube (NG Tube)

- Patient will not be able to eat food or drink fluids by mouth while the nasogastric tube is in place
- Enteral feedings can be disconnected temporarily for mobility
- Exercise requiring movements of the head and neck should be avoided, especially forward bending

Gastrostomy Tube (G Tube)

- Distal tubing can inadvertently become caught on items such as furniture and be pulled out
- Enteral feedings should be turned off temporarily prior to and during treatment
- Enteral feedings can be disconnected temporarily for mobility

Urinary Catheters

- Tubes should be placed below the region being drained since the devices rely on gravity
- The collection bag should not be raised above the level of the bladder for any sustained period
- Avoid disrupting, stretching, disconnecting or occluding the tube during exercise

Chest Tubes

- When ambulating, collection bottles should be kept below the level of the inserted tube location
- Monitor the patient for changes in breath sounds before and after intervention
- Avoid pressing directly on the chest tube during mobility activities

Equipment

Mechanical Ventilation

- Alarm may indicate disconnected tube, coughing or change in respiratory pattern
- Develop nonverbal means of communication with the patient
- Patient is at greater risk for developing contractures, skin ulcers, and deconditioning

Supplemental Oxygen Delivery System

- Be aware of signs of respiratory distress (i.e., dyspnea, cyanosis, cramping)
- Monitor SaO_2, PaO_2, and hemodynamics prior to, during, and after physical therapy intervention
- Exercise is possible, but avoid disturbing the tubing

Study Concept 9: Emergent Conditions

According to the Federation of State Boards of Physical Therapy, the NPTE-PT is designed to assess basic entry-level competence of the licensure candidate who has graduated from an accredited program. The primary purpose of the examination is therefore to protect the public from unqualified practitioners. Given the purpose of the examination, it is reasonable to expect that a high percentage of examination items will deal with safety-related issues including the identification and management of potentially emergent conditions. When encountering this type of question, it is critical that candidates are armed with the necessary knowledge to make informed clinical decisions.

The following provides relevant information on three commonly encountered emergent conditions.

Pulmonary Embolism

DESCRIPTION: A blockage of the pulmonary artery or one of its branches, usually precipitated by a blood clot from a vein (venous thrombus) becoming dislodged from its site of formation. The dislodged blood clot then travels to the arterial blood supply of one of the lungs.

CLINICAL PRESENTATION: Difficulty breathing, chest pain that often mimics a heart attack, rapid pulse; in more severe cases circulatory instability and death

RISK FACTORS: Surgery, long periods of inactivity, increased levels of clotting factor in the blood, and abnormal factors in the vessel wall

DIAGNOSIS: Pulmonary angiography is the most accurate method to diagnose pulmonary embolism, however, because the procedure carries inherent risks to the patient, other diagnostic procedures such as chest x-ray, lung scan, and spiral computerized tomography scan are more commonly utilized.

TREATMENT: Anticoagulant medication such as Heparin and Warfarin

NOTES: Pulmonary embolism remains the leading cause of hospital death in the United States.

Hypovolemic Shock

DESCRIPTION: A life-threatening condition caused by insufficient circulating blood volume. Primary causes include hemorrhage or severe burns.

CLINICAL PRESENTATION: Hypotension due to lack of circulating volume, anxiety, altered mental state, cool and clammy skin, rapid and thready pulse, thirst, and fatigue due to inadequate oxygenation

RISK FACTORS: Exposure to severe trauma or burns

DIAGNOSIS: Primarily through the identification of the described clinical presentation

TREATMENT: Management of suspected shock includes activating the emergency medical system. Positional management includes lying in supine with the legs elevated approximately 12 inches in situations where it is tolerated. Management of confirmed shock includes controlling bleeding and attempting to restore blood volume by providing infusions of balanced salt solutions or blood in more severe cases.

NOTES: There are several other common forms of shock including cardiogenic, septic, and anaphylactic. Cardiogenic shock is characterized by failure of the heart to pump effectively. Management includes oxygen therapy and administering cardiac medications. Septic shock is characterized by an overwhelming infection leading to vasodilation. Management includes restoring intravascular volume and identifying and controlling the source of infection. Anaphylactic shock is characterized by a severe and sometimes fatal reaction to an allergen, antigen or drug which causes vasodilation leading to hypotension and increased capillary permeability. Management includes identifying and removing the causative antigen and administering counter-mediators such as anti-histamine.

Autonomic Dysreflexia

DESCRIPTION: A massive sympathetic discharge that can occur in association with a spinal cord injury or disease. The condition is triggered by a variety of noxious stimuli including bladder distention, urinary tract infection, skin ulcers, and bowel impaction.

CLINICAL PRESENTATION: Sweating above the level of the lesion, flushing of the skin above the level of the lesion, elevated blood pressure, and blurred vision

RISK FACTORS: Patients with spinal cord injuries at and above the T6 level

DIAGNOSIS: Primarily through the identification of the described clinical presentation

TREATMENT: Management of autonomic dysreflexia includes immediate determination and removal of the triggering stimuli. Positional management includes sitting the patient upright to lower the elevated blood pressure below dangerous levels. Tight clothing and stockings should also be removed. If the noxious stimuli cannot be identified, medical management may include vasodilators to assist with symptomatic relief.

NOTES: Prevalence rates for autonomic dysreflexia demonstrate that the majority of patients with spinal cord injuries at T6 and above will experience this condition. The occurrence of autonomic dysreflexia is increased as an individual moves out of spinal shock.

Study Concept 10: Assessment

Candidates must carefully assess their examination performance when taking sample examinations. Each of the sample examinations in **PTEXAM: The Complete Study Guide** offers candidates the opportunity to view their performance according to five system and five content outline categories. The shaded areas in the tables below will be used in the performance analysis section to express the number of questions answered correctly in each category, the total number of questions in the category, and the percentage of questions correct.

System Specific Summary	
Musculoskeletal System	
Neuromuscular and Nervous Systems	
Cardiovascular and Pulmonary Systems	
Other Systems	
Non-Systems	

Content Outline Summary	
Physical Therapy Examination	
Foundations for Evaluation, Differential Diagnosis, and Prognosis	
Interventions	
Equipment, Devices, and Technologies; Therapeutic Modalities	
Safety and Protection; Professional Responsibilities; Research	

Candidates should use this information to develop remedial plans to improve performance on sample examinations. Candidates must be familiar with the content contained in each system specific and content outline category and carefully assess how their performance changes over time.

The academic review section of **PTEXAM: The Complete Study Guide** is arranged according to the exact categories used in the system specific summary and therefore serves as an excellent resource for candidates to utilize when initially remediating deficient areas. In some instances, a candidate may determine that it is necessary to access a more formal academic resource such as a textbook to locate information not covered in the review book. In these situations it is important for candidates to stay focused and avoid purely exploring the textbook since often candidates do not emerge for several hours.

The content outline is less intuitive than the system categories since the content outline is not system based, however, it is still very useful given the detailed information available on the NPTE-PT Blueprint. For example, a candidate may find that they tend to perform very well on questions within the "Physical Therapy Examination" category, but have more difficulty on questions within the "Foundations for Evaluation, Differential Diagnosis, and Prognosis" category. By consulting the NPTE-PT Blueprint, a candidate will quickly realize that the "Physical Therapy Examination" category deals primarily with tests and measures, anatomy and physiology, and movement analysis, while the "Foundations for Evaluation, Differential Diagnosis, and Prognosis" category deals primarily with diseases/conditions, pathophysiology, and differential diagnosis. The information from the content outline combined with the system information allows candidates to gain greater insight toward their current performance and should assist them to be more specific when selecting appropriate remedial activities.

Candidates are encouraged to look for general trends in their scoring when taking sample examinations and avoid making a definitive statement on their level of competence in any given category based on the results of a single sample examination. This is especially true in a category where there is a smaller number of questions. As the number of questions in each category diminishes, the category becomes less accurate as a predictor of actual performance. In some instances, candidates will have a few glaring areas of deficiency (e.g., "Musculoskeletal" and "Other Systems"), while in other cases, candidates will demonstrate more consistency. Consistency can be a very good thing if the scores are consistent at a very high level (i.e., a high percentage of questions answered correctly in the majority of areas) or more problematic if the scores are consistent at a very low level (i.e., a low percentage of questions answered correctly in the majority of areas).

In summary, studying for the examination is analogous to developing a plan of care for a patient; the more specific the plan of care is for the particular needs of the patient, the better the patient outcome. In terms of preparing for the examination, the more specific a remedial plan is to the particular needs of a given candidate, the better the candidate's outcome.

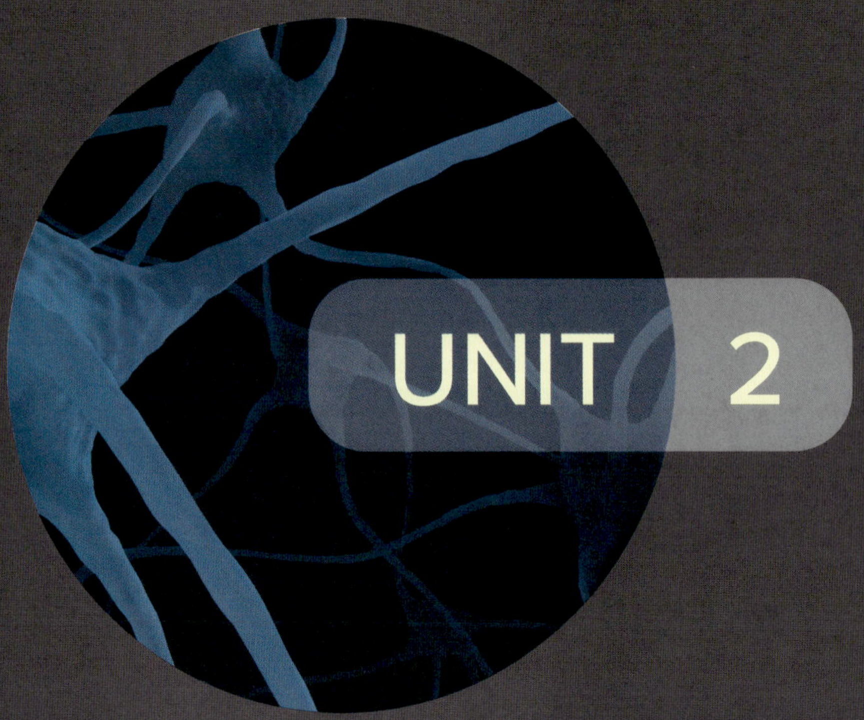

UNIT 2

Academic Review

Academic Review

The academic review section of **PTEXAM: The Complete Study Guide** provides candidates with a method to review essential didactic information from a physical therapy curriculum. Mastery of this core academic information can significantly increase candidates' scores on the NPTE-PT.

Each Chapter of the academic review will have unique elements.

Spotlight on Safety

Spotlight on Safety provides candidates with critical safety information related to relevant physical therapy topics. This information is essential on a licensing examination where the ultimate priority is safe and effective patient care.

Consider This

Consider This offers candidates valuable application driven information related to selected academic content. Candidates use this essential information to increase the breadth and depth of their content knowledge.

Motivational Moments

Even with the fantastic design of the academic review section there will be periods of time when a candidate's focus begins to drift and efficiency precipitously declines. To combat this tendency, we periodically insert Motivational Moments into the academic review. These lighthearted breaks allow candidates to look to the future as a licensed physical therapist or perhaps just chuckle or grin!

Essentials

The Essentials section located at the end of each unit provides a summary of critical topics for candidates to reflect on. Ensuring mastery of this material allows candidates to stay focused on big ticket items and provides a valuable repetition loop to commit information to long term memory.

Proficiencies

The proficiencies provide students with an opportunity to determine their competency in a variety of academic areas. The proficiency activities include image identification, matching, sequencing, and fill in the blank. Candidates should carefully assess their proficiency results and use the information to direct remedial activities.

Clinical Application Templates

Clinical Application Templates (CATs) explore the patient/client management for a wide variety of medical conditions. By utilizing CATS candidates can broaden their experience base and as a result be better prepared to answer examination questions.

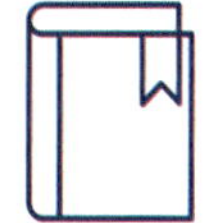

References

The references provide information on the specific resources used to construct the academic review. Scorebuilders uses a wide variety of resources to ensure that the academic review is consistent with current clinical practice.

4

Musculoskeletal System

Scott Giles

Musculoskeletal System represents approximately 51 – 60 questions (25.5% – 30%) of the NPTE-PT.

Contributors

Shawn Paquette
Daniel Lee

CHAPTER 4
Musculoskeletal System

Exercise Physiology

Energy Systems[1]

ATP-PC or Phosphagen System

Anaerobic Glycolysis or Lactic Acid System

Aerobic or Oxygen System

Anaerobic Metabolism

ATP-PC System

This energy system is used for ATP production during high intensity, short duration exercise such as sprinting 100 meters. Phosphocreatine decomposes and releases a large amount of energy that is used to construct ATP. There is two to three times more phosphocreatine in cells of muscles than ATP. This process occurs almost instantaneously, allowing for ready and available energy needed by the muscles. The system provides energy for muscle contraction for up to 15 seconds.

The phosphagen system represents the most rapidly available source of ATP for use by the muscle. The energy system is able to function in the described manner since:

- It does not depend on a long series of chemical reactions.
- It does not depend on transporting the oxygen we breathe to the working muscles.
- Both ATP and PC are stored directly within the contractile mechanisms of the muscle.

Anaerobic Glycolysis

This energy system is a major supplier of ATP during high intensity, short duration activities such as sprinting 400 or 800 meters. Stored glycogen is split into glucose, and through glycolysis, split again into pyruvic acid. The energy released during this process forms ATP. The process does not require oxygen. Anaerobic glycolysis results in the formation of lactic acid, which causes muscular fatigue.

This system is nearly 50% slower than the phosphocreatine system and can provide a person with 30 to 40 seconds of muscle contraction. The energy system is able to function in the described manner since:

- It does not require the presence of oxygen.
- It only uses carbohydrates (glycogen and glucose).
- It releases enough energy for the resynthesis of only small amounts of ATP.

Aerobic Metabolism

The aerobic system is used predominantly during low intensity, long duration exercise such as running a marathon. The oxygen system yields by far the most ATP, but it requires several series of complex chemical reactions. This system provides energy through the oxidation of food. The combination of fatty acids, amino acids, and glucose with oxygen releases energy that forms ATP. This system will provide energy as long as there are nutrients to utilize.

Kinesiology

Anatomical Position[2,3]

The anatomical position is an erect posture of the body with the face forward, feet pointing forward and slightly apart, arms at the side, and palms forward with fingers and thumbs in extension (Figs. 4-1, 4-2). The position serves as a point of reference for definitions and descriptions of movement including the cardinal planes and associated axes.

Planes of the Body[3,4]

Motions are described as occurring in three cardinal planes of the body (frontal, sagittal, transverse). Movement in the cardinal planes occurs around three corresponding axes (anterior-posterior, medial-lateral, vertical).

Frontal plane (coronal)

The frontal (or coronal) plane divides the body into anterior and posterior sections. Motions in the frontal plane, such as abduction and adduction, occur around an anterior-posterior axis.

Sagittal plane

The sagittal plane divides the body into right and left sections. Motions in the sagittal plane, such as flexion and extension, occur around a medial-lateral axis.

Transverse plane

The transverse plane divides the body into upper and lower sections. Motions in the transverse plane, such as medial and lateral rotation, occur around a vertical axis.

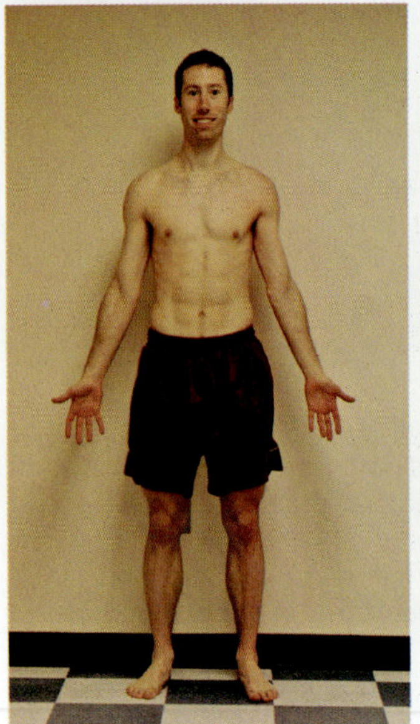

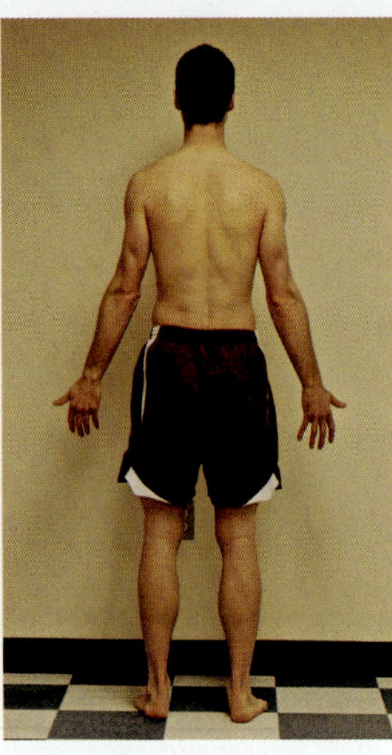

Fig. 4-1 (Left): Anatomical position - anterior view.
Fig. 4-2 (Right): Anatomical position - posterior view.

Classes of Levers[4]

Class 1 Lever

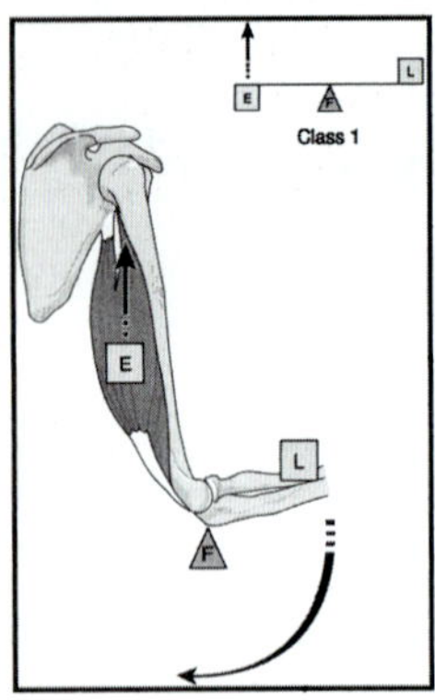

A class 1 lever has the axis of rotation (fulcrum) between the effort (force) and resistance (load). There are very few class 1 levers in the body. A class 1 lever is illustrated with the triceps brachii force on the olecranon with an external counterforce pushing on the forearm. Another example of a class 1 lever is a seesaw.

Class 2 Lever

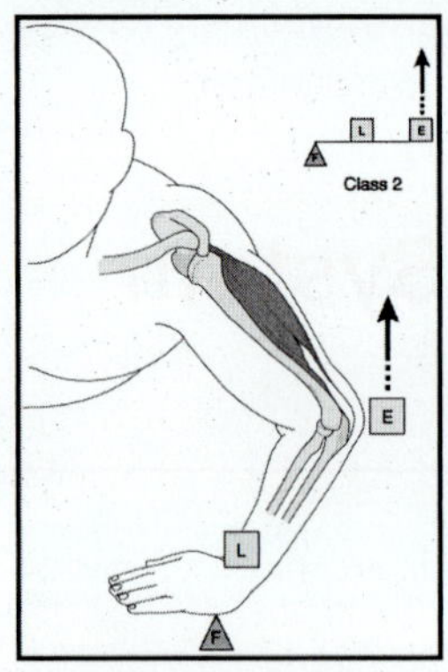

A class 2 lever has the resistance (load) between the axis of rotation (fulcrum) and the effort (force). The length of the effort arm is always longer than the resistance arm. In most instances, gravity is the effort and muscle activity is the resistance, however, there are class 2 levers where the muscle is the effort when the distal attachment is on a weight bearing segment. An example of a class 2 lever is a wheelbarrow.

Class 3 Lever

A class 3 lever has the effort (force) between the axis of rotation (fulcrum) and the resistance (load). The length of the effort arm is always shorter than the length of the resistance arm. Shoulder abduction with weight at the wrist is a class 3 lever. Class 3 levers usually permit large movements at rapid speeds and are the most common type of lever in the body. An example of a class 3 lever is elbow flexion.

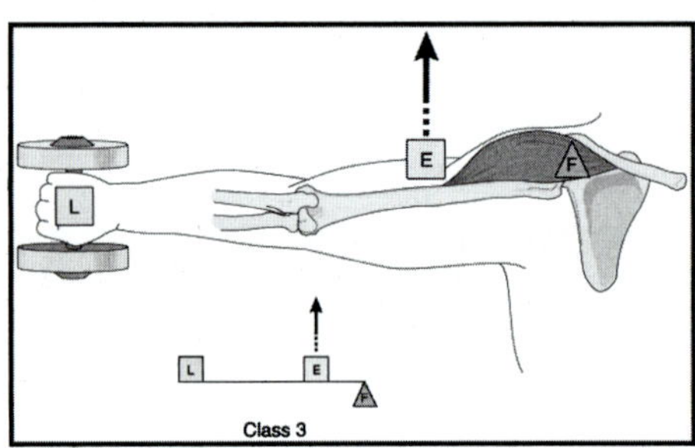

Joint Classification[4,5,6]

Fibrous Joints (Synarthroses)

Fibrous joints are composed of bones that are united by fibrous tissue and are nonsynovial. Movement is minimal to none with the amount of movement permitted at the joint dependent on the length of the fibers uniting the bones.

Suture - (e.g., sagittal suture of the skull)

- Union of two bones by a ligament or membrane
- Immovable joint
- Eventual fusion is termed synostosis

Syndesmosis - (e.g., the tibia and fibula with interosseous membrane)

- Bone connected to bone by a dense fibrous membrane or cord
- Very little motion

Gomphosis - (e.g., a tooth in its socket)

- Two bony surfaces connect as a peg in a hole
- The teeth and corresponding sockets in the mandible/maxilla are the only gomphosis joints in the body
- The periodontal membrane is the fibrous component of the joint

Cartilaginous Joints (Amphiarthroses)

Cartilaginous joints have hyaline cartilage or fibrocartilage that connects one bone to another. These are slightly moveable joints.

Synchondrosis - (e.g., sternum and true rib articulation)

- Hyaline cartilage
- Cartilage adjoins two ossifying centers of bone

- Provides stability during growth
- May ossify to a synostosis once growth is completed
- Slight motion

Symphysis – (e.g., pubic symphysis)

- Generally located at the midline of the body
- Two bones covered with hyaline cartilage
- Two bones connected by fibrocartilage
- Slight motion

Synovial Joints (Diarthroses)

Synovial joints provide free movement between the bones they join. They have five distinguishing characteristics: joint cavity, articular cartilage, synovial membrane, synovial fluid, and fibrous capsule. These joints are the most complex and vulnerable to injury.

They are further classified by the type of movement and shape of the articulating bones.

Uniaxial joint – one motion around a single axis in one plane of the body

- Hinge (ginglymus) – elbow joint
- Pivot (trochoid) – atlantoaxial joint

Biaxial joint – movement occurs in two planes and around two axes through the convex/concave surfaces

- Condyloid – metacarpophalangeal joint of a finger
- Saddle – carpometacarpal joint of the thumb

Multi-axial joint – movement occurs in three planes and around three axes

- Plane (gliding) – carpal joints
- Ball and socket – hip joint

Joint Receptors[1,4]

Free Nerve Endings

Location	Joint capsule, ligaments, synovium, fat pads
Sensitivity	One type is sensitive to non-noxious mechanical stress; other type is sensitive to noxious mechanical or biochemical stimuli
Primary Distribution	All joints

Golgi Ligament Endings

Location	Ligaments, adjacent to ligaments' bony attachment
Sensitivity	Tension or stretch on ligaments
Primary Distribution	Majority of joints

Golgi-Mazzoni Corpuscles

Location	Joint capsule
Sensitivity	Compression of joint capsule
Primary Distribution	Knee joint, joint capsule

Pacinian Corpuscles

Location	Fibrous layer of joint capsule
Sensitivity	High frequency vibration, acceleration, and high velocity changes in joint position
Primary Distribution	All joints

Ruffini Endings

Location	Fibrous layer of joint capsule
Sensitivity	Stretching of joint capsule; amplitude and velocity of joint position
Primary Distribution	Greater density in proximal joints, particularly in capsular regions

Muscle Physiology[5,6]

Classification of Muscle Fibers	
Type I	**Type II**
Aerobic	Anaerobic
Red	Red/White*
Tonic	Phasic
Slow twitch	Fast twitch
Slow-oxidative	Fast-glycolytic

* Type IIa muscle fibers appear red, while Type IIb muscle fibers appear white

Functional Characteristics of Muscle Fibers	
Type I	**Type II**
Low fatigability	High fatigability
High capillary density	Low capillary density
High myoglobin content	Low myoglobin content
Smaller fibers	Larger fibers
Extensive blood supply	Less blood supply
Large amount of mitochondria	Fewer mitochondria
Examples: marathon, swimming	Examples: high jump, sprinting

Muscle Receptors[6,7]

Muscle Spindle

Muscle spindles are distributed throughout the belly of the muscle. They function to send information to the nervous system about muscle length and/or the rate of change of its length. The muscle spindle is important in the control of posture, and with the help of the gamma system, involuntary movements.

Golgi Tendon Organ

Golgi tendon organs are encapsulated sensory receptors through which the muscle tendons pass immediately beyond their attachment to the muscle fibers. They are very sensitive to tension, especially when produced from an active muscle contraction. They function to transmit information about tension or the rate of change of tension within the muscle.

An average of 10-15 muscle fibers are usually connected in series with each Golgi tendon organ. The Golgi tendon organ is stimulated through the tension produced by muscle fibers. Golgi tendon organs provide the nervous system with instantaneous information on the degree of tension in each small muscle segment.

Muscle Action

Head

Temporomandibular Joint

Depress
- Lateral pterygoid
- Suprahyoid
- Infrahyoid

Elevate
- Temporalis
- Masseter
- Medial pterygoid

Protrusion
- Masseter
- Lateral pterygoid
- Medial pterygoid

Retrusion
- Temporalis
- Masseter
- Digastric

Side to Side
- Medial pterygoid
- Lateral pterygoid
- Masseter
- Temporalis

Spine

Cervical Intervertebral Joints

Flexion
- Sternocleidomastoid
- Longus colli
- Scalenus muscles

Extension
- Splenius cervicis
- Semispinalis cervicis
- Iliocostalis cervicis
- Longissimus cervicis
- Multifidus
- Trapezius

Rotation and Lateral Bending
- Sternocleidomastoid
- Scalenus muscles
- Splenius cervicis
- Longissimus cervicis
- Iliocostalis cervicis
- Levator scapulae
- Multifidus

Thoracic and Lumbar Intervertebral Joints

Flexion
- Rectus abdominis
- Internal oblique
- External oblique

Extension
- Erector spinae
- Quadratus lumborum
- Multifidus

Rotation and Lateral Bending
- Psoas major
- Quadratus lumborum
- External oblique
- Internal oblique
- Multifidus
- Longissimus thoracis
- Iliocostalis thoracis
- Rotatores

Upper Extremity

Scapula

Elevation
- Upper trapezius
- Levator scapulae

Depression
- Latissimus dorsi
- Pectoralis major
- Pectoralis minor
- Lower trapezius

Protraction
- Serratus anterior
- Pectoralis minor

Retraction
- Trapezius (middle)
- Rhomboids

Upward Rotation
- Trapezius (upper, lower)
- Serratus anterior

Downward Rotation
- Rhomboids
- Levator scapulae
- Pectoralis minor

Shoulder Joint

Flexion
- Anterior deltoid
- Coracobrachialis
- Pectoralis major (clavicular head)
- Biceps brachii

Extension
- Latissimus dorsi
- Posterior deltoid
- Teres major
- Triceps brachii (long head)

Abduction
- Middle deltoid
- Supraspinatus

Adduction
- Pectoralis major
- Latissimus dorsi
- Teres major

Upper Extremity (continued)

Shoulder Joint (continued)

Horizontal Abduction
- Posterior deltoid
- Infraspinatus
- Teres minor

Horizontal Adduction
- Anterior deltoid
- Pectoralis major

Lateral Rotation
- Teres minor
- Infraspinatus
- Posterior deltoid

Medial Rotation
- Subscapularis
- Teres major
- Pectoralis major
- Latissimus dorsi
- Anterior deltoid

Elbow Joint

Flexion
- Biceps brachii
- Brachialis
- Brachioradialis

Extension
- Triceps brachii
- Anconeus

Radioulnar Joint

Supination
- Biceps brachii
- Supinator

Pronation
- Pronator teres
- Pronator quadratus

Wrist Joint

Flexion
- Flexor carpi radialis
- Flexor carpi ulnaris
- Palmaris longus

Extension
- Extensor carpi radialis longus
- Extensor carpi radialis brevis
- Extensor carpi ulnaris

Radial Deviation
- Extensor carpi radialis longus and brevis
- Flexor carpi radialis
- Extensor pollicis longus and brevis

Ulnar Deviation
- Extensor carpi ulnaris
- Flexor carpi ulnaris

Finger Joints

Flexion
- Flexor digitorum profundus and superficialis
- Flexor digiti minimi (fifth digit)
- Interossei
- Lumbricals

Extension
- Extensor digitorum communis
- Extensor indicis (second digit)
- Extensor digiti minimi (fifth digit)

Abduction
- Dorsal interossei
- Abductor digiti minimi (fifth digit)

Adduction
- Palmar interossei

Thumb Joint

Flexion
- Flexor pollicis longus and brevis
- Opponens pollicis

Extension
- Extensor pollicis longus and brevis
- Abductor pollicis longus

Abduction
- Abductor pollicis longus and brevis

Adduction
- Adductor pollicis

Opposition
- Opponens pollicis
- Flexor pollicis brevis
- Abductor pollicis brevis
- Opponens digiti minimi

Lower Extremity

Hip Joint

Flexion
- Iliopsoas
- Sartorius
- Rectus femoris
- Pectineus

Extension
- Gluteus maximus and medius
- Semitendinosus
- Semimembranosus
- Biceps femoris

Abduction
- Gluteus medius
- Gluteus minimus
- Piriformis
- Obturator internus
- Tensor fasciae latae

Adduction
- Adductor magnus
- Adductor longus
- Adductor brevis
- Gracilis

Medial Rotation
- Tensor fasciae latae
- Gluteus medius
- Gluteus minimus
- Pectineus
- Adductor longus

Lateral Rotation
- Gluteus maximus
- Obturator externus
- Obturator internus
- Piriformis
- Gemelli
- Sartorius

Knee Joint

Flexion
- Biceps femoris
- Semitendinosus
- Semimembranosus
- Sartorius

Extension
- Rectus femoris
- Vastus lateralis
- Vastus intermedius
- Vastus medialis

Ankle Joint

Plantar Flexion
- Tibialis posterior
- Gastrocnemius
- Soleus
- Peroneus longus
- Peroneus brevis
- Plantaris
- Flexor hallucis

Dorsiflexion
- Tibialis anterior
- Extensor hallucis longus
- Extensor digitorum longus
- Peroneus tertius

Inversion
- Tibialis posterior
- Tibialis anterior
- Flexor digitorum longus

Eversion
- Peroneus longus
- Peroneus brevis
- Peroneus tertius

Toe Joints

Flexion
- Flexor digitorum longus and brevis
- Flexor hallucis longus and brevis
- Flexor digiti minimi brevis
- Quadratus plantae
- Lumbricals

Extension
- Extensor digitorum longus and brevis
- Extensor hallucis longus and brevis
- Lumbricals

Abduction
- Abductor hallucis
- Abductor digit minimi
- Dorsal interossei

Adduction
- Adductor hallucis
- Plantar interossei

Specific Joints - Upper Extremity

Shoulder[5,7-11]

The shoulder complex is formed by a series of unique articulations including the glenohumeral joint, sternoclavicular joint, acromioclavicular joint, and scapulothoracic articulation.

Articulations

Glenohumeral joint

The glenohumeral joint is formed by the convex head of the humerus and the concave glenoid fossa of the scapula. The glenohumeral joint is a ball and socket synovial joint with three degrees of freedom. The relatively small articular surface of the glenoid fossa in relation to the size of the humeral head, makes the glenohumeral joint inherently unstable.

Glenohumeral Snapshot
Osteokinematic motions: flexion, extension, abduction, adduction, medial rotation, lateral rotation
Loose packed position: 55 degrees abduction, 30 degrees horizontal adduction
Close packed position: abduction and lateral rotation
Capsular pattern: lateral rotation, abduction, medial rotation

Sternoclavicular joint

The sternoclavicular joint is formed by the medial end of the clavicle and the manubrium of the sternum. The joint is a saddle-shaped synovial joint with three degrees of freedom. A fibrocartilaginous disc between the manubrium and clavicle enhances the stability of the joint. The disc acts as a shock absorber and serves as the axis for clavicular rotation.

Sternoclavicular Snapshot
Osteokinematic motions: elevation, depression, protraction, retraction, medial rotation, lateral rotation
Loose packed position: arm resting by the side
Close packed position: maximum shoulder elevation
Capsular pattern: pain at extremes of range of movement

Acromioclavicular joint

The acromioclavicular joint is formed by the acromion process of the scapula and the lateral end of the clavicle. The joint is a plane synovial joint with three degrees of freedom. The acromioclavicular joint functions to maintain the relationship between the scapula and clavicle during glenohumeral range of motion.

Acromioclavicular Snapshot
Osteokinematic motions: anterior tilting, posterior tilting, upward rotation, downward rotation, protraction, retraction
Loose packed position: arm resting by the side
Close packed position: arm abducted to 90 degrees
Capsular pattern: pain at extremes of range of movement

Scapulothoracic articulation

The scapulothoracic articulation is formed by the body of the scapula and the muscles covering the posterior chest wall. Motion consists of sliding of the scapula on the thorax. The articulation is not a true anatomical joint because it lacks the necessary synovial joint characteristics.

Muscle Action

Shoulder flexion: anterior deltoid, coracobrachialis, pectoralis major (clavicular head), biceps brachii

Shoulder extension: latissimus dorsi, posterior deltoid, teres major, triceps brachii (long head)

Shoulder abduction: middle deltoid, supraspinatus

Shoulder adduction: pectoralis major, latissimus dorsi, teres major

Shoulder lateral rotation: teres minor, infraspinatus, posterior deltoid

Shoulder medial rotation: subscapularis, teres major, pectoralis major, latissimus dorsi, anterior deltoid

Shoulder horizontal abduction: posterior deltoid, infraspinatus, teres minor

Shoulder horizontal adduction: anterior deltoid, pectoralis major

Scapula elevation: upper trapezius, levator scapulae

Scapula depression: latissimus dorsi, pectoralis major, pectoralis minor, lower trapezius

Scapula protraction: serratus anterior, pectoralis minor

Scapula retraction: trapezius (middle), rhomboids

Scapula upward rotation: trapezius (upper, lower), serratus anterior

Scapula downward rotation: rhomboids, levator scapulae, pectoralis minor

Primary Structures

Acromioclavicular ligaments

The acromioclavicular ligaments surround the acromioclavicular joint on all sides and help to control horizontal movements of the clavicle.

Coracoacromial ligament

The coracoacromial ligament attaches between the coracoid process and acromion and forms a "roof" over the humeral head. This ligament helps to limit superior translation of the humeral head and also helps prevent separation of the acromioclavicular joint.

Coracoclavicular ligament

The coracoclavicular ligament attaches between the coracoid process and the clavicle and consists of two different ligaments: the conoid and trapezoid ligaments. The coracoclavicular ligament acts as the primary support of the acromioclavicular joint, limiting superior translation of the clavicle.

Coracohumeral ligament

The coracohumeral ligament attaches proximally to the coracoid process and splits distally to attach to the greater and lesser tuberosities. This ligament is found between and helps to unite the supraspinatus and subscapularis tendons. It limits inferior translation of the humeral head.

Costoclavicular ligament

The costoclavicular ligament attaches between the medial portion of the clavicle and the first rib. This ligament is the primary supporting ligament for the sternoclavicular joint.

Glenohumeral ligaments

The glenohumeral ligaments consist of the superior, middle, and inferior glenohumeral ligaments. The superior glenohumeral ligament limits adduction of the shoulder as well as lateral rotation with the shoulder in 0-45 degrees of abduction. The middle glenohumeral ligament limits lateral rotation with the shoulder in 45-90 degrees of abduction. The inferior glenohumeral ligament has an anterior and a posterior band that limits lateral rotation and medial rotation, respectively, above 90 degrees of abduction. Between the two bands is an axillary pouch that limits inferior translation when the shoulder is above 90 degrees of abduction.

Glenoid labrum

The glenoid labrum is a fibrocartilaginous structure that serves to deepen the glenoid fossa and increases the size of the articular surface. The glenoid labrum consists of a dense fibrous connective tissue that is often damaged with recurrent shoulder instability.

Joint capsule

The joint capsule arises from the glenoid fossa and the glenoid labrum to blend with the muscles of the rotator cuff. The volume of the joint capsule is twice as large as the size of the humeral head. The capsule is reinforced by the glenohumeral ligaments and the coracohumeral ligament.

Rotator interval

The rotator interval is a space in the anterosuperior shoulder that consists of and is bordered by the coracohumeral ligament, superior glenohumeral ligament, joint capsule, and supraspinatus and subscapularis tendons.

Subacromial bursa

The subacromial bursa extends over the supraspinatus tendon and distal muscle belly, beneath the acromion and deltoid muscle. The bursa facilitates movement of the deltoid muscle over the fibrous capsule of the shoulder joint and supraspinatus tendon. The bursa is often involved with impingement beneath the acromial arch.

Subscapular bursa

The subscapular bursa overlies the anterior joint capsule and lies beneath the subscapularis muscle. Anterior shoulder fullness may indicate articular effusion secondary to distention of the bursa.

Transverse humeral ligament

The transverse humeral ligament attaches between the greater and lesser tubercles of the humerus, spanning over the bicipital groove. This ligament helps to maintain the tendon of the long head of the biceps within the bicipital groove.

Elbow[5,8-10]

The elbow joint is a synovial joint consisting of three bones (i.e., humerus, radius, ulna) and three primary articulations (i.e., radiohumeral, ulnohumeral, proximal radioulnar) enclosed within a single joint capsule. The elbow is classified as a hinge joint formed by the articulation of the ulna with the humerus.

Articulations

Radiohumeral joint

The proximal joint surface of the radiohumeral joint is the ball-shaped capitulum of the distal humerus. The distal joint surface is the concave head of the radius.

Radiohumeral Snapshot
Osteokinematic motions: flexion, extension, pronation, supination
Loose packed position: full extension, supination
Close packed position: 90 degrees flexion, 5 degrees supination
Capsular pattern: flexion, extension, supination, pronation

Ulnohumeral joint

The ulnohumeral joint is formed by the hourglass-shaped trochlea of the humerus and the trochlear notch of the ulna.

Ulnohumeral Snapshot
Osteokinematic motions: flexion, extension
Loose packed position: 70 degrees elbow flexion, 10 degrees supination
Close packed position: extension
Capsular pattern: flexion, extension

Proximal radioulnar joint

The proximal radioulnar joint consists of the concave radial notch of the ulna and the convex rim of the radial head.

Proximal Radioulnar Snapshot
Osteokinematic motions: pronation, supination
Loose packed position: 70 degrees elbow flexion, 35 degrees supination
Close packed position: 5 degrees supination
Capsular pattern: supination, pronation

Muscle Action

Elbow flexion: biceps brachii, brachialis, brachioradialis
Elbow extension: triceps brachii, anconeus
Forearm supination: biceps brachii, supinator
Forearm pronation: pronator teres, pronator quadratus

Primary Structures

Annular ligament

The annular ligament consists of a band of fibers that surrounds the head of the radius. It allows the head of the radius to rotate and retain contact with the radial notch of the ulna.

Anterior ligament

The anterior ligament is capsular in nature and function. It stretches from the radial collateral ligament and attaches above the upper edge of the coronoid fossa, extending to just below the coronoid process.

Cubital fossa

The cubital fossa is a triangular space located at the anterior elbow that is bordered by the brachioradialis, pronator teres, brachialis, and a horizontal line passing through the humeral epicondyles. The cubital fossa contains several structures, including the biceps brachii tendon, median nerve, radial nerve, brachial artery, and median cubital vein.

Cubital tunnel

The cubital tunnel is a space formed by the ulnar collateral ligament, the flexor carpi ulnaris, the medial head of the triceps, and the medial epicondyle. The ulnar nerve runs through the cubital tunnel. The cubital tunnel becomes smallest with the elbow held in full flexion.

Olecranon bursa

The olecranon bursa lies posterior to the olecranon process and is considered the main bursa in the elbow. This bursa commonly becomes inflamed with direct trauma to the elbow due to its superficial position.

Posterior ligament

The posterior ligament resembles the anterior ligament. It blends on each side with the collateral ligaments and is attached to the upper portion of the olecranon fossa, and to just below the olecranon process.

Radial collateral ligament (i.e., lateral collateral ligament)

The radial collateral ligament extends from the lateral epicondyle of the humerus to the lateral border and olecranon process of the ulna and to the annular ligament. It is a fan-shaped ligament that prevents adduction of the elbow joint, and provides reinforcement for the radiohumeral articulation.

Ulnar collateral ligament (i.e., medial collateral ligament)

The ulnar collateral ligament runs from the medial epicondyle of the humerus to the proximal portion of the ulna. The ligament prevents excessive abduction of the elbow joint.

CONSIDER THIS
MECHANISMS OF INJURY FOR ELBOW LIGAMENTS

The ulnar and radial collateral ligaments can become stretched, frayed or torn through the stress of repetitive throwing motions. If the force on the soft tissues is greater than the tensile strength of the structure, tiny tears of the ligaments can develop. Months (and even years) of throwing can cause microtears, degeneration, and finally, rupture of the ligaments. Baseball pitchers are the athletes treated most often for this problem. Tennis, track and field, football, ice hockey, and water polo participants have also been reported to injure the collateral ligaments. A fall on an outstretched arm can lead to collateral ligament rupture, often with associated elbow dislocation.

Wrist[5,8,9,10,12]

The wrist complex is formed by the radiocarpal and midcarpal joints. The radiocarpal joint attaches the hand to the forearm. The midcarpal joint is formed by the articulations of the proximal and distal row of carpals.

Articulations

Radiocarpal joint

The proximal joint surface of the radiocarpal joint is formed by the distal radius and the radioulnar articular disc, which connects the medial aspect of the distal radius to the distal ulna. The distal joint surface is formed by the scaphoid, lunate, and triquetrum. The radiocarpal joint has two degrees of freedom. It is encased in a strong capsule reinforced by numerous ligaments shared with the midcarpal joint.

Radiocarpal Snapshot
Osteokinematic motions: flexion, extension, radial deviation, ulnar deviation
Loose packed position: neutral with slight ulnar deviation
Close packed position: extension with radial deviation
Capsular pattern: flexion and extension equally limited

Midcarpal joint

Motion of the wrist results in complex motion between the proximal and distal row of carpals with the exception of the pisiform. The joint surfaces are reciprocally convex and concave.

Muscle Action

Wrist flexion: flexor carpi radialis, flexor carpi ulnaris, palmaris longus

Wrist extension: extensor carpi radialis longus, extensor carpi radialis brevis, extensor carpi ulnaris

Radial deviation: extensor carpi radialis longus and brevis, flexor carpi radialis, extensor pollicis longus, extensor pollicis brevis

Ulnar deviation: extensor carpi ulnaris, flexor carpi ulnaris

Primary Structures

Anatomic snuffbox

The anatomic snuffbox is a depression found on the dorsal surface of the wrist near the distal radius. The snuffbox is bordered by the tendons of the abductor pollicis longus, extensor pollicis brevis, and extensor pollicis longus. This location is often used for palpation of the scaphoid when there is concern for a fracture.

Carpal tunnel

The carpal tunnel is located close to the deep surface of the flexor retinaculum. The median nerve enters the palm through the carpal tunnel. Any condition that significantly reduces the size of the carpal tunnel (e.g., tenosynovitis, inflammation of the flexor retinaculum) may result in compression of the median nerve.

Dorsal radiocarpal ligament

The dorsal radiocarpal ligament is the only major ligament on the dorsal surface of the wrist. The ligament originates on the posterior surface of the distal radius and styloid process of the radius and attaches to the lunate and triquetrum. The ligament serves to limit wrist flexion.

Extensor retinaculum

The extensor retinaculum is a ligamentous structure that crosses the dorsal aspect of the wrist, covering the tendons of the extensor musculature. The retinaculum prevents the tendons from "bowstringing" as the wrist is extended.

Flexor retinaculum

The flexor retinaculum (transverse carpal ligament) is a ligamentous structure that crosses the palmar aspect of the wrist, forming the most anterior aspect of the carpal tunnel. The flexor retinaculum prevents the tendons of the flexor musculature from "bowstringing" as the wrist is flexed. It also serves as an attachment site for the thenar and hypothenar muscles.

Interosseous membrane

The interosseous membrane consists of a dense band of fibrous connective tissue that runs obliquely from the radius to the ulna. The structure spans from the proximal radioulnar joint to the distal radioulnar joint and serves as a stabilizer against axial forces applied to the wrist.

Palmar radiocarpal ligament

The palmar radiocarpal ligament maintains the alignment of the associated joint structures and limits hyperextension of the wrist. The ligament originates from the anterior surface of the distal radius and attaches to the capitate, triquetrum, and scaphoid.

Radial collateral ligament

The radial collateral ligament serves to limit ulnar deviation and becomes taut when the wrist is in extremes of extension and flexion. The ligament originates from the styloid process of the radius and inserts on the scaphoid and trapezium.

Triangular fibrocartilage complex

The triangular fibrocartilage complex is a cartilaginous disc that sits between the ulna, lunate, and triquetrum. The disc provides stability to the wrist joint, connecting the radius and ulna together and allowing for better distribution of forces through the wrist.

Tunnel of Guyon

The tunnel of Guyon is a space that is located between the hook of the hamate, pisiform, palmar carpal ligament, and flexor retinaculum. It provides passage for the ulnar nerve and artery as they enter the hand. Compression of the nerve in this location may result in ulnar tunnel syndrome.

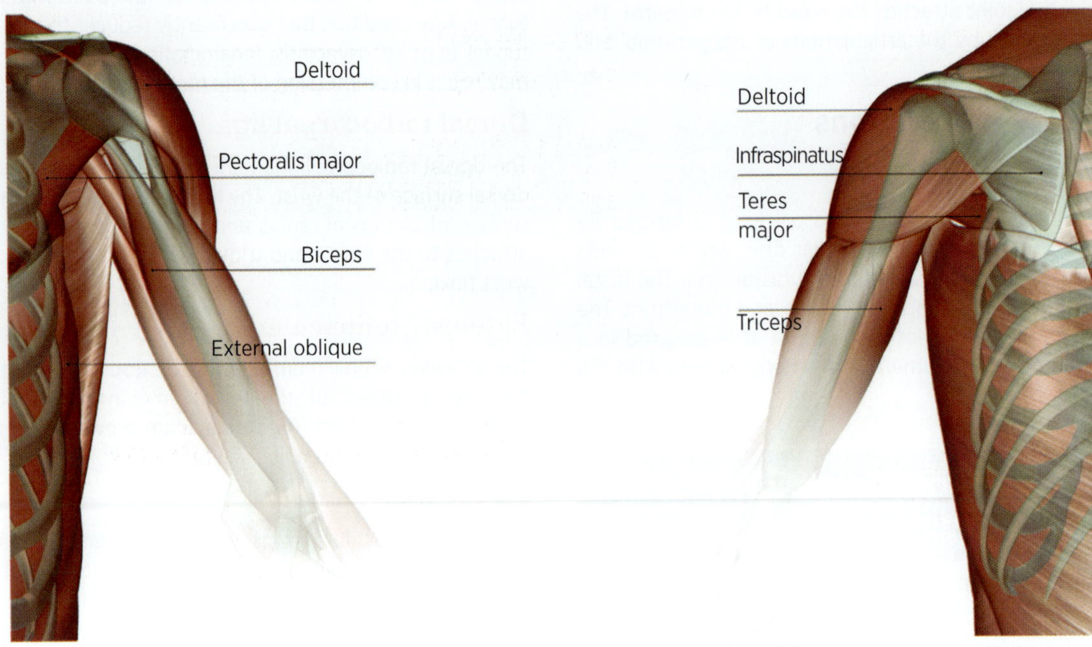

Fig. 4-3: Muscles of the anterior upper limb.

Fig. 4-4: Muscles of the posterior upper limb.

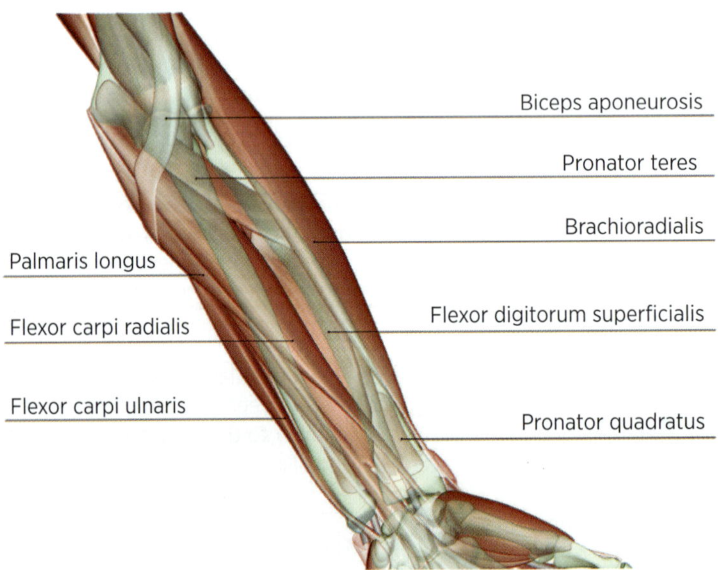

Fig. 4-5: Muscles of the volar surface of the forearm.

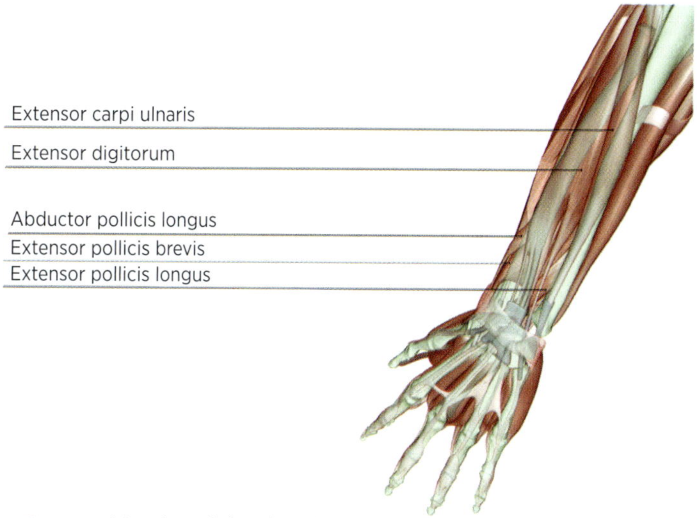
Extensor carpi ulnaris
Extensor digitorum
Abductor pollicis longus
Extensor pollicis brevis
Extensor pollicis longus

Fig. 4-6: Muscles of the dorsal surface of the forearm.

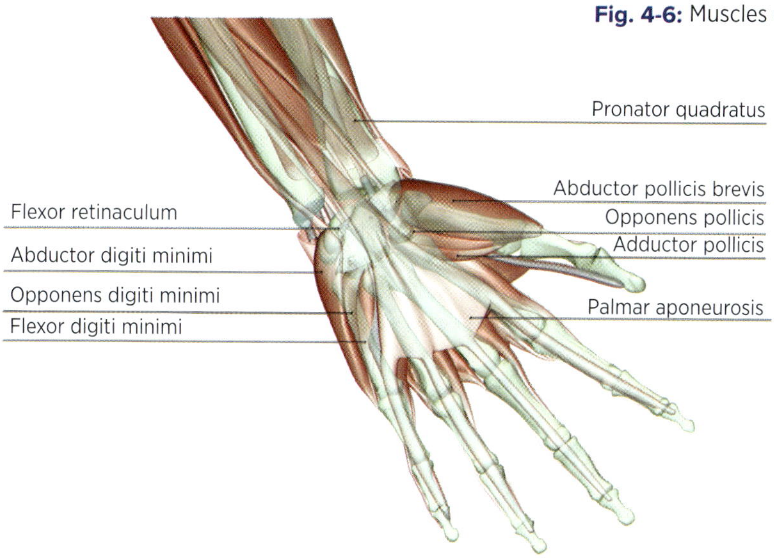
Pronator quadratus
Flexor retinaculum
Abductor pollicis brevis
Opponens pollicis
Adductor pollicis
Abductor digiti minimi
Opponens digiti minimi
Palmar aponeurosis
Flexor digiti minimi

Fig. 4-7: Muscles of the volar surface of the wrist and hand.

Abductor pollicis
Extensor retinaculum
Dorsal
interosseus
Abductor digiti minimi
Extensor digitorum tendons
Extensor digiti minimi tendon

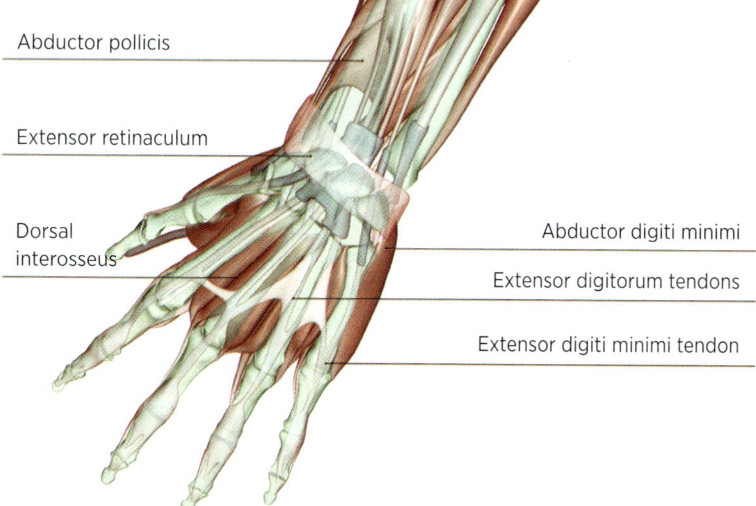

Fig. 4-8: Muscles of the dorsal surface of the wrist and hand.

Specific Joints - Lower Extremity

Hip[5,8-10]

The hip (iliofemoral) joint is a synovial joint formed by the head of the femur and the acetabulum. The hip is classified as a ball and socket joint with three degrees of freedom.

Articulations

Iliofemoral joint

The proximal joint surface of the iliofemoral joint consists of the acetabulum which is oriented laterally, inferiorly, and anteriorly. The distal joint surface consists of the convex head of the femur.

Iliofemoral Snapshot
Osteokinematic motions: flexion, extension, abduction, adduction, medial rotation, lateral rotation
Loose packed position: 30 degrees flexion, 30 degrees abduction, slight lateral rotation
Close packed position: full extension, medial rotation
Capsular pattern: flexion, abduction, medial rotation (sometimes medial rotation is most limited)

Muscle Action

Hip flexion: iliopsoas, sartorius, rectus femoris, pectineus

Hip extension: gluteus maximus, gluteus medius, semitendinosus, semimembranosus, biceps femoris

Hip abduction: gluteus medius, gluteus minimus, piriformis, obturator internus, tensor fasciae latae

Hip adduction: adductor magnus, adductor longus, adductor brevis, gracilis

Hip medial rotation: tensor fasciae latae, gluteus medius, gluteus minimus, pectineus, adductor longus

Hip lateral rotation: gluteus maximus, obturator externus, obturator internus, piriformis, gemelli, sartorius

Primary Structures

Acetabular labrum

The acetabular labrum consists of a fibrocartilaginous rim attached to the margin of the acetabulum. The structure enhances the depth of the acetabulum.

Articular capsule

A strong articular capsule extends from the rim of the acetabulum to the neck of the femur. The capsule is reinforced by the iliofemoral, pubofemoral, and ischiofemoral ligaments.

Bursae

There are several bursae within the hip region, some of which include the iliopsoas, trochanteric, and ischiogluteal bursae. The iliopsoas bursa is located between the anterior joint capsule and iliopsoas tendon. There are multiple trochanteric bursae, all of which lie between the greater trochanter and the different gluteal muscles. The ischiogluteal bursa is located between the ischium and gluteus maximus.

Femoral triangle

The femoral triangle is a space located in the anterior hip that is bordered by the inguinal ligament, sartorius, and adductor longus. Within this space, the femoral artery and lymph glands can be palpated. The femoral nerve and vein also pass through this space.

Iliofemoral ligament

The iliofemoral ligament consists of a thickened portion of the articular capsule that extends from the anterior inferior iliac spine of the pelvis to the intertrochanteric line of the femur. The structure is considered to be the strongest ligament in the body and serves to prevent excessive hip extension and assists to maintain upright posture.

Ischiofemoral ligament

The ischiofemoral ligament consists of a thickened portion of the articular capsule that extends from the ischial wall of the acetabulum to the neck of the femur. The structure is the weakest of the three ligaments, however, it serves to reinforce the articular capsule.

Ligamentum teres

The ligamentum teres (ligament of the head of the femur) is a ligament that provides a physical attachment between the head of the femur and the inferior rim of the acetabulum. Blood vessels and nerves travel with this ligament in a sheath to the head of the femur. The ligament provides minimal stability to the hip.

Pubofemoral ligament

The pubofemoral ligament consists of a thickened portion of the articular capsule that extends from the pubic portion of the rim of the acetabulum to the neck of the femur. The structure serves to prevent excessive abduction of the femur and limits hip extension.

CONSIDER THIS

COMMON MECHANISMS OF INJURY FOR KNEE LIGAMENTS

Stability of the knee is enhanced by the role of four primary ligaments. The ligaments are capable of functioning in isolation or collectively. Due to the unique function of each ligament, it is possible to identify specific mechanisms of injury often associated with a particular ligamentous injury.

Anterior cruciate ligament (ACL)

The ACL may be injured through a noncontact twisting injury associated with hyperextension and varus or valgus stress to the knee. Other mechanisms for ACL damage include the tibia being driven anteriorly on the femur, the femur being driven posteriorly on the tibia or severe knee hyperextension. Special tests designed to assess the integrity of the ACL include the anterior drawer test, Lachman test, lateral pivot shift test, and Slocum test.

Posterior cruciate ligament (PCL)

The PCL may be injured when the superior portion of the tibia is struck while the knee is flexed. A common example of this occurs in a motor vehicle accident when a passenger's leg collides against the dashboard. Other mechanisms for PCL damage include the tibia being driven posteriorly on the femur, the femur being driven anteriorly on the tibia or severe knee hyperflexion. Special tests designed to assess the integrity of the PCL include the posterior drawer test and posterior sag sign.

Medial collateral ligament (MCL)

The MCL may be injured with a pure valgus load at the knee without rotation. This type of injury is often sustained with contact activities such as a lateral blow to the knee during a football game. Injury to the MCL often involves injury to other knee structures such as the ACL or medial meniscus. A valgus stress test can assess the integrity of the MCL.

Lateral collateral ligament (LCL)

The LCL may be injured with a pure varus load at the knee without rotation. This type of injury is often sustained with contact activities such as a medial blow to the knee. The LCL is rarely completely torn without a concurrent injury to the ACL or PCL. A varus stress test can assess the integrity of the LCL.

Knee[8-12]

The knee joint is a synovial joint consisting of three bones (i.e., femur, tibia, patella) and two primary articulations (i.e., tibiofemoral, patellofemoral) enclosed within a single joint capsule. The knee is classified as a hinge joint, formed by the articulation of the tibia with the femur, with two degrees of freedom.

Articulations

Tibiofemoral joint

The proximal joint surface of the tibiofemoral joint is formed by the convex medial and lateral condyles of the distal femur. The distal joint surface is formed by the concave medial and lateral condyles of the proximal tibia.

Patellofemoral joint

The patellofemoral joint is formed by the convex patella and the concave trochlear groove of the femur. The patella slides superiorly in knee extension and inferiorly in knee flexion. Patella rotation and tilting also occur during knee extension and flexion.

Tibiofemoral Snapshot
Osteokinematic motions: flexion, extension, medial rotation, lateral rotation
Loose packed position: 25 degrees flexion
Close packed position: full extension, lateral rotation of tibia
Capsular pattern: flexion, extension

Muscle Action

Knee flexion: biceps femoris, semitendinosus, sartorius, semimembranosus

Knee extension: rectus femoris, vastus lateralis, vastus intermedius, vastus medialis

Primary Structures

Anterior cruciate ligament

The ACL runs from the anterior intercondylar area of the tibia to the medial aspect of the lateral femoral condyle in the intercondylar notch. The ACL prevents anterior displacement of the tibia on the femur.

Arcuate ligament complex

The arcuate ligament complex consists of the arcuate ligament, oblique popliteal ligament, lateral collateral ligament, popliteus tendon, and lateral head of the gastrocnemius. The complex assists the cruciate ligaments in controlling posterolateral rotatory instability of the knee and provides support to the posterolateral joint capsule.

Bursae

The knee has several important bursae including the prepatellar bursa, superficial infrapatellar bursa, and deep infrapatellar bursa. The prepatellar bursa lies over the patella and allows for greater freedom of movement of the skin covering the anterior aspect of the patella. The superficial infrapatellar bursa lies between the patellar tendon and skin, while the deep infrapatellar bursa lies between the patellar tendon and the tibia.

Fat pads

There are three fat pads in the knee: quadriceps, prefemoral, and infrapatellar. The infrapatellar fat pad is the one most commonly affected and can be a source of anterior knee pain when it becomes impinged (e.g., Hoffa's syndrome).

Lateral collateral ligament

The LCL runs from the lateral femoral epicondyle to the fibular head. The LCL prevents excessive varus displacement of the tibia relative to the femur.

Medial collateral ligament

The MCL runs from slightly above the medial femoral epicondyle to the medial aspect of the shaft of the tibia. The deep capsular fibers are attached to the medial meniscus. The MCL prevents excessive valgus displacement of the tibia relative to the femur.

Menisci

The medial and lateral menisci are firmly attached to the proximal surface of the tibia. The menisci are thick at the periphery and thinner at their internal unattached edges. Menisci function to deepen the articular surfaces of the tibia where they articulate with the femoral condyles. The menisci function as shock absorbers and contribute to lubrication and nutrition of the joint.

Pes anserine

The pes anserine is the common insertion point for the gracilis, semitendinosus, and sartorius muscles. The pes anserine is located medial and distal to the tibial tuberosity. Pain and/or swelling in this region may indicate the presence of pes anserine bursitis.

Plicae

Plicae are extensions of the synovial membrane that are sometimes found in the anterior knee, most commonly medial to the patella. They do not serve a specific function, though they can be a source of anterior knee pain.

Posterior cruciate ligament

The PCL runs from the posterior intercondylar area of the tibia to the lateral aspect of the medial femoral condyle in the intercondylar notch. The PCL prevents posterior displacement of the tibia on the femur.

Retinacula

The medial and lateral retinacula are ligamentous structures that attach the patella to the femur, tibia, and menisci. The lateral retinaculum is the stronger of the two and plays a larger role in patellar positioning.

Ankle and Foot[8-12]

The ankle and foot are formed by a series of unique articulations including the distal tibiofibular joint, talocrural joint, subtalar joint, midtarsal joint, and forefoot.

Articulations

Distal tibiofibular joint

The distal tibiofibular joint is formed by a fibrous union between the lateral aspect of the distal tibia and the distal fibula.

Talocrural joint

The talocrural joint is formed by the articulations of the distal tibia, talus, and fibula. The joint is a synovial hinge joint with one degree of freedom. The talocrural joint offers significant stability in dorsiflexion, however, it becomes much more mobile with plantar flexion.

Talocrural Snapshot
Osteokinematic motions: dorsiflexion, plantar flexion
Loose packed position: 10 degrees plantar flexion, midway between maximum inversion and eversion
Close packed position: maximum dorsiflexion
Capsular pattern: plantar flexion, dorsiflexion

Subtalar joint

The subtalar joint is formed by three articulations (anterior, middle, posterior) between the talus and calcaneus. The joint has one degree of freedom. The anterior and middle articulations are formed by two convex facets on the talus and two concave facets on the calcaneus. The posterior articulation is formed by a concave facet on the inferior surface of the talus and a convex facet on the body of the calcaneus.

Subtalar Snapshot
Osteokinematic motions: inversion, eversion
Loose packed position: midway between extremes of range of movement
Close packed position: supination
Capsular pattern: limitation of varus range of movement

Midtarsal joint

The midtarsal (transverse tarsal) joint is formed by the talocalcaneonavicular joint and the calcaneocuboid joint. The joint is considered to have two axes, one longitudinal and one oblique. Motions around both axes are triplanar.

Midtarsal Snapshot
Osteokinematic motions: inversion, eversion
Loose packed position: midway between extremes of range of movement
Close packed position: supination
Capsular pattern: dorsiflexion, plantar flexion, adduction, medial rotation

Forefoot

The forefoot consists of the tarsometatarsal joints, metatarsophalangeal joints, and interphalangeal joints.

Muscle Action

Plantar flexion: tibialis posterior, gastrocnemius, soleus, peroneus longus, peroneus brevis, plantaris, flexor hallucis

Dorsiflexion: tibialis anterior, extensor hallucis longus, extensor digitorum longus, peroneus tertius

Inversion: tibialis posterior, tibialis anterior, flexor digitorum longus

Eversion: peroneus longus, peroneus brevis, peroneus tertius

Primary Structures

Anterior talofibular ligament

The anterior talofibular ligament is taut during plantar flexion and resists inversion of the talus and calcaneus. The ligament also resists anterior translation of the talus on the tibia.

Calcaneofibular ligament

The calcaneofibular ligament is an extracapsular ligament that resists inversion of the talus within the midrange of talocrural motion.

Deltoid ligament

The deltoid ligament is formed by the anterior tibiotalar ligament, tibiocalcaneal ligament, posterior tibiotalar ligament, and tibionavicular ligament. The ligament provides medial ligamentous support by resisting eversion of the talus.

Interosseous membrane

The interosseous membrane consists of a strong fibrous tissue that serves to fixate the fibula to the tibia. Distally, the structure blends into the anterior and posterior tibiofibular ligaments and provides additional support at the distal tibiofibular syndesmosis joint.

Ligaments

The majority of the ligaments in the ankle are areas of increased density within the joint capsule. As a result, damage to the ankle ligaments typically produces damage to the joint capsule and irritation of the synovial lining.

Plantar fascia

The plantar fascia is a thick layer of fascial tissue on the plantar aspect of the foot that originates on the calcaneal tuberosity and inserts into the plantar forefoot. The plantar fascia plays a role in supporting the weight of the body and also helps to support the arch of the foot for improved propulsion during gait.

Posterior talofibular ligament

The posterior talofibular ligament resists posterior displacement of the talus on the tibia.

Retinacula

There are several retinacula within the ankle. The major retinaculum is the extensor retinaculum, which lies on the anterior side of the joint. This structure contains the tendons on the extensor musculature and prevents them from "bowstringing" as the ankle dorsiflexes. There is also a flexor retinaculum and a peroneal retinaculum.

Retrocalcaneal bursa

The retrocalcaneal bursa lies just anterior to the Achilles tendon where it attaches into the superior calcaneus and acts as a cushion between the tendon and the bone. Irritation of the bursa, due to trauma or overuse, can result in retrocalcaneal bursitis.

Sinus tarsi

The sinus tarsi is a space located between the inferior talus, superior calcaneus, and anterior portion of the lateral malleolus. This area contains ligaments that can also be injured during a common inversion ankle sprain.

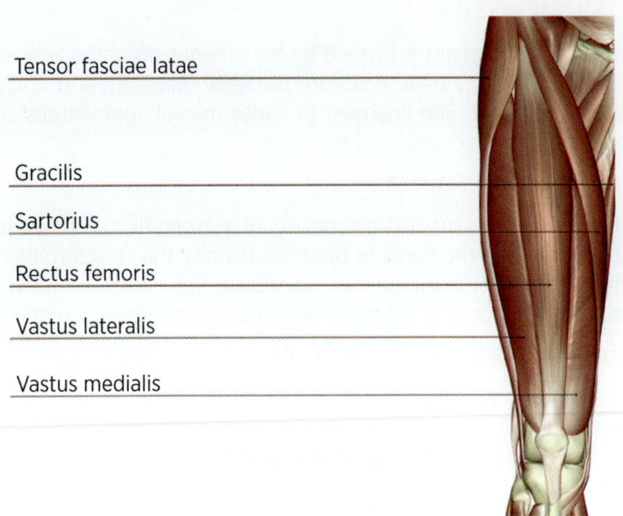

Fig. 4-9: Muscles of the anterior upper leg.

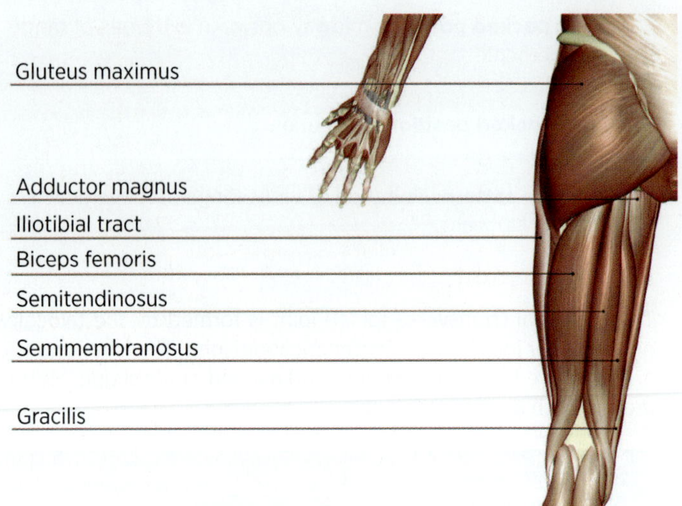

Fig. 4-10: Muscles of the posterior upper leg.

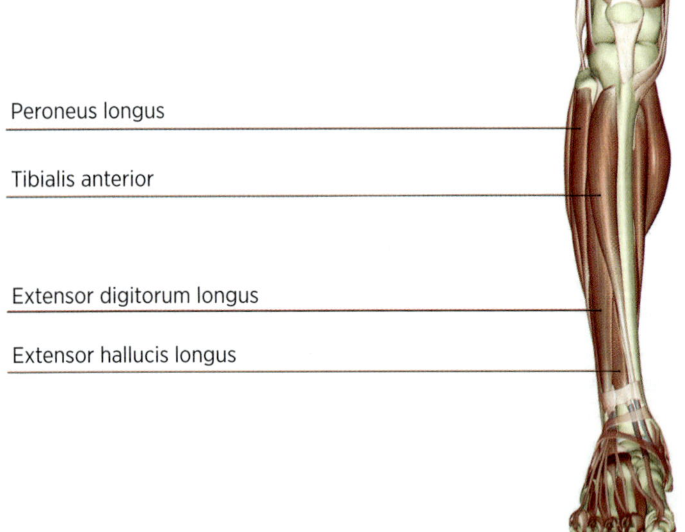

Fig. 4-11: Muscles of the anterior lower leg.

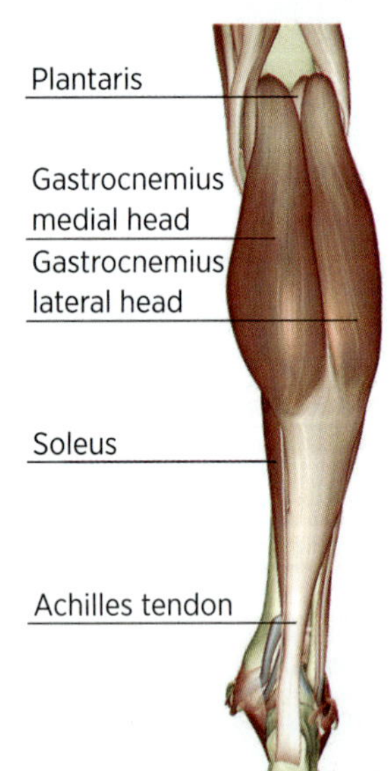

Fig. 4-12: Muscles of the posterior lower leg.

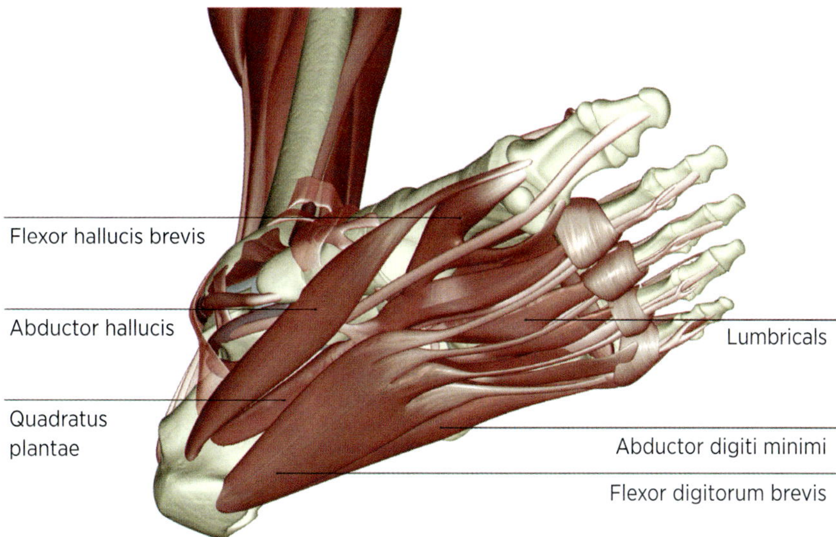

Fig. 4-13: Muscles of the volar surface of the foot.

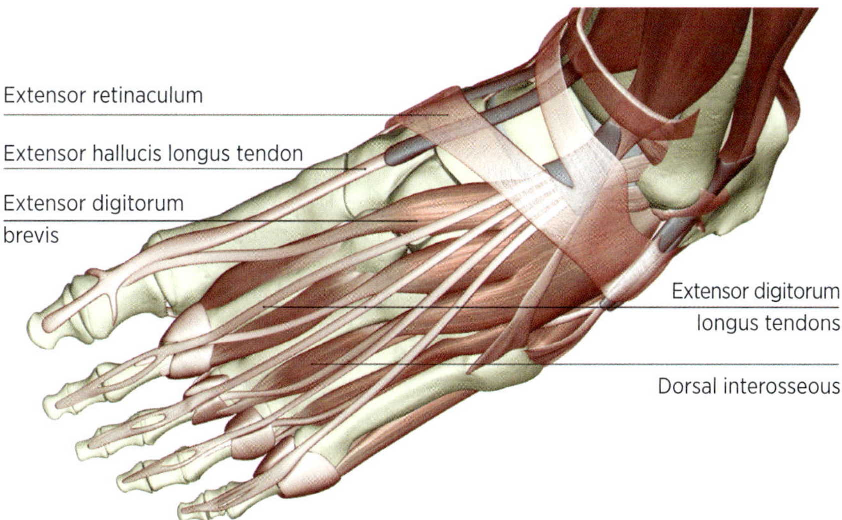

Fig. 4-14: Muscles of the dorsal surface of the foot.

Spine

Cervical Spine[3,10,13,14]

The cervical spine consists of seven cervical vertebrae. The first two, the atlas and axis, are unique. The atlas (C1) supports the weight of the head through two facet joints which form the atlanto-occipital joint. The axis (C2) has a superior projection called the dens. The articulation between the dens and the anterior arch of the atlas forms the atlantoaxial joint.

Articulations

Atlanto-occipital joint

The atlanto-occipital joint is a condylar synovial joint that permits flexion and extension of the cranium. This motion is often noted when nodding the head to say "yes."

Atlantoaxial joints

The atlantoaxial joints are plane synovial joints that permit flexion, extension, lateral flexion, and rotation of the cervical spine. The majority of rotation of the skull on the spinal column occurs at the atlantoaxial joints.

Intervertebral joints

The intervertebral joints are formed by the superior and inferior surfaces of the vertebral bodies and the associated intervertebral disks.

Zygapophyseal joints

The zygapophyseal joints are formed by the right and left superior articular facets of one vertebra and the right and left inferior articular facets of an adjacent superior vertebra.

Muscle Action

Cervical flexion: sternocleidomastoid, longus colli, scalenus muscles

Cervical extension: splenius cervicis, semispinalis cervicis, iliocostalis cervicis, longissimus cervicis, multifidus, trapezius

Cervical rotation and lateral bending: sternocleidomastoid, scalenus muscles, splenius cervicis, longissimus cervicis, iliocostalis cervicis, levator scapulae, multifidus

Primary Structures

Alar ligaments

The alar ligaments attach the dens of the axis to the occipital condyles. These ligaments function to resist flexion, contralateral side bending, and contralateral rotation. They also help to limit sagittal plane translation between the atlas and the occiput.

Anterior longitudinal ligament

The anterior longitudinal ligament limits extension of the spine and reinforces the anterior portion of the intervertebral disks and vertebrae.

Cervical Spine Snapshot
Osteokinematic motions: flexion, extension, lateral flexion, rotation
Loose packed position: midway between flexion and extension
Close packed position: extension
Capsular pattern: lateral flexion and rotation equally limited, extension

Brachial plexus

The brachial plexus arises from the nerve roots of C5 through T1. These nerve roots combine to form trunks, then later divide to form divisions, cords, and finally the peripheral nerves. The nerves that arise from the brachial plexus provide innervation to muscles of the entire upper quarter.

Cruciform ligament

The cruciform ligament has vertical and horizontal portions. The vertical portion connects the dens of the axis to the foramen magnum. The horizontal portion connects the dens with the atlas. This ligament functions to limit upper cervical flexion, as well as translation of the atlas on the axis.

Interspinous ligaments

The interspinous ligaments are located between the spinous processes and serve to limit flexion and rotation of the spine.

Intervertebral disks

Intervertebral disks are formed by a dense layer of collagen fibers and fibrocartilage called the annulus fibrosus as well as a flexible inner layer called the nucleus pulposus. The annulus fibrosus is firmly attached to the adjacent vertebrae and provides tensile strength to the disk during spinal movement. The nucleus pulposus is a gelatinous mass located centrally in the disk. Flexion of a vertebral segment causes the anterior portion of the disk to be compressed and the posterior portion of the disk to be distracted.

Intervertebral foramina

The intervertebral foramina are located in the posterior pillar of each vertebral segment. Spinal nerves and blood vessels exit the spinal canal via the foramina. The size of the intervertebral foramen increases with flexion and contralateral sidebending and decreases with extension and ipsilateral sidebending. Nerve root entrapment can result from closure or narrowing of the intervertebral foramen due to arthritic changes, spurring or narrowing of the intervertebral disks.

Ligamentum flavum

The ligamentum flavum connects the lamina of one vertebra to the lamina of the vertebra above it. The structure serves to limit flexion and rotation of the spine.

Ligamentum nuchae

The ligamentum nuchae restricts flexion in the cervical spine.

Posterior longitudinal ligament

The posterior longitudinal ligament limits flexion of the spine and reinforces the posterior aspect of the intervertebral disks.

Uncovertebral joints

Also known as the uncinate processes or joints of Luschka, the uncovertebral joints are formed between the lateral projections on the inferior surface of one vertebra and the lateral projections on the superior surface of the vertebra below it. These joints are found between C3 and T1. They function to guide motion in the sagittal plane and limit motion in the other two planes.

Thoracolumbar Spine[3,9,10,14-16]

The thoracic spine consists of 12 vertebrae with long prominent spinous processes. The first ten thoracic vertebrae have articular facets on each transverse process where the ribs articulate. The lumbar spine consists of five vertebrae that provide the primary stability for the low back.

Articulations

Intervertebral joints

The intervertebral joints are formed by the superior and inferior surfaces of the vertebral bodies and the associated intervertebral disks.

Zygapophyseal joints

The zygapophyseal joints are formed by the right and left superior articular facets of one vertebra and the right and left inferior articular facets of an adjacent superior vertebra.

Muscle Action

Thoracolumbar flexion: rectus abdominis, internal oblique, external oblique

Thoracolumbar extension: erector spinae, quadratus lumborum, multifidus

Thoracolumbar rotation and lateral bending: psoas major, quadratus lumborum, external oblique, internal oblique, multifidus, longissimus thoracis, iliocostalis thoracis, rotatores

Primary Structures

Anterior longitudinal ligament

The anterior longitudinal ligament limits extension of the spine and reinforces the anterior portion of the intervertebral disks and vertebrae.

Anterior sacroiliac ligament

The anterior sacroiliac ligament connects the anterior surface of the ilium to the anterior sacrum. It is a thickening of the joint capsule and is considered the weakest of the sacroiliac ligaments.

Thoracolumbar Spine Snapshot
Osteokinematic motions: flexion, extension, lateral flexion, rotation
Loose packed position: midway between flexion and extension
Close packed position: extension
Capsular pattern: lateral flexion and rotation equally limited, extension

Coccyx

The coccyx articulates with the sacrum and most often consists of four small, fused vertebral bodies. The coccyx does not have a specific purpose and is most often considered an embryological remnant.

Iliolumbar ligament

The iliolumbar ligament connects the posterior portion of the ilium to the transverse process of the L5 vertebra and functions to limit all motions between L5 and S1.

Interosseous sacroiliac ligament

The interosseous sacroiliac ligament connects the sacrum and ilium and is located deep to the posterior sacroiliac ligament. The ligament is strong and functions to resist anterior and inferior movements of the sacrum.

Interspinous ligaments

The interspinous ligaments are located between the spinous processes and serve to limit flexion and rotation of the spine.

Intervertebral disks

Intervertebral disks are formed by a dense layer of collagen fibers and fibrocartilage called the annulus fibrosus as well as a flexible inner layer called the nucleus pulposus. The annulus fibrosus is firmly attached to the adjacent vertebrae and provides tensile strength to the disk during spinal movement. The nucleus pulposus is a gelatinous mass located slightly posterior to the center of the disk in the lumbar spine. Flexion of a vertebral segment causes the anterior portion of the disk to be compressed and the posterior portion of the disk to be distracted.

Intervertebral foramina

The intervertebral foramina are located in the posterior pillar of each vertebral segment. Spinal nerves and blood vessels exit the spinal canal via the foramina. The size of the intervertebral foramen increases with flexion and contralateral sidebending and decreases with extension and ipsilateral sidebending. Nerve root entrapment can result from closure or narrowing of the intervertebral foramen due to arthritic changes, spurring or narrowing of the intervertebral disks.

Ligamentum flavum

The ligamentum flavum connects the lamina of one vertebra to the lamina of the vertebra above it. The structure serves to limit flexion and rotation of the spine.

Lumbar plexus

The lumbar plexus is formed by the nerve roots of T12 and L1-L4. The plexus innervates the anterior and medial muscles of the thigh and the dermatomes of the medial leg and foot. The largest and most important branches of the plexus are the obturator and femoral nerves.

Posterior longitudinal ligament

The posterior longitudinal ligament limits flexion of the spine and reinforces the posterior aspect of the intervertebral disks.

Posterior sacroiliac ligament

The posterior sacroiliac ligament connects the posterior superior iliac spine with the lateral portions of the 3rd and 4th sacral segments. This ligament is strong and its fibers run in multiple directions, eventually combining with the fibers of the sacrotuberous ligament. This ligament functions to limit all sacral motions, especially posterior rotation of the sacrum.

Pubic symphysis

The pubic symphysis is the joint formed between the end of each pubis bone. The ends of the bones are covered with hyaline cartilage with a fibrocartilage disk between them. Motion at this joint is very limited.

Ribs

Ribs 1-10 articulate with the thoracic vertebrae through the costovertebral joints and the costotransverse joints. Ribs 1-7 are attached to the sternum through costal cartilage and ribs 8-10 join with the costal cartilage of ribs 1-7. Ribs 11-12 articulate only with the vertebral bodies of T11-T12, but not the transverse process of the same vertebrae. Ribs 11-12 are classified as floating because they do not attach to the sternum or the costal cartilage at their distal end.

Sacral plexus

The sacral plexus is formed by the lumbosacral trunk, the ventral rami of S1-S3, and the descending portion of S4. The plexus supplies the muscles of the buttocks, and through the sciatic nerve, innervates the muscles of the posterior thigh and lower leg.

Sacrospinous ligament

The sacrospinous ligament connects the ischial spine to the lateral sacrum and coccyx, and also has fibers that blend with the fibers of the sacrotuberous ligament. This ligament functions to limit anterior rotation of the sacrum on the pelvis.

Sacrotuberous ligament

The sacrotuberous ligament has several attachment sites, including the posterior superior iliac spine, lateral sacrum, coccyx, and ischial tuberosity. The ligament primarily functions to resist sacral anterior rotation and prevent superior translation of the sacrum.

Sacrum

The sacrum is a broad, thick bone consisting of five fused vertebrae that fixate the spinal column to the pelvis. The main functions of the sacrum are to provide an attachment for the iliac bones and to protect the pelvic organs. The sacrum is attached to the pelvis by strong ligaments forming the sacroiliac joint.

Supraspinous ligament

The supraspinous ligament restricts flexion in the thoracic and lumbar spine.

Thoracolumbar fascia

The thoracolumbar fascia is connected to the spinous processes of the lumbar vertebrae, the posterior superior iliac spines, and the iliac crests. The fascia consists of three layers that separate the lumbar muscles into three different compartments. This structure functions to provide stability to the spine, transmit forces, resist lumbar flexion, and provide a site for muscular attachments.

Musculoskeletal System Examination

Upper Quarter Screening[10,13,17-18]

The upper quarter screen provides a rapid assessment of mobility and neurologic function of the cervical spine and upper extremities. The screen is traditionally performed with the patient in sitting.

The following are components of an upper extremity screening:

Posture

- Postural assessment

Range of Motion

- Active range of motion of the cervical spine
- Active range of motion of the upper extremities
- Passive overpressure of the cervical spine and upper extremities, if the patient does not exhibit signs and symptoms of pathology

Resistive Testing (C1 – T1)

Resistive Test	Innervation Level
Cervical rotation	C1
Shoulder elevation	C2 - C4
Shoulder abduction	C5
Elbow flexion	C5 - C6
Wrist extension	C6
Elbow extension	C7
Wrist flexion	C7
Thumb extension	C8
Finger abduction	T1

Reflex Testing (C5 – C7)	
Reflex Test	**Innervation Level**
Biceps	C5
Brachioradialis	C6
Triceps	C7

Dermatome Testing (C2 – T1)	
Area of Skin	**Innervation Level**
Posterior head	C2
Posterior-lateral neck	C3
Acromioclavicular joint	C4
Lateral arm	C5
Lateral forearm and thumb	C6
Palmar distal phalanx – middle finger	C7
Little finger and ulnar border of the hand	C8
Medial forearm	T1

Lower Quarter Screening[10,13,18]

The lower quarter screen provides a rapid assessment of mobility and neurologic function of the lumbosacral spine and lower extremities. The screen is traditionally performed with the patient in standing or sitting.

The following are components of a lower extremity screening:

Posture

- Postural assessment

Range of Motion

- Active range of motion of the lumbosacral spine
- Active range of motion of the lower extremities
- Passive overpressure of the lumbosacral spine and lower extremities, if the patient does not exhibit signs and symptoms of pathology

Functional Testing (L4 – S1)	
Functional Test	**Innervation Level**
Heel walking	L4 - L5
Toe walking	S1
Straight leg raise	L4 - S1

Resistive Testing (L1 – S1)	
Resistive Test	**Innervation Level**
Hip flexion	L1 - L2
Knee extension	L3 - L4
Ankle dorsiflexion	L4 - L5
Great toe extension	L5
Ankle plantar flexion	S1

Reflex Testing (L4 – S1)	
Reflex Test	**Innervation Level**
Patella	L4
Achilles	S1

Dermatome Testing (L2 – S5)	
Area of Skin	**Innervation Level**
Anterior thigh	L2
Middle third of anterior thigh	L3
Patella and medial malleolus	L4
Fibular head and dorsum of foot	L5
Lateral and plantar aspect of foot	S1
Medial aspect of posterior thigh	S2
Perianal area	S3 - S5

Scanning Examination to Rule Out Referral of Symptoms from Other Tissues

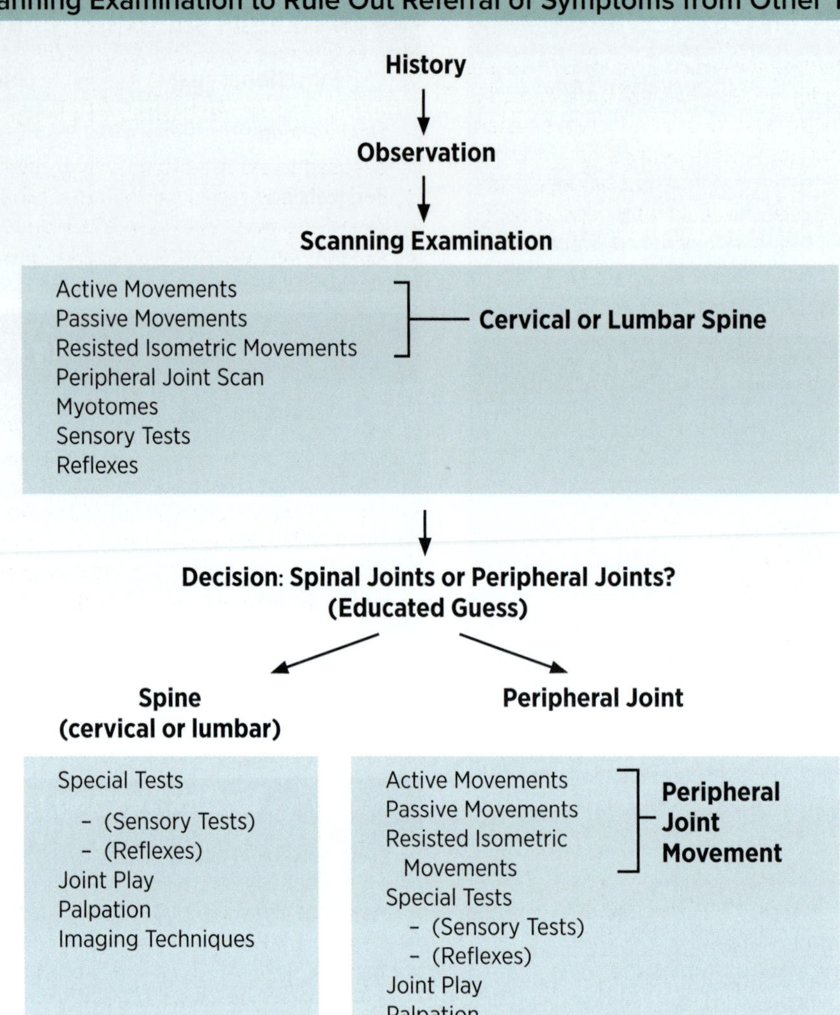

From Magee, DJ: Orthopedic Physical Assessment. W.B. Saunders Company, Philadelphia 2002, p.15, with permission.

Pain[5,9,13,18]

Pain Transmission

Nociceptors are free nerve endings present in most types of tissue that are activated by thermal, mechanical or chemical stimuli. They are the terminal portions of two types of afferent neurons, A-delta fibers and C fibers. A-delta fibers transmit detailed information rapidly from peripheral cutaneous structures. C fibers transmit information from deeper tissues (e.g., joints, viscera) and do so more slowly than A-delta fibers. Because of these differences, A-delta fibers are more likely to transmit pain signals that are sharp and localized, while C fibers transmit pain signals that are dull, aching, and diffuse. These nerve fibers send their impulses to the dorsal horn of the spinal cord, where the impulses are then carried to the thalamus via the spinothalamic tracts. The nerve signal is then projected to the sensory cortex to be interpreted and become a conscious pain sensation.

Gate Control Theory

The gate control theory helps to explain the regulation of pain, specifically how other stimuli can help to decrease the sensation of pain. A-delta and C fibers synapse with a secondary neuron, which sends the pain signal to the brain. However, they also synapse with an inhibitory interneuron at this same junction. A-alpha and A-beta fibers provide input to these inhibitory interneurons. Therefore, nerve transmission through the A-alpha and A-beta fibers can stimulate these interneurons to inhibit pain signals to the brain ("closing the gate"). The use of electrical stimulation and massage as interventions work on this theory by stimulating A-alpha and A-beta fibers.

Endogenous Opioids

Pain regulation is also controlled by endogenous opioids known as opiopeptins (also known as endorphins). These substances bind to opioid receptors, which are located throughout the nervous system, resulting in inhibition of pain signals. Opiopeptins have a direct effect on nerve signals by controlling the amount of calcium and potassium that move into and out of the cell during depolarization. They also have an indirect effect on nerve signals by inhibiting the release of GABA, a substance that normally inhibits the activity of structures that help to control pain, such as A-beta fibers.

McGill Pain Questionnaire

A pain assessment tool that is divided into four parts with a total of 70 questions.

Part 1 Patient marks on a drawing of the body to indicate area and type of pain (internal or external)

Part 2 Patient chooses one word that best describes the pain from each of the twenty categories

Part 3 Patient describes pattern of pain, factors that increase and relieve pain

Part 4 Patient rates the intensity of pain on a scale of zero to five

This tool can be used to establish a baseline, evaluate particular treatment regimens, and monitor progress. It is valid, reliable, and the most widely used pain assessment scale.

Numerical Rating Scale

A tool used to assess pain intensity by rating pain on a scale of 0-10 or 0-100. The 0 represents no discernable pain and the 10 or 100 represent the worst pain ever. The information is used as a baseline and should be reassessed at regular intervals in order to monitor progress. This scale is easy to administer, assess, and monitor.

Visual Analogue Scale

A tool used to assess pain intensity using a 10-15 cm line with the left anchor indicating "no pain" and the right anchor indicating "the worst pain you can have." The level of perceived pain is indicated on the line and is reassessed frequently over the course of physical therapy to record changes and progress, and to predict patient outcome. This scale can be highly sensitive if small increments such as millimeters are used to measure the patient's point of pain on the scale. The visual analogue scale is a valid tool if measurements are taken accurately.

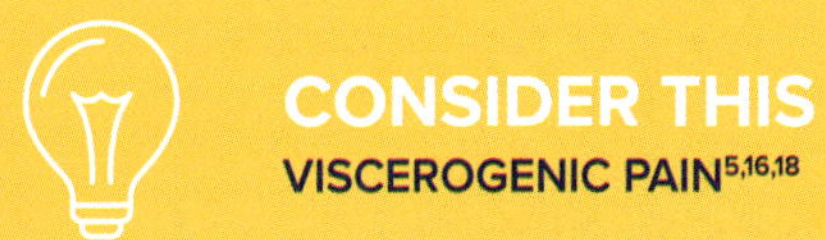

VISCEROGENIC PAIN[5,16,18]

Viscerogenic pain is pain that results from pathology of an internal organ, which can often refer to a site distant from the organ and mimic common patterns of musculoskeletal pain. The mechanism for viscerogenic pain is not fully understood, though viscerosomatic convergence may be one method for explaining this phenomenon. This theory states that the afferent inputs for visceral and somatic structures converge as they approach the central nervous system, and thus the brain interprets viscerogenic pain as originating from a musculoskeletal structure.

Recognizing the pain patterns associated with viscerogenic pain is an important component of the screening process during the patient examination. Viscerogenic pain differs from musculoskeletal pain in many ways. Viscerogenic pain does not change based on movement or positioning of the body part, as would musculoskeletal pain. Because the organs have innervation from multiple spinal cord levels and a low density of nerve receptors, the pain is often diffuse and poorly localized. Additionally, viscerogenic pain may be accompanied by other systemic symptoms, such as nausea, vomiting, weight loss, pallor, profuse sweating, fever, and abnormal vital signs. Common sites for referred viscerogenic pain include the shoulder, scapula, back, chest, pelvis, sacroiliac joint, groin, and hip.

EXAMPLES

Myocardial infarction

The heart is innervated by the C3-T4 spinal segments and thus cardiac pathology can result in referred pain to a variety of areas. A patient having a myocardial infarction may experience pain on the left side of the body in the chest, mid-back, shoulder, arm, neck or jaw.

Kehr's sign

Blood that accumulates in the abdominal cavity, often secondary to rupture of the spleen, can cause irritation of the diaphragm and refer pain to the left shoulder. Pain is referred to this region due to the innervation of the phrenic nerve (i.e., C3-C5). Kehr's sign is positive when pressure to the upper abdomen or supine positioning results in left shoulder pain.

Gallstones

Gallstones, or other gallbladder conditions, can refer pain to the right upper abdomen and interscapular region due to the gallbladder's innervation from mid-thoracic spinal segments. If an inflamed gallbladder leads to irritation of the diaphragm, pain may also refer to the right shoulder.

Body Composition[19]

Body composition is defined as the relative percentage of body weight that is comprised of fat and fat-free tissue. There are multiple methods for testing the percentage of body fat including hydrostatic weighing, skinfold measurements, plethysmography, body mass index, and bioelectrical impedance analysis. A healthy range of body fat is 12-18% for males and 18-23% for females.

Densitometry

Hydrostatic Weighing: This method calculates the density of the body by immersing a person in water and measuring the amount of water that becomes displaced. The percentage of body fat is then determined by calculating the measured amount of water displaced in an equation based on Archimedes' principle. This method is the most widely used laboratory procedure to determine body density. Limitations of this method include the need to account for residual lung volume during submersion and evaluating patients that must tolerate water submersion during the testing. The standard error for this method is estimated at 2 to 2.5%.

Plethysmography: This method calculates the density of the body utilizing the amount of air displacement during testing within a specialized closed chamber. The change in pressure within the chamber is measured and converted to the percentage of body fat using a standardized equation.

Anthropometry

Skinfold Measurement: This method determines the overall percentage of body fat through the measurement of nine standardized sites. The correlation relies on the theory that the amount of subcutaneous fat is proportional to the total fat in the body. Limitations of this method include the requisite of an experienced examiner as well as variance from the standards based on gender, age, and ethnicity. Accuracy of measurement is within +/-3% with appropriate technique and equipment.

Skinfold Measurement Procedure

- All measurements should be taken on the right side of the body
- Take multiple measurements at each site to ensure accuracy and retest if the difference is greater than one to two millimeters
- Skinfold calipers should be positioned one centimeter away from the examiner's fingers when pinching the side, positioned perpendicular to the skinfold, and centered between the base and top of the fold (Fig. 4-15)
- Wait one to two seconds before reading the caliper
- Maintain pinching of the site during the reading of the caliper

Standard Skinfold Sites	
Abdominal	Midaxillary
Triceps *	Subscapular *
Biceps	Suprailiac
Chest/pectoral	Thigh
Medial calf	

There are seven-site and three-site formulas to calculate the percentage of body fat using particular sites. There are also specific formulas for gender, sport, ethnicity, and age.

* Indicates the most commonly utilized sites

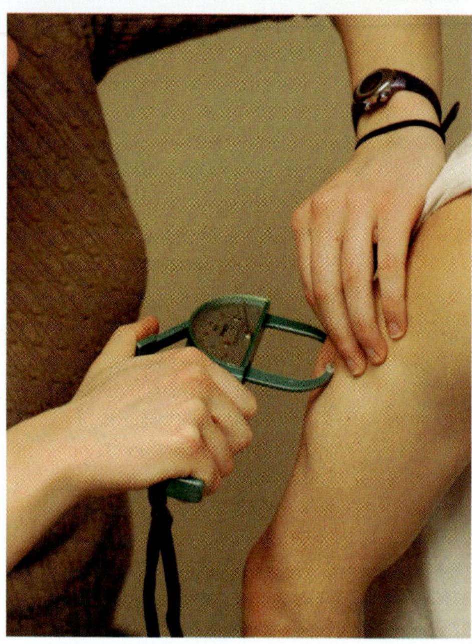

Fig. 4-15: A therapist measuring a skinfold with skinfold calipers at the triceps site.

Other Techniques

Body Mass Index (BMI)

(See Cardiovascular and Pulmonary Systems Unit)

Bioelectrical Impedance Analysis (BIA)

This method of assessing body composition uses a small electrical current and measures the resistance or opposition to the current flow. This technique is based on the principle that resistance to electrical current is inversely related to the composition of water within the body. The formula of height^2/resistance is used for the general population while population-specific equations are also available. The standard error compares to the accuracy of skinfold measurements at approximately +/- 3%. Limitations include the requisite for the subjects to be properly hydrated as well as following all guidelines for the BIA protocol.

BIA Protocol

- Abstain from eating or drinking within four hours prior to testing
- Abstain from vigorous physical activity within 12 hours prior to testing
- Urinate within 30 minutes prior to testing
- Avoid alcohol consumption for 48 hours prior to testing
- Avoid excessive water intake prior to testing

Posture

Good and Faulty Posture: Summary Chart

Good Posture	Part	Faulty Posture
Toes should be straight, that is, neither curled downward nor bent upward. They should extend forward in line with the foot and should not be squeezed together or overlap.	Toes	Toes bend up at the first joint and down at middle joints so that the weight rests on the tips of the toes (hammer toes). This fault is often associated with wearing shoes that are too short. Big toe slants inward toward the midline of the foot (hallux valgus). "Bunion." This fault is often associated with wearing shoes that are too narrow and pointed at the toes.
In standing, the longitudinal arch has the shape of a half dome. Barefoot or in shoes without heels, the feet toe-out slightly. In shoes with heels, the feet are parallel. In walking with or without shoes, the feet are parallel and the weight is transferred from the heel along the outer border to the ball of the foot. In sprinting, the feet are parallel or toe-in slightly. The weight is on the balls of the feet and toes because the heels do not come in contact with the ground.	Foot	Low longitudinal arch or flat foot. Low metatarsal arch, usually indicated by calluses under the ball of the foot. Weight borne on the inner side of the foot (pronation). "Ankle rolls in." Weight borne on the outer border of the foot (supination). "Ankle rolls out." Toeing-out while walking, or while standing in shoes with heels ("slue-footed"). Toeing-in while walking or standing ("pigeon-toed").
Legs are straight up and down. Kneecaps face straight ahead when feet are in good position. Looking at the knees from the side, the knees are straight (i.e., neither flexed or hyperextended).	Knees and Legs	Knees touch when feet are apart (knock-knees). Knees are apart when feet touch (bowlegs). Knee curves slightly backward (hyperextended knee). "Back-knee." Knee bends slightly forward, that is, it is not as straight as it should be (flexed knee). Kneecaps face slightly toward each other (medially rotated femurs). Kneecaps face slightly outward (laterally rotated femurs).
Ideally, the body weight is borne evenly on both feet and the hips are level. One side should not be more prominent than the other as seen from front or back, nor is one hip more forward or backward than the other as seen from the side. The spine does not curve to the left or the right side. (A slight deviation to the left in right-handed individuals and to the right in left-handed individuals is not uncommon. Also, a tendency toward a slightly low right shoulder and slightly high right hip is frequently found in right-handed people, and vice versa for left-handed people.)	Hips, Pelvis, and Spine Back View	One hip is higher than the other (lateral pelvic tilt). Sometimes it is not really higher but appears so because a sideways sway of the body has made it more prominent. (Tailors and dressmakers often notice a lateral tilt because the hemline of skirts or length of trousers must be adjusted to the difference.) The hips are rotated so that one is farther forward than the other (clockwise or counterclockwise rotation).

Good and Faulty Posture: Summary Chart

Good Posture	Part	Faulty Posture
The front of the pelvis and the thighs are in a straight line. The buttocks are not prominent in back but slope slightly downward. The spine has four natural curves. In the neck and lower back the curve is forward; in the upper back and lowest part of the spine (sacral region) it is backward. The sacral curve is a fixed curve while the other three are flexible.	**Spine and Pelvis Side View**	The low back arches forward too much (lordosis). The pelvis tilts forward too much. The front of the thigh forms an angle with the pelvis when this tilt is present. The normal forward curve in the low back has straightened. The pelvis tips backward as in swayback and flat-back postures. Increased backward curve in the upper back (kyphosis or round upper back). Increased forward curve in the neck. Almost always accompanied by round upper back and seen as a forward head. Lateral curve of the spine (scoliosis); toward one side (C-curve), toward both sides (S-curve).
In young children, up to about the age of 10, the abdomen normally protrudes somewhat. In older children and adults it should be flat.	**Abdomen**	Entire abdomen protrudes. Lower part of the abdomen protrudes while the upper part is pulled in.
A good position of the chest is one in which it is slightly up and slightly forward (while the back remains in good alignment). The chest appears to be in a position about halfway between that of a full inspiration and a forced expiration.	**Chest**	Depressed or "hollow-chest" position. Lifted and held up too high, brought about by arching the back. Ribs more prominent on one side than on the other. Lower ribs flaring out or protruding.
Arms hang relaxed at the sides with palms of the hands facing toward the body. Elbows are slightly bent, so forearms hang slightly forward. Shoulders are level and neither one is more forward or backward than the other when seen from the side. Shoulder blades lie flat against the rib cage. They are neither too close together or too wide apart. In adults, a separation of about 4 inches is average.	**Arms and Shoulders**	Arms held stiffly in any position forward, backward, or out from the body. Arms turned so that palms of hands face backward. One shoulder higher than the other. Both shoulders hiked-up. One or both shoulders drooping forward or sloping. Shoulders rotated either clockwise or counterclockwise. Shoulder blades pulled back too hard. Shoulder blades too far apart. Shoulder blades too prominent, standing out from the rib cage (winged scapulae).
Head is held erect in a position of good balance.	**Head**	Chin up too high. Head protruding forward. Head tilted or rotated to one side.

From Kendall F, McCreary E, Provance P: Muscle Testing and Function. Lippincott, William & Wilkins, Baltimore 1993, p.115-116, with permission.

CONSIDER THIS

IDEAL PLUMB LINE ALIGNMENT[10,18]

A plumb line is a tool that consists of a weight suspended at the end of a string to determine verticality. Ideal positioning of selected body parts in relation to the plumb line is described below.

- Slightly posterior to coronal suture
- Through the external auditory meatus
- Through the axis of the odontoid process
- Midway through the tip of the shoulder
- Through the bodies of the lumbar vertebrae
- Slightly posterior to the hip joint
- Slightly anterior to the axis of the knee joint
- Slightly anterior to the lateral malleolus
- Through the calcaneocuboid joint

Although desirable, rarely will a given patient demonstrate ideal alignment with all of the anatomical landmarks listed above. The following pictures provide an example of a patient with "good posture" and a patient with "faulty posture" (Figs. 4-16, 4-17).

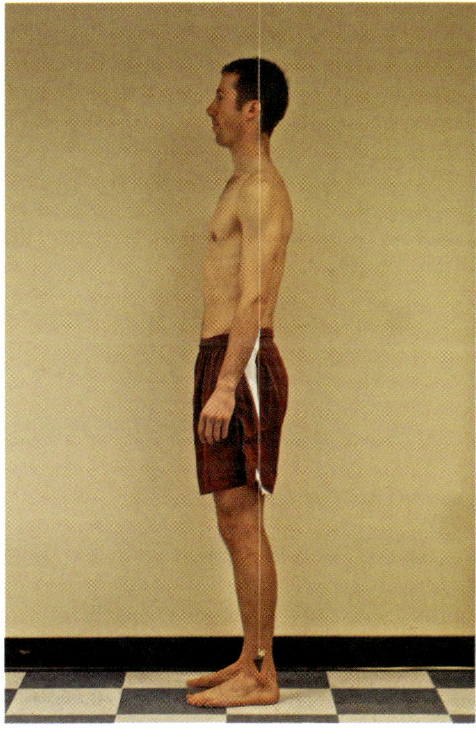

Fig. 4-16: An example of a patient with relatively "good posture" using a plumb line. The image demonstrates several anatomical landmarks in ideal alignment and others that are in close proximity.

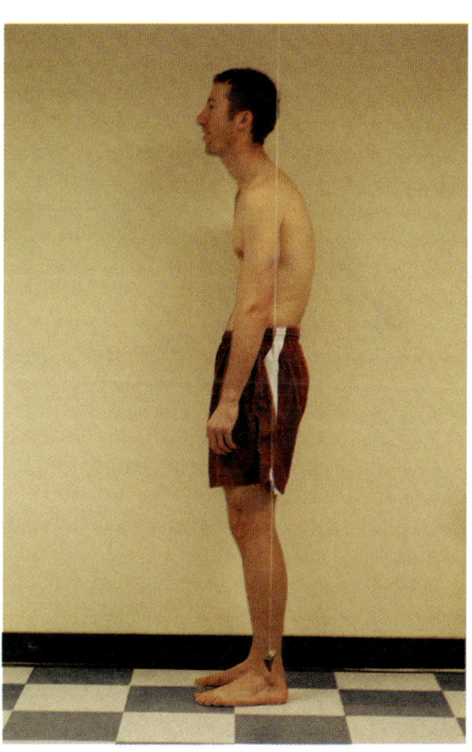

Fig. 4-17: An example of a patient with relatively "faulty posture" using a plumb line.

Positioning of a Joint[10]

Loose Packed Position of Joints	
Joint	**Position**
Facet (spine)	Midway between flexion and extension
Temporomandibular	Mouth slightly open (freeway space)
Glenohumeral	55° abduction, 30° horizontal adduction
Acromioclavicular	Arm resting by side in normal physiological position
Sternoclavicular	Arm resting by side in normal physiological position
Ulnohumeral (elbow)	70° flexion, 10° supination
Radiohumeral	Full extension, full supination
Proximal radioulnar	70° flexion, 35° supination
Distal radioulnar	10° supination
Radiocarpal (wrist)	Neutral with slight ulnar deviation
Carpometacarpal	Midway between abduction - adduction and flexion - extension
Metacarpophalangeal	Slight flexion
Interphalangeal	Slight flexion
Hip	30° flexion, 30° abduction, slight lateral rotation
Knee	25° flexion
Talocrural (ankle)	10° plantar flexion, midway between maximum inversion and eversion
Subtalar	Midway between extremes of range of movement
Midtarsal	Midway between extremes of range of movement
Tarsometatarsal	Midway between extremes of range of movement
Metatarsophalangeal	Neutral
Interphalangeal	Slight flexion

From Magee, DJ: Orthopedic Physical Assessment. W.B. Saunders Company, Philadelphia 2002, p.50, with permission.

Close Packed Position of Joints	
Joint	**Position**
Facet (spine)	Extension
Temporomandibular	Clenched teeth
Glenohumeral	Abduction and lateral rotation
Acromioclavicular	Arm abducted to 90°
Sternoclavicular	Maximum shoulder elevation
Ulnohumeral (elbow)	Extension
Radiohumeral	Elbow flexed 90°, forearm supinated 5°
Proximal radioulnar	5° supination
Distal radioulnar	5° supination
Radiocarpal (wrist)	Extension with radial deviation
Metacarpophalangeal (fingers)	Full flexion
Metacarpophalangeal (thumb)	Full opposition
Interphalangeal	Full extension
Hip	Full extension, medial rotation
Knee	Full extension, lateral rotation of tibia
Talocrural (ankle)	Maximum dorsiflexion
Subtalar	Supination
Midtarsal	Supination
Tarsometatarsal	Supination
Metatarsophalangeal	Full extension
Interphalangeal	Full extension

From Magee, DJ: Orthopedic Physical Assessment. W.B. Saunders Company, Philadelphia 2002, p.50, with permission.

Descriptions of Specific Positions		
	Loose Packed	**Close Packed**
Stress on joint	Minimal	Maximal
Congruency of joint	Minimal	Full
Ligament position	Great laxity	Full tightness
Joint surface	No volitional separation	Compressed

Common Capsular Patterns of Joints[10]

Joint	Restriction*
Temporomandibular	Limitation of mouth opening
Atlanto-occipital	Extension, side flexion equally limited
Cervical spine	Lateral flexion and rotation equally limited, extension
Glenohumeral	Lateral rotation, abduction, medial rotation
Sternoclavicular	Pain at extremes of range of movement
Acromioclavicular	Pain at extremes of range of movement
Ulnohumeral	Flexion, extension
Radiohumeral	Flexion, extension, supination, pronation
Proximal radioulnar	Supination, pronation
Distal radioulnar	Full range of movement, pain at extremes of rotation
Radiocarpal (wrist)	Flexion and extension equally limited
Trapeziometacarpal	Abduction, extension
Metacarpophalangeal and interphalangeal	Flexion, extension

Joint	Restriction*
Thoracic spine	Lateral flexion and rotation equally limited, extension
Lumbar spine	Lateral flexion and rotation equally limited, extension
Sacroiliac, symphysis pubis, and sacrococcygeal	Pain when joints are stressed
Hip**	Flexion, abduction, medial rotation (sometimes medial rotation is most limited)
Knee	Flexion, extension
Tibiofibular	Pain when joint stressed
Talocrural	Plantar flexion, dorsiflexion
Talocalcaneal (subtalar)	Limitation of varus range of movement
Midtarsal	Dorsiflexion, plantar flexion, adduction, medial rotation
First metatarsophalangeal	Extension, flexion
Second to fifth metatarsophalangeal	Variable
Interphalangeal	Flexion, extension

* Movements are listed in order of restriction. ** For the hip: flexion, abduction, and medial rotation are the movements most limited in a capsular pattern.
From Magee, DJ: Orthopedic Physical Assessment. W.B. Saunders Company, Philadelphia 2002, p.28, with permission.

End-Feel[3,20]

Normal End-Feel

End-feel is the type of resistance that is felt when passively moving a joint through the end range of motion. Certain tissues and joints have a consistent end-feel and are described as firm, hard or soft. Pathology can be identified through noting the type of abnormal end-feel within a particular joint.

Firm (stretch)

Examples: Ankle dorsiflexion
Finger extension
Hip medial rotation
Forearm supination

Hard (bone to bone)

Example: Elbow extension

Soft (soft tissue approximation)

Examples: Elbow flexion
Knee flexion

Abnormal End-Feel

Abnormal end-feel consists of any end-feel that is felt at an abnormal or inconsistent point in the range of motion or in a joint that normally presents with a different end-feel.

Empty (cannot reach end-feel, usually due to pain)

Examples: Joint inflammation
Fracture
Bursitis

Firm

Examples: Increased tone
Tightening of the capsule
Ligament shortening

Hard

Examples: Fracture
Osteoarthritis
Osteophyte formation

Soft

Examples: Edema
Synovitis
Ligament instability/tear

Muscle Testing

Manual Muscle Testing Grades[2,21]

Zero (0/5)	The subject demonstrates no palpable muscle contraction.
Trace (1/5)	The subject's muscle contraction can be palpated, but there is no joint movement.
Poor Minus (2-/5)	The subject does not complete range of motion in a gravity-eliminated position.
Poor (2/5)	The subject completes range of motion in a gravity-eliminated position.
Poor Plus (2+/5)	The subject is able to initiate movement against gravity.
Fair Minus (3-/5)	The subject does not complete the range of motion against gravity, but does complete more than half of the range.
Fair (3/5)	The subject completes range of motion against gravity without manual resistance.
Fair Plus (3+/5)	The subject completes range of motion against gravity with only minimal resistance.
Good Minus (4-/5)	The subject completes range of motion against gravity with minimal-moderate resistance.
Good (4/5)	The subject completes range of motion against gravity with moderate resistance.
Good Plus (4+/5)	The subject completes range of motion against gravity with moderate-maximal resistance.
Normal (5/5)	The subject completes range of motion against gravity with maximal resistance.

Positioning for Muscle Testing[2,21]

Supine

Abdominals	Anterior deltoid*
Biceps	Brachioradialis
Finger flexors	Finger extensors
Iliopsoas	Infraspinatus
Lateral rotators of shoulder*	Medial rotators of shoulder*
Neck flexors	Pectoralis major
Pectoralis minor	Peroneals
Pronators	Sartorius
Serratus anterior	Supinators
Tensor fasciae latae	Teres minor
Thumb muscles	Tibialis anterior
Tibialis posterior	Toe extensors
Toe flexors	Triceps*
Wrist extensors	Wrist flexors

Sidelying

Gluteus medius (Fig. 4-22)	Gluteus minimus
Hip adductors (Fig. 4-23)	Lateral abdominals

Prone

Back extensors	Gastrocnemius
Gluteus maximus	Hamstrings*
Lateral rotators of the shoulder*	Latissimus dorsi (Fig. 4-20)
Lower trapezius	Medial rotators of the shoulder*
Middle trapezius	Neck extensors
Posterior deltoid*	Quadratus lumborum
Rhomboids	Soleus
Teres major	Triceps*

Sitting

Coracobrachialis	Deltoid* (Figs. 4-18, 4-19)
Hip flexors* (Fig. 4-21)	Lateral rotators of hip (Fig. 4-24)
Medial rotators of hip	Quadriceps (Fig. 4-25)
Upper trapezius	Serratus anterior*

Standing

Ankle plantar flexors	Serratus anterior*

*Indicates multiple acceptable positions for muscle testing

Manual Muscle Testing

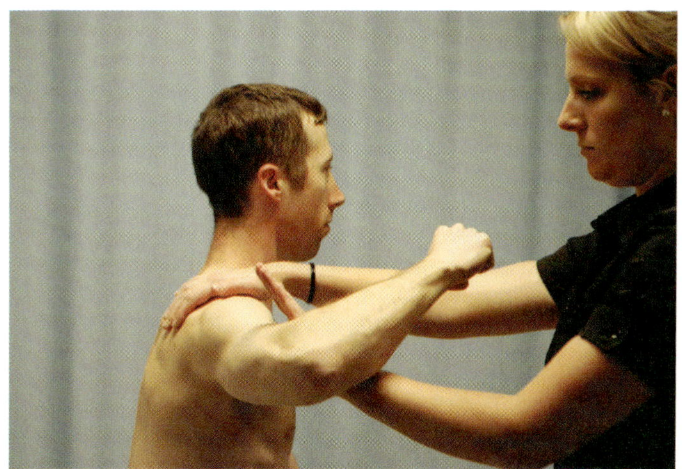

Fig. 4-18: Manual muscle testing of the anterior deltoid.

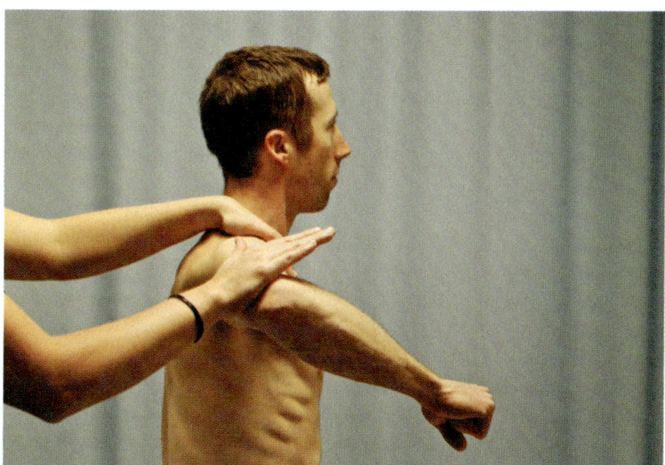

Fig. 4-19: Manual muscle testing of the posterior deltoid.

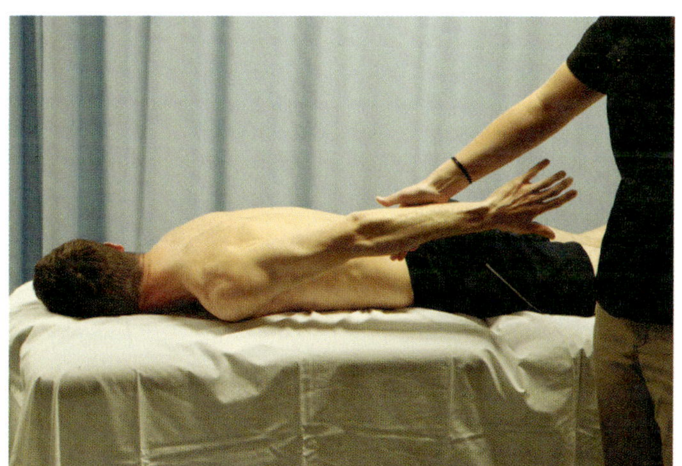

Fig. 4-20: Manual muscle testing of the latissimus dorsi.

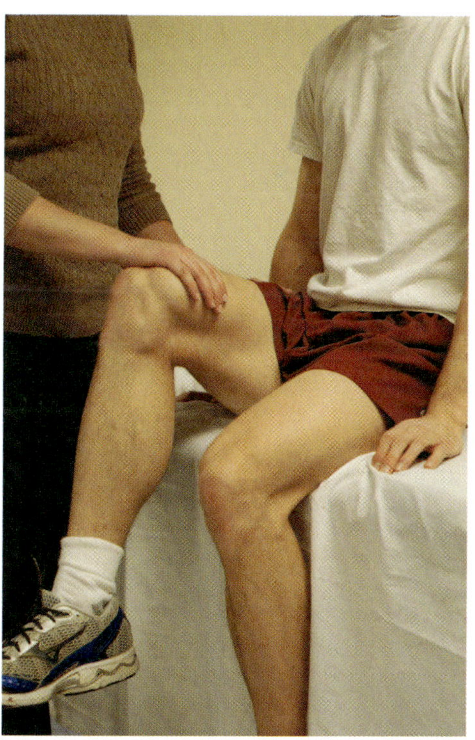

Fig. 4-21: Manual muscle testing of the hip flexors.

Manual Muscle Testing (continued)

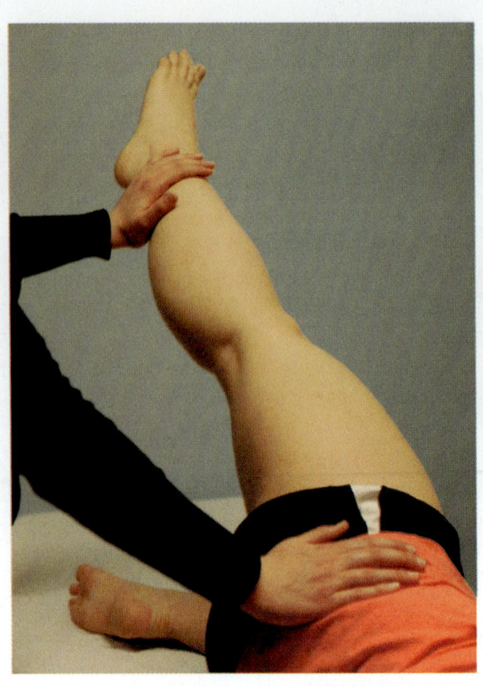

Fig. 4-22: Manual muscle testing of the gluteus medius.

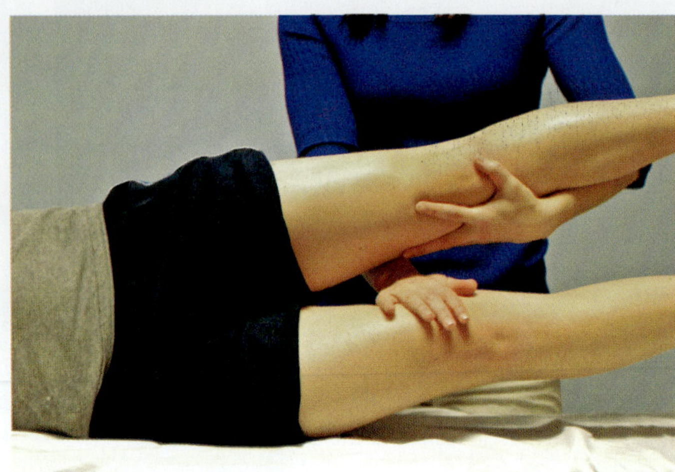

Fig. 4-23: Manual muscle testing of the hip adductors.

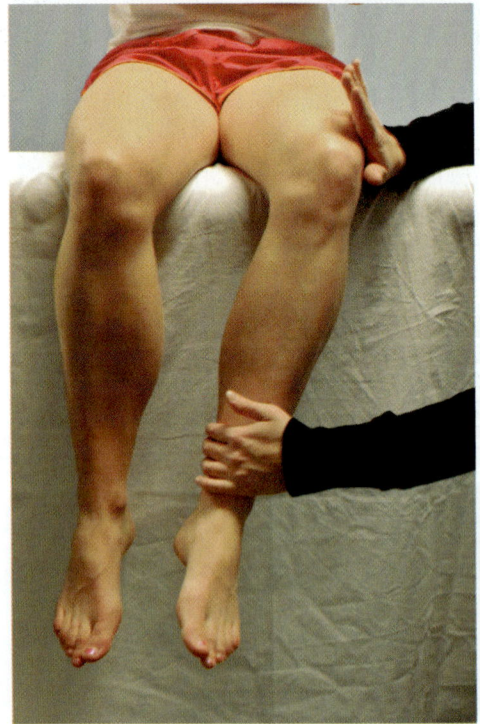

Fig. 4-24: Manual muscle testing of the hip lateral rotators.

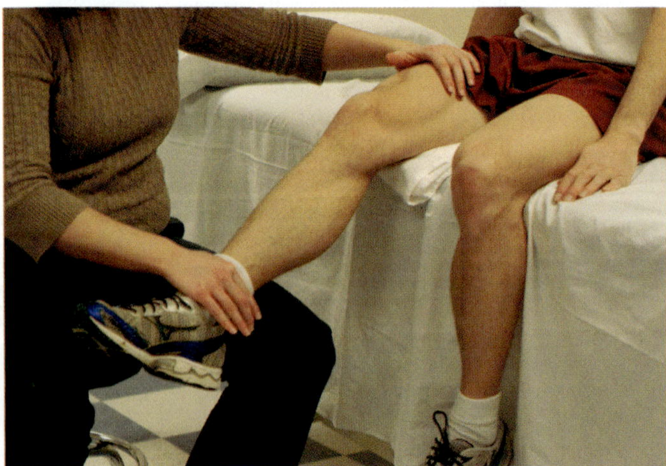

Fig. 4-25: Manual muscle testing of the quadriceps femoris.

Muscle Insufficiency[2,16]

A muscle contraction that is less than optimal due to an extremely lengthened or shortened position of the muscle. There are two types of insufficiency:

Active: when a two-joint muscle is incapable of shortening to the extent required to produce full range of motion at all joints crossed simultaneously

Passive: when a two-joint muscle cannot lengthen to the extent required to allow full range of motion of all joints it crosses simultaneously

Grip[10,18]

Stages of Gripping

1. The hand opens fully, which requires activation of the wrist and finger extensor musculature as well as the hand intrinsics.
2. The fingers position around the object and close to grasp the object, which requires activation of the finger flexor musculature as well as the hand intrinsics.
3. The force of the grasp is modified based on the shape, weight, fragility, and surface characteristics of the object.
4. The object is released by opening the hand, which again requires activation of the extensor musculature.

Types of Grips

A power grip is used when a strong or forceful grip is needed and involves stabilization of the object against the palm of the hand. The fingers are in flexion and the wrist is in ulnar deviation and slight extension. Types of power grips include:

- A cylindrical grasp is characterized by the entire hand wrapping around an object with the thumb on one side and the four fingers on the opposite side of the object. This type of grasp is used for cylindrically shaped objects, such as a soda can.
- A fist grasp is similar to a cylindrical grasp, but involves grasping around a narrower object so that the thumb and fingers overlap. This type of grasp is used for smaller cylindrically shaped objects, such as a hammer.
- A spherical grasp is characterized by the entire hand wrapping around a spherical object. It differs from a cylindrical grasp in that the fingers are separated from one another and there is a greater amount of thumb opposition. This type of grasp is used for spherical objects, such as a baseball.
- A hook grasp is characterized by use of the second and third interphalangeal joints (though it can involve all four fingers) to create a hook to hold an object. A hook grasp is controlled by the forearm flexors and extensors. This type of grasp is used for objects with a handle, such as a pail.

A precision grip (i.e., prehension grip) is used when accurate and precise movements of the hand are needed. This type of grip involves the metacarpophalangeal and interphalangeal joints on the radial side of the hand. Types of precision grips include:

- A digital prehension grip (i.e., three-fingered pinch) is characterized by pulp-to-pulp contact between the thumb, index finger, and middle finger. This type of grip may be used when holding a pencil.
- A lateral prehension grip is characterized by contact between the thumb and lateral side of the index finger. This type of grip may be used when using a key.
- A tip prehension grip (i.e., tip pinch) is characterized by thumb opposition so that the tip of the thumb contacts the tip of another finger. This type of grip may be used when holding a needle.

Dynamometry[10]

Dynamometry is the process of measuring forces that are doing work. A dynamometer is a device that measures strength through the use of a load cell or spring-loaded gauge. There are various kinds of dynamometers that are used based on treatment objectives. Three types of dynamometry that will be discussed here include the handheld dynamometer that measures grip strength, the handheld dynamometer used to measure strength of the extremities through isometric contraction, and the dynamometer used to measure strength through isokinetic contraction. Handheld dynamometry demonstrates intrarater reliability of > .94. The same dynamometer should be used each session and the same tester should consistently measure the patient.

- **A handheld dynamometer** can be used to assess the grip strength of a patient (Fig. 4-26). Normally, a patient's dominant grip strength is five to ten pounds greater than the non-dominant grip strength. Handheld dynamometry is also used to measure muscle group strength by having the patient exert maximal force against the dynamometer. Portable, non-electric units include a hydraulic or spring-load system and display the force on a gauge. Electrical units use load cells or strain gauges and display force digitally. Grip strength is usually recorded in pounds or kilograms.

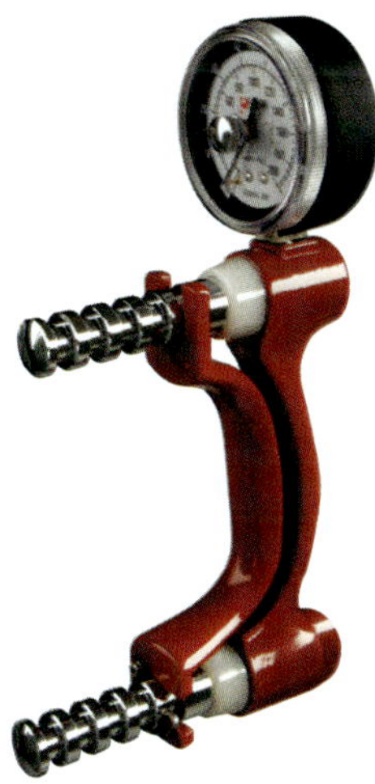

Fig. 4-26: A handheld dynamometer. Courtesy Chattanooga, a DJO Global Company.

- **Isometric dynamometry** measures the static strength of a muscle group without any movement. The extremity is restrained by stabilization straps or stabilized with only verbal instruction (Fig. 4-27).

  Benefits include attaining peak and average force data, reaction time data, rate of motor recruitment, and maximal exertion data. This method is relatively safe, simple to use, easy to interpret data, and cost effective.

  Disadvantages include the inability to convert data to functional activities, as well as the need for caution with patients with acute orthopedic injury, osteoporosis or hernia. This method is contraindicated for patients with fractures and significant hypertension.

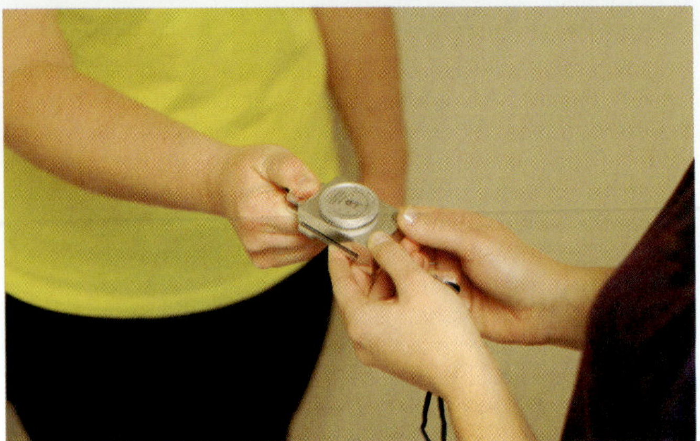

Fig. 4-27: A patient using a pinch grip dynamometer.

- **Isokinetic dynamometry** measures the strength of a muscle group during a movement with constant, predetermined speed. This device will alter the resistance to accommodate for the change in the length-tension ratio and lever arm throughout the entire arc of motion. The muscle group will therefore maximally contract throughout the motion. Common speeds of motion include 60, 120, and 180 degrees per second.

  Benefits include the ability to test the muscle strength at various speeds, the ability to measure the patient's power, and that the patient will never have more resistance than they can handle during the isokinetic testing.

  Disadvantages include the high cost of operation for the device, limitations in patterns of movement, a higher level of understanding required by the patient, and that this method does not truly correlate to function since people do not perform at a constant velocity during daily activities.

Make Test:

A make test is an evaluation procedure where a patient is asked to apply a force against the dynamometer.

Break Test:

A break test is an evaluation procedure where a patient is asked to hold a contraction against pressure that is applied in the opposite direction to the contraction.

Gait

Standard versus Rancho Los Amigos Terminology[4,22]

	Standard Terminology	Rancho Los Amigos Terminology
Stance Phase (60% of gait cycle)	Heel strike Foot flat Midstance Heel off Toe off	Initial contact Loading response Midstance Terminal stance Pre-swing
Swing Phase (40% of gait cycle)	Acceleration Midswing Deceleration	Initial swing Midswing Terminal swing

Standard Terminology[4,23]

Stance Phase

Heel strike: Heel strike is the instant that the heel touches the ground to begin stance phase.

Foot flat: Foot flat is the point in which the entire foot makes contact with the ground and should occur directly after heel strike.

Midstance: Midstance is the point during the stance phase when the entire body weight is directly over the stance limb.

Heel off: Heel off is the point in which the heel of the stance limb leaves the ground.

Toe off: Toe off is the point in which only the toe of the stance limb remains on the ground.

Swing Phase

Acceleration: Acceleration begins when toe off is complete and the reference limb swings until positioned directly under the body.

Midswing: Midswing is the point when the swing limb is directly under the body.

Deceleration: Deceleration begins directly after midswing, as the swing limb begins to extend, and ends just prior to heel strike.

Rancho Los Amigos Terminology[4,22,23]

Stance Phase

Initial contact: Initial contact is the beginning of the stance phase that occurs when the foot touches the ground (Fig. 4-28).

Loading response: Loading response corresponds to the amount of time between initial contact and the beginning of the swing phase for the other leg (Fig. 4-29).

Midstance: Midstance corresponds to the point in stance phase when the other foot is off the floor until the body is directly over the stance limb (Fig. 4-30).

Terminal stance: Terminal stance begins when the heel of the stance limb rises and ends when the other foot touches the ground (Fig. 4-31).

Pre-swing: Pre-swing begins when the other foot touches the ground and ends when the stance foot reaches toe off (Fig. 4-32).

Swing Phase

Initial swing: Initial swing begins when the stance foot lifts from the floor and ends with maximal knee flexion during swing (Fig. 4-33).

Midswing: Midswing begins with maximal knee flexion during swing and ends when the tibia is perpendicular with the ground (Fig. 4-34).

Terminal swing: Terminal swing begins when the tibia is perpendicular to the floor and ends when the foot touches the ground (Fig. 4-35).

Normal Gait

	SWING PHASE 40%			STANCE PHASE 60%				
	Initial Swing	Midswing	Terminal Swing	Initial Contact	Loading Response	Midstance	Terminal Stance	Pre-Swing
Trunk	Erect Neutral	Erect Neutral	Erect Neutral	Erect Neutral	Erect Neutral	Erect Neutral	Erect Neutral	Erect Neutral
Pelvis	Level: Backward Rotation 4-5°	Level: Neutral Rotation	Level: Forward Rotation 4-5°	Level: Maintains Forward Rotation	Level: Less Forward Rotation	Level: Neutral Rotation	Level: Backward Rotation 4-5°	Level: Backward Rotation 4-5°
Hip	Flexion 20°	Flexion 20° - 30°	Flexion 30°	Flexion 30°	Flexion 30°	Extending to Neutral	Apparent Hyperextension 10°	Neutral Extension
	Neutral: Rotation Abduction Adduction	Neutral: Rotation Abduction Adduction	Neutral: Rotation Abduction Adduction	Neutral: Rotation Abduction Adduction	Neutral: Rotation Abduction Adduction	Neutral: Rotation Abduction Adduction	Neutral: Rotation Abduction Adduction	Neutral: Rotation Abduction Adduction
Knee	Flexion 60°	From 60° to 30° Flexion	Extension to 0°	Full Extension	Flexion 15°	Extending to Neutral	Full Extension	Flexion 35°
Ankle	Plantar Flexion 10°	Neutral	Neutral	Neutral Heel First	Plantar Flexion 15°	From Plantar Flexion to 10° Dorsiflexion	Neutral with Tibia Stable and Heel Off Prior to Initial Contact Opposite Foot	Plantar Flexion 20°
Toes	Neutral	Neutral	Neutral	Neutral	Neutral	Neutral	Neutral IP Extended MP	Neutral IP Extended MP

From Rancho Los Amigos National Rehabilitation Center, Downey, California, with permission.

Fig. 4-28: Initial contact **Fig. 4-29:** Loading response **Fig. 4-30:** Midstance **Fig. 4-31:** Terminal stance

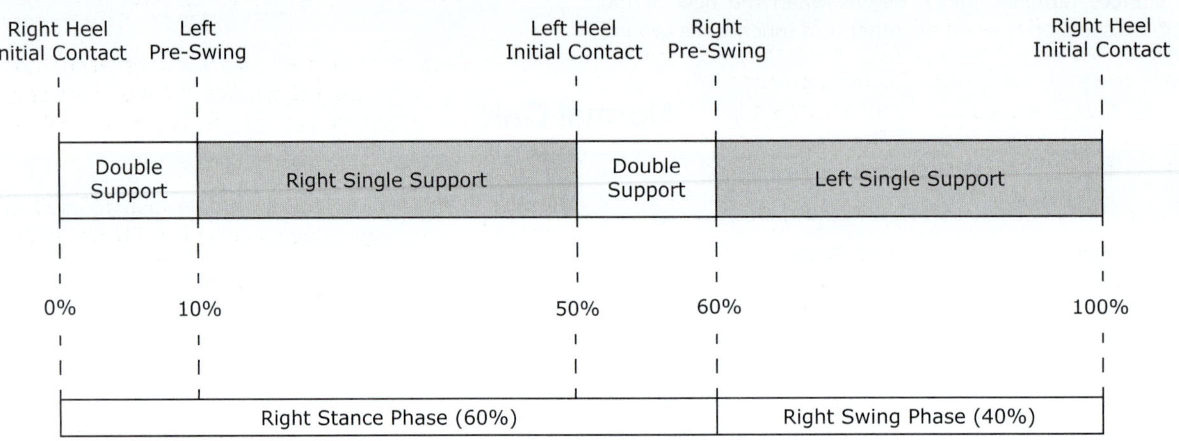

Fig. 4-36: Timing and sequence of the gait cycle.

Range of Motion Requirements for Normal Gait[13,23]

Hip flexion:	**0 - 30 degrees**
Hip extension:	**0 - 10 degrees**
Knee flexion:	**0 - 60 degrees**
Knee extension:	**0 degrees**
Ankle dorsiflexion:	**0 - 10 degrees**
Ankle plantar flexion:	**0 - 20 degrees**

Gait and Muscle Activity[10,13,18]

Initial contact: The ankle dorsiflexors place the ankle in dorsiflexion during heel strike and prepare to lower the foot towards the ground. The quadriceps contract to place the knee in extension while the hamstrings help stabilize the knee and prevent hyperextension. The hip extensors and abductors contract to stabilize the trunk and pelvis over the leg.

Loading response: The ankle dorsiflexors act eccentrically to control lowering of the foot towards the ground. The quadriceps contract eccentrically to control knee flexion as the limb accepts the weight of the body. In the latter portion of this phase, the plantar flexors eccentrically control dorsiflexion as the tibia moves over the foot. Simultaneously, the tibialis posterior eccentrically controls pronation of the foot. The quadriceps contraction becomes concentric to draw the femur forward over the tibia. Throughout the loading response phase, the hip extensors contract concentrically to produce hip extension.

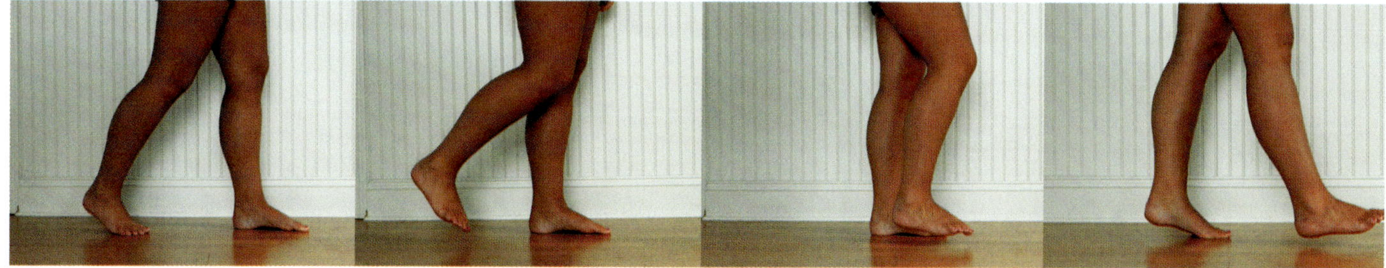

Fig. 4-32: Pre-swing **Fig. 4-33:** Initial swing **Fig. 4-34:** Midswing **Fig. 4-35:** Terminal swing

Midstance: The plantar flexors continue to act eccentrically to control dorsiflexion as the body moves over the stance limb. Activity in the knee musculature is minimal during this phase, though the quadriceps contract concentrically to continue producing closed chain knee extension. The hip abductor muscles stabilize the pelvis and prevent contralateral hip drop. The iliopsoas also begins to contract eccentrically to control hip extension.

Terminal stance: The plantar flexors begin to work concentrically to aid the foot in its propulsion of the body forward. Knee muscle activity remains limited. The hip abductors continue to stabilize the pelvis and the iliopsoas continues to slow the rate of hip extension.

Pre-swing: The plantar flexors are at their peak activity as the foot "toes off" from the ground. The hamstrings begin to produce knee flexion to prepare for the swing phase, though the momentum of the body also aids in this motion. The iliopsoas begins to work concentrically to produce hip flexion, along with other hip flexors (e.g., rectus femoris, sartorius, adductor longus).

Initial swing: The ankle dorsiflexors contract concentrically to clear the foot from the ground, while the hamstrings assist with foot clearance by flexing the knee. The hip flexors continue to produce hip flexion to advance the limb forward.

Midswing: The ankle dorsiflexors continue to contract concentrically to maintain dorsiflexion. Knee and hip muscle activity are minimal during this phase since forward momentum allows for advancement of the limb.

Terminal swing: The ankle dorsiflexors continue to contract concentrically to maintain dorsiflexion. The ankle invertors also contract concentrically to prepare the foot for initial contact. The quadriceps contract concentrically to place the knee in extension for initial contact, while the hamstrings act eccentrically to control the rate of knee extension. The hip extensors eccentrically slow the rate of hip flexion and prepare the limb for initial contact.

Gait Terminology[4,10]

Base of support: The distance measured between the left and right foot during progression of gait. The distance decreases as cadence increases. The average base of support for an adult is two to four inches.

Cadence: The number of steps an individual will walk over a period of time. The average value for an adult is 110–120 steps per minute.

Degree of toe-out: The angle formed by each foot's line of progression and a line intersecting the center of the heel and second toe. The average degree of toe-out for an adult is seven degrees.

Double support phase: The double support phase refers to the two times during a gait cycle where both feet are on the ground. The time of double support increases as the speed of gait decreases. This phase does not exist with running.

Gait cycle: The gait cycle refers to the sequence of motions that occur from initial contact of the heel to the next consecutive initial contact of the same heel.

Pelvic rotation: Rotation of the pelvis occurs opposite the thorax in order to maintain balance and regulate speed. The average pelvic rotation during gait for an adult is a total of 8 degrees (4 degrees forward with the swing leg and 4 degrees backward with the stance leg).

Single support phase: The single support phase occurs when only one foot is on the ground and occurs twice during a single gait cycle.

Step length: The distance measured between right heel strike and left heel strike. The average step length for an adult is 28 inches (Fig. 4-37).

Stride length: The distance measured between right heel strike and the following right heel strike. The average stride length for an adult is 56 inches (Fig. 4-37).

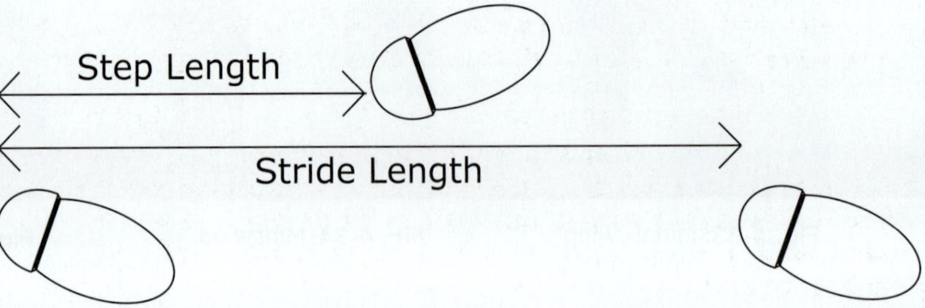

Fig. 4-37: Step and stride length.

Abnormal Gait Patterns[10,23]

Antalgic: A protective gait pattern where the stance time is decreased to avoid weight bearing on the involved side due to pain. This is typically associated with a rapid and shorter swing phase of the uninvolved limb. Causes of antalgic gait include disease (usually bone or joint), joint inflammation, or injuries to muscles, tendons, and/or ligaments.

Ataxic: A gait pattern characterized by staggering and unsteadiness. There is usually a wide base of support and movements are exaggerated.

Cerebellar: A staggering gait pattern seen in cerebellar disease.

Circumduction: A gait pattern characterized by a circular motion to advance the leg during swing phase; this may be used to compensate for insufficient hip or knee flexion or dorsiflexion.

Double step: A gait pattern in which alternate steps are of a different length or at a different rate.

Equine: A gait pattern characterized by high steps; usually involves excessive activity of the gastrocnemius.

Festinating: A gait pattern where a patient walks on toes as though pushed. It starts slowly, increases, and may continue until the patient grasps an object in order to stop.

Hemiplegic: A gait pattern in which patients abduct the paralyzed limb, swing it around, and bring it forward so the foot comes to the ground in front of them.

Parkinsonian: A gait pattern marked by increased forward flexion of the trunk and knees; gait is shuffling with quick and small steps; festinating may occur.

Scissor: A gait pattern in which the legs cross midline upon advancement.

Spastic: A gait pattern with stiff movement, toes seeming to catch and drag, legs held together, and hip and knee joints slightly flexed. Commonly seen in spastic paraplegia.

Steppage: A gait pattern in which the feet and toes are lifted through hip and knee flexion to excessive heights; usually secondary to dorsiflexor weakness. The foot will slap at initial contact with the ground secondary to the decreased control.

Tabetic: A high stepping ataxic gait pattern in which the feet slap the ground.

Trendelenburg: A gait pattern that denotes gluteus medius weakness; excessive lateral trunk flexion and weight shifting over the stance leg.

Vaulting: A gait pattern where the swing leg advances by compensating through the combination of elevation of the pelvis and plantar flexion of the stance leg.

Gait Deviations[10,22,23,25]

Gait Deviations

	Foot slap	Toe down instead of heel strike	Clawing of toes	Heel lift during midstance	No toe off
Ankle and Foot	• Weak dorsiflexors • Dorsiflexor paralysis	• Plantar flexor spasticity • Plantar flexor contracture • Weak dorsiflexors • Dorsiflexor paralysis • Leg length discrepancy • Hindfoot pain	• Toe flexor spasticity • Positive support reflex	• Insufficient dorsiflexion range • Plantar flexor spasticity	• Forefoot/toe pain • Weak plantar flexors • Weak toe flexors • Insufficient plantar flexion range of motion
	Exaggerated knee flexion at contact	**Hyperextension in stance**	**Exaggerated knee flexion at terminal stance**	**Insufficient flexion with swing**	**Excessive flexion with swing**
Knee	• Weak quadriceps • Quadriceps paralysis • Hamstrings spasticity • Insufficient extension range of motion	• Compensation for weak quadriceps • Plantar flexor contracture	• Knee flexion contracture • Hip flexion contracture	• Knee effusion • Quadriceps extension spasticity • Plantar flexor spasticity • Insufficient flexion range of motion	• Flexor withdrawal reflex • Lower extremity flexor synergy
	Insufficient hip flexion at initial contact	**Insufficient hip extension at stance**	**Circumduction during swing**	**Hip hiking during swing**	**Exaggerated hip flexion during swing**
Hip	• Weak hip flexors • Hip flexor paralysis • Hip extensor spasticity • Insufficient hip flexion range of motion	• Insufficient hip extension range of motion • Hip flexion contracture • Lower extremity flexor synergy	• Compensation for weak hip flexors • Compensation for weak dorsiflexors • Compensation for weak hamstrings	• Compensation for weak dorsiflexors • Compensation for weak knee flexors • Compensation for extensor synergy pattern	• Lower extremity flexor synergy • Compensation for insufficient ankle dorsiflexion

Range of Motion

Average Adult Range of Motion - Upper and Lower Extremities; Spine[3]

Upper Extremity	
Shoulder	
Flexion	0-180
Extension	0-60
Abduction	0-180
Medial rotation	0-70
Lateral rotation	0-90
Elbow	
Extension	0
Flexion	0-150
Forearm	
Pronation	0-80
Supination	0-80
Wrist	
Flexion	0-80
Extension	0-70
Radial deviation	0-20
Ulnar deviation	0-30
Thumb	
Carpometacarpal	
Abduction	0-70
Flexion	0-15
Extension	0-20
Opposition	Tip of thumb to base of fifth digit
Metacarpophalangeal	
Flexion	0-50
Interphalangeal	
Flexion	0-80
Digits – Second to Fifth	
Metacarpophalangeal	
Flexion	0-90
Hyperextension	0-45
Proximal interphalangeal	
Flexion	0-100
Distal interphalangeal	
Flexion	0-90
Hyperextension	0-10

Lower Extremity	
Hip	
Flexion	0-120
Extension	0-30
Abduction	0-45
Adduction	0-30
Medial rotation	0-45
Lateral rotation	0-45
Knee	
Flexion	0-135
Ankle (talocrural)	
Dorsiflexion	0-20
Plantar flexion	0-50
Midtarsal (transverse tarsal)	
Inversion	0-35
Eversion	0-15
Subtalar	
Inversion	0-5
Eversion	0-5

Spine	
Cervical Spine	
Flexion	0-45
Extension	0-45
Lateral flexion	0-45
Rotation	0-60
Thoracic and Lumbar Spine	
Flexion	0-80
Extension	0-25
Lateral flexion	0-35
Rotation	0-45

CONSIDER THIS

PROCESS FOR CONDUCTING GONIOMETRIC MEASUREMENT[3]

Goniometric measurement can be reliable (i.e., possessing repeatability of measures) and valid (i.e., meaningful interpretation can be inferred through the measure) when performed by a trained individual following the recommended procedure. The following 12-step process outlines the recommended procedure for conducting goniometric measurement.

1. Place the subject in the recommended testing position.
2. Stabilize the proximal joint segment.
3. Move the distal joint segment through the available range of motion. Make sure that the passive range of motion is performed slowly, the end of the range is attained, and the end-feel is determined.
4. Make a clinical estimate of the range of motion.
5. Return the distal joint segment to the starting position.
6. Palpate bony anatomical landmarks.
7. Align the goniometer.
8. Read and record the starting position. Remove the goniometer.
9. Stabilize the proximal joint segment.
10. Move the distal segment through the full range of motion.
11. Replace and realign the goniometer. Palpate the anatomical landmarks again if necessary.
12. Read and record the range of motion.

Adapted from Norkin and White: Measurement of Joint Motion: A Guide to Goniometry. F.A. Davis Company, Philadelphia, 2003, p.35, with permission.

Goniometric Technique[3,20]

Upper Extremity

Shoulder

Flexion

Patient position: supine

Stabilization: thorax to prevent extension of the spine

End-feel: firm

Axis: acromial process

Stationary arm: midaxillary line of the thorax

Moveable arm: lateral midline of the humerus using the lateral epicondyle of the humerus for reference

Extension

Patient position: prone

Stabilization: thorax to prevent flexion of the spine

End-feel: firm

Axis: acromial process

Stationary arm: midaxillary line of the thorax

Moveable arm: lateral midline of the humerus using the lateral epicondyle of the humerus for reference

Abduction

Patient position: supine

Stabilization: thorax to prevent lateral flexion of the spine

End-feel: firm

Axis: anterior aspect of the acromial process

Stationary arm: parallel to the midline of the anterior aspect of the sternum

Moveable arm: medial midline of the humerus

Adduction

Patient position: supine

Stabilization: thorax to prevent lateral flexion of the spine

End-feel: firm

Axis: anterior aspect of the acromial process

Stationary arm: parallel to the midline of the anterior aspect of the sternum

Moveable arm: medial midline of the humerus

Medial rotation

Patient position: supine with shoulder abducted to 90 degrees and elbow flexed to 90 degrees

Stabilization: distal end of the humerus to maintain the shoulder in 90 degrees of abduction

End-feel: firm

Axis: olecranon process

Stationary arm: parallel or perpendicular to the floor

Moveable arm: ulna using the olecranon process and ulnar styloid process for reference

Lateral rotation

Patient position: supine with shoulder abducted to 90 degrees and elbow flexed to 90 degrees

Stabilization: distal end of the humerus to maintain the shoulder in 90 degrees of abduction

End-feel: firm

Axis: olecranon process

Stationary arm: parallel or perpendicular to the floor

Moveable arm: ulna using the olecranon process and ulnar styloid process for reference

*The supplied stabilization descriptions are for shoulder complex motion. The required stabilization may vary for glenohumeral motions.

Elbow

Flexion (Fig. 4-38)

Patient position: supine

Stabilization: humerus to prevent flexion of the shoulder

End-feel: soft

Axis: lateral epicondyle of the humerus

Stationary arm: lateral midline of the humerus using the center of the acromial process for reference

Moveable arm: lateral midline of the radius using the radial head and radial styloid process for reference

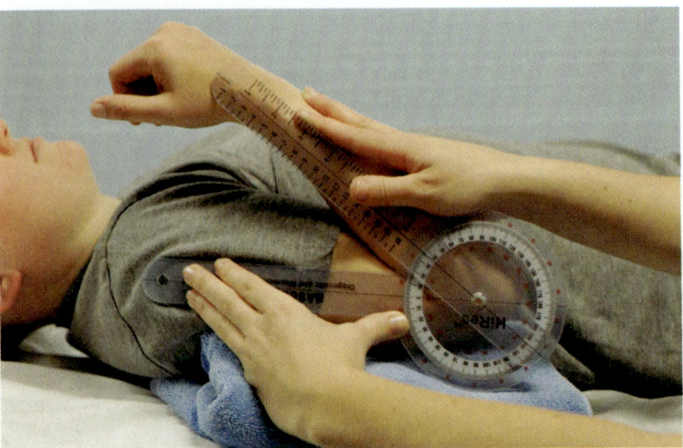

Fig. 4-38: A therapist measuring elbow flexion with a goniometer.

Extension

Patient position: supine

Stabilization: humerus to prevent flexion of the shoulder

End-feel: hard

Axis: lateral epicondyle of the humerus

Stationary arm: lateral midline of the humerus using the center of the acromial process for reference

Moveable arm: lateral midline of the radius using the radial head and radial styloid process for reference

Forearm

Pronation

Patient position: sitting with the elbow flexed to 90 degrees

Stabilization: distal end of the humerus to prevent medial rotation and abduction of the humerus

End-feel: firm or hard

Axis: lateral to the ulnar styloid process

Stationary arm: parallel to the anterior midline of the humerus

Moveable arm: dorsal aspect of the forearm, just proximal to the styloid process of the radius and ulna

Supination

Patient position: sitting with the elbow flexed to 90 degrees

Stabilization: distal end of the humerus to prevent lateral rotation and adduction of the humerus

End-feel: firm

Axis: medial to the ulnar styloid process

Stationary arm: parallel to the anterior midline of the humerus

Moveable arm: ventral aspect of the forearm, just proximal to the styloid process of the radius and ulna

Wrist

Flexion

Patient position: sitting next to a supporting surface with the shoulder abducted to 90 degrees and the elbow flexed to 90 degrees

Stabilization: radius and ulna to prevent supination or pronation

End-feel: firm

Axis: lateral aspect of the wrist over the triquetrum

Stationary arm: lateral midline of the ulna using the olecranon and ulnar styloid process for reference

Moveable arm: lateral midline of the fifth metacarpal

Extension

Patient position: sitting next to a supporting surface with the shoulder abducted to 90 degrees and the elbow flexed to 90 degrees

Stabilization: radius and ulna to prevent supination or pronation

End-feel: firm

Axis: lateral aspect of the wrist over the triquetrum

Stationary arm: lateral midline of the ulna using the olecranon and ulnar styloid process for reference

Moveable arm: lateral midline of the fifth metacarpal

Radial deviation

Patient position: sitting next to a supporting surface with the shoulder abducted to 90 degrees and the elbow flexed to 90 degrees

Stabilization: radius and ulna to prevent supination or pronation

End-feel: firm or hard

Axis: over the middle of the dorsal aspect of the wrist over the capitate

Stationary arm: dorsal midline of the forearm using the lateral epicondyle of the humerus for reference

Moveable arm: dorsal midline of the third metacarpal

Ulnar deviation

Patient position: sitting next to a supporting surface with the shoulder abducted to 90 degrees and the elbow flexed to 90 degrees

Stabilization: radius and ulna to prevent supination or pronation

End-feel: firm

Axis: over the middle of the dorsal aspect of the wrist over the capitate

Stationary arm: dorsal midline of the forearm using the lateral epicondyle of the humerus for reference

Moveable arm: dorsal midline of the third metacarpal

Thumb

Carpometacarpal flexion

Patient position: sitting with the forearm and hand on a supporting surface

Stabilization: carpals, radius, and ulna to prevent wrist motion

End-feel: firm

Axis: over the palmar aspect of the first carpometacarpal joint

Stationary arm: ventral midline of the radius using the ventral surface of the radial head and radial styloid process for reference

Moveable arm: ventral midline of the first metacarpal

Carpometacarpal extension

Patient position: sitting with the forearm and hand on a supporting surface

Stabilization: carpals, radius, and ulna to prevent wrist motion

End-feel: firm

Axis: over the palmar aspect of the first carpometacarpal joint

Stationary arm: ventral midline of the radius using the ventral surface of the radial head and radial styloid process for reference

Moveable arm: ventral midline of the first metacarpal

Carpometacarpal abduction

Patient position: sitting with the forearm and hand on a supporting surface

Stabilization: carpals and second metacarpal to prevent wrist motion

End-feel: firm

Axis: over the lateral aspect of the radial styloid process

Stationary arm: lateral midline of the second metacarpal using the center of the second metacarpophalangeal joint for reference

Moveable arm: lateral midline of the first metacarpal using the center of the first metacarpophalangeal joint for reference

Carpometacarpal adduction

Patient position: sitting with the forearm and hand on a supporting surface

Stabilization: carpals and second metacarpal to prevent wrist motion

End-feel: firm

Axis: over the lateral aspect of the radial styloid process

Stationary arm: lateral midline of the second metacarpal using the center of the second metacarpophalangeal joint for reference

Moveable arm: lateral midline of the first metacarpal using the center of the first metacarpophalangeal joint for reference

Fingers

Metacarpophalangeal flexion

Patient position: sitting with the forearm and hand on a supporting surface

Stabilization: metacarpal to prevent wrist motion

End-feel: firm or hard

Axis: over the dorsal aspect of the metacarpophalangeal joint

Stationary arm: over the dorsal midline of the metacarpal

Moveable arm: over the dorsal midline of the proximal phalanx

Metacarpophalangeal extension

Patient position: sitting with the forearm and hand on a supporting surface

Stabilization: metacarpal to prevent wrist motion

End-feel: firm

Axis: over the dorsal aspect of the metacarpophalangeal joint

Stationary arm: over the dorsal midline of the metacarpal

Moveable arm: over the dorsal midline of the proximal phalanx

Metacarpophalangeal abduction

Patient position: sitting with the forearm and hand on a supporting surface

Stabilization: metacarpal to prevent wrist motion

End-feel: firm

Axis: over the dorsal aspect of the metacarpophalangeal joint

Stationary arm: over the dorsal midline of the metacarpal

Moveable arm: dorsal midline of the proximal phalanx

Metacarpophalangeal adduction

Patient position: sitting with the forearm and hand on a supporting surface

Stabilization: metacarpal to prevent wrist motion

End-feel: firm

Axis: over the dorsal aspect of the metacarpophalangeal joint

Stationary arm: over the dorsal midline of the metacarpal

Moveable arm: dorsal midline of the proximal phalanx

Proximal interphalangeal flexion

Patient position: sitting with the forearm and hand on a supporting surface

Stabilization: proximal phalanx to prevent motion at the metacarpophalangeal joint

End-feel: soft, firm or hard

Axis: over the dorsal aspect of the proximal interphalangeal joint

Stationary arm: over the dorsal midline of the proximal phalanx

Moveable arm: over the dorsal midline of the middle phalanx

Proximal interphalangeal extension

Patient position: sitting with the forearm and hand on a supporting surface

Stabilization: proximal phalanx to prevent motion at the metacarpophalangeal joint

End-feel: firm

Axis: over the dorsal aspect of the proximal interphalangeal joint

Stationary arm: over the dorsal midline of the proximal phalanx

Moveable arm: over the dorsal midline of the middle phalanx

Distal interphalangeal flexion

Patient position: sitting with the forearm and hand on a supporting surface

Stabilization: middle and proximal phalanx to prevent motion at the proximal interphalangeal joint

End-feel: firm

Axis: over the dorsal aspect of the distal interphalangeal joint

Stationary arm: over the dorsal midline of the middle phalanx

Moveable arm: over the dorsal midline of the distal phalanx

Distal interphalangeal extension

Patient position: sitting with the forearm and hand on a supporting surface

Stabilization: middle and proximal phalanx to prevent motion at the proximal interphalangeal joint

End-feel: firm

Axis: over the dorsal aspect of the distal interphalangeal joint

Stationary arm: over the dorsal midline of the middle phalanx

Moveable arm: over the dorsal midline of the distal phalanx

Lower Extremity

Hip

Flexion (Fig. 4-39)

Patient position: supine

Stabilization: pelvis to prevent posterior tilting

End-feel: soft or firm

Axis: over the lateral aspect of the hip joint using the greater trochanter of the femur for reference

Stationary arm: lateral midline of the pelvis

Moveable arm: lateral midline of the femur using the lateral epicondyle for reference

Extension

Patient position: prone

Stabilization: pelvis to prevent anterior tilting

End-feel: firm

Axis: over the lateral aspect of the hip joint using the greater trochanter of the femur for reference

Stationary arm: lateral midline of the pelvis

Moveable arm: lateral midline of the femur using the lateral epicondyle for reference

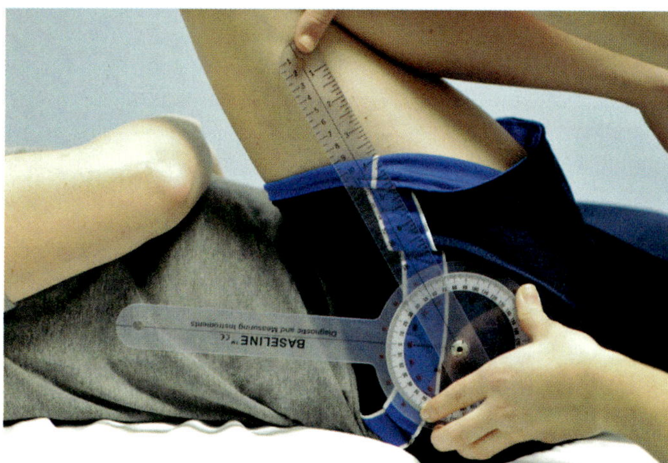

Fig. 4-39: A therapist measuring hip flexion with a goniometer.

Abduction

Patient position: supine

Stabilization: pelvis to prevent lateral tilting and rotation; trunk to prevent lateral flexion

End-feel: firm

Axis: over the anterior superior iliac spine (ASIS) of the extremity being measured

Stationary arm: align with imaginary horizontal line extending from one ASIS to the other ASIS

Moveable arm: anterior midline of the femur using the midline of the patella for reference

Adduction

Patient position: supine

Stabilization: pelvis to prevent lateral tilting

End-feel: firm

Axis: over the anterior superior iliac spine (ASIS) of the extremity being measured

Stationary arm: align with imaginary horizontal line extending from one ASIS to the other ASIS

Moveable arm: anterior midline of the femur using the midline of the patella for reference

Medial rotation

Patient position: sitting

Stabilization: distal end of the femur

End-feel: firm

Axis: anterior aspect of the patella

Stationary arm: perpendicular to the floor or parallel to the supporting surface

Moveable arm: anterior midline of the lower leg using the crest of the tibia and a point midway between the two malleoli for reference

Lateral rotation

Patient position: sitting

Stabilization: distal end of the femur

End-feel: firm

Axis: anterior aspect of the patella

Stationary arm: perpendicular to the floor or parallel to the supporting surface

Moveable arm: anterior midline of the lower leg using the crest of the tibia and a point midway between the two malleoli for reference

Knee

Flexion

Patient position: supine

Stabilization: femur to prevent rotation, abduction, and adduction of the hip

End-feel: soft or firm

Axis: lateral epicondyle of the femur

Stationary arm: lateral midline of the femur using the greater trochanter for reference

Moveable arm: lateral midline of the fibula using the lateral malleolus and fibular head for reference

Extension

Patient position: supine

Stabilization: femur to prevent rotation, abduction, and adduction of the hip

End-feel: firm

Axis: lateral epicondyle of the femur

Stationary arm: lateral midline of the femur using the greater trochanter for reference

Moveable arm: lateral midline of the fibula using the lateral malleolus and fibular head for reference

Ankle (talocrural)

Dorsiflexion

Patient position: sitting with the knee flexed to 90 degrees

Stabilization: tibia and fibula to prevent knee and hip motion

End-feel: firm

Axis: lateral aspect of the lateral malleolus

Stationary arm: lateral midline of the fibula using the head of the fibula for reference

Moveable arm: parallel to the lateral aspect of the fifth metatarsal

Plantar flexion

Patient position: sitting with the knee flexed to 90 degrees

Stabilization: tibia and fibula to prevent knee and hip motion

End-feel: firm or hard

Axis: lateral aspect of the lateral malleolus

Stationary arm: lateral midline of the fibula using the head of the fibula for reference

Moveable arm: parallel to the lateral aspect of the fifth metatarsal

Midtarsal (transverse tarsal)

Inversion (Fig. 4-40)

Patient position: sitting with the knee flexed to 90 degrees

Stabilization: tibia and fibula to prevent knee and hip motion

End-feel: firm

Axis: anterior aspect of the ankle midway between the malleoli

Stationary arm: anterior midline of the lower leg using the tibial tuberosity for reference

Moveable arm: anterior midline of the second metatarsal

Eversion

Patient position: sitting with the knee flexed to 90 degrees

Stabilization: tibia and fibula to prevent knee and hip motion

End-feel: firm or hard

Axis: anterior aspect of the ankle midway between the malleoli

Stationary arm: anterior midline of the lower leg using the tibial tuberosity for reference

Moveable arm: anterior midline of the second metatarsal

Subtalar

Inversion

Patient position: prone with the foot extended over a supporting surface

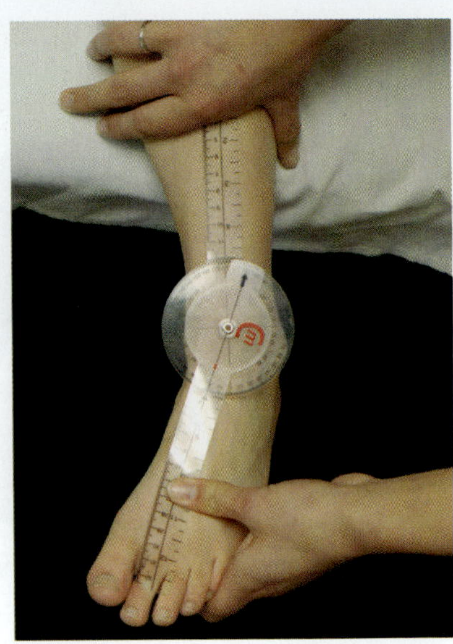

Fig. 4-40: A therapist measuring midtarsal inversion.

Stabilization: tibia and fibula to prevent knee and hip motion

End-feel: firm

Axis: posterior aspect of the ankle midway between the malleoli

Stationary arm: posterior midline of the lower leg

Moveable arm: posterior midline of the calcaneus

Eversion

Patient position: prone with the foot extended over a supporting surface

Stabilization: tibia and fibula to prevent knee and hip motion

End-feel: firm or hard

Axis: posterior aspect of the ankle midway between the malleoli

Stationary arm: posterior midline of the lower leg

Moveable arm: posterior midline of the calcaneus

Spine

Cervical Spine

Flexion

Patient position: sitting with the thoracic and lumbar spine supported

Stabilization: shoulder girdle and chest; the patient's hands should be placed on their knees

End-feel: firm

Axis: over the external auditory meatus

Stationary arm: perpendicular or parallel to the ground

Moveable arm: along the base of the nares or if using a tongue depressor, align the goniometer parallel with the tongue depressor

Extension

Patient position: sitting with the thoracic and lumbar spine supported

Stabilization: shoulder girdle and chest to prevent extension of the thoracic and lumbar spine

End-feel: firm

Axis: over the external auditory meatus

Stationary arm: perpendicular or parallel to the ground

Moveable arm: along the base of the nares, or if using a tongue depressor, align the goniometer parallel with the tongue depressor

Lateral flexion (Fig. 4-41)

Patient position: sitting

Stabilization: shoulder girdle and chest to prevent lateral flexion of the thoracic and lumbar spines

End-feel: firm

Axis: over the spinous process of the C7 vertebra

Stationary arm: with the spinous processes of the thoracic vertebrae so that the arm is perpendicular to the ground

Moveable arm: along the dorsal midline of the head using the occipital protuberance for reference

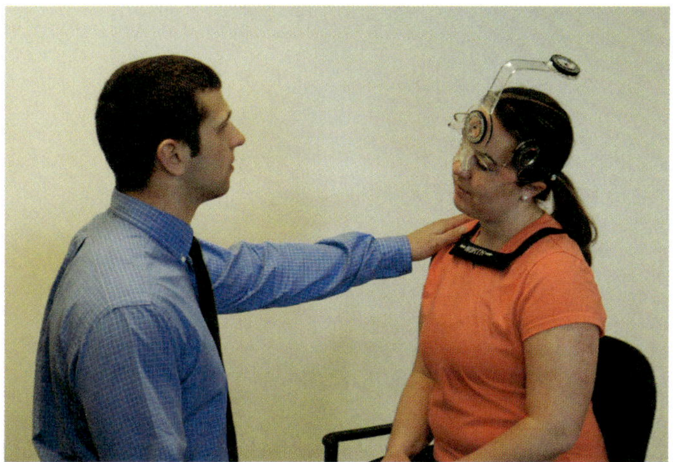

Fig. 4-41: A therapist preparing to measure cervical lateral flexion with a cervical range of motion (CROM) device.

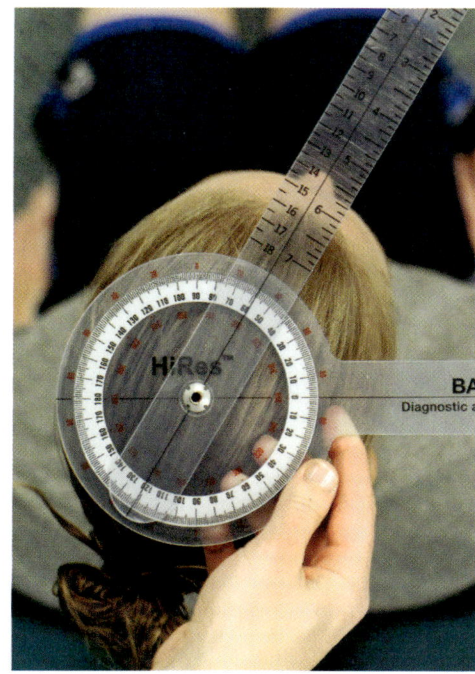

Fig. 4-42: A therapist measuring cervical rotation with a goniometer.

Rotation (Fig. 4-42)

Patient position: sitting with the thoracic and lumbar spine supported

Stabilization: shoulder girdle and chest to prevent rotation of the thoracic and lumbar spines

End-feel: firm

Axis: over the center of the cranial aspect of the head

Stationary arm: parallel to an imaginary line between the two acromial processes

Moveable arm: with the tip of the nose or if using a tongue depressor, align the goniometer parallel with the tongue depressor

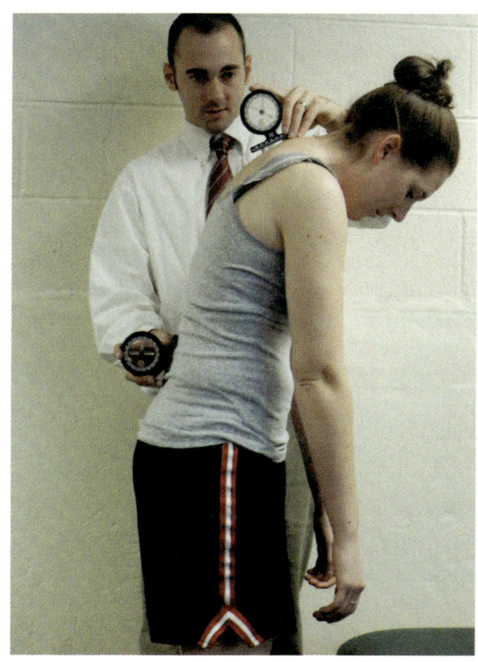

Fig. 4-43: A therapist measuring thoracic and lumbar flexion with a double inclinometer.

Thoracolumbar Spine

Flexion and extension (Fig. 4-43)

Flexion of the thoracic and lumbar spines is most commonly measured with a tape measure instead of a goniometer. The therapist aligns a tape measure between the spinous processes of T1 and S2. The distance is recorded. The patient is then asked to bend forward gradually while the therapist allows the tape measure to unwind. The second distance is recorded. The amount of thoracic and lumbar flexion is determined by calculating the difference between the first and the second measurements. Extension of the thoracic and lumbar spine is measured in a similar manner.

Lateral flexion (Fig. 4-44)

Patient position: standing with the feet shoulder width apart

Stabilization: pelvis to prevent lateral tilting

End-feel: firm

Axis: over the posterior aspect of the spinous process of S2

Stationary arm: perpendicular to the ground

Moveable arm: along the posterior aspect of the spinous process of T1

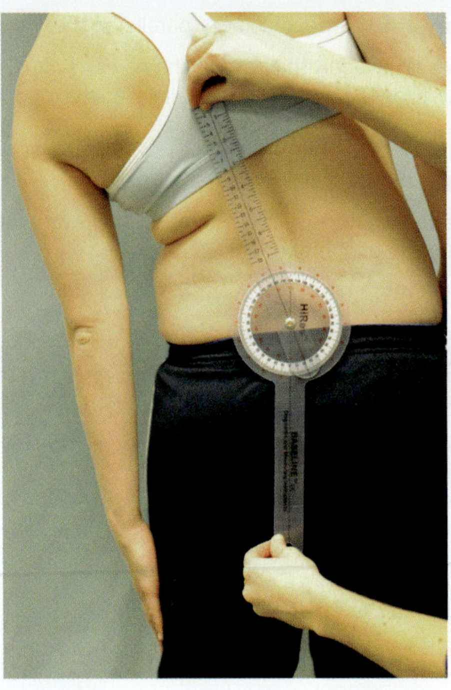

Fig. 4-44: A therapist measuring thoracic and lumbar lateral flexion with a goniometer.

Rotation

Patient position: sitting on a chair without a back with the feet positioned on the floor for pelvic stabilization

Stabilization: pelvis to prevent rotation

End-feel: firm

Axis: over the center of the cranial aspect of the head

Stationary arm: parallel to an imaginary line between the two prominent tubercles on the iliac crests

Moveable arm: along an imaginary line between the two acromial processes

CONSIDER THIS

DOCUMENTATION OF RECORDED MEASURES[3]

Health care providers work in an integrated fashion to deliver patient care. The patient medical record is one of the primary ways that health care providers keep each other informed of current patient status and other relevant information. As a result, it is critical that health care providers document relevant information in the medical record in a timely and accurate manner. Failure to meet this standard potentially results in ineffective medical care and may jeopardize patient safety.

The results of goniometric measurements can be used to illustrate this point. Let's assume that a therapist reviews the medical record of a patient recovering from a motor vehicle accident, in which the patient sustained multiple lower extremity injuries. Upon reviewing the medical record, the therapist determines that in successive notes the patient's right knee range of motion was described as 10-105 degrees and 10-0-105 degrees.

Although the recorded measurements appear extremely similar, they are in fact very different. 10-105 degrees indicates that the patient's range of motion begins at 10 degrees of knee flexion and ends at 105 degrees of knee flexion (95 degrees of total available movement). Conversely, the use of "0" between the starting and ending values indicates the patient has 10 degrees of knee hyperextension and 105 degrees of knee flexion (115 degrees of total available movement).

This type of inaccuracy could cause a variety of potential problems including selecting inappropriate parameters for a device such as a continuous passive motion machine, selecting an inappropriate therapeutic exercise activity based on the patient's available range of motion, and potential reimbursement-related questions concerning the extreme variability in recorded measures.

Special Tests

Special Tests Outline

Upper Extremity

Shoulder

Dislocation

Apprehension test for anterior shoulder dislocation

Apprehension test for posterior shoulder dislocation

Sulcus sign

Biceps Tendon Pathology

Ludington's test

Speed's test

Yergason's test

Rotator Cuff Pathology/Impingement

Drop arm test

Hawkins-Kennedy impingement test

Infraspinatus test

Lateral rotation lag sign

Lift off sign (medial rotation)

Neer impingement test

Supine impingement test

Supraspinatus test

Thoracic Outlet Syndrome

Adson maneuver

Allen test

Costoclavicular syndrome test

Roos test

Wright test (hyperabduction test)

Miscellaneous

Acromioclavicular crossover test

Active compression test (O'Brien's test)

Glenoid labrum tear test

Jerk test

Upper limb tension tests

Elbow

Ligamentous Instability

Valgus stress test

Varus stress test

Epicondylitis

Cozen's test

Lateral epicondylitis test

Medial epicondylitis test

Mill's test

Neurological Dysfunction

Elbow flexion test

Pinch grip test

Tinel's sign

Wrist/Hand

Ligamentous Instability

Ulnar collateral ligament instability test

Vascular Insufficiency

Allen test

Capillary refill test **(See Cardiovascular and Pulmonary Systems Unit)**

Contracture/Tightness

Bunnel-Littler test

Tight retinacular ligament test

Neurological Dysfunction

Carpal compression test (median nerve compression test)

Froment's sign

Phalen's test

Tinel's sign

Miscellaneous

Finkelstein test

Grind test

Murphy sign

Lower Extremity

Hip

Contracture/Tightness

Ely's test

Ober's test

Piriformis test

Thomas test

Tripod sign

90-90 straight leg raise test

Pediatric Tests

Barlow's test

Ortolani's test

Miscellaneous

Anterior labral tear test

Craig's test

Patrick's test (FABER test)

Quadrant scouring test

Trendelenburg test

Knee

Ligamentous Instability

Anterior drawer test

Lachman test

Lateral pivot shift test

Posterior drawer test

Posterior sag sign

Slocum test

Valgus stress test

Varus stress test

Meniscal Pathology

Apley's compression test

Bounce home test

McMurray test

Thessaly test

Swelling

Brush test

Patellar tap test

Miscellaneous

Clarke's sign

Hughston's plica test

Noble compression test

Patellar apprehension test

Ankle

Ligamentous Instability

Anterior drawer test

Lateral rotation stress test (Kleiger test)

Talar tilt test

Miscellaneous

Homans' sign **(See Cardiovascular and Pulmonary Systems Unit)**

Thompson test

Tibial torsion test

True leg length discrepancy test

Spine

Cervical Region

Cervical flexion rotation test

Distraction test

Foraminal compression test

Vertebral artery test

Lumbar/Sacroiliac Region

Gapping test

Sacroiliac joint stress test

Sitting flexion test

Slump test

Standing flexion test

Straight leg raise test

Descriptions of Special Tests

Shoulder

Dislocation

Apprehension test for anterior shoulder dislocation[10,26]

The patient is positioned in supine with the arm in 90 degrees of abduction and 90 degrees of elbow flexion. The therapist laterally rotates the patient's shoulder. A positive test is indicated by a look of apprehension or a facial grimace prior to reaching an end point (Fig. 4-45).

Apprehension test for posterior shoulder dislocation[8,10]

The patient is positioned in supine with the arm in 90 degrees of flexion and medial rotation. The therapist applies a posterior force through the long axis of the humerus. A positive test is indicated by a look of apprehension or a facial grimace prior to reaching an end point.

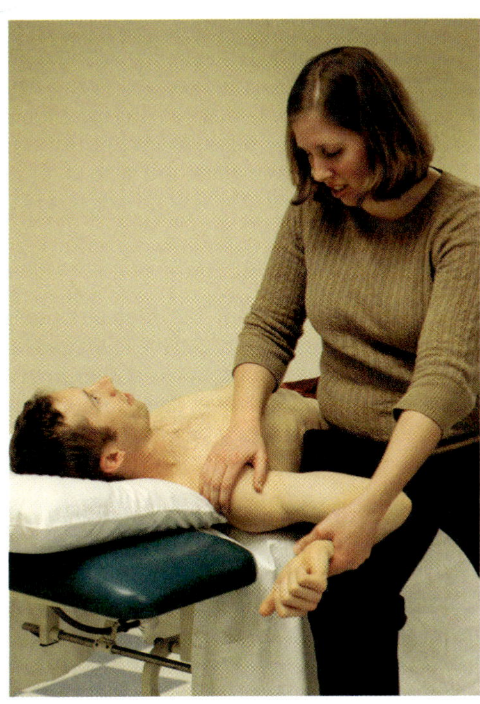

Fig. 4-45: A therapist observing a patient while administering an apprehension test for anterior shoulder dislocation.

Sulcus sign[10,18]

In standing, the therapist positions the patient's arm in 20-50 degrees of abduction. The therapist then grasps the patient's elbow and pulls the arm inferiorly. The test is positive for inferior instability if a sulcus sign (i.e., depression seen between the acromion and humeral head) is noted. The sulcus sign can be graded by measuring the vertical length of the depression. The grades are as follows: 1+ for <1 cm, 2+ for 1-2 cm, and 3+ for >2 cm.

Biceps Tendon Pathology

Ludington's test[10,13]

The patient is positioned in sitting and is asked to clasp both hands behind the head with the fingers interlocked. The patient is then asked to alternately contract and relax the biceps muscles. A positive test is indicated by absence of movement in the biceps tendon and may be indicative of a rupture of the long head of the biceps.

Speed's test[10,26]

The patient is positioned in sitting or standing with the elbow extended and the forearm supinated. The therapist places one hand over the bicipital groove and the other hand on the volar surface of the forearm. The therapist resists active shoulder flexion. A positive test is indicated by pain or tenderness in the bicipital groove region and may be indicative of bicipital tendonitis (Fig. 4-46).

Yergason's test[10,13]

The patient is positioned in sitting with 90 degrees of elbow flexion and the forearm pronated. The humerus is stabilized against the patient's thorax. The therapist places one hand on the patient's forearm and the other hand over the bicipital groove. The patient is directed to actively supinate and laterally rotate against resistance. A positive test is indicated by pain or tenderness in the bicipital groove and may be indicative of bicipital tendonitis.

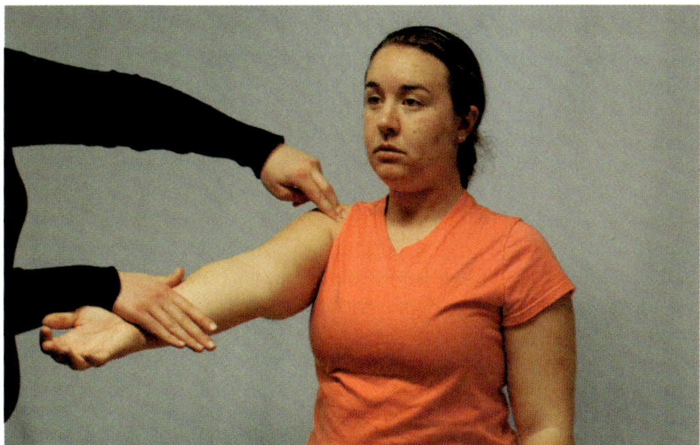

Fig. 4-46: A therapist administering Speed's test. The therapist resists shoulder flexion while palpating the bicipital groove.

Rotator Cuff Pathology/Impingement

Drop arm test[10,26]

The patient is positioned in sitting or standing with the arm in 90 degrees of abduction. The patient is asked to slowly lower the arm to their side. A positive test is indicated by the patient failing to slowly lower the arm to their side or by the presence of severe pain and may be indicative of a tear in the rotator cuff.

Hawkins-Kennedy impingement test[10]

The patient is positioned in sitting or standing. The therapist flexes the patient's shoulder to 90 degrees and then medially rotates the arm. A positive test is indicated by pain and may be indicative of shoulder impingement involving the supraspinatus tendon (Fig. 4-47).

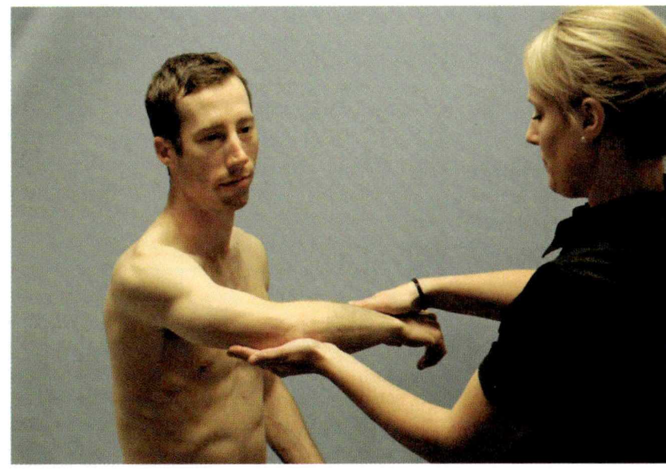

Fig. 4-47: A positive Hawkins-Kennedy impingement test is indicated by the presence of pain.

Infraspinatus test[10,18]

The patient stands with their elbow flexed to 90 degrees and the shoulder in 45 degrees of medial rotation. The patient then resists as the therapist applies a medially directed force to the forearm. Pain or weakness indicates the presence of an infraspinatus strain/tear.

Lateral rotation lag sign[10,18]

With the patient's elbow bent, the therapist passively moves their shoulder into 20 degrees of scaption and near end-range lateral rotation and asks the patient to hold that position. The test is positive for infraspinatus and/or supraspinatus pathology if the patient cannot hold the position (i.e., shoulder moves into more medial rotation). This test can also be performed with the patient's shoulder in varying levels of elevation.

Lift off sign (medial rotation lag sign)[10,18]

The patient stands and places the dorsum of their hand on their low back. The patient is asked to move their hand away from their back. If they are unable to do this, the therapist should passively move the patient's hand away from their back and see if they can hold the position. An inability to hold the position indicates that a subscapularis lesion is present.

Neer impingement test[10,26]

The patient is positioned in sitting or standing. The therapist positions one hand on the posterior aspect of the patient's scapula and the other hand stabilizing the elbow. The therapist elevates the patient's arm through flexion. A positive test is indicated by a facial grimace or pain and may be indicative of shoulder impingement involving the supraspinatus tendon.

Supine impingement test[10,18]

The patient lies supine while the therapist passively moves the shoulder into full flexion. The therapist then laterally rotates and adducts the shoulder so that the arm is near the patient's head. From this position, the therapist medially rotates the shoulder. The test is positive if the patient experiences a significant increase in pain with medial rotation.

Supraspinatus test[10,13]

The patient is positioned with the arm in 90 degrees of abduction followed by 30 degrees of horizontal adduction with the thumb pointing downward. The therapist resists the patient's attempt to abduct the arm. A positive test is indicated by weakness or pain and may be indicative of a tear of the supraspinatus tendon, impingement or suprascapular nerve involvement.

Thoracic Outlet Syndrome

Adson maneuver[10,26]

The patient is positioned in sitting or standing. The therapist monitors the radial pulse and asks the patient to rotate their head to face the test shoulder. The patient is then asked to extend their head while the therapist laterally rotates and extends the patient's shoulder. A positive test is indicated by an absent or diminished radial pulse and may be indicative of thoracic outlet syndrome.

Allen test[10,26]

The patient is positioned in sitting or standing with the test arm in 90 degrees of abduction, lateral rotation, and elbow flexion. The patient is asked to rotate the head away from the test shoulder while the therapist monitors the radial pulse. A positive test is indicated by an absent or diminished pulse when the head is rotated away from the test shoulder. A positive test may be indicative of thoracic outlet syndrome.

Costoclavicular syndrome test[10,18]

The patient is positioned in sitting. The therapist monitors the patient's radial pulse and assists the patient to assume a military posture. A positive test is indicated by an absent or diminished radial pulse and may be indicative of thoracic outlet syndrome caused by compression of the subclavian artery between the first rib and the clavicle.

Roos test[10,18]

The patient is positioned in sitting or standing with the arms positioned in 90 degrees of abduction, lateral rotation, and elbow flexion. The patient is asked to open and close their hands for three minutes. A positive test is indicated by the inability to maintain the test position, weakness of the arms, sensory loss or ischemic pain. A positive test may be indicative of thoracic outlet syndrome.

Wright test (hyperabduction test)[10]

The patient is positioned in sitting or supine. The therapist moves the patient's arm overhead in the frontal plane while monitoring the patient's radial pulse. A positive test is indicated by an absent or diminished radial pulse and may be indicative of compression in the costoclavicular space.

Miscellaneous

Acromioclavicular crossover test[10,13]

The therapist moves the patient's shoulder into 90 degrees of flexion, then fully horizontally adducts the shoulder. The test is positive for an acromioclavicular joint injury if the patient feels pain over the acromioclavicular joint. This test can also be performed actively by the patient.

Active compression test (O'Brien's test)[10,13]

The patient stands with the shoulder flexed to 90 degrees, horizontally adducted 10-15 degrees, and medially rotated so the thumb points downward. The patient resists as the therapist applies a downward force on the arm. The shoulder is then laterally rotated and the same downward force is applied. The test is positive for a superior labral tear if the patient experiences pain when the shoulder is in medial rotation, but has decreased pain with the shoulder laterally rotated. The therapist must ensure the pain is not located over the acromioclavicular joint with this test.

Glenoid labrum tear test[10]

The patient is positioned in supine. The therapist places one hand on the posterior aspect of the patient's humeral head while the other hand stabilizes the humerus proximal to the elbow. The therapist passively abducts and laterally rotates the arm over the patient's head and then proceeds to apply an anterior directed force to the humerus. A positive test is indicated by a clunk or grinding sound and may be indicative of a glenoid labrum tear.

Jerk test[10,13]

The patient is sitting with the shoulder elevated to 90 degrees and in medial rotation with the elbow bent. The therapist provides an axial compression force through the patient's elbow while horizontally adducting the shoulder. A sudden clunk or jerk as the humeral head subluxes posteriorly indicates the presence of posterior instability. A second clunk or jerk may be heard when the shoulder is returned to the starting position as the humeral head reduces. A complaint of pain with this test could indicate the presence of a posterior labral lesion.

Upper limb tension tests[10]

Upper limb tension tests are types of neural provocation maneuvers. The tests require an ordered sequence of movements occurring at the shoulder, arm, elbow, forearm, wrist, and hand. Symptoms and relevant changes in symptoms should be identified after each step. A sensitization test is often employed if symptoms are minimal or absent after the identified sequence. Upper limb tension tests are recommended for patients with symptoms in the arm, head, neck, and thoracic spine. Each test begins with the noninvolved side being tested first.

Upper Limb Tension Tests

	Upper Limb Tension Test 1	Upper Limb Tension Test 2	Upper Limb Tension Test 3	Upper Limb Tension Test 4
Joint Positioning Sequence	shoulder depression with 110 degrees abduction, elbow extension, forearm supination, wrist extension, finger and thumb extension	shoulder depression with 10 degrees abduction, elbow extension, forearm supination, wrist extension, finger and thumb extension, shoulder lateral rotation	shoulder depression with 10 degrees abduction, elbow extension, forearm pronation, wrist flexion and ulnar deviation, finger and thumb flexion, shoulder medial rotation	shoulder depression with 80-110 degrees abduction, elbow flexion, forearm pronation, wrist extension and radial deviation, finger and thumb extension, shoulder lateral rotation
Sensitization Test	contralateral cervical lateral flexion	contralateral cervical lateral flexion	contralateral cervical lateral flexion	contralateral cervical lateral flexion
Nerve Bias	median nerve, anterior interosseous nerve	median nerve, musculocutaneous nerve, axillary nerve	radial nerve	ulnar nerve

Elbow

Ligamentous Instability

Valgus stress test[8,10]

The patient is positioned in sitting with the elbow in 20 to 30 degrees of flexion. The therapist places one hand on the elbow and the other hand proximal to the patient's wrist. The therapist applies a valgus force to test the medial collateral ligament while palpating the medial joint line. A positive test is indicated by increased laxity in the medial collateral ligament when compared to the contralateral limb, apprehension or pain. A positive test may be indicative of a medial collateral ligament sprain.

Varus stress test[8,10]

The patient is positioned in sitting with the elbow in 20 to 30 degrees of flexion. The therapist places one hand on the elbow and the other hand proximal to the patient's wrist. The therapist applies a varus force to test the lateral collateral ligament while palpating the lateral joint line. A positive test is indicated by increased laxity in the lateral collateral ligament when compared to the contralateral limb, apprehension or pain. A positive test may be indicative of a lateral collateral ligament sprain.

Epicondylitis

Cozen's test[10,18]

The patient is positioned in sitting with the elbow in slight flexion. The therapist places their thumb on the patient's lateral epicondyle while stabilizing the elbow joint. The patient is asked to make a fist, pronate the forearm, radially deviate, and extend the wrist against resistance. A positive test is indicated by pain in the lateral epicondyle region or muscle weakness and may be indicative of lateral epicondylitis.

Lateral epicondylitis test[8,10]

The patient is positioned in sitting. The therapist stabilizes the elbow with one hand and places the other hand on the dorsal aspect of the patient's hand distal to the proximal interphalangeal joint. The patient is asked to extend the third digit against resistance. A positive test is indicated by pain in the lateral epicondyle region or muscle weakness and may be indicative of lateral epicondylitis.

Medial epicondylitis test[8,10]

The patient is positioned in sitting. The therapist palpates the medial epicondyle and supinates the patient's forearm, extends the wrist, and extends the elbow. A positive test is indicated by pain in the medial epicondyle region and may be indicative of medial epicondylitis.

Mill's test[10]

The patient is positioned in sitting. The therapist palpates the lateral epicondyle, pronates the patient's forearm, flexes the wrist, and extends the elbow. A positive test is indicated by pain in the lateral epicondyle region and may be indicative of lateral epicondylitis.

Neurological Dysfunction

Elbow flexion test[13,18]

The patient fully flexes both elbows while extending their wrists and holds the position for 3-5 minutes. The test is considered positive for cubital tunnel syndrome if tingling or paresthesia is noted in the ulnar nerve distribution of the forearm and hand.

Pinch grip test[13,18]

The patient is asked to pinch the tips of the index finger and thumb together. If the patient cannot pinch tip-to-tip and instead presses the pads of the fingers together, the test is positive for pathology of the anterior interosseous nerve.

Tinel's sign[10,13]

The patient is positioned in sitting with the elbow in slight flexion. The therapist taps with the index finger between the olecranon process and the medial epicondyle. A positive test is indicated by a tingling sensation in the ulnar nerve distribution of the forearm, hand, and fingers. A positive test may be indicative of ulnar nerve compression or compromise.

Wrist/Hand

Ligamentous Instability

Ulnar collateral ligament instability test[10]

The patient is positioned in sitting. The therapist holds the patient's thumb in extension and applies a valgus force to the metacarpophalangeal joint of the thumb. A positive test is indicated by excessive valgus movement and may be indicative of a tear of the ulnar collateral and accessory collateral ligaments. This type of injury is referred to as gamekeeper's or skier's thumb.

Vascular Insufficiency

Allen test[8,10]

The patient is positioned in sitting or standing. The patient is asked to open and close the hand several times in succession and then maintain the hand in a closed position. The therapist compresses the radial and ulnar arteries. The patient is then asked to relax the hand and the therapist releases the pressure on one of the arteries while observing the color of the hand and fingers. A positive test is indicated by delayed or absent flushing of the radial or ulnar half of the hand and may be indicative of an occlusion in the radial or ulnar artery (Figs. 4-48, 4-49).

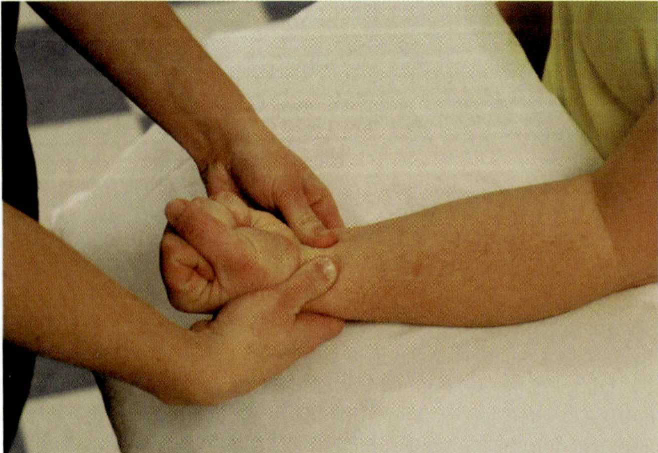

Fig. 4-48: A therapist compresses the radial and ulnar arteries while administering the Allen test.

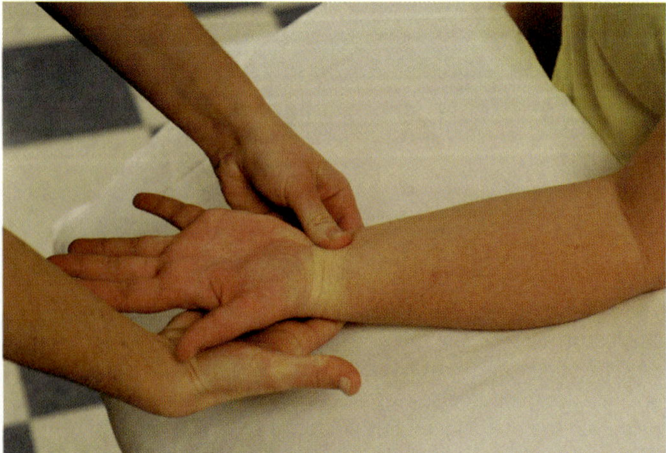

Fig. 4-49: The therapist releases the radial artery and observes the color of the hand and fingers.

Contracture/Tightness

Bunnel-Littler test[10,26]

The patient is positioned in sitting with the metacarpophalangeal joint held in slight extension. The therapist attempts to move the proximal interphalangeal joint into flexion. If the proximal interphalangeal joint does not flex with the metacarpophalangeal joint extended, there may be a tight intrinsic muscle or capsular tightness. If the proximal interphalangeal joint fully flexes with the metacarpophalangeal joint in slight flexion, there may be intrinsic muscle tightness without capsular tightness.

Tight retinacular ligament test[10]

The proximal interphalangeal joint is held in a neutral position while the therapist attempts to flex the distal interphalangeal joint. If the therapist is unable to flex the distal interphalangeal joint, the retinacular ligaments or capsule may be tight. If the therapist is able to flex the distal interphalangeal joint with the proximal interphalangeal joint in flexion, the retinacular ligaments may be tight and the capsule may be normal.

Neurological Dysfunction

Carpal compression test (median nerve compression test)[10,13]

The therapist holds the patient's wrist with both hands and applies pressure over the median nerve in the carpal tunnel for 30 seconds. The test may also be performed by placing the patient's wrist in 60 degrees of flexion before applying pressure. The test is positive for carpal tunnel syndrome if the patient experiences pain or paresthesia in the median nerve distribution.

Froment's sign[10,26]

The patient is positioned in sitting or standing and is asked to hold a piece of paper between the thumb and index finger. The therapist attempts to pull the paper away from the patient. A positive test is indicated by the patient flexing the distal phalanx of the thumb due to adductor pollicis muscle paralysis. If at the same time, the patient hyperextends the metacarpophalangeal joint of the thumb, it is termed Jeanne's sign. Both objective findings may be indicative of ulnar nerve compromise or paralysis (Fig. 4-50).

Fig. 4-50: A positive Froment's sign is indicated by the patient flexing the distal phalanx of the thumb due to adductor pollicis muscle paralysis.

Phalen's test[8,10]

The patient is positioned in sitting or standing. The therapist flexes the patient's wrists maximally and asks the patient to hold the position for 60 seconds. A positive test is indicated by tingling in the thumb, index finger, middle finger, and lateral half of the ring finger and may be indicative of carpal tunnel syndrome due to median nerve compression (Fig. 4-51).

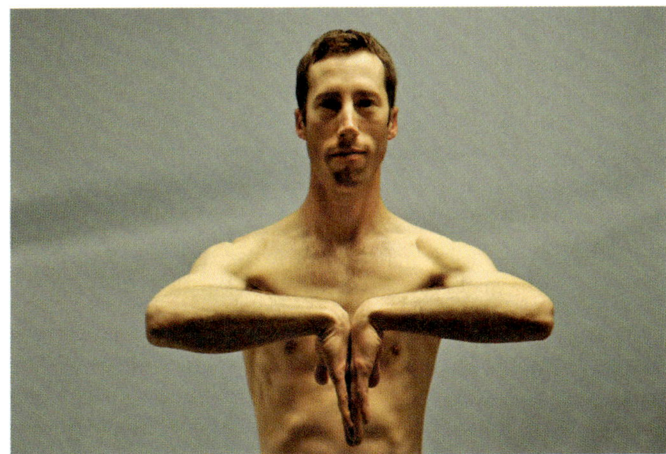

Fig. 4-51: A patient maintains the test position for Phalen's test.

Tinel's sign[10,13]

The patient is positioned in sitting or standing. The therapist taps over the volar aspect of the patient's wrist. A positive test is indicated by tingling in the thumb, index finger, middle finger, and lateral half of the ring finger distal to the contact site at the wrist. A positive test may be indicative of carpal tunnel syndrome due to median nerve compression.

Miscellaneous

Finkelstein test[10,26]

The patient is positioned in sitting or standing and is asked to make a fist with the thumb tucked inside the fingers. The therapist stabilizes the patient's forearm and ulnarly deviates the wrist. A positive test is indicated by pain over the abductor pollicis longus and extensor pollicis brevis tendons at the wrist and may be indicative of tenosynovitis in the thumb (de Quervain's disease) (Fig. 4-52).

Grind test[10]

The patient is positioned in sitting or standing. The therapist stabilizes the patient's hand and grasps the patient's thumb on the metacarpal. The therapist applies compression and rotation through the metacarpal. A positive test is indicated by pain and may be indicative of degenerative joint disease in the carpometacarpal joint.

Murphy sign[10,18]

The patient is positioned in sitting or standing and is asked to make a fist. A positive test is indicated by the patient's third metacarpal remaining level with the second and fourth metacarpals. A positive test may be indicative of a dislocated lunate.

Fig. 4-52: A therapist administers the Finkelstein test to a patient in sitting.

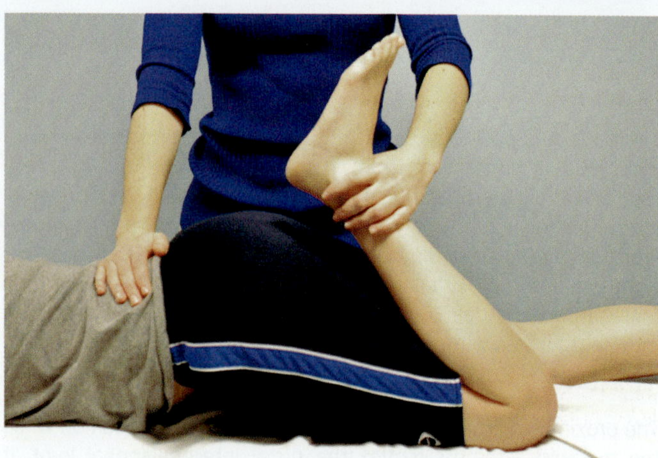

Fig. 4-53: A positive Ely's test is indicated by active hip flexion occurring simultaneously with passive knee flexion.

Hip

Contracture/Tightness

Ely's test[10,13]

The patient is positioned in prone while the therapist passively flexes the patient's knee. A positive test is indicated by spontaneous hip flexion occurring simultaneously with knee flexion and may be indicative of a rectus femoris contracture (Fig. 4-53).

Ober's test[10,26]

The patient is positioned in sidelying with the lower leg flexed at the hip and the knee. The therapist moves the test leg into hip extension and abduction and then attempts to slowly lower the test leg. A positive test is indicated by an inability of the test leg to adduct and touch the table and may be indicative of an iliotibial band or a tensor fasciae latae contracture (Fig. 4-54).

Piriformis test[10,13]

The patient is positioned in sidelying with the test leg positioned toward the ceiling and the hip flexed to 60 degrees. The therapist places one hand on the patient's pelvis and the other hand on the patient's knee. While stabilizing the pelvis, the therapist applies a downward (adduction) force on the knee. A positive test is indicated by pain or tightness, and may be indicative of piriformis tightness or compression on the sciatic nerve caused by the piriformis.

Thomas test[10,26]

The patient is positioned in supine with the legs fully extended. The patient is asked to bring one of their knees to the chest in order to flatten the lumbar spine. The therapist observes the position of the contralateral hip while the patient holds the flexed hip. A positive test is indicated by the straight leg rising from the table and may be indicative of a hip flexion contracture (Fig. 4-55).

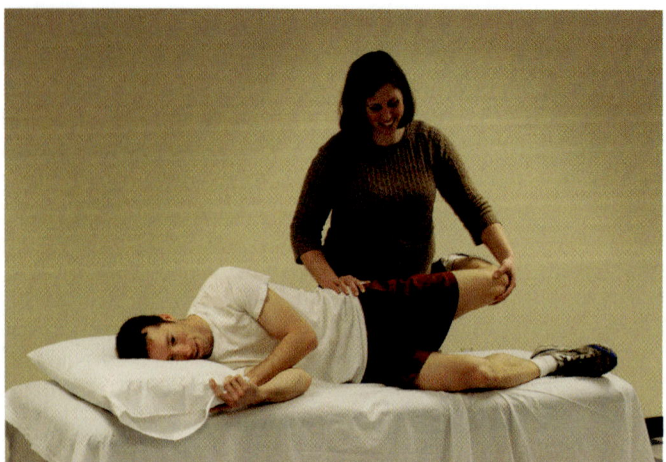

Fig. 4-54: A therapist administers Ober's test by moving the patient's leg into hip extension and abduction, and then attempts to lower the leg towards the table.

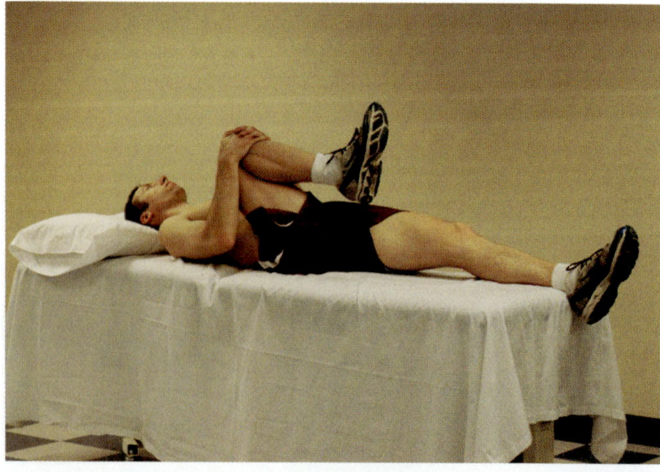

Fig. 4-55: A patient brings the knee towards the chest as part of the Thomas test. A positive test is indicated by the straight leg rising from the table.

Tripod sign[10]

The patient is positioned in sitting with the knees flexed to 90 degrees over the edge of a table. The therapist passively extends one knee. A positive test is indicated by tightness in the hamstrings or extension of the trunk in order to limit the effect of the tight hamstrings.

90-90 straight leg raise test[8,10]

The patient is positioned in supine and is asked to stabilize the hips in 90 degrees of flexion with the knees relaxed. The therapist instructs the patient to alternately extend each knee as much as possible while maintaining the hips in 90 degrees of flexion. A positive test is indicated by the knee remaining in 20 degrees or more of flexion and is indicative of hamstrings tightness.

Pediatric Tests

Barlow's test[10,27]

The patient is positioned in supine with the hips flexed to 90 degrees and the knees flexed. The therapist tests each hip individually by stabilizing the femur and pelvis with one hand while the other hand moves the test leg into adduction. A posteriorly directed pressure is then applied through the knee. A positive test is indicated by a clunk and may be indicative of a hip being dislocated.

Ortolani's test[10,27]

The patient is positioned in supine with the hips flexed to 90 degrees and the knees flexed. The therapist grasps the legs so that their thumbs are placed along the patient's medial thighs and the fingers are placed on the lateral thighs toward the buttocks. The therapist abducts the patient's hips and gentle pressure is applied to the greater trochanters until resistance is felt at approximately 30 degrees. A positive test is indicated by a click or a clunk and may be indicative of a dislocation being reduced.

Miscellaneous

Anterior labral tear test[10,18]

The therapist places the patient's hip in full flexion, lateral rotation, and abduction to begin the test. The therapist then moves the hip into extension, medial rotation, and adduction. A positive test is indicated by the presence of pain and/or a click. The test is used for diagnosing an anterior labral tear, though it may also be indicative of iliopsoas tendonitis or anterior-superior impingement.

Craig's test[10,18]

The patient is positioned in prone with the test knee flexed to 90 degrees. The therapist palpates the posterior aspect of the greater trochanter and medially and laterally rotates the hip until the greater trochanter is parallel with the table. The degree of femoral anteversion corresponds to the angle formed by the lower leg with the perpendicular axis of the table. Normal anteversion for an adult is 8-15 degrees (Fig. 4-56).

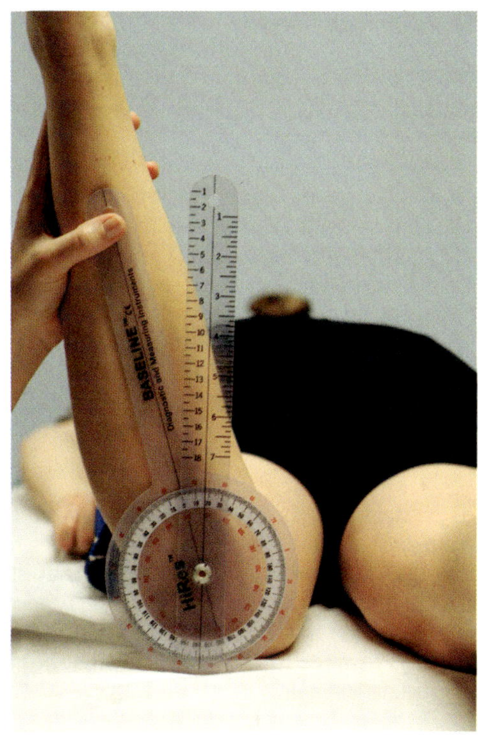

Fig. 4-56: A therapist attempts to quantify the amount of femoral anteversion with a goniometer after administering Craig's test.

Patrick's test (FABER test)[8,10]

The patient is positioned in supine with the test leg flexed, abducted, and laterally rotated at the hip onto the opposite leg. The therapist slowly lowers the test leg through abduction toward the table. A positive test is indicated by failure of the test leg to abduct below the level of the opposite leg and may be indicative of iliopsoas, sacroiliac or hip joint abnormalities.

Quadrant scouring test[10,13]

The patient is positioned in supine. The therapist passively flexes and adducts the hip with the knee in maximal flexion. The therapist applies a compressive force through the shaft of the femur while continuing to passively move the patient's hip. A positive test is indicated by grinding, catching or crepitation in the hip and may be indicative of pathologies such as arthritis, avascular necrosis or an osteochondral defect.

Trendelenburg test[8,10]

The patient is positioned in standing and is asked to stand on one leg for approximately ten seconds. A positive test is indicated by a drop of the pelvis on the unsupported side and may be indicative of weakness of the gluteus medius muscle on the supported side.

Knee

Ligamentous Instability

Anterior drawer test[8,10]

The patient is positioned in supine with the knee flexed to 90 degrees and the hip flexed to 45 degrees. The therapist stabilizes the lower leg by sitting on the forefoot. The therapist grasps the patient's proximal tibia with two hands, places their thumbs on the tibial plateau, and administers an anterior directed force to the tibia on the femur. A positive test is indicated by excessive anterior translation of the tibia on the femur with a diminished or absent end-point and may be indicative of an anterior cruciate ligament injury (Fig. 4-57).

Lachman test[10,26]

The patient is positioned in supine with the knee flexed to 20-30 degrees. The therapist stabilizes the distal femur with one hand and places the other hand on the proximal tibia. The therapist applies an anterior directed force to the tibia on the femur. A positive test is indicated by excessive anterior translation of the tibia on the femur with a diminished or absent end-point and may be indicative of an anterior cruciate ligament injury (Fig. 4-58).

Lateral pivot shift test[8,10]

The patient is positioned in supine with the hip flexed and abducted to 30 degrees with slight medial rotation. The therapist grasps the leg with one hand and places the other hand over the lateral surface of the proximal tibia. The therapist medially rotates the tibia and applies a valgus force to the knee while the knee is slowly flexed. A positive test is indicated by a palpable shift or clunk occurring between 20 and 40 degrees of flexion and is indicative of anterolateral rotatory instability. The shift or clunk results from the reduction of the tibia on the femur.

Posterior drawer test[8,10]

The patient is positioned in supine with the knee flexed to 90 degrees and the hip flexed to 45 degrees. The therapist stabilizes the lower leg by sitting on the forefoot. The therapist grasps the patient's proximal tibia with two hands, places their thumbs on the tibial plateau, and administers a posterior directed force to the tibia on the femur. A positive test is indicated by excessive posterior translation of the tibia on the femur with a diminished or absent end-point and may be indicative of a posterior cruciate ligament injury.

Posterior sag sign[8,10]

The patient is positioned in supine with the knee flexed to 90 degrees and the hip flexed to 45 degrees. A positive test is indicated by the tibia sagging back on the femur and may be indicative of a posterior cruciate ligament injury.

Slocum test[10,13]

The patient is positioned in supine with the knee flexed to 90 degrees and the hip flexed to 45 degrees. The therapist rotates the patient's foot 30 degrees medially to test anterolateral instability. The therapist stabilizes the lower leg by sitting on the forefoot. The therapist grasps the patient's proximal tibia with two hands, places their thumbs on the tibial plateau, and administers an anterior directed force to the tibia on the femur. A positive test is indicated by movement of the tibia occurring primarily on the lateral side and may be indicative of anterolateral instability. The test can also be performed to assess anteromedial instability by rotating the patient's foot 15 degrees laterally.

Valgus stress test[10,13]

The patient is positioned in supine with the knee flexed to 20-30 degrees. The therapist positions one hand on the medial surface of the patient's ankle and the other hand on the lateral surface of the knee. The therapist applies a valgus force to the knee with the distal hand. A positive test is indicated by excessive valgus movement and may be indicative of a medial collateral ligament sprain. A positive test with the knee in full extension may be

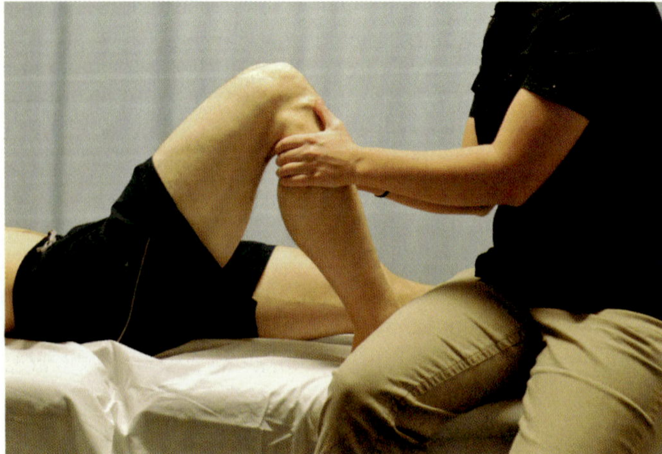

Fig. 4-57: A therapist administers the anterior drawer test to a patient positioned in supine with the hip in 45 degrees of flexion and the knee in 90 degrees of flexion.

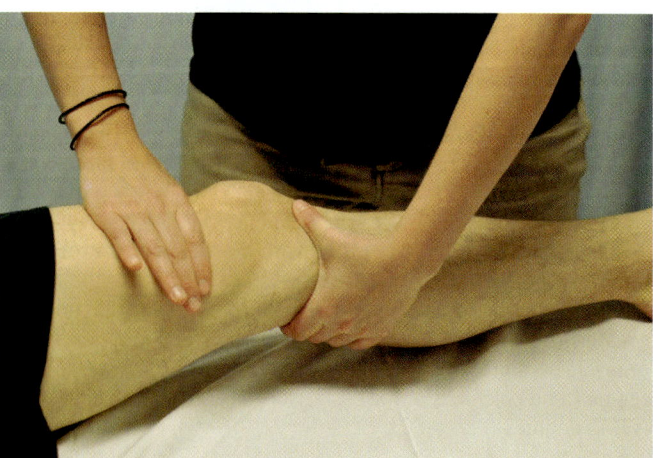

Fig. 4-58: A therapist administers the Lachman test by applying an anterior directed force to the tibia on the femur while stabilizing the distal femur.

indicative of damage to the medial collateral ligament, posterior cruciate ligament, posterior oblique ligament, and posteromedial capsule.

Varus stress test[10,13]

The patient is positioned in supine with the knee flexed to 20-30 degrees. The therapist positions one hand on the lateral surface of the patient's ankle and the other hand on the medial surface of the knee. The therapist applies a varus force to the knee with the distal hand. A positive test is indicated by excessive varus movement and may be indicative of a lateral collateral ligament sprain. A positive test with the knee in full extension may be indicative of damage to the lateral collateral ligament, posterior cruciate ligament, arcuate complex, and posterolateral capsule.

Meniscal Pathology

Apley's compression test[10,18]

The patient is positioned in prone with the knee flexed to 90 degrees. The therapist stabilizes the patient's femur using one hand and places the other hand on the patient's heel. The therapist medially and laterally rotates the tibia while applying a compressive force through the tibia. A positive test is indicated by pain or clicking and may be indicative of a meniscal lesion.

Bounce home test[8,10]

The patient is positioned in supine. The therapist grasps the patient's heel and maximally flexes the knee. The patient's knee is extended passively. A positive test is indicated by incomplete extension or a rubbery end-feel and may be indicative of a meniscal lesion.

McMurray test[8,10]

The patient is positioned in supine. The therapist grasps the distal leg with one hand and palpates the knee joint line with the other. With the knee fully flexed, the therapist medially rotates the tibia and extends the knee. The therapist repeats the same procedure while laterally rotating the tibia. A positive test is indicated by a click or pronounced crepitation felt over the joint line and may be indicative of a posterior meniscal lesion.

Thessaly test[10,18]

The patient stands on one leg with approximately 5 degrees of knee flexion while the therapist provides their hands to assist the patient with their balance. The patient then rotates the femur on the tibia laterally and medially three times. The test is then repeated with a 20 degree knee bend. If the patient has joint line discomfort or catching or locking in the knee, the test is positive for a meniscal tear. This test should be performed on the unaffected extremity first and then the affected extremity.

Swelling

Brush test[10,22]

The patient is positioned in supine. The therapist places one hand below the joint line on the medial surface of the patella and strokes proximally with the palm and fingers as far as the suprapatellar pouch. The other hand then strokes down the lateral surface of the patella. A positive test is indicated by a wave of fluid just below the medial distal border of the patella and is indicative of effusion in the knee.

Patellar tap test[10,22]

The patient is positioned in supine with the knee flexed or extended to a point of discomfort. The therapist applies a slight tap over the patella. A positive test is indicated if the patella appears to be floating and may be indicative of joint effusion.

Miscellaneous

Clarke's sign[8,10]

The patient is positioned in supine with the knees extended. The therapist applies slight pressure distally with the web space of their hand over the superior pole of the patella. The therapist then asks the patient to contract the quadriceps muscle while maintaining pressure on the patella. A positive test is indicated by failure to complete the contraction without pain and may be indicative of patellofemoral dysfunction.

Hughston's plica test[10,22]

The patient is positioned in supine. The therapist flexes the knee and medially rotates the tibia with one hand while the other hand attempts to move the patella medially and palpate the medial femoral condyle. A positive test is indicated by a popping sound over the medial plica while the knee is passively flexed and extended, which may indicate an abnormal or irritated plica.

Noble compression test[8,10]

The patient is positioned in supine with the hip slightly flexed and the knee in 90 degrees of flexion. The therapist places the thumb of one hand over the lateral epicondyle of the femur and the other hand around the patient's ankle. The therapist maintains pressure over the lateral epicondyle while the patient is asked to slowly extend the knee. A positive test is indicated by pain over the lateral femoral epicondyle at approximately 30 degrees of knee flexion and may be indicative of iliotibial band friction syndrome.

Patellar apprehension test[8,10]

The patient is positioned in supine with the knees extended. The therapist places both thumbs on the medial border of the patella and applies a laterally directed force. A positive test is indicated by a look of apprehension or an attempt to contract the quadriceps, in an effort to avoid subluxation and may be indicative of patella subluxation or dislocation.

Ankle

Ligamentous Instability

Anterior drawer test[8,10]

The patient is positioned in supine. The therapist stabilizes the distal tibia and fibula with one hand, while the other hand holds the foot in 20 degrees of plantar flexion and draws the talus forward in the ankle mortise. A positive test is indicated by excessive anterior translation of the talus away from the ankle mortise and may be indicative of an anterior talofibular ligament sprain.

Lateral rotation stress test (Kleiger test)[10,13]

The patient is seated at the edge of a table with their knee in 90 degrees of flexion. The therapist stabilizes the patient's lower leg with one hand and holds the patient's foot in neutral with their other hand. The therapist then applies a lateral rotation force to the foot. If the patient experiences pain over the anterior or posterior tibiofibular ligaments and the interosseous membrane, then the test is positive for a high ankle sprain (i.e., syndesmosis injury). The test is positive for a deltoid ligament tear if the patient has pain medially and the therapist can feel the talus shift away from the medial malleolus.

Talar tilt test[10,22]

The patient is positioned in sidelying with the knee flexed to 90 degrees. The therapist stabilizes the distal tibia with one hand while grasping the talus with the other hand. The foot is maintained in a neutral position. The therapist tilts the talus into inversion and eversion. A positive test is indicated by excessive inversion and may be indicative of a calcaneofibular ligament sprain.

Miscellaneous

Thompson test[8,10]

The patient is positioned in prone with the feet extended over the edge of a table. The therapist asks the patient to relax and proceeds to squeeze the muscle belly of the gastrocnemius and soleus muscles. A positive test is indicated by the absence of plantar flexion and may be indicative of a ruptured Achilles tendon (Fig. 4-59).

Tibial torsion test[10]

The patient is positioned in sitting with the knees over the edge of a table. The therapist places the thumb and index finger of one hand over the medial and lateral malleolus. The therapist then measures the acute angle formed by the axes of the knee and ankle. Normal lateral torsion of the tibia is considered to be 12-18 degrees in an adult.

True leg length discrepancy test[10]

The patient is positioned in supine with the hips and knees extended, the legs 15 to 20 cm apart, and the pelvis in balance with the legs. Using a tape measure, the therapist measures from the distal point of the anterior superior iliac spines to the distal point of the medial malleoli. A positive test is indicated by a bilateral variation of greater than one centimeter and may be indicative of a true leg length discrepancy.

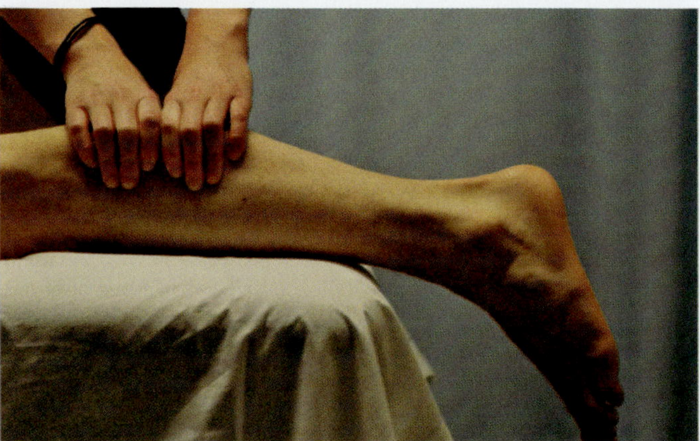

Fig. 4-59: A therapist administers the Thompson test by squeezing the muscle belly of the gastrocnemius and soleus muscles.

Spine

Cervical Region

Cervical flexion rotation test[10,13]

With the patient in supine, the therapist fully flexes the patient's cervical spine. The therapist then rotates the cervical spine in each direction while maintaining flexion. The patient should have approximately 45 degrees of rotation in each direction. If the patient has limited rotation in this position, then the dysfunction is likely occurring at the atlantoaxial joint. This test can also be used as a provocative test for cervicogenic headache.

Distraction test[10,13]

This test is used for patients who are currently experiencing radicular symptoms. With the patient sitting, the therapist places one hand under the patient's chin and the other hand under the occiput. The therapist then applies an upward distraction force. The test is positive for cervical nerve root compression if pain is decreased with the distraction force.

Foraminal compression test[10,22]

The patient is positioned in sitting with the head laterally flexed. The therapist places both hands on top of the subject's head and exerts a downward force. A positive test is indicated by pain radiating into the arm toward the flexed side and may be indicative of nerve root compression.

Vertebral artery test[10,22]

The patient is positioned in supine. The therapist places the patient's head into extension, lateral flexion, and rotation to the ipsilateral side. A positive test is indicated by dizziness, nystagmus, slurred speech or loss of consciousness and may be indicative of compression of the vertebral artery.

Lumbar/Sacroiliac Region

Gapping test[10,13]

The patient lies supine while the therapist crosses their arms and applies pressure in a downward and lateral direction to each anterior superior iliac spine. If the patient experiences pain in the

sacroiliac joint, gluteus or posterior leg, the test is positive for a sprain of the anterior sacroiliac ligaments.

Sacroiliac joint stress test[10]

The patient is positioned in supine. The therapist crosses their arms, placing the palms of the hands on the patient's anterior superior iliac spines. The therapist applies a downward and lateral force to the pelvis. A positive test is indicated by unilateral pain in the sacroiliac joint or gluteal area and may be indicative of sacroiliac joint dysfunction.

Sitting flexion test[10,22]

The patient is positioned in sitting with the knees flexed to 90 degrees and the feet on the floor. The patient's hips should be abducted to allow the patient to bend forward. The therapist places their thumbs on the inferior margin of the posterior superior iliac spines and monitors the movement of the bony structures as the patient bends forward and reaches toward the floor. A positive test is indicated by one posterior superior iliac spine moving farther in a cranial direction and may be indicative of an articular restriction.

Slump test[10,18]

The patient sits at the edge of a table and is asked to "slump" (i.e., move into lumbar and thoracic flexion) and then bring their chin toward their chest. The therapist uses one hand to maintain the position of full spinal flexion while using the other hand to place the patient's ankle in full dorsiflexion. The patient is then asked to actively extend the knee (or this can be done passively). If the patient cannot fully extend the knee because of pain, the therapist asks the patient to extend their neck, and then try to extend the knee again. If symptoms decrease with knee extension or the patient can extend the knee farther, the test is positive for neural tension.

Standing flexion test[10,22]

The patient is positioned in standing with the feet 12 inches apart. The therapist places their thumbs on the inferior margin of the posterior superior iliac spines and monitors the movement of the bony structures as the patient bends forward with the knees extended. A positive test is indicated by one posterior superior iliac spine moving farther in a cranial direction and may be indicative of an articular restriction.

Straight leg raise test[10,18]

With the patient in supine, the therapist flexes the patient's hip while maintaining knee extension and slight medial rotation of the hip. The therapist continues to flex the hip until the patient complains of pain or tightness in the low back or posterior leg. The therapist then lowers the leg until the patient feels no pain or tightness. At this point, the therapist dorsiflexes the ankle (or has the patient flex their neck). If the symptoms return, then the test is positive for neural tension or a lesion within the spinal cord (e.g., disk herniation).

Osteokinematic and Arthrokinematic Motions

Upper Extremity Joints - Osteokinematic and Arthrokinematic Motion[10,14]

Joint	Resting Position	Convex/Concave	Osteokinematic/ Arthrokinematic Motion
Sternoclavicular	Anatomical position	*Elevation/depression* Convex: clavicle Concave: sternum *Protraction/retraction* Convex: sternum Concave: clavicle	Opposite direction Same direction
Glenohumeral	55 degrees abduction, 30 degrees horizontal adduction	Convex: humerus Concave: glenoid	Opposite direction
Ulnohumeral	70 degrees flexion, 10 degrees supination	Convex: humerus Concave: ulna	Same direction
Radiohumeral	Full extension, full supination	Convex: humerus Concave: radius	Same direction
Proximal radioulnar	70 degrees flexion, 35 degrees supination	Convex: radius Concave: ulna	Opposite direction

Upper Extremity Joints - Osteokinematic and Arthrokinematic Motion (continued)

Joint	Resting Position	Convex/Concave	Osteokinematic/ Arthrokinematic Motion
Distal radioulnar	10 degrees supination	Convex: ulna Concave: radius	Same direction
Radiocarpal	Neutral with slight ulnar deviation	Convex: carpals Concave: radius	Opposite direction
Metacarpophalangeal joints of digits 2-5	Slight flexion	Convex: metacarpals Concave: phalanges	Same direction
Proximal and distal interphalangeal joints of digits 2-5	Slight flexion	Convex: proximal phalanges Concave: distal phalanges	Same direction

Lower Extremity Joints - Osteokinematic and Arthrokinematic Motion[10,14]

Joint	Resting Position	Convex/Concave	Osteokinematic/ Arthrokinematic Motion
Hip	30 degrees flexion, 30 degrees abduction, slight lateral rotation	Convex: femur Concave: acetabulum	Opposite direction
Tibiofemoral	25 degrees flexion	Convex: femur Concave: tibia	Same direction
Patellofemoral	25 degrees flexion	Convex: patella Concave: femur	Opposite direction
Proximal tibiofibular	0 degrees plantar flexion	Convex: tibia Concave: fibula	Same direction
Distal tibiofibular	0 degrees plantar flexion	Convex: fibula Concave: tibia	Opposite direction
Talocrural	10 degrees plantar flexion, midway between maximum inversion and eversion	Convex: talus Concave: tibia and fibula	Opposite direction
Subtalar	Midway between extremes of range of movement	Convex: anterior and middle talus Concave: anterior and middle calcaneus Convex: posterior calcaneus Concave: posterior talus	Same direction Opposite direction
Intermetatarsal	Midway between extremes of range of movement	Convex: more medial metatarsals Concave: more lateral metatarsals	Same direction
Metatarsophalangeal	Neutral	Convex: metatarsals Concave: phalanges	Same direction
Interphalangeal joints of the toes	Slight flexion	Convex: proximal phalanges Concave: distal phalanges	Same direction

Miscellaneous Joints - Osteokinematic and Arthrokinematic Motion[10,14]

Joint	Resting Position	Convex/Concave	Osteokinematic/ Arthrokinematic Motion
Temporomandibular	Mouth slightly open (freeway space)	Convex: mandible Concave: temporal bone	Opposite direction

Mobilization[14,16]

Mobilization is a passive movement technique designed to improve joint function.

Indications: restricted joint mobility, restricted accessory motion, desired neurophysiological effects

Contraindications: active disease, infection, advanced osteoporosis, articular hypermobility, fracture, acute inflammation, muscle guarding, joint replacement

Grades of Movement	
Grade I	Small amplitude movement performed at the beginning of range.
Grade II	Large amplitude movement performed within the range, but not reaching the limit of the range and not returning to the beginning of range.
Grade III	Large amplitude movement performed up to the limit of range.
Grade IV	Small amplitude movement performed at the limit of range.
Grade V	Small amplitude, high velocity thrust technique performed to snap adhesions at the limit of range.

Convex-Concave Rule

Determines the direction of decreased joint gliding and the appropriate direction for the mobilizing force.

Convex surface moving on a concave surface:

- Roll and slide occur in the opposite direction
- Mobilizing force should be applied in the opposite direction of the bone movement

Concave surface moving on a convex surface:

- Roll and slide occur in the same direction
- Mobilizing force should be applied in the same direction as the bone movement

Mobilization Technique

- The patient should have a general understanding of the purpose of mobilization.
- The patient should be completely relaxed during treatment.
- The therapist should be in a comfortable position while performing mobilization activities.
- The therapist's position should allow for optimal control of movement. Explain specific mobilization techniques to the patient prior to beginning treatment. Complete a general examination of each patient prior to beginning mobilization activities.
- Use gravity to assist with mobilization whenever possible.
- Mobilization activities are usually performed initially with the joint in a loose packed position.
- Maintain contact with the mobilizing hand as close to the joint space as possible.
- Allow one digit to palpate the joint line when possible.
- Mobilize one joint in one direction at a time.
- Use a mobilization belt or wedge to assist with stabilization when necessary.
- Constantly modify mobilization techniques based on individual patient response.
- Compare the quality and quantity of joint play bilaterally.
- Reassess each patient prior to every treatment session.

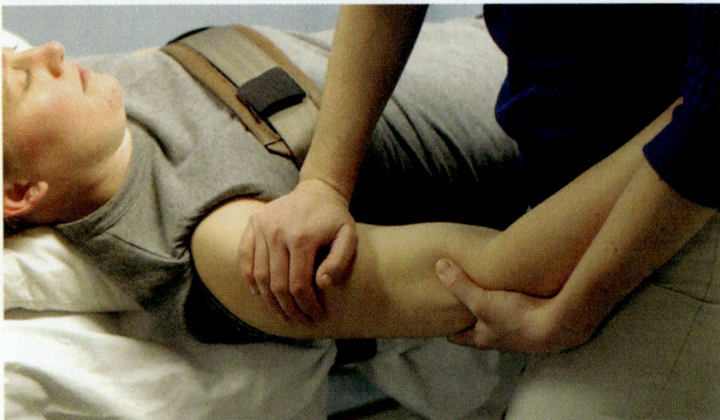

Fig. 4-60: A therapist administers a posterior glide of the humerus on the glenoid. This type of intervention would be most effective to increase glenohumeral flexion, medial rotation, and horizontal adduction range of motion.

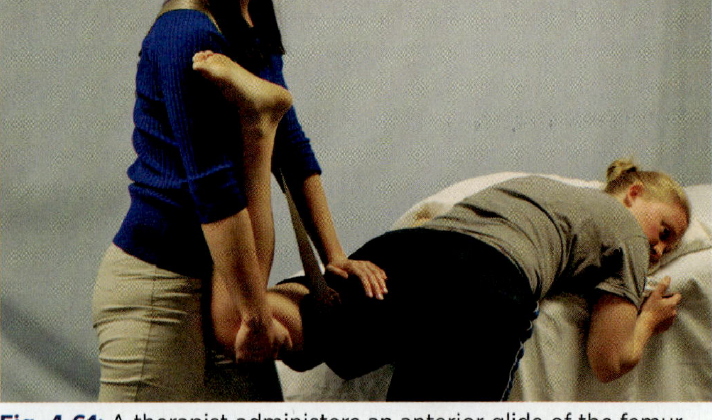

Fig. 4-61: A therapist administers an anterior glide of the femur on the acetabulum. This type of intervention would be most effective to increase hip extension and lateral rotation.

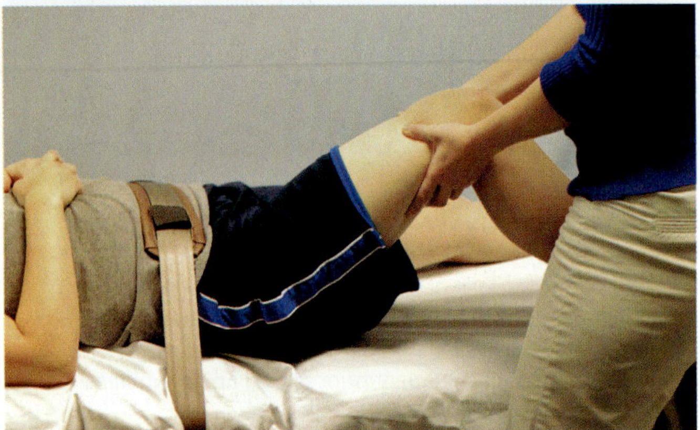

Fig. 4-62: A therapist administers an inferior glide of the femur on the acetabulum. This type of intervention would be most effective to increase hip abduction.

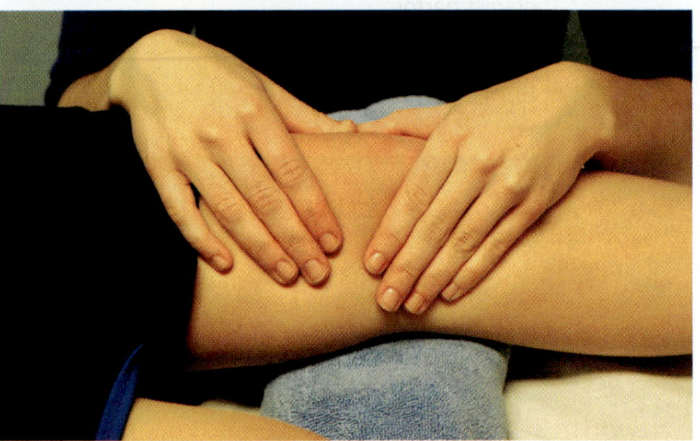

Fig. 4-63: A therapist administers a medial glide of the patella. This type of intervention would be most effective to increase accessory motion of the patellofemoral joint.

Therapeutic Exercise[15,16,17,29]

Range of Motion

Range of motion is defined as the amount of mobility available at a single joint, which may be affected by the structure of the joint or the extensibility of soft tissues that surround the joint. Range of motion is classified as passive, active-assisted or active.

Contraindications: Range of motion activities should not be performed when motion is detrimental to the healing of tissues. However, controlled motion within a pain-free range has been shown to be beneficial in the early stages of healing. Increased pain or inflammation are signs that range of motion activities may be too aggressive.

Passive Range of Motion (PROM)

Definition: PROM is movement that is produced by an external force without muscular activation from the patient. PROM is only performed within the available range of motion. Any movement beyond end-range is considered stretching (Figs. 4-64, 4-65).

Indications:

- the patient is unable to physically move the body segment (e.g., comatose, paralyzed)
- the patient is cognitively impaired and unable to move the body segment
- active movement is contraindicated (e.g., post-operative)
- active movement is painful for the patient
- the therapist is preparing the joint for stretching
- the therapist is teaching an active movement to the patient

Benefits:

- improves the mobility of connective tissues and muscles
- prevents joint contracture formation
- improves circulation
- improves synovial fluid movement for cartilage health
- decreases pain
- improves the patient's awareness of movement

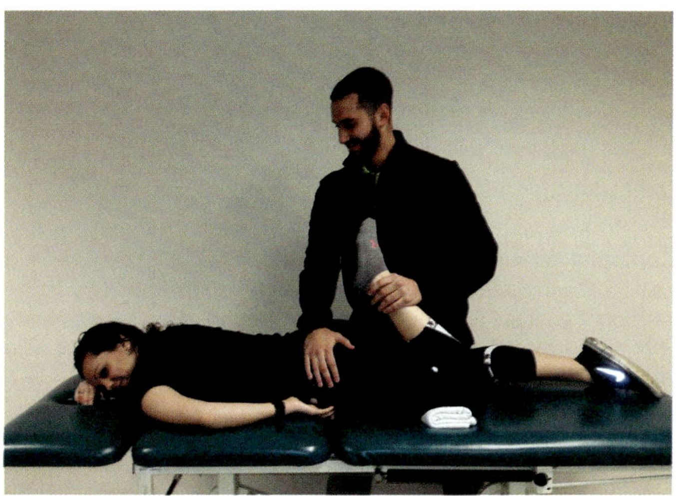

Fig. 4-64: A therapist performs passive knee flexion to stretch the anterior structures of the thigh.

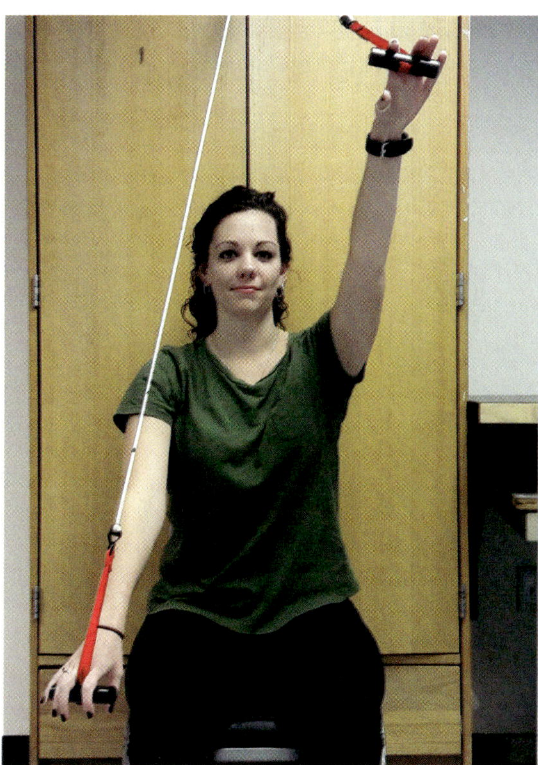

Fig. 4-65: A patient performs passive range of motion of the left upper extremity using an overhead pulley system.

Active-assisted Range of Motion (AAROM)

Definition: AAROM is movement that is produced by the patient through active muscular contraction with some assistance from an external force (Fig. 4-66).

Indications:

- the patient is unable to fully contract a muscle (e.g., paresis, pain)
- full activation of a muscle is contraindicated (e.g., post-operative)
- performed prior to initiating active movement

Benefits:

- improves the mobility of connective tissues and muscles
- prevents joint contracture formation
- improves circulation
- improves synovial fluid movement for cartilage health
- decreases pain
- improves neuromuscular activity
- improves kinesthesia and proprioception

Fig. 4-66: A patient in supine performs active-assisted range of motion of the upper extremities using a dowel.

Active Range of Motion (AROM)

Definition: AROM is movement that is produced by the patient through active muscular contraction without any external assistance (Fig. 4-67).

Indications:

- patient is able to contract a muscle, but demonstrates weakness
- performed prior to initiating resistance training to teach the desired movement

Benefits:

- improves the mobility of connective tissues and muscles
- prevents joint contracture formation

- improves circulation
- improves synovial fluid movement for cartilage health
- decreases pain
- improves neuromuscular activity
- improves kinesthesia and proprioception
- improves strength in very weak muscles (e.g., 3/5 strength)

Fig. 4-67: A patient performs active knee flexion in standing.

Stretching

Stretching is a therapeutic technique used to improve joint range of motion and muscle flexibility by increasing the extensibility of the musculotendinous unit and connective tissues.

Indications: decreased joint range of motion or decreased muscle flexibility

Contraindications: acute inflammation, during soft tissue healing (e.g., following a tendon repair), range of motion limited by bone-on-bone contact, recent fracture, hypermobility, hypomobility that allows for improved function (e.g., tenodesis grip), acute pain associated with stretching

Principles of Stretching

Elasticity: The ability of soft tissue to return to its previous length after a stretch is no longer applied.

Viscoelasticity: A time-dependent property of soft tissue that results in resistance to stretch when it is initially applied, but allows for tissue elongation as the stretch is held for longer durations. As with elasticity, the tissue will return to its previous length after the stretch is no longer applied.

Plasticity: A property of soft tissue that allows for tissue elongation even after a stretch is no longer applied.

Stress-strain curve: A graphic representation that depicts the relationship between the amount of force (stress) applied to connective tissue and the amount of deformation (strain) it experiences (Fig. 4-68).

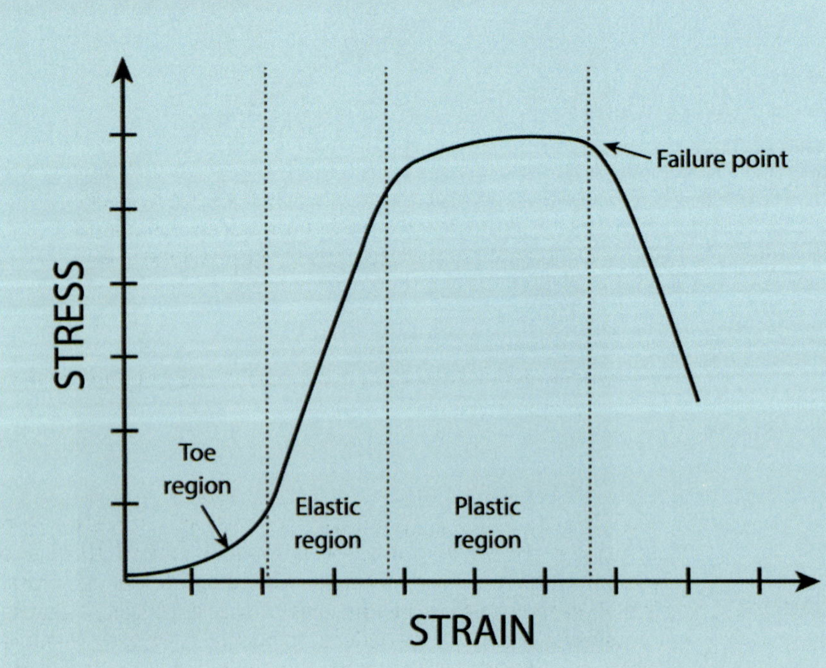

Toe region: Initial stress that results in the wavy collagen fibers becoming straight and aligning with one another.

Elastic region: Added stress to the tissue results in greater deformation, though the tissue returns to its resting length if the stretch force is not maintained. Tissues with greater stiffness will have a steeper slope in this portion of the curve.

Plastic region: The addition of more stress results in permanent deformation even after the stretch force is no longer applied due to the failure of bonds between the collagen fibers.

Fig. 4-68: A stress-strain curve depicting the toe region, elastic region, and plastic region.

Creep: Due to the viscoelastic property, soft tissue that is stretched for a sustained duration will elongate and not return to its original length after the load has been removed. The principle of creep is the basis for stretching.

Stress-relaxation: The longer a stretching force is maintained, the more the tension within the tissue decreases, therefore less force is required to maintain the same tissue length.

Methods of Stretching

Static stretching

Static stretching (Figs. 4-69, 4-70) involves placing the muscle at its maximal length and holding the position against an external force for a prolonged period of time. Static stretching is characterized by low intensity and long duration. It is considered to be the safest form of stretching and results in the greatest gains in tissue extensibility. This form of stretching leads to less activation of the muscle spindles (as compared to ballistic stretching) and thus less resistance to stretch. Though there is no consensus for the optimal duration of static stretching, 30 seconds is a commonly cited value that has been shown to result in significant range of motion gains.

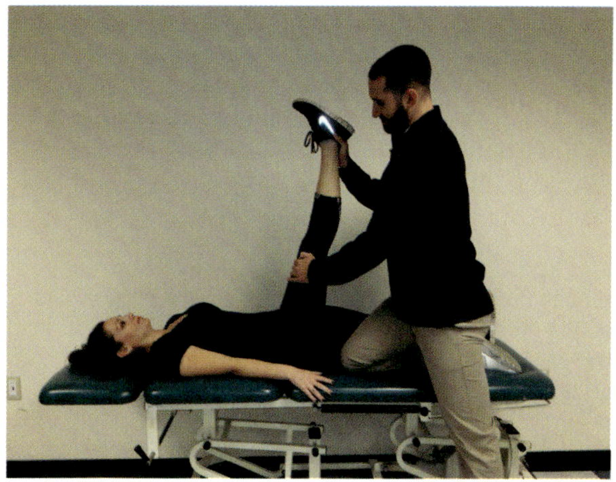

Fig. 4-69: A therapist passively stretching a patient's right hamstrings.

Ballistic stretching

Ballistic stretching (Fig. 4-71) is characterized by quick, jerky movements that result in a rapid change in muscle length. The muscle is placed near its end of range of motion and then the patient bounces back and forth to place repetitive stretch on the muscle (i.e., high intensity, short duration). Because ballistic stretching occurs quickly, it activates the muscle spindles and results in greater resistance to stretch. Therefore, it is not as effective for improving tissue extensibility, though it may be more effective when preparing the muscles for athletic activity. Additionally, ballistic stretching is more likely to lead to muscle soreness and injury due to the high intensity of stretch force.

Fig. 4-71: A patient in standing performs ballistic stretching of the hamstrings by quickly assuming the position depicted in the image resulting in a rapid change in muscle length.

Fig. 4-70: A patient passively stretching the left shoulder using a doorway.

Proprioceptive neuromuscular facilitation (PNF) stretching

PNF incorporates active muscle contractions into stretching techniques. Muscular contraction is thought to lead to muscle relaxation through the principles of autogenic or reciprocal inhibition and results in greater gains in muscle flexibility. Because these techniques exert their effects on muscle fibers, they are more effective at treating range of motion limitations due to muscle spasm as opposed to connective tissue tightness. Other theories for PNF's effects on improved flexibility include increased patient

tolerance to the stretch and length changes secondary to the viscoelastic properties of muscle. Because PNF requires active muscular control from the patient, it is not an effective technique for patients with paralysis or spasticity. Common PNF techniques include contract-relax, agonist contraction, and contract-relax with agonist contraction.

Dynamic stretching

Dynamic stretching involves the patient actively moving a body segment to the end of range (but not beyond this limit) while the antagonist muscle relaxes and stretches. Unlike static stretching, the end-range movement is held only briefly and is performed repeatedly. Dynamic stretching is most commonly used as a "warm-up" to prepare the body for athletic activities. It is more effective at preparing the body for explosive movements when compared to static stretching. Dynamic stretching emphasizes a movement based approach, while ballistic stretching emphasizes bouncing movements.

Resistance Training

Muscle Anatomy

A single muscle is made up of several muscle fibers and the connective tissue layers that surround and lie within the muscle. The endomysium is the innermost connective tissue layer that covers individual muscle fibers. The perimysium is the connective tissue layer that groups bundles of muscle fibers (i.e., a fasciculus) together. The epimysium is the outermost connective tissue layer that surrounds the entire muscle.

Each muscle fiber is its own cell and is made up of several subunits called myofibrils, which are in turn made up of sarcomeres. The sarcomere is the smallest unit of a muscle that gives it the ability to contract. Sarcomeres are composed of the myofilaments actin and myosin. The actin and myosin attach to one another and slide together and apart to allow for muscle contraction and relaxation, respectively.

Resistive and Overload Training

Isometric Exercise: Muscular force is generated without a change in muscle length. Isometric exercises are often performed against an immovable object. Submaximal isometric exercises are traditionally used in rehabilitation programs.

Isotonic Exercise: Muscular contraction is generated with the muscle exerting a constant tension. This can also be thought of as muscle movement with a constant load. Isotonic exercises are performed against resistance, often employing equipment such as handheld weights. There are two types of isotonic contractions: concentric and eccentric. A concentric contraction shortens a muscle, while an eccentric contraction lengthens a muscle.

Isokinetic Exercise: Muscular contraction is generated with a constant maximal speed and variable load. In isokinetic exercise, the reaction force is identical to the force applied to the equipment. Cybex, Biodex, and Lido are a few of the companies making isokinetic exercise equipment.

Resistance Training Parameters

Intensity: The intensity of resistance training is often determined by the amount of weight that is being used, which will in turn determine how many repetitions of the exercise can be performed. The amount of weight being used may be expressed as a percentage of the patient's 1 RM (repetition maximum). The intensity chosen will depend on the goals of the training program. If increased strength is the goal, then lower repetitions (e.g., 6-12) of a higher intensity load should be prescribed. If increased endurance is the goal, then higher repetitions (e.g., 20+) of a lower intensity load should be prescribed. When training for power, low repetitions (e.g., 1-3) of a very high intensity load are used.

Volume: The volume is the total amount of work performed and is calculated as the total number of repetitions multiplied by the intensity of the exercise. The total number of repetitions is inversely related to intensity; if heavier weights are used, the patient will be able to perform fewer total repetitions, as is the case when training to increase power or strength. Two to four sets of repetitions are a common exercise prescription, with the number of repetitions within a single set dependent on the goals of treatment (i.e., strength versus endurance).

Frequency: The frequency refers to the number of times per week resistance exercises are performed and is dependent on the intensity and volume of exercise and the fitness level of the individual. For more intense exercise, training should be performed less frequently (e.g., 2-3 times per week). The same applies for patients with a lower overall fitness level. For patients in a rehabilitation program, exercise can be performed several times per day if the intensity and volume of exercise is kept low. Exercise that is performed too frequently may lead to overtraining and a decline in the patient's condition or performance.

Exercise sequence: The general recommendations for exercise sequencing dictate that large muscle groups should be exercised before small muscle groups, multi-joint exercises should be performed before single joint exercises, and high intensity exercises should be performed before low intensity exercises. However, a therapist may choose to disregard these recommendations if they conflict with the rehabilitation goals of a specific patient.

Rest interval: The recovery period between sets will vary depending on the intensity of the exercise. For high intensity exercise, a longer rest interval is needed (e.g., three or more minutes). For low intensity exercise, a shorter rest interval is adequate (e.g., one to two minutes). Patients who have an overall lower fitness level may also need a longer rest interval when compared to more fit individuals.

Open-Chain: Open-chain activities involve the distal segment, usually the hand or foot, moving freely in space. An example of an open-chain activity is kicking a ball with the lower extremity (Fig. 4-72).

Closed-Chain: Closed-chain activities involve the body moving over a fixed distal segment. An example of a closed-chain activity is a squat lift (Fig. 4-73).

Fig. 4-72: An example of an open-chain exercise.

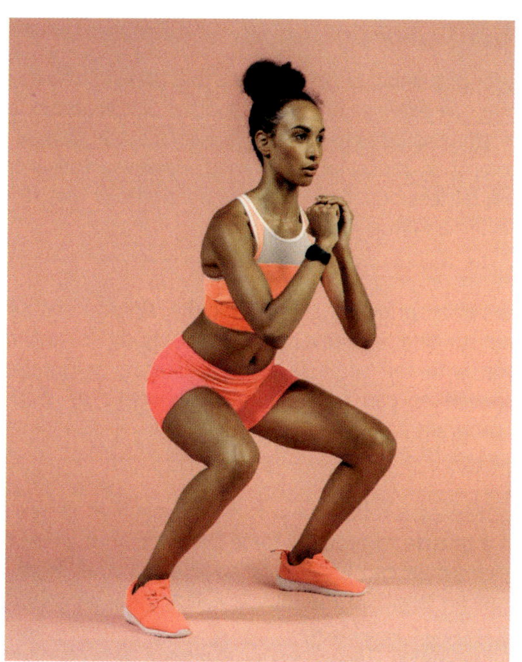

Fig. 4-73: An example of a closed-chain exercise.

Exercise Programs

DeLorme	Protocol	Oxford Technique	Protocol
First Set	10 repetitions x 50% of 10 repetition maximum	First Set	10 repetitions x 100% of 10 repetition maximum
Second Set	10 repetitions x 75% of 10 repetition maximum	Second Set	10 repetitions x 75% of 10 repetition maximum
Third Set	10 repetitions x 100% of 10 repetition maximum	Third Set	10 repetitions x 50% of 10 repetition maximum

Resistance Training Principles

Overload principle

The overload principle states that in order for a muscle to adapt and become stronger, the load that is placed on it must be greater than what it is normally accustomed to. In resistance training, the volume (sets, repetitions) or intensity (resistance) of the exercise can be altered to provide a greater challenge to the muscle.

SAID principle

The SAID principle (Specific Adaptation to Imposed Demands) states that the body will adapt according to the specific type of training that is utilized. To bring about an improvement in a patient's function, the type of training should specifically mirror the desired goal. For example, if a patient needs greater muscular power, the exercises chosen should focus on improving power as opposed to strength or endurance.

Transfer of training principle

The transfer of training principle states that there can be a carryover effect from one exercise or task to another. For example, a patient who performs exercises to improve muscular strength may also see improvements in muscular endurance. However, these carryover effects are far less beneficial than the adaptations that result from more specific training.

Reversibility principle

The reversibility principle states that the adaptations seen with resistance training are reversible if the body is not regularly challenged with the same level of resistance or greater. These reversible effects can begin within 1-2 weeks of stopping an exercise program.

Length-tension relationship

The length-tension relationship is a principle that states that the ability of a muscle to produce force depends on the length of the muscle. A muscle can usually produce a maximal force near its normal resting length. If the muscle is lengthened or shortened, it will likely produce less force.

Force-velocity relationship

The force-velocity relationship is a principle that states that the speed of a muscle contraction affects the force that the muscle can produce. During a concentric contraction, as the speed of contraction increases, the force of contraction decreases. During an eccentric contraction, as the speed of contraction increases, the force of contraction also increases.

Resistance Training Terminology

Endurance: The ability of a muscle to contract repeatedly against a light external load and resist fatigue over a prolonged period of time.

Moment arm: The linear distance from the axis of rotation to the site of the external load.

Muscle performance: The ability of a muscle to perform work. The components of muscle performance include power, strength, and endurance.

Power: The rate at which work is performed (i.e., work divided by time).

Strength: The greatest amount of force that can be produced within a muscle during a single contraction, which may be assessed clinically by determining a patient's 1 RM (i.e., maximum amount of weight that can be lifted once).

Torque: The ability of an external load to produce rotation around an axis, calculated by multiplying the magnitude of the load by the moment arm.

Work: The magnitude of a load (e.g., weight) multiplied by the distance the load is moved (e.g., range of motion used).

Adaptations to Resistance Training

Strength training	Endurance training
• muscle fiber hypertrophy • fiber type remodeling from IIB to IIA • increased neuromuscular activity (number of motor units, firing rate) • decreased or no change in capillary bed density • decreased mitochondrial density • increased stores of ATP, creatine phosphate, and other energy sources • increased tensile strength of tendons and ligaments • increased bone mineral density • increased lean body mass • decreased body fat percentage	• increased capillary bed density • increased mitochondrial density • increased stores of ATP, creatine phosphate, and other energy sources • increased tensile strength of tendons and ligaments • increased bone mineral density • decreased body fat percentage

SPOTLIGHT ON SAFETY

POTENTIAL CONSEQUENCES OF RESISTANCE TRAINING[15,16]

Therapists should carefully monitor patients during and following resistance training in order to avoid undesirable training effects. Three of the more common conditions resulting from resistance training include muscle fatigue, delayed-onset muscle soreness, and the Valsalva maneuver.

Muscle fatigue

Muscle fatigue is characterized by the decreasing ability of a muscle to produce force against a load with increasing repetitions. Muscle fatigue is reversible (i.e., strength will improve after a period of rest). The extent of muscle fatigue will depend on the fiber-type distribution within the muscle. Type I (slow-twitch) muscle fibers are able to generate a low level of force for long durations and therefore are very resistant to fatigue, while type II (fast-twitch) muscle fibers produce large amounts of force over short durations and are therefore more prone to fatigue.

While muscle fatigue may occur during a resistance training program, the therapist should be aware of excessive fatigue and avoid working the patient to this point. Signs and symptoms of excessive muscle fatigue include muscle pain and cramping, tremors, movement that becomes slower or jerky, an inability to complete the full movement pattern, and use of substitution patterns. When these signs or symptoms occur, the therapist should decrease the load being lifted or allow the patient to take a rest break. Allowing the patient to continue exercising in the presence of excessive muscle fatigue could lead to further injury.

For some patients, muscle fatigue does not occur in a normal predictable fashion. Patients with certain neuromuscular disorders (e.g., myasthenia gravis, multiple sclerosis) may fatigue more quickly. Pushing these patients to the point of fatigue may actually result in a worsening of their symptoms. Likewise, patients with cardiovascular or pulmonary diseases fatigue more quickly and may need longer recovery periods during exercise. Therapists should be aware of the fatigue patterns associated with different diseases and treat each patient accordingly.

Delayed-onset muscle soreness

Delayed-onset muscle soreness (DOMS) is a specific type of post-exercise soreness that is thought to result from microtrauma to the muscle and its connective tissues that occurs during resistance training. DOMS is most commonly noted in patients who have engaged in high intensity, eccentric strengthening exercises, especially if the patient has recently begun a resistance training program.

DOMS is characterized by tenderness to palpation in the muscle belly or at the muscle-tendon junction, soreness with passive stretching or active contraction of the muscle, and decreased range of motion and strength. These symptoms usually reach their peak two days after exercise and can last for several days. The soreness will diminish with each successive training session as the muscle adapts to higher levels of stress.

It may be possible to minimize the effect of DOMS by slowly increasing the intensity of a new exercise program. Additionally, performing only concentric and isometric exercises significantly reduces the likelihood that DOMS will occur.

Valsalva maneuver

The Valsalva maneuver is a technique that is often used to increase intra-abdominal and intrathoracic pressures during anaerobic activities that require a large effort, such as lifting a heavy box from the floor. The maneuver is performed by forcefully exhaling against a closed glottis, nose, and mouth while simultaneously contracting the abdominal muscles. The increase in internal pressures helps to stabilize the spine during heavy exertion and is therefore employed during powerlifting to help improve performance.

Though the Valsalva maneuver can be useful in certain situations, it leads to undesirable effects on the cardiovascular system. Because of its negative effects, the Valsalva maneuver should be avoided in all patients, but especially for patients with cardiovascular disease (e.g., hypertension, coronary artery disease, stroke), with intervertebral disk pathology or who have recently undergone eye surgery. To avoid using the Valsalva maneuver, patients should be taught to breathe rhythmically and to exhale during the portion of exercise that requires more exertion.

Pathology of the Musculoskeletal System

Achilles Tendonitis[18,28,29]

Achilles tendonitis is a repetitive overuse disorder resulting in microscopic tears of collagen fibers on the surface or in the substance of the Achilles tendon. The tendon is most often impacted in an avascular zone located two to six centimeters above the insertion of the tendon.

Etiology - Repetitive overload of the Achilles tendon often caused by changes in training intensity or faulty technique. Patients with limited flexibility and strength in the gastrocnemius and soleus complex and patients with a pronated or cavus foot are at increased risk. Activities frequently associated with Achilles tendonitis include running, basketball, gymnastics, and dancing. A history of Achilles tendonitis increases the likelihood of an Achilles tendon rupture later in life.

Signs and Symptoms - aching or burning in the posterior heel, tenderness of the Achilles tendon, pain with increased activity, swelling and thickening in the tendon area, muscle weakness due to pain, morning stiffness

Treatment - Initially RICE (Rest, Ice, Compression, Elevation), nonsteroidal anti-inflammatory medications (NSAIDs), and analgesics as needed. A heel lift and cross training may be used to limit the amount of tensile loading through the tendon. Prevention includes heel cord stretching exercises, use of appropriate soft-soled footwear, eccentric strengthening of the gastrocnemius and soleus complex, and avoiding sudden changes in intensity of training programs.

Adhesive Capsulitis[13,28,29]

Adhesive capsulitis results in a loss of range of motion in active and passive shoulder motion due to soft tissue contracture. The condition is caused by adhesive fibrosis and scarring between the capsule, rotator cuff, subacromial bursa, and deltoid.

Etiology - The onset may be related to a direct injury to the shoulder or may begin insidiously. Peak incidence occurs in individuals between 40 and 60 years of age with females being affected more than males. Patients with diabetes have an increased incidence of adhesive capsulitis. The condition is self-limiting and typically resolves in one to two years, although some individuals have residual loss of motion.

Signs and Symptoms - insidious onset of localized pain often extending down the arm, subjective reports of stiffness, night pain, restricted range of motion in a capsular pattern

Treatment - The focus of treatment is on increasing range of motion with glenohumeral mobilization, range of motion exercises, and palliative modalities. The therapist and patient should avoid overstretching and elevating pain since this can result in further loss of motion. Surgical options include suprascapular nerve block and closed manipulation under anesthesia.

Anterior Cruciate Ligament Sprain[8,13,28]

The anterior cruciate ligament (ACL) runs from the anterior intercondylar area of the tibia to the medial aspect of the lateral femoral condyle in the intercondylar notch. The ligament prevents anterior displacement of the tibia in relation to the femur. The extent of the sprain is classified according to the extent of ligament damage. A grade I sprain involves microscopic tears of the ligament, while a grade III sprain indicates a completely torn ligament.

Etiology - Noncontact twisting injury associated with hyperextension, varus or valgus stress to the knee. An ACL sprain often involves injury to other knee structures such as the medial capsule, medial collateral ligament, and menisci.

Signs and Symptoms - The patient may report a loud pop or feeling the knee "giving way" or "buckling" followed by dizziness, sweating, and swelling. Special tests to identify the presence of an ACL tear include the anterior drawer test, Lachman test, and lateral pivot shift test.

Treatment - Initially RICE, NSAIDs, and analgesics as needed. Conservative treatment includes lower extremity strengthening exercises emphasizing the quadriceps and the hamstrings. Surgery is often warranted for a complete ACL tear (grade III). Surgery most often consists of intra-articular reconstruction using the patellar tendon, iliotibial band or hamstrings tendon. A derotation brace may be beneficial for a patient with an ACL deficient knee, however, it has limited benefit for a patient following surgical reconstruction.

Congenital Hip Dysplasia[27,30]

Congenital hip dysplasia, also known as developmental dysplasia, is a condition characterized by malalignment of the femoral head within the acetabulum. The condition develops during the last trimester in utero.

Etiology - cultural predisposition, malposition in utero, environmental and genetic influences

Signs and Symptoms - Clinical presentation includes asymmetrical hip abduction with tightness and apparent femoral shortening of the involved side. Testing for this condition may include the Ortolani's test, Barlow's test, and diagnostic ultrasound.

Treatment - The focus of treatment is dependent on age, severity, and initial attempts to reposition the femoral head within the acetabulum through the constant use of a harness, bracing, splinting or traction. Open reduction with subsequent application of a hip spica cast may be required if conservative treatment fails. Physical therapy may be indicated after cast removal for stretching, strengthening, and caregiver education.

Congenital Limb Deficiencies[27-30]

A congenital limb deficiency is a malformation that occurs in utero, secondary to an altered developmental course. Congenital limb deficiencies are classified as longitudinal or transverse. A longitudinal limb deficiency refers to a reduction or absence of an element or elements within the long axis of the bone. A transverse limb deficiency refers to a limb that has developed to a particular level beyond which no skeletal elements exist.

Etiology - The majority of congenital limb deficiencies are idiopathic or are genetic in origin. Other possible etiologies include poor blood supply, constricting amniotic bands, infection, and maternal drug exposure.

Signs and Symptoms - structural or acquired abnormality of a limb, phantom limb pain

Treatment - The focus of treatment is on symmetrical movements, strengthening, range of motion, weight bearing activities, and prosthetic training when appropriate.

Congenital Torticollis[30-31]

Congenital torticollis, also known as wry neck, is characterized by a unilateral contracture of the sternocleidomastoid muscle. The condition is most often identified in the first two months of life.

Etiology - The cause is unknown, however, it may be associated with malpositioning in utero (e.g., breech) and birth trauma.

Signs and Symptoms - Clinical presentation includes lateral cervical flexion to the same side as the contracture, rotation toward the opposite side, and facial asymmetries.

Treatment - Initially, treatment is conservative with emphasis on stretching, active range of motion, positioning, and caregiver education. Surgical management is indicated when conservative options have failed and the child is over one year of age. A surgical release followed by physical therapy may be indicated for range of motion and proper alignment.

Glenohumeral Instability[8,13,18,28]

Glenohumeral instability refers to excessive translation of the humeral head on the glenoid during active rotation. Instability involves varying degrees of injuries to dynamic and static structures that function to contain the humeral head in the glenoid. Subluxation refers to joint laxity, allowing for more than 50% of the humeral head to passively translate over the glenoid rim without dislocation. Dislocation is the complete separation of the articular surfaces of the glenoid and the humeral head. Approximately 85% of dislocations detach the glenoid labrum (i.e., Bankart lesion).

Etiology - A combination of forces stress the anterior capsule, glenohumeral ligament, and rotator cuff, causing the humerus to move anteriorly out of the glenoid fossa. An anterior dislocation is the most common and is usually associated with shoulder abduction and lateral rotation.

Signs and Symptoms - Subluxation: feeling the shoulder "popping" out and back into place, pain, paresthesias, sensation of the arm feeling "dead," positive apprehension test, capsular tenderness, swelling; Dislocation: severe pain, paresthesias, limited range of motion, weakness, visible shoulder fullness, arm supported by contralateral limb.

Treatment - Initial immobilization with a sling for three to six weeks. RICE and NSAIDs are often utilized in the early phase. Following immobilization, range of motion, and isometric strengthening should be initiated followed by progressive resistive exercises emphasizing the internal and external rotators, as well as the large scapular muscles.

Impingement Syndrome[8,13,18,28]

Impingement syndrome is one of the most common injuries of the shoulder. It is often caused by repetitive microtrauma from upper extremity activity performed above the horizontal plane. Individuals participating in throwing activities, swimming, and racquet sports are particularly susceptible to impingement syndrome.

Etiology - Impingement syndrome is caused by the humeral head and the associated rotator cuff attachments migrating proximally and becoming impinged on the undersurface of the acromion and the coracoacromial ligament.

Signs and Symptoms - discomfort or mild pain deep within the shoulder, pain with overhead activities, painful arc of motion (i.e., 70-120 degrees abduction), positive impingement sign, tenderness over the greater tuberosity and the bicipital groove

Treatment - Initially RICE, NSAIDs, and activity modification. Once tolerated, treatment includes rotator cuff strengthening and scapular stability exercises. Long-term prevention includes continued strengthening of the rotator cuff and scapula stabilizers, along with improved biomechanics related to sport- specific or relevant work activities.

Juvenile Rheumatoid Arthritis[30,31]

Juvenile rheumatoid arthritis (JRA) is the most common chronic rheumatic disease in children and presents with inflammation of the joints and connective tissues. Classification of JRA includes systemic, polyarticular, and oligoarticular.

Etiology - The exact etiology is unknown, however, it is theorized that an external source such as a virus, infection or trauma may trigger an autoimmune response producing JRA in a child with a genetic predisposition.

Signs and Symptoms - The clinical presentation is based on the classification of JRA. Systemic JRA is the least common type of JRA and presents with acute onset, high fevers, rash, enlargement of the spleen and liver, and inflammation of the lungs and heart. Polyarticular JRA is more common than systemic JRA and presents with high female incidence, significant rheumatoid factor, and arthritis in more than four joints with symmetrical joint involvement. Oligoarticular (pauciarticular) JRA is the most common type of JRA and affects less than five joints with asymmetrical joint involvement.

Treatment - Pharmacological management to relieve inflammation and pain through NSAIDs, corticosteroids, antirheumatics, and immunosuppressive agents. Physical therapy management includes passive and active range of motion, positioning, splinting, strengthening, endurance training, weight bearing activities, postural training, and functional mobility. Pain management includes the use of modalities such as paraffin, ultrasound, warm water, and cryotherapy. Surgical intervention may be indicated secondary to pain, contractures or irreversible joint destruction.

Lateral Epicondylitis[8,28,29]

Lateral epicondylitis refers to an irritation or inflammation of the common extensor muscles at their origin on the lateral epicondyle of the humerus. Individuals who take part in racquet sports or activities requiring throwing are at the greatest risk for developing lateral epicondylitis.

Etiology - The condition is caused by eccentric loading of the wrist extensor muscles, usually the extensor carpi radialis brevis, resulting in microtrauma. Lateral epicondylitis can be precipitated by poor mechanics or faulty equipment such as a tennis racquet with a handle that is too small or with strings that possess too much tension. The condition is most common in individuals between 30 and 50 years of age.

Signs and Symptoms - Pain is present immediately anterior or distal to the lateral epicondyle of the humerus. Pain typically worsens with repetition and resisted wrist extension.

Treatment - Initially RICE, NSAIDs, and activity modification. Physical therapy should attempt to increase strength, flexibility, and endurance of the wrist extensors. A strap placed two to three inches distal to the elbow joint can reduce muscular tension placed on the epicondyle and may diminish or eliminate patient symptoms.

Legg-Calve-Perthes Disease[30,31]

Legg-Calve-Perthes disease is characterized by degeneration of the femoral head due to a disturbance in the blood supply (i.e., avascular necrosis). The disease is self-limiting and has four distinct stages: condensation, fragmentation, re-ossification, and remodeling.

Etiology - trauma, genetic predisposition, synovitis, vascular abnormalities, infection

Signs and Symptoms - pain, decreased range of motion, antalgic gait, positive Trendelenburg sign

Treatment - Activities are variable based on the clinical presentation, but the primary focus is to relieve pain, maintain the femoral head in the proper position, and improve range of motion. Physical therapy may be required intermittently for stretching, splinting, crutch training, aquatic therapy, traction, and exercise. Orthotic devices and surgical intervention may be indicated depending on classification and severity of the condition.

Medial Collateral Ligament Sprain[8,13,28]

The medial collateral ligament (MCL) runs from slightly above the medial femoral epicondyle to the medial aspect of the shaft of the tibia. An MCL sprain often involves injury to other knee structures such as the ACL or medial meniscus.

Etiology - A contact or noncontact, fixed foot, tibial rotational injury associated with valgus force and external tibia rotation can damage the MCL. This injury is often associated with activities such as football, skiing, and soccer.

Signs and Symptoms - Clinical presentation includes knee pain, swelling, antalgic gait, decreased range of motion, and a feeling of instability. A valgus stress test can be used to assess the integrity of the MCL.

Treatment - Initially RICE, NSAIDs, and analgesics as needed. Conservative treatment includes decreasing inflammation, protecting the knee joint and ligament, range of motion, and strengthening exercises as tolerated. Strengthening exercises gradually become more aggressive and functional activities are introduced. Surgery is rarely required since the MCL is well vascularized.

Meniscus Tear[8,13,18,28]

The medial and lateral menisci are firmly attached to the proximal surface of the tibia. The menisci are thick at the periphery and thinner at their internal unattached edges. The medial meniscus is more commonly injured than the lateral meniscus because it is less mobile due to its attachment to the joint capsule. The incidence of medial meniscal tears increases significantly over time with ACL deficiency. Meniscal injuries are definitively diagnosed by arthroscopy or magnetic resonance imaging.

Etiology - Meniscal injuries are usually associated with fixed foot rotation while weight bearing on a flexed knee. This action produces compression and rotational forces on the meniscus.

Signs and Symptoms - The clinical presentation includes joint line pain, swelling, catching or a locking sensation. Special tests to identify the presence of a meniscus tear include Apley's compression test, bounce home test, and McMurray test.

Treatment - Initially RICE, NSAIDs, and analgesics as needed. Conservative treatment consists of palliative modalities and strengthening exercises. Surgery ranging from a partial meniscectomy to a meniscal repair is often warranted for active individuals. Meniscal repairs are typically performed on tears located on the outer edges of the meniscus due to the increased vascularity. Recent advances in technology have increased the incidence of meniscal transplantation.

Osgood-Schlatter Disease[8,13,29]

Osgood-Schlatter disease, also known as traction apophysitis, is a self-limiting condition that results from repetitive traction on the tibial tuberosity apophysis.

Etiology - The condition is caused by repetitive tension to the patellar tendon over the tibial tuberosity in young athletes. This can result in a small avulsion of the tuberosity and subsequent swelling.

Signs and Symptoms - point tenderness over the patella tendon at the insertion on the tibial tubercle, antalgic gait, pain with increasing activity

Treatment - Conservative treatment focuses on education, icing, flexibility exercises, and eliminating activities that place strain on the patella tendon such as squatting, running or jumping.

Osteoarthritis[29,31]

Osteoarthritis is a chronic disease that causes degeneration of articular cartilage, primarily in weight bearing joints. Subsequent deformity and thickening of subchondral bone occur resulting in impaired functional status. Any joint may be involved, however, the most commonly affected sites include the hands and weight bearing joints such as the hips and knees.

Etiology - The cause of osteoarthritis is unknown. The condition typically appears during middle age and affects nearly all individuals to some extent by age 70. Osteoarthritis occurs more commonly in men than women up to age 55, however, it is more common in women later in life. Risk factors include being overweight, fractures or other joint injuries, and occupational or athletic overuse.

Signs and Symptoms - Clinical presentation includes gradual onset of pain present at the affected joint, increased pain after exercise, increased pain with weather changes, enlarged joints, crepitus, stiffness, limited joint range of motion, Heberden's nodes, and Bouchard's nodes. Blood tests are not helpful in diagnosing osteoarthritis, although radiographs may show diminished joint space or a bone spur.

Treatment - The goal of treatment is to reduce pain, promote joint function, and protect the joint. Pharmacological management may include acetaminophen, NSAIDs, and corticosteroids. Some patients benefit from viscosupplementation which is administered through a series of injections of hyaluronic acid into the knee. The goal is to improve lubrication of the knee, reduce pain, and improve range of motion. Physical therapy interventions include passive and active range of motion, heating and cooling agents, patient education, strengthening exercises, transcutaneous electrical nerve stimulation, energy conservation, weight loss, body mechanics, joint protection techniques, and bracing. Surgical intervention can range from arthroscopic surgery to total joint arthroplasty.

Osteogenesis Imperfecta[30,31]

Osteogenesis imperfecta is a connective tissue disorder that affects the formation of collagen during bone development. There are four classifications of osteogenesis imperfecta that vary in level of severity.

Etiology - The cause of osteogenesis imperfecta is genetic inheritance with types I and IV considered autosomal dominant traits and types II and III considered autosomal recessive traits.

Signs and Symptoms - pathological fractures, osteoporosis (i.e., brittle bones), hypermobile joints, bowing of the long bones, weakness, scoliosis, impaired respiratory function

Treatment - Management begins at birth with caregiver education on proper handling and facilitation of movement. Physical therapy will focus on active range of motion emphasizing symmetrical movements, positioning, functional mobility, fracture management, and the use of orthotics. In severe cases where ambulation is not realistic, wheelchair prescription and training are indicated.

Patellofemoral Syndrome[8,13,28,29]

Patellofemoral syndrome is a general term describing pain or discomfort in the anterior knee. The condition is often termed chondromalacia patella, which refers to softening of the articular cartilage of the patella.

Etiology - Patellofemoral syndrome is a repetitive overuse disorder resulting from increased force at the patellofemoral joint. Factors associated with increased patellofemoral forces include decreased quadriceps strength, decreased lower extremity flexibility, patellar instability, increased tibial torsion or femoral anteversion. Patients at increased risk for developing patellofemoral syndrome include females, individuals experiencing a growth spurt, runners who have recently increased mileage, and overweight individuals.

Signs and Symptoms - anterior knee pain, pain with prolonged sitting, swelling, crepitus, pain when ascending and descending stairs

Treatment - The focus of treatment is dependent on the contributing factors associated with the abnormal patellar tracking. Possible treatment options include palliative modalities to decrease inflammation and pain, lower extremity flexibility exercises, medial patella glides, biofeedback, and patella taping. Lower extremity strengthening should emphasize the quadriceps and in particular, the vastus medialis oblique, while minimizing patellofemoral compressive forces.

Plantar Fasciitis[13,28,29]

Plantar fasciitis refers to inflammation of the plantar fascia at the proximal insertion on the medial tubercle of the calcaneus. The plantar fascia is a broad structure comprised of connective tissue which spans from the calcaneus to the metatarsal heads. The structure is designed to provide support to the arch of the foot. Excessive tension over time creates chronic inflammation and microtears at the proximal insertion of the plantar fascia.

Etiology - Plantar fasciitis is often associated with an acute injury from excessive loading of the foot or chronic irritation from an excessive amount of pronation or prolonged duration of pronation. The condition is most common in patients between 40 and 60 years of age.

Signs and Symptoms - Clinical presentation includes tenderness at the insertion of the plantar fascia, presence of a heel spur, pain that is worse in the morning or after periods of prolonged inactivity, difficulty with prolonged standing, and pain when walking in bare feet.

Treatment - Initially RICE, NSAIDs, and analgesics as needed. A heel cup, massage using a tennis ball or rolling pin, medial longitudinal arch taping, and joint mobilization may be helpful. Prevention includes heel cord stretching exercises, use of appropriate soft-soled footwear, and avoiding sudden changes in the intensity of training programs. Orthotics may be used to minimize hyperpronation.

Posterior Cruciate Ligament Sprain[8,13,28]

The posterior cruciate ligament (PCL) runs from the posterior intercondylar area of the tibia to the lateral aspect of the medial femoral condyle in the intercondylar notch. The ligament prevents posterior displacement of the tibia in relation to the femur.

Etiology - The most common causes of a PCL injury are landing on the tibia with a flexed knee or hitting a dashboard in a motor vehicle accident with a flexed knee. Isolated PCL tears are not common and often involve other knee structures such as the ACL, MCL, LCL, and menisci.

Signs and Symptoms - The patient may report feeling as if the femur is sliding off the tibia. Swelling and mild pain may be present, but often the patient is asymptomatic. Special tests to identify the presence of a PCL tear include the posterior drawer test and posterior sag sign.

Treatment - Initially RICE, NSAIDs, and analgesics as needed. Physical therapy treatment includes lower extremity strengthening exercises and functional progression. Surgical treatment can occur, however, the procedure is not as evolved as the procedure for the ACL. If surgery is performed, isolated hamstrings exercises are often avoided for a minimum of six weeks.

Rheumatoid Arthritis[31,34,35]

Rheumatoid arthritis is a systemic autoimmune disorder of unknown etiology. The disease presents with a chronic inflammatory reaction in the synovial tissues of a joint that results in erosion of cartilage and supporting structures within the capsule. Onset of rheumatoid arthritis may initially occur at any joint, but it is common in the small joints of the hand, foot, wrist, and ankle. This disease has periods of exacerbation and remission. Rheumatoid arthritis is diagnosed based on the clinical presentation of involved joints, the presence of blood rheumatoid factor, and radiographic changes.

Etiology - The cause of rheumatoid arthritis is unknown. One to two percent of the American population is affected. Women are affected three times more than men and the most common age of onset falls between 40 and 60 years of age.

Signs and Symptoms - onset may be gradual or immediate, symmetrical involvement, pain and tenderness of affected joints, morning stiffness, warm joints, decrease in appetite, malaise, increased fatigue, swan neck deformity (i.e., DIP flexion, PIP hyperextension), boutonniere deformity (i.e., DIP extension, PIP flexion), low grade fever

Treatment - The goal of treatment is to reduce inflammation and pain, promote joint function, and prevent joint destruction and deformity. Pharmacological management includes NSAIDs to reduce inflammation and pain. Corticosteroid medications may be desirable during severe flare-ups or when the patient's condition is not responding to NSAIDs. Disease-modifying antirheumatic medications are slow-acting and take weeks or months to become effective, however, they have the ability to slow the progression of joint destruction and deformity. Physical therapy interventions include passive and active range of motion, heating and cooling agents, splinting, patient education, energy conservation, body mechanics, and joint protection techniques.

Rotator Cuff Tear[16,29,32,33]

The rotator cuff can be torn due to an acute traumatic incident or as a result of a chronic degenerative pathology. Patients 50 years of age and older are particularly susceptible to tears due to chronic degenerative pathology. Rotator cuff tears are classified as partial-thickness or full-thickness. A partial-thickness tear extends through only a portion of the tendon. A full-thickness tear is a complete tear of the tendon. The size of a tear can range from small (1 centimeter or less) to large (more than 5 centimeters).

Etiology - Intrinsic factors associated with rotator cuff tears include impaired blood supply to the tendon, resulting in degeneration. Extrinsic factors include trauma, repetitive microtrauma, and postural abnormalities.

Signs and Symptoms - arm positioned in internal rotation and adduction, point tenderness at the greater tubercle and acromion, marked limitation in shoulder flexion and abduction with upper trapezius recruitment evident, increased tone in anterior shoulder structures

Treatment - Conservative management includes RICE, NSAIDs, and analgesics as needed. The primary focus of therapy is to prevent adhesive capsulitis and strengthen upper extremity musculature. Surgical management to repair the tendon can be arthroscopic, mini-open with arthroscopic assist or a traditional open approach. Following surgery, the patient will be immobilized in a sling. The amount of immobilization time will vary depending on surgeon preference, surgical procedure, and the size of the tear. A large tear may require four to six weeks of immobilization. Physical therapy begins with passive range of motion and gradually moves to active-assisted motion. Active motion and isometric exercises begin once approved by the surgeon. The patient will gradually become functional with activities of daily living and progress to more aggressive strengthening activities. Return to functional activities requiring dynamic overhead motion occurs in 9-12 months.

Scoliosis[13,28,29]

Scoliosis refers to a lateral curvature of the spine. The condition is most often quantified using the Cobb method with a standing radiograph. Scoliosis is often classified as functional, neuromuscular or degenerative. Functional scoliosis results from abnormalities in the body that indirectly impact the spine (e.g., leg length discrepancy, muscle imbalance, poor posture). This type of scoliosis is often referred to as nonstructural scoliosis since the curves are flexible and can be corrected with lateral bending. Neuromuscular scoliosis results from developmental pathology resulting in alterations within the structure of the spine. This type of scoliosis is often observed in patients with cerebral palsy or Marfan syndrome. Degenerative scoliosis occurs due to the normal aging process and is facilitated by changes such as osteophyte formation, bone demineralization, and disk herniation. Neuromuscular and degenerative scoliosis are considered to be forms of structural scoliosis since the curves are inflexible and do not reduce with lateral bending.

Etiology - The development of scoliosis is typically idiopathic. Idiopathic scoliosis is most commonly diagnosed between 10 and 13 years of age. Girls and boys have a similar risk of developing a mild curve (e.g., 10 degrees or less), however, girls have a significantly greater risk of acquiring a curve greater than 30 degrees.

Signs and Symptoms - Shoulder level asymmetry with or without the presence of a rib hump. Pain is not typically associated with the spinal curvature, rather it is a result of the abnormal forces placed on other tissues of the body due to the curvature.

Treatment - The focus of treatment is determined based on the magnitude of the curve and the degree of progression. If the curve is not progressing, generally no formal action is taken. Physical therapy treatment includes muscle strengthening and flexibility exercises, shoe lifts, and bracing. A spinal orthosis is often warranted with a curve that ranges between 25 and 40 degrees. Surgical intervention may be required with curves greater than 40 degrees.

Talipes Equinovarus[30,31]

Talipes equinovarus, also known as "clubfoot," is a deformity characterized by the heel pointing downward and the forefoot turning inward.

Etiology - The cause is unknown, however, theories postulate familial tendency, positioning in utero or a defect in the ovum. This condition accompanies other neuromuscular abnormalities including spina bifida and arthrogryposis, and may result from the lack of movement in utero.

Signs and Symptoms - The clinical presentation includes adduction of the forefoot, varus positioning of the hindfoot, and equinus at the ankle.

Treatment - Medical management begins shortly after birth and includes splinting and serial casting. The goal of intervention is to restore proper positioning of the foot and ankle. Failed management or severe involvement may require surgical intervention and subsequent casting.

Total Hip Arthroplasty[16,18,29,32,36]

Total hip arthroplasty refers to the removal of the proximal and distal joint surfaces of the hip with subsequent replacement by an acetabular component and a femoral implant. The acetabular component is most often press fit into place, although it is occasionally held in place by screws. Bone is removed from the femur with subsequent shaping to accept the femoral stem with the attached prosthetic femoral head. The surgical procedure can utilize an anterolateral, direct lateral or posterolateral approach. The type of approach selected determines the necessary hip precautions post-operatively.

Fixation can be cemented or cementless. Cemented fixation allows weight bearing as tolerated on the involved lower extremity, often immediately, since the cement achieves maximum fixation in approximately 15 minutes. Cementless and hybrid fixation rely on bone growth and may dictate partial weight bearing or non-weight bearing initially. The level of weight bearing is determined by the surgeon, typically based on the mechanical fixation of the prosthesis within the acetabulum and femur. There are advantages and disadvantages of each type of fixation, however, the primary indication for cementless fixation is a young, active individual (e.g., less than 65 years of age). Minimally invasive surgical techniques require one or two incisions, usually less than 10 centimeters in length. The benefit of minimally invasive procedures is less soft tissue trauma and an accelerated post-operative recovery. The average lifespan for a total hip arthroplasty is 15 to 20 years, and as a result, younger individuals may need one or more revision procedures in their lifetime. Complications for total hip arthroplasty include deep vein thrombosis, infection, pulmonary embolus, heterotopic ossification, femoral fractures, dislocation, and neurovascular injury.

Etiology - Total hip arthroplasty is an elective surgical procedure. Medical conditions often associated with the need for total hip arthroplasty include osteoarthritis, rheumatoid arthritis, osteomyelitis, and avascular necrosis.

SPOTLIGHT ON SAFETY
TOTAL HIP ARTHROPLASTY PRECAUTIONS[16,18,32,36]

The specific surgical approach utilized for total hip arthroplasty is determined based on a variety of factors including patient activity level, co-morbidities, life expectancy, anticipated compliance, and surgeon familiarity. Physical therapists must have an awareness of each type of approach including the structures impacted and the associated hip precautions.

Surgical approaches and associated hip precautions:

Anterolateral approach - Access to the hip occurs through the interval between the tensor fasciae latae and the gluteus medius muscle. Some portion of the hip abductors are released from the greater trochanter and the hip is dislocated anteriorly.

Hip precautions: Avoid extension of the hip, lateral rotation, and adduction.

Direct lateral approach - This approach leaves the posterior portion of the gluteus medius attached to the greater trochanter. It requires longitudinal division of the tensor fasciae latae and vastus lateralis, along with a release of the anterior portion of the gluteus medius. Since the posterior soft tissues and capsule are left intact, the approach minimizes the probability of dislocation and may be ideal for noncompliant patients.

Hip precautions: Avoid flexion of the hip beyond 90 degrees, extension of the hip, lateral rotation, and adduction. If the gluteus medius was repaired, active or resisted hip abduction may need to be avoided for 6-8 weeks.

Posterolateral approach - Access to the hip occurs by splitting the gluteus maximus muscle in line with the muscle fibers. The short external rotators are then released and the hip abductors are retracted anteriorly. This approach maintains the integrity of the gluteus medius and vastus lateralis muscles. The femur is then dislocated posteriorly. Although it is the most commonly used approach for total hip arthroplasty, the procedure results in a higher post-surgical dislocation rate.

Hip precautions: Avoid flexion of the hip beyond 90 degrees, adduction, and medial rotation.

Signs and Symptoms - Prior to surgery, there is severe pain with weight bearing, loss of mobility, gross instability or limitation in range of motion, failure of non-operative management or a previous surgical procedure.

Treatment - Initially physical therapy management focuses on decreasing inflammation and allowing tissues to heal, emphasizing adherence to hip precautions, minimizing muscle atrophy, and regaining full passive range of motion. Treatment may include ankle pumps, quadriceps and gluteal sets, active hip flexion within available range of motion, assistive device training, and progressive ambulation. As the patient progresses, treatment moves toward regaining full strength and endurance and attaining independence in the home setting.

CONSIDER THIS

DISCHARGE GUIDELINES FOLLOWING TOTAL HIP ARTHROPLASTY[16,18,32,36]

Patients may need to remain compliant with a strict set of discharge guidelines, typically for up to three months following total hip arthroplasty. Failure to follow the guidelines potentially jeopardizes the integrity of the surgical procedure and creates an unnecessary safety risk. The specific guidelines that are most critical for a patient upon discharge will be heavily influenced by the surgical approach and the type of fixation utilized.

General guidelines include:

- Avoid crossing the legs when in a sitting position.
- Sit in firm chairs and avoid sitting in low or soft furniture. Limit forward bending when sitting or standing up.
- Stand with the feet in a neutral position (avoid turning the toes inward).
- Use a pillow or splint between the legs when in bed.
- Avoid pulling blankets up in bed with forward bending.
- Place a nightstand on the same side of the bed as the uninvolved side.
- Use a raised toilet seat or portable commode for toileting activities.
- Use a rubber, non-skid bath mat in the shower.
- Use a long handled brush to avoid leaning forward when bathing.
- Remove all throw rugs and always walk with appropriate footwear.
- When walking, turn to the uninvolved side to avoid pivoting on the involved side.
- Walk for short periods and gradually increase the time period to improve endurance.
- When ascending stairs, step up with the uninvolved leg.
- When descending stairs, step down with the involved leg.

*These guidelines apply to traditional total hip arthroplasty and may not be necessary with minimally invasive procedures.

Total Knee Arthroplasty[16,18,29,32,33,36]

Total knee arthroplasty refers to the removal of the proximal and distal joint surfaces of the knee and replacing them with an implant. The procedure is the most commonly performed surgery for advanced arthritis of the knee. Total knee arthroplasty can be classified several different ways. The first classification is based on the number of compartments replaced. Unicompartmental indicates that only the medial or lateral joint surface was replaced. Bicompartmental indicates that the entire surface of the femur and tibia were replaced, while a tricompartmental procedure includes replacement of the femur and tibia along with the patella. The implant design can be classified by the degree of constraint. An unconstrained design offers no inherent stability and relies on soft tissue integrity for stability. This type of design is used primarily with unicompartmental arthroplasty. A semiconstrained design offers some degree of stability without compromising mobility. This is the most common classification of total knee arthroplasty. A fully constrained design offers the most stability by restricting one or more planes of motion. This results in greater implant stress with a higher likelihood of implant problems (e.g., wear, failure, loosening). The average lifespan for a total knee arthroplasty is 15-20 years, and as a result, younger individuals may need one or more revision procedures in their lifetime.

Minimally invasive surgical techniques are becoming more common with total knee arthroplasty. The procedure requires only a 3-5 inch incision instead of the 8-12 inches typically required with a traditional procedure. As a result, there is less soft tissue trauma and minimal damage to the quadriceps muscle, which allows the muscle to initially produce a stronger contraction. This is extremely relevant since quadriceps weakness is correlated with an increased risk of falling. There remains a paucity of research available to determine long-term outcomes associated with the minimally invasive surgical procedure, however, preliminary data suggests positive outcomes including decreased hospital stays, improved range of motion, and improved strength.

Fixation methods include cemented, uncemented (i.e., bone ingrowth), and hybrid. The type of fixation selected is influenced by a variety of factors including patient activity level, co-morbidities, life expectancy, and tightness of fit of the femoral component achieved during surgery. Cemented remains the most common method of fixation. Potential complications of total knee arthroplasty include deep vein thrombosis, infection, pulmonary embolus, peroneal nerve palsy, restricted range of motion, periprosthetic fractures, and chronic joint effusion.

Etiology - Total knee arthroplasty is an elective surgical procedure. Medical conditions often associated with the need for total knee arthroplasty include osteoarthritis and osteomyelitis.

Signs and Symptoms - Prior to surgery there is severe pain with weight bearing, loss of mobility, gross instability or limitation in range of motion, marked deformity of the knee, failure of non-operative management or a previous surgical procedure.

Treatment - Initially, physical therapy treatment focuses on decreasing inflammation and allowing tissues to heal, emphasizing adherence to knee precautions, minimizing muscle atrophy, and regaining full passive range of motion. Knee flexion requires a minimum of 90 degrees for activities of daily living and 105 degrees to rise comfortably from sitting. Therapeutic activities include ankle pumps, quadriceps and gluteal sets, active range of motion within available range, use of a continuous passive motion machine, assistive device training, and progressive ambulation. As the patient progresses, treatment moves toward regaining full strength, endurance, and independence in the home setting. Advanced therapeutic activities include wall slides, controlled lunges, stationary cycling, and step ups.

Orthopedic Surgical Procedures and Considerations[18,28,29,31,32,33]

Spine

Laminectomy

Surgical considerations: A laminectomy is usually performed in the presence of a disk protrusion or spinal stenosis. A complete laminectomy involves the removal of the entire lamina, the spinous process, and the associated ligamentum flavum. A partial laminectomy involves the removal of only one lamina. In cases where a complete laminectomy is performed, the vertebral segment will be much less stable than when a partial laminectomy is performed. Both cervical and lumbar laminectomies are generally performed using a posterior approach.

Rehab considerations: There will likely be restrictions on how much weight can be lifted following surgery. The surgeon may also place restrictions on active motions, especially extension. The physical therapist should emphasize the need for proper body mechanics and posture with the patient.

Spinal fusion

Surgical considerations: Spinal fusion is indicated in the presence of axial pain with unstable spinal segments, advanced arthritis, or uncontrolled peripheral pain. Bone is harvested from the patient's body (often from the iliac crest) and used to help fuse two vertebrae together. Generally the surgeon will use instrumentation (e.g., pedicle screws) to immobilize the segments while a bony callus forms between the segments. Cervical fusion typically uses an anterior approach while lumbar fusion typically uses a posterior approach. Because a fusion creates immobility at one spinal segment, it inherently leads to hypermobility at adjacent segments, which can hasten the onset of degeneration.

Rehab considerations: The surgeon will likely place restrictions on how much can be lifted following surgery. The surgeon may also place restrictions on active motion, such as bending or twisting motions. Early therapy occurs post-operatively in the hospital and involves teaching bed mobility and transfers with the patient to help them become more mobile without compromising the established precautions. Bracing (e.g., cervical collar, thoraco-lumbar-sacral orthosis) may be used to help patients comply with the movement precautions. Bracing is more likely to be used if the surgeon does not use instrumentation to stabilize the segments. Formal outpatient therapy does not usually occur until approximately 6 weeks after the surgery. If instrumentation is used, therapy will usually begin sooner and can be progressed more aggressively. Emphasis should be placed on proper body mechanics and posture, as well as core stabilization exercises.

Upper Extremity

Total shoulder arthroplasty

Surgical considerations: Shoulder arthroplasty is often performed when joint components have become arthritic, though may also be done secondary to fracture or rotator cuff arthropathy. Total shoulder arthroplasty replaces both the glenoid and humeral components, while a shoulder hemiarthroplasty replaces only one of those components. A reverse total shoulder arthroplasty is performed by reversing the concave-convex relationship of the prosthetic components and is used as the surgery of choice when the patient has a dysfunctional rotator cuff. All of these surgeries usually involve an anterior approach in which the subscapularis muscle is detached for easier access to the joint.

Rehab considerations: The patient will be immobilized in a sling for several weeks or longer if there was a repair performed on muscles/tendons (e.g., subscapularis). Protocols vary widely after these surgeries, but there likely will be some movement precautions for a short period of time (e.g., 6-8 weeks). For example, the patient often has to avoid extension and external rotation movements to help protect the healing subscapularis muscle and anterior portion of the capsule. Resisted internal rotation is also avoided for some time for this same reason. There may also be restrictions on weight bearing through the arm and limitations on lifting or carrying weight.

Subacromial decompression

Surgical considerations: This surgery is performed when cases of shoulder impingement have not responded to conservative treatment. The approach can be open (deltoid is detached), a mini-open (deltoid is only split) or arthroscopic. The procedure could involve an acromioplasty, bursectomy, removal of the distal clavicle (in cases where it is degenerated), and release of the coracoacromial ligament.

Rehab considerations: Typically patients experience a rapid recovery from this surgery. A sling will only be used for 1-2 weeks since no repair has been performed. Early rehab focuses on pain control and gentle range of motion, with strength training occurring later in rehab. If a deltoid repair was performed, passive extension is avoided initially to prevent stress on the repair site. Treatment should focus on interventions to reduce the occurrence of impingement (e.g., posture, strengthening scapular upward rotators). A full recovery is typically expected.

Rotator cuff repair

Surgical considerations: Rotator cuff tears are graded according to depth (partial vs. full) and according to width (small <1 cm, medium 1-3 cm, large 3-5 cm, massive >5 cm). Small partial-thickness tears may only require debridement; all others likely require a repair to be performed, in which the tear is reapproximated and fixated using sutures, anchors, tacks or staples. As with a subacromial decompression, the surgery is generally performed arthroscopically, though an open or mini-open approach may be necessary.

Rehab considerations: The patient will be immobilized in a sling for several weeks, and the sling may have an abduction pillow attached to it. Sling use is generally at the discretion of the surgeon and often depends on the extent of the tear/repair. Rehab protocols vary, but therapy usually consists of passive and active-assisted range of motion initially, with strengthening occurring later in the course of therapy. Precautions generally include no active range of motion, lifting, or weight bearing through the arm for several weeks. Depending on which muscle is repaired, there may be precautions set on range of motion for rotation as well. If a deltoid repair was performed, passive extension is avoided initially to prevent stress on the repair site.

Shoulder stabilization surgeries

Surgical considerations: The capsular shift procedure is performed in the presence of chronic shoulder instability. The procedure involves tightening of the joint capsule by cutting the capsule and overlapping the ends to reduce capsular redundancy. There is also an electrothermally assisted capsular shift procedure in which thermal energy is used to shrink and tighten the capsular tissue. The portion of the capsule that is tightened is dependent upon the direction of the instability. Since anterior instability is the most common form of shoulder instability, the anterior capsule is the portion that is most often tightened. In addition to the capsular shift procedure, labral repairs may also be performed since labral tears often accompany dislocation injuries. A Bankart repair involves a repair of the anterior labrum. A SLAP repair involves a repair of the superior labrum. These procedures are generally performed arthroscopically, though can also be done as an open procedure. If the procedure is open then the subscapularis muscle may need to be detached.

Rehab considerations: The type of immobilization used and the precautions will depend on the portion of the capsule that was affected. If the anterior capsule was affected, then the patient will typically utilize a normal sling. They should avoid positions of external rotation, extension, and horizontal abduction. They should also avoid resisted internal rotation if the subscapularis muscle was detached during the surgery. If the posterior capsule was affected, the patient would be immobilized in the "hand shake" position with the shoulder in neutral rotation. The patient should avoid positions of internal rotation, flexion, and horizontal adduction. Active range of motion can begin soon after the surgery. Therapists should not wait for full range of motion before beginning strengthening exercises and should not be overly aggressive in getting full motion early. If a SLAP repair has been performed, the patient should avoid contracting or stretching the biceps since the biceps is attached to the superior labrum.

Lower Extremity

Hip ORIF

Surgical considerations: Proximal hip fractures commonly occur in the femoral neck or in the intertrochanteric region. Femoral neck fractures are intracapsular and may lead to a disruption of the blood supply to the femoral head. Because of this, nonunion and osteonecrosis are more common with these fractures. Intertrochanteric hip fractures are extracapsular and therefore do not affect the blood supply. Though nonunion is less of an issue, implant failure is more of a problem with these fractures since the fixation needed is greater. Fractures can also occur in the subtrochanteric region, which is the region distal to the trochanters. There are several methods of fixation for hip fractures, and the method used depends on fracture location, amount of displacement, and the patient's activity level. Fixation usually occurs with the use of plates and screws or an intramedullary nail. For older patients with poor healing capacity, total hip arthroplasty is often considered. The surgery is always an open procedure. Depending on the approach, the tensor fasciae latae, gluteus medius, and vastus lateralis may be affected. If the fracture site is intracapsular, a capsulotomy will be performed.

Rehab considerations: New advances in this surgery have allowed for early weight bearing, though weight bearing restrictions will be based on age, the location of the fracture, and the bone quality. Early rehab consists of ambulation and range of motion. Isotonic strengthening is usually postponed until the muscles have been given a chance to heal. The muscles affected depend not only on the surgical approach, but also on the site of the fracture. For example, fractures of the greater trochanter will affect the gluteus medius, while fractures of the lesser trochanter will affect the iliopsoas. Therapists should be aware of signs of fixation failure, such as persistent thigh or groin pain, a leg length discrepancy that was not present initially, positioning the limb in external rotation, or a Trendelenburg sign that does not improve with strengthening.

Surgeries to fix articular cartilage defects

Surgical considerations: There are several different options for fixing focal cartilage defects. The microfracture procedure uses an awl to penetrate subchondral bone, which causes an ingrowth of fibrocartilage. Osteochondral autograft transplantation is a procedure in which cartilage is harvested from several non-weight bearing surfaces to form a plug that can fill the chondral defect. Autologous chondrocyte implantation is a procedure in which healthy cartilage is harvested and cultured so it will grow, then later implanted into the cartilage defect.

Rehab considerations: There will likely be weight bearing restrictions, though this is dependent upon the size and location of the lesion. Adherence to weight bearing restrictions is critical to allow healing to occur. The patient will often be in a brace that is initially locked into extension. Range of motion progression will also vary depending on the size and location of the lesion. In general, larger lesions require a slower overall progression.

Anterior cruciate ligament reconstruction

Surgical considerations: This surgery is performed on patients with an anterior cruciate ligament tear that is causing pain and/or instability. The surgery is generally performed arthroscopically.

Use of an autograft is preferred over allograft. A bone-patellar tendon-bone graft is considered the gold standard. Because it uses bone-to-bone healing, it is considered a stronger graft with good fixation. Use of the gracilis and/or semitendinosus is also common, however, the fixation is not as strong since it uses tendon-to-bone healing.

Rehab considerations: Rehab protocols will vary widely, but there generally is some period of immobilization in a hinged brace (initially locked in extension) in addition to weight bearing restrictions. The brace usually is unlocked once the patient can demonstrate good quadriceps control. Range of motion interventions should place an emphasis on achieving full knee extension early in the rehabilitative process. Strengthening exercises can occur soon after surgery and typically include isometric quadriceps strengthening, hamstrings strengthening, and closed-chain exercises. Open-chain exercises between 0-45 degrees of flexion should be avoided since they place excess stress on the graft site. Patients receiving a bone-patellar tendon-bone graft may experience anterior knee pain and should be cautious with quadriceps strengthening. Likewise, those receiving a hamstring graft should be cautious with flexion exercises. It is important for the therapist to remember that the graft tissue is most vulnerable at 6-8 weeks after surgery. As the tendon transforms into ligamentous tissue, it actually becomes weaker before it gets stronger. Failure of the graft site generally happens around that time secondary to poor compliance with the protocol. Graft maturation has been shown to be at 100% around 12-16 months post-operatively, however, most protocols allow for return to sports closer to 6 months. There are several criteria that patients wishing to return to sports must satisfy including no pain or effusion, full range of motion, no instability, quadriceps strength that is 85-90% of the opposite leg, hamstring strength that is 90-100% of the opposite leg, and functional testing (e.g., single leg hop) that is 85-90% of the opposite leg.

Posterior cruciate ligament reconstruction

Surgical considerations: Injuries to the posterior cruciate ligament (PCL) are much less common than anterior cruciate ligament (ACL) injuries. If the PCL injury occurs in isolation, surgery may not be needed. Surgery is indicated if pain and/or instability do not improve with therapy. Options for grafts are similar to those for ACL surgery.

Rehab considerations: In general, the rehab protocol is the same as with ACL surgery. However, the progression with weight bearing and with exercises tends to be more gradual. The therapist should choose exercises that will limit posterior shear forces within the knee. Repetitive knee flexion should also be avoided.

Surgeries for meniscus injuries

Surgical considerations: The surgery for a meniscus tear is generally performed arthroscopically. Meniscus tears can be dealt with surgically in two ways. The first option is a partial meniscectomy in which the torn piece of meniscus is removed. This option is usually chosen for older individuals or when the tear occurs in the inner two-thirds of the meniscus where the healing capacity is poor. The other surgical option is to perform a repair of the meniscus in which the tear is sutured back together. This option is more likely to be chosen in younger patients or when the tear is in the outer third of the meniscus.

Rehab considerations: The rehab protocol will depend on whether or not the meniscus was repaired. Following a meniscus repair, there will likely be a period of restricted weight bearing in addition to bracing. There will also likely be limitations placed on the progression of range of motion, specifically with flexion. Following a partial meniscectomy, the patient is full weight bearing without the use of a brace. There are no rehab restrictions and recovery time is significantly quicker.

Lateral ankle reconstruction

Surgical considerations: Repair of the lateral ankle ligaments is commonly performed secondary to a complete tear of the anterior talofibular ligament or calcaneofibular ligament or secondary to chronic ankle instability. There are two methods for reconstructing the ankle, both of which use an open approach. The first method involves actual repair of the torn ligaments in which they are sutured back together. The second method involves the harvesting of an autograft (usually the peroneus brevis) to replace the torn ligaments. This second option is usually performed when the original ligaments cannot be repaired due to deterioration. The surgery may also include arthroscopy or subchondral drilling since a high percentage of unstable ankles have chondral lesions within the joint.

Rehab considerations: The patient will usually be in a protective cast for a short period of time (e.g., one week), then they are placed in a walking cast or boot for several weeks, followed by a brace. Initially the patient is non-weight bearing while in the protective cast, which is progressed to partial weight bearing and full weight bearing once in the walking boot. Therapy does not usually begin immediately after surgery. Early rehab focuses on increasing the patient's range of motion while still protecting the repaired tissues. Caution should be taken when ranging the ankle into inversion since this will stress the repaired tissues. Bracing may be required long term if the patient plans to return to sports or higher level activities.

Achilles tendon repair

Surgical considerations: This surgery is performed on active patients with an Achilles tendon tear. When the repair is performed within days of the injury, it is generally done arthroscopically. The torn portion of the tendon is sutured back together. However, when the repair is delayed after the injury, the surgery may need to be performed as an open procedure. Additionally, augmentation with use of a graft (e.g., flexor hallucis longus, peroneus brevis, plantaris) may be needed for the repair instead of suturing together the original tendon.

Rehab considerations: The patient will likely be casted with the ankle in slight plantar flexion initially. Additionally, the patient may be non-weight bearing for the first several weeks. Eventually, the patient is transitioned to a cast or boot that places the ankle in neutral and they are allowed to be partial weight bearing. However, in the past few decades, there has been a push for more aggressive rehab following this surgery, in which the ankle is casted in neutral and partial weight bearing is allowed much sooner in the recovery process. Researchers have found that this leads to less restricted range of motion long term. During the healing process, the therapist should take caution with exercises that stretch the Achilles tendon or require active plantar flexion until the tendon is well healed.

Types of Fractures[31]

Avulsion fracture: A portion of a bone becomes fragmented at the site of tendon attachment due to a traumatic and sudden stretch of the tendon.

Closed fracture: A break in a bone where the skin over the site remains intact.

Comminuted fracture: A bone that breaks into fragments at the site of injury.

Compound fracture: A break in a bone that protrudes through the skin.

Greenstick fracture: A break on one side of a bone that does not damage the periosteum on the opposite side. This type of fracture is often seen in children.

Nonunion fracture: A break in a bone that has failed to unite and heal after nine to twelve months.

Stress fracture: A break in a bone due to repeated forces to a particular portion of the bone.

Spiral fracture: A break in a bone shaped like an "S" due to torsion and twisting.

Pharmacological Management of the Musculoskeletal System[37,38,39]

Disease-modifying Antirheumatic Agents

Action: Disease-modifying antirheumatic drugs (DMARD) slow or halt the progression of rheumatic disease. They are used early during the disease process to slow the progression prior to widespread damage of the affected joints. They act to induce remission by modifying the pathology and inhibiting the immune response responsible for rheumatic disease.

Indications: rheumatic disease, preferably during early treatment

Side effects: (depending on classification of DMARD) nausea, headache, joint pain and swelling, toxicity, gastrointestinal distress, sore throat, fever, liver dysfunction, hair loss, potential for sepsis, retinal damage

Implications for PT: Therapists should recognize that many of the agents have a high incidence of toxicity.

Examples: Rheumatrex (methotrexate), Arava (leflunomide), Antimalarial: Aralen (chloroquine), Plaquenil (hydroxychloroquine); Gold compounds: Ridaura (auranofin), Solganal (aurothioglucose); Tumor necrosis factor inhibitors: Humira (adalimumab), Enbrel (etanercept)

Glucocorticoid Agents (Corticosteroids)

Action: Glucocorticoids provide hormonal, anti-inflammatory, and metabolic effects including suppression of articular and systemic diseases. These agents reduce inflammation in chronic conditions that can damage healthy tissue through a series of reactions. Vasoconstriction results from stabilizing lysosomal membranes and enhancing the effects of catecholamines.

Indications: replacement therapy for endocrine dysfunction, anti-inflammatory and immunosuppressive effects; treatment of rheumatic, respiratory, and various other disorders

Side effects: muscle atrophy, gastrointestinal distress, glaucoma, adrenocortical suppression, drug-induced Cushing's syndrome, weakening with breakdown of supporting tissues (bone, ligament, tendon, skin), mood changes, hypertension

Implications for PT: A therapist must wear a mask when working with patients on glucocorticoid therapy since their immune system is weakened. A therapist must be aware of signs of toxicity including moon face, buffalo hump, and personality changes. Patients are at risk for osteoporosis and muscle wasting. Treatment of an injected joint will require special care due to ligament and tendon laxity or weakening.

Examples: Dermacort (hydrocortisone or cortisol), Cordrol (prednisone), Pediapred (prednisolone), Medrol (methylprednisolone), Decadrol (dexamethasone), Nasonex (mometasone)

Nonopioid Agents

Action: Nonopioid agents provide analgesia and pain relief, produce anti-inflammatory effects, and initiate anti-pyretic (reduces fever) properties. These drugs promote a reduction of prostaglandin formation that decreases the inflammatory process, decreases uterine contractions, lowers fever, and minimizes impulse formation of pain fibers.

Indications: mild to moderate pain of various origins, fever, headache, muscle ache, inflammation (except acetaminophen), primary dysmenorrhea, reduction of risk of myocardial infarction (aspirin only)

Side effects: nausea, vomiting, vertigo, abdominal pain, gastrointestinal distress or bleeding, ulcer formation, potential for Reye syndrome in children (aspirin only)

Implications for PT: Patients are at increased risk for masked pain that would allow for movement beyond limitation or false understanding of their level of mobility. Complaints of stomach pain should be taken seriously with a subsequent referral to a physician.

Examples: Tylenol (acetaminophen); Nonsteroidal anti-inflammatories (NSAIDs): Aspirin (acetylsalicylic acid), Aleve (naproxen), Advil (ibuprofen), Celebrex (celecoxib)

Opioid Agents (Narcotics)

Action: Opioid agents provide analgesia for acute severe pain management. The medication stimulates opioid receptors within the CNS to prevent pain impulses from reaching their destination. Certain drugs are also used to assist with dependency and withdrawal symptoms.

Indications: moderate to severe pain of various origins, induction of conscious sedation prior to a diagnostic procedure, management of opioid dependence, relief of severe and persistent cough (codeine)

Side effects: mood swings, sedation, confusion, vertigo, dulled cognitive function, orthostatic hypotension, constipation, incoordination, physical dependence, tolerance

Implications for PT: A therapist must monitor the patient for potential side effects, especially signs of respiratory depression. Treatment that is otherwise painful should be scheduled approximately two hours after administration to maximize the analgesic benefit. A patient may not accurately report if a particular technique is painful.

Examples: Roxanol (morphine), Demerol (meperidine), OxyContin (oxycodone), Sublimaze (fentanyl), Paveral (codeine)

Musculoskeletal System Terminology[2,10,16]

Bursitis: A condition caused by acute or chronic inflammation of the bursae. Symptoms may include a limitation in active range of motion secondary to pain and swelling.

Contusion: A sudden blow to a part of the body that can result in mild to severe damage to superficial and deep structures. Treatment includes active range of motion, ice, and compression.

Edema: An increased volume of fluid in the soft tissue outside of a joint capsule.

Effusion: An increased volume of fluid within a joint capsule.

Genu valgum: A condition where the knees touch while standing with the feet separated. Genu valgum will increase compression of the lateral tibial condyle and increase stress to the medial structures. Genu valgum is also termed knock-kneed.

Genu varum: A condition where there is bowing of the legs with added space between the knees while standing with the feet together. Genu varum will increase compression of the medial tibial condyle and increase stress to the lateral structures. Genu varum is also termed bowleg.

Kyphosis: An excessive curvature of the spine in a posterior direction, usually identified in the thoracic spine. Common causes include osteoporosis, compression fractures, and poor posture secondary to paralysis.

Lordosis: An excessive curvature of the spine in an anterior direction, usually identified in the cervical or lumbar spine. Common causes include weak abdominal muscles, pregnancy, excessive weight in the abdominal area, and hip flexion contractures.

Q angle: The degree of angulation present when measuring from the midpatella to the anterior superior iliac spine and to the tibial tubercle. A normal Q angle measured in supine with the knee straight is 13 degrees for a male and 18 degrees for a female. An excessive Q angle can lead to pathology and abnormal tracking.

Sprain: An acute injury involving a ligament.

- **Grade I** – mild pain and swelling, little to no tear of the ligament
- **Grade II** – moderate pain and swelling, minimal instability of the joint, minimal to moderate tearing of the ligament, decreased range of motion
- **Grade III** – severe pain and swelling, substantial joint instability, total tear of the ligament, substantial decrease in range of motion

Strain: An injury involving the musculotendinous unit that involves a muscle, tendon or their attachments to bone.

- **Grade I** – localized pain, minimal swelling, and tenderness
- **Grade II** – localized pain, moderate swelling, tenderness, and impaired motor function
- **Grade III** – a palpable defect of the muscle, severe pain, and poor motor function

Tendonitis: A condition caused by acute or chronic inflammation of a tendon. Symptoms may include gradual onset, tenderness, swelling, and pain.

Splints[29,33,43,44]

Distal interphalangeal splint

A distal interphalangeal (DIP) splint is a rigid splint that is placed on either the volar or dorsal aspect of the finger and spans from the tip of the finger to the proximal portion of the middle phalanx. This type of splint is used to immobilize the DIP joint to allow injured structures to heal or to rest a painful or inflamed joint. Conditions that may be treated with this splint include mallet finger, a distal phalanx fracture, and DIP joint arthritis. When treating mallet finger, the DIP joint should be placed in neutral or slight hyperextension to allow for healing of the damaged extensor tendon.

Ulnar gutter splint

An ulnar gutter splint is a rigid splint that covers the ulnar side of the forearm and hand as well as the fourth and fifth digits. This type of splint is used to immobilize the metacarpals and phalanges and is commonly used following a fracture to these structures. When splinting, the metacarpophalangeal (MCP) joints are placed in 60-90 degrees of flexion with the interphalangeal (IP) joints in full extension and the wrist in slight extension.

Radial gutter splint

A radial gutter splint is a rigid splint that covers the radial side of the forearm and hand as well as the second and third digits. The splint includes a thenar hole to allow for free movement of the thumb. This type of splint is used to immobilize the metacarpals and phalanges and is commonly used following a fracture of these structures. When splinting, the MCP joints are placed in 60-90 degrees of flexion with the IP joints in full extension and the wrist in slight extension.

Thumb spica splint

A thumb spica splint is a rigid splint that covers the radial side of the forearm and hand as well as the thumb. The splint may cover the entire thumb or may stop at the proximal phalanx of the thumb and thus allow for IP joint motion. This type of splint is used to immobilize the wrist and MCP joint of the thumb and is commonly used for treating gamekeeper's thumb, scaphoid fractures, first metacarpal fractures, de Quervain's syndrome, and other thumb injuries. When splinting, the wrist should be in 20 degrees of extension with the MCP joint in slight flexion.

Volar/dorsal forearm splint

A volar or dorsal forearm splint is a rigid splint that extends from the proximal forearm to the metacarpal heads, allowing for full elbow and MCP joint motion. The splint includes a thenar hole to allow for free movement of the thumb as well. This type of splint is used to immobilize the wrist joint and is commonly used for treating fractures of the carpals, fractures of the distal radius or ulna or soft tissue conditions (e.g., sprain, tendonitis). Positioning of the splint will vary based on the condition being treated. This type of splint can also place the wrist and hand in a functional position to allow for improved grasping for patients with significant weakness of the forearm and hand. By placing the wrist in 20 degrees of extension, the finger flexors are shortened and have an improved mechanical advantage for grasping.

Sugar tong splint

A sugar tong splint is a rigid splint that covers the wrist and elbow joints and allows for greater immobilization than a volar or dorsal forearm splint. The splint limits supination and pronation in addition to any wrist motion. The splint starts on the dorsum of the hand, extends along the dorsal forearm to wrap around the elbow, and continues along the volar forearm to end at the palmar aspect of the hand. When splinting, the elbow should be in 90 degrees of flexion with the wrist and forearm in neutral. This type of splint is commonly used for treating carpal fractures and distal radius or ulna fractures.

Long arm splint

A long arm splint is a rigid splint that covers the elbow joint (typically on the posterior side), spanning from the wrist to the distal humerus. This splint is used to immobilize the elbow joint to allow for healing following injury or surgery. The splint will prevent elbow flexion and extension movements as well as supination and pronation. This may be done following an elbow or proximal forearm fracture or to treat a soft tissue injury (e.g., tendonitis, tendon repair). When splinting, the elbow is typically placed in 90 degrees of flexion with the forearm in neutral.

Orthotics

An orthotic is an external device that provides support or stabilization, improves function, corrects deformities, and distributes pressure from one area to another. Orthotics are made from a variety of materials including plastic, metal, leather, fabric, elastic or hybrid materials. They can be custom made or over-the-counter and are available in various prefabricated sizes. Orthotics should be lightweight, adjustable, and easy to don and doff.

Functions of orthotics include preventing deformity, maintaining proper alignment, inhibiting tone, assisting weak limbs, protecting against injury, and facilitating motion.

Factors to consider when prescribing an orthotic include static versus dynamic, temporary versus permanent, level of support required, energy efficiency, cosmesis, and cost.

Spine[36, 40, 41]

Corset

A corset is constructed of fabric and may have metal uprights within the material to provide abdominal compression and support. Corsets are utilized to provide pressure and relieve pain associated with mid and low back pathologies.

Halo Vest Orthosis

The halo vest is an invasive cervical thoracic orthosis that provides full restriction of all cervical motion. A metal ring with four posts that attach to a vest is placed on a patient and secured by inserting four pins through the ring into the skull. This orthosis is commonly used with cervical spinal cord injuries to prevent further damage or dislocation during the recovery period. A patient will wear a halo vest until the spine becomes stable.

Milwaukee Orthosis

The Milwaukee orthosis is designed to promote realignment of the spine due to scoliotic curvature. The orthosis is custom made and extends from the pelvis to the upper chest. Corrective padding is applied to the areas of severity of the curve.

Taylor Brace

The Taylor brace is a thoracolumbosacral orthosis that limits trunk flexion and extension through a three-point control design.

Thoracolumbosacral Orthosis (TLSO)

A custom molded TLSO is utilized to prevent all trunk motions and is commonly utilized as a means of post-surgical stabilization. The rigid shell is fabricated from plastics in a bivalve style using straps/ Velcro to secure the orthosis.

Lower Extremity[36, 40-42]

Foot Orthosis

A semirigid or rigid insert worn inside a shoe that corrects foot alignment and improves function. May also be used to relieve pain. A foot orthosis is custom molded and is often designed for a specific level of functioning.

Ankle-foot Orthosis (AFO)

A metal ankle-foot orthosis consists of two metal uprights connected proximally to a calf band and distally to a mechanical ankle joint and shoe. The ankle joint may have the ability to be locked and not allow any motion, or set to have limited anterior/posterior capability depending on the patient's need. A plastic ankle-foot orthosis is fabricated by a cast mold of the patient's lower extremity. The use of plastic is more cosmetic, lighter, and requires that if a patient presents with edema it does not significantly fluctuate. Proper fit of a plastic ankle-foot orthosis requires that a patient be casted in a subtalar neutral position. A footplate can be incorporated into the ankle-foot orthosis to assist with tone reduction. Solid ankle-foot orthoses control dorsiflexion/plantar flexion and also inversion/eversion with a trim line anterior to the malleoli. They can be fabricated to keep the ankle positioned at 90 degrees or can be fabricated with an articulating ankle joint. This articulation allows the tibia to advance over the foot during the mid to late stance phase of gait. A posterior leaf spring is a plastic AFO with a trim line posterior to the malleoli. Its primary purpose is to assist with dorsiflexion and prevent foot drop. It requires adequate medial/lateral control by the patient. Ankle-foot orthoses can also influence knee control. A floor reaction AFO assists with knee extension during stance through positioning of a calf band and/or positioning at the ankle. Ankle-foot orthoses are commonly prescribed for patients with peripheral neuropathy, nerve lesions or hemiplegia.

Knee-ankle-foot Orthosis (KAFO)

A knee-ankle-foot orthosis provides support and stability to the knee and ankle. The orthosis can be fabricated using two metal uprights extending from the foot/shoe to the thigh with calf and thigh bands. Plastic knee-ankle-foot orthoses are fabricated by a cast mold of the patient's lower extremity. A plastic thigh shell is connected to a plastic ankle-foot orthosis through metal uprights lateral and medial to the knee joint. Both types allow for a lock mechanism at the knee that provides stability. The ankle is also held in proper alignment.

Craig-Scott Knee-ankle-foot Orthosis

A knee-ankle-foot orthosis designed specifically for persons with paraplegia. This design allows a person to stand with a posterior lean of the trunk.

Hip-knee-ankle-foot Orthosis (HKAFO)

A hip-knee-ankle-foot orthosis is indicated for patients with hip, foot, knee, and ankle weakness. It consists of bilateral knee-ankle-foot orthoses with an extension to the hip joints and a pelvic band. The orthosis can control rotation at the hip and abduction/adduction. The orthosis is heavy and restricts patients to a swing-to or swing-through gait pattern.

Reciprocating Gait Orthosis (RGO)

A reciprocating gait orthosis is a derivative of the HKAFO and incorporates a cable system to assist with advancement of the lower extremities during gait. When the patient shifts weight onto a selected lower extremity, the cable system advances the opposite lower extremity. The orthoses are used primarily for patients with paraplegia.

Parapodium

A parapodium is a standing frame designed to allow a patient to sit when necessary. It is a prefabricated frame and ambulation is achieved by shifting weight and rocking the base across the floor. It is primarily used by the pediatric population.

Shoe Modifications[43,44]

Heel wedge: A heel wedge can be applied to the medial heel to prevent excessive hindfoot eversion or to the lateral heel to prevent excessive hindfoot inversion. Heel wedges can be used to treat symptoms associated with pes planus or pes cavus.

Heel lift: A heel lift is a rigid insert which adds extra height to the heel of a shoe. Heel lifts are commonly used to take pressure off of the Achilles tendon for patients with Achilles tendonitis or a recent repair of the tendon. Heel lifts are also used to help limit the effects of a leg length discrepancy.

Heel cushion: A heel cushion is a soft pad that is placed on the heel of the inner sole to help cushion the heel and thus decrease pain in that region. Heel cushions may be used for a patient with a calcaneal spur or plantar fasciitis.

Heel cup: A heel cup is a rigid insert that covers the plantar surface of the calcaneus and extends upwards on all three sides. A heel cup helps stabilize the calcaneus in a neutral position as well as provide some shock absorption for the heel. It is commonly used for patients with a calcaneal spur or plantar fasciitis.

Metatarsal bar/pad: A metatarsal bar or pad is a flat piece of padding that is placed just posterior to the metatarsal heads either on the outer sole (i.e., bar) or the inner sole (i.e., pad) of the shoe. The placement of the bar/pad helps relieve pressure from the metatarsal heads by transferring it to the metatarsal shafts, thus helping relieve pain for patients with metatarsalgia.

Rocker bar: A rocker bar is similar to a metatarsal bar in its placement, though it consists of a convex strip instead of a flat strip. Because of its shape and position, it assists patients who have difficulty with the terminal stance phase of gait secondary to limited mobility within the foot, especially the great toe. A rocker bar also helps relieve pressure from the metatarsal heads for patients with pain in that region.

Amputations and Prosthetics

Amputations and Prosthetics[46,47,48]

Amputation is the surgical removal of a body part, partial or full extremity, due to disease, trauma or injury. Lower extremity amputations are significantly more common than upper extremity amputations, with peripheral vascular disease serving as the primary etiology. A commonly encountered client with limb loss is an older adult who underwent lower-limb amputation due to vascular disease. Many of these individuals have a comorbid diagnosis of diabetes. Other non-vascular causes of amputations include traumatic, cancer-related, and congenital conditions. Amputation is considered the last course of action, but for many patients with various pathologies, it may become the only viable treatment option.

Prosthetics attempt to replace the missing body part to allow a patient improved function and cosmesis. Physical and occupational therapies are usually indicated for functional retraining with the prosthesis. Rehabilitation of an individual with limb loss requires a multidisciplinary approach typically involving a prosthetist, physical therapist, and occupational therapist.

Types of Upper Extremity Amputations[40,48]

Forequarter (scapulothoracic): Surgical removal of the upper extremity including the shoulder girdle.

Shoulder disarticulation: Surgical removal of the upper extremity through the shoulder.

Transhumeral: Surgical removal of the upper extremity proximal to the elbow joint.

Elbow disarticulation: Surgical removal of the lower arm and hand through the elbow joint.

Transradial: Surgical removal of the upper extremity distal to the elbow joint.

Wrist disarticulation: Surgical removal of the hand through the wrist joint.

Partial hand: Surgical removal of a portion of the hand and/or digits at either the transcarpal, transmetacarpal or transphalangeal level.

Digital amputation: Surgical removal of a digit at either the metacarpophalangeal, proximal interphalangeal or distal interphalangeal level.

Components of an Upper Extremity Prosthesis[40,46,48]

	Transradial	Transhumeral
Socket	• Standard socket covers two-thirds of forearm • Standard socket may be shortened to allow for increased pronation/supination ability • Supracondylar sockets are self-suspending and require no additional harness apparatus	• Standard socket extends to acromion level • Modified design allows for more stability with rotational movements • Lightweight friction units may be used with passive prosthetic arms
Suspension	• Triceps cuff • Harness • Cable system	• Harness • Cable system • Suction
Elbow unit	• Attaches to either triceps cuff or upper arm pad • Flexible or rigid hinge connects socket to proximal component	• Internal or external locking elbow unit
Wrist unit	• Quick change unit • Wrist flexion unit • Ball and socket • Constant friction	• Same as transradial
Terminal device	• Voluntary opening or closing • Body-powered, externally powered, myoelectric or hybrid • Hook, mechanical hand, cosmetic glove	• Same as transradial

Types of Lower Extremity Amputations[40,48]

Hemicorporectomy: Surgical removal of the pelvis and both lower extremities.

Hemipelvectomy: Surgical removal of one half of the pelvis and the lower extremity.

Hip disarticulation: Surgical removal of the lower extremity from the pelvis.

Transfemoral: Surgical removal of the lower extremity above the knee joint.

Knee disarticulation: Surgical removal of the lower extremity through the knee joint.

Transtibial: Surgical removal of the lower extremity below the knee joint.

Syme's: Surgical removal of the foot at the ankle joint with removal of the malleoli.

Transverse tarsal (Chopart's): Amputation through the talonavicular and calcaneocuboid joints. The amputation preserves the plantar flexors, but sacrifices the dorsiflexors often resulting in an equinus contracture.

Tarsometatarsal (Lisfranc): Surgical removal of the metatarsals. The amputation preserves the dorsiflexors and plantar flexors.

Components of a Lower Extremity Prosthesis[44,46,48]

	Transfemoral	Transtibial
Socket	• Quadrilateral socket • Ischial containment socket	• Patella tendon bearing socket (PTB) • Supracondylar patella tendon socket (PTS) • Supracondylar – suprapatellar socket (SC-SP)
Suspension	• Lanyard strap • Shuttle lock • Suction – Seal-in liner suction – Skin fit suction • Partial suction – Silesian bandage – Pelvic belt/band • Vacuum	• Supracondylar cuff • Thigh corset • Supracondylar brim • "Rubber/Neoprene" sleeve suspension • Waist belt with fork strap • Suction with knee sleeve • Shuttle lock • Vacuum
Knee	• Single axis knee • Polycentric knee • Hydraulic Knee • Microprocessor knee	• Not needed
Shank	• Exoskeleton – rigid exterior • Endoskeleton – pylon covered with foam	• Same as transfemoral shank
Foot system	• Solid ankle cushion heel (SACH) • Stationary attachment flexible endoskeleton (SAFE) • Single axis • Multi-axial • Hydraulic • Powered • Dynamic response	• Same as transfemoral foot

Types of Post-Operative Dressings[40,42,43]

Rigid (Plaster of Paris)	
Advantages	**Disadvantages**
• Allows early ambulation with pylon • Promotes circulation and healing • Stimulates proprioception • Provides protection • Provides soft tissue support • Limits edema • Ability to utilize an IPOP (immediate post-operative prosthesis)	• Immediate wound inspection is not possible • Does not allow for daily dressing change • Requires professional application

Non-Weight Bearing Rigid Removable Limb Protectors	
Advantages	**Disadvantages**
• Removable • Accommodates edema fluctuation • Easily applied • Prevents contracture • Provides protection	• Not for ambulatory purposes

Semi-rigid (Unna paste, air splint)	
Advantages	**Disadvantages**
• Reduces post-operative edema • Provides soft tissue support • Provides protection • Easily changeable	• Does not protect as well as rigid dressing • Requires more changing than rigid dressing • May loosen and allow for development of edema

Soft (ACE wrap, shrinker)	
Advantages	**Disadvantages**
• Reduces post-operative edema • Provides some protection • Relatively inexpensive • Easily removed for wound inspection • Allows for active joint range of motion	• Tissue healing is interrupted by frequent dressing changes • Joint range of motion may delay the healing of the incision • Less control of residual limb pain • Cannot control the amount of tension in the bandage • Risk of a tourniquet effect • Shrinker cannot be applied until sutures/ staples are removed

Medicare Classification Levels[45,48,49]

Medicare uses a functional scale called the Medicare Functional Classification Level (MFCL), commonly known as the "K-Level," to classify patients based on functional ability. The level that is assigned plays a primary role in what componentry will be used in a patient's prosthesis. For example, if a patient with a transfemoral amputation is determined to have a K-level of 2, they would be able to traverse low-level barriers such as stairs or curbs. They would be able to ambulate on mostly level surfaces with a non-variable cadence. The type of componentry used in their prosthesis would likely be a polycentric knee with a multi-axial foot and flexible keel. The level is determined by a number of factors, most importantly a patient's current level of function, their potential ability to function, and the patient's particular needs. The K-level can be determined objectively with the use of outcome measures such as the Amputee Mobility Predictor (AMPPRO), or through a thorough history and examination of the patient. Determination of the K-level would be made by the medical doctor, prosthetist, and physical therapist.

Medicare Functional Classification Level Scale[45,48,49]			
K-level	**Description**	**Knee unit**	**Foot/ankle assembly**
0	• Prosthesis will not enhance quality of life or mobility	• Not eligible for prosthesis	• Not eligible for prosthesis
1	• Transfers • Ambulate on level surfaces • Fixed cadence • Limited or unlimited household ambulator	• Single axis • Constant friction mechanism	• SACH • Single axis
2	• Traverse low-level barriers: curbs, stairs, uneven surfaces • Limited community ambulator	• Polycentric • Constant friction mechanism	• Flexible-keel foot • Multi-axial foot/ankle
3	• Variable cadence ambulator • Unlimited community ambulator • Traverse most environmental barriers • Prosthetic use beyond simple locomotion	• Hydraulic/pneumatic • Microprocessor • Variable friction mechanism	• Energy storing • Dynamic response foot • Multi-axial foot/ankle
4	• Exceeds basic ambulation skills • Exhibits high impact, stress, or energy levels • Typical of child, athlete, or active adult	• Any system	• Any system

Influence of Prosthetic Componentry[40,44,49]		
	Description	**Influence**
Knee	Single axis	• Difficult to reciprocate during gait • May or may not have knee extension assist and/or a weight-activated stance phase control • Constant friction mechanism
	Polycentric	• Heavier than a single axis • Reciprocal gait is more fluid • May or may not have a knee extension assist and/or a weight-activated stance phase control • Constant friction mechanism
	Hydraulic	• Variable friction for improved swing and stance phase control
	Microprocessor	• Multiple programs available to accommodate the activity level of the user • Allows for fluid management of descending stairs • Requires charging • Variable friction for improved swing and stance phase control
Foot System	SACH	• Non-articulating with a rigid keel • Inexpensive • Low maintenance • Cushioned heel for shock absorption • Lacks energy return • Cannot accommodate to uneven surfaces
	Single axis	• Allows for motion in a singular plane • Improved knee stability during weight acceptance • Lacks energy return function if not paired with a dynamic response foot
	Dynamic response	• Can be articulating or non-articulating • Keel has the capability to store and return some energy • May have a split keel to allow for improved surface accommodation
	Hydraulic/ microprocessor	• Finer control over the stability/mobility of motions • Improved shock absorption • Not appropriate for all environmental conditions and demands

Managing the Residual Limb and Prosthesis[46,48,49]

Donning and doffing a transtibial or transfemoral prosthesis requires the wearer to make sure they have all of the necessary componentry in addition to the prosthesis itself. Each suspension type has its own requirements and can vary between each individual socket system. The following is a list of the most common categories of componentry when working with individuals with limb loss.

Socket: The socket is the interface between the residual limb and the prosthesis. A properly fitting socket will disperse the pressure experienced in weight bearing throughout the limb, providing total contact with the surface. Certain areas of the residual limb are more pressure tolerant and can handle greater pressure than others (Fig. 4-74). Generally speaking, muscular areas are more tolerant than bony surfaces. Sockets can take on many shapes and sizes, however, the most common design for a transfemoral prosthesis is an ischial containment socket, while one of the more common designs for a transtibial prosthesis is a total surface bearing or patellar tendon-bearing socket.

Liner: A liner plays an important role in the comfort and health of individuals using a prosthesis. Gel liners, commonly made of silicone, are used for a variety of purposes, including cushioning the residual limb and hosting a suspension mechanism such as a pin or lanyard. Some liners are used to maintain suspension through

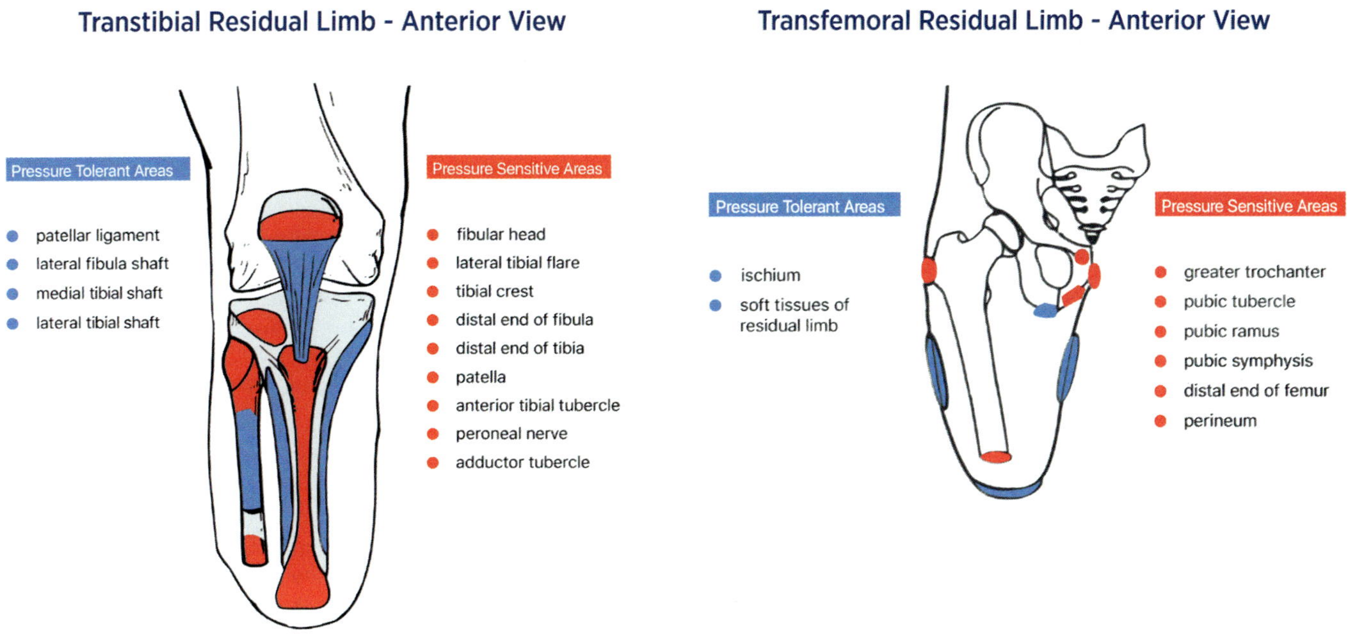

Transtibial Residual Limb - Anterior View

Pressure Tolerant Areas

- patellar ligament
- lateral fibula shaft
- medial tibial shaft
- lateral tibial shaft

Pressure Sensitive Areas

- fibular head
- lateral tibial flare
- tibial crest
- distal end of fibula
- distal end of tibia
- patella
- anterior tibial tubercle
- peroneal nerve
- adductor tubercle

Transfemoral Residual Limb - Anterior View

Pressure Tolerant Areas

- ischium
- soft tissues of residual limb

Pressure Sensitive Areas

- greater trochanter
- pubic tubercle
- pubic ramus
- pubic symphysis
- distal end of femur
- perineum

Fig. 4-74: Pressure Tolerant and Pressure Sensitive Areas
In a posterior view, the hamstrings' tendons are pressure sensitive and the posterior compartment is pressure tolerant.

negative pressure, such as what is seen with a transfemoral seal-in liner. Liners are, for the most part, non-breathable, which means that perspiration can buildup throughout the day. This can result in friction issues and cause irritation on the skin of the residuum. As a result, frequent doffing of the liner may be required to dry it off along with the residual limb. Liners must be carefully washed and dried to maintain a hygienic environment. Gel sheaths can be applied underneath the liner directly on the skin of the residual limb and can serve to relieve irritation when using the prosthesis.

Insert: A flexible or soft insert can be used to accommodate for space in the prosthetic socket. Soft inserts, generally made from a foam material, offer improved cushioning on the residual limb during weight bearing. Flexible inserts are usually made of plastic, and similar to a foam insert, can improve the comfort and fit of the prosthesis. Unlike a foam insert which can offer some shock absorption, the hard insert relieves pressure through a series of buildups and reliefs molded into the insert.

Sock: It is normal for an individual with limb loss to experience a decrease in residual limb volume, especially in the first year. In order to accommodate for this space, prosthetic socks are used to maintain a congruent and comfortable fit. Prosthetic socks come in various sizes and material types, including cotton, wool, and synthetic materials. Commonly encountered plys are 1, 3, and 5 ply. A general rule of thumb is that when the number of ply socks exceeds 12-15, the prosthetist should be notified as a recasting may be required. Some socks are split ply, and will have a greater/lesser ply distally than proximally. Socks must be carefully applied as to eliminate any wrinkles, otherwise the wearer may experience discomfort or breakdown in the area of increased pressure.

Self-Management Considerations[40,46,48,49]

Self-management for an individual with limb loss is a term that describes activities, knowledge, and skills that are related to living with limb loss. Therapists are instrumental in the education and indoctrination of proper self-management abilities during each phase of rehabilitation.

Hygiene: The residual limb should be carefully washed, inspected, and maintained to prevent the formation of wounds or infections. This is of particular importance for individuals with impaired vascular perfusion or a history of wounds or infection. For most patients, once the post-surgical residual limb has fully closed and no evidence of exudate is present, washing with warm water and a mild hypoallergenic soap is appropriate. If lotion use is advised, it should not be petroleum-based and it should not be applied prior to donning the prosthesis since it may inhibit suspension. The residual limb, as well as the contralateral foot, should be inspected daily for areas of breakdown. If an area of breakdown, rash, or wound is identified, it may be necessary to have the area inspected by the prosthetist and/or physician prior to donning the prosthesis.

Wear schedule: While there is no absolute rule for wearing a prosthesis, a "break-in" schedule is normally prescribed for the first few weeks of wear. This allows for careful monitoring of the limb and allows the wearer to slowly accommodate to the sensation of weight bearing through the residuum. A general rule is to start with one hour a day of total wear time, with half of the time spent ambulating. Every 30 minutes or immediately after walking, the skin should be inspected for breakdown. If the wearer is tolerating the prosthesis well and no evidence of breakdown is noted, an hour is added each day while still respecting the 50% rule of rest:use. If the skin is showing no signs of breakdown, the amount of time between inspections is gradually expanded by 15-30 minutes.

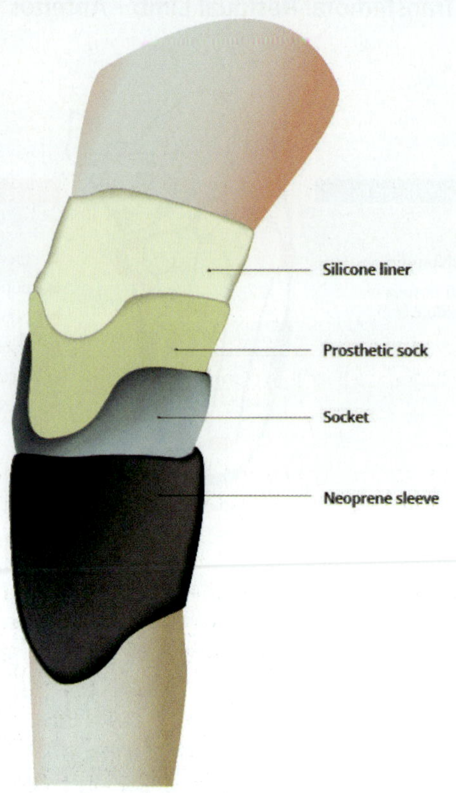

Fig. 4-75: Common components that may be worn when donning a transtibial prosthesis.

Eventually, the wearer will be able to tolerate the prosthesis for extended periods of time without having to remove the prosthesis and inspect the skin.

Fit issues: The most common complaint a new prosthesis wearer makes is regarding the comfort of the socket on the residual limb. Fit issues can be potentially managed through manipulation of sock-ply, alignment of the liners in the socket, and training the patient on how to dynamically adjust the fit to accommodate fluctuations in the size of the residual limb throughout the day (Fig. 4-75). For example, if a patient complains that the prosthesis is fitting too loosely and they are using prosthetic socks to manage their fit, it would be logical to initially adjust the sock ply. If the fit of the socket is too tight, the therapist should determine if the patient has been wearing their shrinker throughout the day when not wearing their prosthesis. If they have been wearing the shrinker, a review of medications and diet may be warranted since they can adversely affect the residual limb volume.

"Red flags": The patient must be educated on how to prevent, identify, and report any issues associated with their residual limb as soon as possible in order to prevent secondary complications. This includes preventing skin breakdown through daily inspections and hygiene, identifying abrasions or wounds that have formed, and discontinuing wearing the prosthesis until the limb has been examined by a physician.

Timeline: The rehabilitation of the individual with limb loss is divided into several phases. Immediately post-amputation is referred to as the pre-prosthetic phase of rehabilitation and will generally last 6 weeks in length. During this timeframe, the therapist focuses on protecting the limb, preventing contractures, developing single limb mobility skills, and preparing the patient for the prosthetic phase of rehabilitation. In some cases, a patient is fit with an immediate post-operative prosthesis (IPOP) which allows for immediate weight bearing using a temporary prosthetic device. More commonly, a patient will be evaluated for their first prosthesis once the sutures/staples have healed and the residual limb skin integrity is intact, usually between 4 and 6 weeks. A patient can begin wearing a shrinker once the sutures are removed. The patient will be sized for the shrinker by the prosthetist. Following the evaluation, the patient will receive their first prosthetic limb, known as the temporary prosthesis. This prosthetic limb is fully functional and allows the wearer to participate in the prosthetic phase of rehabilitation. Modifications may need to be made during this timeframe to improve the comfort and function of the prosthesis during weight bearing activities, which likely involve the prosthetist. After several months of working with the prosthesis, the wearer may feel the comfort and fit is appropriate, and that the residual limb volume fluctuations have stabilized. In this instance, the permanent prosthesis may be manufactured. Medicare supports a new prosthesis every five years, however, based on the activity level of the wearer, repairs/replacement may be needed prior to this period.

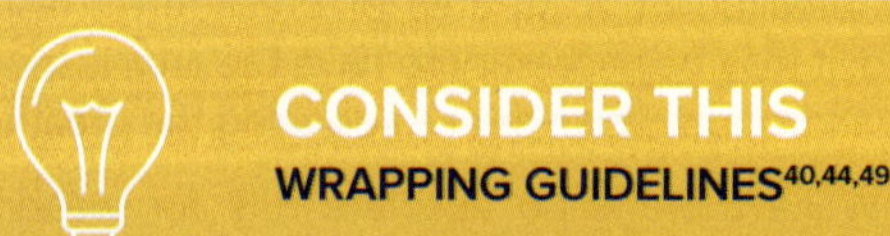

CONSIDER THIS

WRAPPING GUIDELINES[40,44,49]

- Elastic wrap should not have any wrinkles
- Diagonal and angular patterns should be used
- Do not wrap in circular patterns
- Provide pressure distally to enhance shaping
- Anchor wrap above the knee for transtibial amputations
- Anchor wrap around pelvis for transfemoral amputations
- Promote full elbow extension for transradial amputations
- Promote full knee extension for transtibial amputations
- Promote full hip extension for transfemoral amputations
- Secure the wrap with tape; do not use clips
- Use 2-4 inch wrap for upper extremity amputations
- Use 3-4 inch wrap for transtibial amputations
- Use 6 inch wrap for transfemoral amputations
- Rewrap frequently to maintain adequate pressure

SPOTLIGHT ON SAFETY
COMPLICATIONS FOLLOWING AMPUTATION[40,43,44]

There are a multitude of potential complications patients may experience following amputation. Therapists should be aware of the potential signs and symptoms associated with these complications and, when warranted, be prepared to take immediate action.

Several of the more common complications following amputation are discussed.

Contractures
Failure to initiate full range of motion early in the post-operative phase and poor positioning of the residual limb significantly increase the likelihood of a contracture. The joint immediately proximal to the amputation site is the most susceptible. The most likely contractures based on level of amputation are: transmetatarsal and Syme's - equinus deformity; transtibial - knee flexion; transfemoral - hip flexion and abduction.

Deep Vein Thrombosis
A deep vein thrombosis is a blood clot that forms in a vein with the potential to dislodge as an embolism and travel until it blocks an artery. This is a serious medical condition since the embolus may obstruct a selected artery. Heparin is an anticoagulant commonly used to reduce the risk of deep vein thrombosis following surgery.

Hypersensitivity
Hypersensitivity of the residual limb can significantly impede or even prevent the appropriate fit and functional use of a prosthesis. Specific desensitization techniques and early fitting of a temporary prosthesis are key components in post-amputation rehabilitation. Weight bearing, massage, tapping, and residual limb wrapping are all commonly utilized interventions that facilitate desensitization.

Neuroma
A neuroma is a bundle of nerve endings that group together and can produce pain due to scar tissue, pressure from the prosthesis or tension on the residual limb.

Phantom Limb
Phantom limb refers to a painless sensation where the patient feels that the limb is still present. This is common immediately after amputation and will usually subside with desensitization and prosthetic use, however, it may continue for extended periods of time for some patients.

Phantom Pain
Phantom pain refers to the patient's perception of some form of painful stimuli as it relates to the residual limb. The pain can be continuous or intermittent, local or general, and short-term or permanent. This type of pain can disable the patient and interfere with successful rehabilitation. Treatment options include TENS, ultrasound, icing, mirror therapy, relaxation techniques, desensitization techniques, and prosthetic use.

Psychological Impact
It is extremely common for patients to experience a variety of negative thoughts and emotions following amputation. This can include denial, grief, anxiety, depression or suicidal feelings. The intensity of the thoughts and emotions may be elevated in patients following emergency amputation since the patient had insufficient time to mentally prepare for the loss.

Wound Infections
The residual limb can become infected following the surgical procedure. Antibiotics are administered at the time of surgery to reduce the risk of infection.

Considerations for Prosthetic Training[40,43,49]

Forequarter (scapulothoracic)
- Loss of all shoulder, elbow, and hand function
- Most common cause is malignancy
- Functional prosthetic use is common
- A lightweight cosmetic prosthetic is typically well-tolerated

Shoulder disarticulation
- Loss of all shoulder, elbow, and hand function
- Most commonly the result of malignancy or severe electrical injuries
- Functional prosthetic use is possible
- An external prosthetic shoulder joint is typically required

Transhumeral amputation
- Loss of all elbow and hand function
- Most commonly due to trauma
- Typically 7-10 centimeters proximal to the distal humeral condyles
- Trauma associated fracture, dislocation or peripheral nerve injury may delay prosthetic interventions
- Second most common level of upper extremity amputation

Elbow disarticulation
- Loss of all elbow and hand function
- Most commonly due to trauma
- Allows for self-suspending socket
- An external prosthetic elbow joint is typically required

Transradial amputation

- Loss of all hand function
- Must be a minimum of five centimeters proximal to the distal radius
- Typically the result of trauma
- Trauma associated fracture, dislocation or peripheral nerve injury may delay prosthetic interventions
- Functionally preferred over wrist disarticulation or selected partial hand amputations
- Most common level of upper extremity amputation

Wrist disarticulation

- Loss of all hand function
- Relatively uncommon level of amputation
- Cosmetic and functional prosthetic disadvantages

Partial hand amputation

- Loss of a portion of digit/hand function
- Limb sparing technique utilized when functional pinch can be preserved
- Toe transfer to replace a thumb may be considered if prosthesis fails

Digit amputation

- Preserved function is highly variable depending on number of digits involved and level of amputation
- Prostheses are not typically utilized
- A long transradial amputation may be more functional if multiple digits are involved at proximal levels

Hip disarticulation/hemipelvectomy

- All functions of the hip, knee, ankle, and foot are absent
- Most common cause is malignancy
- Does not allow for activation of the prosthesis through a residual limb
- Prosthetic limb advancement initiated through pelvic motion

Transfemoral amputation

- Length of the residual limb with regard to leverage and energy expenditure
- Knee componentry will determine ability to functionally reciprocate gait
- Stance control may not activate until weight bearing occurs through the limb
- Donning can be more difficult than with a transtibial amputation
- Weight bearing through the ischium in an ischial containment socket
- Susceptible to hip flexion contracture
- Adaptation required for balance, weight of prosthesis, and energy expenditure

Knee disarticulation

- Loss of all knee, ankle, and foot function
- The residual limb can weight bear through its end
- Susceptible to hip flexion contracture
- Knee axis of the prosthesis is below the natural axis of the knee
- Gait deviations can occur secondary to the malalignment of the knee axis

Transtibial amputation

- Loss of active foot and ankle motions
- Weight bearing in the prosthesis should be distributed over the total residual limb
- Areas of primary weight bearing should be pressure tolerant
- Adaptations required for balance
- Susceptible to both knee and hip flexion contractures

Syme's amputation

- Loss of all foot functions
- Residual limb can weight bear through its end
- Residual limb is bulbous with a non-cosmetic appearance
- Dog ears must be reduced for proper prosthetic fit
- Adaptation required for the increased weight of the prosthesis
- Adaptation required due to diminished toe off during gait

Transmetatarsal and Chopart's amputation

- Loss of forefoot leverage
- Loss of balance
- Loss of weight bearing surface
- Loss of proprioception
- Tendency to develop equinus deformity

Gait Deviations[40,44,49]

Prosthetic Causes	Amputee Causes
Lateral Bending	
Prosthesis too short Improperly shaped lateral wall High medial wall Prosthesis aligned in abduction	Poor balance Abduction contracture Improper training Short residual limb Weak hip abductors on prosthetic side Hypersensitive and painful residual limb
Abducted Gait	
Prosthesis too long High medial wall Poorly shaped lateral wall Prosthesis positioned in abduction Inadequate suspension Excessive knee friction	Abduction contracture Improper training Adductor roll Weak hip flexors and adductors Pain over lateral residual limb
Circumducted Gait	
Prosthesis too long Excessive knee friction Socket too small Excessive plantar flexion	Abduction contracture Improper training Weak hip flexors Lacks confidence to flex the knee Painful anterior distal residual limb Inability to initiate prosthetic knee flexion

Prosthetic Causes	Amputee Causes
Excessive Knee Flexion During Stance	
Socket set forward in relation to foot Excessive dorsiflexion Stiff heel Prosthesis too long	Knee flexion contracture Hip flexion contracture Pain anteriorly in residual limb Decrease in quadriceps strength Poor balance
Vaulting	
Prosthesis too long Inadequate socket suspension Excessive alignment stability Excessive plantar flexion	Residual limb discomfort Improper training Fear of stubbing toe Short residual limb Painful hip/residual limb
Rotation of Forefoot at Heel Strike	
Excessive toe-out built in Loose fitting socket Inadequate suspension Rigid SACH heel cushion	Poor muscle control Improper training Weak medial rotators Short residual limb
Forward Trunk Flexion	
Socket too big Poor suspension Knee instability	Hip flexion contracture Weak hip extensors Pain with ischial weight bearing Inability to initiate prosthetic knee flexion
Medial or Lateral Whip	
Excessive rotation of the knee Tight socket fit Valgus in the prosthetic knee Improper alignment of toe break	Improper training Weak hip rotators Knee instability

Limb Loss Specific Outcome Measures

There are a variety of outcome measures that can be utilized when assessing an individual with limb loss. The measures are sensitive to needs, adjustments, and functional demands of living with limb loss. While other outcome measures such as the Timed Up and Go (TUG) or the Six-Minute Walk Test are valid measures to use in the limb loss population, the following five measures can provide greater insight into the biopsychosocial factors influencing participation. This list is not exhaustive and is intended to demonstrate some of the many options available.

Functional Outcome Measures

Designed to assess the locomotor or physiological abilities of the patient through physical tasks.

Amputee Mobility Predictor (AMPPRO)

The Amputee Mobility Predictor (AMPPRO) was designed to measure the ambulatory potential of lower-limb prosthesis users. Balance, gait, and transfers are all evaluated as part of the assessment, and the measure is then scored by the test administrator. The score is correlated to a K-level, which can be utilized to inform decision making regarding an appropriate prosthesis prescription. The test may also be performed with individuals who do not have a prosthetic limb (AMPnoPRO).

L-Test

The L-Test is a simple to perform assessment of amputee mobility. The test is very similar to the TUG with three important differences: 1) a 90-degree turn is performed after the initial three meters, 2) the total length ambulated is 20 meters, not six like in the TUG, and 3) four turns are involved. Mean times have been established based on amputation level, age, and use of assistive devices. This is a useful test to supplement or use conjointly along with other functional outcome measures due to its ease of administration.

Patient-Based Outcome Measures

To appreciate the multiple domains influencing participation, it is critical to assess the individual beyond the physical. Specific patient reported outcomes have been established for lower limb prosthesis users and they have been designed to determine the impact of the amputation on the individual's quality of life, societal engagement, and satisfaction. These measures are useful if administered at baseline, and then again prior to discharge to account for the multi-dimensional changes experienced, or not experienced, by the person with limb loss.

Prosthesis Evaluation Questionnaire (PEQ)

The Prosthesis Evaluation Questionnaire was designed to evaluate the prosthesis and life with the prosthesis. The PEQ is composed of nine validated scales that can be administered together or independently. Most questions use a visual analogue scale to assess satisfaction, well-being, frustration, pain, and residual limb health.

Orthotics Prosthetics User Survey (OPUS)

The Orthotics Prosthetics User Survey consists of functional status, quality of life, and satisfaction modules. The survey is simple to administer, and can be performed in part or whole depending on the goals of the clinician.

Trinity Amputation and Prosthesis Experience Scales-revised (TAPES-R)

The Trinity Amputation and Prosthesis Experience Scales-revised is a "multidimensional instrument designed to examine the psychosocial process involved in adjusting to using an amputation and a prosthesis." It consists of four sections: activity restriction, psychosocial adjustment, satisfaction with the prosthesis, and factors influencing health both related to and unrelated to the amputation. The test takes approximately 15 minutes to administer, and may be given in part or whole.

Amputation and Prosthetic Terminology[40,44,49]

Acquired amputation: Refers to the surgical removal of a limb due to disease, trauma, or infection. This can be further defined as traumatic and non-traumatic amputation.

Dysvascular: Refers to the disease of the blood vessels, including peripheral vascular disease, peripheral arterial disease, and complications related to diabetes.

Endoskeletal shank: This type of shank consists of a rigid pylon covered with a material designed to simulate the contour and color of the contralateral limb.

Exoskeletal shank: This type of shank consists of a rigid external frame covered with a thin layer of tinted plastic to match the skin color distally.

Extension assist: A mechanism that assists the knee joint into extension during the swing phase of gait.

Myodesis: The anchoring of muscle tissue or tendon to bone using sutures that are passed through small holes drilled in the bone. This procedure is performed as part of the amputation closure process.

Myoelectric prosthesis: A device using electromyography signals to control movements of the prosthesis with surface electrodes or implantable wires.

Myoplasty: Suturing amputated muscle flaps together over the end of a bone following an amputation.

Non-traumatic amputation: An amputation that is not the result of direct injury. Vascular disease and infection are types of non-traumatic amputations.

Osseointegration (endoprosthesis): The process of implanting a prosthetic device directly into the residual limb of a person with limb loss. This process negates the need for a socket component.

Person with limb loss: This term describes an individual who has lost a limb due to amputation.

Pistoning: The translation of the prosthetic limb from the residual limb. It is the result of inadequate suspension and can result in distal residual limb skin issues.

Polycentric knee: Refers to a knee joint that has multiple axes of rotation that allows for a more natural gait cycle when compared to a single axis knee.

Prosthesis: The term refers to an artificial body part, used as a noun, not an adjective. For example, "My prosthesis is broken."

Prosthetic: The term describes an artificial body part, used as an adjective, not as a noun. For example, "The prosthetic limb is broken."

Pylon: The term used to describe a pipe-like structure used to connect the socket of the prosthesis to the foot/ankle components. The pylon assists with weight bearing and shock absorption.

Residual limb: The term used to describe the remaining extremity following an amputation. The residual limb is characterized based on its location and length.

Residuum: Another commonly used term for the residual limb.

Rotationplasty: An operation where a portion of the limb is removed while the remaining limb below is rotated and reattached. The procedure is often performed as a treatment for distal femoral osteosarcoma.

Shrinker: An elastic sleeve that is placed over the end of the residual limb to control edema and encourage limb shaping.

Stance control (safety): A weight-activated mechanism that maintains knee extension during weight bearing even if the knee joint is not fully extended. If the knee is flexed greater than what the control mechanism is designed for, the mechanism will not engage.

Suspension: The term used to describe how the prosthetic socket is attached to the residual limb. Common types of suspension include vacuum, shuttle lock, suction, waist belt, and harness.

Traumatic amputation: An amputation performed secondary to a direct injury. A car accident or gunshot wound are potential examples of injuries resulting in traumatic amputation.

Clinical Application Templates

Clinical Application Templates* allow candidates to explore many of the elements of patient/client management for a wide variety of medical conditions. Although candidates have been exposed to a variety of medical conditions during their clinical education experiences, it is unlikely they have been exposed to the vast number of medical conditions commonly encountered on the examination. By utilizing Clinical Application Templates students can broaden their experience base and as a result be better prepared to answer examination questions.

Three specific levels of **Clinical Application Templates** (i.e., Gold, Silver, Bronze) will be presented at the conclusion of each system-based chapter.

The GOLD level contains medical conditions that are commonly encountered on the NPTE-PT. As a result, the relative breadth and depth of the template is vast due to the high return on investment.

SILVER

The SILVER level contains medical conditions that are occasionally encountered on the NPTE-PT. As a result, the relative breadth and depth of the template is reduced due to the moderate return on investment.

The BRONZE level contains medical conditions that are infrequently encountered on the NPTE-PT. As a result, the relative breadth and depth of the template is minimal due to the low return on investment.

The basic assumption of this study tool is that candidates should study medical conditions proportionately to the likelihood of seeing the particular condition on the NPTE-PT. An executive summary of selected information for each medical condition is presented at the beginning of each section (i.e., Gold, Silver, Bronze) followed by the completed Clinical Application Template.

Candidates are encouraged to review the templates and carefully reflect on the presented information. Candidates should attempt to make this activity an active learning exercise and resist the urge to simply read each of the templates. By engaging in this type of active learning exercise, candidates are able to further assess their level of preparedness for the examination. Although some candidates may be quite comfortable reviewing selected **Clinical Application Templates**, many candidates learn that they lack necessary knowledge in many others.

Candidates should not rely solely on the presented **Clinical Application Templates** and instead should utilize the template format to potentially review other medical conditions. This type of active learning is best performed by a small group of candidates with a given candidate acting as the facilitator. In this manner candidates can share their individual clinical experiences with the group and at the same time benefit from the knowledge of their classmates.

*The **Clinical Application Template** was adapted from a document by the Academy of Specialty Boards entitled "Preparing Items that Measure More than Recall." The document was originally designed to help item writers develop sample questions for the Physical Therapy Specialty Examinations.

GOLD Level Clinical Application Templates

Level Clinical Application Template Executive Summary

Achilles Tendon Rupture

- Typically occurs within one to two inches above the tendinous insertion on the calcaneus
- Incidence is greatest between 30-50 years of age without history of calf or heel pain
- Patients with an Achilles tendon rupture will typically be unable to stand on their toes and tend to exhibit a positive Thompson test

Adhesive Capsulitis

- Occurs more in the middle-aged population with females having a greater incidence than males
- Arthrogram can assist with diagnosis by detecting decreased volume of fluid within the joint capsule
- Range of motion restriction typically in a capsular pattern (lateral rotation, abduction, medial rotation)

Ankle Sprain - Lateral - Grade II

- Typically occurs due to significant inversion and involves the lateral ligament complex, most commonly damages the anterior talofibular ligament (ATFL)
- Will likely present with significant pain or tenderness along the lateral aspect of the ankle especially at the ATFL
- Should heal fairly quickly if no other structures are involved and will return to the previous functional level within two to six weeks

Anterior Cruciate Ligament Sprain - Grade III

- Injury most commonly occurs during hyperflexion, rapid deceleration, hyperextension or landing in an unbalanced position
- Females involved in selected athletic activities have significantly higher ligament injury rates compared to males
- Approximately two-thirds of complete anterior cruciate ligament tears have an associated meniscal tear

Bicipital Tendonitis

- Increased incidence of injury is associated with selected athletic activities such as baseball pitching, swimming, rowing, gymnastics, and tennis
- Characterized by subjective reports of a deep ache directly in front and on top of the shoulder made worse with overhead activities or lifting
- Examination may reveal a positive Speed's test or Yergason's test

Lateral Epicondylitis

- Characterized by inflammation or degenerative changes at the common extensor tendon that attaches to the lateral epicondyle of the elbow
- Repeated overuse of the wrist extensors, particularly the extensor carpi radialis brevis can produce tensile stress and result in microscopic tearing and damage to the extensor tendon
- Clinical symptoms include difficulty holding or gripping objects and insufficient forearm functional strength

GOLD Level Clinical Application Template Executive Summary

Medial Collateral Ligament Sprain – Grade II

- Grade II injury is characterized by partial tearing of the ligament's fibers resulting in joint laxity when the ligament is stretched
- Mechanism of injury is usually a blow to the outside of the knee joint causing excess force to the medial side of the joint
- Return to previous functional level should occur within four to eight weeks following the injury if no other associated structures are involved

Osteoarthritis

- Degenerative process primarily involving articular cartilage resulting from excessive loading of a healthy joint or normal loading of an abnormal joint
- Typically diagnosed based on the results of a clinical examination and x-ray findings
- Prevalence is higher among women than men later in life, with the large majority of individuals older than 65 years of age demonstrating evidence of osteoarthritis

Osteogenesis Imperfecta

- Classified into four types with a wide range of clinical presentations ranging from normal appearance with mild symptoms to severe involvement that can be fatal during infancy
- Bone densitometry may be used to measure bone mass and estimate the risk of fracture for specific sites within the body
- Children with osteogenesis imperfecta often have delayed developmental milestones secondary to ongoing fractures with immobilization, hypermobility of joints, and poorly developed muscles

Patellofemoral Syndrome

- Causes damage to the articular cartilage of the patella ranging from softening to complete cartilage destruction resulting in exposure of subchondral bone
- Etiology is unknown, however, it is extremely common during adolescence, is more prevalent in females than males, and has a direct association with activity level
- Management includes controlling edema, stretching, strengthening, improving range of motion, and activity modification

Plantar Fasciitis

- Chronic overuse condition that develops secondary to repetitive stretching of the plantar fascia through excessive foot pronation during the loading phase of gait
- Characterized by severe pain in the heel when first standing up in the morning (when the fascia is contracted, stiff, and cold)
- Intervention consists of ice massage, deep friction massage, heel insert, orthotic prescription, activity modification, and gentle stretching program of the Achilles tendon and plantar fascia

Level Clinical Application Template Executive Summary

Rotator Cuff Tear

- May occur as a result of an acute traumatic incident or due to a chronic degenerative pathology such as chronic supraspinatus tendonitis
- The drop arm test and empty can test can assist in identifying supraspinatus pathology which may be indicative of a rotator cuff tear
- Failure to adequately treat a rotator cuff tear may necessitate significant activity modifications, additional surgical management, adhesive capsulitis or degenerative changes

Rotator Cuff Tendonitis

- Caused by an inability of a weak supraspinatus muscle to adequately depress the head of the humerus in the glenoid fossa during elevation of the arm
- Participating in activities that require excessive overhead activity such as swimming, tennis, baseball, painting, and other manual labor activities increases the risk of rotator cuff tendonitis
- Patients may experience a feeling of weakness and identify the presence of a painful arc of motion most commonly occurring between 60 and 120 degrees of active abduction

Scoliosis

- Curvature is usually found in the thoracic or lumbar vertebrae and can be associated with kyphosis or lordosis
- A patient with scoliosis that ranges between 25 and 40 degrees requires a spinal orthosis and physical therapy intervention for posture, flexibility, strengthening, respiratory function, and proper utilization of the spinal orthosis
- Scoliosis does not usually progress significantly once bone growth is complete if the curvature remains below 40 degrees at the time of skeletal maturity

Spondylolisthesis - Degenerative

- Caused by the weakening of joints that allows for forward slippage of one vertebral segment on the one below due to degenerative changes
- Most common site of degenerative spondylolisthesis is the L4-L5 level
- William's flexion exercises may be indicated to strengthen the abdominals and reduce lumbar lordosis

Temporomandibular Joint Dysfunction

- Females are at greater risk than males with the most common age ranging from 20-40 years of age
- Clinical presentation includes pain (persistent or recurring), muscle spasm, abnormal or limited jaw motion, headache, and tinnitus
- Intervention includes patient education, posture retraining, and modalities such as moist heat, ice, biofeedback, ultrasound, electrostimulation, TENS, and massage

GOLD Level Clinical Application Template Executive Summary

Torticollis - Congenital

- Causes the neck to involuntarily contract to one side secondary to contraction of the sternocleidomastoid muscle
- The head is laterally flexed toward the contracted muscle, the chin faces the opposite direction, and there may be facial asymmetries
- Studies indicate that the large majority of patients with congenital torticollis respond to conservative treatment and passive stretching within the first year of life

Total Hip Arthroplasty

- Patients are typically over 55 years of age and have experienced consistent pain that is not relieved through conservative measures which serve to limit the patient's functional mobility
- Posterolateral approach allows the abductor muscles to remain intact, however, there may be a higher incidence of post-operative joint instability due to the interruption of the posterior capsule
- Cemented hip replacement usually allows for partial weight bearing initially, while a noncemented hip replacement requires toe touch weight bearing for up to six weeks

Total Knee Arthroplasty

- Primary indication for total knee arthroplasty is the destruction of articular cartilage secondary to osteoarthritis
- Post-operative care may include a knee immobilizer, elevation of the limb, cryotherapy, intermittent range of motion using a continuous passive motion (CPM) machine, and initiation of knee protocol exercises
- Patient education may include items such as avoid excessive stress to the knee, squatting, quick pivoting, using pillows under the knee while in bed, and low seating

Total Shoulder Arthroplasty

- Surgical candidates typically have irreparable damage, deterioration, and destruction to the humeral head and the glenoid fossa within the shoulder complex
- Surgical complications include mechanical loosening of the prosthesis, instability, rotator cuff tear, implant failure, heterotopic ossification, and intraoperative fracture
- Life expectancy is longer for the shoulder compared to the knee or hip since the shoulder is a non-weight bearing joint

Transfemoral Amputation due to Osteosarcoma

- A highly malignant cancer that begins in the medullary cavity of a bone and leads to the formation of a mass
- A patient status post transfemoral amputation may present with fatigue, loss of balance, phantom pain or sensation, hypersensitivity of the residual limb, and psychological issues regarding the loss of the limb
- Lying in a prone position is beneficial to decrease the incidence of a hip flexion contracture

Level Clinical Application Template Executive Summary

Transtibial Amputation due to Arteriosclerosis Obliterans

- Arteriosclerosis obliterans results in ischemia and subsequent ulceration of the affected tissues
- A patient status post transtibial amputation may have a decrease in cardiovascular status depending on the frequency of intermittent claudication experienced prior to the amputation
- Preprosthetic intervention should focus on strength, range of motion, functional mobility, use of assistive devices, desensitization, and patient education for care of the residual limb

GOLD

Achilles Tendon Rupture

DIAGNOSIS

What condition produces a patient's symptoms?

Rupture of the Achilles tendon normally occurs within one to two inches above its tendinous insertion on the calcaneus. A patient will present with symptoms secondary to the rupture and discontinuity of the Achilles tendon.

An injury was most likely sustained to which structure?

The Achilles tendon is the largest and strongest tendon in the human body and is formed from the tendinous portions of the gastrocnemius and soleus muscles coalescing above the insertion on the calcaneal tuberosity. Theories suggest that an Achilles tendon rupture usually occurs in an Achilles tendon that has undergone degenerative changes. The degenerative changes will begin with hypovascularity in the Achilles tendon area. The impaired blood flow in combination with repetitive microtrauma creates degenerative changes within the tendon and as a result makes the tendon more susceptible to injury.

INFERENCE

What is the most likely contributing factor in the development of this condition?

An Achilles tendon rupture occurs most frequently when pushing off of a weight bearing extremity with an extended knee, through unexpected dorsiflexion while weight bearing or with a forceful eccentric contraction of the plantar flexors. Participation in sports that require quick-changing footwork such as softball, tennis, basketball, and football are high-risk activities. Other contributing factors include poor stretching routine, tight calf muscles, improper shoe wear during high risk activities, and altered biomechanics at the foot during activities (such as a flattened arch). A person over 30 years of age is at a higher risk for rupture secondary to the decrease in blood flow to the area of the tendon associated with aging. A person with a history of corticosteroid injections to the tendon may also have a predisposition for rupture. The highest incidence for rupture is in individuals between 30 and 50 years of age that usually have no history of calf or heel pain and commonly participate in recreational activities.

CONFIRMATION

What is the most likely clinical presentation?

A patient with an Achilles tendon rupture will present with swelling over the distal tendon, a palpable defect in the tendon above the calcaneal tuberosity, and pain and weakness with plantar flexion. The patient may limp and will often complain that during the injury there was a snap or a pop that was associated with the severe pain. A patient will not be able to stand on their toes and in a prone position will not demonstrate any passive plantar flexion with squeezing of the affected calf muscle (the Thompson test). A complete rupture will result in a palpable gap in the tendon prior to the insertion.

What laboratory or imaging studies would confirm the diagnosis?

Confirmation of an Achilles tendon rupture should utilize x-ray to rule out an avulsion fracture or bony injury. MRI can be used to locate the presence and severity of the tear or rupture.

What additional information should be obtained to confirm the diagnosis?

Diagnosis of an Achilles tendon rupture relies on patient history of the event and a positive Thompson's test. Patient history usually reveals a popping sound and a release from the back of the ankle. Physical examination and palpation reveal a discontinuity within the tendon. The O'Brien needle test may be used by the physician to confirm the rupture.

EXAMINATION

What history should be documented?

Important areas to explore include mechanism of present injury, past medical history, medications, current health status, social history and habits, occupation, living environment, and social support system.

What tests/measures are most appropriate?

Anthropometric characteristics: circumferential measurements for edema, palpation to determine ankle effusion

Arousal, attention, and cognition: examine mental status, learning ability, memory, motivation

Assistive and adaptive devices: potential utilization of crutches

Gait, locomotion, and balance: safety with/without an assistive device during gait; biomechanics of gait

Integumentary integrity: assessment of sensation

Joint integrity and mobility: special tests such as Thompson's test

Muscle performance: strength assessment, characteristics of muscle contraction

Pain: pain perception assessment scale

Range of motion: active and passive range of motion

Sensory integration: proprioception and kinesthesia

Self-care and home management: assessment of functional capacity

Achilles Tendon Rupture

GOLD

What additional findings are likely with this patient?

An Achilles tendon rupture is more common in men and in individuals that do not consistently exercise, but are the "weekend warriors." There are risks and benefits to both philosophies of treatment (non-operative and operative) and the physician usually determines the course of treatment on a patient-by-patient basis accounting for the patient's age, activity level, and co-morbidities.

MANAGEMENT

What is the most effective management of this patient?

Medical management of a ruptured Achilles tendon incorporates immobilization through casting or a surgical approach for repair or reconstruction. Pharmacological intervention is not necessary for this condition except to relieve pain through NSAIDs, acetaminophen or narcotics depending on physician preference, and patient profile. Non-surgical treatment includes serial casting for approximately ten weeks followed by the use of a heel lift to ensure maximal healing without stress on the tendon for three to six months. Physical therapy begins when the cast is removed. If a patient requires surgical intervention then a cast or a brace is required for six to eight weeks. Physical therapy intervention is primarily the same for surgical and non-surgical patients and includes range of motion, stretching, icing, assistive device training, endurance programming, gait training, strengthening, plyometrics, and skill specific training. Modalities, pool therapy, and other cardiovascular equipment may assist in the recovery of functional motion and endurance.

What home care regimen should be recommended?

A home care regimen is vital to the success of a patient's recovery. A program must be based on a patient's post-operative impairments and follow the physician's post-surgical protocol. A home program generally incorporates icing and elevation early in the rehabilitation process. A patient is required to continue a home program throughout the six to seven months of rehabilitation. Other areas of focus include range of motion, strengthening, gait, endurance activities, and high-level skill and sport specific tasks.

OUTCOME

What is the likely outcome of a course of physical therapy?

Physical therapy should begin after surgical intervention or when the cast is removed from a non-surgical patient. Assuming an unremarkable recovery, a patient should return to their previous functional level within six to seven months.

What are the long-term effects of the patient's condition?

A patient that manages the Achilles tendon rupture without surgery and allows the tendon to heal on its own has a higher rate of rerupture (40% rerupture the tendon) compared to a patient that has surgical repair of the tendon (0-5% rerupture the tendon). An advantage to non-surgical management is a reduced risk of infection from surgery. However, it may result in an incomplete return of functional performance. A patient that has surgical intervention has a decreased risk for reinjury and a higher rate of return to athletic activities.

COMPARISON

What are the distinguishing characteristics of a similar condition?

Achilles tendonitis can be an acute or chronic condition due to repetitive microtrauma that builds scar tissue in the area over time. A patient initially feels an aching sensation after activity and progresses to pain with walking. There may be localized tenderness and swelling in the area. In the acute stage a patient should utilize anti-inflammatory medications, rest for 2-3 weeks and use a heel lift. In the chronic stage, the symptoms and pain may last beyond six weeks. Examination often reveals a thickened and nodular Achilles tendon. Surgical intervention may be warranted at this stage.

CLINICAL SCENARIOS

Scenario One

A 32-year-old female is playing soccer in a recreational league. A therapist that assists the team observes her kick the ball and then fall to the ground. The therapist examines the patient in the training room and finds that the patient has some plantar flexion in a non-weight bearing position, but is unable to plantar flex the foot while weight bearing. The patient states that something popped while running and palpation indicates a separation in the Achilles tendon.

Scenario Two

A 46-year-old male is referred to physical therapy status post surgical reconstruction of a left Achilles tendon rupture. The patient has been casted for one week and has been using axillary crutches for household mobility. The patient has no significant past medical history. He is employed as a truck driver and resides in a one-story home. The patient sustained the injury while playing tennis.

GOLD

Adhesive Capsulitis

DIAGNOSIS

What condition produces a patient's symptoms?

Adhesive capsulitis (also known as "frozen shoulder") is an enigmatic shoulder disorder characterized by inflammation and fibrotic thickening of the anterior joint capsule of the shoulder. The inflamed capsule becomes adherent to the humeral head and undergoes contracture. This condition is characterized by the symptoms of limitation in glenohumeral motion and pain.

An injury was most likely sustained to which structure?

Adhesive capsulitis is classified as primary or secondary. Primary adhesive capsulitis occurs spontaneously and secondary adhesive capsulitis results from an underlying condition. Inflammation within the joint capsule causes fibrous adhesions to form and the capsule to thicken. A decrease in space within the capsule leads to a decrease of synovial fluid and further irritation to the glenohumeral joint.

INFERENCE

What is the most likely contributing factor in the development of this condition?

Primary adhesive capsulitis has no known etiology, however, it is associated with conditions such as diabetes mellitus, thyroid abnormalities, and cardiopulmonary conditions. Secondary adhesive capsulitis can result from trauma, immobilization, complex regional pain syndrome, rheumatoid arthritis, abdominal disorders, and psychogenic disorders. Orthopedic intrinsic disorders that may initiate this process include supraspinatus tendonitis, partial tear of the rotator cuff, and bicipital tendonitis. Adhesive capsulitis occurs more in the middle-aged population with females having a greater incidence than males.

CONFIRMATION

What is the most likely clinical presentation?

Adhesive capsulitis is characterized by restricted active and passive range of motion at the glenohumeral joint. Characteristics of the acute phase include pain that radiates below the elbow and awakens the patient at night. Passive range of the shoulder is limited during this phase due to pain and guarding. During the chronic phase pain is usually localized around the lateral brachial region, the patient is not awakened by pain, and passive range is limited due to capsular stiffness. Pain is present with a loss of glenohumeral motion, restricted elevation, and lateral rotation.

What laboratory or imaging studies would confirm the diagnosis?

An arthrogram can assist with the diagnosis of adhesive capsulitis by detecting a decreased volume of fluid within the joint capsule. The glenohumeral joint normally holds approximately 16-20 ml of fluid, however, adhesive capsulitis decreases the size of the capsule so it holds only 5-10 ml of fluid. Other tests should only be performed for differential diagnosis.

What additional information should be obtained to confirm the diagnosis?

The diagnosis of adhesive capsulitis is confirmed from clinical evaluation and past medical history. The patient may present with the greatest restriction of glenohumeral motion in abduction and lateral rotation, but all planes of motion are usually affected. There is tightness within the anteroinferior joint capsule, pain with stretching, and restriction with passive and active range of motion.

EXAMINATION

What history should be documented?

Important areas to explore include past medical and surgical history, medications, family history, current symptoms, current health status, social history and habits, occupation, leisure activities, and social support system.

What tests/measures are most appropriate?

Anthropometric characteristics: circumferential measurements of bilateral upper extremities

Arousal, attention, and cognition: examine mental status, learning ability, memory, motivation

Community and work integration: analysis of community, work, and leisure activities

Cranial nerve integrity: assessment of muscle innervation by the cranial nerves, dermatome assessment

Environmental, home, and work barriers: analysis of current and potential barriers or hazards

Integumentary integrity: skin assessment, assessment of sensation

Joint integrity and mobility: assessment of hyper- and hypomobility of a joint, soft tissue swelling and inflammation

Muscle performance: strength assessment, muscle tone assessment

Pain: pain perception assessment scale, visual analogue scale, assessment of muscle soreness

Posture: analysis of resting and dynamic posture

Range of motion: active and passive range of motion

Self-care and home management: assessment of functional capacity

What additional findings are likely with this patient?

A patient with adhesive capsulitis may encounter muscle spasms around the shoulder secondary to muscle guarding. A loss of reciprocal arm swing may be seen and disuse muscle atrophy may occur over time. A thorough examination must be completed to rule out concomitant systemic, rheumatologic, inflammatory, metastatic or infectious disorders.

MANAGEMENT

What is the most effective management of this patient?

Medical management varies with adhesive capsulitis. Adhesive capsulitis is a self-limiting process that can take over 12 months in its course. Pharmacological intervention should emphasize the control of pain through acetaminophen, longer acting analgesics, NSAIDs or narcotics. A physician may inject the shoulder with corticosteroids to assist with recovery of motion. Surgical intervention to break up adhesions or release muscles adhered to the capsule is a last resort if conservative management fails. Physical therapy intervention during the acute phase includes icing or superficial heat, gentle joint mobilization, progressive strengthening, pendulum exercises, and isometric strengthening. During the chronic phase, physical therapy intervention and goals may also include ultrasound, grade III and IV mobilization, increasing the extensibility of the joint capsule, and techniques such as PNF to restore painless functional range of motion.

What home care regimen should be recommended?

A home care regimen during the acute phase should include some self-stretching, but avoid abduction secondary to the risk of damage to subacromial tissue. Once the patient enters the chronic phase, the program should emphasize self-stretching, progressive exercises, posture management, PNF and other exercises such as pendulum exercises and "wall climbing" to assist with improving range of motion.

OUTCOME

What is the likely outcome of a course of physical therapy?

Physical therapy is usually prescribed on an outpatient basis for three to five months after diagnosis. Adhesive capsulitis usually follows a nonlinear pattern of recovery. Spontaneous recovery is said to take 12-24 months in duration.

What are the long-term effects of the patient's condition?

Most patients are able to fully recover over time, but a small percentage of patients experience some permanent loss of range of motion at the shoulder joint. This loss is frequently asymptomatic and may not impair a patient's functional ability.

COMPARISON

What are the distinguishing characteristics of a similar condition?

Acute bursitis is characterized by pain that is intense and sometimes throbbing over the lateral brachial region. This condition may arise secondary to calcific tendonitis. Active and passive motion in all directions is limited by pain. Abduction greater than 60 degrees and flexion greater than 90 degrees usually produce severe pain. Acute bursitis lasts for only a few days and unlike adhesive capsulitis this condition will usually resolve itself within a few weeks.

CLINICAL SCENARIOS

Scenario One

A 29-year-old was diagnosed with primary adhesive capsulitis and referred to outpatient physical therapy. The patient is self-employed as an artist and enjoys outdoor activities. Past medical history includes diabetes mellitus since age six and a femur fracture 11 months ago. The patient noticed reduced range of motion and an increase in pain over the last few weeks.

Scenario Two

A 53-year-old female fell off her bike six months ago while cycling in a road race and sustained an injury to her shoulder complex. The patient attempted to immobilize her arm in a sling for two weeks. The patient states that she was unable to regain functional motion in her shoulder once she stopped using the sling. She saw a physician who diagnosed her with "frozen shoulder." The patient is limited to 10 degrees lateral rotation and 95 degrees of shoulder flexion.

GOLD

Ankle Sprain - Lateral - Grade II

DIAGNOSIS

What condition produces a patient's symptoms?

The vast majority of ankle sprains occur due to significant inversion and involve the lateral ligament complex. This complex resists varus stress and is comprised of the anterior talofibular (ATFL), calcaneofibular (CFL), and posterior talofibular (PTFL) ligaments. The ankle is supported medially by the deltoid ligament which is the strongest of the ankle ligaments. The deltoid ligament is comprised of superficial and deep components and resists valgus stress. Since the deltoid ligament attaches in part to the medial malleolus, significant valgus stress typically causes the medial malleolus to fracture before the deltoid ligament fails mechanically.

An injury was most likely sustained to which structure?

The ATFL resists inversion of the talus and calcaneus as well as anterior translation of the talus on the tibia. The ATFL becomes taut during plantar flexion. The CFL resists inversion of the talus within the midrange of talocrural motion. The PTFL resists posterior translation of the talus and is the strongest of the lateral ligaments. The ATFL is the most likely of the three lateral ligaments to sustain damage during a lateral ankle sprain.

INFERENCE

What is the most likely contributing factor in the development of this condition?

Individuals participating in sport activities requiring high levels of agility (e.g., soccer) or jumping (e.g., basketball, volleyball) are particularly susceptible to lateral ankle sprains. Other factors such as deconditioning, poor proprioception, and obesity may also increase the risk of injury. Recurrent sprains are common and often attributed to a combination of residual ligamentous laxity and decreased proprioceptive responses.

CONFIRMATION

What is the most likely clinical presentation?

A patient with a grade II lateral ankle sprain will likely present with significant pain or tenderness along the lateral aspect of the ankle especially at the ATFL. Pain will typically limit a strength assessment, however, active range of motion should be assessed to rule out an Achilles tendon rupture. Pain will also typically contribute to an antalgic gait pattern and be elicited specifically with passive inversion and end range plantar flexion as this position maximally stretches the ATFL. There is typically discernible laxity with ligamentous testing and joint mobility. Ecchymosis and moderate to severe edema at the ankle are likely and may persist even as pain resolves and function returns.

What laboratory or imaging studies would confirm the diagnosis?

MRI is not typically utilized with suspected lateral ligament involvement without other extenuating circumstances due to the prohibitive cost.

What additional information should be obtained to confirm the diagnosis?

The anterior drawer test for the ankle specifically assesses the integrity of the ATFL during anterior translation of the talus on the tibia. The talar tilt test assesses the integrity of the CFL as the talus is moved into inversion. Though rare, neurovascular complications may accompany the ligamentous injury, therefore distal pulses and sensory integrity should also be assessed.

EXAMINATION

What history should be documented?

Important areas to explore include past medical history, medications, family history, current symptoms, current health status, social history and habits, occupation, leisure activities, and social support system.

What tests/measures are most appropriate?

Anthropometric characteristics: circumferential measurements for edema, palpation to determine ankle effusion

Arousal, attention, and cognition: examine mental status, learning ability, memory, motivation

Assistive and adaptive devices: potential utilization of crutches

Gait, locomotion, and balance: safety with/without an assistive device during gait; biomechanics of gait

Integumentary integrity: assessment of sensation

Joint integrity and mobility: special tests such as Thompson's test

Muscle performance: strength assessment, characteristics of muscle contraction

Pain: pain perception assessment scale

Range of motion: active and passive range of motion

Sensory integration: proprioception and kinesthesia

Self-care and home management: assessment of functional capacity

Ankle Sprain - Lateral - Grade II

GOLD

What additional findings are likely with this patient?

Proprioceptive deficits are common and should be addressed in the plan of care as warranted by examination findings to limit the risk of recurrent injury. Other structural injuries may also accompany a grade II lateral ankle sprain such as osteochondral or chondral injuries of the talar dome, neurovascular disruption, and Achilles tendon rupture.

MANAGEMENT

What is the most effective management of this patient?

Medical management for a grade II lateral ankle sprain usually involves conservative management including R.I.C.E. (rest, ice, compression, elevation). Pharmacological intervention is directed towards pain management through acetaminophen or NSAIDs. Surgical management is not typically indicated unless complications are identified (e.g., fracture, neurovascular disruption). The patient may utilize crutches to limit weight bearing through the involved lower extremity until full weight bearing is tolerated. Physical therapy intervention should be directed towards increasing range of motion and proprioceptive responses, decreasing edema, and beginning light resistive exercises with the involved lower extremity. Passive stretching is recommended to prevent muscle shortening. Range of motion may also be augmented with joint mobilizations if capsular restrictions are noted. Resistive exercises should include a combination of isometric, open-chain, and closed-chain exercises. Resistive exercise should include the peroneal muscles as they provide the ankle with dynamic stability. Proprioception and balance retraining should be addressed with single leg stance activities on variable surfaces. Functional activities such as gait training and stair management should be incorporated. Agility training should be based on sport-specific individual needs. Superficial modalities and electrical stimulation may be utilized to address pain, edema, inflammation, and soft tissue restrictions. Once inflammation has subsided, transverse friction massage may be applied to the healing ligament to assist in preventing the adherence of scar tissue to adjacent structures. A patient should be required to complete a functional progression prior to returning to unrestricted activity.

What home care regimen should be recommended?

The home care regimen should initially consist of R.I.C.E. Range of motion, strengthening, palliative care, and functional activities are also recommended as warranted based on the results of the patient examination. The use of crutches should continue until the patient can tolerate full weight bearing unless otherwise recommended by the referring physician.

OUTCOME

What is the likely outcome of a course of physical therapy?

A grade II lateral ankle sprain should heal fairly quickly if no other structures are involved. A patient should be able to return to their previous functional level within two to six weeks. For patients participating in recreational or competitive athletics, a period of supportive taping or bracing may be recommended to prevent the recurrence of injury.

What are the long-term effects of the patient's condition?

Proper healing time and rehabilitation should allow the patient to return to all forms of activity once the patient demonstrates full pain-free range of motion, minimal pain or tenderness with palpation, normal gait pattern, normal proprioception, and competence with agility testing. Residual laxity will increase the patient's risk of recurrence.

COMPARISON

What are the distinguishing characteristics of a similar condition?

A grade II sprain of one or more of the syndesmotic ligaments is commonly referred to as a "high ankle sprain." The syndesmotic ligaments attach to the tibia and fibula and function to stabilize the ankle mortise. Since the ligaments are deep, a great deal of force is required to cause an injury to the syndesmotic ligaments. The syndesmotic ligaments are often injured in conjunction with an ankle fracture. If the tear is unrecognized and therefore untreated, severe post-traumatic arthritis will likely result. A significant tear will require surgical repair which is not typically true for other ligamentous injuries at the ankle. Management typically is focused on the associated injuries and post-operative rehabilitation with the syndesmotic ligament requiring no specific intervention once repaired.

CLINICAL SCENARIOS

Scenario One

A 35-year-old morbidly obese female is diagnosed with a grade I lateral ligament ankle sprain. The patient was walking on a cobblestone walkway when she had an unrecoverable loss of balance and fell. The patient has enrolled in an exercise-based weight loss program. The program begins in one week and the patient does not want to postpone. The patient resides in a one story home with her mother.

Scenario Two

A 17-year-old basketball player is diagnosed with a grade III lateral ankle sprain. The patient was injured during the third week of an 11 week regular season. The patient has no significant past medical history and would like to return to her starting position before post-season playoffs begin. She is diabetic and resides with her parents in a two-story home with her bedroom on the second floor.

GOLD

Anterior Cruciate Ligament Sprain – Grade III

DIAGNOSIS

What condition produces a patient's symptoms?

The anterior cruciate ligament (ACL) extends from the anterior intercondylar region of the tibia to the medial aspect of the lateral femoral condyle in the intercondylar notch. The ligament prevents anterior translation of the tibia on the fixed femur and posterior translation of the femur on the fixed tibia. The ACL is a broad cord that has long collagen strands that permits up to 500 pounds of pressure prior to rupture. The ligament has a poor blood supply and does not have the ability to heal a complete tear. Injuries to the ACL most commonly occur during hyperflexion, rapid deceleration, hyperextension or landing in an unbalanced position.

An injury was most likely sustained to which structure?

A grade III ACL sprain refers to a complete tear of the ligament with excessive laxity. Tears of the anterior cruciate ligament most often occur in the midsubstance of the ligament and not at the ligament's attachment on the femur or tibia. Laxity rarely occurs solely in a straight plane and instead is often classified as anterolateral or anteromedial.

INFERENCE

What is the most likely contributing factor in the development of this condition?

Participation in athletic activities requiring high levels of agility (soccer, basketball, volleyball) and contact sports increases the incidence of an ACL injury. Studies indicate that women involved in selected athletic activities experience significantly higher ACL injury rates than their male counterparts. Causative factors for ACL disruption include body movement and positioning, muscle strength, joint laxity, Q angle, and a narrow intercondylar notch.

CONFIRMATION

What is the most likely clinical presentation?

The peak incidence of ACL injury occurs between 14 and 29 years of age. This age group corresponds to an overall higher activity level, which increases the risk of injury. A grade III ACL sprain is characterized by significant pain, effusion, and edema that significantly limits range of motion. The patient may be unable to bear weight on the involved extremity resulting in dependence on an assistive device. Ligamentous testing reveals visible laxity in the knee and may exacerbate the patient's pain level.

What laboratory or imaging studies would confirm the diagnosis?

MRI is the preferred imaging tool to identify the presence of an ACL tear and possible disruption of other soft tissue structures such as ligaments and menisci. X-rays may be used to rule out a fracture.

What additional information should be obtained to confirm the diagnosis?

Subjective reports such as hearing a loud pop or feeling as though the knee buckled is often associated with a complete tear of the ACL. Special tests such as the Lachman, anterior drawer, and pivot shift test can be used to confirm the diagnosis. It is important to perform all special tests bilaterally.

EXAMINATION

What history should be documented?

Important areas to explore include mechanism of present injury, current symptoms, past medical history, medications, living environment, social history and habits, and social support system.

What tests/measures are most appropriate?

Anthropometric characteristics: knee effusion and lower extremity circumferential measurements

Arousal, attention, and cognition: examine mental status, learning ability, memory, motivation

Assistive and adaptive devices: analysis of components and safety of a device, potential utilization of crutches

Gait, locomotion, and balance: safety during gait with an assistive device

Integumentary integrity: assessment of sensation (pain, temperature, tactile), skin assessment

Joint integrity and mobility: special tests for ligaments and menisci, Lachman and reverse Lachman test, anterior drawer test, palpation of structures, joint play, soft tissue restrictions, joint pain

Muscle performance: strength and active movement assessment, resisted isometrics, muscle contraction characteristics, muscle endurance

Orthotic, protective, and supportive devices: utilization of bracing, taping or wrapping, foot orthotic assessment

Pain: pain perception assessment scale

Range of motion: active and passive range of motion

Self-care and home management: assessment of functional capacity

Sensory integrity: proprioception and kinesthesia

Anterior Cruciate Ligament Sprain – Grade III

What additional findings are likely with this patient?

Approximately two-thirds of the time the ACL is torn there is an accompanying meniscal tear. The collateral ligaments can also be involved although not as commonly as the menisci. When all three structures (ACL, MCL, and medial meniscus) are damaged it is referred to as the "unhappy triad."

MANAGEMENT

What is the most effective management of this patient?

Management of a patient following a grade III ACL sprain includes controlling edema, increasing range of motion, strengthening, and improving the fluidity of gait. For patients electing to have surgery, the patellar tendon is the most commonly utilized graft for intra-articular reconstruction. Patients often initially present with a knee immobilizer and crutches to protect the reconstructed ligament. Specific parameters are difficult to identify since many orthopedic surgeons utilize very specific protocols. Physical therapy management in the initial post-operative phase includes protecting the integrity of the graft, controlling edema, and improving range of motion. Specific intervention activities include pain modulation, patellar mobility, active range of motion exercises, gait activities, and quadriceps exercises. As patients progress in their rehabilitation program, treatment begins to focus on strengthening activities emphasizing closed-chain exercises and selected functional activities. Closed-chain exercises are considered more desirable than open-chain exercises since they minimize anterior translation of the tibia. Patients should be required to complete a functional progression prior to returning to unrestricted athletics. For patients opting for a conservative (non-operative) approach, it is necessary to begin an aggressive strengthening program once the acute phase of the injury has subsided.

What home care regimen should be recommended?

The home care regimen should consist of range of motion, strengthening, palliative care, and functional activities as warranted based on the results of the patient examination and course (operative versus non-operative) of treatment.

OUTCOME

What is the likely outcome of a course of physical therapy?

It is possible that with an aggressive strengthening program and/or activity modification, patients may be able to participate in light to moderate athletic activities without formal surgical reconstruction. Patients electing to have surgery can expect to return to their previous functional level in four to six months.

What are the long-term effects of the patient's condition?

Patients that sustain a complete tear of the ACL and elect not to have reconstructive surgery will likely be at increased risk for instability and subsequent deterioration of joint surfaces.

COMPARISON

What are the distinguishing characteristics of a similar condition?

A grade III posterior cruciate ligament (PCL) sprain is less common than an ACL sprain. The most common mechanism of injury for a PCL sprain is a "dashboard" injury or forced knee hyperflexion as the foot is plantar flexed. A grade III PCL injury will typically produce effusion, posterior tenderness, and a positive posterior drawer test. Knee extension is often limited due to the effusion and stretching of the posterior capsule and gastrocnemius. The rehabilitation program typically emphasizes strengthening of the quadriceps muscles. Individuals with an isolated PCL sprain may not exhibit any functional performance limitations and as a result, surgical intervention is far less common than with an ACL sprain. A PCL sprain alters the arthrokinematics of the knee joint and as a result a patient will be susceptible to degenerative changes such as arthritis.

CLINICAL SCENARIOS

Scenario One

A 16-year-old gymnast sustains a grade I ACL injury after landing awkwardly on her left leg during a vault. The patient is two days status post injury and has mild effusion in the involved knee. The patient is a competitive gymnast and needs to compete in a regional meet in slightly less than four weeks.

Scenario Two

A 35-year-old male is referred to physical therapy after injuring his knee in a softball game. The patient reports tearing the ACL ten years ago in a skiing accident. The patient is active, however, reports more recent episodes of instability. The physician notes significant arthritic changes in the involved knee including diminished joint space.

GOLD

Bicipital Tendonitis

DIAGNOSIS

What condition produces a patient's symptoms?

Bicipital tendonitis is an inflammatory process of the tendon of the long head of the biceps. Impingement or an inflammatory injury can result in symptoms of shoulder pain. Repeated full abduction and lateral rotation of the humeral head can lead to irritation that produces inflammation, edema, microscopic tears within the tendon, and degeneration of the tendon itself.

An injury was most likely sustained to which structure?

Continuous or repetitive shoulder motions can cause overuse of the biceps tendon. Damaged cells within the tendon do not have time to heal, leading to tendonitis. This is common in sports or work activities that require frequent and repeated use of the upper extremities, especially when the motion is performed overhead. Athletes who throw, swim or swing a racquet or club are at greatest risk. Years of shoulder wear and tear can cause the biceps tendon to become inflamed. Degeneration in a tendon causes a loss of the normal arrangement of the collagen fibers that join together to form the tendon. Some of the individual strands of the tendon become intertwined due to the degeneration, while allowing other fibers to break and the tendon to lose strength.

INFERENCE

What is the most likely contributing factor in the development of this condition?

Bicipital tendonitis is often caused through repetitive overhead activity and motion. There is usually direct trauma to the tendon as the shoulder motion approaches excessive abduction and lateral rotation. Examples of high risk athletes include baseball pitchers, tennis players, gymnasts, rowers, and swimmers. Bicipital tendonitis can also be caused secondary to other shoulder pathology including rotator cuff disease, impingement syndrome or intra-articular pathology such as labral tears.

CONFIRMATION

What is the most likely clinical presentation?

Patients generally report the feeling of a deep ache directly in the front and on the top of the shoulder. The ache may spread down into the biceps muscle and is usually made worse with overhead activities or lifting heavy objects. Resting the shoulder typically reduces the pain. A catching or slipping sensation of the biceps muscle may indicate a tear of the transverse humeral ligament. Bicipital tendinopathy, pain to palpation over the anterior shoulder in the area of the bicipital groove, pain with the biceps resistance test (i.e., shoulder flexion against resistance with elbow extended and forearm supinated), and a positive Yergason's or Speed's test (i.e., pain with resisted supination of the forearm or with the elbow flexed at 90° and the arm adducted against the body) are positive indicators for bicipital tendonitis.

What laboratory or imaging studies would confirm the diagnosis?

There are no laboratory tests to assist with the diagnosis of bicipital tendonitis. Plain x-rays do not diagnose bicipital tendonitis, but may show calcification in the groove or subacromial spurring. Other x-rays of the neck and elbow may be indicated to rule out referred shoulder pain. MRI can view the tendon, but is expensive and not usually used unless the patient is not responding to conservative treatment.

What additional information should be obtained to confirm the diagnosis?

Testing such as the biceps resistance test, Speed's test, and Yergason's test may be performed in conjunction with a full physical examination.

EXAMINATION

What history should be documented?

Important areas to explore include past medical history, medications, current health status, nutritional status, social history and habits, occupation, living environment, and social support system.

What tests/measures are most appropriate?

Arousal, attention, and cognition: examine mental status, learning ability, memory, motivation

Community and work integration: analysis of community, work, and leisure activities

Environmental, home, and work barriers: analysis of current and potential barriers or hazards

Ergonomics and body mechanics: analysis of dexterity and coordination

Joint integrity and mobility: assessment of hyper- and hypomobility of a joint, soft tissue swelling and inflammation

Muscle performance: strength assessment, muscle tone assessment

Pain: pain perception assessment scale, visual analogue scale, assessment of muscle soreness

Posture: analysis of resting and dynamic posture

Range of motion: active and passive range of motion, Speed's test, Yergason's test

Reflex integrity: assessment of deep tendon reflexes

Self-care and home management: assessment of functional capacity

Sensory integrity: assessment of proprioception and kinesthesia

Bicipital Tendonitis

GOLD

What additional findings are likely with this patient?

Patients with long-term chronic tendonitis may experience shoulder instability and subluxation secondary to biceps degeneration. Bicipital tendonitis will also frequently accompany impingement syndrome, rotator cuff tendonitis, and forms of glenohumeral instability.

MANAGEMENT

What is the most effective management of this patient?

The primary goal of medical management is to relieve pain, reduce inflammation, and regain full available range of motion. Rest and/or immobilization using a splint or a removable brace may be indicated initially for a brief period of time. Generally, the patient should avoid all overhead movement, reaching, and lifting of objects. Pharmacological intervention may include nonsteroidal anti-inflammatory medications (NSAIDs) which will reduce both pain and inflammation. Active physical therapy is not often initiated immediately, however, the patient may be referred for instruction in general education of the pathology, guidelines for restrictions, pendulum exercises, and the use of TENS. The application of heat or cold to the affected area can also assist with relief of pain. The patient may benefit from the use of iontophoresis or phonophoresis. As the patient progresses out of the acute phase, physical therapy should focus on an exercise program that stretches and strengthens the affected muscle groups. This can restore the tendon's ability to function properly, improve healing, and prevent future injury. Surgical intervention is only recommended for patients that have not progressed with conservative treatment over a six month period of time. The typical procedure includes arthroscopic decompression and acromioplasty with anterior acromionectomy.

What home care regimen should be recommended?

Patients with bicipital tendonitis are recommended to always perform warm-up activities prior to vigorous exercises, consistently perform passive selective stretching and strengthening, use proper body mechanics, and avoid any painful activity. The ongoing focus of a home program should be on strengthening and endurance surrounding the tendon. Patients will have to consistently participate in an ongoing home exercise program to prevent the risk of recurrence.

OUTCOME

What is the likely outcome of a course of physical therapy?

The goal of physical therapy is to restore full available range of motion without pain. Once the patient does not experience pain or discomfort with activity, they may slowly return to their previous level of activity. Most patients are successful with conservative treatment and are able to return to their activities after an average of six to eight weeks of physical therapy and rehabilitation.

What are the long-term effects of the patient's condition?

Although the overall prognosis depends on the level of involvement, most patients have a positive long-term outcome and are able to return to their previous level of functioning. A small proportion of patients do not achieve a positive outcome and have further deterioration or a rupture of the tendon.

COMPARISON

What are the distinguishing characteristics of a similar condition?

The glenoid labrum is a fibrocartilage rim that surrounds the glenoid cavity, attaches to the glenoid cavity of the scapula to increase its depth, and protects the edge of the bone within the joint capsule. A labral tear is most susceptible with anterior damage or subluxation. A Bankart lesion is the name given to the avulsion of the labral ligamentous complex from the anteroinferior aspect of the glenoid. This is the most common lesion resulting in anterior joint instability. A CT scan can diagnose the tear and surgical intervention is normally successful for repair.

CLINICAL SCENARIOS

Scenario One

A 27-year-old male is referred to physical therapy by his primary care physician for "probable bicipital tendonitis." He went to see his doctor secondary to pain when performing overhead activities and lifting objects of varying weight. He works as an auto mechanic 50 hours per week. He was trying to "work through the pain," but it has worsened over the last month. He resides with his wife and twin girls in a ranch style home.

Scenario Two

A 56-year-old tennis instructor has noticed an increase in pain through a particular arc of motion at her shoulder. She was diagnosed with impingement syndrome years ago, but has not had any recurrence or discomfort again until now. She states that her goal is to return to teaching tennis.

GOLD

Lateral Epicondylitis

DIAGNOSIS

What condition produces a patient's symptoms?

Lateral epicondylitis (tennis elbow) is characterized by inflammation or degenerative changes at the common extensor tendon that attaches to the lateral epicondyle of the elbow. The primary symptom of this condition is pain.

An injury was most likely sustained to which structure?

Repeated overuse of the wrist extensors, particularly the extensor carpi radialis brevis can produce tensile stress and result in microscopic tearing and damage to the extensor tendon. Other muscles that can be affected include the extensor digitorum, extensor carpi radialis longus, and extensor carpi ulnaris.

INFERENCE

What is the most likely contributing factor in the development of this condition?

The exact etiology is uncertain, however, repetitive wrist action against resistance during extension and supination appear to produce this condition. Over time inflammation of the periosteum may develop with formation of adhesions. The continued microtrauma does not allow for proper healing and will continue to injure the tissues. This pattern is best seen while hitting a backhand in tennis, however, overuse with painting, hand tools, gardening, and any repeated activity that involves forceful wrist extension can result in lateral epicondylitis. Men are more likely to develop lateral epicondylitis and it is also more common for individuals in their late 30's and 40's secondary to the normal loss of the extensibility of connective tissue with age.

CONFIRMATION

What is the most likely clinical presentation?

A typical patient with lateral epicondylitis is usually between the third and fifth decades of life and has unilateral involvement of the elbow. Lateral epicondylitis presents with pain along the lateral aspect of the elbow especially over the lateral epicondyle that sometimes radiates into the dorsum of the hand. The pain will increase with wrist flexion with elbow extension, resisted wrist extension, and resisted radial deviation. The patient may also have difficulty holding or gripping objects and insufficient forearm functional strength. Range of motion of the elbow usually remains normal, however, may be limited in severe cases. The patient will have localized tenderness over the lateral epicondyle and may present with localized swelling. The pain usually increases with activity and is noted at night.

What laboratory or imaging studies would confirm the diagnosis?

No lab or imaging studies are required to diagnose lateral epicondylitis. X-ray or MRI may be used to rule out other conditions. Electrodiagnostic tests are only beneficial if there is radial nerve involvement.

What additional information should be obtained to confirm the diagnosis?

Lateral epicondylitis is usually diagnosed based on history, physical examination of the extremity, and several manual maneuvers that specifically identify the presence of lateral epicondylitis. An increase in pain at the lateral epicondyle with resisted wrist extension implies extensor carpi radialis brevis involvement.

EXAMINATION

What history should be documented?

Important areas to explore include past medical history, medications, family history, current symptoms, current health status, social history and habits, occupation, leisure and sport activities, and social support system.

What tests/measures are most appropriate?

Anthropometric characteristics: circumferential measurements of the forearm

Arousal, attention, and cognition: examine mental status, learning ability, memory, motivation

Community and work integration: analysis of community, work, and leisure activities

Environmental, home, and work barriers: analysis of current and potential barriers or hazards

Integumentary integrity: skin assessment, assessment of sensation

Joint integrity and mobility: assessment of hypermobility and hypomobility of a joint, soft tissue swelling and inflammation, quality of movement of the elbow complex, provocative tests for lateral epicondylitis including Cozen's test, Mill's test, and lateral epicondylitis test

Muscle performance: strength assessment, muscle tone assessment, grip test dynamometer

Orthotic, protective, and supportive devices: potential utilization of bracing, splinting

Pain: pain perception assessment scale, visual analogue scale, assessment of muscle soreness

Posture: analysis of resting and dynamic posture

Range of motion: active and passive range of motion of bilateral upper extremities

Reflex integrity: assessment of deep tendon reflexes

Self-care and home management: assessment of functional capacity

Lateral Epicondylitis

GOLD

What additional findings are likely with this patient?

If the patient is involved in tennis or some other potential overuse activity, there should be remediation and modification in training, technique, and equipment to minimize the chance of recurrence.

MANAGEMENT

What is the most effective management of this patient?

Medical management initially treats the pain and inflammation through protection, rest, ice, compression, and elevation. During the initial phase the patient should avoid all activities that aggravate the injury. Pharmacological intervention should include NSAIDs to alleviate pain and inflammation. Modalities may also be used such as phonophoresis with hydrocortisone or iontophoresis with dexamethasone. On occasion, resting splints may be used during the acute stage to relieve tension of the involved muscles. Physical therapy intervention should initiate stretching and strengthening to improve flexibility and increase functional activities. All exercise must remain pain free. Other modalities including electrical stimulation and cryotherapy may be beneficial. Strengthening should include elbow, wrist, and hand exercises. As a patient progresses, resistive, isokinetic, and sport-specific exercises should be introduced. Counter-force bracing in the form of a forearm band may be indicated to reduce the degree of tension in the region of the muscular attachment. A patient should wean from the brace, prior to the completion of rehabilitation so the patient does not depend on it or use it as a replacement for rehabilitation.

What home care regimen should be recommended?

A home care regimen should include the same therapeutic program the patient performs during physical therapy. Patient education should include modification of all activities that exacerbate the symptoms. It is imperative that the patient not rush or advance beyond the parameters of the home program as it will exacerbate the condition. A patient must avoid all activities that produce pain and use ice, elevation, and rest as needed.

OUTCOME

What is the likely outcome of a course of physical therapy?

Physical therapy may be indicated with goals of regaining appropriate strength, flexibility, and endurance while reducing inflammation and pain of the involved muscles. Overall outcome is favorable and a patient should be able to return to all previous functional activities without restrictions.

What are the long-term effects of the patient's condition?

Lateral epicondylitis will commonly recur, however, continued stretching and exercise will decrease the risk of future recurrence. If conservative treatment does not improve symptoms after two to three months, surgical intervention may be indicated.

COMPARISON

What are the distinguishing characteristics of a similar condition?

Medial epicondylitis (golfer's or swimmer's elbow) results from repeated microtrauma to the flexor carpi radialis and/or the humeral head of the pronator teres during pronation and wrist flexion. There is pain with resisted wrist flexion and resisted pronation and point tenderness over the medial epicondyle. Treatment is similar in protocol to lateral epicondylitis, however, is directed at the appropriate location. Complete immobilization is never recommended, however, counter-force bracing or splinting may be indicated.

CLINICAL SCENARIOS

Scenario One

A 27-year-old tennis player is seen in physical therapy diagnosed with right lateral epicondylitis. The patient plays in a competitive league and recently changed his instructor and increased the number of games played per week. He complains of pain and point tenderness over the lateral epicondyle. He is very frustrated, as this pain has had a large impact on his ability to win games.

Scenario Two

A 42-year-old female diagnosed with right lateral epicondylitis has been seen in physical therapy for four weeks. She has a past medical history that includes complex regional pain syndrome two years ago in the right upper extremity and is status post hysterectomy three months ago. She has not had any relief of pain and states that she cannot hold anything in her right hand. She enjoys gardening and works at a vegetable farm.

GOLD

Medial Collateral Ligament Sprain – Grade II

DIAGNOSIS

What condition produces a patient's symptoms?

The medial collateral ligament (MCL) connects the medial epicondyle of the femur to the medial tibia and as a result resists medially directed force at the knee. The MCL is the primary stabilizer of the medial side of the knee against valgus force and lateral rotation of the tibia (especially during knee flexion). This extra-articular ligament is a thick and flat band which attaches proximally on the medial femoral condyle and extends to the medial surface of the tibia approximately six centimeters below the joint line. A common mechanism of injury is a direct blow against the lateral surface of the knee causing valgus stress and subsequent damage to the medial aspect of the knee.

An injury was most likely sustained to which structure?

A grade II injury of the MCL is characterized by partial tearing of the ligament's fibers resulting in joint laxity when the ligament is stretched. Often the medial capsular ligament is involved in a grade II sprain of the MCL.

INFERENCE

What is the most likely contributing factor in the development of this condition?

Individuals participating in contact activities requiring a high level of agility are particularly susceptible to an MCL injury. Mechanism of injury is usually a blow to the outside of the knee joint causing excess force to the medial side of the joint. The MCL can also be injured by a twisting of the knee. Muscle weakness resulting in poor dynamic stabilization may also increase the incidence of this type of injury.

CONFIRMATION

What is the most likely clinical presentation?

A patient with a grade II MCL injury will likely present with an inability to fully extend and flex the knee, pain and significant tenderness along the medial aspect of the knee, possible decrease in strength, potential loss of proprioception, and an antalgic gait. There is typically discernable laxity with valgus testing, instability of the joint, and slight to moderate swelling around the knee. More severe swelling may be indicative of meniscus or cruciate ligament involvement.

What laboratory or imaging studies would confirm the diagnosis?

MRI is a non-invasive imaging technique that can be utilized to view soft tissue structures such as ligaments. The imaging technique is extremely expensive and therefore may not be commonly employed on an individual with a suspected MCL injury without other extenuating circumstances.

What additional information should be obtained to confirm the diagnosis?

A valgus stress test is a technique designed to detect medial instability in a single plane. The examiner applies a valgus stress at the knee while stabilizing the ankle. The test is often performed initially in full extension and then in 30 degrees of flexion. A patient with a grade II MCL sprain may exhibit 5-15 degrees of laxity with valgus stress at 30 degrees of flexion.

EXAMINATION

What history should be documented?

Important areas to explore include mechanism of present injury, current symptoms, past medical history, medications, living environment, occupation, social history and habits, and social support system.

What tests/measures are most appropriate?

Anthropometric characteristics: palpation to determine knee effusion, lower extremity circumferential measurements

Arousal, attention, and cognition: examine mental status, learning ability, memory, motivation

Assistive and adaptive devices: analysis of components and safety of a device, potential utilization of crutches

Community and work integration: analysis of community, work, and leisure activities

Environmental, home, and work barriers: analysis of current and potential barriers or hazards

Gait, locomotion, and balance: safety during gait with an assistive device

Integumentary integrity: assessment of sensation (pain, temperature, tactile), skin assessment

Joint integrity and mobility: special tests for ligaments and menisci, valgus stress test, palpation of structures, joint play, soft tissue restrictions, joint pain

Muscle performance: strength assessment, assessment of active movement, resisted isometrics, muscle contraction characteristics, muscle endurance

Orthotic, protective, and supportive devices: potential utilization of bracing, taping or wrapping

Pain: pain perception assessment scale, visual analogue scale

Range of motion: active and passive range of motion

Self-care and home management: assessment of functional capacity

Sensory integrity: assessment of proprioception and kinesthesia

Medial Collateral Ligament Sprain – Grade II

GOLD

What additional findings are likely with this patient?

Anterior cruciate ligament and/or meniscal damage often accompanies a grade II MCL injury. As a result it is often prudent to perform special tests directed at these particular structures. The MCL normally has a good secondary support system with weight bearing forces compressing the medial side of the joint and adding to the overall stability of the joint. This allows the structures to be protected after injury along with use of a brace.

MANAGEMENT

What is the most effective management of this patient?

Medical management for a grade II MCL sprain usually involves conservative management including R.I.C.E. (rest, icing, compression, elevation). Pharmacological intervention is directed towards pain management through acetaminophen or NSAIDs. The patient may utilize a full-length knee immobilizer or a hinge brace and crutches to limit weight bearing through the involved lower extremity for initial rehabilitation. Physical therapy intervention should be directed towards increasing range of motion in the involved extremity and beginning light resistive exercises. Range of motion exercises may include heel slides or stationary cycling without resistance. Resistive exercises should be directed towards the quadriceps and may include isometrics and closed kinetic chain exercises. Functional activities such as gait and stair climbing should be incorporated into the treatment program. Superficial modalities and electrical stimulation may be utilized to combat pain and inflammation. Transverse friction massage may be applied to the healing ligament so it does not adhere to surrounding and adjacent structures. Care must be taken not to massage the proximal attachment of the MCL due to potential bony periosteal disruption. A patient should be required to complete a functional progression prior to returning to unrestricted activity.

What home care regimen should be recommended?

The home care regimen should consist of range of motion, strengthening, palliative care, and functional activities as warranted based on the results of the patient examination. The use of crutches should continue until the patient can adequately extend the knee joint.

OUTCOME

What is the likely outcome of a course of physical therapy?

A grade II MCL sprain should progress fairly quickly if no other structures (ACL or meniscus) are involved. A patient should be able to return to their previous functional level within four to eight weeks following the injury.

What are the long-term effects of the patient's condition?

Proper healing time and rehabilitation management should allow the patient to return to all forms of activity once the patient demonstrates full range of motion, ambulation without a limp, no visual swelling, and competence with all agility testing. If the patient has residual laxity from the injury the patient may be susceptible to reinjury.

COMPARISON

What are the distinguishing characteristics of a similar condition?

A grade II lateral collateral ligament injury differs from an MCL injury in several ways. The lateral collateral ligament attaches proximally on the lateral femoral condyle and runs distally and posteriorly to insert on the head of the fibula. Lateral collateral ligament injuries are far less common than MCL injuries. Management should focus on the same general goals (range of motion, strengthening, palliative care, functional activities) as those outlined for the MCL injury.

CLINICAL SCENARIOS

Scenario One

A 17-year-old male is diagnosed with a left grade III MCL sprain and a small tear in the medial meniscus. The patient was playing football when he was injured. The patient has no significant past medical history and plans to participate in football at the collegiate level.

Scenario Two

A 20-year-old college field hockey player complains of knee pain after being diagnosed with a grade I MCL sprain. The patient is mildly tender to palpation over the medial joint line and exhibits trace effusion. The patient has no significant past medical history and would like to return to athletic competition as soon as possible.

GOLD

Osteoarthritis

DIAGNOSIS

What condition produces a patient's symptoms?

Osteoarthritis (OA) is a heterogeneous group of conditions resulting in common physiological changes. The most common type of joint disease, OA is a degenerative chronic disorder resulting from the biochemical breakdown of articular cartilage in the synovial joints. Although theories indicate that OA is due to excessive wear and tear, secondary inflammatory changes may also affect the involved joints. OA has been divided into primary and secondary forms.

An injury was most likely sustained to which structure?

The progression of OA begins with degenerative alterations primarily in the articular cartilage. This degenerative process is usually a result of excessive loading of a healthy joint or normal loading of an abnormal joint. External forces create the breakdown of the chondrocytes and cause disruption of the cartilaginous matrix. Loss of cartilage results in the loss of the joint space. Through this process, reactive new bone forms, usually at the margins and subchondral areas of the joint.

INFERENCE

What is the most likely contributing factor in the development of this condition?

The etiology of primary OA is idiopathic occurring within intact joints with no history that supports the initiation of this condition. Primary OA is related to the aging process and typically occurs in older individuals. Secondary OA refers to degenerative disease of the synovial joints that results from some predisposing condition (i.e., trauma) that has adversely altered the articular cartilage and/or subchondral bone of the affected joints. Secondary OA often occurs in relatively young individuals. General risk factors include age, obesity, trauma, infection, repetitive microtrauma, genetic factors, inflammatory arthritis, neuromuscular and metabolic disorders.

CONFIRMATION

What is the most likely clinical presentation?

Potential sites for primary OA include joints of the hands specifically the distal interphalangeal joints (DIP) and interphalangeal joints (PIP), knees, hips, and the spine. Bilateral symmetry is often seen in cases of primary OA, particularly when the hands are affected. A patient with OA may experience a decrease in range of motion accompanied by crepitus within the affected joints. The patient will frequently complain of deep and aching joint pain exacerbated by prolonged activity and use. Heberden's nodes consist of palpable osteophytes in the DIP joints and are usually seen in women, but not men. Pain is the main reason patients seek medical attention. Initially, patients have pain during activity that is alleviated by rest and usually respond to analgesics. Morning stiffness in the affected joints usually occurs with progression of the disease, resulting in an increased pain level even at rest that may not respond to analgesics. Erythema or warmth over the joints is not usually present, but effusion may exist. Malalignment and limitation of the joint may occur as the disease progresses in severity. The patient may also present with a deviated gait pattern, atypical movement patterns, and muscle atrophy.

What laboratory or imaging studies would confirm the diagnosis?

OA is typically diagnosed on the basis of clinical examination and x-ray findings. Laboratory tests will not diagnose OA.

What additional information should be obtained to confirm the diagnosis?

Visual inspection of the affected joints, a thorough examination, and a history of the condition will normally support the diagnosis.

EXAMINATION

What history should be documented?

Important areas to explore include past medical history, medications, current health status, nutritional status, social history and habits, occupation, living environment, and social support system.

What tests/measures are most appropriate?

Aerobic capacity and endurance: assessment of vital signs at rest and with activity, perceived exertion scale, pulse oximetry, auscultation of the lungs

Anthropometric characteristics: circumferential measurements

Arousal, attention, and cognition: mental status exam

Assistive and adaptive devices: analysis of components and safety of a device

Community and work integration: analysis of community, work, and leisure activities

Environmental, home, and work barriers: analysis of current and potential barriers or hazards

Ergonomics and body mechanics: analysis of dexterity and coordination

Gait, locomotion, and balance: static and dynamic balance in sitting and standing, safety during gait with/without an assistive device, Berg Functional Balance Scale, Functional Ambulation Profile

Integumentary integrity: assessment of sensation

Joint integrity and mobility: hypermobility and hypomobility of a joint, soft tissue swelling and inflammation

Motor function: equilibrium and righting reactions, motor assessment scales, coordination

Muscle performance: strength assessment

Pain: pain perception assessment scale, VAS

Posture: analysis of resting and dynamic posture

Range of motion: active and passive range of motion

Self-care and home management: assessment of functional capacity, Functional Independence Measure

Sensory integrity: proprioception and kinesthesia

Osteoarthritis

GOLD

What additional findings are likely with this patient?

In patients greater than 55 years old, the prevalence of OA is higher among women than men. DIP and PIP joint involvement resulting in Heberden's and Bouchard's nodes is also more common in women. Disease progression characteristically is slow, occurring over several years or decades. Pain is usually the initial and principal source of morbidity in OA. The patient can become progressively inactive leading to additional co-morbidities including weight gain. There is also an increased incidence of strains and sprains around joints affected with OA.

MANAGEMENT

What is the most effective management of this patient?

Medical management of a patient with OA is usually multi-faceted based on symptoms and the specific affected joints. Long-term management would include pharmacological intervention using acetaminophen or other NSAIDs to alleviate the pain. Glucocorticoid intra-articular injections may also be prescribed to improve a patient's symptoms, however, must be used sparingly due to the long-term negative effects. Nutritional education and weight reduction may be indicated to reduce the stress on the affected joints. Physical therapy may be indicated intermittently in order to preserve joint motion and flexibility. Other treatment may include posture retraining, work site evaluation, general strengthening, relaxation and endurance activities, icing or heat for pain management, hydrotherapy, modalities, patient education, aquatic therapy, and functional activities. If conservative treatment fails, a patient may be a candidate for joint replacement surgery with the goal of pain relief.

What home care regimen should be recommended?

A home care regimen for OA should include general strengthening to tolerance, AROM exercises, endurance activities, continued use of relaxation techniques, and supportive or assistive devices that would decrease pain and improve functional ability. It is very important that the patient avoid overexertion and fatigue.

OUTCOME

What is the likely outcome of a course of physical therapy?

Physical therapy can assist the patient during periods of exacerbation of the disease process, however, cannot change the ultimate outcome of the condition. OA is a progressive and chronic condition. Physical therapy can assist in minimizing the effects of the process and allow for as much independence as allowed by patient tolerance during functional activities.

What are the long-term effects of the patient's condition?

The large majority of individuals older than 65 years have evidence of primary OA. The degree of disability also depends on the site(s) of involvement and rate of progression. Usually, the pain slowly worsens over time, but it may stabilize. OA of the knee is a leading cause of disability in elderly persons.

COMPARISON

What are the distinguishing characteristics of a similar condition?

Psoriatic arthritis is a rheumatic condition characterized by inflammatory arthritis and is often seen in combination with psoriatic skin lesions. Symptoms include silver or grey scaly spots on the scalp, elbows, knees and spine, pitting of fingernails and toenails, pain and swelling in one or more joints, and swelling of the fingers and toes. Psoriatic arthritis affects men and women of all races and usually occurs between the ages of 20 and 50, but can occur at any age. The etiology is unknown, but theories suggest a relationship to genetic inheritance, psoriasis, and environmental factors.

CLINICAL SCENARIOS

Scenario One

A 71-year-old female is referred to physical therapy with significant OA in her hands, knees, and hips. She is approximately 35 pounds overweight and has lost mobility. She rates her pain as an eight out of ten and wants to have surgery to "fix" her legs. She resides in a two-story home with her husband.

Scenario Two

A 39-year-old male has developed secondary OA as a result of a 15-year career in semi-professional football. The patient lives a very active lifestyle, however, has a significant amount of pain in both knee joints. The patient is currently married and working full-time.

GOLD

Osteogenesis Imperfecta

DIAGNOSIS

What condition produces a patient's symptoms?

Osteogenesis imperfecta (OI) is a rare congenital disorder of collagen synthesis that affects all connective tissue in the body. The genetic defect affects collagen-producing genes and reduces production of collagen from 20-50%. There are many mutations identified and various underlying causes that combine to produce the phenotypic expression of OI in a patient.

An injury was most likely sustained to which structure?

The genes for type I collagen production (COL1A1 and COL1A2) have been identified as the genes that become mutated and result in OI. Since collagen production is vital throughout the body, bones and all forms of connective tissue are compromised. OI can also compromise growth, hearing, cardiopulmonary function, and joint integrity.

INFERENCE

What is the most likely contributing factor in the development of this condition?

Most children inherit OI from parents as either an autosomal dominant or autosomal recessive trait. Twenty-five percent of the time the genetic defect occurs by spontaneous mutation of the genes.

CONFIRMATION

What is the most likely clinical presentation?

OI is classified into four types and has a wide range of clinical presentations ranging from normal appearance with mild symptoms to severe involvement that is fatal during infancy. Type I is the mildest form where a child has near normal growth and appearance with frequency of fractures usually ceasing after puberty. The patient experiences mild or moderate fragility, but most times without deformity. This patient will usually present with blue sclera, easy bruising, triangular face, and possible hearing loss. Type II is the most severe form where a child dies in utero or by early childhood. This child has significant fragility of connective tissue, experiences multiple fractures with extreme deformities, and has a soft skull. Type III is severe, but these children present with greater ossification of the skull. Type III characteristics include significant growth retardation, progressive deformities, ongoing fractures, severe osteoporosis, triangular face, blue sclera, and significant limitations with functional mobility. Type IV is usually a milder course that involves mild to moderate fragility and osteoporosis (but greater than type I). The patient will experience fractures easily prior to puberty, but some children improve at that time. Type IV may or may not have a shorter stature, will have bowing of long bones, a barrel shape of their rib cage, possible hearing loss, brittle teeth, and will present with near normal sclera. These children have a near normal life expectancy.

What laboratory or imaging studies would confirm the diagnosis?

A skin biopsy is used to examine the collagen and determine what type of OI is present. X-rays and bone scans may be used for evidence of deformities and old fractures. Bone densitometry may also be used to measure bone mass and estimate the risk of fracture for specific sites within the body. The diagnosis is made through these tests and in combination with the examination and history.

What additional information should be obtained to confirm the diagnosis?

Diagnosis should be determined based on physical examination, family and personal medical history, and formal testing.

EXAMINATION

What history should be documented?

Important areas to explore include past medical history including falls, medications, family history, current symptoms and health status, and social support system.

What tests/measures are most appropriate?

Arousal, attention, and cognition: examine mental status, learning ability, memory, motivation

Environmental, home, and work barriers: analysis of current and potential barriers or hazards

Ergonomics and body mechanics: analysis of dexterity and coordination

Gait, locomotion, and balance: static/dynamic balance in sitting/standing, safety during gait with/without an assistive device, analysis of wheelchair management

Integumentary integrity: skin and sensation assessment

Joint integrity and mobility: assessment of hypermobility and hypomobility of a joint

Muscle performance: strength assessment of active motion, muscle tone assessment

Neuromotor development and sensory integration: reflex movement patterns and involuntary movements, sensory integration tests, gross/fine motor skills

Orthotic, protective, and supportive devices: analysis of components of a device, analysis of movement while wearing a device

Pain: pain perception assessment scale, visual analogue scale, assessment of muscle soreness

Posture: analysis of resting and dynamic posture, scoliosis assessment

Range of motion: active range of motion only

Self-care and home management: assessment of functional capacity

What additional findings are likely with this patient?

Children with OI often have delayed developmental milestones secondary to ongoing fractures with immobilization, hypermobility and laxity of joints, and poorly developed muscles. Most type I children are community ambulators. Roughly half of type IV children are household ambulators and roughly a quarter are community ambulators. For type III children, only about a quarter become household ambulators.

MANAGEMENT

What is the most effective management of this patient?

Medical management is directed at controlling the symptoms of OI. General goals include maximizing independence with mobility, improving optimal bone mass and muscle strength, and prevention of fractures and deformities. Pharmacological interventions may include bisphosphonate drugs, which are used to increase bone density in children and adults. Children should not be given steroids since it may deplete bone and increase fragility. Nutritional counseling and strong dental care are important in the management of OI. Lightweight orthotics may be indicated early to support the extremities, assist with ambulation, encourage weight bearing, and prevent fractures. Physical therapy intervention initially focuses on parent handling techniques, recognition of fractures, positioning, and activities that facilitate safe movement. Treatment of a child with OI should incorporate developmental activities, strengthening, positioning, weight bearing, and the use of mobility aids (scooters, riding toys or wheelchair). Swimming is also a good alternative for strengthening and exercise. All strengthening exercises should avoid rotational forces, placing weights/resistance near a joint, and using long lever arms. Surgical procedures known as "rodding" may also be indicated if a child has more than two fractures to the same bone within six months or if the angle of the long bone would not allow for stable ambulation.

What home care regimen should be recommended?

A home care regimen will be successful if parents are competent with many of the relevant aspects of care. Handling techniques, recognition of fractures, precautions and contraindications, standing program, and exercise through activities are all key components of a home program for a child with OI. A child needs to continue to move and exercise in a safe fashion in order to optimize strength and bone mass.

OUTCOME

What is the likely outcome of a course of physical therapy?

Physical therapy may be required intermittently over the course of the patient's childhood depending on the severity of OI and the secondary complications. A home program must be established for optimal therapeutic results. Physical therapy may be in an outpatient setting or through the school system. The therapist should work closely with the physician and caregivers for comprehensive care.

What are the long-term effects of the patient's condition?

A patient with OI has outcome potential based on the type of disorder, symptoms, and secondary complications encountered. A strong predictor of a child's ability to ambulate in the future also lies in the child's ability to sit by ten months of age. Some children live normal lives with minimal involvement while others use power wheelchairs for mobility and experience multiple secondary complications.

COMPARISON

What are the distinguishing characteristics of a similar condition?

Arthrogryposis multiplex congenita (AMC) is a non-progressive neuromuscular disorder that results from multiple conditions that ultimately limit fetal movement in an intact skeleton and cause multiple congenital contractures at birth. Children are also born with muscle atrophy and weakness, and articular rigidity. Primary forms of AMC include contracture syndromes, amyoplasia, and distal arthrogryposis. Some children will ambulate and others will require wheelchairs for mobility.

CLINICAL SCENARIOS

Scenario One

A nine-month-old boy is seen in physical therapy with Type IV OI. He currently has a cast on his left lower extremity due to a femur fracture. His mother wants to learn activities in sitting and handling techniques that would help her son.

Scenario Two

A 12-year-old female is seen by a school therapist. She underwent intramedullary rod placement in her right femur six weeks ago. She has type III OI and uses a wheelchair. She also presents with a 45 degree thoracic scoliosis and bowing in her upper extremities.

GOLD

Patellofemoral Syndrome

DIAGNOSIS

What condition produces a patient's symptoms?

Patellofemoral syndrome is caused by an abnormal tracking of the patella between the femoral condyles. The tracking problem places increased and misdirected forces between the patella and femur. This most commonly occurs when the patella is pulled too far laterally during knee extension.

An injury was most likely sustained to which structure?

Patellofemoral syndrome causes damage to the articular cartilage of the patella. The damage can range from softening of the cartilage to complete cartilage destruction resulting in exposure of subchondral bone.

INFERENCE

What is the most likely contributing factor in the development of this condition?

The exact etiology of patellofemoral syndrome is unknown, however, it is extremely common during adolescence, is more prevalent in females than males, and has a direct association with the activity level of the patient. In an older population patellofemoral syndrome is often associated with osteoarthritis. Additional factors associated with patellofemoral syndrome include patella alta, insufficient lateral femoral condyle, weak vastus medialis obliquus, excessive pronation, excessive knee valgus, and tightness in lower extremity muscles (iliopsoas, hamstrings, gastrocnemius, and vastus lateralis).

CONFIRMATION

What is the most likely clinical presentation?

A patient with patellofemoral syndrome often describes a gradual onset of anterior knee pain following an increase in physical activity. The pain is characteristically located behind the patella (retropatellar pain) and may be exacerbated with activities that increase patellofemoral compressive forces (stair climbing, jumping) and also with prolonged static positioning (sitting with the knee flexed at 90 degrees as in a car, plane, theatre). Point tenderness is common over the lateral border of the patella and crepitus may be elicited when the patella is manually compressed into the trochlear groove. Visible quadriceps atrophy may be noted in the involved lower extremity particularly along the vastus medialis obliquus. The patient may also complain of burning pain when sitting for prolonged periods of time or when ascending stairs.

What laboratory or imaging studies would confirm the diagnosis?

Laboratory or imaging studies are not commonly used to diagnose patellofemoral syndrome. X-rays are often used to rule out a fracture, examine the configuration of the patellofemoral joint, and identify potential osteophytes, joint space narrowing, patella alta, and arthritic changes. Arthrogram and arthroscopy can be used to examine the articular cartilage.

What additional information should be obtained to confirm the diagnosis?

Special tests such as Clarke's sign can be useful when attempting to confirm the diagnosis. The test is performed by applying pressure immediately proximal to the upper pole of the patient's patella. The physician/therapist then asks the patient to isometrically contract the quadriceps. A positive test is indicated by a failure to fully contract the quadriceps or by the presence of retropatellar pain. The test should be performed at varying degrees of flexion and extension. It is helpful to determine the patient's Q angle and examine the alignment of the patient's feet, as these factors can contribute to the causative factors.

EXAMINATION

What history should be documented?

Important areas to explore include past medical history, medications, current symptoms and health status, social history, occupation/recreational activities, living environment, and social support system.

What tests/measures are most appropriate?

Anthropometric characteristics: knee effusion, lower extremity circumferential measurements

Arousal, attention, and cognition: examine mental status, learning ability, memory, motivation

Assistive and adaptive devices: components and safety of a device, potential utilization of crutches

Environmental, home, and work barriers: analysis of current and potential barriers or hazards

Gait, locomotion, and balance: safety during gait with an assistive device

Integumentary integrity: assessment of sensation (pain, temperature, tactile), skin assessment

Joint integrity and mobility: Clarke's sign, patella grind test (active and passive), dynamic patella tracking, patella glide test, palpation of structures, joint play, soft tissue restrictions, joint pain

Muscle performance: strength assessment, assessment of active movement, resisted isometrics, muscle contraction characteristics, muscle endurance

Orthotic, protective, and supportive devices: potential utilization of bracing, taping or wrapping

Pain: pain perception assessment scale

Range of motion: active and passive range of motion

Self-care and home management: functional capacity

Sensory integrity: proprioception and kinesthesia

Patellofemoral Syndrome

GOLD

What additional findings are likely with this patient?

Patients diagnosed with patellofemoral syndrome often have an increased Q angle. The normal Q angle is 13 degrees in males and 18 degrees in females. The Q angle is measured using the anterior superior iliac spine, the midpoint of the patella, and the tibial tubercle. Differential diagnosis should rule out other problems such as referred pain from the hip, Osgood-Schlatter syndrome, neuroma, patellar tendonitis, plica syndrome, and infection of the knee joint.

MANAGEMENT

What is the most effective management of this patient?

Medical management of patellofemoral syndrome is usually successful with conservative measures, surgical intervention is rare. Pharmacological intervention may include acetaminophen, NSAIDs, and steroid injections into the joint. Physical therapy management includes controlling edema, stretching, strengthening, improving range of motion, and activity modification. Mobilization activities to increase medial glide can be beneficial to increase the flexibility of the lateral fascia. Strengthening activities emphasizing the vastus medialis obliquus in non-weight bearing and weight bearing positions are recommended. Biofeedback can be a useful tool in order to selectively train the muscle. Stretching activities should emphasize the hamstrings, iliotibial band, tensor fasciae latae, and rectus femoris. Strengthening activities may include quadriceps setting exercises, straight leg raising and mini-squats incorporating the hip adductors. Exercises such as deep squats should be avoided since they will tend to aggravate the patient's condition. Patellar taping to improve the position and tracking of the patella during dynamic activities can be useful to limit irritation.

What home care regimen should be recommended?

The home care regimen should consist of range of motion, strengthening, stretching, palliative care, and functional activities. An active patient must decrease their level of activities to relieve the additional stress placed on the patellofemoral joint. A patient must also comply with recommendations for proper footwear and orthotics to improve alignment and lessen aggravation of symptoms, specifically knee pain.

OUTCOME

What is the likely outcome of a course of physical therapy?

A patient with patellofemoral syndrome that undergoes conservative management may be able to return to their previous functioning within four to six weeks.

What are the long-term effects of the patient's condition?

Prognosis for a full recovery is good with successful conservative management, however, failure to adequately address the cause of the patellofemoral syndrome will likely result in a patient's condition further deteriorating. The patient may experience increased irritation of the patellofemoral joint that further impacts their ability to participate in activities of daily living. Periodic exacerbations of the condition most commonly due to an increased activity level may require further physical therapy intervention.

COMPARISON

What are the distinguishing characteristics of a similar condition?

Patellar tendonitis is an overuse condition characterized by inflammatory changes of the patellar tendon. The condition is most prevalent in athletes who participate in activities requiring repetitive jumping skills. The primary complaint is often pain over the anterior portion of the superior tibia with activities such as jumping or ascending/descending stairs. Patients may also experience pain after prolonged sitting and often exhibit point tenderness at the superior pole of the patella tendon. Management of patellar tendonitis incorporates many of the same interventions as patellofemoral syndrome such as range of motion, stretching, and palliative care.

CLINICAL SCENARIOS

Scenario One

A 14-year-old female is referred to physical therapy with patellofemoral syndrome. The patient has mild edema and is sensitive to light touch over the anterior surface of the knee. The patient reports gaining ten pounds and expresses that she is willing to do "anything" to improve her present condition.

Scenario Two

A 45-year-old male is referred to physical therapy after experiencing anterior knee pain for the last week. The patient is 19 weeks status post ACL reconstruction and has recently returned to a softball league. The patient reports an insidious onset of pain and insists that he has been faithful to his home program. A note from the referring physician confirms that the integrity of the graft is fine and he suspects patellofemoral syndrome.

GOLD

Plantar Fasciitis

DIAGNOSIS

What condition produces a patient's symptoms?

The plantar fascia is a thin layer of tough connective tissue that supports the arch of the foot. Plantar fasciitis is an inflammatory process of the plantar fascia (or aponeurosis) at its origin on the calcaneus. Plantar fasciitis is a chronic overuse condition that develops secondary to repetitive stretching of the plantar fascia through excessive foot pronation during the loading phase of gait. This results in stress at the calcaneal origin of the plantar fascia.

An injury was most likely sustained to which structure?

Injury can occur to the plantar fascia itself and cause microtearing, inflammation, and pain. The abductor hallucis, flexor digitorum brevis, and quadratus plantae muscles share the same origin on the medial tubercle of the calcaneus and may also become inflamed and irritated.

INFERENCE

What is the most likely contributing factor in the development of this condition?

Factors that contribute to the development of plantar fasciitis include excessive pronation during gait, tightness of the foot and calf musculature, obesity, and possessing a high arch. A person participating in endurance sports such as running and dancing or a person with an occupation that requires prolonged walking or standing has an increased risk for plantar fasciitis. It is believed that development of plantar fasciitis results from a combination of predisposing factors. Although it is more common in the middle-age population, it also occurs in younger individuals, but usually in combination with calcaneal apophysitis.

CONFIRMATION

What is the most likely clinical presentation?

A patient with plantar fasciitis presents with severe pain in the heel when first standing up in the morning (when the fascia is contracted, stiff, and cold). This pain has also been reported to radiate proximally up the calf and/or distally to the toes. This is the most common symptom that relates directly to the diagnosis of plantar fasciitis. Pain typically subsides for a few hours during the day, but increases with prolonged activity or when the patient has been non-weight bearing and resumes a weight bearing posture. Pain has also been described by patients as "pain that moves around." A patient will typically experience point tenderness and pain with palpation over the calcaneal insertion of the plantar fascia. There may be bony growths in the plantar fascia near its insertion. Plantar fasciitis is usually unilateral and tightness in the Achilles tendon is found in the majority of the patients.

What laboratory or imaging studies would confirm the diagnosis?

Plantar fasciitis is initially treated based on symptoms and physical examination. If pain persists after six to eight weeks of physical therapy intervention, MRI may be used to confirm the diagnosis. Other diagnostic tools may include x-ray and bone scan to rule out a stress fracture, rheumatology workup to rule out systemic etiology, and EMG testing to rule out nerve entrapment.

What additional information should be obtained to confirm the diagnosis?

A thorough history and biomechanical assessment of the foot, observation of the fat pad, examination for Achilles tendon tightness, analysis of footwear, and gait disturbances all assist in diagnosing plantar fasciitis.

EXAMINATION

What history should be documented?

Important areas to explore include mechanism of current injury, training routine, past medical history, medications, social history and habits, occupation, living environment, and social support system.

What tests/measures are most appropriate?

Anthropometric characteristics: circumferential measurements of affected area or extremity

Arousal, attention, and cognition: examine mental status, learning ability, memory, motivation

Community and work integration: analysis of community, work, and leisure activities

Environmental, home, and work barriers: analysis of current and potential barriers or hazards

Gait, locomotion, and balance: biomechanical analysis of gait during walking and running (if appropriate), footprint analysis, dynamic plantar pressure distribution

Integumentary inspection: assessment of sensation, skin assessment

Joint integrity and mobility: assessment of swelling, inflammation, and joint restriction

Muscle performance: strength assessment, muscle endurance

Pain: pain perception scale, visual analogue scale

Orthotic, protective, and supportive devices: potential utilization of taping or use of cushions

Posture: analysis of resting and dynamic posture

Range of motion: active and passive range of motion

Sensory integrity: assessment of proprioception and kinesthesia

Self-care and home management: assessment of functional capacity

Plantar Fasciitis

GOLD

What additional findings are likely with this patient?

Bony hypertrophy can occur at the origin of the plantar fascia resulting in a heel spur. Plantar fasciitis is a relative of heel spur syndrome, but is not the same condition. Heel spurs develop initially as calcium deposits that form due to the repetitive stress and inflammation in the plantar fascia.

MANAGEMENT

What is the most effective management of this patient?

Medical and pharmacological management of a patient with plantar fasciitis usually requires local corticosteroid injections or anti-inflammatory medications to reduce inflammation within the plantar fascia. Physical therapy intervention consists of ice massage, deep friction massage, shoe modification, heel insert application, foot orthotic prescription, modification of activities to include non-weight bearing endurance activities, and a gentle stretching program of the Achilles tendon and plantar fascia. Muscle strengthening exercises for the intrinsic and extrinsic muscles should be implemented once the acute symptoms have subsided. During the acute phase the patient must also modify activities and rest the affected foot. Heel cup prescription and casting may also be indicated.

What home care regimen should be recommended?

A home care regimen for a patient with plantar fasciitis should include ongoing strengthening and stretching exercises (especially stretching of the gastrocnemius and plantar fascia in the morning and prior to and after exercise), maintenance of a fitness program, the use of proper footwear, and the use of foot orthotics and heel inserts if warranted. Night tension splints may be indicated if symptoms persist.

OUTCOME

What is the likely outcome of a course of physical therapy?

Conservative physical therapy intervention on an outpatient basis in combination with a consistent home program should allow the patient to return to a more functional level within eight weeks. Total resolution of symptoms can take up to twelve months. Physical therapy, orthotic prescription, splinting, pharmacological injections, and physician follow-up are all components of the treatment program that may be required for a positive outcome.

What are the long-term effects of the patient's condition?

A patient previously diagnosed with plantar fasciitis is at an increased risk for recurrence, however, successful conservative management, compliance with a home program, and proper footwear will decrease the incidence of any negative long-term effects. If conservative management fails the patient may require surgical intervention, however, this option is relatively rare. A small proportion of patients will develop persistent, chronic, and disabling symptoms.

COMPARISON

What are the distinguishing characteristics of a similar condition?

The tarsal tunnel is the region where the tibial nerve passes between the medial malleolus and the calcaneus. The tibial nerve splits into the medial and lateral plantar nerves while still traversing in the tunnel along with other nerves in this region. Tarsal tunnel syndrome is characterized by pain that is experienced with weight bearing, but not with direct palpation to the plantar fascia. Characteristics of tarsal tunnel syndrome include complaints of numbness, burning pain, tingling, and paresthesias at the heel. Etiology consists of entrapment and compression of the posterior tibial nerve or plantar nerves within the tarsal tunnel due to inflammation or thickening of the flexor retinaculum.

CLINICAL SCENARIOS

Scenario One

A 19-year-old male athlete is referred to physical therapy with bilateral heel pain. The physician has ruled out systemic disorders and diagnosed bilateral mechanical plantar fasciitis. The athlete is a swimmer and began running cross-country last fall. The patient is otherwise healthy, but wants to return to athletic activities as soon as possible.

Scenario Two

A 56-year-old female is referred to physical therapy with left plantar fasciitis. The patient is mildly obese and works the night shift at a paper mill. She stands at her station throughout the shift and is required to walk between the two buildings every hour. The patient has a history of mild asthma and a cardiac murmur. She is anxious to obtain relief from her symptoms since she feels that her employment may be jeopardized.

GOLD

Rotator Cuff Tear

DIAGNOSIS

What condition produces a patient's symptoms?

A rotator cuff tear may occur as a result of an acute traumatic incident or due to a chronic degenerative pathology such as chronic supraspinatus tendonitis. Tears may be classified as partial-thickness, full-thickness, acute, chronic or degenerative. Rotator cuff tears most commonly involve the supraspinatus tendon. However, with more severe or traumatic etiologies, the infraspinatus and subscapularis may also sustain damage.

An injury was most likely sustained to which structure?

The rotator cuff is comprised of the supraspinatus, infraspinatus, subscapularis, and teres minor. The muscles collectively function to provide dynamic stability to the glenohumeral (GH) joint. All four muscles originate from points on the ipsilateral scapula and insert on the proximal humerus. The muscles assist with shoulder mobility to some degree, however, support and mobility demands are greatest for the supraspinatus. This muscle assists with GH abduction and depression of the humeral head. The infraspinatus is primarily a GH lateral rotator, but also assists with GH extension. The subscapularis primarily assists with depression of the humeral head during GH mobility. The teres minor assists with GH lateral rotation.

INFERENCE

What is the most likely contributing factor in the development of this condition?

In older populations, age-related decreases in tissue elasticity and vascularity increase susceptibility to injury with the performance of everyday tasks. In younger populations, traumatic injury or repetitive high demand muscle use (e.g., professional baseball pitcher) are more typically associated with tearing.

CONFIRMATION

What is the most likely clinical presentation?

Pain and weakness are the most common complaints of a rotator cuff tear. Generalized pain exacerbated by specific movements or functional tasks is typically reported in the lateral aspect of the shoulder with radiating symptoms into the upper arm and deltoid region. Pain symptoms are likely to be more acute and specific with traumatic etiologies. Pain complaints are typically greatest with partial tearing due to increased tension on the remaining muscle fibers and associated neural tissue. A patient with a small partial-thickness tear may retain most functional abilities while a patient with a large partial-thickness or full-thickness tear will likely demonstrate significant functional deficits especially with tasks involving GH lateral rotation and abduction. Other symptoms may include complaints of shoulder instability or stiffness, a sense of GH grinding with mobility, crepitus, night pain, and discomfort when lying on the affected side.

What laboratory or imaging studies would confirm the diagnosis?

MRI is typically utilized to detect the location, size, and general characteristics of a rotator cuff tear as well as damage to adjacent structures. X-rays may also be used to assess possible bone spurs within the joint capsule.

What additional information should be obtained to confirm the diagnosis?

The drop arm test and empty can test can assist in identifying supraspinatus pathology which may be indicative of a rotator cuff tear. Pain with resisted muscle testing is likely to be greatest with a partial-thickness tear.

EXAMINATION

What history should be documented?

Important areas to explore include past medical history, medications, family history, current symptoms, current health status, social history and habits, occupation, leisure activities, and social support system.

What additional findings are likely with this patient?

Rotator cuff tears often present in association with other shoulder pathologies including chronic scapular instability, GH instability or impingement (e.g., supraspinatus tendon, long head of the biceps tendon, subacromial bursa, suprascapular nerve). In young, active individuals, the tear may be accompanied by a small avulsion fracture at the greater tuberosity of the humerus.

What tests/measures are most appropriate?

Anthropometric characteristics: circumferential measurements for upper extremity edema, palpation to determine deformity and effusion

Arousal, attention, and cognition: examine mental status, learning ability, memory, and motivation

Assistive and adaptive devices: analysis of components and safety of a device

Integumentary integrity: skin assessment, assessment of sensation

Joint integrity and mobility: soft tissue swelling and inflammation, assessment of joint play, palpation of the joint, empty can test, drop arm test

Muscle performance: strength assessment, characteristics of muscle contraction

Pain: pain perception assessment scale, visual analogue scale, assessment of muscle soreness

Posture: analysis of resting and dynamic posture

Range of motion: active and passive range of motion

Reflex integrity: assessment of deep tendon reflexes

Self-care and home management: assessment of functional capacity

MANAGEMENT

What is the most effective management of this patient?

Medical management of a rotator cuff tear usually includes pharmacological intervention with analgesics and anti-inflammatory agents including oral NSAIDs and local cortisone injections. In older patients or chronic injuries, conservative management including physical therapy is typically attempted prior to considering surgical intervention. Surgery without conservative management may be indicated depending on the etiology, severity of symptoms, and size of the tear. Surgical interventions using an arthroscopic or open technique may include subacromial decompression, repair of the torn tendon or both. Specific parameters for post-operative protocols are difficult to identify since many orthopedic surgeons utilize very specific protocols. Patients who have undergone surgical repair are typically immobilized using a sling for a period of time to protect the repaired tissue. The acute phase of physical therapy should include cryotherapy, activity modification, range of motion, rest, and gentle isometric exercises. As surgical and non-surgical patients progress, treatment begins to focus on restoration of normal mobility with joint mobilizations, range of motion, progressive strength exercises, and palliative modalities. Activities that promote scapular stability, postural re-education, and modification of functional, work, and recreational activities are emphasized.

What home care regimen should be recommended?

A home care regimen, including the patient's adherence to post-operative mobility restrictions, is vital to a successful functional recovery. The home care regimen may vary initially for conservative versus surgically managed patients. Typical activities include palliative care, range of motion, and strengthening exercises as warranted based on the established protocol.

OUTCOME

What is the likely outcome of a course of physical therapy?

Physical therapy should begin immediately for conservatively managed patients. Depending on the surgeon's preference, patients may begin physical therapy immediately following surgical intervention or after a period of immobilization. The course of rehabilitation is variable depending on the size of the tear, treatment approach (e.g., conservative versus surgical), persistence of symptoms, patient age, patient goals, and prior level of function. In cases where the tear is especially large or complicated, repair options are often limited and patients may never fully recover shoulder function. Assuming an unremarkable recovery, a patient typically will regain functional use of the shoulder in four to six months, however, dynamic overhead activities may be restricted for as long as one year. The timeframe for a full return to sport activities may extend beyond a year.

What are the long-term effects of the patient's condition?

Failure to adequately treat a rotator cuff tear may necessitate significant activity modifications, additional surgical management, or result in the development of adhesive capsulitis or degenerative changes. Since the tendon itself does not heal, but rather forms scar tissue, there will be an increased risk of rupture or an increase in the size of the original tear. These risks are typically greater among patients who are conservatively managed.

COMPARISON

What are the distinguishing characteristics of a similar condition?

A biceps tendon rupture most commonly involves the long head of the biceps tendon (LHBT) occurring either at the bony attachment or tendon-labral junction. The injury is most prevalent among men between 40 and 60 years of age secondary to chronic inflammatory or degenerative conditions. In younger individuals, the injury is typically related to sporting activities, trauma or heavy weightlifting. Pain is a primary characteristic with some patients reporting severe pain that worsens at night and is exacerbated by overhead or repetitive activities. A palpable and often visible mass is typically noted in the upper arm where the muscle mass has retracted. A conservative or surgical treatment approach may be indicated as well as referral to physical therapy depending largely on functional deficits.

CLINICAL SCENARIOS

Scenario One

A 21-year-old male collegiate pitcher has experienced persistent supraspinatus tendonitis which has caused him to discontinue all throwing activities. He received several cortisone injections to assist with pain management. The patient is currently limited by pain with abduction and lateral rotation resistance testing and demonstrates active shoulder abduction to 60 degrees.

Scenario Two

A 73-year-old female dislocated her left shoulder during a recent fall. After four weeks of physical therapy, she continues to complain of limited functional mobility due to weakness and pain. Recent testing reveals that the drop arm test and empty can test are both positive. The patient's goal is to return to recreational swimming.

GOLD

Rotator Cuff Tendonitis

DIAGNOSIS

What condition produces a patient's symptoms?

Repetitive overhead activities can produce impingement of the supraspinatus tendon immediately proximal to the greater tubercle of the humerus. The impingement is caused by an inability of a weak supraspinatus muscle to adequately depress the head of the humerus in the glenoid fossa during elevation of the arm. As a result the humerus translates superiorly due to the disproportionate action of the deltoid muscle. Primary impingement occurs from intrinsic or extrinsic factors within the subacromial space. Secondary impingement describes symptoms that occur from poor mechanics or instability at the shoulder joint.

An injury was most likely sustained to which structure?

The supraspinatus muscle has the most commonly involved tendon in rotator cuff tendonitis. The muscle originates on the supraspinatus fossa of the scapula and inserts on the greater tubercle of the humerus. Bicipital and infraspinatus tendonitis as well as bursitis may also coexist as other contributing factors.

INFERENCE

What is the most likely contributing factor in the development of this condition?

Individuals participating in activities that require excessive overhead activity such as swimming, tennis, baseball, painting, and other manual labor activities are at increased risk for rotator cuff tendonitis. Excessive use of the upper extremity following a prolonged period of inactivity also can produce this condition. Statistically, individuals from 25-40 years of age are the most likely to develop this condition.

CONFIRMATION

What is the most likely clinical presentation?

A patient with rotator cuff tendonitis often reports difficulty with overhead activities and a dull ache following periods of activity. The patient may experience a feeling of weakness and identify the presence of a painful arc of motion most commonly occurring between 60 and 120 degrees of active abduction. The patient usually presents with pain with palpation of the musculotendinous junction of the involved muscle and/or with stretching or resisted contraction of the muscle. Pain often increases at night resulting in difficulty sleeping on the affected side. The patient will often have difficulty with dressing and repetitive shoulder motions such as lifting, reaching, throwing, swinging or pushing and pulling with the involved upper extremity.

What laboratory or imaging studies would confirm the diagnosis?

Magnetic resonance imaging can be used to identify the presence of rotator cuff tendonitis, however, due to the high cost it is not commonly employed prior to the initiation of formal treatment. X-rays with the shoulder laterally rotated can be used to identify the presence of calcific deposits or other bony abnormalities.

What additional information should be obtained to confirm the diagnosis?

A number of specific special tests including the empty can test (i.e., Jobe test), Neer impingement test, and Hawkins-Kennedy impingement test can be used to confirm the presence of rotator cuff tendonitis or impingement.

EXAMINATION

What history should be documented?

Important areas to explore include past medical history, family history, medications, history of symptoms, current health status, living environment, social history and habits, occupation, and social support system.

What tests/measures are most appropriate?

Anthropometric characteristics: upper extremity circumferential measurements
Arousal, attention, and cognition: examine mental status, learning ability, memory, motivation
Assistive and adaptive devices: analysis of components and safety of a device
Community and work integration: analysis of community, work, and leisure activities
Integumentary integrity: skin assessment, assessment of sensation
Joint integrity and mobility: soft tissue swelling and inflammation, assessment of joint play, palpation of the joint, empty can test, Neer impingement test, Hawkins-Kennedy impingement test
Motor function: posture and balance
Muscle performance: strength assessment
Pain: pain perception assessment scale
Posture: analysis of resting and dynamic posture
Range of motion: active and passive range of motion
Reflex integrity: assessment of deep tendon reflexes
Self-care and home management: assessment of functional capacity

Rotator Cuff Tendonitis

What additional findings are likely with this patient?

Rotator cuff tendonitis often presents in association with impingement syndrome. Impingement syndrome typically involves the supraspinatus tendon, glenoid labrum, long head of the biceps, and subacromial bursa. It is extremely difficult to determine through examination the exact level of involvement of each of the identified structures.

MANAGEMENT

What is the most effective management of this patient?

Medical management of acute rotator cuff tendonitis usually includes pharmacological intervention and physical therapy. Pharmacological intervention will focus on pain relief through analgesics and NSAIDs. Acute physical therapy intervention guidelines should include cryotherapy, activity modification, range of motion, and rest. As the acute phase subsides the patient is often instructed in strengthening exercises. Since the rotator cuff muscles are dependent on adequate blood supply and oxygen, it is essential that all range of motion and strengthening exercises are pain free. Range of motion exercises using a pulley system or a cane can serve as an effective intervention. Strengthening exercises are initiated with the arm at the patient's side in order to prevent the possibility of impingement. Elastic tubing or handheld weights are often the preferred equipment of choice. It is important for the entire rotator cuff to be strong prior to initiating overhead activities. Shoulder shrugs and push-ups with the arms abducted to 90 degrees can effectively be used to strengthen the upper trapezius and serratus anterior. This type of activity promotes elevation of the acromion without direct contact with the rotator cuff.

What home care regimen should be recommended?

The home care regimen should consist of range of motion, strengthening, palliative care, and functional activities as warranted based on the results of the patient examination.

OUTCOME

What is the likely outcome of a course of physical therapy?

A patient with rotator cuff tendonitis should be able to return to their previous level of functioning with conservative management within four to six weeks. Outcome can be dependent, however, on the patient's classification of stage I, II or III impingement syndrome. Stage I is usually found in the population less than 25 years of age and consists of localized inflammation, edema, and minimal bleeding around the rotator cuff. Stage II represents progressive deterioration of the tissues surrounding the rotator cuff and is common in 25 to 40-year-old patients. Stage III represents the end-stage and is usually found in patients over 40 years of age. There is usually disruption and/or rupture of numerous soft tissue structures.

What are the long-term effects of the patient's condition?

Failure to adequately treat rotator cuff tendonitis may necessitate significant activity modification or more aggressive surgical management such as subacromial decompression. Prolonged inflammation of the rotator cuff tendon may facilitate eventual tearing of the rotator cuff musculature.

COMPARISON

What are the distinguishing characteristics of a similar condition?

A rotator cuff tear is usually the result of repetitive microtrauma but can also result suddenly from a single traumatic event. Partial tears often occur in a younger population while complete tears more commonly occur in older individuals. The mechanism of injury is often a fall on an outstretched arm or a sudden strain applied to the shoulder during pushing or pulling activities. Diagnosis is made through MRI to identify the tear. Surgical repair of the rotator cuff is often required and may be done with arthroscopy or through a traditional open technique. The shoulder is usually protected by a sling and small abduction pillow for the first six weeks post surgery. Rehabilitation and return to full function can take upwards of six months, heavy lifting may be restricted for six to twelve months following surgery.

CLINICAL SCENARIOS

Scenario One

A 23-year-old female diagnosed with rotator cuff tendonitis is referred to physical therapy after experiencing pain while swimming the breaststroke in a competitive swim meet one week ago. The patient participates on a school swim team and a private club and practices four to six times per week. A few days after experiencing shoulder pain the patient was back in the pool, however, was unable to return to her previous training regimen.

Scenario Two

A 45-year-old male employed as a pipe fitter is referred to physical therapy after subacromial decompression. The patient is one week status post surgery and is anxious to "test" his involved shoulder. Prior to surgery the patient was placed on "light duty." It has been six months since the patient was able to perform his job without restrictions. The patient presently denies any pain in the involved shoulder.

GOLD

Scoliosis

DIAGNOSIS

What condition produces a patient's symptoms?

A patient with scoliosis presents with a lateral curvature of the spine. The curvature is usually found in the thoracic or lumbar vertebrae and can be associated with kyphosis or lordosis. The curvature of the spine may be towards the right or towards the left and rotation of the spine may or may not occur. Typically, the rotation will occur towards the convex side of the major curve.

An injury was most likely sustained to which structure?

The injury or deformity begins when the vertebrae of the spine deviate from the normal vertical position. The curvature disrupts normal alignment of the ribs and muscles and can create compensatory curves that attempt to keep the body in proper alignment. The vertebral column, rib cage, supporting ligaments, and muscles are all affected by a scoliosis of the spine.

INFERENCE

What is the most likely contributing factor in the development of this condition?

Idiopathic scoliosis, termed for its unknown etiology, accounts for the large majority of cases. Upwards of 1 in 10 children are affected by some form of scoliosis with 1 in 4 requiring treatment for the curvature. The age of onset determines the subset of classification as infantile (0 to 3), juvenile (4 to puberty), adolescent (12 for girls and 14 for boys) or adult (skeletal maturation) scoliosis. Non-structural scoliosis is a reversible curve that can change with repositioning. This type of curve is non-progressive and is usually caused by poor posture or leg length discrepancy. Structural scoliosis cannot be corrected with movement and can be caused by congenital, musculoskeletal, and neuromuscular reasons. Contributing factors of a structural curve include altered development of the spine in utero, association with neuromuscular diseases (cerebral palsy, muscular dystrophy, congenital defect of the vertebrae), and inheritance as an autosomal dominant trait. Research indicates a predisposition for scoliosis with a multifactorial etiology.

CONFIRMATION

What is the most likely clinical presentation?

A patient with a structural curve will present with asymmetries of the shoulders, scapulae, pelvis, and skinfolds. Juvenile idiopathic scoliosis is characterized by a thoracic curve with convexity towards the right. This curve may progress quickly and develop compensatory curves above and below. As the curve progresses there will be a rib hump posteriorly over the thoracic region on the convex side of the curve. The patient does not typically experience pain or other subjective symptoms until the curve has progressed. Adolescent scoliosis of greater than 30 degrees is far more common in females than males. Curves that are less than 20 degrees rarely cause a person to experience significant problems or impairments.

What laboratory or imaging studies would confirm the diagnosis?

X-rays should be taken in an anterior and lateral view with the patient standing and with the patient bending over. A device called a scoliometer can be used to measure the angle of trunk rotation. The Cobb method can be used to determine the angle of curvature. A bone scan or MRI can be used to determine and rule out conditions such as infections, neoplasms, spondylolysis, disk herniations or compression fractures.

What additional information should be obtained to confirm the diagnosis?

Physical examination allows visual inspection of the curvature and physical asymmetries. A scoliometer can assist with measurement and the examiner can determine if the curve is non-structural or structural.

EXAMINATION

What history should be documented?

Important areas to explore include past medical history, family history, medications, current health status, living environment, school activities, and social support system.

What tests/measures are most appropriate?

Aerobic capacity and endurance: assessment of vital signs at rest and with activity, perceived exertion scale

Arousal, attention, and cognition: examine mental status, learning ability, memory, motivation

Ergonomics and body mechanics: analysis of dexterity and coordination

Integumentary integrity: skin and sensation assessment

Gait, locomotion, and balance: static and dynamic balance in sitting and standing, safety during gait with/without an assistive device, analysis of wheelchair management

Joint integrity and mobility: assessment of hypermobility and hypomobility of a joint

Muscle performance: strength assessment

Orthotic, protective, and supportive devices: analysis of components of a device, analysis of movement while wearing a device

Pain: assessment of muscle soreness

Posture: analysis of resting and dynamic posture

Range of motion: active and passive range of motion

Self-care and home management: assessment of functional capacity

Scoliosis

GOLD

What additional findings are likely with this patient?

Common postural findings with scoliosis include increased spacing between the elbow and trunk during standing, leg length discrepancy, uneven shoulder and hip heights, and prominence on one side of the pelvis or breast (due to rotation of the curve). If a progressive scoliosis is untreated, the deformity can increase to an angle in excess of 60 degrees and cause pulmonary insufficiency, significant pain, impairment in lung capacity, and degenerative changes including arthritis and disk pathology. Early screening, detection, and treatment are necessary to control the curvature and avoid surgical intervention.

MANAGEMENT

What is the most effective management of this patient?

Medical management of scoliosis is based on the type and severity of the curve, patient age, and previous management. Patients with scoliosis may utilize electrical stimulation to alleviate pain and biofeedback for education with proper posture and positioning. A patient with scoliosis that is less than 25 degrees should be monitored every three months. Breathing exercises and a strengthening program for the trunk and pelvic muscles are indicated. A patient with scoliosis that ranges between 25 and 40 degrees requires a spinal orthosis and physical therapy intervention for posture, flexibility, strengthening, respiratory function, and proper utilization of the spinal orthosis. A patient with scoliosis that is greater than 40 degrees usually requires surgical spinal stabilization. One method to surgically correct scoliosis is through posterior spinal fusion and stabilization with a Harrington rod. Physical therapy intervention after surgical fusion is indicated for breathing exercises, posture, flexibility, general strengthening, and respiratory muscle strengthening.

What home care regimen should be recommended?

A home care regimen is based on the type and severity of the curve. Exercise, stretching, posture, and flexibility are important components of an exercise program.

OUTCOME

What is the likely outcome of a course of physical therapy?

Physical therapy intervention should improve a patient's condition through patient education and therapeutic exercise. Physical therapy may be indicated for implementation of a home program, pain management, posture retraining, orthotic training or following surgical stabilization.

What are the long-term effects of the patient's condition?

Prognosis for structural scoliosis is based on the age of onset and the severity of the curve. Early intervention results in the best possible outcome. Scoliosis does not usually progress significantly once bone growth is complete if the curvature remains below 40 degrees at the time of skeletal maturity. If the curvature is over 50 degrees there likely will be ongoing progression of the curve each year of life.

COMPARISON

What are the distinguishing characteristics of a similar condition?

Torticollis is a deformity of the neck that is caused by shortened or spastic sternocleidomastoid muscles. The patient presents with a bending of the neck towards the affected side and rotation of the head towards the unaffected side. Causative factors include damage to the sternocleidomastoid muscle, malpositioning in utero, spasms secondary to central nervous system impairment or psychogenic origin. Conservative treatment for acquired torticollis includes heat, traction, massage, stretching, positioning, and bracing. Surgical intervention may be indicated if conservative management fails.

CLINICAL SCENARIOS

Scenario One

An 11-year-old female is seen in physical therapy with diagnosis of a 30-degree right thoracic scoliosis. The physician has prescribed a spinal orthosis and physical therapy. The patient denies any pain, but states that she has soreness in her back. The patient is in the marching band and plays basketball. There is no past medical history and her parents are very supportive.

Scenario Two

A seven-year-old boy is referred to physical therapy with a 12-degree right thoracic scoliosis. The physical therapy prescription requests evaluation for a home exercise program. The patient has type 1 diabetes mellitus and a low I.Q. The mother is present for the evaluation and appears to be supportive.

GOLD

Spondylolisthesis - Degenerative

DIAGNOSIS

What condition produces a patient's symptoms?

Spondylolisthesis is the forward slippage of one vertebra on the vertebra below. There are several types of spondylolisthesis classified by the actual cause for the slippage. Classifications include congenital, isthmic, degenerative, post-traumatic, and pathologic spondylolisthesis. Degenerative spondylolisthesis (DS) is caused by the weakening of joints that allows for forward slippage of one vertebral segment on the one below due to degenerative changes. These changes include segmental ligamentous instability and subluxation of the hypertrophic facet joints which can result in stenosis of the spinal canal.

An injury was most likely sustained to which structure?

The most common site of DS is the L4-L5 level. The slippage causes cauda equina symptoms secondary to stenosis of the canal. It is theorized that ischemia and poor nourishment secondary to the stenosis deprives the associated spinal nerves and results in pain. The L4 nerve root is compressed in an L4-L5 spondylolisthesis. Other structures that can be irritated include the intervertebral disk, posterior and anterior longitudinal ligaments, and vertebral periosteum and bone.

INFERENCE

What is the most likely contributing factor in the development of this condition?

DS is caused by arthritis and degenerative changes in the spine. The intervertebral disk loses some of its ability to resist motion and as a result the vertebral facets increase in size and develop bone spurs to compensate. This condition can actually produce spinal stenosis and weaken the spine itself resulting in the slippage of a vertebrae. Since all structures of the spine remain intact the slippage is usually limited due to the secondary bony restraints of the spine.

CONFIRMATION

What is the most likely clinical presentation?

DS usually affects individuals over 50 years of age. It is more common with African Americans and women also have a higher incidence of occurrence than men. Back pain is a primary symptom that is said to increase with exercise, lifting overhead, prolonged standing, getting out of bed or a car, walking up stairs or an incline, and positioning in extension. The pain may be severe and radiate depending on the area of stenosis secondary to the vertebral slippage. Sensory and motor loss may be significant and follow a myotomal and/or dermatomal distribution. Most patients do not have significant neurologic deficits, however, a few do experience severe changes.

What laboratory or imaging studies would confirm the diagnosis?

Plain radiographs of the vertebral column are adequate to confirm the diagnosis of DS. CT scan or MRI may be indicated to rule out any other contributing conditions or to further assess nerve impingement.

What additional information should be obtained to confirm the diagnosis?

Physical and neurological examinations in combination with a full medical history usually provide adequate information for probable diagnosis, however, X-rays are required for definitive diagnosis of DS.

EXAMINATION

What history should be documented?

Important areas to explore include past medical history and previous testing, medications, family history, current symptoms, current health status, social history and habits, occupation, leisure activities, and social support system.

What tests/measures are most appropriate?

Arousal, attention, and cognition: examine mental status, learning ability, memory, motivation

Assistive and adaptive devices: analysis of components and safety of a device

Community and work integration: analysis of community, work, and leisure activities

Environmental, home, and work barriers: analysis of current and potential barriers or hazards

Ergonomics and body mechanics: analysis of dexterity and coordination, evaluation of proper lifting techniques

Gait, locomotion, and balance: static and dynamic balance in sitting and standing, safety during gait with/without an assistive device, Functional Ambulation Profile

Joint integrity and mobility: assessment of hyper- and hypomobility of a joint, soft tissue swelling and inflammation

Muscle performance: strength assessment

Pain: pain perception assessment scale, visual analogue scale, assessment of muscle soreness

Posture: analysis of resting and dynamic posture

Range of motion: active and passive range of motion

Self-care and home management: assessment of functional capacity

Sensory integrity: assessment of sensation

Spondylolisthesis - Degenerative

GOLD

What additional findings are likely with this patient?

A patient with DS may or may not have additional slippage of the vertebra over time. If the slippage of the vertebra worsens it does not necessarily correspond to an increase in symptoms. Symptoms may increase with or without marked degenerative changes and vice versa. A patient that does experience ongoing neurological deficits will require surgical intervention regardless of the amount of slippage.

MANAGEMENT

What is the most effective management of this patient?

Medical management of a patient diagnosed with DS should initially include education, medication, activity modification, and physical therapy intervention. Pharmacological intervention should include NSAIDs to decrease acute inflammation. Corticosteroids may be indicated for severe symptoms. Epidural steroid injections and selective nerve root injections are sometimes indicated if oral medications fail. Activity modification and rest should be instituted to further allow inflammation to subside and improve overall symptoms. Long-term bed rest, however, should be avoided. Once the acute phase has subsided physical therapy should begin. William's flexion exercises should be performed to strengthen the abdominals and reduce lumbar lordosis. Back school, modalities, postural education, and other exercises that provide core stabilization and increase flexibility should be included in the patient's program. External support such as bracing or wearing of a corset may relieve intradiscal pressure. Surgical intervention is only indicated if conservative treatment fails, the pain becomes disabling or significant neurological impairment exists. Surgical intervention usually involves decompression with or without spinal fusion.

What home care regimen should be recommended?

A patient with DS should initially take NSAIDs and decrease overall activities to allow for a reduction in the acute symptoms. Once a patient is able to tolerate physical therapy the home care regimen should include prescribed exercises to improve abdominal strength and core stabilization, flexibility exercises, and proper positioning. Goals for the home program are to alleviate pain and improve function. A patient should only modify the home program per therapist instruction.

OUTCOME

What is the likely outcome of a course of physical therapy?

The majority of patients with DS are successful with conservative treatment that may include physical therapy, home program, bracing, and use of NSAIDs as needed.

What are the long-term effects of the patient's condition?

The long-term effects of DS vary based on progression and advancement of the slipped vertebrae and/or progression of symptoms. Some patients may be able to manage pain and maintain function without any further associated pathology. If symptoms continue to progress, then surgical intervention may be required.

COMPARISON

What are the distinguishing characteristics of a similar condition?

Congenital spondylolisthesis is the slippage of one vertebra on the vertebra below due to an anomaly or defect in the fusion of the neural arch. This usually occurs in the upper sacral vertebral arches or at the L5 level. The condition is usually diagnosed during the growth spurts between 12 and 16 years of age. Patients are normally pain free prior to this point and begin to express complaints of back pain, "sciatica" pain, and other symptoms. There is a strong genetic association found in this type of spondylolisthesis.

CLINICAL SCENARIOS

Scenario One

A 65-year-old female is seen in physical therapy with a diagnosis of L5 degenerative spondylolisthesis. She complains of pain in her back that can occasionally radiate down her left leg. She resides with her husband in their two-story home and works part-time at a grocery store as a clerk. She also enjoys gardening, but has been having a difficult time with all activities in the last eight weeks secondary to pain.

Scenario Two

A 74-year-old male two weeks status post spinal fusion is examined in a nursing home. The patient was diagnosed six months ago with DS, shortly after he began to exhibit neurological symptoms. The physician prescribes physical therapy daily to improve strength and functional independence.

GOLD

Temporomandibular Joint Dysfunction

DIAGNOSIS

What condition produces a patient's symptoms?

The temporomandibular joint (TMJ) is a complex joint that is classified as a condylar, hinge, and synovial joint. The TMJ contains fibrocartilaginous surfaces and articular discs. Temporomandibular joint dysfunction (TMD) occurs due to a change in the joint structure that can cause multiple symptoms and a limitation in function. In many instances inflammation and muscle spasm surrounding the joint produces symptoms for the patient with TMD.

An injury was most likely sustained to which structure?

TMD results from injury, derangement or incongruence of the TMJ itself, intra-articular disks, and/or supporting surrounding structures. Over time the meniscus of the TMJ becomes compressed and torn allowing for the bony portion of the joint (the ball and socket) to deteriorate secondary to the grinding of bone on bone.

INFERENCE

What is the most likely contributing factor in the development of this condition?

TMD can be classified by three primary etiological factors: predisposing factors, triggering factors, and perpetuating/sustaining factors. TMD can occur secondary to multiple causative factors including injury or trauma to the joint, congenital abnormalities, internal derangement of joint structure, arthritis, dislocation, disk degeneration, metabolic conditions or stress. Risk factors include chewing on one side, eating tough food, clenching, and grinding of teeth. Habits of gum chewing and nail biting may increase the incidence of injury to the TMJ. Patients are typically between 20 to 40 years of age with a greater incidence in women. Research indicates a possible link between gender-specific hormones and the risk for TMD.

CONFIRMATION

What is the most likely clinical presentation?

A patient with TMD will present with symptoms that include pain (persistent or recurring), muscle spasm, abnormal or limited jaw motion, headache, and tinnitus. These symptoms can be unilateral or bilateral. The patient will often complain of feeling and hearing a "clicking or popping" sound with motion at the TMJ. Clinical manifestation of symptoms relates to the actual cause of the TMD.

What laboratory or imaging studies would confirm the diagnosis?

Procedures used in diagnosing TMD and its origin may include x-ray, MRI, mandibular kinesiography, CT scan, and a dental examination.

What additional information should be obtained to confirm the diagnosis?

A physical examination, upper quarter screening, TMJ loading, condyle-meniscus relationship, review of symptoms, and past medical history are all important components in the diagnosis of TMD. An occlusion examination may be indicated to evaluate a patient's bite.

EXAMINATION

What history should be documented?

Important areas to explore include past medical history, medications, family history, current symptoms, current health status, diet, social history and habits, occupation, leisure activities, and social support system.

What tests/measures are most appropriate?

Arousal, attention, and cognition: examine mental status, learning ability, memory, motivation

Community and work integration: analysis of community, work, and leisure activities

Cranial nerve integrity: assessment of muscle innervation by the cranial nerves, dermatome assessment

Integumentary integrity: skin assessment, assessment of sensation

Joint integrity and mobility: assessment of hypermobility and hypomobility of a joint, soft tissue swelling and inflammation, joint play

Muscle performance: strength assessment including mastication, tongue, and lips; upper quarter screening

Pain: pain perception assessment scale, visual analogue scale, assessment of muscle soreness

Posture: analysis of resting and dynamic posture

Range of motion: active and passive range of motion

Self-care and home management: assessment of functional capacity

Ventilation, respiration, and circulation: breathing patterns, respiratory muscle strength, accessory muscle utilization

Temporomandibular Joint Dysfunction

GOLD

What additional findings are likely with this patient?

TMD produces a general clinical presentation that includes pain, headache, muscle spasms, and tinnitus. Specific findings result from the specific cause of the TMD. Other findings can include popping and clicking when opening the mandible, locking of the TMJ, restriction of movement of the unaffected side, and/or pulling of the mandible towards the affected side. Common underlying causes include arthritis, fracture, congenital abnormalities, dislocations, and tension-relieving habits (chewing gum, bruxism, clenching or grinding the teeth).

MANAGEMENT

What is the most effective management of this patient?

Medical management of TMD may include pharmacological intervention, the use of splinting, physical therapy treatment, and possible surgical intervention. Pharmacological treatment of TMD may include analgesics, NSAIDs, muscle relaxants, and antianxiety medications. A patient may also benefit from a splint to assist with realignment of the joint and a guard or bite plate to maintain proper positioning and avoid grinding of the teeth throughout the night. Specific physical therapy intervention is based on the exact etiology of the TMD. Generally, physical therapy intervention includes patient education regarding habits such as nail biting, posture retraining, the use of modalities such as moist heat, ice, biofeedback, ultrasound, electrostimulation, TENS, and massage. Soft tissue manipulation, joint mobilization, ROM, stretching, occlusal appliance prescription, and relaxation techniques are also appropriate. If conservative treatment fails or the exact etiology warrants surgical intervention, the patient may require a condylectomy, osteotomy, arthrotomy, arthroscopy, reduction of subluxation or joint debridement.

What home care regimen should be recommended?

A home care regimen for a patient with TMD should include relaxation techniques, self-stretching, posture retraining exercises, and progressive ROM. A patient should avoid all foods and activities (such as gum chewing) that aggravate and stress the TMJ. The patient should continue with the proper use of an occlusal appliance if indicated. In order to maintain progress the patient must have ongoing consistency with the home program.

OUTCOME

What is the likely outcome of a course of physical therapy?

Physical therapy intervention should improve a patient's condition and decrease the symptoms of the TMD. Physical therapy is usually conducted on an outpatient basis with focus on maximizing function and alleviating pain.

What are the long-term effects of the patient's condition?

A patient previously diagnosed with TMD is at an increased risk of recurrence, however, with successful management, ongoing compliance with the home program, and use of an indicated appliance, the patient may not have any long-term effects. If conservative management fails the patient may require surgical intervention for the underlying cause in order to alleviate the TMD.

COMPARISON

What are the distinguishing characteristics of a similar condition?

Myofascial pain dysfunction (MPD) syndrome is a nonarticular disorder that affects the area surrounding the TMJ, however, symptoms are produced secondary to muscle spasm. MPD occurs more in females and can be of psychophysiologic origin. Habits such as grinding and jaw clenching increase tension in the muscles of mastication and create spasm. MPD can mimic the symptoms of TMD, however, differential diagnosis will rule out true TMJ involvement.

CLINICAL SCENARIOS

Scenario One

A 12-year-old female is referred to physical therapy with a diagnosis of TMD secondary to condylar hyperplasia. The patient required a condylectomy with post-operative orders for physical therapy. The female is motivated and she has very supportive parents.

Scenario Two

A 30-year-old male is referred to physical therapy with a diagnosis of TMD. The physician referral notes inflammation, muscle spasm, and poor posture. The patient states that he will feel clicking when he eats certain foods. The patient has a history of childhood scoliosis that was controlled with exercise and short-term bracing. The patient is a stockbroker and spends a great deal of time talking on the phone.

GOLD

Torticollis - Congenital

DIAGNOSIS

What condition produces a patient's symptoms?

Congenital torticollis is a condition that causes the neck to involuntarily unilaterally contract to one side secondary to contraction of the sternocleidomastoid muscle. The head is laterally flexed toward the contracted muscle, the chin faces the opposite direction, and there may be facial asymmetries. The word torticollis means twisted neck. It is a disease, but also a symptom of many conditions.

An injury was most likely sustained to which structure?

Congenital torticollis is not usually seen immediately at birth. Muscle injury may be due to birth trauma, breech position in utero or other forms of intrauterine malpositioning. Infants born with torticollis appear healthy at delivery, however, over days or weeks they develop swelling over the injured sternocleidomastoid.

INFERENCE

What is the most likely contributing factor in the development of this condition?

The exact etiology of congenital torticollis is unknown, however, congenital torticollis may be caused by local trauma to the soft tissues of the neck just before or during delivery. The most common hypothesis is that birth trauma with resultant hematoma formation results in muscular contracture. Typically, children with congenital torticollis have had breech or difficult forceps delivery. The fibrosis that develops in the muscle may be due to venous occlusion and pressure on the neck in the birth canal secondary to skull and neck position. Another theory includes malpositioning in utero resulting in intrauterine compartment syndrome.

CONFIRMATION

What is the most likely clinical presentation?

The patient's head is laterally flexed towards the shortened muscle's side and the chin is pointed toward the opposite shoulder. Intermittent painful spasms of the sternocleidomastoid, trapezius, and other neck muscles may occur. The neck movements vary from jerky to smooth. The first sign may be a firm nontender enlargement of the sternocleidomastoid muscle visible at birth or within the infant's first few weeks of life. This mass, which is usually localized near the clavicular attachment of the sternocleidomastoid muscle, enlarges during the first few weeks of life, and then gradually decreases in size. Usually, the mass disappears by the sixth month of life and the only remaining clinical finding is the contracture of the sternocleidomastoid muscle that creates the torticollis posturing.

What laboratory or imaging studies would confirm the diagnosis?

Cervical spine x-rays are used to assess potential fracture or subluxation. A CT scan or MRI of the cervical spine can identify the presence of a potential neck mass. An electromyography (EMG) study may be useful in defining the degree of muscle or nerve involvement.

What additional information should be obtained to confirm the diagnosis?

The presence of the mass over the sternocleidomastoid along with the classic posturing will confirm the presence of congenital torticollis.

EXAMINATION

What history should be documented?

Important areas to explore include history of labor and delivery, family history, medications, current health status, and social support system.

What tests/measures are most appropriate?

Arousal, attention, and cognition: examine level of consciousness and alertness

Cranial nerve integrity: assessment of muscle innervation by the cranial nerves, dermatome assessment

Environmental, home, and work barriers: analysis of current and potential barriers or hazards in the home

Integumentary integrity: skin assessment, assessment of sensation

Joint integrity and mobility: assessment of hyper- and hypomobility of a joint, soft tissue swelling and inflammation

Motor function: motor assessment scales, coordination, Barthel Index, Bayley Scale of Infant Development, Denver II Scale, Neonatal Behavioral Assessment, Alberta Infant Motor Scale

Neuromotor development and sensory integration: analysis of reflex movement patterns, assessment of involuntary movements, sensory integration tests

Posture: analysis of resting and dynamic posture

Range of motion: active and passive range of motion

Reflex integrity: assessment of deep tendon and pathological reflexes (e.g., Babinski, ATNR)

Torticollis - Congenital

GOLD

What additional findings are likely with this patient?

Some children with congenital torticollis have congenital dysplasia of the hips. In many instances, these infants will also present with facial asymmetries and plagiocephaly or flattening of the skull.

MANAGEMENT

What is the most effective management of this patient?

Congenital torticollis is usually treated with non-operative intervention for 12-24 months before considering surgical intervention. Pharmacological intervention may include nonsteroidal anti-inflammatory drugs (NSAIDs), benzodiazepines and other muscle relaxants, anticholinergics, and local intramuscular injections of botulinum toxin or phenol. Physical therapy includes family/caregiver education and teaching, passive stretching exercises to the sternocleidomastoid and upper trapezius muscles, massage, local heat, analgesics, sensory biofeedback, and transcutaneous electrical nerve stimulation (TENS). Active range of motion with subsequent strengthening is also indicated to correct the infant's positioning of their head. Family training is extremely beneficial if there is consistency with handling and proper positioning during feeding and sleeping in order to promote stretch and active motion of the sternocleidomastoid muscle. If conservative treatment fails, surgical intervention will consist of unipolar sternocleidomastoid release, bipolar sternocleidomastoid release or selective denervation. Physical therapy is indicated after surgery and should include manual stretching of the neck to maintain the overcorrected position. Manual stretching should be continued three times daily for 3-6 months. A cervical collar may be used for the first 6-12 weeks after surgery.

What home care regimen should be recommended?

The family must continue with the stretching program and the correct handling techniques that are recommended by the therapist. The family will need to include proper positioning for the infant's sleep and alert times in order to maximize the benefits of the intervention.

OUTCOME

What is the likely outcome of a course of physical therapy?

Studies indicate that the large majority of patients with congenital torticollis respond to conservative treatment and passive stretching within the first year of life. The best results for conservative management require the child to have had conservative treatment prior to the age of one. If surgical intervention is required, physical therapy will be required after surgery with an expected positive outcome for the patient.

What are the long-term effects of the patient's condition?

If a child is left untreated, congenital torticollis could have detrimental effects including the impairment of normal growth and development. The vast majority of children with congenital torticollis that receive conservative management are expected to fully recover and live a normal life.

COMPARISON

What are the distinguishing characteristics of a similar condition?

Torticollis can also be acquired at an older age and presents in different forms. Acute wryneck is a term to describe a common type of torticollis that develops overnight without provocation. It is a self-limiting process and usually the symptoms subside within one to two weeks. Infectious torticollis may occur when the surrounding tissues become infected such as with a retropharyngeal abscess, nasopharyngeal abscess, tonsillitis, and sinusitis.

CLINICAL SCENARIOS

Scenario One

A three-week-old infant is referred to outpatient physical therapy with a moderate right torticollis. There is a mass felt over the sternocleidomastoid muscle belly. The parents are concerned with this diagnosis and are very eager to assist with the infant's program. The mother is at home during the day and they have three other children at home.

Scenario Two

A child is referred to physical therapy status post unipolar sternocleidomastoid release two weeks ago. The child is 18 months old and was unsuccessful with conservative treatment for a significant left torticollis. The child resides with his foster mother in a studio apartment. The mother works full-time and the child participates in full-time daycare.

GOLD

Total Hip Arthroplasty

DIAGNOSIS

What condition produces a patient's symptoms?

A total hip arthroplasty (THA) may be warranted secondary to progressive and severe osteoarthritis or rheumatoid arthritis in the hip joint, developmental dysplasia of the hip, tumors, failed reconstruction of the hip or other hip conditions that produce incapacitating pain and disability. A THA may also be required secondary to trauma, avascular necrosis or a nonunion fracture.

An injury was most likely sustained to which structure?

Arthritis causes the hip joint to undergo a degenerative process including destruction of articular cartilage that results in bone-to-bone contact. Degenerative changes are usually apparent in both the acetabulum and the femoral head requiring a THA, however, if the acetabulum does not exhibit degenerative changes then only the femoral head will be replaced in a hemiarthroplasty procedure.

INFERENCE

What is the most likely contributing factor in the development of this condition?

Intra-articular disease or the destruction of articular cartilage may come from arthritis, repetitive microtrauma, obesity, nutritional imbalances, falls or abnormal joint mechanics. Indications for THA include osteoarthritis, rheumatoid arthritis, avascular necrosis, developmental dysplasia, osteomyelitis, failed fixation of a fracture, ankylosing spondylitis, and failed conservative management.

CONFIRMATION

What is the most likely clinical presentation?

A patient that requires a THA will present with decreased range of motion, impaired mobility skills, and persistent pain that increases with motion and weight bearing. The patient is usually over 55 years of age and has experienced consistent pain that is not relieved through conservative measures and limits the patient's functional mobility on a consistent basis.

What laboratory or imaging studies would confirm the diagnosis?

X-ray, computed tomography, and magnetic resonance imaging procedures may be used to view the integrity of the joint. These procedures are also used to rule out a fracture or a tumor.

What additional information should be obtained to confirm the diagnosis?

Patient history, current functional status, and level of pain and disability are important factors in determining the need for surgical intervention. A standardized pain assessment scale and the Arthritis Impact Measurement tool may be used to establish an objective baseline. Relative or absolute contraindications must be considered prior to the recommendation for a THA. Contraindications may include but are not limited to active infection, severe obesity, arterial insufficiency, neuromuscular disease, and certain mental illness.

EXAMINATION

What history should be documented?

Important areas to explore include past medical history, family history, medications, current symptoms, current health status, living environment, social history and habits, occupation, and social support system.

What tests/measures are most appropriate?

Aerobic capacity and endurance: assessment of vital signs at rest and with activity, perceived exertion scale
Anthropometric characteristics: hip circumferential measurements, leg length measurements
Arousal, attention, and cognition: examine mental status, learning ability, memory, motivation
Assistive and adaptive devices: analysis of components and safety of a device
Environmental, home, and work barriers: analysis of current and potential barriers or hazards
Gait, locomotion, and balance: safety during gait with/without an assistive device, Functional Ambulation Profile
Joint integrity and mobility: soft tissue swelling and inflammation
Muscle performance: strength assessment, assessment of active movement
Pain: pain perception assessment scale
Range of motion: active and passive range of motion
Self-care and home assessment: assessment of functional capacity, Barthel Index
Sensory integrity: assessment of sensation

What additional findings are likely with this patient?

A patient that requires a THA may also have arthritis in other areas of the body. The patient may present with low endurance and may be deconditioned secondary to inactivity from the effects of arthritis. Post-surgical complications may include nerve injury, vascular damage, dislocation, pulmonary embolism, myocardial infarction, and CVA. The prosthesis is also at risk for loosening, infection, heterotopic ossification, and fracture.

MANAGEMENT

What is the most effective management of this patient?

Medical management includes choosing a surgical approach that meets the patient's needs and level of activity. A THA that utilizes a posterolateral approach allows the abductor muscles to remain intact, however, there may be a higher incidence of post-operative joint instability due to the interruption of the posterior capsule. This type of surgical approach requires a patient to avoid excessive hip flexion greater than 90 degrees, hip adduction, and hip medial rotation. A patient with a THA that utilizes an anterolateral approach should avoid extension of the hip, lateral rotation, and adduction. A direct lateral approach leaves the posterior portion of the gluteus medius attached to the greater trochanter and the posterior capsule left intact. This method is preferred for patients that may be noncompliant in order to avoid posterior dislocation. Pharmacological intervention status post THA will include anticoagulant therapy and pain medication. The patient's post-operative care includes hip precautions, use of an abduction pillow (with posterolateral approach), initiation of hip protocol exercises, and physical therapy intervention. The hip protocol exercises usually include ankle pumps, quadriceps sets, gluteal sets, heel slides, and isometric abduction. Physical therapy should emphasize patient education regarding hip precautions and weight bearing status, scar management, and soft tissue mobilization. At the time of hospital discharge the patient should be able to extend the hip to neutral and flex the hip to 90 degrees. A cemented hip replacement usually allows for partial weight bearing initially and a noncemented hip replacement requires toe touch weight bearing for up to six weeks. Physical therapy encourages early ambulation training in order to avoid deconditioning and the risk of deep vein thrombosis. A patient must practice all mobility skills using the proper hip precautions. Outpatient physical therapy may be indicated to assist with progression to a cane.

What home care regimen should be recommended?

The patient should be instructed in a home care regimen that includes range of motion, strengthening, and progressive ambulation. The patient must adhere to the hip precaution guidelines for a minimum of three months or until a physician determines that the hip demonstrates adequate stability.

OUTCOME

What is the likely outcome of a course of physical therapy?

A patient status post THA will benefit from physical therapy and should attain an improved functional outcome. The patient should have diminished to no pain, increased strength and endurance, and improved mobility within six to eight weeks after surgery.

What are the long-term effects of the patient's condition?

A THA is a highly successful surgical procedure. Hip prostheses can last more than 20 years, though some patients may require a subsequent replacement. Studies indicate pain relief and improved function with good to excellent results in the large majority of the patients at 15 to 20 years post THA. Validated scoring systems such as the Harris Hip Scoring System or the Special Surgery Rating system are measures used to determine the quality of life after the THA.

COMPARISON

What are the distinguishing characteristics of a similar condition?

A hemiarthroplasty of the hip is a replacement of the femoral head due to a subcapital fracture of the femur or degeneration of the femoral head. This type of surgical intervention is sometimes used as an alternative to a THA for elderly patients that sustain a hip fracture or patients that have a shortened expected lifespan.

CLINICAL SCENARIOS

Scenario One

A patient is seen in physical therapy after THA surgery. The surgeon performed an anterolateral approach and used a noncemented prosthesis. The patient is mildly obese and has a lengthy cardiac history. The patient has osteoarthritis and had progressive pain and difficulty with mobility prior to surgery. The patient complains of soreness in the hip and is anxious to get home.

Scenario Two

A 75-year-old male is seen in physical therapy status post reduction of a dislocated right hip prosthesis. The patient had a THA three weeks ago and dislocated the hip two days ago while bending over to tie his shoes. The patient is currently using a walker for mobility and is toe touch weight bearing. The patient resides alone in a garden apartment and does not have any family in the area.

GOLD

Total Knee Arthroplasty

DIAGNOSIS

What condition produces a patient's symptoms?

A total knee arthroplasty (TKA) may be warranted secondary to progressive and disabling pain within the knee joint. The pain is most often due to severe degenerative osteoarthritic destruction and deformity that can occur within the knee.

An injury was most likely sustained to which structure?

Arthritis causes the knee joint to undergo a degenerative process that includes destruction of articular cartilage and resultant bone-to-bone contact within the joint. The knee presents with decreased joint space and osteophyte formation. Injury occurs to the femoral condyles, tibial articulating surface, and the dorsal side of the patella.

INFERENCE

What is the most likely contributing factor in the development of this condition?

The destruction of articular cartilage secondary to osteoarthritis is the most common indication for a TKA. A patient with a history of participation in high-impact sports or has experienced trauma to the knee is at a higher risk for arthritis and subsequent TKA. Obesity, varus/valgus deformity, previous mechanical derangement, infection, rheumatoid arthritis, hemophilia, crystal deposition diseases, avascular necrosis or bone dysplasia at the knee are some other contributing factors that may warrant a TKA.

CONFIRMATION

What is the most likely clinical presentation?

A patient that requires a TKA will present with severe knee pain that worsens with motion and weight bearing, impaired range of motion, possible deformity of the knee, and impaired mobility skills. Night pain is common and may include localized or diffuse pain. Other symptoms may include stiffness, swelling, locking, and giving way of the affected knee. Patients often attempt conservative treatment measures to address the condition with only limited success.

What laboratory or imaging studies would confirm the diagnosis?

X-ray, computed tomography, and magnetic resonance imaging are used to determine the extent of deterioration and bony abnormalities within the knee joint. Radiographic images can be utilized post-operatively to ensure proper fit and obtain baseline information.

What additional information should be obtained to confirm the diagnosis?

Patient history, current functional status, and level of pain and disability are important factors in determining the need for surgical intervention. A pain assessment scale and the Arthritis Impact Measurement tool may be used to establish an objective baseline.

EXAMINATION

What history should be documented?

Important areas to explore include past medical history, family history, medications, current symptoms, living environment, social history and habits, occupation, current functional status, and social support system.

What tests/measures are most appropriate?

Aerobic capacity and endurance: assessment of vital signs at rest and with activity, perceived exertion scale

Anthropometric characteristics: knee circumferential measurements

Arousal, attention, and cognition: examine mental status, learning ability, memory, motivation

Assistive and adaptive devices: analysis of components and safety of a device

Environmental, home, and work barriers: analysis of current and potential barriers or hazards

Gait, locomotion, and balance: safety during gait/stairs with device, Functional Ambulation Profile

Joint integrity and mobility: soft tissue swelling and inflammation

Muscle performance: strength/active movement assessment

Pain: pain perception assessment scale

Range of motion: active and passive range of motion

Self-care and home assessment: assessment of functional capacity, Barthel Index

Sensory integrity: assessment of sensation

What additional findings are likely with this patient?

A patient that requires TKA may have arthritis in other joints, previous replacement surgeries or previous trauma to the knee joint. Patients with significant osteoarthritis and severe pain may exhibit sleep disorders or depression due to the disease process. Relative or absolute contraindications must be considered prior to the recommendation for a TKA. Contraindications may include but are not limited to active infection of the knee, severe obesity, significant genu recurvatum, arterial insufficiency, neuropathic joint, and certain mental illnesses. Post-surgical complications after a TKA include infection, vascular damage, patellofemoral instability, fracture surrounding the prosthesis, pulmonary embolism, nerve damage, loosening of the prosthesis, and arthrofibrosis.

Total Knee Arthroplasty

GOLD

MANAGEMENT

What is the most effective management of this patient?

Medical management of a patient requiring a TKA includes choosing of the appropriate surgical procedure based on the patient's symptoms and level of activity. Pharmacological intervention status post TKA will require anticoagulant therapy and pain medications. The patient's post-operative care includes a knee immobilizer, elevation of the limb, cryotherapy, intermittent range of motion using a continuous passive motion (CPM) machine, and initiation of knee protocol exercises. A cemented knee prosthesis allows for either partial weight bearing or weight bearing as tolerated post surgery based on the individual physician's discretion. A noncemented knee prosthesis requires toe touch weight bearing for up to six weeks to allow for the bone to grow and affix to the prosthesis. Physical therapy should focus on mobility training with the proper weight bearing status using an appropriate assistive device. Early ambulation training is encouraged in order to avoid deconditioning and the risk of deep vein thrombosis. Physical therapy intervention should emphasize ankle pumps, quad sets, and hamstrings sets as well as range of motion and stretching. A goal of 90 degrees of knee flexion and 0 degrees knee extension is often established prior to discharge from the hospital or rehabilitation facility. The following precautions should be used for several months after surgery to avoid excessive stress to the knee: avoid squatting, avoid quick pivoting, do not use pillows under the knee while in bed, and avoid low seating. Outpatient therapy may be recommended to progress the patient from an assistive device. Once the physician progresses the patient to weight bearing as tolerated, physical therapy intervention should include strengthening with closed-chain exercises and functional activities.

What home care regimen should be recommended?

A home care regimen would typically include range of motion, strengthening, and progressive ambulation exercises. The patient must adhere to precautions, use of an immobilizer, and proper weight bearing status until a physician determines that the knee joint demonstrates adequate stability.

OUTCOME

What is the likely outcome of a course of physical therapy?

A patient status post TKA will benefit from physical therapy and should attain an improved functional capacity. The patient should experience relief of pain that will allow for a full return to previous functional activities within eight to twelve weeks after surgery depending on a cemented or noncemented prosthesis and potential complications that were encountered.

What are the long-term effects of the patient's condition?

A TKA is a highly successful surgical procedure that should significantly reduce pain and increase function. After finishing a rehabilitation protocol, a patient may have only minor limitations in knee range of motion. A knee replacement may loosen over time and require revision, however, knee prostheses can last more than 20 years.

COMPARISON

What are the distinguishing characteristics of a similar condition?

A patellectomy (surgical removal of the patella) is a surgical procedure that is indicated for a comminuted fracture of the patella that cannot be repaired with internal fixation. A patellectomy can include the entire patella or just the inferior or superior pole of the patella. The retinaculum and extensor mechanism are repaired with the surgical procedure and the patient is immobilized for six to eight weeks. Once rehabilitation is initiated the patient starts with range of motion and closed-chain exercises.

CLINICAL SCENARIOS

Scenario One

An 80-year-old female in an acute care hospital is two days status post left TKA. The patient presents with partial hearing loss and moderate dementia. The patient's past medical history includes a right CVA with no residual impairment and hypertension that is controlled by medication. The patient resides with her sister in a ranch style home with three steps to enter.

Scenario Two

A 49-year-old male is referred to outpatient physical therapy seven weeks after surgery. The patient received a noncemented knee prosthesis and has recently advanced to weight bearing as tolerated. The patient's range of motion in the involved knee is 10-85 degrees. The patient is otherwise independent with axillary crutches. No significant past medical history is noted.

GOLD

Total Shoulder Arthroplasty

DIAGNOSIS

What condition produces a patient's symptoms?

A patient that is a candidate for a total shoulder arthroplasty (TSA) will have severe pain and impaired shoulder motion due to deterioration of the glenohumeral joint. These candidates have undergone conservative treatment measures that have failed to improve their condition.

An injury was most likely sustained to which structure?

TSA candidates will have irreparable damage, deterioration, and destruction to the humeral head and the glenoid fossa within the shoulder complex. The joint surfaces are severely damaged or destroyed by wear and tear, inflammation, injury or previous surgery.

INFERENCE

What is the most likely contributing factor in the development of this condition?

Indications for a TSA include severe glenohumeral degenerative joint disease, pain and limited range of motion secondary to osteoarthritis, rheumatoid arthritis, avascular necrosis, fracture or rotator cuff arthropathy. Other patients that may require a TSA would include a patient with a bone tumor, Paget's disease or with recurrent dislocations. A patient will be considered for TSA if conservative treatment of the underlying cause fails.

CONFIRMATION

What is the most likely clinical presentation?

A patient will exhibit impaired range of motion at the shoulder, may lack independence with functional mobility and ADLs, and will experience severe pain. It is this unremitting pain (with failed conservative treatment) that is the primary indication for the TSA. A TSA performed secondary to arthritis is usually performed on patients between 55 and 70 years of age while TSA performed secondary to irreparable damage from dislocation or avascular necrosis is usually performed on patients between 40 and 50 years of age.

What laboratory or imaging studies would confirm the diagnosis?

X-ray will reveal the level of degeneration within the shoulder complex. MRI or CT scan will allow the physician to assess the integrity of the rotator cuff and deltoid muscles surrounding the joint as well as the overall integrity of the shoulder complex.

What additional information should be obtained to confirm the diagnosis?

A full medical history along with a physical examination is a key component that is required in determining if a patient is a candidate for a TSA. The patient must possess motivation, realistic expectations, and appropriate goals regarding outcome.

EXAMINATION

What history should be documented?

Important areas to explore include past medical and family history, medication, current symptoms, surgical precautions/contraindications, rehabilitation protocol, social history and habits, occupation, leisure activities, and social support system.

What tests/measures are most appropriate?

Aerobic capacity and endurance: assessment of vital signs at rest and with activity

Anthropometric characteristics: circumferential measurements of the affected upper extremity

Arousal, attention, and cognition: examine mental status, learning ability, memory, motivation

Community and work integration: analysis of community, work, and leisure activities

Environmental, home, and work barriers: analysis of current and potential barriers or hazards

Integumentary integrity: skin assessment, assessment of sensation

Joint integrity and mobility: assessment of hypermobility and hypomobility of a joint, soft tissue swelling and inflammation

Muscle performance: strength assessment except for surgical extremity

Pain: pain perception assessment scale, visual analogue scale, assessment of muscle soreness

Range of motion: passive range of motion within limits of physician protocol for involved shoulder, active and passive range of motion for all other extremities

Self-care and home management: assessment of functional capacity, Functional Independence Measure (FIM)

Sensory integrity: assessment of proprioception and kinesthesia

Total Shoulder Arthroplasty

GOLD

What additional findings are likely with this patient?

Surgical complications post TSA include mechanical loosening of the prosthesis, instability, rotator cuff tear, implant failure, heterotopic ossification and intraoperative fracture. Risk for complication is dependent on the type of prosthesis (unconstrained, semiconstrained, constrained), surgical skill in reproducing proper alignment, use of cemented prosthesis versus press-fit prosthesis, and integrity of rotator cuff musculature.

MANAGEMENT

What is the most effective management of this patient?

A patient status post TSA will remain hospitalized for an average of two to five days. Medical management of the patient will rely on a team approach including nursing, physician services, and rehabilitation therapies. The success of the TSA will rely on the style of the implant, the quality of the soft tissue and bone, and the rehabilitation program. A CPM may be prescribed by the surgeon for use during the patient's hospitalization. Pharmacological intervention includes anticoagulation and pain medications. Physical therapy is initiated the day after surgery and should follow the shoulder rehabilitation protocol designed by the surgeon. The shoulder usually remains immobilized using a sling during initial rehabilitation. The Neer shoulder protocol advocates initiating isometric shoulder exercises approximately three weeks after surgery and active shoulder exercises approximately six weeks after surgery. PROM and AAROM are indicated but AROM at the shoulder is contraindicated during the first phase of rehabilitation. Physical therapy intervention includes pain management, prevention of adhesions, functional activities, PROM/AAROM/AROM, therapeutic exercise, edema management, patient education in self-ROM and wand/pendulum exercises, and the use of modalities.

What home care regimen should be recommended?

The home care regimen should include a range of motion and therapeutic exercise program that follows the surgeon's shoulder rehabilitation protocol. During initial recovery, pendulum and wand exercises are appropriate as well as self-ROM. A patient must not perform any form of medial rotation or lateral rotation beyond 35 to 40 degrees during the first two to three weeks post surgery. Controlled motion and return to functional activity are incorporated into the home program as directed by the physician protocol. A patient must also continue to manage edema and follow other physician orders regarding precautions.

OUTCOME

What is the likely outcome of a course of physical therapy?

The goal of a TSA is to relieve pain and regain functional motion. Physical therapy should assist the patient to meet these goals unless hindered by post-surgical or other complications.

What are the long-term effects of the patient's condition?

Since the shoulder is a non-weight bearing joint there is a longer life expectancy for the prosthesis than for the knee or hip. There is a high success rate for long-term results with a TSA. Patients should avoid activities such as heavy lifting, chopping wood or contact sports since these can increase the risk of fracture, loosening of the joint replacement or rotator cuff tear.

COMPARISON

What are the distinguishing characteristics of a similar condition?

A shoulder hemiarthroplasty is a similar surgery that involves the replacement of the head and neck of the humerus leaving the glenoid fossa of the scapula intact. This surgery is indicated when the humeral head has deteriorated or fractured without healing. This procedure may also be performed if the patient does not have enough bone density to support the glenoid component or when there are significant rotator cuff deficiencies that exist.

CLINICAL SCENARIOS

Scenario One

A 60-year-old female is 14 days status post left TSA and is currently attending outpatient therapy three days per week. The patient's rehabilitation is complicated by right upper extremity paralysis secondary to a CVA two years ago. The patient is motivated, cooperative, and does not have any residual cognitive deficits.

Scenario Two

A 58-year-old male is one-month status post TSA and has been attending outpatient therapy three days per week. His wife states that he complains of significant pain during his home exercise program. He appears to be progressing otherwise. He has no significant medical history other than the rheumatoid arthritis that created the need for the TSA.

GOLD

Transfemoral Amputation due to Osteosarcoma

DIAGNOSIS

What condition produces a patient's symptoms?

Osteosarcoma (osteogenic sarcoma) is the second most common primary bone tumor. Osteosarcoma is a highly malignant cancer that begins in the medullary cavity of a bone and leads to the formation of a mass. It usually affects bones with an active growth phase such as the femur or tibia and is often located in the metaphysis. Amputation may be necessary to remove the tumor and surrounding tissues to avoid metastatic disease.

An injury was most likely sustained to which structure?

The cancer cells are found in osteoblasts within the primitive mesenchymal cells of the medullary cavity of a bone. The cancer rapidly proliferates, replaces normal bone, and causes tissue destruction. Osteosarcoma will also metastasize to the lungs very early in the disease process.

INFERENCE

What is the most likely contributing factor in the development of this condition?

Osteosarcomas can occur as a primary or secondary cancer and the etiology remains unknown. This form of tumor primarily affects young children (especially males), adolescents, and young adults under 30 years of age. A peak time for incidence is during a growth spurt as an adolescent. Risk factors associated with secondary osteosarcoma include Paget's disease, osteoblastoma, giant cell tumor or chronic osteomyelitis. Environmental and genetic factors have been associated with the disease. In many instances amputation is required to cease the disease process.

CONFIRMATION

What is the most likely clinical presentation?

Osteosarcoma can be found most often in the long bones especially at the site of the most active epiphyseal growth plate, the distal femur, proximal tibia, proximal humerus and pelvis. The knee region accounts for approximately 50% of osteosarcomas. Patients that require amputation secondary to an osteosarcoma will present with a mass often found in the tibia or femur. The most common symptoms of osteosarcoma are pain and swelling within the extremity. Pain may worsen at night or with exercise and a lump may develop in the extremity sometime after the onset of pain. The osteosarcoma may weaken the involved extremity leading to a fracture. In some cases, a fracture may be the first sign of the osteosarcoma. Metastases appear in the lungs early in 90% of the cases.

What laboratory or imaging studies would confirm the diagnosis?

X-ray, MRI, and scintigraphy allow the physician to determine the presence, location, and size of a tumor. The "Codman's triangle" can be seen on x-ray indicating reactive bone at the site where the periosteum has been elevated by the neoplasm. Definitive diagnosis for an osteosarcoma is made through tissue biopsy of the tumor.

What additional information should be obtained to confirm the diagnosis?

Diagnosis of osteosarcoma is confirmed solely through biopsy. The course of treatment and the need for surgical amputation is determined by the size, location of the tumor, and progression of the malignancy.

EXAMINATION

What history should be documented?

Important areas to explore include past medical history, medications, family history, current symptoms and health status, social history and habits, occupation, leisure activities, and social support system.

What tests/measures are most appropriate?

Aerobic capacity and endurance: assessment of vital signs at rest and with activity, auscultation of the lungs, palpation of pulses

Anthropometric characteristics: residual limb circumferential measurements, length of limb

Arousal, attention, and cognition: examine mental status, learning ability, memory, motivation

Assistive and adaptive devices: analysis of components and safety of a device

Community and work integration: analysis of community, work, and leisure activities

Gait, locomotion, and balance: analysis of wheelchair mobility, static and dynamic balance in sitting and standing, safety during gait with an assistive device

Integumentary integrity: skin assessment, assessment of sensation, temperature of limb

Muscle performance: strength and tone assessment

Pain: phantom pain, pain perception assessment scale

Prosthetic requirements: analysis and safety of the prosthesis; alignment, efficiency, and fit of the prosthesis with the residual limb

Range of motion: active and passive range of motion

Self-care and home management: assessment of functional capacity, Barthel Index, Functional Independence Measure (FIM)

Sensory integrity: proprioception and kinesthesia

Transfemoral Amputation due to Osteosarcoma

GOLD

What additional findings are likely with this patient?

A patient status post transfemoral amputation secondary to an osteosarcoma may present with fatigue, loss of balance, phantom pain or sensation, hypersensitivity of the residual limb, and psychological issues regarding the loss of the limb. The patient may also have associated symptoms from chemotherapy that can include anemia, abnormal bleeding, infection, and kidney impairment. The presence of these findings can have a negative influence on a patient's ability to utilize a prosthesis.

MANAGEMENT

What is the most effective management of this patient?

Medical management will focus on adjunctive therapies to treat the osteosarcoma. Pharmacological intervention may include pain medication and other medication to deter effects from cancer treatment. Physical and occupational therapies should begin immediately after the transfemoral amputation. Preprosthetic intervention should focus on range of motion, positioning, strengthening, desensitization, residual limb wrapping, functional mobility, gait training, and patient education for care of the residual limb. Patients with a transfemoral amputation should lie prone for a period of time each day to prevent a hip flexion contracture. Modalities may be used to improve range of motion and decrease pain. Serial casting may be indicated if a contracture develops. Without complication, the patient should be able to return home with support and receive short-term physical therapy for prosthetic training.

What home care regimen should be recommended?

A home care regimen for a patient status post transfemoral amputation should include limb desensitization, stretching, proper positioning, and prone lying. The patient must be independent with residual limb care, skin inspection, and proper wrapping. Endurance activities, strengthening, and mobility with an assistive device are necessary as a precursor to prosthetic training.

OUTCOME

What is the likely outcome of a course of physical therapy?

Physical therapy is necessary for both preprosthetic and prosthetic training. A patient should be able to achieve the established goals and function with a prosthesis for all mobility including ambulation, balance, transfers, and stair activities. The general health, cognition, motivation, and social support system of the patient will influence the patient's functional outcome.

What are the long-term effects of the patient's condition?

The transfemoral amputation should not permanently impair the patient's independence with mobility, self-care or ambulation using a prosthesis. The patient's long-term outcome is dependent on the status of the cancer.

COMPARISON

What are the distinguishing characteristics of a similar condition?

Ewing's sarcoma is a malignant nonosteogenic primary bone tumor that infiltrates the bone marrow and usually affects children and adolescents under 20 years of age. A patient will present with pain of increasing severity, swelling, and fever. This tumor is not found consistently in a specific location within the bone and is extremely malignant with a high frequency of metastases. Ewing's sarcoma requires aggressive treatment that may include amputation and adjunctive chemotherapy.

CLINICAL SCENARIOS

Scenario One

A 10-year-old female is seen in physical therapy after a right transfemoral amputation. The patient was diagnosed with osteosarcoma four months ago. The patient is in good spirits and is anxious to receive "a new leg" and begin walking. Her parents are supportive and are eager to assist her during rehabilitation.

Scenario Two

A 16-year-old male is seen for the first time in physical therapy since a left transfemoral amputation. The boy states that his leg had bothered him for a few weeks and the pain got worse each day. He also stated that he was told that the cancer was now also found in his lungs. He wants to start an exercise program so that he will be ready for his prosthesis when his residual limb heals.

GOLD

Transtibial Amputation due to Arteriosclerosis Obliterans

DIAGNOSIS

What condition produces a patient's symptoms?

Arteriosclerosis obliterans, also known as peripheral arterial disease (PAD), is a form of peripheral vascular disease that produces thickening, hardening, and eventual narrowing and occlusion of the arteries. Arteriosclerosis obliterans results in ischemia and subsequent ulceration of the affected tissues. The affected area may become necrotic, gangrenous, and require amputation.

An injury was most likely sustained to which structure?

Injury will occur to all structures that receive blood supply from vessels that have become occluded. Prolonged ischemia results in tissue death and infection. Arteriosclerosis obliterans is the most common arterial occlusive disease.

INFERENCE

What is the most likely contributing factor in the development of this condition?

Risk factors associated with arteriosclerosis obliterans include age, diabetes, sex, hypertension, high serum cholesterol and low-density lipid levels, smoking, impaired glucose tolerance, obesity, and sedentary lifestyle. Unsuccessful management of peripheral vascular disease may ultimately lead to uncontrolled infection, gangrene, necrosis, and amputation. Males have an overall higher incidence of arteriosclerosis than female counterparts.

CONFIRMATION

What is the most likely clinical presentation?

The patient that requires a transtibial amputation secondary to arteriosclerosis obliterans is typically an individual over 45 years that smokes (75-90%) and will present with intermittent claudication that produces cramps and pain in the affected areas. Intermittent claudication will typically present in the gastrocnemius-soleus complex, secondary to its high oxygen demand. Other characteristics include resting pain, decreased pulses, ischemia, pallor skin, and decreased skin temperature.

What laboratory or imaging studies would confirm the diagnosis?

Arteriosclerosis obliterans can be diagnosed using Doppler ultrasonography, MRI or arteriography. These diagnostic tests examine the degree of blood flow throughout the extremities. A patient with arteriosclerosis obliterans would typically demonstrate poor results including blockage, tissue damage, and tissue death.

What additional information should be obtained to confirm the diagnosis?

The physician should examine the limb for temperature, skin condition, the presence of hair, sensation, and palpable pulses when determining the need for amputation. The physician may perform a selected non-invasive test such as a claudication test that examines the presence of intermittent claudication that can occur with prolonged ambulation. The ankle-brachial index, segmental limb pressures or pulse volume recordings may also be used to assist with the diagnosis.

EXAMINATION

What history should be documented?

Important areas to explore include past medical history, medications, current health status, social history and habits, occupation, living environment, and social support system.

What tests/measures are most appropriate?

Aerobic capacity and endurance: palpation of pulses, pulse oximetry, assessment of vital signs at rest and with activity

Anthropometric characteristics: residual limb circumferential measurements, length of limb

Arousal, attention, and cognition: examine mental status, learning ability, memory, motivation

Assistive and adaptive devices: analysis of components and safety of a device

Gait, locomotion, and balance: analysis of wheelchair mobility, static and dynamic balance in sitting and standing, safety during gait with an assistive device

Integumentary integrity: examine presence of hair growth, color, temperature, assessment of sensation

Muscle performance: strength assessment, muscle tone assessment

Pain: phantom pain, pain perception assessment scale

Prosthetic requirements: (when appropriate) analysis and safety of the prosthesis; assessment of alignment, efficiency, and fit of the prosthesis; assessment of residual limb with the prosthesis

Range of motion: active and passive range of motion

Self-care and home management: assessment of functional capacity, Barthel Index, Functional Independence Measure (FIM)

Sensory integrity: assessment of proprioception and kinesthesia

Transtibial Amputation due to Arteriosclerosis Obliterans

GOLD

What additional findings are likely with this patient?

A patient status post transtibial amputation may have a decrease in cardiovascular status depending on the frequency of intermittent claudication the patient experienced prior to the amputation. The patient may initially experience diminished balance secondary to the loss of the limb. Other issues that directly affect the residual limb include phantom pain, decreased range of motion, poor skin integrity, and hypersensitivity. The presence of any of these findings can have a negative influence on a patient's ability to utilize a prosthesis.

MANAGEMENT

What is the most effective management of this patient?

A patient should be a candidate for inpatient physical therapy services immediately after the transtibial amputation. Preprosthetic intervention should focus on strength, range of motion, functional mobility, use of assistive devices, desensitization, and patient education for care of the residual limb. Intervention should focus on proper positioning in order to avoid the risk of contractures, especially a knee flexion contracture. If the patient does not experience complications they should be able to return home either independently or with support. The patient may receive continued short-term physical therapy for prosthetic intervention once the residual limb has fully healed.

What home care regimen should be recommended?

A home care regimen for a patient status post transtibial amputation should include exercises, limb desensitization, proper positioning, and stretching. Since ambulation with a prosthesis increases the energy cost, the patient should be encouraged to perform cardiovascular activities on a frequent basis. In order to be successful, the patient will need to consistently monitor the residual limb and wrap the limb to ensure proper shaping until the prosthesis is tolerated.

OUTCOME

What is the likely outcome of a course of physical therapy?

Physical therapy for both preprosthetic and prosthetic intervention is typically necessary. A patient should be able to achieve the established goals and function with a prosthesis and an assistive device if warranted. The general health, cognition, motivation, and social support system of the patient will influence the patient's functional outcome.

What are the long-term effects of the patient's condition?

Arteriosclerosis obliterans is a chronic disease that a patient should continue to manage. The current transtibial amputation should not permanently alter a patient's level of functional mobility. The patient should be able to manage all aspects of self-care and functional mobility after prosthetic training with the permanent prosthesis unless hindered by other ailments. Some individuals with arteriosclerosis obliterans will have a myocardial infarction or CVA at some point after diagnosis.

COMPARISON

What are the distinguishing characteristics of a similar condition?

Any amputation would be considered a similar condition, with each level of amputation possessing distinguishing characteristics. Regardless, physical therapy intervention will include desensitization, phantom pain education, proper compression and shaping, strengthening, self-care, and mobility. In most instances, patients status post amputation share the common goal of functional prosthetic use.

CLINICAL SCENARIOS

Scenario One

A two-year-old female born with congenital malformation of the ankle joint and without a foot is referred to physical therapy for a pre-operative evaluation. The child is in good health, active, and has no other past medical history. The child has become increasingly frustrated with her alternate means of mobility. Her parents are supportive and carry her for community mobility. She prefers to scoot and crawl around the house since she cannot bear weight through the affected lower extremity. She is scheduled for a Syme's amputation in one week.

Scenario Two

An 83-year-old male, status post right transtibial amputation secondary to insulin-dependent diabetes mellitus, is admitted to a skilled nursing facility for rehabilitation. The patient is obese and presents with cardiopulmonary insufficiency. The patient previously resided alone with intermittent home health care and requires two liters of oxygen with activity.

SILVER Level Clinical Application Templates

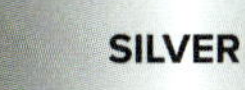

Level Clinical Application Template Executive Summary

Disk Herniation

- Often the result of gradual, age-related changes that cause disk degeneration
- Risk factors include being overweight and having an occupation that requires repetitive lifting, bending or twisting
- Physical therapy may consist of education on activity modification and appropriate body mechanics, soft tissue manipulation, lumbar stabilization exercises, traction, and modalities for pain relief

Glenohumeral Dislocation – Anterior

- Mechanism of injury may vary but typically involves a forceful external blow or loading force when the shoulder is in a position that combines abduction, lateral rotation and extension
- Prior to relocation of the joint, visible deformity, severe pain, and significant range of motion limitations are the most significant characteristics
- Is not life-threatening though recurrent dislocations can have a substantial impact on a patient's lifestyle

Medial Epicondylitis

- Occurs with repetitive wrist or elbow motions or gripping, and is often seen in golfers or those who play throwing or racket sports
- Initial treatment consists of rest, ice, anti-inflammatory medications, massage, stretching, and bracing to help control acute symptoms
- Home care regimen consists of stretching and strengthening exercises, especially for the wrist flexor and forearm pronator muscle groups, as well as icing to help control symptoms

Meniscal Tear

- Often involve twisting of the knee when in a semiflexed position with the foot planted on the ground
- Characterized by joint line pain and tenderness, swelling, loss of range of motion (sometimes with a mechanical block), a complaint of "catching" or "locking" within the joint, and feelings of instability
- Physical therapy focuses on interventions to reduce swelling, normalize range of motion, and improve muscular strength

Osgood-Schlatter Disease

- Refers to traction apophysitis occurring at the tibial tuberosity where symptoms are typically exacerbated by running, jumping, and squatting activities
- Characterized by localized pain and edema with point tenderness over the patella tendon's insertion on the tibial tuberosity
- Limiting symptoms may last for weeks or months before abating, however, the condition typically will resolve in time without intervention

SILVER Level Clinical Application Template Executive Summary

Piriformis Syndrome

- Characterized as the result of compression or irritation to the proximal sciatic nerve due to piriformis muscle inflammation, spasm or contracture
- Location of pain is often imprecise, though typically presents first in the area of the mid-buttock then progresses to radicular complaints in the sciatic nerve distribution
- Patients typically respond well to physical therapy interventions and are able to return to regular activities without restriction

Posterior Cruciate Ligament Sprain

- Occurs when a posteriorly directed force is applied to the tibia in relation to the femur, such as when the knee hits the dashboard in a motor vehicle accident
- Individuals participating in contact activities requiring a high level of agility are particularly susceptible to a posterior cruciate ligament injury
- A large majority of patients that experience a posterior cruciate ligament sprain are able to return to their previous level of function, including participation in athletics

Spinal Stenosis – Lumbar

- Refers to a narrowing of either the lumbar vertebral or intervertebral foramen with symptoms resulting from mechanical compression on either the spinal cord or exiting nerve roots
- Symptoms include a gradual onset and worsening of chronic pain at the midline of the lumbar region, unilateral nerve root radiculopathy, paresthesia, weakness, and diminished reflexes
- Severity of symptoms reported varies widely and directly influences expectations for long-term outcomes of physical therapy interventions

Trochanteric Bursitis

- May occur as a result of acute or cumulative trauma to the lateral hip causing irritation to the trochanteric bursa
- Causative factors may include a true or functional leg length discrepancy, history of lateral hip surgery, and participation in sports with significant running or contact
- Patients typically respond well to conservative interventions and should be able to return fully to their prior level of function including sport activity

Disk Herniation

SILVER

DIAGNOSIS

What condition produces a patient's symptoms?

The most common mechanism of injury for an intervertebral disk herniation is twisting and bending of the spine, often with the addition of some external load (e.g., bending over to lift a heavy object). This injury can occur acutely or gradually over time with repetitive twisting and bending movements.

An injury was most likely sustained to which structure?

The intervertebral disk is composed of two parts: an inner jelly-like material known as the nucleus pulposus and an outer cartilaginous structure known as the annulus fibrosus. A disk herniation occurs when the nucleus pulposus bulges through the exterior wall of the annulus fibrosus. Disk herniations most commonly occur on the posterolateral portion of the disk, where the disk is weakest and most likely to fissure. When the disk herniates, it often will compress nearby nerve roots and cause pain, numbness, and/or weakness into the extremities. The large majority of disk herniations occur at the L4-L5 or L5-S1 vertebral level.

INFERENCE

What is the most likely contributing factor in the development of this condition?

A disk herniation is often the result of gradual, age-related changes that cause disk degeneration. The disks lose water content over time, which makes them less flexible and increases the likelihood of tearing and rupturing of the annulus fibrosus. Risk factors for disk herniation include being overweight and having an occupation that requires repetitive lifting, bending or twisting.

CONFIRMATION

What is the most likely clinical presentation?

The clinical presentation most commonly includes low back pain followed by unilateral radicular leg pain (though bilateral leg pain is possible). Though pain is the most common symptom, the patient may also experience numbness, tingling, and weakness in the distribution of the affected nerve. Symptoms are exaggerated by sitting, walking, standing, and any increase in intra-abdominal pressure (e.g., coughing, sneezing). Though less common, disk herniations can also occur in the cervical spine.

What laboratory or imaging studies would confirm the diagnosis?

Magnetic resonance imaging is the most common imaging technique used to visualize a disk herniation. Electromyography and nerve conduction velocity testing can also be used to determine the extent of nerve damage to peripheral nerves.

What additional information should be obtained to confirm the diagnosis?

Though imaging studies are helpful, an accurate diagnosis can often be made based on a thorough medical history and physical exam. The physical exam will likely include neural provocation testing (e.g., slump test, straight leg raise test), as well as assessment of strength, sensation, and deep tendon reflexes.

MANAGEMENT

What is the most effective management of this patient?

Conservative management, consisting of avoidance of provocative positions and a course of physical therapy, is successful in the large majority of patients. Physical therapy may consist of education on activity modification and appropriate body mechanics, soft tissue manipulation, lumbar stabilization exercises, traction, and modalities for pain relief. Once tolerated, McKenzie extension exercises will likely be incorporated into the exercise program. A variety of pain medications may be administered, including NSAIDs, narcotic medications, nerve pain medications, and muscle relaxants. If conservative treatment is unsuccessful, a cortisone injection may be necessary. A small percentage of patients will eventually need surgery (i.e., microdiscectomy).

What home care regimen should be recommended?

A home care regimen will consist of activity modification and avoidance of provocative positioning, as well as lumbar stabilization exercises. Patients should use pain medications and ice or heat to help control their pain.

OUTCOME

What is the likely outcome of a course of physical therapy?

The large majority of patients will get better with conservative treatment, though complete resolution of symptoms can take months. The effectiveness of physical therapy will be dependent on the extent of disk injury, as well as the patient's age and activity level.

What are the long-term effects of the patient's condition?

The long-term effect of a patient's condition is highly dependent on the extent of the herniation. Individuals with a disk "bulge," in which the annulus fibrosus fibers are unaffected, are less likely to need surgery and more likely to experience a full recovery. Patients that have a larger herniation or rupture of the disk, in which the annulus fibrosus fibers are compromised, are more likely to experience reoccurrence of their symptoms.

SILVER

Glenohumeral Dislocation – Anterior

DIAGNOSIS

What condition produces a patient's symptoms?

An anterior glenohumeral (GH) dislocation occurs when the head of the humerus is traumatically separated from the glenoid fossa. The mechanism of injury may vary, but typically involves a forceful external blow or loading force when the shoulder is in a position that combines abduction, lateral rotation, and extension (e.g., spiking a volleyball, throwing a ball).

An injury was most likely sustained to which structure?

Stability is primarily maintained by the GH joint capsule, ligaments, rotator cuff muscles, and glenoid labrum. Loading or other external forces applied to the joint while it is in a relatively unstable or vulnerable position may cause stretching or tearing of the stabilizing structures, allowing the joint to dislocate. Fracture may also occur.

INFERENCE

What is the most likely contributing factor in the development of this condition?

The shoulder is the most frequently dislocated joint with over 90% of shoulder dislocations occurring anteriorly. It is most common in patients engaged in sporting activities between 18 and 25 years of age. There is also a notable prevalence among the elderly with dislocation predominantly occurring secondary to a fall.

CONFIRMATION

What is the most likely clinical presentation?

Prior to relocation of the joint, visible deformity, severe pain, and significant range of motion limitations are the most significant characteristics. The affected limb will typically be positioned in slight abduction and lateral rotation with the patient unable to touch the opposite shoulder. The normal contour of the affected shoulder will be much more "square" than the unaffected side. The humeral head will typically be palpable anteriorly in the subcoracoid region. Once the dislocation has been reduced, the most severe pain symptoms typically resolve. The patient may continue to demonstrate protective or pain-limited range of motion efforts. A positive apprehension sign is likely. Diminished or absent radial pulses are suggestive of vascular injury and should be addressed immediately. Decreased sensation or motor function in the axillary, musculocutaneous, and radial nerve distributions may also be observed.

What laboratory or imaging studies would confirm the diagnosis?

X-ray imaging is typically performed both before and after the joint is reduced to assess joint position and rule out additional bony pathology. Other diagnostic procedures may also be necessary since adjacent structures may be easily damaged. MRI is typically utilized to assess suspected soft tissue injury and electromyography is utilized to assess nerve injury.

What additional information should be obtained to confirm the diagnosis?

A thorough medical history should be obtained including the mechanism of injury and any prior history of dislocation. Physical examination should include palpation as well as mobility, neurological, vascular, and pain assessments.

MANAGEMENT

What is the most effective management of this patient?

Medical management is initially focused on pharmacological pain management and joint reduction. Acutely, analgesic medications may be used to improve comfort during pre-reduction evaluative procedures and facilitate adequate relaxation of surrounding muscles prior to the reduction. After reduction, patients may require analgesics to effectively manage pain before transitioning to NSAIDs. Surgical management may be necessary if the joint cannot be conservatively reduced or if adjacent structural damage is significant (e.g., Bankart lesion, detached labrum, rotator cuff tear, fracture). Physical therapy intervention may be promptly initiated to assist with pain management and to prevent loss of function. Modalities may be used for palliative goals and to facilitate muscle retraining. Strengthening should initially emphasize isometrics, gradually progressing to resisted activities emphasizing the shoulder stabilizers. Physical therapy intervention may include range of motion, joint mobilizations, stretching, postural education, protective positioning, edema management, and activity modification.

What home care regimen should be recommended?

The home care regimen should include protective positioning, range of motion, and strengthening exercises. Pain management is typically achieved with rest, ice, and NSAIDs.

OUTCOME

What is the likely outcome of a course of physical therapy?

Typically, an aggressive strengthening program and/or activity modification will permit a return to athletic activities. The risk of re-injury is inherently greater in contact sports and is further increased depending on damage sustained to other stabilizing structures. In older or more sedentary populations, a return to prior level of function is possible. Some activity modifications emphasizing joint protection and fall prevention may be recommended.

What are the long-term effects of the patient's condition?

An anterior GH dislocation is not life-threatening though recurrent dislocations can have a substantial impact on a patient's lifestyle. Recurrent dislocations may require surgical intervention and consequently require greater restrictions or complete avoidance of participation in high-risk activities.

Medial Epicondylitis

SILVER

DIAGNOSIS

What condition produces a patient's symptoms?

Medial epicondylitis (also known as golfer's elbow) is a tendonitis that occurs at the medial epicondyle of the elbow. The condition is an overuse injury that occurs when the tendons are overworked and become inflamed, though it can also occur as the result of a traumatic event. Medial epicondylitis commonly occurs with repetitive wrist or elbow motions or gripping, and is often seen in golfers or those who play throwing or racket sports.

An injury was most likely sustained to which structure?

Medial epicondylitis affects the tendons of the muscles in the anterior forearm, which include the forearm pronators, wrist flexors, and finger flexors. The tendons of these muscles share a common tendinous sheath at their origin at the medial epicondyle of the humerus. The tendons of the flexor carpi radialis and pronator teres are most often affected. The ulnar nerve can also become irritated as it passes through the cubital tunnel in this region.

INFERENCE

What is the most likely contributing factor in the development of this condition?

This condition most often results from activities that require repetitive wrist or elbow motions or require lots of gripping. Patients who have poor flexibility, poor strength or poor endurance of the affected muscles are more prone to acquiring medial epicondylitis. Other risk factors for this condition include use of improper equipment (e.g., a racket grip that is the wrong size) or improper technique (e.g., excessive top spin in tennis).

CONFIRMATION

What is the most likely clinical presentation?

The onset of this condition is usually gradual, though it can occur suddenly after a traumatic incident. A patient with medial epicondylitis will report pain and have tenderness over the medial epicondyle. The patient will have pain with resisted wrist flexion and pronation and with gripping. There may also be weakness associated with these movements. If the ulnar nerve is affected, the patient could experience pain and paresthesias into the forearm and fourth and fifth digits.

What laboratory or imaging studies would confirm the diagnosis?

Imaging studies are generally not used in the diagnosis of medial epicondylitis. Radiographs will appear normal, though they will be necessary if the onset was traumatic. Magnetic resonance imaging can be used to identify damage to the soft tissue structures of the medial elbow, however, the diagnosis can usually be made based on the results of the physical examination alone.

What additional information should be obtained to confirm the diagnosis?

A thorough medical history and physical examination is usually enough to confirm the diagnosis of medial epicondylitis. Resisted wrist flexion or passive wrist extension can be used to elicit pain and aid in the diagnosis of medial epicondylitis. The examination should include an assessment of the ulnar collateral ligament since damage to this ligament can mimic symptoms of medial epicondylitis.

MANAGEMENT

What is the most effective management of this patient?

For the large majority of patients, the condition will improve with conservative treatment alone. Initial treatment consists of rest, ice, anti-inflammatory medications, massage, stretching, and bracing to help control acute symptoms. Bracing may involve a counterforce brace applied just distal to the elbow to help limit muscular strain at the epicondyle. Likewise, cock-up splints are sometimes used to limit repetitive movements of the wrist. Once pain subsides, strengthening exercises, especially eccentric exercises for the forearm musculature, can be initiated. A cortisone injection may be used to help alleviate symptoms. For patients who do not respond to conservative treatment, surgery may be necessary. Surgery for medial epicondylitis involves debridement of the degenerated tissue.

What home care regimen should be recommended?

The home care regimen should consist of stretching and strengthening exercises, especially for the wrist flexor and forearm pronator muscle groups, as well as icing to help control symptoms. The patient should be compliant with brace or splint use to help prevent irritation of the tissues.

OUTCOME

What is the likely outcome of a course of physical therapy?

A large majority of patients respond well to conservative treatment and are able to return to their previous functional level. Only a small percentage of patients will end up needing surgical intervention.

What are the long-term effects of the patient's condition?

While a cortisone injection can help to diminish symptoms acutely, it has no long-term effect. To prevent a recurrence of symptoms, it is important that the patient maintain good forearm flexibility and strength. Additionally, the patient should attempt to limit other risk factors by using correct technique and equipment and by limiting the volume of repetitive movements.

SILVER

Meniscal Tear

DIAGNOSIS

What condition produces a patient's symptoms?

Meniscal tears commonly occur as the result of a traumatic injury. The injury will often involve twisting of the knee when it is in a semiflexed position with the foot planted on the ground. Meniscal tears can also occur secondary to a hyperflexion injury. In older patients, meniscal tears are more likely to be caused by degeneration as opposed to acute trauma. When the meniscus has degenerated, a simple pivoting or squatting movement may be enough to cause a meniscus tear.

An injury was most likely sustained to which structure?

The menisci are C-shaped structures made of fibrocartilage that sit on each side of the tibial plateau. The menisci function to absorb shock and distribute loads within the knee joint. Because the medial meniscus is more firmly attached to the tibia, it is more commonly affected than the lateral meniscus. There are several different types of tears that can occur, including oblique, transverse, longitudinal, and complex tears. The location of the tear (e.g., inner meniscus, outer meniscus) is important in determining the most appropriate treatment. Meniscal injuries can occur in isolation or may occur in conjunction with ligamentous injuries (e.g., ACL tear).

INFERENCE

What is the most likely contributing factor in the development of this condition?

Patients who are involved in sports are more likely to experience meniscal tears, especially sports that involve quick cutting and pivoting movements. Older patients are more likely to have degenerative tears of the meniscus since, with increasing age, the cartilage thins and weakens and becomes more prone to tearing. Patients with instability of the knee, secondary to weakness or ligamentous deficiency, are also more prone to meniscal tears.

CONFIRMATION

What is the most likely clinical presentation?

Meniscal tears are characterized by joint line pain and tenderness, swelling, loss of range of motion (sometimes with a mechanical block), a complaint of "catching" or "locking" within the joint, and feelings of instability. Traumatic meniscal tears will result in a sudden onset of symptoms, whereas degenerative tears will have more of a gradual onset.

What laboratory or imaging studies would confirm the diagnosis?

While x-rays will not confirm or deny the presence of a meniscal tear, the diagnostic imaging technique is often performed to rule out other pathology (e.g., arthritis, fracture). Magnetic resonance imaging is the diagnostic test of choice for confirming the presence of a meniscal tear.

What additional information should be obtained to confirm the diagnosis?

In addition to imaging studies, a thorough medical history and physical examination should be performed on patients for whom a meniscus tear is suspected. The physical examination should include palpation, a range of motion assessment, and special tests. Common special tests for diagnosing meniscal tears include the McMurray test, the Apley's compression test, and the Thessaly test.

MANAGEMENT

What is the most effective management of this patient?

There are several considerations that must be made when determining if a patient with a meniscus tear should be treated conservatively or surgically, including the patient's age and activity level, and the location and extent of the tear. Conservative treatment for a meniscus tear involves rest including limited weight bearing, ice, use of anti-inflammatory medications, and physical therapy. Physical therapy will focus on interventions to reduce swelling, normalize range of motion, and improve muscular strength. Since some meniscus tears can heal on their own, conservative treatment is often attempted before considering surgery.

What home care regimen should be recommended?

The home care regimen will consist of rest, ice, and use of anti-inflammatory medications. The exercise program will likely consist of stretching and range of motion exercises to improve knee mobility and strengthening exercises to prevent muscular atrophy.

OUTCOME

What is the likely outcome of a course of physical therapy?

A tear in the outer one-third of the meniscus is more likely to heal spontaneously since this portion of the meniscus is vascular. Conservative treatment in these instances is often successful. If the tear is on the inner two-thirds of the meniscus, surgical intervention may be necessary.

What are the long-term effects of the patient's condition?

If the patient's condition does not respond well to conservative treatment, surgery will likely be considered. For patients who are young and whose lesion is located in the vascular portion of the meniscus, a full repair of the torn meniscus is usually performed. For older patients or for those patients who have a lesion in the avascular portion of the meniscus, a partial meniscectomy, in which the torn tissue is excised, will more likely be performed. Patients who have surgery are eventually able to return to their previous functional level without issue.

Osgood-Schlatter Disease

SILVER

DIAGNOSIS

What condition produces a patient's symptoms?

Osgood-Schlatter disease refers to traction apophysitis occurring at the tibial tuberosity. Symptoms are typically the result of local inflammation at the tibial tuberosity and are exacerbated by running, jumping, and squatting activities.

An injury was most likely sustained to which structure?

The exact etiology is unknown though theories suggest that it may be caused by repeated microtrauma. Repeated tension at the insertion of the patella tendon can cause a small avulsion at the tuberosity thereby producing pain and edema. Over time, heterotopic bone formation may also produce a visible lump over the tibial tuberosity. The onset occurs most commonly in adolescents following a period of rapid long bone growth during which soft tissue tension may be temporarily increased before accommodating to the change in limb length.

INFERENCE

What is the most likely contributing factor in the development of this condition?

Osgood-Schlatter disease is more common in sports that require a great deal of running, jumping, swift directional changes, and repeated knee flexion (e.g., soccer, ballet). The age of onset is typically associated with periods of rapid growth during puberty. The condition is historically more prevalent among boys although the gender gap has lessened as more girls engage in competitive athletics.

CONFIRMATION

What is the most likely clinical presentation?

Osgood-Schlatter disease is characterized by localized pain and edema with point tenderness over the patella tendon's insertion on the tibial tuberosity. Pain symptoms are typically exacerbated by activities that increase traction forces at the tibial tubercle or put pressure directly on the affected area. Symptoms are typically reproducible with resisted knee extension and alleviated with rest or activity restriction. Generalized tightness in hip and knee musculature is common especially in the quadriceps. If heterotopic ossification has occurred, a firm mass will be palpable.

What laboratory or imaging studies would confirm the diagnosis?

X-ray imaging may be utilized to confirm the diagnosis and rule out other pathologies such as abnormal calcification, infection or apophyseal fracture.

What additional information should be obtained to confirm the diagnosis?

A diagnosis of Osgood-Schlatter disease is often made based entirely on symptom history and physical findings, therefore, a thorough examination is essential.

MANAGEMENT

What is the most effective management of this patient?

Medical management of Osgood-Schlatter disease is typically conservative with an emphasis on pain management. Patients should be counseled to modify or avoid pain-producing activities that increase tension on the patella tendon. The use of ice, rest, and over-the-counter medications (e.g., acetaminophen, NSAIDs) are also recommended. A knee immobilizer may be beneficial to facilitate rest during acute phases while an infrapatellar strap may assist in distributing traction forces once acuity is reduced and activity has resumed. Surgical intervention is rare though may be indicated for patients who have not responded to conservative treatment or have developed ossicles in the tendon or on the tibial tuberosity. Physical therapy intervention during an acute exacerbation may include palliative modalities, activity modification, and gentle stretching. Progressive stretching, strengthening, and cross training activities (e.g., swimming, cycling) should begin once acute symptoms have abated.

What home care regimen should be recommended?

A home care regimen should include rest, ice, and prescribed therapeutic exercise. Joint protection and cross training activities should be encouraged. Exacerbating activities should be modified or avoided until symptoms have resolved.

OUTCOME

What is the likely outcome of a course of physical therapy?

Limiting symptoms may last for weeks or months before abating. In some cases, discomfort can last for a number of years until the tibial growth plate has closed. Acute exacerbations are common until the long bones have stopped growing. Physical therapy may assist with reducing the severity of symptoms, however, the condition is typically self-limiting. Conservative treatment is successful in the large majority of cases.

What are the long-term effects of the patient's condition?

Osgood-Schlatter disease is a self-limiting condition that typically has an excellent prognosis. In many patients, a bony lump remains even after symptoms have resolved, though it rarely interferes with function. Complications are uncommon, but may include chronic pain, localized edema, and ossicle formation. Patients with symptoms that continue after reaching skeletal maturity may require surgical intervention.

SILVER

Piriformis Syndrome

DIAGNOSIS

What condition produces a patient's symptoms?

Piriformis syndrome is the result of compression or irritation to the proximal sciatic nerve due to piriformis muscle inflammation, spasm or contracture. It is a common etiology of generalized low back pain and is sometimes referred to as "pseudosciatica" because of the similarity of symptoms.

An injury was most likely sustained to which structure?

The piriformis muscle is a flat oblique muscle that functions to abduct and externally rotate the hip. After exiting the greater sciatic foramen, the sciatic nerve passes inferior to the piriformis before continuing distally along the midline of the posterior thigh. The specific etiology of piriformis syndrome is unknown, however, trauma, mechanical dysfunction, scarring or entrapment due to soft tissue pathology are among the leading theories.

INFERENCE

What is the most likely contributing factor in the development of this condition?

Studies suggest that roughly half of patients diagnosed with piriformis syndrome have a history of local trauma (e.g., contusion, total hip arthroplasty). Abnormal gait mechanics, an exaggerated lumbar lordosis, periods of prolonged sitting, and participation in vigorous physical activity have also been identified as potential contributing factors.

CONFIRMATION

What is the most likely clinical presentation?

The location of pain is often imprecise, though typically presents first in the area of the mid-buttock then progresses to radicular complaints in the sciatic nerve distribution. Hip, coccyx, or groin pain may also be reported. Symptoms are typically exacerbated by prolonged sitting and activities that combine medial rotation and adduction. Pain is typically reproducible on palpation and with positioning into flexion, adduction, and medial rotation. Pain and weakness are likely with resistance testing during lateral rotation with abduction. Radicular symptoms are typically exacerbated with a straight leg raise and alleviated with lower extremity traction. Often piriformis syndrome is misdiagnosed as it has a near identical symptom presentation as L5-S1 radiculopathy, which is due to either a herniated disk or stenosis.

What laboratory or imaging studies would confirm the diagnosis?

Piriformis syndrome is considered a clinical diagnosis of exclusion, therefore no specific laboratory or imaging studies are used for confirmation. X-ray, MRI, and CT scan may be used to rule out other conditions which may mimic symptoms such as disk herniation or spinal stenosis.

What additional information should be obtained to confirm the diagnosis?

A thorough medical history and examination should be obtained to assist in identifying potential etiologies and ruling out similar diagnoses such as trochanteric bursitis or myofascial pain.

MANAGEMENT

What is the most effective management of this patient?

Medical management of piriformis syndrome is typically conservative emphasizing pain management with oral or injectable analgesic agents. Surgical intervention (e.g., piriformis tendon release, sciatic neurolysis) is typically successful but considered only as a last resort when conservative measures fail. Physical therapy intervention typically begins with thermal modalities to improve the quality of subsequent soft tissue mobilizations and stretching. Soft tissue massage, hip joint mobilizations, muscle energy, and strain-counterstrain techniques may further enhance relaxation of the piriformis and surrounding muscles. Existing sacroiliac dysfunction, leg length discrepancy or other biomechanical factors should also be addressed. As symptoms decrease, gradual strengthening of the piriformis and surrounding muscles may be recommended to supplement stretching exercises. Patients returning to athletic activities may benefit from a change in footwear or an orthotic consultation to improve overall lower extremity alignment to reduce the risk of recurrence.

What home care regimen should be recommended?

A home care regimen should include temporary avoidance of aggravating activities and frequent stretching exercises. Superficial ice or heat may be applied palliatively.

OUTCOME

What is the likely outcome of a course of physical therapy?

Patients with piriformis syndrome typically respond well to physical therapy interventions and are able to return to regular activities without restriction. This successful return is often dependent, however, on both the severity and chronicity of symptoms prior to intervention and patient compliance with treatment recommendations.

What are the long-term effects of the patient's condition?

Piriformis syndrome is not life-threatening, but can be disabling in severe cases. Long-term complications are typically related to an incorrect or delayed diagnosis resulting in delayed treatment. Undiagnosed piriformis syndrome often contributes to poor outcomes for patients undergoing surgery for a lumbar disk herniation.

Posterior Cruciate Ligament Sprain

SILVER

DIAGNOSIS

What condition produces a patient's symptoms?

The posterior cruciate ligament (PCL) is an intracapsular ligament that attaches at the posterior tibial plateau and the lateral side of the medial femoral condyle. The PCL prevents posterior translation of the tibia on the femur and provides rotational stability to the knee. PCL injuries generally occur secondary to a traumatic event. They often occur when a posteriorly directed force is applied to the tibia in relation to the femur, such as when the knee hits the dashboard in a motor vehicle accident. Hyperflexion of the knee without a traumatic blow can also lead to a PCL sprain.

An injury was most likely sustained to which structure?

Injuries to the PCL are graded according to the normal 3-point grading scale for sprains, with a grade of 3 indicating complete rupture. Most PCL tears occur where the ligament attaches to the tibia. Isolated PCL injuries are far less common than anterior cruciate ligament (ACL) injuries, in part because the PCL is a stronger ligament. Injuries to the PCL often occur with concurrent damage to the ACL, the collateral ligaments, and/or the menisci.

INFERENCE

What is the most likely contributing factor in the development of this condition?

Individuals participating in contact activities requiring a high level of agility are particularly susceptible to a PCL injury. Muscle weakness resulting in poor dynamic stability may also increase the incidence of this type of injury.

CONFIRMATION

What is the most likely clinical presentation?

When a PCL injury results from acute trauma, the patient may hear an audible "pop" with an immediate onset of pain and swelling. Symptoms will vary depending on the grade of the sprain, however, this injury is generally not as debilitating as an ACL tear. Patients with a PCL sprain may complain of feelings of instability with walking and pain with descending stairs or squatting.

What laboratory or imaging studies would confirm the diagnosis?

While an x-ray will not confirm the presence of a PCL sprain, it can help rule out other pathology (e.g., fracture). An x-ray may also be used to determine if the ligament damage resulted in an associated avulsion injury. Magnetic resonance imaging is used to confirm the presence and determine the extent and location of a PCL sprain.

What additional information should be obtained to confirm the diagnosis?

A thorough medical history and physical examination should be performed. The physical examination will consist of special tests that are used to determine the presence of a PCL sprain, such as the posterior drawer test, the posterior sag sign, and the quadriceps active drawer test. An arthrometer may also be used to identify laxity in the knee and determine the extent of the damage. The examination should consist of an assessment of the other ligaments and the menisci as well since a PCL injury often occurs in conjunction with other pathology.

MANAGEMENT

What is the most effective management of this patient?

A PCL sprain is most often treated conservatively and will likely entail some combination of icing, rest, bracing, anti-inflammatory medications, and physical therapy. Physical therapy should focus on reducing swelling, regaining full range of motion, and strengthening the knee. Strengthening exercises that place a posterior shear force on the knee (e.g., open chain hamstring exercises) should be avoided to allow the ligament to heal.

What home care regimen should be recommended?

The home care regimen will consist of frequent icing and an exercise program. The exercises will focus on regaining mobility and strengthening the knee, specifically with quadriceps strengthening exercises. The patient should also be compliant with any weight bearing restrictions they are given.

OUTCOME

What is the likely outcome of a course of physical therapy?

Patients with a PCL sprain generally do well with conservative treatment, especially if they can improve their quadriceps strength to help stabilize the knee. Patients that have an isolated PCL injury that is a grade 1 or 2 sprain typically do not require surgery and experience a full recovery. If patients do not respond well to conservative treatment, they will likely need surgical intervention to reconstruct the ligament with a tissue graft.

What are the long-term effects of the patient's condition?

The large majority of patients that experience a PCL sprain are able to return to their previous level of function, including participation in athletics. Functional bracing may be needed if a patient plans to return to athletics. As is the case with most ligament-deficient knees, patients with a PCL injury are more prone to meniscal damage in the years following their injury.

SILVER

Spinal Stenosis – Lumbar

DIAGNOSIS

What condition produces a patient's symptoms?

Lumbar spinal stenosis (LSS) refers to a narrowing of either the lumbar vertebral or intervertebral foramina. Symptoms are typically produced as a result of mechanical compression on either the spinal cord or exiting nerve roots and may be further exacerbated by bony degeneration or instability. Primary spinal stenosis accounts for only a small percentage of diagnoses and is the result of a congenital malformation of spinal structures. Secondary spinal stenosis refers to narrowing due to acquired changes in the foramina.

An injury was most likely sustained to which structure?

Structural changes may include degeneration of the vertebral segments, disk herniation, osteophyte formation, and hypertrophy of structures such as the ligamentum flavum. Other etiologies include trauma, compression fracture, systemic conditions (e.g., tumor, ankylosing spondylitis), and iatrogenic factors (e.g., laminectomy, discectomy).

INFERENCE

What is the most likely contributing factor in the development of this condition?

Certain congenital conditions and defects increase the risk of primary spinal stenosis. Age is the primary risk factor for the development of secondary spinal stenosis due to the degenerative changes that are a part of the normal aging process.

CONFIRMATION

What is the most likely clinical presentation?

Typical LSS symptoms include a gradual onset and worsening of chronic pain at the midline of the lumbar region. Other complaints may include unilateral nerve root radiculopathy, paresthesia, weakness, and diminished reflexes. In rare cases, LSS may present bilaterally with bilateral weakness, paresthesia, diminished coordination, ataxic gait, balance dysfunction, bowel/bladder dysfunction, and hyperreflexia. Symptoms are typically exacerbated by activities that increase lumbar extension (e.g., standing upright, lying prone) and are alleviated by rest and activities that increase lumbar flexion (e.g., leaning on a grocery cart, sitting). Many patients adopt a stooped posture to functionally reduce their lumbar lordosis and minimize symptoms.

What laboratory or imaging studies would confirm the diagnosis?

An MRI provides the least invasive and most conclusive means of diagnosing LSS due to its ability to differentiate soft tissue pathologies such as disk damage or neural compression. A CT myelogram utilizes the injection of contrast dye into the spinal column to enhance visualization of the spinal cord, nerve roots, and areas of compression.

What additional information should be obtained to confirm the diagnosis?

A thorough medical history and physical examination should be completed to assist in ruling out similar diagnoses and determine the etiology of LSS in order to best direct treatment.

MANAGEMENT

What is the most effective management of this patient?

Medical management of LSS is typically conservative and focused on palliative pharmacological intervention. NSAIDs are often among the first medications recommended due to their dual action in providing analgesia in low doses and anti-inflammatory benefits. Muscle relaxants may be recommended to assist with sleep-related comfort. Surgical intervention such as lumbar laminectomy may be necessary if conservative measures fail and symptoms become disabling. Physical therapy intervention typically will focus on improving function and pain management. Strength, flexibility, and endurance exercises aim to improve muscular support and spinal stability. Patients who are pain-limited may also benefit from palliative modalities such as TENS to improve their tolerance for activities. Patients who are unable to assume a normal posture without exacerbation of symptoms may benefit from use of an assistive device to ease the excessive strain on postural muscles caused by a forward flexed or kyphotic posture.

What home care regimen should be recommended?

A home care regimen should include regular participation in an exercise program. Palliative home interventions may include hot or cold packs or home TENS use. Weight loss may be recommended and education should include activity modification especially for functional tasks that specifically exacerbate symptoms.

OUTCOME

What is the likely outcome of a course of physical therapy?

The severity of symptoms will vary and directly influence expectations for long-term outcomes. LSS is a progressive condition, however, for patients who are symptomatic, physical therapy can assist in minimizing the effects of the condition and maximizing independence.

What are the long-term effects of the patient's condition?

LSS is not life-threatening and in many patients is never formally diagnosed due to a relative lack of symptoms. In others, LSS can result in significant disability due to chronic pain and muscle weakness.

Trochanteric Bursitis

SILVER

DIAGNOSIS

What condition produces a patient's symptoms?

Trochanteric bursitis may occur from acute or cumulative trauma to the lateral hip causing irritation to the trochanteric bursa. Though symptoms typically include lateral hip pain, the pathology does not involve the actual hip joint.

An injury was most likely sustained to which structure?

The trochanteric bursa is located between the femoral trochanteric process, the gluteus medius, and the iliotibial tract. Acute trauma etiologies typically involve contusion related to direct impact occurring with activities such as falls or impact sports. Cumulative trauma etiologies are typically associated with activities such as running that produce repetitive friction between the bursa and the iliotibial band.

INFERENCE

What is the most likely contributing factor in the development of this condition?

Factors that may contribute to the onset of trochanteric bursitis include a true or functional leg length discrepancy, history of lateral hip surgery, and participation in sports that involve a significant amount of running or contact. The prevalence of the condition is significantly greater among women. Though trochanteric bursitis is more likely to occur in active patients, it is also commonly diagnosed without identifiable etiology in sedentary individuals.

CONFIRMATION

What is the most likely clinical presentation?

The classic symptom of trochanteric bursitis is pain at the lateral hip which may radiate to the lateral aspect of the thigh. Point tenderness and reproduction of pain are typical with palpation. Symptoms are typically exacerbated by weight bearing activity or direct pressure on the affected area. Passive hip movement involving lateral rotation and abduction or resisted hip flexion and abduction are likely to reproduce symptoms. Patients may also complain of pain-related weakness in the affected extremity.

What laboratory or imaging studies would confirm the diagnosis?

An MRI or diagnostic ultrasound may assist in differentiating trochanteric bursitis from gluteus medius tendinitis. X-ray imaging may be utilized to rule out bony pathology or to further assess leg length discrepancies.

What additional information should be obtained to confirm the diagnosis?

A thorough medical history and physical examination should be completed to assist in ruling out similar diagnoses (e.g., sciatic pain, iliotibial band syndrome, femoral head avascular necrosis). The diagnosis is often made based on the patient's symptom history and physical examination findings.

MANAGEMENT

What is the most effective management of this patient?

Pharmacological management typically includes anti-inflammatory or anesthetic agents that may be utilized alone or in combination for local injection of the trochanteric bursa. Many patients require multiple injections, in combination with other conservative interventions in order to attain full symptom resolution. Surgical interventions are uncommon and typically reserved for patients who respond poorly to conservative treatment and develop some degree of disability as a result. Physical therapy interventions emphasize stretching, especially of the iliotibial band, tensor fasciae latae, lateral hip rotators, quadriceps, and hip flexors. Soft tissue massage, iontophoresis, phonophoresis, and palliative interventions such as TENS may also be indicated. Education regarding appropriate stretching techniques and activity modification is indicated. Gait abnormalities such as leg length discrepancies or antalgic gait patterns should be addressed appropriately with assistive devices, orthotics, heel lifts or bracing. Athletes should be educated regarding prevention, ongoing strengthening and stretching, the use of appropriate protective padding for contact sports, and avoidance of excessive unidirectional activities.

What home care regimen should be recommended?

A home care regimen should include rest, ice, and NSAID use as recommended by the patient's physician and therapeutic exercise. Patients should be encouraged to avoid exacerbating activities that may perpetuate inflammatory symptoms during recovery.

OUTCOME

What is the likely outcome of a course of physical therapy?

Patients with trochanteric bursitis typically respond well to conservative interventions. With the resolution of symptoms, patients should be able to return fully to their prior level of function including sport activity.

What are the long-term effects of the patient's condition?

The combination of local injection and physical therapy has been shown to be very successful in the management of trochanteric bursitis. Symptom recurrence is possible especially if patients are not diligent in modifying activities, continuing with therapeutic exercise interventions, and monitoring their response to activity. In some patients, symptoms of pain, altered gait, and sleep disturbances associated with rolling onto the affected side may become chronic.

BRONZE Level Clinical Application Templates

Level Clinical Application Template Executive Summary

Anterior Compartment Syndrome

- Characterized by increased pressure in the lower leg secondary to swelling, which can occlude blood flow and cause ischemia and necrosis of the surrounding nerves and musculature
- Chronic cases may occur secondary to athletic exertion; acute cases are often caused by a traumatic injury and are considered a medical emergency
- Symptoms include tightness and tenderness over the muscle belly of the tibialis anterior, pain with passive stretching or active use of the muscle, and paresthesias and/or numbness in the distribution of the deep peroneal nerve

Colles' Fracture

- Frequently occurs when an individual reaches forward with their hands while attempting to break a fall; characterized by a transverse fracture of the distal radius
- Trauma related to this maneuver is commonly termed a FOOSH "fall on outstretched hand" injury
- X-ray of the wrist is the preferred method of confirming a Colles' fracture and identifying displaced fragments or damage to adjacent bony structures

De Quervain's Tenosynovitis

- Results from an inflammatory process involving the tendons and synovium of the abductor pollicis longus (APL) and extensor pollicis brevis (EPB) at the base of the thumb
- Onset is typically due to repetitive activities involving thumb abduction and extension such as racquet sports and repeated heavy lifting
- Symptom onset may be gradual or sudden depending on the mechanism of injury with report of localized pain and tenderness in the area of the anatomical snuffbox which may radiate

Myositis Ossificans

- Characterized by the calcification of muscle that is usually caused by neglecting to properly treat a muscle strain or contusion
- Development of this condition occurs within a few weeks after the initial injury and may include a noticeable hard lump in the muscle belly, an increase in pain, and a decrease in range of motion
- An x-ray is the primary imaging study used to confirm the diagnosis

Osteochondritis Dissecans

- Condition in which loss of blood flow to subchondral bone causes a piece of bone and its associated cartilage to crack and separate away from the end of the bone
- Symptoms may include pain with functional activities, joint popping or locking, weakness, swelling, and decreased range of motion
- X-ray imaging can be used to confirm the diagnosis

BRONZE Level Clinical Application Template Executive Summary

Osteomyelitis

- An infection that occurs within the bone, most commonly secondary to the Staphylococcus aureus microbe
- Damage to the bone from a surgical procedure, compound fracture or puncture wound that penetrates the bone may directly expose the bone to infectious microbes
- A bone biopsy is the most conclusive procedure for diagnosing osteomyelitis and determining the specific infectious microbe present

Tarsal Tunnel Syndrome

- Occurs as a result of compression of the tibial nerve as it passes through the tarsal tunnel, causing neuropathy in the distribution of the nerve
- Signs and symptoms include pain, numbness, and paresthesias in the foot, muscle atrophy and weakness, diminished light touch and temperature sensation, and an antalgic gait pattern
- Tinel's sign can be used to confirm the presence of the condition, though diagnostic tests (MRI, ultrasound, EMG, NCV) may also be performed

Ulnar Collateral Ligament Sprain – Thumb

- Occurs secondary to a traumatic event in which an excessive valgus force is applied to the metacarpophalangeal joint of the thumb
- The therapist should perform ligament stability testing of the thumb by applying a valgus force to the joint, with a movement of greater than 30-35 degrees indicating a complete tear of the ulnar collateral ligament
- X-rays should be ordered to rule out the existence of a fracture or dislocation

Anterior Compartment Syndrome

BRONZE

DIAGNOSIS

What condition produces a patient's symptoms?

Anterior compartment syndrome occurs when the pressure in the anterior compartment of the lower leg increases secondary to swelling. This increase in pressure results in occlusion of blood flow, which may cause ischemia and necrosis of the surrounding nerves and musculature. Acute compartment syndrome is a medical emergency, often caused by a traumatic injury, that can lead to irreversible muscle damage. Chronic compartment syndrome most often occurs secondary to athletic exertion and is typically not a medical emergency.

An injury was most likely sustained to what structure?

This condition affects the anterior compartment of the lower leg, which consists of the tibialis anterior, extensor hallucis longus, extensor digitorum longus, and peroneus tertius muscles. Because fascia does not stretch, the increase in pressure causes increased compression on the capillaries, nerves, and muscles of the anterior compartment. If not relieved, irreversible damage to the nerves and muscles may result secondary to ischemia.

CONFIRMATION

What is the most likely clinical presentation?

An increase in swelling will cause tightness and tenderness over the muscle belly of the tibialis anterior that does not decrease with elevation or pain medications. Pain increases with passive stretching or active use of the muscle. The patient will also likely experience paresthesias and/or numbness in the distribution of the deep peroneal nerve.

What laboratory or imaging studies would confirm the diagnosis?

Physicians can use compartment pressure testing, in which a needle or catheter is inserted into the affected compartment, to determine the presence of acute compartment syndrome. In the case of chronic compartment syndrome, measurements can be compared before and after exercise.

What additional information should be obtained to confirm the diagnosis?

A thorough medical history and physical examination should be completed to assist in ruling out other similar conditions such as deep venous thrombosis, fracture, and peripheral nerve injury.

Colles' Fracture

BRONZE

DIAGNOSIS

What condition produces a patient's symptoms?

A Colles' fracture frequently occurs when an individual reaches forward with their hands while attempting to break a fall. Trauma related to this maneuver is commonly termed a FOOSH (fall on outstretched hand) injury. Various types of wrist fractures can occur with a FOOSH injury due to the significant momentum and body weight that the wrist absorbs while in a hyperextended position.

An injury was most likely sustained to which structure?

A Colles' fracture is characterized by a transverse fracture of the distal radius, occurring in either an intra or extraarticular location due to direct trauma. The mechanism of injury typically causes the lunate to act as a wedge resulting in a shear force and dorsal displacement of the radius. Damage to structures on the ulnar aspect of the wrist such as the ulnar collateral ligament or styloid process are also common occurrences with a FOOSH injury.

CONFIRMATION

What is the most likely clinical presentation?

A patient with a Colles' fracture will likely present with pain and edema in close proximity to the fracture site. A "dinner fork" or "bayonet" deformity may be present with more severe Colles' fractures as a result of dorsal displacement of the distal radius, carpals, and hand in relation to the forearm. Patients with osteoporosis are at particular risk for acquiring Colles' fractures when falling from a standing position.

What laboratory or imaging studies would confirm the diagnosis?

An x-ray of the wrist is the preferred method of confirming a Colles' fracture and identifying displaced fragments or damage to adjacent bony structures. An x-ray will commonly reveal an area of increased bone density at the fracture site with irregularities in the smooth surface line of the radius. Complete fractures will typically reveal a "dinner fork" deformity on x-ray. An MRI may be utilized if ligamentous or other significant soft tissue damage is suspected.

What additional information should be obtained to confirm the diagnosis?

The patient's subjective report of the mechanism of injury and current symptoms are extremely important when a Colles' fracture is suspected. Visual inspection, a thorough history, and careful examination will typically support the diagnosis.

BRONZE

De Quervain's Tenosynovitis

DIAGNOSIS

What condition produces a patient's symptoms?

De Quervain's tenosynovitis is the result of an inflammatory process involving the tendons and synovium of the abductor pollicis longus (APL) and extensor pollicis brevis (EPB) at the base of the thumb. The onset of de Quervain's tenosynovitis is typically due to repetitive activities involving thumb abduction and extension such as racquet sports and repeated heavy lifting. The associated inflammation results in pain located at the base of the thumb within the anatomical snuffbox.

An injury was most likely sustained to which structure?

The tendons of the APL and EPB are covered by a synovial sheath and pass through the anatomical tunnel that is created by the extensor retinaculum and the radial styloid process. Inflammation of the tendons and synovium results in impingement of the tendons as they move through the tunnel. Direct trauma or structural anomalies in the area can also restrict tendon mobility and cause symptoms of de Quervain's tenosynovitis.

CONFIRMATION

What is the most likely clinical presentation?

Patients will primarily report localized pain and tenderness in the area of the anatomical snuffbox which may occasionally radiate into the forearm. Symptom onset may be gradual or sudden. The degree of reported pain tends to be activity dependent and typically improves with rest and worsens with activity or resisted testing. Edema may be palpable or visible at the base of the thumb. In severe cases, edema may also cause symptoms of nerve entrapment particularly in the superficial branch of the radial nerve. De Quervain's tenosynovitis is more prevalent among women with higher risk among new mothers due to the repetitive lifting and carrying of the infant.

What laboratory or imaging studies would confirm the diagnosis?

There are no laboratory or imaging studies commonly used to assist in the diagnosis of de Quervain's tenosynovitis. A diagnosis is typically made by means of a thorough medical history and physical examination.

What additional information should be obtained to confirm the diagnosis?

Provocative testing using Finkelstein's test should be included in a physical examination to assist with the diagnosis of de Quervain's tenosynovitis. Activities of daily living and functional limitations should also be reviewed in order to identify exacerbating factors.

BRONZE

Myositis Ossificans

DIAGNOSIS

What condition produces a patient's symptoms?

Myositis ossificans is a condition characterized by the calcification of muscle. The condition is typically caused by neglecting to properly treat a muscle strain or contusion. Failing to apply cold therapy after an injury, applying heat after an injury or having intense therapy or massage too soon after injury are precipitating factors that disrupt healing and lead to abnormal bone growth.

An injury was most likely sustained to what structure?

The condition is characterized by bone growth in the muscle belly and often occurs in muscles prone to traumatic injury such as the muscles of the arms and legs (e.g., quadriceps). Bone will begin to grow 2-4 weeks after the injury and will mature within 3-6 months.

CONFIRMATION

What is the most likely clinical presentation?

In the initial stage post injury, the patient will present with the typical symptoms of a contusion. The patient will have pain with functional activities and stiffness and pain after prolonged rest. Swelling, tenderness, and bruising may also be present. Within a few weeks after injury, the development of further symptoms may suggest the presence of myositis ossificans. Symptoms include a noticeable hard lump in the muscle belly, an increase in pain, and a decrease in range of motion that had previously been improving.

What laboratory or imaging studies would confirm the diagnosis?

An x-ray is the primary imaging study used to confirm the diagnosis. This is performed approximately three weeks after the injury when the bone has started to grow. Magnetic resonance imaging and ultrasound imaging can also be used to assist in confirming the diagnosis.

What additional information should be obtained to confirm the diagnosis?

A thorough medical history and physical examination should be performed to assist with the diagnosis of the condition and to rule out the presence of other similar conditions (e.g., osteosarcoma).

Osteochondritis Dissecans

BRONZE

DIAGNOSIS

What condition produces a patient's symptoms?

Osteochondritis dissecans is a condition where subchondral bone and its associated cartilage crack and separate from the end of the bone. In severe cases of the condition, the bone may actually detach from the surrounding area and float freely inside the joint space. There is no definitive etiology, though it is thought the condition occurs secondary to a loss of blood flow to the affected area possibly due to repetitive microtrauma.

An injury was most likely sustained to what structure?

Loss of blood flow causes subchondral bone to die and separate from the surrounding bone. This leaves the associated articular cartilage prone to further damage. This condition primarily affects the knee joint, though is also commonly seen in the elbow and ankle.

CONFIRMATION

What is the most likely clinical presentation?

The clinical presentation varies based on the degree of subchondral bone detachment. Typical symptoms include pain with functional activities, joint popping or locking, weakness, swelling, and decreased range of motion.

What laboratory or imaging studies would confirm the diagnosis?

X-ray imaging may confirm the diagnosis of this condition, though computed tomography and magnetic resonance imaging may also be used to assist in the diagnosis and to better visualize the area of cartilage affected.

What additional information should be obtained to confirm the diagnosis?

A thorough medical history and physical examination should be performed to rule out the existence of other similar conditions (e.g., arthritis). Wilson's test can be performed to detect osteochondritis dissecans of the knee.

Osteomyelitis

BRONZE

DIAGNOSIS

What condition produces a patient's symptoms?

Osteomyelitis refers to an infection that occurs within the bone, most commonly secondary to the Staphylococcus aureus microbe. Exposure to an infectious microbe may occur through direct contamination or secondary to an infection elsewhere in the body such as the bloodstream, a wound or nearby soft tissue.

An injury was most likely sustained to which structure?

Damage to the bone (e.g., result of a surgical procedure, compound fracture or puncture wound that penetrates bone) may directly expose the bone to infectious microbes in the air or contaminating debris. In cases of secondary infection, the location of the primary injury is variable. In either circumstance, prolonged or severe cases of osteomyelitis may result in structural damage to the infected bone which could lead to amputation.

CONFIRMATION

What is the most likely clinical presentation?

Signs and symptoms of osteomyelitis are similar to those of other types of infection. Fever and chills are common systemic complaints. Localized complaints typically include pain, edema, and erythema. A conclusive diagnosis may frequently be delayed since symptoms tend to be generalized or vague. Patients who have a weakened immune system, diabetes, sickle cell disease, who are elderly or are undergoing hemodialysis are at greater risk for developing osteomyelitis. Patients who develop osteomyelitis secondary to a wound infection may show significant changes in observable wound characteristics (e.g., color, amount of exudate, type of exudate, delayed healing) as well as slow or stagnant wound healing.

What laboratory or imaging studies would confirm the diagnosis?

A bone biopsy is the most conclusive procedure for diagnosing osteomyelitis and determining the specific infectious microbe present. Blood tests, x-rays, MRI, ultrasound, CT scans, bone scans, and PET scans may provide additional information (e.g., increased white blood cell count, specific infectious microbe, bone damage), but are not considered diagnostically conclusive.

What additional information should be obtained to confirm the diagnosis?

Medical and surgical history, as well as the patient's current health status should be thoroughly reviewed. If osteomyelitis is suspected, systemic or localized signs and symptoms of infection and potential sources of exposure should be further evaluated.

BRONZE

Tarsal Tunnel Syndrome

DIAGNOSIS

What condition produces a patient's symptoms?

The tarsal tunnel is located on the medial aspect of the ankle and is formed by the flexor retinaculum, the superior aspect of the calcaneus, the medial wall of the talus, and the medial-distal aspect of the tibia. The tibial nerve, posterior tibial artery, and tendons of the flexor hallucis longus, tibialis posterior, and flexor digitorum longus muscles pass through the tarsal tunnel. Tarsal tunnel syndrome occurs as a result of compression of the tibial nerve as it passes through the tarsal tunnel, causing neuropathy in the distribution of the nerve.

An injury was most likely sustained to which structure?

The tibial nerve is injured by compression within the tarsal tunnel causing motor and sensory disturbances. Etiologies are typically classified as either intrinsic (e.g., tumor, scar tissue), extrinsic (e.g., crush injury, severe ankle sprain) or tension factors (e.g., pes planus deformity, hindfoot valgus deformity).

CONFIRMATION

What is the most likely clinical presentation?

Symptoms include pain, numbness, and paresthesias in the foot that may be initially mistaken for plantar fasciitis. An antalgic gait pattern is common when symptoms are exacerbated. Rest typically alleviates, but does not completely resolve symptoms. Muscle atrophy may be visually observed and confirmed using manual muscle testing. Neurological signs may include a positive Tinel's sign with tibial nerve assessment posterior to the medial malleolus. Light touch and temperature sensation may be diminished in the sensory distribution of the tibial nerve and its branches. In severe or long-standing cases, trophic skin changes may also be observed.

What laboratory or imaging studies would confirm the diagnosis?

The presence of neuropathy is typically confirmed through an electromyography (EMG) or nerve conduction velocity (NCV) study. To confirm tarsal tunnel syndrome, however, the etiology of neuropathy must also be confirmed. An MRI or ultrasound may be utilized to assist in identifying compression due to a soft tissue lesion. X-ray may be utilized if bony structures are suspected to contribute to symptoms.

What additional information should be obtained to confirm the diagnosis?

A thorough medical history and physical examination should be completed to assist in ruling out alternative sources of peripheral neuropathy.

BRONZE

Ulnar Collateral Ligament Sprain - Thumb

DIAGNOSIS

What condition produces a patient's symptoms?

An ulnar collateral ligament (UCL) sprain of the thumb is the most common ligament injury in the hand. This injury occurs secondary to a traumatic event in which an excessive valgus force is applied to the metacarpophalangeal (MCP) joint of the thumb. The names "gamekeeper's thumb" and "skier's thumb" are commonly used for this injury and are derived from common mechanisms of the injury.

An injury was most likely sustained to what structure?

The UCL of the thumb is positioned on the medial side of the thumb's MCP joint and acts as an important stabilizer of the thumb. The grade of the sprain indicates the extent of injury to the ligament. With grade 1 and 2 sprains, the majority of the ligament remains intact, while a grade 3 sprain involves a complete tear of the ligament.

CONFIRMATION

What is the most likely clinical presentation?

Signs and symptoms of an UCL sprain include pain, tenderness, ecchymosis, and swelling near the thumb's MCP joint, specifically on the medial side. Other symptoms may include instability of the joint and weakness with grasping objects.

What laboratory or imaging studies would confirm the diagnosis?

X-rays should be ordered to rule out the existence of a fracture or dislocation. Ultrasound or magnetic resonance imaging may be used to determine if a ligament tear is present.

What additional information should be obtained to confirm the diagnosis?

A thorough medical history and physical examination will assist in the diagnosis. The therapist should assess the integrity of the UCL by performing ligament stability testing of the thumb. When applying a valgus force to the MCP joint, a movement of greater than 30-35 degrees indicates a complete tear of the UCL.

Musculoskeletal System Essentials

1. The body's three sources of adenosine triphosphate (ATP) include the ATP-PC (Phosphagen) System, Anaerobic Glycolysis (Lactic Acid) System, and Aerobic (Oxygen) System.

2. The ATP-PC (Phosphagen) System is used for ATP production during high intensity, short duration exercise, such as sprinting 100 meters. The system provides energy for muscle contraction for up to 15 seconds.

3. The anaerobic glycolysis system supplies ATP during high intensity, short duration exercise, such as sprinting 400 or 800 meters. The system provides energy for muscle contraction for 30-40 seconds.

4. The aerobic system supplies ATP during low intensity, long duration activities, such as running a marathon. The amount of ATP production is far greater, but requires a complicated series of chemical reactions.

5. Motion occurs in three cardinal planes of the body (frontal, sagittal, transverse) around three corresponding axes (anterior-posterior, medial-lateral, vertical).

6. Common joint receptors include free nerve endings, Golgi ligament endings, Golgi-Mazzoni corpuscles, Pacinian corpuscles, and Ruffini endings.

7. Golgi tendon organs are encapsulated sensory receptors that are sensitive to tension, especially when produced by active muscle contraction. They function to transmit information about tension or the rate of change of tension within the muscle.

8. Type I muscle fibers are described as aerobic, red, tonic, slow twitch, and slow-oxidative. Type II muscle fibers are described as anaerobic, white, phasic, fast twitch, and fast-glycolytic.

9. Muscle spindles are distributed throughout the belly of the muscle and function to send information to the nervous system about muscle length and/or the rate of change of its length.

10. The upper extremity consists of the shoulder, elbow, and wrist. The shoulder complex is formed by the glenohumeral joint, sternoclavicular joint, acromioclavicular joint, and scapulothoracic articulations. The elbow joint is formed by the radiohumeral joint, ulnohumeral joint, and proximal radioulnar joint. The wrist complex is formed by the radiocarpal and midcarpal joints.

11. The lower extremity consists of the hip, knee, ankle, and foot. The hip joint is a synovial joint formed by the head of the femur and the acetabulum. The knee joint is formed by the tibiofemoral joint and patellofemoral joint. The ankle and foot are formed by the distal tibiofibular joint, talocrural joint, subtalar joint, midtarsal joint, and forefoot.

12. The cervical spine consists of 7 vertebrae. The thoracic spine consists of 12 vertebrae, and the lumbar spine consists of 5 vertebrae.

13. An upper and lower quarter screen should, at a minimum, consist of an assessment of posture, range of motion, resistive testing, reflex testing, and dermatome testing.

14. Body composition refers to the relative percentage of body weight that is comprised of fat and fat-free tissue. A healthy range of body fat is 12-18% for males and 18-23% for females.

15. Common methods to assess body composition include hydrostatic weighing, plethysmography, skinfold measurement, body mass index, and bioelectrical impedance.

16. The loose packed position of a joint is characterized by minimal stress on the joint, minimal joint congruency, and maximum ligament laxity. The close packed position of a joint is characterized by maximal stress on the joint, full joint congruency, and maximum ligament tightness.

17. End-feel refers to the type of resistance felt when passively moving a joint through the end range of motion. An end-feel classified as firm, hard or soft can be normal or abnormal depending on the joint, while an end-feel classified as empty is always abnormal.

18. Manual muscle testing grades range from zero (0/5) to normal (5/5) based on the ability to move a body segment through range with and without varying levels of resistance.

Musculoskeletal System Essentials

19. Active muscle insufficiency occurs when a two-joint muscle contracts across both joints simultaneously. Passive insufficiency occurs when a two-joint muscle is lengthened over both joints simultaneously.

20. Standard gait terminology includes heel strike, foot flat, midstance, heel off, toe off, acceleration, midswing, and deceleration.

21. Rancho Los Amigos gait terminology includes initial contact, loading response, midstance, terminal stance, pre-swing, initial swing, midswing, and terminal swing.

22. The stance phase represents approximately 60% of the gait cycle and the swing phase represents 40% of the gait cycle.

23. Step length refers to the distance measured between right heel strike and left heel strike. Stride length refers to the distance measured between right heel strike and the following right heel strike.

24. Biceps tendon pathology can be identified through Ludington's test, Speed's test, and Yergason's test.

25. Rotator cuff pathology/impairment can be identified through the drop arm test, Hawkins-Kennedy impingement test, Neer impingement test, and supraspinatus test.

26. Contractures, or tightness of the hip, can be identified through Ely's test, Ober's test, piriformis test, Thomas test, tripod sign, and 90-90 straight leg raise test.

27. An anterior cruciate ligament sprain can be identified through the anterior drawer test, Lachman test, and lateral pivot shift test.

28. Meniscal pathology of the knee can be identified through Apley's compression test, bounce home test, and McMurray test.

29. Grades I and IV mobilizations are considered small amplitude movement, while grades II and III are considered large amplitude movements.

30. Grade V manipulation is defined as small amplitude, high velocity thrust technique performed to snap adhesions at the limit of range of motion.

31. The convex/concave rule specifies that when a convex surface is moving on a concave surface, roll and slide occur in the opposite direction. When a concave surface is moving on a convex surface, roll and slide occur in the same direction.

32. Range of motion exercises are designed to improve the mobility of a single joint and may include passive, active-assisted, and active range of motion.

33. Range of motion exercises typically begin with passive range of motion, since it does not require any muscle contraction from the patient, and progress towards active range of motion.

34. Stretching exercises are used to improve muscle flexibility by increasing the extensibility of the musculotendinous unit and connective tissues.

35. Static stretching, characterized by a low intensity and long duration, is the safest form of stretching that results in the greatest gains in tissue extensibility.

36. Proprioceptive neuromuscular facilitation stretching is another stretching technique designed to improve muscle flexibility, while ballistic stretching and dynamic stretching are more often employed as a warm-up prior to initiating activity.

37. A muscle is made up of several muscle fibers and the connective tissue layers that surround and lie within the muscle.

38. Resistive training programs often employ isometric, isotonic, and isokinetic exercise.

39. Open-chain activities involve the distal segment moving freely in space, while closed-chain activities involve the body moving over a fixed distal segment.

40. Strength training parameters, such as intensity, volume, and frequency, will vary according to the desired goal of the strengthening program (e.g., strength, endurance, power).

Musculoskeletal System Essentials

41. Hip precautions following total hip arthroplasty using a posterolateral surgical approach include avoiding hip flexion beyond 90 degrees, adduction, and hip medial rotation.

42. Common types of fractures include avulsion, closed, comminuted, compound, greenstick, nonunion, stress, and spiral.

43. Common pharmacological agents used in the treatment of musculoskeletal disorders include opioid agents, nonopioid agents, glucocorticoid agents, and disease-modifying antirheumatic agents.

44. Kyphosis refers to an excessive curvature of the spine in a posterior direction usually identified in the thoracic spine. Lordosis refers to an excessive curvature of the spine in an anterior direction usually in the cervical or lumbar spine.

45. An orthotic is an external device that provides support or stabilization, improves function, corrects deformities, and distributes pressure from one area to another.

46. Lower extremity amputations are significantly more common than upper extremity amputations with peripheral vascular disease serving as the primary etiology.

47. Components of an upper extremity prosthesis include the socket, suspension, elbow unit, wrist unit, and terminal device.

48. Components of a lower extremity prosthesis include socket, suspension, knee, shank, and foot.

49. Potential complications following amputation include contractures, deep vein thrombosis, hypersensitivity, neuroma, phantom limb, phantom pain, psychological impact, and wound infections.

50. Common gait deviations with a prosthesis include lateral bending, vaulting, forward trunk flexion, medial or lateral whip, abducted gait, circumducted gait, excessive knee flexion during stance, and rotation of the forefoot at heel strike.

Musculoskeletal System Proficiencies

1. Musculoskeletal Upper Extremity Anatomy

Identify the appropriate term for each of the specified locations. Answers must be selected from the Word Bank and can be used only once.

Word Bank: brachioradialis, flexor carpi radialis, flexor carpi ulnaris, flexor digitorum superficialis, palmaris longus, pronator quadratus, pronator teres

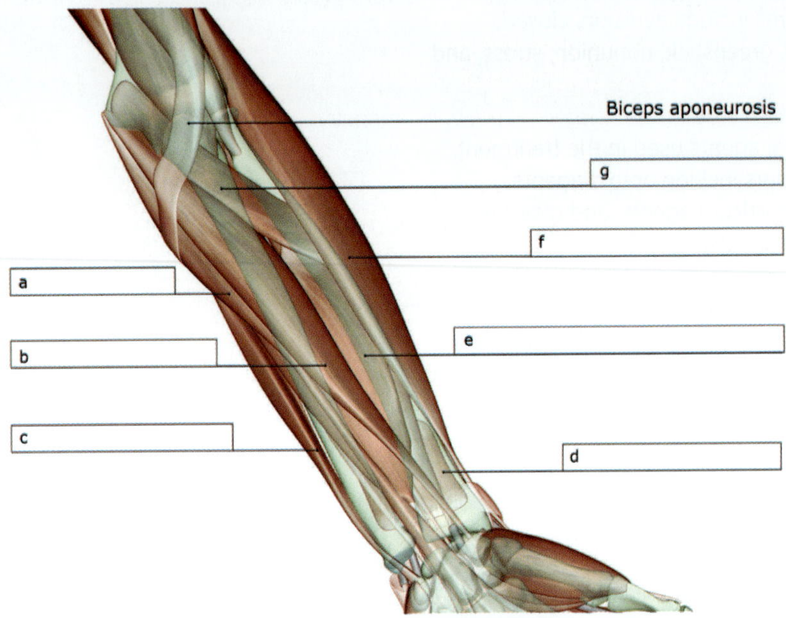

2. Musculoskeletal Lower Extremity Anatomy I

Identify the appropriate term for each of the specified locations. Answers must be selected from the Word Bank and can be used only once.

Word Bank: gracilis, rectus femoris, sartorius, tensor fasciae latae, vastus lateralis, vastus medialis

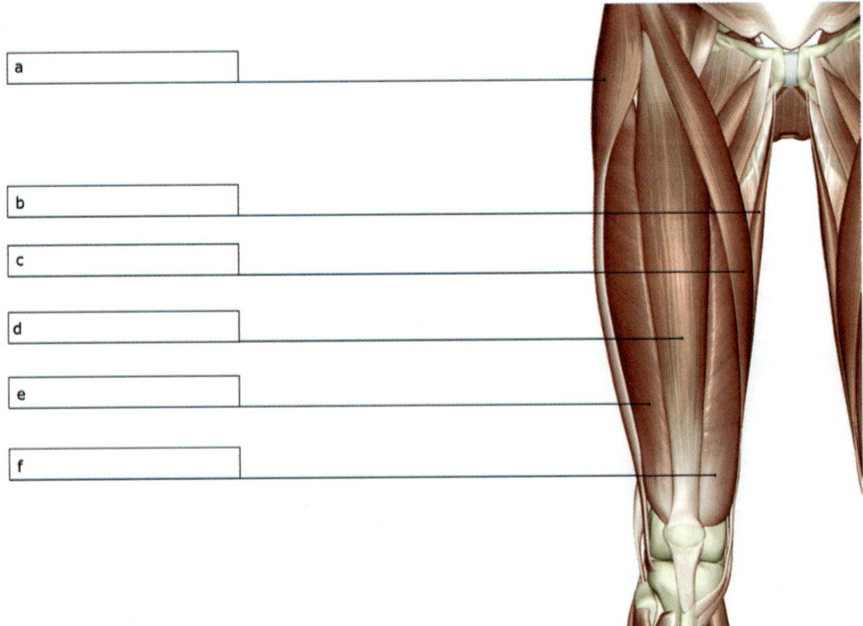

Musculoskeletal System Proficiencies

3. Musculoskeletal Lower Extremity Anatomy II

Identify the appropriate term for each of the specified locations. Answers must be selected from the Word Bank and can be used only once.

Word Bank: abductor digiti minimi, abductor hallucis, flexor digitorum brevis, flexor hallucis brevis, lumbricals, quadratus plantae

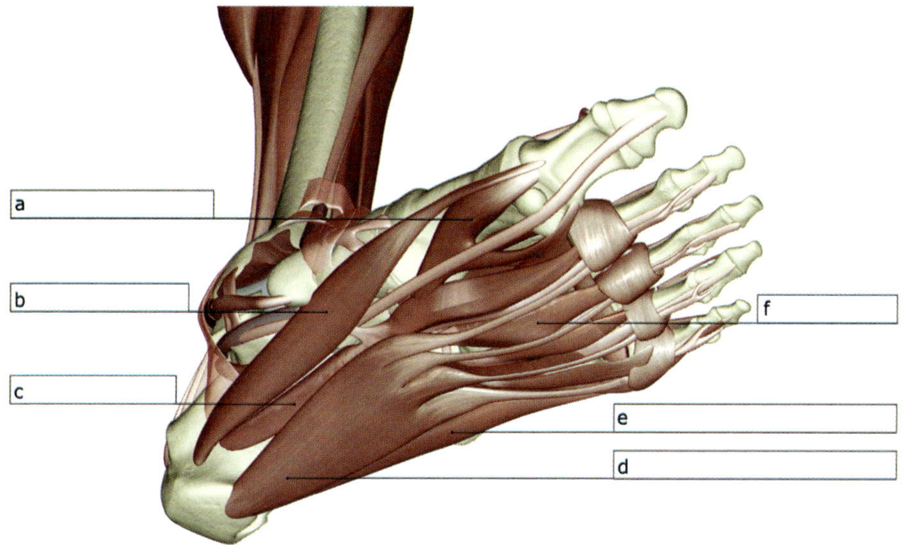

4. Muscle Function - Upper Extremity

Identify the muscle that contributes to performing each of the listed motions. Each muscle in the Word Bank must be used only once. Since a given muscle may contribute to multiple motions, it is essential for answers to be selected in a manner that allows for all muscles to be utilized.

Word Bank: anconeus, brachioradialis, coracobrachialis, extensor carpi ulnaris, flexor carpi radialis, latissimus dorsi, palmaris longus, teres major, teres minor

Shoulder	Muscle
flexion	a
extension	b
lateral rotation	c
medial rotation	d
Elbow	**Muscle**
flexion	e
extension	f
Wrist	**Muscle**
flexion	g
extension	h
radial deviation	i

Musculoskeletal System Proficiencies

5. Muscle Function - Lower Extremity

Identify the muscle that contributes to performing each of the listed motions. Each muscle in the Word Bank must be used only once. Since a given muscle may contribute to multiple motions, it is essential for answers to be selected in a manner that allows for all muscles to be utilized.

Word Bank: biceps femoris, extensor hallucis longus, gluteus medius, gracilis, iliopsoas, peroneus longus, piriformis, tibialis posterior, vastus medialis

Hip	Muscle
flexion	a
adduction	b
lateral rotation	c
medial rotation	d
Knee	**Muscle**
flexion	e
extension	f
Ankle	**Muscle**
dorsiflexion	g
inversion	h
eversion	i

6. Muscle Fibers

Identify the type of muscle fiber most closely associated with each described characteristic. Answers must be selected from the Word Bank.

Word Bank: Type I, Type II

Characteristic	Type
low capillary density	a
aerobic	b
large amount of mitochondria	c
white	d
fast-glycolytic	e
low myoglobin content	f
extensive blood supply	g
slow twitch	h

Musculoskeletal System Proficiencies

7. Manual Muscle Testing

Identify the manual muscle testing grade most closely associated with the supplied description. Answers must be selected from the Word Bank and can be used only once.

Word Bank: zero, trace, poor minus, poor, poor plus, fair minus, fair, fair plus, good minus, good, good plus, normal

Grade	Description
a	The subject does not complete range of motion in a gravity-eliminated position.
b	The subject's muscle contraction can be palpated, but there is no joint movement.
c	The subject does not complete the range of motion against gravity, but does complete more than half of the range.
d	The subject completes range of motion against gravity with maximal resistance.
e	The subject completes range of motion against gravity with minimal-moderate resistance.
f	The subject completes range of motion with gravity eliminated.
g	The subject completes range of motion against gravity with only minimal resistance.
h	The subject completes range of motion against gravity with moderate resistance.

8. Gait - Standard Terminology

Identify the sequence and phase of the gait cycle starting with heel strike and ending with deceleration. Answers must be selected from the Word Bank and can be used only once.

Word Bank: **Sequence** - 2nd, 3rd, 4th, 5th, 6th, 7th

Phase - acceleration, foot flat, heel off, midstance, midswing, toe off

Sequence	Phase	Description
1st	heel strike	The instant the heel touches the ground to begin stance phase.
a	b	The point in which only the toe of the stance limb remains on the ground.
c	d	The point when the swing limb is directly under the body.
e	f	The point in which the entire foot makes contact with the ground.
g	h	Begins when toe off is complete and the reference limb swings until positioned directly under the body.
i	j	The point in which the heel of the stance limb leaves the ground.
k	l	The point during the stance phase when the entire body weight is directly over the stance limb.
8th	deceleration	Begins directly after midswing as the swing limb begins to extend and ends just prior to heel strike.

Musculoskeletal System Proficiencies

9. Abnormal Gait

Identify the abnormal gait pattern most closely associated with the supplied description. Answers must be selected from the Word Bank and can be used only once.

Word Bank: antalgic, circumduction, parkinsonian, scissor, steppage, tabetic, Trendelenburg, vaulting

Gait Pattern	Description
a	A gait pattern in which the feet and toes are lifted through hip and knee flexion to excessive heights.
b	A gait pattern characterized by the legs crossing midline upon advancement.
c	A gait pattern characterized by a circular motion to advance the leg during swing phase.
d	A protective gait pattern where the involved step length is decreased in order to avoid weight bearing on the involved side.
e	A gait pattern where the swing leg advances through a combination of elevation of the pelvis and plantar flexion of the stance leg.
f	A gait pattern characterized by excessive lateral trunk flexion and weight shifting over the stance leg due to gluteus medius weakness.
g	A gait pattern marked by quick and small steps with increased forward flexion of the trunk and knees.
h	A high stepping ataxic gait pattern in which the feet slap the ground.

10. Goniometry

Complete the blank cells with the appropriate information based on the supplied information. The number of desired responses for each cell is identified in parentheses.

Joint	Motion	Axis
shoulder	flexion	a (1)
shoulder	b (2)	olecranon process
c (1)	pronation	lateral to the ulnar styloid process
wrist	radial deviation	d (1)
hip	e (2)	anterior aspect of the patella
ankle	f (2)	lateral aspect of the lateral malleolus
g (1)	h (2)	posterior aspect of the ankle midway between the malleoli

Musculoskeletal System Proficiencies

11. Special Tests

Complete the blank cells with the appropriate information based on the supplied information.

Special Test	Patient Position	Positive Sign
Vertebral artery test	a	b
Speed's test	sitting or standing	c
d	e	failing to slowly lower the arm to their side or by the presence of severe pain
Allen test (thoracic outlet)	f	g
h	i	pain in the lateral epicondyle region or muscle weakness
j	supine	straight leg rising from the table
Ober's test	sidelying	k
Patrick's test	l	m
Anterior drawer test (knee)	supine	n
Apley's compression test	o	pain or clicking
p	q	absence of plantar flexion
Homans' sign	r	s

Musculoskeletal System Proficiencies

12. Osteokinematic and Arthrokinematic Motions

Identify the concave and convex joint surface associated with the listed joints. Answers must be selected from the Word Bank and can be used more than once.

Word Bank: acetabulum, carpals, femur, fibula, glenoid, humerus, radius, talus, tibia

Joint	Concave	Convex
glenohumeral	a (1)	b (1)
radiohumeral	c (1)	d (1)
radiocarpal	e (1)	f (1)
hip	g (1)	h (1)
tibiofemoral	i (1)	j (1)
talocrural	k (2)	l (1)

13. Musculoskeletal System Basics

Mark each statement as True or False. If the statement is False correct the statement in the space provided.

True/False	Statement
a	An end-feel classified as empty can be classified as normal or abnormal depending on the joint.
Correction	
b	The loose packed position of the hip is 30 degrees flexion, 30 degrees abduction, and slight medial rotation.
Correction	
c	Stride length refers to the distance measured between right heel strike and left heel strike.
Correction	

Musculoskeletal System Proficiencies

True/False	Statement
d	The capsular pattern of the glenohumeral joint is lateral rotation, abduction, and medial rotation.
Correction	
e	According to Rancho Los Amigos gait terminology, pre-swing, midswing, and terminal swing are components of swing phase.
Correction	
f	Peak activity of the tibialis anterior occurs during the gait cycle just after heel strike.
Correction	
g	Normal elbow flexion is 0-135 degrees.
Correction	
h	The tensor fasciae latae, gluteus medius, and piriformis function as medial rotators of the hip.
Correction	
i	Muscle testing of the lower trapezius, rhomboids, and latissimus dorsi occurs with the patient positioned in prone.
Correction	
j	Sixty percent of the gait cycle occurs in the stance phase.
Correction	

Musculoskeletal System Answer Key

1. Musculoskeletal Upper Extremity Anatomy

a. palmaris longus
b. flexor carpi radialis
c. flexor carpi ulnaris
d. pronator quadratus
e. flexor digitorum superficialis
f. brachioradialis
g. pronator teres

2. Musculoskeletal Lower Extremity Anatomy I

a. tensor fasciae latae
b. gracilis
c. sartorius
d. rectus femoris
e. vastus lateralis
f. vastus medialis

3. Musculoskeletal Lower Extremity Anatomy II

a. flexor hallucis brevis
b. abductor hallucis
c. quadratus plantae
d. flexor digitorum brevis
e. abductor digiti minimi
f. lumbricals

4. Muscle Function - Upper Extremity

a. coracobrachialis
b. latissimus dorsi or teres major
c. teres minor
d. teres major or latissimus dorsi
e. brachioradialis
f. anconeus
g. palmaris longus
h. extensor carpi ulnaris
i. flexor carpi radialis

5. Muscle Function - Lower Extremity

a. iliopsoas
b. gracilis
c. piriformis
d. gluteus medius
e. biceps femoris
f. vastus medialis
g. extensor hallucis longus
h. tibialis posterior
i. peroneus longus

6. Muscle Fibers

a. Type II
b. Type I
c. Type I
d. Type II
e. Type II
f. Type II
g. Type I
h. Type I

7. Manual Muscle Testing

a. poor minus
b. trace
c. fair minus
d. normal
e. good minus
f. poor
g. fair plus
h. good

8. Gait - Standard Terminology

a. 5th
b. toe off
c. 7th
d. midswing
e. 2nd
f. foot flat
g. 6th
h. acceleration
i. 4th
j. heel off
k. 3rd
l. midstance

9. Abnormal Gait

a. steppage
b. scissor
c. circumduction
d. antalgic
e. vaulting
f. Trendelenburg
g. parkinsonian
h. tabetic

Musculoskeletal System Answer Key

10. Goniometry

a. acromial process
b. lateral rotation and medial rotation
c. forearm
d. over the middle of the dorsal aspect of the wrist over the capitate
e. lateral rotation and medial rotation
f. dorsiflexion and plantar flexion
g. subtalar
h. inversion and eversion

11. Special Tests

a. supine
b. dizziness, nystagmus, slurred speech or loss of consciousness
c. pain or tenderness in the bicipital groove region
d. drop arm test
e. sitting or standing
f. sitting or standing
g. absent or diminished radial pulse
h. lateral epicondylitis test
i. sitting
j. Thomas test
k. inability of the test leg to adduct and touch the table
l. supine
m. failure of the test leg to abduct below the level of the opposite leg
n. excessive anterior translation of the tibia on the femur with a diminished or absent end-point
o. prone
p. Thompson test
q. prone
r. supine
s. pain in the calf

12. Osteokinematic and Arthrokinematic Motions

a. glenoid
b. humerus
c. radius
d. humerus
e. radius
f. carpals
g. acetabulum
h. femur
i. tibia
j. femur
k. tibia and fibula
l. talus

13. Musculoskeletal System Basics*

a. FALSE: Correction - An end-feel classified as empty is always considered abnormal due to the presence of pain.
b. FALSE: Correction - The loose packed position of the hip is 30 degrees flexion, 30 degrees abduction, and slight lateral rotation.
c. FALSE: Correction - Step length refers to the distance measured between right heel strike and left heel strike.
d. TRUE
e. FALSE: Correction - Pre-swing is a component of stance phase. Initial swing, midswing, and terminal swing are components of swing phase.
f. TRUE
g. FALSE: Correction - Normal elbow flexion is 0-150 degrees.
h. FALSE: Correction - The tensor fasciae latae and gluteus medius function as medial rotators of the hip. The piriformis functions as a lateral rotator of the hip.
i. TRUE
j. TRUE

*The correction presented for each false statement is an example of several possible corrections.

Musculoskeletal System References

1. Guyton A. ***Textbook of Medical Physiology.*** W.B. Saunders Company. 1986.
2. Kendall F, McCreary E. Provance P. ***Muscles: Testing and Function with Posture and Pain***. Fifth Edition. Lippincott Williams & Wilkins. 2005.
3. Norkin C, White D. ***Measurement of Joint Motion: A Guide to Goniometry***. Fifth Edition. F.A. Davis Company. 2016.
4. Levangie P, Norkin C. ***Joint Structure and Function: A Comprehensive Analysis***. Fifth Edition. F.A. Davis Company. 2011.
5. Tortora G, Derrickson B. ***Principles of Anatomy and Physiology***. Twelfth Edition. John Wiley & Sons Inc. 2009.
6. Moore K, Dalley A. ***Clinically Oriented Anatomy***. Seventh Edition. Lippincott Williams & Wilkins. 2013.
7. Patton K, Thibodeau G. ***Anatomy and Physiology***. Seventh Edition. Elsevier Inc. 2010.
8. Anderson MK, Hall SJ, Martin M. ***Fundamentals of Sports Injury Management***. Fourth Edition. Lippincott Williams & Wilkins. 2009.
9. Bickley L. ***Bates' Guide to Physical Examination and History Taking***. Twelfth Edition. Wolters Kluwer. 2017.
10. Magee D. ***Orthopedic Physical Assessment***. Sixth Edition. W.B. Saunders Company. 2014.
11. Starkey C, Ryan J. ***Evaluation of Orthopedic and Athletic Injuries***. F.A. Davis Company. 2002.
12. Hoppenfeld S, Thomas H, Hutton R. ***Physical Examination of the Spine and Extremities***. Prentice Hall. 1976.
13. Hertling D, Kessler R. ***Management of Common Musculoskeletal Disorders***. Fourth Edition. Lippincott Williams & Wilkins. 2006
14. Edmond S. ***Joint Mobilization/Manipulation: Extremity and Spinal Techniques***. Third Edition. Mosby Inc. 2016.
15. Brody L, Hall C. ***Therapeutic Exercise: Moving Toward Function***. Fourth Edition. Lippincott Williams & Wilkins. 2018.
16. Kisner C, Colby L, Borstad J. ***Therapeutic Exercise Foundations and Techniques***. Seventh Edition. F.A. Davis Company. 2018.
17. Prentice W, Voight M. ***Techniques in Musculoskeletal Rehabilitation***. McGraw-Hill Inc. 2008.
18. Dutton M. ***Orthopaedic Examination, Evaluation, and Intervention***. Fourth Edition. McGraw-Hill Inc. 2017.
19. American College of Sports Medicine. ***ACSM's Resource Manual for Guidelines for Exercise Testing and Prescription***. Seventh Edition. Lippincott Williams & Wilkins. 2014.
20. Reese N, Bandy WD. ***Joint Range of Motion and Muscle Length Testing***. Second Edition. W.B. Saunders Company. 2009.
21. Hislop HJ, Avers D. ***Daniels and Worthingham's Muscle Testing: Techniques of Manual Examination and Performance Testing***. Ninth Edition, W.B. Saunders Company. 2014.
22. Roy S, Wolf S, Scalzitti D. ***The Rehabilitation Specialist's Handbook***. Fourth Edition. F.A. Davis Company. 2013.
23. Perry J, Burnfield J. ***Gait Analysis: Normal and Pathological Function***. Second Edition. Slack Incorporated. 2010.
24. Hamill J, Knutzen K. ***Biomechanical Basis of Human Movement***. Third Edition. Lippincott Williams & Wilkins. 2008.
25. Oatis C. ***Kinesiology: The Mechanics and Pathomechanics of Human Movement***. Second Edition. Lippincott Williams & Wilkins. 2009.
26. Reider B. ***The Orthopaedic Physical Examination***. W.B. Saunders Company. 1999.
27. Tecklin J. ***Pediatric Physical Therapy***. Fifth Edition. Lippincott Williams & Wilkins. 2015.
28. Birrer R, O'Connor F. ***Sports Medicine for the Primary Care Physician***. Third Edition. CRC Press. 2004.
29. Sueki D, Brechter J. ***Orthopedic Rehabilitation Clinical Advisor***. Mosby Inc. 2010.
30. Palisano R, Orlin M, Shreiber J. ***Campbell's Physical Therapy for Children***. Fifth Edition. Elsevier. 2017.
31. Goodman C, Fuller K. ***Pathology: Implications for the Physical Therapist***. Fourth Edition. W.B. Saunders Company. 2015.
32. Brotzman SB, Wilk KE. ***Clinical Orthopedic Rehabilitation***. Mosby Inc. 2003.
33. Maxey L, Magnusson J. ***Rehabilitation for the Postsurgical Orthopedic Patient***. Mosby Inc. 2001.
34. ***Nurse's 3-Minute Clinical Reference***. Second Edition. Lippincott Williams & Wilkins. 2007.

Musculoskeletal System References

35. Goodman C, Heick J, Lazaro R. ***Differential Diagnosis for Physical Therapists - Screening for Referral***. Sixth Edition. Elsevier. 2018.

36. Cameron M, Monroe L. ***Physical Rehabilitation: Evidence-Based Examination, Evaluation, and Intervention***. W. B. Saunders Company. 2007.

37. Roach S. ***Pharmacology for Health Professionals***. Lippincott Williams & Wilkins. 2005.

38. Gladson B. ***Pharmacology for Physical Therapists***. W. B. Saunders Company. 2006.

39. Ciccone C. ***Pharmacology for Rehabilitation***. Fifth Edition. F.A. Davis Company. 2016.

40. Seymour R. ***Prosthetics and Orthotics: Lower Limb and Spinal***. Lippincott Williams & Wilkins. 2002.

41. Palmer L, Toms J. ***Manual for Functional Training***. Third Edition. F.A. Davis Company. 1992.

42. Radomski MV, Latham CAT. ***Occupational Therapy for Physical Dysfunction***. Sixth Edition. Lippincott, Williams & Wilkins. 2008.

43. Braddom RL. ***Physical Medicine and Rehabilitation***. Third Edition. Saunders. Elsevier. 2007.

44. Tan J. ***Practical Manual of Physical Medicine and Rehabilitation***. Second Edition. Elsevier. 2006.

45. DeRuyter O. ***Clinician's Guide to Assistive Technology***. Mosby Inc. 2002.

46. May B, Lockard M. ***Prosthetics and Orthotics in Clinical Practice: A Case Study Approach***. F.A. Davis Company, 2011.

47. Means K, Kortebein P. ***Geriatrics***. Demos Medical. 2013.

48. Smith D, Michael J, Bowker J. ***Atlas of Amputations and Limb Deficiencies: Surgical, Prosthetic, and Rehabilitation Principles***. American Academy of Orthopaedic Surgeons. 2004.

49. Lusardi M, Milagros J, Nielsen C. ***Orthotics and Prosthetics in Rehabilitation***. Third Edition. Elsevier. 2013.

5

Neuromuscular and Nervous Systems

Therese Giles

Neuromuscular and Nervous Systems represents approximately 44 - 50 questions (22% - 25%) on the NPTE-PT.

Contributors

Scott Giles
Shawn Paquette

CHAPTER 5

Neuromuscular and Nervous Systems

Neuroanatomy: Anatomical Divisions of the Nervous System[1,2,3]

Central Nervous System (CNS)
Brain
forebrain (prosencephalon)
• telencephalon: cerebrum, hippocampus, basal ganglia, amygdala
• diencephalon: thalamus, hypothalamus, subthalamus, epithalamus
midbrain (mesencephalon)
• tectum: superior and inferior colliculi
• tegmentum: cerebral aqueduct, periaqueductal gray, reticular formation, substantia nigra, red nucleus
hindbrain (rhombencephalon)
• metencephalon: cerebellum, pons
• myelencephalon: medulla oblongata
Brainstem
midbrain, pons, medulla oblongata
• Brainstem is noted separately to acknowledge its components since it incorporates the midbrain with specific sections of the hindbrain.
Spinal Cord
• cervical, thoracic, lumbar, sacral, and coccygeal levels
• afferent and efferent tracts
• inner core of gray matter and superficial white matter

Characteristics
• main centers where integration and coordination of nervous system information occur
• covered in a system of meninges and suspended in cerebrospinal fluid for protection
• surrounded by skull and vertebral column for protection
• gray matter - consists of unmyelinated neurons and contains capillaries, glial cells, cell bodies, and dendrites
• white matter - consists of myelinated axons and contains nerve fibers without dendrites
• white matter of the spinal cord is divided into three funiculi: anterior, lateral, and dorsal columns
• brain is divided into left and right cerebral hemispheres
• each hemisphere of the brain contains a frontal lobe, temporal lobe, parietal lobe, and occipital lobe

Peripheral Nervous System (PNS)

Cranial Nerves and Ganglia

- 12 pairs of cranial nerves exit the skull through the foramina

Spinal Nerves and Ganglia/Plexuses

- 31 pairs of spinal nerves exit the vertebral column through the intervertebral foramina
  - 8 cervical, 12 thoracic, 5 lumbar, 5 sacral, 1 coccygeal

Characteristics

- bundles of nerve fibers and axons are supported by connective tissue and conduct information to the CNS
- encased in fibrous sheaths, however, relatively unprotected
- spinal nerves each have an anterior root carrying motor information away from the CNS (efferent fibers)
- spinal nerves each have a posterior root carrying information regarding sensation to the CNS (afferent fibers)
- ganglia are clusters or swellings of cells that give rise to the peripheral and central nerve fibers
- ganglia are divided into sensory ganglia and autonomic ganglia

Autonomic Nervous System (ANS)

Sympathetic Division

- prepares the body for emergency response; norepinephrine neurotransmitter; generally a stimulating response

Parasympathetic Division

- conserving and restoring energy; acetylcholine neurotransmitter; generally an inhibitory response

Characteristics

- anatomically contains portions of the CNS and PNS
- concerned with innervation for involuntary processes, glands, internal organs, and smooth muscle
- emphasis on homeostasis and a person's response to stress
- impulses often do not reach our consciousness
- impulses produce largely automatic responses

Somatic Nervous System (SNS)
• peripheral and motor nerve fibers
Characteristics
• peripheral nerve fibers send sensory information to the CNS • motor nerve fibers send information to skeletal muscles • somatic motor neurons travel directly to skeletal muscle without intervening synapses • all nerve fibers are myelinated • controls voluntary movements and provides the ability to sense touch, smell, sight, taste and sound • all five senses are influenced by the SNS

Limbic System[4]
• corpus callosum, olfactory tract, mammillary bodies, fornix, thalamic nuclei, amygdala, hippocampus, parahippocampal gyrus, cingulate gyrus, hypothalamic nuclei
Characteristics
• involved in the control and expression of mood and emotion, processing and storage of recent memory, olfaction, control of appetite, and emotional responses to food • lesions to the limbic system can also result in a variety of behaviors including aggression, extreme fearfulness, altered sexual behavior, and changes in motivation

CONSIDER THIS

AUTONOMIC NERVOUS SYSTEM DISORDERS[5]

- The autonomic nervous system (ANS) influences all internal organs, blood vessels, pupils and muscles of the eye, as well as sweat, salivary, and digestive glands as it relates to homeostasis. The ANS controls blood pressure, heart and breathing rates, body temperature, digestion, metabolism, electrolyte balance, production of saliva, sweat and tears, urination, defecation, sexual response, and other bodily processes.
- Disorders of the ANS can affect any body part or process. Autonomic disorders may result from outside pathology that damages autonomic nerves, such as diabetes or alcoholism, or there may be primary damage to the system. Autonomic disorders may be reversible or progressive in nature.
- Examples of ANS disorders include constipation, erectile dysfunction, Horner's syndrome, vasovagal syncope, orthostatic hypotension, and postural tachycardia syndrome.
- ANS disorders are typically treated with pharmacological intervention. These disorders may or may not have an impact on the physical therapy plan of care. Therapists need to possess an understanding of the impact of a patient's disorder and modify treatment based on their findings.

Central Nervous System

Brain

Forebrain (Prosencephalon)[1,2,6]

Telencephalon

The telencephalon is the largest division of the human brain and consists of the cerebrum (cerebral cortex), hippocampus, basal ganglia, and amygdala (Fig. 5-1).

Cerebrum

The cerebrum, which encompasses the major portion of the brain, is divided into the right and left cerebral hemispheres (Fig. 5-2). The two hemispheres are joined at the bottom by white matter, termed corpus callosum, which relays information from one side of the brain to the other. The surface of the cerebrum contains billions of neurons and glia that form the cerebral cortex. The outer surface of the cerebrum is termed gray matter and the interior is termed white matter. Sulci and fissures demark the specific lobes of the brain. Each lobe is responsible for different functions.

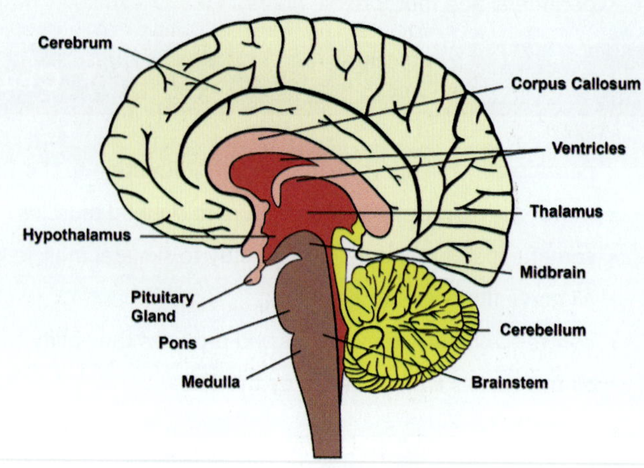

Fig. 5-1: A sagittal view of the human brain.

Fissures

- interhemispheric fissure (medial longitudinal): separates the two cerebral hemispheres
- Sylvian fissure (lateral): anterior portion separates the temporal and frontal lobes; posterior portion separates the temporal and parietal lobes

Sulci

- central sulcus (sulcus of Rolando): separates frontal and parietal lobes laterally
- parieto-occipital sulcus: separates the parietal and occipital lobes medially
- calcarine sulcus: separates the occipital lobe into superior and inferior halves

Hemisphere Specialization/Dominance[6,7]

Left

- Language
- Sequence and perform movements
- Understand language
- Produce written and spoken language
- Analytical
- Controlled
- Logical
- Rational
- Mathematical calculations
- Express positive emotions such as love and happiness
- Process verbally coded information in an organized, logical, and sequential manner

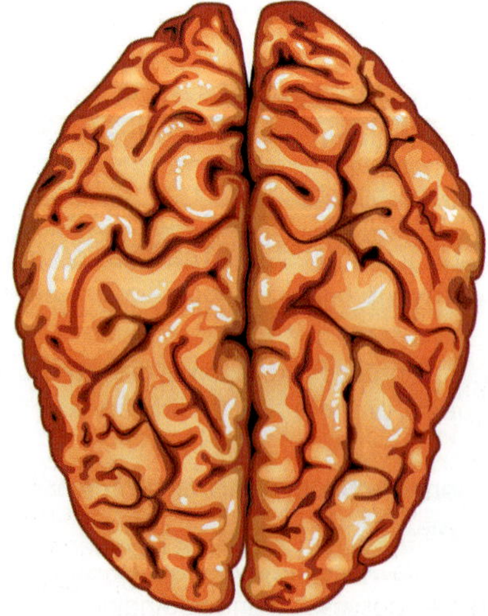

Fig. 5-2: The two hemispheres of the brain and the corresponding characteristics of each.

Right

- Nonverbal processing
- Process information in a holistic manner
- Artistic abilities
- General concept comprehension
- Hand-eye coordination
- Spatial relationships
- Kinesthetic awareness
- Understand music
- Understand nonverbal communication
- Mathematical reasoning
- Express negative emotions
- Body image awareness

Lobes of the Cerebrum[2,7,8]		
Lobe	**Function**	**Impairment**
Frontal	• voluntary movement (primary motor cortex/ precentral gyrus), intellect, orientation • Broca's area (typically located in the left hemisphere): speech, concentration • personality, temper, judgment, reasoning, behavior, self-awareness, executive functions	• contralateral weakness • perseveration, inattention • personality changes, antisocial behavior • impaired concentration, apathy • Broca's aphasia (expressive deficits) • delayed or poor initiation • emotional lability
Parietal	• associated with sensation of touch, kinesthesia, perception of vibration, and temperature • receives information from other areas of the brain regarding hearing, vision, motor, sensory, and memory • provides meaning for objects • interprets language and words • spatial and visual perception	• dominant hemisphere (typically located in the left hemisphere): agraphia, alexia, agnosia • non-dominant hemisphere (typically located in the right hemisphere): dressing apraxia, constructional apraxia, anosognosia • contralateral sensory deficits • impaired language comprehension • impaired taste
Temporal	• primary auditory processing and olfaction • Wernicke's area (typically located in the left hemisphere): ability to understand and produce meaningful speech, verbal and general memory, assists with understanding language • the rear of the temporal lobe enables humans to interpret other people's emotions and reactions	• learning deficits • Wernicke's aphasia (receptive deficits) • antisocial, aggressive behaviors • difficulty with facial recognition • difficulty with memory, memory loss • inability to categorize objects
Occipital	• main processing center for visual information • processes visual information regarding colors, light, and shapes • judgment of distance, seeing in three dimensions	• homonymous hemianopsia • impaired extraocular muscle movement and visual deficits • impaired color recognition • reading and writing impairment • cortical blindness with bilateral lobe involvement

Hippocampus

The hippocampus is deeply embedded within the lower temporal lobe. It is responsible for the process of forming and storing new memories of one's personal history and other declarative memory. It also possesses great importance in learning language. This "memory indexer" sends memories to appropriate areas of the cerebral hemispheres for long-term storage and retrieves memories when needed.

Basal ganglia

The basal ganglia are gray matter masses located deep within the white matter of the cerebrum and include the caudate, putamen, globus pallidus, substantia nigra, and subthalamic nuclei. The basal ganglia are collectively responsible for voluntary movement, regulation of autonomic movement, posture, muscle tone, and control of motor responses. Basal ganglia dysfunction has been associated with conditions including Parkinson's disease, Huntington's disease, Tourette's syndrome, attention-deficit disorder, obsessive-compulsive disorder, and many addictions.

Amygdala

The amygdala is a small, almond-shaped nucleus located within the temporal lobes of each hemisphere of the brain. It lies adjacent to the hippocampus and just beneath the surface of the front, medial portion of the temporal lobe. This positioning results in the bulge on the surface called the uncus. The main function of the amygdala is emotional and social processing. It is involved with fear and pleasure responses, arousal, processing of memory, and the formation of emotional memories.

Diencephalon[9]

The diencephalon is located beneath the cerebral hemispheres and contains the thalamus, hypothalamus, subthalamus, and epithalamus. The diencephalon is the area of the brain where the major motor and sensory tracts synapse. It acts as an interactive site between the central nervous system and the endocrine system, as well as complementing the limbic system.

CONSIDER THIS

TREATMENT CHALLENGES THAT RESULT FROM SPECIFIC LOBE DAMAGE[2,4]

When treating a patient with brain damage, there are predictable patterns of deficits based on the area of the brain that sustained injury. A therapist must recognize the particular concerns as it relates to the affected area(s) of the brain and integrate this into the plan of care.

- Frontal lobe lesions will produce deficits that range from paralysis and apraxia to loss of executive functions and goal-directed behaviors. Modifications to therapy may include response to perseveration, apraxia, and impaired executive functions. Patients with a frontal lobe lesion may present with apathy or may be uninhibited, distractible, and lack judgment.
- Parietal lobe lesions affect sensory awareness, interpretation, and perception. Somatosensory deficits elicit abnormal movement patterns for patients. Deficits in directional concepts hinder movement planning and require modification of therapy.
- Temporal lobe lesions will affect short and long-term memory. Damage to Wernicke's area (left hemisphere) impairs the comprehension of spoken language. Modification to therapy would include a more kinesthetic approach, relying on demonstration. New learning is available, but patients are usually unable to recall the steps that surround the new skill.
- Occipital lobe lesions produce various visual deficits that can hinder therapy. Cortical blindness occurs with damage to the occipital cortex and affects a patient's ability to receive, but not to perceive visual information. Therapy should avoid the use of diagrams, written materials, and reading. Environmental modification is required secondary to visual deficits, field cuts, and potential for visual agnosia.

Thalamus

The thalamus is a relay or processing station for the majority of information that goes to the cerebral cortex. It coordinates sensory perception and movement with other parts of the brain and spinal cord that also have a role in sensation and movement. It receives information from the cerebellum, basal ganglia, and all sensory pathways except for the olfactory tract. The thalamus then relays the information to the appropriate association cortex. Damage to the thalamus can produce thalamic pain syndrome where there is spontaneous pain on the contralateral side of the body to the thalamic lesion.

Hypothalamus

The hypothalamus receives and integrates information from the autonomic nervous system and assists in regulating hormones. The structure also controls functions such as hunger, thirst, sexual behavior, and sleeping. It regulates body temperature, the adrenal glands, the pituitary gland, and many other vital activities. It is located below the thalamus at the base of the diencephalon. Lesions can produce a variety of impairments based on the area of damage including obesity, sexual disinterest, poor temperature control, and diabetes insipidus.

Subthalamus

The subthalamus is located between the thalamus and the hypothalamus and is primarily represented by the subthalamic nucleus. It is important for regulating movements produced by skeletal muscles. It has association with the basal ganglia and substantia nigra.

Epithalamus

The epithalamus is primarily represented by the pineal gland. This gland secretes melatonin and is involved in circadian rhythms, the internal clock, selected regulation of motor pathways, and emotions. It is associated with the limbic system and basal ganglia.

Midbrain (Mesencephalon)[9]

The midbrain is one of the three components of the brainstem and is located at the base of the brain above the spinal cord. The midbrain connects the forebrain to the hindbrain and functions as a large relay area for information passing from the cerebrum, cerebellum, and spinal cord. It is also a reflex center for visual, auditory, and tactile responses. Two key areas of the midbrain include:

- **tectum:** superior and inferior colliculi
- **tegmentum:** cerebral aqueduct, periaqueductal gray, reticular formation, substantia nigra, red nucleus

Hindbrain (Rhombencephalon)[2,3]

The hindbrain consists of the cerebellum, pons, and medulla oblongata. The pons and medulla oblongata are components of the brainstem and control the body's vital functions. The cerebellum coordinates movement and assists with maintaining balance.

Cerebellum

The cerebellum (metencephalon) is located at the posterior of the brain below the occipital lobes and is separated from the cerebrum by the tentorium. The cerebellum is responsible for fine tuning of movement and assists with maintaining posture and balance by controlling muscle tone and positioning of the extremities in space. The cerebellum controls the ability to perform rapid alternating

movements. The cerebellum consists of two hemispheres of gray matter, and is divided into three lobes: the anterior, posterior, and flocculonodular lobes, with the fourth ventricle lying anterior to the lobes. Damage to one side of the cerebellum will produce ipsilateral impairment to the body. Cerebellar lesions may produce ataxia, nystagmus, tremor, hypermetria, poor coordination, and deficits in postural reflexes, balance, and equilibrium depending on the area of cerebellar lesion.

Pons

The pons (also metencephalon) is located below the midbrain and superior to the medulla oblongata. It assists with regulation of respiration rate and is associated with the orientation of the head in relation to visual and auditory stimuli. Cranial nerves V through VIII originate from the pons.

Medulla oblongata

The medulla oblongata (myelencephalon) is cone-shaped, connects to the pons superiorly, and to the spinal cord inferiorly. It's composed of white matter on the surface and gray matter within the interior. The medulla influences autonomic nervous activity and the regulation of respiration and heart rate. Reflex centers for vomiting, coughing, and sneezing are found within the medulla. Damage to motor tracts crossing within the medulla produces contralateral impairment. The medulla is also responsible for relaying somatic sensory information from internal organs and for the control of arousal and sleep. Cranial nerves IX, X, XI, and XII originate from the medulla oblongata.

Brainstem

The brainstem is a separate classification within the brain and is located in front of the cerebellum with connection to the spinal cord. It consists of three structures: the midbrain, pons, and medulla oblongata. These structures are found both within the midbrain and hindbrain. The brainstem works as a relay station, sending messages between various parts of the body and the cerebral cortex. Many of the primitive functions that are essential for survival, such as regulation of heart rate and respiratory rate, are located within the brainstem. The reticular activating system is found within the midbrain, pons, medulla, and a portion of the thalamus. Severe damage to the brainstem will often result in "brain death" secondary to the key functions that are controlled within this area. The majority of cranial nerves originate within the brainstem.

Blood Supply[2,6]

The brain's blood supply consists of the two internal carotid arteries and the two vertebral arteries. The branches of these main arteries form the Circle of Willis (Fig. 5-3).

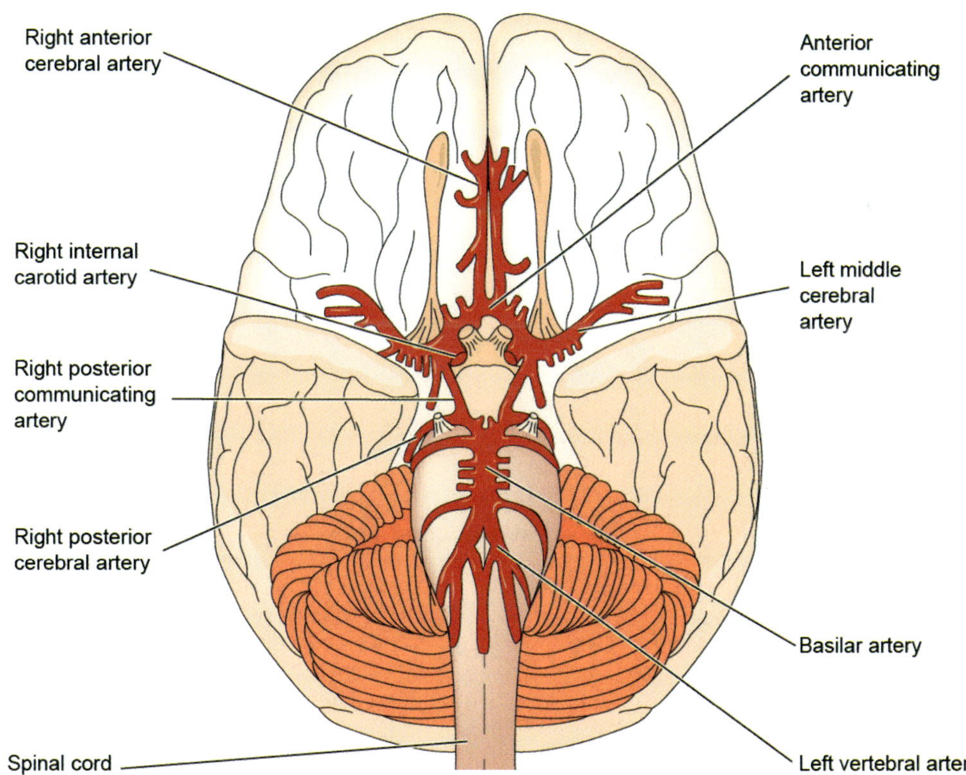

Fig. 5-3: The vascular supply to the brain; Circle of Willis.

Blood Supply to the Brain	
Blood Supply to the Brain	**Expected Possible Impairment Based on Extent of Vascular Involvement**
Anterior cerebral artery (ACA)[10]	
• Anterior frontal lobe • Medial surface of frontal and parietal lobes	• Contralateral lower extremity motor and sensory involvement • Loss of bowel and bladder control • Loss of behavioral inhibition • Significant mental changes • Neglect • Aphasia • Apraxia and agraphia • Perseveration • Akinetic mutism with significant bilateral involvement
Middle cerebral artery (MCA)[11,12]	
• Most of outer cerebrum • Basal ganglia • Posterior and anterior internal capsule • Putamen • Pallidum • Lentiform nucleus	• Most common site of a CVA • Wernicke's aphasia in dominant hemisphere • Homonymous hemianopsia • Apraxia • Flat affect with right hemisphere damage • Contralateral weakness and sensory loss of face and upper extremity with lesser involvement in the lower extremity • Impaired spatial relations • Anosognosia in non-dominant hemisphere • Impaired body schema
Posterior cerebral artery (PCA)[2,6]	
• Portion of midbrain • Subthalamic nucleus • Basal nucleus • Thalamus • Inferior temporal lobe • Occipital and occipitoparietal cortices	• Contralateral pain and temperature sensory loss • Contralateral hemiplegia (central area), mild hemiparesis • Ataxia, athetosis or choreiform movement • Quality of movement is impaired • Thalamic pain syndrome • Anomia • Prosopagnosia with occipital infarct • Hemiballismus • Visual agnosia • Homonymous hemianopsia • Memory impairment • Alexia, dyslexia • Cortical blindness from bilateral involvement
Vertebral-basilar artery[9]	
• Lateral aspect of pons and midbrain together with superior surface of cerebellum • Cerebellum - branches from the basilar artery (posterior inferior cerebellar, anterior inferior cerebellar, and superior cerebellar arteries) • Medulla - posterior inferior cerebellar artery, smaller branches from the vertebral arteries • Pons - branches from the basilar artery • Midbrain and thalamus - posterior cerebral arteries • Occipital cortex - posterior cerebral artery, basilar artery	• Loss of consciousness • Hemiplegia or tetraplegia • Comatose or vegetative state • Inability to speak • Locked-in syndrome • Vertigo • Nystagmus • Dysphagia • Dysarthria • Syncope • Ataxia

CONSIDER THIS

OCCLUSION TO A SPECIFIC ARTERY WILL PRODUCE PREDICTABLE PATTERNS OF IMPAIRMENT[2,10,11]

Blood supply is specific to particular areas within the brain. When a particular artery sustains damage via occlusion or hemorrhage, there is a specific pattern of disability that will occur. The extent of disability is determined by the extent of occlusion, the area of the brain involved, availability of collateral circulation to the affected area of the brain, and if the involved artery produces unilateral or bilateral damage. Bilateral arterial involvement will typically produce the most significant impairments.

Anterior cerebral artery

Bilateral occlusion of the anterior cerebral artery will typically produce paraplegia. Other findings include incontinence, abulic aphasia, frontal lobe symptoms such as personality changes, and potential akinetic mutism (i.e., conscious unresponsiveness).

Middle cerebral artery

Bilateral occlusion of the middle cerebral artery at the stem will produce contralateral hemiplegia and sensory impairment. Dominant hemisphere impairment includes global, Wernicke's or Broca's aphasia. Since the middle cerebral artery supplies the larger portion of the cortex, other impairments are lobe dependent.

Posterior cerebral artery

Two of the most significant impairments with posterior cerebral artery occlusion are thalamic pain syndrome and cortical blindness. Thalamic pain presents with abnormal sensation of pain, temperature, touch, and proprioception. The perceived sensation of pain can become debilitating. Cortical blindness is the loss of vision due to damage to the visual portion of the occipital cortex. Although the affected eye is physically normal, there is full or partial vision loss. The pupil continues to dilate and constrict in response to light since this occurs without influence of the brain.

Vertebral-basilar artery

There is a wide variety of clinical symptoms and syndromes based on the complex vascularity of the vertebral-basilar artery system. Severe impairment can cause locked-in syndrome, coma or vegetative state. Wallenberg syndrome secondary to lateral medullary infarct presents with a variety of symptoms including ipsilateral facial pain and temperature impairment, ipsilateral ataxia, vertigo, contralateral pain and temperature impairment of the body.

Supporting Systems of the Brain and Spinal Cord[2,7]

Meninges

Meninges consist of three layers of connective tissue covering the brain and spinal cord. The meninges provide protection from contusion and infection. There are blood vessels and cerebrospinal fluid (CSF) within the meninges.

- **dura mater:** outermost meninx; has four folds; lines the periosteum of the skull and protects the brain; subdural space separates this from the arachnoid mater
- **arachnoid mater:** the middle meninx; the arachnoid is impermeable; surrounds the brain in a loose manner; subarachnoid space separates this from the pia mater
- **pia mater:** innermost meninx; covers the contours of the brain; forms the choroid plexus in the ventricular system

SPOTLIGHT ON SAFETY

MENINGITIS[1,13]

Meningitis is the inflammation of the meninges of the brain and spinal cord. There are various forms of meningitis with bacterial meningitis being potentially fatal within hours of onset. Acute meningitis is considered to be a medical emergency. A therapist must be aware of the signs and symptoms of meningitis including:

- fever, headache, vomiting
- complaints of a stiff and painful neck, nuchal rigidity
- pain in the lumbar area and posterior thigh
- Brudzinski's sign (flexion of the neck facilitates flexion of the hips and knees)
- Kernig's sign (pain with hip flexion combined with knee extension)
- sensitivity to light

A lumbar puncture is the gold standard for diagnosis. Early diagnosis is essential to avoid permanent neurological damage. Treatment includes antibiotic, antimicrobial, and steroid pharmacological intervention.

Dural Spaces[5,9]

- **epidural space:** an area between the skull and outer dura mater that can be abnormally occupied; also the area in the spinal cord between the dura mater and the periosteum of the vertebrae
- **subdural space:** the area between the dura and arachnoid meninges
- **subarachnoid space:** the area between the arachnoid and pia mater that contains CSF and the circulatory system for the cerebral cortex

Ventricular System[5,9]

The ventricular system is designed to protect and nourish the brain. It is comprised of four fluid-filled cavities called ventricles and multiple foramina that allow the passage of cerebrospinal fluid (CSF). Each ventricle contains specialized tissue called choroid plexus that makes CSF. An excess of CSF in the brain can cause an enlargement in the ventricles causing hydrocephalus; excess fluid within the spinal cord is termed syringomyelia.

Cerebrospinal fluid

Cerebrospinal fluid (CSF) is a clear, fluid-like substance that cushions the brain and spinal cord from injury and provides mechanical buoyancy and support. CSF is produced constantly with a yield of 500-700 ml/day. CSF provides nutrition to the central nervous system, serves as a conduit for removal of metabolites, and is constantly being absorbed and replenished within the brain and spinal cord.

Blood-brain Barrier[5,9]

The blood-brain barrier consists of the meninges, protective glial cells, and capillary beds of the brain. It is responsible for exchange of nutrients between the central nervous system and the vascular system. The blood-brain barrier provides protection for the central nervous system by restricting certain molecules from crossing the barrier while others are able to do so freely.

SPOTLIGHT ON SAFETY
HYDROCEPHALUS[1,14,15]

Hydrocephalus is an increase of CSF within the ventricles of the brain typically due to poor resorption, obstruction of flow or excessive production of CSF. It can be classified as congenital, acquired or idiopathic as well as communicating or non-communicating. Associated conditions and causative factors vary but may include spina bifida, choroid plexus neoplasm, cerebral palsy, tumor, meningitis or encephalocele. Successful treatment includes surgical placement of a shunt or performing an endoscopic third ventriculostomy (ETV). Often repeated neurosurgical procedures are necessary to treat hydrocephalus. Long-term health outcomes for patients with hydrocephalus remain unpredictable.

Signs of hydrocephalus or a blocked shunt include:

- enlarged head or bulging fontanelles in infants
- headache
- changes in vision
- large veins noted on scalp
- behavioral changes
- seizures
- alteration in appetite, vomiting
- "sun setting" sign or downward deviation of the eyes
- incontinence

Physical therapists working with patients with hydrocephalus or at risk for hydrocephalus must be aware of signs and symptoms of the condition as well as shunt malfunction, and when necessary, immediately notify appropriate medical personnel. There must be immediate medical intervention to alleviate the excessive fluid within the brain. Failure to act in a timely manner can result in coma and/or death.

Spinal Cord[6,9]

The spinal cord is a component of the central nervous system and a direct continuation of the brainstem. The spinal cord functions as a relay for information between peripheral structures and the brain in order to process information. The cord is surrounded by meninges and contained within the vertebral canal of the vertebral column (Fig. 5-4). The spinal cord contains both white and gray matter with the largest amount of gray matter found in the lumbar region. The vertebral artery forms the anterior spinal artery and two posterior spinal arteries that all surround the spinal cord. The spinal cord runs from the foramen magnum to the conus medullaris (between the 1st and 2nd lumbar vertebrae). There are 31 segments with a pair of spinal nerves arising from each segment and these nerves are components of the peripheral nervous system. Each spinal nerve contains a dorsal root (sensory) with afferent fibers and a ventral root (motor) with efferent fibers (Fig. 5-5).

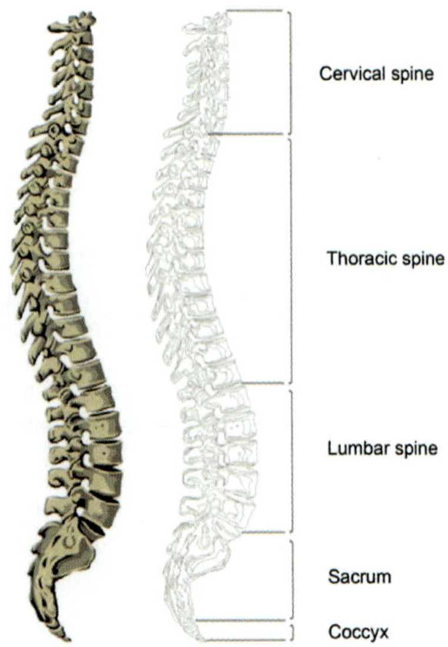

Fig. 5-4: A sagittal view of the spine.

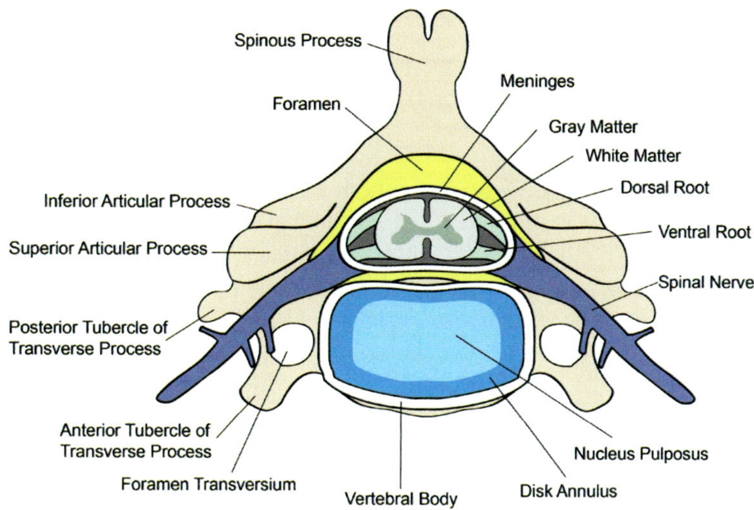

Fig. 5-5: A cross section of a vertebral segment.

Ascending Tracts[7,16,17]

Sensory tracts ascending in the white matter of the spinal cord arise either from cells of spinal ganglia or from intrinsic neurons within the gray matter that receive primary sensory input. Ascending tracts relay sensory feedback to the cerebrum and cerebellum. The primary afferent tracts include:

Cuneocerebellar tract: sensory tract that ascends to the cerebellum for ipsilateral subconscious proprioception of the neck and upper extremities

Fasciculus cuneatus (posterior or dorsal column): sensory tract for trunk, neck, and upper extremity proprioception, vibration, two-point discrimination, and graphesthesia

Fasciculus gracilis (posterior or dorsal column): sensory tract for trunk and lower extremity proprioception, two-point discrimination, vibration, and graphesthesia

Spinocerebellar tract (dorsal and ventral): sensory tract that ascends to the cerebellum for ipsilateral subconscious proprioception, tension in muscles, joint sense, and posture of the trunk and lower extremities

Spino-olivary tract: ascends to the cerebellum and relays information from cutaneous and proprioceptive organs

Spinoreticular tract: the afferent pathway for the reticular formation that influences levels of consciousness

Spinotectal tract: sensory tract providing afferent information for spinovisual reflexes and assists with movement of eyes and head towards a stimulus

Spinothalamic tract (anterior): sensory tract for crude touch and pressure

Spinothalamic tract (lateral): sensory tract for pain and temperature sensation

Descending Tracts[7,16,17]

Tracts descending to the spinal cord are involved with voluntary motor function, muscle tone, reflexes and equilibrium, visceral innervation, and modulation of ascending sensory signals. The largest, the corticospinal tract, originates in the cerebral cortex. Smaller descending tracts originate in nuclei in the midbrain, pons, and medulla oblongata. The primary efferent tracts include:

Corticospinal tract (anterior): pyramidal motor tract responsible for ipsilateral voluntary, discrete, and skilled movements

Corticospinal tract (lateral): pyramidal motor tract responsible for contralateral voluntary fine movement

- Damage to the corticospinal (pyramidal) tracts results in a positive Babinski sign, absent superficial abdominal reflexes and cremasteric reflex, and the loss of fine motor or skilled voluntary movement.

Reticulospinal tract: extrapyramidal motor tract responsible for facilitation or inhibition of voluntary and reflex activity through the influence on alpha and gamma motor neurons

Rubrospinal tract: extrapyramidal motor tract responsible for motor input of gross postural tone, facilitating activity of flexor muscles, and inhibiting the activity of extensor muscles

Tectospinal tract: extrapyramidal motor tract responsible for contralateral postural muscle tone associated with auditory/visual stimuli

Vestibulospinal tract: extrapyramidal motor tract responsible for ipsilateral gross postural adjustments subsequent to head movements, facilitating activity of the extensor muscles, and inhibiting activity of the flexor muscles

- Damage to the extrapyramidal tracts results in significant paralysis, hypertonicity, exaggerated deep tendon reflexes, and clasp-knife reaction.

CONSIDER THIS

BROWN-SEQUARD'S SYNDROME[18,19]

Afferent and efferent pathways provide consistent and predictable deficits with injury. Depending on the location of a lesion and whether or not a pathway crossed or remained on the originating side, symptoms will be noted ipsilaterally or contralaterally to the lesion. Thorough examination of a patient will allow a therapist to potentially target particular pathways that may be damaged.

As an example, Brown-Sequard's syndrome is an incomplete lesion typically caused by a stab wound, which produces hemisection of the spinal cord. There is paralysis and loss of vibratory sense and position sense on the same side as the lesion due to the damage to the corticospinal tracts and dorsal columns. There is a loss of pain and temperature sense on the opposite side of the lesion from damage to the lateral spinothalamic tract.

Peripheral Nervous System

The peripheral nervous system (PNS) contains nerves that originate within the brain and spinal cord, but end peripherally. The PNS consists of motor, sensory, and autonomic neurons that innervate end-organs that include sensory receptors, muscles, and glands. The PNS consists of 12 pairs of cranial nerves, 31 pairs of spinal nerves, and all associated ganglia and sensory receptors. Most peripheral nerves contain motor (efferent) and sensory (afferent) components (Fig. 5-6). Sensory nerves originate in the dorsal root ganglia while motor nerves originate in the anterior horn of the spinal cord. The autonomic neurons are divided into the sympathetic and parasympathetic nerves. The sympathetic nerves originate in the lateral horn of the thoracic spinal cord and the parasympathetic nerves originate from the lateral gray matter of the sacral level of the spinal cord and from the brain itself. Peripheral nerves are typically classified by axon diameter or speed of conduction.

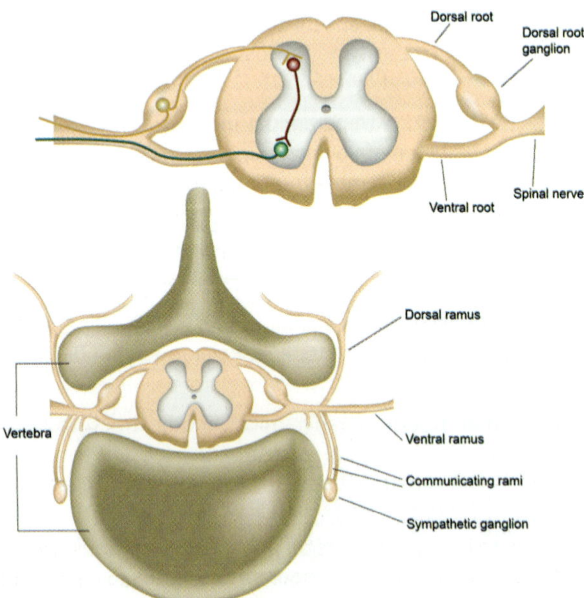

Fig. 5-6: A cross section of the spinal cord noting the spinal nerves.

Cutaneous Sensory End-organ Receptors[20]

- Thermoreceptors
- Nociceptors
- Mechanoreceptors
  - Merkel's disc
  - Ruffini's corpuscle
  - Pacinian corpuscle
  - Meissner's corpuscle
  - muscle spindle
  - free nerve ending
  - Golgi tendon organ
- Chemoreceptors
- Photoreceptors

Peripheral Nervous System Terminology[2,3,20]

Axon: a projection of a nerve away from the cell body that conducts impulses

Dendrite: an extension of the cell body that receives signals from other neurons

Endoneurium: the innermost covering of a peripheral nerve that surrounds each individual axon

Epineurium: the outermost covering of a peripheral nerve that surrounds the entire nerve and provides a buffer for the peripheral nerve

Motor unit: a single motor neuron and all of the muscle fibers that it innervates

Myelin: proteins and lipids that form to create a sheath around particular nerves; increases conductivity of the nerve impulse

Nerve conduction velocity: measures the speed of a nerve impulse along the axon of a nerve

Neurons: nerve cells that receive and send signals to other nerve cells; comprised of a cell body, axon, and dendrites

Nodes of Ranvier: brief gaps in myelination of an axon; serves to facilitate rapid conduction of a nerve impulse via jumping from gap node to gap node

Perineurium: the middle layer of covering surrounding the peripheral nerve that envelopes fascicles or groups of axons and maintains the blood-nerve barrier

Saltatory conduction: an action potential moving along an axon in a jumping fashion from node to node; decreases the use of sodium-potassium pumps and increases speed of conduction

Schwann cell: cells that cover the nerve fibers within the peripheral nervous system and form the myelin sheath

Classification of Peripheral Nerves[20]

A Fibers

- Large fibers
- Myelinated
- High conduction rate
- Alpha, beta, gamma, delta subsets
  - **Alpha:** alpha motor neurons, muscle spindle primary endings, Golgi tendon organs, touch
  - **Beta:** touch, kinesthesia, muscle spindle secondary endings
  - **Gamma:** touch, pressure, gamma motor neurons
  - **Delta:** pain, touch, pressure, temperature
- Sensory components include:
  - **Muscle spindle (primary afferent endings):** primary for low-threshold stretch
  - **Muscle spindle (secondary afferent endings):** receptors that respond to changes in length
  - **Golgi tendon organ:** responds to tension/stretch of a tendon

B Fibers

- Medium fibers
- Myelinated
- Reasonably fast conduction rate
- Preganglionic fibers of the autonomic system

C Fibers

- Small fibers
- Poorly myelinated or unmyelinated
- Slowed conduction rate
- Postganglionic fibers of the sympathetic system
- Exteroceptors for pain, temperature, and touch

Nerve Root Dermatomes, Myotomes, Reflexes, and Paresthetic Areas[21]

Nerve Root	Dermatome*	Muscle Weakness (Myotome)	Reflexes Affected	Paresthesias
C1	Vertex of skull	None	None	None
C2	Temple, forehead, occiput	Longus colli, sternocleidomastoid, rectus capitis	None	None
C3	Entire neck, posterior cheek, temporal area, prolongation forward under mandible	Trapezius, splenius capitis	None	Cheek, side of neck
C4	Shoulder area, clavicular area, upper scapular area	Trapezius, levator scapulae	None	Horizontal band along clavicle and upper scapula
C5	Deltoid area, anterior aspect of entire arm to base of thumb	Supraspinatus, infraspinatus, deltoid, biceps	Biceps, brachioradialis	None
C6	Anterior arm, radial side of hand to thumb and index finger	Biceps, supinator, wrist extensors	Biceps, brachioradialis	Thumb and index finger
C7	Lateral arm and forearm to index, long, and ring fingers	Triceps, wrist flexors	Triceps	Index, long, and ring fingers
C8	Medial arm and forearm to long, ring, and little fingers	Ulnar deviators, thumb extensors, finger flexors	None	Little finger alone or with two adjacent fingers; not ring or long fingers, alone or together (C7)

Nerve Root Dermatomes, Myotomes, Reflexes, and Paresthetic Areas[21]

<table>
<tr><th>Nerve Root</th><th>Dermatome*</th><th>Muscle Weakness (Myotome)</th><th>Reflexes Affected</th><th>Paresthesias</th></tr>
<tr><td>T1</td><td>Medial side of forearm to base of little finger</td><td colspan="3" rowspan="2">Disk lesions at upper two thoracic levels do not appear to give rise to root weakness. Weakness of intrinsic muscles of the hand is due to other pathology (e.g., thoracic outlet pressure, neoplasm of lung, ulnar nerve lesion).</td></tr>
<tr><td>T2</td><td>Medial side of upper arm to medial elbow, pectoral and midscapular areas</td></tr>
<tr><td>T3 - T12</td><td>T3-T6, upper thorax; T5-T7, costal margin; T8-T12, abdomen and lumbar region</td><td colspan="3">Articular and dural signs and root pain are common. Root signs (cutaneous analgesia) are rare and have such indefinite area that they have little localizing value. Weakness is not detectable.</td></tr>
<tr><td>L1</td><td>Back, over trochanter and groin</td><td>None</td><td>None</td><td>Groin; after holding posture, which causes pain</td></tr>
<tr><td>L2</td><td>Back, front of thigh to knee</td><td>Psoas, hip adductors</td><td>None</td><td>Occasionally anterior thigh</td></tr>
<tr><td>L3</td><td>Back, upper buttock, anterior thigh and knee, medial lower leg</td><td>Psoas, quadriceps</td><td>Knee jerk sluggish, PKB positive, pain on full SLR</td><td>Medial knee, anterior lower leg</td></tr>
<tr><td>L4</td><td>Medial buttock, lateral thigh, medial leg, dorsum of foot, big toe</td><td>Tibialis anterior, extensor hallucis</td><td>SLR limited, neck flexion pain, weak or absent knee jerk, side flexion limited</td><td>Medial aspect of calf and ankle</td></tr>
<tr><td>L5</td><td>Buttock, posterior and lateral thigh, lateral aspect of leg, dorsum of foot, medial half of sole, first, second, and third toes</td><td>Extensor hallucis, peroneals, gluteus medius, dorsiflexors, hamstrings, plantar flexors</td><td>SLR limited one side, neck flexion painful, ankle decreased, crossed-leg raising pain</td><td>Lateral aspect of leg, medial three toes</td></tr>
<tr><td>S1</td><td>Lateral and plantar aspect of foot</td><td>Hamstrings, gluteals, peroneals, plantar flexors</td><td>SLR limited, Achilles reflex weak or absent</td><td>Lateral two toes, lateral foot, lateral leg to knee, plantar aspect of foot</td></tr>
<tr><td>S2</td><td>Buttock, thigh, and posterior leg</td><td>Same as S1 except peroneals</td><td>Same as S1</td><td>Lateral leg, knee, and heel</td></tr>
<tr><td>S3</td><td>Groin, posteromedial thigh to knee</td><td>None</td><td>None</td><td>None</td></tr>
<tr><td>S4</td><td>Perineum, genitals, lower sacrum</td><td>Bladder, rectum</td><td>None</td><td>Saddle area, genitals, anus, impotence, massive posterior herniation</td></tr>
</table>

*In any part of which pain may be felt. PKB = prone knee bending; SLR = straight leg raising.

Adapted from Magee, DJ: Orthopedic Physical Assessment. W.B. Saunders Company, Philadelphia 2002, p.16, with permission.

Cranial Nerves and Methods of Testing[21]

Nerve	Afferent (Sensory)	Efferent (Motor)	Test
Olfactory	Smell: Nose		Identify familiar odors (e.g., chocolate, coffee)
Optic	Sight: Eye		Test visual fields Test visual acuity
Oculomotor		Voluntary motor: Levator of eyelid; superior, medial, and inferior recti; inferior oblique muscle of eyeball Autonomic: Smooth muscle of eyeball	Upward, downward, and medial gaze Reaction to light
Trochlear		Voluntary motor: Superior oblique muscle of eyeball	Downward and inward gaze
Trigeminal	Touch, pain: Skin of face, mucous membranes of nose, sinuses, mouth, anterior tongue	Voluntary motor: Muscles of mastication	Corneal reflex Face sensation Clench teeth; push down on chin to separate jaw
Abducens		Voluntary motor: Lateral rectus muscle of eyeball	Lateral gaze
Facial	Taste: Anterior tongue	Voluntary motor: Facial muscles Autonomic: Lacrimal, submandibular, and sublingual glands	Close eyes tight Smile and show teeth Whistle and puff cheeks Identify familiar tastes (e.g., sweet, sour)
Vestibulocochlear (acoustic nerve)	Hearing: Ear Balance: Ear		Hear watch ticking Hearing tests Balance and coordination tests
Glossopharyngeal	Touch, pain: Posterior tongue, pharynx Taste: Posterior tongue	Voluntary motor: Select muscles of pharynx Autonomic: Parotid gland	Gag reflex Ability to swallow
Vagus	Touch, pain: Pharynx, larynx, bronchi Taste: Tongue, epiglottis	Voluntary motor: Muscles of palate, pharynx, and larynx Autonomic: Thoracic and abdominal viscera	Gag reflex Ability to swallow Say "Ahhh"
Accessory		Voluntary motor: Sternocleidomastoid and trapezius muscles	Resisted shoulder shrug
Hypoglossal		Voluntary motor: Muscles of tongue	Tongue protrusion (if injured, tongue deviates toward injured side)

From Magee, DJ: Orthopedic Physical Assessment. W.B. Saunders Company, Philadelphia 2002, p.69, with permission.

Cranial Nerve Testing Procedures[21,22]

The cranial nerves refer to twelve pairs of nerves that have their origin in the brain. Certain cranial nerves contain both sensory and motor fibers, however, many possess either sensory or motor fibers. Since lesions affecting the cranial nerves produce specific and predictable alterations, it is often prudent to perform cranial nerve testing as part of a neurological examination. The following information is a summary of some of the more common methods of testing selected cranial nerves.

Cranial Nerve I - Olfactory

The patient is positioned in sitting with the eyes closed or blindfolded. The therapist places an item with a familiar odor under the patient's nostril and the patient is asked to identify the odor. A positive test may be indicated by an inability to identify familiar odors.

Cranial Nerve II - Optic

The patient is positioned in standing a selected distance from a chart or diagram. The therapist asks the patient to identify objects or read selected items from the chart or diagram. A positive test may be indicated by an inability to identify objects at a reasonable distance.

Cranial Nerve III - Oculomotor

The patient is positioned in sitting and is asked to follow an object such as a writing utensil with their eyes as it is moved vertically, horizontally, and diagonally. The therapist should make sure the patient does not rotate their head during the testing and should inspect the patient's eyes for asymmetry or ptosis. A positive test is indicated by an identified tracking deficit, asymmetry or ptosis.

Cranial Nerve IV - Trochlear (Fig. 5-7)

The patient is positioned in sitting and asked to follow an object such as a writing utensil with their eyes as it is moved in an inferior direction. The therapist should make sure the patient does not move his head downward. A positive test is indicated by an inability to depress the eyes and/or complaints of diplopia.

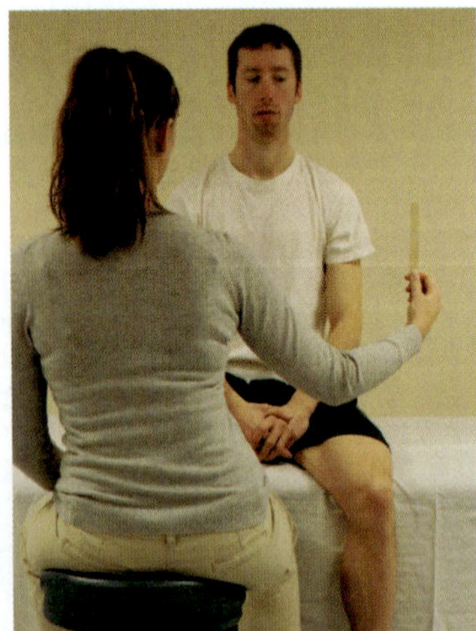

Fig. 5-7: Examination of the trochlear nerve. The patient should be able to follow the tongue depressor as it is moved in an inferior direction without moving the head.

Cranial Nerve V - Trigeminal

The patient is positioned in sitting and is asked to close their eyes. The therapist uses a piece of cotton and a safety pin to alternately touch the patient's face. The patient is asked to classify each contact with the face as "sharp" or "dull." A positive test for the sensory component may be identified by impaired or absent sensation or the inability to differentiate between "sharp" or "dull." The motor component is tested by asking the patient to perform mandibular protrusion, retrusion, and lateral deviation. A positive test may be indicated by an impaired ability to move the mandible through the specified motions.

Cranial Nerve VI - Abducens (Fig. 5-8)

The patient is positioned in sitting. The therapist asks the patient to abduct their eyes without rotating the head. A positive test is indicated by an inability to abduct the eyes.

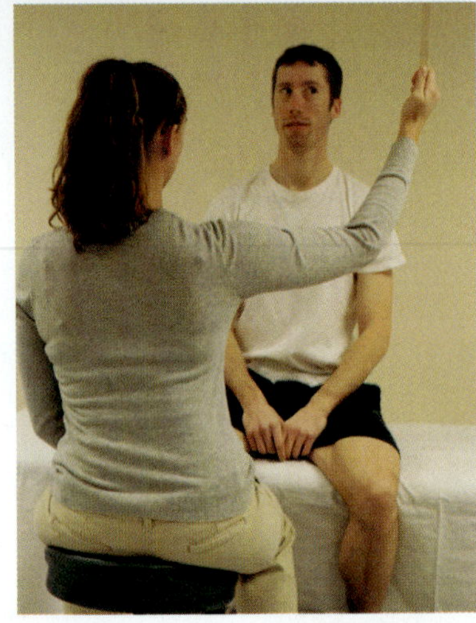

Fig. 5-8: Examination of the abducens nerve. The patient should be able to abduct the eyes without moving the head.

Cranial Nerve VII - Facial (Fig. 5-9)

The patient is positioned in sitting and is asked to distinguish between sweet and salty substances placed on the anterior portion of the tongue. A positive test for the sensory component may be identified by an inability to accurately identify sweet and salty substances. The motor component is tested by performing a manual muscle test of selected muscles involved in facial expression. A positive test for the motor component may be indicated by an inability to mimic selected facial expressions due to muscle impairment.

Fig. 5-9: Examination of the facial nerve. The patient should be able to mimic facial expressions. The sensory component of the nerve distinguishes between sweet and salty taste over the anterior tongue.

Cranial Nerve VIII - Vestibulocochlear

The patient is positioned in sitting in a quiet location. The therapist, positioned behind the patient and to one side, slowly brings a ticking watch toward the patient's ear. The therapist records the distance from the ear when the patient is able to identify the ticking sound. The therapist repeats the procedure on the contralateral ear and compares the measurements. A positive test is indicated by an inability to hear the ticking sound at 18-24 inches or a significant bilateral difference. Alternate tests include the Weber and Rinne tests which require a 512 Hz tuning fork.

Cranial Nerve IX - Glossopharyngeal (Fig. 5-10)

The patient is positioned in sitting. The therapist touches the pharynx with a tongue depressor. A positive test may be indicated by lack of gagging or an inability to feel the tongue depressor touch the back of the throat. The sensory component is tested by assessing the patient's ability to distinguish objects by taste after they are placed on the posterior portion of the tongue. A positive test for the sensory component may be identified by an inability to accurately identify tasted substances, especially sour and bitter substances, placed on the posterior third of the tongue.

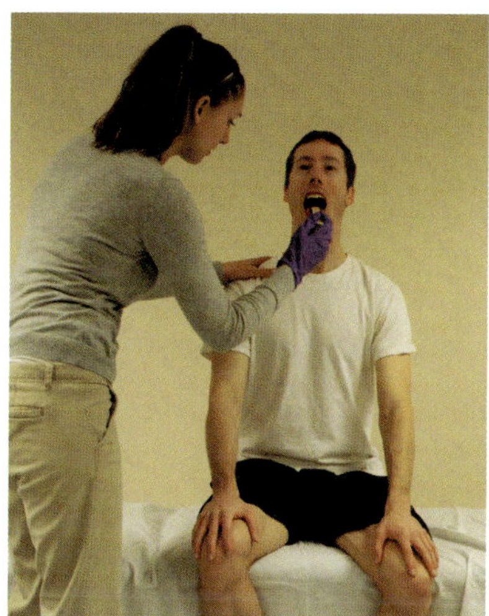

Fig. 5-10: Examination of the glossopharyngeal and vagus nerves. The tongue depressor on the tongue should produce a gag response.

Cranial Nerve X - Vagus (Fig. 5-10)

The patient is positioned in sitting. The therapist touches the pharynx with a tongue depressor. A positive test may be indicated by a lack of gagging or an inability to feel the tongue depressor touch the back of the throat (same description for Cranial Nerve IX - Glossopharyngeal). If the gag reflex is absent the therapist should carefully assess the movement of the soft palate and uvula.

Cranial Nerve XI - Accessory (Fig. 5-11)

The patient is positioned in sitting with the arms at the side. The therapist asks the patient to shrug their shoulders and maintain the position while the therapist applies resistance through the shoulders in the direction of shoulder depression. A positive test may be indicated by an inability to maintain the test position against resistance.

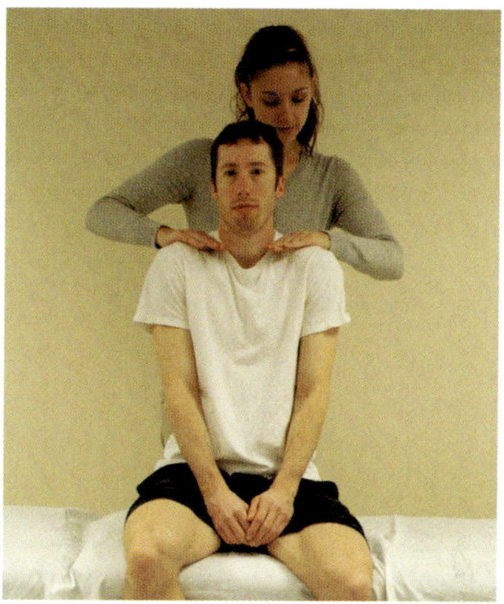

Fig. 5-11: Examination of the accessory nerve. The patient should be able to maintain a shoulder shrug against resistance.

Cranial Nerve XII - Hypoglossal (Fig. 5-12)

The patient is positioned in sitting. The therapist asks the patient to protrude the tongue. A positive test may be indicated by an inability to fully protrude the tongue or the tongue deviating to one side during protrusion.

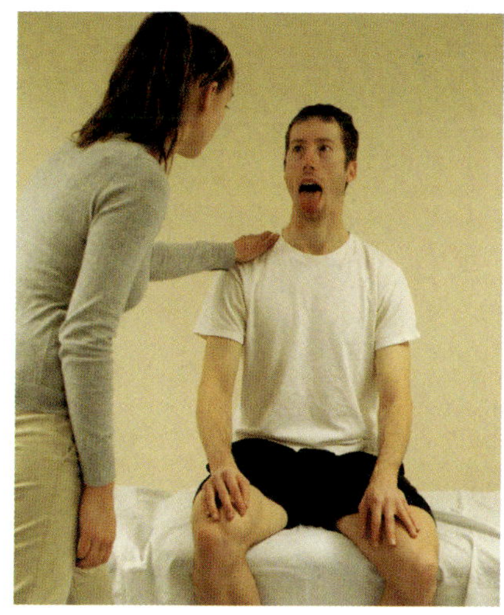

Fig. 5-12: Examination of the hypoglossal nerve. The patient should be able to protrude the tongue in a symmetrical fashion.

Nerves of the Brachial Plexus[23]

Origin	Nerves	Muscles
From the rami of the plexus	Dorsal scapular	Rhomboids, levator scapulae
	Long thoracic	Serratus anterior
From the trunks of the plexus	Nerve to subclavius	Subclavius
	Suprascapular	Infraspinatus, supraspinatus
From the lateral cord of the plexus	Lateral pectoral	Pectoralis major - clavicular head
	Musculocutaneous	Coracobrachialis, biceps brachii, brachialis
	Lateral root of the median	Flexor muscles in the forearm, except flexor carpi ulnaris, and five muscles in the hand
From the medial cord of the plexus	Medial pectoral	Pectoralis major, pectoralis minor
	Ulnar	Flexor carpi ulnaris, flexor digitorum profundus, most small muscles of the hand
	Medial root of the median	Flexor muscles in the forearm, except flexor carpi ulnaris, and five muscles of the hand
From the posterior cord of the plexus	Upper subscapular	Subscapularis
	Thoracodorsal	Latissimus dorsi
	Lower subscapular	Subscapularis, teres major
	Axillary	Deltoid, teres minor
	Radial	Brachioradialis, triceps, supinator, wrist extensors, anconeus

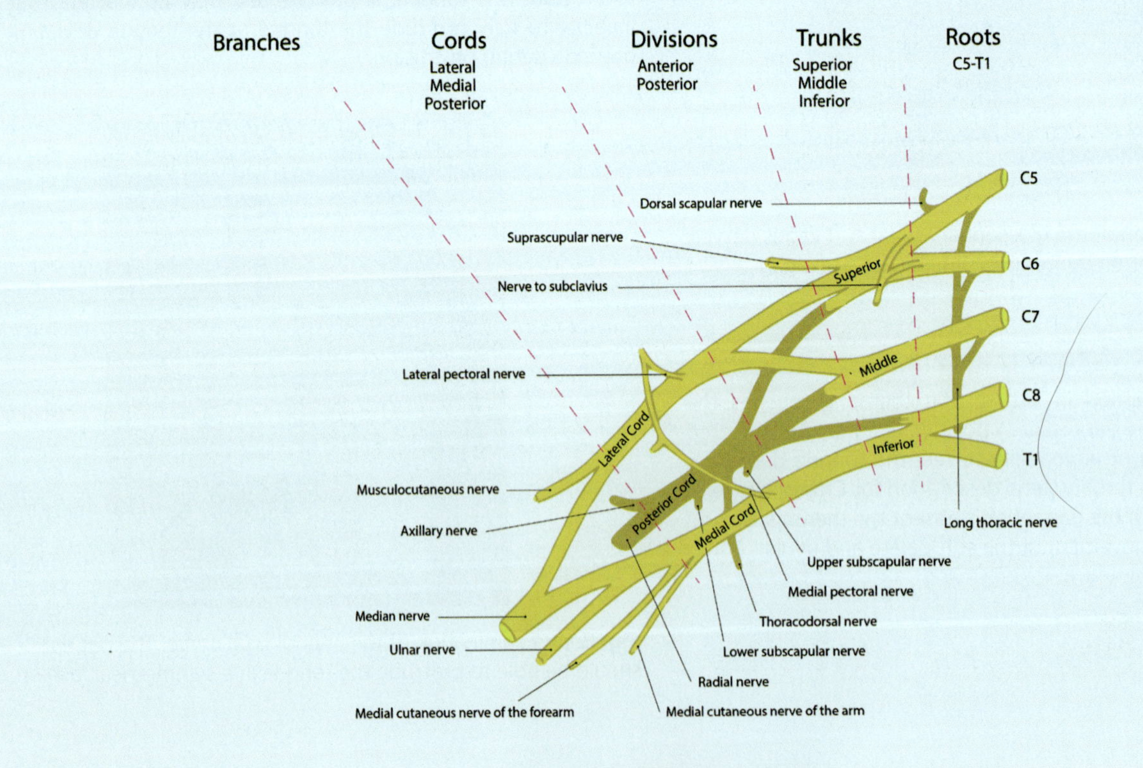

Lower Extremity Innervation[23]

Lumbar Plexus	Sciatic Nerve - Tibial Division
Psoas major Psoas minor Quadratus lumborum	Semitendinosus Semimembranosus Biceps femoris (long head)
Sacral Plexus	**Sciatic Nerve - Common Peroneal Division**
Piriformis Superior gemelli Inferior gemelli Obturator internus Quadratus femoris	Biceps femoris (short head)
Inferior Gluteal Nerve	**Deep Peroneal Nerve**
Gluteus maximus	Tibialis anterior Extensor digitorum longus Extensor hallucis longus Peroneus tertius Extensor digitorum brevis
Superior Gluteal Nerve	**Superficial Peroneal Nerve**
Gluteus medius Gluteus minimus Tensor fasciae latae	Peroneus longus Peroneus brevis
Femoral Nerve	**Medial Plantar Nerve**
Vastus lateralis Rectus femoris Vastus medialis Vastus intermedius Iliacus Sartorius Pectineus	Abductor hallucis Lumbrical I Flexor digitorum brevis Flexor hallucis brevis
Obturator Nerve	**Lateral Plantar Nerve**
Adductor longus Adductor brevis Adductor magnus Obturator externus Gracilis	Abductor digiti minimi Flexor digiti minimi Opponens digiti minimi Dorsal interossei Quadratus plantae Adductor hallucis Lumbrical II, III, IV Plantar interossei
Tibial Nerve	
Soleus Popliteus Plantaris Tibialis posterior Gastrocnemius Flexor hallucis longus Flexor digitorum longus	

Superficial Reflexes[6,22]

A reflex is a motor response to a sensory stimulation that is used to examine the integrity of the nervous system. Superficial reflexes are a response to stimulation of the receptors within the skin. Superficial reflexes are quite different from the muscle stretch (or deep tendon) reflexes since the sensory signal must reach the spinal cord, and must ascend the cord to reach the brain. The motor component also must descend the spinal cord to reach the motor neurons making this a polysynaptic reflex.

Procedure Guidelines for Superficial Reflex Testing[6,22]

- The patient should be relaxed and understand the testing procedure.
- Position the patient properly.
- Reflexes are typically graded as present or absent, although a large difference between left and right will also indicate an abnormal response.
- The examination should provide a comparison of both sides of the body.
- Examination results should assist the therapist to recognize a deficit within the nervous system.

Superficial Reflex Testing[22]

Common Superficial Reflexes	Spinal Level	Procedure	Normal Response
Abdominal reflex	T8-L1	stroke briskly and lightly with a blunt object (tongue depressor) from each quadrant of the abdomen in a diagonal manner towards the umbilicus	contraction of the abdominals and deviation of the umbilicus in the direction of stimulus
Corneal "blink" reflex	trigeminal and facial nerves	ask the patient to look up and away from you; stroke the cornea using a piece of cotton	both eyes will blink with contact to one eye
Cremasteric reflex	L1-L2	scratch the skin of the upper medial thigh	a brisk and brief elevation of the testicle on the ipsilateral side
Gag reflex	glossopharyngeal and vagus nerves	the therapist lightly stimulates each side of the back of the throat and notes the reaction	a gag will occur post stimulation; may be absent in some percentage of the normal population
Plantar reflex (Fig. 5-13)	L5-S1	stroke the lateral aspect of the sole of the foot with the blunt end of a reflex hammer from the heel to the ball of the foot and medially to the base of the great toe	flexion of the toes *Babinski reflex is the abnormal response that indicates CNS lesion (Fig. 5-14)

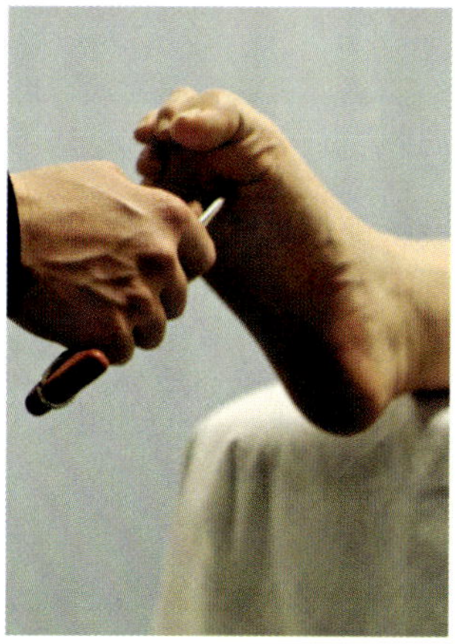
Fig. 5-13: A normal plantar reflex response.

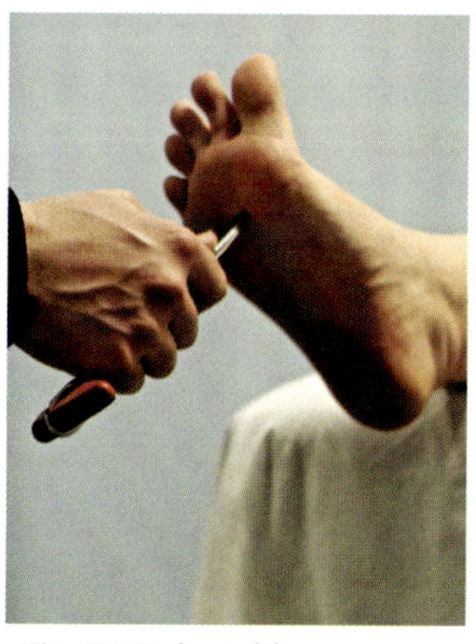
Fig. 5-14: A positive Babinski reflex response.

Deep Tendon Reflexes[6,22,24]

Deep tendon reflexes (DTR) elicit a muscle contraction when the muscle's tendon is stimulated due to the reflex arc involving the spinal or brainstem segment that innervates the specific muscle. Hyperreflexia refers to hyperactivity or clonic reflexes. This can be indicative of a suprasegmental lesion (a lesion above the level of the spinal reflex pathways). Hyporeflexia refers to a diminished or absent response to tapping of the tendon. This can be indicative of disease that involves one or multiple components of the reflex arc itself.

Procedure Guidelines for Deep Tendon Reflex Testing[6,22]

- The patient should be relaxed and understand the testing procedure.
- Position the patient properly and symmetrically with the muscle placed on a slight stretch.
- A reflex hammer should be utilized to deliver a direct strike on the tendon with an anticipated immediate response (Fig. 5-15).
- Avoid "pecking" at the tendon with the hammer as this will not produce valid results.
- Reflexes can be graded as depressed (hypo), normal or exaggerated (hyper) on a scale of 0-4.
- If the therapist has difficulty eliciting a reflex, the Jendrassik maneuver should be employed to distract the patient, increase reflex activity, and decrease guarding. The patient can be directed to perform the Jendrassik maneuver by locking the fingers together and directly pulling against each other immediately prior to the reflex stimulus.
- The examination should provide a comparison of both sides of the body and should include all deep tendon reflexes.
- The examination should provide a comparison of "normal" areas to suspected areas of impairment.
- Examination results should assist the therapist to identify deficits within the nervous system.

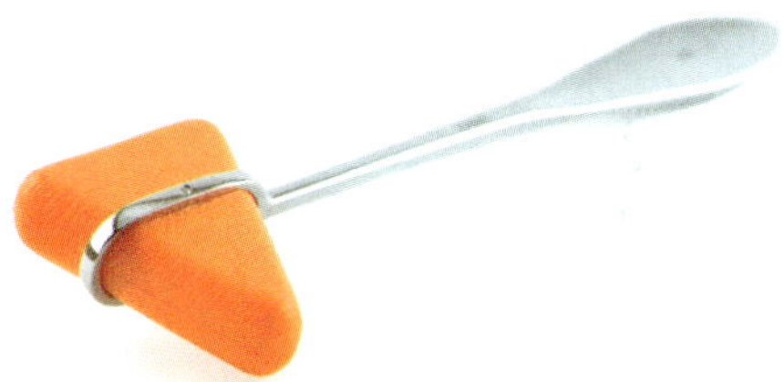
Fig. 5-15: A standard reflex hammer used to assess deep tendon reflexes.

Reflex Grading Scale[25]

Reflex Grading	Interpretation
0 = no response	always abnormal
1+ = diminished/depressed response	may or may not be normal
2+ = active normal response	normal
3+ = brisk/exaggerated response	may or may not be normal
4+ = very brisk/hyperactive	always abnormal

Deep Tendon Reflex Testing[6,22,25]

Biceps tendon (Fig. 5-16) **Spinal Level:** C5-C6 **Procedure:** support the elbow in partial flexion in sitting or supine; place the thumb firmly over the biceps tendon at the elbow and strike the hammer through the thumb **Normal Response:** Contraction of the biceps muscle; flexion of the elbow	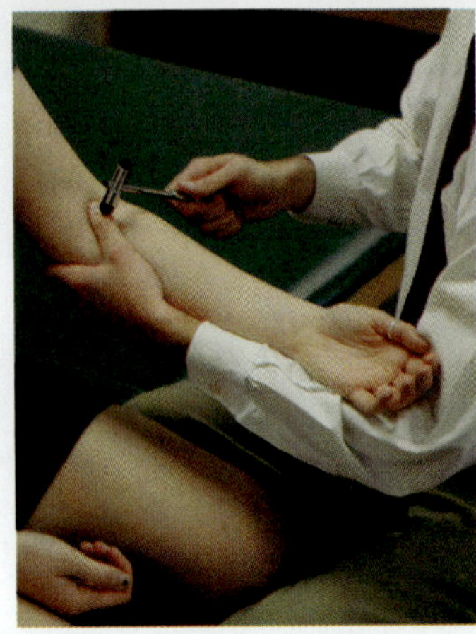 **Fig. 5-16:** Examination of the biceps deep tendon reflex.
Brachioradialis tendon (Fig. 5-17) **Spinal Level:** C5-C6 **Procedure:** rest the hand on the lap in sitting with the forearm supported and in neutral; strike the radius one to two inches superior to the wrist **Normal Response:** Contraction of the brachioradialis muscle; elbow flexion and/or forearm supination	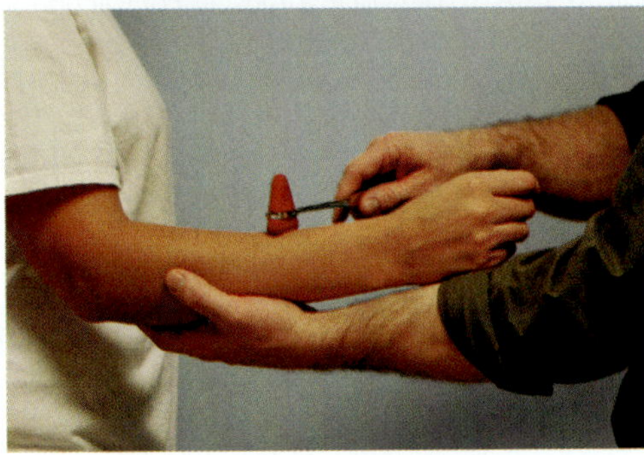 **Fig. 5-17:** Examination of the brachioradialis deep tendon reflex.
Triceps tendon (Fig. 5-18) **Spinal Level:** C6-C7 **Procedure:** support the upper extremity through the humerus and allow the lower portion to hang with elbow flexion; strike the triceps tendon directly above the elbow **Normal Response:** Contraction of the triceps muscle; elbow extension	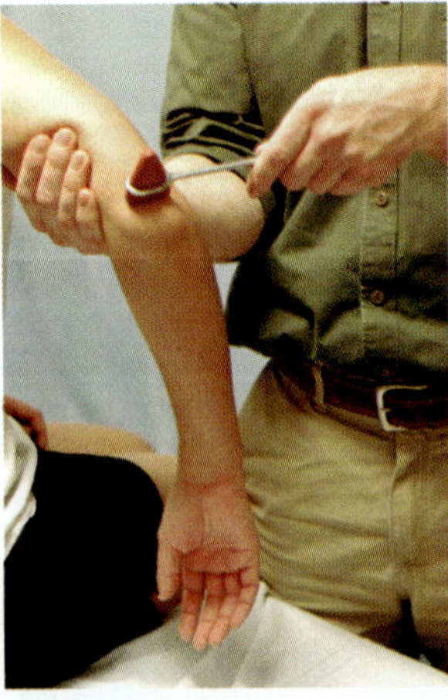 **Fig. 5-18:** Examination of the triceps deep tendon reflex.

Patellar tendon (Fig. 5-19)

Spinal Level: L3-L4

Procedure: supported knee flexion with the patient in sitting or supine; strike the tendon directly inferior to the patella

Normal Response: Contraction of the quadriceps; knee extension

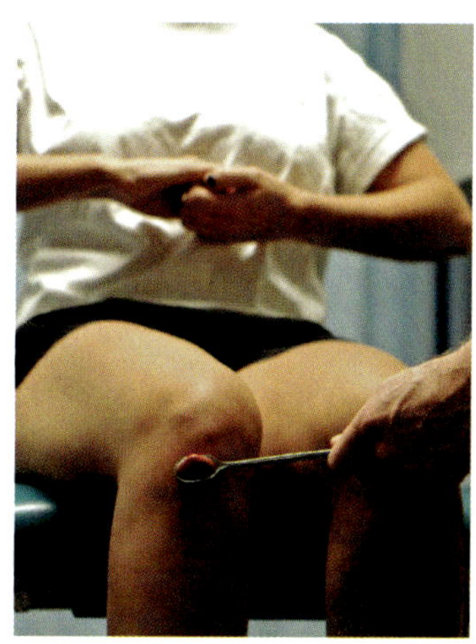

Fig. 5-19: Examination of the patellar deep tendon reflex.

Achilles tendon (Fig. 5-20)

Spinal Level: S1-S2

Procedure: in sitting, flex the foot at the ankle putting the Achilles on stretch; strike the Achilles tendon above the foot

Normal Response: Plantar flexion of the foot

Fig. 5-20: Examination of the Achilles deep tendon reflex.

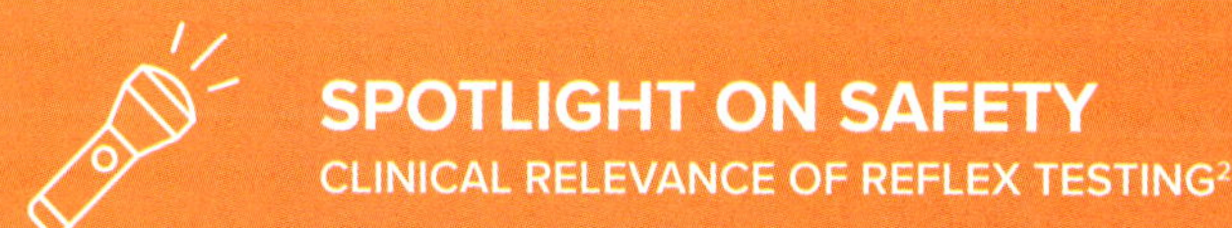

SPOTLIGHT ON SAFETY

CLINICAL RELEVANCE OF REFLEX TESTING[25]

Deep tendon reflex (DTR) testing can assist the therapist in determining the type of pathology that exists. Absent DTRs will indicate a lesion in the reflex arc itself. If absent reflexes accompany sensory loss in the distribution of the nerve that is supplying a particular reflex, the lesion is found within the afferent arc of the reflex and is located in either the nerve or dorsal horn. If an absent DTR accompanies paralysis, fasciculations or atrophy, the lesion is found within the efferent arc of the reflex and may include the efferent nerve, anterior horn cells or both.

Peripheral neuropathy is the most common etiology surrounding absent reflexes. Associated conditions can include diabetes, alcoholism, vitamin deficiencies such as pernicious anemia, certain cancers, and certain toxins (lead, arsenic, vincristine). Neuropathies will typically present with sensory, motor or mixed impairments and may affect all components of the reflex arc.

Hyperactive DTRs are found when there is interruption of the cortical supply to the lower motor neuron (secondary to upper motor neuron lesion). The interruption exists above the segment of the reflex arc, with other findings determining localization of the exact lesion. Assessment of the DTRs can provide information as to the level of lesion that exists within the central nervous system.

Sensation

There are several types of sensation that a physical therapist will evaluate including superficial, deep (proprioceptive), and cortical (combined) sensations. A therapist should examine superficial and deep sensations first, followed by cortical sensations.

- **Superficial:** temperature, light touch, pain
- **Deep:** proprioception, kinesthesia, vibration
- **Cortical:** bilateral simultaneous stimulation, stereognosis, two-point discrimination, barognosis, localization of touch

Procedure Guidelines for Sensory Testing[6,22]

- The patient should be relaxed and understand the expectations of the required response.
- The examination should be conducted in an efficient manner so that the sensory system does not fatigue and allow for unreliable responses.
- The patient's vision should be obscured or the patient blindfolded so that their vision does not influence the perceived sensation.
- The pace of the examination should vary so that the patient does not expect a stimulus or respond merely to the rhythm of the test.
- The therapist should have a complete understanding of areas of the skin that have heightened or decreased sensitivity based on the type of sensation that is tested (i.e., temperature versus light touch).
- The examination should provide a comparison of both sides of the body and should include all extremities and the trunk.
- The examination should provide a comparison of "normal" areas to suspected areas of impairment.
- The examination should provide a comparison of distal versus proximal response for each tested area.
- The therapist may examine dermatomes and peripheral nerve distribution or patterns of sensation such as:
  - bilateral shoulders - C4
  - medial and lateral aspects of bilateral forearms - C6 to T1
  - thumbs and little fingers - C6 and C8
  - bilateral anterior thighs - L2 and L3
  - medial and lateral aspects of bilateral lower legs (calf)- L4 and L5
  - bilateral little toes - S1
  - saddle area - S4
- Examination results should assist the therapist to recognize the deficit as CNS, plexus or peripheral nerve pattern damage.
- Patients with sensory deficits or who are at risk for sensory impairments should be tested using Semmes Weinstein monofilaments for objective data collection regarding protective sensation (Figs. 5-21, 5-22, 5-23).

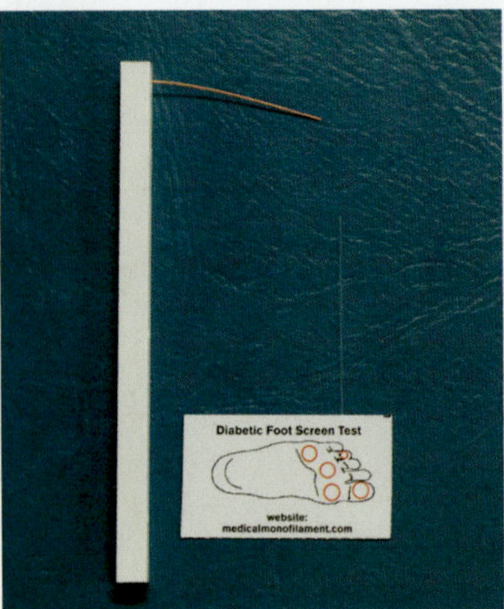

Fig. 5-21: Semmes Weinstein monofilaments.

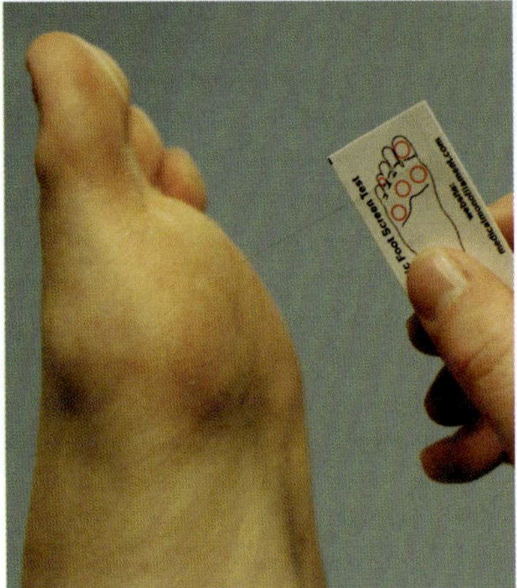

Fig. 5-22: Testing protocol requires the monofilament to be held perpendicular to the surface tested.

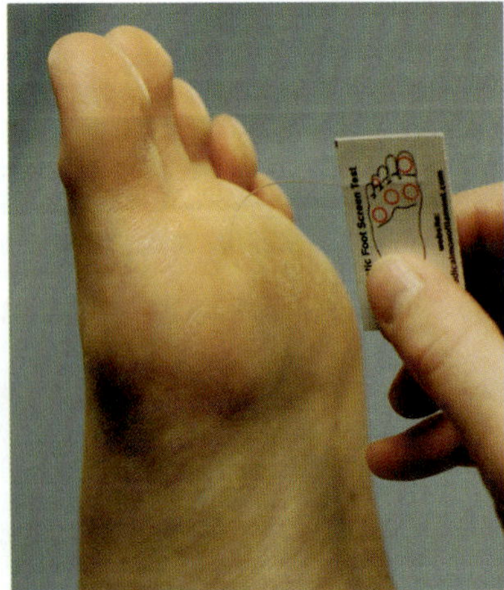

Fig. 5-23: Proper pressure has been applied when the monofilament deforms.

CONSIDER THIS

SCREENING OF SUPERFICIAL, DEEP, AND CORTICAL SENSATIONS[6,26]

When screening a patient's sensation, there are typical stimuli that produce an expected response that measures a patient's sensation as normal or impaired.

- **Barognosis:** perceive the weight of different objects in the hand
- **Deep pain:** squeeze the forearm or calf muscle
- **Graphesthesia:** identify a number or letter drawn on the skin without visual input
- **Kinesthesia:** identify direction and extent of movement of a joint or body part
- **Light touch:** perceive touch through light pressure or use of a cotton ball
- **Localization:** ability to identify the exact location of light touch on the body using a verbal response or gesturing
- **Proprioception:** identify a static position of an extremity or body part
- **Stereognosis:** identify an object without sight (Fig. 5-24)
- **Superficial pain:** perceive noxious stimulus using a pen cap, paper clip end or pin
- **Temperature:** perceive warm and cold test tubes
- **Two-point discrimination:** using a two-point caliper on the skin, identify one or two points without visual input (Fig. 5-25)
- **Vibration:** perceive vibration or pain through a tuning fork

Impairment found with any of the above sensations may designate lesion or pathology to a particular pathway or region of the brain. The therapist can utilize this information to enhance understanding of the neurological impairment as well as to customize the plan of care.

Fig. 5-24: The patient is trying to identify the paper clip without visual feedback and using only the sense of touch. This is an examination of stereognosis.

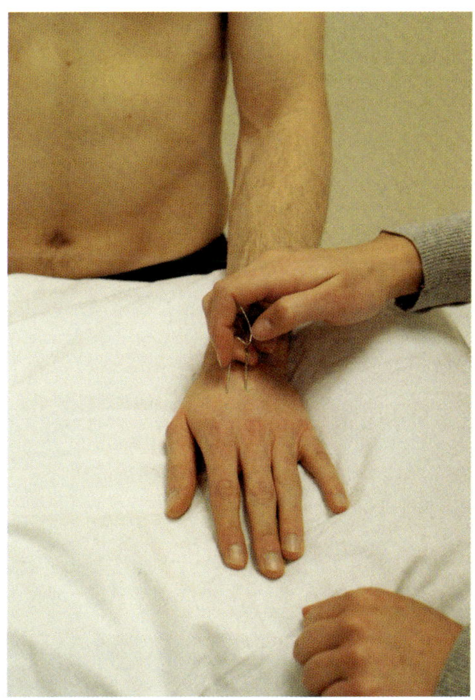

Fig. 5-25: Examination of two-point discrimination.

Sensory Testing[6,22,25]

Light touch (Fig. 5-26)

- instruct and demonstrate the testing procedure to the patient and ask for a response
- attempt to initiate the testing in a normal area so the patient can anticipate what to expect
- performed through touching the skin lightly or using cotton
- with eyes closed, ask patient to identify when they feel a touch
- compare sides of the body, proximal versus distal areas, and identify patterns or innervation level of impairment

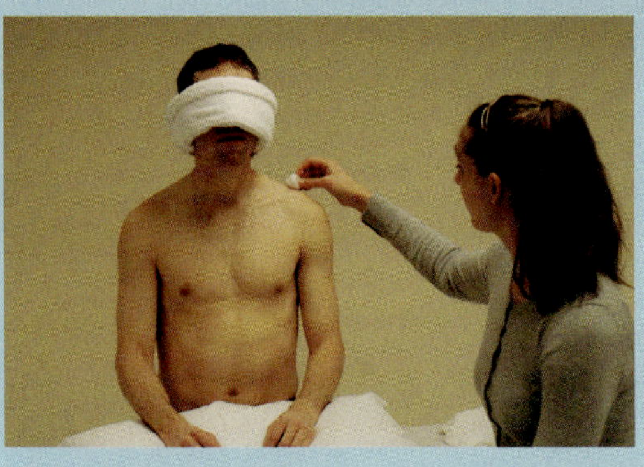

Fig. 5-26: Examination of light touch sensation using a cotton ball.

Pain (Figs. 5-27, 5-28)

- instruct and demonstrate the testing procedure to the patient and have them note the sharp versus dull side of a pin or appropriate instrument such as a Wartenberg pinwheel (Figs. 5-27, 5-28)
- performed through touching the skin while alternating in a random fashion between the sharp and dull ends of the pin
- attempt to initiate the testing in an intact area so the patient can anticipate what to expect
- with eyes closed, ask the patient to identify if they feel a sharp or dull sensation
- allow the patient to make comparisons by asking if the stimulus is the same or different when testing different areas
- compare sides of the body, proximal versus distal areas, identify patterns or innervation level of impairment

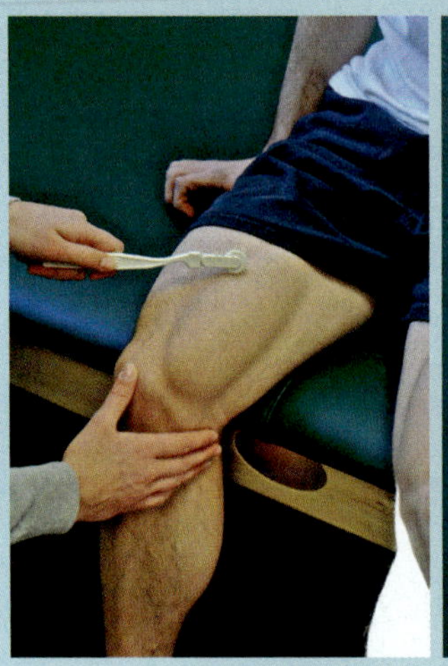

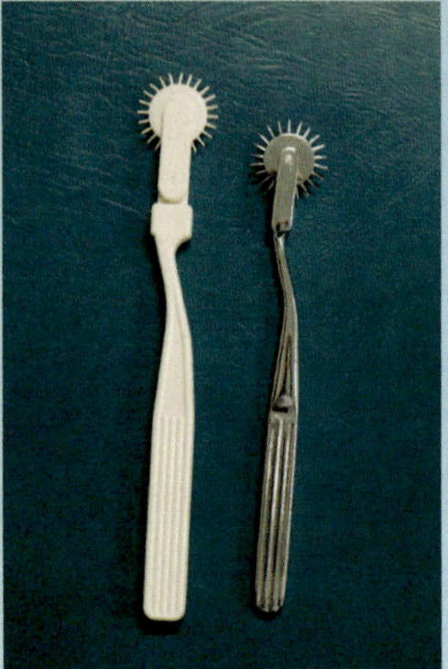

Fig. 5-27 (Left): Examination of sharp versus dull sensation using a Wartenberg pinwheel.

Fig. 5-28 (Right): Wartenberg pinwheels.

Temperature

- temperature discrimination should utilize test tubes, warm water in one and cold water in the other
- avoid extreme temperatures as this is a test of discrimination, not of a patient's tolerance to extreme temperatures
- instruct and demonstrate the testing procedure to the patient with the expectation of a response of "hot" or "cold" for each stimulus
- attempt to initiate the testing in an intact area so the patient can anticipate what to expect
- touch the skin while alternating in a random fashion between the warm and cold test tubes
- with eyes closed, ask the patient to identify if they sense a warm or cold temperature
- allow the patient to make comparisons by asking if the stimulus is the same temperature or a different temperature when testing different areas
- compare sides of the body, proximal versus distal areas, identify patterns or distribution levels of impairment
- testing for temperature discrimination will also predict pain sensation since there are sensory receptors with each modality that overlap

Sensory Testing[6,22,25]

Vibration (Fig. 5-29)

- instruct and demonstrate the testing procedure to the patient
- preferably performed using a 128 Hz tuning fork and alternating the testing with vibration and without vibration (Fig. 5-30)
- initiate the test by tapping the tuning fork to produce vibration and placing it over the interphalangeal joint of a patient's finger or the interphalangeal joint of the great toe
- with eyes closed, ask patient to identify what they feel
- strike the tuning fork tines with each attempt, but stop the vibration on intermittent trials to ensure that the patient will recognize vibration versus touch or pressure
- if there is impairment, test bony prominences proximally including the wrist, elbow, spinous processes, clavicles, medial malleolus, patella, ASIS, etc.
- allow the patient to make comparisons by asking if the stimulus is the same or different when testing the different bony areas of a limb or right versus left sides of the body

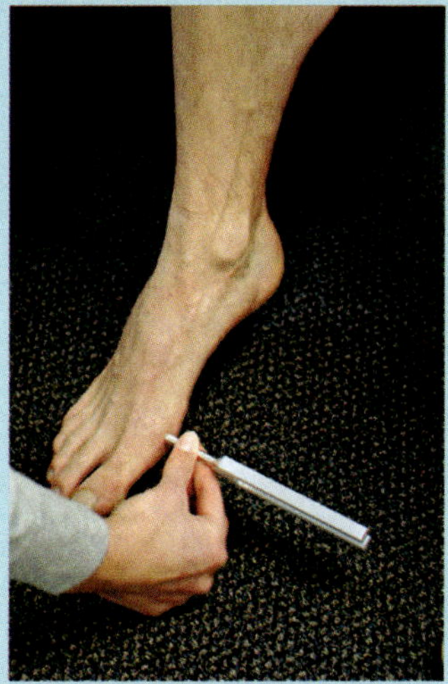

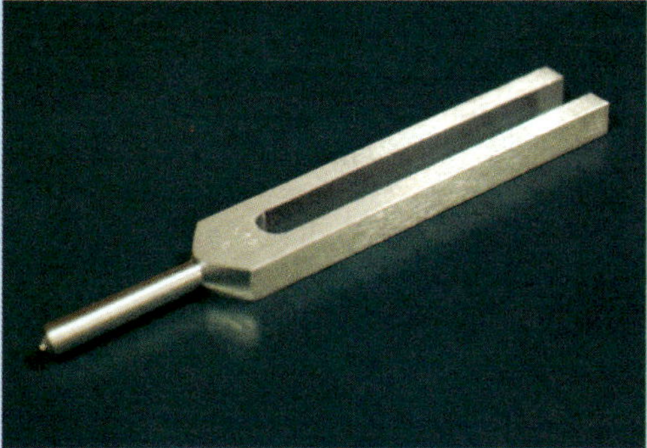

Fig. 5-29 (Above): Examination of vibration using a tuning fork.

Fig. 5-30 (Below): A tuning fork.

Pressure

- instruct and demonstrate the testing procedure to the patient and ask for a response
- attempt to initiate the testing in an intact area so the patient can anticipate what to expect
- touch the skin with a fingertip using direct pressure firm enough to stimulate the deep receptors
- with eyes closed, ask patient to identify when they feel anything
- alternate light touch and deep pressure with the patient responding "light" or "deep"
- compare sides of the body, proximal versus distal areas, identify patterns or distribution level of impairment

CONSIDER THIS

ABNORMALITIES IN SENSORY PERCEPTION[2,17,20]

When treating a patient with peripheral nerve damage, all areas of the face, trunk, and extremities should be assessed for each modality of sensation and documented. Sensation should be tested without the influence of visual feedback to the patient so that the results are not influenced by what a patient anticipates as the response to the stimuli that the therapist provides. Sensory testing requires patience and practice in order to generate the most accurate results.

- **Allodynia:** the sensation of pain in response to a stimulus that would not typically produce pain
- **Analgesia:** the absence of pain while remaining conscious
- **Anesthesia:** the absence of touch sensation
- **Causalgia:** constant, relentless, burning hyperesthesia and hyperalgesia that develops after a peripheral nerve injury
- **Dysesthesia:** distortion of any of the senses, especially the sense of touch
- **Hyperesthesia:** heightened sensation
- **Hyperpathia:** an extreme exaggerated response to pain
- **Hypesthesia:** a diminished sensation of touch
- **Neuralgia:** severe and multiple shock-like pains that radiate from a specific nerve distribution
- **Pallanesthesia:** loss of vibration sensation
- **Paresthesia:** abnormal sensations such as tingling, pins and needles or burning sensations

Peripheral Nerve Lesions[20]

A lesion of the nerve can occur through many mechanisms of injury. Possible etiologies include mechanical (compression injury), crush and percussion (fracture, compartment syndrome), laceration, penetrating trauma (stab wound), stretch (traction injury), high velocity trauma (motor vehicle accident), and cold (frostbite). When there is peripheral nerve degeneration, the voluntary muscles first exhibit an altered response to acetylcholine, with wasting of the sarcoplasm and loss of fibrils. This results in total loss of muscle over time with replacement by fibrous tissues.

Double crush syndrome: existence of two separate lesions along the same nerve that create more severe symptoms than if only one lesion existed

Mononeuropathy: an isolated nerve lesion; associated conditions include trauma and entrapment

Neuroma: abnormal growth of nerve cells; associated conditions include vasculitis, AIDS, and amyloidosis

Peripheral neuropathy: impairment or dysfunction of the peripheral nerves; associated conditions include diabetic peripheral neuropathy, trauma, alcoholism

Polyneuropathy: diffuse nerve dysfunction that is symmetrical and typically secondary to pathology and not trauma; associated conditions include Guillain-Barre syndrome, peripheral neuropathy, use of neurotoxic drugs, and HIV

Wallerian degeneration: degeneration that occurs distally, specifically to the myelin sheath and axon

Classification of Acute Nerve Injuries[9,27]

Neurapraxia

- Mildest form of injury
- Conduction block usually due to myelin dysfunction
- Axonal continuity preserved
- Axons, epineurium, perineurium, and endoneurium intact
- Nerve conduction is preserved proximal and distal to the lesion
- Nerve fibers are not damaged, no evidence of nerve degeneration is noted
- Symptoms include pain, minimal muscle atrophy, numbness or greater loss of motor and sensory function, diminished proprioception
- Recovery is rapid and complete and will occur within 4-6 weeks
- Pressure injuries are the most common

CONSIDER THIS

PERIPHERAL NERVE INJURY: TYPICAL ETIOLOGIES[2,4]

Both upper and lower extremity nerves have typical etiologies that subsequently produce specific patterns of impingement or compression injuries.

In the upper extremity, brachial plexus injuries can result from trauma, penetration, traction or compression. The following lists common etiologies associated with specific nerve injuries.

Axillary: fracture of the neck of the humerus, anterior dislocation of the shoulder

Musculocutaneous: fracture of the clavicle

Radial: compression of the nerve in the radial tunnel, fracture of the humerus

Median: compression in the carpal tunnel, pronator teres entrapment

Ulnar: compression in the cubital tunnel, entrapment in Guyon's canal

In the lower extremity, many nerve injuries for women are secondary to labor, delivery or surgical procedures around the pelvis. The following lists common etiologies associated with specific nerve injuries.

Femoral: total hip arthroplasty, displaced acetabular fracture, anterior dislocation of the femur, hysterectomy, appendectomy

Sciatic: blunt force trauma to the buttocks, total hip arthroplasty, accidental injection to the nerve

Obturator: fixation of a femur fracture, total hip arthroplasty

Peroneal: femur, tibia or fibula fracture, positioning during surgical procedures

Tibial: tarsal tunnel entrapment, popliteal fossa compression

Sural: fracture of the calcaneus or lateral malleolus

Recovery is based on the degree of injury and potential for regeneration of the nerve. The majority of research indicates that children tend to have better outcomes after peripheral nerve damage than adults, although some research sees no difference between the populations. The earlier repair of a nerve yields a better outcome; the more distal the lesion, the better the outcome secondary to the nerve length that requires recovery.

Axonotmesis

- A more severe grade of injury to a peripheral nerve
- Reversible injury to damaged fibers since they maintain an anatomical relationship to each other
- Damage occurs to the axons with preservation of the endoneurium (neural connective tissue sheath), epineurium, Schwann cells, and supporting structures
- Distal Wallerian degeneration can occur
- The nerve can regenerate distal to the site of the lesion at a rate of one millimeter per day
- Recovery is spontaneous and varies from spotty to no recovery; surgery may be required for repair
- Traction, compression, and crush injuries are the most common

Neurotmesis

- The most severe grade of injury to a peripheral nerve
- Axon, myelin, connective tissue components are all damaged or transected
- Irreversible injury; no possibility of regeneration
- Flaccid paralysis and wasting of muscles occur; total loss of sensation to area supplied by the nerve
- All motor and sensory loss distal to the lesion becomes permanently impaired
- No spontaneous recovery; with surgical reattachment, potential regenerating axons may grow at one millimeter per day with proximal recovery first; sensory recovery occurs sooner than motor fibers
- Complete transection of the nerve trunk

Peripheral Nervous System Pathology[2,3,9]

Anterior Horn Cell

- Sensory component intact
- Motor weakness and atrophy
- Fasciculations
- Decreased deep tendon reflexes
- **Example:** amyotrophic lateral sclerosis (ALS), poliomyelitis

Muscle

- Sensory component intact
- Motor weakness; fasciculations are rare
- Normal or decreased deep tendon reflexes
- **Example:** muscular dystrophy

Neuromuscular Junction

- Sensory component intact
- Motor fatigue is greater than actual weakness
- Normal deep tendon reflexes
- **Example:** myasthenia gravis

Peripheral Nerve (Mononeuropathy)

- Sensory loss along the nerve route
- Motor weakness and atrophy in a peripheral distribution; may have fasciculations
- **Example:** trauma

Peripheral Polyneuropathy

- Sensory impairments; "stocking glove" distribution
- Motor weakness and atrophy; weaker distally than proximally; may have fasciculations
- Decreased deep tendon reflexes
- **Example:** diabetic peripheral polyneuropathy

Spinal Roots and Nerves

- Sensory component will have corresponding dermatomal deficits
- Motor weakness in an innervated pattern; may have fasciculations
- Decreased deep tendon reflexes
- **Example:** herniated disk

Upper Motor Neuron Disease

An upper motor neuron disease is characterized by a lesion found in descending motor tracts within the cerebral motor cortex, internal capsule, brainstem or spinal cord. Symptoms include weakness of involved muscles, hypertonicity, hyperreflexia, mild disuse atrophy, and abnormal reflexes. Damaged tracts are in the lateral white column of the spinal cord.

Examples of upper motor neuron lesions include:

- cerebral palsy
- hydrocephalus
- ALS (both upper and lower)
- CVA
- birth injuries
- multiple sclerosis
- Huntington's chorea
- traumatic brain injury
- pseudobulbar palsy
- brain tumors

Lower Motor Neuron Disease

A lower motor neuron disease is characterized by a lesion that affects nerves or their axons at or below the level of the brainstem, usually within the "final common pathway." The ventral gray column of the spinal cord may also be affected. Symptoms include flaccidity or weakness of the involved muscles, decreased tone, fasciculations, muscle atrophy, and decreased or absent reflexes.

Examples of lower motor neuron lesions include:

- poliomyelitis
- ALS (both upper and lower)
- Guillain-Barre syndrome
- tumors involving the spinal cord
- trauma
- progressive muscular atrophy
- infection
- Bell's palsy
- carpal tunnel syndrome
- muscular dystrophy
- spinal muscular atrophy

Upper versus Lower Motor Neuron Disease[1,2,3]

	UMND	LMND
Reflexes	Hyperactive	Diminished or absent
Atrophy	Mild from disuse	Present
Fasciculations	Absent	Present
Tone	Hypertonic	Hypotonic to flaccid

Involuntary Movement/Movement Disorders[1,6,22]

An involuntary movement is defined as a movement that the person does not start or stop at the person's own command or with an observer's command. Muscle fiber contractions of either central or peripheral origin can create small or large scale patterns. Common forms of hypokinesia include apraxia, rigidity, and bradykinesia. Common forms of hyperkinesia include ataxia, athetosis, chorea, tics, tremors, dysmetria, and dystonia. Select movement disorders are highlighted below.

Athetosis

Athetosis is a movement disorder that presents with slow, twisting, and writhing movements that are large in amplitude. Athetoid movement is primarily seen in the face, tongue, trunk, and extremities. When the movements are brief, they merge with chorea (choreoathetosis), and when sustained, they merge with dystonia, and it is typically associated with spasticity. Athetosis is a common finding in several forms of cerebral palsy secondary to basal ganglia pathology.

Chorea

Chorea is a form of hyperkinesia that presents with brief, irregular contractions that are rapid, but not to the degree of myoclonic jerks. Chorea is typically secondary to damage of the caudate nucleus. Chorea is often equated to "fidgeting." Ballism is a form of chorea that includes choreic jerks of large amplitude. Ballism produces flailing movements of the limbs and is typically secondary to damage of the subthalamic nucleus. Huntington's disease is an example of a pathology that presents with chorea.

Dystonia

Dystonia is a syndrome of sustained muscle contractions that frequently causes twisting, abnormal postures, and repetitive movements. All muscles can be affected and the involuntary movements are often accentuated during volitional movement and with progression, can produce overflow. Presentation varies as there are multiple types and etiologies surrounding dystonia. Etiologies range from genetic or acquired to environmental or a secondary effect from medications. Presentations can include sustained contractions of agonist and antagonist muscles; repeatedly persisting within the same muscle group; voluntary movements that create involuntary movement secondary to overflow; torsion spasms that are continual, patterned and twisting; as well as other presentations based on etiology. Common diagnoses that may include dystonia are Parkinson's disease, cerebral palsy, and encephalitis.[13]

Tics

Tics are sudden, brief, repetitive coordinated movements that will usually occur at irregular intervals. There are simple and complex tics that vary from myoclonic jerks to jumping movements that may include vocalization and repetition of other sounds. Tourette syndrome is an example of a pathology that presents with tics.

Tremors

Tremors are involuntary, rhythmic, oscillatory movements that are typically classified into three groupings:

- Resting: Tremors are observable at rest and may or may not disappear with movement; may increase with mental stress. An example is the pill-rolling tremor associated with Parkinson's disease.
- Postural: Tremors are observable during a voluntary contraction to maintain a posture. Examples include the rapid tremor associated with hyperthyroidism, fatigue or anxiety, and benign essential tremor.
- Intention (kinetic): Tremors are absent at rest, but observable with activity and typically increase as the target approaches. These tremors likely indicate a lesion of the cerebellum or its efferent pathways and are typically seen with multiple sclerosis.

Muscle/Movement Impairment Terminology[1,13,24]

Akinesia: The inability to initiate movement; commonly seen in patients with Parkinson's disease.

Asthenia: Generalized weakness, typically secondary to cerebellar pathology.

Ataxia: The inability to perform coordinated movements.

Athetosis: A condition that presents with involuntary movements combined with instability of posture. Peripheral movements occur without central stability.

Bradykinesia: Movement that is very slow.

Chorea: Movements that are sudden, random, and involuntary.

Clasp-knife response: A form of resistance seen during range of motion of a hypertonic joint where there is greatest resistance at the initiation of range that lessens with movement through the range of motion.

Clonus: A characteristic of an upper motor neuron lesion; involuntary alternating spasmodic contraction of a muscle precipitated by a quick stretch reflex.

Cogwheel rigidity: A form of rigidity where resistance to movement has a phasic quality to it; often seen with Parkinson's disease.

Dysdiadochokinesia: The inability to perform rapidly alternating movements.

Dysmetria: The inability to control the range of a movement and the force of muscular activity.

Dystonia: Closely related to athetosis, however, there is larger axial muscle involvement rather than appendicular muscles.

Fasciculation: A muscular twitch that is caused by random discharge of a lower motor neuron and its muscle fibers; suggests lower motor neuron disease, however, can be benign.

Hemiballism: An involuntary and violent movement of a large body part.

Kinesthesia: The ability to perceive the direction and extent of movement of a joint or body part.

Lead pipe rigidity: A form of rigidity where there is uniform and constant resistance to range of motion; often associated with lesions of the basal ganglia.

Rigidity: A state of severe hypertonicity where a sustained muscle contraction does not allow for any movement at a specified joint.

Tremor: Involuntary, rhythmic, oscillatory movements secondary to a basal ganglia lesion. There are various classifications secondary to specific etiology.

CONSIDER THIS

MODIFIED ASHWORTH SCALE FOR GRADING SPASTICITY[20]

The Modified Ashworth Scale is a widely used qualitative scale for the assessment of spasticity; it measures the amount of resistance to passive stretch. Clinical assessment of spasticity may also include muscle grading, deep tendon reflexes (DTRs), and range of motion (ROM) evaluation.

Spasticity is a component of an upper motor neuron lesion, which is also characterized by exaggerated phasic (tendon jerks) and tonic (spastic) stretch reflexes that can occur after injury to the CNS. Spasticity is not a primary condition, but a secondary effect from CNS damage also allowing for a loss of movement dexterity.

Modified Ashworth Scale for Grading Spasticity

Grade	Description
0	no increase in muscle tone
1	slight increase in muscle tone, manifested by a catch and release or by minimal resistance at the end of the range of motion when the affected part(s) is moved in flexion or extension
1+	slight increase in muscle tone, manifested by a catch, followed by minimal resistance throughout the remainder (less than half) of the ROM
2	more marked increase in muscle tone through most of the ROM, but affected part(s) easily moved
3	considerable increase in muscle tone, passive movement difficult
4	affected part(s) rigid in flexion or extension

Other methods for evaluating spasticity include the Bilateral Adductor Tone Score, the Spasm Frequency Score, and electrophysiologic studies, however, most of these methods are time consuming, expensive, and require specialized equipment.

Balance[23,26,28]

Balance can be defined as:

- a state of physical equilibrium
- maintenance and control of the center of gravity
- achieving and maintaining an upright posture

All definitions assume integrated somatosensory, visual, and vestibular information within the central nervous system. Balance is best assessed through investigation of all three components of balance.

Somatosensory Input

Somatosensory receptors are located in the joints, muscles, ligaments, and skin to provide proprioceptive information regarding length, tension, pressure, pain, and joint position. Proprioceptive and tactile input from the ankles, knees, hips, and neck provide balance information to the brain.

- **Challenging the somatosensory system:** examination of pressure and vibration; observation of a patient when changing the surface they are standing on. Examples would be slopes, uneven surfaces, standing on foam (Figs. 5-31, 5-32).

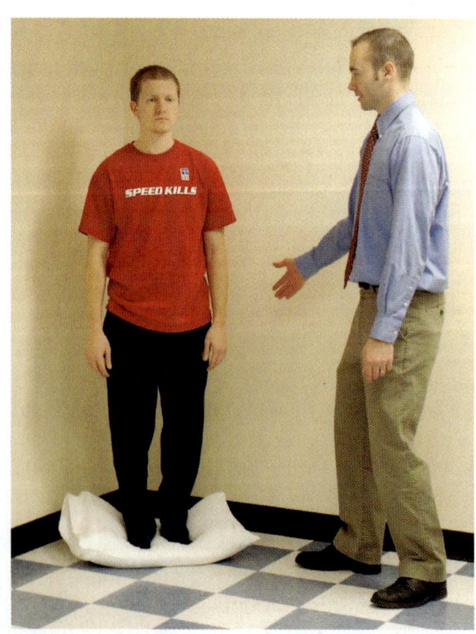

Fig. 5-31: Examination of balance while stressing the somatosensory system by using an altered surface.

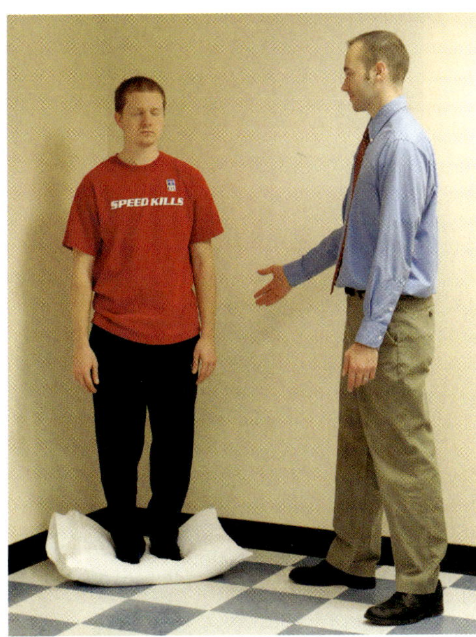

Fig. 5-32: Examination of balance by stressing the somatosensory system by using an altered surface and closing the patient's eyes. This does not allow for visual feedback regarding balance.

Visual Input

Visual receptors allow for perceptual acuity regarding verticality, motion of objects and self, environmental orientation, postural sway, and movements of the head/neck. Children rely heavily on this system for maintenance of balance.

- **Challenging the visual system:** examination of quiet standing with eyes open; observing balance strategies to maintain center of gravity with and without visual input. Assessment of potential visual field cuts, hemianopsia, pursuits, saccades, double vision, gaze control, and acuity is necessary.

Vestibular Input

The vestibular system provides the central nervous system with feedback regarding the position and movement of the head with relation to gravity. The labyrinth consists of three semicircular canals filled with endolymph and two otolith organs. Semicircular canals respond to the movement of fluid with head motion. Otoliths measure the effects of gravity and movement with regard to acceleration/deceleration.

- **Challenging the vestibular system:** examination of balance with movement of the head; testing such as Dix-Hallpike test, bithermal caloric testing, assessment for nystagmus, head thrust sign; testing of the vestibuloocular reflex.

Balance Reflexes

Vestibuloocular reflex (VOR): VOR allows for head/eye movement coordination. This reflex supports gaze stabilization through eye movement that counters movements of the head. This maintains a stable image on the retina during movement.

Vestibulospinal reflex (VSR): VSR attempts to stabilize the body and control movement. The reflex assists with stability while the head is moving as well as coordination of the trunk during upright postures.

Automatic Postural Strategies

Automatic postural strategies are automatic motor responses that are used to maintain the center of gravity over the base of support. These responses always react or respond to a particular stimulus.

Ankle strategy: The ankle strategy is the first strategy to be elicited by a small range and slow velocity perturbation when the feet are on the ground. Muscle groups contract in a distal to proximal fashion to control postural sway from the ankle joint.

Hip strategy: The hip strategy is elicited by a greater force, challenge or perturbation through the pelvis and hips. The hips will move (in the opposite direction from the head) in order to maintain balance. Muscle groups contract in a proximal to distal fashion in order to counteract the loss of balance.

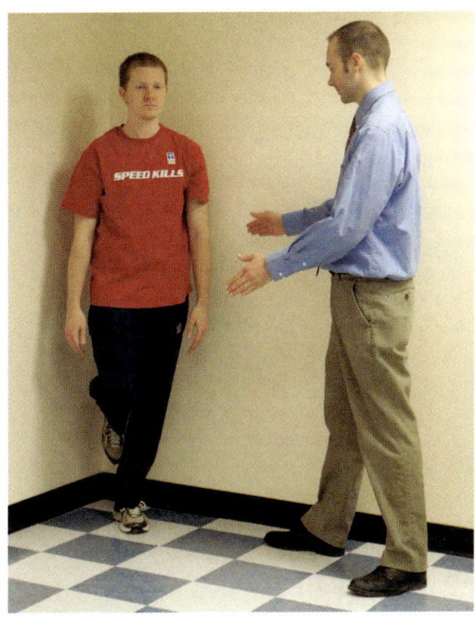

Fig. 5-33: Examination of balance with a decrease in the base of support.

Suspensory strategy: The suspensory strategy is used to lower the center of gravity during standing or ambulation in order to better control the center of gravity. Examples of this strategy include knee flexion, crouching or squatting. This strategy is often used when both mobility and stability are required during a task (such as surfing).

Stepping strategy: The stepping strategy is elicited through unexpected challenges or perturbations during static standing or when the perturbation produces such a movement that the center of gravity is beyond the base of support. The lower extremities step and/or upper extremities reach to regain a new base of support.

Vertigo

Vertigo is used to describe a sense of movement and rotation of oneself or the surrounding environment. It typically is a sensation of spinning, but can also present as linear motion or falling. Vertigo may have a peripheral or central origin.

Characteristics of Central Versus Peripheral Vertigo[1]

Peripheral vertigo	Central vertigo
• episodic and short duration • autonomic symptoms present • precipitating factor • pallor, sweating • nausea and vomiting • auditory fullness (fullness within the ears) • tinnitus	• autonomic symptoms less severe • loss of consciousness can occur • neurological symptoms present including: – diplopia – hemianopsia – weakness – numbness – ataxia – dysarthria

Etiology of Central Versus Peripheral Vertigo[1]

Peripheral	Central
Benign paroxysmal positional vertigo (BPPV)	Meningitis
Meniere's disease	Migraine headache
Infection	Complications of neurologic origin post ear infections
Trauma/tumor	Trauma/tumor
Metabolic disorders (i.e., diabetes mellitus)	Cerebellar degeneration disorders (i.e., alcoholism)
Acute alcohol intoxication	Multiple sclerosis

Benign paroxysmal positional vertigo (BPPV): This condition is comprised of repeated episodes of vertigo that occur subsequent to changes in head position. BPPV only lasts a few seconds and is typically first noted while in a recumbent position since it most commonly affects the posterior semicircular canal. The etiology is usually otoconia (canalith) that loosens and travels into the posterior semicircular canal, causing vertigo. Nystagmus is present and can be noted when assessing a patient using the Dix-Hallpike test. Patients with BPPV typically find it self-limiting and can be successfully treated with canalith repositioning maneuvers which are passive movements used to remove the otoconia from the canals, thus remediating the vertigo.

Dix-Hallpike test: This maneuver is a vertiginous position test used in assessment and treatment. The test stimulates the posterior semicircular canal and attempts to determine if otoconia exist within the canal. If the patient experiences nystagmus and vertigo, the test is performed to determine if a patient presents with BPPV or a central lesion (Figs. 5-34, 5-35, 5-36).

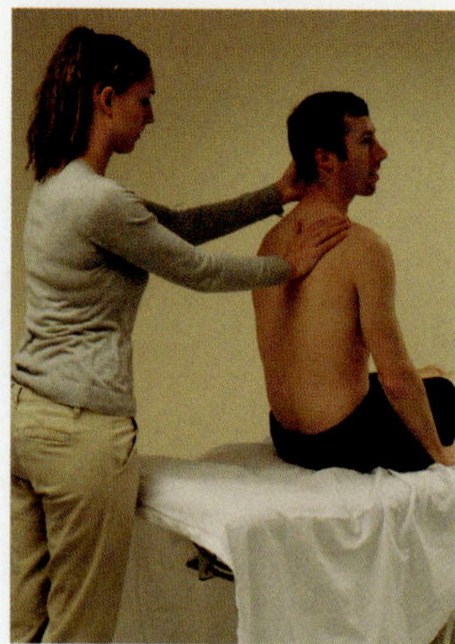

Fig. 5-34: The initial positioning for the Dix-Hallpike test where the patient starts in sitting with the legs extended on the table and head rotated 45 degrees to one side.

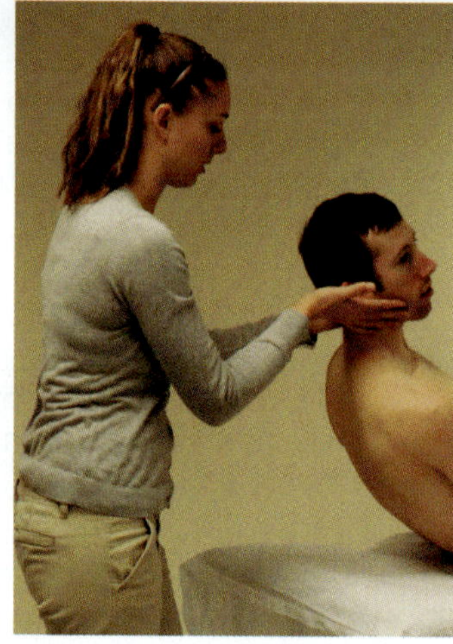

Fig. 5-35: The patient is rapidly moved to a supine position with the head (still in 45 degrees rotation) extended 30 degrees beyond horizontal off the end of the table.

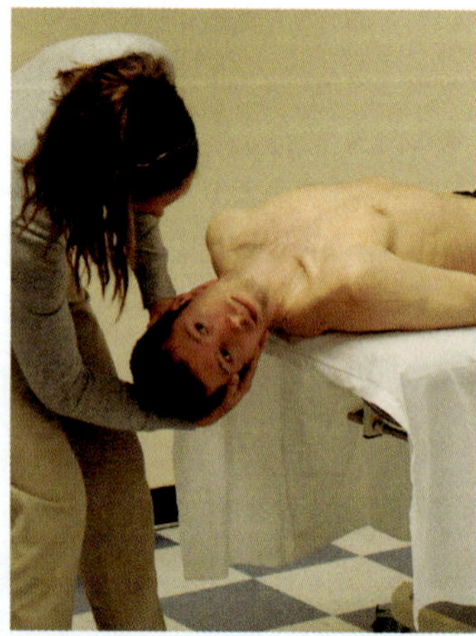

Fig. 5-36: The therapist continues to hold the patient's head in this position for 20-30 seconds observing the potential for nystagmus. If nystagmus exists, the direction of the eyes and appearance of the nystagmus can determine inner ear versus CNS lesion.

Nystagmus is abnormal eye movement that entails nonvolitional, rhythmic oscillation of the eyes. The speed of movement is faster in one direction than the other direction. A patient with nystagmus will also commonly complain of vertigo, nausea, and oscillopsia (movement of objects viewed).

Observation

Eye movement: Horizontal, vertical, rotatory or mixed movements

Type of eye movement: Pendular or jerk

Direction: Bidirectional or unidirectional

Nystagmus movement: Binocular or monocular with symmetrical or dissociated movement. Effects of change of position of the head or posture on nystagmus

Congenital Nystagmus

This form of nystagmus is typically mild and does not change in severity over the person's lifetime. It is not usually associated with other pathology.

Acquired Nystagmus

Spontaneous nystagmus: Nystagmus caused by an imbalance of vestibular signals to the oculomotor neurons that causes a constant drift in one direction that is countered by a quick movement in the opposite direction. This typically occurs after an acute vestibular lesion and will last approximately 24 hours.

Peripheral nystagmus: Nystagmus that occurs with a peripheral vestibular lesion and is inhibited when the patient fixates their vision on an object.

Central nystagmus: Nystagmus that occurs with a central lesion of the brainstem/cerebellum and is not inhibited by visual fixation on an object.

Positional nystagmus: Nystagmus that is induced by a change in head position. The semicircular canals stimulate the nystagmus that typically lasts only a few seconds.

Gaze-evoked nystagmus: Nystagmus that occurs when the eyes shift from a primary position to an alternate position. The nystagmus is caused by the patient's inability to maintain the stable gaze position. This is typically indicative of CNS pathology and is associated with brain injury and multiple sclerosis.

Characteristics of Central Versus Peripheral Nystagmus[24]

Symptoms of Nystagmus	Central Lesion	Peripheral Lesion
Direction	Either bidirectional or unidirectional	Unidirectional with the fast segment of movement indicating the opposite direction of lesion
Visual fixation	No inhibition with fixation	Will inhibit nystagmus and vertigo
Vertigo	Mild	Significant
Length of symptoms	May be chronic	Minutes, days, weeks, but finite period of time; recurrent
Etiology	Demyelination of nerves, vascular lesion, cancer/tumor	Meniere's disease, vascular disorders, trauma, toxicity, infection of inner ear

Balance Tests and Measures[24,29,30]

There are various tests and measures to assess the different facets of balance. Selection of the most appropriate instrument is determined based on clinical diagnosis and patient presentation. Common balance tests and measures are discussed below.

Berg Balance Scale

This is a tool designed to assess a patient's risk for falling. There are 14 tasks, each scored on an ordinal scale from 0-4. These tasks include static activities, transitional movements, and dynamic activities in sitting and standing positions. The maximum score is a 56 with a score less than 45 indicating an increased risk for falling. This tool can be used as a one-time examination or as an ongoing tool to monitor a patient who may be at risk for falls.

Fregly-Graybiel Ataxia Test Battery

A tool that consists of eight test conditions used in the battery with each leg measured on two accounts, the time spent in each test position and the number of steps that a patient takes without falling. Five trials of each condition are performed. The test conditions include:

- stand on beam with eyes open
- stand on beam with eyes closed
- walk on beam with eyes open
- sharpened Romberg (heel-toe static positioning)
- standing with eyes open
- standing with eyes closed
- standing on one leg with eyes closed
- walking on the floor with eyes closed

The therapist scores each condition on a pass/fail basis with normative data for comparison. This tool is best suited for patients with high level motor skills since each condition is challenging. Therapists use this tool to assess and treat balance dysfunction, however, patient performance does not assist the therapist to diagnose the cause of balance dysfunction.

Fugl-Meyer Sensorimotor Assessment of Balance Performance Battery

This tool is designed as a subset of the Fugl-Meyer Physical Performance Battery and is designed to assess balance specifically for patients with hemiplegia. Each of the seven items assessed is scored from 0-2, specific to each item with the maximum score being 14. Even though a 14 is the best score that a person can receive, the patient still may not have normal balance.

Functional Reach Test (Figs. 5-37, 5-38)

A single task screening tool used to assess standing balance and risk of falling. A person is required to stand upright with a static base of support. A yardstick is positioned to measure the forward distance that a patient can reach without moving the feet. Three trials are performed and averaged together.

The following are age-related standard measurements for functional reach:

20 - 40 years: 14.5 - 17 inches

41 - 69 years: 13.5 - 15 inches

70 - 87 years: 10.5 - 13.5 inches

A patient that falls below the age appropriate range for functional reach has an increased risk for falling. The outcome measure demonstrates high test-retest correlation and intrarater reliability.

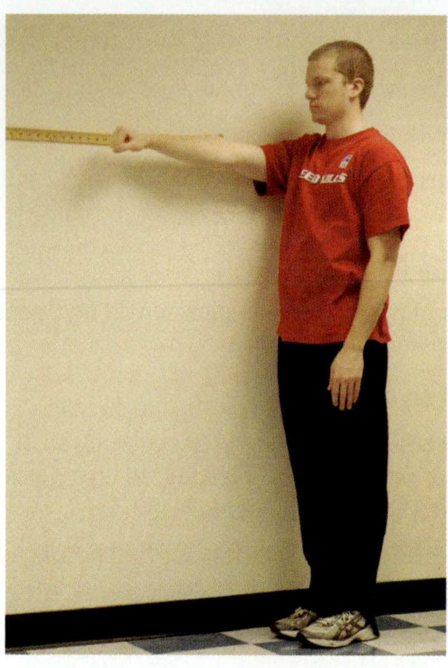

Fig. 5-37: Initial positioning for the Functional Reach Test.

Fig. 5-38: Reaching forward during the Functional Reach Test.

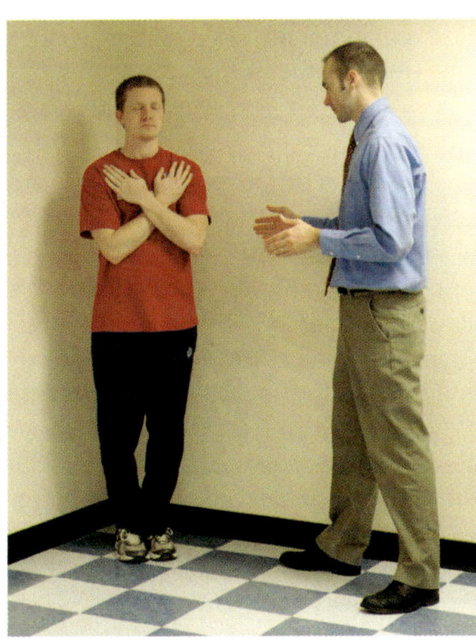

Fig. 5-39: Romberg testing for postural sway with eyes closed.

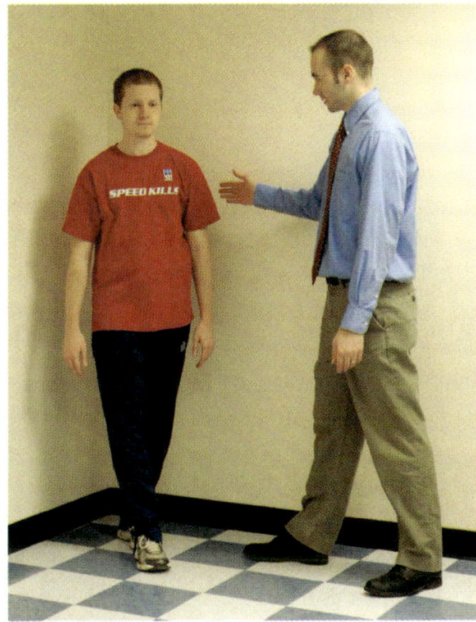

Fig. 5-40: Testing using the sharpened Romberg for postural sway with eyes open.

Romberg Test

This is an assessment tool of balance and ataxia that initially positions the patient in unsupported standing, feet together, upper extremities folded, looking at a fixed point straight ahead with eyes open. With the eyes open, three sensory systems (visual, vestibular, somatosensory) provide input to the cerebellum to maintain standing stability. If there is a mild lesion in the vestibular or somatosensory systems, the patient will typically compensate through the visual sense.

Next the patient maintains the same standing posture, but closes the eyes (Fig. 5-39). A patient receives a grade of "normal" if they are able to maintain the position for 30 seconds. An abnormal response occurs with the inability to maintain balance when standing erect with the feet together and the eyes closed. Patients may exhibit excessive sway or begin to fall. When the visual input is removed, instability will be present if there is a larger somatosensory or vestibular deficit producing the instability. If a patient demonstrates ataxia and has a positive Romberg test, this indicates sensory ataxia and not cerebellar ataxia.

There is also a Sharpened Romberg test where the patient's balance is further assessed by performing in the same manner but with a heel-to-toe stance, typically with the non-dominant foot in front. The patient would first be tested with eyes open (Fig. 5-40) and then with eyes closed. This modification increases the challenge to the vestibular and somatosensory systems.

Timed Get Up and Go Test

This is a functional performance screening tool used to assess a person's level of mobility and balance. The person initially sits in a supported chair with a firm surface, transfers to a standing position, and walks approximately 10 feet. The patient must then turn around without external support, walk back towards the chair, and return to a sitting position. The patient is scored based on amount of postural sway, excessive movements, reaching for support, side stepping or other signs of loss of balance. The 5-point ordinal rating scale designates a score of one as normal and a score of five as severely abnormal. In an attempt to increase overall reliability the use of time was implemented. Patients who are independent can complete the multi-task process in 10 seconds or less. Patients that require over 20 seconds to complete the process are at the limit for functional independence and may be at an increased risk for falling. Patients that require 30 seconds are at a high risk for a fall.

Tinetti Performance Oriented Mobility Assessment

A tool used to screen patients and identify if there is an increased risk for falling. The first section assesses balance through sit to stand and stand to sit from an armless chair, immediate standing balance with eyes open and closed, tolerating a slight push in the standing position, and turning 360 degrees. A patient is scored from 0-2 in most categories with a maximum score of 16. The second section assesses gait at normal speed and at a rapid, but safe speed. Items scored in this section include initiation of gait, step length and height, step asymmetry and continuity, path, stance during gait, and trunk motion. A patient is scored 0-2 for each with a maximum score of 12. The tool has a combined maximum total of 28 with the risk of falling increasing as the total score decreases. A total score less than 19 indicates a high risk for a fall.

Vestibular Rehabilitation

Vestibular rehabilitation is a therapeutic intervention that can be highly successful for patients with vestibular or central balance system disorders. Exercise protocols for vestibular retraining utilize compensation, adaptation, and plasticity to increase the brain's sensitivity, restore symmetry, improve vestibuloocular control, and subsequently increase motor control and movement.

Goals for Vestibular Rehabilitation

- Improve balance
- Improve trunk stability
- Increase strength and range of motion in order to improve musculoskeletal balance responses and strategies
- Decrease the rate and risk of falls
- Minimize dizziness

Vestibuloocular Retraining Therapeutic Guidelines

- Vestibuloocular reflex (VOR) and vestibulospinal reflex (VSR) stimulation exercises
- Ocular motor exercises
- Balance exercises
- Gait exercises
- Combination exercises (obstacle courses, functioning in a public place)
- Habituation training exercises (use only with appropriate patients)
- Individualize each program based on the patient's specific impairments (rehabilitation versus compensation training)
- Use of practice, feedback, and repetition are vital for skill refinement
- Use of gravity, varying surface conditions, visual conditions, and environmental cues should be included in therapeutic planning
- The center of gravity must be controlled at each stage of treatment
- Strategy (hip, ankle, stepping, suspense) training should be implemented during treatment so that strategies become automatic responses
- Force plate systems, electromyographic biofeedback, optokinetic visual stimulation, and videography are all technical systems that can provide feedback to motor learning during vestibular rehabilitation
- Foam, mirrors, rocker boards, BAPS boards, Swiss balls, foam rollers, trampolines, and wedges are lower "tech" treatment tools that are successfully used for vestibular rehabilitation

Communication Disorders

Aphasia[1]

Aphasia is an acquired neurological impairment of processing for receptive and/or expressive language. Aphasia is the result of brain injury, head trauma, CVA, tumor or infection. Diagnosis is based on the site of lesion in the brain and the blood vessels involved. Patients with aphasia are classified based on observation of fluent or non-fluent aphasia.

Prognosis is dependent on the individual patient, location, and extent of the lesion. Typically, the more sudden the onset of damage, as in the case of an acute CVA, the higher extent of aphasia can be expected. The following characteristics associated with aphasia are often associated with a poor prognosis: perseveration of speech, severe auditory comprehension impairments, unreliable yes/no answers, and the use of empty speech without recognition of impairments.

Fluent Aphasia[5,9,31]

- Lesion varies based on the type of fluent aphasia but frequently involves the temporal lobe, Wernicke's area or regions of the parietal lobe
- Word output and speech production are functional
- Prosody is acceptable, but empty speech/jargon
- Speech lacks any substance, use of paraphasias
- Use of neologisms (substitution within a word that is so severe it makes the word unrecognizable)

Non-fluent Aphasia[5,9,31]

- Lesion varies based on the type of non-fluent aphasia, but frequently the frontal lobe (anterior speech center) of the dominant hemisphere is affected
- Poor word output and dysprosodic speech (impairment in the rhythm and inflection of speech)
- Poor articulation and increased effort for speech
- Content is present, but impaired syntactical words

Types of Fluent Aphasia[5,9,31]

Wernicke's Aphasia

- Lesion: posterior region of superior temporal gyrus
- Also known as "receptive aphasia"
- Comprehension (reading/auditory) impaired
- Good articulation, use of paraphasias
- Impaired writing
- Poor naming ability
- Motor impairment not typical due to the distance from Wernicke's area to the motor cortex

Conduction Aphasia

- Lesion: supramarginal gyrus, arcuate fasciculus
- Severe impairment with repetition
- Intact fluency, good comprehension
- Speech interrupted by word-finding difficulties
- Reading intact, writing impaired

Types of Non-fluent Aphasia[5,9,31]

Broca's Aphasia

- Lesion: 3rd convolution of frontal lobe
- Also known as "expressive aphasia"
- Most common form of aphasia
- Intact auditory and reading comprehension
- Impaired repetition and naming skills
- Frustration with language skill errors
- Paraphasias are common
- Motor impairment typical due to proximity of Broca's area to the motor cortex

Global Aphasia

- Lesion: frontal, temporal, parietal lobes
- Comprehension (reading/auditory) is severely impaired
- Impaired naming, writing, repetition skills
- May involuntarily verbalize, usually without correct context
- May use nonverbal skills for communication

Verbal Apraxia[1]

Verbal apraxia is a non-dysarthric and non-aphasic impairment of prosody and articulation of speech. Verbal expression is impaired secondary to deficits in motor planning. A patient is unable to initiate learned movement (articulation of speech) even though they understand the task. Lesions are usually found in the left frontal lobe adjacent to Broca's area.

Dysarthria[1]

Dysarthria is a motor disorder of speech that is caused by an upper motor neuron lesion that affects the muscles that are used to articulate words and sounds. Speech is often noted as "slurred" and there may also be an effect on respiratory or phonatory systems due to the weakness.

SPOTLIGHT ON SAFETY

TREATING APHASIA[8]

Treating a patient with aphasia typically requires a physical therapist to alter the traditional methods of treatment in order to enhance communication and provide a safe and comfortable environment for the patient. The physical therapist may want to co-treat or consult with the speech pathologist to establish the best means of communication with the patient. The following may be considered when treating a patient that presents with aphasia:

- Cueing strategies must avoid verbal input and use tactile and visual cues.
- Attempt to have only one person speak to the patient at a time. Extra noise and multiple voices will only confuse the patient.
- Use concise sentences and yes/no questioning for ease of understanding and response.
- Allow the patient adequate time to process and respond before progressing with treatment.
- Allow for ample time for communication during treatment. If communication is rushed, this can decrease the effectiveness of the therapy session. The patient may also become frustrated with feeling pressure to respond.
- Attempt to allow the patient to perform an activity or segment of therapy without repetitive feedback.

Medical Procedures/Testing for Neurological Dysfunction[32]

Procedure/Test	Rationale
Cerebral angiography	A cerebral angiogram is an invasive procedure that can determine the narrowing or blockage of an artery within the brain. This can be used when diagnosing a potential CVA, brain tumor, aneurysm or vascular malformation. The catheter is threaded up through the body into an artery within the neck and contrast dye is released into the bloodstream. A series of x-rays is then taken.
Computed tomography (CT scan)	Brain scan imaging is typically non-invasive and provides cross sections of the area tested with precise two dimensional views of bones, tissues, and organs. Dyes or contrast are occasionally used to provide the best view of any pathology that may exist within the tissues. A CT scan of the brain or spinal cord is required to rule out vascular malformations, tumors, cysts, herniated disks, hemorrhage, epilepsy, encephalitis, spinal stenosis, intracranial bleeding, and head injury.

Procedure/Test	Rationale
Discography	Invasive procedure to evaluate the integrity and pathology of a spinal disk. Contrast dye is injected and CT scanning is performed in order to better assess suspected damaged areas of intervertebral disks.
Electroencephalography (EEG)	Non-invasive procedure that can continuously measure electrical activity of the brain using multiple electrodes attached to the skull. Baseline electrical activity is determined, and then various stimuli are presented and brain waves are analyzed. An EEG is used to rule out seizure disorders, brain death, brain tumors, brain damage, inflammation, alcoholism, select psychiatric disorders, and degenerative disorders that affect the brain.
Electromyography (EMG)	Invasive procedure that is used to assess nerve and muscle dysfunction or spinal cord disease. EMG records the electrical activity from the brain or spinal cord to the peripheral nerve root being tested. An EMG is used to rule out muscle pathology, nerve pathology, spinal cord disease, denervated muscle, and lower motor neuron injury.
Evoked potentials	Non-invasive procedure using two sets of electrodes that records the time it takes for an impulse to reach the brain. External stimuli (auditory, visual, proprioceptive) are used to evoke electrical potentials within the brain. This is used to rule out multiple sclerosis, brain tumor, acoustic neuroma (small tumors of the inner ear), and spinal cord injury.
Magnetic resonance imaging (MRI)	Brain scan imaging that is typically non-invasive and provides detailed images including tissues, organs, bones, and nerves. A contrast dye may be used to enhance imaging of certain tissues. The MRI is used to rule out tumors of the brain or spinal cord, multiple sclerosis, and head trauma.
Myelography	Invasive procedure of the spinal canal using contrast dye and x-ray imaging. The procedure has a high risk for headache following the spinal tap, but is used to rule out potential abnormalities surrounding the subarachnoid space, spinal nerve injury, herniated disks, fractures, back or leg pathology, and spinal tumors.
Nerve conduction velocity (NCV)	Non-invasive stimulation of a peripheral nerve to determine the nerve action potentials and the nerve's ability to send a signal. NCV rules out peripheral neuropathies, carpal tunnel syndrome, demyelination pathology, and peripheral nerve compression.
Positron emission tomography (PET)	Brain scan imaging that provides two and three-dimensional pictures of brain activity and is used to rule out cerebral circulatory pathology, metabolism dysfunction, tumors, blood flow, and brain changes following injury or drug abuse.
Spinal puncture (lumbar)	Invasive procedure that inserts a needle through lumbar puncture below the level of L1-L2 for cerebral spinal fluid sample. This procedure is most commonly performed at the L3-L4 level. A spinal puncture primarily rules out hemorrhage, inflammation, infection, meningitis, and tumor.

Pharmacology - Neuromuscular Management[13,33]

Antiepileptic Agents

Action: Antiepileptic agents reduce or eliminate seizure activity within the brain. These agents attempt to inhibit the firing of certain cerebral neurons through various effects on the CNS. Chemical classifications include barbiturates, benzodiazepines, carboxylic acids, hydantoins, iminostilbenes, succinimides, and second generation drugs.

Indications: seizure activity (partial seizures, generalized seizures, unclassified seizures)

Side effects: (agent dependent) ataxia, skin issues, behavioral changes, gastrointestinal distress, headache, blurred vision, weight gain

Implications for PT: Therapists must have adequate knowledge of established protocols for responding to a seizure as well as potential side effects of antiepileptic medications. Patients with epilepsy may show greater sensitivity to environmental surroundings such as light or noise level.

Examples: Seconal (secobarbital), Klonopin (clonazepam), Depakote (valproic acid), Dilantin (phenytoin), Tegretol (carbamazepine), Celontin (methsuximide), Neurontin (gabapentin)

Antispasticity Agents

Action: Antispasticity agents promote relaxation in a spastic muscle. Spasticity is an exaggerated stretch reflex of the muscle that can occur after injury to the CNS. Spasticity is not a primary condition, but a secondary effect from CNS damage. Agents bind selectively within the CNS or within the skeletal muscle cells to reduce spasticity.

Indications: increased tone, spasticity, spinal cord injury, CVA, multiple sclerosis

Side effects: drowsiness, confusion, headache, dizziness, generalized muscle weakness, hepatotoxicity potential with Dantrium, tolerance, dependence

Implications for PT: Therapists must balance the need to decrease spastic muscles with the loss of function that a patient may experience with the reduction of hypertonicity. Once spasticity is reduced, therapists should focus on therapeutic handling techniques, facilitation, and strengthening to promote overall mobility. Sedation may also alter the scheduling of therapy to allow for maximal participation.

Examples: Lioresal (baclofen), Valium (diazepam), Dantrium (dantrolene), Zanaflex (tizanidine)

Cholinergic Agents

Action: Cholinergic direct stimulant agents mimic acetylcholine and bind directly to the cholinergic receptor to activate and create a response at the cellular level. Indirect acting cholinergic stimulants increase cholinergic synapse activity through the inhibition of acetylcholinesterase (which normally destroys acetylcholine). The increase of acetylcholine at the synapse increases cholinergic synaptic transmission.

Indications: glaucoma, dementia due to Alzheimer's disease, postoperative decrease in gastrointestinal motility, myasthenia gravis, reversal of anticholinergic toxicity

Side effects: gastrointestinal distress, impaired visual accommodation, bronchoconstriction, bradycardia, flushing, other parasympathetic effects

Implications for PT: Patients may experience a decrease in heart rate and dizziness. Therapists should be aware of characteristics of both sympathetic and parasympathetic systems and notify the physician if a patient begins to exhibit unexpected side effects. Patients with Alzheimer's disease and myasthenia gravis may be better able to participate in therapeutic activities when taking cholinergic agents.

Examples: Direct: Duvoid (bethanechol), Pilocar (pilocarpine); Indirect: Aricept (donepezil), Tensilon (edrophonium), Prostigmin (neostigmine), Cognex (tacrine)

Dopamine Replacement Agents

Action: Dopamine replacement agents assist to relieve the symptoms of Parkinson's disease secondary to the decrease in endogenous dopamine. These agents are able to cross the blood-brain barrier through active transport and transform to dopamine within the brain.

Indications: Parkinson's disease, Parkinsonism

Side effects: arrhythmias (levodopa), gastrointestinal distress, orthostatic hypotension, dyskinesias, mood and behavioral changes, tolerance

Implications for PT: Therapists and patients attain maximal benefit from scheduling therapy one hour after administration of levodopa. Therapists must understand the debilitating effects of drug holidays and should monitor the patient's blood pressure frequently due to the potential for orthostatic hypotension.

Examples: Sinemet or Madopar (levodopa), Symmetrel (amantadine)

Muscle Relaxant Agents

Action: Muscle relaxant agents promote relaxation in muscles that typically present with spasm that is a continuous, tonic contraction. Spasms typically occur secondary to a musculoskeletal or peripheral nerve injury rather than CNS injury.

Indications: muscle spasm

Side effects: (agent dependent) sedation, drowsiness, dizziness, nausea, vomiting, headache, tolerance, dependence

Implications for PT: Therapists must be aware of potential side effects, however, maximize the potential for relaxation through therapeutic techniques and the use of modalities during treatment. Prevention of reinjury through stretching, posture retraining, and education should assist the patient to achieve desired outcomes.

Examples: Valium (diazepam), Flexeril (cyclobenzaprine), Paraflex (chlorzoxazone)

Neuromuscular and Nervous Systems Pathology

Alzheimer's Disease[1,6,24]

Alzheimer's disease is a progressive neurodegenerative disorder that results in deterioration and irreversible damage within the cerebral cortex and subcortical areas of the brain. Neurons that are normally involved with acetylcholine transmission deteriorate within the cerebral cortex. Development of amyloid plaques and neurofibrillary tangles result in further damage to the nervous system.

Etiology – The exact etiology of Alzheimer's disease is unknown, however, hypothesized causes include lower levels of neurotransmitters, higher levels of aluminum within brain tissue, genetic inheritance, autoimmune disease, abnormal processing of the substance amyloid, and virus. The risk of developing Alzheimer's disease increases with age and there is a higher incidence in women.

Signs and symptoms – Alzheimer's disease is initially noted by a change in higher cortical functions such as difficulty with new learning and subtle changes in memory and concentration. Progression includes a loss of orientation, word finding difficulties, depression, poor judgment, rigidity, bradykinesia, shuffling gait, and impaired ability to perform self-care skills. End-stage disease includes severe intellectual and physical destruction, incontinence, functional dependence, and an inability to speak.

Treatment – There is no curative treatment for the disease process. Medications are administered to inhibit acetylcholinesterase, alleviate cognitive symptoms, and control behavioral changes. Tacrine (Cognex), donepezil (Aricept), and rivastigmine (Exelon) are common pharmacological agents, however, the side effects can be substantial. Physical therapy management should focus on maximizing the patient's remaining function and providing family and caregiver education. Many patients require a long-term Alzheimer's care facility secondary to personality changes, aggressive behavior, and end-stage complications.

Amyotrophic Lateral Sclerosis[1,13]

Amyotrophic lateral sclerosis (ALS) is a chronic degenerative disease that produces both upper and lower motor neuron impairments. Significant loss of anterior horn cells in the spinal cord and the motor cranial nerve nuclei in lower brainstem produces weakness and muscle atrophy. Demyelination of corticospinal and corticobulbar tracts produce the upper motor neuron symptoms. The rapid degeneration causes denervation of muscle fibers, muscle atrophy, and weakness.

Etiology – The exact etiology of ALS is unknown, however, theories include genetic inheritance, virus, metabolic disturbances, and toxicity of lead and aluminum. There is a higher incidence in men and the disease typically begins between 40 to 70 years of age.

Signs and symptoms – Early clinical presentation of ALS may include both upper and lower motor neuron involvement. Lower motor neuron signs include asymmetric muscle weakness, fasciculations, cramping, and atrophy within the hands. Weakness spreads in a distal to proximal path. Upper motor neuron symptoms can include incoordination of movement, spasticity, clonus, and a positive Babinski reflex. A patient with ALS will exhibit fatigue, oral motor impairment, motor paralysis, and eventual respiratory paralysis.

Treatment – Effective management of ALS is based on supportive care and symptomatic therapy. Pharmacological intervention may include riluzole (Rilutek). Physical, occupational, speech, respiratory, and nutritional therapies may be warranted with the focus on quality of life and caregiver training.

A therapist must be aware of each patient's medical history and level of orientation prior to treatment. This is achieved through screening of cognition, memory, and judgment regardless of the primary diagnosis. Certain pathologies can cause irreversible dementia including:

Degenerative pathology: Alzheimer's disease, Huntington's disease, multiple sclerosis

Infectious pathology: tuberculosis, AIDS

Vascular pathology: CVA, anoxia, arteriovenous malformation, multi-infarct dementia

Miscellaneous conditions at risk for dementia: head injury, hydrocephalus, toxins, alcoholism

A therapist should modify the plan of care in order to ensure that the therapeutic goals are achieved and the patient remains safe. In early stages of dementia, patients will typically attempt to conceal their shortcomings and this can significantly compromise patient safety. Thorough assessment for at-risk patients will minimize safety risks.

Bell's Palsy[13]

Bell's palsy is a temporary unilateral facial paralysis secondary to trauma with demyelination and/or axonal degeneration of the facial nerve. This is a common clinical condition with the highest incidence in individuals between 15 and 45 years of age.

Etiology – The exact etiology of Bell's palsy is unclear, however, the condition may be secondary to a viral infection, specifically the herpes simplex/herpes zoster virus. Inflammation and subsequent pressure injure the nerve with varying degrees of damage. The inflammation within the auditory canal produces subsequent demyelination of the nerve and if ischemia occurs, there is axonal degeneration of the nerve.

Signs and symptoms – A patient with Bell's palsy will present with an asymmetrical facial appearance with "drooping" of the eyelid and mouth, potential for drooling, dryness of the eye, and inability to close the eyelid due to weakness.

Treatment – The sooner the person is diagnosed and treated, the better the outcome. Some patients have very mild involvement and their symptoms typically resolve within two weeks' time without formal medical intervention. In cases with greater severity, the patient may be treated with anti-viral medications along with high-dose corticosteroids. Physical therapy may be indicated for stimulation of the facial nerve, facial massage and/or exercise, depending on the degree of injury.

Carpal Tunnel Syndrome[13,20]

Carpal tunnel syndrome (CTS) is a peripheral nerve entrapment injury that occurs as a result of compression of the median nerve where it passes through the carpal tunnel. Normal tissue pressure within the tunnel is approximately 2 to 10 mm Hg, but CTS can result in pressure greater than 30 mm Hg with the wrist at rest which produces ischemia within the nerve. This results in sensory and motor disturbances in the median nerve distribution of the hand.

Etiology – The exact etiology of CTS is unclear, however, associated conditions that contribute to CTS include repetitive use, rheumatoid arthritis, pregnancy, diabetes, cumulative trauma disorders, tumor, hypothyroidism, and wrist sprain or fracture.

Signs and symptoms – A patient with CTS will initially present with sensory changes and paresthesia along the median nerve distribution in the hand. It may also radiate into the upper extremity, shoulder, and neck. Symptoms include night pain, weakness of the hand, muscle atrophy, decreased grip strength, clumsiness, and decreased wrist mobility.

Treatment – There is no universally accepted treatment of CTS, however, typically a patient with CTS will initially receive conservative management including splinting, ergonomic measures, local corticosteroid injections, and physical therapy management. Severe cases may require surgical release of the carpal tunnel.

Cerebellar Disorders[1,13,24]

Cerebellar disorders have numerous etiologies and present differently based on etiology and location of the lesion within the cerebellum.

Etiology – Etiologies vary and include congenital malformations, hereditary ataxias, and genetic and acquired conditions.

- **Congenital malformations** manifest early in life and are non-progressive. Manifestations vary depending on the structures involved; ataxia is usually present.
- **Hereditary ataxias** may be autosomal recessive or autosomal dominant. The most common autosomal recessive ataxia is Friedreich's ataxia. Friedreich's ataxia results from a gene mutation causing abnormal repetition of the DNA sequence and ultimately, impaired mitochondrial function. Gait unsteadiness begins early in life and it is followed by upper extremity ataxia, dysarthria, and paresis. Mental function declines and slight tremors may be seen. Reflexes, vibration, and position senses are impaired.
- **Spinocerebellar ataxias** are the main autosomal dominant ataxias. Manifestations vary with many forms affecting multiple areas in the central and peripheral nervous systems. They commonly present with neuropathy, pyramidal signs, ataxia, and restless leg syndrome.
- **Acquired ataxias** may result from nonhereditary neurodegenerative systemic disorders, toxin exposure or can be idiopathic. Systemic disorders include alcoholism, hypothyroidism, and vitamin E deficiency. Toxins include carbon monoxide, heavy metals, and lithium.

Signs and symptoms – Signs and symptoms vary based on etiology, but typically include ataxia.

Treatment – Treatment is diagnosis dependent and typically supportive unless it is acquired and/or reversible. Some systemic disorders such as hypothyroidism and toxin exposure can be treated; surgical intervention may be appropriate for structural lesions (tumor, hydrocephalus), however, the majority of treatment is typically supportive.

Diabetic Neuropathy[13,34]

Diabetic neuropathy is a complication and direct effect of diabetes mellitus. Nerve ischemia results from microvascular disease combined with the direct effects of hyperglycemia on neurons resulting in the impairment of nerve function. There are many forms including cranial neuropathies, radiculopathies, and mononeuropathies. The most common include symmetric polyneuropathy and autonomic neuropathy.

Etiology – The primary etiology is the diagnosis of diabetes mellitus. Continued research attempts to understand the cause and effect of prolonged exposure to high blood glucose and its exact impact on nerve function. There are multiple factors that lead to all forms of diabetic neuropathy including metabolic factors, high blood glucose, duration of diabetes, neurovascular factors, impairment with transport of oxygen and nutrients to the nerves, autoimmune factors, inflammation in nerves, inherited traits, and the impact of environmental and lifestyle choices such as alcohol and smoking.

Signs and symptoms – Symptoms vary depending on the form of diabetic neuropathy, but typically weakness and sensory disturbances occur distally in a symmetrical pattern. Initial symptoms typically include tingling, numbness or pain, especially in the feet. Symptoms can involve the sensory, motor or autonomic systems. Additional symptoms may include wasting of muscles in the feet or hands, "stocking-glove" sensory distribution impairments, orthostatic hypotension, weakness, urinary impairments, and significant pain.

Treatment – Patients require strict monitoring of blood glucose levels to prevent further nerve pathology. Physical therapy is typically indicated to address the various symptoms including pain management, foot care, and overall fitness. Pharmacological intervention may also be warranted.

Epilepsy[13,27,34]

Epilepsy is a chronic condition where there is temporary dysfunction of the brain that results in hypersynchronous electrical discharge of cortical neurons and seizure activity that is typically unprovoked and unpredictable. A seizure is a transient event that is a symptom of interrupted brain functioning. A seizure is the hallmark sign of epilepsy, however, one seizure does not signal epilepsy.

Etiology – There are various classifications of seizures, however, many cases are idiopathic. Other associated conditions that increase risk of epilepsy include genetic influence, head trauma, dementia, CVA, cerebral palsy, Down syndrome, and autism.

Signs and symptoms – Seizure symptoms vary, depending on type and extent of the seizure. Loss of awareness or consciousness and disturbances of movement, sensation, mood or mental function may occur.

Treatment – Many patients require antiepileptic medication to manage seizures, however, there is no current medical treatment to "cure" epilepsy. Initiating antiepileptic medication is a serious decision since side effects can produce a variety of adverse effects. Surgical intervention is sometimes warranted when pharmacological management has failed and there is a high disruption of the quality of the person's life.

Guillain-Barre Syndrome[13,24]

Guillain-Barre syndrome (GBS), or acute polyneuropathy, is a temporary inflammation and demyelination of the peripheral nerves' myelin sheaths, potentially resulting in axonal degeneration. The autoantibodies of GBS attack segments of the myelin sheath of the peripheral nerves. GBS can occur at any age, however, there is a peak in frequency in the young adult population and again in adults that are between their fifth and eighth decades.

Etiology – The exact etiology of GBS is unknown, however, it is hypothesized to be an autoimmune response to a previous respiratory infection, influenza, immunization or surgery. Viral infections, Epstein-Barr syndrome, cytomegalovirus, bacterial infections, surgery, and vaccinations have been associated with the development of GBS.

Signs and symptoms – GBS results in motor weakness in a distal to proximal progression, sensory impairment, and possible respiratory paralysis. A patient with GBS will initially present with distal symmetrical motor weakness, mild distal sensory impairments, and transient paresthesias that progress towards the upper extremities and head. The level of disability usually peaks within two to four weeks after onset. Muscle and respiratory paralysis, absence of deep tendon reflexes, and the inability to speak or swallow may also occur. GBS can be life-threatening with respiratory involvement.

Treatment – Medical management of a patient with GBS typically requires hospitalization for treatment of symptoms. Pharmacological intervention often includes immunosuppressive and analgesic/narcotic medications. Cardiac monitoring, plasmapheresis, and mechanical ventilation may be required. Physical, occupational, and speech therapies are typically indicated. Physical therapy may include pulmonary rehabilitation, strengthening, mobility training, wheelchair and orthotic prescription and/or assistive device training. Intervention and rate of progression are dependent on the ultimate level of disability from GBS.

SPOTLIGHT ON SAFETY

SEIZURES: BEFORE, DURING, AND AFTER[13,27]

Epilepsy is responsible for the majority of seizures. There are various classifications of seizures including partial, generalized, and unclassified; seizures that can be simple or complex (unimpaired versus impaired consciousness), and convulsive versus nonconvulsive. Regardless of the form of seizure, a therapist should be aware of the potential course of the seizure in order to provide safe emergency treatment.

A prodromal period is rare, but can occur days or hours prior to a seizure and may include mood changes, lightheadedness, sleep disturbances, irritability, and difficulty concentrating. An aura will briefly occur within minutes before a complex partial or generalized tonic-clonic seizure. The aura is actually a simple partial seizure and produces symptoms that alert the person that something is about to happen. Symptoms vary but can include restlessness, nervousness, anxiety, heaviness, and a general feeling that something within the body is not quite right.

The therapist should consider the following when attempting to manage a person that is having a seizure:

- Stay calm and prevent injury
- Remove all objects surrounding the person to ensure that there is nothing that could harm the person during the seizure
- Maintain awareness of the length of time of the seizure
- Ensure that the person is as comfortable as possible
- Do not allow other people near the person in an effort to keep the individual isolated
- Consider your safety and do not hold the person down; there is no need for restraint if the person is thrashing during the seizure
- Avoid placing anything into the person's mouth (the person is not capable of swallowing their tongue)
- Avoid providing any water, food or medicine until the person is fully alert
- Be prepared to call 911 if the seizure lasts longer than five minutes

After the seizure is over, place the person on their left side to avoid choking in case the person vomits. The person should remain in this position until they are fully alert. The therapist should stay with the person until they have recovered which typically takes five to twenty minutes. Therapists should be aware of patients that are at-risk for seizure activity in order to avoid any unnecessary safety risks.

Huntington's Disease[13,20]

Huntington's disease (HD), also known as Huntington's chorea, is a neurological disorder of the CNS and is characterized by degeneration and atrophy of the basal ganglia and cerebral cortex within the brain. The neurotransmitters become deficient and are unable to modulate movement.

Etiology – HD is genetically transmitted as an autosomal dominant trait with the defect linked to chromosome four and to the gene identified as IT-15. The disease is usually perpetuated by a person that has children prior to diagnosis. The average age for developing symptoms is between 35 and 55 years, however, symptoms can develop at any age.

Signs and symptoms – HD is a movement disorder that includes affective dysfunction and cognitive impairment. The patient may present with involuntary choreic movements, mild alteration in personality, grimacing, protrusion of the tongue, and ataxia with choreoathetoid movements. Late stage HD includes mental deterioration, decrease in IQ, depression, dysphagia, incontinence, immobility, and rigidity.

Treatment – Medical management of HD requires genetic, psychological, and social counseling for the patient and family. Pharmacological management is initiated once choreiform movement impairs a patient's functional capacity. Physical therapy should maximize endurance, strength, balance, postural control, and functional mobility.

Multiple Sclerosis[13,20,24]

Multiple sclerosis (MS) produces patches of demyelination of the myelin sheaths that surround nerves within the brain and spinal cord. This decreases the efficiency of nerve impulse transmission and symptoms will vary based on the location and the extent of demyelination. There is subsequent plaque development and eventual failure of impulse transmission.

Etiology – The exact etiology of MS is unknown. Genetics, viral infections, and environment all have a role in the development of MS. It is theorized that a slow-acting virus initiates the autoimmune response in individuals that have environmental and genetic factors associated with the disease. MS can occur at any age with the highest incidence between 20-35 years of age.

Signs and symptoms – Symptoms vary based on the type of disease, location, extent of demyelination, and degree of sclerosis. Initial symptoms include visual problems, paresthesias and sensory changes, clumsiness, weakness, ataxia, balance dysfunction, and fatigue. The clinical course usually consists of periods of exacerbations and remissions, with the degree of neurologic dysfunction and subsequent recovery following typical patterns related to the specific type of MS. The frequency and intensity of exacerbations may indicate the speed/course of the disease process.

Treatment – Management of MS includes pharmacological, medical, and therapeutic interventions. The goal is to lessen the length of exacerbations and maximize the health of the patient. Pharmacological intervention is indicated along with physical, occupational, and speech therapies throughout the disease process. Nutritional and psychological counseling are also important components of medical management. Physical therapy intervention includes regulation of activity level, relaxation and energy conservation techniques, normalization of tone, balance and gait training, core stabilization, and adaptive/assistive device training.

Myasthenia Gravis[13,20,24]

Myasthenia gravis is an autoimmune disease resulting in neuromuscular junction pathology. There is a defect specifically in the transmission of nerve impulses to the muscles at the neuromuscular junction. Antibodies block or destroy the receptors that are needed for acetylcholine uptake and this prevents muscle contraction.

Etiology – This is an autoimmune disease process that also has an association with an enlarged thymus. There is also an association with diabetes, rheumatoid arthritis, lupus, and other immune disorders. There are multiple forms of myasthenia gravis that range from mild to severe involvement.

Signs and symptoms – The cardinal signs of myasthenia gravis include extreme fatiguability and skeletal muscle weakness that can fluctuate within minutes or over an extended period. The ocular muscles are typically affected first and approximately half of the patients experience ptosis and diplopia. Dysphagia, dysarthria, and cranial nerve weakness are also common findings.

Treatment – The disease process of myasthenia gravis will fluctuate and a patient will experience remissions and exacerbations. A myasthenia gravis "crisis" is a medical emergency where there is an exacerbation that includes the respiratory muscles and requires a ventilator. Anticholinesterase drug therapy, plasmapheresis, and immunosuppressive therapy may be utilized. Physical and occupational therapies are also indicated intermittently with supportive goals. Physical therapy will typically focus on obtaining a respiratory baseline and pulmonary intervention as needed. Energy conservation techniques and strengthening using isometric contractions are appropriate for most patients. Since patients typically require long-term corticosteroids, physical therapy may also focus on secondary osteoporosis.

Parkinson's Disease[13,20,24]

Parkinson's disease is a primary degenerative disorder and is characterized by a decrease in production of dopamine (neurotransmitter) within the substantia nigra of the basal ganglia. The basal ganglia store the majority of dopamine and are responsible for modulation and control of voluntary movement.

Etiology – Primary Parkinson's disease has an unknown etiology and accounts for the majority of patients with Parkinsonism. Contributing factors that can produce symptoms of Parkinson's disease include genetic defect, toxicity from carbon monoxide, excessive manganese or copper, carbon disulfide, vascular impairment of the striatum, encephalitis, and other neurodegenerative diseases such as Huntington's disease or Alzheimer's disease. The majority of patients are between 50 and 79 years of age, with only a small percentage being diagnosed before 40 years.

CONSIDER THIS

FACTS AND PHYSICAL THERAPY GUIDELINES FOR TREATING MYASTHENIA GRAVIS[13]

Treating a patient with myasthenia gravis requires an understanding of the disease process, precautions, and contraindications to treatment.

Common facts associated with myasthenia gravis include:

- myasthenia gravis encompasses mild to severe symptoms and can fluctuate in severity from hour to hour at times
- proximal muscle groups are typically more affected than distal muscle groups
- difficulty with speech, swallowing, and chewing may persist due to weakness of the pharyngeal muscles and muscles of mastication
- involvement of the cranial nerves may result in eyelid weakness, diplopia, and ptosis
- typified by exacerbations, remissions, and atypically, "crisis" which is life-threatening
- remissions are not typically complete or permanent

Physical therapy guidelines in the treatment of myasthenia gravis should include:

- acquire a baseline for respiratory and neurological status
- monitor respiratory function on a regular basis to ensure that the muscles of respiration are not weakening
- review proper techniques for positioning during meals to prevent aspiration
- observe for signs of a myasthenia "crisis" (e.g., respiratory difficulty, swallowing issues, labored talking or chewing)
- review signs of toxicity and side effects of pharmacological intervention
- educate the patient to plan activity around periods of increased energy
- instruct and review energy conservation techniques
- avoid strenuous exercise and stress
- avoid excessive heat or cold as it exacerbates symptoms
- educate regarding signs of osteoporosis for patients that are using long-term corticosteroids
- initiate strengthening for patients with mild to moderate symptoms using moderate to maximal isometric contractions, while avoiding muscle fatigue
- treatment should always be based on the patient's current symptoms, strength, and level of fatigue

Signs and symptoms – The majority of patients with Parkinson's disease will initially notice a resting tremor in the hands (sometimes called a pill-rolling tremor) or feet that increases with stress and disappears with movement or sleep. Early symptoms can include balance disturbances, difficulty rolling over and rising from bed, and impairment with fine manipulative movements seen in writing, bathing, and dressing. Progression of the disease process includes hypokinesia, sluggish movement, difficulty with initiating (akinesia) and stopping movement, festinating and shuffling gait, bradykinesia, poor posture, dysphagia, and "cogwheel" or "lead pipe" rigidity of skeletal muscles. Patients may also experience "freezing" during ambulation, speech, blinking, and movements of the arms. A patient with Parkinson's disease may also have a mask-like appearance with no facial expression.

Treatment – The medical management of Parkinson's disease relies heavily on pharmacological intervention. Dopamine replacement therapy is most effective in reducing movement disorders, bradykinesia, rigidity, and tremor. Physical, occupational, and speech therapies may be warranted intermittently throughout the course of the disease. Physical therapy intervention should include maximizing endurance, strength, and functional mobility. Verbal cueing and visual feedback are also effective tools to use with this population.

Post-polio Syndrome (PPS)[13]

Poliomyelitis is a viral infection resulting in neuropathy that includes focal and asymmetrical motor impairments. In the United States, this virus was all but eradicated in the 1960s with the development of a vaccine. Post-polio syndrome is a lower motor neuron pathology that affects the anterior horn cells of those previously affected with polio. Surviving axons were originally able to increase the size of their innervation ratio to assist denervated muscle. PPS occurs when the compensated reinnervation fails and results in ongoing muscle denervation.

Etiology – A previous diagnosis of polio is essential to diagnose PPS. Fewer than half of the people with polio experience PPS decades after their initial recovery (average interval is approximately 25 years).

Signs and symptoms – Symptoms vary, however, commonly there is slow and progressive weakness, fatigue, muscle atrophy, pain, and swallowing issues.

Treatment – There is no pharmacological intervention to alter the progression of PPS. Emphasis of treatment surrounds lifestyle modification and symptomatic intervention. Physical therapy should emphasize supervised exercise, functional independence, adaptive equipment, and education to assist patients to maintain as much independence as possible.

Cerebrovascular Accident

A cerebrovascular accident is a specific event that results in a lack of oxygen supply to a specific area of the brain secondary to either ischemia or hemorrhage. The outcome of a CVA greatly varies and is based on etiology, extent of the CVA, the area of the brain that is affected, subsequent collateral damage, and the patient's co-morbidities and overall health status.

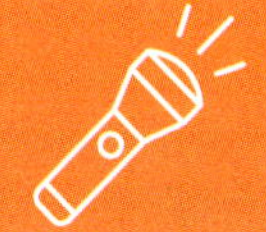

SPOTLIGHT ON SAFETY
RISK FACTORS FOR CEREBROVASCULAR ACCIDENT[13,20,24]

There are a number of primary and secondary risk factors that can lead to the development of a CVA. Patient education regarding risk factors and impairments secondary to CVA should be included in all treatment plans for patients that are at increased risk. Many risk factors are modifiable and can be altered to improve a patient's risk profile and overall health.

Primary	Secondary
Hypertension	Obesity
Cardiac disease or arrhythmias	High cholesterol
Diabetes mellitus	Behaviors related to hypertension (i.e., stress, excessive salt intake)
Cigarette smoking	Physical inactivity
Transient ischemic attacks	Increased alcohol consumption

Types of Cerebrovascular Accidents[13,20,24]

Transient Ischemic Attack (TIA)

A transient ischemic attack is usually linked to an atherosclerotic thrombosis which causes a temporary interruption of blood supply to an area of the brain. The effects may be similar to a CVA, but symptoms resolve quickly, typically within 24 to 48 hours. A TIA most often occurs in the carotid and vertebrobasilar arteries and may indicate future CVA.

Completed Stroke

A CVA that presents with total neurological deficits at the onset.

Stroke in Evolution

A CVA, usually caused by a thrombus that gradually progresses. Total neurological deficits are not seen for one to two days after onset.

Ischemic Stroke

Once there is a loss of perfusion to a portion of the brain (within just seconds), there is a central area of irreversible infarction surrounded by an area of potential ischemia.

- **Embolus**

  Associated with cardiovascular disease, an embolus may be a solid, liquid or gas, and can originate in any part of the body. The embolus travels through the bloodstream to the cerebral arteries causing occlusion of a blood vessel and a resultant infarct. The middle cerebral artery is most commonly affected by an embolus from the internal carotid arteries. Due to the sudden onset of occlusion, tissues distal to the infarct can sustain higher permanent damage than those of thrombotic infarcts. An embolic CVA occurs rapidly with no warning, and often presents with a headache. Common cardiac disorders that can lead to embolism include valvular disease (i.e., rheumatic mitral stenosis), ischemic heart disease, acute myocardial infarction, arrhythmias (i.e., atrial fibrillation), patent foramen ovale, cardiac tumors, and post cardiac catheterization.

- **Thrombus**

  An atherosclerotic plaque develops in an artery and eventually occludes the artery or a branching artery causing an infarct. This type of CVA is extremely variable in onset where symptoms can appear in minutes or over several days. A thrombotic CVA usually occurs during sleep or upon awakening after a myocardial infarction or post-surgical procedure.

Hemorrhage

Hemorrhage is an abnormal bleeding in the brain due to a rupture in blood supply. The infarct is due to disruption of oxygen to an area of the brain and compression from the accumulation of blood. Hypertension is usually a precipitating factor causing rupture of an aneurysm or arteriovenous malformation. Trauma can also precipitate hemorrhage and subsequent CVA. Characteristics include severe headache, vomiting, high blood pressure, and an abrupt onset of symptoms. Hemorrhage usually occurs during the day with symptoms evolving in relation to the speed of the bleed. Roughly half of deaths from hemorrhagic stroke occur within the first 48 hours.

Characteristics of a Cerebrovascular Accident[1,2,30]

Left Hemisphere	Right Hemisphere	Brainstem	Cerebellum
Weakness, paralysis of the right side	Weakness, paralysis of the left side	Unstable vital signs	Decreased balance
Increased frustration	Decreased attention span	Decreased consciousness	Ataxia
Decreased processing	Left hemianopsia	Decreased ability to swallow	Decreased coordination
Possible aphasia (expressive, receptive, global)	Decreased awareness and judgment	Weakness on both sides of the body	Nausea
Possible dysphagia	Memory deficits	Paralysis on both sides of the body	Decreased ability for postural adjustment
Possible motor apraxia (ideomotor and ideational)	Left inattention		Nystagmus
Decreased discrimination between left and right	Decreased abstract reasoning		
Right hemianopsia	Emotional lability		
	Impulsive behaviors		
	Decreased spatial orientation		

Synergy Patterns[35]

When the central nervous system is damaged as with a CVA, the higher centers of the brain are also damaged. The higher centers are responsible for both complex motor patterns and the inhibition of massive gross motor patterns. Synergy patterns result when the higher centers of the brain lose control and the uncontrolled or partially controlled stereotyped patterns of the middle and lower centers emerge.

Upper Limb

	Flexor Synergy	Extensor Synergy
Scapula	Elevation and retraction	Depression and protraction
Shoulder	Abduction and lateral rotation	Medial rotation and adduction
Elbow	Flexion	Extension
Forearm	Supination	Pronation
Wrist	Flexion	Extension
Fingers	Flexion with adduction	Flexion with adduction
Thumb	Flexion and adduction	Flexion and adduction

- The flexor synergy is seen when the patient attempts to lift up their arm or reach for an object.

Lower Limb

	Flexor Synergy	Extensor Synergy
Hip	Abduction and lateral rotation	Extension, medial rotation and adduction
Knee	Flexion	Extension
Ankle	Dorsiflexion with supination	Plantar flexion with inversion
Toes	Extension	Flexion and adduction

- The flexor synergy is characterized by great toe extension and flexion of the remaining toes secondary to spasticity.

CVA Tests and Measures[20,24,29]

There are various tests and measures to assess the different impairments secondary to CVA. Patients are administered specific tests based on clinical diagnosis and patient presentation.

- **National Institute of Health (NIH) Stroke Scale:** assessment of an acute CVA relative to impairment
- **Functional Independence Measure (FIM):** provides a level of burden through assessment of mobility and ADL management
- **Stroke Impact Scale:** assessment of physical and social disability or level of impairment secondary to CVA
- **Fugl-Meyer Assessment of Physical Performance:** motor, sensory, and balance impairment; also assesses pain and range of motion

Neurological Rehabilitation

Neurological rehabilitation may incorporate a variety of treatments based on the patient's pathology, problem list, and deficits. There are many forms of neurological rehabilitation based on each construct's beliefs regarding motor control and motor learning. A therapist must use therapeutic techniques that meet the individual patient's therapeutic objectives and goals. The following are various theories of neurological rehabilitation based on each theory's interpretation of motor control and motor learning.

Motor Control[28,30]

Motor control is the study of the nature of movement; or the ability to regulate or direct essential movement. Historically, control was thought to arise from reflex or hierarchical models where the cortex was perceived as the highest functioning component of the system and spinal level reflexes were the lowest functioning components. New models of motor control challenge these theories and believe that there is a greater distribution of control and that the cortex is not solely at the top of the hierarchy.

Theories in general should provide a framework to interpret the issue or behavior, guide clinical action and treatment, provide new ideas, and utilize working hypotheses for examination and intervention. There are multiple theories of motor control that each embrace abstract ideas regarding the actual control of movement and are based on a specific interpretation of how the brain functions and interacts with other body systems. Some of the motor control theories include the Reflex theory, Hierarchical theory, Motor programming theory, Task-oriented theory, and Ecological theory.

Motor Learning[28,36]

Motor learning is the study of the acquisition or modification of movement. Motor learning differentiates learning versus performance, provides guidelines for appropriate use of feedback, prioritizes the impact of practice as it relates to skill and movement, and also focuses on the transfer of learning across tasks and environments of practice. Two of the initial theories of motor learning include:

- **Adam's closed loop theory:** The first attempt at the creation of a comprehensive motor learning theory with the premise of sensory feedback as an ongoing process for the nervous system to compare current movement with stored information on memory of past movement; high emphasis on the concept of practice.
- **Schmidt's schema theory:** This theory was created in response to the limitations of the closed loop theory. Its main construct relies on open loop control processes and a motor program concept; promotes clinical value of feedback and importance of variation with practice.

Three Stage Model of Motor Learning[7,26,36]

Cognitive Stage: This is the initial stage of learning where there is a high concentration of conscious processing of information. The person will acquire information regarding the goal of the activity and begin to problem solve as to how to attain the goal. A controlled environment is ideal for learning during this stage and participation is a must for the person to progress.

Characterized by:

- large amount of errors
- inconsistent attempts
- repetition of effort allows for improvement in strategies
- inconsistent performance
- high degree of cognitive work: listening, observing, and processing feedback

Associative Stage: This is the intermediate stage of learning where a person is able to more independently distinguish correct versus incorrect performance. The person is linking the feedback that has been received with the movement that has been performed and the ultimate goal. A controlled environment is helpful but at this stage, the person can progress to a less structured or more open environment. Avoid excessive external feedback as the person should have improved internal or proprioceptive feedback for the task at hand.

Characterized by:

- decreased errors with new skill performance
- decreased need for concentration and cognition regarding the activity
- skill refinement
- increased coordination of movement
- large amount of practice yields refinement of the motor program surrounding the activity

Autonomous Stage: This is the final stage of learning or skilled learning where a person improves the efficiency of the activity without a great need for cognitive control. The person can also perform the task with interference from a variable environment.

Characterized by:

- automatic response
- mainly error-free regardless of environment
- patterns of movement are non-cognitive and automatic
- distraction does not impact the activity
- the person can simultaneously perform more than one task if needed
- extrinsic feedback should be very limited or should not be provided
- internal feedback or self-assessment should be dominant

Feedback[36]

Feedback is imperative for the progression of motor learning. A patient will rely on both intrinsic and extrinsic feedback as it relates to movement. Feedback allows for correction and adaptation within the environment. Current research supports reducing the extrinsic feedback (fading of feedback) in order to ultimately enhance learning.

Intrinsic (inherent) feedback: represents all feedback that comes to the person through sensory systems as a result of the movement including visual, vestibular, proprioceptive, and somatosensory inputs.

Extrinsic (augmented) feedback: represents the information that can be provided while a task or movement is in progress or subsequent to the movement. This is typically in the form of verbal feedback or manual contacts.

Knowledge of results: is an important form of extrinsic feedback and includes terminal feedback regarding the outcome of a movement that has been performed in relation to the movement's goals.

Knowledge of performance: is extrinsic feedback that relates to the actual movement pattern that someone used to achieve their goal of movement.

Practice[36]

Practice refers to repeated performance of an activity in order to learn or perfect a skill. Physical practice allows for direct physical experience and kinesthetic stimulation to assist with acquisition of the skill. Mental practice is the cognitive rehearsal of a task or experience without any physical movement.

There are several commonly used terms that describe various types of practice:

Massed practice: The practice time in a trial is greater than the amount of rest between trials.

Distributed practice: The amount of rest time between trials is equal to or is greater than the amount of practice time for each trial.

Constant practice: Practice of a given task under a uniform condition.

Variable practice: Practice of a given task under differing conditions.

Random practice: Varying practice amongst different tasks.

Blocked practice: Consistent practice of a single task.

Whole training: Practice of an entire task.

Part training: Practice of an individual component or selected components of a task.

Key Terminology[28,36]

Closed system model: This is characterized by transfer of information that incorporates multiple feedback loops and larger distribution of control. In this model, the nervous system is seen as an active "participant" with the ability to enable the initiation of movement as opposed to solely "reacting" to stimuli.

Compensation: The ability to utilize alternate motor and sensory strategies due to an impairment that limits the normal completion of a task.

Habituation: The decrease in response that will occur as a result of consistent exposure to non-painful stimuli.

Learning: The process of acquiring knowledge about the world that leads to a relatively permanent change in a person's capability to perform a skilled action.

- **Non-associative:** a single repeated stimulus (habituation, sensitization)
- **Associative:** gaining understanding of the relationship between two stimuli, causal relationships or stimulus and consequence (classical conditioning, operant conditioning)
- **Procedural:** learning tasks that can be performed without attention or concentration to the task; a task is learned by forming movement habits (developing a habit through repetitive practice)
- **Declarative:** requires attention, awareness, and reflection in order to attain knowledge that can be consciously recalled (mental practice)

Motor learning: The ability to perform a movement as a result of internal processes that interact with the environment and produce a consistent strategy to generate the correct movement. It is the acquisition of, or modification of movement.

Motor program: A concept of a central motor pattern that can be activated by sensory stimuli or central processes. Motor programs are seen as containing the rules for creating spatial and temporal patterns of motor activity needed to carry out a given motor task.

Open system model: This is characterized by a single transfer of information without any feedback loop (reflexive hierarchical theory). In this theory, the nervous system is seen as awaiting stimuli in order to react.

Performance: A temporary change in motor behavior seen during a particular session of practice that is a result of many variables, however, only one variable is focusing on the act of learning. Performance is not an absolute measure of learning since there are multiple variables that potentially affect performance.

Plasticity: The ability to modify or change at the synapse level either temporarily or permanently in order to perform a particular function.

Postural control: The ability of the motor and sensory systems to stabilize position and control movement.

Recovery: The ability to utilize previous strategies to return to the same level of functioning.

Sensitization: The increase in response that will occur as a result of a noxious stimulus.

Strategy: A plan used to produce a specific result or outcome that will influence the structure or system.

CONSIDER THIS

MOTOR LEARNING INTERVENTION CONSTRUCTS[28,30,36]

The following are general concepts of motor learning that should be considered when evaluating, developing a plan of care, and treating patients. Many therapists will utilize therapeutic interventions from various theories of neurological rehabilitation based on the individual patient.

- Models of motor control vary based on the interpretation of brain function
- Examination determines the degree of impairment
- Intervention is designed at the level of impairment
- It is essential for a patient to relearn how to perform a functional task in order to maximize recovery and independence
- Sensory, motor, and cognitive strategies should be used to acquire postural control
- Focus is both on recovery and compensatory techniques
- Belief that sensory, motor, and perceptual input contribute to motor control
- Movement is based around a behavioral goal
- Type and amount of feedback (visual, verbal, tactile) should be determined for each individual patient
- Emphasis on postural control, alignment, and sequencing of movements is essential
- Intervention should create multiple ways to solve a movement disorder
- Belief that performance is observed, the act of learning is not
- Environmental factors must be considered with intervention, planning, and implementation

Carr and Shepherd: Motor Relearning Approach[28,37,38]

An approach developed by Janet Carr and Roberta Shepherd in the 1970's that targets normal movement and how it is relearned after neurological insult. Carr and Shepherd's construct is that factors that are involved with learning are also involved with relearning and should include:[28]

- identification of a goal
- inhibition of any unnecessary activity that does not relate to normal movement
- the ability to adjust during activity to the effects of gravity and balance
- proper body alignment
- proper motivation
- incorporate internal or mental practice as well as external or physical practice
- feedback
- knowledge of results

A significant construct of this approach is centered around a therapist's observation of the patient during examination in order to identify the variations in normal movement. Through critical assessment, the therapist is able to identify components of movement that are missing or abnormal and the corresponding interventions. Treatment relies on techniques inherent to this approach as well as other various approaches to neurological rehabilitation. Intrinsic feedback through sensory, visual, proprioceptive or tactile channels as well as external feedback through an observer is necessary for the patient to influence their progress towards their goals.

Key Terminology[30,37,38]

Closed motor skill: A skill that is performed under a stable and unchanging environment.

Knowledge of results: Providing the patient with external feedback regarding a patient's performance of a task. This can include observations as well as objective data and can be positive or negative in nature with the goal of influencing the learner.

Open motor skill: A skill that is performed under a consistently changing environment.

Transfer of learning: An action cannot be separated from the environment that it is performed in. A patient must be able to transfer the skill or motor task into different environments.

CONSIDER THIS

MOTOR RELEARNING INTERVENTION CONSTRUCTS[37,38]

The following are general concepts of motor relearning that should be considered when evaluating, developing a plan of care, and treating patients. Many therapists will utilize therapeutic interventions from various theories of neurological rehabilitation based on the individual patient.

- Utilizes various techniques from other treatment approaches
- Belief that treatment cannot be routine or based on diagnosis, must be individual to the patient
- Developmental sequence may not be necessary in treatment when treating adults
- Practice may include breaking the task into discrete components, followed by practice of the task as a whole
- Use of Bobath techniques for handling, facilitation, inhibitive casting, use of therapeutic ball (Figs. 5-41, 5-42)
- Use of Rood techniques of application of ice, brushing, tapping for facilitation
- Biofeedback should be utilized for decreasing hypertonicity with movement or for targeting facilitation of a muscle group
- Self-correction and self-awareness should be incorporated into treatment through the use of a mirror, verbal feedback, and biofeedback
- Intrinsic and extrinsic (augmented) feedback are important during treatment

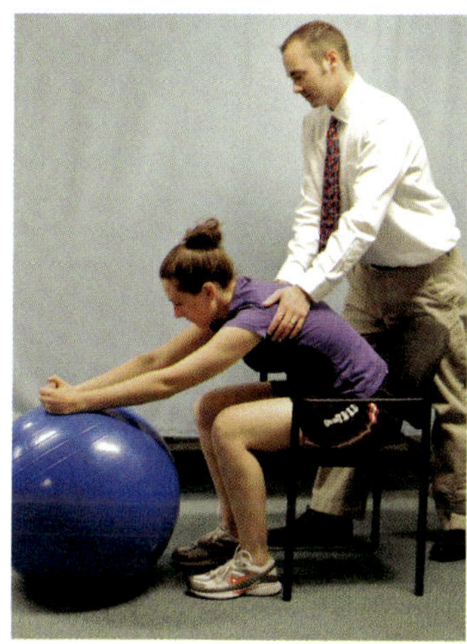

Fig. 5-41: Facilitation of movement patterns using a therapeutic ball.

Fig. 5-42: Therapist uses handling techniques and facilitation to assist with functional activities.

Bobath: Neuro-Developmental Treatment (NDT)[30,39]

An approach developed by Karl and Berta Bobath based on the hierarchical model of neurophysiologic function. Abnormal postural reflex activity and abnormal muscle tone are caused by the loss of central nervous system control at the brainstem and spinal cord levels. The concept recognizes that interference of normal function within the brain caused by central nervous system dysfunction leads to a slowing down or cessation of motor development and the inhibition of righting reactions, equilibrium reactions, and automatic movements. The patient should learn to control movement through activities that promote normal movement patterns that integrate function.

New assumptions that have been incorporated into NDT resulting from current motor control research include:[28]

- Postural control can be learned and modified through experience
- Postural control uses both feedback and feed-forward mechanisms for execution of tasks

- Postural control is initiated from a patient's base of support
- Postural control is required for skill development
- Postural control develops by assuming progressive positions in which there is an increase in the distance between the center of gravity and base of support; the base of support should also decrease

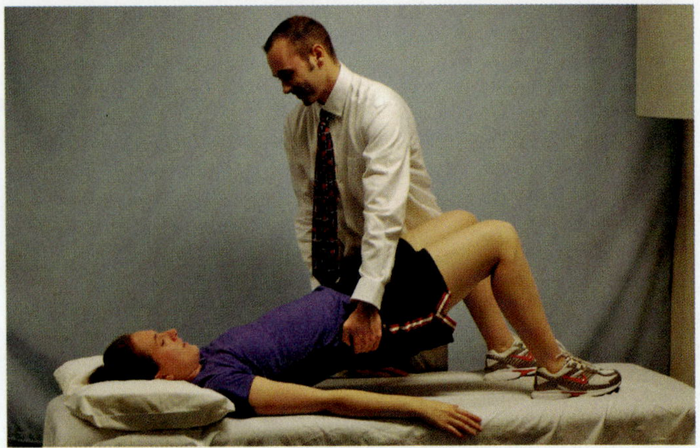

Fig. 5-43: Facilitation using key points of control.

Key Terminology

Facilitation: A technique utilized to elicit voluntary muscular contraction.

Inhibition: A technique utilized to decrease excessive tone or movement.

Key points of control: Specific handling of designated areas of the body (shoulder, pelvis, hand, and foot) will influence and facilitate posture, alignment, and control (Fig. 5-43).

Placing: The act of moving an extremity into a position that the patient must hold against gravity.

Reflex inhibiting posture: Designated static positions that Bobath found to inhibit abnormal tonal influences and reflexes.

CONSIDER THIS

NDT INTERVENTION CONSTRUCTS[30,39]

The following are general concepts of NDT that should be considered when evaluating, developing a plan of care, and treating patients. Many therapists will utilize therapeutic interventions from various theories of neurological rehabilitation based on the individual patient.

- Inhibition of abnormal patterns of movement with simultaneous facilitation of normal patterns
- Alteration of abnormal tone and influencing isolated active movement
- Avoid utilization of abnormal reflexes or associated reactions during treatment
- Utilize manual contact and handling through key points of control for facilitation and inhibition (Fig. 5-44)
- Achieve a balance between muscle groups during therapeutic interventions
- Utilize the developmental sequence, dynamic reflex inhibiting patterns, and functional activities with varying levels of difficulty during therapeutic intervention
- Emphasize the use of rotation during treatment activities (Fig. 5-45)
- Provide the patient with the sensation of normal movement by inhibiting abnormal postural reflex activity
- Treatment should be active and dynamic, incorporating function
- Provide orientation to midline control by moving in and out of midline with dynamic activity (Fig. 5-46)
- Belief that compensation techniques are unnecessary and should be avoided

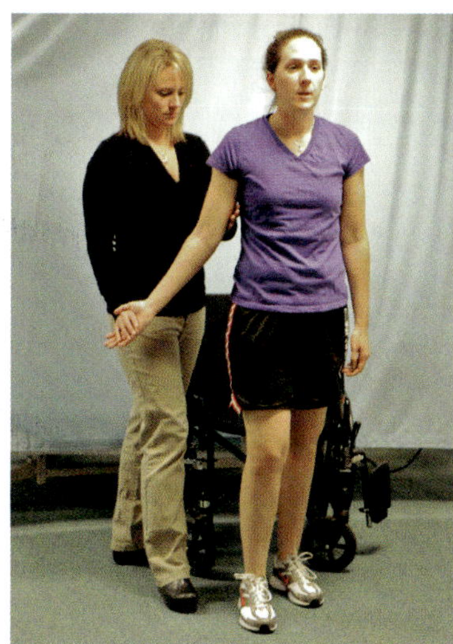

Fig. 5-44: The therapist uses an NDT technique of manual contacts and therapeutic handling to decrease tonal influence during motor output and functional activity. Key points of control can facilitate or inhibit tone based on the therapeutic goals.

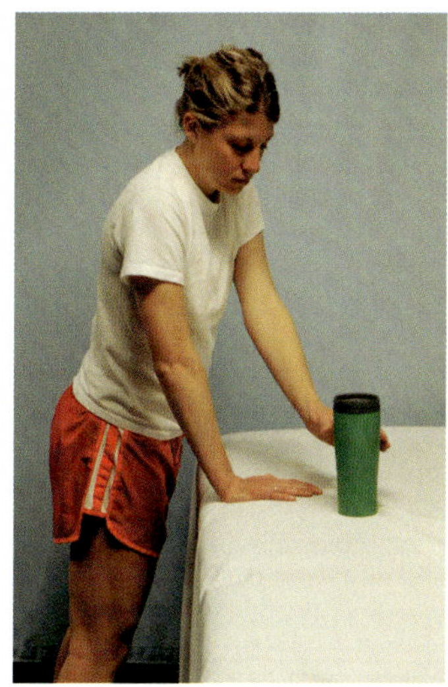

Fig. 5-45: NDT encourages the use of rotation during therapeutic activities.

Fig. 5-46: Using developmental sequence to gain midline control. The therapist can facilitate the patient to move in and out of midline to improve dynamic mobility and control.

Brunnstrom: Movement Therapy in Hemiplegia[24,40,41]

Movement therapy in hemiplegia developed by Signe Brunnstrom is based on the hierarchical model by Hughlings Jackson. This approach created and defined the term synergy and initially encouraged the use of synergy patterns during rehabilitation. The belief was to immediately practice synergy patterns and subsequently develop combinations of movement patterns outside of the synergy. Synergies are considered primitive patterns that occur at the spinal cord level as a result of the hierarchical organization of the central nervous system. Reinforcing synergy patterns is rarely utilized now as research has indicated that reinforced synergy patterns are very difficult to change. Brunnstrom developed the seven stages of recovery, which are used for evaluation and documentation of patient progress.

Key Terminology

Associated reaction: An involuntary and automatic movement of a body part as a result of an intentional active or resistive movement in another body part.

Homolateral synkinesis: A flexion pattern of the involved upper extremity facilitates flexion of the involved lower extremity.

Limb synergies: A group of muscles that produce a predictable pattern of movement in flexion or extension patterns.

Raimiste's phenomenon: The involved lower extremity will abduct or adduct with applied resistance to the uninvolved lower extremity in the same direction.

Souques' phenomenon: Raising the involved upper extremity above 100 degrees with elbow extension will produce extension and abduction of the fingers.

Stages of recovery: Brunnstrom separates neurological recovery into seven separate stages based on progression through abnormal tone and spasticity. These seven stages of recovery describe tone, reflex activity, and volitional movement.

Seven Stages of Recovery[28]

Stage 1: No volitional movement initiated.

Stage 2: The appearance of basic limb synergies. The beginning of spasticity.

Stage 3: The synergies are performed voluntarily; spasticity increases.

Stage 4: Spasticity begins to decrease. Movement patterns are not dictated solely by limb synergies.

Stage 5: A further decrease in spasticity is noted with independence from limb synergy patterns.

Stage 6: Isolated joint movements are performed with coordination.

Stage 7: Normal motor function is restored.

CONSIDER THIS

MOVEMENT THERAPY IN HEMIPLEGIA INTERVENTION CONSTRUCTS[28,41]

The following are general concepts of movement therapy in hemiplegia that should be considered when evaluating, developing a plan of care, and treating patients. Many therapists will utilize therapeutic interventions from various theories of neurological rehabilitation based on the individual patient.

- Evaluation of strength focuses on patterns of movement rather than straight plane motion at a joint
- Sensory examination is required to assist with treating motor deficits
- Initially limb synergies are encouraged as a necessary milestone for recovery
- Encourage overflow to recruit active movement of the weak side
- Repetition of task and positive reinforcement should be emphasized during treatment activities
- A patient will follow the stages of recovery, but may experience a plateau at any point so that full recovery may not be achieved
- Movement combinations that deviate from the basic limb synergies should be introduced in stage 4 of recovery
- Treatment should incorporate only tasks that the patient can master or almost master

Kabat, Knott, and Voss: Proprioceptive Neuromuscular Facilitation (PNF)[30,40]

PNF was introduced in the early 1950's using the hierarchical model as its framework. The original goal of treatment was to establish gross motor patterns within the central nervous system. This approach is based on the premise that stronger parts of the body are utilized to stimulate and strengthen the weaker parts. Normal movement and posture is based on a balance between control of antagonist and agonist muscle groups. Development will follow the normal sequence through a component of motor learning. This theory places great emphasis on manual contacts and correct handling. Short and concise verbal commands are used along with resistance throughout the full movement pattern. The PNF approach utilizes methods that promote or hasten the response of the neuromuscular mechanism through stimulation of the proprioceptors. Movement patterns follow diagonals or spirals that each possess a flexion, extension, and rotatory component and are directed toward or away from midline.

Key Terminology

Chopping: A combination of bilateral upper extremity asymmetrical patterns performed as a closed-chain activity (Fig. 5-47).

Developmental sequence: A progression of motor skill acquisition. The stages of motor control include mobility, stability, controlled mobility, and skill.

Mass movement patterns: The hip, knee, and ankle move into flexion or extension simultaneously.

Overflow: Muscle activation of an involved extremity due to intense action of an uninvolved muscle or group of muscles.

Fig. 5-47: Chopping is a PNF technique using bilateral upper extremity patterns of movement to improve strength, stability, and control.

CONSIDER THIS

PNF INTERVENTION CONSTRUCTS (KABAT, KNOTT, VOSS)[30,40]

The following are general concepts of PNF that should be considered when evaluating, developing a plan of care, and treating patients. Many therapists will utilize therapeutic interventions from various theories of neurological rehabilitation based on the individual patient.

- A patient learns diagonal patterns of movement
- Techniques must have accurate timing, specific commands, and correct hand placement
- Verbal commands must be short and concise
- Repetition of task or activity is important in motor learning
- Resistance given during the movement pattern is greater if the objective is stability (Fig. 5-48), less if the objective is mobility (Fig. 5-49)
- Techniques should utilize isometric and isotonic muscle contractions
- Treatment objectives will dictate the use of techniques through either full movement or at points within the range
- Developmental sequence is used in conjunction with PNF techniques in order to increase the balance between agonists and antagonists
- PNF techniques are implemented to progress a patient through the stages of motor control
- Functional patterns of movement are used to increase control
- Techniques should be utilized that increase strength or improve relaxation by enhancing overflow from the stronger to the weaker muscles

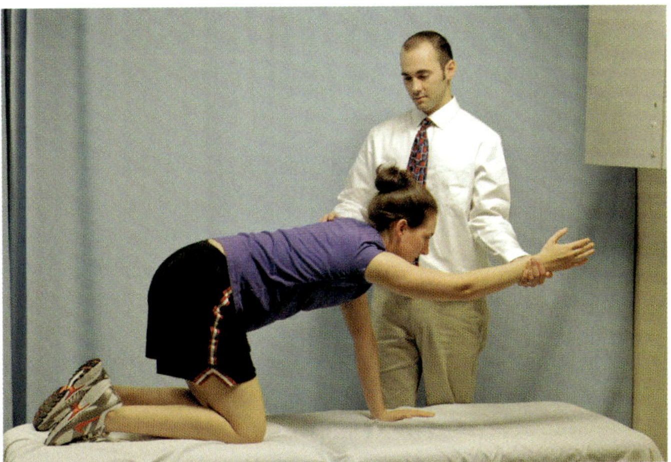

Fig. 5-48: A therapist can provide a graded amount of resistance based on therapeutic goals. This patient is working through the developmental sequence and the therapist is providing a larger amount of resistance to improve stability with a varying base of support.

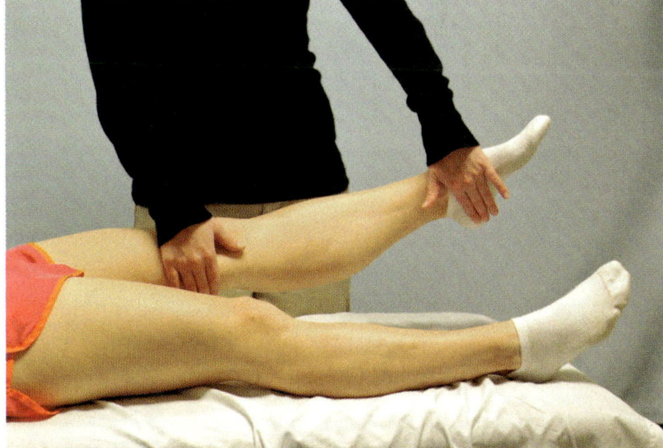

Fig. 5-49: The therapist is using minimal resistance during a lower extremity PNF pattern to improve mobility and active movement.

PNF Diagonal Patterns – Upper Extremity Responses

	D1 Flexion Pattern (Fig. 5-50)	D1 Extension Pattern	D2 Flexion Pattern	D2 Extension Pattern
Scapula	Elevation Abduction Upward rotation	Depression Adduction Downward rotation	Elevation Adduction Upward rotation	Depression Abduction Downward rotation
Shoulder	Flexion Adduction Lateral rotation	Extension Abduction Medial rotation	Flexion Abduction Lateral rotation	Extension Adduction Medial rotation
Elbow	Flexion or extension	Flexion or extension	Flexion or extension	Flexion or extension
Radioulnar	Supination	Pronation	Supination	Pronation
Wrist	Flexion Radial deviation	Extension Ulnar deviation	Extension Radial deviation	Flexion Ulnar deviation
Thumb	Adduction	Abduction	Extension	Opposition

PNF Diagonal Patterns – Lower Extremity Responses

	D1 Flexion Pattern	D1 Extension Pattern	D2 Flexion Pattern (Fig. 5-51)	D2 Extension Pattern
Pelvis	Protraction	Retraction	Elevation	Depression
Hip	Flexion Adduction Lateral rotation	Extension Abduction Medial rotation	Flexion Abduction Medial rotation	Extension Adduction Lateral rotation
Knee	Flexion or extension	Flexion or extension	Flexion or extension	Flexion or extension
Ankle and Toes	Dorsiflexion Inversion	Plantar flexion Eversion	Dorsiflexion Eversion	Plantar flexion Inversion

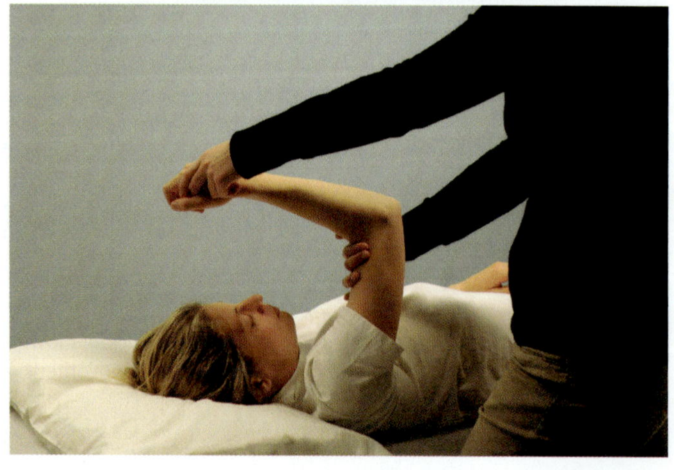

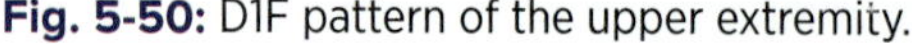

Fig. 5-50: D1F pattern of the upper extremity.

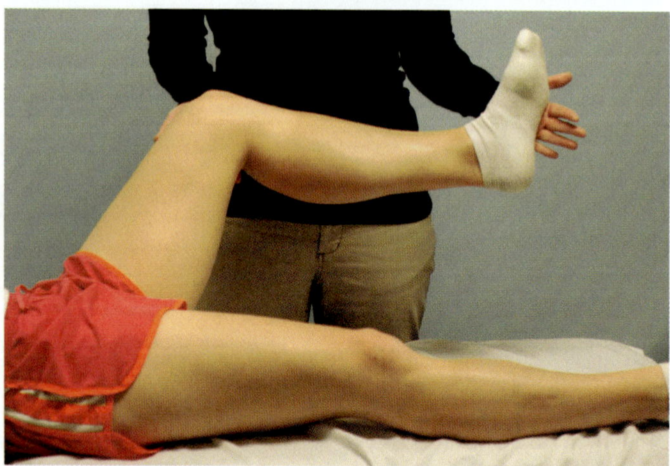

Fig. 5-51: D2F pattern of the lower extremity.

Levels of Motor Control[40]

Mobility

The ability to initiate movement through a functional range of motion.

Stability

The ability to maintain a position or posture through cocontraction and tonic holding around a joint. Unsupported sitting with midline control is an example of stability.

Controlled Mobility

The ability to move within a weight bearing position or rotate around a long axis. Activities in prone on elbows or weight shifting in quadruped are examples of controlled mobility (Fig. 5-52).

Skill

The ability to consistently perform functional tasks and manipulate the environment with normal postural reflex mechanisms and balance reactions. Skill activities include ADLs and community locomotion.

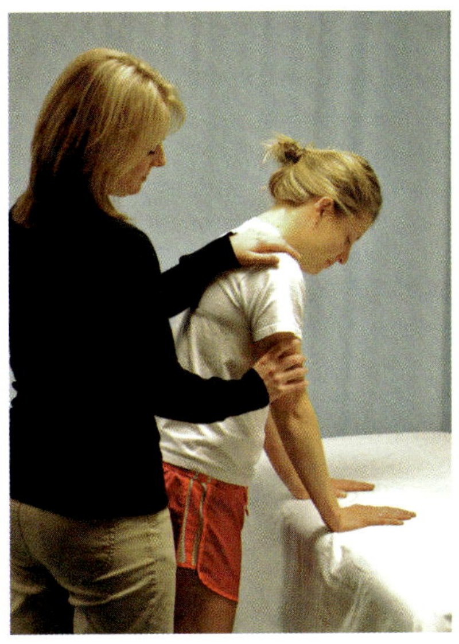

Fig. 5-52: The patient working in modified plantigrade is an example of controlled mobility.

PNF Therapeutic Exercises

Technique	Mobility		Stability	Controlled Mobility	Skill		Strength
	Increased ROM	Initiate Movement			Distal Functional Movement	Proximal Dynamic Stability	
Agonistic Reversals				X		X	
Alternating Isometrics			X				X
Contract-Relax	X						
Hold-Relax	X						
Hold-Relax Active Movement		X					
Joint Distraction	X	X					
Normal Timing					X		
Repeated Contractions		X					X
Resisted Progression						X	X
Rhythmic Initiation		X					
Rhythmical Rotation	X	X					
Rhythmic Stabilization	X		X				
Slow Reversal			X	X	X		
Slow Reversal Hold			X	X	X		
Timing for Emphasis					X		X

PNF Therapeutic Exercise Descriptions

*Blue colored terms indicate the level of developmental sequence.

Agonistic Reversals (AR)

Controlled mobility, skill: An isotonic concentric contraction performed against resistance followed by alternating concentric and eccentric contractions with resistance. AR requires use in a slow and sequential manner, and may be used in increments throughout the range to attain maximum control.

Alternating Isometrics (AI)

Stability: Isometric contractions are performed alternating from muscles on one side of the joint to the other side without rest. AI emphasizes endurance or strengthening.

Contract-Relax (CR)

Mobility: A technique used to increase range of motion. As the extremity reaches the point of limitation, the patient performs a maximal isotonic contraction of the antagonist muscle group, moving the limb through the range of motion against resistance. The therapist resists movement for five to ten seconds with relaxation to follow. The technique is repeated until no further gains in range of motion are noted during the session.

Hold-Relax (HR)

Mobility: A technique used to increase range of motion. As the extremity reaches the point of limitation, the patient performs a maximal isometric contraction of the antagonist muscle group. The therapist resists movement for five to ten seconds with relaxation to follow. The technique is repeated until no further gains in range of motion are noted during the session.

Hold-Relax Active Movement (HRAM)

Mobility: A technique to improve initiation of movement to muscle groups tested at 1/5 or less. An isometric contraction is performed once the extremity is passively placed into a shortened range within the pattern. Overflow and facilitation may be used to assist with the contraction. Upon relaxation, the extremity is immediately moved into a lengthened position of the pattern with a quick stretch. The patient is asked to return the extremity to the shortened position through an isotonic contraction.

Joint Distraction

Mobility: A proprioceptive component used to increase range of motion around a joint. Consistent manual traction is provided slowly and usually in combination with mobilization techniques. It can also be used in combination with quick stretch to initiate movement.

Normal Timing (NT)

Skill: A technique used to improve coordination of all components of a task. NT is performed in a distal to proximal sequence. Proximal components are restricted until the distal components are activated and initiate movement. Repetition of the pattern produces a coordinated movement of all components.

Repeated Contractions (RC)

Mobility: A technique used to initiate movement and sustain a contraction through the range of motion. RC is used to initiate a movement pattern, throughout a weak movement pattern or at a point of weakness within a movement pattern. The therapist provides a quick stretch followed by isometric or isotonic contractions.

Resisted Progression (RP)

Skill: A technique used to emphasize coordination of proximal components during gait. Resistance is applied to an area such as the pelvis, hips or extremity during the gait cycle in order to enhance coordination, strength or endurance.

Rhythmic Initiation (RI)

Mobility: A technique used to assist in initiating movement when hypertonia exists. Movement progresses from passive ("let me move you"), to active assistive ("help me move you"), to slightly resistive ("move against the resistance"). Movements must be slow and rhythmical to reduce the hypertonia and allow for full range of motion.

Rhythmic Stabilization (RS)

Mobility, stability: A technique used to increase range of motion and coordinate isometric contractions. The technique requires isometric contractions of all muscles around a joint against progressive resistance. The patient should relax and move into the newly acquired range and repeat the technique. If stability is the goal, RS should be applied as a progression from AI in order to stabilize all muscle groups simultaneously around the specific body part.

Rhythmical Rotation (RR)

Mobility: A passive technique used to decrease hypertonia by slowly rotating an extremity around the longitudinal axis. Relaxation of the extremity will increase range of motion.

Slow Reversal (SR)

Stability, controlled mobility, skill: A technique of slow and resisted concentric contractions of agonists and antagonists around a joint without rest between reversals. This technique is used to improve control of movement and posture.

Slow Reversal Hold (SRH)

Stability, controlled mobility, skill: Using slow reversal with the addition of an isometric contraction that is performed at the end of each movement in order to gain stability.

Timing for Emphasis (TE)

Skill: Used to strengthen the weak component of a motor pattern. Isotonic and isometric contractions produce overflow to weak muscles.

Rood[28,30]

This theory is based on Sherrington and the reflex stimulus model. Rood believed that all motor output was the result of both past and present sensory input. Treatment is based on sensorimotor learning. It takes into account the autonomic nervous system and emotional factors as well as motor ability. Rood used a developmental sequence, which was seen as "key patterns" in the enhancement of motor control. A goal of this approach is to obtain homeostasis in motor output and to activate muscles to perform a task independent of a stimulus. Exercise is seen as a treatment technique only if the response is correct and if it provides sensory feedback that enhances the motor learning of that response. Once a response is obtained during treatment, the stimulus should be withdrawn. Rood introduced the use of sensory stimulation to facilitate or inhibit responses such as icing and brushing in order to elicit desired reflex motor responses.

Sensory Stimulation Techniques

Facilitation	Inhibition
• Approximation (Fig. 5-53) • Joint compression • Icing • Light touch • Quick stretch • Resistance • Tapping • Traction	• Deep pressure • Prolonged stretch • Warmth • Prolonged cold

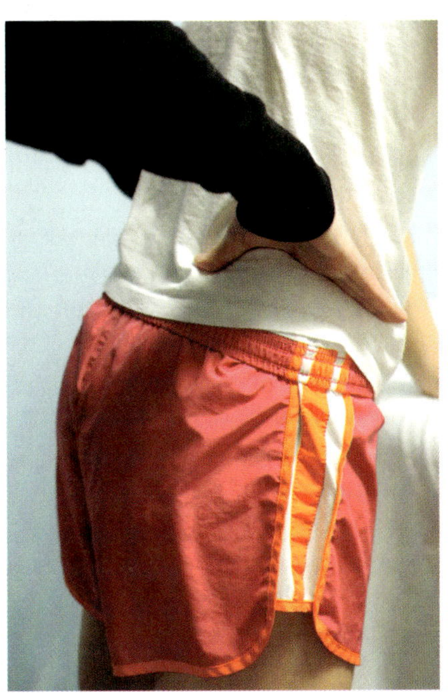

Fig. 5-53: The therapist is providing approximation to the hips while the patient is in standing in order to improve cocontraction around the joint and subsequent stability.

Key Terminology

Heavy work: A method used to develop stability by performing an activity (work) against gravity or resistance. Heavy work focuses on the strengthening of postural muscles.

Light work: A method used to develop controlled movement and skilled function by performing an activity (work) without resistance. Light work focuses on the extremities.

Key patterns: A developmental sequence designed by Rood that directs patients' mobility recovery from synergy patterns through controlled motion.

CONSIDER THIS

ROOD SENSORY INTERVENTION CONSTRUCTS[28,30]

The following are general concepts of Rood that should be considered when evaluating, developing a plan of care, and treating patients. Many therapists will utilize therapeutic interventions from various theories of neurological rehabilitation based on the individual patient.

- Utilization of sensory stimulation to achieve motor output during treatment
- Movement is considered autonomic and noncognitive
- Homeostasis of all systems is essential
- Techniques such as neutral warmth, maintained pressure, and slow rhythmical stroking can be used to calm a patient
- Tactile stimulation is used to facilitate normal movement
- The environment can influence the effects of therapeutic intervention
- Exercise must provide proper sensory feedback in order to be therapeutic
- Belief in techniques used to stimulate the proprioceptive, exteroceptive, and vestibular channels of the central nervous system

Neuromuscular and Nervous Systems Terminology[1,2,3,27]

Agnosia: The inability to interpret information.

Agraphesthesia: The inability to recognize symbols, letters or numbers traced on the skin.

Agraphia: The inability to write due to a lesion within the brain and is typically found in combination with aphasia.

Alexia: The inability to read or comprehend written language secondary to a lesion within the dominant lobe of the brain.

Anosognosia: The denial or unawareness of one's illness; often associated with unilateral neglect.

Aphasia: The inability to communicate or comprehend due to damage to specific areas of the brain.

Apraxia: The inability to perform purposeful learned movements or activities even though there is no sensory or motor impairment that would hinder completion of the task.

Astereognosis: The inability to recognize objects by sense of touch.

Body schema: Having an understanding of the body as a whole and the relationship of its parts to the whole.

Constructional apraxia: The inability to reproduce geometric figures and designs. A person is often unable to visually analyze how to perform a task.

Decerebrate rigidity: A characteristic of a corticospinal lesion at the level of the brainstem that results in extension of the trunk and all extremities (Fig. 5-54).

Decorticate rigidity: A characteristic of a corticospinal lesion at the level of the diencephalon where the trunk and lower extremities are positioned in extension and the upper extremities are positioned in flexion (Fig. 5-55).

Diplopia: Double vision.

Dysarthria: Slurred and impaired speech due to a motor deficit of the tongue or other muscles essential for speech.

Dysphagia: The inability to properly swallow.

Dysprosody: Impairment in the rhythm and inflection of speech.

Emotional lability: A characteristic of a right hemisphere infarct where there is an inability to control emotions and outbursts of laughing or crying that are inconsistent with the situation.

Fluent aphasia: Characteristic of receptive aphasia where speech produces functional output regarding articulation, but lacks content and is typically dysprosodic using neologistic jargon.

Hemiparesis: A condition of weakness on one side of the body.

Hemiplegia: A condition of paralysis on one side of the body.

Homonymous hemianopsia: The loss of the right or left half of the field of vision in both eyes.

Ideational apraxia: The inability to formulate an initial motor plan and sequence tasks where the proprioceptive input necessary for movement is impaired.

Ideomotor apraxia: A condition where a person plans a movement or task, but cannot volitionally perform it. Automatic movement may occur, however, a person cannot impose additional movement on command.

Neologism: Substitution within a word that is so severe that it makes the word unrecognizable.

Non-fluent aphasia: Characteristic of expressive aphasia where speech is non-functional, effortful, and contains paraphasias. Writing is also impaired.

Perseveration: The state of repeatedly performing the same segment of a task or repeatedly saying the same word/phrase without purpose.

Synergy: Mass movement patterns that are primitive in nature and coupled with spasticity due to brain damage.

Unilateral neglect: The inability to interpret stimuli and events on the contralateral side of a hemispheric lesion. Left-sided neglect is most common with a lesion to the right inferior parietal or superior temporal lobes.

Fig. 5-54: Decerebrate positioning.

Fig. 5-55: Decorticate positioning.

Spinal Cord Injury (SCI)

When there is sufficient force exerted on the spinal cord, there can be permanent damage with extensive neurological deficits. Motor vehicle accidents are the largest cause of traumatic SCI. Other etiologies include stabbing, falls, sports injuries, and high-risk behaviors. The mechanism of injury often dictates the predicted pattern of deficits. Flexion injuries occur most often at the C5-C6 level of the spine while extension injuries occur most at the C4-C5 level. Axial loading and rotatory injuries are other mechanisms for spinal cord damage. A spinal cord injury will have an area of primary damage followed by an area of secondary damage that can extend multiple spinal segments beyond the initial segment of injury.

Types of Spinal Cord Injury[18,19,24]

Complete lesion: A lesion to the spinal cord where there is no preserved motor or sensory function below the level of the lesion.

Incomplete lesion: A lesion to the spinal cord with incomplete damage to the cord. There may be scattered motor function, sensory function or both below the level of the lesion.

Specific Incomplete Lesions[18,19,24]

Anterior Cord Syndrome

An incomplete lesion that results from compression and damage to the anterior part of the spinal cord or anterior spinal artery. The mechanism of injury is usually cervical flexion. There is loss of motor function and pain and temperature sense below the lesion due to damage of the corticospinal and spinothalamic tracts.

Brown-Sequard's Syndrome

An incomplete lesion usually caused by a stab wound, which produces hemisection of the spinal cord. There is paralysis and loss of vibratory and position sense on the same side as the lesion due to the damage to the corticospinal tract and dorsal columns. There is a loss of pain and temperature sense on the opposite side of the lesion from damage to the lateral spinothalamic tract. Pure Brown-Sequard's syndrome is rare since most spinal cord lesions are atypical.

Cauda Equina Injuries

An injury that occurs below the L1 spinal level where the long nerve roots transcend. Cauda equina injuries can be complete, however, they are frequently incomplete due to the large number of nerve roots in the area. A cauda equina injury is considered a peripheral nerve injury. Characteristics include flaccidity, areflexia, and impairment of bowel and bladder function. Full recovery is not typical due to the distance needed for axonal regeneration.

Central Cord Syndrome

An incomplete lesion that results from compression and damage to the central portion of the spinal cord. The mechanism of injury is usually cervical hyperextension that damages the spinothalamic tract, corticospinal tract, and dorsal columns. The upper extremities present with greater involvement than the lower extremities and greater motor deficits exist as compared to sensory deficits.

Posterior Cord Syndrome

A relatively rare syndrome that is caused by compression of the posterior spinal artery and is characterized by loss of proprioception, two-point discrimination, and stereognosis. Motor function is preserved.

Spinal Cord Injury Tests and Measures

ASIA Impairment Scale (American Spinal Injury Association)[42]

A =	**Complete:** No sensory or motor function is preserved in sacral segments S4-S5.
B =	**Sensory Incomplete:** Sensory function is preserved below the neurologic level, including S4-S5, AND no motor function is preserved more than 3 levels below the motor level on either side of the body.
C =	**Motor Incomplete:** Motor function is preserved for voluntary anal contraction, OR the patient meets "Sensory Incomplete" status and has motor function more than 3 levels below the motor level on either side of the body. Less than half of key muscle functions below the neurologic level have a muscle grade ≥ 3.
D =	**Motor Incomplete:** "Motor Incomplete" status as defined above, with at least half (half or more) of key muscle functions below the neurologic level having a muscle grade ≥ 3.
E =	**Normal:** Sensory and motor functions are normal in a patient that had prior deficits.

Classification of Level of Injury

Motor level: The motor level is determined by the most caudal key muscles that have muscle strength of 3 or greater with the superior segment tested as normal or 5.

Motor index scoring: Testing each key muscle using the 0-5 scoring, with total points of 25 per extremity for the total possible score of 100.

Sensory level: The sensory level is determined by the most caudal dermatome with a normal score of 2/2 for pinprick and light touch.

Key Muscles Tested

C5	Elbow flexors (biceps, brachialis)
C6	Wrist extensors (extensor carpi radialis longus and brevis)
C7	Elbow extensors (triceps)
C8	Finger flexors (flexor digitorum profundus) to the middle finger
T1	Small finger abductors (abductor digiti minimi)
L2	Hip flexors (iliopsoas)
L3	Knee extensors (quadriceps)
L4	Ankle dorsiflexors (tibialis anterior)
L5	Long toe extensors (extensor hallucis longus)
S1	Ankle plantar flexors (gastrocnemius, soleus)

Potential Complications of Spinal Cord Injury[18,19,24]

Deep Vein Thrombosis (DVT)

Deep vein thrombosis results from the formation of a blood clot that becomes dislodged and is termed an embolus. This is considered a serious medical condition since the embolus may obstruct a selected artery. A patient with a spinal cord injury has a greater risk of developing a DVT due to the absence or decrease in the normal pumping action by active contractions of muscles in the lower extremities. Homans' sign is a special test designed to confirm the presence of a DVT. Prevention of a DVT should include prophylactic anticoagulant therapy, maintaining a positioning schedule, range of motion, proper positioning to avoid excessive venous stasis, and use of elastic stockings.

Symptoms: Swelling of the lower extremity, pain, sensitivity over the area of the clot, and warmth in the area are cardinal symptoms of DVT.

Treatment: Once a DVT is suspected, there should be no active or passive movement performed to the involved lower extremity. Bed rest and anticoagulant pharmacological intervention are usually indicated. Surgical procedures can be performed if necessary.

Sensory Testing for Light Touch and Pinprick

0=Absent, 1=Impaired/hyperesthesia, 2=Intact

Level	Site for Sensory Testing
C2	One cm lateral to occipital protuberance
C3	Supraclavicular fossa
C4	Top of the acromioclavicular joint
C5	Lateral side of antecubital fossa
C6	Dorsal thumb, proximal phalanx
C7	Dorsal middle finger, proximal phalanx
C8	Dorsal little finger, proximal phalanx
T1	Medial side of antecubital fossa
T2	Apex of axilla
T3	Third intercostal space (IS), midclavicular line
T4	Fourth IS (at nipple level), midclavicular line
T5	Fifth IS, midclavicular line
T6	Level of the xiphisternum, midclavicular line
T7	Midway between T6 and T8, midclavicular line
T8	Midway between T6 and T10, midclavicular line
T9	Midway between T8 and T10, midclavicular line
T10	Level of the umbilicus, midclavicular line
T11	Midway between T10 and T12, midclavicular line
T12	Midpoint of inguinal ligament, midclavicular line
L1	Midway between T12 and L2
L2	Anteromedial thigh, midway between T12 and L3
L3	Medial femoral condyle
L4	Medial malleolus
L5	Dorsal surface of third MTP joint
S1	Lateral heel
S2	Popliteal fossa in the midline
S3	Ischial tuberosity
S4-5	Perianal area (taken as 1 level)

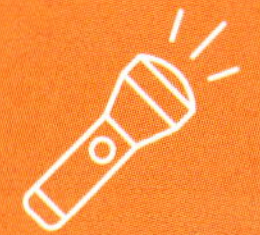

SPOTLIGHT ON SAFETY
AUTONOMIC DYSREFLEXIA: A MEDICAL EMERGENCY[18,43]

Autonomic dysreflexia is perhaps the most dangerous complication of spinal cord injury and can occur in patients with lesions at or above T6. A noxious stimulus below the level of the lesion triggers the autonomic nervous system causing a sudden elevation in blood pressure. Common causes include distended or full bladder, kink or blockage in the catheter, bladder infections, pressure ulcers, extreme temperature changes, tight clothing or even an ingrown toenail. If not treated, this condition can lead to convulsions, hemorrhage, and death.

Symptoms: High blood pressure, severe headache, blurred vision, stuffy nose, profuse sweating, goose bumps below the level of the lesion, and vasodilation (flushing) above the level of injury.

Treatment: The therapist should immediately check the catheter for blockage while having the patient assume or remain in a sitting position. Lying a patient down is contraindicated and will only assist to further elevate blood pressure. The patient should be examined for any other irritating stimuli and potentially checked for bowel impaction. If the cause remains unknown, the patient should receive immediate medical intervention.

Ectopic Bone

Ectopic bone or heterotopic ossification refers to the spontaneous formation of bone in the soft tissue. It typically occurs adjacent to larger joints such as the knees or the hips. Theories regarding etiology range from tissue hypoxia to abnormal calcium metabolism.

Symptoms: Early symptoms include edema, decreased range of motion, and increased temperature of the involved joint.

Treatment: Pharmacological intervention usually involves diphosphates that inhibit ectopic bone formation. Physical therapy and surgery are often incorporated into treatment. Physical therapy should focus on maintaining functional range of motion and allowing the patient the most independent functional outcome possible.

Orthostatic Hypotension

Orthostatic hypotension or postural hypotension occurs due to a loss of sympathetic control of vasoconstriction in combination with absent or severely reduced muscle tone. Venous pooling is fairly common during the early stages of rehabilitation. A decrease in systolic blood pressure greater than 20 mm Hg after moving from a supine position to a sitting position or a decrease in diastolic blood pressure greater than 10 mm Hg is typically indicative of orthostatic hypotension.

Symptoms: Complaints of dizziness, lightheadedness, nausea, and "blacking out" when going from a horizontal to a vertical position are primary symptoms of this condition.

Treatment: Monitoring vital signs assists with minimizing the effects of orthostatic hypotension. The use of elastic stockings, Ace wraps to the lower extremities, and abdominal binders are common. Gradual progression to a vertical position using a tilt table is often indicated. Pharmacological intervention may be indicated in order to increase blood pressure.

Pressure Ulcers

A pressure ulcer is caused by sustained pressure, friction, and/or shearing to a surface. The most common areas susceptible to pressure ulcers are the coccyx, sacrum, ischium, trochanters, elbows, buttocks, malleoli, scapulae, and prominent vertebrae. Pressure ulcers require immediate medical intervention and often can significantly delay the rehabilitation process.

SPOTLIGHT ON SAFETY
SCI: PREVENTION OF PRESSURE ULCERS[13,18,19]

Studies show that more than half of the people with SCI develop a pressure ulcer within their lifetime. Patients with spinal cord injury potentially experience many of the risk factors associated with the development of a pressure ulcer including:

- immobility
- decreased or absent sensation
- prolonged pressure to an area
- shearing forces
- poor positioning
- poor nutrition

Prevention should include:

Proper positioning while sitting and in bed: protecting all bony prominences, equal distribution of weight, use of equipment such as specialized cushions, mattress pads, and other pressure relief devices

Proper skin care: full cleansing and drying of skin, consistently inspect all skin and monitor any red areas closely; use of skin care products that are recommended by health care professionals

Proper changing of position: consistently change position every two hours; need to weight shift in sitting at a minimum of every 15-20 minutes

Proper nutrition: attain adequate nutrition and calories each day, drink the recommended amount of water, limit empty calories and alcohol intake

Clothing: wear clothing that is not high risk for skin breakdown (e.g., zippers), avoid tight clothing; clothing should be breathable with a comfortable fit

Mobility: daily activity is recommended and should include a cardiovascular component; however, avoid activities with a high shear or drag component

Symptoms: Primarily there is a reddened area that persists or an open area of the skin.

Treatment: Prevention is of greatest importance. A patient should change position frequently, maintain proper skin care, sit on an appropriate cushion, consistently weight shift, and maintain proper nutrition and hydration. Surgical intervention is often necessary with advanced pressure ulcers.

Spasticity

Spasticity can occasionally be useful to a patient with a spinal cord injury, however, more often serves to interfere with functional activities. Spasticity can be enhanced by both internal and external sources such as stress, decubiti, urinary tract infections, bowel or bladder obstruction, temperature changes or touch.

Symptoms: Increased involuntary contraction of muscle groups, increased tonic stretch reflexes, and exaggerated DTRs.

Treatment: Medications are usually administered in an attempt to reduce the degree of spasticity (Dantrium, Baclofen, Lioresal). Aggressive treatment includes phenol blocks, rhizotomies, myelotomies, and other surgical interventions. Physical therapy intervention includes positioning, aquatic therapy, weight bearing, functional electrical stimulation, range of motion, resting splints, and inhibitive casting.

Functional Outcomes for Complete Lesions[24]

Functional Skills	Level of Assistance Required (by SCI level groups)			
	High Tetraplegia (C1-C5)	Mid-level Tetraplegia (C6)	Low Tetraplegia (C7-C8)	Paraplegia
Bed Mobility • Rolling side to side • Rolling supine/prone • Supine/sitting • Scooting all directions	– Dependent (C1-C4) – Moderate to maximal assistance (C5) – Verbally direct	– Minimal assistance to modified independent with equipment – Verbally direct	– Independent with all	– Independent
Transfers • Bed • Car • Toilet • Bath equipment • Floor • Upright wheelchair	– Dependent (C1-C4) – Maximal assistance with level sliding board transfers (C5) – Verbally direct	– Minimal assistance to modified independent for sliding board transfers – Dependent with wheelchair loading in car – Dependent with floor transfers and uprighting wheelchair – Verbally direct	– Modified independent to independent with level surface transfer (sliding board) – Moderate assistance to modified independent with car transfer – Maximal to moderate assistance with floor transfers and uprighting wheelchair – Verbally direct	– Independent with level surface and car transfers (depression) – Minimal assistance to independent with floor transfers and uprighting wheelchair – Verbally direct
Weight Shifts • Pressure relief • Repositioning in wheelchair	– Setup to modified independent with power recline/tilt weight shift – Dependent with manual recline/tilt/lean weight shift – Verbally direct	– Modified independent with power recline/tilt weight shift – Minimal assistance to modified independent with side to side/forward lean weight shift – Verbally direct	– Modified independent with side to side/forward lean, or depression weight shift	– Modified independent with depression weight shift
Wheelchair Management • Wheel locks • Armrests • Footrests/legrests • Safety strap(s) • Cushion adjustment • Anti-tip levers • Wheelchair maintenance	– Dependent with all – Able to verbally direct	– Some assistance required – Able to verbally direct	– May require assistance with cushion adjustment, anti-tip levers, and wheelchair maintenance – Able to verbally direct	– Independent with all

Functional Outcomes for Complete Lesions[24]

Functional Skills	Level of Assistance Required (by SCI level groups)			
	High Tetraplegia (C1-C5)	**Mid-level Tetraplegia (C6)**	**Low Tetraplegia (C7-C8)**	**Paraplegia**
Wheelchair Mobility • Smooth surfaces • Up/down ramps • Up/down curbs • Rough terrain • Up/down steps (manual wheelchair only)	– Supervision/ setup to modified independent on smooth, ramp, and rough terrain with power wheelchair – Modified independent with manual wheelchair on smooth surface in forward direction (C5) – Maximal assistance to dependent with manual wheelchair in all other situations (C5) – Able to verbally direct	– Modified independent in smooth, ramp, and rough terrain with power wheelchair – Dependent to maximal assistance up/down curb with power wheelchair – Modified independent on smooth surfaces with manual wheelchair – Moderate to minimal assistance on ramps and rough terrain with manual wheelchair – Maximal to moderate assistance up/down curbs with manual wheelchair – Able to verbally direct	– Modified independent on smooth, ramp, and rough terrain with power wheelchair – Dependent to maximal assistance up/down curb with power wheelchair – Modified independent on smooth surfaces and up/ down ramps with manual wheelchair – Minimal assistance to modified independent on rough terrain – Moderate to minimal assistance up/down curbs with manual wheelchair – Dependent to maximal assistance up/down steps with manual wheelchair – Can verbally direct	– Minimal assistance to modified independent up/ down 6" curbs with manual wheelchair – Modified independent with descending steps with manual wheelchair – Maximal to minimal assistance to ascend steps with manual wheelchair – Able to verbally direct
Gait • Don/doff orthoses • Sit/stand • Smooth surfaces • Up/down ramps • Up/down curbs • Up/down steps • Rough terrain • Safe falling	– Not applicable	– Not applicable	– Not applicable	Abilities range from: – exercise only with KAFOs* – household gait with KAFOs – limited community gait with KAFOs or AFOs* – functional community ambulation with or without orthoses
ROM/Positioning • PROM to trunk, legs, and arms • Pad/position in bed	– Dependent – Able to verbally direct	– Moderate assistance to modified independent with all – Able to verbally direct	– Minimal assistance to modified independent with all – Able to verbally direct	– Independent
Feeding • Drinking • Finger feeding • Utensil feeding	– Dependent (C1-C4) – Minimal assistance with adaptive equipment (C5) – Able to verbally direct	– Modified independent with adaptive equipment	– Modified independent with adaptive equipment (C7)	– Independent

Functional Outcomes for Complete Lesions[24]

Functional Skills	Level of Assistance Required (by SCI level groups)			
	High Tetraplegia (C1-C5)	Mid-level Tetraplegia (C6)	Low Tetraplegia (C7-C8)	Paraplegia
Grooming • Face • Teeth • Hair • Makeup • Shaving face	– Dependent (C1-C4) – Minimal assistance with adaptive equipment for face, teeth, makeup/ shaving (C5) – Maximal/moderate assistance for hair grooming (C5) – Able to verbally direct	– Modified independent with adaptive equipment	– Modified independent	– Independent
Dressing • Dressing and undressing (in bed or wheelchair) • Upper body/lower body (in bed or wheelchair)	– Dependent – Able to verbally direct	– Modified independent for upper body in bed or wheelchair – Minimal assistance with lower body dressing in bed – Moderate assistance with lower body undressing in bed – Able to verbally direct	– Modified independent for upper/lower body dressing in bed – Minimal assistance with lower body dressing/ undressing in wheelchair (C7) – Modified independent for upper/lower body dressing/undressing in wheelchair (C8) – Able to verbally direct	– Modified independent
Bathing • Bathing and drying off • Upper body and lower body	– Dependent – Able to verbally direct	– Minimal assistance for upper body bathing and drying – Moderate assistance for lower body bathing and drying – Use of shower or tub chair – Able to verbally direct	– Modified independent with all using shower or tub chair	– Modified independent with all on tub bench or tub bottom cushion
Bowel/Bladder Problems • Intermittent catheterization • Leg bag care • Condom application • Clean up • In bed/wheelchair (bladder) • Feminine hygiene • Bowel program	– Dependent – Able to verbally direct	**Bladder:** – Minimal assistance for male in bed or wheelchair – Moderate assistance for female in bed **Bowel:** – Moderate assistance with use of equipment – Able to verbally direct	**Bladder:** – Modified independent for male in bed or wheelchair – Modified independent for female in bed; moderate assistance for female in wheelchair **Bowel:** – Minimal assistance to modified independent with use of equipment – Able to verbally direct	**Bladder:** – Modified independent for male and female **Bowel:** – Modified independent for male and female

*KAFO = knee-ankle-foot orthosis; AFO = ankle-foot orthosis
From Umphred DA: Neurological Rehabilitation. Mosby-Year Book, Inc. 1995, p. 502-505, with permission.

Spinal Cord Injury Terminology[18,19,24]

Cauda equina injury: A term used to describe injuries that occur below the L1 level of the spine. A cauda equina injury is considered to be a lower motor neuron lesion.

Dermatome: Designated sensory areas based on spinal segment innervation.

Head-hips relationship: A principle of mechanics used during mobility training with upper extremity weight bearing used as a fulcrum for activity. This technique requires the head to move in the opposite direction from the hips.

Myelotomy: A surgical procedure that severs certain tracts within the spinal cord in order to decrease spasticity and improve function.

Myotome: Designated motor areas based on spinal segment innervation.

Neurectomy: A surgical removal of a segment of a nerve in order to decrease spasticity and improve function.

Neurogenic nonreflexive bladder: The bladder is flaccid as a result of a cauda equina or conus medullaris lesion. The sacral reflex arc is damaged.

Neurogenic reflexive bladder: The bladder empties reflexively for a patient with an injury above the level of T12. The sacral reflex arc remains intact.

Neurologic level: The lowest segment (most caudal) of the spinal cord with intact strength and sensation. Muscle groups at this level must receive a grade of fair.

Paradoxical breathing: A form of abnormal breathing that is common in tetraplegia where the abdomen rises and the chest is pulled inward during inspiration. On expiration the abdomen falls and the chest expands.

Paraplegia: A term used to describe injuries that occur at the level of the thoracic, lumbar or sacral spine.

Rhizotomy: A surgical resection of the sensory component of a spinal nerve in order to decrease spasticity and improve function.

Sacral sparing: An incomplete lesion where some of the innermost tracts remain innervated. Characteristics include sensation of the saddle area, movement of the toe flexors, and rectal sphincter contraction.

Spinal shock: A physiologic response that occurs between 30 and 60 minutes after trauma to the spinal cord and can last up to several weeks. Spinal shock presents with total flaccid paralysis and loss of all reflexes below the level of injury.

Tenodesis: Patients with tetraplegia that do not possess motor control for grasp can utilize the tight finger flexors in combination with wrist extension to produce a form of grasp.

Tenotomy: A surgical release of a tendon in order to decrease spasticity and improve function.

Tetraplegia (quadriplegia): A term adopted by the American Spinal Injury Association to describe injuries that occur at the level of the cervical spine.

Zone of partial preservation: A term used to describe the area below the neurologic level of injury that contains partial sensory or motor innervation.

CONSIDER THIS

SPINAL CORD INJURY INTERVENTION CONSTRUCTS[13,20,24]

Patients with spinal cord injury will likely have a unique course of rehabilitation based on their primary diagnosis, secondary complications, co-morbidities, and level of impairment. The following guidelines, however, reflect areas that should be incorporated into the plan of care for patients with spinal cord injury.

- Positioning
- Prevention of pressure ulcers
- Pressure relief techniques and equipment
- Range of motion
- Family/caregiver teaching
- Bowel and bladder programming
- Respiratory training/airway clearance
  - Assisted cough and secretion clearance
  - Breathing exercises
  - Abdominal binders
  - Mechanical ventilation
  - Glossopharyngeal breathing (GPB)
- Wheelchair, cushion (Figs. 5-56, 5-57), and orthotic prescriptions
- Wheelchair mobility
- Balance and center of gravity retraining
- Motor function retraining (transitioning between positions, seated scooting) (Figs. 5-58, 5-59)
- Mobility training including floor transfers if appropriate (Figs. 5-60, 5-61, 5-62)
- Pain management
- Use of FES, biofeedback, TENS if appropriate
- Self-care skills
- Gait training (T9 or lower)

Fig. 5-56: Roho high profile specialized cushion with cover.

Fig. 5-57: Roho high profile specialized cushion for wheelchair seating.

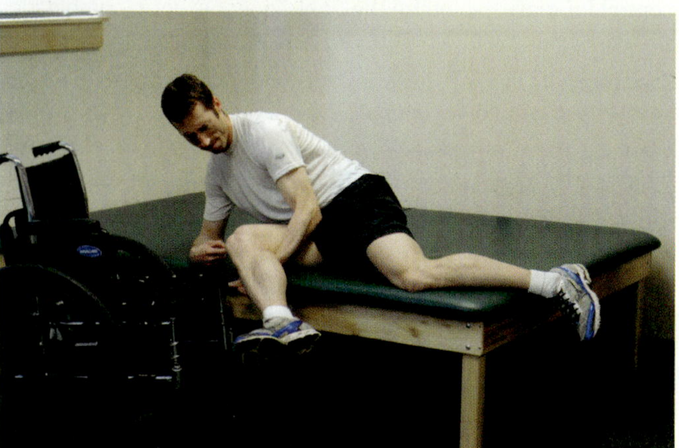

Fig. 5-58: Functional retraining of a patient with spinal cord injury, specifically transfers from the wheelchair to the mat surface.

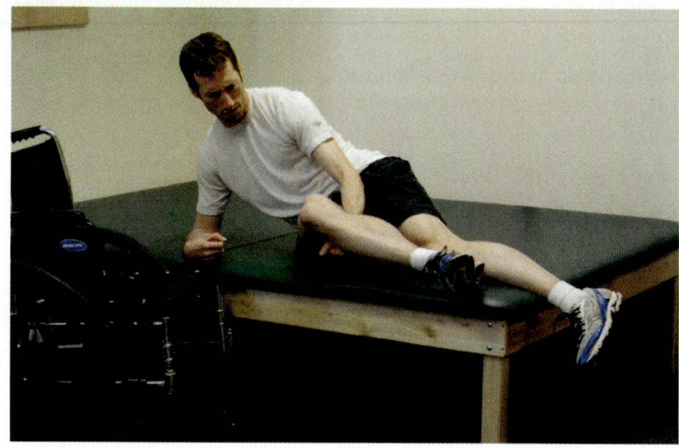

Fig. 5-59: The patient must compensate by looping the upper extremity under the lower extremity in combination with momentum in order to swing the lower extremity onto the mat surface.

Fig. 5-60: The patient initiates the roll by manually crossing legs, using the upper extremities to create movement and momentum.

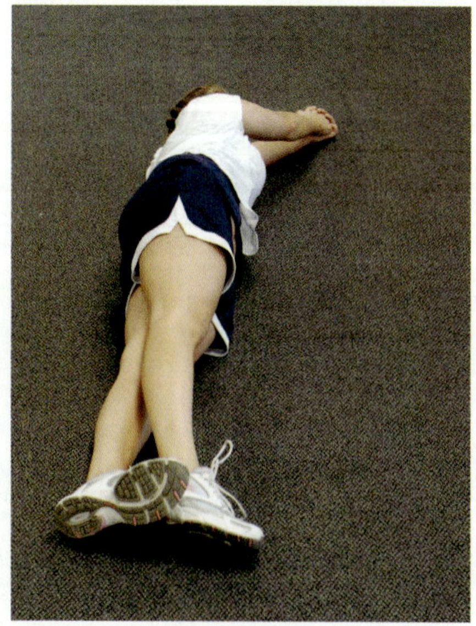

Fig. 5-61: The patient begins to roll using momentum and gravity.

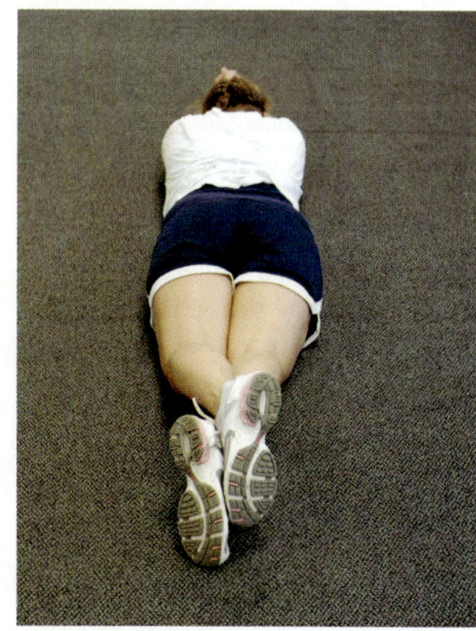

Fig. 5-62: The patient ends in prone position as anticipated.

Traumatic Brain Injury

The leading risk factors for a traumatic brain injury include motor vehicle accidents, falls, high risk behaviors, and gunshot wounds. Brain injury is classified as open versus closed with primary and secondary brain damage. Secondary damage within the brain can be significant due to the widespread areas that are affected.

Types of Brain Injury[20,44]

Open Injury

An injury of direct penetration through the skull to the brain. Location, depth of penetration, and pathway determine the extent of brain damage. Examples include gunshot wound, knife or sharp object penetration, skull fragments, and direct trauma.

Closed Injury

An injury to the brain without penetration through the skull. Examples include concussion, contusion, hematoma, injury to extracranial blood vessels, hypoxia, drug overdose, near drowning, and acceleration or deceleration injuries.

Primary Injury

Initial injury to the brain sustained by impact. Examples include skull penetration, skull fractures, and contusions to gray and white matter.

Coup lesion: A direct lesion of the brain under the point of impact. Local brain damage is sustained.

Contrecoup lesion: An injury that results on the opposite side of the brain. The lesion is due to the rebound effect of the brain after impact.

Secondary Injury

Brain damage that occurs as a response to the initial injury. Examples include hematoma, hypoxia, ischemia, increased intracranial pressure, and post-traumatic epilepsy.

Epidural hematoma: A hemorrhage that forms between the skull and dura mater.

Subdural hematoma: A hemorrhage that forms due to venous rupture between the dura and arachnoid.

Levels of Consciousness[20,44]

Coma: A state of unconsciousness and a level of unresponsiveness to all internal and external stimuli.

Stupor: A state of general unresponsiveness with arousal occurring from repeated stimuli.

Obtundity: A state of consciousness that is characterized by a state of sleep, reduced alertness to arousal, and delayed responses to stimuli.

Delirium: A state of consciousness that is characterized by disorientation, confusion, agitation, and loudness.

Clouding of consciousness: A state of consciousness that is characterized by quiet behavior, confusion, poor attention, and delayed responses.

Consciousness: A state of alertness, awareness, orientation, and memory.

A concussion can occur as a result of injury, specifically a blow to the head. This may or may not produce a temporary loss of consciousness. There is damage to the reticular activating system that allows for immediate changes in vital signs. Concussions occur frequently secondary to acute trauma such as motor vehicle accidents or through athletics.

The American Academy of Neurology classifies concussions as:

Grade 1 – A concussion that results from head injury where there was no loss of consciousness but typically some transient confusion by the patient. Symptoms will typically resolve within 15 minutes of the event. The patient may exhibit full memory of the event. An athlete should be removed from the competition and return only if symptom free after one week of rest.

Grade 2 – A concussion that results from a moderate head injury with transient confusion that will last longer than 15 minutes. The patient may exhibit poor concentration and retrograde and anterograde amnesia. An athlete should be removed immediately from the competition and receive a medical evaluation. CT scan is indicated if symptoms worsen and return to play should be deferred until the athlete is asymptomatic for two weeks at rest and with exertion.

Grade 3 – A concussion that results from head injury with any form of loss of consciousness. A patient should require transport to the emergency room for full neurological evaluation. Hospitalization is warranted if altered consciousness or mental status persists. An athlete should be withheld from competition after a grade 3 concussion once symptom free for a minimum of one month. This form of concussion is secondary to diffuse axonal injury and, if severe, can result in coma.

Traumatic Brain Injury Tests and Measures

Rancho Los Amigos Levels of Cognitive Functioning[24]

I. NO RESPONSE

Patient appears to be in a deep sleep and is completely unresponsive to any stimuli.

II. GENERALIZED RESPONSE

Patient reacts inconsistently and non-purposefully to stimuli in a nonspecific manner. Responses are limited and often the same regardless of stimulus presented. Responses may be physiological changes, gross body movements, and/or vocalization.

III. LOCALIZED RESPONSE

Patient reacts specifically, but inconsistently to stimuli. Responses are directly related to the type of stimulus presented. May follow simple commands such as closing the eyes or squeezing the hand in an inconsistent, delayed manner.

IV. CONFUSED-AGITATED

Patient is in a heightened state of activity. Behavior is bizarre and non-purposeful relative to the immediate environment. Does not discriminate among persons or objects; is unable to cooperate directly with treatment efforts. Verbalizations frequently are incoherent and/or inappropriate to the environment; confabulation may be present. Gross attention to environment is very brief; selective attention is often nonexistent. Patient lacks short and long-term recall.

V. CONFUSED-INAPPROPRIATE

Patient is able to respond to simple commands fairly consistently. However, with increased complexity of commands or lack of any external structure, responses are non-purposeful, random, or fragmented. Demonstrates gross attention to the environment, but is highly distractible and lacks the ability to focus attention on a specific task. With structure, may be able to converse on a social automatic level for short periods of time. Verbalization is often inappropriate and confabulatory. Memory is severely impaired; often shows inappropriate use of objects; may perform previously learned tasks with structure, but is unable to learn new information.

VI. CONFUSED-APPROPRIATE

Patient shows goal-directed behavior, but is dependent on external input or direction. Follows simple directions consistently and shows carryover for relearned tasks such as self-care. Responses may be incorrect due to memory problems, but they are appropriate to the situation. Past memories show more depth and detail than recent memory.

VII. AUTOMATIC-APPROPRIATE

Patient appears appropriate and oriented within the hospital and home setting. Goes through daily routine automatically, but frequently robot-like. Patient shows minimal to no confusion and has shallow recall of activities. Shows carryover for new learning, but at a decreased rate. With structure is able to initiate social or recreational activities; judgment remains impaired.

VIII. PURPOSEFUL-APPROPRIATE

Patient is able to recall and integrate past and recent events and is aware of and responsive to environment. Shows carryover for new learning and needs no supervision once activities are learned. May continue to show a decreased ability relative to premorbid abilities, abstract reasoning, tolerance for stress, and judgment in emergencies or unusual circumstances.

*A revised Rancho Los Amigos Levels of Cognitive Functioning Scale offers further clarification on Purposeful Appropriate by adding **IX Purposeful Appropriate - Stand-by Assistance on Request** and **X Purposeful Appropriate - Modified Independent**.

Glasgow Coma Scale[24]

A neurological assessment tool used initially after injury to determine arousal and cerebral cortex function. A total score of eight or less correlates to severe brain injury or coma. Scores of 9 to 12 indicate moderate brain injuries and scores from 13 to 15 indicate mild brain injuries.

Eye Opening	**E**
Spontaneous	4
To speech	3
To pain	2
Nil	1
Best Motor Response	**M**
Obeys commands	6
Localizes pain	5
Withdraws	4
Abnormal flexion	3
Extensor response	2
Nil	1
Verbal Response	**V**
Oriented	5
Confused conversation	4
Inappropriate words	3
Incomprehensible sounds	2
Nil	1
Coma Score (E+M+V) = 3 to 15	

Memory Impairments

Anterograde amnesia: The inability to create new memory. Anterograde memory is usually the last to recover after a comatose state. Contributing factors include poor attention, distractibility, and impaired perception of stimuli.

Post-traumatic amnesia: The time between the injury and when the patient is able to recall recent events. The patient does not recall the injury or events up until this point of recovery. Post-traumatic amnesia is used as an indicator of the extent of damage.

Retrograde amnesia: An inability to remember events prior to the injury. Retrograde amnesia may progressively decrease with recovery.

CONSIDER THIS

TRAUMATIC BRAIN INJURY INTERVENTION CONSTRUCTS[20,24,44]

Patients with brain injury will likely have a unique course of rehabilitation based on their primary diagnosis, secondary complications, co-morbidities, and level of impairment. The following guidelines, however, reflect areas that should be incorporated into the plan of care for patients with a brain injury.

- Emphasis on motivation
- Promote independence
- Therapy should be goal-directed and functional
- Focus on orientation and behavior modification activities
- Repetition is typically helpful
- Educate patient in compensatory strategies for success
- Structure is essential depending on the level of the patient
- Avoid overstimulation during therapy using a calm voice and simple commands
- Perform activities that are both familiar and enjoyable for the patient
- Family education and support can enhance and assist the rehabilitation process
- Flexibility in treatment is needed based on patient's immediate needs and state of mind
- Intervention should include:
  - Cognitive and orientation training
  - Therapeutic exercise
  - Positioning
  - Sensory integration
  - Balance and vestibular training
  - Range of motion
  - Motor function training
  - Wheelchair and adaptive equipment prescription
  - Splinting and serial casting
  - Mobility training

Pediatrics and Development

Apgar Score

Apgar Sign	0	1	2
Appearance (skin color)	Blue; pale	Normal body color, except blue hands and feet	Normal color "pink"
Pulse	Absent	Below 100 beats per minute	Above 100 beats per minute
Grimace (reflex irritability)	No response to stimulation	Minimal response to stimulation	Pulls away, sneeze or cough
Activity (muscle tone)	No movement, "floppy"	Flexing of the arms and legs	Active movement
Respiration	Absent	Slow, irregular	Vigorous cry

The Apgar score is a method for objectively reporting the health of a newborn shortly after it is delivered. The score is determined by rating five different criteria: **A**ppearance (skin color), **P**ulse rate, **G**rimace (reflex irritability), **A**ctivity, and **R**espiration. Each criterion is graded on a scale from 0-2, with a score of 2 indicating a normal response.

Total scores are calculated at one minute and at five minutes following birth. A newborn is considered to be in good condition if they have a score of 7-10. A score of 3 or below is considered to be low and is an indicator that the newborn requires immediate medical attention.

Concepts of Development[45,46]

Cephalic to Caudal: A person develops head and upper extremity control prior to trunk and lower extremity control. There is a general skill acquisition from the direction of head to toe.

Gross to Fine: A general trend for large muscle movement acquisition with progression to small muscle skill acquisition.

Mass to Specific: A general trend for a person to acquire simple movements and progress towards complex movements.

Proximal to Distal: A concept that uses the midline of the body as the reference point. Trunk control (midline stability) is acquired first with subsequent gain in distal control (extremities).

Infant Reflexes and Possible Effects if Reflex Persists Abnormally[47]

Primitive Reflex	Possible Negative Effect on Movement with Abnormal Persistence of Reflex
Asymmetrical Tonic Neck Reflex (ATNR)	
Stimulus: Head position, turned to one side **Response:** Arm and leg on face side are extended, arm and leg on scalp side are flexed, spine curved with convexity toward face side **Normal age of response:** Birth to 6 months	**Interferes with:** • Feeding • Visual tracking • Midline use of hands • Bilateral hand use • Rolling • Development of crawling • Can lead to skeletal deformities (e.g., scoliosis, hip subluxation, hip dislocation)
Symmetrical Tonic Neck Reflex (STNR)	
Stimulus: Head position, flexion or extension **Response:** When head is in flexion, arms are flexed, legs extended. When head is in extension, arms are extended, legs are flexed **Normal age of response:** 6 to 12 months	**Interferes with:** • Ability to prop on arms in prone position • Attaining and maintaining hands-and-knees position • Crawling reciprocally • Sitting balance when looking around • Use of hands when looking at object in hands in sitting position
Tonic Labyrinthine Reflex (TLR)	
Stimulus: Position of labyrinth in inner ear - reflected in head position **Response:** In the supine position, body and extremities are held in extension; in the prone position, body and extremities are held in flexion **Normal age of response:** Birth to 6 months	**Interferes with:** • Ability to initiate rolling • Ability to prop on elbows with extended hips when prone • Ability to flex trunk and hips to come to sitting position from supine position • Often causes full body extension, which interferes with balance in sitting or standing
Galant Reflex	
Stimulus: Touch to skin along spine from shoulder to hip **Response:** Lateral flexion of trunk to side of stimulus **Normal age of response:** 30 weeks of gestation to 2 months	**Interferes with:** • Development of sitting balance • Can lead to scoliosis

Infant Reflexes and Possible Effects if Reflex Persists Abnormally[47]

Primitive Reflex	Possible Negative Effect on Movement with Abnormal Persistence of Reflex
Palmar Grasp Reflex	
Stimulus: Pressure in palm on ulnar side of hand **Response:** Flexion of fingers causing strong grip **Normal age of response:** Birth to 4 months	**Interferes with:** • Ability to grasp and release objects voluntarily • Weight bearing on open hand for propping, crawling, protective responses
Plantar Grasp Reflex	
Stimulus: Pressure to base of toes **Response:** Toe flexion **Normal age of response:** 28 weeks of gestation to 9 months	**Interferes with:** • Ability to stand with feet flat on surface • Balance reactions and weight shifting in standing
Rooting Reflex	
Stimulus: Touch on cheek **Response:** Turning head to same side with mouth open **Normal age of response:** 28 weeks of gestation to 3 months	**Interferes with:** • Oral-motor development • Development of midline control of head • Optical righting, visual tracking, and social interaction
Moro Reflex	
Stimulus: Head dropping into extension suddenly for a few inches **Response:** Arms abduct with fingers open, then cross trunk into adduction; cry **Normal age of response:** 28 weeks of gestation to 5 months	**Interferes with:** • Balance reactions in sitting • Protective responses in sitting • Eye-hand coordination, visual tracking
Startle Reflex	
Stimulus: Loud, sudden noise **Response:** Similar to Moro response, but elbows remain flexed and hands closed **Normal age of response:** 28 weeks of gestation to 5 months	**Interferes with:** • Sitting balance • Protective responses in sitting • Eye-hand coordination, visual tracking • Social interaction, attention
Positive Support Reflex	
Stimulus: Weight placed on balls of feet when upright **Response:** Stiffening of legs and trunk into extension **Normal age of response:** 35 weeks of gestation to 2 months	**Interferes with:** • Standing and walking • Balance reactions and weight shift in standing • Can lead to contractures of ankles into plantar flexion
Walking (Stepping) Reflex	
Stimulus: Supported upright position with soles of feet on firm surface **Response:** Reciprocal flexion/extension of legs **Normal age of response:** 38 weeks of gestation to 2 months	**Interferes with:** • Standing and walking • Balance reactions and weight shifting in standing • Development of smooth, coordinated reciprocal movements of lower extremities

From Ratliffe KT: Clinical Pediatric Physical Therapy: A Guide for the Physical Therapy Team. Mosby Inc., Philadelphia 1998, p.266, with permission.

Developmental Gross and Fine Motor Skills[47]

Gross Motor Skills	Fine Motor Skills
Newborn to 1 Month	
Prone Physiological flexion Lifts head briefly Head to side **Supine** Physiological flexion Rolls partly to side **Sitting** Head lag in pull to sit **Standing** Reflex standing and walking	Regards objects in direct line of sight Follows moving object to midline Hands fisted Arm movements jerky Movements may be purposeful or random
2 to 3 Months	
Prone Lifts head 90 degrees briefly Chest up in prone position with some weight through forearms Rolls prone to supine **Supine** Asymmetrical tonic neck reflex (ATNR) influence is strong Legs kick reciprocally Prefers head to side **Sitting** Head upright, but bobbing Variable head lag in pull to sitting position Needs full support to sit **Standing** Poor weight bearing Hips in flexion, behind shoulders	Can see farther distances Hands open more Visually follows through 180 degrees Grasp is reflexive Uses palmar grasp
4 to 5 Months	
Prone Bears weight on extended arms Pivots in prone to reach toys **Supine** Rolls from supine to side position Plays with feet to mouth **Sitting** Head steady in supported sitting position Turns head in sitting position Sits alone for brief periods **Standing** Bears all weight through legs in supported standing	Grasps and releases toys Uses ulnar-palmar grasp
6 to 7 Months	
Prone Rolls from supine to prone position Holds weight on one hand to reach for toy **Supine** Lifts head **Sitting** Lifts head and helps when pulled to sitting position Gets to sitting position without assistance Sits independently **Mobility** May crawl backward	Approaches objects with one hand Arm in neutral when approaching toy Radial-palmar grasp "Rakes" with fingers to pick up small objects Voluntary release to transfer objects between hands

Developmental Gross and Fine Motor Skills[47]

Gross Motor Skills	Fine Motor Skills
8 to 9 Months	
Prone Gets into hands-knees position **Supine** Does not tolerate supine position **Sitting** Moves from sitting to prone position Sits without hand support for longer periods Pivots in sitting position **Standing** Stands at furniture Pulls to stand at furniture Lowers to sitting position from supported stand **Mobility** Crawls forward Walks along furniture (cruising)	Develops active supination Radial-digital grasp develops Uses inferior pincer grasp Extends wrist actively Points with index finger Pokes with index finger Release of objects is more refined Takes objects out of container
10 to 11 Months	
Standing Stands without support briefly Pulls to stand using half-kneel intermediate position Picks up object from floor from standing with support **Mobility** Walks with both hands held Walks with one hand held Creeps on hands and feet (bear walk)	Fine pincer grasp developed Puts objects into container Grasps crayon adaptively

Gross Motor Skills	Fine Motor Skills
12 to 15 Months	
Walks without support Fast walking Walks sideways Bends over to look between legs Creeps or hitches upstairs Throws ball in sitting	Marks paper with crayon Builds tower using two cubes Turns over small container to obtain contents
16 to 24 Months	
Squats in play Walks backward Walking upstairs and downstairs with one hand held using both feet on step Propels ride-on toys Kicks ball Throws ball Throws ball forward Picks up toy from floor without falling	Folds paper Strings beads Stacks six cubes Imitates vertical and horizontal strokes with crayon on paper Holds crayon with thumb and fingers
2 Years	
Rides tricycle Walks on tiptoe Runs on toes Walks downstairs alternating feet Catches large ball Hops on one foot	Turns knob Opens and closes jar Able to button large buttons Uses child-size scissors with help Does 12 to 15 piece puzzles Folds paper or clothes

Developmental Gross and Fine Motor Skills[47]

Gross Motor Skills	Fine Motor Skills
Preschool Age (3 to 4 Years)	
Throws ball 10 feet Walks on a line 10 feet Hops 2-10 times on one foot Jumps distances of up to two feet Jumps over obstacles up to 12 inches Throws and catches small ball Runs fast and avoids obstacles	Controls crayons more effectively Copies a circle or cross Matches colors Cuts with scissors Draws recognizable human figures with head and two extremities Draws squares May demonstrate hand preference
Early School Age (5 to 8 Years)	
Skips on alternate feet Gallops Can play hopscotch, balance on one foot, controlled hopping, and squatting on one leg Jumps with rhythm, control (jump rope) Bounces large ball Kicks ball with greater control Limbs growing faster than trunk allowing greater speed, leverage	Hand preference is evident Prints well, starting to learn cursive writing Able to button small buttons
Later School Age (9 to 12 Years)	
Mature patterns of movement in throwing, jumping, running Competition increases, enjoys competitive games Improved balance, coordination, endurance, attention span Boys may develop preadolescent fat spurt Girls may develop prepubescent and pubescent changes in body shape (hips, breasts)	Develops greater control in hand usage Learns to draw Handwriting is developed
Adolescence (13 Years+)	
Rapid growth in size and strength, boys more than girls Puberty leads to changes in body proportions, center of gravity rises toward shoulders for boys, lowers to hips for girls Balance and coordination skills, eye-hand coordination, endurance may plateau during growth spurt	Develops greater dexterity in fingers for fine tasks (knitting, sewing, art, crafts)

From Ratliffe KT: Clinical Pediatric Physical Therapy: A Guide for the Physical Therapy Team. Mosby Company Inc., Philadelphia 1998, p.45-47, with permission.

Pediatric Therapeutic Positioning

Proper positioning is essential to obtain maximum function for the pediatric population. Positioning is used for many purposes including facilitation of desired patterns of movement, inhibition of abnormal reflexes, normalization of tone, midline orientation, enhancement of respiratory capacity, pulmonary hygiene, maintaining skin integrity, and prevention of contractures.

Ideal Positioning[47]

	Supine	Prone	Sidelying	Sitting
Pelvis and Hips	Pelvis in line with trunk. Hips in 30 to 90 degrees of flexion. Neutral rotation of pelvis. Hips symmetrically abducted 10 to 20 degrees.	Pelvis in line with trunk. Hips in extension. Neutral rotation of pelvis. Hips symmetrically abducted 10 to 20 degrees.	Pelvis in line with trunk. Hips in flexion. Neutral rotation. Hips in 10 to 20 degrees abduction.	Pelvis in line with trunk. Hips at 90 degrees flexion. Neutral rotation of pelvis. Hips symmetrically abducted 10 to 20 degrees.
Trunk	Straight. Shoulders in line with hips. Neutral rotation of trunk.	Straight. Shoulders in line with hips. Neutral rotation.	Straight. Shoulders in line with hips. Slight sidebending okay.	Straight. Shoulders over hips. Not rotated.
Head and Neck	Head in neutral position. Facing forward. Slight cervical flexion.	Head in neutral position. Facing to one side. Slight cervical flexion.	Head in neutral position. Facing forward. Slight cervical flexion.	Head in neutral position. Facing forward. Head evenly on shoulders.
Shoulders and Arms	Arms fully supported. Arms forward of trunk. Forearms rest on trunk or pillow.	Arms fully supported. Arms forward of trunk. Flexion at shoulders. Flexion at elbows.	Both arms supported. Lower arm forward, not lying on point of shoulders. Lower arm neutral rotation. Upper arm may have 0 to 40 degrees medial rotation.	Arms fully supported. Elbows in flexion. 0 to 45 degrees internally rotated shoulders.
Legs and Feet	Knees supported in flexion. Feet positioned at 90 degrees.	Knees extended. Feet positioned at 90 degrees.	Knees in flexion. Feet positioned at 90 degrees. Pillow between knees.	Knees at 90 degrees. Ankles at 90 degrees. Feet fully supported. Thighs fully supported.

From Ratliffe KT: Clinical Pediatric Physical Therapy: A Guide for the Physical Therapy Team. Mosby Inc., Philadelphia 1998, p.266, with permission.

Neuromuscular and Nervous Systems Pediatric Pathology

Arthrogryposis Multiplex Congenita (AMC)[45,46,47]

Arthrogryposis multiplex congenita is a non-progressive neuromuscular disorder that is estimated to occur during the first trimester in utero. The restriction in utero allows for fibrosis of muscles and structures within the joints.

Etiology – An exact etiology of AMC is unknown, however, causative factors include poor movement during early development due to myopathic, neuropathic or joint abnormalities. The causative factor for a small percentage of children with this condition is genetic inheritance as an autosomal dominant trait.

Signs and symptoms – AMC characteristics include cylinder-like extremities with minimal definition, significant and multiple contractures, dislocation of joints, and muscle atrophy.

Treatment – The goal of treatment is to attain the maximum level of developmental skills through positioning, stretching, strengthening, splinting, and use of adaptive equipment. Significant family involvement is required for the home program. Surgical intervention may be indicated.

Autism Spectrum Disorder[13,46]

Autism spectrum disorder (ASD) is a group of complex brain development disorders that are characterized by difficulties with social interaction, communication, and repetitive behaviors. Children with ASD can vary widely in their functional level since ASD is an umbrella term that includes four previously isolated disorders: autistic disorder, childhood disintegrative disorder, pervasive development disorder (not otherwise specified), and Asperger syndrome.

Etiology – The etiology for ASD is not well understood, but it is thought to have a multifactorial cause that includes genetic and environmental influences.

Signs and Symptoms – Initial signs and symptoms generally become apparent around the age of two or three. These often include nonpurposeful speech or the complete absence of speech, diminished facial expressions, an inability to understand nonverbal cues, limited interest or awkwardness in social interactions, a lack of empathy, defensiveness or indifference towards sensory stimulation, repetitive self-stimulating behaviors, perseverations, preoccupation with routines and rituals, and decreased coordination. Children that have more severe forms of ASD may be significantly limited in their ability to participate in expected social roles, while children with mild ASD (e.g., Asperger syndrome) may have relatively few limitations and only be recognized as being socially awkward. Many children with ASD have exceptional talents in music, art, and academic skills.

Treatment – Generally multidisciplinary and may focus on improving social communication and decreasing nonpurposeful movements and vocalizations. Sensory integration therapy may also be used to help those patients that have difficulty with sensory processing. The prognosis for patients with ASD is directly related to the severity of the condition.

Cerebral Palsy (CP)[13,45,46,47]

Cerebral palsy is an umbrella term used to describe movement disorders due to brain damage that are non-progressive and are acquired in utero, during birth or infancy. The brain damage decreases the brain's ability to monitor and control nerve and voluntary muscle activity.

Etiology – CP can occur before or during birth secondary to a lack of oxygen, maternal infections, drug or alcohol abuse, placental abnormalities, toxemia, prolonged labor, prematurity, and Rh incompatibility. The etiology of acquired cerebral palsy includes meningitis, CVA, seizures, and brain injury.

Signs and symptoms – Characteristics vary from mild and undetectable to severe loss of control accompanied by profound intellectual disability. All types of cerebral palsy demonstrate abnormal muscle tone, impaired modulation of movement, presence of abnormal reflexes, and impaired mobility.

Cerebral Palsy Primary Motor Patterns (mixed motor patterns exist)

- **Spastic** - indicating a lesion in the motor cortex of the cerebrum; upper motor neuron damage
- **Athetoid** - indicating a lesion involving the basal ganglia

Distribution of Involvement

- **Monoplegia** - one extremity
- **Diplegia** - bilateral lower extremity involvement, however, upper extremities may be affected
- **Hemiplegia** - unilateral involvement of the upper and lower extremities
- **Quadriplegia** - involvement of the entire body

Treatment – Treatment of cerebral palsy is a lifelong process. Intervention includes ongoing family and caregiver education, normalization of tone, stretching, strengthening, motor learning and developmental milestones, positioning, weight bearing activities, and mobility skills. Splinting, assistive devices, and specialized seating may be indicated. Surgical intervention may be required for orthopedic management or reduction of spasticity.

Down Syndrome[45,46,47]

Down syndrome is a genetic abnormality consisting of an extra twenty-first chromosome, termed trisomy 21.

Etiology – The etiology of Down syndrome includes incomplete cell division of the 21st pair of chromosomes due to nondisjunction, translocation or mosaic classification. Advanced maternal age increases the risk of genetic imbalance.

Signs and symptoms – Signs and symptoms of this syndrome include intellectual disability, hypotonia, joint hypermobility, flattened nasal bridge, narrow eyelids with epicanthal folds, small mouth, feeding impairments, flat feet, scoliosis, congenital heart disease, and visual and hearing loss.

Treatment – Treatment should emphasize exercise and fitness, stability, maximizing respiratory function, and education for caregivers. Surgical intervention may be indicated for cardiac abnormalities.

Duchenne Muscular Dystrophy[13,45,46,47]

Duchenne muscular dystrophy is a progressive disorder caused by the absence of the gene required to produce the muscle proteins dystrophin and nebulin. Without dystrophin and nebulin, cell membranes weaken, myofibrils are destroyed, and muscle contractility is lost. Fat and connective tissue eventually replace muscle, and death usually occurs from cardiopulmonary failure prior to age 25, usually in the teenage years.

Etiology – The causative factor is inheritance as an X-linked recessive trait. The child's mother is a silent carrier and only male offspring will manifest the disease.

Signs and symptoms – Characteristics usually manifest between two and five years of age. Progressive weakness, disinterest in running, falling, toe walking, excessive lordosis, and pseudohypertrophy of muscle groups are common symptoms. Progressive impairment with ADLs and mobility begins around age five and the inability to ambulate follows.

Treatment – Intervention focuses on family and caregiver education, respiratory function, submaximal exercise, mobility skills, splinting, orthotics, and adaptive equipment. Medical management includes the use of immunosuppressants, steroids, and surgical intervention for orthopedic impairments.

Prader-Willi Syndrome[45,46,47]

Prader-Willi syndrome is a genetic condition that is diagnosed by physical attributes and patterns of behavior rather than genetic testing.

Etiology – The causative factor is a partial deletion of chromosome 15.

Signs and symptoms – Characteristics include physical and behavioral attributes such as small hands, feet, and sex organs, hypotonia, almond-shaped eyes, obesity, and a constant desire for food. This child will present with coordination impairments and intellectual disability.

Treatment – Physical therapy includes postural control, exercise and fitness, and gross and fine motor skills training.

Spina Bifida[13,45,46,47]

Spina bifida is a developmental abnormality due to insufficient closure of the neural tube by the 28th day of gestation. This defect usually occurs in the low thoracic, lumbar or sacral regions and affects the central nervous, musculoskeletal, and urinary systems.

Etiology – A single etiology has not been identified, however, causative factors include genetic predisposition, environmental influence, low levels of maternal folic acid, maternal hyperthermia, and certain classifications of drugs. Classifications of spina bifida include:

Spina Bifida Occulta - An impairment and non-fusion of the spinous processes of a vertebra, however, the spinal cord and meninges remain intact. There is usually no associated disability.

Spina Bifida Cystica - Presents with a cyst-like protrusion through the non-fused vertebrae, which results in impairment.

Forms of Spina Bifida Cystica

- **Meningocele** - Herniation of meninges and cerebrospinal fluid into a sac that protrudes through the vertebral defect. The spinal cord remains within the canal.
- **Myelomeningocele** - A severe form characterized by herniation of meninges, cerebrospinal fluid, and the spinal cord extending through the defect in the vertebrae. The cyst may or may not be covered by skin.

Signs and symptoms – Characteristics and associated impairments of myelomeningocele include motor loss below the level of the defect in the spinal cord, sensory deficits, hydrocephalus, Arnold-Chiari Type II malformation, osteoporosis, clubfoot, scoliosis, tethered cord syndrome, latex allergy, bowel and bladder dysfunction, and learning disabilities.

Treatment – Physical therapy treatment emphasizes significant family teaching regarding positioning, handling, range of motion, and therapeutic exercise. Additional therapeutic activities include facilitation of developmental milestones, skin care, strengthening, balance and mobility training, adaptive equipment, splinting, orthotic prescription, and wheelchair prescription. Physical therapy is ongoing through adolescence and is based on the severity of impairments and needs of the child.

Spinal Muscular Atrophy (SMA)[13,45,46,47]

Spinal muscular atrophy is characterized by progressive degeneration of the anterior horn cell.

Etiology – The causative factor of spinal muscular atrophy is an autosomal recessive genetic inheritance. Certain types of this disease involve a mutation on chromosome 5. Categories of spinal muscular atrophy include:

Acute Infantile SMA (Type 1-Werdnig-Hoffmann disease) - Occurs between birth and two months of age. Motor degeneration progresses quickly and life expectancy is less than one year.

Chronic Childhood SMA (Type 2-Chronic Werdnig-Hoffmann disease) - Presents after six months to one year and has slower progression than infantile SMA. Impairment is steady, however, a child can survive into adulthood.

Juvenile SMA (Type 3-Kugelberg-Welander SMA) - Occurs later in childhood from 4-17 years of age. Children with juvenile SMA typically survive into adulthood.

Signs and symptoms – Characteristics for all categories of the disease are the same, and vary in onset and speed of progression. Characteristics include progressive muscle weakness and atrophy, diminished or absent deep tendon reflexes, normal intelligence, intact sensation, and end-stage respiratory compromise.

Treatment – Treatment includes positioning, vestibular and visual stimulation, and access to play. Treatment for the slower progressing categories is primarily supportive including educating caregivers, mobility training, and use of assistive devices and adaptive equipment.

Legislation Acts and Amendments for the Education of Children with Disabilities[48]

There have been various forms of legislation that have been enacted in order to improve health care, medical benefits, and education specifically for children. The largest reforms are listed below.

Education for All Handicapped Children Act (enacted 1975)

The groundbreaking law was intended to support states and localities in protecting the rights of, meeting the individual needs of, and improving the results for infants, toddlers, children, and youths with disabilities and their families. This is the origin of the Individuals with Disabilities Education Improvement Act (IDEA).

Carl D. Perkins Vocational Education Act of 1984

Each state was required to meet the special needs of individuals with handicaps or adults that are disadvantaged, adults in need of training and retraining, single parents or homemakers, programs designed to eliminate sex bias/stereotyping, and criminal offenders.

Perkins Vocational and Applied Technology Act (enacted 1990)

Reauthorization and modification of the Education for All Handicapped Children Act (EHA). Provides free, appropriate education in the least restrictive environment for individuals with disabilities from age 3-21.

IDEA (Individuals with Disabilities Education Improvement Act) Amendments (enacted 1991)

Reauthorized early intervention; established Federal Interagency Coordination Council.

Rehabilitation Act Amendments (enacted 1992)

Transition planning at high school graduation includes coordination of assistive technology services and the rehabilitation system.

IDEA Amendments (enacted 1997)

Restructuring of IDEA into four distinct and individual parts. It defines the responsibilities of school districts in providing services to ensure that children with certain specified disabilities receive free, appropriate education. School districts must prepare an Individualized Education Program (IEP) for each eligible child. Related services most commonly include speech, physical, and occupational therapies, and child counseling.

No Child Left Behind Act (enacted 2002)

The most sweeping reform of the Elementary and Secondary Education Act since its enactment in 1965. This act redefines the federal role in K-12 education. It requires accountability for all children, including student groups based on poverty, race and ethnicity, disability, and limited English proficiency (LEP). Its goal is to close the achievement gap between disadvantaged, disabled, and minority students and their peers.

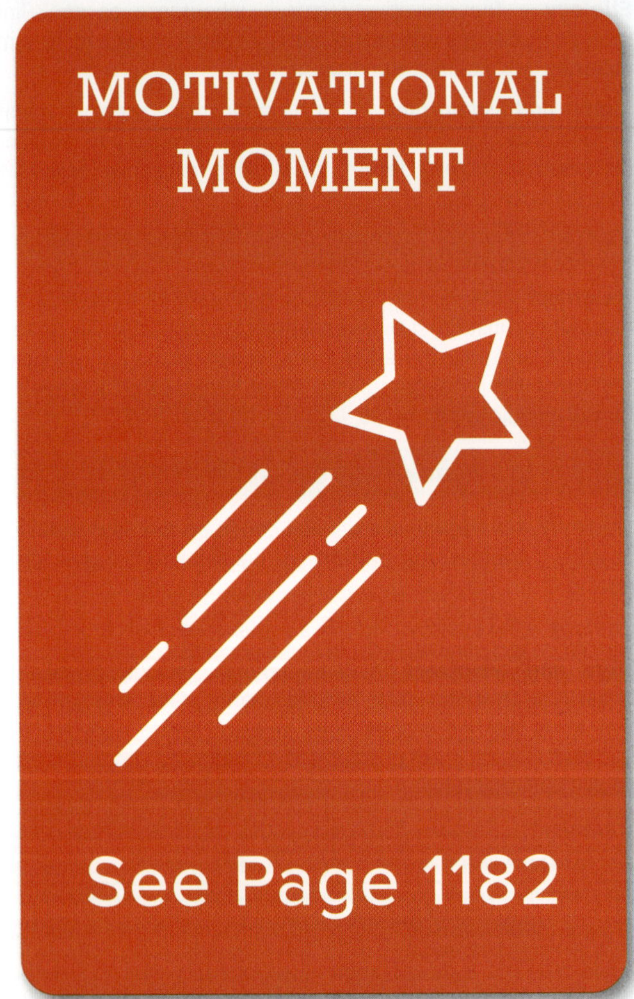

GOLD Level Clinical Application Templates

GOLD Level Clinical Application Template Executive Summary

Alzheimer's Disease

- Progressive neurological disorder that results in deterioration and irreversible damage within the cerebral cortex and subcortical areas of the brain
- Disease is initially noted by a change in higher cortical functions characterized by subtle changes in memory, impaired concentration, and difficulty with new learning
- Typical course of the disease averages between 7-11 years with death resulting from infection or dehydration

Amyotrophic Lateral Sclerosis

- Risk is higher in males than females and usually occurs between 40-70 years of age
- Clinical presentation may include both upper and lower motor neuron involvement with weakness occurring in a distal to proximal progression
- Average course of the diagnosis is two to five years with roughly a quarter of patients surviving longer than five years

Carpal Tunnel Syndrome

- Incidence is higher in females than males with the most common age being from 35-55 years of age
- Muscle atrophy is often noted in the abductor pollicis brevis muscle and later in the thenar muscles
- Electromyography studies, Tinel's sign, and Phalen's test can be used to assist with confirming the diagnosis

Central Cord Syndrome

- An incomplete spinal cord lesion that most often results from a cervical hyperextension injury
- Clinical presentation involves motor loss that is greater in the upper extremities than the lower extremities
- Most common incomplete spinal cord lesion accounting for approximately 30% of all incomplete forms of tetraplegia

Cerebral Palsy

- Spastic cerebral palsy involves upper motor neuron damage; athetoid cerebral palsy involves damage to the basal ganglia
- Clinical presentation includes motor delays, abnormal muscle tone and motor control, reflex abnormalities, poor postural control, and balance impairments
- Intellectual disability and epilepsy are present in 50-60% of children diagnosed with cerebral palsy

Cerebrovascular Accident

- Types of CVA include ischemic stroke (thrombus, embolus, lacunar) and hemorrhagic stroke (intracerebral, subdural, subarachnoid)
- Left CVA may present with weakness or paralysis to the right side, impaired processing, heightened frustration, aphasia, dysphagia, and motor apraxia
- Right CVA may present with weakness or paralysis to the left side, poor attention span, impaired awareness and judgment, spatial deficits, memory deficits, emotional lability, and impulsive behavior

GOLD Level Clinical Application Template Executive Summary

Down Syndrome

- Clinical manifestations include hypotonia, flattened nasal bridge, Simian line (palmar crease), epicanthal folds, enlargement of the tongue, and developmental delay
- Medical management of Down syndrome is a team approach that requires lifelong intervention and should be directed toward achieving maximum potential and level of function
- Exercise is essential for a child with Down syndrome in order to avoid inactivity and obesity

Duchenne Muscular Dystrophy

- X-linked recessive trait manifesting in only male offspring while female offspring become carriers
- Clinical presentation includes waddling gait, proximal muscle weakness, toe walking, pseudohypertrophy of the calf, and difficulty climbing stairs
- There is usually rapid progression of this disease with the inability to ambulate by ten to twelve years of age with death occurring as a teenager or less frequently in the 20's

Erb's Palsy

- Muscles affected are supplied by cervical roots C5 and C6 which result in a loss of function of the rotator cuff, deltoid, brachialis, coracobrachialis, and biceps brachii
- Brachial plexus injury in a newborn usually occurs during a difficult delivery, due to a large baby, a breech presentation with a prolonged labor or with the use of forceps
- Results in flaccid paralysis nicknamed the "waiter's tip deformity" (characterized by a loss of shoulder function, loss of elbow flexion, loss of forearm supination, and the hand positioned in a pinch grip manner)

Guillain-Barre Syndrome

- Results in motor weakness in a distal to proximal progression, sensory impairment, and possible respiratory paralysis
- Etiology of the disease is unknown, however, it is hypothesized to be an autoimmune response to a previous respiratory infection, influenza, immunization or surgery
- Majority of patients experience full recovery, 20% have remaining neurologic deficits, and 3-5% of patients die from respiratory complications

Huntington's Disease

- Chronic progressive genetic disorder that is fatal within 15 to 20 years after clinical manifestation
- Characterized by degeneration and atrophy of the basal ganglia (specifically the striatum) and cerebral cortex within the brain
- Clinical presentation includes enlarged ventricles secondary to atrophy of the basal ganglia, mental deterioration, speech disturbances, and ataxic gait

GOLD Level Clinical Application Template Executive Summary

Multiple Sclerosis

- Characterized by demyelination of the myelin sheaths that surround nerves within the brain and spinal cord resulting in plaque development, decreased nerve conduction velocity, and eventual failure of impulse transmission
- Clinical symptoms may include visual problems, paresthesias, sensory changes, clumsiness, weakness, ataxia, balance dysfunction, and fatigue
- Intervention includes regulation of activity level, relaxation and energy conservation techniques, normalization of tone, balance activities, gait training, and core stabilization

Parkinson's Disease

- Degenerative disorder characterized by a decrease in production of dopamine (neurotransmitter) within the substantia nigra of the basal ganglia
- Clinical presentation may include hypokinesia, difficulty initiating and stopping movement, festinating and shuffling gait, bradykinesia, poor posture, and "cogwheel" or "lead pipe" rigidity
- Medical management includes dopamine replacement therapy (Levodopa, Sinemet, Madopar) which is designed to minimize bradykinesia, rigidity, and tremor

Sciatica Secondary to a Herniated Disk

- The sciatic nerve experiences an inflammatory response and subsequent damage secondary to compression from the herniated disk
- Sciatica is characterized by low back and gluteal pain that typically radiates down the back of the thigh along the sciatic nerve distribution
- Pain will increase in a sitting position or when lifting, forward bending or twisting

Spina Bifida – Myelomeningocele

- Classifications include occulta (incomplete fusion of the posterior vertebral arch with no neural tissue protruding), meningocele (incomplete fusion of the posterior vertebral arch with neural tissue/meninges protruding outside the neural arch), and myelomeningocele (incomplete fusion of the posterior vertebral arch with both meninges and spinal cord protruding outside the neural arch)
- Approximately 75% of vertebral defects are found in the lumbar/sacral region most often at L5-S1
- Prenatal testing of alpha-fetoprotein (AFP) in the blood will show an elevation in levels that indicate a probable neural tube defect at approximately week 16 of gestation

Spinal Cord Injury – Complete C7 Tetraplegia

- Clinical presentation includes impaired cough and ability to clear secretions, altered breathing pattern, and poor endurance
- Outcomes at this level include independence with feeding, grooming, dressing, self-range of motion, independent manual wheelchair mobility, independent transfers, and independent driving with an adapted automobile
- The triceps, extensor pollicis longus and brevis, extrinsic finger extensors, and flexor carpi radialis will remain the lowest innervated muscles

Level Clinical Application Template Executive Summary

Spinal Cord Injury – Complete L3 Paraplegia

- Patients possess at least partial innervation of the gracilis, iliopsoas, quadratus lumborum, rectus femoris, and sartorius with full upper extremity use
- Additional findings that can exist include sexual dysfunction, a nonreflexive bladder, the need for a bowel program, urinary tract infections, muscle contractures, and pressure sores
- Patients with L3 paraplegia should be able to live independently with education regarding the management of their disability

Thoracic Outlet Syndrome

- Results from compression and damage to the brachial plexus nerve trunks, subclavian vascular supply, and/or the axillary artery
- Contributing factors in the development of the condition include the presence of a cervical rib, an abnormal first rib, postural deviations, hypertrophy or spasms of the scalene muscles, and an elongated cervical transverse process
- Females are at a greater risk than males, with the most common age ranging from 30-40 years of age

Traumatic Brain Injury

- Occurs due to an open head injury where there is penetration through the skull or closed head injury where the brain makes contact with the skull secondary to a sudden, violent acceleration or deceleration
- Brain injury may include swelling, axonal injury, hypoxia, hematoma, hemorrhage, and changes in intracranial pressure
- High risk groups include ages 0-4, 15-19, and greater than 65 (males are at greater risk in each category)

Vestibular Disorders

- Occurs when there is a disruption of the sensory information processed by the inner ear and brain with respect to the body's control of balance and eye movements
- Classified as either peripheral or central, with the majority of cases diagnosed as peripheral
- Effects can be quite diverse ranging from spontaneous recovery to permanent disability

GOLD

Alzheimer's Disease

DIAGNOSIS

What condition produces a patient's symptoms?

Alzheimer's disease is a progressive neurological disorder that results in deterioration and irreversible damage within the cerebral cortex and subcortical areas of the brain. The loss of neurons results from the breakdown of several processes that would normally sustain the brain cells.

An injury was most likely sustained to which structure?

Neurons that are normally involved with acetylcholine transmission deteriorate within the cerebral cortex of the brain. Postmortem biopsy reveals neurofibrillary tangles within cytoplasm, amyloid plaques, and cerebral atrophy. Amyloid plaques contain fragmented axons, altered glial cells, and cellular waste that result in an inflammatory response that causes further damage to the nervous system. Amyloid can also cause atrophy of the smooth muscle of the arteries of the brain, predisposing them to rupture.

INFERENCE

What is the most likely contributing factor in the development of this condition?

The exact etiology of Alzheimer's disease is unknown, however, hypothesized causes include lower levels of neurotransmitters, higher levels of aluminum within brain tissue, genetic inheritance, autoimmune disease, abnormal processing of the substance amyloid, and virus. The risk of developing Alzheimer's disease increases with age and there is a higher incidence in women. The prevalence of Alzheimer's disease increases significantly over the age of 80.

CONFIRMATION

What is the most likely clinical presentation?

Alzheimer's disease is initially noted by a change in higher cortical functions characterized by subtle changes in memory, impaired concentration, and difficulty with new learning. These symptoms progress in the early stages and there is a loss of orientation, word finding difficulties, emotional lability, depression, poor judgment, and impaired ability to perform self-care skills. During the middle stages of Alzheimer's disease the patient will develop behavioral and motor problems characterized by neurological symptoms such as aphasia, apraxia, perseveration, agitation, and violent or socially unacceptable behavior that can include wandering. Eventually all ability to learn is lost and long-term memory also disappears. End-stage Alzheimer's disease is characterized by severe intellectual and physical destruction. Patients in this stage will present with vegetative symptoms including incontinence, functional dependence, the inability to speak, and seizure activity.

What laboratory or imaging studies would confirm the diagnosis?

Alzheimer's disease presently cannot be confirmed until a postmortem biopsy reveals the neurofibrillary tangles and amyloid plaques. MRI can be used to assess any abnormalities or signs of atrophy within the brain that is associated with Alzheimer's disease or to rule out other medical conditions. Single photon emission computed tomography (SPECT) may be used to determine brain activity and predict potential for Alzheimer's disease. Blood work, urine, and spinal fluid may be required to rule out other diseases that may cause signs of dementia.

What additional information should be obtained to confirm the diagnosis?

A physical examination, neurological examination, and neuropsychological testing are required for diagnosis of probable Alzheimer's disease. The patient must demonstrate at least two deficits of cognition, memory, and related cognitive functioning with the absence of all other brain disease or disturbances in consciousness that may contribute to the identified deficits. Family history and symptoms may provide insight into the expected speed of progression of the disease.

EXAMINATION

What history should be documented?

Important areas to explore include past medical history, family history, history of current symptoms, current health status, living environment, social history and habits, occupation, and social support system.

What tests/measures are most appropriate?

Aerobic capacity and endurance: assessment of vital signs at rest and with activity

Arousal, attention, and cognition: examine mental status, learning ability, memory, motivation, Mini-Mental State Examination, level of consciousness

Assistive and adaptive devices: analysis of components and safety of a device

Environmental, home, and work barriers: analysis of current and potential barriers or hazards

Gait, locomotion, and balance: static and dynamic balance in sitting and standing, safety during gait with/without an assistive device, Functional Ambulation Profile, Berg Balance Scale

Motor function: equilibrium and righting reactions, coordination, physical performance scales

Muscle performance: strength assessment

Posture: analysis of resting and dynamic posture

Range of motion: active and passive range of motion

Reflex integrity: assessment of deep tendon and pathological reflexes (e.g., Babinski, ATNR)

Self-care and home management: assessment of functional capacity, Functional Independence Measure (FIM), Barthel Index

Alzheimer's Disease

GOLD

What additional findings are likely with this patient?

A patient with end-stage Alzheimer's disease is at high risk for infection and pneumonia. These patients may experience complications from a persistent vegetative state such as contractures, decubiti, fracture, and pulmonary compromise.

MANAGEMENT

What is the most effective management of this patient?

Medical management of Alzheimer's disease may include pharmacological intervention during the early stages of the disease process. Medications are administered to inhibit acetylcholinesterase, alleviate cognitive symptoms, and control behavioral changes. Drug therapies are usually short-term in effect lasting six to nine months. Tacrine (Cognex), donepezil (Aricept), and rivastigmine (Exelon) are common pharmacological agents used to treat Alzheimer's disease, however, the side effects can be substantial. Physical therapy management should focus on maximizing the patient's remaining function and providing family and caregiver education. The therapist should attempt to create an emotional and physical environment that provides the patient with the opportunity to experience success. Modifying the layout of the patient's living space in order for the patient to easily find items is one example of creating an environment that encourages success. Safety with functional mobility and gait training may be indicated in the early stages of the disease. Later stages may require ongoing caregiver education regarding assistance with mobility, range of motion, and positioning. Many patients require a long-term care facility that specializes in Alzheimer's disease secondary to personality changes, aggressive behavior, and end-stage complications.

What home care regimen should be recommended?

During the early stages of Alzheimer's disease a patient should continue with activity as tolerated and utilize a memory book or other compensatory strategies at home. As the disease progresses, a patient will rely on caregiver support to assist with a daily exercise program. The patient should be encouraged to exercise, ambulate, and participate in everyday activities such as folding laundry, making beds, and assisting with dinner in order to avoid restlessness and wandering.

OUTCOME

What is the likely outcome of a course of physical therapy?

Physical therapy may be indicated intermittently throughout the course of the disease, however, the therapy will not alter or cease the progression of the disease process.

What are the long-term effects of the patient's condition?

Alzheimer's disease is a chronic and progressive disorder and is the fourth leading cause of death in adults. The typical course of the disease averages between seven and eleven years. The leading cause of death of a patient with Alzheimer's disease is infection or dehydration.

COMPARISON

What are the distinguishing characteristics of a similar condition?

Multi-infarct dementia produces symptoms in a step-like manner secondary to ongoing cerebral infarcts. This form of dementia is usually found in patients that are over 70 years of age and is more common in males. Hypertension is a primary risk factor and depression is common. A patient may also experience neurological deficits such as hemiplegia and emotional lability.

CLINICAL SCENARIOS

Scenario One

A 65-year-old female is referred to physical therapy for gait disturbances. The patient resides alone and drives on a regular basis. During the examination the patient reveals that she is sometimes confused when driving. The patient complains that she has difficulty managing her time around the house and requires an extended amount of time to get ready in the morning.

Scenario Two

A 79-year-old male is seen by a therapist in an Alzheimer's residential facility. The physician recommends gait training with a walker. The patient enjoys walking around the unit, however, has fallen several times within the last month.

GOLD

Amyotrophic Lateral Sclerosis

DIAGNOSIS

What condition produces a patient's symptoms?

Amyotrophic lateral sclerosis (ALS) is a chronic degenerative disease that produces both upper and lower motor neuron impairments. Demyelination, axonal swelling, and atrophy within the cerebral cortex, premotor areas, sensory cortex, and temporal cortex cause the symptoms of ALS.

An injury was most likely sustained to which structure?

Rapid degeneration and demyelination occur in the giant pyramidal cells of the cerebral cortex and affect areas of the corticospinal tracts, cell bodies of the lower motor neurons in the gray matter, anterior horn cells, and areas within the precentral gyrus of the cortex. The rapid degeneration causes denervation of muscle fibers, muscle atrophy, and weakness.

INFERENCE

What is the most likely contributing factor in the development of this condition?

The exact etiology of ALS is unknown, however, there are multiple theories of causative factors that include genetic inheritance as an autosomal dominant trait, a slow acting virus, metabolic disturbances, and theories of toxicity of lead and aluminum. Risk for ALS is higher in men and usually occurs between 40 to 70 years of age.

CONFIRMATION

What is the most likely clinical presentation?

Early clinical presentation of ALS may include both upper and lower motor neuron involvement. Early lower motor neuron signs include asymmetric muscle weakness, cramping, and atrophy that are usually found within the hands. Muscle weakness due to denervation eventually causes significant fasciculations, atrophy and wasting of the muscles. The weakness spreads throughout the body over the course of the disease and generally follows a distal to proximal path. Upper motor neuron symptoms occur due to the loss of inhibition of the muscle. Incoordination of movement, spasticity, clonus, and a positive Babinski reflex are some of the indicators of upper motor neuron involvement. Bulbar involvement is characterized by dysarthria, dysphagia, and emotional lability. Initially a person may have either upper or lower motor neuron involvement, but eventually both categories are affected. A patient with ALS will exhibit fatigue, oral motor impairment, fasciculations, spasticity, motor paralysis, and eventual respiratory paralysis.

What laboratory or imaging studies would confirm the diagnosis?

There are multiple tests used to assist with diagnosing ALS. Electromyography assesses fibrillation and muscle fasciculations. Muscle biopsy verifies lower motor neuron involvement rather than muscle disease and a spinal tap may reveal a higher protein content in some patients with ALS. CT scan will appear normal until late in the disease process.

What additional information should be obtained to confirm the diagnosis?

Diagnosis relies heavily on symptoms that determine both upper and lower motor neuron involvement. A patient that presents with motor impairment without sensory impairment is a primary indicator of ALS. Definitive diagnosis also first requires a physician to rule out other neurological conditions such as multiple sclerosis, spinal cord tumors, progressive muscular dystrophy, Lyme disease, and syringomyelia.

EXAMINATION

What history should be documented?

Important areas include past medical history, family history, history of current symptoms, current health status, living environment, social history and habits, occupation, and social support system.

What tests/measures are most appropriate?

Aerobic capacity and endurance: assessment of vital signs at rest and with activity, perceived exertion scale

Anthropometric characteristics: weight and height

Arousal, attention, and cognition: examines mental status, learning ability, memory, motivation

Assistive and adaptive devices: analysis of components and safety of a device

Environmental, home, and work barriers: analysis of current and potential barriers or hazards

Gait, locomotion, and balance: static and dynamic balance in sitting and standing, safety during gait with/without an assistive device

Motor function: motor assessment scales, coordination, equilibrium and righting reactions

Muscle Performance: strength assessment, muscle endurance, muscle tone assessment, muscle atrophy

Neuromotor development and sensory integration: analysis of reflex movement patterns, assessment of involuntary movements, sensory integration tests, gross and fine motor skills

Posture: analysis of resting and dynamic posture

Range of motion: active and passive range of motion

Reflex integrity: assessment of deep tendon and pathological reflexes (e.g., Babinski, ATNR)

Self-care and home management: Barthel Index

Ventilation, respiration, and circulation: respiratory muscle strength, accessory muscle utilization, assessment of cough

What additional findings are likely with this patient?

During the initial stages of ALS there are various effects on the body. Progression of the disease allows for significant deterioration within the brain and spinal cord and a patient may exhibit paralysis of vocal cords, swallowing impairment, contractures, decubiti, and breathing difficulty that requires ventilatory support. Throughout the course of ALS, however, sensation, eye movement, and bowel and bladder function remain preserved.

MANAGEMENT

What is the most effective management of this patient?

Effective management of ALS is based on supportive care and symptomatic therapy. Pharmacological intervention may include riluzole (Rilutek). This drug appears to have an effect on the progression of the disease process, however, its long-term effects are unknown. Symptomatic therapy may include anticholinergic, antispasticity, and antidepressant medications. Physical, occupational, speech, respiratory, and nutritional therapies may be warranted. Physical therapy intervention should focus on the quality of life and should include a low-level exercise program, range of motion, mobility training, assistive/adaptive devices, wheelchair prescription, bronchial hygiene, and energy conservation techniques. Patient, family, and caregiver training are important as the disease continues to progress.

What home-care regimen should be recommended?

A home care regimen for a patient with ALS must consider the rate of disease progression and level of respiratory involvement. Goals should focus on maximizing the patient's functional capacity. A low-level exercise program may be indicated as long as the patient does not exercise to fatigue and promote further weakness. Family involvement is encouraged to support the patient through the course of the disease and assist with mobility, pacing skills, energy conservation techniques, and overall safety. During the latter part of the disease the family and caregivers must be competent with positioning, bronchial hygiene, range of motion, and assistance with mobility.

OUTCOME

What is the likely outcome of a course of physical therapy?

Physical therapy intervention may assist with current issues, however, therapy does not hinder progression of ALS. Therapeutic goals will consider disease progression and focus on teaching for the patient and caregivers.

What are the long-term effects of the patient's condition?

ALS is usually a rapidly progressing neurological disease with an average course of two to five years, with roughly a quarter of patients surviving longer than five years. Research indicates that although there is no structured course of this disease process, if a patient is diagnosed before 50 years of age, the disease is usually longer in course. Death usually occurs from respiratory failure.

COMPARISON

What are the distinguishing characteristics of a similar condition?

Muscular dystrophy (MD) is the term for a group of inherited disorders that are progressive and exhibit degeneration of muscles without sensory or neural impairment. Progressive weakness occurs to the muscle fibers secondary to the absence of dystrophin within the skeletal muscles. This group of disorders presents early in life and usually shortens life expectancy. Disuse atrophy, muscle deterioration, contractures, and cardiac and respiratory weakness are common characteristics of this disease process. A patient with MD usually dies from respiratory/cardiac complications secondary to the primary disease process.

CLINICAL SCENARIOS

Scenario One

A 56-year-old male is diagnosed with ALS and presents with mild atrophy of the hand. The patient owns his own business as a painter and wants to continue working for as long as he can. The patient is referred to physical therapy for a home exercise program.

Scenario Two

A 60-year-old female is referred to physical therapy secondary to a left CVA. The patient was also diagnosed with ALS two years ago, requires the use of a wheelchair for mobility, and occasionally chokes while eating. The patient has assistance at home from her husband who is in good health.

GOLD

Carpal Tunnel Syndrome

DIAGNOSIS

What condition produces a patient's symptoms?

The carpal tunnel is created by the transverse carpal ligament, the scaphoid tuberosity and trapezium, the hook of the hamate and pisiform, and the volar radiocarpal ligament and volar ligamentous extensions between the carpal bones. The median nerve, four flexor digitorum profundus tendons, four flexor digitorum superficialis tendons, and the flexor pollicis longus tendon pass through the carpal tunnel. Carpal tunnel syndrome (CTS) occurs as a result of compression of the median nerve where it passes through the carpal tunnel.

An injury was most likely sustained to which structure?

The median nerve is injured by compression within the carpal tunnel at the wrist. Normal tissue pressure within the tunnel is 2 to 10 mm Hg, but CTS can result in pressure above 30 mm Hg, which further increases with flexion and extension of the wrist. The increase in pressure produces ischemia in the nerve. This results in sensory and motor disturbances in the median nerve distribution of the hand.

INFERENCE

What is the most likely contributing factor in the development of this condition?

Any condition such as edema, inflammation, tumor or fibrosis may cause compression of the median nerve within the carpal tunnel and result in ischemia. The exact etiology of CTS is unclear, however, conditions that produce inflammation of the carpal tunnel that can contribute to CTS include repetitive use, rheumatoid arthritis, pregnancy, diabetes, trauma, tumor, hypothyroidism, and wrist sprain or fracture. Other etiologies include a congenital narrowing of the tunnel and vitamin B6 deficiency.

CONFIRMATION

What is the most likely clinical presentation?

Most patients are diagnosed between 35 and 55 years of age with greater prevalence in women. A patient with CTS will initially present with sensory changes and paresthesia along the median nerve distribution in the hand. It may also radiate into the upper extremity, shoulder, and neck. Symptoms include night pain, weakness of the hand, muscle atrophy, decreased grip strength, clumsiness, and decreased wrist mobility. Initially, muscle atrophy is often noted in the abductor pollicis brevis muscle and progresses to the thenar muscles.

What laboratory or imaging studies would confirm the diagnosis?

Electromyography and electroneurographic studies can be used to diagnose a motor conduction delay along the median nerve within the carpal tunnel. MRI is sometimes used to identify inflammation of the median nerve, altered tendon or nerve positioning within the tunnel or thickening of the tendon sheath.

What additional information should be obtained to confirm the diagnosis?

Physical examination, history, and review of symptoms are extremely important when diagnosing CTS. Provocation testing such as a positive Tinel's sign, a positive Phalen's test, and a positive tethered median nerve stress test along with the other symptoms will assist to confirm the diagnosis.

EXAMINATION

What history should be documented?

Important areas to explore include past medical history, medications, history of symptoms, current health status, occupation, living environment, social history and habits, leisure activities, and social support system.

What tests/measures are most appropriate?

Anthropometric characteristics: wrist and hand circumferential measurements

Arousal, attention, and cognition: examine mental status, learning ability, memory, motivation

Community and work integration: analysis of community, work, and leisure activities

Environmental, home, and work barriers: analysis of current and potential barriers or hazards

Ergonomics and body mechanics: analysis of dexterity and coordination

Integumentary integrity: skin and nailbed assessment, assessment of sensation

Joint integrity and mobility: assessment of hypomobility of a joint, assessment of soft tissue swelling/inflammation, Tinel's sign, Phalen's test, tethered median nerve stress test

Muscle performance: strength assessment including hand musculature

Orthotic, protective, and supportive devices: potential utilization of bracing or splinting

Pain: pain perception assessment scale

Range of motion: active and passive range of motion

Self-care and home management: assessment of functional capacity

Carpal Tunnel Syndrome

GOLD

What additional findings are likely with this patient?

Advanced CTS can present with muscle atrophy of the hand, radiating pain in the forearm and shoulder, and nerve damage with motor and sensory loss. Unrelieved compression creates initial neurapraxia with some demyelination of the axons. This results in eventual axonotmesis and Wallerian degeneration within the nerve distribution. The patient may present with ape hand deformity caused by atrophy of the thenar musculature and first two lumbricals.

MANAGEMENT

What is the most effective management of this patient?

A patient with CTS will initially receive conservative management including local corticosteroid injections, splinting, and physical therapy management. Recent pharmacological intervention has included Methylprednisolone injected proximally to the tunnel. Physical therapy is one aspect of conservative management and includes splinting, carpal mobilization, and gentle stretching. Biomechanical analysis and adaptation of a patient's occupation, work place, leisure activities, and living environment may be necessary.

If conservative treatment fails the patient may require surgery to release the carpal ligament and decompress the median nerve. Newer surgical techniques allow for smaller incisions, less manipulation of the nerve, and are highly successful for long-term relief of symptoms. Post-surgical physical therapy intervention should include the use of moist heat with electrical stimulation, iontophoresis, cryotherapy, gentle massage, desensitization of the scar, tendon gliding exercises, and active range of motion. A patient should initially avoid wrist flexion and a forceful grasp. After four weeks, a patient can progress with active wrist flexion, gentle stretching, putty exercises, light progressive resistive exercise, and continued modification of body mechanics. Radial deviation against resistance should be avoided due to the tendency for irritation and inflammation. Post-surgical rehabilitation usually lasts six to eight weeks.

What home care regimen should be recommended?

A home care regimen should consist of continued stretching and strengthening exercises. The patient must be competent and compliant regarding the use of a splint and follow all work and leisure modifications.

OUTCOME

What is the likely outcome of a course of physical therapy?

Physical therapy intervention should improve a patient's condition and decrease symptoms of CTS within four to six weeks. If conservative treatment fails and the patient requires surgical intervention, rehabilitation may last six to eight weeks.

What are the long-term effects of the patient's condition?

CTS can have minor effects on some patients while having debilitating effects on others. The overall long-term effects are dependent on the degree of involvement, the amount of permanent damage, and the level of success with conservative or surgical management. It is possible to have no long-term effects from this condition if the patient responds positively to physical therapy and the rehabilitation process. Other patients may be left with permanent motor and sensory impairments along the median nerve distribution.

COMPARISON

What are the distinguishing characteristics of a similar condition?

Compression in the tunnel of Guyon occurs with inflammation to the ulnar nerve between the hook of the hamate and the pisiform. This condition occurs from tasks such as leaning during extended handwriting, leaning on bike handles while riding, repetitive gripping activities or trauma. The patient will present with paresthesias along the ulnar distribution, weakness and atrophy of the hypothenar musculature, decreased mobility of the pisiform, and impaired grip strength. This condition can be treated with conservative management or surgical intervention.

CLINICAL SCENARIOS

Scenario One

A 26-year-old female is seen in physical therapy with a diagnosis of bilateral CTS. The patient has not been treated previously for this syndrome and is employed as a telephone sales specialist. The patient complains of pain in her hands, numbness when sleeping and while performing at work, and muscle soreness in both hands.

Scenario Two

A 45-year-old male with CTS is referred to physical therapy ten days after surgical decompression. The patient's post-operative routine includes resting the hand, using a splint, icing, and elevation. Minimal edema is noted at the wrist. The patient is anxious to return to work.

GOLD

Central Cord Syndrome

DIAGNOSIS

What condition produces a patient's symptoms?

Central cord syndrome (CCS) is an incomplete spinal cord lesion that most often results from a cervical hyperextension injury. Symptoms are secondary to damage to the central aspect of the spinal cord. CCS usually occurs from a fall but can occur from other forms of trauma such as a motor vehicle accident.

An injury was most likely sustained to which structure?

The spinal cord sustains bleeding into the central gray matter that causes damage to the centrally located cervical tracts. Injury is caused by a ligamentum flavum (hyperextension) injury or otherwise from anterior compression of the cord due to osteophyte formation. Studies often reveal axonal disruption in the lateral columns at the level of injury with preservation of the gray matter.

INFERENCE

What is the most likely contributing factor in the development of this condition?

The most common mechanism of injury for CCS is a hyperextension injury of the cervical spine. Other potential contributing factors in the development of CCS include cervical spondylosis, narrowing or congenital defect of the spinal canal, tumor, rheumatoid arthritis or syringomyelia. CCS predominantly affects the population over 50 years of age with a greater incidence in men.

CONFIRMATION

What is the most likely clinical presentation?

CCS presents with motor loss that is greater in the upper extremities than the lower extremities and is most severe distally in the upper extremities. This presentation is due to the damage that occurs within the central location of the spinal cord. Sensory loss found below the level of the lesion is usually limited, but can be variable. Lumbar, thoracic, and cervical components proceed medially in order towards the center of the spinal cord. Sacral segments are usually unaffected since they are located laterally within the spinal cord.

What laboratory or imaging studies would confirm the diagnosis?

MRI is used to assess spinal cord impingement from bone or disk. CT scan of the spine will assess spinal canal compromise and the degree of impingement. X-rays can be utilized to assess potential fractures, dislocations, and degree of spondylotic deterioration.

What additional information should be obtained to confirm the diagnosis?

Diagnosis is made using results of MRI, CT scan, and x-ray findings. Information may be obtained from past medical history and mechanism of injury that usually supports the diagnosis of CCS.

EXAMINATION

What history should be documented?

Important areas to explore include past medical history, medications, family history, current symptoms, mechanism of injury, social history and habits, occupation, leisure activities, and social support system.

What tests/measures are most appropriate?

Aerobic capacity and endurance: autonomic responses to positional changes, assessment of vital signs at rest/activity

Arousal, attention, and cognition: examine mental status, learning ability, memory, motivation

Assistive and adaptive devices: analysis of components and safety of a device, wheelchair prescription

Community and work integration: analysis of community, work, and leisure activities

Environmental, home, and work barriers: analysis of current and potential barriers or hazards

Gait, locomotion, and balance: static and dynamic balance in sitting and standing, safety during gait with/without an assistive device, Berg Balance Scale, Tinetti Performance Oriented Mobility Assessment, wheelchair management

Integumentary integrity: skin assessment, American Spinal Injury Association (ASIA)-Standard Neurological Classification of Spinal Cord Injury Sensory Examination

Motor function: equilibrium and righting reactions, posture and balance in sitting

Muscle performance: ASIA-Standard Neurological Classification of Spinal Cord Injury Motor Examination, muscle tone examination

Neuromotor development and sensory integration: analysis of reflex movement patterns

Pain: assessment of neuropathic pain

Posture: analysis of resting and dynamic posture

Range of motion: active and passive range of motion

Reflex integrity: assessment of deep tendon and pathological reflexes (e.g., Babinski, ATNR)

Self-care and home management: assessment of functional capacity, Functional Independence Measure (FIM), Barthel Index

Ventilation, respiration, and circulation: breathing patterns, auscultation of the lungs and heart

What additional findings are likely with this patient?

Each patient with CCS will present differently based on location and extent of injury to the spinal cord. Potential side effects and complications include autonomic dysreflexia, spasticity, neurogenic bladder and bowel, allodynia, and pressure ulcers.

MANAGEMENT

What is the most effective management of this patient?

Rehabilitation services are initiated once the patient is medically stable. Medical management should include physiatry, physical therapy, occupational therapy, vocational counseling, and social services. Methylprednisolone should be administered within eight hours of injury to assist with neurologic recovery. Other pharmacological intervention may include blood pressure medication to combat autonomic dysreflexia, antispasticity medication for treatment of spasticity, anticonvulsants for treatment of neurogenic pain, prophylactic anticoagulants, and antidepressants if warranted. Physical therapy intervention should include patient and caregiver education, range of motion, strengthening, endurance activities, balance retraining, proximal stabilization exercises, and functional mobility based on the patient's current functional status. Adaptive devices may be required to assist with overall mobility. If a patient ambulates, a platform attachment walker may initially be indicated since hand function is usually poor for grasp. Surgical intervention is rare, but may be indicated if compression within the spinal cord persists or progress ceases without cause.

What home care regimen should be recommended?

A home care regimen should include a continuation of exercise, endurance, and functional mobility training based on the patient's current functional abilities. Outpatient physical therapy may be warranted and should modify the home program as necessary.

OUTCOME

What is the likely outcome of a course of physical therapy?

Physical therapy can assist a patient with CCS to attain maximum functional outcome based on level and extent of injury. Overall outcome, however, is based on age, motivation, compliance, and extent of injury.

What are the long-term effects of the patient's condition?

CCS is the most common incomplete spinal cord lesion. The majority of patients with CCS will ambulate, while roughly half will regain bowel and bladder control and some hand function. Older patients do not tend to recover as well as younger ones. Favorable long-term prognostic factors for a good outcome include early hand function, improvement of strength in all extremities during the inpatient stay, and little to no lower extremity involvement.

COMPARISON

What are the distinguishing characteristics of a similar condition?

Anterior cord syndrome (ACS) normally affects two-thirds of the spinal cord and can occur from a cervical flexion injury or anterior spinal artery embolization. There is a complete loss of motor function as well as pain and temperature below the level of the lesion due to damage of the spinothalamic and corticospinal tracts. Preservation of the posterior columns allow for intact vibration and proprioception. ACS has the worst prognosis for all the spinal cord syndromes.

CLINICAL SCENARIOS

Scenario One

A 22-year-old female is admitted to the rehabilitation floor with CCS secondary to an MVA. She has some motion in her lower extremities, shoulders, and trace motion at the elbows. She only wants to practice walking and refuses therapy for any other treatment. She also is currently refusing any form of adaptive equipment for use during ambulation and with dressing. The patient is currently living with her friend and planned to move out of state in six weeks. She is employed as a teacher assistant at a local middle school.

Scenario Two

A 79-year-old male is diagnosed with CCS after being admitted through the emergency room secondary to a fall down his basement steps. He complains of severe neck pain and currently is not able to initiate movement in all four extremities. He is anxious and wants to return home to his second floor apartment as soon as he can. He misses his wife of 60 years who he has cared for since her stroke three years ago.

GOLD

Cerebral Palsy

DIAGNOSIS

What condition produces a patient's symptoms?

Cerebral palsy (CP) is an umbrella term used to describe a group of non-progressive movement disorders that result from brain damage. CP is the most common cause of permanent disability in children.

An injury was most likely sustained to which structure?

There is a wide variety of neurological damage that can occur with injury. Autopsy reports have indicated lesions that include hemorrhage below the lining of the ventricles, damage to the central nervous system that caused neuropathy and anoxia, and hypoxia that caused encephalopathy. Hypoxic and ischemic injuries disrupt normal metabolism that results in global damage to the developing fetus. CP is classified by neurological dysfunction and extremity involvement. Spastic CP involves upper motor neuron damage; athetoid CP involves damage to the basal ganglia.

INFERENCE

What is the most likely contributing factor in the development of this condition?

The etiology may be multifactorial and is sometimes unknown. Risk factors are categorized as prenatal (80%) or perinatal and postnatal (20%) cases. Prenatal risk factors include Rh incompatibility, maternal malnutrition, hypothyroidism, infection, diabetes, and chromosome abnormalities. Perinatal factors include multiple or premature births, breech delivery, low birth weight, prolapsed cord, placenta abruption, and asphyxia. Postnatal factors include CVA, head trauma, neonatal infection, and brain tumor. The most common causative factor of CP is prenatal cerebral hypoxia.

CONFIRMATION

What is the most likely clinical presentation?

CP is the second most common neurological impairment seen in children (following intellectual disability). CP is a neuromuscular disorder of posture and controlled movement, however, clinical presentation is highly variable based on the area and extent of CNS damage. A child may present with high tone, low tone or athetoid movement. CP is classified as monoplegia (one involved extremity), hemiplegia (unilateral involvement of the upper and lower extremities), and quadriplegia (involvement of all extremities). CP is also classified as mild, moderate, and severe. General characteristics include motor delays, abnormal muscle tone and motor control, reflex abnormalities, poor postural control, high risk for hip dislocations, and balance impairments. Intellect, vision, hearing, and perceptual skills are usually altered in conjunction with CP. All other characteristics of CP are classification dependent.

What laboratory or imaging studies would confirm the diagnosis?

If CP is suspected through clinical findings, including seizures, an electroencephalography (EEG) may be performed. X-ray of the hip may rule out hip dislocation; blood and urine tests can be used to investigate a metabolic cause of CP. Observation usually will diagnose CP secondary to the observed outward characteristics.

What additional information should be obtained to confirm the diagnosis?

Diagnosis of CP is regularly confirmed through an extensive neurological evaluation, patient observation, and patient history including developmental progress, and the presence of pathological reflexes. Differential diagnosis is performed to rule out other potential disorders.

EXAMINATION

What history should be documented?

Important areas to explore include past medical history, risk factors, maternal course of pregnancy, medications, family history, current characteristics, social history, and social support system.

What tests/measures are most appropriate?

Aerobic capacity and endurance: assessment of vital signs at rest and with activity, auscultation of the lungs

Arousal, attention, and cognition: examine mental status, learning ability, memory, motivation

Assistive and adaptive devices: analysis of components and safety of a device

Environmental, home, and work barriers: analysis of current and potential barriers or hazards

Gait, locomotion, and balance: static/dynamic balance

Integumentary integrity: skin assessment, assessment of sensation

Joint integrity and mobility: assessment of hyper- and hypomobility of a joint

Motor function: equilibrium and righting reactions, coordination, posture and balance, sensorimotor integration, Barthel Index, Bayley Scale of Infant Development, Bruininks-Oseretsky Test of Motor Proficiency, Alberta Infant Motor Scale, Pediatric Evaluation of Disability Inventory

Muscle performance: muscle tone assessment, strength assessment if appropriate

Neuromotor development and sensory integration: analysis of reflex movement patterns, assessment of involuntary movements, sensory integration tests, gross and fine motor skills, developmental milestones

Orthotic, protective, and supportive devices: analysis of components of a device

Pain: adapted pain scale

Posture: analysis of resting and dynamic posture

Range of motion: active and passive range of motion, assessment of contractures

Reflex integrity: assessment of deep tendon and pathological reflexes (e.g., Babinski, ATNR, Moro)

Sensory integrity: proprioception and kinesthesia

Ventilation, respiration, and circulation: breathing patterns, respiratory strength, accessory muscle utilization

What additional findings are likely with this patient?

Specific additional findings are dependent on the classification and extent of CP. Generally, complications can include aspiration, pneumonia, contractures, scoliosis, and constipation. Intellectual disability and epilepsy are also often present in children diagnosed with CP. Common co-morbidities include learning disabilities, seizure disorders, vision and hearing impairments, bowel and bladder dysfunction, microcephalus, and hydrocephalus. Secondary impairments may include psychosocial issues for the patient and family members.

MANAGEMENT

What is the most effective management of this patient?

Effective medical management of CP requires a life-long team approach. Pharmacological intervention may require antianxiety, antispasticity, and anticonvulsant medications. Physical therapy for CP often uses neurodevelopmental treatment and sensory integration techniques. Treatment should include normalization of tone, patient and caregiver education, motor learning, developmental milestones, positioning, stretching, strengthening, balance, and mobility skills. Adaptive equipment, specialized wheelchair seating, and orthotic prescription may be indicated. Surgical management may be required and include hip correction, contracture release, motor point block, dorsal rhizotomy or correction of scoliosis.

What home care regimen should be recommended?

A home care regimen for a patient with CP is also a life-long process that will require ongoing modification to meet the progression of goals. Family and caregiver involvement are vital for patients with moderate to severe CP. A home program may include patient and caregiver education, exercise, positioning, stretching, mobility training, and strengthening.

OUTCOME

What is the likely outcome of a course of physical therapy?

Physical therapy will attempt to maximize a patient's level of current function and prevent secondary loss. If a patient is going to ambulate, this will usually occur by the age of eight. The ability or inability to ambulate will have a large impact on the direction and goals of therapeutic intervention.

What are the long-term effects of the patient's condition?

CP is a non-progressive, but permanent condition. The long-term effects and overall functional outcome depend on the extent of injury, associated impairments, and caregiver support. Prognosis for mild to moderate CP is a near normal lifespan. Roughly half of children with severe CP die by the age of ten.

COMPARISON

What are the distinguishing characteristics of a similar condition?

Arthrogryposis multiplex congenita (AMC) occurs in utero and is also considered to be non-progressive. AMC is a neuromuscular syndrome classified into three forms. The infant is born with multiple contractures and may have fibrous bands that developed in place of muscle. A patient with AMC should have a normal life expectancy and is typically of normal intelligence. It is usually difficult for these individuals to live independently due to their level of physical disability.

CLINICAL SCENARIOS

Scenario One

A two-year-old female diagnosed with moderate spastic quadriplegia is seen in physical therapy. She is delayed in developmental milestones and beginning to acquire contractures. The parents are very supportive and the child appears happy and cooperative. The child's chart indicates normal intelligence.

Scenario Two

A nine-year-old male is seen in physical therapy at the request of his parents. The patient is diagnosed with moderate low tone quadriplegia, has minimal impairments with intelligence, and has acquired a 30-degree left thoracic scoliosis. The parents requested the evaluation since the child remains nonambulatory.

GOLD

Cerebrovascular Accident

DIAGNOSIS

What condition produces a patient's symptoms?

Cerebrovascular accident (CVA) occurs when there is an interruption of cerebral circulation that results in cerebral insufficiency, destruction of surrounding brain tissue, and subsequent neurological deficit. The ischemia occurs from either a stroke in evolution (the infarct slowly progresses over one to two days) or as a completed stroke (an abrupt infarct with immediate neurological deficits).

An injury was most likely sustained to which structure?

CVA results from prolonged ischemia to an artery within the brain. This condition can cause subsequent neurological damage relative to the size and location of the infarct. Disruption of blood flow to a certain artery will lead to damage of a specific area of the brain and its functions. There are different types of CVA that include ischemic stroke (thrombus, embolus, lacunar) and hemorrhagic stroke (intracerebral, subdural, subarachnoid).

INFERENCE

What is the most likely contributing factor in the development of this condition?

The primary risk factors for CVA are classified as modifiable and non-modifiable. Modifiable factors include hypertension, atherosclerosis, heart disease, diabetes, elevated cholesterol, smoking, and obesity. Hypertension is the most prevalent modifiable cause of CVA. Non-modifiable risk factors include age, race, family history, and sex. Age constitutes the greatest risk for CVA, with the majority of patients sustaining a stroke being greater than 65 years of age.

CONFIRMATION

What is the most likely clinical presentation?

The clinical presentation of a CVA is determined by the location and extent of the infarct. Typical characteristics can include hemiplegia or hemiparesis, sensory, visual, and perceptual impairments, balance abnormalities, dysphagia, aphasia, cognitive deficits, incontinence, and emotional lability.

What laboratory or imaging studies would confirm the diagnosis?

Computed tomography can confirm an area of infarct in the brain and its vascular origin, however, it can present as negative for up to a few days after the event. MRI allows for the diagnosis of ischemia within the brain almost immediately after onset. Positron emission tomography (PET) can provide information regarding cerebral perfusion and cell function. Ultrasonography identifies areas of diminished blood flow in vessels and angiography may identify a clot and determine if surgical intervention is necessary.

What additional information should be obtained to confirm the diagnosis?

A chest x-ray may be warranted to rule out lung disease, while an electrocardiogram is used to examine potential cardiac abnormalities. Diagnosis is usually based upon patient history, physical and neurological examinations, symptoms, and diagnostic testing.

EXAMINATION

What history should be documented?

Important areas to explore include past medical history, medications, risk factor profile, current health status, social history and habits, occupation, living environment, and social support system.

What tests/measures are most appropriate?

Arousal, attention, and cognition: examine mental status, learning ability, memory, motivation, Mini-Mental State Exam, Boston Diagnostic Aphasia Examination

Assistive and adaptive devices: analysis of components and safety of a device

Gait, locomotion, and balance: static and dynamic balance in sitting and standing, safety during gait with an assistive device, Berg Balance Scale, Tinetti Performance Oriented Mobility Assessment, Functional Ambulation Profile

Integumentary integrity: skin and sensation assessment

Motor function: equilibrium and righting reactions, coordination, motor assessment scales

Muscle performance: muscle tone assessment, assessment of active movement, Stroke Rehabilitation Assessment of Movement (STREAM)

Neuromotor development and sensory integration: assess involuntary movements, sensory integration, gross and fine motor skills, reflex movement patterns

Orthotic, protective, and supportive devices: analysis of components of a device, analysis of movement while wearing a device

Posture: analysis of resting and dynamic posture

Pain: pain perception assessment scale

Range of motion: active and passive range of motion

Reflexes: assessment of pathological reflexes (e.g., Babinski, ATNR)

Self-care and home management: assessment of functional capacity, Rankin Scale, NIH Stroke Scale, Functional Independence Measure (FIM)

Sensory integrity: proprioception and kinesthesia

What additional findings are likely with this patient?

A patient with a left CVA may present with weakness or paralysis to the right side, impaired processing, heightened frustration, aphasia, dysphagia, motor apraxia, and right hemianopsia. A patient with a right CVA may present with weakness or paralysis to the left side, poor attention span, impaired awareness and judgment, spatial deficits, memory deficits, left inattention, emotional lability, impulsive behavior, and left hemianopsia. Coma and death are the most severe consequences of a CVA. It is common for patients post CVA to have residual complications and deficits that persist.

MANAGEMENT

What is the most effective management of this patient?

Medical management will initially include medically stabilizing the patient through medication and surgical intervention. Pharmacological intervention can include thrombolytic agents, anticoagulants (contraindicated for hemorrhagic CVA), diuretics, antihypertensives, and potential long-term use of aspirin. Respiratory care must also be a priority during acute rehabilitation. Physical therapy during the acute phase focuses on positioning, pressure relief, sensory awareness and integration, ROM, weight bearing, facilitation, muscle re-education, balance, and postural control. The therapist is responsible for implementing the most appropriate therapeutic strategies based on the degree of impairment. There are many approaches to neurological rehabilitation that include, but are not limited to Bobath's Neuro-Developmental Treatment (NDT), motor control, Brunnstrom's Movement Therapy in Hemiplegia, Rood, and Kabat, Knott, and Voss' Proprioceptive Neuromuscular Facilitation (PNF). Many therapists integrate facets from multiple approaches based on the patient's response to selected interventions.

What home care regimen should be recommended?

The majority of patients require ongoing therapy services as part of their home care regimen. A therapeutic program should be designed for a patient to continue at home independently or with the required level of assistance. Fall prevention, control of spasticity, endurance training, and optimizing functional mobility are important components of a successful home program.

OUTCOME

What is the likely outcome of a course of physical therapy?

A patient that experiences neurological deficits due to a CVA may require physical therapy to assist with motor re-education, sensory stimulation, and functional mobility. The outcome is dependent on the patient's overall health, level of cognition and motivation, motor recovery, residual deficits, and family support.

What are the long-term effects of the patient's condition?

The effects of a CVA can be quite diverse ranging from spontaneous recovery to permanent disability requiring compensatory strategies and techniques in order to function. The first three months of recovery typically reveals the most measurable neurologic recovery and is usually a good indicator of the long-term outcome. Long-term outcome is based on several factors including the site and extent of CVA, premorbid status, age, potential for plasticity of the nervous system, and motivation. Research indicates that a patient can continue to improve the control of movement and show progress for an average of two to three years post CVA.

COMPARISON

What are the distinguishing characteristics of a similar condition?

A transient ischemic attack (TIA) is also characterized by diminished blood supply to the brain, however, it is transient. Although the patient may present with similar symptoms of a CVA, the symptoms last for only a brief period of time. Unlike a CVA, the TIA does not cause permanent residual neurological deficits. A TIA is an indication, however, of future risk for a CVA.

CLINICAL SCENARIOS

Scenario One

A 43-year-old male is diagnosed with a left hemorrhagic CVA due to an aneurysm of the middle cerebral artery. The patient resides with his wife and two teenage sons.

Scenario Two

A 79-year-old female is diagnosed with a right CVA involving the anterior cerebral artery. The patient was unconscious for two days and is functioning at a very low-level. The patient was residing in an independent living facility where she had meals provided for her in the dining area.

GOLD

Down Syndrome

DIAGNOSIS

What condition produces a patient's symptoms?

Down syndrome (trisomy 21) occurs when there is an error in cell division either through nondisjunction (the large majority of cases), translocation or mosaicism and the cell nucleus results in 47 chromosomes. Nondisjunction occurs when faulty cell division results in three specific chromosomes instead of two and extra chromosomes are then replicated for every cell. Translocation occurs when part of a chromosome breaks off during cell division and attaches to another chromosome. The total number of chromosomes remains 46, but Down syndrome exists. Mosaicism occurs right after fertilization when nondisjunction occurs in the initial cell divisions. This results in a mixture of cells with 46 and 47 chromosomes.

An injury was most likely sustained to which structure?

The pair of 21st chromosomes is responsible for Down syndrome when nondisjunction, translocation or mosaicism occurs during cell division.

INFERENCE

What is the most likely contributing factor in the development of this condition?

The exact etiology of Down syndrome is currently unknown. Some theories suggest that an increase in maternal age (and age of the oocyte) may cause predisposition to errors in meiosis. Environmental factors such as virus, paternal age, medical exposure, reproductive medications, and intrinsic predispositions have been associated with Down syndrome.

CONFIRMATION

What is the most likely clinical presentation?

Down syndrome is the most common cause of intellectual disability. Other clinical manifestations include hypotonia, flattened nasal bridge, almond-shaped eyes, abnormally shaped ears, Simian line (palmar crease), epicanthal folds, enlargement of the tongue, congenital heart disease, developmental delay, and a variety of musculoskeletal disorders.

What laboratory or imaging studies would confirm the diagnosis?

During pregnancy a female can be tested for Alpha-fetoprotein, human chorionic gonadotropin, and unconjugated estrogen levels (the triple screen). Three diagnostic studies include chorionic villus sampling, amniocentesis or percutaneous umbilical blood sampling. Detection of Down syndrome occurs in the majority of women tested that are carrying a baby with Down syndrome. After birth a chromosome analysis called a karyotype can be performed to confirm the suspected diagnosis.

What additional information should be obtained to confirm the diagnosis?

In most cases, diagnosis of Down syndrome is made through the physical attributes that are present at birth. Chromosomal testing is used to determine the exact chromosomal pathogenesis.

EXAMINATION

What history should be documented?

Important areas to explore include past medical history including cardiac status, family history, history of seizures, current health status, physical attributes, developmental delay, and social support system.

What tests/measures are most appropriate?

Arousal, attention, and cognition: mental status, learning ability, memory, intelligence testing

Environmental, home, and work barriers: analysis of current and potential barriers or hazards

Ergonomics and body mechanics: analysis of dexterity and coordination

Gait, locomotion, and balance: static and dynamic balance in sitting and standing, safety during gait with/without an assistive device

Integumentary integrity: skin and sensation assessment

Joint integrity and mobility: assessment of hypermobility and hypomobility of a joint, ligamentous laxity

Motor function: equilibrium and righting reactions, motor assessment scales, coordination, posture and balance in sitting, assessment of sensorimotor integration, Peabody Developmental Motor Scales

Muscle performance: strength and tone assessment

Neuromotor development and sensory integration: analysis of reflex movement patterns, assessment of involuntary movements, sensory integration tests, gross and fine motor skills, Bayley Scales of Infant Development

Posture: analysis of resting and dynamic posture

Range of motion: active and passive range of motion

Reflex integrity: assessment of deep tendon and pathological reflexes (e.g., Babinski, ATNR)

Self-care and home management: assessment of functional capacity, WEE-FIM

Ventilation, respiration, and circulation: assessment of cough and clearance of secretions, breathing patterns, respiratory muscle strength, accessory muscle utilization and vital capacity, perceived exertion scale, pulse oximetry, palpation of pulses, pulmonary function testing, auscultation of the lungs and heart

Down Syndrome

GOLD

What additional findings are likely with this patient?

There are many associated impairments that a child with Down syndrome may inherit. Potential manifestations and secondary complications that are associated with Down syndrome include atlantoaxial instability, sensory, hearing, and visual impairments, umbilical hernia, respiratory compromise, and Alzheimer's disease. Persons with Down syndrome also have an increased incidence of celiac disease, epilepsy, constipation, as well as blood, dermatologic, and musculoskeletal disorders.

MANAGEMENT

What is the most effective management of this patient?

Medical management of Down syndrome is a team approach that requires lifelong intervention and should be directed toward the specific medical and developmental goals. The overall goal of treatment is to achieve maximum potential and level of function. Pharmacological intervention is based on a particular characteristic or complication such as leukemia or a seizure disorder. Physical therapy intervention plays an important role in the treatment of Down syndrome. Developmental delay, hypotonia, laxity of the ligaments, and poor strength are key areas for the focus of physical therapy treatment. A child with Down syndrome will also require learning strategies based on his or her level of intellectual disability. Children with Down syndrome regularly have significant verbal-motor impairments when they verbally respond to a stimulus. Physical therapy will not accelerate developmental milestones, but will help the patient avoid compensatory patterns with static positioning and mobility.

What home care regimen should be recommended?

A home care regimen should be multifaceted with caregivers being proficient with all aspects of care. A routine of exercise is highly important for a child with Down syndrome in order to avoid inactivity and obesity. Positioning and handling are key components in order to maximize proper alignment and to minimize pathological reflexes, malalignment, and instability.

OUTCOME

What is the likely outcome of a course of physical therapy?

Physical therapy will assist a child by teaching optimal movement patterns during developmental activities and by improving strength. Physical therapy will be indicated on an intermittent basis based on level of function and secondary complications. Strengthening and endurance activities should be encouraged within a home program.

What are the long-term effects of the patient's condition?

Individuals with Down syndrome today have a longer life expectancy secondary to advances in medical care, however, it is still less than standard life expectancy. Higher mortality results from issues such as congenital heart defects and gastrointestinal anomalies. Immune system dysfunction, repeated respiratory infections, onset of leukemia, pulmonary hypertension, and complications from Alzheimer's disease all contribute to a higher overall mortality rate compared to the general population. The large majority of patients with Down syndrome reach the age of 55.

COMPARISON

What are the distinguishing characteristics of a similar condition?

Prader-Willi syndrome is a genetic disorder that occurs when there is a partial deletion of chromosome 15. Characteristics include hypotonia, difficulties with feeding during infancy, short stature, excessive appetite, and obesity through childhood. Learning disabilities also exist.

CLINICAL SCENARIOS

Scenario One

A six-month-old boy with Down syndrome is evaluated for outpatient physical therapy. Moderate hypotonia exists and the child does not roll or sit with support. The child's chart indicates atlantoaxial instability with minimal subluxation between C1 and C2. The boy's parents are supportive but both work full-time and are concerned about the competence of the daycare provider.

Scenario Two

A 12-year-old-girl with Down syndrome is seen in physical therapy two times per week at her school. The child is status post right femur fracture and the cast was taken off two weeks ago. The physician orders strengthening and cardiovascular endurance activities. The child has mild scoliosis and minimal learning deficits. The child is moderately obese and complains of pain consistently during treatment.

GOLD

Duchenne Muscular Dystrophy

DIAGNOSIS

What condition produces a patient's symptoms?

Duchenne muscular dystrophy (DMD) is a progressive neuromuscular degenerative disorder that manifests symptoms once fat and connective tissue begin to replace muscle that has been destroyed by the disease process. The mutation of the dystrophin gene causes the symptoms of DMD.

An injury was most likely sustained to which structure?

A patient with DMD is born with a mutation in the dystrophin gene Xp21 that normally codes for the muscle membrane protein dystrophin. This gene is found on the X-chromosome and since it is a recessive trait, only males are affected while females are carriers. The lack of dystrophin allows for damage within the sarcolemma with contraction of the muscle. The mutated gene causes weakening of cell membranes, destruction of myofibrils, and loss of muscle contractility. The destroyed muscle cells are replaced with fatty deposits.

INFERENCE

What is the most likely contributing factor in the development of this condition?

The etiology of DMD is inheritance as an X-linked recessive trait. The mother is the silent carrier of this disorder. Since it is a recessive trait, only male offspring will manifest the disorder while female offspring become carriers.

CONFIRMATION

What is the most likely clinical presentation?

Diagnosis of DMD usually occurs between two and five years of age. The first symptoms include a waddling gait, proximal muscle weakness, clumsiness, toe walking, excessive lordosis, pseudohypertrophy of the calf and other muscle groups, and difficulty climbing stairs. DMD primarily affects the shoulder girdle musculature, pectorals, deltoids, rectus abdominis, gluteals, hamstrings, and calf muscles, and is initially identified when a child begins to have difficulty getting off the floor, needing to use the Gowers' maneuver. During this technique a patient uses his hands to stabilize and walk up his legs in order to attain an upright posture. Approximately one-third of patients have some form of learning disability secondary to the dystrophin abnormalities. The disabilities usually present as subtle cognitive and/or behavioral deficits. There is usually rapid progression of this disease with the inability to ambulate by ten to twelve years of age.

What laboratory or imaging studies would confirm the diagnosis?

Electromyography is used to examine the electrical activity within the muscles. A muscle biopsy can be performed to determine the absence of dystrophin and evaluate the muscle fiber size. DNA analysis and high serum creatinine kinase levels in the blood also assist with confirming the diagnosis.

What additional information should be obtained to confirm the diagnosis?

Clinical examination, current symptoms, and family history are used to assist in the diagnosis, the type, and progression of the disease. Definitive diagnosis is made from clinical findings along with EMG and muscle biopsy results.

EXAMINATION

What history should be documented?

Important areas to explore include past medical history, family history, medications, current symptoms, current health status, living and school environment, and social support system.

What tests/measures are most appropriate?

Anthropometric characteristics: circumferential measurements to monitor muscle atrophy

Aerobic capacity and endurance: assessment of vital signs at rest and with activity

Arousal, attention, and cognition: examine mental status, learning ability, memory, motivation

Assistive and adaptive devices: analysis of components and safety of a device

Environmental, home, and work barriers: analysis of current and potential barriers or hazards

Gait, locomotion, and balance: static and dynamic balance in sitting and standing, safety during gait with/without an assistive device

Joint integrity: assessment of hypermobility and hypomobility of a joint, assessment of deformity

Muscle performance: assessment of active movement

Orthotic, protective, and supportive devices: analysis of components of a device, analysis of movement while wearing a device

Pain: pain perception assessment scale

Posture: analysis of resting and dynamic posture

Range of motion: active and passive range of motion, contracture assessment

Ventilation, respiration, and circulation: breathing patterns, respiratory muscle strength, accessory muscle utilization, pulmonary function testing

Duchenne Muscular Dystrophy

GOLD

What additional findings are likely with this patient?

Additional findings occur with progression of the disease. Disuse atrophy, contractures, scoliosis, inability to ambulate, weight gain/obesity, cardiac and respiratory impairments, musculoskeletal deformity, and gastrointestinal dysfunction are the most common findings. Respiratory problems and scoliosis progress once the child is utilizing a wheelchair.

MANAGEMENT

What is the most effective management of this patient?

Medical management of DMD focuses on maintaining function of the unaffected musculature for as long as possible. Pharmacological intervention may include glucocorticoids and immunosuppressant medications. Physical therapy intervention is initially indicated to assist a young child with progression through the developmental milestones. Once a child presents with impairments, physical therapy should focus on maintaining available strength, encouraging mobility, adapting to the loss of function, and promoting family involvement in a home program. Manual muscle testing and range of motion should be evaluated on a consistent basis to determine the pattern and rate of disability. Orthotic prescription, adaptive devices, and wheelchair prescription are areas that will require attention during the course of the disease. Respiratory care will also become a vital part of the plan of care as the patient weakens and strength diminishes. As DMD progresses, treatment will include range of motion, prevention of contracture/deformity, positioning, pain management, breathing exercises and postural drainage, and the use of a wheelchair or adaptive equipment. Ongoing emotional support for the child/family is necessary.

What home care regimen should be recommended?

A home care regimen relies on family involvement for a successful home program. Proper positioning, range of motion, submaximal exercise, and breathing exercises are all important aspects that assist a child to maintain function for as long as possible.

OUTCOME

What is the likely outcome of a course of physical therapy?

Physical therapy is an important aspect in the care of a child with DMD, however, it will not alter the degenerative process of the disease. The goals of physical therapy throughout the course of the disease are to maintain present function, adapt to the progressive loss of mobility skills, and educate the patient and family. It is the role of the therapist to ensure that full and proper training has been completed on all aspects of a patient's care to ensure the highest level of function.

What are the long-term effects of the patient's condition?

DMD is a progressive disorder that occurs early in childhood and progresses rapidly. DMD usually affects cardiac muscle in the later stages of the disease. Death occurs primarily from cardiopulmonary complications due to cardiac muscle involvement or respiratory muscle dysfunction. Death usually takes place by the time a patient is a teenager or less frequently into their 20's.

COMPARISON

What are the distinguishing characteristics of a similar condition?

Facioscapulohumeral dystrophy (FSHD), also known as Landouzy-Dejerine dystrophy, is a form of muscular dystrophy that is also inherited, but the exact genetic origin is unclear. This disease presents later in a child's life, usually between seven and twenty years of age. Characteristics include facial and shoulder girdle weakness, weakness lifting the arms over the head, and difficulty closing the eyes. This disease is more common in males than females. Females tend to be carriers of the disorder. Lifespan remains normal.

CLINICAL SCENARIOS

Scenario One

A three-year-old male was recently diagnosed with DMD. The mother reports that the child can ambulate, but prefers to be carried. The child crawls up the stairs and has been falling more frequently. The patient has two sisters at home and resides in a two-story home. At present, both parents work full-time and the child is enrolled in a home daycare.

Scenario Two

A 12-year-old male diagnosed with DMD is referred to physical therapy secondary to increased weakness and frequent falls. The patient is currently ambulating with bilateral Lofstrand crutches. There is evidence of pseudohypertrophy and a mild plantar flexion contracture. The patient's mother is concerned that he is at risk for serious injury while ambulating at school.

GOLD

Erb's Palsy

DIAGNOSIS

What condition produces a patient's symptoms?

Erb's palsy is a term used to denote an upper brachial plexus injury or palsy that usually results from a difficult birth. This type of injury is the most common palsy related to the brachial plexus. It primarily affects the muscles of the shoulder and elbow.

An injury was most likely sustained to which structure?

The brachial plexus is damaged with the most common avulsion located at Erb's point (which is an area in the anterolateral neck). This damages the nerves supplying the ipsilateral upper limb and shoulder. The muscles affected are those supplied by cervical roots C5 and C6: axillary, lateral pectoral, upper and lower subscapular, suprascapular and partial paralysis of the long thoracic and the musculocutaneous nerves. The result is loss of rotator cuff, deltoid, brachialis, coracobrachialis, and biceps brachii function.

INFERENCE

What is the most likely contributing factor in the development of this condition?

A brachial plexus injury in a newborn usually occurs during a difficult delivery, due to a large baby with a breech presentation, with a prolonged labor or with the use of forceps. One side of the baby's neck is stretched which damages the nerves. If the upper nerves are affected the condition is termed Erb's palsy. One theory suggests that congenital chicken pox or amniotic bands may also produce this condition. When it occurs in adults, the cause typically is an injury that has caused stretching, tearing or other trauma to the upper brachial plexus network.

CONFIRMATION

What is the most likely clinical presentation?

There are four types of brachial plexus injuries: avulsion, rupture, neuroma, and neurapraxia. The clinical presentation is a flaccid paralysis that is nicknamed the "waiter's tip deformity," characterized by a loss of shoulder function, loss of elbow flexion, loss of forearm supination, and the hand positioned in a pinch grip manner.

What laboratory or imaging studies would confirm the diagnosis?

An x-ray or magnetic resonance imaging (MRI) may be performed to see if there is any damage to the bones and joints of the neck and shoulder. The physician may also use an electromyogram (EMG) or nerve conduction studies (NCS) to see if any nerve signals are present in the upper extremity muscles. In complete injuries, motor and sensory nerve conduction studies of median, ulnar, and radial nerves may be conducted.

What additional information should be obtained to confirm the diagnosis?

A complete history from the patient or parent should be taken regarding upper extremity weakness. Other testing that may assist with diagnosis includes the active movement scale, Gilbert Shoulder Classification, and the Pediatric Outcomes Data Collection Instrument.

EXAMINATION

What history should be documented?

Important areas to explore include past medical history including labor and delivery (infant patients), mechanism of injury (adult patients), medications, current health status, nutritional status, social history, occupation, living environment, and support system.

What tests/measures are most appropriate?

Anthropometric characteristics: circumferential measurements of the extremities

Cranial nerve integrity: assessment of muscle innervation by the cranial nerves, dermatome assessment

Environmental, home, and work barriers: analysis of current and potential barriers or hazards (adult cases)

Integumentary integrity: assessment of sensation

Joint integrity and mobility: assessment of hypermobility and hypomobility of a joint

Motor function: equilibrium and righting reactions, motor assessment scales, coordination, posture and balance in sitting, assessment of sensorimotor integration, physical performance scales

Muscle performance: strength assessment, muscle tone assessment

Neuromotor development and sensory integration: analysis of reflex movement patterns, assessment of involuntary movements, sensory integration tests, gross and fine motor skills

Posture: analysis of resting and dynamic posture

Range of motion: active and passive range of motion

Reflex integrity: assessment of deep tendon and pathological reflexes (e.g., Babinski, ATNR)

Self-care and home management: assessment of functional capacity

Sensory integrity: proprioception and kinesthesia

Erb's Palsy

GOLD

What additional findings are likely with this patient?

If amniotic bands were the congenital cause for the brachial plexus injury, the child may exhibit characteristics such as an underdeveloped extremity or deformed area. The patient may also experience glenohumeral subluxation or dislocation, skeletal deformity, poor bone growth, and a learned pattern of non-use of the upper extremity. Overall, the chance of a child having a brachial plexus palsy is equally distributed according to gender, gestational age, and race. It occurs frequently in normal and healthy infants.

MANAGEMENT

What is the most effective management of this patient?

Physical therapy is recommended for a patient with Erb's palsy with the goal of developing a program that focuses on increasing active and passive movement and promoting use of the weak upper extremity for functional activities. Occupational and physical therapies are usually indicated immediately when the patient is diagnosed. The length of treatment will depend on the patient's recovery of active movements. If a patient has spontaneous recovery (full active movements) within three to four months, the caregivers are usually given a home program. However, if spontaneous recovery does not occur within that timeframe, the patient may continue in therapy with close monitoring of progress. If conservative management fails, surgery may be indicated. Surgery will not restore normal function. After surgery, the infant will wear a splint for approximately three to four weeks. Caregiver education is very important regarding positioning to avoid any further traction during the child's daily activities. Other treatment techniques may include adaptation of developmental milestones, weight bearing activities, and other sensory techniques.

What home care regimen should be recommended?

The patient's caregivers must be competent with all aspects of the home program and must perform the program in a consistent fashion. The program should include AROM, PROM, general strengthening, functional activities and integration of the weakened upper extremity into all functional activities.

OUTCOME

What is the likely outcome of a course of physical therapy?

The therapeutic management of a patient with Erb's palsy must begin in infancy (or immediately) in order to achieve optimal functional return. Nerve regeneration remains at a constant speed, however, physical therapy intervention can assist with overall strength and function during recovery.

What are the long-term effects of the patient's condition?

Approximately nine out of ten infants with brachial plexus palsy can recover with conservative treatment. The final functional outcome will depend on the degree of damage to the nerves and the caregiver's ability to maintain their motion and their level of interest towards the affected upper extremity during the initial first few months of life. Since nerves grow at a rate of one inch per month, it may take several months or even years for nerves repaired at the cervical spine to reach the muscles of the hand.

COMPARISON

What are the distinguishing characteristics of a similar condition?

Klumpke's palsy is the name for the brachial plexus palsy where there is an injury from childbirth affecting the spinal nerves C7, C8, and T1. It is uncommon and can be contrasted to Erb's palsy, which affects C5 and C6. Classically, it produces flexion and supination of the elbow, extension of the wrist, hyper-extension of the metacarpophalangeal joints, and flexion of the interphalangeal joints allowing for a "claw hand" posture. The mechanism of injury is traction of the upper extremity while in an abducted position.

CLINICAL SCENARIOS

Scenario One

A six-week-old infant is seen in outpatient physical therapy with a recent diagnosis of Erb's palsy. The mother has taken a leave of absence from her job in order to assist her infant. She also has a set of three-year-old twins and her husband has been deployed for 12 months for duty in Iraq.

Scenario Two

A 56-year-old farmer was admitted to the hospital with a humeral fracture and traction injury to the upper brachial plexus. The injuries were sustained while the farmer was using a piece of faulty equipment. He cannot use the muscles in the C5-C6 distribution and is very anxious to return to work.

GOLD

Guillain-Barre Syndrome

DIAGNOSIS

What condition produces a patient's symptoms?

Guillain-Barre syndrome (GBS) or acute polyneuropathy is a temporary inflammation and demyelination of the peripheral nerves' myelin sheaths, potentially resulting in axonal degeneration. GBS results in motor weakness in a distal to proximal progression, sensory impairment, and possible respiratory paralysis.

An injury was most likely sustained to which structure?

The autoantibodies of GBS attack segments of the myelin sheath of the peripheral nerves. The infecting organism is of similar structure to molecules found on the surface of myelin sheaths. The antibodies produced attack both the organism of infection as well as the Schwann cells due to the similar structure. This decreases nerve conduction velocity and results in weakness or paralysis of the involved muscles. The demyelination that is initiated at Ranvier's nodes occurs secondary to macrophage response and inflammation, and as a result, destruction of the myelin. The body responds to this process and attempts to repair the damage through Schwann cell division and myelinization of the damaged nerves. Motor fibers are predominantly affected.

INFERENCE

What is the most likely contributing factor in the development of this condition?

The exact etiology of GBS is unknown, however, it is hypothesized to be an autoimmune response to a previous respiratory infection, influenza, immunization or surgery. Viral infections, Epstein-Barr syndrome, cytomegalovirus, bacterial infections, surgery, and vaccinations have been associated with the development of GBS.

CONFIRMATION

What is the most likely clinical presentation?

GBS can occur at any age, however, there is a peak in frequency in the young adult population and again in adults that are between their fifth and eighth decades. Incidence is slightly greater in males than females and in Caucasians than African Americans. A patient with GBS will initially present with distal symmetrical motor weakness and will likely experience mild distal sensory impairments and transient paresthesias. The weakness will progress towards the upper extremities and head. The level of disability usually peaks within two to four weeks after onset. Muscle and respiratory paralysis, absence of deep tendon reflexes, and the inability to speak or swallow may also occur. GBS can be life threatening if there is respiratory involvement. There are multiple subtypes of GBS, but the classic type involves acute onset of symptoms with peak impairment within four weeks, followed by a two to four week static period and gradual recovery that can take months to years.

What laboratory or imaging studies would confirm the diagnosis?

GBS can be diagnosed through a cerebrospinal fluid sample that contains high protein levels and little to no lymphocytes. Electromyography will result in abnormal and slowed nerve conduction.

What additional information should be obtained to confirm the diagnosis?

A physical and neurological examination, strength testing, and a review of relevant medical history are all important in the diagnosis of GBS. The National Institute of Neurologic and Communicative Disorders and Stroke has established criteria to assist with the diagnosis of GBS.

EXAMINATION

What history should be documented?

Important areas to explore include past medical, family, and surgical history, recent illness, medications, immunizations, current symptoms and health status, social history and habits, occupation, living environment, and social support system.

What tests/measures are most appropriate?

Aerobic capacity and endurance: vital signs at rest/activity, responses to positional changes

Arousal, attention, and cognition: examine mental status, learning ability, memory, motivation

Assistive and adaptive devices: analysis of components and safety of a device

Cranial nerve integrity: assessment of muscles innervated by the cranial nerves, dermatome assessment

Community and work integration: analysis of community, work, and leisure activities

Gait, locomotion, and balance: static and dynamic balance in sitting and standing, safety during gait with/without an assistive device, Berg Balance Scale, Tinetti Performance Oriented Mobility Assessment, analysis of wheelchair management

Integumentary integrity: skin and sensation assessment

Motor function: equilibrium and righting reactions, coordination, motor assessment scales

Muscle performance: strength and tone assessment

Orthotic, protective, and supportive devices: potential utilization of bracing

Pain: pain perception assessment scale

Range of motion: active and passive range of motion

Reflex integrity: assessment of deep tendon and pathological reflexes

Self-care and home management: assessment of functional capacity

Ventilation, respiration and circulation: pulmonary function tests, assessment of cough and secretions

What additional findings are likely with this patient?

The extent of impairment for each patient depends on the clinical course of the GBS. The patient may also experience pelvic floor muscle weakness, deep muscle pain, and autonomic nervous system involvement including arrhythmia, tachycardia, postural hypotension, heart block, and absent reflexes. Up to 30% of patients require mechanical ventilation during the acute stage. Respiratory assistance can last as long as 50-60 days.

MANAGEMENT

What is the most effective management of this patient?

Medical management of a patient with GBS may require hospitalization for treatment of symptoms. Pharmacological intervention often includes immunosuppressive and analgesic/narcotic medications. Corticosteroids are controversial and usually contraindicated. Cardiac monitoring, plasma exchange (through plasmapheresis), and mechanical ventilation may be required. A tracheostomy may be performed for ventilation. Physical, occupational, and speech therapies are indicated to facilitate neurological rehabilitation. Physical therapy should be initiated upon admission to the hospital with focus on passive range of motion, positioning, and light exercise. During the acute stage a therapist must limit overexertion and fatigue to avoid exacerbation of symptoms. As the patient progresses, intervention may include orthotic, wheelchair or assistive device prescription, exercise and endurance activities, family teaching, functional mobility and gait training, and progressive respiratory therapy. The therapeutic pool may be indicated to initiate movement without the effects of gravity.

What home care regimen should be recommended?

A home care regimen should include breathing exercises and incentive spirometry for respiratory involvement. A patient, along with the caregiver, must continue with therapeutic exercise, ongoing functional mobility training, and endurance activities as tolerated.

OUTCOME

What is the likely outcome of a course of physical therapy?

Physical therapy may assist with recovery, but it cannot alter the course of the disease. Physical therapy intervention may be required on an ongoing basis to assist with recovery that can last from 3-12 months.

What are the long-term effects of the patient's condition?

GBS is an autoimmune response that varies in severity from person to person. Recovery is slow and can last up to two years after onset. Although the majority of patients experience full recovery, some patients will have remaining neurologic deficits, while a very small percentage of patients die from respiratory complications.

COMPARISON

What are the distinguishing characteristics of a similar condition?

Polyneuropathy is a progressive condition that affects the nerves. The most common etiology is metabolic conditions such as diabetes mellitus. Polyneuropathy develops slowly, bilaterally, and symmetrically. The first symptom is often sensory impairment of the distal lower extremities. Pain, diminished deep tendon reflexes, and motor loss are other symptoms of this condition that is marked by exacerbations and remissions. Medical management will focus on stabilizing the underlying metabolic condition.

CLINICAL SCENARIOS

Scenario One

A 25-year-old female has been hospitalized for one week with a diagnosis of GBS. The patient's strength assessment reports 3-/5 bilateral hip strength, 2+/5 bilateral knee strength, and 2-/5 bilateral ankle strength. The patient is anxious to improve and is eager to begin physical therapy. The patient resides alone in a second floor apartment and works as a bank teller.

Scenario Two

A 43-year-old male was admitted to the hospital one month ago with GBS. The patient had significant paralysis and was ventilator dependent. The patient began to improve two weeks ago and was taken off the ventilator. The patient was in good health prior to admission and worked as an independent international sales representative. The patient is diabetic and has a history of alcoholism. He is divorced with no children.

GOLD

Huntington's Disease

DIAGNOSIS

What condition produces a patient's symptoms?

Huntington's disease (HD), also known as Huntington's chorea, is a neurological disorder of the CNS and is characterized by degeneration and atrophy of the basal ganglia (specifically the striatum) and cerebral cortex within the brain.

An injury was most likely sustained to which structure?

HD affects the basal ganglia and cerebral cortex of the brain. The ventricles of the brain become enlarged secondary to atrophy of the basal ganglia and there is extensive loss of small and medium sized neurons. There appears to be an overall decrease in the quantity and activity of gamma-aminobutyric acid (GABA) and acetylcholine neurons that are produced in these areas. The identified neurotransmitters become deficient and are unable to modulate movement. Loss of neurons creates dysfunction in inhibition that results in the symptoms of chorea, bradykinesia, and rigidity. The thalamus is also believed to contribute to the movement disorders associated with the disease process.

INFERENCE

What is the most likely contributing factor in the development of this condition?

HD is genetically transmitted as an autosomal dominant trait with the defect linked to chromosome four and to the gene identified as IT-15. The disease is usually perpetuated by a person that has children prior to the normal onset of symptoms and without knowledge that he/she possesses the defective gene. Genetic testing is able to identify the defective gene for HD prior to the onset of symptoms.

CONFIRMATION

What is the most likely clinical presentation?

The average age for developing symptoms ranges between 35 and 55 years, however, symptoms can develop at any age. HD is a disease that produces a movement disorder, affective dysfunction, and cognitive impairment. The patient will initially present with involuntary choreic movements and a mild alteration in personality. Unintentional facial expressions such as a grimace, protrusion of the tongue, and elevation of the eyebrows are common. As the disease progresses gait will become ataxic and a patient experiences choreoathetoid movement of the extremities and the trunk. Speech disturbances and mental deterioration are common. Late stage HD is characterized by a decrease in IQ, dementia, depression, dysphagia, incontinence, inability to ambulate or transfer, and progression from choreiform movements to rigidity.

What laboratory or imaging studies would confirm the diagnosis?

Magnetic resonance imaging (MRI) or computed tomography (CT scan) may indicate atrophy or abnormalities within the cerebral cortex as well as the basal ganglia. Positron emission tomography (PET) may be used to augment other testing and obtain information regarding blood flow, oxygen uptake, and metabolism of the brain. A DNA marker study may be administered to determine if the autosomal dominant trait is present for HD.

What additional information should be obtained to confirm the diagnosis?

A physical examination, review of symptoms, and family history are important components in the diagnosis of HD.

EXAMINATION

What history should be documented?

Important areas to explore include past medical history, medications, family history, current symptoms, health status, social history/habits, occupation, living environment, and social support system.

What tests/measures are most appropriate?

Aerobic capacity and endurance: assessment of vital signs at rest and with activity

Arousal, attention, and cognition: examine mental status, learning ability, memory, motivation

Gait, locomotion, and balance: static/dynamic balance in sitting/standing, safety during gait, Functional Reach Test, Tinetti Performance Oriented Mobility Assessment, Functional Ambulation Profile

Motor function: equilibrium/righting reactions, coordination

Muscle performance: strength and tone assessment, tremor assessment, testing for dysdiadochokinesia

Neuromotor development and sensory integration: analysis of reflex movement patterns, assessment of involuntary movements

Posture: analysis of resting and dynamic posture

Range of motion: active and passive range of motion

Self-care and home management: assessment of functional capacity, Functional Independence Measure (FIM), Barthel Index

Huntington's Disease

GOLD

What additional findings are likely with this patient?

Dementia and other psychological changes usually occur after neurological symptoms appear. The emotional disorder worsens with progression and may require admission to a psychiatric facility for severe depression and/or suicidal attempts. Secondary complications that can occur from symptoms of HD include loss of range of motion, deformity, pain, communication breakdown, aspiration and choking, fatigue, and weakness from weight loss.

MANAGEMENT

What is the most effective management of this patient?

Medical management of HD requires a team approach including genetic, psychological, and social counseling for the patient and family. Education regarding disease process, coping strategies, and genetic consequences should be initiated immediately following diagnosis. Medical treatment will focus on symptoms and pharmacological management. Drug classes such as anticonvulsants and antipsychotics may assist as these block dopamine transmission, however, have very serious side effects. Commonly utilized drugs include Perphenazine, Haloperidol (Haldol), and Reserpine. Physical, occupational, and speech therapy interventions may be warranted intermittently throughout the course of the disease and should focus on current problems with mobility and self-care skills. Physical therapy should maximize endurance, strength, balance, postural control, and functional mobility. Intervention should focus on motor control and utilize techniques including coactivation of muscles, trunk stabilization, the use of biofeedback, and relaxation in an attempt to maintain a patient's functional status. Patient education should include prone lying, stretching, prevention of deformity and contracture, and safety with mobility. As the disease progresses, the degree of dementia will influence treatment and goals. The therapist must continue to emphasize family involvement and caregiver teaching. As the patient continues to lose function the caregiver will require education regarding posture, seating, assistance with transfers, mobility, and the use of adaptive equipment.

What home care regimen should be recommended?

A home care regimen should include an exercise routine, functional mobility skills, relaxation techniques, range of motion, stretching exercises, and endurance activities. Participation in a home care regimen can assist to maintain the optimal quality of life during the progression of the disease process.

OUTCOME

What is the likely outcome of a course of physical therapy?

Physical therapy is recommended on an intermittent basis throughout the course of the disease. Physical therapy will not prevent further degeneration, however, it will maximize the patient's functional potential and safety. The goal of physical therapy is to attain an optimal functional outcome within the limitations of the disease process.

What are the long-term effects of the patient's condition?

HD is a chronic progressive genetic disorder that is fatal within 15 to 20 years after clinical manifestation. Late stages of the disease result in total physical and mental incapacitation. The patient usually requires an extended care facility due to the burden of care and physical, cognitive, and emotional dysfunction.

COMPARISON

What are the distinguishing characteristics of a similar condition?

Athetoid (dyskinetic) cerebral palsy is a non-progressive motor disorder caused by central nervous system damage specifically to the basal ganglia. Clinical manifestations include slow and involuntary movements, choreiform movements, severe dysarthria, and an increased risk of aspiration pneumonia. The involuntary movements will increase with stress and fatigue and subside with sleep. Physical therapy intervention should focus on motor control and mobility deficits in order to attain the highest level of functioning.

CLINICAL SCENARIOS

Scenario One

A 48-year-old attorney is referred for physical therapy home services. The patient was diagnosed with HD two years ago and resides in a two-story home. The patient has a significant other and they reside together. The patient's primary complaint is a loss of balance while ambulating. The patient refuses to utilize an assistive device.

Scenario Two

A 45-year-old female is referred to physical therapy. She was diagnosed with HD seven years ago and has recently fallen multiple times. According to family members the patient is short-tempered, irritable, and occasionally demonstrates poor judgment. The physician requests physical therapy for an evaluation and home program.

GOLD

Multiple Sclerosis

DIAGNOSIS

What condition produces a patient's symptoms?

Multiple sclerosis (MS) produces patches of demyelination that decreases the efficiency of nerve impulse transmission. Symptoms vary based on the location and the extent of demyelination.

An injury was most likely sustained to which structure?

Multiple sclerosis is characterized by demyelination of the myelin sheaths that surround the nerves within the brain and spinal cord. Myelin breakdown results in plaque development, decreased nerve conduction velocity, and eventual failure of impulse transmission. Lesions are scattered throughout the central nervous system and do not follow a particular pattern.

INFERENCE

What is the most likely contributing factor in the development of this condition?

The exact etiology of MS is unknown. Genetics, viral infections, and environment all have a role in the development of MS. It is theorized that a slow acting virus initiates the autoimmune response in individuals that have environmental and genetic factors for the disease. The incidence of MS is higher in Caucasians between the ages of 20 and 35 years and is nearly twice as common in women as in men. There is also a higher incidence of MS in temperate climates.

CONFIRMATION

What is the most likely clinical presentation?

The prevalence of MS differs by geographic area, sex, and race. The highest incidence is 20-35 years of age, however, MS can occur at any age. MS can be classified as relapsing-remitting MS (85%), secondary-progressive MS, primary-progressive MS or progressive-relapsing MS. The clinical presentation varies based on the type of disease, the location, extent of demyelination, and degree of sclerosis. Initial symptoms can include visual problems, paresthesias and sensory changes, clumsiness, weakness, ataxia, balance dysfunction, and fatigue. The clinical course usually consists of periods of exacerbations and remissions, however, the degree of neurologic dysfunction and subsequent recovery will follow typical patterns of the specific type of MS. The frequency and intensity of exacerbations may indicate the speed/course of the disease process.

What laboratory or imaging studies would confirm the diagnosis?

There is not a single testing procedure to diagnose MS early in the disease. MRI may assist with observation and establishing a baseline for lesions, evoked potentials may demonstrate slowed nerve conduction, and cerebrospinal fluid can be analyzed for an elevated concentration of gamma globulin and protein levels.

What additional information should be obtained to confirm the diagnosis?

Clinical presentation and reliable patient history of symptoms are vital in the diagnosis of MS. Guidelines indicate that a clinically definitive diagnosis of MS can be made if a person experiences two separate attacks and shows evidence of two separate lesions. Other diagnoses (having specific criteria) include laboratory-supported definite MS, clinically probable MS, and laboratory-supported probable MS.

EXAMINATION

What history should be documented?

Important areas to explore include past medical history, history of symptoms, medications, current health status, social history, occupation, living environment, and social support system.

What tests/measures are most appropriate?

Aerobic capacity and endurance: assessment of vital signs at rest and with activity

Arousal, attention and cognition: examine mental status, learning ability, memory, and motivation, Mini-Mental State Examination

Assistive and adaptive devices: analysis of components and safety of a device

Community and work integration: analysis of community, work, and leisure activities

Gait, locomotion, and balance: static/dynamic balance in sitting/standing, Tinetti Performance Oriented Mobility Assessment, Berg Balance Scale

Motor function: assessment of dexterity and coordination; assessment of postural, equilibrium, and righting reactions; gross and fine motor skills

Muscle performance: strength and tone assessment, tremor assessment, muscle endurance, Modified Fatigue Impact Scale

Neuromotor development and sensory integration: analysis of reflex movement patterns

Pain: pain perception assessment scale

Posture: resting/dynamic posture, potential contracture

Range of motion: active and passive range of motion

Self-care and home management: Barthel Index, assessment of functional capacity and safety, Kurtzke Expanded Disability Status Scale

What additional findings are likely with this patient?

A low percentage of patients experience benign MS and have little to no long-term disability. The majority experience progressive degeneration through periods of exacerbations and remissions. As the disease advances exacerbations leave greater ongoing disability and the length of remissions decrease. Ongoing symptoms can include emotional lability, depression, dementia, psychological problems, spasticity, tremor, weakness, paralysis, sexual dysfunction, and loss of bowel and bladder control.

MANAGEMENT

What is the most effective management of this patient?

Management of MS includes pharmacological, medical, and therapeutic intervention. The goal of medical treatment of MS is to lessen the length of exacerbations and maximize the health of the patient. Pharmacological intervention is quite complex and can include ABC drugs (approved in the treatment of MS) that are classified as immunomodulatory medications. Physical, occupational, and speech therapies are indicated throughout the clinical course of the disease and well as nutritional and psychological counseling. Physical therapy intervention includes regulation of activity level, relaxation and energy conservation techniques, normalization of tone, balance activities, gait training, core stabilization and control, and adaptive/assistive device training. Patient and caregiver education regarding safety, energy conservation, patterns of fatigue, and the use of adaptive devices is vital to the quality of life.

What home care regimen should be recommended?

A home care regimen should include a submaximal exercise/ endurance program. Exercise in the morning when the patient is rested is advisable to avoid fatigue. The patient may need frequent rest periods throughout the day and may benefit from breaking a task into smaller steps to avoid fatigue. Ongoing ambulation and mobility activities are important to maintain endurance and prevent disuse atrophy. Aquatic therapy may also be beneficial to this population.

OUTCOME

What is the likely outcome of a course of physical therapy?

Physical therapy is indicated intermittently throughout the clinical course of MS with the goal of maximizing functional capacity and the quality of life. Physical therapy will not alter the progression of the disease process, but rather treat the current symptoms and assist the patient to attain the highest level of function. Factors that influence exacerbations include heat, stress, infection, trauma, and pregnancy.

What are the long-term effects of the patient's condition?

MS is generally a progressive degenerative disease process that creates permanent damage and disability. Factors that influence exacerbations include heat, stress, and trauma. Most patients live with MS for many years and die from secondary complications such as disuse atrophy, pressure sores, contractures, pathological fractures, renal infection, and pneumonia. If left untreated 50% of patients will require a wheelchair within 15 years post diagnosis. Overall mortality rate and long-term outcome correlates to age at diagnosis, number of attacks and exacerbations, frequency and duration of remissions, and type of MS. Suicide is also seven times greater when compared to the same age control group without MS.

COMPARISON

What are the distinguishing characteristics of a similar condition?

Dystonia is a neurologic syndrome that presents with involuntary and sustained muscle contractions that cause repetitive movements. Idiopathic dystonia has a genetic basis and accounts for two-thirds of all cases. Secondary dystonia usually results from brain damage or CNS damage. There are no definitive tests to diagnose dystonia. Treatment is based on current symptoms and includes pharmacological intervention, physical therapy, and occasional surgical intervention.

CLINICAL SCENARIOS

Scenario One

A 28-year-old female has recently had visual difficulty, urinary urgency, tingling, and upper extremity weakness on two separate occasions. The patient has an aunt with MS, however, has no other significant medical history. The patient was referred to physical therapy by her primary physician.

Scenario Two

A 42-year-old male with MS is referred to physical therapy. The patient has experienced several exacerbations and remissions with full recovery in the past. The patient presently appears to have an exacerbation of symptoms including excessive fatigue. He lives alone and works in a library.

GOLD

Parkinson's Disease

DIAGNOSIS

What condition produces a patient's symptoms?

Parkinsonism syndrome is used to describe a group of disorders within subcortical gray matter of the basal ganglia that produces a similar disturbance of balance and voluntary movements. This syndrome occurs as a secondary effect or disorder from another disease process. Parkinson's disease is a primary degenerative disorder and is characterized by a decrease in production of dopamine (neurotransmitter) within the substantia nigra portion of the basal ganglia. The degeneration of the dopaminergic pathways creates an imbalance between dopamine and acetylcholine. This process produces the symptoms of Parkinson's disease.

An injury was most likely sustained to which structure?

Injury occurs to the subcortical gray matter within the basal ganglia, specifically the substantia nigra and the corpus striatum. The basal ganglia store the majority of dopamine and are responsible for modulation and control of voluntary movement. A patient with Parkinson's disease exhibits degeneration of dopaminergic neurons that results in depletion of dopamine production within the basal ganglia. Change in the neurochemical production damages the complex loop between the basal ganglia and the cerebrum.

INFERENCE

What is the most likely contributing factor in the development of this condition?

Primary Parkinson's disease has an unknown etiology and accounts for the majority of patients with Parkinsonism. Contributing factors that can produce symptoms of Parkinson's disease include genetic defect, toxicity from carbon monoxide, excessive manganese or copper, carbon disulfide, vascular impairment of the striatum, encephalitis, and other neurodegenerative diseases such as Huntington's disease or Alzheimer's disease.

CONFIRMATION

What is the most likely clinical presentation?

Roughly half of the patients with Parkinsonism are diagnosed specifically with Parkinson's disease. The risk for developing Parkinson's disease increases with age. The majority of patients are between 50 and 79 years of age, with a small proportion diagnosed before 40 years of age. The majority of patients with Parkinson's disease will initially notice a resting tremor in the hands (sometimes called a pill-rolling tremor) or feet that increases with stress and disappears with movement or sleep. Early in the disease process a patient may attribute symptoms to "old age" such as balance disturbances, difficulty rolling over and rising from bed, and impairment with fine manipulative movements seen in writing, bathing and dressing. A patient's symptoms slowly progress and often include hypokinesia, sluggish movement, difficulty with initiating (akinesia) and stopping movement, festinating and shuffling gait, bradykinesia, poor posture, dysphagia, and "cogwheel" or "lead pipe" rigidity of skeletal muscles. Patients may also experience "freezing" during ambulation, speech, blinking, and movements of the arms. A patient with Parkinson's disease will also have a mask-like appearance with no facial expression.

What laboratory or imaging studies would confirm the diagnosis?

There are no laboratory or imaging studies that initially diagnose Parkinson's disease. CT scan or MRI may be used to rule out other neurodegenerative diseases and obtain a baseline for future comparison.

What additional information should be obtained to confirm the diagnosis?

Definitive diagnosis is difficult during the early stages of the disease. Parkinson's disease is believed to progress slowly over 25 to 30 years prior to the onset of pharmacological intervention. Diagnosis is made from patient history, history of symptoms, and differential diagnosis to rule out other potential disorders. There are evaluation tools that are utilized to classify a patient by stage of the disease process.

EXAMINATION

What history should be documented?

Important areas to explore include past medical history, medications, current symptoms, current health status, social history and habits, occupation, living environment, and social support system.

What tests/measures are most appropriate?

Aerobic capacity and endurance: assessment of vital signs at rest and with activity

Arousal, attention, and cognition: examine mental status, learning ability, memory, motivation, and Mini-Mental State Examination

Environmental, home, and work barriers: analysis of current and potential barriers or hazards

Gait, locomotion, and balance: static and dynamic balance in sitting and standing, Functional Reach Test, Tinetti Performance Oriented Mobility Assessment, Berg Balance Scale, outcome measurement tools, safety with/without an assistive device during gait

Joint integrity and mobility: analysis of quality of movement, examine joint hypermobility and hypomobility

Motor function: assessment of dexterity, coordination and agility, assessment of postural, equilibrium, and righting reactions

Muscle performance: strength assessment, muscle tone assessment, and tremor assessment

Posture: analysis of resting and dynamic posture

Range of motion: active and passive range of motion

Self-care and home management: functional capacity, Barthel Index, safety assessments, Parkinson's disease Questionnaire (PDQ-39)

Sensory integration: assessment of combined sensation, assessment of proprioception and kinesthesia
Ventilation, respiratory, and circulation: assessment of chest wall mobility, expansion, and excursion

What additional findings are likely with this patient?

Since Parkinson's disease is a progressive condition there are ongoing physical and cognitive impairments. A patient may develop a stooped posture and an increased risk for falling. Progression of the disease may result in dysphagia, difficulty with speech, and pulmonary impairment. Greater attention is required for skin care once nutrition and mobility are further compromised. Many patients with Parkinson's disease die from complications of bronchopneumonia.

MANAGEMENT

What is the most effective management of this patient?

The medical management of Parkinson's disease relies heavily on pharmacological intervention. Dopamine replacement therapy, (levodopa, Sinemet, Madopar) is the most effective treatment in reducing the symptoms of Parkinson's disease such as movement disorders, bradykinesia, rigidity, and tremor. Antihistamines, anticholinergics, and antidepressants are also utilized. Physical, occupational, and speech therapies may be warranted intermittently throughout the course of the disease. Physical therapy intervention should include maximizing endurance, strength, and functional mobility. Verbal cueing and oral/visual feedback are effective tools to use with this population. Family teaching, balance activities, gait training, stretching, trunk rotation activities, assistive device training, relaxation techniques, and respiratory therapy are all important components in the treatment of Parkinson's disease. Psychological and nutritional counseling are recommended.

What home care regimen should be recommended?

A home care regimen should include an exercise routine, functional mobility skills, the use of relaxation techniques, range of motion and stretching exercises, and endurance activities. A competent caretaker is vital to the success of the home program and must continuously motivate the patient to continue with mobility and endurance activities in order to avoid deleterious effects of the disease process.

OUTCOME

What is the likely outcome of a course of physical therapy?

Physical therapy is recommended on an intermittent basis throughout the course of the disease and will focus on current symptoms that arise. Physical therapy will not prevent further degeneration or cure the movement disorder, however, it will assist the patient to maximize their level of function and quality of life.

What are the long-term effects of the patient's condition?

Parkinson's disease does not significantly alter a patient's lifespan if the patient is diagnosed with a generalized form between 50 and 60 years of age. As the disease progresses, however, there will be an exacerbation of all symptoms and significant loss of mobility. The inactivity and deconditioning allow for complications and eventual death.

COMPARISON

What are the distinguishing characteristics of a similar condition?

Wilson's disease is inherited as an autosomal recessive trait and causes a defect in the metabolism of copper. The accumulation of copper within the erythrocytes, liver, brain, and kidneys produces the associated degenerative changes. The patient presents with hepatic insufficiency, tremor, choreoathetoid movements, dysarthria, and progressive rigidity.

CLINICAL SCENARIOS

Scenario One

A 35-year-old female is sent to physical therapy shortly after being diagnosed with Parkinson's disease. She is presently having difficulty maintaining a grasp on items from an assembly line at work and complains of frequently tripping.

Scenario Two

A 42-year-old male was diagnosed with Parkinson's disease four years ago. The patient requires physical therapy to reassess gait and prescribe an assistive device. The son states that the patient sits a great deal at home and lacks motivation to engage in exercise.

GOLD

Sciatica Secondary to a Herniated Disk

DIAGNOSIS

What condition produces a patient's symptoms?

A herniated disk is an intervertebral disk that bulges and protrudes posterolaterally against a nerve root. Sciatica is the diagnosis of compression of the sciatic nerve (L4, L5, S1, S2, S3) secondary to a herniated disk causing a patient's symptoms. Other causes for sciatica include tumor, infection, spondylolisthesis, narrowing of the canal, and blood clots.

An injury was most likely sustained to which structure?

As a patient gets older there are natural and significant alterations in the composition of the intervertebral disks and supporting structures. In a herniated disk the nucleus pulposus has bulged posterolaterally secondary to a weakening of the outer annulus fibrosis and posterior longitudinal ligament. The sciatic nerve experiences an inflammatory response and subsequent damage secondary to the compression from the herniated disk.

INFERENCE

What is the most likely contributing factor in the development of this condition?

The most common contributing factor for this condition is the natural aging process. Each decade the composition of the annulus fibrosus and nucleus pulposus is altered and decreases in overall stability. Once there is adequate structural breakdown within the disk, a patient becomes a high risk for injury. A "normal mechanical load on a normal disk" is now an "excessive load on a compromised disk." As expected, sciatica secondary to a herniated disk is most often seen in patients between 40 and 60 years of age.

CONFIRMATION

What is the most likely clinical presentation?

Sciatica is characterized by low back and gluteal pain that typically radiates down the back of the thigh along the sciatic nerve distribution. Sciatic pain occurs from nerve root compression and can be dull, aching or sharp. Pain may have a sudden onset or develop gradually over time. Early sciatica may involve discomfort or pain limited to the low back and gluteal region. Leg pain can become greater than the back pain and can radiate the entire length of the nerve to the toes. The patient may also experience intermittent numbness and tingling localized to the dermatomal distribution, limited thoracolumbar range of motion in all planes, tenderness to palpation at the segment of herniation, and muscle guarding.

What laboratory or imaging studies would confirm the diagnosis?

Radiologic testing of the spine and electrophysiologic studies are initially performed to assist with diagnosis. Other imaging may include myelogram, discography, CT scan or MRI. Blood work may assist with differential diagnosis.

What additional information should be obtained to confirm the diagnosis?

A full examination should be performed that includes history (trauma, osteoporosis, corticosteroid use), functional assessment, inspection, palpation, and special tests. The straight leg raise test will reproduce symptoms in the case of a herniated disk. The exam should also include testing for non-organic back pain to rule out psychological factors.

EXAMINATION

What history should be documented?

Important areas to explore include past medical history and treatment, history of trauma and accidents, medications, family history, current symptoms, current health status, social history and habits, occupation, leisure activities, and social support system.

What tests/measures are most appropriate?

Arousal, attention, and cognition: examine mental status, learning ability, memory, motivation

Assistive and adaptive devices: analysis of components and safety of a device

Community and work integration: analysis of community, work, and leisure activities

Environmental, home, and work barriers: analysis of current and potential barriers or hazards

Ergonomics and body mechanics: analysis of dexterity and coordination

Gait, locomotion, and balance: static and dynamic balance in sitting and standing, Functional Ambulation Profile

Integumentary integrity: skin assessment, assessment of sensation, dermatome testing of the lower extremities

Joint integrity and mobility: assessment of hypermobility and hypomobility of a joint, soft tissue swelling and inflammation

Muscle performance: strength assessment, resisted isometrics, straight leg raise testing

Pain: Oswestry Function Test, McGill Pain Questionnaire, visual analogue scale

Posture: analysis of resting and dynamic posture

Range of motion: active and passive movement of the spine, combined movements, segmental mobility testing

Reflex integrity: assessment of deep tendon and pathological reflexes (clonus)

Self-care and home management: assessment of functional capacity, Functional Independence Measure

What additional findings are likely with this patient?

Sciatica will produce pain that increases with certain positions due to an increase in intradiskal pressure. Pain will increase in a sitting position or when lifting, forward bending or twisting. Sneezing and coughing can also exacerbate the pain. Although a patient may want to stop all activity to relieve pain, prolonged bed rest is contraindicated and will not relieve pain on a long-term basis.

MANAGEMENT

What is the most effective management of this patient?

Medical management of sciatica due to a herniated disk includes short-term bed rest, overall reduction of intradiskal pressure, patient education, physical therapy, medications, and in rare instances surgical intervention. Pharmacological intervention will incorporate NSAIDs initially to relieve pain followed by epidural injections of cortisone and local anesthetics that may be indicated for temporary relief, however, do not alter the root of the problem. Physical therapy intervention should include patient education on positioning and biomechanics, pain management, traction, heat, lumbar stabilization exercises, McKenzie exercises, stretching, and endurance activities. Swimming, stationary bicycling and walking are indicated within tolerance. Lifting, squatting, and climbing are contraindicated due to the significant increase in intradiskal pressure. Most herniations will spontaneously decrease in size with conservative treatment. Research indicates that the majority of patients improve with two to four months of conservative treatment. For those who fail conservative treatment, surgical intervention may include laminectomy, discectomy, chemonucleolysis, laser discectomy or laminotomy.

What home care regimen should be recommended?

A home care regimen should include ongoing caution regarding positioning and constant effort to decrease intradiskal pressure. A home exercise program including stabilization exercises is indicated as well as other aerobic/endurance activities to tolerance.

OUTCOME

What is the likely outcome of a course of physical therapy?

Most patients improve with conservative treatment over a two to four month period. Physical therapy intervention combined with a consistent home program will provide the patient with the necessary tools to relieve pain and improve function.

What are the long-term effects of the patient's condition?

Sciatica secondary to a herniated disk can be corrected through rest and physical therapy intervention. Healing of the disk can also occur and scarring can reinforce the posterior aspect and annular fibers so that it is protected from further protrusion. Restoration of functional mobility is plausible, however, surgical intervention may be required if neurological symptoms increase or no progress is made with conservative measures.

COMPARISON

What are the distinguishing characteristics of a similar condition?

Spinal stenosis is another condition that can be a causative factor of sciatica. Symptoms that would indicate spinal stenosis include lower extremity weakness with or without sciatica, back and leg pain after ambulating a short distance, increasing symptoms with continued ambulation, and relief of symptoms through flexion. Radiologic results reveal disk narrowing and degenerative spondylolisthesis. Surgery is only recommended as a last resort when conservative treatment fails.

CLINICAL SCENARIOS

Scenario One

A 42-year-old female is referred to physical therapy with an L5 herniated disk and sciatica. The patient injured her back skiing three months ago. She presently works 50 hours per week at a daycare facility. Current symptoms include radiating pain down the left leg, a "feeling of weakness," and an inability to sleep at night due to pain.

Scenario Two

A 65-year-old male has been seen in physical therapy for three months with sciatica secondary to a L4 herniated disk. The patient states that he experiences constant pain. The therapist questions the patient's overall compliance with his established home exercise program. The physician orders are prescribed as physical therapy three times per week.

GOLD

Spina Bifida – Myelomeningocele

DIAGNOSIS

What condition produces a patient's symptoms?

Spina bifida is a congenital neural tube defect that generally occurs in the lumbar spine but can also occur at the sacral, cervical, and thoracic levels. Spina bifida has three classifications that include spina bifida - occulta (incomplete fusion of the posterior vertebral arch with no neural tissue protruding), spina bifida - meningocele (incomplete fusion of the posterior vertebral arch with neural tissue/meninges protruding outside the neural arch), and spina bifida - myelomeningocele (incomplete fusion of the posterior vertebral arch with both meninges and spinal cord protruding outside the neural arch).

An injury was most likely sustained to which structure?

Spina bifida - myelomeningocele is characterized by a sac or cyst that protrudes outside the spine and contains a herniation of meninges, cerebrospinal fluid, and the spinal cord through the defect in the vertebrae. The cyst may or may not be covered by skin. Spina bifida results from failure of neural tube closure by day 28 of gestation when the spinal cord is expected to form. Approximately 75% of vertebral defects are found in the lumbar/sacral region, typically L5-S1 with injury to the structures at that level and below. Defects can also occur in the cervical or thoracic spine, however, this is rare.

INFERENCE

What is the most likely contributing factor in the development of this condition?

The incidence varies by socioeconomic status, geographic area, and ethnic background. The overall incidence is declining due to improved prenatal care. The exact etiology for spina bifida - myelomeningocele has not been identified, however, causative and risk factors include genetic predisposition, environmental influence (certain solvents, lead, herbicides, glycol ethers), insulin-dependent diabetes, low levels of maternal folic acid, alcohol, maternal hyperthermia, and certain classifications of drugs (teratogenic exposure and vitamin A toxicity). Theories suggest that the cause is multifactorial rather than a single source of etiology. Prenatal care including recommended amounts of folic acid, especially in the first six weeks of pregnancy, appears to be the most effective way to prevent neural tube defects.

CONFIRMATION

What is the most likely clinical presentation?

Myelomeningocele is a severe condition that is characterized by a sac that is seen on an infant's back protruding from a specific area of the spinal cord. Impairments associated with myelomeningocele include motor and sensory loss below the vertebral defect, hydrocephalus, Arnold-Chiari type II malformation, clubfoot, scoliosis, bowel and bladder dysfunction, and learning disabilities. The higher the neural lesion the worse the prognosis is for survival. The infant will require surgical intervention to close the lesion and in the large majority of cases a shunt is required for hydrocephalus. Approximately two-thirds of children with myelomeningocele and shunted hydrocephalus have normal intelligence and the other third demonstrate only mild intellectual disabilities. Regardless of intelligence, children with myelomeningocele exhibit difficulties with perceptual abilities, attention, problem solving, and memory.

What laboratory or imaging studies would confirm the diagnosis?

Prior to birth a fetal ultrasound may identify the myelomeningocele defect in the spine. Prenatal testing of alpha-fetoprotein (AFP) in the blood will show an elevation in levels that indicate a probable neural tube defect at approximately week 16 of gestation. At birth an obvious sac will be present over the spinal defect. Spinal films and CT scan can evaluate for the presence of defects and hydrocephalus.

What additional information should be obtained to confirm the diagnosis?

Diagnosis is confirmed through prenatal testing or upon visual observation at birth. Past medical history of the mother, history of the pregnancy, and family history of neural tube defects may be noted.

EXAMINATION

What history should be documented?

Important areas to explore with the parents include past medical history, current symptoms and health status, medications, past surgical procedures, living environment, and social support system.

What tests/measures are most appropriate?

Aerobic capacity and endurance: assessment of vital signs at rest and with activity

Arousal, attention, and cognition: examine mental status, learning ability, memory, motivation

Assistive and adaptive devices: use of appropriate devices, analysis of components/safety of a device

Ergonomics and body mechanics: analysis of dexterity and coordination

Gait, locomotion, and balance: developmental milestones assessment, static/dynamic balance in prone and sitting, analysis of wheelchair management, standing with frame, gait with assistive device

Integumentary integrity: skin and sensation assessment

Motor function: equilibrium and righting reactions, motor assessment scales, balance in sitting

Muscle performance: assessment of active movement, muscle tone assessment

Orthotic, protective, and supportive devices: analysis of components of a device, analysis of movement while wearing a device

Range of motion: active and passive range of motion

Reflex integrity: assessment of deep tendon and pathological reflexes (e.g., Babinski, ATNR)

Spina Bifida – Myelomeningocele

GOLD

What additional findings are likely with this patient?

Immediately after birth, an infant with myelomeningocele has an increased risk of meningitis, hemorrhage, and hypoxia, however, surgical intervention may significantly reduce the risks. Ongoing additional findings with myelomeningocele include hydrocephalus, clubfoot, neuropathic fracture, visual problems, osteoporosis, kyphosis, hip dislocations, and latex allergy.

MANAGEMENT

What is the most effective management of this patient?

Medical management of a patient with myelomeningocele begins with immediate surgical intervention to repair and close the defect and for placement of a shunt to alleviate hydrocephalus. Orthopedic surgical intervention may be warranted throughout a patient's life to correct deformities such as clubfoot, hip dysplasia, and scoliosis. Pharmacological intervention may include medications that assist in the management of bowel and bladder dysfunction. Physical and occupational therapies are important components in the management of myelomeningocele. Physical therapy is initiated immediately and focuses on family education regarding positioning, handling techniques, range of motion, and therapeutic play. Long-term physical therapy attempts to maximize functional capacity and may include range of motion, facilitation of developmental milestones, therapeutic exercise, skin care, strengthening, balance, and mobility training. Physical therapy will also assist with wheelchair prescription, assistive and adaptive device selection, and the use of orthotics and splinting.

What home care regimen should be recommended?

A home care regimen should include a formal exercise program, range of motion, and mobility training. Family and caregiver involvement are important in assisting a patient through their exercise program. The home program will require modification as the child matures and goals change.

OUTCOME

What is the likely outcome of a course of physical therapy?

Physical therapy initially evaluates and documents the baseline information regarding the patient's motor and sensory function and level of ability. Physical therapy is ongoing through adolescence and is based on the severity of impairments and the needs of the child. Physical therapy is usually initiated based on symptoms, functional problems, and disability.

What are the long-term effects of the patient's condition?

A patient with myelomeningocele has a near normal life expectancy as long as the patient receives consistent and thorough health care. Functional outcome of the patient depends on the level of injury, the amount of associated impairments, and the caregiver support that is provided.

COMPARISON

What are the distinguishing characteristics of a similar condition?

Anencephaly is a condition that is characterized by failed closure of the cranial end of the neural tube. The cerebral hemispheres do not form and some neural tissue may protrude through the defect. This type of neural tube defect cannot be repaired. Many infants with this condition are stillborn, while others only survive a short time after birth.

CLINICAL SCENARIOS

Scenario One

A six-month-old boy is seen in physical therapy after revision of a ventriculoperitoneal shunt. The parents state that the child has been responsive at home and has been doing well. The child can position himself in prone on elbows and is able to sit with support.

Scenario Two

An 11-year-old girl with a T12 spinal cord lesion is seen in outpatient physical therapy. The patient presently uses a wheelchair for mobility, however, indicates that her goal is to walk in her home. The patient's upper body strength is good and intellect is normal.

GOLD

Spinal Cord Injury – Complete C7 Tetraplegia

DIAGNOSIS

What condition produces a patient's symptoms?

The majority of traumatic spinal cord injuries result from compression, flexion or extension of the spine with or without rotation. Spinal cord injuries are classified as a concussion, contusion or laceration, and injury results in primary and secondary neural destruction. Traumatic injury to the spinal cord produces a physiological and biochemical chain of events that results in vascular impairment and permanent tissue and nerve damage.

An injury was most likely sustained to which structure?

A patient sustains primary damage to the spinal cord and surrounding tissues at the C7 level through disruption of the membrane, displacement or compression of the spinal cord, and subsequent hemorrhage and vascular damage. Secondary damage occurs beyond the level of injury due to biochemicals that are released as a result of the initial damage. This process destroys adjacent cells and neural tracts due to the acute inflammation and can last for days or even weeks. After injury, C7 is the most distal segment of the spinal cord that both the motor and sensory components remain intact.

INFERENCE

What is the most likely contributing factor in the development of this condition?

Statistics from the National Spinal Cord Injury Database (NSCID) indicate that motor vehicle accidents, violence, and falls are the top causes of traumatic spinal cord injury. Statistics also indicate a higher ratio of injury in men and Caucasians. The highest incidence of age of injury occurs between 15 and 30 years of age.

CONFIRMATION

What is the most likely clinical presentation?

Spinal shock, which is the total depression of all nervous system function below the level of lesion, occurs immediately following injury and may last for days. Presentation includes total flaccid paralysis and loss of all reflexes and sensation. Surgical intervention may be required after injury in order to stabilize the spinal cord through decompression and fusion at the site of injury. A Halo device is commonly used with cervical injuries to stabilize the spine. As spinal shock subsides, a patient will experience an increase in muscle tone below the level of lesion and neurologic reflexes reappear. Spasticity will evolve and may become problematic. Autonomic dysreflexia and loss of thermoregulation are other impairments that occur secondary to autonomic nervous system dysfunction. A patient with C7 tetraplegia will also present with impaired cough and ability to clear secretions, altered breathing pattern, and poor endurance. The patient is at high risk for contractures and impaired skin integrity.

What laboratory or imaging studies would confirm the diagnosis?

X-rays of the cervical spine observe the positioning and damage of the involved vertebrae. The results of imaging determine subsequent medical intervention including stabilization of the spine. A myelogram or tomogram may be useful to confirm the extent of surrounding damage at the level of the injury.

What additional information should be obtained to confirm the diagnosis?

Other information commonly obtained in order to support the diagnosis includes physician conducted interviews regarding the mechanism of injury as well as a full neurological examination.

EXAMINATION

What history should be documented?

Important areas to explore include past medical history, medications, mechanism of injury, precautions, current health status, social history and habits, occupation or school responsibilities, living environment, and social support system.

What tests/measures are most appropriate?

Aerobic capacity and endurance: autonomic responses to positional changes, vital signs at rest/activity

Arousal, attention, and cognition: examine mental status, learning ability, memory, motivation

Assistive and adaptive devices: analysis of components and safety of a device, wheelchair prescription, adaptive devices, environmental controls

Integumentary integrity: skin assessment, American Spinal Injury Association (ASIA) - Standard Neurological Classification of Spinal Cord Injury Sensory Examination

Motor function: posture and balance in sitting

Muscle performance: ASIA - Standard Neurological Classification of Spinal Cord Injury Motor Examination, muscle tone assessment

Neuromotor development and sensory integration: analysis of reflex movement patterns

Pain: dysesthetic pain (deafferentation pain), nerve root pain, musculoskeletal pain

Posture: positioning, resting and dynamic posture

Range of motion: active and passive range of motion

Reflex integrity: assessment of deep tendon reflexes and pathological reflexes

Sensory integrity: proprioception and kinesthesia

Ventilation, respiration, and circulation: assessment of cough and clearance of secretions, breathing patterns, respiratory muscle strength, accessory muscle utilization, pulmonary function tests

Spinal Cord Injury – Complete C7 Tetraplegia

GOLD

What additional findings are likely with this patient?

There are many additional findings that can exist with a C7 injury, but the most common complications include orthostatic hypotension, pressure sores, spasticity, heterotopic ossification, and autonomic dysreflexia. Autonomic dysreflexia is considered a medical emergency and requires immediate attention to remove the noxious stimuli and lower the blood pressure or the patient will be at risk for subarachnoid hemorrhage. Other findings that require management include sexual dysfunction, respiratory complications, and pain management (neurogenic, central cord, peripheral nerve or musculoskeletal pain).

MANAGEMENT

What is the most effective management of this patient?

Medical management of a SCI injury has both an acute and rehabilitation phase. The acute phase begins at injury and includes medically stabilizing the patient. Pharmacological intervention is started immediately using methylprednisolone (corticosteroid), lipid peroxidation inhibitors, and drugs that block opiate receptors. These drugs appear to control the amount of secondary damage and improve neurological outcome. Once a patient is medically stable, inpatient rehabilitation, which is typically six to eight weeks, should initially focus on range of motion, positioning in bed, and respiratory management such as cough, clearance of secretions, postural drainage, and incentive spirometry. Compensatory techniques, strengthening, muscle substitution, the use of momentum, and the head-hips relationship should be utilized during all activities. Ongoing intervention should include mat and endurance activities, pressure relief training, wheelchair skills, self-range of motion, transfer skills, and community reintegration.

What home care regimen should be recommended?

A home care regimen should include breathing exercises, incentive spirometry, stretching, and mobility skills. Physical therapy intervention may be indicated for continuation of community skills and furthering the patient's independence within the boundaries of the physical limitations.

OUTCOME

What is the likely outcome of a course of physical therapy?

A patient diagnosed with C7 tetraplegia will require extensive physical therapy with projected outcomes based upon the C7 level of motor and sensory innervation. Typical outcomes at this level include independence with feeding, grooming, and dressing, self-range of motion, independent manual wheelchair mobility, independent transfers, and independent driving with an adapted automobile. Independent living with adaptive equipment is possible.

What are the long-term effects of the patient's condition?

At this time there is no cure for a complete spinal cord injury, therefore a patient with a complete C7 injury will not regain innervation below this level. The triceps, extensor pollicis longus and brevis, extrinsic finger extensors, and flexor carpi radialis will remain the lowest innervated muscles. There will be ongoing musculoskeletal and cardiopulmonary deficits that can increase the risk for other health issues. The latest research suggests, however, that approximately 40% of the spinal cord injured population have a life expectancy over 45 years of age.

COMPARISON

What are the distinguishing characteristics of a similar condition?

Brown-Sequard's syndrome is a condition that results from injury to one side of the spinal cord. Motor function, proprioception, and vibration are lost ipsilateral to the lesion and vibration, pain, and temperature are absent contralateral to the lesion.

CLINICAL SCENARIOS

Scenario One

A patient is diagnosed with T12 paraplegia after a motor vehicle accident. Neurological examination reveals no active movement or sensation below T12. The patient is a chemistry teacher and coaches basketball. He is otherwise in good health.

Scenario Two

A 25-year-old male was injured when he was hit from behind. The blow produced cervical hyperextension and bleeding within the central gray matter of the spinal cord. The patient was diagnosed with central cord syndrome and referred to physical therapy. The patient resides alone in a second floor apartment and is a full-time graduate student.

GOLD

Spinal Cord Injury – Complete L3 Paraplegia

DIAGNOSIS

What condition produces a patient's symptoms?

The majority of traumatic spinal cord injuries result from compression, flexion or extension of the spine with or without rotation. Spinal cord injuries are classified as a concussion, contusion or laceration, and injury results in primary and secondary neural destruction. Traumatic injury to the spinal cord produces a physiological and biochemical chain of events that results in vascular impairment and permanent tissue and nerve damage.

An injury was most likely sustained to which structure?

The forces responsible for spinal fractures are compression, flexion, extension, rotation, shear or distraction forces or a combination of these. A patient sustains primary damage to the spinal cord and surrounding tissues at the L3 level through the disruption of the membrane, displacement or compression of the spinal cord, and subsequent hemorrhage and vascular damage. Secondary damage occurs beyond the level of injury due to biochemicals that are released as a result of the initial damage. This process destroys adjacent cells and neural tracts due to the acute inflammation that can last for days or even weeks. After a complete injury at this level, L3 is the most distal segment of the spinal cord that both the motor and sensory components remain intact.

INFERENCE

What is the most likely contributing factor in the development of this condition?

Statistics from the National Spinal Cord Injury Database (NSCID) indicate that motor vehicle accidents, violence, and falls are the top causes of traumatic spinal cord injury. Statistics also indicate a higher ratio of injury in men and Caucasians. The highest incidence of age of injury occurs between 15 and 30 years of age.

CONFIRMATION

What is the most likely clinical presentation?

Spinal shock occurs immediately after the injury and can last for days. Surgical intervention may be required for stabilization of the spine. The patient is usually required to wear a spinal orthosis to maintain stability. As spinal shock subsides, a patient will experience an increase in muscle tone below the level of lesion and neurologic reflexes reappear. Spasticity will evolve and may become problematic. Patients specifically with a complete lesion at the L3 level typically have at least partial innervation of the gracilis, iliopsoas, quadratus lumborum, rectus femoris, and sartorius. Patients have full use of their upper extremities and have hip flexion, adduction, and knee extension.

What laboratory or imaging studies would confirm the diagnosis?

The evaluation of a patient with an acute lumbar spine fracture should include routine laboratory tests, such as CBC, and electrolytes. X-rays, CT scan, and MRI allows for bony and ligamentous injury diagnosis.

What additional information should be obtained to confirm the diagnosis?

A detailed neurological evaluation should include evaluation of sensory level, posterior column function, normal and abnormal reflexes, and examination of rectal tone and perianal sensation. The cutaneous abdominal reflex, bulbocavernosus reflex, and the presence of the Babinski sign also should be examined.

EXAMINATION

What history should be documented?

Important areas to explore include past medical history, medications, mechanism of injury, precautions, current health status, nutritional status, social history, living environment occupation, and social support system.

What tests/measures are most appropriate?

Aerobic capacity and endurance: autonomic responses to positional changes, vital signs at rest/activity

Arousal, attention, and cognition: examine mental status, memory, motivation, level of consciousness

Assistive and adaptive devices: analysis of components and safety of a device, wheelchair prescription, adaptive devices, environmental controls

Community and work integration: analysis of community, work, and leisure activities

Environmental, home, and work barriers: analysis of current and potential barriers or hazards

Gait, locomotion, and balance: static and dynamic balance in sitting, analysis of wheelchair management

Integumentary integrity: skin assessment, American Spinal Injury Association (ASIA) – Standard Neurological Classification of Spinal Cord Injury Sensory Examination

Motor function: equilibrium and righting reactions, posture and balance in sitting

Muscle performance: ASIA – Standard Neurological Classification of Spinal Cord Injury Motor Examination, muscle tone assessment

Neuromotor development and sensory integration: analysis of reflex movement patterns

Orthotic, protective, and supportive devices: analysis of components of a device and movement with a device

Pain: dysesthetic pain (deafferentation pain), nerve root pain, musculoskeletal pain

Range of motion: active and passive range of motion

Reflex integrity: assessment of deep tendon and pathological reflexes

Self-care and home management: assessment of functional capacity, Functional Independence Measure

Sensory integrity: proprioception and kinesthesia

Spinal Cord Injury – Complete L3 Paraplegia

What additional findings are likely with this patient?

There are many additional findings that can exist with a L3 injury including sexual dysfunction, a nonreflexive bladder, and the need for a bowel program. These patients usually present with flaccid paralysis below the level of lesion and are at risk for pain, urinary tract infections, muscle contractures, and pressure sores.

MANAGEMENT

What is the most effective management of this patient?

Medical emergency management of a patient with a L3 SCI is initiated by stabilization of the patient's airway in order to secure adequate oxygenation. As soon as the patient is stabilized all patients with spinal cord injuries should immediately receive intravenous methylprednisolone since it has proven to control the amount of secondary damage and improve the neurological outcome. The patient may be placed in a thoracolumbar orthosis (TLSO) with restriction of activities or undergo stabilization surgery followed by the use of a TLSO. Once the patient's spine is stable, rehabilitation should be initiated on an inpatient basis for approximately four to eight weeks. Rehabilitation management may include physical, occupational, vocational therapies, physiatry, nutritional consult, counseling services, and case management. Physical therapy should initially focus on mobility including transfers, bed mobility, and wheelchair mobility. Range of motion and selective strengthening programs, endurance activities, and balance activities should be performed on an ongoing basis in order to optimize functional outcomes. Orthotic prescription (KAFOs or AFOs) is recommended once the patient has gained strength to assist with ambulation using crutches. Community reintegration must be a component of the overall rehabilitation program.

What home care regimen should be recommended?

A home care regimen for a patient with L3 SCI should include continued selective strengthening, selective stretching, endurance activities, balance and postural control training, and continued use of all orthotics and assistive/adaptive devices. The patient must continue with a home program in order to attain and maintain the highest level of functioning and endurance.

OUTCOME

What is the likely outcome of a course of physical therapy?

A patient with L3 SCI will usually participate in four to eight weeks of inpatient rehabilitation immediately after injury and stabilization. The patient should be able to function independently from a wheelchair level and ambulation level. Outcome is based on the degree of injury, the patient's mental capacity, outside support, emotional stability, motivation, and co-morbidities.

What are the long-term effects of the patient's condition?

Patients with SCI are always at a greater risk for osteoporosis, pressure ulcers, hypertension, and heterotopic ossification. The leading cause of death at present is pneumonia, followed by nonischemic heart disease and sepsis. Patients with L3 paraplegia should be able to live independently with education regarding the management of their disability.

COMPARISON

What are the distinguishing characteristics of a similar condition?

There are various outcomes from spinal cord injuries that occur in the lumbosacral region. Fractures of the thoracolumbar junction can produce a mixture of cord and root syndromes caused by lesions of the conus medullaris and lumbar nerve roots. Complete damage of the conus medullaris presents with no motor function or sensation below L1. Patients with complete damage to the sacral portion of the cord have no control of bowel and bladder function and sacral motor paralysis.

CLINICAL SCENARIOS

Scenario One

A 16-year-old male involved in an MVA sustained a complete L4 injury that required surgery to stabilize his spine. He has just been transferred to rehabilitation and has a TLSO for support. His parents are divorced and he lives between their two homes.

Scenario Two

A 23-year-old male sustained a conus medullaris injury in an MVA. He was admitted to the acute care hospital and has been having complications regulating his blood glucose level. The patient was diagnosed with type 1 diabetes mellitus when he was seven years old. The patient resides in a two-story condominium.

GOLD

Thoracic Outlet Syndrome

DIAGNOSIS

What condition produces a patient's symptoms?

Thoracic outlet syndrome is a term used to describe a group of disorders that presents with symptoms secondary to neurovascular compression of fibers of the brachial plexus. This usually occurs between the points of the interscalene triangle and the inferior border of the axilla. Compression of the nerves and blood supply can also occur as they pass over the first rib.

An injury was most likely sustained to which structure?

Thoracic outlet syndrome results from compression and damage to the brachial plexus nerve trunks, subclavian vascular supply, and/or the axillary artery. Nerve injury can result in neurapraxia with segmental degeneration and progress to axonotmesis due to continued and unrelieved compression.

INFERENCE

What is the most likely contributing factor in the development of this condition?

Contributing factors in the development of thoracic outlet syndrome include the presence of a cervical rib, an abnormal first rib, postural deviations or changes, body composition, chronic hyperabduction of the arm, hypertrophy or spasms of the scalene muscles, degenerative disorders, and an elongated cervical transverse process.

CONFIRMATION

What is the most likely clinical presentation?

A patient with thoracic outlet syndrome will present with symptoms based on nerve and/or vascular compression. Typical symptoms include diffuse pain in the arm most often at night, paresthesias in the fingers and through the upper extremities, weakness and muscle wasting, poor posture, edema, and discoloration. If the upper plexus is involved, pain will be reported in the neck that may radiate to the face and may follow the lateral aspect of the forearm into the hand. If the lower plexus is involved, pain is reported in the back of the neck and shoulder, which will radiate over the ulnar distribution to the hand. A patient's symptoms are usually enhanced with behaviors that aggravate the symptoms such as poor posture, lifting activities, and movements overhead.

What laboratory or imaging studies would confirm the diagnosis?

X-ray will confirm the presence of a cervical rib or other bony abnormality. Nerve conduction velocity testing may be valuable if a neuropathy exists. Otherwise, diagnosis relies solely on a thorough history of patient symptoms, provocative testing, and a physical examination. Other testing should be used for differential diagnosis to rule out cervical radiculopathy, RSD, myofascial pain syndrome, tumor, carpal tunnel syndrome, brachial plexus injury, ulnar nerve compression, and angina.

What additional information should be obtained to confirm the diagnosis?

A patient can be diagnosed with thoracic outlet syndrome following a thorough history of symptoms, physical examination, and provocative testing that includes Adson maneuver, Wright test, Roos test, Halstead maneuver, Allen test, and the costoclavicular and hyperabduction tests.

EXAMINATION

What history should be documented?

Important areas to explore include past medical history, family history, medications, history of symptoms, current health status, living environment, social history and habits, occupation, and social support system.

What tests/measures are most appropriate?

Anthropometric characteristics: upper extremity circumferential measurements

Arousal, attention, and cognition: examine mental status, learning ability, memory, motivation

Community and work integration: analysis of community, work, and leisure activities

Cranial nerve integrity: assessment of muscles innervation by the cranial nerves, dermatome assessment

Environmental, home, and work barriers: analysis of current and potential barriers or hazards

Ergonomics and body mechanics: analysis of dexterity and coordination

Integumentary integrity: skin assessment, assessment of sensation

Joint integrity and mobility: soft tissue swelling and inflammation, assessment of joint play, palpation of the joint

Motor function: posture and balance; upper quarter screening

Muscle performance: strength assessment

Pain: pain perception assessment scale, assessment of interscalene triangle point tenderness

Posture: analysis of resting and dynamic posture

Range of motion: active and passive range of motion

Reflex integrity: assessment of deep tendon and pathological reflexes (e.g., Babinski, ATNR)

Self-care and home management: assessment of functional capacity

What additional findings are likely with this patient?

A patient with thoracic outlet syndrome may have difficulty sleeping due to excessive pillows or malpositioning of the arm. The patient may have difficulty at work with carrying items on the affected side or with driving a car. Thoracic outlet syndrome most commonly affects the population between 30 and 40 years of age with women being affected more than men.

MANAGEMENT

What is the most effective management of this patient?

Initial medical management of thoracic outlet syndrome takes a conservative approach. If conservative management fails, it is followed by surgical intervention. A patient with thoracic outlet syndrome requires physical therapy intervention to assist with modification of posture, breathing patterns, positioning in bed and at the work site, and gentle stretching. Physical therapy should focus on pain management, strengthening (especially the trapezius, levator scapulae, and rhomboids), joint mobilization, body mechanics, flexibility, and postural awareness. A therapist may utilize modalities such as transcutaneous nerve stimulation, ultrasound, and biofeedback to attain goals. Work site analysis and subsequent activity modification may be necessary to relieve the pain and other symptoms. A patient may benefit from anti-inflammatory agents in combination with physical therapy. If physical therapy management fails, the patient may require surgical decompression of bony or fibrotic abnormalities. The exact type of surgical intervention and approach are chosen by the surgeon based on symptoms and current damage.

What home care regimen should be recommended?

A home care regimen for a patient with thoracic outlet syndrome should include stretching, strengthening, and postural awareness. The patient should utilize these strategies on an ongoing basis at work and with recreational activities in order to promote pain free movement and limit undesirable symptoms associated with the condition.

OUTCOME

What is the likely outcome of a course of physical therapy?

Most patients with thoracic outlet syndrome have positive results from physical therapy intervention and are able to return to their previous level of function within four to eight weeks.

What are the long-term effects of the patient's condition?

If a patient has positive results from physical therapy intervention, there will not be any long-term impairments. However, if the patient's symptoms persist for three to four months, surgical intervention may be warranted. The majority of patients post surgery have a positive response, however, complications from surgery can include winging of the scapula, pneumothorax, and nerve compression. Research indicates no significant long-term difference between surgical resection of the first rib and successful conservative management.

COMPARISON

What are the distinguishing characteristics of a similar condition?

A radial nerve lesion may be caused by direct trauma, excessive traction, entrapment or compression. A patient presents with an inability to extend the wrist, thumb, and fingers. The patient will also present with impaired grip strength and coordination. Splinting is recommended to maintain proper positioning. Passive range of motion is necessary to prevent secondary impairments such as contractures within the hand.

CLINICAL SCENARIOS

Scenario One

A 35-year-old female is seen in physical therapy secondary to pain and paresthesias throughout the left upper extremity. The patient's work history reveals that she is employed as a telemarketer and is required to hold the phone between her ear and shoulder throughout her shift. The patient carries a five-pound brief case with a shoulder strap as she walks one-half mile to work. The patient has a one-year-old child.

Scenario Two

A 45-year-old female is referred to physical therapy secondary to pain when reaching overhead and carrying objects. The patient recently complains of waking up during the night with pain and paresthesias in the involved arm. The patient is very anxious and concerned because she is required to carry items and place them above her head as part of her job at a local production mill.

GOLD

Traumatic Brain Injury

DIAGNOSIS

What condition produces a patient's symptoms?

Traumatic brain injury (TBI) occurs due to an open head injury where there is penetration through the skull or closed head injury where the brain makes contact with the skull secondary to a sudden, violent acceleration or deceleration impact. Traumatic brain injury can also occur secondary to anoxia as with cardiac arrest or near drowning.

An injury was most likely sustained to which structure?

Any structure within the brain is vulnerable to injury; however, primary damage will occur at the site of impact. Secondary damage occurs as a result of metabolic and physiologic reactions to the trauma. Brain injury may include swelling, axonal injury, hypoxia, hematoma, hemorrhage and changes in intracranial pressure (ICP).

INFERENCE

What is the most likely contributing factor in the development of this condition?

Statistics from the Centers for Disease Control indicate that falls and motor vehicle accidents are the two leading causes of TBI. High risk groups include ages 0-4, 15-19, and greater than 65 years of age. Males are at greater risk in each demographic category.

CONFIRMATION

What is the most likely clinical presentation?

The clinical presentation of a TBI varies due to the type, area, extent of injury, and secondary damage within the brain. Characteristics of a TBI may include altered consciousness (coma, obtundity, delirium), cognitive and behavioral deficits, changes in personality, motor impairments, alterations in tone, and speech and swallowing issues.

What laboratory or imaging studies would confirm the diagnosis?

Diagnostic imaging such as CT scan or MRI should be performed immediately in order to rule out hemorrhage, infarction, and swelling. X-rays taken of the cervical spine can be used to rule out fracture and potential for subluxation. An electroencephalogram (EEG), positron emission tomography (PET), and cerebral blood flow mapping (CBF) may also be utilized for diagnosis and baseline data.

What additional information should be obtained to confirm the diagnosis?

A full neurological evaluation by a physician should include a mental examination, cranial nerve assessment, tonal assessment and pupillary reactivity assessment. The physician will classify the patient using the Glasgow Coma Scale and indicate severe (coma), moderate or mild brain injury. The Rancho Los Amigos Levels of Cognitive Functioning can also be used to classify injury and assist with developing an appropriate plan of care.

EXAMINATION

What history should be documented?

Important areas to explore include past medical history, medications, family history, current symptoms, level of cognitive functioning, social history and habits, occupation, leisure activities, and social support system.

What tests/measures are most appropriate?

Aerobic capacity and endurance: vital signs at rest/activity, pulse oximetry, auscultation of lungs

Arousal, attention, and cognition: using Rancho Los Amigos Levels of Cognitive Functioning

Assistive and adaptive devices: analysis of components and safety of a device

Cranial nerve integrity: muscle innervation by the cranial nerves, dermatome assessment

Environmental, home, and work barriers: analysis of current and potential barriers or hazards

Gait, locomotion, and balance: static and dynamic balance in sitting and standing, safety during gait with/without an assistive device, Berg Balance Scale, Tinetti Performance Oriented Mobility Assessment, analysis of wheelchair management

Integumentary integrity: skin and sensation assessment

Joint integrity and mobility: assessment of hypermobility and hypomobility of a joint

Motor function: equilibrium and righting reactions, motor assessment scales, coordination, posture and balance in sitting, assessment of sensorimotor integration, physical performance scales

Muscle performance: strength assessment, muscle tone assessment

Neuromotor development and sensory integration: analysis of reflex movement patterns, assessment of involuntary movements, sensory integration tests, gross and fine motor skills

Orthotic, protective, and supportive devices: analysis of components and movement while wearing a device

Pain: pain perception assessment scale, visual analogue scale, assessment of muscle soreness

Posture: analysis of resting and dynamic posture

Range of motion: active and passive range of motion

Reflex integrity: assessment of deep tendon and pathological reflexes (e.g., Babinski, ATNR)

Self-care and home management: assessment of functional capacity, Functional Independence Measure (FIM), Barthel Index, Rankin Scale, Rivermead Motor Assessment

What additional findings are likely with this patient?

There are multiple impairments that can develop secondary to TBI. Intracranial pressure must be monitored initially since it is at risk to increase or develop hemorrhage. A patient can develop heterotopic ossification, contractures, skin breakdown, seizures, and deep vein thrombosis. A patient with a severe TBI may remain in a persistent vegetative state.

MANAGEMENT

What is the most effective management of this patient?

Medical management is initiated at the site of injury or in the emergency room for life preserving measures. The initial goal is to stabilize the patient, control intracranial pressure, and prevent secondary complications. Surgical intervention may be required in attempt to regain homeostasis within the brain secondary to hemorrhage or fracture. Once a patient is medically stable, physical therapy rehabilitation is initiated. Treatment of a patient with TBI usually includes a team approach with goals based on the patient's level of injury. Pharmacological intervention may include cerebral vasoconstrictive agents, psychotropic agents, hypertensive agents, antispasticity agents, and medication to assist with cognition and attention. Physical therapy will focus on sensory stimulation and PROM for a comatose patient or pathfinding and high-level balance activities for a patient with a mild injury. Physical therapy may include functional mobility training, behavior modification, serial casting, compensatory strategies, vestibular rehabilitation, task specific activities, wheelchair seating, and pulmonary intervention.

What home care regimen should be recommended?

A home care regimen should include ongoing therapeutic activities that focus on goals associated with the patient's current Rancho Los Amigos level. Consistency is vital to the success of a home program. The patient may also participate in a community re-entry based program for the TBI population if warranted by their level of current function.

OUTCOME

What is the likely outcome of a course of physical therapy?

A patient diagnosed with TBI does not have a specific projected outcome. Outcome is based on the degree of primary and secondary damage and the extent of cognitive and behavioral impairments. Physical therapy should continue in all settings until the patient has attained all realistic goals.

What are the long-term effects of the patient's condition?

Long-term effects are determined by the extent of injury and impairments resulting from the TBI. Many patients experience lifelong deficits that do not allow them to return to their pre-injury lifestyle.

COMPARISON

What are the distinguishing characteristics of a similar condition?

Meningitis is a bacterial or viral infection that spreads through the cerebrospinal fluid to the brain. The meninges of the brain become inflamed as well as the meningeal membranes. The patient will have a headache and may complain of stiffness in the neck. The patient may also show symptoms of confusion, fatigue, and irritability. As the virus progresses the patient may experience seizures and may progress into a coma. Medical treatment varies based on the causative strain of the virus/bacteria.

CLINICAL SCENARIOS

Scenario One

A 22-year-old male with TBI is admitted to an inpatient rehabilitation hospital. The patient is presently classified as Rancho Los Amigos Level IV. The patient required surgical decompression after the TBI. The patient's parents are with the patient almost constantly.

Scenario Two

A 42-year-old female sustained a severe TBI in a motor vehicle accident and is presently classified as Rancho Los Amigos Level II. The accident was two weeks ago. Prior to admission the patient was healthy and worked full-time. She has a supportive husband.

GOLD

Vestibular Disorders

DIAGNOSIS

What condition produces a patient's symptoms?

A vestibular disorder occurs when there is a disruption of the sensory information processed by the inner ear and brain with respect to the body's control of balance and eye movements. Typically, disease or injury to these processing areas will result in a vestibular disorder, however, genetic, environmental, and idiopathic etiologies have been recognized as well.

An injury was most likely sustained to which structure?

A vestibular disorder may encompass numerous specific diagnoses including Meniere's disease, benign paroxysmal positional vertigo (BPPV), labyrinthitis, ototoxicity, and acoustic neuroma. Vestibular disorders are classified as either peripheral (e.g., dysfunction of the auditory or vestibular structures in the inner ear) or central (e.g., dysfunction of the nervous system in processing spatial and balance information) with the majority of cases diagnosed as peripheral. However, not all etiologies of dizziness (e.g., due to hyperventilation, dehydration, stress, fatigue) or altered balance (e.g., peripheral neuropathy) are classified as vestibular disorders.

INFERENCE

What is the most likely contributing factor in the development of this condition?

Ear infection, whiplash injury, and head injury are among the most common causes of vestibular disorders in younger individuals. In many individuals, especially those over 50 years of age, the onset of symptoms is idiopathic.

CONFIRMATION

What is the most likely clinical presentation?

The clinical presentation of a vestibular disorder may vary greatly. Symptoms may be intermittent or persistent presenting as either a single attack or repeatedly over time. In many cases, symptoms will diminish or resolve without intervention as the body either heals or compensates for deficits. Typical characteristics can include vertigo, dizziness, nausea, altered balance, auditory changes, and difficulties with cognition, memory or coordination. Less common symptoms include migraine headaches, muscle aches, motion sickness, photosensitivity, auditory sensitivity, and fatigue.

What laboratory or imaging studies would confirm the diagnosis?

A vestibular disorder is typically diagnosed based on a patient's past medical history and a clinical examination. MRI may be utilized to rule out soft tissue abnormalities such as tumor, acoustic neuroma or CVA. Depending on the patient's presentation, laboratory blood and allergy testing may also assist in ruling out differential diagnoses.

What additional information should be obtained to confirm the diagnosis?

Various auditory and vestibular tests may assist in the confirmation of a vestibular disorder. Vestibular testing typically emphasizes assessment of the vestibuloocular reflex (e.g., Dix-Hallpike test, electronystagmography, videonystagmography) and an assessment of balance reactions (e.g., gait on varied surfaces, postural sway with eyes closed). Auditory testing is typically performed formally by an audiologist.

EXAMINATION

What history should be documented?

Important areas to explore include past medical history, medications, family history, current symptoms, current health status, social history and habits, occupation, leisure activities, and social support system.

What tests/measures are most appropriate?

Arousal, attention, and cognition: examine mental status, learning ability, memory, motivation, and level of consciousness

Assistive and adaptive devices: analysis of components and safety of a device

Community and work integration: analysis of community, work, and leisure activities

Cranial nerve integrity: assessment of motor and sensory responses

Environment, home, and work barriers: analysis of current and potential barriers or hazards

Gait, locomotion, and balance: static and dynamic balance in sitting and standing, safety during gait with/without an assistive device, Berg Balance Scale, Sensory Organization Test, Timed Up and Go Test, Unipedal Stance Test, limits of stability testing

Integumentary integrity: assessment of sensation

Motor function: equilibrium and righting reactions, coordination, posture and balance in sitting, assessment of sensorimotor integration

Muscle performance: strength assessment, muscle tone assessment

Reflex integrity: assessment of deep tendon and vestibuloocular reflexes

Self-care and home management: assessment of functional capacity

Sensory integrity: assessment of proprioception and kinesthesia

What additional findings are likely with this patient?

Vestibular deficits can become so severe in some patients that functional mobility is impaired. Patients may experience numerous falls or near falls resulting in additional injuries. Persistent long-term symptoms may cause the patient to experience increased irritability, a loss of self-esteem or depression.

Vestibular Disorders

GOLD

MANAGEMENT

What is the most effective management of this patient?

Medical management may include pharmacological intervention, nutritional counseling, psychological counseling, and surgical intervention depending on the etiology and severity of the patient's symptoms. Pharmacological intervention emphasizes symptom management and is typically only recommended either with the initial onset of symptoms, once differential diagnoses have been ruled out or during an acute exacerbation of symptoms. Commonly used medications include vestibular suppressants (e.g., benzodiazepines, anticholinergics, antihistamines) and steroids (e.g., prednisone). Long-term suppression of symptoms is not typically recommended since the body must experience symptoms in order to develop compensatory strategies. For specific etiologies, antibiotic or antiviral medications may also be prescribed. Nutritional counseling typically emphasizes regulation of the body's fluid balance to stabilize the volume and electrolyte concentrations of the inner ear's endolymph fluid. This may include altering the intake of substances such as sodium and sugar, managing fluid intake, eliminating caffeine and alcohol, and avoiding substances likely to trigger symptoms (e.g., nicotine, aspirin, NSAIDs). Psychological counseling is recommended if a patient is having difficulty coping with or has become disabled by symptoms or is experiencing depression, stress, anxiety or feelings of isolation. For patients who have been unsuccessful in conservatively managing symptoms, surgical options do exist, however, they may be limited depending on the specific etiology. Vestibular rehabilitation includes specific physical therapy interventions designed to assist the patient to habituate (e.g., become less sensitive) to symptoms through adaptation, substitution, cognitive, and symptom prediction strategies. Activities to retrain balance reactions, proprioception, and the vestibuloocular reflex are typically key components of a treatment plan. Examples include gaze stabilization with head movements, single leg stance on variable surfaces, gait with head movement, and maintaining balance with eyes closed. Goals typically include improved static and dynamic balance, decreased reports of dizziness, decreased symptom-related anxiety, and reduced dependence on visual and somatosensory information. Patients undertaking a vestibular rehabilitation program should be counseled regarding the likelihood that symptoms will temporarily worsen with therapeutic interventions before they begin to improve.

What home care regimen should be recommended?

The home care regimen should include activities which facilitate symptom accommodation and habituation. Activities should be assigned as warranted based on the results of the patient examination with the physical therapist ensuring that each task can be performed safely and without debilitating symptom exacerbation.

OUTCOME

What is the likely outcome of a course of physical therapy?

Vestibular rehabilitation is typically recommended if a patient's symptoms have not resolved within an extended timeframe. However, the risk of falling and incidence of falls may be reduced when therapy interventions are initiated closer to the onset. Though largely dependent on the location and severity of damage, vestibular exercises have been shown to be effective in most patients. To attain successful outcomes, goals must be set realistically. This typically requires an emphasis on habituation to symptoms rather than full symptom resolution. Failure to progress may be attributed to the etiology or severity of injury or the patient's unwillingness to therapeutically exacerbate symptoms so that accommodation can be learned.

What are the long-term effects of the patient's condition?

The effects of vestibular disorders can be quite diverse ranging from spontaneous recovery to permanent disability.

COMPARISON

What are the distinguishing characteristics of a similar condition?

Symptoms of orthostatic hypotension may include dizziness, blurred vision, confusion, and loss of balance. The symptoms are typically triggered by a change in body position that temporarily reduces blood flow to the brain (e.g., rapidly moving from supine to standing). Though symptoms may mimic some vestibular disorders, they are not vestibular in origin and typically resolve quickly as blood pressure adapts to the change in position.

CLINICAL SCENARIOS

Scenario One

A 14-year-old sustained a head injury in a motor vehicle accident. She was later diagnosed with benign paroxysmal positional vertigo. She reports that her symptoms are worse when rolling over or getting out of bed. Symptoms have persisted for more than three months.

Scenario Two

A 75-year-old is diagnosed with Meniere's disease. His vertigo symptoms are episodic, but debilitating when present. He has fallen twice at home while experiencing vertigo and has previously declined vestibular rehabilitation, not wanting to exacerbate symptoms further. His spouse is concerned that if he continues to fall, he will eventually sustain a serious injury.

SILVER Level Clinical Application Templates

Level Clinical Application Template Executive Summary

Anterior Cord Syndrome

- An incomplete spinal cord lesion in which the anterior two-thirds of the spinal cord is damaged
- Occurs through a traumatic incident that causes compression or damage to the anterior spinal artery, most often associated with fracture or dislocation
- Typically presents with complete loss of motor function and loss of pain and temperature sensation bilaterally below the level of the lesion due to the damage to the corticospinal and spinothalamic tracts

Bell's Palsy

- Refers to an acute onset of sensory and motor deficits in structures supplied by the facial nerve
- Primarily affects the muscles associated with facial expression, however, it can also impact saliva and tear production
- Is a self-limiting condition that is not life-threatening with majority of patients experiencing a spontaneous recovery that occurs within weeks to months

Cauda Equina Syndrome

- Considered to be a peripheral nerve injury and results from damage and loss of function involving two or more nerves of the cauda equina
- May result from compression on the cauda equina nerve roots, including spinal structure pathology, trauma, infectious conditions, tumor or iatrogenic factors
- Is a self-limiting condition, however, the longer a patient is symptomatic prior to intervention, the less likely the patient is to achieve a complete recovery

Myasthenia Gravis

- An autoimmune disorder that affects the transmission of neuromuscular signals
- Primary feature is muscle weakness within the skeletal muscles, with other neurologic findings being normal (e.g., reflexes, sensation)
- Muscles affected commonly include the ocular muscles and limb musculature (proximal greater than distal)

Post-Polio Syndrome

- 25-50% of patients with poliomyelitis will eventually develop post-polio syndrome.
- Symptoms of post-polio syndrome include muscle weakness, atrophy, fatigue, and sometimes muscular or joint pain
- Treatment is generally multidisciplinary and aimed at controlling symptoms and improving daily function

SILVER

Anterior Cord Syndrome

DIAGNOSIS:

What condition produces a patient's symptoms?

Anterior cord syndrome is an incomplete spinal cord lesion in which the anterior two-thirds of the spinal cord is damaged. Since the dorsal columns are not affected, it is considered an incomplete spinal cord injury or syndrome. The mechanism of injury is typically a cervical flexion injury or through infarction of the anterior spinal artery.

An injury was most likely sustained to which structure?

A flexion injury to the cervical spine can result in the anterior structures becoming compressed and damaged, specifically the anterior spinal artery. The anterior spinal artery supplies blood to the anterior two-thirds of the spinal cord. Damage to this artery results in decreased perfusion to the spinal tracts that it supplies, including the anterior and lateral corticospinal tracts and spinothalamic tracts. The corticospinal tracts are responsible for motor function while the spinothalamic tracts are responsible for the sensations of pain and temperature.

INFERENCE:

What is the most likely contributing factor in the development of this condition?

Anterior cord syndrome can occur through a traumatic incident that causes compression or damage to the anterior spinal artery, most often associated with fracture or dislocation. However, decreased perfusion and vascular insufficiencies can also occur through non-traumatic etiologies. Atherosclerosis, external compression such as a disk protrusion or mass, and aortic pathology have caused anterior cord syndrome.

CONFIRMATION:

What is the most likely clinical presentation?

The patient will typically present with complete loss of motor function and loss of pain and temperature sensation bilaterally below the level of the lesion due to the damage to the corticospinal and spinothalamic tracts. Sensations controlled through the dorsal columns (e.g., proprioception, vibration) remain intact. Autonomic dysfunction such as loss of bowel and bladder function and sexual function is likely, though this is dependent on the level of the lesion. Respiratory function may also be affected.

What laboratory or imaging studies would confirm the diagnosis?

MRI is used to determine the location and extent of the injury. X-rays may be used to determine if there is a fracture or dislocation of a vertebral segment. CT scan may also be used as it is more sensitive than x-ray in detecting injuries to the spine and spinal canal.

What additional information should be obtained to confirm the diagnosis?

Though imaging studies will be used to confirm the presence of anterior cord syndrome, a thorough neurological examination should be performed. Special attention should be given to sensory and motor testing. The ASIA impairment scale can be used to determine the extent of the patient's spinal cord injury.

MANAGEMENT:

What is the most effective management of this patient?

Medical management of a SCI has both an acute and rehabilitation phase. Initial management will consist of medical immobilization and stabilization of the patient. Pharmacological management is immediate and includes methylprednisolone administered in high doses to limit swelling and secondary damage and improve potential neurological outcome. An orthosis (e.g., halo, Minerva) may be used for continued immobilization if a cervical fracture has occurred. Acute physical therapy intervention should include range of motion, respiratory management, pressure relief, skin care education and management, and functional mobility. During the rehabilitation phase, physical therapy consists of strengthening, transfer training, adaptive device training, and ambulation and/or wheelchair management. Compensatory techniques, muscle substitution, the use of momentum, and the head-hips relationship should be utilized during all activities. Most patients with anterior cord syndrome will need to be trained to utilize a wheelchair.

What home care regimen should be recommended?

A home care regimen should consist of exercise such as range of motion and strengthening, functional mobility, and skin care management. Community skill training may be appropriate and participation in an outpatient physical therapy program may be warranted.

OUTCOME:

What is the likely outcome of a course of physical therapy?

A patient with anterior cord syndrome will require extensive physical therapy with projected outcomes based on the actual level of injury. Physical therapy can assist patients to compensate for the injury, however, only minor improvement in motor function is anticipated. Significant neurological recovery following spinal cord infarct is unusual.

What are the long-term effects of the patient's condition?

Currently, there is no cure for a spinal cord injury, though there can be some level of recovery that occurs for 1-2 years after the initial injury. The prognosis for anterior cord syndrome is best when recovery is noted within the first 24 hours after the injury. Otherwise, the prognosis is poor compared to other spinal cord injury syndromes. It is associated with high mortality and poor functional outcomes.

Bell's Palsy

SILVER

DIAGNOSIS

What condition produces a patient's symptoms?

Bell's palsy refers to an acute onset of sensory and motor deficits in structures supplied by the facial nerve. Bell's palsy is typically the result of abnormal pressure on the facial nerve, commonly associated with edema or inflammation. It primarily affects the muscles associated with facial expression, however, it can also impact saliva and tear production.

An injury was most likely sustained to which structure?

The facial nerve (cranial nerve VII) is sometimes referred to as the "nerve of facial expression." It is associated with taste sensation on the anterior aspect of the tongue and voluntary motor control of most facial muscles. The nerve originates in the brainstem, traveling with the vestibulocochlear nerve (cranial nerve VIII) around middle ear structures before exiting through the stylomastoid foramen and passing through the parotid gland where it divides into five major branches.

INFERENCE

What is the most likely contributing factor in the development of this condition?

The etiology of Bell's palsy is typically viral and most frequently caused by the herpes simplex virus, though it has also been linked to the Epstein-Barr virus, varicella zoster virus, and HIV. After initial exposure, the virus may remain dormant for a period of time. Once reactivated, it reproduces and travels along the nerve, infecting the Schwann cells that surround the nerve. The immune system's inflammatory response produces abnormal pressure on the nerve resulting in subsequent symptoms.

CONFIRMATION

What is the most likely clinical presentation?

The onset of Bell's palsy may occur suddenly or progress over a few days. Symptoms typically affect only one side of the face and often begin with a feeling of generalized stiffness or tightness. A facial droop is the most recognizable characteristic of the condition. Other symptoms include difficulties with motor skills that may interfere with eye and mouth closure, eating, and facial expressions (e.g., one-sided smile). Decreased taste sensation, altered tear and saliva production, and increased auditory sensitivity may also be reported.

What laboratory or imaging studies would confirm the diagnosis?

An MRI or CT scan may assist in identifying the presence of an infection or structural abnormality (e.g., tumor, fracture) which may be the cause of pressure on the facial nerve. Blood tests and imaging may be used to rule out conditions which may mimic Bell's palsy, such as Lyme disease and CVA.

What additional information should be obtained to confirm the diagnosis?

A thorough medical history should be obtained to assist in ruling out similar diagnoses and identifying conditions associated with an increased incidence of Bell's palsy. Electromyogram (EMG) may be utilized to evaluate the extent and severity of nerve damage. The preliminary diagnosis is typically made based on a functional assessment of facial muscle performance and symmetry with activities such as smiling, frowning, closing the eyes, baring the teeth, and raising the eyebrows.

MANAGEMENT

What is the most effective management of this patient?

Medical management is typically limited to education, monitoring, and the use of anti-inflammatory medications intended to relieve pressure on the facial nerve. Physical therapy interventions are directed at the prevention of long-term deficits which may occur with paralysis-related muscle shortening, and recovery-related muscle weakness or diminished coordination. Massage, stretching, and moist heat assist in maintaining pliable musculature and increasing comfort. Biofeedback and NMES can assist in targeting specific muscles during strength and coordination retraining activities.

What home care regimen should be recommended?

A home care regimen should consist of massage, strengthening, and stretching interventions as warranted based on the results of the patient examination. Moist heat and the use of NSAIDs often help to relieve mild musculoskeletal discomfort. For patients who are unable to fully close an affected eye or have reduced tear production, protective measures must be taken to prevent permanent eye injury. Lubricating eye drops or ointments may be necessary. Eye protection is especially important during sleep to shield the eye from debris and injury that may cause corneal scratching.

OUTCOME

What is the likely outcome of a course of physical therapy?

Bell's palsy is a self-limiting condition that is not life-threatening. The majority of patients experience a spontaneous recovery which may occur in a matter of weeks. Depending on the severity of the condition, full recovery can take up to six months.

What are the long-term effects of the patient's condition?

Once recovery is complete, patients do not typically have residual functional deficits of the condition. Though uncommon, long-term complications may occur. These may include an altered sense of taste, partial to total paralysis due to nerve damage, synkinesis resulting from abnormal nerve regeneration or partial to complete blindness due to eye injuries.

SILVER

Cauda Equina Syndrome

DIAGNOSIS

What condition produces a patient's symptoms?

Cauda equina syndrome (CES) is considered to be a peripheral nerve injury and results from damage and loss of function involving two or more nerves of the cauda equina. CES is associated with numerous mechanisms of injury and typically presents as a complex of symptoms.

An injury was most likely sustained to which structure?

The spinal cord typically extends to L1, terminating with the conus medullaris. Paired lower lumbar, sacral, and coccygeal nerve roots extend beyond the conus medullaris and are termed the cauda equina. The cauda equina provides sensory innervation to the "saddle area" of the lower extremities, lower extremity motor innervation, parasympathetic innervation to the bowel and bladder, and voluntary control over the associated sphincters. The nerves of the cauda equina are more susceptible to damage than most other nerve root pairs due to a poorly developed protective epineurium and the tendency to form edema even with mild injury.

INFERENCE

What is the most likely contributing factor in the development of this condition?

CES may result from any source of compression on the cauda equina nerve roots, including spinal structure pathology (e.g., ruptured disk, fracture, stenosis), trauma (e.g., fall, gunshot wound), infectious conditions (e.g., abscess or tuberculosis), tumor or iatrogenic factors.

CONFIRMATION

What is the most likely clinical presentation?

CES may develop slowly or rapidly depending on the underlying pathology. For patients with gradual onset, diagnosis may be difficult since early symptoms may be poorly defined or mimic other conditions. Altered reflexes, pain, and decreased strength and sensation are common symptoms. Other symptoms can include severe back pain, functional impairment, diminished sensation in the saddle distribution, bowel and bladder dysfunction (e.g., retention or incontinence), and sexual dysfunction. The incidence of CES is higher in adults, however, children with spinal birth defects may also be at an increased risk.

What laboratory or imaging studies would confirm the diagnosis?

MRI studies are able to identify the widest range of potential etiologies as they are able to best delineate soft tissue structures and pathology (e.g., tumor, abscess). Compression due to bony abnormalities, such as narrowed disk spaces, altered bony alignment or arthritic changes are more readily identified with x-ray imaging or a CT scan.

What additional information should be obtained to confirm the diagnosis?

A thorough medical history should be obtained and a physical examination performed if CES is suspected. The physical examination should include an assessment of lower extremity muscle strength, sensation, and deep tendon reflexes. Perineal sensation, reflexes, and rectal tone should also be assessed.

MANAGEMENT

What is the most effective management of this patient?

Surgical and medical interventions are typically directed toward nerve root decompression. Though CES is not fatal, it can signal a surgical emergency since delayed intervention may limit long-term outcomes. Medical management may include radiation therapy or chemotherapeutic agents for tumor-related compression. Other pharmaceutical agents may also be used for compression (e.g., anti-inflammatory, antibiotic agents). Physical therapy interventions should emphasize maximal functional return and accommodation for residual deficits. Therapeutic exercise, functional mobility training, coordination activities, sensory stimulation, orthotics, and adaptive equipment training are typical components of the plan of care. Physical therapists may also provide education related to bowel and bladder retraining. Modalities such as biofeedback and neuromuscular electrical stimulation may assist in targeted muscle retraining.

What home care regimen should be recommended?

A home care regimen should be consistent with physical therapy interventions, including therapeutic exercise and activities that emphasize functional independence with adaptive equipment.

OUTCOME

What is the likely outcome of a course of physical therapy?

A patient with CES does not have a specific projected outcome. Outcomes are based on the degree of primary and secondary damage and the extent of motor and sensory impairments. Physical therapy should continue until the patient has attained realistic goals.

What are the long-term effects of the patient's condition?

Long-term effects are determined by the extent of injury and the resulting impairments. CES is a self-limiting condition, however, the longer a patient is symptomatic prior to intervention, the less likely the patient is to achieve a complete recovery. Morbidity is typically associated with long-term effects including weakness and bowel or bladder dysfunction. Other complications may include the development of decubitus ulcers or thrombus formation.

Myasthenia Gravis

SILVER

DIAGNOSIS

What condition produces a patient's symptoms?

Myasthenia gravis is an autoimmune disorder that affects the transmission of neuromuscular signals. The immune system produces antibodies that attack nerve receptors. Because neuromuscular function is decreased, patients with myasthenia gravis have symptoms of weakness and fatigue.

An injury was most likely sustained to which structure?

The pathology associated with myasthenia gravis occurs at the neuromuscular junction. Normally, there are receptors on the motor end plate that accept acetylcholine, which results in the transmission of an action potential. In patients with myasthenia gravis there are fewer receptors on the motor end plate, secondary to the immune system attacking these receptors, which results in an inefficient nerve transmission process.

INFERENCE

What is the most likely contributing factor in the development of this condition?

Though there is no known cause for myasthenia gravis, abnormalities with thymus function likely plays a role. The majority of patients with myasthenia gravis have abnormalities of the thymus (e.g., tumor, hyperplasia), and it is thought that dysfunction of this gland may cause an autoimmune reaction within the body. Women tend to develop the condition in their twenties and thirties while men develop it in their fifties and sixties. In general, women are more likely to be affected by this condition.

CONFIRMATION

What is the most likely clinical presentation?

The primary feature of myasthenia gravis is muscle weakness within the skeletal muscles, with other neurologic findings being normal (e.g., reflexes, sensation). The muscles fatigue rapidly with activity, however, rest quickly improves muscle function. Muscles affected commonly include the ocular muscles and limb musculature (proximal greater than distal). Because the ocular muscles are commonly affected, the patient can experience diplopia and ptosis. Myasthenia gravis can also affect the muscles involved in facial expression, chewing, swallowing, and speech. Triggers that may make a patient's symptoms worse include activity, heat, stress, illness, certain medications, menstruation, and pregnancy. A myasthenic crisis refers to an episode in which the respiratory muscles experience paralysis and the patient needs ventilation to assist with respiration.

What laboratory or imaging studies would confirm the diagnosis?

There are several tests that can be performed to confirm the presence of myasthenia gravis. Laboratory testing of the blood can be used to identify the presence of the antibodies that attack the acetylcholine receptors. Electromyography can be used to identify the characteristic symptom of myasthenia gravis, rapid fatigue with repeated muscle stimulation. Edrophonium chloride, a drug that blocks the degradation of acetylcholine, can be administered to determine if symptoms temporarily improve secondary to increased acetylcholine uptake. Imaging studies (e.g., x-ray, CT scan, MRI) may be performed if the presence of a thymus tumor is suspected.

What additional information should be obtained to confirm the diagnosis?

A thorough medical history and physical examination should be performed to identify the characteristic symptoms of myasthenia gravis and differentiate this condition from other similar conditions, such as hyperthyroidism or botulism. The physical examination will likely consist of an assessment of the ocular and facial muscles, as well as other neurologic testing including sensory, strength, and reflex testing. The examination may also include pulmonary function testing to determine if the respiratory muscles have been affected.

MANAGEMENT

What is the most effective management of this patient?

Patients with myasthenia gravis are often administered a medication that helps to inhibit acetylcholinesterase, the enzyme that breaks down acetylcholine. This allows acetylcholine to build up at the neuromuscular junction, which diminishes the symptoms of weakness and fatigue. Though this medication helps to improve symptoms, it only does so temporarily. Other medications, such as corticosteroids, can help suppress the immune system, thereby improving symptoms. Surgical intervention to remove the thymus gland is another possible treatment to reduce symptoms, especially for those patients who have a thymus tumor. In serious cases with acute worsening of symptoms, plasmapheresis can be performed to remove the antibodies from the blood. Physical therapy should focus on strength and endurance training with caution to avoid overexertion. Therapy may also involve training in breathing techniques to improve respiratory function.

What home care regimen should be recommended?

The home care regimen should consist of a general exercise program to help improve strength and endurance. The patient should follow energy conservation techniques to avoid overexertion.

OUTCOME

What is the likely outcome of a course of physical therapy?

Physical therapy will not be the primary intervention for patients with myasthenia gravis, though a course of physical therapy can help patients to improve muscular strength and endurance and improve functioning with daily activities. Patients will also be instructed in energy conservation techniques.

What are the long-term effects of the patient's condition?

With appropriate treatment, the prognosis for myasthenia gravis is fairly good. Symptoms are generally most severe within the first few years of diagnosis. Afterwards, symptoms either plateau or improve. Though complete remission is rare, symptoms can be well controlled and patients can experience a high quality of life. Removal of the thymus can result in complete remission of symptoms in some patients. Overall, mortality rates are very low.

SILVER

Post-Polio Syndrome

DIAGNOSIS

What condition produces a patient's symptoms?

Poliomyelitis is a neurologic condition characterized by asymmetric weakness and/or paralysis caused by a viral infection. Vaccines for the virus were created in the 1950s resulting in eradication of the disease in developing countries. However, for patients who had poliomyelitis and recovered, new neuromuscular symptoms can appear years after their recovery. This new onset of weakness is termed post-polio syndrome.

An injury was most likely sustained to which structure?

The original condition involved a viral attack on the nervous system, specifically on the anterior horn cells within the spinal cord. With the death of anterior horn cells, the motor nerves degrade and the muscles experience atrophy. Recovery of strength in these patients was thought to occur secondary to collateral sprouting to help reinnervate denervated muscles (i.e., a single nerve innervates a larger proportion of muscle fibers). Though the collateral sprouting allows for a period of recovery, the increased demands placed on the remaining nerves leads to deterioration of these nerves over time, leading to a new onset of weakness.

INFERENCE

What is the most likely contributing factor in the development of this condition?

Post-polio syndrome only occurs in individuals previously diagnosed with poliomyelitis. It is estimated that 25-50% of patients with poliomyelitis will eventually develop post-polio syndrome. It is thought that patients who have a more serious initial onset of poliomyelitis (i.e., greater motor involvement) are more likely to develop post-polio syndrome. Women are also more likely to develop post-polio syndrome.

CONFIRMATION

What is the most likely clinical presentation?

The main symptoms of post-polio syndrome include muscle weakness, atrophy, fatigue, and sometimes muscular or joint pain. Weakness can also affect axial musculature and result in difficulties with breathing or swallowing. Post-polio syndrome tends to primarily affect the muscles that were affected during the initial poliomyelitis attack, though it can affect previously unaffected muscles. Pain and weakness generally increase with physical activity and with exposure to cold. The patient will experience decades of recovery after their initial acute poliomyelitis attack before the symptoms of post-polio syndrome begin. With the onset of post-polio syndrome, weakness progresses slowly over the course of years and is interspersed with periods of stability where there is no progression of symptoms.

What laboratory or imaging studies would confirm the diagnosis?

Laboratory and imaging studies are used to exclude the presence of other similar conditions that may be causing neuromuscular symptoms. Electromyography can be performed to determine if muscles have become newly denervated. Muscle biopsy may be utilized for this same reason.

What additional information should be obtained to confirm the diagnosis?

The diagnosis of post-polio syndrome is a clinical diagnosis confirmed primarily through the exclusion of other similar diseases. Because the diagnosis is made clinically, a thorough medical history and physical examination are very important. Patients diagnosed with post-polio syndrome must have a previous history of poliomyelitis that was followed by years of recovery and then a gradual onset of new symptoms.

MANAGEMENT

What is the most effective management of this patient?

There is no cure for post-polio syndrome, therefore treatment is generally multidisciplinary and aimed at controlling symptoms and improving daily function. Medications to combat fatigue (e.g., anticholinesterases, intravenous immunoglobulin) may be prescribed, however, these medications have only shown moderate success in patients with post-polio syndrome. Physical therapy interventions focus on improving overall conditioning. Intense exercise that leads to fatigue or exhaustion should be avoided since this can result in worsening of symptoms. Patients with post-polio syndrome should be taught energy conservation techniques to allow for improved function. Training in the use of assistive devices or orthoses may also be necessary.

What home care regimen should be recommended?

The patient's home care regimen should focus on aerobic exercises as well as strengthening exercises to help improve overall strength and endurance. Exercise is typically performed every other day to allow for adequate rest and recovery.

OUTCOME

What is the likely outcome of a course of physical therapy?

Physical therapy has been shown to help patients with post-polio syndrome improve their levels of strength and endurance, leading to greater daily function and quality of life. Additionally, patients who engage in physical activity demonstrate better gait quality than those who do not.

What are the long-term effects of the patient's condition?

Post-polio syndrome is generally not a life-threatening disease, though this may not be true for those patients who have respiratory involvement. Despite the fact that the majority of patients have a normal lifespan, the disease can still greatly affect a patient's quality of life. Symptoms generally slowly progress over a long period of time, though periods of progression are usually interspersed with periods of stability, which can last years without any progression of symptoms.

BRONZE Level Clinical Application Templates

BRONZE Level Clinical Application Template Executive Summary

Epilepsy

- Injury to the brain can cause abnormal activity of the brain's nerve cells in which the electrical discharge of the neurons becomes hypersynchronous, resulting in epileptic seizures
- Symptoms vary widely depending on the type of seizure (e.g., tonic, clonic) and may include mood disturbances, staring, loss of consciousness, uncontrollable jerking of the arms and legs, stiffening of muscles, and loss of muscle control
- An electroencephalogram measures electrical activity of the brain and is the most common test used to confirm the diagnosis of epilepsy

Polyneuropathy

- Characterized by damage or disease that affects multiple peripheral nerves, which is most commonly caused by diabetes mellitus
- Polyneuropathy often starts in the distal lower extremities, generally symmetrically, and may progress to include the hands and more proximal portions of the limbs
- Electromyography and nerve conduction testing are often used to determine the location and extent of nerve damage

Trigeminal Neuralgia

- Typically the result of abnormal pressure on or irritation of the trigeminal nerve
- Symptoms are typically unilateral and may be either episodic or constant; sudden pain described as sharp, jolting, stabbing or shock-like or persistent aching or burning sensations
- Diagnostic testing is often inconclusive with a diagnosis typically made based on the patient's reported symptoms

Epilepsy

BRONZE

DIAGNOSIS

What condition produces a patient's symptoms?

Epilepsy is a chronic central nervous system disorder characterized by epileptic seizures due to abnormal neuronal activity within the brain. Epilepsy has no identifiable etiology in approximately half of the population with the condition. Known conditions that can cause epilepsy include brain injury (e.g., head trauma, stroke, tumor), infectious disease (e.g., AIDS, meningitis), genetic influence, and developmental disorders (e.g., cerebral palsy).

An injury was most likely sustained to what structure?

Injury to the brain can cause abnormal activity of the brain's nerve cells in which the electrical discharge of the neurons becomes hypersynchronous. This abnormal neuronal activity precipitates the patient's seizure symptoms.

CONFIRMATION

What is the most likely clinical presentation?

Seizures are often unpredictable and unprovoked and vary widely in their presentation depending on the type of seizure (e.g., simple focal, absence, tonic, clonic). Symptoms may include mood disturbances, staring, loss of consciousness, uncontrollable jerking of the arms and legs, stiffening of muscles, and loss of muscle control. A seizure is the hallmark sign of epilepsy, though one seizure does not signify that a patient has epilepsy.

What laboratory or imaging studies would confirm the diagnosis?

An electroencephalogram measures electrical activity of the brain and is the most common test used to confirm the diagnosis of epilepsy. It is common for patients to have abnormal brain wave patterns even when they are not experiencing a seizure. Other imaging and laboratory studies, such as magnetic resonance imaging, computed tomography, and blood tests, may be used to identify the cause of the seizures.

What additional information should be obtained to confirm the diagnosis?

A thorough medical history, physical examination, and neurological examination may assist in the diagnosis of epilepsy and rule out other similar conditions (e.g., syncope, metabolic conditions, movement disorders, migraine).

Polyneuropathy

BRONZE

DIAGNOSIS:

What condition produces a patient's symptoms?

Polyneuropathy is a condition characterized by damage or disease that affects multiple peripheral nerves. The most common etiology of polyneuropathy is diabetes mellitus (both type 1 and type 2). Other causes include advanced age, certain drugs (e.g., chemotherapy), alcohol abuse, AIDS, environmental toxins, and inherited neurological conditions.

An injury was most likely sustained to what structure?

Polyneuropathy typically affects peripheral nerves, especially distally in the extremities, though it can also affect cranial nerves and nerves of the autonomic nervous system. Polyneuropathy can affect solely the sensory nerves, solely the motor nerves, or both. Neuropathy may involve damage to the axon, the myelin sheath or the nerve's cell body depending on the cause of the neuropathy.

CONFIRMATION

What is the most likely clinical presentation?

Polyneuropathy often starts in the distal lower extremities, typically symmetrically, and may progress to include the hands and more proximal portions of the limbs. Symptoms include numbness, tingling, and pain in a "stocking" and "glove" pattern. Additional symptoms include loss of position and vibration sense as well as ataxia. If motor nerves are affected, the condition will involve muscle weakness, and possibly atrophy. Autonomic symptoms include constipation, loss of bowel and bladder control, and orthostatic hypotension.

What laboratory or imaging studies would confirm the diagnosis?

Electromyography and nerve conduction testing are often used to determine the location and extent of nerve damage. Other laboratory testing (e.g., blood tests) may be performed to determine the cause of the neuropathy.

What additional information should be obtained to confirm the diagnosis?

The physician can often diagnose the condition based on a thorough medical history and a neurological examination. The examination consists of assessments of sensation (superficial and deep), strength, deep tendon reflexes, and coordination.

BRONZE

Trigeminal Neuralgia

DIAGNOSIS

What condition produces a patient's symptoms?

Trigeminal neuralgia is typically the result of abnormal pressure on or irritation of the trigeminal nerve. Common etiologies for abnormal pressure include tumor or a swollen blood vessel. Irritation of the nerve is more commonly associated with conditions that cause demyelination such as multiple sclerosis. In some cases, the continuous pulsations and consequent friction of a blood vessel in contact with the nerve can cause demyelination and subsequent symptoms over time.

An injury was most likely sustained to which structure?

The trigeminal nerve (cranial nerve V) is a mixed sensory and motor nerve that originates in the brainstem and branches into the ophthalmic, mandibular, and maxillary nerves. Pressure or demyelination injury produces a chronic pain condition which may impact the entire nerve distribution depending on the specific location and severity of the pathology. The most common location of injury is in the narrow space where the nerve exits the brainstem.

CONFIRMATION

What is the most likely clinical presentation?

Symptoms of trigeminal neuralgia are typically unilateral and may be either episodic or constant. Episodic symptoms most commonly present as a sudden onset of pain described as sharp, jolting, stabbing or shock-like. Spasms or tics may also occur. Episodic symptoms may be triggered by touch or sound with attacks that often result from activities of daily living such as shaving, chewing or oral care. Chronic symptoms are more commonly described as persistent aching or burning sensations which may be exacerbated by the same type of daily activities that trigger an episodic attack. Symptoms of either form can be progressive and in severe cases, may be debilitating. Trigeminal neuralgia is more common among women and individuals over the age of 50.

What laboratory or imaging studies would confirm the diagnosis?

Magnetic resonance angiography utilizes a colored dye to visualize blood flow near the brainstem and identify vessel pathology that may be causing compression of the trigeminal nerve.

What additional information should be obtained to confirm the diagnosis?

A thorough medical history should be obtained to identify potential sources of trigeminal nerve trauma (e.g., recent sinus or oral surgery, stroke, facial trauma). Diagnostic testing is often inconclusive with a diagnosis typically made based on the patient's reported symptoms.

Neuromuscular and Nervous Systems Essentials

1. The nervous system is composed of specialized cells that function to receive, integrate, control, and transmit information throughout the body. Components of the nervous system include the central nervous system (CNS), peripheral nervous system (PNS), autonomic nervous system (ANS), somatic nervous system (SNS), and limbic system.

2. The central nervous system anatomically consists of the brain and the spinal cord. There are two hemispheres of the brain and each hemisphere includes a frontal, temporal, parietal, and occipital lobe. The brain can also be divided into the forebrain, midbrain, and hindbrain. Each area is responsible for interpretation and control of certain biological processes and movement.

3. The peripheral nervous system consists of 12 pairs of cranial nerves and 31 pairs of spinal nerves. These nerves all have afferent and efferent fibers for communication between the body and the central nervous system.

4. The autonomic nervous system (ANS) consists of two divisions: the sympathetic division (generally a stimulating response) and the parasympathetic division (generally an inhibitory response). Anatomically, the ANS contains portions of the CNS and PNS. Impulses to the ANS typically do not reach the level of consciousness and instead produce automatic responses.

5. The somatic nervous system (SNS) regulates body movement through sensory and motor neurons that transmit information from the brain to muscle fibers throughout the body. The SNS controls voluntary movement, influences the five senses, and is responsible for reflex arcs such as deep tendon reflexes.

6. The limbic system is found within the brain and is involved with control and expression of mood, processing, memory, appetite, and olfaction. Lesions to this area can produce aggression, fearlessness, alterations in motivation, and other behaviors.

7. The forebrain consists of the telencephalon (cerebral cortex, hippocampus, basal ganglia, amygdala) and the diencephalon (thalamus, hypothalamus, subthalamus, epithalamus).

8. The cerebrum consists of gray matter on the surface and white matter interiorly, while sulci and fissures demark the specific lobes.

9. The left hemisphere has specific responsibilities including the ability to understand language, sequencing of movements, producing written and spoken language, expression of positive emotions, and the ability to be analytical, controlled, and logical. The right hemisphere has specific responsibilities including nonverbal processing, artistic expression, comprehension of general concepts, spatial relationships, kinesthetic awareness, mathematical reasoning, and body image awareness.

10. Each lobe of the brain has specific responsibilities: Frontal: intellect, orientation, voluntary movement, Broca's area, executive functions; Parietal: receives information associated with touch, kinesthesia, vibration; Temporal: auditory processing, Wernicke's area, production of meaningful speech; Occipital: visual processing, judgment of distance, vision in three dimensions.

11. The midbrain is located at the base of the brain above the spinal cord. It consists of the tectum and tegmentum and serves as a relay area, connecting the forebrain to the hindbrain. It is also a reflex center for visual, auditory, and tactile responses.

12. The hindbrain consists of the cerebellum, pons, and medulla oblongata. The cerebellum coordinates movement and assists with maintenance of balance. The pons and medulla assist with control of the body's vital functions.

13. From the Circle of Willis, the anterior cerebral artery, middle cerebral artery, posterior cerebral artery, and vertebral-basilar artery perfuse different regions of the brain and will produce impairments with vascular pathology specific to each artery.

14. The meninges are three layers of connective tissue that provide covering and protection for the brain and spinal cord. The dura mater is the outermost layer, followed by the arachnoid, and the pia mater (innermost layer). Dural spaces are areas normally surrounding meninges that may contain cerebrospinal fluid.

Neuromuscular and Nervous Systems Essentials

15. Cerebrospinal fluid is a clear fluid-like substance that cushions the brain and spinal cord and provides nutrition to the CNS. The ventricular system assists to produce and circulate CSF.

16. The spinal cord is a component of the CNS and a direct continuation of the brainstem. It serves as a relay for information between the brain and peripheral structures. Spinal nerves each possess afferent and efferent fibers for transmission of information through ascending and descending tracts of the spinal cord.

17. The peripheral nervous system contains nerves that have sensory, motor, and autonomic responsibilities. Cutaneous sensory end organs include thermoreceptors, nociceptors, mechanoreceptors, chemoreceptors, and photoreceptors that provide feedback through different channels of stimulation.

18. Peripheral nerve fibers may be classified as A, B or C fibers. A fibers are large and myelinated with a high conduction speed. B fibers are medium and myelinated with a moderate speed. C fibers are small and unmyelinated or poorly myelinated with a slow speed.

19. Nerve roots from C1 through S4 each innervate a particular region for sensation (dermatome), and for motor innervation (myotome), and provide a pattern of anticipated weakness with impairment.

20. The cranial nerves include olfactory, optic, oculomotor, trochlear, trigeminal, abducens, facial, vestibulocochlear, glossopharyngeal, vagus, accessory, and hypoglossal nerves. Each has a specific testing protocol to ensure accuracy of results.

21. The brachial plexus innervates the muscles of the upper extremity while the lower extremity is innervated by the lumbar plexus and sacral plexus.

22. Superficial reflexes are a response to stimulation of the receptors within the skin. The sensory signal must reach the spinal cord and ascend to the brain for processing. Common superficial reflexes include the abdominal, corneal, cremasteric, gag, and plantar reflexes. The Babinski reflex is an abnormal plantar reflex.

23. Deep tendon reflexes (DTR) elicit a muscle contraction through stimulation of the muscle's tendon through a reflex arc. DTRs are graded from 0 to 4+ and results of testing may be indicative of a lesion to the reflex arc or a suprasegmental lesion.

24. Superficial sensations include light touch, temperature, and pain. Deep sensations include kinesthesia, proprioception, and vibration. Cortical sensations include localization of touch, bilateral simultaneous stimulation, two-point discrimination, stereognosis, and barognosis.

25. Acute injury to a peripheral nerve will produce neurapraxia (the mildest form of injury with axons preserved and recovery rapid and complete), axonotmesis (more severe injury with reversible damage, potential for spontaneous recovery), and neurotmesis (most severe damage, axon and myelin are damaged, irreversible injury, no spontaneous recovery, surgery may allow for some recovery).

26. Upper motor neuron lesions are found within the motor cortex, internal capsule, brainstem or spinal cord. Hyperactive reflexes, mild atrophy, and increased tone are characteristic findings with this form of pathology.

27. Lower motor neuron lesions are found in nerves or their axons at or below the level of the brainstem. Hypoactive or absent reflexes, atrophy, fasciculations, and decreased tone are characteristic findings with this form of pathology.

28. Tremors, tics, chorea, dystonia, and athetosis are all forms of movement disorders that present with involuntary movements.

29. Balance is the state of physical equilibrium with maintenance and control of the center of gravity. There are somatosensory, visual, and vestibular systems that provide feedback to the CNS regarding balance.

30. The vestibuloocular reflex (VOR) supports gaze stabilization through eye movement that counters movements of the head. The vestibulospinal reflex (VSR) attempts to stabilize the body while the head is moving in order to manage upright posture.

Neuromuscular and Nervous Systems Essentials

31. Vestibular rehabilitation is targeted for patients with central or peripheral balance disorders and can include VOR and VSR exercises, ocular motor exercises, habituation training, balance training, center of gravity control, varying environments, visual conditions, and use of gravity to challenge the balance system.

32. Communication disorders can include all forms of aphasia, verbal apraxia, and dysarthria. Aphasia is typically classified as receptive, expressive or global. Treatment will be modified based on the patient's ability to communicate or understand alternative forms of communication.

33. Common pharmacological agents used in the treatment of neurological disorders include antiepileptic agents, antispasticity agents, cholinergic agents, dopamine replacement agents, and muscle relaxant agents.

34. A cerebrovascular accident (CVA) is a specific event that results in a lack of oxygen to a specific area of the brain secondary to ischemia or hemorrhage. CVAs are typically termed a completed stroke, stroke in evolution, transient ischemic attack, ischemic stroke or hemorrhage.

35. A patient presents with predictable patterns of impairment when ischemia occurs secondary to a CVA in the left hemisphere, right hemisphere, brainstem or cerebellum.

36. The flexor synergy for the upper extremity includes scapular elevation and retraction; shoulder abduction and lateral rotation; elbow flexion; forearm supination; wrist flexion; and finger and thumb flexion with adduction. The extensor synergy for the upper extremity includes scapular depression and protraction; shoulder adduction and medial rotation; elbow extension; forearm pronation; wrist extension; and finger and thumb flexion with adduction.

37. The flexor synergy for the lower extremity includes hip abduction and lateral rotation; knee flexion; ankle dorsiflexion with supination; and toe extension. The extensor synergy for the lower extremity includes hip extension, medial rotation, and adduction; knee extension; ankle plantar flexion with inversion; and toe flexion and adduction.

38. Neurological rehabilitation may incorporate a variety of treatments based on the patient's pathology and goals. The variety of constructs base each of the theories of rehabilitation on their particular interpretation of motor control and motor learning.

39. Motor control is the study of the nature of movement and the ability to direct essential movement. Motor learning is the study of the acquisition or modification of movement. Stages of motor learning include the cognitive stage, associative stage, and autonomous stage. Feedback is imperative for the progression of motor learning.

40. Practice is integral to motor learning. Various types of practice include massed and distributed practice; constant and variable practice; random and blocked practice; and whole training and part training.

41. Bobath developed Neuro-Developmental Treatment based on the hierarchical model of neurophysiologic function. This approach includes facilitation and inhibition of tone, reflex inhibiting postures, key points of control, proximal control, and the use of rotation during treatment.

42. Brunnstrom's Movement Therapy in Hemiplegia utilizes synergy patterns to assist with developing movement combinations outside of synergy patterns. Raimiste's phenomenon and Souques' phenomenon are used in treatment along with associated reactions, stages of recovery, overflow, and limb synergies.

43. Proprioceptive Neuromuscular Facilitation (PNF) is based on establishing gross motor patterns within the CNS, allowing for stronger parts to stimulate and strengthen the weaker parts. Treatment emphasizes developmental sequence, mass movement patterns, and diagonal patterns.

44. Rood's theory of neurological rehabilitation is based on the reflex stimulus model where motor output is the result of past and present sensory input. The goal of homeostasis is achieved using key patterns to enhance motor control. Treatment includes sensory stimulation to facilitate or inhibit a response.

Neuromuscular and Nervous Systems Essentials

45. Spinal cord injury (SCI) refers to permanent damage that can occur to the spinal cord after a sufficient force has been exerted on the spinal cord itself. Motor vehicle accidents have the highest incidence for SCI. There are complete and incomplete lesions with regard to motor and sensory function.

46. Incomplete lesions can include anterior cord syndrome, Brown-Sequard's syndrome, central cord syndrome, posterior cord syndrome, and cauda equina injuries.

47. The ASIA Impairment Scale is widely used for assessment of a patient with a SCI. This tool classifies complete versus incomplete lesions along with key muscles to test.

48. Autonomic dysreflexia is a common complication of a SCI and is considered a medical emergency. An excessive and uncontrolled increase in blood pressure places the patient at risk. A kinked catheter is the most typical stimulus for this condition.

49. Functional outcomes are anticipated for each level of spinal cord injury. A physical therapist must be able to recognize a patient's potential based on expected functional outcomes.

50. Traumatic brain injury is classified as either open or closed with primary and secondary brain damage. Primary injuries typically consist of coup and contrecoup lesions with secondary injury typically due to an epidural or subdural hematoma.

51. The Glasgow Coma Scale is used to assess patients with suspected head injury in order to classify the injury from mild to severe.

52. Rancho Los Amigos Levels of Cognitive Functioning Scale will also assist to classify the level of injury based on where the patient best meets the criteria of each level. The levels include: no response; generalized response; localized response; confused-agitated; confused-inappropriate; confused-appropriate; automatic-appropriate; and purposeful-appropriate.

53. The concepts of development include cephalic to caudal; gross to fine; mass to specific; and proximal to distal.

54. Primitive reflexes are elicited with a predictable stimulus that causes a predictable response until the time when the primitive reflex is integrated. When reflexes do not integrate, there is typically interference with progressing through the developmental milestones.

55. Developmental milestones for gross and fine motor skills follow a tentative schedule that children will follow through the teenage years. Developmental delay and other pediatric pathology may cause the child to experience difficulty progressing through the milestones.

56. Therapeutic positioning is essential to obtain maximum function for the pediatric population and is used to facilitate desired movement, inhibit unwanted tonal influences, normalize tone, prevent contractures, enhance midline orientation, and improve respiratory capacity.

57. Legislation such as the Individuals with Disabilities Education Improvement Act (IDEA), Rehabilitation Act, and No Child Left Behind Act have provided improved services and benefits for children with disabilities. These laws have been updated and amended to improve services for children with disabilities.

Neuromuscular and Nervous Systems Proficiencies

1. Brain Anatomy

Identify the appropriate term for each of the specified locations. Answers must be selected from the Word Bank and can be used only once.

Word Bank: fornix, hypothalamus, medulla oblongata, midbrain, olfactory bulb, pineal gland, pituitary gland

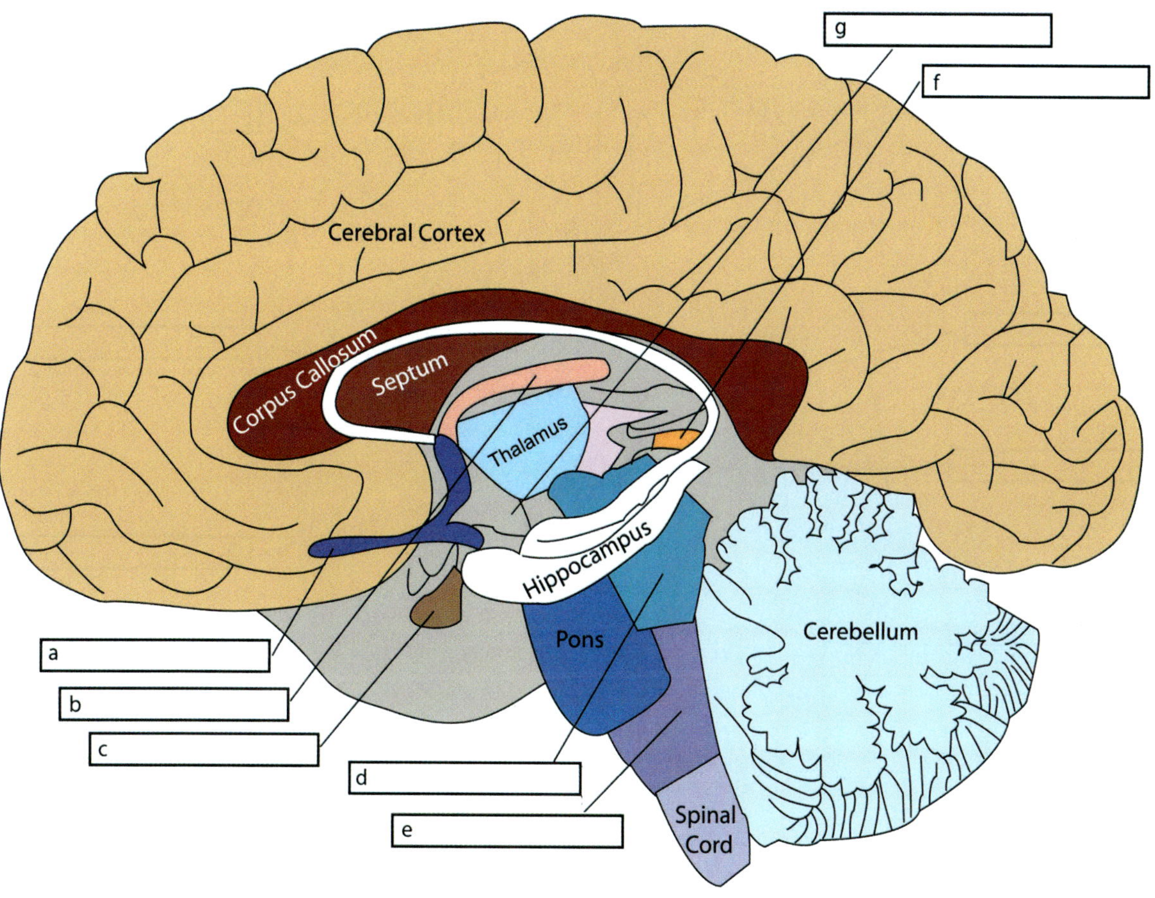

Neuromuscular and Nervous Systems Proficiencies

2. Circle of Willis

Identify the appropriate term for each of the specified locations. Answers must be selected from the Word Bank and can be used only once.

Word Bank: anterior communicating artery, arterial circle, basilar artery, left middle cerebral artery, left vertebral artery, right anterior cerebral artery, right internal carotid artery, right posterior cerebral artery, right posterior communicating artery

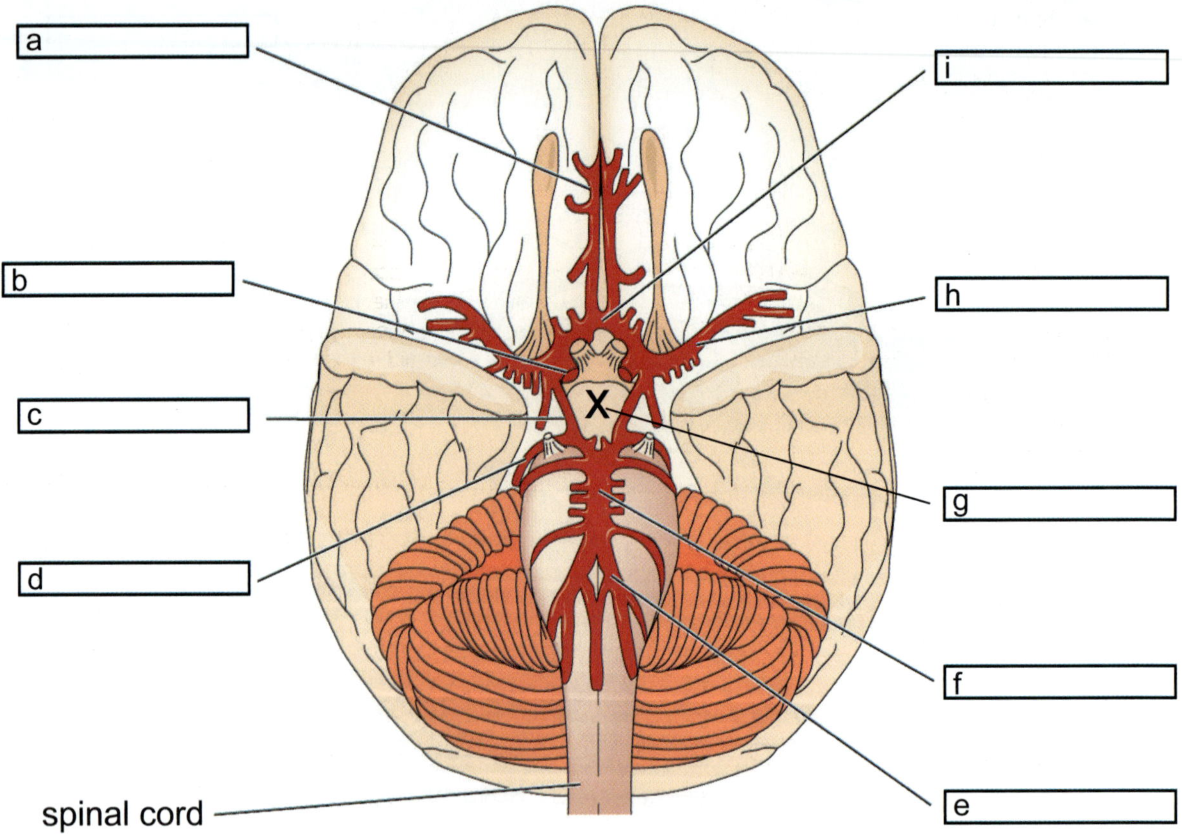

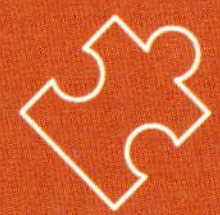

Neuromuscular and Nervous Systems Proficiencies

3. Cranial Nerve Function

Indicate "yes" or "no" in each cell based on the presence or absence of a sensory (afferent) and/or motor (efferent) component for each cranial nerve.

Cranial Nerve	Sensory	Motor
Olfactory	a	b
Optic	c	d
Oculomotor	e	f
Trochlear	g	h
Trigeminal	i	j
Abducens	k	l
Facial	m	n
Vestibulocochlear	o	p
Glossopharyngeal	q	r
Vagus	s	t
Accessory	u	v
Hypoglossal	w	x

4. Cranial Nerve Testing

Identify the most appropriate method of testing for each of the cranial nerves. Answers must be selected from the Word Bank and can be used more than once if indicated.

Word Bank: downward and inward gaze; face sensation; familiar odors; familiar tastes; gag reflex (2); hearing test; lateral gaze; resisted shoulder shrug; tongue protrusion; upward, downward, and medial gaze; visual fields

Cranial Nerve	Cranial Nerve Test
Olfactory	a
Optic	b
Oculomotor	c
Trochlear	d
Trigeminal	e
Abducens	f
Facial	g
Vestibulocochlear	h
Glossopharyngeal	i
Vagus	j
Accessory	k
Hypoglossal	l

Neuromuscular and Nervous Systems Proficiencies

5. Hemispheric Specialization

Identify the specific hemisphere most closely associated with each described function. Answers must be selected from the Word Bank and can be used more than once.

Word Bank: left, right

Hemisphere	Function
a	logical and rational
b	understand nonverbal communication
c	understand and express language
d	spatial relationships
e	artistic abilities
f	mathematical calculations
g	body image awareness
h	express positive emotions
i	express negative emotions

6. Innervation Levels

Identify the primary innervation level most closely associated with the described myotome, dermatome or reflex. Answers must be selected from the Word Bank and can be used more than once.

Word Bank: C4, C5, C6, C7, C8, L4, L5, S1, S3

Myotome	Innervation Level
trapezius	a
triceps	b
extensor hallucis longus	c
gastrocnemius-soleus	d
Dermatome	**Innervation Level**
deltoid area	e
radial side of hand to thumb and index finger	f
medial arm and forearm to long, ring, and little fingers	g
groin, medial thigh to knee	h
Reflex	**Innervation Level**
biceps	i
triceps	j
patellar	k
Achilles	l

Neuromuscular and Nervous Systems Proficiencies

7. Sensory Testing

Identify the type of sensory testing most closely associated with the supplied description. Answers must be selected from the Word Bank and can be used only once.

Word Bank: deep pain, graphesthesia, kinesthesia, light touch, proprioception, temperature, two-point discrimination, stereognosis, superficial pain, vibration

Sensation	Description
a	squeeze the forearm or calf muscle
b	use a tuning fork
c	identify a static position of an extremity
d	use a cotton ball applied to the skin
e	identify direction and extent of movement of a body part
f	use hot and cold test tubes
g	draw a letter on the skin with a finger
h	identify one or two points without sight
i	identify an object without sight
j	use a paper clip end or a pen cap

8. Upper versus Lower Motor Neuron Lesions

Indicate whether each pathology is an upper motor neuron or lower motor neuron lesion. Answers must be selected from the Word Bank and can be used more than once.

Word Bank: upper motor neuron, lower motor neuron

Pathology	Type of Lesion
multiple sclerosis	a
traumatic brain injury	b
Bell's palsy	c
Guillain-Barre syndrome	d
Huntington's chorea	e
muscular dystrophy	f
poliomyelitis	g
cerebral palsy	h
CVA	i

Neuromuscular and Nervous Systems Proficiencies

9. Brunnstrom's Stages of Recovery

Identify the appropriate sequence of Brunnstrom's Stages of Recovery based on the supplied description. Answers must be selected from the Word Bank and can be used only once.

Word Bank: Sequence - 1, 2, 3, 4, 5, 6, 7

Sequence	Description
a	The synergies are performed voluntarily; spasticity increases.
b	Normal motor function is restored.
c	The appearance of basic limb synergies. The beginning of spasticity.
d	Spasticity begins to decrease. Movement patterns are not dictated solely by limb synergies.
e	No volitional movement initiated.
f	A further decrease in spasticity is noted with independence from limb synergy patterns.
g	Isolated joint movements are performed with coordination.

10. Sensory Stimulation Techniques

Identify whether the sensory stimulation technique is used for facilitation or inhibition. Answers must be selected from the Word Bank and can be used more than once.

Word Bank: facilitation, inhibition

Technique	Use
icing	a
deep pressure	b
warmth	c
joint compression	d
prolonged stretch	e
quick stretch	f
tapping	g
light touch	h

Neuromuscular and Nervous Systems Proficiencies

11. Pediatric Reflexes I

Identify the type of pediatric reflex associated with the supplied stimulus. Answers must be selected from the Word Bank and can be used only once.

Word Bank: asymmetrical tonic neck reflex, Galant reflex, Moro reflex, palmar grasp reflex, plantar grasp reflex, positive support reflex, rooting reflex, startle reflex, symmetrical tonic neck reflex, walking (stepping) reflex

Reflex	Stimulus
a	touch on the cheek
b	head position, turned to one side
c	loud, sudden noise
d	head position, flexion or extension
e	head dropping into extension suddenly for a few inches
f	touch to the skin along the spine from the shoulder to the hip
g	weight placed on the balls of the feet when upright
h	pressure to the base of the toes
i	pressure in the palm on the ulnar side of the hand
j	supported upright position with the soles of the feet on a firm surface

12. Pediatric Reflexes II

Identify the type of pediatric reflex associated with the described response. Answers must be selected from the Word Bank and can be used only once.

Word Bank: asymmetrical tonic neck reflex, Galant reflex, Moro reflex, palmar grasp reflex, plantar grasp reflex, positive support reflex, rooting reflex, symmetrical tonic neck reflex, tonic labyrinthine reflex, walking (stepping) reflex

Reflex	Response
a	arms abduct with fingers open, then cross trunk into adduction; cry
b	arm and leg on the face side are extended; arm and leg on the scalp side are flexed
c	when the head is in flexion, the arms are flexed and the legs are extended
d	when in a supine position, the body and the extremities are held in extension
e	flexion of the fingers causing a strong grip
f	lateral flexion of the trunk to the side of the stimulus
g	toe flexion
h	reciprocal flexion and extension of the legs
i	turning the head to the same side with the mouth open
j	stiffening of the legs and the trunk into extension

Neuromuscular and Nervous Systems Proficiencies

13. Neuromuscular and Nervous Systems Terminology

Identify the neuromuscular term most closely associated with the supplied description. Answers must be selected from the Word Bank and can be used only once.

Word Bank: agraphia, alexia, aphasia, constructional apraxia, dysprosody, emotional lability, hemiparesis, homonymous hemianopsia, ideomotor apraxia, neologism, perseveration, unilateral neglect

Terminology	Description
a	Substitution within a word that is so severe that it makes the word unrecognizable.
b	The state of repeatedly performing the same segment of a task or repeatedly saying the same word/phrase without purpose.
c	The inability to write due to a lesion within the brain.
d	The inability to control emotion with outbursts of laughing or crying that are inconsistent with the situation.
e	The loss of the right or left half of the field of vision in both eyes.
f	The inability to interpret stimuli and events on the contralateral side of a hemispheric lesion.
g	Impairment in the rhythm and inflection of speech.
h	A condition where a person plans a movement or task, but cannot volitionally perform it.
i	The inability to communicate or comprehend due to damage to specific areas of the brain.
j	A condition of weakness on one side of the body.
k	The inability to reproduce geometric figures and designs.
l	The inability to read or comprehend written language.

14. Neuromuscular and Nervous Systems Basics

Mark each statement as True or False. If the statement is False, correct the statement in the space provided.

True/False	Statement
a	The occipital lobe of the cerebrum contains the primary motor cortex and Broca's area.
Correction	

Neuromuscular and Nervous Systems Proficiencies

True/False	Statement
b	The meninges consist of three distinct layers termed the dura mater, arachnoid, and pia mater.
Correction	
c	The fasciculus gracilis is a motor tract responsible for voluntary, discrete, and skilled movement.
Correction	
d	The axillary and radial nerves originate from the posterior cord of the brachial plexus.
Correction	
e	The plantar reflex is assessed by stroking the lateral aspect of the sole of the foot to the ball of the foot toward the base of the great toe.
Correction	
f	A reflex grade of 1+ is indicative of a brisk or exaggerated response.
Correction	
g	Elbow flexion and/or forearm supination is a normal response when eliciting the brachioradialis deep tendon reflex.
Correction	
h	Graphesthesia refers to the ability to perceive the weight of different objects placed in the hand.
Correction	

Neuromuscular and Nervous Systems Proficiencies

True/False	Statement
i	A grade of 0 on the Modified Ashworth Scale is indicative of no increase in muscle tone.
Correction	
j	Slopes, uneven surfaces, and standing on foam could be used to challenge the somatosensory system during a balance assessment.
Correction	
k	Crouching or squatting is an example of the suspensory postural strategy.
Correction	
l	The Berg Balance Scale consists of fourteen tasks, each scored on an ordinal five point scale.
Correction	
m	Patients with Brown-Sequard's syndrome present with a loss of pain and temperature sense on the ipsilateral side of the lesion.
Correction	
n	Guillain-Barre syndrome results in motor weakness in a proximal to distal progression.
Correction	
o	The Glasgow Coma Scale has a minimum score of 0 and a maximum score of 15.
Correction	

Neuromuscular and Nervous Systems Answer Key

1. Brain Anatomy

a. olfactory bulb
b. fornix
c. pituitary gland
d. midbrain
e. medulla oblongata
f. pineal gland
g. hypothalamus

2. Circle of Willis

a. right anterior cerebral artery
b. right internal carotid artery
c. right posterior communicating artery
d. right posterior cerebral artery
e. left vertebral artery
f. basilar artery
g. arterial circle
h. left middle cerebral artery
i. anterior communicating artery

3. Cranial Nerve Function

a. yes
b. no
c. yes
d. no
e. no
f. yes
g. no
h. yes
i. yes
j. yes
k. no
l. yes
m. yes
n. yes
o. yes
p. no
q. yes
r. yes
s. yes
t. yes
u. no
v. yes
w. no
x. yes

4. Cranial Nerve Testing

a. familiar odors
b. visual fields
c. upward, downward, and medial gaze
d. downward and inward gaze
e. face sensation
f. lateral gaze
g. familiar tastes
h. hearing test
i. gag reflex
j. gag reflex
k. resisted shoulder shrug
l. tongue protrusion

5. Hemispheric Specialization

a. left
b. right
c. left
d. right
e. right
f. left
g. right
h. left
i. right

6. Innervation Levels

a. C4
b. C7
c. L5
d. S1
e. C5
f. C6
g. C8
h. S3
i. C5
j. C7
k. L4
l. S1

7. Sensory Testing

a. deep pain
b. vibration
c. proprioception
d. light touch

Neuromuscular and Nervous Systems Answer Key

e. kinesthesia
f. temperature
g. graphesthesia
h. two-point discrimination
i. stereognosis
j. superficial pain

8. Upper versus Lower Motor Neuron Lesions

a. upper motor neuron
b. upper motor neuron
c. lower motor neuron
d. lower motor neuron
e. upper motor neuron
f. lower motor neuron
g. lower motor neuron
h. upper motor neuron
i. upper motor neuron

9. Brunnstrom's Stages of Recovery

a. 3
b. 7
c. 2
d. 4
e. 1
f. 5
g. 6

10. Sensory Stimulation Techniques

a. facilitation
b. inhibition
c. inhibition
d. facilitation
e. inhibition
f. facilitation
g. facilitation
h. facilitation

11. Pediatric Reflexes I

a. rooting reflex
b. asymmetrical tonic neck reflex
c. startle reflex
d. symmetrical tonic neck reflex
e. Moro reflex
f. Galant reflex
g. positive support reflex
h. plantar grasp reflex
i. palmar grasp reflex
j. walking (stepping) reflex

12. Pediatric Reflexes II

a. Moro reflex
b. asymmetrical tonic neck reflex
c. symmetrical tonic neck reflex
d. tonic labyrinthine reflex
e. palmar grasp reflex
f. Galant reflex
g. plantar grasp reflex
h. walking (stepping) reflex
i. rooting reflex
j. positive support reflex

13. Neuromuscular and Nervous Systems Terminology

a. neologism
b. perseveration
c. agraphia
d. emotional lability
e. homonymous hemianopsia
f. unilateral neglect
g. dysprosody
h. ideomotor apraxia
i. aphasia
j. hemiparesis
k. constructional apraxia
l. alexia

14. Neuromuscular and Nervous Systems Basics*

a. FALSE: Correction - The frontal lobe of the cerebrum contains the primary motor cortex and Broca's area.
b. TRUE
c. FALSE: Correction - The corticospinal tract is a motor tract responsible for voluntary, discrete, and skilled movement.
d. TRUE
e. TRUE
f. FALSE: Correction - A reflex grade of 1+ is indicative of a diminished or depressed response.
g. TRUE
h. FALSE: Correction - Barognosis refers to the ability to perceive the weight of different objects placed in the hand.
i. TRUE

Neuromuscular and Nervous Systems Answer Key

j. TRUE

k. TRUE

l. TRUE

m. FALSE: Correction - Patients with Brown-Sequard's syndrome present with a loss of pain and temperature sense on the contralateral side of the lesion.

n. FALSE: Correction - Guillain-Barre syndrome results in motor weakness in a distal to proximal progression.

o. FALSE: Correction - The Glasgow Coma Scale has a minimum score of 3 and a maximum score of 15.

*The correction presented for each false statement is an example of several possible corrections.

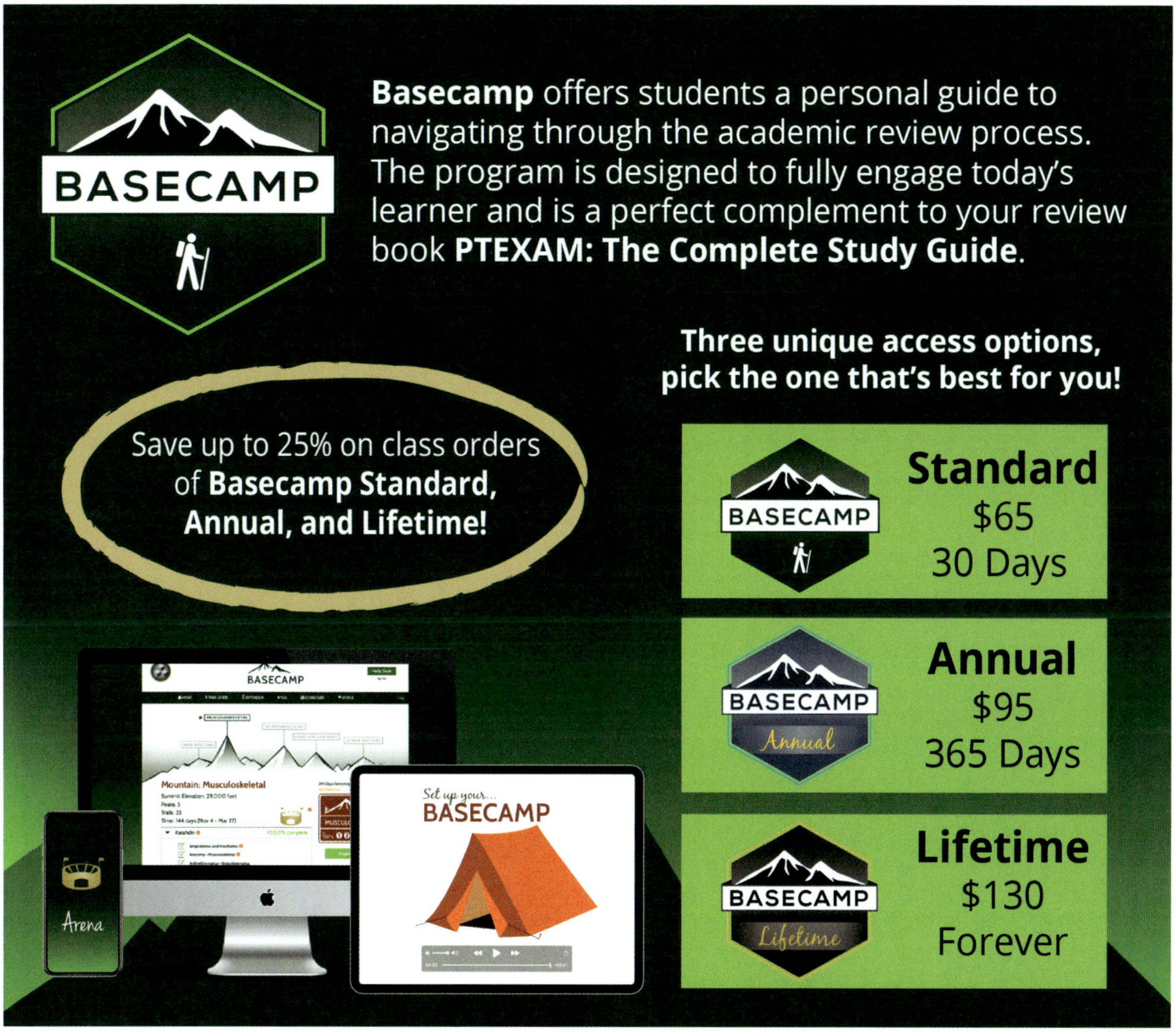

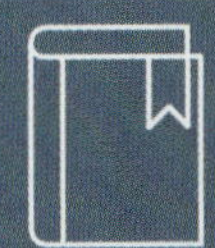

Neuromuscular and Nervous Systems References

1. Rowland LP, Pedley TA. ***Merritt's Neurology***. 12th Edition. Lippincott Williams & Wilkins. 2009.
2. Snell RS. ***Clinical Neuroanatomy***. 7th Edition. Philadelphia, PA: Lippincott Williams & Wilkins. 2009.
3. Lundy-Ekman L. ***Neuroscience: Fundamentals for Rehabilitation***. Fifth Edition. Elsevier. 2018.
4. McCaffrey P. The Corpus Striatum, Rhinencephalon, Connecting Fibers, and Diencephalon. www.csuchico.edu/~pmccaffrey/syllabi/CMSD%20320/362unit5.html Neuroscience on the Web Series. November, 2010. Accessed March, 2011.
5. Cohen H. ***Neuroscience for Rehabilitation***. JB Lippincott Company. 1993.
6. DeMyer W. ***Technique of the Neurologic Examination***. Fifth Edition. McGraw-Hill Companies. 2004.
7. Bertoti, DB. ***Functional Neurorehabilitation Through the Life Span***. F.A. Davis. 2004.
8. Gillen G, Burkhardt A. ***Stroke Rehabilitation: A Functional Approach***. Mosby. 1998.
9. Conn PM. ***Neuroscience in Medicine***. JB Lippincott Company. 2008.
10. Freemon FR. Akinetic Mutism and Bilateral Anterior Cerebral Artery Occlusion. http://www.ncbi.nlm.nih.gov/pmc/articles/PMC1083504/ Journal of Neurology, Neurosurgery, and Psychiatry. Accessed March, 2011.
11. Dawson VL, Hsu CY, Liu TH, Dawson TM, Wamsley JK. Receptor alterations in subcortical structures after bilateral middle cerebral artery infarction of the cerebral cortex. http://www.ncbi.nlm.nih.gov/pubmed/8070526. Accessed April, 2011.
12. Slater D, Curtin S, Johns J. Middle cerebral artery stroke. http://emedicine.medscape.com/article/323120-overview. Accessed March 2011.
13. Goodman C, Fuller K. ***Pathology: Implications for the Physical Therapist***. Fourth Edition. W.B. Saunders Company. 2015.
14. Palisano R, Orlin M, Shreiber J. ***Campbell's Physical Therapy for Children***. Fifth Edition. Elsevier. 2017.
15. Campbell S. ***Decision Making in Pediatric Neurologic Physical Therapy***. Churchill Livingstone. 1999.
16. Human Nervous System. Encyclopedia Britannica Online, http://www.britannica.com/EBchecked/topic/409709/human-nervous-system. Updated 2010. Retrieved November 29, 2010.
17. Gutman S. ***Quick Reference Neuroscience for Rehabilitation Professionals***. Second Edition. Slack Inc. 2008.
18. Field-Fote E. ***Spinal Cord Injury Rehabilitation***. F.A. Davis Company. 2009.
19. Sisto SA, Druin E, Macht-Sliwinski M. ***Spinal Cord Injuries Management and Rehabilitation***. Mosby Elsevier. 2009.
20. Cameron M, Monroe L. ***Physical Rehabilitation: Evidence-Based Examination, Evaluation, and Intervention***. W. B. Saunders Company. 2007.
21. Magee DJ. ***Orthopedic Physical Assessment***. Sixth Edition. W. B. Saunders Company. 2014.
22. Bickley L. ***Bates' Guide to Physical Examination and History Taking***. Twelfth Edition. Wolters Kluwer. 2017.
23. Kendall F, McCreary E, Provance, P. ***Muscles Testing and Function with Posture and Pain***. Fifth Edition. Lippincott Williams & Wilkins. 2005.
24. Umphred D. ***Neurological Rehabilitation***. Sixth Edition. Mosby Inc. 2013.
25. Walker HK, Hall WD, Hurst JW. ***Clinical Methods: The History, Physical, and Laboratory Examinations***. Third Edition. Butterworths. 1990.

Neuromuscular and Nervous Systems References

26. O'Sullivan S, Schmitz T, Fulk G. ***Physical Rehabilitation: Assessment and Treatment***. Sixth Edition. F.A. Davis Company. 2014.
27. Roy S, Wolf S, Scalzitti D. ***The Rehabilitation Specialist's Handbook***. Fourth Edition. F.A .Davis Company. 2013.
28. Montgomery PC, Connolly BH. ***Clinical Applications for Motor Control***. Slack, Incorporated. 2003.
29. ***Physical Therapist's Clinical Companion***, Springhouse Corporation. 2000.
30. Bennett S, Karnes J. ***Neurological Disabilities: Assessment and Treatment***. Lippincott-Raven Publishers. 1998.
31. Barnes M, Dobkin B, Bogousslavsky J. ***Recovery after Stroke***. Cambridge University Press. 2005.
32. Neurological Diagnostic Tests and Procedures. National Institute of Neurological Disorders and Stroke, National Institutes of Health. http://www.ninds.nih.gov/disorders/misc/diagnostic_tests.htm. Accessed June 2011.
33. Ciccone C. ***Pharmacology in Rehabilitation***. Fifth Edition. F.A.Davis Company. 2016.
34. ***Miller-Keane: Encyclopedia and Dictionary of Medicine, Nursing, and Allied Health***. Seventh Edition. W.B. Saunders Company. 2003.
35. Davies PM. ***Steps to Follow: The Comprehensive Treatment of Patients with Hemiplegia***. Springer-Verlag. 2004.
36. Shumway-Cook A, Woollacott M. ***Motor Control: Translating Research into Clinical Practice***. Fourth Edition. Lippincott Williams & Wilkins. 2011.
37. Carr J, Shepherd R. ***Neurologic Rehabilitation: Optimizing Motor Performance***. Churchill Livingstone. 2010.
38. Carr J, Shepard R. ***Stroke Rehabilitation: Guidelines for Exercise and Training to Optimize Motor Skill***. Elsevier Science Limited. 2003.
39. Bobath B. ***Adult Hemiplegia: Evaluation and Treatment***. Third Edition. Butterworth-Heinemann. 1990.
40. Sullivan P, Markos P. ***Clinical Decision Making in Therapeutic Exercise***. Appleton & Lange. 1995.
41. Brunnstrom S. ***Movement Therapy in Hemiplegia***. Harper and Row Publishers Inc. 1992.
42. Mesulam MM. Motor Exam Guide and Key Sensory Points. National Institute of Health http://www.asia-spinalinjury.org/# American Spinal Injury Association (ASIA). Accessed June 2011.
43. Goodman C, Heick J, Lazaro R. ***Differential Diagnosis for Physical Therapists – Screening for Referral***. Sixth Edition. Elsevier. 2018.
44. Campbell M. ***Rehabilitation for Traumatic Brain Injury: Physical Therapy Practice in Context***. Churchill Livingstone. 2000.
45. Long T, Toscano K. ***Handbook of Pediatric Physical Therapy***. Second Edition. Lippincott Williams & Wilkins. 2002.
46. Tecklin J. ***Pediatric Physical Therapy***. Fifth Edition. Lippincott Williams & Wilkins. 2015.
47. Ratliffe KT. ***Clinical Pediatric Physical Therapy: A Guide for the Physical Therapy Team***. Mosby Inc. 1998.
48. Special Education and Rehabilitative Services. ehttp://www2.ed.gov/policy/speced/leg/edpicks.jhtml?src=ln. The US Department of Education. Accessed June 2011.

6

Cardiovascular and Pulmonary Systems

Michael Fillyaw

Cardiovascular and Pulmonary Systems represents approximately 23 - 28 questions (11.5% - 14%) on the NPTE-PT.

Contributors

Scott Giles
Shawn Paquette

CHAPTER 6
Cardiovascular and Pulmonary Systems

Anatomy and Physiology of the Cardiovascular System

Heart

Topology of the Heart

Apex: The lowest part of the heart formed by the inferolateral part of the left ventricle. It projects anteriorly and to the left at the level of the 5th intercostal space and the left midclavicular line.

Base: The upper border of the heart involving the left atrium, part of the right atrium, and the proximal portions of the great vessels. It lies approximately below the second rib at the level of the second intercostal space.

Endocardium: The endothelial tissue that lines the interior of the heart chambers and valves.

Epicardium: The serous layer of the pericardium. The epicardium contains the epicardial coronary arteries and veins, autonomic nerves, and lymphatics.

Myocardium: The thick contractile middle layer of muscle cells that forms the bulk of the heart wall.

Pericardium: A double-walled connective tissue sac that surrounds the outside of the heart and great vessels.

Great Vessels of the Heart

Aorta: The body's largest artery and the central conduit of blood from the heart to the body. The aorta begins at the upper part of the left ventricle, and after ascending for a short distance arches backward and to the left (arch of the aorta). It then descends within the thorax (thoracic aorta) and passes into the abdominal cavity (abdominal aorta).

Inferior vena cava: The vein that returns venous blood from the lower body and viscera to the right atrium.

Pulmonary arteries: The arteries that carry deoxygenated blood from the right ventricle to the left and right lungs.

Pulmonary veins: The veins that carry oxygenated blood from the right and left lungs to the left atrium.

Superior vena cava: The vein that returns venous blood from the head, neck, and arms to the right atrium.

Heart Chambers and Valves

The superior chambers of the heart are the right atrium (RA) and left atrium (LA). The wall between the atria is the atrial septum. The two inferior chambers of the heart are the right ventricle (RV) and left ventricle (LV). The wall between the ventricles is the ventricular septum. The right chambers collect blood from the body and pump it to the lungs. The left chambers collect blood from the lungs and pump it to the rest of the body.

The heart has four valves that function to maintain unidirectional blood flow (Fig. 6.1). The atrioventricular valves (AV) are between the atria and ventricles and are named by the number of leaflets or cusps. The right AV valve, or tricuspid valve, has three leaflets. It controls blood flow between the RA and RV. The left AV valve, or mitral valve, has two leaflets. It controls blood flow between the LA and LV. The aortic valve is between the LV and aorta; the pulmonary valve is between the RV and pulmonary artery.

Venous blood from the superior and inferior vena cava enters the RA and is pumped through the tricuspid valve into the RV. The tricuspid valve closes while the RV contracts to pump blood through the pulmonary valve and into the pulmonary trunk, which divides into right and left pulmonary arteries serving the right and left lungs, respectively. After picking up oxygen and releasing carbon dioxide in the pulmonary capillaries, oxygenated blood returns via the pulmonary veins to the LA. Contraction of the LA forces blood through the mitral valve into the LV. The mitral valve closes when the LV contracts to pump blood through the aortic valve into the aorta where it is distributed into the coronary circulation and systemic circulation (Fig. 6-1).

Coronary Arteries

The coronary arteries are a network of progressively smaller vessels that carry oxygenated blood to the myocardium. The right and left coronary arteries arise from the ascending aorta just beyond where the aorta leaves the left ventricle. These arteries and their branches supply all parts of the myocardium (Fig. 6-2).

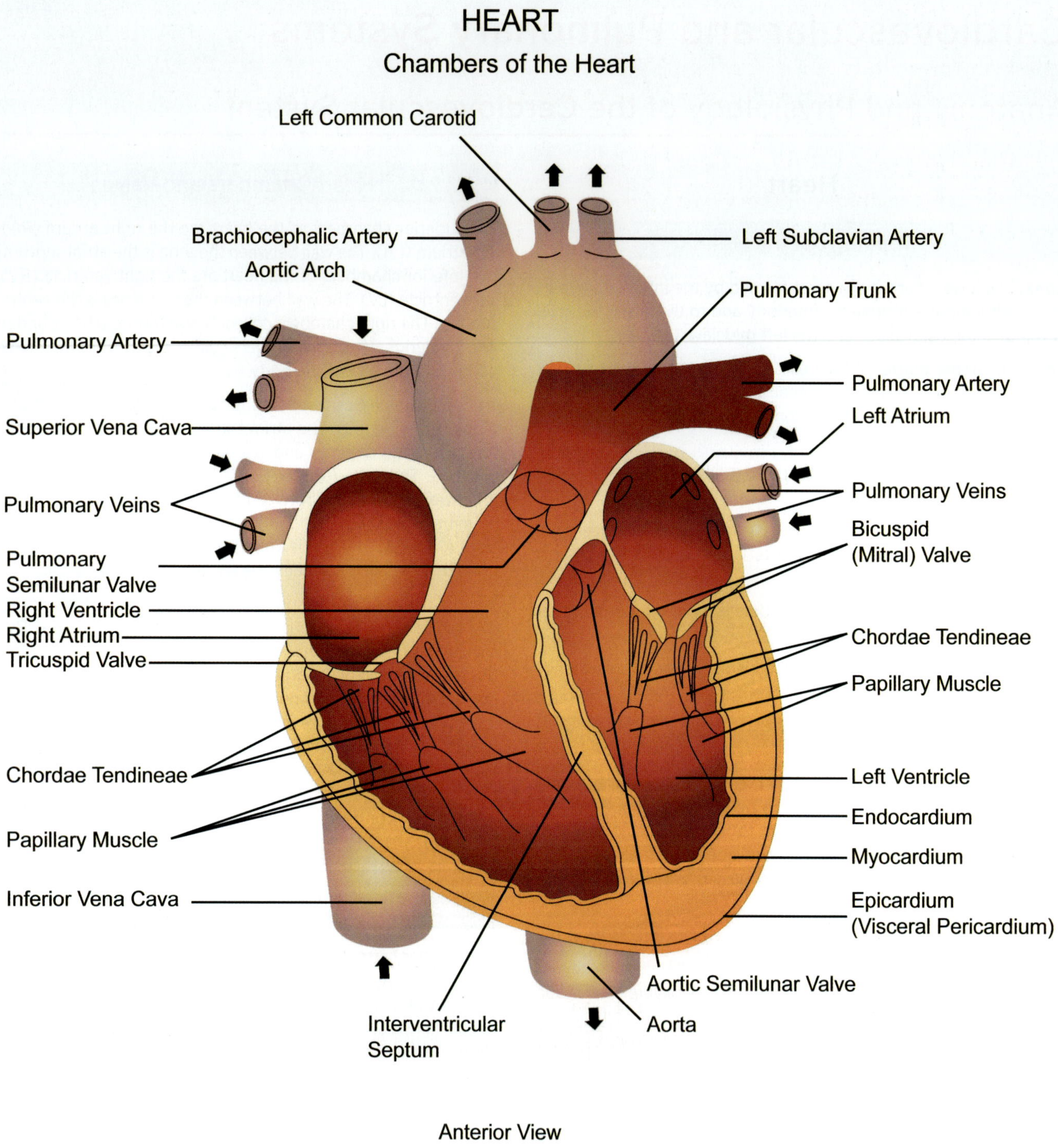

HEART

Chambers of the Heart

Left Common Carotid

Brachiocephalic Artery

Left Subclavian Artery

Aortic Arch

Pulmonary Trunk

Pulmonary Artery

Pulmonary Artery

Superior Vena Cava

Left Atrium

Pulmonary Veins

Pulmonary Veins

Pulmonary Semilunar Valve

Bicuspid (Mitral) Valve

Right Ventricle

Right Atrium

Tricuspid Valve

Chordae Tendineae

Papillary Muscle

Chordae Tendineae

Papillary Muscle

Left Ventricle

Endocardium

Myocardium

Inferior Vena Cava

Epicardium (Visceral Pericardium)

Aortic Semilunar Valve

Interventricular Septum

Aorta

Anterior View

Fig. 6-1: Cross section of the anterior of the heart showing the chambers and valves.

Coronary Artery and Main Branches	Areas Supplied
Right coronary artery	
Sinus node artery	Right atrium
Right marginal artery	Right ventricle
Posterior descending artery	Inferior walls of both ventricles Inferior portion of the interventricular septum
Left coronary artery	
Circumflex artery	Left atrium Posterior and lateral walls of the left ventricle Anterior and inferior walls of the left ventricle
Left anterior descending artery	Anterior portion of the interventricular septum

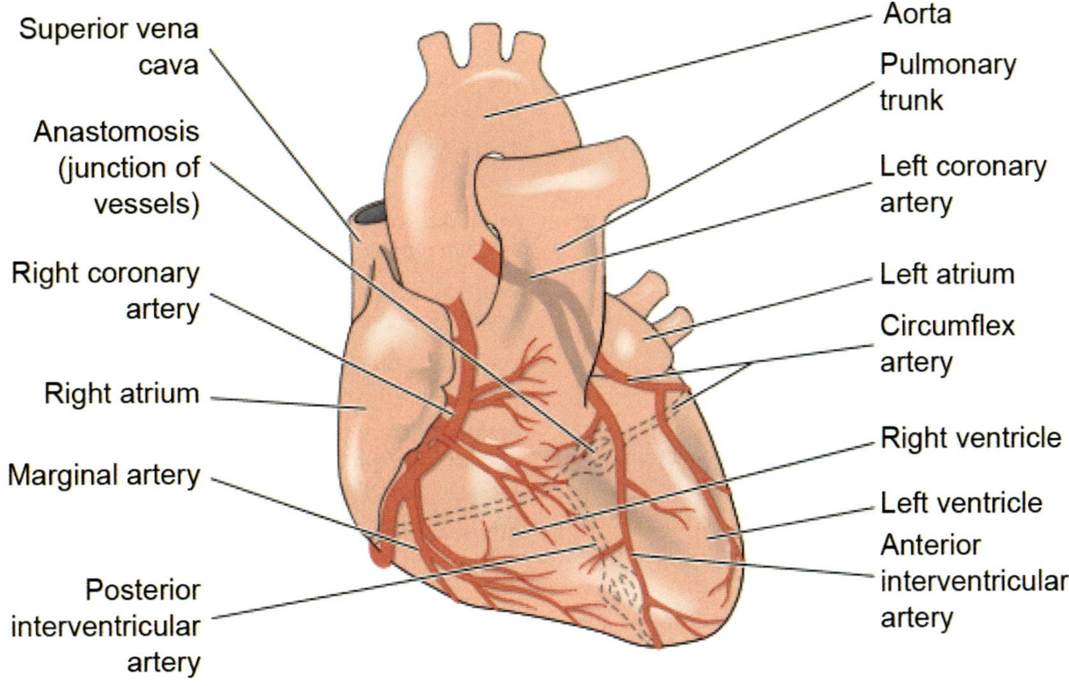

Fig. 6-2: Anterior surface of the heart showing the great vessels and coronary arteries.

Coronary Veins

The coronary venous circulation includes the coronary sinus, cardiac veins, and thebesian veins. The great cardiac vein, along with the small and middle cardiac veins, drain into the coronary sinus, emptying into the right atrium. The thebesian veins arise in the myocardium and drain into all chambers of the heart, but primarily into the right atrium and right ventricle.

Cardiac Conduction System

The components of the cardiac conduction system include the sinoatrial (SA) node, internodal tracts, atrioventricular (AV) node, common AV bundle or bundle of His, right and left bundle branches, and Purkinje fibers. Each cardiac myocyte has an intrinsic ability to depolarize and propagate electrical impulses from cell to cell without nerve stimulation.

The SA node is the normal pacemaker of the heart. Specialized conduction tracts conduct the cardiac impulse between the SA node and AV node and to the atrial musculature. The Bachmann bundle appears to conduct the cardiac impulse preferentially from the right to the left atrium. At the lower end of the AV node, the nodal fibers form the common bundle of His which passes to the interventricular septum and divides into right and left bundle branches. The branches divide into the Purkinje fibers that extend into both ventricular walls.

Innervation of the Heart

Although cardiac automaticity is intrinsic to the SA node; heart rate, rhythm, and contractility are also influenced by the autonomic nervous system. The vagus and sympathetic cardiac nerves converge to form the cardiac plexus at the base of the heart.

- The sympathetic influence is achieved by release of epinephrine and norepinephrine. Sympathetic nerves stimulate the chambers to beat faster (chronotropic effect) and with greater force of contraction (inotropic effect).
- The parasympathetic influence is achieved via acetylcholine release from the vagus nerve. Parasympathetic nerves slow the heart rate (chronotropic effect) primarily through their influence on the SA node.

Neural Reflexes and Circulatory Control

The balance between the sympathetic and parasympathetic components of the autonomic nervous system determines cardiovascular responses.

Baroreceptor reflex: Baroreceptors are mechanoreceptors that detect changes in pressure. The reflexes by which blood pressure is maintained are collectively known as the baroreflex, which includes arterial baroreceptors (high pressure receptors located in the carotid sinus, aortic arch, and origin of the right subclavian artery) and cardiopulmonary receptors (low pressure receptors). Sympathetic activation leads to increased cardiac contractility, increased heart rate, venoconstriction, and arterial vasoconstriction, ultimately leading to increased blood pressure via elevation of total peripheral resistance and cardiac output. Parasympathetic activation leads to a decrease in heart rate and a small decrease in contractility, resulting in a decrease in blood pressure.

Bainbridge reflex: An increase in venous return stretches receptors in the wall of the right atrium which sends vagal afferent signals to the cardiovascular center within the medulla. The signals inhibit parasympathetic activity, resulting in an increased heart rate.

Chemoreceptor reflex: Chemosensitive cells located in the carotid bodies and the aortic body respond to changes in pH status and blood oxygen tension. At an arterial partial oxygen pressure of less than 50 mm Hg or in conditions of acidosis, the chemoreceptors stimulate the respiratory centers and increase the depth and rate of ventilation. In addition, the ensuing activation of the parasympathetic system reduces heart rate and myocardial contractility. In the case of persistent hypoxia, the CNS will be directly stimulated with a resultant increase in sympathetic activity.

Valsalva maneuver: Forced expiration against a closed glottis produces increased intrathoracic pressure, increased central venous pressure, and decreased venous return. The resultant decrease in cardiac output and blood pressure is sensed by baroreceptors, which reflexively increase heart rate and myocardial contractility through sympathetic stimulation. When the glottis opens, venous return increases and blood pressure and heart contractility increase. The increase in blood pressure is sensed by baroreceptors, which reflexively decrease the heart rate through the parasympathetic efferent pathways.

Cardiac Cycle

The cardiac cycle refers to the sequence of events that occur when the heart beats.

Atrial systole: The contraction of the right and left atria pushing blood into the ventricles.

Atrial diastole: The period between atrial contractions when the atria are repolarizing.

Ventricular systole: Contraction of the right and left ventricles pushing blood into the pulmonary arteries and aorta.

Ventricular diastole: The period between ventricular contractions when the ventricles are repolarizing.

Preload: Refers to the tension in the ventricular wall at the end of diastole. It reflects the venous filling pressure that fills the left ventricle during diastole.

Afterload: Refers to the forces that impede the flow of blood out of the heart, primarily the pressure in the peripheral vasculature, the compliance of the aorta, and the mass and viscosity of blood.

Stroke volume (SV): Refers to the volume of blood ejected by each contraction of the left ventricle. Normal SV ranges from 60 to 80 ml depending on age, sex, and activity.

Cardiac output (CO): The amount of blood pumped from the left or right ventricle per minute. It is equal to the product of stroke volume and heart rate. Normal CO for an adult male at rest is 4.5 to 5.0 L/min with women producing slightly less. CO can increase up to 25 L/min during exercise.

Venous return: The amount of blood that returns to the right atrium each minute. This is similar in volume to the CO. Because the cardiovascular system is a closed loop, venous return must equal CO when averaged over time.

Systemic Circulation

The systemic arterial circulation carries oxygenated blood from the left ventricle through the aorta, arteries, and arterioles to the capillaries in the tissues of the body. From the capillaries, deoxygenated blood returns through a series of venules and veins. The veins of the upper and lower extremities are subdivided into superficial and deep. The superficial veins are beneath the skin between the two layers of superficial fascia; the deep veins accompany the arteries. Both types of veins have valves, but they are more numerous in the deep veins than in the superficial veins and in lower extremity veins more than upper extremity veins.

Blood and Components of Blood[1]

Blood transports oxygen and nutrients to the cells of the body and returns waste products from these cells. Normal blood volume of an adult is between 4.5 and 5.0 L, with women's volume being slightly less than men. Hypovolemia refers to decreased blood volume, specifically the volume of plasma. Causes of hypovolemia include bleeding, dehydration from vomiting, diarrhea, sweating, severe burns, and diuretic medications used to treat hypertension. Signs and symptoms of hypovolemia include orthostatic hypotension, tachycardia, and elevated body temperature. Hypervolemia, or fluid overload, refers to increased blood plasma. Causes of hypervolemia include excess intake of fluids (e.g., IV or blood transfusion) and sodium or fluid retention (e.g., heart failure, kidney disease). Signs and symptoms of hypervolemia include swelling in the legs, ascites (fluid in the abdomen), and fluid in the lungs.

Plasma

Plasma is the liquid component of blood, in which the blood cells and platelets are suspended. Plasma consists of water, electrolytes, and proteins, and accounts for more than half of the total blood volume. Plasma is important in regulating blood pressure and temperature.

Red blood cells

Red blood cells (i.e., erythrocytes) make up approximately 40% of blood volume. Red blood cells contain hemoglobin, a protein that gives blood its red color and enables it to bind with oxygen. When the number of red blood cells is too low (anemia), the blood carries less oxygen, resulting in fatigue and weakness. If the number of red blood cells is too high (polycythemia), the blood is too thick, increasing the risk of stroke or heart attack.

Blood platelets

Blood platelets (i.e., thrombocytes) assist in blood clotting by clumping together at a bleeding site and forming a plug that helps to seal the blood vessel. A low number of platelets (thrombocytopenia) increases the risk for bruising and abnormal bleeding. A high number of platelets (thrombocythemia) increases the risk of thrombosis, which may result in a stroke or heart attack.

White blood cells

White blood cells (i.e., leukocytes) protect against infection. A low number of white blood cells (leukopenia) increases the risk of infection. An abnormally high number of white blood cells (leukocytosis) can indicate an infection or leukemia. There are five main types of white blood cells (Fig. 6-3):

Neutrophils: help protect the body against infections by ingesting bacteria and debris.
Lymphocytes: consist of three main types - T lymphocytes and natural killer cells, which help protect against viral infections and can detect and destroy some cancer cells, and B lymphocytes, which develop into cells that produce antibodies.
Monocytes: ingest dead or damaged cells and help defend against infectious organisms.
Eosinophils: kill parasites, destroy cancer cells, and are involved in allergic responses.
Basophils: participate in allergic responses.

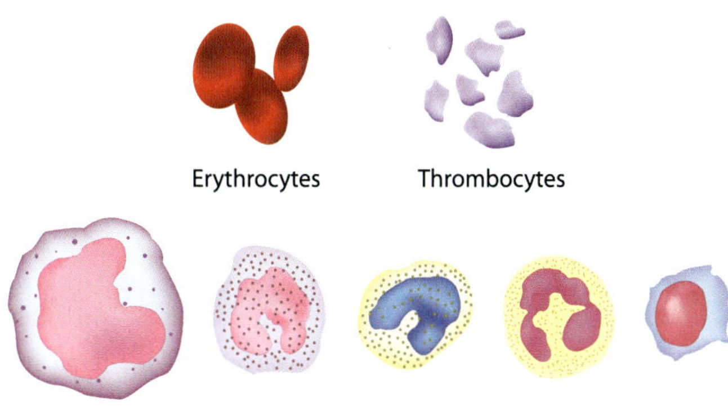

Fig. 6-3: Blood cells. Left to right: top row - erythrocytes and thrombocytes; bottom row – monocyte, basophil, eosinophil, neutrophil, lymphocyte.

Anatomy and Physiology of the Respiratory System

Thorax

The bony thorax encloses and protects the heart, lungs and other organs and provides attachment sites for ventilatory muscles and other muscles. The thorax is bounded posteriorly by the 12 thoracic vertebrae, intervertebral disks, and ribs; anteriorly by the sternum, costal cartilages, and ribs; and laterally by the ribs. Although not considered part of the thorax, the clavicles and scapulae provide attachment sites for the accessory muscles of inspiration.

Sternum

The sternum consists of three parts – manubrium, body, and xiphoid process. The manubrium, the superior portion, articulates with the right and left clavicles at the clavicular notch. The manubrium articulates with the body of the sternum forming the sternal angle (angle of Louis). A notch at the junction of the manubrium and body provides for the articulation of the second rib. The xiphoid process is the inferior portion of the sternum.

Ribs

Most of the bony thorax is formed by the 12 pairs of ribs. Anteriorly, ribs 1 through 7 (true ribs) attach to the sternum by costal cartilage. The costal cartilages of ribs 8 through 10 (false ribs) attach to the cartilage of the rib above and do not reach the sternum. The ventral ends of ribs 11 and 12 (floating ribs) have no skeletal attachment.

Thoracic vertebrae

Except for ribs 1, 10, 11, and 12, which articulate only with one vertebra, the head of each rib has both a superior and inferior facet for articulation with the bodies of two adjacent thoracic vertebrae. The inferior facet articulates with the superior costal facet of the vertebra of the same number. The superior facet articulates with the inferior costal facet of the vertebra numbered one lower. The transverse process of each vertebra has a transverse costal facet that articulates with the facet on the tubercle of the rib forming the costotransverse joints.

Muscles of Inspiration

The diaphragm and external intercostals are considered the principal muscles of inspiration. The diaphragm is a dome-shaped muscle that separates the thoracic cavity from the abdominal cavity. Contraction of the diaphragm causes the chest to expand longitudinally and the lower ribs to elevate to allow for inspiration.

The intercostal muscles occupy the spaces between the ribs. External intercostal muscles are oriented obliquely upward and backward from the upper border of one rib to the lower border of the rib above. Internal intercostal muscles are oriented obliquely upward and forward from the upper border of one rib to the lower border of the rib above. Contraction of the external and internal intercostal muscles elevates the ribs. Upward movement of the upper ribs increases the anterior-posterior (A-P) diameter of the chest; elevation of the lower ribs increases the transverse diameter.

Other muscles that attach to the sternum and ribs and ordinarily contribute to movement of the chest wall only during high levels of ventilation are considered accessory muscles of inspiration. These include the sternocleidomastoid, scalenes, pectoralis major (sternocostal portion), pectoralis minor, and serratus anterior.

Muscles of Exhalation

During quiet breathing, exhalation results from passive recoil of the lungs and rib cage. During forceful breathing, the rectus abdominis, external oblique, internal oblique, and transverse abdominis depress the lower ribs and compress the abdominal contents, thus pushing up the diaphragm and assisting with active exhalation.

Upper Respiratory Tract

The upper respiratory tract includes the nasal cavity, pharynx (nasopharynx, oropharynx, laryngopharynx), and larynx. In addition to serving as gas conduits, these passages humidify, cool or warm inspired air, and filter foreign matter before it can reach the alveoli. The hairs in the nostrils filter out many particles while the remaining particles settle on mucous membranes in the nose or near the tonsils and adenoids.

Lower Respiratory Tract

The lower respiratory tract extends from the larynx to the alveoli in the lungs and consists of the conducting airways and the terminal respiratory units. Between the trachea and the alveoli, the airways divide approximately 23 times.

Trachea

Beginning at the larynx (approximately at the base of the neck) and ending at the carina (at the level of the fourth thoracic vertebra and the sternal angle) the trachea consists of a series of horseshoe-shaped rings of cartilage which support the anterior and lateral walls. Posteriorly, the trachea is composed of longitudinal bundles of smooth muscle, fibrous and elastic tissues, and numerous mucous glands. The trachea divides at the carina into the right and left main bronchi.

Lung Lobes and Segments

The lungs are located on either side of the mediastinum, each within its own pleural cavity. The right lung has three lobes (upper, middle, and lower) and the left lung has two lobes (upper and lower). The lingula of the left upper lobe is analogous to the right middle lobe (Fig. 6-4).

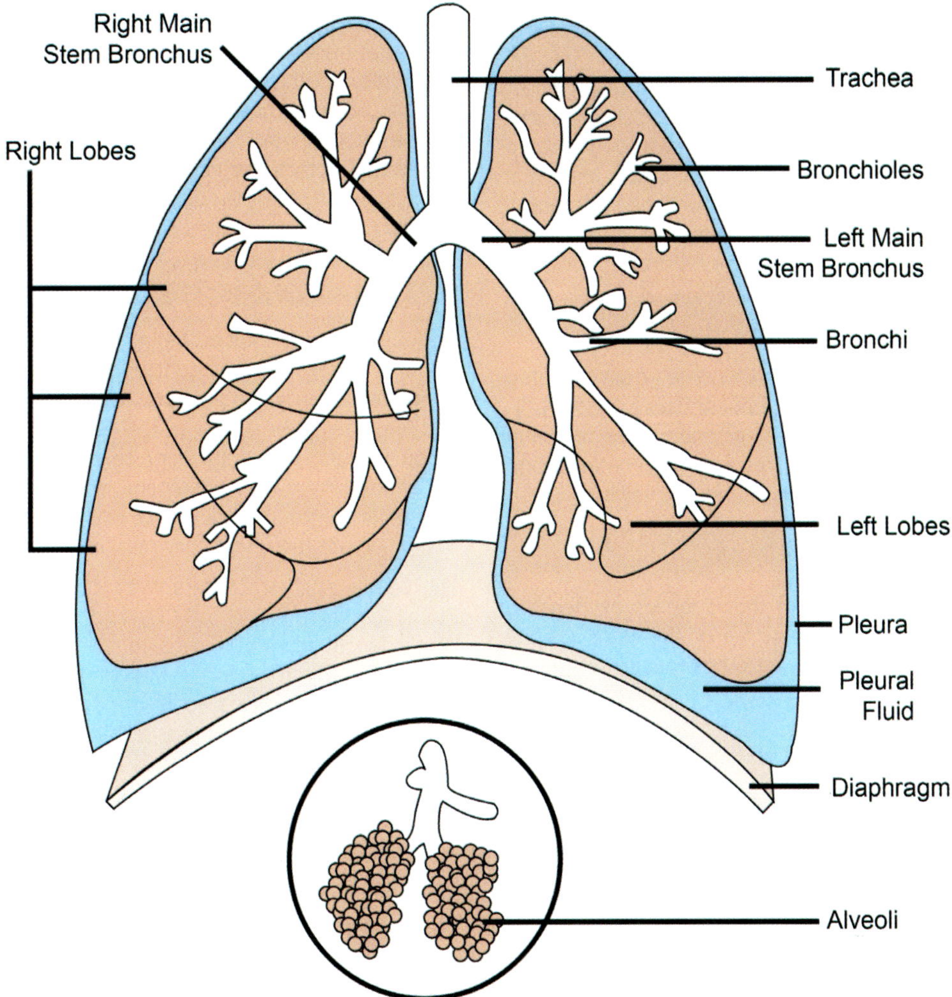

Fig. 6-4: Diagram of the human lungs.

Bronchopulmonary segments

The bronchopulmonary segments are the topographic units of the lungs. There are ten bronchopulmonary segments in the right lung and eight bronchopulmonary segments in the left lung. The right and left main bronchi branch into lobar bronchi. Each lobar bronchus branches into segmental bronchi, corresponding to the bronchopulmonary segments of the right and left lungs, which branch into bronchioles and end in terminal bronchioles.

Right lung

The right main bronchus gives rise to the superior, middle, and inferior lobar bronchi. The right superior lobar bronchus divides into three segmental bronchi: apical, anterior, and posterior. The right middle lobar bronchus divides into two segmental bronchi: medial and lateral. The right inferior lobar bronchus divides into five segmental bronchi: superior, medial basal, anterior basal, lateral basal, and posterior basal.

Left lung

The left main bronchus divides into the superior and inferior lobar bronchi, which correspond to the upper and lower lobes, respectively. The left superior lobar bronchus subdivides into a superior division and an inferior (lingular) division. The superior division divides into the anterior segmental bronchus and the apicoposterior segmental bronchus (corresponding to the apical and posterior segmental bronchi of the right upper lobe). The inferior or lingular division subdivides into the superior segmental bronchus and inferior segmental bronchus. The left inferior lobar bronchus divides into the superior, lateral basal, posterior basal, and anteromedial basal segmental bronchi (corresponding to the anterior and medial segmental bronchi of the right lower lobe).

Alveolar–capillary units

The bronchi branch many times before terminating in the acinus or respiratory unit of the lung. Oxygen diffuses across the alveolar-capillary septum into the red blood cells in the lung capillaries where it combines with hemoglobin to be transported back to the heart. Carbon dioxide diffuses in the opposite direction.

Pleurae

A membranous serous sac called visceral pleura covers each lung. The pleura covering the surface of the lungs is called the visceral pleura. The pleural tissue covering the inner surfaces of the chest wall, ribs, vertebrae, diaphragm, and mediastinum is called parietal pleura. Normally, the two pleurae remain in contact throughout the respiratory cycle, separated only by serous fluid. Under abnormal circumstances, the pleural space may contain air (pneumothorax), blood (hemothorax), pus or increased amounts of serous fluid, which compress the lung and cause respiratory distress.

Pulmonary Circulation

The portion of the circulatory system that carries deoxygenated blood from the heart to the lungs via the pulmonary arterial trunk, right and left pulmonary arteries, lobar arteries, arterioles, and capillaries. The pulmonary circulation returns oxygenated blood from the lungs to the left atrium via the pulmonary veins.

Bronchial Circulation

The portion of the circulatory system that supplies oxygenated blood to the bronchi and connective tissue of the lungs via the bronchial arteries, which drain directly into the bronchial veins.

Innervation of the Lungs

The lungs, trachea, and bronchi are innervated by both sympathetic and parasympathetic nerves containing efferent and afferent fibers. Postganglionic sympathetic fibers innervate the smooth muscles of the bronchi and pulmonary blood vessels. Parasympathetic innervation of these structures is via the vagus nerve. The nerves to the lungs reach the pulmonary vessels and lung tissue through the anterior and posterior pulmonary plexuses.

Control of Breathing[2]

Although spontaneous breathing is largely an involuntary process, also it is under voluntary control. Breathing control is achieved by integrated activity of the central respiratory center in the brainstem and peripheral receptors in the lungs, airways, chest wall, and blood vessels. The respiratory center integrates the information transmitted from the central and peripheral chemoreceptors and mechanoreceptors in the chest wall to stimulate motor neurons that innervate the respiratory muscles.

The central chemoreceptors in the medulla respond to increases in the partial pressure of CO_2 and hydrogen ion by increasing ventilation. In addition to sensing changes in the partial pressure of CO_2 and hydrogen ion concentration, the peripheral chemoreceptors in the carotid bodies also respond to hypoxemia by increasing ventilation. Mechanoreceptors inhibit muscle activity when the force of contraction reaches potentially injurious levels.

Lung Volumes and Capacities	
Anatomic dead space volume (VD)	The volume of air that occupies the non-respiratory conducting airways.
Expiratory reserve volume (ERV)	The maximal volume of air that can be exhaled after a normal tidal exhalation. ERV is approximately 15% of total lung volume.
Forced expiratory volume (FEV)	The maximal volume of air exhaled in a specified period of time: usually the 1st, 2nd, and 3rd second of a forced vital capacity maneuver.
Forced vital capacity (FVC)	The volume of air expired during a forced maximal expiration after a forced maximal inspiration.
Functional residual capacity (FRC)	The volume of air in the lungs after normal exhalation. FRC = ERV + RV. FRC is approximately 40% of total lung volume.
Inspiratory capacity (IC)	The maximal volume of air that can be inspired after a normal tidal exhalation. IC = TV + IRV. IC is approximately 60% of total lung volume.
Inspiratory reserve volume (IRV)	The maximal volume of air that can be inspired after normal tidal volume inspiration. IRV is approximately 50% of total lung volume.
Minute volume ventilation (VE)	The volume of air expired in one minute. VE = TV x respiratory rate.
Peak expiratory flow (PEF)	The maximum flow of air during the beginning of a forced expiratory maneuver.
Residual volume (RV)	The volume of gas remaining in the lungs at the end of a maximal expiration. RV is approximately 25% of total lung volume.
Tidal volume (TV)	Total volume inspired and expired with each breath during quiet breathing. TV is approximately 10% of total lung volume.
Total lung capacity (TLC)	The volume of air in the lungs after a maximal inspiration; the sum of all lung volumes. TLC = RV + VC or TLC = FRC + IC.
Vital capacity (VC)	The volume change that occurs between maximal inspiration and maximal expiration. VC = TV + IRV + ERV. VC is approximately 75% of total lung volume.

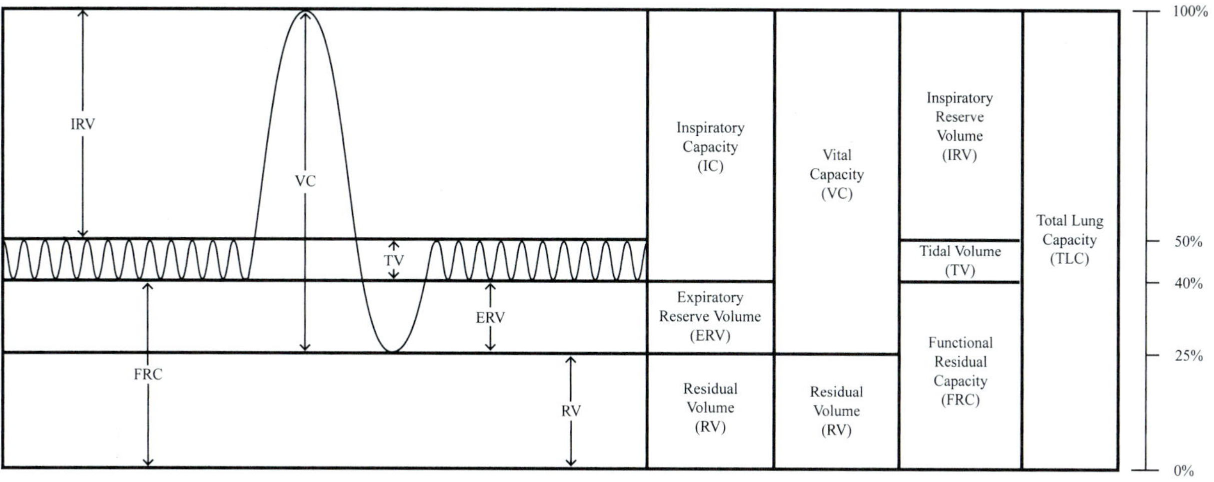

ERV = ~15% total volume
IRV = ~50% total volume
FRC = ~40% total volume
VC = ~75% total volume

RV = ~25% total volume
IC = ~60% total volume
TV = ~10% total volume
TLC = 100% volume

Fig. 6-5: Spirogram showing lung volumes and capacities.

Oxygen and Carbon Dioxide Transport

Oxygen is physically dissolved in the blood plasma and chemically combined with hemoglobin in red blood cells. Much more oxygen is combined with hemoglobin than is dissolved in the plasma. Only about 0.3 mL O_2 is dissolved in 100 mL of arterial blood. However, the physically dissolved oxygen contributes to the PaO_2, which determines how much oxygen combines chemically with hemoglobin.

Carbon dioxide is physically dissolved in the blood, chemically combined with the amino acids of hemoglobin as carbamino compounds, and as bicarbonate ions. About 5-10% of the total carbon dioxide transported by the blood is dissolved in physical solution. A similar percentage is in the form of carbamino compounds. The remaining 80-90% of the carbon dioxide is transported by the blood as bicarbonate ions.

Pathology of the Heart and Blood Vessels

Aneurysm[3]

A localized abnormal dilation of a blood vessel, usually an artery. Common sites include the thoracic and abdominal aorta and vessels within the brain.

Etiology – Congenital defect; weakness in the wall of the vessel often due to chronic hypertension; connective tissue disease (e.g., Marfan syndrome); trauma; infection.

Signs and symptoms – Variable based on the site. Aortic aneurysms are usually asymptomatic, but may include generalized abdominal or low back pain. Abdominal aortic aneurysms may cause pulsations near the navel. A cerebral aneurysm can cause a sudden and severe headache, nausea and vomiting, stiff neck, seizure, loss of consciousness, and double vision.

Treatment – Antihypertensive medications may be recommended for hypertension. Surgery is recommended to repair large aortic aneurysms and consists of replacing the aneurysm with a synthetic fabric graft. Two surgical options for ruptured brain aneurysms are surgical clipping and endovascular coiling.

Angina Pectoris[3]

A transient precordial sensation of pressure or discomfort resulting from myocardial ischemia. Common types of angina pectoris are:

- **Stable angina** - Occurs at a predictable level of exertion, exercise or stress and responds to rest or nitroglycerin.
- **Unstable angina** - Usually is more intense, lasts longer, is precipitated by less exertion, occurs spontaneously at rest, is progressive, or any combination of these features.
- **Prinzmetal (variant) angina** - Occurs due to coronary artery spasm most often associated with coronary artery disease.

Etiology – Inadequate blood flow and oxygenation of the heart muscle mostly due to coronary artery disease.

Signs and symptoms – Usually described as pressure, heaviness, fullness, squeezing, burning or aching behind the sternum, but may also be felt in the neck and back, jaw, shoulders, and arms. The sensation may be associated with difficulty breathing, nausea or vomiting, sweating, anxiety or fear (anginal equivalents). It is typically triggered by exertion or strong emotion and subsides with rest.

Treatment – Treatments for acute angina include supplemental oxygen, nitroglycerin, and rest. Chronic or recurring angina pectoris is treated with long-acting nitrates, beta blockers, and calcium channel blockers. Angioplasty with stenting of the coronary arteries or coronary artery bypass surgery may be performed when medications are not effective.

Atherosclerosis[3]

A slow progressive accumulation of fatty plaques on the inner walls of arteries. Over time the plaque can restrict blood flow, causing a blood clot.

Etiology – Although the exact cause is unknown, the process may begin with damage or injury to the inner wall of the artery from hypertension, high cholesterol, smoking or diabetes. Over time, fatty plaques made of cholesterol and other cellular waste products build up at the site of the injury and harden, narrowing the artery and impeding blood flow (Fig. 6-6).

Signs and symptoms – Varies based on the severity of disease and the artery affected. When the coronary arteries are affected, angina pectoris may result. When cerebral arteries are affected, numbness or weakness of the arms or legs, difficulty speaking or slurred speech, or drooping face muscles may result. When peripheral arteries are affected, intermittent claudication may result.

Treatment – Lifestyle changes, medications, and surgery may be recommended. Lifestyle changes include smoking cessation, regular exercise, healthy diet, and stress management. Medications may include antihypertensive, antiplatelet, and antilipidemic agents. Surgical procedures may include: angioplasty, endarterectomy, and bypass surgery.

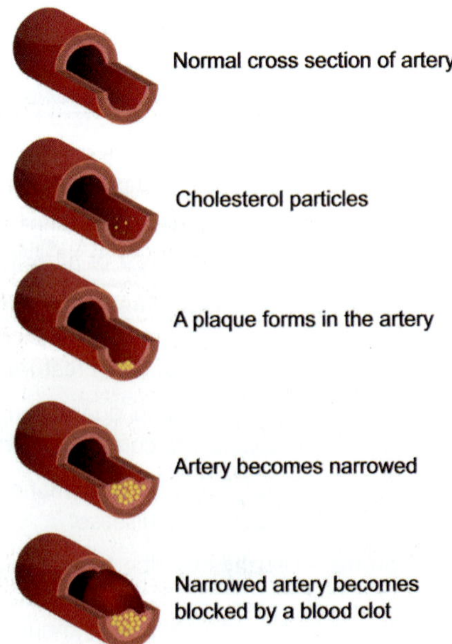

Fig. 6-6: Changes in an artery due to atherosclerosis.

Cardiomyopathy[3]

Cardiomyopathy refers to a group of conditions that affect the myocardium, impairing the ability of the heart to contract and relax. Three types of cardiomyopathy are dilated, hypertrophic, and restrictive.

Etiology – There are many causes of cardiomyopathy, including coronary artery disease and valvular heart disease.

Signs and symptoms – None during the early stages. As the condition progresses, signs and symptoms include breathlessness with exertion or even at rest; swelling of the legs, ankles and feet; bloating of the abdomen due to fluid buildup; fatigue; irregular heartbeat; dizziness, lightheadedness and fainting.

Treatment – Variable depending on type of cardiomyopathy.

- **Dilated cardiomyopathy** – Common medications include ACE inhibitors, beta blockers, digoxin, and diuretics. Surgical intervention may include a biventricular pacemaker or an implantable cardioverter-defibrillator for patients at risk for serious arrhythmias.
- **Hypertrophic cardiomyopathy** – Medications to slow the heart rate and stabilize its rhythm. Common medications include Lopressor and calcium channel blockers. If medications are unsuccessful, surgical interventions may include septal myectomy (removal of the thickened interventricular septum); septal alcohol ablation (destruction of the interventricular septum by alcohol injection); pacemaker implantation; and implantable cardioverter-defibrillator.
- **Restrictive cardiomyopathy** – Medications focus on improving symptoms and may include diuretics, antihypertensives, and antiarrhythmics. In severe cases, surgical options include a ventricular assist device or a heart transplant.

Chronic Venous Insufficiency (CVI)[3]

A condition in which the veins and valves in the lower extremity are damaged and cannot keep blood flowing toward the heart. This causes the veins to remain filled with blood.

Etiology – Weak or damaged valves inside the veins. Risk factors include age, female gender, obesity, pregnancy, and prolonged sitting or standing.

Signs and symptoms – Leg swelling, varicose veins, aching, heaviness or cramping, itching, redness or skin ulcers of the legs and ankles.

Treatment – Compression stockings and elevation of the legs help decrease chronic swelling. Varicose vein stripping may be performed for cases with persistent leg pain or skin ulcers due to poor circulation.

Congenital Heart Defects[3]

A malformation of the interior walls or valves of the heart or the major arteries and veins near the heart that are present at birth. Blood flow through the heart may be slowed, blocked or misdirected. Congenital heart defects are the most common type of major birth defect.

Atrial septal defect (ASD)

A hole in the wall of the heart separating the right and left atria. In fetal circulation, there is normally an opening between the two atria to allow blood to bypass the lungs. This opening is termed foramen ovale and usually closes at birth. If the ASD persists, blood continues to flow from the left to the right atrium and is called a shunt. In severe cases, blood may flow from the right to the left atrium.

Etiology – Congenital heart defects arise from errors early in the heart's development. Genetics and environmental factors may play a role.

Signs and symptoms – Small to moderate sized defects may produce no symptoms or symptoms that appear after 30 years of age. Large or long-standing atrial septal defects may cause:

- Heart murmur
- Shortness of breath, especially when exercising
- Fatigue
- Swelling of the legs, feet or abdomen
- Heart palpitations
- Frequent lung infections
- Stroke
- Cyanosis of the skin

Treatment – Surgical closure is recommended if the defect is large, the heart is swollen or symptoms occur. A non-surgical procedure involves placing a closure device into the heart and across the ASD using a catheter.

Coarctation of the aorta

A congenital heart defect in which the aorta is narrowed near the ductus arteriosus. The coarctation may range from mild to severe and may not be detected until adulthood, depending on the amount of narrowing. It usually occurs along with other congenital defects including patent ductus arteriosus, ventricular septal defect, and bicuspid aortic valve.

Etiology – Congenital heart defects arise from errors early in the heart's development, but there is often no clear cause. Genetics and environmental factors may play a role. Rarely, it may develop later in life due to atherosclerosis or inflammation of the aorta.

Signs and symptoms – Depend on the severity of the narrowing. In infants with severe narrowing, pale skin, sweating, and shortness of breath are noted soon after birth. In older children and adults, the most common sign is high blood pressure in the arms, but low blood pressure in the legs. Other signs and symptoms may include shortness of breath during exercise, intermittent claudication, weakness, and headache.

Treatment – Depends on age when diagnosed and the degree of narrowing of the aorta, but usually consists of surgical repair (resection, patch, bypass), or balloon angioplasty.

Patent ductus arteriosus (PDA)

A congenital heart defect in which the ductus arteriosus, which normally shunts blood from the pulmonary artery directly to the descending aorta in utero, does not close after birth.

Etiology – Congenital heart defects arise from errors early in the heart's development, but there is often no clear cause. Genetics and environmental factors may play a role. Risk factors include premature birth, other heart defects, family history, rubella infection or diabetes during pregnancy, and exposure to alcohol, drugs, chemicals or radiation during pregnancy.

Signs and symptoms – A small ductus may be asymptomatic, whereas a large ductus may present with tachycardia, respiratory distress, poor eating, weight loss, and congestive heart failure.

Treatment – Non-surgical treatments to reduce the size of the ductus include diuretics and indomethacin. Surgical repair may be necessary for a large ductus or when initial management fails. Left untreated, a PDA can cause pulmonary hypertension, heart failure, and other complications.

Ventricular septal defect (VSD)

A hole in the septum separating the right and left ventricles. If the hole is large, too much blood will be pumped to the lungs, leading to heart failure.

Etiology – Congenital heart defects arise from errors early in the heart's development, but there is often no clear cause. Genetics and environmental factors may play a role. Risk factors include rubella or diabetes during pregnancy, exposure to alcohol, drugs, chemicals, and radiation during pregnancy.

Signs and symptoms – A small defect may have no symptoms and the hole may eventually close as the interventricular wall continues to grow after birth. A large defect may cause:

- Cyanosis of the skin, lips, and fingernails
- Poor eating, failure to thrive
- Fast breathing or breathlessness
- Fatigue
- Swelling of the legs, feet or abdomen
- Rapid heart rate (i.e., tachycardia)

Treatment – A common approach involves surgical patching or stitching to close the hole.

Tetralogy of Fallot

A combination of four heart defects including: (1) ventricular septal defect (VSD); (2) pulmonary stenosis; (3) right ventricular hypertrophy; (4) aorta overriding the ventricular septal defect. It is often diagnosed during infancy, but may not be detected until later in life, depending on the severity of the defects and symptoms.

Etiology – In most cases the cause is unknown. Risk factors include poor maternal nutrition, viral illness or genetic disorders.

Signs and symptoms – Depend on the obstruction of blood flow from the right ventricle, but may include:

- Cyanosis of the skin
- Shortness of breath and rapid breathing, especially during feeding
- Fainting
- Clubbing of fingers and toes
- Poor weight gain

- Tiring easily during play
- Irritability and prolonged crying
- Heart murmur

Treatment - Surgery is the only effective treatment. Usually, cardiac surgery involves placing a patch over the VSD and widening the pulmonary valve and pulmonary arteries. Untreated cases usually develop severe complications including infective endocarditis, which may result in death or disability by early adulthood.

Cor Pulmonale[4]

Cor pulmonale, also known as pulmonary heart disease, refers to hypertrophy of the right ventricle caused by altered structure or function of the lungs.

Etiology - Pulmonary hypertension from chronically increased resistance in the pulmonary circulation.

Signs and symptoms - The cardinal symptom is progressive shortness of breath, especially with exertion. Other signs and symptoms are fatigue, palpitations, atypical chest pain, swelling of the lower extremities, dizziness, and syncope.

Treatment - Supplemental oxygen sufficient to maintain SaO_2 > 90% and/or PaO_2 > 60 mm Hg. General measures include diuretics and anticoagulation.

Coronary Artery Disease (CAD)[3]

CAD is the narrowing or blockage of the coronary arteries due to atheromatous plaques resulting in diminished blood flow.

Etiology - CAD is thought to begin with damage or injury to the inner layer of a coronary artery. Once the inner wall is damaged, fatty plaques made of cholesterol and other cellular waste products tend to accumulate at the site of injury. If a plaque ruptures, platelets will clump at the site to try to repair the artery. This clump can block the artery, leading to a heart attack. Risk factors for CAD are the same as those for atherosclerosis: high blood levels of LDL cholesterol, low blood levels of HDL cholesterol, type 2 diabetes mellitus, smoking, obesity, and physical inactivity. Genetic factors, hypertension, and hypothyroidism also contribute to risk.

Signs and symptoms - The degree of stenosis required to produce signs and symptoms varies with the oxygen demand. The diminished blood flow may cause angina, shortness of breath or other symptoms, which may not be felt until >70% of the lumen is occluded. A complete blockage can cause a heart attack.

Treatment - Aggressive modification of atherosclerosis risk factors to slow progression and induce regression of existing plaques and restore or improve coronary blood flow. This includes smoking cessation; weight loss; a heart-healthy diet low in saturated fat, cholesterol and sodium; regular exercise; modification of serum lipids; and control of hypertension and diabetes. Drug therapy includes: antiplatelet agents (e.g., aspirin, Clopidogrel), ACE inhibitors, angiotensin II receptor blockers, and statins. Percutaneous angioplasty and coronary artery bypass graft surgery are considered for patients at high risk of mortality.

Deep Vein Thrombosis (DVT)[3]

A condition in which a blood clot forms in one or more of the deep veins, usually in the lower extremities. DVT is a serious condition because the clot can break loose and travel to the lungs, resulting in a pulmonary embolism.

Etiology - Any condition that impairs normal circulation or normal blood clotting. Many factors increase the risk of a DVT including prolonged sitting or bed rest, inherited blood clotting disorders, injury or surgery of the veins, pregnancy, cancer, birth control or hormone replacement therapy, being overweight, obesity, and smoking.

Signs and symptoms - About 50% of DVT cases are asymptomatic. When signs and symptoms occur they can include swelling, pain, redness, and warmth in the affected leg.

Treatment - The goal of treatment is to prevent the blood clot from getting bigger and to prevent it from breaking loose and causing a pulmonary embolism. Medications include anticoagulant and thrombolytic agents. "Filters" may be surgically inserted into the vena cava to prevent clots from reaching the lungs. Compression stockings may be recommended to reduce blood pooling.

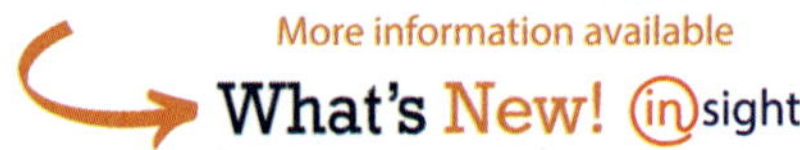

Endocarditis[3]

Endocarditis is inflammation of the endothelium that lines the heart and cardiac valves. If left untreated, endocarditis can damage or destroy heart valves and become life-threatening.

Etiology - Caused by bacteria that may enter the blood from catheters or needles, dental procedures, gum disease, sexually transmitted disease or inflammatory bowel disease. Individuals with a damaged heart valve, an artificial heart valve or other heart defects are at the greatest risk.

Signs and symptoms - May develop slowly, depending on the cause of the infection and if the heart is affected, but can include fever, chills, heart murmur, fatigue, shortness of breath, weight loss, blood in urine, and skin petechiae.

Treatment - Antibiotics are the first line of treatment. Surgery may be needed to treat persistent infections or replace a damaged heart valve.

Heart Failure[5]

Also known as congestive heart failure, heart failure is a progressive condition in which the heart cannot maintain a normal cardiac output to meet the body's demands for blood and oxygen. Heart failure often develops after other conditions have damaged or weakened the heart. The ventricles weaken and dilate to the point that the heart can't pump efficiently. It can affect the right side, left side or both sides of the heart, but typically begins with the left ventricle. The term "congestive heart failure" comes from blood backing up into the liver, abdomen, lower extremities, and lungs. The condition can be acute or chronic.

Etiology - Coronary artery disease, hypertension, diabetes mellitus, myocardial infarction, abnormal heart valves, and cardiomyopathy.

Signs and symptoms – Shortness of breath; fatigue and weakness; swelling in the legs, feet and abdomen; rapid or irregular heartbeat with S3 or S4 heart sound; persistent cough or wheezing; and weight gain from fluid retention.

Treatment – Sometimes treating the underlying cause can correct heart failure (e.g., repairing a damaged heart valve or controlling an abnormal heart rhythm). In most cases, treatment is a balance of medications, devices, and lifestyle changes to help the heart contract normally. Medications include anticoagulants, antihypertensives, and digitalis to increase the strength of contraction. In severe cases, surgery and medical devices may be needed to correct the underlying cause of the heart failure. These include coronary artery bypass graft, heart valve repair, implantable cardioverter-defibrillator (ICD), biventricular pacemaker, left ventricular assist device, and heart transplant. Lifestyle changes include smoking cessation, restricting sodium intake, maintaining healthy weight, limiting alcohol and fluids, stress reduction, and moderate exercise.

Heart Murmur[3]

An abnormal swishing or whooshing sound heard by auscultation sometime during the cardiac cycle.

Etiology – Innocent heart murmurs occur when blood flows rapidly through the heart due to activity, pregnancy, fever, and anemia. Abnormal heart murmurs may be caused by turbulent blood flow through a damaged or narrowed heart valve or a hole in one of the heart's walls. Other causes include rheumatic fever, endocarditis, calcified valves, and mitral valve prolapse.

Signs and symptoms – Innocent murmurs are not usually associated with other signs or symptoms. Abnormal murmurs may be associated with cyanosis, limb edema, shortness of breath, enlarged neck veins, weight gain, chest pain, dizziness, and fainting.

Treatment – Innocent murmurs usually do not require treatment. Treatment for abnormal heart murmurs depends on the underlying cause and can include medications or surgery. Common medications are: digoxin, anticoagulants, diuretics, and other antihypertensive agents. Surgical procedures include valve replacement or patching atrial or ventricular septal defects.

Hypertension[6]

Normal blood pressure is defined as systolic blood pressure less than 120 mm Hg and diastolic blood pressure less than 80 mm Hg. Levels of hypertension include Elevated, Stage 1, and Stage 2.

Etiology – Primary or essential hypertension has no known cause. Hypertension with an identified cause (usually renal disease) is called secondary hypertension.

Signs and symptoms – Hypertension is often asymptomatic until complications develop in the organs. An S4 heart sound is an early sign. Severe hypertension (DBP > 120 mm Hg) can cause significant CNS symptoms (e.g., confusion, cortical blindness, hemiparesis, seizures), cardiovascular symptoms (e.g., chest pain, dyspnea), and renal involvement.

Treatment – Recommendations include lifestyle modifications (aerobic physical activity at least 30 min/day most days of the week; weight loss to a body mass index of 18.5 to 24.9; smoking cessation; reduced intake of dietary sodium and alcohol; increased consumption of fruits, vegetables, and low-fat dairy products with reduced saturated and total fat content); and medications. Classes of medications for hypertension include diuretics, beta blockers, calcium channel blockers, ACE inhibitors, angiotensin II receptor blockers, and direct vasodilators.

Classification of Hypertension in Adults

BP Classification	SBP mm Hg	DBP mm Hg
Normal	<120 (and)	<80
Elevated	120–129 (and)	<80
Stage 1	130–139 (or)	80–89
Stage 2	at least 140 (or)	at least 90

Blood pressure guidelines update – November 2017.
American Heart Association and American College of Cardiology.

Myocardial Infarction (MI)[8]

Also known as a heart attack, a MI occurs when the blood flow through one or more of the coronary arteries is severely reduced or cut off completely. This causes irreversible necrosis to the portion of myocardium supplied by the blocked artery.

Etiology – Most heart attacks occur when a ruptured atherosclerotic plaque or blood clot blocks the flow of blood through a coronary artery. An uncommon cause is a spasm of a coronary artery.

Signs and symptoms – Chest discomfort with pressure, squeezing or pain; shortness of breath; discomfort in the upper body including the arms, shoulder, neck or back; nausea, vomiting, dizziness, sweating, and palpitations.

Treatment – Treatment of a MI varies from medication to surgery, or both, depending on the severity and the amount of heart damage. Medications used to treat the acute MI include anticoagulants and thrombolytic agents, pain relievers, antihypertensives, and cholesterol-lowering medications. Surgical procedures may include coronary angioplasty with stenting or coronary artery bypass surgery. Recommended lifestyle changes include smoking cessation, moderate exercise, maintaining a healthy diet and weight, stress reduction, and consuming alcohol only in moderation.

Heart attack symptoms vary. Not all people who have heart attacks experience the same symptoms or experience them to the same degree. Some heart attacks are sudden and intense, but most start slowly, with mild pain or discomfort. Signs that can indicate a heart attack include:

- Discomfort in the center of the chest that lasts more than a few minutes, or that goes away and comes back. It can feel like uncomfortable pressure, squeezing, fullness or pain.
- Pain or discomfort in one or both upper extremities, the back, neck, jaw or stomach.
- Shortness of breath with or without chest discomfort.
- Breaking out in a cold sweat, nausea or lightheadedness.

The most common heart attack symptom is chest pain or discomfort in both men and women. Women are somewhat more likely than men to experience shortness of breath, nausea/vomiting, and back or jaw pain.

Often people affected aren't sure what's wrong and wait too long before getting help. Even if a patient or therapist is not sure it's a heart attack, they should have it checked by a doctor. Patients should not wait more than five minutes to call 911 or an emergency response number. It is best to call Emergency Medical Services (EMS) for rapid transport to an emergency room. EMS staff can begin treatment when they arrive and can revive someone whose heart has stopped.

Myocarditis

Myocarditis refers to inflammation and weakness of the myocardium. Myocarditis can cause the myocardium to become thick and swollen, which can lead to symptoms of heart failure.

Etiology - Usually caused by a viral (e.g., influenza, coxsackie virus, adenovirus) or bacterial (e.g., polio, rubella, Lyme disease) infection.

Signs and symptoms - Depend on the cause and severity of the disease. Common symptoms include arrhythmias, chest pain, shortness of breath, fatigue, and signs of fever (headache, muscle aches, sore throat, diarrhea or rashes).

Treatment - Treatment focuses on the underlying cause and may include antibiotics, anti-inflammatory agents, diuretics, beta blockers, and calcium channel blockers to reduce the workload of the heart. Severe cases may require surgical implantation of a ventricular assist device or intra-aortic balloon pump.

Pericarditis[3]

Pericarditis refers to an inflammation of the pericardium of the heart. The pericardium has an inner and outer layer with a small amount of lubricating fluid between them. When the pericardium becomes inflamed, the amount of fluid between the two layers increases (pericardial effusion). This condition may be acute or chronic, both of which can disrupt the heart's normal rhythm and/or function and possibly, although rarely, lead to death.

Etiology - Usually a complication of viral infections (e.g., coxsackie, influenza, HIV), but it can also result from bacterial and fungal infections. Other causes include heart attack, chest trauma, surgery, immunosuppressive medications, and radiation to the chest.

Signs and Symptoms - Chest pain, shortness of breath, dry cough, anxiety, fatigue, and fever.

Treatment - Analgesics or anti-inflammatory medications are given to relieve pain; antibiotics are prescribed if the pericarditis is due to a bacterial infection. Most cases are mild and clear up on their own or with rest and simple treatment. More intense treatment may be needed to prevent complications like cardiac tamponade. Cardiac tamponade occurs when fluid in the pericardium creates pressure on the heart preventing the heart from properly filling with blood. As a result, less blood leaves the heart, which causes a sharp drop in blood pressure. If left untreated, cardiac tamponade can be fatal. Treatment consists of pericardiocentesis, in which a needle or catheter is inserted to remove excess fluid in the pericardium.

Peripheral Arterial Disease[9]

Stenotic, occlusive, and aneurysmal diseases of the aorta and peripheral arteries.

Etiology - Caused primarily by atherosclerosis and thromboembolic processes that alter the structure and function of the aorta and its branches.

Signs and symptoms - Fatigue, aching, numbness, or pain primarily in the buttock, thigh, calf, or foot at rest or when walking; poorly healing wounds of the legs or feet; distal hair loss, trophic skin changes, and hypertrophic nails.

Treatment - For patients with asymptomatic disease, treatment consists of smoking cessation, lipid lowering medications, and control of diabetes and hypertension (with beta blockers). For patients with disabling intermittent claudication, treatment consists of revascularization procedures (e.g., angioplasty, stent, lasers, atherectomy devices) and surgery (e.g., aortobifemoral bypass, aortoiliac bypass, aortofemoral bypass, iliofemoral bypass) may be recommended. Supervised exercise training should be performed for a minimum of 30 to 45 minutes, at least three times per week, for a minimum of 12 weeks.

Rheumatic Fever[3]

An inflammatory disease that can develop as a complication of untreated or poorly treated strep throat from group A streptococcus bacteria. Rheumatic fever can damage the heart valves and cause heart failure.

Etiology – Streptococcus pyogenes or group A streptococcus that cause strep throat or scarlet fever.

Signs and symptoms – Result from the inflammation of the heart, joints, skin or central nervous system and may include red, swollen, fever, and painful joints, heart palpitations, chest pain, shortness of breath, and skin rash.

Treatment – The goals of treatment are to destroy group A streptococcal bacteria, relieve symptoms, and control inflammation. Medications include antibiotics and anti-inflammatory agents.

Valvular Heart Disease[10]

Damage to one or more of the heart's valves results in regurgitation or stenosis of blood flow. In regurgitation, also known as insufficiency or incompetence, the blood leaks backward through the damaged valve. Stenosis happens when the leaflets thicken, stiffen or fuse together and do not open wide enough to allow adequate blood flow through the valve.

Etiology – Congenital defects, calcific degeneration, infective endocarditis, coronary artery disease, myocardial infarction, and rheumatic fever.

Signs and symptoms – Varies based on the type and severity of valve disease, but may include heart palpitations, shortness of breath, chest pain, coughing, ankle swelling, and fatigue.

Treatment – Patients with minimal symptoms may not require treatment. Treatment for moderate cases includes medications to reduce the workload of the heart, regulate the heart rhythm, and prevent clotting. These medications may include digitalis, diuretics, antiplatelet and anticoagulant agents, beta blockers, and calcium channel blockers. Severe cases may require balloon valvuloplasty or surgery to repair or replace the affected valve.

Pathology of the Airways and Lungs

Acute Respiratory Distress Syndrome (ARDS)[3]

ARDS is sudden respiratory failure due to fluid accumulation in the alveoli. ARDS usually occurs in people who are already critically ill or who have significant injuries. Severe shortness of breath develops within a few hours to a few days after the original disease or trauma. ARDS is fatal in 25 to 40 percent of the people who develop it. Survivors of ARDS may not regain full lung function for a year or more.

Etiology – The mechanical cause of ARDS is fluid leaking from the smallest blood vessels in the lungs into the alveoli. Normally, a protective membrane keeps this fluid in the vessels, however, inflammation undermines the membrane's integrity, leading to the fluid leakage. A number of conditions can injure the lungs and lead to inflammation including:

- Severe viral or bacterial pneumonia
- Infection spreading through the blood (sepsis)
- Heart failure
- Multiple or massive blood transfusions
- A serious head or chest injury
- Fractures of long bones, which cause a fat embolism
- Prolonged use of large volumes of supplemental oxygen
- Accidental inhalation of vomit or chemicals, such as ammonia or chlorine
- Smoke inhalation
- Near drowning
- An adverse reaction to cancer drugs or other medications
- Drug overdose, most commonly with heroin
- Shock from any cause

Signs and symptoms – Varies based on the cause and severity of ARDS. They include severe shortness of breath, labored and unusually rapid breathing, hypotension, confusion, extreme fatigue, cough, and fever.

Treatment – It is important to determine the cause of ARDS because it can determine treatment and predict the chances for survival. The first goal of treatment is to get oxygen to the lungs and organs. Most people will be treated with supplemental oxygen and mechanical ventilation. Treating the underlying condition then becomes equally important. Medications are given to prevent and treat infection, relieve pain, provide sedation, and prevent blood clot formation.

Asthma[11]

Asthma is a chronic inflammation of the airways caused by an increased airway hypersensitivity to various stimuli.

Etiology – Factors that trigger asthma include respiratory infections; allergens such as pollen, mold, animal dander, feathers, dust, food, and cockroaches; exposure to cold air or sudden temperature change; cigarette smoke; excitement/stress; and exercise.

Signs and symptoms – Range from mild to severe depending on the level of airway restriction. A mild attack presents with wheezing, chest tightness, and slight shortness of breath. A severe attack presents with dyspnea, flaring nostrils, diminished wheezing, anxiety, cyanosis, and the inability to speak. A severe attack can result in respiratory failure if left untreated.

Treatment – Reducing exposure to known triggers is a critical step toward controlling asthma. Two classes of medications are used to treat asthma: anti-inflammatory agents and bronchodilators. Anti-inflammatory agents interrupt bronchial inflammation and have a preventive action. These agents include inhaled corticosteroids, cromolyn sodium, and leukotriene modifiers. Bronchodilators dilate the airways by relaxing bronchial smooth muscle. They include beta-adrenergic agonists, methylxanthines, and anticholinergics. Physical therapy management includes caregiver education, airway clearance, breathing exercises, relaxation, and endurance and strength training.

Atelectasis[12]

A condition in which one or more areas of the lungs collapse or do not inflate properly.

Etiology – Conditions and factors that prevent deep breathing and coughing can cause atelectasis. These include post-operative pain, pleural effusion, tumor, ARDS, asthma, COPD, and cystic fibrosis.

Signs and symptoms – If a small area of the lung is affected, there may be no signs or symptoms. If a large area is affected, there may be cyanosis, shortness of breath, increased breathing rate, and increased heart rate.

Treatment – Treatments vary based on the underlying cause of the atelectasis. Deep breathing, changing positions, and airway clearance techniques assist to fully expand the lungs. Positive end-expiratory pressure or continuous positive airway pressure devices use mild air pressure to help keep the airways and alveoli open. Medications include supplemental oxygen, nebulized bronchodilators, and mucolytic agents. Bronchoscopy may be used to remove foreign objects or mucous plugs blocking the airways.

Bronchiectasis[12]

A progressive obstructive lung disease that produces abnormal dilation of a bronchus. This is an irreversible condition usually associated with chronic infections, aspiration, cystic fibrosis or immune system impairment. The bronchial walls weaken over time due to infection and allow for permanent dilation of bronchi and bronchioles.

Etiology – Injury to the airways or lung infection (pneumonia, whooping cough, measles, tuberculosis, fungal infections).

Signs and symptoms – Consistent productive cough, hemoptysis, weight loss, anemia, crackles, wheezes, and loud breath sounds.

Treatment – Medications include antibiotics, bronchodilators, expectorants, and mucolytics.

Bronchitis[3]

Bronchitis is an inflammation of the bronchi characterized by hypertrophy of the mucus secreting glands, increased mucus secretions, and insufficient oxygenation due to mucus blockage. Chronic bronchitis is characterized by a productive cough for three months over the course of two consecutive years.

Etiology – Acute bronchitis may be caused by cold viruses and exposure to smoke and other air pollutants. Cigarette smoking is the primary cause of chronic bronchitis, but exposure to air pollutants, dust, or toxic gases in the environment or workplace can also contribute.

Signs and symptoms – Persistent cough with production of thick sputum, increased use of accessory muscles of breathing, wheezing, dyspnea, cyanosis, and increased pulmonary artery pressure. Patients with chronic bronchitis present with a cough that is worse in the morning and in damp weather and may experience frequent respiratory infections.

Treatment – Focuses on relieving symptoms and improving breathing. For acute bronchitis, treatment includes rest, fluids, breathing warm and moist air, cough suppressants, and acetaminophen or aspirin. For chronic bronchitis, treatments include antibiotics, anti-inflammatory agents, and bronchodilators. Recommended lifestyle changes include smoking cessation, avoiding respiratory irritants, using an air humidifier, using a cold-air face mask if cold air aggravates cough and promotes shortness of breath, and pulmonary rehabilitation (airway clearance, breathing exercises, and endurance and strength training).

Chronic Obstructive Pulmonary Disease (COPD)[3]

COPD refers to a group of lung diseases that block airflow due to narrowing of the bronchial tree. Emphysema and chronic bronchitis are the two main conditions that make up COPD. COPD can also refer to damage caused by chronic asthmatic bronchitis. Progression of the disease includes alveolar destruction and subsequent air trapping. Patients have an increased total lung capacity with a significant increase in residual volume.

Etiology – In the majority of cases, COPD is caused by long-term smoking or exposure to secondhand smoke. Other irritants can cause COPD, including air pollution and certain occupational fumes. In rare cases, COPD results from a genetic disorder that causes low levels of the protein alpha-1-antitrypsin.

Signs and symptoms – Excessive mucus production, chronic productive cough, wheezing, shortness of breath, fatigue, and reduced exercise capacity.

Treatment – Medications include bronchodilators, inhaled steroids, supplemental oxygen, and antibiotics (if a bacterial infection is present). Surgery may include lung volume reduction surgery, bullectomy, and lung transplantation. Lifestyle modifications include smoking cessation, influenza shots, avoiding respiratory irritants, maintaining good nutrition, and pulmonary rehabilitation (airway clearance, breathing exercises, and endurance and strength training).

Cystic Fibrosis (CF)[13]

CF is an autosomal recessive genetic disease of the exocrine glands that primarily affects the lungs, pancreas, liver, intestines, sinuses, and sex organs. People who have CF inherit two faulty CF genes, one from each parent.

Etiology – The causative factor is a mutation of the cystic fibrosis transmembrane conductance regulator on chromosome 7. A defective gene and its protein product cause the body to produce unusually thick, sticky mucus that leads to life-threatening lung infections, obstructs the pancreas, and inhibits normal digestion and absorption of food.

Signs and symptoms – Symptoms vary with the progression of the disease and may include salty tasting skin, persistent and productive coughing, frequent lung infections, wheezing, shortness of breath, poor growth/weight gain in spite of a good appetite, and frequent greasy, bulky stools.

Treatment – Medications include antibiotics, nutritional supplements, pancreatic enzyme replacements, mucolytics, and bronchodilators. Physical therapy includes airway clearance, breathing techniques, assisted cough, and ventilatory muscle training. General exercise is indicated to improve overall strength and endurance, except with severe lung disease.

Emphysema[3]

In emphysema, the alveolar walls are gradually destroyed and the alveoli are turned into large, irregular pockets with gaping holes in the walls. In addition, the elastic fibers that hold open the bronchioles are destroyed, so that they collapse during exhalation, not letting air escape from the lungs. The alveoli are permanently overinflated and dead space increases within the lungs.

Etiology – Smoking is the leading cause of emphysema. One to two percent of individuals with emphysema have a genetic disorder that causes low levels of the protein alpha-1-antitrypsin, which protects the elastic structures in the lungs. Without this protein, enzymes can cause progressive lung damage, eventually resulting in emphysema.

Signs and symptoms – Shortness of breath, wheezing, chronic coughing, orthopnea, barrel chest, increased use of accessory muscles, increased respiration rate, fatigue, and reduced exercise capacity.

Treatment – Medications include bronchodilators, inhaled steroids, supplemental oxygen, and antibiotics (if a bacterial infection is present). Surgery may include lung volume reduction surgery, bullectomy, and lung transplantation. Lifestyle modifications include smoking cessation, annual influenza inoculation, avoiding respiratory irritants, maintaining good nutrition, and pulmonary rehabilitation (airway clearance, breathing exercises, and endurance and strength training).

Pleural Effusion[3]

A pleural effusion is a buildup of fluid in the pleural space between the lungs and chest cavity. The excess fluid can push the pleura against the lung making it hard to breathe and, in some cases, causing an atelectasis. If the fluid gets infected and turns into an abscess, the condition is called empyema.

Etiology – Pleuritis, or inflammation of the visceral and parietal pleura. Pleuritis can be caused by a viral infection, pneumonia, pulmonary embolism, and autoimmune diseases such as lupus and rheumatoid arthritis.

Signs and symptoms – Shortness of breath. If the fluid becomes infected, dry cough, fever, and chills may appear.

Treatment – Treatment is directed at the underlying condition causing the signs and symptoms. For example, if the pleuritis is caused by a bacterial pneumonia, an antibiotic will be used to treat the infection. Most viral infections run their course without requiring treatment. Nonsteroidal anti-inflammatory drugs may help relieve some of the signs and symptoms. If the fluid buildup is large, a chest tube may be inserted to drain the fluid.

Pneumonia[3]

Pneumonia refers to inflammation of the lungs (Fig. 6-7).

Etiology – Usually caused by bacterial, viral, fungal, or parasitic infection.

Signs and symptoms – Symptoms are variable depending on the cause of the infection. Common signs and symptoms include fever, cough, shortness of breath, sweating, shaking chills, chest pain that fluctuates with breathing, headache, muscle pain, and fatigue.

Treatment – Variable depending on the severity of the symptoms and the type of pneumonia. Antibiotics are used for bacterial and mycoplasma pneumonias. Antiviral agents are used to treat a few forms of viral pneumonia. Antifungal agents are used to treat fungal pneumonia. Lifestyle remedies include rest and drinking plenty of liquids.

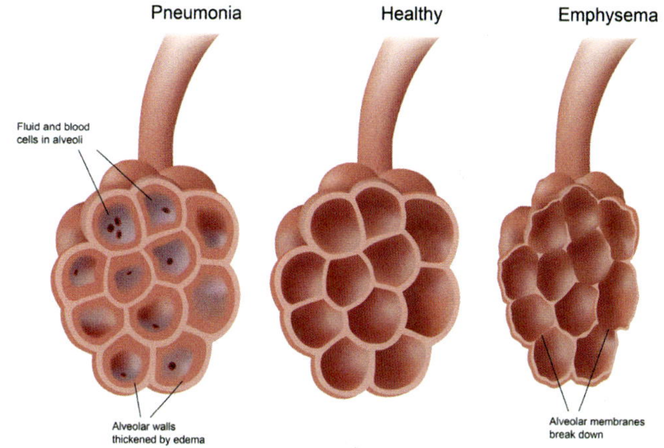

Fig. 6-7: Changes in alveoli with pneumonia and emphysema.

Pulmonary Edema[3]

Pulmonary edema occurs when fluid collects in the alveoli within the lungs, making it difficult to breathe. Acute pulmonary edema is a medical emergency.

Etiology – In most cases, pulmonary edema occurs when the left ventricle is unable to pump blood adequately (e.g., left-sided heart failure). As a result, pressure increases inside the left atrium and then in the pulmonary veins and capillaries, causing fluid to be pushed through the capillary walls into the alveoli. In noncardiac pulmonary edema, fluid leaks from the capillaries within the alveoli since the capillaries themselves become more permeable. This may result from pneumonia, exposure to certain toxins and medications, smoke inhalation, respiratory distress syndrome, and living at high elevations.

Signs and symptoms – Depending on the cause, symptoms can develop suddenly or slowly. Signs and symptoms that come on suddenly may include extreme shortness of breath and difficulty breathing; a feeling of suffocating or drowning; wheezing or gasping for breath; anxiety; restlessness; a sense of apprehension; coughing; frothy, blood-tinged sputum; chest pain (if a cardiac cause); and a rapid, irregular pulse.

Treatment – Variable depending on the underlying cause, but often includes supplemental oxygen and medications.

SPOTLIGHT ON SAFETY
SIGNS AND SYMPTOMS OF ACUTE PULMONARY EDEMA[3]

Acute pulmonary edema is life-threatening. Call 911 or emergency medical services immediately if any of the following signs or symptoms develop:

- Extreme shortness of breath or difficulty breathing with profuse sweating
- A bubbly, wheezing or gasping sound during breathing
- A cough that produces frothy sputum that may be tinged with blood
- Cyanotic skin color
- A rapid, irregular pulse
- A severe drop in blood pressure

Pulmonary Embolism (PE)[3]

PE is a condition where one or more arteries in the lungs become blocked. PE can be life-threatening, but prompt treatment with anti-clotting medications can greatly reduce the risk of death.

Etiology – In most cases, PE is caused by blood clots from the lower extremities.

Signs and Symptoms – Symptoms can vary greatly, depending on how much of the lung is involved, the size of the clot, and overall health of the patient (especially the presence or absence of underlying lung disease or heart disease). Common signs and symptoms include sudden onset of shortness of breath; chest pain that becomes worse with deep breathing, coughing, eating or bending; and coughing up bloody or blood-streaked sputum. Other signs and symptoms include wheezing, lower extremity swelling, excessive sweating, rapid or irregular pulse, and lightheadedness or fainting.

Treatment – Pulmonary embolism can be life-threatening, but prompt treatment with anticoagulants and thrombolytic agents greatly reduces the risk of death. Surgery may be done to remove the clot or insert a filter into the inferior vena cava. Preventing clot formation in the deep leg veins reduces the risk of PE. Prevention includes compression stockings, pneumatic compression, physical activity, and drinking fluids.

Pulmonary Fibrosis[3]

A condition in which microscopic damage to the alveoli causes irreversible scarring of the interstitial tissue. Normally, the tissue is highly elastic, expanding and contracting with each breath. Scarring makes the interstitial tissue stiff and thick and the alveoli less flexible, making breathing more difficult.

Etiology – In most cases, the cause is unknown (idiopathic pulmonary fibrosis). Chronic exposure to silica dust (silicosis), asbestos fibers (asbestosis), grain dust, sugar cane, and bird and animal droppings can cause pulmonary fibrosis. Radiation for lung or breast cancer, chemotherapy drugs (methotrexate, cyclophosphamide), certain antiarrhythmic medications (amiodarone, propranolol), and some antibiotics (nitrofurantoin, sulfasalazine) can also cause fibrosis.

Signs and Symptoms – The most common symptoms are shortness of breath, especially during or after physical activity, and a dry cough, which usually does not appear until the disease is advanced and irreversible lung damage has already occurred. Other symptoms include fatigue, unexplained weight loss, and aching muscles and joints.

Treatment – Although the lung scarring is irreversible and no current treatment has proven effective in stopping the progression of the disease, some treatments may improve symptoms temporarily and improve quality of life. A combination of corticosteroids and immunosuppressive agents are often prescribed initially. Lung transplantation may be used in cases of advanced disease. Other treatments to reduce symptoms and improve quality of life include supplemental oxygen and pulmonary rehabilitation (breathing exercises, nutrition counseling, emotional support).

Restrictive Lung Dysfunction (RLD)[14]

RLD is an abnormal reduction in lung expansion and pulmonary ventilation.

Etiology – RLD is caused by abnormal lung parenchyma (e.g., atelectasis, pneumonia, pulmonary fibrosis, pulmonary edema, acute respiratory distress syndrome), abnormal pleura (e.g., pleural effusion, pleural fibrosis, pneumothorax, hemothorax), and disorders affecting ventilatory pump function (e.g., decrease in respiratory drive, neurologic and neuromuscular diseases, muscle disease or weakness, thoracic deformity or trauma, connective tissue disorders affecting the thoracic joints, pregnancy, obesity, and ascites).

Signs and Symptoms – Dyspnea on exertion, a persistent non-productive cough, increased respiratory rate, hypoxemia, decreased vital capacity, abnormal breath sounds, and reduced exercise tolerance.

Treatment – Variable depending on the etiology (e.g., antibiotics for pneumonia, treatment of edema, reversal of CNS depression). Additional supportive measures include mechanical ventilation, supplemental oxygen, nutrition support, and pulmonary rehabilitation (airway clearance, breathing exercise, respiratory muscle training, endurance and strength training).

Common Laboratory Tests

Arterial Blood Gas (ABG)

Arterial blood gases are collected to evaluate acid–base status (pH), ventilation ($PaCO_2$), and oxygenation of arterial blood (PaO_2). The partial pressure of oxygen in arterial blood (PaO_2) and the percent oxygen saturation of hemoglobin (SaO_2) provide information about how well the lungs are functioning to oxygenate the blood. The partial pressure of carbon dioxide in arterial blood ($PaCO_2$) provides information on how well the lungs are able to remove carbon dioxide. Changes in $PaCO_2$ directly affect the balance of pH in the body. Blood pH is tightly regulated, as an imbalance in either direction can affect the nervous system and can cause convulsions or coma. Bicarbonate (HCO_3-) is an important component of the chemical buffering system that keeps the blood from becoming too acidic or basic and is often part of an ABG test.

Mean (range) of adult normal ABG values:

pH: 7.4 (7.35 - 7.45)

$PaCO_2$: 40 mm Hg at sea level breathing ambient air (35 - 45 mm Hg)

PaO_2: 97 mm Hg at sea level breathing ambient air (80 - 100 mm Hg)

HCO_3-: 24 mEq/L (22 – 26 mEq/L)

SaO_2: 95 - 98%

By convention, ABG results are written or spoken in the following order: pH→$PaCO_2$→PaO_2→HCO_3- (e.g., 7.4/40/97/24)

Acidemia: elevated acidity of blood (pH < 7.35)

Alkalemia: decreased acidity of blood (pH > 7.45)

Eucapnia: normal level of CO_2 in arterial blood ($PaCO_2$ 35 - 45 mm Hg)

Hypercapnia: elevated level of CO_2 in arterial blood ($PaCO_2$ > 45 mm Hg)

Hypocapnia: low level of CO_2 in arterial blood ($PaCO_2$ < 35 mm Hg)

Hypoxemia: low level of O_2 in arterial blood (PaO_2 < 80 mm Hg)

Mild hypoxemia: PaO_2 60 - 79 mm Hg

Moderate hypoxemia: PaO_2 40 - 59 mm Hg

Severe hypoxemia: PaO_2 < 40 mm Hg

Hypoxia: low level of O_2 in the tissue despite adequate perfusion of the tissue

Cardiac Biomarkers[15]

Certain enzymes leak out of the heart cells and into the blood after a myocardial infarction. Cardiac enzyme studies measure the levels of creatine phosphokinase (CK) and the protein troponin in the blood. CK-MB is a relatively specific test for myocardial infarction. It appears in blood approximately four hours after infarction, peaks at 12–24 hours, and declines over 48–72 hours. Cardiac troponin-I is also a specific marker for infarction, and unlike CK-MB levels, it remains elevated for 5–7 days.

Cholesterol Test[15]

Also called a lipid panel or lipid profile, a cholesterol test measures the amount of cholesterol and triglycerides in the blood in order to determine the risk of atherosclerosis. Cholesterol is carried in the circulation in association with lipoproteins. A complete lipid profile includes the measurement of four types of lipids in the blood: total cholesterol, high-density lipoprotein (HDL) cholesterol, low-density lipoprotein (LDL) cholesterol, and triglycerides. HDL cholesterol is referred to as the "good" cholesterol because it helps carry away LDL cholesterol and is protective against atherogenesis. LDL cholesterol is referred to as the "bad" cholesterol since it is associated with the buildup of fatty plaques within the arteries which reduce blood flow. The body converts any calories it does not need to use right away into triglycerides, which are stored in adipose tissue. High levels of triglycerides are seen in overweight people, in those consuming too many sweets or too much alcohol, and in people with diabetes who have elevated blood sugar levels.

Complete Blood Count (CBC)[15]

A CBC measures red blood cell count, total white blood cell count, white blood cell differential, platelets, hemoglobin, and hematocrit. A CBC is performed to assess health, to diagnose and monitor a medical condition, and to monitor the effects of medical treatment.

Hematocrit (HCT)[15]

Hematocrit is the percentage of red blood cells in total blood volume. A low hematocrit may indicate anemia, blood loss, and vitamin or mineral deficiencies. A high hematocrit may indicate dehydration or polycythemia vera, a condition that causes an overproduction of red blood cells.

CONSIDER THIS

SYSTEMATIC ANALYSIS OF ARTERIAL BLOOD GAS

Using a standard approach to interpreting arterial blood gas values improves the therapist's understanding of the patient's acid-base, ventilation, and oxygenation status.

STEP 1
Examine pH to assess acid-base balance

pH < 7.40 indicates acidosis

pH > 7.40 indicates alkalosis

STEP 2
Examine the $PaCO_2$ as an indicator of ventilatory status

$PaCO_2$ = 35 – 45 mm Hg indicates adequate ventilation; no respiratory problem and no respiratory compensation for metabolic problem

$PaCO_2$ < 30 mm Hg indicates alveolar hyperventilation

$PaCO_2$ > 50 mm Hg indicates alveolar hypoventilation, ventilatory failure

STEP 3
Interpret $PaCO_2$ in relation to pH

$PaCO_2$ > 45 mm Hg and pH < 7.40 indicate respiratory acidosis

$PaCO_2$ > 45 mm Hg and pH > 7.40 indicate retention of CO_2 to compensate for metabolic alkalosis

$PaCO_2$ < 35 mm Hg and pH > 7.40 indicate respiratory alkalosis

$PaCO_2$ < 35 mm Hg and pH < 7.40 indicate elimination of CO_2 to compensate for metabolic acidosis

STEP 4
Interpret the HCO_3- in relation to pH

HCO_3- = 22 – 26 mEq/L indicates no primary metabolic problem and no metabolic compensation for a respiratory problem

HCO_3- < 22 mEq/L and pH < 7.40 indicate metabolic acidosis

HCO_3- < 22 mEq/L and pH > 7.40 indicate renal compensation for a respiratory alkalosis

HCO_3- > 26 mEq/L and pH > 7.40 indicate metabolic alkalosis

HCO_3- > 26 mEq/L and pH < 7.40 indicate renal compensation for respiratory acidosis

STEP 5
Interpret the PaO_2 and SaO_2

Normal: PaO_2 80 – 100 mm Hg at sea level with SaO_2 > 95%

Mild hypoxemia: PaO_2 60 – 79 mm Hg; SaO_2 90% – 95% (if no shift in oxyhemoglobin curve)

Moderate hypoxemia: PaO_2 40 – 59 mm Hg; SaO_2 60% – 90% (if no shift in oxyhemoglobin curve)

Severe hypoxemia: PaO_2 < 40 mm Hg; SaO_2 < 60% (if no shift in oxyhemoglobin curve)

Reference Values in Hematology

	Conventional Units	SI Units
Erythrocytes		
Adult males	4.3 - 5.6 x 10^6/ml	4.3 - 5.6 x 10^{12}/L
Adult females	4.0 - 5.2 x 10^6/ml	4.0 - 5.2 x 10^{12}/L
Leukocytes		
Total	3.54 - 9.06 x 10^3/mm^3	3.54 - 9.06 x 10^9/L
Differential Blood Count		
Neutrophils	0.40 - 0.70	40 - 70%
Lymphocytes	0.20 - 0.50	20 - 50%
Monocytes	0.04 - 0.08	4 - 8%
Eosinophils	0.00 - 0.06	0 - 6%
Basophils	0.00 - 0.02	0 - 2%
Platelet Count	165 - 415 x 10^3/mm^3	165 - 415 x 10^9/L
Partial Thromboplastin Time (PTT)	26.3 - 39.4 sec	26.3 - 39.4 sec
Hematocrit		
Adult males	0.388 - 0.464	38.8 - 46.4%
Adult females	0.354 - 0.444	35.4 - 44.4%
Hemoglobin		
Adult males	13.3 - 16.2 gm/dL	13.3 - 16.2 g/dL
Adult females	12.0 - 15.8 gm/dL	12.0 - 15.8 g/dL

Reference Values in Clinical Chemistry

	Conventional Units		SI Units
Serum Cholesterol			
Total	< 200 mg/dL	Desirable	< 5.17 mmol/L
	200 - 239 mg/dL	Borderline	5.17 - 6.20 mmol/L
	> 240 mg/dL	High	≥ 6.21 mmol/L
LDL cholesterol	< 100 mg/dL	Optimal	< 2.59 mmol/L
	100 - 129 mg/dL	Near optimal	2.59 - 3.35 mmol/L
	130 - 159 mg/dL	Borderline	3.36 - 4.12 mmol/L
	160 - 189 mg/dL	High	4.13 - 4.90 mmol/L
	≥ 190 mg/dL	Very high	≥ 4.91 mmol/L
HDL cholesterol	< 40 mg/dL	Low	< 1.03 mmol/L
	≥ 60 mg/dL	High	≥ 1.55 mmol/L
Triglyceride	< 150 mg/dL	Desirable	< 1.70 mmol/L
	150 - 199 mg/dL	Borderline	1.70 - 2.25 mmol/L
	200 - 499 mg/dL	High	2.26 - 5.63 mmol/L
	≥ 500 mg/dL	Very high	> 5.64 mmol/L

The values are for illustrative purposes. Each clinical laboratory establishes its own reference values.

Adapted from: Kratz A, Pesce MA, Fink DJ. Reference Values for Laboratory Tests. In: Fauci A, Braunwald E, Kasper D, Hauser, Longo D, Jameson J, Loscalzo J. Harrison's Manual of Medicine, 17th ed. New York, NY: McGraw-Hill Medical; 2009.

Partial Thromboplastin Time (PTT) and Prothrombin Time (PT)[15]

PTT and PT tests measure how quickly the blood clots. The tests are commonly used to monitor oral anticoagulant therapy or to screen for selected bleeding disorders. The tests examine all of the clotting factors of the intrinsic pathway with the exception of platelets. Partial thromboplastin time is more sensitive than prothrombin time in detecting minor deficiencies.

Common Diagnostic Procedures

Ambulatory Electrocardiography[5]

Also known as Holter monitoring, ECG electrodes are placed on the chest and attached to a small battery-operated recording monitor carried in a pocket or in a small pouch around the neck (Fig. 6-8). The ECG is recorded for 24 to 48 hours or longer to evaluate cardiac rhythm, the efficacy of medications, and pacemaker function. It is then correlated with a diary of the patient's symptoms and activities.

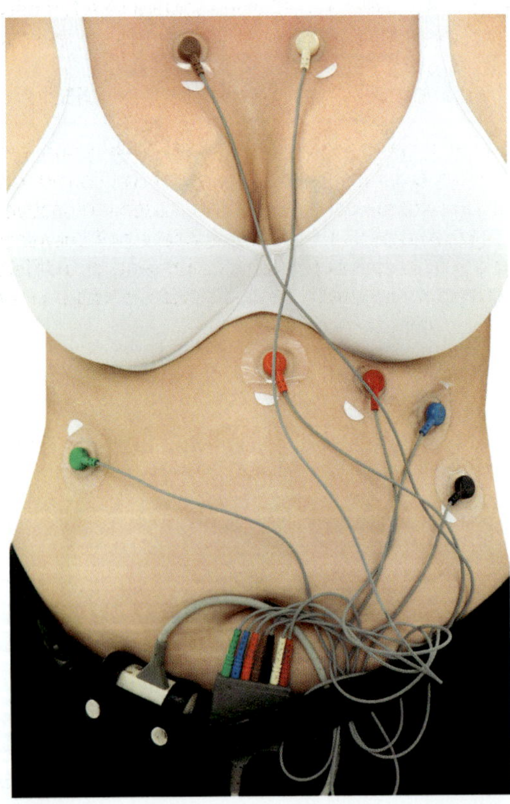

Fig. 6-8: Woman wearing a Holter monitor.

Angiography[15]

A radiologic examination that injects a contrast medium into the blood vessels. Coronary angiograms are part of the group of procedures known as cardiac catheterization. An angiogram can show the location of plaques in the coronary arteries and the extent of occlusion.

Bronchoscopy[15]

A procedure for direct visualization of the bronchial tree performed for diagnostic and therapeutic purposes. A bronchoscope is a fiber optic instrument that transmits an image to an eyepiece or video camera and can identify tumors, bronchitis, foreign bodies, and bleeding. Tissue specimens may be removed from the lungs by biopsy or bronchoalveolar lavage.

Cardiac Catheterization[5]

A thin catheter inserted into an artery in the leg or arm is advanced to the coronary arteries where a contrast dye is injected. The test can evaluate narrowing or occlusion of the coronary arteries and measure blood pressure in the heart and oxygen in the blood. Some treatments, such as coronary angioplasty, are performed using cardiac catheterization.

Carotid Ultrasound[5]

A procedure that uses sound waves to examine and visualize the structure and function of the carotid arteries. The purposes are to screen for blockages that may indicate an increased risk of stroke and to evaluate the placement of a stent or the function of the artery after carotid endarterectomy.

Chest Radiograph[5]

Chest radiographs are used to visualize the location, size, and shape of the heart, lungs, blood vessels, ribs, and bones of the spine. Chest radiographs can also reveal fluid in the lungs or pleural space, pneumonia, emphysema, cancer, and other conditions.

Computed Tomography (CT scan)[5]

A CT scan is a diagnostic test that uses an x-ray machine that rotates around a patient lying on a table. A computer processes the information from the scanner and creates a picture of the organ and surrounding structures. The pictures are slices of the body called tomograms and each picture is called a computed tomograph. The newest models of CT scanners allow pictures of the coronary arteries to be taken without the need, in some cases, for catheterization.

Echocardiography[5]

An echocardiogram uses high frequency sound waves non-invasively to evaluate the functioning of the heart via real time images. An echocardiogram can provide information on the size and function of the ventricles, thickness of the septums, and function of the walls, valves, and chambers of the heart. Transthoracic echocardiography (TTE) is a noninvasive procedure using a handheld ultrasound transducer placed on the chest. In transesophageal echocardiography (TEE), the ultrasound transducer is passed into the esophagus. The transducer provides a more detailed image of the heart because the esophagus lies in extremely close proximity.

Electrophysiologic Testing[5]

An electrophysiology study evaluates the rhythm or electrical conduction abnormalities of the heart using three to five catheters inserted into a blood vessel and threaded to the heart. The recordings help to locate abnormal tissue that causes cardiac arrhythmias.

Fluoroscopy[5]

A continuous x-ray procedure that shows the heart and lungs. Because fluoroscopy involves a relatively high dose of radiation, it has been largely replaced by echocardiography and other diagnostic tests. It is still a component of cardiac catheterization and electrophysiological testing.

Invasive Hemodynamic Monitoring[14]

Continuous monitoring of cardiovascular status is performed by intra-arterial catheters and intravenous lines that measure pressure, volume, and temperature. A balloon catheter, also known as a Swan-Ganz catheter, is placed in the pulmonary artery to obtain the pulmonary artery wedge pressure and left atrial pressure. A thermodilution catheter can be used to measure cardiac output. A central venous pressure (CVP) line measures pressure in the vena cava or right atrium.

Magnetic Resonance Imaging (MRI)[15]

MRI uses a magnetic field and radio waves to create 3-D images of the heart and blood vessels to assess the size and function of the chambers, thickness and movement of the walls, extent of damage caused by myocardial infarction or heart disease, structural problems in the aorta (e.g., aneurysms, dissections), and the presence of plaques and blockages in blood vessels. MRI is also used to image masses located in the mediastinum, but is of limited value for imaging the lungs.

Myocardial Perfusion Imaging (MPI)[16]

Also known as radionuclide stress test and nuclear stress test, the test shows how well the heart muscle is perfused at rest and under exercise stress. A radionuclide agent is injected into the blood at rest and at a maximum level of exercise. Images of the heart reveal areas that have reduced blood supply due to narrowing of one or more coronary arteries.

Pharmacologic Stress Test[16]

A diagnostic procedure in which cardiovascular stress is induced by pharmacologic agents when contraindications to a routine exercise stress test exist, or when the patient is unable to exercise due to injury or another debilitating condition. It is used in combination with imaging modalities such as radionuclide imaging and echocardiography. Pharmacologic agents used include adenosine, dipyridamole, and dobutamine.

Phonocardiography[17]

A diagnostic test that creates a graphic record, or phonocardiogram, of the sounds produced by the heart and great vessels. The phonocardiogram supplements auscultation and improves the detection of S3 and S4 heart sounds in the diagnosis of heart failure.

Pleuroscopy[3]

A procedure that includes examination of the lung surfaces, pleura, and pleural space using a small video camera inserted between the ribs into the pleural space. A tissue sample may be taken to biopsy.

Positron Emission Tomography (PET)[15]

A PET scan is an imaging test in which a small amount of radioactive material is injected, inhaled or swallowed, depending on the organ or tissue being studied. Increased radioactive material tends to accumulate in areas with high levels of chemical activity corresponding to areas of disease. This presents as a different color or brighter spots on the scan. A PET scan is useful in evaluating heart disease and cancer.

Thoracentesis[3]

A procedure that includes removal of fluid from the pleural space with a needle for microbiologic and cytologic studies.

Venography[3]

A radiopaque dye is injected into a vein while an x-ray procedure creates an image of the vein to detect a clot or blockage.

Ventilation–Perfusion Scan[15]

Also known as a lung scan or V/Q scan, the study uses small amounts of radioactive material to study airflow and blood flow within the lungs. It is used most commonly in the diagnosis of pulmonary embolism.

Pharmacological Management of Heart and Vascular Diseases

Alpha Adrenergic Antagonist Agents[18,19]

Action: Alpha adrenergic antagonist agents reduce peripheral vascular tone by blocking alpha-1-adrenergic receptors. This action causes dilation of arterioles and veins and decreases blood pressure.

Indications: hypertension, benign prostatic hyperplasia

Side effects: dizziness, palpitations, orthostatic hypotension, drowsiness

Implications for PT: Use caution when rising from a sitting or lying position due to the risk of dizziness and/or orthostatic hypotension. Closely monitor patient during exercise.

Examples: Cardura (doxazosin), Minipress (prazosin), Hytrin (terazosin)

Angiotensin-Converting Enzyme (ACE) Inhibitor Agents[18,19]

Action: ACE inhibitor agents decrease blood pressure and afterload by suppressing the enzyme that converts angiotensin I to angiotensin II.

Indications: hypertension, congestive heart failure

Side effects: hypotension, dizziness, dry cough, hyperkalemia, hyponatremia

Implications for PT: Avoid sudden changes in posture due to the risk of dizziness and fainting from hypotension. Patients with heart failure should avoid rapid increases in physical activity.

Examples: Capoten (captopril), Vasotec (enalapril), Prinivil (lisinopril), Altace (ramipril)

Angiotensin II Receptor Antagonist Agents[18,19]

Action: Angiotensin II receptor antagonists block angiotensin II receptors which limit vasoconstriction and stimulation of vascular tissue.

Indications: hypertension, congestive heart failure

Side effects: dizziness, back and leg pain, angina pectoris

Implications for PT: Minimal implications for physical therapy.

Examples: Cozaar (losartan), Atacand (candesartan), Diovan (valsartan)

Antiarrhythmic Agents[18,19]

Action: Antiarrhythmic agents are divided into four classes. **Class I** (sodium channel blockers) - control cardiac excitation and conduction. **Class II** (beta blockers) - inhibit sympathetic activity by blocking ß-adrenergic receptors. **Class III** (potassium channel blockers) - prolong repolarization by inhibiting both potassium and sodium channels and are often considered the most effective antiarrhythmic agent. **Class IV** (calcium channel blockers) - depress depolarization and slow conduction through the AV node.

Indications: cardiac arrhythmias

Side effects: unique to the specific antiarrhythmic agent; exacerbation of cardiac arrhythmias, dizziness, hypotension

Implications for PT: Encourage patients to adhere to the prescribed dosing schedule and immediately report any adverse reactions to a healthcare professional.

Examples: Sodium channel blockers: quinidine (generic), Xylocaine (lidocaine); Beta blockers: Tenormin (atenolol); Prolonged repolarization: Cordarone (amiodarone); Calcium channel blockers: Cardizem (diltiazem)

Anticoagulant Agents[18,19]

Action: Anticoagulant agents inhibit platelet aggregation and thrombus formation.

Indications: post percutaneous transluminal coronary angioplasty and coronary artery bypass graft surgery, prevention of venous thromboembolism and cardioembolic events in patients with atrial fibrillation and prosthetic heart valves

Side effects: hemorrhage, increased risk of bleeding, gastrointestinal distress with oral medication

Implications for PT: A therapist must be careful to avoid injury secondary to the risk of excessive bleeding or bruising. Patient education regarding common side effects is also indicated to protect the patient.

Examples: Heparin, Coumadin (warfarin), Lovenox (enoxaparin)

Antihyperlipidemia Agents[18,19]

Action: There are five categories of lipid-modifying agents. The most commonly used drugs, the statins, inhibit enzyme action in cholesterol synthesis, break down low density lipoproteins, decrease triglyceride levels, and increase HDL levels. The other categories are bile acid sequestrants, nicotinic acid, cholesterol absorption inhibitors, and fibric acid derivatives.

Indications: hyperlipidemia, atherosclerosis, prevent coronary events in patients with existing coronary disease, diabetes or peripheral vascular disease

Side effects: headache, gastrointestinal distress, myalgia, rash

Implications for PT: Aerobic exercise can increase high density lipoproteins and maximize the effects of drug therapy.

Examples: Lipitor (atorvastatin), Zocor (simvastatin), Tricor (fenofibrate)

Antithrombotic (Antiplatelet) Agents[18,19]

Action: Antithrombotic agents inhibit platelet aggregation and clot formation.

Indications: post-myocardial infarction, atrial fibrillation, prevent arterial thrombus formation

Side effects: hemorrhage, thrombocytopenia, potential liver toxicity with the use of aspirin, gastrointestinal distress

Implications for PT: A therapist must be careful to avoid injury secondary to the risk of excessive bleeding. Patient education regarding common side effects is also indicated to protect the patient.

Examples: Bayer (aspirin), Plavix (clopidogrel), Persantine (dipyridamole)

Beta Blocker Agents (Beta-Adrenergic Blocking Agents)[18,19]

Action: Beta blocker agents decrease the myocardial oxygen demand by decreasing heart rate and contractility by blocking β-adrenergic receptors.

Indications: hypertension, angina, arrhythmias, heart failure, migraines, essential tremor

Side effects: bradycardia, cardiac arrhythmias, fatigue, depression, dizziness, weakness, blurred vision

Implications for PT: Heart rate and blood pressure response to exercise will be diminished. Rate of perceived exertion may be used to monitor exercise intensity. Closely monitor patients during positional changes due to an increased risk for orthostatic hypotension.

Examples: Tenormin (atenolol), Lopressor (metoprolol), Inderal (propranolol)

Calcium Channel Blocker Agents[18,19]

Action: Calcium channel blocker agents decrease the entry of calcium into vascular smooth muscle cells resulting in diminished myocardial contraction, vasodilation, and decreased oxygen demand of the heart.

Indications: hypertension, angina pectoris, arrhythmias, congestive heart failure

Side effects: dizziness, headache, hypotension, peripheral edema

Implications for PT: Heart rate and blood pressure response to exercise will be diminished. Monitor patient closely when moving to an upright position secondary to dizziness and/or orthostatic hypotension. Observe the patient for signs and symptoms of congestive heart failure such as worsening peripheral edema, dyspnea or weight gain.

Examples: Norvasc (amlodipine), Procardia (nifedipine), Calan (verapamil), Cardizem (diltiazem)

Diuretic Agents[18,19]

Action: Diuretic agents increase the excretion of sodium and urine. This causes a reduction in plasma volume which decreases blood pressure. Classifications include thiazide, loop, and potassium sparing agents.

Indications: hypertension, edema associated with heart failure, pulmonary edema, glaucoma

Side effects: dehydration, hypotension, electrolyte imbalance, polyuria, increased low-density lipoproteins, arrhythmias

Implications for PT: Positioning changes can increase the risk of dizziness and falls due to decreased blood pressure. Monitor patients closely for signs and symptoms of electrolyte imbalance and muscle weakness or cramping.

Examples: Thiazide: Diuril (chlorothiazide); Loop: Lasix (furosemide); Potassium sparing: Dyrenium (triamterene)

Nitrate Agents[18,19]

Action: Nitrate agents decrease ischemia through smooth muscle relaxation and dilation of peripheral vessels.

Indications: angina pectoris

Side effects: headache, dizziness, orthostatic hypotension, reflex tachycardia, nausea, vomiting

Implications for PT: Patients must be educated to come to a standing position slowly to minimize the risk of orthostatic hypotension. Sublingual administration of nitroglycerin is the preferred method to treat an acute angina attack.

Examples: Nitrostat (nitroglycerin), Isordil (isosorbide dinitrate), Amyl nitrite solution for inhalation

Positive Inotropic Agents[18,19]

Action: Positive inotropic agents increase the force and velocity of myocardial contraction, slow the heart rate, decrease conduction velocity through the AV node, and decrease the degree of activation of the sympathetic nervous system.

Indications: heart failure, atrial fibrillation

Side effects: cardiac arrhythmias, gastrointestinal distress, dizziness, blurred vision

Implications for PT: Therapists should monitor heart rate during activity, teach the patient and family to take the patient's pulse, and seek health care provider's advice for rates less than 60 beats/minute or more than 100 beats/minute.

Examples: Lanoxin (digoxin)

Thrombolytic Agents[18,19]

Action: Thrombolytic agents facilitate clot dissolution through conversion of plasminogen to plasmin. Plasmin breaks down clots and allows occluded vessels to reopen to maintain blood flow.

Indications: acute myocardial infarction, pulmonary embolism, ischemic stroke, arterial or venous thrombosis

Side effects: hemorrhage (specifically intracranial in certain populations), allergic reaction, cardiac arrhythmia

Implications for PT: Therapists must be careful to avoid situations that may cause trauma due to altered clotting activity.

Examples: Kinlytic (urokinase), Activase (alteplase)

Medical Procedures for Heart and Vascular Diseases

Atherectomy[8]

A surgical procedure similar to angioplasty except that the catheter has a rotating shaver to cut away plaque from the artery and increase blood flow.

Automatic Implantable Cardioverter-Defibrillator (AICD)[15]

A surgically implanted device similar to a pacemaker that continuously monitors the heart rhythm and delivers electrical shocks to restore a normal heart rhythm when necessary.

Balloon Angioplasty[15]

Angioplasty involves temporarily inserting a small balloon-tipped catheter into a stenotic artery and expanding the balloon at the site of blockage to help widen a narrowed artery (Fig. 6-9). Angioplasty is usually combined with implantation of a small metal coil called a stent in the narrowed artery to help prop it open and decrease the chance of restenosis.

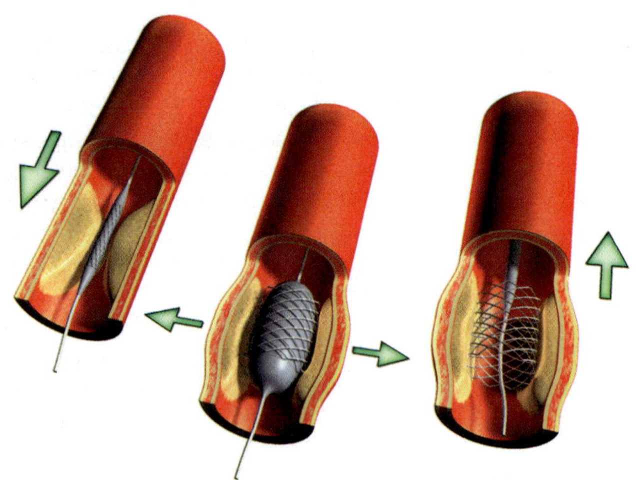

Fig. 6-9: Balloon angioplasty.

Balloon Valvuloplasty[3]

This surgical procedure uses cardiac catheterization to treat stenotic heart valves. A balloon-tipped catheter is threaded through the veins to the faulty heart valve, then inflated to open the narrowed valve and increase blood flow.

Cardiac Ablation[15]

A surgical procedure that uses radio frequencies or chemicals to destroy areas of the myocardium that have been identified by electrophysiologic testing to be causing cardiac arrhythmia. Ablation is an option for patients with tachyarrhythmias that cannot be controlled by medication or who have arrhythmias that respond well to ablation, such as Wolff-Parkinson-White syndrome.

Cardiac Pacemaker[14]

A pacemaker is a surgically implanted battery-powered device placed under the skin, usually in the left anterior chest wall. Pacemakers are a standard treatment for conditions affecting the electrical conduction system including a slow heart rate and arrhythmias. By preventing a slow heart rate, pacemakers can treat fatigue, lightheadedness, and fainting.

Pacemaker modes and functions are described by a 5-position format known as the NBG code.

Cardioversion[15]

Cardioversion is performed to restore a normal heart rhythm for tachyarrhythmias that do not respond to medication. Electrical shocks are delivered by a defibrillator through electrodes on the chest.

Coronary Artery Bypass Graft Surgery (CABG)[15]

CABG surgery is performed to treat coronary arteries that are narrowed or occluded in an attempt to revascularize the myocardium. In this procedure, blood is rerouted around the affected artery joining the patient's own saphenous vein, internal thoracic/mammary artery, or radial artery to connect the affected artery above and below the occlusion.

Enhanced Extracorporeal Counterpulsation (EECP)[14]

A noninvasive procedure in which inflation of pressure cuffs on the lower extremities compresses the veins and assists with venous return to the heart.

Heart Transplant[15]

A surgical procedure in which a failing, diseased heart is replaced with a healthier donor heart. A heart transplant is reserved for patients with end-stage heart failure for whom other treatments have not been successful (e.g., patients with cardiomyopathy, coronary artery disease, valvular disease, and congenital heart disease).

Intra-aortic Balloon Counterpulsation (IABP)[14]

Inflation and deflation of a balloon surgically placed in the aorta provides circulatory assistance for patients after infarction or with cardiogenic shock.

Valve Replacement[14]

A surgical procedure in which a prosthetic valve is implanted in the heart to replace a leaky or narrowed heart valve. Prosthetic valves may be either mechanical (e.g., ball-in-cage, tilting disc, bileaflet) or tissue grafts from the same patient, a cadaver or a pig.

NBG Pacemaker Code				
I	II	III	IV	V
Chamber paced	Chamber sensed	Response sensed	Rate modulation	Multisite pacing
V=Ventricle A= Atrium D=Dual (A+V) O=None	V=Ventricle A= Atrium D=Dual (A+V) O=None	T=Triggered I=Inhibited D=Dual (A+V) O=None	R=Rate modulation O=None	V=Ventricle A= Atrium D=Dual (A+V) O=None

Ventricular Assist Devices (VAD)[15]

A VAD is a miniature pump that is implanted in the chest to provide mechanical support to the ventricle. A right ventricular device (RVAD) attaches to the right atrium and pulmonary artery, bypassing the right ventricle. A left ventricular device (LVAD) attaches to the left atrium, bypassing the left ventricle. With a biventricular device (BiVAD), both ventricles are bypassed. VADs are commonly used as a temporary treatment for people waiting for a heart transplant and increasingly as a permanent treatment for heart failure.

Pharmacological Management of Airway and Lung Diseases

Antihistamine Agents[18,19]

Action: Antihistamine agents block the effects of histamine resulting in a decrease in nasal congestion, mucosal irritation, and symptoms of the common cold, sinusitis, conjunctivitis, and allergies.

Indications: respiratory seasonal allergies, rhinitis and sneezing from the common cold, allergic conjunctivitis, motion sickness, and Parkinson's disease

Side effects: arrhythmias, postural hypotension, gastrointestinal distress, dizziness, drowsiness, headache, blurred vision, fatigue, nausea, thickening of bronchial secretions

Implications for PT: Increase guarding when rising from a sitting or lying position due to the risk of orthostatic hypotension. Closely monitor patient during exercise.

Examples: Benadryl (diphenhydramine), Allegra (fexofenadine), Zyrtec (cetirizine HCL), Claritin (loratadine)

Anti-Inflammatory Agents[18,19]

Action: Inhaled corticosteroids, leukotriene modifiers, and mast-cell stabilizers help prevent inflammatory-mediated bronchoconstriction by inhibiting production of inflammatory cells, suppressing release of inflammatory mediators (cytokines, prostaglandins, leukotrienes), and reversing capillary permeability, in turn reducing airway edema.

Indications: bronchospasm, asthma

Side effects: Corticosteroid: systemic side effects are decreased with the inhaled form of corticosteroids, but may include damage of supporting tissues, skin breakdown, osteoporosis, decreased bone density, glaucoma, and delayed growth. Local effects include nasal irritation and dryness, sneezing, and bloody mucus; Leukotriene modifier: liver dysfunction; Mast-cell stabilizer: bronchospasm, throat and nasal irritation, cough, gastrointestinal distress.

Implications for PT: Instruct the patient in the correct use of the inhaler and to rinse their mouth with water after use to avoid irritation of local mucosa. Advise the patients that these agents are not bronchodilators and should not be used to treat acute episodes of asthma. Inform patients to contact their health care provider immediately if they experience signs and/or symptoms of liver dysfunction (e.g., fatigue, flu-like symptoms, jaundice, lethargy).

Examples: Corticosteroid: Qvar (beclomethasone dipropionate), Pulmicort (budesonide), AeroBid (flunisolide); Leukotriene modifier: Zyflo (zileuton); Mast-cell stabilizer: Nasalcrom (cromolyn sodium)

Bronchodilator Agents[18,19]

Action: Bronchodilator agents relieve bronchospasm by stimulating the receptors that cause bronchial smooth muscle relaxation or by blocking the receptors that trigger bronchoconstriction. Primary classifications of bronchodilators include anticholinergic, sympathomimetics, and xanthine derivatives.

Indications: bronchospasm, wheezing, and shortness of breath in asthma and COPD

Side effects: (depending on class of drug) paradoxical bronchospasm, dry mouth, gastrointestinal distress, chest pain, palpitations, tremor, nervousness. Long-acting sympathomimetics, including salmeterol, increase the risk of asthma-related death.

Implications for PT: Therapists should advise patients to take their bronchodilator medication as prescribed before therapy and to bring their short acting sympathomimetics (rescue medications)

with them. Cardiac or vision abnormalities may indicate toxicity, and the physician should be notified immediately.

Examples: Anticholinergic: Atrovent (ipratropium), Spiriva (tiotropium); Sympathomimetics: Ventolin (albuterol), Primatene mist (epinephrine), Serevent (salmeterol); Xanthine derivative: Theo-Dur (theophylline), Aminophylline

Expectorant Agents[18,19]

Action: Expectorant agents increase respiratory secretions which help to loosen mucus. Reducing the viscosity of secretions and increasing sputum volume improves the efficiency of the cough reflex and of ciliary action in removing accumulated secretions.

Indications: cough associated with respiratory tract infections and related conditions such as sinusitis, pharyngitis, bronchitis, and asthma, when complicated by tenacious mucus or mucus plugs and congestion

Side effects: gastrointestinal distress, drowsiness

Implications for PT: Therapists can exploit the effects of expectorant agents by performing airway clearance interventions within one hour after drug administration. Therapists should encourage the patient to take the medication with a glass of water.

Examples: Mucinex (guaifenesin), terpin hydrate

Mucolytic Agents[18,19]

Action: Mucolytic agents decrease the viscosity of mucus secretions by altering their composition and consistency, making them easier to expectorate. They are administered by a nebulizer.

Indications: viscous mucus secretions due to pneumonia, emphysema, chronic bronchitis, and cystic fibrosis

Side effects: pharyngitis, oral mucosa inflammation, rhinitis, chest pain

Implications for PT: Therapists can exploit the effects of mucolytic agents by performing airway clearance interventions within one hour after drug administration. Patients should be instructed in the proper use and maintenance of the nebulizer and compressor system used in its delivery.

Examples: Pulmozyme (dornase alpha), Mucosil or Mucomyst (acetylcysteine)

Medical Procedures for Airway and Lung Diseases

Airway Adjuncts[14]

A variety of devices are used to maintain or protect the airway, to provide mechanical ventilation or to promote airway clearance.

Oral pharyngeal airway: A plastic tube shaped to fit the curvature of the soft palate and tongue that holds the tongue away from the back of the throat and maintains the patency of the airway.

Nasal pharyngeal airway: A latex or rubber tube inserted through the nose to allow for nasotracheal suctioning.

Endotracheal tube: A plastic tube inserted in the trachea from the mouth or nose to provide an airway and to allow for mechanical ventilation.

Tracheostomy tube: An artificial airway inserted into the trachea from an incision in the neck below the vocal cords used in patients needing prolonged mechanical ventilation.

Airway Suctioning[14]

Suctioning is the mechanical aspiration of secretions from the nasopharynx, oropharynx, and trachea using a suction catheter. Endotracheal suctioning refers to the mechanical aspiration of pulmonary secretions from a patient with an artificial airway in place. Nasotracheal suctioning refers to the insertion of a suction catheter through the nasal passage and pharynx into the trachea without a tracheal tube or tracheostomy to aspirate accumulated secretions or foreign material. Indications for suctioning include increased or thickened secretions and inadequate cough. The frequency of suctioning is dependent on the amount of secretion produced.

Bullectomy[3]

A surgical procedure in which one or more of the large air spaces called bullae that form when the alveoli are destroyed by emphysema are removed. The procedure can improve breathing.

Lobectomy[3]

Surgical removal of a lobe of one lung.

Lung Transplant[3]

A surgical procedure to replace one or both diseased or failing lungs with healthy donor lungs. A lung transplant is reserved for patients with end-stage COPD, interstitial pulmonary fibrosis, cystic fibrosis, and other serious lung diseases, but who do not have serious comorbidities.

Lung Volume Reduction Surgery[3]

A surgical procedure in which a portion of lung tissue damaged by emphysema is removed. This creates extra space in the chest so that the remaining lung tissue and the diaphragm work more efficiently, enabling the patient to breathe more easily.

Mechanical Ventilation[14]

Patients with severe pulmonary dysfunction may need assistance to breathe from a positive pressure mechanical ventilator or breathing machine. The positive pressure from the ventilator provides the force that delivers air into the lungs by increasing intrathoracic pressure. Mechanical ventilation involves an automatic cycling ventilator connected to a tracheostomy tube or mask to assist or breathe for the patient.

Oxygen Therapy[14]

Liquid or gaseous oxygen is indicated for the treatment of acute and chronic hypoxemia in patients with a $PaO_2 \leq 55$ mm Hg, or an oxygen saturation ≤ 88% while seated at rest, or a PaO_2 of 56 to 59 mm Hg, or oxygen saturation of 89% in the presence of cor pulmonale or polycythemia. A number of devices are available to deliver the supplemental oxygen to the patient including nasal cannula, simple face mask, partial rebreathing mask, nonrebreathing mask, aerosol face mask, Venturi mask, and transtracheal catheter.

Thoracotomy[20]

A surgical incision cutting the chest wall to access the heart, great vessels, lungs, esophagus, and diaphragm for diagnostic and therapeutic purposes. The incision may be made under the arm (axillary thoracotomy), through the sternum (median sternotomy), from the back to the side (posterolateral thoracotomy) or under the breast (anterolateral thoracotomy).

Tracheostomy[15]

A surgically created hole through the neck into the trachea below the level of the vocal cords. The term for the surgical procedure to create the opening is tracheotomy. There are two primary indications for tracheostomy: airway obstruction at or above the level of the larynx and respiratory failure requiring prolonged mechanical ventilation. The tracheostomy can be surgically closed when it is no longer needed.

Physical Therapy Tests and Measures

Angina Pain Scales

A number of pain scales are used to grade the severity of angina pectoris.[21,22] One of the more commonly used angina scales rates angina pain from one to four.

Rating	Description
1	Mild, barely noticeable
2	Moderate, bothersome
3	Moderately severe, very uncomfortable
4	Most severe or intense pain ever experienced

Ankle-Brachial Index (ABI)[15]

Also known as the ankle-arm index, the ABI compares systolic blood pressures at the ankle and arm to check for peripheral artery disease.

Procedure

- Systolic blood pressures are measured in both brachial arteries and both tibialis posterior arteries with a sphygmomanometer and a handheld Doppler ultrasound device.
- The ABI is calculated by dividing the higher of the two blood pressure measurements in the ankles by the higher of the two systolic blood pressure measurements at the arms.

Interpretation

> 1.4	Indicates rigid arteries and the need for an ultrasound test to check for peripheral artery disease
1.0 - 1.30	Normal; no blockage
0.8 - 0.99	Mild blockage; beginnings of peripheral artery disease
0.4 - 0.79	Moderate blockage; may be associated with intermittent claudication during exercise
< 0.4	Severe blockage suggesting severe peripheral artery disease; may have claudication pain at rest

Arterial Blood Pressure[6]

Noninvasive measurement of arterial blood pressure (BP) with a pneumatic cuff and sphygmomanometer is considered one of the "vital signs" and an important indicator of health (Fig. 6-10). Deviations from normal pressure provide important information regarding a variety of cardiovascular conditions.

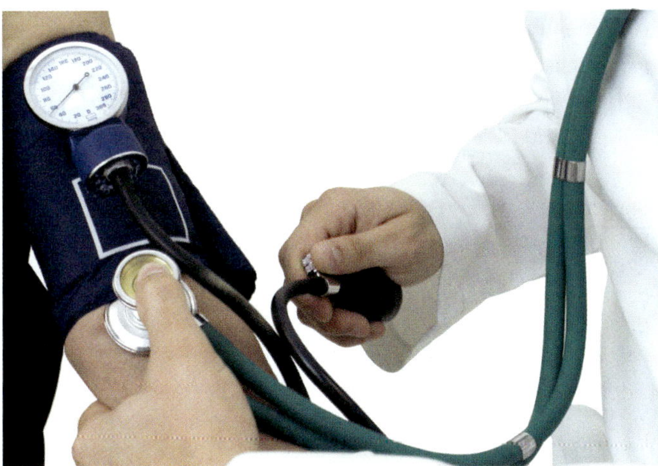

Fig. 6-10: Checking blood pressure at the brachial artery with a sphygmomanometer and stethoscope.

Procedure

- Use the appropriate sphygmomanometer cuff for the size of the body part. The bladder inside the cuff should encircle 80% of the arm in adults and 100% of the arm in children younger than 13 years old. If the bladder is too small, false high readings may result. If in doubt, use a larger cuff.
- The brachial artery is occluded by a sphygmomanometer cuff wrapped snugly around the upper arm and inflated to above the anticipated systolic pressure.
- As the cuff is slowly deflated (no more than 2-3 mm Hg per second), pulsatile blood flow is re-established and accompanied by sounds that can be detected by a stethoscope held over the artery.
- The sounds, known as Korotkoff sounds, originate from a combination of turbulent blood flow and oscillations of the arterial wall. As the pressure is reduced, the sounds change in quality and intensity.

    Phase I - first appearance of clear tapping sounds corresponding to the appearance of a palpable pulse; Phase I corresponds to systolic blood pressure (SBP)

    Phase II - sounds become softer and longer

    Phase III - sounds become crisper and louder

    Phase IV - sounds become muffled and softer

    Phase V - sounds disappear completely; the diastolic pressure (DBP) is the pressure at the last audible sound

Interpretation

In November of 2017, the American Heart Association and the American College of Cardiology released new guidelines that lowered the standards for high blood pressure. The result is that high blood pressure will now be treated earlier with lifestyle changes and in some cases medication. The new guidelines represent the first significant change in blood pressure guidelines since 2003.

- **In adults:**

    Normal BP: < 120 mm Hg SBP and < 80 mm Hg DBP

    Elevated: 120 - 129 mm Hg SBP and < 80 mm Hg DBP

    Stage 1 Hypertension: 130 - 139 mm Hg SBP or 80-89 mm Hg DBP

    Stage 2 Hypertension: at least 140 mm Hg SBP or at least 90 mm Hg DBP

    Hypertensive Crisis: greater than 180 mm Hg SBP and/or greater than 120 mm Hg DBP

Auscultation of Heart Sounds[23]

Listening to the intensity and quality of heart sounds over the surface of the chest can provide useful information about the condition and function of the heart. Although considered an advanced skill, with supervised practice, the therapist should be able to differentiate normal heart sounds from blatantly abnormal sounds such as loud murmurs and gallops.

Procedure

The bell or diaphragm of the stethoscope is held directly on the patient's bare skin with enough pressure to provide a skin seal while the patient breathes quietly through the nose.

- Listen over four designated auscultatory areas (Fig. 6-11):

    Aortic area - 2nd intercostal space at the right sternal border

    Pulmonic area - 2nd intercostal space at the left sternal border

    Mitral area - 5th intercostal space, medial to the left midclavicular line

    Tricuspid area - 4th intercostal space at the left sternal border

- Listen to the overall rate and rhythm of the heart sounds.
- Listen separately to each sound and each pause in the cardiac cycle for as many beats as necessary to evaluate the sounds in one area before moving to the next area.
- Listen for extra sounds or murmurs while concentrating on systole and diastole.

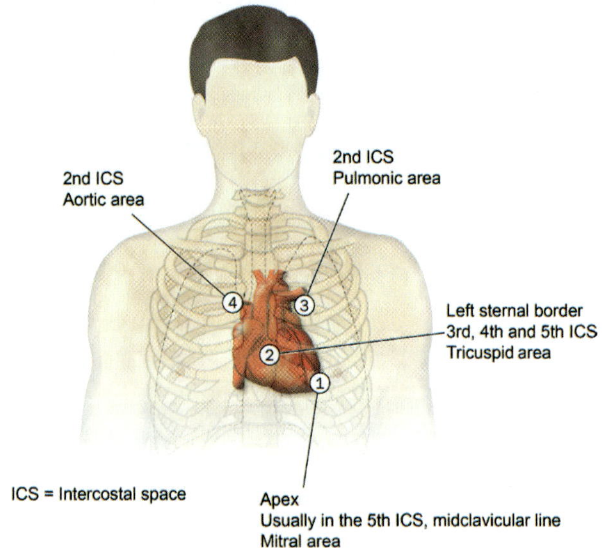

Fig. 6-11: Four areas to auscultate for heart sounds generated from the aortic, pulmonic, tricuspid, and mitral valves.

Interpretation

S1 (lub)

- 1st heart sound - closure of the mitral and tricuspid (atrioventricular) valves at the onset of ventricular systole.
- High frequency sound with lower pitch and longer duration than S2.

S2 (dub)

- 2nd heart sound - closure of the aortic and pulmonary (semilunar) valves at the onset of ventricular diastole.
- High frequency sound with higher pitch and shorter duration than S1 (Fig. 6-12).

S3

- 3rd heart sound - vibrations of the distended ventricle walls due to passive flow of blood from the atria during the rapid filling phase of diastole.
- Normal in healthy young children; termed "physiologic" 3rd heart sound.
- Abnormal in adults; may be associated with heart failure; often called "ventricular gallop."

S4

- 4th heart sound - pathological sound of vibration of the ventricular wall with ventricular filling and atrial contraction.
- May be associated with hypertension, stenosis, hypertensive heart disease or myocardial infarction; often called an "atrial gallop".

Murmurs

- Heart murmurs are vibrations of longer duration than the heart sounds and are often due to disruption of blood flow past a stenotic or regurgitant valve; the sounds are variably described as soft, blowing or swishing.
- When the leaflets of the heart valves are thickened, the forward flow of blood is restricted; when the leaflets lose competency and fail to close tightly, blood can flow backwards (regurgitation).

Auscultation of Lung Sounds[24]

Movement of air in the tracheobronchial tree produces sounds that can be heard with a stethoscope. Auscultation of lung sounds and voice sounds is performed to assist in diagnosis and to evaluate the effects of treatment. Lung or breath sounds are characterized by pitch, intensity, quality, and the duration of the inspiratory and expiratory phases.

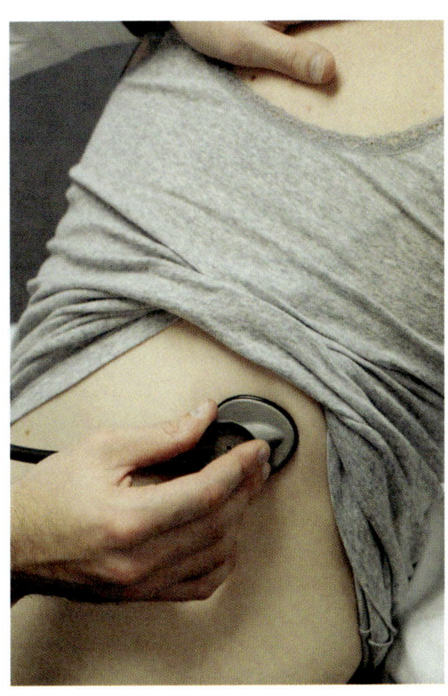

Fig. 6-13: Auscultation of lung sounds from the posterior thorax.

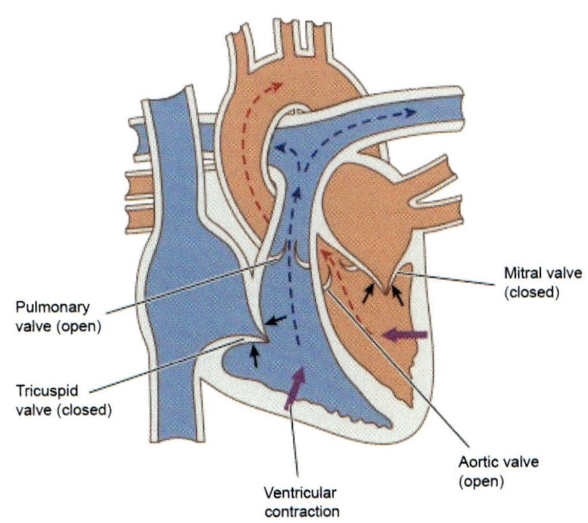

The first heart sound (S1), is caused by the closure of the mitral and tricuspid valves at the beginning of ventricular contraction (systole).

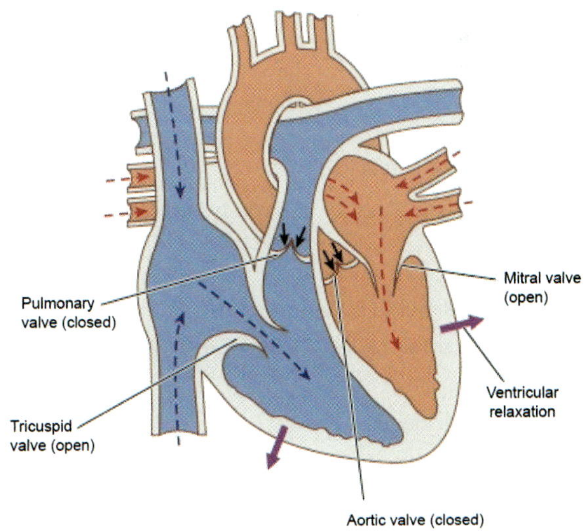

The second heart sound (S2), is caused by the closure of the aortic and pulmonary valves at the onset of ventricular diastole.

Fig. 6-12: Origin of the first and second heart sounds, S1 and S2, respectively.

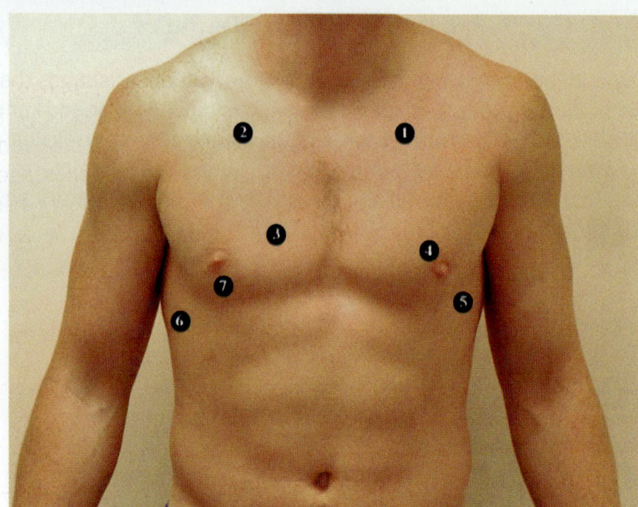

Fig. 6-14: Areas to auscultate for lung or breath sounds on the anterior thorax. Listen to at least one breath sound in each bronchopulmonary segment comparing the sounds from the left and right sides.

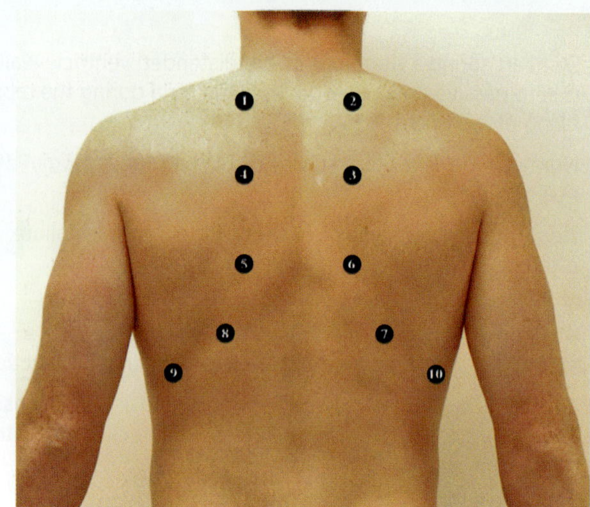

Fig. 6-15: Areas to auscultate for lung sounds on the posterior thorax.

Procedure

- Place the diaphragm of the stethoscope in firm contact with the patient's unclothed chest wall (Fig. 6-13).
- Start at the apices and work downward, comparing symmetrical points sequentially (Figs. 6-14, 6-15).
- Have the patient breathe in and out through the mouth, a little deeper than normal.
- Listen to at least one cycle of inspiration and expiration in each pulmonary segment.

If abnormal sounds are suspected:

- Compare the intensity, pitch, and quality of the sounds heard on one side with sounds heard in the same location on the other side.
- Identify the breath sounds as vesicular, bronchovesicular bronchial or absent by the duration of inspiration and expiration, and by the quality and pitch.
- Note the presence or absence of adventitious (extra) sounds.

Interpretation

Normal breath sounds

These are sounds that are heard in their normal location or phase of respiration.

- Tracheal and bronchial sounds
  - Loud, tubular sounds normally heard over the trachea.
  - Inspiratory phase is shorter than the expiratory phase and there is a slight pause between them.

    Note: Bronchial sounds heard over distal airways are abnormal and represent consolidation or compression of lung tissue that facilitates transmission of sound.
- Vesicular breath sounds
  - High pitched, breezy sounds normally heard over the distal airways in healthy lung tissue.
  - Inspiratory phase is longer than expiratory phase and there is no pause between them.

Abnormal breath sounds

These are sounds that are heard outside of their normal location or phase of respiration.

Adventitious breath sounds

Abnormal breath sounds heard with inspiration and/or expiration that can be continuous or discontinuous.

Crackle (formerly rales)

- An abnormal, discontinuous, high-pitched popping sound heard more often during inspiration. May be associated with restrictive or obstructive respiratory disorders.
- Typically represents the movement of fluid or secretions during inspiration (wet crackles) or occurs from the sudden opening of closed airways (dry crackles). Crackles that occur during the latter half of inspiration typically represent atelectasis, fibrosis, pulmonary edema or pleural effusion. Crackles due to the movement of secretions are usually low-pitched and can be heard during inspiration and/or expiration like the sound of hairs being rubbed together between the thumb and forefinger.
- Pulmonary edema may produce fine crackles as air bubbles through fluid in the distal small airways.
- Often heard in the bases of lungs with interstitial lung disease, atelectasis, pneumonia, bronchiectasis, and pulmonary edema.

Pleural friction rub

- Dry, crackling sound heard during both inspiration and expiration.
- Occurs when inflamed visceral and parietal pleurae rub together.
- Heard over the spot where the patient feels pleuritic pain.

Rhonchi

- Continuous low-pitched sounds described as having a "snoring" or "gurgling" quality that may be heard during both inspiration and expiration.
- Caused by air passing through an airway which is obstructed by inflammatory secretions or liquid, bronchial spasm or neoplasms in the smaller (sibilant rhonchi) or larger (sonorous rhonchi) airways.

Stridor

- Continuous high-pitched wheeze heard with inspiration or expiration.
- Indicates upper airway obstruction.

Wheeze

- Continuous "musical" or whistling sound composed of a variety of pitches.
- Heard during both inspiration and/or expiration, but variable from minute to minute and area to area.
- Arise from turbulent airflow and the vibrations of the walls of small airways due to narrowing by bronchospasm, edema, collapse, secretions, neoplasm or foreign body.

Bronchial breath sounds

Abnormal breath sounds when heard in locations where vesicular sounds are normally present. Pneumonia may produce these sounds.

Decreased or diminished sounds

A less audible sound may indicate severe congestion, emphysema or hypoventilation.

Absent breath sounds

Absent lung sounds may indicate pneumothorax or lung collapse.

Voice Sounds

In the normal lung, transmission of spoken sounds is usually muffled; whispered words are faint and the syllables are not distinct, except over the main bronchi. Increases in loudness and distinctness indicate consolidation, atelectasis or fibrosis, all of which improve transmission of vibrations through lung tissue. Whispered and spoken voice sounds are somewhat more valuable than breath sounds in detecting pulmonary consolidation, infarction, and atelectasis.

Bronchophony:

Increased vocal resonance with greater clarity and loudness of spoken words (e.g., "99").

Egophony:

A form of bronchophony in which the spoken long "E" sound changes to a long, nasal-sounding "A."

Whispered pectoriloquy:

Recognition of whispered words "1, 2, 3."

Body Mass Index (BMI)[25]

BMI describes relative weight for height and is a measurement used to identify increased risk for mortality and morbidity due to excess weight and obesity. It can also monitor changes in body weight from treatment. Although BMI can be used for most men and women, it may overestimate body fat in athletes and others who have a muscular build and underestimate body fat in older persons and others who have lost muscle.

Procedure

- Measure the subject's standing height and body weight.
- BMI = weight [kg] ÷ height [m^2] OR BMI = weight [lb] ÷ height [in^2] x 703

Interpretation

Adult BMI	Classification
< 18.5	Underweight
18.5 - 24.9	Normal
25.0 - 29.9	Overweight
30.0 - 34.9	Obesity (Class 1)
35.0 - 39.9	Obesity (Class 2)
≥ 40.0	Extreme obesity (Class 3)

Classifications do not apply to children and adolescents as BMI changes with age and sex:

- BMI between the 85th and 95th percentile for age and sex is considered at risk for becoming overweight.
- BMI ≥ the 95th percentile is considered overweight or obese.

Capillary Refill Time[23]

The time it takes the capillary bed to refill after it is occluded by pressure is an indicator of impaired perfusion to the extremities.

Procedure

- Apply firm pressure over a nail bed or bony prominence (e.g., chin, forehead, or sternum) until the nail or skin blanches.
- Release the pressure.
- Observe the time for the nail or skin to regain its full color.

Interpretation

- Normal - Full color returns in < 2 seconds
- Abnormal - Refill time is > 2 seconds; indicates capillary blood flow is compromised (e.g., arterial occlusion, hypovolemic shock, hypothermia)

Claudication Test[28]

Claudication is a cardinal symptom of peripheral artery disease. Claudication occurs when skeletal muscle oxygen demand during exercise exceeds blood oxygen supply. This results from stimulation of local sensory receptors by accumulating lactate or other metabolites. It is characterized by pain, aches, cramping, sense of fatigue or other discomfort in the affected muscle group, which limit the ability to exercise.

Procedure

Patient walks on a flat track at maximum speed or on a treadmill at 2.0 mph at a constant grade between 0 - 12%.

Interpretation

Scoring:

- Initial claudication distance (ICD) = pain-free walking distance
- Absolute claudication distance (ACD) = maximum distance walked when test is terminated due to pain
- Speed of walking

Grading scale for claudication pain:[21]

- Grade 1 - Definite discomfort or pain, but only of initial or modest levels
- Grade 2 - Moderate discomfort or pain from which the patient's attention can be diverted
- Grade 3 - Intense pain from which the patient's attention cannot be diverted
- Grade 4 - Excruciating and unbearable pain

The location of the symptoms often corresponds to the site of the most proximal stenosis:

- Pain in the buttock, hip or thigh occurs with obstruction of the aorta and iliac arteries
- Pain in the calf occurs with stenosis of the femoral and popliteal arteries
- Pain in the ankle or foot occurs with disease of the tibial or peroneal arteries

Dyspnea Scales

Dyspnea is an uncomfortable awareness of breathing that may result from decreased oxygenation, hypoventilation, hyperventilation, or increased work of breathing due to changes in respiratory mechanics or anxiety. A number of scales are available to rate dyspnea.[21, 29-31]

Borg Dyspnea Scale[29]	
0	No breathlessness at all
0.5	Very, very slight
1	Very slight
2	Slight breathlessness
3	Moderate
4	Somewhat severe
5	Severe breathlessness
6	
7	Very severe breathlessness
8	
9	Very, very severe breathlessness
10	Maximal

Electrocardiogram (ECG)[32]

The ECG is a graphic representation of the heart's electrical activity recorded from electrodes on the surface of the body. The ECG provides insight into the electrical behavior of the heart and its modification by physiologic, pharmacologic, and pathologic events. A 12-lead ECG provides 12 views of the heart. It is used to assess cardiac rhythm, to diagnose the location, extent, and acuteness of myocardial ischemia and infarction, and to evaluate changes with activity (Fig. 6-16).

Procedure

The resistance between skin and electrode is reduced by removing skin oils and cutaneous debris with an alcohol-saturated gauze pad, then abrading the skin sites to remove the superficial layer of skin.

Apply ECG electrodes to the anatomic locations.

- Anatomic locations of limb electrodes for limb leads:

  Right arm (RA) - Infraclavicular fossa medial to the right deltoid muscle

  Left arm (LA) - Infraclavicular fossa medial to the left deltoid muscle

  Left leg (LL) - Left side of the abdomen below the rib cage

  Right leg (RL) - Right side of the abdomen (ground electrode)

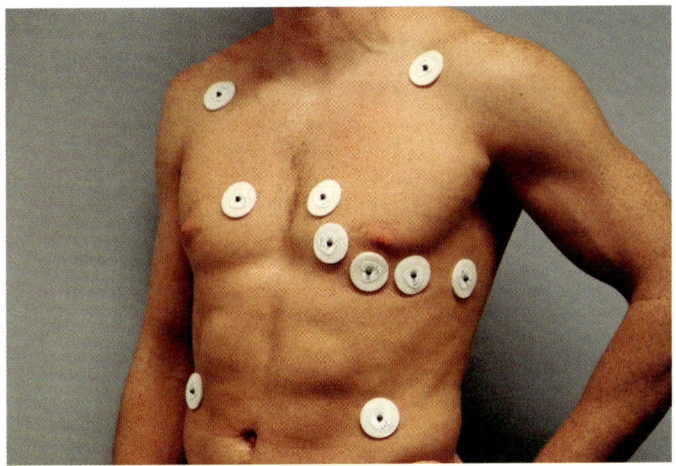

Fig. 6-16: Anatomic locations of limb and chest electrodes for a 12-lead ECG recording.

- Anatomic locations of chest electrodes for precordial leads:
  - V1 - 4th intercostal space at right sternal border
  - V2 - 4th intercostal space at left sternal border
  - V3 - Midway between V2 and V4
  - V4 - 5th intercostal space at left midclavicular line
  - V5 - Left anterior axillary line at V4 level
  - V6 - Left midaxillary line at V4 and V5 levels

Connect the electrodes to their corresponding lead wires to form three bipolar limb leads, three augmented unipolar limb leads, and six unipolar leads.

Location of Electrodes and Lead Connections for 12-Lead ECG		
Lead	**Positive Input**	**Negative Input**
Bipolar Limb Leads		
Lead I	Left arm	Right arm
Lead II	Left leg	Right arm
Lead III	Left leg	Left arm
Augmented Unipolar Limb Leads		
aVR	Right arm	Left arm and left leg
aVL	Left arm	Right arm and left leg
aVF	Left leg	Right arm and left arm
Unipolar Precordial Leads		
V1	4th intercostal space at right sternal border	Central terminal*
V2	4th intercostal space at left sternal border	Central terminal
V3	Midway between V2 and V4	Central terminal
V4	5th intercostal space at left midclavicular line	Central terminal
V5	Left anterior axillary line at V4 level	Central terminal
V6	Left midaxillary line at V4 and V5 levels	Central terminal

*Negative or reference input is composed of a compound electrode formed by electrically combining the output of the left arm, right arm, and left leg electrodes.

Interpretation

Waveforms and Intervals (Fig. 6-17)

- **P wave:** Atrial depolarization
- **PR interval:** Time for atrial depolarization and conduction from the SA node to the AV node. Normal duration is 0.12 to 0.20 seconds
- **QRS complex:** Ventricular depolarization and atrial repolarization. Normal duration is 0.06 to 0.10 seconds
- **QT interval:** Time for both ventricular depolarization and repolarization. Normally ranges from 0.20 to 0.40 seconds, depending on heart rate
- **ST segment:** Isoelectric period following QRS when the ventricles are depolarized
- **T wave:** Ventricular repolarization

Sinus Node Rhythms

- **Normal sinus rhythm:** Atrial depolarization begins in the SA node and spreads normally throughout the electrical conduction system with a heart rate between 60 and 100 beats/minute
- **Sinus bradycardia:** Sinus rhythm with a heart rate less than 60 beats/minute (in adults)
- **Sinus tachycardia:** Sinus rhythm with a heart rate more than 100 beats/minute (in adults)
- **Sinus arrhythmia:** A sinus rhythm, but with quickening and slowing of impulse formation in the SA node resulting in a slight beat-to-beat variation of the rate
- **Sinus arrest:** A sinus rhythm, except with intermittent failure of either SA node impulse formation or AV node conduction that results in the occasional complete absence of P or QRS waves

Atrial Dysrhythmias

Premature atrial contractions (PAC)

- Occur when an ectopic focus in the atrium initiates an impulse before the SA node
- The P wave is premature with abnormal configuration

Clinical Significance:

- PACs are very common and generally benign, but may progress to atrial flutter, tachycardia or fibrillation
- May occur with a normal heart (from caffeine, stress, smoking, alcohol) and any type of heart disease

Atrial flutter

- An ectopic, very rapid atrial tachycardia
- Atrial rate of 250–350 beats per minute; ventricular rate dependent upon AV node conduction
- Saw-tooth shaped P waves (also known as flutter waves) are characteristic

Clinical Significance:

- Occurs with valvular disease (especially mitral), ischemic heart disease, cardiomyopathy, hypertension, acute myocardial infarction, chronic obstructive lung disease, and pulmonary emboli
- Signs and symptoms include palpitations, lightheadedness, and angina due to a rapid rate
- Stagnation of blood may predispose to thrombi in the atria

Atrial fibrillation

- A common arrhythmia where the atria are depolarized between 350 and 600 times/min
- ECG shows characteristically irregular undulations of ECG baseline without discrete P waves

Clinical Significance:

- Occurs in healthy hearts and in patients with coronary artery disease, hypertension, and valvular disease
- Symptoms may include palpitations, fatigue, dyspnea, lightheadedness, syncope, and chest pain
- Stagnation of blood may predispose to thrombi in the atria

Atrioventricular Conduction Blocks

1st degree atrioventricular block

- PR interval is longer than 0.2 seconds, but relatively constant from beat to beat

Clinical Significance:

- No symptoms or significant change in cardiac function
- PR interval may become prolonged for many reasons including medications that suppress AV conduction

2nd degree atrioventricular block

- AV conduction disturbance in which impulses between the atria and ventricles fail intermittently
- Two major types: Mobitz type I block (also called Wenckebach block) and Mobitz type II block

Clinical Significance:

- Mobitz I – progressive prolongation of PR interval until one impulse is not conducted (generally benign)
- Mobitz II – consecutive PR intervals are the same and normal followed by nonconduction of one or more impulses (a more serious condition). If heart rate is slow, cardiac output will decrease with the blocked impulse. Also, 2nd degree AV block may progress to 3rd degree AV block

3rd degree atrioventricular block (complete heart block)

- All impulses are blocked at the AV node and none are transmitted to the ventricles
- The atria and ventricles are paced independently; atrial rate > ventricular rate

Clinical Significance:

- Considered a medical emergency requiring a pacemaker
- If the ventricular rate is too slow, the cardiac output drops and the patient may faint
- Common causes include degenerative changes of the conduction systems, digitalis, heart surgery, and acute MI

Ventricular Arrhythmias

Premature ventricular complex (PVC)

- Premature depolarization arising in the ventricles due to an ectopic focus
- Unifocal PVCs arise from the same ectopic focus and have the same configuration
- Multifocal PVCs arise from different ectopic foci and have different configurations
- On ECG, the P wave is usually absent and the QRS complex has a wide and aberrant shape
- Bigeminy – Normal sinus impulse is followed by a PVC
- Trigeminy – PVC occurs after every two normal sinus impulses

Clinical Significance:

- A common arrhythmia that occurs in healthy and diseased hearts
- Patient may be asymptomatic or have palpitations
- Common causes include anxiety, caffeine, stress, smoking, and all forms of heart disease

Ventricular tachycardia (v-tach)

- 3 or more consecutive PVCs at a ventricular rate of > 150 beats/minute
- P waves are absent and QRS complexes are wide and aberrant in appearance

Clinical Significance:

- V-tach longer than 30 seconds is a life-threatening arrhythmia and requires immediate medical intervention
- Patients are not able to maintain an adequate blood pressure and eventually become hypotensive
- V-tach may degenerate into ventricular fibrillation causing cardiac arrest
- Common causes include: MI, cardiomyopathy, and valvular disease

Ventricular fibrillation (v-fib)

- Ventricles do not beat in a coordinated fashion, but fibrillate or quiver asynchronously and ineffectively
- No cardiac output; patient becomes unconscious
- ECG shows characteristic fibrillatory waves with an irregular pattern that is either coarse or fine

Clinical Significance:

- A lethal tachyarrhythmia requires immediate defibrillation
- Additional measures include medications to support the circulation and intravenous antiarrhythmic agents
- Common causes include heart disease of any type, MI, and cocaine use

Ventricular asystole

- Ventricular standstill with no rhythm
- ECG records a straight-line pattern

Clinical Significance:

- Requires immediate CPR and medications to stimulate cardiac activity
- Common causes include acute MI, ventricular rupture, cocaine use, lightning strikes, and electrical shock

Signs of Myocardial Ischemia and Infarction

ST segment depression

- A depressed ST segment is a sign of subendocardial ischemia, but also can be due to digitalis toxicity or hypokalemia
- The segment is evaluated relative to isoelectric baseline at 0.08 seconds after the J point (junction between the end of the QRS complex and the beginning of the ST segment)
- Deviations from the isoelectric baseline are expressed as ST segment depression of 1 mm, 2 mm, etc.

ST segment elevation

- Earliest sign of acute transmural infarction
- Can also indicate a benign early repolarization pattern in a normal heart
- Deviations from the isoelectric baseline are expressed as ST segment elevation of 1 mm, 2 mm, etc.

Q wave

- A characteristic marker of infarction; signifies the loss of positive electrical voltages due to necrosis
- A significant or abnormal Q wave is longer than 0.04 msec and larger than 1/3 the amplitude of the R wave

T wave inversion

- Occurs hours or days after an MI as the result of a delay in repolarization produced by the injury
- May also occur with right and left bundle branch blocks, after a CVA, and as a normal juvenile T wave pattern in children and some adults

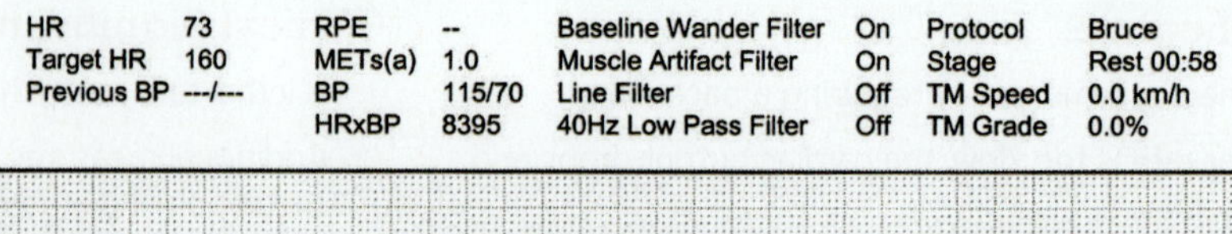

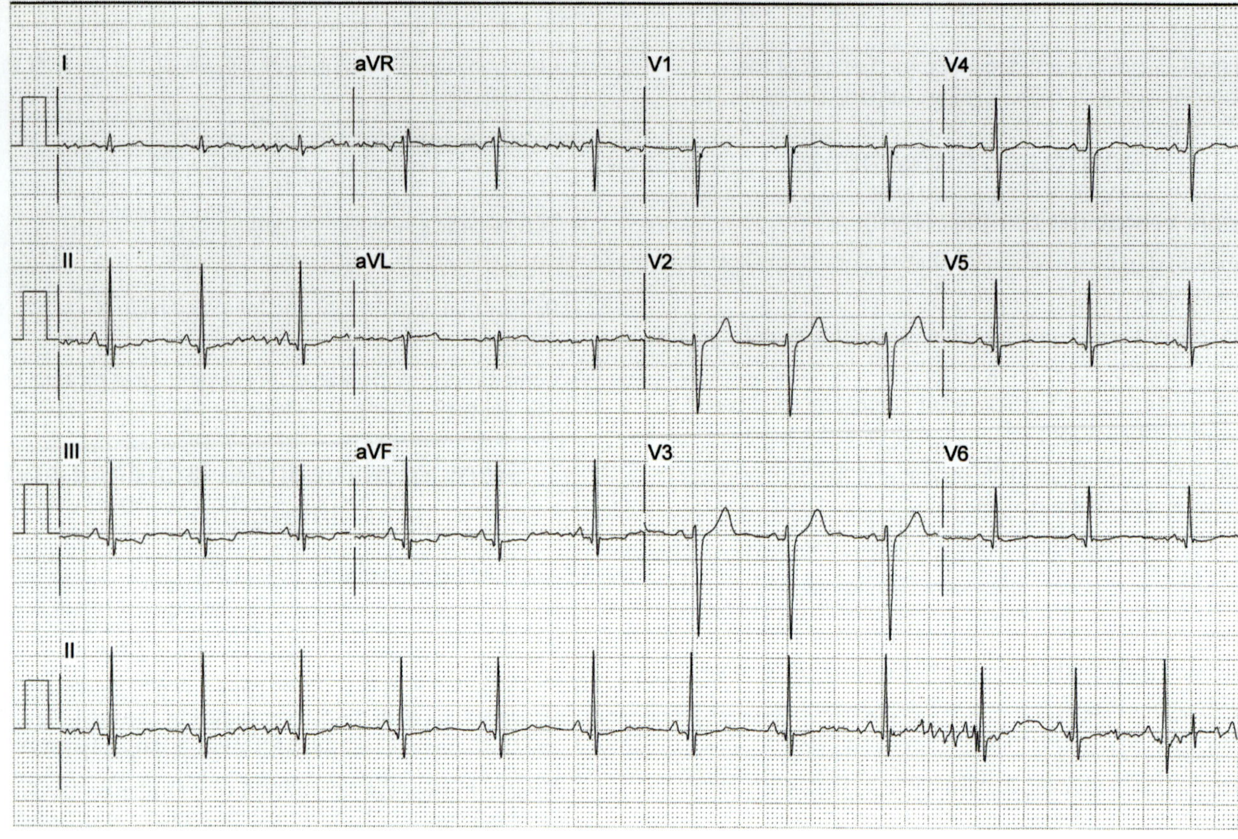

Fig. 6-17: Example of a normal 12-lead ECG recorded after 58 seconds of resting just prior to a graded exercise test using a Bruce protocol.

Exercise Stress Testing[21]

Exercise stress tests are used to assess the patient's ability to tolerate increasing intensity of exercise while ECG, BP, HR, and symptoms are monitored for evidence of myocardial ischemia, abnormal electrical conduction, or other abnormal signs and symptoms of exertion. They may be used to evaluate disease severity and prognosis and to determine functional capacity, especially for exercise prescription and counseling. A number of exercise protocols are available using a treadmill, cycle ergometer or upper extremity ergometer.

Procedure

- Generally, the patient is required to exercise at progressively greater increments of work, by varying the speed and grade of the treadmill, or the speed and resistance to pedaling an upper extremity or cycle ergometer.
- HR, BP, ECG, RPE, and signs and symptoms are monitored before, during, and after the test
- Absolute indications for terminating an exercise test:
  - Drop in SBP > 10 mm Hg from baseline despite increase in workload with other evidence of ischemia
  - Moderately severe angina (three on a scale of four)
  - Increasing nervous system symptoms (e.g., ataxia, dizziness)
  - Signs of poor perfusion (cyanosis, pallor)
  - Sustained ventricular tachycardia
  - > 1.0 mm ST elevation in leads without diagnostic Q waves
- Relative indications for terminating an exercise test:
  - Drop in SBP > 10 mm Hg from baseline despite increase in workload without other evidence of ischemia
  - > 2 mm ST displacement (horizontal or downsloping)
  - Arrhythmias other than sustained ventricular tachycardia, including multifocal PVCs, supraventricular tachycardia, heart block or bradyarrhythmias
  - Fatigue, shortness of breath, wheezing, leg cramps, and claudication
  - Development of bundle branch block or intraventricular conduction delay
  - Increasing chest pain
  - Hypertensive response (SBP > 250 mm Hg and/or DBP > 115 mm Hg)

CONSIDER THIS

SYSTEMATIC APPROACH FOR ANALYZING ECG RHYTHM STRIPS[14]

1. Scan rhythm strip	• Is rate unusually slow or fast? • Does rhythm appear to be regular? • Are there any abnormal looking beats?
2. Determine the heart rate	• Regular rhythm: divide 300 by number of large squares (including fraction of a square) between two consecutive P waves • Irregular rhythm: count the number of QRS complexes in a 6 second strip; multiply by 10
3. Evaluate the rhythm by comparing R to R intervals	• Regular rhythm: R to R intervals are within 0.04 seconds • If irregular, is there a pattern, or is it totally irregular?
4. Evaluate P waves	• Present versus absent • Identical in shape? Upright in leads I, II, and III? • Each P wave followed by a QRS complex?
5. If P waves are present, measure PR interval to evaluate for conduction blocks	• Normal: 0.12 to 0.20 seconds
6. Examine QRS complexes to determine if conduction is normal through the ventricles	• Normal: QRS width is 0.04 to 0.10 seconds in all leads • Identical in shape?
7. Assess ST segment 0.08 seconds after the J point	• Is segment at isoelectric baseline, depressed, or elevated?

Interpretation

A negative test indicates a low probability of coronary artery disease; a positive test indicates a high probability of coronary artery disease.

Prognosis can be assessed using various multivariate indices (e.g., Duke Treadmill Test score and Veteran's Administration Score).

An aerobic exercise prescription can be determined from performance on the exercise test (see also Physical Therapy Procedural Interventions - Cardiac Rehabilitation).

Homans' Sign for Deep Vein Thrombosis[33]

Homans' sign is a test to detect deep vein thrombosis (DVT) in the lower leg.

Procedure

Passively dorsiflex the foot at the ankle with the knee straight.

Interpretation

Homans' sign is positive for DVT if the maneuver produces pain in the calf or popliteal space.

Clinical findings alone are insensitive and nonspecific and cannot be relied on to confirm or exclude the diagnosis of DVT.

Despite the lack of specificity, a positive Homans' sign warrants further evaluation.

Mediate Percussion[23]

Mediate percussion is the act of tapping the surface of the body to identify areas of altered density.

Procedure

- Percuss the back with the patient sitting and the anterior chest with the patient sitting or supine.
- Facing the patient, place the palmar surface of the middle finger of one hand firmly against the chest wall in the

intercostal space parallel to the ribs; other fingers remain off the chest.

- Strike this finger with a quick, sharp blow using the middle finger of the other hand.
- Two or three consecutive blows are struck in one place, before moving the finger to another intercostal space.
- Compare the sounds from each space from left and right sides.

Interpretation

Percussion sounds are evaluated for loudness (intensity) and pitch. Unilateral abnormalities are easier to identify than bilateral abnormalities because there will be a difference in the sounds from side to side in unilateral disease.

The percussion sounds progress from tissues of high density to tissues of low density in the following sequence:

- **Flat or dull** – sound elicited by percussion of the thigh muscles; in the upper lung, suggests neoplasm, atelectasis or consolidation of the lung.
- **Resonance** – percussion sound from the normal air-filled lung.
- **Hyperresonance** – intermediate sound between resonance and tympany; percussion note emitted by the emphysematous lung; suggests pulmonary emphysema or pneumothorax.
- **Tympany** – hollow sound vaguely resembling a drumbeat; occurs almost exclusively with a large pneumothorax.

Palpation of Peripheral Arterial Pulses

The peripheral pulse is a periodic fluctuation in the flow of blood through a peripheral artery caused by the ejection of blood with each heartbeat. Normal pulses are strong and regular. The pulse will be irregular with a cardiac arrhythmia and weak and difficult to palpate in peripheral artery disease. A higher intensity pulse will be present when stroke volume is increased (e.g., exercise, fever).

Procedure

- Heart rate and rhythm, as well as blood flow in the extremity, are assessed by palpating over the artery with the tip of the index or middle finger with enough pressure to feel the pulse, but without obstructing blood flow.
- Common arteries used include brachial, carotid, dorsal pedal, femoral, popliteal, posterior tibial, radial, and temporal.
- Note the time between pulsations.
- For regular rhythms (i.e., time between pulsations is approximately equal), count the pulses in 15 seconds and multiply by four.
- For irregular rhythms (i.e., time between pulsations is not equal), count the pulses in 60 seconds.
- Note the volume and quality of the pulse and any differences between the pulses in the two limbs.

Pulse Points of Selected Peripheral Arteries

Artery	Pulse Point
Carotid	The medial aspect of the sternocleidomastoid muscle in the lower half of the neck (Fig. 6-18)
Brachial	Medial to the biceps tendon and lateral to the medial epicondyle of the humerus
Radial	At the wrist, lateral to the flexor carpi radialis tendon (Fig. 6-19)
Ulnar	At the wrist, between the flexor digitorum superficialis and the flexor carpi ulnaris tendons
Femoral	In the upper thigh, one-third of the distance from the pubis to the anterior superior iliac spine
Popliteal	In the popliteal space of the posterior knee
Posterior tibial	In the space between the medial malleolus and the Achilles tendon, above the calcaneus
Dorsalis pedis	Near the center of the long axis of the foot, between the first and second metatarsal bones (Fig. 6-20)

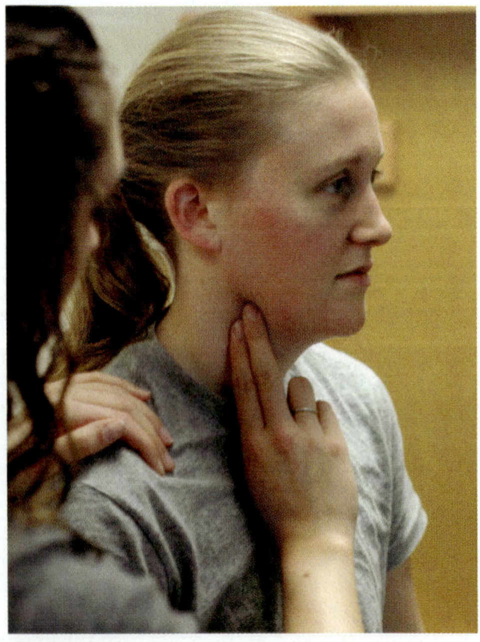

Fig. 6-18: Palpating the carotid artery.

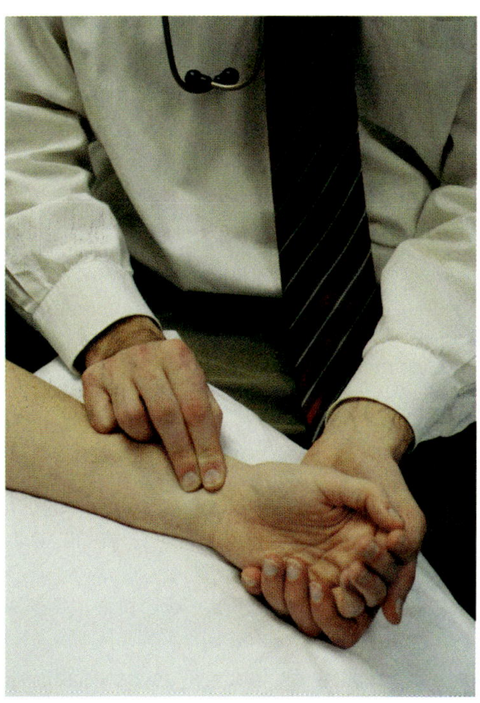

Fig. 6-19: Palpating the radial artery.

Interpretation

Characterize the heart rate	
Normal infant	100 to 130 beats/minute
Normal child	80 to 100 beats/minute
Normal adult	60 to 100 beats/minute
Bradycardia	< 60 beats/minute
Tachycardia	> 100 beats/minute
Characterize the volume or amplitude of the pulse[34]	
3+	= large or bounding pulsation
2+	= normal or average pulsation
1+	= small or reduced pulsation
0	= absence of pulsation

Pulmonary Function Testing (PFT)[35]

Pulmonary function testing measures the volume or flow of air during inhalation and exhalation (Fig. 6-21). The measurements include, but are not limited to, forced vital capacity (FVC), and other forced expiratory flow measurements such as peak expiratory flow (PEF), the forced expiratory volume in the first second (FEV_1), and the mid-expiratory flow (FEF 25-75%).

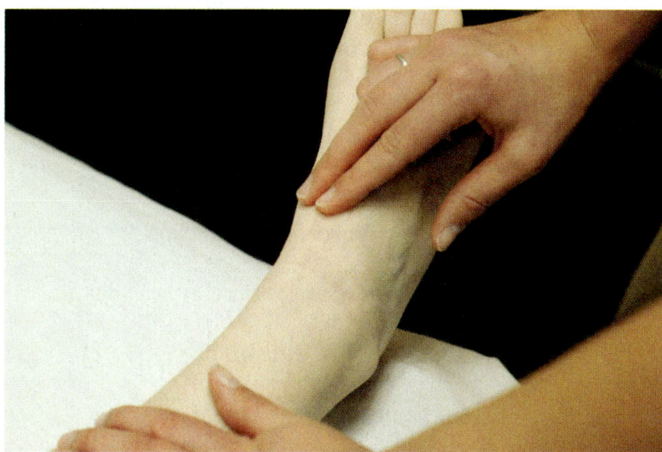

Fig. 6-20: Palpating the dorsalis pedis artery.

Procedure

- While maintaining an upright posture, the subject exhales into the spirometer mouthpiece as hard and as fast as possible for six seconds until no more air can be expelled.
- An adequate FVC test requires three acceptable maneuvers.
- Modern spirometers calculate "predicted normal" values, (i.e., the test value the patient should normally attain based on age, sex, height, weight, and race).

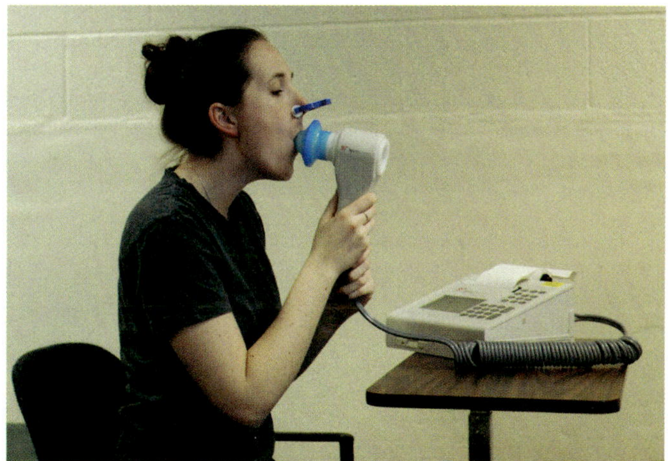

Fig. 6-21: Performing a pulmonary function test with a bedside digital spirometer.

Interpretation[36]

Obstructive ventilatory impairment

- Characterized by decreased expiratory flows.
- Airway narrowing during exhalation causes a disproportionate reduction of maximal air flow compared to the maximal volume displaced from the lungs.
- $FEV_1/FVC < 70\%$ is the primary indicator of an obstructive impairment.

Obstruction can be classified as:	
> 100%	= possible normal variant
70 - 100%	= mild obstruction
60 - 70%	= moderate obstruction
50 - 60%	= moderate to severe obstruction
< 50%	= severe obstruction

- Pathologies include asthma, emphysema, and chronic bronchitis

Restrictive ventilatory impairment

- Characterized by reduced lung volumes (total lung capacity, FVC, FEV_1) and relatively normal expiratory flow rates.
- Inferred from spirometry when FVC is reduced and FEV_1/FVC is normal or > 80%.
- Pathologies include interstitial lung disease, pleural diseases, chest wall deformities, obesity, pregnancy, neuromuscular disease, and tumor.

Pulse Oximetry[37]

A pulse oximeter estimates the percent of arterial oxygen saturation of hemoglobin by placing a sensor on the finger or earlobe (Fig. 6-22). The sensor measures the differential absorption of light by oxygenated and nonoxygenated hemoglobin. This estimate is denoted as SpO_2, which is an indication of the partial pressure of oxygen in arterial blood.

Procedure

- Apply the sensor to the earlobe or fingertip.
- Assess the strength of the waveform or pulse amplitude to assure that the oximeter is detecting adequate arterial blood flow.
- Holding the finger dependent and motionless and covering the finger sensor to occlude ambient light improves the quality of readings.

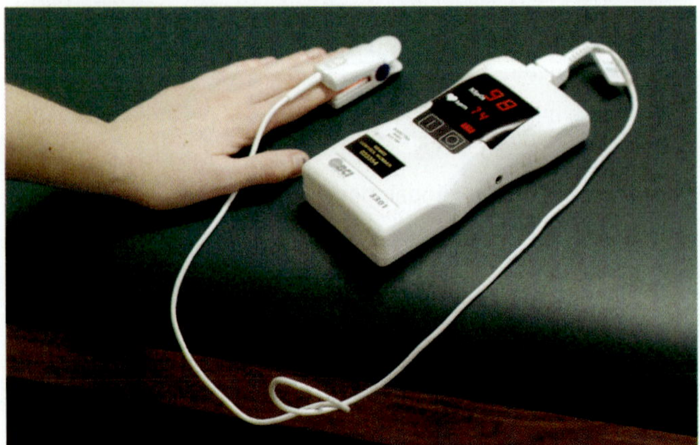

Fig. 6-22: A pulse oximeter.

Interpretation

SpO_2 is only an estimate of the arterial O_2 saturation; actual arterial oxygen saturation is ± 4% of SpO_2. A number of factors limit the accuracy of oximeter readings:

- Motion artifact
- Abnormal hemoglobin
- Intravascular dyes
- Exposure of probe to ambient light during measurement
- Poor cutaneous perfusion at the measurement site due to hypotension, hypothermia, low cardiac output or vasoconstrictor medications
- Skin pigmentation
- Nail polish or nail coverings (with finger probe)

If SpO_2 < 90% in acutely ill patients or < 85% in patients with chronic lung disease, activity should be stopped and a discussion with the physician should take place to consider adding or increasing supplemental oxygen.

Rate Pressure Product (RPP)[14]

RPP, or double-product, is an index of myocardial oxygen consumption and coronary blood flow. RPP provides an easy to measure physiologic correlate to the onset of angina pectoris or the development of ECG abnormalities in patients with heart disease. These signs and symptoms of myocardial ischemia generally occur at a reproducible RPP value.

Procedure

- Measure SBP and heart rate (HR) during the same exercise workload
- RPP = HR x SBP
- RPP is usually reported as a two digit number x 10^3 (e.g., if HR = 150 and SBP = 170, RPP = $25.5 \cdot 10^3$).

Interpretation

In patients with fixed-threshold angina:

- A relatively constant level of activity will precipitate angina.
- RPP obtained during an exercise test may be used to guide the exercise prescription.
- Keeping the intensity of exercise below the RPP value will reduce the risk of developing angina.

Rating of Perceived Exertion (RPE)[38]

The RPE is used to quantify the subject's overall sense of effort during activity. The reported RPE provides the therapist with an idea of the amount of strain or level of exertion the patient is experiencing.

Procedure

- There are two RPE scales that are widely used: the original 6 - 20 scale and the revised 0 - 10 scale. These scales are often referred to as the Borg Scale.
- Recommended instructions for administering the RPE scale:[29]

"While doing physical activity, we want you to rate your perception of exertion. This feeling should reflect how heavy and strenuous the exercise feels to you, combining all sensations and feelings of physical stress, effort, and fatigue. Do not concern yourself with any one factor such as leg pain or shortness of breath, but try to focus on your total feeling of exertion."

"Choose the number that best describes your level of exertion. This will give you a good idea of the intensity level of your activity. Try to appraise your feeling of exertion as honestly as possible, without thinking about what the actual physical load is. Your own feeling of effort and exertion is important, not how it compares to other people's."

Original RPE Scale		Revised RPE Scale	
6		0	Nothing at all
7	Very, very light	0.5	Very, very weak
8		1	Very weak
9	Very light	2	Weak
10		3	Moderate
11	Fairly light	4	Somewhat strong
12		5	Strong
13	Somewhat hard	6	
14		7	Very strong
15	Hard	8	
16		9	
17	Very hard	10	Very, very strong
18		• Maximal	
19	Very, very hard		
20			

Interpretation

RPE of 13 - 14 represents about 70% of maximum heart rate during exercise on a treadmill or cycle ergometer. RPE of 11 - 13 corresponds to the upper limit of prescribed training heart rates early in cardiac rehabilitation. RPE can substitute for HR in prescribing the intensity of exercise when:[39]

- Ability to monitor HR is compromised (e.g., sensory deficits)
- Patients begin an exercise-based rehabilitation program without a preliminary exercise test
- The HR response to exercise is altered (e.g., cardiac transplant)
- Physical activities other than cardiorespiratory endurance activity are assessed
- Clinical status or medical therapy changes

Ratings can be influenced by psychological state, environmental conditions, mode of exercise, and age.

Respiratory Rate, Rhythm, and Pattern

A complete assessment of respiration considers four parameters: rate, rhythm, depth, and character. Respiratory rate is the number of breaths per minute. Rhythm refers to the regularity of inspirations and expirations. Depth of respiration refers to the volume of air exchanged with each breath. The character of respirations refers to the effort and sound produced during breathing.

Procedure

- Observe the patient's breathing at rest for 60 seconds (an alternate method is to place your hand over the patient's upper thorax or abdomen and observe and feel movement with each respiration).
- Document the rate, rhythm, depth, and character of respiration.

Interpretation

Resting respiratory rates for healthy individuals[40]

- **Newborn:** 33 - 45 breaths/minute
- **1 year:** 25 - 35 breaths/minute
- **10 years:** 15 - 20 breaths/minute
- **Adult:** 12 - 20 breaths/minute

Respiratory rhythm

- **Normal:** Inspiration (I) is half as long as expiration (E); I:E ratio is 1:2
- **COPD:** I:E ratio reflects a longer expiration phase; 1:3 or 1:4

Depth of respiration

- Characterized as deeper or shallower than normal tidal volume

Character of respiration

- Normal breathing is quiet and effortless
- Labored breathing is evident by the use of accessory muscles of respiration
- Wheezes and crackles are abnormal sounds produced by changes in the airways

Common Breathing Patterns[23]	
Apnea	absence of spontaneous breathing
Biot's	irregular breathing; breaths vary in depth and rate with periods of apnea; often associated with increased intracranial pressure or damage to the medulla
Bradypnea	slower than normal respiratory rate; < 12 breaths/minute in adults; may be associated with neurologic or electrolyte disturbance, infection or high level of cardiorespiratory fitness
Cheyne-Stokes (periodic)	decreasing rate and depth of breathing with periods of apnea; can occur due to central nervous system damage
Eupnea	normal rate and depth of breathing
Hyperpnea	increased rate and depth of breathing
Hypopnea	decreased rate and depth of breathing
Kussmaul's	deep and fast breathing; often associated with metabolic acidosis
Paradoxical	chest wall moves in with inhalation and out with exhalation; due to chest trauma or paralysis of the diaphragm
Tachypnea	faster than normal respiratory rate; > 20 breaths/minute in adults

Six-Minute Walk Test (6MWT)[41]

The 6MWT is used to measure functional status and to document treatment outcomes in patients with heart and lung disease as well as healthy and older adults.

Procedure

- Walk on a measured "track" at least 100 feet (30 meters) in length.
- Subjects may self-administer any medications ordinarily taken before activity, may use supplemental O_2 at their prescribed flow rate for exercise, and may use any assistive device for walking.
- Three walks are recommended with at least 15 minutes of rest between each walk.
- BP, HR, RR, RPE, and O_2 saturation may be measured before and immediately after the test.
- Standard instructions are given:

  "The purpose of this test is to find out how far you can walk in six minutes. You will start from this point and follow the hallway to the marker at the end, then turn around and walk back. You will go back and forth as many times as you can in the six-minute period. You may stop and rest, if you need to, just remain where you are until you can go on again. The most important thing is that you cover as much ground as you possibly can during the six minutes. I will tell you the time, and I will let you know when the six minutes are up. When I say 'stop', stand right where you are."
- Standard words of encouragement are provided at regular intervals (e.g., "you're doing well," "keep up the good work," "you have three minutes to go").

Interpretation

The therapist should record the distance walked and the number of rest stops.

Waist Circumference[25]

Waist circumference is a practical anthropometric measurement for assessing abdominal fat before and during weight loss treatment. Monitoring changes in waist circumference may be helpful, in addition to measuring BMI, since it can provide an estimate of decreased abdominal fat even in the absence of a change in BMI. The measurement of waist-to-hip ratio provides no advantage over waist circumference alone.

Procedure

- With the subject standing, a measuring tape is placed snugly in a horizontal plane around the abdomen at the level of the iliac crest at the end of a normal exhalation.
- It is not necessary to measure waist circumference in individuals with BMI ≥ 35 kg/m^2 since it adds little to the predictive power of the disease risk classification of BMI.

Interpretation

- An increased risk for type 2 diabetes, dyslipidemia, hypertension, and cardiovascular disease is associated with a circumference > 102 centimeters (> 40 inches) for men and > 88 centimeters (> 35 inches) for women.
- Individuals with waist circumferences greater than these values should be considered one risk category above that defined by their BMI.

Physical Therapy Procedural Interventions

Aerobic Exercise Prescription[21,39]

Aerobic exercise, or cardiorespiratory endurance exercise, refers to submaximal, rhythmic repetitive exercise of large muscle groups during which adenosine triphosphate is synthesized primarily by the long-term energy system and the utilization of inspired oxygen.

Indications

- Reduced cardiorespiratory endurance
- Primary and secondary prevention of cardiovascular disease

Precautions/Contraindications

- Appropriate screening or health appraisal should be performed prior to beginning exercise training to identify known diseases, risk factors for coronary artery disease, and other factors that will optimize adherence, minimize risk, and maximize benefits.
- Avoid Valsalva maneuver

Procedure

Effective aerobic exercise training and improvement in VO_{2max} is directly related to the intensity, frequency, and duration of aerobic activity interacting with the two major principles of exercise training: overload and specificity. The overload principle states that to improve its function, a tissue or organ must be exposed to a stress or load greater than that which it normally encounters. The principle of specificity states that the long-term adaptations to the metabolic and physiologic systems derived from exercise are specific to the exercises performed and the muscles involved.

Mode

- Rhythmic activities that use large muscle groups and can be performed continuously and safely (e.g., walking, hiking, running, jogging, bicycling, cross-country skiing, aerobic dance/calisthenics, rope skipping, rowing, skating, stair climbing, swimming, and various endurance game activities).

Intensity

- A target heart rate (THR) zone is established from lower and upper heart rate limits calculated using different percentage training intensities depending on the individual's age, fitness level, health status, and goals.
- **Method 1:** Percent of maximum heart rate (HRmax)

  Lower THR = HRmax x 55%

  Upper THR = HRmax x 90%

- **Method 2:** Heart rate reserve (HRR) or Karvonen formula

  Lower THR = [(HRmax – HRrest) x 40%] + HRrest

  Upper THR = [(HRmax – HRrest) x 85%] + HRrest

  – HRmax = maximum heart rate measured during a graded exercise test or estimated by 220 - age

  – HRrest = resting heart rate

Duration

- Duration is dependent on the intensity of the activity.
- 20 – 60 minutes of continuous or intermittent activity (minimum of 10-minute bouts accumulated throughout the day).
- Lower intensity activity should be performed over a longer period of time (≥ 30 minutes).
- Higher intensity activity should be performed for 20 minutes or longer.
- Moderate intensity activity of longer duration is recommended for adults not training for athletic competition due to the potential hazards and adherence problems associated with high-intensity activity.

Frequency

- 3 – 5 days per week

Expected Outcomes

The therapist should be aware of the normal cardiorespiratory responses to aerobic exercise as well as the chronic adaptations that occur from a successful long-term aerobic exercise training program.

Normal Cardiorespiratory Response to Acute Aerobic Exercise

- Increased oxygen consumption due to increased cardiac output, increased blood flow, and oxygen utilization in the exercising skeletal muscles.
- Linear increase in SBP with increasing workload (8 to 12 mm Hg per MET)
- No change or moderate decrease in DBP
- Increased respiratory rate and tidal volume

Chronic Adaptations to Aerobic Exercise

- VO_{2max}: increased at maximal exercise
- HR: no change or decrease at maximal exercise; decreased at submaximal exercise
- Arteriovenous oxygen difference: increased at maximal exercise; no change at submaximal exercise
- SBP and DBP: no change or slight increase at maximal exercise; no change or slight decrease at submaximal exercise
- Blood lactate: increased at maximal exercise; decreased at submaximal exercise
- Oxidative capacity of muscle: increase in mitochondrial number and size, capillary density, and oxidative enzymes
- Maximal voluntary ventilation: increased at maximal exercise
- Plasma volume: increased
- Skeletal muscle blood flow: increase at maximum exercise; no change at submaximal exercise

- Reduced body mass and body fat and increase in fat free body mass
- Improved body heat transfer due to larger plasma volume and more responsive thermoregulatory mechanisms
- Psychological benefits: reduced anxiety, stress, and depression; improved mood, and self-esteem

Airway Clearance Techniques

Airway clearance techniques are intended to manage or prevent the consequences of impaired mucociliary transport or the inability to protect the airway (e.g., impaired cough). The techniques may include breathing strategies, manual and mechanical techniques, and postural drainage.

Indications for airway clearance[42]

- Retained secretions in the central airways
- Prophylaxis against postoperative pulmonary complications
- Obtain sputum for diagnostic analysis
- Difficulty clearing secretions
- Atelectasis caused by or suspected of being caused by mucus plugging

Active cycle of breathing

The active cycle of breathing (ACB) technique was developed under the name "forced expiratory technique" to assist secretion clearance in patients with asthma. The name of the technique was changed to "active cycle of breathing" to emphasize that ACB always couples breathing exercise with the huff cough. It includes three phases: breathing control, thoracic expansion exercises, and forced expiratory technique.[43]

Procedure

- Breathing control:
  - Gentle, relaxed breathing (may be diaphragmatic breathing at patient's tidal volume and resting respiratory rate for 5 – 10 seconds, or as long as the patient needs in order to prepare for the next phase).
- Thoracic expansion exercise:
  - Three to four deep, slow, relaxed inhalations to inspiratory reserve with passive exhalation
  - Chest percussion, vibration or shaking may be combined with exhalation
- Forced expiratory technique:
  - One or two huffs at mid to low lung volumes with the glottis open into the expiratory reserve volume
  - A brisk adduction of the upper arms may be added to self-compress the thorax

Precautions/Contraindications

- Splinting postoperative incisions to achieve adequate expiratory force
- Bronchospasm or hyperreactive airways

Autogenic drainage (AD)

AD uses controlled breathing to mobilize secretions by varying expiratory airflow without using postural drainage positions or coughing. The theory is to improve airflow in small airways to facilitate the movement of mucus. AD requires patience to learn, so this may not be suitable for young children and patients who are not motivated or easily distracted. Because AD does not require the assistance of another person or equipment, it can be performed anywhere and during activities of daily living.[43]

Procedure

- The patient is sitting upright in a chair with back support.
- Controlled breathing at three lung volumes
  - "Unsticking phase": slowly breathe in through the nose at low-lung volumes followed by a two to three second breath-hold to allow collateral ventilation to get air behind the secretions, then exhale down into the expiratory reserve volume
  - "Collecting phase": breathe at tidal volume, interspersed by two to three second breath-holds
  - "Evacuating phase": deeper inspirations from low-to-mid inspiratory reserve volume, with breath holding followed by a huff
- Exhalation through pursed lips may be used to control expiratory flow rate.
- An average treatment is 30 to 45 minutes.

Precautions/Contraindications

- Requires motivation and concentration to learn

Directed cough and huffing[44]

A directed cough tries to compensate for the patient's physical limitations to elicit a maximum forced exhalation.

Huffing is a forced expiratory maneuver performed with the glottis open. The maneuver is similar to fogging a pair of glasses with your breath. Although a huff does not produce the same airflow velocity as a cough, the potential for airway collapse is less. Huffing may be reinforced by a quick adduction of the arms to self-compress the chest wall.

Procedure

Cough

- Inhale maximally, close the glottis and hold breath for two to three seconds.
- Contract the expiratory muscles to produce increased intra-thoracic pressure against the closed glottis.
- Cough sharply two to three times through a slightly open mouth.
- Post-surgical patients may need to splint the chest or abdomen by applying pressure over the incision with a pillow or blanket roll.

Huff

- Inhale deeply through an open mouth.
- Contract the abdominal muscles during a rapid exhalation with the glottis open, saying, "Ha, ha, ha."

Precautions/Contraindications

- Inability to control possible transmission of infection from patients suspected or known to have pathogens transmittable by droplets
- Elevated intracranial pressure or known intracranial aneurysm
- Reduced coronary artery perfusion (e.g., acute myocardial infarction)
- Acute unstable head, neck or spine injury
- Potential for regurgitation/aspiration
- Acute abdominal pathology, abdominal aortic aneurysm, hiatal hernia or pregnancy
- Untreated pneumothorax
- Osteoporosis
- Flail chest

High-frequency airway oscillation[43]

The Acapella® and Flutter® are handheld devices that combine positive expiratory pressure and high frequency airway vibrations to mobilize mucus secretions in the airways.

Procedure

- Place the device in the mouth with the lips firmly sealed around the mouthpiece
- Inhale slowly to 75% of a full breath
- Hold the breath for two to three seconds
- Exhale through the device for three to four seconds
- Repeat 10 to 20 breaths
- Remove the device and perform two or three coughs or huffs to raise secretions

Precautions/Contraindications

- Patient tolerance of increased work of breathing (acute asthma, COPD)
- Intracranial pressure >20 mm Hg
- Hemodynamic instability
- Recent facial, oral, or skull surgery or trauma
- Acute sinusitis
- Nosebleed
- Esophageal surgery
- Active hemoptysis
- Nausea
- Known or suspected tympanic membrane rupture or other middle ear pathology
- Untreated pneumothorax

Postural drainage, percussion, and vibration[42]

Postural drainage consists of positioning the patient so that gravity will help drain bronchial secretions from specific lung segments toward the central airways where they can be removed by cough or mechanical aspiration.

Percussion, also known as cupping and clapping, is the rhythmic clapping or striking of the thorax with a cupped hand or mechanical percussor directly over the lung segment being drained. This rhythmic sequence should last for several minutes and should not be painful.

Vibration is the application of a fine, tremulous action on the chest wall over the lung segment being drained in the direction the ribs move during exhalation. It may be performed manually or with a mechanical vibrator. Vibration should be performed during exhalation.

Procedure for postural drainage

- The patient assumes the appropriate position for the affected lung segment (Figs. 6-23 A-J).
- Standard positions may be modified as the patient's condition and tolerance warrant.
- Maintain each position for two to three minutes.

Precautions/Contraindications

All positions are contraindicated for:

- Intracranial pressure > 20 mm Hg
- Head and neck injury until stabilized
- Active hemorrhage with hemodynamic instability
- Recent spinal surgery (e.g., laminectomy) or acute spinal injury
- Active hemoptysis
- Empyema
- Bronchopleural fistula
- Pulmonary edema associated with congestive heart failure
- Large pleural effusion
- Pulmonary embolism
- Confused or anxious patients who do not tolerate position changes
- Rib fracture, with or without flail chest
- Surgical wound or healing tissue

Trendelenburg position is contraindicated for:

- Uncontrolled hypertension
- Distended abdomen
- Esophageal surgery
- Recent gross hemoptysis related to lung carcinoma treated surgically or with radiation therapy
- Uncontrolled airway at risk for aspiration (e.g., tube feeding or recent meal)

Postural Drainage Positioning

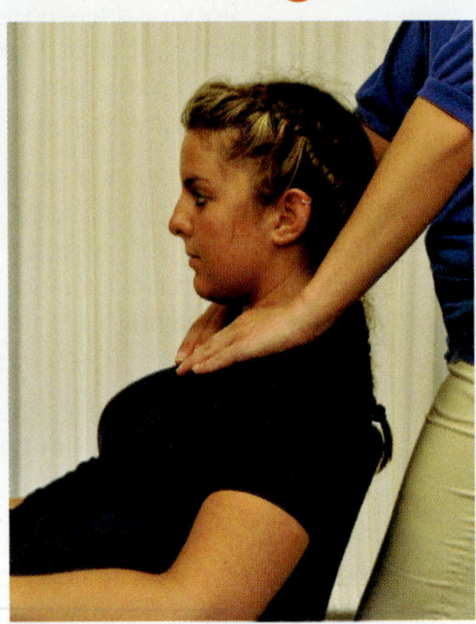

Fig. 6-23A: Apical segments right and left upper lobes: The patient is in a sitting position, leaning back 30-40 degrees. Percussion and vibration are performed above the clavicles.

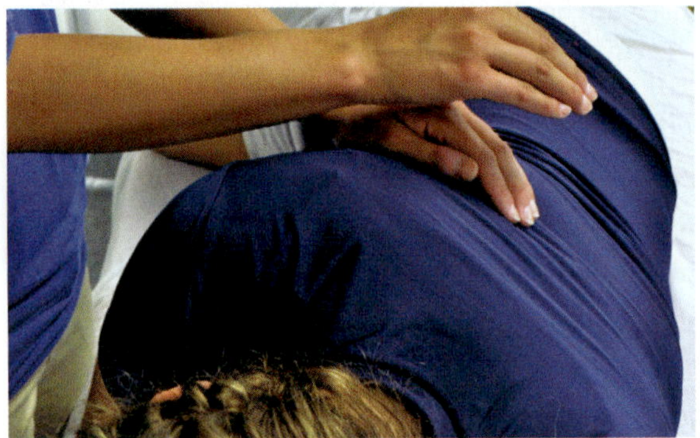

Fig. 6-23B: Posterior segment right upper lobe: The patient is turned ¼ from prone on the left side with the bed horizontal and the head and shoulders raised on a pillow. Percussion and vibration are performed around the medial border of the right scapula.

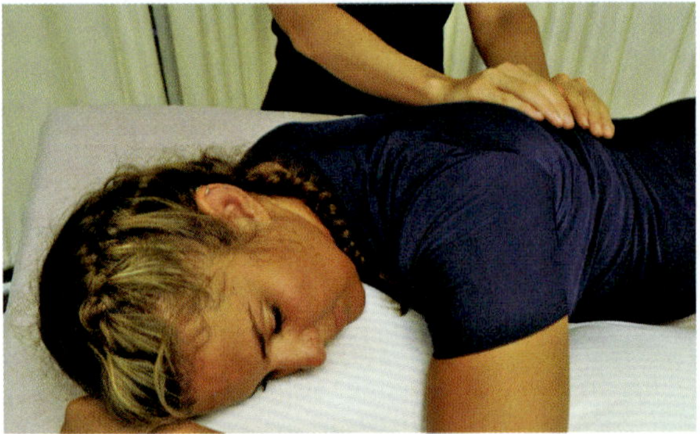

Fig. 6-23C: Posterior segment left upper lobe: The patient is turned ¼ from prone on the right side with the head of the bed elevated 45 degrees and the head and shoulders raised on a pillow. Percussion and vibration are performed around the medial border of the left scapula.

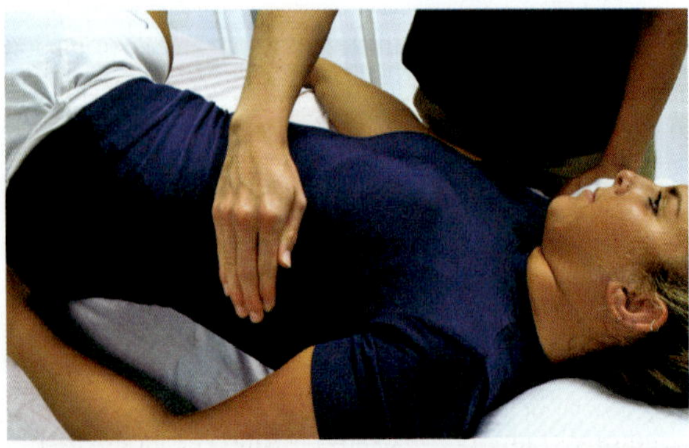

Fig. 6-23D: Lingula left upper lobe: The patient is turned ¼ from supine on the right side with the foot of the bed elevated 12 inches. Percussion and vibration are performed over the left chest between the axilla and the left nipple.

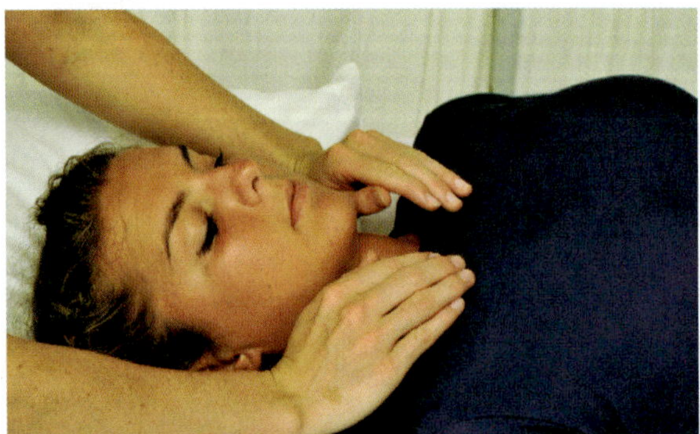

Fig. 6-23E: Anterior segments right and left upper lobes: The patient is in supine with the bed horizontal. Percussion and vibration are performed below the clavicles.

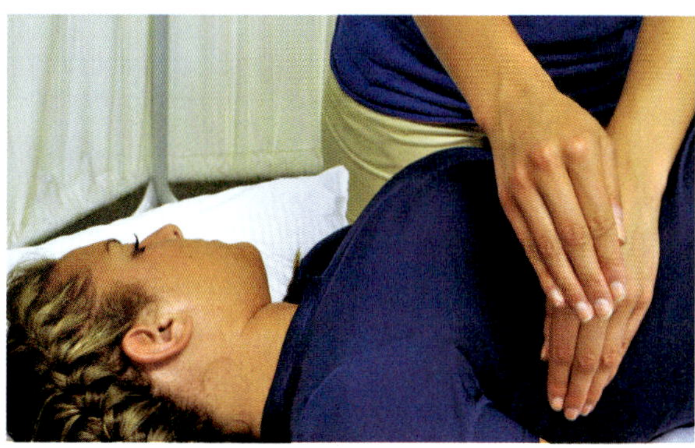

Fig. 6-23F: Right middle lobe: The patient is turned ¼ from supine on the left side with the foot of the bed elevated 12 inches. Percussion and vibration are performed over the right chest between the axilla and the right nipple.

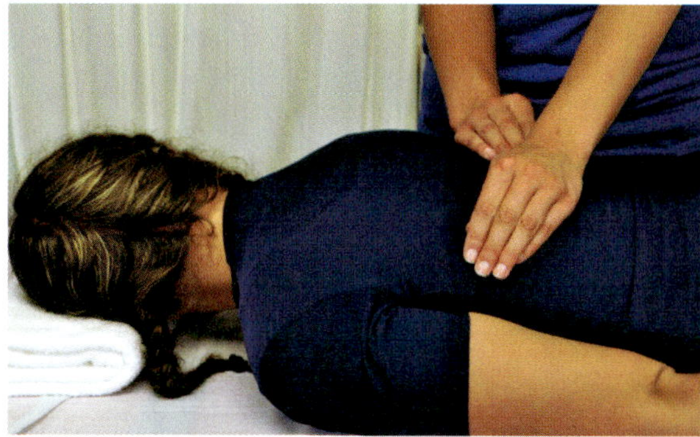

Fig. 6-23G: Superior segments left and right lower lobes: The patient is prone with the bed horizontal. Percussion and vibration are performed below the inferior border of the left and right scapulae.

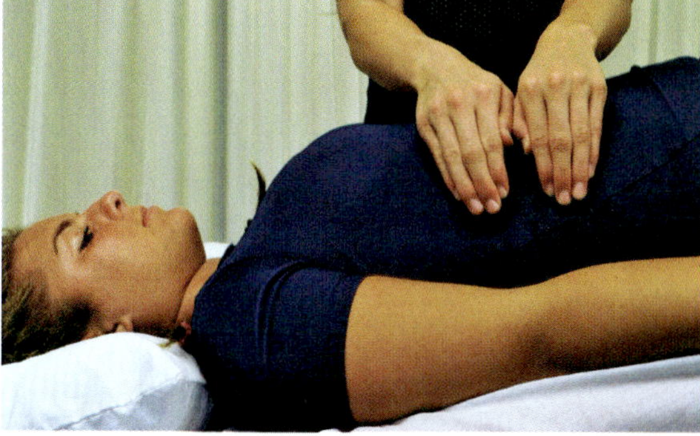

Fig. 6-23H: Anterior basal segments left and right lower lobes: The patient is in supine with the foot of the bed elevated 18 inches. Percussion and vibration are performed over the lower ribs on the left and right side.

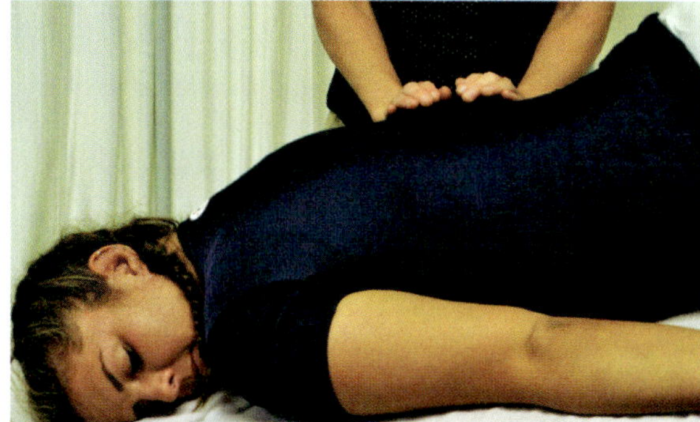

Fig. 6-23I: Posterior basal segments left and right lower lobes: The patient is in prone with the foot of the bed elevated 18 inches. Percussion and vibration are performed over the lower ribs on the left and right side of the chest.

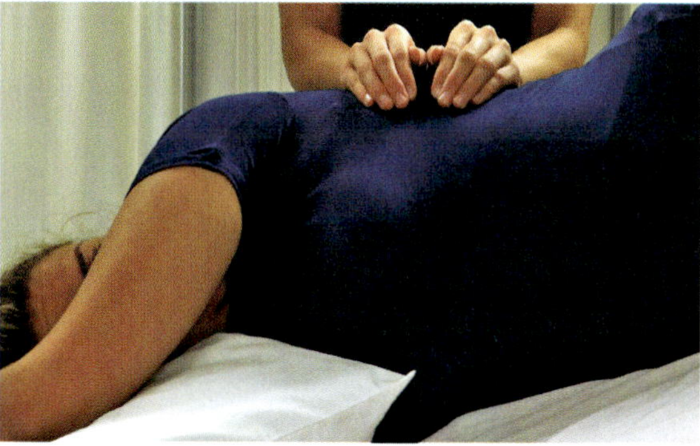

Fig. 6-23J: Lateral basal segments lower lobes: The patient is in sidelying with the foot of the bed elevated 18 inches. Percussion and vibration are performed over the lower ribs. The image shows the position for the lateral segment of the left lower lobe with the patient lying on the right side. For the lateral segment of the right lower lobe, the patient lies on the left side.

Procedure for percussion and vibration

- Place the patient in the appropriate postural drainage position.
- Cover the skin overlying the affected segment with a thin material (towel, t-shirt, hospital gown).
- Therapist rhythmically strikes the chest with a cupped hand for two to three minutes per lung segment (Fig. 6-24).
- Therapist places one hand on top of the other over affected area or one hand on each side of the rib cage.
- Vibrate the chest wall as the patient exhales by tensing the muscles of the hands and arms while applying moderate pressure downward.
- The maneuver is performed in the direction in which the ribs move on expiration.
- Encourage the patient to cough or huff after two or three vibrations.

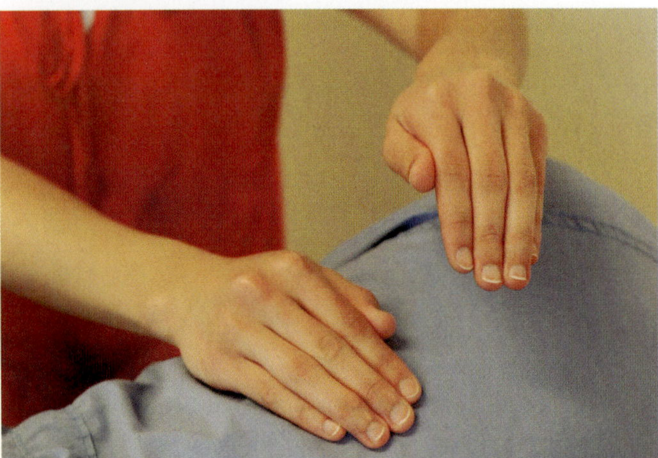

Fig. 6-24: Percussion of the thorax during postural drainage.

Precautions/Contraindications

- All contraindications listed for postural drainage
- Subcutaneous emphysema
- Recent epidural spinal infusion or spinal anesthesia
- Recent skin grafts, or flaps, on the thorax
- Burns, open wounds, and skin infections of the thorax
- Recently placed transvenous or subcutaneous pacemaker
- Suspected pulmonary tuberculosis
- Lung contusion
- Bronchospasm
- Osteomyelitis of the ribs
- Osteoporosis
- Complaint of chest wall pain

Expected outcomes of airway clearance

- Easier clearance of secretions and increased volume of secretions during and after treatments
- Improved breath sounds in the lungs being treated
- Increase in sputum production
- Change in vital signs - moderate changes in respiratory rate and/or pulse rate are expected
- Resolution or improvement of atelectasis and localized infiltrates observed with chest x-ray
- Improvement in arterial blood gas values or oxygen saturation

Breathing Exercises

Diaphragmatic breathing (DB)[45,46]

DB involves breathing predominantly with the diaphragm while minimizing the action of accessory muscles and motion of the upper rib cage during inspiration (Fig. 6-25).

Indications

- Post-surgical patient with pain in the chest wall or abdomen, or restricted mobility
- Patient learning active cycle of breathing or autogenic drainage airway clearance techniques
- Dyspnea at rest or with minimal activity
- Inability to perform ADLs due to dyspnea or inefficient breathing pattern

Precautions/Contraindications

- Moderate to severe COPD and marked hyperinflation of the lungs without diaphragmatic movement
- Patients with paradoxical breathing patterns, or who demonstrate increased inspiratory muscle effort, and increased dyspnea during DB

Procedure

- Semi-Fowler's position is a good starting position.
- Sniffing can be used to facilitate contraction of the diaphragm.
- Have the patient place one hand on the upper chest and the other just below the rib cage.
- Instruct the patient to:

"Breathe in slowly through your nose so that your stomach moves out against your hand. The hand on your chest should remain as still as possible. Feel your abdomen gently rise into your hand. Exhale through pursed lips, let the hand on your abdomen descend, while the hand on your upper chest remains still."

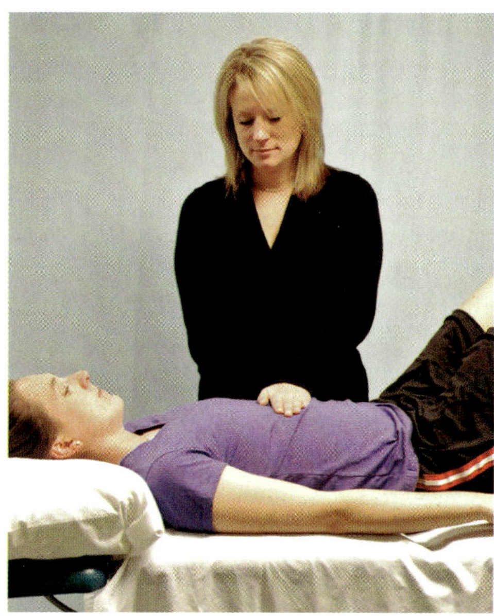

Fig. 6-25: A physical therapist teaches diaphragmatic breathing.

Expected Outcomes

- Decrease respiratory rate
- Decrease use of accessory muscles of inspiration
- Increase tidal volume
- Decrease respiratory flow rate
- Subjective improvement of dyspnea
- Improve tolerance for activity

Inspiratory muscle training (IMT)[45,47,48]

IMT attempts to strengthen the diaphragm and intercostal muscles. Two different IMT devices provide different modes of training: flow resistive breathing and threshold breathing. During flow resistive breathing, the patient inspires through a mouthpiece and adapter with an adjustable diameter. Decreasing the diameter increases the resistance to breathing, provided that breathing rate, tidal volume, and inspiratory time are kept constant. Threshold loading requires a buildup of negative pressure before flow occurs through a valve that opens at a critical pressure. Threshold breathing provides consistent and specific pressure for IMT, regardless of how quickly or slowly patients breathe.

Indications

- Impaired inspiratory muscle strength and/or a ventilatory limitation to exercise performance

Precautions/Contraindications

- Clinical signs of inspiratory muscle fatigue (in characteristic order of appearance)
  - Tachypnea
  - Reduced tidal volume
  - Increased $PaCO_2$
  - Bradypnea and decreased minute ventilation

Procedure

- Measure the patient's maximum inspiratory pressure (MIP) with a manometer. Use the measured MIP to calculate the training load.

Using the Threshold® Inspiratory Muscle Trainer

- Have the patient place the mouthpiece in his or her mouth and inhale with enough force to open the valve.
- Adjust the spring tension by turning the control knob to adjust the pressure indicator to the prescribed setting.
- The device is marked every 2 centimeters H_2O. The higher the setting the greater the effort needed.
- Begin training with the setting that elicits 30% to 40% of the patient's MIP.
- The patient breathes against that resistance at resting respiratory rate and tidal volume for 5 to 15 minutes, two to three times daily, as tolerated.
- Resistance can be increased in small increments by adjusting the tension on the spring until the training load reaches 40 to 60% of MIP over a four to six week period.

Using the PFLEX® Inspiratory Muscle Trainer

- Have the patient place the PFLEX® in his or her mouth and breathe at tidal volume.
- Turn the dial selector to regulate the resistance to breathing - setting 1 provides the least resistance.
- Begin training with the setting that elicits the 30% to 40% level of MIP for 10 to 15 minutes daily, gradually increasing to 20 to 30 minutes, three to five days per week.
- Once the patient can easily tolerate 30 minutes at one resistance, increase the resistance to the next setting.

Expected Outcomes

- Increase inspiratory muscle strength and endurance
- Decrease dyspnea at rest and during exercise
- Increase functional exercise capacity

Paced breathing and exhale with effort[45]

Paced breathing is a strategy to decrease the work of breathing and prevent dyspnea during activity. It allows anyone who experiences shortness of breath to become less fearful of activity and exercise.

Exhale with effort is a breathing strategy employed during activity to prevent a patient from holding their breath. The technique breaks any activity into one or more breaths with inhalation during the resting or less active phase of the activity and exhalation during the movement or more active phase of the activity.

Indications

- Patients with dyspnea at rest or with minimal activity
- Inability to perform activity due to pulmonary limitation
- Inefficient breathing pattern during activity

Precautions/Contraindications

- Avoid Valsalva maneuver during activity

Procedure

- Perform activity at a tempo that does not exceed the patient's breathing limitations.
- Find a comfortable inspiration to expiration (I:E) time to synchronize with the exertion phase of activity.
- Synchronize breathing with components of the activity:
  - inhale before or during the easier component of the activity
  - exhale during the more vigorous component of the activity
- Do not hold breath or rush through the activity.

Walking:

- Inhale through the nose while walking two steps and then pause; exhale through pursed lips while walking four steps

Climbing stairs:

- Inhale through the nose while standing
- Exhale through pursed lips while stepping up (or down) one or two stairs
- Remain on the step until breathing control is restored

Lifting:

- Inhale through the nose while standing or sitting; exhale through pursed lips while bending to reach the object
- Pause
- Inhale through the nose while grabbing the object; exhale through pursed lips while standing up

Expected Outcomes

- Complete activity without dyspnea
- Decrease patient's fear of becoming short of breath during activity

Pursed-lip breathing (PLB)[49]

PLB is a simple technique to reduce respiratory rate, reduce dyspnea, and maintain a small positive pressure in the bronchioles, which may help prevent airway collapse in patients with emphysema. Any patient who is short of breath may use this technique.

Indications

- Tachypnea
- Dyspnea

Precautions/Contraindications

- Forcing exhalation

Procedure

- Semi-Fowler's is a good position to initiate the breathing technique.
- Instruct the patient to:

"Breathe in slowly through your nose with the mouth closed for two counts. Pucker, or purse your lips as if you were going to whistle, then gently breathe out through pursed lips, as if trying to make a candle flame flicker, for a four count. Do not blow with force."

Expected Outcomes

- Decrease respiratory rate
- Relieve dyspnea
- Reduce arterial partial pressure of carbon dioxide ($PaCO_2$)
- Improve tidal volume
- Improve oxygen saturation
- Prevent airway collapse in patients with emphysema
- Increase activity tolerance

Segmental breathing[45,50]

Segmental breathing, also known as localized breathing or thoracic expansion exercise, is intended to improve regional ventilation and prevent and treat pulmonary complications after surgery. It is based on the presumption that asymmetrical chest wall motion may coincide with underlying pathology (e.g., pneumonia, pleuritic chest wall pain, retained secretions) and that inspired air can be directed to a particular area by facilitation or inhibition of chest wall movement through proper hand placements, verbal cues or coordination of breathing.

Indications

- Decreased intrathoracic lung volume
- Decreased chest wall lung compliance
- Increased flow resistance from decreased lung volume
- Ventilation: perfusion (V:Q) mismatch

Precautions/Contraindications

- None

Procedure

- Position the patient:
  - Sitting position for basal atelectasis
  - Sidelying with affected lung uppermost
  - Postural drainage positions with affected lung uppermost to assist with secretion removal
- Therapist applies firm pressure at the end of exhalation to the patient's chest wall overlying the area to be expanded.
- Patient inhales deeply and slowly expands the rib cage under the therapist's hands.
- Therapist reduces hand pressure during the patient's inhalation.

Expected Outcomes

- Increase chest wall mobility
- Expand collapsed alveoli via airflow through collateral ventilation channels
- Assist with secretion removal

Sustained maximal inhalation with incentive spirometer[51]

In a sustained maximal inspiration (SMI), a maximal inspiratory effort is held for three or more seconds at the point of maximum inspiration before exhalation. Many airway clearance techniques include SMI to compensate for asynchronous ventilation, to promote air passage past mucus obstructions in airways, and to maximize alveolar expansion. SMI is also called incentive spirometry when using a device that provides visual or other feedback to encourage the patient to take long, slow, deep inhalations (Fig. 6-26).

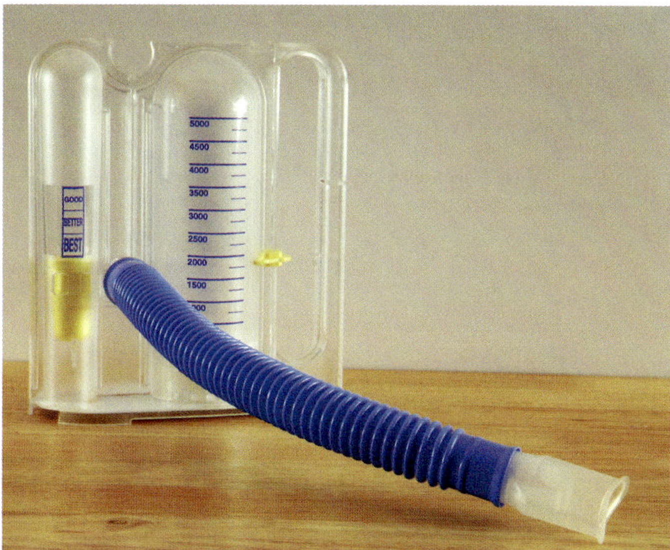

Fig. 6-26: Incentive spirometer.

Indications

- Decreased intrathoracic lung volume
- Decreased chest wall lung compliance
- Increased flow resistance from decreased lung volume
- Ventilation:perfusion (V:Q) mismatch
- Atelectasis or risk of atelectasis due to thoracic and upper abdominal surgery
- Restrictive lung defect associated with quadriplegia and/or dysfunctional diaphragm

Precautions/Contraindications

- Patient is not cooperative or is unable to understand or demonstrate proper use of the incentive spirometer.
- Patient is unable to deep breathe effectively (e.g., with vital capacity less than 10 mL/kg or inspiratory capacity less than one-third of predicted).
- Patients with moderate to severe COPD with increased respiratory rate and hyperinflation.

Procedure

- Hold the incentive spirometer in a vertical position.
- Have the patient exhale completely, then seal his lips around the mouthpiece.
- Breathe in slowly and deeply through the mouth, raising the ball or piston of the spirometer.
- Encourage the patient to move the diaphragm and expand the lower chest, not the upper chest.
- Hold the breath for at least three seconds and note the highest level the piston reaches.
- Perform SMI independently five to ten breaths per hour when awake.

Expected Outcomes

- Absence of or improvement in signs of atelectasis
- Decreased respiratory rate
- Resolution of fever
- Normal pulse rate
- Normal chest x-ray
- Improved PaO_2
- Increased forced vital capacity and peak expiratory flows

Positions to Relieve Dyspnea

A number of positions may be used to provide relief from dyspnea. The choice of position will depend on the circumstances at the time. The forward leaning position often provides relief of dyspnea to patients with lung disease.

Forward leaning with arm support optimizes the length-tension relationship of the diaphragm and allows the pectoralis minor and pectoralis major muscles to assist in elevating the rib cage during inspiration. The positions may be combined with other breathing techniques.

Reverse Trendelenburg position

The opposite of the Trendelenburg position, the reverse Trendelenburg position places a person in supine with their head above their trunk and lower extremities, decreasing the weight of the abdominal contents on the diaphragm and reducing the resistance to movement during breathing.

Semi-Fowler's position

The semi-Fowler's position places a patient in supine with the head of the bed elevated to 45 degrees and pillows under the knees for support and maintenance of a proper lumbar curve. This position is used often for patients with congestive heart failure or other cardiac conditions.

Cardiac Rehabilitation[21,52,53]

Cardiac rehabilitation services are multidisciplinary, long-term programs involving medical evaluation, prescribed exercise, cardiac risk factor modification, education, and counseling. The goals are to limit the physiological and psychological effects of cardiac illness, reduce the risk for sudden death or reinfarction, control cardiac symptoms, stabilize or reverse the atherosclerotic process, and enhance the psychosocial and vocational status of selected patients. Services are provided along a continuum of care, beginning with early assessment and mobilization in the inpatient setting, through early outpatient rehabilitation, to long-term maintenance and follow-up.

Clinical indications for inpatient and outpatient cardiac rehabilitation

- Medically stable post-myocardial infarction
- Stable angina pectoris
- Coronary artery bypass surgery
- Percutaneous transluminal coronary angioplasty (PTCA)
- Compensated heart failure
- Cardiomyopathy
- Heart transplant
- Other cardiac surgery (e.g., valve repair, pacemaker)
- Peripheral arterial disease
- High risk for coronary artery disease with diagnosis of diabetes mellitus, dyslipidemia, hypertension or obesity
- End-stage renal disease

Clinical contraindications for inpatient and outpatient cardiac rehabilitation

- Unstable angina
- Resting systolic pressure > 200 mm Hg or resting diastolic pressure > 110 mm Hg
- Orthostatic blood pressure drop of > 20 mm Hg with symptoms
- Critical aortic stenosis
- Acute systemic illness or fever
- Uncontrolled atrial/ventricular arrhythmias
- Third-degree atrial ventricular block without pacemaker
- Active pericarditis or myocarditis
- Recent embolism
- Thrombophlebitis
- Resting ST segment depression or elevation > 2 mm
- Uncompensated congestive heart failure
- Orthopedic or metabolic conditions that would prohibit exercise

Physical therapist role in cardiac rehabilitation

- Develop an individualized exercise prescription considering mode, intensity, duration, and frequency
- Monitor heart rate, blood pressure, ECG, RPE, and signs and symptoms
- Supervise exercise and promote proper technique and breathing patterns (Fig. 6-27)

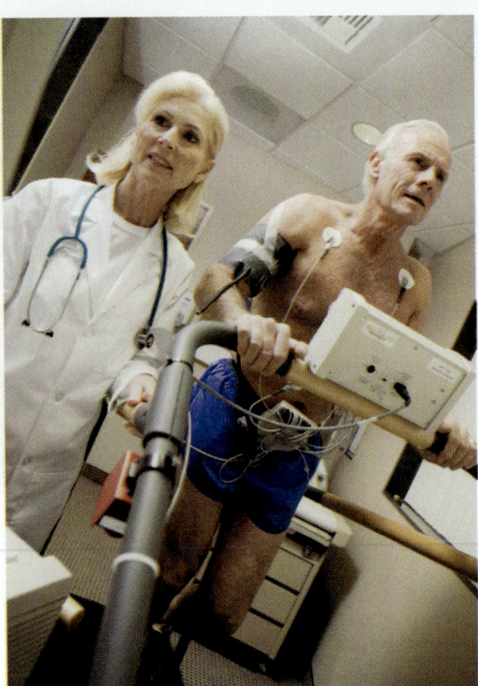

Fig. 6-27: A physical therapist monitoring a patient during cardiac rehabilitation.

Inpatient Cardiac Rehabilitation (Phase I)

Phase I begins with the physician referral to cardiac rehabilitation when the patient is medically stable. Phase I consists of patient and family education, self-care evaluation, continuous monitoring of vital signs, group discussions, and low-level exercise. Exercise activities include active range of motion, ambulation, and self-care. Exercise intensity is often prescribed according to heart rate and by rating on a perceived exertion scale. The trend toward early hospital discharge following a cardiac event has resulted in Phase I programs averaging three to five days.

Procedure

Medical evaluation

- A patient may begin rehabilitation when considered medically stable by the referring physician:
  - No new or recurrent chest pain in eight hours
  - No new signs of uncompensated heart failure (e.g., dyspnea at rest with bilateral basilar crackles)
  - No new significant, abnormal heart rhythm or ECG changes in eight hours
  - Stable creatine kinase and troponin levels

Monitoring and safety

- Ask patient to report any chest discomfort, dyspnea or faintness that occurs during activity
- Discontinue exercise for any of the following adverse responses:
  - Heart rate > 130 beats/minute or > 30 beats/minute above resting heart rate

– DBP ≥ 110 mm Hg
– Decrease in SBP > 10 mm Hg
– Significant ventricular or atrial dysrhythmias
– 2nd or 3rd degree heart block
– Signs or symptoms including angina, marked dyspnea, and ECG changes suggestive of ischemia

Active exercise

- Active upper and lower extremity exercises may begin 24 hours after bypass graft surgery and two days after infarction.
- Active exercises progress from sitting to standing (1 - 4 METs).
- Upper extremity exercise should not stress the incisions of post-surgical patients.

Aerobic exercise[21,52]

- Mode:
  – Progressive, supervised level walking (2 – 3 METs) to walking up and down steps or treadmill walking (3 – 4 METs).
- Intensity:
  – RPE < 13 (6-20 scale)
  – Post infarction: heart rate < 120 beats/minute OR < 20 beats/minute above resting heart rate
  – Post surgery: < 30 beats/minute above resting heart rate
- Duration:
  – Intermittent bouts of three to five minutes, progressing to 10 to 15 minutes of continuous activity.
- Frequency:
  – First three days: three to four times per day
  – After three days: two times per day with increased duration
- Progression:
  – Progress varies according to patient tolerance and risk stratification
  – Activity may be progressed provided:
    - Adequate increase in heart rate
    - Adequate rise in systolic blood pressure (10 - 40 mm Hg)
    - No new dysrhythmias or ST changes on the ECG
    - No cardiac symptoms are observed (e.g., palpitations, dyspnea, angina, excessive fatigue)

Expected outcomes of inpatient cardiac rehabilitation

- Prevent the harmful physiological and psychological effects of bed rest during hospitalization
- Walk 5 to 10 minutes continuously, or 1000 feet, four times daily
- Walk down and up one flight of stairs independently
- Know safe heart rate and RPE limits for exercise
- Recognize abnormal signs and symptoms suggesting intolerance to activity
- Promote a more rapid and safe return to activities of daily living within the limits imposed by their disease
- Prepare the patient and home support system to optimize recovery following discharge

Immediate Outpatient (Phase II)

Outpatient cardiac rehabilitation is a comprehensive program that includes prescribed exercise, cardiac risk factor modification, education, and counseling about diet and disease management. A Phase II program can begin immediately after hospitalization and last up to 12 weeks.

Procedure

Medical evaluation

An exercise test with ECG is recommended for patients entering an outpatient program, and as changes in the patient's condition warrant, to assess:

- Heart rate and rhythm
- Signs and symptoms
- ST segment changes
- Exercise capacity
- Risk stratification
- Target heart rate for exercise
- Initial level of work for exercise

Before beginning formal physical activity, a physical examination of the patient should include:

- Medical history
- Cardiovascular disease risk profile
- Body mass index or waist-hip ratio
- Resting ECG and blood pressure
- Auscultation of lung sounds
- Palpation and inspection of extremities for arterial pulses, edema, and skin integrity
- Examination of chest and leg wounds in patients after CABG or PTCA
- Orthopedic and neuromuscular status (e.g., ROM, strength, posture, balance, activities of daily living)

Monitoring and safety

- For low risk patients with known stable coronary artery disease, 6 to 12 sessions of ECG and BP monitoring and medical supervision are recommended to ascertain desirable exercise levels.
- For patients at moderate to high risk and/or unable to self-regulate or to understand recommended activity levels, continuous ECG and BP monitoring and medical supervision are recommended until safety is established, usually ≥ 12 sessions.

SPOTLIGHT ON SAFETY
ACTIVITY GUIDELINES FOR THE PATIENT WITH ANGINA PECTORIS

A rating of one on the angina scale is the recommended end-point to cease activity during inpatient and outpatient cardiac rehabilitation.

Individuals who experience angina during activity should discontinue the activity immediately and rest in a sitting or recumbent position until the discomfort is resolved.

Individuals with medication for angina should be encouraged to use the medication as directed.

If angina is not relieved by termination of activity or by three sublingual nitroglycerin tablets (one taken every five minutes), transport the individual to the nearest emergency center.

The exercise target heart rate for aerobic exercise training should be ≥ 10 beats/minute below the known ischemic or anginal threshold.

- Discontinue exercise for any of the following adverse responses:
  - Plateau or decrease in HR with increase in work
  - SBP plateaus or falls with increase in work or > 250 mm Hg
  - DBP > 115 mm Hg
  - ST segment depression > 1 mm
  - 2nd or 3rd degree heart block
  - Ventricular dysrhythmias
  - Angina or other symptoms of cardiovascular insufficiency

Aerobic exercise

Mode

- Rhythmic activities that use large muscle groups and can be performed continuously and safely (e.g., walking, hiking, running, jogging, bicycling, cross-country skiing, aerobic dance/calisthenics, rope skipping, rowing, skating, stair climbing, swimming, and various endurance game activities).

Intensity

- Intensity can be prescribed based on heart rate, METs, and RPE
- Heart rate (HR)
  - For patients without an entry exercise test, an exercise HR equal to standing resting heart rate + 20 beats/minute may be used with caution. A period of continuous ECG monitoring is recommended with the intensity gradually increased provided there are no symptoms, abnormal hemodynamics, ventricular dysrhythmias or ECG changes indicative of myocardial ischemia.
  - Usually, a target heart rate (THR) zone is established from lower and upper heart rate limits calculated using different percentage training intensities depending on the individual's age, fitness level, health status, and goals.
  - Percent of maximum heart rate (HRmax)

    Lower THR = HRmax x 55%

    Upper THR = HRmax x 90%
  - Heart rate reserve (HRR) or Karvonen formula

    Lower THR = [(HRmax – HRrest) x 40%] + HRrest

    Upper THR = [(HRmax – HRrest) x 85%] + HRrest

    HRmax = maximum heart rate measured during a graded exercise test or estimated by 220 - age

    HRrest = resting heart rate
- Metabolic equivalents (METs)
  - 1 MET is the energy expended while sitting quietly (3.5 mL O_2/kg/min or 1 kcal/kg/h)
  - To establish a MET level training zone, maximum METs must be measured during an exercise test. Lower and upper MET limits are calculated using the same percentage training intensities as the Karvonen formula

    Lower METs = [(MaxMETs – RestMETs) x 40%] + RestMETs

    Upper METs = [(MaxMETs – RestMETs) x 85%] + RestMETs

Rating of perceived exertion (RPE)

- RPE is a useful guide for rating exercise intensity, especially when heart rate cannot be used to regulate intensity (e.g., after heart transplant, patients taking beta blockers, individuals who do not have an exercise test prior to entering cardiac rehabilitation, individuals who cannot feel their pulse, and for patients whose clinical status or medical therapy changes).
- RPE of 11 to 13 ("fairly light" to "somewhat hard") is an appropriate upper limit during the initial phases of outpatient cardiac rehabilitation.
- RPE of 14 to 16 may be appropriate for higher intensity training later in cardiac rehabilitation if there are no signs or symptoms of ischemia or serious dysrhythmias.
- RPE is specific to the mode of exercise.

Duration

- 15 to 20 minutes of continuous or intermittent exercise during the first month (initial training phase).
- 25 to 30 minutes during the next three or four months (improvement stage).
- 40 minutes or longer after six months (maintenance phase).
- Interval training (exercise bouts of three to five minutes duration followed by equal rest periods) may be appropriate for patients who cannot exercise continuously.

CONSIDER THIS

MET VALUES OF COMMON PHYSICAL ACTIVITIES[14]

Once the appropriate MET levels for exercise are determined for the patient, activities with the desired aerobic requirement can be selected from a published table of MET values.

Light	Moderate	Vigorous
Walking, Jogging, Running		
Walking slowly at home or office = 2.0	Walking 3 mph = 3.0 – 4.0 Walking 4 mph = 4.5 – 7.0	Walking 4.5 mph = 6.3 Jogging 5 mph = 8.0 Running 7 mph = 11.5
Self-care, Household, and Occupation		
Toileting = 1.0 – 2.0 Driving a car = 1.0 – 2.0 Working at a computer or desk = 1.5 Making bed, washing dishes = 2.0 Bathing = 2.0 – 3.0 Cooking = 2.0 – 3.0	Washing windows or car = 3.0 Sweeping, vacuuming = 3.0 – 3.5 Light gardening = 3.0 – 4.0 Carrying, stacking wood = 5.5 Power lawn mowing = 5.5	Shoveling = 7.0 Carrying heavy loads = 7.5 Heavy farm work = 8.0 Digging ditches = 9.5
Leisure Time and Sports		
Playing cards, arts, and crafts = 1.5 Playing musical instrument = 2.0 – 2.5 Fishing (sitting) = 2.5	Slow dancing = 3.0 Table tennis = 4.0 Fast dancing = 4.5 Basketball shooting around = 4.5 Sexual intercourse = 4.0 – 5.0 Golf (walking) = 4.0 – 7.0 Swimming = 4.0 – 8.0 Tennis doubles = 5.0 Bicycling (flat) 10 – 12 mph = 6.0	Backpacking = 5.0 – 11.0 Basketball game = 8.0 Bicycling (flat) 12 – 14 mph = 8.0 Bicycling (flat) 14 – 16 mph = 10.0

SPOTLIGHT ON SAFETY

ENVIRONMENTAL CONSIDERATIONS FOR EXERCISE[21]

Physical therapists should be aware of the special problems encountered during exercise in hot and cold environments and at high altitudes.

Exercise in Hot Environments

Activity in hot environments should be modified to include access to fluids, increased frequency/duration of rest breaks, and shorter exercise time.

Moderate dehydration (loss of ≥ 6% of body weight) contributes to a drop in exercise performance and increases the risk of heat illness. To maintain hydration, measure body weight before and after exercise and drink at least one pint of fluid for each pound of body weight lost.

Wear clothing with a high wicking capacity to assist in evaporative heat loss. Remove clothing and equipment to permit heat loss, especially head gear.

Signs and symptoms of heat-related illnesses:

Heat stroke: disorientation, dizziness, apathy, headache, nausea, vomiting, hyperventilation, dry skin

Heat exhaustion: low blood pressure, elevated heart rate and respiratory rate, wet and pale skin, weakness, dizziness

Heat syncope: decreased heart rate and respiratory rate, pale skin, weakness, vertigo, nausea

Heat cramps: localized muscle spasms progressing to debilitating muscle cramps

Exercise in Cold Environments

Exercise in the cold may lower the angina threshold and increase the risk of death or injury in individuals with heart disease. Inhalation of cold air may exacerbate asthma.

Signs and symptoms of cold-related illnesses:

Frostbite: Loss of feeling and a white or pale appearance in fingers, toes, ear lobes, and the tip of the nose

Hypothermia: Body temperature < 97° Fahrenheit, shivering, confusion, disorientation, incoherence, poor coordination, slurred speech

Hypothermia develops when heat loss exceeds heat production. Factors that increase the risk of developing hypothermia include water immersion, rain, wet clothing, low body fat, age ≥ 60 years, and hypoglycemia.

Clothing should be adjusted during activity to minimize sweating and reduce sweat accumulation.

Exercise in High-Altitude Environments

The decreased atmospheric pressure at ≥ 5000 feet reduces the partial pressure of oxygen in the air, resulting in decreased arterial oxygen levels. The immediate compensatory responses include increases in ventilation and heart rate and a decrease in performance.

Acclimatization to altitude is the best prevention and treatment for altitude-related illness. Staging, or living at a moderate elevation for as long as one week before ascending to the final elevation, minimizing activity, and maintaining hydration and food intake reduce risk and facilitate recovery. If severe signs and symptoms persist, descending to a lower altitude is effective.

Signs and symptoms of altitude-related illnesses:

Acute mountain sickness: headache, nausea, fatigue, poor appetite and sleep, mild swelling in hands, feet or face

High altitude pulmonary edema: crackles/rales in the lungs, cyanosis of lips and nail beds

- As fitness improves and the patient gains confidence, increase the duration of the exercise periods.

Frequency

- Three to five days per week

Expected outcomes of outpatient cardiac rehabilitation

- Promote an active lifestyle through increased participation in domestic, occupational, and recreational activities
- Improved functional capacity through enhanced aerobic capacity, muscular endurance and strength, flexibility, and weight management
- Lower cardiovascular risk factors
- Improve symptoms and physiological responses to physical challenges
- Modification of unhealthy behaviors and psychosocial characteristics
- Improve patient understanding of safety issues during exercise

Pulmonary Rehabilitation[55-57]

Pulmonary rehabilitation is a medically supervised, multidisciplinary program for patients with chronic respiratory impairment. Comprehensive services include exercise training, education, psychosocial and behavioral interventions, nutritional therapy, and outcome assessment to assist the patient to manage and cope with progressive dyspnea.

Clinical indications for pulmonary rehabilitation

Pulmonary rehabilitation is indicated in the presence of respiratory impairments including dyspnea at rest or with exertion, hypoxemia, hypercapnia, reduced exercise tolerance or a decline in the ability to perform activities of daily living due to:

- Chronic bronchitis
- Emphysema
- Asthma
- Interstitial lung disease (sarcoidosis, occupational or environmental lung disease)
- Bronchiectasis
- Cystic fibrosis
- Lung cancer
- Chest wall disease
- Neuromuscular disease (Parkinson's, amyotrophic lateral sclerosis, multiple sclerosis)
- Preoperative and postoperative lung resection, transplantation or volume reduction
- Ventilator dependency

Clinical contraindications/precautions for pulmonary rehabilitation

- Ischemic cardiac disease
- Congestive heart failure
- Acute cor pulmonale
- Severe pulmonary hypertension
- Significant hepatic dysfunction
- Metastatic cancer
- Renal failure
- Severe cognitive deficit that interferes with memory and compliance
- Visual, hearing or orthopedic impairments are not contraindications, but may require the exercise program to be modified

Physical therapist role in pulmonary rehabilitation

- Administer a Six-Minute Walk Test or other appropriate exercise tests
- Develop an individualized exercise prescription considering mode, intensity, duration, and frequency
- Monitor heart rate, blood pressure, dyspnea, and signs and symptoms
- Supervise exercise and promote proper technique and breathing patterns
- Perform airway clearance and breathing exercises, as needed
- Instruct patient in energy conservation techniques

Procedure

Medical evaluation[56]

- Before beginning formal physical activity, a patient examination should include:
  - Medical history
  - Nutritional assessment
  - Spirometry
  - Resting arterial blood gas
  - Arterial oxygen saturation by pulse oximeter
  - Chest x-ray
  - Resting ECG
  - Exercise test (e.g., Six-Minute Walk Test or graded exercise test)
  - Complete blood count
  - Height and weight
  - Resting blood pressure, heart rate, and respiratory rate
  - Temperature
  - Breathing pattern
  - Auscultation of lung sounds

- Auscultation of breath sounds
- Palpation and inspection of extremities for arterial pulses, edema, and skin integrity
- Orthopedic and neuromuscular status (ROM, strength, posture)
- Functional status
- Anxiety and depression

Monitoring and safety

- Remind patients not to hold their breath during exercise and to exhale during the exertion phase of the activity
- Clinical monitoring during exercise includes:
  - Signs and symptoms of exercise intolerance
  - Heart rate and blood pressure
  - ECG, if the patient has heart disease
  - RPE and dyspnea
  - Oxygen saturation via pulse oximeter

Aerobic exercise

- Mode
  - Rhythmic activities that use large muscle groups and can be performed continuously and safely (e.g., walking, hiking, running, jogging, bicycling, cross-country skiing, aerobic dance/calisthenics, rope skipping, rowing, skating, stair climbing, swimming and various endurance games).
- Intensity
  - Target heart rate ranges used by healthy individuals or in cardiac rehabilitation generally are not applicable to patients with chronic lung disease who stop exercise at low heart rates due to ventilatory limits
  - There is no known threshold exercise intensity for training; intensity is determined primarily by patient tolerance and safety
  - Guidelines for exercise intensity include:
    - ≥ 50% of peak oxygen consumption determined from an exercise test
    - Using a dyspnea rating reported at a submaximal exercise level during an exercise test
    - 60% to 80% of the peak work rate achieved determined from an exercise test
    - An RPE of 4 to 6 on the 0 - 10 scale, or 12 to 16 on the 6 - 20 scale
    - Maintaining oxygen saturation > 90% as measured by pulse oximetry
- Duration
  - A minimum of 30 minutes of accumulated exercise per session is recommended
  - Interval training (exercise bouts of 30 seconds to three minutes followed by equal rest periods) may be appropriate for patients who cannot exercise continuously
  - As fitness improves and the patient gains confidence, increase the duration of the exercise periods
- Frequency
  - Three to five days per week

Expected outcomes of pulmonary rehabilitation

- Increase exercise tolerance
- Increase peak oxygen uptake
- Increase endurance time during submaximal testing
- Increase functional walking distance
- Increase muscle strength and endurance
- Reduce exertional dyspnea
- Improve ability to perform activities of daily living
- Improve health-related quality of life
- Reduce anxiety and depression

GOLD Level Clinical Application Templates

GOLD Level Clinical Application Template Executive Summary

Congestive Heart Failure

- Common etiologies contributing to CHF include arrhythmia, pulmonary embolism, hypertension, valvular heart disease, myocarditis, unstable angina, renal failure, and severe anemia
- Left-sided heart failure is generally associated with signs of pulmonary venous congestion; right-sided heart failure is associated with signs of systemic venous congestion
- Diminished cardiac output causes compensatory changes including an increase in blood volume, cardiac filling pressure, heart rate, and cardiac muscle mass

Cystic Fibrosis

- Causes the exocrine glands to overproduce thick mucus which causes subsequent obstruction
- Autosomal recessive genetic disorder (both parents are carriers of the defective gene) located on the long arm of chromosome seven
- The most common cause of death is respiratory failure

Emphysema

- Results from a long history of chronic bronchitis, recurrent alveolar inflammation or from genetic predisposition of a congenital alpha 1-antitrypsin deficiency
- Clinical presentation may include barrel chest appearance, increased subcostal angle, rounded shoulders secondary to tight pectorals, and rosy skin coloring
- Symptoms of emphysema worsen with the progression of the disease and include a persistent cough, wheezing, difficulty breathing especially with expiration, and an increased respiration rate

Myocardial Infarction

- Myocardial infarction occurs when there is poor coronary artery perfusion, ischemia, and subsequent necrosis of the cardiac tissue usually due to thrombus, arterial blockage or atherosclerosis
- Risk factors include patient or family history of heart disease, smoking, physical inactivity, stress, hypertension, elevated cholesterol, diabetes mellitus, and obesity
- Clinical presentation may include deep pain or pressure in the substernal area with or without pain radiating to the jaw or into the left arm or the back

Peripheral Vascular Disease

- Characterized by narrowing of the lumen of blood vessels causing a reduction in circulation usually secondary to atherosclerosis
- Risk factors include phlebitis, injury or surgery, autoimmune disease, diabetes mellitus, smoking, hyperlipidemia, inactivity, hypertension, positive family history, increased age, and obesity
- Patient education is paramount regarding the disease process, limb protection, foot and skin care, and risk factor reduction (smoking cessation, avoid cold exposure)

Level Clinical Application Template Executive Summary

Restrictive Lung Disease

- Classification of disorders caused by a pulmonary or extrapulmonary restriction that produces impairment in lung expansion and an abnormal reduction in pulmonary ventilation
- Pulmonary restriction of the lungs can be caused by tumor, interstitial pulmonary fibrosis, scarring within the lungs, pleural effusion, chest wall stiffness, structural abnormality, and respiratory muscle weakness
- Pathogenesis includes a decrease in lung and chest wall compliance, decrease in lung volumes, and an increase in the work of breathing

GOLD

Congestive Heart Failure

DIAGNOSIS

What condition produces a patient's symptoms?

Congestive heart failure (CHF) occurs when the heart can no longer meet the metabolic demands of the body. The heart's inability to pump a sufficient amount of blood occurs when there is insufficient or defective cardiac filling and/or impaired contraction and emptying of the heart. The impairment in cardiac output causes the body to compensate for this deficit and this results in an increase in blood volume, cardiac filling pressure, heart rate, and cardiac muscle mass.

An injury was most likely sustained to which structure?

CHF is not an independent disease process but rather a symptom of pathology within the heart muscle itself or in the cardiac valves. Injury within the heart can be left-sided, right-sided or both. The abnormal retention of fluids and diminished blood flow causes further stress and injury to the cardiac system.

INFERENCE

What is the most likely contributing factor in the development of this condition?

There are many pathologies (reversible and irreversible) that can contribute to CHF. Common etiologies shown to contribute to CHF include arrhythmia (e.g., atrial fibrillation), pulmonary embolism, hypertension, valvular heart disease, myocarditis, unstable angina, renal failure, medication-induced problems, high salt intake, and severe anemia. CHF occurs when there is a decrease in cardiac output, abnormalities in skeletal muscle metabolism, impaired left ventricular function or all of the above.

CONFIRMATION

What is the most likely clinical presentation?

A patient with CHF will initially show signs of tachycardia. Other signs include venous congestion, high catecholamine levels, and finally impaired cardiac output. As the severity of CHF increases, signs of venous congestion usually become apparent. Left-sided heart failure is generally associated with signs of pulmonary venous congestion; right-sided heart failure is associated with signs of systemic venous congestion. Impairment to either ventricle can affect the other, leading to both systemic and pulmonary venous congestion. A patient may present with pulmonary edema, nocturnal dyspnea, orthopnea, S3 gallop, dry cough, exertional dyspnea with low level exercise, sudden weight gain, possible cyanotic extremities, cardiac hypertrophy, and shortness of breath.

What laboratory or imaging studies would confirm the diagnosis?

Lab tests including urinalysis and a CBC count that includes electrolyte, thyroid stimulating hormone, blood urea nitrogen (BUN), and serum creatinine levels should be performed. A chest x-ray, electrocardiogram, and echocardiogram are also recommended. A Doppler echocardiogram can determine systolic and diastolic performance, the cardiac output (ejection fraction), and pulmonary artery and ventricular filling pressures.

What additional information should be obtained to confirm the diagnosis?

A patient history and administration of cardiac questionnaires will assist with diagnosis of CHF. In the Framingham classification system, the diagnosis of CHF requires that either two major criteria or one major and two minor criteria be present concurrently. The New York Heart Association Functional Capacity Classification also classifies heart disease based on symptomology as it relates to physical activity.

EXAMINATION

What history should be documented?

Important areas to explore include past medical history, medications, current health status, nutritional status, social history and habits, occupation, living environment, and social support system.

What tests/measures are most appropriate?

Aerobic capacity and endurance: assessment of vital signs at rest and with activity, perceived exertion scale, pulse oximetry, auscultation of the lungs

Anthropometric characteristics: circumferential measurements

Arousal, attention, and cognition: examine mental status, learning ability, memory, motivation

Community and work integration: analysis of community, work, and leisure activities

Environmental, home, and work barriers: analysis of current and potential barriers or hazards

Gait, locomotion, and balance: static and dynamic balance in sitting and standing, safety during gait with/without an assistive device

Integumentary integrity: skin assessment

Muscle performance: strength assessment

Pain: pain perception assessment scale, VAS

Range of motion: active and passive range of motion

Self-care and home management: assessment of functional capacity, Functional Independence Measure

Sensory integrity: proprioception and kinesthesia

Ventilation, respiration, and circulation: assessment of cough and clearance of secretions, breathing patterns, vital capacity, perceived exertion scale, pulse oximetry, palpation of pulses, auscultation of the lungs and heart

What additional findings are likely with this patient?

Diagnoses such as left ventricular infarction, aortic or mitral valve disease, and hypertension create pulmonary congestion that may result in left-sided CHF. Over time, however, fluid accumulation spreads and ankle edema, congestive hepatomegaly, ascites, and pleural effusion occur. This leads the patient to develop right-sided CHF as well. Later stages of CHF are characterized by symptoms of low cardiac output.

MANAGEMENT

What is the most effective management of this patient?

A patient with CHF will be treated based on the root cause of the heart failure. Medical management includes the use of diuretics, nitrates, cardiac glycosides, analgesics, and angiotensin-converting enzyme inhibitor agents. Medications play a vital role in the optimal management of this disease process. Therapists must be aware of the potential side effects such as digitalis toxicity when treating this population. The patient may be referred to physical therapy for generalized conditioning and mobility. Primary goals include improving exercise tolerance and increasing knowledge of the disease process. Therapeutic intervention has to be individualized by each patient since the etiology, current medications, and overall health play a role in the plan of care. Walking is commonly used to initiate an exercise program with cardiac patients. Patients can progress their overall endurance following their own heart rate and perceived exertion guidelines. Caregiver education and instruction may also be appropriate. Psychosocial support, nutritional counseling (no salt diet and no alcohol), and caretaker education are also important components of the plan of care.

What home care regimen should be recommended?

A patient will usually follow a similar program at home once they are discharged from the hospital or in addition to their outpatient therapy. The patient should continue energy conservation and pacing techniques with all activities. The family and patient must be fully educated as to the signs and symptoms of concern as well as potential medication toxicity.

OUTCOME

What is the likely outcome of a course of physical therapy?

A patient can live with CHF and should benefit from physical therapy in order to improve endurance and strength after a decline in function from hospitalization or bed rest. Physical therapy will improve skeletal muscle function, blood flow, metabolic capacity, and overall exercise tolerance. Physical therapy, however, will not cure CHF or its cause.

What are the long-term effects of the patient's condition?

The prognosis for CHF is poor. Despite the heart's compensatory mechanisms, the ability of the heart to contract and relax progressively worsens and eventually fails. The most significant predictors of mortality for patients with CHF include decreasing left ventricular ejection fraction, worsening NYHA functional status, degree of hyponatremia, decreasing peak exercise oxygen uptake, decreasing hematocrit, widened QRS on ECG, chronic hypotension, resting tachycardia, renal insufficiency, intolerance to conventional therapy, and refractory volume overload. End-stage CHF without pharmaceutical or surgical intervention (e.g., transplantation) will result in death.

COMPARISON

What are the distinguishing characteristics of a similar condition?

Cor pulmonale is a form of right-sided heart failure but is normally seen as a consequence of chronic obstructive pulmonary disease. Sustained hypoxia produces an increase in pulmonary artery pressure that leads to right ventricular hypertrophy and finally, right-sided heart failure. When the right side fails, the left side does not receive adequate amounts of blood and then cannot sustain a normal cardiac output. This is not congestive in nature, however, as there is no fluid buildup within the lungs. The right-sided heart failure also does not present with an audible S3 gallop.

CLINICAL SCENARIOS

Scenario One

A 69-year-old male has been hospitalized for five days with congestive heart failure. He was diagnosed last year with the condition and has been doing well on medication. He started having shortness of breath and noted a six pound weight gain. His medications have been adjusted and he is motivated to get home to his wife. The physician requests a physical therapy consult for baseline data and a home exercise program.

Scenario Two

An 82-year-old female resides in a nursing home since her husband who cared for her passed away last summer. She was diagnosed with a left CVA three years ago that resulted in moderate weakness of her right upper extremity and as a result she requires assistance for ADLs. She requires a quad cane and supervision for ambulation. She has been in bed for the last month due to pneumonia and she currently has been diagnosed with CHF.

GOLD

Cystic Fibrosis

DIAGNOSIS

What condition produces a patient's symptoms?

Cystic fibrosis (CF) is an inherited disease that affects the ion transport of the exocrine glands resulting in impairment of the hepatic, digestive, respiratory, and reproductive systems. The disease causes the exocrine glands to overproduce thick mucus (that causes subsequent obstruction), overproduce normal secretions or overproduce sodium and chloride.

An injury was most likely sustained to which structure?

CF affects multi-systems within the body, however, the respiratory and gastrointestinal systems are usually the most involved in the disease process. There is an underlying impermeability of epithelial cells to chloride that results in viscosity of mucous gland secretions within the lungs, sweat glands, pancreas, and intestines. CF creates an elevation of sodium chloride and pancreatic enzyme insufficiency.

INFERENCE

What is the most likely contributing factor in the development of this condition?

CF is an autosomal recessive genetic disorder (both parents are carriers of the defective gene) and is located on the long arm of chromosome seven. This disorder creates an abnormality in the CF transmembrane conductance regulator (CFTR) protein. CFTR normally is involved with the process that allows for chloride to pass through the plasma membrane of epithelial cells.

CONFIRMATION

What is the most likely clinical presentation?

CF is more common in Caucasian children than in African American children. CF can be diagnosed shortly after birth, however, it is sometimes not diagnosed for years. The most consistent symptom is the finding of high concentrations of sodium and chloride in the sweat. Parents will notice a salty taste when kissing their child. Other symptoms vary depending on the systems that are affected by the disease and the course of progression. These systems include pulmonary, gastrointestinal, digestive (liver, intestinal, pancreatic), genitourinary, and musculoskeletal impairments. Early symptoms may include a persistent cough, salty skin, sputum production, wheezing, poor weight gain, and recurrent infections.

What laboratory or imaging studies would confirm the diagnosis?

Neonates' meconium can be tested as a screening tool for increased albumin. The quantitative pilocarpine iontophoresis sweat test is the sole diagnostic tool in determining the presence of CF. Sodium and chloride amounts greater than 60 mEq/l (standard value is 40 mEq/l) is a positive diagnosis for CF. The sweat test should be performed twice to ensure accuracy.

What additional information should be obtained to confirm the diagnosis?

Additional information in the diagnosis of CF is found through a positive family history, genetic screening of the parents, a previous diagnosis of failure to thrive, and in the manifestation of symptoms.

EXAMINATION

What history should be documented?

Important areas to explore include past medical history (if diagnosed after birth), medications, current health status, developmental milestones, living environment, and social support system.

What tests/measures are most appropriate?

Aerobic capacity and endurance: assessment of vital signs at rest and with activity, perceived exertion scale

Arousal, attention, and cognition: examine mental status, learning ability, memory, motivation

Assistive and adaptive devices: analysis of components and safety of a device

Integumentary integrity: skin assessment, sweat test findings, clubbing of the digits

Muscle performance: active motion, strength assessment

Posture: analysis of resting and dynamic posture, especially thorax and shoulder girdle

Range of motion: active and passive range of motion, chest wall mobility

Self-care and home management: functional capacity

Ventilation, respiration, and circulation: assess cough and clearance of secretions, pulmonary function testing (FEV_1 and FVC), pulse oximetry, auscultation of the lungs, accessory muscle utilization and vital capacity

What additional findings are likely with this patient?

The most common complication of CF is an exacerbation of obstructive pulmonary disease. Pulmonary function testing results in a decreased forced expiratory volume (FEV_1) and forced vital capacity (FVC). The functional residual capacity (FRC) and residual volume (RV) become increased. Hypoxemia and hypercapnia develop due to the alteration in perfusion. Chronic pulmonary infections and poor absorption often lead to barrel chest, pectus carinatum, and kyphosis deformities. Approximately 90% of patients have pancreatic enzyme deficiency, degeneration, and eventual progressive fibrosis of the pancreas. This process interferes with digestion and absorption of nutrients. Airway obstruction can cause pulmonary hypertension, atelectasis, pneumonia, and lung abscess. Severe complications can include cirrhosis, diabetes mellitus, pneumothorax, cardiac pathology, pancreatitis, cor pulmonale, and intestinal obstruction.

MANAGEMENT

What is the most effective management of this patient?

Medical management of CF is a multidisciplinary approach that should focus on the quality of life, providing emotional and psychosocial support, and controlling symptoms. Nutritional support is necessary throughout the patient's life to ensure adequate nutrition. Pharmacological intervention is required to treat infections, thin mucus secretions, replace pancreatic enzymes, reduce inflammation, and assist with breathing. Psychological counseling is indicated as needed. Gene therapy is experimental and attempts to correct the defect in CF cells. Physical therapy intervention is essential for management of the disease. Chest physical therapy should be performed several times per day and includes postural drainage, percussion, vibration, breathing and assistive cough techniques, and ventilatory muscle training. Posture training, mobilization of the thorax, and breathing exercises must be incorporated into the overall program. A patient may also be trained to use autogenic drainage, a positive expiratory pressure (PEP) device or Flutter valve therapy to assist with independent postural drainage. General exercise and stretching are indicated to optimize overall function. Family and patient education are vital to the survival of the patient.

What home care regimen should be recommended?

A home care regimen for a patient with CF requires an ongoing routine performing postural drainage and chest physical therapy several times each day. Family members are trained to provide this ongoing support at home. Mechanical percussors may be used to ease the time and energy spent on manual percussion by the care provider. Mechanical percussors also offer the patient control and independence with treatment. Physical conditioning including exercise and endurance training are indicated except with severe lung disease. Exercise programs may improve pulmonary function, increase maximal work capacity, improve mucus expectoration, and increase self-esteem.

OUTCOME

What is the likely outcome of a course of physical therapy?

A patient with CF will require intermittent physical therapy throughout his or her life. The goals of physical therapy are to maximize secretion clearance from the lungs, optimize pulmonary function, and maximize the patient's quality of life.

What are the long-term effects of the patient's condition?

CF is a terminal disease, however, the median age of death has increased dramatically due to early detection and comprehensive management. Mean life expectancy of individuals born with CF today is projected to be well into their forties. The most common cause of death for patients with CF remains respiratory failure. A child that initially presents with gastrointestinal symptoms generally has a good clinical course whereas a child that initially presents with pulmonary symptoms is more likely to clinically deteriorate at a faster pace. Males generally have a better prognosis than females.

COMPARISON

What are the distinguishing characteristics of a similar condition?

There is no other respiratory disease that is similar to the etiology of CF, however, chronic obstructive pulmonary disease (COPD) has similar lung characteristics. COPD is characterized by altered pulmonary function tests, difficulty with expiration, cough, sputum production, and physical damage to specific portions of the lungs. Chest physical therapy and pharmacological intervention are indicated for moderate to advanced COPD.

CLINICAL SCENARIOS

Scenario One

A four-week-old infant is referred to physical therapy after being diagnosed with CF. The infant has a pleasant disposition and does not have any observable discomfort, however, the parents are very anxious. The patient has three siblings that do not have CF.

Scenario Two

A 26-year-old female with CF is referred to physical therapy with a severe respiratory infection. The patient recently moved into an apartment with her boyfriend and works 30 hours per week in a hair salon. Prior to the infection the patient was living at home and was able to manage the disease with occasional assistance from family members. The physical therapy referral is for chest physical therapy.

GOLD

Emphysema

DIAGNOSIS

What condition produces a patient's symptoms?

Emphysema refers to a pathologic accumulation of air in the lungs found with chronic obstructive pulmonary disease (COPD). There are three classifications of emphysema that include centrilobular emphysema, panlobular emphysema, and paraseptal emphysema. Emphysema results from a long history of chronic bronchitis, recurrent alveolar inflammation or from genetic predisposition of a congenital alpha 1-antitrypsin deficiency.

An injury was most likely sustained to which structure?

Emphysema results from a non-reversible injury and destruction of elastin protein within the alveolar walls. This process causes permanent enlargement of the air spaces distal to the terminal bronchioles within the lungs. Anatomical changes include loss of elastic recoil, excessive airway collapse during exhalation, and chronic obstruction of airflow. Progression of the disease includes further destruction of the alveolar walls, collapse of the peripheral bronchioles, and impaired gas exchange. Emphysema causes pockets of air to form between the alveolar spaces, (known as blebs), and within the lung parenchyma (known as bullae). This results in an increase in dead space within the lungs that diminishes gas exchange.

INFERENCE

What is the most likely contributing factor in the development of this condition?

The primary risk factors for the development of emphysema include chronic bronchitis, lower respiratory infections, cigarette smoking, and genetic predisposition. Environmental influence includes air pollution and other airborne toxins. The risk of acquiring emphysema increases with age.

CONFIRMATION

What is the most likely clinical presentation?

Emphysema can be asymptomatic until middle age and is most often diagnosed between 55 and 60 years of age. Centrilobular emphysema usually destroys the bronchioles in the upper lungs while the alveolar sacs usually remain intact. Panlobular emphysema destroys the air spaces of the acinus and is usually found in the lower lungs. Paraseptal emphysema destroys the alveoli in the lower lobes resulting in blebs along the lung periphery. Symptoms of emphysema worsen with the progression of the disease and include a persistent cough, wheezing, difficulty breathing especially with expiration, and an increased respiration rate. Advanced disease symptoms include increased use of accessory muscles, severe dyspnea, cor pulmonale, and cyanosis.

What laboratory or imaging studies would confirm the diagnosis?

X-ray is utilized to visually evaluate the shape and spacing of the lungs. Other imaging studies include a planogram to detect bullae and a bronchogram to evaluate mucus ducts and detect possible enlargement of the bronchi. Arterial blood gases may indicate a decreased PaO_2.

What additional information should be obtained to confirm the diagnosis?

A physical examination, thorough patient history (including cigarette smoking), and pulmonary function tests are required for diagnosis. Pulmonary function testing will result in impaired forced expiratory volume (FEV_1), vital capacity (VC), and forced vital capacity (FVC). Total lung capacity (TLC), residual volume (RV), and functional residual capacity (FRC) will be increased.

EXAMINATION

What history should be documented?

Important areas to explore include past medical history, history of smoking, medications, current health status, social history and habits, occupation, living environment, and social support system.

What tests/measures are most appropriate?

Aerobic capacity and endurance: assessment of vital signs at rest and with activity, perceived exertion scale, Six-Minute Walk Test, Three-Minute Step Test

Arousal, attention, and cognition: examine mental status, learning ability, memory, motivation

Assistive and adaptive devices: analysis of components and safety of a device

Environmental, home, and work: analysis of current and potential barriers or hazards

Gait, locomotion, and balance: static and dynamic balance in sitting and standing, safety during gait with/without an assistive device

Muscle performance: strength assessment, assessment of active movement, and muscle endurance

Posture: analysis of resting and dynamic posture

Self-care and home management: functional capacity

Ventilation, respiration, and circulation: assessment of thoracoabdominal movement, auscultation of vesicular sounds/potential rhonchi, pulse oximetry, pulmonary function testing, accessory muscle utilization

What additional findings are likely with this patient?

A patient with emphysema may present with a barrel chest appearance, an increased subcostal angle, rounded shoulders secondary to tight pectorals, rosy skin coloring, and may utilize pursed-lip breathing to assist with ventilation. Patients will also have high rates of anxiety associated with difficulty breathing and may present with claustrophobia, insomnia, and depression. Complications such as the formation and rupture of bullae and blebs can lead to pneumothorax. Cor pulmonale is a serious complication that can occur with advanced emphysema.

MANAGEMENT

What is the most effective management of this patient?

Medical management of a patient with emphysema includes pharmacological intervention, oxygen therapy, and physical therapy. Pharmacological intervention promotes bronchodilation, improved oxygenation, and ventilation. Drugs such as oral/inhaled bronchodilators, anti-inflammatory agents, mucolytic expectorants, mast cell membrane stabilizers, and antihistamines may be used in the treatment of emphysema. Preventative immunizations against influenza and pneumonia are also recommended. Physical therapy intervention is based on the severity of the disease process and can include general exercise and endurance training, breathing exercises including pursed-lip breathing, ventilatory muscle strengthening, chest wall exercises, and patient education on posture, airway secretion clearance, and energy conservation techniques. Pulse oximetry should be used to monitor a patient's oxygen saturation during activities and exercise. This will assist with patient education and deter the effects of hypoxemia. Chest physical therapy is required during advanced stages of emphysema.

What home care regimen should be recommended?

The home care regimen should include breathing strategies and exercises, energy conservation, pacing techniques, and general strength and endurance training.

OUTCOME

What is the likely outcome of a course of physical therapy?

A patient with emphysema may require physical therapy intermittently as the disease progresses. The goals of physical therapy are to maximize the patient's functional abilities and optimize pulmonary function.

What are the long-term effects of the patient's condition?

Emphysema is a chronic progressive disease process. Patients require ongoing medical care and intermittent physical therapy intervention. Life expectancy decreases to less than five years with severe expiratory slowing measured at a rate of <1L of air during forced expiratory volume (FEV_1).

COMPARISON

What are the distinguishing characteristics of a similar condition?

Bronchiectasis is inherited or acquired and is characterized by chronic inflammation and dilation of bronchi and destruction of the bronchial walls. This disease is associated with chronic bacterial infections and is an extreme form of bronchitis. Incidence within the United States is low. Bronchiectasis has a higher risk for development in patients with cystic fibrosis, sinusitis, Kartagener's syndrome, and endobronchial tumors. Characteristics include a chronic cough with sputum, hemoptysis, wheezing, dyspnea, and recurrent respiratory infections. Primary treatment includes physical therapy, bronchodilators, and antibiotics.

CLINICAL SCENARIOS

Scenario One

A 65-year-old male is referred to physical therapy after recently being diagnosed with emphysema. The patient works in an oil refinery part-time and manages a small dairy farm. The patient's past medical history is negative for smoking and consists of recurrent respiratory infections and chronic cough. The patient complains of shortness of breath with exertion, however, pulmonary function testing indicates only minimal impairment in lung volumes.

Scenario Two

A 75-year-old female requires physical therapy for management of emphysema. The patient has a history of smoking cigarettes for over 40 years and continues to smoke approximately one pack per day. The patient has an oxygen saturation rate of 94% at rest and requires two liters of oxygen with exertion. The patient has moderate impairment in pulmonary function testing and a persistent cough. The patient presently resides in a two-story home and assists with the care of her disabled husband.

GOLD

Myocardial Infarction

DIAGNOSIS

What condition produces a patient's symptoms?

Myocardial infarction (MI) occurs when there is poor coronary artery perfusion, ischemia, and subsequent necrosis of the cardiac tissue usually due to thrombus, arterial blockage or atherosclerosis. The location and severity of the infarct will determine symptoms and the overall acute clinical picture.

An injury was most likely sustained to which structure?

A MI produces ischemia and subsequent necrosis to a portion of the myocardium. The extent of the damage to the myocardium is dependent on the duration of ischemia and on the thickness of the tissue involved. A transmural MI involves the full-thickness of the myocardium while a nontransmural MI involves the subendocardial area (inner third of the myocardium). The myocardium has three zones that form concentric circles around the point of infarct termed zone of infarct, zone of hypoxic injury, and zone of ischemia. Thrombosis of the anterior descending branch of the left coronary artery is the most common location of infarct and affects the left ventricle. A right coronary artery thrombosis can result in an infarct of the posteroinferior portion of the left ventricle and can potentially affect the right ventricular myocardium.

INFERENCE

What is the most likely contributing factor in the development of this condition?

The primary risk factors for MI include patient or family history of heart disease, smoking, physical inactivity, stress, hypertension, elevated cholesterol, diabetes mellitus, and obesity. The use of cocaine and aortic stenosis may also cause a MI. It has been documented that a MI will occur more frequently in the morning hours and during the November to December holiday season.

CONFIRMATION

What is the most likely clinical presentation?

MI occurs in 1.5 million individuals each year within the United States with a mortality rate of 500,000 deaths annually. Approximately two-thirds of patients experience prodromal symptoms days to weeks before the event, including unstable angina, shortness of breath, and fatigue. A patient that is experiencing a MI will initially present with deep pain or pressure in the substernal area. The pain may or may not radiate to the jaw and down the left arm or to the back. The patient cannot alleviate the pain with rest or nitroglycerin and the pain may last for hours. The patient is usually anxious, pale, sweating, fatigued, and may present with nausea and vomiting. Symptoms of a MI frequently do not follow a typical pattern, especially in females. There are also instances of a silent MI where no symptoms are noted.

What laboratory or imaging studies would confirm the diagnosis?

The primarily tool to detect a MI is a 12-lead electrocardiogram. An inverted T wave indicates myocardial ischemia, elevated ST segment indicates acute infarction, and a depressed ST segment indicates a pending subendocardial or transmural infarction. A blood serum analysis can be utilized to determine the level of selected cardiac enzymes. The level of selected enzymes such as creatine phosphokinase (CPK), aspartate transferase (AST), and lactic dehydrogenase (LDH) can be dramatically altered during and after a MI. A complete blood count (CBC), chest radiograph, radionuclide imaging, and amylase level may be ordered to assist with the diagnosis.

What additional information should be obtained to confirm the diagnosis?

Additional information in the diagnosis of a MI is found through the manifestation of symptoms and clinical examination including a thorough past medical history and history of current symptoms.

EXAMINATION

What history should be documented?

Important areas to explore include past medical history, family history, medications, current health status, living environment, social history and habits, occupation, and social support system.

What tests/measures are most appropriate?

Aerobic capacity and endurance: vital signs at rest and during activity, palpation of pulses, perceived exertion scale, electrocardiogram analysis, auscultation of the heart and lungs, pulse oximetry

Arousal, attention, and cognition: examine mental status, learning ability, memory, motivation

Assistive and adaptive devices: analysis of components and safety of a device

Environmental, home, and work: analysis of current and potential barriers or hazards

Gait, locomotion, and balance: assessment of static and dynamic balance in sitting and standing, safety during gait with/without an assistive device

Muscle performance: strength assessment through active movement only (no manual muscle testing)

Pain: pain perception scale, visual analogue scale

Posture: analysis of resting and dynamic posture

Self-care and home management: assessment of functional capacity, Barthel Index

Ventilation, respiration, and circulation: ventilation, respiration, and circulation; assessment of pulses

What additional findings are likely with this patient?

A patient status post MI is at risk for complications that include arrhythmias, hypotension, pericarditis, impaired cardiac output, pulmonary edema, congestive heart failure, cardiogenic shock, recurrent infarction, and sudden death. Arrhythmias occur in 90% of patients post MI and are caused by ischemia, ANS impairment, electrolyte imbalances, conduction defects, and other chemical imbalances.

MANAGEMENT

What is the most effective management of this patient?

Initial medical management of a MI is to stabilize the patient and initiate pharmacological intervention to hinder the evolution of the MI. Anticoagulants, beta-blockers, thrombolytic agents, angiotensin-converting enzyme inhibitors, vasodilators, and estrogen (in women) may be used. Once stable, the patient is managed through a cardiac rehabilitation program. Surgical intervention including angioplasty, stenting, endarterectomy, and bypass grafting may be indicated based on the underlying cause of the MI. Exercise testing is performed within three days of the MI in order to establish baseline guidelines for patients that are cleared to exercise and do not exhibit any arrhythmias or angina. Physical therapy intervention usually follows a multi-phase cardiac rehabilitation program and continues in an outpatient setting once the patient is discharged from the hospital. Low-level therapeutic exercise, functional activities, relaxation, breathing techniques, endurance training, and continuous monitoring of vital signs are key components of this program. Patient education regarding reduction of risk factors, return to activity, and commitment to fitness and health are also important to the success of physical therapy intervention.

What home care regimen should be recommended?

A home care regimen should follow the guidelines indicated for each phase of cardiac rehabilitation. A patient must continue with safe exercise and integration of risk factor reduction. Symptom recognition and nutritional strategies are also important in a daily routine.

OUTCOME

What is the likely outcome of a course of physical therapy?

Cardiac rehabilitation is recommended status post MI. The patient should start in the coronary care unit (CCU) and progress through each of the phases of cardiac rehabilitation. The goal is successful completion of a cardiac rehabilitation program allowing the patient to resume all activities of daily living and recreational pursuits. Upon completion, the patient should possess self-management skills associated with symptoms/risk factors of heart disease.

What are the long-term effects of the patient's condition?

A patient that has experienced a MI may be able to return to all previous activities after successful completion of a cardiac rehabilitation program. A patient must continue to reduce the modifiable risk factors and maintain an appropriate level of exercise in order to limit a possible subsequent MI. Long-term outcome is dependent on prior functional ability, the extent and damage to the heart, and factors that negatively affect prognosis such as age, cardiovascular disease, hypotension, the presence of co-morbidities, and an abnormal treadmill exercise test.

COMPARISON

What are the distinguishing characteristics of a similar condition?

Angina pectoris is a myocardial ischemic disorder that occurs when there is an oxygen deficit to the coronary arteries. Coronary artery disease accounts for 90% of all cases of angina. Angina is classified as stable, post-infarction, Prinzmetal's, resting, unstable, nocturnal or variant. Symptoms often occur during exertion and include chest pain that may radiate. Rest or nitroglycerin normally provides relief of the symptoms. Treatment of the underlying cause is essential to prevent further damage to the heart.

CLINICAL SCENARIOS

Scenario One

A 51-year-old male is referred to a phase I cardiac rehabilitation program after a transmural MI two days ago. The patient has hypertension, high cholesterol, smokes, and is obese. The patient currently supervises a local automobile dealership. The patient is divorced and lives in a two-story home.

Scenario Two

A 78-year-old female is status post nontransmural MI. The patient is very active and plays golf. The patient's past medical history includes treatment for a cardiac arrhythmia, obesity, and diabetes mellitus. The physician referred the patient for cardiac rehabilitation.

GOLD

Peripheral Vascular Disease

DIAGNOSIS

What condition produces a patient's symptoms?

Peripheral vascular disease (PVD) is a condition where there has been narrowing of the lumen of blood vessels causing a reduction in circulation usually secondary to atherosclerosis. This can be compounded by either emboli or thrombi.

An injury was most likely sustained to which structure?

PVD, also known as arteriosclerosis obliterans, is primarily the result of atherosclerosis. Damage can occur to the walls of both arteries and veins from fatty plaque buildup that creates hard and narrow vessels. The atherosclerotic process will gradually progress to significant or complete occlusion of medium and large arteries.

INFERENCE

What is the most likely contributing factor in the development of this condition?

The primary factor for developing PVD is atherosclerosis. Other etiologies and risk factors that have been associated with the development of PVD may include phlebitis, injury or surgery, autoimmune disease, diabetes mellitus, smoking, hyperlipidemia, inactivity, hypertension, positive family history, increased age, and obesity.

CONFIRMATION

What is the most likely clinical presentation?

Symptoms and clinical presentation will differ depending on which vessel or blood flow has been compromised. During the early stages of PVD intermittent claudication may be the only manifestation. Symptoms are precipitated by walking a predictable distance and are normally relieved by rest. Claudication also may present as buckling or "giving out" of the lower extremity after a certain period of exertion and may not demonstrate the typical symptom of pain on exertion. Other symptoms may include tingling and numbness of the affected extremities, pain at rest and during sleep, slowed healing, changes in skin coloring, a decrease in skin temperature, absence of hair on the extremity, and a weak or absent pulse.

What laboratory or imaging studies would confirm the diagnosis?

Routine blood tests generally are indicated and include CBC, BUN, creatinine, and electrolytes studies. Doppler ultrasound studies are used to determine flow status. MRI, angiogram or arteriogram can also be used to assist with the diagnosis.

What additional information should be obtained to confirm the diagnosis?

The ankle-brachial index (ABI) can be used to provide a ratio of systolic blood pressure of the lower extremity compared to the upper extremity. A rubor of dependency test, transcutaneous oximetry, and treadmill exercise test may also assist with baseline information and diagnosis of insufficiency.

EXAMINATION

What history should be documented?

Important areas to explore include past medical history, medications, current health status, nutritional status, social history and habits, occupation, living environment, and social support system.

What tests/measures are most appropriate?

Aerobic capacity and endurance: assessment of vital signs at rest and with activity, perceived exertion scale, pulse oximetry, auscultation of the lungs

Arousal, attention, and cognition: examine mental status, memory, motivation

Assistive and adaptive devices: analysis of components and safety of a device

Community and work integration: analysis of community, work, and leisure activities

Environmental, home, and work barriers: analysis of current and potential barriers or hazards

Gait, locomotion, and balance: static and dynamic balance in sitting and standing, safety during gait with/without an assistive device, Functional Ambulation Profile

Integumentary integrity: skin assessment, assessment of sensation

Muscle performance: strength assessment

Pain: pain perception assessment scale, visual analogue scale, assessment of muscle soreness

Posture: analysis of resting and dynamic posture

Range of motion: active and passive range of motion

Self-care and home management: assessment of functional capacity, Functional Independence Measure

Sensory integrity: proprioception and kinesthesia

Ventilation, respiration, and circulation: palpation of pulses, pulse oximetry, ABI, capillary refilling test

What additional findings are likely with this patient?

Ischemic rest pain can occur from the combination of PVD and inadequate perfusion. It is fairly common for a patient with PVD to be diagnosed with coronary artery disease or diabetes mellitus. There is a higher risk for complications such as deep vein thrombosis, insufficiency ulcers, gangrene, and amputation.

MANAGEMENT

What is the most effective management of this patient?

The medical management of a patient with PVD should include a physician, psychiatrist or psychologist, nurse, nutritionist, occupational therapist, physical therapist, vocational therapist, and case manager. Pharmacological intervention may be utilized to reduce morbidity and prevent complications. Anticoagulants such as heparin, antiplatelet agents and thrombolytics may be indicated. Patient education is paramount regarding the disease process, limb protection, foot and skin care, and risk factor reduction (smoking cessation, avoid cold exposure). Physical therapy is an important component in the treatment of PVD. A walking program will initially have the patient walk until near maximal pain and then rest until the pain is relieved. The goal is to have the patient achieve longer walking periods with less rest, eventually walking for 30 minutes continuously. Non-weight bearing exercises such as swimming or stationary cycling can supplement the program. After 4-6 weeks of therapy including isometric and active range exercises, the patient should tolerate the implementation of resistive exercise. Physical rehabilitation, involving dynamic aerobic exercise and resistance training improves cardiovascular endurance and demonstrates a positive impact on patient function and independence. In more severe cases, surgical intervention may be required. Common procedures include balloon angioplasty, endarterectomy, stent implantation or bypass surgery.

What home care regimen should be recommended?

A patient must continue with their walking program and a generalized exercise program to tolerance. They should perform skin and foot inspections daily and continue with smoking cessation and a low cholesterol diet. For patients with pain at rest, particularly at night, the head of the bed should be elevated 4-6 inches, which should improve lower extremity perfusion by the effects of gravity on blood flow.

OUTCOME

What is the likely outcome of a course of physical therapy?

Physical therapy can be instrumental in managing PVD through education of the disease process, implementing a walking program that allows for the development of collateral circulation, and designing an exercise program that allows the patient to gain strength and endurance for activities. The patient must have the desire, discipline, and motivation to continue with habit modification and maintain their exercise regimen in order to be successful.

What are the long-term effects of the patient's condition?

PVD can be controllable with pharmacological treatment, risk factor reduction, and in some cases, surgical intervention. Patients with PVD are at a higher risk overall for complications such as permanent numbness, tingling or weakness in lower extremities and/or feet, permanent sensory changes such as burning or aching pain, gangrene, and amputation of the affected body part. Patients with PVD are also at higher risk of heart attack and stroke.

COMPARISON

What are the distinguishing characteristics of a similar condition?

Coronary artery disease (CAD) is the narrowing or blockage due to fatty build up (cholesterol) within the artery walls reducing the overall blood flow to the cardiac muscle. Patient symptoms will vary based on the location and severity of blockage. Patients range from asymptomatic to symptoms at rest. These symptoms can include nausea, vomiting, heartburn, shortness of breath, and profuse sweating. Risk factors include hypertension, smoking, obesity, stress, elevated cholesterol, and sedentary lifestyle. Electrocardiograms and angiograms are typically used to diagnose CAD.

CLINICAL SCENARIOS

Scenario One

A 66-year-old male is seen in physical therapy with a new diagnosis of PVD. The patient's past medical history consists of L5 disc herniation with surgical stabilization and type 2 diabetes mellitus. The patient complains of increasing lower extremity pain with ambulation while at his job as a surveyor. The patient lives alone and has two dogs.

Scenario Two

An 82-year-old female is seen in physical therapy in an acute care hospital with orders for whirlpool secondary to an ulcer on her right lower extremity. The patient has moderate to severe PVD affecting both lower extremities. She presents with sensory loss and significant pain with ambulation greater than 20 feet. She also complains of pain at night. She resides with her husband in a first floor apartment.

GOLD

Restrictive Lung Disease

DIAGNOSIS

What condition produces a patient's symptoms?

Restrictive lung disease (RLD) is a classification of disorders caused by a pulmonary or extrapulmonary restriction that produces impairment in lung expansion and an abnormal reduction in pulmonary ventilation. There are multiple conditions that can cause restrictive lung disease. Many symptoms are common regardless of the underlying etiology and other symptoms are disease-specific.

An injury was most likely sustained to which structure?

Pulmonary restriction of the lungs can be caused by tumor, interstitial pulmonary fibrosis, scarring within the lungs, and pneumonia. Extrapulmonary restrictions of the lungs include pleural effusion, chest wall stiffness, structural abnormality, postural deformity, respiratory muscle weakness, and central nervous system injury.

INFERENCE

What is the most likely contributing factor in the development of this condition?

There are varying etiologies for the group of disorders that cause restrictive lung disease. Musculoskeletal etiology includes scoliosis, pectus excavatum or other chest wall deformity, rib fractures, ankylosing spondylitis, and kyphosis. Pulmonary etiology includes idiopathic pulmonary fibrosis, pneumonia, pleural effusion, sarcoidosis, hyaline membrane disease, and tumor within the lungs. Other etiologies include inhalation of toxic fumes, drug therapy, asbestos, rheumatoid arthritis, systemic lupus erythematosus, muscular dystrophy, spinal cord injury, obesity, and other neurologic and neuromuscular diseases.

CONFIRMATION

What is the most likely clinical presentation?

The clinical presentation varies based on the underlying cause or disease process. The pathogenesis of RLD includes a decrease in lung and chest wall compliance, decrease in lung volumes and an increase in the work of breathing. Generally, restrictive lung disease is characterized by a reduction of lung volumes (total lung capacity, vital capacity, inspiratory reserve volume, tidal volume, expiratory reserve volume, and inspiratory capacity) due to impaired lung expansion. A patient with restrictive lung disease will present with decreased chest mobility, decreased breath sounds, shortness of breath, hypoxemia, a rapid and shallow respiratory pattern (tachypnea), respiratory muscle weakness, ineffective cough, and increased use of accessory muscles.

What laboratory or imaging studies would confirm the diagnosis?

A chest radiograph is utilized to evaluate lung structure and evidence of fibrosis, infiltrates, tumor, and deformity. Arterial blood gas analysis may indicate a decrease in PaO_2.

What additional information should be obtained to confirm the diagnosis?

Pulmonary function testing will result in impaired vital capacity (VC), forced vital capacity (FVC), and total lung capacity (TLC). The patient will usually present with normal residual volume (RV) and expiration flow rates. Expiratory reserve volume (ERV) and functional residual capacity (FRC) are often decreased. Arterial blood gas analysis examines the presence of hypoxemia and hypocapnia.

EXAMINATION

What history should be documented?

Important areas to explore include past medical history, medications, current health status, social history and habits, occupation, living environment, and social support system.

What tests/measures are most appropriate?

Aerobic capacity and endurance: assessment of vital signs at rest and with activity, perceived exertion scale, pulse oximetry, auscultation of the lungs

Arousal, attention, and cognition: examine mental status, learning ability, memory, motivation

Assistive and adaptive devices: analysis of components and safety of a device

Environmental, home, and work barriers: analysis of current and potential barriers or hazards

Gait, locomotion, and balance: static and dynamic balance in sitting and standing, safety during gait with/without an assistive device, Berg Balance Scale, Tinetti Performance Oriented Mobility Assessment, Functional Ambulation Profile

Motor function: assessment of dexterity, coordination and agility, assessment of postural, equilibrium, and righting reactions

Muscle performance: strength assessment, active movement

Posture: analysis of resting and dynamic posture

Range of motion: active and passive range of motion

Self-care and home management: assessment of functional capacity

Ventilation, respiration, and circulation: auscultation of breath sounds, thoracoabdominal movement, pulmonary function testing, perceived exertion scale, assessment of cough and clearance of secretions

What additional findings are likely with this patient?

A patient with restrictive lung disease may become incapable of deep inspiration due to poor lung expansion. As restrictive lung disease progresses, respiratory muscle fatigue will lead to impaired alveolar ventilation and carbon dioxide retention. A patient will initially present with exertional dyspnea and progress to dyspnea at rest if the restriction progresses. Hypoxemia, pulmonary hypertension, cor pulmonale, severe decrease in oxygenation, and ventilatory failure are complications and outcomes of advanced restrictive lung disease.

MANAGEMENT

What is the most effective management of this patient?

Medical management of restrictive lung disease includes treatment of the underlying cause through pharmacological intervention, physical therapy, and potential surgical intervention. Physical therapy intervention is based on the severity of the condition, but is consistently oriented toward the goals of maximizing gas exchange and obtaining maximal functional capacity. Physical therapy intervention may include body mechanics, posture training, diaphragm and ventilatory muscle strengthening, relaxation and energy conservation techniques, and the use of these techniques during functional mobility. Breathing exercises, coughing techniques, and airway secretion clearance are often components of a comprehensive care plan.

What home care regimen should be recommended?

A home care regimen should include breathing strategies and exercises, proper positioning, energy conservation and pacing techniques, general strengthening and endurance activities, and postural awareness with mobility. Low-level general strengthening and endurance training are indicated as tolerated.

OUTCOME

What is the likely outcome of a course of physical therapy?

Physical therapy intervention is specific to the underlying cause of the restrictive lung disease. Outcome is based on the etiology of the restrictive lung disease and patient response to physical therapy intervention. Treatment goals should include improving oxygenation and obtaining the maximal level of functioning.

What are the long-term effects of the patient's condition?

Long-term effects from restrictive lung disease are also specific to the underlying cause. Some disorders require surgical intervention that alleviates the condition while other conditions are progressive and irreversible. Some patients with end-stage disease may be candidates for lung transplantation, however, most eventually progress to ventilatory failure. Idiopathic pulmonary fibrosis is a restrictive lung disease that has a high mortality rate within four to six years of diagnosis whereas many conditions that cause restrictive lung disease are alleviated through appropriate management.

COMPARISON

What are the distinguishing characteristics of a similar condition?

Tuberculosis is an infectious and inflammatory systemic disease that can result in restrictive lung disease. The condition is a chronic pulmonary and extrapulmonary disease that causes fibrosis within the lungs. It is caused by the mycobacterium tuberculosis (tubercle bacillus) and transmitted through infected airborne droplets that are inhaled. Pulmonary symptoms include fatigue, weakness, an initial non-productive cough, and dyspnea with exertion. The disease also can affect other systems within the body including the lymph nodes and organs. Pharmacological intervention is the primary means of treating a patient with tuberculosis.

CLINICAL SCENARIOS

Scenario One

A 32-year-old male shows signs of restrictive lung disease. The patient is slightly short of breath with activity, has difficulty with deep inspiration, and complains of a non-productive cough. The patient had prolonged exposure to asbestos at his last place of employment and is under a physician's care. The physician referred the patient to physical therapy to improve the patient's general pulmonary status.

Scenario Two

A 65-year-old female is seen in physical therapy for restrictive lung disease secondary to the removal of a benign tumor from the left lung. The patient reports having difficulty breathing, limited inhalation capability, and a productive cough. The patient has not been able to perform self-care and home activities secondary to breathing difficulties and relies solely on her 72-year-old husband.

SILVER Level Clinical Application Templates

Level Clinical Application Template Executive Summary

Angina Pectoris

- Results from diminished myocardial perfusion, most commonly caused by narrowing of one or more of the coronary arteries (e.g., due to embolism, atherosclerosis, inflammation)
- Described as an uncomfortable or painful feeling of tightness, pressure, fullness or squeezing in the center of the chest
- Medical management varies greatly with symptom severity and type (i.e., stable versus unstable), focusing primarily on the underlying pathology

Coronary Artery Disease

- Occurs as a result of atherosclerotic plaque buildup within the coronary arteries; develops slowly, often going unnoticed for years before producing symptoms
- Risk factors include hypertension, diabetes, obesity, chronic kidney disease, elevated cholesterol and triglyceride levels, and a family history of the condition
- Cardiac rehabilitation is recommended and upon completion, the patient should possess self-management skills associated with symptom recognition and reduction of risk factors

Hypertension

- A condition in which blood pressure is persistently elevated; Stage 1 hypertension: 130–139 mm Hg systolic blood pressure or 80–89 mm Hg diastolic blood pressure; Stage 2 hypertension: at least 140 mm Hg systolic blood pressure or at least 90 mm Hg diastolic blood pressure
- Symptoms may not be recognized until blood pressure becomes dangerously high producing a headache, confusion, visual changes, fatigue, arrhythmia or tinnitus
- Medical management is largely focused on risk reduction through modifiable risk factors and pharmacological intervention

SILVER

Angina Pectoris

DIAGNOSIS

What condition produces a patient's symptoms?

Angina pectoris results from diminished myocardial perfusion, most commonly caused by narrowing of one or more of the coronary arteries (e.g., due to embolism, atherosclerosis, inflammation). When the tissue's oxygen demand is greater than that provided by the coronary arteries, myocardial ischemia results producing characteristic chest pain. This specific type of pain is termed angina pectoris and is most commonly associated with underlying coronary artery disease (CAD).

An injury was most likely sustained to which structure?

Angina pectoris is not an independent disease process, but rather a symptom of myocardial ischemia. Damage to the myocardial tissue is dependent on the location, extent, and duration of the ischemia. Certain etiologies may also result in localized vessel damage, as well as narrowing or blockages that can produce angina.

INFERENCE

What is the most likely contributing factor in the development of this condition?

Risk factors for angina pectoris are consistent with those of CAD and include a family history of heart disease, smoking, physical inactivity, stress, hypertension, elevated cholesterol, diabetes mellitus, and obesity.

CONFIRMATION

What is the most likely clinical presentation?

Angina pectoris is typically described as an uncomfortable or painful feeling of tightness, pressure, fullness or squeezing in the center of the chest. Symptoms will typically present on the left side of the body in the back, arm, shoulder, neck or jaw when accompanied by radiating pain. Shortness of breath and unexplained fatigue are also frequently reported. Angina pectoris may be classified as either stable or unstable. Stable angina occurs predictably in response to activities that increase the oxygen demands of myocardial tissue (e.g., exercise, stress, cold weather, large meals). Stable angina symptoms typically do not last longer than 15 minutes and are relieved with rest or nitroglycerin. Unstable angina is typically considered to be more serious since it occurs without cause and is often unresponsive to nitroglycerin.

What laboratory or imaging studies would confirm the diagnosis?

A 12-lead electrocardiogram (ECG) is most commonly used to diagnose angina pectoris with an inverted T wave indicating myocardial ischemia. In patients with normal resting ECG readings, a more provocative exercise ECG or stress test may be required. A diagnosis of angina pectoris is most often confirmed by first diagnosing the underlying pathology causing the ischemia.

What additional information should be obtained to confirm the diagnosis?

A thorough medical history should be completed to assist in identifying cardiac risk factors. The patient's history of symptoms should include detail regarding exacerbating and alleviating factors. A thorough clinical examination should also be performed in order to rule out similar diagnoses.

MANAGEMENT

What is the most effective management of this patient?

The medical management of angina pectoris varies greatly with symptom severity and type (i.e., stable versus unstable), focusing primarily on the underlying pathology. Pharmacological intervention may target vessel relaxation, heart rate, the blood's clotting ability or cholesterol levels. Aspirin, nitrates, beta-blockers, statins, calcium channel blockers, and ACE inhibitors may be used in the treatment of angina. The goal of surgical intervention is typically to widen a coronary artery in order to improve blood flow. Angioplasty, stent placement, endarterectomy, and coronary artery bypass graft are common surgical procedures. Lifestyle changes such as smoking cessation, weight management, increased activity level, and stress management are recommended. Physical therapy intervention usually follows a multi-phase cardiac rehabilitation program for patients with stable angina.

What home care regimen should be recommended?

A home care regimen should follow the guidelines indicated for each phase of cardiac rehabilitation. Patients should continue to safely exercise and incorporate the reduction of modifiable risk factors. Symptom recognition and nutritional management are also important in a daily routine.

OUTCOME

What is the likely outcome of a course of physical therapy?

Cardiac rehabilitation is recommended for patients with angina pectoris. Patients with stable angina that are managed with lifestyle changes and medication may initiate cardiac rehabilitation in an outpatient setting. The goal is successful completion of the cardiac rehabilitation program, allowing the patient to resume all activities of daily living and recreational pursuits.

What are the long-term effects of the patient's condition?

Patients with angina pectoris typically have some degree of pre-existing cardiac pathology. These patients are at an increased risk for developing cardiac arrhythmias or experiencing a myocardial infarction or cardiac arrest. The severity of risk is linked to the severity of the underlying disease process as well as prior cardiac history and the patient's response to pharmaceutical management.

Coronary Artery Disease

SILVER

DIAGNOSIS

What condition produces a patient's symptoms?

Coronary artery disease (CAD) occurs as a result of atherosclerotic plaque buildup within the coronary arteries. The plaque is primarily comprised of fatty deposits containing cholesterol and other blood products that accumulate over time. CAD typically develops slowly and often goes unnoticed for years before producing symptoms.

An injury was most likely sustained to which structure?

The right and left coronary arteries are branches of the ascending aorta. The right coronary artery primarily supplies the right atrium and ventricle and the left coronary artery primarily supplies the left atrium and ventricle. As plaques develop, the arteries harden and narrow, decreasing the volume of blood available to perfuse cardiac tissue when demand is increased. Diminished perfusion significantly increases the risk of myocardial ischemia and permanent cardiac damage.

INFERENCE

What is the most likely contributing factor in the development of this condition?

The risk factors for CAD include hypertension, diabetes, obesity, chronic kidney disease, elevated cholesterol and triglyceride levels, and family history. Modifiable risk factors include smoking, inactivity, alcohol abuse, and stress.

CONFIRMATION

What is the most likely clinical presentation?

Certain patients with CAD never develop symptoms or complications from the disease. In others, symptoms typically develop when arteries are no longer able to adequately perfuse cardiac tissue resulting in ischemia. The severity of symptoms varies with the exacerbating activity and degree of occlusion. A partial occlusion may cause exertion-related shortness of breath, weakness or angina pectoris and is often the initial indicator of underlying pathology. In some cases, however, the first symptom of CAD may be as severe as a myocardial infarction secondary to plaques that have completely occluded an artery.

What laboratory or imaging studies would confirm the diagnosis?

Cardiac catheterization with coronary angiography introduces contrast dye via small catheters into the coronary arteries for x-ray imaging. This invasive diagnostic procedure provides the most accurate information regarding both the location and severity of CAD. CT scan and magnetic resonance coronary angiograms provide a less invasive means of visualizing the coronary arteries with contrast dye introduced either intravenously or via injection.

What additional information should be obtained to confirm the diagnosis?

A thorough medical history should be completed to assist in identifying cardiac risk factors. The patient's history should include details of symptoms including alleviating and exacerbating factors, frequency, and duration. A thorough clinical examination should also be performed in order to rule out similar diagnoses.

MANAGEMENT

What is the most effective management of this patient?

The medical management of CAD is largely focused on risk reduction and pharmacological intervention. Lifestyle changes are typically recommended to address modifiable risk factors. Pharmacological agents facilitate vessel relaxation, modify heart rate or reduce the blood's clotting ability or cholesterol levels. Aspirin, nitrates, beta-blockers, statins, calcium channel blockers, and ACE inhibitors may be used alone or in combination. Surgical intervention is typically performed to widen one or more of the coronary arteries in order to improve blood flow. Angioplasty, stent placement, endarterectomy, and coronary artery bypass are common surgical procedures. Physical therapy intervention is typically provided through a formal multi-phase cardiac rehabilitation program. Patients who have undergone surgical intervention will begin during their inpatient stay. Others may begin cardiac rehabilitation on an outpatient basis. Patients should be educated regarding target heart rate zones and self-monitoring of cardiac status during exercise.

What home care regimen should be recommended?

A home care regimen should follow the guidelines indicated for each phase of cardiac rehabilitation. Patients should continue to safely exercise and incorporate healthy habits. Nutritional management and the ability to recognize symptoms of cardiac distress are also important in a daily routine.

OUTCOME

What is the likely outcome of a course of physical therapy?

Cardiac rehabilitation is recommended for patients diagnosed with CAD. At the conclusion of physical therapy, the patient should possess self-management skills associated with symptom recognition and the reduction of cardiac risk factors.

What are the long-term effects of the patient's condition?

Patients diagnosed with CAD are at increased risk of developing angina pectoris, heart failure, cardiac arrhythmias, and cardiac arrest. The severity of risk is linked to the severity of disease. The patient's response to pharmacological and lifestyle interventions can also influence the overall risk of complications.

SILVER

Hypertension

DIAGNOSIS

What condition produces a patient's symptoms?

Hypertension (HTN) is a condition in which blood pressure is persistently elevated. Primary HTN occurs without an identifiable cause and typically develops slowly over time. Secondary HTN occurs as a result of underlying pathology (e.g., pre-eclampsia, kidney disease, congenital vessel defects, atherosclerosis, stress) or as a side effect of certain medications.

An injury was most likely sustained to which structure?

Blood pressure measures represent the force of blood against interior arterial walls. The systolic component represents the maximum pressure exerted as the heart contracts. The diastolic component represents the minimum pressure exerted when the heart is at rest. In patients with primary HTN, increased forces may cause damage to the arteries, increasing the risk of more serious comorbidities such as CVA or MI. For patients with secondary HTN, structural injuries may also be linked to the specific underlying pathology.

INFERENCE

What is the most likely contributing factor in the development of this condition?

Patients of African descent, men, post-menopausal women, and those with a family history of HTN have a higher risk of developing HTN. Risk increases further with age. Certain conditions (e.g., pregnancy, diabetes, sleep apnea) and modifiable risk factors (e.g., obesity, sedentary lifestyle, stress, tobacco use, excessive alcohol use, excess dietary sodium) are also associated with HTN.

CONFIRMATION

What is the most likely clinical presentation?

Hypertension is classified based on the degree of elevation. Classifications include Stage 1 hypertension, Stage 2 hypertension, and hypertensive crisis. Both systolic and diastolic values are relevant, however, many patients over 50 years of age demonstrate significantly elevated systolic measures with normal diastolic findings. This is referred to as isolated systolic hypertension (ISH). Patients do not typically report symptoms due to the slow onset of primary HTN. Secondary HTN may present with or without symptoms depending on the specific etiology and how quickly the condition progresses. Symptoms may not be recognized until blood pressure becomes dangerously high producing a headache, confusion, visual changes, fatigue, arrhythmia or tinnitus.

What laboratory or imaging studies would confirm the diagnosis?

There are no specific laboratory or imaging studies used to diagnose HTN. Specific testing (e.g., electrocardiogram, urinalysis, blood cholesterol) may be used to identify underlying pathologies so that medical management may be specifically targeted.

What additional information should be obtained to confirm the diagnosis?

A thorough medical history and physical examination should be completed to assist in identifying risk factors associated with the development of HTN. This is typically diagnosed by assessing blood pressure at least twice to determine if hypertension exists. Some patients may be asked to monitor their blood pressure at home if a medical office is felt to be stressful and contributing to elevated readings.

MANAGEMENT

What is the most effective management of this patient?

The medical management of HTN is largely focused on risk reduction through modifiable risk factors and pharmacological intervention. Lifestyle changes are recommended to address modifiable risk factors associated with HTN. Pharmacological agents may be used to decrease preload, dilate peripheral vessels or alter heart rate. Diuretics, beta-blockers, calcium channel blockers, and angiotensin-converting enzyme inhibitors may be used alone or in combination, depending on the pathology. Physical therapy intervention is typically focused on risk factor modification through progressive exercise and education. A patient may also qualify for a formal cardiac rehabilitation program depending on the degree of hypertension and existence of other comorbidities.

What home care regimen should be recommended?

A home care regimen should include progressive exercise and a comprehensive plan emphasizing risk reduction through lifestyle modification.

OUTCOME

What is the likely outcome of a course of physical therapy?

Patient compliance in a home care regimen is essential in reducing hypertension and associated risk factors. With appropriate management and controlled hypertension, most patients are able to participate in functional and recreational activities without limitation.

What are the long-term effects of the patient's condition?

Most patients are able to effectively manage HTN through risk factor modification and medication management. For patients with secondary HTN, further intervention may be necessary to treat the underlying pathology. Morbidity and mortality are typically associated with poorly controlled HTN which increases the risk for metabolic syndrome, myocardial infarction, heart failure, cerebrovascular accident, aneurysm, cognitive changes, kidney dysfunction, and visual impairment.

BRONZE Level Clinical Application Templates

BRONZE Level Clinical Application Template Executive Summary

Aneurysm

- Abnormal balloon-like bulge in the wall of a blood vessel (most often the aorta) that occurs when the blood vessel becomes weakened and can no longer handle the pressure of the blood
- Symptoms will differ based on the site of the aneurysm (e.g., thoracic versus abdominal aorta) and whether the aneurysm has ruptured or not
- Symptoms include low back, abdominal or groin pain, nausea and vomiting, lightheadedness, and a rapid heart rate; symptoms of a thoracic aortic aneurysm include jaw, neck, back or chest pain, coughing or hoarseness, and shortness of breath

Atelectasis

- Occurs when the alveoli within the lung become deflated, resulting in the complete or partial collapse of a lung and a reduction in gas exchange
- Conditions that prevent coughing and deep breathing (e.g., pleural effusion, surgical anesthesia) increase the risk for atelectasis
- When large portions of the lung are affected, signs and symptoms include coughing, fast and shallow breathing, increased heart rate, cyanosis, reduced oxygen saturation levels, and occasionally chest pain

Chronic Venous Insufficiency

- Typically affects the distal lower extremities and is characterized by venous incompetence and resultant venous hypertension
- Symptoms include edema, feelings of heaviness, tingling sensations, and dull, aching pain in the distal lower extremities
- Symptoms generally improve and may resolve fully with elevation, however, reappear once dependent positioning is resumed

Cor Pulmonale

- Occurs when the right ventricle is unable to effectively pump blood due to the prolonged presence of pulmonary hypertension and increased right ventricular afterload
- Initially, symptoms are primarily associated with the underlying pulmonary pathology; as the condition advances, symptoms may include peripheral pitting edema and jugular vein distention
- Most commonly diagnosed by means of clinical findings, medical history, echocardiogram, laboratory tests, chest x-ray, and electrocardiography

Pericarditis

- Characterized by swelling and irritation of the pericardium that is often caused by viral infections
- Symptoms include a sharp chest pain that can radiate to the neck or shoulder, pain that intensifies with coughing, lying down or inhaling deeply, shortness of breath, heart palpitations, weakness and fatigue, fever, and a cough
- A pericardial rub is the sound heard during auscultation when the pericardial layers rub against one another

BRONZE Level Clinical Application Template Executive Summary

Pleural Effusion

- Occurs when excess fluid accumulates in the pleural cavity secondary to medical conditions that result in increased fluid production or decreased fluid absorption
- Patients with a large effusion may experience shortness of breath, chest pain, cough, and fever
- Common tests used to identify the condition include chest x-ray, computed tomography, and ultrasound imaging

Pneumothorax

- Occurs when air accumulates in the pleural cavity and causes a collapsed lung
- Symptoms vary widely depending on the type and size of the pneumothorax, but may include chest pain, shortness of breath, hypoxemia, cyanosis, and hypotension
- Tension pneumothorax is a specific type of pneumothorax that results in large increases in pressure in the pleural cavity and is considered a medical emergency

Pulmonary Edema

- Characterized by excess fluid in the lungs that often occurs when the left ventricle is unable to adequately pump blood to the systemic circulation
- Acute pulmonary edema is considered a medical emergency and is characterized by extreme shortness of breath, wheezing or gasping, anxiety, a cough that produces frothy sputum, chest pain, and palpitations
- A chest x-ray is the primary imaging study to confirm the presence of fluid in the lungs

Pulmonary Embolism

- Occurs most commonly as a result of venous thrombi that have detached and traveled from elsewhere in the body before lodging in a pulmonary artery
- Symptoms include a sudden onset of dyspnea, coughing, hypoxia, and chest pain which may mimic myocardial infarction
- Pulmonary angiogram is the most conclusive means of identifying a pulmonary embolism, however, complication risks are high and so it is used only when other diagnostic methods are inconclusive

Respiratory Acidosis

- Refers to a state in which the pH of body fluids is abnormally low indicating acidemia
- Hypoventilation prevents adequate removal of CO_2 from the body causing hypercapnia and as a result, bicarbonate (HCO_{3-}) levels decrease altering the body's acid-base balance
- Initial symptoms are often vague and more closely related to the underlying pathology; as the condition worsens, symptoms include lethargy, confusion, altered mental status, and cyanosis

Respiratory Alkalosis

- Refers to a state in which the pH of body fluids is abnormally high indicating alkalemia
- Hyperventilation removes more CO_2 from the body than can be produced causing hypocapnia and as a result, hydrogen (H+) levels decrease altering the body's acid-base balance
- Initial symptoms are often vague and more closely related to the underlying pathology, however, tachypnea, tachycardia, hyperventilation, and dizziness are commonly observed

BRONZE Level Clinical Application Template Executive Summary

Sarcoidosis

- A condition characterized by the growth of small, abnormal collections of inflammatory cells, known as granulomas, within the body's organs
- The cause of sarcoidosis is not known, though it is thought to be the result of an abnormal immune system response to a foreign substance
- Symptoms will vary based on what organs are affected, most commonly the lungs, lymph nodes, and skin

Tuberculosis

- Highly contagious infectious disease spread via airborne transmission primarily caused by the Mycobacterium tuberculosis bacteria
- Active TB typically presents with generalized symptoms of infection including fever, chills, fatigue, weight loss, decreased appetite, and night sweats; left untreated can be fatal
- Diagnosed based on a skin test where a small amount of the substance tuberculin is injected at a forearm site with the skin's reaction then assessed 48 to 72 hours later

Venous Thrombosis

- The formation of a blood clot within a vein, most commonly occurring in the deep veins of the lower extremities
- Signs and symptoms include swelling, redness, warmth, and pain in the affected leg, though it can occur without any noticeable symptoms
- Ultrasound imaging is most commonly used to identify the presence of a venous thrombus

Aneurysm

BRONZE

DIAGNOSIS

What condition produces a patient's symptoms?

An aneurysm is an abnormal balloon-like bulge in the wall of a blood vessel. An aneurysm occurs when the wall of the blood vessel becomes weakened and can no longer tolerate the pressure of the blood, thus leading to bulging of the wall. There are many factors which may lead to damage or weakening of the blood vessel walls, including smoking, high blood pressure, atherosclerosis, infections, genetic conditions (e.g., Marfan syndrome), trauma, and advanced age.

An injury was most likely sustained to what structure?

This condition involves injury to the wall of a blood vessel, typically an artery. Most aneurysms occur in the aorta, and are labeled thoracic aortic aneurysms (TAA) or abdominal aortic aneurysms (AAA) based on the portion of the aorta affected. Aneurysms also occur in the brain, specifically in the Circle of Willis circulation, or in any peripheral artery.

CONFIRMATION

What is the most likely clinical presentation?

Symptoms will differ based on the site of the aneurysm and whether the aneurysm has ruptured or not. Symptoms of a ruptured AAA include low back, abdominal or groin pain, nausea and vomiting, lightheadedness, and a rapid heart rate. The internal bleeding from a ruptured AAA will typically lead to hypovolemic shock and is fatal in the large majority of cases. Symptoms of a TAA include jaw, neck, back or chest pain, coughing or hoarseness, and shortness of breath. A brain aneurysm may cause fatigue, loss of balance, and speech and vision problems. A ruptured brain aneurysm will result in a subarachnoid hemorrhage. Symptoms may include severe headache, loss of vision or double vision, loss of consciousness, vomiting, change in mental status, and seizure. This is a medical emergency.

What laboratory or imaging studies would confirm the diagnosis?

The imaging studies that may be performed to detect an aneurysm include ultrasound, computed tomography, magnetic resonance imaging, echocardiography, and angiography.

What additional information should be obtained to confirm the diagnosis?

A thorough medical history and physical examination should be performed to rule out other similar conditions. With a large AAA, palpation may reveal a throbbing mass in the abdominal area. If a ruptured brain aneurysm is suspected, a lumbar puncture may be performed to detect blood within the cerebrospinal fluid.

Atelectasis

BRONZE

DIAGNOSIS

What condition produces a patient's symptoms?

Atelectasis is the complete or partial collapse of a lung that results in reduced gas exchange. Conditions that prevent deep breathing and coughing increase the risk of atelectasis as the lungs are unable to fill with air in the normal manner. The most common cause of atelectasis is surgical anesthesia, which reduces the normal deep breathing pattern and diminishes the urge to cough. Patients' breathing patterns may also be disrupted secondary to airway obstruction (e.g., mucus secretions, airway narrowing) or from pressure outside of the lungs (e.g., pleural effusion, pneumothorax, chest trauma, tumor).

An injury was most likely sustained to what structure?

Atelectasis occurs when the alveoli within the lung become deflated and cause all or part of the lung to collapse. The amount of lung tissue involved is variable depending on the origin of the condition. If large portions of the lung are involved, the patient may not be able to deliver enough oxygen to the blood.

CONFIRMATION

What is the most likely clinical presentation?

If atelectasis only affects a small portion of the lung, the patient will likely be asymptomatic. When larger portions of the lung are affected, signs and symptoms include coughing, fast and shallow breathing, increased heart rate, cyanosis, reduced oxygen saturation levels, and occasionally chest pain.

What laboratory or imaging studies would confirm the diagnosis?

Atelectasis is typically diagnosed with a chest x-ray. Computed tomography can also be used to aid in the diagnosis. Ultrasound imaging and bronchoscopy may be used to better identify the cause of the atelectasis.

What additional information should be obtained to confirm the diagnosis?

A thorough medical history and physical examination should be performed to rule out the existence of other similar conditions (e.g., pneumothorax, pleural effusion, lung cancer). Auscultation will reveal diminished or absent breath sounds. A therapist may also use pulse oximetry to determine the oxygen saturation level of the blood.

BRONZE

Chronic Venous Insufficiency

DIAGNOSIS

What condition produces a patient's symptoms?

Chronic venous insufficiency (CVI) typically affects the distal lower extremities and is characterized by venous incompetence and resultant venous hypertension. CVI increases fluid volume within interstitial spaces, eventually overloading the lymphatic system resulting in edema. The accumulation of protein-rich fluid causes local inflammation, hypoxia, and fibrotic changes within the tissues. These changes are significant factors in the development of venous stasis ulcers and delayed healing.

An injury was most likely sustained to which structure?

Typically, the bicuspid valves prevent the back flow within vessels returning blood from the periphery to the heart. Malfunctioning valves create venous incompetence and allow blood to pool within the vessels causing venous hypertension. At the capillary level, venous hypertension alters the pressure gradient between the capillaries and interstitium, impeding reabsorption and blood flow.

CONFIRMATION

What is the most likely clinical presentation?

Patients typically report symptoms more closely associated with resultant venous hypertension and stasis than the CVI itself. Symptoms include edema, feelings of heaviness, and dull, aching pain in the distal lower extremities. Symptoms generally improve and may resolve fully with elevation, however, they reappear once dependent positioning is resumed. Untreated venous hypertension and stasis related symptoms will cause a brawny skin discoloration and hyperkeratosis. Chronic inflammation can lead to poor wound healing and fibrotic changes in the subcutaneous tissue.

What laboratory or imaging studies would confirm the diagnosis?

Diagnosis will often include bidirectional or color-flow studies using venous ultrasonography to visualize structures and flow patterns and to identify reflux. A medical history and a thorough physical examination are also indicated.

What additional information should be obtained to confirm the diagnosis?

A complete medical history and description of daily activities is important. Patients who are obese, have vessel damage or who are pregnant are at greater risk for developing CVI due to structural or tissue impedance of venous structures. Patients who spend extended periods in sitting or standing are also at increased risk.

BRONZE

Cor Pulmonale

DIAGNOSIS

What condition produces a patient's symptoms?

Cor pulmonale, or right-sided heart failure, occurs when the right ventricle is unable to effectively pump blood due to the prolonged presence of pulmonary hypertension and increased right ventricular afterload. This results in ventricular hypertrophy and dilation, as well as changes in blood pressure. Cor pulmonale may be associated with conditions which cause prolonged decreases in blood oxygen levels such as COPD. Cor pulmonale may also be caused by congenital heart conditions that impede blood flow through the pulmonary arteries or increase blood viscosity, such as pulmonary embolism or sickle cell anemia.

An injury was most likely sustained to which structure?

Cor pulmonale is typically a chronic condition resulting from long-term hypertension in the pulmonary arteries. Cor pulmonale can also occur acutely as a result of emergent conditions such as pulmonary embolism (PE) or acute respiratory distress syndrome (ARDS). In both instances, the right ventricle's ability to effectively pump blood becomes significantly limited.

CONFIRMATION

What is the most likely clinical presentation?

Initially, patients with cor pulmonale present with symptoms that are primarily associated with their underlying pulmonary pathology (e.g., cough, tachypnea, increased chest diameter, hyperresonance with chest percussion, dyspnea with exertion). As the condition advances, visible signs related more specifically to cor pulmonale may include peripheral pitting edema and jugular vein distention.

What laboratory or imaging studies would confirm the diagnosis?

Cor pulmonale is most commonly diagnosed by means of clinical findings, medical history, and minimally invasive procedures such as echocardiogram, laboratory tests, chest x-ray, and electrocardiography. These tests provide valuable information regarding etiology and severity of the condition. Cor pulmonale treatment is often directed at the underlying cause. Right cardiac catheterization is the most accurate method of confirming cor pulmonale, however, it is often considered unnecessarily invasive.

What additional information should be obtained to confirm the diagnosis?

A complete medical history should be obtained with suspected cor pulmonale. Pulmonary function tests may be utilized to identify previously undiagnosed pulmonary pathology.

Pericarditis

BRONZE

DIAGNOSIS

What condition produces a patient's symptoms?

Pericarditis is the swelling and irritation of the pericardium, the sac-like membrane which surrounds the heart. This condition is often caused by viral infections, though can also occur secondary to myocardial infarction, systemic inflammatory disorders, trauma, medications, and radiation to the chest.

An injury was most likely sustained to what structure?

The pericardium is a double-layered membrane that surrounds the heart and contains a small amount of fluid. As the pericardium becomes inflamed, the membrane layers rub against one another. The sharp chest pain felt with this condition is a result of the friction between the membranous layers.

CONFIRMATION

What is the most likely clinical presentation?

Pericarditis is characterized by sharp chest pain that can radiate to the neck or shoulder. The pain can intensify with coughing, lying down or inhaling deeply. Additional symptoms often include shortness of breath, heart palpitations, weakness, fatigue, fever, and coughing. Pericarditis may be acute or chronic. Most cases are mild and typically improve on their own.

What laboratory or imaging studies would confirm the diagnosis?

A diagnosis is confirmed based on a medical history, physical examination, and auscultation of heart sounds. Pericarditis is characterized by a pericardial rub, which is the sound heard during auscultation when the pericardial layers rub against one another. Other tests used to assist in the diagnosis include electrocardiogram, chest x-ray, echocardiogram, and computed tomography.

What additional information should be obtained to confirm the diagnosis?

A thorough medical history and physical examination should be performed to rule out the presence of other similar conditions, including angina, myocardial infarction, and pulmonary embolism. Blood tests may also be administered to determine if a viral infection is present.

Pleural Effusion

BRONZE

DIAGNOSIS

What condition produces a patient's symptoms?

Pleural effusion is the excess fluid that accumulates in the space surrounding the lungs. The condition occurs secondary to a variety of medical conditions and is the result of increased fluid production, decreased fluid absorption or both. Some of the medical conditions that may precipitate pleural effusion include congestive heart failure, pneumonia, renal or liver disease, cancer, pulmonary embolism, and autoimmune disorders.

An injury was most likely sustained to what structure?

The pleural cavity is bordered by the visceral and parietal pleurae and contains a small volume of pleural fluid (about one milliliter). Excess fluid accumulation in this space can impair breathing by limiting the expansion of the lungs. The exact type of fluid entering the pleural cavity is dependent on the cause of the effusion and may include serous fluid, lymphatic fluid, blood or pus.

CONFIRMATION

What is the most likely clinical presentation?

Pleural effusion is often asymptomatic. If the effusion is large in size or if inflammation is present, symptoms may include shortness of breath, chest pain, cough, and fever. Additional symptoms are more likely the result of the underlying condition which caused the pleural effusion.

What laboratory or imaging studies would confirm the diagnosis?

Common tests used to identify a pleural effusion include chest x-ray, computed tomography, and ultrasound imaging. Once identified, a fluid sample is usually obtained via thoracentesis for further testing to determine the etiology of the effusion.

What additional information should be obtained to confirm the diagnosis?

In addition to laboratory and imaging studies, the physician will perform a thorough medical history and physical examination to assist in the diagnosis. Auscultation will reveal decreased breath sounds, decreased fremitus, egophony, and a pleural friction rub.

BRONZE Pneumothorax

DIAGNOSIS

What condition produces a patient's symptoms?

A pneumothorax is an accumulation of air in the pleural cavity that results in a collapsed lung. A primary pneumothorax is one that occurs without a known etiology, while a secondary pneumothorax occurs in the presence of existing lung pathology. Causes of secondary pneumothorax include trauma, airway disease (e.g., cystic fibrosis, emphysema), lung infections (e.g., pneumonia, tuberculosis), lung disease (e.g., sarcoidosis, pulmonary fibrosis), connective tissue disease (e.g., rheumatoid arthritis, systemic sclerosis), and cancer.

An injury was most likely sustained to what structure?

A pneumothorax occurs when air leaks into the pleural cavity. The pleural cavity refers to the space between the lungs and chest wall. The increase in pressure in the pleural space causes partial collapse of the lung, which results in impaired gas exchange and decreased oxygenation of the blood. If the pneumothorax is large, it can cause a shift in position of the mediastinum.

CONFIRMATION

What is the most likely clinical presentation?

The presentation varies widely, from asymptomatic to life-threatening, depending on the type and size of the pneumothorax. Symptoms include chest pain, shortness of breath, hypoxemia, cyanosis, and hypotension. A tension pneumothorax occurs when damaged tissue causes a one-way valve into the chest and results in large increases in pressure. A tension pneumothorax is a medical emergency that leads to significant impairment of respiration and circulation and requires immediate medical attention.

What laboratory or imaging studies would confirm the diagnosis?

A chest x-ray is typically the first imaging study performed to confirm the diagnosis of pneumothorax. Computed tomography and ultrasound imaging can also be useful in providing more detailed information regarding the condition.

What additional information should be obtained to confirm the diagnosis?

A thorough medical history and physical examination should be performed to rule out the existence of other similar conditions (e.g., pulmonary embolism, acute respiratory distress syndrome). Auscultation of the lungs typically reveals decreased breath sounds and decreased fremitus.

BRONZE Pulmonary Edema

DIAGNOSIS

What condition produces a patient's symptoms?

Pulmonary edema is a condition characterized by excess fluid within the lungs. This often occurs when the left ventricle is unable to adequately pump blood to the systemic circulation (e.g., left-sided heart failure). This causes fluid to back up into the pulmonary circulation and the lungs. Other causes of fluid buildup within the lungs include living at high elevations, respiratory distress syndrome, pulmonary embolism, adverse drug reactions, viral infections, smoke inhalation, and exposure to toxins. Acute pulmonary edema is considered a medical emergency.

An injury was most likely sustained to what structure?

When the left ventricle is unable to adequately pump blood to the systemic circulation, fluid backs up into the left atrium and then into the pulmonary circulation. As the pressure in the pulmonary circulation increases, the fluid moves from the lung capillaries into the alveoli, which makes breathing more difficult. In noncardiogenic pulmonary edema, the fluid buildup in the alveoli is not caused by an increase in pressure in the pulmonary circulation, but rather an increase in permeability of the capillaries themselves.

CONFIRMATION

What is the most likely clinical presentation?

Depending on the etiology, symptoms can develop slowly or suddenly. Acute pulmonary edema is characterized by extreme shortness of breath (especially when lying down), wheezing or gasping, anxiety, a cough that produces frothy sputum (may be tinged with blood), chest pain, and palpitations. Chronic pulmonary edema is characterized by shortness of breath that worsens when lying down or during physical activity, wheezing, weight gain, lower extremity swelling, and fatigue.

What laboratory or imaging studies would confirm the diagnosis?

A chest x-ray is the primary imaging study used to confirm the presence of fluid within the lungs. Other tests may be ordered to determine the cause of the pulmonary edema, including blood tests, electrocardiogram, and echocardiogram.

What additional information should be obtained to confirm the diagnosis?

A thorough medical history and physical examination should be performed to rule out other similar conditions that may cause shortness of breath (e.g., asthma, chronic obstructive pulmonary disease, pulmonary embolism).

Pulmonary Embolism

BRONZE

DIAGNOSIS

What condition produces a patient's symptoms?

An embolism that blocks a pulmonary artery is referred to as a pulmonary embolism (PE). A PE occurs as a result of venous thrombi that have detached and traveled from elsewhere in the body before lodging in a pulmonary artery. In most cases, multiple thrombi must be present to create a blockage large enough to produce PE symptoms.

An injury was most likely sustained to which structure?

A PE will cause decreased perfusion in the lung tissue supplied by the blocked vessel. As a result, the tissue becomes ischemic and fails to provide adequate oxygen for the body. Localized damage to venous structures associated with the initial thrombus formation may also occur.

CONFIRMATION

What is the most likely clinical presentation?

Signs and symptoms of PE include a sudden onset of dyspnea, coughing, hypoxia, and chest pain which may mimic myocardial infarction. Dyspnea presents both at rest and with activity. Complaints of chest pain typically worsen with coughing, eating, deep breathing or bending activities. Coughing may produce blood tinged sputum. Other signs and symptoms may include unilateral lower extremity edema, cyanosis, wheezing, diaphoresis, fainting, and a rapid or weak pulse.

What laboratory or imaging studies would confirm the diagnosis?

A ventilation-perfusion scan (V-Q scan) uses nuclear imaging of inhaled and injected radioactive substances to visualize air and blood flow through the lungs and identify blockages. The 3-D images produced by a spiral CT scan may be used to confirm the presence and location of a PE. MRI or diagnostic ultrasound may also be ordered to rule out the presence of additional thrombi, especially in the lower extremities. A pulmonary angiogram is the most conclusive and accurate means of identifying a PE, however, complication risks are high and so it is typically used only when other diagnostic methods are inconclusive.

What additional information should be obtained to confirm the diagnosis?

A complete medical and surgical history should be obtained in order to identify PE risk factors. Patients who are elderly or have certain inherited blood abnormalities (e.g., fibrinogen anomalies, antithrombin III deficiency) are at increased risk for developing a PE. Acquired risk factors are typically identified through the patient's history. These include extended periods of immobility, recent surgery, pregnancy, estrogen replacement use, smoking, and heart disease.

Respiratory Acidosis

BRONZE

DIAGNOSIS

What condition produces a patient's symptoms?

Respiratory acidosis refers to a state in which the pH is abnormally low indicating acidemia. Hypoventilation prevents adequate removal of CO_2 from the body causing hypercapnia. As a result, bicarbonate (HCO_3-) levels decrease altering the body's acid-base balance. Common etiologies include pulmonary disease, medications that suppress breathing, structural factors that limit effective lung expansion (e.g., severe scoliosis, morbid obesity), and conditions that cause respiratory muscle weakness (e.g., Guillain-Barre syndrome, amyotrophic lateral sclerosis).

An injury was most likely sustained to which structure?

Respiratory acidosis is not an independent disease process, but rather a symptom of some other underlying condition or disease. Injuries sustained vary with the etiology of the altered respiratory state and associated acidosis.

CONFIRMATION

What is the most likely clinical presentation?

Initial signs and symptoms of respiratory acidosis are often vague and more closely related to the underlying pathology. As the condition worsens, patients may present with lethargy, confusion, altered mental status, and cyanosis. Respiratory acidosis may present as a chronic or acute condition. Patients with chronic respiratory acidosis are likely to become stable if renal function is normal and HCO_3- excretion can be modulated to compensate for respiratory-induced acidemia. This renal compensation will be reflected in laboratory values that typically show a near normal pH and partial pressure of CO_2 ($PaCO_2$) measures toward the upper limits of normal. Acute respiratory acidosis is considered an emergent condition due to the rapid buildup of CO_2. This results in acidemia and $PaCO_2$ levels above the normal reference range.

What laboratory or imaging studies would confirm the diagnosis?

Laboratory analysis of arterial blood gases (e.g., serum CO_2 and O_2 levels), metabolic panel blood analysis (e.g., serum electrolytes), and urine pH are used to identify abnormal acidity and differentiate between respiratory and metabolic acidosis.

What additional information should be obtained to confirm the diagnosis?

A thorough medical history is necessary to assist in identifying conditions or medications which may contribute to alveolar hypoventilation and respiratory acidosis. Physical examination should include assessments of posture and respiratory muscle strength as well as mechanics.

BRONZE

Respiratory Alkalosis

DIAGNOSIS

What condition produces a patient's symptoms?

Respiratory alkalosis refers to a state in which the pH is abnormally high indicating alkalemia. Hyperventilation removes more CO_2 from the body than can be produced causing hypocapnia. As a result, hydrogen (H+) levels decrease altering the body's acid-base balance. Numerous conditions (e.g., pulmonary embolism, hyperthyroidism, sepsis), medications (e.g., catecholamines, nicotine), external influences (e.g., high altitude), and internal influences (e.g., CNS response to trauma, pain, anxiety, fever) can induce hyperventilation and subsequent alkalosis.

An injury was most likely sustained to which structure?

Respiratory alkalosis is not an independent disease process, but rather a symptom of some other underlying condition or disease. Injuries sustained vary with the etiology of the altered respiratory state and associated alkalosis.

CONFIRMATION

What is the most likely clinical presentation?

Initial signs and symptoms of respiratory alkalosis may be vague and are often closely related to the underlying pathology. Tachypnea, tachycardia, hyperventilation, and dizziness are commonly observed. In severe cases, a patient may develop seizures. If the patient is also hypoxic, cyanosis may be observed. Respiratory alkalosis may present as either a chronic or acute condition. As a chronic condition, lab values will reflect a partial pressure of CO_2 ($PaCO_2$) measure below normal reference values and serum pH alkalemia. Acute respiratory alkalosis will also reflect a $PaCO_2$ measure below normal reference values while serum pH will be normal or near normal.

What laboratory or imaging studies would confirm the diagnosis?

Laboratory analysis of arterial blood gases (e.g., serum CO_2 and O_2 levels), metabolic panel blood analysis (e.g., serum electrolytes), and urine pH are used to identify abnormal alkalinity and differentiate between respiratory and metabolic alkalosis.

What additional information should be obtained to confirm the diagnosis?

A thorough medical history is necessary to assist in identifying conditions or medications which may contribute to alveolar hyperventilation and respiratory alkalosis. Additional diagnostic testing may be required to identify a patient's underlying etiology so that respiratory alkalosis treatment interventions may be specifically targeted.

BRONZE

Sarcoidosis

DIAGNOSIS

What condition produces a patient's symptoms?

Though the etiology of sarcoidosis is unknown, it is thought the condition is the result of an abnormal immune system response to some foreign substance, such as an inhaled bacterium, virus, chemical or allergen. Sarcoidosis is characterized by the growth of small, abnormal collections of inflammatory cells, known as granulomas, within the body's organs.

An injury was most likely sustained to what structure?

Sarcoidosis can affect any of the body's organs, though it typically affects certain organs more than others, specifically the lungs, lymph nodes, and skin. When multiple granulomas form within an organ, it will affect how the organ functions leading to a variety of signs and symptoms depending on the organ affected. If the condition affects the heart or brain, serious complications may result.

CONFIRMATION

What is the most likely clinical presentation?

Many people with sarcoidosis have no signs or symptoms or only mild ones. Signs and symptoms will present differently depending on the organ(s) affected. Because the condition most commonly affects the lungs, signs and symptoms typically include wheezing, coughing, shortness of breath, and chest pain. Other symptoms may include fatigue, weight loss, blurry vision, enlarged lymph nodes, sores or areas of discolored skin, and painful, swollen joints. Sarcoidosis may present with a specific set of signs and symptoms known as Lofgren's syndrome, which is an acute form of sarcoidosis.

What laboratory or imaging studies would confirm the diagnosis?

There is no specific test used to diagnose sarcoidosis since it is diagnosed as a matter of exclusion. However, a chest x-ray is often performed since the large majority of patients with the condition will have an abnormal chest x-ray. A biopsy may also be ordered to check for the presence of granulomas.

What additional information should be obtained to confirm the diagnosis?

Since the signs and symptoms of this condition vary widely based on the organ(s) affected and can mimic the signs and symptoms of several other conditions, performing a thorough medical history and physical examination are very important in the diagnosis of this condition.

Tuberculosis

BRONZE

DIAGNOSIS

What condition produces a patient's symptoms?

Tuberculosis (TB) is a highly contagious infectious disease spread via airborne transmission. The infection is primarily caused by the Mycobacterium tuberculosis bacteria. Multiple antibiotic-resistant strains of the bacteria have been identified. Patients with latent TB are infected, however, it is not contagious and produces no symptoms. Active TB will produce symptoms and may develop from the latent bacteria or from a recent exposure to a contagious individual.

An injury was most likely sustained to which structure?

TB typically affects the lungs. Less common infection sites include the brain, spine, and kidneys with each producing different clinical symptoms. Patients with a weakened immune system are most likely to contract TB.

CONFIRMATION

What is the most likely clinical presentation?

Patients with active TB in the lungs typically present with symptoms including fever, chills, and fatigue. Weight loss, decreased appetite, and night sweats are also common. Complaints of a persistent cough for greater than three weeks, bloody sputum, and chest pain associated with deep breathing or coughing may be present. Physical examination will reveal abnormal lung sounds suggestive of pleural effusion and enlarged lymph nodes which may be tender with palpation. Clubbing of the digits may also be observed in patients with advanced TB. Patients who have been on an appropriate pharmacological regimen for at least two weeks are no longer considered contagious. Most recover from TB without long-term effects, however, untreated TB can spread to other areas of the body and become fatal.

What laboratory or imaging studies would confirm the diagnosis?

TB is typically diagnosed based on the results of a skin test. A small amount of the substance tuberculin is injected at a forearm site and the skin's reaction is then assessed 48 to 72 hours later. This diagnostic tool is, however, known to produce false results especially in patients who have previously had a TB vaccination or have recently been infected.

What additional information should be obtained to confirm the diagnosis?

A thorough medical history should be obtained to assist in identifying risk factors and ruling out similar diagnoses. Social history may also be significant if the patient has a high risk of occupational exposure or has ever visited or lived abroad.

Venous Thrombosis

BRONZE

DIAGNOSIS

What condition produces a patient's symptoms?

Venous thrombosis is a condition characterized by the formation of a blood clot (thrombus) within a vein. Any condition which slows or changes the flow of blood within a vein can increase the risk for thrombus formation. These risk factors include prolonged immobility, recent surgery, pregnancy, obesity, cigarette smoking, medications (e.g., birth control, hormone replacement), blood conditions characterized by "thick" blood (e.g., polycythemia), blood-clotting disorders, cancer, and certain autoimmune disorders.

An injury was most likely sustained to what structure?

Venous thrombosis most commonly affects the deep veins of the lower extremities. A thrombus can break off from its site of origin and travel within the bloodstream (i.e., embolus) to the brain, lungs or heart and cause severe damage.

CONFIRMATION

What is the most likely clinical presentation?

Signs and symptoms include swelling, redness, warmth, and pain in the affected leg, most commonly in the calf, though the condition can occur without any noticeable symptoms.

What laboratory or imaging studies would confirm the diagnosis?

Ultrasound imaging is most commonly used to identify the presence of a venous thrombus. Blood tests will also be ordered to detect elevated levels of clot-dissolving substances. Other imaging studies less often used include magnetic resonance imaging, computed tomography, and venography.

What additional information should be obtained to confirm the diagnosis?

A thorough medical history and physical examination should be performed to help diagnose the presence of a venous thrombus. Homans' sign may be performed as part of the physical examination, though further evaluation should be performed due to the poor diagnostic value of this test.

Cardiovascular and Pulmonary Systems Essentials

1. The components of the cardiac conduction system include the sinoatrial (SA) node, internodal tracts, atrioventricular (AV) node, common AV bundle or bundle of His, right and left bundle branches, and Purkinje fibers.
2. Sympathetic nerves stimulate the heart to beat faster (chronotropic effect) and with greater force of contraction (inotropic effect). Parasympathetic nerves slow the heart rate (chronotropic effect) primarily through their influence on the SA node.
3. The Valsalva maneuver produces increased intrathoracic pressure, increased central venous pressure, and decreased venous return and should be avoided, especially by patients with heart, blood vessel or lung disease.
4. Ventricular systole denotes contraction of the ventricles; ventricular diastole denotes the relaxation phase.
5. Cardiac output is the product of heart rate and stroke volume. It is approximately 5.0 – 5.5 L/min in resting adults, but can increase fivefold during exercise.
6. The components of blood are plasma, red blood cells, white blood cells, and platelets.
7. Oxygen is both dissolved in the blood plasma and chemically combined to hemoglobin in red blood cells. Only about 0.3 mL O_2 is dissolved in 100 mL of arterial blood; the rest is attached to hemoglobin.
8. The diaphragm is the primary muscle of inspiration. Secondary muscles of inspiration are the internal and external intercostals, sternocleidomastoids, and scalenes.
9. The bronchopulmonary segments are the topographic units of the lungs. There are ten bronchopulmonary segments in the right lung and eight in the left lung.
10. The most common sign of a heart attack in both men and women is chest pain or discomfort.
11. Blood pressure classifications include normal, elevated, Stage 1 hypertension, Stage 2 hypertension, and hypertensive crisis.
12. Pulmonary edema can be fatal if not treated. Seek immediate emergency medical assistance if the signs or symptoms of acute pulmonary edema develop including extreme shortness of breath or difficulty breathing, a feeling of suffocating or drowning, wheezing or gasping for breath, anxiety, restlessness or a sense of apprehension or a cough that produces frothy sputum tinged with blood.
13. Arterial blood gases evaluate acid–base status (pH), ventilation ($PaCO_2$), and oxygenation (PaO_2). Mean arterial blood gas values in adults at sea level are: pH = 7.4; $PaCO_2$ = 40 mm Hg; PaO_2 = 97 mm Hg; HCO_3- = 24 mEq/L.
14. A complete blood count (CBC) measures red blood cell count, total white blood cell count, white blood cell differential, platelets, hemoglobin, and hematocrit.
15. Antihypertensive medications include diuretics, calcium channel blockers, ACE inhibitors, angiotensin II blockers, ß-adrenergic blockers, and alpha adrenergic antagonists.
16. Bronchodilator agents work to relieve bronchospasm by stimulating the receptors that cause bronchial smooth muscle relaxation or by blocking the receptors that trigger bronchoconstriction. Primary classifications of bronchodilators include anticholinergic, sympathomimetics, and xanthine derivatives.
17. BMI describes relative weight for height and is a useful measurement for identifying adults at increased risk for mortality and morbidity due to being overweight and obese. BMI = weight [kg] ÷ height [m^2].
18. Normal heart sounds are S1 (closing of the mitral and tricuspid valves) and S2 (closing of the aortic and pulmonic valves).
19. ST segment depression on the ECG may indicate ischemia of the myocardium.
20. Adventitious inspiratory or expiratory breath sounds include crackles, pleural friction rub, rhonchi, stridor, and wheeze.

Cardiovascular and Pulmonary Systems Essentials

21. Pulmonary function tests help to differentiate obstructive and restrictive forms of lung dysfunction. Obstructive defects are characterized by decreased expiratory flows ($FEV_1/FVC < 70\%$). Restrictive defects are characterized by reduced lung volumes and relatively normal expiratory flow rates (FVC is reduced and FEV_1/FVC is normal or increased).

22. If the percent of arterial oxygen saturation of hemoglobin falls below 90% in acutely ill patients or below 85% in patients with chronic lung disease, activity should be stopped and a discussion with the physician should take place to consider adding or increasing supplemental oxygen.

23. The rate pressure product (RPP), the product of heart rate and systolic blood pressure, is a clinical index of myocardial oxygen consumption that provides an easy to measure physiologic correlate to the onset of angina pectoris or the development of ECG abnormalities in patients with previous heart disease.

24. Active cycle of breathing and autogenic drainage are breathing techniques that patients can perform independently to assist with airway clearance.

25. Huffing is a forced expiratory maneuver performed with the glottis open that can be used instead of a cough.

26. Pursed-lip breathing helps to reduce respiratory rate, reduce dyspnea, and prevent airway collapse in patients with emphysema. Any patient who is short of breath may use this technique.

27. An incentive spirometer provides visual or other feedback to encourage the patient to take long, slow, deep inhalations, which is especially important after thoracic and abdominal surgery.

28. Intensity of aerobic exercise can be regulated by heart rate, MET level, and RPE.

29. During inpatient cardiac rehabilitation, exercise intensity is usually limited to:
    - RPE < 13 (6 - 20 scale)
    - Exercise heart rate < 120 beats/minute OR < 20 beats/minute above resting heart rate for patients post infarction
    - Exercise heart rate < 30 beats/minute above resting heart rate for patients after heart surgery

30. The target heart rate zone for exercise can be calculated using the Karvonen formula:
    - Lower THR = [(HRmax – HRrest) x 40%] + HRrest
    - Upper THR = [(HRmax – HRrest) x 85%] + HRrest

31. The exercise target heart rate should be ≥ 10 beats/minute below the patient's known anginal threshold.

32. One MET is the energy expended while sitting quietly (3.5 mL O_2/kg/min or 1kcal/kg/h).

33. The target MET zone for exercise can be calculated using the Karvonen formula:
    - Lower METs = [(MaxMETs – RestMETs) x 40%] + RestMETs
    - Upper METs = [(MaxMETs – RestMETs) x 85%] + RestMETs

34. RPE of 11 - 13 corresponds to the upper limit of prescribed training heart rates for patients in the early phase of outpatient cardiac rehabilitation.

35. There is no optimal exercise intensity for the aerobic exercise training of patients in pulmonary rehabilitation. Intensity is determined primarily by patient tolerance and safety.

Cardiovascular and Pulmonary Systems Proficiencies

1. Heart Anatomy

Identify the appropriate term for each of the specified locations. Answers must be selected from the Word Bank and can be used only once.

Word Bank: inferior vena cava, left ventricle, left atrium, left pulmonary veins, left pulmonary arteries, left subclavian artery, left cardiac vein, left common carotid artery, right pulmonary veins, right atrium, right coronary artery, superior vena cava

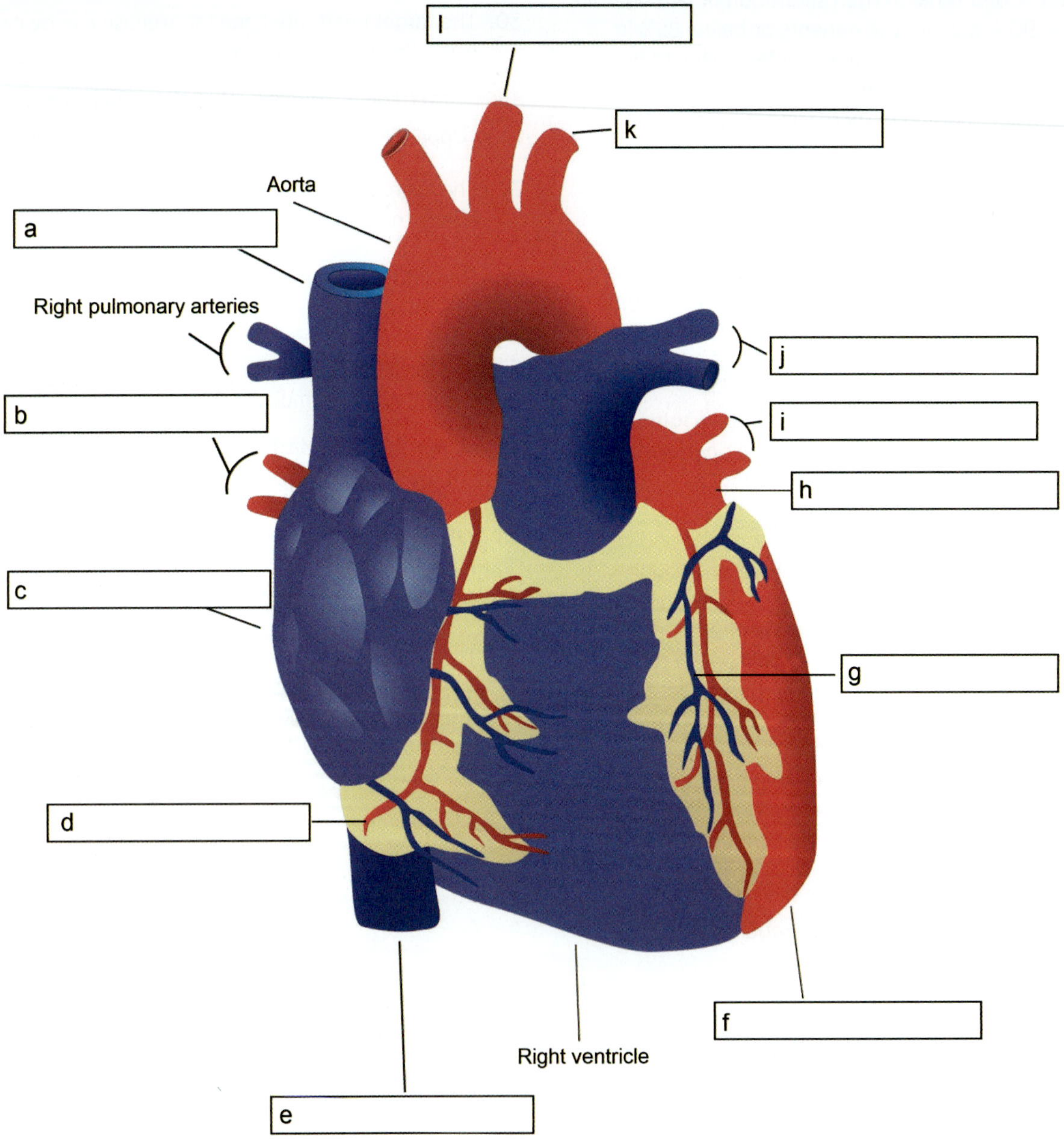

l

k

Aorta

a

Right pulmonary arteries

j

b

i

h

c

g

d

f

Right ventricle

e

Cardiovascular and Pulmonary Systems Proficiencies

2. Heart Circulation

Identify the appropriate term for each of the specified locations. Answers must be selected from the Word Bank and can be used only once.

Word Bank: aortic valve, deoxygenated blood from body, deoxygenated blood to left lung, deoxygenated blood to right lung, left atrium, left ventricle, mitral valve, oxygenated blood from left lung, oxygenated blood to body, pulmonary valve, right atrium, right ventricle, tricuspid valve

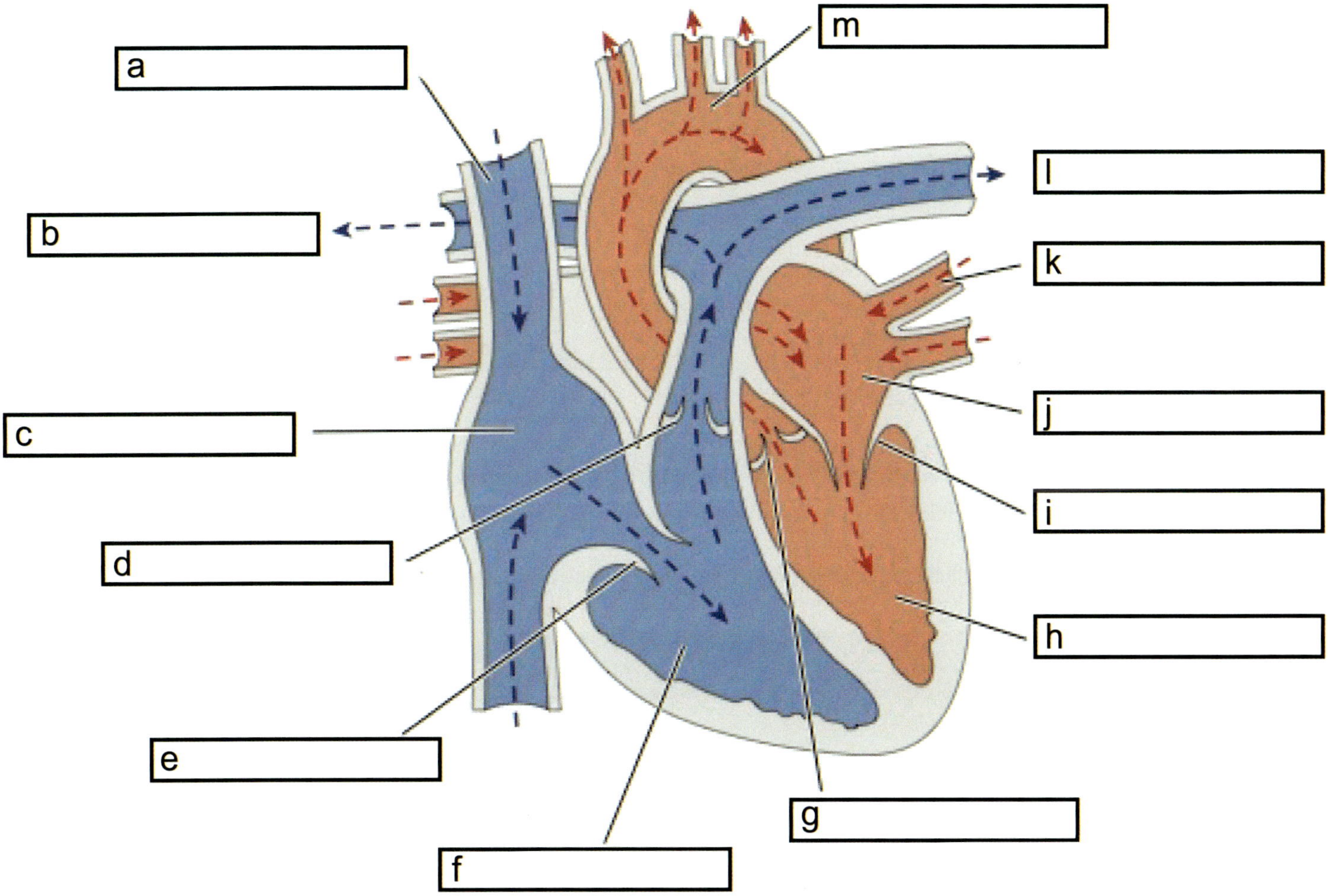

a
m
l
b
k
c
j
i
d
h
e
g
f

Cardiovascular and Pulmonary Systems Proficiencies

3. Vessels of the Heart

Identify the appropriate vessel of the heart based on the described function. Answers must be selected from the Word Bank and can each be used only once.

Word Bank: aorta, inferior vena cava, pulmonary arteries, pulmonary veins, superior vena cava

Great Vessel	Description
a	returns blood to the right atrium from the head, neck and arms
b	takes blood away from the right ventricle to the left and right lungs
c	returns blood from the left and right lungs to the left atrium
d	takes blood away from the left ventricle
e	returns blood to the right atrium from the lower body and viscera

4. Heart Valves

Identify the areas associated with each valve. Answers must be selected from the Word Bank. Answers can be used more than once.

Word Bank: aorta, left atrium, left ventricle, pulmonary artery, right atrium, right ventricle

a. The tricuspid valve controls blood flow between the ____________ and the ____________.

b. The pulmonary valve controls blood flow between the ____________ and the ____________.

c. The aortic valve controls blood flow between the ____________ and the ____________.

d. The mitral valve controls blood flow between the ____________ and the ____________.

5. Lung Capacities

Identify the components of each of the listed lung capacities. The sum of the identified components must equal the stated capacity. A list of possible components is provided in the Word Bank. The components can be used more than once.

Word Bank: Expiratory Reserve Volume (ERV), Functional Residual Capacity (FRC), Inspiratory Capacity (IC), Inspiratory Reserve Volume (IRV), Residual Volume (RV), Tidal Volume (TV), Vital Capacity (VC)

Measure	Components
functional residual capacity	a
inspiratory capacity	b
total lung capacity	c
vital capacity	d

Cardiovascular and Pulmonary Systems Proficiencies

6. Lung Volumes and Capacities

Identify the volumes and capacities most closely associated with the supplied descriptions. Answers must be selected from the Word Bank and can each be used only once.

Word Bank: anatomic dead space volume, expiratory reserve volume, forced vital capacity, functional residual capacity, inspiratory capacity, inspiratory reserve volume, residual volume, tidal volume, total lung capacity, vital capacity

Volumes and Capacities	Description
a	The maximal volume of air that can be inspired after a normal tidal exhalation.
b	The volume of air in the lungs after normal exhalation.
c	The maximal volume of air that can be exhaled after a normal tidal exhalation.
d	The volume change that occurs between maximal inspiration and maximal expiration.
e	The volume of air in the lungs after a maximal inspiration; the sum of all lung volumes.
f	The volume of gas remaining in the lungs at the end of a maximal expiration.
g	The volume of air expired during a forced maximal expiration after a forced maximal inspiration.
h	Total volume inspired and expired with each breath during quiet breathing.
i	The volume of air that occupies the non-respiratory conducting airways.
j	The maximal volume of air inspired after normal tidal volume inspiration.

7. Pathology of the Cardiovascular and Pulmonary Systems

Identify the appropriate medical condition based on the supplied descriptions. Answers must be selected from the Word Bank and can each be used only once.

Word Bank: acute respiratory distress syndrome, angina pectoris, asthma, atelectasis, atherosclerosis, bronchitis, cor pulmonale, cystic fibrosis, endocarditis, myocarditis, pulmonary edema, rheumatic fever

Pathology	Description
a	hypertrophy of the right ventricle caused by altered structure or function of the lungs
b	an inflammatory disease that can develop as a complication of strep throat
c	inflammation of the bronchi characterized by hypertrophy of the mucus secreting glands
d	fluid collects in the alveoli in the lungs making it difficult to breathe
e	a transient precordial sensation of pressure or discomfort resulting from myocardial ischemia
f	one or more areas of the lungs collapse or fail to properly inflate
g	inflammation of the endothelium that lines the heart and cardiac valves
h	a slow progressive accumulation of fatty plaques on the inner walls of arteries
i	chronic inflammation of the airways caused by increased airway sensitivity to various stimuli
j	inflammation and weakness of the heart muscle
k	an autosomal recessive genetic disease of the exocrine glands
l	respiratory failure due to fluid accumulation in the alveoli

Cardiovascular and Pulmonary Systems Proficiencies

8. Arterial Blood Gas Values

Identify the appropriate arterial blood gas measure for each of the supplied values. Answers must be selected from the Word Bank and can each be used only once.

Word Bank: HCO_3-, $PaCO_2$, PaO_2, pH, SaO_2

Measure	Value
a	7.35 - 7.45
b	40 mm Hg
c	97 mm Hg
d	24 mEq/L
e	95-98%

9. Arterial Blood Gas Analysis

Identify the anticipated change in pH, $PaCO_2$, and HCO_3- based on the listed medical conditions. Place an ↑ or ↓ in each of the provided spaces.

Partially Compensated	pH	$PaCO_2$	HCO_3-
respiratory acidosis	a	b	c
respiratory alkalosis	d	e	f
metabolic acidosis	g	h	i
metabolic alkalosis	j	k	l

10. Pharmacology of the Cardiovascular and Pulmonary Systems

Identify the appropriate medication based on the supplied descriptions. Answers must be selected from the Word Bank and can each be used only once.

Word Bank: alpha adrenergic antagonist agents, angiotensin-converting enzyme inhibitor agents, anticoagulant agents, anti-inflammatory agents, beta blocker agents, calcium channel blockers, diuretics, expectorant agents, nitrates, positive inotropic agents

Drug	Action
a	decrease the entry of calcium into vascular smooth muscle cells
b	increase the excretion of sodium and urine
c	decrease blood pressure and afterload by suppressing a specific enzyme
d	decrease ischemia through smooth muscle relaxation and dilation of peripheral vessels
e	reduce peripheral vascular tone causing dilation of arterioles and veins resulting in decreased blood pressure
f	decrease myocardial oxygen demand by decreasing heart rate and contractility
g	increase respiratory secretions which help to loosen mucus
h	inhibit platelet aggregation and thrombus formation
i	prevent inflammatory-mediated bronchoconstriction
j	increase the force and velocity of myocardial contraction, slow the heart rate, and decrease conduction through the AV node

Cardiovascular and Pulmonary Systems Proficiencies

11. Hypertension

Next to each value state whether the BP is normal, elevated, stage 1 hypertension, or stage 2 hypertension. Classification should be made based on the November 2017 Blood Pressure Guidelines. Answers must be selected from the Word Bank and can each be used more than once.

Word Bank: normal, elevated, stage 1 hypertension, stage 2 hypertension

Blood Pressure Value	Classification
125/89 mm Hg	a
170/105 mm Hg	b
155/95 mm Hg	c
110/75 mm Hg	d
142/105 mm Hg	e
135/82 mm Hg	f

12. Heart Sounds

Identify the appropriate heart sounds for each of the supplied descriptions. Answers must be selected from the Word Bank and can each be used only once.

Word Bank: S1, S2, S3, S4, murmur

Heart Sound	Definition
a	closure of the aortic and pulmonary valves at the onset of diastole
b	closure of the mitral and tricuspid valves at the onset of systole
c	pathological sound of vibration of the ventricle walls with ventricular filling and atrial contraction
d	vibrations of the distended ventricle walls due to passive flow of blood from the atria during diastole
e	vibrations of longer duration than the heart sounds due to disrupted blood flow past a stenotic or regurgitant valve

13. Abnormal Breath Sounds

Identify the appropriate abnormal breath sound for each of the supplied descriptions. Answers must be selected from the Word Bank and can each be used only once.

Word Bank: crackle, pleural friction rub, rhonchi, stridor, wheeze

Breath Sound	Definition
a	dry, crackling sound heard during inspiration and expiration
b	continuous low-pitched sounds resembling snoring or gurgling during inspiration and expiration
c	continuous high-pitched wheeze heard with inspiration or expiration
d	discontinuous high-pitched popping sound heard during inspiration
e	continuous musical or whistling sound composed of a variety of pitches

Cardiovascular and Pulmonary Systems Proficiencies

14. Waveforms and Intervals for an Electrocardiogram

Identify the appropriate waveform or interval for each of the supplied descriptions. Answers must be selected from the Word Bank and can each be used only once.

Word Bank: P Wave, PR Interval, QRS Complex, QT Interval, ST Segment, T Wave

Segment	Electrical Activity
a	time for both ventricular depolarization and repolarization
b	ventricular repolarization
c	atrial depolarization
d	time for atrial depolarization and conduction from the SA node to the AV node
e	isoelectric period following the QRS complex
f	ventricular depolarization and atrial repolarization

15. Peripheral Pulses

Identify the appropriate artery based on the supplied descriptions. Answers must be selected from the Word Bank and can each be used only once.

Word Bank: brachial, carotid, dorsalis pedis, femoral, popliteal, posterior tibial, radial, ulnar

Artery	Pulse Location
a	the medial aspect of the sternocleidomastoid muscle in the lower half of the neck
b	at the wrist, lateral to the flexor carpi radialis tendon
c	in the upper thigh, one-third of the distance from the pubis to the anterior superior iliac spine
d	in the space between the medial malleolus and the Achilles tendon, above the calcaneus
e	medial to the biceps tendon and lateral to the medial epicondyle of the humerus
f	at the wrist, between the flexor digitorum superficialis and the flexor carpi ulnaris tendons
g	in the popliteal space of the posterior knee
h	near the center of the long axis of the foot, between the first and second metatarsal bones

16. Cardiovascular and Pulmonary Systems Basics

Mark each statement as True or False. If the statement is False correct the statement in the space provided.

True/False	Statement
a	Cardiac output refers to the volume of blood ejected by each contraction of the left ventricle.
Correction:	

Cardiovascular and Pulmonary Systems Proficiencies

True/False	Statement
b	Preload refers to the tension in the ventricular wall at the end of diastole.
Correction:	
c	The radial artery is assessed at the wrist, medial to the flexor carpi radialis tendon.
Correction:	
d	The dorsalis pedis artery is assessed near the center of the long axis of the foot, between the second and third metatarsals.
Correction:	
e	White blood cells, also known as leukocytes, protect the body from infection by ingesting bacteria and debris.
Correction:	
f	Minute volume ventilation is calculated by multiplying total lung capacity and respiratory rate.
Correction:	
g	The pulmonic area of the heart is auscultated by placing the diaphragm of the stethoscope over the fourth intercostal space at the left sternal border.
Correction:	
h	A body mass index of 27.5 would be classified as normal.
Correction:	
i	When observing an electrocardiogram, the P wave represents atrial depolarization.
Correction:	

Cardiovascular and Pulmonary Systems Proficiencies

True/False	Statement
j	A drop in systolic blood pressure greater than 5 mm Hg from baseline would warrant terminating an exercise stress test.
Correction:	
k	A rating of 14 on a rate of perceived exertion scale represents approximately 50% of the maximum heart rate during exercise on a treadmill.
Correction:	
l	Eupnea refers to the absence of spontaneous breathing.
Correction:	
m	When performing pursed-lip breathing, the inspiratory phase is twice as long in duration as the expiratory phase.
Correction:	
n	Activities requiring 3-6 metabolic equivalents would be considered moderate level activity.
Correction:	
o	The S4 heart sound is a pathological sound often associated with hypertensive heart disease or myocardial infarction.
Correction:	

Cardiovascular and Pulmonary Systems Answer Key

1. Heart Anatomy

a. superior vena cava
b. right pulmonary veins
c. right atrium
d. right coronary artery
e. inferior vena cava
f. left ventricle
g. left cardiac vein
h. left atrium
i. left pulmonary veins
j. left pulmonary arteries
k. left subclavian artery
l. left common carotid artery

2. Heart Circulation

a. deoxygenated blood from body
b. deoxygenated blood to right lung
c. right atrium
d. pulmonary valve
e. tricuspid valve
f. right ventricle
g. aortic valve
h. left ventricle
i. mitral valve
j. left atrium
k. oxygenated blood from left lung
l. deoxygenated blood to left lung
m. oxygenated blood to body

3. Vessels of the Heart

a. superior vena cava
b. pulmonary arteries
c. pulmonary veins
d. aorta
e. inferior vena cava

4. Heart Valves

a. The tricuspid valve controls blood flow between the right atrium and the right ventricle.
b. The pulmonary valve controls blood flow between the right ventricle and the pulmonary artery.
c. The aortic valve controls blood flow between the left ventricle and the aorta.
d. The mitral valve controls blood flow between the left atrium and the left ventricle.

5. Lung Capacities

a. FRC = ERV + RV
b. IC = TV + IRV
c. TLC = RV + VC or TLC = FRC + IC
d. VC = TV + IRV + ERV

6. Lung Volumes and Capacities

a. inspiratory capacity
b. functional residual capacity
c. expiratory reserve volume
d. vital capacity
e. total lung capacity
f. residual volume
g. forced vital capacity
h. tidal volume
i. anatomic dead space volume
j. inspiratory reserve volume

7. Pathology of the Cardiovascular and Pulmonary Systems

a. cor pulmonale
b. rheumatic fever
c. bronchitis
d. pulmonary edema
e. angina pectoris
f. atelectasis
g. endocarditis
h. atherosclerosis
i. asthma
j. myocarditis
k. cystic fibrosis
l. acute respiratory distress syndrome

8. Arterial Blood Gas Values

a. pH
b. $PaCO_2$
c. PaO_2
d. HCO_3-
e. SaO_2

Cardiovascular and Pulmonary Systems Answer Key

9. Arterial Blood Gas Analysis

a. pH ↓
b. $PaCO_2$ ↑
c. HCO_3- ↑
d. pH ↑
e. $PaCO_2$ ↓
f. HCO_3- ↓
g. pH ↓
h. $PaCO_2$ ↓
i. HCO_3- ↓
j. pH ↑
k. $PaCO_2$ ↑
l. HCO_3- ↑

10. Pharmacology of the Cardiovascular and Pulmonary Systems

a. calcium channel blockers
b. diuretics
c. angiotensin-converting enzyme inhibitor agents
d. nitrates
e. alpha adrenergic antagonist agents
f. beta blocker agents
g. expectorant agents
h. anticoagulant agents
i. anti-inflammatory agents
j. positive inotropic agents

11. Hypertension

a. stage 1 hypertension
b. stage 2 hypertension
c. stage 2 hypertension
d. normal
e. stage 2 hypertension
f. stage 1 hypertension

12. Heart Sounds

a. S2
b. S1
c. S4
d. S3
e. murmur

13. Abnormal Breath Sounds

a. pleural friction rub
b. rhonchi
c. stridor
d. crackle
e. wheeze

14. Waveforms and Intervals for an Electrocardiogram

a. QT Interval
b. T Wave
c. P Wave
d. PR Interval
e. ST Segment
f. QRS Complex

15. Peripheral Pulses

a. carotid
b. radial
c. femoral
d. posterior tibial
e. brachial
f. ulnar
g. popliteal
h. dorsalis pedis

16. Cardiovascular and Pulmonary Systems Basics*

a. FALSE: Correction - Stroke volume refers to the volume of blood ejected by each contraction of the left ventricle.
b. TRUE
c. FALSE: Correction - The radial artery is assessed at the wrist, lateral to the flexor carpi radialis tendon.
d. FALSE: Correction - The dorsalis pedis artery is assessed near the center of the long axis of the foot, between the first and second metatarsal.
e. TRUE
f. FALSE: Correction - Minute volume ventilation is calculated by multiplying tidal volume and respiratory rate.
g. FALSE: Correction - The tricuspid area of the heart is auscultated by placing the diaphragm of the stethoscope over the fourth intercostal space at the left sternal border.

Cardiovascular and Pulmonary Systems Answer Key

h. FALSE: Correction - A body mass index of 18.5 - 24.9 would be considered normal.

i. TRUE

j. FALSE: Correction - A drop in systolic blood pressure greater than 10 mm Hg from baseline would warrant terminating an exercise stress test.

k. FALSE: Correction - A rating of 14 on a rate of perceived exertion scale represents approximately 70% of the maximum heart rate during exercise on a treadmill.

l. FALSE: Correction - Apnea refers to the absence of spontaneous breathing. Eupnea refers to the normal rate and depth of breathing.

m. FALSE: Correction - When performing pursed-lip breathing, the expiratory phase is twice as long in duration as the inspiratory phase.

n. TRUE

o. TRUE

*The correction presented for each false statement is an example of several possible corrections.

Cardiovascular and Pulmonary Systems References

1. Components of Blood. The Merck Manuals Online Medical Library. http://www.merckmanuals.com/home/sec14/ch169/ch169b.html#sec14-ch169-ch169b-4. Updated August 2006. Accessed January 3, 2011.
2. DePalo VA, McCool F D. Pulmonary Anatomy & Physiology. In: Hanley ME, Welsh CH, eds. ***CURRENT Diagnosis & Treatment in Pulmonary Medicine***. New York, NY: McGraw-Hill; 2003. http://0-www.accessmedicine.com.lilac.une.edu/content.aspx?aID=575000. Accessed January 3, 2011.
3. Diseases and Conditions. Mayo Clinic Web site. http://www.mayoclinic.com/health/DiseasesIndex/DiseasesIndex. Accessed January 3, 2011.
4. Lawrence EC, Brigham KL. Chronic Cor Pulmonale. In: Fuster V, O'Rourke RA, Walsh RA, Poole-Wilson P, eds. ***Hurst's the Heart***, 12th ed. New York, NY: McGraw-Hill; 2008. http://0-www.accessmedicine.com.lilac.une.edu/content.aspx?aID=3070848. Accessed January 13, 2011.
5. Diagnostic tests and procedures. American Heart Association Web site. http://www.heart.org/HEARTORG/Conditions/HeartAttack/SymptomsDiagnosisofHeartAttack/Diagnostic-Tests-Procedures_UCM_303929_Article.jsp. Updated November 3, 2010. Accessed January 2, 2011.
6. Chobanian AV, Bakris GL, Black HR, et al. Seventh report of the joint national committee on prevention, detection, evaluation, and treatment of high blood pressure: the JNC 7 complete report. ***Hypertension***. 2003; 42: 1206–1252.
7. The Seventh Report of the Joint National Committee on Prevention, Detection, Evaluation, and Treatment of High Blood Pressure (JNC 7). National Heart Lung and Blood Institute Web site. http://www.nhlbi.nih.gov/guidelines/hypertension/jnc7full.pdf. Accessed January 3, 2011.
8. Cardiac procedures and surgeries. American Heart Association Web site. http://www.heart.org/HEARTORG/Conditions/HeartAttack/PreventionTreatmentofHeartAttack/Cardiac-Procedures-and-Surgeries_UCM_303939_Article.jsp. Updated November 3, 2010. Accessed January 2, 2011.
9. ACC/AHA 2005 Practice guidelines for the management of patients with peripheral arterial disease (lower extremity, renal, mesenteric, and abdominal aortic) ***Circulation*** 2006; 113:1474-1547.
10. Valve disease. Texas Heart Institute Web site. http://www.texasheartinstitute.org/HIC/Topics/Cond/valvedis.cfm Updated July 2010. Accessed January 3, 2011.
11. Asthma. American Lung Association website. http://www.lungusa.org/lung-disease/asthma/. Accessed January 3, 2011.
12. Diseases and conditions index. National Heart Lung and Blood Institute Web site. http://www.nhlbi.nih.gov/health/dci/index.html. Updated June 2010. Accessed January 3, 2010.
13. About cystic fibrosis. Cystic Fibrosis Foundation Web site. http://www.cff.org/AboutCF/. Accessed January 3, 2011.
14. Watchie J. ***Cardiovascular and Pulmonary Physical Therapy. A Clinical Manual.*** 2nd ed. St. Louis, MO: Saunders Elsevier; 2010.
15. Tests and procedures. Mayo Clinic Web site. http://www.mayoclinic.com/health/tests-and-procedures/Test Procedure Index. Accessed January 3, 2011.
16. Fuster V, O'Rourke RA, Walsh RA, Poole-Wilson P. Nuclear Cardiology. In: Fuster V, O'Rourke RA, Walsh RA, Poole-Wilson P, eds. Hurst's The Heart, 12th ed. New York, NY: McGraw-Hill; 2008. http://0-www.accessmedicine.com.lilac.une.edu/content.aspx?aID=3059284. Accessed January 13, 2011.
17. Chang AM, Maisel AS, Hollander JE. Diagnosis of heart failure. ***Heart Failure Clinics***. 2009; 5:25-35.DOI: 10.1016/j.hfc.2008.08.013.
18. Drug Facts and Comparison. Facts and Comparisons Web site. http:www.factsandcomparisons.com. Accessed January 3, 2011.
19. Monographs A-Z. Clinical Pharmacology Web site. http://www.clinicalpharmacology.com/?epm=2_1. Accessed January 3, 2011.
20. Nason KS, Maddaus MA, Luketich JD. Chest Wall, Lung, Mediastinum, and Pleura. In: Brunicardi FC, Andersen DK, Billiar TR, Dunn DL, Hunter JG, Matthews JB, Pollock RE, eds. ***Schwartz's Principles of Surgery***, 9th ed. New York, NY: McGraw-Hill; 2010. http://0-www.accessmedicine.com.lilac.une.edu/content.aspx?aID=5016069. Accessed January 3, 2010.
21. American College of Sports Medicine. ***ACSM's Resource Manual for Guidelines for Exercise Testing and Prescription***. Seventh Edition. Lippincott Williams & Wilkins. 2014.
22. Campeau L. The Canadian Cardiovascular Society grading of angina pectoris revisited 30 years later. ***Can J Cardiol***. 2002:18:371-9.
23. Seidel HM, Ball JW, Dains JE, Benedict GW. ***Mosby's Guide to Physical Examination***. Fifth Edition. St. Louis, MO: Mosby; 2003.
24. LeBlond RF, DeGowin RL, Brown DD. Cardiovascular and Respiratory Signs. DeGowin's Diagnostic Examination. 9th ed. New York: McGraw-Hill Medical; 2009. http://0-www.accessmedicine.com.lilac.une.edu/content.aspx?aID=3661627. Accessed January 3, 2011.
25. Assessing your weight and health risk. National Heart Lung and Blood Institute website. http://www.nhlbi.nih.gov/health/public/heart/obesity/lose_wt/risk.htm. Accessed January 3, 2011.
26. Zuther JE. Lymphedema Management. ***The Comprehensive Guide for Practitioners***. New York, NY: Thieme; 2005
27. ***Guide to Physical Therapist Practice***. 2nd ed. Phys Ther. 2001; 81:583.

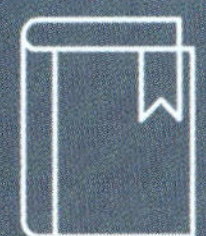

Cardiovascular and Pulmonary Systems References

28. Wullink M, Stoffers HE, Kuipers H. A primary care walking exercise program for patients with intermittent claudication. ***Med Sci Sports Exerc***. 2001; 33:1629-1634.
29. Borg G. Borg's Perceived Exertion and Pain Scales. Champaign IL: Human Kinetics; 1998.
30. Prasad SA, Randall SD, Balfour-Lynn IM. Fifteen-count breathlessness score: an objective measure for children. ***Pediatr Pulmonol***. 2000 30(1):56-62.
31. American Thoracic Society. Dyspnea. Mechanisms, assessment, and management: A consensus statement. ***Am J Respir Crit Care Med***. 1999; 159:3321-340.
32. Goldberger AL. ***Clinical Electrocardiography: A Simplified Approach***. 7th ed. Philadelphia, PA: Mosby Elsevier; 2006.
33. American Thoracic Society. The diagnostic approach to acute venous thromboembolism. Clinical practice guideline. ***Am J Respir Crit Care Med***. 1999; 160:1043-1066.
34. O'Rourke RA, Shaver JA, Silverman ME. The History, Physical Examination, and Cardiac Auscultation. In: Fuster V, O'Rourke RA, Walsh RA, Poole-Wilson P, eds. ***Hurst's The Heart***, 12th ed. New York, NY: McGraw-Hill; 2008. http://0-www.accessmedicine.com.lilac.une.edu/content.aspx?aID=3057120. Accessed January 3, 2011.
35. Miller MR, Hankinson J, Brusasco V, Burgos R, et al. Standardisation of spirometry. ***Eur Respir J.*** 2005; 26: 319-338.
36. American Thoracic Society. Lung function testing: Selection of reference values and interpretative strategies. ***Am Rev Respir Dis***. 1991; 144:1202-1218.
37. AARC Clinical Practice Guideline: Exercise testing for evaluation of hypoxemia and/or desaturation. ***Respir Care***. 1992; 37: 907-912.
38. Borg GAV: Psychophysical bases of perceived exertion. ***Med Sci Sports Exerc.*** 1982;14:377.
39. Wallace J. Principles of cardiorespiratory endurance programming. In: ***ACSM's Resource Manual for Guidelines for Exercise Testing and Prescription***. Philadelphia, PA: Lippincott Williams & Wilkins; 2006; 336-349.
40. Krider SJ. Vital Signs. In: Wilkins RL, Krider SJ, Sheldon RL, eds. ***Clinical Assessment in Respiratory Care***, 4th ed. St. Louis, MO: Mosby; 2000.
41. ATS statement: Guidelines for the six-minute walk test. ***Am J Respir Crit Care Med***. 2002; 166:111-117.
42. AARC Clinical Practice Guideline. Postural drainage therapy. ***Respir Care***. 1991; 36:1418-1426
43. Hardy KA. A review of airway clearance: new techniques, indications and recommendations. ***Respir Care***. 1994; 39:440.
44. AARC Clinical Practice Guideline. Directed cough. ***Respir Care***. 1993; 38:495-499
45. Levenson CR. Breathing exercises. In: ***Pulmonary Management in Physical Therapy***. In: Zadai CC. Ed. New York, NY; 1992: 135-155.
46. Cahalin LP, Braga M, Matsuo Y, Hernandez ED. Efficacy of diaphragmatic breathing in persons with chronic obstructive pulmonary disease: a review of the literature. ***J Cardiopulm Rehabil.*** 2002; 22:7-21.
47. Shekleton M, Berry JK, Covey MK. Respiratory muscle weakness and training. In: Frownfelter D, Dean E, eds. ***Principles and Practice of Cardiopulmonary Physical Therapy***. Fifth ed. St. Louis, Mo: Mosby; 2012: 443-452.
48. Lotters F, van Tol B, Kwakkel G, Gosselink R. Effects of controlled inspiratory muscle training in patients with COPD: a meta-analysis. ***Eur Respir***. 2002; 20:570-576.
49. Gosselink R. Controlled breathing and dyspnea in patients with chronic obstructive pulmonary disease (COPD) ***J Rehabil Res Dev.*** 2003;40(5): Suppl 2:25-33.
50. Humberstone N, Tecklin JS. Respiratory treatment. In: Irwin S, Tecklin JS, eds. ***Cardiopulmonary Physical Therapy***. 3rd ed. St. Louis, Mo: Mosby; 1995; 356-374.
51. AARC Clinical Practice Guideline. Incentive spirometry. ***Respir Care***. 1991; 36:1402-1405.
52. American Association of Cardiovascular & Pulmonary Rehabilitation. ***Guidelines for Cardiac Rehabilitation and Secondary Prevention Programs.*** 4th ed. Champaign,IL: Human Kinetics; 2004.
53. Balady GJ, Ades PA, Comoss P, Limacher M, et al. Core components of cardiac rehabilitation/secondary prevention programs: A statement for healthcare professionals from the American Heart Association and the American Association of Cardiovascular and Pulmonary Rehabilitation. ***Circulation***. 2000;102:1069-1073.
54. Keteyian SJ, Brawner CA. Cardiopulmonary Adaptations to Exercise. In: Kaminsky LA, ed. ACSM's ***Resource Manual for Guidelines for Exercise Testing and Prescription***. 5th ed. Baltimore, MD: Williams & Wilkins; 2006.
55. AARC Clinical Practice Guideline Pulmonary Rehabilitation. ***Respir Care*** 2002; 47:617-625.
56. American Association of Cardiovascular & Pulmonary Rehabilitation. ***Guidelines for Pulmonary Rehabilitation Programs***. 3rd ed. Champaign, IL: Human Kinetics; 2004.
57. Troosters T, Casaburi R, Gosselink R, Decramer M. Pulmonary rehabilitation in chronic obstructive pulmonary disease. Am J Respir Crit Care Med 2005:172:19-38.

7

Other Systems

Therese Giles
Scott Giles

Other Systems represents approximately 32 - 53 questions (16% - 26.5%) on the NPTE-PT.

Contributors

Shawn Paquette
Daniel Lee
Danielle Cowan
Ryan Bailey

CHAPTER 7
Other Systems

Integumentary System

Foundational Science: Integumentary System

The integumentary system (or skin) is the body's largest organ consisting of stratified dermal and epidermal layers, hair follicles, nails, sebaceous glands, and sweat glands. The avascular epidermis is the most superficial layer of skin. The dermis, known as the true skin, is well vascularized, and is characterized as elastic, flexible, and tough (Fig. 7-1).[1]

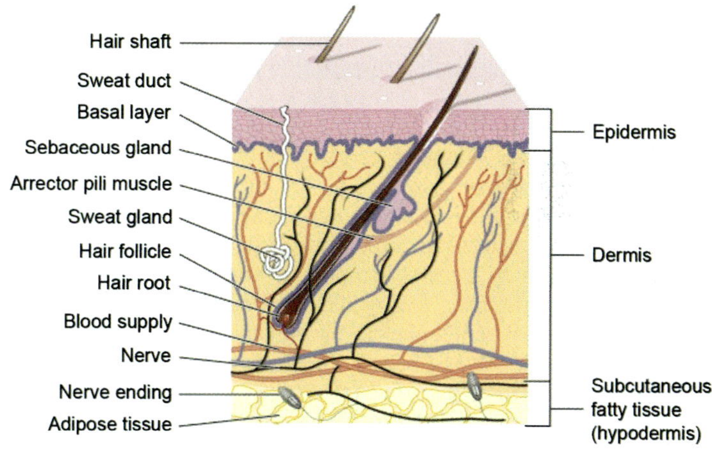

Fig. 7-1: Anatomy of the skin.

Key Functions of the Integumentary System

- Protection
- Sensation
- Thermoregulation
- Excretion of sweat
- Vitamin D synthesis

Phases of Normal Wound Healing[1,2]

Normal wound healing occurs as damaged tissues move through distinct yet overlapping phases of repair. In chronic wounds, this progression is either interrupted or delayed causing the wound to become "stuck" in a particular phase of healing.

Inflammatory Phase (1 to 10 days)[3,4]

Inflammation is the immune system's initial response to a wound. Temporary repair mechanisms rapidly re-establish hemostasis through platelet activation and the clotting cascade. Debris and necrotic tissue are removed and bacteria are killed by mast cells, neutrophils, and leukocytes. Processes occurring in the inflammatory phase establish a clean wound bed which signals tissue restoration and permanent repair processes to begin. Re-epithelialization typically begins within 24 hours at the wound borders, though visible signs are usually not observed earlier than three days after injury.

Proliferative Phase (3 to 21 days)[3,4]

The formation of new tissue signals the beginning of the proliferative phase. Capillary buds and granulation tissue begin to fill the wound bed creating a support structure for the migration of epithelial cells. Keratinocytes, endothelial cells, and fibroblasts are active and the collagen matrix is formed. Skin integrity is restored in the proliferative phase with wound closure occurring through epithelialization and wound contraction.

Maturation Phase (7 days to 2 years)[3,4]

The maturation, or remodeling phase is initiated when granulation tissue and epithelial differentiation begin to appear in the wound bed. As the maturation phase progresses, mechanisms of fiber reorganization and contraction shrink and thin the scar. An immature scar will appear red, raised, and rigid while a mature scar will appear pale, flat, and pliable. Scar tissue is remodeled and strengthened through the processes of collagen lysis and synthesis. Newly repaired tissues have approximately 15% of pre-injury tensile integrity and should be protected to prevent re-injury. Over time, tensile integrity may increase to as much as 80% of the pre-injury strength. Hypertrophic scarring, especially in relation to burn injuries, can significantly impact maturation phase progression. A burn without hypertrophic scarring will typically mature within four to eight weeks; burns with hypertrophic scarring, however, may require up to two years to reach maturity.

CONSIDER THIS
THE INFLAMMATORY PHASE AND CHRONIC WOUNDS[2]

An abnormal inflammatory response (e.g., chronic or delayed) is believed to be the most significant factor in delayed wound healing and chronicity. Re-injury, infection, poor tissue perfusion or the body's failure to initiate appropriate responses may prolong the inflammatory phase. Inflammation that persists chronically for weeks or months interferes with the initiation of proliferative phase processes and increases the risk of infection.

Anti-inflammatory or immunosuppressive medications, arterial insufficiency or conditions that alter immune responses (e.g., diabetes mellitus, alcoholism, AIDS) can limit the body's response to a wound. This can occur to the extent that the healing process is never truly initiated, resulting in a chronic wound. Differing from chronically inflamed wounds, chronic wounds show little if any of the usual inflammatory phase characteristics and fail to progress.

Healing by Intention[2,4]

Primary Intention

Healing by primary intention most commonly occurs in acute wounds with minimal tissue loss. Smooth clean edges are reapproximated and closed with sutures, staples or adhesives to facilitate re-epithelialization. Superficial partial-thickness wounds, such as abrasions or blisters, also heal by primary intention with epithelial migration over the wound bed frequently completed within 72 hours. Wounds healing by primary intention typically have minimal scarring and heal quickly in an uncomplicated and orderly progression (e.g., surgical incision, laceration, puncture, and superficial and partial-thickness wounds).

Secondary Intention

Healing by secondary intention permits wounds to close on their own without superficial closure. Wounds with characteristics such as significant tissue loss or necrosis, irregular or nonviable wound margins that cannot be reapproximated, infection or debris contamination typically heal by secondary intention. These wounds are often associated with pathology such as diabetes, ischemic conditions, pressure damage or inflammatory disease. A layer of granulation tissue will gradually fill the wound bed to the level of the surrounding skin, with closure occurring by wound contraction and scar formation. Wounds healing by secondary intention require ongoing wound care and have significantly larger scars than those healing by primary intention (e.g., neuropathic, arterial, venous or pressure ulcers, most full-thickness wounds, and chronically inflamed wounds).

Tertiary Intention

Healing by tertiary intention may also be referred to as delayed primary intention healing. Wounds at risk for developing complications, such as sepsis or dehiscence, may be temporarily left open. Once risk factors have been alleviated (e.g., wounds with significant edema, contamination from debris, at high risk for infection or with questionable vascular integrity) the wound is closed by the usual primary intention methods.

Factors Influencing Wound Healing

There are a variety of factors, not inherent to the wound itself, which can significantly impact the rate and degree of wound healing. Physical therapists should encourage patients to make positive changes with modifiable factors and assist them in compensating for unmodifiable factors.

Age: The epidermis thins and flattens as part of the aging process, making it more fragile and susceptible to injury from friction and shear. Decreased metabolism in older adults is also correlated with a decrease in the overall rate of wound healing.[2,4]

Co-morbidities: Medical co-morbidities such as cardio-pulmonary disease, vascular conditions, and diabetes mellitus can significantly delay wound healing. This is often attributed to poor tissue perfusion which limits the wound's ability to sustain cellular activity. Co-morbidities which suppress or compromise the immune system can result in altered inflammatory responses and increased risk of infection.[1,2]

Edema: Some degree of edema is considered a normal part of the body's inflammatory response to a wound. However, increased tissue pressure from excessive edema, such as with venous insufficiency or lymphedema, can negatively impact both tissue perfusion and the removal of cellular waste. This alteration in hemodynamics decreases the availability of oxygen and nutrients thus delaying healing and increasing the risk of infection.[1,2]

Harsh or Inappropriate Wound Care: Failure to use appropriate technique or best-practice interventions in wound care can contribute to wound healing delays. Vigorous wound irrigation, aggressive debridement, prolonged whirlpool exposure or the use of harsh cleansing techniques and agents can impair healing by further damaging peripheral and granulating tissues.[4]

Infection: Wound infection negatively impacts the restorative processes necessary for wound healing. Immune responses become overwhelmed as infectious bacteria compete with the body's own cells for available nutrients. Infectious bacteria can also release toxins into the wound causing further tissue damage and increasing the rate of cellular necrosis.[1,2]

Lifestyle: Regular physical activity and good nutrition facilitate wound healing by enhancing tissue perfusion and the availability of nutrients needed to sustain cellular activity. In contrast, smoking dramatically impedes wound healing by limiting the blood's oxygen carrying capacity. The resulting wound hypoxia slows healing and creates an ideal environment for anaerobic bacteria growth, thereby increasing the risk of wound infection.[1,2]

Medication: Medications from a variety of pharmacological classes can negatively impact wound healing. Common classes include anti-inflammatory, immunosuppressive, anti-coagulant, anti-neoplastic, steroid, and oral contraceptive agents. Undesirable physiologic effects may include a poor or prolonged inflammatory response, reduced blood supply, delayed collagen synthesis, and decreased tensile strength of repaired tissues.[1,2]

Obesity: Obesity is associated with numerous medical co-morbidities in addition to various inherent factors that may negatively impact wound healing. Poor periwound skin quality is susceptible to fissuring which increases the risk of wound infection. Increased skin tension heightens the risk of skin tears and limits options for reapproximation. Large skin folds create moist, warm environments contributing to skin maceration and bacterial growth which may lead to both the onset and perpetuation of wounds in skin crevasses.[2,5]

CONSIDER THIS

CONTAMINATED, COLONIZED OR INFECTED?[4]

Contamination: The presence of non-replicating bacteria on a wound surface that causes no additional tissue injury and does not stimulate an inflammatory immune response.

Colonization: The presence of replicating bacteria on a wound surface that does not invade or further injure tissues and does not stimulate an inflammatory immune response. Colonization can delay wound healing, however, colonized bacteria occasionally benefit wound healing by preventing more virulent organisms from proliferating in the wound bed.

Infection: The presence of replicating bacteria that invades viable tissue beyond the wound surface causing a visible inflammatory immune response. Infection will significantly delay wound healing and, if untreated, can progress to sepsis, osteomyelitis, and gangrene.

Wound Types

Acute Wounds[2]

Abrasion: An abrasion is a wound caused by a combination of friction and shear forces, typically over a rough surface, resulting in the scraping away of the skin's superficial layers.

Avulsion: A soft tissue avulsion, sometimes referred to as degloving, is a serious wound resulting from tension that causes skin to become detached from underlying structures.

Incisional wound: An incisional wound is most often associated with surgery and is created intentionally by means of a sharp object such as a scalpel or scissors.

Laceration: A laceration is a wound or irregular tear of tissues often associated with trauma. Lacerations can result from shear, tension or high force compression with the resultant wound characteristics dependent on the mechanism of injury.

Penetrating: A penetrating wound can result from various mechanisms of injury and is described as a wound that enters the interior of an organ or cavity.

Puncture: A puncture wound is made by a sharp pointed object as it penetrates the skin and underlying tissues. Typically, there is relatively little tissue damage beyond the wound tract, however, the risks of contamination and infection can be significant.

Skin tear: A skin tear often results from trauma to fragile skin such as bumping into an object, adhesive removal, shear or friction forces. The severity of a skin tear can range from a flap-like tear, that may or may not remain viable, to full-thickness tissue loss.

Ulcers

Arterial Insufficiency Ulcers[1,2]

Wounds resulting from arterial insufficiency occur secondary to inadequate circulation of oxygenated blood (e.g., ischemia) often due to complicating factors such as atherosclerosis.

General Recommendations:

- Rest
- Limb protection
- Risk reduction education
- Inspect legs and feet daily
- Avoid unnecessary leg elevation
- Avoid using heating pads or soaking feet in hot water
- Wear appropriately sized shoes with clean, seamless socks

CONSIDER THIS

ASSESSING PROTECTIVE SENSATION[4]

The loss of protective sensation in individuals with peripheral neuropathy can significantly increase the risk of tissue damage. Monofilament testing is a reliable method of assessing and documenting changes in protective sensation. Monofilament testing kits contain a variety of filament thicknesses which are applied perpendicular to the skin and held in place for one second with enough force to bend the filament into a "C" shape (Fig. 7-2).

Failure to perceive the application of a 10 gm monofilament indicates a loss of protective sensation (e.g., inability to feel a small pebble in a shoe or a developing blister) and places a patient at increased risk for developing a neuropathic ulcer. Failure to perceive a 75 gm monofilament indicates that an area is insensate.[4]

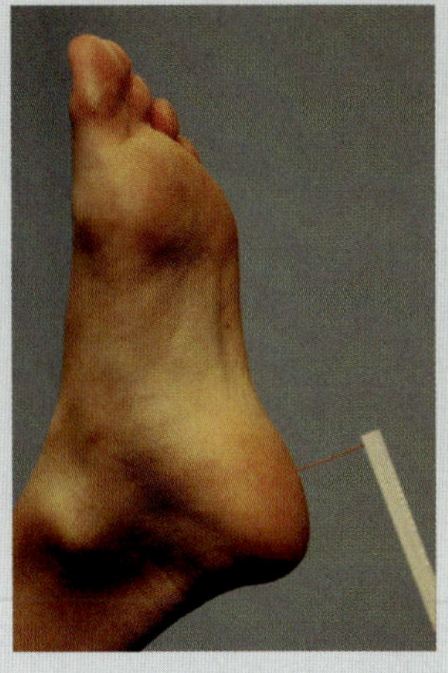

Fig. 7-2: A monofilament applied perpendicular to the target area.

Venous Insufficiency Ulcers[1,2]

Wounds resulting from venous insufficiency occur secondary to impaired functioning of the venous system resulting in inadequate circulation and eventual tissue damage and ulceration.

General Recommendations:

- Limb protection
- Risk reduction education
- Inspect legs and feet daily
- Compression to control edema
- Elevate legs above the heart when resting or sleeping
- Attempt active exercise including frequent range of motion
- Wear appropriately sized shoes with clean, seamless socks

Neuropathic Ulcers[1,2]

Neuropathic ulcers are a secondary complication usually associated with a combination of ischemia and neuropathy. Neuropathic ulcers are often associated with diabetes mellitus, however, any form of peripheral neuropathy poses an increased risk of wound development.

General Recommendations:

- Limb protection
- Risk reduction education
- Inspect legs and feet daily
- Inspect footwear for debris prior to donning
- Wear appropriately sized off-loading footwear with clean, cushioned, seamless socks

Pressure Ulcers[1,2]

Pressure ulcers, also referred to as decubitus ulcers, result from sustained or prolonged pressure on tissue at levels greater than that of capillary pressure. Skin covering bony prominences is particularly susceptible to localized ischemia and tissue necrosis due to pressure. Pressure injuries to deeper tissues may initially present as bruising or purple blisters under intact skin before opening to reveal full-thickness damage. Factors contributing to pressure ulcers include shearing forces, moisture, heat, friction, medications, muscle atrophy, malnutrition, and debilitating medical conditions. Valid and reliable pressure injury risk assessment tools are readily available (e.g., Braden Scale, Norton Scale) and typically include intervention recommendations based on the level of risk assessed.

General Recommendations:

- Repositioning every two hours in bed
- Management of excess moisture
- Off-loading with pressure relieving devices
- Inspect skin daily for signs of pressure damage
- Limit shear, traction, and friction forces over fragile skin

Characteristics of Lower Extremity Ulcers[1,2,4]			
	Arterial Insufficiency Ulcers	**Venous Insufficiency Ulcers**	**Neuropathic Ulcers**
Location	Lower one-third of leg, toes, web spaces (distal toes, dorsal foot, lateral malleolus)	Proximal to the medial malleolus	Areas of the foot susceptible to pressure or shear forces during weight bearing
Appearance	Smooth edges, well defined; lack granulation tissue; tend to be deep	Irregular shape; shallow	Well-defined oval or circle; callused rim; cracked periwound tissue; little to no wound bed necrosis with good granulation
Exudate	Minimal	Moderate/heavy	Low/moderate
Pain	Severe	Mild to moderate	None, however dysesthesia may be reported
Pedal Pulses	Diminished or absent	Normal	Diminished or absent; unreliable ankle-brachial index with diabetes
Edema	Normal	Increased	Normal
Skin Temperature	Decreased	Normal	Decreased
Tissue Changes	Thin and shiny; hair loss; yellow nails	Flaking, dry skin; brownish discoloration	Dry, inelastic, shiny skin; decreased or absent sweat and oil production
Miscellaneous	Leg elevation increases pain	Leg elevation lessens pain	Loss of protective sensation

** Additional detail regarding pressure injury characteristics and the National Pressure Ulcer Advisory Panel (NPUAP) descriptions are found in the Wound Assessment section.

Wound Assessment

Wound Classification by Depth of Injury[4]

Wounds that are not categorized as pressure or neuropathic ulcers (e.g., skin tears, surgical wounds, venous stasis ulcers) are classified based on the depth of tissue loss.

Superficial wound

A superficial wound causes trauma to the skin with the epidermis remaining intact, such as with a non-blistering sunburn. A superficial wound will typically heal as part of the inflammatory process.

Partial-thickness wound

A partial-thickness wound extends through the epidermis and possibly into, but not through, the dermis. Examples include abrasions, blisters, and skin tears. A partial-thickness wound will typically heal by re-epithelialization or epidermal resurfacing depending on the depth of injury.

Full-thickness wound

A full-thickness wound extends through the dermis into deeper structures such as subcutaneous fat. Wounds deeper than 4 millimeters are typically considered full-thickness and heal by secondary intention.

Subcutaneous wound

Subcutaneous wounds extend through integumentary tissues and involve deeper structures such as subcutaneous fat, muscle, tendon or bone. Subcutaneous wounds typically require healing by secondary intention.

Wagner Ulcer Grade Classification Scale	
Grade	**Description**
0	No open lesion, but may possess pre-ulcerative lesions; healed ulcers; presence of bony deformity
1	Superficial ulcer not involving subcutaneous tissue
2	Deep ulcer with penetration through the subcutaneous tissue; potentially exposing bone, tendon, ligament or joint capsule
3	Deep ulcer with osteitis, abscess or osteomyelitis
4	Gangrene of digit
5	Gangrene of foot requiring disarticulation

Wagner Ulcer Grade Classification System[1,2]

The Wagner Ulcer Grade Classification System categorizes dysvascular ulcers based on wound depth and the presence of infection. Most commonly associated with the assessment of diabetic foot ulcers, the scale can be appropriately used to categorize most ulcers arising from neuropathic, ischemic or arterial etiology.

Pressure Injury Staging

A pressure injury is localized damage to the skin and underlying soft tissue usually over a bony prominence or related to a medical or other device. The injury can present as intact skin or an open ulcer and may be painful. The injury occurs as a result of intense and/or prolonged pressure with or without shear. The tolerance of soft tissue for pressure and shear may also be affected by microclimate, nutrition, perfusion, and co-morbidities.

Stage 1 Pressure Injury: Non-blanchable erythema of intact skin

Intact skin with a localized area of non-blanchable erythema. Presence of blanchable erythema or changes in sensation, temperature, or firmness may precede visual changes. Color changes do not include purple or maroon discoloration; these may indicate deep tissue pressure injury.

Stage 2 Pressure Injury: Partial-thickness skin loss with exposed dermis

Partial-thickness loss of skin with exposed dermis. The wound bed is viable, pink or red, moist, and may also present as an intact or ruptured serum-filled blister. Adipose is not visible and deeper tissues are not visible. Granulation tissue, slough and eschar are not present. These injuries commonly result from adverse microclimate and shear over the pelvis and shear in the heel. This stage should not be used to describe moisture associated skin damage (MASD) including incontinence associated dermatitis (IAD), intertriginous dermatitis (ITD), medical adhesive related skin injury (MARSI), or traumatic wounds.

Stage 3 Pressure Injury: Full-thickness skin loss

Full-thickness loss of skin, in which adipose is visible in the ulcer and granulation tissue and epibole (rolled edges) are often present. Slough and/or eschar may be visible. The depth of tissue damage varies by anatomical location; areas of significant adiposity can develop deep wounds. Undermining and tunneling may occur. Fascia, muscle, tendon, ligament, cartilage and/or bone are not exposed. If slough or eschar obscures the extent of tissue loss, this is an Unstageable Pressure Injury.

Stage 4 Pressure Injury: Full-thickness skin and tissue loss

Full-thickness skin and tissue loss with exposed or directly palpable fascia, muscle, tendon, ligament, cartilage or bone in the ulcer. Slough and/or eschar may be visible. Epibole (rolled edges), undermining and/or tunneling often occur. Depth varies by anatomical location. If slough or eschar obscures the extent of tissue loss this is an Unstageable Pressure Injury.

Unstageable Pressure Injury: Obscured full-thickness skin and tissue loss

Full-thickness skin and tissue loss in which the extent of tissue damage within the ulcer cannot be confirmed because it is obscured by slough or eschar. If slough or eschar is removed, a Stage 3 or Stage 4 pressure injury will be revealed. Stable eschar (i.e. dry, adherent, intact without erythema) on the heel or ischemic limb should not be softened or removed.

Deep Tissue Pressure Injury: Persistent non-blanchable deep red, maroon or purple discoloration

Intact or non-intact skin with localized area of persistent non-blanchable deep red, maroon, purple discoloration or epidermal separation revealing a dark wound bed or blood filled blister. Pain and temperature change often precede skin color changes. Discoloration may appear differently in darkly pigmented skin. This injury results from intense and/or prolonged pressure and shear forces at the bone-muscle interface. The wound may evolve rapidly to reveal the actual extent of tissue injury, or may resolve without tissue loss. If necrotic tissue, subcutaneous tissue, granulation tissue, fascia, muscle or other underlying structures are visible, this indicates a full-thickness pressure injury (Unstageable, Stage 3 or Stage 4). Do not use deep tissue pressure injury to describe vascular, traumatic, neuropathic, or dermatologic conditions.

Adapted from NPUAP's Pressure Ulcer Staging System, Revised 2016

SPOTLIGHT ON SAFETY

INTEGUMENTARY INJURY AND AUTONOMIC DYSREFLEXIA[3]

Ingrown toenails, burns, pressure ulcers, blisters, and other integumentary trauma can trigger an episode of autonomic dysreflexia when occurring below the level of a patient's spinal cord injury.

Since this is a potentially life-threatening condition, it is important for therapists to recognize signs, symptoms, and causative factors of the condition as well as how to immediately and appropriately intervene. If symptoms do not begin to resolve after the patient has been assisted into a sitting position with catheter obstruction ruled out, the therapist should activate the emergency response system and begin to assess for other potential sources of noxious stimuli.

Bony Prominences Associated with Pressure Injuries[1]

Supine	Prone	Sidelying	Sitting (Chair)
Occiput	Forehead	Ears	Spine of the scapula
Spine of scapula	Anterior portion of acromion process	Lateral portion of acromion process	Vertebral spinous processes
Inferior angle of scapula	Anterior head of humerus	Lateral head of humerus	Ischial tuberosities
Vertebral spinous processes	Sternum	Lateral epicondyle of humerus	
Medial epicondyle of humerus	Anterior superior iliac spine	Greater trochanter	
Posterior iliac crest	Patella	Head of fibula	
Sacrum	Dorsum of foot	Lateral malleolus	
Coccyx		Medial malleolus	
Heel			

Exudate Classification[1]

Serous: Presents with a clear, light color and a thin, watery consistency. Serous exudate is considered to be normal in a healthy healing wound and is observed during the inflammatory and proliferative phases of healing.

Sanguineous: Presents with a red color and a thin, watery consistency. The red appearance of sanguineous exudate is due to the presence of blood which may become brown if allowed to dehydrate. Sanguineous exudate may be indicative of new blood vessel growth or the disruption of blood vessels.

Serosanguineous: Presents with a light red or pink color and a thin, watery consistency. Serosanguineous exudate is considered to be normal in a healthy healing wound and is typically observed during the inflammatory and proliferative phases of healing.

Seropurulent: Presents as cloudy or opaque, with a yellow or tan color and a thin, watery consistency. Seropurulent exudate may be an early warning sign of an impending infection and is always considered an abnormal finding.

Purulent: Presents with a yellow or green color and a thick, viscous consistency. Purulent exudate is generally an indicator of wound infection and is always considered an abnormal finding.

CONSIDER THIS

COMPONENTS OF WOUND EXAMINATION AND DOCUMENTATION[4]

There are a number of important areas that therapists must thoroughly assess and document when examining a wound. Each element provides the therapist with potentially useful information that can guide the therapist when developing an individualized plan of care (Fig. 7-3).

- etiology
- location
- wound type and classification
- clinical signs of infection
- area, depth, and shape of wound
- condition of wound margins/edges
- undermining or tunneling
- involvement of underlying structures (e.g., tendon/bone/muscle)
- stage of healing
- color of base
- odor
- exudate type and volume
- chronicity
- response to previous treatment
- surrounding skin/scar assessment
- presence of necrosis

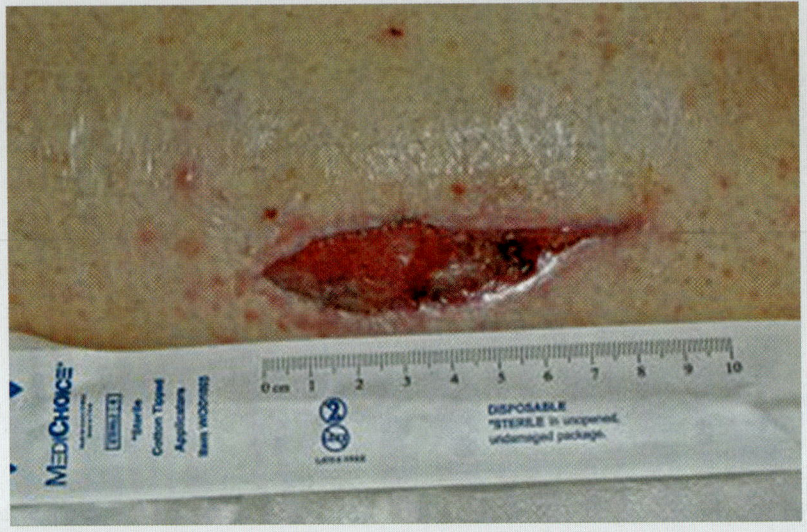

Fig. 7-3: Quantifying the area of a wound.

Necrotic Tissue Types[1,4]

Necrotic tissue is dead tissue resulting from the localized physiological and enzymatic changes associated with cell death. Necrotic tissue is often documented and named by the specific type observed, and may also be referred to as devitalized or nonviable tissue. The color, consistency, and adherence of necrotic tissue varies depending on other wound characteristics such as hydration and bacterial activity.

Eschar: Eschar is described as hard or leathery, black/brown, dehydrated tissue that tends to be firmly adhered to the wound bed.

Gangrene: Gangrene refers to the death and decay of tissue resulting from an interruption in blood flow to an area of the body. Some types of gangrene are also characterized by the presence of bacterial infection. Gangrene most commonly affects the extremities, but can also occur in muscles and internal organs.

Hyperkeratosis: Hyperkeratosis, also referred to as callus, is typically white/gray in color and can vary in texture from firm to soggy depending on the moisture level in surrounding tissue.

Slough: Slough is described as moist, stringy or mucinous, white/yellow tissue that tends to be loosely attached in clumps to the wound bed.

Wound Healing Interventions

Red-Yellow-Black System[2]

Red-Yellow-Black System		
Color	**Wound Description**	**Goals**
Red	Pink granulation tissue	Protect wound; maintain moist environment
Yellow	Moist, yellow slough	Remove exudate and debris; absorb drainage
Black	Black, thick eschar firmly adhered	Debride necrotic tissue

Selective Debridement[2]

Selective debridement involves the removal of only nonviable tissues from a wound. Selective debridement is most often performed by sharp debridement, enzymatic debridement or autolytic debridement.

Sharp Debridement

Sharp debridement requires the use of a scalpel, scissors, and/or forceps to selectively remove devitalized tissue, foreign material or debris from a wound. Sharp debridement is most often used for wounds with large amounts of thick, adherent, necrotic tissue; however, it may also be used in the presence of cellulitis or sepsis. Sharp debridement is the most expedient form of removing necrotic tissue. Physical therapists are permitted to perform sharp, selective debridement as a procedural intervention.

Enzymatic Debridement

Enzymatic debridement refers to the topical application of an enzymatic preparation to necrotic tissue. Enzymatic debridement can be used on infected and non-infected wounds with necrotic tissue. This type of debridement may be used for wounds that have not responded to autolytic debridement or in conjunction with other debridement techniques. Enzymatic debridement can be slow to establish a clean wound bed and should be discontinued once devitalized tissue is removed to avoid damage to adjacent healthy tissue.

Autolytic Debridement

Autolytic debridement refers to the use of the body's own mechanisms to remove nonviable tissue. Common methods of autolytic debridement include the use of transparent films, hydrocolloids, hydrogels, and alginates. Autolytic debridement establishes a moist wound environment that rehydrates necrotic tissue and eschar, facilitating enzymatic digestion of the nonviable tissue. This type of debridement is non-invasive and pain free. Autolytic debridement can be used with any amount of necrotic tissue, however, requires a longer healing period and is not commonly performed on infected wounds.

Non-selective Debridement[1,2,4]

Non-selective debridement involves the removal of both viable and nonviable tissues from a wound. Non-selective debridement is often termed "mechanical debridement" and is most commonly performed via wet-to-dry dressings, wound irrigation, and hydrotherapy (whirlpool).

Wet-to-dry Dressings

Wet-to-dry dressings refer to the application of a moistened gauze dressing over an area of necrotic tissue. The dressing is allowed to dry completely and is later removed, along with any necrotic tissue that has adhered to the gauze. Wet-to-dry dressings are most often used to debride wounds with moderate amounts of exudate and necrotic tissue. This type of debridement should be used sparingly on wounds containing both necrotic and viable tissue since granulation tissue will be traumatized in the process. Removal of dry dressings from granulation tissue may cause bleeding and be extremely painful.

Wound Irrigation

Wound irrigation removes necrotic tissue from the wound bed using pressurized fluid. Pulsatile lavage is an example of wound irrigation that uses a pressurized stream of irrigation solution. This type of debridement is most desirable for wounds that are infected or have loose debris. Many devices permit variable pressure settings and provide suction for the removal of exudate and debris.

Hydrotherapy

Hydrotherapy is most commonly employed using a whirlpool tank with agitation directed toward a wound requiring debridement. This process softens and loosens adherent necrotic tissue. Physical therapists must be aware of potential hydrotherapy side effects such as maceration of viable tissue, edema from dependent lower extremity positioning, and systemic effects such as hypotension.

Modalities and Physical Agents[1,2,5]

Negative Pressure Wound Therapy (NPWT)

NPWT, also referred to as vacuum-assisted closure (V.A.C.), is a non-invasive wound care modality used to facilitate healing and manage drainage (Fig. 7-4). A sterile foam dressing is placed in the wound and sealed with an airtight secondary dressing which attaches via tubing to a vacuum pump with a reservoir container. Treatment protocols vary depending on wound characteristics.

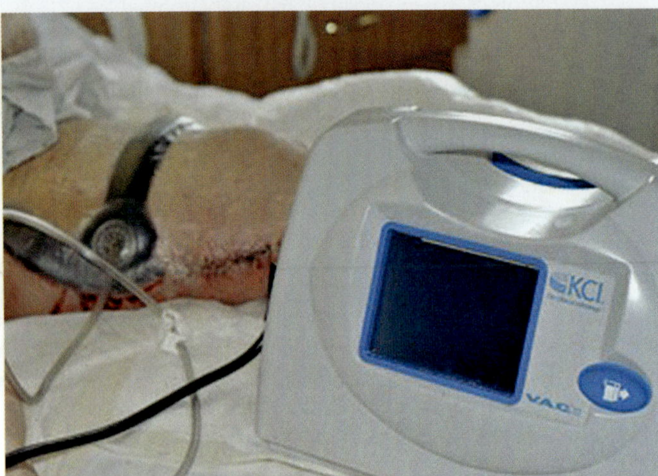

Fig. 7-4: Negative pressure wound therapy applied to the lower extremity.

Indications

Chronic or acute wounds which cannot be closed by primary intention such as dehisced surgical incisions, full-thickness wounds, partial-thickness burns, heavily draining granular wounds, flaps, grafts, and most ulcer types.

Contraindications

Malignancy within the wound, insufficient vascularity to sustain wound healing, large amounts of necrotic tissue with eschar present, untreated osteomyelitis, fistulas to organs or body cavities, exposed arteries or veins, and uncontrolled pain.

Advantages

- Provides management of wound drainage
- Maintains a moist wound environment
- Decreases interstitial edema
- Decreases bacterial colonization
- Increases capillary blood flow
- Increases granular tissue formation
- Enhances epithelial cell migration

Disadvantages

- Requires special supplies and training
- Treatment can be painful
- Not reimbursed in acute or long-term care settings

Hyperbaric Oxygen

Hyperbaric oxygen refers to the inhalation of 100% oxygen delivered at pressures greater than one atmosphere. Hyperbaric oxygen treatment is delivered in a closed chamber typically at pressures two to three times that of the atmosphere, effectively reducing edema and hyperoxygenating tissues.

Indications

Osteomyelitis, diabetic wounds, crush injuries, compartment syndromes, necrotizing soft tissue infection, thermal burns, radiation necrosis, and compromised flaps and grafts.

Contraindications

Terminal illness, untreated pneumothorax, active malignancy, pregnancy, seizure disorder, emphysema, and use of certain chemotherapy agents.

Advantages

- Antibiotic effects
- Stimulation of fibroblast production and collagen synthesis
- Stimulation of growth factor release and epithelialization

Disadvantages

- Specialized equipment is not widely available
- Cannot be used with active malignancy

Growth Factors

Growth factors used in wound healing are derived from naturally occurring protein factors. These substances facilitate healing by stimulating the activity of specific cell types (e.g., neutrophils, endothelial cells, fibroblasts). Currently, only a limited number of growth factors have been approved by the Food and Drug Administration for topical wound healing applications.

Indications

Neuropathic ulcers extending into or through subcutaneous tissue with adequate circulation to sustain wound healing.

Contraindications

Wounds closed by primary intention, patients with known hypersensitivity to any component of the product or a history of neoplasm at the application site.

Advantages:

- Adjunct to promote wound healing environment
- Increases growth rate of new tissue
- Promotes cell division

Disadvantages

- Costly
- Poor reimbursement
- Additional research is needed
- Secondary dressing required
- Requires refrigeration
- Limited number of products have been approved by the Food and Drug Administration

CONSIDER THIS

THERAPEUTIC MODALITIES WITH WOUND HEALING APPLICATIONS[1]

Therapeutic ultrasound applied at a low intensity with pulsed duty cycle has been shown to enhance all phases of wound healing. During the inflammatory and proliferative phases, fibroblast, endothelial, and white blood cell activity are stimulated by ultrasound. Ultrasound use during these early stages of repair has been shown to enhance the strength and elasticity of scar tissue. Recommended treatment protocols vary depending on the phase of healing and intended outcome (e.g., restarting the inflammatory phase of healing in a chronic ulcer vs. dispersing ecchymosis associated with skin tears or contusions to reduce pain and edema).

High-voltage pulsed current (HVPC) electrical stimulation has been shown to enhance healing in numerous types of wounds including chronic ulcers, burns, and donor and graft sites. The application of monophasic direct current stimulates angiogenesis and epithelial migration, decreases bacterial activity and wound pain, and increases oxygen perfusion and tensile strength. HVPC is typically applied using a sensory or sub-sensory intensity. Treatment protocols vary widely depending on the stage of healing or presence of infection.

Types of Dressings[1,2,4]

Dressings may be defined as either primary or secondary. A primary dressing is one that comes into direct contact with a wound. A number of primary dressings include a self-adhesive backing and do not require a secondary dressing. Secondary dressings are placed directly over the primary dressing to provide additional protection, absorption, occlusion, and/or to secure the primary dressing in place.

Alginates

Alginate dressings are derived from a seaweed extraction, specifically, the calcium salt component of alginic acid. Alginates are highly absorptive, but are also highly permeable and non-occlusive. As a result, they require a secondary dressing. Alginate dressings act as a hemostat and create a hydrophilic gel through the interaction of calcium ions in the dressing and sodium ions in the wound exudate.

Indications

Alginates are typically used on partial or full-thickness draining wounds such as pressure or venous insufficiency ulcers. Alginates are often used on infected wounds due to the likelihood of excessive drainage.

Advantages

- High absorptive capacity
- Enables autolytic debridement
- Offers protection from microbial contamination
- Can be used on infected or non-infected wounds
- Non-adhering to wound

Disadvantages

- May require frequent dressing changes based on level of exudate
- Requires a secondary dressing
- Cannot be used on wounds with an exposed tendon, joint capsule or bone

Foam Dressings

Foam dressings are comprised of a hydrophilic polyurethane base that contacts the wound surface and a hydrophobic outer layer. The dressings allow exudate to be absorbed into the foam through the hydrophilic layer. The dressings are most commonly available in sheets or pads with varying degrees of thickness. Semipermeable foam dressings are produced in adhesive and non-adhesive forms. Non-adhesive forms require a secondary dressing.

Indications

Foam dressings are used to provide protection and absorption over partial and full-thickness wounds with varying levels of exudate. They can also be used as secondary dressings over amorphous hydrogels.

Advantages

- Provides a moist environment for wound healing
- Available in adhesive and non-adhesive forms
- Provides prophylactic protection and cushioning
- Encourages autolytic debridement
- Provides moderate absorption

Disadvantages

- May tend to roll in areas of excessive friction
- Adhesive form may traumatize periwound area upon removal
- Lack of transparency makes inspection of wound difficult

Gauze

Gauze dressings are manufactured from yarn or thread and are the most readily available dressing used in inpatient environments. Gauze dressings come in many shapes and sizes (e.g., sheets, squares, rolls, packing strips). Impregnated gauze is a variation of woven gauze in which various materials such as petrolatum, zinc or antimicrobials have been added.

Indications

Gauze dressings are commonly used on infected or non-infected wounds of any size. The dressings can be used for wet-to-wet, wet-to-moist or wet-to-dry debridement.

Advantages

- Readily available and cost effective short-term dressings
- Can be used alone or in combination with other dressings and topical agents
- Can modify number of layers to accommodate for changing wound status
- Can be used on infected or non-infected wounds

Disadvantages

- Has a tendency to adhere to the wound bed traumatizing viable tissue on removal
- Highly permeable
- Requires frequent dressing changes
- Prolonged use decreases cost effectiveness
- Increased infection rate compared to occlusive dressings

Hydrocolloids

Hydrocolloid dressings consist of gel-forming polymers (e.g., carboxymethylcellulose, gelatin, pectin) backed by a strong film or foam adhesive. The dressing does not attach to the wound itself but instead anchors to the intact surrounding skin. The dressings absorb exudate by swelling into a gel-like mass and vary in permeability, thickness, and transparency.

Indications

Hydrocolloids are useful for partial and full-thickness wounds. The dressings can be used effectively with granular or necrotic wounds.

Advantages

- Provides a moist environment for wound healing
- Enables autolytic debridement
- Offers protection from microbial contamination
- Provides moderate absorption
- Does not require a secondary dressing
- Provides a waterproof surface

Disadvantages

- May traumatize surrounding intact skin upon removal
- May tend to roll in areas of excessive friction
- Cannot be used on infected wounds

Hydrogels

Hydrogels consist of varying amounts of water and gel-forming materials such as glycerin. The dressings are typically available in both sheet and amorphous forms.

Indications

Hydrogels are moisture retentive and commonly used on superficial and partial-thickness wounds (e.g., abrasions, blisters, pressure ulcers) that have minimal drainage.

Advantages

- Provides a moist environment for wound healing
- Enables autolytic debridement
- May reduce pressure and diminish pain
- Can be used as a coupling agent for ultrasound
- Minimally adheres to wound
- Some products have absorptive properties

Disadvantages

- Potential for dressings to dehydrate
- Cannot be used on wounds with significant drainage
- Typically requires a secondary dressing

Transparent Film

Transparent film dressings are thin membranes made from transparent polyurethane with water-resistant adhesives. The dressings are permeable to vapor and oxygen, but are largely impermeable to bacteria and water. They are highly elastic, conform to a variety of body contours, and allow easy visual inspection of the wound since they are transparent.

Indications

Film dressings are useful for superficial or partial-thickness wounds with minimal drainage (e.g., scalds, abrasions, lacerations).

Advantages

- Provides a moist environment for wound healing
- Enables autolytic debridement
- Allows visualization of the wound
- Resistant to shearing and frictional forces
- Cost effective over time

Disadvantages

- Excessive exudate accumulation can result in periwound maceration
- Adhesive may traumatize periwound area upon removal
- Cannot be used on infected wounds

CONSIDER THIS

COMBINATION DRESSINGS USING SILVER AND IODINE[1,2]

Silver and iodine are elemental broad-spectrum antimicrobial agents that have become valuable adjuncts to wound healing interventions. First used in topical applications (e.g., powder, ointment, cream), these elements control microorganism activity in wound beds without damaging viable tissue. Many silver and iodine-impregnated dressings also help to maintain a moist wound healing environment.

Absorbency and recommended frequency of dressing changes are product dependent with many requiring a secondary dressing.

Moisture and Occlusion[2,4]

A dry wound bed slows normal metabolic functions, impeding the healing process. Dry peripheral tissues are at risk for developing cracks or fissures that can become open avenues for infection. Conversely, prolonged excessive moisture (e.g., from poorly managed exudate or incontinence) will cause maceration damage and erosion of intact peripheral tissues.

In an appropriately moist wound environment, macrophages appear earlier and in greater numbers helping to reduce the risk of infection. Collagen synthesis and epithelialization rate are enhanced, facilitating more rapid wound closure. In exudating wounds, moisture must be well managed to prevent damage to surrounding tissue. In dry wounds, moisture must be added in order to maintain hydration and sustain cellular activity. Maintaining an appropriately moist wound bed requires a delicate balance often necessitating specialized dressings to appropriately manage exudate and provide some level of occlusion.

Occlusion refers to the ability of a dressing to transmit moisture, vapor or gases between a wound bed and the atmosphere. A fully occlusive substance would be completely impermeable (e.g., latex gloves), while a non-occlusive substance would be completely permeable (e.g., gauze pads). Wound dressings are typically classified according to this occlusion continuum or by their moisture retention properties.

Dressings from Most Occlusive to Non-Occlusive	Dressings from Most to Least Moisture Retentive
Hydrocolloids	Alginates
Hydrogels	Semipermeable foams
Semipermeable foam	Hydrocolloids
Semipermeable film	Hydrogels
Impregnated gauze	Semipermeable films
Alginates	
Traditional gauze	

CONSIDER THIS

INCONTINENCE AND TISSUE INJURY[5]

Incontinence refers to the inability to control urination or defecation. A patient who is incontinent is at a significantly increased risk of tissue injury or in the presence of existing tissue injury, may experience additional complications including delayed healing.

- Urine and feces are typically acidic in composition and can contribute to tissue irritation and erosion.
- Skin shear and friction are increased in the presence of mild to moderate moisture.
- Macerated skin has decreased epidermal resilience to shear and friction forces.
- Harsh cleansers, hot water, and scrubbing will make delicate tissues more friable.
- Mild cleansers, warm water, and minimal friction should be used when cleansing to minimize irritation.
- Topical agents should be employed both to maintain the skin's natural moisture and act as a barrier to excessive moisture from incontinence.
- Emollient creams and ointments are typically better choices for skin moisturizers than watery lotions as they tend to have higher concentrations of solids and oils requiring less frequent reapplication and providing better barrier protection.

Skin Care Products[2,3]

Therapeutic moisturizers: (e.g., lotion, cream) Lotions are largely water-based and best used to replace skin moisture that has been lost either to the air or as a result of frequent hand washing. Creams are thicker water-based substances with higher concentrations of solids and oils than lotions, making the need for reapplication less frequent. Therapeutic moisturizers are intended to maintain the skin's natural moisture and prevent tissue cracking due to dryness, but do not typically protect the skin from excessive moisture.

Moisture barriers: (e.g., ointment) Moisture barriers are designed to adhere to the skin and repel excess moisture from protected areas. They are frequently used to protect surrounding skin from a heavily draining wound or perineal tissues from exposure to incontinence.

Liquid skin protectants: (e.g., skin sealant) Liquid skin protectant is applied to skin and when dry it creates a thin plastic film protecting the skin from adhesive-related tissue damage. This thin barrier also offers some degree of moisture protection. Skin protectant application varies slightly depending on packaging (e.g., swab, wipes, tube, bottle). Regardless, once applied to the skin it should be allowed to dry fully before an adhesive product is applied over it.

Skin cleansers: Skin cleansers are liquid agents typically intended for use on the skin of patients at risk for breakdown. Ingredients often have a pH balancing component that is especially beneficial for perineal cleansing in patients who are incontinent. Skin cleansers are designed to be less drying to the skin and more effective than usual soap or detergent skin products.

Wound cleansers: Wound cleansers vary from simple saline solutions to more complex compositions with cytotoxicity. Many wound cleansers have the potential to cause inflammation, however, this quality is product dependent. Wound cleansers are not typically designed to remove necrotic tissue, but rather associated wound substances such as foreign materials, exudate and dried blood.

Wound Terminology[1,2,4,5]

Contusion: An injury, usually caused by a blow, that does not disrupt skin integrity. The injury is characterized by pain, edema, and discoloration which appears as a result of blood seepage under the surface of the skin.

Dehiscence: The separation, rupture or splitting of a wound closed by primary intention. This disruption of previously approximated surfaces may be superficial or involve all layers of tissue.

Dermis: The vascular layer of skin located below the epidermis containing hair follicles, sebaceous glands, sweat glands, lymphatic and blood vessels, and nerve endings.

Desiccated: The drying out or dehydration of a wound. Desiccation often results from poor dressing selection that does not control the evaporation of wound bed moisture.

Desquamation: The peeling or shedding of the outer layers of the epidermis. Desquamation normally occurs in small scales, although certain conditions, injuries, and medications may cause peeling in larger scales or sheets and extend to deeper layers of the skin.

Ecchymosis: The discoloration occurring below intact skin resulting from trauma to underlying blood vessels and blood seeping into tissues. The discoloration is typically blue-black, changing in time to a greenish brown or yellow color. An area where ecchymosis is present is commonly referred to as a bruise.

Epidermis: The superficial, avascular epithelial layer of the skin that includes flat, scale-like squamous cells, round basal cells, and melanocytes which produce melanin and give skin its color.

Erythema: A diffuse redness of the skin often resulting from capillary dilation and congestion or inflammation.

Friable: Tissue that readily tears, fragments or bleeds when gently palpated or manipulated.

Hematoma: A localized swelling or mass of clotted blood confined to a tissue, organ or space usually caused by a break in a blood vessel.

Hypergranulation: Increased thickness of the granular layer of the epidermis that exceeds the surface height of the skin.

Hyperpigmentation: An excess of pigment in a tissue that causes it to appear darker than surrounding tissues.

Hypertrophic scar: An abnormal scar resulting from excessive collagen formation during healing. A hypertrophic scar is typically raised, red, and firm with disorganized collagen fibers.

Keloid: An abnormal scar formation that is out of proportion to the scarring required for normal tissue repair and is comprised of irregularly distributed collagen bands. A keloid scar typically exceeds the boundaries of the original wound appearing red, thick, raised, and firm.

Maceration: The skin softening and degeneration that results from prolonged exposure to water or other fluids.

Normotrophic scar: A scar characterized by the organized formation of collagen fibers that align in a parallel fashion.

Turgor: The relative speed with which the skin resumes its normal appearance after being lightly pinched. Turgor is an indicator of skin elasticity and hydration and normally occurs more slowly in older adults.

Ulcer: An open sore or lesion of the skin accompanied by sloughing of inflamed necrotic tissue.

Burns

Types of Burns[6]

Thermal burn: Caused by conduction or convection. Examples include burns resulting from contact with a hot liquid, fire or steam.

Electrical burn: Caused by the passage of electrical current through the body. Typically there is an entrance and an exit wound. Complications can include cardiac arrhythmias, respiratory arrest, renal failure, neurological damage, and fractures. A burn caused by a lightning strike is an example of an electrical burn.

Chemical burn: Occurs when certain chemical compounds come in contact with the body. The reaction will continue until the chemical compound is diluted at the site of contact. Compounds that cause chemical burns include sulfuric acid, lye, hydrochloric acid, and gasoline.

Radiation burn: Occurs most commonly with exposure to external beam radiation therapy. DNA is altered in exposed tissues and ischemic injury may be irreversible. Complications may include severe blistering and desquamation, non-healing wounds, tissue fibrosis, permanent discoloration, and new malignancies.

Zones of Injury[3]

Zone of coagulation: The area of the burn that received the most severe injury with irreversible cell damage.

Zone of stasis: The area of less severe injury that possesses reversible damage and surrounds the zone of coagulation.

Zone of hyperemia: The area surrounding the zone of stasis that presents with inflammation, but will fully recover without any intervention or permanent damage.

Burn Classification[3,6]

The extent and severity of a burn is dependent on gender, age, duration of burn, type of burn, and affected area. Burns are most appropriately classified according to the depth of tissue destruction.

Superficial burn: A superficial burn involves only the outer epidermis. The involved area may be red with slight edema. Healing occurs without peeling or evidence of scarring in two to five days.

Superficial partial-thickness burn: A superficial partial-thickness burn involves the epidermis and the upper portion of the dermis. The involved area may be extremely painful and exhibit blisters. Healing occurs with minimal to no scarring in 5-21 days.

Deep partial-thickness burn: A deep partial-thickness burn involves complete destruction of the epidermis and the majority of the dermis. The involved area may appear to be discolored with broken blisters and edema. Damage to nerve endings may result in only moderate levels of pain. Hypertrophic or keloid scarring may occur. In the absence of infection, healing will occur in 21-35 days.

SPOTLIGHT ON SAFETY
IONTOPHORESIS RELATED BURNS[7]

Chemical burns from iontophoresis occur when skin pH increases or decreases beyond the range of normal tolerance. Chemical burns are typically more severe under the negative electrode where pooling of the alkaline medium can occur. This can begin to erode the insulating epidermis. With skin resistance reduced, electrical current delivery increases, further accelerating skin erosion.

Factors contributing to chemical burns from iontophoresis include treatment delivered with excessive current, prolonged duration, and electrode placement over defective skin areas with lower resistance.

Poor iontophoresis electrode placement can contribute to a thermal burn in cases of excessive impedance or poor electrode contact.

Full-thickness burn: A full-thickness burn involves complete destruction of the epidermis and dermis along with partial damage to the subcutaneous fat layer. The involved area typically presents with eschar formation and minimal pain. Patients with full-thickness burns require grafts and are susceptible to infection. Healing time varies significantly with smaller areas healing in a matter of weeks, with or without grafting, and larger areas requiring grafting and potentially months to heal.

Subdermal burn: A subdermal burn involves the complete destruction of the epidermis, dermis, and subcutaneous tissue. Subdermal burns may involve muscle and bone and as a result, often require multiple surgical interventions and extensive healing time.

Rule of Nines

Allows for a gross approximation of the percentage of the body affected by a burn. The rule of nines does not account for severity.

Adult Values

Head and neck	**9%**
Anterior trunk	**18%**
Posterior trunk	**18%**
Bilateral anterior arm, forearm, and hand	**9%**
Bilateral posterior arm, forearm, and hand	**9%**
Genital region	**1%**
Bilateral anterior leg and foot	**18%**
Bilateral posterior leg and foot	**18%**

Child Values

A child under one year has 9% taken from the lower extremities and added to the head and neck region. Each year of life, 1% is distributed back to the lower extremities until the age of nine when the head is considered to be the same proportion as an adult.

Anticipated Deformities Based on Burn Location

Area	Anticipated deformity	Splinting type
Anterior neck	Flexion with possible lateral flexion	Soft collar, molded collar, Philadelphia collar
Anterior chest and axilla	Shoulder adduction, extension, and medial rotation	Axillary or airplane splint, shoulder abduction brace
Elbow	Flexion and pronation	Gutter splint, conforming splint, three-point splint, air splint
Hand and wrist	Extension or hyperextension of the MCP joints; flexion of the IP joints; adduction and flexion of the thumb; flexion of the wrist	Wrist splint, thumb spica splint, palmar or dorsal extension splint
Hip	Flexion and adduction	Anterior hip spica, abduction splint
Knee	Flexion	Conforming splint, three-point splint, air splint
Ankle	Plantar flexion	Posterior foot drop splint, posterior ankle conforming splint, anterior ankle conforming splint

CONSIDER THIS

CALCULATING BURN SEVERITY[6]

Like the rule of nines, the Lund and Browder method also provides an estimated calculation of the extent of body surface area burned based on assigned percentages. This method, however, offers a more detailed calculation for children under the age of seven.

While both the rule of nines and the Lund and Browder method provide a gross surface area burned calculation method, neither offer indications of severity or prognosis. Prognostic burn indexes have been developed as more thorough evaluative tools used to predict medical attention needs, outcomes, and mortality by taking into account both the surface area burned and the severity of burns.

Scar Management[3,6]

Hypertrophic scarring is the result of an imbalance between collagen synthesis and lysis during healing, and can occur with any integumentary injury. The development of hypertrophic scarring is particularly common in relation to severe burn injuries. Complications of hypertrophic scarring may include contracture, adhesions, hypersensitivity, functional limitation, and poor cosmesis.

Scar assessment: Assessment devices, such as a tonometer, and rating scales aid in quantifying scar characteristics. A number of rating scales are available to objectively document observed characteristics. These tend to be more helpful in the assessment and re-assessment of an individual rather than for comparative assessment of a group. General characteristics that should be documented include location, sensation, texture, pigmentation, vascularity, pliability, and height.

Scar massage: Friction massage is advocated to loosen adhesions between cutaneous scar tissue and underlying structures. Reported benefits include decreased sensitivity and improved pliability. Caution should be taken not to begin scar massage too soon or too aggressively due to the risk of causing re-injury or re-initiating the inflammatory phase of healing. Massage techniques should be slow and firm using perpendicular, parallel, circular, and/or rolling strokes to mobilize tissue layers.

Compression garments: Compression therapy to reduce hypertrophic scarring is typically recommended for burns requiring greater than 14 days to heal. The use of sustained compression from 15-35 mm Hg is believed to create an environment that facilitates the balance of collagen synthesis and lysis, improving scar structure. Compression is applied by custom-made garments worn for 22-23 hours per day until the scar has matured. Silicone or foam inserts may be necessary to provide sufficient pressure over small areas or concave surfaces. For optimal effect, it is recommended that the use of compression garments begins between two weeks and two months after wound closure or grafting, continuing for up to two years.

CONSIDER THIS

DESENSITIZATION TECHNIQUES[8]

As with some patients status post amputation, patients who have sustained severe burns are susceptible to developing hypersensitivity that can become functionally limiting. Incorporating desensitization techniques into the plan of care and a patient's self-care routine can significantly improve a patient's tolerance to variable temperatures, touch, pressure, and vibration, thereby decreasing discomfort and improving functional abilities.

Desensitization interventions typically include variable texture, pressure, and vibratory sensations applied to the affected area by either rubbing, tapping or rolling motions. The use of particle contact (e.g., container of dry beans, popcorn kernels or fluidotherapy) can be beneficial in desensitizing distal extremities. Compression and TENS have also been shown to have clinical applications for desensitization goals.

It is recommended that desensitization interventions be performed for five to ten minutes, three to four times daily. Each session should begin with a sensation that is slightly irritating, but tolerable, and progress to more noxious stimuli. A textural progression may include: feather, cotton ball, chamois cloth, soft terry cloth, corduroy cloth, rough terry cloth, wool.

Topical Agents Used in Burn Care[9]

Topical Agent	Advantages	Disadvantages
Silver Sulfadiazine	Can be used with or without dressings Painless Can be applied to wound directly Broad-spectrum Effective against yeast	Does not penetrate into eschar
Silver Nitrate	Broad-spectrum Non-allergenic Dressing application is painless	Poor penetration Discolors, making assessment difficult Can cause severe electrolyte imbalances Removal of dressings is painful
Povidone-iodine	Broad-spectrum Antifungal Easily removed with water	Not effective against pseudomonas May impair thyroid function Painful application
Mafenide Acetate	Broad-spectrum Penetrates burn eschar May be used with or without occlusive dressings	May cause metabolic acidosis May compromise respiratory function May inhibit epithelialization Painful application
Gentamicin	Broad-spectrum May be covered or left open to air	Has caused resistant strains Ototoxic Nephrotoxic
Nitrofurazone	Bacteriocidal Broad-spectrum	May lead to overgrowth of fungus and pseudomonas Painful application

From Trofino, RB: Nursing Care of the Burn-Injured Patient. F.A. Davis Company, Philadelphia 1991, p.46, with permission.

Skin Graft Terminology[6]

Allograft (homograft): A temporary skin graft taken from another human, usually a cadaver, in order to cover a large burned area.

Autograft: A permanent skin graft taken from a donor site on the patient's own body.

Donor site: A site where healthy skin is taken and used as a graft.

Escharotomy: A surgical procedure that opens or removes eschar from a burn site to reduce tension on a surrounding structure, relieve pressure from interstitial edema, and subsequently enhance circulation.

Full-thickness graft: A skin graft that contains the dermis and epidermis.

Heterograft (xenograft): A temporary skin graft taken from another species.

Mesh graft: A skin graft that is altered to create a mesh-like pattern in order to cover a larger surface area.

Recipient site: A site that has been burned and requires a graft.

Sheet graft: A skin graft that is transferred directly from the unburned donor site to the prepared recipient site.

Split-thickness graft: A skin graft that contains only a superficial layer of the dermis in addition to the epidermis.

Z-plasty: A surgical procedure to eliminate a scar contracture. An incision in the shape of a "z" allows the contracture to change configuration and lengthen the scar.

Integumentary Pathology[1,4,10]

Cellulitis

Cellulitis is a fast spreading inflammation that occurs as a result of a bacterial infection of the skin and connective tissues. It can develop anywhere under the skin, but will typically affect the extremities.

Etiology – Cellulitis is caused by particular bacterial infections including streptococci or staphylococci. Predisposing factors to cellulitis include an increased age, immunosuppression, trauma, the presence of wounds or venous insufficiency.

Signs and Symptoms – Symptoms may include localized redness that may spread quickly, skin that is warm or hot to touch, local abscess or ulceration, tenderness to palpation, chills, fever, and malaise.

Treatment – A patient with suspected cellulitis should be immediately referred to a physician for further assessment. Cellulitis requires pharmacological intervention using systemic antibiotics. Differential diagnosis should attempt to rule out deep vein thrombosis and contact dermatitis. Physical therapy may be warranted for wound care. Cellulitis can lead to sepsis or gangrene if not properly treated.

Contact Dermatitis

Contact dermatitis is a superficial irritation of the skin resulting from localized irritation (e.g., poison ivy, latex, soap, jewelry sensitivity). This condition can be acute or chronic based on exposure to the precipitating agent. Contact dermatitis is a very common skin disease that can occur at any age.

Etiology – Contact dermatitis occurs with exposure to mechanical, chemical, environmental or biological agents. Nickel, rubber, latex, and topical antibiotics are common precipitating agents.

Signs and Symptoms – Patients experience intense itching, burning, and red skin in areas corresponding to the location of the topical irritation. Edema may also occur in the area of sensitivity and symptoms can expand beyond the initial point of topical irritation.

Treatment – The focus of treatment should be on identifying and removing the source of irritation. Topical steroid application is commonly employed. Acute lesions should resolve with treatment once exposure to the external irritant has been removed.

Eczema

Eczema, also referred to as dermatitis, is used to describe a group of disorders that cause chronic skin inflammation typically due to an immune system abnormality, allergic reaction or external irritant.

Etiology – Eczema's etiology is based on the particular form of the disorder. Infants and children are at higher risk for eczema, however, many outgrow the condition with age. The geriatric population is also at an increased risk for many forms of eczema.

Signs and Symptoms – Red or brown-gray, itchy, lichenified skin plaques that may be exacerbated by some topical agents such as soaps and lotions. The younger population will also frequently experience oozing and crusting of the patchy areas of irritation.

Treatment – Pharmacological interventions are variable ranging from topical or oral corticosteroids to oral antibiotics and antihistamines. Cold compresses and other modalities may assist with reducing the itching. Stress management techniques and avoidance of extreme temperatures should be employed to avoid potential exacerbations of the condition.

Gangrene (Dry)

Gangrene is referred to as "dry" when there is a loss of vascular supply resulting in local tissue death. Fingers, toes, and limbs are most often affected. The hardened tissue is not painful, however, there may be significant pain at the line of demarcation. Dry gangrene typically develops slowly and in some cases results in auto-amputation.

Etiology - Dry gangrene occurs most commonly in blood vessel disease, such as diabetes mellitus or atherosclerosis. It develops when blood flow to an affected area is impaired, typically as a result of poor circulation. Infection is typically not present in dry gangrene, however, dry gangrene can progress to wet gangrene if infection occurs.

Signs and Symptoms - Dry gangrene presents as dark brown or black nonviable tissue that eventually becomes a hardened mass (mummified). The patient may complain of cold or numb skin and they may present with pain.

Treatment - Gangrene is a serious medical condition and requires immediate medical intervention. Depending on the severity, gangrene is treated by pharmacological intervention, surgery, and hyperbaric oxygen therapy.

Gangrene (Wet)

Gangrene is referred to as "wet" if there is an associated bacterial infection in the affected tissue. Gangrene may develop as a complication of an infected untreated wound. Swelling resulting from the bacterial infection causes a sudden stoppage of blood flow.

Etiology - Wet gangrene can develop after a severe burn, frostbite or injury and requires immediate treatment since it tends to spread very quickly and can be fatal. There is cessation of blood flow that starts a chain of events including invasion by bacteria at the affected site. As a result of the occluded blood supply, the white blood cells are unable to fight the infection.

Signs and Symptoms - swelling and pain at the site of infection, change in skin color from red to brown to black, blisters that produce pus, fever, and general malaise

Treatment - Wet gangrene is a serious medical condition and requires immediate medical intervention. Surgical debridement of the gangrene and intravenous antibiotic treatment are typical interventions for wet gangrene. Depending on the severity, gangrene is treated by pharmacological intervention, surgery, and hyperbaric oxygen therapy.

Onychomycosis

Onychomycosis refers to a fungal infection that primarily affects the toenails and nailbeds. Onychomycosis is divided into subtypes, but are typically medically treated in a similar fashion.

Etiology - Acquiring a fungal infection can be a fairly common occurrence. Risk factors include manicures and pedicures with unsterile utensils, possessing nail injuries or deformities, excess skin moisture, wearing closed toe shoes, and an impaired immune response.

Signs and Symptoms - yellow or brown nail discoloration; hyperkeratosis and hypertrophy of the nail causing it to partially detach from the nailbed

Treatment - Manual debridement of the nail and topical antifungal medications are primary interventions. Fungal infections may return to the nailbeds and in some cases, the nails may have permanent damage.

Psoriasis - Plaque

Plaque psoriasis is a chronic autoimmune disease of the skin and is the most common of the five types of psoriasis. T cells trigger inflammation within the skin and produce an accelerated rate of skin cell growth. The skin cells accumulate in raised red patches on the surface of the skin.

Etiology - Some patients have a genetic predisposition to plaque psoriasis. Other factors may trigger psoriasis, such as injury to the skin, insufficient or excess sunlight, stress, excessive alcohol, HIV infection, smoking, and certain medications.

Signs and Symptoms - The primary symptom is red raised blotches that typically present in a bilateral fashion for example over both knees or elbows. These plaques can appear anywhere on the body and will tend to itch and flake. Complications can include arthritis, pain, severe itching, secondary skin infections, and side effects secondary to pharmacological interventions.

Treatment - The primary goal for treatment of plaque psoriasis is to control the symptoms and prevent secondary infection. Treatment varies widely from topical applications to systemic medications and phototherapy. Plaque psoriasis is a life-long condition that can be effectively managed and controlled through the various stages and exacerbations.

Tinea Pedis

Tinea pedis, commonly referred to as athlete's foot, is a superficial fungal infection which causes epidermal thickening and a scaly skin appearance. This fungus is opportunistic and will rapidly multiply in a warm and moist environment (e.g., between the toes).

Etiology - Risk factors include wearing closed toe shoes that don't allow airflow, prolonged periods of moisture or wetness, excessive sweating, and possessing small nail or skin abrasions. This infection is contagious through direct contact or when making contact with a surface containing the tinea pedis infection.

Signs and Symptoms - itching, redness, peeling skin between the toes, pain, odor, and in more severe cases breaks in skin continuity

Treatment - Pharmacological intervention includes topical or oral antibiotics depending on the severity of symptoms. Tinea pedis may persist or recur and more long-term management may be required. Prevention includes thorough drying of the feet when bathing or swimming, wearing sandals around public pools or showers, changing socks frequently, proper hygiene, and avoiding shoe wear that creates a moist environment.

Metabolic and Endocrine Systems

Metabolic System

Key Functions of the Metabolic System[11]

The metabolic system governs the chemical and physical changes that take place within the body enabling it to grow and function. Metabolism involves breakdown of the body's complex organic compounds in order to generate energy for all bodily processes. It also generates energy for the synthesis of complex substances that form tissues and organs. During metabolism, organic compounds are broken down by a process called catabolism, while anabolism is the process that combines simple molecules for tissue growth. Many metabolic processes are facilitated by enzymes. The overall speed at which an organism carries out its metabolic processes is termed its metabolic rate (or when the organism is at rest, its basal metabolic rate).

Metabolic System Pathology

Inherited Metabolic Disorders[10]

Metabolic disorders are classified by the particular building block that is affected. An enzyme deficiency leads to accumulation of the substrate and a subsequent deficiency in the intended enzyme's product. There are many different disorders that can occur genetically and these are grouped according to the substrate that has been affected (i.e., carbohydrates, amino acids). Inherited metabolic disorders can be diagnosed in utero via amniocentesis or chorionic villus sampling. Many inherited metabolic disorders will produce symptoms in a newborn including lethargy, apnea, poor feeding, tachypnea, vomiting, hypoglycemia, urine changes, and seizures. Symptoms that are immediately apparent indicate a more dangerous disorder.

Phenylketonuria (amino acid/organic acid metabolic disorder)[12]

Phenylketonuria (PKU) is a syndrome that consists of intellectual disability as well as behavioral and cognitive issues secondary to an elevation of serum phenylalanine. There is a deficiency in the enzyme phenylalanine hydroxylase. Normally, excessive phenylalanine is converted to tyrosine by phenylalanine hydroxylase. When this process does not occur and there is an excess of phenylalanine, the brain is the primary organ that becomes affected. Children in the United States are tested at birth for PKU and levels greater than 6 mg/dl of phenylalanine require some form of treatment.

Etiology – This is an autosomal recessive inherited trait and is most common in Caucasian populations.

Signs and symptoms – Symptoms will typically present within a few months of birth as the phenylalanine accumulates. If left untreated, severe intellectual disability will occur. These children may also experience gait disturbances, hyperactivity, psychoses, abnormal body odor, and display features that are lighter in coloring when compared to other family members.

Treatment – Phenylketonuria is treated through dietary restriction of phenylalanine throughout the person's lifetime. Adequate prevention will avoid all manifestations of the disease.

Tay-Sachs Disease (lysosomal storage disorder)[10]

Tay-Sachs disease is the absence or deficiency of hexosaminidase A. This produces an accumulation of gangliosides (GM2) within the brain.

Etiology – This disease is an autosomal recessive inherited trait and carried primarily in the Eastern European (Ashkenazi) Jewish population.

Signs and symptoms – At approximately six months of age, the child will start to miss developmental milestones and will continue to deteriorate in motor and cognitive skills. As symptoms progress, the patient develops significant intellectual disability and paralysis, and will usually die by the age of five.

Treatment – There is currently no effective treatment for this condition. Genetic testing in high risk populations to identify the carriers prior to pregnancy is important in order to avoid this disorder.

Mitochondrial Disorders[10]

There are over one hundred different forms of mitochondrial disease and each produces a different spectrum of disability and clinical manifestations.

Etiology – Mitochondrial disorders result from genetically inherited or spontaneous mutations in the DNA that lead to impaired function of proteins found within the mitochondria.

Signs and symptoms – Symptoms vary depending on the type of mitochondrial disorder, however, can include loss of muscle coordination, muscle weakness, visual and hearing problems, learning disabilities, heart, liver, and kidney disease, respiratory, neurological, and gastrointestinal disorders, and dementia.

Treatment – These diagnoses are relatively new and treatment is as varied as the symptomatology and presentation of the disease. Treatment is aimed at alleviating the current symptoms and slowing the progression of the disease process.

Wilson's Disease (hepatolenticular degeneration)[10]

Wilson's disease is a rare inherited disorder that is most common in eastern Europeans, Sicilians, and southern Italians, but may occur in any group. Wilson's disease typically appears in people under 40 years old and symptoms can develop in children typically between four and six years of age.

Etiology – Wilson's disease is an autosomal recessive inherited trait that produces a defect in the body's ability to metabolize copper. The copper accumulates over time within the brain, liver, cornea, kidney, and other tissues.

Signs and symptoms – Symptoms typically appear between the ages of four to six and include Kayser-Fleischer rings surrounding the iris of the eye secondary to copper deposits, degenerative changes in the brain (especially within the basal ganglia), hepatitis, cirrhosis of the liver, athetoid movements, and ataxic gait patterns. There may also be emotional and behavioral changes as the copper continues to accumulate. Over time, and with severe disease, there will be deformities of the musculoskeletal system, pathologic fractures, osteomalacia, muscle atrophy, and contractures.

Treatment – Treatment consists of continual pharmacological intervention using vitamin B6 and D-penicillamine as both promote the excretion of excess copper from the body. Treatment will also focus on prevention of hepatic disease since a patient will die from hepatic failure if the condition is left untreated.

Rehabilitation Considerations for Patients with Inherited Metabolic Disorders[10]

- Must have an awareness of dietary restrictions
- Patient and family training to prevent deleterious effects from the metabolic disease
- Adapt treatment to facilitate developmental milestones within patient tolerance

Acid-Base Metabolic Disorders[13]

The process of metabolism is regulated by the endocrine and nervous systems. The rate of metabolism can be influenced by body temperature, exercise, hormone activity, and digestion activity. If proper fluid or acid-base balance is compromised, it can alter metabolic function and cause many signs and symptoms of the dysfunction.

Metabolic Alkalosis[13]

Metabolic alkalosis is a condition that occurs when there is an increase in bicarbonate accumulation or an abnormal loss of acids. As a result, the pH rises above 7.45.

Etiology – Metabolic alkalosis commonly occurs when there has been continuous vomiting, ingestion of antacids or other alkaline substances or diuretic therapy. It may also be associated with hypokalemia or nasogastric suctioning.

Signs and symptoms – Symptoms include nausea, diarrhea, prolonged vomiting, confusion, muscle fasciculations, muscle cramping, neuromuscular hyperexcitability, convulsions, paresthesias, and hypoventilation. If left untreated the patient can become comatose, experience seizures, and respiratory paralysis.

Treatment – The most important interventions include managing the underlying cause, correcting coexisting electrolyte imbalances, and administering potassium chloride to the patient.

Metabolic Acidosis[13]

Metabolic acidosis is a condition that occurs when there is an accumulation of acids due to an acid gain or bicarbonate loss. As a result, the pH drops below 7.35.

Etiology – Metabolic acidosis commonly occurs with conditions such as renal failure, lactic acidosis, starvation, diabetic or alcoholic ketoacidosis, severe diarrhea or poisoning by certain toxins.

Signs and symptoms – Symptoms include compensatory hyperventilation, vomiting, diarrhea, headache, weakness and malaise, hyperkalemia, and cardiac arrhythmias. If left untreated the continued increase in acid can induce coma and eventual death.

Treatment – Treatment includes managing the underlying cause, correcting any coexisting electrolyte imbalances, and administering sodium bicarbonate.

Rehabilitation Considerations for Patients with Acid-Base Disorders[10,13]

- Recognize higher risk populations for imbalances such as patients with renal, cardiovascular, pulmonary disease; burns, fever, and sepsis; patients on mechanical ventilation; diabetes mellitus; patients currently vomiting with diarrhea or enteric drainage
- Recognize signs of dehydration in a diabetic patient
- Injury prevention during involuntary muscular contractions secondary to metabolic alkalosis
- Recognize that patients using diuretic therapy may be at risk for potassium depletion
- Recognize that Trousseau's sign during blood pressure measurements may indicate calcium deficiency and the early stages of tetany

Metabolic Bone Disease[10]

Metabolic bone disease is a classification for particular diagnoses where there has been a disruption in normal metabolism within the skeletal system. The skeletal system houses calcium and phosphorus. It also continuously balances the remodeling of the cortical and trabecular bone in order to optimize the structure of the skeleton. Disruption in the homeostasis of skeletal metabolic processes will result in deformity, bone loss, fracture, softening of the bone, arthritis, and pain.

Osteomalacia[10]

Osteomalacia is a metabolic condition where bones become soft secondary to a calcium or phosphorus deficiency. There is adequate bone matrix, however, there is insufficient calcification of the matrix due to the deficiency.

Etiology – Calcium is typically lost secondary to inadequate intestinal absorption and the phosphorus is lost secondary to an increase in renal excretion. A deficiency in vitamin D will also cause osteomalacia.

CONSIDER THIS

LOW BONE MASS[12]

Certain medical conditions may present with low bone mass as an associated clinical feature. A patient may report such conditions while detailing their medical history, but not be aware of the condition's potential influence on bone mass. Physical therapists should be aware of such conditions, regardless of an accompanying osteopenia or osteoporosis diagnosis, in order to best incorporate preventative interventions and education into the plan of care.

Medical conditions which may cause low bone mass include: Cushing's syndrome, osteomalacia, hyperthyroidism, hyperparathyroidism, celiac disease, rheumatoid arthritis, renal failure, hypogonadism, and osteogenesis imperfecta.

Signs and symptoms – Osteomalacia can include a vague presentation of aching, fatigue, and weight loss. Myopathy and sensory polyneuropathy may also occur along with periarticular tenderness and pain, thoracic kyphosis deformity, and bowing of the lower extremities. The patient may also struggle to perform transfers and assume a standing position.

Treatment – Specific intervention will focus on the underlying etiology. Increased nutrition is recommended and pharmacological intervention may include vitamin D or phosphate supplements.

Osteoporosis[10]

Osteoporosis is a metabolic condition that presents with a decrease in bone mass that subsequently increases the risk of fracture. Osteoporosis primarily affects trabecular and cortical bone where the rate of bone resorption accelerates while the rate of bone formation declines. Declining osteoblast function coupled with the loss of calcium and phosphate salts will cause the bones to become brittle.

Etiology – Primary osteoporosis can include idiopathic, post-menopausal or involutional (senile) osteoporosis. Secondary osteoporosis can occur as a result of another primary condition or with use of certain medications.

Signs and symptoms – Symptoms include compression and other bone fractures, low thoracic or lumbar pain, loss of lumbar lordosis, deformities such as kyphosis, decrease in height, dowager's hump, and postural changes.

Treatment – Management of primary osteoporosis includes vitamin and pharmacological intervention, proper nutrition, assistive and adaptive device prescription, and patient education. Surgical intervention may be required for fracture stabilization.

Paget's Disease[10]

Paget's disease is a metabolic condition characterized by heightened osteoclast activity. This process of excessive bone formation lacks true structural integrity. The bone appears enlarged, but lacks strength due to the high turnover of bone secondary to abnormal osteoclastic proliferation.

Etiology – This disease has a genetic component as well as geographical incidence, and most commonly affects patients over 50 years of age.

Signs and symptoms – Symptoms include musculoskeletal pain accompanied by bony deformities (kyphosis, coxa varus, bowing of the long bones, vertebral compression). The skull, clavicle, pelvis, femur, spine and tibia are common sites that will exhibit bony changes. Symptoms of advanced progression of the disease include continued pain, headache, vertigo, hearing loss, mental deterioration, fatigue, increased cardiac output, and heart failure (secondary to an increased cardiac output).

Treatment – Management relies heavily on pharmacological intervention using bisphosphonates in order to inhibit bone resorption and improve the quality of the involved bone. Exercise, weight control, and cardiac fitness are all key components in a program to maintain strength and motion.

Rehabilitation Considerations for Patients with Metabolic Bone Disease[10]

- Must have awareness of signs of compression fracture and of patients at higher risk for all forms of fracture
- Focus on both resistance training and endurance training to build bone density and increase strength
- Avoid treatments that exacerbate the condition or place patients at risk for fracture

Metabolic System Terminology[10, 14-16]

Aerobic metabolism: The ATP producing metabolic processes that are dependent on oxygen transported via the circulatory system. Aerobic metabolic functions typically provide energy for low intensity and/or longer duration activities.

Anabolism: The metabolic process in which simple molecules (e.g., nucleic acids, polysaccharides, amino acids) are combined to create the complex molecules (e.g., proteins) needed for tissue and organ growth.

Anaerobic metabolism: Metabolic functions that do not require the presence of oxygen and produce energy for high intensity, shorter duration activities.

Adenosine triphosphate (ATP): The molecular unit within the body which transports the chemical compounds used for cellular metabolism.

CONSIDER THIS

OSTEOPOROSIS RISK FACTORS AND PREVENTION[12,14,15]

Bone mineral density (BMD) is used to diagnose osteoporosis and other low bone mass disorders. BMD is measured via dual-energy x-ray absorptiometry and expressed in terms of T-score and Z-score. T-score refers to how many standard deviations above or below average healthy young adult norms an individual's BMD is. Z-score refers to how many standard deviations above or below average age and gender adjusted norms an individual's BMD is. The World Health Organization reports that in women, a T-score lower than -1 standard deviation (SD) but greater than -2.5 SD is indicative of osteopenia. A score that is -2.5 SD or lower is indicative of osteoporosis, and a score at or below -2.5 SD with one or more related fractures is considered severe osteoporosis.

Physical therapists are often the primary educator with patients who have either sustained or are at risk for osteoporotic fractures. Therapists should therefore have a sound understanding of non-modifiable and modifiable risk factors so that education topics and treatment planning may be adapted to address both.

Non-modifiable risk factors associated with the development of low bone mass include age, early menopause, history of previous fracture, slender build, family history of low bone mass, female gender, and being of either Asian or Caucasian descent. Certain conditions and medications, such as glucocorticoids, may also be considered non-modifiable if discontinuing such medications is medically ill-advised.

Modifiable risk factors associated with the development of low bone mass include insufficient dietary intake of vitamin D and calcium, estrogen deficiency, cigarette smoking, alcohol use in excess of two drinks per day, caffeine intake in excess of two servings per day, and sedentary lifestyle.

Treatment interventions and educational topics are similar for both osteopenia and osteoporosis. Prevention of osteoporosis associated fractures is a primary goal of therapeutic interventions for at-risk individuals of all ages. Specific interventions, however, may be emphasized or excluded depending on the patient's age and associated risk factors.

Interventions for Children and Adolescents

Osteoporosis prevention is important to begin during childhood by ensuring adequate nutrition, especially with regard to calcium intake, since malnutrition and undernutrition negatively impact bone development. Bone mass density typically peaks during an individual's mid-20's. Younger patients should be encouraged to participate regularly in physical activity to promote bone strength. The adverse effects of smoking and excessive alcohol consumption on bone development should also be addressed with younger patient populations. Adherence to recommendations may be the greatest challenge in addressing osteoporosis in younger populations.

Interventions for Adults

Once peak BMD has been reached, maintaining this during the processes of ongoing remodeling is paramount in minimizing the eventual imbalance between bone formation and remodeling. Maintaining good nutrition, including recommended calcium and vitamin D intake, is a key factor in managing the risk of osteoporotic fractures. Regular weight bearing exercise is strongly recommended in addition to avoiding smoking and heavy drinking. Postural education and fall prevention activities are also increasingly important during later years when fracture risk is heightened.

Catabolism: The metabolic process in which complex materials (e.g., proteins, lipids) are broken down in the body for the purpose of creating and releasing heat and energy.

DNA (deoxyribonucleic acid): A double helix molecule that contains the genes that provide the blueprint for all of the structures and functions of a living being.

Gene: A fundamental unit of heredity.

Metabolism: The physical and chemical processes of cells burning fuel to produce and use energy. Examples include digestion, elimination of waste, breathing, thermoregulation, muscular contraction, brain function, and circulation.

Mitochondria: The part of the cell that is responsible for energy production. The mitochondria are also responsible for converting nutrients into energy and other specialized tasks.

Osteopenia: A condition presenting with low bone mass that is not severe enough to qualify as osteoporosis. Individuals with osteopenia may not have actual bone loss, but a naturally lower bone density than established norms.

Osteopetrosis: A group of conditions characterized by impaired osteoclast function which causes bone to become thickened but fragile. Osteopetrosis is an inherited condition that can vary widely in symptoms and severity.

pH: A measure of the hydrogen ion concentration in body fluid.

Endocrine System

Key Functions of the Endocrine System[12]

The endocrine system consists of endocrine glands (specialized ductless glands) that secrete hormones that travel through the bloodstream to signal specific target cells throughout the body. The hormones travel throughout the body to the target organs upon which they act. They will bind selectively to receptor sites on the surface of the receptor cells. The endocrine system and nervous system both function to achieve and maintain stability of the internal environment (homeostasis). The systems are capable of working alone or in concert with each other. The endocrine and nervous systems work together to regulate metabolism, response to stress, sexual reproduction, blood pressure, and water and salt balances.

Endocrine System

- Secreting cells send hormones through the bloodstream to signal specific target cells
- Hormones diffuse into the blood and travel long distances to virtually every area of the body
- Endocrine effectors consist of virtually all tissues
- Regulatory effects are slow and tend to last for long periods

Nervous System

- Neurons secrete neurotransmitters to signal nearby cells that have an appropriate receptor site
- Neurotransmitters are sent very short distances across a synapse
- Nervous effectors are limited to muscle and glandular tissue
- Regulatory effects appear rapidly and are often short lived

Glands of the Endocrine System[10,12]

Hypothalamus

The hypothalamus is part of the diencephalon located below the thalamus and cerebral hemisphere. The hypothalamus connects to the pituitary gland through the infundibular or pituitary stalk. It is responsible for regulation of the autonomic nervous system (body temperature, appetite, sweating, thirst, sexual behavior, rage, fear, blood pressure, sleep) and other endocrine glands through its impact on the pituitary gland.

Pituitary Gland

The pituitary gland is normally the size of a pea and is located at the base of the brain just beneath the hypothalamus. The pituitary gland consists of two separate glands, the adenohypophysis (anterior) and the neurohypophysis (posterior). The pituitary gland is considered the most important part of the endocrine system since it releases hormones that regulate several other endocrine glands. This "master gland" is influenced by factors such as seasonal changes or emotional stress. The pituitary gland secretes endorphins that act on the nervous system and reduce a person's sensitivity to pain. It also controls ovulation and works as a catalyst for the testes and ovaries to create sex hormones.

Thyroid Gland

The thyroid gland is located on the anterior and lateral surfaces of the trachea immediately below the larynx and is shaped like a "bow tie" or "butterfly" with two halves (lobes); a right lobe and a left lobe joined by an isthmus. The thyroid produces thyroxine and triiodothyronine that act to control the rate at which cells burn the fuel from food. An increase in thyroid hormones will increase the rate of the chemical reactions within the body.

Parathyroid Glands

There are four parathyroid glands found on the posterior surface of the thyroid's lateral lobes. These glands produce parathyroid hormone, which functions as an antagonist to calcitonin and is important for the maintenance of normal blood levels of calcium and phosphate. Parathyroid hormone increases the reabsorption of calcium and phosphate from bones to the blood. Secretion of parathyroid hormone is stimulated by hypocalcemia and inhibited by hypercalcemia. Normal clotting, neuromuscular excitability, and cell membrane permeability are dependent on normal calcium levels.

Adrenal Glands

The two adrenal glands are located on top of each kidney; the outer portion is called the adrenal cortex and the inner portion is called the adrenal medulla. The adrenal cortex and the adrenal medulla secrete different hormones. The adrenal cortex produces corticosteroids that will regulate water and sodium balance, the body's response to stress, the immune system, sexual development and function, and metabolism. The adrenal medulla produces epinephrine that increases heart rate and blood pressure when there is an increase in stress.

Pancreas

The pancreas is located in the upper left quadrant of the abdominal cavity, extending from the duodenum to the spleen. The pancreas includes both endocrine and exocrine tissues. The islets of Langerhans are the hormone-producing cells of the pancreas. Alpha cells produce glucagon and beta cells produce insulin. These hormones work in combination to ensure a consistent level of glucose within the bloodstream and properly maintain stores of energy within the body.

Ovaries

The ovaries are located in the pelvic cavity on each side of the uterus. The ovaries provide estrogen and progesterone that contribute to regulation of the menstrual cycle and pregnancy. Estrogen is secreted by the ovarian follicles and is responsible for the development and maintenance of female sex characteristics such as breast development and the cycles of the female reproductive system. Progesterone is produced by the corpus luteum and functions to maintain the lining of the uterus at a level necessary for pregnancy.

Testes

The testes are located in the scrotum between the upper thighs. The testes secrete androgens (most importantly testosterone) that regulate body changes associated with sexual development and support the production of sperm.

Classes of Hormones[10, 12, 16]

Steroid hormones (e.g., prostaglandins)

All cells create prostaglandins from the phospholipids of the cell membrane. They are unique from other hormones since they do not circulate in the blood and instead exert their effects only where they are produced. Prostaglandins are capable of producing a wide variety of effects; some effects as it pertains to rehabilitation are related to inflammation, pain mechanisms, vasodilation, vasoconstriction, nutrient metabolism, and blood clotting.

Amine hormones (e.g., catecholamines)

Catecholamines (epinephrine, norepinephrine, and dopamine) are synthesized from chromaffin cells within the adrenal medulla. Sympathetic nervous system stimulation releases the catecholamines into the bloodstream. Epinephrine has one of the largest effects on the sympathetic nervous system and creates the "fight or flight" response. The target areas for epinephrine are receptor sites in the cardiovascular and metabolic systems. Other functions of catecholamines include increasing cardiac contraction, constriction of blood vessels, activation of glycogen breakdown, blocking of insulin secretion, increasing metabolic rate, and dilation of the airways within the lungs.

Peptide hormones (e.g., insulin)

Insulin is a hormone secreted by the beta cells of the islets of Langerhans within the pancreas. Insulin is released when there is an elevation in the level of blood glucose. The insulin produces an increase in cellular uptake of glucose for metabolism. Insulin also stimulates the skeletal muscle and liver to store the glucose and increases amino acid transport across hepatic, muscle, and adipose tissues. Insulin release affects all systems of the body with its primary goal of reducing blood glucose levels.

Endocrine System: Hormone, Function, and Regulation of Secretion[10,12]

Hormone	Function	Regulation of Secretion
Hypothalamus		
Growth hormone-releasing hormone Target: pituitary gland	Increases the release of growth hormone	Central nervous system feedback; circulating levels of hormones
Growth hormone-inhibiting hormone Target: pituitary gland	Decreases the release of growth hormone	Central nervous system feedback; circulating levels of hormones
Gonadotropin-releasing hormone Target: pituitary gland	Increases the release of luteinizing hormone and follicle-stimulating hormone	Central nervous system feedback; circulating levels of hormones
Thyrotropin-releasing hormone Target: pituitary gland	Increases the release of thyroid-stimulating hormone	Central nervous system feedback; circulating levels of hormones
Corticotropin-releasing hormone Target: pituitary gland	Increases the release of adrenocorticotropic hormone	Central nervous system feedback; circulating levels of hormones
Prolactin-releasing hormone Target: pituitary gland	Stimulates the release of prolactin	Central nervous system feedback; circulating levels of hormones
Prolactin-inhibitory factor; dopamine Target: pituitary gland	Decreases the release of prolactin	Central nervous system feedback; circulating levels of hormones

Hormone	Function	Regulation of Secretion
Pituitary		
Growth hormone Target: bone and muscle	Promotes growth and development; increases the rate of protein synthesis	Hypothalamus
Follicle-stimulating hormone Target: ovaries and testes	Promotes follicular development and the creation of estrogen in females; promotes spermatogenesis in males	Hypothalamus
Luteinizing hormone Target: ovaries and testes	Promotes ovulation along with estrogen/progesterone synthesis from the corpus luteum in females; promotes testosterone synthesis in males	Hypothalamus
Thyroid-stimulating hormone Target: thyroid gland	Increases the synthesis of thyroid hormones T3 and T4	Hypothalamus
Adrenocorticotropic hormone Target: adrenal cortex	Increases cortisol synthesis (adrenal steroids)	Hypothalamus
Prolactin Target: mammary glands	Allows for the process of lactation	Hypothalamus
Oxytocin Target: uterus and mammary glands	Increases contraction of uterine muscles; promotes release of milk from mammary glands	Nerve impulses from the hypothalamus; stretching of cervix; nipple stimulation
Antidiuretic hormone Target: kidneys	Increases water reabsorption; conserves water; increases blood pressure through stimulating contraction of muscles in small arteries	Decreased water content
Adrenal Cortex		
Androgen Target: ovaries and testes	Increases masculinization; promotes growth of pubic hair in males and females	Influenced by the hypothalamic production and release of GnRH and luteinizing hormone (LH)
Aldosterone (mineralocorticoid) Target: kidneys	Increases reabsorption of sodium ions by the kidneys to the blood; increases excretion of potassium ions by the kidney into the urine	Low blood sodium level; high blood potassium level
Cortisol (glucocorticoid) Target: gastrointestinal system	Influences metabolism of food molecules; anti-inflammatory effect in large amounts	Adrenocorticotropic hormone
Adrenal Medulla		
Epinephrine Target: cardiovascular and metabolic systems	Increases heart rate and force of contraction; increases energy production; vasodilation in skeletal muscle	Sympathetic impulses from the hypothalamus in stress situations
Norepinephrine Target: cardiovascular and metabolic systems	Vasoconstriction in skin, viscera, and skeletal muscles	
Ovaries		
Estrogen, progesterone Target: uterus and mammary glands	Involved in regulation of the female reproductive system and female sexual characteristics	Cyclical rise and fall of hormone levels

Hormone	Function	Regulation of Secretion
Pancreas		
Glucagon Target: liver	Increases blood glucose by stimulating the conversion of glycogen to glucose	Hypoglycemia
Insulin Target: all body systems	Decreases blood glucose and increases the storage of fat, protein, and carbohydrates	Hyperglycemia
Parathyroids		
Parathormone Target: bone, kidney, intestinal mucosa	Increases blood calcium	Hypocalcemia
Testes		
Testosterone Target: pituitary gland	Involved in the process of spermatogenesis and male sexual characteristics	Influenced by pituitary release of LH
Thyroid		
Thyroxine (T4), Triiodothyronine (T3) Target: all tissues	Involved with normal development; increases cellular level metabolism	Thyroid-stimulating hormone
Calcitonin Target: plasma	Increases calcium storage in bone; decreases blood calcium levels	Hypercalcemia

Endocrine System Dysfunction General Signs and Symptoms[10,12]

Neuromuscular

- Muscle weakness
- Periarthritis
- Myalgia
- Arthralgia
- Stiffness
- Osteoarthritis
- Muscle atrophy
- Adhesive capsulitis

Systemic

- Polydipsia
- Growth dysfunction
- Skin pigmentation dysfunction
- Polyuria
- Increased vital signs
- Hair dysfunction
- Nervousness or anxiety

Endocrine System Pathology[10,12]

The endocrine system is multifaceted and can develop pathology in one or more areas due to hyperfunction or hypofunction of one or more glands. In many instances, it is the hypothalamus or the pituitary gland that affects the function of other endocrine glands when they experience direct or indirect dysfunction.

Hyperfunction of an endocrine gland: usually secondary to overstimulation of the pituitary gland. This can also occur due to hyperplasia or neoplasia of the gland itself.

Hypofunction of an endocrine gland: usually secondary to understimulation of the pituitary gland. This can also occur from congenital or acquired disorders.

There are other instances where direct damage to the hypothalamus or pituitary gland creates dysfunction:

Hypothalamus Dysfunction

- Hypothalamus tumors (i.e., ependymomas)
- Inflammatory processes (i.e., sarcoidosis)
- Surgical transection
- Trauma (i.e., skull fracture)

Pituitary Dysfunction

- Pituitary tumors (i.e., adenomas)
- Ischemic necrosis or infarction of the pituitary gland
- Infiltrative disorders (i.e., hemochromatosis)
- Inflammatory processes (i.e., meningitis)
- Iatrogenic (i.e., irradiation)

Hypopituitarism: This condition occurs when there is a decreased or absent hormonal secretion from the anterior pituitary gland. This is a rare disorder and symptoms are dependent on the age of the affected person and deficit hormones. Typical disorders may include short stature (dwarfism), delayed growth and puberty, sexual and reproductive disorders, and diabetes insipidus. Treatment is also based on the deficit hormones and usually includes pharmacological replacement therapy.

Hyperpituitarism: This condition occurs when there is an excessive secretion of one or more hormones under the pituitary gland's control (frequently growth hormone that produces acromegaly in adults). Disorders and symptoms are dependent on the hormone(s) that are affected. Some disorders include gigantism or acromegaly, hirsutism, galactorrhea (abnormal lactation in males or females), amenorrhea, infertility, and impotence. Treatment is hormone and site dependent and can include tumor resection, surgery, radiation therapy, and hormone suppression or replacement (if gland becomes dysfunctional after treatment).

Rehabilitation Considerations for Patients with Pituitary Dysfunction[10]

- Ambulation/exercise encouraged within 24 hours of surgery (post tumor/gland removal)
- Must demonstrate increased awareness for signs of hypoglycemia
- Bilateral carpal tunnel syndrome, arthritis, osteophyte formation are common with hyperpituitarism
- Orthostatic hypotension may be present with hypopituitarism
- Bilateral hemianopsia that can occur with hypopituitarism requires special consideration during treatment

Adrenal Dysfunction

Addison's Disease[12]

Addison's disease is a form of adrenal dysfunction that presents with hypofunction of the adrenal cortex. Subsequently, there is decreased production of both cortisol (glucocorticoid) and aldosterone (mineralocorticoid).

Etiology – When the adrenal cortex produces insufficient cortisol and aldosterone hormones it is termed Addison's disease.

Signs and symptoms – Symptoms include a widespread metabolic dysfunction secondary to cortisol deficiency as well as fluid and electrolyte imbalances secondary to aldosterone dysfunction. The person may experience hypotension, weakness, anorexia, weight loss, altered pigmentation, and if left untreated this condition will result in shock and possible death.

Treatment – Treatment primarily consists of long-term pharmacological intervention using synthetic corticosteroids and mineralocorticoids.

Cushing's Syndrome[12]

Cushing's syndrome is a form of adrenal dysfunction that presents with hyperfunction of the adrenal gland, allowing for excessive amounts of cortisol (glucocorticoid) production.

Etiology – When the pituitary gland produces excessive adrenocorticotropic hormone (ACTH) with subsequent hypercortisolism, it is termed Cushing's syndrome.

Signs and symptoms – Symptoms evolve over years and can include persistent hyperglycemia, growth failure, truncal obesity, purple abdominal striae, "moon shaped face," "buffalo hump" posteriorly at the base of the neck, weakness, acne, hypertension, and male gynecomastia. Mental changes can include depression, poor concentration, and memory loss.

Treatment – Treatment may include pharmacological intervention to block the production of the hormones, radiation therapy, chemotherapy or surgery.

Rehabilitation Considerations for Patients with Adrenal Dysfunction[10]

- Recognize signs of stress or exhaustion and avoid treatments that exacerbate the condition
- Notify the physician with any signs of illness or increased intracranial pressure (e.g., papilledema); medications may need to be altered
- Orthostatic hypotension is common secondary to long-term cortisol therapy
- Report sleep disturbances to the physician
- Increased incidence of osteoporosis, bone fractures, degenerative myopathy, tendon ruptures, ataxic gait
- Delayed wound healing may be common

Thyroid Dysfunction[11]

Hypothyroidism: This condition occurs when there are decreased levels of thyroid hormones in the bloodstream, slowing metabolic processes within the body. Symptoms may include fatigue, weakness, decreased heart rate, weight gain, constipation, delayed puberty, and retarded growth and development. Common causes of hypothyroidism are Hashimoto's thyroiditis or an underdeveloped thyroid gland. Treatment includes oral thyroid hormone replacement therapy.

Hyperthyroidism: This condition occurs when there are excessive levels of thyroid hormones in the bloodstream. Symptoms can include an increase in nervousness, excessive sweating, weight loss, increase in blood pressure, exophthalmos, myopathy, chronic periarthritis, and an enlarged thyroid gland. Treatment may include pharmacological intervention, radioactive iodine, and surgery.

CONSIDER THIS

POSTPARTUM THYROIDITIS[14]

Postpartum thyroiditis refers to a painless inflammation of the thyroid occurring in some women after childbirth. The presentation of this condition is typically defined by two phases. Initially, a state of hyperthyroidism will present within the first one to four months following childbirth. This is followed by a shift to hypothyroidism four to eight months following delivery.

Signs of the hyperactive phase of postpartum thyroiditis may include tachycardia, unexplained weight loss, anxiety, irritability, fatigue, and heat sensitivity. Unfortunately, the initial signs of this hyperactive thyroid phase may be misinterpreted as typical postpartum symptoms, thereby delaying diagnosis. More frequently, postpartum thyroiditis is detected after the onset of the hypoactive phase. Symptoms in this phase are consistent with other hypothyroidism disorders including dry skin, hoarse voice, depression, cold sensitivity, and poor exercise tolerance. Risk factors for postpartum thyroiditis include a history of autoimmune disorders, thyroid dysfunction, prior postpartum thyroiditis or a family history of thyroid dysfunction. Blood tests are used to confirm a diagnosis in either phase.

Timely diagnosis and treatment of women with postpartum thyroiditis can impact both physical therapy outcomes and the patient's quality of life. Physical therapists should be cautious not to dismiss symptoms of fatigue and irritability as typical postpartum occurrences, especially if other signs of thyroid dysfunction can be identified. Therapists should also be mindful that pharmacological interventions (e.g., beta blockers, thyroid replacement hormones) may further influence a patient's exercise tolerance and anticipated outcomes.

Graves' Disease[10]

Graves' disease is the most specific cause of hyperthyroidism. Graves' disease is most common in women over age 20, however, it occurs in men as well and can affect any age group.

Etiology – Graves' disease is caused by an autoimmune disease in which certain antibodies produced by the immune system stimulate the thyroid gland causing it to become overactive.

Signs and symptoms – Symptoms are consistent with hyperthyroid presentation. The classic signs of Graves' disease include mild enlargement of the thyroid gland (goiter), heat intolerance, nervousness, weight loss, tremor, and palpitations.

Treatment – Management includes pharmacological intervention and/or removal of the thyroid gland using radiation or surgical intervention.

Hypothyroidism[17]	Hyperthyroidism[17]
Depression and/or anxiety, increased lethargy, fatigue, headache, slowed speech, slowed mental function, impaired short-term memory	Tremors, hyperkinesis, nervousness, increased DTRs, emotional lability, insomnia, weakness, atrophy
Proximal muscle weakness, carpal tunnel syndrome, trigger points, myalgia, increased bone density, cold intolerance, paresthesias	Chronic periarthritis, heat intolerance, flushed skin, hyperpigmentation, increased hair loss
Dyspnea, bradycardia, CHF, respiratory muscle weakness, decreased peripheral circulation, angina, increase in cholesterol	Tachycardia, palpitations, increased respiratory rate, increase in blood pressure, arrhythmias
Anorexia, constipation, weight gain, decreased absorption of food and glucose	Hypermetabolism, increased appetite, increased peristalsis, nausea, vomiting, diarrhea, dysphagia
Infertility, irregular menstrual cycle, increased menstrual bleeding	Polyuria, infertility, increased first trimester miscarriage, amenorrhea

Rehabilitation Considerations for Patients with Thyroid Dysfunction[10]

- Recognize reduced exercise capacity and fatigue are typical
- Avoid treatments that exacerbate the condition such as exercise in a hot aquatic or gym setting due to heat intolerance (Graves' disease)
- Avoid cardiovascular stress to eliminate secondary complications from hypotension, goiter, Graves' disease
- Provide close monitoring of vital signs
- Recognize the effects of radioiodine therapy
- Recognize the risk of rhabdomyolysis (hypothyroidism)

Parathyroid Dysfunction[10]

Hypoparathyroidism: This condition occurs due to hyposecretion or low-level production of parathyroid hormone by the parathyroid gland. Symptoms may include hypocalcemia, neurological symptoms such as seizures, cognitive defects, short stature, tetany, muscle pain, and cramps. Treatment of acute hypoparathyroidism requires rapid elevation in serum calcium levels through intravenous calcium. Long-term treatment includes pharmacological management and dietary modifications.

Hyperparathyroidism: This condition occurs due to excessive levels of hormone production by the parathyroid gland that leads to disruption of calcium, phosphate, and bone metabolism. Symptoms may include renal stones and kidney damage, depression, memory loss, muscle wasting, bone deformity, and myopathy. Acute treatment may include pharmacological intervention that produces an immediate lowering of serum calcium using diuretics or antiresorptive medications. Surgical intervention is usually required to remove the diseased parathyroid gland. Pharmacological intervention may be used prior to surgery or for long-term management.

Rehabilitation Considerations for Patients with Parathyroid Dysfunction[10]

- Must be familiar with all signs and symptoms of parathyroid dysfunction in order to refer patients to a physician if a change in their status occurs
- Recognize symptoms of excessive or inadequate pharmacological treatment and side effects of the agents
- Avoid treatments that exacerbate the condition
- Recognize effects of hypercalcemia (hyperparathyroidism) and hypocalcemia (hypoparathyroidism)
- Recognize the increased risk for fractures and effects from osteogenic synovitis (Achilles, triceps, and obturator tendons most affected)

Hypoparathyroidism[17]	Hyperparathyroidism[17]
Decreased bone resorption	Increased bone resorption
Hypocalcemia	Hypercalcemia
Elevated serum phosphate levels	Decreased serum phosphate levels
Shortened 4th and 5th metacarpals (pseudohypoparathyroidism)	Osteitis fibrosa, subperiosteal resorption, arthritis, bone deformity
Compromised breathing due to intercostal muscle and diaphragm spasms	Nephrocalcinosis, renal hypertension, and significant renal damage
Cardiac arrhythmias and potential heart failure	Gout
Increased neuromuscular activity that can result in tetany	Decreased neuromuscular irritability

Pancreas Dysfunction[12]

Type 1 Diabetes Mellitus (DM)

This form of DM occurs when the pancreas fails to produce enough or any insulin. This form of diabetes is normally diagnosed in childhood, but can occur at any age. It is also known as insulin-dependent diabetes or juvenile diabetes.

Etiology - The exact cause is unknown, but genetic predisposition in combination with exposure to a viral or environmental trigger is believed to cause an immune reaction that damages the pancreas with subsequent failure in secretion of endogenous insulin.

Signs and symptoms - Symptoms of DM include a rapid onset of symptoms, polyphagia, weight loss, ketoacidosis, polyuria, polydipsia, blurred vision, dehydration, and fatigue.

Treatment - Management includes exogenous insulin injections that are required to maintain proper glucose blood levels and avoid complications. Proper nutritional management is also required for blood glucose control. Insulin pumps may be indicated for continuous administration of insulin. Presently, there is no cure for type 1 DM and as a result, the goal is to control the regulation of blood glucose levels (Fig. 7-5).

Type 2 Diabetes Mellitus (DM)

This form of DM typically occurs in the population over the age of 45, however, there has been an increase in children diagnosed with type 2 DM secondary to a rise in childhood obesity. This form of DM typically retains the ability to produce some endogenous insulin.

Etiology - Type 2 DM occurs secondary to an array of dysfunctions resulting from the combination of resistance to insulin action and inadequate insulin secretion. This disorder is characterized by hyperglycemia when the body cannot properly respond to insulin. Obesity is found to contribute to this condition by increasing insulin resistance.

Signs and symptoms - Symptoms are relatively the same as with type 1, however, ketoacidosis does not occur since insulin is still typically produced.

Treatment - Treatment of type 2 diabetes includes blood glucose control through diet, exercise, oral medications or insulin injections when necessary.

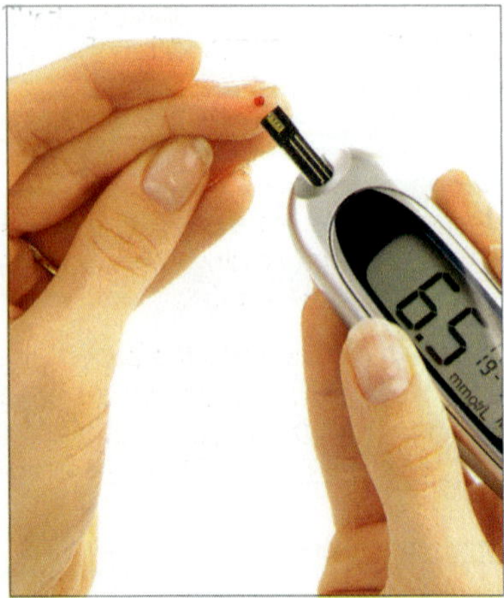

Fig. 7-5: Self-monitoring of blood glucose levels.

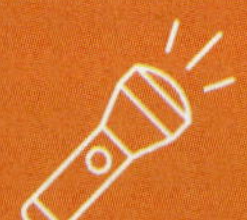

SPOTLIGHT ON SAFETY
BLOOD GLUCOSE LEVELS – EXERCISE RESPONSE[11,18]

For patients with diabetes mellitus (DM), an awareness of how to manage blood glucose levels is imperative to prevent the potentially life threatening effects of hyper or hypoglycemia. Both patients and physical therapists must be aware of the signs and symptoms of these emergent conditions, how to respond, and how therapy interventions may be either a causative or alleviating factor.

Hyperglycemia

Unaddressed hyperglycemia is a significant factor in the development of DM related complications. In addition to blood glucose measures, early signs of hyperglycemia that can occur when blood glucose is >180-200 mg/dl include increased thirst and frequent urination. Recognition of these early signs is crucial in preventing the dangerous onset of ketoacidosis, often referred to as a "diabetic coma." Most commonly occurring in patients with type 1 DM, ketoacidosis is a life-threatening condition requiring immediate medical attention. Symptoms include dyspnea, a fruity breath odor, dry mouth, nausea, vomiting, confusion, and an eventual loss of consciousness.

Hypoglycemia

It is equally important to recognize the initial signs of hypoglycemia so that early intervention may prevent more serious symptoms. Early signs of hypoglycemia that may occur when blood glucose is <70 mg/dl include hunger, sweating, shaking, dizziness, clumsiness, and headache. If unaddressed, patients who become hypoglycemic may lose consciousness, at which point immediate medical attention is necessary. Hypoglycemia is often counteracted simply by ingestion of a glucose or carbohydrate-rich substance (e.g., sugar, honey, juice, crackers). Patients with significant hypoglycemic issues may be advised by their physician to carry a glucose source or injectable glucagon with them at all times.

Exercise Response

A regular exercise program offers numerous benefits to patients with DM. The weight and stress management aspects of exercise are particularly beneficial with regard to controlling blood glucose levels. Physical and mental stressors have been shown to elevate blood glucose levels making long term management more challenging for patients with DM. Exercise provides positive dual influences of aiding stress management and increasing blood glucose uptake by the muscles without significantly impacting insulin levels. Physical therapists, however, must be alert to signs of exercise induced hypoglycemia which may occur with strenuous or prolonged exercise tasks. The risk of symptom onset can often be reduced by ingestion of a carbohydrate snack prior to exercise in order to compensate for increased glucose demands and/or increased insulin absorption.

Type 1 Diabetes Mellitus[12] (insulin-dependent, juvenile diabetes)	Type 2 Diabetes Mellitus[12] (non-insulin dependent, adult onset diabetes)
Onset: usually less than 25 years of age	Onset: usually older than 45 years of age
Abrupt onset	Gradual onset
5-10% of all cases	90-95% of all cases
Etiology: destruction of islets of Langerhans cells secondary to possible autoimmune or viral causative factor	Etiology: resistance at insulin receptor sites usually secondary to obesity; ethnic prevalence
Insulin production: very little or none	Insulin production: variable
Ketoacidosis can occur	Ketoacidosis will rarely occur
Treatment includes insulin injection, exercise, and diet	Treatment includes weight loss, oral insulin, exercise, and diet

Rehabilitation Considerations for Patients with Diabetes Mellitus[10]

- Recognize the risk for peripheral neuropathies, small vessel angiopathy, tissue ischemia and ulceration, impaired wound healing, tissue necrosis, and amputation
- Recognize acute metabolic changes
- Recognize the signs of sudden hypoglycemia and necessary treatment
- Focus on consistent management of insulin intake, diet, and physical activity
- Provide education for proper skin care, shoe evaluation, and shoe wear

Gestational Diabetes

Gestational diabetes is a condition characterized by an increase in insulin resistance and therefore an increase in blood glucose levels that occurs during pregnancy. This condition generally develops in the last trimester. The etiology of the condition is not known, but it is thought that hormones that assist the fetus to grow and develop also lead to insulin resistance. The large majority of women with gestational diabetes return to normal glucose metabolism after the pregnancy. If glucose intolerance persists for more than six weeks after childbirth, the patient should be reclassified to another form of diabetes mellitus.

Babies born to women with gestational diabetes have increased glucose levels and are at an increased risk for macrosomia (i.e., larger than average size), which makes delivery more difficult and potentially more dangerous. The baby may also experience breathing difficulties, jaundice, and hypoglycemia following birth. In childhood and adolescence, these children are more likely to experience insulin resistance, obesity, behavior health issues such as hyperactivity disorders, and delays in gross and fine motor skills.

Diabetes Testing

There are several different methods of testing for diabetes mellitus (DM). Testing is generally performed on two different occasions to confirm a diagnosis of DM. Some of the various testing procedures include:

Fasting plasma glucose – Blood glucose testing that occurs at least eight hours after a patient's last intake of food or drink. Testing is positive for DM if the blood glucose level is >125 mg/dL (normal is <100 mg/dL).

Oral glucose tolerance test – Blood glucose testing that occurs two hours after ingestion of a sugary drink. Testing is positive for DM if the blood glucose level is 200 mg/dL or greater (normal is <140 mg/dL).

A1c testing – A blood test based on the attachment of glucose to hemoglobin that measures the patient's average blood glucose level over the past 2-3 months. Testing is positive for DM if the A1c level is 6.5% or greater (normal is <5.7%).

A diagnosis of DM may also be made if a patient has classic signs and symptoms of DM (e.g., polydipsia, polyuria) along with a casual (random) glucose test of 200 mg/dL or greater. Casual glucose testing can be performed at any time of day without regard to food or drink intake.

Testes and Ovaries Dysfunction[10]

In males, the hypothalamus produces gonadotropin-releasing hormone (GnRH) and the pituitary responds by producing luteinizing hormone (LH) and follicle-stimulating hormone (FSH). The Leydig cells of the testes respond to these hormones with the production of testosterone. This cycle normally occurs on a daily basis.

In females, the hypothalamus produces GnRH and the pituitary responds by producing LH and FSH. In the ovaries, LH acts on theca and interstitial cells to produce progestins and androgens, and FSH acts on granulosa cells to stimulate the precursor steroids to estrogen.

Male hypogonadism: Primary hypogonadism is defined as a deficiency of testosterone secondary to failure of the testes to respond to FSH and LH (produced by the pituitary and hypothalamus). The most common cause of primary hypogonadism is Klinefelter's syndrome. Secondary hypogonadism occurs when there is a failure of the hypothalamus or pituitary to produce the hormones that will subsequently stimulate the production of testosterone. If a male experiences this prior to puberty, symptoms will include sparse body hair, underdevelopment of skeletal muscles, and long arms and legs secondary to a delay in the closure of the epiphyseal growth plates. Adult-onset testosterone deficiency will present with a decreased libido, erectile dysfunction, infertility, decreased cognitive skills, mood changes, and sleep disturbances. Treatment includes hormone replacement pharmacological intervention.

Female hypogonadism: Primary hypogonadism results if the gonad does not produce the amount of sex steroid sufficient to suppress secretion of LH and FSH at normal levels. The most common cause of primary hypogonadism is Turner syndrome. Secondary hypogonadism occurs when there is a failure of the hypothalamus or pituitary to produce the hormones that subsequently stimulate the production of estrogen. If a female experiences this prior to puberty symptoms will include gonadal dysgenesis, a short stature, failure to progress through puberty or primary amenorrhea, and premature gonadal failure. When hypogonadism occurs in postpubescent females, secondary amenorrhea is the primary symptom. Treatment includes hormone replacement pharmacological intervention.

Pharmacology - Endocrine Management[19]

Endocrine pharmacological intervention will either consist of replacement therapy that will provide the deficient hormones or hyperfunction therapy which inhibits the oversecretion of the target hormones. The following is an overview highlighting only the general process for treatment.

Bone Mineral Regulating Agents

Action: Bone mineral regulating agents attempt to enhance and maximize bone mass along with preventing bone loss or rate of bone resorption. Typical agents can include estrogens, calcium and vitamin D, bisphosphonates, calcitonin, and anabolic agents.

Indications: Paget's disease, osteoporosis, hyperparathyroidism, rickets, hypoparathyroidism, osteomalacia

Side effects: (agent dependent) gastrointestinal distress, dyspepsia, dysphagia, anorexia, bone pain, cardiac arrhythmias

Implications for PT: Patients with bone mineralization deficit are at risk for fracture and side effects from drug therapy. Therapists must be aware of potential side effects and should attempt to augment drug therapy through ambulation and other weight bearing activities that stimulate bone formation.

Examples: Estrogens: Premarin (conjugated estrogen); Calcium and vitamin D: Tums (calcium carbonate), Calderol (calcifediol); Bisphosphonates: Fosamax (alendronate sodium), Boniva (ibandronate); Calcitonin: Cibacalcin (human calcitonin)

Hormone Replacement Agents

Action: These agents restore normal endocrine function when endogenous production of a particular hormone is deficient or absent.

Indications: decrease in endogenous hormone secretion

Side effects: Vary by exogenous or synthetic hormone replacement used for treatment

Implications for PT: Therapists must be aware of signs and symptoms of hormone deficit and side effects of hormone therapy.

Examples: see specific hormone categories, pg. 524-526

Hyperfunction Agents

Action: These agents manage hyperactive endocrine function to allow for inhibition of hormone function. This is accomplished through negative feedback loops or through hormone antagonists.

Indications: hyperactive or excessive endocrine function, excessive hormone levels

Side effects: Vary depending on the use of exogenous or synthetic hormone therapy

Implications for PT: Therapists must be aware of signs of hyperfunction of particular hormones and side effects from agents that attempt to regulate and normalize hormone functioning.

Examples: see specific hormone categories, pg. 524-526

Gastrointestinal System

Gastrointestinal System

The gastrointestinal system is responsible for the process of digestion. It breaks down food into its components, absorbs nutrients, and discards the waste.

Gastrointestinal Anatomy and Function[10]

Upper GI	
Mouth	Initiation of mechanical and chemical digestion
Esophagus	Transports food from the mouth to the stomach
Stomach	Grinding of food, secretion of hydrochloric acid and other exocrine functions, secretion of hormones that release digestive enzymes from the liver, pancreas, and gallbladder to assist with digestion

Lower GI – Small Intestine	
Duodenum	Neutralizes acid in food from the stomach and mixes pancreatic and biliary secretions with food
Jejunum	Absorbs water, electrolytes, and nutrients
Ileum	Absorbs bile and intrinsic factors to be recycled

Lower GI – Large Intestine	
Ascending colon **Transverse colon** **Descending colon** **Sigmoid colon** **Rectum** **Anus**	Continues to absorb water and electrolytes, stores and eliminates undigested food as feces

Gland Organs	
Gallbladder	Stores and releases bile into the duodenum to assist with digestion
Liver	Bile is produced and is necessary for absorption of lipid soluble substances, assists with red blood cell and vitamin K production, regulates serum level of carbohydrates, proteins, and fats
Pancreas	Exocrine - secretes bicarbonate and digestive enzymes into the duodenum; Endocrine - secretes insulin, glucagon, and other hormones into the blood to regulate serum glucose level

Gastrointestinal System Pathology

GI Components	Common Pathologies
Esophagus	Hiatal hernia, gastroesophageal reflux disease, esophageal cancer, dysphagia, esophageal varices, Barrett's esophagus
Stomach	Gastritis, peptic ulcer disease, gastric cancer, gastrointestinal hemorrhage, motility and emptying disorders
Intestines	Malabsorption syndrome, appendicitis, irritable bowel syndrome, Crohn's disease, ulcerative colitis, colon cancer, intestinal hernia, diverticular diseases
Rectum and anus	Rectal or anal cancer, hemorrhoids, anorectal fistula, rectal fissure
Gallbladder	Gallstones (cholelithiasis), cholecystitis, gallbladder cancer
Liver	Cirrhosis, jaundice, hepatitis (A, B, C, D, E, G), ascites, hepatic encephalopathy, liver cancer, hepatomegaly
Pancreas	Pancreatitis (acute and chronic), diabetes mellitus, pancreatic cancer

Rehabilitation Considerations for Patients with Gastrointestinal Disease[10]

- Recognize electrolyte imbalances from diarrhea, vomiting, and weight loss
- Recognize the potential for orthostatic hypotension secondary to electrolyte imbalances
- Increased risk for muscle cramping secondary to alteration in the sodium-potassium pumps
- Potential for difficulty swallowing secondary to disk protrusion or esophageal pathology
- Recognize that back pain and/or shoulder pain may be secondary to an acute ulcer or GI bleed
- Observation of Kehr's sign indicates free air or blood within the abdominal cavity

Esophagus

Gastroesophageal Reflux Disease (GERD)[10,17]

GERD is the result of an incompetent lower esophageal sphincter (LES) that allows reflux of gastric contents. This backwards movement of stomach acids and contents can cause esophageal tissue injury over time as well as other pathology.

Etiology – The etiologies of GERD include weakness of the LES, intermittent relaxation of the LES, direct damage of the LES through NSAIDs, alcohol, infectious agents, smoking, and certain prescription medications.

Signs and symptoms – Clinical symptoms include heartburn, regurgitation of gastric contents, belching, chest pain, hoarseness and coughing, esophagitis, and hematemesis. If GERD is left untreated, the patient may develop esophageal strictures, esophagitis, aspiration pneumonia, asthma, Barrett's esophagitis, and esophageal adenocarcinoma.

Treatment – Treatment is primarily through pharmacological intervention.

Rehabilitation Considerations for Patients with GERD[10,17]

- Avoid certain exercise secondary to an increase in symptoms with activity; recumbency will induce symptoms
- Recognize increased incidence of neck and head discomfort secondary to perception of a lump in the throat and subsequent compensation
- Left sidelying preferred since right sidelying may promote acid flowing into the esophagus
- Recognize conditions such as chronic bronchitis, asthma, and pulmonary fibrosis may all present with GERD
- Recognize that tight clothing, exercise, and constipation may all precipitate GERD
- Consider that certain positioning during postural drainage may encourage acid to move into the esophagus

Stomach

Gastritis[10,17]

Gastritis is the inflammation of the gastric mucosa or inner layer of the stomach. Symptoms are similar to GERD, however, they tend to have a higher intensity. Gastritis is classified as erosive or non-erosive based on the level and zone of injury.

Erosive Gastritis (acute gastritis)[10,17]

Etiology – Etiology includes bleeding from the gastric mucosa secondary to stress, NSAIDs, alcohol utilization, viral infection or direct trauma.

Signs and symptoms – Symptoms include dyspepsia, nausea, vomiting, and hematemesis. At times, the patient may be asymptomatic.

Treatment – Treatment is supportive with removal of the stimulus of the disease process and pharmacological intervention. Surgical procedures may be required if the bleeding continues.

Non-erosive Gastritis (chronic type B gastritis)[10,17]

Etiology – This condition is typically a result of a helicobacter pylori infection (H. pylori).

Signs and symptoms – The patient is usually asymptomatic but will show symptoms if the gastritis progresses.

Treatment – H. pylori is a carcinogen and must be treated aggressively. Pharmacological intervention is most common and typically includes a proton pump inhibitor and antibiotics.

Rehabilitation Considerations for Patients with Gastritis[10,17]

- Patients with gastritis secondary to chronic NSAID use may be asymptomatic
- Knowledge of blood in the stool should result in physician referral
- Educate each patient to take medications with food and avoid certain types of food and drink
- The patient should avoid all aspirin-containing compounds

Peptic Ulcer Disease[10,17]

Peptic ulcer disease is a condition where there is a disruption or erosion in the gastrointestinal mucosa. There is an imbalance between the protective mechanisms of the stomach and the secretion of acids within the stomach.

Etiology – Many ulcers are caused by the H. pylori infection and chronic NSAID use. Irritants that increase risk of ulcer include stress, alcohol, particular medications, foods, and smoking.

Signs and symptoms – Symptoms are dependent on the location and severity of ulceration (gastric or duodenal) and can include epigastric pain, burning or heartburn, nausea, vomiting, bleeding, bloody stools, and pain that comes in waves that may be relieved or exacerbated by eating. Symptoms specific to the etiology of H. pylori can also include halitosis, rosacea, and flushing. Complications can include hemorrhage, perforation, obstruction (secondary to scarring), and malignancy.

Treatment – Treatment is primarily through pharmacological intervention, however, in more severe cases, surgical intervention may be required.

Rehabilitation Considerations for Patients with Peptic Ulcer Disease[10]

- Asymptomatic patients with history of ulcer should be monitored for signs of bleeding
- Fatigue level, pallor, and exercise tolerance must be monitored for signs of bleeding
- Recognize that heart rate increase or blood pressure decrease may be signs of bleeding
- Recognize that back pain is a sign of a perforated ulcer located on the posterior wall of the stomach and duodenum
- Recognize that pain that radiates from the midthoracic area to the right upper quadrant and shoulder may signify blood and acid within the peritoneal cavity secondary to a perforated and bleeding ulcer

Diarrhea/Constipation[10]

Diarrhea is defined as an abnormal frequency or volume of stool and can appear as a symptom of certain gastrointestinal pathologies. Constipation is defined as the infrequent or difficult passage of stool, secondary to an increase in the hardness of the stool, and can also appear as a symptom of certain gastrointestinal pathologies.

Conditions Associated with Diarrhea and Constipation[17]

Diarrhea	Constipation
• Irritable bowel syndrome	• Multiple sclerosis
• Hyperthyroidism	• Spinal cord tumors
• Electrolyte imbalance	• Irritable bowel syndrome
• Endocrine disorder	• Duchenne muscular dystrophy
• Incomplete obstruction of the bowel	• Endocrine disorder
• Diverticulitis	• Diverticulitis
• Certain medications	• Inactivity
• Caffeine	• Bowel obstruction or fecal impaction
• Diet	• Pregnancy
• Malabsorption	• CVA
• Pelvic inflammatory disease	• Certain medications

Intestines

Malabsorption Syndrome[10,17]

Malabsorption syndrome is a condition characterized by a group of pathologies where there is reduced intestinal absorption and inadequate nutrition. Celiac disease, cystic fibrosis, pancreatic carcinoma, pernicious anemia, AIDS, Crohn's disease, and Addison's disease are a few pathologies that may present with malabsorption syndrome.

Etiology – Malabsorption syndrome occurs secondary to defects in digestion and/or the inability of the intestinal mucosa to absorb the nutrients from digested food.

Signs and symptoms – Although each patient's symptoms are based on the root pathology and co-morbidities that may exist, the primary symptoms are weight loss, chronic diarrhea, and anemia. Other symptoms can include fatigue, abdominal bloating, steatorrhea (oil covered stools), abdominal cramps, indigestion, bone pain, and excessive gas.

Treatment – Once diagnosed, treatment includes avoidance of the underlying cause for the malabsorption, probiotics, antibiotics, dietary modification, and nutritional support including vitamins, minerals, and electrolytes.

Rehabilitation Considerations for Patients with Malabsorption Syndrome[10]

- Recognize increased risk for osteoporosis and pathologic fractures
- Monitor fatigue level, pallor, bone pain, and exercise tolerance
- Recognize weight loss and abdominal bloating
- Recognize increased risk for muscle spasms secondary to electrolyte imbalances
- Recognize increased risk for generalized swelling secondary to protein depletion

Irritable Bowel Syndrome (IBS)[10,17]

Irritable bowel syndrome consists of recurrent symptoms of the upper and lower gastrointestinal system that interfere with the normal functioning of the colon.

Etiology – The etiology is unknown, but one theory believes that the colon or large intestine may be sensitive to certain foods or stress. Other theories hypothesize that the immune system, serotonin, and bacterial infections may all be causative factors. Females have a slightly higher rate of incidence which may be triggered by food sensitivities, stress, anxiety, caffeine, smoking, alcohol or high fat intake.

Signs and symptoms – Symptoms can include abdominal pain, bloating or distention of the abdomen, nausea, vomiting, anorexia, changes in form and frequency of stool, and passing of mucus in the stool.

Treatment – IBS is normally a diagnosis of exclusion from other GI diagnoses and treatment is usually multifactorial. Change in lifestyle and nutrition, decrease in stress, pharmacological intervention, adequate sleep, exercise, and psychotherapy may all assist in alleviating symptoms. Patients with IBS should avoid large meals, milk, wheat, rye, barley, alcohol, and caffeine. Although the symptoms can be severe, it does not lead to serious disease. Symptoms can typically be controlled by diet, pharmacological intervention, and stress management.

Rehabilitation Considerations for Patients with Irritable Bowel Syndrome[10]

- Emphasize physical activity to assist with bowel function and relieve stress
- Emphasize breathing techniques to assist in stress reduction and with breath-holding patterns
- Recognize that biofeedback training may be beneficial

Diverticulitis[10,17]

Diverticulitis is the condition of having inflamed or infected diverticula. This occurs in roughly a quarter of the population that has diverticulosis. Diverticulosis is the condition of having diverticula. These are pouch-like protrusions occurring in the colon. The large majority of individuals with diverticulosis are asymptomatic, however, those with symptoms may experience bloating, mild cramping, and both diarrhea and constipation. Treatment includes an increased amount of dietary fiber (20-35 grams per day recommended) to avoid diverticulitis.

Etiology – The exact etiology of diverticulitis is unknown; however, a dominant theory is that the disease results from a low fiber diet.

Signs and symptoms – Abdominal pain is the primary symptom of diverticulitis. Tenderness over the left side of the lower abdomen, cramping, constipation or diarrhea, nausea, fever, chills, and vomiting can also occur.

Treatment – Treatment includes diet modification, controlling the underlying infection, and lowering internal colonic pressure through increased fiber intake. In more severe cases, a nasogastric tube may be required to give the intestines a rest. Surgical intervention is indicated for severe obstruction, perforation or necrosis. Complications can include bleeding infections, intestinal blockage, abscess, perforations or tears in the colon, fistulas or peritonitis.

Rehabilitation Considerations for Patients with Diverticular Disease[10]

- Physical activity assists the bowel function and is extremely important during periods of remission
- Breathing techniques will assist in stress reduction and with breath-holding patterns
- Avoid any increase in intra-abdominal pressure with exercise or activity
- Back pain and/or referred hip pain must be examined for possible medical diseases

Liver

Hepatitis[10,17]

Hepatitis is an inflammatory process within the liver. Viral hepatitis is most common and is classified as hepatitis A, B, C, D, E or G. Hepatitis A, B, and C are the most common and discussed briefly below.

Etiology – Many instances of hepatitis are viral in nature. Other etiologies include a chemical reaction, drug reaction or alcohol abuse. Other viruses that can cause hepatitis include Epstein-Barr virus, herpes virus I and II, varicella-zoster virus, and measles.

Signs and symptoms – Symptoms of hepatitis include fever, flu symptoms, abrupt onset of fatigue, anorexia, headache, jaundice, darkened urine, lighter stool, enlarged spleen and liver, and intermittent pruritus.

Treatment – Acute viral hepatitis usually resolves with medical treatment, but can become chronic in some cases. Chronic hepatitis may result in the need for liver transplant.

Hepatitis A (HAV)

Hepatitis A is a virus that affects the liver and its function. Transmission occurs by close personal contact with someone that has the infection or through the fecal-oral route (i.e., contaminated water and food sources). The flu-like symptoms represent an acute infection; this form does not progress to chronic disease or cirrhosis of the liver. Patients usually recover in six to ten weeks. Treatment is supportive and the virus is self-limiting.

Hepatitis B (HBV)

Hepatitis B is a virus that affects the liver and its function. Transmission of this virus occurs through the sharing of needles, intercourse with an infected person, exposure to an infected person's blood, semen or maternal-fetal exposure. A small proportion of cases progress to chronic hepatitis since the body cannot always rid itself of HBV. Treatment includes hepatitis B immunoglobulin (HBIG) for the unvaccinated patient within 24 hours of exposure. The patient should then receive the vaccination series at one and six months. If the patient is already vaccinated, they may require another dose of the HBV vaccine. Chronic hepatitis is now being treated with interferon alfa-2b, providing remission for some patients.

Hepatitis C (HCV)

Hepatitis C is a virus that affects the liver and its function. It is one of the primary etiologies for chronic liver disease and eventual liver failure. Transmission of this virus occurs through the sharing of needles, intercourse with an infected person, exposure to an infected person's blood, semen, body fluids or maternal-fetal exposure. The virus accounts for the large majority of post transfusion hepatitis cases. Like hepatitis B, this virus is often asymptomatic and the acute infection can be mild. Patients with hepatitis C have an increased frequency of manifesting conditions such as Hashimoto's thyroiditis, diabetes mellitus, and corneal ulceration. Treatment may include the use of interferon alfa-2b to reduce the inflammation and liver damage but only a small percentage of patients with hepatitis C benefit from the medication. There is no vaccine to prevent this virus and no immunoglobulin fully effective in treating the infection. Chronic hepatitis occurs in about half of the cases, with some of those cases progressing to cirrhosis of the liver.

Rehabilitation Considerations for Patients with Hepatitis[10]

- Health care workers that are at risk for contact with hepatitis should receive all immunizations for HBV, and if exposed to blood or body fluids of an infected person must receive immunoglobulin therapy immediately
- Standard precautions should be followed at all times for protection
- Enteric precautions are required for patients with hepatitis A and E
- Recognize that arthralgias may be noted, especially in older patients, and will not typically respond to traditional therapeutic intervention
- Energy conservation techniques and pacing skills should be incorporated into therapy
- Balance activities along with periods of rest, avoid prolonged bed rest, and provide patient education regarding signs of relapse or chronic hepatitis

Cirrhosis of the Liver[10,17]

Cirrhosis of the liver is a condition where the healthy tissue of the liver is replaced with scar tissue that blocks the flow of blood through the organ and prevents the liver from properly functioning.

Etiology – The etiology is usually alcoholism or hepatitis C. Alcohol tends to block the normal metabolism of protein, fats, and carbohydrates. This condition will normally occur after a patient has been heavily drinking for more than a decade. Inflammation of the liver secondary to hepatitis C is also a large causative factor for cirrhosis. Persistent inflammation and slow damage to the liver will result in cirrhosis of the liver after several decades of infection. Other causes include hepatitis B and D, certain drugs, infections, and toxins, specific hereditary diseases, nonalcoholic steatohepatitis, and blocked bile ducts.

Signs and symptoms – Symptoms include fatigue, decreased appetite, nausea, weakness, abdominal pain, spider angiomas, and weight loss. Common complications from cirrhosis include ascites (water accumulation in the abdomen secondary to decreased production of albumin by the liver), edema in the lower extremities, jaundice, gallstones, increased itching, ecchymosis, bleeding, an increase in sensitivity to medications, accumulation of toxins in the brain, portal vein hypertension, development of varices (enlarged blood vessels in the stomach and esophagus), immune system dysfunction, encephalopathy, and liver cancer.

Treatment – Treatment cannot reverse the process or damage, but can slow the process. Treatment is based on the causative factors and is implemented until symptoms cannot be controlled. A liver transplant may be necessary to sustain life.

Pancreas

Diabetes Mellitus

Please refer to the endocrine section on page 530 and the clinical application templates on diabetes mellitus on pages 606 and 608.

Rehabilitation Considerations for Patients with Cirrhosis of the Liver[10]

- Recognize that ascites may develop as well as fluid accumulation in the ankles and feet
- Report any blood loss through nose bleeds, gum bleeds, tarry stools or excessive bruising
- Avoid all activities that produce the Valsalva maneuver (increase in intra-abdominal pressure)
- Adequate rest is required to lower the demands on the liver and improve circulation; avoid unnecessary fatigue with therapeutic or daily activities

Gallbladder

Cholecystitis and Cholelithiasis[10,17]

Cholecystitis refers to inflammation of the gallbladder that may be acute or chronic.

Etiology – The most common etiology is gallstones (cholelithiasis) that have become impacted within the cystic duct. Gallstones develop from hypomobility of the gallbladder, supersaturation of the bile with cholesterol or crystal formation from bilirubin salts. These stones can also cause infection which exacerbate the condition.

Signs and symptoms – Many times gallstones are asymptomatic, however, the most common symptom is right upper quadrant pain. If the gallstone becomes lodged within the cystic duct, then the patient can experience many problems including severe right upper quadrant pain with muscle guarding, tenderness, and rebound pain. These symptoms can radiate to the interscapular region. Other symptoms include jaundice, fever, nausea, vomiting, anorexia, and abdominal rigidity.

Treatment – Treatment is not recommended for the patient with asymptomatic gallstones, but a low-fat diet can decrease gallbladder stimulation if mild symptoms are present. If patients are symptomatic, a lithotripsy procedure can be used in an attempt to break up and dissolve the stones. Primary treatment is a laparoscopic cholecystectomy to remove the gallbladder and the lodged stones from the ducts. Acute cholecystitis should resolve itself within a week with analgesics, antibiotics, and intravenous alimentary feedings.

Rehabilitation Considerations for Patients with Cholecystitis and Cholelithiasis[10]

- Must be familiar with all signs and symptoms of cholecystitis in order to refer patients to a physician if a change in their status occurs
- Post-surgical exercises and ambulation are appropriate post laparoscopic cholecystectomy such as breathing exercises, splinting while coughing, and mobility training

Pharmacology - Gastrointestinal Management[19]

Pharmacological intervention is normally related to gastrointestinal disorders that are caused by gastric acid secretion and abnormal food movement through the gastrointestinal tract.

Antacid Agents

Action: Antacid agents are used to chemically neutralize gastric acid and increase the intragastric pH. Primary antacids are classified as aluminum-containing, calcium carbonate-containing, magnesium-containing or sodium bicarbonate-containing.

Indications: episodic minor gastric indigestion or heartburn, peptic ulcer, gastroesophageal reflux disease (GERD)

Side effects: acid rebound phenomenon, constipation or diarrhea (depending on the antacid), may affect metabolism of other medication, electrolyte imbalances

Implications for PT: Since these agents are well tolerated, there are typically no side effects that interfere with physical therapy. Patients are more likely to participate in therapy with effective management of gastrointestinal issues using these agents.

Examples: Aluminum-containing: Basaljel (aluminum carbonate gel); Calcium carbonate-containing: Tums (calcium carbonate); Magnesium-containing: Milk of Magnesia (magnesium hydroxide); Sodium bicarbonate-containing: Bromo seltzer (sodium bicarbonate)

Antibiotics

Action: Antibiotics are prescribed to treat H. pylori infection with the goal of facilitating more rapid healing of associated gastric ulcerations.

Indications: H. pylori bacteria

Side effects: hypersensitivity, diarrhea, nausea

Implications for PT: Physical therapists should be aware of potential side effects in order to respond appropriately especially with regard to severe dermatologic and respiratory reactions which may be associated with hypersensitivity.

Examples: metronidazole, tetracycline, clarithromycin, amoxicillin

Anticholinergics

Action: Anticholinergics block the effects of acetylcholine on parietal cells in the stomach and decrease the release of gastric acid.

Indications: gastric ulcers

Side effects: dry mouth, confusion, constipation, urinary retention

Implications for PT: Physical therapists should be aware of potential side effects in order to respond appropriately to changes in cognition or complaints of dry mouth, constipation or urinary retention.

Examples: Gastrozepin (pirenzepine), muscarinic cholinergic antagonist

Antidiarrheal Agents

Action: Antidiarrheal agents are used to slow the serious debilitating effects of dehydration associated with prolonged diarrhea. There are multiple classes of antidiarrheal agents.

Indications: prolonged diarrhea

Side effects: constipation, abdominal discomfort

Implications for PT: Since these agents are well tolerated there are typically no side effects that interfere with physical therapy. Patients are more likely to participate in therapy with effective management of gastrointestinal issues using these agents.

Examples: Donnagel (attapulgite), Kapectolin (kaolin), Pepto-Bismol (bismuth subsalicylate), Motofen (difenoxin), Imodium (loperamide)

Antiemetic Agents

Action: Antiemetic agents are used to decrease symptoms of nausea and vomiting.

Indications: nausea associated with motion sickness, anesthesia, pain or oncology treatments

Side effects: side effects are agent dependent, but can include sedation, dysrhythmias, and pain.

Implications for PT: Antiemetic agents frequently cause sedative effects which can be limiting to physical therapy interventions. Many other antiemetic agents are typically well tolerated and should not significantly interfere with therapy interventions.

Examples: Scopolamine (anticholinergic agent), Meclizine (antihistamine agent), Dolasetron (5-HT3 receptor antagonist agent), Phenergan (promethazine hydrochloride)

Emetic Agents

Action: Emetic agents are used to induce vomiting.

Indications: to induce vomiting; usually after ingestion of a toxic substance

Side effects: dehydration, electrolyte imbalance, and upper GI erosion may occur with inappropriate or prolonged usage

Implications for PT: The medical concerns associated with administration of an emetic agent should be addressed prior to initiation or resumption of therapy interventions. Therapy should also be deferred if a patient is actively vomiting.

Examples: Apomorphine, Ipecac

H_2 Receptor Blockers

Action: H_2 receptor blockers bind specifically to histamine receptors to prevent the histamine-activated release of gastric acid normally stimulated during food intake.

Indications: dyspepsia, acute and long-term treatment of peptic ulcer, GERD

Side effects: headache, dizziness, mild gastrointestinal distress, tolerance, arthralgia, acid rebound with discontinuation of agent

Implications for PT: Since these agents are well tolerated there are typically no side effects that interfere with physical therapy. Patients are more likely to participate in therapy with effective management of gastrointestinal issues using these agents.

Examples: Tagamet (cimetidine), Pepcid (famotidine), Zantac (ranitidine)

CONSIDER THIS

REFERRED VISCERAL PAIN MAY MIMIC MUSCULOSKELETAL CONDITIONS[17]

Visceral pain refers to pain caused by pathology in the visceral organs (e.g., organ cancer, small bowel obstruction, kidney stones). Pain originating from organs is often difficult to localize due to the tendency to perceive the pain in locations other than the organ source. Due to the overlap in sensory and visceral nerve pathways, symptoms will often refer to soft tissue within the dermatome that corresponds to the organ's spinal cord innervation. The left arm or jaw pain commonly associated with myocardial infarction is a well known example of referred visceral pain. With lesser known symptoms, however, referred pain patterns may result in a delayed diagnosis. Many referred visceral pain patterns mimic musculoskeletal symptoms. Therefore physical therapists must be diligent in assessing pain of an unknown origin. Since visceral pain is transmitted via the autonomic nervous system, this is especially true when pain is accompanied by autonomic responses such as nausea, vomiting, pallor or sweating.

Laxative Agents

Action: Laxative agents are used to facilitate bowel evacuation and should be used sparingly.

Indications: to promote defecation

Side effects: nausea, abdominal discomfort, cramping, electrolyte imbalance, dehydration, dependence with prolonged use

Implications for PT: If the laxative was recently ingested, physical discomfort may temporarily limit patient participation in therapy interventions. Patients may also express concern about treatment occurring in areas that do not have easy access to restroom facilities.

Examples: Citrucel (methylcellulose), Metamucil (psyllium), Colace (docusate), Fleet Glycerin suppository (glycerin), Phillips' Milk of Magnesia (magnesium hydroxide), Correctol (bisacodyl), Senokot (senna)

Proton Pump Inhibitors (PPI)

Action: Proton pump inhibitor agents inhibit the H+/K+-ATPase enzyme, blocking secretions of acid from gastric cells into the stomach. These agents prevent erosive esophagitis and may also possess antibacterial effects against H. pylori.

Indications: dyspepsia, GERD

Side effects: acid rebound phenomenon when discontinued after prolonged use

Implications for PT: Since these agents are well tolerated, there are typically no side effects that interfere with physical therapy. Patients are more likely to participate in therapy with effective management of gastrointestinal issues using these agents.

Examples: Prevacid (lansoprazole), Nexium (esomeprazole), Prilosec (omeprazole), Protonix (pantoprazole), AcipHex (rabeprazole)

Abdominal Pain Quadrant and Potential Etiologies[17,20]

Left upper quadrant	Right upper quadrant	Left lower quadrant	Right lower quadrant
Gastric ulcer	Hepatomegaly	Perforated colon	Kidney stone
Perforated colon	Duodenal ulcer	Ileitis	Ureteral stone
Pneumonia	Cholecystitis	Sigmoid diverticulitis	Meckel diverticulum
Spleen injury	Pneumonia	Kidney stone	Appendicitis
Spleen rupture	Hepatitis	Ureteral stone	Cholecystitis
Aortic aneurysm	Biliary stones	Intestinal obstruction	Intestinal obstruction

Gastrointestinal System Terminology

Adhesion: Fibrous bands of tissue that bind together normally separate anatomic structures.

Anastomosis: Joining of two ducts, blood vessels or bowel segments to allow flow from one to the other. An anastomosis may be naturally occurring or may be created during embryonic development, surgery or by pathologic means.

Ascites: Fluid in the peritoneal cavity, usually causing abdominal swelling.

Barium: A substance that, when swallowed or given rectally as an enema, makes the upper gastrointestinal tract visible on x-ray.

Biopsy: Removal of a sample of tissue taken from the body for study, usually under a microscope.

Colectomy: The surgical removal of part or all of the colon.

Colonoscopy: Visual inspection of the interior of the colon with a flexible, lighted instrument inserted through the rectum.

Colostomy: The surgical creation of an opening from the colon through the abdominal wall.

Constipation: Infrequent or difficult passage of stool, secondary to an increase in the hardness of the stool.

Diarrhea: Abnormal frequency or volume of stool that often appears as a symptom of certain gastrointestinal pathologies.

Endoscopy: A method of physical examination using a lighted, flexible instrument that allows a physician to examine the inside of the digestive tract.
Endosonography: A diagnostic tool used to visualize the gastrointestinal organs using high-frequency sound waves.
Enema: Injection of fluid into the rectum and colon to induce a bowel movement.
Esophagus: A muscular tube connecting the pharynx with the stomach.
Fecal diversion: Surgical creation of an opening of part of the colon or small intestine to the surface of the skin to allow for stool to exit the body.
Fecal incontinence: Inability to retain stool, resulting in leakage of stool from the rectum.
Fecal occult blood test: A lab test used to check a stool sample for blood.
Fistula: An abnormal or surgically made passage that forms between two internal organs or between two different parts of the intestine.
Gas: A product of digestion that is made primarily of odorless vapors.
Gastrectomy: Surgical procedure in which all or part of the stomach is removed.
Gastric: Pertaining to the stomach.
Gastroscopy: Procedure to examine the upper gastrointestinal tract using an endoscope which is passed through the mouth and into the stomach.
Heartburn: A form of indigestion
Helicobacter pylori: A type of bacterium that causes infection in the stomach. The bacterium is often the causative agent in peptic ulcers.
Ileocolectomy: Surgical removal of a section of the ileum and ascending colon.
Ileostomy: The surgical creation of an opening from the ileum through the abdominal wall.
Jaundice: A condition in which the skin and eyes turn yellow because of increased levels of bilirubin in the blood.
Laparoscopy: A surgical diagnostic procedure utilizing a fiber optic instrument inserted through the abdominal wall to view organs.
Large intestine: The portion of the digestive tract made up of the ascending colon, transverse colon, descending colon, sigmoid colon, and appendix. The large intestine receives the liquid contents from the small intestine and absorbs the water and electrolytes from this liquid to form feces or waste.
Laxative: Medications that increase the action of the intestines or stimulate the addition of water to the stool to facilitate bowel evacuation.
Mesentery: A fold of the peritoneum that carries blood vessels and lymph glands, and attaches various organs to the abdominal wall.
Paracentesis: The removal of accumulated fluid from the abdomen.
Peristalsis: Involuntary contraction and relaxation of the muscles of the intestines which propel food.
Polyps (colon): Small, non-cancerous growths on the inner lining of the colon.
Small intestine: The portion of the digestive tract that first receives food from the stomach. The small intestine is comprised of the duodenum, jejunum and ileum.
Stoma: An artificial opening of the intestine through the abdominal wall.
Thrombosis: The formation of a blood clot in a blood vessel.
Ulcers: A break in the lining of the stomach or in the duodenum.
Varices: Large, swollen veins that develop in the esophagus or stomach, often causing internal bleeding.
Vomiting: The forcible expulsion of the contents of the stomach through the mouth.

Genitourinary System

Genitourinary System

The genitourinary system consists of all the reproductive organs and the urinary organs. These are often considered together due to their common embryological origin.

Genitourinary Anatomy and Function

The genitourinary system is supported by the pelvic floor consisting of muscle, fascia, and ligament.

Muscles of the Pelvic Floor[20,21]	
Pelvic diaphragm	Levator ani: pubococcygeus, puborectalis, iliococcygeus, and coccygeus (ischiococcygeus)
Urogenital diaphragm	Deep transverse perineal, urethrae sphincter
Urogenital triangle	Female: bulbocavernosus, ischiocavernosus, superficial transverse perineal Male: bulbospongiosus, ischiocavernosus, superficial transverse perineal
Anal triangle	Internal anal sphincter, external anal sphincter

Genital System

The genital system consists of the male and female gonads and associated ducts, external genitalia, and associated hormones that all function for reproduction.

Female Genital System[20-22]	
External genitalia Mons pubis, labia majora, labia minora, clitoris, vestibule of vagina, bulbs of vestibule, greater vestibular (Bartholin's) glands, Skene's gland	• Provides protection and hydration of vaginal tissue and urethra
Vagina Musculomembranous tube connected to the cervix	• Receptacle for male sperm • Birth canal • Excretory duct for menstrual fluid
Uterus Hollow muscular organ	• Houses the fetus during development
Uterine tubes Extend laterally from the ovaries to the uterus	• Provides transport for the ovum from the ovary for fertilization and implantation within the uterus
Ovaries Almond-shaped glands suspended in the broad ligaments	• Produce hormones such as estrogen and progesterone • Storage of oocytes prior to ovulation

Male Genital System[20]	
Penis	• External genitalia that expels urine during voiding and semen during the act of copulation
Scrotum	• Cutaneous fibromuscular external sac for the testes, ductus deferens, epididymis, nerves, and blood vessels
Testes	• Produce sperm and hormones such as testosterone
Ductus/vas deferens	• Carries sperm from the testes to the seminal vesicle to form the ejaculatory duct
Epididymis	• Encased within the scrotum • Stores sperm
Seminal vesicles	• Internal tubes that secrete a thick fluid to combine with sperm within the ejaculatory duct
Prostate	• Internal organ lying inferior to the bladder • Produces and secretes fluid to combine with sperm, seminal vesicle fluid, and bulbourethral gland fluid to create semen

Renal System

The renal system consists of two kidneys, two ureters, the urinary bladder, and the urethra that function to form and eliminate urine.

Renal System[20,21]	
Kidneys	• Remove water, salt, and metabolic waste from the blood through excretion of urine • Contribute to homeostasis including: acid-base balance, regulation of electrolyte concentrations, control of blood volume, and regulation of blood pressure through the control of hormones secreted into the bloodstream
Ureters	• Muscular tubes connecting the kidneys to the urinary bladder to transport urine
Urinary bladder	• Temporary muscular reservoir for urine
Urethra	• Muscular tube for excretion of urine • Semen transport during ejaculation in males

Genitourinary System Pathology

Genital Components	Common Pathologies[20,21]
Uterus	Cervical cancer*, endometriosis, uterine prolapse
Vagina	Dyspareunia, vulvodynia, vulvovaginal candidiasis (yeast infection)
Prostate	Prostatitis, prostate cancer*
Penis	Erectile dysfunction
Renal Components	**Common Pathologies[20,21]**
Kidneys	Glomerulonephritis, nephrolithiasis, renal failure
Bladder	Cystocele, dysuria, hematuria, interstitial cystitis, neurogenic bladder, nocturia, polyuria, urgency, frequency, urinary incontinence, urinary tract infections

*For more information on cervical and prostate cancer see pages 558-559.

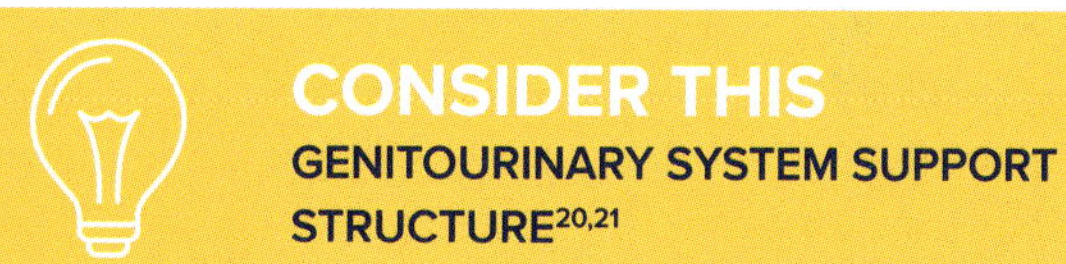

CONSIDER THIS

GENITOURINARY SYSTEM SUPPORT STRUCTURE[20,21]

The pelvic floor muscles' primary functions include bladder/bowel control and sexual function. In addition, the pelvic floor muscles support the pelvic organs by holding the organs in position in conjunction with ligaments and surrounding fascia. The muscles are made up of two different fiber types, type I (slow twitch) and type II (fast twitch). When the pelvic floor muscles are weak or have poor endurance due to pregnancy, trauma, surgery, repetitive straining or genetics they are not able to support the pelvic organs leading to organ prolapse. Affected structures may include the bladder, uterus, cervix, intestines, and rectum. This may result in urgency, frequency, urinary or fecal incontinence due to the muscle imbalance during increased intra-abdominal pressure.

Uterus

Endometriosis[21,23]

Endometriosis is the development of endometrial tissue, which normally lines the uterus, in extrauterine locations within the abdomen and pelvis. The most common location of extrauterine endometrial growth occurs at the uterosacral ligaments. The level of pain does not always correlate with the severity of extrauterine tissue growth.

Etiology – The exact etiology of endometriosis is unknown. During each menstrual cycle the endometrial tissue bleeds causing subsequent scarring and adhesions.

Signs and symptoms – Symptoms can vary, but typically include moderate to severe lower abdominal, pelvic or low back pain before or during menstruation, irregular menstrual cycles, premenstrual spotting, dyspareunia, pain during defecation, and infertility.

Treatment – Physical therapy treatment may include manual techniques such as myofascial release, visceral mobilization and soft and deep tissue massage to break up scar tissue and adhesions. Mobility exercises are performed to sustain elongation of tissues. Relaxation exercises such as breathing routines and restorative poses are performed to regulate the pain cycle. TENS is also indicated. Pharmacological intervention may be indicated to alter hormonal balance using oral contraceptives and antigonadotropins. Surgery to remove extrauterine endometrial tissue, scarring, and adhesions; and a total hysterectomy may be recommended when pregnancy is no longer desired.

Uterine Prolapse[24,25]

Uterine prolapse is the descent of the uterus and cervix into the vagina. The Baden-Walker System is the most widespread classification of prolapse using a five-point grading system ranging from no prolapse to maximum descent of vaginal tissue outside of the body.

Etiology – The etiology typically consists of genetics, denervation or direct muscle trauma (i.e., labor and delivery).

Signs and symptoms – Primary symptoms vary, but can include pelvic pressure that increases with exertion, urgency, frequency, urinary incontinence, incomplete bladder emptying, discomfort, vaginal dryness or irritation, dyspareunia, and lower back pain that is relieved by lying down.

Treatment – Physical therapy treatment may include pelvic floor muscle training using biofeedback, Kegel exercises, core strengthening exercises, body mechanics, and symptom dependent lifestyle modifications. In more severe cases, an intravaginal mechanical support device called a pessary may be indicated. The patient may require reconstructive or obliterative surgery, if conservative treatment fails.

Prostate

Prostatitis[24]

Prostatitis is an inflammation of the prostate gland.

Etiology – The most common etiologies include bacterial infection or the backup of prostate secretions within the gland. Classification of prostatitis includes acute bacterial prostatitis (I), chronic bacterial prostatitis (II), chronic pelvic pain syndrome (III), and asymptomatic inflammatory prostatitis (IV).

Signs and symptoms – Common symptoms include watery urethral discharge, urgency, frequency, discomfort with urination, and pain with ejaculation. Chronic pelvic pain syndrome manifests as pain in the perineum, rectum, prostate, penis, testicles, and abdomen. Asymptomatic inflammatory prostatitis is characterized by prostate inflammation in the absence of genitourinary tract symptoms.

Treatment – Management includes lifestyle modifications, biofeedback training, stretching exercises, myofascial techniques, and bladder retraining. Pharmacological intervention such as antibiotics, alpha blockers or nonsteroidal anti-inflammatory medication for pain may be indicated.

Penis

Erectile Dysfunction (ED)[10,20,24]

Erectile dysfunction, also known as impotence, is more prevalent in men with diabetes when compared to the general population. Onset of ED in individuals with diabetes usually occurs 10-15 years earlier than in men without diabetes.

Etiology – There are various causative factors for ED. Diabetes is a primary etiology, while other risk factors include coronary heart disease, hypertension, hypothyroidism, hypopituitarism, multiple sclerosis, psychiatric disorders, excessive alcohol consumption, smoking, vessel disease, kidney disease, pharmacological side effects, and hormonal imbalances.

Signs and symptoms – The primary symptom is the consistent inability to maintain an erection adequate for sexual intercourse.

Treatment – Treatment varies and includes pharmacological intervention, surgical intervention, injections directly to the penis, and Kegel exercises.

Kidneys

Renal Failure[10,24]

Renal failure is a condition where the kidneys experience a decrease in glomerular filtration rate and fail to adequately filter toxins and waste from the blood. There are two forms: acute renal failure and chronic renal failure.

Etiology – Renal pathology typically occurs secondary to diabetes mellitus or hypertension, but can also occur from poison, trauma, and genetics. The nephrons are usually damaged and they lose their ability to filter the blood. Renal failure can be classified as:

- Acute (damage occurs quickly)
- Chronic (damage occurs slowly)
- End-stage (nearly total or total renal failure, dialysis required)

Acute Renal Failure (ARF)

- Sudden decline in renal function
- Increase in BUN and creatinine
- Oliguria, hyperkalemia, sodium retention
- Prerenal etiology is secondary to a decrease in blood flow typically due to shock, hemorrhage, burn or pulmonary embolism
- Postrenal etiology is secondary to obstruction distal to the kidney due to neoplasm, kidney stone or prostate hypertrophy
- Intrarenal etiology is secondary to primary damage of renal tissue due to toxins, intrarenal ischemia or vascular disorders

Chronic Renal Failure (CRF)

- Progressive deterioration in renal function
- Diabetes mellitus
- Severe hypertension
- Glomerulopathies
- Obstructive uropathy
- Interstitial nephritis
- Polycystic kidney disease

Stages of Kidney Disease According to the National Kidney Foundation

Stage 1 kidney damage with normal GFR (90 or greater)
Stage 2 mild decrease in GFR (60-89)
Stage 3 moderate decrease in GFR (30-59)
Stage 4 severe reduction in GFR (15-29)
Stage 5 kidney failure (GFR less than 15)

Signs and symptoms – Symptoms of renal failure vary based on severity of the condition and can include nausea, vomiting, lethargy, weakness, hiccups, anorexia, ulceration within the GI tract, sleep disorders, headache, peripheral neuropathy, anemia, pruritus, osteomalacia, ecchymosis, pulmonary edema, seizures, and coma.

Treatment – Treatment of ARF includes management of primary etiology, pharmacological intervention, diuretics, nutritional support, hydration, hemodialysis and/or transfusions if applicable. Treatment of CRF includes conservative management and renal replacement therapy. Conservative management assists with slowing the process and assisting the body in its compensation. Nutritional support, hydration, avoidance of protein, and pharmacological intervention are usually the primary basis of intervention. Renal replacement therapy includes some form of hemodialysis and/or organ transplant. Peritoneal dialysis is a form of renal replacement therapy that uses the peritoneal cavity as a semi-permeable membrane between the dialysate fluid and blood vessels of the abdominal cavity.

Hemodialysis

Hemodialysis is a treatment process for patients with advanced and permanent kidney failure. Kidney failure creates excess toxic waste, increased blood pressure, retention of excess body fluids, and a decrease in red blood cell production. Hemodialysis removes the blood from the body along with waste, excess sodium, and fluids. The process cleanses the blood and returns it to the body. A patient requires this process on average three times per week and each visit requires three to five hours to complete the treatment. Side effects that may be associated with dialysis include anemia, renal osteodystrophy, pruritus (itching), sleep disorders ("restless legs"), and dialysis-related amyloidosis.

Rehabilitation Considerations for Patients with Renal Failure/Dialysis[10,24]

- Modify treatment plan based on fluid and electrolyte status
- Standard precautions should be followed at all times for protection
- Recognize patient's abilities post dialysis and potential for dehydration and hypotension
- Monitor vital signs closely, however, avoid placement of the blood pressure cuff over the fistula
- Avoid mobilization activities as they are contraindicated during dialysis
- Energy conservation techniques and pacing skills should be incorporated into therapy

Bladder

Neurogenic Bladder[10,24]

Neurogenic bladder is a dysfunction where there is damage to the cerebral control that allows for urinary dysfunction. If the urine cannot be properly released, there may be an increase in urinary tract infections and kidney damage.

Etiology – The etiology of neurogenic bladder can include diabetes, diminished bladder capacity, hyperactive detrusor muscle, CVA, other disease processes, infection, and nerve damage.

Signs and symptoms – Symptoms include frequent urinary tract infections, leakage of urine, inability to empty the bladder or loss of the urge to urinate when the bladder is full. Diagnosis should include an evaluation by a physician, X-rays, and urodynamics to assist with diagnosis.

Treatment – Management is dependent on the actual etiology with a goal of preventing bladder overdistention, UTIs, and renal damage. Patient education, bladder techniques, lower abdominal massage, temporary catheterization, pharmacological intervention, and a timed urination program may be indicated.

Urinary Incontinence[10,24]

Urinary incontinence is an involuntary loss of urine that is great enough to be problematic for the person and typically occurs when bladder pressure exceeds sphincter resistance. Below are four classifications of urinary incontinence. General treatment includes pelvic floor muscle training using biofeedback, lifestyle modifications, bladder retraining, prompted voiding programs, urge suppression strategies, myofascial release, visceral mobilization, body mechanics, abdominal strengthening, and stretching exercises of surrounding muscles. Pharmacological intervention to address urgency, injection therapy of a "bulking" agent, and surgical intervention for urethral and bladder positioning may also be indicated. These interventions may not apply to all types of urinary incontinence and should be determined on a per patient basis.

Stress Urinary Incontinence (SUI)

SUI is the loss of urine due to activities that increase intra-abdominal pressure, such as sneezing, coughing, laughing, running, and jumping. *Please refer to clinical application template on page 628 for more information.*

Urge Urinary Incontinence (UUI)

UUI is the loss of urine after a sudden, intense urge to void due to the detrusor muscle of the bladder involuntarily contracting during bladder filling. UUI is the most common incontinence in the geriatric population and among residents in long-term care facilities.

Etiology – The most common etiologies are detrusor muscle overactivity, overactive bladder also known as "urgency-frequency" syndrome, changes in the smooth muscle of the bladder, increased afferent activity, increased sensitivity of the detrusor to acetylcholine, and idiopathic. There is also association with the following neurological disorders: multiple sclerosis, spinal cord injury, cerebrovascular accident, and Parkinson's disease.

CONSIDER THIS

LIFESTYLE MODIFICATIONS TO ADDRESS BLADDER SYMPTOMS[24]

- Daily fluid intake should be 2,500 mL, or 10 cups, to regulate excessively high or low fluid intake.
- Reduce bladder irritants including carbonated, caffeinated, and alcoholic beverages, spicy foods, citrus juices, and artificial sweeteners. Caffeine reduction should be tapered slowly to avoid severe headaches.
- Schedule voiding for every 3-4 hours to reduce bladder distention. An average person voids 6-8 times in a 24-hour period. A bladder diary assists with baseline measurements and goal setting.
- Regulate bowel function to prevent constipation and straining during bowel movements by monitoring dietary fiber, fluid intake, and exercise.
- Avoid fluid intake 2-3 hours prior to bedtime to reduce nocturia.
- A smoking cessation program may decrease the occurrence of coughing and subsequent bladder leakage.
- A weight loss program, if moderately obese, may decrease pressure on the pelvic tissues and organs.

Signs and symptoms – For many people, UUI is triggered by certain events due to a conditioned reflex. Two of the most common triggers are "key-in-the-lock" when arriving home and running water.

Treatment – Behavior modification is the primary goal of treatment for this condition. Biofeedback, pelvic floor strengthening, and bladder retraining (scheduled voiding) are key components in resolving UUI. Pharmacological intervention may also be warranted.

Overflow Urinary Incontinence (OUI)

OUI is the loss of urine when the intra-bladder pressure exceeds the urethra's capacity to remain closed due to urinary retention.

Etiology – This condition is caused by outflow obstruction secondary to a narrowed or obstructed urethra that results from a prolapsed pelvic organ, a stricture, an enlarged prostate, chronic constipation or neurological disease.

Signs and Symptoms – Individuals who present with OUI may also experience difficulty initiating the urine stream. Once the stream is initiated, it is weak and presents with post void dribble.

Treatment – Treatment will likely include surgical intervention if there is an obstruction. If there is weakness of the detrusor muscles, double voiding is recommended for these patients as well as other strengthening measures. Failed intervention may result in intermittent catheterization.

Functional Urinary Incontinence (FUI)

FUI is the loss of urine due to the inability or unwillingness of a person to use the bathroom facilities prior to involuntary bladder release.

Etiology – A decreased level of mental awareness or a decrease in mobility are the two primary causative factors for FUI. FUI is rarely seen without another bladder issue or neurological involvement.

Signs and symptoms – These patients will typically present with impaired cognition and/or mobility and will experience incontinence secondary to the inability to successfully use a bathroom to void.

Treatment – Since there is typically no urologic pathology associated with functional incontinence, treatment should be directed to alleviate the underlying issue. Improving mobility, modifying clothing style, increasing independence with ambulation and with function will assist with decreasing functional incontinence. Patients may also require a behavioral toileting schedule or program to decrease incontinence.

SPOTLIGHT ON SAFETY

FUNCTIONAL INCONTINENCE AND AT-RISK POPULATIONS[2]

When working with patients within the acute care, long-term care or home care settings there are many factors contributing to functional incontinence that pose an added safety risk.

- Restricted mobility or dexterity: Patients may have difficulty or the inability to get to the bathroom in a timely fashion due to underlying physical disabilities or limitations such as a spinal cord injury, rheumatoid arthritis or acute illness.
- Environmental barriers: Patients may not be able to reach the restroom or toilet due to stairs, lack of handrails or narrow doorways that do not accommodate wheelchairs or walkers.
- Mental and psychosocial disability: Patients may not realize they have to urinate or may be confused over the location of the restroom.
- Pharmacological intervention: Patients may take medications that affect awareness, mobility, and dexterity.

Urinary Tract Infections (UTI)[10,24]

Urinary tract infections are very common and occur within the general population, however, there is a higher incidence in women and the geriatric population. UTIs can be classified as uncomplicated, complicated, recurrent or chronic.

Etiology – Urinary tract infections (UTI) occur when bacteria infiltrate the urethra (termed urethritis) or further into the bladder itself (cystitis). Untreated, this type of infection can spread and cause a kidney infection (pyelonephritis). Diagnosis is confirmed with urinalysis. Frequent UTIs may require ultrasound, intravenous pyelogram, and cystoscopy to further assess the function of the bladder.

Signs and symptoms – Symptoms of a UTI include increased frequency of urination, pain and/or burning with urination, cloudy urine, pressure above the pubic bone in women, shakiness, fever, back pain, and fatigue.

Treatment – Early treatment has the best results; delay in treatment may allow for serious infection to occur. Pharmacological treatment includes bacteria-specific antibiotics based on the bacteria found in the bladder. Patients are also encouraged to drink an excess of fluids to assist with treatment of the infection.

CONSIDER THIS

ADVANCED PHYSICAL THERAPY INTERVENTIONS[21,23,24]

Other treatment techniques that are not entry-level for pelvic floor dysfunction may include:

- Perineal massage both by the practitioner and patient
- Scar tissue massage both by the practitioner and patient
- Intravaginal soft tissue massage (also known as Thiele massage)
- Intravaginal trigger point release and myofascial release
- Intravaginal self-stretching techniques including the use of a dilator
- Prostate massage

These techniques may be used for, but are not limited to patients who have dyspareunia, vulvodynia, prostatitis, interstitial cystitis, urgency, urge incontinence, levator ani syndrome, coccydynia, and perineal pain from pregnancy.

Obstetrics

Obstetric Pathology

Coccydynia[21]

After childbirth the joint between the coccyx and sacrum can become hypermobile causing the soft tissue surrounding the coccyx to become painful.

Etiology – Subluxation during delivery, adherence to tear or episiotomy scar.

Signs and symptoms – Difficulty sitting on hard surfaces, referred pain to the low back, sacroiliac joint, hip, buttock, groin or rectum areas, pain with bowel movements, dyspareunia, and formation of hemorrhoids.

Treatment – Treatment may include heat, external joint mobilization, myofascial release, muscle energy techniques, biofeedback for pelvic floor muscle relaxation, postural training, abdominal strengthening exercises, stretching exercises for surrounding muscles, and the use of a cushion for sitting.

Diastasis Recti[21,22,25]

Diastasis recti is a separation of the rectus abdominis muscle along the linea alba that can occur during pregnancy. Testing for diastasis recti should be performed on all pregnant women prior to prescribing exercises that require the use of the abdominals.

Etiology – The exact cause is unknown, however, theories indicate biomechanical and hormonal changes in women may cause the separation. The therapist must note how many fingers fit into the separation and modify treatment accordingly.

Signs and symptoms – A patient is considered to have diastasis recti if the therapist detects a separation greater than the width of two fingers when the woman lifts her head and shoulders off the plinth (Figs. 7-6, 7-7).

Treatment – Treatment will include stabilization and support with abdominal strengthening exercises, postural awareness exercises, and body mechanics training. A newborn can also have diastasis recti secondary to incomplete development, however, in infants this condition usually resolves itself without intervention.

Piriformis Syndrome[21]

Piriformis syndrome refers to a persistent, severe radiating low back and buttock pain spanning from the sacrum to the hip and posterior thigh. However, controversy exists over piriformis syndrome's efficacy as an accurate diagnosis.

Etiology – During pregnancy the piriformis may shorten or spasm due to postural changes and hip lateral rotation while walking.

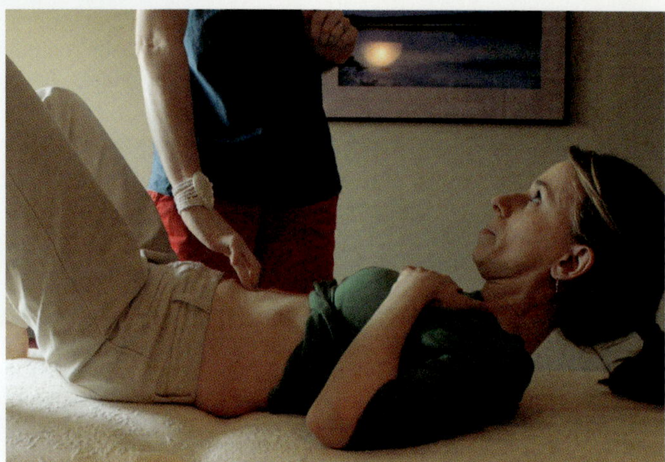

Fig. 7-6: Testing for a diastasis recti.

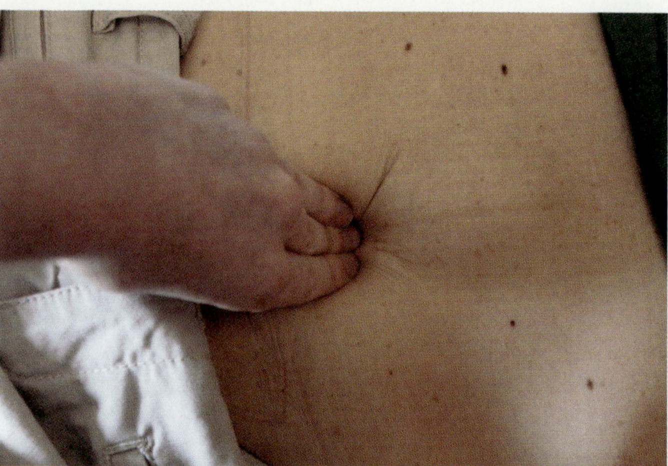

Fig. 7-7: A three finger separation at the linea alba.

Signs and symptoms – The primary symptom is sciatic paresthesia due to nerve entrapment as the sciatic nerve passes under or through the piriformis muscle.

Treatment – Manual techniques for correcting pelvic or sacral alignment such as muscle energy techniques, joint mobilization, self-correction techniques for alignment, heat application, deep tissue massage, myofascial release, strain-counterstrain, abdominal strengthening, stretching exercises for both the piriformis and surrounding muscles, body mechanics, and postural education.

Symphysis Pubis Pain[21]

To prepare for delivery, the symphysis pubis joint becomes mobile in order to allow the joint to slightly separate during delivery.

Etiology – Postural adaptations, ligamentous laxity, and complications during delivery or birthing of a large infant can result in more severe injury to the soft tissues surrounding the joint.

Signs and symptoms – Severe pain in the symphysis pubis and sacroiliac joints as well as blood in the urine due to injury to the urethra or bladder neck.

Treatment – Medical treatment includes pharmacological intervention for pain and surgical intervention based on the degree of separation in the joint. Treatment may also include heat or ice if acute, manual techniques for correcting pelvic or sacral alignment such as muscle energy techniques, self-correction techniques for alignment, education on positioning, postural training, gait training, pelvic and lumbar stabilization exercises, and the use of a lumbo-pelvic brace or binder.

Physiological and Postural Changes during Pregnancy[21,22,25]

- Weight gain between 25 and 35 pounds; anemia may occur
- Uterus ascends into the abdominal cavity becoming an abdominal organ
- Ribs expand to accommodate the uterine ascent; respiratory diaphragm elevates four centimeters
- Increased depth of respiration, tidal volume, and minute ventilation
- Increased oxygen consumption (15-20%), blood volume (40-50%), and cardiac output (30-60%)
- Hypotension in supine position during pregnancy from pressure on the inferior vena cava
- Abdominals become overstretched; ligaments become lax secondary to hormonal changes
- Joints may become hypermobile

Exercise & Pregnancy[21,22,25-27]

Pregnant women are encouraged to continue with exercise activity at a moderate rate during a low risk pregnancy. Guidelines permit women to remain at 50-60% of their maximal heart rate for approximately thirty minutes per session. Women must monitor their heart rate intermittently to ensure that they are maintaining their target heart rate. Non-weight bearing activities are preferred due to the continuous change in the center of gravity and balance. Loose clothing is advised to allow for adequate heat loss, and adequate fluids are required during exercise. Women should avoid becoming overtired and should not exercise in the supine position after the first trimester.

Pelvic Floor Muscle Exercises[21,25]

Once the pelvic floor muscles have been assessed for strength, an exercise routine can be created based on the findings. Some factors to consider are: position, endurance, and repetitions. Introduce new positions transitioning from gravity-assisted to standing as the strength and awareness of the pelvic floor muscles increase. The goal is for the patient to be able to perform the contractions with functional tasks.

Recommendations vary from 80-100 contractions per day combining quick, long hold, and functional contractions. Quick contractions are important to withstand increased intra-abdominal pressure. The patient typically begins with three sets of ten quick contractions daily, holding for two seconds and resting for four seconds. Long hold contractions are for endurance training and are important for maintaining proper posture and pelvic support. The patient typically begins with three sets of five long hold contractions daily, holding for five seconds and resting for ten seconds, gradually increasing the contraction time to ten seconds. Make sure the patient fully relaxes after each contraction. Variations of contractions will depend on each patient's diagnosis, awareness, and ability.

CONSIDER THIS

BACK PAIN DURING PREGNANCY[21,22]

Back pain is experienced by the majority of women who are pregnant, ranging from minor strain to significant structural deformities. Back pain is often caused by physical changes associated with pregnancy including weight gain, altered muscle tone, increased lordosis, changes in center of gravity and laxity within pelvic ligaments. Typically excessive bending, lifting and walking can produce back pain especially if there is a history of prior back pain or obesity.

Minor back pain can be relieved through education related to body mechanics, postural awareness, and stretching and strengthening exercises. More severe pain should not be dismissed as simply a side effect of pregnancy. Etiology of severe back pain may include pregnancy-induced osteoporosis, disk disease or herniated disk, vertebral osteoarthritis, and septic arthritis. Patients with both minor and severe back pain should be examined to determine if the source of the pain is mechanical, muscular, joint or discogenic.

SPOTLIGHT ON SAFETY

CONTRAINDICATIONS TO EXERCISE DURING PREGNANCY[27]

Participating in a wide range of recreational activities and exercise appears to be safe during and after pregnancy. Exercise programs are designed to minimize impairments and help maintain function during pregnancy. Certain circumstances exist where exercise is not safe during pregnancy. Below is a list of relative and absolute contraindications to exercise.

Relative

- Severe anemia
- Unevaluated maternal cardiac dysrhythmia
- Chronic bronchitis
- Poorly controlled type 1 diabetes
- Extreme morbid obesity
- Extreme underweight (BMI <12)
- History of extremely sedentary lifestyle
- Intrauterine growth restriction in current pregnancy
- Poorly controlled hypertension
- Orthopedic limitations
- Poorly controlled seizure disorder
- Poorly controlled hyperthyroidism
- Heavy smoker

Absolute

- Hemodynamically significant heart disease
- Restrictive lung disease
- Incompetent cervix/cerclage
- Multiple gestation at risk for premature labor
- Persistent second or third trimester bleeding
- Placenta previa after 26 weeks of gestation
- Premature labor during the current pregnancy
- Ruptured membranes
- Preeclampsia/pregnancy-induced hypertension

American College of Obstetricians and Gynecologists (ACOG) Recommendations for Exercise in Pregnancy and Postpartum[27]

1. During pregnancy, women can continue to exercise and derive health benefits even from mild to moderate exercise routines. Regular exercise (at least three times per week) is preferable to intermittent activity.

2. Women should avoid exercise in the supine position after the first trimester. Such a position is associated with decreased cardiac output in most pregnant women. Since the remaining cardiac output will be preferentially distributed away from splanchnic beds (including the uterus) during vigorous exercise, such regimens are best avoided during pregnancy. Prolonged periods of motionless standing should be avoided.

3. Women should be aware of the decreased oxygen available for aerobic exercise during pregnancy. They should be encouraged to modify the intensity of their exercise according to maternal symptoms. Pregnant women should stop exercising when fatigued and not exercise to exhaustion. Weight bearing exercises may, under some circumstances, be continued at intensities similar to those prior to pregnancy throughout pregnancy. Non-weight bearing exercises, such as cycling or swimming, will minimize the risk of injury and facilitate the continuation of exercise during pregnancy.

4. Morphologic changes in pregnancy should serve as a relative contraindication to types of exercise in which loss of balance could be detrimental to maternal or fetal well-being, especially in the third trimester. Further, any type of exercise involving the potential for even mild abdominal trauma should be avoided.

5. Pregnancy requires an additional 300 kcal/day in order to maintain metabolic homeostasis. Thus, women who exercise during pregnancy should be particularly careful to ensure an adequate diet.

6. Pregnant women who exercise in the first trimester should augment heat dissipation by ensuring adequate hydration, appropriate clothing, and optimal environmental surroundings during exercise.

7. Many of the physiological and morphological changes of pregnancy persist 4 to 6 weeks postpartum. Thus, pre-pregnancy exercise routines should be resumed gradually based upon a woman's physical capability.

From American College of Obstetricians and Gynecologists. Physical Activity and Exercise During Pregnancy and the Postpartum Period. (No. 804). Washington, DC, copyrights ACOG, 2020.

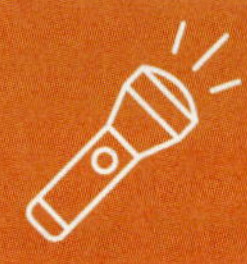

SPOTLIGHT ON SAFETY

MANAGEMENT GUIDELINES AND PRECAUTIONS FOR HIGH-RISK PREGNANCIES[25]

A pregnancy is designated as high-risk based on complications from disease or pathology that place the mother and fetus at risk for illness or death. Medical intervention is focused on prevention of preterm delivery through the prescription of bed rest, activity restriction, and medications.

Physical therapy can enhance the well-being and quality of life of the pregnant woman with a high-risk pregnancy. The physical therapist should closely monitor the patient during all activities, reassess after each treatment, and develop an individualized exercise program addressing the patient's needs. The patient should also be instructed in self-monitoring techniques during activities to avoid adverse reactions.

The following guidelines can assist in working with high-risk patients:

- Left sidelying is the position of choice to reduce the pressure on the inferior vena cava, maximize cardiac output to enhance maternal and fetal circulation, and reduce the risk of incompetent cervix.
- Abdominal exercises may stimulate uterine contractions. The therapist should modify or discontinue the exercises.
- Keep exercises simple, slow, smooth, and with minimal exertion.
- Avoid the Valsalva maneuver by discontinuing activities that increase intra-abdominal pressure.
- Provide instruction on proper body mechanics and postural instruction to limit straining during abdominal contractions.
- Encourage maximum muscle efficiency during each movement.
- Educate the women about Cesarean delivery rehabilitation.
- Monitor and report any uterine contraction, bleeding or amniotic fluid loss.

Pharmacology - Genitourinary Management[19]

Pharmacological intervention is used for treating bladder symptoms related to urgency, frequency, infection, and pain.

Diuretic Agents

See Cardiac pharmacology

Hormones

See Metabolic and Endocrine pharmacology

Overactive Bladder Agents

Action: Overactive bladder agents relieve the symptoms of an overactive bladder. This condition is noted by involuntary contractions of the bladder (detrusor muscle).

Indications: urinary urgency, urinary frequency, urge incontinence, nocturia

Side effects: widely vary based on drug classification; typically gastrointestinal distress, nausea, dizziness, photosensitivity, headache, constipation, pulmonary reactions

Implications for PT: Therapists should be aware of the adverse effects of these agents, however, these agents do not typically interfere with rehabilitation. A therapist should communicate any signs of pulmonary impairment or distress to the physician.

Examples: Ditropan (oxybutynin chloride), Detrol (tolterodine tartrate)

Urinary Anti-infective Agents

Action: Urinary anti-infective agents treat urinary tract infections, but are not traditional antibiotics or sulfonamide agents. These agents can be used independently or in combination to treat urinary infections.

Indications: cystitis, urinary urgency, burning with urination, urinary tract infection, nocturia

Side effects: widely vary based on drug classification; gastrointestinal distress, nausea, dizziness, photosensitivity, headache, constipation, rash

Implications for PT: Therapists should be aware of the adverse effects of these agents, however, these agents do not typically interfere with rehabilitation.

Examples: Cinobac (cinoxacin), Furadantin (nitrofurantoin)

CONSIDER THIS

HORMONE REPLACEMENT THERAPY FOR MENOPAUSAL SYMPTOMS[23]

Hormone replacement therapy (HRT), including estrogen and progestin replacement, has been approved by the Food and Drug Administration (FDA) for treatment of menopausal symptoms and osteoporosis.

The Women's Health Initiative (WHI) trial of HRT found the benefits for hormone replacement to be reduction in hot flash frequency and severity, improvement in atrophic vaginitis and UTIs, and prevention of osteoporosis and fractures. Studies suggest women going through menopausal transition who are experiencing depression and memory loss may also benefit from HRT, however, this remains a controversial claim.

The risks of participating in HRT include pulmonary embolus, stroke, deep vein thrombosis, gallbladder disease, and a small increase in breast cancer.

Over the past 30 years, there has been an increase in HRT for post-menopausal women who also have cardiovascular disease (CVD). The primary and secondary prevention of CVD using HRT has not been demonstrated in randomized treatment trials leading to much controversy. However, studies also indicate that early initiation of HRT may inhibit the progression of CVD.

The decision to use HRT should be individualized based on the woman's goals for therapy. Each woman should consult her physician to discuss the benefits and risks, and should reevaluate periodically to ensure the benefits continue to favor hormone use.

Genitourinary System Terminology[10,20,24]

Anuria: Inadequate urine output in a 24-hour period; less than 100 ml (e.g., severe dehydration, shock, end-stage renal disease).

Benign prostatic hypertrophy: A non-cancerous enlargement of the prostate gland that is progressive. Common in males over 60 and can interfere with normal voiding.

Cystocele: Bulging of the bladder into the vagina.

Ectopic: Implantation of a fertilized ovum outside of the uterus. The fallopian tube is the most common site of an ectopic pregnancy.

Endometrium: The inner lining of the uterus that is shed monthly in response to hormonal influence.

Glomerular filtration rate: An estimate of the filtering capacity of the kidneys; volume of filtrate produced per minute by the kidneys.

Glomerulus: The specialized tuft of capillaries that are needed for the filtration of fluid as blood passes through the arterioles of the kidneys.

Hematuria: Presence of blood in the urine (e.g., cancer, faulty catheterization, serious disease).

Impotence: Impairment with ejaculation, orgasm, erection, and/or libido.

Myometrium: The muscular outer layer of the uterus.

Nephrolithiasis: The condition of developing kidney stones. There are various types of crystal formations that create stones.

Nocturia: Urinary frequency at night (e.g., diabetes mellitus, congestive heart failure).

Oliguria: Inadequate urine output in a 24-hour period; less than 400 ml (e.g., acute renal failure, diabetes mellitus).

Polyuria: Large volume of urine excreted at one time (e.g., diabetes mellitus, chronic renal failure).

Perimetrium: The serous peritoneal coat of the uterus.

Radical mastectomy: A surgical procedure in which the entire breast, pectoral muscles, axillary lymph nodes, and some skin are removed usually secondary to breast cancer.

Rectocele: The bulging of the anterior wall of the rectum into the vagina secondary to weakening of the pelvic supporting structures.

Seminiferous tubules: Coiled tubes found within each lobe of the testes where spermatogenesis takes place.

Urea: Major nitrogen-containing end product of protein metabolism normally cleared from the blood by the kidney into the urine.

Urinary frequency: Voiding more than eight times in a 24-hour period. Etiology may include overactive bladder, reduced bladder capacity, painful bladder syndrome or increased urine output caused by uncontrolled diabetes mellitus.

Urinary urgency: The sudden desire to urinate that is stronger than usual and difficult to defer. Etiology may include detrusor overactivity, bladder infection, inflammation or the presence of a foreign body such as stones or tumors. Urgency may lead to urinary urge incontinence.

Lymphatic System

Anatomy and Physiology

The primary functions of the lymphatic system include collection and transportation of fluids and other materials that are not reabsorbed by the venous system, maintenance of fluid balance within the body, and immune system defense.

Lymph is the fluid transported by the lymphatic system. It originates as a component of the interstitial fluid and primarily consists of water, proteins, fatty acids, and cellular components. The lymphatic system consists of a network of both superficial and deep lymph vessels that transport lymph throughout the body. These lymph vessels are located anywhere that a blood supply exists, except for the brain and spinal cord.

The first lymph vessel within the lymphatic system is the smallest vessel and is known as the initial lymph vessel. These initial lymph vessels are located near blood capillaries and are responsible for collecting fluid from the interstitium that is not picked up by the venous system. The lymphatic system also transports the majority of extracellular proteins since they are often too large to be transported by the venous system. The lymphatic system is normally responsible for collecting 10-20% of the interstitial fluid, while the venous system collects the other 80-90%.

From the initial lymph vessels, lymph is transported towards larger lymph vessels known as lymph collectors. The lymph collectors then transport lymph to even larger lymph vessels known as lymphatic trunks. The two main lymphatic trunks are the right lymphatic duct, which drains lymph from the right arm and right side of the head, and the thoracic duct, which drains lymph from the remainder of the body. These vessels empty lymph directly into the venous system via the subclavian veins.

The lymphatic system is under the control of the autonomic nervous system, which produces contractions of smooth muscle within the lymph vessel walls to help move the lymph fluid along. Skeletal muscle contraction can also help to compress the lymph vessels and move lymph. One-way valves help maintain the unidirectional flow of lymph throughout the entire lymphatic system.

Lymph nodes are specialized structures contained throughout the lymphatic system, but found most commonly in the neck, axilla, chest, abdomen, and groin. The lymph nodes collect lymph from several adjacent areas and function primarily to filter waste products and foreign materials from the lymph (e.g., bacteria, viruses) and provide immune system defense with the use of T and B lymphocytes.

Other components of the lymphatic system include the thymus, bone marrow, spleen, tonsils, and Peyer patches in the small intestine. These structures are involved in the production of lymphocytes, which are important to the functioning of the immune system.

Lymphedema

Lymphedema is a chronic, incurable condition and is characterized by the accumulation of protein-rich fluid (i.e., lymph) in the body. The result is edema that typically presents in the extremities, but can occur anywhere in the body including the face, neck, abdomen, genitalia, and trunk. Fluid accumulation occurs secondary to damage to the lymph structures, which affects the normal flow of lymph. Lymphedema is categorized as either primary or secondary based on the etiology.

Primary lymphedema occurs due to an abnormal development of the lymphatic system. Though this may occur from birth, it may take several years before the patient becomes symptomatic. Abnormalities of the lymph system may include the absence of lymph vessels, a decrease in the number or size of lymph vessels, and/or an increased size of lymph vessels, which makes the valves incompetent. This type of lymphedema occurs more frequently in females and is usually seen in the lower extremities.

Secondary lymphedema occurs as a result of some other disease or injury that causes damage to the lymphatic system. This may include trauma, surgery, radiation, tumor growth, multiparity, chronic venous insufficiency or infection. In the United States, breast cancer surgery and treatment is the most common cause for secondary lymphedema. When a patient has treatment for breast cancer, the risk for lymphedema increases significantly with axillary lymph node dissection and/or radiation therapy. More radical mastectomy procedures are also associated with an increased risk of developing lymphedema.

There are three types of insufficiencies in the lymphatic system that can lead to lymphedema. Dynamic insufficiency is the most common type of insufficiency and occurs when there is excess lymph circulating in the lymphatic system that exceeds the transport capacity of the system. Dynamic insufficiency results in pitting edema. Examples of this type of insufficiency include chronic venous insufficiency, congestive heart failure, and pregnancy. Mechanical insufficiency occurs when the transport capacity of the system is reduced due to damage to the lymph system. This type of insufficiency results in the more protein-rich lymphedema (i.e., non-pitting). Combined insufficiency is the third type of insufficiency that occurs when there is both an increase in lymph fluid as well as a decrease in transport capacity.

The primary sign of lymphedema is swelling in the extremities. Because the lymphatic system can no longer handle the volume of fluid that it normally would, excess fluid builds up in the interstitium and leads to enlargement of the affected limb. Patients will complain of achiness, fullness, and heaviness of the affected limb. As lymphedema progresses, the valves expand and become incompetent, which leads to further fluid accumulation. If the fluid

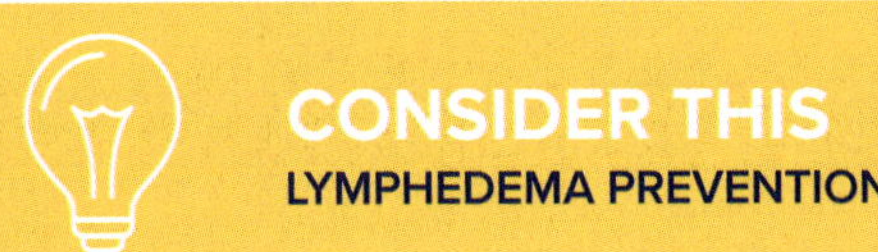

CONSIDER THIS
LYMPHEDEMA PREVENTION

Individuals at greater risk for lymphedema (e.g., lymph node removal, extensive chest surgeries, radiation therapy, obesity) can significantly limit their risk by following specific guidelines.

1. Avoid injury to the skin to help reduce the risk of infection. This may include treating cuts and abrasions properly, caution with use of razors or nail clippers, applying moisturizer to the skin, and avoiding skin punctures (e.g., blood draws) on the affected limb.
2. Avoid any constriction of the extremity. This may include wearing loose fitting clothing and avoiding having blood pressure measurements performed on the affected limb.
3. Diet and exercise to maintain a healthy weight. Being overweight significantly increases a patient's risk for developing lymphedema.
4. When exercising, carefully observe any changes in the size of the limb to ensure that increased activity is not causing negative side effects. It is also advisable to take frequent rest breaks during periods of intense activity.
5. Avoid extreme hot and cold temperatures as they can lead to fluctuations in limb edema.
6. Wear compression garments during periods of strenuous activity, when standing for prolonged periods of time or when traveling on an airplane.

stasis continues, the proteins begin to degrade which leads to the development of chronic inflammation and eventually fibrotic changes to the surrounding tissues. Fibrosis results in local hypoxia in the tissues, which causes further chronic inflammation and an increased risk for infection.

Diagnosis

Imaging Techniques

Lymphedema is typically diagnosed from a thorough medical history and physical examination, though imaging techniques can be useful in identifying the cause of the condition.

Direct lymphography: This technique involves injection of a contrast medium into a lymph vessel that allows for visualization of the entire lymph system through radiography. It is not commonly used due to complications caused by the contrast medium.

Indirect lymphography: This technique involves injection of a contrast medium (water-soluble) just under the skin to allow for visualization of the smaller superficial lymph vessels.

Lymphoscintigraphy: This technique involves injection of radioactive material that allows for visualization of the lymphatic system through nuclear medical imaging. The radioactive material is traced throughout the system to determine how effectively lymph is being transported. This method is preferred over direct lymphography since there are fewer complications.

MRI and CT scan: These imaging techniques can be used to identify tumors that may be the cause of a patient's lymphedema.

Physical Therapy Tests and Measures

Tests and measures used by therapists for lymphedema commonly include comparative measurements for limb size. Changes in limb size help determine the progression of the disease and the effectiveness of treatment. The most common method for measuring lymphedema is circumferential measurements.

Circumferences for Limb Edema[26]

Circumference measurements made at a number of points along the limb at specified distances from an anatomical landmark are an accepted technique to detect limb enlargement and to provide a quantitative assessment of changes in limb size due to edema, lymphedema, and joint effusion.

Procedure

- Measurements should be made on a measuring board.
- Measurements should be from a standard point of reference on the extremity that is replicable (e.g., every 5 or 10 centimeters along the extremity or a specified distance from a bony prominence).
- Seven circumferences are recommended for the upper and lower extremities to deduce that the fluid has been removed and not just redistributed.

Interpretation

The opposite limb, when available, is used for comparison. A difference of two or three centimeters between four comparative circumferences on bilateral upper extremities is evidence of lymphedema.

Classification for lymphedema[27]

Mild: < 3 centimeters difference between the affected and unaffected limbs

Moderate: 3 to 5 centimeters difference between the affected and unaffected limbs

Severe: > 5 centimeters difference between the affected and unaffected limbs

Other tests and measures that may be part of the examination include volumetric measurements, goniometry, manual muscle testing, pain assessment, sensory testing, skin inspection, bioelectrical impedance, and gait and balance assessments.

Staging of Lymphedema	
Stage	**Description**
0	This stage is known as the latent (or preclinical) stage. There is no visible edema, though the transport capacity of the lymph system has been affected.
1	This stage is known as the reversible lymphedema stage. Pitting edema is present and increases with activity or heat, but will diminish with elevation and rest.
2	This stage is known as the spontaneously irreversible lymphedema stage. The edema is now non-pitting and does not change with elevation or rest. The skin begins to demonstrate fibrotic changes and the risk for infection increases. Stemmer's sign is positive at this stage.
3	This stage is known as the lymphostatic elephantiasis stage. It is characterized by extensive non-pitting edema, significant fibrotic changes to the skin, and the presence of papillomas, deep skinfolds, and hyperkeratosis. Infection is common at this stage. Stemmer's sign remains positive at this stage.

Treatment

Once a diagnosis has been made, formal intervention is recommended in order to assist patients in managing their symptoms at the lowest possible level. Early, appropriate intervention and ongoing self-care significantly decrease the risk of infection and other negative sequelae associated with poor symptom management. Complete decongestive therapy (CDT) is the standard of care for patients with lymphedema.

Complete Decongestive Therapy

CDT is a treatment model that occurs in two different phases. Phase I is the intensive acute treatment phase and is typically provided in an outpatient setting by a certified lymphedema therapist for 4-6 weeks. Phase II is the self-management phase and consists of long-term management of symptoms utilizing various components of CDT. Patients may need to return to phase I treatment whenever a significant change in symptoms is noted. CDT consists of manual lymphatic drainage, compression therapy, exercise, and skin care.

Manual lymphatic drainage: Manual lymphatic drainage (MLD) involves techniques designed to move lymph around blockages in the lymphatic system and into desired areas where it can be drained. Treatment should first be directed at uninvolved areas to prepare those areas for new lymph flow, then be directed towards the involved areas. It is important for therapists to know the location of lymph nodes since this will affect where they decide to perform manual strokes and in what direction. It is also important to know if lymph nodes are intact and functioning.

Compression therapy: Compression therapy helps to maintain the reduction in edema that is achieved with MLD. Compression therapy helps reduce limb size by improving the reabsorption ability of the capillaries and reducing the filtration of fluids into the interstitium. It can also help soften fibrotic tissues that may have formed. In phase I treatment, compression bandages are typically used. Short-stretch bandages are used for treating lymphedema since they have a low resting pressure and therefore do not constrict lymph flow like long-stretch bandages would. In phase II treatment, a combination of compression garments (during the day) and compression bandages (during the night) are used. Compression garments should only be fitted once edema levels have plateaued. Bandages and garments should have higher pressures in distal regions (i.e., graded compression).

Exercise: Exercise can help improve lymph flow by increasing lymph vessel contractions, increasing fluid uptake in the initial lymph vessels, improving the "muscle pump" to stimulate lymph flow, and increasing deep breathing which improves lymph flow in the thoracic duct. Because some patients can have a negative response to exercise, they must be monitored carefully when initiating an exercise program and their program should be gradually progressed. Low impact, aerobic activities are generally recommended at the onset since they are less likely to exacerbate the patient's lymphedema. Basic guidelines for an exercise session include starting with trunk exercises followed by extremity exercises and working from the proximal joints to the distal joints. The session should finish with additional trunk exercises and deep breathing to enhance lymphatic flow. Compression bandages/garments should be used when exercising.

Skin care: The skin is more prone to damage since the protein-rich fluid of lymphedema impairs immune system function allowing for bacterial and fungal growth. Infections can lead to worsening of a patient's lymphedema. Prevention is therefore of primary importance. The limb should be inspected and cleansed thoroughly each day and patients should frequently apply moisturizing lotion. Any soaps or moisturizers used should have a low or neutral pH to avoid damage to the skin.

Other Treatments

There are currently no medications or surgical procedures that are effective in the treatment of lymphedema. Debulking is a surgical procedure that may be done for a patient with lymphedema to help remove the excessive skin that forms in the later stages of the disease. However, this procedure must be performed with caution as it can damage existing lymph vessels and further accelerate the course of the disease.

Intermittent pneumatic compression devices may be used as a part of compression therapy. However, there are some concerns that exist when using these devices on patients with lymphedema. If the pressure is too high, lymphatic vessels may be damaged, and these devices often deliver pressures that are inconsistent with the desired settings. Another concern is that patients may develop genital edema since the fluids are moved proximally.

SPOTLIGHT ON SAFETY
CONTRAINDICATIONS TO COMPLETE DECONGESTIVE THERAPY

There are several precautions and relative contraindications to complete decongestive therapy. Failure to recognize the presence of these medical conditions has the potential to significantly compromise patient safety.

- Acute infection
- Cardiac edema
- Diabetes
- Hypertension
- Malignancy
- Renal insufficiency
- Deep vein thrombosis

Lymphatic System Terminology

Filariasis: A disease caused by a parasitic infection that is most often seen in tropical climates. It is one of the most common causes of secondary lymphedema worldwide.

Hyperkeratosis: Thickening of the outermost layer of the skin, which is typically observed with stage 3 lymphedema.

Lymphadenitis: Infection and inflammation of a lymph node, which may be acute or chronic.

Lymphadenomegaly: Enlargement of lymph nodes, which commonly occurs secondary to cancer, infections, and allergic reactions.

Lymphadenopathy: Any disease that affects the size, number or consistency of the lymph nodes.

Lymphangitis: Infection and inflammation of the lymphatic system pathways.

Milroy's disease: An inherited type of primary lymphedema that typically presents in infancy. Bilateral lower extremity edema is the most common symptom of this disease.

Non-pitting edema: Fluid accumulation that is "harder" and not compressible when pressure is applied. This type of edema is observed in the later stages of lymphedema.

Papilloma: A benign wart-like skin growth that is typically observed with stage 3 lymphedema.

Pitting edema: Fluid accumulation that can be compressed and demonstrates an indentation with applied pressure. This type of edema may be observed in the early stages of lymphedema.

Spleen: An organ located in the upper left quadrant of the abdomen that is responsible for the filtration of red blood cells as well as the production of antibodies to help fight infection.

Stemmer's sign: A test used to aid in the diagnosis of lymphedema. Stemmer's sign is positive if the skin at the dorsal base of the second toe/finger can't be easily lifted away from the bone, which indicates thickening of the skin due to fibrotic changes.

Thymus: An organ located posterior to the sternum and anterior to the heart that produces T cells and T lymphocytes to help combat infection.

System Interactions

Oncology[28,29]

Cancer, malignancy, neoplasm, and tumor are all terms referring to abnormal uncontrolled cell growth within the body. There are more than one hundred different cancers of various types and tissue origins currently recognized, including lymphoma and hematologic cancers. Malignant cancer cells are characterized by their ability to grow uncontrollably, invade other tissues, remain undifferentiated, initiate growth at distant sites, and avoid detection and destruction by the body's immune system. The origins of malignant cells vary widely from environmental factors and lifestyle choices to genetic predisposition.

Carcinoma is a malignancy originating from the epithelial cells of organs. Carcinomas in specific organs may be named more specifically depending on the characteristics present. For example, large cell carcinoma, adenocarcinoma, and squamous cell carcinoma are all subsets of lung carcinoma. The large majority of cancers in the United States are carcinomas.

Risk Factors[28]	
• Increasing age	• Poor diet
• Tobacco use	• Stress
• Alcohol use	• Occupational hazards
• Gender	• Ethnic background
• Virus exposure	• Genetic influence
• Environmental influence	• Sexual/reproductive behavior

General Signs and Symptoms of Cancer

C - Change in bowel/bladder routine
A - A sore that will not heal
U - Unusual bleeding/discharge
T - Thickening/lump develops
I - Indigestion or difficulty swallowing
O - Obvious change in wart/mole
N - Nagging cough/hoarseness

Unexplained weight loss, fatigue, anorexia, anemia, pain, and/or weakness are other general symptoms that may indicate cancer.[28]

Cancer Prevention[28]

Primary Prevention	• Elimination of modifiable risk factors • Use of natural agents (i.e., teas, vitamins) to prevent cancer • Cancer vaccine
Secondary Prevention	• Early detection • Selective preventative pharmacological agents (e.g., Tamoxifen) • Multifactorial risk reduction
Tertiary Prevention	• Prevent disability that can occur secondary to cancer and its treatment • Manage symptoms • Limit complications

Tissue and Tumor Classification[30]

Tissue Classification	Examples	Tumor Classification
Epithelium Protect, absorb, and excrete	– Skin – Lines internal cavities – Mucous membrane – Lining of bladder	Carcinoma Adenocarcinoma (glandular tissue)
Pigmented Cells	– Moles	Malignant melanoma
Connective Tissues Elastic, collagen, fibrous	– Striated muscle – Blood vessels – Bone – Cartilage – Fat – Smooth muscle	Sarcoma Fibrosarcoma Liposarcoma Chondrosarcoma Osteosarcoma Hemangiosarcoma Leiomyosarcoma Rhabdomyosarcoma
Nerve Tissues Neurons, nerve fibers, dendrites, glial cells	– Brain – Nerves – Spinal cord – Retina	Astrocytoma Glioma Neurilemma sarcoma Neuroblastoma Retinoblastoma
Lymphoid Tissues	– Wherever lymph tissue is present throughout the body – Lymph nodes – Spleen – Can appear in stomach, intestines, skin, CNS, bone, and tonsils	Lymphoma
Hematopoietic Tissues	– Bone marrow – Plasma cells	Leukemia Myelodysplasia Myeloproliferative syndromes Multiple myeloma

SPOTLIGHT ON SAFETY
MUSCULOSKELETAL PAIN AND ONCOLOGY[30]

Musculoskeletal pain complaints should not be taken lightly in oncology populations. Bony or soft tissue pain complaints can be heralding signs of disease progression or adverse treatment effects.

Bony pain complaints may relate to a primary site of malignancy, such as with osteosarcoma, or new metastasis to a bony area. New back pain complaints of unclear origin, for example, should be evaluated immediately as this pain may be indicative of spinal metastasis which may result in neurological deficits.

Soft tissue complaints may relate to medication side effects or physiological changes in the tissue itself as a result of oncological interventions. Women who have received radiation treatment for breast cancer and develop axillary web syndrome or radiation fibrosis, for example, may experience considerable discomfort along with palpable tissue changes and functional limitations in the affected upper quadrant.

Diagnostic Tools[28]

• Family history	• Pap smear
• Physical examination	• Blood tests
• Radiography	• Biopsy
• CT scan	• Mammography
• Bone scan	• Endoscopy
• Stool guaiac	• Isotope scan

Staging[31,32]

The stage of a malignancy is determined by evaluating the extent of the disease, lymph node involvement, and existence of metastasis. Staging data is utilized in the selection of treatment interventions, to assist in goal setting, and in the prediction of outcomes and prognosis for both oncological and physical therapy interventions. Staging data and responses to treatment are also typically reported to a tumor registry. The aggregate data maintained by a tumor registry supplies medical providers with information regarding treatment outcomes that can be compared nationally. Numerous staging systems exist with some used for many cancer types and others being type specific such as for cancers of the blood or lymphatic system.

The TNM system is one of the most commonly used methods of determining tumor stage. The system describes a malignancy based on the size and extent of the primary tumor (T), lymph node involvement (N), and presence of metastasis (M). For most cancers, the TNM combination will correspond to a stage designation that further defines the severity of the disease. Lower numbered stages are considered to have a better overall prognosis.

National Cancer Institute Staging[31]

Stage	Definition
Stage 0	Early malignancy that is present only in the layer of cells in which it began. For most cancers, this is referred to as carcinoma in situ. Not all cancers have a stage 0.
Stage I	Malignancy limited to the tissue of origin with no lymph node involvement or metastasis.
Stage II	Malignancy spreading into adjacent tissues; lymph nodes may show signs of micrometastases.
Stage III	Malignancy that has spread to adjacent tissue showing signs of fixation to deeper structures. The likelihood of metastatic lymph node involvement is high.
Stage IV	Malignancy that has metastasized beyond the primary site, for example, to bone or another organ.

Adapted from National Cancer Institute, www.cancer.gov

Clinical staging refers to the estimated extent of malignancy present based on the findings of a patient's physical examination, laboratory values, imaging tests, and biopsy. Clinical staging is a key component in determining a patient's optimal course of treatment and also establishes a baseline for comparison used in assessing the response to treatment.

Pathologic staging refers to staging based on the pathology findings of tissue samples obtained during surgery. Often surgery is performed to remove a malignant mass and/or nearby lymph nodes, or for an exploratory assessment and tissue sample removal. In some cases, the pathologic stage may differ from the clinical stage (e.g., if surgery reveals that the cancer has spread more than expected in relation to the clinical staging). The pathological stage gives the health care team more precise information which can be used to more definitively predict treatment responses and prognosis.

Oncology Pathology

Brain Cancer[10,32]

Brain cancer may occur as a primary tumor arising from astrocytes, meninges, nerve cells, or tissues within the brain. Metastatic brain cancer occurs when a brain tumor develops as a consequence of cancer in another primary area of the body.

Etiology - Most primary cancers outside of the brain metastasize to the brain during progression of the cancer.

Signs and symptoms - Symptoms are dependent on the location of the tumor and typically progress rapidly. Symptoms include headache, seizures, increased intracranial pressure, cognitive and emotional impairment, and decreased motor and sensory function.

Treatment - Surgical resection along with radiation or other combined therapies are typically indicated.

Breast Cancer[10,32]

Breast cancer is the most common female malignancy, but can also occur in men. The majority of cases are classified as adenocarcinoma and it is the second leading cause of female death from cancer. Common metastases are found in the lymph nodes, lungs, bones, skin, and brain. If the cancer recurs, it is usually within two years of the initial diagnosis.

Etiology - Risk factors include genetics, gender, age, menstrual history, and geography.

Signs and symptoms - Breast cancer presents as a lump and is usually found by the woman. The mass is typically firm, irregular, and non-painful. The patient may also present with signs including nipple discharge, erythema or a change in breast shape.

Treatment - Treatment may include surgery, radiation, chemotherapy or hormonal manipulation. It is curable if diagnosed prior to metastases; survival rate decreases as the stage of the cancer increases. The current 5-year survival rate for localized tumors is 92%; this drops substantially if there is nodal involvement.

Bronchial Carcinoma[3]

Bronchial carcinoma refers to any epithelial carcinoma occurring in the bronchopulmonary tree. Cancers are broadly divided into two main groups: small cell lung carcinomas and non-small cell lung carcinomas, including squamous cell carcinoma, adenocarcinoma, and large cell carcinoma.

Etiology - Smoking is the primary cause of the majority of lung cancers, but it can occur in people who have never smoked or had prolonged exposure to secondhand smoke. In these cases, the exact etiology may be unknown.

Signs and symptoms - A new cough or changes in a chronic cough, coughing up blood, shortness of breath, wheezing, weight loss, and bone pain. Typically, signs and symptoms are not present until the disease is advanced.

Treatment - Surgery (wedge resection, segmental resection, lobectomy, pneumonectomy), chemotherapy, and radiation therapy.

Cervical Cancer[10,32]

Cervical cancer starts in the cells on the surface of the cervix, typically squamous cells. This precancerous condition is called dysplasia and is easily treatable. Annual cervical screening is recommended; diagnosis is made through a Pap test (smear). Prognosis is good with timely intervention. If dysplasia goes undetected, changes can develop into cervical cancer and metastasize to the bladder, intestines, lungs, and liver.

Etiology - The human papilloma virus (HPV) is the primary cause of cervical cancer; it is slow growing. Risk factors include smoking, maternal use of diethylstilbestrol (DES), African American ethnicity, oral contraceptive use, and certain sexually transmitted diseases.

Signs and symptoms - Asymptomatic during the early stages; however, symptoms can include abnormal bleeding, pelvic and low back pain, impairment with bladder and bowel function.

Treatment - Treatment is dependent on staging of the cancer and may include laser therapy, excision, cryotherapy or hysterectomy with adjunct chemotherapy or radiation.

Colorectal Cancer[10,32]

Most colorectal cancers start as a growth on the inner lining of the colon or rectum (i.e., polyp). Some polyps can change into cancer over time, while others do not. Adenocarcinoma and primary lymphoma account for the majority of intestinal cancers.

Etiology - Risk factors include increasing age, history of polyps, ulcerative colitis, Crohn's disease, family history, and a diet high in fat and low in fiber.

Signs and symptoms - Colon cancer does not provide early signs of disease and the most prominent symptom is a continuous change in bowel habits. Bright red blood from the rectum is another prominent sign of colon cancer. The patient may experience symptoms of fatigue, weight loss, anemia, and overt rectal bleeding.

Treatment - Treatment is based on the type and staging of the cancer and may include surgical resection of the tumor and potentially a portion of the bowel, with subsequent radiation therapy and/or chemotherapy; colostomy may be required. Prognosis is good for early diagnosis if the cancer is contained; prognosis is poor if it has metastasized.

Lung Cancer[10,32]

Lung cancer is cancer of the epithelium within the respiratory tract. It is the most frequent cause of death from all cancers. Rapid metastasis can occur through the pulmonary vascular system, adrenal gland, brain, bone, and liver.

Etiology - Risk factors include smoking, environment, geography, occupational hazards, age, and family history.

Signs and symptoms - Early symptoms include cough, sputum, and dyspnea. Progression may include symptoms of adventitious breath sounds, chest pain, and hemoptysis.

Treatment - There is a poor prognosis secondary to expedited metastasis (less than 14% for a five-year survival rate). Surgical intervention along with combination therapies may be required.

CONSIDER THIS

EXERCISE GUIDELINES FOR PATIENTS UNDERGOING CANCER TREATMENT[30]

The combination of surgical, medical, and radiation oncology interventions can produce a variety of unpleasant symptoms which may significantly impact a patient's quality of life during treatment. Common side effects include pain, fatigue, depression, anxiety, altered body image, sleep disturbances, lymphedema, and gastrointestinal distress. With therapeutic exercise, physical therapists have the ability to positively impact both symptoms and quality of life. In planning exercise interventions, therapists should consider the following:

- Always check physician orders prior to treating a patient with bone metastases to verify weight bearing status and clearance to perform mobility
- Monitor a patient's blood values daily, especially platelet and hematocrit counts, to ensure that it is safe for the patient to participate in therapy activities
- Exercise should be conducted at a range of 40-65% of the peak heart rate, heart rate reserve, and VO_{2max} or below the anaerobic threshold
- During exercise, perceived exertion should not exceed a 12 using the Borg's Rating of Perceived Exertion Scale
- Treatment visits should be scheduled during the time of day when the patient's energy is at peak levels
- Treatment should be modified as needed to accommodate any side effects of medical treatment

Lymphoma (Hodgkin, non-Hodgkin disease)[10,32]

Lymphoma is classified as cancer found in the lymphatic system and lymph tissues; lymphomas are categorized as Hodgkin disease or non-Hodgkin lymphoma.

Etiology – Risk factors for Hodgkin disease include association with Epstein-Barr virus, drug abuse, immunosuppressant use, obesity, chronic or autoimmune diseases. Risk factors for non-Hodgkin lymphoma include exposure to benzene (i.e., cigarette smoke), auto emissions, and pollution.

Signs and symptoms – A painless lump is typically the first sign and general symptoms include fever, chills, and fatigue. Hodgkin disease is distinguished by the presence of Reed-Sternberg cancer cells. Both forms can metastasize.

Treatment – Hodgkin disease is one of the most curable cancers depending on age, disease stage, overall health, and responsiveness to treatment. Treatment options are based on the patient's age and staging classification and include chemotherapy, radiation, stem cell transplant, and highly active antiretroviral therapy. Non-Hodgkin progression varies based on classification, co-morbidities, and treatment response.

Pancreatic Cancer[10,32]

Pancreatic cancer is a prominent type of cancer with an extremely high mortality rate. Cancer of the exocrine cells within the ducts is the most common form of pancreatic cancer. It will metastasize to the liver, lungs, pleura, colon, stomach, and spleen.

Etiology – Risk factors include tobacco use, gender, increasing age, and cholecystectomy.

Signs and symptoms – Symptoms are very vague during the initial stages of the disease which often results in delayed diagnosis. Common symptoms include weight loss, jaundice, and epigastric pain that can radiate to the thoracic region. Advanced cancer may present with severe pain that may indicate the cancer has metastasized.

Treatment – Treatment is usually directed to assist in the relief of symptoms. Pancreatic cancer has a very poor survival rate with a mortality rate of almost 100%. Surgical resection along with chemotherapy and radiation assist to relieve symptoms.

Prostate Cancer[10,32]

Adenocarcinoma is the most common type of prostate cancer. Prostate cancer typically affects men over 50 years old; it is the second highest cause of death from cancer in men. Diagnosis is found through prostate biopsy and prognosis is good with appropriate treatment. There is an approximate 10% fatality from this diagnosis.

Etiology – Risk factors include increased age, high fat diet, genetic predisposition, African American descent, and exposure to cadmium.

Signs and symptoms – Most times this is asymptomatic until the cancer reaches the advanced stages. Symptoms include urinary obstruction, pain, urgency, and decreased stream/flow of urine.

Treatment – Treatment varies and may include surgical incision of the prostate gland, radiation, or hormonal therapy; can metastasize to the bladder, musculoskeletal system, lungs, and lymph nodes.

Skin Cancer[10,32]

Basal Cell Carcinoma

Basal cell carcinoma is a slow growing form of skin cancer that rarely metastasizes. It originates from the epidermis and is the most common form of skin cancer.

Etiology – Sun exposure is a common cause, with risk factors including frequent sun exposure, light eyes, and fair skin.

Signs and symptoms – Open sores that can bleed or crust and remain for three or more weeks, reddish patches of skin, a shiny bump on the skin that is often pink, or a scar-like area that has poorly defined borders

Treatment – Prognosis is good; basal cell carcinoma can routinely be cured. Surgical excision may be required to remove the cancer cells.

Malignant Melanoma

Malignant melanoma originates from melanocytes and can be classified as: superficial spreading, nodular, lentigo maligna or acral lentiginous melanomas. Peak incidence is between 40-60 years of age. Early diagnosis is vital to prognosis, as it can spread and metastasize quickly. Areas of metastases include the brain, lungs, liver, bone, and skin.

Etiology – Risk factors for malignant melanoma include a history of blistering sunburns prior to 20 years of age, family history, immunosuppression, light eyes, fair skin, and a previous history of cancer.

Signs and symptoms – Lesions can be elevated on the surface of the skin and appear keratotic or scaly. Other symptoms when observing the skin or a mole may include asymmetry, irregular borders, varied color, and a diameter of greater than six millimeters.

Treatment – This form of cancer is 100% curable with early diagnosis. Excision may solely be required with early treatment. If melanoma has metastasized, surgical intervention along with combination therapies may be required.

Pediatric Oncology Pathology[34,35]

Astrocytoma

Astrocytoma is a classification that accounts for approximately fifty percent of pediatric brain tumors. The etiology of pediatric cancers is usually unknown.

Etiology – Etiology includes genetic predisposition, environmental influence, radiation and toxin exposure, and association with certain childhood disorders.

Signs and symptoms – There are two types of astrocytoma with characteristics as follows:

- **Cerebellar** - clumsiness, ataxic gait, headache, change in personality, and vomiting
- **Supratentorial** - headache, seizures, change in personality, visual impairments, and vomiting

Treatment – Surgical resection of cerebellar tumors offers an 80-90% cure rate. Supratentorial tumors also require surgery to resect the tumor with radiation and/or chemotherapy.

Leukemia

Leukemia is a cancer of the blood that occurs when leukocytes change into malignant cells. These immature cells proliferate, accumulate in bone marrow, and ultimately cease the production of normal cells. This process will spread to lymph nodes, liver, spleen, and other areas of the body.

Etiology – The exact etiology is unknown, however, causative factors include environmental, chemical or toxin exposure, genetic predisposition, and viral association. There are many types of leukemia with acute lymphoblastic leukemia (ALL) and acute myelogenous leukemia (AML) occurring most frequently in children.

Signs and symptoms – Characteristics include an abrupt onset with high fever, bleeding, enlarged lymph nodes and spleen, progressive weakness, fatigue, and painful joints. Blood work will indicate anemia, a leukocyte count greater than 500,000 mm^3 and thrombocytopenia.

Treatment – Treatment will vary based on the type and degree of leukemia. Options include immunotherapy, cytotoxic agents, chemotherapy or radiation, and bone marrow transplant. Over 90% of patients with ALL achieve complete remission with treatment, while 70-80% of patients with AML achieve complete remission with treatment.

Neuroblastoma

A neuroblastoma is a tumor that initiates from primitive ectodermal cells of the neural plate and is found within the sympathetic nervous system, primarily seen in the adrenal glands or paraspinal ganglia. This is the most common malignant tumor seen in children.

Etiology – The etiology remains unknown, but causative factors include genetic predisposition, familial incidence, environmental influence, radiation and toxin exposure or viral association.

Signs and symptoms – Characteristics vary with the site and include an abdominal mass, change in personality, anemia, sweating, pain, and diarrhea.

Treatment – Treatment includes surgical resection, chemotherapy, and radiation. Prognosis is best for children diagnosed in the first year of life. A neuroblastoma will spontaneously regress in rare cases.

Osteogenic Sarcoma

An osteogenic sarcoma is a cancer that occurs at the epiphyses of long bones. Osteogenic sarcoma is the most common form of bone cancer in children with a peak incidence between the ages of 10 and 20.

Etiology – Exact etiology is unknown, however, there is a correlation between immunoincompetence and rate of tumor progression. Osteogenic sarcoma can metastasize quickly.

Signs and symptoms – Characteristics include presence of a mass, rapid metastases, and associated pain. Diagnosis can be made with a biopsy.

Treatment – Treatment includes amputation with proximal resection to ensure proper removal of affected tissue or surgical procedures that attempt to resect the tumor and salvage the limb. Chemotherapy is beneficial, however, radiation is not effective with this type of tumor.

Wilms' Tumor

Wilms' tumor is an embryonal nephroblastoma found in the kidney. Most cases are diagnosed between one and four years of age.

Etiology – Etiology includes genetic inheritance as an autosomal dominant disease or a non-inherited form with an unknown etiology.

CONSIDER THIS

CHEMOTHERAPY RELATED ALTERED BLOOD COUNTS[38]

Many chemotherapeutic agents include side effects that alter a patient's normal blood count which may result in conditions such as anemia, thrombocytopenia, and neutropenia. These conditions are diagnosed based on the laboratory results from a complete blood count.

Anemia refers to hemoglobin and hematocrit levels below normal gender specific laboratory reference values. In severe cases, a blood transfusion may be necessary. Symptoms may include dyspnea, heart palpitations, and dizziness. Patients who are anemic are advised to change positions slowly, rest frequently during activity, and allow themselves full nights of sleep.

Thrombocytopenia refers to platelet levels below normal reference laboratory values. Patients with thrombocytopenia will bruise very easily. Other symptoms may include petechiae, epistaxis, bleeding gums, and black or bloody stool. Patients with thrombocytopenia are advised to consult a physician before using over the counter medications that may further affect platelets such as aspirin and ibuprofen. Other precautions include avoiding contact sports, working with or around sharp objects, and tight fitting clothing or accessories.

Neutropenia refers to a neutrophil count below normal laboratory reference values placing a patient at risk for developing a serious infection. The severity of neutropenia may be categorized as mild, moderate or severe. An individual's risk of infection is typically a factor of the severity and duration of neutropenia. Patients who are neutropenic do not typically present with observable signs or symptoms. In hospitals, patients with neutropenia are typically assigned a private room with precautions instituted to decrease a patient's risk of exposure to infection from visitors, staff or unhygienic conditions. Patients with neutropenia who are not in medical facilities are advised to maintain excellent hand and body hygiene, closely self monitor for signs and symptoms of infection, wear shoes even in the home, and avoid exposure to potentially infectious environmental factors (e.g., crowds or people with illnesses, litter boxes, bird cages, fish tanks, flowers and plants, stagnant water, manicures/pedicures, jacuzzis/hot tubs).

Signs and symptoms – Characteristics include an abdominal mass, pain, hematuria, fever, nausea, and vomiting.

Treatment – Treatment includes resection of the kidney and the associated lymphatic tissue followed by chemotherapy and/or radiation. Dactinomycin is also administered due to the drug's antitumor properties. The five-year cure rate is approximately 75%.

Oncology Treatment Options[28,36,37]

Surgery

Surgery is often used to resect and excise a defined area of malignancy, but may be indicated for prophylactic, diagnostic, curative or palliative goals. Surgical interventions usually require a combination of other treatment modalities secondary to the potential for metastases. These adjunct therapies function to destroy any residual malignant cells. Common side effects include fatigue, pain, deformity, scar tissue formation, and infection.

Radiation

Radiation is administered as either ionizing radiation or particle radiation and can be delivered by teletherapy (external beam), brachytherapy (a sealed and/or implanted source) or system therapy (unsealed source). Radiation destroys the hydrogen bonds between the DNA strands of malignant cells. Radiation may be curative, adjuvant or palliative in its use. It may be used prior to surgical intervention, palliatively to shrink a malignant mass or post-surgically to ensure destruction of residual malignant cells. Radiation is most useful with localized malignancy. Common side effects include headache, bone marrow suppression, skin reactions, neuropathy, visual disturbances, nausea, vomiting, urinary frequency, diarrhea, delayed wound healing, and infection.

Chemotherapy

Chemotherapy consists of a group of drugs that are administered to destroy malignant cells. Chemotherapeutic agents include alkylating agents, antimetabolite agents, steroid hormones, plant alkaloid agents, interferons, and antitumor antibiotics. Each class of chemotherapeutic agents has a different mechanism of action to destroy malignant cells. Chemotherapy is most useful with widespread and metastatic malignancies, but is also used to induce remission, cure and/or eradicate residual malignant cells. The drugs may be administered orally, subcutaneously, intramuscularly, intravenously or intracavitary. Common side effects include nausea, vomiting, electrolyte imbalance, sexual dysfunction, hair loss, pain, and a decrease in platelet, red, and white blood cell counts.

Biotherapy (Immunotherapy)

Biotherapy utilizes various agents and/or techniques to change the relationship between the malignancy and its host. Biologic response modifiers are commonly utilized for biotherapy and act to strengthen a patient's biological response to the malignant cells. Common agents or procedures used with this treatment include interferons, interleukin-2, bone marrow transplant, stem cell transplant, monoclonal antibodies, hormonal therapy, and colony-stimulating factors. Common side effects include fever, chills, nausea, vomiting, anorexia, central nervous system impairment, inflammatory reactions, leukopenia, and fatigue.

Antiangiogenic Therapy

Antiangiogenic therapy focuses on the use of thalidomide and its suppression of blood supply formation. It has had initial success in the treatment of multiple myeloma. There is research that supports blocking the process of growth, as opposed to destruction of an already formed mass, as a means of inhibiting growth of primary malignant masses.

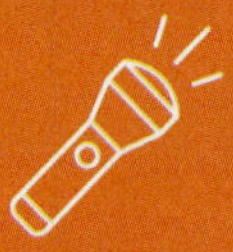

SPOTLIGHT ON SAFETY
REHABILITATION CONSIDERATIONS FOR PATIENTS UNDERGOING CHEMOTHERAPY AND RADIATION[30]

- Strenuous activity should be initially avoided following implantation of radioactive seeds utilized for brachytherapy. Communication with the radiation oncologist and/or referring physician is imperative as further activity contraindications or precautions may be advised depending on the individual case.
- Skin tattoos are used to guide beam alignment with external beam radiation. Physical therapists must be cautious and defer interventions which may alter the position of alignment tattoos (e.g., taping interventions, certain soft tissue or myofascial mobilizations).
- Irradiated skin requires special care to protect tissues prone to erythema, rash, and dry desquamation, as well as more painful wet desquamation and superficial burns.
- Massage and heat are contraindicated over irradiated areas for a minimum of 12 months.
- Certain chemotherapy agents may cause the patient to have a level of toxicity that requires staff and visitors to take additional precautions before making physical contact.
- Patient vomiting during therapy should be reported to the nurse/physician, especially if the patient is taking antiemetic medication to control nausea and vomiting.

Other Pharmacologic Therapies

Hormone therapy is a systemic intervention that is utilized with some types of cancer which rely on a particular hormone to grow (e.g., estrogen). Prescribed agents typically alter the body's production or action of specific hormones, preventing malignant cells from using the hormone they need to grow. Examples of hormone types used in oncology interventions include anti-estrogens, aromatase inhibitors, progestins, estrogens, anti-androgens, and corticosteroids. Targeted therapies refer to drugs designed to specifically target cancer cells. More specific in their action than systemic chemotherapeutic agents, targeted therapies attack mutated versions of a gene or the cells carrying the mutation. Targeted therapies may be a part of the primary oncological interventions or used to help maintain remission.

Palliative Treatment[39,40]

Palliative treatment emphasizes symptom management as opposed to curative efforts. Palliative oncology interventions may include radiation, chemotherapy, physical therapy, chiropractic, acupuncture, alternative and homeopathic medicines, relaxation, biofeedback, pharmacological intervention, and hospice. Palliative treatment may be provided at any time in the disease process with goals of maintaining comfort and dignity through appropriate symptom management. Palliative services can be differentiated into patient support and caregiver support. Patient focused goals may include pain management, emotional and spiritual support, and management of symptoms such as confusion, fatigue, dyspnea, nausea, weakness, and bowel/bladder concerns. Caregiver support may include respite care, education, assistance with transportation, home management, and accessing social services.

Pharmacology - Oncology Management[19,41]

Alkylating Agents

Action: Alkylating agents bind the DNA strands together to prevent replication. If the DNA cannot untwist, then it cannot divide and replicate its genetic code. These agents initiate cell death by disrupting DNA function and releasing enzymes that destroy the cell.

Indications: various malignancies

Side effects: vary by class of drugs and by specific agent; multi-system involvement with mild to severe side effects, however, potential risks are typically warranted secondary to the diagnosis of malignancy

Implications for PT: Therapists must be aware of the chemotherapy regimen and modify treatment based on the patient's symptoms and side effects from cancer treatment. Extreme fatigue, gastrointestinal distress, cancer pain, and blood disorders are common. Therapists must provide support and encouragement without pushing the patient beyond their abilities.

Examples: Mustargen (mechlorethamine), Busulfex (busulfan), Leukeran (chlorambucil)

SPOTLIGHT ON SAFETY
MODALITIES AND PALLIATIVE CARE[39]

Numerous electrotherapeutic, thermal, and mechanical modalities are considered to be contraindicated for use with the oncology population. Physical therapists should be aware of the specifics of these contraindications in order to avoid limiting appropriate treatment options. For example, most heat and electrotherapeutic modalities are contraindicated for use over an active malignancy, but are not necessarily contraindicated for use elsewhere on the body. The therapist's ability to interpret information with respect to an individual's disease status, and when appropriate to seek physician guidance, is imperative when treating patients undergoing oncological interventions.

The use of heat and electrical modalities are typically contraindicated for direct use over malignancies due to the potential for facilitating growth of a malignant mass or hematogenous spread. With physician guidance, these contraindications often may be overlooked in lieu of palliative goals for terminally ill patients. This is especially true in hospice environments where curative efforts have been discontinued and end of life is imminent. However, therapists are advised to be mindful of and adhere to contraindications which may cause a terminally ill patient additional discomfort (e.g., the potential for neuromuscular electrical stimulation causing a pathological fracture in a patient with bone metastasis).

CONSIDER THIS

"CHEMO BRAIN": COGNITIVE CHANGES ASSOCIATED WITH CANCER TREATMENT[42]

Many patients and medical professionals recognize that treatment related cognitive changes in the oncology population are common occurrences. Referred to as "chemo brain" or "chemo fog," these colloquial names are misleading as research has not definitively connected impaired cognition with chemotherapy interventions. A number of factors make defining "chemo brain" difficult. For example, many patients still perform well on formal cognitive assessments, and most do not undergo baseline cognitive testing prior to beginning cancer treatment. Likewise, it is difficult for researchers to truly delineate if cognitive changes are due to the disease process itself, the treatment interventions or side effects of treatment (e.g., depression, fatigue, hormonal changes, altered blood counts, stress).

Regardless, the collection of symptoms commonly associated with "chemo brain" are openly acknowledged in the medical community and anecdotally supported by millions of patients. Physical therapists must be aware of and sensitive to these potential cognitive changes so that they may alter treatment interventions and teaching methods appropriately.

Common "chemo brain" complaints may include feelings of "foggy cognition," confusion, fatigue, limited attention span or short-term memory, and an unusual degree of difficulty with concentration, word finding, multi-tasking, and organization.[28]

Antibiotic Agents

Action: Certain antibiotic agents are used with treatment of cancer due to their high toxicity and ability to interfere with DNA and RNA synthesis and subsequent cell division.

Indications: various malignancies

Side effects: vary by class of drugs and by specific agent; multi-system involvement with mild to severe side effects, however, potential risks are typically warranted secondary to the diagnosis of malignancy; shortness of breath, dysrhythmias, blood disorders, myelosuppression, pedal edema

Implications for PT: Therapists must be aware of the chemotherapy regimen and modify treatment based on the patient's symptoms and side effects from cancer treatment. Extreme fatigue, gastrointestinal distress, cancer pain, and blood disorders are common. Therapists must provide support and encouragement without pushing the patient beyond their abilities.

Examples: Adriamycin (doxorubicin), Mithracin (plicamycin), Cosmegen (dactinomycin)

Antimetabolite Agents

Action: Antimetabolite agents impair biosynthesis of genetic material and interrupt the cellular pathways that synthesize DNA and RNA. These agents create an impostor to the endogenous metabolites within the body to form a nonfunctional genetic product that is incapable of reproduction.

Indications: various malignancies, particularly rapidly dividing neoplastic cells

Side effects: vary by class of drugs and by specific agent; multi-system involvement with mild to severe side effects, however, potential risks are typically warranted secondary to the diagnosis of malignancy

Implications for PT: Therapists must be aware of the chemotherapy regimen and modify treatment based on the patient's symptoms and side effects from cancer treatment. Extreme fatigue, gastrointestinal distress, cancer pain, and blood disorders are common. Therapists must provide support and encouragement without pushing the patient beyond their abilities.

Examples: Leustatin (cladribine), Adrucil (fluorouracil), Fludara (fludarabine), Trexall (methotrexate)

Biologic Response Modifier Agents

Action: Biologic response modifier agents include interferons, interleukin-2, and monoclonal antibodies that are responsible for enhancing the body's own ability to respond to neoplastic growth. These agents are not cytotoxic, but facilitate the patient's immune response to destroy malignant tissues.

Indications: various malignancies, particularly leukemias, lymphomas, Kaposi sarcoma, organ and tissue malignancies

Side effects: vary by class of drugs and by specific agent; multi-system involvement with mild to severe side effects, however, potential risks are typically warranted secondary to the diagnosis of malignancy

Implications for PT: Therapists must be aware of the chemotherapy regimen and modify treatment based on the patient's symptoms and side effects from cancer treatment. Extreme fatigue, gastrointestinal distress, cancer pain, and blood disorders are common. Therapists must provide support and encouragement without pushing the patient beyond their abilities.

Examples: Proleukin (aldesleukin), Avastin (bevacizumab), Intron-A (interferon alfa-2b)

Heavy Metal Compounds

Action: Heavy metal compounds used as antineoplastic agents are also known as platinum coordination complexes. They act as alkylating agents that inhibit DNA translation and replication.

Indications: various malignancies; particularly epithelial malignancies, ovarian cancer, testicular cancer, bladder cancer

Side effects: vary by class of drugs and by specific agent; multi-system involvement with mild to severe side effects, however, potential risks are typically warranted secondary to the diagnosis of malignancy

Implications for PT: Therapists must be aware of the chemotherapy regimen and modify treatment based on the patient's symptoms and side effects from cancer treatment. Extreme fatigue, gastrointestinal distress, cancer pain, and blood disorders are common. Therapists must provide support and encouragement without pushing the patient beyond their abilities.

Examples: Platinol (cisplatin), Paraplatin (carboplatin), Eloxatin (oxaliplatin)

Hormones

Action: Certain hormones can exacerbate or facilitate proliferation of particular forms of cancer while other hormones can attenuate particular cancers. Hormones are typically used as adjunct therapy along with other forms of treatment specific to the malignancy.

Indications: various malignancies, particularly hormone sensitive neoplasms

Side effects: vary by class of drugs and by specific agent; multi-system involvement with mild to severe side effects, however, potential risks are typically warranted secondary to the diagnosis of malignancy; masculinization in women, hot flashes, general catabolic effects

Implications for PT: Therapists must be aware of the chemotherapy regimen and modify treatment based on the patient's symptoms and side effects from cancer treatment. Extreme fatigue, gastrointestinal distress, cancer pain, and blood disorders are common. Therapists must provide support and encouragement without pushing the patient beyond their abilities.

Examples: Nolvadex (tamoxifen citrate), Lupron (leuprolide acetate), Casodex (bicalutamide)

Plant Alkaloid Agents (Mitotic Inhibitors)

Action: Agents in this classification are nitrogen-based and largely derived from plants. They directly target the replication process prior to and during mitosis to inhibit cell division. This limits cell division and cancer growth in various types of malignancy.

Indications: various malignancies

Side effects: vary by class of drugs and by specific agent; multi-system involvement with mild to severe side effects, however, potential risks are typically warranted secondary to the diagnosis of malignancy

Implications for PT: Therapists must be aware of the chemotherapy regimen and modify treatment based on the patient's symptoms and side effects from cancer treatment. Extreme fatigue, gastrointestinal distress, cancer pain, and blood disorders are common. Therapists must provide support and encouragement without pushing the patient beyond their abilities.

Examples: Oncovin (vincristine sulfate), Taxotere (docetaxel), Taxol (paclitaxel)

Oncology Terminology[16,31,32]

Adjuvant: Treatment provided, in addition to other cure-focused interventions, with the intention of preventing cancer recurrence.

Benign neoplasm: An abnormal cell growth that is usually slow growing and harmless, closely resembling the composition of adjacent tissues.

Cancer: A group of diseases characterized by uncontrolled cell proliferation with mutation and spreading of the abnormal cells. The etiology is based on the type and location of the cancer. The most common causes include cigarette smoking, diet and nutrition, chemical agents, physical agents, environmental causes, viral causes, and genetics.

Differentiated cells: Cells that have matured from a less specific to a more specific cell type.

Dysplasia: An abnormal development of cells or tissue that is often an early sign of neoplasia.

Hyperplasia: An increase in cell number that may be normal or abnormal depending on additional characteristics.

Malignant neoplasm: An abnormal uncontrolled cell growth that invades and destroys adjacent tissues and may metastasize to other sites and systems of the body.

Metaplasia: A change in a cell from one type to another that may be normal or abnormal.

Neoadjuvant: Chemotherapy or radiation given prior to surgical oncology intervention.

Tumor (neoplasm): An abnormal new growth of tissue that increases the overall tissue mass. Tumors are benign (non-cancerous) or malignant (cancerous) as well as primary or secondary. Primary tumors form from cells that belong to the area of the tumor. Secondary tumors grow from cells that have metastasized (spread) from another affected area within the body. Tumor classification is defined by cell type, tissue of origin, amount of differentiation, benign versus malignant, and anatomic site.

Undifferentiated cells: Cells which have not differentiated into a specific type (e.g., primitive, embryonic) or have no special structure or function.

Psychological Disorders[10,32,43]

Affective Disorders

Affective disorders are classified by disturbances in mood or emotion. States of extreme happiness or sadness occur and mood can alternate without cause. These extreme emotions can become intense and unrealistic.

Bipolar

- Alternating periods of depression and mania
- Females are at greater risk; typically begins in a patient's twenties

Depression

- Slower mental and physical activity; poor self-esteem
- Immobilized from everyday activities; sadness, hopelessness, and helplessness
- Desire to withdraw; delusions in severe cases

Mania

- Constantly active
- Impulses immediately expressed
- Unrealistic activity
- Elation and self-confidence
- Disagreement with a patient may produce patient aggression
- Disorganized thoughts and speech
- Very few patients are diagnosed with only a manic disorder

Dissociative Disorders

Dissociative disorders develop when a person unconsciously dissociates (separates) one part of the mind from the rest.

Multiple Personality

- A rare dissociative disorder; includes two or more independent personalities
- Each personality may or may not know about the other
- Causative factors are not understood; believed to allow a person to engage in behaviors that are against the patient's morality and normally produce guilt

Psychogenic Amnesia

- Produced by the mind with no physical cause
- Forgets all aspects of the past

Neuroses Disorders

Neuroses refer to a group of disorders that are characterized by individuals exhibiting fear and maladaptive strategies in dealing with stressful or everyday stimuli. Patients with neuroses are not dealing with psychosis, do not have delusions, and usually realize that they have a problem.

Anxiety Disorder

- Constant high tension; overreacts in certain instances
- Presents with apprehension and chronic worry
- Acute anxiety attacks
  - Lasts a few minutes in duration
  - Excitation of the sympathetic autonomic nervous system
  - Fear of impending doom or death
  - Shortness of breath, heart palpitations, dizziness, nausea
  - Initiated by unconscious and internal mechanisms

Obsessive-compulsive Disorder

- Obsessions – persistent thoughts that will not leave
- Compulsions – repetitive ritual behaviors the patient cannot stop performing
- Thoughts or ritual behaviors that interfere with daily living
- Unable to control irrational behavior
- Most commonly begins in young adulthood

Phobia Disorder

- Excessive fear of objects, occurrences or situations that is considerably out of proportion/irrational
- Fear creates difficulty in everyday life
- Subclassifications include agoraphobia, social phobia, and simple phobia; simple phobia is easiest to treat
- May develop from traumatic experiences, observation, classical conditioning

Personality Disorders

A personality disorder is classified by observing a patient's pattern of behavior, dysfunctional view of society, and level of sadness. Personality disorders are usually ongoing patterns of dysfunctional behavior.

Antisocial Behavior

- Results from particular causes (e.g., need for attention or involvement in a gang)
- Typically has some concern for others
- Blames other institutions (e.g., family, school) for their actions
- Symptoms are typically seen before 16 years of age
- Violates the rights of others; lacks responsibility and emotional stability

Borderline Behavior

- Instability in all aspects of life
- Can identify self from others
- Uses projection, denial, defensiveness; unpredictable mood or behavior
- Intense and uncontrolled anger; chronic feelings of emptiness

Narcissistic Behavior

- Incapable of loving others
- Self-absorbed; obsessed with success and power
- Unrealistic perception of self-importance

Psychopathic Personality

- Low morality, poor sense of responsibility, no respect for others
- Impulsive behavior for immediate gratification; high frustration
- Little guilt or remorse for all actions; inability to alter behavior, even with punishment
- Expert liar

Schizophrenia Disorders

Schizophrenia disorders are psychotic in nature and present with disorganization of thought, hallucinations, emotional dysfunction, anxiety, and perceptual impairments. Causative factors include traumatic events, genetic inheritance, biochemical imbalances, and environmental influence.

Catatonic Schizophrenia

- Motor disturbances with rigid posturing
- Episodes consist of uncontrolled movements, however, patients remain aware during episodes
- Medications are required to regulate episodes

Disorganized Schizophrenia

- Usually progressive and irreversible with inappropriate emotional responses; mumbled talking

Paranoid Schizophrenia

- Delusions of grandeur; delusions of persecution
- May believe they possess special powers

Somatoform Disorders

Somatoform disorders are classified based on the physical symptoms present in each disorder.

Conversion Disorder

- Physical complaints of neurological basis with no underlying cause
- Paralysis is the most common finding; other findings include deafness, blindness, paresthesia
- Freud believed this is mental anxiety transformed into physical symptoms
- Diagnosis can be made once testing is negative for physical ailments

Hypochondriasis Disorder

- Excessive fear of illness
- Believes that minor illnesses or medical problems indicate a serious or life threatening disease

Somatization Disorder

- Primarily in women, has familial association, and often chronic and long lasting
- Complaints of symptoms with no physiological basis
- Symptoms usually lead to medications and medical visits and alter the patient's life
- Resembles hypochondriasis disorder

Pharmacology - Psychiatric Management[19,43]

Antianxiety Agents

Action: Antianxiety agents collectively target the CNS through facilitating the effects of GABA or targeting dopamine and serotonin within the brain. Benzodiazepines, azapirones, and certain selective serotonin reuptake inhibitor (SSRI) antidepressants treat various anxiety disorders.

Indications: general anxiety disorder, social anxiety, panic disorder, obsessive-compulsive disorder, post-traumatic stress syndrome

Side effects: drowsiness, sedation, withdrawal symptoms including rebound anxiety

Implications for PT: Similar concerns as with sedative-hypnotic agents; therapists can also implement alternate methods to decrease stress and anxiety including exercise and physical activity, massage, relaxation techniques, and stress management education.

Examples: Benzodiazepines: Xanax (alprazolam), Valium (diazepam), Ativan (lorazepam); Azapirones: BuSpar (buspirone); SSRIs: Effexor (venlafaxine), Paxil (paroxetine)

Antidepressant Agents (Tricyclic, SSRI, MAOI, Other)

Action: Antidepressant agents are classified as tricyclic, monoamine oxidase inhibitors (MAOI), and selective serotonin reuptake inhibitors (SSRI), as well as miscellaneous agents that attempt to increase aminergic transmission and normalize neurotransmission activity.

Indications: depression, certain agents also treat anxiety disorders

Side effects: vary by class of drugs and by specific agent; sedation, blurred vision, tachycardia, dry mouth, insomnia, weight gain, sexual dysfunction

Implications for PT: Therapists should typically see improvement in a patient's affect with pharmacological treatment for depression. Therapists must be aware of side effects such as sedation, fatigue, hypertension or orthostatic hypotension. Therapists must also look for any signs of further depression or suicidal tendencies.

Examples: Tricyclics: Elavil (amitriptyline), Pamelor (nortriptyline); MAOIs: Nardil (phenelzine); SSRIs: Wellbutrin (bupropion), Prozac (fluoxetine), Paxil (paroxetine)

Antipsychotic Agents (Neuroleptic Agents)

Action: Most antipsychotic agents block dopamine receptors and reduce the overactivity of dopamine typically transmitted in areas such as the limbic system. The agents will bind to the dopamine receptors, but will not allow for activation. There are traditional and newer "atypical" antipsychotic agents used for schizophrenia and other various psychosis disorders.

Indications: schizophrenia, various psychotic disorders, Alzheimer's disease (certain cases)

Side effects: traditional agents produce increased extrapyramidal (motor) side effects, tardive dyskinesia, pseudoparkinsonism, akathisia, sedation, constipation, dry mouth; atypical agents can produce substantial weight gain, diabetes mellitus, hyperlipidemia

Implications for PT: These agents assist patients to participate in physical therapy by decreasing their symptoms of psychoses and allowing for an increased attention span, diminished agitation and restlessness, improved sense of reality, and an overall normalization of their behavior and affect. The largest barrier is the influence of extrapyramidal effects on therapy. Early detection of these effects can allow for prompt medical and pharmacological management.

Examples: Traditional: Haldol (haloperidol), Thorazine (chlorpromazine); Atypical: Risperdal (risperidone), Abilify (aripiprazole)

Bipolar Disorder Agents

Action: Bipolar disorder agents focus on the prevention of manic episodes in order to avoid the extreme mood swings that follow. The primary agent used in this treatment is lithium. Certain antiseizure and antipsychotic medications may assist as mood stabilizers with bipolar disorder.

Indications: bipolar or manic-depressive disorders

Side effects: in general, gastrointestinal distress, tardive dyskinesia, fatigue, confusion, ataxia, nystagmus, lethargy, tremor, Parkinsonism, seizures, diabetes insipidus, toxicity, coma, risk of death

Implications for PT: Therapists should become familiar with the side effects of medications that treat bipolar disorder, especially symptoms of toxicity as it relates to lithium. Long-term use of lithium may result in osteoporosis which will impact the physical therapy plan of care.

Examples: Lithobid (lithium); Antipsychotics: Clozaril (clozapine), Risperdal (risperidone); Antiseizures: Tegretol (carbamazepine), Neurontin (gabapentin)

Sedative-hypnotic Agents (Benzodiazepine and Non-benzodiazepine)

Action: Sedative agents produce a calming and relaxation while hypnotic agents induce sleep. Benzodiazepines have properties to promote sleep through increasing inhibitory effects at the CNS synapses where GABA (gamma-aminobutyric acid) is found. Non-benzodiazepines include barbiturates and other drugs that also provide CNS depression through the inhibitory effects of GABA.

Indications: anxiety, preoperative sedation, insomnia

Side effects: residual effects can produce drowsiness and decreased motor performance, anterograde amnesia, tolerance, dependency, rebound insomnia with withdrawal; barbiturates are highly addictive and can be fatal

Implications for PT: Therapists may find it beneficial to treat a patient when peak blood levels of the agent exist so that the patient is calm, relaxed, and can focus on the treatment regimen, however, this may become problematic if the patient experiences side effects of drowsiness and impairments in motor control. The risk of falling increases with use of these agents.

Examples: Benzodiazepine: Halcion (triazolam), Dalmane (flurazepam); Non-benzodiazepine: Luminal (phenobarbital), Sonata (zaleplon), Ambien (zolpidem)

SPOTLIGHT ON SAFETY
RESPECTFUL MANAGEMENT OF ESCALATING PATIENT BEHAVIORS[32]

Patients with or without a psychiatric diagnosis may exhibit escalating behaviors from time to time. The financial, social, physical, and mental stress that accompanies injury or illness can be frustrating enough to cause even mild mannered patients to become agitated or combative. When dealing with patients in these challenging situations, physical therapists should be respectful in their de-escalation attempts, but also mindful of maintaining a safe environment for everyone involved.

Many health care facilities offer training in non-verbal de-escalation techniques which are helpful in defusing a potentially threatening situation. Guiding principles for safe use of these techniques include an understanding that attempting to reason with an escalating patient may make matters worse, and that calm reasoning in a threatening situation is counterintuitive to our own "fight or flight" response. Successful non-verbal de-escalation requires the provider to maintain self-control and a protective yet non-threatening physical presence while facilitating the de-escalation conversation.

Tips for interacting with an escalating patient:

- Be empathetic when setting boundaries
- Use a low, calm tone of voice when speaking
- Do not respond defensively to patient comments
- Offer choices, options or small concessions if appropriate
- Do not force constant eye contact, allow the patient to look away
- Be respectful and acknowledge the patient's complaints or frustration
- When speaking, wait for the patient to pause rather than raising your voice to be heard
- Be aware of your supportive resources, including the option to leave the area if necessary
- Avoid physical contact
- Do not turn your back to an agitated or escalating patient
- Do not allow an agitated or escalating patient to block your exit route
- Maintain more space than usual between yourself and the patient for safety
- Stand at an angle facing the patient so that it is easier to sidestep if necessary
- Always stay at the same eye level as the patient (e.g., both standing, both sitting)
- Keep hands out of your pockets both for self-protection and to avoid the appearance of concealment

Geriatrics

Gerontology[51]

Gerontology is defined as the study of aging in older adults. It is expected that the average age of individuals in the United States will increase due to improvements in health care and the aging of the baby-boomer generation. In general, women will outlive men and make up the greatest percentage of adults over 85 years of age. Knowing how to provide skilled care to an aging adult requires specific knowledge of the biological, psychological, and social influences affecting the patient.

Optimal Aging[52]

Aging occurs along a spectrum, from successful to usual to sub-optimal. Successful aging is defined as the absence of disease and disability, high cognitive and physical functioning, and maintaining active engagement with life. This is a somewhat restrictive definition of aging since statistically there is a greater chance of incurring a functional limitation or disease with increasing age. Optimal aging is a term perhaps more appropriate for a health care practitioner to use. It is defined as the capacity to function across many domains - physical, functional, cognitive, emotional, social, and spiritual - to one's satisfaction and despite one's medical conditions. This definition deliberately avoids the importance of aging without disease and instead embraces the health variations that can occur while still maintaining a meaningful engagement in a chosen lifestyle. This is different than aging sub-optimally, which occurs when an individual does not engage in preventative health care and experiences the deleterious effects of normal physiological aging along with that of preventable pathology. An example of this would be an individual who develops emphysema, heart disease, and diabetes secondary to lifestyle choices.

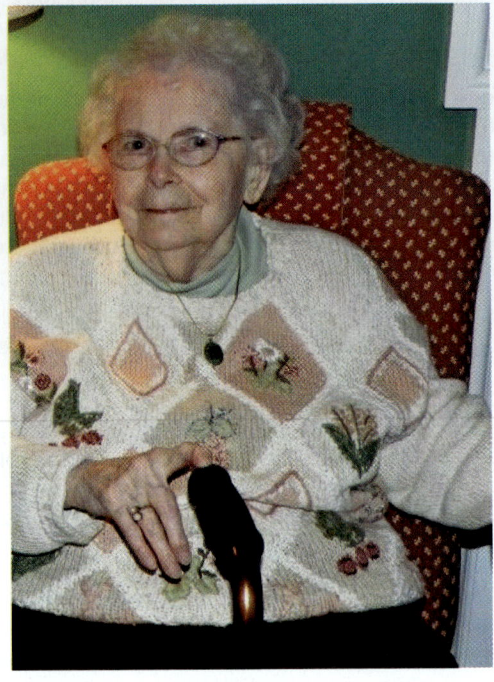

Fig. 7-8: An older adult at rest.

The Body Systems[10,53,54]

Individuals reach their greatest physical health in their 20s and early 30s. Afterwards, age-related changes begin to occur that result in a decrease in physical and cognitive functioning. Aging affects all physiologic processes within the body. The rate of age-related changes is relatively constant, though the patient is typically more symptomatic later in life. Many of the physiologic changes that occur with aging also occur with a decrease in activity, therefore exercise may help to attenuate some of these changes.

CONSIDER THIS

AGEISM[51]

Ageism is a form of discrimination based on stereotypes regarding age. While this can be directed at any specific age group, older adults often encounter prejudice because of myths and stereotypes perpetuated by cultural beliefs, personal beliefs, and media representations. Ageism can impact the ability of a caretaker or health professional to provide unbiased care, where treatment is instead based on preconceived notions. Examples include when a therapist refers to an older adult as "honey" or "sweetie," thereby infantilizing the older adult despite good intentions. Another example of ageism is when an older adult presents to physical therapy with a family member, and the therapist directs questions to the family member rather than the patient. This minimalizes the patient's role in the rehabilitation program, potentially reducing their motivation. Finally, ageism can present itself as the routine delivery of care for all patients over a specific age, instead of applying sound principles of clinical decision making. Recognizing inherent beliefs and prejudices allow practitioners to provide objective, unbiased care, and meet the needs of the patient.

Musculoskeletal System

Age-related changes that occur within the musculoskeletal system lead to an overall decrease in a patient's physical functioning. Muscles atrophy and decrease in their ability to regenerate (i.e., sarcopenia), both of which result in a loss of strength. Additionally, the number of motor units decreases so that each motor neuron must innervate a larger number of muscle fibers, resulting in motor unit hypertrophy. An increase in fat mass occurs as an older adult's lean body mass decreases. This infiltration of fat is a predictor of mobility restriction.

Fig. 7-9: An older adult exercising with assistance from a therapist.

Older adults also begin to experience a decrease in bone mass in their 40s or 50s, a change that occurs due to an increase in bone resorption without an equivalent increase in bone deposition. Due to the decrease in bone density, older adults are at a higher risk for fractures secondary to falls, especially when combined with sarcopenia. With increasing age, there are also changes noted in the patient's joints and connective tissues. Articular cartilage loses much of its water content and begins to degenerate leading to arthritis, especially in weight bearing joints. Intervertebral disks also begin to lose their water content, which results in an overall decrease in height and an increased incidence of disk-related pathology. Connective tissues such as fascia, ligaments, and tendons lose their extensibility, which results in an overall decrease in the patient's range of motion and flexibility. These changes can contribute to the development of frailty syndrome, which is identified in older adults who have three out of the five following symptoms: unintentional weight loss, muscle weakness, slow walking speed, exhaustion, and low physical activity. Many of the changes that occur in the musculoskeletal system with aging can be mitigated with exercise.

Age-Related Changes Impacting the Musculoskeletal System

- Type IIb fibers are denervated and remaining motor units hypertrophy
- Approximately 10% decline in strength per decade, especially during the sixth and seventh decades
- Decreased muscle mass (sarcopenia)
- Decreased velocity of muscular contraction
- Decreased cross-sectional area of type II muscle fibers
- Decreased ability to perform forceful and alternating movements
- Increased muscular fat infiltration
- Decreased skeletal bone mass after the fourth decade
- Women have lower bone mass compared to men
- Women experience the greatest level of bone mass loss following menopause
- Decreased articular cartilage thickness
- Increased collagen stiffness due to cross linkage between fibers

Neuromuscular and Nervous Systems

Changes with age occur in both the central and peripheral nervous systems. Changes in the central nervous system include an overall decrease in brain size due to atrophy of brain tissue and a decrease in nerve conduction velocity that results in an overall decrease in central processing. These changes can result in alterations with the patient's movement as well as their cognition. In the peripheral nervous system, there is also a decrease in processing time that affects nociceptors and other peripheral receptors. As a result, older adults have decreased ability to sense pain, decreased joint proprioception and coordination, decreased somatosensory input, impaired balance reactions and reflexes, and increased gait instability. Balance is also negatively affected by changes that occur within the vestibular system, primarily due to a loss of vestibular receptor cells. The result of these changes leads to diminished capacity to react to environmental challenges and disturbances to postural stability. Combined with the musculoskeletal changes normally experienced with age, this leaves an older adult at greater risk for falls.

Age-Related Changes Impacting the Neuromuscular and Nervous Systems

- Decreased brain volume with an increased ventricular size
- Decreased peripheral nerve conduction velocity
- Decreased reaction speed

Cardiovascular and Pulmonary Systems

With increasing age, cardiac output decreases making older adults less tolerant to exercise secondary to decreased perfusion of the peripheral tissues. Several factors lead to this decrease in cardiac output, including decreased venous return, arteriosclerosis which increases afterload (especially in the aorta), fibrotic changes within the myocardium that make it less compliant, and a decreased response to cardiac hormones. Cardiac output may also be decreased due to a diminished arteriovenous oxygen difference (A-VO2) secondary to the musculoskeletal changes experienced as part of aging. However, if stroke volume can be maintained or increased as a result of exercise, overall cardiac output can be sustained despite the diminished maximum heart rate. Other changes in the cardiovascular system that occur with aging include increased blood pressure, an increased risk for postural hypotension, decreased resting heart rate, and an increased risk for cardiac dysrhythmias. The increase in myocyte volume of the ventricles encroaches on the vasculature of the myocardium, increasing the risk for myocardial ischemia. Due to these cardiovascular changes, older adults are at greater risk for stroke, coronary artery disease, and congestive heart failure. Greater than 50% of all older adults have some form of heart disease.

Age-Related Changes Impacting the Cardiovascular and Pulmonary Systems

- Decreased myocyte density with increased myocyte volume
- Decreased sinoatrial node pacemaker cells
- Increased cardiac afterload
- Decreased sensitivity to beta-adrenergic stimulation
- Increased calcification and fibrosis of heart valves
- Increased vascular tone leading to increased systolic blood pressure
- Decreased arterial elasticity and compliance
- Increased mucosal thickening in combination with decreased mucosal transport
- Increased physiological "dead space"
- Decreased inspiratory muscle strength
- Decreased FEV_1
- Increased residual volume following maximal expiration

There are several changes within the pulmonary system that occur with aging that result in a decrease in overall gas exchange. The chest wall becomes stiffer and less compliant and the elasticity and recoil of the lungs also decreases. In combination with an increased thoracic kyphosis and weakened inspiratory muscles, these changes result in a diminished musculoskeletal pump. The result is a decrease in the vital capacity of the lungs. As vital capacity decreases, residual volume increases (since total lung capacity stays roughly the same). Other changes that occur in the pulmonary system include decreased number and size of alveoli, decreased expiratory flow rates, decreased ciliary function in the upper airways (which increases the risk for infections like pneumonia), and decreased strength and effectiveness of coughing.

Integumentary System

The integumentary system experiences several changes associated with aging. A decrease in thickness of the dermal layer as well as a loss of elastin fibers causes the skin to wrinkle and sag and makes it more prone to damage (e.g., bruising, cuts). A loss of collagen also makes the skin more prone to damage from shear forces. Pressure ulcers are more common in this population, especially since vascular changes further delay wound healing, making education and prevention strategies essential. A reduction in blood vessels within the dermis makes the skin appear paler and also impairs thermoregulation. These changes make older adults more prone to hypothermia and hyperthermia. A decrease in the number and structure of sweat glands decreases perspiration and further impairs thermoregulation. When using thermal modalities, great care must be taken to monitor an older adult's tolerance in order to prevent injury. An older adult may present with a blunted fever response, making it difficult to diagnose certain pathologies for which elevated body temperature is a symptom.

Age-Related Changes Impacting the Integumentary System

- Decreased fever response
- Decreased autonomic regulation of thermoregulatory responses
- Decreased vascularity, thickness, and elasticity of the dermis
- Increased pain threshold
- Decreased subcutaneous adipose tissue
- Decreased sensory perception

Metabolic and Endocrine Systems

There are a variety of changes that occur within the metabolic and endocrine systems as a person ages. In general, basal metabolism decreases with age, which may be a result of the decrease in lean body mass. Changes also occur with acid-base balance in the body, which can have a negative effect on metabolic function. In the endocrine system, there is a general decrease in hormone production and function. Older adults tend to exhibit higher blood glucose levels secondary to a reduction in the number and function of beta cells within the pancreas as well as an increase in peripheral resistance to insulin. Elevated blood glucose is one of the contributing factors to the development of metabolic syndrome, a condition that is prevalent in greater than half of all older adults. Loss of bone mass occurs secondary to an increase in bone resorption and has also been linked to hormonal changes, especially in older adult women.

Age-Related Changes Impacting the Metabolic and Endocrine Systems

- Decreased insulin sensitivity
- Decreased hepatic insulin release control
- Decreased sensitivity to beta-adrenergic stimulation

Gastrointestinal System

Physiologic changes with aging occur along the entire length of the gastrointestinal tract. Decreased taste and smell sensations may affect the patient's desire to eat, and loss of alveolar bone mass and other dental issues may make the act of mastication more difficult to perform. Decreased salivation leads to dry mouth, which may further affect a patient's appetite. This can result in malnutrition and dehydration, which will adversely affect all of the body's systems. Loss of motility (i.e., peristalsis) begins in the esophagus and continues throughout the digestive tract. In the esophagus, this can lead to dysphagia and gastroesophageal reflux disease. Intestinal motility issues are common (especially in the large intestine) and lead to an increased incidence of constipation and diverticulosis. Aging is also associated with a loss of control of the anal sphincters (i.e., internal, external), which increases the risk for fecal incontinence.

Age-Related Changes Impacting the Gastrointestinal System

- Decreased energy metabolism
- Decreased drug metabolism
- Increased risk of adverse side effects from medications
- Decreased gastric acid production
- Decreased bowel mobility

Genitourinary System

With increasing age, the kidneys become less effective at removing wastes from the blood. This occurs secondary to anatomic and physiologic changes such as decreased blood flow to the kidneys, fewer nephrons and glomeruli, and an overall decrease in the size of the kidney. Due to these changes, the glomerular filtration rate decreases and the kidneys become less effective at concentrating and diluting urine. This affects the regulation of sodium levels within the blood as well as clearance of certain medications from the body. Another change that occurs with aging is decreasing capacity of the bladder which increases the likelihood of urinary frequency and nocturia. Sensation associated with the need to urinate is often delayed or nonexistent in older adults, which results in an increased incidence of incontinence. Certain medical conditions such as Alzheimer's disease and Parkinson's disease result in detrusor muscle instability, which leads to an overactive bladder and urge incontinence. Conversely, some older adults require assistance to ambulate to the bathroom and may be unable to reach the bathroom before voiding (i.e., functional incontinence). Finally, some older adults may decrease their water intake or hold their urine to limit the number of trips to the bathroom. This can lead to urinary tract infections and sepsis if untreated. In men, the prostate enlarges, which can cause issues with voiding completely.

Age-Related Changes Impacting the Genitourinary System

- Prostate enlargement
- Increased incontinence
- Decreased kidney function and filtration rate
- Decreased bladder capacity

The Five Senses[53,54]

Hearing

The progressive loss of hearing experienced in older adults is called presbycusis. Hearing loss begins around the fourth decade and accelerates in the decades that follow. Older adults tend to have difficulty differentiating between sounds. For example, they often have trouble following a conversation when they are in a crowded room. When working with patients with hearing loss, the therapist should reduce background noise, speak loudly and slowly, and pronounce their words carefully. The therapist should attempt to communicate in a lower frequency range since older adults can distinguish lower frequencies better than higher frequencies. Tinnitus is another common hearing impairment that is associated with increasing age.

Vision

As an individual ages, the degree of visual impairment will increase, especially in those older than 75 years of age. Visual impairment is associated with falls, depression, and functional decline. There are several specific changes that occur in the visual system with increased age. Visual acuity, the visual field, and peripheral vision all decrease. The pupils become smaller and are less responsive to changes in light, making it more difficult to see in the dark. Older adults have an increase in the amount of time it takes to accommodate to a brighter or darker environment. Loss of contrast sensitivity and depth perception can result in an increased risk of falling when navigating stairs or uneven surfaces. Common eye diseases that occur with aging include cataracts, glaucoma, macular degeneration, and diabetic retinopathy.

Visual impairments can be mitigated through environmental and behavioral modifications that can reduce the risk of injury associated with visual decline.

- Use contrasting colors to highlight the edge of steps, thresholds, and transition areas.
- Remove throw rugs that are not secured at the edges to the floor.
- Use diffuse lighting instead of direct lighting throughout the home.
- Use night lights for maintaining low level illumination during the night.
- Allow for extra time when transitioning from a bright atmosphere to a dark atmosphere, and vice-versa, to accommodate to the change.
- Maintain clear hallways and rooms, including removing any wires across the walkway.
- Have handrails, preferably two, for stairwells both in and outside of the home.

Taste and Smell

The senses of taste and smell both interact to play a role in the enjoyment of food. With increasing age, the number and size of taste buds decrease resulting in a decreased sensitivity to all five tastes (e.g., sour, sweet). Additionally, less saliva is produced and causes a dry mouth, which can also decrease taste sensitivity. A decrease in the ability to detect odors also occurs with increased age. The combination of decreased taste and smell result in a diminished desire for older adults to eat, which can affect their nutritional health.

Touch

Older adults have decreased sensitivity to a variety of sensations including touch, pain, vibration, pressure, proprioception, and temperature. Changes in sensation make older adults more prone to injury (e.g., burns, pressure ulcers). A decrease in somatosensation contributes to balance impairments. These impairments can be exacerbated due to the influence of age-related visual impairments.

Cognition[51,53]

Memory

Memory loss is the most common cognitive impairment that is associated with aging. Memory is made up of numerous constructs, and only some of the facets of memory are affected by aging. Short-term memory is affected, and as a result older adults may have difficulty recalling information they have just learned. This is exacerbated by trying to remember more complex or lengthy memories. Working memory also declines in older age. This is the memory type where individuals use relevant information while in the middle of an activity (e.g., remembering items on a shopping list while shopping). Episodic memory (i.e., personally experienced events) tends to be affected to a greater degree than semantic memory (i.e., knowledge of facts) or procedural memory (i.e., performance of skills).

Attention

Older adults demonstrate significant loss of divided attention, which is the ability to process two or more sources of information at the same time. This is known as dual-tasking and a deficit in this ability can be associated with a greater risk for falls in older adults. They also show a decreased ability to switch their attention between two different tasks. However, other forms of attention do not show a decline with age, such as sustained attention (i.e., maintaining attention over a long period of time on a single task) and selective attention (i.e., the ability to disregard sources of information that are irrelevant to the task).

Intelligence

With increasing age, intelligence declines though this construct is difficult to study due to generational differences. General intelligence begins to decline sometime between the 50s and 70s. Crystalized intelligence, which is the accumulation of knowledge and skills, has the tendency to be maintained, or even improve, as an individual ages. However, fluid intelligence, which is the speed and ability to reason and problem solve, begins to decline.

Mild Cognitive Impairment

Mild cognitive impairment (MCI) is defined as having lower than expected cognitive performance when compared to others in the age group. It generally does not interfere with activities of daily living. Having MCI does not infer that an individual will progress towards developing dementia.

Dementia

Dementia is a process of cognitive decline that eventually influences the individual's ability to participate in daily activities. Difficulty comprehending language, impaired problem solving, behavioral disturbances, and memory deficits are all commonly associated with dementia. Alzheimer's disease, a progressive form of dementia, is found largely in older adults. The incidence of dementia is shown to increase with age.

Delirium

Delirium is different from dementia in that it is a transient state of fluctuating cognitive abilities. Memory, orientation, and arousal may all be affected. The condition is commonly experienced after a hospitalization, post-surgically, during the course of an untreated medical condition or as a side effect of certain medications. While the symptoms of delirium can mimic other conditions (e.g., dementia), it is important to consider that the patient's cognitive status may change from day to day. Daily orientation and cognitive evaluations are key components of skilled geriatric physical therapy. Risk factors for developing delirium include age greater than 70, having a diminished cognitive status, depression, and alcohol abuse.

CONSIDER THIS
GOAL SETTING IN OLDER ADULTS

Assumptions about older adults and their capabilities can result in discrepancies between the patient's goals and the therapist's goals. It is imperative that a therapist designing a care plan for an older adult incorporate relevant patient goals. Therapists should avoid developing generic goals (e.g., "Patient will ambulate 150 feet with rolling walker on level surfaces.") and instead focus on goals that the patient has explicit interest in performing (e.g., "Patient will ambulate 20 feet with two turns using a single point cane to simulate their daily routine of getting the newspaper."). Setting goals that are appropriate for the patient, not for their age, will strengthen the bond between the therapist and the patient.

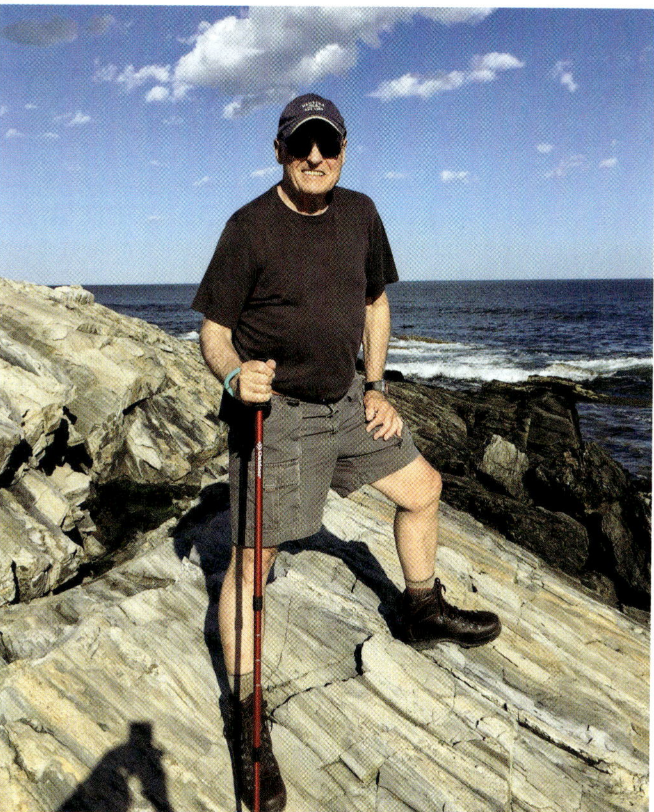

Fig. 7-10: An active older adult on a hike.

Medication Safety[10,19,51]

Pharmacology Considerations in Geriatrics

Older adults process medication differently than younger adults, therefore an awareness of the pharmacokinetic and pharmacodynamic changes is necessary. This section discusses the differences experienced with aging and how they can impact patient care.

Pharmacokinetics

Pharmacokinetics is the study of what happens to the drug once it is in the human body. There are four major parameters that are influenced by pharmacokinetics: absorption, distribution, metabolism, and excretion. As an individual ages, the ability to process a drug changes and it can greatly influence the effect of the medication. Absorption refers to the movement of a drug into the bloodstream. Decreased acidity in the stomach, along with slower emptying times and decreased motility can alter the absorption of the drug. It also can predispose the stomach to developing ulcerations from maintaining prolonged contact with the medication.

Distribution of the medication refers to the transport of the drug to various tissues. Certain drugs are lipophilic or hydrophilic, and as such the distribution will be influenced based on the older adult's body composition. Considering older adults demonstrate a decrease in total body water, an increase in adipose tissue, and a decrease in muscle mass, certain drugs will be influenced greater by their distribution characteristics than others. Additionally, since there is a potential decrease in serum albumin levels in older adults, certain drugs may become more concentrated in the bloodstream, which will result in intensified drug effects.

Metabolism is a component of drug clearance and it occurs primarily in the liver. Since metabolism of a drug is dependent on the mass of the liver, enzyme levels, and blood flow, any changes to the hepatic system can influence the body's ability to break down the drug. Older adults are more predisposed to side effects as the half-life of the drug is extended.

The final component of pharmacokinetics is excretion. Excretion is primarily performed by the renal system. Kidney function is the most quantifiable determining factor of drug clearance from the body. In the older adult the kidneys have diminished ability to excrete drugs from the body due to decreases in kidney size, renal blood flow, and glomerular filtration rate. These changes result in medications acting for a longer period of time in the body (i.e., increased half-life), which can result in drug toxicity if dosages are not adjusted accordingly.

Pharmacodynamics

Pharmacodynamics refers to the study of how a drug exerts its therapeutic effects on the body at the cellular or organ level. It refers to the relationship between the concentrations of the drug in the body to the individual's response to the drug. Pharmacodynamics is influenced primarily by the age-related pharmacokinetic alterations to the body, but also by a decrease of neurotransmitters and receptors. When treating an older adult, a therapist must consider that the same dosage amount and time schedule will likely produce different effects based on variables such as age and body composition.

Polypharmacy

Polypharmacy can be defined as taking multiple medications. There are two primary forms of polypharmacy: rational and irrational. Rational polypharmacy is when an individual takes multiple medications to treat multiple medical issues, or to treat a single medical issue where each drug works together to control symptoms. Irrational polypharmacy occurs when excessive, duplicate or contraindicated medications are prescribed to treat a medical condition.

Older adults are at an increased risk of experiencing medication-related problems (MRP). Two of the most common MRPs are discussed here in more detail.

Non-adherence is an issue of not being compliant with a prescribed drug regimen. In older adults, this is more common for a number of reasons. First, many older adults cannot afford their medication, therefore they may need to make decisions regarding which medications they take and in what amount. Second, older adults may become confused or forgetful about their routine, and as a result lose track of when or if they have taken their medication. Third, if health literacy and education are minimal, the older adult may not understand the influence of failing to comply with the medication regimen.

An adverse drug reaction (ADR) is a serious condition that results from an undesirable response associated with the use of a drug. ADRs can range from minor to life-threatening. Common adverse reactions include nausea and vomiting, diarrhea, constipation, nervousness, drowsiness, confusion, delirium, depression, tachycardia, orthostatic hypotension, falls, weakness, and dyskinesia. Three drugs in particular are responsible for one-third of all emergency department visits for older adults: digoxin, warfarin, and insulin. Therapists must be alert to identify signs and symptoms commonly associated with ADRs.

End-of-Life Care Terminology

Advance directives: Documents that are completed by a patient prior to the onset of an illness that dictate how the patient wants their end-of-life care to be carried out. Advance directives are important since illness may take away a patient's ability to communicate their wishes concerning their own health care as they get older. A durable power of attorney and a living will are two types of advance directives.

Do not resuscitate: A medical order written by a doctor that documents a patient's wishes to not be resuscitated with cardiopulmonary resuscitation (CPR) if they stop breathing or their heart stops beating. This order only applies to CPR; it does not apply to the administration of medication or other health care treatments.

Durable power of attorney: A legal document in which a patient authorizes another person to make their health care decisions when the patient can no longer make their own decisions.

Hospice: A form of palliative care for terminally ill patients who have a limited life expectancy that focuses on the management of their pain and other symptoms as well as the acceptance of their own death. The goal of hospice care is to allow the patient to remain in their home as they near death, though there are inpatient facilities that provide these services as well.

Living will: A legal document in which a patient dictates their preferences for health care treatment, which becomes especially important if the patient becomes terminally ill and can no longer express their wishes.

Palliative care: An approach to a patient's care (typically patients with serious illnesses) that aims to relieve their pain and suffering, as well as address any psychological, social, and spiritual problems, with the goal of improving the patient's quality of life.

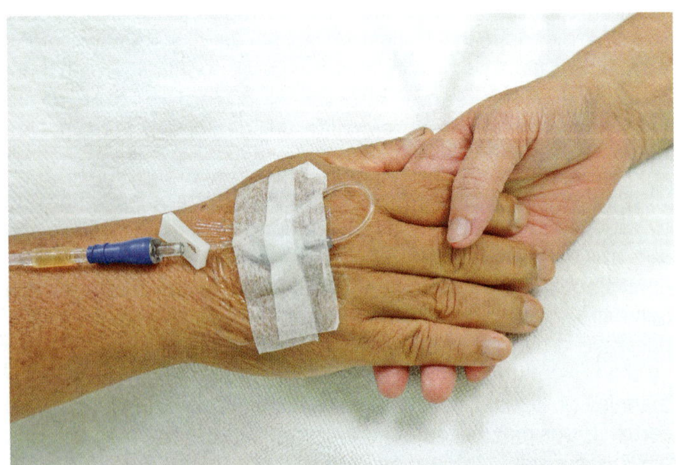

Fig. 7-11: A therapist holding the hand of an older adult.

Bariatrics[44-46]

Obesity refers to the state of excessive adipose tissue accumulation in the body contributing to a variety of chronic conditions that negatively impact multiple body systems and overall health. Obesity is most commonly the result of a prolonged imbalance between an individual's energy intake through diet and energy expenditure through activity and metabolic functions. The prevalence of obesity has reached pandemic proportions and has in recent years become viewed as a chronic progressive disease. Obesity is a modifiable morbidity and mortality risk factor second only to smoking.

Risk Factors for Developing Obesity[44-46]

• Sedentary lifestyle	• Medications that increase appetite or food cravings
• High glycemic diet	• Genetic or familial predisposition
• Environmental and lifestyle factors: smoking cessation, stress, history of abuse	• Underlying illness (e.g., hypothyroidism, polycystic ovary syndrome, Cushing's syndrome, Prader-Willi syndrome)

Anatomic and Physiologic Changes Commonly Associated with Obesity[45]

Cardiac	Cardiomyopathy (e.g., heart failure), abnormal ventricular remodeling (e.g., hypertrophy), atrial fibrillation, dysrhythmias
Pulmonary	Asthma, obstructive sleep apnea, hypoventilation syndrome
Kidneys	Decreased renal perfusion
Genitourinary	Urinary incontinence, infertility
Integumentary	Infection, hyperkeratosis, acanthosis nigricans
Vascular	Increased total blood volume, altered stroke volume and cardiac output, hypertension, venous insufficiency, varicosities
Musculoskeletal	Osteoarthritis, altered mobility patterns
Adipose tissue	Increased production of adipokines (e.g., leptin, interleukin-6, angiotensinogen)
Liver	Non-alcoholic fatty liver disease, non-alcoholic steatohepatitis
Pancreas	Insulin resistance, type 2 diabetes mellitus

CONSIDER THIS
CHILDHOOD OBESITY

The behaviors and systemic changes associated with childhood obesity can set children and adolescents on an unfortunate path toward lifelong health problems. The rise of childhood obesity has had a significant impact on the development of co-morbidities and risk factors previously associated only with adults (e.g., hypertension, type 2 diabetes mellitus, sleep disorders, metabolic syndrome). Adding to the physical health concerns of the condition, children and adolescents that are obese have also been shown to be at increased risk for a number of social and emotional issues including bullying, low self-esteem, depression, and behavioral problems.[47,48]

Because of the rapid developmental changes and variations in body type associated with this younger population, health care providers and caregivers must be cautious not to assume that all children who appear to be carrying extra weight are truly overweight or obese. At various points in normal development children and adolescents are expected to carry differing proportions of body fat. For parents, a conversation with their child's pediatrician is usually the best way to determine if the appearance of extra weight is truly a long term health concern. In general, a child is considered overweight if their age-appropriate BMI is between the 85th and 94th percentiles. Childhood obesity is characterized by an age-appropriate BMI greater than or equal to the 95th percentile.[49,50]

Behavioral risk factors for developing childhood obesity are similar to those in adult populations. Increased dietary intake, decreased activity levels, and psychological factors such as stress and boredom are most frequently attributed to childhood obesity. Some children may be more susceptible to weight gain due to genetic factors, however, genetic predisposition is often erroneously blamed for childhood obesity. Prader-Willi syndrome is an example of a condition where children are more likely to become obese. However, given the prevalence of childhood obesity, the greater influence of diet, activity, behavioral habits, and environmental factors must be both clearly acknowledged and addressed.[49,50]

CONSIDER THIS

OBESITY, LIPEDEMA OR BOTH?[33,46]

Lipedema is a disease with undefined etiology that affects the physical size and distribution of adipose cells in the body. The condition is most simply described as a bilateral, symmetrical, soft swelling most frequently appearing in the lower extremities of women. Many times a hereditary trend can be identified. Initial symptoms tend to present at times of significant hormonal change (e.g., menarche, menopause or during pregnancy). Women affected earlier in life often comment that their "big legs" have always seemed disproportionate to their body.

Patients with lipedema are often frustrated by the failure of weight loss efforts to alter the general shape and proportion of their affected lower extremities. This frustration can be compounded by the failure of health care professionals to recognize lipedema and instead continue to advise weight loss to patients who, in the absence of lipedema, would likely be of normal weight. In obese populations, weight loss is a reasonable expectation that does positively impact lipedema symptoms. However, patients should be educated regarding realistic outcome expectations so as not to assume that weight loss will "fix" their overall morphological proportions.

Signs and symptoms of lipedema include exquisite tenderness to palpation in the affected extremities, column-like or "riding breeches" fat distribution in the lower extremities, and increased edema as the day progresses which subsides overnight. Ongoing healthy weight management and complete decongestive therapy interventions are most often recommended to patients with lipedema as symptom management options.

Diagnostic Tools[2,35]

Body Mass Index (BMI) estimates an individual's body fat percentage and weight related health risks based on a calculation using height and weight measures. An adult would be considered underweight with a BMI less than 18.5, of desirable weight between 18.5 and 24.9, and obese with a BMI greater than 30. There are some limitations in correlating BMI with potential health risks, for example, an individual who is very muscular may have a BMI over 30 despite being extremely fit and healthy. Because of this, therapists cannot rely solely on BMI when characterizing a patient's weight related health risks. Other important factors in determining these risks are the patient's morphological distribution of body fat, waist circumference, and hip-to-waist ratio. These additional factors are primarily utilized as indicators of visceral fat distribution.

A peripheral fat distribution, also referred to as pear shape or gluteofemoral obesity, is more common in women and typically associated with a lower relative incidence of obesity related risk factors. A central fat distribution, also referred to as apple shape or abdominal obesity, is much more highly correlated with significant risk factors such as cardiovascular disease and type 2 diabetes mellitus. This is in part attributed to the presence of a much higher percentage of metabolically active visceral fat.

Research suggests that waist circumference measures may be better predictors of diabetes and cardiovascular risks than BMI alone, even though waist circumference measures are correlated with BMI. Waist measurements greater than 40 inches for adult males and greater than 36 inches for adult females are considered to be indicative of central obesity. Waist to hip ratio has also been found to show positive correlation to obesity related risks of death and disease; a ratio of greater than 1.0 in males and greater than 0.85 in females is suggestive of central obesity.

Bariatric Interventions[45,46]

Medical Management: Due to the multi-system health risks associated with obesity, physician involvement is imperative for support on many levels. With physician monitoring, patients are more likely to have appropriate medical management of co-morbidities as well as access to education or program referrals which may assist in weight loss goals. For patients who do not elect to attempt weight loss, the physician role typically becomes more focused on the medical management of co-morbidities. Most bariatric surgical teams include a physician specialist, often an internist, responsible for the medical assessment and monitoring of patients throughout the weight loss process.

Behavioral Therapy: Typically there is some degree of psychological influence associated with the behaviors that lead to obesity. Identifying and addressing these influences can significantly improve long-term outcomes that could otherwise be limited by underlying issues of motivation and compliance. Behavioral therapy may be provided in individualized or support group formats with topics including stimulus control, goal setting and problem solving strategies, social support, and/or strategies to improve self-monitoring of dietary intake and physical activity. Patients hoping to undergo bariatric surgery are typically required to participate in some form of behavioral counseling prior to surgery.

Increased Activity: Increased activity levels are essential for long term weight loss and weight management. For obese individuals, increased activity in the first six months of weight loss efforts has not been shown to significantly impact weight reduction. Patient education and support should be offered so as to prevent frustration and diminished motivation in attempts to make long-term modifications in activity level. Patients should be advised to begin increasing activity levels with gentle modes of exercise, such

CONSIDER THIS

EATING DISORDERS - THE OTHER END OF THE WEIGHT SPECTRUM[44]

Weight related health risks are not exclusive to overweight and obese populations. The Centers for Disease Control and Prevention consider individuals with a BMI of less than 18.5 to be underweight. While some patients may be naturally more slender, physical therapists should be cognizant of the signs, symptoms, and health concerns associated with eating disorders. Due to the significant roles of both physical and psychological factors in low-weight eating disorders, treatment in a partial-hospitalization or inpatient program is often recommended.

Bulimia nervosa refers to a binge-purge cycle that can cause chemical and enzyme imbalances that can lead to multiple organ dysfunction. Major health concerns include heart failure due to electrolyte imbalance, gastric rupture during purging, esophageal inflammation and tooth decay due to frequent vomiting, dehydration, peptic ulcers, pancreatitis, and bowel irregularity.

Anorexia nervosa refers to a self-imposed starvation that forces the body to either slow or shut down normal systemic processes. Major health concerns include heart failure due to slowed heart rate and decreased blood pressure, kidney failure due to dehydration, osteoporosis, and muscle atrophy.

as walking or swimming, performed at a tolerable pace. A general target of thirty minutes of increased activity daily is recommended and may be spread out into smaller intervals over the course of a day. Caution should be taken to prevent injury as intensity level and exercise duration increase. Research suggests that increased activity levels can positively influence the body's insulin sensitivity and fasting blood glucose to a measurable degree even in the absence of weight loss.

Dietary Modifications: In obese populations, a 500-1000 kcal/day reduction in dietary intake is usually sufficient to produce a 1-2 pounds per week weight loss. This rate can typically be maintained for six months before slowing or plateauing. Patients often have the misconception that reducing fat intake alone will produce the desired weight loss result. While this is a component of dietary modification, reduction of carbohydrate intake and overall calories are equally important. It is recommended that patients who are obese and wish to lose weight consult both a physician and dietician to ensure a medically safe and nutritionally sound approach to weight loss.

Pharmacology: The Food and Drug Administration (FDA) has approved a number of pharmacological weight loss agents for short-term adjunct use with diet, activity, and behavioral modifications. Classes of approved medications include appetite suppressants and lipase inhibitors. Appetite suppressants function to either reduce feelings of hunger or increase feelings of fullness. Lipase inhibitors decrease the body's ability to absorb dietary fats, thereby decreasing overall caloric intake. Though not specifically approved for weight loss by the FDA, some antidepressant, seizure, and diabetes medications are prescribed for short-term use to assist weight loss goals.

Community Resources: A variety of community-based weight loss programs are in existence, each with their own structured approach. Program commonalities include advocating increased activity and decreased caloric intake. Patients often cite geographical, philosophical or financial concerns as barriers to participating in a formal program. Well known community-based programs include Weight Watchers, Jenny Craig, Take Off Pounds Sensibly (TOPS), and Food Addicts Anonymous.

Bariatric Surgery: Bariatric surgery is a consideration for some patients who are morbidly obese and is often considered the intervention of last resort. Pre-operatively, patients must meet a number of requirements in order to be considered a surgical candidate. This typically includes a BMI greater than 40, or greater than 35 with additional co-morbidities, and evidence that other weight loss interventions have been largely unsuccessful. Most bariatric programs require a pre-operative commitment to support group attendance or individual counseling as well as some degree of substantive weight loss by more traditional methods. Pre- and post-operatively, a multidisciplinary team is responsible for providing support and assessing a number of pre-operative factors (e.g., co-morbidities, behavioral history, extent of adiposity). This bariatric specialty team commonly includes an internist, surgeon, psychologist, dietician, and program coordinator.

Bariatric surgical procedures may be classified as restrictive, malabsorptive or a combination of the two. The most common bariatric procedure is the invasive Roux-en-Y gastric bypass which facilitates weight loss through a combination of restriction and malabsorption. Due to the nature of the procedure, the risk of both post-operative and long-term complications is high. In contrast, the most common restrictive procedure is also the least invasive. Laparoscopic gastric banding, often referred to as a "lap-band" procedure, has a low risk of complications and can be adjusted or removed as needed.

Nutrition[10,19,32]

Macronutrients

Macronutrients are the nutrients that have caloric value and provide the body with energy. These nutrients make up a greater proportion of our diet since they are needed in large amounts. The three macronutrients are carbohydrates, fats, and proteins.

Carbohydrates: Carbohydrates are the preferred fuel source for high-intensity exercise. Without adequate carbohydrate intake, the body will start to consume protein (i.e., muscle) as its fuel source. Carbohydrates are also the main source of fuel for the central nervous system. Carbohydrates can be broken down into simple and complex carbohydrates. Simple carbohydrates are made up of smaller molecules that increase blood glucose levels rapidly. Complex carbohydrates are made up of larger molecules that need to be broken down before they can be used, therefore they increase blood glucose levels much more slowly over a longer period of time. The glycemic index is a measure of how quickly a specific food will raise blood glucose levels.

Fats: Fats act as an energy reserve in the body and are the primary fuel source for low-intensity exercise. Fats also play a role in insulating the body, protecting organs, and assisting in the transport of fat-soluble vitamins. Fats are made up of fatty acids, which can be classified as saturated, monounsaturated or polyunsaturated. Saturated fats are commonly found in animal fats and tend to increase levels of bad cholesterol (i.e., low-density lipoprotein) within the body, while unsaturated fats are more commonly found in plant fats and tend to increase levels of good cholesterol (i.e., high-density lipoprotein).

Proteins: Proteins make up the structure of the body and are responsible for the growth and maintenance of the body's tissues. Proteins are abundant in collagen fibers which are present in structures such as skin, ligaments, and skeletal muscle. Adults should consume 0.8 grams of protein per kilogram of body weight. If the body is not receiving adequate carbohydrate or fat intake, protein may also be used as a fuel source. Proteins are made up of smaller subunits known as amino acids. There are 20 amino acids, 9 of which cannot be produced by the body and must be consumed in the diet (i.e., essential amino acids).

Vitamins

Vitamins are essential non-caloric nutrients that are required in small amounts for certain metabolic functions and cannot be manufactured by the body. Vitamins are most often classified as fat-soluble or water-soluble.

Fat-Soluble Vitamins

Fat-soluble vitamins include vitamins A, D, E, and K. After being absorbed by the intestinal tract, the vitamins are stored in the liver and fatty tissues. Fat-soluble vitamins require protein carriers to move through body fluids and excesses are stored in the body. Since they are not water-soluble, it is possible that the vitamins may reach toxic levels.

Vitamin A

Vitamin A is essential to the eyes, epithelial tissue, normal growth and development, and reproduction.

- Common food sources containing vitamin A include green, orange, and yellow vegetables, liver, butter, egg yolks, and fortified margarine.
- Symptoms of deficiency include night blindness, rough and dry skin, and growth failure.
- Symptoms of toxicity include appetite loss, hair loss, and enlarged liver and spleen.

Vitamin D

Vitamin D increases the blood flow levels of minerals, notably calcium and phosphorus.

- Common food sources containing vitamin D include fortified milk, fish oils, and fortified margarine.
- Symptoms of deficiency include faulty bone growth, rickets, and osteomalacia.
- Symptoms of toxicity include calcification of soft tissues and hypercalcemia.

Vitamin E

Vitamin E functions as an antioxidant in cell membranes and is especially important for the integrity of cells that are constantly exposed to high levels of oxygen such as the lungs and red blood cells.

- Common food sources containing vitamin E include vegetable oils, wheat germ, nuts, and fish.
- Symptoms of deficiency include breakdown of red blood cells, however, this is relatively rare in adults.
- Symptoms of toxicity include decreased thyroid hormone levels and increased triglycerides.

Vitamin K

Vitamin K is necessary for the synthesis of at least two of the proteins involved in blood clotting.

- Common food sources containing vitamin K include dark green leafy vegetables, cheese, egg yolks, and liver.
- Symptoms of deficiency include hemorrhage and defective blood clotting.
- Toxicity has not been reported.

Water-Soluble Vitamins

Water-soluble vitamins are not stored in the body in any significant amount and therefore need to be included in the diet on a daily basis. Toxicity is less common than with fat-soluble vitamins.

Vitamin B2 (Riboflavin)

Vitamin B2 facilitates selected enzymes involved in carbohydrate, protein, and fat metabolism.

- Common food sources containing vitamin B2 include milk, green leafy vegetables, eggs, and peanuts.
- Symptoms of deficiency include inflammation of the tongue, sensitive eyes, and scaling of the skin.
- Toxicity has not been reported.

Vitamin B3 (Niacin)

Vitamin B3 facilitates several enzymes that regulate energy metabolism.

- Common food sources containing vitamin B3 include meats, whole grains, and white flour.
- Symptoms of deficiency include pellagra and gastrointestinal disturbances.
- Symptoms of toxicity include abnormal glucose metabolism, nausea, vomiting, and gastric ulceration.

Vitamin B6 (Pyridoxine)

Vitamin B6 is essential in the metabolism of proteins, amino acids, carbohydrates, and fat.

- Common food sources containing vitamin B6 include liver, red meats, whole grains, and potatoes.
- Symptoms of deficiency include peripheral neuropathy, convulsions, and depression.
- Symptoms of toxicity include sensory damage, numbness of the extremities, and ataxia.

Vitamin B12 (Cobalamin)

Vitamin B12 is essential for the functioning of all cells and aids in hemoglobin synthesis.

- Common food sources containing vitamin B12 include meats, whole eggs, and egg yolks.
- Symptoms of deficiency include pernicious anemia and various psychological disorders.
- Toxicity has not been reported.

Vitamin C

Vitamin C assists the body to combat infections and facilitates wound healing. The vitamin is necessary for the development and maintenance of bones, cartilage, connective tissue, and blood vessels.

- Common food sources containing vitamin C include citrus fruits, tomatoes, and cantaloupe.
- Symptoms of deficiency include anemia, swollen gums, loose teeth, and scurvy.
- Symptoms of toxicity include urinary stones, diarrhea, and hypoglycemia.

Biotin

Biotin is necessary for the action of many enzyme systems.

- Common food sources containing biotin include liver, meats, and milk.
- Symptoms of deficiency include anemia, depression, and muscle pain.
- Toxicity has not been reported.

SPOTLIGHT ON SAFETY
ADVERSE EFFECTS OF COMPLIMENTARY AND ALTERNATIVE MEDICATIONS (CAM)[19]

Patients have ready access to countless vitamin, mineral, herbal, and other natural supplements. Often these supplements are sought out for preventative means, to support or to replace more traditional pharmacological interventions. While the use of many of these substances cause mild to no side effects, some supplements can reach toxic levels or impact the actions of other medications causing significant adverse effects. More specifically, some natural supplements interfere with the metabolism, absorption, and excretion of prescription medications. This is typically due to interference with liver function, which can prevent drugs from reaching therapeutic levels or cause them to metabolize either too quickly or too slowly. Given the prevalence and underreporting of CAM use it is important for physical therapists to address this topic when taking a patient's history and be aware of potential interactions.

Garlic: reported to exacerbate bleeding issues for patients who are taking prescription anticoagulants

Ginkgo biloba: reported to increase the risk of hemorrhage in patients using other anticoagulants

Ginseng: reported to reduce the effects of anticoagulants and exaggerate the effects of medications such as insulin and oral antidiabetic medications

Kava: reported to cause liver toxicity

St. John's wort: reported to accelerate metabolism of some medications (e.g., warfarin, cyclosporine) and prevent numerous others from reaching therapeutic levels

Choline

Choline is a component of compounds necessary for nerve function and lipid metabolism.

- Choline is synthesized from methionine which is an amino acid.
- Symptoms of deficiency only occur when intake of methylamine is low.
- Toxicity has not been reported.

Folacin (Folic acid)

Folacin is involved in the formation of red blood cells and in the functioning of the gastrointestinal tract.

- Common food sources containing folacin include yeast, dark green leafy vegetables, and whole grains.
- Symptoms of deficiency include impaired cell division and alteration of protein synthesis.
- Toxicity has not been reported.

Pantothenic Acid

Pantothenic acid is an integral component of complex enzymes involved in the metabolism of fatty acids.

- Common food sources containing pantothenic acid include liver, eggs, and whole grains.
- Symptoms of deficiency include headache, fatigue, and poor muscle coordination.
- Symptoms of toxicity include diarrhea.

Minerals

Minerals are organic elements that fulfill essential roles in the metabolic process.

Major Minerals

Calcium (Ca)

Calcium facilitates muscle contraction and relaxation, builds strong bones and teeth, and aids in coagulation.

- Common food sources containing calcium include milk, green leafy vegetables, and soy products.
- Calcium deficiency may lead to poor bone growth, rickets, osteomalacia, and osteoporosis.
- Symptoms of toxicity include kidney stones.

Chloride (Cl)

Chloride facilitates the maintenance of fluid and acid-base balance.

- Common food sources containing chloride include table salt, fish, and vegetables.
- Chloride deficiency may lead to a disturbance of acid-base balance.
- Toxicity has not been reported.

Magnesium (Mg)

Magnesium builds strong bones and teeth, activates enzymes, and helps regulate heartbeat.

- Common food sources containing magnesium include raw dark vegetables, nuts, soybeans, milk, and cheese.
- Symptoms of deficiency include confusion, apathy, muscle weakness, and tremors.
- Symptoms of toxicity include increased calcium excretion.

Phosphorus (P)

Phosphorus strengthens bones, assists in the oxidation of fats and carbohydrates, and aids in maintaining acid-base balance.

- Common food sources containing phosphorus include milk, milk products, meats, whole grains, and soft drinks.
- Symptoms of deficiency include weakness, stiff joints, and fragile bones.
- Symptoms of toxicity include muscle spasms.

Potassium (K)

Potassium maintains fluid and acid-base balance.

- Common food sources containing potassium include apricots, bananas, oranges, grapefruit, and milk.
- Symptoms of deficiency include impaired growth and diminished heart rate.
- Symptoms of toxicity include hyperkalemia and cardiac disturbances.

Sodium (Na)

Sodium facilitates the maintenance of acid-base balance, transmits nerve impulses, and helps control muscle contractions.

- Common food sources containing sodium include salt and milk.
- Deficiency and toxicity have not been reported.

Sulfur (S)

Sulfur facilitates enzyme activity and energy metabolism.

- Common food sources containing sulfur include meat, eggs, milk, and cheese.
- Deficiency is extremely rare.
- Toxicity has not been reported.

Trace Minerals

Chromium (Cr)

Chromium controls glucose metabolism.

- Common food sources containing chromium include whole grains, meats, and cheese.
- Symptoms of deficiency include weight loss and central nervous system abnormalities.
- Symptoms of toxicity include liver damage.

Cobalt (Co)

Cobalt is an essential component of vitamin B12 and functions to activate enzymes.

- Common food sources containing cobalt include figs, cabbage, and spinach.
- Symptoms of deficiency include pernicious anemia.
- Symptoms of toxicity include polycythemia and increased blood volume.

Copper (Cu)

Copper facilitates hemoglobin synthesis and lipid metabolism.

- Common food sources containing copper include shellfish, liver, meat, and whole grains.
- Symptoms of deficiency include anemia, central nervous system abnormalities, and abnormal electrocardiograms.
- Symptoms of toxicity include Wilson's disease.

Fluorine (F)

Fluorine aids in the formation of bones and teeth and prevents osteoporosis.

- Common food sources containing fluorine include fish and water.
- Symptoms of deficiency include increased susceptibility of dental cavities.
- Symptoms of toxicity include fluorosis.

Iodine (I)

Iodine assists with the regulation of cell metabolism and basal metabolic rate.

- Common food sources containing iodine include iodized salt and seafood.
- Symptoms of deficiency may include goiters.
- Toxicity has not been reported.

Iron (Fe)

Iron assists in oxygen transport and cell oxidation.

- Common food sources containing iron include red meats and liver.
- Symptoms of deficiency include anemia.
- Symptoms of toxicity include hemochromatosis.

Manganese (Mn)

Manganese facilitates proper bone structure and functions as an enzyme component in general metabolism.

- Common food sources containing manganese include cereals and whole grains.
- There are no known symptoms of deficiency.
- Toxicity has not been reported.

Selenium (Se)

Selenium is a synergistic antioxidant with vitamin E.

- Common food sources containing selenium include meat, eggs, milk, seafood, and garlic.
- Symptoms of deficiency include Keshan's disease.
- Symptoms of toxicity include physical defects of fingernails and toenails, nausea, and abdominal pain.

Molybdenum (Mo)

Molybdenum is a component of three enzymes in particular, that are necessary for normal cell functioning.

- Common food sources containing molybdenum include meats, whole grains, and dark green vegetables.
- Symptoms of deficiency include vomiting and tachypnea.
- Toxicity has not been reported.

Zinc (Zn)

Zinc aids in immune function and cell division.

- Common food sources containing zinc include seafood, liver, milk, cheese, and whole grains.
- Symptoms of deficiency include depressed immune functions and impaired skeletal growth.
- Symptoms of toxicity include anemia, nausea, and vomiting.

Healthy Eating

MyPlate is a program created by the United States Department of Agriculture (USDA) that is designed to teach people how to create and maintain a healthy diet and healthy eating habits. General principles of MyPlate include making healthy choices from all of the food groups, eating the correct number of calories based on age, gender, size, and activity level, and limiting saturated fats, sodium, and added sugars. The MyPlate diet is broken down into six different food groups: fruits, vegetables, grains, protein foods, dairy, and oils.

Fruits: Any fruit or 100% fruit juice is considered to be in the "fruit" category. Whole fruits are a more ideal source of fruit when compared to fruit juices. Fruit intake should be 1.5-2 cups per day for an adult. A cup is equal to one cup of fruit or fruit juice or half a cup of dried fruit.

Vegetables: Any vegetable or 100% vegetable juice is considered to be in the "vegetable" category. Vegetables are categorized into five subgroups: dark green vegetables, starchy vegetables, red and orange vegetables, beans and peas, and other vegetables. A healthy diet should consist of a variety of these different vegetable subgroups. Vegetable intake should be 2.5-3 cups per day for an adult. A cup is equal to one cup of vegetables or vegetable juice or two cups of raw leafy green vegetables.

Grains: Any food made from wheat, barley, oats, cornmeal, rice or another cereal grain is considered to be in the "grain" category. Grains are divided into two subgroups: whole grains and refined grains. Whole grains contain the entire grain kernel; examples include whole wheat flour and oatmeal. Refined grains have been processed and only contain part of the grain kernel; examples include white flour and white rice. Grain intake should be 5-8 ounce equivalents per day for an adult. An ounce equivalent is equal to a slice of bread, one cup of cereal or half a cup of cooked pasta or rice. It is recommended that half of the grain intake come from whole grains.

Protein foods: Any food made from meat, poultry, seafood, eggs, soy products, beans and peas (also in the vegetable category), nuts, and seeds is considered to be in the "protein food" category. Protein intake should be 5-6.5 ounce equivalents per day for an adult. An ounce equivalent is equal to one ounce of meat, poultry or fish, an egg, half an ounce of nuts or seeds or a quarter cup of cooked beans. Protein intake should be varied among the different groups. Meat and poultry choices should be lean or low-fat. To limit sodium intake, nuts and seeds should be unsalted and processed meats should be limited.

Dairy: Fluid milk products and foods made from milk are considered to be in the "dairy" category. Dairy intake should be 3 cups per day for an adult. A cup is equal to one cup of milk or yogurt, 1.5 ounces of natural cheese or 2 ounces of processed cheese. It is recommended that most dairy choices be fat-free or low-fat.

Oils: Oils are fats that are liquid at room temperature. Oils are not a separate food group, though they do provide essential nutrients and are therefore important to consume. Oil intake should be 5-7 teaspoons per day for an adult. Commonly eaten oils include canola oil, olive oil, and safflower oil. Some foods are naturally high in oils, like fish, nuts, olives, and avocados. It is recommended that oils consumed in the diet should be high in unsaturated fats and low in saturated fats.

Nutrition Facts

Serving Size 1/2 cup (115g)
Servings Per Container About 4

Amount Per Serving	
Calories 250	**Calories from Fat** 130
	% Daily Value*
Total Fat 14g	**22%**
Saturated Fat 9g	**45%**
Cholesterol 55mg	**18%**
Sodium 75mg	**3%**
Total Carbohydrate 26g	**9%**
Dietary Fiber 0g	**0%**
Sugars 26g	
Protein 4g	
Vitamin A 10%	Vitamin C 0%
Calcium 10%	Iron 0%

* Percent Daily Values are based on a 2,000 calorie diet.

Fig. 7-12: A traditional nutritional label.

Nutrition Label

Serving size: The serving size is located at the top of the nutrition label (Fig. 7-12) and should be where an individual starts when examining the nutritional content of food. The serving size is standardized into familiar units (e.g., cups, pieces) to allow for easy comparison with other similar food items. The nutritional values given on the label are in reference to a single serving. The serving size is the number of servings within the entire package. These two numbers can be used together to determine the nutritional content of the entire package of food or just the food that is consumed.

Calories: Below the serving size section is the caloric information. The number of calories given is the total number of calories per serving. To the right of the total calorie count is the number of calories that are derived from fat. These two numbers can be used to determine the percentage of calories that are coming from fat.

Macronutrients: The macronutrient section contains information on the metric amounts (i.e., grams) for total fat, saturated fat, cholesterol, sodium, total carbohydrate, dietary fiber, sugar, and protein.

Micronutrients: Below the macronutrient section is a small box with four micronutrients: vitamin A, vitamin C, calcium, and iron. While the micronutrients do not contain a metric amount, they do each have a Percent Daily Value.

Percent Daily Value: To the right of the various nutrients and their metric amount is the Percent Daily Value. The Percent Daily Value is the percentage of a person's daily intake that one serving will represent, based on the recommendations for that specific nutrient. The values are based on a 2,000-calorie diet. The Percent Daily Value helps give added meaning to the metric numbers. For example, a person may not know if 75 milligrams of sodium is high or low, but they will know that 3% of daily intake represents a small proportion and therefore the food has low sodium content. A Percent Daily Value of 5% or less is considered low and 20% or more is considered high. For nutrients that should be limited (e.g., saturated fat, sodium), individuals should not surpass 100% with their daily intake. For nutrients that should be encouraged (e.g., fiber), individuals should reach or surpass 100% intake.

Pharmacology Basics[19,32]

Methods of Drug Administration

There are two basic methods for the administration of drugs:

- **Enteral Administration** – involves use of the gastrointestinal tract for administration of a drug.
- **Parenteral administration** – involves any form of drug administration that does not involve the gastrointestinal tract.

Enteral administration

Oral: Oral administration involves swallowing a medication so it passes through the esophagus and stomach and is eventually absorbed into the body by the intestines. It is the most common and easiest method for administering a drug. Absorption by the gastrointestinal tract allows for a gradual increase in drug levels within the body. A disadvantage to oral administration is that the compound must be lipid-soluble so that the intestinal tract can absorb it. This can be achieved by placing a nonlipid-soluble medication inside a lipid-soluble capsule for ingestion. Other disadvantages include gastric irritation from the drug, metabolism and degradation of a drug by the liver before reaching its target tissue, and factors that affect intestinal absorption and thus make bioavailability unpredictable.

Sublingual: Sublingual administration involves passage of a drug through the sublingual mucosa (under the tongue) or buccal mucosa (between the cheek and gums). After being absorbed, the drug travels from the venous circulation directly to the heart, where it enters the systemic circulation. Sublingual administration allows for faster introduction of a drug in cases of acute pain (e.g., angina) and allows drugs to bypass the liver so they are not overly metabolized before reaching their target tissue.

Rectal: Rectal administration involves the insertion of a suppository into the rectum and absorption of the drug within the rectal cavity. Rectal administration is advantageous for patients who cannot take drugs orally (e.g., unconscious, vomiting). As with sublingual medications, these drugs also bypass the liver. However, drugs are not absorbed as well through the rectal cavity when compared to sublingual and oral administrations.

Parenteral administration

Inhalation: Drugs can be inhaled for administration if they are in a gaseous or aerosol form. Inhalation is advantageous since the lungs have a large surface area for absorption and therefore the drug can enter the systemic circulation rapidly. Additionally, this method of administration is often used when treating pulmonary pathologies. A potential disadvantage of inhalation is that the respiratory tract can become irritated.

Topical: Topical administration involves application of a drug directly to the skin or mucous membranes. Because drugs are poorly absorbed through the skin into the systemic circulation, this method is reserved for treating localized skin, ear, eye or nose disorders. Mucous membranes have a larger capacity for drug absorption and thus drugs applied to mucous membranes (e.g., nasal mucosa) can be used to treat systemic conditions.

Transdermal: Transdermal administration involves application of a drug directly to the skin. Unlike topical administration, the intent is that the drug will absorb through the skin and enter the systemic circulation. Transdermal administration allows for a slow, controlled release of the drug into the circulation over a long period of time. This form of administration often occurs with the use of patches (e.g., fentanyl), though iontophoresis and phonophoresis also use the transdermal route. Drugs that cannot penetrate the skin or that are degraded by dermal enzymes cannot be administered with this method.

Injection: There are a variety of administration methods that involve injection of a medication. Injection can be used to administer a drug either locally or systemically. A disadvantage is that injection is invasive and therefore can cause infection. Additionally, it may be difficult for patients to self-administer drugs via injection. The various forms of injection include:

- **Intravenous:** Intravenous (IV) administration involves injection of a medication into a peripheral vein so it can enter the bloodstream. An advantage of IV administration is that the drug can enter the circulation and reach the target tissue rapidly, though this can become dangerous if an inaccurate dosage is given. IV administration is a more accurate method of administering a drug since it is considered 100% bioavailable.

CONSIDER THIS
FACTORS THAT AFFECT PHARMACOKINETICS

Age: As age increases, the incidence of adverse drug reactions tends to increase. There may be several reasons for this including a decrease in lean body mass, a decrease in serum proteins, a reduction in renal and liver function, and interactions with other drugs. Infants and young children also require alterations in dosing to avoid adverse reactions since their organs are not fully developed and are unable to metabolize drugs in the same manner.

Weight: Dosages are typically based on a 150-pound individual. Patients who fall far above or below this value may need their drug dosage altered to achieve the desired therapeutic effect.

Genetics: Because genes control the production of enzymes, genetic mutations may result in an abnormal response to the administration of a drug. Differences in drug effectiveness or the elimination of a drug may be seen among different ethnic groups.

Disease: Disease of the kidneys or liver can result in reduced ability to metabolize or eliminate a drug and may cause toxic effects. Viral infections may also affect a drug's half-life by exerting a negative effect on enzymatic activity.

Exercise: Exercise can affect many factors that have an influence on drug activity, including blood flow, pH, body temperature, gastrointestinal function, metabolism, and excretion. The effects of exercise on drug action can vary based on the type and intensity of exercise, the type of drug, the method of administration, and the dosing schedule. Because the interactions are so complex, there is not a clear consensus on the exact effects that exercise exerts on drug action.

Medications: The effectiveness of a drug may be altered when it is taken in combination with other drugs. These drug-drug interactions can be antagonistic or synergistic. For example, taking aspirin may reduce the effectiveness of a diuretic (i.e., antagonistic), or taking a sedative while also drinking alcohol may result in excessive central nervous system depression (i.e., synergistic).

Food: The presence of food in the stomach can slow the rate of absorption of a drug. Drugs may be taken on an empty stomach to speed their absorption into the bloodstream, while other drugs may be taken in combination with food to avoid gastric irritation. Specific food-drug interactions are generally insignificant, though there are several examples of foods that affect the bioavailability of a drug. Foods or beverages that are acidic (e.g., soda) may affect the absorption of some drugs within the gastrointestinal tract. Grapefruit juice is a commonly identified drink that affects enzymatic activity within the gastrointestinal tract and thus changes the metabolism of certain drugs.

- **Intra-arterial:** Intra-arterial administration involves injection of a medication into an artery so that it can travel directly to the target tissue. This type of injection is difficult to perform, though may be necessary in instances where the drug is intended to act at a specific site without affecting other tissues (e.g., chemotherapy).
- **Subcutaneous:** Subcutaneous administration involves injection of a drug directly under the skin into the subcutaneous fat or connective tissue. This form of administration can be useful when a slow release of medication into the systemic circulation is required (e.g., insulin). Patients have the ability to self-administer these medications if they are trained. However, the rate of absorption of these drugs can be affected by a variety of factors. Some factors, such as immobility of the limb or the application of cold, may slow the absorption rate while other factors, such as massage or the application of heat, may speed absorption.
- **Intramuscular:** Intramuscular (IM) administration involves injection of a drug into skeletal muscle. IM injections are often used when treating localized muscular problems (e.g., botulinum toxin for spasticity). Absorption of a drug via IM injection is more rapid than subcutaneous injection, while still allowing for a steady release of the drug into the systemic circulation. A disadvantage of IM injections is that they tend to cause localized muscle soreness and pain at the site of injection.
- **Intrathecal:** Intrathecal administration involves injection of a drug into a sheath, such as the subarachnoid space of the spinal meninges. This form of administration is advantageous because it allows for the introduction of a drug into the central nervous system without having to pass through the blood-brain barrier.

Pharmacology Terminology

Bioavailability: Bioavailability refers to the percentage of a drug that makes it into the systemic circulation from the site of original administration. Bioavailability will vary depending on how much the drug becomes degraded before reaching the systemic circulation. A drug that is injected intravenously is 100% bioavailable.

Chemical name: The name for the drug's specific compound structure (e.g., N-acetyl-p-aminophenol).

Dose-response curve: The dose-response curve (Fig. 7-13) is a graphic representation of the relationship between the dosage of a drug and the body's response to that drug. As the dosage of a drug increases, more receptors for the drug become activated which increases the body's response to the drug. However, the body's response will plateau at a certain dosage. The dose-response curve can be used to compare the potency of two different drugs.

Generic name: The official name given to a drug that is derived from its chemical name (e.g., acetaminophen).

Half-life: The half-life of a drug refers to the rate of elimination of the drug. If a drug has a half-life of two hours and 4,000 units of the drug are administered initially, then only 2,000 units will remain after two hours, and only 1,000 units will remain after four hours.

Controlled substances are drugs that are considered to have the potential for abuse. The Comprehensive Drug Abuse Prevention and Control Act of 1970 placed these drugs into five classifications depending on their likelihood for abuse. These classifications are as follows:

Schedule I drugs have a high potential for abuse and high risk for addiction and are therefore used for research purposes, not medical treatment. Examples of schedule I drugs include heroin and LSD.

Schedule II drugs have a high potential for abuse and high risk of addiction, though they are still approved for medical uses. Automatic prescription refills are not allowed for these drugs. Examples of schedule II drugs include opioids, amphetamines, and some barbiturates.

Schedule III drugs have a lower potential for abuse than schedule II drugs, but have a moderate risk for physical dependence and a high risk for psychological dependence. Automatic prescription refills are allowed for these drugs, though there are limitations set on these refills. Examples of schedule III drugs include opioids that are combined with non-opioids (e.g., a narcotic mixed with acetaminophen) and anabolic steroids.

Schedule IV drugs have a lower potential for abuse than schedule III drugs and only a mild risk for physical or psychological dependence. There are still some limitations set on automatic refills for these drugs. Examples of schedule IV drugs include antianxiety drugs and certain barbiturates (e.g., phenobarbital).

Schedule V drugs have the lowest potential for abuse and addiction. In some states, these drugs may even be available without a prescription. Examples of schedule V drugs include cough and cold medicines that have low doses of opioids.

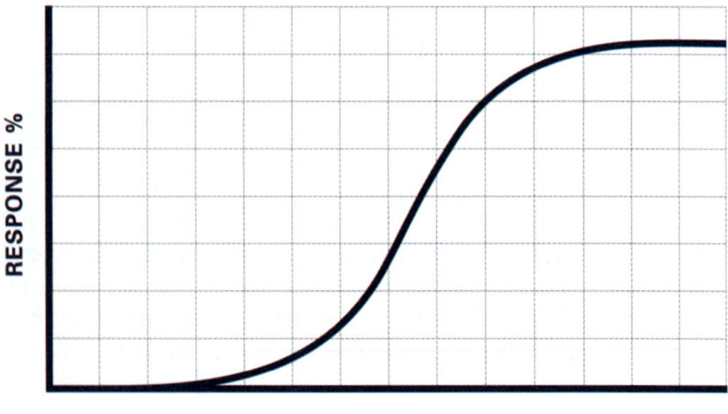

Fig. 7-13: A dose-response curve.

CONSIDER THIS

DRUG DEVELOPMENT

The Food and Drug Administration (FDA) is the government agency that is responsible for the development, approval, and regulation of drugs. Drugs are regulated by the FDA to ensure that they are both safe and effective for the patient. The development of a new drug involves a five-step process:

Preclinical testing involves testing of the drug at the cellular and organ levels as well as testing the drug on animals. Preclinical trials are used to determine if the drug is safe and to identify any adverse effects that the drug will have on the body. These trials are also used to identify the pharmacokinetics and pharmacodynamics of the drug.

Phase 1 is the first stage of human testing in which the safety of the drug is tested on a small number of patients. Researchers identify toxicity effects as well as the safe dosing range.

Phase 2 is the next stage of drug development in which the effectiveness of the drug is tested on a small number of patients. Researchers identify if the drug is effective and at what dosing level. Adverse effects of the drug are also studied.

Phase 3 is similar to the phase 2 trials, but involves a much larger sample size of patients. If phase 3 trials are successful, the drug company can file a new drug application and apply through the FDA to start marketing and prescribing the drug.

Phase 4 occurs once the drug has been approved and is being used by members of the public. The FDA begins to monitor the safety of the drug in real-life scenarios. This phase is also known as post-marketing surveillance.

Pharmacodynamics: The study of how a drug exerts its therapeutic effect on the body at the cellular or organ level.

Pharmacotherapeutics: The division of pharmacology that deals with the use of drugs for preventing, treating, and diagnosing diseases.

Pharmacokinetics: The study of how drugs are absorbed, distributed, metabolized, and eliminated by the body.

Therapeutic index: The therapeutic index (TI) is a measurement of the safety of a drug. It is calculated as a ratio and compares the effectiveness of a drug against its lethal effects. A drug with a low TI indicates that the drug is less safe, resulting in patients taking these drugs being frequently monitored for adverse reactions.

Toxicology: The division of pharmacology that studies the adverse effects of drugs.

Trade name: The brand name of a drug that is assigned by the pharmaceutical company (e.g., Tylenol); there can be several trade names for a single drug if there are multiple companies manufacturing the same drug.

Pharmacology Effects on Specific Systems

Musculoskeletal System

General anesthesia: Therapists may encounter patients who are post-surgery and dealing with the side effects of general anesthesia. These effects can last for several days in some patients. Confusion and muscle weakness are two of the more common side effects associated with anesthesia. Since anesthesia can result in retained pulmonary secretions, the therapist may need to initiate breathing exercises or postural drainage with the patient.

Local anesthesia: Patients that receive a local or spinal nerve block during surgery may have diminished sensation and motor function following surgery. Exercise should be performed cautiously since the patient may not fully feel pain. Additionally, bracing may be needed during ambulation if the patient is lacking motor control. Local anesthesia may also be administered in the form of transdermal patches to help control pain (e.g., lidocaine). Therapists should not apply heating modalities on or near the patch as it can accelerate the rate of absorption of the medication leading to toxic effects.

Opioid analgesic agents: These drugs provide significant pain relief that may allow a patient to tolerate more aggressive physical therapy interventions. Therapy sessions should be scheduled to coincide with peak effectiveness of the drug. Side effects that may affect therapy interventions include sedation and respiratory depression. The patient's respiratory response to physical activity may be decreased.

Nonsteroidal anti-inflammatory agents: These drugs can provide analgesia while avoiding the side effects that are associated with opioid analgesics (e.g., sedation). However, these drugs will not provide the same level of pain relief as compared to opioid analgesics. The side effects associated with nonsteroidal anti-inflammatory drugs, primarily gastrointestinal discomfort, are unlikely to have a negative effect on physical therapy sessions.

Antiarthritic agents: Side effects of these drugs will vary depending on the specific drug that is administered. Glucocorticoid drugs have catabolic effects and can lead to the breakdown of tendon, bone or skin. Therapists should be cautious with aggressive stretching and strengthening exercises to eliminate the risk for fractures or soft tissue injuries. Care must also be taken when applying orthotic devices to prevent skin breakdown. The use of some antirheumatic drugs can result in an increase in joint pain and swelling, which should be considered when choosing therapy interventions.

Neuromuscular and Nervous Systems

Antiepileptic agents: Cerebellar side effects (e.g., ataxia) are common with antiepileptic drugs and the loss of coordination may significantly affect therapeutic activities. Additionally, these drugs may cause specific skin conditions (e.g., dermatitis). Any modalities used in therapy that may exacerbate these conditions should be used cautiously.

Skeletal muscle relaxants: These drugs reduce muscle spasm and spasticity and therefore can improve a patient's ability to participate in and benefit from rehabilitation activities. However, these effects can be detrimental for patients who rely on spasticity to improve their function (e.g., using extensor tone to help with standing transfers). Physical therapy plays an important role in assisting these patients to adapt to a sudden decrease in spasticity by improving their strength and motor control. Sedation and muscle weakness are common side effects of these drugs and should be taken into consideration when scheduling therapy sessions.

Anti-Parkinson's agents: Therapy sessions should be scheduled to coincide with maximum effectiveness of anti-Parkinson's drugs (roughly an hour after administration for levodopa). Therapists should closely monitor blood pressure for these patients since the drugs may produce orthostatic hypotension and increase the risk for falls.

Cardiovascular and Pulmonary Systems

Antihypertensive agents: Patients taking these drugs to lower blood pressure are at increased risk for orthostatic hypotension. Therapists should be alert for hypotensive symptoms, especially when patients are changing position. Interventions that cause widespread vasodilation, such as whirlpool therapy, should be avoided in patients who are taking vasodilating drugs. Patients taking beta blockers may have a diminished heart rate response to exercise, therefore other means of assessing exercise intensity (e.g., rating of perceived exertion) should be used.

Antianginal agents: Drugs taken to treat symptoms of angina pectoris can have a variety of effects on the cardiovascular system. Some patients will have an increase in exercise tolerance since they will not be limited by episodes of angina. Other patients, especially those taking beta blockers or calcium channel blockers, will have a diminished heart rate response to exercise and therefore may not be able to tolerate higher workloads. As stated with antihypertensive drugs, patients taking drugs to treat angina are also at an increased risk for orthostatic hypotension due to the vasodilating properties of the drug.

Antiarrhythmic agents: While these drugs are used to treat cardiac arrhythmias, they can sometimes lead to an increase in arrhythmias or a change in the type of arrhythmia the patient is experiencing. Arrhythmias can be identified using electrocardiography or palpation of peripheral pulses. If beta blockers or calcium channel blockers are used to treat cardiac arrhythmias, therapists should be aware of the risk for orthostatic hypotension.

Congestive heart failure agents: Side effects of these drugs will depend on the specific drug used to treat congestive heart failure. Patients taking diuretics may experience fatigue and muscle weakness associated with diminished fluid and electrolyte levels, which may affect their ability to actively participate in therapy sessions. Vasodilating drugs will increase the risk for orthostatic hypotension and therefore exercise or modalities that produce widespread vasodilation should be avoided.

Anticoagulant agents: Patients taking anticoagulant drugs are at an increased risk for bleeding. Physical therapy interventions that increase the risk for tissue trauma, such as soft tissue massage or chest percussion, should be performed with caution. Likewise, wound care interventions (e.g., dressing changes) should be performed carefully to avoid excessive bleeding.

Respiratory agents: Patients who use bronchodilator drugs may experience cardiac arrhythmias, confusion, and tremors, all of which may be signs of toxicity and should be closely monitored by therapists. There are no significant side effects noted with the use of mucolytic and expectorant drugs, however, therapists should be aware of the patient's dosing schedule. Mucolytics and expectorants should be taken 30-60 minutes prior to chest physical therapy to maximize treatment effectiveness.

Other Systems

Sedative-hypnotic and antianxiety agents: These drugs initially create a calming effect that may make a patient more willing to participate in physical therapy. However, when the drugs reach their peak effectiveness, the patient may experience a level of drowsiness that makes it difficult to actively participate. Scheduling patients a few hours after taking these medications should be avoided since the therapy session will be less effective. It is also important to note that patients taking these medications have an increased risk for falls and subsequent injury.

Antidepressant agents: These drugs are associated with a variety of side effects that may negatively affect therapy sessions. Some antidepressant drugs, such as lithium and the tricyclics, produce sedation and muscle weakness, making it more difficult for a patient to actively participate in therapy sessions. Some antidepressants increase the risk for orthostatic hypotension, while others result in hypertension. Therapists should monitor patients' blood pressure regularly to avoid drastic increases or decreases during exercise.

Antipsychotic agents: The most common side effects associated with antipsychotic drugs are extrapyramidal symptoms, which are abnormal movement patterns such as dyskinesia or dystonia. Therapists should be alert for changes in the patient's posture, balance or movement pattern and notify personnel immediately. Early intervention can diminish the risk for long-term motor dysfunction.

Gastrointestinal agents: These drugs do not have any side effects that would significantly affect physical therapy treatment. Some minor side effects include dizziness, fatigue, and gastrointestinal disturbances.

Adrenocorticosteroid agents: Glucocorticoid drugs have catabolic effects and can lead to the breakdown of tendon, bone or skin. These effects are more pronounced in patients that are older, are inactive, and have poor nutrition habits. Therapists should be cautious with aggressive stretching and strengthening exercises to eliminate the risk for fractures or soft tissue injuries. Care must also be taken when applying orthotic devices to prevent skin breakdown. However, strengthening and moderate intensity weight bearing activities can be beneficial in decreasing the catabolic effects of these drugs. Both glucocorticoid and mineralocorticoid drugs lead to water retention and can contribute to hypertension. Therapists should routinely monitor blood pressure for these patients.

Sex hormone replacement therapy: Use of estrogens, progesterones, and androgens lead to salt and water retention and can contribute to hypertension. Therapists should routinely monitor blood pressure for these patients to help prevent a hypertensive crisis.

Thyroid agents: Drugs used to treat hypothyroidism or hyperthyroidism often produce side effects associated with symptoms of the opposite condition. Therapists should avoid interventions that can exacerbate symptoms of thyroid dysfunction. For example, patients with hypothyroidism symptoms may have decreased cardiac function and may not tolerate heavy workloads. Drugs used to treat parathyroid dysfunction can produce side effects that affect therapy as well. For example, calcium supplementation may result in cardiac arrhythmias when used in excessive amounts. Therapists should monitor cardiac function to help identify inappropriate dosing and prevent drug toxicity.

Insulin replacement therapy: Patients taking insulin to control diabetes mellitus may experience symptoms of hypoglycemia, especially if they have not eaten or are participating in strenuous physical activity. Therapists should be aware of the signs of hypoglycemia (e.g., confusion, nausea) and monitor patients closely during and after therapy sessions. If the patient begins to experience hypoglycemia, the therapist can administer a source of glucose (e.g., fruit juice) to help improve blood glucose levels.

Antibacterial agents: Certain antibacterial drugs may cause hypersensitivity of the skin or respiratory tract. Therapists should be cautious when using ultraviolet light as part of therapy treatments to avoid the potential for adverse skin reactions.

Chemotherapy agents: These drugs can have a number of adverse side effects that will affect physical therapy treatment. The most significant side effect is severe fatigue that may make it impossible for a patient to participate in therapy sessions. It is important for the therapist to recognize that there will be days when the patient is unable to tolerate even a light therapy session. These drugs may also cause toxic effects on both the central and peripheral nervous systems. Therapists should be aware of any nervous system abnormalities that may affect treatment, such as peripheral neuropathy or ataxia.

Immunomodulating agents: While immunosuppressant drugs can have a positive effect on rehabilitation by decreasing the debilitating effects of autoimmune disorders, they also have numerous adverse side effects. Some immunosuppressant drugs have a catabolic effect on muscle, tendon, and bone, therefore therapists must be cautious with treatments that could lead to further breakdown of these tissues. Other immunosuppressant drugs have neurotoxic effects, which may affect a patient's ability to participate in balance or gait activities secondary to peripheral neuropathy or central nervous system damage.

Pharmacology - Systems Side Effects

Review of Systems: Side Effects/Subjective Complaints
(In Order of Most Common Occurrence)

Gastrointestinal Distress: dyspepsia, heartburn, nausea, vomiting, abdominal pain, constipation, diarrhea, bleeding		
• Salicylates • Skeletal muscle relaxants • Antiarrhythmic agents • Theophylline • Calcium-channel blockers • Cholesterol-lowering agents • Antidepressants (TCAs and MAOIs, lithium)	• Opioids • ACE inhibitors • Neuroleptics • NSAIDs • Diuretics • Estrogens and progestins	• ß-Blockers • Nitrates • OCAs • Corticosteroids • Digoxin • Antiepileptic agents
Pulmonary: bronchospasm, shortness of breath, respiratory depression		
• Salicylates • NSAIDs	• Opioids • ß-Blockers	• ACE inhibitors
Central Nervous System: dizziness, drowsiness, insomnia, headaches, hallucinations, confusion, anxiety, depression, muscle weakness		
• NSAIDs • Nitrates • Antiepileptic agents • Corticosteroids • Antianxiety agents	• Opioids • Digoxin • Estrogens and progestins • Calcium-channel blockers • Neuroleptics	• ß-Blockers • Antidepressants (TCAs and MAOIs) • Skeletal muscle relaxants • ACE inhibitors • OCAs
Dermatologic: skin rash, itching, flushing of face		
• NSAIDs • Nitrates • Antiepileptics • ACE inhibitors • Estrogens and progestins	• ß-Blockers • Antiarrhythmic agents • Corticosteroids • Cholesterol-lowering agents	• Calcium-channel blockers • OCAs • Opioids • MAOIs and lithium
Musculoskeletal: weakness, fatigue, cramps, arthritis, decreased exercise tolerance, osteoporosis		
• Corticosteroids • Antianxiety agents • ACE inhibitors • Neuroleptic agents	• Calcium-channel blockers • Antidepressants • Digoxin	• Diuretics • ß-Blockers • Antiepileptic agents
Cardiac: bradycardia, ventricular irritability, AV block, CHF, PVCs, ventricular tachycardia		
• Opioids • TCAs • Calcium-channel blockers	• ß-Blockers • Oral antiasthmatic agents • Antiarrhythmic agents	• Digoxin • Diuretics • Neuroleptics
Vascular: claudication, hypotension, peripheral edema, cold extremities		
• NSAIDs • Nitrates • Corticosteroids • Antidepressants (TCAs and MAOIs)	• Diuretics • Neuroleptics • ß-Blockers • OCAs	• Calcium-channel blockers • Estrogens and progestins • ACE inhibitors
Genitourinary: sexual dysfunction, urinary retention, urinary incontinence		
• Opioids • OCAs • Neuroleptics	• ß-Blockers • Diuretics • Antidepressants (TCAs and MAOIs)	• Estrogens and progestins • Antiarrhythmic agents
HEENT: tinnitus, loss of taste, headache, lightheadedness, dizziness		
• Salicylates • Calcium-channel blockers • Antiepileptic agents • Nitrates • Antidepressants (TCAs and MAOIs)	• Opioids • Digoxin • NSAIDs • ACE inhibitors	• ß-Blockers • Antianxiety agents • Skeletal muscle relaxants • Antiarrhythmic agents

**Abbreviations: ACE, angiotensin-converting enzyme; MAOIs, monoamine oxidase inhibitors; NSAIDs, nonsteroidal anti-inflammatory drugs; OCAs, oral contraceptive agents; TCAs, tricyclic antidepressants. From Boissonnault, WG: Examination in Physical Therapy Practice: Screening for Medical Disease. W.B. Saunders Company, Philadelphia 1995, p.350-351, with permission.

GOLD Level Clinical Application Templates

GOLD Level Clinical Application Template Executive Summary

Ankylosing Spondylitis

- Systemic condition characterized by inflammation of the spine and the larger peripheral joints
- Males are at two to three times greater risk than females with peak onset observed between 20-40 years of age
- Clinical presentation initially includes recurrent and insidious onset of back pain, morning stiffness, and impaired spinal extension

Arterial Insufficiency Ulcer

- Characterized by the narrowing of arterial vessels that impedes the delivery of oxygenated blood to tissues
- Peripheral artery disease is typically linked to the development of arterial insufficiency ulcers; risk factors include atherosclerosis, hypertension, obesity, diabetes mellitus, and smoking
- Typically heal by secondary intention with adequate blood supply and wound healing interventions

Breast Cancer

- May spread to the lymphatic system and commonly metastasizes to the brain, lungs, bones, adrenals, and liver
- Breast cancer makes up approximately one quarter of all female cancers and is the second leading cause of cancer death for females in the United States
- Prognosis and ten-year survival rates for breast cancer decrease as the stage of disease increases secondary to tumor progression and lymph node involvement

Burn - Full Thickness

- Burn causes immediate cellular and tissue death and subsequent vascular destruction
- Eschar forms from necrotic cells and creates a dry and hard layer that requires debridement
- Absent sensation and pain due to destruction of free nerve endings, however, there may be pain from adjacent areas that experience partial-thickness burns

Burn - Partial Thickness

- Superficial partial-thickness burn involves the epidermis and upper portion of the dermis; deep partial-thickness burn involves the epidermis, majority of the dermis, and structures within the dermis
- Superficial partial-thickness burn is characterized by a red color that will blanch when touched; deep partial-thickness burn is characterized by red discoloration, however, it will not blanch
- Will typically heal without residual deficits in the absence of infection or other factors that may complicate or delay healing

GOLD Level Clinical Application Template Executive Summary

Complex Regional Pain Syndrome

- Increase in sympathetic activity causes a release of norepinephrine in the periphery and subsequent vasoconstriction of blood vessels resulting in pain and an increase in sensitivity to peripheral stimulation
- Affects all age groups, but is most likely found in individuals 35-60 years of age, with females more likely affected than males
- Patients experience intense burning and chronic pain in the affected extremity that eventually spreads in a proximal direction

Diabetes Mellitus - Type 1

- Insulin is functionally absent due to the destruction of the beta cells of the pancreas; where the insulin would normally be produced
- Starts in children ages four years or older, with the peak incidence of onset coinciding with early adolescence and puberty
- Common symptoms include polyuria, polydipsia, polyphagia, nausea, weight loss, fatigue, blurred vision, and dehydration

Diabetes Mellitus - Type 2

- Characterized by an inappropriate cellular response to insulin, preventing adequate absorption of blood glucose; excess blood glucose results in a persistent hyperglycemic state
- May develop slowly prior to showing initial symptoms that can include polydipsia, polyuria, blurred vision, delayed healing, frequent infections, and acanthosis nigricans
- Medical management is typically focused on lifestyle changes and pharmaceutical intervention through various oral or injectable pharmacological agents

Fibromyalgia Syndrome

- Nonarticular rheumatic condition with pain caused by tender points within muscles, tendons, and ligaments
- Greater incidence in females potentially affecting any age
- Widespread history of pain that exists in all four quadrants of the body (above and below the waist)

Human Immunodeficiency Virus

- Primary risk factors for contracting HIV include unprotected sexual intercourse (anal or vaginal), intravenous drug use, or mother to fetus transmission
- Without treatment, HIV advances in three stages: 1) acute HIV infection, 2) clinical latency, and 3) AIDS (acquired immunodeficiency syndrome)
- Leading cause of death for patients with the virus are, in order of prevalence, AIDS-related (i.e., opportunistic infections), non-AIDS-defining cancers, liver disease, and cardiovascular disease

GOLD Level Clinical Application Template Executive Summary

Juvenile Rheumatoid Arthritis

- Autoimmune disorder found in children less than 16 years of age that occurs when the immune cells mistakenly begin to attack the joints and organs causing local and systemic effects throughout the body
- Girls have a higher incidence of JRA and are most commonly diagnosed as toddlers or in early adolescence
- Clinical symptoms include persistent joint swelling, pain, and stiffness

Lymphedema Post-Mastectomy

- Caused by an excess load of lymph fluid or inadequate transport capacity within the lymphatic system secondary to the loss of homeostasis
- Primary contributing factor in the development of lymphedema following a mastectomy is the damage and/or removal of the axillary lymph nodes and vessels
- Intervention should focus on manual lymph drainage, short stretch compression bandages, retrograde massage, exercise, compression therapy, and use of a mechanical pump

Neuropathic Ulcer

- Occurs most frequently in the diabetic population and are often referred to as diabetic ulcers
- At-risk areas include those that are routinely subjected to pressure during normal weight bearing, atypical stresses due to structural changes or improper fitting footwear
- Will typically heal by secondary intention with appropriate wound healing interventions and the absence of complications (e.g., infection, severe arterial insufficiency)

Osteoporosis

- Metabolic bone disorder where the rate of bone resorption accelerates while the rate of bone formation slows down
- Patients may complain of low thoracic or lumbar pain and experience compression fractures of the vertebrae
- Bone mineral density test accounts for 70% of bone strength and is the easiest way to determine osteoporosis

Pressure Ulcer

- Unrelieved pressure deprives the tissues of oxygen which causes ischemia, subsequent cell death, and tissue necrosis
- High risk areas for pressure ulcers include the occiput, heels, greater trochanters, ischial tuberosities, sacrum, and epicondyles of the elbow
- Impaired cognition, poor nutrition, altered sensation, incontinence, decreased lean body mass, and infection contribute to the development of a pressure ulcer

Level Clinical Application Template Executive Summary

Rheumatoid Arthritis

- Systemic autoimmune disorder of the connective tissue that is characterized by chronic inflammation within synovial membranes, tendon sheaths, and articular cartilage
- Incidence is greater in females than males and is diagnosed most frequently between 30-50 years of age
- Blood work assists with the diagnosis of rheumatoid arthritis through evaluation of the rheumatoid factor, white blood cell count, erythrocyte sedimentation rate, hemoglobin, and hematocrit values

Systemic Lupus Erythematosus

- Connective tissue disorder caused by an autoimmune reaction in the body
- Females are at greater risk than males with the most common age group ranging from 15-40 years of age
- Clinical presentation includes a red butterfly rash across the cheeks and nose, a red rash over light exposed areas, arthralgias, alopecia, pleurisy, kidney involvement, seizures, and depression

Urinary Stress Incontinence

- Occurs during activities where there is an increase in abdominal pressure through straining, sneezing, coughing or lifting
- Risk factors include pregnancy, vaginal delivery, episiotomy, prostate or pelvic surgery, aging, diabetes mellitus, central nervous system dysfunction, and recurrent urinary infection
- Accounts for the majority of incontinence cases and is manifested solely by the involuntary loss of urine with any form of exertion or increased abdominal pressure

Venous Insufficiency Ulcer

- Typically results from venous hypertension which may present idiopathically, secondary to valve incompetence or peripheral impedance
- Pain complaints are typically mild and relieved with elevation or use of compression garments
- Treatment of a venous insufficiency ulcer and the underlying pathology should allow for a normal course of recovery without residual deficits

GOLD

Ankylosing Spondylitis

DIAGNOSIS

What condition produces a patient's symptoms?

Ankylosing spondylitis (AS), also known as Marie-Strumpell disease, is a systemic condition that is characterized by inflammation of the spine and larger peripheral joints. The chronic inflammation causes destruction of the ligamentous-osseous junction with subsequent fibrosis and ossification of the area.

An injury was most likely sustained to which structure?

AS primarily affects the sacroiliac joint, intervertebral disks, spine, costovertebral and apophyseal joints, connective tissue, and larger peripheral joints (hips, knees, and shoulders). Ossification can occur within all affected joints resulting in pain and deformity.

INFERENCE

What is the most likely contributing factor in the development of this condition?

AS is a progressive systemic disorder with uncertain etiology. Research supports the possibility of genetic inheritance combined with environmental influence. Gender, race, age, and family history are all factors to consider regarding risk for developing AS. A person born with a histocompatibility antigen HLA-B27 has a high risk for the disease. Almost all patients with AS are HLA-B27 positive, but only a very small percent of individuals that are HLA-B27 positive develop AS. HLA-B27 is more common in Caucasians than it is in African Americans. Men are at a greater risk than women and onset is typically seen between 20 and 40 years of age.

CONFIRMATION

What is the most likely clinical presentation?

A patient with early AS will present with recurrent and insidious episodes of low back pain, morning stiffness, impaired spinal extension, and limited range of motion in the affected joints for over a three-month period of time. As the disease progresses pain will become severe, consistent, and extending to the midback, and sometimes towards the neck. The natural lumbar curve will eventually flatten due to muscle spasms. Other manifestations include fixed flexion at the hips, spinal kyphosis, fatigue, weight loss, and peripheral joint involvement. If the costovertebral joints are affected a patient will present with impaired chest mobility, compromised breathing, and decreased vital capacity.

What laboratory or imaging studies would confirm the diagnosis?

X-ray of the spine may be negative in the initial stage of AS but with progression will reveal areas of erosion, demineralization, calcification, and syndesmophyte formation (ossification of the outside of the intervertebral disks). In the later stages of the disease x-ray will reveal fusion of the sacroiliac joint, calcification of apophyseal joints and spinal ligaments, and a bamboo appearance of the spine. Blood work can be used to rule out other diseases and assists with the diagnosis since the majority of patients with AS possess the HLA-B27 antigen and many of them have an elevated erythrocyte sedimentation rate.

What additional information should be obtained to confirm the diagnosis?

Physical examination may reveal joint tenderness, pain, and/or limitation of the sacroiliac joint and the spine. Family inheritance and a thorough history of a patient's symptoms assist with the diagnosis of AS.

EXAMINATION

What history should be documented?

Important areas to explore include past medical history, medications, current health status, family inheritance, living environment, occupation, leisure activities, social history and habits, and social support system.

What tests/measures are most appropriate?

Aerobic capacity and endurance: assessment of vital signs at rest and with activity, perceived exertion scale, pulse oximetry, auscultation of the lungs

Anthropometric characteristics: circumferential measurements

Arousal, attention, and cognition: examine mental status, learning ability, memory, motivation

Community and work integration: analysis of community, work, and leisure activities

Environmental, home, and work barriers: analysis of current and potential barriers or hazards

Gait, locomotion, and balance: static and dynamic balance in sitting and standing, safety during gait with/without an assistive device

Integumentary integrity: skin assessment

Muscle performance: strength assessment

Pain: pain perception assessment scale, VAS

Range of motion: active and passive range of motion

Self-care and home management: assessment of functional capacity, Functional Independence Measure

Sensory integrity: proprioception and kinesthesia

Ventilation, respiration, and circulation: assessment of cough and clearance of secretions, breathing patterns, vital capacity, perceived exertion scale, pulse oximetry, palpation of pulses, auscultation of the lungs and heart

Ankylosing Spondylitis

GOLD

What additional findings are likely with this patient?

Long-term AS will present with progressive symptoms and multiple complications. Iritis, uveitis, osteoporosis, fracture, atlantoaxial subluxation, and complete spinal fusion can occur in severe long-standing cases of AS. Pericarditis, cardiac pathology, pulmonary fibrosis, cardiac arrhythmias, amyloidosis, and aortic insufficiency have also been noted as potential complications.

MANAGEMENT

What is the most effective management of this patient?

The goals of medical management are to reduce inflammation, maintain functional mobility, and relieve pain. Pharmacological intervention may include NSAIDs, disease-modifying drugs such as methotrexate, analgesics, and specifically Indomethacin to relieve pain. Physical therapy intervention should include postural exercises emphasizing extension, general range of motion, pain management, and energy conservation techniques. Low-impact and aerobic exercise with emphasis on extension and rotation are appropriate for a patient with AS. High-impact and flexion exercises are contraindicated. Patient education should include posture retraining, positioning for sleeping, and lifting techniques. Excessive exercise should be avoided as it can increase the inflammatory response and injury. Swimming is a highly recommended activity. Surgical intervention is rarely indicated to correct or stabilize a musculoskeletal deformity.

What home care regimen should be recommended?

A home care regimen for a patient with AS should include a daily low-impact therapeutic exercise program. Range of motion should focus on spinal movement in all directions. The patient requires a firm sleeping surface and competence with proper positioning and use of pillows to maintain optimal alignment. Ongoing breathing exercises and posture retraining will assist with overall level of function.

OUTCOME

What is the likely outcome of a course of physical therapy?

Physical therapy cannot modify the progression of AS, however, it may assist to alleviate pain and improve a patient's functional capacity. A patient may require physical therapy on an intermittent basis for secondary complications throughout the disease process.

What are the long-term effects of the patient's condition?

AS progresses slowly over a 15–25 year period and may remain isolated to the spine and sacroiliac joint or spread to larger peripheral joints. Stiffness and joint limitation are common long-term effects of AS that can negatively impact a patient's functional mobility. The extent of disability varies greatly, though complete remission is rare. The normal course includes periods of exacerbations and remissions. Hip disease with AS is a marker for a severe form of AS and is more likely to occur in a patient that is diagnosed at a young age.

COMPARISON

What are the distinguishing characteristics of a similar condition?

Sjogren's syndrome, like AS, is classified as a spondyloarthropathy. Sjogren's is a chronic arthritis and autoimmune disease that also can affect several organs. Lymphocytes attack healthy tissues and organs and are usually found in combination with RA or lupus. Postmenopausal women are affected most often with over two to four million individuals in the United States living with the disease. It does not have a cure, but can be managed through medications, exercise, and proper nutrition. Exercise should follow general guidelines for the treatment of RA.

CLINICAL SCENARIOS

Scenario One

A 28-year-old male is seen in physical therapy shortly after being diagnosed with AS. The patient complains of sacroiliac pain and tenderness. The patient has a negative family history and is currently employed as a high school maintenance technician.

Scenario Two

A 60-year-old female is seen in physical therapy with advanced AS. The patient has bilateral hip flexion contractures and kyphosis. The patient resides alone and receives daily assistance from her two sisters who live locally. The patient has previously refused recommendations to utilize an assistive device for ambulation.

GOLD

Arterial Insufficiency Ulcer

DIAGNOSIS

What condition produces a patient's symptoms?

An arterial insufficiency ulcer is caused by inadequate perfusion of oxygenated blood in the affected tissue. Over time, diminished blood flow is no longer able to meet the metabolic demands of the tissue resulting in cell death and tissue necrosis. Arterial insufficiency ulcers typically occur due to underlying pathology such as progressive atherosclerosis or an arterial embolism.

An injury was most likely sustained to which structure?

An arterial insufficiency ulcer can affect different structures based on the depth of tissue injury. A superficial ulceration is associated with damage to the epidermis. Damage from a partial-thickness ulceration will extend through the epidermis and possibly into, but not through, the dermis. A full-thickness ulceration extends through the dermis and into deeper layers such as the subcutaneous fat layer.

INFERENCE

What is the most likely contributing factor in the development of this condition?

Peripheral artery disease (PAD) is typically linked to the development of arterial insufficiency ulcers. The condition is characterized by the narrowing of arterial vessels that impedes the delivery of oxygenated blood to tissues. Risk factors for the development of PAD include atherosclerosis, hypertension, obesity, diabetes mellitus, and smoking.

CONFIRMATION

What is the most likely clinical presentation?

A patient will typically develop an arterial insufficiency ulcer distally on the lower one-third of the lower extremity. Common sites include the dorsum of the foot, the lateral malleolus, and the toes. Wound edges may initially be slightly irregular, however, they soon progress to the more characteristic smooth and defined appearance. A clean wound bed is typically light pink in color though a grayish undertone may be observed. Minimal bleeding is noted with manipulation of the wound and debridement. Discoloration may be noted in the nails (e.g., yellow), nail beds (e.g., cyanotic), and surrounding skin (e.g., pale). Intact surrounding skin may be cool to the touch, thin, shiny, and hairless. Distal pulses are usually diminished or absent with palpation and often require assessment via Doppler ultrasound. In more advanced cases, muscle wasting may also be observed. Pain complaints are typically significant. Limb-related pain is most commonly positional, occurring when the limb is in a non-dependent position or with activity that results in intermittent claudication.

What laboratory or imaging studies would confirm the diagnosis?

Diagnosis of an arterial insufficiency ulcer is made based on the characteristics of the observed wound and diagnosis of the underlying condition. Duplex ultrasonography is the least invasive method of assessing arterial blood flow. It determines the speed and direction of blood flow and narrowing of the vessels. An angiogram (e.g., arteriogram, venogram) utilizes a contrast dye and x-ray imaging to identify narrowed, blocked, malformed or enlarged arterial vessels.

What additional information should be obtained to confirm the diagnosis?

The ankle-brachial index (ABI) assists in predicting the severity of arterial occlusion. An ABI of 0.79 or less is indicative of a moderate arterial blockage, increasing the likelihood of ulcer development and symptoms of intermittent claudication with activity.

EXAMINATION

What history should be documented?

Important areas to explore include past medical history, medications, family history, current symptoms, current health status, social history and habits, occupation, leisure activities, and social support system.

What tests/measures are most appropriate?

Anthropometric characteristics: circumferential measurements
Arousal, attention, and cognition: examine mental status, learning ability, memory, and motivation
Assistive and adaptive devices: analysis of components and safety of a device
Gait, locomotion, and balance: static and dynamic balance in sitting and standing, safety during gait with/without an assistive device
Integumentary integrity: skin assessment, assessment of sensation, assessment of wound characteristics, photographic documentation
Muscle performance: strength assessment, muscle tone assessment
Pain: pain perception assessment scale, visual analogue scale, claudication pain
Range of motion: active and passive range of motion
Reflex integrity: assessment of deep tendon reflexes
Self-care and home management: assessment of functional capacity
Ventilation, respiration, and circulation: assessment of pulse oximetry, palpation of pulses, capillary refill, ankle-brachial index

Arterial Insufficiency Ulcer

GOLD

What additional findings are likely with this patient?

Arterial insufficiency ulcers are likely to become chronic without adequate perfusion to the wound bed and surrounding tissue. Patients may develop multiple ulcers concurrently. Complications that may further impact healing include gangrene, osteomyelitis, sepsis, and pain.

MANAGEMENT

What is the most effective management of this patient?

Medical management typically includes monitoring the severity of the underlying disease process, counseling regarding modifiable risk factors, pharmaceutical intervention, and potential surgical intervention. Surgical debridement will typically convert a chronic ulceration to an acute wound thereby reactivating the normal healing process. In cases with more significant arterial occlusion, surgical revascularization (e.g., femoral-popliteal bypass) will typically allow the wound to heal. For larger wounds, grafting may be indicated once normal circulation has been restored. If vascular integrity cannot be restored, amputation is typically recommended. Physical therapy management emphasizes skin protection and wound healing interventions. The ulcer may require cleansing agents and/or debridement (e.g., enzymatic, mechanical, autolytic, sharp) and should be regularly monitored for signs of infection. Packing may be necessary to fill the wound space as part of the dressing application depending on the wound depth. Arterial insufficiency ulcers typically produce minimal exudate, therefore, it is important to select dressings which both protect the wound and assist in maintaining a moist wound healing environment. Photo documentation is recommended to supplement written documentation describing wound characteristics (e.g., area, depth, odor, exudate, color).

What home care regimen should be recommended?

The home care regimen is dependent on the size and characteristics of the arterial ulcer. Patients who do not require debridement may appropriately manage routine dressing changes at home. All patients should be diligent with hygiene and skin protection to limit the risk of infection.

OUTCOME

What is the likely outcome of a course of physical therapy?

An arterial insufficiency ulcer will typically heal by secondary intention with adequate blood supply and wound healing interventions. Patients typically will not experience residual deficits from the wound itself, but may have increased morbidity and mortality secondary to the underlying pathology.

What are the long-term effects of the patient's condition?

Treatment of an arterial insufficiency ulcer and the underlying pathology should allow for a normal course of recovery without residual deficits. Infection or other healing complications may require additional pharmacological, medical or surgical intervention. If infection is pervasive or vascular integrity cannot be adequately restored, additional ulcerations, gangrene or amputation may result.

COMPARISON

What are the distinguishing characteristics of a similar condition?

Venous insufficiency ulcers are typically the result of tissue changes associated with venous hypertension. These ulcers commonly develop in the distal lower extremities, as with arterial insufficiency ulcers, however, the underlying pathology and ulcer characteristics are markedly different. Venous insufficiency ulcers are typically shallow with irregular edges and moderate to heavy exudate. Pain complaints are usually mild to moderate, most notable with prolonged dependent positioning, and relieved with elevation. On examination, pedal pulses are typically intact, however, they may be difficult to assess if edema is significant. Skin is often dry and flaky with a brownish discoloration (e.g., hemosiderin staining). Specific wound care interventions emphasize skin and wound protection, establishing a clean wound bed, exudate management, and the selection of optimal primary and secondary dressings. Successful treatment typically will require some degree of graded compression to manage edema and support normal tissue healing. The regular use of compression is recommended to reduce the risk of future ulcer development.

CLINICAL SCENARIOS

Scenario One

A 91-year-old female is referred to physical therapy by her vascular surgeon for wound care. She has an ABI of 0.7 and small ulceration on her left great toe which is covered with firmly adhered eschar. The patient complains of significant pain during the examination. She resides with her daughter in a second floor apartment.

Scenario Two

A 67-year-old male is a two pack per day smoker with a history of hypertension and atherosclerosis. He has developed large ulcerations on the dorsum of his right foot and proximal to the lateral malleolus. The physical therapist notes an ABI of 0.45 and cyanotic nail beds. He is a general contractor and lives alone in a one story home.

GOLD

Breast Cancer

DIAGNOSIS

What condition produces a patient's symptoms?

Breast cancer's primary symptom is a painless mass within the breast tissue. This mass is composed of malignant altered cells that proliferate and spread uncontrollably. A malignancy can occur anywhere within the breast tissue, however, the lump is usually found directly behind the areola in men and is usually located behind the areola or in the outer upper quadrant of the breast in women. There may or may not be generalized discomfort in the area of the mass.

An injury was most likely sustained to which structure?

Injury occurs initially at the cellular level within the breast tissue. Breast cancer either begins in the lobules, which are the milk producing glands, or in the ducts that bring the milk to the nipples. Breast cancer can spread into the lymphatic system and will commonly metastasize to the brain, lungs, bones, adrenals, and liver.

INFERENCE

What is the most likely contributing factor in the development of this condition?

The etiology of breast cancer is unknown, however, estrogen is believed to have some relationship to the disease process. Risk factors include gender, age, young menarche, late menopause, family history of breast cancer, high alcohol intake, high fat diet, radiation exposure, and past history of cancer. Breast cancer can occur in both males and females, however, males account for less than 1% of all breast cancer cases.

CONFIRMATION

What is the most likely clinical presentation?

Breast cancer makes up approximately one quarter of all female cancers and is the second leading cause of cancer death for females within the United States. The majority of all breast cancer occurs in women over the age of 50. A patient with breast cancer will present with a lump in the breast that is often noticed by a physician or by the patient through self-examination. Breast cancer is initially otherwise asymptomatic. As the disease progresses the breast may become painful, change shape, bleed from the nipple, and dimple over the area of the mass. Symptoms associated with metastases may include bone pain, upper extremity edema, and weight loss.

What laboratory or imaging studies would confirm the diagnosis?

Mammography is used to detect the location and growth of a mass, however, definitive diagnosis of breast cancer is made only after microscopic examination of a suspected mass by needle or excision biopsy. Ultrasound can also be used to detect if a lump is filled with fluid or a solid mass. Sentinel lymph node mapping is used upon diagnosis to identify exact lymph node involvement.

What additional information should be obtained to confirm the diagnosis?

Additional information such as family history of cancer, past medical history, and history of self-examination is helpful in support of a definitive diagnosis. This information is usually obtained prior to mammography and biopsy.

EXAMINATION

What history should be documented?

Important areas to explore include past medical history, family history of cancer, medications, current health status, social history and habits, hand dominance, occupation, living environment, and social support system.

What tests/measures are most appropriate?

Aerobic capacity and endurance: assessment of vital signs at rest and with activity

Anthropometric characteristics: upper extremity circumferential measurements

Arousal, attention, and cognition: examine mental status, learning ability, memory, motivation

Community and work integration: analysis of community, work, and leisure activities

Gait, locomotion, and balance: assess static/dynamic balance in sitting and standing, safety during gait

Integumentary integrity: assessment for potential infection of surgical incision

Muscle performance: strength assessment

Pain: pain perception assessment scale, visual analogue scale

Range of motion: active and passive range of motion

Self-care and home management: assessment of self-care and home management skills, assessment of functional capacity, Barthel Index

Sensory integrity: assessment of superficial and combined sensations, proprioception, and kinesthesia

What additional findings are likely with this patient?

Additional findings are dependent on the stage of the cancer (I, II, III, IV) and course of treatment. If a patient has undergone surgical resection or mastectomy the patient may experience pain, edema, fatigue, and psychological issues. Patients that are diagnosed with advanced breast cancer may experience pleural effusion, pathological fractures, and spinal compression.

MANAGEMENT

What is the most effective management of this patient?

The medical management of breast cancer is based on the size and the stage of the mass and corresponding involvement of the lymph nodes. Surgical management may range from excision of the mass (lumpectomy) to total radical mastectomy with axillary dissection. Chemotherapy, radiation therapy, and hormone therapies may be used in isolation or after a surgical procedure. Physical therapy may be indicated to assist with lymphedema management, post-surgical breathing exercises, positioning, pain management, strengthening and endurance activities, range of motion exercises, massage, intermittent compression, and patient education.

What home care regimen should be recommended?

A home care regimen should include education, positioning, and techniques to manage lymphedema. Range of motion exercises, energy conservation techniques, as well as general exercise and endurance activities should continue on a regular basis at home.

OUTCOME

What is the likely outcome of a course of physical therapy?

Physical therapy may be indicated for post-surgical management to assist with impairments and promote independence with self-care and functional skills.

What are the long-term effects of the patient's condition?

The long-term effects of breast cancer are varied. The risk of recurrence is always present and should be monitored closely. Post-surgical lymphedema may persist and require ongoing home management. The prognosis and ten-year survival rates for breast cancer decrease as the stage of disease increases, secondary to tumor progression and lymph node involvement. The overall mortality rate decreases annually within the United States secondary to changes in lifestyle, improved self-examination, earlier diagnosis, and better treatment.

COMPARISON

What are the distinguishing characteristics of a similar condition?

Fibrocystic breast disease (mammary dysplasia) usually occurs in both breasts and is characterized by nodular lumps within the breast tissue. The cysts are benign and become tender immediately prior to menstruation. Fibrocystic breast disease is the most common breast disorder in women. Other symptoms include aching and burning within the breast. Symptoms normally disappear after menstruation is over. Although benign, fibrocystic breast disease increases a patient's risk for breast cancer later in life.

CLINICAL SCENARIOS

Scenario One

A 65-year-old female is seen by a therapist 24 hours after total mastectomy. The patient was active prior to the surgery and walked for exercise two miles every day. The patient's past medical history is positive for fibrocystic breast disease, diabetes mellitus, and skin cancer. The patient reports pain with coughing. The patient resides alone in a retirement village and lost her husband to cancer last year. She has three supportive children that reside in the local area.

Scenario Two

A 45-year-old female is referred to outpatient physical therapy with lymphedema secondary to stage III breast cancer and radical mastectomy three months ago. The patient is fatigued and anxious about the increased size of her arm and limitation in range of motion. The patient runs a daycare center out of her home and is active in her church. Past medical history includes endometriosis and pharmacological treatment for depression.

GOLD

Burn - Full-Thickness

DIAGNOSIS

What condition produces a patient's symptoms?

Full-thickness burns can be caused by thermal (fire, hot fluids, steam), chemical (acid, alkalis, vesicants) or electrical (lightning, high voltage, faulty wiring) agents. This severe burn causes immediate cellular and tissue death and subsequent vascular destruction. The patient will experience primary and secondary symptoms secondary to the extent and area of injury.

An injury was most likely sustained to which structure?

A full-thickness burn indicates complete destruction of the epidermis, dermis, hair follicle, and nerve endings within the dermis; and also affects the subcutaneous fat layer and underlying muscles, resulting in red blood cell destruction. There is irreversible damage sustained to all epithelial elements.

INFERENCE

What is the most likely contributing factor in the development of this condition?

The majority of burns are a direct result of the patient's actions. There is a higher risk for burns in children between one and five years of age as well as individuals over 70 years of age. Males have a higher overall frequency of injury than females.

CONFIRMATION

What is the most likely clinical presentation?

A full-thickness burn is characterized by a variable appearance of deep red, black or white coloring. Eschar forms from necrotic cells and creates a dry and hard layer that requires debridement. Edema is present at the site of injury and in surrounding tissues. Hairs within the region of the burn are easily pulled from the follicle due to the destruction. An area of full-thickness burn does not have sensation or pain due to destruction of free nerve endings, however, there may be pain from adjacent areas that experience partial-thickness burns. During the initial stages the patient will experience thermoregulation impairment, shortness of breath, electrolyte disturbances, poor urine output, and variation in level of consciousness.

What laboratory or imaging studies would confirm the diagnosis?

Blood work should include a complete blood count, electrolytes, blood urea nitrogen, creatinine, bilirubin, and arterial blood gases. This will indicate baseline data, systemic changes, level of shock, and metabolic complications. Bronchoscopy and pulmonary function tests may be indicated to assess airway damage and pulmonary insufficiency.

What additional information should be obtained to confirm the diagnosis?

Diagnosis is primarily based on observation and assessment regarding the extent and depth of the burn. The rule of nines and the Lund-Browder charts grossly approximate the percentage of the body affected by a burn.

EXAMINATION

What history should be documented?

Important areas to explore include past medical history, mechanism of injury, medications, family history, type and percentage of burn, current symptoms and health status, social history and habits, occupation, leisure activities, and social support system.

What tests/measures are most appropriate?

Aerobic capacity and endurance: assessment of vital signs, perceived exertion scale, pulse oximetry

Anthropometric characteristics: circumferential measurements of affected areas

Arousal, attention, and cognition: examine mental status, learning ability, memory, motivation

Cranial nerve integrity: dermatome assessment

Gait, locomotion, and balance: static and dynamic balance in sitting and standing

Integumentary integrity: sensation assessment, assessment of burn, size, color, eschar, hair follicle integrity, wound mapping

Joint integrity and mobility: assessment of contracture, hypomobility of joints, soft tissue swelling

Muscle performance: strength and tone assessment

Pain: pain perception assessment scale, visual analogue scale to the area of the burn and surrounding tissues

Posture: analysis of resting and dynamic posture

Range of motion: active and passive range of motion

Reflex integrity: assessment of deep tendon and pathological reflexes (e.g., Babinski, ATNR)

Self-care and home management: functional capacity, Functional Independence Measure (FIM)

Ventilation, respiration, and circulation: cough and clearance of secretions, auscultation of the lungs, breathing patterns, respiratory muscle strength, accessory muscle utilization, vital capacity, pulse oximetry and palpation, pulmonary function testing

Burn - Full-Thickness

GOLD

What additional findings are likely with this patient?

A patient with a full-thickness burn will present with multiple secondary effects based on the mechanism of the burn, size of the burn, and location of the burn. Infection, hypertrophic scarring, and contractures are the most common complications. Other secondary damage may include impairments of the cardiovascular system, renal system, gastrointestinal system, respiratory system and/or immune system. Damage to these vital areas can result in metabolic disorders, acidosis, sepsis, and dehydration.

MANAGEMENT

What is the most effective management of this patient?

The initial management includes medically stabilizing the patient followed by a full assessment of primary and secondary damage. This emergent phase lasts 48-72 hours and concludes with regaining capillary permeability and hemodynamic stability. An autograft procedure is usually required for full-thickness burns. The rehabilitation phase is a long-term commitment that includes all aspects of functional recovery. Physical therapy intervention begins immediately following skin grafting and includes wound care, pulmonary exercises, positioning, splinting, and immobilization for the first three to five days. A therapist will also provide education regarding skin care, positioning, and contracture prevention. Early ambulation and mobility activities should be incorporated as soon as possible in order to decrease complications such as atelectasis, pneumonia, and contracture. Continued physical therapy management will involve edema control, monitoring of any elastic garments, massage, stretching, hydrotherapy, ROM, debridement, relaxation techniques, progressive exercise, ambulation, and functional mobility training.

What home care regimen should be recommended?

A patient must continue with the established splinting and positioning schedule at home. Physical therapy may initially be warranted for continued pulmonary management, stretching, and functional mobility. A home program is vital to the patient's continued success and should include strengthening exercises, massage, scar management, positioning, and stretching. As the patient progresses, participation in wound management, activities of daily living, and functional activities should be incorporated into the daily routine.

OUTCOME

What is the likely outcome of a course of physical therapy?

Patient outcome is dependent on location, extent, and secondary complications of the burn. Physical therapy will provide the patient with education for an ongoing therapeutic program. Therapeutic exercise, stretching, compression garments, and other modalities will enhance the probability of a positive outcome.

What are the long-term effects of the patient's condition?

The mortality rate has decreased over the last two decades due to improvement in burn care, prevention of infection, and advances in grafting procedures. Mortality rates are highest for children under four and adults over 65 years of age. Overall prognosis is dependent on factors such as cardiac pathology, alcoholism, peripheral vascular disease, and obesity. Other factors that also require consideration are depression, social and emotional shock, and level of difficulty reintegrating into a daily routine (with employment, spouse, children, community). Long-term outcome is also based on the extent of secondary effects such as scarring and contractures. Garments may be worn up to two years after injury. Without significant complications a patient should achieve independence within a few months post injury.

COMPARISON

What are the distinguishing characteristics of a similar condition?

A superficial partial-thickness burn damages the epidermis and the papillary layer of the dermis (the dermis remains largely intact). This burn presents with blister formation, bright red coloring, intact blanching, moderate edema, and pain. The burn will heal without surgical intervention within 5-21 days with minimal to no scarring noted.

CLINICAL SCENARIOS

Scenario One

A 32-year-old female six weeks status post full-thickness burns to 50% of her right arm and 70% of her right leg is referred to physical therapy. She wears compression garments and has decreased range of motion. She resides alone in a two-story home and is employed as a cook.

Scenario Two

A three-year-old boy is referred to physical therapy 48 hours after an autograft for a full-thickness burn on the left side of his thorax. The chart review notes the mechanism of injury as pulling a cup of coffee off a table. Other medical history includes developmental delay, seizures, and hydrocephaly.

GOLD

Burn - Partial-Thickness

DIAGNOSIS

What condition produces a patient's symptoms?

Partial-thickness burns can be caused by thermal (e.g., fire, hot fluid, steam), chemical (e.g., acid, alkali, vesicant) or electrical (e.g., lightning, high voltage, faulty wiring) agents. They are differentiated as superficial partial-thickness and deep partial-thickness burns based on the depth of tissue destruction. The area and extent of the injury determine the primary and secondary symptoms experienced by the patient.

An injury was most likely sustained to which structure?

A superficial partial-thickness burn involves the epidermis and the upper portion of the dermis. Free nerve endings are exposed making this depth of burn extremely painful. A deep partial-thickness burn involves complete destruction of the epidermis, the majority of the dermis, and the structures within the dermis (e.g., hair follicles, sebaceous glands, sweat glands). As a result of damage to nerve endings, there is less pain than would be associated with a superficial partial-thickness burn. Irreversible epithelial damage is sustained with a deep partial-thickness burn which may result in hypertrophic or keloid scarring.

INFERENCE

What is the most likely contributing factor in the development of this condition?

The majority of burns are a direct result of the patient's actions. There is a higher risk for burns in children between one and five years of age as well as individuals over 70 years of age. Males have a higher overall frequency of injury than females.

CONFIRMATION

What is the most likely clinical presentation?

A superficial partial-thickness burn is characterized by a red color that will blanch when touched and then return to red indicating that capillary refill is intact. Blisters and superficial moisture are typically present with hair follicles remaining intact. The preservation of deeper dermal tissues will allow for epithelial regeneration during healing. A deep partial-thickness burn is also characterized by red discoloration, however, when touched it will not blanch. This indicates the absence of capillary refill and damage to deeper blood vessels. Edema typically accumulates between the epidermal and dermal layers. Cellular necrosis is typical, especially in the upper dermal layer. Healing occurs either with scar tissue formation or grafting.

What laboratory or imaging studies would confirm the diagnosis?

Diagnosis of a partial thickness-burn is typically based on a physical examination. Depending on the total area burned and the depth of damage, the burn may still be considered quite severe. In this case, blood work (e.g., complete blood count, electrolytes, blood urea nitrogen, arterial blood gases) may be indicated to establish baseline data, systemic changes, level of shock, and metabolic complications. Bronchoscopy and pulmonary function tests may be indicated to assess airway damage and pulmonary insufficiency.

What additional information should be obtained to confirm the diagnosis?

Diagnosis is primarily based on observation and assessment regarding the extent and depth of the burn. The rule of nines and the Lund-Browder charts grossly approximate the percentage of the body affected by the burn. Prognostic burn indices provide a more thorough evaluative tool to assist caregivers in the prediction of medical attention needs, outcomes, and mortality by taking into account both the surface area burned and the severity of burns.

EXAMINATION

What history should be documented?

Important areas to explore include past medical history, medications, family history, current symptoms, current health status, social history and habits, occupation, leisure activities, and social support system.

What tests/measures are most appropriate?

Aerobic capacity and endurance: assessment of vital signs, perceived exertion scale, pulse oximetry

Anthropometric characteristics: circumferential measurements of affected areas

Arousal, attention, and cognition: examine mental status, learning ability, memory, and motivation

Cranial nerve integrity: dermatome assessment

Gait, locomotion, and balance: static and dynamic balance in sitting and standing

Integumentary integrity: sensation assessment, assessment of burn size, color, hair follicle integrity, surface characteristics (e.g., blisters), wound mapping

Joint integrity and mobility: assessment of contracture, joint hypomobility, soft tissue swelling

Muscle performance: strength and tone assessment

Pain: pain perception assessment scale, visual analogue scale for the burn and surrounding tissues

Posture: analysis of resting and dynamic posture

Range of motion: active and passive range of motion

Reflex integrity: assessment of deep tendon and pathological reflexes (e.g., Babinski, ATNR)

Self-care and home management: assessment of functional capacity, Functional Independence Measure (FIM), Barthel ADL Index

Ventilation, respiration, and circulation: assessment of cough and clearance of secretions, breathing patterns, respiratory muscle strength, accessory muscle utilization and vital capacity, pulse oximetry, palpation of pulses, pulmonary function testing, auscultation of the lungs

What additional findings are likely with this patient?

Partial-thickness burns may present with secondary effects based on the mechanism of the burn, the overall size, and the location of the burn. Infection, hypertrophic scarring, and contracture may occur with deep partial-thickness burns, but are not typically associated with superficial partial-thickness burns.

MANAGEMENT

What is the most effective management of this patient?

Medical management of a partial-thickness burn begins with a full assessment of primary and secondary damage. Since the dermis is not fully destroyed, the patient is typically able to maintain hemodynamic stability even with large areas affected. A superficial partial-thickness burn will typically re-epithelialize with little to no scarring within five to twenty-one days, though larger areas may require a longer period even with a normal healing progression. Management primarily involves protection of the damaged area and maintenance of an appropriate moisture balance with the use of specialized dressings and topical agents. Medical follow-up is not typically required unless the patient develops complications such as an infection. No additional consults, including physical therapy, are indicated. A deep partial-thickness burn will typically heal through the formation of scar tissue although in some cases may require grafting. Uncomplicated healing will typically occur within twenty-one to thirty-five days. Like superficial partial-thickness burns, tissue protection and maintenance of an appropriate moisture balance are emphasized and supported with the use of specialized dressings. A surgical consult may be indicated to determine if a skin graft is necessary. Physical therapy may be indicated to assist in preventing hypertrophic or keloid scarring and contractures if the burns include joint involvement. Physical therapy intervention may Include edema management, splinting and positioning, scar mobilization techniques, massage, range of motion, stretching, dressing management, wound care, monitoring elastic garment use, and functional mobility training.

What home care regimen should be recommended?

A patient should continue with any established wound management, splinting, positioning, massage, exercise, and scar management techniques at home. This is especially important for patients with deep partial-thickness burns due to the increased likelihood of infection, scarring, and contractures. As the patient progresses, normal activities of daily living and functional activities should be resumed.

OUTCOME

What is the likely outcome of a course of physical therapy?

Physical therapy is not typically indicated for a patient with a superficial partial-thickness wound. A patient with a deep partial-thickness wound may benefit from physical therapy to address wound and edema management and prevent the formation of hypertrophic or keloid scarring.

What are the long-term effects of the patient's condition?

Both types of partial-thickness burns will typically heal without residual deficits in the absence of infection or other factors that may complicate or delay healing (e.g., smoking, diabetes mellitus). A full functional return is expected.

COMPARISON

What are the distinguishing characteristics of a similar condition?

A subdermal burn is typically severe and life-threatening, involving the complete destruction of the epidermis, dermis, subcutaneous tissue, and larger blood vessels. The burned tissue has a charred appearance and is not painful due to the complete destruction of local nerve fibers. A subdermal burn may involve muscle and bone and as a result is highly susceptible to infection and other healing complications. Multiple surgical interventions (e.g., debridement, grafting) are typically required and associated with extensive healing times.

CLINICAL SCENARIOS

Scenario One

A 22-year-old female sunburns a large percentage of her body during a beach vacation. She reports significant skin discomfort and pain with even light palpation. Blisters have formed on her upper chest and forearms due to the extent of the sun damage. She is a college student who resides in student housing.

Scenario Two

A 43-year-old-male is referred to physical therapy for wound management. During a motorcycle accident he sustained a deep partial-thickness burn to his posterior-medial ankle from the tailpipe. His gait is antalgic and the physical therapist observes both dorsiflexion and plantar flexion range of motion limitations at the ankle. The patient resides with his wife and two children and is employed as a lineman for a phone company.

GOLD

Complex Regional Pain Syndrome

DIAGNOSIS

What condition produces a patient's symptoms?

Complex regional pain syndrome is usually found in an extremity that has experienced some form of trauma. Symptoms result from a disturbance in the functioning of the sympathetic nervous system. The increase in sympathetic activity causes a release of norepinephrine in the periphery and subsequent vasoconstriction of blood vessels. This results in pain and an increase in sensitivity to peripheral stimulation.

An injury was most likely sustained to which structure?

Complex regional pain syndrome results from injured sensory nerve fibers at one somatic level that initiates sympathetic efferent activity that affects many segmental levels. The extremity of origin sustains injury as well as areas adjacent to the extremity.

INFERENCE

What is the most likely contributing factor in the development of this condition?

The exact etiology of complex regional pain syndrome is unknown, however, predisposing factors include trauma, surgery, CVA, TBI, repetitive motion disorders, and lower motor neuron and peripheral nerve injuries. While many cases of complex regional pain syndrome resolve, others progress and become a disabling disorder. Complex regional pain syndrome can affect all age groups, but is most likely found in the age group of 35-60 years, with females more likely to be affected by the condition than males.

CONFIRMATION

What is the most likely clinical presentation?

A patient with complex regional pain syndrome will experience intense, burning, and chronic pain in the affected extremity that will eventually spread proximally. Early in the syndrome, the degree of pain is greater than expected based on the amount of trauma that the tissue sustained. Edema, thermal changes, discoloration, stiffness, and dryness are seen during stage I (acute stage) of complex regional pain syndrome. Progression to stage II (dystrophic stage) is characterized by worsening and constant pain, continued edema, and trophic skin changes. X-rays may reveal bone loss, osteoporosis, and subchondral bone erosion in the affected extremity. Stage III (atrophic stage) is characterized by pain that continues to spread, hardened edema, decreased limb temperature, and atrophic changes to fingertips or toes. X-rays at this stage may reveal demineralization and ankylosis. Motor disorders such as tremor, spasms, and atrophy may also be present throughout each stage of complex regional pain syndrome.

What laboratory or imaging studies would confirm the diagnosis?

Imaging studies that can assist with the diagnosis of complex regional pain syndrome include x-rays, thermographic studies, a three-phase bone scan, and laser Doppler flowmetry.

What additional information should be obtained to confirm the diagnosis?

Complex regional pain syndrome is diagnosed primarily through a complete physical examination and a patient's complete medical history including a history and course of illness.

EXAMINATION

What history should be documented?

Important areas to explore include past medical history, medications, family history, current symptoms, current health status, social history and habits, occupation, leisure activities, and social support system.

What tests/measures are most appropriate?

Anthropometric characteristics: circumferential measurements of affected area or extremity

Arousal, attention, and cognition: examine mental status, learning ability, memory, motivation

Environmental, home, and work barriers: analysis of current and potential barriers or hazards

Gait, locomotion, and balance: static and dynamic balance in sitting and standing, safety during gait

Integumentary integrity: skin assessment, assessment of sensation, skin temperature changes

Joint integrity and mobility: assessment of hypermobility and hypomobility of a joint, soft tissue swelling

Motor function: motor assessment scales, assessment of sensorimotor integration, physical performance scales

Muscle performance: strength assessment, muscle tone assessment

Pain: pain perception scale, visual analogue scale, assessment of muscle soreness, McGill Pain Questionnaire

Reflex integrity: assessment of deep tendon and pathological reflexes

Posture: analysis of resting and dynamic posture

Range of motion: active and passive range of motion

Sensory integrity: assessment of proprioception and kinesthesia

Self-care and home management: assessment of functional capacity

Complex Regional Pain Syndrome

GOLD

What additional findings are likely with this patient?

Complex regional pain syndrome will affect a patient's function throughout the progression of this neurovascular syndrome. Complex regional pain syndrome may progress to the point of bone demineralization and joint ankylosis (seen in stage III). Muscle atrophy, contractures, spasms, and incoordination will also contribute to functional decline. Depression and anxiety are also frequently seen and require medical attention. Malingering for secondary gain has been documented in some cases and should be monitored by the rehabilitation team.

MANAGEMENT

What is the most effective management of this patient?

Complex regional pain syndrome requires prolonged medical management. Treatment is based on identifying the underlying cause and stage of complex regional pain syndrome at the time of diagnosis. Pharmacological intervention may include NSAIDs and corticosteroids for pain relief in early stages. Amitriptyline may be used for sleep and calcium channel blockers used for increasing peripheral circulation. Baclofen has been used as a long-term intervention to assist motor function. Bisphosphonate administration is warranted in later stages to combat bone loss. Surgical interventions such as sympathetic blocks or a sympathectomy are used to alleviate pain. Physical therapy intervention is a key component in the management of complex regional pain syndrome. Pain control, patient education, skin care, joint mobilization, desensitization, and functional activity training are vital to the program. Modalities, pool therapy, relaxation training, and a home program all assist a patient with management of this syndrome.

What home care regimen should be recommended?

A home program is vital to the management of complex regional pain syndrome. Stretching and ROM, light weight bearing activities, ice and/or heat, TENS, and light exercise for conditioning are all key components of a home program. The patient must be educated and encouraged to use the involved extremity as tolerated. Edema management using a pump or compression garments may be indicated. Functional activities must also be encouraged.

OUTCOME

What is the likely outcome of a course of physical therapy?

Overall prognosis is better for a patient that begins treatment early in the cycle of the disease process. Physical therapy attempts to break the pain cycle and allows for a patient to continue with functional activities. Outcome is also dependent on a patient's motivation to maintain all aspects of a home program.

What are the long-term effects of the patient's condition?

Complex regional pain syndrome can spontaneously resolve, continue with ongoing symptoms that can last for years or follow a pattern of remissions and recurring symptoms that develop from subsequent injuries. A patient's long-term outcome is dependent on how early the complex regional pain syndrome was detected and treated. Research indicates a better prognosis if treatment is initiated within the first six months of the disease process.

COMPARISON

What are the distinguishing characteristics of a similar condition?

Sympathetically maintained pain (SMP) is a pain syndrome that is maintained by sympathetic efferent activity and is caused by a partial peripheral nerve lesion. SMP occurs less than complex regional pain syndrome and is characterized by pain that is produced by a non-painful stimulus, vasomotor disturbances, and trophic changes. These symptoms remain localized to the affected nerve and the pain can usually be temporarily alleviated by sympathetic nerve block. Physical therapy intervention is warranted to assist with pain control through the use of modalities.

CLINICAL SCENARIOS

Scenario One

A 39-year-old female is seen in physical therapy with stage I (acute) complex regional pain syndrome. The patient complains of burning pain in her left arm and presents with mild edema. The patient injured her shoulder two months ago. Past medical history includes being diagnosed with fibromyalgia two years ago. She is a team manager for a photography company and works approximately 50 hours per week.

Scenario Two

A 62-year-old female is evaluated in physical therapy. She was diagnosed with complex regional pain syndrome 13 months ago. She complains of significant pain in her right lower extremity and cannot walk without a walker. She has both hip and knee flexion contractures and significant swelling of the affected lower extremity

GOLD

Diabetes Mellitus - Type 1

DIAGNOSIS

What condition produces a patient's symptoms?

Type 1 diabetes mellitus (DM) is a multi-system disease with both biochemical and anatomical consequences. There is persistent hyperglycemia due to diminished or absent production of insulin. In type 1 DM, insulin is functionally absent due to the destruction of the beta cells of the pancreas where the insulin would normally be produced.

An injury was most likely sustained to which structure?

Type 1 DM is characterized as an autoimmune disease in which circulating insulin is very low or absent, plasma glucose is elevated, and the pancreatic beta cells fail to respond to all insulin producing stimuli. The pancreas shows lymphocytic infiltration and destruction of insulin-secreting cells of the islets of Langerhans, causing insulin deficiency. Patients need exogenous insulin to reverse this catabolic condition, prevent ketosis, decrease hyperglycemia, and normalize lipid and protein metabolism.

INFERENCE

What is the most likely contributing factor in the development of this condition?

The exact etiology of type 1 DM is unknown, however, there are several theories. It is an autoimmune process with a strong genetic component. It is also believed that the genetic predisposition in combination with an unknown factor, potentially environmental, triggers the ongoing cycle of destruction of the beta cells of the pancreas.

CONFIRMATION

What is the most likely clinical presentation?

Type 1 DM usually starts in children ages 4 years or older, with the peak incidence of onset at 11-13 years of age, coinciding with early adolescence and puberty. Also, a relatively high incidence exists in people in their late 30s and early 40s, when it tends to present in a less aggressive manner. The most common symptoms of type 1 DM are polyuria, polydipsia, and polyphagia, along with nausea, weight loss, fatigue, blurred vision, and dehydration. A fasting glucose reading of 126 mg/dl is also a sign of DM. The disease onset is usually sudden or within a short period of time. It is not unusual for type 1 DM to present with ketoacidosis.

What laboratory or imaging studies would confirm the diagnosis?

A test of blood glucose levels will be necessary. In asymptomatic patients, physicians use the American Diabetes Association (ADA) recommendation of two different fasting plasma glucose levels of greater than 125 mg/dl. In symptomatic patients, a random glucose of 200 mg/dl suggests DM. Other testing includes urinalysis for glucose, ketones, and protein and a white blood cell count as well as blood and urine cultures to rule out infection.

What additional information should be obtained to confirm the diagnosis?

A detailed history and exam should provide the physician with confirmation of the previously mentioned symptoms that present with type 1 DM. Diagnosis is based on one of the subsequent factors: fasting glucose levels, two-hour post-load glucose levels or symptoms of DM.

EXAMINATION

What history should be documented?

Important areas to explore include past medical history, medications, current health status, history of incontinence, recent polyuria, polydipsia, nocturia or weight loss, nutritional status, social history and habits, occupation, living environment, and social support system.

What tests/measures are most appropriate?

Arousal, attention, and cognition: examine mental status, learning ability, memory, motivation

Community and work integration: analysis of community, work, and leisure activities

Environmental, home, and work barriers: analysis of current and potential barriers or hazards

Gait, locomotion, and balance: static and dynamic balance in sitting and standing, safety during gait

Integumentary integrity: skin assessment, assessment of sensation

Motor function: equilibrium and righting reactions, coordination, posture and balance in sitting

Muscle performance: strength assessment, muscle tone assessment

Posture: analysis of resting and dynamic posture

Range of motion: active and passive range of motion

Self-care and home management: assessment of functional capacity, Functional Independence Measure

Diabetes Mellitus - Type 1

GOLD

What additional findings are likely with this patient?

Complications of type 1 DM include hypoglycemia and hyperglycemia, diabetic ketoacidosis, increased risk of infections, cardiovascular and peripheral vascular disease, retinopathy, nephropathy, impotence, and acceleration of atherosclerosis. DM is the major cause of blindness in adults aged 20-74 years, as well as the leading cause of non-traumatic lower extremity amputation and end-stage renal disease.

MANAGEMENT

What is the most effective management of this patient?

Patients with type 1 DM require insulin therapy to control initial hyperglycemia and maintain serum electrolytes and hydration. At times, the first incidence of ketoacidosis is followed by a symptom-free period where patients do not need treatment. Pharmacological intervention includes the use of exogenous insulin per physician orders. Type 1 DM typically requires insulin delivery subcutaneously via continuous pump or self-administered injection. Supplemental insulin may also be delivered by oral or nasal route. Medical management should also include regular self-monitoring of blood glucose levels through finger stick samples and urine testing. Patient education and counseling is appropriate for nutritional components, weight loss if obese, the disease process, complications, medications, and long-term effects. Physical therapy may be indicated for a home exercise program and the patient may be seen intermittently for change and update of their program. Exercise is an important aspect in management of DM. Patients should be taught general exercise and strengthening, stretching, and self-monitoring of their cardiac status. The therapist should coordinate exercise sessions around the patient's meal schedule in order to avoid hypoglycemia and optimize exercise tolerance. Patients should exercise at 50-60% of their predicted maximum heart rate unless directed by a physician otherwise.

What home care regimen should be recommended?

A patient with type 1 DM requires a good nutritional program, regular self-monitoring of blood glucose levels, and adequate and consistent daily exercise.

OUTCOME

What is the likely outcome of a course of physical therapy?

Physical therapy may be indicated initially for a patient with goals of optimizing exercise endurance and implementing a home exercise program. Otherwise, patients are usually seen in physical therapy for co-morbidities or due to complications from DM. Physical therapy attempts to maximize patients' functional and health status, but cannot alter the disease process.

What are the long-term effects of the patient's condition?

Type 1 DM is associated with a high morbidity and premature mortality due to complications. As a result of these complications, people with diabetes have an increased risk of developing ischemic heart disease, cerebral vascular disease, peripheral vascular disease (that sometimes leads to amputation), chronic renal disease, reduced visual acuity and blindness, and autonomic and peripheral neuropathy.

COMPARISON

What are the distinguishing characteristics of a similar condition?

Type 2 DM is more common in the United States than type 1. Type 2 usually involves a defect in the insulin release sites within the pancreas or a resistance to the insulin due to impairment of the receptor sites in the peripheral tissues. In contrast to type 1, type 2 is usually diagnosed in a patient older than 40 years of age. This form of DM is significantly linked to a person's lifestyle, weight, and age. A patient with type 2 can present with the symptoms of type 1, but can also include paresthesias, visual changes, recurrent infections, inadequate wound healing, and cold extremities. In most cases, oral hypoglycemics are used instead of insulin injections.

CLINICAL SCENARIOS

Scenario One

A three-year-old girl is seen in physical therapy that has just been diagnosed with type 1 DM. She also has a greenstick fracture of the left tibia secondary to an auto accident, but otherwise is in good health. Her mother has stated that her blood sugar levels were not yet regulated and it has been difficult for the physician to find the correct amount and timing of insulin.

Scenario Two

A 35-year-old male was just diagnosed with type 1 DM after he visited his physician for a routine check-up. He did note polyuria, polydipsia, and visual changes over the last six months. He is referred to physical therapy for a home exercise program. The physician also recommended a nutritional consult as the patient is approximately 40 pounds overweight.

GOLD

Diabetes Mellitus - Type 2

DIAGNOSIS

What condition produces a patient's symptoms?

Type 2 diabetes mellitus (DM) is a chronic disease with biochemical and anatomical consequences. Normally, insulin facilitates the absorption of glucose from the bloodstream into liver, fat, and muscle cells where it may be used immediately or stored for energy. Type 2 DM is characterized by an inappropriate cellular response to insulin, preventing adequate absorption of blood glucose. Excess blood glucose results in a persistent hyperglycemic state.

An injury was most likely sustained to which structure?

Type 2 DM is characterized by an alteration in the metabolism of glucose. This is typically due to either an inadequate supply or cellular resistance to insulin. Excess body fat interferes with the body's ability to metabolize insulin correctly and is often a key characteristic of type 2 DM. Decreased insulin production and the insulin resistance that may accompany it, may result from factors including stress, advanced age, sedentary lifestyle, comorbidities, and certain prescribed medications.

INFERENCE

What is the most likely contributing factor in the development of this condition?

Patients with a family history of type 2 DM, who are over 45 years of age or who are of African, Asian, Hispanic or American Indian descent are at increased risk for developing type 2 DM. Patients who are overweight, sedentary, pre-diabetic or had gestational diabetes are also at increased risk.

CONFIRMATION

What is the most likely clinical presentation?

Type 2 DM may develop slowly over time prior to manifestation of initial symptoms. Common symptoms include polydipsia, polyuria, blurred vision, delayed healing and frequent infections. Type 2 DM was formerly referred to as "adult-onset diabetes mellitus," however, there has been a statistically significant rise in the incidence of type 2 DM in patients between 10 and 19 years of age in recent decades. This is largely attributed to increasingly sedentary habits among adolescents and epidemic childhood obesity.

What laboratory or imaging studies would confirm the diagnosis?

A diagnosis of type 2 DM is based on blood glucose measures. The glycated hemoglobin (A1C) test measures the average blood glucose level over a two to three month period and is typically used to confirm the diagnosis. A random blood glucose measure of 200 mg/dL or higher is suggestive of DM. Fasting blood glucose measures greater than 125 mg/dL on two separate tests is considered to be indicative of DM. The rate of blood glucose metabolism may be more specifically assessed with an oral glucose tolerance test.

What additional information should be obtained to confirm the diagnosis?

A thorough history and examination should be performed to confirm relevant risk factors and rule out similar diagnoses.

EXAMINATION

What history should be documented?

Important areas to explore include past medical history, medications, current health status, history of incontinence, recent polyuria, polydipsia, nocturia, nutritional status, social history and habits, occupation, living environment, and social support system.

What tests/measures are most appropriate?

Arousal, attention, and cognition: examine mental status, learning ability, memory, motivation

Community and work integration: analysis of community, work, and leisure activities

Environmental, home, and work barriers: analysis of current and potential barriers or hazards

Gait, locomotion, and balance: static and dynamic balance in sitting and standing, safety during gait

Integumentary integrity: skin assessment, assessment of sensation

Motor function: equilibrium and righting reactions, coordination, posture and balance in sitting

Muscle performance: strength assessment, muscle tone assessment

Posture: analysis of resting and dynamic posture

Range of motion: active and passive range of motion

Self-care and home management: assessment of functional capacity, Functional Independence Measure

What additional findings are likely with this patient?

Complications of type 2 DM include hypoglycemia and hyperglycemia, increased risk of infections, cardiovascular and peripheral vascular disease, retinopathy, nephropathy, impotence, and acceleration of atherosclerosis. DM is the major cause of blindness in adults aged 20-74 years, as well as the leading cause of nontraumatic lower extremity amputation and end-stage renal disease.

MANAGEMENT

What is the most effective management of this patient?

Medical management is typically focused on lifestyle changes and pharmaceutical intervention. Patient education and counseling are appropriate to address the disease process, nutrition, and long-term effects. Many patients are able to manage type 2 DM through lifestyle changes that impact modifiable risk factors. Increased physical activity increases insulin sensitivity, assisting cells to better absorb and utilize blood glucose as an appropriate source of energy. Stress management is also an important focus as prolonged stress can impact the body's ability to properly produce and metabolize insulin. Various oral or injectable pharmacological agents may be prescribed depending on individual factors. Patients should be instructed in general exercise, including strengthening and stretching activities. Education should address common signs and symptoms of hyperglycemia or hypoglycemia, foot care, susceptibility to infection, and the potential for delayed healing.

What home care regimen should be recommended?

A home care regimen should emphasize management of modifiable risk factors including nutrition, exercise, stress management, and self-monitoring for complications such as neuropathy, hyperglycemia, and hypoglycemia.

OUTCOME

What is the likely outcome of a course of physical therapy?

Physical therapy may be indicated initially to assist patients in optimizing outcomes relating to weight management, increasing activity levels, and stress management goals. Physical therapy should maximize function and support management of the condition. More commonly, patients are treated for comorbidities or complications that result from poor management of type 2 DM.

What are the long-term effects of the patient's condition?

In the United States, DM is the leading cause of kidney failure, new cases of blindness, and non-traumatic lower extremity amputation in adults. Type 2 DM accounts for greater than 90% of all DM cases diagnosed and is one of the conditions included in the diagnostic criteria for metabolic syndrome. Patients with type 2 DM are at an increased risk of developing numerous systemic comorbidities such as neuropathy, kidney damage, osteoporosis, and cardiac and vessel disease.

COMPARISON

What are the distinguishing characteristics of a similar condition?

Type 1 DM is less common in the United States than type 2. Type 1 is caused by a diminished or absent production of insulin due to destruction of the beta cells within the pancreas. In contrast to type 2, type 1 is typically diagnosed in adolescence, though some patients are diagnosed in adulthood (i.e., 30s to 40s). Though the exact etiology is unknown, it is thought to be an autoimmune condition that has both genetic and environmental influences. Signs and symptoms between the two conditions are similar, though a patient with type 1 DM is far more likely to experience diabetic ketoacidosis. Because patients with type 1 DM do not produce insulin, they require exogenous insulin, which is usually administered via self-injections.

CLINICAL SCENARIOS

Scenario One

A 65-year-old male with type 2 DM is being seen in physical therapy for balance training. Examination reveals that the patient has decreased protective sensation on the plantar surface of both feet and an inability to maintain static stance with his eyes closed. The patient's gait is slow and cautious and characterized by decreased step length.

Scenario Two

A 70-year-old female with type 2 DM is being seen in physical therapy for gait training with a new prosthesis. The patient had a transtibial amputation ten weeks ago and is just beginning to ambulate with a single point cane. The patient admits that they are not compliant with taking their medications or controlling their blood glucose levels.

GOLD

Fibromyalgia Syndrome

DIAGNOSIS

What condition produces a patient's symptoms?

Fibromyalgia syndrome (FMS) is classified as a rheumatology syndrome or a nonarticular rheumatic condition. Pain is the primary symptom caused by tender points within muscles, tendons, and ligaments.

An injury was most likely sustained to which structure?

The exact etiology of FMS is unknown. Theories suggest potential biochemical, metabolic or immunologic pathology. Researchers believe it to be multifactorial in origin and suggest a link to a dysfunction within the stress system, autonomic nervous system, immune system and/or reproductive and hormone systems.

INFERENCE

What is the most likely contributing factor in the development of this condition?

Since the exact etiology of FMS is unknown there is speculation linking many factors to the development of this condition. Factors include diet, sleep disorders, viral infections, psychological distress, occupational and environmental factors, hypothyroidism, trauma, and potential hereditary links. Many individuals diagnosed with FMS note multiple causative factors, however, there are individuals diagnosed with FMS that possess none of the theorized causative factors.

CONFIRMATION

What is the most likely clinical presentation?

FMS has a greater incidence in females and can affect any age, but most frequently is diagnosed between 14 and 68 years of age. FMS is diagnosed when a patient exhibits the criteria authored by the American College of Rheumatology. There is a widespread history of pain that exists in all four quadrants of the body (above and below the waist). The patient may also complain of fatigue, memory and visual impairment, sleep disturbances, irritable bowel syndrome, headaches, and anxiety/depression.

What laboratory or imaging studies would confirm the diagnosis?

FMS has been commonly misdiagnosed as myofascial pain, systemic lupus erythematosus, fibrositis, and chronic fatigue syndrome. There are no specific tests used to diagnose FMS. Radiographs are negative and blood work often appears normal except for a possible alteration in the levels of substance P. This substance is a chemical involved with pain transmission. Image studies and other lab testing are performed only for differential diagnosis.

What additional information should be obtained to confirm the diagnosis?

FMS is diagnosed according to the criteria from the American College of Rheumatology. A dolorimeter is used for reliability when testing the tender points by providing a consistent pressure (4 kg/cm^2). If the patient meets the criteria and has experienced symptoms for greater than three months, then a patient may be diagnosed with FMS. Diagnostic written tools that can assist with diagnosis include the Beck Depression Inventory and the Fibromyalgia Impact Questionnaire.

EXAMINATION

What history should be documented?

Important areas to explore include past medical history, medications, family history, current symptoms, current health status, social history and habits, occupation, leisure activities, and social support system.

What tests/measures are most appropriate?

Aerobic capacity and endurance: assessment of vital signs at rest and with activity, perceived exertion scale, pulse oximetry, auscultation of the lungs

Arousal, attention, and cognition: examine mental status, learning ability, memory, motivation

Community and work integration: analysis of community, work, and leisure activities

Environmental, home, and work barriers: analysis of current and potential barriers or hazards

Ergonomics and body mechanics: analysis of dexterity and coordination

Gait, locomotion, and balance: static and dynamic balance in sitting and standing, safety during gait

Integumentary integrity: skin assessment, assessment of sensation

Joint integrity and mobility: assessment of hypermobility and hypomobility of a joint, effusion, edema

Muscle performance: strength assessment, muscle tone assessment

Neuromotor development and sensory integration: analysis of reflex movement patterns, assessment of involuntary movements, sensory integration tests, gross and fine motor skills

Pain: pain perception assessment scale, visual analogue scale, assessment of muscle soreness and tender points

Posture: analysis of resting and dynamic posture

Range of motion: active and passive range of motion

Self-care and home management: assessment of functional capacity

What additional findings are likely with this patient?

The aforementioned symptoms can progress over time. Certain symptoms intensify and cause the patient to lose functional independence secondary to increased pain, decreased range of motion, and severe fatigue.

MANAGEMENT

What is the most effective management of this patient?

FMS is best treated with a multidisciplinary approach including education, medical management, and exercise. Medical management will attempt to normalize various dysfunctions of the autonomic nervous system, hormonal imbalances, and metabolic abnormalities. Physicians must address sleep disorders (which can be common) and pharmacological intervention based on symptoms. Psychotherapy may be warranted for anxiety or depression and must incorporate stress management and coping strategies into the plan of care. Physical therapy intervention may include relaxation techniques, energy conservation, gentle stretching, moist heat, ultrasound, posture and body mechanics, biofeedback, and exercise to tolerance. Aquatic therapy is recommended to improve a patient's fitness level and an ergonomic evaluation should be performed at the patient's work place. This population should not work through pain. They require short exercise sessions initially (three to five minutes) due to a low tolerance for exertion.

What home care regimen should be recommended?

A home care regimen should include short duration exercise, aquatic therapy (if indicated), energy conservation strategies, the use of proper positioning, proper body mechanics, and gentle stretching. Patient education is the key to success. Exercises that strain muscles such as weight lifting should be avoided. A comprehensive plan should also include lifestyle management, nutritional support, and stress management.

OUTCOME

What is the likely outcome of a course of physical therapy?

A patient with FMS may benefit from multidisciplinary intervention. Patient compliance with a home program increases the overall success rate. In many cases, symptoms can remain unchanged even with intervention and patient compliance. Some patients will report improvement in areas of fatigue, sleep, and self-reported pain.

What are the long-term effects of the patient's condition?

FMS is presently not "curable." Many patients that have mild symptoms do not require multidisciplinary intervention and have a good long-term outcome. The majority of patients diagnosed with FMS exhibit moderate levels of symptoms and usually continue to experience these symptoms for years or even their entire lifetime.

COMPARISON

What are the distinguishing characteristics of a similar condition?

Myofascial pain syndrome (MPS) is often misdiagnosed for FMS. MPS is characterized by trigger points rather than tender points and lacks associated symptoms. MPS is a localized musculoskeletal condition that is specific to a muscle. FMS, on the other hand, is a systemic condition. MPS is usually caused by overuse, reduced muscle activity or repetitive motions.

CLINICAL SCENARIOS

Scenario One

A 32-year-old female recently diagnosed with FMS is seen in physical therapy. Her chief complaints are fatigue, pain throughout her body, and difficulty with sleeping which has affected her employment as a mail carrier. She has been on disability for the last six months and under a physician's care for depression.

Scenario Two

A 45-year-old construction worker is referred to physical therapy with diagnosis of FMS. His history reveals mild symptoms for the last year. He has seen specialists and was diagnosed last week by a rheumatologist. He exhibits tender points throughout his body and denies any sleep disturbances or other medical history. He is currently working and appears motivated for therapy.

Human Immunodeficiency Virus

DIAGNOSIS

What condition produces a patient's symptoms?

The human immunodeficiency virus (HIV) is a retrovirus that initially invades and destroys cells within the immune system, specifically CD4+ T-lymphocytes (T-cells). This virus also affects monocytes, macrophages, and B-cells. Once the T-cells decrease beyond a specific level a patient will begin to demonstrate symptoms of the HIV infection.

An injury was most likely sustained to which structure?

HIV infects T-cells within the immune system. Other cells that eventually house HIV include monocytes, macrophages, microglia, cervical cells, and epithelial cells of the GI tract. HIV uses and destroys the cells that possess the antigen CD4 on their surface in order to replicate HIV, and as a result the immune system becomes weaker and unable to function.

INFERENCE

What is the most likely contributing factor in the development of this condition?

HIV is transmitted through contact with blood, semen, vaginal secretions, and breast milk. Contact can be sexual, perinatal or through contact with blood or body fluids that carry infected cells. Risk factors for contracting HIV include unprotected sexual relations, intravenous drug use or mother to fetus transmission. The largest risk factor for HIV transmission is unprotected sex.

CONFIRMATION

What is the most likely clinical presentation?

Without treatment, HIV advances in three stages: Acute HIV infection, Clinical Latency/Asymptomatic HIV, and AIDS. Stage 1: Acute HIV infection: This stage occurs 2-4 weeks after initial transmission. Patients can range from being asymptomatic to experiencing severe flu-like symptoms including fever, rash, myalgia, arthralgia, and headaches. During this stage, large amounts of the virus are being produced, CD4 cells fall rapidly, and the patient is at the highest risk of transmitting the virus to others. Stage 2: Clinical latency/Asymptomatic HIV/Chronic HIV infection: Patients on antiretroviral therapy (ART) can live with clinical latency for several decades as the treatment keeps the virus in check. Clinical latency for people not taking ART typically lasts 10 years before progressing to AIDS. Stage 3: AIDS: When the number of CD4 cells falls below 200 cells/mm^3 and the person has other AIDS-defining illnesses, a person is considered to have progressed to AIDS. Without treatment, people typically survive with AIDS about 3 years. Once a person has an opportunistic illness, life expectancy without treatment falls to about 1 year. Manifestations of HIV may lead to other infections, malignancies, neurological dysfunction, cognitive decline, and cardiopulmonary pathologies.

What laboratory or imaging studies would confirm the diagnosis?

HIV is diagnosed through various blood tests such as the enzyme-linked immunosorbent test or Western blot test. Once diagnosed the lab results can also assist with classifying the stage of HIV infection.

What additional information should be obtained to confirm the diagnosis?

Definitive diagnosis is made through blood tests, however, the physician should ascertain accurate medical and social history. Accurate drug use and sexual partner history will allow for appropriate patient education in order to cease the spread of the virus. A positive diagnosis will allow the patient to notify others at risk.

EXAMINATION

What history should be documented?

Important areas to explore include past medical history–especially antiretroviral therapy (ART), medications, family history, current symptoms, current health status, social history and habits, occupation, leisure activities, and social support system.

What tests/measures are most appropriate?

Aerobic capacity and endurance: assessment of vital signs, perceived exertion scale, auscultation of the lungs

Arousal, attention, and cognition: examine mental status, learning ability, memory, and level of motivation

Community and work integration: analysis of community, work, and leisure activities

Environmental, home, and work barriers: analysis of current and potential barriers or hazards

Gait, locomotion, and balance: static and dynamic balance in sitting and standing, safety during gait with/without an assistive device, Tinetti Performance Oriented Mobility Assessment, analysis of wheelchair management

Integumentary integrity: skin assessment and sensation assessment

Motor function: equilibrium and righting reactions, motor assessment scales, coordination, posture and balance in sitting, assessment of sensorimotor integration, physical performance scales

Muscle performance: strength assessment, muscle tone assessment

Pain: pain perception assessment scale

Range of motion: active and passive range of motion

Reflex integrity: assessment of deep tendon and pathological reflexes (e.g., Babinski, ATNR)

Self-care and home management: assessment of functional capacity

Ventilation, respiration, and circulation: pulmonary function testing, breathing patterns, perceived exertion scale, assessment of cough

What additional findings are likely with this patient?

The Centers for Disease Control classifies HIV into three categories based on the T-cell count. Symptoms and secondary illnesses occur as the T-cell count decreases. The onset of AIDS occurs when the T-cell count falls below 200 cells per mm^3 (normal ranges 500-1,200 cells) or when one of 26 specific AIDS defining disorders is present or both. A patient may experience musculoskeletal, neuromuscular, cardiopulmonary, integumentary, and other impairments secondary to HIV.

MANAGEMENT

What is the most effective management of this patient?

Early detection is important so that pharmacological intervention can be initiated and slow the progression of the virus. There is no cure for HIV, however, proper medical intervention can allow the virus to remain a manageable chronic condition. With proper medical management, people living with HIV have equal life expectancies as their HIV-negative counterparts. Current guidelines recommend antiretroviral therapy for all HIV-infected individuals, regardless of CD4 count, to reduce HIV-related morbidity and mortality. Medical management will institute antiretroviral therapy (HAART) when T-cells drop below 500 mm^3. The goal of drug therapy is to significantly decrease the virus' ability to replicate, and therefore decrease the progression of the disease. Drugs may include nucleoside analogs, protease inhibitors, and non-nucleoside reverse transcriptase inhibitors. Physical therapy intervention may be indicated during the course of HIV/AIDS due to secondary impairments. Physical therapy goals and intervention include the promotion of optimal fitness, flexibility, energy conservation, stress management, ADL equipment, relaxation, aquatic therapy, modalities, positioning, pain management, breathing exercises, and neurological rehabilitation.

What home care regimen should be recommended?

A patient with HIV must follow a home regimen including medication, proper nutrition and sleep, and fitness in order to remain as healthy as possible. A physical therapy home program can also minimize the negative effects on functional ability and improve the overall independence and quality of life.

OUTCOME

What is the likely outcome of a course of physical therapy?

Physical therapy may be warranted for periods of time throughout the progression of HIV/AIDS. Physical therapy cannot alter the progression of the virus, but can foster improvement in functional mobility, conditioning, and overall independence.

What are the long-term effects of the patient's condition?

Studies indicate that psychosocial factors influence progression of the virus as well as survival. Presently, the leading causes of death, in order of prevalence, are AIDS-related (i.e., opportunistic infections), non-AIDS-defining cancers, liver disease, and cardiovascular disease.

COMPARISON

What are the distinguishing characteristics of a similar condition?

Hepatitis B (HBV) is a form of viral hepatitis that produces inflammation and damage to the liver. Like HIV, hepatitis B is transmitted parenterally through intravenous drug use, sexual relations, blood transfusions, perinatal transmission or dialysis. A vaccine is available for prevention and blood tests are used for diagnosis. Almost all of those infected with HBV will fully recover, however, a small proportion of these individuals become carriers. Some of the carriers develop chronic liver disease and may die prematurely.

CLINICAL SCENARIOS

Scenario One

A 19-year-old female is seen in outpatient physical therapy secondary to weakness and balance impairments. She was diagnosed with HIV two years ago, but the physician believes that she was infected at least one to two years prior to diagnosis by IV drug use. Her T-cell count is 404 mm^3 using HIV drug therapies.

Scenario Two

A 58-year-old male was diagnosed with AIDS one year ago and has lost significant weight. He presents with general muscle atrophy and is having difficulty with ambulation and ADLs. The patient is referred to physical therapy for adaptive and assistive devices. He lives with his spouse in a ranch style home and is on medical disability.

GOLD

Juvenile Rheumatoid Arthritis

DIAGNOSIS

What condition produces a patient's symptoms?

Juvenile rheumatoid arthritis (JRA) is a form of arthritis found in children less than 16 years of age. JRA causes inflammation and stiffness to multiple joints for a period of greater than six weeks. The inflammatory process affects the tissues surrounding the affected synovial joints causing symptoms of JRA.

An injury was most likely sustained to which structure?

JRA, like adult rheumatoid arthritis, is an autoimmune disorder that occurs when the immune cells mistakenly begin to attack the joints and organs causing local and systemic effects throughout the body. The severity of ongoing injury is based on the specific classification and subtype of the disease.

INFERENCE

What is the most likely contributing factor in the development of this condition?

The etiology for JRA is currently unknown. Research postulates that JRA develops in children with a genetic predisposition for the disease. The predisposition may be triggered by environmental factors or a viral or bacterial infection. Girls have a higher incidence of JRA and it is found to begin most commonly in the toddler or adolescent.

CONFIRMATION

What is the most likely clinical presentation?

JRA is an umbrella term for three specific classifications and subtypes of childhood arthritis. Classification is based on the number of joints involved, symptoms, presence of the rheumatoid factor (RF) or antinuclear antibody (ANA), and systemic involvement. General symptoms include persistent joint swelling, pain, and stiffness. Pauciarticular JRA involves four or less joints, is asymmetric, and is usually a mild form of JRA. This is the most common form of JRA, with girls under eight most likely to develop this subtype. ANA can be found in some of these patients and correlates with eye disease. Polyarticular JRA involves more than four joints, is usually symmetrical, involves the joints of the hands and feet as well as larger joints, and has potential for severe destruction. This subtype is less common than pauciarticular JRA and children may have the IgM rheumatoid factor (RF) similar to adult RA. Systemic JRA is the least common of the cases and is otherwise known as Still's disease. Onset includes a high fever, chills, and a rash that may last for weeks, followed by severe myalgia and polyarthritis. This form presents with severe extraarticular manifestations including anemia, hepatosplenomegaly, lymphadenopathy, pericarditis, and myocarditis. Most children in this subtype are negative for RF or ANA antibodies.

What laboratory or imaging studies would confirm the diagnosis?

There is not a single test to identify the presence of JRA. Blood tests may include serum evaluation to measure inflammation and detect RF, ANA or HLA-B27 (human leukocyte antigen). Only a small percentage of patients with JRA possess RF or ANA. An erythrocyte sedimentation rate (ESR or "sed rate") may also indicate rheumatic disease. Other tests or procedures may be used to rule out other conditions such as Lyme disease, lupus, infection, and cancers.

What additional information should be obtained to confirm the diagnosis?

Diagnosis is made largely through physical examination, a patient's past and present medical status, and meeting the criteria set forth by the American Rheumatoid Association regarding the diagnosis and classification of JRA.

EXAMINATION

What history should be documented?

Important areas to explore include past medical history, medications, family history, current symptoms, current health status, social history and habits, leisure activities, and social support system.

What tests/measures are most appropriate?

Aerobic capacity and endurance: vital signs at rest and with activity, timed walk, aerobic endurance, VO_{2max}

Anthropometric characteristics: circumferential measurements of all affected joints

Arousal, attention, and cognition: examine mental status, learning ability, memory, motivation

Assistive and adaptive devices: analysis of components and safety of a device

Environmental and home barriers: analysis of current and potential barriers or hazards

Ergonomics and body mechanics: analysis of dexterity and coordination

Gait, locomotion, and balance: static/dynamic balance in sitting and standing, visual inspection of gait with and without shoes, timed walk, gait over level and unlevel surfaces, gait analysis with videography

Integumentary integrity: skin and sensation assessment

Joint integrity and mobility: active joint count, joint effusion, articular tenderness

Motor function: equilibrium and coordination

Muscle performance: break testing of isometric contractions, manometer method of strength testing, dynamic muscle strength using repetition maximum (only if pain free)

Neuromotor development and sensory integration: analysis of reflex movement patterns, assessment of involuntary movements, sensory integration tests, gross and fine motor skills

Orthotic, protective, and supportive devices: analysis of components and movement using a device

Pain: Pediatric Pain Questionnaire (PPQ), visual analogue scale
Posture: analysis of resting and dynamic posture, scoliosis screening
Range of motion: active/passive range of motion for extremities, active motion only for cervical spine, angular deformities and joint play assessments
Self-care and home management: Pediatric Evaluation of Disability Inventory (PEDI), Child Health Assessment Questionnaire (CHAQ), Juvenile Arthritis Functional Status Index (JASI)

What additional findings are likely with this patient?

Potential complications are dependent on the subtype of JRA and the presence (or absence) of RF or ANA. Joint swelling, stiffness, and pain are the most common symptoms. Eye inflammation and development of iritis/uveitis can be a significant complication. Some patients have periods of exacerbations and remissions while other patients' symptoms will persist.

MANAGEMENT

What is the most effective management of this patient?

A pediatric rheumatologist is ideal to direct a multidisciplinary team in the complex care of JRA. Primary goals of treatment are to maintain a high level of physical functioning and quality of life. Pharmacological intervention may include NSAIDS, immunosuppressive medications, disease-modifying antirheumatic drugs, and corticosteroids. Physical therapy intervention is a key component and should include range of motion, exercise, and pain control. Functional mobility, strengthening, endurance, and aerobic training will assist a patient in overall function. Range of motion exercises, modalities, splints and orthotics, patient/family education, and the integration of recreational activities should optimize the quality of life. Surgical intervention is sometimes warranted for severe contractures or irreversible joint destruction. Soft tissue release, supracondylar osteotomy, and arthroplasty are the most common surgical procedures.

What home care regimen should be recommended?

A home care regimen should provide an individualized exercise program. The program should be simple and take no more than 20 minutes to complete in order to optimize compliance. Swimming is also a beneficial activity for a child with JRA.

OUTCOME

What is the likely outcome of a course of physical therapy?

Physical therapy may be indicated periodically throughout a patient's childhood based on symptoms and complications. Ongoing education and revision of a home program is vital to promote patient compliance. Physical therapy outcome is variable depending on the severity of the patient's symptoms.

What are the long-term effects of the patient's condition?

Long-term effects of JRA are dependent on subtype, symptoms, and any complications encountered. Some patients "outgrow" JRA and are not affected as adults while others experience pain and other manifestations of the disease on a consistent and long-term basis.

COMPARISON

What are the distinguishing characteristics of a similar condition?

Infectious bacterial arthritis most often develops within a joint secondary to systemic corticosteroid use, trauma, HIV or alcohol/drug abuse. If treated immediately, long-term prognosis is good. If left uncontrolled, toxemia and septicemia can be fatal. Inflammation and pannus within the synovium erodes articular cartilage. There is an acute onset of swelling, tenderness, and loss of range of motion. A child will usually not bear weight through the involved joint.

CLINICAL SCENARIOS

Scenario One

A 12-year-old boy diagnosed with systemic JRA is seen in physical therapy two days status post soft tissue release of the bilateral heel cords. The patient primarily uses a wheelchair for mobility.

Scenario Two

A six-year-old girl is seen in physical therapy shortly after diagnosis of pauciarticular JRA two months ago. The patient's primary complaint is pain in the right ankle with any weight bearing activity. The patient enjoys playing outside and participates in soccer in the fall.

GOLD

Lymphedema Post-Mastectomy

DIAGNOSIS

What condition produces a patient's symptoms?

Lymphedema following a mastectomy is termed secondary lymphedema and is the result of damage to the lymphatic nodes and vessels during surgery. Excessive accumulation of lymph fluid within the soft tissues is caused by an excess load of lymph fluid or inadequate transport capacity within the lymphatic system secondary to the loss of homeostasis.

An injury was most likely sustained to which structure?

The lymphatic system is damaged as a result of the mastectomy, the surgical removal of the breast, whereby the lymph nodes and vessels are removed or damaged. The lymphatic system is unable to compensate, the lymph vessels dilate, and the valve flaps are not able to fully stop lymph flow. This allows for backflow of lymph into the tissues. This chain reaction causes further injury, chronic inflammation and progression including fibrosis, hypoxia within the tissues, and an increased risk of infection.

INFERENCE

What is the most likely contributing factor in the development of this condition?

The most likely contributing factor in the development of lymphedema following a mastectomy is the damage and/or removal of the axillary lymph nodes and vessels in an attempt to prevent the spread of breast cancer. If the lymphatic nodes have not been removed, but have received radiation they may stop functioning due to chronic inflammation, fibrosis, and scarring. Globally, the parasitic infection called filariasis is the most common cause of secondary lymphedema. Other causes include severe infection, crush injuries, burns or repeated pregnancies. For primary lymphedema, only a small percent of cases are present at birth, with the large majority of cases acquired from adolescence through midlife years. Females are affected more frequently than males.

CONFIRMATION

What is the most likely clinical presentation?

The clinical presentation of lymphedema includes edema in an affected area/extremity that increases with dependent positioning. The patient usually does not experience pain, but rather a tight or heavy sensation. Lymphedema is classified into three stages that present differently based on the severity of the condition. Stage I is characterized by pitting edema that reduces with elevation overnight and does not exhibit any fibrotic changes. Stage II is identified by some fibrotic changes that begin to occur and an increase in non-pitting edema that does not reduce with elevation. Stage III is characterized by skin changes, frequent infections, and severe edema that is non-pitting and fibrotic.

What laboratory or imaging studies would confirm the diagnosis?

Diagnosis is confirmed through history, observation, and several diagnostic tools to rule out other potential disorders. A Doppler study of the affected area is able to rule out a deep vein thrombosis. A CT scan or MRI may be performed before treatment of lymphedema is initiated to rule out malignancy. A lymphoscintigram is a nuclear medicine procedure that tests the function of the lymphatic system.

What additional information should be obtained to confirm the diagnosis?

A medical evaluation should include a thorough history including all illnesses, hospitalizations, and surgeries. History should be noted regarding the current edema and its course. Date of onset, progression, and symptoms associated with the edema are important to attain and note in the patient's record.

EXAMINATION

What history should be documented?

Important areas to explore include past medical history and surgical history, medications, history of swelling, family history, current symptoms, current health status, living environment, social history and habits, occupation, and social support system.

What tests/measures are most appropriate?

Aerobic capacity and endurance: assessment of vital signs at rest and with activity, perceived exertion scale, pulse oximetry, auscultation of the lungs

Anthropometric characteristics: circumferential and volumetric measurements of involved areas, skinfold measurements

Arousal, attention, and cognition: examine mental status, learning ability, memory, motivation

Community and work integration: analysis of community, work, and leisure activities

Environmental, home, and work barriers: analysis of current and potential barriers or hazards

Gait, locomotion, and balance: static and dynamic balance in sitting and standing, safety during gait with/without an assistive device

Integumentary integrity: skin assessment, assessment of sensation, nailbed assessment

Joint integrity and mobility: soft tissue swelling and inflammation

Muscle performance: strength and tone assessment

Pain: pain perception assessment scale

Range of motion: active and passive range of motion

Lymphedema Post-Mastectomy

GOLD

Self-care and home management: assessment of functional capacity
Ventilation, respiration, and circulation: assessment of brachial and radial pulses, capillary refill assessment

What additional findings are likely with this patient?

Additional findings are based on the etiology, stage, and progression of the lymphedema. Complications can include ulcer formation, increased risk for fungal and bacterial infections, loss of range, fatigue, and fibrotic edema with atrophic skin changes. If left untreated a patient could progress to stage III "lymphostatic elephantiasis."

MANAGEMENT

What is the most effective management of this patient?

Effective medical management of secondary lymphedema may involve pharmacological intervention or natural substances that increase proteolysis and macrophage activity, however, there is no particular class of drugs that can "cure" lymphedema. Surgery is used in the treatment of severe lymphedema, but only achieves limited results since the cause remains unchanged. Physical therapy intervention usually follows a treatment approach termed complete decongestive therapy (CDT). The philosophy of lymphatic management includes patient education in skin care, hygiene, bandaging, self-massage, and exercise. Therapeutic intervention should focus on manual lymph drainage, short stretch compression bandages, retrograde massage, and exercise.

What home care regimen should be recommended?

A home care regimen is vital to the success of the CDT treatment of lymphedema. A patient must understand and comply with skin care, bandaging, self-massage, lymphatic drainage techniques, compression therapy, and an exercise program. Each patient must also understand the lifetime precautions that can increase lymphedema such as sunburn, air travel, excessive exercise, poor nutrition, and obesity.

OUTCOME

What is the likely outcome of a course of physical therapy?

Comprehensive lymphedema intervention such as CDT has shown significant reduction in lymphedema during treatment and continued reduction with an ongoing home program over time.

What are the long-term effects of the patient's condition?

Lymphedema is progressive if left untreated, but can be managed through intervention and education. Patients must comply with a home program and must remain aware of all activities that place the patient at an increased risk for lymphedema.

COMPARISON

What are the distinguishing characteristics of a similar condition?

Lipedema is a condition where there appears to be swelling throughout the bilateral lower extremities from the hips to the ankle joints. This swelling is actually subcutaneous adipose tissue. This condition is sometimes confused with lymphedema, but does not affect the lymphatic system. It most often occurs in women with hormonal disorders and is believed to have a family history in some cases. Medical management treats the hormonal imbalance and assists with nutritional guidance to allow for effective weight management.

CLINICAL SCENARIOS

Scenario One

A 39-year-old female status post right mastectomy secondary to malignancy develops lymphedema in her right arm four months after surgery. She resides alone and is employed as a web design consultant. She complains of heaviness in the arm, but denies pain. She was referred by her oncologist for outpatient physical therapy.

Scenario Two

A 68-year-old male is seen in physical therapy with stage II lymphedema in his right lower extremity. He underwent total hip arthroplasty two months ago and experienced immediate swelling and discomfort. His history includes multiple abdominal surgeries with edema present after each surgery. He presents with non-pitting edema that does not reduce with elevation.

GOLD

Neuropathic Ulcer

DIAGNOSIS

What condition produces a patient's symptoms?

A neuropathic ulcer typically develops due to a combination of peripheral neuropathy, atherosclerotic changes, and pressure. Neuropathic ulcers occur most frequently in the diabetic population and are often referred to as diabetic ulcers. This form of ulcer may also develop in association with other peripheral neuropathy etiologies.

An injury was most likely sustained to which structure?

A neuropathic ulcer can affect various tissue structures based on the depth of injury. A superficial ulceration is associated with damage to the epidermis only. Damage from a partial-thickness ulceration will extend through the epidermis and possibly into, but not through the dermis. A full-thickness ulceration extends through the dermis and into deeper layers such as the subcutaneous fat layer. Damage from a subcutaneous ulcer extends through all layers of integumentary tissue typically exposing deeper tissue layers such as tendon, muscle or bone.

INFERENCE

What is the most likely contributing factor in the development of this condition?

Neuropathic ulcers are most prevalent among patients with diabetes mellitus. Peripheral neuropathy impacts both motor and sensory function which contributes to the development of neuropathic ulcers. Motor neuropathy, for example, may cause weakness of the intrinsic foot muscles allowing the forefoot to splay during weight bearing and altering the fit of footwear. Decreased coordination within the muscles of the lower leg, ankle, and foot further contributes to increased stress over bony prominences during weight bearing. The loss of protective sensation impairs the patient's ability to detect discomfort from these altered physical pressures and is often the most significant contributing factor to ulcer development.

CONFIRMATION

What is the most likely clinical presentation?

A patient will typically develop a neuropathic ulcer in the distal lower extremity. At-risk areas include those that are routinely subjected to pressure during normal weight bearing, atypical stresses due to structural changes or improper fitting footwear. Common sites include the heel, tips of prominent toes, tips of hammer toes, plantar surface of the metatarsal heads, dorsal aspect of hammer toes, and bunions. The wound typically presents with a well-defined oval or round shape surrounded by a rim of hypertrophic callus. The wound bed typically shows evidence of granular tissue with little evidence of necrosis. Exudate production is typically minimal. Pain complaints are minimal, however, dysesthesia may be reported. Surrounding intact skin tends to be shiny, dry, and inelastic. Distal pulses may be diminished or absent. Ankle-brachial index measures may be unreliable especially for patients with diabetes mellitus who are likely to develop vessel rigidity. The loss of protective sensation is a significant characteristic and should be well documented.

What laboratory or imaging studies would confirm the diagnosis?

A neuropathic ulcer is diagnosed primarily based on the physical characteristics of the ulcer and the diagnosis of underlying conditions. Laboratory blood analysis may be warranted to assist in identifying the etiology of the ulcer, ruling out infection, and identifying additional conditions which may impede wound healing. Imaging is typically utilized to determine vascular integrity, to rule out infection or to identify bony changes such as demineralization or deformity which may contribute to ulcer formation.

What additional information should be obtained to confirm the diagnosis?

A complete medical history should be obtained to assist in identifying conditions which may contribute to the development of an ulcer or impede ulcer healing. Both the ulcer and general condition of the extremities should be thoroughly examined. Testing to determine the extent of the peripheral neuropathy and potential vascular insufficiency should also be performed.

EXAMINATION

What history should be documented?

Important areas to explore include past medical history, medications, family history, current symptoms, current health status, social history and habits, occupation, leisure activities, and social support system.

What tests/measures are most appropriate?

Anthropometric characteristics: circumferential measurements

Arousal, attention, and cognition: mental status, learning ability, memory, motivation, and level of consciousness

Assistive and adaptive devices: analysis of components and safety of a device

Gait, locomotion, and balance: static and dynamic balance in sitting and standing, safety during gait with/without an assistive device

Integumentary integrity: skin assessment, assessment of sensation, Wagner Ulcer Grade Classification Scale, assessment of wound characteristics, exudate, surrounding skin, photo documentation

Joint integrity and mobility: assessment of hypermobility and hypomobility of a joint, swelling and inflammation

Muscle performance: strength assessment, muscle tone assessment, signs of muscle atrophy

Orthotic, prosthetic, and supportive devices: analysis of components of a device, analysis of movement while wearing a device

Pain: pain perception assessment scale, visual analogue scale

Range of motion: active and passive range of motion
Reflex integrity: assessment of deep tendon and pathological reflexes (e.g., Babinski, ATNR)
Self-care and home management: assessment of functional capacity
Sensory integrity: assessment of proprioception and kinesthesia, Semmes-Weinstein monofilament testing
Ventilation, respiration, and circulation: pulse oximetry, palpation of pulses, ankle-brachial index, capillary refill

What additional findings are likely with this patient?

Neuropathic ulcer staging is based on the extent of soft tissue and osseous involvement. Neuropathic ulcers which extend to bony surfaces are associated with a high risk of osteomyelitis. Physical examination is likely to reveal numerous abnormalities associated with peripheral neuropathy and arterial changes. Neuropathic ulcers are often slow to heal due to the systemic impact of the associated underlying conditions.

MANAGEMENT

What is the most effective management of this patient?

Medical management typically emphasizes management of contributing factors (e.g., blood glucose, hypertension, hyperlipidemia, obesity, atherosclerosis, renal insufficiency) through lifestyle modifications (e.g., dietary changes, stress management) and pharmaceutical intervention. Pharmaceutical interventions specifically directed toward wound management may include the use of platelet-derived growth factors (PDGF) or, in the presence of infection, antimicrobial or antibiotic agents. Activity restrictions, total contact casting or specialized footwear may be indicated to protect the extremity as the wound heals. Surgical management may include debridement for wounds with heavy necrosis, grafting for non-healing wounds, stabilization or revision of bony structures to reduce pressure points, and restoration of vascular integrity. Physical therapy management emphasizes skin protection through footwear assessment, moisturizers, skin inspection, and wound healing interventions. The ulcer may require cleansing agents and/or debridement (enzymatic, autolytic, mechanical non-selective or sharp) and should be closely monitored for signs of infection. Deep wounds or those with significant tunneling or tracts may specifically benefit from debridement by means of pulsatile lavage and packing may be indicated as a part of the dressing application. Neuropathic ulcers do not typically produce significant volumes of exudate, therefore, if a neuropathic ulcer begins to produce significant volumes of exudate, infection should be ruled out. If an infection is confirmed, the use of dressings impregnated with antimicrobial or antibiotic agents (e.g., silver or iodine) may be indicated. Dressings should be selected to appropriately manage the increased exudate and prevent maceration of adjacent tissue. For more severe wounds, healing interventions may also include vacuum-assisted closure or hyperbaric oxygen treatment. Photo documentation is recommended to supplement written documentation describing wound characteristics.

What home care regimen should be recommended?

The home care regimen is dependent on the size and characteristics of the neuropathic ulcer. Many patients who do not require debridement may appropriately manage routine dressing changes at home. All patients should be diligent with skin hygiene, protection, and inspection to limit the risk of infection and the formation of additional wounds.

OUTCOME

What is the likely outcome of a course of physical therapy?

A neuropathic ulcer will typically heal by secondary intention with appropriate wound healing interventions and the absence of complications (e.g., infection, severe arterial insufficiency). Patients will not typically experience residual deficits from the wound itself, but may have increased morbidity and mortality risks associated with the underlying pathology.

What are the long-term effects of the patient's condition?

Treatment of a neuropathic ulcer and the underlying pathology should allow for a normal course of recovery without residual deficits. Complicated wounds may require additional orthotic, pharmacological, medical or surgical intervention.

COMPARISON

What are the distinguishing characteristics of a similar condition?

A pressure ulcer results from ischemia that is caused by unrelieved tissue pressure. Pressure ulcers typically occur over bony prominences that are likely to be subjected to sustained pressure such as the sacrum or heels. Pressure ulcers are staged based on the depth of tissue damage and may vary widely in their general characteristics.

CLINICAL SCENARIOS

Scenario One

A 44-year-old male with peripheral neuropathy develops a neuropathic ulcer on the plantar surface of the third metatarsal head. The patient is a postal carrier and resides alone. He attempted to manage the wound, however, examination reveals visible bone at the base of the wound bed and moderate production of purulent exudate.

Scenario Two

A 63-year-old patient was diagnosed with type 1 diabetes mellitus as an adolescent. The patient has an extensive history of non-compliance resulting in visual deficits, Charcot foot deformity, and a neuropathic ulcer on the plantar surface of the midfoot. The patient resides alone in an apartment building with an elevator.

GOLD

Osteoporosis

DIAGNOSIS

What condition produces a patient's symptoms?

Osteoporosis is a metabolic bone disorder where the rate of bone resorption accelerates while the rate of bone formation slows down; osteoclast activity exceeds osteoblast activity. This reduction of bone mass decreases the overall bone density and strength. Primary osteoporosis includes classifications such as idiopathic osteoporosis, involutional (senile) osteoporosis, and postmenopausal osteoporosis. Secondary osteoporosis occurs due to a primary disease process or as a result of taking certain medications.

An injury was most likely sustained to which structure?

Osteoporosis primarily affects trabecular bone in a postmenopausal patient, however, is primarily seen in both trabecular and cortical bone in the geriatric population. Impaired bone formation due to declining osteoblast function in addition to the loss of calcium and phosphate salts within the bone structure cause brittle and porous bones that easily fracture. All bones can be affected with fractures of the vertebrae, distal radius/ulna, and femoral neck being the most common.

INFERENCE

What is the most likely contributing factor in the development of this condition?

The exact cause of primary osteoporosis is unknown, however, risk factors include inadequate dietary calcium, smoking, excessive caffeine, high intake of alcohol or salt, small stature, Caucasian race, inactive lifestyle, family history or history of chronic disease. Secondary osteoporosis may be caused by prolonged drug therapies of heparin or corticosteroid use, endocrine disorders, malnutrition, and other disease processes. Postmenopausal osteoporosis targets women approximately 50-60 years of age. Involutional (senile) osteoporosis usually targets men and women >70 years of age. Idiopathic osteoporosis can occur in both genders at all ages.

CONFIRMATION

What is the most likely clinical presentation?

Osteoporosis is the most frequently seen metabolic bone disease. The prevalence is expected to increase with the increase in the aging population. A patient diagnosed with osteoporosis may complain of low thoracic or lumbar pain, experience compression fractures of the vertebrae, and complain of back pain. Vertebral and other crush fractures may occur with little to no trauma. Pain is acute and increases with weight bearing and palpation. A patient may also present with deformities such as kyphosis, Dowager's hump, a decrease in height, and other postural changes.

What laboratory or imaging studies would confirm the diagnosis?

There is not an accurate measure of overall bone strength or standards for routine screening that have been established, however, X-rays are taken to investigate the amount of degeneration and the decrease in density of a particular area. A bone mineral density test accounts for 70% of bone strength and is the easiest way to determine osteoporosis. Photon absorptiometry is used to measure bone mass particularly of the vertebrae, hips, and extremities. Quantitative CT scans may be used to aid diagnosis by examining the bone density of the spine.

What additional information should be obtained to confirm the diagnosis?

Differential diagnosis including lab testing and urinalysis must exclude other disease processes through examination and testing. A patient's past medical history, current symptoms, and location of pain all play a role in diagnosing osteoporosis.

EXAMINATION

What history should be documented?

Important areas to explore include past medical history, medications, family history, current symptoms, current health status, social history and habits, occupation, leisure activities, and social support system.

What tests/measures are most appropriate?

Aerobic capacity and endurance: assessment of vital signs at rest and with activity, perceived exertion scale

Arousal, attention, and cognition: examine mental status, learning ability, memory, motivation

Assistive and adaptive devices: analysis of components and safety of a device

Environmental, home, and work barriers: analysis of current and potential barriers or hazards

Ergonomics and body mechanics: analysis of dexterity and coordination

Gait, locomotion, and balance: static and dynamic balance in sitting and standing, safety during gait with/without an assistive device, Berg Balance Scale, functional capacity evaluation

Integumentary integrity: skin and sensation assessment

Motor function: coordination, posture/balance in sitting

Muscle performance: strength of active range of motion only

Pain: pain perception scale, visual analogue scale

Posture: analysis of resting and dynamic posture

Range of motion: active range of motion

Self-care and home management: assessment of functional capacity

Osteoporosis

GOLD

What additional findings are likely with this patient?

Once osteoporosis progresses in severity it can affect areas other than weight bearing bones such as the skull, long bones, and ribs. Spontaneous fractures and skeletal deformities may increase due to the continuing bone loss. A single fracture significantly increases the risk for subsequent fractures and skeletal deformities such as kyphosis.

MANAGEMENT

What is the most effective management of this patient?

Effective management of osteoporosis includes vitamin and pharmaceutical supplements, proper nutrition, education and physical therapy intervention. Hormone replacement therapy is recommended for postmenopausal patients. Calcium supplements, vitamin D, Raloxifene, and Fosamax (prevents bone resorption) may be recommended in the treatment of osteoporosis. Physical therapy intervention should include patient education regarding exercise, positioning, pain management, nutrition, and fall prevention. Physical therapy should include an exercise program that emphasizes weight bearing activities as tolerated. A patient may require a corset or lumbar support if at risk for vertebral fractures and many patients will require training with an assistive device. Aquatic therapy will assist with conditioning, however, should not replace weight bearing activities. Surgical intervention may be indicated for a patient requiring fracture stabilization.

What home care regimen should be recommended?

The home care regimen for osteoporosis includes a consistent home exercise program that combines exercise, walking, and other activities within a patient's tolerance. Exercise is crucial to slow the bone resorption process and increase bone development. Patients should be educated to avoid heavy resistive exercise, excessive flexion during exercise or household activities, and the use of ballistic movements. Light resistance such as small dumbbells or Theraband can be used with caution after consulting with the physician.

OUTCOME

What is the likely outcome of a course of physical therapy?

Physical therapy should prescribe an exercise program that the patient can follow independently. Patient education should allow for independent decision making regarding proper nutrition and activities that incorporate precautions and fall prevention techniques. This level of patient competency should assist in decreasing the risk of fractures and other complications. Physical therapy cannot cease the process, but can empower the patient to effectively manage this bone disorder.

What are the long-term effects of the patient's condition?

Osteoporosis will create thin and porous bones that will fracture easily and result in direct and indirect complications. Deformity and pain can become long-term effects of osteoporosis. Early detection and management of osteoporosis is important to limit the long-term effects of the disease.

COMPARISON

What are the distinguishing characteristics of a similar condition?

Paget's disease (osteitis deformans) is a chronic bone disease of unknown etiology where there is thickened, spongy, and abnormal bone formation. Large multinucleated osteoblasts, fibrous tissue, and thickened lamellae and trabeculae form and create weak and brittle bones. Bone pain, headache, hearing loss, fatigue, and stiffness are some early characteristics of Paget's disease. Progression of the disease includes bowing of long bones, an increase in skull size, bone deformities, and fractures (especially of the vertebrae).

CLINICAL SCENARIOS

Scenario One

A 63-year-old female is seen in outpatient physical therapy for a home exercise program. She is postmenopausal and does not take hormone replacement therapy. She has been recently diagnosed with osteoporosis and x-rays revealed three old vertebral fractures. The patient's major complaints are pain and stiffness.

Scenario Two

A 92-year-old male was admitted to the hospital for internal fixation of a femoral neck fracture. The patient's history reveals osteoporosis, diabetes, and anxiety. He wants to be discharged home to care for his cat. The physician orders are for physical therapy two times per week with the goal of returning home alone.

GOLD

Pressure Ulcer

DIAGNOSIS

What condition produces a patient's symptoms?

A pressure ulcer is a type of ulcer or wound caused by unrelieved pressure to a specific area that results in damage to the underlying tissues. The unrelieved pressure deprives the tissues of oxygen, which causes ischemia to the site, subsequent cell death, and tissue necrosis. A definition of unrelieved pressure is >32 mm Hg of pressure to an area for more than two hours.

An injury was most likely sustained to which structure?

A pressure ulcer can affect different structures based on the degree or staging of the ulcer. Damage can be contained to only the epidermis in stage I ulcers, while stage IV ulcers will include damage to the epidermis, dermis, the fascia and deeper, potentially damaging muscles, ligaments, tendons and/or bones. The most high risk areas for pressure ulcers include the occiput, heels, greater trochanters, ischial tuberosities, sacrum, and epicondyles of the elbow.

INFERENCE

What is the most likely contributing factor in the development of this condition?

A pressure ulcer can occur at any time secondary to unrelieved pressure, but there are certain populations and risk factors that are associated with its development. Immobility is a leading factor and is seen with populations such as spinal cord injury, other paralysis, and hemiplegia. Impaired cognition, poor nutrition, altered sensation, incontinence, decreased lean body mass, and infection are other contributing factors in the development of a pressure ulcer. At the cellular level, the interface pressure, shear and/or friction are the contributing factors in the development of a pressure ulcer.

CONFIRMATION

What is the most likely clinical presentation?

A patient will usually develop a pressure ulcer over a bony prominence with common sites including the greater trochanter, ischium, sacrum, and heel. A stage I pressure ulcer is classified as an area of nonblanchable erythema of intact skin. There may also be an increase in warmth to the site or altered coloration. Stage II is classified as a partial thickness wound involving the epidermis, dermis or both. This ulcer does not extend through the entire dermis. Stage III is classified as an ulcer that has extended into subcutaneous tissue, but not through fascia. Stage IV is classified as an ulcer that extends through the fascia and deeper. It is a full thickness wound that may damage muscles, bones, ligaments and/or tendons. Pressure ulcers will vary in color, odor, drainage, and volume.

What laboratory or imaging studies would confirm the diagnosis?

A diagnosis is made from visual inspection, however, blood studies such as a CBC, electrolyte, and protein levels, as well as tests for bacteremia or sepsis may be indicated. Urinalysis and stool samples may be indicated to determine contributing factors in the development of the ulcer. Coagulation studies and tissue sampling may also be indicated.

What additional information should be obtained to confirm the diagnosis?

Extensive examination and photography of the site are necessary for accurate baseline data. A patient's history and current status are also important factors in designing the plan of care. Diagnosis of staging of the ulcer requires the use of the Braden Scale, Gosnell Scale or Norton Scale along with baseline measurements of size and depth of the ulcer.

EXAMINATION

What history should be documented?

Important areas to explore include past medical history, medications, current health status, history of incontinence, nutritional status, social history, living environment, occupation, and social support system.

What tests/measures are most appropriate?

Aerobic capacity and endurance: assessment of vital signs at rest and with activity

Arousal, attention, and cognition: examine mental status, learning ability, memory and motivation

Environmental, home, and work barriers: analysis of current and potential barriers or hazards

Gait, locomotion, and balance: static and dynamic balance in sitting and standing, safety during gait with/without an assistive device

Integumentary integrity: skin assessment, assessment of sensation, Braden Scale, Norton Scale, photography of ulcer, eschar, granulation formation, Gosnell Scale

Joint integrity and mobility: assessment of hypermobility and hypomobility of a joint, soft tissue swelling and inflammation

Muscle performance: strength assessment

Pain: pain perception assessment scale, visual analogue scale

Posture: analysis of resting and dynamic posture

Range of motion: active and passive range of motion

Sensory integrity: proprioception and kinesthesia

What additional findings are likely with this patient?

Complications that may prevent healing of the ulcer include infection, osteomyelitis, sepsis, pain, spasticity, malnutrition, incontinence, and depression. Patients at high risk may also develop multiple ulcers at once.

MANAGEMENT

What is the most effective management of this patient?

Patient and caregiver education for the prevention of subsequent pressure ulcers is very important and should include skin inspection, positioning, and pressure relief techniques. The use of pressure reducing devices such as seat cushions, multipodus boots or specialized mattresses is also an important aspect to the overall care of ulcers. Pharmacological intervention may include antimicrobials and antibiotics to fight infection and allow for proper healing. Dressings for the ulcer may include nonocclusive or occlusive types of dressings. Nonocclusive dressings include dry to dry, wet to wet, wet to dry or composite dressings. Occlusive dressings include semipermeable films, hydrocolloids, hydrogels, semipermeable foams, and alginates. The ulcer may require cleansing agents, and/or debridement (enzymatic, mechanical non-selective or sharp). Mobility training and proper positioning for the patient will also be vital in order to decrease forces of shear and friction upon the site of the ulcer. A general exercise program should be initiated as well as mobility training to tolerance. Skin inspection should be provided daily and photography should be documented regularly to track the progress of healing. Patients should avoid the use of hot water and the use of massage surrounding the site. The therapist should promote proper positioning techniques (such as positioning of the bed at less than a 45 degree angle) in order to decrease friction and shear forces.

What home care regimen should be recommended?

The home care regimen is dependent on the size and staging of the pressure injury. The patient should continue with the appropriate schedule for dressings and follow physician orders. The patient should maintain an appropriate activity level, use correct positioning, and receive adequate protein and calorie intake to assist with the healing process. The patient should use a mild cleansing agent, dry and wrinkle free sheets for their bed, and appropriate moisturizers.

OUTCOME

What is the likely outcome of a course of physical therapy?

Many people that develop a pressure ulcer completely recover with no residual impairments. While each patient will respond differently to physical therapy treatment, there are certain factors which will improve the opportunity for successful healing of a pressure ulcer. These factors include adequate redistribution of pressure to the affected area (i.e., through positioning or support surfaces), adequate blood supply to the affected area, absence of infection, and proper nutrient intake.

What are the long-term effects of the patient's condition?

Treatment of a pressure ulcer should provide a normal path of recovery without any residual deficits. If there is infection or complications to healing, the patient may have to undergo additional treatment such as further pharmacological intervention or surgical procedures. If the patient is in a high risk group for skin breakdown the patient may require the ongoing use of a pressure relief seating system or air mattress for the bed.

COMPARISON

What are the distinguishing characteristics of a similar condition?

A neuropathic ulcer is an ulcer that develops due to the lack of neural function, which occurs commonly in patients with diabetes mellitus. Other high risk groups include spinal cord injury, stroke, spina bifida, sensory neuropathies, and tumors. The feet are the prime region for neuropathic ulcers in the diabetic patient. These ulcers occur in areas of weight bearing where there are mechanical shear forces such as under the metatarsal heads. These ulcers are usually round in shape and are not painful. It is believed that these ulcers occur not only due to motor neuropathy, but also impairment of the sensory and autonomic systems. Approximately 15% of patients with diabetes mellitus will develop a foot ulcer. Treatment is usually the same as with a pressure ulcer, but care must be taken to continually assess progress since there is usually motor and sensory damage surrounding the ulcer site.

CLINICAL SCENARIOS

Scenario One

A 31-year-old male has been in the hospital for four weeks secondary to a motor vehicle accident. He was in a coma for ten days and was required to stay in bed due to multiple fractures for three of the four weeks. He developed a stage two pressure ulcer on his right heel and has orders for whirlpool treatment. He is being discharged home alone in two weeks to his two-story home and is currently NWB on the right lower extremity and WBAT on the left lower extremity.

Scenario Two

An 85-year-old female is admitted to the hospital due to a stage four pressure ulcer on her sacrum. She had been cared for at home by her husband since her stroke four months ago. The husband states that the wife remained in bed most of the time, has lost over 30 pounds, and presents with some mild cognitive deficits.

GOLD

Rheumatoid Arthritis

DIAGNOSIS

What condition produces a patient's symptoms?

Rheumatoid arthritis (RA) is a systemic autoimmune disorder of the connective tissue that is characterized by chronic inflammation within synovial membranes, tendon sheaths, and articular cartilage. The acute and chronic inflammatory changes produce the symptoms of this condition.

An injury was most likely sustained to which structure?

Smaller peripheral joints are usually the first to be affected by RA, however, all connective tissue may become involved. Inflammation is present within the synovial membrane and granulation tissue forms as a result of the synovitis. The granulation tissue and protein degrading enzymes erode articular cartilage resulting in destruction, adhesions, and fibrosis within the joint.

INFERENCE

What is the most likely contributing factor in the development of this condition?

The etiology of RA is unknown, however, there appears to be evidence of genetic predisposition with viral or bacterial triggers. Approximately 80% of individuals diagnosed with RA possess a positive rheumatoid factor (RF). RF represents the presence of autoantibodies that conflict with immunoglobulin antibodies found in the blood. The incidence of RA in women is greater than the incidence in men.

CONFIRMATION

What is the most likely clinical presentation?

This condition is characterized by periods of exacerbations and is diagnosed most frequently between 30 and 50 years of age. RA will vary in onset and progression from patient to patient. Onset of RA may be sudden or develop over a period of weeks. Early characteristics include fatigue, bilateral involvement, tenderness of smaller joints, and low-grade fever. Patients often experience pain with motion, stiffness including prolonged morning stiffness, and progression of symptoms to larger synovial joints. In late stages of the disease the heart can become affected and deformities, subluxations, and contractures can occur.

What laboratory or imaging studies would confirm the diagnosis?

Blood work assists with the diagnosis of RA through evaluation of the rheumatoid factor (RF), white blood cell count, erythrocyte sedimentation rate, hemoglobin, and hematocrit values. A synovial fluid analysis evaluates the content of synovial fluid within a joint. X-rays can be used to evaluate the joint space and the extent of decalcification.

What additional information should be obtained to confirm the diagnosis?

Physical examination and patient history of symptoms are required to confirm the diagnosis. The American Rheumatoid Association has designed diagnostic criteria for RA that can be used as a guide to determine a definite, possible, probable or classic diagnosis.

EXAMINATION

What history should be documented?

Important areas to explore include past medical history, family history, medications, current symptoms and health status, living environment, social history and habits, occupation, and social support system.

What tests/measures are most appropriate?

Aerobic capacity and endurance: assessment of vital signs at rest and with activity, timed walk, VO_{2max}

Anthropometric characteristics: circumferential measurements of all affected joints

Arousal, attention, and cognition: examine mental status, learning ability, memory, motivation

Community and work integration: analysis of community, work, and leisure activities

Ergonomics and body mechanics: analysis of dexterity and coordination

Environmental, home, and work barriers: analysis of current and potential barriers or hazards

Gait, locomotion, and balance: safety during gait with/without an assistive device, Functional Ambulation Profile, gait over level/unlevel surfaces, visual inspection of gait with and without shoes

Integumentary integrity: skin and sensation assessment

Joint integrity and mobility: assessment of joint hypomobility, soft tissue inflammation, presence of deformity, active joint count, articular tenderness

Motor function: equilibrium and righting reactions, motor assessment scales, coordination, posture and balance in sitting, physical performance scales

Muscle performance: break testing of isometric contractions, manometer method of strength testing

Orthotic, protective, and supportive devices: potential utilization of bracing, analysis of movement while wearing a device

Pain: pain perception assessment scale

Range of motion: active and passive range of motion

Self-care and home management: assessment of functional capacity

Sensory integrity: assessment of sensation, kinesthesia, and proprioception

What additional findings are likely with this patient?

Extraarticular manifestations with RA can include pericarditis, anemia, tearing of tendons and musculature, osteoporosis, swan neck and/or boutonniere deformities, compression neuropathies, peripheral neuropathies, depression, pleurisy, skin changes, and anorexia.

MANAGEMENT

What is the most effective management of this patient?

Early medical management of a patient with RA is critical to improve the long-term outcomes of the disease. Medical treatment will focus on pain relief, reduction of edema, and preservation of joint integrity. Pharmacological intervention is required to decrease inflammation and retard the progression of the disease. NSAIDs, corticosteroids, and disease-modifying medications such as methotrexate are indicated. Physical therapy management during the acute stage or exacerbation includes patient education regarding regular rest, pain relief, relaxation, positioning, joint protection techniques, splinting, energy conservation, and body mechanics. Treatment may include gentle massage, hydrotherapy, hot pack, paraffin or cold modalities, gentle isometrics, and instruction in the use of assistive devices. Treatment during the acute stage should avoid resistive exercise, deep heating modalities, and any form of active stretching since these activities will further exacerbate the arthritis. Physical therapy management during the chronic stage or remission focuses on improving overall functional capacity, endurance, and strength. Treatment consists of low-impact conditioning through swimming or the stationary bicycle. Gentle stretching may be indicated to maintain available range of motion, however, aggressive stretching is contraindicated.

What home care regimen should be recommended?

A home care regimen for a patient with RA must maintain a delicate balance between activity and rest. The patient should perform low-level exercise, utilize relaxation and energy conservation techniques, and use splints as needed. The patient should recognize when total rest is indicated due to an acute exacerbation.

OUTCOME

What is the likely outcome of a course of physical therapy?

Physical therapy cannot halt the progression of RA, however, it can improve a patient's ability to function. Physical therapy may be indicated intermittently throughout the disease process with goals that focus on pain relief, relaxation, improving motion, and preventing deformity.

What are the long-term effects of the patient's condition?

RA is a chronic disease process that currently does not have a known cure, progresses at a varied rate, creates irreversible damage and deformity, and results in disability. As the disease progresses there is bilateral and symmetrical involvement of joints. Systemic effects include insomnia, fatigue, and organ involvement including the heart and lungs.

COMPARISON

What are the distinguishing characteristics of a similar condition?

Osteoarthritis is a chronic degenerative condition that usually develops secondary to repetitive trauma, disease or obesity. The hyaline cartilage in the joint softens and breaks apart allowing bone-to-bone contact that results in joint deformity, crepitus, impaired range of motion, and pain. Pain typically increases with prolonged activity. Joints become swollen and tender and joint deformity develops. Women have a slightly greater risk for OA than men. Surgical procedures including osteotomy and joint replacement may be indicated if conservative treatment is unsuccessful.

CLINICAL SCENARIOS

Scenario One

A 38-year-old female diagnosed with RA is seen in an outpatient clinic. The patient history reveals fatigue and malaise for two to three weeks and pain in the fingers and wrists. The patient has difficulty caring for herself at home and is on medical leave from her job. The patient does not have any other significant past medical history and resides alone.

Scenario Two

A 74-year-old male diagnosed with RA is treated by a therapist. The patient presents with multi-joint involvement, deformities of the hands and feet, poor endurance, stiffness, and pain. The patient is ambulatory, however, is currently in a wheelchair secondary to pain from an exacerbation. The patient is oriented and has a history of COPD.

GOLD

Systemic Lupus Erythematosus

DIAGNOSIS

What condition produces a patient's symptoms?

Systemic lupus erythematosus (SLE) is a connective tissue disorder caused by an autoimmune reaction in the body. The primary manifestation of the condition is the production of destructive antibodies that are directed at the individual's own body. The chronic inflammatory disorder produces a variety of symptoms depending on the severity and extent of involvement.

An injury was most likely sustained to which structure?

SLE is an autoimmune disorder that creates high levels of autoantibodies (antinuclear antibodies) that attack various cells and tissues within the body. The autoantibodies form immune complexes that produce an inflammatory response and cause further tissue destruction. Proliferation of immune complexes precipitates inflammation responses that in turn destroy cells, tissues, and organs. Specific injury is organ or system dependent depending on which areas of the body are affected by SLE.

INFERENCE

What is the most likely contributing factor in the development of this condition?

The exact etiology of SLE is unknown, however, it is described as an immunoregulatory disturbance from genetic, environmental, viral, and hormonal contributing factors. Environmental factors associated with SLE include ultraviolet light exposure, infection, antibiotics (specifically penicillin and sulfa drugs), extreme stress, immunization, and pregnancy. SLE can occur at any age, but the most common age group is 15 to 40 years of age. The disorder is far more common in women than in men.

CONFIRMATION

What is the most likely clinical presentation?

A patient with SLE will have diverse symptoms based on the involvement of the connective tissue throughout the body. Symptoms will appear with exacerbations and disappear with remissions throughout the course of the disease. Symptoms such as arthralgias, malaise, and fatigue may persist even during a remission period. A patient may initially see a physician for symptoms that include fever, malaise, rash, arthralgias, headache, and weight loss. Common clinical presentation throughout the course of SLE includes a red butterfly rash across the cheeks and nose, a red rash over light exposed areas, arthralgias, alopecia, pleurisy, kidney involvement, seizures, depression, fibromyalgia, and cardiac involvement. SLE can affect the skin, joints, kidneys, lungs, heart, and other organs and tissues within the body. Patients can also have CNS involvement that can lead to neuropsychiatric manifestations that present with depression, irritability, emotional instability, and seizures.

What laboratory or imaging studies would confirm the diagnosis?

Microscopic fluorescent techniques are indicated to detect the presence of the antinuclear antibody (ANA) within the blood. A positive ANA test warrants an additional test for antideoxyribonucleic acid antibodies. These two tests in combination with the physical presentation support the presence of SLE. Other testing including erythrocyte sedimentation rate, complete blood count, and urinalysis.

What additional information should be obtained to confirm the diagnosis?

The American Rheumatism Association has designated criteria to confirm the diagnosis of SLE. A patient requires at least four of fourteen characteristics that occur during the same period of time. A patient evaluation including a thorough history and current symptoms assists with confirming a diagnosis of SLE.

EXAMINATION

What history should be documented?

Important areas to explore include past medical and family history, medications, current symptoms and health status, living environment, social history and habits, occupation, and social support system.

What tests/measures are most appropriate?

Aerobic capacity and endurance: assessment of vital signs at rest/activity, auscultation of the lungs/heart

Arousal, attention, and cognition: examine mental status, learning ability, memory, motivation

Assistive and adaptive devices: analysis of components and safety of a device

Community and work integration: analysis of community, work, and leisure activities

Environmental, home, and work barriers: analysis of current and potential barriers or hazards

Ergonomics and body mechanics: analysis of dexterity and coordination

Gait, locomotion, and balance: static/dynamic balance in sitting and standing, safety during gait, Tinetti Performance Oriented Mobility Assessment, Berg Balance Scale, Functional Ambulation Profile

Integumentary integrity: skin assessment, assessment of sensation, presence and assessment of rash

Joint integrity and mobility: soft tissue swelling and inflammation, presence of deformity

Motor function: posture and balance

Muscle performance: strength assessment

Neuromotor development and sensory integration: analysis of reflex movement patterns, sensory integration tests, gross and fine motor skills
Orthotic, protective, and supportive devices: potential utilization of bracing
Pain: pain perception assessment scale
Range of motion: active and passive range of motion
Self-care and home management: assessment of functional capacity

What additional findings are likely with this patient?

SLE can produce skeletal deformities such as ulnar deviation and subluxed interphalangeal joints. Kidney involvement and cardiovascular impairments such as endocarditis, myocarditis, and pericarditis can occur during an exacerbation. Patients that experience nephritis, myocarditis or neurological implications have a poor prognosis. Modifiable risk factors for exacerbation include high stress, limited emotional and social support, and psychological distress.

MANAGEMENT

What is the most effective management of this patient?

Medical management of SLE focuses on reversing the autoimmune response in order to avoid complications and exacerbations of symptoms. Pharmacological intervention for a patient with mild SLE will include salicylates, Indomethacin or NSAIDs. Antimalarial medications, corticosteroids, and immunosuppressive therapy may be used. General management of SLE includes good nutrition, ongoing medical supervision, and avoidance of ultraviolet exposure. Physical therapy intervention is usually indicated after a period of exacerbation and includes a slow resumption of physical activity, energy conservation techniques, gradual endurance activities and significant patient education regarding skin care, pacing, exercise, and strengthening to tolerance.

What home care regimen should be recommended?

A home care regimen during an acute exacerbation of SLE should include relaxation and energy conservation techniques, stress reduction strategies, therapeutic exercise as tolerated, and pain management.

OUTCOME

What is the likely outcome of a course of physical therapy?

Physical therapy cannot cease or alter the clinical course of SLE, however, it may assist in controlling the debilitating effects during an acute phase/exacerbation of the disease. Goals include focus on pain relief, relaxation, strengthening, and preventing deformity.

What are the long-term effects of the patient's condition?

The clinical course of SLE is highly unpredictable. A patient may only exhibit symptoms for skin and joint involvement or may exhibit multi-system involvement. Periods of remission may last years and the prognosis depends on the severity and the extent of the disease process. The overall prognosis for SLE is good, although in rare cases the disease process can remain acute and become fatal within a short period of time. There is a high ten-year survival rate with SLE. Death is usually attributed to kidney failure or secondary infections.

COMPARISON

What are the distinguishing characteristics of a similar condition?

Systemic sclerosis, also termed scleroderma, is a chronic disease that primarily affects the skin, but can involve articular structures and internal organs. There is long-term hardening and shrinking of the affected connective tissues. The two subtypes of this disease are systemic scleroderma and localized scleroderma. Etiology is unknown and the disease varies in course (months, years or a lifetime) and progression.

CLINICAL SCENARIOS

Scenario One

A 25-year-old female is referred to physical therapy for a therapeutic exercise program. The patient was diagnosed last year with SLE and has not exercised since that time. The patient is currently taking corticosteroids and antimalarial medications to manage a recent exacerbation.

Scenario Two

A 43-year-old female was seen in outpatient physical therapy to assist with pain management. The patient was diagnosed five years ago with SLE and has recently experienced increased difficulty using her hands secondary to deformity and pain. The patient's goal is to reduce the pain in her hands.

GOLD

Urinary Stress Incontinence

DIAGNOSIS

What condition produces a patient's symptoms?

Urinary incontinence is the involuntary loss of urine. There are five classifications that include functional incontinence, stress incontinence, urge incontinence, mixed incontinence, and overflow incontinence. Urinary stress incontinence may occur during activities when there is an increase in abdominal pressure through straining, sneezing, coughing or lifting.

An injury was most likely sustained to which structure?

Urinary stress incontinence usually occurs from loss of strength and/or integrity of the contractile and noncontractile tissues that maintain bladder control. Urinary stress incontinence is caused by weakness of the pelvic floor musculature (urogenital diaphragm, levator ani muscle group), damage of the pudendal nerve, malposition of the urethra, and/or urethral sphincter incompetence.

INFERENCE

What is the most likely contributing factor in the development of this condition?

Risk factors for the development of urinary stress incontinence include pregnancy, vaginal delivery, episiotomy, prostate or pelvic surgery, aging, diabetes mellitus, central nervous system and peripheral nervous system dysfunction, and recurrent urinary tract infections. A prolapsed bladder, uterus or bowel may contribute to leakage and is seen in women that have had multiple vaginal deliveries. Medications that treat other illnesses can sometimes contribute to incontinence especially with the older population. Obesity is another risk factor that is believed to increase the risk of stress incontinence due to increased intra-abdominal pressure and the effect of obesity on the neuromuscular function of the genitourinary tract.

CONFIRMATION

What is the most likely clinical presentation?

Urinary stress incontinence accounts for the majority of incontinence cases and is manifested solely by the involuntary loss of urine with any form of exertion or increased abdominal pressure. The amount of urine that leaks is typically less than 50 milliliters with coughing, sneezing or straining. Physical activity or exercise can also produce leakage due to exertion with these activities. Other manifestations may include dribbling of urine, urgency, frequency, nocturia, and a weak stream while voiding.

What laboratory or imaging studies would confirm the diagnosis?

Cystometry is used to evaluate bladder capacity, control, contractility, and sensation. During this procedure, provocative stress testing will be performed when stress incontinence is suspected. Urodynamic testing observes the stability of the bladder and electromyography observes bladder contractions. Urinalysis is used for differential diagnosis to rule out infection, diabetes, and other conditions.

What additional information should be obtained to confirm the diagnosis?

Urinary stress incontinence can be determined through history, pelvic examination, and noted loss of urine with straining activities. The Marshall-Marchetti test utilizes finger elevation of the paraurethral vaginal tissues at the neck of the bladder in order to stop the leakage of urine during coughing, sneezing or straining. Baseline exam should include the amount of time that a patient can hold urine, repetitions performed of a holding contraction, and the amount of pelvic floor contractions a patient can perform.

EXAMINATION

What history should be documented?

Important areas to explore include past medical history, childbirth history, medications, current health status, fluid intake, social history, occupation, living environment, and social support system.

What tests/measures are most appropriate?

Aerobic capacity and endurance: assessment of vital signs at rest and with activity, perceived exertion scale

Arousal, attention, and cognition: examine mental status, learning ability, memory, motivation, Urge Impact scale

Community and work integration: analysis of community, work, and leisure activities

Environmental, home, and work barriers: analysis of current and potential barriers or hazards

Ergonomics and body mechanics: analysis of dexterity and coordination, assessment of lifting techniques (intra-abdominal pressure)

Integumentary integrity: skin assessment, examination of the pelvic floor

Muscle performance: strength assessment of the pelvic floor and abdominal muscles, muscle tone assessment

Pain: pain perception assessment scale

Posture: analysis of resting and dynamic posture

Range of motion: active and passive range of motion

Self-care and home management: assessment of functional capacity, bladder diary, fluid intake

Urinary Stress Incontinence

GOLD

What additional findings are likely with this patient?

A patient with urinary stress incontinence may be at increased risk for a urinary tract infection with subsequent skin breakdown. Pelvic floor weakness, uterine prolapse, and kidney infection may all relate to urinary stress incontinence. A patient that has poor diet and nutrition, constipation, inadequate hydration, and urinary frequency will further promote incontinence.

MANAGEMENT

What is the most effective management of this patient?

Medical management of urinary incontinence usually consists of conservative measures (physical therapy) as a first line of defense followed by pharmacological and surgical interventions depending on the underlying cause and response to conservative treatment. Physical therapy intervention for pelvic floor muscle weakness that is tested as 0/5 - 2/5 includes biofeedback, electrical stimulation, bladder retraining, and therapeutic exercise. Pelvic floor muscle strengthening at this level includes facilitation and tapping of the pelvic floor muscles, overflow exercises using the buttocks, adductors, and lower abdominals, and implementation of Kegel exercises. Physical therapy intervention for pelvic floor muscle weakness that is tested as 3/5 - 5/5 includes continued biofeedback and bladder retraining, weighted vaginal cones for resistance training, and implementation of pelvic floor muscle exercise during activities.

What home care regimen should be recommended?

A home care regimen for a patient with urinary stress incontinence should emphasize an active exercise program that includes pelvic floor strengthening in order to regain control of the flow of urine. Patients are encouraged to perform the recommended exercises throughout the day and integrate the pelvic exercises during activities that may trigger an increase in abdominal pressure within their daily routine. In addition to exercise, patients are advised to make behavioral and dietary modifications based on their personal bladder diary.

OUTCOME

What is the likely outcome of a course of physical therapy?

Outpatient physical therapy for urinary stress incontinence should alleviate pelvic floor weakness and involuntary leakage of urine within eight to twelve weeks. If a patient requires surgical intervention or presents with multiple impairments then physical therapy may be warranted for a longer period of time to assist with gaining bladder control.

What are the long-term effects of the patient's condition?

The long-term effects of urinary stress incontinence depend on the exact cause for the incontinence and the responsiveness to therapeutic intervention. Some patients do not have any long-term effects upon successful completion of physical therapy while other patients do not benefit from physical therapy intervention and require surgical intervention for the underlying cause. Compliance with the home exercise program is required when the underlying cause is weakness of the pelvic floor musculature.

COMPARISON

What are the distinguishing characteristics of a similar condition?

Bowel incontinence can occur from birth defects, trauma to the rectum, spinal cord injuries, fecal impaction, and tumor. Conservative treatment is preferred and includes diet, pharmacological agents, and strengthening of the sphincter muscles through exercise, electrical stimulation, and biofeedback. Surgical intervention may be warranted.

CLINICAL SCENARIOS

Scenario One

A 32-year-old female is referred to physical therapy with a diagnosis of incontinence. The patient gave birth to her fourth child six weeks ago. The patient reports involuntary leakage of urine with exertion. The patient has no significant past medical history, however, reports that she is very anxious about participating in physical therapy.

Scenario Two

A 68-year-old female complains to her doctor during her annual examination that she has difficulty controlling her bladder since a kidney infection six months ago. The patient states that she is unable to hold her urine if she sneezes or coughs and cannot perform any activity of exertion without wearing feminine pads due to leakage. The physician referred the patient to physical therapy for Kegel exercises.

GOLD

Venous Insufficiency Ulcer

DIAGNOSIS

What condition produces a patient's symptoms?

A venous insufficiency ulcer typically results from venous hypertension which may present idiopathically, secondary to valve incompetence (e.g., damaged from a deep vein thrombosis) or peripheral impedance (e.g., obesity). The resultant distension of the capillary beds impedes the exchange of oxygen and nutrients at the capillary level. This results in relative stasis of the interstitial fluid and significant edema. Over time, increased protein and fibrinogen content in the interstitium facilitates fibrotic changes further impeding capillary exchange. The formation of an ulcer results from a combination of increased tissue pressure that decreases skin resilience and endothelial damage that allows enzyme and free radical leakage into the tissue.

An injury was most likely sustained to which structure?

A superficial ulceration is associated with damage to the epidermis only. Damage from a partial-thickness ulceration will extend through the epidermis and possibly into, but not through, the dermis. A full-thickness ulceration extends through the dermis and into deeper layers such as the subcutaneous fat layer. Damage from a subcutaneous ulcer extends through all layers of integumentary tissue typically exposing tendon, muscle or bone.

INFERENCE

What is the most likely contributing factor in the development of this condition?

A venous insufficiency ulcer forms as a result of an underlying condition which impedes normal venous blood flow and capillary exchange. Diagnoses of venous hypertension and chronic venous insufficiency are commonly associated with venous insufficiency ulcers. Patients who are obese are more likely to develop a venous insufficiency ulcer.

CONFIRMATION

What is the most likely clinical presentation?

A patient will typically develop a venous insufficiency ulcer on the medial surface of the lower leg in the area between the mid-calf and malleolus. Venous insufficiency ulcers are typically larger in area and more shallow in depth than arterial or neuropathic ulcers. Wound borders are typically irregular. The wound bed is typically moist with evidence of red granulation tissue. The wound bed may initially be obscured by a moist layer of yellow-white slough requiring debridement. Both the wound borders and bed will typically bleed easily with disruption (e.g., palpation, debridement, dressing changes) due to distended and fragile superficial capillaries. Serous or serosanguineous exudate is typically moderate to heavy. Signs of stasis dermatitis may be observed in the surrounding skin including a dry, flaky appearance and a ruddy, brownish skin discoloration termed hemosiderin staining. Distal lower extremity pulses are typically intact and pain complaints are typically mild and associated with the increased tissue tension caused by edema. Pain complaints are typically relieved with elevation or use of compression garments.

What laboratory or imaging studies would confirm the diagnosis?

A diagnosis of venous insufficiency ulcer is made based on the characteristics of the observed wound and diagnosis of the underlying condition. Duplex ultrasonography produces two-dimensional color images and is the least invasive method of assessing venous blood flow.

What additional information should be obtained to confirm the diagnosis?

An ankle-brachial index (ABI) should be obtained since compression is typically desirable when treating a venous insufficiency ulcer. The use of compression may be limited or contraindicated depending on the severity of occlusion.

EXAMINATION

What history should be documented?

Important areas to explore include past medical history, medications, family history, current symptoms, current health status, social history and habits, occupation, leisure activities, and social support system.

What tests/measures are most appropriate?

Anthropometric characteristics: circumferential measurements

Arousal, attention, and cognition: examine mental status, learning ability, memory, and motivation

Assistive and adaptive devices: analysis of components and safety of a device

Gait, locomotion, and balance: static and dynamic balance in sitting and standing, safety during gait with/without an assistive device

Integumentary integrity: skin assessment, assessment of sensation, assessment of wound characteristics, photo documentation, assessment of edema

Pain: pain perception assessment scale, visual analogue scale

Range of motion: active and passive range of motion

Reflex integrity: assessment of deep tendon reflexes

Self-care and home management: assessment of functional capacity

Ventilation, respiration, and circulation: assessment of pulse oximetry, palpation of pulses, capillary refill, ankle-brachial index

Venous Insufficiency Ulcer

GOLD

What additional findings are likely with this patient?

With chronic venous insufficiency, the same conditions that impede capillary exchange are also likely to locally overwhelm the lymphatic system. With impaired lymphatic function, the patient is at increased risk for developing a significant infection (e.g., cellulitis, wound infection, osteomyelitis). Impaired lymphatic function is also associated with fibrotic tissue changes. Over time, this may further limit normal exchange functions of both the capillaries and lymphatic vessels.

MANAGEMENT

What is the most effective management of this patient?

Medical management typically includes monitoring the severity of the underlying disease process and counseling regarding modifiable risk factors (e.g., weight, edema management). Other medical interventions may include procedures that either chemically (e.g., sclerotherapy) or thermally (e.g., ablation) close abnormal veins thereby redirecting venous blood return to better functioning vessels. Pharmacological intervention may include diuretics, antibiotics or antimicrobial agents. Surgical intervention typically targets the underlying pathology and may include vein stripping, bypass, valve repair, angioplasty or stent placement. Grafting may be indicated when the wound bed is unable to support normal healing and conservative measures have failed. Physical therapy management emphasizes edema management, skin protection, and wound healing interventions. Successful healing of venous insufficiency ulcers typically will include graded compression (e.g., garments, bandaging, Unna boot). The surrounding skin should be kept well moisturized and appropriate exudate management is essential to prevent breakdown of surrounding tissue. The ulcer may require cleansing agents and/or debridement (enzymatic, mechanical non-selective, sharp or autolytic). A venous insufficiency ulcer typically produces moderate to heavy volumes of exudate, therefore, it is important to select dressing components which protect the wound and maintain an appropriate moisture balance. Photo documentation is recommended to supplement written documentation describing wound characteristics (e.g., area, depth, odor, exudate, color).

What home care regimen should be recommended?

The home care regimen is dependent on the size and characteristics of the venous insufficiency ulcer. Patients who do not require debridement may appropriately manage routine dressing changes at home. All patients should be diligent with edema management, hygiene, and skin protection to limit the risk of infection.

OUTCOME

What is the likely outcome of a course of physical therapy?

A venous insufficiency ulcer will typically heal by secondary intention with appropriate management and an uncomplicated course of healing. Patients will not typically experience residual deficits from the wound itself, but may have increased morbidity and mortality risks associated with the wound's underlying pathology.

What are the long-term effects of the patient's condition?

Treatment of a venous insufficiency ulcer and the underlying pathology, in addition to edema management, should allow for a normal course of recovery without residual deficits. Infection or other complications to healing may require additional pharmacological, medical or surgical intervention. If infection is pervasive, osteomyelitis or sepsis may result.

COMPARISON

What are the distinguishing characteristics of a similar condition?

An arterial insufficiency ulcer is typically the result of inadequate perfusion of oxygenated blood causing cell death and tissue necrosis. Ulcers typically form on the distal lower extremities with smooth borders giving the wound a punched out appearance. Exudate is typically minimal, however, pain may be severe especially when the limb is not in a dependent position. On examination, pedal pulses are typically diminished. Skin is cool with a shiny, hairless appearance. Specific wound care interventions emphasize skin and wound protection as well as maintenance of a moist wound environment to facilitate healing. Medical or surgical intervention is typically required to address decreased blood supply to the area before healing can be supported.

CLINICAL SCENARIOS

Scenario One

A 53-year-old morbidly obese male presents with multiple small venous insufficiency ulcers on both lower legs. The wound beds are clean and granulating, however, exudate regularly saturates the gauze dressings. The patient reports that the ulcers have not healed in six months. The patient must walk distances with his job and does not have proper footwear.

Scenario Two

A 68-year-old active female is diagnosed with venous hypertension due to valve incompetence. She is referred to physical therapy for wound management after developing a shallow lower extremity ulceration. The wound bed is loosely covered in moist yellow-white slough and exudate is primarily serous.

SILVER Level Clinical Application Templates

SILVER Level Clinical Application Template Executive Summary

Cellulitis

- Refers to a noncontagious bacterial skin infection occurring in the dermal and subcutaneous layers
- Typically presents with visible signs of inflammation including localized redness, warmth, tenderness, and edema that progressively worsens
- Early detection and treatment are vital in reducing complications and systemic infection; untreated cellulitis can spread, causing potentially fatal septicemia

Chronic Fatigue Syndrome

- Complex condition with an unknown etiology; potential etiologies include a viral origin, an immune response to inflammation with the nervous system, or a combination of lifestyle factors
- Best managed using a multidisciplinary approach including education, medical management, cognitive behavioral therapy, and exercise
- There is no cure; symptom presentation, progression, and resolution can be highly variable making outcomes difficult to predict

Diastasis Recti

- Refers to a separation of the right and left sides of the rectus abdominis
- The condition is not exclusively seen in women who are pregnant, however, there is a significant prevalence among this population
- Most patients improve with conservative treatment focused on corrective exercise and do not suffer long-term functional deficits associated with the condition

Graves' Disease

- Most common form of hyperactive thyroid disorder and is the result of an autoimmune attack on the thyroid gland causing overproduction of the hormone thyroxine (T4)
- General complaints may include heat intolerance, increased appetite, increased sweating, frequent bowel movements, physical fatigue, weakness, tremor, weight loss, and insomnia
- Typically responds well to pharmacological intervention that regulates T4 hormone production

SILVER

Cellulitis

DIAGNOSIS

What condition produces a patient's symptoms?

Cellulitis refers to a noncontagious bacterial skin infection occurring in the dermal and subcutaneous layers. Streptococcus and Staphylococcus microbes are most commonly associated with cellulitis. Other microbes including pneumococcus, pseudomonas, and clostridium may also cause cellulitis.

An injury was most likely sustained to which structure?

The integumentary system functions to protect underlying tissues from external debris and infectious microbes. When there is compromise of this protective barrier (e.g., insect bite, surgical wound, abrasion), vulnerable tissues are more easily exposed to bacteria resulting in infection. Without timely treatment the infection can spread to adjacent tissues and systemically through the bloodstream and lymphatic system. Repeated cellulitis infections and the associated edema can cause permanent damage to the lymphatic system.

INFERENCE

What is the most likely contributing factor in the development of this condition?

The body's immune response prevents external microbes from causing infection in exposed tissues. Patients with a weakened immune system secondary to medication (e.g., corticosteroids, chemotherapy agents) or other medical conditions (e.g., HIV, leukemia) are more susceptible to cellulitis. High-risk patients also include those with conditions that impede immune responses due to impaired blood or lymphatic flow (e.g., chronic venous insufficiency, lymphedema, obesity). Although a break in the skin's protective barrier is typically associated with cellulitis, some patients, such as those with diabetes, may develop cellulitis without an identifiable cause.

CONFIRMATION

What is the most likely clinical presentation?

Cellulitis typically presents with visible signs of inflammation including localized redness, warmth, tenderness, and edema that progressively worsens. Red streaks leading away from the primary site of infection, weeping, and serous drainage may also be observed. As the condition worsens, other systemic signs and symptoms of infection may develop including fever, aches, chills, and swollen or tender lymph nodes.

What laboratory or imaging studies would confirm the diagnosis?

Blood sample analysis may be used to evaluate the patient's white blood cell count. When elevated, it is suggestive of infection, but alone is not conclusive. A wound culture can assist in identifying the specific infectious microbe present so that treatment can be specifically targeted.

What additional information should be obtained to confirm the diagnosis?

A thorough medical history should be obtained, including a detailed history of current symptoms and the identification of known cellulitis risk factors. Physical examination should include an examination of the integumentary system.

MANAGEMENT

What is the most effective management of this patient?

Early detection is important to prevent the infection from spreading systemically. Pharmacological intervention with antibiotic therapy is the primary mode of medical management. The antibiotic selected will vary depending on the type of bacteria involved. Typically, antibiotics are administered orally, allowing the patient to self-medicate and care for themselves. In more severe cases (e.g., patients who are immunocompromised or have a high fever), inpatient treatment and intravenous antibiotics may be required. Physical therapy interventions may be indicated if an integumentary injury requires ongoing wound care. Patients who demonstrate functional limitations due to pain from severe inflammation are likely to benefit from adaptive equipment instruction to assist with mobility or self-care activities until symptoms resolve. Education regarding risk reduction, skin protection, and appropriate skin hygiene practices may also be components of a physical therapy plan of care.

What home care regimen should be recommended?

With antibiotic intervention, symptoms should begin to resolve within a few days. Until this time, rest and elevation of the affected area may assist in reducing edema and discomfort caused by inflammation. Skin protection and skin hygiene are important both while recovering and after symptoms have resolved to prevent recurrence in at-risk patients. Patients should be educated regarding risk factors, appropriate care following future skin compromise, and early recognition of signs or symptoms suggesting recurrence.

OUTCOME

What is the likely outcome of a course of physical therapy?

Physical therapy interventions for cellulitis are primarily palliative to assist in improving comfort and function during recovery. Appropriate antibiotic intervention will typically resolve symptom complaints and any associated limitations.

What are the long-term effects of the patient's condition?

Recurrences of cellulitis are common among patients with comorbidities that increase the risk of infection. Early detection and treatment are vital in reducing complications and systemic infection. Untreated cellulitis can spread, causing potentially fatal septicemia.

Chronic Fatigue Syndrome

SILVER

DIAGNOSIS

What condition produces a patient's symptoms?

Chronic fatigue syndrome (CFS) is a complex condition with unknown etiology. Potential etiologies include a viral origin, an immune response to inflammation within the nervous system or a combination of lifestyle factors (e.g., stress, environment), non-modifiable factors (e.g., age, genetics), and comorbidities.

An injury was most likely sustained to which structure?

Since the exact etiology of CFS is unknown, the condition cannot be linked specifically to one structure or system.

INFERENCE

What is the most likely contributing factor in the development of this condition?

There is speculation linking many potential factors to CFS. Factors include environmental and genetic influences, viral infection, immunological dysfunction, nutritional deficiency, hormonal imbalance, depression, anemia, allergens, hypotension, and autoimmune response.

CONFIRMATION

What is the most likely clinical presentation?

Patients must meet several specific criteria in order to meet the diagnostic criteria set forth by the Centers for Disease Control and Prevention. These criteria include a history of at least six months of unexplained, prolonged, and severe fatigue that is not relieved by rest. This must be accompanied by at least four of eight additional symptoms, including self-reported memory or concentration deficits severe enough to interfere with daily activities, persistent or recurrent sore throat, painful or enlarged axillary or cervical lymph nodes, unexplained muscle pain, migrating joint pain without visible signs of inflammation, complaints of malaise lasting more than 24 hours after physical or mental exertion, and headache that exhibits changes in pattern or severity.

What laboratory or imaging studies would confirm the diagnosis?

The etiology of CFS is unknown, therefore no specific diagnostic tests exist to confirm the diagnosis. Since CFS is considered a diagnosis of exclusion, laboratory and imaging studies are frequently used to rule out other conditions known to produce severe and prolonged fatigue (e.g., hypothyroidism, multiple sclerosis, cancer, mononucleosis).

What additional information should be obtained to confirm the diagnosis?

A thorough medical history should be obtained to assist in ruling out other conditions that may mimic the symptoms of CFS, including psychological disorders, sleep apnea, eating disorders, substance abuse, and morbid obesity. Additional diagnostic testing may be warranted if a specific alternative pathology is suspected.

MANAGEMENT

What is the most effective management of this patient?

CFS is best managed using a multidisciplinary approach including education, medical management, cognitive behavioral therapy, and exercise. Medical management will attempt to reestablish homeostasis for any systemic abnormalities contributing to CFS symptoms (e.g., sleep apnea, metabolic conditions). Pharmacological intervention is typically symptom-based and psychotherapy may be warranted to treat depression or assist with stress management. Physical therapy intervention may include relaxation techniques (e.g., deep breathing exercises, biofeedback), energy conservation, and exercise. Patients with CFS have a low tolerance for physical exertion, however, avoidance of exercise may exacerbate symptoms. As a result, exercise should begin with low-level, short duration sessions. A gradual progression of regular exercise is beneficial for patients with CFS especially with improving tolerance for moderate daily activities.

What home care regimen should be recommended?

A home care regimen should include short duration exercise, energy conservation strategies, and relaxation techniques (e.g., hypnosis, meditation). Complementary therapies such as massage, acupuncture, yoga or Tai Chi may also provide patients with alternative methods to address exercise and relaxation goals. A comprehensive plan of care should include lifestyle management, nutritional support, and stress management.

OUTCOME

What is the likely outcome of a course of physical therapy?

A patient with CFS may benefit from a multidisciplinary approach to assist with symptom management, however, interventions are not considered curative. In some cases, symptoms may remain unchanged despite dedicated efforts on the part of the patient.

What are the long-term effects of the patient's condition?

Presently there is no cure for CFS. Some patients are able to manage symptoms adequately to allow continued participation in household, social, and occupational activities while others become significantly debilitated. Patients may experience complete symptom resolution in as little as six months or experience persistent symptoms for years, never fully returning to their pre-illness state.

SILVER

Diastasis Recti

DIAGNOSIS

What condition produces a patient's symptoms?

Diastasis recti refers to a separation of the right and left sides of the rectus abdominis. This is typically the result of anteriorly directed sustained internal pressure which weakens and eventually splits the connective tissue between the two sides of the muscle. The result is an alteration in the alignment and mechanics of the rectus abdominis which may lead to trunk instability and, in severe cases, abdominal hernia.

An injury was most likely sustained to which structure?

The medial aspects of the right and left rectus abdominis are connected by a fibrous band extending from the xiphoid process to the pubic symphysis. This seam of connective tissue is referred to as the linea alba. Sustained pressure within the abdomen that is directed anteriorly weakens the fibers of the linea alba causing it to stretch and in some cases split. This may occur in a segment of the fibrous line or along the full length depending on the duration and force of the pressure.

INFERENCE

What is the most likely contributing factor in the development of this condition?

Though the condition is not exclusively seen in women who are pregnant, there is a significant prevalence among this population. The risk of developing or exacerbating the condition increases with multiple pregnancies. Diastasis recti is often observed and considered a normal characteristic in premature infants. Obese adults of both sexes are also at increased risk of developing diastasis recti.

CONFIRMATION

What is the most likely clinical presentation?

The degree of muscle separation is highly variable. A visible separation can be observed in one or more positions (e.g., sitting, standing, supine), though this varies widely based on the patient's body morphology. Abdominal weakness, decreased lumbar stability, and low back pain complaints are often noted due to the altered mechanics associated with the rectus separation. Abdominal pain may be present if excessive stretching has caused microtearing within the muscle tissue.

What laboratory or imaging studies would confirm the diagnosis?

There are no specific laboratory or imaging tests used to diagnose diastasis recti.

What additional information should be obtained to confirm the diagnosis?

A thorough medical history and physical examination should be completed. Diastasis recti is typically diagnosed on the basis of the physical examination. The patient should be positioned in hooklying and asked to lift their head and shoulders from the supporting surface. While in this position, a palpable separation of greater than two finger widths is considered to signify the presence of diastasis recti.

MANAGEMENT

What is the most effective management of this patient?

The management of diastasis recti is typically conservative and includes physical therapy. Abdominal muscle support and corrective exercise interventions assist in improving comfort and facilitating healing. A gentle progression of corrective abdominal exercises may begin within 24 hours of delivery for patients who developed the condition during pregnancy. Patients should be instructed to use their hands or other external assistance such as a towel or bed sheet wrapped around the abdominals to facilitate approximation of the muscles during exercise. This approximation allows muscles to heal and strengthen in an anatomically and mechanically correct position. Abdominal crunches should be avoided until healing has reduced the separation to less than two finger widths. Rotational exercises should be avoided until there is no separation. While healing, patients should avoid moving from supine directly to long sitting (e.g., jack knife) and double leg lifts in order to avoid further injury to the rectus abdominis and low back. In severe cases, surgical intervention for diastasis recti may be warranted to prevent complications associated with abdominal herniation.

What home care regimen should be recommended?

Patients should continue at home with a corrective abdominal exercise progression as recommended by the physical therapist. An abdominal binder may be recommended to assist in maintaining approximation of the healing abdominal muscles and to provide lumbar support. Patients should be advised to limit lifting activities while healing.

OUTCOME

What is the likely outcome of a course of physical therapy?

Most patients improve with conservative treatment focused on corrective exercise and do not suffer long-term functional deficits associated with the condition.

What are the long-term effects of the patient's condition?

Some degree of diastasis recti may persist despite appropriate conservative intervention. Functional mobility and stability are not typically impaired. In cases where pain persists or hernia related complications develop, surgical intervention may be necessary.

Graves' Disease

SILVER

DIAGNOSIS

What condition produces a patient's symptoms?

Graves' disease is the most common form of hyperactive thyroid disorder and is the result of an autoimmune attack on the thyroid gland causing overproduction of the hormone thyroxine (T4). Abnormally high levels of T4 increase the body's metabolic rate producing subsequent symptoms. The etiology of Graves' disease is currently unknown.

An injury was most likely sustained to which structure?

The thyroid gland is a part of the endocrine system, located anteriorly in the neck just below the larynx. It is butterfly-shaped and responsible for the release of the T4 and triiodothyronine (T3) hormones which control metabolism and influence factors such as weight, mood, and general energy levels. Patients with Graves' disease have an abnormal presence of the thyroid-stimulating hormone receptor antibody (TRAb). TRAb mimics the effect of the thyroid-stimulating hormone (TSH) released by the pituitary gland that results in an increased production of T4.

INFERENCE

What is the most likely contributing factor in the development of this condition?

The cause of Graves' disease is currently unknown, however, research suggests that stress, smoking, pregnancy, and a family history of the disease may be contributing factors. The condition is most prevalent in women over 20 years of age.

CONFIRMATION

What is the most likely clinical presentation?

Patients with Graves' disease typically present with a variety of multi-systemic symptoms. General complaints may include heat intolerance, increased appetite, increased sweating, frequent bowel movements, physical fatigue, weakness, tremor, weight loss, and insomnia. Visual complaints typically stem from exophthalmos, which may cause excessive tear production, double vision, light sensitivity, and eye irritation. Cardiopulmonary complaints may include dyspnea with exertion, palpitations, tachycardia, and arrhythmias. Cognitive changes may include increased anxiety, mental fatigue, and difficulty with concentration.

What laboratory or imaging studies would confirm the diagnosis?

Graves' disease is typically diagnosed through blood analysis of T3 and T4 hormone levels as well as TSH released by the pituitary gland. An elevated T4 level in combination with low TSH is considered indicative of Graves' disease. Thyroid function may be further evaluated via a radioactive iodine uptake test. A high uptake of radioactive iodine is indicative of excess T4 production, as occurs with Graves' disease.

What additional information should be obtained to confirm the diagnosis?

A thorough medical history should be obtained and physical examination completed, including a detailed assessment of reported symptoms.

MANAGEMENT

What is the most effective management of this patient?

Medical management of Graves' disease is primarily focused on pharmacological intervention. Antithyroid medications reduce thyroid production and assist in regulating T4 levels within the body. Other medications such as beta-blockers and corticosteroids may be used temporarily to manage symptoms such as tachycardia or exophthalmos while thyroid-regulating medications are being introduced. In some cases, surgical intervention or radioactive iodine treatment may be components of treatment. Since these interventions effectively damage or remove portions of the thyroid gland, lifelong pharmacological management (e.g., hormone replacement) will be necessary. Though physical therapy intervention is not typically indicated for the treatment of Graves' disease, physical therapists should be adept in recognizing signs and symptoms of the condition. Physical therapists should be cautious to select interventions that will not exacerbate symptoms. Cardiovascular stress and exercise in a hot environment may lead to secondary complications for patients with Graves' disease. During physical therapy intervention, vital signs should be closely monitored and modifications made to accommodate for reduced exercise tolerance or excess fatigue.

What home care regimen should be recommended?

A home care regimen should include pharmacological management and close monitoring of symptoms. Patients should be conscientious to avoid activities or environments that exacerbate symptoms.

OUTCOME

What is the likely outcome of a course of physical therapy?

Physical therapy is not typically indicated for patients with Graves' disease. Patients treated in physical therapy with a comorbidity of Graves' disease may have limited tolerance for exercise activity, however, the condition will not typically interfere with overall outcomes.

What are the long-term effects of the patient's condition?

Patients typically respond well to pharmacological intervention that regulates T4 hormone production. Side effects of antithyroid medications may include joint aches, itching, rash, liver dysfunction, and reduced white blood cell count.

BRONZE Level Clinical Application Templates

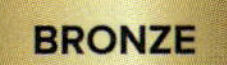

BRONZE Level Clinical Application Template Executive Summary

Addison's Disease

- Adrenal insufficiency that occurs due to dysfunction of the adrenal cortex resulting in decreased production of glucocorticoid and mineralocorticoid hormones
- Glucocorticoid hormones assist in regulation of cardiovascular function, metabolism, and stress; mineralocorticoid hormones assist in regulation of fluid and electrolyte balances
- Laboratory results of the rapid adrenocorticotropic hormone (ACTH) test are considered to be definitive in the diagnosis of Addison's disease

Appendicitis

- An inflammation of the inner lining of the appendix which may spread to other areas
- Abdominal pain is most commonly reported with symptoms beginning as either umbilical or gastric pain that migrates to the right lower quadrant
- Examination findings typically include abdominal rebound tenderness, pain with percussion, guarding, and rigidity

Crohn's Disease

- A specific form of inflammatory bowel disease in which the lining of the gastrointestinal (GI) tract becomes abnormally inflamed
- Typical signs and symptoms range from mild to significantly debilitating to life-threatening
- Symptoms may develop gradually or rapidly and typically include abdominal pain, cramping, diarrhea, blood in the stool, GI tract ulcers, diminished appetite, and weight loss

Cushing's Syndrome

- Results from abnormally high levels of cortisol which may occur due to endogenous overproduction of cortisol or excessive exogenous use of corticosteroids
- Typically present with hallmark physical signs including weight gain, purple striae, and a ruddy complexion
- May be diagnosed by laboratory analysis of cortisol levels in urine, saliva or blood

Diverticular Disease

- Benign condition characterized by the presence of outpocketings of the colon wall (i.e., diverticula)
- Risk factors include constipation, a diet low in fiber, obesity, a lack of exercise, connective tissue disorders, and advanced age
- Patients are often asymptomatic, though may experience abdominal pain and tenderness, fever, nausea, vomiting, constipation or diarrhea

Electrolyte Imbalances

- Commonly involve one of the following minerals: calcium, chloride, magnesium, phosphate, potassium, and sodium
- Symptoms vary depending on the mineral(s) involved and may include a change in mental status or behavior, dehydration, poor skin elasticity, rapid heart rate, and sunken eyes
- Blood tests and urinalysis can be used to detect abnormalities in electrolyte levels

BRONZE Level Clinical Application Template Executive Summary

Endometriosis

- A condition in which the cells of the uterine lining begin to grow outside of the uterine cavity, resulting in scar tissue and adhesions forming within the pelvic and abdominal cavities
- Primary symptom is pelvic pain, which worsens during menstruation and can spread to the abdomen or lower back
- Laparoscopy, a surgical procedure where a camera is inserted into the abdominal cavity to directly visualize the lesions, is used to definitively diagnose this condition

Gastroesophageal Reflux Disease

- Gastroesophageal reflux refers to the abnormal movement of partially digested solids, liquids, and gastric acid from the stomach into the esophagus
- Most common complaints include heartburn, acid reflux, nausea after eating, and feeling as though food remains trapped in the esophagus
- Typically diagnosed by reported symptoms and physical examination with additional testing for patients who do not respond to initial treatment

Gout

- Considered a complex form of arthritis resulting from an abnormally high uric acid level (hyperuricemia) in the body
- Greater prevalence among males with the great toe, knee, and ankle being the most commonly affected joints; may present as a chronic condition or a series of acute attacks
- Identification of uric acid crystals in synovial fluid, collected via synovial biopsy, may be used to confirm the diagnosis

Herpes Zoster

- Varicella-zoster virus (VZV) is responsible for outbreaks of "chickenpox" in children and herpes zoster "shingles" in adults
- Highly contagious especially to patients with a compromised immune system
- Symptoms typically begin with a unilateral painful itching or burning sensation caused by the virus' initial attack on the nerve fibers

Irritable Bowel Syndrome

- Characterized by gastrointestinal distress and alterations in bowel habits, such as constipation and diarrhea, which may be triggered by foods, stress or illness
- There are three main types of the condition: diarrhea-predominant, constipation-predominant, and alternating diarrhea and constipation symptoms
- Diagnosis is based on symptoms and the exclusion of other similar conditions

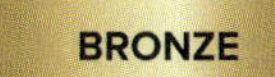

BRONZE Level Clinical Application Template Executive Summary

Lung Cancer

- Smoking, or exposure to smoke, is the leading cause of lung cancer
- Signs and symptoms that may suggest lung cancer include wheezing, coughing, hemoptysis, shortness of breath, chest pain, weight loss, fever, clubbing of the fingernails, and fatigue
- X-ray imaging is often used to detect an abnormal mass or nodule within the lungs, though computed tomography may be used to detect smaller lesions that cannot be seen on x-ray

Malabsorption Syndrome

- Condition in which the gastrointestinal tract fails to properly absorb nutrients from ingested food, which often results in malnutrition
- Symptoms differ depending on the nutrients not absorbed, though may include abdominal distention and bloating, flatulence, diarrhea, steatorrhea, foul-smelling stools, weight loss, weakness, fatigue, anemia, edema, muscle cramps, and excess bleeding
- There is no diagnostic testing for malabsorption syndrome, though the condition should be considered if a patient suffers from chronic diarrhea, nutritional deficiencies, and significant weight loss despite having a normal diet

Malignant Melanoma

- A form of skin cancer considered to be especially serious due to the high likelihood of metastasis that develops in the melanin-producing cells responsible for giving skin its color
- The first sign is a suspicious change in the appearance of a freckle or mole through asymmetry, irregular borders, uneven coloration or increased diameter
- Diagnosis of malignant melanoma is typically confirmed by an analysis of biopsied tissue

Metabolic Acidosis

- A state in which the pH of body fluids is abnormally low, which may result from overproduction or inadequate excretion of hydrogen ions or excessive excretion of bicarbonate ions
- Common signs and symptoms include tachypnea, confusion, and lethargy, though other signs and symptoms may present depending on the underlying pathology
- Laboratory analysis of arterial blood gases, serum electrolytes, and urine pH is used to identify abnormal acidity and differentiate between respiratory and metabolic acidosis

Metabolic Alkalosis

- A state in which the pH of body fluids is abnormally elevated, which may result from inadequate excretion of bicarbonate ions, ingestion of large amounts of bicarbonate or excessive excretion of hydrogen ions
- Common signs and symptoms include bradypnea and symptoms of hypokalemia (e.g., weakness, myalgia, polyuria), though other signs and symptoms may present depending on the underlying pathology
- Laboratory analysis of arterial blood gases, serum electrolytes, and urine pH is used to identify abnormal alkalinity and differentiate between respiratory and metabolic alkalosis

BRONZE Level Clinical Application Template Executive Summary

Multiple Organ Dysfunction Syndrome

- Characterized by the physiologic dysfunction of two or more organs or organ systems that can be caused by infection, injury, hypermetabolism or circulatory shock
- Clinical presentation varies depending on the severity of the condition as well as the organs or organ systems affected
- Laboratory and imaging studies are used to identify the source of the condition and may include x-ray, computed tomography, ultrasonography, blood testing or lumbar puncture

Peptic Ulcer Disease

- Peptic ulcers form when the balance of protective and erosive factors is disrupted to such an extent that epithelial injury occurs and subsequent erosion extends to the muscularis mucosa
- Primary symptom of a burning epigastric pain that occurs after eating; other symptoms include dyspepsia, chest discomfort, heartburn, fatty food intolerance, and hematemesis
- Upper GI endoscopy is typically the diagnostic tool of choice allowing for visualization and tissue biopsy

Prostate Cancer

- Prostate cancer is generally a slow-growing cancer, though it can metastasize to other parts of the body, especially the lymph nodes and bones
- Symptoms are more likely to be present in the advanced stages of the disease and may include difficulty urinating, nocturia, erectile dysfunction, blood in the urine or semen, pelvic or low back pain, and bone pain, if metastasized
- The prostate-specific antigen (PSA) test is a blood test used to determine the presence of elevated levels of PSA, which can be indicative of prostate cancer

Systemic Sclerosis

- A connective tissue disease characterized by excess collagen deposition which leads to changes of the skin and internal organs
- Symptoms vary based on the organs affected but may include itching, skin that appears tight, reddish or scaly, Raynaud's phenomenon, muscle weakness, joint pain, decreased lung function, pulmonary hypertension, gastroesophageal reflux, decreased gastric or intestinal motility, intestinal malabsorption, and renal disease
- Blood tests can be performed to detect elevated levels of certain autoantibodies and a skin biopsy can be performed to determine changes in the skin

Ulcerative Colitis

- An inflammatory bowel disease that results in chronic inflammation and the formation of ulcers in the large intestine
- Symptoms may include abdominal pain and cramping, diarrhea, blood in the stools, urgency to defecate, weight loss, fatigue, and fever
- The best test for diagnosing ulcerative colitis is endoscopy, which allows for direct visualization of the colon

Level Clinical Application Template Executive Summary

Urinary Tract Infection

- The urinary tract is normally a sterile environment, but under certain conditions infectious organisms from internal or external sources can proliferate and cause infection
- Characterized by a strong and persistent urge to urinate, as well as a burning sensation with urination
- Urinalysis and urine culture are most commonly used to diagnose a urinary tract infection, however, patients who suffer recurrent urinary tract infections may require more invasive diagnostic testing

Uterine Cancer

- The most common type of uterine cancer affects the endometrium, which is thought to occur when an imbalance of hormones causes the endometrium to grow thicker
- Unexpected vaginal bleeding is the most common symptom associated with uterine cancer, especially when it occurs after menopause
- The only method to confirm the diagnosis of uterine cancer is through a tissue biopsy, which is obtained during a procedure known as dilation and curettage

BRONZE

Addison's Disease

DIAGNOSIS

What condition produces a patient's symptoms?

Addison's disease refers to a specific form of adrenal insufficiency that occurs due to dysfunction of the adrenal cortex resulting in decreased production of glucocorticoid (e.g., cortisol) and mineralocorticoid (e.g., aldosterone) hormones. Glucocorticoid hormones assist with regulation of cardiovascular function, metabolism, and the body's response to stress. Mineralocorticoid hormones assist in the regulation of fluids and electrolytes.

An injury was most likely sustained to which structure?

The most common etiology of Addison's disease is idiopathic autoimmune adrenocortical insufficiency. The chronic condition is the result of an abnormal autoimmune response which causes atrophy, fibrosis, and infiltration of lymphocytes within the adrenal cortex. Etiologies of acute Addison's disease include stress due to infection, trauma, emotional distress, adrenal hemorrhage, and adrenal artery embolism or thrombosis.

CONFIRMATION

What is the most likely clinical presentation?

Characteristics of Addison's disease typically mimic signs and symptoms of glucocorticoid and mineralocorticoid deficiency. Hyperpigmentation of the skin and mucous membranes is typically the first symptom to present, with changes most notable over areas frequently exposed to the sun. Vitiligo, gastrointestinal symptoms, syncope, weakness, fatigue, and myalgias are also common. Idiopathic autoimmune Addison's disease is most prevalent among females, typically between 30 and 50 years of age. Patients may experience an adrenal crisis presenting with significant nausea and vomiting while appearing confused and cyanotic. Abdominal symptoms may be acute including abdominal distention, pain, and tenderness.

What laboratory or imaging studies would confirm the diagnosis?

Laboratory results of the rapid adrenocorticotropic hormone (ACTH) test are considered to be definitive in the diagnosis of Addison's disease. Other laboratory studies may include a complete metabolic panel, complete blood count, antibody testing, and thyroid-stimulating hormone (TSH) test.

What additional information should be obtained to confirm the diagnosis?

A complete medical history should be obtained. Information regarding a familial history of adrenal insufficiency and commonly occurring comorbidities such as Graves' disease, type 1 diabetes mellitus or celiac disease should also be reviewed.

BRONZE

Appendicitis

DIAGNOSIS

What condition produces a patient's symptoms?

Appendicitis refers to an inflammation of the inner lining of the appendix which may spread to other areas. The inflammation may occur for a number of reasons, however, infection and obstruction of the appendiceal lumen are among the most commonly reported causes. Both etiologies result in increased pressure as bacteria multiply and fluids stagnate within the appendix. Eventually, the walls of the appendix become ischemic compromising their integrity and allowing for bacterial invasion which can lead to perforation, gangrene, peritonitis or abscess.

An injury was most likely sustained to which structure?

The appendix extends from the cecum as a worm-like projection. Though its position is not fixed, it is most commonly located in a dorsomedial position in the right lower quadrant. The actual position of an individual's appendix can considerably alter the clinical presentation of appendicitis.

CONFIRMATION

What is the most likely clinical presentation?

Presentation may vary depending on the age of the patient, position of the appendix, and degree of inflammation. Abdominal pain is most commonly reported with symptoms beginning as either umbilical or gastric pain that migrates to the right lower quadrant. Patients will often try to remain still, lying down with the hips flexed in an attempt to avoid exacerbating movements. Nausea, vomiting, and anorexia are also often reported. The duration of symptoms is typically less than 48 hours in adults, but may be longer in elderly patients or in instances when the appendix has perforated. Examination findings typically include abdominal rebound tenderness, pain with percussion, guarding, and rigidity.

What laboratory or imaging studies would confirm the diagnosis?

Laboratory tests are utilized to confirm the presence of infection or inflammation. Tests typically include a complete blood count, C-reactive protein test, urinalysis, and in some cases liver and pancreatic function tests. Imaging studies such as ultrasonography, CT scan, and MRI may be used.

What additional information should be obtained to confirm the diagnosis?

A thorough medical and symptom history should be obtained to assist in ruling out similar diagnoses. Specific questions regarding recent gastroenterologic and genitourinary conditions should be included as well as a gynecologic history for female patients.

Crohn's Disease

BRONZE

DIAGNOSIS

What condition produces a patient's symptoms?

Crohn's disease is a specific form of inflammatory bowel disease in which the lining of the gastrointestinal (GI) tract becomes abnormally inflamed. Symptoms can involve any aspect of the GI tract, however, typically present in lower structures (e.g., small bowel, colon). Symptom complaints are typically associated with an exacerbation of the inflammatory process or complications such as fibrosis or obstruction.

An injury was most likely sustained to which structure?

The etiology of Crohn's disease is idiopathic, but likely the result of an imbalance between anti-inflammatory and pro-inflammatory mediators within the GI tract. Structural injury typically begins with ulceration, hyperemia, and edema of the GI tract's superficial mucosal lining. The inflammatory process may cause adhesions, fibrosis, thickening, and may also spread to deeper mucosal layers forming granulomas or abscesses.

CONFIRMATION

What is the most likely clinical presentation?

The typical signs and symptoms range from mild to significantly debilitating to life-threatening. Symptoms may develop gradually or rapidly and typically include abdominal pain, cramping, and diarrhea. Other symptoms may include blood in the stool, GI tract ulcers, diminished appetite, and weight loss. Over time, some patients may develop complications including anal fissures, intestinal fistula, malnutrition, and bowel obstruction. The chronic inflammatory process may also precipitate symptoms such as gallstones, kidney stones, arthritis, and osteoporosis. Children with Crohn's disease typically experience delays in normal growth and development.

What laboratory or imaging studies would confirm the diagnosis?

Blood tests may be utilized to determine the presence of infection, anemia or abnormal antibodies and also typically include a fecal occult blood test. Invasive imaging procedures such as colonoscopy and sigmoidoscopy allow for lower GI visualization and the collection of tissue samples. X-ray, MRI, and CT scan may be visually enhanced using barium to assist in the identification of affected intestinal segments.

What additional information should be obtained to confirm the diagnosis?

A medical history should be completed to rule out similar diagnoses such as colon cancer, irritable bowel syndrome, and diverticulitis. Patients with a family history of Crohn's disease, who smoke, or who maintain a diet high in fat are at greater risk for developing the condition.

Cushing's Syndrome

BRONZE

DIAGNOSIS

What condition produces a patient's symptoms?

Cortisol is a glucocorticoid hormone produced by the adrenal cortex which assists in the regulation of cardiovascular function, metabolism, and the body's response to stress. Cushing's syndrome is a condition resulting from abnormally high levels of cortisol due to endogenous overproduction of cortisol or excessive exogenous use of corticosteroids.

An injury was most likely sustained to which structure?

The most common endogenous etiology of hypercortisolism is a pituitary or adrenal gland tumor. Pituitary tumors are typically benign and linked to increased production of the adrenocorticotropic hormone (ACTH) which stimulates cortisol overproduction. This condition is termed Cushing's syndrome. A benign adrenal cortex tumor may also cause cortisol overproduction independent of ACTH influence. Less common endogenous etiologies include genetics and malignancy. Exogenous etiologies are linked to high doses of corticosteroids typically used for inflammatory conditions.

CONFIRMATION

What is the most likely clinical presentation?

Patients with Cushing's syndrome typically present with hallmark physical signs including weight gain, purple striae, and a ruddy complexion. Weight gain is accompanied by increased adipose tissue distribution in the face (e.g., "moon face"), upper back (e.g., "buffalo hump"), torso (e.g., central obesity), and supraclavicular region. Other symptoms include fatigue, depression, emotional lability, excessive hair growth, bruising, and proximal muscle weakness. Systemically, Cushing's syndrome may contribute to conditions such as hypertension, diabetes mellitus, peptic ulcer disease, osteopenia, and immune system impairment. There is a significantly greater prevalence among women with the onset of symptoms between 25 and 40 years of age.

What laboratory or imaging studies would confirm the diagnosis?

Cushing's syndrome may be diagnosed by laboratory analysis of cortisol levels in urine, saliva or blood. Laboratory studies detailing the body's response to a low dose of dexamethasone, alone or in combination with ACTH stimulation, are also considered to be diagnostically valid.

What additional information should be obtained to confirm the diagnosis?

A thorough medical history and physical examination should be completed to rule out similar diagnoses and identify characteristics commonly associated with the condition.

BRONZE

Diverticular Disease

DIAGNOSIS

What condition produces a patient's symptoms?

Diverticulosis is a benign condition characterized by the presence of outpocketings of the colon wall (i.e., diverticula). The condition develops secondary to increased pressure within the colon. Diverticulitis is the condition characterized by the inflammation or infection of the diverticula. Risk factors for this condition include constipation, a diet low in fiber, obesity, a lack of exercise, connective tissue disorders (e.g., Marfan syndrome, Ehlers-Danlos syndrome), and advanced age.

An injury was most likely sustained to what structure?

The condition is characterized by outpocketings of the colon wall, most often in the sigmoid colon. When the colon experiences an increase in pressure, pockets develop in areas where the wall of the colon is weak (i.e., herniations). If these pockets become further damaged or rupture, they may become infected (i.e., diverticulitis).

CONFIRMATION

What is the most likely clinical presentation?

Patients with diverticulosis will likely be asymptomatic. They may experience abdominal pain and tenderness (often in the left lower quadrant), fever, nausea, vomiting, constipation or diarrhea. More serious complications of the condition include rectal bleeding, colonic obstruction, and infection of the abdominal cavity.

What laboratory or imaging studies would confirm the diagnosis?

Computed tomography is the most commonly used tool to identify the presence of diverticulitis. A colonoscopy can be performed to directly visualize the diverticula and surrounding structures, though it should not be conducted during or shortly after an acute episode of diverticulitis.

What additional information should be obtained to confirm the diagnosis?

A thorough medical history and physical examination should be performed to rule out other pathologies that may cause abdominal pain. The physical examination would include palpation of the abdomen to check for areas of tenderness.

BRONZE

Electrolyte Imbalances

DIAGNOSIS

What condition produces a patient's symptoms?

Electrolytes are minerals that carry an electrical charge and are present within the fluids of the body. They are critical to many of the body's processes, including nerve and muscle function and maintenance of fluid balance. Electrolyte imbalances occur when these minerals are not maintained within a specific range. There are several causes for electrolyte imbalances including medications, vomiting, diarrhea, inadequate diet or malabsorption, trauma, burns, cancer, thyroid disorders, endocrine or metabolic disorders, renal disease, liver disease, congestive heart failure, alcoholism, and eating disorders.

An injury was most likely sustained to what structure?

Electrolyte imbalances commonly involve one of the following minerals: calcium, chloride, magnesium, phosphate, potassium, and sodium. The body structures affected as a result of this condition will depend on which electrolyte is too low or high in concentration. For example, skeletal muscles may be affected if there are abnormalities in the concentration of magnesium, potassium, calcium or sodium.

CONFIRMATION

What is the most likely clinical presentation?

The clinical presentation will vary depending on the mineral(s) involved. General symptoms that may occur include dizziness, fatigue, nausea, constipation, diarrhea, decreased urine output, dark urine, dry mouth, decreased perspiration, muscle weakness, muscle cramping or spasm, irregular heartbeat, and headache. A change in mental status or behavior, poor skin elasticity, rapid heart rate, and sunken eyes are signs and symptoms indicative of dehydration and require immediate medical care.

What laboratory or imaging studies would confirm the diagnosis?

Blood tests and urinalysis are used to detect abnormalities in electrolyte levels. If abnormalities are detected, other testing (e.g., electrocardiogram for heart problems, ultrasound or x-ray for kidney problems) may be warranted.

What additional information should be obtained to confirm the diagnosis?

A thorough medical history and physical examination should be performed to rule out the existence of other similar conditions. The physical examination will vary depending on which electrolyte imbalance is suspected, but may include assessment of vital signs, strength, and reflexes.

Endometriosis

BRONZE

DIAGNOSIS

What condition produces a patient's symptoms?

Endometriosis is a condition in which the endometrial cells that line the inside of the uterus begin to grow outside of the uterine cavity. The exact etiology is unknown. The most widely accepted theory is the retrograde menstruation theory, in which the menstrual blood flows backwards in the fallopian tubes and into the pelvic cavity.

An injury was most likely sustained to what structure?

Endometriosis is the growth of endometrial cells outside the uterine cavity. Scar tissue and adhesions form within the pelvic and abdominal cavities. The displaced endometrial cells continue to function normally by breaking down and bleeding since the blood has no way to exit the body. The structures most commonly affected include the ovaries, fallopian tubes, uterine ligaments, intestines, urinary bladder, and ureters. Endometrial tissue rarely spreads beyond the pelvic and abdominal regions.

CONFIRMATION

What is the most likely clinical presentation?

The primary symptom associated with this condition is pelvic pain, which worsens during menstruation and can spread to the abdomen or lower back. The intensity of pain is not indicative of the extent of the endometriosis. Other signs and symptoms may include pain with intercourse, pain with urination or bowel movements, diarrhea, constipation, excessive bleeding, fatigue, and infertility.

What laboratory or imaging studies would confirm the diagnosis?

The only test that can definitively diagnose endometriosis is laparoscopy, a surgical procedure where a camera is inserted into the abdominal cavity to directly visualize the lesions. Ultrasound may also be used to aid in the diagnosis, though it is only effective in identifying large cysts.

What additional information should be obtained to confirm the diagnosis?

A thorough medical history and physical examination should be performed to rule out the presence of other similar conditions (e.g., pelvic inflammatory disease, irritable bowel syndrome). The physical examination will likely include a pelvic examination where the physician palpates in and around the pelvic area to detect the presence of endometrial growths.

Gastroesophageal Reflux Disease

BRONZE

DIAGNOSIS

What condition produces a patient's symptoms?

Gastroesophageal reflux occurs in the upper gastrointestinal tract and refers to the abnormal movement of partially digested solids, liquids, and gastric acid from the stomach into the esophagus. This back flow of highly acidic stomach contents irritates the lining of the esophagus causing acid indigestion. Occasional reflux is common, however, chronic recurrences are typically indicative of gastroesophageal reflux disease (GERD).

An injury was most likely sustained to which structure?

The esophagus has both an upper esophageal sphincter (UES) and a lower esophageal sphincter (LES) which function to prevent regurgitation. A weak or abnormally functioning LES that fails to close completely will allow stomach contents to reflux into the esophagus. Persistent reflux, as is characteristic of GERD, can cause significant irritation of the esophageal lining and eventual esophagitis leading to more severe damage and additional symptoms such as esophageal erosion and bleeding.

CONFIRMATION

What is the most likely clinical presentation?

Patients with GERD can present with a variety of symptoms that typically occur more than twice weekly and interfere to some degree with daily life. The most common complaints include heartburn, acid reflux, nausea after eating, and feeling as though food remains trapped in the esophagus. Other symptoms may include a sour taste in the mouth, dysphagia, chest pain, dry cough, hoarseness, and the sensation of a lump in the throat. GERD symptoms are often increased with bending, stooping or supine positioning and tend to worsen at night.

What laboratory or imaging studies would confirm the diagnosis?

A barium swallow with x-ray imaging of the upper GI tract may be used to identify structural or anatomical problems within the esophagus. An upper GI endoscopy may be used to visualize and identify esophageal irritation or damage. GERD is typically diagnosed by reported symptoms and physical examination with additional testing pursued in patients who do not respond to initial treatment.

What additional information should be obtained to confirm the diagnosis?

A thorough medical history should be obtained with a detailed symptom history. Patients at increased risk for developing GERD include those who are obese, pregnant, use cigarettes, abuse alcohol or present with a hiatal hernia or scleroderma.

BRONZE — Gout

DIAGNOSIS

What condition produces a patient's symptoms?

Gout is a complex form of arthritis resulting from an abnormally high uric acid level in the body. This most commonly occurs secondary to the underexcretion of uric acid, but can also result from overproduction of uric acid or a combination of both. As uric acid levels increase around joints, needle-like crystals form and accumulate causing inflammation and joint swelling.

An injury was most likely sustained to which structure?

Uric acid is formed as the body breaks down foods that are high in purine. The etiology of hyperuricemia is often idiopathic, however, a number of medical conditions (e.g., ketoacidosis, hypothyroidism) and side effects of certain medications are also associated with hyperuricemia. Some individuals with hyperuricemia fail to develop symptoms of gout while others may be asymptomatic for years prior to the first acute gout attack. Structural damage is more commonly associated with chronic gout.

CONFIRMATION

What is the most likely clinical presentation?

Gout has a significantly greater prevalence among males with the great toe, knee, and ankle being the most commonly affected joints. Gout may present as a chronic condition or a series of acute attacks. An acute attack typically involves a single joint and presents with signs of inflammation including pain, redness, and warmth. Pain tends to be severe and is described as throbbing, crushing or excruciating. The onset of acute symptoms typically begins with a rapid progression of discomfort, often occurring at night time, which then gradually eases over time. In chronic gout, multiple joints tend to be affected with less intense symptoms. Chronic gout may go unrecognized initially with symptoms attributed to arthritis. Firm, lumpy deposits of uric acid that form under the skin, referred to as tophi, are typically associated with chronic gout.

What laboratory or imaging studies would confirm the diagnosis?

The identification of uric acid crystals in synovial fluid, collected via synovial biopsy, may be used to confirm the diagnosis. Abnormal systemic levels of uric acid may be assessed through laboratory analysis of blood and urine samples.

What additional information should be obtained to confirm the diagnosis?

A thorough medical history and physical examination should be completed. Conditions such as obesity, kidney disease, diabetes mellitus or insipidus, leukemia, and sickle cell anemia are associated with an increased incidence of gout.

BRONZE — Herpes Zoster

DIAGNOSIS

What condition produces a patient's symptoms?

The varicella-zoster virus (VZV) is responsible for "chickenpox" in children and herpes zoster (shingles) in adults. Once exposed, the virus can remain dormant for years. Herpes zoster is highly contagious especially to patients with a compromised immune system. VZV exposure in childhood may offer some protection, but it does not guarantee immunity against a herpes zoster outbreak as an adult.

An injury was most likely sustained to which structure?

After exposure, VZV typically lies dormant within neural tissue where it may never reactivate. Reactivation and a resultant herpes zoster outbreak commonly occur when the immune system has been weakened. As the reactivated virus reproduces, the infection attacks and damages nerve fibers while moving along the nerve toward the skin's surface. Once the virus reaches the surface, a characteristic blistered rash will appear. Though external outbreaks of herpes zoster are most readily recognized, internal structures such as organ surfaces, the mouth, and the inner eye may also be affected.

CONFIRMATION

What is the most likely clinical presentation?

Symptoms of herpes zoster typically begin with a unilateral painful itching or burning sensation caused by the virus' initial attack on the nerve fibers. Numbness or skin sensitivity may also be reported. Initial symptoms are followed by a painful, blistered rash. General symptoms may also include fever, body aches, chills, and fatigue. As the infection progresses, the blisters will break open and drain. VZV transmission occurs through direct contact with open sores created by the broken blisters. Once the sores have scabbed over, the patient is no longer considered contagious. Post-herpetic neuralgia, due to scarring or destruction of nerve tissue, is the most common herpes zoster complication. Other potential complications tend to be specific to the area affected such as vision loss, balance deficits or facial paralysis.

What laboratory or imaging studies would confirm the diagnosis?

Blood samples may show the presence of VZV antibodies and an increased white blood cell count, but these findings are not considered to be diagnostic.

What additional information should be obtained to confirm the diagnosis?

A medical history should be obtained including any history of exposure to VZV. Herpes zoster is diagnosed based on physical examination and reported symptoms.

Irritable Bowel Syndrome

BRONZE

DIAGNOSIS

What condition produces a patient's symptoms?

Irritable bowel syndrome (IBS) is a condition characterized by gastrointestinal distress and alterations in bowel habits, such as constipation and diarrhea. The exact etiology of IBS is not known. Theories include an overgrowth of bacteria in the small intestine and altered signaling between the brain and gastrointestinal tract. Triggers for the condition include foods, stress, and illness.

An injury was most likely sustained to what structure?

IBS is a condition that affects the gastrointestinal tract, specifically the large intestine. The walls of the intestines are lined with muscular layers which contract and relax to pass food along the tract. When the contractions are longer or stronger than normal, symptoms of gastrointestinal distress (e.g., bloating, flatulence) may result. When the contractions are too weak, stools may become hard and dry and lead to constipation. Unlike other gastrointestinal disorders (e.g., Crohn's disease, ulcerative colitis), IBS does not result in structural changes to the intestinal tissue.

CONFIRMATION

What is the most likely clinical presentation?

IBS is characterized by abdominal pain and discomfort, bloating, flatulence, and constipation and/or diarrhea. There are three main types of the condition: diarrhea-predominant (IBS-D), constipation-predominant (IBS-C) or alternating diarrhea and constipation symptoms (IBS-A). Typically, IBS is a chronic condition that will require lifetime management of symptoms.

What laboratory or imaging studies would confirm the diagnosis?

There are no laboratory or imaging studies that diagnose IBS. Colonoscopy or computed tomography may be performed to rule out other conditions that produce abdominal pain and gastrointestinal distress. Blood tests and stool tests may also be performed for this reason.

What additional information should be obtained to confirm the diagnosis?

A thorough medical history and physical examination should be performed since this condition is diagnosed based on symptoms and the exclusion of other similar conditions. Abdominal pain that improves with defecation and changes in stool consistency are two symptoms that often suggest the presence of IBS.

Lung Cancer

BRONZE

DIAGNOSIS

What condition produces a patient's symptoms?

Lung cancer is a malignant tumor within the lungs that is characterized by uncontrolled cell growth. Smoking or exposure to smoke is the leading cause of lung cancer, however, lung cancer can occur in individuals that have never smoked. Other causes of lung cancer may include genetic factors and exposure to radon gas, asbestos or air pollution.

An injury was most likely sustained to what structure?

Lung cancer arises when carcinogens damage the epithelial cells of the lungs. Initially, the body is able to repair the cell damage, though cumulative damage causes genetic mutation to the DNA of the cells and leads to development of a tumor. As the cells divide and proliferate, they may metastasize to other areas of the body. Lung cancer metastasizes early, making it a very difficult cancer to treat. Common locations of metastasis include the adrenal glands, liver, brain, and bones.

CONFIRMATION

What is the most likely clinical presentation?

Signs and symptoms that may suggest lung cancer include wheezing, coughing, hemoptysis, shortness of breath, chest pain, weight loss, fever, clubbing of the fingernails, and fatigue. Signs and symptoms often only present in the more advanced stages of the disease, which results in a poor prognosis.

What laboratory or imaging studies would confirm the diagnosis?

X-ray imaging is often used to detect an abnormal mass or nodule within the lungs, though computed tomography may be used to detect smaller lesions that cannot be seen on x-ray. If cancer is suspected, a tissue biopsy may be performed to determine the presence of malignant cells. If the patient presents with a cough that produces sputum, the sputum can also be tested to identify the presence of malignant cells. A bone scan may be performed to determine the level of metastasis.

What additional information should be obtained to confirm the diagnosis?

A thorough medical history and physical examination is helpful in identifying signs and symptoms that may be suspicious for lung cancer. Once lung cancer has been diagnosed, the physician will "stage" the cancer (i.e., the extent of metastasis) to determine what treatment is most appropriate.

BRONZE

Malabsorption Syndrome

DIAGNOSIS

What condition produces a patient's symptoms?

Malabsorption syndrome is a condition in which the gastrointestinal tract fails to properly absorb nutrients from ingested food, which often results in malnutrition. There are a variety of reasons that the body may not properly absorb nutrients including infectious agents (e.g., HIV, Giardia), structural defects (e.g., Crohn's disease, diverticula), mucosal abnormalities (e.g., celiac disease), enzyme deficiencies (e.g., lactose intolerance), digestive insufficiencies (e.g., cystic fibrosis, pancreatitis), and systemic diseases (e.g., diabetes mellitus).

An injury was most likely sustained to what structure?

The purpose of the gastrointestinal tract is to absorb macronutrients, micronutrients, water, and electrolytes. The process of absorbing nutrients includes digestion (within the lumen of the intestines), absorption (across the mucosa of the intestines), and transport (events occurring after mucosal absorption). Malabsorption occurs when this sequence of digestion-absorption-transport is disrupted.

CONFIRMATION

What is the most likely clinical presentation?

The clinical presentation may differ depending on the nutrients that are not properly absorbed. Common signs and symptoms of malabsorption syndrome include abdominal distention and bloating, flatulence, diarrhea, steatorrhea (i.e., presence of fat in the feces), foul-smelling stools, weight loss, weakness, and fatigue. Signs of nutrient deficiency may include anemia, edema, muscle cramps, and excess bleeding.

What laboratory or imaging studies would confirm the diagnosis?

Laboratory studies used to diagnose this condition include blood testing and sampling of stool. Tests that measure the fat content in the stool are the most reliable. A biopsy may be performed if an abnormality in the wall of the bowel is suspected.

What additional information should be obtained to confirm the diagnosis?

There is no specific test used to diagnose malabsorption syndrome, therefore a diagnosis is often made based on the patient's signs and symptoms. The condition should be strongly considered if the patient suffers from chronic diarrhea, nutritional deficiencies, and significant weight loss despite having a normal diet.

BRONZE

Malignant Melanoma

DIAGNOSIS

What condition produces a patient's symptoms?

Malignant melanoma is a form of skin cancer considered to be especially serious due to the high risk of metastasis. The cancer develops in the melanin-producing cells responsible for giving skin its color. The disease is most commonly diagnosed among patients with light complexions. Visible changes in skin markings may be more difficult to detect in darker skin tones leading to a delay in diagnosis and a less favorable prognosis.

An injury was most likely sustained to which structure?

Injury occurs at the cellular level with an alteration in melanocyte DNA causing cell overproduction and the formation of a malignant mass. The exact etiology of this abnormality is unclear, however, exposure to ultraviolet radiation is regarded to be the most significant risk factor.

CONFIRMATION

What is the most likely clinical presentation?

Most melanomas develop in areas of skin that have been extensively exposed to ultraviolet radiation such as the face, chest, back, arms, and legs. Typically, the first sign of melanoma is a suspicious change in the appearance of a freckle or mole. Asymmetry, irregular borders, uneven coloration or increased diameter of a skin marking may all be signs of malignancy. Many melanomas do not exclusively occur in areas exposed to ultraviolet radiation. Occurrences in these areas are often difficult to detect due to limited visibility or overlooked due to their uncommon location. Consequently, detection is often delayed increasing the likelihood of metastasis occurring before a diagnosis is made.

What laboratory or imaging studies would confirm the diagnosis?

A diagnosis of malignant melanoma is typically confirmed by an analysis of biopsied tissue. The type of biopsy utilized depends on the location, type of skin involved, and specific presentation. If melanoma is confirmed, a sentinel node biopsy is typically recommended to determine if the cancerous cells have metastasized to nearby lymph nodes.

What additional information should be obtained to confirm the diagnosis?

A thorough medical history and physical examination should be completed. Factors that increase the risk of developing melanoma include living at high altitudes close to the equator, history of sunburns or ultraviolet radiation exposure, excessive number of moles, fair skin, weakened immune system, and a family history of melanoma. Regular skin examinations are recommended for early identification of suspicious skin marks.

Metabolic Acidosis

BRONZE

DIAGNOSIS

What condition produces a patient's symptoms?

Metabolic acidosis refers to a state in which the pH of body fluids is abnormally low indicating acidemia. This may result from overproduction or inadequate excretion of hydrogen ions (H+) or excessive excretion of bicarbonate ions (HCO_3^-). Conditions such as ketoacidosis and lactic acidosis are common forms of metabolic acidosis related to H+ overproduction. Impaired kidney function is most often associated with metabolic acidosis due to inadequate H+ excretion. The kidneys may also play a role in excessive HCO_3^- excretion, however, severe diarrhea is more often the etiology of excessive HCO_3^- excretion.

An injury was most likely sustained to which structure?

Metabolic acidosis is not an independent disease process, but rather a symptom of some other underlying condition or disease. Injuries sustained vary with the etiology of the acidosis.

CONFIRMATION

What is the most likely clinical presentation?

Tachypnea is often observed as the body tries to regulate its acid-base balance by inducing respiratory alkalosis through hyperventilation. Confusion or lethargy is likely to occur as acid levels increase. Other signs and symptoms are typically related more to the underlying pathology than the resultant acid-base imbalance. Depending on the etiology, metabolic acidosis can cause a variety of nonspecific symptoms including tinnitus, cardiac arrhythmia, chest pain, headache, visual changes, vomiting, abdominal pain, generalized weakness, and hyperventilation. Metabolic acidosis may present as either an acute or chronic condition and can be fatal if left untreated.

What laboratory or imaging studies would confirm the diagnosis?

Laboratory analysis of arterial blood gases, serum electrolytes, and urine pH is used to identify abnormal acidity and differentiate between respiratory and metabolic acidosis.

What additional information should be obtained to confirm the diagnosis?

A thorough medical history should be obtained in order to identify conditions which may contribute to systemic H+ increases (e.g., uncontrolled diabetes, alcoholism, salicylate poisoning), inadequate H+ excretion (e.g., renal failure) or excessive HCO_3^- loss (e.g., severe diarrhea, intestinal fistula).

Metabolic Alkalosis

BRONZE

DIAGNOSIS

What condition produces a patient's symptoms?

Metabolic alkalosis refers to a state in which the pH of body fluids is abnormally elevated indicating alkalemia. This typically results from inadequate excretion of bicarbonate ions (HCO_3^-), ingestion of large amounts of bicarbonate (e.g., antacids) or excessive excretion of hydrogen ions (H+). Renal dysfunction is typically the etiology of metabolic alkalosis due to inadequate HCO_3^- excretion. Metabolic alkalosis due to excessive H+ excretion is most frequently attributed to the use of diuretics or activities that decrease the body's volume of acidic substances (e.g., gastric acid) such as vomiting and nasogastric suctioning.

An injury was most likely sustained to which structure?

Metabolic alkalosis is not an independent disease process, but rather a symptom of some other underlying condition or disease. Injuries sustained vary with the etiology of the alkalosis.

CONFIRMATION

What is the most likely clinical presentation?

Bradypnea is typically observed as the body tries to regulate its acid-base balance by inducing respiratory acidosis through hypoventilation. In patients with other pulmonary impairments, this may also cause hypoxemia. In severe cases, metabolic alkalosis can cause seizure, tetany, altered mental status or arrhythmia. Patients with metabolic alkalosis typically present with symptoms of hypokalemia (e.g., weakness, myalgia, polyuria). Other signs and symptoms tend to be nonspecific and related more to the underlying pathology of the acid-base imbalance. Metabolic alkalosis may present as either an acute or chronic condition and can be fatal if untreated.

What laboratory or imaging studies would confirm the diagnosis?

Laboratory analysis of arterial blood gases, serum electrolytes, and urine pH are used to identify abnormal alkalinity and differentiate between respiratory and metabolic alkalosis.

What additional information should be obtained to confirm the diagnosis?

A thorough medical history should be obtained in order to identify conditions which may contribute to systemic increases in HCO_3^- (e.g., blood transfusion, significant alkali ingestion) or decreases in H+ (e.g., bulimia, hypertension).

BRONZE

Multiple Organ Dysfunction Syndrome

DIAGNOSIS

What condition produces a patient's symptoms?

Multiple organ dysfunction syndrome (MODS) is a clinical syndrome characterized by the physiologic dysfunction of two or more organs or organ systems. The condition can be caused by infection, injury, hypermetabolism or circulatory shock. Infection and/or a systemic inflammatory response leads to sepsis which eventually leads to MODS.

An injury was most likely sustained to what structure?

There must be dysfunction of two or more organs or organ systems to be classified as MODS. Any organ or organ system in the body can be affected, however, there are six organ systems that are typically considered when characterizing the condition. These include the respiratory, cardiovascular, renal, hepatic, neurologic, and hematologic systems. Histologic changes to these organs include edema, inflammation, fibrosis, and tissue ischemia and necrosis.

CONFIRMATION

What is the most likely clinical presentation?

The clinical presentation will depend on where the patient falls on the continuum of the condition, from the onset of an inflammatory response to eventual MODS. Fever, chills, sweating, altered mental function, and hyperventilation are common symptoms that occur when sepsis is present. Other symptoms are dictated by the systems affected and may include earache, sore throat, sinus pain, swollen lymph glands, productive cough, chest pain, dyspnea, abdominal pain, nausea, vomiting, diarrhea, pelvic or flank pain, vaginal/urethral discharge, and urgency or frequency of urination.

What laboratory or imaging studies would confirm the diagnosis?

There are several laboratory and imaging studies that may be performed since the condition affects multiple systems. X-ray, computed tomography, and ultrasonography are often used to help determine the source of infection or insult. A complete blood cell count may be performed to assist with diagnosis and also to ensure that hemoglobin levels are adequate in the presence of shock. A lumbar puncture may be performed if meningitis or encephalitis is suspected.

What additional information should be obtained to confirm the diagnosis?

A thorough medical history and physical examination should be performed to rule out the presence of other similar conditions (e.g., respiratory distress syndrome, renal failure). The physical examination will likely involve assessment of all vital signs.

BRONZE

Peptic Ulcer Disease

DIAGNOSIS

What condition produces a patient's symptoms?

Peptic ulcer disease affects the gastrointestinal (GI) tract and encompasses both gastric and duodenal ulcers. H. pylori infection and use of high-dose NSAIDs are the two most prevalent etiologies linked to peptic ulcer disease. Other etiologies include psychological stress, advanced age, genetics, and certain comorbidities (e.g., COPD, celiac disease, Crohn's disease).

An injury was most likely sustained to which structure?

The protective lining of the stomach and duodenum is comprised of various cells which normally prevent the erosion of the underlying tissue. Peptic ulcers form when the balance of these protective and erosive factors is disrupted to such an extent that epithelial injury occurs and subsequent erosion extends to the muscularis mucosa.

CONFIRMATION

What is the most likely clinical presentation?

Patients with peptic ulcer disease typically present with the gnawing or burning epigastric pain that occurs after eating. Other general symptoms include dyspepsia, chest discomfort, heartburn, and hematemesis. Patients with a bleeding ulcer may also present with symptoms of anemia. A patient with a gastric ulcer will typically report pain shortly after eating, while a patient with a duodenal ulcer may have relief immediately after eating, but will typically report pain two to three hours after a meal often waking at night with pain. Patients who present with sudden or more severe symptoms may have developed a perforated ulcer and should be promptly evaluated by a physician. Symptoms of perforation include abdominal guarding, rigidity or rebound tenderness with palpation, and a more generalized but sharp abdominal pain that worsens with movement. The condition should be considered emergent if perforation is suspected and the patient displays any signs of septic shock such as anuria, hypotension or tachycardia.

What laboratory or imaging studies would confirm the diagnosis?

Upper GI endoscopy is typically the diagnostic tool used for visualization and tissue biopsy. This tool may also be used to rule out gastric cancer or H. pylori infection.

What additional information should be obtained to confirm the diagnosis?

A thorough medical history should be completed to assist in ruling out similar diagnoses and identifying factors which may contribute to the development or exacerbation of peptic ulcer disease.

Prostate Cancer

BRONZE

DIAGNOSIS

What condition produces a patient's symptoms?

Prostate cancer is the growth of malignant cancer cells within the prostate gland. There is no known etiology for prostate cancer, but factors increasing the risk for acquiring prostate cancer include advanced age, African American descent, family history of prostate or breast cancer, and obesity.

An injury was most likely sustained to what structure?

The prostate is a gland found in the male reproductive system that is responsible for the production of seminal fluid. Prostate cancer is generally a slow-growing cancer, though it can metastasize to other parts of the body, especially the lymph nodes and bones.

CONFIRMATION

What is the most likely clinical presentation?

In its early stages, prostate cancer is generally asymptomatic. Symptoms are more likely present during the advanced stages of the disease. Because of the prostate's position surrounding the urethra, prostate cancer may result in difficulty urinating, nocturia, erectile dysfunction, blood in the urine or semen, pelvic or low back pain, and bone pain, if metastasized.

What laboratory or imaging studies would confirm the diagnosis?

The prostate-specific antigen (PSA) test is a blood test used to determine the presence of elevated levels of PSA, which may be indicative of prostate cancer. If prostate cancer is suspected, a physician may decide to perform a tissue biopsy of the prostate to further assist with diagnosis. Imaging studies that may be used include transrectal ultrasound or magnetic resonance imaging.

What additional information should be obtained to confirm the diagnosis?

A thorough medical history and physical examination should be performed to rule out other similar conditions (e.g., benign prostatic hypertrophy) and assist with diagnosis. The physical examination involves a prostate examination to determine abnormalities in the texture, shape or size of the prostate gland.

Systemic Sclerosis

BRONZE

DIAGNOSIS

What condition produces a patient's symptoms?

Systemic sclerosis (or scleroderma) is a connective tissue disease characterized by excess collagen deposition which leads to changes of the skin and internal organs. Though the exact etiology of the disease is unknown, an abnormal immune response appears to play a critical role in the overproduction of collagen.

An injury was most likely sustained to what structure?

Limited scleroderma is characterized by thickening of the skin without involvement of the internal organs. This form tends to affect the extremities distal to the knees and elbows, and may also affect the face. Diffuse scleroderma affects the skin on all areas of the body, though it also affects the internal organs such as the lungs, kidneys, heart, and gastrointestinal tract.

CONFIRMATION

What is the most likely clinical presentation?

The presentation of systemic sclerosis will differ depending on the organ(s) affected. Signs and symptoms may include itching, skin that appears tight, reddish or scaly, Raynaud's phenomenon, muscle weakness, joint pain, decreased lung function, pulmonary hypertension, gastroesophageal reflux, decreased gastric or intestinal motility, intestinal malabsorption, and renal disease. Involvement of the kidneys, lungs or heart generally leads to a poor prognosis.

What laboratory or imaging studies would confirm the diagnosis?

Blood tests can be performed to detect elevated levels of certain autoantibodies. A biopsy of the skin may also be performed to determine changes in the skin that may indicate presence of the condition. Other tests may include x-ray or computed tomography of the lungs, pulmonary function testing, and an echocardiogram of the heart.

What additional information should be obtained to confirm the diagnosis?

Due to the large variation in presentation, the disease can be very difficult to diagnose. A thorough medical history and physical examination are important in diagnosing the condition and ruling out other similar conditions that may cause hardening of the skin.

BRONZE Ulcerative Colitis

DIAGNOSIS

What condition produces a patient's symptoms?

Ulcerative colitis is an inflammatory bowel disease that results in chronic inflammation and the formation of ulcers in the gastrointestinal tract. There is no known etiology for this condition, though it is thought to be an autoimmune condition that results from an exaggerated response to a bacterium or virus. There is also a presumed genetic component to the condition.

An injury was most likely sustained to what structure?

Ulcerative colitis affects the innermost lining of the large intestine (most often the sigmoid colon) and rectum, as opposed to Crohn's disease which may affect any portion of the gastrointestinal tract. The severity of the patient's symptoms is directly related to the extent of the colon that is affected.

CONFIRMATION

What is the most likely clinical presentation?

The clinical presentation will be determined by the location and severity of inflammation. Signs and symptoms may include abdominal pain and cramping, diarrhea, blood in the stools, urgency to defecate, weight loss, fatigue, and fever. Symptoms are often intermittent, alternating between periods of exacerbation and remission. Because the condition is considered an autoimmune disorder, other systemic symptoms can also occur (e.g., arthritic joints, skin disorders, visual issues).

What laboratory or imaging studies would confirm the diagnosis?

The primary test for diagnosing ulcerative colitis is endoscopy, which allows for direct visualization of the colon. Biopsies of the mucosa may also be performed to definitively diagnose the condition. Other testing may include stool samples and blood tests.

What additional information should be obtained to confirm the diagnosis?

A thorough medical history and physical examination should be performed to rule out the presence of other similar conditions (e.g., Crohn's disease, irritable bowel syndrome, diverticulitis).

BRONZE Urinary Tract Infection

DIAGNOSIS

What condition produces a patient's symptoms?

The urinary tract is normally a sterile environment. Under certain conditions, however, infectious organisms from internal or external sources can proliferate causing a urinary tract infection (UTI). The Escherichia coli (E. coli) bacteria and the sexually transmitted microorganisms chlamydia and mycoplasma are most commonly associated with UTI.

An injury was most likely sustained to which structure?

The urinary system is comprised of the kidneys and ureters in the upper urinary tract and the bladder and urethra in the lower urinary tract. An infection can occur anywhere within the system although the lower urinary tract is more commonly involved. A UTI may be more specifically named based on the location of the infection.

CONFIRMATION

What is the most likely clinical presentation?

A UTI is typically characterized by a strong and persistent urge to urinate, as well as a burning sensation with urination. Frequent voiding tends to produce only small volumes of cloudy, strong smelling urine. Other general symptoms that may be associated with UTI include fever and body aches. Cognitive changes are commonly observed in elderly and cognitively impaired patients. UTIs are more prevalent among women, especially those who are pregnant or menopausal due to the associated hormonal and body chemistry changes.

What laboratory or imaging studies would confirm the diagnosis?

Urinalysis and urine culture are most commonly used to diagnose a UTI. Urinalysis details the urine's physical (e.g., color, clarity, odor), microscopic (e.g., white blood cell, red blood cell, and bacterial counts), and chemical (e.g., acidity, concentration, glucose level) characteristics with comparison to established norms. A urine culture is used to identify the specific organism causing the infection so that treatment interventions may be targeted accordingly. Patients who suffer recurrent UTIs may require more invasive diagnostic testing.

What additional information should be obtained to confirm the diagnosis?

A thorough medical history should be obtained. Patients with urinary catheters are at an increased risk of developing a UTI as are those with conditions which impede the normal flow of urine (e.g., benign prostate hypertrophy, kidney stones) or impact kidney function (e.g., diabetes mellitus).

Uterine Cancer

BRONZE

DIAGNOSIS

What condition produces a patient's symptoms?

Uterine cancer (i.e., endometrial cancer) is the malignant growth of any cells that comprise the tissue of the uterus. The exact etiology of uterine cancer is unknown, though risk factors for the disease involve elevated levels of estrogen without similar levels of progesterone. Common risk factors include advanced age, obesity, diabetes, family history of uterine cancer, radiation therapy to the pelvis, medications (e.g., estrogen, tamoxifen), early onset of menstruation or late onset of menopause, and nulliparity.

An injury was most likely sustained to what structure?

The most common type of uterine cancer affects the endometrium, which is the inner lining of the uterus. When there is an imbalance of hormones (i.e., estrogen and progesterone), the endometrium becomes thicker over time. As the condition progresses, cancerous cells may start to develop. If metastasized, these cancerous cells can invade the lymph nodes, lungs, liver, bones or brain.

CONFIRMATION

What is the most likely clinical presentation?

Unexpected vaginal bleeding is the most common symptom associated with uterine cancer, especially when it occurs after menopause. Other signs and symptoms may include abnormal menstrual cycles (in premenopausal women), vaginal discharge (in postmenopausal women), pelvic or lower abdominal pain, painful urination, and painful intercourse.

What laboratory or imaging studies would confirm the diagnosis?

The only method to confirm the diagnosis of uterine cancer is through a tissue biopsy, which is obtained during a procedure known as dilation and curettage. The physician may perform a transvaginal ultrasound or hysteroscopy for imaging. Diagnostic imaging can also be used (e.g., MRI, CT scan) to determine if the cancer has metastasized.

What additional information should be obtained to confirm the diagnosis?

A thorough medical history and physical examination should be performed to rule out the presence of other similar conditions (e.g., endometriosis). The physical examination will typically involve a pelvic examination, in which the physician palpates for changes in the size, shape or consistency of the uterus.

Other Systems Essentials

Integumentary System

1. The integumentary system or "skin" is the largest organ of the body and consists of dermal and epidermal layers, hair follicles, nails, sebaceous glands, and sweat glands.

2. The normal phases of healing are overlapping and progressive beginning with an inflammatory response and ending with scar maturity.

3. Healing can occur through primary, secondary or tertiary intention. Most wounds requiring formal wound care interventions will heal by secondary intention.

4. Maintaining the balance of moisture in and around healing wounds is paramount. A wound that is too dry will have delayed healing; a wound with excessive moisture is at risk for additional tissue deterioration.

5. Infection is the most common cause of wound chronicity.

6. Certain types of wound exudate typically occur during the various stages of wound healing while others may be signs of impending infection or other complications.

7. Ulcers have primary classification as arterial, venous, neuropathic or pressure. Causative factors are ulcer specific and treatment is dependent on classification and severity of the ulcer.

8. Wounds that are not classified as pressure or neuropathic can be classified by depth of tissue loss.

9. Wound color, depth, exudate, and infection status must be considered in order to select the most appropriate wound dressing for a patient.

10. Wagner Ulcer Grade Classification System categorizes dysvascular ulcers based on wound depth and the presence of infection.

11. Pressure injury staging typically includes stage 1,2,3,4, Suspected Deep Tissue Injury, and Unstageable.

12. Exudate is typically classified as serous, sanguineous, serosanguineous, seropurulent, and purulent.

13. Physical therapists provide selective debridement through sharp, enzymatic or autolytic debridement interventions. Non-selective debridement typically includes wet-to-dry dressings, hydrotherapy, and wound irrigation interventions.

14. Modalities and physical agents such as negative pressure wound therapy, hyperbaric oxygen, and growth factors promote and facilitate healing, improve oxygenation and blood flow, increase collagen synthesis, minimize edema, and decrease drainage from the wound.

15. Therapeutic modalities such as ultrasound and high-voltage pulsed current have clinical applications and parameters which can assist through all stages of healing.

16. A fully occlusive substance would be completely impermeable while a non-occlusive dressing permits bacteria and fluid contamination of the wound bed increasing the risk for infection and delaying the healing process.

17. Classification of dressings includes hydrocolloids, hydrogels, foam dressings, transparent film, gauze, and alginates. Each dressing classification has advantages and disadvantages and is used based on the wound characteristics and goals for the dressing.

18. The major classifications of burn injury include thermal, electrical, chemical, and radiation burns. The extent of burn-related tissue damage in each zone of injury will significantly impact the overall healing prognosis.

19. The level of pain secondary to a burn varies based on the depth of the burn with superficial partial-thickness burns typically exhibiting the highest level of pain.

20. The Rule of Nines is well recognized for its use in estimating the amount of total surface area damaged by a burn injury. However, this calculation does not reflect wound severity and therefore cannot predict prognosis or outcomes.

21. Numerous scar assessment scales are available to assess characteristics such as scar height, thickness, pliability, banding/adherence, color, vascularity, texture, and size.

Other Systems Essentials

22. Burns sustained in proximity to joints are at particular risk for developing limiting contractures as patients will tend to assume a position of comfort. Splints should be used to support limbs in a neutral or slight stretch position to prevent deformity.

23. Principles of burn scar management, such as scar massage and desensitization techniques, are valuable tools for managing non-burn related scars that may be painful or otherwise restrictive.

Metabolic and Endocrine

24. The metabolic system is responsible for generating the energy required to fuel all bodily functions.

25. Catabolism refers to metabolic processes which provide heat and energy to the body while anabolism refers to processes involved with tissue growth and repair.

26. Inherited metabolic disorders, though present at birth, may not immediately show symptoms.

27. Metabolic acidosis occurs when the body's pH drops below 7.35 as a result of an acid and bicarbonate imbalance which allows acid to accumulate.

28. Metabolic alkalosis occurs when the body's pH rises above 7.45 as a result of a bicarbonate and acid imbalance which allows bicarbonate to accumulate.

29. Osteoporosis or osteopenia may be an underlying clinical feature of various other metabolic or systemic disorders.

30. A diagnosis of osteopenia may not be due to bone loss, but rather a naturally occurring bone density that is lower than established norms.

31. General classes of hormones controlled by the endocrine system include prostaglandins, catecholamines, and insulin.

32. Endocrine pathology most commonly relates to either hyper or hypofunction of endocrine glands and the effect of their targeted hormone secretions.

33. Patients with hyperthyroidism may present with exercise limitations associated with heat intolerance caused by hypermetabolism.

34. Patients with hypothyroidism often present with limited exercise tolerance due to a hypofunctioning metabolism and subsequent energy deficits.

35. Untreated, both hyperglycemia and hypoglycemia are life threatening conditions.

36. Type 1 diabetes mellitus occurs when the pancreas fails to produce insulin to regulate blood glucose levels in the body.

37. Type 2 diabetes mellitus occurs when the body becomes insulin resistant and is unable to effectively utilize the insulin that is present to control blood glucose levels.

38. Patients with diabetes mellitus must be cautious to avoid becoming hypoglycemic with exercise as a result of increased glucose uptake with increased muscle activity.

39. Patients with type 1 diabetes mellitus are at the greatest risk for becoming hyperglycemic and developing life threatening ketoacidosis.

Gastrointestinal

40. The gastrointestinal system is responsible for the process of digestion. It breaks down food into its components, absorbs nutrients, and discards the waste.

41. Diverticula, or pouch-like protrusions that occur in the colon, can become infected causing diverticulitis. A high fiber diet will help to avoid this condition.

42. The hepatitis B vaccine is administered in three doses and may be used prophylactically or as treatment for an unvaccinated patient who has been exposed.

43. Health care workers that are at risk for contact with hepatitis should receive all immunizations for HBV, and if exposed to blood or body fluids of an infected person must receive immunoglobulin therapy immediately.

44. Physical therapists must be diligent in assessing pain of an unknown origin. This is especially true when pain is accompanied by autonomic responses such as nausea, vomiting, pallor or sweating.

45. For numerous gastrointestinal disorders, lifestyle changes are the primary intervention recommended for symptom management.

Other Systems Essentials

Genitourinary

46. The pelvic floor complex attaches to the pelvis and serves the genitourinary system through three primary functions: support, sphincteric function, and sexual function.

47. The genitourinary system consists of female and male genital organs and the urinary organs.

48. Physical therapy intervention for all bladder pathologies includes behavioral modification to address healthy bladder habits.

49. A woman's body transitions through multiple physiological and postural changes during pregnancy that may lead to impairments and functional limitations.

50. Relative and absolute contraindications need to be considered when developing an exercise program for a pregnant woman.

51. The goal of pelvic floor muscle strengthening exercises is to be able to perform a contraction during functional tasks.

Lymphatic

52. The lymphatic system is responsible for collecting and transporting fluids that are not collected by the venous system, as well as immune system defense for the body.

53. Lymphedema is a chronic, incurable condition and is characterized by the accumulation of protein-rich fluid (i.e., lymph) in the body, especially in the extremities.

54. Primary lymphedema occurs due to abnormal development of the lymphatic system, while secondary lymphedema occurs as a result of some other disease or injury that causes damage to the lymphatic system (e.g., mastectomy, radiation therapy).

55. Signs and symptoms of lymphedema can range from mild pitting edema that reverses with elevation and rest to severe non-pitting edema that results in fibrotic changes to the skin and an increased risk for infections.

56. Complete decongestive therapy is the standard of care for patients with lymphedema, which consists of manual lymphatic drainage, compression therapy, exercise, and education in proper skin care.

57. Circumferential measurements are commonly used by therapists to determine the progression of lymphedema and the effectiveness of treatment.

58. Lymphedema is not curable, however, symptoms can be managed if patients are treated early and maintain ongoing self-care using the principles of complete decongestive therapy.

Oncology

59. Cancers are typically named based on the cell type involved and the tissue of origin.

60. A significant percentage of cancer related risk factors are modifiable.

61. The American Cancer Society names cancer as the leading cause of death in the United States.

62. Musculoskeletal pain in patients with cancer may be indicative of metastasis and should be promptly evaluated.

63. Physical therapists should be aware of the general signs and symptoms of cancer and refer patients back to the referring physician when signs and symptoms are observed in patients without a cancer diagnosis.

64. Staging of a malignancy is most commonly based on factors relating to the size of the primary tumor, lymph node involvement, and the presence of metastasis.

65. Staging assists multidisciplinary care providers to establish an optimal plan of care with appropriate goals and interventions.

66. Patients being treated for a cancer diagnosis with chemotherapy, radiation, and/or surgical interventions are at an increased risk for developing lymphedema.

67. Palliative treatment emphasizes symptom relief and may be provided in any care setting at any time during the course of a disease process.

68. Hospice care includes palliative interventions and goals, but is specifically reserved for patients at the end of life when curative efforts are no longer being pursued.

Other Systems Essentials

69. The usual modality contraindications relating to a cancer diagnosis may be occasionally disregarded in lieu of palliative goals for some patients at the end of life.

70. Cognitive changes related to oncological interventions are widely recognized and acknowledged despite limited definitive research on the subject.

71. The prevention of infection in patients who are neutropenic is imperative to prevent potentially life threatening complications.

Psychological Disorders

72. Affective disorders relate to changes in mood or emotion and include depression, mania, and bipolar disorder.

73. Neuroses disorders are characterized by irrational fears or maladaptive responses to everyday stimuli and include phobias, psychogenic amnesia, multiple personality, obsessive-compulsive, anxiety, and dissociative disorders.

74. Somatoform disorders are classified by the presenting physical characteristics and include somatization, conversion, and hypochondriasis disorders.

75. Schizophrenic disorders are psychotic in nature and vary widely in presentation. Classifications of schizophrenia include catatonic, paranoid, disorganized, and undifferentiated.

76. Personality disorders are classified based on behavior patterns and include psychopathic, antisocial, narcissistic, and borderline personalities.

77. The side effects of numerous medications can have a significant impact on a patient's willingness and ability to effectively participate in physical therapy treatment.

Geriatrics

78. Ageism can impact the ability of a caretaker or health professional to provide unbiased care, instead basing their treatment on preconceived notions.

79. Older adults experience specific age-related changes that impact the five senses (hearing, vision, taste and smell, touch, cognition).

80. Older adults are at an increased risk of experiencing medication-related problems such as non-adherence and adverse drug reactions.

81. Older adults process medication differently than younger adults, therefore it is critical to be aware of pharmacokinetic and pharmacodynamic changes.

Bariatrics

82. The morphological distribution of a patient's adipose tissue often correlates to their overall health risk factors.

83. Therapists may be the first health care providers to initiate a conversation about weight loss with a patient and should therefore be well informed of both appropriate community and medical resources so that a referral may be made as needed.

84. Waist-to-hip ratio measures are highly correlative to body mass index and indicators of central obesity.

85. Failure to address psychological influences associated with obesity, or eating disorders of any kind, will limit the potential for positive long-term success.

86. Significant weight loss cannot be achieved or maintained in a healthful way through a single mode of intervention.

87. With regard to weight loss, an individual's readiness and commitment to altering behavior is a significant factor in predicting long-term outcomes and success.

88. Options for bariatric surgical interventions vary from minimally invasive, reversible procedures to highly invasive procedures which significantly impact the body's anatomy and gastrointestinal function.

89. When initiating an exercise program for a morbidly obese patient special care should be taken to prevent injury and ensure safe, appropriate systemic responses.

Nutrition

90. Macronutrients are the nutrients that provide the body with energy and consist of carbohydrates, fats, and proteins.

Other Systems Essentials

91. Carbohydrates are the energy source for high-intensity exercise, fats are the energy source for low-intensity exercise, and proteins are responsible for the growth and maintenance of the body's tissues.

92. Vitamins are commonly classified as either fat-soluble or water-soluble.

93. Fat-soluble vitamins are more likely to reach toxic levels in the body.

94. Water-soluble vitamins are not stored in significant amounts within the body.

95. Some complementary and alternative medicine supplements can interfere with the action of pharmaceutical agents and reach toxic levels within the body.

96. Minerals and vitamins are necessary to support the body's metabolic functions.

97. MyPlate is a program that is designed to teach people how to create and maintain a healthy diet and includes recommendations for intake of the six major food groups: fruits, vegetables, grains, protein foods, dairy, and oils.

98. The nutrition label on food and drink products should be used to determine the health content of the product and will include information such as the number of calories, macronutrients, and micronutrients that the product contains.

Pharmacology Basics

99. Drugs can be administered via enteral routes (i.e., within the gastrointestinal tract) or parenteral routes (i.e., outside the gastrointestinal tract).

100. Oral administration is the most common type of enteral administration since it is easy for the patient to perform this method on their own and it allows for a slow, controlled release of the drug into the patient's system.

101. Intravenous injection is a common form of drug administration that allows for rapid administration of a drug to the target tissue and is one of the only methods that ensures 100% bioavailability of the drug.

102. There are several factors that can affect how a drug acts within the body, including a patient's age, weight, and ethnicity, the presence of disease or infection, drug-drug interactions, and food-drug interactions.

103. The Food and Drug Administration is the government agency that is responsible for the development and approval of new drugs, a process that typically occurs in five different phases over the course of several years.

104. All drugs are categorized into one of five different classifications (i.e., Schedule I-V) depending on their potential for abuse and their risk for addiction, with Schedule I drugs having the highest risk for abuse and addiction.

Other Systems Proficiencies

1. Integumentary Anatomy

Select the appropriate term for each of the specified locations. Answers must be selected from the Word Bank and can be used only once.

Word Bank: adipose tissue, arrector pili muscle, blood supply, dermis, epidermis, hair follicle, nerve, nerve ending, sebaceous gland, subcutaneous fatty tissue, sweat duct, sweat gland

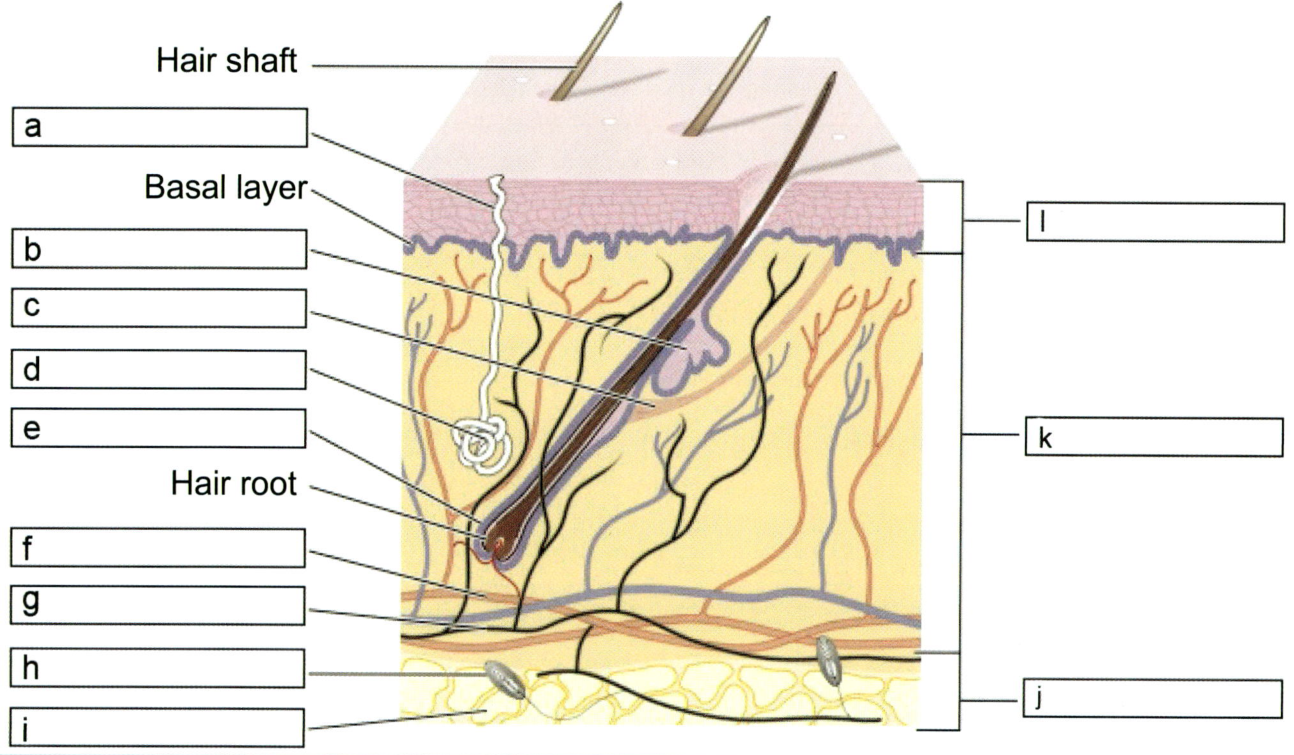

2. Ulcer Characteristics

Identify the type of ulcer that is most associated with the supplied description. Answers must be selected from the Word Bank and can be used more than once.

Word Bank: arterial, neuropathic, venous

Type of Ulcer	Clinical Finding
a	ulcer located proximal to the medial malleolus
b	normal pedal pulse
c	leg elevation diminishes pain
d	absence of pain
e	evidence of increased edema
f	evidence of hair loss in tissue

Other Systems Proficiencies

3. Pressure Injury Staging

Identify the pressure injury stage that is most associated with the supplied description. Answers must be selected from the Word Bank and can be used more than once.

Word Bank: 1, 2, 3, 4

Stage	Clinical Finding
a	slough is present, but does not obscure depth of tissue loss
b	subcutaneous fat is visible, but bone, tendon or muscles are not exposed
c	extends into the joint capsule
d	intact skin with non-blanchable redness
e	tunneling with muscle visible
f	intact serum filled blister
g	shallow ulcer with a red wound bed

4. Pressure Injuries

Identify the position or positions, most likely to cause a pressure injury over the identified bony prominence. The number of desired responses for each bony prominence is identified in parentheses. Answers must be selected from the Word Bank and can be used more than once.

Word Bank: sidelying, sitting, supine, prone

Bony Structure	Position(s)	
patella	a	(1)
dorsum of foot	b	(1)
ear	c	(1)
ischial tuberosity	d	(1)
vertebral spinous process	e	(2)
sternum	f	(1)
head of fibula	g	(1)
anterior superior iliac spine	h	(1)

Other Systems Proficiencies

5. Debridement

Classify each of the debridement techniques as selective or non-selective debridement.

Type of Debridement	Classification
autolytic	a
enzymatic	b
hydrotherapy	c
sharp debridement	d
wet-to-dry	e
wound irrigation	f

6. Wound Terminology

Identify the wound terminology most closely associated with the supplied description. Answers must be selected from the Word Bank and can be used only once.

Word Bank: contusion, dehiscence, desiccated, ecchymosis, erythema, friable, hematoma, keloid, maceration, turgor

Terminology	Description
a	The separation, rupture or splitting of a wound closed by primary intention.
b	Tissue that readily tears, fragments or bleeds when gently palpated or manipulated.
c	A diffuse redness of the skin often resulting from either capillary dilation and congestion or inflammation.
d	Skin softening and degeneration that results from prolonged exposure to water or other fluids.
e	The drying out or dehydration of a wound.
f	A localized swelling or mass of clotted blood confined to a tissue, organ or space usually caused by a break in a blood vessel.
g	The discoloration occurring below intact skin resulting from trauma to underlying blood vessels and blood seeping into tissue.
h	An abnormal scar formation that is out of proportion to the scarring required for normal tissue repair.
i	The relative speed with which the skin resumes its normal appearance after being lightly pinched.
j	An injury, usually caused by a blow, that does not disrupt the skin integrity.

Other Systems Proficiencies

7. Rule of Nines

Identify the percentage of the total body surface affected based on the description of the area involved. Answers must be selected from the Word Bank and can be used more than once. Not all answers will be used.

Word Bank: 10%, 18%, 19%, 22.5%, 23.5%, 28%, 36%, 54%, 55%, 63%, 64%

% of Body	Areas Affected
a	anterior right arm, forearm, and hand; anterior trunk
b	bilateral legs and feet
c	anterior trunk, genital region, bilateral legs and feet
d	posterior head and neck; posterior trunk
e	bilateral arms, forearms, and hands; entire trunk
f	genital region, anterior left leg and foot

8. Integumentary System Basics

Mark each statement as True or False. If the statement is False, correct the statement in the space provided.

True/False	Statement
a	A patient with a deep partial-thickness burn would typically experience more pain than a patient with a superficial partial-thickness burn.
Correction:	
b	Patients with venous insufficiency ulcers should avoid unnecessary leg elevation.
Correction:	
c	Enzymatic debridement refers to the use of the body's own mechanisms to remove nonviable tissue.
Correction:	

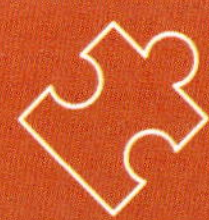

Other Systems Proficiencies

True/False	Statement
d	The epidermis thickens as part of the aging process, making it more resilient and therefore less susceptible to injury from friction and shear.
Correction:	
e	Healing by primary intention permits wounds to close on their own without superficial closure.
Correction:	
f	Patients with arterial insufficiency ulcers should avoid heating pads or soaking their feet in hot water.
Correction:	
g	A full-thickness burn involves complete destruction of the epidermis and dermis, along with partial damage to the subcutaneous fat layer.
Correction:	
h	The goal of treatment with a wound classified as "Red" using the Red-Yellow-Black System is to remove exudate and debris.
Correction:	
i	A superficial partial-thickness burn involves the epidermis and the upper portion of the dermis.
Correction:	
j	A grade of 3 on the Wagner Ulcer Grade Classification scale is indicative of a superficial ulcer not involving subcutaneous tissue.
Correction:	

Other Systems Proficiencies

9. Pathology of the Metabolic and Endocrine Systems

Identify the appropriate medical condition based on the supplied descriptions. Answers must be selected from the Word Bank and can only be used once.

Word Bank: Cushing's syndrome, Graves' disease, Klinefelter's syndrome, osteoporosis, Paget's disease, phenylketonuria, diabetes mellitus - type 1, Wilson's disease

Pathology	Description
a	Adrenal dysfunction that produces excessive cortisol as well as a "moon-shaped face" and "buffalo hump."
b	Metabolic bone disease that affects trabecular and cortical bone resulting in decreased bone mass and increased risk for fracture.
c	Hypofunction of the pancreas where there is failure to produce adequate endogenous insulin.
d	Primary hypogonadism that presents with a deficiency of testosterone secondary to a failure of the testes to respond to follicle stimulating and luteinizing hormones.
e	Autosomal recessive inherited trait in which an enzyme deficiency permits excessive phenylalanine accumulation within the brain.
f	Autosomal recessive inherited trait that produces a defect in the body's ability to metabolize copper allowing it to accumulate in the brain and other tissues.
g	Autoimmune disease that produces thyroid hypersecretion resulting in heat intolerance, tremor, weight loss, and nervousness.
h	Metabolic bone disease characterized by heightened osteoclast activity resulting in excessive bone formation that lacks true structural integrity.

10. Metabolic Acidosis versus Metabolic Alkalosis

Identify characteristics of each condition. Answers must be selected from the Word Bank and can be used only once.

Word Bank: <7.35, >7.45, compensatory hyperventilation, continuous vomiting, potassium chloride, renal failure, slowed breathing, sodium bicarbonate

Metabolic Acidosis		Metabolic Alkalosis
a	**Possible etiologies**	e
b	**pH**	f
c	**Symptoms**	g
d	**Treatment**	h

Other Systems Proficiencies

11. Glands of the Endocrine System and Hormones Secreted

Identify the endocrine gland or associated hormones. Answers must be selected from the Word Bank and can be used only once.

Word Bank: adrenal gland, estrogen and progesterone, glucagon and insulin, parathyroid gland, testes, thyroxine and triiodothyronine

Endocrine Gland	Associated Hormones
a	testosterone and other androgens
ovaries	b
thyroid	c
pancreas	d
e	parathyroid hormone
f	corticosteroids and epinephrine

12. Diabetes: Type 1 or Type 2

Identify the characteristic as Type 1 or Type 2 diabetes mellitus. Answers must be selected from the Word Bank and can be used more than once.

Word Bank: Type 1, Type 2

Type	Characteristic
a	treatment includes insulin injections or insulin pump
b	etiology unclear, but a genetic predisposition with a viral or environmental trigger is believed to facilitate onset
c	typically controlled through diet, exercise, and oral medications
d	obesity contributes to the condition by increasing insulin resistance
e	increased incidence in children due to rise in childhood obesity
f	typically there is some ongoing production of endogenous insulin
g	exogenous insulin injections are typically required
h	ketoacidosis rarely occurs
i	less common form of diabetes mellitus
j	gradual onset
k	destruction of the islet of Langerhans cells

Other Systems Proficiencies

13. Other Systems Basics

Mark each statement as True or False. If the statement is False, correct the statement in the space provided.

True/False	Statement
a	Catabolism is the process that combines simple molecules for tissue growth.
Correction	
b	Hormones secreted by endocrine glands travel through the bloodstream and signal specific target organs in order to maintain homeostasis of the internal environment.
Correction	
c	Norepinephrine is the catecholamine that creates the "fight or flight" response.
Correction	
d	Gastroesophageal reflux disease occurs as the result of an incompetent lower esophageal sphincter and allows for backwards movement of stomach acids into the esophagus.
Correction	
e	Diverticulitis is a condition with inflamed diverticula (pouch-like protrusions within the colon).
Correction	
f	Cirrhosis of the liver is a condition where the blood vessels dilate and allow for excess blood flow within the liver.
Correction	
g	The ovaries provide storage of oocytes prior to ovulation and secrete both estrogen and progesterone.
Correction	

Other Systems Proficiencies

True/False	Statement
h	Hemodialysis is a treatment for patients with end-stage renal disease in order to cleanse the blood and is typically performed one time per week.
Correction	
i	Functional urinary incontinence is the loss of urine secondary to increased intra-abdominal pressure from activities such as sneezing or coughing.
Correction	
j	Diastasis recti is the separation of the rectus abdominis along the linea alba.
Correction	
k	Hypertension in supine during late pregnancy is secondary to compression of the inferior vena cava.
Correction	
l	Incompetent cervix, placenta previa, restrictive lung disease, and preeclampsia are absolute contraindications for exercise during pregnancy.
Correction	
m	A melanoma is a malignancy originating from connective tissues such as fat, cartilage, bone or muscle.
Correction	
n	Affective disorders include diagnoses such as obsessive-compulsive, anxiety, and phobia disorders.
Correction	
o	A body mass index of greater than 30 is indicative of obesity.
Correction	

Other Systems Proficiencies

14. Other Systems Terminology

Identify the term most closely associated with the supplied description. Answers must be selected from the Word Bank and can be used only once.

Word Bank: anorexia nervosa, anuria, cystocele, erectile dysfunction, gastritis, gene, glomerular filtration rate, hypoglycemia, insulin, lymphoma, mitochondria, neoplasm, osteopenia, pH, seminiferous tubules, urgency

Terminology	Description
a	bulging of the bladder into the vagina
b	self-imposed starvation that results in impairment or "shut down" of systemic processes
c	the measure of the hydrogen ion concentration in body fluid
d	a fundamental unit of heredity
e	a group of oncology diagnoses referring to cancers that involve uncontrolled lymphocyte proliferation in the lymph nodes
f	a part of the cell that is responsible for energy production
g	synonymous with impotence
h	an abnormal new growth of tissue that can be classified as benign or malignant
i	a condition that presents with decreased bone mass, but not severe enough to be classified as osteoporosis
j	an estimate of the volume of filtrate produced per minute by the kidneys
k	a condition where blood sugar levels decrease below 70 mg/dL
l	the sudden strong desire to urinate that is difficult to defer
m	inflammation of the gastric mucosa of the inner layer of the stomach
n	hormone secreted by the islets of Langerhans within the pancreas
o	inadequate urine output in a 24-hour period of less than 100 ml
p	coiled tubes found within each lobe of the testes where spermatogenesis occurs

Other Systems Proficiencies

15. Staging of Cancer

Identify the appropriate sequence of staging based on the supplied description. Answers must be selected from the Word Bank and can be used only once.

Word Bank: 0, I, II, III, IV

Stage	Description
a	Malignancy that has spread to adjacent tissue showing signs of fixation to deeper structures. The likelihood of metastatic lymph node involvement is high.
b	Malignancy that has metastasized beyond the primary site, for example, to bone or another organ.
c	Malignancy spreading into adjacent tissues; lymph nodes may show signs of micrometastases.
d	Early malignancy that is present only in the layer of cells in which it began. For most cancers, this is referred to as carcinoma in situ.
e	Malignancy limited to the tissue of origin with no lymph node involvement or metastasis.

16. Pharmacology for Other Systems

Identify the appropriate medication based on the supplied descriptions. Answers must be selected from the Word Bank and can be used only once.

Word Bank: antacid agents, antimetabolite agents, bipolar disorder agents, bone mineral regulating agents, chemotherapy, emetic agents, endocrine hyperfunction agents, insulin, laxative agents, proton pump inhibitors

Drug	Action
a	prevents histamine-activated release of gastric acid
b	administered to destroy malignant cells
c	administered as mood stabilizers preventing manic episodes and extreme swings in mood
d	facilitate bowel evacuation
e	administered via injection to maintain blood glucose levels
f	used to induce vomiting
g	promote inhibition of hormone function
h	chemically neutralize gastric acid and increase the intragastric pH
i	impair biosynthesis of genetic material by interrupting cellular pathways that synthesize DNA and RNA
j	enhance and maximize bone mass while preventing bone loss or rate of bone reabsorption

Other Systems Proficiencies

17. Vitamins and Potential Food Sources

Identify the appropriate vitamin based on the supplied potential food sources. Answers must be selected from the Word Bank. Each answer can be used only once.

Word Bank: A, B12, C, D, E, K

Vitamin	Potential Food Sources
a	fortified milk, fish oils, salmon
b	green, orange, yellow vegetables, liver
c	citrus fruits, tomatoes, cantaloupe
d	vegetable oils, nuts, fish
e	meats, whole eggs
f	dark green leafy vegetables, cheese, egg yolks

18. Minerals and their Function

Identify the appropriate mineral based on the supplied function. Answers must be selected from the Word Bank. Each answer can be used only once.

Word Bank: calcium, chromium, copper, iodine, iron, sodium, sulfur, zinc

Mineral	Function
a	assists with glucose metabolism
b	facilitates the maintenance of acid-base balance, transmits nerve impulses, and assists to control muscle contractions
c	facilitates muscle contraction and relaxation, builds strong bones, aids in coagulation
d	facilitates enzyme activity and energy metabolism
e	assists with regulation of cell metabolism and basal metabolic rate
f	facilitates hemoglobin synthesis and lipid metabolism
g	assists in oxygen transport and cell oxidation
h	aids in immune function and cell division

Other Systems Answer Key

1. Integumentary Anatomy

a. sweat duct
b. sebaceous gland
c. arrector pili muscle
d. sweat gland
e. hair follicle
f. blood supply
g. nerve
h. nerve ending
i. adipose tissue
j. subcutaneous fatty layer
k. dermis
l. epidermis

2. Ulcer Characteristics

a. venous
b. venous
c. venous
d. neuropathic
e. venous
f. arterial

3. Pressure Injury Staging

a. 3
b. 3
c. 4
d. 1
e. 4
f. 2
g. 2

4. Pressure Injuries

a. prone
b. prone
c. sidelying
d. sitting
e. supine, sitting
f. prone
g. sidelying
h. prone

5. Debridement

a. selective
b. selective
c. non-selective
d. selective
e. non-selective
f. non-selective

6. Wound Terminology

a. dehiscence
b. friable
c. erythema
d. maceration
e. desiccated
f. hematoma
g. ecchymosis
h. keloid
i. turgor
j. contusion

7. Rule of Nines

a. 22.5%
b. 36%
c. 55%
d. 22.5%
e. 54%
f. 10%

8. Integumentary System Basics*

a. FALSE: Correction - A patient with a deep partial-thickness burn would typically experience less pain than a patient with a superficial partial-thickness burn.
b. FALSE: Correction - Patients with venous insufficiency ulcers should elevate the legs when possible.
c. FALSE: Correction - Autolytic debridement refers to the use of the body's own mechanisms to remove nonviable tissue.
d. FALSE: Correction - The epidermis thins as part of the aging process, making it less resilient and therefore more susceptible to injury from friction and shear.
e. FALSE: Correction - Healing by secondary intention permits wounds to close on their own without superficial closure.
f. TRUE
g. TRUE
h. FALSE: Correction - The goal of treatment with a wound classified as "Red" using the Red-Yellow-Black System is to protect the wound and maintain a moist wound environment.
i. TRUE
j. FALSE: Correction - A grade of 3 on the Wagner Ulcer Grade Classification scale is indicative of a deep ulcer with osteitis, abscess or osteomyelitis.

*The correction presented for each false statement is an example of several possible corrections.

Other Systems Answer Key

9. Pathology of the Metabolic and Endocrine Systems

a. Cushing's syndrome
b. osteoporosis
c. diabetes mellitus - type 1
d. Klinefelter's syndrome
e. phenylketonuria
f. Wilson's disease
g. Graves' disease
h. Paget's disease

10. Metabolic Acidosis versus Metabolic Alkalosis

a. renal failure
b. <7.35
c. compensatory hyperventilation
d. sodium bicarbonate
e. continuous vomiting
f. >7.45
g. slowed breathing
h. potassium chloride

11. Glands of the Endocrine System and Hormones Secreted

a. testes
b. estrogen and progesterone
c. thyroxine and triiodothyronine
d. glucagon and insulin
e. parathyroid gland
f. adrenal gland

12. Diabetes: Type 1 or Type 2

a. Type 1
b. Type 1
c. Type 2
d. Type 2
e. Type 2
f. Type 2
g. Type 1
h. Type 2
i. Type 1
j. Type 2
k. Type 1

13. Other Systems Basics

a. FALSE: Correction - Catabolism is the process of breaking down organic compounds during metabolism.
b. TRUE
c. FALSE: Correction - Epinephrine is the catecholamine that creates the "fight or flight" response.
d. TRUE
e. TRUE
f. FALSE: Correction - Cirrhosis of the liver is a condition where tissue of the liver is replaced with scar tissue that blocks blood flow within the liver resulting in decreased functioning.
g. TRUE
h. FALSE: Correction - Hemodialysis is a treatment for patients with end-stage renal disease in order to cleanse the blood and is typically performed three times per week.
i. FALSE: Correction - Stress urinary incontinence is the loss of urine secondary to increased intra-abdominal pressure from activities such as sneezing or coughing.
j. TRUE
k. FALSE: Correction - Hypotension in supine during late pregnancy is secondary to compression of the inferior vena cava.
l. TRUE
m. FALSE: Correction - A sarcoma is a malignancy originating from connective tissues such as fat, cartilage, bone or muscle.
n. FALSE: Correction - Neuroses disorders would include diagnoses such as obsessive-compulsive, anxiety, and phobia disorders. Affective disorders include depression, mania, and bipolar disorders.
o. TRUE

*The correction presented for each false statement is an example of several possible corrections.

14. Other Systems Terminology

a. cystocele
b. anorexia nervosa
c. pH
d. gene
e. lymphoma
f. mitochondria
g. erectile dysfunction
h. neoplasm
i. osteopenia
j. glomerular filtration rate
k. hypoglycemia
l. urgency
m. gastritis
n. insulin
o. anuria
p. seminiferous tubules

Other Systems Answer Key

15. Staging of Cancer

a. III
b. IV
c. II
d. 0
e. I

16. Pharmacology for Other Systems

a. proton pump inhibitors
b. chemotherapy
c. bipolar disorder agents
d. laxative agents
e. insulin
f. emetic agents
g. endocrine hyperfunction agents
h. antacid agents
i. antimetabolite agents
j. bone mineral regulating agents

17. Vitamins and Potential Food Sources

a. D
b. A
c. C
d. E
e. B12
f. K

18. Minerals and their Function

a. chromium
b. sodium
c. calcium
d. sulfur
e. iodine
f. copper
g. iron
h. zinc

Other Systems References

1. Sussman C, Bates-Jensen B. ***Wound Care: A Collaborative Practice Manual for Health Professionals***. Fourth Edition. Wolters Kluwer Health/Lippincott Williams & Wilkins. 2012.
2. Irion G. ***Comprehensive Wound Management***. Second Edition. SLACK Inc. 2010.
3. O'Sullivan S, Schmitz T, Fulk G. ***Physical Rehabilitation: Assessment and Treatment*** Fifth Edition. F.A. Davis Company. 2014.
4. Baranoski S, Ayello EA. ***Wound Care Essentials: Practice Principles.*** Second Edition. Lippincott Williams & Wilkins. 2008.
5. Milne CT, Corbett LQ, Dubuc DL. ***Wound, Ostomy, and Continence Nursing Secrets***. Hanley & Belfus. 2003.
6. Herdon DN. ***Total Burn Care***. Third Edition. Saunders Elsevier. 2007.
7. Prentice W. ***Therapeutic Modalities in Rehabilitation***. Fifth Edition. McGraw-Hill Inc. 2018.
8. Stanley BG, Tribuzi SM. ***Concepts in Hand Rehabilitation***. F.A. Davis Company. 1992.
9. Trofino RB. ***Nursing Care of the Burn-Injured Patient***. F.A. Davis Company. 1991.
10. Goodman C, Fuller KS. ***Pathology: Implications for the Physical Therapist***. Fourth Edition. W.B. Saunders Company. 2015.
11. Gould BE, Dyer RM. ***Pathophysiology for the Health Professions***. Fourth Edition. Saunders Elsevier. 2011.
12. McDermott MT. ***Endocrine Secrets***. Fifth Edition. Mosby Elsevier. 2009.
13. ***Fluids & Electrolytes: An Incredibly Easy Pocket Guide***. Lippincott Williams & Wilkins. 2006.
14. About Osteoporosis. National Osteoporosis Foundation Website. http://www.nof.org/aboutosteoporosis. Updated 2010. Accessed September 15, 2010.
15. About Osteoporosis. International Osteoporosis Foundation Website. http://www.iofbonehealth.org/health-professionals/about-osteoporosis.html. Updated 2010. Accessed September 15, 2010.
16. ***Stedman's Medical Dictionary***. 27th Edition. Lippincott Williams & Wilkins. 2000.
17. Goodman C, Heick J, Lazaro R. ***Differential Diagnosis for Physical Therapists – Screening for Referral***. Sixth Edition. Elsevier. 2018.
18. Blood Glucose Control. American Diabetes Association Website. http://www.diabetes.org/living-with-diabetes/treatment-and-care/blood-glucose-control/?utm_source=WWW&utm_medium=DropDownLWD&utm_content=BGC&utm_campaign=CON. Accessed October 4, 2010.
19. Ciccone C. ***Pharmacology in Rehabilitation***. Fifth Edition. F.A. Davis Company. 2016.
20. Moore K, Dalley A. ***Clinically Oriented Anatomy***. Seventh Edition. Lippincott Williams & Wilkins. 2013.
21. Stephenson R, O'Connor L. ***Obstetric and Gynecologic Care in Physical Therapy***. Second Edition. Slack Inc. 2000.
22. Cunningham FG, Leveno KJ, Bloom SL, Hauth JC, Rouse DJ, Spong CY. ***Williams Obstetrics***. 23rd Edition. McGraw Hill Medical. 2010.
23. Gibbs RS, Karlan BY, Kaney AF, Nygaard I. ***Danforth's Obstetrics and Gynecology***. Tenth Edition. Lippincott Williams & Wilkins. 2008.
24. Newman DK, Wein AJ. ***Managing and Treating Urinary Incontinence***. Second Edition. Health Professions Press. 2009.
25. Kisner C, Colby L, Borstad J. ***Therapeutic Exercise Foundations and Techniques***. Seventh Edition. F.A. Davis Company. 2018.
26. American College of Sports Medicine. ***ACSM's Resource Manual for Guidelines for Exercise Testing and Prescription***. Seventh Edition. Lippincott Williams & Wilkins. 2014.
27. American College of Obstetricians and Gynecologists: Physical Activity and Exercise During Pregnancy and the Postpartum Period. ACOG, No. 804. 2020.
28. Gates RA, Fink RM. ***Oncology Nursing Secrets***. Third Edition. Mosby Elsevier. 2008.
29. Disease Information. Leukemia and Lymphoma Society Website. http://www.leukemia-lymphoma.org/all_toplevel.adp?item_id=4187. Accessed September 24, 2010.
30. Schneider CM, Dennehy CA, Carter SD. ***Exercise and Cancer Recovery***. Human Kinetics Publishing. 2003.
31. Staging: Questions and Answers. National Cancer Institute Website. http://www.cancer.gov/cancertopics/factsheet/Detection/staging. Reviewed September 22, 2010. Accessed September 29, 2010.
32. ***The Merck Manual***. 18th Edition. Merck Research Laboratories. 2006.
33. Foldi M, Foldi E. ***Foldi's Textbook of Lymphology for Physicians and Lymphedema Therapists***. Second Edition. Mosby Elsevier. 2006.
34. Tecklin J. ***Pediatric Physical Therapy***. Fifth Edition. Lippincott Williams & Wilkins. 2015.
35. Palisano R, Orlin M, Shreiber J. ***Campbell's Physical Therapy for Children***. Fifth Edition. Elsevier. 2017.
36. Paz J, West MP. ***Acute Care Handbook for Physical Therapists***. Fourth Edition. W. B. Saunders Company. 2014.

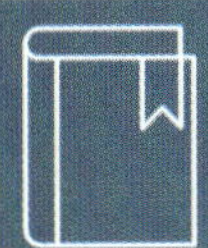

Other Systems References

37. Cancer Facts and Figures 2010. American Cancer Society Website. http://www.cancer.org/acs/groups/content/@epidemiologysurveilance/documents/document/acspc-026238.pdf. Reviewed 2010. Accessed September 24, 2010.
38. Understanding Your Complete Blood Count. Clinical Center National Institute of Health Website. http://www.cc.nih.gov/ccc/patient_education/pepubs/cbc97.pdf. Updated November 2008. Accessed September 26, 2010.
39. Cooper J. ***Occupational Therapy in Oncology and Palliative Care***. Second Edition. John Wiley & Sons. 2007.
40. JAMA Patient Page: Palliative Care. Journal of the American Medical Association Website. http://jama.ama-assn.org/cgi/reprint/296/11/1428.pdf. Updated September 20, 2006. Accessed September 26, 2010.
41. Chemotherapy Principles: An Indepth Discussion. American Cancer Society Website. http://www.cancer.org/Treatment/TreatmentsandSideEffects/TreatmentTypes/Chemotherapy/ChemotherapyPrinciplesAnIn-depthDiscussionoftheTechniquesanditsRoleinTreatment/index. Updated September 28, 2010. Accessed October 1, 2010.
42. Chemo Brain. Mayo Clinic Website. http://www.mayoclinic.com/health/chemo-brain/DS01109. Updated October 10, 2010. Accessed October 15, 2010.
43. Bickley L. ***Bates' Guide to Physical Examination and History Taking***. Twelfth Edition. Wolters Kluwer. 2017.
44. American College of Sports Medicine. ***ACSM's Resource Manual for Guidelines for Exercise Testing and Prescription***. Seventh Edition. Lippincott Williams & Wilkins. 2014.
45. Alvarez A, Brodsky JB, Lemmens HJM, Morton JM. ***Morbid Obesity: Peri-operative Management***. Second Edition. Cambridge University Press. 2010.
46. Clinical Guidelines on the Identification, Evaluation, and Treatment of Overweight and Obesity in Adults: The Evidence Report. National Heart, Lung, and Blood Institute Website. http://www.nhlbi.nih.gov/guidelines/obesity/ob_gdlns.pdf. 1998.
47. Childhood Obesity: Risk Factors. Mayo Clinic Website. http://www.mayoclinic.com/health/childhood-obesity/DS00698/DSECTION=risk%2Dfactors. Reviewed October 9, 2010. Accessed October 14, 2010.
48. Childhood Overweight and Obesity. Centers for Disease Control Website. http://www.cdc.gov/obesity/childhood/index.html. Reviewed March 31, 2010. Accessed October 9, 2010.
49. Childhood Obesity. Mayo Clinic Website. http://www.mayoclinic.com/health/childhood-obesity/DS00698. Updated October 9, 2010. Accessed October 11, 2010.
50. Childhood Overweight and Obesity. Centers for Disease Control and Prevention Website. http://www.cdc.gov/obesity/childhood/index.html. Updated March 31, 2010. Accessed September 24, 2010.
51. Robnett R, Chop W. ***Gerontology for the Healthcare Practitioner***. Third Edition. Jones & Bartlett Publishing. 2015.
52. Lewis C, Bottomley J. ***Geriatric Rehabilitation: A Clinical Approach.*** Third Edition. Prentice Hall. 2007
53. Guccione A, Wong R, Avers D. ***Geriatric Physical Therapy***. Third Edition. Mosby. 2011.
54. Kauffman T, Scott R, Barr J. ***A Comprehensive Guide to Geriatric Rehabilitation***. Third Edition. Elsevier. 2014.

8

Equipment, Devices, and Technologies; Therapeutic Modalities

Scott Giles

Equipment, Devices, and Technologies represents approximately 5 - 6 questions (2.5% - 3%) on the NPTE-PT.

Scott Giles

Therapeutic Modalities represents approximately 6 - 8 questions (3% - 4%) on the NPTE-PT.

CHAPTER 8

Equipment, Devices, & Technologies; Therapeutic Modalities

Mobility

Preparation for Treatment

In order to create an effective and successful treatment environment, the patient must be informed regarding all expectations of the upcoming treatment as well as have all questions answered prior to initiating the actual hands-on intervention. The therapist must obtain informed consent from the patient and document consent in the patient's chart. The therapist must also determine if there are any potential limitations to treatment due to a patient's religious or cultural beliefs. The patient must be notified as to appropriate clothing for therapy, and subject areas such as draping must also be discussed prior to the initiation of therapy in order to ensure a patient's comfort during treatment.

Draping

Draping is a technique utilized by health care providers to ensure the patient's privacy and modesty when treating particular areas of the body. Draping assists to keep the patient warm during treatment, adequately expose the area of treatment, and protect open areas, wounds, scars, and the patient's personal belongings from being soiled or injured during treatment. Draping materials may include gowns, towels, and sheets that must be secured in a manner that will properly expose the area of the body that requires treatment, while maintaining a patient's modesty and overall level of comfort during treatment.

Bed Mobility Guidelines[1,2]

- A patient that is dependent must be repositioned in bed at least every two hours
- Skin should be inspected for redness or breakdown with each position change
- A dependent patient must be lifted when changing positions in order to avoid shearing of the skin across the bed
- Use pillows, towels or blankets when positioning a patient in order to support and maintain a particular position
- A patient should always be encouraged to participate in all mobility and positioning
- Practice moving segmentally from one side of the bed to the other
- Utilize the "bridging" position of hip flexion and knee flexion with feet flat on the surface to assist with movement and rolling
- Move from a supine to sitting position by rolling into sidelying and placing the feet over the edge; with assist as needed
- All components of bed mobility are complete only when the patient ends in a comfortable and safe position

Transfers

Communication During Transfers

The patient should be informed about the transfer itself and their responsibility during the transfer. The explanation should be understood by the patient and should occur prior to performing the transfer.

Commands and counts are used to synchronize the actions of the participants involved in the transfer. The therapist at the head of the patient should give the commands during transfers when more than one person is involved (Fig. 8-1).

Levels of Physical Assistance[1,3]

Independent: The patient does not require any assistance to complete the task.

Supervision: The patient requires a therapist to observe throughout completion of the task.

Contact Guard: The patient requires the therapist to maintain contact with the patient to complete the task. Contact guard is usually needed to assist if there is a loss of balance.

Minimal Assist: The patient requires 25% assist from the therapist to complete the task.

Moderate Assist: The patient requires 50% assist from the therapist to complete the task.

Maximal Assist: The patient requires 75% assist from the therapist to complete the task.

Dependent: The patient is unable to participate and the therapist must provide all of the effort to perform the task.

Transfer Guidelines

- Evaluate the patient's level of cognition and mobility
- When in doubt, utilize a second person to maintain patient/therapist safety
- Obtain all appropriate equipment prior to initiating the transfer
- Utilize a safety belt
- Educate the patient regarding the expectations and transfer sequence through verbal explanation and demonstration
- Instruct the patient in smaller segments of the transfer, if necessary, prior to performing the entire transfer all at once
- Position yourself correctly around the patient and maintain a large base of support; use proper body mechanics throughout the transfer

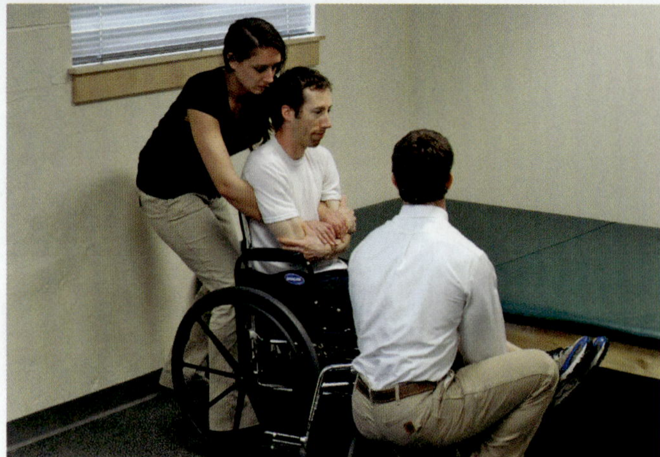
Fig. 8-1: The therapist at the head verbally initiates the transfer.

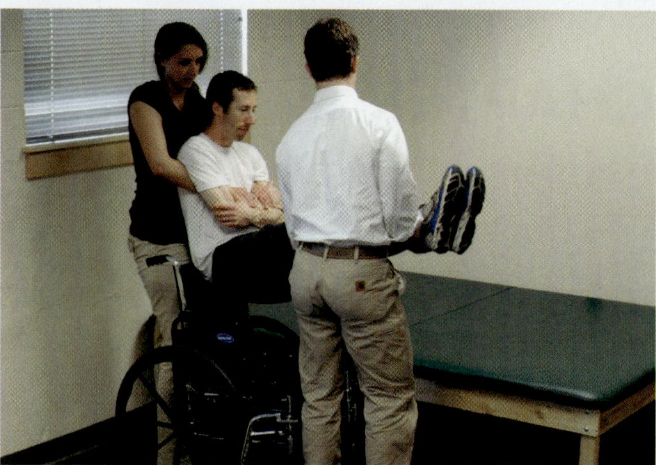
Fig. 8-2: The therapists lift the patient from the wheelchair in a coordinated fashion.

- Vary the amount of assistance as needed
- Utilize manual contacts with the patient to direct their participation during the transfer
- Complete the transfer with the patient positioned comfortably and safely

Types of Transfers[1,3]

Dependent Transfers

Three-person carry/lift

The three-person carry or lift is used to transfer a patient from a stretcher to a bed or treatment plinth. Three therapists carry the patient in a supine position; one therapist supports the head and upper trunk, the second therapist supports the trunk, and the third supports the lower extremities. The therapist at the head is the one to initiate commands. The therapists flex their elbows that are positioned under the patient and roll the patient on their side towards them. The therapists then lift on command and move in a line to the destination surface, lower, and position the patient properly.

Two-person lift

The two-person lift is used to transfer a patient between two surfaces of different heights or when transferring a patient to the floor. Standing behind the patient, the first therapist should place their arms underneath the patient's axilla. The therapist should grasp the patient's left forearm with their right hand and grasp the patient's right forearm with their left hand. The second therapist places one arm under the mid to distal thighs and the other arm is used to support the lower legs. The therapist at the head usually initiates the command to lift and transfer the patient out of the chair to the destination surface (Figs. 8-1, 8-2, 8-3, 8-4).

Dependent squat pivot transfer

The dependent squat pivot transfer is used to transfer a patient who cannot stand independently, but can bear some weight through the trunk and lower extremities. The therapist should position the patient at a 45-degree angle to the destination surface. The patient places their upper extremities on the therapist's shoulders, but should not be allowed to pull on the therapist's neck. The

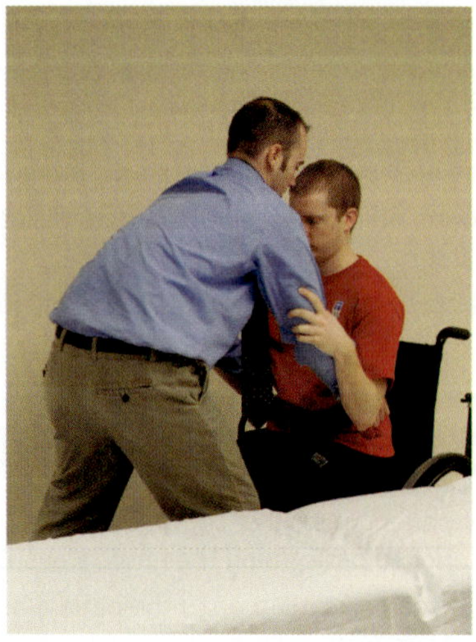
Fig. 8-5: A therapist prepares to initiate a dependent squat pivot transfer.

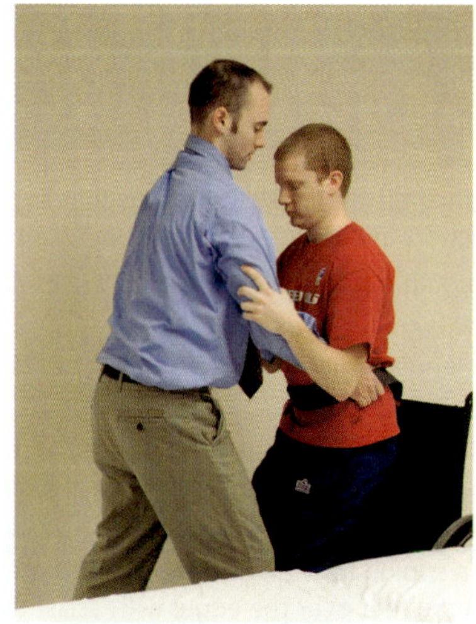
Fig. 8-6: The therapist moves the patient from the chair to a supported squatting position. The patient can bear some weight through the lower extremities.

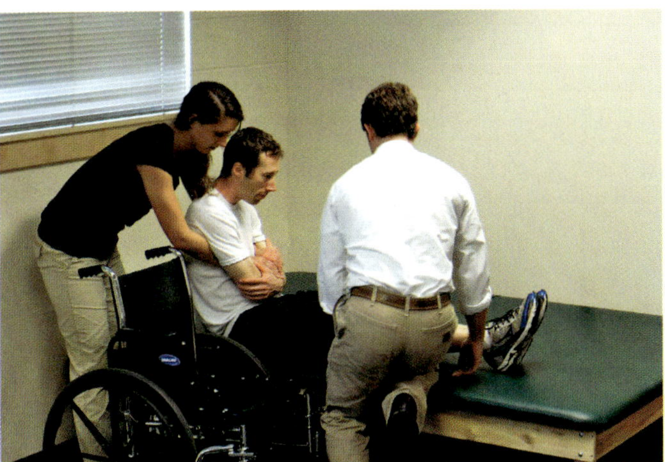

Fig. 8-3: The patient is slowly lowered to the mat table.

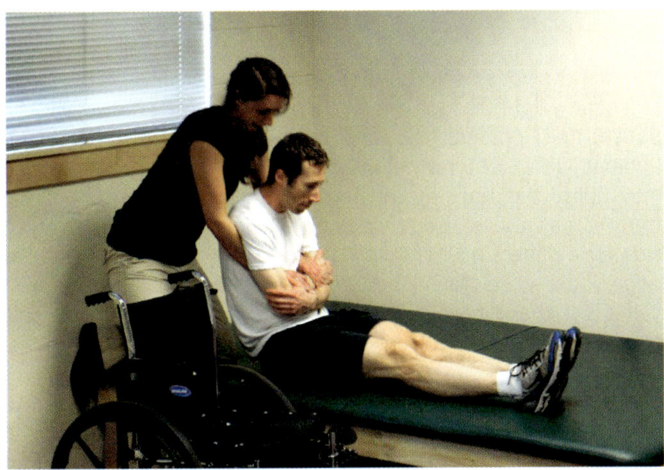

Fig. 8-4: The patient must be in a comfortable and safe position before the therapist concludes the transfer.

therapist should position the patient at the edge of the surface, hold the patient around the hips and under the buttocks, and block the patient's knees in order to avoid buckling while standing. The therapist should utilize momentum, straighten their legs, and raise the patient or allow the patient to remain in a squatting position. The therapist should then pivot and slowly lower the patient to the destination surface (Figs. 8-5, 8-6, 8-7, 8-8).

Hydraulic lift

The hydraulic lift is a device used for dependent transfers when a patient is obese, there is only one therapist available to assist with the transfer or the patient is totally dependent. The hydraulic lift needs to be locked in position before the transfer. The therapist positions a webbed sling under the patient and attaches the S-ring to the bars on the lift. Once all attachments are checked, the therapist should pump the handle on the device in order to elevate the patient. When the patient is elevated, the therapist can navigate the lift with the patient to the destination surface. The chains should be removed once the patient has been transferred, however, the webbed sling should remain in place in preparation for the return transfer.

Assisted Transfers

Sliding board transfer

The sliding board transfer is used for a patient who has some sitting balance, some upper extremity strength, and can adequately follow directions. The patient should be positioned at the edge of the wheelchair or bed and should lean to one side while placing one end of the sliding board sufficiently under the proximal thigh. The other end of the sliding board should be positioned on the destination surface. The patient should not hold onto the end of the sliding board in order to avoid pinching the fingers. The patient should place the lead hand four to six inches away from the sliding board and use both arms to initiate a push-up and scoot across the board. The therapist should guard in front of the patient and assist as needed as the patient performs a series of push-ups across the board. The therapist should be careful to avoid direct contact between the patient's skin and the sliding board to avoid shearing force and potential skin breakdown.

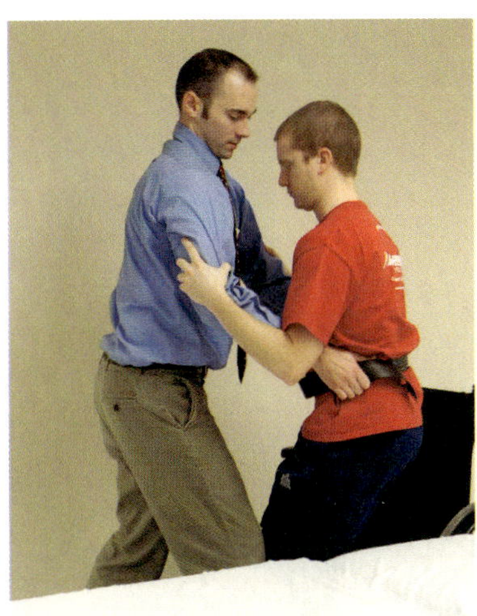

Fig. 8-7: The therapist blocks the patient's knees in order to provide additional stability during the transfer.

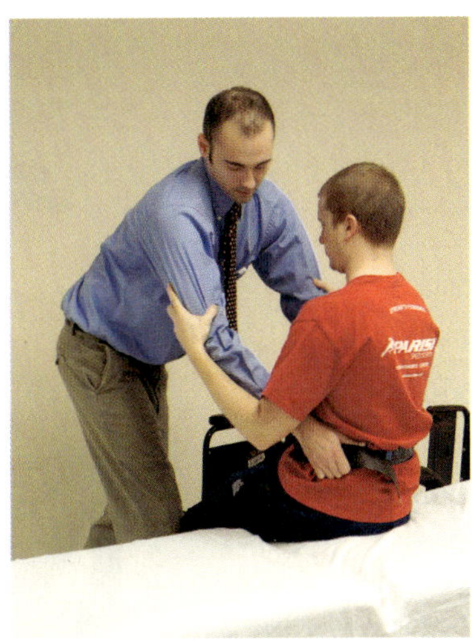

Fig. 8-8: The therapist pivots and slowly lowers the patient to the plinth.

Stand pivot transfer

The stand pivot transfer is used when a patient is able to stand and bear weight through one or both of the lower extremities. The patient must possess functional balance and the ability to pivot. Patients with unilateral weight bearing restrictions or hemiplegia may utilize this transfer and lead with the uninvolved side. The transfer may also be used therapeutically, leading with the involved side for a patient post CVA. A patient should be positioned at the edge of the wheelchair or bed to initiate the transfer. The therapist can assist the patient to keep their feet flat on the floor while bringing the head and trunk forward. The therapist should assist the patient as needed with their feet. The therapist must guard or assist the patient through the transfer and instruct the patient to reach back for the surface before they begin to sit down. Once the stand pivot is performed, the therapist should assist as needed to ensure control with lowering the patient to the destination surface.

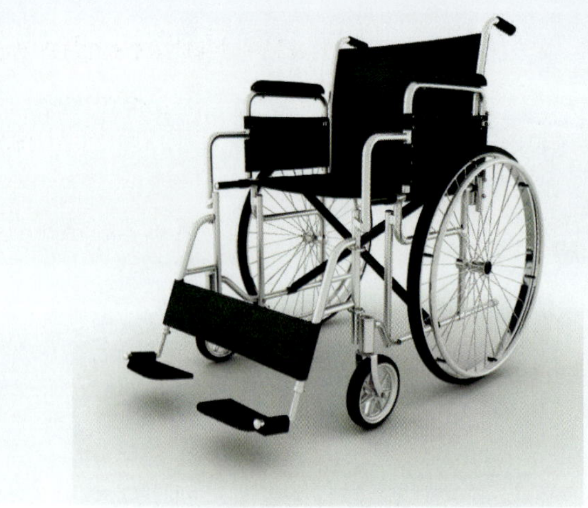

Fig. 8-9: A manual wheelchair.

Stand step transfer

The stand step transfer is used with a patient who has the necessary strength and balance to weight shift and step during the transfer. The patient requires guarding or supervision from the therapist and performs the transfer as a stand pivot transfer except the patient actually takes a step to maneuver and reposition their feet instead of a pivot.

Wheelchairs

Wheelchairs can be manually propelled or externally powered. Manual wheelchairs require patients to possess sufficient strength to propel the wheelchair independently (Fig. 8-9). Powered wheelchairs are propelled by an external energy source, usually a battery, that provides stored energy to one or more belts that propel the wheelchair (Fig. 8-10). Considerations when selecting an appropriate wheelchair include the patient's physical needs, physical abilities, cognition, coordination, and endurance.

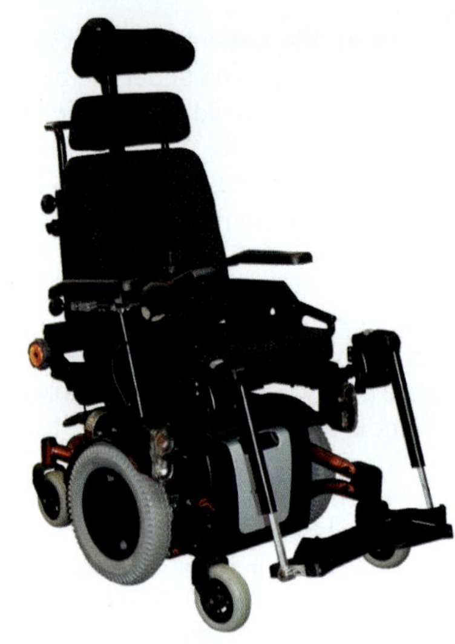

Fig. 8-10: A powered wheelchair.

Wheelchair Measurements[4]

A = total height
B = seat depth
C = armrest height
D = seat height from floor
E = seat and back width
F = back height

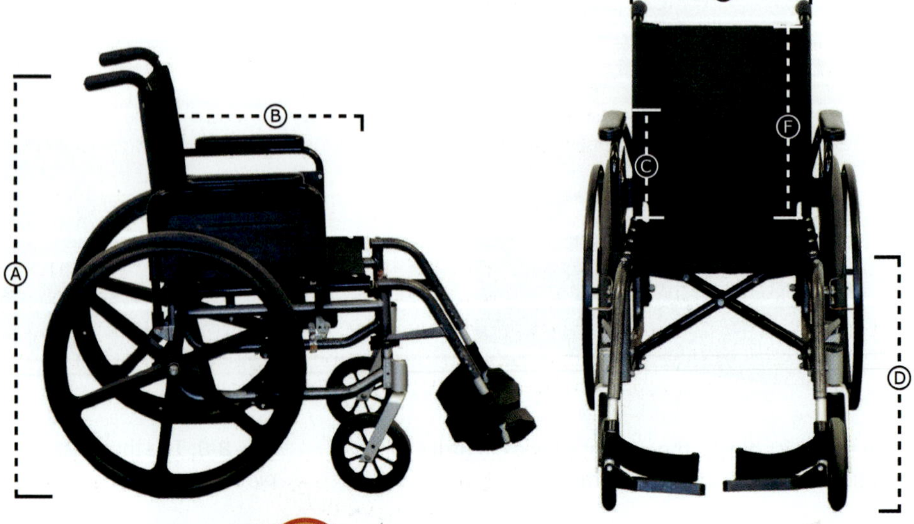

Fig. 8-11: Common wheelchair measurements.

Standard Wheelchair Measurements for Proper Fit[1]

Measurement	Instructions	Average Adult Size
Seat Height	Measure from the user's heel to the popliteal fold and add 2 inches to allow clearance of the footrest.	19.5 to 20.5 inches
Seat Depth	Measure from the user's posterior buttock, along the lateral thigh to the popliteal fold; then subtract approximately 2 inches to avoid pressure from the front edge of the seat against the popliteal space. 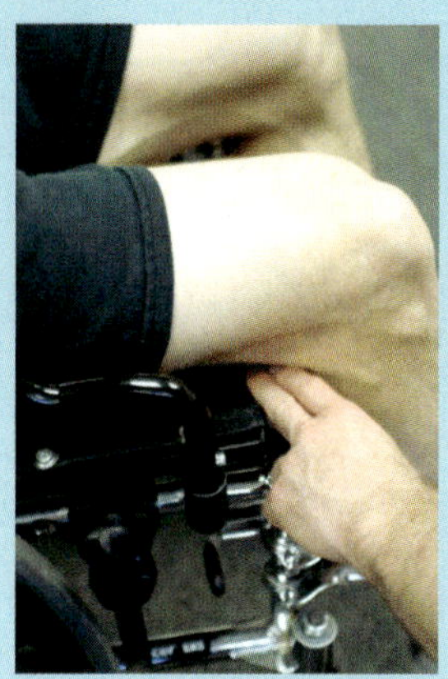 **Fig. 8-12:** A therapist assesses the depth of a wheelchair.	16 inches
Seat Width	Measure the widest aspect of the user's buttocks, hips or thighs and add approximately 2 inches. This will provide space for bulky clothing, orthoses or clearance of the trochanters from the armrest side panel. 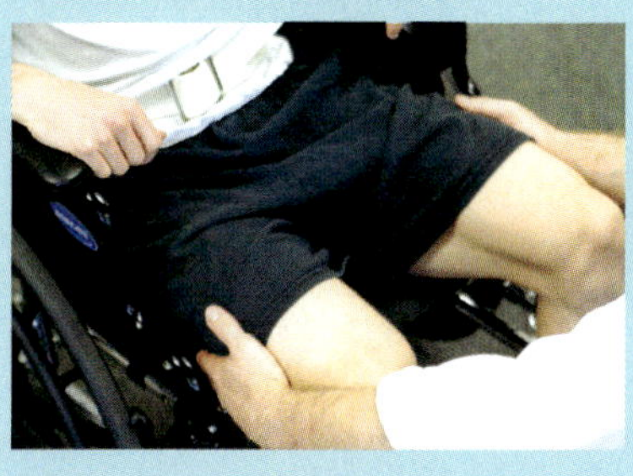 **Fig. 8-13:** A therapist assesses the width of a wheelchair.	18 inches
Back Height	Measure from the seat of the chair to the floor of the axilla with the user's shoulder flexed to 90 degrees and then subtract approximately 4 inches. This will allow the final back height to be below the inferior angles of the scapulae. (Note: This measurement will be affected if a seat cushion is to be used. The person should be measured while seated on the cushion or the thickness of the cushion must be considered by adding that value to the actual measurement.)	16 to 16.5 inches
Armrest Height	Measure from the seat of the chair to the olecranon process with the user's elbow flexed to 90 degrees and then add approximately 1 inch. (Note: This measurement will be affected if a seat cushion is to be used. The person should be measured while seated on the cushion or the thickness of the cushion must be considered by adding that value to the actual measurement.)	9 inches above the chair seat

From Pierson, FM: Principles and Techniques of Patient Care. W.B. Saunders Company, Philadelphia 2002, p.168, with permission.

Common Components of Wheelchair Prescription[5-8]	
Wheelchair Component	**Clinical Indication**
Wheelchair Frame	
Ultralight frame	Patient is highly active with no need for postural supports; used for sports
Standard or lightweight frame	Patient is able to self propel using both upper extremities; adequate lower extremity ROM and sitting ability for comfortable seating
Hemi frame	Patient is able to self propel using lower extremities
One-hand drive frame	Patient is able to self propel using one upper extremity
Amputee frame	Patient is able to self propel, but center of gravity is shifted posteriorly due to amputation
Power wheelchair	Patient is not able to self propel, but is able to safely operate a power mobility device; patient may have transfer, sitting and/or upper extremity functional limitations
Geri chair	Patient is not able to self propel or safely operate a power mobility device; requires assistance for seated mobility
Reclining frame	Patient is unable to perform weight shifting tasks and/or is unable to sit upright for extended periods; moderate to severe trunk involvement
Backward tilt-in-space frame	Patient is unable to sit upright or perform weight shifts, but also has issues with sliding or extensor tone
Headrest	
Planar (flat) posterior	Patient uses a reclining or tilt-in-space frame or patient tends to maintain a hyperextended head/neck position in upright sitting
Curved headrest	Patient tends to maintain backward listing and/or lateral head and neck position in sitting; side panels may be indicated for more aggressive support
Back Inserts	
Sling back	Patient requires no postural support and has no neuromuscular deficits; not typically intended for long term use
Planar back insert	Patient requires mild to moderate trunk support due to tone, strength or deformity related postural concerns
Curved back insert	Patient requires moderate trunk support due to tone, strength or deformity related postural concerns

Common Components of Wheelchair Prescription[5-8]

Wheelchair Component	Clinical Indication
Custom molded insert	Patient requires significant trunk support due to severe postural concerns
Removable back insert	Wheelchair must be able to fold
Back height below inferior angle of scapula	Patient is able to self propel and has good trunk control
Back height above inferior angle of scapula	Patient is either able to self propel, but requires some spinal support or uses a power mobility device with or without poor trunk control
Seat Inserts	
Sling seat	Patient requires no postural support and has no neuromuscular deficits; not typically intended for long term use
Planar seat	Patient has no seated deformity
Curved seat	Patient requires mild to aggressive supportive curvature to provide increased contact between the lower body and seat
Custom molded seat	Patient requires customized seat support to correct for pelvic obliquity or a fixed asymmetrical deformity
Removable seat insert	Wheelchair must be able to fold
Bevel (undercut) front edge of seat	Patient self propels using lower extremities
Trunk Supports	
Planar lateral supports	Patient requires mild to moderate lateral support due to listing or scoliosis
Contoured or curved lateral supports	Patient requires total contact lateral support for significant lateral listing or scoliosis
Chest strap	Patient requires trunk support to correct for anterior listing
Chest harness	Patient requires both trunk and shoulder support to correct for anterior listing

Common Components of Wheelchair Prescription[5-8]	
Wheelchair Component	**Clinical Indication**
Armrests	
Removable	Patient transfers via slide board or two person maximal assist; patient requires access to wheels for propulsion
No armrests	Patient does not require any upper extremity or trunk support
Full length arms	Patient performs sit to stand transfers; patient requires additional postural support; patient utilizes a lap board
Tubular or single posted arms	Patient requires minimal support for the upper extremities; patient requires easy access to wheels for propulsion; patient requires easy removal of arms
Fixed/non-removable	Patient requires durable upper extremity support
Wheel locks/brakes	
Toggle/lever brakes (push or pull)	Patient has coordinated motor ability to operate brakes
Brake extension	Patient requires additional leverage to operate a toggle/lever brake; patient has limited ability to reach brake mechanism
Attendant operated brakes	Patient does not possess the ability to safely or independently operate brakes
Handrims	
Small diameter	Patient has adequate strength to efficiently propel chair without adaptation; typically suggested for patients requiring speed for tasks
Large diameter	Patient has some degree of weakness in the upper extremities; typically suggested for patients requiring the ability to propel with more power
Rim projections	Patient has grip deficits or hand deformity which limits the ability to functionally grip rims
Covered rims	Patient requires assist for adequate grasp or friction when hands are in contact with wheel rims
Footrests	
Standard	Patient has full ROM available through feet and ankles

Common Components of Wheelchair Prescription[5-8]

Wheelchair Component	Clinical Indication
Adjustable angle	Patient has some degree of deformity in feet and/or ankles
One-piece footboard	Patient requires a supportive surface to maximize strength and/or stability; patient requires additional lateral foot support
Custom foot box	Patient's lower extremities are not aligned with body midline as with a windswept deformity; individualized height, angle or support needs are identified
Power Mobility Controls	
Joystick control	Joysticks options vary widely and can be adapted for operation by numerous body parts (e.g., hand, chin, foot)
Proportional control	Allows user to modulate speed of device based on the displacement of the joystick; 360 degree directionality
Non-proportional control	Device moves at a pre-set speed regardless of joystick displacement; user must release joystick in order to change directions
Sip-and-puff control	A switch based system often used for patients with high level spinal cord injuries; patient controls direction based on the force of inhalation/exhalation into a small tube positioned near the patient's mouth
Head control	Head controls may be proportional or non-proportional and operate via an electronic switch system; configurations vary
Other Considerations	
Bariatric wheelchair	Bariatric wheelchairs are available in a variety of weight ratings and dimensions to accommodate patient needs. Weight limits for bariatric wheelchairs typically range between 300 and 1,000 pounds.
Solid cushions (viscoelastic, polyurethane or honeycomb foam)	Solid cushions vary greatly in density and stiffness depending on the product selected. Solid cushions are typically lightweight, however, can produce high shear forces. Examples include Sunmate, Stimulite, and T-foam cushions.
Liquid cushions (gel or water filled)	Liquid cushions vary greatly in the density and stiffness depending on the product selected. Liquid cushions are typically heavier than other alternatives, but serve to limit shear forces. Examples include Jay, Flo-fit, Avanti, and Action cushions.
Air filled cushions	Air filled cushions vary in average shear forces depending on the product selected. Common characteristics include being lightweight with pressure influenced by altitude. Air filled cushions require diligent monitoring of inflation levels. Examples include the Roho and Bye Bye Decubiti cushions.

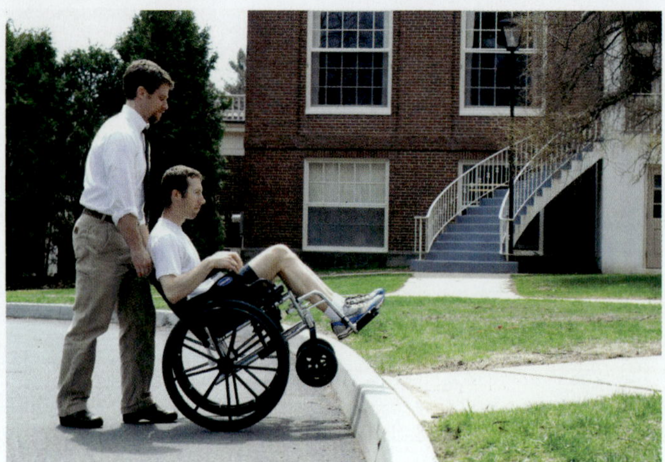

Fig. 8-14: A therapist tips a wheelchair backwards.

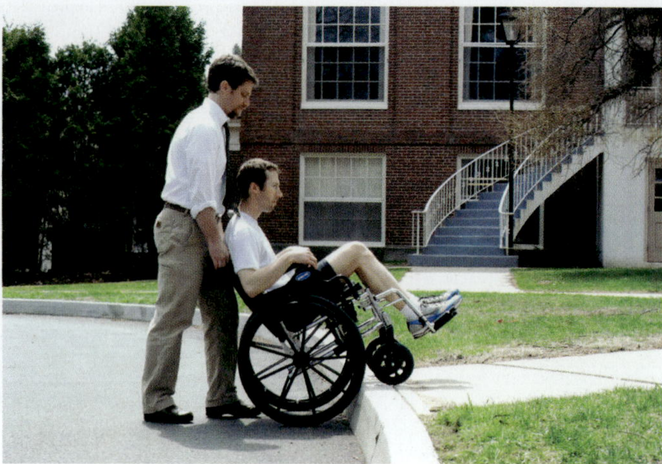

Fig. 8-15: The wheelchair is moved forward until the rear wheels come in contact with the curb.

Wheelchair Mobility[1,3]

Ascending a curb with a forward approach

1. Elevate the front casters of the wheelchair by tipping the wheelchair backwards (Fig. 8-14).
2. Move the wheelchair forward until the rear wheels are in contact with the curb and the casters are above the curb (Fig. 8-15).
3. Lower the casters on the elevated surface and ascend the curb with the real wheels until the rear wheels and the casters are in contact with the elevated surface (Figs. 8-16, 8-17).

Ascending a curb with a backward approach

1. Position the patient facing away from the curb.
2. Standing on the upper surface, lift and roll the rear wheels backward up the curb.
3. Continue to roll the wheelchair backwards until the casters are in contact with the upper surface.

Descending a curb with a forward approach

1. Position the casters close to the elevated edge of the curb.
2. Tip the wheelchair backwards and slowly roll the wheelchair forward until the rear wheels are in contact with the lower surface.
3. Gently lower the casters to the lower surface.

Descending a curb with a backward approach

1. Position the patient facing away from the curb.
2. Move the wheelchair backwards and slowly lower the rear wheels to the lower surface maintaining contact with the curb.
3. Continue to roll the wheelchair backwards and gently lower the casters to the lower surface.

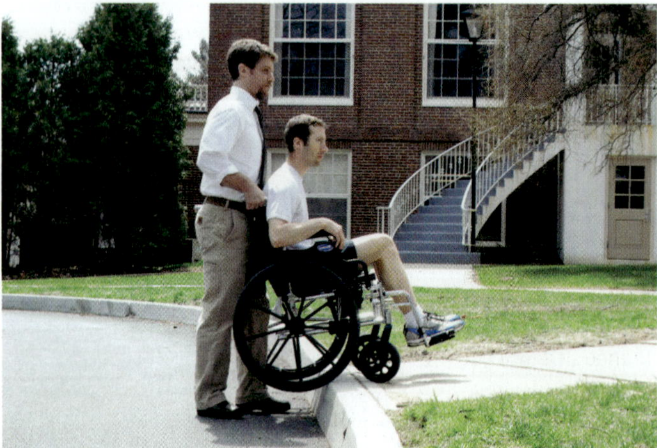

Fig. 8-16: The casters are lowered and the rear wheels ascend the curb.

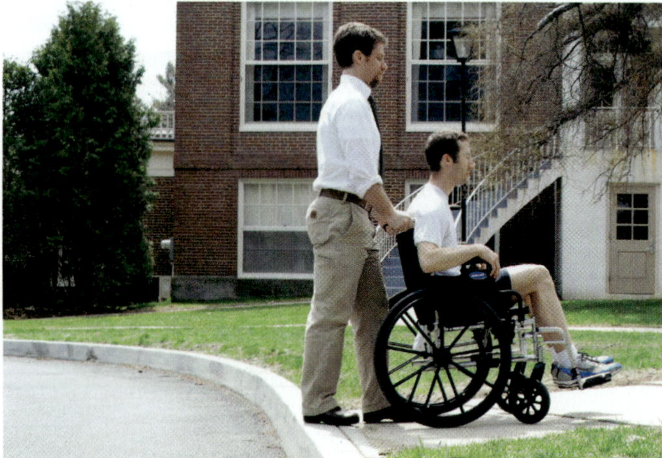

Fig. 8-17: The rear wheels and casters are positioned on the elevated surface.

CONSIDER THIS

EQUIPMENT FOR ACTIVITIES OF DAILY LIVING[9]

Physical therapists should be aware of equipment available to assist patients to perform activities of daily living as effectively and efficiently as possible. The most appropriate equipment for each patient will depend on the patient's medical status and their current living condition.

A listing of some of the more commonly used equipment for activities of daily living is presented.

Bed safety rails - Externally applied rails assist patients with bed mobility.

Button hook - A device that allows individuals with limited dexterity to button clothing using a handheld device. Individuals unable to utilize the device effectively can use Velcro instead of buttons.

Commode chair - A chair with a cut out seat for personal hygiene and a removable pan for commode use. The device is elevated above the level of a standard commode and the armrests increase safety during transfers.

Door knob extenders - A device that increases leverage when opening and closing doors making it easier for individuals with diminished strength and dexterity to function independently.

Grab bars - Stable, mounted bars designed to provide individuals with a handgrip for added stability during functional tasks.

Fig. 8-18: Grab bars positioned around a toilet.

Handwriting aids - Writing devices can be enlarged using a triangular grip or cylindrical foam. This adaptation makes it easier for patients with limited dexterity and pinch strength to write.

Long straw - A long plastic straw enables individuals to drink from a glass without lifting the glass from the surface.

Reacher - The device consists of a long, lightweight aluminum surface with a trigger which activates a grip closure enabling an individual to reach upward or downward without excessive bending.

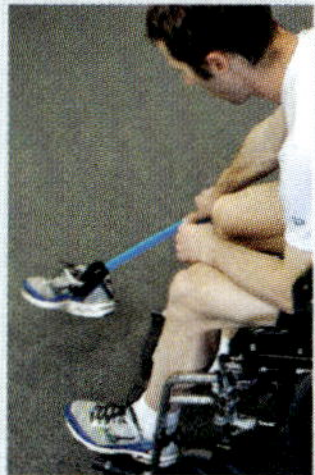

Fig. 8-19: A patient using a reacher to retrieve a shoe.

Rocker knife - This type of knife has a curved blade with an enlarged handle which allows an individual to cut food using a rocking motion.

Sock aids/shoe aids - Devices designed to assist individuals to independently apply socks and shoes using some type of a plastic or wire frame. The devices work by maintaining the sock in an open position or providing a funnel for the patient to use when placing the foot into a shoe.

Tub bench - A bench that allows an individual to sit on a firm, stable surface when bathing.

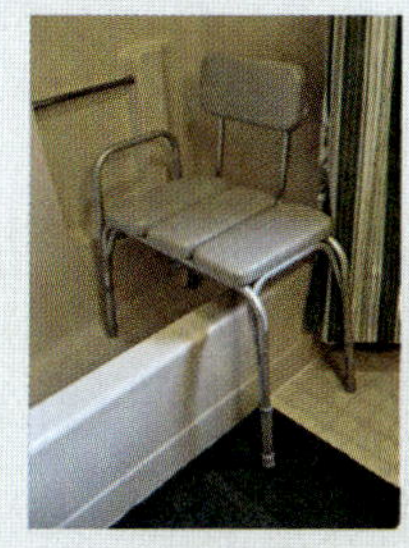

Fig. 8-20: A tub bench positioned in a bathtub.

Zipper pull - A device that allows individuals with inadequate strength in the arms and fingers to pull a zipper using a loop.

Ambulation

Assistive Devices

Primary indications for using an assistive device during ambulation include:

- Decreased weight bearing on the lower extremities
- Muscle weakness of the trunk or lower extremities
- Decreased balance or impaired kinesthetic awareness
- Pain

Assistive Device Selection[1,3,10]

Parallel Bars

Parallel bars provide maximum stability and security for a patient during the beginning stages of ambulation or standing. Proper fit includes bar height that allows for 20–25 degrees of elbow flexion while grasping on the bars approximately four to six inches in front of the body. A patient must progress out of the parallel bars as quickly as possible to increase overall mobility and decrease dependence using the parallel bars.

Walker

A walker can be used with all levels of weight bearing. The walker has a significant base of support and offers good stability (Fig. 8-21). The walker should allow for 20–25 degrees of elbow flexion to ensure proper fit. The standard walker has many variations including rolling, hemi, reciprocal, folding, or adjustable walker with brakes, upper extremity attachments and/or a seat platform. The walker is used with a three-point gait pattern.

Fig. 8-21: A standard walker.

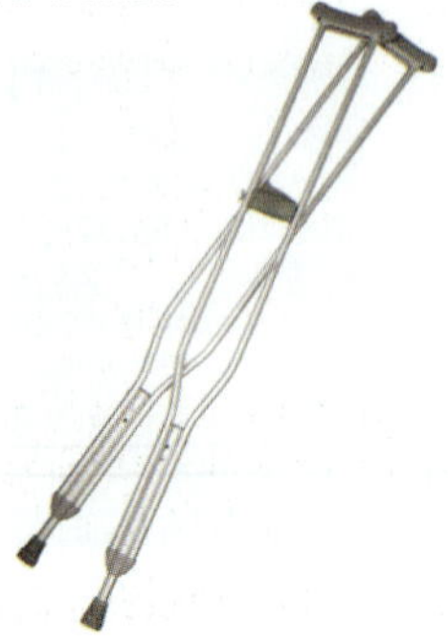

Fig. 8-22: Axillary crutches.

Axillary Crutches

Axillary crutches can be used with all levels of weight bearing, however, require higher coordination for proper use (Fig. 8-22). Proper fit includes positioning with the crutches six inches in front and two inches lateral to the patient. The crutch height should be adjusted no greater than three finger widths from the axilla (Fig. 8-23). The handgrip height should be adjusted to the ulnar styloid process and allow for 20–25 degrees of elbow flexion while grasping the handgrip (Fig. 8-24). A platform attachment can be utilized with this device. Axillary crutches can be used with two-point, three-point, four-point, swing-to, and swing-through gait patterns.

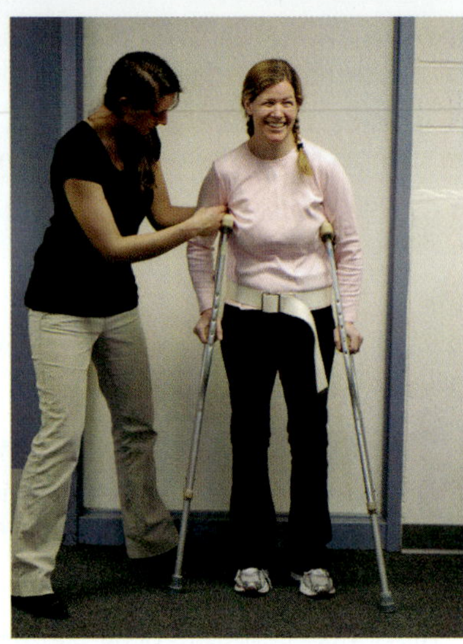

Fig. 8-23: A therapist assesses crutch height by determining the distance from the top of the crutch to the base of the axilla.

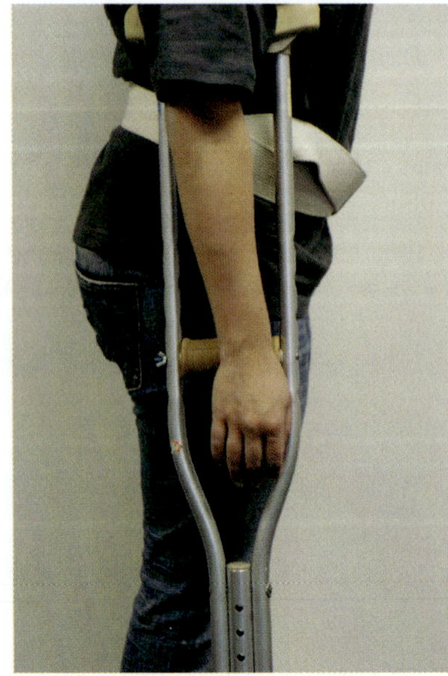

Fig. 8-24: The handgrip of an axillary crutch should be at the approximate level of the ulnar styloid process.

Lofstrand (forearm) Crutches

Lofstrand crutches can be used with all levels of weight bearing, however, require the highest level of coordination for proper use (Fig. 8-25). Proper fit includes 20–25 degrees of elbow flexion while holding the handgrip with the crutches positioned six inches in front and two inches lateral to the patient's foot. The arm cuff should be positioned one to one and one half inches below the olecranon process so it does not interfere with elbow flexion. A platform attachment can be utilized with this device if necessary. The Lofstrand crutches can be used with two-point, three-point, four-point, swing-to, and swing-through gait patterns.

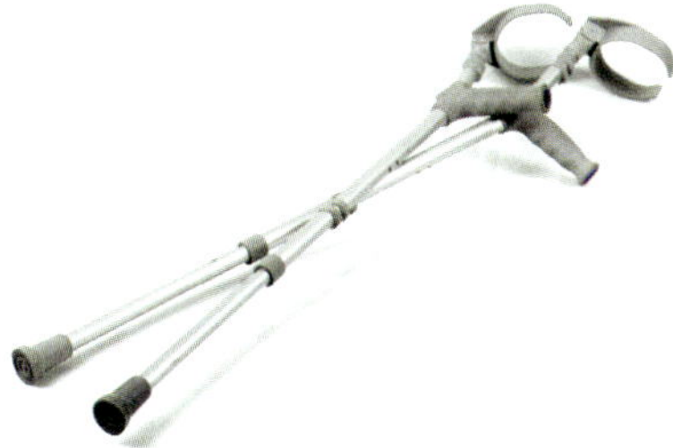

Fig. 8-25: Lofstrand crutches.

Cane

A cane provides minimal stability and support for patients during ambulation activities. The straight cane provides the least support and is used primarily for assisting with balance. A straight cane should not be utilized for patients that are partial weight bearing. The small base and large base quad canes provide a larger base of support and can better assist with limiting weight bearing on an involved lower extremity and improving balance on unlevel surfaces, curbs, and stairs. The cane is typically used on the opposite side of an involved lower extremity. Proper fit includes standing the cane at the patient's side and adjusting the handle to the level of the wrist crease at the ulnar styloid (Fig. 8-26). The patient should have 20–25 degrees of elbow flexion while grasping the handgrip. The straight cane can be used with the two-point, four-point, modified two-point, and modified four-point gait patterns.

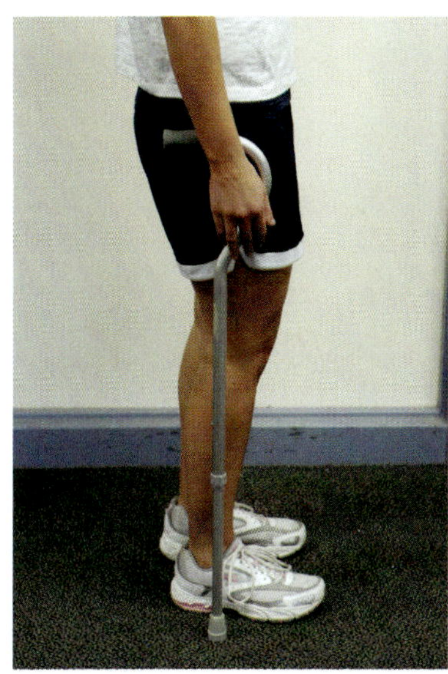

Fig. 8-26: The handle of a cane should be at the approximate level of the ulnar styloid process.

Levels of Weight Bearing[3]

Non-weight bearing (NWB): A patient is unable to place any weight through the involved extremity and is not permitted to touch the ground or any surface. An assistive device is required.

Toe touch weight bearing (TTWB): A patient is unable to place any weight through the involved extremity, however, may place the toes on the ground to assist with balance. An assistive device is required.

Partial weight bearing (PWB): A patient is allowed to put a particular amount of weight through the involved extremity. The amount of weight bearing is expressed as allowable pounds of pressure or as a percentage of total weight. A therapist must monitor the amount of actual weight transferred through the involved foot during partial weight bearing (Fig. 8-27). An assistive device is required.

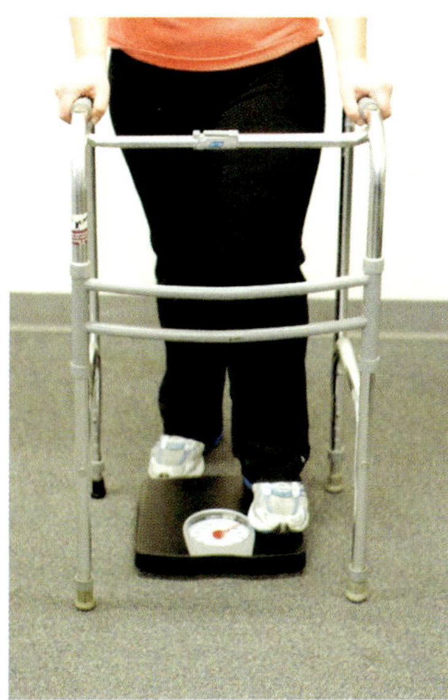

Fig. 8-27: A patient using a scale to determine the approximate amount of weight bearing.

Weight bearing as tolerated (WBAT): A patient determines the proper amount of weight bearing based on comfort. The amount of weight bearing can range from minimal to full. An assistive device may or may not be required.

Full weight bearing (FWB): A patient is able to place full weight on the involved extremity. An assistive device is not required at this level, but may be used to assist with balance.

Guarding

Guarding During Ambulation

A therapist must consider the patient's size, weight, and level of impairment prior to initiating ambulation activities. The following are general guarding recommendations:

- Stand to the side (usually the affected side) and slightly behind the patient.

- Grasp the safety belt with one hand; place the other hand on the patient's shoulder.
- Avoid grasping the arm since it can interfere with the patient's ability to use the extremity.
- Move the lead foot forward when the patient moves; the back leg should advance as the patient ambulates.
- Attempt to anticipate potential hazards during ambulation and take appropriate precautions when possible.
- Utilize a second therapist when needed.

Gait Patterns[1,3]

An appropriate gait pattern is determined by the amount of weight bearing permitted and the severity of the patient's overall condition. Commonly used gait patterns include two-point, three-point, four-point, swing-to, and swing-through.

Two-point gait

This is a pattern in which a patient uses two crutches or canes. The patient ambulates moving the left crutch forward while simultaneously advancing the right lower extremity and vice versa. Each step is one point and a complete cycle is two points.

Three-point gait

This pattern can be seen with a walker or crutches. It involves one injured lower extremity that may have decreased weight bearing. The assistive device is advanced followed by the injured lower extremity and then the uninjured lower extremity. The assistive device and each lower extremity are considered separate points.

Four-point gait

This pattern is very similar to the two-point pattern. The primary difference is that the patient does not move the lower extremities simultaneously with the device, but rather waits and advances the opposite leg once the crutch/cane has been advanced. This gait pattern may be prescribed when a patient exhibits impaired coordination, balance or significant strength deficits. Each advancement of the crutch or cane as well as the bilateral lower extremities indicates a single point, thus allowing for a four-point gait pattern.

Swing-to gait

A gait pattern where a patient with trunk and/or bilateral lower extremity weakness, paresis or paralysis uses crutches or a walker and advances the lower extremities simultaneously only to the point of the assistive device.

Swing-through gait

A gait pattern where the patient performs the same sequence as a swing-to gait pattern, however, advances the lower extremities beyond the point of the assistive device.

Guarding During Curbs and Stairs[1,11]

Ascending

- When using a handrail, stand to the opposite side and behind the patient.
- When a handrail is not available, stand behind the patient slightly toward the affected side (Fig. 8-28).
- Grasp the safety belt with one hand and have the opposite hand available to support the trunk as needed.
- The therapist should position one foot on the step the patient is starting from and the other on the step below. The therapist should maintain a wide base of support.
- Remain static when the patient is moving, then advance keeping the feet in stride position.

Descending

- When using a handrail, stand to the opposite side and in front of the patient.
- When a handrail is not available, stand in front of the patient slightly toward the affected side.
- Grasp the safety belt with one hand and have the opposite hand available to support the trunk as needed.
- The therapist should position one foot on the step the patient will step to and the other on the step below. The therapist should maintain a wide base of support.
- Remain static when the patient is moving, then advance keeping the feet in stride position.

Fig. 8-28: A patient ascending a curb with a quad cane.

CONSIDER THIS

ASCENDING AND DESCENDING STAIRS WITH AN ASSISTIVE DEVICE[1,11]

Patients can ascend and descend stairs with a number of different assistive devices. Regardless of the specific assistive device utilized, when ascending stairs the patient should place the uninvolved lower extremity on the higher stair since it will generate the force needed to propel the body. The involved lower extremity and the assistive device then move to the same stair. When descending stairs, the uninvolved lower extremity generates the force needed to lower the involved extremity with the assistive device to the next step.

Additional factors for therapists to consider when using various assistive devices on stairs are listed.

Walker

Ascending - The patient should place the walker on the opposite side of the handrail and turn the walker sideways. The patient should then grasp the handrail with one hand and the top of the walker's handpiece with the other hand. Using the handrail and walker for stability, the patient takes a step up with the uninvolved extremity. The involved extremity is then advanced to the same step and the walker follows.

Descending - The walker is positioned in a similar manner as described previously. The patient uses the handrail and top of the walker for stability while lowering the involved lower extremity. The uninvolved lower extremity is then lowered and the walker follows.

Axillary Crutches

Ascending - The patient should use the handrail and turn the crutch sideways. This will result in the patient grasping the handrail and the crutch with the same hand. The patient should use the handrail and advance the uninvolved lower extremity to the next step. The patient will then advance the involved lower extremity followed by the other crutch.

Descending - The patient uses the handrail and turns the crutch sideways as described previously. The patient lowers the involved lower extremity and the crutch to the next step followed by the uninvolved extremity.

The patient may alternately elect to ascend and descend stairs holding the handrail with one hand and the two crutches in the other hand.

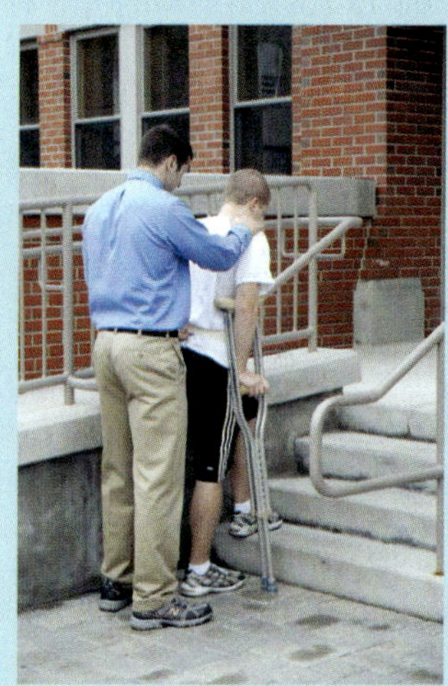

Fig. 8-29: A patient ascending stairs with axillary crutches using the alternate method.

Cane

Ascending - The patient should use the handrail and turn the cane sideways. This will result in the patient grasping the handrail and the cane with the same hand. The patient should use the handrail and advance the uninvolved lower extremity to the next step. The patient will then advance the involved lower extremity.

Descending - The patient uses the handrail and turns the cane sideways as described previously. The patient lowers the involved lower extremity to the next step followed by the uninvolved extremity.

SPOTLIGHT ON SAFETY

LOSS OF BALANCE DURING STAIR TRAINING[1]

Physical therapists take many precautions to avoid unnecessary safety risks when instructing patients in a variety of functional activities. Despite these precautions, on occasion adverse events still occur. In these instances, therapists must be prepared to take immediate action to avoid or minimize the potential impact of an adverse event.

The most appropriate therapist action when a patient experiences a loss of balance during stair training is described. The descriptions are based on the therapist being positioned behind the patient when ascending the stairs and in front of the patient when descending the stairs.

Forward loss of balance

Ascending: Pull backwards on the safety belt and attempt to move the trunk backwards with the opposing hand. If the patient cannot regain balance, transition the patient toward the handrail or lower the patient slowly toward the stairs.

Descending: Use one hand to apply a posterior directed force to the patient's trunk. The therapist may elect to use both hands to stabilize the patient or may use one hand to grasp the handrail while stabilizing the trunk with the opposing hand. If the patient cannot regain balance, the therapist should attempt to move them to a sitting position.

Backward loss of balance

Ascending: Attempt to stabilize the patient's trunk by applying an anterior directed force while maintaining a wide base of support. If the patient cannot regain balance, transition the patient toward the handrail or lower the patient slowly toward the stairs.

Descending: Pull forwards on the safety belt using one hand to grasp the handrail. If the patient cannot regain balance, transition the patient toward the handrail or attempt to move them to a sitting position.

Sideways loss of balance toward the therapist

Ascending: Use one hand or your trunk to stabilize the patient and use the other hand to grasp the handrail. If the patient cannot regain balance, transition the patient toward the handrail or lower the patient slowly toward the stairs.

Descending: Use one hand or your trunk to stabilize the patient and use the other hand to grasp the safety belt or handrail. If the patient cannot regain balance, transition the patient toward the handrail or attempt to move them to a sitting position.

Sideways loss of balance away from the therapist

Ascending: Use one hand to pull the safety belt toward you and use the other to stabilize the trunk or grasp the handrail. If the patient cannot regain balance, transition the patient toward the handrail or lower the patient slowly toward the stairs.

Descending: Use one hand to pull the safety belt toward you and use the other to stabilize the trunk or grasp the handrail. If the patient cannot regain balance, transition the patient toward the handrail or attempt to move them to a sitting position.

Medical Equipment

Feeding Devices[1,12]

Nasogastric tube (NG tube)

A nasogastric tube is a plastic tube inserted through a nostril that extends into the stomach. The device is commonly used for short-term liquid feeding, medication administration or to remove gas from the stomach. The position of the tube in the nostril and back of the throat can inhibit a cough and be irritating for the patient.

Gastric tube (G tube)

A gastric tube is a tube inserted through a small incision in the abdomen into the stomach. The tube can be used for long-term feeding in the presence of difficulty with swallowing due to an anatomic or neurologic disorder or to avoid the risk of aspiration.

Jejunostomy tube (J tube)

A jejunostomy tube is a tube inserted through endoscopy into the jejunum via the abdominal wall. The tube can be used for long-term feeding for patients that are unable to receive food by mouth.

Intravenous system (IV)

An intravenous system consists of a sterile fluid source, a pump, a clamp, and a catheter to insert into a vein (Fig. 8-30). An intravenous system can be used to infuse fluids, electrolytes, nutrients, and medication. Intravenous lines are most commonly inserted into superficial veins such as the basilic, cephalic or antecubital. Intravenous infusion lines permit nutrients to be introduced when the gastrointestinal tract is not able to digest and absorb food.

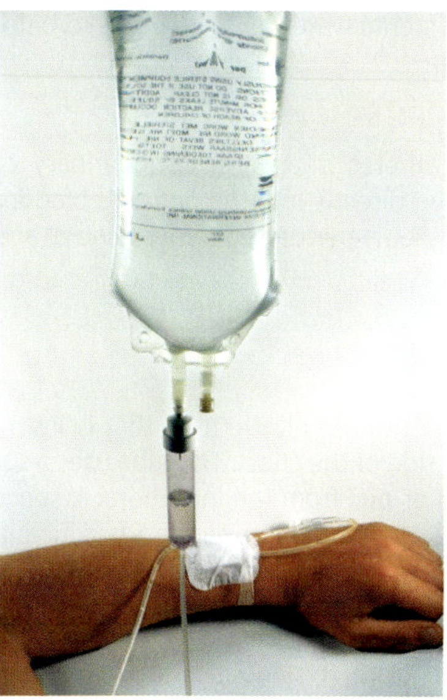

Fig. 8-30: An intravenous system.

Monitoring Devices[1,12,13]

Arterial line

An arterial line is a monitoring device consisting of a catheter that is inserted into an artery and attached to an electronic monitoring system. An arterial line is used to measure blood pressure or to obtain blood samples. The device is considered to be more accurate than traditional measures of blood pressure and does not require repeated needle punctures. If an arterial line is displaced, a therapist should apply direct pressure to limit blood loss and call for assistance.

Central venous pressure catheter

A central venous pressure catheter is used for measuring pressures in the right atrium or the superior vena cava by means of an indwelling venous catheter and a pressure manometer. It is used to evaluate the right ventricular function, right atrial filling pressure, and circulating blood volume. The use of the catheter significantly reduces the need for repeated venipuncture.

Indwelling right atrial catheter (Hickman)

An indwelling right atrial catheter is inserted through the cephalic or internal jugular vein and threaded into the superior vena cava and right atrium. The catheter is used for long-term administration of substances into the venous system such as chemotherapeutic agents, total parenteral nutrition, and antibiotics.

Intracranial pressure monitor

An intracranial pressure monitor measures the pressure exerted against the skull using pressure sensing devices placed inside the skull. Excessive pressure can be produced by a closed head injury, cerebral hemorrhage, overproduction of cerebrospinal fluid or brain tumor. Types of intracranial pressure monitors include epidural sensor, subarachnoid bolt, and intraventricular catheter.

Oximeter

An oximeter is a photoelectric device used to determine the oxygen saturation of blood. The device is most commonly applied to the finger or the ear. Oximetry is often used by therapists to assess activity tolerance. Therapists should monitor changes in oxygen saturation during exercise and position changes.

Pulmonary artery catheter (Swan-Ganz catheter)

A pulmonary artery catheter is a soft, flexible catheter that is inserted through a vein into the pulmonary artery. The device is used to provide continuous measurements of pulmonary artery pressure. The patient should avoid excessive movement of the head, neck, and extremities to avoid disrupting the line at the insertion site.

Oxygen Therapy[1,12]

Nasal cannula

A nasal cannula consists of tubing extending approximately one centimeter into each of the patient's nostrils. The tubing is connected to a common tube that is attached to an oxygen source. This method of oxygen therapy is capable of delivering up to six liters of oxygen per minute.

Oronasal mask

An oronasal mask consists of a facepiece designed to cover the nose and mouth with small vent holes to expel exhaled air along with a breathing tube and connector. The device is used most often for oxygen therapy, however, can be used to administer medications, mucolytic detergents, or humidity, by the use of an accessory nebulizer.

Tent

An oxygen tent refers to a canopy placed over the head and shoulders or the entire body for the purpose of delivering oxygen at a higher level than normal.

Tracheostomy mask

A tracheostomy mask is placed over a stoma or tracheostomy for the purpose of administering supplemental oxygen. The mask is held in place by an elastic strap placed around the patient's neck.

Skeletal Traction[12]

Balanced suspension

Balanced suspension traction requires pins, screws, and wires to be surgically inserted into bone for the purpose of applying a traction force using an externally applied weight. This type of traction is most often utilized with comminuted femur fractures. Balanced suspension traction requires prolonged immobilization and therefore increases the incidence of secondary complications such as contractures or skin breakdown.

External fixation

External fixation refers to a surgical procedure where holes are drilled into uninjured areas of bone surrounding the fracture. The fracture is then set in the desired anatomical configuration using specialized wires, pins, bolts, and screws. An external frame is used

to maintain the bony fragments in the desired alignment (Fig. 8-31). External fixation enhances stability and allows for earlier mobility while maintaining the desired alignment.

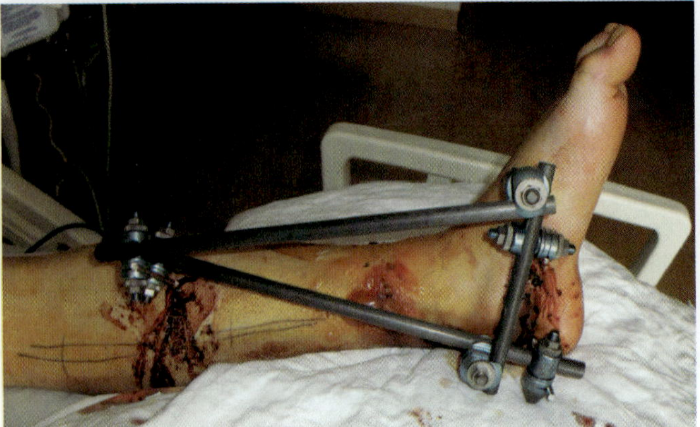

Fig. 8-31: An external fixation device applied to a tibial fracture sustained in a motor vehicle accident.

Internal fixation

Internal fixation refers to a surgical procedure that attempts to promote the healing process of bone without appliances being applied external to the skin. Common types of internal fixation include metal plates, rods, wires, screws, and nails. Internal fixation is often employed with comminuted or displaced fractures. The procedure provides needed stability to healing joints which allows earlier mobility and less postoperative complications.

Urinary Catheters[1,12]

External catheter

An external catheter is applied over the shaft of the penis and is held in place by a padded strap or adhesive tape.

Foley catheter

A Foley catheter is an indwelling urinary tract catheter that has a balloon attachment at the indwelling end. The balloon which is filled with air or sterile water must be deflated before the catheter can be removed.

Suprapubic catheter

A suprapubic catheter is an indwelling urinary catheter that is surgically inserted directly into the patient's bladder. Insertion of a suprapubic catheter is performed under general anesthesia.

Miscellaneous[1,12]

Chest tube

A chest tube is a flexible plastic tube that is inserted through an incision into the side of the chest. The tube uses a suction system to remove air, fluid or pus from the intrathoracic space. A chest tube can cause significant discomfort and result in inhibition of a cough, deep breathing, and mobility.

Mechanical ventilator

A mechanical ventilator produces a controlled flow of gas into a patient's airways. The flow of gas provides positive pressure that produces lung inflation. Patients with acute illness, trauma, and severe chronic illness may require mechanical ventilation. The most common type of ventilators include volume cycled and pressure cycled. Volume cycled ventilators deliver a predetermined amount of gas based on the patient's needs during the inspiratory phase. This type of ventilation is most commonly used for patients that require long-term support. Pressure cycled ventilators deliver a predetermined maximum pressure of gas during respiration. When the established pressure is reached, the inspiratory phase ends. The expiratory phase is passive with both volume cycled and pressure cycled ventilators.

Ostomy device

An ostomy device provides a method for collection of waste from a surgically produced opening in the abdomen. The removal of the waste occurs through a stoma extending into the small intestine. The waste is collected in a plastic bag or pouch covering the stoma. Ostomy systems are typically air and water-tight and allow the user to lead an active normal lifestyle.

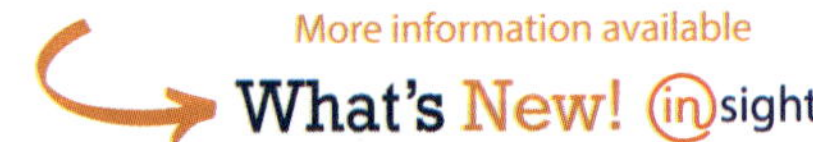

Diagnostic Imaging[12,14,30]

Arteriography

Arteriography (i.e., angiography) is an invasive procedure that uses x-ray imaging and an injected contrast dye to visualize blood vessels (Fig. 8-32). This technique can visualize the major systemic arteries as well as the arterial systems that perfuse the major organs (e.g., brain, heart). A catheter is inserted into an artery, either at the groin or in the arm, and is guided up to the heart. The test can be used to identify arteriosclerosis, aneurysm, vascular malformations, tumors or blockages.

Advantages:

- useful in the diagnosis of vascular abnormalities

Disadvantages:

- invasive procedure
- contrast dye may cause an allergic reaction

Arthrography

Arthrography is an invasive procedure that uses x-ray imaging and an injected contrast dye to visualize joint structures. A long needle is used to inject the dye directly into the joint (i.e., direct arthrography). Alternatively, the dye can be injected into a blood vessel and then absorbed into the joint space (i.e., indirect arthrography). X-rays are then taken with the joint in different positions. Arthrography is useful in identifying pathology of joint structures (e.g., ligament damage, capsular tears). Soft tissue disruption can be identified by leakage of fluid from the joint cavity. The test is commonly used at peripheral joints such as the hip, knee, ankle, shoulder, elbow, and wrist. Arthrography is commonly used with x-ray imaging, though it can also be used with fluoroscopy, MRI, and CT imaging.

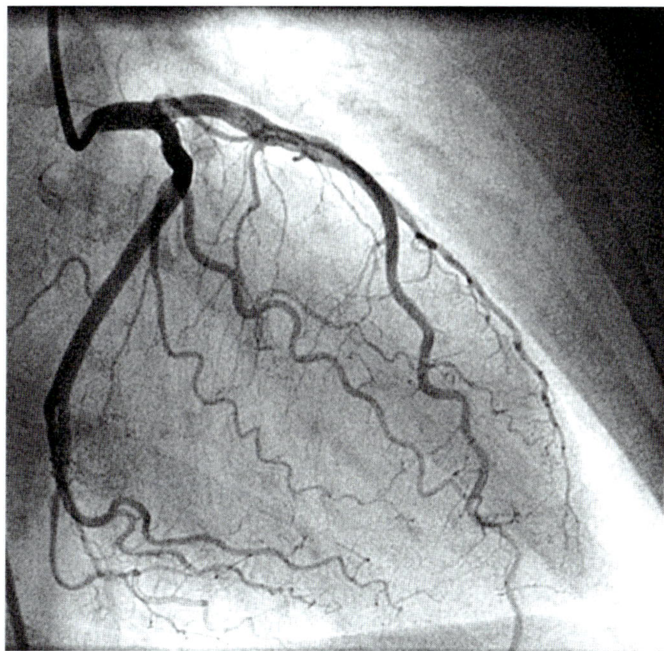

Fig. 8-32: Blood vessels as depicted using arteriography.

Advantages:

- provides a more detailed image of a joint compared to a standard x-ray

Disadvantages:

- invasive procedure
- contrast dye may cause an allergic reaction (especially with indirect arthrography)
- patient may experience joint swelling after the procedure
- not recommended for patients with active arthritis or joint infection

Bone scan

A bone scan (i.e., skeletal scintigraphy) is an invasive procedure used specifically to provide detailed information on bony structures, such as stress fractures, infection, and bone cancer or metastasis (Fig. 8-33). A bone scan involves the injection of a radionuclide into the body. The body is then scanned with a gamma camera to see which bones have taken up the radioactive material. The image produced during the scan shows areas that have high levels of bone remodeling since the radionuclide is taken up by the osteoblast cells within the bone. Bone scans can identify bone disease or stress fractures with as little as 4-7% bone loss.

Advantages:

- provides information on bone pathology that is not identified on x-ray
- low dose of radiation used
- less expensive than PET scans

Disadvantages:

- invasive procedure
- requires a 2-3 hour waiting period between injection and imaging
- patient must lie still for long periods of time
- radionuclide may cause an allergic reaction
- not recommended for patients who are pregnant

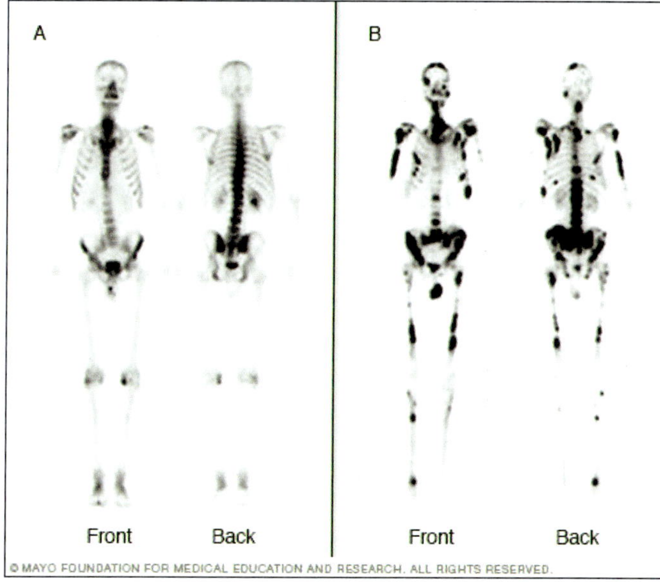

Fig. 8-33: Bone scan images depicting high levels of bone remodeling.

Computed tomography

Computed tomography (CT) is a non-invasive imaging procedure in which x-ray images are taken from multiple angles using a large circular scanner (Fig. 8-34). The images are then combined using computer analysis to produce cross-sectional images. Some types of CT scans use a contrast medium, which can be swallowed or injected, to improve the image quality. CT scans produce images of any structure within the body and therefore have a wide range of uses. CT scans are most commonly used to diagnose spinal lesions and in diagnostic studies of the brain.

Advantages:

- offers quick results and is useful in emergent situations
- generates images of multiple structures at the same time
- produces more detailed images than x-ray

Disadvantages:

- uses a higher dosage of radiation than other imaging techniques
- not recommended for patients who are pregnant
- contrast dye may cause an allergic reaction
- patient is in a small space and may become claustrophobic

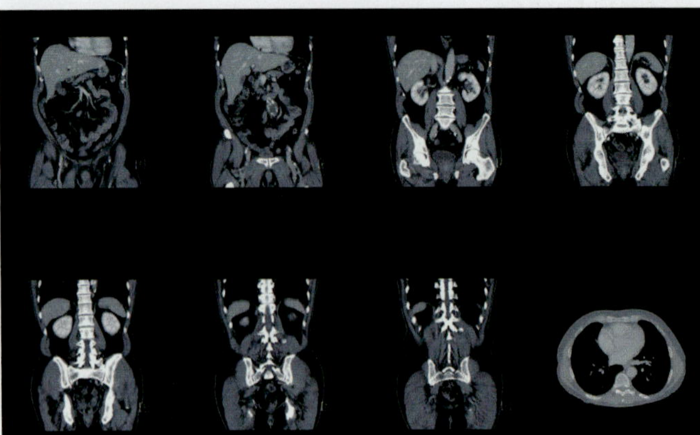

Fig. 8-34: Computed tomography image series.

Electrocardiography

Electrocardiography (ECG) is a procedure used to record the electrical activity of the heart. This form of diagnostic imaging is covered in detail in Chapter 6: Cardiovascular and Pulmonary Systems.

Electroencephalography

Electroencephalography (EEG) is a non-invasive procedure used to record the electrical activity of the brain. Several electrodes are placed on the scalp and are used to record the electrical impulses that result from brain activity. The electrical activity is recorded and displayed as characteristic waveforms on a monitor. Brain disorders, such as epilepsy or narcolepsy, can be diagnosed based on abnormalities in these waveforms. Evoked potential studies are a form of EEG in which brain activity is measured in response to various stimuli (e.g., light, sound).

Advantages:

- useful in diagnosing brain disorders by measuring electrical activity directly as opposed to measuring blood flow or metabolic activity
- noninvasive procedure
- detects changes over the course of milliseconds, as opposed to seconds or minutes with other imaging techniques (e.g., MRI)
- costs less than other imaging techniques

Disadvantages:

- less effective at providing information on exact location of the pathology compared to other imaging techniques (e.g., MRI)
- several factors can affect the accuracy of the results (e.g., medications, caffeine, hypoglycemia, hair products, small movements)
- in some patients with epilepsy, use of an evoked potential study may cause a seizure

Electromyography

Electromyography (EMG) is the recording of the electrical activity of a selected muscle or muscle groups at rest and during voluntary contraction. This form of diagnostic imaging is covered in detail in Chapter 8: Equipment, Devices, and Technologies; Therapeutic Modalities.

Fluoroscopy

Fluoroscopy is designed to show motion within the body with the use of x-ray imaging and injection of a contrast dye. The technique permits objects placed between a fluorescent screen and a roentgen tube to become visible. Instead of a single x-ray image being taken, the x-ray beam is passed through the body continuously to allow for the visualization of movement. Fluoroscopy can show motion within joints or movement of the dye within the digestive tract. A barium swallow exam is a specific type of fluoroscopy procedure used to assess the gastrointestinal tract. The procedure can also be used during the insertion of medical devices (e.g., pacemakers).

Advantages:

- can visualize movement within the body

Disadvantages:

- invasive procedure
- higher dose of radiation than x-rays
- not recommended for patients who are pregnant
- contrast dye may cause an allergic reaction

Lumbar puncture

Lumbar puncture is an invasive procedure that is used to diagnose problems with the spine or brain. The procedure is performed by inserting a needle into the subarachnoid space in the lumbar spine and drawing cerebrospinal fluid (CSF) out to be tested. Lumbar puncture can be used to diagnose conditions such as encephalitis, meningitis, and Guillain-Barre syndrome. Lumbar puncture can also be used to measure the pressure of the CSF.

Advantages:

- useful in diagnosing a variety of brain and spinal cord pathologies

Disadvantages:

- invasive procedure
- should not be performed in the presence of increased intracranial pressure
- leakage of CSF can cause a headache
- small risk of bleeding occurring in epidural and subarachnoid spaces
- patient must remain inactive after the procedure

Magnetic resonance imaging

Magnetic resonance imaging (MRI) is a noninvasive procedure that utilizes magnetic fields and radio waves to produce cross-sectional images of the body (Figs. 8-35, 8-36). The MRI scanner is a large cylindrical device with a hollow tunnel in the center where the patient lies. MRI can be used to visualize almost any structure within the body, but is most often used for imaging soft tissue structures, such as muscles, menisci, ligaments, tumors, and internal organs. MRI provides excellent contrast detail, therefore contrast dyes rarely need to be used, though they may still be used in certain types of imaging to improve the image quality.

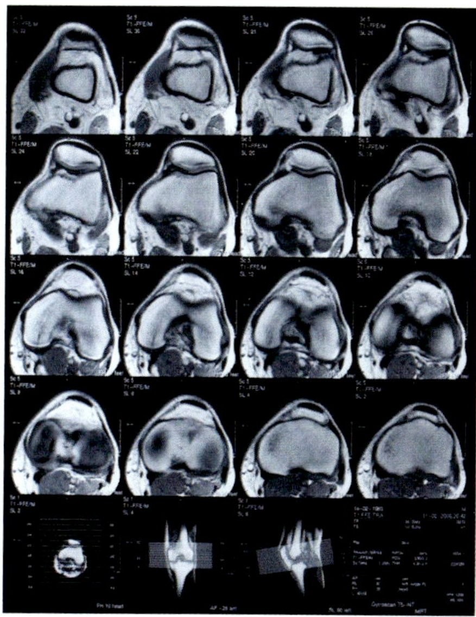

Fig. 8-35: Magnetic resonance imaging of the knee.

Advantages:

- useful in imaging a wide variety of structures, especially soft tissue structures
- noninvasive procedure
- does not use radiation
- safe for use on patients who are pregnant
- contrast dye used is unlikely to cause an allergic reaction

Disadvantages:

- cannot be used if there is metal in the body
- interferes with functioning of internal devices (e.g., pacemaker, cochlear implant)
- patient must lie still for long periods of time
- patient is in a small space and may become claustrophobic
- high cost compared to other tests

Myelography

Myelography is an invasive procedure that combines x-ray/fluoroscopy or computed tomography with use of a contrast dye to evaluate spinal structures, specifically the spinal cord, nerve roots, and meninges. The contrast dye is injected directly into the epidural space by lumbar puncture. Myelography is used to identify bone displacement, spinal stenosis, disk herniation, spinal cord compression, infection/inflammation of the meninges or tumors.

Advantages:

- provides better detail of spinal structures than x-ray
- provides imaging of spinal structures for those patients who cannot have MRI
- low dose of radiation

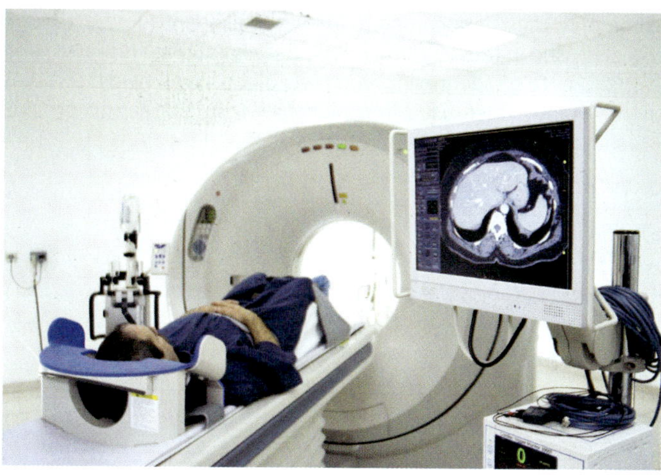

Fig. 8-36: A magnetic resonance imaging unit.

Disadvantages:

- invasive procedure
- contrast dye may cause an allergic reaction
- may cause headache if cerebrospinal fluid leaks out
- small risk of seizure since dye is injected into cerebrospinal fluid

Nerve conduction velocity test

A nerve conduction velocity (NCV) test is a procedure used to determine the extent of nerve damage by measuring the speed of an electrical impulse through the nerve. Two surface electrodes are attached on the skin over the course of the nerve. The first electrode stimulates the nerve while the second electrode measures the speed of the electrical impulse. NCV is often used in conjunction with electromyography testing. Performing both tests allows the health care practitioner to determine if the condition is related to nerve pathology or muscle pathology. NCV is helpful in the diagnosis of conditions such as Guillain-Barre syndrome, carpal tunnel syndrome, and peripheral neuropathy.

Advantages:

- effective at diagnosing nerve-related pathology
- noninvasive procedure
- offers quick results

Disadvantages:

- precautions need to be taken for patients with a pacemaker

Positron emission tomography

Positron emission tomography (PET) is an invasive procedure that uses radiography and an injected radionuclide to determine the metabolic activity of an organ or tissue. The radionuclide is attached to a substance that would be used by the organ of interest (e.g., attached to glucose when studying the brain). A scanner is used to determine the amount of radionuclide taken up by the organ, thereby determining how metabolically active the organ is. PET is commonly used in oncology to identify malignant tumors, though it is also used in the neurology (e.g., identifying brain diseases) and cardiology (e.g., identifying impaired blood flow) fields. PET has more recently been used in conjunction with CT scan to provide greater detail on tumors and other lesions.

Advantages:

- images the function of an organ as opposed to just its anatomy
- detects pathological changes at the cellular level
- identifies the onset of disease processes before other imaging techniques
- low dose of radiation

Disadvantages:

- invasive procedure
- radionuclide may cause an allergic reaction
- not recommended for patients who are pregnant
- results may be affected by high blood glucose levels, medications, caffeine, alcohol or tobacco
- patient must lie still for long periods of time
- patient is in a small space and may become claustrophobic

Ultrasound

Ultrasound is a noninvasive procedure that uses sound waves to produce images of structures within the body, especially the internal organs (e.g., liver, kidneys). A transducer is placed on the skin and sends sound waves into the body, where they reflect off the internal structures and are then received and processed by the transducer. This information is converted into an image based on the different speeds at which the sound waves travel. Ultrasound shows not only an image of a structure, but also the movement of that structure since it is performed in real time. Doppler ultrasound is a specific form of ultrasound that evaluates blood flow in the major veins, arteries, and cerebrovascular system. In comparison to a standard ultrasound, Doppler ultrasound can provide auditory output in addition to the visual projection.

Advantages:

- shows movement of internal structures in real time
- noninvasive procedure
- does not use radiation
- can be used on patients who are pregnant
- safer and less expensive than other procedures (e.g., arteriography)

Disadvantages:

- quality of images highly dependent on the skill of the operator
- cannot image structures filled with air (e.g., stomach, intestines) or structures behind bone (e.g., brain)
- not as effective for patients who are obese due to subcutaneous fat

Venography

Venography is an invasive procedure that uses x-ray imaging and an injected contrast dye to visualize the venous system. A catheter is inserted into a vein in the foot so that the contrast dye can be injected. This test is most often used for visualizing the veins in the leg, though it can also be used for the upper extremities or the inferior vena cava. Venography is helpful for diagnosing deep vein thrombosis, tumors, valve dysfunction or other pathology of the venous system.

Advantages:

- effective in visualizing the venous system
- low dose of radiation

Disadvantages:

- invasive procedure
- contrast dye may cause an allergic reaction

X-ray

X-ray is a radiographic image commonly used to assist with the diagnosis of issues related to the bones, such as fractures, dislocations, arthritis, and bone infections (Fig. 8-37). Chest x-rays may be performed to help diagnose lung conditions, such as pneumonia or chronic obstructive pulmonary disease. An x-ray uses radiation to penetrate the body and create a two-dimensional picture. Structures with low density (e.g., soft tissue structures) do not absorb x-rays as well and therefore do not show up on a radiograph. X-ray produces only two-dimensional images and as a result often requires images to be taken in multiple planes in order to visualize a lesion's location and size.

Advantages:

- useful in diagnosing bone and joint pathology
- noninvasive procedure
- low dose of radiation
- low cost and rapid results

Disadvantages:

- cannot image soft tissue structures
- not recommended for patients who are pregnant

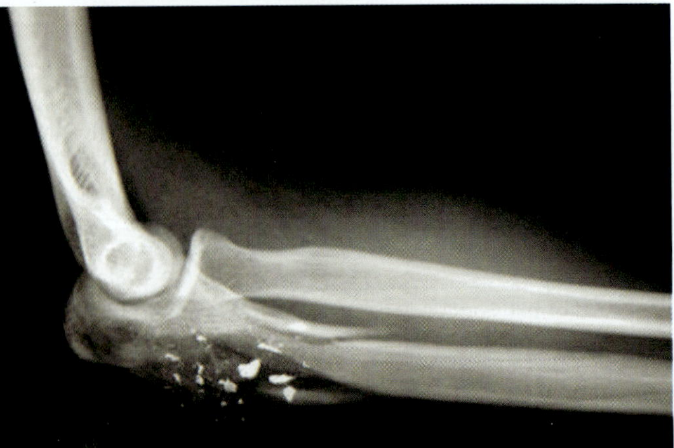

Fig. 8-37: An x-ray image depicting a comminuted fracture.

Therapeutic Modalities

Therapeutic modalities is a broad term describing a variety of agents used in the rehabilitation of patients. Therapeutic modalities include thermal agents (e.g., hot pack, ultrasound), mechanical agents (e.g., traction, compression), and electromagnetic agents (e.g., electrical stimulation, diathermy). In a rehabilitation program, therapeutic modalities are primarily used as adjuncts to other interventions, such as therapeutic exercise.

Indications for Therapeutic Modalities[16,17,18]
Inflammation and repair: Modalities can alter circulation, chemical reactions, flow of body fluids, and cell function throughout all phases of healing. Modalities can enhance and accelerate the healing process and reduce the risk of adverse effects associated with inflammation.
Pain: Modalities can assist with controlling pain by altering the origin of the pain or altering the process of pain perception.
Restriction in motion: Modalities are used to enhance extensibility of collagen to allow for greater range of motion and tolerance to stretch.
Abnormal tone: Modalities can influence tonal abnormalities that are due to pain, musculoskeletal pathology or neurological pathology. Alterations in nerve conduction, pain, and biomechanical properties of muscle can normalize tone and enhance functional outcomes.

Principles of Heat Transfer[16,18]

Therapeutic modalities result in the transfer of heat to or from a patient's body. Heating agents transfer heat to the body, while cooling agents transfer heat away from the body. Methods of heat transfer include conduction, convection, conversion, evaporation, and radiation.

Conduction

Conduction refers to the gain or loss of heat resulting from direct contact between two materials at different temperatures. Heat is conducted from a material of higher temperature to a material of lower temperature. Heat transfer continues until the temperature and speed of molecular movement of both materials become equal. The rate of heat transfer will accelerate when there is a large temperature difference between a heating or cooling agent and the body part being treated. Materials with high thermal conductivity transfer heat faster than those with low thermal conductivity. For example, water transfers heat faster than air since it possesses higher thermal conductivity. Metal has extremely high thermal conductivity, which is the rationale for removing all metal jewelry prior to initiating treatment with a conductive thermal agent.

Examples of modalities that utilize conduction include hot pack, cold pack, paraffin, ice massage, and Cryo Cuff.

Convection

Convection refers to the gain or loss of heat resulting from air or water moving in a constant motion across the body. Since the thermal agent is in motion and new parts of the agent are constantly coming into contact with the target area, heating by convection is capable of transferring large amounts of heat. For example, blood circulating in the body maintains body temperature by convection. As a result, when circulation is compromised, the relative risk of thermal injury significantly increases.

Examples of modalities that utilize convection include fluidotherapy, hot whirlpool, and cold whirlpool.

Conversion

Conversion refers to heating that occurs when nonthermal energy (e.g., mechanical, electrical) is absorbed into tissue and transformed into heat. The rate of heat transfer with conversion is determined by the power of the energy source. For example, the power of ultrasound would be determined by the selected intensity. Heating by conversion is not affected by the temperature of the thermal agent as it is with conduction and convection. Heat transfer does not require direct contact between the thermal agent and the target area, however, it does require a medium that allows transmission of the particular type of energy. In the case of ultrasound, the medium may be gel, lotion or water.

Examples of modalities that utilize conversion include diathermy and ultrasound.

Evaporation

Evaporation refers to the transfer of heat that occurs as a liquid absorbs energy and changes form into a vapor. In the case of a vapocoolant spray, the liquid spray is applied to a patient's body. The vapocoolant spray is then heated by the warmer skin of the body, causing the liquid to change into a vapor. The evaporation of sweat is another example of this cooling phenomenon.

An example of a modality that utilizes evaporation is vapocoolant spray.

Radiation

Radiation refers to the direct transfer of heat from a radiation energy source of higher temperature to one of cooler temperature. In order for heating by radiation to occur, there must be a difference in temperature between the energy source and the target area. This difference must exist without the energy source being in direct contact with the target area. The rate of heat transfer will be influenced by a number of factors including the intensity and size of the energy source, the target area, the angle of the radiation in relation to the target area, and the distance between the energy source and the target area.

Examples of modalities that utilize radiation include infrared lamp, laser, and ultraviolet light.

Examples of Heat Transfer by Category				
Conduction	**Convection**	**Conversion**	**Evaporation**	**Radiation**
Cold pack	Cold whirlpool	Diathermy	Vapocoolant spray	Infrared lamp
Cryo Cuff	Fluidotherapy	Ultrasound		Laser
Ice massage	Hot whirlpool			Ultraviolet light
Hot pack				
Paraffin				

Cryotherapy

Cryotherapy refers to the local or general use of low temperatures in rehabilitation. Cryotherapy generates therapeutic effects by influencing hemodynamic (e.g., blood flow), metabolic (e.g., metabolic rate), and neuromuscular processes (e.g., nerve conduction velocity). Common examples of modalities used for cryotherapy include ice massage, cold pack, cold bath, controlled cold compression unit, Cryo Cuff, and vapocoolant spray. The type of cryotherapeutic agent selected is influenced by numerous variables including the size of the target area, anatomical location, desired magnitude of cooling, and the patient's medical history.

Therapeutic Effects[16,18]	
• Decreased blood flow to the treatment area • Decreased edema • Decreased local temperature • Decreased metabolic rate	• Decreased nerve conduction velocity • Decreased tone • Increased pain threshold
Indications[16,18]	
• Abnormal tone • Acute or chronic pain • Acute or subacute inflammation • Bursitis • Muscle spasm	• Musculoskeletal trauma • Myofascial trigger points • Tendonitis • Tenosynovitis
Contraindications[16,18]	
• Cold intolerance • Cold urticaria • Cryoglobulinemia • Infection • Over an area of compromised circulation	• Over regenerating peripheral nerves • Paroxysmal cold hemoglobinuria • Peripheral vascular disease • Raynaud's phenomenon • Skin anesthesia

Ice Massage

Ice massage is typically performed by freezing water in a paper cup and then applying the ice directly to the treatment area. A wooden tongue depressor can be frozen in water to form an ice popsicle. Ice massage is ideal for small or contoured areas and is easily integrated into a home exercise program. In addition to the anti-inflammatory effects, ice massage can be used as a stimulus to facilitate a desired motor response in patients with impaired motor control. In this scenario, ice is applied with direct pressure over a muscle belly for 3-5 seconds or quickly stroked over the targeted muscle belly to enhance contraction.[16]

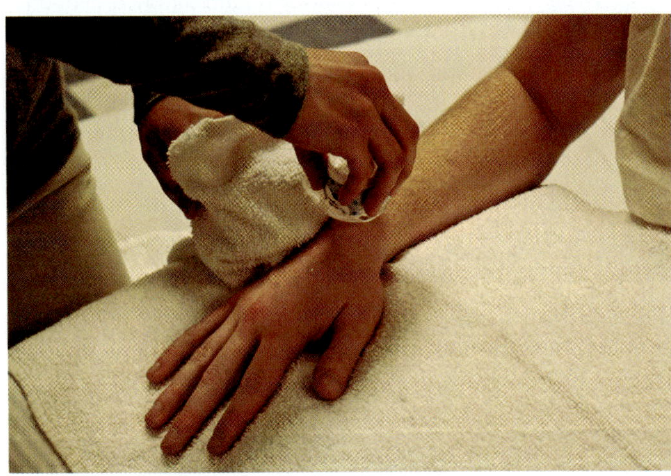

Fig. 8-38: Using a towel to absorb excess water during ice massage.

Ice massage should be applied with the patient in a relaxed and comfortable position. Clothing and jewelry should be removed from the treatment area. The top third of the paper cup should be removed leaving the base of the cup covered for the therapist or patient to grip. A towel should be used to absorb dripping water as melting occurs. Ideally, the body part to be treated should also be elevated (Fig. 8-38).

The ice should be applied using small, overlapping circles or strokes. An area 10 cm by 15 cm can be covered in 5-10 minutes (Fig. 8-39).[17] Patients will typically progress through a series of unique sensations during ice massage including intense cold, burning, aching, and analgesia.[17] These sensations are thought to be caused by increased stimulation of thermal receptors and pain receptors, followed by blocking of sensory nerve conduction as the tissue temperature decreases.

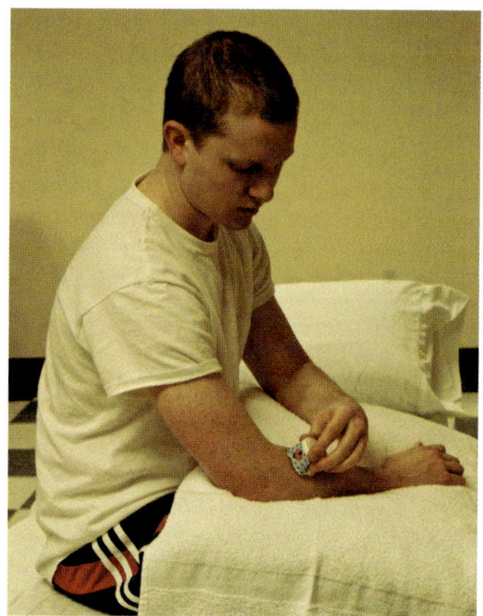

Fig. 8-39: Ice massage being self administered.

Ice massage should continue until the patient reports analgesia. The exact amount of time for analgesia to occur will depend largely on the size of the treatment area, however, 5-10 minutes is typically adequate.[17] Maintaining skin temperature above 59 degrees Fahrenheit will minimize the risk of damaging tissue or producing frostbite.[16]

Ice massage typically cools tissues more rapidly than other types of cryotherapy, including an ice pack or ice bag. The therapist should inspect the skin during treatment and after the completion of treatment. Normally, the skin should appear to be red or dark pink. An abnormal response is most often noted by the presence of wheals or a rash.[16]

Cold Pack

A cold pack typically contains silica gel and is available in a variety of shapes and sizes. The gel remains in a semisolid form even at relatively low temperatures, which allows the cold pack to conform to the contour of the body. Cold packs are typically stored in a specialized cooling unit at approximately 25 degrees Fahrenheit (Fig. 8-40).[17] Cold packs should be cooled for at least 30 minutes between uses and for two or more hours prior to the initial use.[17]

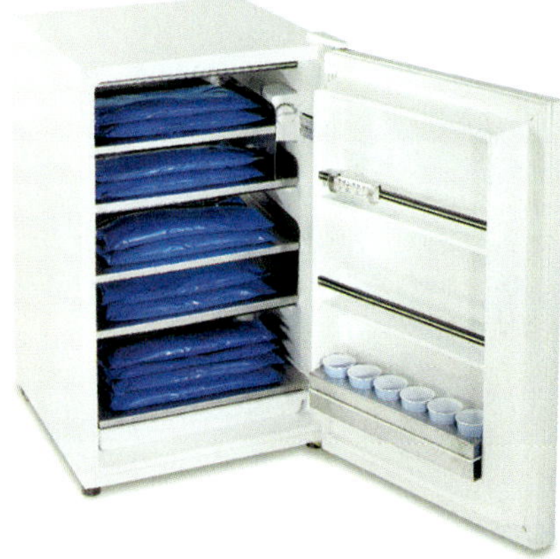

Fig. 8-40: A specialized cooling unit containing cold packs and cups for ice massage. Courtesy Chattanooga, a DJO Global Company.

The therapist should thoroughly inspect the targeted area prior to initiating treatment. Clothing and jewelry should be removed from the treatment area. If edema is present, the involved extremity can be elevated. The cold pack should be applied over a moist, cold towel to increase the initial magnitude of cooling (Fig. 8-41). The moist towel increases the conduction by minimizing the influence of air, which is a poor conductor.[17] Warm water can be used to moisten the towel when using a cold pack on a patient who is sensitive to cold, since it allows for a more gradual onset of cold. The cold pack can be applied using an elastic wrap to increase the surface contact between the cold pack and the target area. The patient should be given a bell or another type of call device in the event they need assistance during treatment.

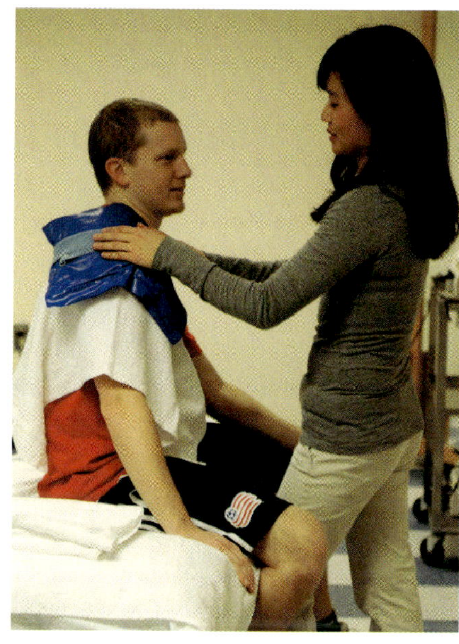

Fig. 8-41: Application of a cold pack to a patient's shoulder.

A cold pack should be applied for approximately 20 minutes.[18] Applying a cold pack for this duration reduces the temperature of the skin and subcutaneous tissues up to two centimeters in depth. Additional treatment time may be necessary when applying the cold pack over bandages or other types of wraps to allow the cold to adequately penetrate through the additional layers. The therapist should inspect the skin during and after the completion of treatment. Normally, the skin should appear red or dark pink. An abnormal response is most often noted by the presence of wheals or a rash.[16]

Cold packs can be applied every one to two hours for the reduction of inflammation and pain control. Patients can use a variety of substitute cryotherapeutic agents at home, such as a bag of frozen vegetables or a plastic bag filled with crushed ice.

Application may extend to 30 minutes if the treatment goal is spasticity reduction.[17] In this scenario, the skin would require inspection every ten minutes. Treatment beyond 20 minutes may require replacing the original cold pack.

Cold Bath

A cold bath is commonly used for the immersion of the distal extremities. Unlike many other forms of cryotherapy, a cold bath allows for circumferential contact with the cooling agent. In the presence of edema, therapists should be mindful of the influence of a gravity-dependent position on the involved extremity during treatment.

A cold bath requires water temperature ranging from 55-64 degrees Fahrenheit.[19] A whirlpool or container of water with crushed ice can be used (Fig. 8-42). The body part should be immersed for 15-20 minutes to attain the desired therapeutic effects.[19] The lower the temperature selected, the shorter the duration of treatment. The intervention is often used as a component of a home exercise program.

Fig. 8-42: Immersion of a hand in a cold bath.

Controlled Cold Compression Unit

A controlled cold compression unit circulates cooled water through a sleeve that is applied to an extremity. The water can be maintained at temperatures ranging from 50-77 degrees Fahrenheit.[19] Compression is applied intermittently by inflating the sleeve with air with the goal of controlling inflammation and reducing edema in the extremity. In post-operative situations, the sleeve may be placed on the patient's involved extremity immediately after surgery. The combined use of cold and compression is more effective than cold or compression alone in controlling inflammation.[18]

Cryo Cuff

A Cryo Cuff is a cold water circulating unit that combines the benefits of cold with compression. The Cryo Cuff consists of a nylon sleeve that is connected to a specialized gallon container via a plastic tube. Water from the container flows via gravity into the sleeve when the gallon container is elevated approximately 15-18 inches above the level of the sleeve (Fig. 8-43). This action provides cooling from the cold water and compression from the increased pressure in the sleeve. The water is drained from the sleeve via gravity by placing the container below the level of the sleeve (Fig. 8-44). The water in the container must be recooled periodically in order to maintain the desired therapeutic temperature.

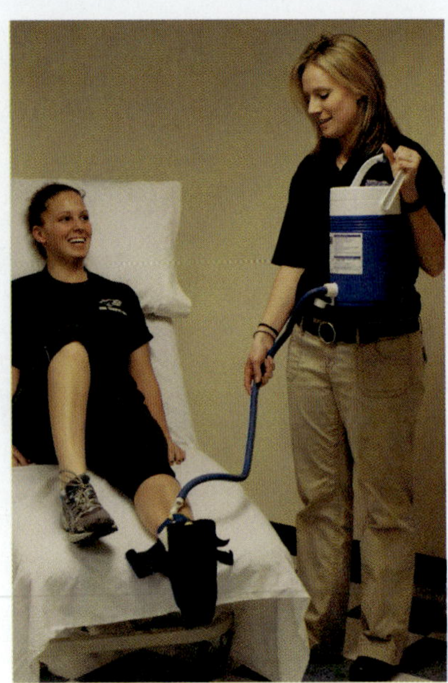

Fig. 8-43: Filling an ankle Cryo Cuff.

The device can provide hours of mild cooling at levels far below the intensity of other cryotherapeutic agents, such as ice massage or cold packs.[20] The Cryo Cuff is most commonly used on the knee, however, it is available for a number of other areas of the body including the shoulder and the ankle. The device is commonly employed post-operatively with the goal of decreasing pain and the need for analgesic medications.

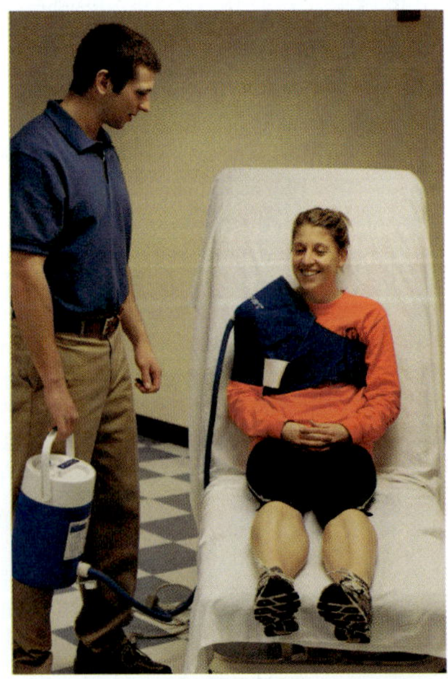

Fig. 8-44: Draining water from a shoulder Cryo Cuff.

CONSIDER THIS

CRYOTHERAPY AGENTS - ADVANTAGES AND DISADVANTAGES[16,17,18]

There are a variety of cryotherapy agents that provide similar therapeutic effects. Therapists should consider the nuances associated with the patient's current condition, as well as the advantages and disadvantages of each cryotherapy agent, when selecting an appropriate mode of intervention.

The following table illustrates several advantages and disadvantages of commonly used cryotherapy agents.

Cryotherapy Agent	Advantages	Disadvantages
Ice massage	Effective for small or irregular areas Target area can be observed during treatment Short duration of treatment Available for home use	Intensity of cooling may not be tolerated by the patient Time consuming for large areas Requires active participation from the therapist or patient
Cold pack	Covers moderate to large areas Can be applied in conjunction with elevation Available for home use	May not maintain good contact on small or severely contoured areas Patient may not tolerate the weight of the pack Difficult to observe target area directly during treatment
Cold bath	Effective for cooling the distal extremities Allows for circumferential contact with water Available for home use	Requires the extremity to remain in a gravity-dependent position
Controlled cold compression unit	Allows simultaneous application of cold and compression Temperature and compression force can be accurately controlled Can be combined with other interventions, such as electrotherapy	Difficult to observe target area directly during treatment Limited to extremity use
Cryo Cuff	Allows simultaneous application of cold and compression Provides hours of mild cooling Available for home use	Difficult to precisely control temperature and compression force
Vapocoolant spray	Localized area of application Brief duration of cooling Effectively treats trigger points Increases range of motion	Difficult to apply spray uniformly Risk of frostbite if skin is not rewarmed between repeated treatments Limited in scope of use

Vapocoolant Spray[16,18,20]

A vapocoolant spray produces rapid cooling through evaporation, with temperature changes occurring superficially in the epidermis. This therapeutic modality is most commonly used in the treatment of trigger points, which are described as deep and hypersensitive, localized spots in a muscle that cause a referred pain pattern. Vapocoolant sprays produce a counter-irritant stimulus to the cutaneous thermal afferent nerves that overlay the muscles. This causes a reduction in motor neuron activity and a decrease in the resistance to stretch. This may break the pain cycle and allow the muscle to be stretched to its normal length.

The use of vapocoolant spray to treat trigger points is often termed "spray and stretch" based on the work of Janet Travell. When using spray and stretch, therapists should identify the trigger point and make three to four sweeps with the spray in the direction of the muscle fibers. The spray must be applied in one direction only and not in a back and forth motion. Special care must be taken to cover the patient's eyes, nose, and mouth if spraying near the face. The spray should be applied at a 30 degree angle at a distance of 12-18 inches from the skin.

Stretching should begin while applying the spray and continue after the spray has been applied (Fig. 8-45).[18] Repeated applications during the same treatment are safe if the skin is rewarmed between applications.

When using vapocoolant sprays to increase range of motion without the presence of trigger points, the spray is applied along the muscle from the proximal to the distal attachment. Clinical conditions that may respond to treatment with vapocoolant sprays include torticollis, neck or low back pain caused by muscle spasm, acute bursitis, and hamstrings tightness.

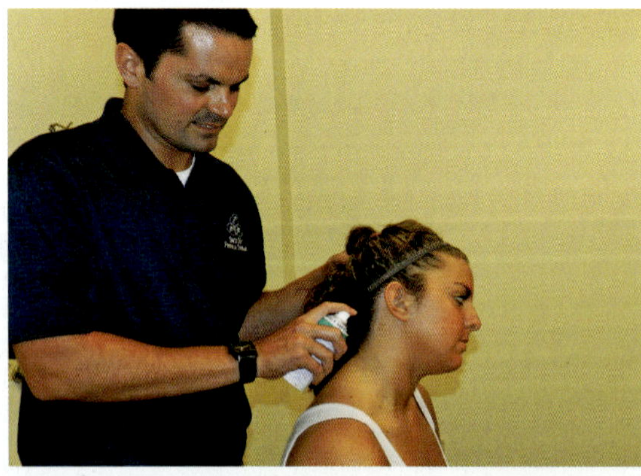

Fig. 8-45: Vapocoolant spray applied to the right upper quadrant.

Superficial Thermotherapy

Superficial thermotherapy refers to the local or general use of high temperatures in rehabilitation with the goal of increasing skin temperature and superficial subcutaneous tissue to depths of up to two centimeters. Superficial thermotherapy generates therapeutic effects by influencing hemodynamic (e.g., blood flow), metabolic (e.g., metabolic rate), and neuromuscular processes (e.g., nerve conduction velocity). Common examples of modalities used for superficial thermotherapy include hot packs, warm water baths, fluidotherapy, infrared lamp, and paraffin. Relative changes in skin temperature and superficial subcutaneous tissue will be influenced by the intensity of the heating agent, duration of the exposure, and thermal conductivity of the tissues.

Therapeutic Effects[16,18]	
• Decreased muscle spasm • Decreased tone • Increased blood flow to the treatment area • Increased capillary permeability • Increased collagen extensibility	• Increased local temperature • Increased metabolic rate • Increased muscle elasticity • Increased nerve conduction velocity • Increased pain threshold
Indications[16,18]	
• Abnormal tone • Decreased range of motion • Muscle guarding • Muscle spasm	• Myofascial trigger points • Subacute or chronic pain • Subacute or chronic inflammatory conditions
Contraindications[16,18]	
• Acute musculoskeletal trauma • Arterial disease • Bleeding or hemorrhage • Over an area of compromised circulation	• Over an area of malignancy • Peripheral vascular disease • Thrombophlebitis

Hot Packs

A hot pack consists of a canvas or nylon-covered pack filled with bentonite, a hydrophilic silicate gel that provides a moist heat. The size and shape of the hot pack varies depending on the size and contour of the treatment area. A standard size hot pack measures 12 inches by 12 inches and is used for the majority of body segments. A double size hot pack measures 24 inches by 24 inches and is generally used for the low back or buttocks. A cervical hot pack measures 6 inches by 18 inches.

Hot packs transmit heat to the body through conduction, since hot packs have a much higher temperature than the surface of the skin. The primary therapeutic effects include decreased pain, increased tissue extensibility, and reduced muscle spasm. A hot pack is easy to use, inexpensive, and can cover large areas. Limitations of hot packs include the need for close monitoring of the skin, the inability to maintain total contact in contoured areas, and the patient's inability to move during treatment.

Hot packs are stored in water between 158 and 167 degrees Fahrenheit.[16] The water is housed in a thermostatically controlled container that maintains the water at a relatively constant

Fig. 8-46: Hot pack removal from a hydrocollator unit using tongs.

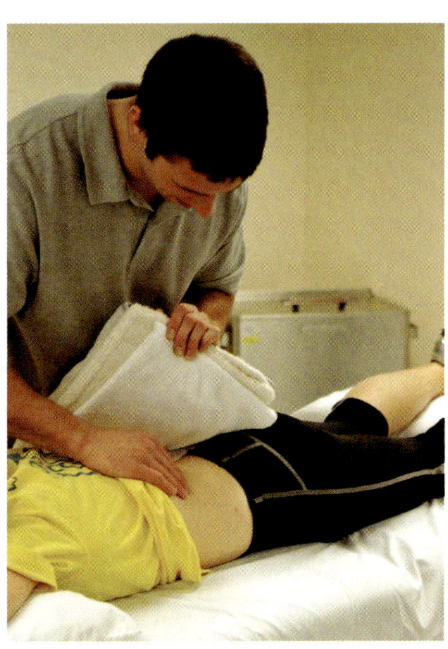

Fig. 8-47: Skin checks should be performed frequently when using hot packs.

temperature. The hot pack should be removed from the container with tongs due to the high water temperature (Fig. 8-46). The therapist should thoroughly inspect the target area prior to initiating treatment. Clothing and jewelry should be removed from the target area. Application requires six to eight layers of towels between the hot pack and skin.[16] If commercial hot pack covers are used, they typically are equivalent to two to three layers of towels.

The hot pack should be applied on top of the treatment area. The therapist should not permit the patient to lie on top of the hot pack since this action tends to remove some of the water from the hot pack, which can result in an accelerated rate of heating and an increased risk for burns. In addition, lying directly on the hot pack can reduce local circulation through compression of vessels resulting in reduced circulatory convective cooling.[17] If a patient cannot tolerate the weight of the hot pack directly on the target area (e.g., the low back while positioned in prone), the hot pack can be applied in sidelying with a strap or tied sheet.

The patient should feel a mild to moderate heating sensation from the hot pack.[17] Skin checks for excessive redness, blistering or other signs of a burn are required after five minutes (Fig. 8-47). The treatment area of fair-skinned individuals may turn bright pink or red, while darker-skinned individuals may exhibit areas of lighter or darker color. The maximum surface temperature is reached within 6-8 minutes, making it critical to perform frequent skin checks during the first 10 minutes of treatment.[17] The patient should be given a bell or another type of call device in the event that they need assistance during treatment.

Hot packs require approximately 15-20 minutes to achieve the desired effects.[18] If a patient reports that the heat is too intense, the therapist may elect to add towel layers. If the patient reports insufficient warming, the therapist may elect to remove towels prior to administering a hot pack at the next treatment session. Towels should not be removed during the current session since the increased skin temperature may diminish the patient's thermal sensitivity and the ability to accurately assess the intensity of the heat. A hot pack can take up to two hours to initially heat in the hydrocollator unit and 30 minutes to reheat after use.

Fluidotherapy

Fluidotherapy consists of a container that circulates warm air and small cellulose particles (Fig. 8-48). The superficial heating modality generates dry heat through forced convection. The dry cellulose medium does not irritate the skin and allows for higher treatment temperatures than hydrotherapy. Fluidotherapy units come in a variety of sizes and shapes and are most often used to treat the distal extremities.

The therapist must thoroughly inspect the area to be treated and have the patient remove all clothing and jewelry. The extremity is placed into the container and a protective shield is applied to prevent the escape of the cellulose particles. Direct contact between the skin and the cellulose particles is desired since this will maximize heat transfer. Open wounds should be covered with a plastic barrier to prevent the cellulose particles from becoming embedded in the wound bed.

The fluidotherapy unit contains a separate portal that provides the therapist with access to the extremity during treatment. The temperature should be set between 100-118 degrees Fahrenheit.[16] The maximum temperature rise during treatment occurs after approximately 15 minutes. Treatment time is usually 15-20 minutes.[18] The level of agitation (i.e., air speed) can be controlled for patient comfort or for use as part of a desensitization program. Some units provide other treatment options including the ability to preheat or select a pulse mode. The therapeutic effects of fluidotherapy include the promotion of tissue healing, skin desensitization, and edema management.

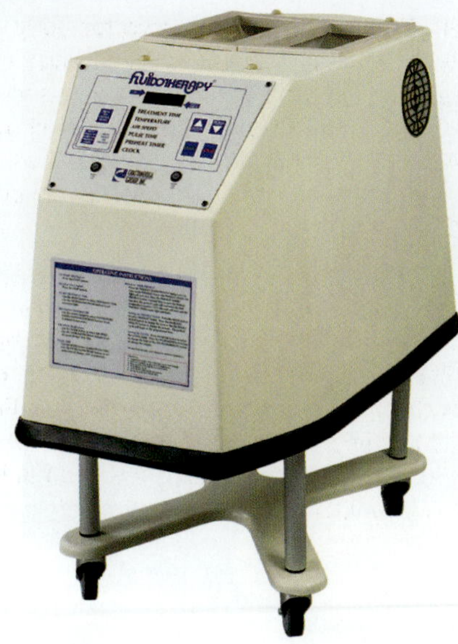

Fig. 8-48: A fluidotherapy unit. Courtesy Chattanooga, a DJO Global Company.

Heated air is circulated in the unit causing cellulose particles to become suspended and move rapidly within the unit. The result is a fluidized bed of cellulose particles that take on the properties of a liquid. Patients often report that the body part feels like it is suspended in a moving liquid. Patients can perform active exercise of the distal extremity during treatment, however, therapists should avoid placing the extremity in a gravity-dependent position whenever possible.[19]

Infrared Lamp

An infrared lamp produces superficial heating of tissue through radiant heat. Infrared radiation has a wavelength that lies between visible light and microwaves on the electromagnetic spectrum. Infrared lamps used in the clinical setting have a wavelength ranging from 780 to 1500 nanometers.[16] The majority of infrared radiation is absorbed within the first few millimeters of human tissue. Human skin allows maximum penetration of infrared radiation with a wavelength of 1200 nm.[16]

Infrared allows for constant observation of the skin since it does not require contact with the treatment area. The main therapeutic effect is the enhancement of soft tissue healing. The amount of tissue temperature increase is directly proportional to the amount of radiation that penetrates the tissue. The amount of radiation is influenced by the power and wavelength of the radiation, the distance of the radiation source from the target area, the angle of incidence, and the absorption coefficient of the target area.[16]

The therapist must thoroughly inspect the area to be treated and have the patient remove all clothing and jewelry. Opaque goggles should be worn by the therapist and the patient to avoid potential irradiation of the eyes. The patient should be positioned approximately 20 inches from the source to produce a comfortable level of warmth.[18] Protective toweling should be applied to tissues outside of the target area. Optimal absorption occurs when the infrared radiation strikes perpendicular to the target area. Darker tissue absorbs more radiation than lighter tissue.

The therapist should record the distance from the infrared lamp to the target area. The patient should be periodically monitored during the session and instructed to avoid moving closer or further away from the lamp since this will alter the amount of radiation reaching the target area. Treatment duration is generally 15-30 minutes and is influenced by the distance from the infrared lamp to the target area.[16] Infrared radiation tends to dry the skin more than other superficial heating agents and results in uneven heating when the target area is nonuniform.

Paraffin

Paraffin wax is a commonly used heating source for the distal extremities. There are several internal characteristics of paraffin that make it an effective superficial heating agent. Paraffin has a low melting point that can be lowered further by adding mineral oil. As a result, paraffin can provide a more even distribution of heat to areas, such as the fingers and toes. Secondly, paraffin has a low specific heat, that enhances a patient's ability to tolerate heat from paraffin compared to heat from water at the same temperature.

Therapists must have patients remove jewelry and thoroughly wash the body part being treated to minimize the chance of paraffin bath contamination. Paraffin cannot be applied to areas with open wounds or infected skin lesions. The temperature of the paraffin mixture should be maintained between 113 and 122 degrees Fahrenheit.[16]

There are three methods of paraffin application: dip-wrap, dip-reimmersion, and paint application.

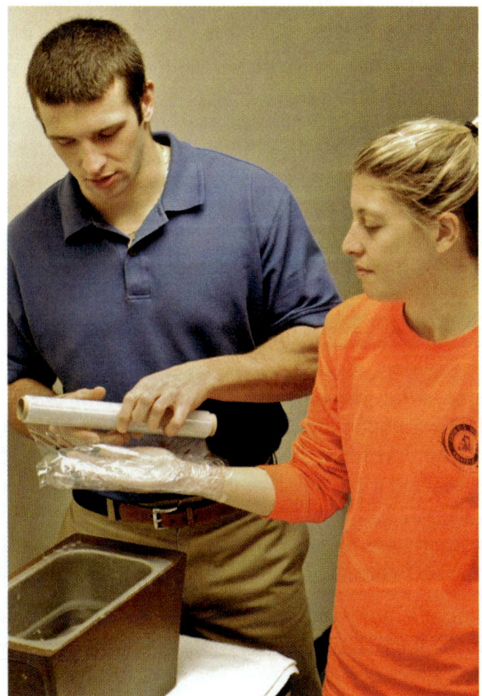

Fig. 8-49: Application of a plastic wrap to the hand following paraffin application.

Dip-wrap: The patient is required to maintain a static position as the distal extremity dips into the paraffin bath and is removed. After waiting briefly for the paraffin to harden, the extremity should be redipped 6-10 times and then immediately placed into a plastic bag (Fig. 8-49).[16] A towel should be wrapped around the bag to slow the paraffin cooling. The paraffin should be left in place for 10-15 minutes.[16]

Dip-reimmersion: After the initial 6-10 dips, the distal extremity should remain in the paraffin bath for the duration of treatment. The paraffin unit should be turned off during the treatment session to prevent the sides and the bottom of the unit from becoming too hot. It may also be necessary to use a temperature closer to the lower limit (i.e., 113 degrees Fahrenheit) since the affected extremity will remain in the bath for up to 20 minutes.[16]

Paint application: The paint method is used for body parts that cannot be immersed into the paraffin bath. A layer of paraffin is painted on the body with a brush. After a few seconds, 6-10 additional layers are applied. The area is then covered by a plastic bag or plastic wrap with a towel wrapped around it as described in the dip-wrap method. The paraffin should be left in place for approximately 20 minutes.[16]

Removal of the paraffin is the same for all forms of application. Paraffin should be peeled off after treatment and either placed back into the container to melt or discarded.[18] A paraffin bath can be reused unless it becomes contaminated. Some paraffin units have the ability to elevate the temperature to 212 degrees Fahrenheit, which will destroy bacteria that can grow in the paraffin.[18] In the absence of contamination, the contents of the paraffin bath must be changed at least every six months.

CONSIDER THIS
DOCUMENTATION OF THERAPEUTIC MODALITIES

The primary purpose of physical therapy patient care documentation is to communicate relevant information to other health care providers who are concurrently treating the same patient. The failure to document relevant patient care information in a clear, objective, and timely manner can result in professional negligence.

Documentation of therapeutic modalities must provide other health care providers with a clear understanding of the intervention performed and the associated parameters used. Appropriate documentation will allow another therapist treating the same patient to perform the identical intervention.

Relevant information when documenting therapeutic modalities includes:

- Body part to be treated (e.g., knee, anterior thigh, low back)
- Modality used (e.g., ultrasound, TENS)
- Treatment duration (e.g., 10 minutes, 20 minutes)
- Parameters (e.g., intensity, duty cycle, pulse rate)
- Patient response to treatment (e.g., skin color, pain level, sensitivity)
- Outcome measure (e.g., goniometry, circumferential measurements, visual analogue pain scale)

The following is an example of a documented ultrasound treatment in S.O.A.P. note format. Abbreviations were not used in the S.O.A.P. note below to increase clarity.

S: Patient reports the absence of knee pain during a recent exercise session.

O: Ultrasound to the anterior midline of the knee over the peri-patellar tendon region at 0.5 W/cm2, pulsed 20% duty cycle, 7 minutes.

A: Patient tolerated treatment without adverse effects.

P: Continue ultrasound treatment as described for three additional sessions. Continue to increase the intensity of exercise activities.

Deep Thermotherapy

Deep thermotherapy refers to the local or general use of energy (i.e., sound, electromagnetic) in rehabilitation with the goal of increasing tissue temperature.[16,18] Deep heating agents are capable of heating to depths of three to five centimeters.[21] Deep thermotherapy generates therapeutic effects by influencing mechanical (e.g., microstreaming), muscular (e.g., muscle heating), connective tissue (e.g., tendon, ligament), hemodynamic (e.g., blood flow), metabolic (e.g., metabolic rate), and neuromuscular processes (e.g., nerve conduction velocity).[16,18] Common examples of modalities used for deep thermotherapy include ultrasound and diathermy.

Relative changes in tissue temperature will be influenced by the intensity of the heating agent, the duration of the exposure, and the thermal conductivity of the tissues.

Ultrasound

Ultrasound is a common deep heating agent that transfers heat through conversion and elevates tissue temperature to depths up to five centimeters (Fig. 8-50). The modality uses high frequency acoustic mechanical vibrations to produce thermal and nonthermal effects. Ultrasound has a frequency above 20,000 hertz (Hz).[16] Therapeutic ultrasound typically has a frequency between 0.75 and 3 megahertz (MHz).[18]

Indications[16,18]	
• Acute and post-acute conditions (ultrasound with nonthermal effects) • Calcium deposits • Chronic inflammation • Delayed soft tissue healing	• Dermal ulcers • Joint contracture • Muscle spasm • Myofascial trigger points • Pain • Plantar warts • Scar tissue • Tissue regeneration

Contraindications[16,18]	
• Acute and post-acute conditions (ultrasound with thermal effects) • Areas of active bleeding • Areas of decreased temperature sensation • Areas of decreased circulation • Deep vein thrombosis • Infection • Malignancy • Over breast implants • Over carotid sinus or cervical ganglia	• Over epiphyseal areas in young children • Over eyes, heart, and genitalia • Over methyl methacrylate cement or plastic • Over pelvic, lumbar or abdominal areas in pregnant women • Over a pacemaker • Thrombophlebitis • Vascular insufficiency

Fig. 8-50: An ultrasound machine. Courtesy Chattanooga, a DJO Global Company.

An ultrasound machine uses an alternating electrical current, generated at the same frequency as the crystal resonance, to create a mechanical vibration of the piezoelectric crystal located in the transducer. This action converts electrical energy to acoustic energy and generates ultrasound at the desired frequency.

Thermal effects[16,18]

Thermal effects of ultrasound include acceleration of metabolic rate, modulation of pain, reduction of muscle spasm, decreased joint stiffness, alteration of nerve conduction velocity, increased circulation, and increased soft tissue extensibility. The extent of the thermal effects is dependent on the intensity, duration, and frequency selected.

Nonthermal effects[16,18]

Nonthermal effects of ultrasound include increased cell and skin membrane permeability, increased intracellular calcium levels, facilitation of tissue repair, and promotion of normal cell function. The nonthermal effects occur as a result of cavitation and acoustic microstreaming.

Fig. 8-51: Coupling agents used with ultrasound.

Cavitation refers to the formation of gas-filled bubbles that expand and compress secondary to pressure changes caused by ultrasound.[18] Cavitation can be classified as stable or unstable. During stable cavitation, the bubbles oscillate in size in response to pressure changes, but do not burst. During unstable cavitation, the bubbles change in size over several cycles and then suddenly burst. Unstable cavitation is possible with high intensity, low frequency ultrasound, however, it does not typically occur with therapeutic ultrasound. Acoustic microstreaming refers to the unidirectional movement of fluids along the boundaries of cell membranes caused by ultrasound.[18]

Ultrasound Parameters

Technique

A transducer housing a piezoelectric crystal is used to administer ultrasound. Transducers vary in size, but most often range from 5-10 cm^2. Ultrasound waves do not travel through air and, as a result, a coupling agent is required. Coupling agents are designed to decrease acoustical impedance by eliminating as much air as possible between the transducer and the target area. Coupling agents can be direct or indirect and include gels, gel pads, mineral oil, water, and lotions (Fig. 8-51).

Direct coupling agents (e.g., gel, lotion) should be applied to the treatment area and the transducer before the power is turned on. The face of the transducer must be parallel with the surface of the skin so that ultrasound waves will be introduced at a 90 degree angle.[18] Failure to maintain the integrity of the transducer-skin interface will result in a large percentage of the ultrasound energy being reflected and may damage the ultrasound's piezoelectric crystal.

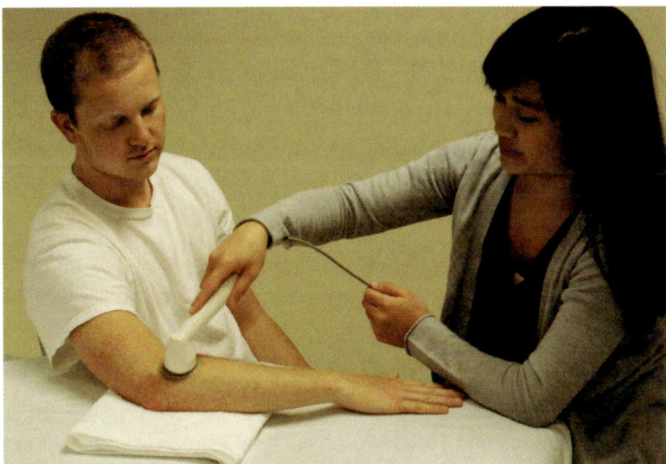

Fig. 8-52: Ultrasound applied to the dorsal surface of the forearm.

Indirect coupling agents are often employed when the treatment area is excessively small, irregularly shaped or unable to tolerate direct pressure from the transducer. Water immersion is an indirect coupling method requiring the treatment area to be immersed in a basin of water (Fig. 8-54). The basin should be made of rubber or plastic to minimize the amount of reflection present with metals. The transducer should be moved parallel to the treatment surface at a distance of 0.5 - 3.0 centimeters away from the skin.[21] Air bubbles occurring on the transducer and the patient's skin should be wiped away by the therapist since they will interfere with ultrasound transmission.[17] Increased intensity, as much as 50%, may be necessary when using the underwater technique due to dispersion and ultrasound energy absorption by the water. Other methods of indirect coupling include gel or water-filled bladders and gel pads. This type of indirect coupling is often referred to as "cushion contact."

Administration of ultrasound can occur with a stationary or moving (i.e., dynamic) technique (Fig. 8-52). The stationary technique is used sparingly in clinical practice due to the potential for uneven heating and other undesirable effects, such as subjective reports of pain or tissue damage. Justification for use of the stationary technique may include a very small treatment area or when pulsed ultrasound is used with low intensity. When using a moving technique the transducer should be moved slowly in a small, rhythmical pattern. Longitudinal stroking or overlapping circular motions are the most common application method (Fig. 8-53). The transducer should be moved at an approximate rate of 4 centimeters per second.[16]

Intensity

Intensity measures the quantity of energy delivered per unit area. The power generated from ultrasound is not uniform and therefore, some portions of the ultrasound beam are more intense than others as it leaves the transducer. Effective radiating area (ERA) refers to the area of the transducer that transmits ultrasound energy.[16] The ERA is always smaller than the total size of the transducer head. Spatial-averaged intensity refers to the intensity of the ultrasound beam averaged over the area of the transducer.[18] It is computed by dividing the power output in watts by the total effective radiating area of the soundhead in cm^2. Spatial-averaged intensity is labeled as intensity on an ultrasound unit and is expressed in watts per square centimeter (W/cm^2). Spatial-peak intensity refers to the intensity of the ultrasound beam at its highest point.[18]

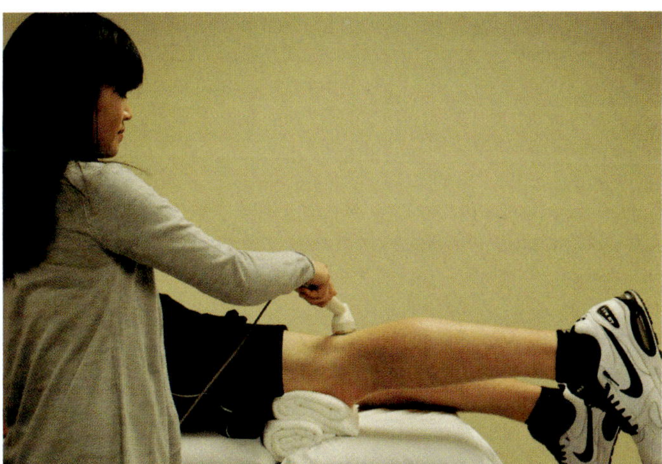

Fig. 8-53: Ultrasound applied to the posterior knee region combined with gravity assisted passive stretching.

Beam nonuniformity ratio (BNR) is the ratio between the spatial-peak intensity and spatial-averaged intensity. The BNR is derived from the intrinsic factors and quality of the piezoelectric crystal. The higher the quality of the crystal, the lower the BNR. A lower BNR is more favorable since patients will be less likely to experience hot spots and discomfort during treatment.[20] The BNR of an ultrasound unit is required to be listed on the device for consumer education and awareness. BNR values should range between 2:1 and 8:1, however, most devices often fall in the 5:1 or 6:1 range.[21] The higher the beam nonuniformity ratio, the more critical it is to move the transducer more rapidly to avoid undesirable effects, such as pain, caused by periosteal irritation.[16]

Frequency

Frequency is the primary determinant in the depth of ultrasound penetration. Attenuation is a term that describes the inevitable decrease in energy intensity as the ultrasound travels through various tissues. Tissues that are high in water content, such as blood plasma, have a low rate of absorption while more dense tissues high in protein, such as bone, have a high rate of absorption.[18]

Ultrasound delivered at a higher frequency is absorbed more rapidly than ultrasound delivered at a lower frequency. As a result, ultrasound at higher frequencies affects more superficial tissues and ultrasound at lower frequencies affects deeper tissues. A frequency setting of 1 MHz is used for deeper tissues (up to five centimeters) while a setting of 3 MHz is used for more superficial tissues (one to two centimeters).[18]

Duty Cycle

Ultrasound can be administered using a continuous or pulsed mode. In continuous mode, ultrasound intensity remains constant throughout the treatment. In pulsed mode, the ultrasound intensity is periodically interrupted. The portion of treatment time that ultrasound is generated during the entire treatment is referred to as the duty cycle.

$$\text{Duty cycle} = \frac{\text{on time}}{\text{on time + off time}} \quad (*100)$$

Duty cycle is calculated by dividing the time sound is delivered (on time) by the total time (on time + off time).[17] For example, if the on time was 1 msec and the off time was 4 msec, the duty cycle would be 20%.

Continuous ultrasound (i.e., 100% duty cycle) generates constant ultrasound waves producing thermal effects at higher intensities and nonthermal effects at lower intensities. Continuous ultrasound is more effective in elevating tissue temperature, while pulsed ultrasound minimizes the thermal effects.

Pulsed ultrasound with a duty cycle of 20% generates ultrasound 20% of the total treatment time (on time + off time). Pulsed ultrasound results in a reduced average heating of the tissues and is therefore used primarily for nonthermal effects. When using pulsed ultrasound for nonthermal effects, most resources recommend a 20% or lower duty cycle.

The duty cycle impacts the total quantity of energy generated. Ultrasound using a pulsed mode requires an intensity measure that takes the duty cycle into consideration. Spatial-temporal averaged intensity refers to the ultrasound beam averaged over the on time and off time of the pulse.[16] This measure allows therapists to compare energy outputs between continuous and pulsed ultrasound, however, it is not frequently used in clinical practice. Instead, therapists often describe the intensity based on the spatial-averaged intensity and then specify a duty cycle.

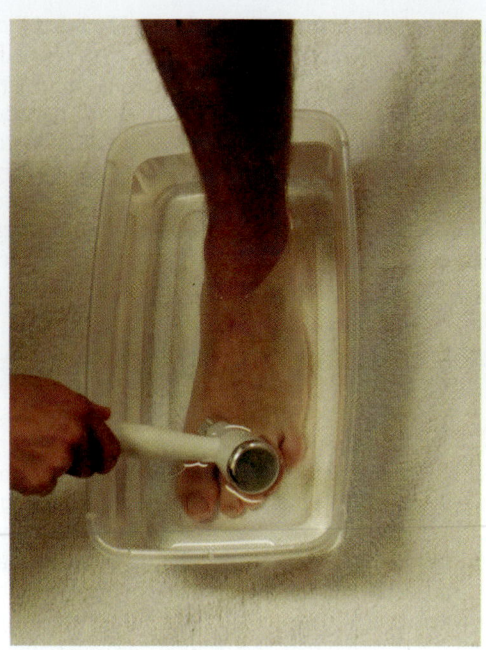

Fig. 8-54: Ultrasound applied to the dorsal surface of the foot using water immersion.

Duration

Duration of ultrasound is determined based on a number of variables including the size of the treatment area, the depth of penetration, and the desired therapeutic effects. An area two to three times the size of the transducer typically requires a duration of five minutes.[17,18] Longer duration may be necessary when using lower intensities or lower frequencies or when the therapeutic objective is higher tissue temperatures. Ultrasound should not be used to treat areas larger than four times the effective radiating area (ERA) of the transducer. Areas larger than this would require excessively long treatment times making the application of ultrasound impractical.

Number of Treatments

The number of ultrasound treatments is primarily dependent on the established therapeutic objectives, the level of acuity, and the patient response. Ultrasound using thermal effects is usually applied later in the healing process and is most commonly administered two to three times a week. Ultrasound using nonthermal effects is usually applied earlier in the healing process, as frequently as once a day. A positive response to ultrasound should be evident within three sessions. Failure to observe a desired response within this time frame provides justification to change the ultrasound parameters or select an alternate intervention. Research has indicated that more than 14 ultrasound treatments within a single episode of care can reduce red and white blood cell counts.[18]

Patient Safety and Effectiveness

Safe and effective ultrasound treatment is dependent on the therapist's ability to identify relevant contraindications to ultrasound and select appropriate treatment parameters. The therapist must comfortably position the patient and seek feedback from the patient throughout the course of treatment. The therapist should periodically inspect the patient's skin during treatment and attempt to determine the relative effect of the intervention. The effectiveness of ultrasound can be assessed through a variety of subjective and objective measures. Examples of positive findings include decreased pain, diminished tenderness to palpation, increased range of motion, and enhanced functional levels.

Ultrasound units must be inspected by qualified personnel at the manufacturer's recommended interval or minimally on an annual basis. Many of the parameters, including intensity output, must conform to established performance standards.

Phonophoresis

Phonophoresis describes the use of ultrasound for the transdermal delivery of medication. Ultrasound enhances the distribution of medication through the skin, provides a high concentration of the drug directly to the treatment site, and avoids risks that may be associated with the injection of medication.[18] Medications regularly used in phonophoresis include anti-inflammatory agents and analgesics. Phonophoresis can be used with both continuous and pulsed techniques. Phonophoresis is not likely to produce burns or damage skin since the technique transports whole molecules instead of ions into the body's tissue (i.e., iontophoresis). Therapists using phonophoresis must carefully select coupling agents that are effective conductors of acoustic energy and are compatible with the medication selected. There is a limited amount of evidence in the literature that supports the efficacy of phonophoresis.

Diathermy

Diathermy is a deep heating agent that converts high frequency electromagnetic energy into therapeutic heat (Fig. 8-55). Electrical energy produces a molecular vibration within tissue that generates heat and elevates tissue temperature.

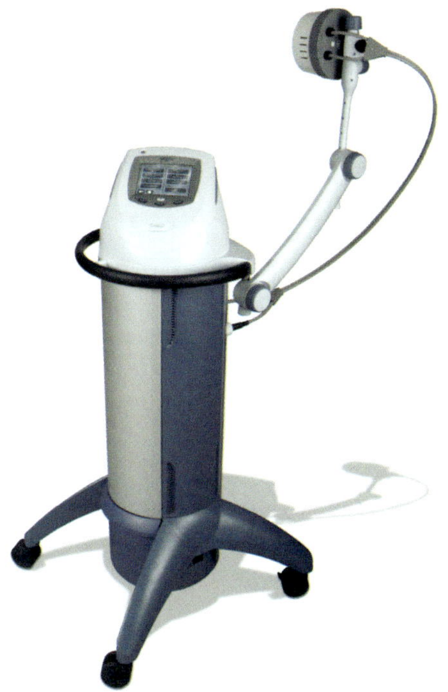

Fig. 8-55: A diathermy unit. Courtesy Chattanooga, a DJO Global Company.

Therapeutic Effects[16,18]	
• Altered cell membrane function • Increased collagen extensibility • Increased metabolic rate • Increased muscle elasticity	• Increased nerve conduction velocity • Increased pain threshold • Increased temperature • Vasodilation

Indications[16,18]	
• Bursitis • Chronic inflammation • Chronic inflammatory pelvic disease • Decreased collagen extensibility • Degenerative joint disease • Increased metabolism	• Joint stiffness • Muscle guarding • Myofascial trigger points • Pain • Peripheral nerve regeneration • Tissue healing

Contraindications[16,18]	
• Acute infection • Acute inflammation • Cardiac pacemaker • Hemophilia • Internal and external metal objects • Intrauterine device • Ischemic tissue • Low back, abdomen or pelvis of a pregnant woman	• Malignant area • Moist wound dressing • Over a hemorrhagic region • Over the eyes • Over the testes • Pain and temperature sensory deficits

Shortwave diathermy can be delivered in a continuous or pulsed mode. A pulsed mode is typically utilized to attain nonthermal effects while a continuous mode is used for thermal effects. Pulsed diathermy is produced by discontinuing the output of continuous shortwave diathermy at regular intervals. The output during the on time is adequate to produce tissue heating, however, the length of the off time allows the heat to dissipate.

The most common frequency used for shortwave diathermy is 27.12 MHz.[17] Shortwave diathermy can utilize a capacitance technique or inductance technique. Capacitive plate applicators produce a high frequency electrical current that alternates between the plates. The patient becomes part of the electrical circuit and the oscillation of ions increases tissue temperature.

Inductive coil applicators utilize a coil that generates alternating electric current, creates a magnetic field perpendicular to the coil, and produces eddy currents within the tissues. Eddy currents cause the oscillation of ions that increase tissue temperature. Inductive coil applicators are bundled as cables that wrap around an extremity or as a drum applicator.

CONSIDER THIS

HEATING AGENTS - ADVANTAGES AND DISADVANTAGES[16,17,18]

Therapists should consider the nuances associated with the patient's current condition and the advantages and disadvantages of each heating agent when selecting an appropriate intervention.

The following table illustrates several advantages and disadvantages of commonly used heating agents.

Heating Agent	Advantages	Disadvantages
Fluidotherapy	Temperature and agitation of the dry particles can be controlled Patient can perform active exercise during treatment Minimal pressure applied to the treatment area Can be used for desensitization of distal extremities	Constant heat source can result in overheating Some patients are intolerant of the dry particles and the enclosed container Some units require the extremity to be in a dependent position
Hot pack	Moist, comfortable heat Variety of shapes and sizes Available for home use	May not maintain good contact on small or contoured areas Patient may not tolerate the weight of the pack Difficult to observe target area directly during treatment
Infrared lamp	Target area can be observed during treatment Does not require direct contact with the treatment area	Difficult to ensure uniform heating in all treatment areas Difficult to localize to a specific treatment area Tends to dry the skin more than other superficial heating agents
Paraffin	Low specific heat allows for application at higher temperatures than water Low thermal conductivity allows for slower heating of tissues which reduces the risk of overheating Maintains good contact with contoured areas Oils used in the wax add moisture to the skin	Effective only in distal extremities Risk of cross-contamination if the paraffin is reused Cannot be used over an open skin lesion
Diathermy	Capable of reaching deeper tissues Can produce thermal and nonthermal effects Covers large areas Heat is applied in a more uniform fashion since the application is performed statically Rate of tissue cooling is slower than other deep heating agents	Difficult to target small treatment areas effectively Requires patient to subjectively classify their heat sensation response Relatively large number of contraindications
Ultrasound	Capable of reaching deeper tissues Can produce thermal and nonthermal effects Amount of energy delivered per unit area can be quantified Covers small areas effectively Short duration of treatment	May not maintain good contact on small or contoured areas causing uneven heating Patient may not tolerate direct contact with the ultrasound transducer Rate of tissue cooling is faster than other deep heating agents

Capacitive Plate Method[16]

- Metal encased in a plastic housing produces an electric field from one plate to the other
- Field radiation consists of a strong electrical field and a weak magnetic field
- Heating pattern is superficial with the majority of energy absorbed within the skin
- Application is generally over areas of low fat content

Inductive Coil Method[16]

- Rigid metal encased coil produces a magnetic field perpendicular to the coil
- Field radiation consists of a strong magnetic field and a weak electrical field
- Heating pattern is deeper with the majority of energy absorbed within the deeper structures (i.e., tissues with the highest electrical conductivity, such as muscle and synovial fluid)
- Application is generally over areas of high water content

A therapist should first select the most appropriate diathermy technique and device based on patient examination. The patient must remove all metal and jewelry in the area surrounding the treatment site. The therapist should position the patient and clean and dry the patient's skin thoroughly. Nonmetal clothing does not need to be removed before treatment since the magnetic fields will penetrate through clothing, however, when using continuous mode, clothes should be removed so that sweat can be absorbed with towels.

When using an inductive applicator, the therapist must wrap the coils around the extremity that has been covered by a towel. When using a drum, the therapist should place the drum directly over the treatment area. When using a capacitive applicator, place the two plates over both sides of the treatment area ensuring equal distance from the plates to the skin (2-10 centimeters).[16] The patient must remain in the same position throughout treatment for complete and consistent heating.

The amount of energy delivered and corresponding temperature increase can be variable with continuous diathermy. As a result, therapists need to rely on the patient's subjective heat sensation response. The following dosage guidelines are commonly used in clinical practice.

Dose I – No sensation of heat

Dose II – Mild heating sensation

Dose III – Moderate heating sensation

Dose IV – Vigorous heating that is tolerable below the pain threshold

The patient should have a call bell and should be checked within the first few minutes of treatment. Treatment time with diathermy is approximately 20 minutes for thermal effects and may last as long as 30-60 minutes for nonthermal effects.[16]

Diathermy is not used as commonly as other therapeutic modalities, however, there are several scenarios where the use of diathermy may be particularly beneficial. These include when an increase in temperature is required at tissue depths greater than those achieved with superficial heating agents and when the target area will not tolerate direct contact from a thermal agent.

Diathermy also offers several potential advantages compared to ultrasound. Diathermy can effectively heat surfaces of up to 25 times the size of a typical ultrasound transducer.[18] Heat is applied to the target area in a more uniform fashion with diathermy since the application is performed statically. In addition, the rate of tissue cooling following heating with diathermy is significantly slower than the rate of tissue cooling with ultrasound. As a result, the therapist has additional time to perform interventions that are enhanced by the increased tissue temperature (e.g., stretching).

Additional Physical Agents

Ultraviolet Light

Ultraviolet light is a form of energy that is used therapeutically and is divided into UV-A, UV-B, and UV-C according to wavelength and location on the electromagnetic spectrum.[17] Ultraviolet light is absorbed one to two millimeters into the skin and is most commonly used to treat skin disorders.

Therapeutic Effects[16,18]	
• Bacteriocidal effects • Exfoliation • Facilitate healing	• Increased pigmentation • Thickening of the epidermis • Vitamin D production
Indications[16,18]	
• Acne • Chronic ulcer/wound • Osteomalacia	• Psoriasis • Sinusitis • Vitamin D deficiency
Contraindications[16,18]	
• Areas receiving radiation • Diabetes mellitus • Herpes simplex • Pellagra	• Photosensitive medications • Skin cancer • Systemic lupus erythematosus • Tuberculosis

Ultraviolet Dosage

The ultraviolet dosage is classified according to the patient's response. Dosage categories include:[16]

Dose	Description
Suberythemal dose	The absence of erythema 24 hours after ultraviolet exposure.
Minimal erythemal dose	The smallest dose that produces erythema that appears in 1-8 hours and fades without trace within 24 hours.
First-degree erythemal dose	A dose that results in erythema that lasts 1-3 days with clear redness and mild desquamation. The dose is approximately 2.5 times the minimal erythemal dose and should be used only if the target area is less than 20% of the total body surface.
Second-degree erythemal dose	A dose that results in intense erythema, edema, peeling, pigmentation, and itching. The dose is approximately five times the minimal erythemal dose.
Third-degree erythemal dose	A dose that results in erythema with severe blistering, peeling, and exudation. The dose is approximately 10 times the minimal erythemal dose and should be used on areas less than 10 square inches.

Treatment parameters are based on diagnosis, desired effects, and minimal erythemal dose. Sensitivity to radiation varies greatly from person to person and is primarily influenced by age, pigmentation, prior exposure to ultraviolet radiation, and the use of photosensitive medications.

The therapist must thoroughly inspect the area to be treated and have the patient remove all jewelry. Polarized goggles should be worn by the therapist and the patient. A therapist should initially determine the patient's minimal erythemal dose (MED). The MED is tested by placing a piece of paper with five one-inch cut outs over a patient's anterior forearm. The patient should have all other non-treatment areas covered. Once the lamp is warmed up it should be positioned at a 90-degree angle to the area of treatment (for maximum absorption) and at a distance between 24 and 40 inches from the forearm.[18] The squares should be exposed sequentially in 15 second increments for 15, 30, 45, 60, and 75 seconds.[18] Visual inspection after an 8-hour period will determine the MED. The MED for patients being treated with psoralen-based topical and systemic drugs should be determined after the patient has taken psoralen orally or bathed in psoralen.

Parameters including distance from the lamp, position of the lamp at a 90-degree angle to the treatment site, and the MED must remain consistent over the course of treatment. The treatment time should increase each consecutive treatment day. Patients will build up tolerance to ultraviolet radiation with repeated exposure due to darkening of the skin with tanning and thickening of the skin caused by epidermal hyperplasia. Instead of increasing the treatment time, the therapist may elect to move the lamp closer to the target area. The intensity of the radiation reaching the target area increases as the lamp moves closer according to the inverse square law. For example, the intensity of the radiation increases by a multiple of four if the distance from the lamp to the target area is halved.

The therapist should utilize a stopwatch and continue with ongoing visual inspection during all treatment sessions. The response to ultraviolet radiation must be reassessed if an alternate lamp is used in a subsequent session since even a slight difference in the frequency of the radiation can significantly change the patient response.

Hydrotherapy

Hydrotherapy transfers heat through conduction or convection and is administered in tanks of varying size, ranging from extremity whirlpools to Olympic size pools. The main therapeutic effects of hydrotherapy include wound care, unloading of weight, and reduction of edema. The specific equipment and parameters used depend on the treatment objectives and site of the pathology.

Therapeutic Effects[16,18]	
• Decreased abnormal tone • Increased blood flow • Increased core temperature	• Pain relief • Relaxation • Vasodilation • Wound debridement
Indications[16,18]	
• Arthritis • Burn care • Edema • Decreased range of motion • Desensitization of residual limb	• Joint stiffness • Muscle spasm/spasticity • Muscle strain • Pain • Sprain • Wound care
Contraindications[16,18]	
• Advanced cardiovascular or pulmonary disease • Active bleeding • Diminished sensation • Gangrene • Impaired circulation	• Incontinence • Maceration • Peripheral vascular disease • Renal infection • Severe infection • Severe mental disorders

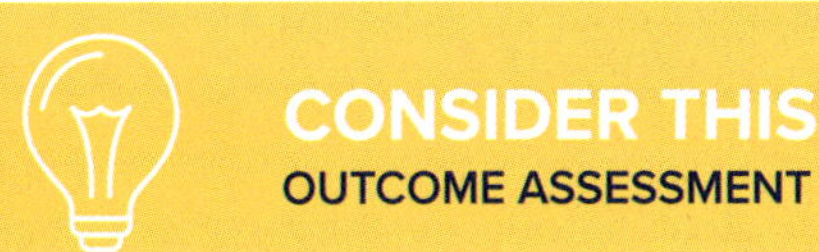

Physical therapists must continually assess the effectiveness of selected interventions, including therapeutic modalities. There are a variety of subjective and objective measures that can assist the therapist to determine the relative value of each intervention.

Consider the following scenarios:

Scenario 1

A physical therapist administers continuous ultrasound at 1.4 W/cm^2 for seven minutes to the right shoulder of a patient diagnosed with adhesive capsulitis.

1. Administer a visual analogue pain scale prior to and at the conclusion of treatment.
2. Perform periodic shoulder goniometric measurements to quantify the relative change in range of motion.

Scenario 2

A physical therapist administers an ice pack to the knee of a patient positioned in supine with the lower extremity elevated. The patient is two weeks status post anterior cruciate ligament reconstruction.

1. Perform circumferential measurements at predetermined knee landmarks at regular intervals.
2. Administer a visual analogue pain scale prior to and at the conclusion of treatment.

It is often difficult to discern the effectiveness of a given intervention in isolation since, in most cases, patients are treated with several interventions addressing the same therapeutic objective. Despite this fact, it remains important for therapists to attempt to assess the relative effectiveness of selected interventions.

Properties of Water[22]

Buoyancy

Archimedes' principle of buoyancy states that there is an upward force on the body when immersed in water equal to the amount of water that has been displaced by the body.

Resistance

Water molecules tend to attract to each other and provide resistance to movement of the body in water. The resistance of water increases in proportion to the speed of motion.

Specific Gravity

The specific gravity of water is equal to 1.0. The human body varies based on size and somatotype, but typically it has a specific gravity of less than 1.0 (average .974). Therefore, a person will generally float when fully submerged in water.

Specific Heat

The specific heat is the measure of the ability of a fluid to store heat. This is calculated as the amount of thermal energy required to increase the fluid's temperature by one unit. Water has a specific heat of 1.0 calorie/gram while air has a specific heat of .001 calorie/gram. Water, therefore, retains heat 1,000 times more than an equivalent volume of air.

Total Drag Force

The total drag force is comprised of profile drag, wave drag, and surface drag forces. This is a hydromechanic force exerted on a person submerged in water that normally opposes the direction of the body's motion.

Viscosity

Viscosity refers to the magnitude of the cohesive forces between the molecules specific to the fluid. The greater the viscosity of the fluid, the greater the force required to create movement in the fluid.

Water Motion

The primary determinants of water motion include speed, viscosity, and turbulence. The movement of water includes laminar flow and turbulent flow. Laminar flow occurs when each particle of a fluid follows a smooth path without crossing paths. Typically, laminar flow rates are slow since when water moves quickly even minor oscillations create uneven flow. Turbulent flow occurs when fluids flow in erratic, small whirlpool-like circles called eddy currents or eddies. Movement in water at rest will encounter minimal turbulence. Movement against turbulent water will encounter greater resistance.

Types of Hydrotherapy Equipment

Extremity tank[17]

An extremity tank is used for a distal upper or lower extremity. Approximate dimensions for an extremity tank are a depth of 18-24 inches, a length of 28-32 inches, and a width of 15 inches (10-45 gallons).

Lowboy tank[17]

A lowboy tank is used for larger parts of the extremities and permits long sitting with water up to the midthoracic level. Approximate dimensions for a lowboy tank are a depth of 18 inches, a length of 52-65 inches, and a width of 24 inches (90-105 gallons).

Highboy tank[17]

A highboy tank is used for larger parts of the extremities and the trunk. This tank permits sitting in chest-high water with the hips and knees flexed (Fig. 8-56). Approximate dimensions for the highboy tank are a depth of 28 inches, a length of 36-48 inches, and a width of 20-24 inches (60-105 gallons).

Hubbard tank[16]

The Hubbard tank is used for full-body immersion. Approximate dimensions for the Hubbard tank are a depth of four feet, a length of eight feet, and a width of six feet. Contraindications specific to full-body immersion include unstable blood pressure and incontinence. The temperature should not exceed 100 degrees Fahrenheit (425 gallons).

Therapeutic pool[16]

A therapeutic pool is used for exercising in a water medium. The temperature should range from 79-97 degrees Fahrenheit depending on patient age, health status, and goals.

Treatment Temperature Guidelines

Degrees F	Purpose
32 - 79 °F	Acute inflammation of distal extremities
79 - 92 °F	Exercise
92 - 96 °F	Wound care, spasticity
96 - 98 °F	Cardiopulmonary compromise, treatment of burns
99 - 104 °F	Pain management
104 - 110 °F	Chronic rheumatoid or osteoarthritis, increased range of motion

Adapted from Cameron M: *Physical Agents in Rehabilitation: From Research to Practice*, Third Edition, WB Saunders Company, 2008.

Whirlpool

A whirlpool consists of a tank that holds water with an attached motor, called a turbine, that provides agitation and aeration to create the "whirlpool effect." The turbine assembly typically allows the height and the lateral position of the turbine to be adjusted. This feature allows the therapist to direct the flow of water directly toward or away from the body part being treated. Whirlpools come in a variety of sizes and can accommodate an isolated body part or the entire body.

Prior to treatment the therapist should explain the sensations the patient will experience during treatment. Water temperature should be selected based on the patient diagnosis and goals. The therapist should assist the patient into a comfortable position and turn on the turbine. The patient's vital signs and reported level of comfort should be periodically assessed. Treatment time ranges between 10 and 30 minutes.[17] Exercise can be performed during whirlpool treatment as indicated. After treatment, dry and inspect the treated area. The tank must be thoroughly cleaned after each use with a disinfectant and antibacterial agent.

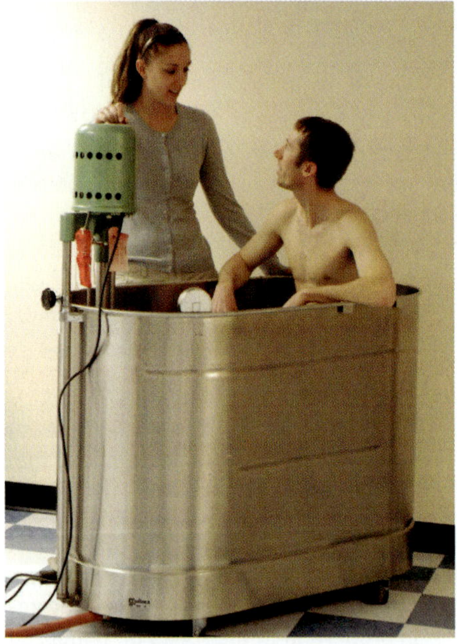

Fig. 8-56: A patient immersed in a whirlpool tank.

Pool Therapy

Advantages of pool therapy include decreased weight bearing due to buoyancy, improved therapist handling, enhanced control over the amount of resistance during exercise, and diminished risk of falling with activity. The therapist should assist the patient as needed into the pool and throughout treatment. The therapist must remain with the patient and monitor vital signs and tolerance to activity. Recommended populations for pool therapy include patients with arthritis, musculoskeletal injuries, neurological deficits, spinal cord injury, CVA, multiple sclerosis, and selected cardiopulmonary diagnoses.

SPOTLIGHT ON SAFETY

SAFETY CONSIDERATIONS WITH HYDROTHERAPY

All physical therapy interventions, including hydrotherapy, have inherent safety risks. It is essential for therapists to be aware of potential risks in order to ensure patient safety and limit any potential liability. This section identifies specific risks associated with hydrotherapy and offers proactive strategies to assist therapists to minimize their level of risk.

Drowning

Personnel in charge of therapeutic pools should be trained in personal water safety techniques, as well as current cardiopulmonary resuscitation and first aid. The pool area should be equipped with emergency equipment including a spine board, blanket, life ring, and resuscitation devices. The entire staff should be aware of the facility's emergency action plan and be aware of the supervisory needs of each patient.

Electrical safety

All electrical equipment should be inspected by qualified personnel according to the manufacturer's recommendations. Ground fault circuit interrupters (GFCI) are required for all hydrotherapy units. GFCIs are designed to cut off electrical supply to equipment when any form of leakage or ground-fault is identified. Whirlpool tanks should be properly grounded and should use a hospital grade plug for the turbine.

Burns

Therapists must carefully screen patients to identify any potential contraindications to hydrotherapy. Therapists treating patients with a warm or hot whirlpool must correctly determine an appropriate temperature range to achieve the established therapeutic objectives. Prior to immersing the body part in water, the therapist must measure the temperature of the water. Therapists must be aware of medical and environmental conditions that may compromise a patient's ability to adequately dissipate heat.

Fainting

Patients are at an increased risk for fainting due to hypotension when large body areas are immersed in warm or hot water. This risk can be exaggerated in an aquatic environment due to the relative increase in ambient temperature. Patients taking antihypertensive medications such as beta blockers are also at an increased risk for becoming hypotensive. To minimize this risk, therapists should closely monitor patients during hydrotherapy and only immerse body parts in water that require treatment.

Falls

The presence of water on floors can result in a slippery surface that places patients at an increased risk of falling. Therapists should be diligent to dry any wet surfaces once they are identified.

Contrast Bath

A contrast bath utilizes alternating heat and cold in order to decrease edema in a distal extremity (Fig. 8-57). The alternating vasodilation and vasoconstriction is theorized to allow the benefits of heat, such as decreased pain and increased flexibility, while avoiding the risk of increased edema. The technique provides good contact over irregularly shaped areas, allows for movement during treatment, and assists with pain management. Limitations of contrast baths include potential intolerance to cold, dependent positioning, and a lack of credible research supporting the efficacy of contrast baths.

The therapist should position the patient so that both baths are easily accessible for the patient. The treatment should begin with the patient's distal extremity immersed in the hot bath with a temperature between 104-106 degrees Fahrenheit for 3-4 minutes.[17] The patient should then place the distal extremity into the cold bath with a temperature between 50 and 60 degrees Fahrenheit for one minute.[17] The patient should repeat this hot/cold sequence for 25-30 minutes.[16] The degree of temperature increase desired often determines whether the treatment ends in the hot or cold water.

Contrast baths are utilized primarily with arthritis of the smaller joints, musculoskeletal sprains and strains, complex regional pain syndrome, and residual limb desensitization.

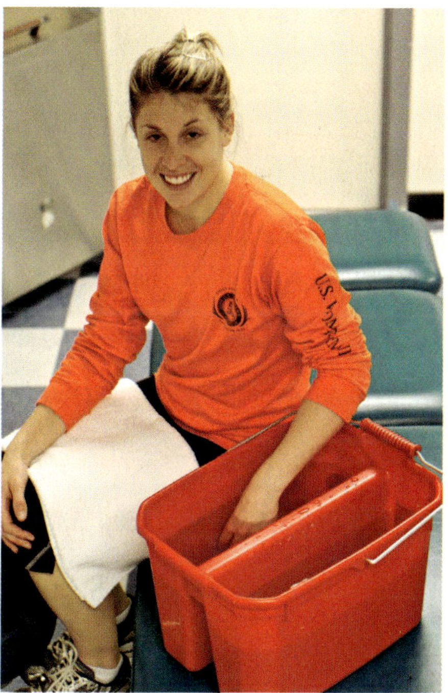

Fig. 8-57: A patient immersing their hand in hot water as part of a contrast bath.

Mechanical Agents

Traction

Traction is a modality that applies forces to the body to separate joint surfaces and decrease pressure. The force can be applied manually by the therapist, passively by the patient or mechanically by a machine. Types of traction include manual traction, mechanical traction, positional traction, gravity-assisted traction, and inversion traction. Traction is indicated for many diagnoses and allows for variation and adjustment of the established protocol based on individual patient needs. Traction affects many of the body's systems and requires ongoing monitoring and reassessment of treatment parameters.

Therapeutic Effects[16,18]	
• Decreased disk protrusion • Decreased pain • Increased joint mobility • Increased muscle relaxation	• Increased soft tissue elasticity • Promote arterial, venous, and lymphatic flow
Indications[16,18]	
• Disk herniation • Joint hypomobility • Muscle guarding • Muscle spasm • Narrowing of the intervertebral foramen • Nerve root impingement	• Osteophyte formation • Spinal ligament and other connective tissue contractures • Subacute joint inflammation • Subacute pain
Contraindications[16,18]	
• Acute inflammation • Acute sprains or strains • Aortic aneurysm • Bone diseases • Cardiac or pulmonary problems • Conditions where movement significantly increases symptoms • Conditions where movement is contraindicated • Dislocation • Fracture • Hiatal hernia • Increased pain or radicular symptoms with traction • Infections in bones or joints	• Meningitis • Osteoporosis • Peripheralization of symptoms • Positive alar ligament test* • Positive vertebral artery test* • Pregnancy** • Rheumatoid arthritis–advanced* • Subluxation • Temporomandibular joint pain or dysfunction (use of halter)* • Trauma–if diagnostic tests have not ruled out other medical conditions • Tumors • Vascular conditions • Vertebral joint instability

* Cervical traction only **Lumbar traction only

Mechanical Lumbar and Cervical Traction Procedures

Lumbar Traction

Procedure for mechanical lumbar traction

1. Determine the patient position

Mechanical lumbar traction is performed with the patient in a supine or prone position. The position chosen is often based on the medical diagnosis and patient tolerance. A flexed position of the spine (i.e., traction in supine) results in greater separation of the posterior structures including the facet joints and intervertebral foramen.[18] An extended position of the spine (i.e., traction in prone) results in greater separation of the anterior structures including the disk spaces.[18]

Traction is most often performed in the supine position, however, the prone position offers the therapist the opportunity to apply other modalities simultaneously and assess the amount of spinous process separation.

Certain medical diagnoses are characteristically treated in a specific position. For example, spinal stenosis is most often treated with a flexed spine since this position increases the intervertebral foramen opening.[17] Disk protrusions are most often treated with the patient positioned in prone since the spine can extend and the forces on the disk are directed anteriorly.[17] This is beneficial since the majority of disk herniations occur in a posterolateral direction.

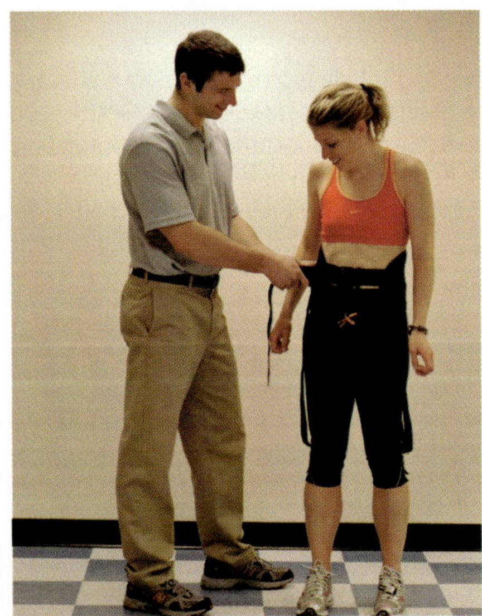

Fig. 8-58: Application of a traction harness.

2. Apply the traction harness

Mechanical lumbar traction requires the use of a traction harness. The harness is necessary to stabilize the trunk while the lumbar spine is placed under traction. The non-slip belt surface should be applied directly on the patient's skin in a standing position (Fig. 8-58).[18] This will allow the harness to better adhere to the skin and allow the therapist to adequately secure the harness with minimal active patient participation. The traction harness can also be applied by placing it on the traction table and having the patient lie on top of it. Once secured, the traction harness should be connected to the traction unit (Fig. 8-59).

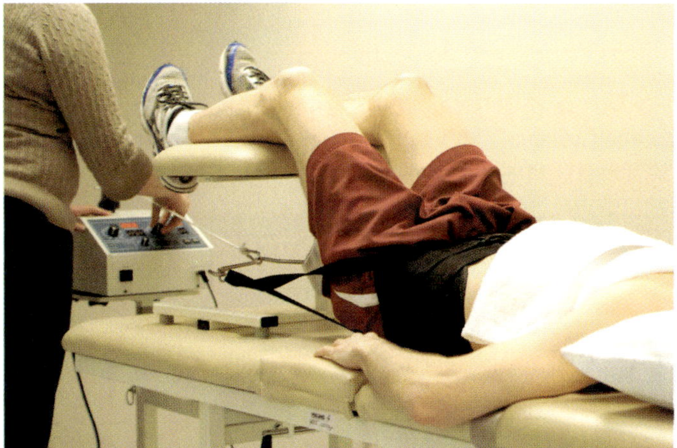

Fig. 8-59: A therapist setting the parameters for mechanical lumbar traction.

3. Select the traction parameters

Static versus intermittent traction

Traction can be applied in a static or intermittent form. Static refers to consistent force being applied throughout the treatment. Static traction may be desirable if the patient's symptoms are slightly exaggerated by movement.[17] Intermittent refers to varying force applied throughout the treatment. Intermittent traction may be desirable for joint mobilization or for patients who cannot tolerate static traction.[17] Intermittent traction requires the therapist to select the amount of force used during the hold and relax periods. The maximum force is applied during the hold period and the minimum force is applied during the relax period. The force during the relax period usually approximates 50% of the force used during the hold period.[16] There is little evidence to guide the timing of the hold and relax periods. The relax period should be relatively short, but must provide a sufficient interval to allow the patient to feel relaxed prior to the next traction cycle.

Force

The force of lumbar traction is dependent on the goals of treatment and is influenced by a number of variables including friction. Friction refers to the force that arises to oppose motion. The amount of friction when performing lumbar traction can be approximated by using the coefficient of friction, which refers to the constant frictional forces when applying traction between surfaces. The coefficient of friction of the human body on a mattress is 0.5.[17] The amount of friction can be estimated by multiplying the percentage of the body weight below L3 (i.e., 50%) and the coefficient of friction (0.5). The result is 25%, meaning that a force of approximately 25% of the patient's body weight is necessary to overcome the force of friction.[17]

The use of a split traction table can eliminate the majority of friction between the patient's body and the treatment table. When the two sections of the split traction table are unlocked and traction is applied, the lower portion of the table slides away from the upper portion. If intermittent traction is used, the table should be split during the second or third hold period when the traction approaches its maximum force.[16]

The literature varies in the exact amount of force necessary when performing mechanical lumbar traction. The majority of sources indicate that a maximum of 30 pounds should be used for the initial traction session.[18] A force of 25% of total body weight may be adequate to stretch soft tissue and treat muscle spasm or disk protrusion.[16] A force of approximately 50% of the body weight is required for actual separation of the vertebrae.[18]

Many traction units provide therapists with the option to progressively increase or decrease the traction force in a series of predetermined steps. The gradual increase or decrease in pressure may be more comfortable for a patient since it allows the patient to gradually accommodate to the traction force and therefore, stay more relaxed throughout the duration of treatment.

Duration

The research does not offer specific guidance on the duration of lumbar traction. In general, treatment times vary from 5-30 minutes.[16] When treating disk-related symptoms, treatment time is generally 10 minutes or less and may extend up to 30 minutes with other spinal conditions.[18] Patient tolerance and changes in symptoms are the primary determining factors when selecting the duration of traction.

Cervical Traction

Procedure for mechanical cervical traction

1. Determine the patient position

Mechanical cervical traction is performed with the patient in a supine or sitting position. The position chosen is often based on the medical diagnosis and patient tolerance. A supine position is used more often since the traction force does not have to overcome the force exerted by gravity and the position allows the patient to attain a more relaxed state, minimizing the opposition to force. A flexed position of the spine results in greater separation of the posterior structures including the facet joints and intervertebral foramen.[16] An extended position of the spine results in greater separation of the anterior structures including the disk spaces.[16]

In a supine position, the therapist can adjust cervical flexion, rotation, and sidebending to focus on a specific target area and to promote comfort. In sitting, the amount of cervical flexion and extension can be controlled to a limited extent by the direction the patient is positioned in relation to the traction force. A patient positioned toward the traction force will exhibit more flexion than a patient positioned away from the traction force.

The relative amount of flexion in the cervical spine allows therapists to target specific spinal levels: upper cervical spine = 0-5 degrees of flexion; midcervical spine = 10-20 degrees of flexion; lower cervical spine = 25-35 degrees of flexion.[17]

2. Apply the head halter

Mechanical cervical traction requires the use of a head halter or padded board attached to a frictionless trolley that moves up

and down a bar attached to the traction unit. The head halter is necessary to stabilize the head while the cervical spine is placed under traction (Fig. 8-60). The head halter should be applied so that the majority of traction pull is placed on the occiput and not the chin.[16] Therapists must be extremely careful when using the head halter since the device can place considerable force on the temporomandibular joints.

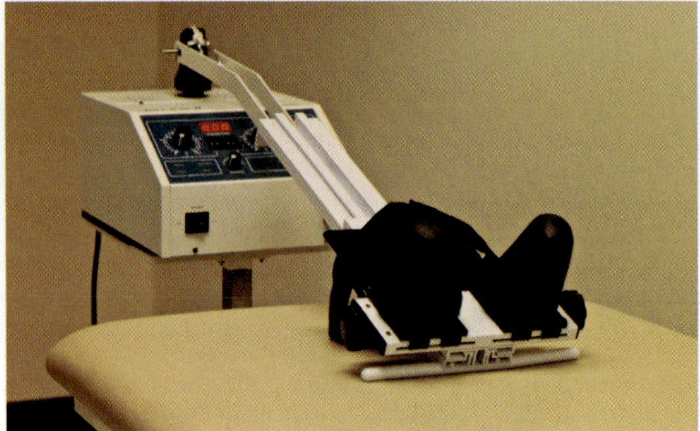

Fig. 8-60: A mechanical cervical traction unit.

3. Select the traction parameters

Static versus intermittent traction

The therapist should select static or intermittent traction. Intermittent traction may be more effective for reducing pain and increasing cervical range of motion.

Force

The force of cervical traction is dependent on the goals of treatment and is influenced by a number of variables including patient position. The literature varies as to the exact amount of force necessary when performing mechanical cervical traction. The majority of sources indicate that a force of up to 10 pounds should be used for the initial traction session.[16] A force of 7-10% of a patient's body weight (11-15 pounds) may be adequate to stretch soft tissue or treat muscle spasm and disk protrusion.[16] A force of 13-20% of a patient's body weight (20-30 pounds) may be necessary for joint distraction.[16] A traction force applied to the cervical spine should typically not exceed 30 pounds.

Duration

The research does not offer specific guidance on the duration of mechanical cervical traction. In general, treatment time varies from 5-30 minutes.[16] When treating disk-related symptoms, treatment time is generally 10 minutes or less, but may extend up to 30 minutes with other spinal conditions.[18] Patient tolerance and changes in symptoms are the primary determining factors when deciding the duration of traction.

Patient safety for mechanical lumbar and cervical traction

The therapist should assess the patient's initial response to traction within the initial five minutes of treatment. If the patient's symptoms worsen or peripheralize, the traction should be temporarily discontinued. The therapist may attempt to modify the traction parameters, however, if undesirable symptoms persist, traction is not likely a viable treatment option. The patient should be supplied with a call bell or safety switch to turn off the traction in the event that traction increases symptoms or becomes uncomfortable.

Compression

Compression refers to the application of a mechanical force to increase pressure on the treated body part. Compression works to keep venous and lymphatic flow from pooling in the venous system and interstitial space.

Therapeutic Effects[16,18]	
• Control of peripheral edema • Management of scar formation • Prevention of deep vein thrombosis	• Promote lymphatic and venous return • Shaping of the residual limb
Indications[16,18]	
• Edema • Hypertrophic scarring • Lymphedema	• New residual limb • Risk for deep vein thrombosis • Stasis ulcers
Contraindications[16,18]	
• Circulatory obstruction • Deep vein thrombosis • Heart failure • Infection of treated area	• Malignancy of treated area • Unstable or acute fracture • Pulmonary edema

Static Compression

Static compression can be used to shape residual limbs, control edema, prevent abnormal scar formation, and reduce the risk of deep vein thrombosis. Examples of static compression devices include compression bandages and compression garments.

Compression bandages

Compression bandages increase external pressure on a body part by exerting resting pressure and working pressure. Resting pressure is produced when an elastic bandage is placed on stretch.[16] Pressure can be exerted when the patient is active or at rest. Working pressure is produced by an active muscle contracting against an inelastic bandage.[16] Pressure is only exerted when the patient is active.

Compression bandages are designed to offer greater pressure distally than proximally and must be applied using a figure-eight pattern. The bandages should not be applied in a circular pattern since this can result in uneven pressure and may actually inhibit edema management. In some instances, a liner may be applied under the bandages to minimize the probability of the bandages slipping on the skin.

There are a variety of different types of compression bandages including:

Long-stretch bandages provide the greatest resting pressure and are capable of applying 60-70 mm Hg of pressure.[16] The elasticity of the bandage allows them to extend up to 200% of their pre-stretch length.[16] This type of bandage provides very little working pressure since the bandages stretch when the muscles expand. Long-stretch bandages are most often used to apply compression in patients who are immobile.

Short-stretch bandages produce low pressure at rest and high working pressure when the muscles expand. These bandages can be moderately effective while a patient is active or at rest since they produce both resting and working pressure. Short-stretch bandages are most often used during exercise.[16] Patients must have a functional calf muscle and a functional gait pattern to maximally benefit from short-stretch bandages in the lower extremities.[16] The bandages are not effective in a flaccid or inactive limb.

Multi-layered bandages produce moderate to high resting pressure through the use of several bandages containing elastic and inelastic layers. The multiple layers of bandages provide protection, absorption, and compression. Multi-layered bandages are most commonly used to treat venous stasis ulcers.[16]

Semirigid bandages most often consist of treated gauze applied to a distal extremity. The treated gauze is initially wet and later dries into a hardened form. The bandages are often used in the treatment of venous stasis ulcers. An Unna boot is an example of a semirigid bandage made of zinc oxide impregnated gauze. The boot is capable of providing a sustained compression force of 35-40 mm Hg.[16]

Compression garments

Compression garments provide varying degrees of resting pressure and working pressure through elasticity. Compression garments are most often used to control edema, limit scar formation after burns, and improve venous circulation in active patients.[16,23] The garments consist of off-the-shelf and custom fit offerings for all parts of the body. Off-the-shelf garments (e.g., antiembolism stockings) provide a compression force of 16-18 mm Hg and are used to prevent deep vein thrombosis in patients on bed rest.[16] The stockings should be worn at all times unless bathing. Compression garments offering 20-30 mm Hg pressure are used for scar tissue control while 30-40 mm Hg pressure is typically required for edema control.[23]

Compression garments should be fit when the level of edema is minimal. An appropriately fit compression garment will fit tightly to the affected body part and can be challenging for some patients to don and doff without assistance. The average life expectancy of a compression garment is six months, although changes may be required sooner if there is a significant change in the size of the limb.[16]

Intermittent Compression

Intermittent compression refers to the use of compression at specified cyclical intervals to control edema. Intermittent compression is most often delivered using an intermittent pneumatic compression pump.

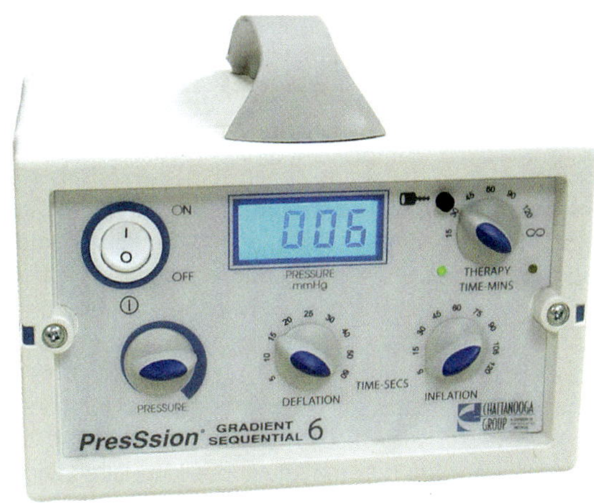

Fig. 8-61: An intermittent compression unit. Courtesy Chattanooga, a DJO Global Company.

Intermittent pneumatic compression pump

Intermittent compression with a pneumatic device is primarily used to reduce chronic or post-traumatic edema. The therapist has the ability to adjust treatment parameters including inflation pressure, on/off ratio, and total treatment time (Fig. 8-61).

The therapist must ask the patient to remove all jewelry and ensure appropriate fit of the compression sleeve prior to treatment. The patient should be placed in a comfortable position with the extremity elevated. Blood pressure and girth measurements should be recorded. The therapist should then apply a stockinette over the extremity and adjust the compression sleeve. The literature provides little definitive guidance on parameters such as on/off time, inflation time, and deflation time. As a result, patient comfort and the desired therapeutic effects are often the most important variables to consider.

Inflation pressure generally ranges from 30-80 mm Hg and typically should not exceed the patient's diastolic blood pressure.[16] Arterial capillary pressure is approximately 30 mm Hg, and therefore, inflation pressure below this value will not typically have any significant therapeutic value. Inflation pressure greater than the patient's systolic blood pressure may restrict arterial blood flow and create a medical emergency.

Treatment of the upper extremities generally requires 30-60 mm Hg of inflation pressure while treatment of the lower extremities generally requires 40-80 mm Hg of inflation pressure.[16] Treatment time varies from 30 minutes to four hours based on diagnosis. Intermittent compression is utilized from three times per week up to four times per day.[16] The patient should have a call bell and be monitored throughout treatment. When treatment is complete, the therapist should reassess the extremity and measure blood pressure. Girth measurements should be recorded and compared to the values obtained before treatment.

Compression may be coupled with therapeutic cold and electrical stimulation.[18] When using electrical stimulation in combination with compression, the current intensity should be adjusted only after the sleeve is fully inflated since this can significantly impact electrode contact with the skin.

Continuous Passive Motion Machine

The continuous passive motion machine (CPM) is a mechanical device designed to provide continuous motion for a particular joint using a predetermined range and speed (Fig. 8-62). Robert Salter first developed this device based on research that continuous passive motion had beneficial healing effects for injured joints and surrounding soft tissues. Subsequent studies examining the efficacy of using a CPM versus not using a CPM vary in conclusion.[23] Some studies show no significant difference in short-term outcomes for CPM use versus alternate forms of early motion. Others show benefits from using CPM including earlier motion of joints resulting in shorter hospitalizations. The primary indication for CPM is to improve range of motion that may have been impaired secondary to a surgical procedure. Any joint may be indicated for CPM, however, the knee is the most commonly treated.

Therapeutic Effects	
• Decrease post-operative pain • Improve the rate of recovery • Increase range of motion	• Lessen the debilitating effects from immobilization • Reduce edema by assisting venous and lymphatic return • Stimulate tissue healing
Indications	
• Pain • Limited range of motion • Edema	• Susceptibility to contractures or adhesions • Muscle or joint stiffness
Contraindications	
• Increase in pain after use • Particular anticoagulants may increase the risk for intracompartment hematoma	• Unwanted translation of opposing bones

A continuous passive motion machine is often utilized immediately after surgery. The patient's joint must be aligned with the fulcrum of the CPM in order to receive effective and safe treatment. Proximal and distal stabilization straps stabilize the patient's upper and lower leg in the device and assist to maintain the desired alignment. The patient must be instructed in the use of the CPM and all associated safety information.

Specific protocols apply for each individual joint regarding time of use and degrees of motion. Initially, a small arc of motion is utilized and patients gradually increase the range of motion as tolerated or as allowed based on their current medical status. A rate of two cycles per minute typically allows patients to tolerate the CPM without difficulty. CPMs may be utilized at home after discharge from the hospital. A patient or caregiver must be independent with the CPM protocol for home use.

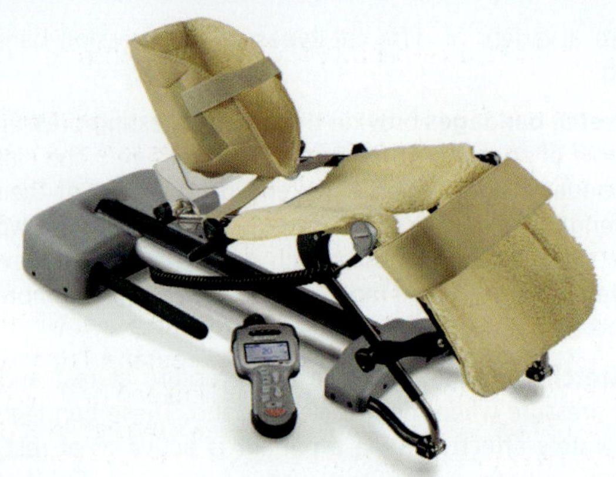

Fig. 8-62: A continuous passive motion machine. Courtesy Chattanooga, a DJO Global Company.

Electrotherapy

Electrotherapy is a commonly used therapeutic modality capable of producing a wide variety of therapeutic effects including muscle strengthening, pain management, muscle re-education, and stimulation of denervated muscle. Therapists must possess a thorough understanding of the mechanism by which electrical stimulation affects tissue as well as the advantages and disadvantages of the various electrotherapeutic agents available.

Therapeutic Effects[16,17,18,21]	
• Decreased edema • Decreased pain • Eliminate disuse atrophy • Facilitate bone repair • Facilitate wound healing	• Improved range of motion • Increased local circulation • Muscle re-education • Muscle strengthening • Relaxation of muscle spasm
Indications[16,17,18,21]	
• Bell's palsy • Decreased range of motion • Facial neuropathy • Fracture • Idiopathic scoliosis • Joint effusion • Labor and delivery	• Muscle atrophy • Muscle spasm • Muscle weakness • Open wound/ulcer • Pain • Stress incontinence • Shoulder subluxation
Contraindications[16,17,18,21]	
• Cardiac arrhythmia • Cardiac pacemaker • Malignancy • Osteomyelitis • Over a pregnant uterus	• Over carotid sinus • Patient with a bladder stimulator • Phlebitis • Seizure disorders

Muscle and Nerve Cell Excitation

Physical therapists must possess a thorough understanding of muscle and nerve cell membranes and their response to electrical stimulation. Muscles and nerve cells are excitable because of the ability to produce action potentials. Action potentials refer to the recorded change in the electrical potential between the inside and outside of a nerve cell.[18] The muscle and nerve cell membranes regulate the exchange of substances between the inside of the cell and the environment outside of the cell. The potential difference in the concentration and permeability of sodium and potassium ions is termed the resting potential. Creating an impulse in a muscle or nerve cell requires the resting potential to be reduced below a threshold level causing changes in the membrane's permeability. The described change creates an action potential that results in depolarization. For an action potential to be evoked using electrical stimulation, the amplitude of the stimulus and pulse duration must be sufficient to overcome the established threshold.

Principles of Electricity

Current (i.e., electrical) refers to the directed flow of charge from one place to another. In order to produce electrical current, there must be a source of electrons, a material that allows passage of the electrons (i.e., conductor), and a driving force of electrons (i.e., electromotive force).[17,18] Current is measured in amperes. One ampere is equal to 6.25×10^{18} electrons per second. A milliampere is one thousandth of an ampere, while a microampere is one millionth of an ampere.[18]

Voltage is a measure of electromotive force or the electrical potential difference.[17,18] Electrons will only flow between two points when there is a difference in the quantity of electrons between the two points. The magnitude of the difference between the positive and negative poles is the voltage. Voltage is measured in volts.

Resistance describes the ability of a material to oppose the flow of ions through it. Resistance is measured in ohms.[17,18] The resistance of a material can be calculated using Ohm's law.

$$\text{Resistance} = \frac{\text{Voltage}}{\text{Current}}$$

Ohm's law states that the current in a conductor varies in proportion to the voltage and inversely with the resistance.[17] An electromotive force of one volt is required to drive one ampere of current across a resistance of one ohm.

Therapeutic Currents

Direct current[17,18]

Direct current is characterized by a constant flow of electrons from the anode (i.e., positive electrode) to the cathode (i.e., negative electrode) for a period of greater than one second without interruption (Fig. 8-63). Polarity remains constant and is determined by the therapist based on treatment goals. Direct current can be modulated for therapeutic use by interrupting the current flow after one second, reversing the polarity or gradually increasing or decreasing the amplitude. Clinically, direct current is most often used with iontophoresis.

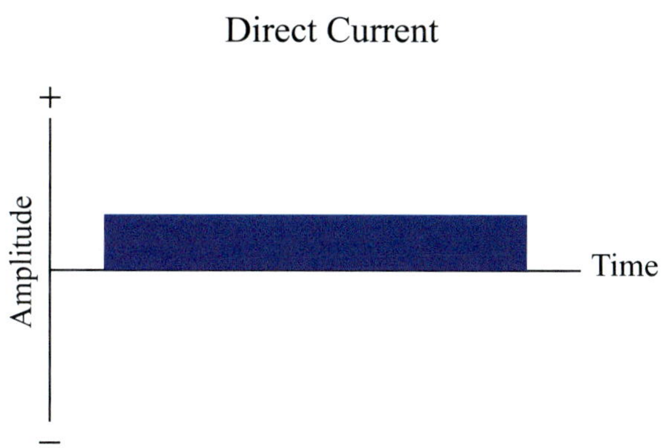

Fig. 8-63: Direct current is characterized by a constant flow of electrons from the anode to the cathode.

Alternating current[17,18]

Alternating current is characterized by polarity that continuously changes from positive to negative with the change in direction of current flow (Fig. 8-64). Alternating current is biphasic, symmetrical or asymmetrical, and is characterized by a waveform that is sinusoidal in shape. The frequency of cycles of alternating current is measured in cycles per second or hertz. Alternating current is used most frequently in a modulated form as burst or time-modulated.

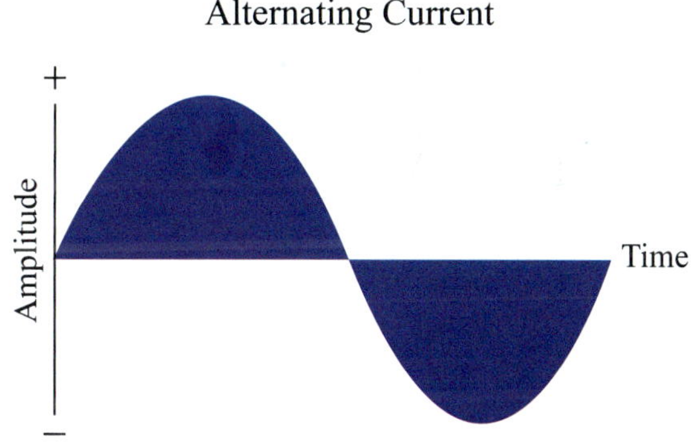

Fig. 8-64: Alternating current is characterized by a continuous bidirectional flow of current.

Pulsatile current[17,18]

Pulsatile current is characterized by the non-continuous flow of direct or alternating current. A pulse is defined as a discrete electrical event separated from other pulses by a period of time in which no electrical activity exists. Most pulse waveforms are either monophasic or biphasic. Monophasic pulsed current has one phase for each pulse and therefore, the waveform is either positive or negative (Fig. 8-65). Monophasic pulsed current produces a polarity effect since the current flows through the tissues in only one polarity (i.e., positive or negative) for a given period of time.

Biphasic pulsed current has two phases, one which is positive and one which is negative (Fig. 8-66). Biphasic waveforms can be described as symmetric or asymmetric and balanced or unbalanced (Fig. 8-67).

Fig. 8-65: Monophasic pulsatile current has one phase for each pulse.

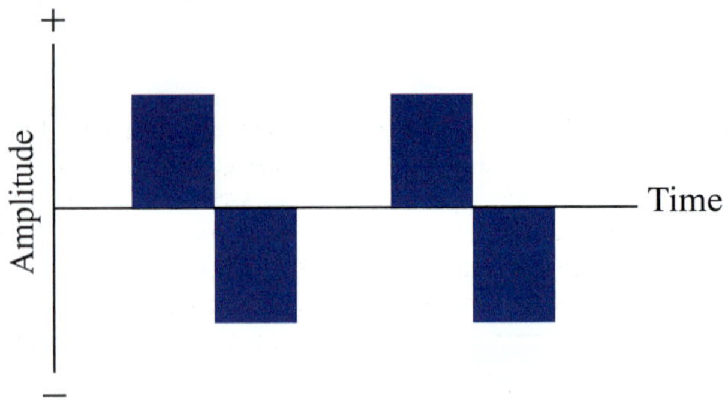

Fig. 8-66: Biphasic pulsatile current has two phases for each pulse.

Fig. 8-67: Balanced and unbalanced biphasic pulsatile current.

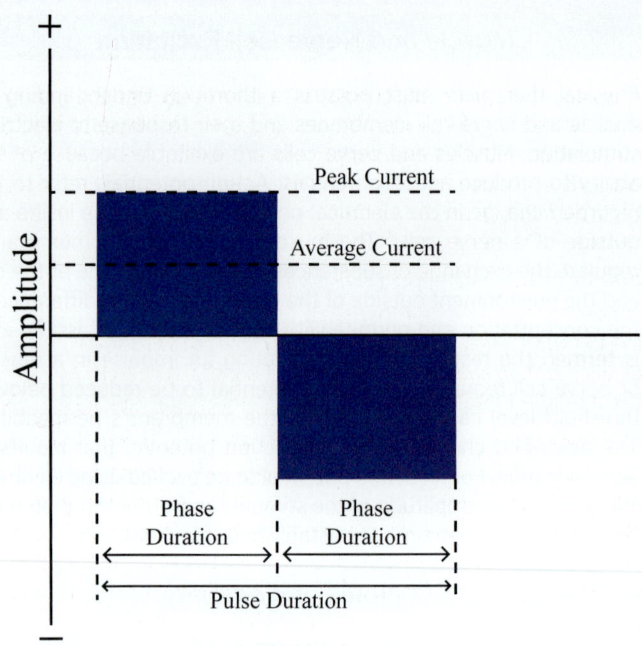

Fig. 8-68: Characteristics of pulsatile current.

Waveforms of Therapeutic Currents[18]

An oscilloscope can be used to create a graphical representation of the shape, direction, amplitude, duration, and pulse frequency of the electrical current being produced by an electrotherapeutic device. On an oscilloscope, an individual waveform is referred to as a pulse. Waveforms of monophasic, biphasic, and pulsatile currents include sine, square, rectangular or spiked (Fig. 8-69).

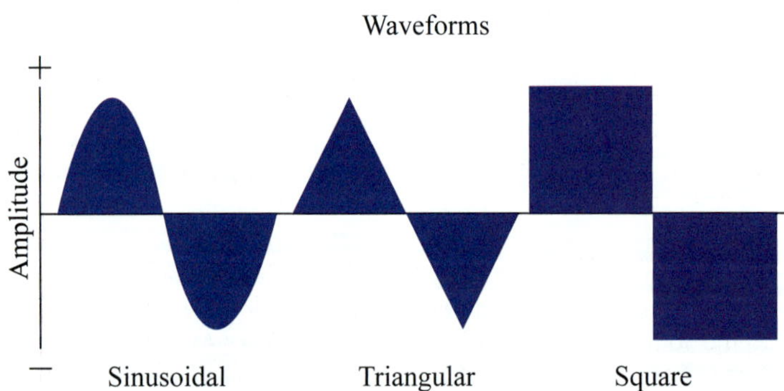

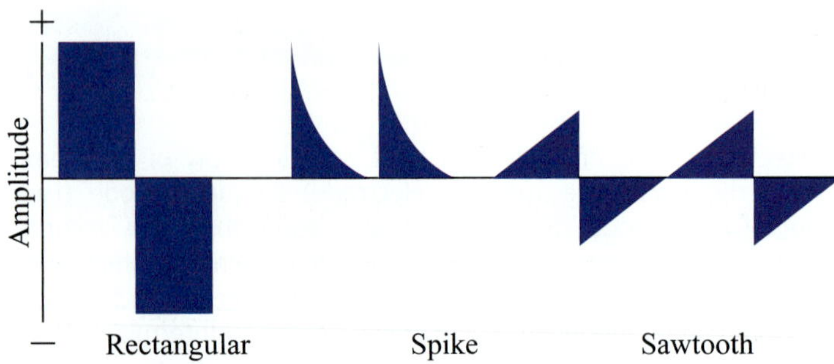

Fig. 8-69: Common types of electrical waveforms.

Electrodes

Administering electrical current to a body requires the use of at least two electrodes of opposing charges. When direct current or a monophasic pulsed waveform is used, one electrode will remain the cathode (negative) and the other the anode (positive) throughout the treatment. In an alternating current, the cathode and anode are constantly changing.

Proper cleaning of the skin and electrode application will facilitate conductance and limit impedance. Prior to applying the electrodes, the patient's skin must be thoroughly cleansed with soap and water or a suitable cleansing wipe. Ideally, hair should be removed from the identified treatment area, however, this is not required.

Electrodes are typically flexible with a self-adhesive gel coating and are intended for one time use. Reusable electrodes are typically made of carbon-silicon rubber. This type of electrode requires application of a gel or coupling spray to ensure appropriate contact. Since they are not self-adhesive, reusable electrodes must be secured on the patient with tape or elastic straps. Therapists should closely monitor the patient's skin since it is fairly common to develop irritation under the electrodes. Some patients may also exhibit an allergic reaction to the material or selected polymers from an electrode.[16] In these instances, the therapist may elect to utilize a different type of electrode, modify the location of the electrode placement or discontinue treatment.

Small electrodes are used for electrotherapy treatments for small areas of the body or small muscles that require relatively low levels of stimulation. Large electrodes are used for larger areas of the body or larger muscles of the body that require high levels of stimulation.[17] Current density is influenced by the size of the electrodes and the distance they are apart. When the same size electrodes are used, the current density under each electrode is the same. When unequal size electrodes are used, the current will be more concentrated in the smaller electrode. Current density can also refer to the concentration of current within the tissues.[20] If the electrodes are in close proximity, the current is more dense in the superficial tissues. If the electrodes are relatively farther apart, the current is more dense in the deeper tissues.[20]

Characteristics of Electrical Current Based on Electrode Size

Small Electrodes	Large Electrodes
Increased current density	Decreased current density
Increased impedance	Decreased impedance
Decreased current flow	Increased current flow

Electrode Placement

The two primary methods of electrode placement are monopolar and bipolar.

Monopolar technique: The stimulating or active electrode is placed over the target area. A second dispersive electrode is placed at another site away from the target area. Typically, the active electrode is smaller than the dispersive electrode. This technique is used with wounds, iontophoresis, and in the treatment of edema.[24]

Bipolar technique: Two active electrodes are placed over the target area. Typically, the electrodes are equal in size. This technique is used for muscle weakness, neuromuscular facilitation, spasms, and range of motion.[24]

Parameters of Electrical Stimulation

The law of Dubois Reymond specifies that the effectiveness of a current to target specific excitable tissue is dependent on three major factors:[20]

1. Adequate intensity to reach the threshold (i.e., amplitude)
2. Current onset fast enough to reduce accommodation (i.e., rise time)
3. Duration long enough to exceed the capacitance of the tissue (i.e., phase duration)

The specific parameters selected for electrotherapy determine the anticipated therapeutic effects. Common parameters available on most electrotherapy devices include:

Amplitude[16,18]

Amplitude refers to the magnitude of current. Average amplitude refers to the average amount of current supplied over a period of time, while peak amplitude refers to the maximum positive or negative point from zero where the pulse is maintained.[20] The peak amplitude must be large enough to exceed the threshold for the nerve or muscle cell. Amplitude controls are often labeled intensity or voltage and can be expressed in volts, microvolts or millivolts. The higher the amplitude, the greater the peak amplitude.

Rise time[16,18]

Rise time is the time it takes for the current to move from zero to the peak intensity within each phase (Fig. 8-71). Fast rise times are necessary with low capacitance tissues, such as large motor nerves. Rise times are typically very short, ranging from nanoseconds to milliseconds. By observing the graphical representation of a given pulse generated from an oscilloscope, therapists can gain a general sense of the rise time. For example, a sine wave would exhibit a more gradual increase in amplitude compared to a rectangular wave which has an almost instantaneous increase in amplitude. Decay time is the time it takes for the current to move from the peak intensity to zero.

Phase duration[16,18]

Phase duration is the amount of time it takes for one phase of a pulse. The phase begins when the current departs from the zero line and ends as the current returns to the zero line. Pulse duration is the amount of time it takes for two phases of a pulse with biphasic current (Fig. 8-68). In monophasic current, the phase duration and the pulse duration are the same. If the current is biphasic, there are two phase durations for each pulse. The length of the phase duration must be sufficient to exceed the capacitance of the targeted nerve in order to cause an action potential. Phase duration is typically measured in microseconds. The interpulse interval is the time between two successive phases of a pulse.

Frequency[16,18]

Frequency determines the number of pulses delivered through each channel per second. Frequency controls are often labeled as rate and are expressed in pulses per second or hertz. The frequency affects the number of action potentials elicited during the stimulation. Although the same number of fibers are recruited, a higher frequency causes them to fire at a more rapid rate.

Current modulation[18,24]

Current modulation refers to any alteration in the amplitude, duration or frequency of the current during a series of pulses or cycle.

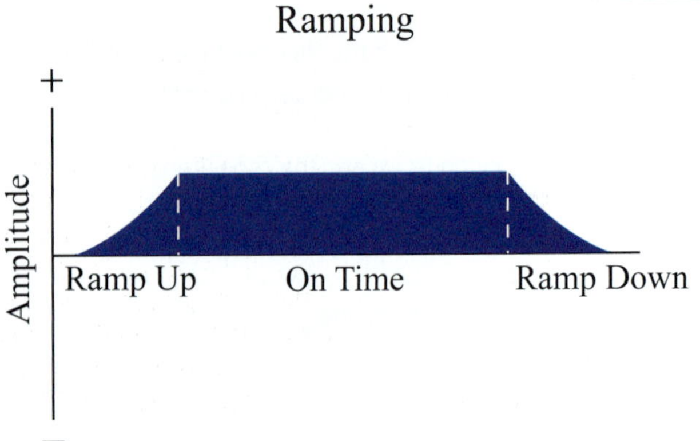

Fig. 8-70: Current modulation using a ramp.

Common categories of modulation include bursts, interrupted pulses, and ramps (Fig. 8-70). Bursts occur when pulsed current flows for several milliseconds and then ceases to flow for several milliseconds in a repeated cycle. The minimal length of the interruptions is too short to allow for a true interruption of muscle contraction. Interrupted pulses allow for a true

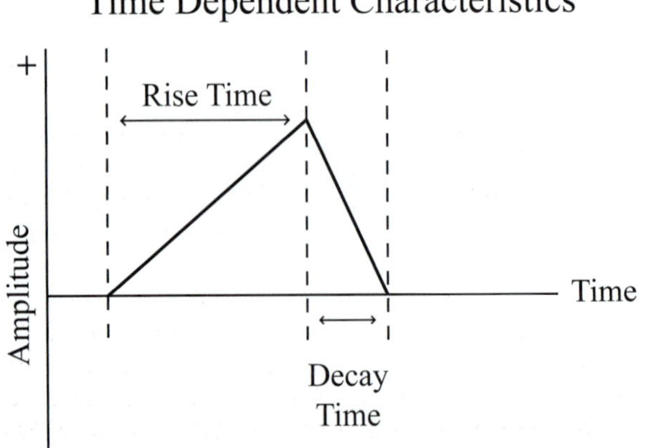

Fig. 8-71: Determining rise time and decay time.

interruption by using an on time and off time. This type of modulation is commonly used with muscle strengthening due to the necessity for a rest period. Ramps allow current amplitude to gradually increase to a preset maximum and then gradually decrease. Ramping is commonly used to make the onset of stimulation more comfortable and is frequently utilized with muscle strengthening.[24]

Neuromuscular Electrical Stimulation

Neuromuscular electrical stimulation (NMES) is a technique used to facilitate skeletal muscle activity (Fig. 8-72). Stimulation of an innervated muscle occurs when an electrical stimulus of appropriate intensity and duration is administered to the corresponding peripheral nerve. Electrical stimulation of a denervated muscle has been used in an attempt to maintain the muscle, however, there is little documented evidence that supports this treatment option. Functional electrical stimulation (FES) uses electrical stimulation to create or enhance the performance of a functional activity.[17] An example of FES is the stimulation of the anterior tibialis to produce dorsiflexion during the swing phase of gait.

Fig. 8-72: A neuromuscular electrical stimulation unit. Courtesy Chattanooga, a DJO Global Company.

NMES is a commonly used therapeutic technique to facilitate the return of controlled functional muscular activity or to maintain postural alignment until recovery occurs. When performing NMES the patient should be positioned comfortably (Fig. 8-73). The therapist should place the electrodes over the muscle to be stimulated so that the electrodes are aligned in parallel. This alignment will allow the current to travel parallel to the direction of the muscle fibers. Ideally, one of the electrodes should be placed over the muscle's motor point since this will produce the strongest contraction with the least amount of current. The electrodes should be separated by a minimum of two inches.[17]

Parameters for applying NMES for muscle strengthening

Current amplitude: The amount of current amplitude is dependent on the desired strength of the contraction (Fig. 8-74). For example, a therapist would want a much more forceful muscle contraction for a patient participating in general muscle strengthening than for a patient recovering from a recent surgery.

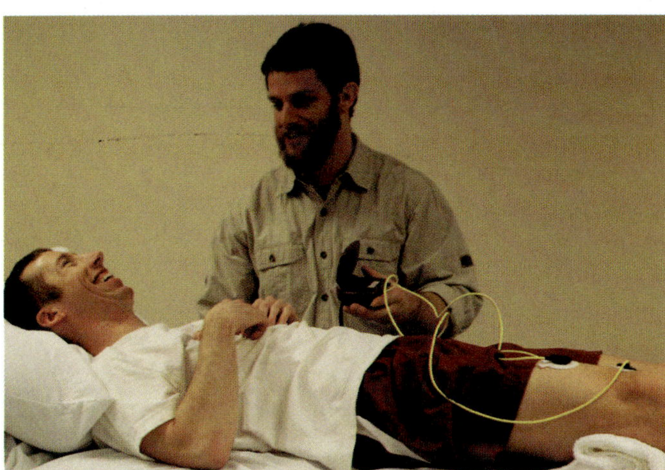

Fig. 8-73: A therapist discussing the use of a neuromuscular electrical stimulation unit with a patient.

Pulse duration: The pulse duration should be high enough to overcome the relatively low capacitance of motor nerve fibers. Despite the low capacitance, the relative depth of the muscle fibers requires a high pulse duration.[20] Patients often find shorter pulse durations more comfortable when targeting smaller muscles and longer pulse durations more comfortable when treating larger muscles.[17] Therapists should recognize that as the pulse duration is shortened, a greater current amplitude will be required to produce the same strength of contraction.

Frequency: The frequency should be sufficient to produce a tetanic contraction. A smooth tetanic contraction is usually produced at a frequency of 35-50 pulses per second.[20] Higher frequencies will not produce a stronger contraction, but instead will promote more rapid fatigue.

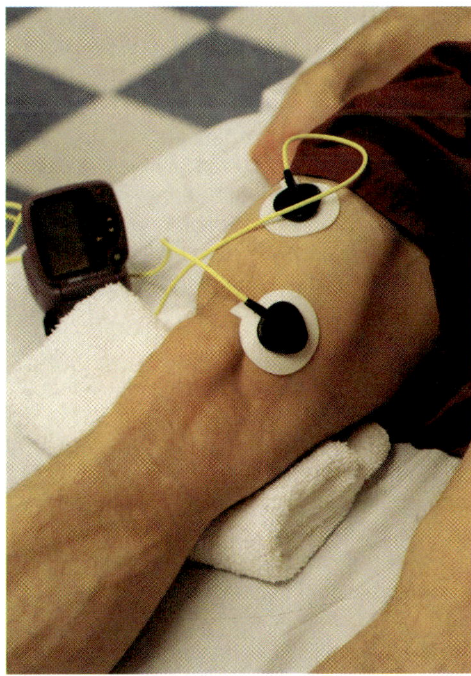

Fig. 8-74: A forceful quadriceps femoris contraction using a neuromuscular electrical stimulation unit.

Duty cycle: A duty cycle must be used when applying NMES to provide the muscle with relaxation time and limit the influence of fatigue. On time should range from 6-10 seconds while off time should be approximately five times longer.[20] The therapist may elect to decrease the length of the off time in subsequent sessions based on patient progress.

Ramp time: A ramp allows current amplitude to gradually increase to a preset maximum and then gradually decrease. Ramping is commonly used to make the onset of stimulation more comfortable when performing muscle strengthening. Based on an on time of 6-10 seconds, a ramp up time of 1-4 seconds would be recommended.

Treatment time: Patients should complete a minimum of 10 contractions and a maximum of 20 contractions. Based on typical on and off times, performing 10 contractions would take approximately 10 minutes while 20 contractions would take 20 minutes. Treatment should ideally take place a minimum of three times per week.[18]

Transcutaneous Electrical Nerve Stimulation (TENS)

Transcutaneous electrical nerve stimulation is widely used for acute and chronic pain management. Areas of use include obstetrics, temporomandibular joint pain, and post-operative pain. The main therapeutic effects of TENS include pain relief through the gate control theory of pain or the endogenous opiate pain control theory. TENS units are portable and indicated for home use (Fig. 8-75). The most commonly used modes of TENS include conventional, acupuncture-like, brief intense, and noxious.[16,25]

Conventional TENS[17,21,24]

Conventional TENS is characterized by delivery of electrical pulses having short duration and high frequency with low current amplitude. The current amplitude should be sufficient to generate a sensory response, but should be below the motor threshold. Electrodes should be placed over the painful area. The majority of patients report a mild tingling sensation under and between the electrodes. Pain relief is usually brief and only occurs when the current is being generated. Conventional TENS is most often used to relieve pain during activities of daily living. Treatment time is highly variable depending on the duration of the activity.

Acupuncture-like TENS[17,21,22]

Acupuncture-like TENS is characterized by the delivery of electrical pulses that have long duration and low frequency with moderate current amplitude. The current amplitude should be sufficient to generate muscle twitching. Electrodes should be placed over the area of pain or a related area, such as an acupuncture point. The majority of patients report the stimulus as uncomfortable or burning. Pain relief can last for several hours after stimulation. Acupuncture-like TENS is most often used for patients requiring longer lasting pain relief. It is not often used during activities of daily living since the muscle twitching can interfere with functional tasks. Treatment time is usually 20-45 minutes.

Common TENS Techniques and Recommended Parameters[17]				
Technique	**Amplitude**	**Pulse Frequency**	**Pulse Duration**	**Treatment Time**
Conventional	Sufficient for a sensory response	High (30-150 pps)	Short (50-100 μsec)	Variable based on the duration of the activity
Acupuncture-like	Sufficient to produce muscle twitching	Low (2-4 pps)	Long (100-300 μsec)	20-45 minutes
Brief Intense	Sufficient for strong paresthesia or a motor response	High (60-200 pps)	Long (150-500 μsec)	15 minutes
Noxious	Highest tolerated stimulus	High or Low	Long (250 μsec up to 1 second)	30-60 seconds for each point

Adapted from Michlovitz S: *Thermal Agents in Rehabilitation,* Fourth Edition, FA Davis Company, 2005

**This table demonstrates a typical range for each type of TENS, however, there are discrepancies that exist from author to author regarding the appropriate settings for TENS. Given this fact, it is more important to have a basic understanding of TENS parameters (e.g., short, long, low, high) than it is to memorize an exact pulse frequency or pulse duration.

Brief intense TENS[17,21,24]

Brief intense TENS is characterized by delivery of electrical pulses having long duration and high frequency with moderate current amplitude. This mode of TENS is referred to as brief intense TENS since the application is shorter and the current amplitude is higher than some of the other presented modes. The current amplitude should be sufficient for strong paresthesia or a motor response. Brief intense TENS is often used to minimize pain during therapeutic activities that may be painful. Treatment time is usually 15 minutes.

Fig. 8-75: A transcutaneous electrical nerve stimulation unit. Courtesy Chattanooga, a DJO Global Company.

Noxious TENS[17,24]

Noxious TENS is characterized by high density current that is described by patients as uncomfortable or painful. This mode of TENS is administered with a small probe type applicator or electrode. Stimulation is delivered in 30-60 second intervals to motor, acupuncture or trigger points. Noxious level stimulation should be applied to patients only after the therapist has thoroughly explained the expected sensation.[17]

The waveforms used are monophasic pulsatile current or biphasic pulsatile current with a spiked, square, rectangular or sine waveform. Electrode placement may be based on sites of nerve roots, trigger points, acupuncture sites or key points of pain and sensitivity.[24] Net polarity is normally equal to zero. If the waveform is unbalanced there will be an accumulation of charges that will lead to skin irritation under the electrodes.

Interferential Current

Interferential current combines two medium frequency alternating waveforms that are biphasic. The two waveforms are delivered through two sets of electrodes from separate channels of the same stimulator. When the currents intersect, they produce a higher amplitude when both currents are in the same phase and a lower current when they are in opposite phases. This continuous sequence produces envelopes of pulses known as beats.[16] Interferential current is often comfortable for patients since a low amplitude current is delivered through the skin and a higher amplitude current is delivered to deeper tissues. Interferential current is most often used for pain relief, increased circulation, and muscle stimulation.[20]

Methods of Interferential Current Delivery

Bipolar delivery[20]

Bipolar delivery utilizes two electrodes connected to a single channel with two medium sinusoidal currents. The interference between the two currents creates an amplitude modulated interferential current with a beat frequency (beats per second). The beat frequency is the net difference between the two currents. The bipolar method allows for the interferential current to be modulated prior to delivery of the current to the electrodes. Bipolar delivery creates an oval-shaped field of interferential current.

Quadripolar delivery[20]

Quadripolar delivery utilizes four electrodes with each pair connected to a single channel. The interference between the currents using this method occurs at the level of the treatment area within the targeted tissues. When the currents intersect at a 90 degree angle, the maximum resultant amplitude occurs halfway between the two lines of current. The current treatment area creates a four-leaf clover shaped treatment field within the area between all four electrodes (Fig. 8-76).

Quadripolar with automatic vector scan[21]

The quadripolar method with automatic vector scan is used when there is a need to increase the size of the field of current that is created by the quadripolar method. One of the circuits is allowed to vary in amplitude and this allows the field pattern to automatically rotate between the two lines of current. The field is circular in shape, as opposed to the cloverleaf, and allows for an overall larger field of current.

Some interferential units include suction electrodes that attach to the skin surface through mild suctioning. This feature can be desirable since the electrodes stay in place throughout treatment without having to be strapped to the body surface. Interferential current can be used in combination with other modalities, such as ice or heat. Treatment time is variable and is primarily influenced by the established goals (e.g., pain relief, increased circulation, muscle stimulation).

Interferential Current

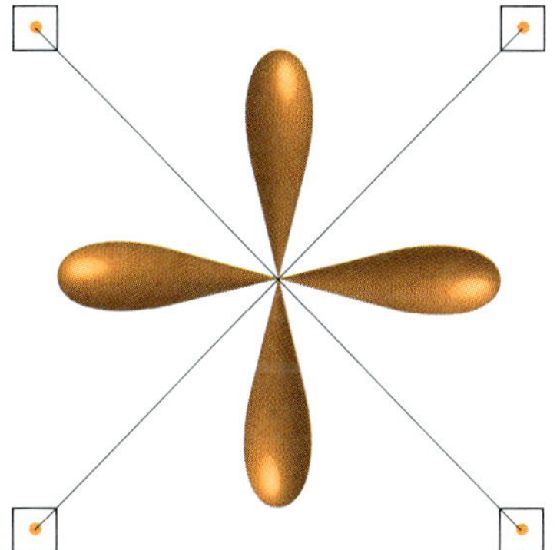

Fig. 8-76: Interaction of two medium frequency alternating wave-forms using interferential current with a quadripolar technique.

Iontophoresis

Iontophoresis is the process by which ions are introduced into the body through the skin by means of continuous direct current electrical stimulation (Fig. 8-77). Iontophoresis is based on the theory that like charges repel and, as a result, ions in a solution of similar charge will move away from the electrical source and into the body. Positively charged ions are carried into the body's tissue from the positive pole (anode) and negatively charged ions are carried into the body's tissue from the negative pole (cathode). The rate of ion delivery is determined by the concentration of the ion, the pH of the solution, the current density, and the duration of the treatment.[18] The specific therapeutic effects of iontophoresis are determined based on the ion selected.

SPOTLIGHT ON SAFETY

SAFETY CONSIDERATIONS WITH ELECTROTHERAPY[18,21,24]

Electrical equipment used in health care can pose a significant potential risk to both the patient and therapist. Therapists should be aware of these potential risks in order to ensure safety and limit any potential liability. This section identifies several safe practices that minimize risk when using electrotherapy.

- All electrotherapy equipment should be inspected by qualified personnel at or before the manufacturer's suggested service dates.
- Any electrotherapy equipment that may have been damaged (e.g., dropped on the floor) or is functioning improperly should be inspected by qualified personnel before subsequent use.
- Ensure all line-powered equipment has a testing seal (maximum leakage of a current < 1 milliampere).
- A sticker should be placed on equipment noting the last inspection/maintenance date.
- Maintain an updated log for all equipment used in the physical therapy department.
- Maintain electrotherapy equipment operation manuals in an accessible location for staff members to use as a resource.
- Electrotherapy equipment should only be used by qualified personnel who have read the operating manual and are familiar with how to properly operate the equipment.
- All electrotherapy devices should have a hospital grade three-pronged plug that has a safety ground attached to an earth ground.
- Electrical outlets should be equipped with ground fault circuit interrupters (GFCIs). GFCIs are designed to cut off electrical supply to equipment when any form of leakage or ground-fault is identified.
- Extension cords or multiple adapters should not be used.
- Plugs should be removed from the wall by gripping and pulling the plug and not by pulling the cable.
- Unplug all powered-line devices at the end of each day.
- Always turn the intensity dial to zero before unplugging electrotherapy equipment.
- Instruct patients to avoid all contact with the controls of an electrotherapy device unless otherwise instructed.
- Thoroughly instruct patients on the type of sensations typically experienced with a specific electrotherapy device.
- Avoid placing containers of liquid (e.g., coffee, soda) on top of the casing of electrical equipment.
- Keep electrotherapy equipment 3-5 meters from each other when in use to minimize the possibility of electrical interference.

Indications[16,17,18]	
• Pain	• Keloids
• Calcium deposits	• Muscle spasm
• Fungal infection	• Myositis ossificans
• Hyperhidrosis	• Plantar warts
• Inflammation	• Scar tissue
• Ischemia	• Wounds
Contraindications[16,17,18]	
• Drug allergies	• Skin sensitivity reactions to specific ions

The amount of electricity used when performing iontophoresis is measured in milliamp minutes (mA-min). This value is often termed "dosage" and is determined by multiplying current amplitude and time. Dosage ranges from 40-80 mA-min with iontophoresis.[16,17]

A dosage of 40 mA-min could be delivered in 10 minutes with a current amplitude of 4.0 mA. The same dosage could be delivered using a lower current amplitude with a longer duration. A lower current amplitude and a longer duration will be less likely to cause skin irritation or burns.[17]

The current amplitude should be adjusted to be comfortable for the patient. Current amplitudes typically range from 1.0-4.0 mA.[16,17] Once the current amplitude is determined, the therapist can select an appropriate amount of time to ensure the appropriate mA-min dosage level. Many iontophoresis units will automatically calculate the duration of the treatment session based on the preset dosage and the current amplitude.

Iontophoresis procedures

The therapist must identify any known patient allergies or the potential for adverse reactions based on the ion used. The skin should be thoroughly cleaned with soap or isopropyl alcohol. The patient should be positioned comfortably, but should not lie on top of the electrodes. The unit should be set to continuous direct current. Polarity should be set to the same polarity as the ion solution.[16] The ion solution is placed into a small chamber located on a self-adhesive electrode placed at the treatment site.

The electrode containing the ion solution is referred to as the active electrode.[18] A second electrode, referred to as the dispersive electrode, is placed away from the active electrode. The recommended spacing between the active and dispersive electrodes should be minimally equivalent to the diameter of the active electrode.[18] As the spacing between the electrodes increases, the current density in the superficial tissues decreases, resulting in a diminished risk for burns. Smaller electrodes have higher current density and are often used to treat a specific lesion, while larger electrodes are used when the treatment area is less well defined.[18]

The therapist should make sure the electrodes are appropriately secured and slowly increase the intensity towards a maximum of four milliamperes. Treatment should last 10-20 minutes.[18] Additional time may be required for treatment at an intensity of less than four milliamperes. The therapist must monitor the patient every 3-5 minutes during treatment to ensure that the patient is not exhibiting signs of skin irritation or burns under the electrode.[18]

Acidic reaction: A patient may have an acidic reaction from the iontophoresis treatment as a result of hydrochloric acid forming under the positive electrode (anode).[18]

Alkaline reaction: A patient may have an alkaline reaction from the iontophoresis treatment as a result of sodium hydroxide forming under the negative electrode (cathode).

Acidic and alkaline reactions often cause significant discomfort, skin irritation or chemical burns.[18]

The likelihood of a burn can be decreased by increasing the size of the cathode relative to the anode, decreasing the current density, and increasing the space between the electrodes.[18]

Upon completion of treatment, the therapist must slowly decrease the intensity and remove the electrodes. It is common for patients to have redness of the skin under the active electrode. In some cases, the active electrode can be left in place for 12-24 hours after treatment to facilitate further diffusion of ions through the skin.

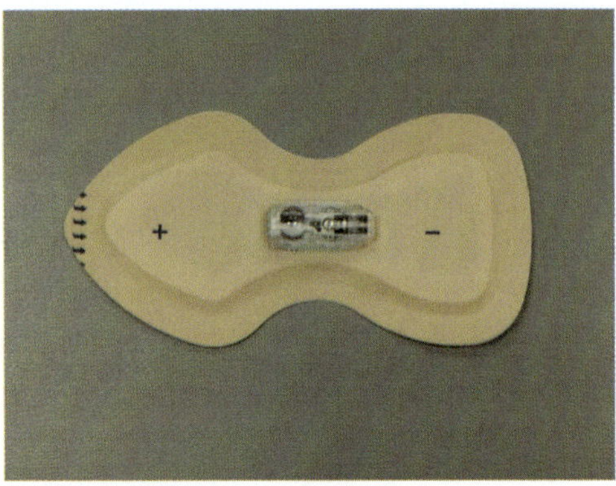

Fig. 8-77: An electrode with an integrated battery for iontophoresis drug delivery.

The frequency of treatment depends on the ion selected, the underlying condition, patient tolerance, and the relative effectiveness of the treatment.[17] Iontophoresis should be applied no more frequently than every other day due to the potential side effects from using direct current.[17] A therapist should be able to make a relative determination of the effectiveness of iontophoresis within three to five treatment sessions.

Ions Used with Iontophoresis[16,17,18]		
Medication	**Indications**	**Polarity**
Acetic acid	Calcific deposits, myositis ossificans	Negative
Calcium chloride	Scar tissue, keloids, muscle spasms	Negative
Copper sulfate	Fungal infection	Positive
Dexamethasone	Inflammation	Negative
Iodine	Scars, adhesive capsulitis	Negative
Lidocaine	Analgesia, inflammation	Positive
Magnesium sulfate	Muscle spasms, ischemia	Positive
Salicylates	Muscle and joint pain, plantar warts	Negative
Zinc oxide	Healing, dermal ulcers, wounds	Positive

Electromyography

Electromyography (EMG) is the science of evaluating motor units (the anterior horn cell and its axon, neuromuscular junctions, and muscle fibers innervated by the unit) through the use of intramuscular needle electrodes or surface electrodes. EMG involves the recording of action potentials from muscle fibers during voluntary movement and potentially spontaneous action potentials from muscle fibers at rest.[24] Indwelling electrodes (i.e., intramuscular EMG) are used for small or deep muscles or when there is a need to record a single motor unit potential. Surface electrodes (i.e., biofeedback) are used to monitor larger muscle groups.

Intramuscular EMG

Intramuscular EMG involves insertion of a needle electrode into the muscle by a trained professional, most often a neurologist, physiatrist or physical therapist. In some licensing jurisdictions, physical therapists may not be able to perform intramuscular EMG due to the established practice act.

The area of skin over the muscle to be tested should be thoroughly cleaned. The needle is inserted into the muscle at rest while the oscilloscope is observed. The insertional irritability should last only a few milliseconds. A normal relaxed muscle should exhibit electrical silence (i.e., no electrical potentials).[26] Spontaneous potentials during rest are abnormal findings and may indicate nerve or muscle damage.[26] When the muscle is voluntarily contracted, action potentials begin to appear. The size, shape, and frequency of the motor unit potentials should be assessed. As the strength of the contraction increases, a greater number of muscle fibers produce action potentials. During full muscle contraction, a disorderly group of action potentials of varying rates and amplitudes is observed. A nerve conduction velocity test is often performed in conjunction with an EMG.

Abnormal Potentials

Spontaneous[24]

Fibrillation potentials: indicative of lower motor neuron disease

Positive sharp wave: denervated muscle disorders at rest, primary muscle disease such as muscular dystrophy

Fasciculations: irritation/degeneration of anterior horn cell, nerve root compression or muscle spasms

Repetitive discharges: myopathies, lesion of anterior horn cells and peripheral nerves

Voluntary[24]

Polyphasic potentials: myopathies, muscle or peripheral nerve involvement

Abnormal results from intramuscular EMG can be associated with a variety of medical conditions including amyotrophic lateral sclerosis, carpal tunnel syndrome, Duchenne muscular dystrophy, Guillain-Barre syndrome, myasthenia gravis, peripheral neuropathy, and poliomyelitis.

Common Muscles used for Insertion of Needle Electrodes			
Upper Extremity		**Lower Extremity**	
C5-6	Lateral deltoid	**L2, 3, 4**	Vastus medialis
C5-6	Biceps brachii	**L4-5**	Tibialis anterior
C6-7	Triceps brachii	**L4-5, S1**	Tensor fasciae latae
C6-7	Flexor carpi radialis	**L5-S1**	Peroneus longus
C7-8	Extensor indicis proprius	**L5, S1-2**	Gluteus maximus
C8-T1	Abductor pollicis brevis	**L5, S1-2**	Hamstrings
C8-T1	First dorsal interossei	**S1-2**	Gastrocnemius

Biofeedback

Biofeedback refers to the use of instrumentation to bring specific events to conscious awareness (Fig. 8-78). Biofeedback can be utilized to receive information related to motor performance, kinesthetic performance or physiological response.[16] Electromyographic biofeedback is the most commonly used biofeedback modality in the clinical setting. Biofeedback allows patients to make small changes in performance and receive immediate feedback. By successfully rewarding small changes incrementally, larger changes can potentially be achieved.

Biofeedback does not measure muscle contraction, but rather the electrical activity associated with muscle contraction. There is not a standard measurement scale when reporting electrical activity using a biofeedback unit. The electrical activity is most commonly presented as visual and/or auditory feedback. Visual feedback is often presented as a series of colored lights that go on and off in a linear fashion based on the strength of the incoming signal. Auditory feedback is often presented as a buzzing, clicking or beeping sound that changes in intensity as the strength of the incoming signal increases or decreases.

Prior to treatment the therapist should ensure that the patient's skin is clean and dry. Biofeedback requires the use of surface electrodes which provide less specific information than indwelling electrodes, however, surface electrodes are more effective in quantifying muscle activity in several muscles or a group of muscles. The electrodes can be disposable or non-disposable. Disposable electrodes typically are designed with the appropriate amount of gel and an adhesive that allows the electrode to firmly adhere to the skin. Non-disposable electrodes require gel and need to be adequately secured to the skin by the therapist.

Therapeutic Effects[18, 20]	
• Decreased accessory muscle use • Decreased muscle spasm • Decreased pain	• Improved muscle strength • Muscle relaxation • Neuromuscular control
Indications[18, 20]	
• Bowel incontinence • Cerebral palsy • Hemiplegia • Impaired motor control • Muscle spasm	• Muscle weakness • Pain • Spinal cord injury • Urinary incontinence
Contraindications[18, 20]	
• Conditions where muscle contraction is detrimental	• Skin irritation at the electrode site

The two active electrodes should be placed parallel to the muscle fibers and close to each other.[18] The reference or ground electrode can be placed anywhere on the body, but is often secured between the two active electrodes. The signals are transmitted to a differential amplifier and information is conveyed through visual and auditory feedback. The described setup can minimize "noise," which refers to the extraneous electrical activity not produced by the contraction of the muscle.

Fig. 8-78: A biofeedback unit. Courtesy Chattanooga, a DJO Global Company.

The therapist can control the relative signal sensitivity during treatment. A high sensitivity will detect extremely small amounts of electrical activity while a low sensitivity setting will detect only large amounts of electrical activity. As a result, high sensitivity settings are used when the treatment objective is relaxation and low sensitivity settings are used when the treatment objective is muscle re-education.[18]

Muscle relaxation

The treatment for muscle relaxation requires a high sensitivity setting with active electrodes initially positioned close to each other. As the patient improves with relaxation, the electrodes should be placed further apart and the sensitivity setting should be increased. A decrease in audio or visual feedback would be considered a positive sign. The patient may also benefit from adjunct relaxation techniques, such as imagery. Treatment duration of 10-15 minutes is usually adequate to attain relaxation.

Muscle re-education

The treatment for muscle re-education should begin with the patient performing a maximal muscle contraction. The sensitivity of the biofeedback unit should be set at a low sensitivity setting and adjusted so that the patient can perform the repetitions at a ratio of two-thirds of the maximal muscle contraction. Isometric contractions should continue for 6-10 seconds with relaxation in between each contraction. An increase in audio or visual feedback would be considered a positive sign. Treatment duration for a single muscle group is 5-10 minutes.[18] As the patient is able to demonstrate greater recruitment of the target muscle, more complex activities are added to the program.

Massage

Massage is a manual therapeutic modality that produces physiologic effects through different types of stroking, rubbing, and pressure (Fig. 8-79). Massage is capable of producing mechanical and reflexive effects.

Therapeutic Effects[27,28,29]	
• Altered pain transmission • Decreased anxiety and tension • Decreased muscle atrophy • Decreased muscle spasm • Facilitate healing • Improved circulation	• Increased lymphatic circulation • Loosen adhesions • Reduction of edema • Relaxation • Removal of metabolic waste • Stimulate reflexive effects
Indications[27,28,29]	
• Adhesion • Bursitis • Decreased range of motion • Edema • Intermittent claudication • Lactic acid excess • Migraine or headache	• Muscle spasm and cramping • Pain • Raynaud's phenomenon • Scar tissue • Tendonitis • Trigger point
Contraindications[27,28,29]	
• Acute injury • Arteriosclerosis • Cancer • Cellulitis	• Embolus • Infection • Thrombus

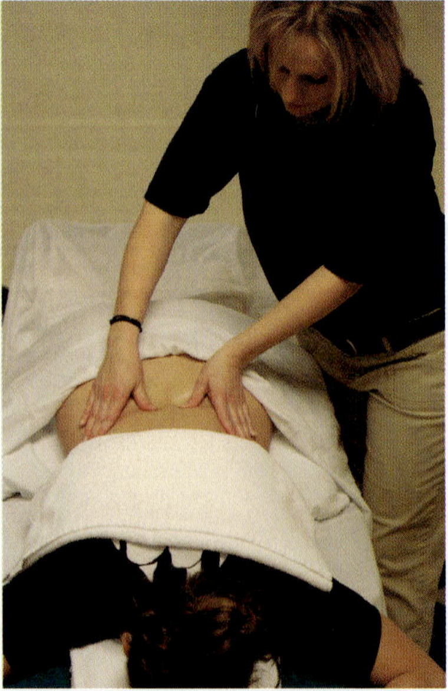

Fig. 8-79: Application of massage to the low back of a properly draped patient.

Massage Parameters[28]

There are a variety of different massage techniques described in the literature. Each technique varies in relation to a number of important variables.

Direction – The general movement pattern of the massage stroke. Direction can be described as centrifugal or centripetal. Centrifugal is moving from the center of the body out. Centripetal is moving in from the extremities toward the center of the body.

Duration – The length of time a massage technique is performed. Duration is highly variable depending on the characteristics of the massage technique, established therapeutic objectives, and patient tolerance.

Frequency – The rate at which the massage technique repeats itself in a given time frame. The variety of massage techniques are repeated several times prior to transitioning to a different technique.

Pressure – The relative amount of compressive stress applied to the body. Pressure is usually described by terms such as light, moderate, deep or variable (Fig. 8-80).

Rhythm – The relative regularity of the massage technique. A massage technique applied at regular consistent intervals would be considered rhythmic. If the technique was applied at inconsistent intervals, it would be considered non-rhythmic.

Speed – The general rate the therapist's hands move. Speed is usually described as slow, moderate, fast or variable.

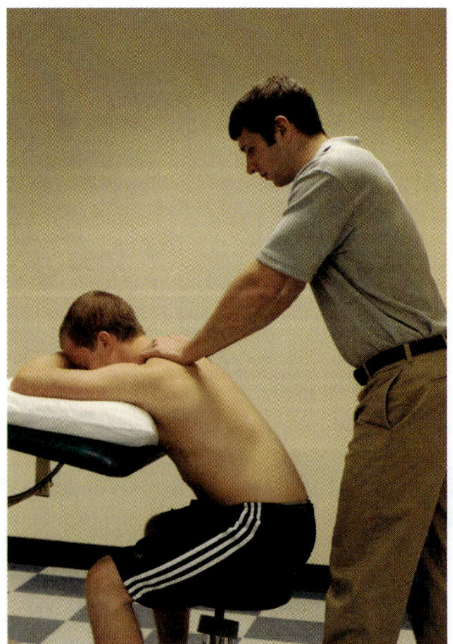

Fig. 8-80: Massage applied to the upper back of a patient in supported sitting.

Massage Techniques[27,28,29]

Effleurage

Effleurage is a massage technique that is characterized by a light stroke that produces a reflexive response. The technique is performed at the beginning and end of a massage to allow the patient to relax. Strokes should be directed towards the heart. Effleurage can also be applied as a deep stroke to produce both a mechanical and a reflexive response.

Friction

Friction is a massage technique that incorporates small circular motions over a trigger point or muscle spasm. This is a deep massage technique that penetrates into the depth of a muscle and attempts to reduce edema, loosen adhesions, and relieve muscle spasm. Friction massage is used frequently with chronic inflammation or with overuse injuries (Fig. 8-81).

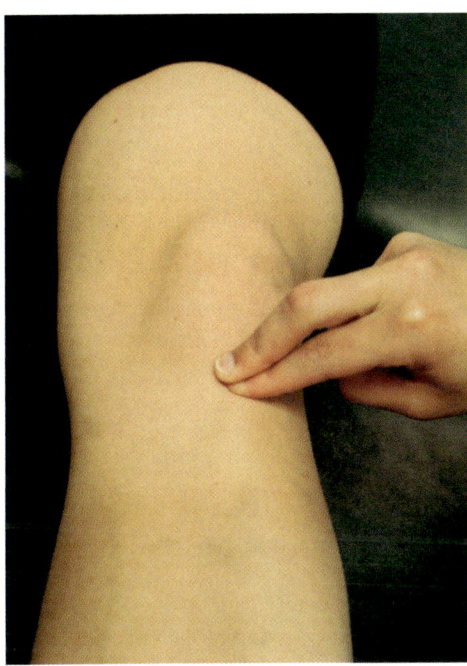

Fig. 8-81: Transverse friction massage applied to the patellar tendon.

Petrissage

Petrissage is a massage technique described as kneading, where the muscle is squeezed and rolled under the therapist's hands. The goal of petrissage is to loosen adhesions, improve lymphatic return, and facilitate removal of metabolic waste from the treatment area. Petrissage should be performed in a distal to proximal sequence. Petrissage can be performed with two hands over larger muscle groups or with as few as two fingers over smaller muscles.

Tapotement

Tapotement is a massage technique that provides stimulation through rapid alternating movements such as tapping, hacking, cupping, and slapping. The primary purpose of tapotement is to enhance circulation and stimulate peripheral nerve endings.

Vibration

Vibration is a massage technique that places the therapist's hands or fingers firmly over an area and utilizes a rapid, shaking motion that causes vibration to the treatment area. The therapist initiates this motion from the forearm while maintaining firm contact on the treatment area. Vibration is used primarily for relaxation.

Massage Procedure

Prior to initiating massage, a therapist must obtain patient consent. Components of consent when performing massage would minimally include:

1. A description of the proposed massage.
2. The relative risks and benefits.
3. The expectations of the patient during the massage.
4. The opportunity to consent to or refuse the proposed intervention.

Massage should occur in a room with air temperature of 72-75 degrees Fahrenheit.[28] This temperature range will allow the patient to relax and minimize undesired muscular tension. The patient should be comfortably positioned and properly draped prior to the initiation of treatment. Standard bed linens are most often used for draping. The therapist should attempt to leave only the area of the body being massaged exposed, while the remainder of the body should be draped. Pillows, towels, bolsters, foam, and blankets can be used to ensure patient comfort.

The therapist's hands must be clean, dry, and warm. A therapist will typically use a lubricant to reduce friction on the skin during massage. The primary exception to using lubricant would be when performing friction massage. The lubricant should be applied to the therapist's hands and gently warmed by rubbing the hands together prior to patient application.

The therapist must be positioned in an efficient posture during treatment to maintain the required pressure and rhythm based on the goals of treatment. The massage should start with the effleurage technique. The amount of time required for each treatment is dependent on the body part and therapeutic goal. Generally, the back requires 15 minutes as opposed to a smaller area or joint that requires 8-10 minutes. The intensity should progressively increase and then decrease, using effleurage again to end the treatment session.

Equipment, Devices, and Technologies; Therapeutic Modalities Essentials

Equipment, Devices, and Technologies

1. Communication between the therapist and patient is essential in performing safe and effective mobility tasks.
2. A patient who is dependent should be repositioned at least every two hours to prevent skin breakdown.
3. Shear and friction forces should be minimized during mobility and transfer tasks to prevent integumentary injury.
4. The level of physical assistance required during a mobility or transfer task is a function of the amount of assistance the therapist must provide in order for the patient to safely complete the task.
5. Levels of physical assistance for transfers include independent, supervision, contact guard, minimal assist, moderate assist, maximal assist, and dependent.
6. Dependent transfers may be performed either with physical assistance from staff or a mechanical lift device.
7. Dependent transfers include three-person carry/lift, two-person lift, dependent squat pivot transfer, and hydraulic lift.
8. Assisted transfers include sliding board transfer, stand pivot transfer, and stand step transfer.
9. The adult standard wheelchair seat specifications are 18 inches wide, 16 inches deep, and 20 inches high.
10. A patient's physical and mental abilities and limitations must be considered when making recommendations for wheelchair prescription.
11. Parallel bars provide the most stable environment for patients who are beginning to initiate standing and ambulation activities.
12. Levels of weight bearing include non-weight bearing, toe touch weight bearing, partial weight bearing, weight bearing as tolerated, and full weight bearing.
13. An appropriately fit walker, crutches or cane requires 20-25 degrees of elbow flexion.
14. A straight cane is not appropriate for patients who are partial weight bearing.
15. When using an assistive device, the gait pattern utilized should be dependent on the patient's weight bearing status and overall condition.
16. Gait patterns include two-point, three-point, four-point, swing-to, and swing-through.
17. Guidelines for guarding a patient during ambulation activities may require modification or the assist of a second therapist depending on the patient's size, impairments, and abilities.
18. During stair training, the physical therapist should be positioned behind the patient while ascending and in front of the patient when descending.
19. An arterial line is a monitoring device consisting of a catheter that is inserted into an artery. The device is used to measure blood pressure or to obtain blood samples.
20. A nasal cannula is a commonly used device for oxygen therapy, capable of delivering up to six liters of oxygen per minute.
21. A suprapubic catheter is an indwelling urinary catheter that is surgically inserted directly into the patient's bladder.
22. Doppler ultrasonography is a non-invasive test that evaluates blood flow in the major veins, arteries, and cerebrovascular system.
23. Magnetic resonance imaging is a non-invasive technique that utilizes magnetic fields to produce an image of bone and soft tissue.

Therapeutic Modalities

24. Methods of heat transfer include conduction, convection, conversion, evaporation, and radiation.
25. Ice massage should be applied using small, overlapping circles or strokes. An area 10 centimeters by 15 centimeters can be covered in 5 to 10 minutes.
26. Patients typically progress through a series of different sensations during ice massage including intense cold, burning, aching, and analgesia.
27. Ice massage typically cools tissues more rapidly than other types of cryotherapy such as an ice pack or ice bag. The cold pack should be applied over a moist cold towel to increase the initial magnitude of cooling.
28. Cold baths allow for circumferential contact with the cooling agent, however, they require the lower extremity to be in a gravity-dependent position.

Equipment, Devices, and Technologies; Therapeutic Modalities Essentials

29. Controlled cold compression units combine cryotherapy and compression. The units allow therapists to precisely control the temperature of the cold and the amount of compression.
30. A Cryo Cuff is a commercially available device used to provide mild cooling and compression. The device consists of a nylon sleeve connected to a container using a plastic tube.
31. Vapocoolant sprays produce very rapid cooling through evaporation with temperature changes occurring only in the epidermis. The primary use of vapocoolant sprays is to treat trigger points.
32. Relative changes in surface tissue temperature will be influenced by the intensity of the heating agent, time of the exposure, and thermal conductivity of the tissues.
33. Superficial heating agents produce the largest temperature elevation within 0.5 centimeters from the skin surface.
34. Application of a hot pack requires six to eight towel layers. If commercial hot pack covers are used, they typically are equivalent to two or three layers of towels.
35. A patient should not lie on top of a hot pack since this tends to remove water from the hot pack. This can result in an accelerated rate of heating and an increased risk of burns.
36. Fluidotherapy is a superficial heating agent that generates dry heat through forced convection by circulating warm air and small cellulose particles.
37. An infrared lamp produces superficial heating of tissue through radiant heat. Optimal absorption occurs when the infrared radiation strikes the target area perpendicularly.
38. Paraffin has a low specific heat which enhances a patient's ability to tolerate heat compared to heat from water at the same temperature.
39. Paraffin can be applied using the dip-wrap method, dip-reimmersion method or paint application method.
40. Thermal effects of ultrasound include acceleration of metabolic rate, modulation of pain, reduction of muscle spasm, decreased joint stiffness, alteration of nerve conduction velocity, increased circulation, and increased soft tissue extensibility.
41. Nonthermal effects of ultrasound include increased cell and skin membrane permeability, increased intracellular calcium levels, facilitation of tissue repair, and promotion of normal cell function.
42. A frequency setting of 1 MHz when using ultrasound is used for deeper tissues (up to five centimeters) while a setting of 3 MHz is used for more superficial tissues (one to two centimeters).
43. An area two to three times the size of the ultrasound transducer typically requires a duration of five minutes.
44. The duty cycle of ultrasound is calculated by dividing the time during which sound is delivered (on time) by the total time (on time + off time) and multiplying the result by 100.
45. Phonophoresis is not likely to produce burns or damage skin since the technique transports whole molecules instead of ions into the body's tissue.
46. Shortwave diathermy can be delivered in a continuous or pulsed mode. A pulsed mode is typically utilized to attain nonthermal effects while a continuous mode is used for thermal effects.
47. The patient's subjective heat sensation response is used to estimate the amount of energy delivered and corresponding temperature increase with continuous diathermy.
48. The minimal erythemal dose refers to the smallest dose of ultraviolet light needed to produce an area of mild redness within eight hours of ultraviolet exposure that disappears within 24 hours after exposure.
49. The properties of water essential for physical therapists to understand include buoyancy, resistance, specific gravity, specific heat, total drag force, and viscosity.
50. Hydrotherapy can be administered using a variety of equipment including an extremity tank, lowboy tank, highboy tank, Hubbard tank, and therapeutic pool.
51. A flexed position of the spine results in greater separation of the posterior structures including the facet joints and intervertebral foramen when using mechanical lumbar traction. An extended position of the spine results in greater separation of the anterior structures including the disk spaces.
52. Static traction may be desirable for more acute conditions or if the patient's symptoms are slightly exaggerated by movement.

Equipment, Devices, and Technologies; Therapeutic Modalities Essentials

53. Intermittent traction may be desirable for joint mobilization or for patients who cannot tolerate static traction.
54. A force of 25% of a patient's body weight may be adequate to treat muscle spasm, disk protrusion, and stretch soft tissue when using mechanical lumbar traction. A force of up to 50% of the body weight is required for actual separation of the vertebrae.
55. A supine position is used more often for cervical traction since the traction force does not have to overcome the force exerted by gravity.
56. A force of 7-10% of a patient's body weight (11-15 pounds) may be adequate to treat muscle spasm, stretch soft tissue, and reduce disk protrusion using cervical traction.
57. A force of 13-20% of a patient's body weight (20-30 pounds) may be necessary for joint distraction using cervical traction.
58. Compression garments are most often used to control edema, limit scar formation after burns, and improve venous circulation in active patients.
59. An intermittent pneumatic compression pump is primarily used to reduce chronic or post-traumatic edema and requires adjusting the parameters of inflation pressure, on/off ratio, and total treatment time.
60. A patient's joint must be aligned correctly with the axis of the CPM to receive safe and effective treatment. A rate of two cycles per minute allows most patients to tolerate the CPM without difficulty.
61. For an action potential to be evoked using electrical stimulation, the amplitude of the stimulus and pulse duration must be sufficient to overcome the established threshold.
62. Direct current is characterized by a constant flow of electrons from the anode to the cathode (for a period of greater than one second) without interruption.
63. Alternating current is characterized by polarity that continuously changes from positive to negative with a change in direction of current flow.
64. Pulsatile current is characterized by the non-continuous flow of direct or alternating current.
65. Small electrodes exhibit increased current density, increased impedance, and decreased current flow. Large electrodes exhibit decreased current density, decreased impedance, and increased current flow.
66. The effectiveness of a current to target specific excitable tissue is dependent on adequate intensity to reach the threshold, current onset fast enough to reduce accommodation (i.e., rise time), and duration long enough to exceed the capacitance of the tissue (i.e., phase duration).
67. Neuromuscular electrical stimulation (NMES) is a technique used to facilitate skeletal muscle activity. Functional electrical stimulation (FES) uses electrical stimulation to create or enhance the performance of a functional activity.
68. The most commonly used modes for TENS include conventional, acupuncture-like, brief intense, and noxious.
69. Interferential current combines two medium frequency alternating waveforms that are biphasic. Interferential current is most often used for pain relief, increased circulation, and muscle stimulation.
70. Iontophoresis is based on the theory that like charges repel and as a result, ions in a solution of similar charge will move away from the electrical source and into the body. The rate of ion delivery is determined by the concentration of the ion, the pH of the solution, the current density, and the duration of the treatment.
71. The likelihood of a burn using iontophoresis can be decreased by increasing the size of the cathode relative to the anode, decreasing the current density, and increasing the space between the electrodes.
72. Indwelling electrodes (i.e., intramuscular EMG) are used for small or deep muscles or when there is a need to record a single motor unit potential. Surface electrodes (i.e., biofeedback) are used to monitor larger muscle groups.
73. Biofeedback can be utilized to receive information related to motor performance, kinesthetic performance or physiological response. A high sensitivity setting will detect extremely small amounts of electrical activity while a low sensitivity setting will detect only large amounts of electrical activity.
74. Descriptive characteristics of massage techniques include direction, duration, frequency, pressure, rhythm, and speed.
75. Commonly used massage techniques include effleurage, friction, petrissage, tapotement, and vibration.

Equipment, Devices, and Technologies; Therapeutic Modalities Proficiencies

Equipment, Devices, and Technologies Proficiencies

1. Levels of Physical Assistance

Identify the level of physical assistance associated with each of the descriptions. Answers must be selected from the Word Bank and can be used only once.

Word Bank: dependent, independent, maximal assist, minimal assist, moderate assist, supervision

Level	Description
a	The patient requires a therapist to observe throughout the completion of the task.
b	The therapist exerts all of the effort to perform the task.
c	The patient requires 50% assist from the therapist to complete the task.
d	The patient does not require any assistance to complete the task.
e	The patient requires 25% assist from the therapist to complete the task.
f	The patient requires 75% assist from the therapist to complete the task.

2. Wheelchair Measurements

Identify the most appropriate wheelchair component associated with each of the obtained measurements. Answers must be selected from the Word Bank and can be used only once. Secondly, identify the final value in inches for each component based on the obtained measurement.

Word Bank: armrest height, back height, seat depth, seat height, seat width

Component	Obtained Measurement	Final Value
a	7 inches from the seat of the chair to the olecranon process with the elbow flexed to 90 degrees.	b
c	18 inches from the user's heel to the popliteal fold.	d
e	18 inches from the posterior buttock, along the lateral thigh to the popliteal fold.	f
g	20 inches from the seat of the chair to the floor of the axilla with the user's shoulder flexed to 90 degrees.	h
i	17 inches represents the widest aspect of the user's buttocks, hips or thighs.	j

Equipment, Devices, and Technologies; Therapeutic Modalities Proficiencies

Equipment, Devices, and Technologies Proficiencies

3. Levels of Weight Bearing

Identify the level of weight bearing associated with each of the descriptions. Answers must be selected from the Word Bank and can be used only once.

Word Bank: full weight bearing, non-weight bearing, partial weight bearing, toe touch weight bearing, weight bearing as tolerated

Level	Description
a	A patient using axillary crutches is able to transmit approximately 25% of their weight through the involved lower extremity.
b	A patient uses a single cane during ambulation.
c	A patient is permitted to vary the amount of weight bearing based on their relative comfort level and the amount of pain present.
d	A patient is unable to transmit weight through the involved lower extremity, but may place a portion of the involved foot on the ground to assist with balance.
e	A patient is unable to transmit weight through the involved extremity or have the foot come in contact with the floor.

4. Assistive Device Selection

Identify the most appropriate assistive device for each patient based on the supplied description. Answers must be selected from the Word Bank and can be used only once.

Word Bank: axillary crutches, cane, Lofstrand crutches, parallel bars, walker

Level	Description
a	A 34-year-old male in an acute care hospital prepares to ambulate for the first time following a compound tibia fracture treated with internal fixation.
b	An 83-year-old female that often experiences transient periods of dizziness while walking in the home.
c	A 21-year-old female that is toe touch weight bearing following a grade II knee sprain.
d	A 74-year-old female that experiences subtle balance changes when walking on uneven ground.
e	A 28-year-old male that is partial weight bearing on the right ankle following an ankle sprain. The patient is unable to tolerate pressure in the axillary region due to recent removal of a benign cyst.

Equipment, Devices, and Technologies; Therapeutic Modalities Proficiencies

Equipment, Devices, and Technologies Proficiencies

5. Wheelchair Frame

Identify the most appropriate wheelchair frame for each patient based on the supplied description. Answers must be selected from the Word Bank and can be used only once.

Word Bank: amputee frame, hemi frame, one-hand drive frame, power wheelchair frame, reclining frame, ultralight frame

Frame	Description
a	Patient is able to independently propel the wheelchair, however, the center of gravity is shifted posteriorly.
b	Patient is able to independently propel the wheelchair using one or both of the lower extremities.
c	Patient is involved in sports activities without the need for postural supports.
d	Patient is able to independently propel the wheelchair using one upper extremity.
e	Patient is unable to independently propel the wheelchair.
f	Patient is unable to sit upright for extended periods of time.

Equipment, Devices, and Technologies; Therapeutic Modalities Proficiencies

Equipment, Devices, and Technologies Proficiencies

6. Equipment and Devices Basics

Mark each statement as True or False. If the statement is False, correct the statement in the space provided.

True/False	Statement
a	A dependent squat pivot transfer is used to transfer a patient who cannot stand independently and is unable to bear any weight through the lower extremities.
Correction:	
b	The standard adult wheelchair has 16 inches of seat width, 18 inches of seat depth, and 20 inches of seat height.
Correction:	
c	Wheelchair seat depth is determined by measuring from the posterior buttock, along the lateral thigh to the popliteal fold and adding two inches.
Correction:	
d	An appropriately fit axillary crutch should result in the patient having 20-25 degrees of elbow flexion when grasping the hand grip.
Correction:	
e	A custom molded wheelchair seat is warranted for patients with pelvic obliquity or fixed asymmetrical deformity.
Correction:	

Equipment, Devices, and Technologies; Therapeutic Modalities Proficiencies

Equipment, Devices, and Technologies Proficiencies

True/False	Statement
f	A cane can be used to improve balance in patients that are partial weight bearing.
Correction:	
g	Lofstrand crutches can be used with a variety of gait patterns including four-point, swing-to, and swing-through.
Correction:	
h	A gastric tube is a plastic tube inserted through a nostril that extends into the stomach.
Correction:	
i	A suprapubic catheter is applied over the shaft of the penis and is held in place by a padded strap or adhesive tape.
Correction:	
j	Myelography utilizes a contrast medium that is injected into the epidural space by spinal puncture.
Correction:	

Equipment, Devices, and Technologies; Therapeutic Modalities Proficiencies

Therapeutic Modalities Proficiencies

7. Heat Transfer

Identify the type of heat transfer utilized by each therapeutic modality. Answers should be selected from the Word Bank. Answers can be used more than once.

Word Bank: conduction, convection, conversion, evaporation, radiation

Modality	Heat Transfer
fluidotherapy	a
paraffin	b
vapocoolant spray	c
hot pack	d
whirlpool	e
ultrasound	f
diathermy	g
ice massage	h
ultraviolet light	i

8. Therapeutic Effects of Cryotherapy

Potential therapeutic effects of cryotherapy are listed. Mark each statement as True or False.

True/False	Effects
a	increased metabolic rate
b	decreased nerve conduction velocity
c	decreased tone
d	decreased pain threshold
e	decreased blood flow to the treatment area

Equipment, Devices, and Technologies; Therapeutic Modalities Proficiencies

Therapeutic Modalities Proficiencies

9. Indications/Contraindications of Cryotherapy

Mark each condition as an indication or contraindication of cryotherapy.

Indication/Contraindication	Condition
a	bursitis
b	infection
c	cold urticaria
d	tendonitis
e	tenosynovitis
f	skin anesthesia
g	Raynaud's phenomenon
h	muscle spasm

10. Cooling Agents Matching

Assign each of the descriptions to the most appropriate cooling agent. More than one of the descriptions may apply to each cooling agent. The number of desired responses for each cooling agent is identified in parentheses.

1. Effective for small and irregular contoured areas
2. Allows simultaneous application of cold and compression
3. Short duration time (i.e., 10 minutes or less)
4. Unable to observe target area during treatment
5. Difficult to apply spray uniformly
6. Requires the extremity to be in a gravity dependent position

Cooling Agent	Description
cold bath	a (1)
controlled cold compression unit	b (2)
Cryo Cuff	c (2)
ice massage	d (2)
vapocoolant spray	e (1)

Equipment, Devices, and Technologies; Therapeutic Modalities Proficiencies

Therapeutic Modalities Proficiencies

11. Therapeutic Effects of Superficial Thermotherapy

Potential therapeutic effects of superficial thermotherapy are listed. Mark each statement as True or False.

True/False	Effects
a	increased tone
b	decreased collagen extensibility
c	increased pain threshold
d	decreased nerve conduction velocity
e	increased metabolic rate

12. Indications/Contraindications of Superficial Thermotherapy

Mark each condition as an indication or contraindication of superficial thermotherapy.

Indication/Contraindication	Condition
a	decreased range of motion
b	over an area of malignancy
c	subacute or chronic pain
d	muscle spasm
e	arterial disease
f	subacute or chronic inflammatory conditions
g	peripheral vascular disease
h	thrombophlebitis

Equipment, Devices, and Technologies; Therapeutic Modalities Proficiencies

Therapeutic Modalities Proficiencies

13. Heating Agents Matching

Assign each of the descriptions to the most appropriate heating agent. More than one of the descriptions may apply to each heating agent. The number of desired responses for each heating agent is identified in parentheses.

1. Can produce thermal and nonthermal effects
2. Provides a moist, comfortable heat
3. Tends to dry skin
4. Useful for desensitization of the distal extremities
5. Does not require direct contact with the treatment area
6. May serve to moisturize the skin
7. Capable of reaching deeper tissues

Heating Agent	Description
diathermy	a (2)
fluidotherapy	b (1)
hot pack	c (1)
infrared lamp	d (2)
paraffin	e (1)
ultrasound	f (2)

Equipment, Devices, and Technologies; Therapeutic Modalities Proficiencies

Therapeutic Modalities Proficiencies

14. Parameters and Procedures

Mark each statement as True or False. If the statement is False, correct the statement in the space provided.

True/False	Statement
a	The Cryo Cuff should be held approximately 6-8 inches above the level of the sleeve during filling.
Correction:	
b	A vapocoolant spray should be applied perpendicular to the direction of the muscle fibers.
Correction:	
c	6-8 layers of towels are necessary for hot pack application.
Correction:	
d	Ultrasound frequency of 3 MHz heats deep tissue (up to 5 cm), while 1 MHz heats superficial tissue (1-2 cm).
Correction:	
e	The temperature of a paraffin bath should be maintained between 107 and 112 degrees Fahrenheit.
Correction:	
f	A 20% duty cycle with an on time of 1 second would have an off time of 5 seconds.
Correction:	
g	An area two to three times the size of the ultrasound transducer typically requires a treatment duration of five minutes.
Correction:	

Equipment, Devices, and Technologies; Therapeutic Modalities Proficiencies

Therapeutic Modalities Proficiencies

True/False	Statement
h	A patient's subjective heat sensation response is an important factor when determining the amount of energy delivered with diathermy.
Correction:	
i	The minimal erythemal dose is characterized by a dose that results in erythema that lasts 1-3 days with clear redness and mild desquamation.
Correction:	
j	Buoyancy refers to the magnitude of the cohesive forces between the molecules specific to the fluid.
Correction:	
k	Hot packs are required to be in place for 5-10 minutes to achieve the desired therapeutic effects.
Correction:	
l	An infrared lamp's primary therapeutic effect is the enhancement of deep tissue healing.
Correction:	
m	During application of fluidotherapy, patients can perform active exercises of the distal extremity.
Correction:	
n	The rate of tissue cooling following heating with diathermy is significantly slower than the rate of tissue cooling with ultrasound.
Correction:	
o	Ultraviolet light is absorbed 1-2 centimeters into the skin.
Correction:	

Equipment, Devices, and Technologies; Therapeutic Modalities Proficiencies

Therapeutic Modalities Proficiencies

15. Electrotherapy Terminology

Identify the electrotherapy term most closely associated with the supplied description. Answers must be selected from the Word Bank and can be used only once.

Word Bank: alternating current, current, direct current, frequency, phase duration, pulsatile current, pulse duration, resistance, rise time, voltage

Terminology	Description
a	The time it takes for the current to move from zero to the peak intensity within each phase.
b	Characterized by a constant flow of electrons from the anode (i.e., positive electrode) to the cathode (i.e., negative electrode) for a period of greater than one second without interruption.
c	The number of pulses delivered through each channel per second.
d	The ability of a material to oppose the flow of ions through it.
e	Characterized by polarity that continuously changes from positive to negative with the change in the direction of current flow.
f	The amount of time it takes for two phases of a pulse with biphasic current.
g	A measure of the electromotive force or the electrical potential difference.
h	Characterized by the non-continuous flow of direct or alternating current.
i	The directed flow of charge from one place to another.
j	The amount of time it takes for one phase of a pulse.

Equipment, Devices, and Technologies; Therapeutic Modalities Proficiencies

Therapeutic Modalities Proficiencies

16. Electrical Current and Electrode Size

Identify the relevant influence of small electrodes versus large electrodes on selected elements of electrical current. Place the word "increased" or "decreased" in each of the blank cells.

	Small Electrodes	Large Electrodes
current density	a	b
impedance	c	d
current flow	e	f

17. TENS Parameters

Identify the specific TENS technique most closely associated with the supplied description. The specific technique should be selected from the Word Bank. A specific technique can be used more than once or not at all.

Word Bank: acupuncture-like, brief intense, conventional, noxious

Technique	Description
a	characterized by high pulse frequency and short pulse duration
b	often administered with a small probe applicator
c	the duration is 30-60 seconds for each point
d	the amplitude is sufficient for strong paresthesia
e	characterized by high density current that is described as uncomfortable or painful
f	the amplitude is sufficient for a sensory response
g	characterized by high pulse frequency and long pulse duration with moderate current amplitude

Equipment, Devices, and Technologies; Therapeutic Modalities Proficiencies

Therapeutic Modalities Proficiencies

18. Iontophoresis

Complete the blank cells with the correct information related to each medication. Answers should be selected from the Word Bank and can be used more than once. The number of desired responses is indicated in parentheses.

Word Bank: Indications: analgesia, calcific deposits, dermal ulcers, fungal infection, inflammation, muscle and joint pain
Polarity: positive, negative

Medication	Indications	Polarity
acetic acid	a (1)	b (1)
copper sulfate	c (1)	d (1)
dexamethasone	e (1)	f (1)
lidocaine	g (2)	h (1)
salicylates	i (1)	j (1)
zinc oxide	k (1)	l (1)

19. Massage Techniques

Identify the specific massage technique most closely associated with the supplied description. Answers must be selected from the Word Bank and can be used only once.

Word Bank: effleurage, friction, petrissage, tapotement, vibration

Technique	Description
a	A technique described as kneading, where the muscle is squeezed and rolled under the therapist's hands.
b	A technique that provides stimulation through rapid alternating movements such as tapping, hacking, cupping, and slapping.
c	A technique characterized by a light stroke that produces a reflexive response.
d	A technique that incorporates small circular motions over a trigger point or muscle spasm.
e	A technique that places the therapist's hands or fingers firmly over an area and utilizes a rapid, shaking motion.

Equipment, Devices, and Technologies; Therapeutic Modalities Answer Key

Equipment, Devices, and Technologies

1. Levels of Physical Assistance

a. supervision
b. dependent
c. moderate assist
d. independent
e. minimal assist
f. maximal assist

2. Wheelchair Measurements

a. armrest height
b. 8 inches
c. seat height
d. 20 inches
e. seat depth
f. 16 inches
g. back height
h. 16 inches
i. seat width
j. 19 inches

3. Levels of Weight Bearing

a. partial weight bearing
b. full weight bearing
c. weight bearing as tolerated
d. toe touch weight bearing
e. non-weight bearing

4. Assistive Device Selection

a. parallel bars
b. walker
c. axillary crutches
d. cane
e. Lofstrand crutches

5. Wheelchair Frame

a. amputee frame
b. hemi frame
c. ultralight frame
d. one-hand drive frame
e. power wheelchair frame
f. reclining frame

6. Equipment and Devices Basics*

a. FALSE: Correction: A dependent squat pivot transfer is used to transfer a patient who cannot stand independently, but is able to bear some weight through the trunk and lower extremities.
b. FALSE: Correction: The standard adult wheelchair has 18 inches of width, 16 inches of depth, and 20 inches of height.
c. FALSE: Correction: Wheelchair seat depth is determined by measuring from the posterior buttock, along the lateral thigh to the popliteal fold and subtracting two inches.
d. TRUE
e. TRUE
f. FALSE: Correction: A cane can be used to improve balance, however, does not permit partial weight bearing.
g. TRUE
h. FALSE: Correction: A gastric tube is a tube inserted through a small incision in the abdomen into the stomach.
i. FALSE: Correction: A suprapubic catheter is an indwelling urinary catheter that is surgically inserted directly into a patient's bladder.
j. TRUE

*The correction presented for each false statement is an example of several possible corrections.

Therapeutic Modalities

7. Heat Transfer

a. convection
b. conduction
c. evaporation
d. conduction
e. convection
f. conversion
g. conversion
h. conduction
i. radiation

8. Therapeutic Effects of Cryotherapy

a. FALSE
b. TRUE
c. TRUE
d. FALSE
e. TRUE

Equipment, Devices, and Technologies; Therapeutic Modalities Answer Key

9. Indications/Contraindications of Cryotherapy

a. indication
b. contraindication
c. contraindication
d. indication
e. indication
f. contraindication
g. contraindication
h. indication

10. Cooling Agents Matching

a. 6
b. 2,4
c. 2,4
d. 1,3
e. 5

11. Therapeutic Effects of Superficial Thermotherapy

a. FALSE
b. FALSE
c. TRUE
d. FALSE
e. TRUE

12. Indications/Contraindications of Superficial Thermotherapy

a. indication
b. contraindication
c. indication
d. indication
e. contraindication
f. indication
g. contraindication
h. contraindication

13. Heating Agents Matching

a. 1,7
b. 4
c. 2
d. 3,5
e. 6
f. 1,7

14. Parameters and Procedures*

a. FALSE - Correction: The Cryo Cuff should be held 15-18 inches above the level of the sleeve during filling.
b. FALSE - Correction: A vapocoolant spray should be applied parallel to the direction of the muscle fibers.
c. TRUE
d. FALSE - Correction: Ultrasound frequency of 3 MHz heats superficial tissue (1-2 cm), while 1 MHz heats deep tissue (up to 5 cm).
e. FALSE - Correction: The temperature of a paraffin bath should be maintained between 113 and 122 degrees Fahrenheit.
f. FALSE - Correction: A 20% duty cycle with an on time of 1 second would have an off time of 4 seconds (duty cycle = on time / on + off time x 100).
g. TRUE
h. TRUE
i. FALSE - Correction: First-degree erythemal dose is characterized by a dose that results in erythema that lasts 1-3 days with clear redness and mild desquamation.
j. FALSE - Correction: The supplied definition describes viscosity. The principle of buoyancy states that there is an upward force on the body when immersed in water equal to the amount of water that has been displaced by the body.
k. FALSE - Correction: Hot packs are required to be in place for 15-20 minutes to achieve desired therapeutic effects.
l. FALSE - Correction: An infrared lamp's main therapeutic effect is the enhancement of superficial tissue healing.
m. TRUE
n. TRUE
o. FALSE - Correction: Ultraviolet light is absorbed 1-2 millimeters into the skin.

*The correction presented for each false statement is an example of several possible corrections.

Equipment, Devices, and Technologies; Therapeutic Modalities Answer Key

15. Electrotherapy Terminology

a. rise time
b. direct current
c. frequency
d. resistance
e. alternating current
f. pulse duration
g. voltage
h. pulsatile current
i. current
j. phase duration

16. Electrical Current and Electrode Size

a. increased
b. decreased
c. increased
d. decreased
e. decreased
f. increased

17. TENS Parameters

a. conventional
b. noxious
c. noxious
d. brief intense
e. noxious
f. conventional
g. brief intense

18. Iontophoresis

a. calcific deposits
b. negative
c. fungal infection
d. positive
e. inflammation
f. negative
g. analgesia, inflammation
h. positive
i. muscle and joint pain
j. negative
k. dermal ulcers
l. positive

19. Massage Techniques

a. petrissage
b. tapotement
c. effleurage
d. friction
e. vibration

Equipment, Devices, and Technologies; Therapeutic Modalities References

Equipment, Devices, and Technologies References

1. Fairchild S, O'Shea R, Washington R. ***Pierson and Fairchild's Principles and Techniques of Patient Care***. Sixth Edition. Elsevier. 2018.
2. ***Nurse's 3-Minute Clinical Reference***. Second Edition. Lippincott Williams & Wilkins. 2007.
3. Minor M, Minor S. ***Patient Care Skills***. Seventh Edition. Prentice Hall. 2014.
4. Roy S, Wolf S, Scalzitti, D. ***The Rehabilitation Specialist's Handbook***. Fourth Edition. F.A. Davis Company. 2013.
5. Batavia M. ***The Wheelchair Evaluation: A Clinician's Guide***. Second Edition. Jones and Bartlett Publishers. 2010.
6. Cook AM, Hussey SM, Polgar JM. ***Cook & Hussey's Assistive Technologies: Principles and Practice.*** Mosby Elsevier. 2008.
7. Olson DA, DeRuyter F. ***A Clinician's Guide to Assistive Technology***. Mosby Elsevier. 2002.
8. Tan J. ***Practical Manual of Physical Medicine and Rehabilitation***. Second Edition. Mosby Inc. 2006.
9. Pendleton H, Schultz-Krohn W. ***Occupational Therapy Practice Skills for Physical Dysfunction***. Sixth Edition. Mosby. 2006.
10. Cameron M, Monroe L. ***Physical Rehabilitation: Evidence-Based Examination, Evaluation, and Intervention***. W.B. Saunders Company. 2007.
11. Prentice W, Voight M. ***Techniques in Musculoskeletal Rehabilitation***. McGraw-Hill Inc. 2008.
12. Paz J, West MP. ***Acute Care Handbook for Physical Therapists***. Fourth Edition. W.B. Saunders Company. 2014.
13. Hillegass E, Sadowsky S. ***Essentials of Cardiopulmonary Physical Therapy***. Fourth Edition. W.B. Saunders Company. 2017.
14. Magee D. ***Orthopedic Physical Assessment***. Sixth Edition. W.B. Saunders Company. 2014.
15. Dutton M. ***Orthopaedic Examination, Evaluation, and Intervention***. Fourth Edition. McGraw-Hill Inc. 2017.

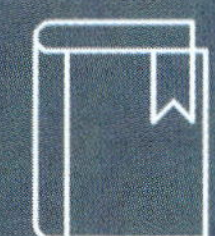

Equipment, Devices, and Technologies; Therapeutic Modalities References

Therapeutic Modalities References

16. Cameron M. ***Physical Agents in Rehabilitation: An Evidence-Based Approach to Practice.*** Fifth Edition. Elsevier. 2018.
17. Bellew J, Michlovitz S, Nolan T. ***Modalities for Therapeutic Intervention***. Sixth Edition. F.A. Davis Company. 2016.
18. Prentice W. ***Therapeutic Modalities in Rehabilitation***. Fourth Edition. McGraw-Hill Inc. 2011.
19. Bracciano A. ***Physical Agent Modalities. Theories and Application for the Occupational Therapist***. Second Edition. Slack Inc. 2008.
20. Denegar C. ***Therapeutic Modalities for Musculoskeletal Injuries***. Second Edition. Human Kinetics. 2005.
21. Belanger AY. ***Evidence-Based Guide to Therapeutic Physical Agents***. Lippincott Williams & Wilkins. 2003.
22. Ruoti RG, Morris DM. ***Aquatic Rehabilitation***. Lippincott Williams & Wilkins. 1997.
23. Cameron M, Monroe L. ***Physical Rehabilitation: Evidence Based Examination, Evaluation, and Intervention***. W.B. Saunders Company. 2007.
24. Nelson R, Hayes K, Currier D. ***Clinical Electrotherapy***. Third Edition. Appleton & Lange. 1999.
25. Kitchen S. ***Electrotherapy. Evidence-Based Practice***. Churchill Livingstone. 2002.
26. Robinson A, Snyder-Mackler L. ***Clinical Electrophysiology***. Third Edition. Williams & Wilkins. 2007.
27. De Domenico G, Wood E. ***Beard's Massage***. Fifth Edition. W.B. Saunders Company. 2007.
28. Fritz S. ***Mosby's Fundamentals of Therapeutic Massage***. Second Edition. Mosby, Inc. 2000.
29. Houglum P. ***Therapeutic Exercise for Athletic Injuries***. Human Kinetics. 2001.
30. McKinnis L. ***Fundamentals of Musculoskeletal Imaging***. Fourth Edition. F.A. Davis. 2014.

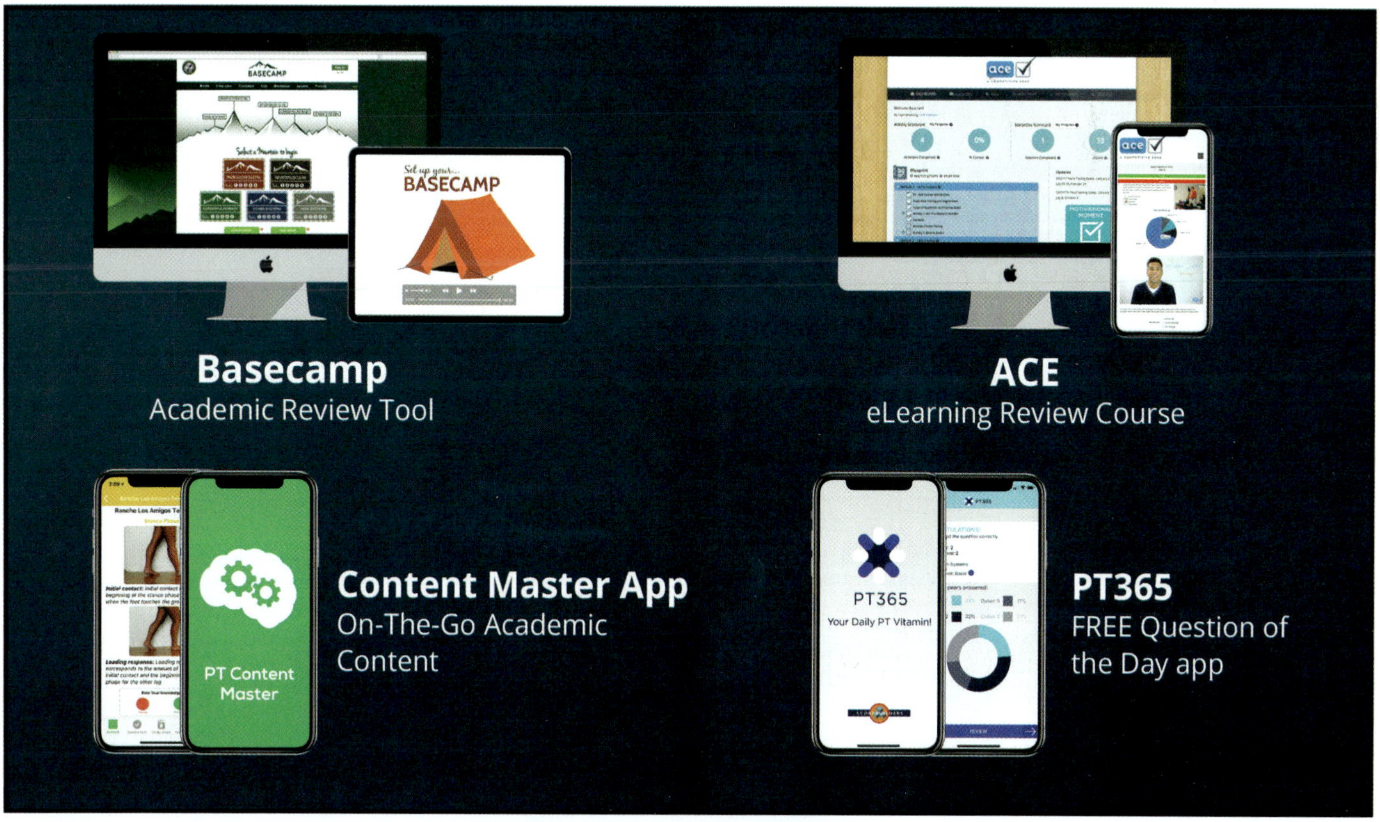

9

SAFETY AND PROTECTION; PROFESSIONAL RESPONSIBILITIES; RESEARCH

Scott Giles
Michael Fillyaw

Safety and Protection represent approximately 5 - 6 questions (2.5% - 3%) on the NPTE-PT.

Professional Responsibilities represent approximately 4 - 5 questions (2% - 2.5%) on the NPTE-PT.

Research and Evidence-based Practice represent approximately 3 - 5 questions (1.5% - 2.5%) on the NPTE-PT.

Contributors

Shawn Paquette

CHAPTER 9

Safety and Protection; Professional Responsibilities; Research

Safety and Protection

Infection Control

Infectious Disease

Infectious disease is defined as a condition where an organism invades a host and develops a parasitic relationship with the host. The invasion and multiplication of the microorganisms produces an immune response with subsequent signs and symptoms.

Potential Symptoms of Infectious Disease	
• Fever, chill, malaise	• Headache
• Rash, skin lesion	• Stiff neck
• Bleeding from gums	• Myalgia
• Joint effusion	• Convulsions
• Diarrhea	• Confusion
• Frequency, urgency	• Tachycardia
• Cough, sore throat	• Hypotension
• Nausea, vomiting	

Chain of Transmission for Infection

1. Causative agent, bacteria, pathogen, virus
2. Reservoir of humans, animals, inanimate objects
3. Portal of exit through blood, intestinal tract, respiratory tract, skin/mucous membrane, open lesion, excretions, tears or semen
4. Transmission through airborne, contact, vector, vehicle or droplet modes
5. Portal of entry through non-intact skin, blood, mucous membrane, inhalation, ingestion or percutaneous injection
6. Susceptible host regarding age, health status, nutrition, and environmental status

Standard Precautions[3,4]

Standard precautions are guidelines designed for the care of all patients regardless of infection or diagnosis. These precautions apply to blood, all body fluids, secretions, and excretions (except sweat), nonintact skin, and mucous membranes. They protect healthcare providers from infection and prevent the spread of infection between patients.

Hand Hygiene

Alcohol-based hand sanitizers are the preferred method for cleaning your hands in most situations since they are the most effective at decontaminating the hands. Healthcare providers should wash their hands with soap and water whenever they are visibly dirty, before eating, and after using the restroom.

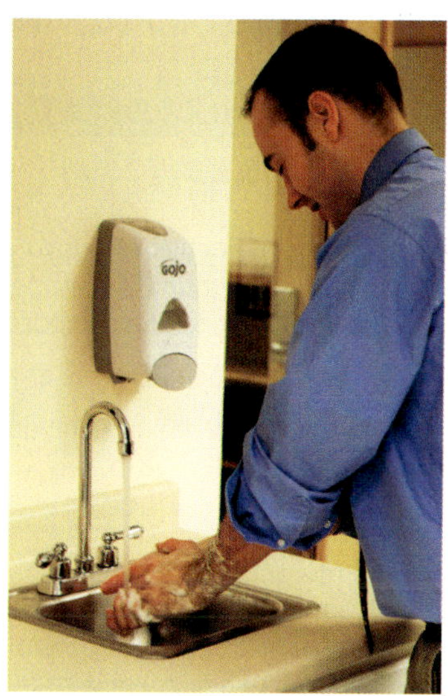

Fig. 9-1: A therapist washing his hands prior to initiating treatment.

Use an Alcohol-Based Hand Sanitizer

- ✓ Before and after touching a patient or their environment.
- ✓ Before performing an aseptic task (e.g., wound care) or handling invasive medical devices.
- ✓ Before moving from work on a soiled body site to a clean body site.
- ✓ After contact with blood, body fluids or contaminated surfaces.
- ✓ After glove removal.

When using alcohol-based hand sanitizer:

- Remove jewelry from the hands and wrists.
- Put the sanitizer on your hands and rub your hands together.
- Cover all surfaces until your hands feel dry (around 20 seconds).

Use Soap and Water

✓ When hands are visibly dirty or soiled.

✓ After caring for a person with known or suspected infectious diarrhea.

✓ After known or suspected exposure to spores (e.g., C. difficile).

When using soap and water:

- Remove jewelry from the hands and wrists.
- Wet your hands with warm water, then apply the soap to your hands.
- Rub your hands together briskly for at least 20-30 seconds, covering all surfaces of the hands and fingers.
- Rinse your hands with water and use disposable towels to dry, then use a clean towel to turn off the faucet.

Personal Protective Equipment (PPE)

General principles

✓ Wear PPE when patient interaction may involve contact with blood or body fluids. The extent of PPE usage should be proportional to the level of anticipated exposure.

✓ Before leaving the patient's room, remove and discard PPE.

✓ Prevent contamination of clothing and skin during the process of removing PPE.

Gloves

✓ Wear gloves any time contact with contaminated items, blood, body fluids, secretions, excretions (except sweat), mucous membranes, nonintact skin or potentially contaminated intact skin (e.g., patient with fecal/urinary incontinence) may occur.

✓ Gloves are not a substitute for hand hygiene. Perform hand hygiene prior to donning gloves and immediately after removing gloves.

✓ Change gloves and perform hand hygiene during patient care if:

- the gloves become damaged.
- the gloves become visibly soiled.
- moving from work on a soiled body site to a clean body site.

✓ Never wear the same pair of gloves for more than one patient.

Gowns

✓ Wear a gown to protect and prevent the contamination of exposed skin or clothing during patient care activities when contact with blood, body fluids, secretions or excretions (except sweat) may occur.

✓ Remove the gown and perform hand hygiene before leaving the patient's environment.

✓ Do not reuse gowns, even for repeated contacts with the same patient.

Masks and protective eyewear

✓ Use PPE (e.g., mask, goggles, face shield) to protect the mucous membranes of the eyes, nose, and mouth during patient care activities that are likely to generate splashes or sprays of blood, body fluids, secretions or excretions (except sweat).

Patient care equipment

✓ Handle all patient equipment in a manner that prevents transfer of microorganisms. Ensure that all reusable equipment is properly sanitized prior to reuse.

✓ Vigilance is required when handling/disposing of sharp instruments. Never recap needles or remove syringes by hand. All sharps disposals should use puncture-resistant containers.

✓ Mouthpieces, resuscitation bags, and ventilation devices should be used as an alternative to mouth-to-mouth resuscitation.

Transmission-based Precautions[3,4]

Transmission-based precautions are updated guidelines for the particular care of specified patients infected with epidemiologically important pathogens transmitted by airborne, droplet or contact modes. These are additional precautions that should be implemented in addition to standard precautions.

Airborne Precautions

Airborne precautions reduce the risk of airborne transmission of infectious agents through evaporated droplets in air or dust particles containing infectious agents.

- Private room with monitored negative air pressure; door should stay closed.
- If private room is not an option, place together patients who are presumed to have the same infection in areas of the facility that are away from other patients.
- Wear an N95 or higher level respirator when entering the room; patient should be wearing a surgical mask with others in the room.
- Limit patient's transport outside of the room for only essential purposes; patient should wear a mask during transport.

Examples
Measles, varicella (chickenpox), tuberculosis, SARS

Droplet Precautions

Droplet precautions reduce the risk of droplet transmission of infectious agents through contact of the mucous membranes of the mouth and nose, contact with the conjunctivae, and through coughing, sneezing, talking or suctioning. This transmission requires close contact, as the infectious agents do not suspend in the air and travel only 3-6 feet or less.

- Private room; door may remain open.
- If private room is not an option, place together patients who are presumed to have the same infection.
- Ensure that patients are physically separated (i.e., at least 3 feet apart) from each other; draw the privacy curtain between beds.
- Don a mask upon entry into the patient's room; patient should also be wearing a mask.
- Wear a mask whenever within 3-6 feet of the patient.
- Limit the patient's transport outside of the room for only essential purposes; patient should wear a mask during transport.

Examples
Haemophilus influenzae (including meningitis, pneumonia, sepsis), *Neisseria meningitidis* (including meningitis, pneumonia, sepsis), pertussis, influenza, diphtheria, mumps, rubella, streptococcal infections (group A)

Contact Precautions

Contact precautions reduce the risk of transmission of infectious agents through direct or indirect contact. Direct contact involves skin-to-skin transmission; indirect contact involves a contaminated intermediate object, usually within the patient's environment.

- Private room.
- If private room is not an option, place together patients who are presumed to have the same infection.
- Ensure that patients are physically separated (i.e., at least 3 feet apart) from each other; draw the privacy curtain between beds.
- Don gloves upon entry into the room; change gloves after direct contact with infectious material.
- Wear a gown if you will have substantial close contact with the patient or contaminated objects.
- Take gloves/gown off prior to leaving the room and perform proper hand hygiene.
- Limit the patient's transport outside of the room for only essential purposes; infected or colonized areas of the patient's body should be covered.
- Dedicate non-critical patient care equipment to one patient; do not share between patients, or disinfect properly prior to use on another patient.

Examples
Gastrointestinal, respiratory, skin or wound infections, presence of stool incontinence (including patients with norovirus, rotavirus, or *Clostridium difficile*), enterohemorrhagic *Escherichia coli*, MRSA, herpes simplex virus, scabies, impetigo

Sequence for Donning/Doffing Personal Protective Equipment[3]

Donning

1. Perform hand hygiene.
2. Don the gown, making sure it covers from the neck to the knees, the entire arm down to the wrist, and wraps fully around the back. Fasten the ties at both the neck and the waist.
3. Don the mask, securing the ties (if present) at both the head and the neck. Then press the flexible band around the nose bridge to secure the mask to the face.
4. Place the goggles or face shield over your face and eyes and adjust it to fit.
5. Don the gloves and extend them up over the wrists of the gown.

Doffing

1. Remove the gloves, being mindful that the outside of the gloves is contaminated. Grasp the outside of one glove with the opposite hand and peel it off so it is inside out. Slide the fingers of your ungloved hand on the inside of the remaining glove. Peel that glove off without touching the outside of the glove. Discard the gloves.
2. Remove the goggles or face shield by touching the clean portion of the headband or earpieces in the back. Discard the goggles or face shield (if the item is not reusable).
3. Remove the gown, being mindful that the front of the gown and the sleeves are contaminated. Untie both the neck and waist ties, then peel the gown down the arms and away from your body, touching only the inside of the gown. As you peel downward, the gown will turn inside out. Roll the gown into a ball and discard it.
4. Remove the mask, being mindful that the front of the mask is contaminated. If using ties, untie the bottom tie first, then the top tie. Only hold the mask by the ties when discarding it.
5. Perform hand hygiene.

Emergent Conditions

Allergic Reaction

Recognition: A mild to moderate allergic reaction is typically not life-threatening and may include itchy skin, skin redness, rash, hives, areas of swelling, itchy and watery eyes, runny nose, sneezing, and headache. A severe allergic reaction may include swelling of the face or mouth, difficulty swallowing or speaking, wheezing and difficulty breathing, chest tightness and pressure, tachycardia, abdominal pain, nausea and vomiting, altered mental status, and dizziness or syncope. Common allergens include pollen, dust, eggs, shellfish, milk, wheat, soy, nuts, insect stings, chemicals, latex, and medications.

Response: A severe allergic reaction can be life-threatening and requires prompt medical attention. The therapist should first try to remove the source of the allergic reaction if possible. The therapist should check the patient's airway to assess if it is compromised and begin cardiopulmonary resuscitation if necessary. If the patient uses an emergency allergy medication (e.g., EpiPen), the therapist should assist the patient to ingest or inject the medication. If the patient is having trouble breathing, the patient should not take medications orally. Emergency medical services should be called if the patient is having difficulty breathing or swallowing.

Autonomic Dysreflexia

Recognition: This condition is commonly seen in patients with a complete spinal cord injury above the level of T6 in response to some noxious stimulus (e.g., bladder distention, tight clothing). Signs and symptoms include severe hypertension, bradycardia, profuse sweating above the level of the lesion, headache, nausea, piloerection, and red and blotchy skin.

Response: The patient should first be placed in an upright position (e.g., sitting, semirecumbent) and the therapist should attempt to identify and remove the noxious stimulus. For example, a kink in the catheter may prevent urine from draining from the bladder and cause a systemic response. The therapist should then monitor the patient's vital signs and call for medical assistance.

Burns

Recognition: There are several causative factors that can result in burns including heat, chemicals, and electricity. The therapist should identify the source of the burn, the location, and extent of the burn. Burns can be classified according to depth and according to the surface area affected (e.g., rule of nines).

Response: The therapist should initially attempt to remove the source of the burn if still present. If the burn has been caused by a chemical, water should be used to dilute the substance. However, be cautious not to wash the chemical onto an unaffected portion of skin. Also, if the chemical is a dry powder, it should be brushed off the skin. If it is a thermal burn, run the affected part under a cool tap for several minutes. However, if the burn covers a large surface area, cold water should not be used as this can increase the risk for hypothermia. If it is an electrical burn, assess the patient's heart rate and respiration and monitor for signs of cardiac arrest. For all burns, the therapist should remove any clothing or jewelry near the burn, however, should not attempt to remove clothing if it has become part of the wound. A clean towel or dressing should be placed over the wound to prevent infection. If the burn is extensive, involves the face, hands, perineum or feet or involves the respiratory system, emergency medical services should be called.

Concussion

Recognition: A concussion is a mild traumatic brain injury that occurs secondary to a blow to the head. Signs and symptoms include loss of memory, confusion, drowsiness, behavior or personality changes, light or noise sensitivity, headache, impaired vision, nausea or vomiting, lack of coordination, dizziness, and loss of consciousness. Symptoms typically occur immediately after the injury, however, they can also occur hours or days later.

Response: If a patient demonstrates signs and symptoms of a concussion, they should not be allowed to return to physical activity until cleared by a medical professional. Emergency medical services should be contacted immediately if the patient demonstrates any of the following symptoms: extreme drowsiness or loss of consciousness, a headache that will not improve, one pupil that is larger than the other, slurred speech, weakness, numbness, loss of coordination, repeated vomiting or nausea, convulsions or seizures, and increasing confusion, restlessness or agitation.

Fractures

Recognition: Observe the site of the injury and the position of the extremity. A visible deformity and the presence of bruising and/or swelling may indicate that a fracture has occurred. Other signs and symptoms include pain, tenderness, and limited movement.

Response: Peripheral pulses and sensation should be assessed distal to the injury to determine the extent of injury to nerves and blood vessels. The therapist should apply support to the site with a firm object (e.g., flat piece of wood) to stabilize the position of the extremity. The splint should immobilize the affected area as well as the adjacent joints. The patient should avoid movement of the extremity and the therapist should not try to realign the fracture. If the fracture site is open, cover it with a sterile towel or dressing. If a spinal fracture is suspected, do not move the patient.

Heat Illness

Recognition: The two primary types of heat illness are heat exhaustion and heat stroke. Heat exhaustion is a less serious condition, but can progress to heat stroke, which is a medical emergency if not treated properly. The signs and symptoms of heat exhaustion include profuse sweating, moist and pale skin, nausea, headache, dizziness, muscle cramps, weakness, rapid and shallow breathing, and a weak and rapid pulse. The signs and symptoms of heat stroke include dry skin, a flushed color, nausea, headache, labored breathing, a strong and rapid pulse, elevated temperature, contraction and dilation of the pupils, convulsions, altered mental status, and possible loss of consciousness.

Response: For any form of heat illness, the patient should be placed in a shaded or covered area and the therapist should monitor vital signs. Remove or loosen any outer clothing layers and use an ice bag or cold compress on the patient's forehead, neck, and/or groin. Water or a solution with electrolytes can be given if the person is still conscious. Do not give the patient salt tablets as this can negatively affect the electrolyte balance. Emergency medical services should be called if the patient is experiencing heat stroke or if their condition is worsening.

Heart Attack/Cardiac Arrest

Recognition: The onset of a heart attack may be sudden or gradual. Signs and symptoms typically include chest discomfort that may feel like pressure, squeezing, fullness or pain. This discomfort may spread to the arms, back, neck, jaw or stomach. Other signs and symptoms include shortness of breath, abnormal heart rate and blood pressure, sweating, nausea, lightheadedness, and anxious behavior. If a heart attack progresses to cardiac arrest, there will be a sudden loss of responsiveness and/or consciousness.

Response: If a patient is experiencing a heart attack or cardiac arrest, the therapist should first determine if the patient is responsive. If unresponsive, the therapist should call emergency medical services and have a second person locate an automated external defibrillator (AED). Cardiopulmonary resuscitation (CPR) should be initiated until an AED or emergency medical personnel arrive. To use the AED, the therapist should expose the patient's chest so the pads can be applied. Once ready the AED will analyze the patient's heart rhythm. The therapist should follow the prompts from the AED. If the AED plans to "shock" the patient, the therapist should move away from the patient and clear the immediate area.

Hypothermia/Frostbite

Recognition: Hypothermia occurs when a person has been exposed to cold temperatures for a prolonged period of time. Signs and symptoms of hypothermia include shivering, exhaustion, decreased motor function, slurred speech, drowsiness, confusion, memory loss, and decreased vital signs. Infants will present with low energy and their skin will be cold and bright red. When exposed to freezing temperatures, frostbite may occur. Symptoms of frostbite include white or grayish-yellow skin that is numb and feels firm or waxy.

Response: The therapist should assess the patient's body temperature via palpation, as well as assess the patient's verbal and motor responses. To treat hypothermia, the patient should be moved into a warm room and remove any wet clothing. The therapist should attempt to warm the patient, starting with the core of the body, with dry towels or blankets or with skin-to-skin contact. If the patient loses consciousness or if their body temperature is below 95 degrees Fahrenheit, emergency medical services should be contacted immediately. For cases of frostbite, the affected area should be immersed in warm (not hot) water or be warmed using body heat. Massage should not be used over the affected areas since the additional pressure can increase the amount of tissue damage.

Insulin-related Illness

Recognition: Hypoglycemia is caused by low blood glucose and has a rapid onset. Signs and symptoms include pale and moist skin, rapid heart rate, shallow breathing, dizziness, headache, altered vision, hunger, excited and agitated behavior, confusion, seizure, and loss of consciousness. Hyperglycemia is caused by elevated blood glucose and has a slower onset. When hyperglycemia is left untreated for long periods of time, it can lead to ketoacidosis and diabetic coma, which are life-threatening conditions. Signs and symptoms of hyperglycemia include thirst, frequent urination, and glucose in the urine. Symptoms of ketoacidosis include fruity smelling breath, deep, labored breathing, nausea and vomiting, and a dry tongue.

Response: In cases of hypoglycemia, the patient should ingest some form of sugar (e.g., orange juice). If the patient is not conscious, an intravenous glucose injection should be administered by a medical professional. The patient should rest as much as possible until blood glucose levels have returned to normal. In cases of ketoacidosis, emergency medical services should be called as the patient will likely need to be injected with insulin. The therapist should avoid giving the patient any form of sugar.

Laceration (External Bleeding)

Recognition: Lacerations can vary in severity depending on the size, depth, and location of the laceration. Arterial bleeding is characterized by spurting blood that is bright red in appearance, while venous bleeding is characterized by flowing blood that is more purple in appearance.

Response: A therapist should apply gloves if available before applying pressure to the wound with a sterile towel. Direct pressure should be maintained over the laceration until bleeding ceases. If arterial bleeding occurs, then intermittent pressure may need to be applied to the artery just proximal to the site of the injury. If blood flow is excessive, the extremity should be elevated above the level of the heart. Prolonged pressure with use of a tourniquet should be avoided. Emergency medical services should be called if a cut is bleeding severely, blood is spurting out or the bleeding does not stop after ten minutes of steady pressure.

Obstructed Airway

Recognition: Ask the patient if they are choking. If they can speak, cough or breathe, do not attempt to intervene, but stay close by. If they cannot speak, cough or breathe, the therapist should provide assistance.

Response: The therapist should first check the patient's mouth and attempt to remove any foreign objects. The therapist should then position themselves behind the patient with their hands clasped (i.e., one hand in a closed fist with the other hand covering it) over the patient's abdomen (i.e., above the umbilicus and below the diaphragm). The therapist then gives forceful, abrupt thrusts inward and upward. This is done until the object becomes dislodged. If the patient becomes unconscious, the patient should be placed in supine and the therapist should perform rescue breathing and abdominal thrusts. When treating a child under the age of one, the child should be placed in a recumbent prone position over the therapist's forearm with the head supported while the therapist provides four forceful blows to the interscapular region with the heel of the hand. The therapist then turns the child over and provides four thrusts to the lower sternum with two fingers. This cycle is repeated until the object is expelled.

Orthostatic Hypotension

Recognition: Orthostatic hypotension occurs when a patient attempts to stand from a sitting or supine position. As a result of reduced venous return, perfusion of the brain decreases and results in symptoms of dizziness or syncope. Other symptoms may include weakness, altered vision, nausea, and confusion.

Response: Treatment for this condition is similar to that of shock, in that the patient should be positioned in a supine position with the legs elevated so that the blood supply can better perfuse the brain.

Pulmonary Embolism

Recognition: The common signs and symptoms of a pulmonary embolism include shortness of breath, a cough (sometimes with bloody sputum), and chest pain that worsens with deep breathing. Other signs and symptoms may include lightheadedness or dizziness, tachypnea, a rapid and irregular heart rate, fever, diaphoresis, anxious behavior, cyanosis, clammy skin, and leg pain and swelling.

Response: Emergency medical services should be called immediately, especially if the onset of symptoms is sudden. The therapist should continue to monitor vital signs until emergency medical personnel arrive.

Seizures

Recognition: There are several different types of seizures including myoclonic, tonic, clonic, tonic-clonic, atonic, and absence. Each form of seizure will present differently. Symptoms may include convulsions, muscle rigidity, loss of consciousness, jerking movements or loss of muscle tone.

Response: The therapist should place the patient in a safe location and position without trying to constrain the patient's movements. The patient's respiratory rate and quality should be monitored. The therapist should ensure that the airway stays patent, though an object should not be placed in the patient's mouth. When the convulsions subside, the patient's head should be turned to one side in case vomiting occurs.

Shock

Recognition: Shock is caused by the loss of perfusion to the body's organs, often from excessive bleeding, excessive heat or movement from a supine to a vertical position. Signs and symptoms of shock include pale, moist, cool skin, diaphoresis, shallow and irregular breathing, a weak and rapid pulse, hypotension, low body temperature, weakness, dizziness, nausea and vomiting, dilated pupils, anxiety, altered mental status, and syncope.

Response: The therapist should initially attempt to remove the source of the shock, as well as monitor the patient's blood pressure, heart rate, and respiration. Cardiopulmonary resuscitation should be performed if necessary. The patient should be placed in supine with the feet elevated above the level of the head, assuming they do not have injuries to the head, spine, trunk or legs. For comfort, a cold compress may be applied to the forehead or a blanket may be used to prevent loss of body heat. The patient should avoid exertion until symptoms have been relieved.

Stroke

Recognition: Signs and symptoms typically include drooping or numbness on one side of the face, numbness or weakness of one arm, slurred speech, altered vision, headache, dizziness, lack of coordination, confusion, and loss of consciousness.

Response: If the therapist recognizes that a stroke is occurring, emergency medical services should be called immediately. The therapist should note the time that the initial symptoms appeared since treatment is dependent on the amount of time that has elapsed. If the patient's symptoms go away after a few minutes, they should still seek treatment since they have likely experienced a transient ischemic attack, which is also a serious condition.

SPOTLIGHT ON SAFETY

SUMMARY OF KEY BASIC LIFE SUPPORT COMPONENTS FOR ADULTS, CHILDREN, AND INFANTS

Component	Adults	Children	Infants
Recognition	Scan the scene for safety Check that the victim is unresponsive Shout for nearby help and/or activate the EMS Get an AED if available (For children/infants, if sudden collapse is not witnessed, perform 5 cycles of CPR before EMS/AED)		
	No breathing or only gasping		
	No pulse palpated within 10 seconds		
CPR sequence	Compression – Airway – Breathing		
Compression rate	100-120 compressions/minute		
Compression depth	At least 2 inches	At least 1/3 AP depth About 2 inches	At least 1/3 AP depth About 1.5 inches
	Allow complete recoil between compressions		
Hand placement	Heel of one hand on top of the other Pressure over lower half of the sternum	Heel of one hand on top of the other (or one hand only) Pressure over lower half of the sternum	Using two fingers Pressure over the sternum, just below the intermammary line
Compression interruptions	Minimize interruptions in chest compressions HCPs rotate compressors every 2 minutes Attempt to limit interruptions to <10 seconds		
Airway	Head tilt – chin lift (if trauma is suspected, perform a jaw thrust)		
Compression-to-ventilation ratio	30:2 (1 or 2 rescuers)	30:2 (1 rescuer), 15:2 (2 HCP rescuers)	
	Perform only compressions when HCP is not proficient in CPR Perform only compressions once an advanced airway is placed		
Ventilations	1 second per breath Visible chest rise		
Ventilations with advanced airway	Asynchronous with chest compressions 1 breath every 6 seconds (10 breaths/minute)		
Ventilations only (circulation is present)	1 breath every 5-6 seconds	1 breath every 3-5 seconds	
Defibrillation	Attach and use an AED as soon as possible Minimize interruptions in chest compressions before/after shock Resume CPR beginning with compressions immediately after each shock		

AED = automated external defibrillator; AP = anterior-posterior; CPR = cardiopulmonary resuscitation; HCP = healthcare provider

Source: American Heart Association CPR and ECC Guidelines. American Heart Association website, https://eccguidelines.heart.org/circulation/cpr-ecc-guidelines/. Accessed April 2020.

Ergonomics

Ergonomic Guidelines[1]

Workstation Recommendations

- ✓ 18-20 inch monitor
- ✓ Easily adjustable monitor to angle or tilt
- ✓ Split keyboard preferred
- ✓ Adjustable feet for the keyboard
- ✓ Monitor display should be directed ten degrees below the horizontal
- ✓ Monitor should be placed at least twenty inches away from the eyes
- ✓ Chair should swivel 360 degrees for easy access
- ✓ Wrist rests should match the front edge of the keyboard in order to maximize comfort
- ✓ Hands-free telephone set preferred
- ✓ Use a mouse that contours to the hand
- ✓ 30 second exercise break every hour while at a desk
- ✓ Space under the desk should be at least 30 inches wide, 19 inches deep, and 27 inches in height; there should be 2-3 inches between the top of the thighs and the desk

Workstation Posture

Head: level, facing forward, in line with trunk
Shoulders: relaxed, arms at side
Elbows: remain close to trunk, bent 90-120 degrees
Forearms, wrists, hands: parallel to the floor, straight
Trunk: maintain normal curves of the spine with appropriate lumbar support, shoulders and pelvis are level
Hips, thighs: well supported with contoured seat, parallel to the floor
Knees: maintain a level position with a 90 degree angle of flexion, knees generally at the same height as the hips
Feet: place feet flat on the floor or supported in a slight incline

Body Mechanics[2,3]

A therapist must consistently use proper body mechanics when treating patients and avoid unnecessary stress and strain by maintaining proper alignment within the musculoskeletal system.

Principles of Proper Body Mechanics

- Use the shortest lever arm possible
- Stay close to the patient when possible
- Use larger muscles to perform heavy work
- Maintain a wide base of support
- Avoid any rotary movement when lifting
- Attempt to maintain your center of gravity and the patient's center of gravity within the base of support

Lifting Guidelines[2,3]

- ✓ Always attempt to increase your base of support
- ✓ Maintain a proper lumbar curve as you lift
- ✓ Pivot your feet when lifting; do not twist your back to turn
- ✓ Maintain a slow and consistent speed while lifting
- ✓ Only lift an object as a last resort

Deep Squat Lift (Figs. 9-2, 9-3, 9-4)

1. Begin with the hips below the level of the knees
2. Assume a wide base of support
3. Straddle the object
4. Grasp the object from each side or from beneath
5. The trunk should remain vertical
6. Maintain a lumbar lordosis and anterior pelvic tilt

Half-Kneeling Lift (Figs. 9-5, 9-6, 9-7, 9-8)

1. Begin in a half-kneel position
2. The bottom leg should be positioned behind and to the side of the object
3. Maintain a normal lumbar lordosis
4. Lift the object onto the knee and draw it closer to the trunk
5. Continue the lift by holding the object close as you assume a standing position

One Leg Stance Lift

1. Used for lifting light objects that can be lifted with one extremity
2. Face the object in a lunge position
3. Shift weight onto the forward extremity
4. Flex the forward extremity and lower to reach the object
5. The hind leg rises off the ground to counterbalance the shift in weight
6. Maintain a neutral spine throughout the lift

Power Lift

1. Begin with the hips above the level of the knees
2. Assume a wide base of support behind the object with the feet parallel to each other
3. Grasp the object from each side or from underneath
4. The trunk should remain in a vertical position
5. Maintain a lumbar lordosis and anterior tilt

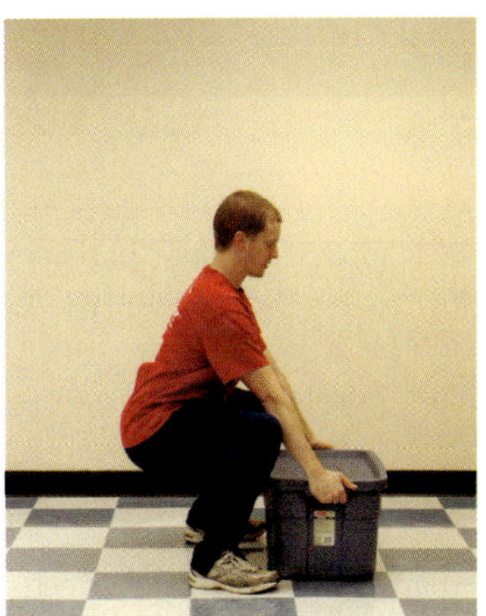

Fig. 9-2: A patient begins a deep squat lift with the hips below the knees.

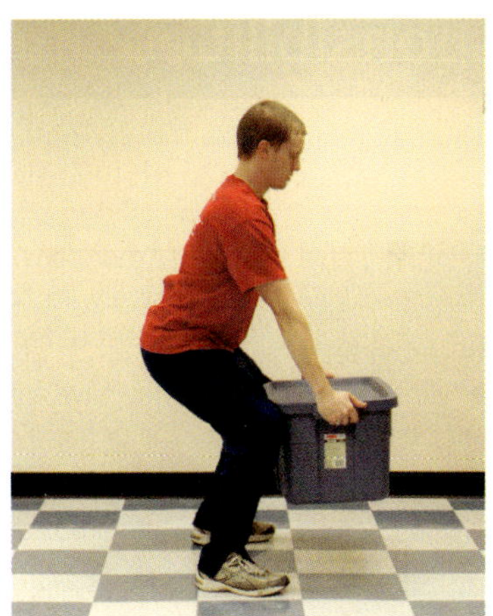

Fig. 9-3: The patient lifts the container while maintaining the trunk in a vertical position.

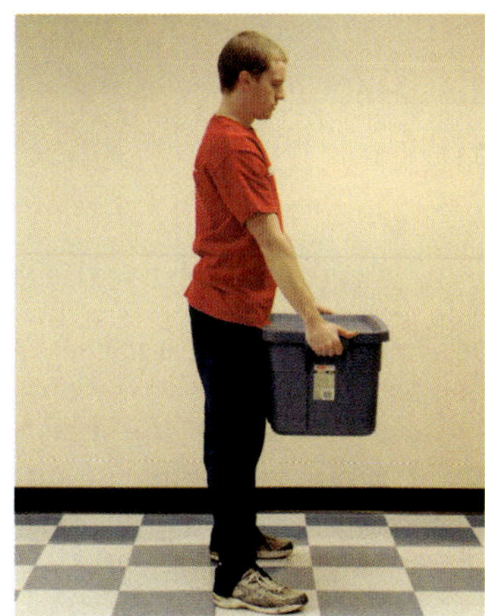

Fig. 9-4: The patient completes the lift by achieving a fully erect position.

Traditional Lift

1. Begin with the lower extremities in a full squat facing the object
2. The feet are positioned in an anterior-posterior manner on each side of the object
3. Grasp the object and flex the upper extremities to initiate the lift
4. Use bilateral lower extremities to provide the work of the lift
5. Keep the object close to the trunk during the lift
6. Maintain normal lumbar lordosis
7. Do not lift with the back

Pushing or Pulling an Object

- ✓ Use a semi-squat position to push or pull
- ✓ Apply the force parallel to the surface that the object should be moved upon
- ✓ Exert an initial force that is adequate to overcome the counterforce of inertia and friction
- ✓ Attempt to push, pull, slide or roll the object prior to lifting or carrying an object

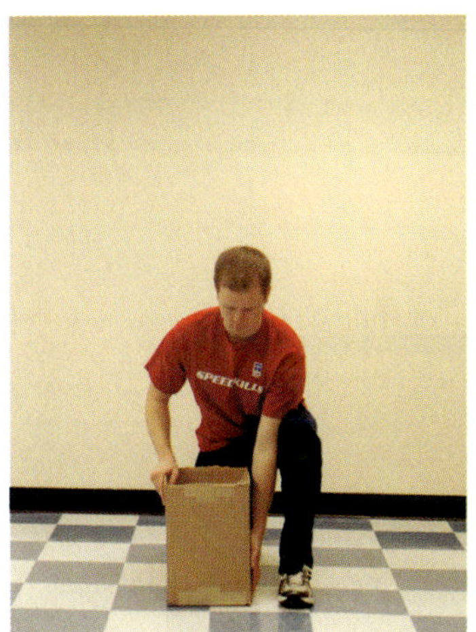

Fig. 9-5: The patient begins a half-kneeling lift while grasping the box in a half-kneeling position.

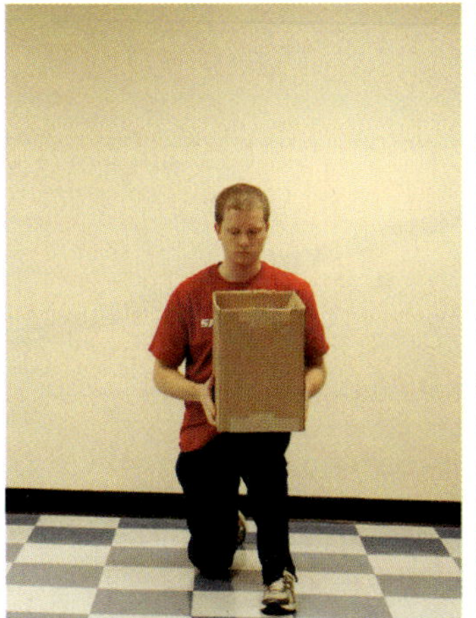

Fig. 9-6: The patient lifts the box onto the knee while maintaining normal lordosis.

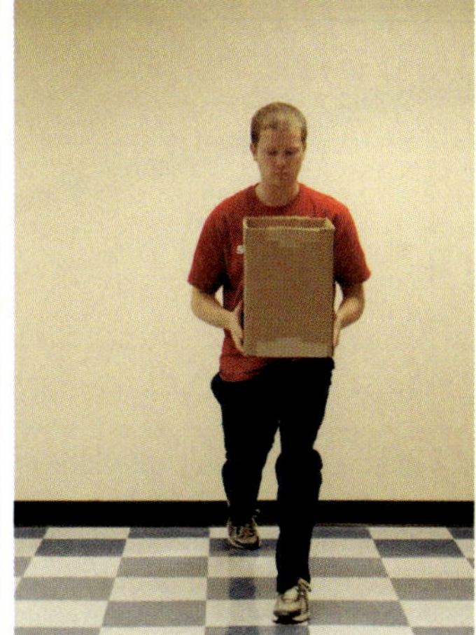

Fig. 9-7: The patient gradually assumes a standing position.

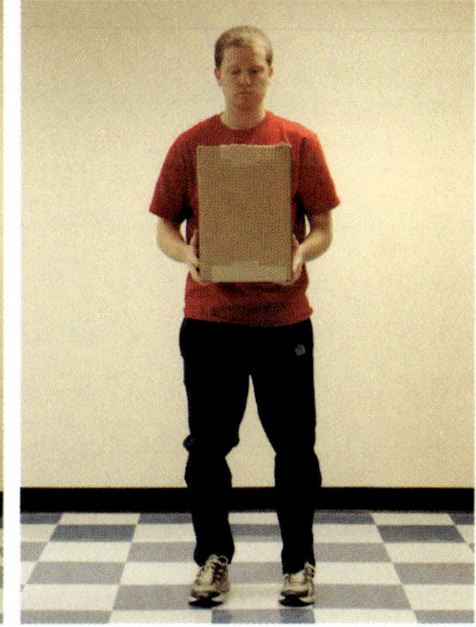

Fig. 9-8: The patient completes the lift by achieving a fully erect position.

Professional Responsibilities

Accessibility

Americans with Disabilities Act[1,2]

The Americans with Disabilities Act is designed to provide a clear and comprehensive national mandate for the elimination of discrimination. The Americans with Disabilities Act is federal legislation that was signed into law on July 26, 1990.

The Americans with Disabilities Act is divided into five titles:

Title I	Employment
Title II	Public Services
Title III	Public Accommodations
Title IV	Telecommunications
Title V	Miscellaneous

The Americans with Disabilities Act applies primarily, but not exclusively, to "disabled" individuals. An individual is "disabled" if they meet at least one of the following criteria:

- They have a physical or mental impairment that substantially limits one or more of their major life activities.
- They have a record of such an impairment.
- They are regarded as having such an impairment.

The Employment provisions (Title I) apply to employers of fifteen employees or more. The Public Accommodations provisions (Title III) apply to all businesses, regardless of the number of employees.

Employers are required to make reasonable accommodations for qualified individuals with a disability, who are defined by the Americans with Disabilities Act as individuals who satisfy the job-related requirements of a position held or desired, and who can perform the "essential functions" of such position with or without reasonable accommodation. The Americans with Disabilities Act does not require employers to make accommodations that pose an "undue hardship." "Undue hardship" is defined as significantly difficult or expensive accommodations.

Individuals unable to utilize stairs often rely on ramps. A ramp should possess twelve inches of horizontal run for each inch of vertical rise which is equivalent to an 8.3% grade (Fig. 9-9).

Ramp Specifications

Landing

Rise

Landing

Horizontal Run

Fig. 9-9: A diagram of a ramp depicting the relative relationship of rise to run.

Percent grade reflects the angle of inclination. A percent grade of 100% would be completely vertical and a percent grade of 0% would be completely horizontal. The percent grade is determined by taking the rise, dividing the value by the run, and then multiplying the number by 100 to convert the value to a percentage.

A ramp should be a minimum of 36 inches wide and should be equipped with handrails if the ramp has a rise of greater than 6 inches or a horizontal run of greater than 72 inches. The ramp should have a level landing at the top and bottom. If a ramp changes direction, the landing area must be a minimum of five feet by five feet (i.e., 60 inches x 60 inches).

Accessibility Requirements[1,2,5]

Doorway (Fig. 9-10)	Minimum 32 inch width Maximum 24 inch depth
Threshold	Less than ¾ inch for sliding doors Less than ½ inch for other doors
Carpet	Requires ½ inch pile or less
Hallway clearance (Fig. 9-10)	36 inch width
Wheelchair turning radius (U-turn) (Fig. 9-11)	60 inch width 78 inch length
Forward reach in wheelchair (Fig. 9-12)	Low reach 15 inches High reach 48 inches
Side reach in wheelchair	Reach over obstruction to 24 inches
Bathroom sink	Not less than 29 inch height Not greater than 40 inches from floor to bottom of mirror or paper dispenser 17 inch minimum depth under sink to back wall
Bathroom toilet	17-19 inches from floor to top of toilet Not less than 36 inch grab bar length Grab bars should be 1¼ - 1½ inches in diameter 1½ inch spacing between grab bars and wall Grab bar placement 33-36 inches up from floor level
Hotel	Approximately 2% total rooms must be accessible
Parking space	96 inch width 240 inch length Approximately 2% of the total spaces must be accessible

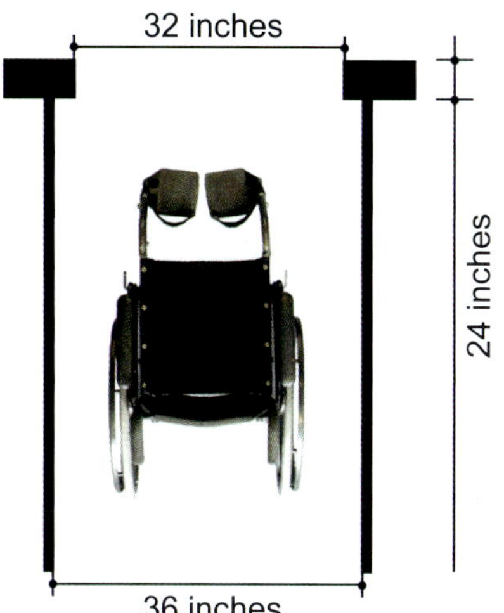

Fig. 9-10: An overhead image of the minimum required doorway width and hallway width.

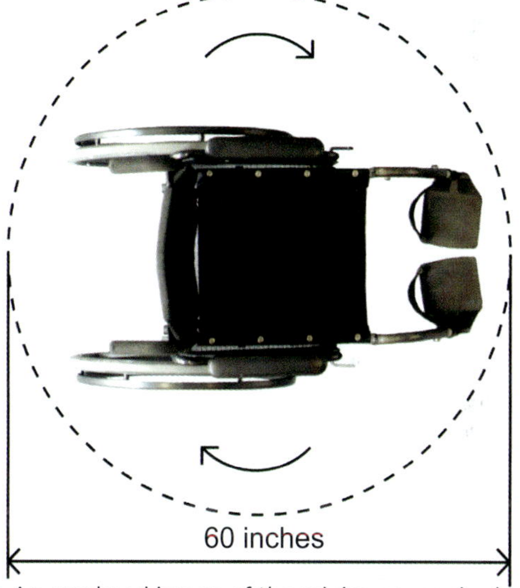

Fig. 9-11: An overhead image of the minimum required width for turning a wheelchair.

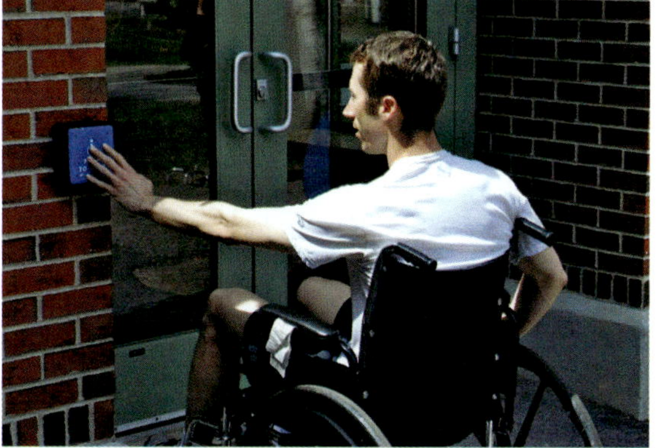

Fig. 9-12: A patient in a wheelchair activating an automatic door opener.

Documentation[6,7]

Purpose of Documentation

- Communicate with other treating professionals
- Assistance with discharge planning
- Reimbursement
- Assistance with utilization review
- A legal document regarding the course of therapy

Types of Documentation

Record

- An increase in specialization of care and multidisciplinary treatment increases the need for medical records to serve as a means of communication among clinicians.
- Progress notes and referrals related directly to patient care are examples of clinical records.
- Departmental statistics and records are examples of administrative records.

Referral

- Acceptable forms of referral range from a signed prescription form to a highly structured checklist. The referral must include the name of the patient and be signed and dated by the referring physician.
- Referrals commonly include some indication as to the number and frequency of treatments desired and any special precautions or instructions.

Progress Note

- Improvement of patient care is the most important function of progress notes.
- Progress notes allow members of all health services to know what the patient is accomplishing in each given area.
- Progress notes should contain patient identification, the date, and the signature of the therapist.
- Progress notes should be written when the patient's condition changes during the course of treatment.
- Specific frequency of progress notes is usually dictated by department policy.
- Appropriate forms of documentation include diagrams, videotapes, and flow sheets as well as many other less frequently used media.

S.O.A.P. Note

A commonly used record to write daily notes is the S.O.A.P. note. S.O.A.P. stands for:

S: Subjective

O: Objective

A: Assessment

P: Plan

Subjective: Refers to information the patient communicates to the therapist. This could include social or medical history not previously recorded. It could also include the patient's statements or complaints.

Objective: Refers to information the therapist observes. Common examples include range of motion measurements, muscle strength, and functional abilities. It also includes manual techniques and equipment used during treatment.

Assessment: Allows the therapist to express their professional opinion. Changes in the treatment program are often expressed in this section.

Plan: Includes ideas for future physical therapy sessions. Frequency and expected duration of physical therapy services can also be incorporated into this section.

Discharge Summary

A discharge summary should provide a capsule view of the patient's progress during therapy. The discharge summary is usually conducted on the day of the patient's last therapy session.

Guidelines: Physical Therapy Documentation Of Patient/Client Management[8]

Preamble

The American Physical Therapy Association (APTA) is committed to meeting the physical therapy needs of society, to meeting the needs and interests of its members, and to developing and improving the art and science of physical therapy, including practice, education, and research. To help meet these responsibilities, APTA's Board of Directors has approved the following guidelines for physical therapy documentation. It is recognized that these guidelines do not reflect all of the unique documentation requirements associated with the many specialty areas within the physical therapy profession. Applicable for both handwritten and electronic documentation systems, these guidelines are intended to be used as a foundation for the development of more specific documentation guidelines in clinical areas, while at the same time providing guidance for the physical therapy profession across all practice settings. Documentation may also need to address additional regulatory or payer requirements.

Finally, be aware that these guidelines are intended to address documentation of patient/client management, not to describe the provision of physical therapy services. Other APTA documents, including APTA Standards of Practice for Physical Therapy, Code of Ethics and Guide for Professional Conduct, and the Guide to Physical Therapist Practice, address provision of physical therapy services and patient/client management.

APTA Position On Documentation

Documentation Authority For Physical Therapy Services

Physical therapy examination, evaluation, diagnosis, prognosis, and plan of care (including interventions) shall be documented, dated, and authenticated by the physical therapist who performs the service. Interventions provided by the physical therapist or selected interventions provided by the physical therapist assistant under the direction and supervision of the physical therapist are documented, dated, and authenticated by the physical therapist or, when permissible by law, the physical therapist assistant.

Other notations or flow charts are considered a component of the documented record but do not meet the requirements of documentation in or of themselves.

Students in physical therapist or physical therapist assistant programs may document when the record is additionally authenticated by the physical therapist or, when permissible by law, documentation by physical therapist assistant students may be authenticated by a physical therapist assistant.

Operational Definitions

Guidelines

APTA defines a "guideline" as a statement of advice.

Authentication

The process used to verify that an entry is complete, accurate and final. Indications of authentication can include original written signatures and computer "signatures" on secured electronic record systems only.

The following describes the main documentation elements of patient/client management: 1) initial examination/evaluation, 2) visit/encounter, 3) reexamination, and 4) discharge or discontinuation summary.

Initial Examination/Evaluation

Documentation of the initial encounter is typically called the "initial examination," "initial evaluation," or "initial examination/evaluation." Completion of the initial examination/evaluation is typically completed in one visit, but may occur over more than one visit. Documentation elements for the initial examination/evaluation include the following:

Examination: Includes data obtained from the history, systems review, and tests and measures.

Evaluation: Evaluation is a thought process that may not include formal documentation. It may include documentation of the assessment of the data collected in the examination and identification of problems pertinent to patient/client management.

Diagnosis: Indicates level of impairment, activity limitation and participation restriction determined by the physical therapist. May be indicated by selecting one or more preferred practice patterns from the Guide to Physical Therapist Practice.

Prognosis: Provides documentation of the predicted level of improvement that might be attained through intervention and the amount of time required to reach that level. Prognosis is typically not a separate documentation element, but the components are included as part of the plan of care.

Plan of care: Typically stated in general terms, includes goals, interventions planned, proposed frequency and duration, and discharge plans.

Visit/Encounter

Documentation of a visit or encounter, often called a progress note or daily note, documents sequential implementation of the plan of care established by the physical therapist, including changes in patient/client status and variations and progressions of specific interventions used. Also may include specific plans for the next visit or visits.

Reexamination

Documentation of reexamination includes data from repeated or new examination elements and is provided to evaluate progress and to modify or redirect intervention.

Discharge or Discontinuation Summary

Documentation is required following conclusion of the current episode in the physical therapy intervention sequence to summarize progression toward goals and discharge plans.

General Guidelines

Documentation is required for every visit/encounter.

- All documentation must comply with the applicable jurisdictional/regulatory requirements.
- All handwritten entries shall be made in ink and will include original signatures. Electronic entries are made with appropriate security and confidentiality provisions.
- Charting errors should be corrected by drawing a single line through the error and initialing and dating the chart or through the appropriate mechanism for electronic documentation that clearly indicates that a change was made without deletion of the original record.
- All documentation must include adequate identification of the patient/client and the physical therapist or physical therapist assistant:
  - The patient's/client's full name and identification number, if applicable, must be included on all official documents.
  - All entries must be dated and authenticated with the provider's full name and appropriate designation:
    - Documentation of examination, evaluation, diagnosis, prognosis, plan of care, and discharge summary must be authenticated by the physical therapist who provided the service.
    - Documentation of intervention in visit/encounter notes must be authenticated by the physical therapist or physical therapist assistant who provided the service.
    - Documentation by physical therapist or physical therapist assistant graduates or other physical therapists and physical therapist assistants pending receipt of an unrestricted license shall be authenticated by a

licensed physical therapist, or, when permissible by law, documentation by physical therapist assistant graduates may be authenticated by a physical therapist assistant.

  - Documentation by students (SPT/SPTA) in physical therapist or physical therapist assistant programs must be additionally authenticated by the physical therapist or, when permissible by law, documentation by physical therapist assistant students may be authenticated by a physical therapist assistant.

- Documentation should include the referral mechanism by which physical therapy services are initiated. Examples include:
  - Self-referral/direct access
  - Request for consultation from another practitioner
- Documentation should include indication of no shows and cancellations.

Initial Examination/Evaluation

Examination (History, Systems Review, and Tests and Measures)

History:

Documentation of history may include the following:

- General demographics
- Social history
- Employment/work (job/school/play)
- Growth and development
- Living environment
- General health status (self-report, family report, caregiver report)
- Social/health habits (past and current)
- Family history
- Medical/surgical history
- Current condition(s)/chief complaint(s)
- Functional status and activity level
- Medications
- Other clinical tests

Systems Review:

Documentation of systems review may include gathering data for the following systems:

Cardiovascular/Pulmonary

- Blood pressure
- Edema
- Heart rate
- Respiratory rate

Integumentary

- Pliability (texture)
- Presence of scar formation
- Skin color
- Skin integrity

Musculoskeletal

- Gross range of motion
- Gross strength
- Gross symmetry
- Height
- Weight

Neuromuscular

- Gross coordinated movement (e.g., balance, locomotion, transfers, and transitions)
- Motor function (motor control, motor learning)

Documentation of systems review may also address communication ability, affect, cognition, language, and learning style:

- Ability to make needs known
- Consciousness
- Expected emotional/behavioral responses
- Learning preferences (e.g., education needs, learning barriers)
- Orientation (person, place, time)

Tests and Measures:

Documentation of tests and measures may include findings for the following categories:

Aerobic Capacity/Endurance

Examples of examination findings include:

- Aerobic capacity during functional activities
- Aerobic capacity during standardized exercise test protocols
- Cardiovascular signs and symptoms in response to increased oxygen demand with exercise or activity
- Pulmonary signs and symptoms in response to increased oxygen demand with exercise or activity

Anthropometric Characteristics

Examples of examination findings include:

- Body composition
- Body dimensions
- Edema

Arousal, Attention, and Cognition

Examples of examination findings include:

- Arousal and attention
- Cognition
- Communication
- Consciousness
- Motivation
- Orientation to time, person, place, and situation
- Recall

Assistive and Adaptive Devices

Examples of examination findings include:

- Assistive or adaptive devices and equipment use during functional activities
- Components, alignment, fit, and ability to care for the assistive or adaptive devices and equipment
- Remediation of impairments, activity limitations and participation restrictions with use of assistive or adaptive devices and equipment
- Safety during use of assistive or adaptive devices and equipment

Circulation (Arterial, Venous, Lymphatic)

Examples of examination findings include:

- Cardiovascular signs
- Cardiovascular symptoms
- Physiological responses to position change

Cranial and Peripheral Nerve Integrity

Examples of examination findings include:

- Electrophysiological integrity
- Motor distribution of the cranial nerves
- Motor distribution of the peripheral nerves
- Response to neural provocation
- Response to stimuli, including auditory, gustatory, olfactory, pharyngeal, vestibular, and visual
- Sensory distribution of the cranial nerves
- Sensory distribution of the peripheral nerves

Environmental, Home, and Work (job/school/play) Barriers

Examples of examination findings include:

- Current and potential barriers
- Physical space and environment

Ergonomics and Body Mechanics

Examples of examination findings for ergonomics include:

- Dexterity and coordination during work
- Functional capacity and performance during work actions, tasks, or activities
- Safety in work environments
- Specific work conditions or activities
- Tools, devices, equipment, and workstations related to work actions, tasks, or activities

Examples of examination findings for body mechanics include:

- Body mechanics during self-care, home management, work, community, or leisure actions, tasks, or activities

Gait, Locomotion, and Balance

Examples of examination findings include:

- Balance during functional activities with or without the use of assistive, adaptive, orthotic, protective, supportive, or prosthetic devices or equipment
- Balance (dynamic and static) with or without the use of assistive, adaptive, orthotic, protective, supportive, or prosthetic devices or equipment
- Gait and locomotion during functional activities with or without the use of assistive, adaptive, orthotic, protective, supportive, or prosthetic devices or equipment
- Gait and locomotion with or without the use of assistive, adaptive, orthotic, protective, supportive, or prosthetic devices or equipment
- Safety during gait, locomotion, and balance

Integumentary Integrity

Examples of examination findings include:

- Activities, positioning, and postures that produce or relieve trauma to the skin
- Assistive, adaptive, orthotic, protective, supportive, or prosthetic devices and equipment that may produce or relieve trauma to the skin
- Skin characteristics

Wound

Examples of examination findings include:

- Activities, positioning, and postures that aggravate the wound or scar or that produce or relieve trauma
- Burn
- Signs of infection
- Wound characteristics
- Wound scar tissue characteristics

Joint Integrity and Mobility

Examples of examination findings include:

- Joint integrity and mobility
- Joint play movements
- Specific body parts

Motor Function

Examples of examination findings include:

- Dexterity, coordination, and agility
- Electrophysiological integrity
- Hand function
- Initiation, modification, and control of movement patterns and voluntary postures

Muscle Performance

Examples of examination findings include:

- Electrophysiological integrity
- Muscle strength, power, and endurance
- Muscle strength, power, and endurance during functional activities
- Muscle tension

Neuromotor Development and Sensory Integration

Examples of examination findings include:

- Acquisition and evolution of motor skills
- Oral motor function, phonation, and speech production
- Sensorimotor integration

Orthotic, Protective, and Supportive Devices

Examples of examination findings include:

- Components, alignment, fit, and ability to care for the orthotic, protective, and supportive devices and equipment
- Orthotic, protective, and supportive devices and equipment use during functional activities
- Remediation of impairments, activity limitations, and participation restrictions with use of orthotic, protective, and supportive devices and equipment
- Safety during use of orthotic, protective, and supportive devices and equipment

Pain

Examples of examination findings include:

- Pain, soreness, and nocioception
- Pain in specific body parts

Posture

Examples of examination findings include:

- Postural alignment and position (dynamic)
- Postural alignment and position (static)
- Specific body parts

Prosthetic Requirements

Examples of examination findings include:

- Components, alignment, fit, and ability to care for prosthetic device
- Prosthetic device use during functional activities
- Remediation of impairments, activity limitations, and participation restrictions with use of the prosthetic device
- Residual limb or adjacent segment
- Safety during use of the prosthetic device

Range of Motion (including muscle length)

Examples of examination findings include:

- Functional ROM
- Joint active and passive movement
- Muscle length, soft tissue extensibility, and flexibility

Reflex Integrity

Examples of examination findings include:

- Deep reflexes
- Electrophysiological integrity
- Postural reflexes and reactions, including righting, equilibrium, and protective reactions
- Primitive reflexes and reactions
- Resistance to passive stretch
- Superficial reflexes and reactions

Self-care and Home Management (including activities of daily living and instrumental activities of daily living)

Examples of examination findings include:

- Ability to gain access to home environments
- Ability to perform self-care and home management activities with or without assistive, adaptive, orthotic, protective, supportive, or prosthetic devices and equipment
- Safety in self-care and home management activities and environments

Sensory Integrity

Examples of examination findings include:

- Combined/cortical sensations
- Deep sensations
- Electrophysiological integrity

Ventilation and Respiration

Examples of examination findings include:

- Pulmonary signs of respiration/gas exchange
- Pulmonary signs of ventilatory function
- Pulmonary symptoms

Work (job/school/play), Community, and Leisure Integration or Reintegration (including instrumental activities of daily living)

Examples of examination findings include:

- Ability to assume or resume work (job/school/play), community, and leisure activities with or without assistive, adaptive, orthotic, protective, supportive, or prosthetic devices and equipment
- Ability to gain access to work (job/school/play), community, and leisure environments
- Safety in work (job/school/play), community, and leisure activities and environments

Evaluation

Evaluation is a thought process that may not include formal documentation. However, the evaluation process may lead to documentation of impairments, activity limitations, and participation restrictions using formats such as:

- A problem list
- A statement of assessment of key factors (e.g., cognitive factors, comorbidities, social support) influencing the patient/client status

Diagnosis

Documentation of a diagnosis determined by the physical therapist may include impairment, activity limitation, and participation restrictions.

Examples include:

- Impaired Joint Mobility, Motor Function, Muscle Performance, and Range of Motion Associated With Localized Inflammation
- Impaired Motor Function and Sensory Integrity Associated With Progressive Disorders of the Central Nervous System
- Impaired Aerobic Capacity/Endurance Associated With Cardiovascular Pump Dysfunction or Failure
- Impaired Integumentary Integrity Associated With Partial-Thickness Skin Involvement and Scar Formation

Prognosis

Documentation of the prognosis is typically included in the plan of care.

Plan of Care

Documentation of the plan of care includes the following:

- Overall goals stated in measurable terms that indicate the predicted level of improvement in functioning
- A general statement of interventions to be used
- Proposed duration and frequency of service required to reach the goals
- Anticipated discharge plans

Visit/Encounter

Documentation of each visit/encounter shall include the following elements:

- Patient/client self-report (as appropriate)
- Identification of specific interventions provided, including frequency, intensity, and duration as appropriate

Examples include:

  - Knee extension, three sets, ten repetitions, 10 pound weight
  - Transfer training bed to chair with sliding board
  - Equipment provided

- Changes in patient/client impairment, activity limitation, and participation restriction status as they relate to the plan of care
- Response to interventions, including adverse reactions, if any
- Factors that modify frequency or intensity of intervention and progression of goals, including patient/client adherence to patient/client related instructions
- Communication/consultation with providers/patient/client/family/significant other
- Documentation to plan for ongoing provision of services for the next visit(s), which is suggested to include, but not be limited to:
  - The interventions with objectives
  - Progression parameters
  - Precautions, if indicated

Reexamination

Documentation of reexamination shall include the following elements:

- Documentation of selected components of examination to update patient's/client's functioning, and/or disability status
- Interpretation of findings and, when indicated, revision of goals
- When indicated, revision of plan of care, as directly correlated with goals as documented

Discharge/Discontinuation Summary

Documentation of discharge or discontinuation shall include the following elements:

- Current physical/functional status
- Degree of goals achieved and reasons for goals not being achieved
- Discharge/discontinuation plan related to the patient's/client's continuing care

Examples include:

  - Home program
  - Referrals for additional services
  - Recommendations for follow-up physical therapy care
  - Family and caregiver training
  - Equipment provided

BOD G03-05-16-41 Updated: 5/19/2014 American Physical Therapy Association, web site 2017

CONSIDER THIS

DOCUMENTATION RECOMMENDATIONS[9]

Physical therapists are responsible for completing daily documentation on patients throughout the episode of care. Documentation should be completed in a timely manner and accurately describe the patient's status, physical therapy management, and outcome of care.

The American Physical Therapy Association provides therapists with insight on how to improve physical therapy documentation and promote reimbursement from third party payers.

Top 10 Tips for Defensible Documentation	Top 10 Payer Complaints Regarding Documentation
1. Limit use of abbreviations	1. Poor legibility
2. Date and sign all entries	2. Incomplete documentation
3. Document legibly	3. No documentation for date of service
4. Report progress towards goals regularly	4. Abbreviations, too many, cannot understand
5. Document at the time of the visit when possible	5. Does not demonstrate skilled care
6. Clearly identify note types (e.g., progress reports, daily notes)	6. Documentation does not support the billing code
7. Include all related communications	7. Does not support medical necessity
8. Include missed or cancelled visits	8. Does not demonstrate progress
9. Demonstrate skilled care and medical necessity	9. Repetitious daily notes showing no change in patient status
10. Demonstrate discharge planning through the episode of care	10. Interventions with no clarification of time, frequency, duration

Symbols Commonly Used in Clinical Practice

=	Equal	±	Very slight trace or reaction, indefinite
≠	Unequal	+	Slight trace or reaction, positive, plus excess, acidic reaction
>	Greater than	++	Trace or notable reaction
<	Less than	+++	Moderate amount of reaction
↑	Increase	++++	Large amount or pronounced reaction
↗	Increasing	#	Number, pound, has been given or done
↓	Decrease	→	Yields, leads to
↘	Decreasing	←	Resulting from or secondary to
–	Negative, minus, deficiency, alkaline reaction	1°, 2°	Primary, secondary

From Miller-Keane: Encyclopedia and Dictionary of Medicine, Nursing, and Allied Health. W.B. Saunders Company, Philadelphia 1997, p.1802, with permission.

Military Time

The 24-hour clock (military time) is used to standardize time in the medical record.

Standard Time	Military Time
Noon	1200 hours
1:00 PM	1300 hours
2:00 PM	1400 hours
3:00 PM	1500 hours
4:00 PM	1600 hours
5:00 PM	1700 hours
6:00 PM	1800 hours
7:00 PM	1900 hours
8:00 PM	2000 hours
9:00 PM	2100 hours
10:00 PM	2200 hours
11:00 PM	2300 hours
Midnight	2400 hours

Measurement

Length	
1 cm	= 0.3937 inch
1 m	= 39.37 inches = 3.28 ft = 1.09 yds
1 km	= 0.62 mile
1 inch	= 2.54 centimeters (cm) = 25.4 millimeters (mm) = 0.0254 meters (m)
1 foot	= 30.48 cm = 304.8 mm = 0.304 m
1 mile	= 5280 ft = 1760 yds = 1609.35 m = 1.61 kilometers (km)

Temperature	
0°C	= 32°F = 273°K
100°C	= 212°F
°C	= (°F - 32) x 5/9
°F	= (°C x 9/5) + 32

Weight	
1 ounce (oz)	= 0.0625 pounds (lb) = 28.35 grams (g) = 0.028 kilograms (kg)
1 pound (lb)	= 16 oz = 454 g = 0.454 kg
1 g	= 0.035 oz = 0.0022 lb = 0.001 kg
1 kg	= 35.27 oz = 2.2 lb = 1000 g

Energy and Work	
1 kcal	= 3086 foot-pounds (ft/lbs) = 426.4 kilogram-meter (kg-m) = 4.184 kilojoules (kJ)
1 kJ	= 1000 joules (J) = 0.239 kcal
1 liter O_2 consumed	= 5.05 kcal = 15.575 ft/lbs = 2153 kg-m = 21.237 kJ
1 MET	= 3.5 mL O_2/kg/min = 0.0175 kcal/kg = 0.0732 kJ/kg
1 ft-lb	= 0.1383 kg-m
1 kg-m	= 7.23 ft/lbs

Metric versus United States Units of Measure					
1 inch	=	2.54 centimeters	1 kilogram	=	2.2 pounds
1 foot	=	30.5 centimeters	1 pound	=	4.45 Newtons
1 mile	=	1.61 kilometers	1 liter	=	.2642 gallons
1 meter	=	3.28 feet	1 milliliter	=	.0338 ounce
1 gram	=	.0353 ounce	1 gallon	=	3.785 liters
1 ounce	=	28.35 grams	1 calorie	=	4.18 Joules
1 pound	=	454 grams			
°C	=	(°F - 32) X 5/9	Boiling	=	212 °F/100°C
°F	=	(°C x 9/5) + 32	Freezing	=	32 °F/0 °C

Management

Quality Management Process[12,13]

- Review selected patient medical records
- Prioritize adverse event outcomes
- Conduct a thorough review of care
- Identify problematic areas of care
- Develop a plan to change identified aspects of care
- Implement the plan
- Monitor the plan
- Determine if the implemented change results in a measurable difference

Quality Improvement[12,13]

Quality improvement is a form of objective self-examination designed to improve the quality of services. Quality measures should assess the structure, process, and outcome of physical therapy care. According to the American Physical Therapy Association structure, process, and outcome are defined as follows:

Structure

A review of structure is an assessment of organization, staffing and staff qualifications, rules and policies governing physical work, records, equipment, and physical facilities. The assessment may include a judgment of the adequacy as well as the presence of the element of structure being examined.

Process

Process assessment is based on the degree or extent to which the therapist conforms to accepted professional practices in providing services. The various approaches to care and their application, efficacy, adequacy, and timeliness are considered. A process review requires that considerable attention be given to developing and specifying the standards to be used in the assessment.

Outcome

Outcome assessment is based on the condition of the patient at the conclusion of care in relation to the goals of treatment. Assessment of outcome provides a means of reviewing the practitioner, the services, and events that led to the results of care. The results of outcome assessment ultimately may lead to the evaluation of the basic treatment procedures and modalities of physical therapy and validation of the approaches to patient care. Outcomes are the ultimate manifestations of effectiveness and quality of care.

Models of Disability

The Nagi Model[14]

This model was originally designed in 1965 by a social worker named Saad Nagi as an alternative to the medical model of disease. It describes health status as a product of the relationship between health and function and is defined by four primary concepts:

Pathology: An interruption or interference in the body's normal processes and the simultaneous efforts of the systems to regain homeostasis. Pathology occurs at the cellular level.

Impairment: The loss or abnormality at the tissue, organ or body system level. This can be of an anatomic, physiologic, mental or emotional nature. Each pathology will present with an impairment, however, impairments can exist without pathology (e.g., congenital defects). Impairments occur at the organ level.

Functional Limitation: The inability to perform an action or skill in a normal manner due to an impairment. Functional limitations are at the level of the whole person.

Disability: Any restriction or inability to perform a socially defined role within a social or physical environment due to an impairment. Environmental barriers impose disability.

Example: A patient with progressive weakness presents with paralysis of the trunk and lower extremities. The patient is diagnosed with a T12 spinal cord tumor. The patient utilizes a wheelchair for mobility and requires assistance with self-care. Prior to hospitalization, the patient worked as a delivery man.

Pathology: Spinal cord tumor at T12

Impairment: Loss of motor function below T12

Functional Limitation: Unable to ambulate

Disability: Cannot continue to work as a delivery person

International Classification of Functioning, Disability and Health (ICF) Model[15]

The International Classification of Functioning, Disability and Health (ICF) is a classification of health and health-related domains. These domains are classified from body, individual, and societal perspectives by means of two lists: one list of body functions and structure and one list of domains of activity and participation. Since an individual's functioning and disability occurs in a context, the ICF also includes a list of environmental factors.

The ICF is the World Health Organization's (WHO) latest framework, endorsed in 2001, for measuring health and disability at both individual and population levels. The WHO's previous model, known as the ICIDH, was defined by the primary concepts of disease, impairment, disability, and handicap. The WHO is also responsible for the creation and implementation of the International Classification of Diseases (ICD-10).

The ICF's constructs acknowledge that every human being can experience some degree of disability. It shifts focus from cause to impact and takes into account the social aspects of disability and acknowledges environmental factors that can impact a person's functioning.

ICF Primary Concepts:

Body Functions: physiological functions of body systems including psychological functions

Body Structures: anatomical parts of the body such as organs, limbs and their components

Impairments: problems in body function or structure such as a significant deviation or loss

Activity: the execution of a task or action by an individual

Participation: involvement in a life situation

Activity Limitations: difficulties an individual may have in executing activities

Participation Restrictions: problems an individual may experience in involvement in life situations

Environmental Factors: physical, social, and attitudinal environment in which people live

Categories that fall under each domain include:

Body Function

- Mental functions
- Sensory functions and pain
- Voice and speech functions
- Functions of the cardiovascular, hematological, immunological, and respiratory systems
- Functions of the digestive, metabolic, and endocrine systems
- Genitourinary and reproductive functions
- Neuromuscular and movement-related functions
- Functions of the skin and related structures

Body Structure

- Structures of the nervous system
- The eye, ear, and related structures
- Structures involved in voice and speech
- Structures of the cardiovascular, immunological, and respiratory systems
- Structures related to the digestive, metabolic, and endocrine systems
- Structures related to the genitourinary and reproductive systems
- Structures related to movement
- Skin and related structures

Activities and Participation

- Learning and applying knowledge
- General tasks and demands
- Communication
- Mobility
- Self-care
- Domestic life
- Interpersonal interactions and relationships
- Major life areas
- Community, social, and civic life

Environmental Factors

- Products and technology
- Natural environment and human-made changes to environment
- Support and relationships
- Attitudes
- Services, systems, and policies

Example: A patient status post motor vehicle accident diagnosed with C6 complete tetraplegia is wheelchair dependent for mobility and resides in a town without public transportation. He was very active in his church choir and taught Sunday school prior to his motor vehicle accident.

Health Condition: Complete spinal cord injury - tetraplegia

Impairment: Paralysis

Activity Limitation: Incapable of using public transportation

Participation Restriction: Lack of accommodations in public transportation leads to no participation in religious activities

Ethics

"Morality cannot be legislated, but behavior can be regulated. Judicial decrees may not change the heart, but they can restrain the heartless." —*Martin Luther King Jr.*

Ethics is a branch of philosophy that emphasizes morality, justice, honesty, right versus wrong, and free will. Ethics is defined as a principle of good conduct or a body of right principles and specific moral choices. We respond to each instance that we face as health care providers based on specific moral choices. These are specific to each person and are based on cultural, religious, environmental, and personal values.

Ethical Principles and Terminology[10,11]

Autonomy: Requires that the wishes of competent individuals must be honored. Autonomy is often referred to as self-determination.

Beneficence: A moral obligation of health care providers to act for the benefit of others.

Confidentiality: The holding of professional secrets or discussions. Keeping client information within appropriate limits.

Duty: The obligations that individuals have to others in society.

Fidelity: Related to confidentiality and is defined as the moral duty to keep commitments that have been promised.

Justice: The quality of being just and fair; righteousness.

Nonmaleficence: The obligation of health care providers to above all else, do no harm.

Paternalism: A term used when someone fails to recognize another individual's rights and autonomy.

Rights: The ability to take advantage of a moral entitlement to do something or not to do something.

Veracity: Obligation of health care providers to tell the truth.

Ethical Theories and Issues

Teleological theory (consequentialism)[10]

This ethical theory believes that the outcome or consequences of a particular action should come from answering the question "What should I do?" The person judges the good and bad outcome based on answering "Which decision would bring the best consequences?" When the decision cannot be made from these questions, a person will choose the course of action that brings the most good and least harm. This theory supports paternalistic behavior if no harm is done. The worth of an action is judged by the consequences and the goal will be that the end result justifies the means.

Deontologism theory[10]

This ethical theory does not focus on the consequences of an action, but on the action itself and if the action follows moral principles. The theory believes that a person's obligations should determine the ethical course of action. There is a strict following of the principles of ethics (autonomy, nonmaleficence, beneficence, and justice).

Professional Behaviors

✓ Organization	**L**- Listen
✓ Professional presentation	**E**- Explain
✓ Dependability	**A**- Acknowledge
✓ Initiative	**R**- Recommend
✓ Empathy	**N**- Negotiate
✓ Cooperation	
✓ Clinical reasoning	
✓ Written communication	
✓ Verbal communication	

Malpractice[11]

Claims of malpractice usually stem from the theory of negligence. Negligence describes a substandard level of care for the particular profession. Negligence deals with a particular conduct, not state of mind.

In order to prove malpractice through negligence, there are four elements:

1. A duty to act in a particular manner
2. Conduct that breaches that particular duty
3. Damage that occurs from that conduct
4. Conduct that is substandard, causing injury

Legal

Health Insurance Portability and Accountability Act

The Health Insurance Portability and Accountability Act (HIPAA) is a law that was passed in 1996 with the purpose of setting guidelines for the protection of patients' health information. This law applies to all covered entities, including health plans, health care providers, and billing services. Within Title II of HIPAA, there are several separate "rules" that dictate how protected health information (PHI) can be used.

PHI is considered to be any individually identifiable health information that is used by a covered entity. Individually identifiable health information is any health information that relates to the patient's health condition, the provision of their care or the payment for services, and that can be linked to the patient via a patient identifier (e.g., name, address, social security number, birthdate).

The Privacy Rule sets guidelines for the disclosure of PHI as needed for efficient and effective patient care. For example, health care providers can share PHI with other health care providers to facilitate treatment without the consent of the patient. At the same time, the Privacy Rule ensures that the patient's PHI is properly protected and the patient has rights concerning their own PHI. For example, when disclosing PHI, a covered entity must disclose only the minimum information that is necessary to facilitate treatment. Additionally, covered entities must maintain patient confidentiality at all times by de-identifying PHI, unless patient identification is necessary.

The Security Rule deals specifically with how electronic PHI should be protected and is divided into administrative, physical, and technical safeguards. Administrative safeguards address how the covered entity will protect electronic PHI, including creating policies and procedures and training staff members. Physical safeguards focus on controlling physical access to electronic PHI, including limiting access to the health care facility as well as limiting access to employee workstations. Technical safeguards include protecting access to electronic devices (e.g., use of passwords) and protecting information that is transmitted electronically.

OSHA

The Occupational Safety and Health Act is a law that was passed in 1970 to help protect employees from being physically harmed in the workplace. The law created the Occupational Safety and Health Administration (OSHA), an agency that sets and enforces workplace safety and health standards. These standards may include:

- Limiting exposure to hazardous chemicals
- Creating a materials safety data sheet
- Use of personal protective equipment
- Creating emergency action plans
- Providing protection against falls
- Keeping record of workplace injuries and illnesses

In addition to having a safe workplace, employees also have other rights. Employers must provide training for their employees concerning any and all workplace hazards. Additionally, employees have the right to file a complaint with OSHA without workplace retaliation.

Sexual Harassment

Sexual harassment is a form of discrimination that is based on a person's sex/gender. This type of harassment was made illegal in Title VII of the Civil Rights Act of 1964. Sexual harassment may include unwelcome sexual advances, requests for sexual favors or other verbal and physical conduct of a sexual nature. To be considered sexual harassment, the conduct must interfere with an individual's employment or work performance or must create a hostile or intimidating work environment.

There are many scenarios in which sexual harassment may occur. The perpetrator may be a boss or supervisor, though is not always in a position of power over the victim. Additionally, victims may include the person being harassed and other individuals who find the conduct offensive. The perpetrator can be a man or a woman, and the victim does not necessarily have to be a person of the opposite gender.

In cases of sexual harassment, the victim should attempt to inform the perpetrator that the behavior is unwelcome and that it needs to stop. The victim should file an official complaint with their employer if the behavior continues. Retaliation against employees that file a complaint is illegal. Prevention is the best tool in stopping sexual harassment. Employers should provide training on sexual harassment and establish an effective grievance process.

Elements of a Risk Management Program

- Management involvement
- Risk management organization
- Incident reporting and investigation
- Inspections
- Communications

Recommendations to Avoid Litigation[11]

- Conduct a thorough examination
- Seek consultation when in doubt
- Check the condition of your equipment
- Instruct patients thoroughly
- Keep the referring physician informed
- Obtain proper consent for treatment
- Do not delegate to unqualified individuals
- Keep accurate and timely written records

Legal Terminology[11]

Abandonment: Unacceptable one-sided termination of services by a health care professional without patient consent or agreement.

Administrative law: Administrative agencies at the federal and state level develop rules and regulations to supplement statutes and executive orders.

Common law: Refers to court decisions in the absence of statutory law. Common law often creates legal precedent in areas where statutes have not been enacted.

Constitutional law: Involves law that is derived from the federal Constitution. The United States Supreme Court is responsible for ultimately interpreting and enforcing the Constitution.

Informed consent: The patient is required to sign a document and give permission to the health care professional to render treatment. This should be obtained from the patient in accordance with the standards of practice prior to initiation of treatment. The patient has the right to full disclosure of treatment procedures, risks, expected outcomes, and goals.

Malpractice: The failure to exercise the skills that would normally be exercised by other members of the profession with similar skills and training. This can include areas of professional negligence, breach of contract issues, and intentional conduct by a health care professional.

Negligence: The failure to do what a reasonable and prudent person would ordinarily have done under the same or similar circumstances for a given situation. In order to prove negligence, the plaintiff must prove all of the following:

- There was a duty owed to the plaintiff by the defendant.
- There was a breach of that duty under conditions that constituted negligence and the negligence was the proximate cause of the breach.
- There was damage to the plaintiff's person or property.

Risk management: The identification, analysis, and evaluation of risks and the selection of the most advantageous method for treating them.

Statutory law: Congress and state legislatures are responsible for enacting statutes. Examples of federal statutes affecting health care include the Americans with Disabilities Act and the Family and Medical Leave Act.

Tort: A private or civil wrong or injury, involving omission and/or commission.

Delegation and Supervision[16]

Direction and Supervision of the Physical Therapist Assistant

Physical therapists have a responsibility to deliver services in ways that protect the public safety and maximize the availability of their services. They do this through direct delivery of services in conjunction with responsible utilization of physical therapist assistants who assist with selected components of intervention. The physical therapist assistant is the only individual permitted to assist a physical therapist in selected interventions under the direction and supervision of a physical therapist.

Direction and supervision are essential in the provision of quality physical therapy services. The degree of direction and supervision necessary for assuring quality physical therapy services is dependent upon many factors, including the education, experiences, and responsibilities of the parties involved, as well as the organizational structure in which the physical therapy services are provided.

Regardless of the setting in which the physical therapy service is provided, the following responsibilities must be borne solely by the physical therapist:

1. Interpretation of referrals when available.
2. Initial examination, evaluation, diagnosis, and prognosis.
3. Development or modification of a plan of care which is based on the initial examination or reexamination and which includes the physical therapy goals and outcomes.
4. Determination of when the expertise and decision-making capability of the physical therapist requires the physical therapist to personally render physical therapy interventions and when it may be appropriate to utilize the physical therapist assistant. A physical therapist shall determine the most appropriate utilization of the physical therapist assistant that provides for the delivery of service that is safe, effective, and efficient.
5. Reexamination of the patient/client in light of their goals, and revision of the plan of care when indicated.
6. Establishment of the discharge plan and documentation of discharge summary/status.
7. Oversight of all documentation for services rendered to each patient/client.

The physical therapist remains responsible for the physical therapy services provided when the physical therapist's plan of care involves the physical therapist assistant to assist with selected interventions. Regardless of the setting in which the service is provided, the determination to utilize physical therapist assistants for selected interventions requires the education, expertise, and professional judgment of a physical therapist as described by the *Standards of Practice, Guide to Professional Conduct*, and *Code of Ethics.*

In determining the appropriate extent of assistance from the physical therapist assistant (PTA), the physical therapist considers:

- The PTA's education, training, experience, and skill level.
- Patient/client criticality, acuity, stability, and complexity.
- The predictability of the consequences.
- The setting in which the care is being delivered.
- Federal and state statutes.
- Liability and risk management concerns.
- The mission of physical therapy services for the setting.
- The needed frequency of reexamination.

Physical Therapist Assistant

Definition: The physical therapist assistant is a technically educated health care provider who assists the physical therapist in the provision of physical therapy. The physical therapist assistant is a graduate of a physical therapist assistant associate degree program accredited by the Commission on Accreditation in Physical Therapy Education (CAPTE).

Utilization: The physical therapist is directly responsible for the actions of the physical therapist assistant related to patient/client management. The physical therapist assistant may perform selected physical therapy interventions under the direction and at least general supervision of the physical therapist. In general supervision, the physical therapist is not required to be on-site for direction and supervision, but must be available at least by telecommunications. The ability of the physical therapist assistant to perform the selected interventions as directed shall be assessed on an ongoing basis by the supervising physical therapist. The physical therapist assistant makes modifications to selected interventions either to progress the patient/client as directed by the physical therapist or to ensure patient/client safety and comfort.

The physical therapist assistant must work under the direction and at least general supervision of the physical therapist. In all practice settings, the performance of selected interventions by the physical therapist assistant must be consistent with safe and legal physical therapist practice, and shall be predicated on the following factors: complexity and acuity of the patient's/client's needs; proximity and accessibility to the physical therapist; supervision available in the event of emergencies or critical events; and type of setting in which the service is provided.

When supervising the physical therapist assistant in any off-site setting, the following requirements must be observed:

1. A physical therapist must be accessible by telecommunications to the physical therapist assistant at all times while the physical therapist assistant is treating patients/clients.
2. There must be regularly scheduled and documented conferences with the physical therapist assistant regarding patients/clients, the frequency of which is determined by the needs of the patient/client and the needs of the physical therapist assistant.
3. In those situations in which a physical therapist assistant is involved in the care of a patient/client, a supervisory visit by the physical therapist will be made:
    a. Upon the physical therapist assistant's request for a reexamination, when a change in the plan of care is needed, prior to any planned discharge, and in response to a change in the patient's/client's medical status.
    b. At least once a month, or at a higher frequency when established by the physical therapist, in accordance with the needs of the patient/client.
    c. A supervisory visit should include:
        i. An on-site reexamination of the patient/client.
        ii. On-site review of the plan of care with appropriate revision or termination.
        iii. Evaluation of need and recommendation for utilization of outside resources.

HOD P06-05-18-26 Updated: 08/07/12 American Physical Therapy Association, web site 2017.

Health Care Professionals[17]

Audiologists

Audiologists assess patients with suspected hearing disorders. The audiologist can educate patients on how to make the best use of their available hearing and assist them in selecting and fitting appropriate aids. Audiologists are required to possess a master's degree or equivalent. The vast majority of states require audiologists to obtain a license to practice.

Chiropractors

Chiropractors diagnose and treat patients whose health problems are associated with the body's muscular, nervous, and skeletal systems. Patient care activities include manually adjusting the spine, ordering and interpreting X-rays, performing postural analysis, and administering various physical agents. Chiropractors are required to complete a four-year chiropractic curriculum leading to the Doctor of Chiropractic degree. All states require chiropractors to obtain a license to practice.

Home Health Aides

Home health aides provide health-related services to the elderly, disabled, and ill in their homes. Patient care activities include performing housekeeping duties, assisting with ambulation or transfers, and promoting personal hygiene. A registered nurse, physical therapist, or social worker is often the health care professional that assigns specific duties and supervises the home health aide. The federal government has established guidelines for home health aides whose employers receive reimbursement from Medicare. The National Association for Home Care offers voluntary national certification for home health aides.

Licensed Practical Nurses

Licensed practical nurses care for the sick, injured, convalescent, and disabled under the direction of physicians and registered nurses. Patient care activities include taking vital signs, performing transfers, applying dressings, administering injections, and instructing patients and families. In some states, licensed practical nurses can administer prescribed medications or start intravenous fluids. Experienced licensed practical nurses may supervise nursing assistants and aides. Educational programs for licensed practical nurses are approximately one year in length and include classroom study and supervised clinical practice. All states require a license to practice.

Medical Assistants

Medical assistants perform routine administrative and clinical tasks in a medical office. Administrative duties include answering telephones, updating patient files, completing insurance forms, and scheduling appointments. Clinical duties include taking medical histories, measuring vital signs, and assisting the physician during treatment. Educational programs for medical assistants are typically one to two years in length.

Occupational Therapists

Occupational therapists help people improve their ability to perform activities of daily living, work, and leisure skills. The educational preparation of occupational therapists emphasizes the social, emotional, and physiological effects of illness and injury. Occupational therapists most commonly work with individuals who have conditions that are mentally, physically, developmentally or emotionally disabling. Occupational therapists can enter the field with bachelors, masters, or doctoral degrees. All states require occupational therapists to obtain a license to practice.

Occupational Therapy Aides

Occupational therapy aides work under the direction of occupational therapists to provide rehabilitation services to persons with mental, physical, developmental or emotional impairments. Occupational therapy aides often prepare materials and assemble equipment used during treatment and may be responsible for a variety of clerical tasks. The majority of training for occupational therapy aides occurs on the job.

Occupational Therapy Assistants

Occupational therapy assistants work under the direction of occupational therapists to provide rehabilitation services to persons with mental, physical, developmental or emotional impairments. Occupational therapy assistants perform a variety of rehabilitative activities and exercises as outlined in an established treatment plan. To practice as an occupational therapy assistant, individuals must complete an associate degree or certificate program from an accredited academic institution. Occupational therapy assistants are regulated in the majority of states.

Physical Therapists

Physical therapists provide services to help restore function, improve mobility, relieve pain, and prevent or limit permanent physical disabilities of patients suffering from injuries or disease. Physical therapists engage in examination, evaluation, diagnosis, prognosis, and intervention in an effort to maximize patient outcomes. Physical therapists currently enter the field with a doctorate degree.

Physical Therapy Aides

Physical therapy aides are considered support personnel who may be involved in support services directed by physical therapists. Physical therapy aides receive on the job training under the direction and supervision of a physical therapist and are permitted to function only with continuous on-site supervision by a physical therapist or in some cases, a physical therapist assistant. Support services are limited to methods and techniques that do not require clinical decision making by the physical therapist or clinical problem solving by the physical therapist assistant.

Physical Therapist Assistants

Physical therapist assistants perform components of physical therapy procedures and related tasks selected and delegated by a supervising physical therapist. Physical therapist assistants may modify an intervention only in accordance with changes in patient status and within the established plan of care developed by the physical therapist. Physical therapist assistants are the only paraprofessionals that perform physical therapy interventions. Typically, physical therapist assistants have an associate degree from an accredited physical therapist assistant program. The vast majority of states require physical therapist assistants to obtain a license to practice.

Physicians

Physicians diagnose illnesses and prescribe and administer treatment for people suffering from injury or disease. The term physician encompasses both the Doctor of Medicine (MD) and the Doctor of Osteopathic Medicine (DO). The role of the MD and DO are very similar, however, the DO tends to place special emphasis on the body's musculoskeletal system, preventive medicine, and holistic patient care. All states require physicians to obtain a license to practice.

Physician Assistants

Physician assistants provide health care services with supervision by physicians. The supervising physician and established state law determine the specific duties of the physician assistant. In the vast majority of states physician assistants may prescribe medication. Physician assistants work with the supervision of a physician. All states require physician assistants to obtain a license to practice.

Psychologists

Psychologists use various techniques including interviewing and testing to advise people how to deal with problems of everyday life. In the health care setting, psychologists may be involved in counseling programs designed to help people achieve goals such as weight loss or smoking cessation. A doctoral degree is usually required for employment as a licensed clinical or counseling psychologist. All states require psychologists to obtain a license to practice.

Recreational Therapists

Recreational therapists provide treatment services and recreation activities to individuals with disabilities or illness. In acute care hospitals and rehabilitation hospitals, recreational therapists work closely with other health care professionals to treat and rehabilitate individuals with specific medical conditions. In long-term care settings, recreational therapists function primarily by offering structured group sessions emphasizing leisure activities. Recreational therapists are required to have a bachelor's degree in order to be eligible for certification as certified therapeutic recreation specialists.

Registered Nurses

Registered nurses work to promote health, prevent disease, and help patients cope with illness. Patient care activities are extremely diverse including tasks such as assisting physicians during treatments and examinations, administering medications, recording symptoms and reactions, and instructing patients and families. Registered nurse programs include associates, bachelors, and diploma programs. All states require registered nurses to obtain a license to practice.

Respiratory Therapists

Respiratory therapists evaluate, treat, and care for patients with breathing disorders. The vast majority of respiratory therapists are employed in hospitals. Patient care activities include performing postural drainage techniques, measuring lung capacities, administering oxygen and aerosols, and analyzing oxygen and carbon dioxide concentrations. Educational programs for respiratory therapists are offered by hospitals, colleges, universities, vocational-technical institutes, and the military. The vast majority of states require respiratory therapists to obtain a license to practice.

Social Workers

Social workers help patients and their families to cope with chronic, acute or terminal illnesses and attempt to resolve problems that stand in the way of recovery or rehabilitation. A bachelor's degree is often the minimum requirement to qualify for employment as a social worker, however, in the health field, the master's degree is often required. All states have licensing, certification or registration requirements for social workers.

Speech-Language Pathologists

Speech-language pathologists evaluate speech, language, cognitive-communication, and swallowing skills of children and adults. The majority of practitioners provide direct clinical services to individuals with communication disorders. Speech-language pathologists are required to possess a master's degree or equivalent. The vast majority of states require speech-language pathologists to obtain a license to practice.

Regulatory Groups

American Physical Therapy Association (APTA): The APTA is the professional organization that represents physical therapists, physical therapist assistants, and physical therapy students. The goal of the APTA is to advance physical therapist practice, education, and research and increase the awareness of how physical therapy can play a role in health care. The APTA is responsible for creating and promoting ethical principles and standards of conduct for physical therapy practitioners and for influencing public policy that will affect the practice of physical therapy. Each state has its own APTA chapter, and there are also several special-interest sections (e.g., orthopedics, women's health) that exist within the APTA.

Federation of State Boards of Physical Therapy (FSBPT): The FSBPT is an organization that aims to protect the public by ensuring that physical therapists and physical therapist assistants provide safe and competent physical therapy services. They create the National Physical Therapy Examinations and determine necessary scoring requirements for PTs and PTAs to obtain licensure.

State licensing boards: State licensing boards are responsible for providing professional licenses to physical therapists and physical therapist assistants. Eligibility to acquire a license can vary widely from state to state, but it is generally based on a criminal background check, completion of an accredited physical therapy or physical therapist assistant educational program, and the ability to pass the National Physical Therapy Examinations provided by the FSBPT. State licensing boards also create and maintain the rules surrounding licensure renewal.

Commission on Accreditation of Rehabilitation Facilities (CARF): CARF is a nonprofit organization that provides accreditation services for institutions that provide health and human services, which may include behavioral health services, aging services, medical rehabilitation facilities, and opioid treatment programs. Institutions that are accredited by CARF commit to providing high quality health care services to ensure the satisfaction of consumers.

The Joint Commission: The Joint Commission, formerly the Joint Commission on Accreditation of Healthcare Organizations (JCAHO), is a nonprofit organization that provides accreditation and certification services to a variety of health care organizations, which may include hospitals, doctor's offices, nursing homes, home care companies, and behavioral health facilities. Organizations that are accredited by the Joint Commission agree to meet certain performance standards in their provision of health care services to ensure that members of the public are receiving the highest quality health care.

Health Care Settings

Acute care: This type of care is typically provided in a hospital for patients who have a serious injury or medical condition or who are recovering from a surgery. The inpatient stay is as short as possible; patients are typically discharged as soon as they are medically stable and able to transfer to a rehabilitation hospital, a skilled nursing facility, or home.

Long-term acute care: This type of care is provided for patients who need an extended hospital stay due to a chronic illness or injury. These patients require constant medical supervision (e.g., patient needing mechanical ventilation) and thus are not ready to be discharged to another facility. These types of facilities may be stand-alone hospitals or may exist as a unit within an acute care hospital.

Acute rehabilitation: This type of care occurs in a specific type of hospital that requires patients to participate in therapies (e.g., physical, occupational, speech) for at least three hours a day. Patients recovering from an injury or surgery are often discharged to a rehabilitation hospital from an acute care hospital once they are medically stable. The goal of this setting is to improve the patient's function so they can be discharged back to their home, though some patients may need long-term care in a nursing facility.

Sub-acute rehabilitation: This type of care provides similar services as an acute rehabilitation hospital, though the intensity of rehabilitation services is less. This setting is appropriate for patients of a lower functional level who need therapy services, but cannot tolerate three hours of therapy each day (i.e., receive one to two hours per day).

Nursing home: This type of care occurs in an inpatient setting that provides care for patients who are at a lower functional level and require assistance with their activities of daily living. These patients no longer need to be in a hospital, but they still require medical care and supervision that cannot be provided at home. Care may be provided on a long-term basis or for short periods of time (e.g., post-operative). A skilled nursing facility is a specific type of nursing home that provides skilled nursing and rehabilitation services.

Hospice care: This type of care is provided to patients who have an incurable disease and are nearing the end of their life. Health care in this setting is focused on managing a patient's pain and maximizing their function. Hospice care is often provided in a patient's home, though there are inpatient facilities that also provide these services.

Home health: In this setting, rehabilitation and nursing services are provided in the patient's home as opposed to an inpatient or outpatient setting. This setting is appropriate for patients who no longer need the constant medical care and supervision of an inpatient setting, but who are still limited in their physical ability to access outpatient services (e.g., unable to drive, inability to walk community distances).

Ambulatory care: This type of outpatient care is designed for patients that are typically at a higher functional level. The patients are well enough that they can travel to the clinic to attend their treatment session and return home the same day. Outpatient physical therapy is usually provided in a private practice clinic or in a hospital's outpatient department.

Physical Therapy Practice

The Physical Therapist Patient/Client Management Model[14]

Examination: The process of obtaining a history, performing a systems review, and selecting and administering tests and measures to gather data about the patient/client. The initial examination is a comprehensive screening and specific testing process that leads to a diagnostic classification. The examination process also may identify possible problems that require consultation with, or referral to, another provider.

Evaluation: A dynamic process in which the physical therapist makes clinical judgments based on data gathered during the examination. This process also may identify possible problems that require consultation with, or referral to, another provider.

Diagnosis: Both the process and the end result of evaluating examination data, which the physical therapist organizes into defined clusters, syndromes or categories to help determine the prognosis (including the plan of care) and the most appropriate intervention strategies.

Prognosis (including plan of care): Determination of the level of optimal improvement that may be attained through intervention and the amount of time required to reach that level. The plan of care specifies the interventions to be used and their timing and frequency.

Intervention: Purposeful and skilled interaction of the physical therapist with the patient/client and, if appropriate, with other individuals involved in the care of the patient/client, using various physical therapy methods and techniques to produce changes in the condition that are consistent with the diagnosis and prognosis. The physical therapist conducts a re-examination to determine changes in patient/client status and to modify or redirect intervention. The decision to re-examine may be based on new clinical findings or on lack of patient/client progress. The process of re-examination also may identify the need for consultation with, or referral to, another provider.

Outcomes: Results of patient/client management, which include the impact of physical therapy interventions in the following domains: pathology/pathophysiology (disease, disorder or condition); impairments, functional limitations and disabilities, risk reduction/ prevention, health, wellness, and fitness; societal resources; and patient/client satisfaction.

From Guide to Physical Therapist Practice 3.0. American Physical Therapy Association, 2014.

Standards of Practice for Physical Therapy[18]

Preamble

The physical therapy profession is committed to transforming society by optimizing movement to improve the human experience. Physical therapists pursue excellence in a professional scope of practice that includes optimizing physical function, health, quality of life, and well-being across the lifespan, and they work to improve population health in the communities where they practice. The American Physical Therapy Association (APTA) attests to this commitment by adopting and promoting the following *Standards of Practice for Physical Therapy*. These standards are the profession's statement of conditions and performances that are essential for provision of high-quality professional service to society, and they provide a foundation for assessment of physical therapist practice.

I. Ethical/Legal Considerations

A. Ethical Considerations

The physical therapist practices according to the APTA *Code of Ethics for the Physical Therapist*.

The physical therapist assistant complies with the APTA *Standards of Ethical Conduct for the Physical Therapist Assistant*.

B. Legal Considerations

The physical therapist complies with all the legal requirements of jurisdictions regulating the practice of physical therapy.

The physical therapist assistant complies with all the legal requirements of jurisdictions regulating the work of the physical therapist assistant.

II. Administration of the Physical Therapy Service

A. Statement of Mission, Purposes, Goals, Objectives, and Scope of Services

The physical therapy service has a statement of mission, purposes, goals, objectives, and scope of services that is reviewed annually and reflects the needs and interests of the patients and clients served, the physical therapy personnel affiliated with the service, and the community.

B. Organizational Plan

The physical therapy service has a written organizational plan.

The organizational plan:

- Describes relationships among components within the physical therapy service and, where the service is part of a larger organization, between the service and the other components of that organization;
- Ensures that a physical therapist provides the clinical direction of physical therapist services;

- Defines supervisory structures within the service; and
- Reflects current personnel functions.

C. Policies and Procedures

The physical therapy service has written policies and procedures that are reviewed regularly and revised as necessary; reflect the operation, mission, purposes, goals, objectives, and scope of the service; are legally compliant with federal and state law; and are guided by the association's positions, standards, guidelines, policies, and procedures.

D. Administration

Guided and informed by APTA positions, standards, guidelines, policies, and procedures, the physical therapist responsible for the clinical direction of physical therapist services ensures:

- Compliance with local, state, and federal requirements;
- Services are provided in accordance with established policies and procedures;
- The process for assignment and reassignment of physical therapist staff (handoff communication) supports individual physical therapist responsibility to their patients and clients and meets the needs of the patients and clients; and
- Continuing competence of physical therapists and physical therapist assistants by providing training consistent with their respective roles.

E. Fiscal Management

The physical therapist responsible for physical therapist services, in consultation with physical therapy staff and appropriate administrative personnel, participates in the planning for and allocation of resources. Fiscal planning and management of the service is based on sound accounting principles.

The fiscal management plan:

- Includes a budget that provides for optimal use of resources;
- Ensures accurate recording and reporting of financial information;
- Allows for cost-effective utilization of resources;
- Follows billing processes that are consistent with federal regulations and payer policies, charge reasonable fees for physical therapist services, and encourage physical therapists to be knowledgeable of service fee schedules, contractual relationships, and payment methodologies; and
- Considers options for providing *pro bono* services.

F. Improvement of Quality of Care and Performance

The physical therapy service has a written plan for continuous improvement of quality of care and performance of services.

The improvement plan:

- Provides evidence of ongoing review and evaluation of services; and
- Provides a mechanism for documenting improvement in quality of care and performance and is consistent with requirements of external agencies, as applicable.

G. Staffing

The physical therapy personnel affiliated with the physical therapy service have demonstrated competence, and are sufficient to achieve the mission, purposes, goals, objectives, and scope of the service.

The physical therapy service:

- Ensures that the level of expertise within the service is appropriate to the needs of the patients and clients served, and consistent with the scope of the services provided; and
- Provides appropriate professional and support personnel to meet the needs of the patient and client population.

H. Staff Development

The physical therapy service has a written plan that provides for appropriate and ongoing staff development.

The staff development plan:

- Includes strategies for lifelong learning and professional and career development that include self-assessment, individual goal setting, and organizational needs;
- Includes mechanisms to foster mentorship activities;
- Includes information regarding evidence-based practice and relevant clinical practice guidelines; and
- Includes education regarding use of clinical practice guidelines, reflective reasoning, clinical reasoning, metacognition, and the value of mentoring.

I. Physical Setting

The physical setting, where applicable, is designed to provide a safe and accessible environment that facilitates fulfillment of the mission, purposes, goals, objectives, and scope of the physical therapy service. It is appropriate for the number and type of patients and clients served. The equipment is safe and sufficient to achieve the purposes and goals of the physical therapy service.

J. Coordination

Physical therapy personnel collaborate with all health services providers and with patients, clients, caregivers, and others as appropriate; and use a team and person-centered approach in coordinating and providing physical therapist services.

III. Patient and Client Management

Physical therapist practice incorporates all components of evidence-based practice, integrating best available research evidence, clinical expertise, and an individual's values and circumstances to make decisions regarding services for patients and clients, practice management, and health policy.

A. Physical Therapist of Record

The physical therapist of record is the therapist who assumes responsibility for patient and client management and is accountable for the coordination, continuation, and progression of the plan of care.

B. Patient and Client Collaboration

Within the patient and client management process, the physical therapist, the individual, and their caregiver(s) establish and maintain an ongoing collaborative process of decision-making that exists throughout the provision of services and can extend over the lifespan.

C. Initial Examination/Evaluation/Diagnosis/ Prognosis

The physical therapist performs an initial examination and evaluation to establish a diagnosis and prognosis prior to intervention. Wellness and prevention visits or encounters may occur without the presence of disease, illness, impairments, activity limitations, or participation restrictions. Physical therapist services include the use of assessments to identify the presence of risk factors, and cognitive and environmental barriers and opportunities that may be targets for health promotion activities.

The physical therapist examination:

- Is documented and dated by the physical therapist who performed it;
- Identifies the physical therapy and as indicated other health needs of the patient or client;
- Incorporates appropriate diagnostic procedures, tests, and measures to facilitate outcome measurement;
- Produces data that are sufficient to allow evaluation, diagnosis, prognosis, and the establishment of a plan of care;
- May result in recommendations for additional services to meet the needs of the patient or client; and
- Includes, when appropriate and available, results from imaging, laboratory testing, and neurologic testing, to assist with clinical decision-making.

D. Plan of Care

The plan of care consists of statements that specify the goals, predicted level of optimal improvement, interventions to be used, proposed duration and frequency of the interventions that are required to reach the goals and outcomes, and plans as appropriate for referral, consultation, or co-management with other providers.

The physical therapist involves the patient or client and appropriate others in the planning, goals and outcomes, proposed frequency and duration, and implementation of the plan of care. Consideration is given to clinical practice guidelines when they are in alignment with the patient or client diagnosis and/or prognosis.

Prevention and wellness interactions, particularly at a community level, may not require a plan of care.

E. Intervention

The physical therapist provides or directs and supervises intervention consistent with results of the examination, evaluation, diagnosis, prognosis, and plan of care. Intervention is focused on optimizing functional independence, emphasizes patient or client instruction, and promotes proactive, wellness-oriented lifestyles. It may be provided in an episode of care, or in a single visit or encounter such as for wellness and/or prevention, specialty consultation, or follow-up after an episode of care. Services also may be provided intermittently over longer periods of time in cases of managing chronic conditions or as needed in the case of a lifelong patient or client relationship with the physical therapist.

An *episode of care* is the managed care provided for a specific problem or condition during a set time period. The episode can be given either for a short period or on a continuous basis, or it may consist of a series of intervals marked by 1 or more brief separations from care.

The intervention:

- Is provided at a level that is consistent with best available evidence and current physical therapist practice;
- Is in direct alignment with the patient's or client's desired outcomes and goals;
- Is altered in accordance with changes in response or status; and
- Is provided in such a way that directed and supervised responsibilities are commensurate with the qualifications and legal limitations of the physical therapist assistant.

F. Lifelong and Long-Term Patient and Client Relationships

Physical therapists foster and encourage lifelong and long-term patient and client relationships. Where feasible, physical therapists, as entry-point providers, provide services within the community that are available to patients or clients over a lifetime. Efforts are made to address movement system disorders and to maintain optimal health and wellness through physical therapist intervention as needed.

Lifelong and long-term patient and client relationships:

- Foster continuity of service over patients' and clients' lifespans by addressing changes in the movement system, health status, or disabilities as they arise;
- Empower patients and clients to advocate for their own health;
- Empower the physical therapist to advocate on behalf of patients and clients within the health services system; and
- Foster identification by patients and clients that they have their own physical therapist among various health professions.

G. Reexamination

The physical therapist reexamines the patient or client as necessary to evaluate progress or change in status. Reexamination may occur during an episode of care, during follow-up visits or encounters after an episode of care, or periodically in the case of chronic care management or lifelong and long-term relationships with patients and clients. During reexamination the physical therapist modifies the plan of care accordingly, refers the patient or client to another health services provider for consultation, or concludes the episode of care.

H. Conclusion of an Episode of Care

The physical therapist concludes an episode of care when the goals and outcomes for the patient or client have been achieved, when the patient or client is unable to continue to progress toward goals, or when the physical therapist determines that the patient or client will no longer benefit from physical therapy. Conclusion of a single episode of care may not, in many settings or circumstances, signal the end of a patient or client provider relationship.

I. Communication/Coordination/Documentation

The physical therapist communicates, coordinates, and documents all aspects of patient and client management including the results of the initial examination and evaluation, diagnosis, prognosis, plan of care, intervention, responses to intervention, changes in patient or client status relative to the intervention, reexamination, and episode of care summary. The physical therapist of record is responsible for "handoff" communication and follows "handoff" procedures developed by the physical therapy service. As appropriate, patient records and data are recorded using a method that allows for collective analysis.

J. Co-management/Consultation/Referral

At any point in an episode of care, or in a long-term or lifelong physical therapist-patient or client relationship, a physical therapist may engage in 1 or more of the following actions related to involvement of other providers in the management process. Other providers may be those in other professions and also may be physical therapist colleagues, some with advanced practice credentials or board certification in a clinical specialty.

- Co-management: The physical therapist shares responsibility for the individual with another professional who is also managing that individual.
- Consultation: In some cases, the physical therapist renders professional expert opinion or advice by applying highly specialized knowledge and skills to identify problems, recommend solutions, or produce a specified outcome or product in a given amount of time on behalf of an individual. In other cases, the physical therapist seeks consultative services from another provider to inform the physical therapist plan of care and/or to obtain services for the individual that are beyond the professional or personal scope of practice of the physical therapist. In these cases, the physical therapist shares responsibility for the individual with the consultant.
- Referral: The physical therapist may:
  - Refer an individual to another provider and either conclude care or not develop a plan of care;
  - Refer an individual to another provider and continue the plan of care at the same time;
  - Receive an individual referred from another provider who chooses not to continue services for the individual; or
  - Receive an individual from another provider who continues to provide services to the individual (if the physical therapy episode of care is ongoing, the physical therapist shares responsibility for the individual).

IV. Education

The physical therapist is responsible for individual professional development. The physical therapist assistant is responsible for individual career development.

- The physical therapist and the physical therapist assistant, under the direction and supervision of the physical therapist, participate in the education of peers, other health services providers, and students.
- The physical therapist educates and provides consultation to consumers and the general public regarding the purposes and benefits of physical therapy.
- The physical therapist educates and provides consultation to consumers and the general public regarding the roles of the physical therapist and the physical therapist assistant.

V. Advocacy

The physical therapist and the physical therapist assistant will participate in advocacy for patients' and clients' rights with respect to:

- Physical therapy being an entry-point for patients into the health services system;
- Physical therapists serving in primary care roles;
- Appropriate access to needed health services including physical therapist services; and
- Communities creating safe and accessible built environments, where population health is a priority.

VI. Research

The physical therapist applies research findings to practice and encourages, participates in, and promotes activities that establish the outcomes of patient and client management provided by the physical therapist.

The physical therapist:

- Remains current in their knowledge of literature related to practice;
- Protects the rights of research subjects and maintains the integrity of research;
- Participates in research as appropriate to individual education, experience, and expertise;
- Educates physical therapists, physical therapist assistants, students, other health professionals, and the general public about new evidence from research and the outcomes of physical therapist practice; and
- Accesses and translates knowledge in support of clinical decisions, and uses literature based on its quality and appropriateness.

VII. Community Responsibility

The physical therapist demonstrates community responsibility by participating in community and community agency activities, educating the public, formulating public policy, and providing *pro bono* physical therapist services.

HOD S06-19-29-50, Updated: September 2019. American Physical Therapy Association website, accessed April 2020.

Code of Ethics for the Physical Therapist[19]

Preamble

The Code of Ethics for the Physical Therapist (Code of Ethics) delineates the ethical obligations of all physical therapists as determined by the House of Delegates of the American Physical Therapy Association (APTA). The purposes of this Code of Ethics are to:

1. Define the ethical principles that form the foundation of physical therapist practice in patient/client management, consultation, education, research, and administration.
2. Provide standards of behavior and performance that form the basis of professional accountability to the public.
3. Provide guidance for physical therapists facing ethical challenges, regardless of their professional roles and responsibilities.
4. Educate physical therapists, students, other health care professionals, regulators, and the public regarding the core values, ethical principles, and standards that guide the professional conduct of the physical therapist.
5. Establish the standards by which the American Physical Therapy Association can determine if a physical therapist has engaged in unethical conduct.

No code of ethics is exhaustive nor can it address every situation. Physical therapists are encouraged to seek additional advice or consultation in instances where the guidance of the Code of Ethics may not be definitive.

This Code of Ethics is built upon the five roles of the physical therapist (management of patients/clients, consultation, education, research, and administration), the core values of the profession, and the multiple realms of ethical action (individual, organizational, and societal). Physical therapist practice is guided by a set of seven core values: accountability, altruism, compassion/caring, excellence, integrity, professional duty, and social responsibility. Throughout the document the primary core values that support specific principles are indicated in parentheses. Unless a specific role is indicated in the principle, the duties and obligations being delineated pertain to the five roles of the physical therapist. Fundamental to the Code of Ethics is the special obligation of physical therapists to empower, educate, and enable those with impairments, activity limitations, participation restrictions, and disabilities to facilitate greater independence, health, wellness, and enhanced quality of life.

Principles

Principle #1: Physical therapists shall respect the inherent dignity and rights of all individuals. (Core Values: Compassion, Integrity)

1A. Physical therapists shall act in a respectful manner toward each person regardless of age, gender, race, nationality, religion, ethnicity, social or economic status, sexual orientation, health condition or disability.

1B. Physical therapists shall recognize their personal biases and shall not discriminate against others in physical therapist practice, consultation, education, research, and administration.

Principle #2: Physical therapists shall be trustworthy and compassionate in addressing the rights and needs of patients/clients. (Core Values: Altruism, Compassion, Professional Duty)

2A. Physical therapists shall adhere to the core values of the profession and shall act in the best interests of patients/clients over the interests of the physical therapist.

2B. Physical therapists shall provide physical therapy services with compassionate and caring behaviors that incorporate the individual and cultural differences of patients/ clients.

2C. Physical therapists shall provide the information necessary to allow patients or their surrogates to make informed decisions about physical therapy care or participation in clinical research.

2D. Physical therapists shall collaborate with patients/clients to empower them in decisions about their health care.

2E. Physical therapists shall protect confidential patient/client information and may disclose confidential information to appropriate authorities only when allowed or as required by law.

Principle #3: Physical therapists shall be accountable for making sound professional judgments. (Core Values: Excellence, Integrity)

3A. Physical therapists shall demonstrate independent and objective professional judgment in the patient's/client's best interest in all practice settings.

3B. Physical therapists shall demonstrate professional judgment informed by professional standards, evidence (including current literature and established best practice), practitioner experience, and patient/client values.

3C. Physical therapists shall make judgments within their scope of practice and level of expertise and shall communicate with, collaborate with or refer to peers or other health care professionals when necessary.

3D. Physical therapists shall not engage in conflicts of interest that interfere with professional judgment.

3E. Physical therapists shall provide appropriate direction of and communication with physical therapist assistants and support personnel.

Principle #4: Physical therapists shall demonstrate integrity in their relationships with patients/clients, families, colleagues, students, research participants, other health care providers, employers, payers, and the public. (Core Value: Integrity)

4A. Physical therapists shall provide truthful, accurate, and relevant information and shall not make misleading representations.

4B. Physical therapists shall not exploit persons over whom they have supervisory, evaluative or other authority (e.g., patients/clients, students, supervisees, research participants, or employees).

4C. Physical therapists shall discourage misconduct by health care professionals and report illegal or unethical acts to the relevant authority, when appropriate.

4D. Physical therapists shall report suspected cases of abuse involving children or vulnerable adults to the appropriate authority, subject to law.

4E. Physical therapists shall not engage in any sexual relationship with any of their patients/clients, supervisees, or students.

4F. Physical therapists shall not harass anyone verbally, physically, emotionally, or sexually.

Principle #5: Physical therapists shall fulfill their legal and professional obligations. (Core Values: Professional Duty, Accountability)

5A. Physical therapists shall comply with applicable local, state, and federal laws and regulations.

5B. Physical therapists shall have primary responsibility for supervision of physical therapist assistants and support personnel.

5C. Physical therapists involved in research shall abide by accepted standards governing protection of research participants.

5D. Physical therapists shall encourage colleagues with physical, psychological or substance-related impairments that may adversely impact their professional responsibilities to seek assistance or counsel.

5E. Physical therapists who have knowledge that a colleague is unable to perform their professional responsibilities with reasonable skill and safety shall report this information to the appropriate authority.

5F. Physical therapists shall provide notice and information about alternatives for obtaining care in the event the physical therapist terminates the provider relationship while the patient/client continues to need physical therapy services.

Principle #6: Physical therapists shall enhance their expertise through the lifelong acquisition and refinement of knowledge, skills, abilities, and professional behaviors. (Core Value: Excellence)

6A. Physical therapists shall achieve and maintain professional competence.

6B. Physical therapists shall take responsibility for their professional development based on critical self-assessment and reflection on changes in physical therapist practice, education, health care delivery, and technology.

6C. Physical therapists shall evaluate the strength of evidence and applicability of content presented during professional development activities before integrating the content or techniques into practice.

6D. Physical therapists shall cultivate practice environments that support professional development, lifelong learning, and excellence.

Principle #7: Physical therapists shall promote organizational behaviors and business practices that benefit patients/clients and society. (Core Values: Integrity, Accountability)

7A. Physical therapists shall promote practice environments that support autonomous and accountable professional judgments.

7B. Physical therapists shall seek remuneration as is deserved and reasonable for physical therapist services.

7C. Physical therapists shall not accept gifts or other considerations that influence or give an appearance of influencing their professional judgment.

7D. Physical therapists shall fully disclose any financial interest they have in products or services that they recommend to patients/clients.

7E. Physical therapists shall be aware of charges and shall ensure that documentation and coding for physical therapy services accurately reflect the nature and extent of the services provided.

7F. Physical therapists shall refrain from employment arrangements, or other arrangements, that prevent physical therapists from fulfilling professional obligations to patients/clients.

Principle #8: Physical therapists shall participate in efforts to meet the health needs of people locally, nationally or globally. (Core Value: Social Responsibility)

8A. Physical therapists shall provide pro bono physical therapy services or support organizations that meet the health needs of people who are economically disadvantaged, uninsured, and underinsured.

8B. Physical therapists shall advocate to reduce health disparities and health care inequities, improve access to health care services, and address the health, wellness, and preventive health care needs of people.

8C. Physical therapists shall be responsible stewards of health care resources and shall avoid overutilization or underutilization of physical therapy services.

8D. Physical therapists shall educate members of the public about the benefits of physical therapy and the unique role of the physical therapist.

HOD S06-09-07-12 Updated: June, 2009. American Physical Therapy Association, web site 2017.

Health Insurance

There are three major classifications of health insurance companies. They include private health insurance companies, independent health plans, and government health insurance.

Private Health Insurance Companies

Private health insurance companies include stock companies, mutual companies, and non-profit insurance plans. Reimbursement for physical therapy services is usually on a fee for service basis.

Stock companies: Operated nationally and are owned by independent stockholders.

Mutual companies: Operated nationally and are owned by the individual policyholders.

Non-profit insurance plans: Operate in a specific geographic region and are subject to specific state regulations. They are classified as tax exempt due to their non-profit status.

Fee for Service versus Managed Care[20,21]

Fee for Service:	Managed Care:
Payers assume primary financial risk	Providers share in financial risk
Provides enrollees with freedom of choice	Services provided by a specific pool of providers
Unlimited access to specialty providers	Primary care provider serves as a gatekeeper
Co-payments often in the form of 80% / 20%	Provides services for a fixed, prepaid monthly fee
Limited internal/external cost controls	Formal quality assurance and utilization review
Minimal emphasis on health promotion and education	Health education and preventive medicine emphasized

Independent Health Plans[20,21]

Independent health plans are organized into various groups. Health maintenance organizations and self-insurance plans are examples of independent health plans. Reimbursement is typically based on fee for service or a predetermined fixed fee.

Managed care: A concept of health care delivery where subscribers utilize health care providers that are contracted by the insurance company at a lower cost. Health maintenance organizations (HMO) and preferred provider organizations (PPO) are two examples of a managed care system. This concept attempts to attain the highest quality of care at the lowest cost.

Health maintenance organization: Subscribers to these insurance plans agree to receive all of their health care services through the predetermined providers of the HMO. The primary physician of the subscriber controls health care access through a referral system. Cost containment is a high priority and subscribers cannot receive care from providers outside of the plan except in an emergency.

Preferred provider organization: Subscribers can choose their health care services from a list of providers that contract with the insurance plan. These contracts provide extreme discounts for health care. Subscribers can use a health care provider that is not associated with the PPO, however, they will absorb a greater portion of the cost.

Government Health Insurance[12,20,21]

Government health insurance programs such as Medicare and Medicaid are administered by the federal government. The government uses private contractors to manage the payment process of each health plan.

Medicare

Medicare provides health insurance for individuals over 65 years of age and the disabled. Medicare is a nationwide program operated by the Centers for Medicare and Medicaid Services.

Established in 1966, Medicare was the second mandated health insurance program in the United States (Workers' Compensation was the first). In 1972, Medicare coverage was expanded to include certain categories of the disabled, renal dialysis, and transplant patients.

Medicare Part A:

Provides benefits for care provided in hospitals, extended care facilities, hospice, and short-term care at home required by an illness for which the patient is hospitalized.

Enrollment in Medicare Part A is automatic and funding is through payroll taxes (i.e., no monthly premiums for those who qualify).

Medicare Part B:

Provides benefits for outpatient care, physician services, and services ordered by physicians such as diagnostic tests, medical equipment, and supplies.

Enrollment in Medicare Part B is voluntary and funding is through premiums paid by beneficiaries and general federal tax revenues.

Medicare Part C:

Provides "bundled" benefits known as Medicare Advantage plans that cover all Medicare services (Part A and Part B) as an alternative choice to traditional Medicare plans. Medicare Advantage plans usually include prescription drug (Part D) coverage and may offer extra coverage (e.g., vision, hearing, dental) as well.

Enrollment in Medicare Part C is voluntary and is offered by private companies approved by Medicare. The cost of monthly premiums as well as additional out-of-pocket expenses will vary based on the plan chosen. Companies offering Medicare Advantage plans must follow rules set by Medicare.

Medicare Part D:

Provides at least a standard level of benefits for prescription drug coverage. Medicare prescription drug plans provide a list of medications that are covered known as a formulary. The formulary typically includes at least two drugs in the most commonly prescribed classes of medications.

Enrollment in Medicare Part D is voluntary and funding is through premiums paid by beneficiaries. Medicare prescription drug plans can charge different out-of-pocket costs, including annual deductibles and copayments, depending on the plan chosen.

The Medicare program requires beneficiaries to share in the costs of health care through deductibles and coinsurance.

- Deductibles require beneficiaries to reach a predetermined amount of personal expenditure each 12 month period before Medicare payment is activated.
- Coinsurance is required on a per day basis for Part A for any hospital stay that lasts longer than 60 days; Part B coinsurance typically requires that 20% of the Medicare-approved amount for medical services is covered by the patient.

Medicare sets limits on the total days of hospital care that will be paid based on a lifetime pool of days limit. Medicare payments for post hospital stays in extended care facilities are limited to 100 days.

Providers are reimbursed for Medicare services through intermediaries such as Blue Cross. In order for services to be reimbursed under Medicare Part B benefit, they may not be provided by a physical therapy aide regardless of the level of supervision. Only services provided by physical therapists and physical therapist assistants are considered skilled care and reimbursable under Medicare rules and regulations.

Medicaid

Medicaid provides basic medical services to the economically indigent population who qualify by reason of low income or who qualify for welfare or public assistance benefits in the state of their residence. Medicaid is a jointly funded program through the federal and state governments.

Established in 1965, Medicaid is funded through personal income, corporate, and excise taxes. Federal and state support is shared based on the state's per capita income.

Rate setting formulas, procedures, and policies vary widely among states. All state Medicaid operations must be approved by the Centers for Medicare and Medicaid Services. The Medicaid program reimburses providers directly.

The Medicaid program covers inpatient and outpatient hospital services, physician services, diagnostic services, nursing care for older adults, home health care, preventative health screening services, and family planning services.

Workers' Compensation

First designed in 1911 to provide protection for employees that were injured on the job. This legislation provides continued income as well as paid medical expenses for employees injured while working. Workers' Compensation is a joint federal and state program that is regulated at the state level. Case managers are typically involved in this system by monitoring the rehabilitation process and controlling potential abuse.

Employers with ten or more employees or high-risk employers must pay a percentage of each employee salary to the Workers' Compensation board of the state. The exact payment is based on the risk rating of the job or institution.

Reimbursement Coding

Current Procedural Terminology Codes

Current Procedural Terminology (CPT) codes are procedure codes used by physical therapists and other health care professionals to describe the interventions that were provided to a given patient. The majority of codes used by physical therapists are in the CPT 97000 series. Examples of commonly used CPT codes by physical therapists include: 97530 – Therapeutic Activities; 97035 – Ultrasound; 97012 – Traction, mechanical. CPT is a registered trademark of the American Medical Association.

In January 2017, three new CPT codes were created for billing evaluations (as opposed to one previously). The new codes were created to account for evaluating patients of different complexities, and they are as follows: 97161 (low complexity), 97162 (moderate complexity), and 97163 (high complexity). There is also a new code that is replacing the old code for re-evaluations (97164).

There are two types of CPT codes: timed and untimed. Timed codes are billed based on the amount of time spent performing that intervention, generally one unit per 15-minute interval. If a patient performs therapeutic exercise for 45 minutes, they would be billed for three units of that code (i.e., 97110). Untimed codes are billed for one unit regardless of the time spent performing the intervention. For example, whether a patient has unattended electrical stimulation (i.e., CPT code 97014) for 15 minutes or 30 minutes, they will still only be billed one unit for that code.

When using timed codes, Medicare (and other insurance companies that follow Medicare guidelines) state that at least eight minutes of an intervention must be performed to bill a unit of that code. To calculate the total number of units, take the total time spent performing the intervention and divide by 15. If there is a remainder of eight or greater, an extra unit can be billed for that code. For example, if a therapist performs manual therapy for 40 minutes, they should bill for three units of that code (40/15 = 2 units and 10 extra minutes), since the remaining extra time is greater than eight minutes.

Reimbursement rates for CPT codes vary widely according to the insurance company that is being billed. Each insurance company creates a contract with the medical facility to dictate what they will be willing to pay for each code. Though a therapist may bill the exact same treatment codes to two different insurance companies, the reimbursement rates from those two companies may be drastically different.

International Classification of Diseases

The International Classification of Diseases (ICD) codes are designed to describe a patient's infirmity through specific categories based on etiology and affected anatomical systems. ICD-10 was the 10th revision of this ICD coding system and it officially replaced ICD-9 in 2015. The change to ICD-10 included an overall expansion in the number of possible codes, a switch from numeric to alphanumeric coding (e.g., 755.12 vs. M25.712), and a switch from 5-character codes to 6-character codes (or 7-character, in some cases). The increase in the number of codes occurred due to the addition of symptom-based codes (e.g., M25.651 for "stiffness of the right hip"), the addition of codes defining the external cause of the injury (e.g., W10.1 for "fall from a sidewalk curb") and social circumstance it occurred in (e.g., Y93.66 for "soccer"), and a new option for defining laterality (i.e., coding right vs. left). Physicians are required to make the medical diagnosis, however, in some cases a physical therapist may need to utilize the ICD manual to determine an appropriate ICD code. This action is within a physical therapist's scope of practice and would not be considered equivalent to making a medical diagnosis.

Teaching & Learning

Maslow's Hierarchy of Needs[22]

Maslow's hierarchy of needs hypothesizes that there is a hierarchy of biogenic and psychogenic needs that individuals must progress through. In order to move to a higher level of needs, an individual must attain the objectives associated with the previous level. In essence, an individual must achieve basic or fundamental needs before moving to upper level needs.

Self-actualization needs: The need to realize one's full potential as a human being.

Esteem needs: The need to feel good about oneself and one's capabilities, to be respected by others, and to receive recognition and appreciation.

Affiliative needs: The need for security, stability, and a safe environment.

Physiological needs: The need for basic things necessary in order to survive such as food, water, and shelter.

Classical Conditioning (Pavlov)[22]

Classical conditioning is a process where learning occurs when an unconditioned stimulus (food) is repeatedly preceded by a neutral stimulus (bell). The neutral stimulus serves as a conditioned stimulus and the learned reaction that results is termed the conditioned response. In order to maintain a conditioned response, the conditioned and unconditioned stimuli must occasionally be paired.

Operant Conditioning (B.F. Skinner)[22]

Operant conditioning is a process where learning occurs when an individual engages in specific behaviors in order to receive certain consequences.

Positive reinforcement: Administering desirable consequences to individuals who perform a specific behavior.

Negative reinforcement: Removing undesirable consequences from individuals who perform a specific behavior.

Extinction: Removing selected variables that reinforce a specific behavior.

Punishment: Administering negative consequences to individuals who perform undesirable behaviors.

Reinforcement Frequency and Schedules

Continuous reinforcement: A behavior is reinforced every time it occurs.

Partial reinforcement: A behavior is reinforced intermittently.

Fixed-interval schedule: The period of time between the occurrences of each instance of reinforcement is fixed or set.

Variable-interval schedule: The amount of time between reinforcements varies around a constant average.

Levels of Prevention

Health care prevention is defined as the actions taken to reduce the potential risks to one's health. Prevention activities fall into one of three categories: primary, secondary or tertiary.

Primary prevention: Interventions that occur before the onset of a disease or condition with the goal of preventing the disease/condition. This may be accomplished by preventing exposure to substances that may cause a disease or by modifying behavior to prevent risk factors associated with a disease.

> **Examples:** receiving immunizations, educating patients on exercise and healthy eating, legislation aimed at banning the use of hazardous materials

Secondary prevention: Interventions that aim to diagnose a condition early in its onset and prevent complications from occurring. Though this form of prevention cannot stop the onset of disease, it can stop or slow the progression of the disease by treating it early.

> **Examples:** screening adolescents for scoliosis, performing self-testicular examinations, blood glucose testing for diabetes

Tertiary prevention: Interventions that occur after a disease has already been diagnosed with the goal of minimizing the long-term effects of the disease. This form of prevention typically occurs once a patient has already become symptomatic. The goal is to help the patient manage their condition and maximize their quality of life.

> **Examples:** rehabilitation after a spinal cord injury, palliative care for end-of-life patients, support groups for patients with HIV

Health Behavior Models[23]

Change in behavior is a complex process that is difficult to attain and sustain. There has been significant research that has resulted in many different models for understanding behavior change and specific interventions. The following are a few commonly used models.

Health Belief Model

The Health Belief Model is one of the initial theories for behavior change. It is based on the belief that change in behavior depends upon the following factors:

Perceived susceptibility: one is at risk for the problem

Perceived severity: the health problem is serious

Perceived benefit: changing the behavior will reduce the threat

Perceived barriers: recognize obstacles required to change a behavior

Cues to action: strategies to activate readiness for change

Self-efficacy: the ability to change a behavior

The model provides insight as to why patients make health decisions and outlines a process to encourage change. Limitations of this model may include socioeconomic status, previous experiences, and cultural factors.

Social Cognitive Theory (Social Learning Theory)

This theory assesses the cognitive and emotional aspects of behavior for understanding behavioral change. The Social Cognitive Theory also attempts to explain how patients acquire and continue with particular behavioral patterns as well as providing a basis for intervention strategies. According to this theory, the environment, personal factors, and behavior are constantly influencing each other. The concepts of the Social Cognitive Theory include:

- **Behavior capability:** The process of learning how to make a change in behavior. Possessing the knowledge and skill to perform a given behavior; promote mastery learning through skills training.
- **Emotional coping responses:** Strategies or tactics that are used by a person to deal with emotional stimuli. To provide training in problem solving and stress management.
- **Environment:** Factors physically external to the person. The environment provides opportunities and social support.
- **Expectancies:** The value that is placed on the expected results. The values that the person places on a given outcome or incentives. Expectancies also represent present outcomes of change that have functional meaning.
- **Expectations:** Anticipatory outcomes of a behavior. To model positive outcomes of healthful behavior.
- **Observational learning:** Behavioral acquisition that occurs by watching the actions and outcomes of others' behavior. This will include credible role models of the targeted behavior.
- **Reinforcement:** Responses that are either positive or negative consequences of behavior. These are responses to a person's behavior that increase or decrease the likelihood of reoccurrence. Reinforcement promotes self-initiated rewards and incentives.
- **Reciprocal determinism:** The relationship between an individual and their environment. The dynamic interaction of the person, the behavior, and the environment in which the behavior is performed; consider multiple avenues to behavioral change, including environmental, skill, and personal change.
- **Self-control:** Personal regulation of goal-directed behavior or performance. Self-control will provide opportunities for self-monitoring, goal setting, problem solving, and self-reward.
- **Self-efficacy:** The belief in one's ability to successfully change a behavior. The person's confidence in performing a particular behavior. Approach behavioral change in small steps to ensure success.
- **Situation:** Perception of the environment; correct misperceptions and promote healthful forms.

It is believed that a patient's reality is formed through the interaction of the environment and a person's cognitions (which change with experience and time). Social comparison of a patient's performance to others is also a strong source of self-efficacy. This theory is used when studying a variety of health pathologies, medical management compliance, alcohol abuse, and other health-related issues. A limitation to this theory is that its complexity can make it difficult to use.

Trans-theoretical Model (Stages of Change)

The Trans-theoretical Model is a model of intentional change. It focuses on the decision making process of the individual. The theory differs from many others in its belief that change implies a process over time, not an isolated event. The process of change includes progressing through five stages:

1. **Precontemplation:** not intending to change
2. **Contemplation:** intending to change behavior in the near future
3. **Preparation:** making a plan to change behavior
4. **Action:** implementing the plan to change behavior
5. **Maintenance:** continuation of behavior change

This process for behavior change is not linear as individuals can enter and exit at any point or may repeat stages several times. The model can be useful to health programs and the process of moving a patient through various stages.

Culture is characterized by the set of shared beliefs, values, attitudes, and customs that exist within a specific ethnic, religious or social group. As the cultural makeup of the United States becomes more diverse, it is important that health care professionals have an understanding of how a patient's unique culture may impact their health care experience. The following factors should be considered when working with patients of different cultural backgrounds.

Communication: Many Americans speak English as a second language or may not speak English at all. It is important for these patients to have adequate access to interpreter services so that they can effectively communicate with their health care provider. Therapists should realize that even with the use of an interpreter, some information can still be lost in translation, which could influence the patient's treatment. In addition to language barriers, other aspects of communication may vary from one culture to another, such as nonverbal communication, the use of silence during conversations, and the appropriateness of eye contact. In some cultures, patients choose to avoid any form of conflict with authority figures. A patient may disagree with their treatment plan but never verbalize it, which likely will lead to poor patient compliance.

Social roles: A patient's social role within their family or relationship may affect how they approach health care decisions. In some cultures, a patient may rely heavily on their family in the decision-making process. In other cultures, the patriarchal figure may be the sole party responsible for making health care decisions. It is important for therapists to include family members in appropriate aspects of a patient's care.

Modesty: Cultural influences may affect a patient's comfort level when it comes to being touched by their health care provider or being physically close to the provider. In some cultures, being touched by someone of the opposite gender is unacceptable. Before working with someone, it is important for the therapist to determine the patient's level of modesty to allow for maximum patient comfort during treatment.

Health care beliefs: A patient's culture may affect how they view their diagnosis and how they approach treatment for their diagnosis. Patients with strong religious beliefs may assume that their condition is controlled by a higher power and thus they may deny formal treatment. Other cultures may choose to seek treatment, though they may do so through "alternative" forms of medicine (e.g., herbal remedies, acupuncture). This may be done in isolation, or in conjunction with conventional treatments. In some cultures, reporting pain is considered a sign of weakness. These patients may appear to have a higher pain tolerance or neglect to report some of their symptoms, which could negatively impact their recovery.

End-of-life care: The approach towards a patient's end-of-life care may vary depending on the patient's cultural background. Some religions encourage prolonging a patient's life through whatever medical interventions are available, while other religions oppose this practice and believe the patient should die "naturally" (e.g., taking a comatose patient off life support). Cultural traditions may also dictate where a terminally ill patient chooses to spend their remaining days (e.g., hospital, home).

Patient Education

Adult Learning

- Therapists must strive to make patient education sessions practical and useful for the patient.
- Failure to identify the relevance of the presented information will promote disinterest and decrease compliance.

Guidelines to Promote Adult Learning

- Design learning activities that will incorporate the patient's past experiences.
- Encourage the learner to play an active role in their educational program.
- Attempt to demonstrate the relevance of selected learning activities.
- Provide ample opportunities for practice and feedback.
- Recognize skill acquisition or objective improvement in patient performance.

Domains of Learning

Domains of learning are educational terms that describe various aspects of human behavior. The three most commonly recognized domains of learning are the cognitive, psychomotor, and affective domains. Recognizing the various levels of each of the domains can assist therapists to plan appropriate patient learning activities.

Affective domain: The affective domain is primarily concerned with attitudes, values, and emotions.

The domain consists of five specific levels: receiving, responding, valuing, organization, and characterization.

Cognitive domain: The cognitive domain is primarily concerned with knowledge and understanding.

The domain consists of six specific levels: knowledge, comprehension, application, analysis, synthesis, and evaluation.

Psychomotor domain: The psychomotor domain is primarily concerned with physical action or motor skill.

The domain consists of seven specific levels: perception, set, guided response, mechanism, complex overt response, adaptation, and origination.

Learning Style

Therapists can often obtain information related to a patient's preferred learning style by asking a few basic questions.

- Do you prefer to learn new information by observing, reading, listening or experiencing?
- Are you more comfortable learning in an active or passive manner?
- What increases your motivation to learn?

Teaching Methods

Individual

- Therapists most commonly instruct patients on an individual basis.
- The individual approach allows the therapist to focus on the needs of the learner and is the model of choice when the objectives of the session are unique to an individual patient.
- The individual approach allows the therapist to strengthen the patient/therapist bond and provides additional opportunities for specific feedback.

Group

- Therapists often instruct patients in a group.
- Group teaching may occur with patients, family members, staff, and support persons.
- Group teaching can be difficult if patients are not supportive of each other or if the learning needs of the group are diverse.
- Some patients may be intimidated by selected group members and tend to withdraw, while others may attempt to take control of the group.
- Since individuals typically receive less individual attention in a group, it is critical for the therapist to regularly assess individual patient progress.
- Group teaching allows participants to support each other in the educational process and permits therapists to effectively use scarce resources such as time or money.
- Patients participating in group activities often feel a sense of camaraderie interacting with others who have similar personal experiences.

Patient Communication[24,25]

- Verbal commands should focus the patient's attention on specifically desired actions.
- Instruction should remain as simplistic as possible and should not incorporate confusing medical terminology.
- The therapist should describe to the patient the general sequence of events that will occur prior to initiating treatment.
- The therapist should ask the patient questions during treatment in order to establish a rapport with the patient and to provide feedback as to the status of the current treatment.
- The therapist should speak clearly and vary their tone of voice as required by the situation.

Guidelines for Effective Patient Education[10,25]

- Attempt to establish a positive rapport with the patient.
- Assess the patient's readiness and motivation to learn.
- Attempt to identify the patient's preferred learning style and available resources.
- Identify potential barriers to patient progress.
- Design an individualized education program for the patient based on their medical condition and personal goals.
- Coordinate education with the other members of the health care team.
- Focus the majority of available time on the most important concepts.
- Provide clear and succinct communication to the patient.
- Use repetition to improve patient learning.
- Provide frequent feedback to the patient.
- Utilize appropriate teaching resources to facilitate patient learning.
- Assess the effectiveness of patient education.
- Modify the patient education program based on the assessment results.

Principles of Motivation[25,26]

- Readiness to learn significantly influences motivation.
- Individuals respond differently to selected motivational strategies.
- Success is more motivating than failure.
- Internal motivation has a greater potential to contribute to meaningful and lasting change than external motivation.
- A positive patient/therapist relationship enhances motivation.
- Limited anxiety may serve to motivate, while excessive anxiety may debilitate.
- Affiliation and approval can be motivating.

Culture[26]

- Understanding cultural differences in patients can assist therapists to function as more effective educators.
- Patient culture is influenced and shaped by society, community, family, personal values, and attitudes.
- Language barriers, nonverbal communication, and limited personal experience can serve as obstacles when educating patients with significant cultural differences.
- Therapists should embrace cultural diversity and avoid efforts to make patients conform to any particular norm or standard.
- Therapists must be cautious when interpreting specific language or behavior and avoid labeling patients as unmotivated or disinterested.
- Therapists should use available resources such as experienced staff members, interpreters or consultants as necessary to achieve desired outcomes.

Designing Effective Patient Education Materials

- Design the materials to convey only the necessary information.
- Emphasize essential information.
- Utilize active instructions such as "you" and avoid passive terms such as "patient."
- Larger print may be more desirable than smaller print.
- Avoid long sentences or complex medical terminology.
- Pictures or graphics should be used where appropriate to complement written information.
- Incorporate answers to frequently asked questions.
- Written materials should flow in a logical sequence.
- Written materials should utilize a reading level appropriate for the target audience.

Teaching Guidelines for Specific Patient Categories[25,26,27]

Therapists often vary their approach when educating patients of various ages and abilities. It is difficult to develop recommendations that apply to all patients in a given category, however, the following represent general guidelines for therapists to consider when treating selected patient categories.

Infants/Children

- Therapists should try to make therapy sessions with infants/children interactive.
- Sessions should include structured play and should be of relatively short duration.
- Frequent breaks and positive reinforcement will serve to increase the patient's level of participation.

Adolescents

- Therapists should try to assume the role of an advocate when working with adolescents.
- It is important for therapists to establish patients' trust and incorporate patient goals into the plan of care.
- Adolescents prefer to be treated like adults and may resent the presence of parents during therapy sessions.
- Therapists should provide patients with clear and concise instructions and offer frequent positive reinforcement.

Adults

- Therapists should involve adults in determining education outcomes.
- The education program should be compatible with the patient's daily routine and goals.
- Emphasizing the relevance of educational activities will serve to increase patient compliance.
- Therapists should be aware of the available patient support system and identify any barriers to progress.

Elderly

- Therapists may find it necessary to introduce new information gradually when working with the elderly.
- Special attention should be paid to identify signs of hearing loss or visual impairments.
- The elderly population often benefits from the social benefits of group activities.
- Education sessions for the elderly should not be longer in duration, however, the achievement of selected outcomes may require additional sessions.

Terminally Ill

- Therapists should incorporate patient goals as an integral component of any educational session for patients with terminal illness.
- Family members and other support personnel should be encouraged to participate in the educational session, however, it is important to provide the patient with the opportunity to make independent decisions whenever possible.
- Goals for the terminally ill patient often include maximizing function, safety, and comfort.
- Therapists may alter their teaching methods based on the current mental and physical well-being of the patient.

Cognitively Impaired

- The therapist should focus on the education of the caregiver and incorporate the patient whenever possible.
- When incorporating the patient in the session, instructions should be clear and concise and should be summarized through demonstration and pictures.
- Therapists should encourage the patient to compensate for any memory deficit.

Illiteracy

- Therapists should attempt to determine the literacy level of their patients.
- If a patient is determined to be illiterate, the therapist may elect to modify language to use basic wording and short sentences.
- Demonstration, repetition, and pictures should be incorporated into educational sessions.
- Therapists may include more detailed written information in educational sessions if the patient has adequate support at home.

Stages of Dying[10,24]

Elizabeth Kubler-Ross identified five stages in coming to terms with death after interviewing a large number of terminally ill patients. The stages Kubler-Ross identified were denial, anger, bargaining, depression, and acceptance.

Denial

The denial stage is characterized by a failure of the individual to believe that their condition is terminal. Therapists should attempt to establish trust with a patient in this stage and avoid trying to make the patient accept their condition.

Anger

The anger stage is characterized by frustration and negative emotional feelings often directed at anyone the individual comes in contact with. Individuals often ask "Why me?" Therapists should avoid taking the anger personally and recognize that expressing anger is often a useful step for the individual to move beyond this stage.

Bargaining

The bargaining stage is characterized by the individual trying to negotiate with fate. The individual may try to make a deal with a higher being based on good behavior, compliance with an exercise program or dedication of their life to a specific cause. Therapists should facilitate discussion with the patient and serve as a good listener.

Depression

The depression stage is characterized by the individual expressing the depths of their anguish. The individual is often deeply depressed and may show little interest in any form of medical intervention. Therapists should listen to the individual and exhibit a great deal of patience during this stage.

Acceptance

The acceptance stage is characterized by the individual coming to terms with their fate. The individual may attempt to resolve any unfinished business and may experience a sense of inner peace. Therapists should encourage the individual and family to ask questions and attempt to spend meaningful time with the individual.

Education Concepts

Team Models[28]

Unidisciplinary: A single discipline provides patient care services.

Multidisciplinary: Several different disciplines are involved in providing patient care, however, the disciplines tend to function independently and communication occurs primarily through the medical record.

Interdisciplinary: Several different disciplines are involved in providing patient care. The disciplines function independently, however, they routinely report to each other and may coordinate patient care.

Transdisciplinary: Numerous disciplines function as a collective unit to provide patient care services. Team goals are established rather than individual discipline goals and as a result, discipline specific boundaries tend to erode.

Research

Evidence-Based Practice (EBP)

Evidence-based medicine has been defined as the integration of the best clinically relevant research with clinical expertise and patient values.[29] In recognition of the movement's adoption by other health care practitioners, the concept has evolved into evidence-based practice (EBP). The term "practice" recognizes the expansion of the framework to physical therapy, nursing, and other aspects of health care beyond medicine.

Best research evidence refers to clinically relevant, patient-centered clinical research about the accuracy of diagnostic tests, prognostic factors, and the efficacy of interventions. Clinical expertise refers to the clinician's use of past experiences to make clinical judgments. Patient values refer to the preferences and expectations of the patient that are considered in clinical decisions about health care.[29] In physical therapy, the goal of evidence-based practice is to help therapists make sense of knowledge derived from research and use the information as a basis for making decisions about their patients.

Steps to Practicing Evidence-Based Physical Therapy[29]

1. Identify a problem or area of uncertainty about prevention, diagnosis, prognosis or therapy.
2. Formulate a focused clinical question for a specific patient problem.
3. Search the literature for relevant clinical articles to answer that question.
4. Critically appraise each article to determine its validity (closeness to the truth), impact (size of the effect), and applicability (usefulness in clinical practice).
5. Integrate the relevant findings in clinical practice along with clinical expertise and patient values.
6. Assess the outcomes of the selected action.

Using P-I-C-O to Ask a Focused Clinical Question

The focused clinical question needs to be directly relevant to the patient's problems and phrased in a way that directs the search of the literature to relevant answers. The focused question makes it relatively easy to combine the appropriate terms to search the databases. A well-built clinical question usually contains four elements that form the acronym PICO.[30]

Patient or Problem – What is the target patient population or the problem of interest?

Intervention – What intervention or form of therapy needs to be evaluated? Alternatively, if intervention is not the area of interest, the "I" could refer to diagnosis or prognosis.

Comparison – What comparison or control treatments (e.g., placebo or other treatments) are being compared to the primary intervention?

Outcome – What changes or results would suggest an intervention is effective, a prognostic factor is important, or a diagnostic test is accurate?

How to Evaluate Individual Studies about Therapy

Individual studies about therapy must be evaluated to determine if the results of the study are valid, important, and applicable to the patient.[31]

1. Determine if the results of the study can be considered valid:
   - Were patients assigned to treatment randomly and was the randomization list concealed?
   - Was the follow-up of patients long enough and complete?
   - Was an intention-to-treat analysis performed?
   - Were patients and clinicians kept blind to patient assignment to group?
   - Except for the experimental therapy, were patients treated equally?
   - Were the groups similar at the start of the study?
2. Determine if the results of the study can be considered important:
   - What is the magnitude of the treatment effect?
   - How precise is the estimate of the treatment effect?
3. Determine if the valid and important results are applicable to the patient?
   - Is the patient so different from those in the study that the results cannot apply?
   - Is the treatment feasible in the clinical setting?
   - What are the potential benefits and harms from the therapy?
   - What are the patient's values and expectations for the treatment?

Practice Guidelines

Practice guidelines are statements developed by panels of experts to help health care professionals and patients make decisions about screening, prevention or treatment of a specific health condition.[32] These rigorously developed evidence-based guidelines assist health care providers to make the best decision about treatment for a particular patient and to limit potential harm. It is important to remember that guidelines cannot account for individual variation among patients and, therefore, cannot replace clinician judgment with respect to particular patients or special clinical situations.

A number of practice guidelines related to physical therapy may be accessed through "Collections" at the website of *Physical Therapy* – Journal of the American Physical Therapy Association.[33] Also, the Agency for Healthcare Research and Quality of the US Department of Health and Human Services offers a searchable database of clinical practice guidelines online.[34]

Levels of Evidence for Articles about Therapy/Intervention

The hierarchy of "levels of evidence" refers to how different categories of studies are ranked and should be considered when decisions need to be made about interventions. To evaluate the strength of the different types of clinical evidence, studies or clinical trials are ranked according to the strength of the design (Fig. 9-13).[35] In many cases, it is not possible to find the best level of evidence to answer a particular research question. In these instances, a clinician will need to consider moving down the pyramid to other types of studies, however, clinicians must be aware of the limitations incurred as the strength of the evidence diminishes.

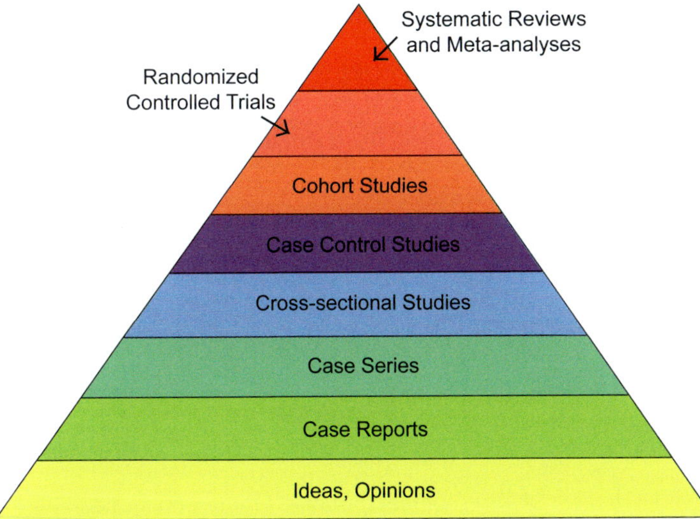

Fig. 9-13: Levels of evidence pyramid for studies about interventions.

Systematic Review

A comprehensive review of the medical literature that uses explicit methods to systematically search, identify, appraise, and summarize all literature on a specific issue. For example, a Cochrane Systematic Review is a type of review aimed at providing evidence specifically in health care and health policy.[29]

Meta-analysis

A systematic review that uses a statistical technique to derive an estimate of effect size by combining the results of several randomized controlled trials to determine the overall effectiveness of a treatment. This strategy can minimize the problem of small sample size from individual studies since the pooling of trials increases the overall sample size.[36]

Randomized Controlled Trial (RCT)

A form of experimental research used to assess the relative effect of a specific intervention compared to a control condition. Patients are randomized into a control group and at least one experimental group. The control group receives either no treatment or a standard default treatment. Ideally, the groups will be identical except for the intervention they have been randomized to receive. Random assignment reduces the risk of bias and increases the probability that differences between the groups can be attributed to the intervention.[33]

Cohort Study

A type of longitudinal, observational study in which individuals with a risk factor or exposure are followed over time to compare the occurrence of a disease in the exposed group to that of the group of unexposed individuals. The measure of association between exposure and disease in cohort studies is the relative risk (i.e., the ratio of the incidence rate of exposed individuals to that of the controls). Cohort studies can be performed prospectively or retrospectively from historical records. Limitations of cohort studies include the excessive length of time a study can take and the influence of other lifestyle variables that invariably result in the two groups being uniquely different.[36]

Case Control Study

A type of retrospective, observational study in which individuals who already have a particular disease are matched with a comparison group of individuals without the disease. The history of exposure or other characteristics prior to the onset of the disease is recorded through interview and other sources and compared between the two groups. The control group provides an estimate of the frequency and amount of exposure in subjects in the population without the disease being studied. The measure of association between exposure and occurrence of disease in case control studies is the odds ratio (i.e., the ratio of odds of exposure in diseased subjects to the odds of exposure in non-diseased subjects).[36]

Cross-Sectional Study

A type of observational study where the data or observations are made at only one point in time and all subjects are tested at relatively the same time.[5] A cross-sectional study aims to describe relationships between a disease or condition and factors of interest that exist in a specified population at a given time. These studies can describe the prevalence of disease or conditions and demonstrate associations, but they cannot distinguish between newly occurring and long-established conditions, nor can they identify causal relationships about what may have precipitated the disease or condition.

Case Report or Case Series

A case report is an in-depth description of an individual's condition or response to treatment. A case series consists of a collection of observations of similar cases. Case reports may be used to generate theories and hypotheses for future research. They cannot test hypotheses or establish cause-and-effect relationships.[36]

Types of Research

A number of methods are used to classify research. One way is to view research along a continuum reflecting the type of question the research is intended to answer. On this continuum, research is classified as descriptive, experimental or exploratory.[36]

Descriptive research: Recording, analyzing, and interpreting conditions that exist for the purpose of classification and understanding a clinical phenomenon. Examples include developmental research, normative research, qualitative research, case report, and case series.

Experimental research: Comparing two or more conditions for the purpose of determining cause-and-effect relationships between independent and dependent variables. Examples include randomized controlled trials, quasi-experimental studies, and single-subject designs.

Exploratory research: Examines the dimensions of a phenomenon of interest and its relationships to other factors. Examples include cohort studies, case control studies, historical research, and methodological studies.

Another method of categorizing research is to distinguish it by qualitative and quantitative methods.

Characteristics of Qualitative and Quantitative Research

	Qualitative Research	Quantitative Research
Definition	Data are from observation, interviews or verbal interactions and focus on the meanings and interpretations of the participants.	Data are measurements of outcomes that can be subjected to analysis by traditional inferential statistics.
Purpose	To gain an understanding of underlying reasons and motivations of prevalent trends in thought and opinion. May generate hypotheses for subsequent quantitative research.	To quantify data and generalize results from a sample to a population.
Rationale	Human behavior must be bound to the context in which the behavior occurs and therefore must be studied in the manner it occurs, rather than being manipulated.	Social reality can be reduced to variables that when tightly controlled, allow researchers to examine how other variables are influenced.
Type of Research Question	Probing, global	Non-probing, specific
Sample	A small number of subjects.	A large number of subjects representing the population of interest.
Researcher Role	Active participant who becomes immersed in the activity for the purpose of maximizing learning.	Objective observer that does not participate in or influence what is being studied.
Data Analysis	Non-statistical	Statistical
Training of the Researcher	Background is most often in the social sciences with specialized training and skills in interviewing.	Background is most often in statistics and mathematics.
Outcome	Exploratory or investigative. Develop an initial understanding for further decision making. Findings are not conclusive and cannot be used to make generalizations about the population.	Used to recommend a final course of action.

Ethics of Human Subjects Research

Assent: A child's affirmative agreement to participate in research. A child's failure to object should not be construed as agreement.[37]

Belmont Report: In 1974, the National Research Act established the National Commission for the Protection of Human Subjects of Biomedical and Behavioral Research. This Commission, in turn, published The Belmont Report which articulated the three ethical principles that guide human subjects' research:[37]

- **Respect for persons:** Refers to the individual's right of self-determination and the right to make decisions about their medical care as an autonomous person. Respect for persons requires that people with diminished autonomy be provided special protection.
- **Beneficence:** Refers to the obligation of the researcher to provide for the well-being of their subjects and to maximize the possible benefits and minimize the possible harm in research.
- **Justice:** Refers to the fair treatment of subjects including the equitable distribution of burdens and benefits in research.

Confidentiality: An ethical principle that requires the researcher to not disclose any information revealed by the subject or discovered by the researcher to ensure that data is accessible only to authorized individuals.

Generalizable knowledge: Although used in the definition of research, the Code of Federal Regulations does not define the term. Most Institutional Review Boards operationally define it to be information or conclusions of research that have the potential to be applied to individuals and settings beyond those that were the focus of the original research.

Human subject: A living individual about whom an investigator conducting research obtains data through intervention or interaction with the individual or identifiable private information.[37]

Informed consent: The process by which a person is given important facts about the possible risks, benefits, and limits of the procedure, treatment, trial or testing before deciding whether or not to participate.[37]

Institutional Review Board (IRB): A group of scientists and non-scientists charged with protecting the rights and welfare of persons participating in research and authorized to review and approve research involving human subjects.[37]

Minimal risk: The probability and magnitude of harm or discomfort anticipated in the research are not greater than those ordinarily encountered in daily living or during the performance of routine physical or psychological examinations or tests.[37]

Research: A systematic investigation including research development, testing, and evaluation, designed to develop or contribute to generalizable knowledge.[37]

Vulnerable populations: Populations in which a voluntary informed consent process could be compromised are considered "vulnerable." Several populations are typically considered vulnerable including minors (under 18 years of age), subjects with a diminished capacity to consent, pregnant women, human fetuses, neonates and products of labor and delivery, non-English speaking subjects, prisoners or other involuntarily institutionalized persons, and students.[37]

CONSIDER THIS
INFORMED CONSENT

In keeping with the principle of Respect for Persons, researchers must obtain the informed consent of the subject or the subject's legally authorized representative under circumstances that provide the opportunity to consider whether or not to participate without undue influence or coercion. Informed consent should contain all of the following:[37]

1. A statement that the study involves research.
2. An explanation of the purpose(s) of the research.
3. A description of the procedures to be followed, including the duration of participation, and identification of any experimental procedures.
4. A description of any reasonably foreseeable risks or discomforts to the subject.
5. A description of any benefits to the subject or to others that may reasonably be expected.
6. A disclosure of any appropriate alternative procedures or treatments that might be advantageous.
7. A description of who will have access to records that identify the subjects, and how confidentiality of those records will be maintained.
8. For research involving greater than minimal risk, an explanation of any compensation and an explanation of any medical treatments that are available if injury occurs, and what they consist of, or where further information may be obtained.
9. Identification of whom to contact for answers to questions about the research and subjects' rights, and whom to contact in the event of a research-related injury to the subject, along with contact information.
10. A statement that participation is voluntary and that the subject may refuse to participate or discontinue participation at any time without penalty.

Types of Data and Measurement

Data

Data are the numeric and non-numeric information that represent the quantitative or qualitative attributes of an object, event or person.[38] Types of data include:

Continuous data: Data that can assume any value along a continuous scale that covers a range of values without gaps or interruptions. Values are limited by the degree of accuracy of the measuring instrument. Examples of continuous variables are range of motion (degrees), distance (m), weight (kg), and time (s).[36]

Discrete data: Data that is measured in whole units.[36] Examples include heart rate, patients diagnosed with cancer, and number of visits to a physical therapy clinic.

Dichotomous data: A type of discrete data limited to only two values.[36] Examples include gender (male or female) and smoking status (smoker or non-smoker).

Qualitative data: Also known as categorical data, these data represent different categories distinguished by a non-numeric characteristic.[38] Examples include eye color, blood type, and hand dominance.

Quantitative data: Data consisting of numbers that represent counts or measurements.[38] A measurement is the numeral assigned to an object, event or person, or the category to which an object, event or person is assigned according to rules.[11]

Scales of Measurement

Nominal: Also known as the classification scale because the values of the variable are mutually exclusive and exhaustive categories, so that each object or person can be assigned to only one category. Nominal scales are qualitative rather than quantitative. Examples of nominal scale measurements in physical therapy include blood type, type of breath sound, and type of arthritis.[39]

Ordinal: This scale of measurement is also known as a ranking scale. The data are ranked on the basis of a property of the variable, but the intervals between the ranks may not be equal or known. Examples of ordinal scale measurements in physical therapy include manual muscle test grades, levels of assistance, pain, and joint laxity grades.[39]

Interval: A measurement scale where the intervals between adjacent values are equal, but there is no true zero point. Examples of interval scale measurements in physical therapy include temperature (e.g., body, skin, whirlpool) on the Fahrenheit or Celsius scale and some developmental and functional status tests.[39]

Ratio: A measurement scale where the intervals between adjacent values are equal and there is a true zero point. Examples of ratio scale measurements in physical therapy include range of motion (degrees), distance walked (m), time to complete an activity (s), and nerve conduction velocity (m/sec).[39]

Measurement Reliability

Reliability is the reproducibility or repeatability of measurements.[39] Examples of different forms of reliability include:

Alternate forms reliability: Also known as parallel forms reliability, it assesses the consistency or agreement of measurements obtained with different forms of a test. Alternate forms reliability is essential if the different forms of the test are to be used interchangeably.[39] For example, different forms of standardized tests like the SAT, GRE, and NPTE can be administered each year as long as the different versions of the tests are considered equivalent measures.

Internal consistency: The extent to which items or elements that contribute to a measurement reflect one basic phenomenon or dimension.[39] For example, in physical therapy, a functional assessment scale should only include items that relate to patients' physical function.[36]

Intrarater reliability: The consistency or equivalence of repeated measurements made by the same person over time.[39]

Interrater reliability: The consistency or equivalence of measurements made by more than one person. Interrater reliability indicates the agreement of measurements taken by different examiners.[39]

Test-retest reliability: The consistency or equivalence of repeated measurements made on the same individual on separate occasions.[39] Test-retest reliability can be affected by the interval between tests, effects of fatigue or learning, and changes in the characteristic being measured.[36]

Measurement Validity

Validity is the degree to which a useful or meaningful interpretation can be inferred from a measurement.[39] Examples of different types of measurement validity include:

Face validity: The degree to which a measurement appears to test what it is supposed to.[36] Although face validity is insufficient documentation of validity, it is an important form of validity because patients may not be compliant with repeated testing if they don't see how the measurements derived from the tests relate to their specific problem.

Content validity: The degree to which a measurement reflects the meaningful elements of a construct and the items in a test adequately reflect the content domain of interest and not extraneous elements.[39] For example, the McGill Pain Questionnaire may have greater content validity than a visual analogue pain scale because, in addition to pain intensity, it assesses the location, quality, and duration of pain.[36]

Construct validity: The degree to which a theoretical construct is measured by a test or measurement. Evidence of construct validity is through logical argument based on theoretical and research evidence.[39] For example, manual muscle test (MMT) scores would have construct validity as indicators of innervation status of muscle if there was a relationship between MMT scores and the results of electromyographic testing.

Criterion-related validity: The validity of the measurement is established by comparing it to either a different measurement often considered to be a "gold standard" or data obtained by different forms of testing.[39] Examples of criterion-related validity include:

- **Concurrent validity:** A form of criterion-related validity in which an interpretation is justified by comparing a measurement to a "gold standard" measurement at approximately the same time.[39] For example, heart rate measurements made by palpation of peripheral pulses will have concurrent validity if the heart rate measurements by palpation are associated with the heart rates measured simultaneously from an ECG.
- **Predictive validity:** A form of criterion-related validity in which the measurement is considered to be valid because it is predictive of a future behavior or event.[39] For example, the use of a student's GPA or GRE as admission criteria for graduate school is based on their presumed ability to predict future academic success.
- **Prescriptive validity:** A form of criterion-related validity in which the measurement suggests the form of treatment the person should receive. The prescriptive validity of the measurement is judged based on the successful outcome of the treatment.[39] For example, the measurement of asystole on the ECG could be said to have prescriptive validity if patients with this arrhythmia are successfully revived by cardiopulmonary resuscitation techniques.

Research Subjects and Sampling

Population: The complete collection of elements to be studied. The group to which the results of research are intended to be generalized.[38]

Sample: A subset of elements drawn from a population to draw conclusions or make estimates about the larger population.[36]

Sampling error: The chance difference between the statistic calculated from a sample and the true value of the parameter in the population. Sampling error is inherent in the use of sampling methods.[36]

Sampling with replacement: A sampling method in which each unit that is selected for the sample is put back into the population before the next unit is drawn from the sample. This results in each unit truly having an equal chance of being selected throughout the sampling process. This method of sampling is rarely used in research on human subjects.[36]

Sampling without replacement: A sampling method in which a unit selected from the population is not returned to the population and therefore, cannot be selected again for the same sample. Thus, the size of the population decreases as the size of the sample increases.[36]

Probability sampling: A method of sampling that uses some form of random selection. Every member of the population must have the same probability of being selected for the sample, since the sample should be free of bias and representative of the population.[8] Examples of probability sampling methods include:

- **Simple random sampling:** Subjects have an equal chance of being selected for the sample. The sampling method often relies on a table of random numbers or a random number generator on a computer to determine the sample. However, simple random sampling is not the most statistically efficient method of sampling and may not result in a representative sample, since it is the luck of the draw.[36]
- **Systematic sampling:** Subjects are selected by taking every n^{th} subject from the population. The size of the interval is based on the size of the population and the desired sample size. The greatest advantage associated with this sampling technique is its simplicity.[36]
- **Stratified random sampling:** Also called proportional or quota random sampling, the population is divided into homogenous subgroups (strata) and then a simple random sample is drawn from each. Stratified random sampling assures that the sample will be representative of key subgroups of the population in addition to the overall population.[36]
- **Cluster sampling:** The population is divided into clusters or areas (usually along geographic boundaries) and a random sample of the clusters is selected. Then, all of the units in the selected samples are measured. The sampling technique is less costly and more efficient than simple random sampling, especially when the population is spread across a wide geographic region.[36]

Non-probability sampling: Any method of sampling that does not involve random selection of subjects.[36] Examples of non-probability sampling methods include:

- **Convenience sampling:** As the name suggests, the sample is selected from subjects who are convenient or readily available to the researcher.[36]
- **Purposive sampling:** Subjects are deliberately selected based on predefined criteria chosen by the investigators.[36]
- **Quota sampling:** Similar to stratified random sampling, except that subjects from each subgroup are not selected randomly. After identifying the subgroups or strata of interest from the population, the researcher uses convenience sampling to select the required number of subjects from each stratum.[36]
- **Snowball sampling:** Subjects are identified by asking existing subjects to identify the names of other potential participants. Snowball sampling is used when the characteristic to be studied is rare and it would be extremely difficult and costly to identify individuals with this characteristic.[36]

Experimental Designs

The essence of an experiment is to demonstrate a cause and effect relationship between an intervention or condition (independent variable) and an outcome or response (dependent variable).

Clinical trial: A type of research design that tests how well methods of screening, prevention, diagnosis or treatment of a disease work in people.[36]

Completely randomized design: A type of research design in which subjects are randomly assigned to different groups and each group receives a unique intervention. The outcomes of the different groups are compared at the end of the trial. This method is also known as a parallel groups design.[36]

Crossover design: A type of research design where the subject receives both treatments (e.g., treatment and control) in random order separated by a period of no treatment. In this design, each subject serves as their own control.[36]

Factorial design: A type of research design in which two or more independent variables are investigated with different subjects assigned to the various combinations of levels of the independent variables.[36]

Pretest-posttest control group design: A type of research design that compares the outcomes of two or more groups formed by random assignment by testing all groups before and after the treatment. This represents the basic format of a randomized controlled trial.[36]

Posttest only control group design: A type of research design that compares the outcomes of two or more groups formed by random assignment by testing all groups only after the treatment.[36]

Randomized controlled trial (RCT): A clinical trial in which a group of individuals is randomly assigned to an experimental group and a control group.[29]

Repeated measures design: A type of research design in which subjects are tested under all conditions, therefore, each person acts as their own control. This is also known as a within-subjects design.[36]

Sequential clinical trial: A type of research design in which the data are analyzed as they become available so the trial can be stopped as soon as the evidence is sufficient to show a significant difference between treatments.[36]

Single-subject design: A type of research design that permits drawing conclusions about the effects of treatment based on the responses of a single patient. Single-subject designs are characterized by the use of repeated measurement of a response over time and at least two test periods or phases: a baseline phase (A) prior to treatment and an intervention phase (B) after treatment. The baseline and intervention phases may be replicated to create a number of designs (e.g., A-B; A-B-A; A-B-A-B).[36]

Quasi-experimental design: A type of research design without a control group, random assignment of subjects to groups, or both.

- **One-group pretest-posttest design:** A type of quasi-experimental research design in which measurements are made on one group of subjects before and after treatment. Time is the independent variable, with two levels (pretest and posttest).[36]
- **One-way repeated measures design over time:** An extension of the one-group pretest-posttest design in which measurements are made on one group of subjects at multiple, prescribed time intervals. The intervention may be administered once or it may be repeated. If more than two measurements are made, trends over time may be evaluated by polynomial contrasts.[36]
- **Time series design:** A type of quasi-experimental research design in which multiple measurements are made before and after treatment to observe patterns or trends during the pretreatment and posttreatment periods.[36]

Experimental Controls

An experiment is said to have internal validity when there is confidence that the intervention caused the outcome. To achieve this result, the researcher will design the experiment to control extraneous variables and sources of bias that could reduce the validity of the results.[36] There are a number of methods for researchers to help increase the internal validity of an experiment.

Blinding: A term used to describe conditions that are imposed to keep groups of individuals from knowing which subjects have or have not received an intervention. Sometimes called masking, blinding is used to reduce bias and the placebo effect. There are several different types of blinding:[36]

- **Single blind:** The subjects are unaware of the research hypothesis and the group to which they were assigned until the end of the study.
- **Double blind:** The subjects and certain members of the research team are unaware of the research hypothesis and the group to which each subject was assigned until the end of the study.
- **Triple blind:** The subject, certain members of the research team, and data analyzers are unaware of the research hypothesis and the group to which each subject was assigned until the end of the study.

Control group: In a clinical trial, a group against which the treatment group is compared. The control group should be statistically identical to the treatment group, except for the variable of interest that is being evaluated in the experiment. Control groups are used to help isolate the effect of the independent variable and eliminate the unintended influence of extraneous factors that can confound the results. The two most common forms of control are placebo and active.[36]

- **Active control:** A known effective form of treatment in a clinical trial against which the experimental treatment is compared. When an effective treatment is available, it is unethical to use a placebo control for comparison to the experimental treatment.[36]
- **Placebo control:** An inactive substance or treatment that looks the same as, and is administered in the same way as an active drug or treatment.[36]

Matching/pairing: In research, a strategy for attempting to control for differences between subjects. Investigators identify pairs of subjects who have identical characteristics (e.g., weight, age, race) before randomizing them to ensure that the resultant groups are balanced on important variables that may affect the outcome. Using identical twins is a classic example of matching.[36]

Intention-to-treat analysis: A method of analysis in which all subjects randomly assigned to one of the treatments are analyzed together, regardless of whether they received or completed that treatment. The method preserves the original balance of subject groups achieved through randomization.[29]

External validity: The degree to which results of the research study are generalizable to populations or circumstances beyond those included in the study. Threats to external validity include the interaction of treatment with the specific type of subjects tested and the place (setting) and time (history) in which the experiment is performed.[36]

Internal validity: The degree to which an intervention being evaluated (independent variable) is the cause of the outcome measured in the study (dependent variable) and not the result of extraneous factors. Threats to internal validity include history, maturation, attrition, testing, instrumentation, and regression toward the mean.[36]

Randomization: A means of assigning subjects to groups in an experiment so that each subject has an equal chance of being assigned to each group. The most robust method of random assignment is accomplished by computer-generated random numbers or random number tables.[36]

Hawthorne effect: An untreated subject experiences a change simply from participating in a research study. The tendency for individuals to change their behavior in response to the fact that they are being observed or studied.[36]

Placebo effect: A phenomenon in which an inactive treatment or procedure that is intended to mimic a real treatment causes an improvement in the patient's condition simply because the patient has the expectation that it will be helpful.

Hypothesis Testing

In hypothesis testing, the researcher examines the probability that some estimate calculated from sample data might have occurred by chance.

Hypothesis: A tentative statement to explain certain observations or facts that requires further experimentation to be verified.[36]

- **Alternate hypothesis (H_a or H_1):** Also known as the experimental hypothesis, the alternate hypothesis is a statement that the population parameter has a value that differs from the null hypothesis. In hypothesis testing, the alternate hypothesis is accepted when the null hypothesis is rejected.[38]
- **Null hypothesis (H_o):** Also known as the statistical hypothesis, the null hypothesis is a statement that the value of a population parameter (e.g., mean, proportion or correlation coefficient) is equal to some claimed value.[38] The null hypothesis is tested statistically by inferential statistics.

Independent variable: The variable that is presumed to have caused or influenced the dependent variable. In research, the independent variable is what is controlled or manipulated by the researcher.[36]

Dependent variable: The response or outcome assumed to be caused by the effect of the independent variable.[36]

p-value: The probability that a particular statistical result could have happened by chance. When the p-value is smaller than the stated value of alpha, or level of significance, the null hypothesis is rejected. When the p-value is larger than the stated value of alpha, or level of significance, the null hypothesis is not rejected.[38]

Alpha level (a level): Also known as the significance level, the probability of rejecting the null hypothesis when it is true, or the chance of committing a Type 1 error. Traditional values for alpha are 0.05 and 0.01.[38]

Steps in Testing a Statistical Hypothesis[38]

1. State the null hypothesis and alternate hypothesis
2. Select the appropriate test statistic
3. Select the level of significance for the statistical test (e.g., $p < 0.05$)
4. Calculate the test statistic from the sample data
5. Interpret the results: Compare the p-value associated with the test statistic to the significance level.
   - If the p-value is ≤ the level of significance, reject the null hypothesis in favor of the alternate hypothesis
   - If the p-value is > the level of significance, do not reject the null hypothesis

Type I error (alpha error): The error the researcher makes when wrongly deciding to reject the null hypothesis, concluding that there is a difference or relationship when there is not. If the level of significance is set at 0.01, there is a 1% chance of a Type I error occurring. A Type I error is a false positive finding.[38]

Type II error (beta error): The error the researcher makes when wrongly deciding not to reject the null hypothesis, concluding that there is no difference or relationship when there is. A Type II error is a false negative finding.[38]

Statistically significant: A statistical conclusion made when the probability is small that the difference between groups or the relationship between variables happened by chance.[38]

Statistical power: Refers to the chance that a statistical test will lead to rejection of a false null hypothesis (i.e., find a "statistically significant" result).[38]

Effect size (ES): A measure of the magnitude of the difference between two treatments or the magnitude of the relationship between two variables. The larger the ES, the more likely it will be statistically significant. ES is one of the statistical elements used to estimate sample size and perform a power analysis.[36]

Effect size index: A statistic that represents effect size using a standardized value. Generally, the effect size index is calculated by taking the difference between the two groups (e.g., the mean of the treatment group minus the mean of the control group) and dividing it by the standard deviation of one of the groups.

To interpret the resulting index, this general guide is used:[36]

< 0.1 = trivial effect

0.1 - 0.3 = small effect

0.3 - 0.5 = moderate effect

> 0.5 = large effect

Minimal clinically important difference (MCID): The smallest difference in a patient's condition that the patient or clinician considers worthwhile and that would, in the absence of side effects and excessive cost, warrant a change in the patient's management. The MCID is an important concept for judging if changes reported in a research study indicate a meaningful or trivial effect on the patient's status. The MCID is also known as the minimal clinically significant difference (MCSD).[36]

Minimal detectable difference (MDD): The minimum detectable change in a patient's condition beyond the threshold of measurement error. MDD represents the smallest difference or change that would be statistically significant. The standard error of measurement is a common statistic used to determine the MDD. MDD is also known as minimal detectable change (MDC).[36]

Parameter: A numerical measurement describing some characteristic of a population.[38] Parameters are rarely known and usually estimated by statistics computed from a sample. In research publications, Greek letters are used to designate parameters. For example, μ (mu) is the symbol for the mean of the population and σ (sigma) is the symbol for the standard deviation of the population.

Statistic: A numerical measurement describing some characteristic of a sample.[38] Statistics are used to estimate population parameters. In research publications, English letters are used to designate statistics. For example, $\overline{x}$ or M is the symbol for the sample mean and s is the symbol for the sample standard deviation.

Describing Data with Graphs

Bar graph: A type of graph used to show the magnitude or frequency of categories of the data. Data in each category are represented by vertical bars, with the length of the bars proportional to the magnitude or frequency on a vertical y-axis (Fig. 9-14).[40]

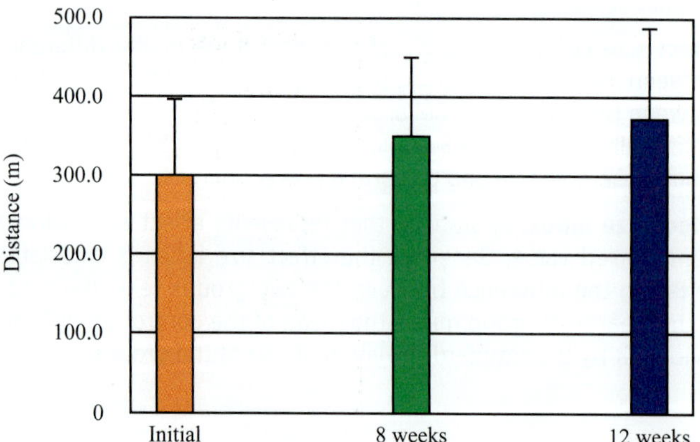

Fig. 9-14: Example of a bar graph showing the average distance walked by 31 subjects at three time periods. Values are means +1 standard deviation.

Box and whisker plot: A type of graph that illustrates the distribution of values within a group through five numbers: minimum score, lower quartile (Q1), median (Q2), upper quartile (Q3), and maximum score. Outliers are shown as circles (Fig. 9-15).[38]

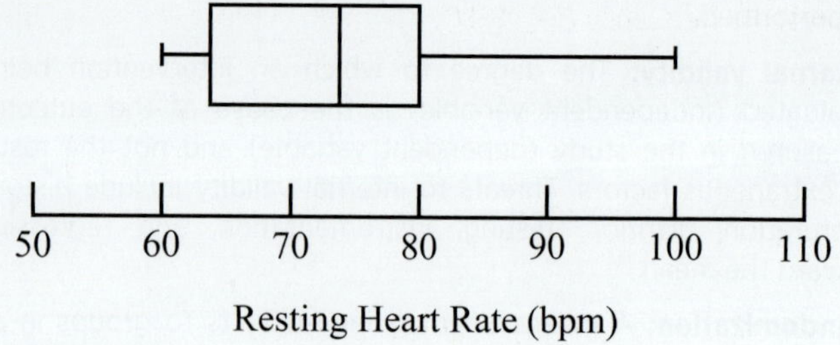

Fig. 9-15: Example of a box and whisker plot for 22 subjects. Minimum = 60; lower quartile (Q1) = 64; median (Q2) = 74; upper quartile (Q3) = 80; maximum = 100. No outliers are shown.

Forest plot: A type of graph used in a meta-analysis that shows the results of the individual studies as well as a cumulative summary of all studies. The graph plots the point estimate of the measure of effect (e.g., odds ratio, relative risk) for each study as a square along a horizontal line, the width of which represents the confidence interval of the effect. The area of each square is proportional to the study's weight in the meta-analysis. The measure of effect for all studies combined is plotted as a diamond. The center of the diamond represents the point estimate for the cumulative effect and the width of the horizontal line represents the upper and lower confidence limits. A vertical line represents no effect or the null value. A forest plot is also known as a blobbogram (Fig. 9-16).

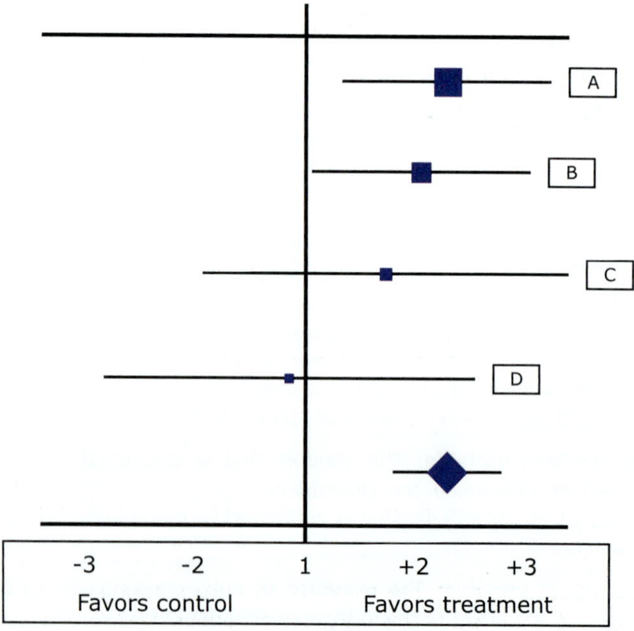

Fig. 9-16: Example of a forest plot depicting the odds ratios from four studies (A, B, C, D) and a cumulative summary of all the studies combined (diamond) from a meta-analysis.

Histogram: A graphical display of a frequency distribution. Histograms display the distribution of data by plotting the frequency (count or percentages) of observations (y-axis) for each interval represented on the x-axis. Histograms use continuous bars of equal widths determined by the x-axis intervals, where bar height represents frequency (Fig. 9-17).[38]

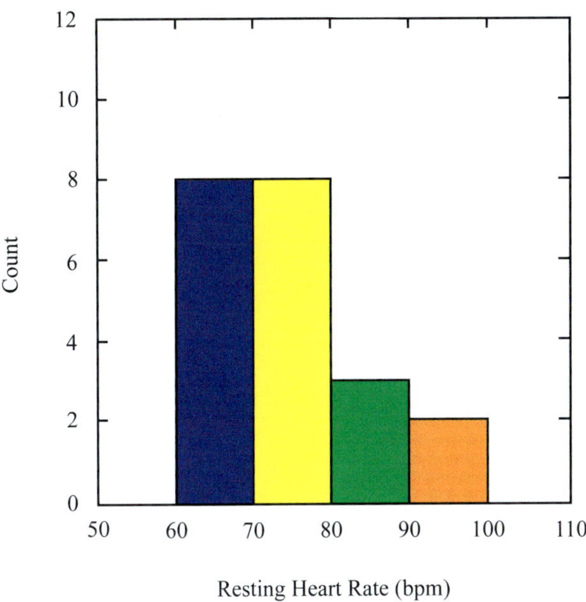

Fig. 9-17: Example of a histogram for resting heart rate of 21 subjects.

Line graphs: A graph that demonstrates the relationship between two or more quantitative variables. Line graphs usually are designed with the dependent variable on the y-axis and the independent variable on the x-axis and are ideal for showing trends in data over time. The data points are connected by curves (Fig. 9-18).[40]

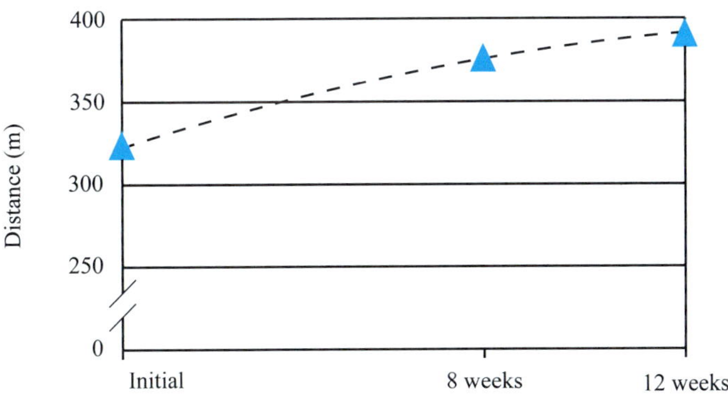

Fig. 9-18: Example of a line graph showing the curvilinear increase in average distance walked in a 6-minute walk test performed by 31 patients measured at three time periods.

Scatter plot: A graphical display that illustrates the relationship between two quantitative variables. Each paired (x,y) value is plotted on the graph as a single point. A line of best fit generated mathematically may be fitted to the data to show the relationship among the variables (Fig. 9-19).[38]

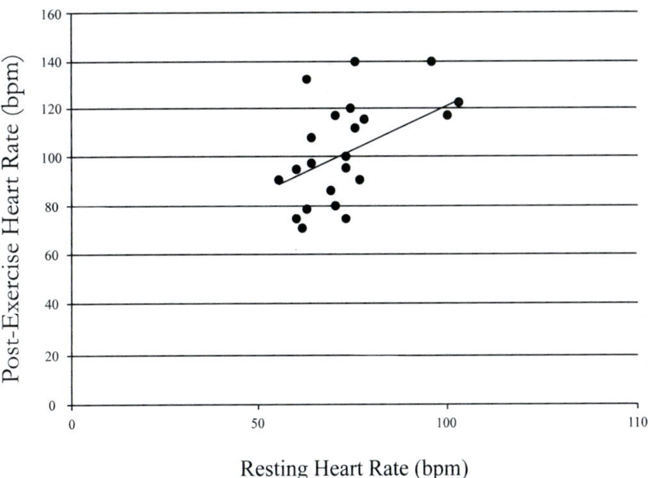

Fig. 9-19: Example of a scatter plot showing the relationship between resting heart rate and post-exercise heart rate in 22 subjects with the linear regression line.

Stem and leaf plots: A graphical display which enables the reader to observe the entire distribution of data without losing any information. Most commonly this is done by organizing data into categories (e.g., 20-29, 30-39), and then dividing a number into two digits. The first digit is placed to the left side of a vertical line (stem) and the second digit is placed on the right side of the vertical line (leaves) (Fig. 9-20).[38]

5	359
6	47888
7	27899
8	1124
9	247
10	23

Fig. 9-20: Example of a stem and leaf plot showing heart rate data for each of 22 subjects.

Descriptive Statistics

Descriptive statistics summarize or describe important characteristics of a population. Typically, data from the population are examined for measures of center, distribution, and variation.

Measures of Center

Values that describe the center of the data.

Mean: The arithmetic average; the sum of all the values divided by number of values.[38]

Median: The point on a distribution at which 50% of the values fall above and below. It is the 50th percentile. The median is identified by first rank ordering the values. If the number of values is odd, the median is the middle value. If the number of values is even, the median is the mean of the two middle values.[38]

Mode: The value that occurs most frequently. A distribution with two modes is termed bimodal. A distribution with more than two modes is termed multimodal.[38]

Measures of Distribution

Values that describe the shape of the data.

Kurtosis: Refers to the "peakedness" of a distribution. It is a measure of whether the data are peaked or flat relative to a normal distribution. A high kurtosis distribution has a sharper peak and longer, fatter tails, while a low kurtosis distribution has a more rounded peak and shorter, thinner tails.[38]

Normal: A bell-shaped curve with the majority of data clustered around the mean. The mean, median, and mode are the same (Figs. 9-21, 9-22, 9-23).[38]

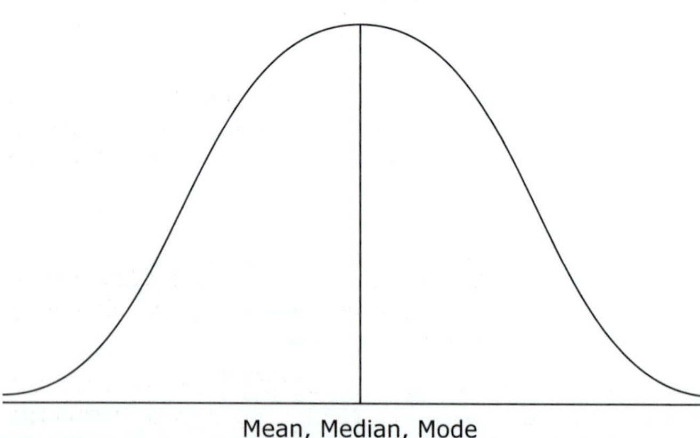

Fig. 9-21: Location of the mean, median, and mode in a normal distribution.

- Approximately 68% of all values fall within one standard deviation above and below the mean.
- Approximately 95% of all values fall within two standard deviations above and below the mean.
- Approximately 99% of all values fall within three standard deviations above and below the mean.

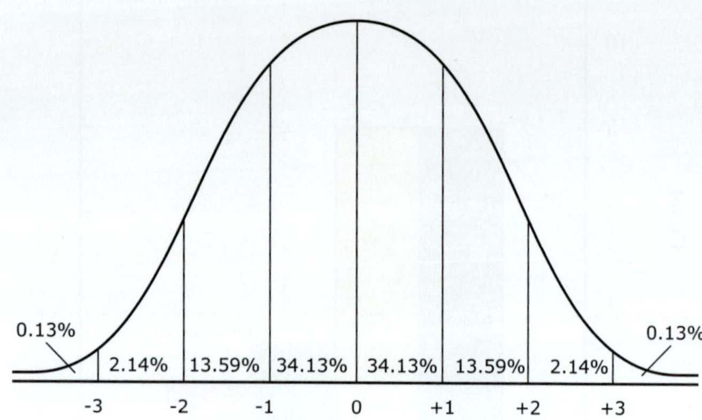

Fig. 9-22: Areas under the curve of a normal distribution represented by each standard deviation between -3 and +3.

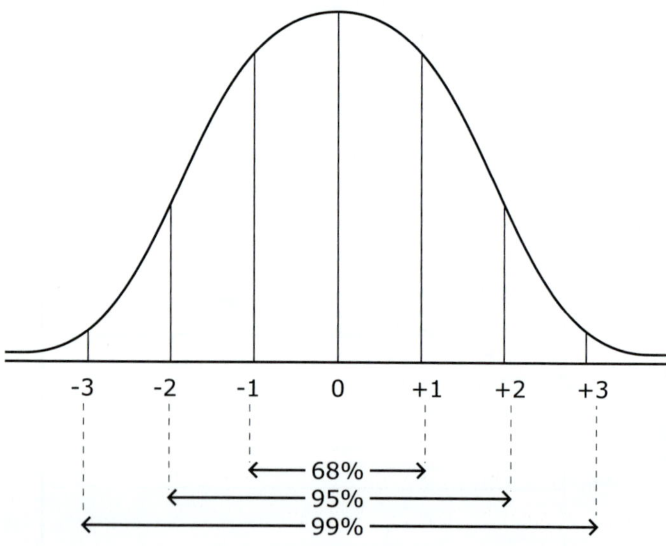

Fig. 9-23: The approximate areas of a normal distribution bounded by ±1, ±2, and ±3 standard deviations from the mean.

Skewness: Refers to the asymmetry in the shape of a distribution. In a negatively skewed distribution, the mean and median are to the left of the mode and the left tail is elongated (Fig. 9-24). In a positively skewed distribution, the mean and median are to the right of the mode and the right tail is elongated (Fig. 9-25).[38]

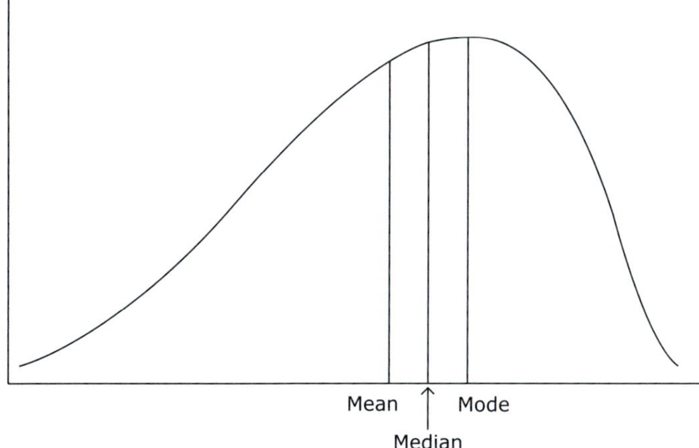

Fig. 9-24: Negatively skewed distribution.

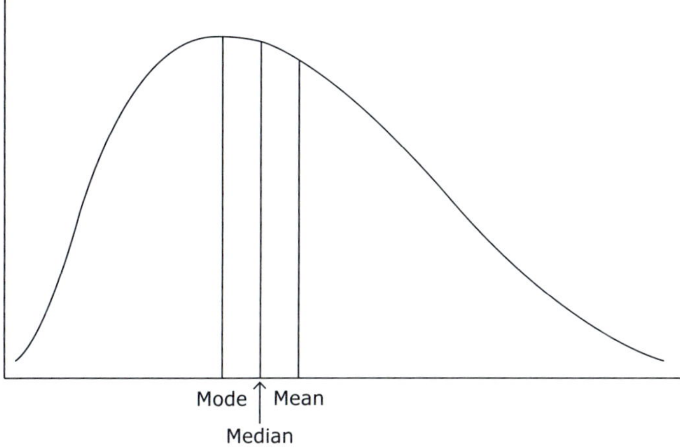

Fig. 9-25: Positively skewed distribution.

Measures of Variation

Values that describe how the data vary.

Coefficient of variation (CV): The CV is the ratio of the standard deviation of a distribution to the mean, expressed as a percentage. CV = (s / mean) x 100.[38]

Percentiles: The value below which a certain percent of observations within a distribution will fall. For example, the 20th percentile is the value or score below which 20% of scores are found.[38]

Quartiles: Quartiles divide the data into four equal parts, so that each part represents one fourth of the sampled population. The 25th percentile is also known as the first quartile (Q1), the 50th percentile as the median or second quartile (Q2), and the 75th percentile as the third quartile (Q3).[38]

Range: The difference between the maximum and minimum values.[38]

Standard deviation: A descriptive measure of the spread or dispersion of data; the positive square root of the variance. Describing data by means of standard deviation implies that the data are normally distributed.

Variance: The sum of the squared deviations of each data point from the mean, divided by the number of observations in the sample.[38] The variance equals the standard deviation squared, and therefore is expressed as squared units of the data. Because squared units are difficult to make sense of, the variance is often not reported. The formula for the variance (S^2) of a sample is:

$$S^2 = \frac{\sum (X-M)^2}{N}$$

where X is a single score, M is the sample mean, and N is the number of scores.

Inferential Statistics

Inferential statistics are a branch of statistics that use sample data to make inferences about a population. Inferential statistics are used to test hypotheses. Two types of inferential statistics are parametric and nonparametric.

Parametric Statistics

Parametric statistics assume that samples come from populations that are normally distributed and there is homogeneity of variance. Parametric statistical tests are applied to both interval and ratio level data.[38]

Analysis of variance (ANOVA)

Analysis of variance is an inferential statistical procedure used to test the equality of means between two or more populations by analyzing sample variances.

One-way analysis of variance: A statistical procedure similar to the independent t-test, however, the test is designed to accommodate two or more population means. One-way refers to the fact that the sample data are separated into different groups on the basis of one characteristic or factor; only one independent variable is examined in the analysis.[38]

Two-way analysis of variance: A statistical procedure used to compare two or more population means with two or more independent variables. Two-way refers to the fact that the sample data are separated into different groups on the basis of two characteristics or factors. Both independent variables are examined in the analysis, which also examines the interaction of the two independent variables.[38]

Repeated measures analysis of variance: An analysis of variance procedure where all individuals are measured under a number of different experimental conditions. It is an appropriate analysis to perform for variables where practice or carryover effects are minimal. Repeated measures ANOVA can also be used when individuals have been matched according to an important characteristic.[36]

Regression analysis: A set of statistical procedures to examine the relationship between a dependent variable (Y) and one or more independent predictor variables (X). Regression analysis predicts how a change in one or more of the independent variables affects the dependent variable.[36]

Confidence intervals

Confidence interval (CI): A range of values used to estimate a population parameter. CI is also known as the interval estimate.[38]

Confidence level: The probability, usually expressed as a percentage, that the confidence interval actually contains the unknown population parameter. With repeated sampling, the interval would contain the true parameter value with the probability at the stated confidence level. For example, a 95% confidence level means that if the same population is sampled 100 times and CIs are calculated on each sample, 95 of the resulting CIs would be expected to contain the true population parameter.[38]

Point estimate: A single value calculated from a sample that best approximates a population parameter of interest. For example, the sample mean is the point estimate for the mean of the population.

Correlation

A statistical measure of the strength of association among two or more variables. Two variables may be correlated for a number of reasons, so correlation does not imply causation.[36]

Intraclass correlation (ICC): A form of correlation coefficient that assesses both the degree of correspondence and agreement among scores. The ICC ranges from 0.0 to 1.0 and is calculated from variance estimates derived from an analysis of variance.[36]

Pearson product moment correlation (r): A correlation coefficient that measures the magnitude and direction of the linear relationship of two variables on the interval scale. The test yields a value between -1.0 and +1.0. The sign indicates the direction of the relationship and the number indicates the magnitude of the relationship. A positive sign indicates that the two variables increase or decrease together; a negative sign indicates that an increase in one variable is associated with a decrease in the other. A value of +1.0 or -1.0 indicates that the sample values fall in a straight line, while a value of 0 indicates no relationship.[38]

t-test

An inferential statistical procedure for estimating a population mean or comparing two means when the population is normally distributed and the population variance is not known.[38]

Dependent or paired t-test: A parametric statistical procedure used to compare the means of two groups that are correlated. A paired sample t-test is used when the samples are matched pairs.[38]

Independent t-test: A parametric statistical procedure used to compare the means of two independent groups. The groups are considered independent if members of each group are different. For example, the independent sample t-test is appropriate when testing differences between males and females because a person cannot be in both groups.[38]

One sample t-test: A statistical procedure used to compare the mean of a sample to an expected or reference mean of the population to make a statistical decision as to whether or not the sample mean is different from the population.[38]

One-tailed test: A test of statistical significance in which deviations from the null hypothesis in only one direction are considered. When using a significance level of 0.05, a one-tailed test apportions 0.05 to either the right or left tail of the distribution of the test statistic. This only applies when the test statistic is symmetrically distributed (e.g., z, t). The use of a one-tailed test implies that the intervention could have only one effect (i.e., beneficial or harmful).[38]

Two-tailed test: A test of statistical significance in which deviations from the null hypothesis in either direction are considered. When using a significance level of 0.05, a two-tailed test apportions 0.025 to each tail of the distribution of the test statistic. This only applies when the test statistic is symmetrically distributed (e.g., z, t).[38]

z-test

A statistical procedure for estimating the mean of a population or comparing two means when the population is normally distributed and the population variance is known.[38]

Nonparametric Statistics

Nonparametric statistics do not assume that samples come from populations that are normally distributed and do not assume homogeneity of variance. Nonparametric statistical tests are commonly applied to nominal or ordinal level data, or interval or ratio data that are not normal.[38]

Chi-Square test: A nonparametric statistical procedure for nominal data. The test evaluates the difference between observed and expected frequencies to examine the association or independence between categorical variables.[38]

Kruskal-Wallis test: A statistical procedure used to determine if three or more independent samples come from the same population. It is the nonparametric version of the one-way analysis of variance.[38]

Mann-Whitney test: A statistical procedure used to compare two independent samples with ordinal level data. It is the nonparametric alternative of the independent t-test and is equivalent to the Wilcoxon signed rank test.[38]

Spearman rank correlation coefficient: A type of correlation to test for the association between two variables. The data are ranks (ordinal level) or can be converted to ranks. It is the nonparametric equivalent to the Pearson product moment correlation. The test yields a value between -1.0 and +1.0.[38]

Wilcoxon Signed Rank test: A nonparametric statistical procedure used to compare two dependent samples with ordinal level data. It is the nonparametric alternative of the dependent or paired t-test.[38]

Statistical Measures of Validity for Diagnostic and Screening Tests

Sensitivity: When referring to a medical test, sensitivity refers to the percentage of people who test positive for a specific disease among a group of people who have the disease.[36]

Specificity: When referring to a medical test, specificity refers to the percentage of people who test negative for a specific disease among a group of people who do not have the disease.[36]

False negative test: A test that indicates a person does not have a specific disease or condition when the person actually does have the disease or condition.[36]

False positive test: A test that indicates a person has a specific disease or condition when the person actually does not have the disease or condition.[36]

Negative predictive value: The ability of a diagnostic test to correctly determine the proportion of patients without the disease from all the patients with negative test results.[29]

Positive predictive value: The ability of a diagnostic test to correctly determine the proportion of patients with the disease from all the patients with positive test results.[29]

SpPin: A mnemonic used to remember the relationship between a diagnostic or screening test with a high specificity value and the confidence we have in ruling in the diagnosis. In a test with high specificity, a positive diagnostic test rules in the diagnosis.

SnNout: A mnemonic used to remember the relationship between a diagnostic or screening test with a high sensitivity value and the confidence we have in ruling out the diagnosis. In a test with high sensitivity, a negative diagnostic test rules out the diagnosis.

Epidemiology

Epidemiology is the study of the causes, distribution, transmission, and control of disease in groups of people.[36]

Risk factor: Something that increases the chance of developing a condition or disease.[36]

Measures of disease frequency

Incidence: The number of new cases of a particular disease or condition in the population at risk during a specified time interval. Often expressed as the number of new cases per 100,000 people at risk.[36]

Prevalence: The number of existing cases of a disease or condition at a point in time, including new and pre-existing cases.[36] Often expressed as the number of existing cases per 100,000 people at risk.

Measures of association and risk

Relative risk (RR): A measure of the risk of a certain event happening in one group compared to the risk of the same event happening in another group. Typically, this is the ratio of incidence of disease among individuals exposed to some disease risk factor to the incidence of disease among individuals who were not exposed. Like the odds ratio, a RR of 1.0 means that the event is equally probable in both groups. A RR greater than 1.0 implies that exposure increases the risk and a RR less than 1.0 implies that the exposure decreases the risk. The RR is also known as the risk ratio.[34]

Odds ratio (OR): A measure of the odds of an event happening in one group compared to the odds of the same event happening in another group. In research, odds ratios are most often used in case control (backward looking) studies to find out if being exposed to a certain substance or other risk factor increases the risk of developing a certain disease. An OR of 1.0 means that the exposure probably does not increase the risk of developing the disease. An OR > 1.0 means that the exposure may increase the risk of getting the disease, and an OR < 1.0 means that the exposure may reduce the risk. The OR is also known as the relative odds.[34]

Number needed to treat (NNT): The number of patients that need to be treated to prevent one bad outcome or result in one additional good outcome.[29] The ideal NNT is one, where everyone improves with treatment. The higher the NNT, the less effective is the treatment.

Institutional policies and procedures on research with human subjects are designed to comply with the Code of Federal Regulations[9] as well as state and local laws to protect individuals involved in research participation.

The Code of Ethics for the Physical Therapist sets forth principles for the ethical practice of physical therapy as determined by the House of Delegates of the American Physical Therapy Association.[13] Principle 5C of the Code of Ethics states: Physical therapists involved in research shall abide by accepted standards governing protection of research participants.

Safety and Protection; Professional Responsibilities; Research Essentials

Safety and Protection

1. Standard precautions combine universal precautions and body substance isolation precautions. Standard precautions apply to all blood/body fluids, secretions, and excretions.

2. Transmission-based precautions offer guidelines for the care of specified patients infected with selected pathogens transmitted by airborne, droplet or contact modes.

3. Airborne precautions reduce the risk of airborne transmission of infectious agents through evaporated droplets in air or dust particles.

4. Droplet precautions reduce the risk of droplet transmission of infectious agents through contact of the mucous membranes of the mouth and nose, contact with the conjunctivae, and through coughing, sneezing, talking or suctioning.

5. Contact precautions reduce the risk of transmission of infectious agents through direct or indirect contact. Direct contact involves skin-to-skin transmission; indirect contact involves a contaminated intermediate object, usually within the patient's environment.

6. Personal protective equipment (e.g., gowns, lab coats, masks, gloves, goggles, spill kits, mouthpieces) are used as barriers to protect someone who is assisting a patient with a potentially infectious disease.

7. A sterile field is a designated area that is considered void of all contaminants and microorganisms. Specific protocols are required to develop and maintain the sterile field.

Professional Responsibilities

8. The Americans with Disabilities Act is federal legislation designed to provide a clear and comprehensive national mandate for the elimination of discrimination.

9. A ramp must possess twelve inches of length for each inch of vertical rise (i.e., 8.3% grade).

10. A S.O.A.P. note is a commonly used format for daily notes. The S.O.A.P. acronym stands for: S = Subjective, O = Objective, A = Assessment, P = Plan.

11. Quality improvement refers to a form of objective self-examination designed to improve the quality of services.

12. The Nagi Model describes health status as a product of the relationship between health and function and is defined by four primary concepts: pathology, impairment, functional limitation, and disability.

13. Negligence refers to the failure to do what a reasonable and prudent person would ordinarily have done under the same or similar circumstances for a given situation.

14. Risk management refers to the identification, analysis, and evaluation of risks and the selection of the most advantageous method for treating them.

15. Responsibilities delegated to support personnel by physical therapists must be commensurate with their qualifications. This includes experience, education, and training of the individuals to whom the responsibilities are being assigned.

16. A physical therapist assistant is a technically educated health care provider who assists the physical therapist in the provision of physical therapy. The physical therapist assistant, under the direction and supervision of the physical therapist, is the only paraprofessional who provides physical therapy interventions.

17. A physical therapy aide is a non-licensed worker who is specifically trained under the direction and supervision of a physical therapist. The physical therapy aide may be involved in the provision of physical therapist directed support services.

18. The Physical Therapist Patient/Client Management Model includes examination, evaluation, diagnosis, prognosis (including plan of care), intervention, and outcomes.

19. Criteria for Standards of Practice for Physical Therapy serve as the profession's statement of conditions and performances that are essential for provision of high quality professional service to society, and provide a foundation for assessment of physical therapist practice.

Safety and Protection; Professional Responsibilities; Research Essentials

20. The Code of Ethics for the Physical Therapist published by the American Physical Therapy Association sets forth principles for the ethical practice of physical therapy. All physical therapists are responsible for maintaining and promoting ethical practice.

21. Medicare provides health insurance for individuals over 65 years of age and the disabled. Medicaid provides basic medical services for individuals with low income or who qualify for welfare or public assistance benefits in the state of their residence.

22. Workers' Compensation provides protection for employees that are injured on the job. This legislation provides continued income as well as paid medical expenses for employees injured while working.

23. Current Procedural Terminology (CPT) codes are procedure codes used by physical therapists and other health care professionals to describe the interventions that were provided to a given patient.

24. The International Classification of Diseases (ICD) codes are designed to describe a patient's infirmity through categories based on etiology and affected anatomical systems.

25. Maslow's Hierarchy of Needs includes self-actualization needs, esteem needs, affiliative needs, and physiological needs.

26. Classical conditioning refers to a process where learning occurs when an unconditioned stimulus is repeatedly preceded by a neutral stimulus. The neutral stimulus serves as a conditioned stimulus and the learned reaction that results is termed the conditioned response.

27. Operant conditioning refers to a process where learning occurs when an individual engages in specific behaviors in order to receive certain consequences.

28. Common Health Behavior Models include the Health Belief Model, Social Cognitive Theory (Social Learning Theory), and Trans-theoretical Model (Stages of Change).

29. Domains of learning are educational terms that describe various aspects of human behavior. The three most commonly recognized domains of learning are the cognitive, psychomotor, and affective domains.

30. The Stages of Dying describe five stages in coming to terms with death. The stages include denial, anger, bargaining, depression, and acceptance.

Research

31. Evidence-based practice refers to the physical therapist's reliance on patient-centered clinical research, clinical expertise and past experiences, and the patient's values when making clinical decisions about the patient's physical therapy plan of care.

32. When searching the literature for patient-centered clinical research, the physical therapist should ask a focused clinical question that is directly relevant to the patient's problems and phrased in a way that directs the search of the literature. A focused clinical question usually contains four elements that form the acronym P-I-C-O.

    Patient or Problem – The target patient population or the problem of interest

    Intervention – The intervention or form of therapy to evaluate

    Comparison – The comparison/control treatments to be compared to the primary intervention

    Outcome – The measurements that would suggest the intervention or therapy is effective

33. Before accepting the results of a study about an intervention, therapists should determine if the results of the study are valid, important, and applicable to their patients.

34. There is a hierarchy for the levels of evidence for studies about therapy/intervention, diagnosis, and prognosis. For studies about therapy/interventions, systematic reviews and meta-analyses are considered to be the highest forms of evidence followed by randomized controlled trials.

35. Physical therapists involved in clinical research must adhere to the principles and practices that govern the planning and implementation of research when working with human subjects. These are summarized in the Belmont Report.

36. The three basic ethical principles relevant to research involving human subjects are the principles of respect of persons, beneficence, and justice.

Safety and Protection; Professional Responsibilities; Research Essentials

37. Reliability and validity are important properties of measurements. Physical therapists should select tests and measurements which have been investigated for appropriate forms of reliability and validity.

38. Selecting a representative sample of subjects from the population is an important step in the research process to ensure that the results of the research can be generalized to the population of interest.

39. Probability samples involve some form of random selection; non-probability samples do not.

40. A number of different experimental designs are available to test hypotheses in clinical research. The randomized controlled trial (RCT) is considered the gold standard of true experimental designs.

41. Blinding, controls, randomization, and intention-to-treat analysis are important means researchers use to control extraneous variables and sources of bias that could reduce the validity of their results.

42. Researchers use the hypothesis testing procedure to test hypotheses of differences or relationships between variables.

43. When the results of a study report a p-value that is smaller than the stated value of alpha, or level of significance, the null hypothesis is rejected and the result is said to be statistically significant. When the p-value is larger than the stated value of alpha, the null hypothesis is not rejected and the result is not statistically significant.

44. When evaluating the effectiveness of interventions, physical therapists must consider the clinical importance in addition to the statistical significance. The minimal clinically important difference (MCID) for the test or measurement, if known, provides a guide to assess the meaningfulness of the change in patient status.

45. Descriptive statistics (e.g., measures of center, distribution, and variability) summarize or describe important characteristics of a population.

46. Inferential statistics are used to test hypotheses and to make inferences from the sample to the population.

47. The t-test and analysis of variance are examples of parametric inferential statistics used to test the significance of the differences in two or more means.

48. The intraclass correlation coefficient and Pearson product moment correlation coefficient are examples of parametric inferential statistics used to test the significance of the relationships between variables.

49. The validity of screening and diagnostic tests is assessed by measures of sensitivity, specificity, negative predictive value, and positive predictive value.

50. The odds ratio and risk ratio are statistical measures used to assess the association between exposure to a risk factor and developing a disease.

Safety and Protection; Professional Responsibilities; Research Proficiencies

Safety and Protection; Professional Responsibilities Proficiencies

1. Accessibility Requirements

Determine if each provided measurement is consistent with established accessibility standards. If a given measurement satisfies existing standards, it is considered acceptable. If the measurement fails to satisfy existing standards, it is considered unacceptable.

Determine if each measurement is acceptable or unacceptable, and identify the established accessibility standard for each measurement.

Word Bank: acceptable, unacceptable

Acceptable/Unacceptable	Measurement
a	A ramp with a grade of 9.8%.
Standard:	
b	A ramp that is 20 feet in length with a 24 inch vertical rise.
Standard:	
c	A ramp with a width of 36 inches.
Standard:	
d	A doorway with a width of 34 inches.
Standard:	
e	A hallway with a width of 32 inches.
Standard:	
f	A bathroom sink with 30 inches of height from the floor.
Standard:	
g	A bathroom toilet with 18 inches of height from the floor to the top of the toilet.
Standard:	

Safety and Protection; Professional Responsibilities; Research Proficiencies

Safety and Protection; Professional Responsibilities Proficiencies

2. S.O.A.P. Notes

Identify the appropriate portion of the S.O.A.P. note for each entry. Answers must be selected from the Word Bank.

Word Bank: subjective, objective, assessment, plan

Section	Entry
a	The patient reports hurting the knee after falling down a flight of stairs.
b	Right knee active range of motion is 0-126 degrees.
c	The patient received instructions for shoulder strengthening using elastic tubing.
d	The patient denies pain when coughing.
e	The patient may not have exhibited maximal effort during resistive testing.
f	The patient exhibits 5/5 strength in the left iliopsoas.
g	The patient indicates a desire to return home with her husband after discharge.
h	The patient demonstrated appropriate use of pacing techniques during ambulation.
i	The patient's cardiac status may diminish the patient's rate of recovery.
j	The patient will be referred to a speech-language pathologist.

3. The Nagi Model

Identify the appropriate concept from the Nagi Model based on each description. Answers must be selected from the Word Bank and can be used more than once.

Word Bank: disability, impairment, functional limitation, pathology

Concept	Description
a	lateral collateral ligament sprain
b	diminished knee range of motion
c	difficulty ascending a flight of stairs
d	unable to work as a housekeeper
e	diminished upper extremity sensation
f	unable to propel a wheelchair on level ground

Safety and Protection; Professional Responsibilities; Research Proficiencies

Safety and Protection; Professional Responsibilities Proficiencies

4. Scope of Practice

Determine if each described activity is consistent with the scope of practice for the identified health care provider. Appropriate activities should be labeled acceptable and inappropriate activities should be labeled unacceptable.

Word Bank: acceptable, unacceptable

Acceptable/Unacceptable	Entry
a	A physical therapist assistant completes a discharge summary.
b	A physical therapist instructs a physical therapist assistant to teach an existing patient to utilize axillary crutches.
c	A physical therapist assistant describes a patient's exercise tolerance in the medical record.
d	A physical therapy aide guards a patient ascending stairs.
e	A physical therapist assistant discontinues an existing exercise session due to safety concerns.
f	A physical therapist assistant completes a re-examination on a patient.
g	A physical therapy aide monitors a patient's vital signs during exercise.
h	A physical therapist assistant increases the weight a patient uses on an existing upper extremity progressive resistive exercise.
i	A physical therapy aide returns a previously used hot pack to the hydrocollator unit.

Safety and Protection; Professional Responsibilities; Research Proficiencies

Safety and Protection; Professional Responsibilities Proficiencies

5. Health Care Disciplines

Identify the health care discipline most closely associated with the supplied description. Answers must be selected from the Word Bank and can be used only once.

Word Bank: home health aides, occupational therapists, physical therapist assistants, physical therapists, physical therapy aides, respiratory therapists, social workers, speech-language pathologists

Discipline	Description
a	These individuals provide health related services to the elderly, disabled, and ill in their homes. Patient care activities include performing housekeeping duties, assisting with ambulation or transfers, and promoting personal hygiene.
b	These individuals are considered support personnel who may be involved in support services directed by physical therapists. They are permitted to function only with continuous on-site supervision by a physical therapist, or in some cases a physical therapist assistant.
c	These individuals evaluate, treat, and care for patients with breathing disorders. Patient care activities include performing postural drainage techniques, measuring lung capacities, administering oxygen and aerosols, and analyzing oxygen and carbon dioxide concentrations.
d	These individuals help people improve their ability to perform activities of daily living, work, and leisure skills. Educational preparation emphasizes the social, emotional, and physiological effects of illness and injury.
e	These individuals provide services to help restore function, improve mobility, relieve pain, and prevent or limit permanent physical disabilities of patients suffering from injuries or disease.
f	These individuals evaluate speech, language, cognitive-communication, and swallowing skills of children and adults.
g	These individuals perform components of physical therapy procedures and related tasks selected and delegated by a supervising physical therapist.
h	These individuals help patients and their families to cope with chronic, acute or terminal illnesses and attempt to resolve problems that stand in the way of recovery or rehabilitation.

Safety and Protection; Professional Responsibilities; Research Proficiencies

Safety and Protection; Professional Responsibilities Proficiencies

6. Safety and Professional Roles Basics

Mark each statement as True or False. If the statement is False, correct the statement in the space provided.

True/False	Statement
a	A computer monitor in a work station should be a minimum of 12 inches away from the eyes.
Correction:	
b	When performing a transfer with a patient that requires assistance, a physical therapist should attempt to be as close to the patient as possible and use a long lever arm.
Correction:	
c	Sterile gowns are only considered sterile in the front from the waist level upwards.
Correction:	
d	If an object on a sterile field becomes contaminated, the entire field is considered non-sterile.
Correction:	
e	A patient with droplet precautions would require a physical therapist to wear a mask if they were within ten feet of the patient.
Correction:	
f	A ramp that is 20 inches in elevation should be a minimum of 20 feet in length.
Correction:	

Safety and Protection; Professional Responsibilities; Research Proficiencies

Safety and Protection; Professional Responsibilities Proficiencies

True/False	Statement
g	A discharge summary should provide a capsule view of the patient's progress during therapy.
Correction:	
h	One inch is equivalent to 3.28 centimeters.
Correction:	
i	Autonomy refers to the moral obligation of health care providers to act for the benefit of others.
Correction:	
j	Prognosis refers to the anticipated level of optimal improvement that may be attained through intervention and the amount of time required to reach that level.
Correction:	
k	The Consolidated Omnibus Budget Reconciliation Act provides protection for employees that are injured on the job.
Correction:	
l	Medicare Part A provides benefits for outpatient care, physician services, and services ordered by physicians such as diagnostic tests, medical equipment, and supplies.
Correction:	
m	International Classification of Diseases Codes are procedure codes used by physical therapists and other health care professionals to describe specific interventions provided to a given patient.
Correction:	

Safety and Protection; Professional Responsibilities; Research Proficiencies

Safety and Protection; Professional Responsibilities Proficiencies

7. Domains of Learning

Identify the appropriate domain of learning for each described activity. Answers must be selected from the Word Bank and can be used more than once.

Word Bank: affective, cognitive, psychomotor

Domain	Description
a	A patient lists three postoperative contraindications following total hip arthroplasty.
b	A patient reports being fearful that they will reinjure their knee after returning to athletic activities.
c	A patient performs a D2 flexion pattern using the right upper extremity.
d	A patient verbally summarizes the activities included in a home exercise program with their physical therapist.
e	A patient demonstrates a sliding board transfer using the appropriate technique.
f	A patient is extremely cautious when weight bearing on the involved lower extremity.

8. Stages of Dying

Identify the appropriate stage of dying for each description. Answers must be selected from the Word Bank and can be used only once.

Word Bank: acceptance, anger, bargaining, denial, depression

Stage	Description
a	This stage is characterized by an individual trying to negotiate with fate.
b	This stage is characterized by frustration and negative emotional feelings often directed at anyone the individual comes in contact with.
c	This stage is characterized by the individual expressing the depths of their anguish and showing little interest in any form of medical intervention.
d	This stage is characterized by the individual coming to terms with their fate.
e	This stage is characterized by a failure of the individual to believe that their condition is terminal.

Safety and Protection; Professional Responsibilities; Research Proficiencies

Safety and Protection; Professional Responsibilities Proficiencies

9. Teaching and Learning Basics

Mark each statement as True or False. If the statement is False, correct the statement in the space provided.

True/False	Statement
a	According to Maslow's Hierarchy of Needs, esteem needs refer to the need to realize one's full potential as a human being.
Correction:	
b	Therapists should attempt to identify the patient's preferred learning style and available resources.
Correction:	
c	Therapists should attempt to design learning activities that will incorporate the patient's past experiences.
Correction:	

Safety and Protection; Professional Responsibilities; Research Proficiencies

Research Proficiencies

10. Levels of Evidence

Assign a number to each category based on the strength of the design. An assignment of "1" would indicate the most desirable or highest level of evidence from the available options while an assignment of "5" would indicate the least desirable or lowest level of evidence.

Study	Rank
randomized controlled trial	a
case control study	b
systematic review	c
cohort study	d
case report	e

11. Scales of Measurement

Identify the appropriate scale of measurement for each of the following types of data. Answers must be selected from the Word Bank and can be used more than once.

Word Bank: interval, nominal, ordinal, ratio

Data	Scale
range of motion	a
body temperature on the Celsius scale	b
distance walked	c
blood type	d
manual muscle test grades	e
type of breath sounds	f
transfer levels of assistance	g
nerve conduction velocity	h

Safety and Protection; Professional Responsibilities; Research Proficiencies

Research Proficiencies

12. Validity

Identify the type of validity most closely associated with the supplied definition. Answers must be selected from the Word Bank and can be used only once.

Word Bank: face validity, construct validity, content validity, criterion related validity

Type of Validity	Definition
a	The degree to which a measurement reflects the meaningful elements of a construct and the items in a test adequately reflect the content domain of interest and not extraneous elements.
b	The degree to which a theoretical construct is measured by a test or measurement.
c	The validity of the measurement is established by comparing it to either a different measurement, often considered to be a "gold standard" or data obtained by different forms of testing.
d	The degree to which a measurement appears to test what it is supposed to.

13. Sampling

Identify the type of sampling most closely associated with the supplied definition. Answers must be selected from the Word Bank and can be used only once.

Word Bank: convenience, purposive, simple random, snowball, stratified random, systematic

Type of Sampling	Definition
a	Subjects are identified by asking existing subjects to identify the names of other potential participants.
b	Subjects are selected from those readily available to the researcher.
c	Subjects are selected from a population that has been divided into homogenous subgroups or strata and then a simple random sample is drawn from each.
d	Subjects have an equal chance of being selected for the sample.
e	Subjects are deliberately selected based on predefined criteria chosen by the investigators.
f	Subjects are selected by taking every n^{th} subject from the population.

Safety and Protection; Professional Responsibilities; Research Proficiencies

Research Proficiencies

14. Testing a Statistical Hypothesis

Identify the appropriate sequence when testing a statistical hypothesis. Assign a "1" for the first step in the process and a "5" for the last step in the sequence.

Step	Sequence
calculate the test statistic from the sample data	a
interpret the results	b
state the null hypothesis and alternative hypothesis	c
select the level of significance for the statistical test	d
select the appropriate test statistic	e

15. Statistics

Identify the type of statistic most closely associated with the supplied definition. Answers must be selected from the Word Bank and can be used only once.

Word Bank: mean, median, mode, range, standard deviation, variance

Type of Statistic	Definition
a	The sum of the squared deviations of each data point from the mean, divided by the number of observations in the sample.
b	The arithmetic average; the sum of all the values divided by the number of values.
c	A descriptive measure of the spread or dispersion of data; the positive square root of the variance.
d	The point on a distribution at which 50% of the values fall above and below.
e	The value that occurs most frequently.
f	The difference between the maximum and minimum values.

Safety and Protection; Professional Responsibilities; Research Proficiencies

Research Proficiencies

16. Normal Distribution

Assuming a normal distribution, determine what percentage of values would fall within the specified values. Answers must be selected from the Word Bank and can be used only once.

Word Bank: 34%, 50%, 68%, 95%, 99%

Percentage	Interval
a	between plus one and minus one standard deviations
b	between the mean and plus one standard deviation
c	between plus three and minus three standard deviations
d	between the mean and a point beyond three standard deviations above the mean
e	between plus two and minus two standard deviations

17. Research Basics

Mark each statement as True or False. If the statement is False, correct the statement in the space provided.

True/False	Statement
a	A false negative test indicates a person does not have a specific disease or condition when the person actually does have the disease or condition.
Correction:	
b	Specificity refers to the percentage of people who test positive for a specific disease among a group of people who have the disease.
Correction:	
c	Incidence refers to the number of existing cases of a disease or condition at a point in time, including new and pre-existing cases.
Correction:	

Safety and Protection; Professional Responsibilities; Research Proficiencies

Research Proficiencies

True/False	Statement
d	A two-tailed test is a test of statistical significance in which deviations from the null hypothesis in either direction are considered.
Correction:	
e	Alpha level refers to the probability of rejecting the null hypothesis when it is true or the chance of committing a type 2 error.
Correction:	
f	In research, the dependent variable is controlled or manipulated by the researcher.
Correction:	
g	A single blind study indicates that the subjects are unaware of the research hypothesis and the group to which they were assigned.
Correction:	
h	Interrater reliability refers to the consistency or equivalence of measurements made by more than one person.
Correction:	
i	Beneficence refers to the fair treatment of subjects including the equitable distribution of burdens and benefits in research.
Correction:	
j	Qualitative research typically uses a relatively large number of subjects and data is analyzed using statistical measures.
Correction:	

Safety and Protection; Professional Responsibilities; Research Answer Key

Safety and Protection; Professional Responsibilities

1. Accessibility Requirements

a. Unacceptable: Guideline - A ramp should have a maximum grade of 8.3%.

b. Unacceptable: Guideline - A ramp should possess twelve inches of horizontal run for each inch of vertical rise.

c. Acceptable: Guideline - A ramp should have a minimum width of 36 inches.

d. Acceptable: Guideline - A doorway should have a minimum width of 32 inches.

e. Unacceptable: Guideline - A hallway should have a minimum width of 36 inches.

f. Acceptable: Guideline - A bathroom sink should have a minimum of 29 inches of height from the floor.

g. Acceptable: Guideline - A bathroom toilet should have 17-19 inches of height from the floor to the top of the toilet.

2. S.O.A.P. Notes

a. subjective
b. objective
c. objective
d. subjective
e. assessment
f. objective
g. subjective
h. objective
i. assessment
j. plan

3. The Nagi Model

a. pathology
b. impairment
c. functional limitation
d. disability
e. impairment
f. functional limitation

4. Scope of Practice

a. unacceptable
b. acceptable
c. acceptable
d. unacceptable
e. acceptable
f. unacceptable
g. unacceptable
h. acceptable
i. acceptable

5. Health Care Disciplines

a. home health aides
b. physical therapy aides
c. respiratory therapists
d. occupational therapists
e. physical therapists
f. speech-language pathologists
g. physical therapist assistants
h. social workers

6. Safety and Professional Roles Basics*

a. FALSE: Correction: A computer monitor of a work station should be a minimum of 20 inches away from the eyes.

b. FALSE: Correction: When performing a transfer with a patient that requires assistance, a physical therapist should attempt to be as close to the patient as possible and use a short lever arm.

c. TRUE

d. TRUE

e. FALSE: Correction: A patient with droplet precautions would require a physical therapist to wear a mask if they were within three feet of the patient.

f. TRUE

g. TRUE

h. FALSE: Correction: One inch is equivalent to 2.54 centimeters.

i. FALSE: Correction: Beneficence refers to the moral obligation to health care providers to act for the benefit of others.

j. TRUE

k. FALSE: Correction: The Consolidated Omnibus Budget Reconciliation Act allows an employee to remain under an employer's group plan for a period of time after the loss of a job, death of a spouse, a decrease in hours or a divorce.

l. FALSE: Correction: Medicare Part B provides benefits for outpatient care, physician services, and services ordered by physicians such as diagnostic tests, medical equipment, and supplies.

m. FALSE: Correction: Current procedural terminology codes are procedure codes used by physical therapists and other health care professionals to describe specific interventions provided to a given patient.

*The correction presented for each false statement is an example of several possible corrections.

7. Domains of Learning

a. cognitive
b. affective
c. psychomotor

Safety and Protection; Professional Responsibilities; Research Answer Key

d. cognitive
e. psychomotor
f. affective

8. Stages of Dying

a. bargaining
b. anger
c. depression
d. acceptance
e. denial

9. Teaching and Learning Basics*

a. FALSE: Correction: According to Maslow's Hierarchy of Needs, self-actualization refers to the need to realize one's full potential as a human being.
b. TRUE
c. TRUE

*The correction presented for each false statement is an example of several possible corrections.

Research

10. Levels of Evidence

a. 2
b. 4
c. 1
d. 3
e. 5

11. Scales of Measurement

a. ratio
b. interval
c. ratio
d. nominal
e. ordinal
f. nominal
g. ordinal
h. ratio

12. Validity

a. content validity
b. construct validity
c. criterion-related validity
d. face validity

13. Sampling

a. snowball
b. convenience
c. stratified random
d. simple random
e. purposive
f. systematic

14. Testing a Statistical Hypothesis

a. 4
b. 5
c. 1
d. 3
e. 2

15. Statistics

a. variance
b. mean
c. standard deviation
d. median
e. mode
f. range

16. Normal Distribution

a. 68%
b. 34%
c. 99%
d. 50%
e. 95%

17. Research Basics*

a. TRUE
b. FALSE: Correction: Sensitivity refers to the percentage of people who test positive for a specific disease among a group of people who have the disease.
c. FALSE: Correction: Prevalence refers to the number of existing cases of a disease or condition at a point in time, including new and pre-existing cases.
d. TRUE
e. FALSE: Correction: Alpha level refers to the probability of rejecting the null hypothesis when it is true or the chance of committing a type 1 error.
f. FALSE: Correction: In research, the independent variable is controlled or manipulated by the researcher.
g. TRUE
h. TRUE
i. FALSE: Correction: Justice refers to the fair treatment of subjects including the equitable distribution of burdens and benefits in research.
j. FALSE: Correction: Quantitative research typically uses a relatively large number of subjects and data is analyzed using statistical measures.

*The correction presented for each false statement is an example of several possible corrections.

Safety and Protection; Professional Responsibilities; Research References

1. Cameron M, Monroe L. ***Physical Rehabilitation: Evidence Based Examination, Evaluation, and Intervention***. W.B. Saunders Company. 2007.
2. Minor M, Minor S. ***Patient Care Skills***. Seventh Edition. Pearson Education, Inc. 2014.
3. Fairchild S, O'Shea R, Washington R. ***Pierson and Fairchild's Principles and Techniques of Patient Care***. Sixth Edition. Elsevier. 2018.
4. Guide to Infection Prevention for Outpatient Settings: Minimum Expectations for Safe Care version 2.3. Centers for Disease Control and Prevention Web Site. http://www.cdc.gov Updated September 2016. Accessed May 22, 2017.
5. Roy S, Wolf S, Scalzitti D. ***The Rehabilitation Specialist's Handbook***. Fourth Edition, F.A. Davis Company. 2013.
6. Kettenbach G. ***Writing SOAP Notes***. Second Edition. F.A. Davis Company. 1995
7. Shamus E, Stern D. ***Effective Documentation for the Physical Therapy Professional***. Second Edition. McGraw-Hill Inc. 2011.
8. Guidelines: Physical Therapy Documentation of Patient/Client Management. BOD G03-05-16-41, updated 5/19/14. American Physical Therapy Association Web Site. Accessed May 22, 2017.
9. Defensible Documentation Elements. American Physical Therapy Association Web Site. http://www.apta.org/Documentation/DefensibleDocumentation/. Updated 12/8/2015. Accessed May 22, 2017.
10. Davis C. ***Patient Practitioner Interaction***. Fourth Edition. Slack Inc. 2006.
11. Scott R. ***Promoting Legal and Ethical Awareness***. Mosby Inc. 2009.
12. Nosse L, Friberg D. ***Managerial and Supervisory Principles for Physical Therapists***. Third Edition. Lippincott Williams & Wilkins. 2010.
13. Buchbinder S, Shanks N. ***Introduction to Health Care Management***. Jones and Bartlett Publishers. 2007.
14. ***Guide to Physical Therapist Practice*** 3.0. American Physical Therapy Association. 2014.
15. International Classification of Functioning, Disability and Health (ICF). World Health Organization Web Site. http://www.who.int/classifications/icf/en/. Accessed May 22, 2017.
16. Direction and Supervision of the Physical Therapist Assistant. HOD P06-05-18-26, updated 08/07/12. American Physical Therapy Association Web Site. Accessed May 22, 2017.
17. ***Mosby's Dictionary of Medicine, Nursing and Health Professions***. Eighth Edition, Mosby. 2009.
18. Standards of Practice for Physical Therapy. HOD S06-19-29-50, updated September 2019. American Physical Therapy Association website. Accessed April 5, 2020.
19. Code of Ethics for the Physical Therapist. HOD S06-09-07-12, updated June 2009. American Physical Therapy Association Web Site. Accessed May 22, 2017.
20. Curtis K: ***The Physical Therapist's Guide to Health Care***. Slack Inc. 1999.
21. Sandstrom R, Lohman H. ***Health Services: Policy and Systems for Therapists***. Prentice Hall. 2003.
22. Sadock B, Sadock V. ***Kaplan & Sadock's Comprehensive Textbook of Psychiatry***. Ninth Edition. Lippincott Williams & Wilkins. 2009.
23. Edelman C, Mandle C. ***Health Promotion Throughout the Lifespan***. Fifth Edition. Mosby. 2002.
24. Purtilo R, Haddad A. ***Health Professional and Patient Interaction***. Eighth Edition. Elsevier. 2014.
25. Falvo D. ***Effective Patient Education***. Fourth Edition. Jones and Bartlett Publishers. 2011.
26. Haggard A. ***Handbook of Patient Education***. Aspen Publishers. 1989.
27. Arends R. ***Learning to Teach***. Third Edition, McGraw-Hill Inc. 2005.

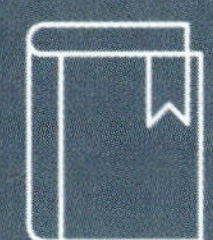

Safety and Protection; Professional Responsibilities; Research References

28. Scott R. ***Foundations of Physical Therapy: A 21st Century-Focused View of the Profession***. McGraw-Hill Inc. 2002.

29. Sackett DL, Straus SE, Richardson WS, Rosenburg W, Haynes RB. ***Evidence-Based Medicine. How to Practice and Teach EBM***. 2nd ed. Edinburgh, Scotland; Churchill Livingstone. 2000.

30. Asking focused questions. Centre for Evidence-Based Medicine Web Site. http://www.cebm.net/index.aspx?o=1036. Updated April 7, 2009. Accessed October 7, 2010.

31. Critical appraisal. Centre for Evidence-Based Medicine Web Site. http://www.cebm.net/index.aspx?o=1157 Updated December 16, 2010. Accessed October 7, 2010.

32. Practice Guidelines. ***Physical Therapy*** Web Site. http://ptjournal.apta.org/cgi/collection/practice_guidelines Accessed October 3, 2010.

33. Guidelines by Topic. National Guideline Clearinghouse Web Site. http://www.guideline.gov/. Accessed October 3, 2010.

34. Levels of evidence. Centre for Evidence-Based Medicine Web Site. http://www.cebm.net/index.aspx?o=1025. Updated September 16, 2010. Accessed October 3, 2010.

35. Portney L, Watkins MP. ***Foundations of Clinical Research: Applications to Practice***. Third Edition. Prentice Hall. 2015.

36. Glossary of Statistical Terms. National Cancer Institute Web Site. http://www.cancer.gov/statistics/glossary. Accessed October 3, 2010.

37. Code of Federal Regulation Title 45. Public Welfare. Part 46. Protection of Human Subjects. US Department of Health and Human Services Web Site. http://www.hhs.gov/ohrp/humansubjects/guidance/45cfr46.htm. Accessed October 3, 2010.

38. Triola MF. ***Elementary Statistics***. 9th ed. Boston, MA: Pearson Addison Wesley. 2004.

39. Rothstein JM, Echternach JL. ***Primer on Measurement: An Introductory Guide to Measurement Issues***. Alexandria, VA; American Physical Therapy Association. 1993.

40. Iverson C, Christiansen S, Flanagin A, et al. ***AMA Manual of Style: A Guide for Authors and Editors***. 10th ed. New York, NY: Oxford University Press. 2007.

Jumpstart Your Academic Review!

Basecamp

Basecamp offers students a personal guide to navigating through the academic review process. The program is a perfect complement to our best-selling review book **PTEXAM: The Complete Study Guide**.

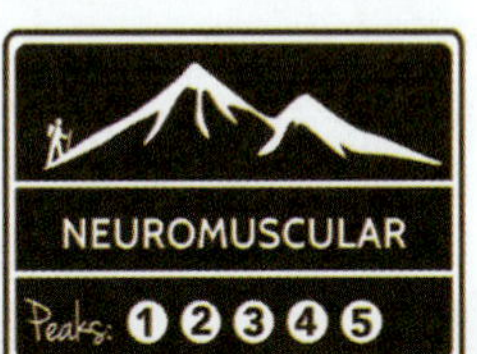

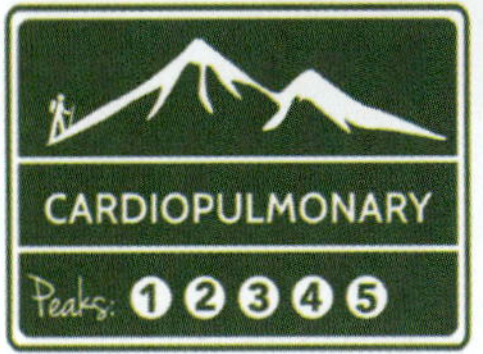

Basecamp - Start Climbing!

We created a completely new learning tool called **Basecamp** that provides you with an incredibly efficient method to review academic content within ***PTEXAM: The Complete Study Guide***. The content is organized in five distinct Mountains (Musculoskeletal, Neuromuscular, Cardiopulmonary, Other Systems, and Non-Systems) and 140 Trails. Each trail has dedicated assignments, video, and exams. **A $25 off coupon for Basecamp is included within Insight. Purchase Basecamp today and start climbing!**

Enter The Basecamp Arena

Our newest **Basecamp** features, **King of the Mountain** and **Climb**, allow students to challenge one another in real-time. The player to answer the most consecutive questions wins! Our **Basecamp Arena app** provides students with the opportunity to play the competitive games anytime and anywhere. Access over 6,000 content-based questions and see how you stack up against the competition. Students can explore their performance data using the **Arena-Scorecard**. See if you have the knowledge to survive in the **Arena**.

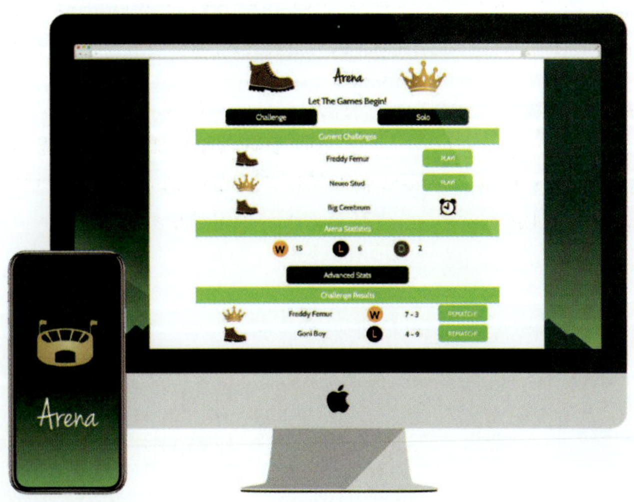

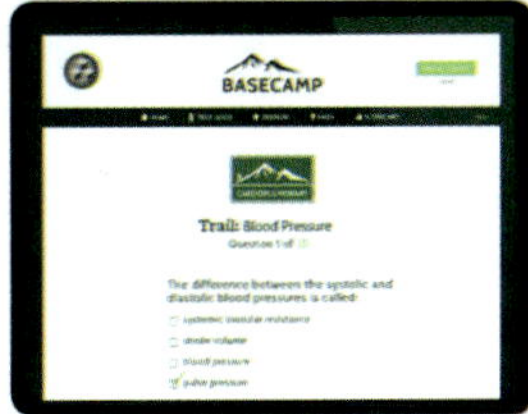

Scalability

Basecamp is designed to fully engage today's students utilizing a variety of forms of media and the latest in eLearning technology. The program is fully accessible on computers, tablets, and mobile devices.

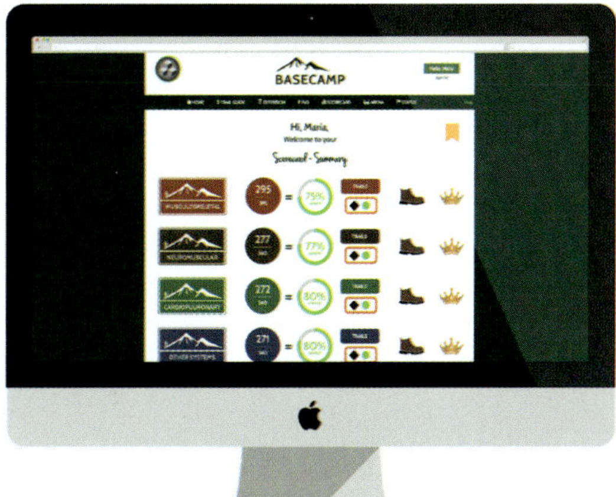

Scorecard

An advanced Scorecard section allows students to monitor their performance in each of the Mountains and the associated Trails. By identifying areas of deficiency students are able to develop appropriate remedial plans and enhance core academic content in needed areas.

BASECAMP PURCHASING OPTIONS

Basecamp - Standard (30 day access) $65.00

The 30 day option is ideal for students attempting to engage in a meaningful review of core academic content prior to the NPTE-PT. Various extension options are available.

Basecamp - Annual (One year access) $95.00 (Save up to 25% on class orders)

The one year option provides students and faculty with an ideal method to enhance learning throughout the academic program. Improved content mastery and retention can significantly increase academic performance in the classroom and on the NPTE-PT.

Basecamp – Lifetime (Forever access) $130.00 (Save up to 25% on class orders)

The forever option allows students and physical therapists to enjoy **Basecamp** during their academic training and well after they have successfully passed the NPTE-PT. Take advantage of this tremendous value and let **Basecamp** assist you to stay in tip-top academic shape throughout your physical therapy career.

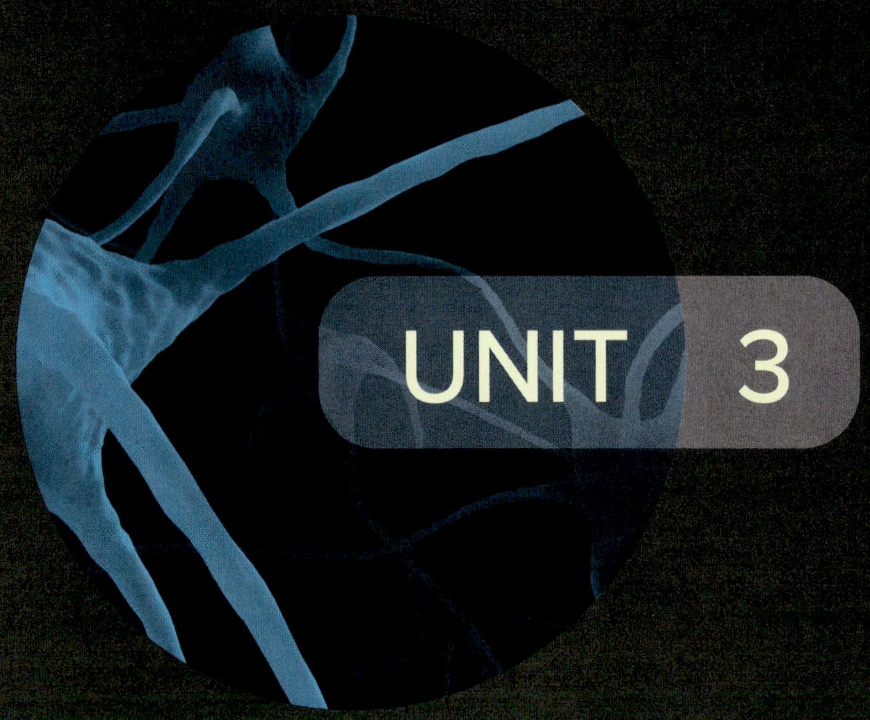

Examinations Answer Key

Examinations Answer Key

This unit includes an **answer key for the three, 200 question sample examinations** located on our eLearning site called Insight. Candidates should take the examinations using Insight and then consult the answer key. It is important that candidates avoid "browsing" through the answer key prior to taking the sample examinations since any prior exposure to the questions will significantly influence examination scoring.

Candidates who are exposed to numerous sample examinations have several distinct opportunities that otherwise may not be available.

- Candidates have the opportunity to assess their current level of preparedness prior to the actual examination.
- Candidates have the opportunity to refine their test taking skills with sample questions that are similar in design and format to actual examination questions.
- Candidates have the opportunity to build their endurance and stamina when answering multiple-choice questions.

The sample examinations include questions representative of each of the categories and subcategories of the current content outline of the **NPTE-PT**. A sophisticated performance analysis section offers candidates detailed feedback on their examination performance according to five system areas and five content outline areas.

System Specific Areas	Content Outline Areas
Musculoskeletal System	Physical Therapy Examination
Neuromuscular and Nervous Systems	Foundations for Evaluation, Differential Diagnosis, and Prognosis
Cardiovascular and Pulmonary Systems	Interventions
Other Systems	Equipment, Devices, and Technologies; Therapeutic Modalities
Non-Systems	Safety and Protection; Professional Responsibilities; Research

The answer key in **PTEXAM: The Complete Study Guide** offers a variety of features that can assist students to assess their examination performance and to direct remedial efforts.

Access the sample examinations included with **PTEXAM: The Complete Study Guide** by registering your code located on the inside front cover of the book at:

https://insight-sb.com

Visit our Synapse Center in Insight and let Scott Giles, President of Scorebuilders, show you how to use performance data to improve your examination performance.

PTEXAM ONE: QUESTION 160

Examinations Answer Key Components

A physical therapist treats an infant diagnosed with torticollis with marked lateral flexion of the neck to the right. As part of the infant's plan of care the therapist performs passive stretching activities to improve the patient's range of motion. The MOST appropriate stretch for the patient is:

1. **Lateral flexion to the right and rotation to the right**
2. **Lateral flexion to the left and rotation to the left**
3. **Lateral flexion to the right and rotation to the left**
4. **Lateral flexion to the left and rotation to the right**

Question

Correct Answer and Resource

Correct Answer: 4 (Palisano p. 184) 

Video Explanation

Torticollis is characterized by lateral flexion of the head toward the affected side and rotation toward the unaffected side. The condition is caused by a contracture of the sternocleidomastoid muscle.

General Statement

1. Stretching in lateral flexion to the right would be inappropriate since the question indicates that the patient presents with marked lateral flexion of the neck to the right. The direction of the stretch for the rotation component is accurate.
2. Stretching in lateral flexion to the left would be beneficial, however, patients with torticollis present with rotation to the opposite side. As a result, the rotation component should be stretched to the right and not the left.
3. This option more accurately characterizes the clinical presentation of the patient than it does the necessary stretch. The question indicates that the patient presents with marked lateral flexion of the neck to the right and therefore it would not make sense to stretch to the right. The direction of stretch for the rotation component is also inaccurate.
4. **Stretching the patient in lateral flexion to the left and rotation to the right is the correct answer since it is opposite of the patient's current contracture (i.e., marked lateral flexion of the neck to the right and rotation to the left).**

Explanation of the Correct and Incorrect Options

System: Musculoskeletal System
Content Outline: Interventions

System and Content Outline Assignment

Test Taking Tip: It is possible for a candidate to eliminate two of the presented options without having any specific knowledge related to torticollis. The question indicates that the patient presents with marked lateral flexion of the neck to the right. Based on the that particular clinical finding it becomes apparent that the stretch would need to be in the opposite direction (i.e., to the left). Often when presented with information that is unfamiliar, candidates fail to recognize that they can still narrow down the presented options. It is critically important for candidates to use this valuable skill since it can significantly increase the probability of identifying the correct response.

Test Taking Tip

Level Analysis

Academic Focus Area

Examinations Answer Key Components Explained

Question

Our questions are designed to replicate the style, format, and difficulty level of the questions on the NPTE-PT. The questions are located within our eLearning site Insight. All examinations should be taken using Insight to best simulate the actual NPTE-PT.

Correct Answer and Resource

This section provides the correct answer and the author name and page number that substantiates the correct answer. A bibliography provides complete information on each resource including the edition used.

Video Explanation

Video explanations provide candidates with the opportunity to watch videos that compare and contrast good, better, and best options for selected examination questions.

General Statement

This section introduces relevant subject matter and offers related value added information.

Explanation of the Correct and Incorrect Options

The explanations offer incredibly detailed information supporting why the correct answer is correct and why each incorrect answer is incorrect. This feature is critically important to enhance decision making when choosing between good, better, and best options

System and Content Outline Assignment

This section assigns a system and content outline category to each question allowing candidates to assess examination performance in unique areas.

Test Taking Tip

This section offers unique Test Taking Tips, when possible, to assist candidates to use deductive reasoning strategies when academic knowledge alone is not adequate to correctly answer a question.

Level Analysis

This feature allows candidates to analyze their examination performance according to three different levels of questions.

Level 1 – Questions require candidates to possess basic foundational academic knowledge.

Level 2 – Questions require candidates to integrate numerous pieces of information or to apply knowledge in a given clinical scenario.

Level 3 – Questions require candidates to systematically analyze and often interpret information to determine an appropriate course of action. The questions tend to have some degree of subjectivity and candidates are required to assign varying degrees of importance to different variables.

Candidates have the ability to direct remedial efforts by examining their performance in each of the unique levels.

Academic Focus Area

This feature immediately directs the user to critical pieces in the academic review section related to the particular subject matter. Not all questions will have an academic focus area since some questions are situationally dependent and rely more on decision making than recollection of factual information.

Insight

Insight is a technological marvel that offers candidates an unprecedented look into their sample examination performance.

Performance Analysis

After taking each of the examinations in Insight, candidates utilize the sophisticated performance analysis features to assess their examination performance. A brief description of some of the more prominent performance analysis features is presented.

Candidate Score

A candidate's score reflects the number of questions answered correctly for a given examination.

Mean Score

The mean score allows candidates to compare their score to the average score of thousands of other candidates taking the same examination. The mean score accounts for the relative difficulty of the examination and is a critical piece of data for candidates when assessing examination performance.

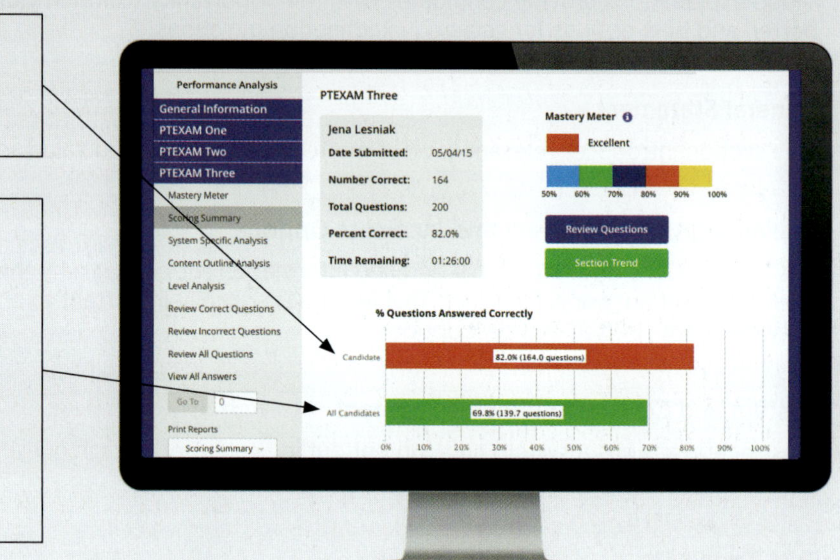

Item Analysis

The item analysis feature allows candidates to identify the percentage of candidates answering the question correctly and the specific percentages of candidates selecting each of the four options. Candidates can utilize this information to critically evaluate their approach to answering questions and improve future decision making. Video explanations provide candidates with a deeper understanding of academic concepts addressed in selected examination questions.

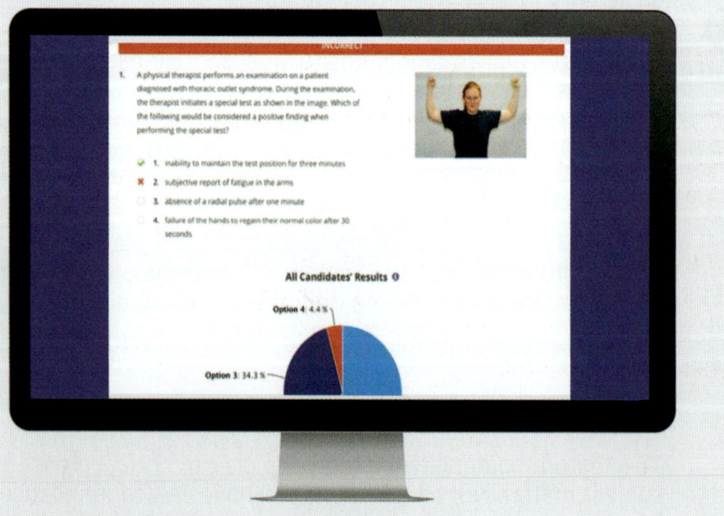

Mastery Meter

The Mastery Meter assigns candidates a level of mastery in each category based on the percentage of questions answered correctly. Candidates should strive to achieve a score of “Superior” or “Excellent” on the Mastery Meter in each category.

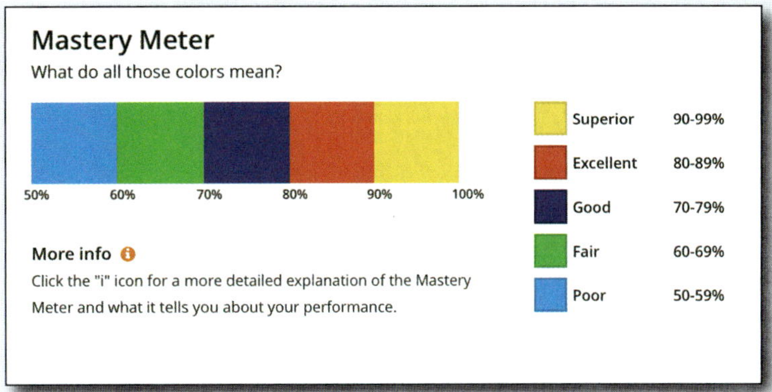

System and Content Outline Analyses

The system and content outline analyses offer candidates an immediate analysis of their performance in specific areas of the NPTE-PT. Candidates can click on a given area and immediately review their performance in relation to the mean score of other users. They also have the ability to selectively review questions only within specific system and content outline areas.

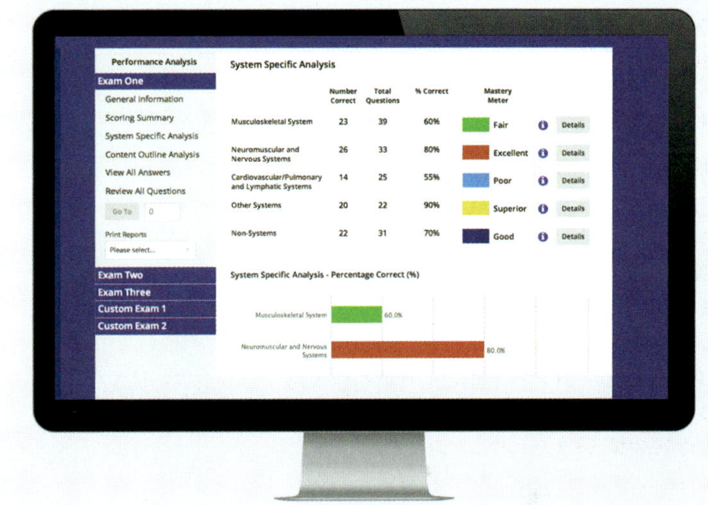

Study Stack

Our Study Stack feature allows candidates to tag specific questions that they would like to review at a later time. Candidates can easily add or remove questions from their Study Stack by simply clicking the bookmark icon. Review a created Study Stack in its entirety or by System area. Customization of remedial activities is a great way to boost examination scores!

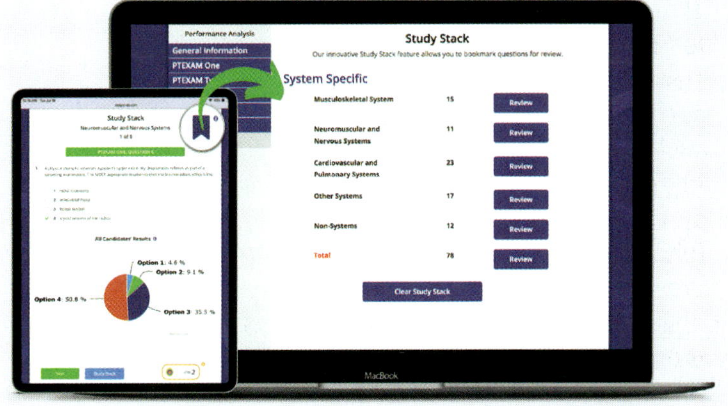

10

PHYSICAL THERAPY EXAM ONE ANSWER KEY

Scott Giles

PHYSICAL THERAPY EXAM ONE ANSWER KEY

STRATEGY

"Good fortune is what happens when opportunity meets preparation."

— Thomas Edison

Candidates need to have a strategy or plan to prepare for the NPTE-PT. An important component of any comprehensive study plan involves answering multiple-choice questions and carefully analyzing the results. Identifying strengths and weaknesses in the various system and content outline areas can be a useful activity to direct remedial activities.

PTEXAM ONE: QUESTION 1

A physical therapist inspects a wound over a patient's sacrum. The therapist would MOST accurately classify the presented wound as which of the following pressure injury stages?

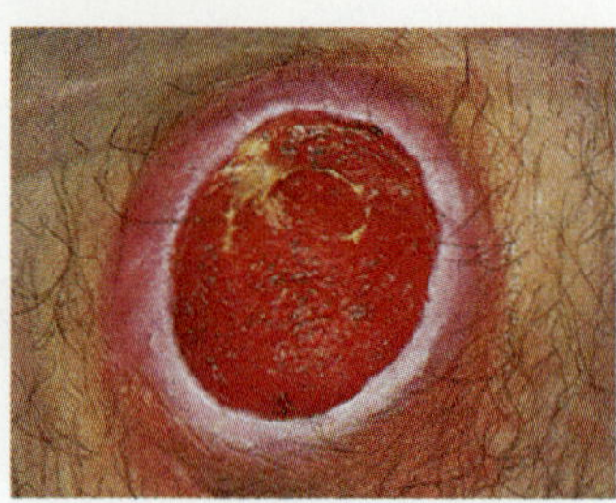

1. 1
2. 2
3. **3**
4. 4

Correct Answer: 3 (Sussman p. 236)

The National Pressure Ulcer Advisory Panel pressure ulcer staging criteria was developed for use with pressure injuries. The staging criteria range from 1–4.

1. A stage 1 pressure injury is characterized by an observable pressure related alteration of intact skin whose indicators, as compared to an adjacent or opposite area on the body, may include changes in skin color, skin temperature, skin stiffness or sensation.
2. A stage 2 pressure injury is characterized by partial-thickness skin loss that involves the epidermis and/or dermis. The ulcer is superficial and presents clinically as an abrasion, a blister or a shallow crater.
3. **A stage 3 pressure injury is characterized by full-thickness skin loss that involves damage or necrosis of subcutaneous tissue that may extend down to, but not through, underlying fascia. The ulcer presents clinically as a deep crater with or without undermining adjacent tissue. Visible subcutaneous fat without muscle, tendon or bone is consistent with a stage 3 pressure injury.**
4. A stage 4 pressure injury is characterized by full-thickness skin loss with extensive destruction, tissue necrosis or damage to muscle, bone or supporting structures (e.g., tendon, joint capsule).

System: Other Systems
Content Outline: Physical Therapy Examination

 Level 1  p. 504

PTEXAM ONE: QUESTION 2

A physical therapist reviews the medical record of a patient who has experienced recurrent angina. A recent entry indicated that an exercise stress test ordered by the physician was positive. What is the MOST accurate interpretation of this finding?

1. Presence of balanced oxygen demand and supply
2. **Presence of ischemia**
3. Presence of normal vital signs
4. Presence of cardiac arrhythmias

Correct Answer: 2 (Hillegass p. 279)

An exercise stress test is used to determine the ability of the cardiovascular system to accommodate for increasing metabolic demand. Patients are typically tested using a bicycle ergometer, treadmill or upper extremity ergometer. This form of testing provides a general link between a patient's impairment and overall functional capacity.

1. A patient that performs an exercise stress test and demonstrates a balanced oxygen supply and demand would typically have a negative stress test. A negative stress test shows that a patient's cardiovascular system was able to handle the expected increasing metabolic demands without any form of ischemia present.
2. **An exercise stress test is used to determine the presence of ischemia and evaluate the overall functional capacity of a patient. The patient is typically monitored through a 12-lead electrocardiogram and vital signs. An echocardiogram is often used to further assess perfusion. Determination of the presence of ischemia is the goal of the exercise stress test.**
3. Since an exercise stress test attempts to determine the presence of ischemia, a positive test would typically be characterized by abnormal vital signs appearing at some point during the testing procedure.
4. Cardiac arrhythmias are not necessary to have a positive stress test. The exercise stress test is designed to determine the presence of ischemia.

System: Cardiovascular and Pulmonary Systems
Content Outline: Physical Therapy Examination

 Level 2  p. 428-429

PTEXAM ONE: QUESTION 3

During a patient interview, a physical therapist determines that the mechanism of injury was forced ankle dorsiflexion with eversion. The patient reports pain and a popping sensation in the posterolateral ankle. The therapist observes swelling and ecchymosis in the posterolateral ankle and notes apprehension with both active and resisted eversion. These findings are **MOST** consistent with which of the following conditions?

1. Lateral ankle sprain
2. Tibialis posterior tenosynovitis
3. **Fibularis tendon subluxation**
4. Tarsal tunnel syndrome

Correct Answer: 3 (Dutton p. 1097)

Forced ankle dorsiflexion with eversion of the foot is the typical mechanism of injury for fibularis (peroneal) tendon subluxation. Conditions increasing the likelihood of fibularis tendon subluxation include absent or shallow fibula groove, pes planus, hindfoot valgus, and a lax or ruptured fibular retinaculum.

1. The typical mechanism of injury for a lateral ankle sprain is plantar flexion, inversion, and adduction of the foot and ankle. A patient with a lateral ankle sprain will likely present with significant pain or tenderness along the lateral aspect of the ankle, especially over the anterior talofibular ligament. Ecchymosis and edema at the lateral ankle are likely, however, a popping sensation in the ankle would not be anticipated.
2. The typical mechanism of injury associated with tibialis posterior tenosynovitis is overuse with a pronated foot and flattened medial longitudinal arch. The patient will typically present with pain on resisted ankle plantar flexion and inversion, with tenderness to palpation along the tendon posterior to the medial malleolus. Swelling may be present in the posteromedial aspect of the ankle.
3. **The clinical presentation of fibularis (peroneal) tendon subluxation includes pain and a popping sensation at the posterior lateral ankle, swelling, ecchymosis, apprehension, and the inability to evert the foot against resistance. Chronic subluxation can both mimic and coexist with chronic lateral ankle instability. Subluxation may be provoked by forceful ankle dorsiflexion with eversion.**
4. The tarsal tunnel is located on the medial aspect of the ankle and is formed by the flexor retinaculum, the superior aspect of the calcaneus, the medial wall of the talus, and the medial-distal aspect of the tibia. Tarsal tunnel syndrome occurs as a result of compression of the tibial nerve as it passes through the tarsal tunnel, causing neuropathy in the distribution of the nerve.

System: Musculoskeletal System
Content Outline: Foundations for Evaluation, Differential Diagnosis, and Prognosis

p. 55, 65

PTEXAM ONE: QUESTION 4

A physical therapist teaches a patient in the supine position to posteriorly rotate the pelvis. The patient has full active and passive range of motion in the upper extremities, but is unable to achieve full shoulder flexion while maintaining a posterior pelvic tilt. Which of the following impairments could BEST explain this finding?

1. Capsular tightness
2. **Latissimus dorsi tightness**
3. Pectoralis minor tightness
4. Quadratus lumborum tightness

Correct Answer: 2 (Kendall p. 325)

A posterior pelvic tilt results in the posterior superior iliac spines of the pelvis moving posteriorly and inferiorly. This motion results in hip extension and lumbar spine flexion.

1. The capsular pattern at the glenohumeral joint is lateral rotation, abduction, and medial rotation. A capsular pattern of restriction at the glenohumeral joint would limit range of motion, however, would not be influenced by the position of the pelvis.
2. **Shortening of the latissimus dorsi often results in a limitation of shoulder flexion or abduction due to the muscle's origin on the external lip of the iliac crest and its insertion on the intertubercular groove of the humerus.**
3. Pectoralis minor tightness may have a direct effect on shoulder range of motion, however, would not be influenced by the position of the pelvis. Pectoralis minor tightness is often best identified by positioning a patient in supine with the arms at their side and the palms facing upward. The relative tightness of the muscle is determined by the extent to which the shoulder is raised from the table and the amount of resistance felt to downward pressure on the shoulder.
4. Quadratus lumborum tightness may affect the ability of the pelvis to achieve the posterior pelvic tilt position required in the question, however, would not affect shoulder range of motion since the muscle does not directly attach to the shoulder joint.

System: Musculoskeletal System
Content Outline: Interventions

PTEXAM ONE: QUESTION 5

A patient diagnosed with a cerebrovascular accident involving the anterior cerebral artery is referred to physical therapy. Based on this diagnosis, which of the following interventions should the physical therapist **MOST** anticipate needing to incorporate into the plan of care?

1. **Progression of lower extremity strengthening exercises and gait activities**
2. Facilitation techniques for weakness of upper extremity and facial muscles
3. Coordination/balance activities and referral to speech therapy for aphasia
4. Inhibitory techniques for upper extremity spasticity and synergy patterns

Correct Answer: 1 (O'Sullivan p. 597)

Occlusion of the anterior cerebral artery (ACA) will typically produce contralateral hemiparesis and sensory loss with greater involvement of the lower extremity. Other findings may include incontinence, abulia or akinetic mutism, and frontal lobe symptoms such as personality changes.

1. **Progression of lower extremity strengthening and gait activities would be the most anticipated intervention of the presented options since lower extremity weakness and sensory loss is the most common presentation associated with a cerebrovascular accident (CVA) involving the ACA.**
2. Facilitation techniques for weakness of upper extremity and facial muscles would be the most anticipated intervention to treat a patient diagnosed with a CVA involving the middle cerebral artery (MCA). Occlusion of the MCA will typically produce contralateral weakness and sensory loss of the face and upper extremity with lesser involvement of the lower extremity. Dominant hemisphere involvement includes global, Wernicke's or Broca's aphasia.
3. Coordination/balance activities would be most anticipated as an intervention for a CVA involving the cerebellum. The cerebellum is located in the posterior portion of the brain below the occipital lobes. It is responsible for fine tuning of movement and assists with maintaining posture and balance by controlling muscle tone and positioning of the extremities in space. Additionally, referral to speech therapy for aphasia, although potentially necessary, would be more likely for a CVA involving the MCA than the ACA.
4. Inhibitory techniques for upper extremity spasticity and synergy patterns would be most anticipated as an intervention for a CVA involving the MCA since the upper extremity and facial muscles are typically more involved. The MCA is the most common site of a CVA.

System: Neuromuscular and Nervous Systems
Content Outline: Interventions

Level 2  p. 239-241

PTEXAM ONE: QUESTION 6

When performing range of motion exercises with a patient who sustained a head injury, a physical therapist determines that the patient lacks full elbow extension and classifies the end-feel as hard. The presence of which of the following findings is the **MOST** likely cause?

1. **Heterotopic ossification**
2. Spasticity of the biceps
3. Anterior capsular tightness
4. Triceps weakness

Correct Answer: 1 (Goodman – Pathology p. 1287) 

Heterotopic ossification refers to abnormal bone growth in tissue and is relatively common in patients following head injury. Signs and symptoms include decreased range of motion, local swelling, and warmth.

1. **The presence of abnormal bone growth in tissue (i.e., heterotopic ossification) could result in an end-feel that is classified as hard due to the bony contact.**
2. Spasticity of the biceps would tend to produce a firm end-feel due to the presence of increased muscle tone.
3. Anterior capsular tightness would tend to produce a firm end-feel. Other common examples of a firm end-feel include muscular, ligamentous, and fascial shortening.
4. Muscle weakness would not be associated with an end-feel of any type since by definition end-feel is a passive assessment.

System: Musculoskeletal System
Content Outline: Foundations for Evaluation, Differential Diagnosis, and Prognosis

 Level 2  p. 79, 297

PTEXAM ONE: QUESTION 7

A physical therapist examines a patient who has adhesive capsulitis of the shoulder. Given the capsular pattern of the shoulder, which functional activity would be the **MOST** difficult for the patient?

1. Reaching across the body
2. Reaching into the back hip pocket
3. Performing a push-up
4. **Combing their hair**

Correct Answer: 4 (Dutton p. 585)

Patients with adhesive capsulitis (i.e., frozen shoulder) will typically demonstrate range of motion restrictions consistent with the capsular pattern of the affected joint. For the shoulder, the capsular pattern involves maximal loss of external rotation, moderate loss of abduction, and minimal loss of internal rotation.

1. Reaching across the body is a functional activity that involves shoulder horizontal adduction. Horizontal adduction is not a motion included in the capsular pattern of the shoulder.
2. Reaching into the back hip pocket is a functional activity that involves shoulder internal rotation, extension, and adduction. Shoulder extension and adduction are not motions included in the capsular pattern of the shoulder. Shoulder internal rotation is part of the capsular pattern, but it is typically only minimally affected.
3. Impairment in the ability to perform a push-up is usually secondary to a strength deficit, not a range of motion limitation. The push-up position generally requires approximately 90 degrees of flexion at the shoulder. A patient with adhesive capsulitis would likely possess the necessary range of motion to perform a push-up.
4. **Combing the hair is a functional activity that involves shoulder abduction and external rotation. These two motions are the most limited in patients with adhesive capsulitis of the shoulder.**

System: Musculoskeletal System
Content Outline: Foundations for Evaluation, Differential Diagnosis, and Prognosis

 Level 2  p. 79, 122, 156-157

PTEXAM ONE: QUESTION 8

A physical therapist inspects a patient's wheelchair and identifies that the wheel axle is aligned further posterior than it typically would be in a standard wheelchair. This type of alignment would **MOST** likely result in which of the following outcomes?

1. Decreased rolling resistance
2. Increased ability to balance on the rear wheels
3. Decreased turning radius
4. **Increased energy required for propulsion**

Correct Answer: 4 (Tan p. 313) 

Posterior alignment of the wheel axle is often utilized for patients with bilateral amputations to increase stability and compensate for the change in the center of gravity. This type of adaptation may also be utilized in a recliner or tilt wheelchair.

1. The posterior alignment of the wheel axle increases the amount of rolling resistance which serves to decrease the mechanical efficiency of the wheelchair.
2. The posterior alignment of the wheel axle decreases the ability of the patient to perform a "wheelie." Patients with spinal cord injuries may have the wheel axle moved forward to make it easier to perform a "wheelie" since this position moves the axle closer to the patient's center of gravity.
3. The posterior alignment of the wheel axle increases the turning radius of the wheelchair since the distance from the wheel axle to the casters increases. An increased turning radius reduces the maneuverability of the wheelchair.
4. **The posterior alignment of the wheel axle increases the amount of energy required for propulsion which serves to decrease the patient's ability to propel the wheelchair.**

System: Non-Systems
Content Outline: Equipment, Devices, and Technologies; Therapeutic Modalities

 Level 2   p. 684-687

PTEXAM ONE: QUESTION 9

A physical therapist orders a wheelchair for a patient who has C4 tetraplegia. Which wheelchair would be the **MOST** appropriate for the patient?

1. Manual wheelchair with friction surface handrims
2. Manual wheelchair with handrim projections
3. **Power wheelchair with sip and puff controls**
4. Power wheelchair with joystick controls

Correct Answer: 3 (O'Sullivan p. 883) 

A patient with C4 tetraplegia would require a power wheelchair with sip and puff, head, mouth or chin controls. The wheelchair would also require a tilt-in-space frame to allow for pressure relief.

1. Friction surface handrims are used when patients do not have a functional grip or the strength necessary to adequately propel a wheelchair. Patients with C6-C7 tetraplegia commonly rely on this feature.
2. Handrim projections add depth to the wheel and allow the patient to more easily propel the wheelchair. This is indicated with C5 tetraplegia where the lowest innervation includes the biceps, brachialis, brachioradialis, deltoids, rhomboids, and supinator. Although a patient with C5 tetraplegia may utilize handrim projections, the necessary energy expenditure may necessitate the use of a power wheelchair for mobility.
3. **A patient with C4 tetraplegia will have innervation of the face and neck, diaphragm, and trapezius muscles. The patient should be able to verbally direct all aspects of wheelchair management and would be a candidate for a power wheelchair with head or mouth controls.**
4. A patient with C5 tetraplegia is appropriate for a power wheelchair with joystick controls. Patients utilize a power wheelchair for community mobility secondary to the high energy expenditure of using a manual wheelchair with handrim projections.

System: Neuromuscular and Nervous Systems
Content Outline: Interventions

 **Level 2** **p. 298-300, 684-687**

PTEXAM ONE: QUESTION 10

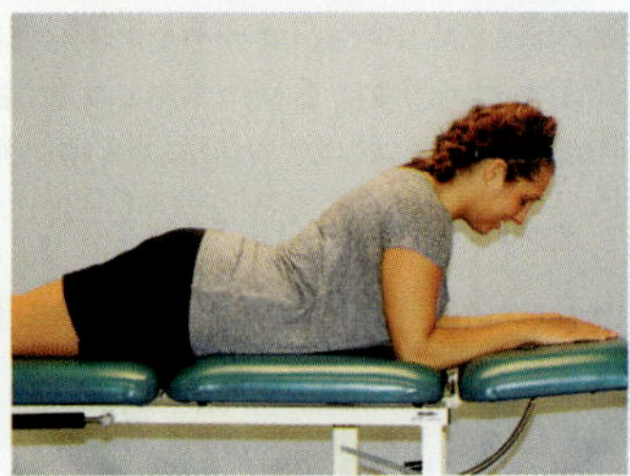

A physical therapist works with a patient who has a moderate disk protrusion on an extension progression. 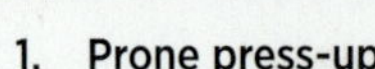 Which position would have immediately preceded the position shown in the image?

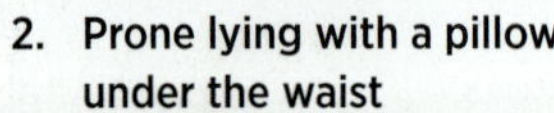

1. Prone press-up
2. Prone lying with a pillow under the waist
3. Standing extension
4. **Prone lying**

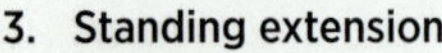

Correct Answer: 4 (Dutton p. 1485) 

The patient in the picture is demonstrating prone on elbows. A patient assumes the position by lying in prone with their elbows directly under their shoulders. The patient then moves their sternum away from the surface as the spine moves up and away from the shoulder blades. The extension progression sequence from least provocative to most provocative is: 1. prone with a pillow under the waist; 2. prone; 3. prone on elbows; 4. prone press-up; 5. standing extension.

1. A patient performing a prone press-up lies in prone with their palms on the surface. The patient performs a press-up by straightening their arms as much as possible while keeping the pelvis flat on the surface.
2. Prone with a pillow under the waist is often the most comfortable position for a patient since the pillow allows the spine to assume a more flexed position.
3. Standing extension occurs with the patient in standing with their feet slightly separated. The patient places their hands on the small of the back with the fingers pointing downward and the thumbs pointing anteriorly. The patient then bends backwards at the waist.
4. **A prone position refers to a patient lying on their stomach. This position requires the spine to be in a slightly extended position.**

System: Musculoskeletal System
Content Outline: Interventions

 **Level 2**

PTEXAM ONE: QUESTION 11

A physical therapist works with a patient status post right CVA with left hemiparesis. In the presented image, the patient is stabilizing the upper trunk and shifts weight onto the right ischium. Which description is **MOST** consistent with the described weight shift?

1. **Lower body left-side initiated lateral weight shift**
2. Lower body right-side initiated lateral weight shift
3. Lower body initiated anterior weight shift
4. Lower body initiated posterior weight shift

Correct Answer: 1 (Umphred p. 732)

Therapists will typically work with patients on both upper and lower body initiated movements while in sitting. Posterior, anterior, and lateral weight shifts produce different outcomes when initiated by the upper body versus the lower body. The upper body is stable while holding a ball in the presented image, while the lower body is initiating a lateral weight shift.

1. **In sitting, a lower body left-side initiated lateral weight shift produces lateral flexion on the left with concentric lateral activity on the left and eccentric lateral activity on the right. The therapist is attempting to facilitate a lower body initiated weight shift in the presented image. There is unweighting on the left ischium and increased weight bearing on the right ischium with elongation of the trunk on the right side.**
2. In sitting, a lower body right-side initiated lateral weight shift would produce similar movement to the opposite side as the presented image. The right side would demonstrate lateral flexion and decreased weight bearing on the right ischium and subsequent increased weight bearing on the left ischium with left trunk elongation. A therapist would focus more on lower body right-side initiated lateral weight shift with a patient that exhibits right hemiparesis.
3. In sitting, a lower body initiated anterior weight shift will facilitate spinal extension through concentric activity of the trunk extensors in order to maintain upright posture. A lower body initiated anterior movement would produce forward weight shift into an anterior tilt of the pelvis.
4. In sitting, a lower body initiated posterior weight shift will facilitate spinal flexion through concentric activity of the trunk flexors in order to maintain upright posture. A lower body initiated posterior movement would produce backward weight shift into a posterior tilt of the pelvis.

System: Neuromuscular and Nervous Systems
Content Outline: Interventions

 Level 2

PTEXAM ONE: QUESTION 12

A patient post stroke affecting the right hemisphere displays signs consistent with pusher syndrome. While practicing seated balance reactions, this patient would **MOST** likely lean in which direction?

1. Forward
2. Backward
3. To the right
4. **To the left**

Correct Answer: 4 (O'Sullivan p. 619) 

Pusher syndrome (also known as ipsilateral pushing) is an abnormal motor behavior sometimes encountered in patients who have had a stroke. The condition is characterized by the patient pushing with the stronger extremities toward the hemiparetic side. Pusher syndrome is caused by a misperception of body orientation in relation to gravity.

1. The misperception of body orientation with pusher syndrome causes the patient to inaccurately judge a vertical position resulting in a strong lateral lean. A patient with pusher syndrome would not lean forward.
2. The misperception of body orientation with pusher syndrome causes the patient to inaccurately judge a vertical position resulting in a strong lateral lean. A patient with pusher syndrome would not lean backward.
3. A patient with pusher syndrome would lean laterally to the hemiparetic side. A patient with a stroke affecting the left hemisphere would have right hemiparesis and would lean to the right side.
4. **A patient with pusher syndrome would lean laterally to the hemiparetic side. A patient with a stroke affecting the right hemisphere would have left hemiparesis and would lean to the left side. The patient would also resist attempts to passively correct their posture to midline.**

System: Neuromuscular and Nervous Systems
Content Outline: Interventions

 Level 2

PTEXAM ONE: QUESTION 13

A physical therapist identifies a limitation in movement after performing a straight leg raise test on a patient in the supine position. The therapist then passively flexes the patient's knee on the test leg, but is unable to gain any additional hip flexion range of motion. Which of the following conditions should the therapist MOST likely suspect?

1. **Gluteal bursitis**
2. Hamstrings strain
3. Sciatic nerve pathology
4. Trochanteric bursitis

Correct Answer: 1 (Magee p. 728)

The sign of the buttock test is used to determine if a patient's buttock pain has its origin in the buttock or is referred pain from the hip, sciatic nerve or hamstring muscles. The therapist administers the test by completing a straight leg raise to the patient's point of limitation. The therapist then flexes the knee and assesses the amount of hip flexion. If the amount of hip flexion does not increase, the test is considered to be positive for buttock pathology.

1. **Gluteal bursitis is an example of a condition that would result in buttock pathology and a positive sign of the buttock test. Other conditions that may also yield a positive test include an abscess, tightness of the gluteus maximus, and tightness of the posterior capsule.**
2. A hamstrings strain would likely produce a limitation in movement during the straight leg raise test, however, flexing the knee would significantly shorten the hamstring muscles allowing for increased hip flexion.
3. Sciatic nerve pathology would likely produce a limitation in movement during the straight leg raise test due to stretching of the sciatic nerve. The straight leg raise test will reproduce sciatic pain if the nerve is compressed or inflamed. Flexing the knee would decrease sciatic tension and allow for increased hip flexion.
4. Trochanteric bursitis may occur as a result of acute or cumulative trauma to the lateral hip causing irritation to the trochanteric bursa. Symptom complaints typically include lateral hip pain, however, limitations in movement are not typically present.

System: Musculoskeletal System
Content Outline: Physical Therapy Examination

Level 2

PTEXAM ONE: QUESTION 14

A physical therapist examines a patient who reports fullness of the left lower extremity, a sensation of tightening skin, and overall aching of the left lower extremity. As part of the examination, the therapist attempts to pinch and pick up a fold of skin at the base of the left second toe, but is unable to do so. This type of objective finding is BEST known as which of the following signs?

1. **Stemmer's**
2. Froment's
3. Tripod
4. Homans'

Correct Answer: 1 (Goodman – Pathology p. 682)

The described scenario is consistent with the clinical presentation of lymphedema. Lymphedema is the swelling of soft tissues that occurs secondary to the accumulation of fluid within the extracellular spaces. This occurs due to a decreased lymphatic transport capacity or an overload of lymphatic fluid within the system. Primary lymphedema has an unknown etiology, while secondary lymphedema is due to a known injury and disruption to the lymphatic system.

1. **A positive Stemmer's sign is characterized by the inability to squeeze and pick up a skinfold at the base of the second toe. This test is typically used to determine the presence of primary lymphedema. If the therapist was able to pinch a skinfold, the test would be negative.**
2. Froment's sign is associated with adductor pollicis muscle paralysis. The testing procedure requires that a patient hold a piece of paper between the thumb and index finger while the therapist attempts to pull the paper away from the patient. A positive Froment's sign is indicated by the patient flexing the distal phalanx of the thumb due to adductor pollicis muscle paralysis. This may be indicative of ulnar nerve compromise or paralysis.
3. The tripod sign is associated with tight hamstrings. The testing procedure requires that a patient is positioned in sitting with the knees flexed to 90 degrees over the edge of a table. The therapist passively extends one knee. A positive tripod sign is indicated by tightness in the hamstrings or extension of the trunk in order to limit the effect of the tight hamstrings.
4. Homans' sign is associated with a potential deep venous thrombosis (DVT). The testing procedure requires that a therapist passively dorsiflex the patient's foot at the ankle with the knee kept straight. A positive Homans' sign is characterized by pain in the calf or popliteal space. This determines risk for DVT. Clinical findings alone cannot confirm the diagnosis of DVT, but rather promote the need for further testing, typically using a Doppler ultrasound.

System: Other Systems
Content Outline: Physical Therapy Examination

p. 554-555

PTEXAM ONE: QUESTION 15

A physical therapist observes that a patient has difficulty controlling the affected lower extremity during the loading response. This phase of gait is characterized by which of the following muscle activity responses?

1. Increased quadriceps activity and increased hamstrings activity
2. **Increased quadriceps activity and decreased hamstrings activity**
3. Decreased quadriceps activity and increased hamstrings activity
4. Decreased quadriceps activity and decreased hamstrings activity

Correct Answer: 2 (Dutton p. 299)

Rancho Los Amigos stages of gait include initial contact, loading response, midstance, terminal stance, pre-swing, initial swing, midswing, and terminal swing. Loading response corresponds to the period between initial contact and the beginning of the swing phase for the opposite leg.

1. The goal of the loading response phase is to accept body weight onto the stance limb in a manner that ensures limb stability and permits forward progression. The acceptance of body weight relies heavily on the quadriceps while the hamstrings are less active.
2. **The loading response phase requires increased quadriceps activity to limit the rate of knee flexion. Hamstrings activity, particularly of the semimembranosus and semitendinosus, is decreased since the muscles are no longer needed to prevent knee hyperextension.**
3. Decreased quadriceps activity during the loading response phase could result in an excessive rate of knee flexion causing buckling or instability at the knee. The hamstrings are less active in the loading response phase than in other phases of the gait cycle such as during terminal swing.
4. Quadriceps activity is increased as the limb accepts body weight during the loading response phase, however, hamstrings activity is diminished.

System: Musculoskeletal System
Content Outline: Physical Therapy Examination

 **Level 2**  **p. 86-87**

PTEXAM ONE: QUESTION 16

A patient has weakness of the quadriceps secondary to a femoral nerve injury. When examining the patient's gait from heel strike to foot flat, the physical therapist would **MOST** likely observe the patient compensate for this injury with which of the following gait deviations?

1. Excessive dorsiflexion
2. **Forward trunk lean**
3. Excessive knee flexion
4. Vaulting on the contralateral limb

Correct Answer: 2 (O'Sullivan p. 234)

During the heel strike to foot flat phase of gait, the quadriceps work concentrically to hold the knee in extension, then eccentrically to control the amount of flexion. When the quadriceps are weak and cannot oppose the flexion moment at the knee, the knee goes into excessive flexion. Compensations may be observed at this point in the gait cycle to counteract the effect of the quadriceps weakness.

1. Patients with quadriceps weakness would be more likely to compensate with excessive plantar flexion during the heel strike to foot flat phase. Plantar flexion at the ankle reduces the flexion moment at the knee, which helps compensate for the quadriceps weakness.
2. **A patient with quadriceps weakness may use a forward trunk lean to compensate for their impairment. A forward trunk lean reduces the flexion moment at the knee and helps compensate for the quadriceps weakness.**
3. A patient with quadriceps weakness will likely demonstrate excessive knee flexion during the heel strike to foot flat phase of gait due to the quadriceps' inability to counteract the flexion moment at the knee. However, excessive knee flexion is a result of quadriceps weakness, not an attempt to compensate for the muscular weakness.
4. Vaulting on the contralateral limb is a compensation used to help clear the ipsilateral limb from the ground during the swing phase of gait. Not only is quadriceps weakness not a cause for contralateral vaulting, the described scenario would not occur during the swing phase of gait.

System: Neuromuscular and Nervous Systems
Content Outline: Foundations for Evaluation, Differential Diagnosis, and Prognosis

 **Level 2**  **p. 86-87, 251**

PTEXAM ONE: QUESTION 17

A physician analyzes the results of a magnetic resonance imaging (MRI) study to determine the extent of a patient's lung cancer. When staging the patient's cancer using the TNM system, which of the following factors would **NOT** be considered?

1. Size of the tumor
2. Involvement of the lymphatic system
3. **Rate of growth of the cancer cells**
4. Presence of metastasis

Correct Answer: 3 (Goodman – Pathology p. 368)

The TNM system is one of the most commonly used methods for staging cancer. The system describes a malignancy based on the size and extent of the primary tumor, lymph node involvement, and presence of metastasis. For most cancers, the TNM combination will correspond to a stage designation that further defines the severity of the disease.

1. The "T" in the TNM system refers to the size and extent of the primary tumor. Tumors that are larger in size will generally result in a poorer prognosis for the patient.
2. The "N" in the TNM system refers to the extent of lymph node involvement. Cancer that involves the lymph nodes generally results in a poorer prognosis for the patient.
3. **The rate of growth of cancer cells is highly variable depending on the actual type of cancer. This variable is determined by examining cancer cells using a microscope. The rate of growth of cancer cells, although extremely relevant, is not considered when using the TNM system to stage a patient's cancer.**
4. The "M" in the TNM system refers to the presence of metastasis of the cancer cells. Cancer that involves metastasis to other areas of the body generally results in a poorer prognosis for the patient.

System: Other Systems
Content Outline: Foundations for Evaluation, Differential Diagnosis, and Prognosis

 Level 1  p. 557

PTEXAM ONE: QUESTION 18

A physical therapist administers the Functional Reach Test to a patient who has a neurological disorder. What bony landmark would be the **MOST** appropriate for the therapist to utilize when measuring the distance the patient reached during each trial?

1. Distal tip of the third digit
2. **Third metacarpal**
3. Radial styloid process
4. Ulnar styloid process

Correct Answer: 2 (O'Sullivan p. 216)

The Functional Reach Test was developed to assess standing balance and the risk for falls. The test is reliable, however, the standard error of measurement may be relatively high and the test measures sway only in a forward direction. A person is required to stand upright against a wall with a static base of support. The patient is then asked to make a fist and raise the arm nearest the wall to 90 degrees of shoulder flexion. The therapist records the beginning position on a yardstick. The patient is then asked to lean forward as far as possible and the ending position is recorded. The beginning position is then subtracted from the ending position to obtain the final value.

1. The distal tip of the third digit is in the midline of the hand, but is not the identified landmark used on the Functional Reach Test.
2. **The Functional Reach Test requires the therapist to measure the position of the patient's third metacarpal on the yardstick after making a fist.**
3. The radial styloid process is located on the lateral side of the distal radius with the hand in the anatomic position. The most prominent part of the radial styloid process is just proximal to the carpal joint.
4. The ulnar styloid process is located on the medial side of the ulna with the hand in the anatomic position. The ulna articulates with the distal radius, but does not articulate with the carpals.

System: Neuromuscular and Nervous Systems
Content Outline: Physical Therapy Examination

 Level 1  p. 268

PTEXAM ONE: QUESTION 19

A 22-year-old patient who sustained multiple injuries, including a fractured tibia and a traction injury to the brachial plexus, is ready to begin gait training. The patient is partial weight bearing and has good upper extremity strength. Which of the following assistive devices is the **MOST** appropriate for the physical therapist to select for this patient?

1. Axillary crutches
2. **Lofstrand crutches**
3. Walker with platform attachment
4. Cane

Correct Answer: 2 (Fairchild p. 216) 

Physical therapists often have to consider a variety of factors when determining an appropriate assistive device for a patient. In this particular question, the therapist has to consider the patient's brachial plexus injury and the present weight bearing status.

1. Axillary crutches would accommodate the patient's weight bearing status, however, have the potential to transmit pressure through the axillary region which could exacerbate the brachial plexus injury.
2. **Lofstrand or forearm crutches avoid transmitting pressure to the brachial plexus area and accommodate for the weight bearing status of the involved lower extremity. The patient's age and upper extremity strength make Lofstrand crutches the most appropriate device.**
3. A walker with a platform attachment would be an appropriate option for the patient, however, given the patient's age and upper extremity strength, the device may offer more stability than the patient requires.
4. A cane or bilateral canes do not permit partial weight bearing and instead are used to promote balance.

System: Neuromuscular and Nervous Systems
Content Outline: Interventions

 Level 2  p. 690-691

PTEXAM ONE: QUESTION 20

A patient informs a physical therapist how frustrated they feel after being examined by their physician. The patient explains that they become so nervous that they cannot ask any questions during scheduled office visits. Which of the following actions is the **MOST** appropriate for the therapist to utilize?

1. Offer to go with the patient to their next scheduled physician visit
2. Offer to call the physician and ask any relevant questions
3. **Suggest that the patient write down questions for the physician and bring them to the next scheduled visit**
4. Tell the patient it is a very normal response to be nervous in the presence of a physician

Correct Answer: 3 (Purtilo p. 90) 

The physical therapist should attempt to identify a strategy or strategies that the patient can use to take a more active role during visits with the physician.

1. It is probably not realistic for the physical therapist to go with the patient to their next scheduled visit. In addition, the action places the burden on the therapist and does not promote a long-term change in the patient's current behavior.
2. Offering to call the physician and ask any relevant questions is similar to the previous option, however, may be slightly more practical. The action, however, does not require the patient to take a more active role and instead uses the physical therapist as an intermediary.
3. **Writing down questions allows the patient to reflect on the information they would like to gather in advance and provides the structure necessary to reduce the influence of the patient's anxiety during office visits.**
4. Acknowledging that many people are nervous in the presence of a physician may make the patient momentarily feel better, however, it does not provide the patient with a viable method to change their current behavior.

System: Non-Systems
Content Outline: Safety and Protection; Professional Responsibilities; Research

 Level 3

PTEXAM ONE: QUESTION 21

A physical therapist reviews a patient's medical record and identifies that the patient was recently placed on a corticosteroid medication. Which of the following conditions would MOST warrant the use of this type of pharmacological agent?

1. **Dermatitis**
2. **Folliculitis**
3. **Melanoma**
4. **Rosacea**

Correct Answer: 1 (Goodman – Pathology p. 422)

Corticosteroids provide hormonal, anti-inflammatory, and metabolic effects. These agents reduce inflammation in conditions that can damage healthy tissue through a series of reactions. Vasoconstriction results from stabilizing lysosomal membranes and enhancing the effects of catecholamines.

1. **Dermatitis is a broad term covering many different disorders characterized by a rash accompanied by pruritus and erythema. Patients with dermatitis are often treated with corticosteroids, antihistamines or immunomodulators. Actions to avoid dermatitis include wearing loose fitting natural fiber clothing, avoiding wearing plated jewelry, and lubricating the skin after bathing.**
2. Folliculitis is a common skin condition where the hair follicles become inflamed usually due to a bacterial or fungal infection. Patients with folliculitis are often treated with antiseptic cleansers or antibiotics. Actions to avoid folliculitis include shaving with care, keeping the skin moist and well hydrated, and avoiding unsanitary hot tubs and pools.
3. Melanoma is a malignancy originating from connective tissues such as fat, cartilage, bone or muscle. Patients with melanoma are often treated with surgery, chemotherapy, radiation therapy or immunotherapy. Actions to avoid melanoma include limiting ultraviolet radiation exposure and examining the skin on a regular basis.
4. Rosacea is an inflammatory skin disorder that causes facial erythema. Patients with rosacea are often treated with antibiotics, vitamin A derivatives or laser surgery. Actions to avoid rosacea include avoiding spicy and oily foods, reducing sun exposure, and limiting alcohol consumption.

System: Other Systems
Content Outline: Foundations for Evaluation, Differential Diagnosis, and Prognosis

Level 2

p. 132, 517

PTEXAM ONE: QUESTION 22

An athlete is forced to contemplate knee surgery after spraining the anterior cruciate ligament (ACL) while playing soccer. Which scenario provides the MOST direct support for an anterior cruciate ligament reconstruction?

1. **Grade III ACL sprain with a grade I posterior cruciate ligament (PCL) sprain**
2. **Grade III ACL sprain with a lateral meniscus tear**
3. **Grade II ACL sprain with a medial meniscus tear**
4. **Functional instability**

Correct Answer: 4 (Kisner p. 812) 

Surgical intervention is based on the amount of functional instability, however, is also influenced by a number of other variables including skeletal maturity, previous ligament injury, activity level, and age.

1. A grade III ACL sprain refers to a complete tear of the ACL. A grade I PCL sprain refers to a mild injury to the PCL without discernable laxity.
2. A grade III ACL sprain refers to a complete tear of the ACL. The addition of a lateral meniscus tear would likely enhance the instability already caused by the complete tear of the ACL.
3. A grade II ACL sprain refers to a moderate tear of the ACL with discernable laxity with the presence of an endpoint. The amount of laxity would be compounded by the presence of the medial meniscus tear. Meniscal tears contribute to knee instability since the menisci, when healthy, contribute to the stability of the knee.
4. **Many individuals are able to continue to function at high levels despite a variety of ligamentous and meniscal injuries, therefore functional instability provides the most direct support for an anterior cruciate ligament reconstruction.**

System: Musculoskeletal System
Content Outline: Foundations for Evaluation, Differential Diagnosis, and Prognosis

Level 2

p. 122, 130-131, 160-161

PTEXAM ONE: QUESTION 23

A physical therapist assesses a patient in a long-term care facility to help determine the need for skilled therapy services. The therapist utilizes a screening tool that examines a patient's ability to perform a variety of activities of daily living independently. Which screening tool has the therapist **MOST** likely used?

1. **Barthel Index**
2. Berg Balance Scale
3. Functional Reach Test
4. Tinetti Performance Oriented Mobility Assessment

Correct Answer: 1 (O'Sullivan p. 253)

There are a vast number of available screening tools utilized in physical therapy. A selected screening tool must be both valid and reliable and the individuals administering the tool must be qualified and capable in order to obtain meaningful results.

1. **The Barthel Index consists of ten activities of daily living and is often used as a screening tool in rehabilitation, long-term care settings, and home care. Scoring ranges from 0-100 in increments of 5. A score of 100 indicates that the patient is independent.**
2. The Berg Balance Scale consists of 14 tasks of everyday life activities that are scored according to a 0-4 scale. The maximum total score possible is 56, with a score of less than 45 indicating the patient is at risk for multiple falls.
3. The Functional Reach Test was developed to assess standing balance and the risk for falls. A person is required to stand upright against a wall with a static base of support. The patient is asked to make a fist and raise the arm nearest the wall to 90 degrees of shoulder flexion. The patient is then asked to lean forward as far as possible. The beginning position is subtracted from the ending position in order to obtain the final value.
4. The Tinetti Performance Oriented Mobility Assessment measures balance and gait using an ordinal scale of 0-2. The test has a total possible score of 28. Patients scoring less than 19 are considered to be at high risk for falling.

System: Neuromuscular and Nervous Systems
Content Outline: Physical Therapy Examination

 Level 2

PTEXAM ONE: QUESTION 24

A physical therapist uses the rule of nines on a three-year-old child to determine the approximate percentage of the total body surface area affected by a burn. When using this assessment tool, which area of the child's body would be given a higher percentage value compared to an adult?

1. **The head**
2. The trunk
3. The legs
4. The genitalia

Correct Answer: 1 (Sussman p. 407) 

The rule of nines is an assessment tool used to determine the total surface area of the body that is affected by a burn. The body is divided into 11 areas, with each area representing 9% of the total surface area, and the genitalia representing the additional 1%. When using the rule of nines, the surface area percentages must be altered if the patient is an infant or child.

1. **The head of an infant makes up a larger percentage of the total surface area as compared to an adult. For an adult, the front and the back of the head each comprise 4.5% of the total surface area.**
2. The trunk of an infant is similar in percentage value to that of an adult. For an adult, the front and the back of the trunk each comprise 18% of the total surface area (36% total for the entire trunk).
3. The legs of an infant make up a smaller percentage of the total surface area as compared to an adult. For an adult, the front and the back of a leg each comprise 9% (18% total for an entire leg) of the total surface area.
4. The genitalia of an infant are similar in percentage value to that of an adult. For an adult, the genitalia comprise 1% of the total surface area.

System: Other Systems
Content Outline: Physical Therapy Examination

 Level 1  p. 514-515

PTEXAM ONE: QUESTION 25

A physical therapist completes a respiratory assessment on a patient with T2 paraplegia. As a component of the assessment, the therapist measures the amount of chest excursion during inspiration. Which position is the **MOST** appropriate for the therapist to place the patient in to conduct the measurement?

1. Sitting
2. **Supine**
3. Prone
4. Sidelying

Correct Answer: 2 (Umphred p. 481)

The primary muscles of inspiration are the diaphragm and external intercostals. The primary muscles of expiration are the abdominals and internal intercostals. Normal mechanics of inspiration allow for an increase in the diameter of the thorax. Normal mechanics of resting expiration is through recoil of the lungs, however, the abdominals and intercostals contribute in several ways. The loss of these muscles significantly decreases the overall respiratory efficiency. Supine is the most appropriate position to assess chest excursion and initially strengthen.

1. The sitting position is a higher level activity for patients with any form of respiratory weakness and compromise. Patients should be assessed and initiate strengthening in the supine position with the goal of progressing to a sitting position. Abdominal binders assist the patient with respiration in sitting by maintaining pressure that is normally lost in patients with lesions at T12 or above.
2. **The supine position creates support and resistance to the diaphragm. There is a direct correlation between the amount of chest expansion and intercostal strength.**
3. The prone position would not be recommended for a patient with a spinal cord injury due to the patient's body weight and force of gravity upon the weakened muscles of respiration.
4. The sidelying position would not be indicated for measurement of chest excursion during inspiration since one portion of the thorax would be supported by the surface that the patient is sidelying on.

System: Cardiovascular and Pulmonary Systems
Content Outline: Physical Therapy Examination

Level 2

PTEXAM ONE: QUESTION 26

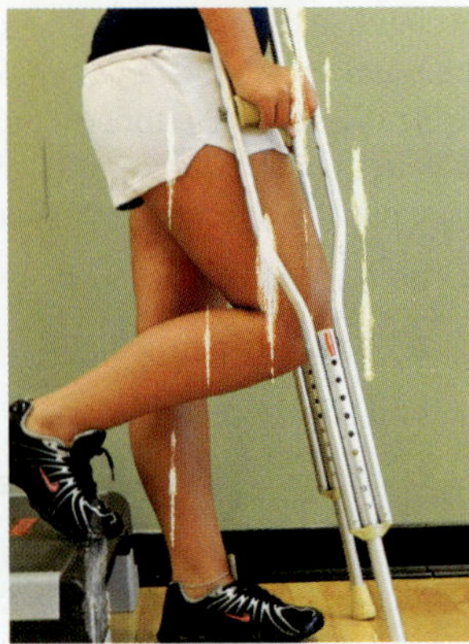

A physical therapist instructs a patient in the appropriate sequence for descending a step with axillary crutches as shown in the image. Based on the image, which of the following patient scenarios is the **MOST** likely?

1. **Partial weight bearing secondary to a left lateral ankle sprain**
2. Partial weight bearing secondary to a right lateral ankle sprain
3. Toe touch weight bearing secondary to a left lateral ankle sprain
4. Toe touch weight bearing secondary to a right lateral ankle sprain

Correct Answer: 1 (Fairchild p. 248)  

When descending a step with axillary crutches the involved lower extremity and crutches are moved from the step to the ground, while the upper extremities and the uninvolved lower extremity are used to slowly lower the body.

1. **The patient should use the upper extremities and the uninvolved lower extremity to slowly lower the body when descending a step. As a result, the patient's left ankle would be the involved ankle. Partial weight bearing occurs when a patient is allowed to put a particular amount of weight through the involved extremity.**
2. If the right ankle was the involved ankle, the patient would use the upper extremities and the left lower extremity to slowly lower the body when descending a step.
3. The patient's left ankle is the involved ankle, however, the picture does not depict toe touch weight bearing. Toe touch weight bearing occurs when a patient is unable to place any weight through the involved extremity, however, can place the toes on the ground to assist with balance.
4. The right ankle is not the involved ankle and the depicted weight bearing status is better described as partial weight bearing.

System: Musculoskeletal System
Content Outline: Interventions

Level 2  p. 692-694

PTEXAM ONE: QUESTION 27

A physical therapist treats a patient who had a reverse total shoulder arthroplasty. What is the **MOST** likely reason the patient had this surgical procedure as opposed to a total shoulder arthroplasty?

1. Fracture of the humerus
2. Glenohumeral osteoarthritis
3. Significant deltoid weakness
4. **Irreparable supraspinatus tear**

Correct Answer: 4 (Kisner p. 559)

Severe deterioration of the glenohumeral joint caused by osteoarthritis, rheumatoid arthritis, traumatic arthritis, rotator cuff tear arthropathy or a proximal humeral fracture is the most common indication for a glenohumeral arthroplasty. Arthroplasty of the glenohumeral joint falls into several categories including total shoulder arthroplasty, hemireplacement arthroplasty, and reverse total shoulder arthroplasty. The reverse total shoulder arthroplasty changes the ball and socket location of the shoulder so that the glenoid surface is convex and the humeral surface is concave.

1. A fracture of the humerus is one reason that a surgeon may elect to perform a glenohumeral arthroplasty. However, a fracture of the humerus would not necessarily provide justification for a reverse total shoulder arthroplasty.
2. Glenohumeral osteoarthritis is a common indication for glenohumeral arthroplasty. However, the presence of glenohumeral osteoarthritis would not necessarily provide justification for a reverse total shoulder arthroplasty.
3. Significant deltoid weakness alone is not an indication for reverse total shoulder arthroplasty. In fact, this procedure relies on the deltoid muscle, instead of the rotator cuff muscles, to position and elevate the arm.
4. **In cases where a rotator cuff tear cannot be repaired, a reverse total shoulder replacement is indicated. The inverted alignment of the joint surface components allows for greater congruency and stability of the joint surfaces, decreased translation of the humeral component, and an increased deltoid moment arm. These features allow the patient to elevate their arm in the presence of an insufficient rotator cuff.**

System: Musculoskeletal System
Content Outline: Foundations for Evaluation, Differential Diagnosis, and Prognosis

Level 2

p. 129, 192-193

PTEXAM ONE: QUESTION 28

A physical therapist assesses a patient's sensation of light touch in the lower extremities. The therapist documents that the patient has impaired sensation of the entire right leg, yet normal sensation of the left leg. Which injury is **MOST** likely present?

1. Compression of a lower extremity peripheral nerve
2. Compression of a lumbar nerve root
3. Spinal cord transection
4. **Left hemisphere stroke**

Correct Answer: 4 (O'Sullivan p. 622)

An important component of a sensory examination is to determine the pattern of an identified sensory impairment. The pattern of impairment will provide the therapist with information on the structure most likely involved.

1. Sensory impairments caused by a peripheral nerve injury will follow the distribution of the involved nerve. Peripheral nerves generally innervate small, irregularly shaped segments of the skin. A single peripheral nerve would not innervate the entire leg.
2. Sensory impairments caused by a nerve root injury will follow the distribution of the involved dorsal nerve root (i.e., dermatome). Nerve roots generally innervate small, irregularly shaped segments of the skin. A single nerve root would not innervate the entire leg.
3. Depending on the level of the lesion, a patient with a spinal cord injury may present with sensory impairment in the entire right leg. However, because the spinal cord is completely transected, the sensory impairment would be seen bilaterally.
4. **Patients status post stroke often have impairments of superficial and/or deep sensations. The type of impairment found is related to the location of the vascular lesion. A patient with a left hemisphere lesion will have sensory impairments on the right side of the body and can involve the face, upper extremity, and lower extremity.**

System: Neuromuscular and Nervous Systems
Content Outline: Foundations for Evaluation, Differential Diagnosis, and Prognosis

Level 2

p. 236, 280

PTEXAM ONE: QUESTION 29

A physical therapist treats a patient diagnosed with spinal stenosis. As part of the treatment plan, the patient lies in the prone position on a treatment plinth with a hot pack draped over the low back. Which of the following methods is the **MOST** effective for the therapist to use to monitor the patient during application of the hot pack?

1. Check on the patient at least every ten minutes
2. **Supply the patient with a bell to ring if the hot pack becomes too hot**
3. Instruct the patient to remove the hot pack if it becomes too hot
4. Select an alternate superficial heating modality

Correct Answer: 2 (Bellew p. 70) 

A hot pack consists of a canvas or nylon covered pack filled with a hydrophilic silicate gel that provides a moist heat. A hot pack must be stored in hot water between 158 to 167 degrees Fahrenheit (70 to 75 degrees Celsius). Application requires six to eight layers of towels around the hot pack. Given the potential for burns, formal measures must be adopted to ensure safe use throughout the treatment session.

1. Checking on a patient on a frequent basis is desirable, however, ten minutes is not frequent enough, particularly when considering that the duration of treatment with a hot pack may only be 15-20 minutes.
2. **Supplying the patient with a bell to ring if the hot pack becomes too intense provides a form of instant communication with the therapist. The use of a bell does not negate the need for the physical therapist to formally check on the patient frequently.**
3. It may be challenging for the patient to independently remove the hot pack based on the selected positioning. In addition, this option places the burden solely on the patient to make a definitive decision on whether or not to continue using the hot pack. This decision should be made by the therapist with feedback from the patient.
4. There is no need to discontinue a selected intervention in the absence of data to support this decision. Hot packs can be a safe and effective form of superficial heat when applied with the necessary precautions.

System: Non-Systems
Content Outline: Equipment, Devices, and Technologies; Therapeutic Modalities

 Level 3  p. 706-707

PTEXAM ONE: QUESTION 30

A physical therapist treats a patient who has a stage 3 pressure injury over the left ischial tuberosity. The patient's pressure injury has healed over time and currently shows the characteristics of a stage 1 pressure injury. What pressure injury stage should the therapist assign to the wound?

1. Stage 1 pressure injury
2. Modified stage 1 pressure injury
3. **Stage 3 pressure injury**
4. Modified stage 3 pressure injury

Correct Answer: 3 (Fairchild p. 296) 

A pressure Injury describes a localized injury to the skin and/or underlying tissue, usually over a bony prominence, as a result of pressure or pressure in combination with shear and/or friction forces. The National Pressure Ulcer Advisory Panel pressure ulcer staging criteria was developed for use with pressure Injuries. The staging criteria range from 1–4.

1. A stage 1 pressure injury is characterized by an observable pressure-related alteration of intact skin whose indicators, as compared to an adjacent or opposite area on the body, may include changes in skin color, skin temperature, skin stiffness or sensation. Pressure ulcers cannot be classified regressively as they heal. Therefore, an ulcer that had been graded as a stage 3 would still be known as a stage 3 pressure injury as it heals.
2. Terms such as "modified" would not be used to describe the healing status of a wound. Instead the percentage of the wound that has healed is often reported.
3. **A stage 3 pressure injury is characterized by full-thickness skin loss that involves damage or necrosis of subcutaneous tissue that may extend down to, but not through, underlying fascia. The ulcer presents clinically as a deep crater with or without undermining adjacent tissue.**
4. The ulcer would remain a stage 3 pressure injury, however, terms such as "modified" would not be used to describe the healing status of the wound. Instead the percentage of the wound that has healed is often reported.

System: Other Systems
Content Outline: Physical Therapy Examination

 Level 1  p. 504

PTEXAM ONE: QUESTION 31

A physical therapist examines superficial reflexes on a patient who has an upper motor neuron lesion. When assessing the cremasteric reflex, what is the MOST appropriate stimulus for the therapist to utilize?

1. Stroke the skin beneath the costal margins and above the inguinal ligament
2. **Stroke the skin of the superior and medial thigh**
3. Prick the skin of the perianal region
4. Prick the skin of the glans penis

Correct Answer: 2 (Goodman - Differential Diagnosis p. 630)

The physical therapist should stroke the skin in the area of the superior and medial thigh in order to elicit the cremasteric reflex. The anticipated response is elevation of the testicle on the same side as the stimulus.

1. Stroking the skin beneath the costal margins and above the inguinal ligament assesses the abdominal reflex. A normal response will produce a contraction of the abdominal muscles in the stimulated quadrant.
2. **Stroking of the skin of the superior and medial thigh will elicit the cremasteric reflex. Upper and lower motor neuron disorders as well as a spinal injury at the L1-L2 level can cause the reflex to be absent.**
3. Pricking the skin of the perianal region assesses the superficial anal reflex. A normal response will produce a contraction of the rectal sphincter.
4. Pricking the skin of the glans penis assesses the bulbocavernosus reflex. A normal response will produce a contraction of the bulbous urethra.

System: Neuromuscular and Nervous Systems
Content Outline: Physical Therapy Examination

 p. 252

PTEXAM ONE: QUESTION 32

A physical therapist assesses a pressure injury and identifies the presence of tunneling. This observation is MOST consistent with which pressure injury stages?

1. Stage 1 and 3
2. Stage 2 and 4
3. **Stage 3 and 4**
4. Stage 2 and unstageable

Correct Answer: 3 (Sussman p. 78)

Pressure injuries, also referred to as decubitus ulcers, result from sustained or prolonged pressure on tissue at levels greater than that of capillary pressure. Skin covering bony prominences is particularly susceptible to localized ischemia and tissue necrosis due to pressure. Factors contributing to pressure injuries include shearing forces, moisture, heat, friction, medications, muscle atrophy, malnutrition, and debilitating medical conditions. Tunneling refers to channels that extend from a wound into and through subcutaneous tissue or muscle.

1. A stage 1 pressure injury is characterized by intact skin with a localized area of non-blanchable erythema. As a result, this type of ulcer would not present with tunneling due to the lack of depth of the tissue injury. Tunneling may occur in stage 3 pressure injuries since they are characterized by full-thickness skin loss.
2. A stage 2 pressure injury is characterized by partial-thickness skin loss with exposed dermis. As a result, this type of ulcer would not present with tunneling due to the lack of depth of the tissue injury. Tunneling may occur in stage 4 pressure injuries since they are characterized by full-thickness skin loss.
3. **Stage 3 and 4 pressure injuries both may exhibit tunneling since they are characterized by full-thickness skin loss. The incidence of tunneling is greater in stage 4 pressure injuries.**
4. A stage 2 pressure injury is characterized by partial-thickness skin loss with exposed dermis. As a result, this type of ulcer would not present with tunneling due to the lack of depth of the tissue injury. An unstageable pressure injury is characterized by full-thickness skin and tissue loss in which the extent of tissue damage within the ulcer cannot be confirmed because it is obscured by slough or eschar. Since this type of pressure injury is characterized by full-thickness skin loss, tunneling often occurs.

System: Other Systems
Content Outline: Foundations for Evaluation, Differential Diagnosis, and Prognosis

 p. 504

PTEXAM ONE: QUESTION 33

A physical therapist prepares to work on standing balance with a patient who is post abdominal surgery. The patient has been on extended bed rest following the surgical procedure and has only been out of bed a few times. Which of the following objective measures is the MOST important for the therapist to assess after assisting the patient from a supine to sitting position?

1. **Systolic blood pressure**
2. Diastolic blood pressure
3. Perceived exertion
4. Oxygen saturation rate

Correct Answer: 1 (Fairchild p. 333) 

Orthostatic hypotension results from an inability to compensate quickly for changes in blood pressure. When a person stands up suddenly, gravity tends to cause blood to pool in the veins of the legs and lower body. As a result, the amount of blood returned to the heart is reduced and blood pressure falls. Dizziness or light headedness is the most common symptom. Normally, the body quickly responds to a decrease in blood pressure, however, compensatory mechanisms may malfunction or function too slowly in patients who have been on extended bed rest.

1. **During bed rest, when the leg muscles are not used regularly, blood pools in the leg veins and is not pumped back to the heart. This results in diminished blood volume which serves to reduce blood pressure. Systolic blood pressure is the maximum arterial pressure during systole or contraction of the left ventricle. It is the most important measure to assess after prolonged bed rest due to the risk of orthostatic hypotension. A decrease in systolic blood pressure of 20 mm Hg or greater with vertical positioning or a decrease in diastolic blood pressure greater than 10 mm Hg is indicative of orthostatic hypotension.**
2. Diastolic blood pressure refers to the arterial pressure during diastole (between ventricular contractions), therefore, it is not as useful a measure to assess the patient's response to vertical positioning.
3. Rating of perceived exertion is a subjective measure of how hard the body is working. It is based on the sensations experienced during physical activity including increased heart rate, respiration rate, sweating, and muscle fatigue. It is not a useful measure to assess the patient's response to vertical positioning.
4. Oxygen saturation measures the percentage of hemoglobin binding sites in the blood bound to oxygen. It is not affected by changing positions.

System: Other Systems
Content Outline: Interventions

 Level 2  p. 419-420, 766

PTEXAM ONE: QUESTION 34

Prior to initiating an ultrasound treatment, a physical therapist formally measures the target area as 12 cm^2. Based on the therapist's measurements, what is the MOST appropriate size of soundhead to utilize during the treatment?

1. 1 cm^2
2. 3 cm^2
3. **5 cm^2**
4. 8 cm^2

Correct Answer: 3 (Prentice p. 385) 

An accepted guideline is that ultrasound can be administered to an area two to three times the size of the effective radiating area (ERA) of the transducer face in a five minute period. This recommendation equates to roughly twice the size of the transducer face since the ERA is always slightly smaller than the total size of the transducer's soundhead. The most commonly used transducers are 5 and 10 cm^2.

1. A soundhead size of 1 cm^2 is extremely small and would not be practical to use given the size of the target area.
2. A soundhead size of 3 cm^2 is one fourth of the size of the target area and therefore would be slightly smaller than the optimal soundhead size.
3. **A soundhead size of 5 cm^2 is slightly less than half the size of the target area. This size soundhead would allow the therapist to achieve the desired therapeutic effects within a reasonable amount of time.**
4. A soundhead size of 8 cm^2 is two thirds the size of the target area and therefore would be slightly larger than the optimal soundhead size.

System: Non-Systems
Content Outline: Equipment, Devices, and Technologies; Therapeutic Modalities

 Level 2  p. 710-713

PTEXAM ONE: QUESTION 35

A physical therapist palpates the lunate bone on a patient post wrist injury. Which wrist motion will **BEST** allow the therapist to facilitate palpation of the lunate?

1. Extension
2. **Flexion**
3. Radial deviation
4. Ulnar deviation

Correct Answer: 2 (Dutton p. 781) 

The lunate is located in the center of the proximal row of carpals between the scaphoid and the triquetrum. The lunate is distinguished by its crescent-like outline and is just proximal to the capitate.

1. Extension and flexion of the wrist can be helpful to identify the lunate and capitate articulation, however, extension in isolation would not facilitate palpation of the lunate.
2. **The lunate is palpable just distal to the radial tubercle. Flexion of the wrist facilitates palpation of the lunate.**
3. Radial deviation would not be helpful to facilitate palpation of the lunate because the carpal bone is a midline structure.
4. Ulnar deviation would not be helpful to facilitate palpation of the lunate. Ulnar deviation can be used to facilitate palpation of the scaphoid since the motion causes the scaphoid to slide out from under the radial styloid process.

System: Musculoskeletal System
Content Outline: Physical Therapy Examination

 Level 1

PTEXAM ONE: QUESTION 36

A patient post CVA is exhibiting significant perceptual deficits. Which anatomical region would **MOST** likely be affected by this type of impairment?

1. Primary motor cortex
2. **Somatosensory cortex**
3. Basal ganglia
4. Cerebellum

Correct Answer: 2 (O'Sullivan p. 86)

A lesion affecting the somatosensory cortex often results in numerous impairments including loss of sensation, perception, proprioception, and diminished motor control.

1. The primary motor cortex is located in the precentral gyrus within the frontal lobe and contains the largest concentration of corticospinal neurons. This area lies directly in front of the central sulcus and primarily controls contralateral voluntary movements.
2. **The somatosensory cortex occupies the postcentral gyrus which is directly behind the central sulcus. The structure is responsible for complex processing of sensory information and damage can cause severely impaired perception. The somatosensory cortex receives information regarding touch, temperature, pain, and discriminative senses including stereognosis and position sense.**
3. The basal ganglia are a group of nuclei (putamen, caudate nucleus, substantia nigra, subthalamic nuclei, globus pallidus) that are located at the base of the cerebral cortex. The basal ganglia influence movement and postural control.
4. The cerebellum regulates movement, muscle tone, and postural control. Symptoms of a cerebellar lesion include ataxia, tremor, hypotonia, and asthenia.

System: Neuromuscular and Nervous Systems
Content Outline: Foundations for Evaluation, Differential Diagnosis, and Prognosis

 Level 2

PTEXAM ONE: QUESTION 37

A physical therapist examines a patient who has Achilles tendonitis and observes that the foot and ankle appear to be pronated. Which motions combine to create pronation in a non-weight bearing foot?

1. **Abduction, dorsiflexion, eversion**
2. Adduction, dorsiflexion, inversion
3. Abduction, plantar flexion, eversion
4. Adduction, plantar flexion, inversion

Correct Answer: 1 (Magee p. 896)

Pronation and supination are triplanar multi-joint motions that occur between the hindfoot, the midfoot, and the forefoot. A non-weight bearing foot is synonymous with the term open-chain.

1. **Pronation of the foot consists of abduction of the forefoot, dorsiflexion of the subtalar and midtarsal joints, and eversion and inward rotation of the heel.**
2. Pronation requires abduction of the forefoot and eversion of the heel, instead of adduction of the forefoot and inversion of the heel.
3. Pronation requires dorsiflexion and not plantar flexion of the subtalar and midtarsal joints.
4. Supination of the foot consists of adduction of the forefoot, plantar flexion of the subtalar and midtarsal joints, and inversion and outward rotation of the heel.

System: Musculoskeletal System
Content Outline: Physical Therapy Examination

 Level 1

PTEXAM ONE: QUESTION 38

A physical therapist reviews the results of a patient's pulmonary function test prior to examining a patient. The therapist notes that the patient's total lung capacity is significantly increased when compared to established norms. Which of the following medical conditions would MOST likely produce this type of result?

1. Chronic bronchitis
2. **Emphysema**
3. Spinal cord injury
4. Pulmonary fibrosis

Correct Answer: 2 (Frownfelter p. 86)

Emphysema is a chronic obstructive pulmonary disease characterized by an abnormal and permanent enlargement of the air spaces distal to the terminal bronchiole, accompanied by destructive changes in their walls. Changes in lung tissue resulting from these anatomic changes include loss of elastic recoil, collapse of airways during exhalation, and airflow obstruction.

1. In chronic bronchitis there is hypertrophy of the submucosal glands in the large and small bronchi and trachea with hypersecretion of mucus sufficient to cause a productive cough. Pulmonary function tests demonstrate a forced expiratory volume in one second (FEV_1) of < 65% of the predicted value. Total lung capacity is not increased in true chronic bronchitis.
2. **As a result of the pathologic changes to the lung tissue in emphysema, the lungs become hyperinflated. Due to the loss of elastic recoil, obstruction to airflow is seen as an increase in total lung capacity, residual volume, and functional residual capacity.**
3. Spinal cord injury is a neuromuscular cause of restrictive lung dysfunction. Characteristic changes in pulmonary function tests may include decreases in total lung capacity, vital capacity, and inspiratory capacity.
4. Pulmonary fibrosis is an inflammatory process affecting the alveoli that grossly distorts the architecture of the lung. These changes cause a decrease in lung compliance and a decrease in lung volumes including total lung capacity, vital capacity, functional residual capacity, and residual volume.

System: Cardiovascular and Pulmonary Systems
Content Outline: Foundations for Evaluation, Differential Diagnosis, and Prognosis

Level 2  p. 407, 458-459

PTEXAM ONE: QUESTION 39

A patient who has a left shoulder injury performs a resistive exercise as shown in the image. Which muscle would be **PRIMARILY** emphasized when performing the pictured isometric exercise?

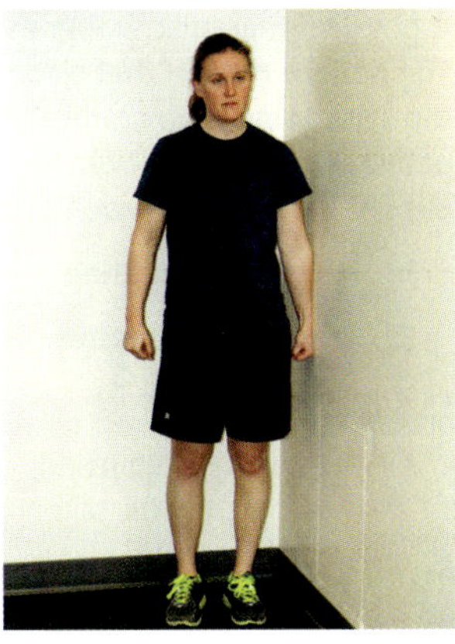

1. Pectoralis major
2. **Supraspinatus**
3. Teres major
4. Teres minor

Correct Answer: 2 (Magee p. 287) 

The image shows a patient performing an isometric shoulder exercise emphasizing shoulder abduction. An isometric exercise utilizes isometric contractions that occur when tension develops, but there is no change in the length of the muscle.

1. The clavicular head of the pectoralis major originates on the anterior surface of the medial half of the clavicle. The sternocostal head originates on the anterior surface of the sternum and six costal cartilages and the aponeurosis of the external oblique muscle. The muscles insert on the lateral lip of the intertubercular groove of the humerus. The clavicular head acts to flex the humerus while the sternocostal head extends the humerus. Collectively, the muscle adducts and medially rotates the humerus.
2. **The supraspinatus originates on the middle two-thirds of the supraspinous fossa of the scapula and inserts on the greater tubercle of the humerus. The muscle acts to abduct the shoulder and stabilize the head of the humerus in the glenoid fossa.**
3. The teres major originates on the dorsal surface of the inferior angle of the scapula and the lower third of the border of the scapula. The muscle inserts on the lesser tubercle of the humerus. The muscle acts to medially rotate, adduct, and extend the shoulder.
4. The teres minor originates on the upper two-thirds of the dorsal surface of the lateral border of the scapula and inserts on the greater tubercle of the humerus. The muscle acts primarily to laterally rotate the shoulder.

System: Musculoskeletal System
Content Outline: Interventions

Level 1

PTEXAM ONE: QUESTION 40

A physical therapist instructs a patient to squeeze a piece of paper between the index and middle fingers while the therapist attempts to pull it away. This type of testing would be the **MOST** appropriate to assess which of the following myotomes?

1. C6
2. C7
3. C8
4. **T1**

Correct Answer: 4 (Dutton p. 1284)

Involvement of a specific nerve root often results in predictable impairments including muscle weakness, diminished sensation, and impaired reflexes. Testing of the myotomes using resisted muscle testing allows the therapist to gain insight into the spinal level affected.

1. Involvement of the C6 myotome would most likely result in weakness of elbow flexion and wrist extension.
2. Involvement of the C7 myotome would most likely result in weakness of elbow extension and wrist flexion.
3. Involvement of the C8 myotome would most likely result in weakness of thumb extension.
4. **Involvement of the T1 myotome would most likely result in weakness of finger abduction and adduction.**

System: Neuromuscular and Nervous Systems
Content Outline: Physical Therapy Examination

  p. 105, 245-246

PTEXAM ONE: QUESTION 41

A physical therapist assesses an infant by performing a pull-to-sit maneuver. During the maneuver, the therapist observes that the infant has learned to lead with the head as soon as the stimulus of being pulled to sitting occurs. Which muscle group would be the LEAST instrumental in performing the described activity?

1. Abdominals
2. Cervical flexors
3. Hip flexors
4. **Scapular stabilizers**

Correct Answer: 4 (Tecklin p. 37)

The pull-to-sit maneuver involves the physical therapist moving a child to sitting by gently pulling the infant's upper extremities at the wrists. During the maneuver, the therapist observes the position of the head in relation to the body. The head of an infant without adequate head control will fall backward while they are pulled toward a sitting posture. To accomplish the pull-to-sit sequence the patient must utilize the abdominals, cervical flexors, and hip flexors.

1. The abdominals are necessary since the infant demonstrated the described anticipatory reaction (i.e., leading with the head) as the pull-to-sit maneuver was initiated.
2. The cervical flexors are necessary in the pull-to-sit maneuver to overcome the tendency of the head to fall backward due to the force of gravity. Active head control in the pull-to-sit maneuver cannot occur without adequate strength of the cervical flexors.
3. The hip flexors begin to actively flex the lower extremities during the pull-to-sit maneuver. This action assists the infant with the described anticipatory reaction (i.e., leading with the head) as the pull-to-sit maneuver is initiated. In addition, the hip flexors contribute to the core stability necessary for the described activity.
4. **The scapular stabilizers are not as critical as the other listed muscles when performing the pull-to-sit maneuver since the therapist applies the force necessary to move the infant by pulling the infant's upper extremities at the wrists. In addition, the scapular stabilizers are not necessary to overcome the force of gravity or to generate the flexion moment required at the neck, trunk or lower extremities during the pull-to-sit maneuver.**

System: Neuromuscular and Nervous Systems
Content Outline: Physical Therapy Examination

Level 2

PTEXAM ONE: QUESTION 42

A physical therapist examines a patient who has multiple sclerosis. The patient reports that since being diagnosed four years ago, the symptoms have gradually gotten worse without any plateau or lessening in severity. Which type of multiple sclerosis does this patient MOST likely have?

1. Relapsing-remitting
2. **Primary-progressive**
3. Secondary-progressive
4. Progressive-relapsing

Correct Answer: 2 (O'Sullivan p. 665)

Multiple sclerosis is a chronic disease caused by inflammation and demyelination within the central nervous system. The disease is highly variable from patient to patient with the majority of individuals following one of the four major disease courses (i.e., relapsing-remitting, primary-progressive, secondary-progressive, and progressive-relapsing).

1. Relapsing-remitting multiple sclerosis is the most common type of multiple sclerosis and is characterized by disease relapses, periods of acute symptom exacerbation, followed by remissions, periods without symptoms and without further progression of the disease.
2. **Primary-progressive multiple sclerosis is characterized by a continuous worsening of symptoms from the onset without distinct relapses or remissions.**
3. Secondary-progressive multiple sclerosis is characterized by an initial onset of the relapsing-remitting presentation, followed by a progression of the disease at a variable rate that may include minor relapses and remissions.
4. Progressive-relapsing multiple sclerosis is characterized by a progression of the disease from the initial onset, as well as acute relapses. In between relapses, the disease continues to progress.

System: Neuromuscular and Nervous Systems
Content Outline: Foundations for Evaluation, Differential Diagnosis, and Prognosis

Level 2  p. 277, 342-343

PTEXAM ONE: QUESTION 43

A patient diagnosed with piriformis syndrome is referred to physical therapy for one visit for instruction in a home exercise program. After examining the patient, the physical therapist feels the patient's rehabilitation potential is excellent, but is concerned that one visit will not be sufficient to meet the patient's needs. Which of the following actions is the **MOST** appropriate for the therapist to implement?

1. Schedule the patient for treatment sessions as warranted by the results of the examination
2. Explain to the patient that recent health care reforms have drastically reduced the frequency of physical therapy visits covered by third party payers
3. Explain to the patient that they can continue with physical therapy beyond the initial session, but will be liable for all expenses not covered by their insurance
4. **Contact the referring physician and request approval for additional physical therapy visits**

Correct Answer: 4 (Criteria for Standards of Practice)

A physical therapist has an ethical and legal obligation to act in the patient's best interest.

1. Scheduling the patient for treatment sessions based on the results of the examination is appropriate, however, the physical therapist should contact the referring physician and attempt to have the visits approved.
2. Health care reforms have, in many cases, limited the frequency of physical therapy visits covered by third party payers, however, there is no indication that the patient would not have coverage for the additional visits.
3. Patients should understand that they may be responsible for the cost of unreimbursed physical therapy services, however, the physical therapist should take the necessary steps to ensure that the services are both necessary and authorized by the referring physician.
4. **The physical therapist will need to seek physician approval for the additional visits in order to be working under a physician referral. Although this does not guarantee that the visits will be approved by the physician or that the visits will be covered by the third party payer, it provides the therapist with the opportunity to act in the patient's best interest.**

System: Musculoskeletal System
Content Outline: Foundations for Evaluation, Differential Diagnosis, and Prognosis

Level 3

PTEXAM ONE: QUESTION 44

A physical therapist observing a patient complete a leg curl exercise notices two prominent tendons visible on the posterior surface of the patient's knee as shown in the image. The visible medial and lateral tendons are **MOST** likely associated with which muscles?

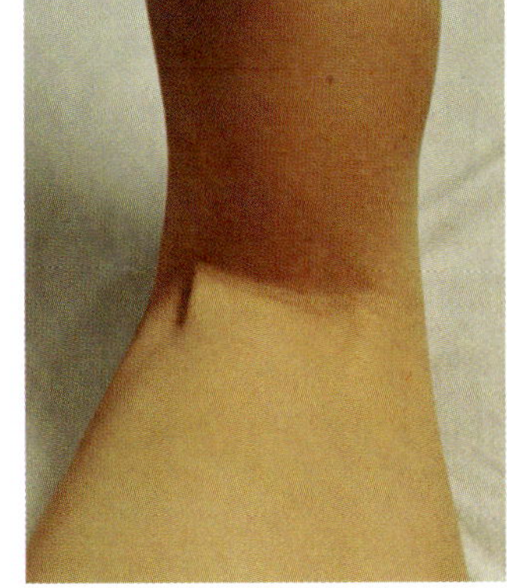

1. Semimembranosus and semitendinosus
2. **Semitendinosus and biceps femoris**
3. Popliteus and semitendinosus
4. Semimembranosus and biceps femoris

Correct Answer: 2 (Kendall p. 418) 

The hamstring muscles include the semitendinosus, semimembranosus, and biceps femoris. The muscles' primary action is to flex the knee. As a result, the tendons of each of the hamstring muscles become more prominent with resisted knee flexion.

1. The semimembranosus and semitendinosus are hamstring muscles that act to flex the knee joint, however, they are both located on the medial aspect of the posterior knee joint. The image shows two tendons, one that is located on the medial aspect of the posterior surface of the knee joint and the other on the lateral aspect.
2. **The semitendinosus and biceps femoris are hamstring muscles whose tendons become prominent when performing a leg curl. The biceps femoris is the lateral tendon, while the semitendinosus is the medial tendon.**
3. The popliteus muscle is located deep within the posterior surface of the knee joint and would not appear as a tendinous cord-like structure. The semitendinosus is a medial hamstrings muscle that would be prominent on the medial aspect of the posterior surface of the knee joint.
4. The semimembranosus muscle is a medial hamstrings muscle, however, the muscle's tendon is not nearly as prominent as the semitendinosus. The biceps femoris is a lateral hamstrings muscle that would be prominent on the lateral aspect of the posterior surface of the knee joint.

System: Musculoskeletal System
Content Outline: Physical Therapy Examination

Level 1

PTEXAM ONE: QUESTION 45

A patient diagnosed with Guillain-Barre syndrome works on weight shifting activities while standing in the parallel bars. The PRIMARY objective of this activity is to improve which stage of motor control?

1. Mobility
2. Stability
3. **Controlled mobility**
4. Skill

Correct Answer: 3 (Sullivan p. 77)

Functional training uses postures and activities to improve motor control. Physical therapists select activities for patients that are designed to progressively increase the effects of gravity and body weight.

1. Mobility, the first stage of motor control, refers to the ability to initiate movement through a functional range of motion.
2. Stability, the second stage of motor control, refers to the ability to maintain a position or posture through cocontraction and tonic holding around a joint.
3. **Controlled mobility, the third stage of motor control, refers to the ability to move within a weight bearing position or rotate around a long axis.**
4. Skill, the fourth stage of motor control, refers to the ability to consistently perform functional tasks and manipulate the environment with normal postural reflex mechanisms and balance reactions. Skill activities include ADLs and community locomotion.

System: Neuromuscular and Nervous Systems
Content Outline: Interventions

 Level 1 p. 291

PTEXAM ONE: QUESTION 46

A physical therapist directs a physical therapist assistant to complete a lower extremity isokinetic test on a patient. The assistant is willing to complete the test, however, indicates it has been quite some time since they have set up the isokinetic device. Which of the following actions is the MOST appropriate for the therapist to take?

1. Provide verbal cueing for the physical therapist assistant prior to beginning the set up
2. Instruct the physical therapist assistant to refer to the owner's manual
3. **Observe the physical therapist assistant complete the set up**
4. Ask another physical therapist assistant to complete the set up

Correct Answer: 3 (Standards of Practice) 

A physical therapist should establish and maintain an ongoing professional relationship with a physical therapist assistant. The physical therapist should delegate appropriate patient care duties to the physical therapist assistant that are within their established scope of practice. The physical therapist assistant must clearly communicate their needs to the physical therapist and work in a collaborative manner.

1. Verbal cueing allows the physical therapist to assist the physical therapist assistant to set up the isokinetic device through verbal input, however, it does not ensure that the device is set up correctly.
2. Referring the physical therapist assistant to the owner's manual provides the physical therapist assistant with a general reference to guide them through the set up, but like the previous option does not ensure that the device is set up correctly.
3. **Observing the physical therapist assistant complete the set up allows the physical therapist to assist the physical therapist assistant as needed and at the same time ensures the device is set up correctly. Direct involvement of the physical therapist is collaborative and may assist the physical therapist assistant to complete the set up independently in the future.**
4. The physical therapist assistant is capable of completing the set up with assistance. As a result, it is not necessary to secure another physical therapist assistant to complete the set up. In addition, the question does not provide direct evidence that another physical therapist assistant is available who possesses the requisite knowledge to complete the activity.

System: Musculoskeletal System
Content Outline: Physical Therapy Examination

 Level 3  p. 784-785

PTEXAM ONE: QUESTION 47

A physical therapist administers ultrasound over a patient's anterior thigh. After one minute of treatment, the patient reports feeling a slight burning sensation under the soundhead. Which of the following actions is the **MOST** appropriate for the therapist to take?

1. Explain to the patient that what they feel is not out of the ordinary when using ultrasound
2. **Temporarily discontinue treatment and examine the amount of coupling agent utilized**
3. Discontinue treatment and contact the referring physician
4. Continue with treatment utilizing the current parameters

Correct Answer: 2 (Bellew p. 98) 

A patient report of a slight burning sensation under the soundhead can be due to inadequate coupling, loosening of the crystal or hot spots due to a high beam nonuniformity ratio.

1. A complaint of a slight burning sensation would be an abnormal response when using ultrasound. As a result, it would be inappropriate to inform the patient that what they feel is "not out of the ordinary." It may be normal to feel a dull warming, however, a slight burning sensation would require an immediate response.
2. **The complaint of a slight burning sensation may indicate improper coupling. By temporarily discontinuing the treatment and examining the amount of coupling agent used, the physical therapist may be able to continue with treatment. If the physical therapist adds coupling agent and the patient reports a similar sensation, the intervention should be discontinued and the ultrasound unit should be formally inspected by a qualified technician.**
3. Discontinuing treatment would be an acceptable option, however, there is not presently a need to contact the referring physician. A physical therapist may elect to contact the physician in situations where the patient has been injured by a physical therapy intervention or if there has been a change in the patient's medical status.
4. Continuing with treatment utilizing the current parameters is not appropriate since the patient has already reported a slight burning sensation. Failure to respond specifically to the patient's subjective report creates an unnecessary safety risk.

System: Non-Systems
Content Outline: Equipment, Devices, and Technologies; Therapeutic Modalities

 Level 3  p. 710-713

PTEXAM ONE: QUESTION 48

A physical therapist receives a referral for a patient with back pain associated with an L3 vertebral compression fracture. Which information collected from the patient interview would be associated with this medical diagnosis?

1. History of intravenous drug abuse for over ten years
2. Onset of numbness in the saddle region when sitting on a bike seat
3. **Prednisone use for the management of systemic lupus erythematosus**
4. Unintentional weight loss of 20 pounds within the last six months

Correct Answer: 3 (Ciccone p. 241)

As part of a comprehensive examination, physical therapists routinely collect information on a patient's past medical history and their current condition. This information will provide the physical therapist with needed guidance when selecting appropriate examination procedures and physical therapy interventions.

1. History of intravenous drug abuse for over ten years increases the risk of developing a number of infectious diseases including the human immunodeficiency virus and hepatitis C.
2. Onset of numbness in the saddle region when sitting on a bike seat is often associated with cauda equina syndrome. This condition is considered to be a peripheral nerve injury and results from damage and loss of function involving two or more nerves of the cauda equina. Symptoms associated with this condition include altered reflexes, pain, diminished sensation in the saddle distribution, bowel and bladder dysfunction, and decreased strength and sensation.
3. **Prednisone is an oral, synthetic corticosteroid used to suppress the immune system and control inflammation. Side effects of long-term use include a decrease in the formation of new bone, an increase in the breakdown of old bone, and a decrease in the body's ability to absorb calcium from food. As a result, long-term prednisone use would increase the incidence of vertebral compression fractures.**
4. Unintentional weight loss of 20 pounds within the last six months would be abnormal and is often associated with cancer. Other signs and symptoms associated with cancer include a change in bowel/bladder routine, unusual bleeding/discharge, nagging cough, a sore that will not heal, and an obvious change in a wart/mole.

System: Musculoskeletal System
Content Outline: Foundations for Evaluation, Differential Diagnosis, and Prognosis

 Level 2  p. 132, 585-588

PTEXAM ONE: QUESTION 49

A physical therapist works with a patient who sustained burns to the left axilla and shoulder. The therapist would most likely fabricate a splint for the patient in order to avoid which of the following deformities?

1. Shoulder abduction contracture and webbing of the axillary folds
2. **Shoulder adduction contracture and webbing of the axillary folds**
3. Shoulder flexion and medial rotation contracture
4. Thoracic kyphosis secondary to flexion forces

Correct Answer: 2 (Lusardi p. 420)

A burned area is at high risk for either hypertrophic or keloid scar formation during the healing process. Contractures result when a portion of the shortening scar becomes fixed or semifixed. The axilla is one of the most common sites of scar contracture formation. Splinting should promote proper positioning of the joint in order to avoid the potential for a contracture.

1. The preferred position for a burn surrounding the shoulder is shoulder abduction and lateral rotation. Burns to the shoulder and axilla would not typically produce a shoulder abduction contracture, however, they can create webbing of the axillary folds if the joint is not splinted properly.
2. **A burn involving the shoulder and axilla may result in a shoulder adduction contracture and webbing of the axillary folds if the joint is not splinted properly. Ideally, the splint would conform to the entire arm from the wrist, through the axillary area, and down the trunk to the waist in order to provide the necessary support. The splint should be molded to the patient and secured with wraps, pads, and other strapping.**
3. A burn involving the shoulder and axilla may result in a contracture into medial rotation, however, a shoulder flexion contracture is not typical with this type of burn.
4. A patient with a burn to the anterior trunk is at risk for developing a kyphosis deformity secondary to the flexion forces associated with this area of burn. Splinting should counteract these forces by maintaining a position of retraction and upright posture. This scenario is inconsistent with a burn to the left axilla and shoulder.

System: Other Systems
Content Outline: Interventions

Level 1  p. 514

PTEXAM ONE: QUESTION 50

A patient is currently taking Neurontin (gabapentin) for the treatment of seizures. Based on the prescribed medication, the patient may have the **MOST** difficulty when performing interventions that attempt to improve which of the following components?

1. **Coordination**
2. Verbal comprehension
3. Strength
4. Flexibility

Correct Answer: 1 (Ciccone p. 122)

Neurontin (gabapentin) is used to prevent and control seizures. It is also used to relieve nerve pain following shingles, trigeminal neuralgia, and in the treatment of diabetic neuropathy. Primary side effects include fatigue, sedation, dizziness, and ataxia.

1. **Ataxia is a common side effect of Neurontin. Ataxia is a cerebellar deficit that may impair the patient's ability to perform coordinated movements and participate in functional activities. Physical therapists should include coordination activities in the plan of care if ataxia is present.**
2. Poor verbal comprehension is not a typical side effect of Neurontin. Pathologies such as cerebrovascular accident are more likely to result in receptive aphasia.
3. A patient taking Neurontin may experience fatigue and sedation, however, the patient should still benefit from scheduled exercise that allows for gains in strength. Neurontin does not affect the body's ability to gain strength with appropriate training.
4. A patient taking Neurontin may experience fatigue and sedation, however, the patient should still benefit from a flexibility program. Neurontin does not affect the patient's ability to improve flexibility with appropriate stretching activities.

System: Other Systems
Content Outline: Interventions

 Level 2  p. 273

PTEXAM ONE: QUESTION 51

A patient post CVA ambulates with a large base quad cane. The patient presents with left neglect and diminished proprioception. Which of the following actions is the **MOST** appropriate to ensure patient safety?

1. Provide continuous verbal cues
2. Utilize visual cues and demonstration
3. **Offer manual assistance on the left side**
4. Offer manual assistance on the right side

Correct Answer: 3 (O'Sullivan p. 1198) 

A physical therapist must carefully consider a patient's current limitations and identify remedial strategies to assist the patient to achieve established goals. The presence of left neglect and diminished proprioception requires the therapist to take formal action to avoid jeopardizing patient safety.

1. Verbal cues may be beneficial for the patient, however, without concurrent manual assistance the patient would likely still have increased difficulty with ambulation and may be at increased risk for a fall.
2. Demonstration prior to practice is important, however, this type of educational strategy would not directly address the left neglect and diminished proprioception.
3. **The physical therapist should offer manual assistance on the patient's left side during ambulation activities. The manual assistance can facilitate motor activity and weight bearing, as well as proprioception on the affected side. Manual contact significantly reduces the risk for fall or injury.**
4. The patient presents with left neglect and as a result manual assistance would not typically be necessary on the right side of the body.

System: Neuromuscular and Nervous Systems
Content Outline: Interventions

 Level 2  p. 691-692

PTEXAM ONE: QUESTION 52

A physical therapist employed in a rehabilitation hospital creates a professional development plan as part of their annual performance appraisal. Which of the following methods for attending continuing education courses would be the **MOST** appropriate plan to facilitate the therapist's development in their present practice setting?

1. Attend courses approved by the Federation of State Boards of Physical Therapy
2. Attend courses featuring nationally recognized experts
3. Attend a minimum of two courses annually
4. **Attend courses related to primary patient care responsibilities**

Correct Answer: 4 (Guide for Professional Conduct)

Facilitating the physical therapist's development in their present practice setting requires the physical therapist to attend continuing education courses related to their primary care responsibilities. Continuing education courses allow the physical therapist to refine existing skills and learn new skills. By taking courses related to primary patient care responsibilities the therapist will be able to immediately integrate selected skills into their daily practice.

1. The Federation of State Boards of Physical Therapy does not approve continuing education courses.
2. Attending continuing education courses featuring nationally recognized experts does not ensure that the courses will be more beneficial to the therapist than courses taught by less known speakers. The physical therapist should evaluate each course based on its relevant merit and the direct relevance to their patient care duties.
3. The quality of the continuing education courses a physical therapist attends is a more important variable to consider than the actual number of courses attended. For example, a physical therapist could attend several courses with little direct relevance to their present patient care duties and as a result receive little practical benefit.
4. **The physical therapist should attend continuing education courses that directly relate to their primary patient care responsibilities. Developing this particular skill set will allow the physical therapist to improve the quality of patient care within their current practice setting.**

System: Non-Systems
Content Outline: Safety and Protection; Professional Responsibilities; Research

 Level 2

PTEXAM ONE: QUESTION 53

A patient who has a left ventricular assist device reports experiencing signs and symptoms consistent with thoracic outlet syndrome. Which provocative test would be the MOST appropriate to test for thoracic outlet syndrome given the presence of the left ventricular assist device?

1. **Roos test**
2. Adson maneuver
3. Allen test
4. Wright test

Correct Answer: 1 (Dutton p. 1299)

A left ventricular assist device (LVAD) is an implantable mechanical pump that helps pump blood from the left ventricle to the rest of the body. It is typically used in patients with heart failure to augment the function of the failing left ventricle. Most LVADs are continuous flow, meaning pulses will not be palpable. This would make any of the provocative tests for thoracic outlet syndrome in which the radial pulse is palpated an ineffective choice.

1. **To perform the Roos test, the patient is positioned in sitting or standing with the arms positioned in 90 degrees of abduction, lateral rotation, and elbow flexion. The patient is asked to open and close their hands for three minutes. The test is considered positive if the patient demonstrates an inability to maintain the test position, weakness of the arms, and sensory loss or ischemic pain and it may be indicative of thoracic outlet syndrome. This would be the most appropriate provocative test for thoracic outlet syndrome in this scenario since palpation of the radial pulse is not required.**
2. To perform the Adson maneuver, the patient is positioned in sitting or standing while the therapist monitors the radial pulse and then asks the patient to rotate their head towards the test shoulder. The patient is then asked to extend their head while the therapist laterally rotates and extends the patient's shoulder. This test would not be appropriate in this scenario since monitoring the radial pulse is required.
3. To perform the Allen test, the patient is positioned in sitting or standing with the test arm in 90 degrees of abduction, lateral rotation, and elbow flexion. The patient is asked to rotate the head away from the test shoulder while the therapist monitors the radial pulse. This test would not be appropriate in this scenario since monitoring the radial pulse is required.
4. To perform the Wright test, the patient is positioned in sitting or supine. The therapist moves the patient's arm into maximum abduction while monitoring the patient's radial pulse. This test would not be appropriate in this scenario since monitoring the radial pulse is required.

System: Musculoskeletal System
Content Outline: Physical Therapy Examination

p. 102, 354-355, 417

PTEXAM ONE: QUESTION 54

A physical therapist treats a patient diagnosed with metabolic syndrome for general deconditioning. Which of the following signs or symptoms would the patient LEAST likely demonstrate?

1. Elevated triglyceride levels
2. **Abnormal blood pH**
3. Insulin resistance
4. Elevated blood pressure

Correct Answer: 2 (Goodman – Differential Diagnosis p. 411)

Metabolic syndrome is a group of signs and symptoms that are risk factors for cardiovascular disease, diabetes, and stroke. During the patient's examination, the therapist can screen for this condition through the identification of red flags, such as a BMI greater than 30, elevated blood pressure, increased waist circumference, and signs of insulin resistance.

1. Dyslipidemia (i.e., increased triglyceride levels, increased low-density lipoprotein levels, decreased high-density lipoprotein levels) is one of the signs associated with metabolic syndrome.
2. **Metabolic syndrome is not generally associated with abnormal blood pH since the syndrome represents only a collection of risk factors. However, if the risk factors associated with metabolic syndrome progressed to a specific pathology (e.g., diabetic ketoacidosis), abnormal blood pH would be more likely.**
3. Insulin resistance is one of the signs associated with metabolic syndrome. Excess body fat and physical inactivity are risk factors that may predispose patients to insulin resistance.
4. Elevated blood pressure is a sign associated with metabolic syndrome. The significance of this finding is related to the extent of the blood pressure increase. Hypertension is classified as stage 1 hypertension, stage 2 hypertension, and hypertensive crisis.

System: Other Systems
Content Outline: Foundations for Evaluation, Differential Diagnosis, and Prognosis

PTEXAM ONE: QUESTION 55

A physical therapist works on balance reeducation activities to improve a patient's independence with functional activities in the kitchen. Which of the following tests would provide the therapist with the **MOST** useful information on the patient's ability to safely perform meal preparation?

1. **Multi-Directional Reach Test**
2. Timed Get Up and Go Test
3. Romberg Test
4. Tinetti Performance Oriented Mobility Assessment

Correct Answer: 1 (O'Sullivan p. 217)

Balance requires integration of somatosensory, visual, and vestibular information within the central nervous system. Balance tests investigate the contribution of input from each system and assess a patient's risk for falling. Selection of an appropriate balance test is dependent on clinical diagnosis and patient presentation.

1. **The Multi-Directional Reach Test measures the distance a patient can reach in a forward, backward or lateral direction. This test will provide the physical therapist with information on a patient's ability to maintain their balance when reaching in and out of the base of support.**
2. The Timed Get Up and Go Test is a measure of dynamic balance and mobility. The Timed Get Up and Go test is a reliable, quick screen to identify fall risk, but it is not specific to the functional task of reaching which is required when performing kitchen activities.
3. The Romberg Test is performed to determine the impact of proprioception on standing balance. This test provides useful information to a physical therapist assessing a patient's risk of falling, however, it is not specific to balance during the task of reaching which is required during meal preparation.
4. The Tinetti Performance Oriented Mobility Assessment is a tool used to screen patients to assess risk of falling. This test assesses both static and dynamic balance by using two subtests which assess balance and gait. The assessment offers a quick and reliable measure of a patient's risk of falling, however, the test does not specifically address balance during reaching.

System: Neuromuscular and Nervous Systems
Content Outline: Foundations for Evaluation, Differential Diagnosis, and Prognosis

 **Level 2**

PTEXAM ONE: QUESTION 56

A physical therapist attends an in-service entitled "Principles of Exercise for the Obstetric Patient." During the session, the speaker identifies several conditions that are considered to result in high risk pregnancies. Which of the following conditions would result in the **LOWEST** risk to the pregnancy?

1. **Diastasis recti**
2. Incompetent cervix
3. Pre-eclampsia
4. Multiple gestation

Correct Answer: 1 (Kisner p. 1012)

Diastasis recti refers to a separation of the two halves of the rectus abdominis muscle at the linea alba. This condition is often associated with pregnancy during the second and third trimesters, however, does not place a pregnancy at high risk.

1. **The etiology of diastasis recti is unknown, with separation greater than two centimeters considered significant. This condition is not considered high risk for pregnancy, however, can produce low back pain due to a limited ability of the abdominal muscles to stabilize the pelvis and lumbar spine.**
2. The increase in pressure associated with pregnancy may cause the cervix to open prematurely. An incompetent cervix may lead to miscarriage or premature delivery and results in a high risk pregnancy. Causative factors include previous cervical surgeries, damage during a previous birth, malformed cervix or diethylstilbestrol (DES) exposure.
3. Pre-eclampsia is a rapidly progressing condition characterized by high blood pressure and protein in the urine. Swelling, sudden weight gain, headaches, and changes in vision are common symptoms. The condition is considered a medical emergency with high risk to both the mother and baby.
4. Multiple gestation pregnancies are considered high risk since the fetal mortality rate for twins is four times that of single births. Twins have increased frequency of congenital anomalies, placenta previa, abruptio placentae, pre-eclampsia, cord accidents, and malpresentations.

System: Other Systems
Content Outline: Foundations for Evaluation, Differential Diagnosis, and Prognosis

 **Level 1**  **p. 547-548, 636**

PTEXAM ONE: QUESTION 57

A physical therapist determines that a patient is at an increased fall risk after being prescribed a new medication that tends to promote postural hypotension. Which of the following medications is the MOST consistent with the described scenario?

1. **ACE inhibitor agents**
2. Antiepileptic agents
3. Anticoagulant agents
4. Antispasticity agents

Correct Answer: 1 (Roy p. 655)

There are a variety of pharmacological agents that can significantly increase a patient's fall risk. Mechanisms contributing to the increased risk include postural hypotension, sedation, dizziness, altered vision, and disorientation. Physical therapists must be aware of common side effects of pharmacological agents in order to avoid unnecessarily jeopardizing patient safety.

1. **ACE inhibitor agents decrease blood pressure and afterload by suppressing the enzyme that converts angiotensin I to angiotensin II. Patients taking ACE inhibitors should avoid sudden changes in position due to the risk of dizziness and fainting from hypotension.**
2. Antiepileptic agents reduce or eliminate seizure activity within the brain. These agents attempt to inhibit the firing of certain cerebral neurons through various effects on the central nervous system. Patients taking antiepileptic agents may be at increased fall risk due to ataxia, confusion, and cognitive impairments.
3. Anticoagulant agents inhibit platelet aggregation and thrombus formation. The side effects associated with anticoagulant agents, such as hemorrhage, increased risk of bleeding, and gastrointestinal distress with oral medication, would not tend to increase fall risk.
4. Antispasticity agents promote relaxation in a spastic muscle. Patients taking antispasticity agents may be at increased fall risk due to drowsiness, confusion, and dizziness.

System: Cardiovascular and Pulmonary Systems
Content Outline: Foundations for Evaluation, Differential Diagnosis, and Prognosis

 Level 2  p. 414

PTEXAM ONE: QUESTION 58

A patient admitted to an acute care hospital is not able to attend a scheduled physical therapy session due to suspected critical limb ischemia. Which of the following symptoms is MOST commonly associated with this condition?

1. **Severe pain in the legs and feet at rest**
2. Increased temperature in the lower leg and foot
3. Bounding lower extremity peripheral pulses
4. Flaking skin on the legs with brownish discoloration

Correct Answer: 1 (Goodman – Pathology p. 641) 

Critical limb ischemia refers to a severe obstruction of the arteries which markedly reduces blood flow to the extremities. The condition is considered the advanced stage of peripheral artery disease which results from a progressive buildup of plaque that narrows or blocks blood flow. Critical limb ischemia is a serious medical condition that potentially threatens the sustainability of the limb.

1. **Critical limb ischemia is characterized by severe pain in the legs and feet at rest. A patient often experiences the pain when in bed and may be able to diminish the intensity of pain by hanging the legs over the edge of the bed or getting up to walk around.**
2. Critical limb ischemia is characterized by a significant decrease in temperature of the lower legs and feet due to the significant decrease in blood flow.
3. A bounding pulse refers to a full and spring-like pulse on palpation as a result of cardiac contraction or excessive volume of circulating blood within the vascular system. Critical limb ischemia is characterized by absent or diminished peripheral pulses in the legs or feet.
4. Flaking skin on the legs with brownish discoloration is more characteristic of venous insufficiency. Critical limb ischemia is characterized by shiny, smooth, dry skin on the legs or feet.

System: Cardiovascular and Pulmonary Systems
Content Outline: Foundations for Evaluation, Differential Diagnosis, and Prognosis

Level 2

PTEXAM ONE: QUESTION 59

A physical therapist treating a patient who has cerebral palsy would like to utilize a reverse walker to help with the observed gait impairments. Which of the following findings would **BEST** explain the therapist's rationale for prescribing a reverse walker instead of a traditional walker for this patient?

1. Trendelenburg gait pattern
2. Excessive upper extremity weakness
3. **Forward trunk lean with gait**
4. Excessive extensor tone

Correct Answer: 3 (Tan p. 298) 

Reverse walkers, also known as posterior walkers, are designed differently from traditional walkers in that the support system is behind the patient. As a result, the patient tends to hold the device with the shoulders in more extension and the scapulae in more depression and retraction, which leads to improved thoracic extension. Reverse walkers have also proven to be more energy efficient than traditional walkers.

1. A Trendelenburg gait pattern is characterized by contralateral hip drop and ipsilateral trunk lean and is caused by weak hip abductor musculature. A reverse walker would not be any more effective at correcting a Trendelenburg gait pattern than would a traditional walker.
2. Upper extremity weakness could affect a patient's ability to use an assistive device. Depending on the area of weakness, modifications to the assistive device may need to be made (e.g., platform attachment). However, a reverse walker would not be any easier to use than a traditional walker for a patient with upper extremity weakness.
3. **Patients with cerebral palsy may demonstrate a crouched gait pattern where they walk with a forward trunk lean and the lower extremity joints are held in flexion. A reverse walker would potentially be effective for a patient with cerebral palsy to help increase thoracic extension and therefore improve upright posture.**
4. A patient with excessive extensor tone would not benefit from a reverse walker, as this device would facilitate extension and lead to a further increase in their tone. A traditional walker may be more beneficial for patients with excessive extensor tone.

System: Non-Systems
Content Outline: Equipment, Devices, and Technologies; Therapeutic Modalities

Level 2

PTEXAM ONE: QUESTION 60

A physical therapist needs to determine the target heart rate range for a patient before beginning aerobic exercise training. The patient's resting heart rate is recorded as 60 beats per minute and the maximal heart rate is 180 beats per minute. Using the heart rate reserve method (Karvonen formula) and a range of 60-80 percent intensity, which of the following ranges **BEST** represents the patient's target heart rate when using this method?

1. 96–120 beats per minute
2. **132–156 beats per minute**
3. 144–174 beats per minute
4. 164–185 beats per minute

Correct Answer: 2 (ACSM – Resource Manual p. 473)

There are a number of formulas used to prescribe exercise intensity based on heart rate. The heart rate (HR) reserve method, also known as the Karvonen method, uses resting heart rate subtracted from the maximal heart rate to obtain the heart rate reserve. Adding 60% and 80% of the heart rate reserve to resting heart rate results in the target heart rate range. Target heart rate range = [(HRmax – HRrest) *0.60 and 0.80]+ HRrest

1. 96–120 beats per minute is less than the target heart rate range calculated using the Karvonen formula and the patient's maximal and resting heart rates.
2. **Target heart rate range = [(180 – 60) * 0.60 and 0.80] + 60 = [120*0.60 and 120*0.80] + 60 = (72 + 60) and (96 + 60) = 132–156 beats per minute**
3. 144–174 beats per minute overlaps with a portion of the target heart rate range calculated from the Karvonen formula and the patient's maximal and resting heart rates, but is too high at the lower and upper ends.
4. 164–185 beats per minute is more than the target heart rate range calculated using the Karvonen formula and the patient's maximal and resting heart rates.

System: Cardiovascular and Pulmonary Systems
Content Outline: Interventions

Level 1

p. 435-436

PTEXAM ONE: QUESTION 61

A patient who has left hemiplegia post CVA is referred for orthotic examination. Significant results of manual muscle testing include: hip flexion 3+/5, hip extension 3/5, knee flexion 3+/5, knee extension 3+/5, ankle dorsiflexion 2/5, and ankle inversion and eversion 1/5. Sensation is intact and no abnormal tone is noted. Which of the following orthoses is the MOST appropriate for this patient?

1. Knee-ankle-foot orthosis with a locked knee
2. **Plastic articulating ankle-foot orthosis**
3. Metal upright ankle-foot orthosis locked in neutral
4. Prefabricated posterior leaf spring orthosis

Correct Answer: 2 (Seymour p. 382)

The goal of an orthotic is to correct abnormal movement patterns and improve function using the least amount of intervention. A plastic ankle-foot orthosis (AFO) with an articulating ankle joint is the most appropriate orthotic based on the patient's strength, sensation and tone.

1. A knee-ankle-foot orthosis (KAFO) with a locked knee would be most appropriate for a patient that had no voluntary knee control. The locked knee ensures that the knee joint remains in an extended position and avoids genu recurvatum or collapsing of the knee during stance phase.
2. **The patient's strength at the hip and knee allows for an ankle-foot orthosis (AFO) to be used. A plastic AFO is appropriate since there is intact sensation and an articulating ankle joint is recommended to improve biomechanics during gait since there is an absence of tonal abnormalities.**
3. A metal upright AFO is normally prescribed for a patient that has fluctuating tone and/or a sensory deficit. An AFO may be locked in neutral at the ankle joint if an increase in tone exists or in the absence of voluntary motion.
4. A posterior leaf spring orthosis provides a dorsiflexion assist during gait. This type of AFO provides a spring-like dorsiflexion assist during terminal stance. Since the trim lines are posterior to the malleoli, dorsiflexion and plantar flexion can still occur during gait. The posterior leaf spring orthosis would not offer enough stability for the patient.

System: Neuromuscular and Nervous Systems
Content Outline: Interventions

Level 2

PTEXAM ONE: QUESTION 62

A patient with T10 paraplegia is discharged from a rehabilitation hospital following 12 weeks of intense rehabilitation. Which of the following pieces of equipment should the physical therapist expect to be the MOST essential to assist the patient with functional mobility?

1. Lofstrand crutches
2. Lofstrand crutches and ankle-foot orthoses
3. Lofstrand crutches and knee-ankle-foot orthoses
4. **Manual wheelchair**

Correct Answer: 4 (Roy p. 369)

A patient with a lesion above T12 would not be a functional ambulator due to the extreme energy demands and therefore would utilize a wheelchair as their primary mode of mobility.

1. A patient with an incomplete lesion may ambulate without an orthotic using Lofstrand crutches, however, this would not be an option for a complete spinal cord lesion.
2. A patient with a complete lesion at L4 or L5 would typically ambulate with crutches or canes and bilateral AFOs. The extensor digitorum, medial hamstrings, posterior tibialis, quadriceps, tibialis anterior, and low back muscles would be the lowest innervated muscles.
3. A patient with a complete lesion at L2 or L3 would typically ambulate with crutches and bilateral KAFOs. Patients at this level of injury may also use a manual wheelchair for energy conservation and convenience. The gracilis, iliopsoas, quadratus lumborum, rectus femoris, and sartorius would be the lowest innervated muscles.
4. **A patient with T10 paraplegia will require a wheelchair for community ambulation due to the increased energy expenditure associated with ambulation. The lower abdominals and intercostals would be the lowest innervated muscles.**

System: Neuromuscular and Nervous Systems
Content Outline: Interventions

Level 2  p. 298-300

PTEXAM ONE: QUESTION 63

A physical therapist instructs a patient's spouse to remove and reapply a bandage. Which of the following instructional methods would be the **MOST** appropriate to ensure that the task is performed appropriately?

1. Have the patient instruct the spouse how to remove and reapply the bandage
2. Provide written instructions on how to remove and reapply the bandage
3. **Instruct the spouse to remove and reapply the bandage and observe their performance**
4. Instruct the spouse to contact the physical therapy department if they have specific questions on how to remove or reapply the bandage

Correct Answer: 3 (Brody p. 41) 

The physical therapist should observe the removal and reapplication of the bandage in order to determine if the spouse is capable of performing the task. Although this will not ensure the task is done appropriately in the future, it will provide the patient with the opportunity for feedback based on their current performance.

1. If the patient instructs the spouse how to remove and reapply the bandage, the therapist can conclude that the patient can explain the task, but this does not ensure that the spouse can independently perform the task.
2. Written instructions are helpful for the patient and spouse as a resource, but will not ensure independence. Demonstration is the best instructional method to ensure proper technique and independence.
3. **Patient and family education is a critical component of a comprehensive plan of care. Direct observation of the spouse's performance is the best method to increase the probability that the activity will be performed correctly.**
4. The physical therapist would be exercising poor judgment if they requested the patient to call the department with questions on bandaging without providing additional instruction. The therapist must provide instruction and observe the family members' performance to ensure competence.

System: Other Systems
Content Outline: Interventions

 Level 3  p. 798-799

PTEXAM ONE: QUESTION 64

A physical therapist treats a patient for a pressure injury on the ischial tuberosity and is concerned about the risk of infection caused by the patient's weakened immune system. Which of the following patients would have the **LOWEST** risk for infection?

1. A 55-year-old patient with malabsorption syndrome
2. A 50-year-old patient with acquired immune deficiency syndrome
3. A 60-year-old patient receiving monthly cortisone injections
4. **A 65-year-old patient with iron-deficiency anemia**

Correct Answer: 4 (Goodman – Pathology p. 276)

There are several factors that can influence the strength of the immune system, including age, nutrition, trauma, surgery, certain medical conditions, use of immunosuppressive drugs, sleep deprivation, and stress. In general, increased age is associated with a weaker immune system.

1. A patient with malabsorption syndrome has difficulty digesting and absorbing nutrients. Poor nutritional status is one factor that can significantly affect immune system function. Deficiencies of protein, vitamin A, vitamin E or zinc can result in reduced function of the T cells and B cells, which aid in immune function.
2. Human immunodeficiency virus (HIV) and acquired immune deficiency syndrome (AIDS) are two related diseases that result in reduced functioning of the immune system. AIDS is characterized by the destruction of lymphocytes, which play a major role in defending the body from invading organisms.
3. Cortisone is a corticosteroid medication that is used in the treatment of inflammatory conditions (e.g., bursitis). A common side effect of cortisone is suppression of the immune system. Long-term or frequent use of these medications can result in immunosuppression.
4. **Anemia is a condition characterized by reduced oxygen-carrying capacity of the blood. This condition is not associated with any change in immune system function. Though this patient is older than the other options (i.e., 65 years old), this small difference in age would not make up for the fact that this patient has no other risk factors for immunosuppression.**

System: Other Systems
Content Outline: Foundations for Evaluation, Differential Diagnosis, and Prognosis

 Level 3  p. 500-501

PTEXAM ONE: QUESTION 65

A patient presents with left upper extremity lymphedema post mastectomy. The physical therapist plans to initiate lymphatic drainage exercises as part of the plan of care. Which of the following breathing exercises is the **MOST** appropriate for the therapist to teach the patient to perform prior to initiating lymphatic drainage exercises?

1. Segmental breathing
2. **Diaphragmatic breathing**
3. Paced breathing
4. Inspiratory muscle training

Correct Answer: 2 (Kisner p. 1035)

Lymphatic drainage exercises can help improve lymph flow by increasing lymph vessel contractions, increasing fluid uptake in the initial lymph vessels, improving the "muscle pump" to stimulate lymph flow, and increasing deep breathing, which improves lymph flow in the thoracic duct.

1. Segmental breathing is intended to improve regional ventilation and prevent and treat pulmonary complications after surgery. It is based on the presumption that asymmetrical chest wall motion may coincide with underlying pathology (e.g., pneumonia, pleurisy) and that inspired air can be directed to a particular area by facilitation or inhibition of chest wall movement.
2. **Diaphragmatic breathing should be performed prior to lymphatic drainage exercises. Diaphragmatic breathing can assist in the movement of lymphatic fluid as the diaphragm descends during inspiration to increase the thoracic cavity volume and then the abdominals contract to assist with a controlled expiration. Changes in intra-abdominal and intra-thoracic pressures help create a continual, gentle pumping action that moves fluid in the lymphatic vessels. The use of diaphragmatic breathing is an important component throughout the exercise regimen for the management of lymphedema.**
3. Paced breathing is a strategy to decrease the work of breathing and prevent dyspnea during activity. It allows anyone who experiences shortness of breath to become less fearful of activity and exercise. Shortness of breath is not typically associated with lymphedema.
4. Inspiratory muscle training (IMT) attempts to strengthen the diaphragm and intercostal muscles. Two different IMT devices provide different modes of training: flow resistive breathing and threshold breathing. Indications for IMT include impaired inspiratory muscle strength and/or a ventilatory limitation to exercise performance. This strengthening exercise would not be essential prior to initiating lymphatic drainage exercises.

System: Other Systems
Content Outline: Interventions

Level 2  **p. 440-441, 552-555, 616-617**

PTEXAM ONE: QUESTION 66

A physical therapist instructs a patient in pelvic floor muscle strengthening exercises. Which of the following verbal cues would be the **MOST** effective to assist the patient to perform a pelvic floor contraction?

1. Tighten your muscles like you were trying to expel a large amount of urine in a very short amount of time
2. **Pull your muscles upward and inward as if attempting to stop the flow of urine**
3. Tighten your abdominal muscles and anteriorly rotate your pelvis
4. Gently push out as if you had to pass gas

Correct Answer: 2 (Brody p. 498)

The pelvic floor muscles support the pelvic organs against intra-abdominal pressure, provide closure of the urethra and rectum for continence, and support sexual function. Pelvic floor exercises, also known as Kegel exercises, assist to maintain the strength and function of the pelvic floor muscles.

1. Placing a downward pressure on the pelvic floor serves to increase intra-abdominal pressure and encourages protrusion or prolapse of the pelvic organs.
2. **The correct technique for pelvic floor exercises includes pulling the pelvic floor muscles up and in. Isometric contractions should be held for five to ten seconds with complete relaxation after each contraction. Five to ten contractions should be performed in a series and three to four series should be performed each day.**
3. Tightening the abdominal muscles will trigger reflexive contraction of the pelvic floor, however, anteriorly rotating the pelvis will lengthen the abdominal muscles. Performing both actions simultaneously will reduce the strength of any pelvic floor contraction.
4. The act of "gently pushing out as if you had to pass gas" places a downward pressure on the pelvic floor muscles. This action is opposite of the necessary action for pelvic floor strengthening.

System: Other Systems
Content Outline: Interventions

 **Level 2**  **p. 548**

PTEXAM ONE: QUESTION 67

According to proponents of evidence-based medicine, which type of research provides the **BEST** source of information upon which to make clinical decisions about therapy for an individual patient?

1. Cohort study
2. Randomized controlled trial
3. **Systematic review**
4. Case report

Correct Answer: 3 (Straus p. 98) 

The hierarchy of evidence ranks the strength of the different types of clinical evidence, studies or clinical trials from those with the least amount of bias to those with the potential for the greatest amount of bias.

1. Cohort studies are observation studies in which subjects are classified according to the presence or absence of a particular risk factor or exposure and followed over time to determine disease outcomes. Cohort studies do not evaluate the effect of therapy.
2. In a randomized controlled trial, patients are randomized into an experimental and a control group. Both groups are followed up for the variables or outcomes of interest. Randomized-control trials provide strong evidence for or against a therapy, but are not considered to be the highest level of evidence.
3. **Systematic reviews are summaries of the medical literature that use explicit methods to perform a thorough literature search, a critical appraisal of individual studies, and statistical techniques to combine results. Systematic reviews are considered to provide the highest level of evidence for or against a therapy.**
4. A case report is an in-depth description of an interesting condition or response to treatment. A case report is the least rigorous form of research because of its inherent lack of control and limited generalizability.

System: Non-Systems
Content Outline: Safety and Protection; Professional Responsibilities; Research

 **Level 1**  **p. 803**

PTEXAM ONE: QUESTION 68

A patient exercising in an outpatient clinic informs the physical therapist that they are experiencing chest pain. After resting for 20 minutes the patient's condition is unchanged, however, they insist it is something that they can work through. Which of the following actions is the **MOST** appropriate for the therapist to take?

1. Allow the patient to resume exercise and continue to monitor the patient's condition
2. Reduce the intensity of the exercise and continue to monitor the patient's condition
3. Discontinue the treatment session and encourage the patient to make an appointment with their physician
4. **Discontinue the treatment session and call an ambulance**

Correct Answer: 4 (Hillegass p. 535) 

Changes in anginal symptoms may reflect a change in coronary status. Any increase or change in anginal symptoms should be recorded and receive immediate medical attention.

1. Continued angina after 20 minutes of rest is cause for concern since it may indicate a serious change in the patient's coronary status. The patient should not be allowed to exercise, even if the patient indicates they can work through it.
2. Reducing the intensity of exercise does not negate the fact that the patient has continued angina after 20 minutes of rest.
3. Discontinuing the treatment session is necessary, however, encouraging the patient to make an appointment with their physician does not ensure that the patient will receive immediate medical attention.
4. **If anginal symptoms are not relieved by stopping exercise, or the use of three sublingual nitroglycerin tablets (one taken every five minutes), the patient should be transported to the nearest hospital emergency center.**

System: Cardiovascular and Pulmonary Systems
Content Outline: Interventions

 **Level 3**  **p. 399-400, 446, 468**

PTEXAM ONE: QUESTION 69

A physical therapist attempts to determine the number of known risk factors a patient has for coronary artery disease prior to initiating an aerobic exercise program. Which of the following objective findings would serve as the **MOST** relevant risk factor?

1. Blood pressure = 128/78 mm Hg
2. **Waist-hip ratio = 1.15**
3. Low-density lipoproteins = 96 mg/dL
4. Body mass index = 23.9 kg/m^2

Correct Answer: 2 (ACSM – Resource Manual p. 291)

Coronary artery disease is a condition characterized by a narrowing or blockage of the coronary arteries. Signs and symptoms of this condition include angina and, if it progresses, myocardial infarction. Risk factors for coronary artery disease include advanced age, cigarette smoking, sedentary lifestyle, obesity, hypertension, dyslipidemia, and prediabetes.

1. Stage 1 hypertension is characterized by systolic blood pressure from 130-139 mm Hg or diastolic blood pressure from 80-89 mm Hg. A blood pressure of 128/78 mm Hg would be classified as elevated and would not be considered as relevant a risk factor for coronary artery disease as a waist-hip ratio of 1.15.
2. **Waist-hip ratio is the ratio of the circumference of the waist to that of the hips. A waist-hip ratio of greater than 0.9 is an indication of central obesity and a risk factor for coronary artery disease. The patient's value of 1.15 is well above this level.**
3. Low-density lipoproteins (LDL) are the major carriers of cholesterol in plasma. High levels of LDL cholesterol increase the risk of coronary artery disease. The optimal level of low-density lipoprotein cholesterol is less than 100 mg/dL. The patient's low-density lipoprotein value is below this threshold.
4. The body mass index (BMI) is used to assess weight relative to height and is calculated by dividing body weight (kilograms) by height (meters squared). A BMI of greater than 30 is associated with an increased risk of hypertension, hypercholesterolemia, coronary artery disease, and mortality. A BMI from 18.5 - 24.9 is considered normal.

System: Other Systems
Content Outline: Physical Therapy Examination

 **Level 2**  **p. 402, 434, 469, 576**

PTEXAM ONE: QUESTION 70

A physical therapist treats a patient with several injuries impacting the upper extremity including mallet finger. The therapist notes that the affected finger is immobilized using a static splint. Which position of the finger would be the **MOST** essential when splinting?

1. 5 degrees of flexion at the distal interphalangeal joint
2. 5 degrees of flexion at the proximal interphalangeal joint
3. **5 degrees of hyperextension at the distal interphalangeal joint**
4. 5 degrees of hyperextension at the proximal interphalangeal joint

Correct Answer: 3 (Higgins p. 770)

Mallet finger refers to an injury of the extensor digitorum tendon at the distal interphalangeal joint. The injury most often occurs when the finger is abruptly forced into flexion at the distal interphalangeal joint.

1. Splinting in 5 degrees of flexion at the distal interphalangeal joint would serve to lengthen the extensor tendon. Once the extensor tendon has healed in a lengthened position, full extension of the distal interphalangeal joint cannot be achieved.
2. The position of the proximal interphalangeal joint is not as critical when treating mallet finger since the injury affects the distal interphalangeal joint. If the patient has a swan neck deformity, it may be necessary to splint the proximal interphalangeal joint in slight flexion while simultaneously splinting the distal interphalangeal joint in slight hyperextension.
3. **Splinting in 5 degrees of hyperextension allows the extensor tendon to heal in an optimal position without becoming excessively lengthened. The amount of hyperextension should be very slight since too much can cause ischemia to the skin. Splinting may be required for as long as 6-8 weeks.**
4. The position of the proximal interphalangeal joint is not as critical when treating mallet finger since the injury affects the distal interphalangeal joint.

System: Musculoskeletal System
Content Outline: Foundations for Evaluation, Differential Diagnosis, and Prognosis

 **Level 1**

PTEXAM ONE: QUESTION 71

A physical therapist treats a patient with a peroneal tendon subluxation. To observe the subluxation, which of the following motions is the **MOST** appropriate to reproduce the subluxation?

1. Active ankle plantar flexion and inversion
2. **Active ankle dorsiflexion and eversion**
3. Passive ankle plantar flexion and inversion
4. Passive ankle dorsiflexion and eversion

Correct Answer: 2 (Higgins p. 328) 

Peroneal tendon subluxation occurs when the peroneus longus and/or peroneus brevis displace from the retromalleolar groove with peroneal tendon loading. The initial cause of the subluxation may occur during an inversion ankle sprain when the peroneals are forcefully stretched, damaging the retinaculum that maintains the tendons in the retromalleolar groove. Patients with a peroneal tendon subluxation often describe a painful "snapping" or "popping" sensation at the lateral malleolus. Patients with this condition often present with lateral ankle effusion and tenderness to palpation in the retromalleolar groove.

1. The peroneus longus and brevis act as strong evertors of the ankle. As a result, inversion would not be useful to reproduce the subluxation.
2. **Active ankle dorsiflexion and eversion often serve as the preferred action to reproduce the subluxation. Plantar flexion or circumduction may also be useful. Although reproducing the subluxation is not necessarily desirable, it is important for the therapist to initially observe the subluxation.**
3. The peroneus longus and brevis act as strong evertors of the ankle. As a result, inversion would not be useful to reproduce the subluxation. In addition, since the tendon is a contractile structure, active range of motion is necessary.
4. Ankle dorsiflexion and eversion are often used to reproduce the subluxation, however, active motion is required since the tendon is a contractile structure.

System: Musculoskeletal System
Content Outline: Foundations for Evaluation, Differential Diagnosis, and Prognosis

Level 1

PTEXAM ONE: QUESTION 72

A patient with chronic edema in the extremities is told that they have a form of primary lymphedema. Which of the following conditions is an example of primary lymphedema?

1. Filariasis
2. Mastectomy
3. **Milroy's disease**
4. Lymphadenitis

Correct Answer: 3 (Hillegass p. 658)

Lymphedema is categorized as either primary or secondary lymphedema based on the etiology. Primary lymphedema occurs due to an abnormal development of the lymphatic system. Secondary lymphedema occurs as a result of some other disease or injury that causes damage to the lymphatic system.

1. Filariasis is a disease that is caused by a parasitic infection and can lead to lymphedema. Because the parasitic infection is what causes the lymphedema, it is considered a form of secondary lymphedema.
2. Mastectomy refers to the surgical removal of breast tissue, which is often performed because of breast cancer. When a mastectomy is performed, lymph nodes may be removed or damaged, which can lead to lymphedema. Because it is the surgical procedure that causes the lymphedema, it is considered a form of secondary lymphedema.
3. **Milroy's disease is an inherited disease that presents during infancy and is characterized by lymphedema. Because the lymphedema is caused by developmental abnormalities of the lymphatic system, it is considered a form of primary lymphedema.**
4. Lymphadenitis is a condition that is characterized by infection and inflammation of a lymph node. Though this condition also affects the lymphatic system, it is not a form of lymphedema.

System: Other Systems
Content Outline: Foundations for Evaluation, Differential Diagnosis, and Prognosis

Level 1  p. 552-555

PTEXAM ONE: QUESTION 73

A patient post hip surgery receives opioids through patient-controlled analgesia. Which objective finding would be the MOST responsible for a decision to terminate opioid use?

1. Oxygen saturation rate of 94%
2. **Respiratory rate of 9 breaths per minute**
3. Resting pulse rate of 80 beats per minute
4. Body temperature of 99.4 degrees Fahrenheit

Correct Answer: 2 (Ciccone p. 211) 

Patient-controlled analgesia allows the patient to manage their pain by delivering an intravenous analgesic dose with preset parameters. Opioids are often the self-administered medication used with patient-controlled analgesia.

1. Oxygen saturation rate measures the amount of oxygen bound to hemoglobin in the blood. Normal oxygen saturation is 95-98 percent. An oxygen saturation rate of 94% would be only slightly below the normal value and therefore would not be associated with a decision to terminate opioid use.
2. **Opioids are central nervous system depressants that are commonly administered with patient-controlled analgesia. Opioids tend to decrease respiratory rate. A rate below 10 breaths per minute is typically used as a guideline to terminate opioid use. A normal resting respiratory rate in an adult is 12-20 breaths per minute.**
3. A resting pulse rate of 80 beats per minute is within the normal range of 60-100 beats per minute for an adult and therefore would not be associated with a decision to terminate opioid use.
4. Normal body temperature is 98.6 degrees Fahrenheit or 37 degrees Celsius. An increase or decrease of one degree Fahrenheit for a given individual can be considered normal. As a result, a temperature of 99.4 degrees Fahrenheit would not be associated with a decision to terminate opioid use.

System: Non-Systems
Content Outline: Safety and Protection; Professional Responsibilities; Research

 **Level 2** **p. 132-133, 585**

PTEXAM ONE: QUESTION 74

A physical therapist witnesses a motor vehicle accident in which a passenger is badly injured and appears to have sustained a partial amputation of the lower leg. The patient is able to move their arms and legs, however, the therapist is concerned that the victim is experiencing symptoms of shock. What type of shock is the MOST consistent with this scenario?

1. Septic
2. Neurogenic
3. Cardiogenic
4. **Hypovolemic**

Correct Answer: 4 (Goodman – Pathology p. 706)

Shock is a condition that occurs when blood flow to the organs becomes diminished. There are several causes of shock including sepsis, cardiac problems, injury to the central nervous system, hypovolemia, and anaphylaxis. Shock is characterized by hypotension, tachycardia, hyperventilation, diaphoresis, pallor, confusion, and anxiety.

1. Sepsis, which is a systemic infection, is one possible cause for the onset of shock. Though the victim has an open wound and could have acquired an infection, it is unlikely that the infection would have spread through the body and resulted in symptoms of shock immediately after the accident.
2. Neurogenic shock occurs when there is an insult to the neurological system, specifically the central nervous system. It does not appear that the victim has acquired a spinal cord injury since it states that they are able to move their arms and legs.
3. Cardiogenic shock occurs when cardiac problems lead to poor perfusion of the organs, as may occur with heart failure or a myocardial infarction. There is nothing in the scenario that indicates the victim is experiencing cardiac problems.
4. **Hypovolemic shock occurs when severe blood loss results in decreased perfusion of the organs. The scenario states that the patient has a partial amputation of the leg and thus they have likely lost a high volume of blood.**

System: Non-Systems
Content Outline: Safety and Protection; Professional Responsibilities; Research

 **Level 3**  **p. 44, 766**

PTEXAM ONE: QUESTION 75

A patient with a transfemoral amputation is assigned a K-level of 1. Based on the K-level assignment, which functional task would represent the patient's **HIGHEST** anticipated level of function?

1. Propelling a manual wheelchair
2. **Walking short distances in the home**
3. Negotiating six stairs
4. Walking down a sloped driveway to a mailbox

Correct Answer: 2 (May p. 107)

K-levels are used by Medicare based on an individual's ability or potential to ambulate and navigate their environment. The rating system consists of a 0-4 scale and is used to inform decisions on the type of prosthetic device provided and the payment for the device.

1. A K-level of 1 indicates that ambulation on level surfaces is possible and therefore propelling a manual wheelchair would not represent the highest anticipated functional level.
2. **Walking short distances in the home is characteristic of a K-level of 1. Specifically, a K-level of 1 is characterized by the ability to transfer using the prosthesis and ambulate on level surfaces with a fixed cadence.**
3. The ability to traverse low level barriers (e.g., curbs, stairs, uneven surfaces) is characteristic of a K-level of 2 or above.
4. Walking down a sloped driveway to a mailbox would require the patient to safely traverse on an uneven surface. This functional task would require a minimum K-level of 2.

System: Musculoskeletal System
Content Outline: Physical Therapy Examination

 Level 1  p. 138-139

PTEXAM ONE: QUESTION 76

A physical therapist informs a patient that a ramp needed to access the patient's home with a wheelchair will require two separate sections with a landing area. What variable would have **MOST** likely influenced this decision?

1. Slope of the ramp
2. Angle of inclination of the ramp
3. **Length of the ramp**
4. Width of the ramp

Correct Answer: 3 (Minor p. 19) 

Physical therapists routinely conduct home visits to determine accessibility needs. During a home visit, a variety of standard measurements are taken and then compared to acceptable accessibility guidelines established by the Americans with Disabilities Act. Although the guidelines established by the Americans with Disabilities Act are not enforced in a patient's home, they are nonetheless useful when attempting to determine obstacles to accessibility.

1. The slope of the ramp describes the relative relationship of rise to run. The slope should be no greater than one inch of rise for every 12 inches of run. Slope is a critical factor in ramp design, but is not directly linked to the number of sections of a ramp.
2. The angle of inclination of the ramp is an alternate method for expressing slope. The angle of inclination is expressed as a percent grade. A percent grade of 100% would be completely vertical while a percent grade of 0% would be completely horizontal. The percent grade is determined by taking the rise, dividing the value by the run, and then multiplying the number by 100 to convert the value to a percentage.
3. **The length of the ramp is the most critical variable to consider when determining the number of sections of a ramp. Any ramp with more than 30 consecutive feet of horizontal run would require more than one section and a transitional landing area.**
4. The width of the ramp would not be a relevant variable when determining the necessary sections of a ramp. A ramp should be a minimum of 36 inches wide according to the Americans with Disabilities Act.

System: Non-Systems
Content Outline: Safety and Protection; Professional Responsibilities; Research

 Level 3  p. 770-771

PTEXAM ONE: QUESTION 77

An employee with a disclosed disability informs their employer that they are unable to perform an essential function of their job unless their workstation is modified. Which of the following would provide the employer with a legitimate reason for denying the employee's request?

1. **The accommodation would cost hundreds of dollars**
2. **The accommodation would require an expansion of the employee's present workstation**
3. **The accommodation would fundamentally alter the operation of the business**
4. **The accommodation would not address the needs of other employees**

Correct Answer: 3 (Fairchild p. 349) 

The Americans with Disabilities Act was designed to provide a clear and comprehensive national mandate for the elimination of discrimination. Employers are required to make reasonable accommodations for qualified individuals with a disability who satisfy the job-related requirements of a position held or desired.

1. An accommodation that costs hundreds of dollars does not necessarily indicate that the accommodation is unreasonable or creates an "undue hardship" for the employer.
2. Workstation modifications are common and are most often designed to allow a qualified employee or applicant to perform an essential job function.
3. **An accommodation that fundamentally alters the operation of a business would be considered an "undue hardship."**
4. The Americans with Disabilities Act applies primarily, but not exclusively, to "disabled" individuals. It is not necessary to ensure that an accommodation made for a qualified individual addresses the needs of other employees.

System: Non-Systems
Content Outline: Safety and Protection; Professional Responsibilities; Research

Level 2 p. 770

PTEXAM ONE: QUESTION 78

A physical therapist prepares to measure a patient's blood pressure prior to treatment. Which of the following values describes the MOST appropriate rate to release the pressure when obtaining the blood pressure measurement?

1. **2-3 mm Hg per second**
2. **3-5 mm Hg per second**
3. **5-7 mm Hg per second**
4. **8-10 mm Hg per second**

Correct Answer: 1 (Fairchild p. 60) 

Deflating the cuff at a rate of 2-3 mm Hg per second is recommended to identify normal Korotkoff sounds and obtain a valid measure of the patient's blood pressure. Rates faster than 2-3 mm Hg per second will tend to increase the measurement error.

1. **After inflating the cuff to 20 mm Hg above the estimated systolic pressure, the therapist should carefully unscrew (open) the valve and deflate the bladder no more than 2-3 mm Hg per second while listening for the Korotkoff sounds.**
2. 3-5 mm Hg per second is faster than the recommended rate of 2-3 mm Hg per second.
3. 5-7 mm Hg per second is more than twice as fast as the recommended rate of 2-3 mm Hg per second.
4. 8-10 mm Hg per second is more than three times as fast as the recommended rate of 2-3 mm Hg per second.

System: Cardiovascular and Pulmonary Systems
Content Outline: Physical Therapy Examination

 Level 1  p. 419-420

PTEXAM ONE: QUESTION 79

A physician prescribes a spinal brace for a patient with chronic low back pain. Which of the following braces would be the **MOST** appropriate if the objective is to allow spinal motion while increasing intra-abdominal pressure?

1. Taylor
2. Milwaukee
3. Jewett
4. **Corset**

Correct Answer: 4 (Tan p. 240) 

Spinal braces may be used to stabilize, support, and/or realign the trunk. Additionally, they can be used to protect the spine after a traumatic event or surgery. The specific brace selected should be based on the established therapeutic objectives.

1. A Taylor brace is a thoracolumbosacral orthosis (TLSO) that consists of two posterior rigid struts that attach inferiorly to a pelvic band and superiorly to axillary straps. The brace primarily limits trunk motion in the sagittal plane.
2. A Milwaukee brace is a cervicothoracolumbosacral orthosis (CTLSO) that consists of a TLSO with an upward extension to the mandible and mastoid. This brace is primarily used to help correct scoliotic curvatures.
3. A Jewett brace is a TLSO that has two plates anteriorly, at the sternal and suprapubic regions, and one plate posteriorly, at the lumbar region. The brace primarily limits trunk flexion and encourages an erect posture.
4. **A corset brace is a non-rigid spinal orthosis that is made of fabric and contains pouches for the optional addition of flexible vertical stays. Because of this, it will not restrict spinal motion like rigid braces will. However, because corset braces fit more snugly to the body, they are more effective at increasing intra-abdominal pressure than are rigid orthoses.**

System: Non-Systems
Content Outline: Equipment, Devices, and Technologies; Therapeutic Modalities

 **Level 1** **p. 134-135**

PTEXAM ONE: QUESTION 80

A patient exhibits a compensatory contralateral step-to gait pattern and persistent left knee pain. Which of the following conditions would **MOST** likely result in this type of long-term compensatory gait pattern?

1. **Degenerative joint disease**
2. Anterior cruciate ligament sprain
3. Osgood-Schlatter disease
4. Patellofemoral syndrome

Correct Answer: 1 (Dunleavy p. 79)

A compensatory contralateral step-to gait pattern for a patient with left knee pain refers to a shortened swing phase on the right when the left limb is in the stance phase of gait. Protective gait patterns (e.g., antalgic gait) are often the result of disease (usually bone or joint), joint inflammation or injuries to muscles, tendons, and/or ligaments.

1. **Osteoarthritis is a chronic disease that causes degeneration of articular cartilage, primarily in weight bearing joints (e.g., knee, hip). Subsequent deformity and thickening of subchondral bone occur resulting in impaired functional status. As the disease progresses in severity, the patient may present with a deviated gait pattern, atypical movement patterns, and muscle atrophy. The described gait deviation would most likely occur over time with the progression of degenerative joint disease.**
2. An anterior cruciate ligament sprain is characterized by significant knee pain, effusion, and edema that significantly limit range of motion. The patient may be unable to bear weight on the involved extremity resulting in dependence on an assistive device. Although a patient may exhibit an antalgic gait with a contralateral step-to gait pattern in the early stages of an anterior cruciate ligament sprain, this compensatory gait pattern would not be expected over the long term.
3. Osgood-Schlatter disease refers to traction apophysitis occurring at the tibial tuberosity. It typically affects adolescents involved in sports that require a great deal of running, jumping, swift directional changes, and repeated knee flexion (e.g., soccer, ballet). Although an antalgic gait pattern may likely occur with Osgood-Schlatter disease, it is a self-limiting condition that typically has an excellent prognosis.
4. Patellofemoral syndrome is caused by an abnormal tracking of the patella (usually laterally) between the femoral condyles. Prognosis for a full recovery is good with successful conservative management of patellofemoral syndrome. Long-term gait compensation is more likely to occur with degenerative joint disease.

System: Musculoskeletal System
Content Outline: Foundations for Evaluation, Differential Diagnosis, and Prognosis

PTEXAM ONE: QUESTION 81

A physical therapist prepares a patient for a graded exercise test using an arm cycle ergometer instead of a treadmill due to a lower extremity injury. Which objective finding is the MOST accurate when using the arm cycle ergometer instead of the treadmill?

1. The results of the testing will be more heavily influenced by patient motivation.
2. **The obtained maximum oxygen consumption will be significantly lower.**
3. The work level associated with the point of volitional fatigue will be greater.
4. The incremental work levels will be progressively shortened during testing.

Correct Answer: 2 (ACSM – Resource Manual p. 331)

A treadmill is the most commonly used equipment for clinical exercise testing. Arm cycle ergometry is an acceptable alternative for patients without the ability to engage in exercise using the legs.

1. All forms of graded exercise testing are heavily influenced by patient motivation, however, this limitation is not necessarily exaggerated with arm cycle ergometry.
2. **The obtained maximum oxygen consumption with arm cycle ergometry is typically 20-30% lower than the value obtained with treadmill testing. The lower maximum oxygen consumption with arm cycle ergometry is due to the smaller muscle mass of the arms compared to the larger muscle mass of the legs.**
3. The work level associated with the point of volitional fatigue is generally smaller with arm cycle ergometry than with treadmill testing due to the smaller muscle mass of the arms compared to the larger muscle mass of the legs.
4. The incremental work levels are not necessarily shortened with arm cycle ergometry and instead are determined based on the patient's perceived functional capacity. Typically, work levels are chosen so that the total test time ranges between 8 and 12 minutes.

System: Cardiovascular and Pulmonary Systems
Content Outline: Physical Therapy Examination

 Level 2  p. 435-436

PTEXAM ONE: QUESTION 82

A physical therapist assesses the vital signs of a patient with a blood disorder. The therapist records the patient's blood pressure as 150/85 mm Hg. Which of the following conditions is the MOST likely cause of the abnormal blood pressure measurement?

1. Anemia
2. Thrombocytosis
3. Leukopenia
4. **Polycythemia**

Correct Answer: 4 (Goodman – Differential Diagnosis p. 215)

Normal blood pressure is defined as systolic blood pressure less than 120 mm Hg and diastolic blood pressure less than 80 mm Hg. There are several different underlying mechanisms that may result in hypertension.

1. Anemia is defined as a reduction in the oxygen-carrying capacity of the blood due to an abnormality in the quantity or quality of the red blood cells. Signs and symptoms include skin pallor, fatigue, dyspnea, angina, headache, and dizziness. In patients with anemia, diastolic blood pressure may be lower than normal, though systolic blood pressure is usually unaffected.
2. Thrombocytosis is defined as an increase in the platelet count of the blood. Blood viscosity becomes increased due to the high platelet count, which results in an increased risk for thrombosis. Despite the increase in blood viscosity, this condition is not associated with an increase in blood pressure.
3. Leukopenia is defined as a reduction in the number of white blood cells. This condition can result from chemotherapy or radiation therapy, dietary deficiencies, infectious diseases, and autoimmune diseases. Signs and symptoms include fever, chills, sweating, mucous membrane ulcerations, and infections. Patients with leukopenia will not typically experience abnormalities in blood pressure, assuming the absence of other relevant medical conditions.
4. **Polycythemia is defined as an increase in the number of red blood cells and concentration of hemoglobin. This condition results in increased blood viscosity and increased blood volume, thus resulting in elevated blood pressure measurements. Other signs and symptoms include fatigue, dyspnea, headache, dizziness, irritability, blurred vision, decreased mental acuity, and sensory disturbances.**

System: Cardiovascular and Pulmonary Systems
Content Outline: Foundations for Evaluation, Differential Diagnosis, and Prognosis

 Level 2  p. 395, 419-420

PTEXAM ONE: QUESTION 83

A physical therapist prepares to assess the blink reflex in a patient with suspected neurological involvement. Which cranial nerve components are assessed with this reflex?

1. **Afferent cranial nerve V; efferent cranial nerve VII**
2. Afferent cranial nerve VII; efferent cranial nerve V
3. Afferent cranial nerve IX; efferent cranial nerve X
4. Afferent cranial nerve X; efferent cranial nerve IX

Correct Answer: 1 (Umphred p. 1011) 

The corneal (i.e., blink) reflex refers to an involuntary blinking of the eyelids elicited by stimulation of the cornea. The stimulus is typically applied with a wisp of cotton or a cotton swab. The normal response is concurrent blinking of the eyes with contact to the sclera. Afferent nerves are considered to be sensory nerves, while efferent nerves are considered to be motor nerves.

1. **The afferent cranial nerve V (trigeminal) is associated with face sensation. The efferent cranial nerve VII (facial) is responsible for closing the eyes.**
2. The afferent cranial nerve VII (facial) is associated with taste on the anterior tongue. The efferent cranial nerve V (trigeminal) is responsible for the muscles of mastication.
3. The afferent cranial nerve IX (glossopharyngeal) is associated with taste on the posterior tongue. The efferent cranial nerve X (vagus) is responsible for muscles of the palate, pharynx, and larynx.
4. The afferent cranial nerve X (vagus) is associated with taste receptors on the palate and epiglottis. The efferent cranial nerve IX (glossopharyngeal) is responsible for muscles of the pharynx.

System: Neuromuscular and Nervous Systems
Content Outline: Physical Therapy Examination

 Level 1  p. 247-249, 252

PTEXAM ONE: QUESTION 84

A physical therapist designs a training program for a patient without cardiovascular pathology. The therapist calculates the patient's age-predicted maximal heart rate as 175 beats per minute. Which of the following target heart rates would be the **MOST** appropriate for the patient during cardiovascular exercise?

1. 93 beats per minute
2. **135 beats per minute**
3. 169 beats per minute
4. 195 beats per minute

Correct Answer: 2 (ACSM – Resource Manual p. 473) 

The target heart rate for exercise can be approximated using a percentage of the maximum heart rate, which can be estimated as 220 – age. With this approach, 70-85% of maximum heart rate or 50-70% of maximum oxygen uptake (VO_{2max}) is the recommended exercise intensity according to the American College of Sports Medicine. If the maximal heart rate is 175 beats per minute, the target heart rate range is (70% x 175) to (85% x 175), or 123 to 149 beats per minute. Some sources recommend a more broadly defined target heart rate range of 60-90%. In either case, the correct answer would be option 2.

1. 93 beats per minute is below the recommended range for exercise intensity. 93 beats per minute corresponds to 53% of the maximum heart rate.
2. **135 beats per minute is within the recommended range for exercise intensity. 135 beats per minute corresponds to 77% of the maximum heart rate.**
3. 169 beats per minute is above the recommended range for exercise intensity. 169 beats per minute corresponds to 97% of the maximum heart rate.
4. 195 beats per minute is above the recommended range for exercise intensity. 195 beats per minute corresponds to 111% of the maximum heart rate.

System: Cardiovascular and Pulmonary Systems
Content Outline: Interventions

 Level 1  p. 435-436

PTEXAM ONE: QUESTION 85

A patient with complete C5 tetraplegia works on a forward raise for pressure relief. The patient utilizes loops that are attached to the back of the wheelchair to assist with the forward raise. Which muscles should be particularly strong in order for the patient to be successful with the forward raise?

1. **Brachioradialis, brachialis**
2. **Rhomboids, levator scapulae**
3. **Biceps, deltoids**
4. **Triceps, flexor digitorum profundus**

Correct Answer: 3 (Roy p. 363)

A patient with C5 tetraplegia would not have muscles innervated below the C5 level. Primary innervations and actions for each of the muscles are listed.

1. The brachioradialis (C5-C6) and brachialis (C5-C6) would both be innervated. The primary action of the brachioradialis and brachialis is to flex the elbow.
2. The rhomboids (C4-C5) and levator scapulae (C3-C5) would both be innervated. The rhomboids adduct and rotate the scapula downward. The levator scapulae elevate and rotate the scapula downward.
3. **The biceps (C5-C6) and deltoids (C5-C6) would both be innervated. The deltoids (anterior, middle, posterior) assist with all shoulder motions with the exception of adduction. The biceps act to flex the shoulder, flex the elbow, and supinate the forearm.**
4. The triceps (C7-C8) and flexor digitorum profundus (C8-T1) would not be innervated in a patient with C5 tetraplegia.

System: Neuromuscular and Nervous Systems
Content Outline: Interventions

 **Level 2**  **p. 70-71, 245-246**

PTEXAM ONE: QUESTION 86

A patient is referred to physical therapy for fall prevention training. The physical therapist determines that the patient has difficulty adapting their vision from low lighting to bright environments. Which of the following home modifications would be the MOST appropriate based on this information?

1. **Use unfiltered direct lighting**
2. **Replace bathroom light bulbs with red bulbs**
3. **Use diffuse lighting**
4. **Use only dim lighting**

Correct Answer: 3 (Kaufman p. 361)

Glare sensitivity is a common visual impairment experienced by aging adults. This makes transitioning between bright and dark areas more difficult, and can result in loss of balance or falling if not accommodated for.

1. Unfiltered direct light would provoke glare sensitivity, therefore the use of filtered light (e.g., diffused through a lampshade or blinds) is preferable.
2. The color of the light is not an issue, however, the directness of the light is. Therefore, standard bulbs are most appropriate, as long as the light is well diffused.
3. **Diffuse (filtered) lighting decreases sensitivity to glare and reduces the home adaptations that an individual needs to make when transitioning between rooms. It is recommended to use blinds and lampshades to help filter light in the home.**
4. Dim lighting would create its own fall hazard as objects would not be fully visualized. Instead, diffuse lighting should be used uniformly throughout the house.

System: Non-Systems
Content Outline: Safety and Protection; Professional Responsibilities; Research

 **Level 3**  **p. 572**

PTEXAM ONE: QUESTION 87

A patient two weeks post transtibial amputation is instructed by their physician to remain at rest for two days after contracting bronchitis. Which of the following positions is the **MOST** appropriate for the patient while in bed?

1. Supine with a pillow under the patient's knees
2. Supine with a pillow under the thighs and knees
3. **Supine with the legs extended**
4. Sidelying in the fetal position

Correct Answer: 3 (Seymour p. 145) 

It is important for a patient with a transtibial amputation to keep the knee extended in order to prevent shortening of the hamstring muscles and avoid developing a flexion contracture at the knee.

1. Lying in supine with a pillow under the knees is a comfortable position for the patient after transtibial amputation. However, placing a pillow under the knee puts the knee in a partially flexed position. This promotes the development of hamstrings muscle tightness, which may lead to a flexion contracture at the knee.
2. Lying in supine with a pillow under the thighs and knees puts the hip and knee in a flexed position. This promotes the development of hip flexor and hamstrings muscle tightness, which may lead to flexion contractures at the hip or knee.
3. **The supine position with the legs extended is the most appropriate position since it promotes lengthening of the hip flexors and hamstring muscles and prevents the development of flexion contractures.**
4. Sidelying in the fetal position places the hips and knees in a flexed position. This promotes the development of hip flexor and hamstrings muscle tightness, which may lead to flexion contractures at the hip or knee.

System: Other Systems
Content Outline: Interventions

 Level 2  p. 140-143

PTEXAM ONE: QUESTION 88

A physical therapist works with a patient who has paraplegia on how to react in the event of a backward fall. The patient is instructed to place one hand behind the head and the other across the lap as seen in the image. Placing the hand across the lap is important for which of the following reasons?

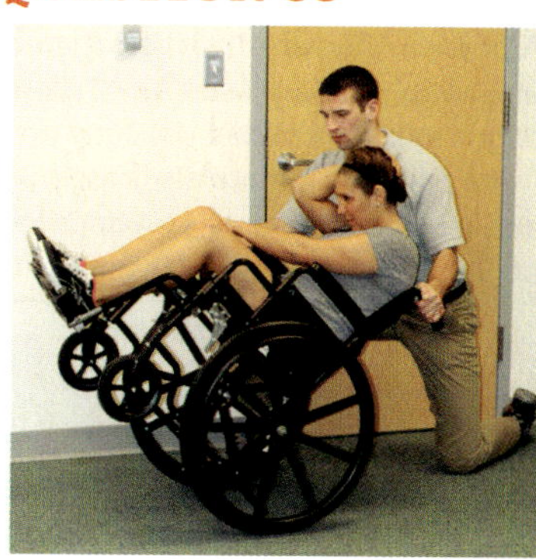

1. Allows the patient to remain within the chair upon landing
2. Allows the patient to hold onto one armrest to stabilize the wheelchair
3. **Prevents the lower extremities from hitting the patient's face**
4. Allows the patient to secure the brake to slow the fall

Correct Answer: 3 (Fairchild p. 166) 

Patients that use wheelchairs as their primary mode of mobility should be proficient with all aspects of wheelchair mobility, including a backward fall. Patients with tetraplegia and paraplegia must stabilize their lower extremities during a backward fall to avoid injury secondary to the backward momentum. Patients can also learn how to return the wheelchair to an upright position, however, this is unrealistic for the majority of patients with a complete spinal cord injury.

1. The patient will likely not remain completely within the chair after a backward fall secondary to limited trunk control and lower extremity paralysis.
2. Holding the armrest is a preventative measure to decrease the movement of the lower extremities, not to stabilize the wheelchair.
3. **The primary goal of placing one arm across the lap is to limit the movement of the lower extremities with the forearm so that they do not fall into the patient's face during the backward fall.**
4. Even if the patient is able to reach the brake with the hand placed across the lap, this would not slow the progression of the fall and is not the primary purpose of placing one arm across the lap.

System: Non-Systems
Content Outline: Equipment, Devices, and Technologies; Therapeutic Modalities

 Level 2

PTEXAM ONE: QUESTION 89

A physical therapist treats a patient that was diagnosed with amyotrophic lateral sclerosis 18 months ago. The patient is experiencing increased difficulty performing activities of daily living and their strength is grossly 3/5 for the lower extremities and the upper extremities. Which intervention would be the MOST appropriate to include in the patient's plan of care?

1. Passive range of motion
2. **Active range of motion**
3. Resistance exercise program
4. Endurance training

Correct Answer: 2 (O'Sullivan p. 733)

Amyotrophic lateral sclerosis (ALS) is a chronic degenerative disease that produces both upper and lower motor neuron impairments. Significant loss of anterior horn cells produces weakness and muscle atrophy. The rapid degeneration causes denervation of muscle fibers, muscle atrophy, and weakness, with death typically due to respiratory failure within two to five years from the onset of symptoms. The patient's clinical presentation is most consistent with the "middle" stage of ALS.

1. Passive range of motion is more appropriate as a primary activity for the "late" stage of ALS when active exercise is no longer feasible. A therapist may incorporate stretching activities at the current stage, but this would not be a primary emphasis.
2. **Active range of motion may be indicated to assist with activities of daily living as long as the patient does not exercise to the point of fatigue. Active exercise at low-intensity levels has been found to be beneficial for patients through the "early" and "middle" stages of ALS.**
3. Resistance exercise is not indicated for patients with ALS that demonstrate existing weakness in muscles of 3/5 or below since it is likely to result in overuse fatigue. A weak muscle is more susceptible to overuse damage during resistive exercise since the muscle is already functioning near its maximal limit.
4. Endurance training is used cautiously during the "early" stage of the disease process and can be effective when managed properly. In the "middle" stage of ALS, the duration of the disease process and the loss of functional mobility make endurance training too aggressive for most patients.

System: Neuromuscular and Nervous Systems
Content Outline: Interventions

 Level 3  p. 274, 322-323

PTEXAM ONE: QUESTION 90

A patient three weeks status post transtibial amputation exhibits intact skin integrity of the residual limb with normally appearing sutures. What is the MOST appropriate covering to apply to the residual limb to minimize the incidence of a knee contracture?

1. Residual limb shrinker
2. Prosthetic sock
3. Elastic wrap bandage
4. **Rigid dressing**

Correct Answer: 4 (May p. 62)

Preventing a knee flexion contracture is the priority when managing a patient's lower limb following a transtibial amputation. Contractures are best prevented with the use of rigid dressings, such as a plaster cast or an external immobilizer.

1. Elastic shrinkers are contraindicated if sutures are present. Shrinkers are useful for shaping the limb and maintaining the residual limb volume when the limb is not in the prosthesis, but not for preventing contractures.
2. Prosthetic socks do not prevent contractures from forming. They are commonly used to protect the skin during periods when wearing a shrinker is not indicated.
3. Elastic bandages are appropriate at this stage of recovery, but are not effective at preventing contractures. They help to shape the limb, albeit not as uniformly as a shrinker.
4. **Rigid dressings help to prevent contractures and are appropriate for an individual with an intact and well healing residual limb.**

System: Musculoskeletal System
Content Outline: Interventions

 Level 2  p. 137-138

PTEXAM ONE: QUESTION 91

A physical therapist reviews a laboratory report for a patient who sustained burns to over 25 percent of the total body surface area. Assuming the patient exhibits hypovolemia, which of the following laboratory values would be the **MOST** significantly affected?

1. **Hematocrit**
2. Erythrocyte sedimentation rate
3. Oxygen saturation rate
4. Prothrombin time

Correct Answer: 1 (Paz p. 287)

Hypovolemia refers to a state of decreased blood volume, most often related to a decrease in blood plasma. The reduction of blood volume often occurs following a burn due to the shift in fluid to the interstitium, which reduces plasma and intravascular fluid volume. This results in a variety of hemodynamic and circulatory changes, however, hematocrit would likely be the laboratory value most affected.

1. **Hematocrit is the volume percentage of red blood cells in whole blood. The hematocrit rises immediately after a severe burn and gradually decreases with fluid replacement.**
2. Erythrocyte sedimentation rate is a non-specific test for inflammatory disorders often associated with conditions such as cancer, autoimmune diseases, and infection. The test is based on how quickly red blood cells sink to the bottom of a test solution containing anticoagulated blood.
3. Oxygen saturation rate indicates the saturation of hemoglobin with oxygen. Normal oxygen saturation is 95-98 percent. Oxygen saturation is not related to total blood volume.
4. Prothrombin time is most commonly used to monitor oral anticoagulant therapy or to screen for selected bleeding disorders.

System: Other Systems
Content Outline: Foundations for Evaluation, Differential Diagnosis, and Prognosis

 Level 2  p. 409

PTEXAM ONE: QUESTION 92

A physical therapist performs autolytic debridement in an attempt to remove nonviable tissue from a stage 4 pressure injury. Autolytic debridement removes necrotic tissue from the wound by using which of the following methods?

1. A sharp instrument
2. An externally applied force
3. **The body's own mechanisms**
4. A commercially prepared enzyme

Correct Answer: 3 (Sussman p. 445) 

Autolytic debridement is typically performed using a moisture-retentive dressing. The dressing maintains a moist wound environment which promotes rehydration of viable tissue and allows the body's enzymes to digest necrotic tissue.

1. Sharp debridement requires the use of scalpel, scissors, and/or forceps to selectively remove nonviable tissue, foreign material or debris from a wound.
2. Wound irrigation removes nonviable tissue from the wound bed using pressurized fluid which serves as an externally applied force. Pulsatile lavage is an example of a specific wound irrigation technique.
3. **Autolytic debridement refers to using the body's own mechanisms to remove nonviable tissue. Common methods of autolytic debridement include transparent films, hydrocolloids, hydrogels, and alginates.**
4. Enzymatic debridement requires the application of a commercially prepared enzyme to the surface of nonviable tissue. The applied enzyme attempts to degrade the nonviable tissue through gradual digestion.

System: Other Systems
Content Outline: Interventions

 Level 2  p. 507

PTEXAM ONE: QUESTION 93

A physical therapist treats a patient post knee surgery. The therapist performs goniometric measurements to quantify the extent of the patient's extension lag. Which of the following findings would NOT provide a plausible rationale for the extension lag?

1. **Muscle weakness**
2. **Bony obstruction**
3. **Inhibition by pain**
4. **Patient apprehension**

Correct Answer: 2 (Kisner p. 776) 

Patients that demonstrate an extension lag have greater passive extension than active extension. The difference in the passive and active extension range of motion is used to quantify the amount of the lag.

1. Muscle weakness would provide a plausible rationale for an extension lag since force production is necessary to produce active motion. Inability to produce adequate force to move the tibia on the femur while performing active extension would produce the lag.
2. **A bony obstruction would not produce an extension lag since passive range of motion and active range of motion would be equal. In essence, the obstruction would interfere with the ability to perform both passive and active knee extension.**
3. Inhibition by pain would provide a plausible rationale for an extension lag. The amount of pain produced during an active muscle contraction may make it impossible for the muscle to generate the required amount of force to actively extend the tibia on the femur. The difference in the passive extension versus the active extension would determine the amount of the extension lag.
4. Patient apprehension would provide a plausible rationale for an extension lag since the patient may be unwilling to actively move the knee through the available active range of motion due to fear or anxiety.

System: Musculoskeletal System
Content Outline: Physical Therapy Examination

Level 2

PTEXAM ONE: QUESTION 94

A physical therapist completes a developmental assessment on an infant. Assuming normal development, which of the following positions would typically be the LAST to occur?

1. **Modified plantigrade**
2. **Quadruped**
3. **Ring sitting**
4. **Bridging**

Correct Answer: 1 (Tecklin p. 19) 

Physical therapists can use existing neurodevelopmental postures to assess normal development and to accomplish a variety of specific therapeutic objectives. These objectives include, but are not limited to, influencing tone, balance reactions, stability, and weight bearing.

1. **Modified plantigrade typically occurs at 10 months with an age range of 10-12 months. Modified plantigrade is characterized by lower extremity weight bearing in supported standing while leaning with upper extremity support on a table or weight bearing surface.**
2. Quadruped typically occurs at 8 months with an age range of 7-9 months. Quadruped describes a position where body weight is supported by both upper extremities as well as both lower extremities (i.e., hands and knees).
3. Ring sitting typically occurs at 6 months with an age range of 5-7 months. Ring sitting refers to an independent sitting position where the lower extremities form the shape of a ring. The position allows the infant to use their upper extremities for reaching or grasping objects.
4. Bridging typically occurs at 5 months with an age range of 5-7 months. Bridging occurs when a patient positioned in hooklying lifts their buttocks and low back from a fixed surface.

System: Neuromuscular and Nervous Systems
Content Outline: Physical Therapy Examination

Level 1  p. 291

PTEXAM ONE: QUESTION 95

A patient four weeks post anterior cruciate ligament reconstruction using a patellar tendon autograft informs their therapist that they are going on vacation for a week in a tropical location. Which of the following recommendations would be the **MOST** beneficial for the patient to protect their scar from the sun?

1. **Keep the scar covered when outside in the sun**
2. Apply sunscreen with a minimum of 15 SPF directly to the scar
3. Apply sunscreen with a minimum of 30 SPF directly to the scar
4. Apply sunscreen with a minimum of 50 SPF directly to the scar

Correct Answer: 1 (Sussman p. 421) 

An anterior cruciate ligament reconstruction using a patellar tendon autograft is a common surgical procedure that requires a 3-4 inch vertical incision over the anterior surface of the knee. It is imperative for the patient to protect the sensitive scar tissue from the sun since exposure can result in thickening and discoloration of the healing tissue.

1. **Keeping the scar covered when outside in the sun provides the best form of protection. This is particularly important in the presented scenario since it has only been four weeks since surgery and the scar is still maturing. Scars should be covered with clothing or a bandage that allows air to circulate. As scars mature, they typically fade in color and become softer, flatter, and less sensitive. Scars are considered to be mature in 12-18 months.**
2. Applying sunscreen with a minimum of 15 SPF directly to the scar provides limited protection from the potentially harmful effects of the sun. SPF stands for sun protection factor and refers to the theoretical amount of time an individual can stay in the sun without being sunburned. A SPF of 15 would allow an individual to stay in the sun 15 times longer than they would be able to without protection.
3. Applying sunscreen with a minimum of 30 SPF to the scar is typically the minimum SPF recommended when protecting a scar from the sun. This recommendation, however, would be more appropriate for a scar that is more mature.
4. Applying sunscreen with a minimum of 50 SPF directly to the scar offers greater protection than the other listed SPF options, however, it is not as desirable as covering the four-week-old scar when outside in the sun.

System: Other Systems
Content Outline: Foundations for Evaluation, Differential Diagnosis, and Prognosis

Level 2

PTEXAM ONE: QUESTION 96

A physical therapist is asked to provide a presentation on the dangers of anabolic steroid use to a group of adolescent male athletes. Which risk factor associated with steroids would be unique to the target audience?

1. Deepened voice
2. **Growth cessation**
3. Liver damage
4. Testicular atrophy

Correct Answer: 2 (Ciccone p. 471)

Anabolic steroids are the synthetic derivatives of the naturally occurring male anabolic hormone testosterone. Adolescents may elect to use steroids to increase body weight, accelerate the growth of muscle tissue, and reduce recovery time.

1. A deepened voice would most likely be associated with a female using anabolic steroids since the steroids create a "masculinization effect" in females. The presented scenario indicates that the presentation is provided to adolescent males.
2. **Rising levels of testosterone and other sex hormones trigger the growth spurt associated with adolescence. When these hormones reach a specific level, they signify the conclusion of growth. Adolescents using anabolic steroids exhibit artificially increased levels of sex hormones that may trigger the cessation of bone growth prematurely.**
3. Liver damage occurs with anabolic steroid use as the liver cells attempt to break down the foreign agents. The extent of the damage depends on the type of anabolic steroid and the amount and length of time the steroid was used. Liver damage is a relevant risk of steroid use for individuals of all ages and is not unique to an adolescent population.
4. Anabolic steroids inhibit the release of follicle-stimulating hormone and luteinizing hormone from the pituitary gland, which contributes to testicular atrophy. Testicular atrophy is a relevant risk of steroid use for males of all ages and is not unique to an adolescent population.

System: Other Systems
Content Outline: Foundations for Evaluation, Differential Diagnosis, and Prognosis

Level 2

PTEXAM ONE: QUESTION 97

A patient successfully completes 10 anterior lunges. The physical therapist would like to modify the activity to maximally challenge the patient in the sagittal plane. Which of the following modifications would be the **MOST** appropriate to accomplish this goal?

1. Anterior lunge with concurrent bilateral elbow flexion to 45 degrees with five pound weights
2. **Anterior lunge with concurrent bilateral shoulder flexion to 90 degrees with five pound weights**
3. Anterior lunge with concurrent unilateral shoulder flexion to 90 degrees with a five pound weight
4. Anterior lunge with concurrent bilateral shoulder abduction to 45 degrees with five pound weights

Correct Answer: 2 (Norkin p. 6) 

The sagittal plane divides the body into left and right halves. Motions in the sagittal plane include flexion and extension. In order to maximally challenge the patient in this plane, therapists should choose the option that moves the patient's center of gravity furthest outside the base of support in the sagittal plane.

1. Bilateral elbow flexion would challenge the patient in the sagittal plane, however, the movement would not significantly change the center of gravity since the upper extremities would be held close to the body.
2. **Bilateral shoulder flexion would create the largest forward movement and would therefore provide the greatest challenge for the patient due to the center of gravity moving forward outside the base of support.**
3. Unilateral shoulder flexion would challenge the patient in the sagittal plane, however, it would not provide as much of a challenge as the bilateral shoulder flexion due to the decreased amount of mass moving outside the base of support (one upper extremity versus two upper extremities).
4. Bilateral shoulder abduction would challenge the patient in the frontal plane.

System: Musculoskeletal System
Content Outline: Interventions

Level 2 p. 49

PTEXAM ONE: QUESTION 98

A patient is treated using pulsed wave ultrasound at 1.2 W/cm^2 for 7 minutes. The specific parameters of the pulsed wave are 2 msec on time and 8 msec off time for one pulse period. The duty cycle should be recorded as what percentage?

1. 10%
2. **20%**
3. 25%
4. 50%

Correct Answer: 2 (Cameron p. 194) 

Duty cycle is defined as the ratio of the on time to the total time. When ultrasound is used in a pulsed mode with a 20% or lower duty cycle, the heat produced during the on time of the cycle is dispersed during the off time and as a result, there is no measurable net increase in temperature. Ultrasound using a 20% or lower duty cycle would typically be used for nonthermal effects.

1. A 10% duty cycle would result if the parameters of the pulsed wave were 1 msec on time and 9 msec off time. Duty cycle = 1 msec / (1 msec + 9 msec) = .10 (100) = 10%.
2. **The question indicates that the parameters of the pulsed wave are 2 msec on time and 8 msec off time for one pulse period. As a result, duty cycle = 2 msec / (2 msec + 8 msec) = .20 (100) = 20%.**
3. This option may have been a common response for candidates who incorrectly answered the question since it is intuitive to take the on time and divide it by the off time. This calculation would be as follows: 2 msec / 8 msec = .25 (100) = 25%. Although the math is correct, the option remains incorrect since by definition duty cycle is defined as the ratio of the on time to the total time (not only the off time).
4. A 50% duty cycle would result any time the on time was the same as the off time (e.g., if the parameters of the pulsed wave were 2 msec on time and 2 msec off time). In this scenario, duty cycle equals 2 msec / (2 msec + 2 msec) = .50 (100) = 50%.

System: Non-Systems
Content Outline: Equipment, Devices, and Technologies; Therapeutic Modalities

  Level 2 p. 710-713

PTEXAM ONE: QUESTION 99

A physical therapist observes a patient's postural strategies following a series of perturbations. What strategy is **BEST** illustrated in the presented image?

1. Ankle
2. **Hip**
3. Suspensory
4. Stepping

Correct Answer: 2 (O'Sullivan p. 211) 

Automatic postural strategies are automatic motor responses that are used to maintain the center of gravity over the base of support. These responses occur in a predictable pattern based on the magnitude of the perturbation.

1. The ankle strategy is the first strategy to be elicited by a small range and slow velocity perturbation when the feet are on the ground. Muscle groups contract in a distal to proximal progression to control postural sway from the ankle joint.
2. **The presented image is an example of the hip strategy which is elicited by a greater force, challenge or perturbation. The hips will move (in the opposite direction from the head) in order to maintain balance. Muscle groups contract in a proximal to distal progression in order to counteract the loss of balance.**
3. The suspensory strategy is used to lower the center of gravity during standing or ambulation in order to better control the center of gravity. Examples of this strategy include knee flexion, crouching or squatting. This strategy is often used when both mobility and stability are required during a task (e.g., surfing).
4. The stepping strategy is elicited through unexpected challenges or perturbations during static standing or when the perturbation produces a movement that displaces the center of gravity beyond the base of support. The lower extremities step and/or upper extremities reach to regain a new base of support.

System: Neuromuscular and Nervous Systems
Content Outline: Physical Therapy Examination

 Level 1  p. 265

PTEXAM ONE: QUESTION 100

A physical therapist works with a patient who has left-sided hemiparesis as depicted in the image. As the therapist facilitates an anteriorly directed weight shift, the patient shifts weight onto the left lower extremity through which of the following mechanisms?

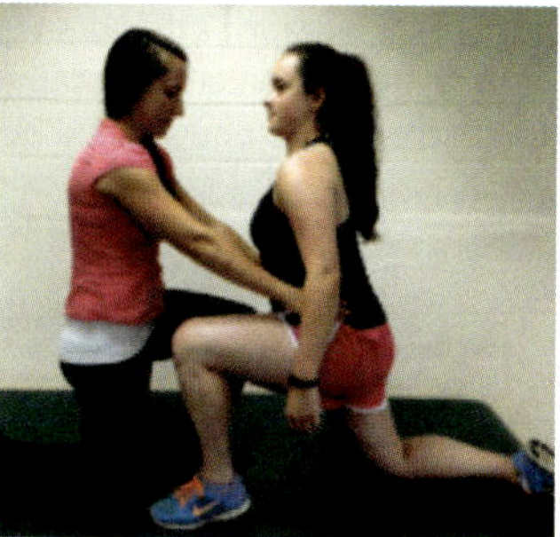

1. Concentric activity of the left quadriceps and soleus
2. **Eccentric activity of the left quadriceps and soleus**
3. Concentric activity of the right quadriceps and soleus
4. Eccentric activity of the right quadriceps and soleus

Correct Answer: 2 (Sullivan p. 51)

Kneeling and half-kneeling are upright postures that are transitional activities typically performed for the assumption of standing or when moving to the ground from a standing position. In half-kneeling, there is weight bearing through the hips, the posterior knee, and the anterior foot. This position allows for a base of support that is angled between the anterior flexed limb and the posterior supporting limb.

1. A patient positioned in half-kneeling as depicted in the image would not use concentric activity of the left quadriceps and soleus when weight shifting anteriorly. An anterior weight shift would promote increased hip flexion, knee flexion, and dorsiflexion, not knee extension and plantar flexion.
2. **A patient positioned in half-kneeling as depicted in the image would use eccentric control of the left quadriceps and soleus when weight shifting anteriorly. This activity also reinforces right hip extension with knee flexion and proximal control of the posterior extremity.**
3. A patient positioned in half-kneeling as depicted in the image would not use concentric activity of the right quadriceps and soleus when weight shifting anteriorly. The right posterior extremity uses hip extensors to maintain proximal control when shifting weight anteriorly so that the patient does not lose balance in a forward direction.
4. A patient positioned in half-kneeling as depicted in the image would not use eccentric activity of the right quadriceps and soleus when weight shifting anteriorly. Eccentric activity of the right quadriceps would be seen if the patient was to sit back on the right heel in a controlled manner.

System: Neuromuscular and Nervous Systems
Content Outline: Interventions

 Level 3

PTEXAM ONE: QUESTION 101

A physical therapist attempts to assess the temperature of a patient's skin in an area susceptible to a pressure ulcer. Which area of the therapist's body would be the **MOST** appropriate to utilize when assessing the patient's skin temperature?

1. **Dorsum of the hand**
2. Hypothenar eminence
3. Thenar eminence
4. Second and third finger pads

Correct Answer: 1 (Goodman – Differential Diagnosis p. 162)

Physical therapists routinely assess the temperature of a patient's skin. Altered skin temperature can be indicative of impaired circulation or an active disease process. Typically, the therapist will compare and contrast symmetrical body parts.

1. **The dorsum of the hand is most sensitive to temperature changes in the body. The relative superficial nature of the area and the available cutaneous receptors allow even subtle temperature changes to be detected.**
2. The hypothenar eminence consists of the opponens digiti minimi, flexor digiti minimi, and abductor digiti minimi muscles. The hypothenar eminence would not typically be used to assess skin temperature.
3. The thenar eminence consists of the abductor pollicis brevis, flexor pollicis brevis, and opponens pollicis. The thenar eminence would not typically be used to assess skin temperature.
4. The second and third finger pads are the most common area of the hand used for palpation, but are not as sensitive to temperature change as the dorsum of the hand. The finger pads are useful in assessing fine tactile discrimination, skin moisture, and texture.

System: Other Systems
Content Outline: Physical Therapy Examination

 Level 1  p. 297-298, 502, 504, 622-623

PTEXAM ONE: QUESTION 102

A patient reports experiencing tenderness and sensitivity to pressure in the area of the hand consistent with the marking in the image. This subjective finding is **MOST** consistent with which of the following medical conditions?

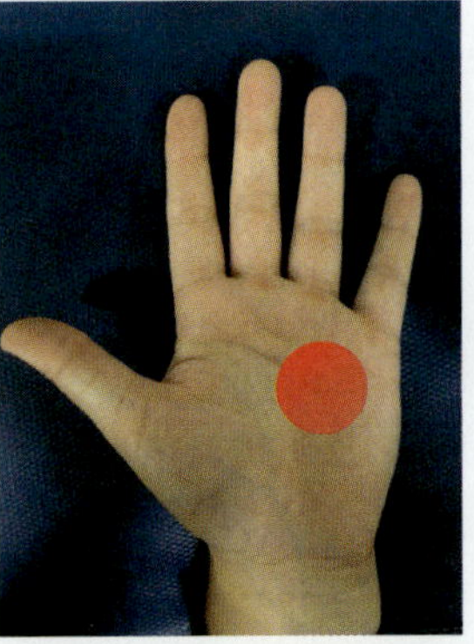

1. Carpal tunnel syndrome
2. **Dupuytren's contracture**
3. De Quervain's disease
4. Ulnar nerve entrapment

Correct Answer: 2 (Sarwark p. 447) 

Medical conditions often have several characteristic signs and symptoms that can help distinguish the condition from other similar conditions. Knowledge of this information can assist physical therapists to develop appropriate plans of care and maximize patient outcomes.

1. Carpal tunnel syndrome (CTS) is a peripheral nerve entrapment injury that occurs as a result of compression of the median nerve where it passes through the carpal tunnel. A patient with CTS will initially present with sensory changes and paresthesias along the median nerve distribution in the hand. The sensory changes and paresthesias may also radiate into the upper extremity, shoulder, and neck.
2. **Dupuytren's contracture is a contracture of the palmar fascia of the hand which results in a flexion deformity of involved metacarpophalangeal and proximal interphalangeal joints. This deformity most commonly affects the fourth and fifth digits. The condition is characterized initially by nodules and thickened tissue near the distal palmar crease in the palm region below the ring finger and little finger. This area is often tender and sensitive to pressure.**
3. De Quervain's disease refers to inflammation of the sheath that surrounds the abductor pollicis longus and extensor pollicis brevis tendons at the wrist. This condition is likely to produce pain or discomfort in the area of the distal radius.
4. Ulnar nerve entrapment occurs due to compression, injury or irritation of the ulnar nerve. A patient with ulnar nerve entrapment at the wrist will often report weakness and numbness in the ulnar nerve distribution, but would be less likely to experience tenderness and sensitivity to pressure. This condition is more common at the elbow than the wrist.

System: Musculoskeletal System
Content Outline: Foundations for Evaluation, Differential Diagnosis, and Prognosis

 Level 1

PTEXAM ONE: QUESTION 103

A physical therapist attempts to identify an appropriately sized wheelchair for a patient. The therapist determines that the patient's hip width in the sitting position and the measurement from the back of the buttocks to the popliteal space are each 16 inches. Given these measurements, which of the following wheelchair specifications would **BEST** fit this patient?

1. Seat width 16 inches, seat depth 14 inches
2. Seat width 18 inches, seat depth 18 inches
3. Seat width 16 inches, seat depth 18 inches
4. **Seat width 18 inches, seat depth 14 inches**

Correct Answer: 4 (Fairchild p. 137) 

Seat width is determined by measuring the widest aspect of the user's buttocks, hips or thighs and adding two inches. Seat depth is measured from the user's posterior buttock, along the lateral thigh to the popliteal fold, then subtracting two inches. In the described scenario, seat width and depth should be calculated as follows: seat width = hip width (16 inches) + 2 inches = 18 inches; seat depth = posterior buttock to the popliteal space (16 inches) - 2 inches = 14 inches.

1. The described wheelchair would have inadequate seat width, however, the seat depth would be appropriate. Inadequate seat width could result in the development of a pressure sore.
2. The described wheelchair would have appropriate seat width, however, the seat depth would be excessive. Excessive seat depth could result in increased pressure in the popliteal area leading to discomfort or circulatory compromise.
3. The described wheelchair would have inadequate seat width and the seat depth would be excessive.
4. **A seat width of 18 inches and a seat depth of 14 inches are consistent with the presented formula based on the obtained measurements.**

System: Non-Systems
Content Outline: Equipment, Devices, and Technologies; Therapeutic Modalities

 Level 1  p. 682-683

PTEXAM ONE: QUESTION 104

A physical therapist utilizes the shoulder abduction test with the patient in the sitting position and the patient's hand resting on the top of their head. The test position reduces the patient's symptoms. Based on this finding, which of the following conditions should the therapist **MOST** suspect?

1. **Cervical radiculopathy**
2. Thoracic outlet syndrome
3. Impingement syndrome
4. Subacromial bursitis

Correct Answer: 1 (Dutton p. 1297)

The shoulder abduction test is used to assess the symptoms of cervical radiculopathy. The patient is typically positioned in sitting and asked to actively abduct the arm until the hand rests on top of the head. A positive test finding is relief or reduction of the patient's ipsilateral radicular symptoms in this position. Other clinical tests that may also help confirm the presence of cervical radiculopathy include the Spurling test and the cervical distraction test.

1. **Cervical radiculopathy refers to compression or irritation of a nerve root in the cervical spine, often caused by a herniated disk or degenerative changes. Symptoms of radiculopathy often include pain, paresthesias, and weakness depending on the severity of compression. Reduced tension on the nerve root is the most probable rationale for pain relief associated with the shoulder abduction test.**
2. Thoracic outlet syndrome is a term used to describe a group of disorders that presents with symptoms secondary to neurovascular compression of fibers of the brachial plexus. This usually occurs between the points of the interscalene triangle and the inferior border of the axilla. The shoulder abduction test position would most likely worsen the symptoms of thoracic outlet syndrome due to increased pressure in the interscalene triangle.
3. Impingement syndrome is one of the most common injuries of the shoulder. It is often caused by repetitive microtrauma from upper extremity activity performed above the horizontal plane. A painful arc of motion typically occurs between 70-120 degrees. The shoulder abduction test would typically worsen the symptoms.
4. The subacromial bursa extends over the supraspinatus tendon and distal muscle belly, beneath the acromion and deltoid muscle. Inflammation of the bursa is often caused by impingement beneath the acromial arch. The shoulder abduction test would typically worsen the pain associated with subacromial bursitis.

System: Musculoskeletal System
Content Outline: Examination

 Level 1

PTEXAM ONE: QUESTION 105

A physical therapist reads in the medical record that a patient developed a hematoma in their lower leg. Which diagnostic imaging method would have MOST likely been used to identify the presence of the hematoma?

1. **X-ray**
2. **Bone scan**
3. **Arteriography**
4. **Ultrasound**

Correct Answer: 4 (Dutton p. 363)

A hematoma is characterized by a localized swelling or mass of clotted blood confined to a tissue, organ or space, usually caused by a break in a blood vessel. Imaging such as ultrasound, magnetic resonance imaging, and computed tomography can be useful in diagnosing this condition.

1. An x-ray is a radiographic image commonly used to assist with the diagnosis of issues related to the bones, such as fractures, dislocations, arthritis, and bone infections. An x-ray would not be used to identify the presence of a hematoma.
2. A bone scan (i.e., skeletal scintigraphy) is an invasive procedure used specifically to provide detailed information on bony structures, such as stress fractures, infection, and bone cancer or metastasis. A bone scan involves the injection of a radionuclide into the body, which is then scanned with a gamma camera to see which bones have taken up the radioactive material. A bone scan would not be used to identify the presence of a hematoma.
3. Arteriography (i.e., angiography) is an invasive procedure that uses x-ray imaging and an injected contrast dye to visualize blood vessels. This technique can visualize the major systemic arteries as well as the arterial systems that perfuse the major organs. Arteriography would not be used to identify the presence of a hematoma.
4. **Ultrasound is a noninvasive procedure that uses sound waves to produce images of structures within the body, especially the internal organs (e.g., liver, kidneys). A transducer placed on the skin sends sound waves into the body, where they are reflected off the internal structures. The sound waves are then processed and ultimately used to create visual images. Ultrasound is often used to identify the presence of a hematoma.**

System: Non-Systems
Content Outline: Equipment, Devices, and Technologies; Therapeutic Modalities

Level 1

p. 512, 700

PTEXAM ONE: QUESTION 106

A physical therapist assesses a patient's upper extremity deep tendon reflexes as part of a screening examination. Which of the following locations is the MOST appropriate to elicit the brachioradialis reflex?

1. **Radial tuberosity**
2. **Antecubital fossa**
3. **Biceps tendon**
4. **Styloid process of the radius**

Correct Answer: 4 (Magee p. 58)

The brachioradialis muscle is innervated by the radial nerve via the C5-C6 nerve root, however, the reflex is largely a function of C6. The brachioradialis muscle is the only muscle in the body that extends from the distal end of one bone to the distal end of another.

1. The radial tuberosity is an oval projection from the medial surface of the radius, immediately distal to the radial neck. The biceps brachii tendon inserts on the radial tuberosity.
2. The antecubital fossa is a triangular cavity of the elbow that contains the tendon of the biceps, the median nerve, and the brachial artery.
3. The biceps reflex (C5-C6) is tested by tapping over the biceps tendon or the thumb of the therapist placed directly over the biceps tendon in the antecubital fossa.
4. **The brachioradialis reflex is tested by tapping the brachioradialis tendon at the distal end of the radius with the flat edge of the reflex hammer.**

System: Neuromuscular and Nervous Systems
Content Outline: Physical Therapy Examination

Level 1

p. 253-255

PTEXAM ONE: QUESTION 107

A physical therapist reads in the medical record that a patient has recently been prescribed nitrates due to angina. What is the **PRIMARY** action of this pharmacological agent?

1. **Decrease cardiac preload and decrease cardiac afterload**
2. Decrease cardiac preload and increase cardiac afterload
3. Increase cardiac preload and decrease cardiac afterload
4. Increase cardiac preload and increase cardiac afterload

Correct Answer: 1 (Ciccone p. 335)

Nitrates are administered to produce a general vasodilation throughout the body. Nitrates decrease the amount of blood returning to the heart as well as the amount of work the heart must perform, which decreases myocardial oxygen demand. Cardiac preload refers to the amount of blood in the ventricle at the end of the diastolic phase and is directly related to venous return. Cardiac afterload refers to the force the left ventricle must generate during the systolic phase and is directly related to the resistance in the aorta and peripheral arteries.

1. **Nitrates produce their primary effects by producing a general vasodilation in vasculature throughout the body. Cardiac preload is diminished by dilation of the systemic venous system. Cardiac afterload is diminished by dilation of the systemic peripheral arteries which decreases the pressure against which the heart must pump.**
2. Nitrates decrease cardiac preload, however, would not increase cardiac afterload due to the dilation of the systemic peripheral arteries.
3. Nitrates do not increase cardiac preload due to the general vasodilation in vasculature throughout the body. However, they would decrease cardiac afterload.
4. Nitrates do not increase cardiac preload due to the general vasodilation in vasculature throughout the body and also would not increase cardiac afterload due to the dilation of the systemic peripheral arteries.

System: Cardiovascular and Pulmonary Systems
Content Outline: Foundations for Evaluation, Differential Diagnosis, and Prognosis

p. 399-400, 414-415, 468

PTEXAM ONE: QUESTION 108

A physical therapist works on standing balance activities with a patient following a right transtibial amputation. Assuming the patient is not yet utilizing a prosthesis, what impact would the amputation have on the location of the patient's center of mass?

1. Move inferior and to the right of midline
2. Move inferior and to the left of midline
3. Move superior and to the right of midline
4. **Move superior and to the left of midline**

Correct Answer: 4 (Johansson p. 46)

The center of mass is the average position of all parts of the system, weighted according to their masses. In a standing position, the normal center of mass is located just anterior to the second sacral vertebra.

1. The center of mass moving inferior and to the right of midline would occur if weight was added to the right lower extremity such as through a cast or orthosis, or if weight was removed from the left upper extremity.
2. The center of mass moving inferior and to the left of midline would occur if weight was added to the left lower extremity such as through a cast or orthosis, or if weight was removed from the right upper extremity.
3. The center of mass moving superior and to the right of midline would occur if weight was added to the right side of the abdomen or the right upper extremity. This scenario could also occur if weight was removed from the left lower extremity.
4. **The center of mass moving superior and to the left of midline would occur if weight was added to the left side of the abdomen or the left upper extremity. This scenario could also occur if weight was removed from the right lower extremity. A right transtibial amputation is consistent with weight being removed from the right lower extremity.**

System: Musculoskeletal System
Content Outline: Foundations for Evaluation, Differential Diagnosis, and Prognosis

p. 136-146

PTEXAM ONE: QUESTION 109

A physical therapist instructs a patient post thoracic surgery how to produce an effective cough. Which of the following patient positions would be the MOST appropriate to initiate treatment?

1. **Standing**
2. **Sitting**
3. **Sidelying**
4. **Hooklying**

Correct Answer: 2 (Hillegass p. 544)

An effective cough requires an inspiration greater than tidal volume, followed by closure of the glottis, abdominal muscle contraction, and sudden opening of the glottis for the forceful expulsion of the inspired air.

1. Although it is possible to perform a maximal inhalation needed for an effective cough, the standing position would not be the most appropriate position to initiate treatment after thoracic surgery.
2. **Sitting upright will maximize all of the steps needed to produce an effective cough.**
3. The sidelying position does not promote the maximal inhalation needed for an effective cough.
4. Hooklying refers to a position where the patient is lying in supine with their hips and knees bent and the feet flat on the floor with the arms positioned at their side. The hooklying position does not promote the maximal inhalation needed for an effective cough.

System: Cardiovascular and Pulmonary Systems
Content Outline: Interventions

 Level 2 p. 436-437

PTEXAM ONE: QUESTION 110

A physical therapist provides pre-operative instructions for a patient scheduled for a total hip arthroplasty. As part of the session, the therapist discusses the importance of preventing deep vein thrombosis post surgery. Which of the following findings is the BEST indicator that the patient is at minimal risk of acquiring a deep vein thrombosis?

1. **Ability to perform ankle pumps and muscle setting exercises**
2. **Ability to ambulate on a frequent schedule**
3. **Ability to achieve full hip range of motion within the allowable limits**
4. **Ability to utilize pneumatic compression devices and elastic stockings**

Correct Answer: 2 (Kisner p. 367) 

Deep vein thrombosis results from the formation of a blood clot that becomes dislodged and is termed an embolus. This is a serious medical condition since the embolus may obstruct a selected artery. Patients are often at risk for acquiring a deep vein thrombosis after surgery. Other risk factors include advanced age, obesity, infection, tobacco, and air travel.

1. Ankle pumps and muscle setting exercises are beneficial, but would not produce the magnitude of muscle pumping action compared to an activity such as ambulation since the exercises tend to involve muscles working in relative isolation.
2. **The ability to ambulate on a frequent schedule requires a significant amount of muscle pumping action generated from contraction of the lower extremity muscles. The initiation of this activity signifies that the patient is progressing toward a more dynamic state which significantly decreases the risk of acquiring deep vein thrombosis.**
3. Range of motion is a desirable activity following surgery since it requires muscle activity and promotes circulation, however, the intensity of the activity is relatively low when compared to ambulation.
4. Pneumatic compression devices and elastic stockings are often utilized following surgery since they can help to prevent coagulation and the formation of a thrombus. The interventions are less desirable than an activity like ambulation, however, can be successfully integrated into a comprehensive program to prevent deep vein thrombosis.

System: Other Systems
Content Outline: Interventions

 Level 2  p. 402, 481

PTEXAM ONE: QUESTION 111

A group of physical therapists design a research study that examines the reliability of the Functional Independence Measure. The therapists utilize a test-retest design to measure reliability. What is the MOST significant source of error with this type of research design?

1. Sampling error
2. Tendency to rate too strictly or leniently
3. Change in test forms due to sampling of items
4. **Change in subject situation over time**

Correct Answer: 4 (Portney p. 85)

The repeatability of scores on the Functional Independence Measure (FIM) from one test administration to another provides evidence of test-retest reliability.

1. Sampling error refers to the differences between samples drawn from the same population due to chance. This is not an issue in test-retest design for reliability because the same individuals are tested each time.
2. In a test-retest design for reliability, the therapists rating the patients use the same scoring rules on each occasion.
3. In a test-retest design for reliability, the FIM would be administered both times, therefore the form of the test would not change.
4. **Because test-retest design necessitates an interval of time between test administrations, a real change in the patient's function during this time would adversely affect the reliability score.**

System: Non-Systems
Content Outline: Safety and Protection; Professional Responsibilities; Research

 Level 2  p. 806

PTEXAM ONE: QUESTION 112

A physical therapist treats a patient post femur fracture with external fixation. While monitoring the patient during an exercise session, the therapist observes clear drainage from a distal pin site. Which of the following actions is the MOST appropriate for the therapist to take?

1. Discontinue the exercise session and contact the referring physician
2. Use a gauze pad to absorb the drainage and notify nursing
3. **Use a gauze pad to absorb the drainage and continue with the exercise session**
4. Document the finding and discontinue the exercise session

Correct Answer: 3 (Fairchild p. 284) 

External fixation devices provide stabilization to fracture sites through the use of pins that are inserted into bone fragments. Clear drainage from a pin site is not uncommon and should not be viewed as a sign of infection or any other serious medical complication.

1. Clear drainage from a distal pin site would not warrant discontinuing the exercise session or contacting the referring physician. If the scenario offered compelling data suggestive of infection, it would be appropriate to notify the referring physician and/or the nurse.
2. The gauze pad is an acceptable method to absorb the drainage. The observation of clear drainage from a distal pin site is relatively common and therefore would not require consultation with nursing.
3. **The exercise session can continue after the drainage has been absorbed. The physical therapist may be required to use multiple gauze pads throughout the session, however, this should not impact the overall exercise routine.**
4. Documenting the observation would be acceptable, however, the presented scenario does not provide adequate justification for discontinuing the exercise session.

System: Other Systems
Content Outline: Interventions

 Level 3

PTEXAM ONE: QUESTION 113

A patient diagnosed with multiple sclerosis uses extensor tone to assist them to successfully complete a sit to stand transfer. Which pharmacological agent would **MOST** limit the patient's ability to complete the transfer?

1. Calcium carbonate
2. **Dantrolene sodium**
3. Levodopa
4. Secobarbital

Correct Answer: 2 (Umphred p. 591)

Physical therapists must possess an awareness of commonly used pharmacological agents, their indications, and potential side effects. This awareness must extend to the unique clinical presentation of each patient and the established physical therapy plan of care.

1. Calcium carbonate is a bone mineral regulating agent that attempts to enhance and maximize bone mass along with preventing bone loss or decreasing the rate of bone resorption. Side effects of this medication include nausea, decreased appetite, constipation, and dry mouth. This pharmacological agent would not have a significant impact on the patient's ability to complete the transfer.
2. **Dantrolene sodium is a post-synaptic muscle relaxant that exerts its effects directly on the skeletal muscle cells. This pharmacological agent is most commonly used to treat spasticity by interfering with the release of calcium. Side effects include drowsiness, confusion, and generalized muscle weakness. Reducing the patient's spasticity may significantly impact their ability to complete the transfer since it will likely reduce the patient's extensor tone which is presently being relied upon to complete the transfer.**
3. Levodopa is a dopamine replacement agent that assists to relieve the symptoms of Parkinson's disease. Side effects of this medication include arrhythmias, gastrointestinal distress, orthostatic hypotension, and dyskinesias. The potential for orthostatic hypotension and dyskinesias could impact the patient's ability to complete the transfer, but it is unlikely that this impact would be as significant as the reduced extensor tone associated with the use of a muscle relaxant.
4. Secobarbital is an antiepileptic agent that reduces or eliminates seizure activity within the brain. These agents attempt to inhibit the firing of certain cerebral neurons within the central nervous system. Side effects of this medication include drowsiness, dizziness, and ataxia. This medication would not have a significant impact on the patient's ability to complete the transfer.

System: Neuromuscular and Nervous Systems
Content Outline: Foundations for Evaluation, Differential Diagnosis, and Prognosis

p. 273, 586

PTEXAM ONE: QUESTION 114

A physical therapist collects data as part of a research project that requires direct observation of children performing selected gross motor activities. The therapist is concerned about the influence of an observer on the children's performance. Which of the following strategies would be the MOST effective to control for this source of error?

1. Provide initial and refresher observer training
2. Increase observer awareness of the influence of their background
3. **Have an observer spend time with the children before direct observation**
4. Ask the children to ignore the presence of the observer

Correct Answer: 3 (Portney p. 310) 

A research project should be designed to eliminate as many extraneous variables as possible. Failure to eliminate or at least reduce the potential impact of an observer on the children's performance would be a significant limitation of the study.

1. Observer training would be beneficial in order to provide the observers with a better sense of their purpose, role, and actions. This action would be desirable, but would not address the nuance of the observer for the children.
2. An individual's background can influence their observations particularly when the data collected is open for interpretation. This option also focuses on the observer and not the children.
3. **Spending time with the children prior to direct observation will allow the children to feel more at ease and as a result their performance may be more reflective of their current abilities.**
4. Asking the children to ignore the presence of the observer would likely serve to bring additional attention to the observer and therefore influence behavior.

System: Musculoskeletal System
Content Outline: Physical Therapy Examination

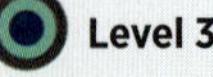

PTEXAM ONE: QUESTION 115

A physical therapist discusses the importance of proper posture with a patient post back surgery at the L3-L4 spinal level. Which body position would place the **MOST** pressure on the lumbar spine?

1. Standing in the anatomical position
2. Standing with 45 degrees of hip flexion
3. **Sitting in a chair slouching forward**
4. Sitting in a chair with reduced lumbar lordosis

Correct Answer: 3 (Hertling p. 880)

A study by Nachemson examined intradiskal pressures in the lumbar spine (L3 disk) as they relate to specific body positions. The order of body positions from the lowest total load to the greatest total load is as follows: lying in supine, sidelying, standing in the anatomical position, standing with 45 degrees of hip flexion, sitting in a chair with reduced lumbar lordosis, and sitting in a chair slouching forward.

1. Standing in the anatomical position resulted in a greater total load than the load associated with lying in supine or sidelying.
2. Standing with 45 degrees of hip flexion resulted in a greater total load than the load associated with lying in supine, sidelying, and standing in the anatomical position.
3. **Sitting in a chair slouching forward resulted in a greater total load than any of the other five body positions measured.**
4. Sitting in a chair with reduced lumbar lordosis had the greatest total load of the positions measured with the only exception being sitting in a chair slouching forward.

System: Musculoskeletal System
Content Outline: Interventions

PTEXAM ONE: QUESTION 116

A physical therapist works on transfer activities with a patient who has a complete C5 spinal cord injury. Which of the following muscles would the patient **MOST** likely be able to utilize during the training session?

1. **Brachioradialis**
2. Pronator teres
3. Extensor carpi radialis brevis
4. Latissimus dorsi

Correct Answer: 1 (Kendall p. 294) 

A patient with C5 tetraplegia would be able to utilize muscles innervated at or above the C5 spinal level.

1. **The brachioradialis is innervated by the radial nerve (C5-C6) and acts to flex the elbow joint and assists in pronating and supinating the forearm when these movements are resisted.**
2. The pronator teres is innervated by the median nerve (C6-C7) and acts to pronate the forearm and assists in flexion of the elbow joint.
3. The extensor carpi radialis brevis is innervated by the radial nerve (C6, C7, C8) and acts to extend the wrist and assists in wrist abduction.
4. The latissimus dorsi is innervated by the thoracodorsal nerve (C6, C7, C8) and with the origin fixed acts to medially rotate, adduct, and extend the shoulder joint.

System: Neuromuscular and Nervous Systems
Content Outline: Foundations for Evaluation, Differential Diagnosis, and Prognosis

 p. 250, 298-300

PTEXAM ONE: QUESTION 117

A physical therapist assesses the deep tendon reflexes of a patient as part of a lower quarter screening examination. The therapist determines that the right and left patellar tendon reflex and the left Achilles tendon reflex are 2+, while the right Achilles tendon reflex is absent. This finding is **MOST** associated with which of the following medical conditions?

1. Cerebral palsy
2. Multiple sclerosis
3. **Peripheral neuropathy**
4. Intermittent claudication

Correct Answer: 3 (Goodman – Differential Diagnosis p. 623)

A reflex is a motor response to a sensory stimulation that can be used to assess the integrity of the nervous system. Deep tendon reflexes (DTR) elicit a muscle contraction when the muscle's tendon is stimulated. A grade of 2+ would be considered a normal response.

1. Cerebral palsy is a neuromuscular disorder of posture and controlled movement, however, the clinical presentation is highly variable based on the area and extent of central nervous system damage. It is unlikely that a reflex would be absent in an upper motor neuron disorder such as cerebral palsy.
2. Multiple sclerosis is a chronic autoimmune inflammatory disease of the central nervous system characterized by demyelination of the myelin sheaths that surround nerves within the brain and spinal cord. Symptoms can include visual problems, paresthesias and sensory changes, clumsiness, weakness, ataxia, balance dysfunction, and fatigue. Deep tendon reflexes would not typically be absent with multiple sclerosis since it is an upper motor neuron disorder.
3. **Peripheral neuropathy is a broad term that describes a lesion to a peripheral nerve. Patients with peripheral neuropathy may exhibit motor, sensory, and autonomic changes including extreme sensitivity to touch, loss of sensation, muscle weakness, and loss of vasomotor tone. Deep tendon reflexes may be asymmetrical based on the location of the involved peripheral nerve and usually present as diminished or absent.**
4. Intermittent claudication occurs as a result of insufficient blood supply and ischemia in active muscles. Symptoms most commonly include pain and cramping in muscles distal to the occluded vessel. Deep tendon reflexes would not typically be affected.

System: Neuromuscular and Nervous Systems
Content Outline: Foundations for Evaluation, Differential Diagnosis, and Prognosis

Level 2

p. 253-255, 260-262

PTEXAM ONE: QUESTION 118

A patient is directed to reach for an object beyond arm's length during therapeutic activities emphasizing core training and balance activities as depicted in the image. Which response would be **MOST** desirable when performing this activity?

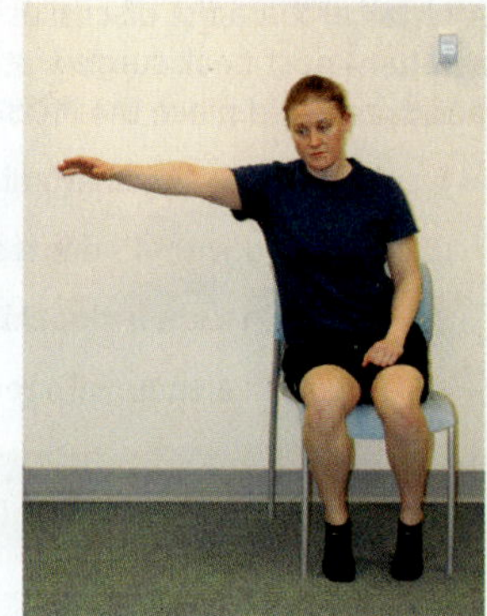

1. Left trunk elongation, left weight shift, right hip hiking
2. Right trunk elongation, right weight shift, right hip hiking
3. Left trunk elongation, left weight shift, left hip hiking
4. **Right trunk elongation, right weight shift, left hip hiking**

Correct Answer: 4 (O'Sullivan p. 387)

When treating patients, therapists must be cognizant of the goals of specific activities and use therapeutic interventions that relate to the goal. For example, reaching above shoulder level will produce trunk elongation and weight shift ipsilaterally and reaching towards the floor will produce trunk elongation and weight shift contralaterally.

1. A patient that presents with left trunk elongation, left weight shift, and right hip hiking is likely reaching for an object just beyond their reach at shoulder height or higher on their left side.
2. A patient that presents with right trunk elongation and right weight shift would typically be reaching for an object beyond arm's length at shoulder level or higher on their right side. They would, however, present with left hip hiking, not right hip hiking.
3. A patient that presents with left trunk elongation and left weight shift would typically be reaching for an object beyond arm's length at shoulder level or higher on their left side. They would, however, present with right hip hiking, not left hip hiking.
4. **A patient that presents with right trunk elongation, right weight shift, and left hip hiking is likely reaching for an object just beyond reach at shoulder height or higher on their right side.**

System: Neuromuscular and Nervous Systems
Content Outline: Interventions

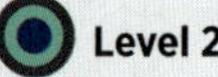
Level 2

PTEXAM ONE: QUESTION 119

A physical therapist attempts to palpate the tibialis posterior tendon. Which of the following activities should the therapist do to facilitate palpation of this structure?

1. **Ask the patient to invert and plantar flex the foot**
2. Ask the patient to evert and dorsiflex the foot
3. Ask the patient to invert and dorsiflex the foot
4. Passively evert and plantar flex the foot

Correct Answer: 1 (Kendall p. 411) 

A tendon is a band of dense fibrous tissue forming the termination of a muscle which attaches the muscle to a bone. A tendon becomes more prominent when the associated muscle is active. The tendon of the tibialis posterior can be palpated posterior and inferior to the medial malleolus.

1. **The tibialis posterior originates on the interosseous membrane, lateral portion of the posterior surface of the tibia, and proximal two thirds of the medial surface of the fibula. The muscle acts to invert the foot and assists with plantar flexion of the ankle joint. As a result, the tendon is more prominent with active inversion and plantar flexion.**
2. Eversion and dorsiflexion are opposite of the action of the tibialis posterior. As a result, the active movement would not facilitate palpation of the muscle's tendon.
3. The tibialis anterior acts to dorsiflex the ankle joint and assists with inversion of the foot. As a result, the tendon is more prominent with active dorsiflexion and inversion. The tendon of the muscle is easily palpated where it crosses the ankle joint to its insertion on the medial aspect of the base of the first metatarsal and the medial cuneiform bone.
4. Passive movement would not be as desirable as active movement to facilitate palpation of the tendon since muscular activity is necessary to make the tendon prominent. In addition, the tibialis posterior inverts the foot and assists with plantar flexion of the ankle joint.

System: Musculoskeletal System
Content Outline: Physical Therapy Examination

PTEXAM ONE: QUESTION 120

A physical therapist participating in a research project uses a simple random sample to create a sample from the population. By selecting this type of sample, the therapist ensures which of the following outcomes?

1. The data collected from the sample will be normally distributed
2. The sample size will be large
3. The sample will have proportional representation from all parts of the population
4. **Every member of the population has an equal opportunity of being chosen**

Correct Answer: 4 (Portney p. 148)

Probability samples are created through a process of random selection. Each selection is independent and every member of the population has an equal chance of being selected for the sample.

1. Simple random sampling does not ensure that the data collected will be normally distributed. The shape of the distribution of the data collected from the sample is independent of the type of sample.
2. Simple random sampling does not determine the size of the sample.
3. To ensure that the sample will have proportional representation from all parts of the population, the therapist would create a proportional stratified sample.
4. **A simple random sample is unbiased; each member of the population has an equal chance of being chosen.**

System: Non-Systems
Content Outline: Safety and Protection; Professional Responsibilities; Research

 p. 807

PTEXAM ONE: QUESTION 121

A physical therapist examines the heart sounds of a patient post coronary artery bypass graft. During auscultation, what heart sound is associated with closing of the mitral and tricuspid valves?

1. **S1**
2. S2
3. S3
4. S4

Correct Answer: 1 (Hillegass p. 98)

The heart sounds are the noises generated by the beating heart and the resultant flow of blood through it. The therapist uses a stethoscope to listen for these sounds, which provide important information about the condition of the heart.

1. **The first heart sound, S1 (the lub of the lub-dub), is associated with the closing of the mitral and tricuspid valves, corresponding to the onset of ventricular systole.**
2. The second heart sound, S2, (the dub of the lub-dub), is associated with the closing of the aortic and pulmonary valves, corresponding to the onset of ventricular diastole.
3. A third heart sound, S3, occurs early in diastole while the ventricle is rapidly filling. The sound occurs immediately after S2 (lub-dub-dub). The S3 sound may occur in healthy children and young adults, and is referred to as a physiologic third heart sound. It also indicates a loss of ventricular compliance in the presence of heart disease or heart failure. In this case, it is called a ventricular gallop.
4. A fourth heart sound, S4, occurs late in diastole just before S1 (la-lub-dub) and is associated with atrial contraction and an increased resistance to ventricular filling. The heart sound is referred to as an atrial gallop. The sound is common in patients with hypertension, a history of myocardial infarction or coronary bypass surgery.

System: Cardiovascular and Pulmonary Systems
Content Outline: Physical Therapy Examination

Level 1  p. 420-421

PTEXAM ONE: QUESTION 122

During a balance assessment of a patient with left hemiplegia, it is noted that in sitting the patient requires minimal assistance to maintain the position and cannot accept any additional challenge. What grade should the physical therapist use to document this patient's sitting balance?

1. Normal
2. Good
3. Fair
4. **Poor**

Correct Answer: 4 (O'Sullivan p. 212)

Sitting balance can be graded in an objective manner by using a scale that ranges from poor to normal. A patient that requires assistance to maintain a sitting position would be graded as having poor sitting balance.

1. A grade of normal is indicative of a person that is able to sit unsupported, move in and out of the base of support, and accept maximal challenge without loss of balance.
2. A grade of good is indicative of a person that is able to sit unsupported, move in and out of the base of support, and accept some challenge without loss of balance.
3. A grade of fair is indicative of a person that is able to maintain their balance in sitting unsupported, but cannot accept any challenge or go outside of their base of support without loss of balance.
4. **A grade of poor is indicative of a person that is unable to maintain their balance in sitting without external support or assistance.**

System: Neuromuscular and Nervous Systems
Content Outline: Physical Therapy Examination

 Level 1

PTEXAM ONE: QUESTION 123

A physical therapist is treating a patient with a head injury who begins to perseverate. The therapist should do which of the following activities in order to refocus the patient and achieve the desired therapeutic outcome?

1. Focus on the topic of perseveration for a short period of time in order to appease the patient
2. **Guide the patient into an interesting new activity and reward successful completion of the task**
3. Take the patient back to their room for quiet time and attempt to resume therapy once they have stopped perseverating
4. Continue with repetitive verbal cues to cease perseveration

Correct Answer: 2 (O'Sullivan p. 605) 

Perseveration is the continued repetition of a word, phrase or movement. Initiating a new activity during therapy may allow the patient to redirect attention and subsequently receive positive reinforcement for attending to the selected task.

1. It is not necessary to attempt to appease the patient since the patient cannot independently move beyond whatever they are perseverating on. Staying with the topic will not assist in moving forward.
2. **Patients with a lesion in the premotor or prefrontal cortex often exhibit perseveration. Since the patient typically continues the repetition of a word, phrase or movement after the cessation of the original stimulus, the best intervention would be to redirect the patient away from the current activity.**
3. The patient will not benefit from "quiet time" since the patient is not perseverating due to a behavioral issue. Redirecting the patient may successfully allow the patient to move forward and continue with therapy without interruption.
4. Verbal cueing is not an effective technique to cease perseveration. The patient typically requires a redirection of their attention to another activity or environment.

System: Neuromuscular and Nervous Systems
Content Outline: Interventions

PTEXAM ONE: QUESTION 124

A male physical therapist examines a female patient who has subacromial bursitis. After taking a thorough history, the therapist asks the patient to change into a gown. The patient seems very uneasy about this suggestion, but finally agrees to use the gown. Which of the following actions is the **MOST** appropriate for the therapist to take?

1. Continue with treatment as planned
2. Attempt to treat the patient without using the gown
3. **Bring a female staff member into the treatment room and continue with treatment**
4. Offer to transfer the patient to a female physical therapist

Correct Answer: 3 (Nosse p. 217) 

The physical therapist should be sensitive to the patient's apparent discomfort with the situation, however, must also take appropriate steps to manage their relative risk. Physical therapists must be willing to modify their approach with each patient encounter based on the unique presented circumstances.

1. The patient's original reluctance to wear the gown makes it prudent to have a witness present during treatment. The decision to continue with treatment without any formal action places the physical therapist at unnecessary risk.
2. Failure to wear the gown may make it more difficult for the physical therapist to treat the patient or depending on the chosen intervention, could risk damaging or soiling the patient's clothes.
3. **The male physical therapist should bring a female staff member into the treatment room. The presence of a witness is a form of risk management that protects the physical therapist in the event of any alleged misconduct and may make the patient more comfortable.**
4. It would be impractical to transfer a patient to another physical therapist simply because the patient seemed to be uncomfortable when asked to change into the gown. In addition, the female physical therapist may have similar concerns which would still require another staff member to be present.

System: Musculoskeletal System
Content Outline: Physical Therapy Examination

Level 3

PTEXAM ONE: QUESTION 125

A physical therapist treats a patient status post stroke. Which of the following actions would be the **MOST** likely to facilitate elbow extension in a patient who has hemiplegia?

1. **Turn the head to the affected side**
2. Turn the head to the unaffected side
3. Extend the lower extremities
4. Flex the lower extremities

Correct Answer: 1 (O'Sullivan p. 177)

Patients status post CVA are likely to exhibit abnormal tonic reflexes. Eliciting the reflexes will produce sustained posturing and abnormal movement patterns.

1. **The asymmetrical tonic neck reflex produces extension of the affected upper extremity when the patient's head is turned toward the affected side. The upper extremity on the skull side will flex.**
2. If the patient's head is turned toward the unaffected side, the unaffected upper extremity will extend and the affected upper extremity will flex due to the influence of the asymmetrical tonic neck reflex (ATNR).
3. The tonic labyrinthine reflex (TLR) promotes a tendency for extension when a patient is in supine and reduced extensor influence when the patient is in prone. TLR would not facilitate elbow extension in isolation as noted with ATNR.
4. Flexion of the lower extremities does not have a direct influence on upper extremity flexion or extension.

System: Neuromuscular and Nervous Systems
Content Outline: Interventions

 Level 2  p. 306-307

PTEXAM ONE: QUESTION 126

A physical therapist examines a patient three days post shoulder surgery. The patient reports general malaise and has had a slightly elevated body temperature during the last 24 hours. Physical examination reveals an edematous shoulder that is warm to the touch. A small amount of yellow fluid is observed seeping from the incision. Which of the following actions is the **MOST** appropriate for the therapist to take in this situation?

1. Send the patient to the emergency room
2. **Communicate the information to the referring physician**
3. Document the findings in the medical record
4. Ask the patient to make an appointment with the referring physician

Correct Answer: 2 (Goodman – Pathology p. 319) 

Physical therapists must be aware of any signs or symptoms of infection, particularly in patients following surgery. Common signs of infection include elevated body temperature, purulent exudate, swelling, edema, and redness.

1. The patient's presentation requires the physical therapist to take formal action, but would not be indicative of an emergent condition that requires the patient to be seen in the emergency room.
2. **The possibility of infection in a patient three days status post surgery warrants immediate consultation with the referring physician.**
3. The subjective and objective information gathered by the physical therapist should be documented in the medical record, however, this action would not address the primary issue which is the possibility of an infection.
4. Asking the patient to make an appointment with the physician is not an appropriate action since it places the burden solely on the patient. The physical therapist is responsible for communicating any potential change in a patient's medical status to the physician in a timely manner.

System: Other Systems
Content Outline: Interventions

Level 3

PTEXAM ONE: QUESTION 127

A patient with an acute burn is referred to physical therapy less than 24 hours after being admitted to the hospital. The patient's burns range from superficial partial-thickness to deep partial-thickness and encompass approximately 35 percent of the patient's total body surface area. Which of the following findings would be the MOST predictable based on the patient's injury?

1. **Increased oxygen consumption**
2. Hypernatremia
3. Increased intravascular fluid
4. Decreased core temperature

Correct Answer: 1 (Paz p. 287)

An acute burn produces hypermetabolism that results in increased oxygen consumption, increased minute ventilation, and an increased core temperature. Intravascular, interstitial, and intracellular fluids are all diminished.

1. **Pulmonary function is affected by the presence of a burn injury. In addition to increased oxygen consumption, the patient can also experience increased minute ventilation up to five times the normal value.**
2. Hyponatremia or low sodium concentration, initially occurs (within the first 36 hours) secondary to extracellular changes from the increased cellular permeability. In patients that sustain burns above 20% of the total body surface area, fluid and electrolyte replacement is a component of immediate medical management in order to control the hypermetabolic cycle that results from the burn.
3. Intravascular fluid will decrease due to the increased vascular permeability and overall hematologic changes. Cardiac output can decrease secondary to a combination of an increase in blood viscosity, decrease in intravascular fluid, and an overall increase in peripheral resistance.
4. A patient with a significant burn injury is at risk for an increased core temperature due to the increased metabolic and catabolic activity. The one to two degree increase occurs secondary to the "recalibrating" of the hypothalamic temperature centers in the brain. Patients that have sustained extensive burns require a warmer ambient temperature in order to reduce their metabolic rate. Average room temperature will create continued heat loss and perpetuate the hypermetabolic state.

System: Other Systems
Content Outline: Foundations for Evaluation, Differential Diagnosis, and Prognosis

Level 2

PTEXAM ONE: QUESTION 128

A patient sustains a deep partial-thickness burn to the anterior surface of the right upper extremity and a superficial partial-thickness burn to the anterior surface of the trunk. According to the rule of nines, the patient has burns over what percentage of total body surface area?

1. 13.5%
2. **22.5%**
3. 27.0%
4. 36.0%

Correct Answer: 2 (Roy p. 551) 

The rule of nines is commonly utilized to assess the percentage of the body surface affected by a burn. Each area of the body has a specific percentage allocated to it in order to approximate the total percentage of the body surface affected. The values are as follows: head (9%), each upper extremity (9%), the trunk (36%), each lower extremity (18%), and the genital area (1%).

1. A value of 13.5% is less than the percentage of body surface affected. A candidate may have generated an answer of 13.5% by allocating only 9% for the anterior trunk instead of 18% and then adding 4.5% for the anterior surface of the upper extremity.
2. **The anterior surface of the right upper extremity equals 4.5% and the anterior surface of the trunk equals 18% (4.5% + 18% = 22.5%).**
3. A value of 27% is greater than the percentage of body surface affected in the described scenario. A candidate may have generated an answer of 27% by incorrectly allocating 9% for the anterior surface of the right upper extremity and then adding 18% for the anterior surface of the trunk.
4. The entire trunk is valued at 36% of the body using the rule of nines.

System: Other Systems
Content Outline: Physical Therapy Examination

Level 1

p. 514

PTEXAM ONE: QUESTION 129

A physical therapist examines the posture of a patient from a lateral view using a plumb line. Which of the following medical conditions would be the LEAST likely to result in the external auditory meatus being anterior to the plumb line?

1. Ankylosing spondylitis
2. **Graves' disease**
3. Osteoporosis
4. Parkinson's disease

Correct Answer: 2 (Kendall p. 60) 

When assessing a patient's posture, a plumb line can be used as a line of reference to determine areas of abnormal posture and the extent of these abnormalities. In normal posture, the stationary plumb line runs through the external auditory meatus.

1. Ankylosing spondylitis is a systemic condition that is characterized by inflammation of the spine and larger peripheral joints. Symptoms include back pain, morning stiffness, and impaired spinal extension. The tendency of a patient with ankylosing spondylitis to exhibit a forward flexed posture would result in the external auditory meatus being anterior to the stationary plumb line.
2. **Graves' disease is an autoimmune disease in which certain antibodies produced by the immune system stimulate the thyroid gland causing it to become overactive. Symptoms are consistent with hyperthyroidism including mild enlargement of the thyroid gland (goiter), heat intolerance, nervousness, tremor, and palpitations. Graves' disease is not typically associated with postural changes.**
3. Osteoporosis is a metabolic condition that presents with a decrease in bone mass that subsequently increases the risk of fracture. Symptoms include compression and other bone fractures, loss of lumbar lordosis, deformities such as kyphosis, and postural changes. The tendency of a patient with osteoporosis to exhibit a forward flexed posture would result in the external auditory meatus being anterior to the stationary plumb line.
4. Parkinson's disease is a movement disorder caused by the progressive degeneration of the dopamine-producing cells in the basal ganglia. Symptoms include difficulty initiating and stopping movement, festinating, and shuffling gait. The tendency of a patient with Parkinson's disease to exhibit a forward flexed posture would result in the external auditory meatus being anterior to the stationary plumb line.

System: Other Systems
Content Outline: Foundations for Evaluation, Differential Diagnosis, and Prognosis

 **Level 1**  **p. 75-77, 528, 637**

PTEXAM ONE: QUESTION 130

A patient with complete paraplegia discusses accessibility issues with an employer in preparation for return to work. The patient is concerned about the ability to navigate a wheelchair in certain areas of the building. What is the MINIMUM space required to turn 180 degrees in a standard wheelchair?

1. 32 inches
2. 48 inches
3. **60 inches**
4. 72 inches

Correct Answer: 3 (Roy p. 24)

The Americans with Disabilities Act was designed to provide a clear and comprehensive national mandate for the elimination of discrimination. Title III provides information on public accommodations including minimum accessibility standards.

1. Thirty-two inches is the minimum required width of a doorway for wheelchair clearance, however, this space would not be adequate to turn 180 degrees in a standard wheelchair.
2. Forty-eight inches would be 12 inches less than the minimum required space to turn 180 degrees in a standard wheelchair.
3. **Sixty inches is the minimum required width to turn 180 degrees in a standard wheelchair according to the Americans with Disabilities Act.**
4. Seventy-two inches would be adequate to turn 180 degrees in a standard wheelchair, however, this value exceeds the minimum required space by 12 inches.

System: Non-Systems
Content Outline: Safety and Protection; Professional Responsibilities; Research

 **Level 1**  **p. 770-771**

PTEXAM ONE: QUESTION 131

A physical therapist treats a patient who has spastic diplegia that recently underwent an iliopsoas tendon release. Which of the following findings is MOST likely associated with the need for this surgical procedure?

1. **Crouched gait**
2. **Lower limb scissoring**
3. **Equinovarus deformity**
4. **Knee flexion contracture**

Correct Answer: 1 (Tan p. 515)

The treatment of spasticity will follow a continuum from conservative to aggressive based on the degree to which the spasticity interferes with overall function. Surgical procedures may be appropriate for patients that have been unsuccessful with more conservative treatment. Goals of surgery include lengthening of muscles and tendons, improving function, increasing range of motion, and correcting deformity.

1. **A crouched gait results from spasticity in the hip flexors and is associated with compensatory hip and knee flexion as well as lumbar hyperlordosis. The iliopsoas tendon is released from the lesser trochanter while maintaining its capsular attachments. This will effectively weaken the iliopsoas and decrease crouching.**
2. Lower limb scissoring results from spasticity of the hip adductors. A partial obturator neurectomy is performed if contracture is not the cause of the gait deviation. This will effectively weaken the hip adductors and decrease the scissoring during gait.
3. Equinovarus deformity is the most common deformity of the lower extremity and results from spasticity of the gastrocnemius, soleus, and anterior tibialis. A split anterior tibialis tendon transfer (SPLATT) procedure is performed to create an eversion force in an attempt to rebalance the forefoot deformity.
4. A knee flexion contracture results from spasticity of the hamstrings. The distal hamstring muscles are released along with a transfer of the distal hamstrings' insertion if necessary.

System: Musculoskeletal System
Content Outline: Foundations for Evaluation, Differential Diagnosis, and Prognosis

Level 2

PTEXAM ONE: QUESTION 132

A physical therapist plans to apply ultrasound over an extremely irregular body surface area. Which method of ultrasound administration would be the MOST appropriate?

1. **Direct contact with a gel coupling agent**
2. **Direct contact without a gel coupling agent**
3. **Water immersion with a gel coupling agent**
4. **Water immersion without a gel coupling agent**

Correct Answer: 4 (Bellew p. 98) 

Ultrasound waves do not travel through air and, as a result, a coupling agent is required. Coupling agents are designed to decrease acoustical impedance by eliminating as much air as possible between the transducer and the target area. Coupling agents can be direct or indirect and include gels, gel pads, mineral oil, water, and lotions.

1. Direct contact requires the face of the transducer to be parallel with the surface of the skin so that ultrasound waves will be introduced at a 90 degree angle. This method of administration requires a coupling agent, however, is potentially problematic with extremely irregular body surface areas.
2. Direct contact requires the face of the transducer to be parallel with the surface of the skin so that ultrasound waves will be introduced at a 90 degree angle. This method of administration requires a coupling agent.
3. Water immersion is an indirect coupling method requiring the treatment area to be immersed in water. This method of administration is ideal for irregular surfaces since the transducer does not need to be in direct contact with the treatment area. A gel coupling agent is not required since water serves as the coupling agent. A coupling agent would be more appropriate when using direct contact.
4. **Water immersion is an indirect coupling method requiring the treatment area to be immersed in water. This method of administration is ideal for irregular surfaces since the transducer does not need to be in direct contact with the treatment area. A gel coupling agent is not required with water immersion since water serves as the coupling agent.**

System: Non-Systems
Content Outline: Equipment, Devices, and Technologies; Therapeutic Modalities

Level 2

p. 710-713

PTEXAM ONE: QUESTION 133

A physical therapist examines the breath sounds of a patient diagnosed with pulmonary disease. The therapist identifies crackles during both inspiration and expiration. This finding is MOST representative of which of the following conditions?

1. **Pleural effusion**
2. **Pulmonary fibrosis**
3. **Impaired secretion clearance**
4. **Localized stenosis**

Correct Answer: 3 (Hillegass p. 521)

Auscultation of the lungs with a stethoscope is an examination procedure physical therapists use to identify abnormalities in lung sounds. Abnormal lung sounds may suggest problems with ventilation or airway clearance.

1. Pleural effusion is the accumulation of fluid in the pleural space. Lung sounds are usually decreased, but a pleural friction rub may be heard if the pleural surfaces are inflamed.
2. Pulmonary fibrosis is a type of restrictive lung dysfunction characterized by changes to the alveoli and lung architecture from an inflammatory process. The inflammatory changes cause scarring and fibrotic lesions in the lungs which result in decreased lung compliance, lung volumes, diffusing capacity, increased pulmonary arterial pressure, and work of breathing. Auscultation often reveals decreased breath sounds.
3. **Crackles or rales are abnormal breath sounds heard during auscultation of the lungs with a stethoscope. Crackles are extra sounds caused by the "popping open" of small airways blocked by secretions or fluid and may be heard during both the inspiratory and expiratory phases of the breathing cycle.**
4. Localized stenosis is not a term associated with breath sounds.

System: Cardiovascular and Pulmonary Systems
Content Outline: Foundations for Evaluation, Differential Diagnosis, and Prognosis

 **Level 2**  **p. 421-423**

PTEXAM ONE: QUESTION 134

As part of the medical history, a patient reports a sudden onset of pain. Which medical condition is MOST consistent with this clinical presentation?

1. **Bicipital tendonitis**
2. **Hamstrings strain**
3. **Osgood-Schlatter disease**
4. **Peripheral vascular disease**

Correct Answer: 2 (Dutton p. 942) 

The patient interview provides a physical therapist with an opportunity to identify specific characteristics of pain. Subjective pain descriptors can provide valuable information related to a patient's medical condition. Characteristics to explore may include location, intensity, description, duration, and pattern.

1. Bicipital tendonitis is an inflammatory process of the tendon of the long head of the biceps. The condition is characterized by subjective reports of a deep ache directly in front and on top of the shoulder, made worse with overhead activities or lifting. Pain tends to come on gradually over time and can be heavily influenced by activity.
2. **The hamstrings consist of the semimembranosus, semitendinosus, and biceps femoris muscles. A hamstrings strain is typically caused by muscle overload that occurs when one or more of the muscles is stretched beyond its capacity or challenged with a sudden load. Pain varies based on the severity of the injury, but is usually described as a sudden, sharp pain in the back of the thigh.**
3. Osgood-Schlatter disease, also known as traction apophysitis, is a self-limiting condition that results from repetitive traction on the tibial tuberosity apophysis. The condition is caused by repetitive tension to the patellar tendon and commonly occurs in young athletes. Pain often occurs in the form of point tenderness over the patella tendon at the insertion on the tibial tubercle. Pain tends to come on gradually and is typically made worse with increasing activity.
4. Peripheral vascular disease (PVD) is a condition where there is narrowing of the lumen of blood vessels causing a reduction in circulation usually secondary to atherosclerosis. Symptoms will differ depending on which blood vessel has been compromised. During the early stages of PVD, intermittent claudication may be the only manifestation. In later stages, the patient may experience tingling and numbness of the affected extremities along with pain at rest and during sleep.

System: Musculoskeletal System
Content Outline: Foundations for Evaluation, Differential Diagnosis, and Prognosis

 **Level 1**

PTEXAM ONE: QUESTION 135

A patient attending outpatient physical therapy for right shoulder pain has a positive sulcus sign. This finding would **MOST** likely be present in which of the following medical conditions?

1. Early-onset Alzheimer's disease
2. Rupture of the biceps tendon
3. **Cerebrovascular accident**
4. Duchenne muscular dystrophy

Correct Answer: 3 (Fell p. 174)

A positive sulcus sign at the shoulder can be indicative of glenohumeral instability. This is identified by a depression below the acromion when the arm is held at the side and distracted manually.

1. Alzheimer's disease is a progressive neurological disorder that results in deterioration and irreversible damage within the cerebral cortex and subcortical areas of the brain. The disease is initially noted by a change in higher cortical functions characterized by subtle changes in memory, impaired concentration, and difficulty with new learning. A positive sulcus sign is not associated with this medical condition.
2. A biceps tendon rupture is an injury that causes the tendinous attachment of the biceps to separate from the bone. The biceps may rupture proximally (i.e., shoulder) or distally (i.e., elbow). Although the biceps muscle significantly influences movement at the shoulder and elbow, this injury is not associated with a positive sulcus sign.
3. **A cerebrovascular accident (CVA) is a specific event that results in a lack of oxygen supply to a specific area of the brain secondary to either ischemia or hemorrhage. The outcome of a CVA greatly varies and is based on etiology, extent of the CVA, the area of the brain that is affected, subsequent collateral damage, and the patient's co-morbidities and overall health status. A common finding is weakness or paralysis contralateral to the side of the lesion, often leading to a flaccid shoulder and potentially a positive sulcus sign even after the patient has completed a rehabilitative program.**
4. Duchenne muscular dystrophy is a progressive disorder caused by the absence of the gene required to produce the muscle proteins dystrophin and nebulin. The causative factor is inheritance as an X-linked recessive trait. Characteristics usually manifest between two and five years of age. Progressive weakness, disinterest in running, falling, toe walking, excessive lordosis, and pseudohypertrophy of muscle groups are common symptoms. A positive sulcus sign is not typically observed with Duchenne muscular dystrophy despite the progressive weakness associated with this disorder.

System: Neuromuscular and Nervous Systems
Content Outline: Foundations for Evaluation, Differential Diagnosis, and Prognosis

Level 2

p. 101, 279-280, 330-331

PTEXAM ONE: QUESTION 136

A physical therapist examines a patient who has limited cervical range of motion. As part of the examination, the therapist attempts to screen the patient for possible vertebral artery involvement, but is unable to position the patient's head and neck in the recommended test position. Which of the following actions is the **MOST** appropriate for the therapist to take?

1. Complete the vertebral artery test with the head and neck positioned in approximately 50 percent of the available cervical range of motion
2. **Complete the vertebral artery test as far into the available cervical range of motion as tolerated**
3. Avoid completing the vertebral artery test until the patient has full cervical range of motion
4. Avoid all direct cervical treatment techniques until the vertebral artery test can be assessed at the limits of normal cervical range of motion

Correct Answer: 2 (Dutton p. 1252) 

The vertebral artery test is performed with the patient positioned in supine. The therapist places the patient's head in extension, lateral flexion, and rotation to the ipsilateral side. A positive test is indicated by dizziness, nystagmus, slurred speech or loss of consciousness and may be indicative of compression of the vertebral artery.

1. The vertebral artery test should be administered using the available cervical range of motion and as a result it would not make sense to utilize only a portion of the available range of motion.
2. **The physical therapist should perform the test and clear the patient's vertebral artery for their available range of motion. As the patient gains additional range of motion the test can be readministered.**
3. The vertebral artery test can be performed on patients that possess less than full cervical range of motion.
4. Direct cervical treatment techniques are often employed on patients with less than full cervical range of motion. In many cases it is still necessary to clear the vertebral artery using the patient's available cervical range of motion.

System: Musculoskeletal System
Content Outline: Physical Therapy Examination

Test Taking Tip: In some cases two options express different ways of saying the exact same thing. When this happens the options often mutually exclude each other since it would be impossible for one of the respective options to be correct and the other to be incorrect. In this particular question, option 3 and option 4 imply that the vertebral artery test, and therefore direct cervical treatment techniques, cannot be performed until the patient possesses full cervical range of motion.

Level 3

p. 110

PTEXAM ONE: QUESTION 137

A physical therapist treats a patient who has benign paroxysmal positional vertigo. Which of the following physical therapy treatments would MOST benefit this patient?

1. Dix-Hallpike maneuver
2. **Canalith repositioning maneuvers**
3. Singular neurectomy
4. Gaze stability exercises

Correct Answer: 2 (Goodman – Pathology p. 1644)

Benign paroxysmal positional vertigo (BPPV) is an intense and intermittent vertigo that occurs in relation to rapid movement of the head in a particular direction and is believed to be a mechanical disorder of the labyrinths. Canaliths develop and float into the semicircular canals causing the brain to interpret their presence as an intense rotation of the head.

1. Dix-Hallpike maneuver is not a treatment for BPPV but rather a diagnostic tool. A patient that presents with BPPV will have torsional nystagmus when performing this maneuver. The patient moves from an upright posture to supine with the head hanging over the surface extended and rotated to 45 degrees. Nystagmus will occur in this position when the affected ear is toward the floor and should fatigue within 60 seconds.
2. **Canalith repositioning maneuvers are a highly effective treatment for BPPV and are designed to dislodge the provoking canaliths. This treatment technique attempts to move the canalith debris out of the affected semicircular canal and back to the otolith. Canalith repositioning maneuvers begin in the Dix-Hallpike position to provoke vertigo. Repeated head rolling utilizes gravity to assist with movement of the debris. Treatment continues until no further nystagmus is noted.**
3. A singular neurectomy is a surgical procedure that can assist with BPPV, but is rarely performed. This is not a physical therapy treatment but rather a selective surgical transection of the nerve supply to the posterior canal.
4. Gaze stability exercises are frequently used in the treatment of unilateral vestibular hypofunction with the goal of improving the vestibuloocular reflex and other systems that provide gaze stability while the head is in motion.

System: Neuromuscular and Nervous Systems
Content Outline: Interventions

 Level 2  p. 266

PTEXAM ONE: QUESTION 138

A physical therapist inspects the static wrist and hand position of a patient who has advanced rheumatoid arthritis. Which positioning would MOST likely be observed based on the medical diagnosis?

1. Radial deviation of the radiocarpal joint and radial deviation of the fingers
2. **Radial deviation of the radiocarpal joint and ulnar deviation of the fingers**
3. Ulnar deviation of the radiocarpal joint and radial deviation of the fingers
4. Ulnar deviation of the radiocarpal joint and ulnar deviation of the fingers

Correct Answer: 2 (Sarwark p. 429)

Rheumatoid arthritis is a systemic autoimmune disorder of unknown etiology. The disease presents with a chronic inflammatory reaction in the synovial tissues of a joint that results in erosion of cartilage and supporting structures within the capsule. Rheumatoid arthritis is diagnosed based on the clinical presentation of involved joints, the presence of blood rheumatoid factor, and radiographic changes.

1. Patients with advanced rheumatoid arthritis tend to exhibit radial deviation of the radiocarpal joint, however, the fingers would tend to be positioned in ulnar deviation.
2. **Patients with advanced rheumatoid arthritis tend to exhibit radial deviation of the radiocarpal joint and ulnar deviation of the fingers. The radiocarpal changes include a distinct loss of joint space and erosive bone changes. Ulnar displacement of the extensor tendons and an increased ulnar approach of the flexor tendons contribute to the ulnar deviation of the fingers.**
3. Patients with advanced rheumatoid arthritis tend to exhibit radial deviation of the radiocarpal joint and ulnar deviation of the fingers. This option is opposite of the typical positioning of a wrist and hand affected by rheumatoid arthritis.
4. Patients with advanced rheumatoid arthritis tend to exhibit radial deviation of the radiocarpal joint. They would, however, exhibit ulnar deviation of the fingers.

System: Musculoskeletal System
Content Outline: Foundations for Evaluation, Differential Diagnosis, and Prognosis

 Level 1  p. 126, 624-625

PTEXAM ONE: QUESTION 139

A physical therapist instructs a patient in a self-stretching activity using the FABER test position. This position would be **MOST** useful to stretch which of the following groups of muscles at the hip?

1. Abductors
2. Flexors
3. External rotators
4. **Internal rotators**

Correct Answer: 4 (Kisner p. 752) 

The FABER or figure-4 position occurs with the patient assuming a supine position with the involved leg flexed, abducted, and externally rotated at the hip so that the ankle is resting on the opposite leg. FABER stands for flexion, abduction, and external rotation.

1. The hip abductors are stretched when the hip is positioned in adduction. The FABER position requires the hip to be in abduction.
2. The hip flexors are stretched when the hip is positioned in extension. The FABER position requires the hip to be in flexion.
3. The hip external rotators are stretched when the hip is positioned in internal rotation. The FABER position requires the hip to be in external rotation.
4. **The hip internal rotators are stretched when the hip is positioned in external rotation. The FABER position requires the hip to be in external rotation.**

System: Musculoskeletal System
Content Outline: Interventions

 Level 1  p. 107

PTEXAM ONE: QUESTION 140

As part of a cognitive assessment, a physical therapist asks a patient to count from one to twenty-five by increments of three. What component of cognitive function does this task **MOST** accurately assess?

1. **Attention**
2. Constructional ability
3. Abstract ability
4. Orientation

Correct Answer: 1 (O'Sullivan p. 79)

Attention is defined as the capacity of the brain to process information from the environment or from long-term memory. The complexity and familiarity of the task determines the degree of attention required to complete the task.

1. **Attention can be assessed by asking a patient to count from one to twenty-five by increments of three. The task should be relatively easy for most individuals, however, it requires the person to exert a sustained, consistent effort. Attention deficits are common with many neurological disorders including brain injury, stroke, and dementia.**
2. Constructional ability can be assessed by asking a person to copy figures consisting of varying sizes and shapes or to draw a known item such as a clock.
3. Abstract ability can be assessed by asking a person to interpret a common proverb or to describe similarities or differences between two objects.
4. Orientation can be assessed by asking a person to identify time (e.g., day, month, season), person (e.g., name), and place (e.g., city, state).

System: Neuromuscular and Nervous Systems
Content Outline: Physical Therapy Examination

 Level 2

PTEXAM ONE: QUESTION 141

A physical therapist treats a patient who sustained an acute wound to the anterior surface of the forearm. Which of the following types of cells would have been the FIRST to arrive at the injury site immediately following the incident?

1. Endothelial cells
2. Fibroblasts
3. Leukocytes
4. **Platelets**

Correct Answer: 4 (Roy p. 546)

Normal wound healing occurs as damaged tissues move through distinct yet overlapping phases of repair. The phases of repair occur in a predictable sequence with complex cellular activity and chemical reactions occurring at each phase.

1. Endothelial cells stimulate the production of new blood vessels as well as transport oxygen and nutrients into the wound environment. Endothelial cells are most active in the proliferative phase of wound healing.
2. Fibroblasts produce a wound matrix that consists of collagen, elastin, and proteoglycans. Fibroblast activity is facilitated by macrophages that are present from the inflammatory phase. Fibroblasts are most active in the proliferative phase of wound healing.
3. Leukocytes (i.e., white blood cells) arrive at the wound site in response to the coagulation cascade. Leukocytes include both monocytes and granulocytes. Leukocytes are most active in the inflammatory phase of wound healing, however, they arrive at the wound site after the platelets.
4. **Platelets are the first cells to arrive at the wound site. The cells attach to exposed collagen at the injury site and release chemicals that attract more platelets. Collectively, the platelets form a platelet plug to temporarily stop the bleeding. Platelets are most active in the hemostasis phase of wound healing.**

System: Other Systems
Content Outline: Physical Therapy Examination

 Level 1  p. 395, 499

PTEXAM ONE: QUESTION 142

A physical therapist reads in the medical record that radiographs confirmed the presence of a reverse Hill-Sachs fracture. What injury would MOST likely be associated with this type of fracture?

1. Anterior glenohumeral dislocation
2. **Posterior glenohumeral dislocation**
3. Rotator cuff tear
4. Biceps tendon rupture

Correct Answer: 2 (Sarwark p. 320)

A reverse Hill-Sachs fracture (i.e., reverse Hill-Sachs lesion) is an impaction fracture of the anterior medial humeral head. Management of this injury is primarily based on the size of the impression defect.

1. A Hill-Sachs fracture, sometimes referred to as a Hill-Sachs lesion, is characterized as an impaction fracture of the posterior superior humeral head and is frequently diagnosed in patients who have repeatedly sustained anterior glenohumeral dislocations. Approximately 95% of dislocations occur in an anterior direction.
2. **A reverse Hill-Sachs fracture is typically associated with a posterior glenohumeral dislocation. Patients with a posterior glenohumeral dislocation typically present holding their arm medially rotated and adducted and may exhibit flattening of the anterior shoulder and a prominent coracoid process.**
3. A fracture of the greater tuberosity can result in a rotator cuff tear, however, this is not associated with a reverse Hill-Sachs fracture.
4. A biceps tendon rupture is an injury that occurs to the biceps tendon causing the attachment to separate from the bone. The biceps may rupture proximally (i.e., shoulder) or distally (i.e., elbow). A biceps tendon rupture is rarely associated with a fracture.

System: Musculoskeletal System
Content Outline: Foundations for Evaluation, Differential Diagnosis, and Prognosis

 Level 1

PTEXAM ONE: QUESTION 143

A physical therapist uses the Modified Ashworth Scale when assessing a patient post stroke. Which of the following assessment procedures would be the **MOST** appropriate when using the Modified Ashworth Scale?

1. Strength testing
2. Deep tendon reflex testing
3. Active range of motion
4. **Passive range of motion**

Correct Answer: 4 (O'Sullivan p. 146)

The Modified Ashworth Scale (MAS) is an instrument that is used to assess muscle spasticity. The MAS uses ordinal scoring, with a grade of "0" indicating the absence of spasticity and a grade of "4" indicating the presence of rigidity.

1. Strength testing may be used for patients who have had a stroke to determine which muscles have been affected as a result of the neurological damage. However, strength testing would not provide valuable information when using the MAS since the instrument is used to assess spasticity.
2. Deep tendon reflex testing may be used for patients who have had a stroke to determine if the patient has hyporeflexia or hyperreflexia as a result of the neurological damage. However, deep tendon reflex testing would not provide valuable information when using the MAS since the instrument is used to assess spasticity.
3. Active range of motion may be used for patients who have had a stroke to determine the patient's functional use of their extremities. However, active range of motion would not provide valuable information when using the MAS since the instrument is used to assess spasticity, which requires a passive assessment.
4. **The MAS is an assessment tool that is used to grade spasticity. Spasticity is defined as increased resistance to passive stretch that is velocity-dependent, therefore, passive range of motion would be the most appropriate method for measuring spasticity.**

System: Neuromuscular and Nervous Systems
Content Outline: Physical Therapy Examination

 Level 1  p. 264

PTEXAM ONE: QUESTION 144

A physical therapist treats a patient who has lower extremity weakness due to a laceration injury to the tibial nerve. Which movement would **LEAST** likely be affected by this nerve injury?

1. Plantar flexion of the ankle
2. **Extension of the great toe**
3. Flexion of the great toe
4. Flexion of toes 2-5

Correct Answer: 2 (Kendall p. 364) 

The tibial nerve is a branch of the sciatic nerve that supplies innervation to the muscles of the posterior lower leg. In the foot, the tibial nerve branches into the medial and lateral plantar nerves.

1. Ankle plantar flexion is performed by several muscles that are innervated by the tibial nerve, including the gastrocnemius, soleus, plantaris, tibialis posterior, flexor hallucis longus, and flexor digitorum longus. A patient with a tibial nerve injury would have significant difficulty performing ankle plantar flexion.
2. **Extension of the great toe is performed by the extensor hallucis longus and extensor hallucis brevis. These muscles are innervated by the deep peroneal nerve, which is a branch of the common peroneal nerve. A patient with a tibial nerve injury would have no difficulty performing extension of the great toe.**
3. Flexion of the great toe is performed by the flexor hallucis longus and flexor hallucis brevis. These muscles are innervated by the tibial nerve. A patient with a tibial nerve injury would have significant difficulty performing flexion of the great toe.
4. Flexion of toes 2-5 is performed by the flexor digitorum longus and flexor digitorum brevis. These muscles are innervated by the tibial nerve. A patient with a tibial nerve injury would have significant difficulty performing flexion of toes 2-5.

System: Neuromuscular and Nervous Systems
Content Outline: Physical Therapy Examination

 Level 1  p. 251

PTEXAM ONE: QUESTION 145

A physical therapist treats a patient following knee arthroscopy after observing a limitation in knee flexion range of motion when the patient was positioned in hooklying. The therapist uses a contract-relax stretching technique to improve the patient's range of motion. Which clinical scenario would **MOST** benefit from this intervention?

1. Stiffness of the joint capsule
2. Decreased flexibility of the rectus femoris
3. Bony obstruction due to arthritic joint surfaces
4. **Increased quadriceps muscle spasm**

Correct Answer: 4 (Kisner p. 103)

Contract-relax is a proprioceptive neuromuscular facilitation (PNF) technique used to increase range of motion. As the extremity reaches the point of limitation, the patient performs a maximal contraction of the antagonistic muscle group. The therapist resists movement for eight to ten seconds followed by relaxation. The technique is repeated until no further gains in range of motion are noted during the session.

1. Stiffness within the joint capsule is a common cause of joint range of motion limitation. However, the contract-relax method tends to exert its effects on the muscle fibers and therefore would not be as effective at treating connective tissue tightness.
2. The rectus femoris is a two-joint muscle that crosses the knee and hip joints. It would not likely limit flexion range of motion in a hooklying position since the muscle would be "on slack" at the hip joint. Additionally, the contract-relax method results in increased range of motion through relaxation of the muscle fibers. If the rectus femoris is truly inflexible, the patient would likely need to perform static stretching over a longer period of time to see range of motion gains.
3. If the patient's range of motion is limited secondary to bony obstruction, stretching would be unlikely to result in improvements in range of motion.
4. **The contract-relax method is thought to lead to muscle relaxation through the principles of autogenic or reciprocal inhibition. Because the technique exerts its effects on the muscle fibers, it is more effective at treating range of motion limitations due to muscle hypertonicity or spasm as opposed to connective tissue tightness.**

System: Musculoskeletal System
Content Outline: Interventions

  p. 116-118, 291-292

PTEXAM ONE: QUESTION 146

A patient informs a physical therapist that additional therapy visits will not be covered by their medical insurance provider. The patient is 12 weeks post anterior cruciate ligament reconstruction and has had an unremarkable post-operative progression. Which of the following actions is the **MOST** appropriate for the therapist to take?

1. Offer to treat the patient pro bono
2. Devise an affordable payment plan
3. Request additional visits from the third party payer
4. **Discharge the patient with a home exercise program**

Correct Answer: 4 (Kisner p. 820) 

Physical therapists should discharge patients from physical therapy when the anticipated goals or expected outcomes have been achieved or the patient is no longer benefitting from physical therapy services.

1. Physical therapists are not permitted to offer pro bono services to selected patients based on factors such as reimbursement or the ability to pay. Therapists should strive to treat all patients equitably.
2. A payment plan permits a patient to pay for incurred physical therapy services in a gradual manner. This may be a more desirable option when a patient requires ongoing physical therapy services, but does not have adequate financial resources.
3. Requesting additional physical therapy visits from the third party payer is a possible option, however, based on the patient's diagnosis and post-operative progression additional visits may not be warranted.
4. **A patient 12 weeks status post anterior cruciate ligament reconstruction that has experienced an unremarkable recovery should be able to function independently using a well designed home exercise program. The program should incorporate activities such as jogging, strengthening, and agility drills.**

System: Musculoskeletal System
Content Outline: Interventions

PTEXAM ONE: QUESTION 147

A physical therapist reads in a patient's medical chart that the patient has been prescribed albuterol. Which of the following conditions would **MOST** likely require the use of this medication?

1. Breast cancer
2. Angina pectoris
3. **Exercise-induced asthma**
4. Spinal cord injury

Correct Answer: 3 (Ciccone p. 405) 

Albuterol is a beta-adrenergic agonist, a class of medications that stimulate beta-2 adrenergic receptors. Stimulation of these receptors results in relaxation of the bronchiole smooth muscles leading to bronchodilation.

1. There are several classes of drugs that can be used to treat breast cancer, some of which include alkylating agents, antimetabolites, anticancer antibiotics, antimicrotubule agents, and anticancer hormones. Albuterol would not be used to treat cancer or its associated symptoms.
2. Angina pectoris refers to chest pain that occurs secondary to ischemia of the heart musculature. The most common classes of drugs used to treat this condition include organic nitrates, beta blockers, and calcium channel blockers. Albuterol would not be used to treat angina pectoris.
3. **Exercise-induced asthma occurs when the bronchioles constrict in response to exercise, resulting in shortness of breath and wheezing. Albuterol is a medication that is commonly prescribed for conditions that result from bronchoconstriction, such as asthma or chronic obstructive pulmonary disease.**
4. There are a large variety of medications used to treat the symptoms that occur secondary to a spinal cord injury. Antispasticity medications (e.g., baclofen) are commonly prescribed to help control the spasticity and resultant pain that occur secondary to a spinal cord injury. Albuterol would not be used to treat symptoms of a spinal cord injury.

System: Cardiovascular and Pulmonary Systems
Content Outline: Foundations for Evaluation, Differential Diagnosis, and Prognosis

 Level 1  p. 405, 414-415

PTEXAM ONE: QUESTION 148

A patient is referred to physical therapy with a C6 nerve root injury. Which of the following clinical findings would be the **LEAST** expected with this type of injury?

1. Diminished sensation on the anterior arm and the index finger
2. Weakness in the biceps and supinator
3. Diminished brachioradialis reflex
4. **Paresthesias of the long and ring fingers**

Correct Answer: 4 (Magee p. 24)

Involvement of a specific nerve root often results in predictable impairments including diminished sensation, muscle weakness, impaired reflexes, and paresthesias.

1. Diminished sensation on the anterior arm and index finger is characteristic of a C6 nerve root injury and is assessed using light touch from a cotton ball.
2. Weakness in the biceps and supinator muscles is characteristic of a C6 nerve root injury and is assessed through resistive testing as part of an upper quarter screening examination and/or specific manual muscle testing.
3. A diminished brachioradialis reflex is characteristic of a C6 nerve root injury and is assessed by striking the blunt end of a reflex hammer at the distal end of the radius with the patient's elbow flexed to 90 degrees and the upper extremity supported by the therapist.
4. **Paresthesias of the long and ring fingers are commonly associated with the C7 nerve root. Other findings of a C7 nerve root injury include weakness of the triceps and wrist flexors, and a diminished triceps reflex.**

System: Neuromuscular and Nervous Systems
Content Outline: Foundations for Evaluation, Differential Diagnosis, and Prognosis

 Level 1  p. 245-246, 250

PTEXAM ONE: QUESTION 149

A patient post traumatic brain injury is presently at the confused-appropriate level of cognitive functioning. The patient has progressed well in therapy, however, has been bothered by diplopia. Which of the following treatment strategies would be the **MOST** appropriate to address diplopia?

1. Provide non-verbal instructions within the patient's direct line of sight
2. **Place a patch over one of the patient's eyes**
3. Ask the patient to turn their head to one side when experiencing diplopia
4. Instruct the patient to carefully focus on a single object

Correct Answer: 2 (O'Sullivan p. 1184)

Diplopia refers to double vision resulting from defective function of the extraocular muscles that is typically caused by damage to the brain. A patient with diplopia is often instructed to wear a patch alternately over one of their eyes. Specific strengthening exercises of the extraocular muscles can serve to improve the patient's vision.

1. Verbal instruction is often more desirable than non-verbal instruction since double vision would tend to minimize the effectiveness of non-verbal instruction.
2. **A patient with diplopia will actually see two sets of the environment. If wearing the patch over the alternate eye does not resolve the problem, the patient may require prism glasses.**
3. The patient will not alleviate diplopia through positioning of the head. Double vision can result from damage to the brain and requires strengthening and the use of an eye patch.
4. A patient with diplopia can use the extraocular muscles of each eye, but they are not in focus. Verbal cueing to "focus" on a single object will not alleviate diplopia since strengthening is required.

System: Neuromuscular and Nervous Systems
Content Outline: Interventions

 Level 3

PTEXAM ONE: QUESTION 150

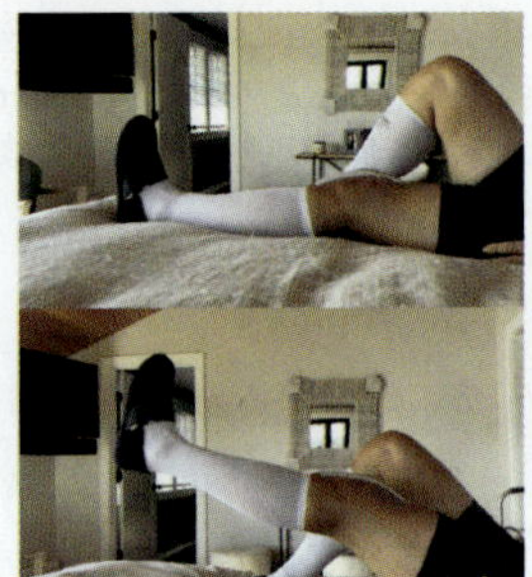

A physical therapist works with a patient in their home following knee surgery. Which documentation would be **MOST** consistent with the depicted starting and ending points of the exercise shown in the image assuming the patient has full passive knee extension?

1. **Straight leg raise to 30 degrees with 10 degree extension lag**
2. Straight leg raise to 30 degrees with 20 degree extension lag
3. Straight leg raise to 60 degrees with 10 degree extension lag
4. Straight leg raise to 60 degrees with 20 degree extension lag

Correct Answer: 1 (Kisner p. 785)

A supine straight leg raise (SLR) combines isotonic hip flexion with an isometric quadriceps contraction to maintain knee extension. The rectus femoris is the primary muscle activated during the SLR exercise. An extension lag of the knee is a common impairment observed post-operatively due to muscle weakness caused by joint effusion or pain that inhibits the function of the quadriceps. When the patient is unable to fully extend the knee despite having full passive extension range of motion, the difference in the active versus passive range of motion is the amount of the extension lag.

1. **A supine SLR is the exercise depicted in the image with the opposite hip flexed to 45 degrees, knee flexed to 90 degrees, and the foot stabilized on the supporting surface (e.g., bed). It is clear in the image that the end point of the SLR is below the height of the opposite knee with only a slight extension lag of the involved knee. Therefore, an SLR to 30 degrees with a 10 degree extension lag represents the documentation that would be most consistent with the depicted image.**
2. Although the amount of hip flexion at the end point of the SLR exercise depicted in the image is 30 degrees, the extension lag at the knee is less severe (i.e., 10 degrees) than the 20 degree extension lag recorded in this option.
3. Although the 10 degree extension lag recorded in this option is correct, documenting the SLR to 60 degrees would be inaccurate since the end point of hip flexion is below the opposite lower extremity as depicted in the image.
4. Documenting the exercise depicted in the image as an SLR to 60 degrees with a 20 degree extension lag would be inaccurate for both the end point of the SLR and the amount of extension lag at the knee. The end point of hip flexion depicted in the SLR is more representative of 30 degrees than 60 degrees and the extension lag is better recorded as 10 degrees than 20 degrees.

System: Musculoskeletal System
Content Outline: Interventions

 Level 2

PTEXAM ONE: QUESTION 151

A physician orders an electrocardiogram (ECG) for a patient diagnosed with congestive heart failure. The medical record indicates the patient is currently taking digitalis. What effect would digitalis **MOST** likely have on the patient's ECG?

1. Sinus tachycardia
2. **Lengthened PR interval**
3. Lengthened QT interval
4. Elevated ST segment

Correct Answer: 2 (Ciccone p. 362)

Digitalis is a medication given to increase the force of myocontractility and is often prescribed for patients with heart failure. Increased contractility increases cardiac output and decreases preload, cardiac workload, and myocardial oxygen demand, thus reducing the clinical effects of congestive heart failure. Therapists should be aware of the potential for digitalis toxicity when using this medication.

1. Sinus tachycardia is a fast heart rate (greater than 100 bpm) that has its origin in the SA node.
2. **Digitalis prolongs the PR interval on the ECG by increasing conduction time through the AV node.**
3. The QT interval measures the depolarization and repolarization time of the ventricles and extends from the beginning of the QRS complex to the end of the T wave. Digitalis may produce shortening of the QT interval.
4. The ST segment represents the beginning of ventricular repolarization and is generally isoelectric. The ST segment is elevated in an acute myocardial infarction, however, digitalis may produce sagging in the ST segment.

System: Cardiovascular and Pulmonary Systems
Content Outline: Foundations for Evaluation, Differential Diagnosis, and Prognosis

 Level 2  p. 402-403, 405

PTEXAM ONE: QUESTION 152

A physical therapist completes an examination on a patient who has Duchenne muscular dystrophy. The referral indicates that the patient was diagnosed with the disease less than one year ago. Assuming a normal progression, which of the following findings would be the **FIRST** to occur?

1. Distal muscle weakness
2. **Proximal muscle weakness**
3. Impaired respiratory function
4. Inability to perform activities of daily living

Correct Answer: 2 (Ratliffe p. 241) 

Duchenne muscular dystrophy is an inherited disorder, characterized by rapidly worsening muscle weakness that starts in the proximal muscles of the lower extremities and pelvis, and later affects all voluntary muscles.

1. Distal muscles are affected later in the course of the disease process.
2. **Muscle weakness and atrophy begin in the proximal muscles of the lower extremities and pelvis, then progress to the muscles of the shoulders and neck, followed by loss of upper extremity muscles and respiratory muscles.**
3. The muscles of respiration are not initially affected in patients with Duchenne muscular dystrophy.
4. As the condition progresses, weakness begins to interfere with activities of daily living.

System: Musculoskeletal System
Content Outline: Foundations for Evaluation, Differential Diagnosis, and Prognosis

 Level 2   p. 313, 334-335

PTEXAM ONE: QUESTION 153

A physical therapist obtains an x-ray of a patient recently referred to physical therapy after experiencing an increase in back pain following activity. The patient previously participated in competitive gymnastics, however, reports that their back was unable to tolerate the intensity of training. Based on the presented x-ray, the therapist should expect the patient's medical diagnosis to be which of the following clinical conditions?

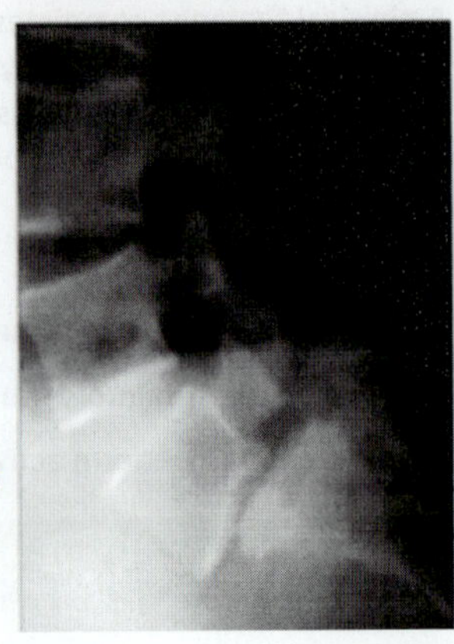

1. Spondylitis
2. Spondylolysis
3. **Spondylolisthesis**
4. Spondyloptosis

Correct Answer: 3 (Magee p. 569) 

There are a variety of commonly encountered medical conditions that significantly impact the lumbar spine. Physical therapists should be familiar with the clinical presentation and management of these medical conditions.

1. Spondylitis refers to inflammation of a vertebra.
2. Spondylolysis refers to a defect in the pars interarticularis or the arch of the vertebra. This is most common in the L5 vertebra, but can also occur in other lumbar or thoracic vertebrae.
3. **Spondylolisthesis refers to the forward displacement of one vertebra over another. The x-ray involves spondylolisthesis at the L5-S1 level. Individuals involved in physical activities such as weight lifting, gymnastics or football are particularly susceptible to this condition. The severity of the spondylolisthesis is classified on a scale of 1-5 based on how much a given vertebral body has slipped forward over the vertebral body beneath it.**
4. Spondyloptosis refers to the condition where a vertebral body has shifted completely off of the adjacent vertebral body (grade 5).

System: Musculoskeletal System
Content Outline: Foundations for Evaluation, Differential Diagnosis, and Prognosis

 Level 2  p. 182-183

PTEXAM ONE: QUESTION 154

A physical therapist treats a patient diagnosed with cystic fibrosis. As part of the treatment session the therapist attempts to improve the efficiency of the patient's breathing. Which of the following techniques is the **MOST** appropriate to encourage full expansion at the base of the lungs?

1. Manual percussion over the posterior portion of the ribs with the patient in prone
2. **Manual contacts with pressure over the lateral borders of the ribs with the patient in supine**
3. Manual vibration over the lateral portion of the ribs with the patient in sidelying
4. Manual cues over the epigastric area with the patient in supine

Correct Answer: 2 (Frownfelter p. 362)

Applying direct pressure with the hands on the lateral borders of the ribs with the patient in supine can promote a more efficient breathing pattern. Physical therapy management for a child with cystic fibrosis may include postural drainage techniques, chest percussion, vibration, and suctioning.

1. Manual percussion over the posterior ribs with the patient in prone describes the postural drainage position and technique used for airway clearance, not expansion, of the posterior basal lung segments.
2. **Direct pressure of the hands over the lateral ribs can facilitate expansion of the basal lobes of the lungs.**
3. Manual vibration over the lateral portion of the ribs in sidelying describes the postural drainage position and technique used for airway clearance, not expansion, of the lateral basal lung segments.
4. The epigastric area refers to the upper central region of the abdomen. Manual cues on this area would not encourage expansion at the base of the lungs.

System: Cardiovascular and Pulmonary Systems
Content Outline: Interventions

 Level 2  p. 440-443

PTEXAM ONE: QUESTION 155

A physical therapist treats a patient who sustained deep partial-thickness burns to the anterior surface of both lower extremities. After identifying an irregularity in the patient's laboratory results, the referring physician discusses with the therapist the possibility of discontinuing the use of the topical medication silver sulfadiazine. Which of the following findings is MOST likely related to the use of silver sulfadiazine?

1. **Leukopenia**
2. Peripheral edema
3. Hypokalemia
4. Altered pH balance

Correct Answer: 1 (Paz p. 316)

Silver sulfadiazine is a topical antibiotic that works by interfering with bacterial nucleic acid production by disrupting folic acid synthesis in susceptible bacteria. The antibiotic is a broad spectrum agent that can be applied directly to the skin. Additional problems encountered with sulfa drugs include gastrointestinal distress and allergic reactions.

1. **Silver sulfadiazine is a sulfa drug that can produce a decrease in the number of circulating white blood cells (leukopenia), usually below 5,000 mm^3.**
2. Peripheral edema refers to the swelling of tissues in the lower limbs due to the accumulation of fluid. Peripheral edema frequently is associated with heart failure, venous insufficiency, pregnancy, kidney disease, and selected pharmacological agents, however, it is not a side effect of silver sulfadiazine.
3. Hypokalemia refers to an abnormally low potassium concentration in the blood. The condition can be caused by vomiting, diarrhea, burns, uncontrolled diabetes mellitus, diuretic therapy, and steroid therapy, however, it is not a side effect of silver sulfadiazine.
4. The pH is a measure of the degree to which a solution is acidic or alkaline. A pH of 7.0 indicates neutrality, a pH of less than 7.0 indicates acidity, a pH of more than 7.0 indicates alkalinity. The body's fluids are usually between 7.35-7.45. Topical agents such as mafenide acetate would be more likely to alter pH.

System: Other Systems
Content Outline: Interventions

 Level 3

 p. 516

PTEXAM ONE: QUESTION 156

A physical therapist reviews the medical record of a patient who has atrial flutter. Which characteristic of atrial flutter BEST differentiates this condition from atrial fibrillation?

1. **The regularity of the atrial rhythm**
2. The irregularity of the atrial rhythm
3. The rapid rate of atrial depolarization
4. The slow rate of atrial depolarization

Correct Answer: 1 (Hillegass p. 320)

Atrial flutter is a frequently occurring abnormal heart rhythm characterized by rapid atrial tachycardia. This rapid rate creates decreased filling time of the ventricles resulting in diminished amounts of blood being ejected from the heart. Atrial fibrillation is an arrhythmia characterized by erratic electrical conductivity within the atria.

1. **In atrial flutter, the heart beats fast, but in a very regular rhythm producing sawtooth P waves. In atrial fibrillation, the heart also beats fast, however, the rhythm is irregular.**
2. Atrial flutter is characterized by a rapid rate of atrial contraction (i.e., 250-350 beats per minute) in a consistent and predictable rhythm. An irregularity of the atrial rhythm is characteristic of atrial fibrillation.
3. Both atrial flutter and atrial fibrillation are characterized by extremely rapid rates of atrial depolarization. This rapid rate creates decreased filling time of the ventricles resulting in diminished amounts of blood being ejected from the heart.
4. Both atrial flutter and atrial fibrillation are characterized by extremely rapid rates of atrial depolarization. A slow rate of atrial depolarization would be more characteristic of bradycardia which refers to a heart rate of less than 60 beats per minute.

System: Cardiovascular and Pulmonary Systems
Content Outline: Foundations for Evaluation, Differential Diagnosis, and Prognosis

 Level 1

 p. 426-427

PTEXAM ONE: QUESTION 157

A note in the medical record indicates that a patient was recently prescribed Lasix (furosemide). Which of the following medical conditions is MOST commonly associated with the use of this medication?

1. **Atrial flutter**
2. **Deep vein thrombosis**
3. **Hyperlipidemia**
4. **Congestive heart failure**

Correct Answer: 4 (Goodman – Pathology p. 599)

Lasix (furosemide) is a loop diuretic often used in the treatment of edema or hypertension. Lasix increases the excretion of sodium and chloride in the kidneys, thereby increasing urination and decreasing the volume of fluid that is retained within the body.

1. Atrial flutter is a type of cardiac arrhythmia characterized by a rapid contraction rate of the atria. Digoxin is an example of a medication that may be used to treat atrial flutter.
2. Deep vein thrombosis is a condition where a blood clot forms in a vein, most commonly in the lower extremities. Thrombolytic drugs would be administered to help break up an already existing blood clot.
3. Hyperlipidemia is a condition characterized by high levels of lipids (i.e., triglycerides, cholesterol) within the blood. Atorvastatin (Lipitor) is an example of a medication that may be used to treat hyperlipidemia.
4. **Congestive heart failure is a condition characterized by an inability of the heart to effectively pump blood to meet the metabolic demands of the body. Chronic heart failure can result in pulmonary edema or peripheral edema, depending on the side of the heart that is affected. Lasix is a medication that is commonly prescribed to help lessen the edema associated with chronic heart failure.**

System: Cardiovascular and Pulmonary Systems
Content Outline: Foundations for Evaluation, Differential Diagnosis, and Prognosis

Level 2  p. 402-403, 415, 454-455

PTEXAM ONE: QUESTION 158

A physical therapist instructs a patient to expire maximally after taking a maximal inspiration. The therapist can use these instructions to assess which of the following lung measures?

1. **Expiratory reserve volume**
2. **Inspiratory reserve volume**
3. **Total lung capacity**
4. **Vital capacity**

Correct Answer: 4 (Frownfelter p. 139) 

Vital capacity is the maximum volume of gas that can be exhaled after a maximum inhalation.

1. Expiratory reserve volume (ERV) is the additional volume of air that can be exhaled beyond the normal tidal exhalation. ERV is one component of vital capacity.
2. Inspiratory reserve volume (IRV) is the additional volume of air that can be inhaled beyond the normal tidal inhalation. IRV is one component of vital capacity.
3. Total lung capacity is the maximum volume to which the lungs can be expanded. It is the sum of vital capacity and residual volume: TLC = VC + RV.
4. **Vital capacity is the maximum volume of gas that can be exhaled after a maximum inhalation. It is equal to the sum of inspiratory reserve volume, tidal volume, and expiratory reserve volume: VC = IRV + TV + ERV.**

System: Cardiovascular and Pulmonary Systems
Content Outline: Physical Therapy Examination

 Level 1  p. 398-399

PTEXAM ONE: QUESTION 159

A patient's medical record indicates the presence of a significant electrolyte imbalance. Which of the following conditions would MOST commonly be associated with an increased risk of cardiac arrest if left untreated?

1. Hypercalcemia
2. **Hyperkalemia**
3. Hypermagnesemia
4. Hypernatremia

Correct Answer: 2 (Paz p. 358)

Electrolytes play a critical role in maintaining homeostasis within the body. Examples of critical roles played by electrolytes include regulating cardiac function, fluid balance, acid-base balance, and neurologic activity. The most serious electrolyte imbalances involve abnormalities in the level of calcium, potassium, and sodium.

1. Hypercalcemia refers to an excessive level of calcium in the blood. Normal serum calcium is 8.4-10.2 mg/dL. The condition is most commonly associated with hyperparathyroidism since excessive parathyroid hormone raises the level of circulating calcium above normal. Symptoms typically include constipation, pain, nausea, and vomiting.
2. **Hyperkalemia refers to an excessive level of potassium in the blood. Normal serum potassium is 3.5-5.0 mEq/L. Levels higher than 7 mEq/L can have significant hemodynamic and neurologic consequences, while levels exceeding 8.5 mEq/L can cause respiratory paralysis or cardiac arrest. Symptoms typically are related to abnormalities in muscular or cardiac function.**
3. Hypermagnesemia refers to an excessive level of magnesium in the blood. Normal serum magnesium is 1.5-2.0 mEq/L. This condition is relatively rare since the kidneys are able to eliminate excess magnesium by rapidly reducing its tubular absorption. Hypermagnesemia is most often caused by renal failure. Symptoms typically include hypotension and respiratory depression.
4. Hypernatremia refers to an excessive level of sodium in the blood. Normal serum sodium is 135-145 mEq/L. The condition results when there is a net water loss or a sodium gain and reflects too little water in relation to total body sodium and potassium. Hypernatremia is most often caused by impaired thirst or restricted access to water and can be facilitated by pathologic conditions with increased fluid loss. The primary symptom of this condition is thirst.

System: Other Systems
Content Outline: Foundations for Evaluation, Differential Diagnosis, and Prognosis

 **Level 2** p. 646

PTEXAM ONE: QUESTION 160

If the forced expiratory volume in one second (FEV_1) test is negative for airway obstruction in 99 percent of individuals without lung disease, then the measurement of FEV_1 BEST represents which of the following research terms?

1. Sensitive
2. **Specific**
3. Reliable
4. Valid

Correct Answer: 2 (Portney p. 620)

The validity of a diagnostic test, such as the FEV_1 test, is evaluated by its accuracy in assessing the presence or absence of a target condition such as airway obstruction. A test is considered to be specific when the test is negative in persons who do not have the disease. A highly specific test will rarely be positive when a person does not have the disease.

1. Sensitivity is the probability of obtaining a positive test among individuals who have the disease. In this example, neither condition was met: the test result was negative for airway obstruction and the individuals tested did not have lung disease.
2. **Specificity is the probability of obtaining a negative test among individuals without the disease (who should test negative). Since 99 of 100 individuals without lung disease had a negative FEV_1 test for airway obstruction, the test is highly specific.**
3. Reliability refers to the extent to which a test or measurement is consistent or yields the same result on repeated trials. In this example, there is no indication that the FEV_1 was administered more than once, therefore no estimate of reliability is possible.
4. Validity refers to the degree to which a test or measurement accurately reflects or assesses the specific concept the clinician is attempting to measure. Validity is concerned with the success at measuring what was set out to be measured. In this example, the data does not provide useful information for assessing the extent to which FEV_1 is a valid way to identify airway obstruction.

System: Cardiovascular and Pulmonary Systems
Content Outline: Physical Therapy Examination

 **Level 1**  p. 815

PTEXAM ONE: QUESTION 161

A physical therapist applies an automated external defibrillator (AED) to a patient in cardiac arrest. In addition to ventricular fibrillation, what condition is MOST likely to be identified and treated with the AED?

1. Atrial fibrillation
2. Premature atrial contractions
3. **Ventricular tachycardia**
4. First degree ventricular heart block

Correct Answer: 3 (Le Baudour p. 205)

An AED is a portable electronic device that automatically diagnoses the potentially life-threatening cardiac arrhythmias of ventricular fibrillation and ventricular tachycardia. The electrical current potentially stops the abnormal rhythm and allows the heart to begin to beat normally by administering an electrical shock.

1. Atrial fibrillation is a common arrhythmia where the atria are depolarized between 350 and 600 times/minute. Atrial fibrillation occurs in healthy hearts and in patients with coronary artery disease, hypertension, and valvular disease.
2. Premature atrial contractions occur when an ectopic focus in the atrium initiates an impulse before the SA node. Premature atrial contractions are relatively common and generally benign.
3. **Ventricular tachycardia refers to three or more consecutive premature ventricular contractions occurring at a ventricular rate of > 150 beats/minute. Ventricular tachycardia longer than 30 seconds is a life-threatening arrhythmia and requires immediate medical intervention. This type of abnormal heart rhythm can be recognized and potentially treated by an AED.**
4. First degree ventricular heart block is characterized by a PR interval that is longer than 0.2 seconds, but relatively constant from beat to beat. First degree ventricular heart block results in no associated symptoms or significant changes in cardiac function.

System: Non-Systems
Content Outline: Safety and Protection; Professional Responsibilities; Research

Level 1

p. 427, 765

PTEXAM ONE: QUESTION 162

A physical therapist examines a patient with low back pain of unknown etiology. The patient describes cramping and pain in the legs that is exacerbated by activity and diminished with rest. During the examination, the therapist observes that the patient's pain level improves with positioning in flexion and extension. This scenario is MOST consistent with which of the following medical conditions?

1. Facet joint irritation
2. Ankylosing spondylitis
3. Disk herniation
4. **Neurogenic claudication**

Correct Answer: 4 (Dutton p. 1447)

Physical therapists should be familiar with the unique characteristics of commonly encountered medical conditions. This knowledge should include information such as actions which improve or exacerbate a patient's symptoms.

1. The facet joints are paired joints located on the posterior aspect of the spine at each spinal level. Patients with facet joint irritation tend to experience less discomfort when in a flexed position since an extended position is consistent with the close packed position of the joint (i.e., maximal congruence between joint surfaces). However, facet joint irritation would not likely result in cramping and pain in the legs.
2. Ankylosing spondylitis is a systemic condition that is characterized by inflammation of the spine and larger peripheral joints. The clinical presentation of ankylosing spondylitis initially includes recurrent and insidious onset of back pain, morning stiffness, and impaired spinal extension. The patient may exhibit flexion at the hips, spinal kyphosis, fatigue, weight loss, and peripheral joint involvement. Cramping and pain in the legs are not typically associated with ankylosing spondylitis.
3. Disk herniation refers to a condition when the disk is pushed outside of its normal position between the vertebrae, often resulting in pressure being applied to adjacent spinal nerves. Patients with disk herniation tend to experience less discomfort when in an extended position and more discomfort when in a flexed position.
4. **Neurogenic claudication is a common side effect of spinal stenosis where the spinal nerves become compressed by narrowing of the spinal column. The condition is characterized by weakness, cramping, and pain in the legs that is often exacerbated by positioning in extension. Patients with neurogenic claudication tend to experience less discomfort when positioned in flexion.**

System: Neuromuscular and Nervous Systems
Content Outline: Foundations for Evaluation, Differential Diagnosis, and Prognosis

Level 2

PTEXAM ONE: QUESTION 163

A physical therapist observes a patient standing in a pool immersed in water to the level of the neck performing a number of upper extremity exercises. Which of the following active movements would be the MOST resisted by buoyancy with the patient starting with the upper extremity positioned at the side and the elbow in 90 degrees of flexion?

1. Elbow flexion
2. **Elbow extension**
3. Shoulder abduction
4. Shoulder medial rotation

Correct Answer: 2 (Coburn p. 67) 

Archimedes' principle of buoyancy states that there is an upward force on the body when immersed in water equal to the amount of water that has been displaced by the body. When an individual exercises in water, the buoyant force works in opposition to the gravitational force.

1. Elbow flexion is a sagittal plane motion that would best be classified as buoyancy assisted since the motion occurs in the same direction as the buoyant force. As a result, the buoyant force would make performing elbow flexion significantly easier for the patient.
2. **Elbow extension is a sagittal plane motion that would best be classified as buoyancy resisted since the motion occurs in the opposite direction as the buoyant force. As a result, the buoyant force would make performing elbow extension more difficult for the patient.**
3. Shoulder abduction is a frontal plane motion that would best be classified as buoyancy assisted since the motion occurs in the same direction as the buoyant force. As a result, the buoyant force would make performing shoulder abduction easier for the patient.
4. Shoulder medial rotation is a transverse plane motion that would best be classified as buoyancy supported since the motion occurs parallel to the bottom of the pool. The buoyant force would assist to support the arm, but would not be resisted by buoyancy.

System: Musculoskeletal System
Content Outline: Interventions

 Level 2  p. 717

PTEXAM ONE: QUESTION 164

A physician orders x-rays for a patient who has shoulder pain. Which of the following medical conditions would MOST likely be confirmed using this type of diagnostic imaging?

1. Bicipital tendonitis
2. **Calcific tendonitis**
3. Supraspinatus impingement
4. Subacromial bursitis

Correct Answer: 2 (Hertling p. 304)

The greater the density of the tissue, the more visible it will appear on x-ray. The majority of inflammatory conditions of the shoulder would be formally diagnosed using magnetic resonance imaging.

1. Bicipital tendonitis is an inflammatory process of the tendon of the long head of the biceps. The condition is characterized by subjective reports of a deep ache directly in front and on top of the shoulder, made worse with overhead activities or lifting. Repeated full abduction and lateral rotation of the humeral head can lead to irritation that produces inflammation, edema, microscopic tears within the tendon, and degeneration of the tendon itself.
2. **Calcific tendonitis is often visible on x-ray due to the relative density of calcium. The greater the density of the tissue, the more visible it will appear on x-ray. The supraspinatus and infraspinatus tendons are common sites for calcific tendonitis.**
3. Supraspinatus impingement is caused by an inability of a weak supraspinatus muscle to adequately depress the head of the humerus in the glenoid fossa during elevation of the arm. The patient may experience a feeling of weakness and identify the presence of a painful arc of motion most commonly occurring between 60 and 120 degrees of active abduction.
4. Subacromial bursitis refers to inflammation of the subacromial bursa which lies between the deltoid muscle, supraspinatus tendon, and the fibrous capsule of the shoulder joint. The clinical presentation of the condition is very similar to the clinical presentation of supraspinatus impingement.

System: Musculoskeletal System
Content Outline: Foundations for Evaluation, Differential Diagnosis, and Prognosis

 Level 2  p. 700

PTEXAM ONE: QUESTION 165

A physical therapist designs a research study that will examine the effect of high voltage galvanic electrical stimulation on edema following arthroscopic knee surgery. Which of the following methods is the MOST appropriate to collect the necessary data?

1. **Anthropometric measurements**
2. **Circumferential measurements**
3. **Goniometric measurements**
4. **Volumetric measurements**

Correct Answer: 2 (Hertling p. 501)

Physical therapists must utilize appropriate tests and measures to quantify the relative effectiveness of selected interventions. Therapists should carefully consider the reliability and validity of selected tests and measures when analyzing the collected data.

1. Common anthropometric measurements used for adults include height, weight, body mass index (BMI), waist-to-hip ratio, and percentage of body fat. These measures are then compared to reference standards to assess items such as weight status and the risk for various diseases.
2. **Circumferential measurements using a flexible tape measure allow physical therapists to obtain a gross estimate of edema in the knee. Pre-test and post-test measurements provide information on the effect of the electrical stimulation on the edema.**
3. Goniometric measurements are obtained with a goniometer and are designed to quantify available range of motion. If electrical stimulation is effective in reducing the edema, the patient may have improved range of motion, however, this would still not directly quantify the relative change in edema.
4. Volumetric measurements are often used to quantify the presence of edema in the wrist and hand by examining the amount of water displaced following immersion. Comparison with the uninvolved extremity provides a baseline measure. It would be impractical to attempt this type of measurement at the knee joint.

System: Musculoskeletal System
Content Outline: Physical Therapy Examination

Level 2

PTEXAM ONE: QUESTION 166

A patient diagnosed with ankylosing spondylitis reports progressive stiffening of the spine and associated pain for more than five years. Which of the following descriptions best represents the patient's MOST typical and anticipated standing posture?

1. **Posterior thoracic rib hump**
2. **Flattened lumbar curve, exaggerated thoracic curve**
3. **Excessive lumbar curve, flattened thoracic curve**
4. **Lateral curvature of the spine with fixed rotation of the vertebrae**

Correct Answer: 2 (Goodman – Differential Diagnosis p. 447)

Ankylosing spondylitis is a form of systemic rheumatic arthritis that is associated with an increase in thoracic kyphosis and loss of the lumbar curve. Ankylosing spondylitis occurs three times more often in males than females with a typical age of onset of 20-40 years.

1. A posterior thoracic rib hump is characteristic of scoliosis. The rotated vertebrae cause a rotation in the corresponding rib segments and result in posterior displacement of the rib cage.
2. **The clinical presentation of ankylosing spondylitis initially includes recurrent and insidious onset of back pain, morning stiffness, and impaired spinal extension. Chronic inflammation causes destruction of the ligamentous-osseous junction with subsequent fibrosis and ossification. The patient may exhibit flexion at the hips, spinal kyphosis, fatigue, weight loss, and peripheral joint involvement. If the costovertebral joints are affected there may be impaired chest mobility, compromised breathing, and decreased vital capacity.**
3. Excessive lumbar curve with a flattened thoracic curve is opposite from the typical clinical presentation of ankylosing spondylitis.
4. Lateral curvature of the spine with fixed rotation of the vertebrae is descriptive of scoliosis.

System: Musculoskeletal System
Content Outline: Foundations for Evaluation, Differential Diagnosis, and Prognosis

Level 2

p. 594-595

PTEXAM ONE: QUESTION 167

A physical therapist monitors the vital signs of a patient running on a treadmill at a series of steadily increasing speeds. A change in which variable would be **MOST** responsible for an observed increase in pulse pressure during the exercise session?

1. Heart rate
2. **Systolic blood pressure**
3. Diastolic blood pressure
4. Cardiac output

Correct Answer: 2 (ACSM – Resource Manual p. 500)

Pulse pressure, which is the difference between systolic and diastolic pressure, generally increases in direct proportion to the intensity of exercise since systolic pressure increases with exercise and diastolic pressure tends to stay the same. In a healthy adult, it is common to see a 40-50 mm Hg change in systolic pressure with intense exercise.

1. Heart rate is determined by the number of ventricular contractions per minute. Heart rate increases with an increase in exercise intensity, but would not be directly responsible for the observed increase in pulse pressure.
2. **Systolic blood pressure is the maximum arterial pressure during systole. Systolic pressure initially increases with exertion in a linear progression, often at a rate of 8-12 mm Hg per metabolic equivalent. The relative increase in systolic blood pressure, combined with stable diastolic blood pressure, results in an increase in pulse pressure.**
3. Diastolic blood pressure refers to the arterial pressure during diastole. Diastolic blood pressure remains relatively stable during exercise and therefore would not be responsible for the observed increase in pulse pressure.
4. Cardiac output refers to the amount of blood pumped from the left or right ventricle per minute. It is equal to the product of stroke volume and heart rate. Cardiac output can increase dramatically during exercise, however, is not used as a variable to determine pulse pressure.

System: Cardiovascular and Pulmonary Systems
Content Outline: Foundations for Evaluation, Differential Diagnosis, and Prognosis

p. 42, 435-436

PTEXAM ONE: QUESTION 168

A physical therapist treats a patient with a sacral pressure ulcer by applying a foam dressing impregnated with charcoal. This type of dressing would be MOST beneficial in treating which type of wound?

1. A dry wound that is infected
2. A dry wound that has a fetid odor
3. A heavily exuding wound that is infected
4. **A heavily exuding wound that has a fetid odor**

Correct Answer: 4 (Sussman p. 511)

Foam dressings can be made up of a single layer or multiple layers and are usually made from a polyurethane material. These dressings are ideal for absorbing exudate and maintaining a wound bed with a normal moisture level. Foam dressings can be used as a primary or secondary dressing.

1. A foam dressing should not be used on a dry wound since it is a highly absorptive dressing. Other dressings may be more appropriate for dry wounds, such as hydrogels.
2. The charcoal impregnated into the foam dressing can be beneficial in treating wounds that have strong odors. However, a foam dressing should not be used on a dry wound due to its absorptive properties.
3. Foam dressings are useful in treating heavily exuding wounds since they have high absorbency. However, the charcoal would not be beneficial in treating infection. Dressings impregnated with silver may be more useful in treating infection secondary to the antimicrobial properties of silver.
4. **A foam dressing would be beneficial for treating a heavily exuding wound due to its absorptive properties. The charcoal in the dressing is beneficial for decreasing fetid odors associated with the wound.**

System: Other Systems
Content Outline: Interventions

p. 509-510

PTEXAM ONE: QUESTION 169

A patient is instructed to perform the depicted exercise in sidelying. What muscles are targeted when performing this exercise?

1. **Gluteus maximus and adductor magnus**
2. **Gluteus medius and sartorius**
3. **Gluteus minimus and pectineus**
4. **Tensor fasciae latae and semimembranosus**

Correct Answer: 2 (Kisner p. 757)

A clamshell exercise requires a patient positioned in sidelying with the knee flexed to abduct and laterally rotate the hip against the resistance offered by the weight of the limb and gravity. Progression of the exercise occurs by using an elastic band placed around the distal femurs.

1. The gluteus maximus acts to extend and laterally rotate the hip. The adductor magnus acts to adduct the hip. The gluteus maximus is innervated by the inferior gluteal nerve, while the adductor magnus is innervated by the obturator nerve.
2. **The gluteus medius is responsible for hip abduction and medial rotation. The sartorius acts to flex, abduct, and laterally rotate the hip. This combination of muscles is the only option that incorporates both of the motions (i.e., abduction, lateral rotation) required for the clamshell exercise. The gluteus medius is innervated by the superior gluteal nerve, while the sartorius is innervated by the femoral nerve.**
3. The gluteus minimus acts to abduct and medially rotate the hip. The pectineus acts to medially rotate the hip. The gluteus minimus is innervated by the superior gluteal nerve, while the pectineus is innervated by the femoral nerve.
4. The tensor fasciae latae acts to abduct the hip and the semimembranosus acts to extend the hip and flex the knee. The tensor fasciae latae is innervated by the superior gluteal nerve, while the semimembranosus is innervated by the sciatic nerve.

System: Musculoskeletal System
Content Outline: Interventions

 **Level 1** **p. 53-55, 62**

PTEXAM ONE: QUESTION 170

A physical therapist observes a patient during gait training. The patient has normal strength and equal leg length. The patient slightly vaults and exhibits early heel off during midstance. Which of the following impairments is the MOST likely cause of this deviation?

1. **Weakness of the dorsiflexors**
2. **Weakness of the hip abductors**
3. **Limited plantar flexion**
4. **Limited dorsiflexion**

Correct Answer: 4 (Magee p. 1007) 

A patient with limited dorsiflexion may compensate with a vault or bounce through mid to late stance. Approximately ten degrees of dorsiflexion is required for late stance through toe off.

1. Weakness of the dorsiflexors will typically create a "steppage gait pattern." The patient will present with foot slap at initial contact and compensate by lifting the knee higher than normal to clear the foot and avoid dragging the toe.
2. Weakness of the hip abductors (gluteus medius and minimus) will typically create a contralateral dip of the pelvis during the stance phase of the weak side, also known as a Trendelenburg gait pattern. The patient will typically compensate with excessive lateral trunk flexion and weight shifting over the stance leg.
3. Limited plantar flexion would not result in a vaulting gait pattern. The patient would require plantar flexion to vault (ascend onto the toes) during gait. Plantar flexion of 0-20 degrees is required for normal gait biomechanics with approximately 15 degrees during the loading response and 20 degrees during the pre-swing phase.
4. **Limited dorsiflexion will typically result in premature elevation of the heel during midstance. The patient will appear to have a bounce during gait secondary to the gastrocnemius-soleus tightness.**

System: Musculoskeletal System
Content Outline: Foundations for Evaluation, Differential Diagnosis, and Prognosis

 **Level 2**  **p. 88**

PTEXAM ONE: QUESTION 171

A physical therapist treats a patient with Parkinson's disease who has been receiving levodopa therapy for two years. Which of the following side effects would MOST likely be present due to the chronic use of this medication?

1. Bradykinesia
2. **Choreoathetosis**
3. Shuffling gait
4. Rigidity

Correct Answer: 2 (Ciccone p. 137)

Parkinson's disease is a movement disorder caused by the progressive degeneration of the dopamine-producing cells in the basal ganglia. The disease is characterized by difficulties in planning, initiation, and execution of movement. Levodopa is a medication commonly used to improve motor function and general mobility in patients with Parkinson's disease.

1. Bradykinesia (i.e., slowness of movement) is a common characteristic of Parkinson's disease which would improve with the administration of levodopa.
2. **Choreoathetosis is a type of dyskinesia characterized by uncontrolled, involuntary movements. The onset of dyskinesias can occur as soon as three months after first receiving levodopa therapy.**
3. Shuffling gait is a common characteristic of Parkinson's disease which would improve with the administration of levodopa.
4. Rigidity is a common characteristic of Parkinson's disease which would improve with the administration of levodopa.

System: Neuromuscular and Nervous Systems
Content Outline: Foundations for Evaluation, Differential Diagnosis, and Prognosis

 Level 2  p. 263, 273, 344-345

PTEXAM ONE: QUESTION 172

A physical therapist concludes that the Lachman test is negative in a patient with a suspected anterior cruciate ligament injury. Which finding would MOST likely contribute to a potential false negative?

1. Moderate effusion of the knee joint capsule
2. 12 millimeters of anterior translation of the tibia on the femur
3. **Protective muscle guarding of the hamstring muscles**
4. Previous injury involving the anterior cruciate ligament

Correct Answer: 3 (Dutton p. 1003) 

The Lachman test is designed to assess the integrity of the anterior cruciate ligament. The test is performed with the patient positioned in supine with the knee flexed to 20-30 degrees. The therapist stabilizes the distal femur with one hand and places the other hand on the proximal tibia. The therapist applies an anterior directed force to the tibia on the femur. A positive test is indicated by excessive anterior translation of the tibia on the femur with a diminished or absent end-point. A false negative in this scenario refers to a negative Lachman test when there is in fact an anterior cruciate ligament injury.

1. Moderate effusion of the knee joint capsule would not likely contribute to a false negative when performing the Lachman test. A more dramatic change in the volume of fluid in the knee (i.e., hemarthrosis) would likely be necessary.
2. Twelve millimeters of anterior translation of the tibia on the femur would be considered serious knee instability and therefore would not likely contribute to a false negative when performing the Lachman test. Mild instability = 5 millimeters or less; moderate instability = 5-10 millimeters; severe instability = greater than 10 millimeters.
3. **The semitendinosus and semimembranosus insert on the posteromedial surface of the proximal tibia, while the biceps femoris inserts on the lateral condyle of the tibia and the head of the fibula. Protective muscle guarding of the hamstring muscles could limit the translation of the tibia on the femur and contribute to a false negative when performing the Lachman test.**
4. A previous injury involving the anterior cruciate ligament would make a positive Lachman test more likely and therefore would not contribute to a false negative when performing this test.

System: Musculoskeletal System
Content Outline: Physical Therapy Examination

 Level 2  p. 63, 108

PTEXAM ONE: QUESTION 173

A physical therapist observes an infant exhibiting a high guard position when sitting. Which of the following muscles would be the MOST essential for the infant to maintain this position?

1. Pectoralis major
2. **Rhomboids**
3. Serratus anterior
4. Lower trapezius

Correct Answer: 2 (Tecklin p. 45)

High guard position is characterized by the arms being held near shoulder level with retraction of the scapulae. The position increases midline trunk stability against the pull of gravity. High guard positioning may be observed in a number of different postures including sitting, tall kneeling or erect standing.

1. The pectoralis major acts to adduct and medially rotate the humerus. The muscle receives dual motor innervation by the medial pectoral nerve and the lateral pectoral nerve. The pectoralis major would likely be active when assuming a high guard position, however, would not be as essential as the rhomboids.
2. **The rhomboids act to adduct and downwardly rotate the scapula. The muscle originates on the nuchal ligaments and spinous processes of the C7-T5 vertebrae and inserts on the medial border of the scapula. The rhomboids are innervated by the dorsal scapular nerve. The rhomboids' ability to adduct the scapula provides assistance to the trunk extensors when maintaining an upright posture.**
3. The serratus anterior acts to protract and upwardly rotate the scapula during humeral elevation. The serratus anterior is innervated by the long thoracic nerve. A high guard position requires retraction of the shoulder, not protraction.
4. The trapezius is a large superficial muscle that consists of three different components (i.e., upper, middle, lower). The lower fibers depress and upwardly rotate the scapula and would not allow for the necessary adduction of the scapula required for the high guard position. The middle fibers of the trapezius would be a better option since they function to adduct the scapula. The middle fibers originate on the spinous processes of the first through fifth thoracic vertebrae and insert on the spine of the scapula.

System: Neuromuscular and Nervous Systems
Content Outline: Interventions

Level 2

PTEXAM ONE: QUESTION 174

A physical therapist examines a patient diagnosed with cerebral palsy. The therapist has limited experience treating patients who have cerebral palsy and is concerned about their ability to provide appropriate treatment. Which of the following actions is the MOST appropriate for the therapist to utilize?

1. Inform the patient of your area of expertise
2. **Co-treat the patient with another more experienced therapist**
3. Treat the patient
4. Refuse to treat the patient

Correct Answer: 2 (Guide for Professional Conduct)

Physical therapists must make decisions that are consistent with their professional training. Since the therapist is concerned about their ability to provide appropriate treatment, they are in need of some form of external assistance.

1. Informing the patient of their area of expertise would likely make the patient question the therapist's competence.
2. **By co-treating the patient, the therapist receives external assistance and at the same time improves their skills with a particular patient population.**
3. The question states that the therapist is concerned about their ability to treat the patient. This type of admission makes it inappropriate to simply treat the patient without utilizing available resources.
4. Refusing to treat the patient would not be necessary since the therapist has available resources to offer assistance.

System: Neuromuscular and Nervous Systems
Content Outline: Interventions

Level 3  **p. 792-793**

PTEXAM ONE: QUESTION 175

A physical therapist treating a patient rehabilitating from spinal surgery four days ago observes the patient's incision. What type of healing is **BEST** depicted in the image?

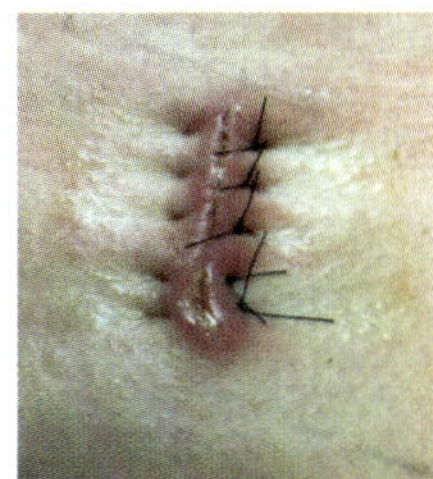

1. **Primary intention**
2. Delayed primary intention
3. Secondary intention
4. Tertiary intention

Correct Answer: 1 (Sussman p. 215)

Healing by intention refers to the method by which a wound heals. Wound characteristics such as etiology, depth, border integrity, and wound bed contamination are typically considered when determining which closure method is most appropriate.

1. **Healing by primary intention is most commonly associated with acute wounds which have minimal associated tissue loss (e.g., surgical wound, laceration, puncture wound). In these wounds, clean edges are reapproximated and closed with sutures, staples or adhesives to facilitate re-epithelialization.**
2. Healing by delayed primary intention is most commonly associated with acute wounds that have minimal associated tissue loss, but are at high risk for developing complications (e.g., infection, dehiscence). These wounds are temporarily left open until risk factors have been alleviated and then are closed by usual primary intention methods.
3. Healing by secondary intention is most commonly associated with wounds that have significant tissue loss, necrosis or borders that cannot be reapproximated (e.g., full-thickness wound, pressure ulcer). These wounds are left open and typically require specialized dressings and ongoing wound care to facilitate healing.
4. Healing by tertiary intention is synonymous with healing by delayed primary intention. Risk factors such as wound bed contamination, infection, and significant local edema increase the risk of healing complications and must be addressed before the wound can be appropriately closed by usual primary intention methods.

System: Other Systems
Content Outline: Foundations for Evaluation, Differential Diagnosis, and Prognosis

 Level 2  p. 500

PTEXAM ONE: QUESTION 176

A physical therapist monitors a patient's vital signs while exercising in a phase I cardiac rehabilitation program. The patient is post myocardial infarction and has progressed without difficulty while involved in the program. Which of the following vital sign recordings would exceed the typical limits of a phase I program?

1. Heart rate elevated 18 beats per minute above resting level
2. Respiration rate of 18 breaths per minute
3. **Systolic blood pressure decreased by 25 mm Hg from resting level**
4. Diastolic blood pressure less than 100 mm Hg

Correct Answer: 3 (Hillegass p. 573)

Physical therapists should closely monitor the response to exercise of patients in a phase I cardiac rehabilitation program. Any abnormal responses observed during the cardiac rehabilitation program should be documented and shared with other members of the medical team.

1. An increase in heart rate of 18 beats per minute above resting heart rate is acceptable. Most guidelines for phase I cardiac rehabilitation recommend that heart rate not exceed 130 beats per minute or a heart rate more than 20 beats above resting for post myocardial infarction patients or a heart rate more than 30 beats above resting for post-surgical patients.
2. Dyspnea is a reason to terminate exercise during phase I exercise. However, a respiration rate of 18 breaths per minute is at the upper limit of the normal range and would not typically cause a patient to report a sense of dyspnea.
3. **A decrease in systolic pressure of 25 mm Hg exceeds the 10 mm Hg limit allowed during exercise in a phase I cardiac rehabilitation program.**
4. A diastolic blood pressure of 110 mm Hg is considered the upper limit for exercise in phase I cardiac rehabilitation. A diastolic pressure less than 110 mm Hg is acceptable.

System: Cardiovascular and Pulmonary Systems
Content Outline: Interventions

 Level 2  p. 444-446

PTEXAM ONE: QUESTION 177

A physical therapist is treating a patient in an acute care setting with a hematologic disorder. Which of the following test results would be the MOST appropriate to monitor on a daily basis in order to ensure patient safety during physical therapy?

1. Hemoglobin
2. **Complete blood count**
3. Arterial blood gas
4. Blood glucose

Correct Answer: 2 (Paz p. 195) 

When treating a patient with a hematologic disorder, a physical therapist should monitor a patient's complete blood count (CBC) along with the coagulation profile to determine the potential risk for bruising, decreased oxygen carrying capacity at rest or with exercise, or thrombus formation. This information will allow a therapist to modify or defer physical therapy intervention if warranted secondary to abnormal lab values.

1. Hemoglobin is the iron-containing pigment in red blood cells that functions to carry oxygen in the blood. Low hemoglobin may indicate anemia or blood loss; elevated hemoglobin suggests polycythemia or dehydration. Hemoglobin is important to monitor, but not in isolation. A patient with a hematologic disorder requires monitoring of all components of a CBC to assess the patient's status.
2. **A CBC measures red blood cell count, total white blood cell count, white blood cell differential, platelets, hemoglobin, and hematocrit. A CBC is performed to assess health, to diagnose and monitor a medical condition, and to monitor the effects of medical treatment. A patient with a hematologic disorder requires daily monitoring of a CBC to allow the therapist to determine trends and to recognize abnormal lab values that may require modification or deferment of services.**
3. Arterial blood gases are collected to evaluate acid-base status (pH), ventilation ($PaCO_2$), and oxygenation of arterial blood (PaO_2). This profile is typically not affected by a hematologic disorder and therefore would not require daily monitoring in this scenario.
4. Blood glucose refers to sugar that is transported through the bloodstream to supply energy to all the cells. Daily monitoring of blood glucose is most appropriate for a patient diagnosed with diabetes mellitus. This is imperative to prevent the effects of hyperglycemia or hypoglycemia. This profile is typically not affected by a hematologic disorder and therefore would not require daily monitoring in this scenario.

System: Other Systems
Content Outline: Physical Therapy Examination

 **Level 2**  **p. 409**

PTEXAM ONE: QUESTION 178

A physical therapist treats a patient with a colostomy that is capable of producing solid stool on a fairly regular schedule. Which type of colostomy would be the MOST consistent with this description?

1. Ascending
2. Descending
3. **Sigmoid**
4. Transverse

Correct Answer: 3 (Smeltzer p. 1104)

A colostomy is a surgical opening in the colon created for the elimination of feces. This type of procedure can be required when an injury or pathology prohibits the colon from functioning properly. There are several unique types of colostomies including ascending, transverse, descending, and sigmoid. The farther along the intestinal tract that fecal material travels, the more it resembles the consistency of normal stool.

1. The ascending colon, located on the right side of the abdomen, is the beginning portion of the large intestine. The ascending colon extends upward to a bend in the colon called the hepatic flexure. An ascending colostomy results in only a very short portion of the colon remaining active and as a result the output is primarily liquid containing many digestive enzymes.
2. The descending colon, located on the left side of the abdomen, follows the transverse colon and the splenic flexure. A descending colostomy results in a large portion of the colon remaining active and therefore the output is often firm, although tends to be somewhat irregular.
3. **The sigmoid colon is the final portion of the large intestine and serves as a connection to the rectum. A sigmoid colostomy is the most common type of colostomy, located a few inches lower than a descending colostomy. As a result, this type of colostomy has additional working colon. A sigmoid colostomy produces normal stool consistency and discharge can be regulated.**
4. The transverse colon, located across the upper portion of the abdomen, follows the ascending colon and the hepatic flexure. The transverse colon ends with a bend in the colon called the splenic flexure. A transverse colostomy may produce soft or loose stool at infrequent intervals.

System: Other Systems
Content Outline: Foundations for Evaluation, Differential Diagnosis, and Prognosis

Level 1

PTEXAM ONE: QUESTION 179

A physical therapist obtains a gross measurement of hamstrings length by passively extending the lower extremity of a patient in short sitting. Which of the following substitutions is the MOST common to attempt to exaggerate hamstrings length?

1. Weight shift to the contralateral side
2. Anterior rotation of the pelvis
3. **Posterior rotation of the pelvis**
4. Hiking of the contralateral hip

Correct Answer: 3 (Magee p. 674) 

The hamstring muscles consist of the semitendinosus, semimembranosus, and biceps femoris. The semitendinosus and semimembranosus are considered the medial hamstrings since they insert on the medial surface of the tibia. The biceps femoris is considered the lateral hamstrings since the muscle inserts on the lateral surface of the tibia and the lateral surface of the head of the fibula.

1. Weight shifting to the contralateral side in short sitting without other compensatory movement would have minimal impact on measured hamstrings length.
2. Anterior rotation of the pelvis would tend to make the apparent hamstrings length shorter than the actual length due to the hamstrings origin on the tuberosity of the ischium.
3. **Posterior rotation of the pelvis would tend to make the apparent hamstrings length longer than the actual length due to the hamstrings origin on the tuberosity of the ischium. Patients often attempt to posteriorly rotate the pelvis in short sitting by leaning backwards.**
4. Hip hiking of the contralateral limb may cause the patient to weight shift toward the involved side. This adaptation would have minimal impact on measured hamstrings length.

System: Musculoskeletal System
Content Outline: Physical Therapy Examination

PTEXAM ONE: QUESTION 180

A physical therapist prepares to formally assess the balance of a patient with a neurological disorder. Which of the following methods is the MOST appropriate to assess the vestibular component of balance?

1. Assess cutaneous sensation
2. **Apply a perturbation to alter the body's center of gravity**
3. Examine proprioception in a weight bearing posture
4. Quantify visual acuity and depth perception

Correct Answer: 2 (Goodman – Pathology p. 1631)

Balance requires complex integration of the vestibular, visual, and somatosensory systems. Each system is responsive to specific stimuli and therefore can be assessed individually or collectively.

1. Cutaneous sensation is commonly assessed as part of a neurological examination, however, would not be directly associated with the vestibular system. Cutaneous sensory receptors include free nerve endings, Ruffini endings, hair follicle endings, and Meissner's corpuscles.
2. **The vestibular system reports information to the brain regarding the position and movement of the head with respect to gravity and movement. Assessment of the vestibular system often includes perturbations that require the body to make automatic adjustments that restore normal alignment.**
3. The somatosensory system provides information about the relative orientation and movement of the body in relation to the support surface. Examining proprioception in a weight bearing posture would be a common method used for assessment of the somatosensory system.
4. The visual system allows individuals to perceive movement and detect the relative orientation of the body in space. Visual receptors allow for perceptual acuity regarding verticality, motion of objects and self, environmental orientation, postural sway, and movements of the head and neck. Visual acuity and depth perception contribute to the feedback gathered by the visual system.

System: Neuromuscular and Nervous Systems
Content Outline: Physical Therapy Examination

 p. 264-265

PTEXAM ONE: QUESTION 181

A physical therapist uses metabolic equivalents (METs) as a method to establish exercise intensity for a 36-year-old patient. The patient is recreationally active and has no relevant past medical history. Which of the following MET levels would be the MOST consistent with the patient's anticipated maximal aerobic capacity?

1. 3
2. 6
3. **10**
4. 15

Correct Answer: 3 (Nyland p. 127)

One metabolic equivalent is the amount of oxygen consumed at rest and is equal to approximately 3.5 milliliters of oxygen per kilogram of body weight per minute. This measure allows therapists to describe the energy requirements of an activity as a multiple of the metabolic rate.

1. Maximal aerobic capacity of 3 METs is extremely low regardless of age and gender. For example, walking three miles per hour on a level, firm surface is approximately 3.5 METs. A maximal aerobic capacity of 3 METs is likely associated with significant pathology or illness.
2. Maximal aerobic capacity for older men and women typically ranges from 5-8 METs. The patient's age and activity level make it likely that the patient's maximal aerobic capacity is significantly greater than 6 METs.
3. **Maximal aerobic capacity for men and women typically ranges from 8-12 METs. The patient's age and activity level make it likely that the individual's anticipated maximal aerobic capacity would fall within this range.**
4. Maximal aerobic capacity for highly trained men and women has been shown to reach 15-20 METs. This is unlikely for the described patient given the available information.

System: Cardiovascular and Pulmonary Systems
Content Outline: Interventions

Level 2  p. 446-447

PTEXAM ONE: QUESTION 182

A physical therapist makes footwear recommendations for a patient with foot pathology. The recommendations include a high and wide toe box, small to no heel, medial arch support, and a contoured posterior counter. This type of shoe prescription would be the MOST beneficial for a patient diagnosed with which of the following conditions?

1. Sesamoiditis
2. **Hallux valgus**
3. Pes cavus
4. Metatarsalgia

Correct Answer: 2 (Lusardi p. 173)

Hallux valgus, or bunion, is a prominent bony formation on the medial aspect of the first metatarsophalangeal (MTP) joint that results from lateral deviation of the hallux and foot pronation. This disorder is typically the result of wearing shoes with a triangular toe box over a sustained period of time.

1. Sesamoiditis refers to the inflammation surrounding the sesamoid bones under the first metatarsal head. Shoe prescription would include a transverse metatarsal bar to redistribute pressure from the metatarsal heads to the metatarsal shafts. A rocker sole can be used to reduce motion of the painful joint.
2. **Shoe prescription for hallux valgus would include a high and wide toe box to reduce friction and pressure to the first MTP joint. Medial support is required to decrease pronation, while reduced heel height decreases forefoot pressure. A contoured posterior counter of the shoe better controls the subtalar joint.**
3. Pes cavus refers to an exaggerated longitudinal arch that results in a plantar flexed forefoot, retracted toes, and increased weight bearing stress to the metatarsal heads and heel. Shoe prescription would include a cushion sole to absorb shock, a metatarsal bar to shift weight from the metatarsal heads, and a lateral flare to increase overall stability.
4. Metatarsalgia refers to pain around the metatarsal heads secondary to compression of the plantar digital nerve. Shoe prescription would be identical to the recommendations described for sesamoiditis.

System: Musculoskeletal System
Content Outline: Interventions

 Level 2  p. 75

PTEXAM ONE: QUESTION 183

A physical therapist observes thenar atrophy when examining a patient's hand. In the absence of other relevant findings, this could BEST be explained by which of the following conditions?

1. **C8 nerve root lesion**
2. Paralysis of the interossei
3. Radial nerve lesion
4. Ulnar nerve lesion

Correct Answer: 1 (Dutton p. 809)

Atrophy refers to the partial or complete wasting of muscle tissue in a defined anatomical region. Atrophy is often classified as disuse or neurogenic. Causes of atrophy can potentially include loss of innervation, impaired circulation or diminished activity.

1. **A C8 or T1 nerve root lesion often results in atrophy of the thenar eminence. The muscles associated with the thenar eminence include the abductor pollicis brevis, flexor pollicis brevis, and opponens pollicis. The nerves that innervate each of the muscles arise from the C8-T1 nerve roots. The abductor pollicis brevis and opponens pollicis are innervated by the median nerve. The superficial head of the flexor pollicis brevis is innervated by the median nerve and the deep head is innervated by the ulnar nerve.**
2. Paralysis of the interossei often results in a deformity characterized by hyperextension of the metacarpophalangeal joints.
3. A radial nerve lesion often results in a deformity characterized by wrist drop with increased flexion of the wrist, flexion of the metacarpophalangeal joints, and extension of the distal interphalangeal joints.
4. An ulnar nerve lesion often results in a deformity characterized by atrophy of the hypothenar eminence and a clawed hand with flexion of the fourth and fifth digits.

System: Neuromuscular and Nervous Systems
Content Outline: Foundations for Evaluation, Differential Diagnosis, and Prognosis

p. 245-246

PTEXAM ONE: QUESTION 184

A physical therapist inspects the skin of a patient who recently sustained a scald burn to the torso. The burn is moist and red with several areas of blister formation. The burn covers an area approximately four inches by three inches and blanches with direct pressure. Based on this description, what is the MOST likely burn classification?

1. Superficial
2. **Superficial partial-thickness**
3. Deep partial-thickness
4. Full-thickness

Correct Answer: 2 (Goodman – Pathology p. 454) 

The extent and severity of a burn is dependent on a variety of factors including age, duration of burn, type of burn, and affected area. Burns are most appropriately classified according to the depth of tissue destruction.

1. A superficial burn involves only the outer epidermis. The involved area may be red with slight edema. Healing occurs without evidence of scarring.
2. **A superficial partial-thickness burn involves the epidermis and the upper portion of the dermis. Healing occurs with minimal to no scarring in approximately two weeks. A superficial partial-thickness burn is relatively common since many scalding water burns and intense sunburns fall into this category. The primary difference in appearance between superficial and superficial partial-thickness burns is the presence of blistering. This category of burn is the most painful since all nerve endings remain intact.**
3. A deep partial-thickness burn involves complete destruction of the epidermis and the majority of the dermis. The involved area may appear discolored with broken blisters and edema. Damage to nerve endings may result in only moderate levels of pain. Healing occurs with hypertrophic scars and keloids.
4. A full-thickness burn involves complete destruction of the epidermis and dermis along with partial damage of the subcutaneous fat layer. The involved area often presents with eschar formation and minimal pain. Patients with full-thickness burns require grafts and may be susceptible to infection.

System: Other Systems
Content Outline: Foundations for Evaluation, Differential Diagnosis, and Prognosis

p. 513

PTEXAM ONE: QUESTION 185

A patient informs a physical therapist that at a recent doctor visit the physician recommended healthy lifestyle changes to reduce blood pressure, however did not prescribe a blood pressure lowering medication. Which blood pressure value would BEST support the physician's action?

1. Systolic blood pressure = 116 mm Hg
2. Systolic blood pressure = 142 mm Hg
3. **Diastolic blood pressure = 86 mm Hg**
4. Diastolic blood pressure = 92 mm Hg

Correct Answer: 3 (O'Sullivan p. 29) 

Recent revisions in blood pressure guidelines have resulted in more aggressive treatment for hypertension. Treatment typically includes lifestyle modifications and medication. Common lifestyle modifications include aerobic physical activity at least 30 minutes per day most days of the week; weight loss to a body mass index of 18.5 to 24.9; smoking cessation; reduced intake of dietary sodium and alcohol; and increased consumption of fruits, vegetables, and low-fat dairy products with reduced saturated and total fat content. Classes of medications for hypertension include diuretics, beta blockers, calcium channel blockers, ACE inhibitors, angiotensin II receptor blockers, and direct vasodilators.

1. A systolic blood pressure value of 116 mm Hg is considered "normal" since the value is less than 120 mm Hg. As a result, reducing blood pressure is not necessary.
2. A systolic blood pressure value of 142 mm Hg is greater than 140 mm Hg and is therefore indicative of Hypertension – Stage 2. Recommended treatment for this stage of hypertension includes healthy lifestyle changes and blood pressure lowering medication.
3. **A diastolic blood pressure value of 86 mm Hg is greater than 80 mm Hg and less than 90 mm Hg. As a result, the diastolic blood pressure value is indicative of Hypertension – Stage 1. Recommended treatment for this stage of hypertension focuses primarily on healthy lifestyle changes and is unlikely to include blood pressure lowering medication unless the patient has a significant risk of heart disease and stroke.**
4. A diastolic blood pressure value of 92 mm Hg is greater than 90 mm Hg and is therefore indicative of Hypertension – Stage 2. Recommended treatment for this stage of hypertension includes healthy lifestyle changes and blood pressure lowering medication.

System: Cardiovascular and Pulmonary Systems
Content Outline: Foundations for Evaluation, Differential Diagnosis, and Prognosis

 **Level 2** **p. 403, 414-415, 419-420, 470**

PTEXAM ONE: QUESTION 186

A physical therapist reviews the medical record of a patient who sustained a spinal cord injury four weeks ago in a diving accident. Which of the following medical diagnoses would result in the patient being the MOST susceptible to autonomic dysreflexia?

1. **T4 paraplegia**
2. T12 paraplegia
3. Cauda equina injury
4. Posterior cord syndrome

Correct Answer: 1 (O'Sullivan p. 861)

Autonomic dysreflexia is caused when a noxious stimulus below the level of the lesion triggers the autonomic nervous system causing a sudden elevation in blood pressure. Symptoms include profuse sweating, bradycardia, goose bumps, headache, and vasodilation (flushing) above the level of the injury. This condition should be treated as a medical emergency.

1. **Autonomic dysreflexia is common in patients with spinal cord lesions above the T6 level. The condition should be treated as a medical emergency. Immediate medical management includes assisting the patient to a sitting position in an attempt to reduce blood pressure and examining the urinary drainage system since this often serves as the noxious stimulus that triggers the autonomic response.**
2. A patient with T12 paraplegia would not typically be at risk for autonomic dysreflexia since the level of the lesion is below T6.
3. Cauda equina injury occurs below the L1 spinal level where the long nerve roots transcend. Characteristics include flaccidity, areflexia, and impairment of bowel and bladder function. Full recovery is not typical due to the distance needed for axonal regeneration.
4. Posterior cord syndrome refers to a relatively rare incomplete lesion caused by compression of the posterior spinal artery and is characterized by loss of proprioception, two-point discrimination, and stereognosis. Motor function is preserved.

System: Neuromuscular and Nervous Systems
Content Outline: Foundations for Evaluation, Differential Diagnosis, and Prognosis

 **Level 2**  **p. 297, 764**

PTEXAM ONE: QUESTION 187

A physical therapist utilizes neuromuscular electrical stimulation by attaching an electrode over the motor point of the peroneus longus. Which of the following locations is the MOST appropriate for placement of the electrode?

1. Along the lateral border of the popliteal fossa
2. **On the anterolateral surface of the lower leg**
3. Proximal to the first metatarsophalangeal joint
4. Immediately inferior to the lateral malleolus

Correct Answer: 2 (Kendall p. 412)

A motor point refers to a point on the skin where the application of an electrical stimulus via an electrode will cause the contraction of an underlying muscle. A physical therapist can attempt to identify a motor point based on their knowledge of a muscle's origin and insertion.

1. The popliteal fossa refers to an area or shallow depression located on the posterior surface of the knee. The area is significantly superior to the origin and insertion of the peroneus longus and therefore could not serve as a motor point for the muscle.
2. **The peroneus longus originates on the head and upper two-thirds of the lateral surface of the fibula and inserts on the lateral side of the base of the first metatarsal and the medial cuneiform. The muscle acts to evert the foot and assists in plantar flexion of the ankle joint. The anterolateral surface of the lower leg is consistent with the muscle's motor point.**
3. A motor point proximal to the first metatarsophalangeal joint would likely be associated with one of the intrinsic muscles of the foot.
4. While the location immediately inferior to the lateral malleolus would correspond to an area that the peroneus longus passes over, by the time the muscle reaches this distal point, it is mostly tendon and therefore an electrical stimulus would not produce the desired motor response.

System: Musculoskeletal System
Content Outline: Interventions

Level 1

PTEXAM ONE: QUESTION 188

A physical therapist evaluates the fall risk of a 73-year-old patient after being placed on a new medication. Which of the following medications would MOST likely contribute to an increased risk of falling?

1. Nonopioid analgesics
2. **Benzodiazepines**
3. Thrombolytics
4. Antidiarrheals

Correct Answer: 2 (Ciccone p. 78)

Many medications can contribute to an increased fall risk, particularly in an elderly population. Evidence is strongest for an association of falls with the use of hypnotic-anxiolytic drugs, particularly benzodiazepines. Other medications commonly associated with an increased fall risk include diuretics, antihypertensives, and selected antiparkinsonian medications.

1. Nonopioid analgesic agents provide analgesia and pain relief, produce anti-inflammatory effects, and initiate anti-pyretic properties. Side effects include nausea, vomiting, vertigo, abdominal pain, gastrointestinal distress or bleeding, and ulcer formation. Common trade names of nonopioid analgesic agents include Tylenol, Advil, and Aleve.
2. **Benzodiazepines promote sleep through increasing inhibitory effects on the central nervous system synapses where GABA (gamma-aminobutyric acid) is found. Side effects include drowsiness, decreased motor performance, anterograde amnesia, and diminished alertness. Common trade names of benzodiazepines include Xanax, Valium, and Klonopin.**
3. Thrombolytics facilitate clot dissolution through conversion of plasminogen to plasmin. Plasmin breaks down clots and allows occluded vessels to reopen to maintain blood flow. Side effects include hemorrhage, allergic reaction, and cardiac arrhythmia. Common trade names of thrombolytics include Activase, Kinlytic, and Streptase.
4. Antidiarrheal agents are used to slow the debilitating effects of dehydration associated with prolonged diarrhea. Side effects include constipation and abdominal discomfort. Common trade names of antidiarrheal agents include Imodium, Motofen, and Pepto-Bismol.

System: Other Systems
Content Outline: Foundations for Evaluation, Differential Diagnosis, and Prognosis

Level 1

p. 566-567

PTEXAM ONE: QUESTION 189

A physical therapist receives a referral for a patient diagnosed with lung cancer. Assuming the patient was diagnosed with cancer two months ago, which of the following pieces of data would provide the therapist with the MOST valuable information when establishing the plan of care and the associated goals?

1. Premorbid lifestyle
2. **Staging of cancer**
3. Past medical history
4. Motivation level

Correct Answer: 2 (Goodman – Pathology p. 368)

Lung cancer is the most frequent form of cancer in the United States and refers to a malignancy of the epithelium of the respiratory tract. The staging of the cancer is used to estimate prognosis and to determine appropriate intervention strategies.

1. The patient's premorbid lifestyle is relevant, however, would not be the primary factor when establishing the plan of care and associated goals.
2. **The TNM Classification System (T=tumor, N=node, M=metastasis) is a commonly used cancer classification system that describes the extent of a particular malignant tumor. "T" refers to the extent of the primary tumor, "N" refers to the absence or presence and extent of regional lymph node metastasis, and "M" refers to the absence or presence of distant metastasis. This type of staging offers guidance to health care professionals when determining treatment options, life expectancy, and prognosis for complete resolution.**
3. Past medical history provides a basic snapshot of a patient's overall health status. This information would be considered when establishing the plan of care and associated goals, but it would not be as critical as other pieces of information (i.e., cancer staging).
4. Motivation level is particularly important once a plan of care is established, however, the patient's motivation level would be of only modest value when establishing the plan of care and associated goals.

System: Other Systems
Content Outline: Foundations for Evaluation, Differential Diagnosis, and Prognosis

 Level 3  p. 557-558

PTEXAM ONE: QUESTION 190

A physical therapist treats a patient post tibial plateau fracture. While completing a resistive exercise, the patient indicates that lifting weights often causes them to void small amounts of urine. Which of the following actions is the MOST appropriate for the therapist to implement?

1. Refer the patient to a support group
2. Instruct the patient in pelvic floor muscle strengthening exercises
3. Discontinue resistive exercises as part of the established plan of care
4. **Educate the patient about incontinence**

Correct Answer: 4 (Brody p. 511) 

Incontinence refers to an inability to control the release of urine, feces or gas and is a common occurrence for many men and women. The causes of incontinence may include weak pelvic floor muscles or medical conditions such as an enlarged prostate, prostatitis, cancer, neurological disorders or obstruction. Proper diagnosis is necessary in order to effectively treat this condition.

1. The use of a support group would be a potential adjunct activity for the patient, however, at this time, education is the appropriate action.
2. It would be inappropriate to begin pelvic floor exercises without a referral from a physician since the cause of the incontinence is unknown.
3. The physical therapist should not discontinue resistive exercises since strengthening is a necessary component of a rehabilitation program for a patient following a tibial plateau fracture. This action also does not directly address the current issue of uncontrolled voiding of urine.
4. **The patient may significantly benefit from formal education about incontinence. The action would provide the patient with necessary information and make the patient more likely to see a physician about this issue. A vast majority of patients with incontinence can be successfully treated with non-invasive measures such as pelvic floor exercises.**

System: Other Systems
Content Outline: Interventions

Level 3  p. 545-546, 628-629

PTEXAM ONE: QUESTION 191

A physical therapist participates in a research study that formally measures an individual's maximum oxygen consumption. Which of the following individuals would be expected to have the largest maximum oxygen consumption?

1. **A 23-year-old male (weight: 240 pounds; height: 72 inches)**
2. A 25-year-old female (weight: 160 pounds; height: 66 inches)
3. A 53-year-old male (weight: 210 pounds; height: 69 inches)
4. A 47-year-old female (weight: 130 pounds; height: 62 inches)

Correct Answer: 1 (ACSM – Resource Manual p. 57)

Maximum oxygen consumption (VO_{2max}) is generally considered the best indicator of cardiorespiratory endurance and aerobic fitness. Maximum oxygen consumption decreases with age at a rate of approximately 10% per decade after the age of 25.

1. **A 23-year-old male (weight: 240 pounds; height: 72 inches) would be expected to have the largest maximum oxygen consumption. Males have a higher maximum oxygen consumption than females and maximum oxygen consumption is directly proportional to height and weight.**
2. A 25-year-old female (weight: 160 pounds; height: 66 inches) would not be expected to have the largest maximum oxygen consumption of the presented options. This individual would, however, likely have a larger maximum oxygen consumption than the 47-year-old female since she is younger, heavier, and taller.
3. A 53-year-old male (weight: 210 pounds; height: 69 inches) would not be expected to have the largest maximum oxygen consumption of the presented options since the other male option is younger, heavier, and taller.
4. A 47-year-old female (weight: 130 pounds; height: 62 inches) would likely have the lowest maximum oxygen consumption of the presented options.

System: Cardiovascular and Pulmonary Systems
Content Outline: Physical Therapy Examination

PTEXAM ONE: QUESTION 192

A patient sustained a grade II strain to the iliopsoas muscle. Which of the following phases of the gait cycle should the physical therapist expect to be the MOST impacted by this injury?

1. **Toe off (pre-swing) and acceleration (initial swing)**
2. Heel strike (initial contact) and acceleration (initial swing)
3. Foot flat (loading response) and deceleration (terminal swing)
4. Midstance and deceleration (terminal swing)

Correct Answer: 1 (Dutton p. 298)

A strain is an injury involving the musculotendinous unit that involves a muscle, tendon or their attachments to the bone. Signs and symptoms associated with a grade II strain include localized pain, moderate swelling, tenderness, and impaired motor function. A grade II strain is likely to negatively influence a patient's gait at the point in the gait cycle where the affected muscle is most active.

1. **The iliopsoas contracts eccentrically beginning at midstance and continues through to toe off (pre-swing). The iliopsoas then switches quickly to a concentric contraction to advance the limb forward at acceleration (initial swing). Therefore, weakness of the hip flexors is best observed during the toe off (pre-swing) and acceleration (initial swing) phases.**
2. During heel strike (initial contact), the hip extensors are active to resist the flexion moment at the hip. The iliopsoas is not active during this phase, but is active during acceleration (initial swing).
3. During foot flat (loading response), the hip extensors work concentrically to extend the hip and then eccentrically during deceleration (terminal swing) to slow the rate of both hip flexion (gluteus maximus) and knee extension (hamstrings). The iliopsoas is not active during either of these phases of gait.
4. The hip abductors are most active at midstance to stabilize the pelvis and prevent contralateral hip drop. The iliopsoas begins to contract eccentrically at midstance to control the rate of hip extension, but is not active during deceleration (terminal swing).

System: Musculoskeletal System
Content Outline: Foundations for Evaluation, Differential Diagnosis, and Prognosis

p. 55, 62, 84-89

PTEXAM ONE: QUESTION 193

A physical therapist consults with a teacher regarding a child who has impairments in sensory processing. Which piece of equipment would be the MOST useful to address the child's dyspraxia?

1. Swing
2. **Weighted vest**
3. Sit and spin
4. Rocking chair

Correct Answer: 2 (Tecklin p. 415)

Sensory integration is the process in which the central nervous system accepts, organizes, and modulates afferent sensory information and produces a response. A child with sensory integration dysfunction has difficulty processing sensory information and producing an appropriate response. Therapists can provide children with opportunities to experience sensory input in a controlled environment using sensory modulation. Dyspraxia refers to difficulty planning a new motor act and is often caused by difficulty interpreting and modulating tactile input.

1. Swings are used for children with sensory integration disorders in order to provide vestibular input. The vestibular system plays a role in the development of body posture, muscle tone, ocular-motor control, integration of reflexes, and equilibrium reactions. Addressing the vestibular system would not directly address the child's dyspraxia.
2. **A weighted vest can provide proprioceptive input and can be worn by a child with a sensory processing disorder. The proprioceptive input provides the child with an improved sense of position and understanding of where joints and muscles are in space. Proprioceptive input contributes to the ability to plan movement and would directly address the child's dyspraxia.**
3. A sit and spin can provide vestibular input to a child with a sensory processing disorder. Children with difficulty processing vestibular information may be intolerant to movement. The sit and spin provides them with the opportunity to experience movement in a controlled environment. Addressing the vestibular system would not directly address the child's dyspraxia.
4. A rocking chair can provide vestibular input to a child with a sensory processing disorder. Children with sensory integration dysfunction may have difficulty modulating their behavior, presenting with either hypo-arousal or hyper-arousal. Rocking chairs can be used to provide vestibular input to calm a child who is over-aroused. The additional vestibular input would not address the child's dyspraxia.

System: Neuromuscular and Nervous Systems
Content Outline: Interventions

Level 2

PTEXAM ONE: QUESTION 194

A physical therapist prepares to examine a patient's triceps using a reflex hammer. Which of the following positions for the patient's upper extremity is the MOST appropriate to test the triceps reflex?

1. **Shoulder extension and elbow flexion**
2. Shoulder flexion and elbow extension
3. Shoulder extension and elbow extension
4. Shoulder flexion and elbow flexion

Correct Answer: 1 (Magee p. 201) 

Deep tendon reflexes are performed to test the integrity of the spinal reflex. A physical therapist should assess a deep tendon reflex by placing the tendon on slight stretch. A reflex hammer is used to sharply tap over the tendon. Reflexes can be graded as normal, exaggerated (hyper) or depressed (hypo) or can be graded on a scale of 0-4.

1. **Shoulder extension and elbow flexion would be the most appropriate position to test the triceps reflex. The reflex is best elicited with the patient in sitting or standing with the arm supported by the physical therapist. The therapist strikes the triceps tendon with a reflex hammer where it crosses the olecranon fossa. An acceptable alternate position to test the triceps reflex would be shoulder abduction and elbow flexion.**
2. Shoulder flexion and elbow extension would not place the triceps tendon on adequate stretch to elicit the triceps reflex.
3. Shoulder extension and elbow extension would result in an ineffective position to elicit the triceps reflex since the triceps is already in a maximally shortened position.
4. Shoulder flexion and elbow flexion place the triceps on total stretch secondary to the origin and insertion of the triceps muscle. A deep tendon reflex should be tested with the tendon on slight stretch.

System: Neuromuscular and Nervous Systems
Content Outline: Physical Therapy Examination

Level 1 p. 253-255

PTEXAM ONE: QUESTION 195

A patient sustains a chemical burn on the cubital area of the elbow. What position would be the MOST appropriate for splinting of the involved upper extremity?

1. Elbow flexion and forearm pronation
2. Elbow flexion and forearm supination
3. Elbow extension and forearm pronation
4. **Elbow extension and forearm supination**

Correct Answer: 4 (O'Sullivan p. 1069)

A burn in the cubital area of the elbow would impact the motions at the elbow and the forearm. The general rule for positioning is to place the affected area in a position that is opposite from the impending contracture. The elbow is most susceptible to a flexion contracture and the forearm is most susceptible to a pronation contracture. Physical therapists must be aware of patient positioning following a burn in order to avoid potential contractures. Daily monitoring of the patient's medical status, range of motion, and skin condition will assist health care providers to determine how long specific positions should be maintained and what other modifications may be necessary.

1. Splinting in the position of elbow flexion and forearm pronation would result in the patient being susceptible to elbow flexion and forearm pronation contractures.
2. Splinting in the position of elbow flexion and forearm supination would result in the patient being susceptible to an elbow flexion contracture.
3. Splinting in the position of elbow extension and forearm pronation would result in the patient being susceptible to a forearm pronation contracture.
4. **Splinting in the position of elbow extension and forearm supination will effectively limit contractures and maximize functional use of the upper extremity.**

System: Other Systems
Content Outline: Interventions

p. 514

PTEXAM ONE: QUESTION 196

A patient is placed in the supine position with the hips flexed to 90 degrees and the knees extended. As the patient slowly lowers the extended legs toward the horizontal, there is an increase in the lumbar lordosis. This finding is indicative of weakness of what muscle group?

1. Hip flexors
2. Back extensors
3. Hip extensors
4. **Abdominals**

Correct Answer: 4 (Kendall p. 212) 

Muscle testing is often a standard component of a physical examination and can be useful in differential diagnosis and the treatment of musculoskeletal and neuromuscular conditions.

1. The strength of the hip flexors is assessed with the patient in short sitting. The patient is asked to raise their leg toward the ceiling. The physical therapist stabilizes the iliac crest of the test leg while placing a resistive downward force at the distal end of the femur. Weakness would be indicated by inability to maintain the leg off of the table or attempted substitution.
2. The strength of the back extensors is assessed with the patient in prone. The patient is asked to raise their trunk off of the surface of the table while clasping their hands behind the buttocks or behind the head. The physical therapist stabilizes by providing a downward force to the legs so that they remain firmly on the table. Weakness would be indicated by an inability to maintain the trunk off of the surface of the table or attempted substitution.
3. The strength of the hip extensors, as a group, is assessed in prone. The patient is asked to raise the leg off of the surface of the table, toward the ceiling. The physical therapist stabilizes the pelvis of the test leg while placing a resistive downward force at the distal end of the femur. Weakness would be indicated by an inability to maintain the leg off of the surface of the table.
4. **The supplied description of the resistive test in the question is a standard method to assess the strength of the lower abdominal muscles. Failure to maintain the low back flat on the surface of the table as the legs are lowered is indicative of muscle weakness.**

System: Musculoskeletal System
Content Outline: Physical Therapy Examination

PTEXAM ONE: QUESTION 197

In a clinical trial, patient height is measured in centimeters and weight is measured in kilograms. The physical therapist should recognize that height and weight are measured on which scale of measurement?

1. **Ratio**
2. **Ordinal**
3. **Nominal**
4. **Interval**

Correct Answer: 1 (Portney p. 71) 

The four scales of measurement – nominal, ordinal, interval, and ratio – have different characteristics and a special set of rules for manipulating and interpreting numerical data.

1. **Measurements on the ratio scale have an absolute zero point, meaning a score of 0 represents a total absence of the property being measured. Length in centimeters and mass in kilograms are examples of ratio scale measurements because the numbers represent the actual amount of the attributes being measured.**
2. Measurements on an ordinal scale are rank-ordered according to an operationally defined characteristic or property. The measurements exhibit a greater than – less than relationship. Ordinal scale measurements are common in physical therapy. For example, scales of sensation, balance, and manual muscle test scores.
3. In the nominal scale or classification scale, elements are assigned to mutually exclusive categories according to some criterion. The categories may be coded by a name, number or symbol, which are used as labels for identification, but have no quantitative value. Gender, blood type, and diagnosis are examples of nominal variables.
4. The interval scale has the same rank-order characteristics as an ordinal scale, but also demonstrates known and equal distances or intervals between the units of measurement. Unlike the ratio scale, the interval scale has no true zero point. Temperature measured on the Celsius and Fahrenheit scales are examples of interval measurements.

System: Non-Systems
Content Outline: Safety and Protection; Professional Responsibilities; Research

Level 1

p. 806

PTEXAM ONE: QUESTION 198

A physical therapist attempts to select an appropriate intervention to treat a patient who has a 10 degree limitation in knee extension. Which of the following mobilization techniques would be the MOST appropriate?

1. **Lateral glide of the patella**
2. **Caudal glide of the patella**
3. **Posterior glide of the tibia**
4. **Anterior glide of the tibia**

Correct Answer: 4 (Kisner p. 776)

The patellofemoral articulation consists of a convex patella articulating with the concave femoral condyles. The tibiofemoral articulation consists of a concave tibial plateau articulating with the convex femoral condyles.

1. A lateral glide of the patella may be used to improve accessory motion of the patellofemoral joint, but would not be useful to improve knee extension.
2. A caudal glide refers to a downward glide (i.e., inferior) toward the feet. A caudal glide would not be useful to improve knee extension range of motion since the patella slides superiorly in knee extension.
3. A posterior glide of the tibia on the femur would be used to increase knee flexion range of motion.
4. **An anterior glide of the tibia on the femur would be used to increase knee extension range of motion.**

System: Musculoskeletal System
Content Outline: Interventions

Level 2

p. 111-113

PTEXAM ONE: QUESTION 199

A physical therapist examines a patient post right radial head fracture. The patient's involved elbow range of motion begins at 15 degrees of flexion and ends at 90 degrees of flexion. Which of the following methods of documentation represents how the therapist should record the patient's elbow range of motion?

1. 0-15-90 degrees
2. 15-0-90 degrees
3. **15-90 degrees**
4. 0-90 degrees

Correct Answer: 3 (Norkin p. 35) 

Physical therapists must accurately record the results of goniometric measurements in a manner that is easily interpreted by all health care providers. Any recording of range of motion must include the beginning of the range as well as the end of the range.

1. This style of recording is not acceptable since it is not possible to have two distinct values to the right of the "0".
2. The use of "0" between the starting and ending value indicates the patient has 15 degrees of elbow hyperextension. The total available degrees of movement would be 105 degrees.
3. **The recording depicts a patient who begins in 15 degrees of elbow flexion and ends in 90 degrees of elbow flexion. The total available degrees of movement would be 75 degrees.**
4. The recording depicts a patient who is able to fully extend the elbow and flex the elbow to 90 degrees. The total available degrees of movement would be 90 degrees.

System: Musculoskeletal System
Content Outline: Physical Therapy Examination

p. 98

PTEXAM ONE: QUESTION 200

A physical therapist attempts to improve a patient's lower extremity strength. Which proprioceptive neuromuscular facilitation (PNF) technique would be the MOST appropriate to achieve the therapist's goal?

1. Contract-relax
2. **Repeated contractions**
3. Rhythmic stabilization
4. Hold-relax

Correct Answer: 2 (Sullivan p. 71)

There are a wide variety of proprioceptive neuromuscular facilitation techniques. Each technique is designed with a specific purpose and therapeutic objective. Repeated contractions is designed to initiate movement and promote strength while the other listed options are designed to increase range of motion or promote stability.

1. Contract-relax is a technique used to increase range of motion. As the extremity reaches the point of limitation the patient performs a maximal contraction of the antagonistic muscle group. The therapist resists the movement followed by relaxation and passive movement into newly gained range of motion.
2. **Repeated contractions are used to initiate movement and sustain a contraction through the range of motion. The therapist provides a quick stretch followed by isometric or isotonic contractions. Providing resistance at the point of weakness can enhance the effectiveness of repeated contractions.**
3. Rhythmic stabilization is a technique used to increase range of motion and coordinate isometric contractions. The technique requires isometric contractions of all muscles around a joint against progressive resistance.
4. Hold-relax uses isometric contractions to increase range of motion. The contractions are facilitated for all muscle groups at the limiting point within the range of motion. Relaxation occurs and the extremity moves through the newly acquired range to the next point of limitation.

System: Neuromuscular and Nervous Systems
Content Outline: Interventions

Level 1

p. 291-292

11

PHYSICAL THERAPY EXAM TWO ANSWER KEY

Scott Giles

PHYSICAL THERAPY EXAM TWO ANSWER KEY

DIRECTION

"If you don't know where you are going you could wind up some place else."

— Yogi Berra

Candidates must be proactive throughout the study process and avoid relying on their past accomplishments. Candidates that assess their progress throughout the study plan and make appropriate modifications often outperform candidates that prepare for the NPTE-PT in a more random fashion.

PTEXAM TWO: QUESTION 1

A physical therapist assesses several superficial reflexes as part of a neurological examination. Which grading system is the MOST appropriate when documenting the obtained results?

1. **Present, absent**
2. Ordinal scale from 0-4+
3. Hypoactive, normal, hyperactive
4. Zero, trace, poor, fair, good, normal

Correct Answer: 1 (O'Sullivan p. 148) 

Superficial reflexes are involuntary muscle contractions that follow stimulation of the skin usually by stroking or scratching. Examples of superficial reflexes include the abdominal reflex, cremasteric reflex, corneal reflex, and normal plantar response.

1. **Superficial reflexes are graded as present or absent, although asymmetry should be noted. True asymmetry is almost always pathological.**
2. Deep tendon reflexes are graded on an ordinal scale from 0-4+. 0 = no response, 1+ = diminished/depressed response, 2+ = active normal response, 3+ = brisk/exaggerated response, and 4+ = very brisk/hyperactive; abnormal response.
3. Hypoactive, normal, and hyperactive are general terms to describe the relative responsiveness of deep tendon reflexes to stimulation. Hyperactive reflexes are often associated with upper motor neuron disorders while hypoactive reflexes are often associated with lower motor neuron disorders.
4. Manual muscle testing grades range from zero (0/5) to normal (5/5) based on the ability to move a body segment through range with and without varying levels of resistance. Specifically, manual muscle test grades include zero (0), trace (1), poor (2), fair (3), good (4), and normal (5).

System: Neuromuscular and Nervous Systems
Content Outline: Physical Therapy Examination

Level 1  p. 252

PTEXAM TWO: QUESTION 2

A physical therapist treats a patient diagnosed with myasthenia gravis. Which of the following tests should the therapist MOST likely expect to be abnormal with this condition?

1. Coordination testing
2. Sensory testing
3. Deep tendon reflex testing
4. **Endurance testing**

Correct Answer: 4 (Goodman – Pathology p. 1696) 

Myasthenia gravis is an autoimmune disorder that disrupts neuromuscular transmission and results in muscle weakness and fatigability. The condition is characterized by weakness with repetitive activity that is restored quickly after a period of rest. Other neurologic findings typically are normal in patients with myasthenia gravis.

1. A patient with myasthenia gravis does not typically demonstrate coordination deficits and therefore would not exhibit abnormal findings with coordination testing. A patient with a cerebellar disorder would be more likely to exhibit abnormal findings with coordination testing.
2. A patient with myasthenia gravis does not typically demonstrate sensory deficits and therefore would not exhibit abnormal findings with sensory testing. A patient with a spinal cord injury would be more likely to exhibit abnormal findings with sensory testing.
3. A patient with myasthenia gravis does not typically demonstrate hyporeflexia or hyperreflexia and therefore would not exhibit abnormal findings with deep tendon reflex testing. A patient with a traumatic brain injury would be more likely to exhibit abnormal findings with deep tendon reflex testing.
4. **Myasthenia gravis is a condition that is characterized by muscle weakness and significant muscle fatigability. A patient with myasthenia gravis could demonstrate normal strength with manual muscle testing since it only requires a single muscle contraction. However, the patient would demonstrate significant weakness if required to perform repeated contractions. Endurance testing (e.g., treadmill testing, cycle ergometry) would likely be abnormal for this patient.**

System: Neuromuscular and Nervous Systems
Content Outline: Foundations for Evaluation, Differential Diagnosis, and Prognosis

Level 1  p. 277, 365

PTEXAM TWO: QUESTION 3

A patient post CVA requires an orthosis due to occasional dragging of the toe during the swing phase of gait. The patient presents with weakness of the dorsiflexors and has good medial/lateral stability at the ankle. Which of the following orthotic options is the MOST appropriate for this patient?

1. Solid ankle-foot orthosis
2. Tone reducing foot orthosis
3. **Posterior leaf spring orthosis**
4. Custom articulating ankle-foot orthosis with anterior trim lines

Correct Answer: 3 (Seymour p. 383)

A posterior leaf spring (PLS) orthosis is a type of ankle-foot orthosis that provides a dorsiflexion assist during swing phase. The trim line is posterior to the malleoli and as a result the device offers minimal medial or lateral ankle support.

1. A solid ankle-foot orthosis (AFO) is typically indicated for diminished strength of the dorsiflexors, plantar flexors, and evertors/invertors. The solid AFO will control the ankle and influence the knee joint during gait. The solid AFO maintains the ankle in a static position, however, may assist with tonal influence and lower extremity weakness. The AFO provides more stability than the patient requires.
2. A tone reducing foot orthosis is typically indicated to decrease hypertonicity and normalize tone. The foot orthosis provides total contact under the foot allowing for areas of pressure that function to decrease tone.
3. **The PLS orthosis is designed with flexibility so that both dorsiflexion and plantar flexion can occur during the gait cycle. The PLS allows for improved biomechanics during gait secondary to its flexibility and therefore would be the most appropriate type of orthosis for the patient given their level of medial/lateral stability.**
4. A custom articulating ankle-foot orthosis (AFO) with anterior trim lines typically provides total contact and a significant amount of stability. The articulating joint promotes improved biomechanics allowing the tibia to advance over the foot during stance phase. The patient would not require the level of stability offered by this type of AFO.

System: Neuromuscular and Nervous Systems
Content Outline: Interventions

p. 134-135

PTEXAM TWO: QUESTION 4

A physical therapist treats a patient who was in good health prior to being diagnosed with Guillain-Barre syndrome two weeks ago. Which of the following symptoms would result in the LEAST favorable prognosis for this patient?

1. Weakness that begins in the lower extremities
2. Loss of sensation throughout the extremities
3. **Respiratory impairment**
4. Bladder dysfunction

Correct Answer: 3 (Goodman – Pathology p. 1687)

Guillain-Barre syndrome is an acute polyneuropathy that primarily affects the peripheral nervous system. The condition often occurs following a relatively benign respiratory or gastrointestinal illness. Guillain-Barre syndrome is characterized by ascending weakness that begins distally in the lower extremities and progresses towards the trunk.

1. The primary symptom associated with Guillain-Barre syndrome is ascending weakness, which begins in the distal lower extremities and moves toward the trunk. Patients displaying this symptom are likely experiencing a normal progression of the condition.
2. Though not as common of a symptom as ascending weakness, sensory loss is also a relatively common symptom associated with Guillain-Barre syndrome. Sensory loss usually takes the form of loss of proprioception and areflexia. Loss of pain and temperature sensation are usually mild.
3. **Respiratory impairment is a symptom that can be associated with Guillain-Barre syndrome and is seen in more severe cases of the condition. Patients that have respiratory impairment and require mechanical ventilation are considered to have a poor prognosis compared to those patients that do not require mechanical ventilation. Other poor prognostic factors include advanced age, long hospital stays, and poor upper extremity muscle strength.**
4. Bladder dysfunction is seen in the more severe cases of Guillain-Barre syndrome. Though this symptom is seen in severe cases, it would be less likely to lead to a poor prognosis (i.e., mortality) than would respiratory impairment.

System: Neuromuscular and Nervous Systems
Content Outline: Foundations for Evaluation, Differential Diagnosis, and Prognosis

Level 2

p. 276, 338-339

PTEXAM TWO: QUESTION 5

A physical therapist completes a family training session with a patient rehabilitating from a spinal cord injury. During the training, the patient asks a question regarding their functional ability following rehabilitation. Which of the following responses is the MOST appropriate option for the therapist to utilize?

1. Explain that it is difficult to predict since all patients progress differently
2. **Provide information on the expected prognosis based on the nature and severity of the injury**
3. Refer the patient to the director of rehabilitation
4. Refer the patient to the physiatrist

Correct Answer: 2 (Purtilo p. 31) 

Patients often ask physical therapists questions about their functional abilities following rehabilitation. It is reasonable for the therapist to provide the patient with information on this topic given the patient's level of motor and sensory innervation.

1. The statement, although accurate, does not directly address the patient's question. Physical therapists should attempt to answer questions posed by patients in a direct and forthcoming manner whenever possible.
2. **Physical therapists can share information with patients related to projected functional outcomes following rehabilitation. Physical therapists should be careful to make sure that the topics addressed fall within their scope of practice.**
3. The director of rehabilitation is typically responsible for oversight of the therapy services provided by the various health care disciplines. The position is primarily administrative and therefore the director would not typically be well suited to respond to questions regarding expected patient outcome.
4. Referring the patient to the physiatrist, although appropriate, would be a more attractive option if the question posed by the patient was directly related to their medical management or another similar topic that would fall under the scope of practice of the physiatrist.

System: Neuromuscular and Nervous Systems
Content Outline: Foundations for Evaluation, Differential Diagnosis, and Prognosis

Level 3

PTEXAM TWO: QUESTION 6

A physical therapist reviews the parameters of several pain modulation theories using transcutaneous electrical nerve stimulation (TENS). When comparing sensory stimulation to motor stimulation, sensory stimulation requires which of the following modifications to the parameters?

1. Greater phase duration
2. **Greater frequency**
3. Stronger amplitude
4. Shorter treatment time

Correct Answer: 2 (Cameron p. 258)

Motor stimulation requires sufficient phase charge to elicit a muscle contraction. This is accomplished by using a low frequency and long phase duration. Sensory stimulation, also called conventional TENS, requires a sufficient phase charge to achieve a sensory response, but is below the motor threshold. This is accomplished by using a high frequency and short phase duration.

1. Phase duration is shorter with sensory level stimulation compared to motor level stimulation.
2. **Frequency is significantly greater with sensory level stimulation compared to motor level stimulation.**
3. Sensory level stimulation requires lower amplitude than motor level stimulation.
4. Treatment time is highly variable with sensory and motor stimulation TENS.

System: Non-Systems
Content Outline: Equipment, Devices, and Technologies; Therapeutic Modalities

Level 2  p. 729-730

PTEXAM TWO: QUESTION 7

A patient reports shoulder pain during active shoulder range of motion testing. The pain is most pronounced when the shoulder is in 170 to 180 degrees of abduction. This finding is MOST commonly associated with which of the following conditions?

1. Anterior glenohumeral instability
2. Posterior glenohumeral instability
3. **Acromioclavicular arthritis**
4. Bicipital tendonitis

Correct Answer: 3 (Dutton p. 607)

It is important for physical therapists to collect as much information as possible about a patient's present pain. Many diagnoses have characteristic patterns of pain which can be useful when engaging in differential diagnosis activities.

1. A patient with anterior glenohumeral instability would be more likely to experience pain with terminal shoulder lateral rotation.
2. A patient with posterior glenohumeral instability would be more likely to experience pain with terminal shoulder medial rotation.
3. **A patient with acromioclavicular arthritis would likely experience pain with terminal shoulder abduction. The acromioclavicular joint is a diarthrodial joint formed by the medial margin of the acromion and the lateral end of the clavicle. Degenerative changes of the acromioclavicular joint include narrowing of the joint space and the formation of osteophytes.**
4. A patient with bicipital tendonitis would be more likely to experience pain with shoulder extension with the elbow extended.

System: Musculoskeletal System
Content Outline: Foundations for Evaluation, Differential Diagnosis, and Prognosis

PTEXAM TWO: QUESTION 8

A patient being treated for low back pain indicates that they recently were diagnosed with benign prostatic hyperplasia. Which of the following symptoms is MOST commonly associated with this condition?

1. Epigastric pain
2. Painful urination
3. Painful ejaculation
4. **Urge to urinate frequently**

Correct Answer: 4 (Goodman – Differential Diagnosis p. 369)

Benign prostatic hyperplasia (BPH) is an enlargement of the prostate that commonly occurs in men over 50 years old. The enlargement of the prostate squeezes the urethra and interferes with urinary function and, less frequently, sexual function.

1. BPH is more commonly associated with lower abdominal, low back or thigh pain, not epigastric pain.
2. Though a patient with BPH may experience urinary problems, painful urination is not typically one of the symptoms. Painful urination is more likely with conditions such as prostatitis.
3. Though a patient with BPH may experience sexual dysfunction (e.g., difficulty attaining an erection), painful ejaculation is not typically one of the symptoms. Painful ejaculation is more likely with conditions such as prostatitis.
4. **Patients with BPH typically have issues passing urine due to the enlargement of the prostate and its position next to the urethra. Symptoms include hesitancy of urination, small amounts of urine when voiding, dribbling at the end of urination, urge to urinate frequently, and nocturia.**

System: Other Systems
Content Outline: Foundations for Evaluation, Differential Diagnosis, and Prognosis

p. 551

PTEXAM TWO: QUESTION 9

A physical therapist reviews a patient's medical record prior to beginning treatment. The record indicates the patient was recently placed on amitriptyline (Elavil). Which of the following responses is the MOST common side effect associated with this tricyclic antidepressant?

1. **Sedation**
2. Dysarthria
3. Seizures
4. Blood pressure variability

Correct Answer: 1 (Ciccone p. 92)

Antidepressant medications are classified into groups according to function or chemical criteria. As a group, there are a broad range of side effects including sedation, sexual dysfunction, overstimulation, anxiety, seizure activity, arrhythmias, and orthostatic hypotension. Tricyclic antidepressants are particularly prone to producing sedation.

1. **Sedation is the primary side effect with tricyclic antidepressants, however, other side effects can include confusion and even delirium secondary to the medication's anticholinergic properties. Tricyclic antidepressants have been associated with fatal overdoses and therefore should be used with great caution.**
2. Dysarthria is a motor disorder of speech that is caused by an upper motor neuron lesion that affects the muscles that are used to articulate words and sounds. Speech is often "slurred" due to the muscle weakness. Dysarthria is not a common side effect of tricyclic antidepressants.
3. A variety of antidepressant medications can cause seizure activity, however, this is not a common side effect of tricyclic antidepressants.
4. Selected tricyclic antidepressants can increase the likelihood of orthostatic hypotension, however, this side effect is not nearly as common as sedation.

System: Other Systems
Content Outline: Foundations for Evaluation, Differential Diagnosis, and Prognosis

Level 1

p. 566-567, 585-588

PTEXAM TWO: QUESTION 10

A patient who has been on bed rest for three weeks has developed a plantar flexion contracture. Which phase of the gait cycle would be the MOST problematic for the patient based on the described impairment?

1. Heel strike to foot flat
2. Foot flat to midstance
3. **Midstance to heel off**
4. Heel off to toe off

Correct Answer: 3 (O'Sullivan p. 231)

Normal ankle range of motion needed for the stance phase of gait is 20 degrees of plantar flexion to 15 degrees of dorsiflexion. Limited range of motion is one of several reasons a patient may demonstrate deviations in gait. Patients who are on bed rest may develop a plantar flexor contracture secondary to the positioning of the ankle under the sheets.

1. Heel strike requires 0 degrees of dorsiflexion which progresses to 15 degrees of plantar flexion at foot flat. A patient with a plantar flexion contracture may have difficulty with heel strike, however, they would have greater difficulty with other phases of the gait cycle.
2. Foot flat requires 15 degrees of plantar flexion which progresses to 10 degrees of dorsiflexion at midstance. A patient with a plantar flexion contracture may have difficulty with the end of this phase (i.e., midstance), however, they would have greater difficulty with other phases of the gait cycle.
3. **Midstance requires 10 degrees of dorsiflexion which progresses to 15 degrees of dorsiflexion at heel off. A patient with a plantar flexion contracture would have the most difficulty with this phase of gait since it requires the largest range of motion for dorsiflexion.**
4. Heel off requires 15 degrees of dorsiflexion which progresses to 20 degrees of plantar flexion at toe off. Though heel off requires the maximum amount of dorsiflexion (i.e., 15 degrees), the majority of this phase occurs with the ankle in plantar flexion. Therefore, the patient would have less difficulty with this phase than with the midstance to heel off phase.

System: Musculoskeletal System
Content Outline: Foundations for Evaluation, Differential Diagnosis, and Prognosis

Level 2

p. 84-87

PTEXAM TWO: QUESTION 11

A physical therapist administers iontophoresis to a patient with a lower extremity ulceration in an attempt to promote tissue healing. Which of the following ions would **BEST** meet the stated goal?

1. Acetate
2. Magnesium
3. Lidocaine
4. **Zinc**

Correct Answer: 4 (Prentice p. 195)

Iontophoresis refers to the transcutaneous delivery of ions into the body for therapeutic purposes using an electrical current. Physical therapists must possess an in-depth awareness of the most appropriate ions to treat specific conditions.

1. Acetate, from acetic acid, is a negatively charged ion used to treat calcific deposits.
2. Magnesium, from magnesium sulfate, is a positively charged ion used as a muscle relaxant and vasodilator.
3. Lidocaine, from xylocaine, is a positively charged ion used to treat pain and inflammation associated with acute inflammatory conditions.
4. **Zinc, from zinc oxide, is a positively charged ion used to promote healing, most often with open lesions and ulcerations.**

System: Non-Systems
Content Outline: Equipment, Devices, and Technologies; Therapeutic Modalities

Level 2

p. 731-733

PTEXAM TWO: QUESTION 12

A physical therapist performs segmental breathing exercises with a patient post atelectasis. Which of the following hand placements would be the **MOST** appropriate to emphasize expansion of the lingula?

1. **On the left side of the chest below the axilla**
2. Below the clavicle on the anterior chest wall
3. Over the posterior aspect of the lower ribs
4. On the right side of the chest below the axilla

Correct Answer: 1 (Tan p. 735)

Segmental breathing, also known as localized breathing or thoracic expansion exercise, is intended to improve regional ventilation in patients with pulmonary disease and to prevent and treat pulmonary complications after surgery. The technique combines positioning with tactile and verbal cueing and resistance to enhance expansion of a specific lung segment to facilitate chest wall motion and increase ventilation.

1. **The lingula is a segment of the left upper lobe. Placing the hands on the left side of the chest below the axilla would provide tactile stimulation to facilitate expansion of the chest wall to improve ventilation of the left upper lobe.**
2. Placing the hands below the clavicle on the anterior chest wall would provide tactile stimulation to the anterior segments of the upper lobes, but not the lingula.
3. Placing the hands over the posterior aspect of the lower ribs would provide tactile stimulus over the lateral basal segments of the right and left lower lobes, not the lingula.
4. Placing the hands on the right side of the chest below the axilla would be overlying the right middle lobe, not the lingula.

System: Cardiovascular and Pulmonary Systems
Content Outline: Interventions

Level 2

PTEXAM TWO: QUESTION 13

A physical therapist administers a submaximal exercise test to a patient in a cardiac rehabilitation program. The protocol requires the patient to ride a cycle ergometer for a predetermined amount of time using progressive workloads. In order to predict the patient's maximum oxygen uptake, it is necessary to determine the relationship between which of the following parameters?

1. Heart rate and rate of perceived exertion
2. **Heart rate and workload**
3. Blood pressure and rate of perceived exertion
4. Blood pressure and workload

Correct Answer: 2 (ACSM – Resource Manual p. 342)

Because maximal exercise testing is not always feasible, practitioners often rely on submaximal exercise tests to assess cardiorespiratory fitness. In addition to the heart rate response, it is recommended that the individual's functional response to exercise is examined.

1. Rate of perceived exertion (RPE) is one of the indices commonly measured as a response to exercise. However, oxygen uptake cannot be determined from heart rate and RPE.
2. **The physical therapist can use the heart rate response to one or more submaximal workloads to predict maximum oxygen uptake.**
3. Rate of perceived exertion (RPE) and blood pressure are commonly measured as a response to exercise. However, oxygen uptake cannot be determined from blood pressure and RPE.
4. Blood pressure is one of the indices commonly measured as a response to exercise. However, oxygen uptake cannot be determined from blood pressure and workload.

System: Cardiovascular and Pulmonary Systems
Content Outline: Interventions

 Level 2 p. 435-436

PTEXAM TWO: QUESTION 14

A physical therapist reviews the chart of a 63-year-old patient referred to physical therapy for pulmonary rehabilitation. The chart indicates the patient has smoked one to two packs of cigarettes a day since the age of 25, and notes that the patient's thorax was enlarged with flaring of the costal margins and widening of the costochondral angle. What pulmonary disease does the chart MOST accurately describe?

1. Asthma
2. Bronchiectasis
3. Chronic bronchitis
4. **Emphysema**

Correct Answer: 4 (Goodman - Pathology p. 796)

Due to the pathologic changes in alveoli, patients with emphysema often have increased total lung capacity from "air trapping." Over time, many patients develop a barrel-shaped configuration of the thorax. The anteroposterior diameter enlarges to approximate the transverse diameter. The diaphragm is depressed and the sternum pushed forward with the ribs attached in a horizontal, not angular, fashion. As a result, the chest appears continuously in the inspiratory position.

1. Asthma is a chronic inflammatory disease of the airways. Clinical features include cough, dyspnea, and wheezing, but not an enlarged thorax.
2. Bronchiectasis is a permanent, abnormal dilatation of one or more bronchi caused by destruction of the elastic and muscular components of the bronchial walls. Common clinical features include recurrent pulmonary infections with cough and copious mucopurulent sputum, but not an enlarged thorax.
3. Chronic bronchitis is defined as hypersecretion of mucus sufficient to cause a productive cough on most days for three months during two consecutive years, but not an enlarged thorax.
4. **Emphysema is an obstructive pulmonary disease characterized by destruction of alveoli leading to hyperinflation of the lungs. A barrel-shaped configuration of the thorax is a common clinical feature of the disease.**

System: Cardiovascular and Pulmonary Systems
Content Outline: Foundations for Evaluation, Differential Diagnosis, and Prognosis

 Level 2  p. 407, 458-459

PTEXAM TWO: QUESTION 15

A physical therapist reviews the results of pulmonary function testing on a patient who has emphysema. Assuming the patient's testing was classified as unremarkable, which of the following lung volumes would MOST likely approximate 10 percent of the patient's total lung capacity?

1. **Tidal volume**
2. Inspiratory reserve volume
3. Residual volume
4. Functional residual capacity

Correct Answer: 1 (Hillegass p. 24) 

Tidal volume is the total volume of air inhaled or exhaled during quiet breathing. Total lung capacity is the maximum volume of air to which the lungs can be expanded. Normal tidal volume is approximately 10% of total lung capacity.

1. **While there is wide variability in tidal volume in the normal population, the average for a healthy adult is around 500 mL (± 100 mL). Total lung capacity is the maximum volume of air to which the lungs can be expanded, typically 4,000 – 6,000 mL. Thus, normal tidal volume is approximately 10% of total lung capacity.**
2. Inspiratory reserve volume is the additional volume of air that can be inhaled beyond the normal tidal inhalation. The inspiratory reserve volume varies, however, should represent approximately 55% to 60% of total lung capacity.
3. Residual volume is the volume of air remaining in the lungs after a forced expiratory effort. This volume is usually 1,000 mL and approximates 25% of total lung capacity.
4. Functional residual capacity is the amount of air remaining in the lungs at the end of a normal tidal exhalation. This volume approximates 40% of total lung capacity.

System: Cardiovascular and Pulmonary Systems
Content Outline: Physical Therapy Examination

 Level 1  p. 398-399

PTEXAM TWO: QUESTION 16

A physical therapist prepares to examine a patient with a suspected grade III sprain of the anterior cruciate ligament. Which of the following special tests is considered to have the HIGHEST sensitivity for detecting this type of injury in the acute phase?

1. Anterior drawer
2. McMurray
3. **Lachman**
4. Pivot shift

Correct Answer: 3 (Dutton p. 1003)

The anterior cruciate ligament (ACL) prevents anterior translation of the tibia on the fixed femur and posterior translation of the femur on the fixed tibia. A grade III ACL sprain refers to a complete tear of the ligament with excessive laxity. Sensitivity refers to the ability of a test to correctly identify patients with a condition, or the "true positive" rate. Specificity refers to the ability of a test to correctly identify patients without the condition, or the "true negative" rate.

1. The anterior drawer test is used to detect an anterior cruciate ligament injury by identifying excessive anterior translation of the tibia on the femur with a diminished or absent end-point. Studies have found the anterior drawer test to have low sensitivity, but higher specificity.
2. The McMurray test is a special test used to identify a posterior meniscal lesion and would not be used to identify ACL injuries. Other special tests used to help identify meniscal lesions include Apley's test and the Thessaly test. These tests generally have low sensitivity, although some studies have shown the Thessaly test to have higher sensitivity than other common tests designed to identify meniscal pathology.
3. **The Lachman test is performed in 20-30 degrees of knee flexion, whereas the anterior drawer test is performed in 90 degrees of flexion. The knee position for the Lachman test places the ACL in a more equally taut position than the anterior drawer test and would also be more tolerable in acute lesions. The Lachman test has been shown across multiple sources to be more sensitive than the anterior drawer test for detecting an ACL rupture.**
4. The pivot shift test is used to detect anterolateral rotatory instability of the knee. The structures that are potentially compromised if this test is positive include the ACL, lateral collateral ligament, posterolateral capsule, and arcuate complex. Studies have found the pivot shift test to have high specificity, but relatively low sensitivity. Additionally, the Lachman test would be much easier to perform on an acute injury than the pivot shift test.

System: Musculoskeletal System
Content Outline: Physical Therapy Examination

 Level 1 p. 108-109, 815

PTEXAM TWO: QUESTION 17

A physical therapist asks a patient to lie in the prone position to measure passive knee flexion. Range of motion may be limited in this position due to which of the following reasons?

1. Active insufficiency of the knee extensors
2. Active insufficiency of the knee flexors
3. **Passive insufficiency of the knee extensors**
4. Passive insufficiency of the knee flexors

Correct Answer: 3 (Kisner p. 61)

Passive insufficiency occurs when a two-joint muscle cannot lengthen to the extent required to allow full range of motion of all joints it crosses simultaneously. When the muscle is in a lengthened position, the actin filaments are pulled away from the myosin heads so that they cannot create as many cross-bridges. Active insufficiency occurs when a two-joint muscle is incapable of shortening to the extent necessary to produce full range of motion at all joints crossed simultaneously. When the muscle is in a shortened position the overlap of actin and myosin reduces the number of sites available for cross-bridge formation.

1. Active insufficiency occurs with active movement and not passive movement. The question specifically asks about passive knee flexion.
2. Active insufficiency occurs with active movement and not passive movement.
3. **Passive insufficiency refers to a lack of muscle length. When performing passive knee flexion the two-joint knee extensors are placed on stretch and therefore in the presence of insufficient length, may contribute to a limitation in knee flexion.**
4. When performing passive knee flexion, the knee flexors would shorten and therefore would not limit knee flexion range of motion.

System: Musculoskeletal System
Content Outline: Physical Therapy Examination

 **Level 1** p. 83

PTEXAM TWO: QUESTION 18

A patient sustained a superficial wound that appears as a moderate abrasion on the anterior surface of their thigh approximately four inches above the superior pole of the patella. Which type of wound dressing would MOST likely be utilized?

1. Calcium alginate dressing
2. Hydrocolloid dressing
3. Hydrogel dressing
4. **Transparent film dressing**

Correct Answer: 4 (Sussman p. 504) 

Physical therapists select particular wound dressings based on the established therapeutic objectives. General indications for utilizing a dressing include protecting a wound, managing exudate, preventing infection, reducing pain, and promoting healing.

1. A calcium alginate dressing is highly absorptive and typically utilized with wounds that produce moderate to heavy exudate. A superficial wound such as an abrasion would produce minimal exudate and therefore is unlikely to saturate the alginate to the extent necessary for it to form a beneficial hydrophilic gel.
2. Hydrocolloid dressings consist of gel-forming polymers (e.g., carboxymethylcellulose, gelatin, pectin) backed by a strong film or foam adhesive. The dressings absorb exudate by swelling into a gel-like mass and vary in permeability, thickness, and transparency. A hydrocolloid dressing is not used for a superficial wound, however, is often used on partial and full-thickness wounds.
3. Hydrogel dressings are moisture-retentive primary dressings that are commonly used on superficial and partial-thickness wounds (e.g., abrasions, blisters, pressure ulcers) with minimal drainage. This type of dressing is typically used to prevent a wound from dehydrating and impeding the healing process. Small superficial abrasions with minimal to no drainage are much more commonly treated with transparent film dressings than hydrogel dressings because the transparent nature of the dressing allows for quick and easy inspection of the wound.
4. **Transparent film dressings consist of thin membranes coated with a layer of acrylic adhesive. Since the film is transparent, it allows for frequent assessment of the wound and offers some level of protection. The films are oxygen permeable, however, are impermeable to microorganisms and moisture. The relatively superficial nature and clinical presentation (i.e., abrasion) of the wound result in a transparent film dressing serving as the most appropriate choice.**

System: Other Systems
Content Outline: Interventions

Level 3  p. 501, 503, 510

PTEXAM TWO: QUESTION 19

A pregnant patient indicates that her physician ordered genetic testing. Which condition would be the **LEAST** likely to be identified through the testing process?

1. Cystic fibrosis
2. **Meningitis**
3. Phenylketonuria
4. Tay-Sachs disease

Correct Answer: 2 (Goodman – Pathology p. 1405)

Genetic testing can be used to identify a mutation that confirms a potential risk to an unborn child. Common testing procedures include amniocentesis, ultrasonography, serum marker screening, and genetic screening.

1. Cystic fibrosis is characterized by the exocrine glands overproducing thick mucus that causes subsequent obstruction. The disease is an autosomal recessive genetic disorder located on the long arm of chromosome seven. Testing during pregnancy for cystic fibrosis most commonly includes chorionic villus sampling and amniocentesis.
2. **Meningitis is characterized by inflammation of the meninges of the brain and spinal cord. The condition is caused by a bacterial or viral infection that spreads through the cerebrospinal fluid to the brain. A lumbar puncture is the gold standard for diagnosis. Early diagnosis is essential to avoid permanent neurological damage. Meningitis is not hereditary and therefore would not require genetic testing.**
3. Phenylketonuria is characterized by behavioral and cognitive issues secondary to an elevation of serum phenylalanine. The disease is an autosomal recessive inherited trait and is most common in Caucasians. Testing during pregnancy for phenylketonuria includes chorionic villus sampling and amniocentesis. All newborns in the United States are tested shortly after birth through a blood sample. The testing procedure is used to test for a variety of metabolic disorders including phenylketonuria.
4. Tay-Sachs disease is characterized by the absence or deficiency of hexosaminidase A. This produces an accumulation of gangliosides within the brain. The disease is an autosomal recessive inherited trait that is carried primarily in the Eastern European (Ashkenazi) Jewish population. Testing during pregnancy for Tay-Sachs most commonly includes chorionic villus sampling and amniocentesis.

System: Neuromuscular and Nervous Systems
Content Outline: Foundations for Evaluation, Differential Diagnosis, and Prognosis

Level 2

p. 241

PTEXAM TWO: QUESTION 20

A physical therapist notes that a newborn has extremely limited dorsiflexion. Which positional foot deformity would be the **MOST** likely based on the range of motion limitation?

1. Calcaneovalgus
2. Metatarsus adductus
3. Syndactyly
4. **Talipes equinovarus**

Correct Answer: 4 (Sarwark p. 1025)

Positional deformities are abnormalities that are mechanically produced by the fetal environment. The deformities are most often caused by restrictions in fetal movement or fetal compression. Early identification of the deformities is critical to minimize the impact of the deformities on the developing newborn.

1. Calcaneovalgus is a foot deformity characterized by the forefoot being curved out laterally, the hindfoot positioned in valgus, and full or even excessive dorsiflexion range of motion. Calcaneovalgus is an extremely common positional deformity in newborns most often caused by intrauterine positioning.
2. Metatarsus adductus is a foot deformity characterized by a medially curved forefoot while the hindfoot remains in normal alignment. The condition is believed to be caused by intrauterine positioning. The presence of metatarsus adductus would not impact a patient's dorsiflexion range of motion.
3. Syndactyly refers to the presence of webbed toes or fingers. The genetic condition is most commonly observed between the second and third toes. The presence of syndactyly would not impact a patient's dorsiflexion range of motion.
4. **Talipes equinovarus, also known as "clubfoot," is a deformity characterized by adduction of the forefoot, varus positioning of the hindfoot, and plantar flexion at the ankle. The positioning associated with talipes equinovarus would likely result in a limitation in dorsiflexion range of motion.**

System: Musculoskeletal System
Content Outline: Foundations for Evaluation, Differential Diagnosis, and Prognosis

Level 2

p. 127

PTEXAM TWO: QUESTION 21

A physical therapist observes the gait of a patient following a lateral ankle sprain. The patient walks without crutches, but it is evident that walking is extremely painful. Which of the following descriptions is the MOST accurate when describing the anticipated compensation with the unaffected extremity during gait?

1. **Shorter swing phase and shorter step length**
2. Shorter swing phase and longer step length
3. Longer swing phase and shorter step length
4. Longer swing phase and longer step length

Correct Answer: 1 (Dutton p. 307)

An injury to one extremity will invariably alter the movement pattern in both extremities. Physical therapists must carefully assess the impact of an injury on the entire body.

1. **When an injury occurs to a single extremity, an individual typically attempts to spend less time weight bearing on the affected extremity. This results in a shortening of the stance time on the affected extremity which requires the unaffected extremity to contact the ground sooner (i.e., shorter swing phase). A shorter swing phase on the unaffected extremity typically produces a shorter step length.**
2. A shorter swing phase on the unaffected extremity tends to shorten step length.
3. A longer swing phase on the unaffected extremity is unlikely since this would require the stance phase to be longer on the affected extremity. The amount of pain the patient is experiencing makes this unlikely.
4. A longer swing phase on the unaffected extremity typically produces a longer step length, however, the longer swing phase on the unaffected extremity is unlikely for the reasons discussed in option 3.

System: Musculoskeletal System
Content Outline: Physical Therapy Examination

 Level 2  p. 88

PTEXAM TWO: QUESTION 22

A physical therapist attempts to examine the relationship between scores on a functional independence measure and another measurement whose validity is known. This type of example BEST describes which type of validity?

1. Face
2. Predictive
3. **Concurrent**
4. Content

Correct Answer: 3 (Portney p. 103) 

Concurrent validity refers to the relationship between test scores and either criterion states or measurements whose validity is known.

1. Face validity refers to whether the test "looks valid" to those who take and administer it. It refers, not to what the test actually measures, but to what it appears superficially to measure.
2. Predictive validity is a form of validity that is demonstrated when a score is helpful in predicting a specific future outcome. Examples of tests with predictive validity are career or aptitude tests, which are helpful in determining who is likely to succeed or fail in certain subjects or occupations.
3. **Concurrent validity is demonstrated when a test score correlates well with a measure that has previously been validated. This is the circumstance in the example, where the functional independence measure would have concurrent validity if a strong relationship can be shown between its scores and scores on a previously validated measurement.**
4. Content validity refers to the extent to which a measure represents all facets of a given concept or construct.

System: Non-Systems
Content Outline: Safety and Protection; Professional Responsibilities; Research

 Level 1  p. 806-807

PTEXAM TWO: QUESTION 23

A physical therapist develops a chart detailing expected functional outcomes for a variety of spinal cord injuries. Which is the HIGHEST spinal cord injury level at which independent transfers with a sliding board would be feasible?

1. C4
2. **C6**
3. T1
4. T3

Correct Answer: 2 (O'Sullivan p. 884) 

The ability to independently transfer with a sliding board following a spinal cord injury is primarily dependent on the patient's available motor and sensory innervation. In addition to performing independent sliding board transfers, a patient with a C6 spinal cord injury should be able to perform independent bed mobility, coughing, skin inspection, and pressure relief with equipment and adaptations.

1. A patient with a C4 spinal cord injury would not have adequate upper extremity movement to be capable of completing the transfer. Primary muscles innervated include the diaphragm and trapezius.
2. **A patient with a C6 spinal cord injury would possess the requisite upper extremity strength to make the transfer feasible. Primary muscles innervated include the extensor carpi radialis, infraspinatus, latissimus dorsi, pectoralis major, pronator teres, serratus anterior, and teres minor.**
3. A patient with a T1 spinal cord injury would possess full upper extremity innervation and should be able to complete the transfer. The option is not the correct response since the item asks the highest spinal cord injury level where the transfer is feasible.
4. A patient with a T3 spinal cord injury should also be able to complete the transfer. The patient's clinical presentation would be consistent with the patient at the T1 level.

System: Neuromuscular and Nervous Systems
Content Outline: Foundations for Evaluation, Differential Diagnosis, and Prognosis

 Level 2  p. 245-246, 298-300

PTEXAM TWO: QUESTION 24

An individual is asked to complete the PAR-Q & You. Which scenario would be MOST consistent with the use of this tool?

1. A 13-year-old male with a congenital heart condition
2. **A 62-year-old female planning to become more physically active**
3. A 57-year-old male rehabilitating from a recent cardiac event
4. A 72-year-old female with no known cardiac pathology

Correct Answer: 2 (Frownfelter p. 259) 

The PAR-Q & You (Physical Activity Readiness Questionnaire) is a document designed for individuals 15 to 69 years of age who plan to become much more physically active than they are currently. The survey consists of seven "yes" or "no" questions related to current health and functional status. Answering "yes" to one or more questions indicates that an individual should talk to their doctor before becoming more physically active.

1. A 13-year-old male would be too young to use the PAR-Q & You since the tool is designed for individuals 15 to 69 years of age. In addition, the patient does not express a desire to become more physically active.
2. **A 62-year-old female planning to become more physically active would be an appropriate candidate to complete the PAR-Q & You. The patient is within the recommended age range and the desire to become more physically active is consistent with the purpose of the tool.**
3. A 57-year-old male rehabilitating from a recent cardiac event meets the age criteria for the PAR-Q & You, however, the option does not specify that the patient would like to become more physically active.
4. A 72-year-old female with no known cardiac pathology would be too old to use the PAR-Q & You since the tool is designed for individuals 15 to 69 years of age. The option also does not specify that the patient would like to become more physically active.

System: Cardiovascular and Pulmonary Systems
Content Outline: Physical Therapy Examination

 Level 1 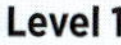

PTEXAM TWO: QUESTION 25

A physical therapist working in an acute care hospital reads in a medical chart that a patient has a blood pH of 7.55. Which of the following scenarios could BEST explain the presence of the abnormal pH?

1. **Prolonged use of antacids**
2. Hypoventilation due to Guillain-Barre syndrome
3. Hypoventilation due to severe scoliosis
4. Diabetic ketoacidosis

Correct Answer: 1 (Goodman – Differential Diagnosis p. 214)

The normal pH of the blood is between 7.35 and 7.45. Acidosis is characterized by a blood pH of less than 7.35. Alkalosis is characterized by a blood pH of greater than 7.45. Acidosis and alkalosis can have either metabolic or respiratory causes.

1. **Ingesting large amounts of bicarbonate (e.g., antacids) causes a buildup of bicarbonate ions, which results in the blood becoming more alkaline. Thus, prolonged use of antacids could be a potential cause of alkalosis (i.e., blood pH >7.45). Other causes of alkalosis include inadequate excretion of bicarbonate ions or excessive excretion of hydrogen ions.**
2. Hypoventilation can be caused by conditions that cause respiratory muscle weakness, such as Guillain-Barre syndrome. Hypoventilation prevents adequate removal of carbon dioxide from the body, which results in the blood becoming more acidic.
3. Hypoventilation can also occur secondary to conditions that cause limited lung expansion, such as severe scoliosis. The cause of the patient's hypoventilation is irrelevant since it is the hypoventilation itself that results in acidosis.
4. Diabetic ketoacidosis occurs when the body breaks down fat cells, which results in the buildup of ketones and causes the blood to become more acidic. Diabetic ketoacidosis is a common cause of metabolic acidosis.

System: Other Systems
Content Outline: Foundations for Evaluation, Differential Diagnosis, and Prognosis

CO_2 = basic/alkaline

O_2 = acidic

Level 2 p. 409-410, 520, 651

PTEXAM TWO: QUESTION 26

A patient reports recurrent ankle pain. As part of the treatment program, the therapist decides to use ultrasound over the peroneus longus and brevis tendons. What location is the MOST appropriate for application of this ultrasound?

1. Inferior to the sustentaculum tali
2. Over the sinus tarsi
3. **Posterior to the lateral malleolus**
4. Anterior to the lateral malleolus

Correct Answer: 3 (Kendall p. 412)

The peroneus longus and brevis are innervated by the superficial peroneal nerve (L4, L5, S1) and act to evert the foot and assist in plantar flexion of the ankle joint. The peroneus longus also acts to depress the head of the first metatarsal.

1. The sustentaculum tali is a horizontal eminence arising from the medial surface of the calcaneus. The bony prominence serves as the attachment for several ligaments including the plantar calcaneonavicular ligament, also known as the spring ligament.
2. The sinus tarsi is a small osseous canal which runs into the ankle under the talus bone. The structure is at the same approximate level as the lateral malleolus.
3. **The peroneus longus and brevis tendons pass posterior to the lateral malleolus. The peroneus longus inserts on the lateral side of the base of the first metatarsal and first cuneiform, while the peroneus brevis inserts on the tuberosity of the fifth metatarsal.**
4. The tendon of the extensor digitorum longus can be palpated slightly anterior to the lateral malleolus.

System: Musculoskeletal System
Content Outline: Interventions

Level 1

PTEXAM TWO: QUESTION 27

A physical therapist treats a patient who has a closed head injury and is presently functioning at the confused-agitated level of cognitive functioning (level IV). The therapist treats the patient in their home for 60 minute sessions, three times per week. Recently the therapist has noticed that the patient becomes increasingly combative as the session progresses and believes the deterioration in behavior is linked to the patient becoming fatigued. Which of the following treatment modifications is the MOST appropriate to assist in reducing patient fatigue?

1. Reduce the treatment sessions to 30 minutes, three times per week
2. Reduce the frequency of the treatment sessions to two times per week
3. **Increase the rest periods during existing treatment sessions**
4. Increase the treatment sessions to 90 minutes, two times per week

Correct Answer: 3 (O'Sullivan p. 827) 

The Rancho Los Amigos Levels of Cognitive Functioning Scale is used to describe cognitive and behavioral recovery in individuals following traumatic brain injury. A patient at level IV is labeled "Confused-Agitated."

1. Reducing the treatment sessions to 30 minutes in length would result in a fifty percent decrease in therapy time. It is possible that this may be necessary, however, the therapist should attempt to modify other parameters of treatment prior to implementing such a drastic reduction in therapy time.
2. Reducing the frequency of the sessions to two times per week would likely have minimal impact on the patient's behavior without reducing the length of the sessions or incorporating more frequent rest periods.
3. **A patient functioning at level IV may be particularly susceptible to changes in behavior based on fatigue. Ideally, the physical therapist should attempt to maintain the integrity of the current treatment regimen, however, if increased rest periods do not produce an observable change in the patient's behavior it may be appropriate to modify other parameters such as the frequency or length of treatment.**
4. It is likely that the length of the session, currently 60 minutes, may be more challenging for the patient than the frequency of the sessions. As a result, increasing the duration of the treatment sessions to 90 minutes would likely exacerbate the current situation.

System: Neuromuscular and Nervous Systems
Content Outline: Interventions

Level 3  p. 305

PTEXAM TWO: QUESTION 28

A physical therapist positions a patient in supine in preparation for goniometric measurements. When measuring medial rotation of the shoulder, the therapist should position the fulcrum over what anatomical landmark?

1. On the lateral midline of the humerus using the lateral epicondyle as a reference
2. Perpendicular to the floor
3. Along the midaxillary line of the thorax
4. **Over the olecranon process**

Correct Answer: 4 (Norkin p. 86) 

According to the American Academy of Orthopaedic Surgeons normal shoulder medial rotation is 0-70 degrees.

1. The lateral midline of the humerus using the lateral epicondyle as a reference should be used to align the moveable arm of the goniometer when measuring shoulder flexion and extension.
2. The stationary arm of the goniometer should be aligned parallel or perpendicular to the floor when measuring medial rotation of the shoulder.
3. The midaxillary line of the thorax should be used to align the stationary arm of the goniometer when measuring shoulder flexion and extension.
4. **The fulcrum of the goniometer should be aligned over the olecranon process. The moveable arm of the goniometer should be aligned with the ulna, using the olecranon and ulnar styloid as a reference when measuring medial rotation of the shoulder.**

System: Musculoskeletal System
Content Outline: Physical Therapy Examination

 Level 1  p. 91-92

PTEXAM TWO: QUESTION 29

A physical therapist examines a patient diagnosed with left-sided heart failure. Which of the following findings is the LEAST likely to be associated with this condition?

1. Pulmonary edema
2. Persistent cough
3. **Dependent edema**
4. Muscular weakness

Correct Answer: 3 (Hillegass p. 87)

Heart failure refers to the heart's inability to maintain a cardiac output that is adequate to meet the demands of the tissues due to an abnormality in the pumping ability of the heart muscle. Left-sided heart failure occurs when the left ventricle fails to pump properly resulting in pulmonary venous congestion. Left-sided failure is frequently caused by myocardial infarction, hypertension or aortic valve disease.

1. Pulmonary edema is the abnormal accumulation of fluid in the alveolar spaces of the lungs. This is the "congestion" of congestive heart failure. It is often caused by increased pulmonary hydrostatic pressure from left-sided heart failure.
2. Patients with left-sided failure may be in respiratory distress and have a cough that produces pink, frothy (blood-tinged) sputum.
3. **Dependent edema is associated with right-sided heart failure. Fluid backs up behind the right ventricle and produces the accumulation of fluid in the liver, abdomen, and ankles.**
4. Muscle weakness, fatigue, and decreased exercise tolerance are universal among patients with left-sided heart failure due to the decreased blood flow to the extremities.

System: Cardiovascular and Pulmonary Systems
Content Outline: Foundations for Evaluation, Differential Diagnosis, and Prognosis

p. 402-403, 454-455

PTEXAM TWO: QUESTION 30

A note in the medical record indicates that a patient is exhibiting extrapyramidal symptoms including tardive dyskinesia. Which of the following conditions would MOST likely be treated with a medication that could produce the described symptoms?

1. Endometriosis
2. Rheumatoid arthritis
3. Hypertension
4. **Psychotic disorder**

Correct Answer: 4 (Ciccone p. 107)

Tardive dyskinesia is an extrapyramidal adverse effect that can routinely occur with administration of neuroleptic (antipsychotic) medications. Tardive dyskinesia presents with involuntary and fragmented choreoathetoid movements. Rhythmic movements of the tongue, mouth, and jaw are often present.

1. Endometriosis refers to the development of endometrial tissue, which normally lines the uterus, in extrauterine locations within the abdomen and pelvis. The most common location of extrauterine endometrial growth occurs at the uterosacral ligaments. Pharmacological intervention may be indicated to alter hormonal balance using oral contraceptives and antigonadotropins. These medications are not associated with tardive dyskinesia.
2. Rheumatoid arthritis is a systemic autoimmune disorder of unknown etiology. The disease presents with a chronic inflammatory reaction in the synovial tissues of a joint that results in erosion of cartilage and supporting structures within the capsule. Pharmacological management includes NSAIDs, corticosteroids, and disease-modifying antirheumatic medications. These medications are not associated with tardive dyskinesia.
3. Hypertension refers to abnormally high blood pressure. It is classified as stage 1 hypertension, stage 2 hypertension, and hypertensive crisis. Classes of medications for hypertension include diuretics, beta blockers, calcium channel blockers, ACE inhibitors, angiotensin II receptor blockers, and direct vasodilators. These medications are not associated with tardive dyskinesia.
4. **Psychosis is a severe mental disorder in which thoughts and emotions are impaired to an extent that contact is lost with external reality. Traditional antipsychotic agents produce increased extrapyramidal (motor) side effects, tardive dyskinesia, pseudoparkinsonism, constipation, and dry mouth. Haldol and Thorazine are two examples of antipsychotic medications that can produce tardive dyskinesia.**

System: Other Systems
Content Outline: Foundations for Evaluation, Differential Diagnosis, and Prognosis

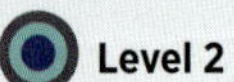

p. 566-567

PTEXAM TWO: QUESTION 31

A three-year-old child with osteogenesis imperfecta participates in an aquatic therapy program. What is the PRIMARY goal of aquatic therapy for a patient diagnosed with this condition?

1. Decrease abnormal tone
2. Decrease bone density
3. Increase range of motion
4. **Increase strength**

Correct Answer: 4 (Palisano p. 236) 

Osteogenesis imperfecta is an autosomal disorder of collagen synthesis that affects bone metabolism. Children with osteogenesis imperfecta often have delayed developmental milestones secondary to ongoing fractures that result in immobilization, hypermobility of joints, and poorly developed muscles. This disorder is classified into four types with diverse clinical presentations ranging from normal appearance with mild symptoms to severe involvement that can be fatal during infancy. Bisphosphonate medication has been reported to reduce the occurrence of fractures, strengthen skeletal structures, and improve bone density with this population.

1. The elevated temperature in certain therapeutic pools would be beneficial to decrease hypertonicity/spasticity, however, children with osteogenesis imperfecta do not exhibit tonal abnormalities. As a result, decreasing abnormal tone would not be the primary goal of aquatic therapy for this patient.
2. Aquatic therapy can have a positive effect on increasing bone density (not decreasing) through weight bearing and resistance exercise. A goal of decreasing bone density would not be appropriate with osteogenesis imperfecta since the associated collagen synthesis disorder already negatively affects bone density.
3. The elevated temperature and properties of buoyancy within therapeutic pools would be beneficial to increase range of motion, however, children with osteogenesis imperfecta do not typically present with decreased range of motion or contractures. As a result, increasing range of motion would not be the primary goal of aquatic therapy for this patient.
4. **Aquatic therapy is an appropriate intervention for a child with osteogenesis imperfecta. It is a safe method of protected strengthening of the muscles due to buoyancy and the physical properties of water. Strengthening in a pool can occur safely in a supported weight bearing position and can be finely graded in terms of exercise intensity. Cardiovascular training and balance training are other benefits of this intervention.**

System: Musculoskeletal System
Content Outline: Interventions

 Level 2  p. 125, 170-171

PTEXAM TWO: QUESTION 32

An entry in the medical record indicates that electromyography revealed denervation of the flexor pollicis longus, flexor digitorum profundus, and pronator quadratus muscles. This finding would MOST likely be associated with which of the following conditions?

1. Anterior compartment syndrome
2. **Anterior interosseous syndrome**
3. Cubital tunnel syndrome
4. Erb's palsy

Correct Answer: 2 (Roy p. 267)

An understanding of the typical clinical presentation of common medical diagnoses is essential in developing an appropriate plan of care and determining realistic outcome expectations.

1. Anterior compartment syndrome is a serious medical condition that causes compression of nerves and blood vessels in the anterior compartment of the lower leg. The result is a dangerous disruption of nerve conduction and blood flow that can threaten the viability of the limb. Anterior compartment syndrome would not impact upper extremity muscles.
2. **Anterior interosseous syndrome is characterized by an injury to the anterior interosseous nerve, a branch of the median nerve which is sometimes pinched or entrapped as it passes between the two heads of the pronator teres muscle. This leads to pain and functional impairment of the flexor pollicis longus, the lateral half of the flexor digitorum profundus, and the pronator quadratus muscles.**
3. Cubital tunnel syndrome is associated with compression of the ulnar nerve at the elbow. Complaints of pain, paresthesia, and muscle weakness are typical in the ulnar nerve distribution (i.e., 4th and 5th digits). The flexor pollicis longus, flexor digitorum profundus, and pronator quadratus muscles would not be affected by involvement of the ulnar nerve.
4. Erb's palsy is a term used to denote an upper brachial plexus injury or palsy that usually results from a difficult birth. The muscles affected are supplied by cervical roots C5 and C6 which results in a loss of function of the rotator cuff, deltoid, brachialis, coracobrachialis, and biceps brachii. The flexor pollicis longus, flexor digitorum profundus, and pronator quadratus muscles receive innervation from the roots of C8-T1.

System: Neuromuscular and Nervous Systems
Content Outline: Foundations for Evaluation, Differential Diagnosis, and Prognosis

 Level 1

PTEXAM TWO: QUESTION 33

A physical therapist treats a patient post CVA who presents with speech and language deficits. The therapist incorporates phonetics into the plan of care. This intervention would be MOST essential for a patient diagnosed with which of the following disorders?

1. Broca's aphasia
2. **Dysarthria**
3. Verbal apraxia
4. Dysphagia

Correct Answer: 2 (O'Sullivan p. 1238)

Phonetics is the study of sound in speech. It focuses on how speech is physically created and received. Phonetics is the primary focus in the treatment of dysarthria since articulatory precision is necessary to improve overall intelligibility.

1. Broca's aphasia, also known as expressive aphasia, occurs with a lesion to the frontal lobe in the dominant (typically left) hemisphere that results in impairment of speech and expression. The treatment emphasis includes family training, group therapy, and compensatory strategies for communication. A task-oriented approach is preferred since it allows for therapeutic intervention through performing familiar tasks. Therapists must avoid activities that require substantial verbal output from the patient and allow adequate time for the patient to process verbal information.
2. **Dysarthria is a motor disorder of speech that is caused by an upper motor neuron lesion. The condition affects the muscles that are used to articulate words and sounds. Speech is often noted as "slurred" and there may also be an effect on respiratory or phonatory systems due to weakness. Treatment focuses on improving the intelligibility of speech by strengthening all aspects of speech production through phonetics. Exercises will also work on coordination and articulatory precision.**
3. Verbal apraxia is a non-dysarthric and non-aphasic impairment of prosody (stress and intonation) and articulation of speech. Verbal expression is impaired due to deficits in motor planning. A patient is unable to initiate learned movement (articulation of speech) even though they understand the task. Intonation drills and rhythmic techniques are used in the treatment of verbal apraxia.
4. Dysphagia is the inability to properly swallow. Treatment focuses on proper body positioning and compensatory strategies to avoid aspiration when swallowing. Educational activities include topics such as the use of thick liquids and conscious swallowing.

System: Neuromuscular and Nervous Systems
Content Outline: Foundations for Evaluation, Differential Diagnosis, and Prognosis

Level 2  p. 271

PTEXAM TWO: QUESTION 34

A physical therapist determines that a patient has 0-135 degrees of passive knee flexion and 0-120 degrees of active knee flexion. Which of the following tests would be the MOST appropriate to help determine the reason for the difference in the range of motion values?

1. Passive joint motion testing
2. Special tests isolating flexibility
3. **Manual muscle testing**
4. Diagnostic imaging

Correct Answer: 3 (Higgins p. 81)

Physical therapists often form a clinical hypothesis and test the established hypothesis using clinical testing. The selected test or tests should help to accept or reject the established hypothesis.

1. Passive joint motion testing is commonly used with a suspected capsular restriction. A capsular restriction would present with decreased passive and active range of motion with pain during motion.
2. Special tests isolating flexibility are commonly used with a suspected musculotendinous limitation. A musculotendinous limitation would present with decreased passive and active range of motion.
3. **Manual muscle testing is commonly used with suspected muscle weakness. Muscle weakness would present with normal passive range of motion and decreased active range of motion. Normal knee flexion is 0-135 degrees.**
4. Diagnostic imaging is commonly used with suspected internal derangement. Internal derangement would present with decreased passive and active range of motion with pain during motion.

System: Musculoskeletal System
Content Outline: Physical Therapy Examination

 Level 2

PTEXAM TWO: QUESTION 35

A patient has a current medical history that includes Graves' disease. Which of the following descriptions BEST explains the pathophysiology associated with this medical condition?

1. Inflammation of the lining of the digestive tract
2. Insufficient insulin production from the pancreas
3. Hypofunction of the adrenal cortex
4. **Hyperactivity of the thyroid gland**

Correct Answer: 4 (Goodman – Pathology p. 484)

A physical therapist should possess a basic understanding of the pathophysiology associated with commonly encountered medical conditions. This information is critical when designing an appropriate plan of care in order to optimize patient outcomes and preserve patient safety.

1. Inflammation of the lining of the digestive tract is associated with Crohn's disease. The condition is a specific form of inflammatory bowel disease. Symptoms may develop gradually or rapidly and typically include abdominal pain, cramping, and diarrhea. Other symptoms may include blood in the stool, gastrointestinal tract ulcers, diminished appetite, and weight loss.
2. Insufficient insulin production from the pancreas is associated with type 1 diabetes mellitus. Symptoms of diabetes mellitus include polyphagia, weight loss, ketoacidosis, polyuria, polydipsia, blurred vision, dehydration, and fatigue.
3. Hypofunction of the adrenal cortex is associated with Addison's disease. Subsequently, there is decreased production of both cortisol and aldosterone. Symptoms may include hypotension, weakness, anorexia, and altered pigmentation.
4. **Hyperactivity of the thyroid gland is associated with Graves' disease. The condition is an autoimmune disease in which certain antibodies produced by the immune system stimulate the thyroid gland causing it to become overactive. Symptoms include mild enlargement of the thyroid gland (goiter), heat intolerance, nervousness, tremor, weight loss, and palpitations.**

System: Other Systems
Content Outline: Foundations for Evaluation, Differential Diagnosis, and Prognosis

p. 528, 637

PTEXAM TWO: QUESTION 36

A physical therapist treats a patient who has rheumatoid arthritis. During the patient interview, the patient indicates that they are diabetic. Which type of pharmacological agent would be the LEAST likely to be used to treat rheumatoid arthritis given the stated comorbidity?

1. Nonopioid analgesic agents
2. **Corticosteroid agents**
3. Biologic response modifiers
4. Disease-modifying antirheumatic agents

Correct Answer: 2 (O'Sullivan p. 1014)

Rheumatoid arthritis is a systemic autoimmune disorder that presents with a chronic inflammatory reaction in the synovial tissues of a joint that results in erosion of cartilage and supporting structures within the capsule. Pharmacological management typically includes nonopioid analgesic agents, corticosteroid agents, disease-modifying antirheumatic agents, and biologic response modifiers.

1. Nonopioid analgesic agents (e.g., acetaminophen, Motrin) provide analgesia and pain relief, produce anti-inflammatory effects, and initiate anti-pyretic (reduces fever) properties. These drugs promote a reduction of prostaglandin formation that decreases the inflammatory process. Nonopioid analgesic agents are not contraindicated for use with diabetes mellitus.
2. **Corticosteroids (e.g., prednisone, Prednisolone) are the most powerful class of anti-inflammatory agents available, however, side effects of short and long-term use can be serious to life-threatening. Patients with diabetes mellitus may be unable to use corticosteroids since a side effect of use is the elevation of blood sugar.**
3. Biologic response modifiers (e.g., Enbrel, Humira) target proteins, cells, and pathways responsible for many of the symptoms associated with rheumatoid arthritis. Biologic response modifiers affect immune system function resulting in patients becoming more susceptible to serious infections. These agents are not contraindicated for use with diabetes mellitus.
4. Disease-modifying antirheumatic agents (e.g., methotrexate, gold) slow or halt the progression of rheumatic disease. They act to induce remission by modifying the pathology and inhibiting the immune response responsible for rheumatic disease. These agents are not contraindicated for use with diabetes mellitus.

System: Other Systems
Content Outline: Foundations for Evaluation, Differential Diagnosis, and Prognosis

p. 126, 132, 624-625

PTEXAM TWO: QUESTION 37

A physical therapist performs postural drainage to the anterior basal segments of the lower lobes. During the treatment session, the patient suddenly complains of dizziness and mild dyspnea. Which of the following actions is the most appropriate INITIAL response for the therapist to take?

1. Reassure the patient that the response is normal
2. Assess the patient's vital signs
3. **Elevate the patient's head**
4. Call for assistance

Correct Answer: 3 (Hillegass p. 541) 

Postural drainage is the assumption of one or more body positions that allow gravity to drain secretions from each of the patient's lung segments. In each position, the segmental bronchus of the area to be drained is positioned perpendicular to the floor. Postural drainage to the anterior basal segment of the lower lobes would require the bottom of the bed to be elevated 18 inches.

1. A subjective complaint of dizziness and mild dyspnea would exceed a "normal" patient response. The physical therapist must act based on the patient's comment even though it would not be entirely unexpected given the necessary patient position for postural drainage of the anterior basal segment of the lower lobes.
2. Assessing the patient's vital signs is a desirable option, however, only after the patient is repositioned with the head elevated.
3. **Dizziness and dyspnea are signs of intolerance to the head down postural drainage position required to drain the anterior basal segments of the lower lobes. Elevating the patient's head will likely relieve the symptoms.**
4. Calling for assistance is not necessary since the patient's symptoms should subside once the head is elevated.

System: Cardiovascular and Pulmonary Systems
Content Outline: Interventions

 Level 3  p. 438-439, 443

PTEXAM TWO: QUESTION 38

A patient is asked to complete a pain questionnaire. The patient selects words such as cramping, dull, and aching to describe the pain. What structure is MOST often associated with this type of pain description?

1. Nerve root
2. **Muscle**
3. Bone
4. Vascular

Correct Answer: 2 (Magee p. 8) 

The patient interview provides a physical therapist with an opportunity to identify specific characteristics of pain. Subjective pain descriptors can provide valuable information related to a patient's condition. Characteristics to explore may include location, intensity, description, duration, and pattern.

1. Nerve root pain is often characterized as sharp, shooting, and burning. The pain tends to travel in the distribution of the specific nerve root.
2. **Muscle pain is often characterized as cramping, dull, and aching. The pain tends to worsen when the involved muscle contracts or is lengthened.**
3. Bone pain is often characterized as deep, intolerable, boring, and highly localized.
4. Vascular pain is often characterized as diffuse, throbbing, aching, and poorly localized. The pain is often referred to other parts of the body.

System: Other Systems
Content Outline: Foundations for Evaluation, Differential Diagnosis, and Prognosis

 Level 1

PTEXAM TWO: QUESTION 39

A physical therapist completes a study that examines the effect of goniometer size on the reliability of passive shoulder joint measurements. The therapist concludes that goniometric measurements of passive shoulder range of motion can be highly consistent when taken by a single therapist, regardless of the size of the goniometer. The results of this study demonstrate a high degree of which of the following measures?

1. Interrater reliability
2. **Intrarater reliability**
3. Internal validity
4. External validity

Correct Answer: 2 (Norkin p. 45) 

Reliability, or the extent to which a measurement is consistent and free from error, is a prerequisite of any measurement. There are a number of types of reliability that may be estimated: test-retest, rater (intrarater and interrater), alternate forms, and internal consistency.

1. Interrater reliability refers to the reproducibility of measurements made by two or more raters who measure the same group of subjects.
2. **Intrarater reliability refers to the reproducibility of measurements made by one individual across two or more trials.**
3. Internal validity focuses on cause and effect relationships. Specifically, is there evidence that, given a statistical relationship between the independent variable and dependent variable in an experiment, one causes the other.
4. External validity refers to the extent to which the results of a study can be generalized beyond the study sample to persons, settings, and times that are different from those employed in the experimental situation. External validity is concerned with the usefulness of the information outside the experimental situation.

System: Musculoskeletal System
Content Outline: Physical Therapy Examination

 Level 1  p. 806

PTEXAM TWO: QUESTION 40

A physical therapist reads in the medical record that a patient has an ejection fraction of 40%. Which class of medication is the patient MOST likely to be taking?

1. **Angiotensin-converting enzyme inhibitor agents**
2. Nitrate agents
3. Anticholinergic agents
4. Thrombolytic agents

Correct Answer: 1 (Hillegass p. 38)

The ejection fraction is a measure of left ventricular contractility. It is determined by dividing stroke volume by left ventricular end-diastolic volume. A normal ejection fraction is approximately 55-70 percent. Anything less than 55 percent of the blood pumped out of the ventricles with each heartbeat is abnormal and indicates impairment in left ventricular function. Ejection fraction is decreased in patients with left-sided congestive heart failure since the left ventricle is unable to maintain a normal cardiac output.

1. **Angiotensin-converting enzyme inhibitor (ACE inhibitor) agents decrease blood pressure and afterload by suppressing the enzyme that converts angiotensin I to angiotensin II. This medication is indicated for medical conditions presenting with a low ejection fraction such as congestive heart failure.**
2. Nitrate agents decrease ischemia through smooth muscle relaxation and dilation of peripheral vessels. Medications from this class are indicated for angina pectoris and would not be prescribed to treat a patient with a decreased ejection fraction.
3. Anticholinergic agents block the effects of acetylcholine on parietal cells in the stomach and decrease the release of gastric acid. This class of medication is indicated for management of gastric ulcers and would not be prescribed to treat a patient with a decreased ejection fraction.
4. Thrombolytic agents facilitate clot dissolution through conversion of plasminogen to plasmin. Plasmin breaks down clots and allows occluded vessels to reopen, restoring blood flow. This class of medication is indicated for conditions such as acute myocardial infarction and ischemic stroke and would not likely be prescribed to treat a patient with a decreased ejection fraction.

System: Cardiovascular and Pulmonary Systems
Content Outline: Foundations for Evaluation, Differential Diagnosis, and Prognosis

 Level 2  p. 402-403, 414, 454-455

PTEXAM TWO: QUESTION 41

A patient who has a peripheral nerve injury is examined in physical therapy. The patient's primary symptoms result from an injury to the superficial peroneal nerve. What location should the physical therapist expect to be the MOST likely area of sensory alteration?

1. Sole of the foot
2. Plantar surface of the toes
3. **Lateral aspect of the leg and dorsum of the foot**
4. Triangular area between the first and second toes

Correct Answer: 3 (Kendall p. 369)

The superficial peroneal nerve innervates the peroneus longus and brevis. It is a branch of the sciatic nerve.

1. The sole of the foot receives cutaneous innervation from the medial and lateral plantar nerves, which are branches of the tibial nerve. The tibial nerve is a branch of the sciatic nerve.
2. The plantar surface of the toes is innervated by the medial and lateral plantar nerves, which are branches of the tibial nerve. The tibial nerve is a branch of the sciatic nerve.
3. **A peripheral nerve injury affecting the superficial peroneal nerve often results in sensory alterations along the lateral aspect of the leg and dorsum of the foot.**
4. The triangular area between the first and second toes is innervated by the deep peroneal nerve. It is a branch of the sciatic nerve.

System: Neuromuscular and Nervous Systems
Content Outline: Physical Therapy Examination

 Level 1  p. 246, 251

PTEXAM TWO: QUESTION 42

A physical therapist receives a referral for a patient diagnosed with systemic lupus erythematosus. Which of the following patient profiles would be MOST consistent with the onset of this medical diagnosis?

1. **A 29-year-old female**
2. A 67-year-old female
3. A 27-year-old male
4. A 61-year-old male

Correct Answer: 1 (Goodman – Pathology p. 306) 

Systemic lupus erythematosus (SLE) is a connective tissue disorder caused by an autoimmune reaction in the body. The primary manifestation of the condition is the production of destructive antibodies that are directed at the individual's own body. The chronic inflammatory disorder produces a variety of symptoms depending on the severity and extent of involvement. SLE can occur at any age, however, is most common during childbearing years. The disorder is more common in women than men.

1. **SLE is more common in females and a 29-year-old is within the period of peak incidence (i.e., 15-40 years of age).**
2. SLE is more common in females, however, a 67-year-old female is significantly older than the period of peak incidence (i.e., 15-40 years of age).
3. SLE is less common in males. A 27-year-old is within the period of peak incidence (i.e., 15-40 years of age), however, the fact that the individual is a male makes this answer less likely to be consistent with the established risk profile.
4. SLE is less common in males. In addition, a 61-year-old is significantly older than the period of peak incidence (i.e., 15-40 years of age).

System: Other Systems
Content Outline: Foundations for Evaluation, Differential Diagnosis, and Prognosis

 Level 1  p. 626-627

PTEXAM TWO: QUESTION 43

A physical therapist prepares to perform volumetric measurements as a means of quantifying edema. Which patient would appear to be the **MOST** appropriate candidate for this type of objective measure?

1. **A 38-year-old female with a Colles' fracture**
2. A 27-year-old male with bicipital tendonitis
3. A 48-year-old male with a rotator cuff tear
4. A 57-year-old male with pulmonary edema

Correct Answer: 1 (Magee p. 478) 

Volumetric measurements are commonly used to measure edema in the distal extremities. The measurement is typically performed by examining the amount of water displaced from a cylinder following immersion of an affected body part. It would be impractical to use this type of measurement in an area other than a distal extremity.

1. **A Colles' fracture refers to a fracture of the distal end of the radius. The injury would likely result in swelling in the wrist and hand which could be quantified with volumetric measurements.**
2. The location of the biceps tendon would require immersion of the upper extremity or the entire shoulder complex. The size of the upper extremity would make this unrealistic.
3. The location of the rotator cuff would require immersion of the entire shoulder complex which would also be unrealistic due to the size of the area.
4. Pulmonary edema refers to swelling or fluid accumulation in the lungs. This condition would be impossible to assess using volumetric measurements.

System: Cardiovascular and Pulmonary Systems
Content Outline: Physical Therapy Examination

 Level 2

PTEXAM TWO: QUESTION 44

A physical therapist is asked by the clinic manager to help develop a fall prevention program. What would be the **FIRST** step when developing this type of program?

1. Set goals and objectives for the program
2. **Identify the intended audience**
3. Identify valid and reliable screening tools
4. Develop a plan for each class

Correct Answer: 2 (Kisner p. 55) 

Primary prevention is aimed at preventing a target problem or condition in individuals that do not currently have the condition, but are at risk. Secondary prevention is aimed at decreasing the duration and/or severity of the target problem or condition. The goal of tertiary prevention is to decrease the degree of disability for individuals with chronic diseases or conditions. There are typically five steps to follow when developing and implementing prevention programs.

1. Setting goals and objectives is the second step to developing and implementing a prevention program. Once the intended audience is identified, the purpose of the program along with the goals and objectives should be clearly established.
2. **The first step in developing and implementing a prevention program is to identify the need for the program, which involves identifying the intended audience. Once the audience is established, the next step is to set the goals and objectives of the program.**
3. Identifying valid and reliable screening tools is part of step number three: develop the intervention. This step involves identifying the appropriate screening tools, developing a plan for each class, including handouts for the participants, as well as establishing the logistics for implementing the program.
4. Developing a plan for each class is also part of step three: develop the intervention. Step four is to implement the intervention and step five (final step) involves evaluating the results or outcomes.

System: Non-Systems
Content Outline: Safety and Protection; Professional Responsibilities; Research

 Level 2

PTEXAM TWO: QUESTION 45

A physical therapist reads in the medical record that the foot progression angle of a four-year-old child was recorded as -10 degrees (minus 10 degrees). Which range of motion measurement at the hip would MOST likely be associated with the obtained foot progression angle?

1. **75 degrees of hip medial rotation and 25 degrees of hip lateral rotation**
2. 35 degrees of hip medial rotation and 70 degrees of hip lateral rotation
3. 30 degrees of hip medial rotation and 20 degrees of hip lateral rotation
4. 45 degrees of hip medial rotation and 45 degrees of hip lateral rotation

Correct Answer: 1 (Palisano p. 295) 

Foot progression angle is defined as the angle between the longitudinal axis of the foot and a straight line progression of the body in walking. The obtained value is expressed as a negative number for in-toeing and a positive number for out-toeing.

1. **Exaggerated hip medial rotation (i.e., 75 degrees) and diminished hip lateral rotation (i.e., 25 degrees) are commonly observed with femoral anteversion which is the most common cause of in-toeing in children. A foot progression angle of -10 degrees indicates 10 degrees of in-toeing.**
2. Diminished hip medial rotation (i.e., 35 degrees) and exaggerated hip lateral rotation (i.e., 70 degrees) are indicative of femoral retroversion. This type of positioning would not be associated with in-toeing and is more characteristic of out-toeing.
3. Diminished hip medial rotation (i.e., 30 degrees) and diminished hip lateral rotation (i.e., 20 degrees) would not necessarily be associated with in-toeing. Although the hip medial rotation value is greater than the hip lateral rotation value, which is characteristic of a negative foot progression angle, both values are well below the expected available range for a four-year-old.
4. 45 degrees of hip medial rotation and 45 degrees of hip lateral rotation do not suggest the presence of a torsional condition. The values are equivalent and only slightly below the expected sum for children of 95-110 degrees for hip medial and lateral rotation.

System: Musculoskeletal System
Content Outline: Physical Therapy Examination

 **Level 2**

PTEXAM TWO: QUESTION 46

A physical therapist performs a chart review of a new patient and finds the patient is positive for the Helicobacter pylori bacterium. The therapist should anticipate that the patient presents with which of the following medical conditions?

1. Meningitis
2. Pneumonia
3. **Gastric ulcer disease**
4. Tetanus

Correct Answer: 3 (Ciccone p. 425)

Bacterial infections can be harmful and potentially life-threatening if left untreated. Bacteria will multiply and utilize nutrients of its host, produce direct tissue damage, and produce an immune response that can ultimately harm the host. Specific medications are used to treat bacteria based on their classification and microorganism.

1. Meningitis is the inflammation of the membranes surrounding the brain and spinal cord. There are multiple forms of meningitis and multiple bacteria that can produce this condition. Neisseria meningitidis is one of the bacterium that is a leading cause of bacterial meningitis. It is treated primarily with penicillin G.
2. Pneumonia refers to inflammation of the lungs due to bacterial, viral, fungal or parasitic infection. The common bacterium in most cases of community-acquired pneumonia is Streptococcus pneumoniae. It is treated primarily with penicillin, ampicillin, or if penicillin-resistant, vancomycin.
3. **Gastric ulcer disease is often caused by the gram-negative bacterium Helicobacter pylori that is found in the upper gastrointestinal tract. This infection is believed to be a potential cause of gastroduodenal ulcers and must be treated with antibiotics. It is treated primarily with amoxicillin or clarithromycin and may be combined with other medications to enhance the healing process of any ulcers that are present.**
4. Tetanus is an acute and often fatal disease if left untreated marked by a continuous state of muscular contraction and rigidity of voluntary muscles. The bacterium Clostridium tetani is a common cause of tetanus and it is treated with penicillin and vancomycin.

System: Other Systems
Content Outline: Foundations for Evaluation, Differential Diagnosis, and Prognosis

 **Level 2**  **p. 535, 652**

PTEXAM TWO: QUESTION 47

A physical therapist examines a patient who reports abdominal pain. The patient's symptoms include left lower quadrant abdominal pain, loss of appetite, and nausea. The clinical presentation is MOST consistent with which of the following medical conditions?

1. **Diverticulitis**
2. Appendicitis
3. Peptic ulcer
4. Pancreatitis

Correct Answer: 1 (Goodman – Differential Diagnosis p. 318)

Gastrointestinal (GI) symptoms can be related to various GI organ disturbances and differ in character depending on the organ which is affected. Some of the most clinically meaningful symptoms reported include abdominal pain, epigastric pain, dysphagia, GI bleeding, constipation/diarrhea, and symptoms affected by food.

1. **Diverticulitis is the infection and inflammation that accompanies the perforation of one of the diverticula, which are weakened areas of the colon. Signs and symptoms of diverticulitis include left lower abdominal pain, nausea, abdominal bloating, flatulence, bloody stools, and either constipation or diarrhea.**
2. Appendicitis is an inflammation of the appendix that occurs most commonly in adolescents and young adults. A patient with appendicitis may experience nausea and loss of appetite, however, their pain would more likely be reported in the right lower quadrant.
3. Peptic ulcer is a loss of tissue lining the lower esophagus, stomach, and/or duodenum. A patient with a peptic ulcer may experience nausea and loss of appetite, however, their pain would more likely be reported in the epigastric region.
4. Pancreatitis is an inflammation of the pancreas that can be acute or chronic. A patient with pancreatitis may experience nausea and loss of appetite, however, their pain would more likely be reported in the epigastric region.

System: Other Systems
Content Outline: Foundations for Evaluation, Differential Diagnosis, and Prognosis

p. 537, 646

PTEXAM TWO: QUESTION 48

A patient reports to physical therapy after being fit for an upper extremity splint. Which type of splint would MOST likely be prescribed for a patient that demonstrates a positive Finkelstein's test?

1. Ulnar gutter
2. **Thumb spica**
3. Radial gutter
4. Dorsal forearm

Correct Answer: 2 (Dutton p. 847)

To perform Finkelstein's test the patient is asked to make a fist with the thumb tucked underneath the fingers. The therapist stabilizes the patient's forearm and ulnarly deviates the wrist. A positive test is indicated by pain over the abductor pollicis longus and extensor pollicis brevis tendons and may be indicative of tenosynovitis in the thumb (i.e., de Quervain's disease).

1. An ulnar gutter splint is a rigid splint that covers the ulnar side of the forearm and hand as well as the fourth and fifth digits. This type of splint is used to immobilize the metacarpals and phalanges and is commonly used following a fracture to these structures, and therefore would not be the most effective option for a patient with de Quervain's disease.
2. **A thumb spica splint is a rigid splint that covers the radial side of the forearm and hand as well as the thumb. The splint may cover the entire thumb or may stop at the proximal phalanx of the thumb, and thus allow for interphalangeal joint motion. This type of splint is used to immobilize the wrist and metacarpophalangeal joint of the thumb and is commonly used for treating gamekeeper's thumb, scaphoid fractures, first metacarpal fractures, and de Quervain's disease.**
3. A radial gutter splint is a rigid splint that covers the radial side of the forearm and hand as well as the second and third digits. The splint includes a thenar hole to allow for free movement of the thumb. This type of splint is used to immobilize the metacarpals and phalanges and is commonly used following a fracture to these structures, and therefore would not be the most effective option for a patient with de Quervain's disease.
4. A dorsal forearm splint is a rigid splint that extends from the proximal forearm to the metacarpal heads, allowing for full elbow and metacarpophalangeal joint motion. The splint includes a thenar hole to allow for free movement of the thumb. This type of splint is used to immobilize the wrist joint and is commonly used for treating fractures of the carpals, fractures of the distal radius or ulna or soft tissue conditions (e.g., sprain, tendonitis). This splint would not be the most effective option for a patient with de Quervain's disease.

System: Musculoskeletal System
Content Outline: Interventions

p. 105, 133-134, 214

PTEXAM TWO: QUESTION 49

A physical therapist attempts to perform mediate percussion over a patient's spleen. Which anatomical structure would be placed firmly on the surface to be percussed?

1. Distal interphalangeal joint of the middle finger of the dominant hand
2. **Distal interphalangeal joint of the middle finger of the nondominant hand**
3. Proximal interphalangeal joint of the middle finger of the dominant hand
4. Proximal interphalangeal joint of the middle finger of the nondominant hand

Correct Answer: 2 (Boissonnault p. 159)

Mediate percussion is used to assess density. The technique requires the physical therapist to place the middle finger of the nondominant hand flat on the desired surface of the body. The dominant hand acts as a fulcrum using the middle finger to strike the middle finger of the nondominant hand positioned on the target area. By analyzing the sound produced, the therapist can determine whether the underlying structure is air-filled, fluid-filled or solid.

1. Mediate percussion requires the nondominant hand to be placed on the surface to be assessed to allow the middle finger of the dominant hand to strike the interphalangeal joint.
2. **The dominant hand acts as a fulcrum using the middle finger to strike the middle finger of the nondominant hand positioned on the target area. The distal interphalangeal joint of the middle finger of the nondominant hand is placed on the surface to be assessed to allow the middle finger of the dominant hand to strike it.**
3. Mediate percussion requires the nondominant hand to be placed on the surface to be assessed to allow the middle finger of the dominant hand to strike the interphalangeal joint.
4. The proximal interphalangeal joint of the middle finger of the nondominant hand would be placed on the skin, but the distal interphalangeal joint of the nondominant hand would be pressed firmly on the skin since it is directly contacted by the middle finger of the dominant hand.

System: Cardiovascular and Pulmonary Systems
Content Outline: Physical Therapy Examination

 **Level 1** **p. 429-430**

PTEXAM TWO: QUESTION 50

A physical therapist enters a private treatment area and observes a patient collapsed on the floor. The patient appears to be moving slightly, however, seems to be in need of medical assistance. Which of the following actions should the therapist perform FIRST?

1. **Check for unresponsiveness**
2. Monitor airway, breathing, and circulation
3. Position the patient
4. Phone emergency medical services

Correct Answer: 1 (Le Baudour p. 190)

The first step in performing a primary survey is to determine responsiveness.

1. **To check for responsiveness, tap the victim on the shoulder and ask, "Are you all right?" If the patient is unresponsive (i.e., no movement or response to stimulation), the therapist should phone 911, get an automated external defibrillator (AED), provide cardiopulmonary resuscitation, and use the AED, if necessary.**
2. Monitoring airway, breathing, and circulation are the primary elements of cardiopulmonary resuscitation. The current recommended sequence when performing CPR is compression, airway, and breathing.
3. Positioning the patient is only necessary if the patient is unresponsive and needs cardiopulmonary resuscitation. If an unresponsive victim is face down, the therapist should roll the victim to a face up position to open the airway.
4. The therapist should phone emergency medical services only after determining the patient is unresponsive.

System: Non-Systems
Content Outline: Safety and Protection; Professional Responsibilities; Research

 **Level 3**  **p. 767**

PTEXAM TWO: QUESTION 51

A physical therapist works with a patient who experiences hyperfunction of the parathyroid glands secondary to a tumor. This condition would MOST likely contribute to the development of which of the following disorders?

1. Cardiac arrhythmias
2. **Osteopenia**
3. Muscle spasms
4. Obesity

Correct Answer: 2 (Goodman – Differential Diagnosis p. 398)

There are two parathyroid glands located on the posterior surface of each thyroid gland. They are responsible for secreting parathyroid hormone (PTH), which regulates the metabolism of calcium and phosphorus. The major cause of hyperparathyroidism is a tumor of the parathyroid gland, which leads to increased secretion of PTH. Elevated levels of PTH cause the release of calcium by the bones and a subsequent accumulation of calcium in the bloodstream.

1. Cardiac arrhythmias are a common side effect of hypoparathyroidism. This condition results in low blood calcium levels, which leads to altered function of many of the body's tissues including cardiac tissue (e.g., arrhythmias).
2. **Hyperparathyroidism results in the demineralization of bones due to the increased secretion of PTH and subsequent loss of bone density and strength (i.e., osteopenia). Other common symptoms include muscle weakness, loss of appetite, weight loss, nausea, vomiting, personality changes, and kidney stones.**
3. Muscle spasms are a common side effect of hypoparathyroidism. The low blood calcium levels lead to altered function of many of the body's tissues including neuromuscular tissue (e.g., muscle spasms).
4. Hyperparathyroidism is more likely to result in diminished appetite and weight loss rather than obesity.

System: Other Systems
Content Outline: Foundations for Evaluation, Differential Diagnosis, and Prognosis

 Level 2  p. 521-522, 529

PTEXAM TWO: QUESTION 52

A physical therapist observes that a patient with a history of recurrent lateral ankle sprains exhibits excessive supination during gait. Which of the following conditions would MOST likely be associated with this type of observation?

1. Tarsal tunnel syndrome
2. **Peroneal tenosynovitis**
3. Plantar fasciitis
4. Posterior tibial tenosynovitis

Correct Answer: 2 (Sarwark p. 779)

Physical therapists should be familiar with the unique characteristics of commonly encountered medical conditions. This knowledge should include awareness of specific biomechanical forces associated with various medical conditions.

1. Tarsal tunnel syndrome is a compression neuropathy where the tibial nerve is compressed as it travels through the tarsal tunnel which is located posterior to the medial malleolus. Tarsal tunnel syndrome is more commonly associated with "flat feet" or pronation since this increases pressure in the tunnel region often resulting in nerve compression.
2. **Peroneal tenosynovitis refers to inflammation of the peroneal tendons. The peroneus longus and brevis tendons are located posterior to the lateral malleolus and are the structures most commonly affected. Peroneal tenosynovitis is typically associated with activities requiring repetitive ankle motion that result in overuse, trauma or recurrent ankle sprains. A supinated gait places additional stress on the peroneal tendons within the groove behind the lateral malleolus.**
3. Plantar fasciitis refers to inflammation of the plantar fascia at the proximal insertion on the medial tubercle of the calcaneus. The plantar fascia is a broad structure comprised of connective tissue which spans from the calcaneus to the metatarsal heads. Plantar fasciitis is often associated with an acute injury from excessive loading of the foot or chronic irritation from an excessive amount of pronation or prolonged duration of pronation.
4. Posterior tibial tenosynovitis refers to an inflammation of the posterior tibial tendon. Patients often experience symptoms immediately inferior to the medial malleolus. The posterior tibial tendon assists to support the arch of the foot. As a result, as the condition progresses the arch of the foot can become significantly flattened. Posterior tibial tenosynovitis is more commonly associated with pronation.

System: Musculoskeletal System
Content Outline: Foundations for Evaluation, Differential Diagnosis, and Prognosis

 Level 2

PTEXAM TWO: QUESTION 53

A physical therapist works with a patient who sustained a torn anterior cruciate ligament (ACL) and a medial meniscus tear. Which of the following scenarios would result in the **GREATEST** likelihood of a successful surgical meniscus repair?

1. A tear involving the inner third of the meniscus with reconstruction of the ACL
2. A tear involving the inner third of the meniscus with conservative management of the ACL
3. **A tear involving the outer third of the meniscus with reconstruction of the ACL**
4. A tear involving the outer third of the meniscus with conservative management of the ACL

Correct Answer: 3 (Dutton p. 973) 

Meniscal tears often occur in conjunction with anterior cruciate ligament injuries. In athletic-related ACL injuries, the incidence of meniscal tears approaches fifty percent. The medial and lateral menisci are firmly attached to the proximal surface of the tibia. The menisci are thick at the periphery and thinner at their internal unattached edges. Menisci function to deepen the articular surfaces of the tibia where they articulate with the femoral condyles.

1. A surgically repaired tear involving the inner third of the medial meniscus is less likely to be successful since the inner third of the meniscus is avascular. Although ACL reconstruction increases success rates, the avascularity of the inner third of the meniscus remains a limiting factor.
2. A surgically repaired tear involving the inner third of the medial meniscus is less likely to be successful since the inner third of the meniscus is avascular. In addition, conservative management (i.e., nonoperative) of the ACL increases the failure rate of the surgically repaired meniscus.
3. **A surgically repaired tear involving the outer third of the medial meniscus is more likely to be successful since the outer third of the meniscus is vascular. In addition, ACL reconstruction increases success rates.**
4. A surgically repaired tear involving the outer third of the medial meniscus is more likely to be successful since the outer third of the meniscus is vascular, however, conservative management (i.e., nonoperative) of the ACL increases the failure rate of the surgically repaired meniscus.

System: Musculoskeletal System
Content Outline: Foundations for Evaluation, Differential Diagnosis, and Prognosis

 Level 2  p. 124, 204

PTEXAM TWO: QUESTION 54

A patient post modified radical mastectomy is referred for treatment of associated soft tissue restrictions and pain. During the examination, the physical therapist becomes concerned since the surgical site is extremely warm to touch, tender, and discolored, as shown in the image. Given the patient's recent history, which of the following conditions is the **MOST** likely cause of this complication?

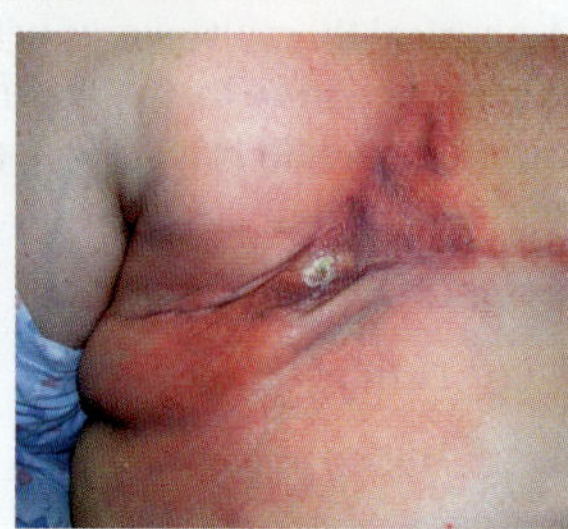

1. Dermatitis
2. **Cellulitis**
3. Mastitis
4. Erysipelas

Correct Answer: 2 (Goodman – Pathology p. 427)

A modified radical mastectomy includes removal of all tissues of the affected breast including the areola, nipple, and most of the axillary lymph nodes. The local lymphatic disruption and resultant impairment of local immune responses increases the likelihood of post-operative cellulitis.

1. Dermatitis presents in numerous forms (e.g., contact, seborrheic, atopic), all of which involve some degree of general skin irritation. Although contact dermatitis may have a visible presentation similar to cellulitis, it would not typically be warm to touch nor is it consistent with the described clinical scenario.
2. **Cellulitis tends to develop in areas where the skin's protective barrier (e.g., surgical site, wound) and lymphatic flow (e.g., lymph node removal, excessive soft tissue, edema) have been disrupted. Cellulitis is a common post-operative complication of surgical breast cancer treatment.**
3. Mastitis is an infection of the fatty breast tissue typically associated with breast feeding. The infection may present with an appearance similar to cellulitis, but is further characterized by painful lumps within the breast tissue.
4. Erysipelas is a specific form of cellulitis caused by streptococcal bacteria. Like cellulitis, the skin is typically warm and tender to the touch, however, it is much more defined in its appearance. Erysipelas is characterized by a raised, sharp demarcation of borders with an unmistakable bright red discoloration.

System: Other Systems
Content Outline: Foundations for Evaluation, Differential Diagnosis, and Prognosis

 Level 2  p. 517, 634

PTEXAM TWO: QUESTION 55

A physical therapist attempts to design an exercise program for a patient with a body mass index (BMI) of 34.5 kg/m^2. Which potential complication of exercise is the MOST relevant for this patient?

1. **Heat intolerance**
2. Asthma
3. Gastroesophageal reflux
4. Orthostatic hypotension

Correct Answer: 1 (Goodman – Pathology p. 38)

BMI describes relative weight for height and is a measurement used to identify increased risk for mortality and morbidity due to excess weight and obesity. Obesity (BMI of 30 kg/m^2 or greater) refers to the state of excessive adipose tissue accumulation in the body contributing to a variety of chronic conditions that negatively impact multiple body systems and overall health.

1. **The excessive adipose tissue in obese patients can act as an extra layer of insulation and not allow heat to dissipate as expected. Obese patients are at high-risk for heat intolerance since they are often unable to appropriately respond to the thermal challenges of exercise.**
2. Asthma is a chronic inflammation of the airways caused by increased airway hypersensitivity to various stimuli. Obese patients are not at increased risk for asthma during exercise.
3. Gastroesophageal reflux is the result of an incompetent lower esophageal sphincter that allows reflux of gastric contents. Obese patients are not at increased risk for gastroesophageal reflux during exercise, however, this is a post-operative complication of bariatric surgery.
4. Orthostatic hypotension occurs due to a loss of sympathetic control of vasoconstriction in combination with absent or severely reduced muscle tone. Obese patients are not at increased risk for orthostatic hypotension during exercise. In fact, they are far more likely to experience an excessive rise in blood pressure during exercise.

System: Other Systems
Content Outline: Interventions

 Level 2  p. 423

PTEXAM TWO: QUESTION 56

A physical therapist assigns a manual muscle test grade of 4 to patient A and a grade of 2 to patient B after assessing the strength of the tibialis anterior. Which of the following descriptions is the BEST interpretation of the patients' strength?

1. Patients A and B have equal strength
2. **Patient A is stronger than patient B**
3. Patient A is twice as strong as patient B
4. Patient B is twice as strong as patient A

Correct Answer: 2 (Portney p. 68) 

Manual muscle test grades are examples of ordinal measurements, which in essence represent labels specifying relative rank or position. Ordinal measurements are rank-ordered into categories that have a "greater than – less than" relationship. The intervals between ranks on an ordinal scale may not be consistent and may not be known.

1. The numerical scale used in manual muscle testing ranks the strength by strongest (equivalent to the grade of 5) and weakest (equivalent to the grade of 0). In this situation, the grades are not equal, 4 does not equal 2, therefore, they cannot have equal strength.
2. **Based on the traditional 0 – 5 manual muscle grading scale, a grade of 4 represents more muscle strength than a grade of 2.**
3. The numerical scale does not provide an "absolute" value, therefore, it is impossible to say that a grade of 4 is two times stronger than a grade of 2. Furthermore, the testing positions of these grades are not the same and as a result they cannot be compared in this manner.
4. The numerical order of the manual muscle testing scale indicates that a grade of 5 is the strongest and a grade of 0 is the weakest. Therefore, a grade of 2 cannot indicate greater strength than a grade of 4.

System: Musculoskeletal System
Content Outline: Physical Therapy Examination

 Level 2  p. 806

PTEXAM TWO: QUESTION 57

A physical therapist inspects a patient's wound prior to applying a dressing. When documenting the findings in the medical record, the therapist classifies the exudate from the wound as serous. Based on the documentation, what is the MOST likely color of the exudate?

1. **Clear**
2. Pink
3. Red
4. Yellow

Correct Answer: 1 (Sussman p. 458) 

It is normal during the stages of healing to observe exudate from a wound. The physical therapist should inspect the exudate and determine whether it is a normal response to healing or an abnormal response that needs to be reported.

1. **Serous exudate is described as a clear or light color fluid with a thin, watery consistency. This particular type of exudate is normal during the inflammatory and proliferative phases of healing.**
2. Serosanguineous (pink) exudate can be a normal exudate in a healthy healing wound.
3. Sanguineous (red) exudate indicates a bloody discharge which may be indicative of either new blood vessel growth (normal healing tissue) or a disruption of blood vessels (abnormal).
4. Purulent (yellow) exudate is generally indicative of infection.

System: Other Systems
Content Outline: Physical Therapy Examination

 Level 1  p. 505

PTEXAM TWO: QUESTION 58

A patient coverage form indicates selective debridement is to be performed on a patient who has a lower extremity burn. Which of the following interventions would the physical therapist MOST likely perform to accomplish this type of treatment?

1. Whirlpool
2. Wet-to-dry dressings
3. **Enzymatic debridement**
4. Wound irrigation

Correct Answer: 3 (Sussman p. 442)

Selective debridement involves removing only nonviable tissues from a wound. Non-selective debridement involves removing both viable and nonviable tissues from a wound.

1. Whirlpool uses a turbine to produce agitation and aeration which creates movement of the water in the tank. The movement of the water results in the softening and loosening of adherent necrotic tissue. The inability to isolate necrotic tissue using whirlpool makes the intervention a form of non-selective debridement.
2. Wet-to-dry dressings refer to the application of a moistened gauze dressing placed in an area of necrotic tissue. The dressing is then allowed to dry completely and is later removed along with the necrotic tissue that has adhered to the gauze. This type of debridement should be used sparingly on wounds with both necrotic tissue and viable tissue since granulation tissue will be traumatized in the process. As a result, a wet-to-dry dressing is a form of non-selective debridement.
3. **Enzymatic debridement is considered to be selective since the topical preparation of the enzymes used (collagenolytic, proteolytic) will greatly influence the treatment outcome.**
4. Wound irrigation removes necrotic tissue from the wound bed using pressurized fluid. Most devices permit varying pressure settings and provide suction for removal of the exudate and debris. Wound irrigation is a form of non-selective debridement.

System: Other Systems
Content Outline: Interventions

 Level 1  p. 507

PTEXAM TWO: QUESTION 59

A physical therapist participates in a community-based screening program designed to identify individuals who have osteoporosis. Which of the following groups would have the HIGHEST risk for developing osteoporosis?

1. **Caucasian females over the age of 60**
2. African American females over the age of 60
3. Caucasian females under the age of 40
4. African American females under the age of 40

Correct Answer: 1 (Goodman – Differential Diagnosis p. 417)

Osteoporosis is a metabolic bone disease characterized by increased bone resorption resulting in a reduction in bone mass. Osteoporosis is more prevalent in females than in males, in older than younger individuals, and in Caucasians than African Americans.

1. **Caucasian females experience an increased incidence of osteoporosis compared to African American females. The relative risk of osteoporosis increases with age since there is decreased production of estrogen and a greater loss of bone density following menopause.**
2. African American females have an increased risk of osteoporosis with increasing age, however, this group is at less risk than Caucasian females because bone mass has a positive correlation to the color and pigmentation of the skin. Therefore, African American females generally have greater bone mass than the statistically equivalent Caucasian females.
3. Caucasian females under the age of 40 are typically not at high risk for osteoporosis. Bone mass will normally peak between 25 and 35 years of age, followed by a progressive increase in bone resorption compared to bone formation that may result, decades later, in osteopenia and osteoporosis.
4. African Americans under the age of 40 are typically not at high risk for osteoporosis. Bone mass will normally peak between 25 and 35 years of age. Bone resorption and bone formation occur in a similar manner as described in option 3.

System: Other Systems
Content Outline: Foundations for Evaluation, Differential Diagnosis, and Prognosis

 Level 1  p. 521-522, 620-621

PTEXAM TWO: QUESTION 60

A 74-year-old individual reports experiencing increased urinary incontinence over the past year. What physiological change is MOST commonly associated with this condition in older adults?

1. Reduced kidney filtration capacity
2. Increased reservoir capacity of the bladder
3. Spasm of the detrusor muscle
4. **Decreased urge sensation**

Correct Answer: 4 (Kaufman p. 387)

Urinary incontinence occurs frequently in older adults due to a combination of physiological changes that may be exacerbated by underlying medical conditions. Commonly, a combination of reduced sensitivity to needing to urinate, along with reduced bladder capacity creates this condition.

1. Kidney function decreases with age, however, it is not the primary reason for incontinence. Decreased kidney function is directly responsible for incomplete excretion of waste products.
2. The bladder capacity does not increase with age, rather it becomes diminished leading to more frequent bouts of urination. However, with proper voiding this is not a major contributing factor in the development of incontinence.
3. The detrusor muscle can become spastic in the company of neurological trauma, however, it is not a common reason for incontinence associated with aging.
4. **Decreased urge sensation is one of the leading reasons for incontinence in older adults. The bladder becomes full, but due to decreased bladder sensitivity the older adult may not recognize this and as a result experiences episodes of incontinence.**

System: Other Systems
Content Outline: Foundations for Evaluation, Differential Diagnosis, and Prognosis

 Level 1  p. 545-546

PTEXAM TWO: QUESTION 61

Before beginning to train for a wheelchair racing event, a 40-year-old patient with complete C7 tetraplegia undergoes a graded exercise test using an upper body ergometer. In the absence of cardiac pathology, which value represents the MOST likely maximum heart rate for this patient given their medical condition?

1. 60 beats per minute
2. 80 beats per minute
3. **120 beats per minute**
4. 180 beats per minute

Correct Answer: 3 (O'Sullivan p. 889)

Because of sympathetic nervous system impairment, patients with T3 or higher complete spinal cord injuries typically have difficulty reaching age-adjusted maximum and target training heart rate zones. Heart rate responses are more variable with injuries between T4-T6, while patients with injuries below T7 are typically able to reach age-adjusted ranges.

1. A heart rate of 60 beats per minute (bpm) or below would be considered bradycardia. Acutely, patients with complete upper thoracic or cervical lesions commonly experience a period of bradycardia due to an interruption of the sympathetic nervous system. However, this typically resolves in a matter of weeks following the initial injury.
2. A patient with C7 complete tetraplegia will typically have a lower maximum heart rate and target training zone as compared to a non-injured individual. 80 bpm may be a value within the target training zone, but is unlikely to be representative of the patient's maximum heart rate.
3. **The sympathetic impairment associated with complete spinal cord injuries will impact numerous aspects of a patient's response to exercise (e.g., heart rate, stroke volume, sweating, vasodilation). In the general population of patients with complete lesions above T3, achieving maximum heart rate values from 110-120 bpm is considered typical.**
4. Based on the patient's age, 180 bpm would be the age-predicted maximum heart rate. However, with a diagnosis of C7 tetraplegia, it is unlikely that the patient will be able to reach this heart rate during the graded exercise test.

System: Neuromuscular and Nervous Systems
Content Outline: Physical Therapy Examination

Level 2

PTEXAM TWO: QUESTION 62

A patient performing a prone knee hang as shown in the image reports direct pressure and discomfort on the patellofemoral region. Which of the following actions would be the MOST appropriate to address the patient's comment and still maintain the goal of this exercise?

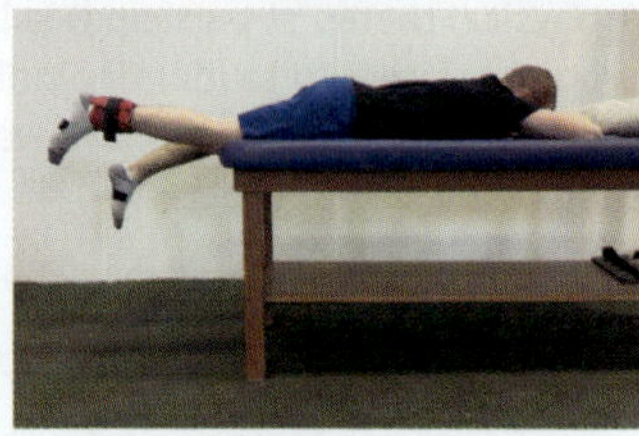

1. **Place a folded towel under the patient's distal femur**
2. Scoot the patient's body further up on the treatment table
3. Decrease the amount of weight in the ankle cuff weight
4. Apply ice to alleviate any discomfort during the stretch

Correct Answer: 1 (Dunleavy p. 126) 

A prone knee hang exercise is a commonly used sustained passive stretching technique for an individual with limited knee extension. The body should be fully supported in the prone position on the treatment table with the end of the table supporting the distal thighs, proximal to the patella to avoid compression on the patellofemoral joint. A cuff weight placed around the ankle creates a sustained passive stretch on the hamstrings as the muscle relaxes, which increases knee extension.

1. **Placing a folded towel under the patient's distal femur would further ensure there is no pressure on the patella and may be more comfortable to the distal femur area. This modification may provide further stabilization to the distal femur as gravity is used to increase knee extension.**
2. Having the patient scoot the body further up on the treatment table would likely result in greater compressive forces on the patella. Use of a folded towel placed under the patient's distal femur is the most appropriate choice to make this technique more comfortable for the patient and limit compressive forces on the patella while still maintaining the sustained stretch into knee extension.
3. Decreasing the amount of weight used in the ankle cuff weight may potentially make the exercise more comfortable by reducing the intensity of the stretch, however, it may also reduce the effectiveness of the exercise. In addition, the patient's report of "direct pressure and discomfort" on the patellofemoral region combined with the proximity of the patella to the end of the plinth in the image result in placement of the towel under the distal femur being the best option.
4. Although applying ice may temporarily alleviate any discomfort, this should not be necessary since the technique can easily be modified to increase patient comfort and limit compressive forces on the patella.

System: Musculoskeletal System
Content Outline: Interventions

Level 2

p. 116-118

PTEXAM TWO: QUESTION 63

A physical therapist uses the Six-Minute Walk Test as a means of quantifying functional status in a patient who has heart disease. During testing the patient expresses to the therapist that they need to rest. Which of the following actions is the **MOST** appropriate for the therapist to utilize in this situation?

1. Allow the patient to rest, however, stop the elapsed time during the rest period
2. **Allow the patient to rest, however, allow the elapsed time to continue**
3. Allow the patient to rest, however, discontinue the test
4. Offer encouragement to the patient in order to avoid or delay the rest period

Correct Answer: 2 (Hillegass p. 688) 

The Six-Minute Walk Test is used to determine a patient's functional exercise capacity. The test is commonly used to monitor progress or decline throughout physical therapy. This tool is administered to various populations including those with cardiac impairments, pulmonary disease, chronic conditions, and patients recovering from orthopedic surgical procedures. The test requires the therapist to measure the distance the patient walks within a six-minute period with rest periods permitted as necessary.

1. Rest periods are permitted as needed during the Six-Minute Walk Test, however, the elapsed time does not stop.
2. **Rest periods are permitted as needed during the Six-Minute Walk Test, however, the elapsed time continues during rest periods. The test measures the distance walked in a six-minute period regardless of the number of rest periods.**
3. Rest periods are permitted as needed during the Six-Minute Walk Test. Following a rest period, the patient should resume walking at a time of their choosing until the elapsed time expires.
4. The therapist should offer words of encouragement (e.g., "you're doing well," "keep up the good work," "you have three minutes to go") at regular intervals. The purpose of the encouragement is to allow the patient to perform to their abilities, not to avoid or delay rest periods.

System: Cardiovascular and Pulmonary Systems
Content Outline: Physical Therapy Examination

 Level 2  p. 434

PTEXAM TWO: QUESTION 64

A patient who has chronic pulmonary dysfunction is placed on a corticosteroid medication to reduce mucosal edema and inflammation. Which of the following cardiovascular side effects is the **MOST** common with use of corticosteroids?

1. Palpitations
2. Arrhythmias
3. **Increased blood pressure**
4. Tachycardia

Correct Answer: 3 (Ciccone p. 408)

Increased blood pressure or hypertension is a side effect that is associated with heavy or prolonged use of corticosteroids (also known as glucocorticoids). Other side effects include osteoporosis, muscle wasting, skin breakdown, cataracts, adrenocorticosuppression, and hyperglycemia.

1. A palpitation is a sensation in which a person is aware of an irregular, hard or fast heartbeat that may skip or beat irregularly. The word palpitation is sometimes used synonymously with arrhythmia, however, a palpitation may or may not be caused by an arrhythmia. Many palpitations are benign, but the underlying cause is important to diagnose.
2. An arrhythmia is defined as a significant deviation from normal sinus rhythm. Many medications have potential side effects of arrhythmias including other cardiac medications, tricyclic antidepressants, and minerals such as calcium.
3. **Corticosteroid use can increase blood pressure secondary to the sodium and water retention properties of the corticosteroid. Long-term use of corticosteroids must be closely monitored due to the stated adverse effects.**
4. Tachycardia refers to a heart rate in excess of 100 beats per minute in an adult. It may occur normally in response to fever, exercise or excitement. Many substances have potential side effects of tachycardia including alcohol, caffeine, nicotine, and certain anti-anxiety and cardiac medications.

System: Cardiovascular and Pulmonary Systems
Content Outline: Foundations for Evaluation, Differential Diagnosis, and Prognosis

 Level 2  p. 132

PTEXAM TWO: QUESTION 65

A physical therapist serves as an accessibility consultant for a local retail store. What is the MINIMUM width in inches required for a patient using a wheelchair to safely traverse through a doorway?

1. 24
2. 30
3. **32**
4. 36

Correct Answer: 3 (Fairchild p. 356) 

The Americans with Disabilities Act was designed to provide a clear and comprehensive national mandate for the elimination of discrimination. Title III provides information on public accommodations including minimum accessibility standards.

1. The seat width in an average adult size wheelchair is 18 inches. As a result, 24 inches would not be nearly sufficient to accommodate the remainder of the wheelchair and still have adequate space available to propel the wheelchair through the doorway.
2. A wheelchair would likely be able to traverse through a doorway that was 30 inches wide, however, it would not meet the minimum width required by the Americans with Disabilities Act.
3. **The Americans with Disabilities Act requires that the minimum width of a doorway is 32 inches.**
4. The Americans with Disabilities Act requires that the minimum width of a corridor (hallway) is 36 inches. This width allows the patient to change the direction of the wheelchair within the corridor.

System: Non-Systems
Content Outline: Safety and Protection; Professional Responsibilities; Research

 Level 1  p. 771

PTEXAM TWO: QUESTION 66

A physical therapist suspects that a patient's upper extremity range of motion limitation may be the result of a fear-based psychological response. Which of the following examination findings would be MOST consistent with the therapist's hypothesis?

1. Decreased passive range of motion; weak but pain-free resistive testing
2. Decreased active range of motion; strong but painful resistive testing
3. Decreased active and passive range of motion; strong and pain-free resistive testing
4. **Decreased active range of motion; decreased effort with resistive testing**

Correct Answer: 4 (Dunleavy p. 84) 

Although pain is certainly related to physiological processes, pain is a subjective experience. The experience of pain is often shaped by a host of psychological factors. Fear-based psychological responses during movement testing typically result in a voluntary limitation of active and resisted motion. Physical therapists should be aware of the potential ability of psychological factors to influence a patient's clinical presentation.

1. Decreased passive range of motion would be unlikely with a fear-based psychological response since the patient does not have to participate. Weak but pain-free resistive testing would more likely be expected with a grade III muscle strain due to the complete rupture of the muscle. Although severe pain is expected when the injury initially occurs, a lack of pain often exists following the acute phase of the injury.
2. Although decreased active range of motion is likely with a fear-based psychological response, a decreased effort with resistive testing would also be expected. Strong but painful resistive testing would be expected with a grade I strain or minor lesion of the musculotendinous unit. Grade I strains present with localized pain, minimal swelling, and tenderness.
3. Although decreased active range of motion would be expected in a fear-based psychological response, decreased passive range of motion would not be expected. A decreased effort with resistive testing would also be expected with a fear-based psychological response rather than strong and pain-free resistive testing.
4. **Decreased active range of motion and decreased effort with resistive testing would be expected with a fear-based psychological response during clinical examination. The voluntary limitation of active motion and the lack of effort with resistive testing are often associated with the fear of pain.**

System: Musculoskeletal System
Content Outline: Physical Therapy Examination

 Level 2  p. 70-72

PTEXAM TWO: QUESTION 67

A physical therapist designs an exercise program aimed at improving a patient's core and lower extremity strength. The physical therapist would like to avoid exercises that may elevate the patient's blood pressure. Which exercise would be the MOST likely to increase the patient's blood pressure?

1. **Wall sits for 15 seconds for 10 repetitions**
2. Leg press for 10 repetitions
3. Walking at 2.0 miles per hour on a treadmill for 10 minutes
4. Standing hip abduction using an elastic band for 10 repetitions

Correct Answer: 1 (ACSM – Resource Manual p. 626) 

Physical therapists often need to carefully consider relevant aspects of a patient's medical history when designing an exercise program. Resistive activities in general can be potentially dangerous for patients with high blood pressure if they are likely to result in the patient holding their breath during the activity (i.e., Valsalva maneuver). The Valsalva maneuver produces increased intrathoracic pressure, increased central venous pressure, and decreased venous return and therefore should be avoided, especially by patients with heart, blood vessel or lung disease.

1. **A wall sit is an isometric exercise targeting the lower extremities and core. This exercise requires isometric control which increases the likelihood of the Valsalva maneuver being used. This action would increase the patient's already elevated blood pressure and may create an unnecessary safety risk.**
2. A leg press is similar to a squat, however, is usually performed in a supine position. A patient is less likely to perform the Valsalva maneuver when performing a leg press than during a wall sit since the exercise requires continuous movement which is more conducive to a synchronized breathing pattern.
3. Walking on a treadmill at a relatively slow rate of speed (i.e., 2.0 miles per hour) for 10 minutes is a low intensity exercise and is therefore unlikely to significantly exacerbate the patient's blood pressure.
4. Standing hip abduction using an elastic band requires significantly less muscular activity than the wall sit or the leg press and is therefore not likely to significantly exacerbate the patient's blood pressure. In addition, the exercise requires continuous movement making use of the Valsalva maneuver less likely.

System: Cardiovascular and Pulmonary Systems
Content Outline: Interventions

 Level 3  p. 118, 121

PTEXAM TWO: QUESTION 68

A patient who has right upper extremity lymphedema post radical mastectomy discusses the cause of lymphedema with her physician. The physician explains that both the venous system and the lymphatic system are responsible for collecting and transporting interstitial fluid. What percentage of interstitial fluid is collected by a normally functioning lymphatic system?

1. **15%**
2. 35%
3. 55%
4. 75%

Correct Answer: 1 (Hillegass p. 651)

The initial lymph vessels in the lymphatic system are located near blood capillaries and are responsible for collecting fluid from the interstitium that is not picked up by the venous system. The lymphatic system also transports the majority of extracellular proteins since they are often too large to be transported by the venous system.

1. **The lymphatic system is normally responsible for collecting 10-20% of the interstitial fluid, while the venous system collects the other 80-90%. A value of 15% would fall within the range for a normally functioning lymphatic system.**
2. The lymphatic system is normally responsible for collecting 10-20% of the interstitial fluid. A value of 35% is above the normal range and may indicate that the venous system is not functioning normally.
3. A value of 55% is far above the range for what the lymphatic system is normally responsible for collecting. This may indicate that the venous system is not functioning normally.
4. A value of 75% is far above the range for what the lymphatic system is normally responsible for collecting. This may indicate that the venous system is not functioning normally.

System: Other Systems
Content Outline: Foundations for Evaluation, Differential Diagnosis, and Prognosis

 Level 1  p. 552

PTEXAM TWO: QUESTION 69

A physical therapist examines a patient with suspected vascular compression in the shoulder region. Which of the following special tests would be the LEAST beneficial to confirm the therapist's suspicions?

1. Adson maneuver
2. Halstead maneuver
3. **Froment's sign**
4. Wright test

Correct Answer: 3 (Magee p. 473)

There are a variety of special tests designed to identify vascular compression in the shoulder. When performing the tests, a positive sign is often indicated by diminution or disappearance of a pulse or reproduction of neurological signs or symptoms.

1. Adson maneuver is performed with the patient in sitting or standing. The therapist monitors the radial pulse and asks the patient to rotate their head to face the test shoulder. The patient is then asked to extend their head while the therapist laterally rotates and extends the patient's shoulder. A positive test is indicated by an absent or diminished radial pulse.
2. The Halstead maneuver is performed with the patient sitting over the edge of a table. The therapist palpates the radial pulse and applies a downward traction on the symptomatic side. The patient is then asked to extend the head and turn away from the tested side. A positive test is indicated by an absent or diminished pulse.
3. **Froment's sign requires a patient to grasp a piece of paper between the thumb and index finger. A positive test is indicated by flexion of the terminal phalanx of the thumb caused by paralysis of the adductor pollicis longus. The test is used to assess the integrity of the ulnar nerve.**
4. The Wright test or hyperabduction test is performed with the patient in sitting or supine. The therapist moves the patient's arm overhead in the frontal plane while monitoring the patient's radial pulse. A positive test is indicated by an absent or diminished radial pulse and may be indicative of compression in the costoclavicular space.

System: Musculoskeletal System
Content Outline: Physical Therapy Examination

 Level 2  p. 105

PTEXAM TWO: QUESTION 70

A physical therapist prepares to treat a patient using continuous ultrasound. What general rule BEST determines the length of treatment time when using ultrasound?

1. Two minutes for an area that is two times the size of the transducer face
2. **Five minutes for an area that is two times the size of the transducer face**
3. Five minutes is the maximum treatment time regardless of the treatment area
4. Ten minutes is the maximum treatment time regardless of the treatment area

Correct Answer: 2 (Cameron p. 185) 

The duration of ultrasound treatment is based on a number of variables including the treatment goal, the size of the area to be treated, and the effective radiating area of the transducer face.

1. Two minutes would not be enough time to use ultrasound in an area that was two times the size of the transducer face.
2. **An accepted recommendation is that ultrasound can be administered to an area two to three times the size of the effective radiating area of the transducer face in a five minute period. This recommendation equates to roughly twice the size of the transducer face.**
3. There is not a specified maximum amount of time when using ultrasound. Most often ultrasound is used for periods ranging from five to eight minutes in duration.
4. Ten minutes is a relatively long duration for treatment with ultrasound, however, this could be plausible in situations where the size of the area to be treated is large.

System: Non-Systems
Content Outline: Equipment, Devices, and Technologies; Therapeutic Modalities

 Level 2  p. 710-713

PTEXAM TWO: QUESTION 71

A physical therapist reviews the medical record of a patient with known cardiovascular pathology. The patient's past medical history includes gastroesophageal reflux disease. Which of the following activities would potentially be the **MOST** problematic for this patient?

1. Performing diaphragmatic breathing exercises in a semi-Fowler position
2. Initiating a progressive ambulation program on a treadmill
3. **Administering percussion to the anterior basal segments of the lower lobes**
4. Assessing tactile fremitus while palpating the chest wall in sitting

Correct Answer: 3 (Goodman – Pathology p. 871) 

Gastroesophageal reflux disease (GERD) is the result of an incompetent lower esophageal sphincter that allows reflux of gastric contents. The backwards movement of stomach acids can cause esophageal tissue injury. Positioning with the head lower than the body significantly increases the likelihood of reflux and therefore should be avoided whenever possible.

1. Diaphragmatic breathing can decrease the work of breathing by lowering respiratory rate, increasing tidal volume, and decreasing the use of accessory muscles by facilitating use of the diaphragm. The semi-Fowler position places a patient in supine with the head of the bed elevated to 45 degrees and pillows under the knees. The position would not be problematic for a patient with GERD since the patient is relatively upright.
2. Ambulation on a treadmill is an appropriate activity for a patient with GERD. The activity is rhythmic, occurs in an upright position, and does not involve excessive movement of the stomach.
3. **To administer percussion to the anterior basal segments of the lower lobes, the patient is positioned in supine with the foot of the bed elevated 18 inches. Percussion is applied over the lower ribs on the left and right side. Positioning with the head lower than the feet would significantly increase the likelihood of reflux.**
4. Tactile fremitus refers to the vibration of spoken words felt through the chest wall. The assessment procedure provides information about the density of the lungs and the thoracic cavity. The option indicates that tactile fremitus is being assessed in an upright position and therefore would not be problematic for a patient with GERD.

System: Cardiovascular and Pulmonary Systems
Content Outline: Interventions

 Level 3  p. 438-439, 534-535, 647

PTEXAM TWO: QUESTION 72

A physical therapist works with a child who has Legg-Calve-Perthes disease. Which of the following medical conditions is **MOST** often associated with this diagnosis?

1. **Avascular necrosis**
2. Congenital hip dysplasia
3. Osteomyelitis
4. Septic arthritis

Correct Answer: 1 (Palisano p. 319)

Legg-Calve-Perthes disease is characterized by degeneration of the femoral head due to a disturbance in the blood supply. Signs and symptoms of Legg-Calve-Perthes disease include pain, decreased range of motion, antalgic gait, and a positive Trendelenburg sign.

1. **Avascular necrosis refers to the death of bone tissue due to a lack of blood supply. The condition most commonly affects the head of the femur, talus, and scaphoid. The medial femoral circumflex artery is the primary vessel responsible for vascular distribution in the head and neck of the femur.**
2. Congenital hip dysplasia is a condition characterized by malalignment of the femoral head within the acetabulum. The condition develops during the last trimester in utero. The condition is not commonly associated with Legg-Calve-Perthes disease.
3. Osteomyelitis is an infection of a bone by bacterial organisms. The condition can result in rapid destruction and deterioration of bone causing permanent damage. Although the condition often affects an adolescent population, it is not commonly associated with Legg-Calve-Perthes disease.
4. Septic arthritis, also known as infectious arthritis, is most often caused by bacteria such as haemophilus influenza, staphylococcus, and streptococcus. The condition often affects only a single joint (e.g., hip, knee) and is most common in extremely young children (i.e., less than two years of age) and the elderly. The condition is not commonly associated with Legg-Calve-Perthes disease.

System: Musculoskeletal System
Content Outline: Foundations for Evaluation, Differential Diagnosis, and Prognosis

Level 2  p. 124

PTEXAM TWO: QUESTION 73

A physical therapist reviews a patient's medical history prior to administering intermittent compression. Which of the following conditions would be considered a contraindication when using this type of mechanical device?

1. Venous stasis ulcer
2. **Acute pulmonary edema**
3. Intermittent claudication
4. Lymphedema

Correct Answer: 2 (Prentice p. 579)

Intermittent compression is effective in controlling edema since it increases the extravascular hydrostatic pressure and circulation. Intermittent compression is most commonly used to control edema due to venous insufficiency or lymphatic dysfunction.

1. Venous stasis ulcers occur secondary to inadequate functioning of the venous system resulting in inadequate circulation and eventual tissue damage and ulceration. Intermittent compression improves venous circulation and facilitates the healing of previously formed ulcers.
2. **Acute pulmonary edema should not be treated with intermittent compression since the shift of fluid from the peripheral to the central circulation may significantly increase stress on the heart.**
3. Intermittent claudication occurs when blood flow is not adequate to meet the demand of the peripheral tissue, most often during activity. The result is ischemia which produces symptoms such as muscle pain, numbness, tingling, and fatigue. Caution should be used when applying compression in the presence of peripheral artery disease, however, intermittent claudication itself would not be a contraindication to intermittent compression.
4. Lymphedema refers to an abnormal accumulation of fluid in the interstitial spaces. Stagnation of the fluid promotes the inflammatory response and increases the probability of infection. Intermittent compression is commonly used to treat lymphedema.

System: Non-Systems
Content Outline: Equipment, Devices, and Technologies; Therapeutic Modalities

 Level 1  p. 722

PTEXAM TWO: QUESTION 74

A physical therapist attempts to prevent alveolar collapse in a patient post thoracic surgery. Which of the following respiratory devices would be the MOST beneficial to achieve the established goal?

1. Inspiratory muscle trainer
2. Mechanical percussors
3. **Incentive spirometer**
4. Flutter valve

Correct Answer: 3 (Hillegass p. 552) 

An incentive spirometer provides visual or in some cases auditory feedback as the patient takes a maximum inspiration. Incentive spirometry increases the amount of air that is inspired and as a result, can be used as a treatment to prevent alveolar collapse after thoracic surgery.

1. Inspiratory muscle trainers are handheld breathing training devices used primarily to increase the strength and endurance of the muscles of inspiration. They are not used to prevent alveolar collapse after thoracic surgery.
2. Mechanical percussors are electronically or pneumatically powered devices employed as a substitute for manual percussion with the hands. They can be used to help mobilize bronchial secretions after thoracic surgery, but only if the patient was retaining secretions.
3. **Incentive spirometers are devices that provide visual or other feedback while the patient performs sustained maximal inspirations. The device is most often used following upper abdominal or thoracic surgery. Indications may include chest wall pain, loss of mobility, weakness of the muscles of inspiration, and the prevention or treatment of atelectasis.**
4. Flutter valves are mucus clearance devices that combine positive expiratory pressure with high frequency oscillations at the airway opening during exhalation.

System: Cardiovascular and Pulmonary Systems
Content Outline: Interventions

 Level 2  p. 440-443

PTEXAM TWO: QUESTION 75

A physical therapist working in the home care setting attempts to obtain the body temperature of a patient. Which of the following methods for obtaining temperature would likely result in the LOWEST obtained value?

1. Tympanic membrane
2. Rectal
3. Oral
4. **Axillary**

Correct Answer: 4 (Fairchild p. 51)

Body temperature represents a balance between the heat produced and the heat lost by the body. Body temperature is measured through a variety of methods including oral temperature, tympanic membrane temperature, temporal artery temperature, axillary temperature, and rectal temperature.

1. Tympanic membrane temperature reads the infrared heat waves released by the ear's tympanic membrane. An accurate measurement requires the examiner to pull the ear backward to straighten the ear canal. The tympanic membrane temperature is typically 0.5-1.0 degree Fahrenheit higher than the oral temperature value.
2. Rectal temperature is obtained by placing a thermometer into the opening of the anus. The rectal (i.e., core) temperature value is typically 0.5-1.0 degree Fahrenheit higher than the oral temperature value.
3. Oral temperature is obtained by placing the tip of a thermometer under one side of the tongue towards the back of the oral cavity. The thermometer is held in place for three minutes with a glass thermometer and approximately 30 seconds with an electronic thermometer. The oral temperature value is typically 0.5-1.0 degree Fahrenheit lower than the rectal temperature value.
4. **Axillary temperature is obtained by placing the tip of a thermometer in the armpit. The arm is then brought to the patient's side holding the elbow against the chest for 4-5 minutes. The axillary temperature value is typically 0.5-1.0 degree Fahrenheit lower than the oral temperature value.**

System: Non-Systems
Content Outline: Equipment, Devices, and Technologies; Therapeutic Modalities

 Level 1

PTEXAM TWO: QUESTION 76

A physical therapist conducts a sensory assessment on numerous areas of a patient's face. What cranial nerve is MOST likely assessed using this type of testing procedure?

1. Facial nerve
2. Oculomotor nerve
3. **Trigeminal nerve**
4. Trochlear nerve

Correct Answer: 3 (Magee p. 86) 

The cranial nerves refer to twelve pairs of nerves that have their origin in the brain. The majority of cranial nerves contain both sensory and motor fibers, however, there are several exceptions including the oculomotor and trochlear nerves.

1. The afferent component of the facial nerve (cranial nerve VII) can be assessed by examining a patient's ability to accurately identify sweet and salty substances. The efferent component is tested by performing a manual muscle test of selected muscles involved in facial expression.
2. The efferent component of the oculomotor nerve (cranial nerve III) can be assessed by asking a patient positioned in sitting to follow an object such as a writing utensil with their eyes as it is moved vertically, horizontally, and diagonally. The therapist should make sure the patient does not rotate their head during the testing and should inspect the patient's eyes for asymmetry or ptosis.
3. **The afferent component of the trigeminal nerve (cranial nerve V) can be assessed by examining sensation of the face and jaw. The efferent component is assessed by examining the muscles of mastication.**
4. The efferent component of the trochlear nerve (cranial nerve IV) can be assessed by asking a patient positioned in sitting to follow an object such as a writing utensil with their eyes as it is moved in an inferior direction. The therapist should make sure the patient does not move their head downward.

System: Neuromuscular and Nervous Systems
Content Outline: Physical Therapy Examination

 Level 1  p. 247-249

PTEXAM TWO: QUESTION 77

A patient who is four months post surgery to repair a torn biceps tendon still lacks 40 degrees of elbow extension. Because conservative efforts have failed, the physician orders serial casting to improve the patient's mobility. After one round of casting, what would be the MOST likely expected increase in range of motion?

1. **5 degrees**
2. 15 degrees
3. 25 degrees
4. 35 degrees

Correct Answer: 1 (Umphred p. 480)

Serial casting is a casting technique that is used to improve range of motion at a joint that has developed a contracture. The procedure consists of placing the joint in a submaximal position and then applying a cast. After wearing the cast for several days, it is removed. With each round of casting, the joint should make modest range of motion gains (e.g., 5-7 degrees). Serial casting can last for a few weeks or several months depending on the extent of the contracture and the relative success of the intervention.

1. **Five degrees is a realistic expectation for the increase in range of motion after a single round of casting. One round of serial casting usually yields roughly a 5-7 degree increase in range of motion.**
2. An increase of 15 degrees would be larger than the normally expected increase in range of motion from a single round of serial casting. This type of range of motion gain would be more likely in 2-3 rounds of serial casting.
3. An increase of 25 degrees would be larger than the normally expected increase in range of motion from a single round of serial casting. This type of range of motion gain would be more likely in 4-5 rounds of serial casting.
4. An increase of 35 degrees would be larger than the normally expected increase in range of motion from a single round of serial casting. This type of range of motion gain would be more likely in 5-7 rounds of serial casting.

System: Non-Systems
Content Outline: Equipment, Devices, and Technologies; Therapeutic Modalities

Level 1

PTEXAM TWO: QUESTION 78

A physical therapist completes a cognitive function test on a patient post CVA. As part of the test, the therapist examines the patient's abstract ability. Which of the following tasks would be the MOST appropriate to assess this type of cognitive function?

1. Orientation to time, person, and place
2. Copy drawn figures of varying size and shape
3. **Discuss how two objects are similar**
4. Identify letters or numbers traced on the skin

Correct Answer: 3 (O'Sullivan p. 140)

A patient with impaired abstract thinking may have involvement of the frontal lobe, diffuse encephalopathy or psychiatric illness.

1. Orientation can be assessed by asking a person to identify time (e.g., day, month, season), person (e.g., name), and place (e.g., city, state). Disorientation is most commonly associated with traumatic brain injury, delirium, and advanced dementia.
2. Copying drawn figures of varying size and shape assesses constructional ability. Impairments in constructional ability are often associated with damage to the parietal lobe or stroke.
3. **Abstract ability is commonly tested using two specific methods. The first method is by asking a patient to describe how two items such as a cat and a mouse are similar. The other method is by asking a patient to interpret the meaning of a proverb such as "a rolling stone gathers no moss." Patients with difficulty in abstract thinking may provide answers that tend to be literal or concrete.**
4. The ability to recognize symbols, letters or numbers traced on the skin refers to graphesthesia. Patients with language or speech disorders secondary to stroke can identify the correct figure by pointing at an image located in a chart instead of through verbal identification.

System: Neuromuscular and Nervous Systems
Content Outline: Physical Therapy Examination

Level 2

PTEXAM TWO: QUESTION 79

A six-month-old patient who has developmental hip dysplasia is fitted with a Pavlik harness to promote proper alignment of the hip joints. Which of the following hip motions would be the MOST restricted with this harness?

1. Flexion and abduction
2. Flexion and adduction
3. Extension and abduction
4. **Extension and adduction**

Correct Answer: 4 (Palisano p. 312) 

A Pavlik harness is the primary method of treating developmental dysplasia of the hip (DDH). DDH is a subluxed or dislocated hip in infancy as a result of abnormal congruency of the femoral head and acetabulum. The Pavlik harness maintains the infant's hips in a position that enhances acetabular development.

1. The Pavlik harness positions the infant's hips in flexion and abduction to maintain the femoral head within the acetabulum and promote acetabular development. The harness would actually promote, not restrict, these motions.
2. The Pavlik harness positions the infant's hips in flexion and abduction, therefore it would restrict hip adduction, though it would promote hip flexion.
3. The Pavlik harness positions the infant's hips in flexion and abduction, therefore it would restrict hip extension, though it would promote hip abduction.
4. **Because the Pavlik harness positions the infant's hips in flexion and abduction, it would restrict the opposing motions (i.e., extension and adduction). Studies have found that the positions of extension and adduction promote hip dislocation. The Pavlik harness attempts to minimize these motions and thus reduce the incidence of hip dislocation.**

System: Non-Systems
Content Outline: Equipment, Devices, and Technologies; Therapeutic Modalities

Level 1

PTEXAM TWO: QUESTION 80

A physical therapist documents in the medical record that a patient has moved from stage 5 to stage 6 of Brunnstrom's Stages of Recovery. This type of transition is characterized by which of the following changes in movement patterns?

1. Absence of associated reactions
2. **Disappearance of spasticity**
3. Voluntary movement begins outside of synergy patterns
4. Return of normal motor function

Correct Answer: 2 (Brunnstrom p. 47) 

Brunnstrom separates neurological recovery into seven separate stages based on progression through abnormal tone and spasticity. The seven stages of recovery describe tone, reflex activity, and volitional movement.

1. In stage 2, movement occurs primarily in the form of associated reactions and spasticity begins to develop. In stage 3, voluntary movement begins within basic limb synergies.
2. **In stage 5, spasticity is still present although it continues to decrease. Stage 6 is characterized by the disappearance of spasticity and the ability to complete isolated joint movements in a coordinated fashion.**
3. In stage 4, movement patterns are not dictated solely by limb synergies and voluntary movement patterns begin outside of limb synergies.
4. In stage 7, normal motor function is restored.

System: Neuromuscular and Nervous Systems
Content Outline: Physical Therapy Examination

 Level 1  p. 287

PTEXAM TWO: QUESTION 81

A patient who is a tennis player is referred to physical therapy after being diagnosed with median nerve entrapment. The patient reports paresthesias in the hand and progressive weakness. Which of the following muscles would MOST likely contribute to the entrapment?

1. Abductor pollicis longus
2. Flexor digiti minimi
3. Flexor digitorum profundus
4. **Pronator teres**

Correct Answer: 4 (Dutton p. 763) 

Median nerve entrapment is often associated with racquet sports or with activities requiring repetitive gripping with pronation of the forearm and extension of the elbow. Patients with median nerve entrapment often experience sensory alterations in the lateral aspect of the hand and lateral three and a half fingers. Motor alterations may be found in the anterior forearm or the hand.

1. The abductor pollicis longus is innervated by the radial nerve and therefore would not contribute to median nerve entrapment.
2. The flexor digiti minimi is innervated by the ulnar nerve and therefore would not contribute to median nerve entrapment.
3. The medial aspect of the flexor digitorum profundus is innervated by the ulnar nerve while the lateral aspect is innervated by the median nerve. Although the lateral aspect of the flexor digitorum profundus is innervated by the median nerve, the muscle would not contribute to median nerve entrapment.
4. **The median nerve arises from the cubital fossa and passes between the two heads of the pronator teres. As a result, the pronator teres can be a possible source of median nerve entrapment.**

System: Neuromuscular and Nervous Systems
Content Outline: Foundations for Evaluation, Differential Diagnosis, and Prognosis

 Level 1  p. 261

PTEXAM TWO: QUESTION 82

A physical therapist examines a patient with a cerebrovascular disorder due to arterial occlusion. The patient exhibits an ataxic gait, intention tremors, and dysmetria. Which of the following arteries is the MOST likely vessel affected?

1. **Anterior inferior cerebellar**
2. Anterior spinal
3. Basilar
4. Middle cerebral

Correct Answer: 1 (Gutman p. 237)

The cerebellum is located at the posterior portion of the brain below the occipital lobes. The cerebellum is responsible for fine tuning of movement, maintaining posture and balance by controlling muscle tone, and positioning of the extremities in space. Blood supply to the cerebellum is from the anterior inferior cerebellar artery, posterior inferior cerebellar artery, and superior cerebellar artery.

1. **The anterior inferior cerebellar artery is one of three vessels that supplies blood to the cerebellum. Occlusion of the artery can result in a variety of symptoms including ataxia, nystagmus, tremor, dysmetria, incoordination, and balance deficits.**
2. The anterior spinal artery supplies blood to the anterior portion of the spinal cord and arises from the vertebral artery in the region of the medulla oblongata. Occlusion of the artery can result in contralateral hemiplegia, deviation of the tongue toward the affected side, dysphagia, and loss of the gag reflex.
3. The basilar artery is part of the posterior cerebral circulation arising from the confluence of the left and right vertebral arteries at the base of the pons. Occlusion of the artery can result in contralateral hemiplegia and ipsilateral sensory loss of the face.
4. The middle cerebral artery is one of three major paired arteries that supplies blood to the cerebrum. Occlusion of the artery can result in contralateral hemiplegia, aphasia, apraxia, and cognitive deficits.

System: Neuromuscular and Nervous Systems
Content Outline: Foundations for Evaluation, Differential Diagnosis, and Prognosis

 Level 2  p. 239-241

PTEXAM TWO: QUESTION 83

A physical therapist prepares to instruct a patient in a home exercise program designed to increase lower extremity flexibility. The therapist is somewhat concerned since the patient has difficulty following multi-step instructions and tends to be overly aggressive on prescribed exercises. Which type of stretching would be the MOST appropriate?

1. Ballistic
2. Dynamic
3. Proprioceptive neuromuscular facilitation
4. **Static**

Correct Answer: 4 (Kisner p. 87) 

Stretching refers to the lengthening of muscles and their associated structures. Stretching helps muscles stay flexible and strong and serves as a form of injury prevention. Common forms of stretching include static, dynamic, ballistic, and proprioceptive neuromuscular facilitation (PNF).

1. Ballistic stretching is characterized by quick, jerky movements that result in a rapid change in muscle length. Because ballistic stretching occurs quickly, it activates the muscle spindles and results in greater resistance to stretch. This type of stretching would likely be problematic for the described patient based on their tendency to be overly aggressive with exercise.
2. Dynamic stretching involves the patient actively moving a body segment to the end of range (but not beyond this limit) while the antagonist muscle relaxes and stretches. Unlike static stretching, the end-range movement is held only briefly and is performed repeatedly. Dynamic stretching is most commonly used as a "warm-up." The patient's difficulty following multi-step directions and aggressiveness make static stretching a more desirable form of stretching.
3. PNF incorporates active muscle contractions into stretching techniques. Muscular contraction is thought to lead to muscle relaxation through the principles of autogenic or reciprocal inhibition. Because these techniques exert their effects on muscle fibers, they are more effective at treating range of motion limitations due to muscle spasm as opposed to connective tissue tightness. The patient's inability to follow multi-step directions makes this form of stretching impractical.
4. **Static stretching involves placing the muscle at its maximal length and holding the position against an external force for a prolonged period of time. It is considered to be the safest form of stretching and results in the greatest gains in tissue extensibility. The relative simplicity of static stretching combined with being the most conservative stretching technique makes this the most appropriate option for the patient.**

System: Musculoskeletal System
Content Outline: Interventions

 Level 3  p. 116-117

PTEXAM TWO: QUESTION 84

A physical therapist attempts to examine a wound with full-thickness skin loss that is obscured by eschar. Which pressure injury stage is BEST depicted by this scenario?

1. Stage 2
2. Stage 3
3. Stage 4
4. **Unstageable**

Correct Answer: 4 (Sussman p. 235) 

Pressure injuries, also referred to as decubitus ulcers, result from sustained or prolonged pressure on tissue at levels greater than that of capillary pressure. Skin covering bony prominences is particularly susceptible to localized ischemia and tissue necrosis due to pressure. Factors contributing to pressure injuries include shearing forces, moisture, heat, friction, medications, muscle atrophy, malnutrition, and debilitating medical conditions.

1. A stage 2 pressure injury describes partial-thickness loss of skin with exposed dermis. The wound bed is viable, pink or red, moist, and may also present as an intact or ruptured serum-filled blister. Adipose and deeper tissues are not visible. Granulation tissue, slough, and eschar are not present. These injuries commonly result from shear over the pelvis and shear in the heel. This stage should not be used to describe moisture-associated skin damage including incontinence-associated dermatitis, intertriginous dermatitis, medical adhesive-related skin injury or traumatic wounds.
2. A stage 3 pressure injury describes full-thickness loss of skin, in which adipose is visible in the ulcer and granulation tissue and epibole are often present. Slough and/or eschar may be visible, but they do not obscure the extent of tissue loss. Fascia, muscle, tendon, ligament, cartilage, and/or bone are not exposed.
3. A stage 4 pressure injury describes full-thickness skin and tissue loss with exposed or directly palpable fascia, muscle, tendon, ligament, cartilage or bone in the ulcer. Slough and/or eschar may be visible, but they do not obscure the extent of tissue loss.
4. **An unstageable pressure injury is characterized by full-thickness skin and tissue loss in which the extent of tissue damage within the pressure injury cannot be determined because it is obscured by slough or eschar. If slough or eschar is removed, a stage 3 or 4 pressure injury will be revealed.**

System: Other Systems
Content Outline: Physical Therapy Examination

 Level 2  p. 504, 622-623

PTEXAM TWO: QUESTION 85

A patient with increased sympathetic output is examined in physical therapy. Which of the following treatment techniques would be the LEAST beneficial in decreasing the level of sympathetic activity?

1. Connective tissue massage
2. Rotating the lower trunk in hooklying
3. **Slow reversal hold of the quadriceps and hamstrings**
4. Gentle manual pressure to the abdomen

Correct Answer: 3 (Sullivan p. 60)

The sympathetic division of the autonomic nervous system prepares the body for stressful situations using the "fight or flight" response. It increases heart rate, dilates the airways, and allows the body to release stored energy. This division also causes the palms to sweat, pupils to dilate, and hair to stand on end.

1. Connective tissue massage is a technique that can be used to decrease sympathetic activity. Massage can influence muscle tension via the circulatory and autonomic systems with noted changes in vital signs and muscle tone.
2. Passive rotation of the lower trunk while in a hooklying position is an example of rhythmical movement which produces reflexive autonomic changes and an overall calming effect.
3. **Slow reversal hold is a proprioceptive neuromuscular facilitation technique used primarily to improve stability surrounding a joint. The technique uses slow and resisted concentric contractions of agonists and antagonists around a joint with an isometric contraction that is performed at the end of each movement. Slow reversal hold would not decrease sympathetic activity.**
4. Maintained touch is used to promote a parasympathetic response and produce a generalized calming effect due to the stimulation of tonic sensory receptors. Gentle manual pressure to the abdomen is an example of maintained touch.

System: Neuromuscular and Nervous Systems
Content Outline: Interventions

Level 2 p. 291-292

PTEXAM TWO: QUESTION 86

A group of physical therapists designs a research study in which they record the shoulder range of motion before and after treatment in three different age groups: adolescents, teenagers, and young adults. The therapists want to determine if there is a difference in the treatment effect based on the age of the patient. What statistical test would MOST likely be used to compare the differences between the three groups?

1. T-test
2. Z-test
3. Chi-square test
4. **Analysis of variance (ANOVA) test**

Correct Answer: 4 (Portney p. 451)

There are a variety of statistical tests that may be used as a means of analyzing data in a research study (e.g., t-test, z-test, chi-square test, analysis of variance test). The statistical test used will depend on the dependent and independent variables that are being investigated.

1. A t-test would be used when a study is comparing the means of two different groups. In the described scenario, the researchers are comparing the means of three different groups (i.e., adolescents, teenagers, young adults), therefore, a t-test could not be used to analyze the data in this study.
2. A z-test is similar to a t-test in that it compares the means of two different groups. However, a z-test would be used in situations where the variance of the population being studied is known. A t-test is used when the variance is not known.
3. A chi-square test is a statistical test used to compare nominal data (e.g., gender, yes-no responses). The described scenario is comparing range of motion values, which would be considered ratio data.
4. **An analysis of variance (ANOVA) test is a statistical test that is used when three or more variables are being compared. In the described scenario, the researchers are comparing the means of three different groups, therefore, an ANOVA test would be the most appropriate statistical test.**

System: Non-Systems
Content Outline: Safety and Protection; Professional Responsibilities; Research

Level 1

p. 813-815

PTEXAM TWO: QUESTION 87

A physical therapist recognizes that a child has significant difficulty flexing the neck while in a supine position. Failure to integrate which of the following reflexes would BEST explain the child's difficulty?

1. **Tonic labyrinthine**
2. Moro
3. Asymmetrical tonic neck
4. Symmetrical tonic neck

Correct Answer: 1 (Ratliffe p. 26) 

The tonic labyrinthine reflex promotes a tendency for extension when a patient is in supine and reduced extensor influence when the patient is in prone. The persistence of a primitive reflex is generally seen with a neurological insult.

1. **The tonic labyrinthine reflex serves to limit the child's ability to flex the neck when in a supine position. The child should lie in sidelying or in supine with hip flexion and/or knee flexion in order to decrease the influence of the reflex.**
2. The Moro reflex is elicited by a sudden change in the position of the head, usually having the head drop backwards. The typical response is crying along with extension and abduction of the upper extremities followed by flexion and adduction across the chest.
3. The asymmetrical tonic neck reflex is elicited through rotation of the neck. If the patient's head is turned, the upper and lower extremities on the face side extend and the upper and lower extremities on the skull side flex. The asymmetrical tonic neck reflex does not influence the child's ability to flex the neck while in a supine position.
4. The symmetrical tonic neck reflex is elicited by flexion or extension of the neck. When the head is flexed, upper extremities flex and lower extremities extend. When the head is extended, upper extremities extend and lower extremities flex. The symmetrical tonic neck reflex does not influence the child's ability to flex the neck while in a supine position.

System: Neuromuscular and Nervous Systems
Content Outline: Physical Therapy Examination

 Level 1 p. 306-307

PTEXAM TWO: QUESTION 88

An older adult is referred to physical therapy secondary to a recent fall. The patient reports difficulty seeing objects directly in front of them. This description is MOST consistent with the presence of which of the following visual impairments?

1. Cataracts
2. **Macular degeneration**
3. Presbyopia
4. Glaucoma

Correct Answer: 2 (Lewis p. 89)

The most common visual impairments experienced by older adults include cataracts, glaucoma, macular degeneration, and the normal loss of lens elasticity known as presbyopia. If left untreated, any of these conditions can result in an increased fall risk.

1. Cataracts cause opacity to the lens of the eye, which in turn results in the patient seeing light streaks and glare from light sources. This can be especially dangerous at night when driving.
2. **Macular degeneration involves the loss of central vision (looking forward) due to degenerative changes to the eyes. Individuals with macular degeneration can effectively see in the periphery of their visual field.**
3. Presbyopia is the normal loss of lens elasticity that is experienced with aging. This is commonly known as farsightedness and can be managed with eyeglasses.
4. Glaucoma is an increase in the intraocular pressure of the eye that can damage the optic nerve. Early stages of glaucoma are characterized by loss of peripheral vision and sparing of central vision.

System: Non-Systems
Content Outline: Safety and Protection; Professional Responsibilities; Research

 Level 1

PTEXAM TWO: QUESTION 89

A note in a patient's medical record indicates a specific drug is taken through enteral administration. Which of the following methods of drug delivery is an example of enteral administration?

1. **Inhalation**
2. **Injection**
3. **Topical**
4. **Oral**

Correct Answer: 4 (Ciccone p. 15)

Enteral administration of drugs involves the esophagus, stomach, and small and large intestines. The most common routes of enteral administration are oral, sublingual, and rectal.

1. Drugs that are in a gaseous or volatile state or that can be suspended as tiny droplets in an aerosol form can be administered through inhalation. Examples are general anesthetics and anti-asthmatic drugs.
2. Injection allows drugs to be introduced systemically or locally. Common types of injection include intravenous, intra-arterial, subcutaneous, intramuscular, and intrathecal. Examples are insulin and narcotic analgesics.
3. Topical administration refers to the application of drugs topically to the surface of the skin or mucous membranes. Topical administration is most often used to treat the outer layer of the skin and not other areas since most medications are absorbed poorly through the epidermis and into the systemic circulation.
4. **Oral administration is considered the easiest form of taking medication when self-medication is required and is relatively safe since drugs enter the system in a fairly controlled manner.**

System: Other Systems
Content Outline: Foundations for Evaluation, Differential Diagnosis, and Prognosis

 Level 1  p. 582-584

PTEXAM TWO: QUESTION 90

A physical therapist designs a home exercise program for a patient who has a lower extremity injury. Which of the following steps would be the MOST appropriate to maximize patient adherence?

1. **Limit the exercise program to 10 minutes**
2. **Select a maximum of five different exercises**
3. **Select exercises consistent with the patient's goals**
4. **Avoid physically demanding exercises**

Correct Answer: 3 (Kisner p. 22) 

Many factors can influence patient adherence with a home exercise program, however, regardless of the construction of the program it is essential that the program is designed to be consistent with the patient's rehabilitation goals.

1. An exercise program that can be completed in a relatively short period of time is more likely to be completed since patients have a better opportunity to fit the program into their existing schedule.
2. Limiting the number of exercises tends to promote adherence since it is easier for the patient to focus and complete each exercise.
3. **Patients are typically highly motivated to complete home exercise programs when they believe the exercises will help them to achieve their personal rehabilitation goals. Options such as limiting the length of the exercise program and limiting the number of exercises are helpful strategies to promote adherence, however, they would not be as critical as aligning the exercises with the patient's rehabilitation goals.**
4. There is no information presented which implies the patient is averse to physically demanding activities.

System: Musculoskeletal System
Content Outline: Interventions

Test Taking Tip: Many items on the NPTE-PT require candidates to differentiate between good, better, and best options. Candidates must therefore carefully assess the relative value of each of the presented options. In this particular item, candidates must differentiate between several options that are plausible and attractive. Candidates must remain open minded when examining each of the options and avoid the tendency to select the first viable option that they encounter since in many cases there is an additional option that may be better.

 Level 3  p. 800-801

PTEXAM TWO: QUESTION 91

A physical therapist completes a series of upper extremity resisted tests on a patient with suspected cervical spine pathology. Which myotome would **BEST** be assessed using the test shown in the image?

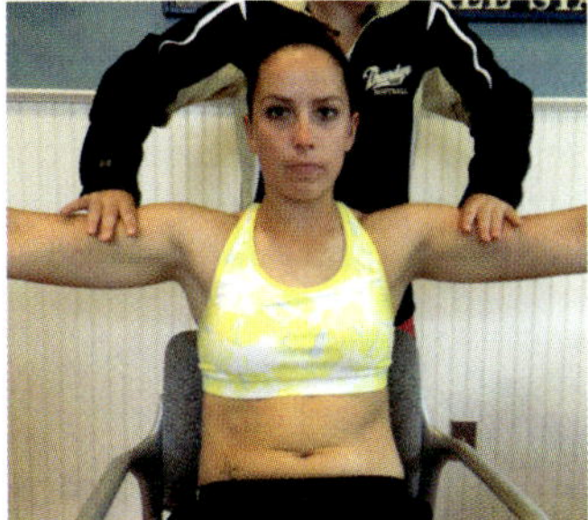

1. C4
2. **C5**
3. C6
4. C7

Correct Answer: 2 (Dutton p. 1282) 

Resisted isometric movements are designed to determine the role of contractile tissue in an injury. The therapist attempts to elicit a strong, static, voluntary muscle contraction. The therapist then classifies the movement as strong or weak and painful or pain-free.

1. The C4 myotome is commonly assessed by examining the diaphragm. The therapist uses a tape measure to quantify the amount of rib expansion that occurs with a deep breath. This measurement is then compared to the same measurement performed with the patient at rest. The C4 myotome can also be assessed by providing manual resistance after the patient completes a shoulder shrug.
2. **The C5 myotome is commonly assessed by performing resisted isometric movements of the shoulder abductors or the shoulder external rotators. The image shows the therapist assessing the shoulder abductors by applying a downward force on the humerus while the patient resists the movement. The deltoid and supraspinatus muscles are the primary muscles active during this resisted test.**
3. The C6 myotome is commonly assessed by performing resisted isometric movements of the elbow flexors or shoulder internal rotators.
4. The C7 myotome is commonly assessed by performing resisted isometric movements of the elbow extensors or wrist flexors.

System: Musculoskeletal System
Content Outline: Physical Therapy Examination

 Level 1  p. 70-71, 245-246

PTEXAM TWO: QUESTION 92

A five-month-old infant is able to sit in a propped position. Which objective finding would be the **MOST** essential for the child to progress to ring sitting?

1. Increased strength of the trunk flexors
2. **Increased strength of the trunk extensors**
3. Integration of the symmetrical tonic neck reflex
4. Integration of the asymmetrical tonic neck reflex

Correct Answer: 2 (Tecklin p. 45)

A propped sitting position is characterized by a forward trunk position where the infant uses their upper extremities to maintain the position. Ring sitting refers to an independent sitting position where the legs form the shape of a ring. The position allows the infant to use their upper extremities for reaching or grasping objects.

1. Increased strength of the trunk flexors would not be useful to assist the infant to progress to ring sitting since the progression would require the infant to sit more upright using the trunk extensors.
2. **Increased strength of the trunk extensors allows the infant to sit more upright with the pelvis remaining perpendicular to the surface. The increased strength of the trunk extensors allows the infant to maintain the sitting position without weight bearing through the upper extremities. The infant may gain additional stability in this position by maintaining a high guard position with the upper extremities.**
3. The symmetrical tonic neck reflex is stimulated by the head moving into flexion or extension. When the head is in flexion, the arms are flexed and the legs are extended. When the head is in extension, the arms are extended and the legs are flexed. Integration of the reflex would not assist with attaining ring sitting, but may assist the infant with reciprocal crawling and the ability to prop on the arms in a prone position.
4. The asymmetrical tonic neck reflex is stimulated when the head is turned to one side. The response is a fencing posture (arm and leg on face side are extended, arm and leg on scalp side are flexed). Integration of the reflex would not assist with attaining ring sitting, but may assist the infant with feeding, use of the hands in midline, and rolling.

System: Neuromuscular and Nervous Systems
Content Outline: Interventions

 Level 2

PTEXAM TWO: QUESTION 93

A physical therapist works with a child who walks with an equinus gait pattern. Which of the following interventions would be the MOST appropriate to address the muscle shortening associated with this gait pattern?

1. Side stepping
2. **Backward stepping**
3. Activities in single leg stance
4. Toe walking

Correct Answer: 2 (Long p. 15)

A child who walks with an equinus gait pattern will have exaggerated plantar flexion during the swing phase and decreased heel strike with forefoot contact during stance. This gait pattern is typically a result of a shortened Achilles tendon from muscular imbalance secondary to spasticity or clubfoot. Hamstrings shortening may also be associated with an equinus gait pattern.

1. Side stepping exercises require the patient to abduct and adduct the legs while moving laterally. These exercises will target the hip abductors and adductors, but will not directly address shortening of the plantar flexors.
2. **The goal of intervention is to restore muscle length in the shortened plantar flexors (i.e., gastrocnemius and soleus muscles). Backward stepping elongates the plantar flexors, along with the hamstrings, which are also typically shortened in children who walk with an equinus gait pattern.**
3. Activities in single leg stance will address standing balance, but do not address lengthening of the plantar flexors.
4. Toe walking is an activity that can be useful to strengthen the plantar flexors or challenge dynamic standing balance, however, it will produce further shortening of the gastrocnemius and soleus muscles.

System: Neuromuscular and Nervous Systems
Content Outline: Interventions

Level 2

PTEXAM TWO: QUESTION 94

A physical therapist reviews the medical record of a patient with a suspected head injury. During testing using the Glasgow Coma Scale, the patient exhibited spontaneous eye opening, was able to follow selected motor commands, and was considered to be "oriented" based on verbal responses. What score should the therapist assign to this patient?

1. 6
2. 12
3. **15**
4. 18

Correct Answer: 3 (O'Sullivan p. 822)

The Glasgow Coma Scale is a neurological assessment tool used initially after injury to determine arousal and cerebral cortex function. The assessment tool utilizes an ordinal scale ranging from 3-15 with a higher score representing a greater level of consciousness. The Glasgow Coma Scale examines eye opening, motor response, and verbal response. The scale was initially used to assess level of consciousness after head injury and is often used on selected patients in acute care or following trauma.

1. A score of 8 or less is indicative of a severe head injury.
2. A score of 9-12 is indicative of a moderate head injury.
3. **A score of 15 is the highest attainable score on the Glasgow Coma Scale. In this scenario, the observed patient response warranted the highest score in each area (i.e., eye opening, motor, verbal). A score of 13-15 is indicative of a mild head injury.**
4. A score of 18 is not possible on the Glasgow Coma Scale since the maximum score is 15.

System: Neuromuscular and Nervous Systems
Content Outline: Physical Therapy Examination

Level 1  p. 304

PTEXAM TWO: QUESTION 95

A physical therapist assesses the end-feel of plantar flexion range of motion. The therapist classifies the end-feel as firm. Which of the following structures does NOT contribute to the firm end-feel?

1. Tension in the anterior joint capsule
2. Tension in the tibialis anterior
3. Tension in the anterior talofibular ligament
4. **Tension in the calcaneofibular ligament**

Correct Answer: 4 (Norkin p. 356)

End-feel refers to the type of resistance that is felt when passively moving a joint through the end range of motion.

1. The anterior joint capsule experiences increased tension with passive plantar flexion range of motion which contributes to a firm end-feel.
2. The tibialis anterior acts to dorsiflex the ankle joint and invert the foot. As a result, the muscle would experience increased tension while lengthening during passive plantar flexion range of motion.
3. The anterior talofibular ligament resists movement into plantar flexion and inversion. The ligament would therefore experience increased tension during passive plantar flexion range of motion.
4. **Tension in the calcaneofibular ligament is often associated with the normal end-feel of dorsiflexion (i.e., firm). Other structures contributing to an end-feel associated with dorsiflexion include the posterior joint capsule, soleus, Achilles tendon, posterior portion of the deltoid ligament, and the posterior talofibular ligament.**

System: Musculoskeletal System
Content Outline: Physical Therapy Examination

 Level 2  p. 64-65, 79

PTEXAM TWO: QUESTION 96

A physical therapist prepares to use phonophoresis as a component of a patient's plan of care, but is concerned about the potential of the ultrasound to exacerbate the patient's current inflammation. Which of the following methods would be the MOST effective to address the therapist's concerns?

1. Utilize ultrasound with a frequency of 1 MHz
2. Limit treatment time to five minutes
3. **Incorporate a pulsed 20% duty cycle**
4. Select an ultrasound intensity less than 1.5 W/cm^2

Correct Answer: 3 (Cameron p. 184) 

Physical therapists must select ultrasound treatment parameters that are consistent with the desired therapeutic outcome. Failure to select appropriate parameters can lead to poor outcomes and potentially jeopardize patient safety.

1. The frequency of ultrasound selected primarily determines the depth of penetration. A frequency setting of 1 MHz is used for heating of deeper tissues (up to five centimeters).
2. Limiting the treatment time to five minutes does effectively control the duration of ultrasound, but it does not address several other critical factors that significantly influence changes in tissue temperature (e.g., duty cycle, intensity).
3. **When ultrasound is used in a pulsed mode with a 20% or lower duty cycle, the heat produced during the on time of the cycle is dispersed during the off time and as a result there is no measurable net increase in temperature. Ultrasound using a 20% or lower duty cycle would typically be used for nonthermal effects.**
4. Limiting the intensity of ultrasound to less than 1.5 W/cm^2 is helpful to avoid exacerbating the patient's current inflammation, however, the patient's condition could still be exacerbated at many intensity levels below 1.5 W/cm^2.

System: Non-Systems
Content Outline: Equipment, Devices, and Technologies; Therapeutic Modalities

 Level 2  p. 710-713

PTEXAM TWO: QUESTION 97

A physical therapist records a patient's resting blood pressure as 115/75 mm Hg prior to initiating running activities on a treadmill. After five minutes of running at speeds ranging from 4.0-6.0 miles per hour, what diastolic blood pressure value would be MOST anticipated?

1. 64 mm Hg
2. **76 mm Hg**
3. 84 mm Hg
4. 98 mm Hg

Correct Answer: 2 (ACSM – Resource Manual p. 500)

The normal blood pressure response to exercise is a progressive increase in systolic blood pressure with increasing workload, while the diastolic blood pressure remains relatively unchanged.

1. A diastolic blood pressure value of 64 mm Hg is 11 mm Hg below the patient's resting diastolic blood pressure value. This significant change in the diastolic blood pressure would require the exercise to be terminated.
2. **A diastolic blood pressure value of 76 mm Hg is 1 mm Hg above the patient's resting diastolic blood pressure value. This change would be very consistent with the anticipated diastolic blood pressure response to exercise.**
3. A diastolic blood pressure value of 84 mm Hg is 9 mm Hg above the patient's resting diastolic blood pressure value. This significant change in the diastolic blood pressure is excessive and would require careful monitoring and potentially termination of the exercise.
4. A diastolic blood pressure value of 98 mm Hg is 23 mm Hg above the patient's resting diastolic blood pressure value. This drastic change in the diastolic blood pressure would require the exercise to be terminated.

System: Cardiovascular and Pulmonary Systems
Content Outline: Interventions

Level 2 p. 435-436

PTEXAM TWO: QUESTION 98

A physical therapist performs a muscle length test for the long head of the triceps. Which of the following findings is the MOST consistent with shortening of this muscle?

1. Limitation of elbow flexion with the shoulder maintained at the end range of extension
2. Limitation of elbow extension with the shoulder maintained at the end range of extension
3. Limitation of elbow extension with the shoulder maintained at the end range of flexion
4. **Limitation of elbow flexion with the shoulder maintained at the end range of flexion**

Correct Answer: 4 (Kisner p. 115)

Muscle length testing involves elongating the muscle in the direction opposite of its actions while assessing resistance to passive movement. Although all three heads of the triceps extend the elbow, the long head originates from the infraglenoid tubercle of the scapula and extends the shoulder as well.

1. Although assessing elbow flexion is appropriate for muscle length testing of the triceps, placing the shoulder at the end range of extension would give slack to the long head of the triceps.
2. A limitation of elbow extension with the shoulder maintained at the end range of extension would be a sign of shortening of the biceps brachii, especially if the forearm is maintained in a pronated position, since the biceps muscle is also a supinator.
3. Although assessing the end range of shoulder flexion is part of muscle length testing for the long head of the triceps, elbow extension places this muscle on slack.
4. **A limitation of elbow flexion while the shoulder is maintained at the end range of flexion is indicative of shortening of the long head of the triceps.**

System: Musculoskeletal System
Content Outline: Physical Therapy Examination

Level 2

p. 116-117

PTEXAM TWO: QUESTION 99

A physical therapist reads in the medical record that a patient has an indurated ulcer on their lower leg. Which method was MOST likely used to identify the induration?

1. Diagnostic imaging
2. Measurement
3. Observation
4. **Palpation**

Correct Answer: 4 (Sussman p. 85) 

Induration refers to an abnormal firmness or hardening of the skin which is typically indicative of pathology. Induration is often due to increased exudate or fibrous tissue in an area near a wound.

1. Diagnostic imaging techniques used with wounds may include x-ray, computed tomography, magnetic resonance imaging, and ultrasonography. Goals of diagnostic imaging may include identifying underlying osseous abnormalities, determining proximity of a wound to hardware or identifying arterial occlusive disease. Diagnostic imaging would not be necessary to identify induration.
2. There are a variety of measurements that can occur with wounds. This includes determining the relative surface area affected by a wound or performing circumferential measurements of an affected body part. Conducting formal measurements would not be necessary in order to identify induration.
3. Observation is routinely used to gather specific information on an ulcer. Items gathered through this process may assist with ulcer staging (e.g., tissue depth, color) and developing an effective plan of care. Observation would be helpful to identify an indurated ulcer, but would not be as critical as palpation.
4. **The key defining characteristic of an indurated ulcer is abnormal firmness or hardening of the skin. Palpation is the most definitive way to assess these wound attributes.**

System: Other Systems
Content Outline: Physical Therapy Examination

PTEXAM TWO: QUESTION 100

A physical therapist attempts to strengthen the lumbricals on a patient who has a low metatarsal arch. Which of the following exercises would be the MOST appropriate?

1. Resisted extension of the metatarsophalangeal joint
2. **Resisted flexion of the metatarsophalangeal joint**
3. Resisted abduction of the metatarsophalangeal joint
4. Resisted adduction of the metatarsophalangeal joint

Correct Answer: 2 (Kendall p. 404) 

The lumbricals act to flex the metatarsophalangeal joints and assist in extension of the interphalangeal joints of the second through fifth digits. The lumbricals are innervated by the tibial nerve.

1. The extensor digitorum longus extends the metatarsophalangeal joints of the second through fifth digits. The extensor digitorum brevis extends the metatarsophalangeal joints of the first through fourth digits.
2. **Resisted flexion of the metatarsophalangeal joint can be used to strengthen the lumbricals. This can be performed with manual resistance or by gathering a towel or another similar object placed on the floor.**
3. The dorsal interossei abduct the second through fourth digits from the axial line through the second digit and assist in flexion of the metatarsophalangeal joints.
4. The plantar interossei adduct the third, fourth, and fifth digits toward the axial line through the second digit and assist in flexion of the metatarsophalangeal joints.

System: Musculoskeletal System
Content Outline: Interventions

PTEXAM TWO: QUESTION 101

A physical therapist designs an exercise program for a patient who is three weeks post cardiac transplantation. Which of the following treatment modifications would be the MOST essential to incorporate into the patient's exercise program based on the transplantation?

1. **Increased warm-up and cool down period**
2. Increased duration of training sessions
3. Increased target heart rate range during exercise
4. Increased monitoring of exercise intensity through heart rate

Correct Answer: 1 (ACSM – Resource Manual p. 629)

The surgical procedure required for cardiac transplantation results in several relevant anatomical and physiological changes that must be carefully considered when designing an exercise program.

1. **A patient with a cardiac transplant would require an increased warm-up and cool down period. For several months after the transplant, the transplanted heart fails to respond normally to sympathetic nervous stimulation. Specifically, the heart rate response to exercise and recovery is delayed, thus requiring the increased warm-up and cool down periods.**
2. A patient with a cardiac transplant would likely be required to have shorter duration training sessions initially due to their general health status. The training sessions would progressively increase based on the patient's exercise tolerance and general medical status.
3. A patient with a cardiac transplant would likely be required to exercise at a decreased target heart rate range. In addition, the abnormal heart rate response following cardiac transplantation makes this measure somewhat less valid as a means of quantifying exercise intensity.
4. Monitoring of exercise intensity is important following cardiac transplantation, however, heart rate is often a less desirable method than perceived exertion due to the abnormal heart rate response to exercise.

System: Cardiovascular and Pulmonary Systems
Content Outline: Interventions

 Level 2

PTEXAM TWO: QUESTION 102

During a patient interview, the physical therapist becomes concerned that a patient might be contemplating suicide based on several verbal statements. The patient was recently prescribed a new medication to treat depression. Which of the following actions would be the MOST appropriate initial step by the therapist?

1. Remind the patient it normally takes a period of time for this type of medication to be helpful
2. Use the impact suicide would have on the patient's family as a deterrent
3. Recommend the patient make an appointment to return to the physician
4. **Ask questions to determine if the patient is considering suicide**

Correct Answer: 4 (Goodman - Pathology p. 116)

Healthcare professionals treat people, not diagnoses, and therefore greater attention is placed on concepts of whole systems healing and integrative care along with prevention. Side effects of antidepressant agents are common and may affect multiple systems. All suicidal thoughts must be taken seriously and responded to appropriately.

1. Although it is true that most drugs used to treat depression take a period of time before reaching a therapeutic dose and elevating mood, reminding the patient of this does not address the therapist's immediate concern for the patient's safety.
2. The temptation to offer reasons for living to the patient or using the impact this might have on the family should be avoided. The patient would benefit most from the therapist conveying without judgement that they care and understand that depression can be treated.
3. Although referral to the physician may certainly be warranted, it is clear that the therapist is concerned that the patient may be contemplating suicide. As a result, the therapist cannot simply rely on the patient making an appointment with the physician. If the option involved the therapist taking a more active role in arranging for a physician visit, this option would be more attractive.
4. **Asking questions to determine if the patient is considering suicide is recommended to determine the seriousness of the concern for suicide. Health professionals should not hesitate to ask whether a person is considering suicide or even if the patient has a plan. The QPR model for suicide prevention involves "Q" (question the person about suicide), "P" (persuade the person to get help), and "R" (refer for help by contacting the individual's physician or making a referral).**

System: Non-Systems
Content Outline: Safety and Protection; Professional Responsibilities; Research

 Level 3  p. 565-567

PTEXAM TWO: QUESTION 103

A physical therapist administers a special test to a patient with suspected hand pathology. The pinch test shown in the image would be used to assess the integrity of which nerve?

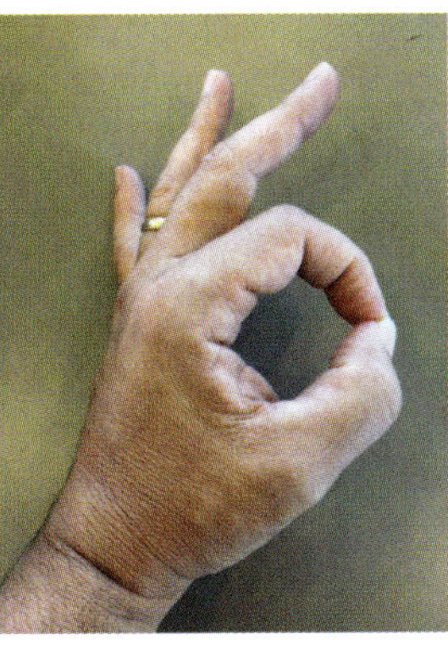

1. Posterior interosseous
2. **Anterior interosseous**
3. Deep radial
4. Ulnar

Correct Answer: 2 (Magee p. 411)

Normal tip-to-tip pinch demonstrates normal function of the anterior interosseous nerve. An abnormal response would be a pad-to-pad pinch due to extension of the distal interphalangeal joint of the index finger and the interphalangeal joint of the thumb.

1. The posterior interosseous nerve is a continuation of the deep branch of the radial nerve after it crosses the supinator muscle. The nerve innervates a majority of the muscles that extend the wrist and hand.
2. **The anterior interosseous nerve is a branch of the median nerve that innervates the deep muscles on the anterior forearm, except the medial half of the flexor digitorum profundus. Inability to maintain tip-to-tip pinch is most likely due to weakness of the flexor pollicis longus.**
3. The radial nerve divides into a superficial and deep branch at the cubital fossa. The deep branch provides motor function to the muscles in the posterior aspect of the forearm, which are primarily the extensor muscles of the wrist and hand.
4. The ulnar nerve innervates the flexor carpi ulnaris and the medial half of the flexor digitorum profundus. The nerve also innervates a large number of muscles acting on the hand.

System: Musculoskeletal System
Content Outline: Physical Therapy Examination

Level 1  p. 104

PTEXAM TWO: QUESTION 104

A physical therapist applies passive overpressure to the spine of a patient with low back pain. The patient reports back and leg symptoms with extension overpressure, however, denies the presence of symptoms with flexion. This finding is **MOST** consistent with which of the following conditions?

1. Lumbar disk lesion
2. Lumbar muscle strain
3. Sacroiliac joint sprain
4. **Spinal stenosis**

Correct Answer: 4 (Nyland p. 121)

Passive overpressure testing provides the physical therapist with information on the integrity of contractile and inert tissue as well as the quality of resistance at end range.

1. A lumbar disk lesion is due to the protrusion of the nucleus pulposus of an intervertebral disk through a weakened area in the annulus fibrosus. Prolapsed tissue from the nucleus pulposus often presses on a nerve root and causes back and leg pain. A lumbar disk lesion is likely to produce back and/or leg pain with flexion overpressure.
2. A lumbar muscle strain occurs when the muscle fibers are abnormally stretched or torn. A lumbar muscle strain is likely to produce back pain with flexion and rotation overpressure.
3. The sacroiliac joint is formed by the sacrum and its connection or articulation to the iliac bones (i.e., pelvis). The sacroiliac joint acts to transfer weight from the spine to the pelvis and allows for a small amount of movement to occur. A sacroiliac joint strain is likely to produce pain with flexion, extension, and rotation overpressure.
4. **Spinal stenosis refers to narrowing of the spinal column that causes pressure on the spinal cord and potentially narrowing of the neural foramina. Patients with spinal stenosis often experience back and leg symptoms with extension overpressure. Flexion overpressure does not typically produce back and leg symptoms.**

System: Musculoskeletal System
Content Outline: Foundations for Evaluation, Differential Diagnosis, and Prognosis

 Level 2  p. 208

PTEXAM TWO: QUESTION 105

While reviewing a patient's medical record that recently underwent total knee arthroplasty, the physical therapist notes that the surgical incision was closed with staples. This form of wound closure is BEST classified as which type of healing by intention?

1. **Primary**
2. Delayed primary
3. Secondary
4. Tertiary

Correct Answer: 1 (Sussman p. 215) 

Healing by intention refers to the method by which a wound heals. Wound characteristics such as etiology, depth, border integrity, and wound bed contamination are typically considered when determining which closure method is most appropriate.

1. **Healing by primary intention is most commonly associated with acute wounds which have minimal associated tissue loss (e.g., surgical wound, laceration, puncture wound). In these wounds, clean edges are reapproximated and closed with sutures, staples or adhesives to facilitate re-epithelialization.**
2. Healing by delayed primary intention is most commonly associated with acute wounds which have minimal associated tissue loss, but are at high risk for developing complications (e.g., infection, dehiscence). These wounds are temporarily left open until risk factors have been alleviated and then are closed by usual primary intention methods.
3. Healing by secondary intention is most commonly associated with wounds which have significant tissue loss, necrosis or borders which cannot be reapproximated (e.g., full-thickness wound, pressure ulcer). These wounds are left open and typically require specialized dressings and ongoing wound care to facilitate healing.
4. Healing by tertiary intention is synonymous with healing by delayed primary intention. Risk factors such as wound bed contamination, infection, and significant local edema increase the risk of healing complications and must be addressed before the wound can be appropriately closed by usual primary intention methods.

System: Other Systems
Content Outline: Foundations for Evaluation, Differential Diagnosis, and Prognosis

 Level 1  p. 500

PTEXAM TWO: QUESTION 106

A physical therapist works with a patient who has been instructed to take non-steroidal anti-inflammatory drugs (NSAIDs) to help control the symptoms of arthritis. The therapist educates the patient that overuse of NSAIDs can result in gastrointestinal damage. This side effect is caused by the inhibition of the production of which hormone?

1. Angiotensin
2. Erythropoietin
3. **Prostaglandins**
4. Gastrin

Correct Answer: 3 (Ciccone p. 224)

The primary side effect of all NSAIDs is gastrointestinal damage. Problems ranging from minor stomach discomfort to gastrointestinal hemorrhage and ulceration are fairly common. Factors such as advanced age, a history of ulcers, use of multiple NSAIDs, and use of other agents (e.g., anticoagulants) appear to increase the risk of gastrointestinal damage.

1. Angiotensin is a hormone involved in the regulation of blood pressure. The release of this hormone causes vasoconstriction, which results in an increase in blood pressure.
2. Erythropoietin is a hormone involved in the production of red blood cells. Under hypoxic conditions, the kidneys will secrete this hormone to increase the production of red blood cells.
3. **Prostaglandins are a group of hormones that help protect the lining of the stomach by inhibiting gastric acid secretion and increasing the production of mucous in the stomach lining. NSAIDs inhibit the production of these protective prostaglandins, which results in the stomach becoming more susceptible to damage from the gastric acids.**
4. Gastrin is a hormone that stimulates the secretion of gastric acid in the stomach. Gastric acid is a fluid composed primarily of hydrochloric acid that aids in the digestion of proteins. If the production of gastrin were inhibited, the result would not be gastrointestinal damage. In fact, there would be less gastrointestinal damage since less gastric acid would be produced.

System: Other Systems
Content Outline: Foundations for Evaluation, Differential Diagnosis, and Prognosis

 Level 2  p. 132

PTEXAM TWO: QUESTION 107

A physical therapist treats a 30-year-old individual who was admitted to the hospital with insidious respiratory issues and small, red granulomas on their face, particularly surrounding the mouth. These clinical findings are typical of which of the following conditions?

1. Systemic sclerosis
2. Bronchiectasis
3. **Sarcoidosis**
4. Phenylketonuria

Correct Answer: 3 (Goodman – Pathology p. 840)

Sarcoidosis is a systemic pathology of unknown etiology. The primary characteristic of the disease is tiny clumps of abnormal tissue (granulomas) that form on certain organs or over certain regions of the body. Granulomas are clusters of immune cells that affect diffuse areas, most commonly the lungs, skin, bones, muscles, and nervous system.

1. Systemic sclerosis, also referred to as scleroderma, is an autoimmune disorder affecting connective tissue that results in fibrosis of the skin, blood vessels, joints, and internal organs. The primary characteristic of the initial stage of the disease is the development of bilateral non-pitting edema that is eventually replaced by a thick, hard skin.
2. Bronchiectasis is a progressive form of obstructive lung disease secondary to a chronic bacterial infection. The chronic inflammatory changes that result from the infection cause irreversible destruction and dilation of the airways. The primary characteristic is a persistent cough along with large amounts of purulent sputum.
3. **Sarcoidosis occurs primarily between the ages of 20 and 40 and has a higher incidence in women than men. It is also more prevalent in African Americans than Caucasians. The impact of sarcoidosis is dependent on the magnitude and region of the granulomas. Prognosis is typically favorable, however, there are some instances where it can be life-threatening.**
4. Phenylketonuria is an autosomal recessive disease that results in a defect in the ability to metabolize the amino acid phenylalanine. If left untreated, manifestations can include intellectual disability, tremors, muscular coordination deficits, and seizures.

System: Other Systems
Content Outline: Foundations for Evaluation, Differential Diagnosis, and Prognosis

 **Level 1** p. 480

PTEXAM TWO: QUESTION 108

A patient attending her third physical therapy session transitions from a hospital bed to standing in preparation for ambulation activities. Which blood pressure response would BEST support the physical therapist's decision to return the patient to a recumbent position?

1. Increase in systolic blood pressure of 18 mm Hg and an increase in diastolic blood pressure of 5 mm Hg
2. **Decrease in systolic blood pressure of 5 mm Hg and a decrease in diastolic blood pressure of 12 mm Hg**
3. Increase in systolic blood pressure of 20 mm Hg and a decrease in diastolic blood pressure of 7 mm Hg
4. Decrease in systolic blood pressure of 13 mm Hg and an increase in diastolic blood pressure of 2 mm Hg

Correct Answer: 2 (Fairchild p. 333) 

Orthostatic hypotension, or postural hypotension, occurs due to a loss of sympathetic control of vasoconstriction in combination with absent or severely reduced muscle tone. This condition commonly occurs in a hospital setting during positional changes due to venous pooling. A decrease in systolic blood pressure greater than 20 mm Hg after moving from a supine position to a sitting or standing position or a decrease in diastolic blood pressure greater than 10 mm Hg is typically indicative of orthostatic hypotension.

1. The increase in systolic (i.e., 18 mm Hg) and diastolic blood pressure (i.e., 5 mm Hg) are not consistent with orthostatic hypotension and would not provide direct support to return the patient to a recumbent position.
2. **The decrease in systolic blood pressure (i.e., 5 mm Hg) is not large enough to be associated with orthostatic hypotension, however, the magnitude of the decrease in diastolic blood pressure (i.e., 12 mm Hg) would provide support for returning the patient to a recumbent position.**
3. The increase in systolic blood pressure (i.e., 20 mm Hg) and decrease in diastolic blood pressure (i.e., 7 mm Hg) are not consistent with orthostatic hypotension and would not provide direct support to return the patient to a recumbent position.
4. A decrease in systolic blood pressure is often precipitated with vertical positioning, however, a decrease of 13 mm Hg is below the 20 mm Hg minimum decrease associated with orthostatic hypotension. The increase in diastolic blood pressure (i.e., 2 mm Hg) is extremely small and would not necessitate any formal action by the therapist.

System: Cardiovascular and Pulmonary Systems
Content Outline: Interventions

 **Level 2**  p. 297, 766

PTEXAM TWO: QUESTION 109

A physical therapist suspects that a patient's chronic lower extremity swelling is due to lymphedema. Which of the following symptoms is the MOST consistent with the later stages of this condition?

1. **Swelling that is relieved by elevation**
2. **Swelling proximal to the site of lymph dysfunction**
3. **Fibrotic changes of the dermis**
4. **Pitting edema**

Correct Answer: 3 (O'Sullivan p. 535)

Lymphedema is a chronic condition characterized by an abnormal accumulation of lymph fluid caused by a mechanical insufficiency of the lymphatic system. Primary lymphedema is caused by a congenital or hereditary condition in which lymph node formation is abnormal. Secondary lymphedema is caused by injury to the lymphatic system (e.g., blockage, dissection, fibrosis).

1. In the early stages of the condition, swelling may be relieved by elevation of the lower extremities. In the later stages, swelling becomes irreversible and is no longer relieved with elevation.
2. Regardless of the stage, lymphedema is characterized by swelling adjacent and distal to the site of lymph dysfunction.
3. **In the later stages of the condition, fibrotic changes occur within the dermal layer of the skin. Fibrosis results in hardening of the limbs which eventually leads to increasing size of the limbs.**
4. Pitting edema is common in the early stages of the condition. However, as fibrotic changes occur in the later stages, the pitting edema evolves into non-pitting edema.

System: Other Systems
Content Outline: Foundations for Evaluation, Differential Diagnosis, and Prognosis

 Level 2  p. 552-555

PTEXAM TWO: QUESTION 110

A physical therapist grades a patient's ankle strength as Good Plus (4+/5) for the dorsiflexors and Fair Plus (3+/5) for the plantar flexors. Assuming that the patient does not compensate for the muscular impairments, which deviation is the therapist MOST likely to observe during the foot flat to midstance phase of gait?

1. **Excessive dorsiflexion**
2. **Foot maintained in plantar flexion**
3. **Inadequate toe off**
4. **Decreased knee flexion**

Correct Answer: 1 (O'Sullivan p. 233)

The gastrocnemius and soleus (i.e., plantar flexors) function concentrically to plantar flex the foot and eccentrically to control dorsiflexion during the gait cycle. Weakness of these muscles can result in a variety of gait deviations.

1. **During the foot flat to midstance phase of gait, the gastrocnemius and soleus function eccentrically to oppose the dorsiflexion moment at the ankle and control the advancement of the tibia. Weakness of these muscles would result in excessive dorsiflexion during this phase of gait, assuming no compensations were made by the patient.**
2. Weakness of the gastrocnemius and soleus would result in excessive dorsiflexion during the stance phase of gait. As a compensation, the patient may attempt to maintain the ankle in a plantar flexed position to avoid the results of the plantar flexor weakness.
3. Weakness of the gastrocnemius and soleus would result in inadequate toe off, however, this would occur during the latter portion of the stance phase, not during the foot flat to midstance phase.
4. The patient would not demonstrate a decrease in knee flexion with weakness of the plantar flexors. The patient would more likely demonstrate an increase in knee flexion due to the lack of control of closed-chain dorsiflexion.

System: Musculoskeletal System
Content Outline: Foundations for Evaluation, Differential Diagnosis, and Prognosis

 Level 2  p. 84-89

PTEXAM TWO: QUESTION 111

A 16-year-old patient walks with a toe-in gait. Which of the following objective findings would MOST likely contribute to this type of gait deviation?

1. 15 degree Q angle
2. 20 degree Q angle
3. **18 degrees of femoral anteversion**
4. 7 degrees of femoral anteversion

Correct Answer: 3 (Magee p. 1013) 

Normal gait most often occurs with the toes pointing forward or slightly outward. A toe-in gait (i.e., pigeon-toed) is most often caused by femoral anteversion, internal tibial torsion or metatarsus adductus.

1. Q angle refers to the degree of angulation present when measuring from the midpatella to the anterior superior iliac spine and to the tibial tubercle. A normal Q angle measured in supine with the knee straight is 13 degrees for a male and 18 degrees for a female. The magnitude of the Q angle does not significantly influence the relative position of the toes.
2. A 20-degree Q angle is slightly more than the average value for a female. An increased Q angle is typically observed in females and is often associated with patellofemoral syndrome. The increased angle alters the quadriceps' line of pull in such a way that the patella tends to track more laterally along the femoral groove.
3. **Femoral anteversion is measured by the angle formed between the femoral neck and femoral condyles. At birth, it is approximately 30 degrees, and decreases to 8-15 degrees by adulthood. A value of 18 degrees of femoral anteversion would be considered excessive and may contribute to a "toe-in" gait.**
4. A value of 7 degrees of femoral anteversion is less than the normal value of 8-15 degrees. As a result, this objective finding would not be associated with a "toe-in" gait.

System: Musculoskeletal System
Content Outline: Physical Therapy Examination

PTEXAM TWO: QUESTION 112

A physical therapist works with a patient diagnosed with congestive heart failure who presents with dyspnea during ambulation. The patient has an ejection fraction of 40 percent. Which of the following interventions would be the MOST appropriate?

1. Instruction in pursed-lip breathing
2. Progressive resistive exercises
3. **Education on energy conservation**
4. Instruction in diaphragmatic breathing

Correct Answer: 3 (O'Sullivan p. 513) 

The ejection fraction is a measure of left ventricular contractility. It is determined by dividing stroke volume by left ventricular end-diastolic volume. Normal ejection fraction is approximately 55-70 percent. Anything less than 55 percent of the blood pumped out of the ventricles with each heartbeat is abnormal and indicates impairment in left ventricular function. Ejection fraction is decreased in patients with left-sided congestive heart failure since the left ventricle is unable to maintain a normal cardiac output.

1. Pursed-lip breathing is a breathing exercise used most often with patients who have chronic obstructive pulmonary disease. The goals of pursed-lip breathing are to reduce respiratory rate, reduce dyspnea, and maintain a small positive pressure in the bronchioles which may help prevent airway collapse. Pursed-lip breathing can be used for any patient with dyspnea, however, it is not the most appropriate intervention for this patient since the underlying cause is not pulmonary.
2. Progressive resistive exercises are not the most appropriate intervention for this patient since resistive exercises do not directly address the patient's dyspnea during ambulation.
3. **The primary goals of treating a patient with congestive heart failure include improving exercise tolerance and increasing knowledge of the disease process. Since the heart is unable to meet the metabolic demands of the body, pacing and energy conservation techniques are necessary for the patient to improve their tolerance for activities of daily living and potentially exercise.**
4. Diaphragmatic breathing is a technique used to improve the patient's ability to enlist the diaphragm for breathing and to minimize the action of the accessory muscles. Diaphragmatic breathing is not the most appropriate intervention for this patient since their dyspnea is not the result of inefficient use of the diaphragm.

System: Cardiovascular and Pulmonary Systems
Content Outline: Interventions

PTEXAM TWO: QUESTION 113

A physical therapist treats a patient who has end-stage renal disease for general deconditioning. Which of the following signs and symptoms would this patient MOST likely demonstrate?

1. **Increased urine output and polycythemia**
2. **Increased urine output and anemia**
3. **Decreased urine output and polycythemia**
4. **Decreased urine output and anemia**

Correct Answer: 4 (Goodman – Differential Diagnosis p. 374)

End-stage renal disease (ESRD), is a state of progressive decline in the kidneys' ability to filter fluids, metabolites, and electrolytes from the body. Individuals with ESRD develop signs and symptoms characteristic of impaired fluid and waste excretion, such as systemic and pulmonary edema.

1. In most cases of renal failure, urine output is significantly decreased or absent. Polycythemia is a condition characterized by an increase in the production of red blood cells. ESRD is more closely associated with a decrease in the production of red blood cells (i.e., anemia).
2. In most cases of renal failure, urine output is significantly decreased or absent. Due to the kidney's role in the production of erythropoietin, a hormone that stimulates the bone marrow to make red blood cells, patients with ESRD often display signs and symptoms of anemia.
3. With renal failure, the kidneys have a reduced ability to adequately filter fluids, therefore, urine output is significantly decreased or absent. However, patients with ESRD are unlikely to have signs and symptoms consistent with polycythemia.
4. **With renal failure, the kidneys have a decreased ability to adequately filter fluids, therefore, urine output is significantly reduced or absent. Due to the kidneys' role in the production of erythropoietin, patients with ESRD often display signs and symptoms of anemia.**

System: Other Systems
Content Outline: Foundations for Evaluation, Differential Diagnosis, and Prognosis

p. 544-545

PTEXAM TWO: QUESTION 114

A physical therapist attempts to determine if a patient with known heart disease is an appropriate candidate for an exercise program. Which of the following findings would MOST likely exclude this patient from participating?

1. **Ejection fraction of 45%**
2. **Uncomplicated myocardial infarction two months ago**
3. **ST segment depression of one millimeter on an electrocardiogram**
4. **Ventricular arrhythmias at rest**

Correct Answer: 4 (O'Sullivan p. 502)

The American Association of Cardiovascular and Pulmonary Rehabilitation (AACVPR) and the American College of Physicians (ACP) have provided a framework for determining a patient's risk of increased morbidity and mortality. Patients are classified as low, moderate or high risk based on a number of factors. These groups have also established guidelines for evaluating patients that are inappropriate for exercise.

1. Normal ejection fraction is between 55% and 70%. A patient with an ejection fraction of 45% would be considered at moderate risk for increased morbidity and mortality. Though this patient may have decreased exercise tolerance due to a reduced ejection fraction, they still would be allowed to engage in an exercise program.
2. A patient with a history of an uncomplicated myocardial infarction and/or cardiac surgery (e.g., angioplasty, coronary artery bypass graft surgery) would be classified as low risk for increased morbidity and mortality. Patients commonly engage in rehabilitation programs following myocardial infarction and therefore would not be excluded from exercise, though they may need increased monitoring by a therapist.
3. A patient with ST segment depression of one millimeter on their electrocardiogram would be classified as moderate risk for increased morbidity and mortality. A patient with marked ST segment depression (i.e., greater than two millimeters) would be classified as high risk. This patient would not be excluded from exercise, though they may need increased monitoring by a therapist.
4. **A patient with ventricular arrhythmias at rest would be classified as high risk for increased morbidity and mortality. Additionally, the AACVPR recommends that patients with uncontrolled arrhythmias be excluded from exercise.**

System: Cardiovascular and Pulmonary Systems
Content Outline: Foundations for Evaluation, Differential Diagnosis, and Prognosis

PTEXAM TWO: QUESTION 115

A physical therapist attempts to implement a formal exercise program for a patient who is three weeks post cardiac transplantation. Which of the following physiologic responses should the therapist MOST anticipate based on the transplantation?

1. **Increased resting heart rate**
2. Increased heart rate response with exercise
3. Increased peak heart rate during exercise
4. Increased age-predicted maximal heart rate

Correct Answer: 1 (ACSM – Resource Manual p. 629)

The medical management of a patient following cardiac transplantation focuses on controlling immune system rejection while minimizing potential side effects. For several months after the transplant, the transplanted heart fails to respond normally to sympathetic nervous stimulation. By one year after surgery, approximately one-third of patients will exhibit a near normal heart rate response to exercise.

1. **The patient would likely experience an increased resting heart rate following cardiac transplantation because of the lack of parasympathetic innervation. The heart rate is usually greater than 80 beats per minute.**
2. The patient would likely experience a decreased heart rate response with exercise following cardiac transplantation. In addition, the initial increase in heart rate that accompanies exercise is often delayed. The abnormal heart rate response makes it necessary to utilize rate of perceived exertion to monitor exercise intensity.
3. The patient would likely experience a decreased peak heart rate during exercise following cardiac transplantation. The peak heart rate in a patient after cardiac transplantation is approximately 150 beats per minute.
4. The patient's age-predicted maximal heart rate is a constant based on their chronological age and therefore would not be influenced by the cardiac transplantation.

System: Cardiovascular and Pulmonary Systems
Content Outline: Physical Therapy Examination

PTEXAM TWO: QUESTION 116

A physical therapist receives a referral for a patient diagnosed with spondylolisthesis. Which of the following scenarios would be MOST consistent with the medical diagnosis?

1. **A 13-year-old female gymnast with no significant medical history**
2. A 17-year-old female tennis player with a 15 degree lateral curvature of the spine
3. A 28-year-old male machinist with a history of recurrent low back pain
4. A 67-year-old male with a previous diagnosis of ankylosing spondylitis

Correct Answer: 1 (Dutton p. 1488)

Spondylolisthesis refers to a condition where one vertebra slips forward on the one below it due to a bilateral fracture of the pars interarticularis. This condition most commonly occurs at L4-L5 or L5-S1.

1. **Children ages 10-15 who are involved in activities such as gymnastics, weight lifting, volleyball, and pole vaulting are particularly susceptible to spondylolisthesis.**
2. Lateral curvature of the spine is indicative of scoliosis and not spondylolisthesis. Scoliosis has many causes including changes in bony structure of the spine (e.g., wedging of a vertebral body), neuromuscular disorders (e.g., cerebral palsy, muscular dystrophy) or an impairment of an extremity (e.g., leg length discrepancy). Scoliosis can also have idiopathic etiology.
3. This patient's age and occupation are not typically consistent with the incidence of spondylolisthesis. The recurrence of the patient's low back pain is more suggestive of a muscular strain than a fracture.
4. Ankylosing spondylitis is a systemic condition that is characterized by inflammation of the spine and larger peripheral joints. The chronic inflammation causes destruction of the ligamentous-osseous junction with subsequent fibrosis and ossification of the area. Men are at a two to three times greater risk than women and onset is typically seen between twenty and forty years of age.

System: Musculoskeletal System
Content Outline: Foundations for Evaluation, Differential Diagnosis, and Prognosis

p. 182-183

PTEXAM TWO: QUESTION 117

A patient diagnosed with Cushing's syndrome is referred to physical therapy. Which of the following signs and symptoms is NOT consistent with this syndrome?

1. Distension of the abdomen
2. Swelling in the facial area
3. **Adrenal hypoplasia**
4. Cardiac hypertrophy

Correct Answer: 3 (Goodman – Pathology p. 500)

Cushing's syndrome is produced by an excess of free circulating cortisol from the adrenal cortex. Physical therapists may be more likely to treat patients who have developed medication-induced Cushing's syndrome, usually after receiving large doses of cortisol or cortisol derivatives.

1. Distention of the abdomen and subsequent central obesity is consistent with Cushing's syndrome. Weakening of the muscles and elastic tissue in combination with abnormal fat distribution results in distention of the abdomen. Thinning of the skin with striae on the breasts, axillary areas, and abdomen are often observed.
2. Swelling in the facial area is a common characteristic of Cushing's syndrome. This condition is often referred to as "moon-shaped face."
3. **Cushing's syndrome is a condition characterized by hyperfunction of the adrenal cortex. Addison's disease is a condition characterized by hypoplasia of the adrenal cortex.**
4. Physiological manifestations of Cushing's syndrome include hypertension caused by potassium depletion, and sodium and water retention. Hypertension can result in left ventricular hypertrophy and increased risk of congestive heart failure or CVA.

System: Other Systems
Content Outline: Foundations for Evaluation, Differential Diagnosis, and Prognosis

 Level 2  p. 527, 645

PTEXAM TWO: QUESTION 118

After palpating a patient's foot and ankle, a physical therapist concludes that the majority of the patient's discomfort is located in an area depicted by the red marking on the image. This type of finding is MOST consistent with which of the following medical conditions?

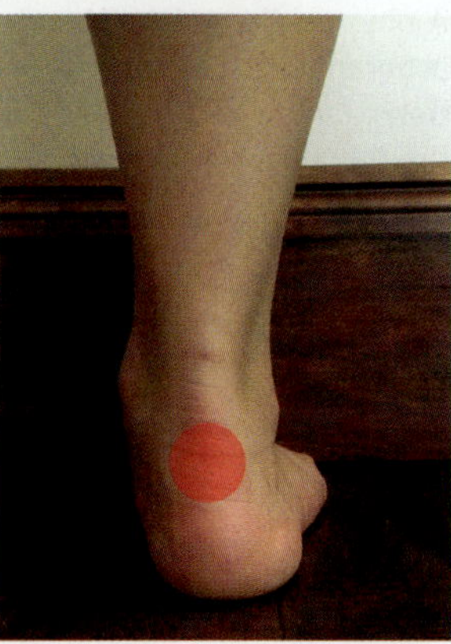

1. Ganglion cyst
2. **Sever's disease**
3. Tarsal tunnel syndrome
4. Plantar fasciitis

Correct Answer: 2 (Dutton p. 1583)

Medical conditions often have several characteristic signs and symptoms that can help distinguish the condition from other similar conditions. Knowledge of this information can assist physical therapists to develop appropriate plans of care and maximize patient outcomes.

1. A ganglion cyst is a benign cyst located on top of a joint or covering of a tendon. Ganglion cysts most commonly occur on the dorsum of the hand at the wrist, however, can also occur on the dorsum of the foot. If pain is present, it is usually caused by motion around a joint impacted by the ganglion cyst.
2. **Sever's disease (i.e., calcaneal apophysitis) is a painful bone disorder that results from inflammation of the growth plate in the heel. The disease most commonly occurs during adolescence and rarely occurs once an individual reaches skeletal maturity. The pain is typically located on the posterior surface of the calcaneus.**
3. Tarsal tunnel syndrome is a compression neuropathy where the tibial nerve is compressed as it travels through the tarsal tunnel, which is located posterior to the medial malleolus. Pain is typically located in and around the ankle region and may extend into the toes.
4. Plantar fasciitis refers to inflammation of the plantar fascia at the proximal insertion on the medial tubercle of the calcaneus. The plantar fascia is a broad structure comprised of connective tissue which spans from the calcaneus to the metatarsal heads. Pain and stiffness are experienced on the bottom of the heel.

System: Musculoskeletal System
Content Outline: Foundations for Evaluation, Differential Diagnosis, and Prognosis

 Level 1

PTEXAM TWO: QUESTION 119

A physical therapist works with a patient who has right hemiplegia post CVA. Which of the following therapeutic positions would be the MOST difficult for this patient to maintain?

1. Half-kneel with involved leg anterior
2. **Half-kneel with involved leg posterior**
3. Bilateral tall kneeling
4. Bilateral lower extremity bridge

Correct Answer: 2 (Sullivan p. 50)

Kneeling and half-kneeling are upright postures where the knees are flexed and the weight bearing occurs through the hips and lower trunk onto the patella tendon and proximal tibia. Half-kneeling also incorporates weight bearing through the anterior foot. Physical therapists must have an understanding of the required base of support as well as the center of mass for each position.

1. Half-kneel with the involved leg anterior provides a base of support that is angled between the anterior flexed leg and the posterior supporting leg. There is some stretch to the one-joint quadriceps in this position, however, the quadriceps are not as inhibited as they are in tall kneeling and can therefore assist the patient to maintain this position. This position is relatively easy to maintain with respect to the other options provided.
2. **Half-kneel with the involved leg posterior is the most difficult position for the patient to maintain since the posterior leg is responsible for increased body weight as compared to tall kneeling. The overall increased stability demands placed on the affected posterior limb provides additional challenge to all of the supporting muscles in order to maintain hip extension and lower trunk control.**
3. Bilateral tall kneeling is an activity that is typically mastered after half-kneeling with the involved leg anterior, but before half-kneeling with the involved leg posterior. The prolonged stretch and maintained pressure on the quadriceps tendons in bilateral tall kneeling will tend to increase the inhibitory influence and limit the effectiveness of the quadriceps. Although the posture is challenging, the ability to assist the involved extremity with the uninvolved extremity in a symmetrical posture makes this slightly less difficult than half-kneel with the involved leg posterior.
4. A bilateral lower extremity bridge would be the easiest activity since there is a large base of support while lying supine on a mat table compared to upright kneeling. The patient also has the ability to utilize the uninvolved lower extremity to assist the weaker extremity. Bridging promotes static and dynamic control in the lower trunk.

System: Neuromuscular and Nervous Systems
Content Outline: Interventions

PTEXAM TWO: QUESTION 120

A physical therapist treats a patient diagnosed with Parkinson's disease. When working on controlled mobility, which of the following activities would BEST describe the therapist's objective?

1. Facilitate postural muscle control
2. **Promote weight shifting and rotational trunk control**
3. Emphasize reciprocal extremity movement
4. Facilitate tone and rigidity

Correct Answer: 2 (Sullivan p. 77)

Controlled mobility refers to the ability to move within a weight bearing position or rotate around a long axis. Controlled mobility is one component of the Stages of Motor Control (mobility, stability, controlled mobility, and skill).

1. Stability refers to the ability to maintain a position or posture through cocontraction and tonic holding around a joint. Unsupported sitting with midline control is an example of stability.
2. **Controlled mobility activities should emphasize weight shifting and trunk control with rotation. This type of activity may serve to decrease rigidity and improve the fluidity of gait in a patient with Parkinson's disease.**
3. A patient must possess prerequisite stability and dynamic postural control in order to perform reciprocal extremity movement. Coordination training often focuses on reciprocal extremity movement.
4. Facilitation techniques are used to increase tone in patients with hypotonia. These techniques are not often used to treat Parkinson's disease since patients with this condition typically exhibit hypertonia or in more severe cases, rigidity.

System: Neuromuscular and Nervous Systems
Content Outline: Interventions

 p. 291

PTEXAM TWO: QUESTION 121

A physical therapist performs a manual muscle test on a patient as shown in the image. This test would be MOST effective to examine the strength of what muscles at the hip?

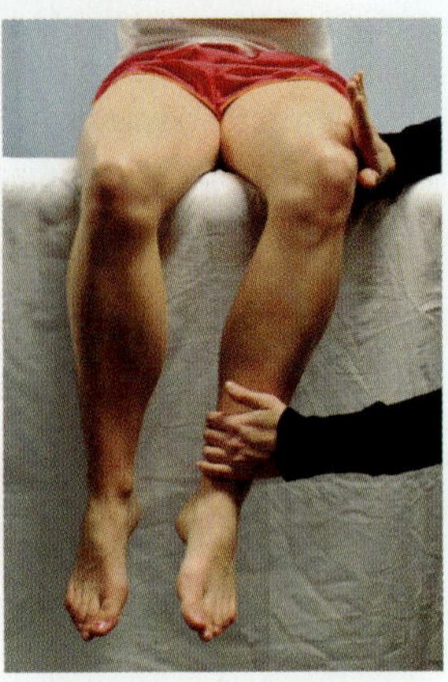

1. **Abductors**
2. **Adductors**
3. **Medial rotators**
4. **Lateral rotators**

Correct Answer: 4 (Kendall p. 430) 

The hip lateral rotators include the gluteus maximus, obturator internus, obturator externus, piriformis, gemelli, and sartorius. Weakness of the lateral rotators usually results in medial rotation of the femur accompanied by pronation of the foot and a tendency toward a valgus position at the knee.

1. The strength of the hip abductors is assessed with the patient in sidelying with the test leg raised. The physical therapist should apply pressure to the distal aspect of the femur, pushing the leg downward in an attempt to adduct the thigh.
2. The strength of the hip adductors is assessed with the patient in sidelying with the test leg closest to the surface adducted. The physical therapist should apply pressure to the distal aspect of the femur, pushing the leg downward in an attempt to abduct the thigh.
3. The strength of the hip medial rotators is assessed with the patient in sitting. The physical therapist should apply pressure to the lateral side of the leg above the ankle, pushing the leg inward in an attempt to rotate the thigh laterally.
4. **The strength of the hip lateral rotators is assessed with the patient in sitting. The physical therapist should apply pressure to the medial side of the leg above the ankle, pushing the leg outward in an attempt to rotate the thigh medially.**

System: Musculoskeletal System
Content Outline: Physical Therapy Examination

 Level 1  p. 80, 82

PTEXAM TWO: QUESTION 122

A physical therapist performs sensation testing on a patient post CVA. During the examination, the therapist identifies significant sensory deficits in the anterolateral spinothalamic system. Which type of sensation should the therapist expect to be the MOST affected?

1. **Barognosis**
2. **Kinesthesia**
3. **Graphesthesia**
4. **Temperature**

Correct Answer: 4 (O'Sullivan p. 87)

Sensory information enters the spinal cord through the dorsal roots and is delivered to higher centers through the spinothalamic system or the dorsal columns. The spinothalamic system is involved with the transmission of nondiscriminative sensations which are activated by mechanoreceptors, thermoreceptors, and nociceptors.

1. Barognosis refers to the recognition of weight. Barognosis is tested by asking a patient to identify the comparative weight of similar sized objects presented in a series. This type of sensory information is transmitted through the dorsal columns.
2. Kinesthesia refers to the ability to identify the direction and extent of movement of a joint or body part. This type of sensory information is transmitted through the dorsal columns.
3. Graphesthesia refers to the ability to recognize symbols, letters or numbers traced on the skin. This type of sensory information is transmitted through the dorsal columns.
4. **Temperature information is transmitted through the spinothalamic system. The system consists of small diameter and relatively slow conducting afferent fibers. Conversely, the dorsal columns consist of large diameter, rapidly conducting afferent fibers.**

System: Neuromuscular and Nervous Systems
Content Outline: Foundations for Evaluation, Differential Diagnosis, and Prognosis

 Level 1  p. 256-257

PTEXAM TWO: QUESTION 123

A 13-year-old girl discusses the possibility of anterior cruciate ligament reconstruction with an orthopedic surgeon. The patient injured her knee while playing soccer and is concerned about the future impact of the injury on her athletic career. Which of the following factors would have the GREATEST influence on her candidacy for surgery?

1. Anthropometric measurements
2. Hamstrings/quadriceps strength ratio
3. **Skeletal maturity**
4. Somatotype

Correct Answer: 3 (Hertling p. 518) 

Physical therapists should possess a general idea of how specific factors such as normal growth and development influence a candidate's eligibility for selected medical and surgical procedures.

1. Common anthropometric measurements used for adults include height, weight, body mass index (BMI), waist-to-hip ratio, and percentage of body fat. These measures are then compared to reference standards to assess items such as weight status and the risk for various diseases.
2. Hamstrings/quadriceps strength ratio is a general measure of the relative strength of the hamstrings compared to the relative strength of the quadriceps. Strength is an important factor both prior to and post surgery, however, it is unlikely that this would influence candidacy for surgery.
3. **Due to the potential impact on future bone growth, lack of skeletal maturity can be a contraindication to anterior cruciate ligament reconstruction surgery.**
4. Somatotype is a term used to classify a system of body typing. The most common classifications of somatotype include endomorph, mesomorph, and ectomorph.

System: Musculoskeletal System
Content Outline: Foundations for Evaluation, Differential Diagnosis, and Prognosis

Level 2

PTEXAM TWO: QUESTION 124

A physical therapist performs reflex testing on a patient with a suspected upper motor neuron lesion. The testing procedure shown in the image would MOST likely assess the status of which of the following nerves?

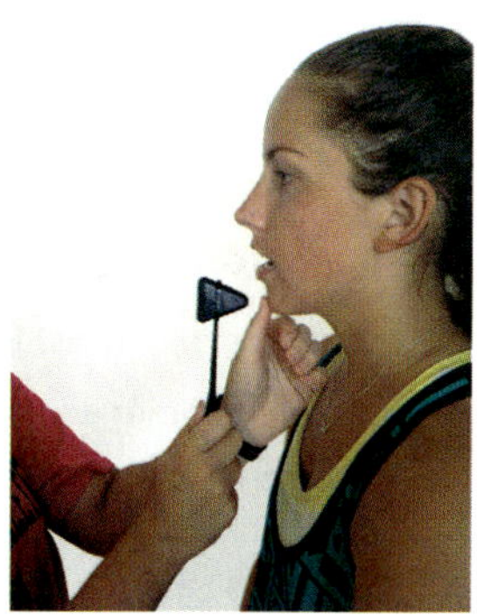

1. Glossopharyngeal
2. Oculomotor
3. **Trigeminal**
4. Trochlear

Correct Answer: 3 (Dutton p. 1366) 

The jaw jerk reflex testing procedure requires the therapist to transmit force with the reflex hammer just below the lips with the mouth slightly open. In most individuals the reflex is absent or very slight, however, in the presence of an upper motor neuron injury the masseter muscles will jerk the mandible upward. The reflex is not standardly assessed as part of a neurologic examination, but can be assessed when there are other signs of damage to the trigeminal nerve.

1. The glossopharyngeal nerve can be assessed by testing the gag reflex. The therapist touches the pharynx with a tongue depressor. A positive test may be indicated by lack of gagging or an inability to feel the tongue depressor touch the back of the throat.
2. The oculomotor nerve can be assessed by asking the patient to follow an object, such as a writing utensil, with their eyes as it is moved vertically, horizontally, and diagonally. A positive test is indicated by an identified tracking deficit, asymmetry or ptosis.
3. **The jaw jerk reflex is a muscle stretch reflex used to assess the trigeminal nerve. Both the sensory and motor components of the reflex are through the trigeminal nerve.**
4. The trochlear nerve can be assessed by asking the patient to follow an object, such as a writing utensil, with their eyes as it is moved in an inferior direction. A positive test is indicated by an inability to depress the eyes and/or complaints of diplopia.

System: Neuromuscular and Nervous Systems
Content Outline: Physical Therapy Examination

Level 1

p. 247-249

PTEXAM TWO: QUESTION 125

A physical therapist treats a patient diagnosed with plantar fasciitis. During the treatment session, the therapist attempts to strengthen the muscles that support the medial longitudinal arch. Which of the following muscles would be MOST important to emphasize in the strengthening program?

1. Gastrocnemius, soleus, and plantaris
2. Fibularis (peroneus) longus and brevis
3. Tibialis anterior and extensor hallucis longus
4. **Tibialis posterior and flexor digitorum longus**

Correct Answer: 4 (Dutton p. 1101)

The plantar fascia is a thin layer of tough connective tissue that supports the arch of the foot. Plantar fasciitis is a chronic overuse condition that develops secondary to repetitive stretching of the plantar fascia through excessive foot pronation during the loading phase of gait. Plantar fasciitis is usually unilateral and often presents with tenderness at the insertion of the plantar fascia, extreme morning pain, and difficulty with prolonged standing.

1. The gastrocnemius, soleus, and plantaris muscles form the superficial posterior compartment of the calf and function to plantar flex the ankle. The gastrocnemius and soleus muscles are more likely to need stretching rather than strengthening since tightness in the Achilles tendon is found in the majority of patients with plantar fasciitis.
2. The fibularis (peroneus) longus and brevis muscles form the lateral compartment of the leg with the tendons lying behind the lateral malleolus. Both muscles function to plantar flex the ankle and evert the foot. Although the fibularis longus crosses underneath the foot, the fibularis brevis inserts into the tuberosity of the fifth metatarsal and does not support the medial arch.
3. The tibialis anterior and extensor hallucis longus, along with the extensor digitorum longus, form the anterior compartment of the leg that collectively functions to dorsiflex the ankle. The extensor hallucis longus extends the big toe. The tibialis anterior and extensor digitorum longus also act to invert the foot. The tibialis anterior does support the medial longitudinal arch, however, the extensor hallucis longus does not.
4. **The tibialis posterior and flexor digitorum longus, along with the flexor hallucis longus, form the deep posterior compartment of the calf. These muscles all provide support to the medial longitudinal arch. Strengthening of these muscles, along with the intrinsic muscles of the foot, is essential in managing plantar fasciitis.**

System: Musculoskeletal System
Content Outline: Foundations for Evaluation, Differential Diagnosis, and Prognosis

Level 1

p. 55, 65, 125, 174-175

PTEXAM TWO: QUESTION 126

A physical therapist designs an exercise program for a patient whose current medical history includes gastroesophageal reflux disease. Which activity would likely be the MOST problematic for the patient?

1. Squatting exercise using a resistance band
2. Walking at 4 to 5 miles per hour on a treadmill
3. Resistive exercise using an upper body ergometer
4. **Strengthening using cuff weights in semi-Fowler's position**

Correct Answer: 4 (Goodman–Pathology p. 871)

Gastroesophageal reflux disease (GERD) is the result of an incompetent lower esophageal sphincter that allows reflux of gastric contents. The backwards movement of stomach acids can cause esophageal tissue injury. GERD symptoms are often increased with bending, stooping or supine positioning and tend to worsen at night. Patients with GERD should sleep on their left side, as this position reduces acid reflux, or elevate the head of the bed if lying in the supine position.

1. Squatting exercise using a resistance band requires the patient to maintain an upright position and therefore should be acceptable for a patient with GERD.
2. Walking at 4 to 5 miles per hour on a treadmill (i.e., fast walking) occurs with the body in an upright position and therefore should be acceptable for a patient with GERD.
3. An upper body ergometer requires a patient to be seated in an upright position. As a result, the upper extremity resistive exercise should be acceptable for a patient with GERD.
4. **Semi-Fowler's position refers to a position in which the head of the patient's bed is raised to an angle between 30 and 45 degrees. Although strengthening exercises using cuff weights would not typically be considered vigorous exercise, the position of the patient (semi-Fowler's) results in the activity being potentially the most problematic of the presented options for a patient with gastroesophageal reflux disease.**

System: Other Systems
Content Outline: Interventions

Level 2

p. 534-535, 647

PTEXAM TWO: QUESTION 127

A physical therapist prepares to initiate an examination procedure by placing a patient in the long sitting position on a mat table. This position would be the MOST appropriate to initiate which of the following tests?

1. Craig's
2. **Dix-Hallpike**
3. Ely's
4. Vertebral artery

Correct Answer: 2 (Goodman – Pathology p. 1644)

Long sitting is a position in which a person sits with the hips flexed to 90 degrees and the knees fully extended on a supporting surface. This position is utilized to initiate the Dix-Hallpike maneuver.

1. Craig's test is performed with the patient in prone and the test knee flexed to 90 degrees. The test is designed to determine the relative amount of femoral anteversion.
2. **Dix-Hallpike test is a diagnostic tool for benign paroxysmal positional vertigo (BPPV). A patient that presents with BPPV will have torsional nystagmus when performing this maneuver. The patient moves from a long sitting position to supine with the head hanging over the surface extended and rotated to 45 degrees. Nystagmus will occur in this position when the affected ear is toward the floor and should fatigue within 60 seconds.**
3. Ely's test is performed with the patient in prone. The therapist passively flexes the patient's knee through the available range of motion. A positive test is indicated by spontaneous hip flexion and may be indicative of a rectus femoris contracture.
4. The vertebral artery test is performed with the patient positioned in supine. The therapist places the patient's head in extension, lateral flexion, and rotation to the ipsilateral side. A positive test is indicated by dizziness, nystagmus, slurred speech or loss of consciousness and may be indicative of compression of the vertebral artery.

System: Neuromuscular and Nervous Systems
Content Outline: Physical Therapy Examination

p. 266

PTEXAM TWO: QUESTION 128

A physical therapist observes a 10-year-old patient attempt to move from the floor to a standing position. During the activity, the patient has to push on their legs with their hands in order to attain an upright position. This finding is MOST commonly associated with which of the following medical conditions?

1. Cystic fibrosis
2. Down syndrome
3. **Duchenne muscular dystrophy**
4. Spinal muscular atrophy

Correct Answer: 3 (Palisano p. 400)

Duchenne muscular dystrophy is a sex-linked disorder characterized by progressive muscular weakness beginning between the ages of two and five. Life expectancy with Duchenne muscular dystrophy is late teens to early twenties due to respiratory or cardiac failure. The described method of standing upright is termed Gowers' sign.

1. Cystic fibrosis is a progressive autosomal recessive genetic disorder of the exocrine glands. The primary findings include pancreatic insufficiency, excessive pulmonary secretions within the lungs, and excessive electrolyte secretion of the sweat glands.
2. Down syndrome (trisomy 21) is a chromosomal disorder that has an increased incidence in children of older parents. A moderate to severe decrease in cognition is typical, however, the mean life expectancy is 50-60 years of age.
3. **Gowers' sign is a descriptive term used to describe a specific method patients with muscular dystrophy often use to assume an upright position. The disease causes mechanical weakening and cell destruction. Pseudohypertrophy of the calf muscles is often the first observed finding, however, all muscles are eventually affected including respiratory and cardiac muscles.**
4. Spinal muscular atrophy is a progressive autosomal recessive genetic disorder characterized by anterior horn cell degeneration, paralysis, and intact cognition. Spinal muscular atrophy–Type 1 (Werdnig-Hoffman disease) has a life expectancy of less than three years while Type 2 has a slower progression and Type 3 (Kugelberg-Welander) has a normal life expectancy.

System: Musculoskeletal System
Content Outline: Foundations for Evaluation, Differential Diagnosis, and Prognosis

p. 313, 334-335

PTEXAM TWO: QUESTION 129

A physical therapist administers the Mini-Mental State Examination to a patient recently admitted to the hospital. What is the MINIMUM patient score necessary in order to avoid being classified as possessing a cognitive impairment?

1. 18
2. **24**
3. 30
4. 34

Correct Answer: 2 (Umphred p. 842)

The Mini-Mental State Examination can be used to screen for cognitive dysfunction or dementia. The 11 question measure assesses five areas of cognitive function: orientation, registration, attention/calculation, recall, and language. The measure takes approximately 5-10 minutes to complete. Possible scores obtained on the Mini-Mental State Examination range from 0-30.

1. A score less than 20 may be associated with dementia, delirium, schizophrenia or an affective disorder.
2. **A score of 24 is the minimum score to avoid being classified as having a cognitive impairment.**
3. A score of 30 is a perfect score and would indicate that the patient is cognitively within normal limits.
4. A score of 34 exceeds the maximum score that can be attained on the Mini-Mental State Examination.

System: Neuromuscular and Nervous Systems
Content Outline: Physical Therapy Examination

Level 1

PTEXAM TWO: QUESTION 130

A physical therapist works with a patient who is post total knee arthroplasty. Which of the following activities would be the MOST appropriate to delegate to a physical therapy aide?

1. Monitoring vital signs
2. Measuring knee range of motion with a goniometer
3. **Observing a patient complete a mat exercise program**
4. Recording modality parameters in the medical record

Correct Answer: 3 (Guide to Physical Therapist Practice)

The physical therapy aide is a non-licensed worker who is specifically trained under the direction and supervision of a physical therapist. Activities performed by the physical therapy aide are limited to those tasks that do not require clinical decision making by the physical therapist.

1. Monitoring vital signs is a skilled activity and therefore would be inappropriate for a physical therapy aide. Failure to accurately monitor vital signs can jeopardize patient safety.
2. Performing goniometric measurements is a skilled activity taught to physical therapists and physical therapist assistants as part of their academic training. A physical therapy aide would therefore not be permitted to perform this type of activity.
3. **Observing a patient complete a mat exercise program could be considered an unskilled activity and therefore appropriate for the physical therapy aide. It would be inappropriate for the physical therapy aide to expand their duties beyond an observational role (i.e., modify, interpret, progress) since this would require clinical decision making.**
4. Physical therapy aides should not make entries in the medical record. Recording parameters associated with a specific intervention should be completed by the physical therapist or in some cases the physical therapist assistant who performed the intervention.

System: Non-Systems
Content Outline: Safety and Protection; Professional Responsibilities; Research

Level 2

p. 784-786

PTEXAM TWO: QUESTION 131

A physical therapist notices a small area of skin irritation under the chin of a patient wearing a Philadelphia collar. The patient reports that the area is not painful, but is becoming increasingly itchy. Which of the following actions is the **MOST** appropriate for the therapist to take?

1. Instruct the patient to apply 1% hydrocortisone cream to the area twice daily
2. Apply powder to the area and instruct the patient to avoid scratching
3. **Provide the patient with a liner to use as a barrier between the skin and the orthosis**
4. Discontinue use of the orthosis until the skin has become less irritated

Correct Answer: 3 (Seymour p. 393) 

Patients can experience itching or skin irritation when using a cervical orthosis. Since an orthosis is applied directly over the skin, it is imperative to utilize a liner that maximizes comfort, promotes cleanliness, limits moisture, and reduces skin irritation. Failure to select an appropriate liner may result in skin breakdown.

1. Hydrocortisone may be used to treat an existing area of irritation, however, it does not address the primary cause of irritation.
2. Powder may assist to temporarily reduce friction over a particular area, but it does not address the primary cause of irritation.
3. **Liners made from lambs' wool are commonly utilized and prevent chafing and irritation of the patient's skin. This liner is easily donned and provides an adequate barrier between the skin and orthosis.**
4. Discontinuing the use of the cervical orthosis would be undesirable since it is prescribed based on medical necessity.

System: Other Systems
Content Outline: Interventions

 Level 3

PTEXAM TWO: QUESTION 132

A patient who has muscle weakness and compromised balance uses a four-point gait pattern with two canes. The physical therapist would like to instruct the patient to ascend and descend the stairs according to the normal flow of traffic. Which of the following methods is the **MOST** appropriate for the therapist to instruct when ascending stairs?

1. **Use the handrail with the right hand and place the two canes in the left hand**
2. Use the handrail with the left hand and place the two canes in the right hand
3. Place one cane in each hand and avoid using the handrail
4. Place the two canes in the left hand and avoid using the handrail

Correct Answer: 1 (Minor p. 405) 

Since the normal flow of traffic assumes ascending on the right and descending on the left, the patient should grasp the railing with the right hand and use the two canes in the left hand when ascending and descending the stairs.

1. **Since the patient does not have unilateral weakness, it is most appropriate to ascend the stairs on the right in order to utilize the handrail and remain consistent with the normal flow of traffic.**
2. Since the normal flow of traffic assumes ascending on the right and descending on the left, the patient would be going against the normal flow of traffic by grasping the handrail with the left hand and using the two canes in the right hand.
3. The patient should use a handrail when available in order to improve stability and balance.
4. Failure to use the handrail would significantly increase the patient's relative risk of falling.

System: Non-Systems
Content Outline: Equipment, Devices, and Technologies; Therapeutic Modalities

 Level 2  p. 692-694

PTEXAM TWO: QUESTION 133

A patient post total hip arthroplasty receives home physical therapy services. The patient is currently full weight bearing and is able to ascend and descend stairs independently. The patient expresses that their goal following rehabilitation is to walk one mile each day. Which of the following actions is the MOST appropriate for the physical therapist to implement to accomplish the patient's goal?

1. Continue home physical therapy services until the patient's goal is attained
2. Refer the patient to an outpatient orthopedic physical therapy clinic
3. **Design a home exercise program that emphasizes progressive ambulation**
4. Recommend admission of the patient to a rehabilitation hospital

Correct Answer: 3 (Guide for Professional Conduct)

The patient's goal of walking one mile each day does not warrant continued physical therapy services. The physical therapist should assist the patient to achieve their individual goals by implementing a home exercise program that includes progressive ambulation.

1. Home physical therapy is warranted for patients that are "homebound." This patient would not qualify for home physical therapy services secondary to their current functional status.
2. Since the patient is now independent in the home and their goal includes ambulating one mile each day, the outpatient orthopedic clinic is not an appropriate setting. The patient can meet their goal independently by following a home program.
3. **The physical therapist can assist the patient with their long-term goal by designing a home exercise program that incorporates ongoing exercise and progressive ambulation activities. This patient would not typically qualify for further physical therapy services.**
4. A rehabilitation hospital is appropriate for patients with functional deficits and acute rehabilitation needs. The patient's current functional status makes the intensity of rehabilitation offered in this setting unnecessary.

System: Musculoskeletal System
Content Outline: Interventions

 Level 3

PTEXAM TWO: QUESTION 134

A physical therapist instructs a patient to perform a stretch as shown in the image. Which muscle is MOST likely stretched when using this technique?

1. **Pectoralis minor**
2. Triceps
3. Middle trapezius
4. Upper trapezius

Correct Answer: 1 (Dutton p. 694)

Physical therapists routinely instruct patients in a variety of self stretching activities. Specific stretching exercises should be prescribed based on the established therapeutic objectives.

1. **The pectoralis minor muscle originates on ribs three to five and inserts on the coracoid process of the scapula. The muscle acts to stabilize the scapula by drawing it inferiorly and anteriorly against the thoracic wall. The pectoralis minor is stretched in a manner similar to the various methods used to stretch the pectoralis major (e.g., corner wall stretch).**
2. The triceps muscle originates on the lateral and medial surface of the humerus and the infraglenoid tubercle of the scapula. The muscle inserts on the olecranon process of the ulna. The triceps muscle acts to extend the elbow and assists in shoulder extension. The triceps can be stretched by placing both arms over the head and bending one elbow so it points toward the ceiling. The patient then grasps the elbow pointing toward the ceiling with the contralateral hand and gently pulls the arm backwards.
3. The middle fibers of the trapezius muscle originate on the spinous processes of the first through fifth thoracic vertebrae and insert on the spine of the scapula. The middle fibers act to adduct the scapula. The middle fibers of the trapezius can be stretched by clasping the hands in front of the body at chest height with the shoulders and upper back rounded forward. The patient should then be instructed to pull the shoulder blades apart.
4. The upper fibers of the trapezius muscle originate from the external occipital protuberance, superior nuchal line, and the ligamentum nuchae. The muscle inserts on the lateral third of the clavicle and acts to assist with scapular elevation. The upper fibers of the trapezius can be stretched by bringing the contralateral arm to the opposite ear and pulling the head towards the contralateral shoulder while keeping the opposite shoulder depressed.

System: Musculoskeletal System
Content Outline: Interventions

 Level 1

PTEXAM TWO: QUESTION 135

A patient requires inpatient physical therapy after sustaining brain damage in a motor vehicle accident. Upon entering the patient's room, the physical therapist finds the patient as shown in the image. Which of the following perceptual deficits is the **MOST** likely cause of the patient's behavior?

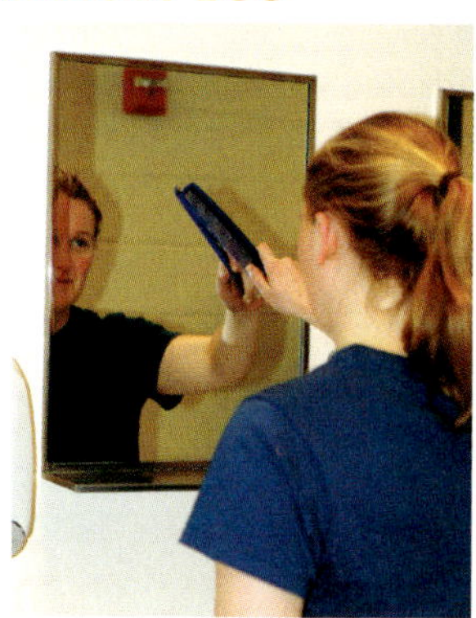

1. Diplopia
2. Apraxia
3. **Somatoagnosia**
4. Anosognosia

Correct Answer: 3 (O'Sullivan p. 1205)

Perception is the integration of sensory impressions into information that is meaningful and that can be interpreted. Perception allows individuals to have awareness of things and experiences in a constantly changing environment. Damage to the central nervous system can produce many forms of perceptual deficits that can significantly influence patient outcomes.

1. Diplopia (i.e., double vision) is a visual deficit where an individual sees two images of the same object. The duplicate image can be seen vertically, horizontally or diagonally in relation to the other image.
2. Apraxia is the inability to perform purposeful learned movements or activities despite the absence of a motor or sensory impairment that would hinder completion of the task.
3. **Somatoagnosia is an impairment of body schema where there is a lack of awareness of a body structure and its relationship to other body parts, to oneself or to others. This patient is attempting to brush their hair, however, does not realize that the mirror image is not the true body part.**
4. Anosognosia is a severe denial or awareness of the presence or severity of one's neurologic defect or illness in general, especially paralysis. Patients may deny that a paretic extremity belongs to them or lie as to the reasons for why an extremity doesn't move as it should.

System: Neuromuscular and Nervous Systems
Content Outline: Foundations for Evaluation, Differential Diagnosis, and Prognosis

Level 2

PTEXAM TWO: QUESTION 136

A physical therapist is treating a patient diagnosed with leukemia who is currently receiving chemotherapy. The patient has been referred to physical therapy to improve their functional mobility and endurance. Which activity would be the **LEAST** desirable to accomplish the stated goal?

1. Yoga
2. Bike riding
3. **Jumping rope**
4. Swimming

Correct Answer: 3 (Palisano p. 394) 

Leukemia is a cancer of the blood that occurs when leukocytes change into malignant cells. These immature cells proliferate, accumulate in bone marrow, and ultimately cease the production of normal cells. This process can spread to the lymph nodes, liver, spleen, and other areas of the body. Treatment will vary based on the type and degree of leukemia, but may include immunotherapy, cytotoxic agents, chemotherapy or radiation, and bone marrow transplant.

1. Yoga is an appropriate low-impact activity that focuses on stretching. Patients undergoing medical treatment for leukemia must work to maintain range of motion and muscle length. Yoga will allow for improvement in range of motion, strength, balance, and cardiovascular endurance.
2. Bike riding is an appropriate endurance activity for a patient undergoing medical treatment for leukemia. This activity will allow for improvement in strength and cardiovascular endurance.
3. **Patients with leukemia are at risk for osteonecrosis, which can occur at the hips, knees, and ankles. Patients may or may not present with symptoms related to osteonecrosis and therefore therapists must be aware of potential risk factors. High-impact activities such as jumping rope should be avoided as an intervention to improve endurance since these types of activities place the patient at risk for further injury.**
4. Swimming is an appropriate low-impact endurance activity that uses buoyancy and the properties of water to minimize weight bearing forces through the lower extremities.

System: Other Systems
Content Outline: Interventions

 Level 3  p. 560

PTEXAM TWO: QUESTION 137

A physical therapist conducts an interview with a patient referred to physical therapy with low back pain. Which subjective statement would BEST support the belief that the pain is of musculoskeletal origin instead of neuromuscular origin?

1. "Physical activity causes pain and tingling in my buttocks and the back of my thighs."
2. "My legs have suddenly become very weak and I have difficulty traversing stairs."
3. **"When I am resting in a comfortable position, my back pain is significantly diminished."**
4. "The pain has not diminished with anti-inflammatories and has become much worse at night."

Correct Answer: 3 (Boissonnault p. 70) 

As part of a comprehensive examination, physical therapists routinely collect information on a patient's past medical history and current condition. This information is helpful when determining if the patient is an appropriate candidate for physical therapy services. It also provides needed guidance when selecting appropriate physical therapy interventions.

1. The statement "physical activity causes pain and tingling in my buttocks and the back of my thighs" is suggestive of pain of neuromuscular origin. Radicular or radiating pain into the lower extremity often occurs along the course of a spinal nerve root.
2. The statement "my legs have suddenly become very weak and I have difficulty traversing stairs" is often suggestive of pain of neuromuscular origin. Pain of musculoskeletal origin tends to have a slower and more predictable onset.
3. **The statement "when I am resting in a comfortable position, my back pain is significantly diminished" is typically associated with pain of musculoskeletal origin. Conversely, pain that is not diminished with a positional change is more likely suggestive of pain of neuromuscular origin.**
4. The statement "the pain has not diminished with anti-inflammatories and has become much worse at night" is suggestive of pain of neuromuscular origin since anti-inflammatories and diminished activity (i.e., at night) both tend to decrease pain of musculoskeletal origin.

System: Musculoskeletal System
Content Outline: Physical Therapy Examination

 Level 3  p. 70-72

PTEXAM TWO: QUESTION 138

A physical therapist discusses the process of learning to drive an adapted van with a patient post spinal cord injury. What is the HIGHEST spinal cord injury level where this activity would be a realistic independent functional outcome?

1. C4
2. **C6**
3. T1
4. T3

Correct Answer: 2 (Umphred p. 473)

A patient with a spinal cord injury would need to have adequate upper extremity active movement to manipulate the hand controls. Prior to driving, an individual would have several unique tests that determine range of motion, strength, vision, and reaction time. The tests are usually performed by a physical therapist, occupational therapist or a certified driving instructor.

1. A patient with a C4 spinal cord injury would not have adequate upper extremity movement to independently manipulate hand controls. The diaphragm and trapezius would be innervated.
2. **A patient with a C6 spinal cord injury would possess the requisite upper extremity movement to drive an adapted van with hand controls and use a lift to get the wheelchair in and out of the vehicle. The extensor carpi radialis, infraspinatus, latissimus dorsi, pectoralis major, pronator teres, serratus anterior, and teres minor would be innervated.**
3. A patient with a T1 spinal cord injury would be able to drive an adapted van. The patient would have full upper extremity innervation including a strong grasp. The option is not the correct response since the question asks the highest spinal cord injury level where driving is a realistic functional outcome.
4. A patient with a T3 spinal cord injury would also be able to drive an adapted van. The patient's clinical presentation would be consistent with the description of the patient at the T1 level.

System: Neuromuscular and Nervous Systems
Content Outline: Foundations for Evaluation, Differential Diagnosis, and Prognosis

 Level 2  p. 298-300

PTEXAM TWO: QUESTION 139

A physical therapist searches the literature to find an appropriate cardiovascular screening test to identify individuals with known cardiovascular disease who should have a medical examination before starting an exercise program. The therapist should choose a screening test that has which of the following characteristics?

1. **High positive predictive value**
2. Low positive predictive value
3. High discriminant validity
4. High internal consistency

Correct Answer: 1 (Portney p. 622)

To be clinically useful, a screening test should be efficient to use and yield accurate responses. The accuracy of the screening test is assessed by its predictive value.

1. **A positive predictive value estimates the probability that a person who tests positive on the screening test actually has the condition the screening test is intended to detect. A test with a high positive predictive value provides a strong estimate of the actual number of patients who have the condition.**
2. A screening test with a low positive predictive value would not be clinically useful as it would not accurately identify individuals with the condition or disease.
3. Discriminant validity is a way to assess the construct validity of a measurement. When measurements that are believed to assess different characteristics are shown to be different, or have a low correlation, then one measurement is said to have discriminant validity with respect to the second measurement. This is not the most important attribute for a screening test.
4. Internal consistency is a form of reliability of a measurement, assessing the degree to which a set of items in an instrument all measure the same trait. This is not the most important attribute for a screening test.

System: Cardiovascular and Pulmonary Systems
Content Outline: Physical Therapy Examination

 Level 1 p. 815

PTEXAM TWO: QUESTION 140

A physical therapist uses repeated contractions to strengthen the quadriceps of a patient who fails to exhibit the desired muscular response throughout a portion of the range of motion. Which of the following methods is the MOST appropriate when applying this proprioceptive neuromuscular facilitation (PNF) technique?

1. Place the extremity into a shortened range within the pattern
2. **Apply at the point where the desired muscular response begins to diminish**
3. Apply at the end of the available range of motion
4. Apply a maximal contraction of the antagonistic muscle group

Correct Answer: 2 (Sullivan p. 71)

Repeated contractions should be applied at the point where the contraction begins to diminish. The technique utilizes an isometric contraction followed by subsequent manual stretching and resisted isotonic movement. Repeated contractions assist with enhancing motor neuron recruitment and strengthening of a muscle or group of muscles.

1. Hold-relax active movement is a technique to improve initiation of movement to muscles tested at 1/5 or less. An isometric contraction is performed once the extremity is passively placed into a shortened range within the pattern. Overflow and facilitation may be used to assist with the contraction. Upon relaxation, the extremity is moved into a lengthened position with a quick stretch. The patient then returns the extremity to the shortened position through an isotonic contraction.
2. **Repeated contractions, alternating isometrics, resisted progression, and timing for emphasis are all examples of PNF techniques that are applied with the goal and purpose of increasing strength.**
3. Hold-relax is a technique that applies an isometric contraction at the end of available range to increase range of motion. The contraction is facilitated for all muscle groups at the limiting point in the range. Relaxation occurs and the extremity moves through the newly acquired range to the next point of limitation until there are no further gains in range of motion.
4. Contract-relax is a technique that applies a maximal contraction of the antagonistic muscle group as the extremity reaches the point of limitation. The therapist resists movement for eight to ten seconds with relaxation to follow. The technique is repeated until there are no further gains in range of motion.

System: Neuromuscular and Nervous Systems
Content Outline: Interventions

  p. 291-292

PTEXAM TWO: QUESTION 141

During palpation, a physical therapist determines that the spine of a patient's scapula is level with the spinous process of T2. Which postural deformity is MOST likely to be associated with this clinical finding?

1. Forward head
2. **Shoulder elevation**
3. Rounded shoulders
4. Scapular winging

Correct Answer: 2 (Dutton p. 604)

Palpation can be used to determine postural abnormalities. The spine of the scapula typically aligns with the spinous process of the T3 vertebra. Variation from the ideal position can indicate muscle imbalances that often correlate with postural abnormalities.

1. Forward head posture is characterized by lengthening of the neck flexors and shortening of the neck extensors, resulting in anterior displacement of the head relative to the shoulders. Forward head posture is not likely to cause significant elevation of the scapula from its normal position.
2. **Shoulder elevation is characterized by a shortening of muscles that cause the scapula to elevate, including the upper trapezius and levator scapulae. Elevation of the scapula commonly results in the spine of the scapula appearing to be level with a spinous process above its normal position at T3.**
3. Palpation of an individual demonstrating a rounded shoulder postural deformity is more likely to reveal scapular protraction. This movement is not likely to cause the spine of the scapula to move cranially.
4. Scapular winging, characterized by the inability to maintain the scapula against the thorax, is more consistent with impairment of the long thoracic nerve or weakness of the serratus anterior muscle. Palpation of an individual with this condition would reveal that although the spine of the scapula is still level with T3, the medial border of the scapula is lifted off of the thorax.

System: Musculoskeletal System
Content Outline: Physical Therapy Examination

Level 2

p. 75-77

PTEXAM TWO: QUESTION 142

A patient with several motor and sensory abnormalities exhibits signs of autonomic nervous system dysfunction. Which of the following physiological responses is a parasympathetic response, rather than an indicator of increased sympathetic involvement?

1. Anxiety, distractibility
2. Mottled, cold, shiny skin
3. **Constriction of the pupils**
4. Rapid, shallow breathing

Correct Answer: 3 (Sullivan p. 60)

The autonomic nervous system (sympathetic and parasympathetic divisions) function together to maintain homeostasis. The sympathetic division prepares the body for stressful situations using the "fight or flight" response. The parasympathetic division ("rest and digest") controls body processes during ordinary situations.

1. Anxiety and distractibility are characteristics seen with an increase in sympathetic activity. Increased sweating, abnormal circulation, a lowered pain threshold, and heightened reflex activity are additional characteristics of a sympathetic response.
2. Skin that appears mottled and shiny is indicative of an increase in sympathetic activity. Other characteristics include hypersensitivity to touch, a rapid heart rate, dilation of the lungs, and increased muscle tension and strength.
3. **Constriction of the pupils is characteristic of a parasympathetic response. The parasympathetic division will also decrease heart rate, stimulate digestion, constrict the lungs, and stimulate other internal organs.**
4. Rapid and shallow breathing is a characteristic of increased sympathetic activity. Treatment techniques to decrease sympathetic stimulation include maintained touch, massage, rocking, deep breathing, generalized warmth, and midline pressure.

System: Other Systems
Content Outline: Foundations for Evaluation, Differential Diagnosis, and Prognosis

Level 1

p. 234

PTEXAM TWO: QUESTION 143

A physical therapist works with a patient who has right hemiparesis post stroke. As the patient lies in the supine position on the mat, the therapist applies resistance to right elbow flexion and notes mass flexion of the right lower extremity as the resistance is applied. The therapist should document this response as which of the following associated reactions?

1. Raimiste's phenomenon
2. Souques' phenomenon
3. Coordination synkinesis
4. **Homolateral synkinesis**

Correct Answer: 4 (Sullivan p. 25)

Homolateral synkinesis is an associated reaction that can occur after neurological damage. Resistance to flexion of the involved upper extremity will cause flexion in the involved lower extremity.

1. Raimiste's phenomenon occurs when the involved lower extremity abducts or adducts with applied resistance to the uninvolved lower extremity in the same direction.
2. Souques' phenomenon is observed when a patient raises the involved upper extremity above 100 degrees with the elbow extended. This action produces extension and abduction of the involved fingers.
3. Coordination synkinesis refers to voluntary contraction of certain muscle groups on the involved side that, in turn, gives rise to involuntary contractions of synergistic muscles.
4. **Homolateral synkinesis is a condition often associated with hemiplegia where there is mutual dependency between the involved upper and lower extremities. Certain theories of neurological rehabilitation avoid utilizing associated reactions while other theories utilize them to increase movement.**

System: Neuromuscular and Nervous Systems
Content Outline: Interventions

 Level 1  p. 287

PTEXAM TWO: QUESTION 144

A child with a unilateral hip disarticulation using a prosthesis works on advanced gait training activities. Which of the following activities would be the **MOST** difficult for the patient to perform?

1. Rising from a wheelchair
2. Ascending stairs with a handrail
3. Descending stairs with a handrail
4. **Ascending a curb**

Correct Answer: 4 (Seymour p. 256)

Patients with amputations experience greater energy use when completing functional skills. The higher the level of amputation, the greater the metabolic demand will be for a given activity. A hip disarticulation refers to the surgical removal of the lower extremity from the pelvis.

1. Rising from a wheelchair is performed with double leg support allowing for use of the arm rests to provide assistance with upward movement during the transfer. This requires less energy expenditure than ascending a curb.
2. Ascending stairs with a handrail is a challenging activity for a patient with a hip disarticulation, however, the presence of a handrail likely provides the patient with the necessary balance and stability to complete the activity.
3. Descending stairs with a handrail is typically slightly less difficult for a patient with a hip disarticulation compared to ascending stairs since the patient does not need to overcome the force of gravity.
4. **A child with a hip disarticulation would have the greatest difficulty ascending a curb during prosthetic training since there are no external supports (handrails) to assist with the activity.**

System: Musculoskeletal System
Content Outline: Foundations for Evaluation, Differential Diagnosis, and Prognosis

 Level 2

PTEXAM TWO: QUESTION 145

A physical therapist assesses a patient who has significant biceps brachii weakness and suspects there may be underlying neurological damage that is causing the weakness. Damage to what cord of the brachial plexus would MOST likely explain this finding?

1. **Lateral**
2. Posterior
3. Medial
4. Anterior

Correct Answer: 1 (Magee p. 23)

The brachial plexus is a grouping of nerves that originate from the C5-T1 nerve roots. The nerve roots merge to form trunks, which then divide again (divisions), and merge once more (cords). There are three cords (lateral, posterior, medial) that eventually branch off to become the peripheral nerves.

1. **The lateral cord branches off to become the musculocutaneous nerve, median nerve, and lateral pectoral nerve. The musculocutaneous nerve innervates the muscles of the anterior upper arm, including the biceps brachii.**
2. The posterior cord branches off to become the axillary nerve, radial nerve, thoracodorsal nerve, and upper and lower subscapular nerves.
3. The medial cord branches off to become the ulnar nerve, median nerve, and medial pectoral nerve.
4. There is no anterior cord, though there are anterior divisions that branch off of each of the trunks (upper, middle, lower).

System: Neuromuscular and Nervous Systems
Content Outline: Physical Therapy Examination

p. 250

PTEXAM TWO: QUESTION 146

A patient rehabilitating from extensive burns to the right upper extremity often reports severe pain in the arm during physical therapy treatment sessions. The present plan of care emphasizes range of motion, stretching, and positioning. Which of the following actions is the MOST appropriate to address the patient's pain intensity?

1. Reduce the frequency and duration of the treatment sessions
2. **Schedule treatment sessions when the patient's pain medication is most effective**
3. Avoid treatment activities that are uncomfortable for the patient
4. Request that the referring physician increase the dosage of the patient's pain medication

Correct Answer: 2 (Paz p. 295) 

Rehabilitation following a burn is extremely painful. Scheduling therapy to coincide with the maximum benefit from pain medication is a high priority. The reduction of pain level will allow for progression with the established plan of care.

1. Reducing the frequency and duration of treatment will not allow for adequate intervention and burn care. Patient participation may decrease as well secondary to pain if they are not treated in coordination with the pain medication schedule.
2. **A patient should receive the optimal benefit of pain medication during their scheduled therapy session. Greater tolerance may allow the patient to make more rapid progress in therapy.**
3. Patients with burns will likely have discomfort with all activities and treatments. Avoiding certain treatments (e.g., stretching) would be negligent.
4. The physician is responsible for prescribing the correct amount of medication. Increasing the dosage of the pain medication may not benefit the patient if physical therapy is not performed at an appropriate time.

System: Other Systems
Content Outline: Interventions

PTEXAM TWO: QUESTION 147

A physical therapist conducts an examination on a patient with suspected ulnar nerve palsy. Which finding is the **MOST** consistent with the hypothesized diagnosis?

1. **Wasting of the hypothenar eminence**
2. Wrist drop with increased flexion of the wrist
3. Increased flexion of the metacarpophalangeal joint
4. Proximal interphalangeal joint hyperextension and slight flexion of the distal interphalangeal joint

Correct Answer: 1 (Dutton p. 809) 

Nerve palsy is a term used to describe a range of nervous disorders resulting in weakness or immobility of a nerve. In some cases, the palsy is only temporary and will dissipate with time, however, in other cases, the palsy may be permanent.

1. **The hypothenar eminence consists of the opponens digiti minimi, flexor digiti minimi, and abductor digiti minimi. These muscles are innervated by the ulnar nerve. An ulnar nerve palsy would result in diminished activity in the hypothenar muscles resulting in atrophy.**
2. Wrist drop with increased flexion of the wrist is more characteristic of a radial nerve palsy. The radial nerve innervates the majority of muscles acting to extend the wrist including the extensor carpi radialis longus, extensor carpi radialis brevis, and extensor digitorum.
3. The interossei muscles assist to flex the metacarpophalangeal joint and are innervated by the deep branch of the ulnar nerve. An ulnar nerve palsy would be unlikely to result in increased flexion of the metacarpophalangeal joint since the muscles would be adversely affected by the nerve palsy.
4. Proximal interphalangeal joint hyperextension and slight flexion of the distal interphalangeal joint are often associated with a rupture of the flexor digitorum superficialis. The muscle's primary action is to flex the proximal interphalangeal joint. A rupture of the flexor digitorum superficialis would tend to result in the proximal interphalangeal joint being positioned in extension.

System: Neuromuscular and Nervous Systems
Content Outline: Foundations for Evaluation, Differential Diagnosis, and Prognosis

 Level 1  p. 250, 261

PTEXAM TWO: QUESTION 148

A physical therapist instructs a patient to perform a standing stretch as shown in the image. This type of stretch would **MOST** likely be used to stretch which of the following tissues?

1. Horizontal abductors
2. **Inferior capsule**
3. Pectoralis major
4. Pectoralis minor

Correct Answer: 2 (Dutton p. 694)

Physical therapists routinely instruct patients in a variety of self-stretching activities. Specific stretching exercises should be prescribed based on the established therapeutic objectives.

1. The horizontal abductors would be stretched by moving the arm into horizontal adduction. Horizontal adduction requires the upper arm to move toward the chest in a transverse plane with the shoulder flexed at 90 degrees.
2. **The capsule encompasses the glenohumeral joint and attaches to the scapula, humerus, and head of the biceps. The inferior portion of the capsule is tightened when the arm is raised overhead. A restriction in the inferior capsule often accompanies prolonged periods of immobilization and results in difficulty lifting the arm overhead.**
3. The pectoralis major consists of a sternocostal head and a clavicular head. Collectively, the muscle horizontally adducts and medially rotates the humerus. As a result, the muscle is stretched by placing the arms in horizontal abduction and lateral rotation. An example of a pectoralis major stretch would be a corner wall stretch.
4. The pectoralis minor stabilizes the scapula by drawing it inferiorly and anteriorly against the thoracic wall. The pectoralis minor is stretched in a manner similar to the various methods used to stretch the pectoralis major (e.g., corner wall stretch).

System: Musculoskeletal System
Content Outline: Interventions

 Level 2

PTEXAM TWO: QUESTION 149

A physical therapist observes that a patient is unable to heel walk during a neurological examination. This objective finding may indicate damage to which spinal tract?

1. **Corticospinal**
2. **Reticulospinal**
3. **Rubrospinal**
4. **Tectospinal**

Correct Answer: 1 (O'Sullivan p. 191)

Tracts descending to the spinal cord are involved with voluntary motor function, muscle tone, reflexes and equilibrium, visceral innervation, and modulation of ascending sensory signals.

1. **The corticospinal tract originates from pyramid-shaped cells in the premotor, primary motor, and primary sensory cortices and is involved in skilled voluntary activity. Damage to the corticospinal (pyramidal) tracts results in a positive Babinski sign, absent superficial abdominal and cremasteric reflexes, and the loss of fine motor or skilled voluntary movement. Heel walking is a commonly utilized functional test to identify corticospinal tract involvement.**
2. The reticulospinal tract is an extrapyramidal motor tract responsible for facilitation or inhibition of voluntary and reflex activity through the influence on alpha and gamma motor neurons.
3. The rubrospinal tract is an extrapyramidal motor tract responsible for motor input of gross postural tone, facilitating activity of flexor muscles, and inhibiting activity of extensor muscles.
4. The tectospinal tract is an extrapyramidal motor tract responsible for contralateral postural muscle tone associated with auditory/visual stimuli.

System: Neuromuscular and Nervous Systems
Content Outline: Foundations for Evaluation, Differential Diagnosis, and Prognosis

Level 2

p. 243

PTEXAM TWO: QUESTION 150

A physical therapist works with a patient who has been on bed rest for one month. Which of the following muscle groups should the therapist anticipate being the MOST affected by the prolonged immobilization?

1. **Extensor muscles of the upper extremities**
2. **Flexor muscles of the upper extremities**
3. **Extensor muscles of the lower extremities**
4. **Flexor muscles of the lower extremities**

Correct Answer: 3 (Nyland p. 6)

Disuse or immobilization results in decreased muscle mass and strength within a relatively short period of time. This occurs primarily due to the lack of normal weight bearing forces acting on the bones and a decrease in the magnitude of muscle contractions. Physical therapists should develop plans of care that attempt to minimize the effects of immobilization and disuse for their patients.

1. Extensor muscles generally tend to be more affected by immobilization than flexor muscles, however, the lower extremities tend to be more affected than the upper extremities.
2. Flexor muscles generally tend to be less affected by immobilization than extensor muscles. The lower extremities tend to be more affected by immobilization than the upper extremities.
3. **The lower extremities tend to be more affected by immobilization than the upper extremities. Research has demonstrated that bed rest for 30 days decreases knee extensor strength by 20 percent while knee flexor strength experiences a nonsignificant decrease. The loss of strength is primarily due to a decrease in muscle mass and cross-sectional area.**
4. The lower extremities tend to be more affected by immobilization than the upper extremities, however, the flexor muscles tend to be less affected than the extensor muscles.

System: Musculoskeletal System
Content Outline: Foundations for Evaluation, Differential Diagnosis, and Prognosis

Level 2

PTEXAM TWO: QUESTION 151

A physical therapist examines a patient recently diagnosed with adhesive capsulitis. Based on the patient's subjective reports and examination findings, the therapist believes the patient is in the acute phase of the condition. Which finding tends to be unique to the acute phase of adhesive capsulitis?

1. **The patient's sleep is disrupted by nocturnal pain**
2. Range of motion is limited by muscle weakness
3. Pain complaints progressively decrease
4. The patient demonstrates a capsular pattern of restriction

Correct Answer: 1 (Hertling p. 315)

Complaints of pain and limited glenohumeral mobility are typical of both the acute and chronic phases of adhesive capsulitis. However, variations in the presentation of these characteristics between the different phases are notable and should be recognized by a physical therapist for optimal treatment planning.

1. **Nocturnal pain is one of the initial signs associated with the onset of adhesive capsulitis. Early pain complaints often include disrupted sleep with resultant fatigue, often adding to the patient's sense of debilitation.**
2. Range of motion in the acute phase of adhesive capsulitis is often limited by pain and/or apprehensive muscle guarding and not muscle weakness.
3. The acute phase of adhesive capsulitis is characterized by pain that is usually associated with an insidious onset. Pain symptoms typically begin to subside and localize during the chronic phase of adhesive capsulitis.
4. Range of motion limitations consistent with a capsular pattern are typical of both the acute and chronic phases.

System: Musculoskeletal System
Content Outline: Foundations for Evaluation, Differential Diagnosis, and Prognosis

p. 122, 156-157

PTEXAM TWO: QUESTION 152

A physical therapist completes a series of resistive movements on a patient with a lower extremity injury. The patient denies pain initially, but reports increasing pain after performing a number of repetitions. This scenario is MOST consistent with which of the following conditions?

1. Complete rupture of a tendon
2. **Intermittent claudication**
3. Ligamentous laxity
4. Emotional hypersensitivity

Correct Answer: 2 (Roy p. 153)

Resistive movements attempt to identify the status of contractile tissue (i.e., muscles, tendons, associated attachments) and the nervous tissue supplying the contractile tissue.

1. A complete rupture of a tendon is characterized by significant muscle weakness. The onset of the weakness would be immediate.
2. **Intermittent claudication occurs as a result of insufficient blood supply and ischemia in active muscles. Symptoms most commonly include pain and cramping in muscles distal to the occluded vessel. Pain tends to progressively worsen with increasing activity.**
3. Ligamentous laxity would not significantly influence resistive movements. Ligamentous laxity is more commonly associated with excessive range of motion.
4. Emotional hypersensitivity may result in an exaggerated pain response with all forms of resistive movements. The exaggerated response would typically be evident immediately.

System: Musculoskeletal System
Content Outline: Foundations for Evaluation, Differential Diagnosis, and Prognosis

Level 2

PTEXAM TWO: QUESTION 153

A physical therapist applies a transparent film dressing to a patient's forearm. Which objective finding would MOST warrant the use of this type of dressing?

1. **Bacterial infection**
2. **Fragile skin**
3. **Minimal drainage**
4. **Peri-wound maceration**

Correct Answer: 3 (Sussman p. 504)

Transparent film dressings are thin membranes made from transparent polyurethane with water-resistant adhesives. They are highly elastic, conform to a variety of body contours, and allow easy visual inspection of the wound since they are transparent. Film dressings are useful for superficial or partial-thickness wounds with minimal drainage (e.g., scalds, abrasions, lacerations).

1. A bacterial infection is a contraindication to the use of transparent film dressings. Alginate dressings are an example of a wound dressing that can be used on infected or non-infected wounds.
2. Fragile skin is often a contraindication to the use of transparent film dressings since the adhesive used to secure the dressing may traumatize the peri-wound area upon removal.
3. **Transparent film dressings are used for wounds with minimal to no drainage. This type of dressing is permeable to water vapor but not water, and therefore moderate or heavy drainage will accumulate under the dressing, resulting in maceration and excessive dressing changes.**
4. The presence of peri-wound maceration often makes it undesirable to use transparent film dressings since the affected area is particularly susceptible to damage from the adhesive. In addition, peri-wound maceration may make it difficult to secure the transparent film dressing.

System: Other Systems
Content Outline: Interventions

 Level 2  p. 510

PTEXAM TWO: QUESTION 154

Members of a community health task force evaluate a proposal for a new adolescent screening program. Several members of the task force raise questions as to the validity of the screening instrument. Which measure of validity examines the instrument's ability to identify individuals with a disease by comparing true positives?

1. **Adaptability**
2. **Selectivity**
3. **Sensitivity**
4. **Specificity**

Correct Answer: 3 (Portney p. 620)

The validity of a diagnostic test is evaluated by its ability to accurately assess the presence or absence of the target condition. A diagnostic test can have four possible outcomes: true positive, true negative, false positive, and false negative.

1. Adaptability is the quality of adjusting to new conditions or modifications for new purpose. It is not a measure of the accuracy or validity of a diagnostic or screening test.
2. Selectivity is the ability to discriminate, refine, discern within a given process. It is not a measure of the accuracy or validity of a diagnostic or screening test.
3. **Sensitivity is a measure of the validity of a screening test, based on the probability that the screening test will be positive in someone with the disease or target condition (i.e., true positive).**
4. Specificity is a measure of the validity of a screening test, based on the probability that the screening test will be negative in someone who does not have the disease or target condition (i.e., true negative).

System: Non-Systems
Content Outline: Safety and Protection; Professional Responsibilities; Research

 Level 1  p. 815

PTEXAM TWO: QUESTION 155

A physical therapist attempts to quantify a patient's endurance level by administering a maximal exercise test. What is the PRIMARY limitation of a maximal exercise test?

1. **It requires participants to exercise to the point of volitional fatigue**
2. **It does not typically allow a steady state heart rate at each work rate**
3. **It is not useful in diagnosing coronary artery disease**
4. **It requires progressive stages of increasing work intensities without rest intervals**

Correct Answer: 1 (Frownfelter p. 282)

The decision to use a maximal or submaximal exercise test depends largely on the reasons for the test and the availability of the appropriate equipment and personnel. Maximal exercise testing offers increased sensitivity for diagnosing coronary artery disease in asymptomatic individuals and provides a better estimate of maximum oxygen uptake than a submaximal test.

1. **The primary limitation of a maximal exercise test is that it requires the individual to exercise to the point of volitional fatigue. Some subjects terminate the exercise test due to fatigue or exercise intolerance before reaching their physiological maximum. This reduces the sensitivity of the estimate of maximum oxygen uptake.**
2. Most standardized exercise test protocols have the individual exercise at two or three minute intervals before increasing to a higher workload. This type of design allows the subject to come to a steady state heart rate for each workload before increasing the workload.
3. Maximal exercise testing is used to help diagnose coronary artery disease and offers better sensitivity than submaximal exercise testing.
4. Most standard exercise test protocols are continuous and do not allow formal rest intervals, however, this is not considered the primary limitation of the test.

System: Cardiovascular and Pulmonary Systems
Content Outline: Physical Therapy Examination

Level 2

PTEXAM TWO: QUESTION 156

A physical therapist prepares to complete a sensory examination on a patient who sustained a lower extremity burn. Which of the following factors would serve as the BEST predictor of altered sensation?

1. **Presence of a skin graft**
2. **Depth of burn injury**
3. **Percentage of body surface affected**
4. **Extent of hypertrophic scarring**

Correct Answer: 2 (Sussman p. 405) 

Patients with burns often experience a number of sensory changes. These changes can include impaired sensation or increased sensitivity. Although many factors contribute to sensory alteration, the depth of the burn appears to be the best predictor.

1. Skin grafts are typically used with full-thickness burns and although there is a predictable pattern of sensory alteration with full-thickness burns, the absence of a skin graft would not be useful to predict sensory changes in less severe burns (i.e., superficial and partial-thickness).
2. **It is possible to predict the relative extent of sensory alteration based on the depth of the burn. For example, a superficial partial-thickness burn is characterized by extreme pain and significant sensitivity to temperature change, while a full-thickness burn is characterized by an absence of pain and inability to identify temperature change.**
3. The percentage of body surface affected provides information on the size or extent of the burn, but does not provide information on other important variables such as the depth or severity of the burn.
4. Hypertrophic scarring refers to an overgrowth of dermal constituents that remain within the boundaries of the wound. This occurs as a result of scar formation when the burn extends into the dermis. Hypertrophic scarring results in poor cosmesis and the development of contractures that may limit function. The presence of hypertrophic scarring provides only limited information regarding the extent of altered sensation.

System: Other Systems
Content Outline: Foundations for Evaluation, Differential Diagnosis, and Prognosis

Level 2

p. 513

PTEXAM TWO: QUESTION 157

A physical therapist would like to minimize the likelihood of a burn when using iontophoresis. Which action would be the MOST consistent with the therapist's objective?

1. **Increase the size of the cathode relative to the anode**
2. Decrease the space between the electrodes
3. Increase the current intensity
4. Decrease the moisture of the electrodes

Correct Answer: 1 (Prentice p. 185)

Current density (mA/cm^2) is calculated by taking the current amplitude (mA) and dividing by the surface area (cm^2). Greater current density will result in an increased risk of an electrochemical burn.

1. **Increasing the size of the cathode relative to the anode serves to decrease current density and therefore reduces the probability of a burn when using iontophoresis. The cathode refers to the negatively charged electrode in a direct current system and the anode refers to the positively charged electrode. The accumulation of positively charged ions in a small area creates an alkaline reaction that is more likely to create tissue damage. As a result, it is desirable to increase the size of the cathode.**
2. Decreasing the space between the electrodes decreases the surface area and therefore increases current density resulting in an increased risk of an electrochemical burn.
3. Increasing the current intensity will increase the force and speed of propulsion of the ions and increase ion uptake. The result of this is increased current density and an increased risk of an electrochemical burn.
4. Commercially produced electrodes most commonly used with iontophoresis have a small chamber covered by a semipermeable membrane which houses the ionized solution. This type of electrode eliminates the need to soak a more traditional electrode in water or saline and instead is simply self-adherent.

System: Non-Systems
Content Outline: Equipment, Devices, and Technologies; Therapeutic Modalities

 Level 2 p. 731-733

PTEXAM TWO: QUESTION 158

A physical therapist reviews a patient coverage form that lists the following parameters used during a recent ultrasound treatment: 1.5 W/cm^2, pulsed 20%, 1 MHz, 6 minutes. If the objective of the ultrasound treatment was to increase tissue temperature, what parameter would be the MOST critical for the therapist to alter?

1. Time
2. **Duty cycle**
3. Frequency
4. Intensity

Correct Answer: 2 (Cameron p. 184) 

Physical therapists must select specific parameters when using ultrasound based on the desired physiological effect. Failure to select the correct parameters will minimize the effectiveness of the session and could potentially jeopardize patient safety in extreme cases.

1. The duration of the ultrasound is an important parameter, however, it is typically determined based on the size of the area to be treated and not by the desired increase in tissue temperature.
2. **Duty cycle is defined as the ratio of the on time to the total time. When ultrasound is used in a pulsed mode with a 20% or lower duty cycle, the heat produced during the on time of the cycle is dispersed during the off time and as a result there is no measurable net increase in temperature. To increase tissue temperature it would be necessary to significantly increase the duty cycle or use a continuous mode.**
3. The frequency of ultrasound selected primarily determines the depth of penetration. A frequency setting of 1 MHz is used for heating of deeper tissues (up to five centimeters). A frequency setting of 3 MHz produces a more rapid heating with a depth of penetration of less than two centimeters.
4. Intensity for continuous ultrasound is normally set between 0.5 to 2.0 W/cm^2 for thermal effects. Pulsed ultrasound is normally set between 0.5 to 0.75 W/cm^2 with a 20% duty cycle for nonthermal effects.

System: Non-Systems
Content Outline: Equipment, Devices, and Technologies; Therapeutic Modalities

 Level 2  p. 710-713

PTEXAM TWO: QUESTION 159

A physical therapist attempts to assess the integrity of the vestibulocochlear nerve by administering the Rinne test on a patient. After striking the tine of the tuning fork to begin vibration, what bony prominence should the therapist utilize to position the stem of the tuning fork?

1. Midline of the skull
2. Occipital protuberance
3. Inion
4. **Mastoid process**

Correct Answer: 4 (Magee p. 133)

The Rinne test is designed to compare bone conduction hearing with air conduction hearing. A therapist uses a vibrating tuning fork placed on the mastoid process and then placed next to the ear. Air conducted sound should be approximately twice as long as bone conducted sound.

1. The Weber test is another commonly used hearing test that requires placing a tuning fork on the midline of the skull on the patient's forehead.
2. The occipital protuberance refers to a prominence on the outer surface of the occipital bone.
3. The inion refers to the most prominent projecting point of the occipital bone at the midline of the base of the skull. The inion marks the center of the superior nuchal line.
4. **The mastoid process refers to a protruding bony area in the lower part of the skull situated behind the ear. This structure is used while performing the Rinne test.**

System: Neuromuscular and Nervous Systems
Content Outline: Physical Therapy Examination

 Level 1

PTEXAM TWO: QUESTION 160

A physical therapist prepares to apply a topical antibiotic to a small portion of the proximal forearm of a patient with a deep partial-thickness burn. When applying the topical antibiotic, the therapist should utilize which form of medical asepsis?

1. Non-sterile gloves
2. **Sterile gloves**
3. Sterile gloves, gown
4. Sterile gloves, gown, mask

Correct Answer: 2 (Paz p. 306)

Topical antibiotics are often utilized in the treatment of burns. They serve to reduce bacterial count, provide a covering for the wound, reduce stiffness, and reduce evaporative loss. Since topical antibiotics are applied directly to the affected area, sterile gloves should be worn.

1. Gloves offer protection to the physical therapist's hands to reduce the likelihood of becoming infected with microorganisms from a patient and reduce the risk of the patient receiving microorganisms from the physical therapist. Non-sterile gloves are typically used with intact skin.
2. **Topical antibiotics are applied directly to the burn and therefore require the use of sterile gloves. Failure to use sterile technique increases the probability of contamination.**
3. A gown is used to protect the physical therapist's clothing from being contaminated or soiled by a contaminant. The gown also reduces the probability of the physical therapist transmitting a microorganism from their clothing to the patient. The size and the location of the burn make it unnecessary to use a gown.
4. A mask is designed to reduce the spread of microorganisms that are transmitted through the air. The mask protects the physical therapist from inhalation of particles or droplets that may contain pathogens and also reduces the transmission of pathogens from the physical therapist to the patient. The mask would not be necessary since there is minimal risk of microorganisms being transmitted through the air in the described scenario.

System: Other Systems
Content Outline: Interventions

 Level 2  p. 761-763

PTEXAM TWO: QUESTION 161

A physical therapist examines a patient with coordination deficits who exhibits excessive involuntary and extraneous movements including hemiballismus. This clinical presentation is MOST consistent with damage or a lesion in what area of the brain?

1. **Cerebellum**
2. **Basal ganglia**
3. **Frontal lobe**
4. **Medulla oblongata**

Correct Answer: 2 (O'Sullivan p. 192)

Ballistic movements refer to large amplitude, involuntary movements affecting the proximal limb musculature, manifested in jerking, flinging movements of the extremity. Ballismus usually results from a lesion in the subthalamic nucleus within the basal ganglia. Often only one side of the body is involved, resulting in hemiballismus.

1. The primary function of the cerebellum is to regulate movement, postural control, and muscle tone. Damage to the cerebellum tends to produce ataxia, not hemiballismus. Ataxia results in difficulty initiating movement, as well as errors in rate, rhythm, and timing of motor responses. Other common cerebellar deficits include dysarthria, dysdiadochokinesia, and nystagmus.
2. **The basal ganglia are gray matter masses located deep within the white matter of the cerebrum and include the caudate, putamen, globus pallidus, substantia nigra, and subthalamic nuclei. In addition to hemiballismus, other basal ganglia deficits include choreoathetosis, hyperkinesis, rigidity, and bradykinesia.**
3. A frontal lobe lesion can produce a wide range of deficits including paralysis, apraxia, and loss of executive and goal-directed behaviors. A patient with a frontal lobe lesion may also be apathetic, uninhibited, distractible, and lack judgment.
4. The medulla oblongata is located within the brainstem. The structure's primary purpose is to control the body's vital functions by influencing autonomic nervous activity and regulating the processes of heart rate, swallowing, and respiration. If there is significant damage to the medulla oblongata, the body would cease to function.

System: Neuromuscular and Nervous Systems
Content Outline: Foundations for Evaluation, Differential Diagnosis, and Prognosis

 **Level 1**  **p. 237, 263**

PTEXAM TWO: QUESTION 162

A patient with Addison's disease reports fatigue and extreme weight loss. What mechanism is the MOST likely cause of this patient's symptoms?

1. **Decreased production of cortisol**
2. **Hyperfunction of the thyroid gland**
3. **Decreased absorption of nutrients within the intestines**
4. **Hyperfunction of the adrenal gland**

Correct Answer: 1 (Goodman – Differential Diagnosis p. 391)

Addison's disease, also known as primary adrenal insufficiency, is characterized by hypofunction of the adrenal glands. The most common cause of adrenal insufficiency is an autoimmune process that causes destruction of the adrenal cortex. Signs and symptoms include dark pigmentation of the skin, hypotension, fatigue, hyperkalemia, gastrointestinal disturbances, weight loss, nausea, vomiting, arthralgias, and hypoglycemia.

1. **The adrenal glands are responsible for the production of cortisol and aldosterone. Decreased production of these hormones results in fatigue and weight loss. Addison's disease can be treated by the administration of exogenous cortisol.**
2. Hyperfunction of the thyroid gland (i.e., hyperthyroidism), as seen in conditions such as Graves' disease, can result in fatigue and weight loss through an elevation in the body's metabolism. However, this is not the mechanism by which Addison's disease occurs.
3. Decreased absorption of nutrients within the intestines, as seen in conditions such as Crohn's disease, can result in weight loss through nutritional deficiencies. Though this is sometimes a secondary side effect of Addison's disease, it is not the primary mechanism by which Addison's disease occurs.
4. Hyperfunction of the adrenal gland (i.e., Cushing's syndrome) results in increased secretion of cortisol. This condition is more likely to result in weight gain than weight loss.

System: Other Systems
Content Outline: Foundations for Evaluation, Differential Diagnosis, and Prognosis

 **Level 2**  **p. 527, 644**

PTEXAM TWO: QUESTION 163

A physical therapist observes a patient complete an arm curl with a dumbbell in the standing position using the starting and ending positions as shown in the image. Which scenario would produce the **GREATEST** power?

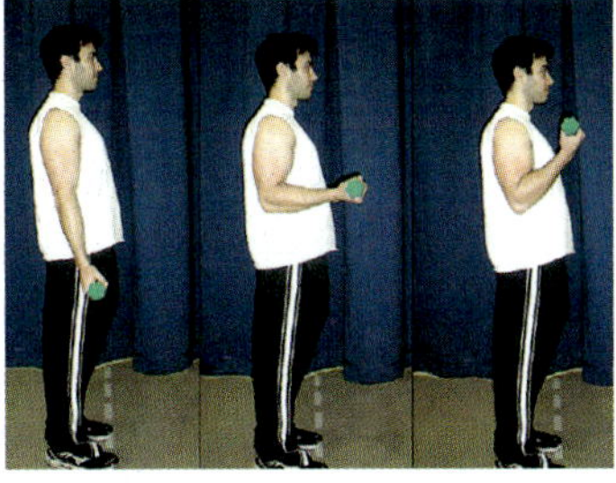

1. Lifting a two pound dumbbell in two seconds
2. Lifting a two pound dumbbell in three seconds
3. **Lifting a four pound dumbbell in one second**
4. Lifting a four pound dumbbell in four seconds

Correct Answer: 3 (Coburn p. 52) 

Power is calculated as the amount of work divided by the time needed to perform the work. Work is defined as the product of force and distance. Each of the presented options involve the same amount of distance, therefore the relevant variables to consider are the weight of the dumbbell and the time to complete the repetition.

1. A 2 pound dumbbell lifted in two seconds would produce more power than the same weight lifted over a longer period of time, however, it would not be as great as a heavier weight (i.e., 4 pounds) lifted over a shorter period of time (i.e., one second).
2. A 2 pound dumbbell lifted in three seconds would produce the smallest amount of power of the presented options since the weight is relatively light (i.e., 2 pounds) and the amount of time to complete the repetition is relatively long (i.e., three seconds).
3. **A 4 pound dumbbell lifted in one second would produce the greatest amount of power since the weight lifted is the heaviest of the presented options and the amount of time to complete the repetition (i.e., one second) is the shortest.**
4. A 4 pound dumbbell lifted in four seconds would produce less power than the same amount of weight lifted over a shorter period of time.

System: Musculoskeletal System
Content Outline: Interventions

 Level 1  p. 120

PTEXAM TWO: QUESTION 164

A physical therapist examines a patient with a suspected injury to the thoracodorsal nerve. Which objective finding would be the **MOST** consistent with this injury?

1. Shoulder medial rotation weakness
2. **Shoulder extension weakness**
3. Paralysis of the rhomboids
4. Paralysis of the diaphragm

Correct Answer: 2 (Kendall p. 324) 

The thoracodorsal nerve (C6, C7, C8) is a branch of the posterior cord of the brachial plexus. The nerve follows the course of the subscapular artery along the posterior wall of the axilla to the latissimus dorsi.

1. The medial rotators of the shoulder include the subscapularis, teres major, pectoralis major, latissimus dorsi, and anterior deltoid. The latissimus dorsi would be affected by an injury to the thoracodorsal nerve, however, the presence of a number of other muscles which act to medially rotate the humerus would be adequate to compensate for any impairment in the latissimus dorsi.
2. **The latissimus dorsi is innervated by the thoracodorsal nerve (C6, C7, C8). Weakness of the latissimus dorsi would produce impaired strength during shoulder extension resistive testing despite the fact that several other muscles also function to extend the shoulder. These muscles include the posterior deltoid and teres major.**
3. The rhomboids are innervated by the dorsal scapular nerve (C4, C5).
4. The diaphragm is innervated by the phrenic nerve (C3, C4, C5).

System: Neuromuscular and Nervous Systems
Content Outline: Physical Therapy Examination

 Level 1  p. 250

PTEXAM TWO: QUESTION 165

A physical therapist works with a patient using a flotation device positioned vertically in the deep end of a pool. Which area of the patient's body would experience the GREATEST amount of hydrostatic pressure?

1. **Shoulders**
2. **Torso**
3. **Hips**
4. **Feet**

Correct Answer: 4 (Cameron p. 342)

Hydrostatic pressure refers to the pressure exerted by a fluid on a body immersed in the fluid. Hydrostatic pressure increases as the depth of immersion increases.

1. When positioned vertically, the shoulders would be only partially immersed since the patient is using a flotation device. The hydrostatic pressure on the shoulders would be negligible.
2. When positioned vertically, the torso will likely be partially or perhaps fully immersed. The hydrostatic pressure on the torso will be greater than the hydrostatic pressure on the shoulders, but less than the hydrostatic pressure on the hips or feet.
3. When positioned vertically, the hips will be fully immersed. The hydrostatic pressure on the hips will be less than the hydrostatic pressure on the feet since the feet are immersed to a greater depth.
4. **When positioned vertically, the feet would experience the greatest amount of hydrostatic pressure since they are the deepest immersed body part.**

System: Other Systems
Content Outline: Interventions

Level 1

PTEXAM TWO: QUESTION 166

A patient utilizing a prosthesis following a right transfemoral amputation demonstrates a right lateral bend during the right stance phase of gait. Which testing procedure would be MOST anticipated based on the observed finding?

1. **Patient is positioned in right sidelying; downward pressure is applied to the distal aspect of the left limb**
2. **Patient is positioned in left sidelying; downward pressure is applied to the distal aspect of the right limb**
3. **Patient is positioned in unsupported sitting; therapist applies a lateral force to the patient's right shoulder**
4. **Patient is positioned in unsupported sitting; therapist applies a lateral force to the patient's left shoulder**

Correct Answer: 2 (Seymour p. 230)

Gait deviations demonstrated with prosthetic limb use can be caused by either the prosthetic device or the individual using the device. Prosthetic causes contributing to lateral bending with gait include a prosthesis that is too short, improperly shaped lateral wall, high medial wall, and prosthesis aligned in abduction. Causes related to the individual using the device include poor balance, abduction contracture, improper training, short residual limb, weak hip abductors on the prosthetic side, and a hypersensitive and painful residual limb.

1. The test scenario described is used to test the strength of the hip abductors on the left side. While hip abductor weakness can contribute to a lateral bend during gait, weakness on the prosthetic (i.e., right) side is more likely the cause of this deviation since the described lateral bend is to the right. Suspected right-sided abductor weakness would be assessed with the patient in left sidelying.
2. **The test scenario described is used to test the strength of the hip abductors on the right side. Weakness of the hip abductors on the prosthetic side is a common cause of this type of gait deviation. Since the patient has a right transfemoral amputation and demonstrates a right lateral bend with gait, it is likely that the right hip abductors are weak.**
3. The test described can be used to grossly assess a patient's trunk strength. This test is not likely to be performed since lateral bending during gait is commonly caused by weak hip abductors, not inadequate strength of the trunk musculature.
4. The test described can be used to grossly assess a patient's trunk strength. This test is not likely to be performed since lateral bending during gait is commonly caused by weak hip abductors, not inadequate strength of the trunk musculature.

System: Musculoskeletal System
Content Outline: Physical Therapy Examination

Level 2

p. 80-82, 86-88, 137, 144-145

PTEXAM TWO: QUESTION 167

A physical therapist completes an examination on a patient diagnosed with Parkinson's disease. Results of the examination include Good (4/5) strength in the lower extremities, 10 degrees flexion contracture at the hips, and exaggerated forward standing posture. The patient has difficulty initiating movement and requires manual assistance for gait on level surfaces. Which of the following activities is the MOST appropriate to incorporate into a home program for this patient?

1. **Prone lying**
2. Progressive relaxation exercises
3. Lower extremity resistive exercises with ankle weights
4. Postural awareness exercises in standing

Correct Answer: 1 (Umphred p. 613)

Prone lying is a commonly employed positional technique designed to stretch the hip flexors in patients with Parkinson's disease. Increased flexibility of the hip muscles will improve standing posture and enable the body's center of gravity to remain within the base of support. Although some of the other options are appropriate, they would not provide the same degree of benefit for the patient based on the described clinical presentation.

1. **Prone lying is a static positioning activity designed to stretch the hip flexors. If the patient was unable to tolerate prone lying, the physical therapist could place one or more pillows under the patient's hips and gradually remove pillows over time as the patient improves their flexibility.**
2. Progressive relaxation exercises can be incorporated using gentle rocking or segmental trunk rotation, however, the patient needs to have adequate range of motion in the hip flexors to optimize their functional status.
3. Strengthening is a restorative intervention used with patients with Parkinson's disease, however, the patient's strength in the lower extremities is already good (i.e., 4/5) and therefore would not be an immediate treatment priority.
4. Postural awareness exercises in standing are an appropriate intervention, however, the relative benefit of the activity is limited without adequate muscle length. By improving the patient's hip flexibility, the patient would be able to exhibit improved standing posture.

System: Neuromuscular and Nervous Systems
Content Outline: Interventions

Level 3

PTEXAM TWO: QUESTION 168

The medical record indicates a patient has been diagnosed with chronic respiratory alkalosis. Which laboratory finding is the MOST consistent with this condition?

1. **Elevated arterial blood pH, low $PaCO_2$**
2. Low arterial blood pH, elevated $PaCO_2$
3. Elevated arterial blood pH, elevated $PaCO_2$
4. Low arterial blood pH, low $PaCO_2$

Correct Answer: 1 (Roy p. 520)

Analysis of arterial blood gases provides information about acid-base balance, ventilation, and oxygenation.

1. **Elevated arterial blood pH and low $PaCO_2$ are consistent with respiratory alkalosis. This condition can be caused by alveolar hyperventilation due to dizziness or syncope.**
2. Low arterial blood pH and elevated $PaCO_2$ are consistent with respiratory acidosis. This condition can be caused by alveolar hypoventilation due to anxiety, confusion, and coma.
3. Elevated arterial blood pH and elevated $PaCO_2$ are consistent with a partially compensated metabolic alkalosis. Causes of metabolic alkalosis include bicarbonate ingestion, vomiting, diuretics, steroids, and adrenal disease.
4. Low arterial blood pH and low $PaCO_2$ are consistent with a partially compensated metabolic acidosis. Causes of metabolic acidosis include metabolic diseases or disturbances such as diabetes, lactic acid, uremic acidosis, and chronic diarrhea.

System: Cardiovascular and Pulmonary Systems
Content Outline: Foundations for Evaluation, Differential Diagnosis, and Prognosis

p. 410, 480

PTEXAM TWO: QUESTION 169

A patient involved in a motor vehicle accident sustains a proximal fibula fracture. The fracture damaged the motor component of the common peroneal nerve. Ankle dorsiflexion and eversion are tested as Poor (2/5). Which of the following interventions is the MOST appropriate to assist the patient with activities of daily living?

1. **Electrical stimulation**
2. **Use of an orthosis**
3. **Exercise program**
4. **Aquatic program**

Correct Answer: 2 (Seymour p. 31)

There are a variety of interventions that can assist patients to perform activities of daily living following a peripheral nerve injury. Physical therapists must select the most appropriate interventions to accomplish each of the established goals. In this particular question, the candidate is asked to identify the most appropriate intervention to assist the patient with activities of daily living.

1. Electrical stimulation can be used to facilitate motor activity within the affected muscle, however, the effectiveness of this intervention may be limited depending on the severity of the damage to the nerve. In addition, the intervention would not immediately assist the patient with activities of daily living.
2. **The use of an orthosis would ensure adequate foot clearance and stability during activities of daily living. This form of intervention would have an immediate impact on the patient's ability to perform activities of daily living.**
3. An exercise program would be beneficial for the patient for a variety of reasons. The patient will need to perform selected movements in a different manner since the lower extremity musculature has been affected. Exercise will also be necessary to strengthen the surrounding musculature to provide additional stability. Despite the stated benefits, the intervention would not provide the same magnitude of benefit as the orthosis when performing activities of daily living.
4. An aquatic program allows the patient to exercise in a decreased weight bearing environment, however, the intervention is unlikely to have an immediate impact on the patient's ability to perform activities of daily living.

System: Other Systems
Content Outline: Interventions

 Level 3 p. 134-135

PTEXAM TWO: QUESTION 170

A physical therapist instructs a patient with chronic pulmonary dysfunction in energy conservation techniques. Which of the following techniques would be the MOST effective when assisting a patient to complete a selected activity without dyspnea?

1. **Diaphragmatic breathing**
2. **Pacing**
3. **Pursed-lip breathing**
4. **Ventilatory muscle training**

Correct Answer: 2 (Hillegass p. 612)

Pacing is a technique that can allow patients to complete functional activities without shortness of breath or dyspnea.

1. Diaphragmatic breathing is a breathing technique that can decrease the work of breathing by lowering respiratory rate, increasing tidal volume, and decreasing the use of accessory muscles of respiration by facilitating use of the diaphragm. Diaphragmatic breathing can be used with pacing when necessary.
2. **Pacing is an integral component of energy-saving techniques used by patients who present with dyspnea during activity. Pacing refers to dividing an activity into component parts so that the patient does not exceed the limits of their breathing capacity throughout each portion of the task. For example, climbing up stairs is performed only on exhalation and by taking only one or two steps at a time.**
3. Pursed-lip breathing is a breathing technique performed by inhaling through the nose and exhaling through pursed lips. Patients with chronic obstructive pulmonary disease have been shown to benefit from pursed-lip breathing by decreasing respiratory rate, increasing tidal volume, and reducing the sense of dyspnea. When used in isolation the technique would not be as effective as pacing to assist the patient to complete the activity without dyspnea.
4. Ventilatory muscle training is accomplished by devices called inspiratory muscle trainers, which strengthen the inspiratory muscles by providing resistance to inspiration.

System: Cardiovascular and Pulmonary Systems
Content Outline: Interventions

 Level 2  p. 440-443

PTEXAM TWO: QUESTION 171

During an examination, a physical therapist notes a yellow discoloration of the patient's skin and sclera of the eye. This discoloration would be LEAST likely observed with which of the following conditions?

1. Cholecystitis
2. **Ulcerative colitis**
3. Pancreatitis
4. Hepatitis

Correct Answer: 2 (Goodman – Differential Diagnosis p. 323)

Pathology of the body's organs or organ systems can develop symptoms that mimic musculoskeletal injuries. Physical therapists should be aware of signs and symptoms of common organ pathologies. Jaundice, a yellow discoloration of the skin, is a sign usually related to hepatic pathology.

1. Cholecystitis is an infection or inflammation of the gallbladder caused by blockage or impaction of gallstones in the cystic duct. Signs and symptoms include jaundice, fever, nausea, vomiting, right upper quadrant pain, and gastrointestinal symptoms.
2. **Ulcerative colitis is an inflammation and ulceration of the inner lining of the colon and rectum. Signs and symptoms include rectal bleeding, diarrhea, nausea, vomiting, weight loss, and fever. Jaundice is not a symptom typically seen with this condition.**
3. Pancreatitis is an inflammation of the pancreas that may result in autodigestion of the organ by its own enzymes. Signs and symptoms include epigastric pain, nausea, vomiting, diarrhea, fever, tachycardia, malaise, and jaundice.
4. Hepatitis is an acute or chronic inflammation of the liver that may be caused by a virus, a chemical, a drug reaction or alcohol abuse. Signs and symptoms vary depending on the type of hepatitis (e.g., viral, nonviral, chronic), however, jaundice is a sign almost always associated with this condition.

System: Other Systems
Content Outline: Foundations for Evaluation, Differential Diagnosis, and Prognosis

Level 2

p. 654

PTEXAM TWO: QUESTION 172

A physical therapist consults with the teacher of a nine-year-old child with dyspraxia. Which of the following school-based activities would likely be the MOST challenging for the child?

1. Maintaining upright sitting posture in a classroom chair
2. **Negotiating a crowded hallway between classrooms**
3. Opening and closing a locker
4. Writing their name

Correct Answer: 2 (O'Sullivan p. 199)

Dyspraxia, or motor incoordination, is associated with developmental coordination disorders. Developmental coordination disorders are disorders in movement without a known medical diagnosis. Children with developmental coordination disorders often present with slow movement times, poor motor sequencing, poor motor memory, and perceptual problems. Learning disabilities, sensory integration disorders, and attention deficit hyperactivity disorders are often associated with developmental coordination disorders.

1. Maintaining an upright sitting posture will not be the most difficult activity for this child since it is a static activity.
2. **A child with dyspraxia will have difficulty maintaining their balance in environments with changing surfaces and many obstacles, such as in a crowded hallway. To accommodate for this, a student may be allowed to leave class a few minutes early in order to transition between classrooms in a less crowded hallway.**
3. Opening and closing a locker is not the most difficult activity for this child since the activity is not as dynamic as traversing through a crowded hallway.
4. Poor written communication will be one of the first signs of developmental coordination disorders in school-aged children. Since this child is nine years of age, any issues with writing their name should have been identified and addressed previously.

System: Neuromuscular and Nervous Systems
Content Outline: Foundations for Evaluation, Differential Diagnosis, and Prognosis

Level 2

PTEXAM TWO: QUESTION 173

A physical therapist works with a patient diagnosed with Down syndrome. The therapist determines that the patient has abnormalities in muscular tone consistent with the diagnosed condition. Which of the following techniques would be the **MOST** beneficial when treating the patient's tone abnormalities?

1. **Quick stretch**
2. Deep pressure
3. Prolonged icing
4. Neutral warmth

Correct Answer: 1 (O'Sullivan p. 167)

There are a variety of stimulation techniques that can be employed to help treat tone abnormalities (i.e., hypertonicity versus hypotonicity). Some of these techniques help facilitate muscular contraction while others help inhibit muscular contraction. Down syndrome is a genetic disorder that typically results in hypotonia (i.e., low tone).

1. **Providing a quick stretch to a muscle helps activate muscle spindles and results in enhanced muscular contraction. For patients with low tone, this technique may help facilitate increased activity in affected muscles.**
2. Deep pressure across the longitudinal axis of tendons helps activate muscle and tactile receptors and results in the inhibition of muscular tone. This would not be a useful technique for a patient who already has low tone.
3. Prolonged icing helps activate thermoreceptors and results in the inhibition of muscular tone. This would not be a useful technique for a patient who already has low tone.
4. Neutral warmth helps activate tactile and thermoreceptors and results in the inhibition of muscular tone. This would not be a useful technique for a patient who already has low tone.

System: Neuromuscular and Nervous Systems
Content Outline: Interventions

 Level 2  p. 293, 312-313, 332-333

PTEXAM TWO: QUESTION 174

A physical therapist treats a patient diagnosed with osteonecrosis of the femoral condyle. Which patient profile is the **MOST** typical with this medical condition?

1. A 42-year-old female with osteonecrosis of the lateral femoral condyle
2. **A 64-year-old female with osteonecrosis of the medial femoral condyle**
3. A 46-year-old male with osteonecrosis of the medial femoral condyle
4. A 68-year-old male with osteonecrosis of the lateral femoral condyle

Correct Answer: 2 (Sarwark p. 689)

Osteonecrosis of the femur occurs when a segment of the bone loses its blood supply. Symptoms include sudden pain on the medial side of the knee, swelling, and sensitivity to touch. The medical condition is diagnosed based on a combination of symptoms and x-ray. The etiology is unknown, however, likely involves a combination of trauma and altered blood flow.

1. Females are more likely than males to experience osteonecrosis of the femoral condyle. Peak incidence is greater at a more advanced age than 42 and the lateral femoral condyle is less likely to be involved than the medial femoral condyle.
2. **Females are more likely than males to experience osteonecrosis of the femoral condyle with peak incidence occurring in women who are over 60 years of age. The medial femoral condyle is more likely to be affected than the lateral femoral condyle due to increased weight bearing forces caused by the center of gravity being medial to the knee.**
3. Males are less likely than females to experience osteonecrosis of the femoral condyle and peak incidence is greater at a more advanced age than 46. The medial femoral condyle is more likely to be affected than the lateral femoral condyle.
4. Males are less likely than females to experience osteonecrosis of the femoral condyle. The patient's age (i.e., over 60) is consistent with peak incidence, however, the lateral femoral condyle is less likely to be involved than the medial femoral condyle.

System: Musculoskeletal System
Content Outline: Foundations for Evaluation, Differential Diagnosis, and Prognosis

 Level 2

PTEXAM TWO: QUESTION 175

A physical therapist reads in the medical record that a patient was recently prescribed a thrombolytic agent. Which condition would be considered a contraindication to this type of pharmacological agent?

1. Myocardial infarction
2. **Hemorrhagic stroke**
3. Pulmonary embolism
4. Venous thrombosis

Correct Answer: 2 (Hillegass p. 455) 

Thrombolytic agents facilitate clot dissolution through the conversion of plasminogen to plasmin. Plasmin breaks down clots and allows occluded vessels to reopen to restore blood flow. Side effects include hemorrhage and cardiac arrhythmia. Physical therapists must be careful to avoid situations that may cause trauma to the patient due to altered clotting activity.

1. Myocardial infarction (i.e., heart attack) occurs when the blood flow through one or more of the coronary arteries is severely reduced or cut off completely causing tissue death in the portion of the myocardium supplied by the blocked artery. Thrombolytic agents are indicated as a management option for this condition.
2. **Hemorrhagic stroke is characterized by abnormal bleeding in the brain due to a rupture in a blood vessel. Thrombolytic agents are contraindicated for individuals experiencing a hemorrhagic stroke as this can result in increased hemorrhaging. However, thrombolytic agents are indicated for the management of ischemic stroke.**
3. Pulmonary embolism is a condition where one or more arteries in the lungs become blocked. Prompt treatment with anticoagulants and thrombolytic agents is indicated to reduce the risk of death.
4. Venous thrombosis is a condition characterized by the formation of a blood clot (thrombus) within a vein. Thrombolytic agents are indicated as a management option for this condition.

System: Cardiovascular and Pulmonary Systems
Content Outline: Foundations for Evaluation, Differential Diagnosis, and Prognosis

 Level 1  p. 279-280, 330-331, 415

PTEXAM TWO: QUESTION 176

A physical therapist treats a patient post traumatic brain injury by applying approximation to the pelvis to increase bilateral lower extremity weight bearing as shown in the image. The patient exhibits significant hypertonicity and the presence of the positive support reflex. Which of the following rationales is the MOST likely reason for why the therapist is using the therapeutic ball?

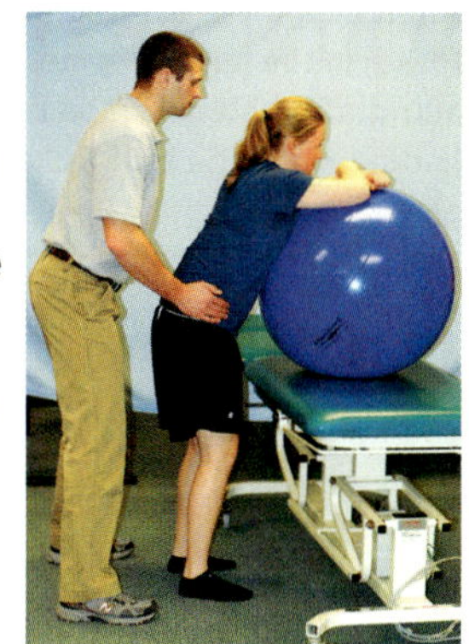

1. **Avoid a mass extensor pattern in standing**
2. Encourage active-assisted range of motion
3. Allow the patient partial weight bearing through the ball
4. Limit range of motion at the shoulder

Correct Answer: 1 (O'Sullivan p. 150)

The positive support reflex is an abnormal reflex that occurs with weight bearing through the ball of the foot. The response produces an increase in extensor tone through the lower extremities and trunk. The use of trunk flexion with lower extremity weight bearing activities using the therapeutic ball assists the patient to avoid a mass extensor pattern in standing. A therapeutic ball can be utilized for facilitation, inhibition, and range of motion.

1. **In this particular scenario, the patient uses the therapeutic ball to allow for supported trunk flexion when standing. This avoids a mass extensor response and allows for weight bearing and weight shifting through the lower extremities.**
2. The therapeutic ball can be used to promote active-assisted range of motion, however, the use of the therapeutic ball in this scenario is more related to supported standing with the trunk flexed to avoid a mass extensor pattern.
3. The therapeutic ball can be used for weight bearing through the upper extremities, however, the use of the therapeutic ball in this scenario is more related to supported standing with the trunk flexed to avoid a mass extensor pattern.
4. The therapeutic ball may be used for increasing range of motion of a given joint, however, it is rarely used to limit range of motion. Decreasing upper extremity range of motion would not be beneficial to limit the mass extensor pattern.

System: Neuromuscular and Nervous Systems
Content Outline: Interventions

 Level 3   p. 306-307

PTEXAM TWO: QUESTION 177

A physical therapist treats a patient rehabilitating from spinal fusion in the lumbar spine. The surgical procedure required a bone autograft to stabilize the lumbar segment. What postoperative finding would be MOST likely based on the utilization of the bone graft?

1. **Hip pain**
2. Spinal hypermobility
3. Hyporeflexia
4. Myotomal weakness

Correct Answer: 1 (Dutton p. 1496)

Spinal fusion is indicated in the presence of axial pain with unstable spinal segments, advanced arthritis or uncontrolled peripheral pain. Generally, the surgeon will use a bone graft and instrumentation (e.g., pedicle screws) to immobilize the desired spinal segment.

1. **Bone grafts are most commonly taken from the anterior or posterior portions of the iliac crest. As a result, harvesting of the bone graft is often associated with postoperative hip pain, bleeding, and increased swelling.**
2. A bone graft is specifically used to fuse two vertebrae together and therefore would not be associated with spinal hypermobility. Spinal instability is the primary indication for spinal fusion.
3. Reflex deficits are not uncommon in patients prior to spinal fusion due to neurologic involvement, however, the presence of a bone graft would not typically impact the integrity of spinal reflexes.
4. Myotomal weakness is not uncommon in patients prior to spinal fusion due to neurologic involvement. Additional weakness would be anticipated postoperatively based on the surgical procedure, however, would not be unique to the presence of a bone graft.

System: Musculoskeletal System
Content Outline: Foundations for Evaluation, Differential Diagnosis, and Prognosis

 Level 2  p. 129

PTEXAM TWO: QUESTION 178

A physical therapist utilizes a special test in which the therapist passively performs the required motion without the need for active participation by the patient. Which test would meet this criterion?

1. Adson maneuver
2. **Hawkins-Kennedy impingement test**
3. Roos test
4. Speed's test

Correct Answer: 2 (Dutton p. 630)

There are a wide variety of special tests commonly employed in physical therapy practice. The tests include active, active-assisted, and passive movement and in some cases a combination of these movements. Physical therapists should be familiar with the standard procedure for utilizing commonly performed special tests.

1. The Adson maneuver is performed with the patient positioned in sitting or standing. The therapist monitors the radial pulse and asks the patient to rotate their head to face the test shoulder. The patient is then asked to extend their head while the therapist laterally rotates and extends the patient's shoulder. An absent or diminished radial pulse is considered a positive test and may be indicative of thoracic outlet syndrome.
2. **The Hawkins-Kennedy impingement test is performed with the patient positioned in sitting or standing. The therapist flexes the patient's shoulder to 90 degrees and then medially rotates the arm. A positive test occurs when there is an onset or exacerbation of pain and may be indicative of shoulder impingement involving the supraspinatus tendon.**
3. Roos test is performed with the patient positioned in sitting or standing with the arms in 90 degrees of abduction, lateral rotation, and elbow flexion. The patient is asked to open and close their hands for three minutes. An inability to maintain the test position, weakness of the arms, and sensory loss or ischemic pain are all considered positive results and may be indicative of thoracic outlet syndrome.
4. Speed's test is performed with the patient positioned in sitting or standing with the elbow extended and the forearm supinated. The therapist places one hand over the bicipital groove and the other hand on the volar surface of the forearm. The therapist resists active shoulder flexion. A positive test consists of pain or tenderness in the bicipital groove region and may be indicative of bicipital tendonitis.

System: Musculoskeletal System
Content Outline: Physical Therapy Examination

 Level 1  p. 101

PTEXAM TWO: QUESTION 179

A physical therapist working in a school system develops long-term goals as part of an Individualized Educational Plan for a child with Down syndrome. Which of the following timeframes is the MOST appropriate to attain these goals?

1. One month
2. Four months
3. Six months
4. **One year**

Correct Answer: 4 (Tecklin p. 723)

An Individualized Educational Plan (IEP) is designed for any school-aged child that requires therapy services. Long-term goals are based on a one-year plan. These services are provided through federal legislation through the Individuals with Disabilities Education Act (IDEA).

1. A goal with a one month timeframe is designed for a patient that requires therapeutic intervention for an injury or condition that will steadily progress and improve. This timeframe is not within the framework of the IEP.
2. A four month timeframe may be an appropriate interval to informally reassess the child and quantify the actual progress towards the established goals, however, it is typically an insufficient amount of time to expect the established goals to be accomplished.
3. A six month timeframe may be an appropriate interval for review of established goals for the IEP since it is a midpoint in the year. This timeframe, however, is not typically sufficient to accomplish the long-term goals.
4. **Federal legislation mandates the review of an IEP on a one year basis. Goals relate to improving a child's educational experience. IDEA also provides for children 0-5 years of age through early intervention programs.**

System: Non-Systems
Content Outline: Safety and Protection; Professional Responsibilities; Research

 Level 2

PTEXAM TWO: QUESTION 180

A physical therapist initiates gait training on a patient who has T10 spina bifida. Initially, the BEST method to teach the patient how to maintain standing is with the use of which of the following devices?

1. Bilateral hip-knee-ankle-foot orthoses (HKAFO) and forearm crutches
2. **Parapodium and the parallel bars**
3. Bilateral knee-ankle-foot orthoses (KAFO) and the parallel bars
4. Bilateral ankle-foot orthoses (AFO) and the parallel bars

Correct Answer: 2 (O'Sullivan p. 1300)

The parapodium provides the necessary amount of support and is optimal to assist with standing activities for children with thoracic and high level lumbar lesions. The parallel bars are the most stable assistive device to initiate standing and gait training.

1. HKAFOs would require a swing-through or reciprocal gait pattern. Using HKAFOs with forearm (Lofstrand) crutches requires a high level of balance and energy expenditure and is not appropriate for initial standing activities.
2. **The parapodium is a HKAFO with a thoracolumbar orthosis that supports the trunk and lower extremities. It has a large base of support and is used with or without an assistive device. This would be ideal for a patient with T10 spina bifida to initiate standing within the parallel bars.**
3. A patient with T10 spina bifida would not initially use KAFOs in the parallel bars when working on standing activities due to the deficits in strength and sensation below the T10 level.
4. A patient with T10 spina bifida would not possess the necessary motor function to use bilateral AFOs.

System: Neuromuscular and Nervous Systems
Content Outline: Interventions

 Level 2  p. 135, 690-691

PTEXAM TWO: QUESTION 181

A physical therapist works on weight shifting activities with a patient who is sitting over the edge of a mat table with the feet positioned on the floor. The therapist facilitates an anterior weight shift through the patient's pelvis. What pattern of activity would be required for the patient to maintain an upright posture?

1. **Spinal extension due to concentric contraction of the spinal extensors**
2. Spinal flexion due to concentric contraction of the spinal flexors
3. Spinal extension due to eccentric contraction of the spinal extensors
4. Spinal flexion due to eccentric contraction of the spinal flexors

Correct Answer: 1 (Umphred p. 732) 

Weight shifting is necessary to maintain upright positioning and perform functional sitting activities. Certain tasks require the ability to stabilize and weight shift through the trunk simultaneously (i.e., upper versus lower trunk). When weakness of the trunk exists, weight shifting and trunk control activities are often included in the plan of care.

1. **When a patient initiates an anterior weight shift through the pelvis, spinal extension must occur in order to maintain an upright posture in sitting. Concentric contraction of the spinal extensors is required to produce spinal extension.**
2. When a patient initiates a posterior weight shift through the pelvis, spinal flexion must occur in order to maintain an upright posture in sitting. Concentric contraction of the spinal flexors is required to produce spinal flexion.
3. Spinal extension is necessary to maintain an upright posture in sitting following an anterior weight shift through the pelvis, however, this would occur as a result of concentric contraction of the spinal extensors.
4. Spinal flexion is necessary to maintain an upright posture in sitting following a posterior weight shift through the pelvis. Concentric contraction of the spinal flexors is required to produce spinal flexion.

System: Neuromuscular and Nervous Systems
Content Outline: Interventions

Level 2

PTEXAM TWO: QUESTION 182

A physical therapist observes a patient running on a treadmill at an intensity of approximately 75 percent of their estimated maximum oxygen consumption. What is the PRIMARY source for the adenosine triphosphate (ATP) produced during this activity?

1. Amino acids
2. **Carbohydrates**
3. Fats
4. Proteins

Correct Answer: 2 (Nyland p. 36)

Assuming adequate availability of nutrients, carbohydrates and fats are the primary sources of energy production while proteins provide the raw materials for making hormones and muscle and facilitating numerous chemical processes. The percentage of carbohydrates and fats utilized are determined by a number of variables including intensity and duration of exercise.

1. Proteins consist of long chains of amino acids. The contribution of amino acids to the production of ATP is minimal during short-term exercise, but increases during prolonged activity.
2. **As exercise intensity increases (e.g., greater than 70% of maximum oxygen consumption), carbohydrates are responsible for the vast majority of ATP production. The transition from the use of fats to carbohydrates as the primary fuel source is referred to as the "crossover" concept. The rate of oxidation during exercise is a function of the rate of carbohydrate utilization and the availability of circulating fatty acids. If activity lasts for a long period of time (e.g., greater than one hour), fats play a greater role in energy metabolism.**
3. At lower levels of exercise intensity, the majority of ATP production comes from fats. As exercise intensity increases, the biochemical processes for fat metabolism are too slow to meet the needs for faster production of ATP, and carbohydrate utilization increases.
4. Proteins are used in ATP production as described in option 1. Protein can be metabolized in more significant amounts during long duration activity or long-term starvation.

System: Cardiovascular and Pulmonary Systems
Content Outline: Foundations for Evaluation, Differential Diagnosis, and Prognosis

Level 1  p. 49, 578

PTEXAM TWO: QUESTION 183

A physical therapist examines several pathological reflexes on a patient with a suspected upper motor neuron disease. What stimulus would be the MOST appropriate when assessing Hoffman's reflex?

1. **Tapping the nail of the middle finger**
2. Stroking the superior and medial thigh
3. Stroking the plantar aspect of the foot
4. Rapidly dorsiflexing the foot

Correct Answer: 1 (Roy p. 326)

Reflexes are often used for diagnosing and localizing nervous system disorders. Categories of reflexes include superficial, deep, visceral, and pathological.

1. **Hoffman's reflex is assessed by tapping or snapping the nail of the middle finger. An abnormal response consists of flexion of the index finger and thumb.**
2. The cremasteric reflex is assessed by stroking the skin in the area of the superior and medial thigh. The anticipated response is elevation of the testicle on the same side as the stimulus.
3. The plantar reflex is assessed by stroking the lateral aspect of the sole of the foot from the heel to the ball of the foot and medially to the base of the great toe with the blunt end of a reflex hammer. An abnormal response, also known as Babinski's sign, consists of extension of the great toe and flexion of the other toes.
4. Clonus is assessed by supporting the knee in a partially flexed position and providing a quick stretch into dorsiflexion. Clonus refers to rhythmic oscillations between plantar flexion and dorsiflexion.

System: Neuromuscular and Nervous Systems
Content Outline: Physical Therapy Examination

Level 1

PTEXAM TWO: QUESTION 184

With the patient positioned in supine, a physical therapist performs an upper limb neural tension test with the arm positioned as shown in the image. Based on this upper extremity positioning, which of the following nerves is MOST likely being assessed?

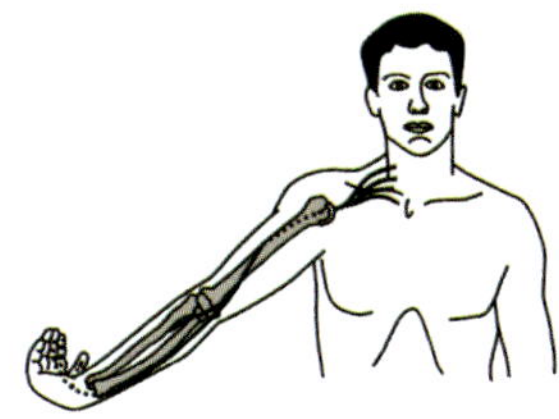

1. Median
2. **Radial**
3. Ulnar
4. Axillary

Correct Answer: 2 (Kisner p. 398)

Upper limb tension tests (ULTTs) require an ordered sequence of movements occurring at the shoulder, elbow, forearm, wrist, and hand. Symptoms and relevant changes in symptoms should be identified after each step.

1. The ULTT for biasing the median nerve involves shoulder girdle depression with 110 degrees abduction, elbow extension, forearm supination, wrist extension, and finger and thumb extension. Since it is clear in the image that the forearm is in pronation and the wrist is in flexion, the median nerve is not the primary nerve being assessed in this scenario.
2. **The ULTT for biasing the radial nerve involves shoulder girdle depression with approximately 10 degrees of abduction, elbow extension, shoulder medial rotation with forearm pronation, wrist flexion, finger and thumb flexion, and finally ulnar deviation of the wrist can be added. The positioning in the image shown is most consistent with the ULTT to assess the radial nerve.**
3. The ULTT for biasing the ulnar nerve involves shoulder girdle depression with 80-110 degrees of abduction, elbow flexion, shoulder lateral rotation with forearm pronation, wrist extension, and finger and thumb extension. Since it is clear in the image that the elbow is in extension, the shoulder in medial rotation, and the wrist in flexion, the ulnar nerve is not the primary nerve being assessed.
4. The ULTT for biasing the axillary nerve, along with the musculocutaneous and median nerves, involves shoulder girdle depression with approximately 10-40 degrees abduction, shoulder lateral rotation, elbow extension, forearm supination, wrist extension, and finger and thumb extension. Since it is clear in the image that the shoulder is in medial rotation with the forearm pronated and the wrist in flexion, the axillary nerve is not the primary nerve being assessed.

System: Neuromuscular
Content: Physical Therapy Examination

Level 1  p. 103

PTEXAM TWO: QUESTION 185

A patient reports to the physical therapist that they have felt nauseous since having their methotrexate medication level altered. Which of the following actions is the MOST appropriate for the therapist to take?

1. **Explain to the patient that nausea is a very common side effect**
2. **Ask the patient to stop taking the prescribed medication**
3. **Request that the patient make an appointment with the physician**
4. **Request that the patient contact the physician's office**

Correct Answer: 4 (Ciccone p. 246) 

Methotrexate is used as a disease-modifying agent in the treatment of rheumatoid arthritis and selected forms of cancer. Adverse effects include nausea, gastrointestinal distress, hemorrhage, cough, shortness of breath, and lower extremity edema. Nausea refers to the sensation of unease and discomfort in the stomach with an urge to vomit. Although nausea is not a medical emergency, it is appropriate for the patient to inform the physician of any persistent side effects as soon as possible.

1. A physical therapist may inform a patient about common side effects of medications, however, the patient's acknowledgement of feeling nauseous after having their medication level altered would still require contact with the physician.
2. A physical therapist is not able to ask a patient to discontinue the use of a prescribed medication. This action is the sole responsibility of the physician.
3. A recommendation to make an appointment with the physician is appropriate, however, would not typically be as timely as contacting the physician's office. Given the patient's present status (i.e., feeling nauseous), it is necessary to advocate for an immediate resolution to the problem.
4. **A patient should contact the physician's office whenever they experience side effects that may be associated with prescribed medication. Direct contact with the physician is an immediate response which makes the physician aware of the patient's present status and allows them to potentially modify or discontinue medication.**

System: Other Systems
Content Outline: Foundations for Evaluation, Differential Diagnosis, and Prognosis

 Level 3

PTEXAM TWO: QUESTION 186

A patient uses patient-controlled analgesia with a lockout interval following an inpatient surgical procedure. Which medication would be MOST consistent with this delivery model?

1. **Atorvastatin (Lipitor)**
2. **Baclofen (Lioresal)**
3. **Meperidine (Demerol)**
4. **Methotrexate (Trexall)**

Correct Answer: 3 (Roy p. 1137) 

Patient-controlled analgesia allows the patient to manage their pain by delivering an intravenous analgesic dose with preset parameters. Opioids are often the medication of choice for patient-controlled analgesia to manage severe acute pain. A lockout interval refers to the period of time in which a patient-controlled analgesia system will not allow the patient to receive medication.

1. Atorvastatin (Lipitor) is a commonly used antihyperlipidemia agent. This class of pharmacological agents consists of five categories of lipid-modifying agents. The most commonly used drugs, the statins, inhibit enzyme action in cholesterol synthesis, break down low-density lipoproteins, decrease triglyceride levels, and increase high-density lipoprotein levels. This medication is not utilized for patient-controlled analgesia.
2. Baclofen (Lioresal) is a commonly used antispasticity agent. This class of pharmacological agents promotes relaxation in spastic muscles by binding selectively within the central nervous system or within the skeletal muscle cells. This medication is not utilized for patient-controlled analgesia.
3. **Meperidine (Demerol) is a commonly used opioid agent. This class of pharmacological agents provides analgesia for acute severe pain management. The medication stimulates opioid receptors within the central nervous system to prevent pain impulses from reaching their destination. The potential serious side effects (e.g., sedation, respiratory depression) and the potential for physical dependence result in the medication often being administered with a lockout interval.**
4. Methotrexate (Trexall) is a commonly used disease-modifying antirheumatic drug that functions by slowing or halting the progression of rheumatic disease. It is used early during the disease process to slow the progression prior to widespread damage of the affected joints. It acts to induce remission by modifying the pathology and inhibiting the immune response responsible for rheumatic disease. This medication is also used to treat various types of cancers, but is not utilized for patient-controlled analgesia.

System: Musculoskeletal System
Content Outline: Foundations for Evaluation, Differential Diagnosis, and Prognosis

 Level 2  p. 132-133

PTEXAM TWO: QUESTION 187

While performing gait analysis on a patient, a physical therapist observes a posterior trunk lean during heel strike (initial contact) to foot flat (loading response). Which of the following interventions would be the MOST appropriate to address the observed gait pattern?

1. Strengthening exercises for the quadriceps
2. **Strengthening exercises for the gluteus maximus**
3. Stretching exercises for the hip extensors
4. Stretching exercises for the hip internal rotators

Correct Answer: 2 (Dutton p. 313)

The gluteus maximus gait, which is a compensation for weakness of the gluteus maximus muscle, is characterized by a posterior trunk lean between heel strike (initial contact) and foot flat (loading response) in an attempt to maintain hip extension. In normal gait, the hip extensors should act concentrically to extend the hip during the early stance phase of the gait cycle.

1. The quadriceps should be activating eccentrically during the early stance phase. Hyperextension of the knee often occurs as a compensation to keep the knee from buckling, which is accomplished by an anterior trunk lean during early stance. Strengthening of the quadriceps would not address the weak hip extensors, primarily the gluteus maximus, that led to the described gait deviation.
2. **Strengthening exercises for the gluteus maximus would be the most appropriate intervention since the gait deviation described is typically a compensation for weak hip extensors, primarily the gluteus maximus. An emphasis on the concentric phase would also be useful due to the role of the hip extensors during this phase of the gait cycle.**
3. Stretching exercises for the hip extensors would not be indicated since the gait deviation is associated with weakness of the hip extensors, not shortening. Stretching may also further weaken these muscles.
4. Stretching exercises for the hip internal rotators would be appropriate if the internal rotators were tight. Tightness in the internal rotators often results in a toe-in gait pattern.

System: Musculoskeletal System
Content Outline: Interventions

 **Level 2**  **p. 84-89**

PTEXAM TWO: QUESTION 188

A physical therapist treats a patient with a suspected rupture of the patellar tendon. Which of the following objective findings would be the MOST indicative of this condition?

1. Marked tenderness along the anterior surface of the knee joint
2. **Inability to actively extend the knee against gravity**
3. Limited ability to complete range of motion due to hemarthrosis
4. Resistive isometrics are strong and painful for knee extension

Correct Answer: 2 (Sarwark p. 697) 

The patellar tendon originates on the patella and inserts on the tibial tuberosity. The structure is a flat ligament approximately 10 centimeters in length. A patellar tendon rupture is often caused by an extremely strong force such as in a fall or during an explosive movement such as jumping. A weakened tendon due to chronic tendonitis, chronic diseases that impact blood supply, and steroid use significantly increases the incidence of a patellar tendon rupture.

1. Marked tenderness along the anterior surface of the knee joint is a possible finding with a patellar tendon rupture particularly in the acute phase. However, there are a variety of other medical conditions such as patellofemoral syndrome, prepatellar bursitis, and patellar tendonitis that are likely to exhibit similar symptoms.
2. **A functioning patellar tendon is essential to successfully extend the knee. When the quadriceps contract, the force is transmitted through the patellar tendon using the patella as a fulcrum. Any lack of continuity in this tendon would significantly influence a patient's ability to actively extend the knee against gravity.**
3. Hemarthrosis refers to an accumulation of blood in a joint or joint cavity. The presence of hemarthrosis would likely limit range of motion, however, hemarthrosis is not necessarily associated with a patellar tendon rupture.
4. Resistive isometrics require active contraction of the surrounding musculature. As a result, if the patellar tendon is completely torn, the resistive isometrics would be weak and pain-free.

System: Musculoskeletal System
Content Outline: Foundations for Evaluation, Differential Diagnosis, and Prognosis

Level 1

PTEXAM TWO: QUESTION 189

A patient sustained a proximal humerus fracture that is non-displaced. Which of the following clinical findings would provide the BEST support for the patient being cleared to perform active-assisted exercise?

1. Hematoma formation
2. Diminished pain
3. **Callus formation**
4. Remodeling

Correct Answer: 3 (Kaufman p. 143)

Proximal humerus fractures are commonly associated with falls, particularly in older adult females due to decreased bone density. Physical therapists should consider a patient's stage of healing when selecting therapeutic activities.

1. A hematoma occurs in the fracture site soon after injury. This occurs in the inflammatory stage of bone healing and would therefore be too early to initiate active-assisted exercise.
2. Diminished pain often accompanies the initiation of more dynamic therapeutic activities following fracture, however, the finding by itself does not provide the necessary information to determine the patient's current stage of healing.
3. **Callus formation is one of the first indications that healing has occurred. The presence of a callus identified through diagnostic imaging allows the patient to progress to active-assisted exercise.**
4. Remodeling is the final stage of bone healing where the fracture has solidly united with woven bone. A patient would begin active-assisted exercise far earlier in the rehabilitation process.

System: Musculoskeletal System
Content Outline: Interventions

Level 2

PTEXAM TWO: QUESTION 190

A physical therapist reviews the medical record of a patient who has been admitted to the intensive care unit. A note from the patient's physician indicates an order for arterial blood gas analysis six times daily. Which of the following indwelling lines would be used to collect the necessary samples?

1. Intravenous
2. **Arterial**
3. Central venous
4. Pulmonary artery

Correct Answer: 2 (Fairchild p. 274)

Samples for blood gas analysis may be obtained from different regions of the vascular bed. Arterial samples are taken from either a needle puncture or indwelling catheter in a peripheral artery.

1. An intravenous line consists of a short catheter inserted through the skin into a peripheral vein. Intravenous lines are used as a route to administer medications or fluids.
2. **An arterial line consists of a catheter inserted through the skin into an artery connected to pressure tubing, a transducer, and a monitor. The device can be used for continuous direct blood pressure readings and to sample arterial blood for arterial blood gas analysis. The radial and brachial arteries are the most common sites for an arterial line.**
3. A central venous line consists of a catheter inserted through the skin into a large vein, usually the superior vena cava or inferior vena cava, or within the right atrium of the heart to measure right atrial pressure. The catheter also may be used as a route for medication or fluid administration, blood sampling, and emergency placement of a pacemaker.
4. A pulmonary artery line is a balloon-tipped catheter introduced via the internal jugular vein or subclavian vein passing through the right atrium, tricuspid valve, right ventricle, pulmonary valve, and into the pulmonary artery. It is used to monitor cardiovascular pressures and to sample mixed venous blood for gas analysis.

System: Cardiovascular and Pulmonary Systems
Content Outline: Foundations for Evaluation, Differential Diagnosis, and Prognosis

Level 1  p. 695

PTEXAM TWO: QUESTION 191

A physical therapist examines a patient with a suspected lesion of the common fibular nerve. Which objective finding would be the MOST useful to rule out the possibility of a sciatic nerve lesion?

1. Inability to actively dorsiflex the foot
2. **Preservation of the Achilles reflex**
3. Presence of a steppage gait
4. Weakness of the quadriceps muscle

Correct Answer: 2 (Roy p. 296)

The sciatic nerve is derived from fibers originating in the anterior primary rami of L4, L5, S1, S2, and S3. The nerve divides into the tibial and common fibular nerves above the level of the popliteal fossa. The common fibular nerve divides into the deep fibular nerve and superficial fibular nerve at the level of the head of the fibula. A lesion of the sciatic nerve can result in impaired functioning of the nerve branches that it supplies.

1. Inability to actively dorsiflex the foot is characteristic of a common fibular nerve injury or a sciatic nerve injury. As a result, the objective finding would not rule out the possibility of a sciatic nerve lesion.
2. **Absence of the Achilles reflex is characteristic of a tibial nerve or sciatic nerve injury. Preservation of the Achilles reflex means that a sciatic nerve injury could not be present though the common fibular nerve could still be affected since this nerve is not responsible for the Achilles reflex.**
3. A steppage gait is characterized by lifting of the feet and toes through exaggerated hip and knee flexion during swing phase. The gait pattern is associated with a common fibular nerve injury or a sciatic nerve injury due to the presence of dorsiflexor weakness.
4. Weakness of the quadriceps muscle would not typically be associated with a common fibular nerve injury or a sciatic nerve injury. Weakness of the quadriceps muscle is more likely associated with involvement of the femoral nerve.

System: Neuromuscular and Nervous Systems
Content Outline: Physical Therapy Examination

Level 2 **p. 251, 255**

PTEXAM TWO: QUESTION 192

A patient sustained a sprained thumb in a volleyball game five weeks ago and continues to have decreased range of motion with carpometacarpal abduction. What direction of glide should the physical therapist use to mobilize the first metacarpal on the trapezium in order to increase carpometacarpal abduction?

1. Medial
2. Lateral
3. Anterior
4. **Posterior**

Correct Answer: 4 (Dutton p. 802)

The movements at the first carpometacarpal joint include flexion/extension, abduction/adduction, and opposition. Flexion and extension occur in the frontal plane around an anterior-posterior axis. In this plane, the metacarpal surface is concave and the trapezium surface is convex. Abduction and adduction occur in the sagittal plane around a medial-lateral axis. In this plane, the metacarpal surface is convex and the trapezium surface is concave.

1. Since abduction occurs in an anterior-posterior direction (i.e., sagittal plane), a medial glide would not be used to increase this motion. A medial glide of the metacarpal would be used to increase carpometacarpal flexion.
2. Since abduction occurs in an anterior-posterior direction (i.e., sagittal plane), a lateral glide would not be used to increase this motion. A lateral glide of the metacarpal would be used to increase carpometacarpal extension.
3. An anterior glide of the metacarpal would be used to increase carpometacarpal adduction. In this plane, a convex surface is moving on a concave surface, so the glide (i.e., anterior) will occur in the opposite direction to the osteokinematic motion of adduction (i.e., posterior).
4. **A posterior glide of the metacarpal would be used to increase carpometacarpal abduction. In this plane, a convex surface is moving on a concave surface, so the glide (i.e., posterior) will occur in the opposite direction to the osteokinematic motion of abduction (i.e., anterior).**

System: Musculoskeletal System
Content Outline: Interventions

Level 2

PTEXAM TWO: QUESTION 193

A physical therapist works with a patient post bone marrow transplant. The patient's platelet count is 25,000 cells/mm^3. Which of the following interventions would be the MOST appropriate?

1. **Log roll training and breathing exercises**
2. **Progressive resistive exercises and infection control**
3. **Bicycling and lower extremity stretching**
4. **Patient education on fall prevention and progressive ambulation**

Correct Answer: 4 (Goodman – Pathology p. 1712)

Thrombocytopenia, or low platelet count, occurs with bone marrow transplants. Platelets function to initiate the clotting sequence to repair damaged blood vessels. Low platelet levels place the patient at risk of bleeding. Normal platelet counts are 150,000-400,000 cells/mm^3. When levels fall below 15,000-20,000 cells/mm^3, serious bleeding can occur. It is important for physical therapists to be aware of the activity restrictions associated with a low platelet count.

1. Log roll training and breathing exercises are more appropriate for a patient following abdominal surgery. Performing a log roll technique during bed mobility allows for improved comfort and diminished incisional pain. Breathing exercises are also important since the patient's breathing pattern often becomes shallow post-operatively secondary to pain.
2. Progressive resistive exercises are allowed for patients with platelet levels greater than 50,000 cells/mm^3. The patient's present platelet level results in progressive resistive exercises being contraindicated. Infection control is important in patients with decreased white blood cells. Decreased white blood cells can be problematic following chemotherapy since they place the patient at risk for opportunistic infections.
3. Bicycling is not recommended for patients with platelet levels below 50,000 cells/mm^3. Based on the patient's diagnosis, muscle length is not expected to be significantly impaired, making this intervention less desirable.
4. **Thrombocytopenia places a patient at an increased risk of bleeding following injury. Fall prevention is an important aspect of patient education for patients with this disorder. Progressive ambulation to tolerance is typically allowed as an activity for patients with platelet levels greater than or equal to 20,000 cells/mm^3.**

System: Other Systems
Content Outline: Foundations for Evaluation, Differential Diagnosis, and Prognosis

 **Level 2** **p. 395, 411**

PTEXAM TWO: QUESTION 194

A physical therapist treats a child with cerebral palsy classified at Level V using the Gross Motor Function Classification System. Which of the following recommendations from the therapist is the MOST likely?

1. **Orthoses and assistive devices for community ambulation**
2. **Orthoses and assistive devices for household ambulation**
3. **Standing frame and orthoses and/or assistive devices for household ambulation**
4. **Standing frame and wheelchair for community ambulation**

Correct Answer: 4 (Palisano p. 450)

The functional abilities of children with cerebral palsy are classified using the Gross Motor Function Classification System (GMFCS). There are five distinct levels of this classification system. Children at Level I are more functional and less severely involved than children at Level V. Children at Level V are severely limited in their functional abilities, are unable to maintain antigravity head and trunk positions, and possess minimal control of the upper and lower extremities.

1. Community ambulation is not likely for a child at Level V. A child at Levels I and II would be more likely to effectively ambulate in the community with orthoses and/or assistive devices.
2. Household ambulation is not likely for a child at Level V. A child at Levels III and IV would be more likely to have some ability to ambulate in the home, but would primarily use a wheelchair for community mobility.
3. A standing frame is a device that allows a child with an inability to maintain antigravity head and/or trunk positioning an opportunity to assume an upright position. A standing frame may be an appropriate option, however, household ambulation is not likely for a child at Level V.
4. **A standing frame is an appropriate recommendation to allow the child to assume an upright position for weight bearing through the lower extremities. The position would also serve to provide a prolonged stretch to the hip flexors and hamstrings. A child at Level V would likely use a wheelchair for both home and community mobility.**

System: Neuromuscular and Nervous Systems
Content Outline: Physical Therapy Examination

 **Level 2**  **p. 312, 328-329**

PTEXAM TWO: QUESTION 195

A patient four weeks post anterior cruciate ligament reconstruction questions a physical therapist as to why they are still partial weight bearing. Which of the following impairments would be the **MOST** likely rationale for the patient's weight bearing status?

1. **The patient lacks full active knee extension**
2. The patient has good (4/5) quadriceps strength
3. The patient has fair (3/5) hamstrings strength
4. The patient has diminished superficial cutaneous sensation

Correct Answer: 1 (Kisner p. 817)

The physician is responsible for determining a patient's weight bearing status following surgery. Physical therapists should possess an understanding of relevant factors associated with the prescribed weight bearing status and understand what is necessary for the patient to progress to full weight bearing.

1. **A patient status post anterior cruciate ligament reconstruction surgery may continue to use an assistive device for weight bearing if they do not possess full active knee extension. Ambulation on a flexed knee can result in excessive irritation of the patellofemoral joint.**
2. The quadriceps control the amount of knee flexion during initial contact (loading response) and then extend the knee toward midstance. The quadriceps also control the amount of knee flexion during pre-swing (heel off to toe off) and prevent excessive heel rise during initial swing. Good quadriceps strength would be adequate for full weight bearing on the involved lower extremity assuming the absence of other relevant clinical findings. A grade of good indicates that the patient completes range of motion against gravity with moderate resistance.
3. The hamstrings are responsible for controlling the forward swing of the leg during terminal swing. The hamstrings provide posterior support to the knee capsule when the knee is extended during stance. Fair hamstrings strength would be adequate for full weight bearing on the involved lower extremity assuming the absence of other relevant clinical findings. A grade of fair indicates that the patient completes range of motion against gravity without manual resistance.
4. Diminished superficial cutaneous sensation is common following surgery particularly in close proximity to an incision. The presence of diminished superficial cutaneous sensation would not influence a patient's weight bearing status.

System: Musculoskeletal System
Content Outline: Interventions

p. 130-131, 160-161

PTEXAM TWO: QUESTION 196

A physical therapist instructs a patient diagnosed with C6 tetraplegia in functional activities. Which of the following activities should the therapist expect the patient to have the **MOST** difficulty performing?

1. Independent raises for skin protection
2. Manual wheelchair propulsion
3. Assisted to independent transfers with a sliding board
4. **Independent self-range of motion of the lower extremities**

Correct Answer: 4 (Umphred p. 473)

A patient with C6 tetraplegia does not have sufficient motor innervation to consistently perform independent self-range of motion of the lower extremities. The lowest motor innervation at the C6 level includes extensor carpi radialis, infraspinatus, latissimus dorsi, pectoralis major, teres minor, pronator teres, and serratus anterior.

1. A patient with C6 tetraplegia can provide pressure relief using a wheelchair with push handles or loops attached.
2. A patient with C6 tetraplegia can perform manual wheelchair propulsion with friction surface handrims or rim projections.
3. A patient with C6 tetraplegia can perform assisted to independent transfers using a sliding board. A patient with C7 tetraplegia is typically independent with transfers with or without a sliding board.
4. **A patient with C6 tetraplegia cannot typically perform self-range of motion of the lower extremities. The activity is more appropriate for a patient with C7 tetraplegia.**

System: Neuromuscular and Nervous Systems
Content Outline: Interventions

p. 298-300

PTEXAM TWO: QUESTION 197

After completing a wheelchair seating and mobility assessment, a physical therapist determines the wheelchair has excessive seat width. Which of the following adverse effects would MOST likely result from excessive seat width?

1. Difficulty changing position within the wheelchair
2. Insufficient trunk support
3. **Difficulty propelling the wheelchair**
4. Increased pressure to the distal posterior thighs

Correct Answer: 3 (O'Sullivan p. 1417) 

Seat width is determined by measuring the widest aspect of the user's buttocks, hips or thighs and adding approximately two inches. This provides space for bulky clothing, orthoses or clearance of the trochanters from the armrest side panel. The standard seat width for an adult wheelchair is 18 inches.

1. Difficulty changing position within the wheelchair may be due to a wheelchair that is too small and constricts movement. A seat with excess width would not prohibit the patient from moving within the wheelchair.
2. Insufficient trunk support may be due to a wheelchair that has less back support than is recommended. Back support is measured from the seat of the chair to the floor of the axilla with the patient's shoulder flexed to 90 degrees. Subtracting approximately four inches will allow the back height to be below the inferior angles of the scapulae. The standard back height is 16–16.5 inches.
3. **Difficulty propelling a wheelchair may be due to excessive seat width. This will require the patient to stabilize at the shoulders and excessively abduct the upper extremities to reach the wheels. This produces a less functional push and increases the difficulty maneuvering through tight spaces.**
4. Increased pressure to the distal posterior thighs typically results from excessive seat depth. Seat depth is measured from the patient's posterior buttocks, along the lateral thigh to the popliteal fold; then subtract approximately two inches to avoid pressure from the front edge of the seat against the popliteal space. The standard seat depth for an adult wheelchair is 16 inches.

System: Non-Systems
Content Outline: Equipment, Devices, and Technologies; Therapeutic Modalities

 Level 2  p. 682-683

PTEXAM TWO: QUESTION 198

An 11-month-old child who has cerebral palsy attempts to maintain a quadruped position. Which of the following reflexes would MOST likely interfere with this activity if it was not integrated?

1. Galant
2. **Symmetrical tonic neck**
3. Plantar grasp
4. Positive support

Correct Answer: 2 (Ratliffe p. 26) 

Primitive reflexes are reflexes which begin in utero or in early infancy. Most of these reflexes become integrated as the infant ages. Integration denotes that the reflex is no longer present when the stimulus is provided. Failure to integrate primitive reflexes can lead to impaired movement.

1. The Galant reflex is stimulated by stroking lateral to the spine. The response is lateral sidebending to the same side as the side of the stimulus. An infant would typically be able to maintain the quadruped position if this reflex was stimulated.
2. **Head positioning is the stimulus for the symmetrical tonic neck reflex. When the head is flexed, the upper extremities flex and the lower extremities extend. When the head extends, the upper extremities extend and the lower extremities flex. The reaction of the extremities would not allow the infant to maintain a quadruped position.**
3. The plantar grasp reflex is stimulated by placing pressure on the ball of the foot, generally in standing. The response is for the toes to curl or flex. The reflex will have no impact on an infant's ability to maintain quadruped since the balls of the feet are not in contact with the floor.
4. The positive support reflex is stimulated by bearing weight through the feet. The response is for the lower extremities to extend, thereby allowing the infant to bear weight through the lower extremities. The reflex will have no impact on an infant's ability to maintain quadruped since they are not bearing weight through the feet.

System: Neuromuscular and Nervous Systems
Content Outline: Interventions

Level 2  p. 306-307

PTEXAM TWO: QUESTION 199

A physical therapist attempts to schedule a patient for an additional therapy session after completing the examination. The physician referral indicates the patient is to be seen two times a week. The therapist suggests several possible times to the patient, but the patient insists they can only come in on Wednesday at 4:30 that week for a second visit. The therapist would like to accommodate the patient, but already has two patients scheduled at that time. Which of the following actions is the **MOST** appropriate for the therapist to take?

1. Schedule the patient on Wednesday at 4:30
2. Attempt to move one of the patients scheduled on Wednesday at 4:30 to a different time
3. **Schedule the patient with another physical therapist on Wednesday at 4:30**
4. Inform the referring physician the patient will only be seen once this week in therapy

Correct Answer: 3 (Guide for Professional Conduct)

The Guide for Professional Conduct published by the American Physical Therapy Association states that physical therapists shall respect the rights and dignity of all individuals. It is therefore necessary for the physical therapist to consider not only what is best for the patient in question, but also what is best for all of the patients being treated by the physical therapist.

1. Scheduling the patient on Wednesday at 4:30 will result in the physical therapist having three patients scheduled at the same time. It is unlikely that the physical therapist will be able to provide the requisite level of care for each patient given the number of patients.
2. Attempting to move a patient who is already scheduled to another appointment is not considerate of the patient's particular needs. It is the physical therapist's responsibility to ensure that each patient in their care is treated with the utmost respect.
3. **Scheduling with another physical therapist will allow the patient to be seen two times per week as indicated on the referral and will accommodate the patient's schedule.**
4. Informing the physician that the patient cannot be seen two times per week in physical therapy is not usually considered necessary information to communicate to the physician. When possible physical therapists should attempt to provide patients with the necessary frequency of physical therapy visits.

System: Non-Systems
Content Outline: Safety and Protection; Professional Responsibilities; Research

Level 3

PTEXAM TWO: QUESTION 200

While reading the Methods section of a research report, a physical therapist notes the investigators used a repeated measures design. This type of experimental design is used to accomplish which of the following outcomes?

1. **Controls for differences between subjects**
2. Keeps the subjects "blind" to the identity of the treatment group
3. Ensures that subjects with similar characteristics are assigned to different treatment groups
4. Selects a homogenous group of subjects

Correct Answer: 1 (Portney p. 172)

Researchers may employ a number of design strategies to manipulate and control variables and measurements to strengthen the validity of their experiment and demonstrate a cause-and-effect relationship between the independent and dependent variables.

1. **In a repeated measures design all subjects experience all levels of the independent variable. This provides an efficient method for controlling differences between subjects because characteristics that may affect the outcomes, such as gender, age and physical characteristics, remain constant for each subject. Differences in outcomes can be attributed to the treatment. Since each subject acts as their own control, a repeated measures design is also called a within-subjects design.**
2. In its most complete form, blinding involves hiding the identity of group assignments from the subjects, from those who provide treatment, from those who measure the outcome variables, and from those who analyze the data. A repeated measures design may or may not include "blinding."
3. The design strategy that ensures that subjects with similar characteristics are assigned to different treatment groups is called matching. A repeated measures design may or may not include matching.
4. By selecting subjects who are homogenous with respect to a specific trait, the researcher eliminates these traits as variables that may interfere with the dependent variable. A repeated measures design may or may not use homogeneous subjects.

System: Non-Systems
Content Outline: Safety and Protection; Professional Responsibilities; Research

Level 1

p. 807-808

12

PHYSICAL THERAPY EXAM THREE ANSWER KEY

Scott Giles

PHYSICAL THERAPY
EXAM THREE ANSWER KEY

EXCELLENCE

"Aiming for perfection is always a goal in progress."

— Thomas J. Watson Jr.

Candidates do not have to be perfect to pass the NPTE-PT, however, should attempt to strive for perfection. The relative importance of the examination makes it imperative that candidates become intolerant of any risk of failure.

PTEXAM THREE: QUESTION 1

Which combination of orthoses and assistive device would be the MOST appropriate for energy efficient ambulation in a seven-year-old child with L1 to L3 level spina bifida?

1. Ankle-foot orthoses (AFO) and rolling walker
2. Ankle-foot orthoses (AFO) and standard walker
3. **Reciprocating gait orthosis (RGO) and rolling walker**
4. Reciprocating gait orthosis (RGO) and standard walker

Correct Answer: 3 (Palisano p. 569)

A child with L1 to L3 level spina bifida most likely has a manual muscle test grade of 3/5 for hip flexors, hip adductors, and knee extensors and a grade of 3 or less for hip extensors and knee flexors. Ambulation would likely be limited to household or short distances because of the amount of energy required.

1. A rolling walker requires less energy to push forward compared to a standard walker, however, an AFO will not provide the level of support needed based on the child's present strength.
2. AFOs will not assist with hip and knee extension and will not assist the child to assume the upright position needed for ambulation. A standard walker requires more energy to pick up and move forward during ambulation compared to a rolling walker.
3. **RGOs assist with hip flexion and hip extension during ambulation, which is typically necessary for children with L1-L3 level spina bifida due to insufficient strength. Since the cables of the RGO assist with hip flexion and hip extension, the child uses less energy compared to traditional hip-knee-ankle-foot orthoses. Using a rolling walker is more efficient than a standard walker.**
4. RGOs assist with the necessary hip flexion and extension as described previously, however, the standard walker would be less energy efficient and more cumbersome.

System: Neuromuscular and Nervous Systems
Content Outline: Interventions

Level 3

p. 135, 313, 348-349

PTEXAM THREE: QUESTION 2

A physical therapist adjusts the on:off time on an electrical stimulation unit prior to beginning treatment. Which on:off ratio is the MOST appropriate when using the unit for muscle re-education initially?

1. 5:1
2. 15:1
3. **1:5**
4. 1:15

Correct Answer: 3 (Prentice p. 130)

The on:off ratio should be determined based on the established therapeutic objectives. The on:off ratio for muscle strengthening is most often expressed as 1:5 while a ratio of 1:1 may be more appropriate for a therapeutic objective such as relieving muscle spasm.

1. On time should be less than off time in order to prevent muscle fatigue. The ratio is expressed in the same order that the words appear in the ratio statement "on:off" and therefore a ratio of 5:1 would result in five times greater on time than off time.
2. A ratio of 15:1 would result in severe muscle fatigue due not only to the excessive period of on time, but also to the inadequate period of off time.
3. **The initial on:off ratio should be 1:5 in order to minimize muscle fatigue. As the patient gets stronger, the on:off ratio may be altered to 1:4 or 1:3.**
4. A ratio of 1:15 would provide excessive periods of rest following each contraction and would result in extremely long treatment sessions.

System: Non-Systems
Content Outline: Equipment, Devices, and Technologies; Therapeutic Modalities

Level 1

p. 728-729

PTEXAM THREE: QUESTION 3

A physical therapist is scheduled to administer a whirlpool treatment to a patient who is HIV positive. The therapist sustained a small paper cut on their ring finger (fourth digit) three hours ago and is concerned about their ability to complete the treatment. Which of the following actions is the MOST appropriate for the therapist to take?

1. Refuse to treat the patient and document the rationale in the medical record
2. **Treat the patient using appropriate medical asepsis**
3. Ask the patient to reschedule their appointment
4. Select another appropriate treatment procedure

Correct Answer: 2 (Fairchild p. 27)

Standard precautions are designed for the care of all patients in hospitals regardless of the medical diagnosis. Health care professionals that follow established standard precautions do not place themselves or the patient at any significant risk for being contaminated or infected by pathogenic microorganisms.

1. A physical therapist cannot refuse to treat patients based on the presence of HIV or any other potentially infectious condition.
2. **A physical therapist should treat a patient that is HIV positive using established medical asepsis techniques to prevent the possible transmission of blood or body fluids.**
3. The physical therapist has an obligation to treat the patient despite their HIV status. Rescheduling the patient without adequate cause would be a violation of the patient's right to receive necessary health care services.
4. The question does not provide any evidence that the current treatment procedure is inappropriate for the patient. As a result, it would be unnecessary to select another treatment procedure.

System: Other Systems
Content Outline: Interventions

 Level 3  p. 761-763

PTEXAM THREE: QUESTION 4

A physical therapist examines a patient diagnosed with anterior compartment syndrome. The patient presents with an inability to dorsiflex the foot and a mild sensory disturbance between the first and second toes. Given the described impairments, which nerve is MOST likely involved?

1. **Deep peroneal**
2. Medial plantar
3. Tibial
4. Lateral plantar

Correct Answer: 1 (Magee p. 943)

Anterior compartment syndrome often affects the deep peroneal nerve as it passes under the extensor retinaculum. The result of nerve compression ranges from a mild sensory disturbance to an inability to dorsiflex the foot.

1. **The deep peroneal nerve innervates the tibialis anterior, extensor hallucis longus, extensor digitorum longus, extensor digitorum brevis, and peroneus tertius muscles.**
2. The medial plantar nerve is the larger of the two branches of the tibial nerve. The nerve supplies cutaneous branches to the medial three and a half digits, and motor branches to the abductor hallucis, flexor digitorum brevis, flexor hallucis brevis, and lumbrical I.
3. The tibial nerve innervates the tibialis posterior, flexor hallucis longus, flexor digitorum longus, soleus, gastrocnemius, plantaris, and popliteus muscles.
4. The lateral plantar nerve is the smaller of the two branches of the tibial nerve. The nerve supplies cutaneous branches to the lateral one and a half toes and motor branches to muscles of the sole of the foot that are not supplied by the medial plantar nerve. These include abductor digiti minimi, flexor digiti minimi, opponens digiti minimi, dorsal interossei, quadratus plantae, adductor hallucis, lumbrical II, III, IV, and plantar interossei.

System: Neuromuscular and Nervous Systems
Content Outline: Physical Therapy Examination

 Level 2  p. 213

PTEXAM THREE: QUESTION 5

A patient is admitted to the hospital following a recent illness. Laboratory testing reveals a markedly high platelet count. This finding is typical with which of the following conditions?

1. **Emphysema**
2. **Metabolic acidosis**
3. **Renal failure**
4. **Malignancy**

Correct Answer: 4 (Goodman – Differential Diagnosis p. 218)

Thrombocytosis refers to an increased number of blood platelets. This condition is usually temporary and can occur as a compensatory measure after severe hemorrhage, surgery, iron deficiency, and as a manifestation of certain cancers.

1. Emphysema is defined as an abnormal permanent enlargement of air spaces distal to the terminal bronchioles. Blood values will include an increase in red blood cells to carry the oxygen and abnormal carbon dioxide and carbon monoxide levels. Pulmonary function tests will show an increase in total lung capacity, functional residual capacity, and residual volume. The vital capacity is decreased.
2. Metabolic acidosis is an acid-base disorder defined as an accumulation of acids or a deficit of bases within the blood. Causes may include renal failure, starvation, diabetic or alcoholic ketoacidosis. Blood values will show a decrease in serum pH due to a decrease in HCO_3- or an increase in H+ ions. An arterial pH < 7.35 in the absence of an elevated $PaCO_2$ is considered metabolic acidosis.
3. Renal failure is defined as an abrupt or rapid decline in renal filtration and function. There are three categories: prerenal, intrinsic, and post renal failure. Typical causes include hypovolemia, congestive heart failure, dehydration, sepsis, and autoimmune diseases. Blood values include hypocalcemia, hyperkalemia, elevated blood urea nitrogen, creatinine, magnesium, and uric acid.
4. **Malignancy is defined as cells that have the ability to spread, invade, and destroy tissue. A tumor that is malignant may or may not respond to treatment or may return after removal. Blood values vary based on type, degree, and location of the malignancy, however, are often increased as a manifestation of an occult neoplasm such as lung cancer.**

System: Other Systems
Content Outline: Foundations for Evaluation, Differential Diagnosis, and Prognosis

Level 2

PTEXAM THREE: QUESTION 6

A physical therapist completes a coordination assessment on a patient with a cerebellar lesion. Which of the following findings would be the LEAST likely to be associated with cerebellar dysfunction?

1. **Dysmetria**
2. **Hypertonia**
3. **Ataxia**
4. **Nystagmus**

Correct Answer: 2 (O'Sullivan p. 193)

Cerebellar pathology is often characterized by incoordinated movement. Specific motor impairments associated with cerebellar pathology include ataxia, hypotonicity, dysmetria, dysdiadochokinesia, nystagmus, tremor, and scanning speech.

1. Dysmetria refers to the inability to control the range of a movement and the force of muscular activity. The result of this is often overshooting or undershooting.
2. **Cerebellar dysfunction would typically be associated with hypotonia and not hypertonia. Hypotonia causes the patient to have difficulty fixating the limb, leading to incoordination with movement.**
3. Ataxia refers to the inability to perform coordinated movements. Ataxia can affect gait, patterns of movement, and posture. The condition increases the incidence of errors in the rate, rhythm, and timing of responses.
4. Nystagmus refers to abnormal eye movement that entails nonvolitional, rhythmic oscillation of the eyes. The speed of movement is typically faster in one direction than the other direction.

System: Neuromuscular and Nervous Systems
Content Outline: Foundations for Evaluation, Differential Diagnosis, and Prognosis

Level 1  p. 238-239, 275

PTEXAM THREE: QUESTION 7

A physical therapist classifies an obtained sputum sample as purulent. Which of the following medical conditions would MOST likely be associated with this type of sputum?

1. Asthma
2. **Lung abscess**
3. Pulmonary edema
4. Tuberculosis

Correct Answer: 2 (Bickley p. 334)

Sputum refers to matter expectorated from the respiratory system usually consisting of saliva, mucus or foreign matter. The relative color and composition of the sputum can provide valuable information to health care providers related to a patient's medical condition. Purulent sputum tends to be yellowish-greenish in color and is most often indicative of infection.

1. Asthma is a chronic inflammatory disease of the airways. Sputum associated with asthma is most often described as mucoid.
2. **A lung abscess refers to necrosis of pulmonary tissue and formation of cavities containing necrotic debris or fluid caused by infection. Sputum associated with a lung abscess is most often described as purulent.**
3. Pulmonary edema refers to an abnormal accumulation of fluid in the alveolar spaces of the lungs. Sputum associated with pulmonary edema is most often described as frothy.
4. Tuberculosis refers to a highly contagious infectious disease spread via airborne transmission. Sputum associated with tuberculosis is often blood-tinged due to damage to the respiratory tract caused by excessive coughing.

System: Cardiovascular and Pulmonary Systems
Content Outline: Physical Therapy Examination

PTEXAM THREE: QUESTION 8

A physical therapist participates in a research study to determine the effect of noise level on the ability to perform a physical skill. In this study, noise is what type of variable?

1. **Independent**
2. Dependent
3. Criterion
4. Extraneous

Correct Answer: 1 (Portney p. 129)

The independent variable is also known as the experimental or predictor variable. It is the condition, intervention or characteristic that will predict or cause an outcome in an experimental study.

1. **Noise level is the independent variable because it is the condition or characteristic that the researcher will manipulate to see how it changes physical skill.**
2. The dependent variable is also known as the outcome variable, which is the response or effect that is presumed to vary with the independent variable. Physical skill is the dependent variable because it is presumed to vary depending on noise level.
3. The term criterion variable is a synonym for dependent variable.
4. An extraneous variable is also known as a nuisance or intervening variable. An extraneous variable is any factor that is not related to the purpose of the study, but that may affect the dependent variable.

System: Non-Systems
Content Outline: Safety and Protection; Professional Responsibilities; Research

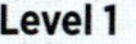

p. 809

PTEXAM THREE: QUESTION 9

A patient with a C6 spinal cord injury is examined in physical therapy. Which of the following objective findings would be the BEST indication that the spinal cord injury is incomplete rather than complete?

1. Intact sensation on the lateral portion of the shoulder
2. Absent triceps reflex
3. **Diminished sensation over the hypothenar eminence**
4. Weakness of the biceps muscle

Correct Answer: 3 (Magee p. 24)

A patient with a complete C6 spinal cord injury would not possess motor, sensory or reflex function below the C6 level. As a result, any identified finding below this level could provide evidence that the injury is not complete.

1. The dermatome associated with the lateral portion of the shoulder is C5 and therefore sensation in this area would typically be intact in a complete spinal cord injury at the C6 level.
2. The triceps reflex is associated with the C7-C8 nerve root and therefore the reflex would be absent in a complete spinal cord injury at the C6 level.
3. **The dermatome that corresponds to the hypothenar eminence is at the C8 level. As a result, the finding of diminished sensation (not absent) at a level below the level of injury (i.e., C6) indicates that the injury is incomplete.**
4. The biceps muscle is innervated by C5-C6 and therefore weakness is often associated with a spinal cord injury at this level.

System: Neuromuscular and Nervous Systems
Content Outline: Foundations for Evaluation, Differential Diagnosis, and Prognosis

 Level 2  p. 245-246, 295-296

PTEXAM THREE: QUESTION 10

A physical therapist reviews the medical record of a 77-year-old patient who was prescribed non-steroidal anti-inflammatory medications (NSAIDs) for pain post arthroscopic surgery. If toxicity is the primary concern, the physician would have likely prescribed an analgesic that possesses which of the following drug characteristics?

1. **A short half-life**
2. A long half-life
3. Minimal biotransformation
4. Limited clearance

Correct Answer: 1 (Ciccone p. 35)

When prescribing medication, the physician should be aware of a variety of factors including absorption, distribution, metabolism, excretion, and pharmacodynamics.

1. **Half-life is defined as the amount of time required for fifty percent of the drug remaining in the body to be eliminated. In general, elderly patients do not metabolize medications as quickly as younger patients which creates higher plasma levels. As a result, the elderly are at a higher risk for toxicity or adverse effects. Medications with a short half-life reduce these risks.**
2. Half-life is typically the most relevant pharmacokinetic parameter that is considered with the prescription of medication. NSAIDs such as Aleve have a long half-life (approximately ten hours) whereas acetaminophen has a short half-life (approximately two hours).
3. Biotransformation refers to the series of chemical changes that take place within a drug following its administration, most often due to enzymatic activity. Biotransformation typically converts the drug to an inactive form and reduces the chance for toxic effects that occur with accumulation or prolonged administration. Minimal biotransformation would not be as effective in preventing drug toxicity as a medication with a shorter half-life.
4. Clearance refers to the rate at which an active drug is removed from the body. Clearance is dependent on the organ's or tissue's ability to extract the drug from the plasma and on the overall perfusion of the organ. If a drug possessed limited clearance, there would be a higher risk for toxicity since it would take the drug longer to be eliminated from the system.

System: Other Systems
Content Outline: Foundations for Evaluation, Differential Diagnosis, and Prognosis

 Level 3  p. 584-585

PTEXAM THREE: QUESTION 11

A physical therapist examines the reflex status of a patient. Which technique should the therapist use to assess the patient's superficial reflexes?

1. Brushing the skin with a light, feathery object
2. Passive joint range of motion
3. **Stroking the skin with a blunt object**
4. Tapping over a muscle tendon

Correct Answer: 3 (O'Sullivan p. 148) 

Superficial cutaneous reflexes are elicited with a light stroke of the skin. The anticipated response is a small or brief contraction of the muscles innervated by a given spinal segment that received the light stroking.

1. Light touch sensation is assessed by brushing the skin with a light, feathery object.
2. Passive joint range of motion is performed to assess the influence of noncontractile structures on range of motion or tone (hypertonicity or hypotonicity).
3. **The plantar reflex (S1, S2) is an example of a superficial reflex. The reflex is elicited by stroking the lateral aspect of the foot from the heel to the ball of the foot with a blunt object. A normal response is indicated by flexion of the great toe, while an abnormal response is indicated by extension of the great toe with fanning of the four other toes (Babinski sign). The Babinski sign is often associated with upper motor neuron damage.**
4. Deep tendon reflexes are performed to test the integrity of the spinal reflex and are elicited by tapping over a muscle tendon. A physical therapist should strike the tendon with a reflex hammer after placing the tendon on slight stretch.

System: Neuromuscular and Nervous Systems
Content Outline: Physical Therapy Examination

 Level 1

 p. 252-253

PTEXAM THREE: QUESTION 12

A physical therapist treats a patient who sustained a back injury two weeks ago. The patient returns to the outpatient clinic two hours after a physical therapy session to report increased back pain. The patient has had three previous therapy visits and has had little difficulty with a program consisting of palliative modalities and pelvic stabilization exercises. Which of the following actions is the MOST appropriate for the therapist to take?

1. Contact the referring physician to discuss the patient's plan of care
2. **Instruct the patient to discontinue the pelvic stabilization exercises and re-examine the patient at the next visit**
3. Refer the patient to the emergency room of a local hospital
4. Instruct the patient to cancel existing physical therapy visits and schedule an appointment with the physician

Correct Answer: 2 (Criteria for Standards of Practice)

Physical therapists must carefully assess a patient's response to physical therapy interventions. The severity of the patient's signs and symptoms combined with the therapist's knowledge of their medical condition assists the therapist to make an informed decision regarding an appropriate course of action.

1. The patient's current complaints do not suggest the need for immediate consultation with the referring physician.
2. **The physical therapist should have the patient discontinue any activities that increase their pain. The therapist can re-examine the patient at the next scheduled visit and determine an appropriate course of action based on the findings.**
3. The patient's current complaints are not severe enough to warrant referral to an emergency room.
4. Physical therapists most often refer patients back to the referring physician due to a change in medical status or failure to make anticipated progress in physical therapy. The patient's recent increase in symptoms does not suggest that the patient is not a candidate for physical therapy.

System: Musculoskeletal System
Content Outline: Interventions

Level 3

PTEXAM THREE: QUESTION 13

An older adult patient reports persistent pain, weakness, and stiffness affecting the pelvis and shoulders. Additionally, the patient has a higher than normal erythrocyte sedimentation rate (ESR). Which of the following medical conditions is the MOST consistent with the described clinical presentation?

1. Pseudogout
2. Gout
3. **Polymyalgia rheumatica**
4. Systemic lupus erythematosus

Correct Answer: 3 (Kaufman p. 132)

Musculoskeletal pain, stiffness, and weakness are common elements of arthritic conditions, which are experienced at a high rate in older adults. Laboratory values can be useful to establish a definitive medical diagnosis.

1. Pseudogout is an inflammatory condition characterized by the deposition of calcium crystals in the articular and periarticular structures. Erythrocyte sedimentation rate would not be used to diagnose this condition. Pseudogout most commonly affects the knee joints.
2. Gout is an inflammatory condition characterized by acute pain due to the deposition of urate crystals in the joint which causes hyperuricemia. This condition most commonly affects the first metatarsophalangeal joint.
3. **Polymyalgia rheumatica is a systemic inflammatory condition that is experienced primarily by older adults. Patients with this condition exhibit a high erythrocyte sedimentation rate (ESR) and pain is most commonly experienced in the pelvic and shoulder girdles.**
4. Systemic lupus erythematosus is an autoimmune condition characterized by numerous organ and joint issues. Typically, a patient with systemic lupus erythematosus exhibits a trademark butterfly rash and experiences joint pain primarily affecting smaller joints.

System: Other Systems
Content Outline: Foundations for Evaluation, Differential Diagnosis, and Prognosis

Level 2

PTEXAM THREE: QUESTION 14

A physical therapist examines a patient who exhibits pain and sensory loss in the posterior thigh, lateral calf, and dorsal foot. Extensor hallucis longus strength is Poor (2/5), however, the Achilles reflex is normal. What spinal level should the therapist expect to be involved?

1. L4
2. **L5**
3. S1
4. S2

Correct Answer: 2 (Magee p. 25)

Involvement of a specific spinal level often results in predictable impairments including diminished sensation, muscle weakness, impaired reflexes, and paresthesias.

1. L4 nerve root:
   Dermatome – medial buttock, lateral thigh, medial leg, dorsum of foot, great toe
   Myotome – tibialis anterior, extensor hallucis
   Reflexes – patellar
2. **L5 nerve root:**
   Dermatome – buttock, posterior and lateral thigh, lateral aspect of leg, dorsum of foot, medial half of sole, first, second, and third toes
   Myotome – extensor hallucis, peroneals, gluteus medius, dorsiflexors, hamstrings, plantar flexors
   Reflexes – medial hamstrings, posterior tibial
3. S1 nerve root:
   Dermatome – lateral and plantar aspect of foot
   Myotome – hamstrings, peroneals, plantar flexors
   Reflexes – Achilles
4. S2 nerve root:
   Dermatome – buttock, thigh, posterior leg
   Myotome – hamstrings, plantar flexors
   Reflexes – Achilles

System: Neuromuscular and Nervous Systems
Content Outline: Physical Therapy Examination

Level 1

p. 71, 245-246, 253-255

PTEXAM THREE: QUESTION 15

When is it considered acceptable for a clinical trial to include a non-treatment control group as a basis for comparison with a new experimental therapy?

1. **When there is no known effective treatment for the patient's condition**
2. **When the experimental therapy has shown positive results in animal studies**
3. **When the study is reviewed by the facility's Institutional Review Board (IRB)**
4. **When subjects are randomly assigned to a group**

Correct Answer: 1 (Portney p. 49)

According to the current Declaration of Helsinki, in research with human beings, a placebo control may be used in clinical conditions for which no treatments have been effective or when the purpose of the research is to determine if a particular treatment is not effective. In all cases, the researcher is obliged to inform the potential human subjects when the study includes a control group.

1. **A non-treatment control group may be used in clinical conditions for which no treatments have been effective.**
2. Positive results in animal studies do not make the use of a non-treatment control group acceptable in research on humans.
3. Federal regulations in the United States require that an Institutional Review Board (IRB) review research proposals using human subjects prior to implementation to ensure that the rights of the subjects are protected. However, review by the IRB does not make the use of a non-treatment control group acceptable.
4. Random assignment to groups is the best way to control for confounding variables that could affect the outcomes of the study. However, it does not make the use of a non-treatment control group acceptable.

System: Non-Systems
Content Outline: Safety and Protection; Professional Responsibilities; Research

 Level 2  p. 808-809

PTEXAM THREE: QUESTION 16

A physical therapist educates a patient on how to apply a transparent film dressing to a wound located on the anterior surface of their thigh. What is the MOST appropriate distance of the dressing's border from the edge of the wound when using this type of dressing?

1. **10 millimeters**
2. **1 centimeter**
3. **3 centimeters**
4. **6 centimeters**

Correct Answer: 3 (Sussman p. 504) 

Transparent film dressings are thin membranes made from transparent polyurethane with water-resistant adhesives. The dressings are permeable to vapor and oxygen, but are largely impermeable to bacteria and water. They are highly elastic, conform to a variety of body contours, and allow for easy visual inspection of the wound since they are transparent. Film dressings are useful for superficial or partial-thickness wounds with minimal drainage (e.g., scalds, abrasions, lacerations).

1. A 10 millimeter border is less than a half inch (i.e., 0.39 inches) and would result in the adherent portion of the transparent film dressing being too close to the wound bed. In addition, moisture around the immediate wound area may make it difficult to secure the dressing.
2. A 1 centimeter border is the same as a 10 millimeter border (i.e., 0.39 inches).
3. **A 3 centimeter border is slightly over one inch (i.e., 1.18 inches). A minimum border of one inch provides sufficient coverage for the wound and ensures that the adherent used to secure the dressing is an adequate distance away from the wound bed. When removing a transparent film dressing, it should be lifted slowly and carefully from the edges to the center to avoid disrupting the epidermal layer of skin.**
4. A 6 centimeter border is over two inches (i.e., 2.36 inches) and would be considered excessive for a transparent film dressing. There would be no clinically viable reason to cover this much of the peri-wound area since the sole purpose of the border is to protect the wound bed and secure the dressing.

System: Other Systems
Content Outline: Interventions

 Level 1  p. 510

PTEXAM THREE: QUESTION 17

A patient is referred to physical therapy with a diagnosis of carpal tunnel syndrome. The patient is scheduled for a diagnostic test that may help to confirm the diagnosis. Which of the following electrodiagnostic tests would be the MOST appropriate?

1. Electroencephalography
2. Evoked potentials
3. **Nerve conduction velocity**
4. Electromyography

Correct Answer: 3 (Tan p. 45)

Carpal tunnel syndrome results from repetitive compression of the median nerve where it passes through the carpal tunnel at the wrist. Nerve conduction velocity is commonly used to diagnose carpal tunnel syndrome. Less formal methods to assist in identifying carpal tunnel syndrome include Phalen's test and Tinel's sign.

1. Electroencephalography is the recording of the electrical activity of the brain. The electrical activity is collected by examining the difference between the electrical potential of two electrodes placed at different locations on the scalp. Electroencephalography is used to assess seizure activity, metabolic disorders, and cerebellar lesions.
2. An evoked potential refers to electrical activity recorded from the presentation of a stimulus. Signals can be recorded from the cerebral cortex, brain stem, spinal cord, and peripheral nerves. Evoked potentials can be used to determine how quickly and completely nerve signals reach the brain and can be used to assist with the diagnosis of several medical conditions including multiple sclerosis.
3. **Nerve conduction velocity refers to the speed by which an action potential travels down a peripheral nerve. The measure is recorded in meters per second. Nerve conduction velocity can be used to diagnose conditions such as carpal tunnel syndrome, peripheral neuropathy, and Guillain-Barre syndrome.**
4. Electromyography is the recording of the electrical activity of a selected muscle or muscle group at rest and during voluntary contraction. Electromyography is performed by inserting a needle electrode percutaneously into a muscle or through the use of surface electrodes. The test is commonly used to assess peripheral nerve injuries and to differentiate between various neuromuscular disorders.

System: Neuromuscular and Nervous Systems
Content Outline: Foundations for Evaluation, Differential Diagnosis, and Prognosis

 Level 2  p. 272, 275, 324-325, 699

PTEXAM THREE: QUESTION 18

A physical therapist performs a goniometric measurement of the wrist on a patient with carpal tunnel syndrome. Based on the presented image, which value would be the MOST anticipated assuming the patient has normal wrist range of motion?

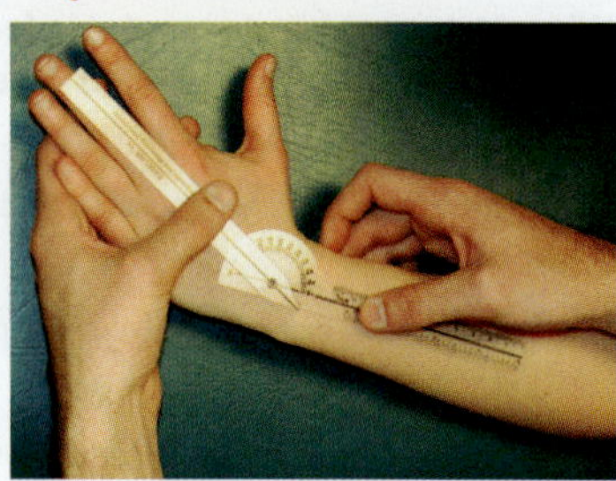

1. **0-20 degrees**
2. 0-30 degrees
3. 0-40 degrees
4. 0-70 degrees

Correct Answer: 1 (Norkin p. 159) 

The presented image depicts a physical therapist measuring radial deviation of the wrist. The measurement is performed with the axis of the goniometer aligned over the middle of the dorsal aspect of the wrist over the capitate. The stationary arm is aligned along the dorsal midline of the forearm using the lateral epicondyle of the humerus for reference. The moving arm is positioned over the dorsal midline of the third metacarpal.

1. **A measurement of 0-20 degrees is consistent with normal wrist radial deviation.**
2. A measurement of 0-30 degrees is consistent with normal wrist ulnar deviation.
3. A measurement of 0-40 degrees would be greater than the normal values of wrist radial or ulnar deviation.
4. A measurement of 0-70 degrees is consistent with normal wrist extension.

System: Musculoskeletal System
Content Outline: Physical Therapy Examination

Level 1  p. 90, 92-93

PTEXAM THREE: QUESTION 19

A physical therapist performs the talar tilt test on a patient who sustained an inversion ankle sprain. Which ligament does the talar tilt test examine?

1. Anterior talotibial
2. **Calcaneofibular**
3. Deltoid
4. Posterior talotibial

Correct Answer: 2 (Magee p. 936)

The talar tilt test requires the patient to be positioned in supine or sidelying with the knee flexed to 90 degrees. The physical therapist stabilizes the distal tibia with one hand while grasping the talus with the other hand. The foot is maintained in a neutral position. The therapist tilts the talus into inversion and eversion. A positive test is indicated by excessive inversion and may be indicative of a calcaneofibular ligament sprain.

1. The anterior talotibial ligament extends from the tip of the medial malleolus to the anterior aspect of the medial surface of the talus. The ligament is extremely strong and resists abduction of the talus when it is in plantar flexion and eversion.
2. **The calcaneofibular ligament is a round cord that passes posteroinferiorly from the tip of the lateral malleolus to the lateral surface of the calcaneus. The integrity of the ligament can be assessed using the talar tilt test.**
3. The deltoid ligament refers to the collective medial ligaments of the ankle. The ligament as a whole attaches proximally to the medial aspect of the medial malleolus and fans out to the various distal attachments. The ligament provides medial ligamentous support by resisting eversion of the talus.
4. The posterior talotibial ligament extends from the medial malleolus to the medial side of the talus and the medial tuberosity of the talus. The ligament resists ankle dorsiflexion and lateral translation and external rotation of the talus.

System: Musculoskeletal System
Content Outline: Physical Therapy Examination

Level 1

p. 110

PTEXAM THREE: QUESTION 20

A patient referred to physical therapy with chronic low back pain has failed to make any progress toward meeting established goals in over three weeks of treatment. The physical therapist has employed a variety of treatment techniques, but has yet to observe any sign of subjective or objective improvement in the patient's condition. Which of the following actions is the MOST appropriate for the therapist to take next?

1. Transfer the patient to another therapist's schedule
2. Re-examine the patient and establish new goals
3. Continue to modify the patient's treatment plan
4. **Alert the referring physician to the patient's status**

Correct Answer: 4 (Criteria for Standards of Practice)

Physical therapists must be willing to consult with a referring physician when there is ample evidence suggesting that the patient is not benefitting from physical therapy services.

1. There is no supporting evidence to suggest that the patient's failure to make progress is influenced by the patient- therapist relationship or the therapist's level of competence.
2. Re-examining the patient and establishing new goals is a viable option, however, failing to make progress during a relatively long period of time (i.e., three weeks) necessitates formal communication with the physician.
3. Modifying an established treatment plan is desirable when progress has not been made or the rate of progress is not satisfactory. Although a desirable option, the length of time the patient has failed to make progress would necessitate formal communication with the physician.
4. **Formal communication should occur with the referring physician when a patient fails to make progress in physical therapy. This is particularly relevant in the described scenario since the physical therapist has employed a variety of treatment techniques and has not observed any sign of subjective or objective improvement.**

System: Musculoskeletal System
Content Outline: Interventions

Level 3

PTEXAM THREE: QUESTION 21

A physical therapist examines a patient who had a cyst removed from the larynx two days ago. The patient's speech sounds very rough and hoarse. Which of the following terms BEST describes this type of abnormal sound?

1. **Dysphonia**
2. Dysarthria
3. Dysphasia
4. Diplopia

Correct Answer: 1 (Magee p. 109)

Laryngeal cysts are rare, generally benign lesions that can affect all age groups.

1. **Dysphonia is a disorder of vocalization characterized by an abnormal production of sounds from the larynx. The principal complaint of dysphonia is hoarseness ranging from mild roughness of the voice to an inability to produce sound.**
2. Dysarthria indicates defects in articulation, enunciation or rhythm of speech. It is usually caused by extraneural problems such as malformation of the oral structures, poor fitting dentures, and impairment of the musculature of the tongue, palate, pharynx or lips because of incoordination. It is characterized by slurring, slowness of speech, indistinct speech, and breaks in normal speech rhythm.
3. Dysphasia refers to the inability to use and understand written and spoken words as a result of disorders involving the cortical centers of speech or their interconnections in the dominant cerebral hemisphere.
4. Diplopia is a condition in which a single object is seen as two rather than one. The condition is caused by defective function of the extraocular muscles or a disorder of the nerves that innervate the muscles.

System: Other Systems
Content Outline: Foundations for Evaluation, Differential Diagnosis, and Prognosis

Level 2

PTEXAM THREE: QUESTION 22

A physical therapist treats a patient diagnosed with gouty arthritis. Which joint should the therapist expect to be the MOST likely affected by this medical condition?

1. Hip
2. Knee
3. Ankle
4. **Toe**

Correct Answer: 4 (Goodman – Differential Diagnosis p. 413)

Gouty arthritis is a condition characterized by excess uric acid in the blood that results in the formation of crystals within the joints, which triggers a painful inflammatory response. Gouty arthritis can affect any of the joints in the body, though it commonly affects the peripheral joints of the lower extremities.

1. Though any joint can be affected by gouty arthritis, the hip is not a joint that is typically affected.
2. Though the knee can be affected by gouty arthritis, it makes up a relatively small percentage of the cases.
3. Though the ankle can be affected by gouty arthritis, it makes up a relatively small percentage of the cases.
4. **The peripheral joints of the feet are the sites most commonly affected by gouty arthritis. The metatarsophalangeal joint of the great toe is affected in 90% of the cases of gouty arthritis.**

System: Other Systems
Content Outline: Foundations for Evaluation, Differential Diagnosis, and Prognosis

Level 1

p. 648

PTEXAM THREE: QUESTION 23

A physical therapist works on community re-integration with a patient prior to discharge to home. Which aspect of gait should the therapist focus on during training to ensure the patient's ability to safely cross the street?

1. Step length
2. **Velocity**
3. Cadence
4. Heel strike

Correct Answer: 2 (O'Sullivan p. 257)

Physical therapists who are working with patients on community re-integration need to have an understanding of distance and time requirements prior to setting goals for functional ambulation. For example, the patient who is re-entering the community may need to be able to walk at a specific velocity to safely cross the street.

1. Step length is the distance between two successive points of contact of the right and left lower extremities during gait. Impaired joint mobility, pain or muscle weakness can result in reduced step length. A reduced step length may increase the time it takes for a patient to cross the street, but improving step length alone does not ensure safety.
2. **Velocity is the rate of forward progression. It is defined as the distance traveled per unit of time. Gait velocity, or gait speed, is the most important measure of a patient's ability to safely cross the street.**
3. Cadence is the number of steps taken per unit of time. Cadence does not specifically address the distance covered per unit of time and would therefore not be the most important aspect of gait to ensure safety when crossing the street.
4. Heel strike is the point when the heel contacts the ground during normal gait. The absence of a heel strike can result in a foot slap or toe walking. These deviations can be caused by flaccid or weak dorsiflexors in the case of a foot slap or shortening or spasticity of the plantar flexors in the case of toe walking. The absence of a heel strike can impact gait and place the patient at a risk of falling, however, it is not the most important aspect of gait to ensure safety when crossing the street.

System: Musculoskeletal System
Content Outline: Interventions

Level 1  p. 84-88

PTEXAM THREE: QUESTION 24

A physical therapist treats a patient receiving supplemental oxygen using a nasal cannula with a flow rate of three liters per minute. Which value BEST approximates the percentage of oxygen delivered to the patient?

1. 25%
2. 29%
3. **33%**
4. 37%

Correct Answer: 3 (Le Baudour p. 175)

A nasal cannula delivers oxygen into the nostrils using two small prongs. Oxygen flow rates typically range from one liter per minute to six liters per minute. Supplemental oxygen is usually mixed with room air which is 21% oxygen. Oxygen concentration is increased by approximately 4% for every one liter per minute increase in oxygen flow.

1. An oxygen flow rate of one liter per minute would result in approximately 25% oxygen delivered.
2. An oxygen flow rate of two liters per minute would result in approximately 29% oxygen delivered.
3. **An oxygen flow rate of three liters per minute would result in approximately 33% oxygen delivered.**
4. An oxygen flow rate of four liters per minute would result in approximately 37% oxygen delivered.

System: Cardiovascular and Pulmonary Systems
Content Outline: Interventions

 Level 2  p. 419, 695

PTEXAM THREE: QUESTION 25

A physical therapist assesses a patient's proximal muscle control by attempting to identify the presence of Gowers' sign. Which position would be the MOST appropriate to administer the active portion of the testing procedure?

1. Hooklying
2. Modified plantigrade
3. **Squatting**
4. Supine

Correct Answer: 3 (Dutton p. 1454) 

Gowers' sign describes a specific method that patients with muscular dystrophy often use to assume an upright position. The presence of Gowers' sign is assessed by having a patient attempt to stand upright from a squatting position. A positive sign (i.e., Gowers' sign) is observed when the patient has to walk their hands up their thighs to achieve the desired upright position.

1. A hooklying position refers to a position in which the patient is lying in supine with their hips and knees bent and their feet flat on the floor with their arms positioned at their side. This position would not be utilized when attempting to identify the presence of Gowers' sign.
2. A modified plantigrade position is characterized by lower extremity weight bearing in supported standing, while leaning with upper extremity support on a table or weight bearing surface. This position would not be utilized when attempting to identify the presence of Gowers' sign.
3. **A squatting position refers to crouching or sitting with the knees bent and the heels close to or touching the buttocks or the back of the thighs. This position is utilized when attempting to identify the presence of Gowers' sign. The individual attempts to move from the squatting position to upright standing. A positive test, or Gowers' sign, occurs when the patient uses their upper extremities to compensate for weakness by walking their hands up their thighs to assist them during the transition from squatting to an upright position.**
4. A supine position refers to lying horizontally with the face and torso facing up. This position would not be utilized when attempting to identify the presence of Gowers' sign.

System: Neuromuscular and Nervous Systems
Content Outline: Physical Therapy Examination

 Level 1   p. 334-335

PTEXAM THREE: QUESTION 26

A physical therapist treating a four-year-old child with cerebral palsy decides to utilize sustained positioning through lower extremity casting. What is the PRIMARY goal of this intervention?

1. Increased standing tolerance
2. Increased core stability
3. **Decreased hypertonicity**
4. Decreased dependent edema

Correct Answer: 3 (Fell p. 639) 

Sustained positioning is a therapeutic technique often utilized with patients with cerebral palsy. Inhibitive casting is a specific type of sustained positioning that incorporates a series of static casts to decrease hypertonicity, increase range of motion, and improve overall function. Patients are often encouraged to trial inhibitive casting as a prerequisite to a custom molded orthosis. The orthosis utilizes tone-reducing properties in order to normalize tone and maintain range of motion.

1. Casting of the lower extremity would not be an intervention used to increase a patient's standing tolerance. Standing while utilizing a standing frame would be an example of an intervention used to increase standing tolerance.
2. Casting of the lower extremity would not be an intervention used to increase a patient's core stability. Therapeutic techniques such as approximation, weight bearing, and rotational activities would be effective interventions to increase core stability.
3. **Casting of the lower extremity allows for sustained positioning at the ankle in a predetermined position. This process is closely monitored and casting is repeated at set intervals to further improve range and decrease the hypertonicity that is often associated with cerebral palsy. The design of the cast integrates pressure points to decrease tone and diminish the influence of spasticity.**
4. Casting of the lower extremity would not be an intervention used to decrease dependent edema. Custom compression stockings to assist with venous return would be an example of an intervention used to decrease dependent edema.

System: Neuromuscular and Nervous Systems
Content Outline: Interventions

 Level 2  p. 312, 328-329

PTEXAM THREE: QUESTION 27

A physical therapist reads a recent entry in a patient's medical record that indicates aspiration was performed in the elbow region. This procedure is MOST commonly associated with which of the following conditions?

1. Dorsal ganglion cyst
2. Lateral epicondylitis
3. Medial epicondylitis
4. **Olecranon bursitis**

Correct Answer: 4 (Dutton p. 753)

Aspiration, also known as arthrocentesis, refers to a technique using a sterile needle to remove fluid from a joint. A local anesthetic is typically utilized prior to the needle puncture to minimize discomfort. The obtained fluid is often sent to a laboratory for further analysis.

1. A dorsal ganglion cyst is a benign cyst located on the back of the wrist or hand. Although aspiration may be appropriate, a dorsal ganglion cyst would not be located at the elbow. The primary rationale for aspirating the cyst would be due to cosmesis.
2. Lateral epicondylitis (i.e., tennis elbow) refers to an irritation or inflammation of the common extensor muscles at their origin on the lateral epicondyle of the humerus. Aspiration is not common with lateral epicondylitis, however, if the condition has not responded to conservative treatment an injection of a corticosteroid may be warranted.
3. Medial epicondylitis (i.e., golfer's or swimmer's elbow) results from repeated microtrauma to the flexor carpi radialis and/or the humeral head of the pronator teres during pronation and wrist flexion. Aspiration is not common with medial epicondylitis, however, if the condition has not responded to conservative treatment an injection of a corticosteroid may be warranted.
4. **Olecranon bursitis is characterized by pain, redness, and swelling around the olecranon caused by inflammation of the elbow's bursa. Aspirating the excess bursa fluid is often performed to relieve the inflammation and prevent further accumulation of fluid. An excessive amount of fluid in this region can inhibit range of motion and functional use of the elbow. The aspirated fluid is often cultured and evaluated for crystals to rule out infection or gout.**

System: Musculoskeletal System
Content Outline: Foundations for Evaluation, Differential Diagnosis, and Prognosis

PTEXAM THREE: QUESTION 28

A patient recently admitted to an acute care hospital is referred to physical therapy. The physical therapist documents the following clinical signs: pallor, cyanosis, and cool skin. These clinical signs are MOST consistent with which of the following conditions?

1. Cor pulmonale
2. **Anemia**
3. Hypertension
4. Diaphoresis

Correct Answer: 2 (Paz p. 183)

Anemia refers to a reduction in the number of circulating red blood cells or a reduction in hemoglobin. Anemia is the most common disorder of the blood. The three main categories of anemia include excessive blood loss (i.e., hemorrhage), excessive blood cell destruction (i.e., hemolysis), and deficient red blood cell production (i.e., hematopoiesis).

1. Cor pulmonale is right-sided heart failure arising from disease of the lungs. Signs of right ventricular failure are elevated central venous pressure with distension of the neck veins and shortness of breath. Ascites (accumulation of fluid in the peritoneal cavity) and peripheral edema of the feet and ankles are common. Individuals with heart failure often experience fatigue and exercise intolerance.
2. **A decrease in the number of red blood cells that carry oxygen in the blood results in a variety of symptoms including pallor, cyanosis, cool skin, vertigo, weakness, headache, and malaise.**
3. Hypertension refers to abnormally high blood pressure. It is classified as stage 1 hypertension, stage 2 hypertension, and hypertensive crisis. Hypertension often goes unrecognized as mild to moderate elevations in blood pressure usually are not symptomatic.
4. Diaphoresis refers to profuse perspiration and is often associated with shock or other emergent medical conditions.

System: Cardiovascular and Pulmonary Systems
Content Outline: Foundations for Evaluation, Differential Diagnosis, and Prognosis

p. 395

PTEXAM THREE: QUESTION 29

A physical therapist instructs a patient in a home stretching program that includes the stretch shown in the image. What tissue is MOST likely targeted in this stretch?

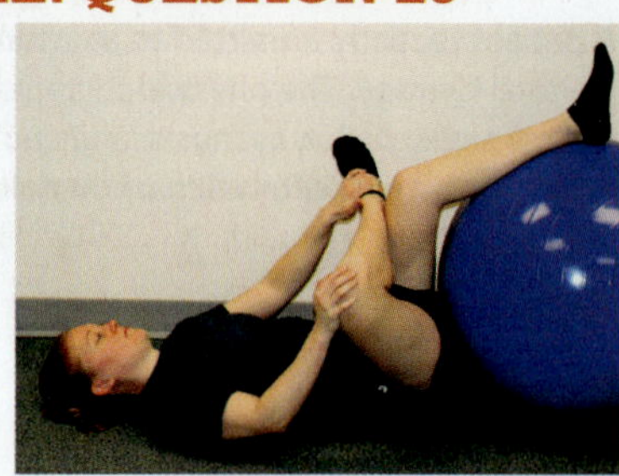

1. **Gluteus medius**
2. **Iliotibial band**
3. **Piriformis**
4. **Rectus femoris**

Correct Answer: 3 (Brody p. 576)

The image shows a patient stretching the right piriformis. The patient uses the left leg to assist with lateral rotation of the right hip. The patient will perceive tension in the right buttock when performing the stretch.

1. The gluteus medius originates on the ilium and inserts on the greater trochanter. The primary action of the muscle is abduction of the hip. As a result, the hip would not be abducted when stretching the gluteus medius.
2. The iliotibial band is a thick tendon-like reinforcement of the tensor fasciae latae that runs from the iliac crest to the lateral condyle of the tibia. The iliotibial band acts to flex and abduct the hip. As a result, the hip would not be in a flexed and laterally rotated position when stretching the iliotibial band.
3. **The piriformis muscle originates on the sacrum and inserts on the greater trochanter. The muscle acts to laterally rotate the femur, however, with the hip flexed more than 60 degrees, the piriformis medially rotates the femur.**
4. The rectus femoris originates on the anterior inferior iliac spine and inserts into the patellar tendon. The muscle acts to flex the hip and extend the knee. As a result, the hip would not be in a flexed position when stretching the rectus femoris.

System: Musculoskeletal System
Content Outline: Interventions

Level 1

PTEXAM THREE: QUESTION 30

A physical therapist examines a two-month-old infant diagnosed with osteogenesis imperfecta. After completing the examination, the therapist discusses the plan of care with the infant's parents. What should be the PRIMARY goal of physical therapy with this disorder?

1. **Improve muscle strength and diminish tone**
2. **Facilitate protected weight bearing**
3. **Promote safe handling and positioning**
4. **Diminish pulmonary secretions**

Correct Answer: 3 (Ratliffe p. 254) 

Osteogenesis imperfecta is an autosomal disorder of collagen synthesis that affects bone metabolism. Children with osteogenesis imperfecta often have delayed developmental milestones secondary to ongoing fractures that result in immobilization, hypermobility of joints, and poorly developed muscles. The disorder is classified into four types with diverse clinical presentations ranging from normal appearance with mild symptoms to severe involvement that can be fatal during infancy.

1. The patient would likely have diminished muscle strength due to atrophy, hypermobility of joints, and multiple fractures. Improving strength is therefore desirable, however, would not be the primary goal of therapy for the patient. In addition, tone is not typically altered with osteogenesis imperfecta.
2. Protected weight bearing is desirable in order to reduce the risks associated with fracture and prevent disuse atrophy. Given the patient's age this goal would not be the primary focus of therapy.
3. **A patient with osteogenesis imperfecta is extremely susceptible to fractures during even basic activities such as being carried or bathing. As a result, safe handling and positioning would be the primary goal. This information would be critical to convey to all caregivers, perhaps most notably, the infant's parents.**
4. Osteogenesis imperfecta is a disorder of collagen synthesis that affects bone metabolism. The disorder would not directly influence pulmonary secretions.

System: Musculoskeletal System
Content Outline: Foundations for Evaluation, Differential Diagnosis, and Prognosis

Level 2  **p. 125, 170-171**

PTEXAM THREE: QUESTION 31

A physical therapist elects to utilize the Six-Minute Walk Test as a means of quantifying endurance for a patient rehabilitating from a lengthy illness. Which variable would be the MOST appropriate to measure when determining the patient's endurance level with this objective test?

1. Perceived exertion
2. Heart rate response
3. Elapsed time
4. **Distance walked**

Correct Answer: 4 (Paz p. 476) 

The Six-Minute Walk Test is used to determine a patient's functional exercise capacity. The test is commonly used upon admission, at discharge, and to monitor progress or decline throughout physical therapy. This tool is administered to various populations including those with cardiac impairments, pulmonary disease, chronic conditions, and patients recovering from orthopedic surgical procedures.

1. The patient is instructed to walk as quickly as they can and attempt to cover as much ground as possible within the six minute period. The therapist does not attempt to record the patient's perceived exertion, however, the patient must let the therapist know if they experience chest pain or dizziness.
2. The heart rate response will likely increase as the intensity and duration of the test increases, however, the test is not designed to examine the heart rate response. Heart rate, blood pressure, oxygen saturation, and a dyspnea score are typically assessed prior to and after the administration of the test.
3. The elapsed time for the Six-Minute Walk Test is six minutes, as the name implies, and therefore does not vary during the administration of the test.
4. **The test requires the therapist to measure the distance the patient walks within a six minute period with rest periods permitted as necessary.**

System: Cardiovascular and Pulmonary Systems
Content Outline: Physical Therapy Examination

 **Level 2**  **p. 434**

PTEXAM THREE: QUESTION 32

A patient reports a chronic history of widespread muscular pain, multiple tender points throughout the body, and excessive fatigue. Upon examination, the physical therapist observes that the patient's tender points are distributed throughout the body and do not refer pain when pressure is applied. What diagnosis should the therapist MOST suspect for this patient?

1. Myofascial pain syndrome
2. Chronic regional pain syndrome
3. **Fibromyalgia**
4. Systemic lupus erythematosus

Correct Answer: 3 (Goodman – Pathology p. 310)

There are several conditions that can result in muscular tenderness, either as a primary or secondary symptom. Tender points are small, localized areas of muscle or tendon that are sensitive to pressure and exist in multiple different areas of the body. Trigger points are similar to tender points, however, they are generally less widespread (i.e., localized to a specific region of the body) and will cause radiation of pain when palpated.

1. Myofascial pain syndrome is a condition characterized by trigger points. Unlike tender points, trigger points will refer pain or paresthesias away from the source of the pain when stimulated. Trigger points tend to occur more locally in a single muscle or group of muscles in the same region of the body. Additionally, myofascial pain will not be accompanied by other systemic symptoms (e.g., fatigue).
2. Chronic regional pain syndrome (CRPS) is a condition characterized by abnormalities in the nervous system's response to injury. CRPS is characterized by hypersensitivity to stimuli that would otherwise not be perceived as painful. The hypersensitivity is typically isolated to a specific region of the body. Though fatigue may be a secondary symptom of CRPS, this condition is not commonly associated with tender points.
3. **Fibromyalgia is a condition characterized by widespread muscular pain with localized tender points that are sensitive to pressure. For a patient to have a diagnosis of fibromyalgia, they must have tender points in multiple different areas of the body. Patients with fibromyalgia typically report sleep disturbances and fatigue.**
4. Systemic lupus erythematosus (SLE) is an autoimmune disorder that has a wide variation of clinical presentations depending on the organ system affected. When the musculoskeletal system is affected, fatigue and malaise may be associated symptoms. However, widespread muscular pain and the presence of tender points are not characteristic of this condition.

System: Other Systems
Content Outline: Foundations for Evaluation, Differential Diagnosis, and Prognosis

 **Level 1**  **p. 610-611**

PTEXAM THREE: QUESTION 33

A physical therapist prepares to complete an assisted standing pivot transfer with a patient who requires moderate assistance. In order to increase a patient's independence with the transfer, which of the following instructions would be the MOST appropriate?

1. "I want you to help me perform the transfer."
2. **"Try to utilize your own strength to complete the transfer."**
3. "Only grab onto me if it is absolutely necessary."
4. "Pretend you were home alone and needed to complete the transfer."

Correct Answer: 2 (Purtilo p. 168) 

When treating a patient there must be clear and specific instructions given prior to the initiation of any task. Failure to offer clear and specific instructions increases the probability of an unwanted action. Requesting that the patient utilize their own strength to complete the transfer is the most appropriate instruction for the patient.

1. The statement, "I want you to help me perform the transfer," states that the therapist wants the patient to assist, but does not give the patient exact expectations on how to perform during the transfer.
2. **The statement, "Try to utilize your own strength to complete the transfer," is a direct statement that explains the exact expectations of the patient during the transfer.**
3. The statement, "Only grab onto me if it is absolutely necessary," does not encourage any kind of active patient participation and allows for a "high risk" behavior of grabbing onto the therapist at the patient's discretion.
4. The statement, "Pretend you were home alone and needed to complete the transfer," would not be appropriate since the patient currently requires moderate assistance and if they were "pretending to be alone" they would not follow the correct and safe method for transferring independently.

System: Musculoskeletal System
Content Outline: Interventions

 Level 3  p. 679-680

PTEXAM THREE: QUESTION 34

A patient presents to the emergency room with multiple burns on the upper extremity and chest. The wounds all appear dry, but vary in size and are poorly defined. Examination reveals significant irregularity in the patient's cardiac rhythm. What type of burn did this patient MOST likely sustain?

1. Friction
2. Chemical
3. **Electrical**
4. Radiation

Correct Answer: 3 (Sussman p. 403)

A burn injury can be caused by heat, chemicals, radiation, friction or electricity and results in damage to the skin and underlying structures. The characteristics of the wound (e.g., pattern, moisture level) can be important indicators as to the source or cause of the burn.

1. A friction burn results from the skin rubbing against a surface and causing an abrasive wound. A friction burn would likely be a single, well-defined wound and would not typically be scattered throughout the entire arm and chest. Additionally, a friction burn would not be associated with an alteration in the patient's cardiac rhythm.
2. A chemical burn is caused by direct contact between the skin and a chemical agent, which can be either acidic or basic. It is possible that a chemical burn could be scattered throughout a large area and be poorly defined. Additionally, a chemical burn could be described as dry, especially if it were caused by an acidic agent. However, a chemical burn would not be associated with an alteration in the patient's cardiac rhythm.
3. **An electrical burn occurs when an electrical current passes through the body. These burns are often spread over a larger area since they contain an entrance wound (i.e., at the site of contact) and several poorly defined exit wounds (i.e., where the current leaves the body). Electrical burns often appear dry, which likely occurs secondary to the electrical cauterization of the blood vessels. If the electrical current passes through the heart, it can also result in the development of cardiac arrhythmias.**
4. A radiation burn occurs as a result of excessive exposure to ionizing radiation (e.g., ultraviolet radiation from the sun). A radiation burn would likely be more uniform in its pattern instead of appearing as multiple scattered burn sites. Additionally, a radiation burn would not be associated with an alteration in the patient's cardiac rhythm.

System: Other Systems
Content Outline: Foundations for Evaluation, Differential Diagnosis, and Prognosis

 Level 1  p. 513, 764

PTEXAM THREE: QUESTION 35

A patient's blood glucose level is measured as 60 mg/dL after ten minutes of exercise on a treadmill. Which symptom would this patient MOST likely experience?

1. Polyuria
2. Hyperventilation
3. Excessive thirst
4. **Headache**

Correct Answer: 4 (Goodman – Differential Diagnosis p. 408)

Blood glucose values below 70 mg/dL may be representative of a hypoglycemic state. Physical therapists should recognize the signs and symptoms associated with this condition and be able to act accordingly.

1. Polyuria (i.e., increased urination) occurs in a hyperglycemic state because the body tries to remove the excess glucose in the blood via increased excretion through the kidneys.
2. If hyperglycemia is left untreated, it may progress to diabetic ketoacidosis. Hyperventilation is a common symptom associated with diabetic ketoacidosis. Hyperventilation occurs as a means to control acidity levels within the blood by expelling excess carbon dioxide.
3. The increased urination associated with a hyperglycemic state results in overall dehydration, which may lead to excessive thirst.
4. **Headache is a symptom commonly associated with a hypoglycemic state. The low level of glucose circulating in the blood results in less glucose reaching the brain. Since the brain uses glucose as its primary source of energy, a lack of glucose can result in a headache.**

System: Other Systems
Content Outline: Physical Therapy Examination

Level 2

p. 530-531, 765

PTEXAM THREE: QUESTION 36

Echocardiographic testing revealed a significant decrease in a patient's anticipated cardiac output. An increase in which variable would MOST likely contribute to this finding?

1. Heart rate
2. Preload
3. **Afterload**
4. Stroke volume

Correct Answer: 3 (O'Sullivan p. 474)

The heart's function is to supply adequate cardiac output, and therefore energy, to meet the body's metabolic demands. Cardiac output is defined as the amount of blood that leaves the heart each minute and is determined by calculating the product of heart rate and stroke volume. Cardiac output is influenced by oxygen supply to the myocardium, contractility of the myocardium, and conduction of electrical impulses within the ventricles.

1. Heart rate is one of the variables used to calculate cardiac output. As heart rate increases, cardiac output will also increase.
2. Preload is the amount of blood in the ventricle at the end of the diastolic phase and is directly related to venous return. As preload increases, stroke volume (and thus cardiac output) will also increase.
3. **Afterload is the force the left ventricle must generate during the systolic phase and is directly related to the resistance in the aorta and peripheral arteries. As afterload increases, stroke volume (and thus cardiac output) will decrease.**
4. Stroke volume is the amount of blood ejected from the heart with each contraction and is one of the variables used to calculate cardiac output. As stroke volume increases, cardiac output will also increase.

System: Cardiovascular and Pulmonary Systems
Content Outline: Physical Therapy Examination

Level 1

p. 394

PTEXAM THREE: QUESTION 37

A physical therapist performs crutch training with a patient post total hip arthroplasty. The patient has orders for partial weight bearing. Which of the following gait patterns would be the MOST appropriate for the patient?

1. **Four-point**
2. **Two-point**
3. **Three-point**
4. **Swing-to**

Correct Answer: 3 (Minor p. 297)

Gait training often includes the introduction of an assistive device such as a cane, crutches or a walker. Impairments that affect normal gait include muscle weakness, spasticity, pain in the weight bearing lower extremity, loss of sensation, and balance deficits. The most appropriate gait pattern for the patient depends on the patient's weight bearing status, as well as their strength, balance, and cognitive abilities.

1. A four-point gait pattern is performed with two crutches or canes. The patient advances the crutch/cane on the left followed by the right leg, then advances the crutch/cane on the right followed by the left leg. This gait pattern does not allow for partial weight bearing status and is most often utilized when a patient has poor balance, incoordination or muscle weakness.
2. With a two-point gait pattern, the patient advances one assistive device and the opposite lower extremity simultaneously. During the beginning of the stance phase of one limb, the assistive device on the opposite side provides support. Each step is one point. This gait pattern requires the patient to have good balance as only two points of floor contact are maintained at any one time. This gait pattern most closely resembles normal gait and would be inappropriate for a patient that is partial weight bearing.
3. **A three-point gait pattern is used when one limb is affected, such as after joint arthroplasty. This pattern is used when the weight bearing orders are for non-weight bearing or partial weight bearing. Three points of support contact the floor with weight borne through each crutch and the uninvolved lower extremity. The crutches are advanced followed by the affected lower extremity, then the unaffected lower extremity.**
4. In a swing-to gait pattern the patient advances the lower extremities simultaneously to the point of the crutches. This gait pattern is used when a patient has trunk and/or bilateral lower extremity weakness, paresis or paralysis. This gait pattern would be inappropriate for a patient following total hip arthroplasty.

System: Non-Systems
Content Outline: Equipment, Devices, and Technologies; Therapeutic Modalities

 **Level 1**  **p. 691-692**

PTEXAM THREE: QUESTION 38

A physical therapist observes a patient rehabilitating from a right cerebrovascular accident circumducting the left lower extremity during the swing phase of gait to advance the involved limb. Which of the following interventions would be MOST appropriate to utilize during acceleration (initial swing) in order to diminish this gait deviation?

1. **Facilitation techniques to the left hip extensors**
2. **Inhibitory techniques to the left hip extensors**
3. **Facilitation techniques to the left hip flexors**
4. **Inhibitory techniques to the left hip flexors**

Correct Answer: 3 (O'Sullivan p. 242)

A hemiplegic gait pattern is characterized by the patient abducting the paralyzed limb, swinging it around (circumduction), and bringing it forward so the foot comes to the ground in front of them. Common causes of this gait deviation in a patient post stroke are weak hip flexors, weak knee flexors, and/or weak ankle dorsiflexors. Circumduction becomes a necessary compensation due to an inability to shorten the limb for clearance during the swing phase of gait.

1. Facilitation techniques to the left hip extensors during initial swing would further lengthen the swing limb and be counterproductive to advancing the swing limb.
2. Inhibitory techniques to the left hip extensors during initial swing might help diminish any lower extremity extensor synergy, but would not provide the necessary facilitation to the antagonists (hip flexors) needed to accelerate and advance the swing limb.
3. **Facilitation techniques to the left hip flexors during initial swing would be most appropriate, as the hip and knee flexors should be active concentrically to advance the limb and help with ground clearance. Techniques to strengthen the hip flexors during acceleration (initial swing) would be beneficial.**
4. Inhibitory techniques to the left hip flexors during initial swing would inhibit the role of the hip flexors to accelerate and advance the swing limb and actually exacerbate the gait deviation.

System: Neuromuscular and Nervous Systems
Content Outline: Interventions

 **Level 2**  **p. 330-331**

PTEXAM THREE: QUESTION 39

A physical therapist attempts to identify a patient's risk factors for coronary artery disease as part of a health screening. The patient's heart rate is recorded as 78 beats per minute and blood pressure as 110/70 mm Hg. Laboratory values indicate a total cholesterol level of 170 mg/dL with high-density lipoproteins reported as 20 mg/dL and low-density lipoproteins as 110 mg/dL. Which of these values would be considered atypical?

1. Heart rate
2. Blood pressure
3. **High-density lipoproteins (HDL)**
4. Low-density lipoproteins (LDL)

Correct Answer: 3 (Paz p. 26)

A value less than 40 mg/dL is considered low for HDL cholesterol. Values of 60 mg/dL or greater are considered high. A low HDL value is strongly associated with an increased risk for coronary artery disease.

1. 78 beats per minute is a normal resting heart rate. The range of normal is 60–100 beats per minute.
2. A systolic blood pressure of 110 mm Hg and a diastolic blood pressure of 70 mm Hg are considered within normal limits.
3. **An HDL cholesterol level of 20 mg/dL is very low and is associated with an increased risk of coronary artery disease. The patient would likely be treated by their physician with pharmacological and non-pharmacological therapies to raise the HDL cholesterol level.**
4. The optimal level of LDL cholesterol is less than 100 mg/dL. LDL values from 100-129 mg/dL are considered near optimal. High levels of LDL cholesterol increase the risk of coronary artery disease.

System: Cardiovascular and Pulmonary Systems
Content Outline: Foundations for Evaluation, Differential Diagnosis, and Prognosis

Level 1

p. 402, 411, 469

PTEXAM THREE: QUESTION 40

A physical therapist works with a patient who has a painful, slow healing wound on the medial lower leg. The affected limb is swollen and appears dark red/purple in color with thickened skin. Which of the following conditions would MOST likely contribute to this type of wound?

1. Diabetes
2. Arterial insufficiency
3. **Venous insufficiency**
4. Prolonged pressure

Correct Answer: 3 (Paz p. 297)

Physical therapists should have a basic understanding of the etiology of different types of wounds and wound healing.

1. Neuropathic ulcers are commonly associated with diabetes. These ulcers are secondary complications of peripheral vascular disease, peripheral neuropathy, and infection. Neuropathic ulcers are painless with absent pedal pulses, decreased lower limb temperature, and shiny skin.
2. Arterial insufficiency can cause ulcers as a result of decreased blood flow or ischemia. These wounds are typically caused by atherosclerosis and as a result show minimal signs of healing and are often gangrenous. Wounds caused by arterial insufficiency usually present in the distal leg where collateral circulation is limited. The wound bed is deep and the edges are distinct and well-defined.
3. **Wounds as a result of venous insufficiency occur when the venous system is not functioning properly, leading to poor nutrition to the tissues. Tissue damage results, eventually leading to tissue death and ulceration. These painful wounds often present proximal to the medial malleolus. Hyperpigmentation of the skin and edema are present on the affected leg. The wound bed is shallow, the edges are irregular, and substantial drainage occurs.**
4. Pressure ulcers, or decubitus ulcers, are caused by ischemia as a result of prolonged pressure. These ulcers are typically located over areas of bony prominences.

System: Other Systems
Content Outline: Foundations for Evaluation, Differential Diagnosis, and Prognosis

Level 2

p. 502-503, 630-631

PTEXAM THREE: QUESTION 41

A physical therapist performs palpation on a patient in the standing position as part of a respiratory assessment. Which assessment procedure would be performed with the therapist positioned behind the patient?

1. **Mediastinum motion**
2. **Upper chest wall motion**
3. **Middle chest wall motion**
4. **Lower chest wall motion**

Correct Answer: 4 (Frownfelter p. 210)

Palpation of chest wall motion is performed segmentally to compare the motion over the upper, middle, and lower lobes while the patient is breathing quietly and while breathing deeply.

1. The physical therapist palpates the mediastinum to evaluate for deviation of the trachea by inserting the tip of the index finger in the suprasternal notch. This is done facing the patient.
2. The physical therapist evaluates upper chest wall expansion by placing the palms of the hands anteriorly over the chest wall from the fourth rib upward. The therapist's fingers are stretched over the trapezius and the thumbs placed together along the midline of the chest. The therapist faces the patient.
3. The physical therapist evaluates middle chest wall expansion by placing the fingers laterally over the posterior axillary folds with the thumbs together along the midline of the chest. The therapist faces the patient.
4. **The lower chest wall expansion is evaluated with the patient's back to the therapist and the therapist's fingers wrapped around the anterior axillary folds with the tips of the thumbs together at the vertebral spines.**

System: Cardiovascular and Pulmonary Systems
Content Outline: Physical Therapy Examination

 **Level 1**

PTEXAM THREE: QUESTION 42

A physical therapist conducts scoliosis screenings on adolescents as part of physical therapy week. Which of the following actions is the MOST appropriate for the therapist to take after identifying an adolescent with a moderate scoliotic curve?

1. **Refer the adolescent for further orthopedic assessment**
2. **Educate the adolescent as to the cause of the scoliosis**
3. **Devise an exercise program for the adolescent**
4. **Instruct the adolescent in the importance of proper posture**

Correct Answer: 1 (Goodman – Pathology p. 1166) 

A patient with moderate scoliosis should be referred to an orthopedic physician since treatment for moderate curves requires a spinal orthosis and physical therapy intervention for posture, flexibility, strengthening, respiratory function, and proper utilization of the spinal orthosis.

1. **Scoliosis is a condition that will respond to treatment best when detected early. Common postural findings with scoliosis include increased spacing between the elbow and trunk during standing, leg length discrepancy, uneven shoulder and hip heights, and prominence on one side of the pelvis or breast (due to rotation of the curve).**
2. Although education regarding scoliosis is important, the most appropriate action when identifying a moderate curve is to refer the patient to a physician for further assessment and treatment. The physician will educate the patient based on their findings regarding the scoliosis.
3. A physician should always evaluate a patient with moderate scoliosis prior to the development and implementation of an exercise program.
4. Postural training will not rectify or maintain a moderate scoliotic curve. Moderate curves require multifaceted treatment and physician involvement.

System: Musculoskeletal System
Content Outline: Interventions

 **Level 3**  **p. 126, 180-181**

PTEXAM THREE: QUESTION 43

A physical therapist attempts to secure a wheelchair for a patient with an incomplete spinal cord injury. The patient is very active and relies on a wheelchair as a primary mode of transportation. Which type of wheelchair design would be the MOST appropriate for the patient?

1. Standard chair with a rigid frame
2. **Lightweight chair with a rigid frame**
3. Standard chair with a folding frame
4. Lightweight chair with a folding frame

Correct Answer: 2 (Roy p. 1059)

A lightweight wheelchair will be significantly easier for the patient to propel and maneuver, while a rigid frame provides the necessary durability and strength required for an active individual.

1. A standard chair would not be optimal secondary to the increased weight of the chair and the patient's decreased strength due to the incomplete spinal cord injury.
2. **A lightweight wheelchair is easier to propel and maneuver. The chair is made from stainless steel or aluminum which also enhances durability. The rigid frame allows for stability and a smoother ride for the patient.**
3. A standard wheelchair with a folding frame would not be optimal secondary to the increased weight of the chair which would necessitate greater effort for mobility and transportation. The folding frame would not possess the durability required for an active individual.
4. The lightweight wheelchair is a better choice for the patient, however, the folding frame is not an optimal choice based on the patient's activity level.

System: Neuromuscular and Nervous Systems
Content Outline: Interventions

 Level 2  p. 684-687

PTEXAM THREE: QUESTION 44

A patient with prediabetes is seen by their primary care physician every three months to review the results of their diabetes tests. The patient recently had a series of tests to determine if their condition has progressed to diabetes mellitus. Which of the following criteria is typically considered a positive result for diabetes mellitus?

1. Oral glucose tolerance test of greater than 140 mg/dL
2. Oral glucose tolerance test of less than 140 mg/dL
3. **A1c test of greater than 6.5%**
4. A1c test of less than 6.5%

Correct Answer: 3 (Goodman – Pathology p. 516)

There are several different methods of testing for diabetes mellitus (DM). Some of the various testing procedures include a fasting plasma glucose test, an oral glucose tolerance test, and A1c testing. Testing is generally performed on two different occasions to confirm a diagnosis of DM.

1. An oral glucose tolerance test measures the blood glucose level two hours after the patient ingests a sugary drink. A positive test is indicated by a blood glucose level of 200 mg/dL or greater.
2. In order for an oral glucose tolerance test to be positive for DM, the blood glucose level would need to be 200 mg/dL or greater. The test is considered normal if the patient's blood glucose level is less than 140 mg/dL.
3. **An A1c test is a blood test that measures the patient's average blood glucose level over the past 2-3 months. This test is positive for DM if the patient's A1c level is 6.5% or greater.**
4. An A1c test would not be positive for DM if the A1c level is less than 6.5%. This test is considered normal if the patient's A1c level is less than 5.7%.

System: Other Systems
Content Outline: Foundations for Evaluation, Differential Diagnosis, and Prognosis

  Level 1  p. 530-531, 606-609

PTEXAM THREE: QUESTION 45

A physical therapist examines a patient with anterior cruciate ligament insufficiency. During the examination, a Lachman test is performed. Ideally, the therapist should perform the test with the knee in how many degrees of flexion?

1. **20-30**
2. 30-40
3. 40-50
4. 80-90

Correct Answer: 1 (Magee p. 817)

The Lachman test is perhaps the most common ligamentous instability test designed to assess the integrity of the anterior cruciate ligament. It is typically performed with the patient in a supine position and the knee flexed 20-30 degrees. The therapist applies an anterior directed force to the tibia on the femur. A positive test is indicated by excessive anterior translation of the tibia on the femur with a diminished or absent end-point and may be indicative of an anterior cruciate ligament injury.

1. **20-30 degrees of knee flexion is generally accepted as the amount of knee flexion used for the Lachman test. The position approximates a functional position and all parts of the anterior cruciate ligament are relatively taut.**
2. 30-40 degrees of knee flexion is slightly greater than the recommended amount of knee flexion for the Lachman test.
3. 40-50 degrees is significantly greater than the recommended amount of knee flexion for the Lachman test.
4. 80-90 degrees of knee flexion more closely approximates the position of the knee when performing the anterior drawer test.

System: Musculoskeletal System
Content Outline: Physical Therapy Examination

 Level 1  p. 108-109

PTEXAM THREE: QUESTION 46

A patient with a cerebellar lesion exhibits signs of dysmetria. Which of the following activities would be the MOST difficult for the patient to perform?

1. **Rapid alternating pronation and supination of the forearms**
2. **Placing feet on floor markers while walking**
3. **Walking at varying speeds**
4. **Marching in place**

Correct Answer: 2 (Umphred p. 637) 

Dysmetria refers to an inability to modulate movement where patients will either overestimate or underestimate their targets. The cerebellum is normally responsible for the timing, force, extent, and direction of the limb movement in order to correctly reach a target.

1. Dysdiadochokinesia refers to the inability to perform rapid alternating movements such as pronation and supination of the forearms. As speed increases there is typically a rapid loss of range of movement and rhythm of movement. This condition is a result of damage to the cerebellum.
2. **Dysmetria occurs with cerebellar lesions and is defined as the inability to appropriately reach a target. An example of dysmetria would be the inability of a patient to place their feet on floor markers successfully while walking.**
3. Difficulty walking at varying speeds is common with cerebellar pathology, however, the activity is not associated with dysmetria.
4. Patients with cerebellar lesions often have difficulty modulating movement. As a result, irregular stepping patterns and poor upright stance make activities such as marching in place difficult.

System: Neuromuscular and Nervous Systems
Content Outline: Interventions

 Level 2  p. 263

PTEXAM THREE: QUESTION 47

A physical therapist examines a patient with a medial collateral ligament sprain. During the examination, the patient appears to be relaxed and comfortable, however, is extremely quiet. Which of the following questions would be the MOST appropriate to further engage the patient?

1. **Is this the first time you have injured your knee?**
2. **Have you ever been to physical therapy before?**
3. **How long after your injury did you see a physician?**
4. **What do you hope to achieve in physical therapy?**

Correct Answer: 4 (Goodman – Differential Diagnosis p. 35)

Physical therapists often use a variety of strategies to increase the level of patient participation in treatment sessions. Open-ended questions allow patients to answer with a myriad of responses, while closed-ended questions can often be answered with a yes or no response.

1. The question can be answered with a simple "yes or no" and therefore would be unlikely to increase patient participation.
2. The question would also require a simple "yes or no" response.
3. The question requires the patient to respond with an amount of time. The response, although not a "yes or no," would be equally unlikely to further engage the patient.
4. **The question requires the patient to provide some level of insight towards their physical therapy goals and may provide a foundation for a meaningful exchange between the patient and therapist. The information obtained by the therapist can be valuable when designing an appropriate plan of care.**

System: Musculoskeletal System
Content Outline: Physical Therapy Examination

PTEXAM THREE: QUESTION 48

A physical therapist presents an inservice on the aging process and its effect on the skin. Which of the following skin changes is the MOST likely to occur as a person ages?

1. **Increase in skin elasticity**
2. **Decrease in skin turgor**
3. **Increase in sebaceous gland activity**
4. **Decrease in skin dryness**

Correct Answer: 2 (Sussman p. 63)

There are several changes that occur within the integumentary system as patients age. These changes combine to create skin that is more fragile and prone to tearing. Physical therapists can use observation and palpation to evaluate a patient's skin texture.

1. As a person ages, skin elasticity will decrease, not increase. Collagen and elastin fibers shrink, leading to a reduction in the elastic response of the skin. These changes result in skin that is more fragile and prone to damage.
2. **As a person ages, skin turgor will decrease. Turgor refers to the resistance of skin to deformation. This can be assessed by pinching the skin and observing how quickly it returns to its resting position. The aging process results in thinning of the epithelial layers and results in a loss of turgor.**
3. As a person ages, the secretions of the sebaceous gland decrease, not increase. A decrease in sebaceous gland activity results in skin that is dry and therefore more easily damaged.
4. As a person ages, skin dryness increases, not decreases. This increase in dryness is a direct result of decreased activity of the sebaceous glands. Dry skin increases the risk that the skin will become damaged.

System: Other Systems
Content Outline: Foundations for Evaluation, Differential Diagnosis, and Prognosis

p. 512, 570

PTEXAM THREE: QUESTION 49

A physician orders compression garments for a patient who is ambulatory but has significant difficulty with lower extremity edema. How much pressure would typically be necessary to control lower extremity edema?

1. 10 mm Hg
2. 18 mm Hg
3. 25 mm Hg
4. **35 mm Hg**

Correct Answer: 4 (Cameron p. 420)

Compression garments are available in different thicknesses and different levels of pressure. The garments offer varying levels of pressure ranging from 10 mm Hg to 50 mm Hg. The amount of pressure selected must be determined based on the intended goals of the therapeutic intervention.

1. A pressure of 10 mm Hg would not be adequate to control lower extremity edema in an ambulatory patient.
2. A pressure of 16-18 mm Hg is characteristic of "off the shelf" stockings used to prevent deep vein thrombosis in patients who are in bed.
3. A pressure of 20-30 mm Hg is used to control scar tissue formation.
4. **A pressure of 30-40 mm Hg is used to control edema in ambulatory patients.**

System: Cardiovascular and Pulmonary Systems
Content Outline: Interventions

 Level 1  p. 722-723

PTEXAM THREE: QUESTION 50

A physical therapist monitors the vital signs of a patient during a graded exercise test. When interpreting the data collected during the exercise test, which finding would serve as the BEST indicator that the patient had exerted a maximal effort?

1. **Failure of the heart rate to increase with further increases in intensity**
2. Rise in systolic blood pressure of 50 mm Hg when compared to the resting value
3. Rating of 12/20 on a perceived exertion scale
4. Rating of 2/4 on the dyspnea scale

Correct Answer: 1 (ACSM – Resource Manual p. 373)

Failure of the heart rate to increase with further increases in intensity occurs when the patient can no longer meet the demands imposed by the exercise, signifying the patient has produced a maximal effort.

1. **Failure of the heart rate to increase with further increases in exercise intensity is an objective indicator that the patient made a maximal effort during graded exercise testing.**
2. The normal response to exercise is a progressive increase in systolic blood pressure, typically 10 mm Hg per metabolic equivalent (MET), with a possible plateau at peak exercise. A rise in systolic blood pressure of 50 mm Hg over the resting rate is common during graded exercise testing, however, it is not necessarily an indication of a maximal effort.
3. A rating of 12 on the 6-20 perceived exertion scale corresponds only to a perception of "fairly light" to "somewhat hard." A rating of > 17 ("very hard") is an indicator of a maximal effort.
4. A rating of 2 out of 4 on the dyspnea scale corresponds to a perception of "moderate, bothersome" degree of breathlessness. This level does not indicate a maximal effort.

System: Cardiovascular and Pulmonary Systems
Content Outline: Interventions

 Level 2  p. 428-429

PTEXAM THREE: QUESTION 51

A physical therapist examines a patient with a dorsal scapular nerve injury. Which muscles should the therapist expect to be the MOST affected by this condition?

1. Serratus anterior, pectoralis minor
2. **Levator scapulae, rhomboids**
3. Latissimus dorsi, teres major
4. Supraspinatus, infraspinatus

Correct Answer: 2 (Kendall p. 348) 

Damage to a peripheral nerve can significantly impair muscle function. The severity of the impact ranges from a mild disturbance to denervation.

1. The serratus anterior is innervated by the long thoracic nerve and the pectoralis minor is innervated by the medial pectoral nerve.
2. **The levator scapulae and rhomboids are innervated by the dorsal scapular nerve.**
3. The latissimus dorsi is innervated by the thoracodorsal nerve and the teres major is innervated by the lower subscapular nerve.
4. The supraspinatus and infraspinatus are innervated by the suprascapular nerve.

System: Neuromuscular and Nervous Systems
Content Outline: Foundations for Evaluation, Differential Diagnosis, and Prognosis

Test Taking Tip: In some cases, a physical therapist may not have a full complement of academic information available to answer a given question, however, may still be able to identify the correct option or at least eliminate one or more of the incorrect options. For example, in option 1 the therapist may know that the serratus anterior is innervated by the long thoracic nerve, but may not know the innervation of the pectoralis minor. By recognizing that at least one of the muscles listed in option 1 is not associated with the dorsal scapular nerve, the therapist can safely eliminate this option. Candidates should not become anxious or unsettled when they identify information that they are not familiar with on the National Physical Therapy Examination and instead attempt to answer the question based on their existing academic knowledge. Candidates can use this strategy to enhance their examination score.

  p. 250

PTEXAM THREE: QUESTION 52

A physical therapist treats a patient with mechanical lumbar traction in the supine position with the hips and knees flexed and the lower legs resting on a stool. This position would be MOST appropriate to treat a patient diagnosed with which of the following conditions?

1. **Spinal stenosis**
2. Herniated disk
3. Osteoporosis
4. Spondylolisthesis

Correct Answer: 1 (Cameron p. 385)

Supine positioning with the hips and knees flexed and the lower legs resting on a stool causes flexion of the lumbar spine and separation of the spinous processes. This movement increases the size of the intervertebral foramen bilaterally.

1. **Spinal stenosis is a condition in which the spinal canal narrows and compresses the spinal cord and nerves. The condition is best treated with the patient positioned in flexion since the position maximizes opening of the intervertebral foramen.**
2. The majority of disk pathology results from herniation in a posterolateral direction. Prone positioning is desirable since it facilitates spinal extension and directs forces on the disk anteriorly.
3. Osteoporosis is a metabolic bone disorder where the rate of bone resorption accelerates while the rate of bone formation decelerates. The condition is considered a contraindication for mechanical lumbar traction.
4. Spondylolisthesis refers to the forward slippage of one vertebral body with respect to the vertebral body below it. Traction can potentially be used on patients with spondylolisthesis depending on the degree of slippage of the vertebral body. The severity of the slippage is most often classified with a lateral x-ray using the Meyerding grading system. Traction is not used to correct the slippage, however, it can effectively reduce neurological deficits from subsequent spinal nerve root impingement. The patient position used with mechanical traction is variable when treating spondylolisthesis.

System: Non-Systems
Content Outline: Equipment, Devices, and Technologies; Therapeutic Modalities

  p. 208, 720-721

PTEXAM THREE: QUESTION 53

A physical therapist attempts to utilize a functional activity as a method to increase a patient's limited wrist passive range of motion due to shortened wrist flexors. Which position would be the MOST appropriate to utilize to achieve the stated objective?

1. Semi-Fowler's
2. **Modified plantigrade**
3. Ring sitting
4. Pivot prone

Correct Answer: 2 (Sullivan p. 54) 

Physical therapists can use positioning through functional activities to address a variety of impairments. These impairments include, but are not limited to, influencing tone, balance reactions, stability, and weight bearing.

1. The semi-Fowler's position places a patient in supine with the head of the bed elevated to 45 degrees and pillows under the knees for support and maintenance of a proper lumbar curve. This position is often utilized for patients with congestive heart failure and other cardiac conditions. This position would not influence muscle length in the upper extremities.
2. **Modified plantigrade is characterized by lower extremity weight bearing in supported standing while leaning with upper extremity support on a table or another weight bearing surface. This most often occurs with an open palm pushing on a fixed surface, resulting in the wrist assuming an extended position with the shortened wrist flexors on stretch.**
3. Ring sitting, an important milestone in early childhood development, refers to an independent sitting position where the lower extremities form the shape of a ring. The position allows the infant to use their upper extremities for reaching or grasping objects, however, it would not influence muscle length in the upper extremities.
4. Pivot prone, another important milestone in early childhood development, is exhibited when the infant is in prone with extension of the neck, spine, and hips as well as retraction of the scapulae with lateral rotation of the shoulders. The upper extremities assume the high guard position with the scapulae adducted, shoulders horizontally abducted, and elbows flexed.

System: Neuromuscular and Nervous Systems
Content Outline: Interventions

 Level 2

PTEXAM THREE: QUESTION 54

A physical therapist instructs a patient to make a fist. The patient can make a fist, but is unable to flex the distal phalanx of the ring finger (4th digit). This clinical finding can BEST be explained by a ruptured tendon of which muscle?

1. Flexor carpi radialis
2. Flexor digitorum superficialis
3. **Flexor digitorum profundus**
4. Extensor digitorum communis

Correct Answer: 3 (Dutton p. 792) 

The flexor digitorum profundus muscle originates on the anterior and medial surfaces of the proximal portion of the ulna, interosseous membrane, and deep antebrachial fascia. The muscle inserts via four tendons into the anterior surface of the bases of the distal phalanges.

1. The flexor carpi radialis muscle acts to flex and abduct the wrist and may assist in pronation of the forearm and in flexion of the elbow.
2. The flexor digitorum superficialis muscle acts to flex the proximal interphalangeal joints of the second through fifth digits, and assists in flexion of the metacarpophalangeal joints and flexion of the wrist.
3. **The flexor digitorum profundus muscle acts to flex the distal interphalangeal joints of the index, middle, ring, and little fingers, and assists in flexion of the proximal interphalangeal and metacarpophalangeal joints. A ruptured flexor digitorum profundus tendon would therefore make it impossible to flex the distal phalanx.**
4. The extensor digitorum communis muscle acts to extend the metacarpophalangeal joints and in conjunction with the lumbricals and interossei, extends the interphalangeal joints of the second through fifth digits. The muscle assists in abduction of the index, ring, and little fingers and in extension and abduction of the wrist.

System: Musculoskeletal System
Content Outline: Foundations for Evaluation, Differential Diagnosis, and Prognosis

Test Taking Tip: Candidates will often benefit from attempting to narrow down the possible options to a given examination question by eliminating options that they know are incorrect. In this particular question, a candidate should recognize that the answer cannot be option 4 since a rupture to an extensor tendon would result in an inability to extend and not to flex. Candidates who can use this type of pragmatic approach often achieve higher scores on the examination.

 Level 1

PTEXAM THREE: QUESTION 55

A physical therapist implements an aquatic program for a patient who has a lower extremity injury. The program requires the patient to run in place using a flotation device while tethered to the side of the pool using an elastic cord. Which action would be the MOST appropriate to increase resistance?

1. Increase the water temperature
2. **Increase the speed of movement**
3. Increase the depth of the water
4. Remove the flotation device

Correct Answer: 2 (Kisner p. 298) 

The therapeutic effects of immersion in water relate to the principles of hydrodynamics and thermodynamics. Some of the more relevant concepts associated with these principles include density, specific gravity, hydrostatic pressure, buoyancy, and viscosity.

1. Changes in the water temperature can influence variables such as oxygen uptake, but would not significantly influence resistance.
2. **The viscosity of water provides resistance to a body in motion. Viscosity refers to the thickness or resistance to the flow of a liquid. The faster the relative speed of the body, the greater the magnitude of resistance.**
3. Increasing the depth of the water would not result in a significant change in resistance since the patient is using a flotation device and therefore their level of immersion would remain relatively constant.
4. Removal of the flotation device would likely increase resistance since the patient may tend to move faster without the flotation device, however, it remains less desirable than simply continuing to use the belt and increasing the speed of movement.

System: Other Systems
Content Outline: Interventions

 Level 2  p. 716-717

PTEXAM THREE: QUESTION 56

A physical therapist reads a recently published case report. Which of the following descriptions represents the MOST important contribution that case reports make to evidence-based practice in physical therapy?

1. Demonstrate a causal relationship between treatment and outcome in a single patient
2. **Provide information that can be used to generate inductive hypotheses for future studies**
3. Provide data on the natural history of disease states
4. Use triangulation to test a hypothesis with more than one source of data

Correct Answer: 2 (Portney p. 316)

Describing interesting, new and unique cases is one means of building a foundation for clinical science. The case report is a practical approach to research in the clinical sciences because it is directly applicable to patient care, but it is also the least rigorous because of its lack of control and limited generalizability.

1. Due to the lack of control and the number of different interventions the patient may receive (medical, surgical, nursing, social, recreational, etc.), it is not reasonable to try to suggest a direct causal relationship between one treatment and the outcome in a single patient.
2. **Case reports are important for generating and testing theory and for providing information that may be used to generate inductive hypotheses that can be tested by exploratory or experimental methods.**
3. Longitudinal studies of many patients followed for a long period of time are the preferred means of studying the natural history of a disease.
4. Case reports do not triangulate data from multiple sources to test hypotheses. In most case reports, the data comes from a single patient.

System: Non-Systems
Content Outline: Safety and Protection; Professional Responsibilities; Research

 Level 1  p. 803

PTEXAM THREE: QUESTION 57

A physical therapist reviews the results of a patient's laboratory testing and notices the erythrocyte sedimentation rate was normal. Which medical condition would typically produce this finding?

1. **Duchenne muscular dystrophy**
2. Hodgkin's lymphoma
3. Systemic lupus erythematosus
4. Polymyalgia rheumatica

Correct Answer: 1 (O'Sullivan p. 1033)

Erythrocyte sedimentation rate is a non-specific test for inflammatory disorders often associated with conditions such as cancer, autoimmune diseases, and infection. The test is based on how quickly red blood cells sink to the bottom of a test solution containing anticoagulated blood.

1. **Duchenne muscular dystrophy is a sex-linked disorder characterized by progressive muscular weakness beginning between the ages of two and five. It is a progressive disorder caused by the absence of the gene required to produce the muscle proteins dystrophin and nebulin. Erythrocyte sedimentation rate is typically not affected with this condition. A creatine phosphokinase determination is the most specific test for muscular dystrophy.**
2. Hodgkin's disease is a type of cancer found in the lymphatic system and lymph tissues. Hodgkin's disease can metastasize to extralymphatic sites including the liver, spleen, and lungs. This condition produces an elevated erythrocyte sedimentation rate.
3. Systemic lupus erythematosus is an autoimmune condition characterized by numerous organ and joint issues. Typically, a patient with systemic lupus erythematosus exhibits a trademark butterfly rash and experiences joint pain primarily affecting smaller joints. This condition produces an elevated erythrocyte sedimentation rate.
4. Polymyalgia rheumatica is a systemic inflammatory condition that is experienced primarily by older adults. It is characterized by aching and stiffness affecting the upper arms, neck, lower back, and thighs. This condition produces an elevated erythrocyte sedimentation rate.

System: Neuromuscular and Nervous Systems
Content Outline: Foundations for Evaluation, Differential Diagnosis, and Prognosis

 Level 1 p. 313, 334-335

PTEXAM THREE: QUESTION 58

A physical therapist treats a patient with a wound impacting the epidermis of the skin. Which structure would be the MOST affected based on the described wound?

1. Arrector pili muscles
2. Meissner's corpuscles
3. **Melanocytes**
4. Sebaceous glands

Correct Answer: 3 (Roy p. 545)

The epidermis refers to the superficial, avascular epithelial layer of the skin that includes flat, scale-like squamous cells, round basal cells, and melanocytes which produce melanin and give skin its color. The dermis refers to the vascular layer of skin located below the epidermis. The dermis includes hair follicles, arrector pili muscles, sebaceous glands, sweat glands, Meissner's corpuscles, lymphatic and blood vessels, and nerve endings. The epidermis and dermis vary in thickness based on the location of the skin. For example, the epidermis is approximately 0.05 millimeters thick on the eyelids and is 1.5 millimeters thick on the palms and soles of the feet.

1. Arrector pili muscles, located in the dermis, are attached to the base of hair follicles. When the follicle is stimulated by cold or fright, the arrector pili muscle pulls on the hair follicle causing it to stand upright.
2. Meissner's corpuscles, located in the dermis, are a type of mechanoreceptor responsible for detecting light touch. They have the highest sensitivity when sensing vibrations lower than 50 hertz.
3. **Melanocytes, located at the base of the epidermis, produce a dark pigment called melanin, which contributes to skin color and provides protection from ultraviolet light.**
4. Sebaceous glands, located in the dermis, are small, sacculated organs that secrete sebum, which is a natural moisturizer of the hair and skin. The glands are more plentiful in the forehead, chin, cheeks, nose, and scalp areas.

System: Other Systems
Content Outline: Physical Therapy Examination

 Level 1  p. 499, 512

PTEXAM THREE: QUESTION 59

A physical therapist discusses pain management for a patient who is post total hip arthroplasty with the patient's nurse. Which objective finding would make the use of patient-controlled analgesia the MOST unrealistic?

1. **Altered cognitive status**
2. Elevated respiratory rate
3. Advanced age
4. History of substance abuse

Correct Answer: 1 (Fairchild p. 285)

Patient-controlled analgesia (PCA) allows the patient to manage their pain by delivering an intravenous analgesic dose with preset parameters. The medication is self-administered by pressing a button to receive a preset dose.

1. **Altered cognitive status would make it problematic for the patient to understand the rationale for the use of PCA and to follow the supplied instructions. PCA is an ineffective form of pain management for patients with altered cognition.**
2. An elevated respiratory rate would not necessarily prohibit the use of PCA. The use of intravenous narcotics through PCA is likely to produce sedation and a decreased respiratory rate.
3. Advanced age would not necessarily prohibit the use of PCA since the ability to follow instructions and physically push the button is not age dependent.
4. A history of substance abuse may make the use of PCA undesirable. However, the ability to control the type of medication, demand dose, and dose interval makes this option remain a possibility depending on the unique circumstances associated with the patient's history of substance abuse.

System: Musculoskeletal System
Content Outline: Foundations for Evaluation, Differential Diagnosis, and Prognosis

PTEXAM THREE: QUESTION 60

A physical therapist treats an infant diagnosed with torticollis with marked lateral flexion of the neck to the right. As part of the infant's plan of care, the therapist performs passive stretching activities to improve the patient's range of motion. The MOST appropriate stretch for the patient should involve which of the following motions?

1. Lateral flexion to the right and rotation to the right
2. Lateral flexion to the left and rotation to the left
3. Lateral flexion to the right and rotation to the left
4. **Lateral flexion to the left and rotation to the right**

Correct Answer: 4 (Palisano p. 184) 

Torticollis is characterized by lateral flexion of the head toward the affected side and rotation toward the unaffected side. The condition is caused by a contracture of the sternocleidomastoid muscle.

1. Stretching in lateral flexion to the right would be inappropriate since the question indicates that the patient presents with marked lateral flexion of the neck to the right. The direction of the stretch for the rotation component is accurate.
2. Stretching in lateral flexion to the left would be beneficial, however, patients with torticollis present with rotation to the opposite side. As a result, the rotation component should be stretched to the right and not the left.
3. This option more accurately characterizes the clinical presentation of the patient than it does the necessary stretch. The question indicates that the patient presents with marked lateral flexion of the neck to the right and therefore it would not make sense to stretch to the right. The direction of stretch for the rotation component is also inaccurate.
4. **Stretching the patient in lateral flexion to the left and rotation to the right is the correct answer since it is opposite of the patient's current contracture (i.e., marked lateral flexion of the neck to the right and rotation to the left).**

System: Musculoskeletal System
Content Outline: Interventions

Test Taking Tip: It is possible for a candidate to eliminate two of the presented options without having any specific knowledge related to torticollis. The question indicates that the patient presents with marked lateral flexion of the neck to the right. Based on the that particular clinical finding it becomes apparent that the stretch would need to be in the opposite direction (i.e., to the left). Often when presented with information that is unfamiliar, candidates fail to recognize that they can still narrow down the presented options. It is critically important for candidates to use this valuable skill since it can significantly increase the probability of identifying the correct response.

p. 123, 186-187

PTEXAM THREE: QUESTION 61

With the patient's eyes closed and the hand held out, a physical therapist places a series of different weights in the patient's hand one at a time. The patient is then asked to identify the comparative weight of the objects. Which type of sensation is the therapist MOST likely testing?

1. **Barognosis**
2. Graphesthesia
3. Recognition of texture
4. Stereognosis

Correct Answer: 1 (O'Sullivan p. 96) 

Barognosis, graphesthesia, recognition of texture, and stereognosis are considered combined cortical sensations.

1. **Barognosis refers to the ability of a patient to identify the comparative weight of objects in a series. This can be done by placing a series of different weights in the same hand or by placing different weights in each hand simultaneously.**
2. Graphesthesia refers to the ability of a patient to verbally identify letters or numbers traced on the palm of the hand typically with a fingertip or the eraser of a pencil.
3. Recognition of texture refers to the ability to differentiate among various textures such as cotton, wool or silk. Items may be identified by name or texture such as rough or smooth.
4. Stereognosis refers to the ability to identify an object without sight. Objects used are typically easily obtainable and familiar such as a coin, key or comb. Patients are asked to verbally identify the object by name.

System: Neuromuscular and Nervous Systems
Content Outline: Physical Therapy Examination

 Level 1  p. 256-257

PTEXAM THREE: QUESTION 62

A physical therapist instructs a patient post motor vehicle accident to ambulate with a platform walker. The patient has poor balance and is presently partial weight bearing. Which of the following impairments would MOST warrant the use of the platform attachment?

1. Upper extremity spasticity
2. Generalized upper extremity muscle weakness
3. **Flexion contracture of the elbow**
4. Impaired upper extremity sensation

Correct Answer: 3 (Tan p. 298)

Platform walkers have a platform type of forearm support which can be attached to a standard or rolling walker. The attachment allows the patient to transmit their body weight through the humerus instead of through the wrist and hand.

1. While a patient with upper extremity spasticity may have difficulty when using an assistive device, a platform walker would provide no added benefit for this patient when compared to other assistive devices.
2. While a patient with upper extremity weakness may have difficulty when using an assistive device, a platform walker would provide no added benefit for this patient when compared to other assistive devices. If the patient exhibited distal extremity weakness (e.g., poor grip strength), a platform walker may have been indicated.
3. **A patient with an elbow flexion contracture would be unable to straighten their arm to use a standard walker. The platform attachment would allow this patient to bear weight through the humerus while maintaining the elbow in a flexed position. This type of assistive device could also be used for patients with pain or deformities in the wrist or hand.**
4. While a patient with impaired sensation to the upper extremity may have difficulty when using an assistive device, a platform walker would provide no added benefit to this patient when compared to other assistive devices.

System: Non-Systems
Content Outline: Equipment, Devices, and Technologies; Therapeutic Modalities

Level 2  p. 690-691

PTEXAM THREE: QUESTION 63

A physical therapist utilizes the services of a physical therapy aide. Which variable BEST determines the extent to which physical therapy aides are involved in patient care activities?

1. The number of years of experience
2. The scope of formal training
3. **The discretion of the physical therapist**
4. The quantity of continuing education courses

Correct Answer: 3 (Guide to Physical Therapist Practice)

The physical therapy aide is a non-licensed worker who is specifically trained under the direction and supervision of a physical therapist. Activities performed by the aide are limited to those tasks that do not require clinical decision making by the physical therapist.

1. Regardless of the number of years of training the aide remains a non-licensed health care provider.
2. The scope of the formal training of the physical therapy aide may influence how the aide is utilized, however, to what extent this factor is considered will depend on the judgment of the physical therapist.
3. **The determination of what tasks are appropriately directed to the aide must be made by the physical therapist or, where allowable by law or regulations, the physical therapist assistant.**
4. The quantity of continuing education courses may provide the physical therapy aide with specialized knowledge in selected areas of clinical practice, however, how this influences the aide's role in patient care activities remains the responsibility of the physical therapist.

System: Non-Systems
Content Outline: Safety and Protection; Professional Responsibilities; Research

 Level 2  p. 784-786

PTEXAM THREE: QUESTION 64

A physical therapist prepares to treat a patient with cystic fibrosis using postural drainage. Which of the following patient positions is the MOST appropriate when treating the superior segments of the lower lobes?

1. Sitting, leaning back at a 30-40 degree angle
2. Head down on left side, 1/4 turn backward
3. Supine with two pillows under the knees
4. **Prone with two pillows under the hips**

Correct Answer: 4 (Roy p. 539) 

Postural drainage for the superior segments of the lower lobes requires the physical therapist to clap over the middle of the back at the tip of the scapula on either side of the spine.

1. Sitting, leaning back 30-40 degrees describes the postural drainage position for the apical segments of the right and left upper lobes.
2. Head down on left side, 1/4 turn backward describes the postural drainage position for the right middle lobe.
3. Supine with two pillows under the knees describes the postural drainage position for the anterior segments of the left and right upper lobes.
4. **Prone with two pillows under the hips describes the postural drainage position for the superior segments of the left and right lower lobes.**

System: Cardiovascular and Pulmonary Systems
Content Outline: Interventions

 Level 1  p. 438-439

PTEXAM THREE: QUESTION 65

A physical therapist reviews the medical record of a patient who recently had a "long" spinal fusion. Which medical condition would MOST likely require this type of surgical procedure?

1. Ankylosing spondylitis
2. **Scoliosis**
3. Spinal disk herniation
4. Spinal segment instability

Correct Answer: 2 (Goodman – Pathology p. 1166)

Spinal fusion is a surgical procedure that creates a solid bridge of bone between two or more adjacent vertebrae. Spinal fusions are classified as long if they occur across many spinal levels and short if they occur across few, most often one, spinal levels.

1. Ankylosing spondylitis is a systemic condition that is characterized by inflammation of the spine and larger peripheral joints. The goals of medical management for this condition are to reduce inflammation, maintain functional mobility, and relieve pain, typically through conservative interventions and pharmacological management.
2. **Scoliosis is characterized by a lateral curvature of the spine. A patient with a primary curve greater than 40 degrees usually requires surgical spinal stabilization. This most often occurs using posterior spinal fusion and stabilization with instrumentation (e.g., Harrington rod). Given the number of spinal segments impacted by the scoliotic curve, the fusion to correct this issue typically involves a large number of spinal segments (i.e., long fusion).**
3. Spinal disk herniation occurs when the nucleus pulposus bulges through the exterior wall of the annulus fibrosus. When the disk herniates, it often results in the compression of nearby nerve roots and causes pain, numbness, and/or weakness into the extremities. The large majority of disk herniations occur at the L4-L5 or L5-S1 vertebral level. When spinal fusion is necessary due to disk herniation, the procedure most often involves only one or two spinal segments.
4. Spinal segment instability describes abnormal movement between adjacent vertebrae. There are a number of possible causes of spinal segment instability including disk degeneration that produces a loss of tension "turgor" and disk bulging that eventually results in abnormal movements between vertebrae. Spinal segment instability may necessitate spinal fusion, however, it would only involve a few vertebrae and therefore would not be considered a long spinal fusion.

System: Musculoskeletal System
Content Outline: Foundations for Evaluation, Differential Diagnosis, and Prognosis

Level 1

p. 126, 129, 180-181

PTEXAM THREE: QUESTION 66

A physical therapist elects to use mechanical lumbar traction for a patient with low back pain. The therapeutic goal of the treatment is to decrease the patient's muscle spasm. What percentage of the patient's body weight is the MOST appropriate force for the therapist to utilize?

1. 10%
2. 15%
3. **25%**
4. 50%

Correct Answer: 3 (Cameron p. 386)

The optimal amount of force when using traction depends on the patient's clinical presentation, the goals of the treatment, and the position selected. There are, however, some general guidelines that physical therapists can use. Guidelines are often expressed in percentages of total body weight instead of strictly an amount of force in pounds or kilograms since this method accommodates for patients of varying sizes.

1. Ten percent of the patient's body weight would be far less than the amount of force needed to accomplish the identified goal of decreasing the patient's muscle spasm.
2. Fifteen percent of the patient's body weight would be less than the amount of force needed, although it is possible that this amount of force could be used as a trial to determine how the patient will tolerate traction. Assuming the patient tolerates fifteen percent, the therapist could then move to twenty-five percent.
3. **Twenty-five percent of the patient's body weight is generally recommended when the goal of treatment is to decrease muscle spasm or stretch soft tissue in the lumbar spine.**
4. Fifty percent of the patient's body weight is required for mechanical separation of the lumbar spine, however, this amount of force would be excessive to diminish muscle spasm.

System: Non-Systems
Content Outline: Equipment, Devices, and Technologies; Therapeutic Modalities

Level 2

p. 720-721

PTEXAM THREE: QUESTION 67

A physical therapist reviews a physician referral form that includes only the patient's name and the referring physician's signature. During the examination, the patient indicates that they had knee surgery two weeks ago, however, is unable to provide more specific details. The therapist attempts to call the physician's office, but is unable to reach anyone. Which of the following actions is the MOST appropriate for the therapist to take?

1. Initiate treatment based on the results of the examination
2. Initiate treatment based on an established protocol following knee surgery
3. Initiate treatment, however, avoid resistive exercises and high-level functional activities
4. **Delay treatment until orders are received from the referring physician**

Correct Answer: 4 (Criteria for Standards of Practice)

Physical therapists should not initiate treatment for patients following surgery until they have adequate medical information to develop an effective plan of care. Presently, the therapist only knows that the patient had knee surgery two weeks ago and was referred to physical therapy by their surgeon.

1. Initiating treatment without specific knowledge of the surgical procedure could be considered a negligent act and may unnecessarily jeopardize the integrity of the surgical procedure.
2. Initiating treatment based on an established protocol following knee surgery is too generic of an approach since there are a multitude of different protocols for each of the various types of commonly performed knee surgeries. It is critical that the physical therapist receives additional information on the surgical procedure directly from the referring physician or an appropriate intermediary (i.e., the referring physician's office).
3. Initiating treatment while avoiding resistive exercises and high-level functional activities limits the scope of the physical therapy session, however, it does not ensure that the chosen interventions are appropriate based on the patient's current status.
4. **Delaying treatment until orders are received from the referring physician ensures that the physical therapist has all of the relevant information prior to developing a plan of care. This action allows the therapist to be fully informed about relevant contraindications and precautions and allows the therapist to develop a plan of care based on the anticipated outcomes.**

System: Non-Systems
Content Outline: Safety and Protection; Professional Responsibilities; Research

p. 792-793

PTEXAM THREE: QUESTION 68

A physical therapist reviews the results of recent laboratory testing before treating a patient. A note in the medical record indicates that the patient was dehydrated at the time the blood sample was taken. Which of the following findings would be the MOST likely based on the patient's hydration status?

1. Increased coagulation time
2. Decreased hematocrit level
3. **Increased blood urea nitrogen level**
4. Decreased hemoglobin level

Correct Answer: 3 (Goodman – Pathology p. 1707)

A blood urea nitrogen (BUN) test measures the amount of nitrogen in the blood that comes from the waste product urea. Urea is made when protein is broken down in the body.

1. Prothrombin time and partial thromboplastin time measure the coagulation of the blood. Increased coagulation time indicates an increased time to form a clot. Neither test is affected by hydration status.
2. Hematocrit measures the percentage of red blood cells in a volume of blood. Hematocrit may be increased when the body's water content is decreased from dehydration, diarrhea, vomiting, excessive sweating, severe burns, and the use of diuretics.
3. **A blood urea nitrogen test is performed to assess kidney function. An increased blood urea nitrogen level can be indicative of dehydration, renal failure or heart failure. Normal blood urea nitrogen levels for adults are 10-20 mg/dL.**
4. Hemoglobin is the iron-containing molecule of red blood cells that binds with oxygen. A low hemoglobin level is indicative of anemia and suggests the oxygen-carrying capacity of the blood is decreased. Hemoglobin may be increased when the body's water content is decreased from dehydration, diarrhea, vomiting, excessive sweating, severe burns, and the use of diuretics.

System: Other Systems
Content Outline: Foundations for Evaluation, Differential Diagnosis, and Prognosis

Level 2

PTEXAM THREE: QUESTION 69

A physical therapist performs transfer training with a patient who is four days post transtibial amputation. Assuming an uncomplicated recovery, which of the following transfers is the MOST appropriate for the therapist to utilize from a wheelchair to a mat table?

1. Two-person lift
2. Hydraulic lift
3. **Stand pivot**
4. Sliding board

Correct Answer: 3 (Seymour p. 160) 

Physical therapists should select transfers for patients based on their unique abilities and limitations. A patient status post transtibial amputation should be able to utilize their uninvolved lower extremity during the transfer and as a result, the therapist would not need to utilize a dependent transfer.

1. A two-person lift is used to transfer a patient between two surfaces of different heights or when transferring a patient to the floor.
2. A hydraulic lift is a device required for dependent transfers when a patient is obese, when there is only one therapist available to assist with the transfer or when the patient is totally dependent.
3. **A stand pivot transfer is used when a patient is able to stand and bear weight through one or both of the lower extremities. The patient must possess functional balance and the ability to pivot.**
4. A sliding board transfer is used for a patient who has sitting balance, some upper extremity strength, and can adequately follow directions.

System: Musculoskeletal System
Content Outline: Interventions

 Level 2 p. 680-682

PTEXAM THREE: QUESTION 70

A patient reports pain during testing of active shoulder range of motion. The physical therapist suspects that the pain may be associated with anterior glenohumeral instability. Which portion of the shoulder range of motion should the therapist expect the pain to be MOST pronounced?

1. 70-80 degrees of lateral rotation
2. **80-90 degrees of lateral rotation**
3. 60-70 degrees of medial rotation
4. 70-80 degrees of medial rotation

Correct Answer: 2 (Dutton p. 607) 

It is important for physical therapists to collect as much information as possible about a patient's present pain. Many diagnoses have characteristic patterns of pain which can be useful when engaging in differential diagnosis activities.

1. 70-80 degrees of lateral rotation may have the potential to result in pain with active motion due to anterior glenohumeral instability, however, the portion of the range is not as provocative as 80-90 degrees of lateral rotation.
2. **80-90 degrees of lateral rotation places the greatest amount of pressure on the anterior structures, therefore, any level of inflammation, irritation or structural damage may be likely to produce pain with active motion.**
3. 60-70 degrees of medial rotation would be more likely to stress the posterior structures of the shoulder. Pain with medial rotation may be associated with posterior glenohumeral instability or suprahumeral impingement.
4. 70-80 degrees of medial rotation would be more likely to place additional stress on the posterior structures of the shoulder. Normal shoulder medial rotation is 0-70 degrees. This option would be more provocative to the posterior shoulder structures than option 3. Pain with medial rotation may be associated with posterior glenohumeral instability or suprahumeral impingement.

System: Musculoskeletal System
Content Outline: Foundations for Evaluation, Differential Diagnosis, and Prognosis

 Level 2  p. 100

PTEXAM THREE: QUESTION 71

A physical therapist examines the abdomen of a patient with suspected referred shoulder pain from the viscera. Which examination component should be assessed FIRST?

1. Superficial palpation
2. Deep palpation
3. Percussion
4. **Auscultation**

Correct Answer: 4 (Goodman - Differential Diagnosis p. 90)

The abdominal cavity consists of four abdominal quadrants formed by two imaginary perpendicular lines running through the umbilicus. Viscera in the right upper quadrant can often refer pain to the right shoulder, while pain in the left upper quadrant can often refer pain to the left shoulder.

1. Superficial palpation can be used to assess for temperature changes, tenderness, and large masses. Superficial palpation should be performed prior to deep palpation since some patients may have difficulty even tolerating superficial palpation.
2. Deep palpation is often performed by placing the flat of the hand on the abdominal wall and applying firm, steady pressure. Deep palpation should start in the quadrant directly opposite the area of pain. The majority of viscera in a normal adult are not palpable unless enlarged. Deep palpation should not be performed unless the patient tolerated superficial palpation.
3. Percussion over abdominal organs is considered a fairly advanced skill even for physicians and is therefore not a typical component of the physical therapy examination. If percussion was performed, it would still occur after auscultation.
4. **Auscultation of the abdomen allows the physical therapist to hear clicks, rumblings, and gurgling sounds throughout the abdomen. Auscultation occurs using the diaphragm of the stethoscope applied directly to the abdominal wall with firm, but gentle pressure. Auscultation should occur prior to palpation and percussion since the act of palpating or percussing may alter the frequency and intensity of bowel sounds.**

System: Other Systems
Content Outline: Physical Therapy Examination

 Level 2

PTEXAM THREE: QUESTION 72

A physical therapist observes a patient utilize a suspensory strategy to regain their balance. Which active movement would be MOST characteristic of this postural strategy?

1. Trunk extension
2. Hip extension
3. **Knee flexion**
4. Ankle plantar flexion

Correct Answer: 3 (O'Sullivan p. 211) 

The suspensory strategy is used to lower the center of gravity during standing or ambulation in order to improve balance and stability. Examples of this strategy include knee flexion, crouching or squatting. This strategy is often used when both mobility and stability are required during a task (e.g., surfing).

1. Trunk extension would not be effective to lower the center of gravity and is therefore not consistent with the suspensory strategy.
2. Hip extension would not be effective to lower the center of gravity and is therefore not consistent with the suspensory strategy. Hip flexion, however, would be consistent with this strategy.
3. **Knee flexion is often the immediate action utilized in standing to lower the center of gravity following a significant perturbation. This action often provides the individual with the ability to regain their balance.**
4. Ankle plantar flexion would not be effective to lower the center of gravity and is therefore not consistent with the suspensory strategy.

System: Neuromuscular and Nervous Systems
Content Outline: Foundations for Evaluation, Differential Diagnosis, and Prognosis

 Level 1  p. 265

PTEXAM THREE: QUESTION 73

A physical therapist positions a patient in supine prior to performing a manual muscle test of the supinator. To isolate the supinator muscle and minimize the action of the biceps, the therapist should place the patient's elbow in which of the following positions?

1. 30 degrees of flexion
2. 60 degrees of flexion
3. 90 degrees of flexion
4. **Terminal flexion**

Correct Answer: 4 (Kendall p. 289) 

The supinator is innervated by the radial nerve (C5, C6, C7) and acts to supinate the forearm. The biceps is innervated by the musculocutaneous nerve (C5-C6) and acts to flex the elbow and supinate the forearm. A therapist can isolate one muscle from another muscle with a similar action by placing the de-emphasized muscle in a shortened position during the testing procedure. This finding is based on the length-tension relationship which specifies that a muscle can generate the greatest tension at its resting length.

1. The biceps is significantly lengthened in this position, however, 30 degrees of elbow flexion allows the biceps to generate a reasonable amount of force.
2. The biceps is slightly lengthened in 60 degrees of elbow flexion, however, the muscle is able to generate a significant amount of force since the position is relatively close to the muscle's resting length.
3. The biceps is typically tested with the elbow in 90 degrees of flexion and therefore this is an undesirable position to minimize the action of the muscle.
4. **Placing the biceps in a maximally shortened position significantly limits the muscle's ability to function as a supinator. Physical therapists should avoid maximum pressure in this position since the shortened position of the biceps can result in significant cramping.**

System: Musculoskeletal System
Content Outline: Physical Therapy Examination

Level 2

PTEXAM THREE: QUESTION 74

A physical therapist treats a patient with Parkinson's disease using whole-body vibration. Which symptom associated with Parkinson's disease would this intervention MOST influence?

1. Dysphagia
2. **Tremor**
3. Akinesia
4. Cognitive impairment

Correct Answer: 2 (Fell p. 664) 

Whole-body vibration consists of transferring vibration of varying frequencies to the body as a whole in one or multiple planes. Vibration training can be utilized as an intervention to improve muscle strength, power, flexibility, and coordination. Common medical conditions treated with whole-body vibration include osteoporosis, balance disorders, and Parkinson's disease.

1. Dysphagia refers to the inability to swallow properly. Treatment of dysphagia does not include whole-body vibration, but rather focuses on proper body positioning and compensatory strategies to avoid aspiration when swallowing. Educational topics include the use of thick liquids and conscious swallowing.
2. **Whole-body vibration has been found to effectively decrease tremors and rigidity in patients with Parkinson's disease. Vibratory input to the muscle spindle biases information about muscle length, resulting in more fluid and purposeful movement during memory-guided activity.**
3. Akinesia refers to the inability to initiate movement. The decrease in tremor and rigidity associated with vibration can allow for improved gait and increased step length, however, the actual inability to initiate movement is not directly affected by this intervention.
4. Cognitive, memory, and language impairments can be associated with Parkinson's disease. These impairments most often involve executive functioning within the brain. Cognitive impairments are not affected with the use of whole-body vibration. Adaptive strategies are most commonly utilized to assist with cognitive deficits.

System: Neuromuscular and Nervous Systems
Content Outline: Interventions

Level 1

p. 263, 277-278, 344-345

PTEXAM THREE: QUESTION 75

A patient in the intensive care unit due to a serious infection is connected to a series of lines and tubes. Which of the following veins would be the MOST appropriate infusion site to administer an intravenous line in the lower extremity?

1. Median cubital
2. Basilic
3. Cephalic
4. **Saphenous**

Correct Answer: 4 (Fairchild p. 279) 

The majority of intravenous insertions are made into superficial veins. Appropriate veins exist in the upper extremity, lower extremity, and scalp.

1. The median cubital vein is the communication between the basilic and cephalic veins in the cubital fossa.
2. The basilic vein is a large and superficial vein of the upper limb that assists with drainage of the hand and forearm.
3. The cephalic vein is located along the anterolateral surface of the biceps and is often visible through the skin.
4. **The saphenous vein is a superficial vein that extends from the foot to the saphenous opening. The vein is the only listed option that is located in the lower extremity.**

System: Cardiovascular and Pulmonary Systems
Content Outline: Foundations for Evaluation, Differential Diagnosis, and Prognosis

Test Taking Tip: On occasion, examination questions appear to be considerably more difficult than they actually are. In this particular item, candidates do not have to possess specific knowledge related to each of the options, rather they need to recognize that only one of the options is located in the lower extremity. Candidates must be sure they interpret each question correctly and attempt to make the question as simple as possible. Candidates who can do this consistently on the examination often score higher than other candidates with similar academic knowledge.

Level 1

PTEXAM THREE: QUESTION 76

A physical therapist administers a neural tension test to a patient with low back pain as shown in the image. Assuming the current testing procedure has been unable to reproduce the patient's symptoms, the MOST appropriate therapist action is to do which of the following steps next?

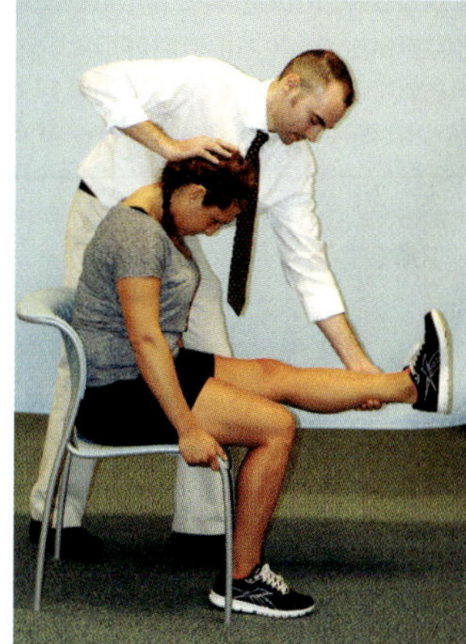

1. Apply passive overpressure to cervical flexion
2. **Apply passive overpressure to left ankle dorsiflexion**
3. Passively extend the right knee
4. Ask the patient to actively extend the right knee

Correct Answer: 2 (Dutton p. 448)

The slump test is a neural provocation test performed with the patient in sitting. The slump test is a series of progressive active and passive movements. At each portion of the test, the therapist asks the patient if they are experiencing symptoms (e.g., radicular pain, numbness, tingling). If symptoms are produced, the test would be considered positive. If symptoms are not produced, the therapist systematically increases the amount of dural stretch. The therapist initiates the test by asking the patient to flex the thoracic and lumbar spine. The patient is then asked to actively flex their cervical spine and the therapist applies overpressure. The therapist next asks the patient to actively extend their knee and then provides overpressure to ankle dorsiflexion.

1. The image already depicts the therapist applying passive overpressure to cervical flexion. As a result, there is no need for the therapist to apply additional pressure.
2. **Although the patient's left ankle appears to be dorsiflexed, applying passive overpressure to left ankle dorsiflexion would increase the amount of neural tension.**
3. The slump test requires the therapist to move through the described progression unilaterally prior to performing a bilateral assessment.
4. Actively extending the right knee would occur when assessing the right lower extremity. The right lower extremity would not be assessed until the described progression has been completed with the left lower extremity.

System: Neuromuscular and Nervous Systems
Content Outline: Physical Therapy Examination

 Level 2  p. 111

PTEXAM THREE: QUESTION 77

A physical therapist examines the foot of a patient with lower extremity pain. After placing the foot in subtalar neutral, the therapist determines that the medial border of the foot along the first metatarsal is higher than the lateral border of the foot along the fifth metatarsal. This position would MOST appropriately be documented as which of the following malalignments?

1. **Forefoot varus**
2. Forefoot valgus
3. Rearfoot varus
4. Rearfoot valgus

Correct Answer: 1 (Magee p. 907)

Malalignment of the foot and ankle can alter the normal biomechanics of gait and distribute abnormal forces to other joints in the kinematic chain. Physical therapists must carefully assess the individual and collective functioning of the rearfoot, midfoot, and forefoot when assessing the foot and ankle.

1. **Forefoot varus refers to an inverted position of the forefoot in relationship to the rearfoot with the subtalar joint in a neutral position. Patients with low arches in weight bearing often exhibit forefoot varus with the subtalar joint in a neutral position.**
2. Forefoot valgus refers to an everted position of the forefoot in relation to the rearfoot with the subtalar joint in a neutral position. Forefoot valgus is often associated with high arches or cavus feet.
3. Rearfoot varus refers to the calcaneus assuming a position of inversion (calcaneus varus) with the subtalar joint in a neutral position. Three to four degrees of inversion is considered to be within normal limits.
4. Rearfoot valgus refers to the calcaneus assuming a position of eversion (calcaneus valgus) with the subtalar joint in a neutral position. Rearfoot valgus is often a result of compensation for forefoot varus.

System: Musculoskeletal System
Content Outline: Physical Therapy Examination

Level 2

PTEXAM THREE: QUESTION 78

A physical therapist prepares to examine a patient admitted to an inpatient rehabilitation hospital. The patient sustained a traumatic head injury in a motor vehicle accident five weeks ago. The medical record indicates that the patient is often disoriented and can frequently become agitated with little provocation. The MOST appropriate setting for the therapist to make initial contact with the patient is in which of the following locations?

1. **Patient's room**
2. Physical therapy gym
3. Private treatment room
4. Physical therapy waiting room

Correct Answer: 1 (Umphred p. 788) 

A patient with a head injury that is confused and can become agitated is likely functioning at level IV on the Rancho Los Amigos Scale.

1. **The patient's room is the most appropriate first meeting place since the patient will be familiar with the surroundings and may therefore be less distractible. The patient may tend to become agitated in the gym due to overstimulation from other patients and the overall level of activity.**
2. The physical therapy gym is a good option for the treatment of the general population, but becomes more difficult following brain injury due to the patient's decreased attention, lack of focus, and potential agitation.
3. A private treatment room may be too isolated if assistance is needed. Since the patient has a poor attention span, it will be helpful to use familiar surroundings, pictures, and personal effects.
4. The physical therapy waiting room is not an appropriate place to treat a patient. This patient would likely have a difficult time adjusting to the various distractions in the waiting room.

System: Neuromuscular and Nervous Systems
Content Outline: Interventions

Level 3

PTEXAM THREE: QUESTION 79

A physical therapist prepares to treat a patient with limited elbow and forearm range of motion. When mobilizing the humeroradial articulation, which of the following statements BEST represents the appropriate treatment plane?

1. In the concave radial head, parallel to the long axis of the radius
2. **In the concave radial head, perpendicular to the long axis of the radius**
3. In the convex radial head, parallel to the long axis of the radius
4. In the convex radial head, perpendicular to the long axis of the radius

Correct Answer: 2 (Kisner p. 148)

The humeroradial joint is a uniaxial hinge joint between the capitulum of the humerus and the head of the radius. The humerus is convex and the radius is concave and therefore osteokinematic motion and arthrokinematic glide are in the same direction. The treatment plane is considered the plane perpendicular to a line running from the axis of rotation to the middle of the concave articular surface. The plane itself is located in the concave partner and is therefore determined by the position of the concave bone.

1. The radial head is the concave partner, however, the treatment plane is perpendicular and not parallel to the long axis of the radius.
2. **The radial head is the concave partner and the treatment plane is perpendicular to the long axis of the radius.**
3. The radial head is the concave partner and not the convex partner. The treatment plane is perpendicular and not parallel to the long axis of the radius.
4. The radial head is the concave partner and not the convex partner, however, the treatment plane is perpendicular to the long axis of the radius.

System: Musculoskeletal System
Content Outline: Interventions

 Level 2  p. 111-113

PTEXAM THREE: QUESTION 80

A physical therapist conducts an inservice on exercise guidelines for a group of senior citizens. As part of the program, the therapist discusses the benefits of improving cardiovascular endurance through a low intensity activity such as a walking program. What frequency of exercise would be the MOST desirable to achieve the stated objective?

1. Twice per day
2. One time per week
3. Three times per week
4. **Five times per week**

Correct Answer: 4 (ACSM – Resource Manual p. 175) 

To minimize medical problems and promote long-term compliance with this population, exercise intensity should start low and progress gradually according to individual tolerance and preference. Exercise performed at a moderate intensity should be performed for 30 minutes on most days of the week. If exercise is at a vigorous level, it should be performed at least three times per week. Since the cited exercise is low intensity, five times per week is the most appropriate option.

1. The therapist can recommend that individuals who have difficulty sustaining exercise for 30 minutes continuously, or who prefer shorter bouts of exercise, should exercise for shorter periods (e.g., 10 minutes) several times each day. This is not the most desirable combination of exercise intensity and frequency, however, to improve cardiovascular status.
2. One time per week is an inadequate frequency to improve cardiovascular fitness when exercising at low intensity.
3. Three times per week is an appropriate frequency if the exercise is at a vigorous level. It would not be the most desirable frequency for low intensity exercise.
4. **Since walking is a low intensity activity, more frequent exercise sessions are needed to improve cardiovascular status. Five times per week is the most desirable option.**

System: Cardiovascular and Pulmonary Systems
Content Outline: Interventions

 Level 2  p. 435-436

PTEXAM THREE: QUESTION 81

A physical therapist would like to implement a formal exercise program for a patient diagnosed with congestive heart failure, but is concerned about the patient's exercise tolerance. Which of the following conditions would be the MOST responsible for the patient's limited exercise tolerance?

1. Diminished lung volumes
2. Arterial oxygen desaturation
3. **Insufficient stroke volume during ventricular systole**
4. Excessive rise in blood pressure

Correct Answer: 3 (Hillegass p. 88)

Congestive heart failure refers to the heart's inability to maintain a cardiac output that is adequate to meet the demands of the tissues due to an abnormality in the pumping ability of the heart muscle.

1. Diminished lung volumes are more commonly associated with obstructive or restrictive lung conditions and are not typically associated with congestive heart failure.
2. The level of arterial oxygenation is not significantly impacted with congestive heart failure, rather the primary issue is that a smaller volume of blood is pumped with each contraction of the ventricles.
3. **Congestive heart failure may be due to a diminished pumping ability of the ventricles due to muscle weakening (systolic dysfunction) or to stiffening of the heart muscle that impairs the ventricles' capacity to relax and fill (diastolic dysfunction). With systolic dysfunction, the weak heart pumps a smaller volume of blood for each contraction of the ventricles (stroke volume), reducing cardiac output. The resultant decrease in the delivery of oxygenated blood to the active tissues limits the patient's ability to exercise.**
4. Most patients with congestive heart failure take multiple medications including diuretics, vasodilators, ACE inhibitors, and beta-blockers. The medications serve to reduce the hemodynamic response to exercise. An excessive increase in blood pressure is therefore unlikely.

System: Cardiovascular and Pulmonary Systems
Content Outline: Foundations for Evaluation, Differential Diagnosis, and Prognosis

 Level 2 p. 402-403, 454-455

PTEXAM THREE: QUESTION 82

A physical therapist measures a patient for a wheelchair. When measuring back height, which method is the MOST accurate?

1. Measure from the seat of the chair to the base of the axilla and subtract two inches
2. **Measure from the seat of the chair to the base of the axilla and subtract four inches**
3. Measure from the seat of the chair to the acromion process and subtract two inches
4. Measure from the seat of the chair to the acromion process and subtract four inches

Correct Answer: 2 (Fairchild p. 137) 

There are a variety of specific measurements that must be performed when fitting a patient for a wheelchair. Failure to obtain accurate measurements can result in a wheelchair that is not appropriately sized. An improperly sized wheelchair can result in increased difficulty with mobility and potential complications such as pressure sores or skin breakdown.

1. Measuring from the seat of the chair to the base of the axilla and subtracting two inches would result in the back height being at the mid-scapular level. This back height would be too high to allow for optimal mobility.
2. **Back height should be determined by measuring from the seat of the chair to the base of the axilla and subtracting four inches. This method will allow the back height to fall below the inferior angle of the scapula. The height of the seat cushion used, if applicable, must be added to the obtained measurement.**
3. Measuring from the seat of the chair to the acromion process and subtracting two inches would result in a back height that is excessive and would significantly restrict the patient's movement.
4. Measuring from the seat of the chair to the acromion process and subtracting four inches is more desirable than option 3, but would still not allow the back height to fall below the inferior angle of the scapula.

System: Non-Systems
Content Outline: Equipment, Devices, and Technologies; Therapeutic Modalities

 Level 1  p. 682-683

PTEXAM THREE: QUESTION 83

A physical therapist plans to perform a sensory examination on a patient with a suspected neurological lesion. Which type of sensation should the therapist assess FIRST?

1. Vibration
2. Two-point discrimination
3. **Temperature**
4. Kinesthesia

Correct Answer: 3 (O'Sullivan p. 89)

When performing a sensory examination, superficial sensations are generally tested first, followed by the deep sensations, then the combined cortical sensations. If assessment of the superficial sensations reveals an impairment, then it would be unnecessary to test the more discriminative sensations (i.e., deep and combined cortical). The superficial sensations must be sufficiently intact to allow meaningful testing of the discriminative sensations.

1. Vibration is a deep sensation and would be assessed after the superficial sensations have been assessed.
2. Two-point discrimination is the ability to perceive two different points applied to the skin simultaneously. Two-point discrimination is a combined cortical sensation and would be assessed after the superficial and deep sensations have been assessed.
3. **Temperature is a superficial sensation and should therefore be assessed prior to the other options. Other superficial sensations include pain, crude touch, and pressure.**
4. Kinesthesia is defined as the awareness of movement. Kinesthesia is a deep sensation and would be assessed after the superficial sensations have been assessed.

System: Neuromuscular and Nervous Systems
Content Outline: Physical Therapy Examination

Level 1

p. 256-257

PTEXAM THREE: QUESTION 84

A patient has been diagnosed with end-stage renal disease. Which of the following comorbidities is the MOST likely to have caused this condition?

1. Chronic hypotension
2. **Diabetes**
3. Peripheral arterial disease
4. Congestive heart failure

Correct Answer: 2 (Goodman – Differential Diagnosis p. 373)

Chronic renal failure, or end-stage renal disease (ESRD), is a state of progressive decline in the kidneys' ability to filter fluids, metabolites, and electrolytes from the body. Individuals with ESRD develop signs and symptoms characteristic of impaired fluid and waste excretion, such as systemic and pulmonary edema.

1. Hypotension (i.e., low blood pressure) is defined as systolic blood pressure less than 90 mm Hg or diastolic blood pressure less than 60 mm Hg. Chronic hypotension is rare and unlikely to affect the functioning of the kidneys. Chronic hypertension, however, is one of the primary causes of ESRD.
2. **Diabetes is the primary cause of ESRD. High blood glucose levels overwork the kidneys by causing them to filter excessive volumes of blood, eventually leading to breakdown of the kidneys (i.e., diabetic nephropathy). When not treated early, this condition can lead to ESRD.**
3. Peripheral arterial disease (PAD) is a condition in which plaque builds up in the arteries that carry blood to the head, organs, and limbs. PAD can affect blood flow to the kidneys (i.e., renal artery disease). Renal artery disease is primarily characterized by impairments in the regulation of blood pressure and is unlikely to result in ESRD.
4. Congestive heart failure (CHF) is a condition in which the heart's function is impaired and the blood supply to the body becomes inadequate. CHF may result in a decrease in blood supply to the kidneys, though it is unlikely to cause ESRD. Conversely, ESRD is a possible cause for the development of CHF.

System: Other Systems
Content Outline: Foundations for Evaluation, Differential Diagnosis, and Prognosis

Level 2

p. 530-531, 544-545

PTEXAM THREE: QUESTION 85

A physical therapist is concerned that a 77-year-old patient who is taking diazepam (Valium) may be a significant fall risk. Which of the following side effects would MOST likely be associated with this increased risk?

1. Ataxia
2. Hemorrhage
3. **Sedation**
4. Postural hypotension

Correct Answer: 3 (Ciccone p. 75)

Diazepam (Valium) is a benzodiazepine that can be used to calm severe anxiety and agitation. In a geriatric population, the liver metabolizes diazepam very slowly and the kidneys excrete it slowly. As a result, the patient may experience potentially toxic medication levels.

1. Ataxia is a side effect more commonly associated with antidepressants, opioid analgesics, and anticonvulsants.
2. Hemorrhage is a side effect more commonly associated with anticoagulant agents and thrombolytic agents.
3. **Sedation is a side effect commonly associated with diazepam. Diazepam remains active in the body for many hours and as a result drowsiness may last into the next day. Other side effects associated with diazepam that can contribute to an increased fall risk include impaired balance, decreased neuromuscular function, and decreased central processing. Diazepam has a high potential for dependence and addiction.**
4. Postural hypotension is commonly associated with an increased fall risk, however, the condition is not a side effect of diazepam. Postural hypotension is a side effect of a large number of antihypertensives (e.g., beta blockers) and cardiac drugs (e.g., nitrates).

System: Other Systems
Content Outline: Foundations for Evaluation, Differential Diagnosis, and Prognosis

 Level 2  p. 566-567

PTEXAM THREE: QUESTION 86

A patient who has infrapatellar tendonitis completes a series of functional activities. After completing the activities, the physical therapist instructs the patient to use ice massage over the anterior surface of the knee. What is the MOST appropriate treatment time in minutes?

1. 3-5
2. **5-10**
3. 10-15
4. 15-20

Correct Answer: 2 (Cameron p. 138)

Ice massage is typically performed by freezing water in paper cups and applying the ice directly to the treatment area. Ice massage tends to create a more intense cooling since the ice is applied directly to a localized target area.

1. Sufficient cooling with ice massage would not occur with a 3-5 minute treatment time.
2. **Ice massage requires a treatment time of 5-10 minutes due to the intensity of the cooling.**
3. A treatment time of 10-15 minutes would be excessive with ice massage and could result in signs and symptoms of cold intolerance.
4. A treatment time of 15-20 minutes would be within the established range for an ice pack, but would not be acceptable for ice massage.

System: Non-Systems
Content Outline: Equipment, Devices, and Technologies; Therapeutic Modalities

 Level 2  p. 702-703

PTEXAM THREE: QUESTION 87

A physical therapist works with a six-year-old patient with hip pathology. Which condition would be the MOST likely based on the patient's age?

1. Apophysitis
2. **Legg-Calve-Perthes disease**
3. Rheumatoid arthritis
4. Slipped capital femoral epiphysis

Correct Answer: 2 (Palisano p. 319)

Physical therapists should be familiar with the unique characteristics of commonly encountered medical conditions. This knowledge should include items such as age of onset and peak incidence.

1. Apophysitis refers to inflammation of an apophysis. An apophysis is a secondary ossification center that functions as an attachment site for the musculotendinous unit. The site is highly susceptible to injury from repetitive stress or an acute injury. Peak incidence of apophysitis occurs in pre-adolescents because exercise and training increase the strength of the muscle and tendon more rapidly than bone in this age group.
2. **Legg-Calve-Perthes disease is characterized by degeneration of the femoral head due to a disturbance in the blood supply (i.e., avascular necrosis). Peak incidence of Legg-Calve-Perthes disease is between five and seven years of age. The condition is more common in boys than girls.**
3. Rheumatoid arthritis is a systemic autoimmune disorder of unknown etiology. The disease presents with a chronic inflammatory reaction in the synovial tissues of a joint resulting in erosion of cartilage and supporting structures within the capsule. Peak incidence of rheumatoid arthritis is between 30 and 50 years of age with females being affected more often than males. Juvenile rheumatoid arthritis would be a more plausible option since this particular type of arthritis affects children less than 16 years of age.
4. Slipped capital femoral epiphysis refers to a separation between the ball of the hip joint and the femur at the growth plate. Peak incidence of slipped capital femoral epiphysis occurs in pre-adolescents who are obese or who have experienced a recent growth spurt.

System: Musculoskeletal System
Content Outline: Foundations for Evaluation, Differential Diagnosis, and Prognosis

 Level 1  p. 124

PTEXAM THREE: QUESTION 88

A physical therapist instructs a patient in the supine position to bring the left leg toward the chest and maintain the position. Assuming the therapist observes the reaction shown in the image, what muscle would MOST likely have insufficient length?

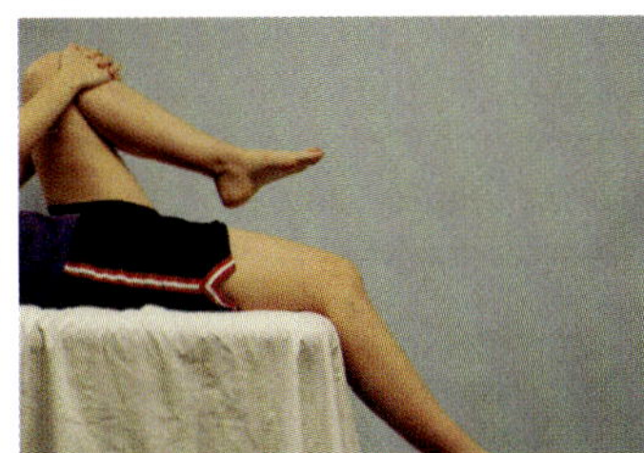

1. Iliopsoas
2. Quadratus lumborum
3. **Rectus femoris**
4. Sartorius

Correct Answer: 3 (Magee p. 728) 

The left hip and knee are flexed to the chest to flatten the lumbar spine and stabilize the pelvis. A hip flexion contracture would be denoted by the right leg rising off the table. The length of the rectus femoris can be assessed by examining the relative position of the knee (i.e., amount of knee flexion).

1. The iliopsoas acts to flex the hip. Tightness in the muscle could be identified using the Thomas test, however, the patient's right leg remains on the table which would be an indication of sufficient length in the iliopsoas.
2. The quadratus lumborum originates on the iliolumbar ligament and the iliac crest. The muscle inserts on the inferior border of the last rib and the transverse processes of the upper four lumbar vertebrae. As a result, the muscle does not act on the hip.
3. **Extension of the right knee is an indication that the patient has tightness in the two-joint rectus femoris muscle. A patient without tightness in the rectus femoris would typically present with the knee in 90 degrees of flexion while maintaining the position.**
4. The sartorius is a two-joint muscle that crosses both the hip and knee. The muscle acts to flex, laterally rotate, and abduct the hip joint. The Thomas test is not specific enough to address tightness in the sartorius due to the diversity of the muscle's action.

System: Musculoskeletal System
Content Outline: Physical Therapy Examination

Level 1

PTEXAM THREE: QUESTION 89

A 16-year-old patient accompanied by her mother receives exercise instructions from a physical therapist. During the treatment session, the mother makes several comments to her daughter that appear to be extremely upsetting and result in the daughter losing concentration. Which of the following actions is the MOST appropriate for the therapist to take?

1. Document the mother's comments in the medical record
2. Ask the patient if her mother is verbally abusive
3. **Ask the mother to return to the waiting area**
4. Discontinue the treatment session

Correct Answer: 3 (Umphred p. 19) 

The physical therapist's primary concern should be to establish an environment that is conducive to instructing the patient in the exercise program. Failure to address the negative interaction between the mother and daughter may limit the effectiveness of the session.

1. Documentation may be an appropriate option, however, it does not address the primary objective which is to allow the patient to receive exercise instructions in an appropriate learning environment.
2. It would be inappropriate to ask the child a question about this topic, particularly in the presence of the mother.
3. **The therapist increases the likelihood that the child will be able to concentrate on the exercise instructions by asking the mother to return to the waiting area. The question provides ample information to hypothesize that the mother's actions may be the reason the child is upset.**
4. The child appears to be upset and is losing concentration, however, there is no indication that the session is hopeless and therefore the decision to discontinue the treatment session would be premature without first trying to modify the current learning environment.

System: Non-Systems
Content Outline: Safety and Protection; Professional Responsibilities; Research

PTEXAM THREE: QUESTION 90

The goals for a patient who is post total knee arthroplasty include general conditioning and independent household mobility. Which component of the patient's treatment would be the MOST appropriate to delegate to a physical therapy aide?

1. Stair training
2. Progressive gait training with a straight cane
3. Patient education regarding the surgical procedure
4. **Ambulation with a walker for endurance**

Correct Answer: 4 (Guide to Physical Therapist Practice)

A physical therapy aide is a non-licensed worker, trained under the direction of a physical therapist, who requires continuous on-site supervision. A physical therapist is required, before delegating any component of a treatment plan, to have an understanding of the physical therapy aide's level of training as well as the patient's current abilities.

1. Stair training is a skilled activity that requires the constant supervision of a licensed physical therapist. The term "training" implies that the patient is being taught a new skill. Delegating this type of skilled activity to a physical therapy aide is inappropriate and would potentially jeopardize patient safety.
2. Progressive gait training implies that there will be some progression within the activity based on the patient's performance. The decision to progress a patient during an activity is the responsibility of the physical therapist and would be inappropriate for a physical therapy aide.
3. Patient education regarding the surgical procedure requires an individual to possess specific knowledge of the actual surgical procedure performed by the surgeon. A physical therapy aide does not possess the educational background to provide the patient with this information.
4. **A physical therapist, and in some jurisdictions a physical therapist assistant, may delegate ambulation activities to an aide if the physical therapist feels the aide's training is adequate to complete the activity. This decision would be heavily influenced by the patient's current status and competence with ambulation. Ambulation for endurance implies that the patient already possesses basic competence with the activity.**

System: Non-Systems
Content Outline: Safety and Protection; Professional Responsibilities; Research

 p. 784-786

PTEXAM THREE: QUESTION 91

A patient is admitted to the hospital with a stage 3 pressure injury over the right ischial tuberosity. The patient's past medical history includes severe chronic obstructive pulmonary disease. Which of the following positions is the MOST appropriate for the patient?

1. Supine with pillows under the knees
2. Prone with pillows under the knees
3. **Left sidelying with pillows between the knees**
4. Right sidelying with pillows between the knees

Correct Answer: 3 (Frownfelter p. 515) 

Left sidelying would be the position of choice in order to relieve pressure on the ulcer and maximize the patient's respiration. Recognizing contraindications for chronic obstructive pulmonary disease as well as positioning for pressure relief will allow for safe and effective positioning to enhance recovery.

1. Although the supine position with pillows under the knees is a comfortable position that reduces lumbar lordosis and strain, there would be pressure directly over the right ischial tuberosity and this would hinder progress or worsen the pressure injury.
2. A prone position would allow for pressure relief over the right ischial tuberosity, however, the patient has severe chronic obstructive pulmonary disease and should not lie in prone as breathing would be very difficult. Pillows are also not typically placed under the knees when a patient is in prone.
3. **Left sidelying does not compromise respiration and avoids placing stress on the right ischial tuberosity.**
4. A right sidelying position would assist the patient with breathing and would not compromise overall respiration, however, there would be significant pressure over the right ischial tuberosity.

System: Other Systems
Content Outline: Interventions

 Level 2  p. 504

PTEXAM THREE: QUESTION 92

A patient who found relief from low back pain with single knee to chest and double knee to chest exercises undergoes a laminectomy without spinal fusion. Which pathology would have MOST likely precipitated the surgical procedure?

1. Anterior disk protrusion
2. Quadratus lumborum strain
3. Spondylolisthesis
4. **Lumbar stenosis**

Correct Answer: 4 (Cameron – Physical Rehabilitation p. 146)

Laminectomy is a surgical procedure that is commonly performed on individuals who have symptoms related to arthritis or stenosis of the spine. A complete laminectomy involves removing the entire lamina, the spinous process, and the associated ligamentum flavum. A partial laminectomy involves the removal of only one lamina.

1. While a laminectomy can provide relief for symptoms caused by disk pathologies, this is more commonly performed for posterior disk protrusions because of the position of the lamina in relation to the displaced disk. A microdiscectomy is more likely to be performed for an anterior disk protrusion.
2. While single knee and double knee to chest exercises will likely provide relief for an individual with a quadratus lumborum strain, a muscle strain of the low back rarely warrants surgical intervention.
3. Spondylolisthesis is characterized by the forward slippage of one vertebral segment on the one below it. While flexion exercises are indicated for this pathology, surgical intervention commonly involves decompression and spinal fusion.
4. **Spinal stenosis is characterized by narrowing of the vertebral or intervertebral foramen. This can result in compression of the spinal cord or exiting nerve roots. A laminectomy is often performed in patients experiencing spinal stenosis to relieve pressure on affected nerves.**

System: Musculoskeletal System
Content Outline: Foundations for Evaluation, Differential Diagnosis, and Prognosis

 Level 2  p. 129, 208

PTEXAM THREE: QUESTION 93

A 13-year-old patient diagnosed with juvenile rheumatoid arthritis experiences an acute exacerbation of their condition. The physical therapist recommends a custom splint in order to prevent a knee flexion contracture. Which type of splint is the MOST appropriate to support this goal?

1. Functional
2. Dynamic
3. **Resting**
4. Serial

Correct Answer: 3 (Cameron – Physical Rehabilitation p. 911)

Patients diagnosed with juvenile rheumatoid arthritis (JRA) may benefit from different splinting options depending on the acuity of symptoms and degree of inflammation present. Splints may be custom or non-custom and often support a variety of treatment goals.

1. A functional splint is typically utilized to support, protect, and stabilize a joint during specific activities (e.g., holding a writing or eating utensil) in order to improve efficiency and functional performance of a task.
2. A dynamic splint typically includes a spring or elastic component utilized to exert force on a joint. This force may be utilized to facilitate passive or assisted movement of a joint or to resist movement in the direction opposite the line of pull. Dynamic splints are not typically indicated during acute exacerbations.
3. **A resting splint is typically utilized to maintain a joint in an appropriate position during an acute exacerbation of symptoms, allowing the joint to rest while limiting the risk of contracture development.**
4. A serial splint is a form of corrective splinting utilized to immobilize a joint in order to increase range of motion while correcting a deformity such as a soft tissue contracture.

System: Non-Systems
Content Outline: Equipment, Devices, and Technologies; Therapeutic Modalities

Level 1

PTEXAM THREE: QUESTION 94

A physical therapist performs a special test on a patient injured in a soccer contest. The patient is presently able to flex the knee to only 80 degrees. Which test would be LEAST affected by the patient's range of motion limitation?

1. Anterior drawer test
2. Apley's compression test
3. Craig's test
4. **Thompson test**

Correct Answer: 4 (Magee p. 940)

There are a wide variety of special tests commonly employed in physical therapy practice. Physical therapists should be familiar with the testing procedures associated with these tests and be able to select appropriate special tests based on a patient's current functional status and limitations.

1. The anterior drawer test is performed with the patient positioned in supine with the knee flexed to 90 degrees and the hip flexed to 45 degrees. The therapist grasps the patient's proximal tibia with two hands, places their thumbs on the tibial plateau, and administers an anterior directed force to the tibia on the femur. A positive test is indicated by excessive anterior translation of the tibia on the femur with a diminished or absent end-point and may be indicative of an anterior cruciate ligament injury.
2. Apley's compression test is performed in prone with the knee flexed to 90 degrees. The therapist stabilizes the patient's femur using one hand and places the other hand on the patient's heel. The therapist medially and laterally rotates the tibia while applying a compressive force through the tibia. A positive test is indicated by pain or clicking and may be indicative of a meniscal lesion.
3. Craig's test is performed with the patient positioned in prone with the knee flexed to 90 degrees. The therapist palpates the greater trochanter and medially and laterally rotates the hip until the greater trochanter is parallel with the table. The degree of femoral anteversion corresponds to the angle formed by the lower leg with the perpendicular axis of the table. Normal anteversion for an adult is 8-15 degrees.
4. **The Thompson test is performed with the patient positioned in prone with the legs extended and the feet hanging over the edge of a table. The therapist asks the patient to relax and proceeds to squeeze the muscle belly of the gastrocnemius and soleus muscles. A positive test is indicated by the absence of plantar flexion and may be indicative of a ruptured Achilles tendon. The knee remains in an extended position throughout the testing procedure.**

System: Musculoskeletal System
Content Outline: Physical Therapy Examination

Level 1

p. 110

PTEXAM THREE: QUESTION 95

A physical therapist recommends a wheelchair for a patient post CVA with the goal of independent mobility. The left upper and lower extremities are flaccid and present with edema. There is Normal (5/5) strength on the right, however, the patient's trunk is hypotonic. The patient is cognitively intact. Which of the following wheelchairs is the MOST appropriate for this patient?

1. Solid seat, solid back, elevating legrests, and anti-tippers
2. Sling seat, sling back, arm board, and elevating legrests
3. **Light weight, solid seat, solid back, arm board, and elevating legrests**
4. Light weight, solid seat, solid back, arm board, and standard footrests

Correct Answer: 3 (Fairchild p. 141)

A physical therapist must carefully select a wheelchair for a patient that possesses the necessary adaptations to meet the patient's unique needs. Failure to select an adequately equipped wheelchair can significantly compromise the patient's progress in rehabilitation.

1. The flaccid upper extremity would need to be supported using an arm board. Anti-tippers would not typically be necessary for this patient.
2. A sling seat and sling back promote poor positioning and would not provide the necessary stability the patient requires.
3. **Independent propulsion is facilitated by the use of a light-weight wheelchair, while a solid seating system assists with posture and activities. An arm board allows the flaccid upper extremity to be supported and an elevating legrest will assist to decrease dependent edema.**
4. The wheelchair is appropriate for the patient, however, the presence of lower extremity edema makes it desirable to incorporate elevating legrests.

System: Neuromuscular and Nervous Systems
Content Outline: Interventions

 Level 2  p. 684-687

PTEXAM THREE: QUESTION 96

A physical therapist participates in a formal gait analysis using three-dimensional analysis software for a patient with cerebral palsy. Which objective finding would LEAST likely be obtained through this process?

1. Decreased swing phase
2. Decreased walking velocity
3. **Decreased quadriceps strength**
4. Decreased knee extension range of motion

Correct Answer: 3 (Levangie p. 525)

Formal gait analysis can objectively measure the magnitude of gait deviations in children with disabilities. Kinematics in gait analysis most often utilize either two or three dimensions and rely on external markers serving as reference points to analyze motion. The collected information can be utilized to quantify spatial and temporal variables associated with gait, evaluate the effectiveness of treatment, and examine the influence of medications, bracing or surgical interventions.

1. The amount of time spent in stance phase or swing phase can be determined through gait analysis. The stance phase of the gait cycle typically occupies approximately 60% of the gait cycle and the swing phase occupies approximately 40%.
2. Walking velocity refers to the rate of walking or the distance traversed in a specified length of time. Velocity is often expressed as stride length divided by cycle time and is routinely measured during gait analysis. Normalization methods are used when comparing different velocities due to the correlation with leg length.
3. **Muscle weakness cannot be measured directly with gait analysis. Although gait analysis may include electromyography, this measure would not provide specific information on muscle strength. A thorough knowledge of muscle function and normal gait combined with the results of manual muscle testing provides the therapist with the necessary information to assess muscle weakness.**
4. Range of motion can be quantified at a variety of joints throughout the gait cycle using gait analysis. Diminished range of motion in an individual with cerebral palsy could be due to a static contracture or a dynamic contracture caused by spasticity.

System: Musculoskeletal System
Content Outline: Physical Therapy Examination

 Level 1

PTEXAM THREE: QUESTION 97

A patient's medical chart indicates that a patient has a lesion in the posterior portion of the spinal cord. Which of the following impairments would MOST likely be observed?

1. **Inability to determine joint position**
2. Inability to distinguish between hot and cold
3. Inability to distinguish between sharp and dull
4. Inability to feel light touch

Correct Answer: 1 (O'Sullivan p. 82)

Sensory information is transmitted to the brain either by the spinothalamic tract or the dorsal column-medial lemniscus tract. The spinothalamic tract is located in the anterior and lateral portions of the spinal cord and the dorsal column-medial lemniscus tract is located in the posterior portion of the spinal cord. The spinothalamic tract primarily transmits nondiscriminative sensations (e.g., temperature, pain, touch), while the dorsal column-medial lemniscus tract transmits more discriminative sensations (e.g., discriminative touch, stereognosis, kinesthesia).

1. **Proprioception is the sense of static joint position. Proprioceptive information is transmitted to the brain via the dorsal column-medial lemniscus tract.**
2. Temperature awareness is the ability to distinguish between hot and cold stimuli. Temperature sense information is transmitted to the brain via the anterolateral spinothalamic tract.
3. Pain perception is determined by the ability to distinguish between sharp and dull sensations. Pain perception information is transmitted to the brain via the anterolateral spinothalamic tract.
4. Touch awareness is the ability to perceive the sensation of touch. Touch awareness information is transmitted to the brain via the anterolateral spinothalamic tract. If the patient were required to determine the location of the touch (i.e., tactile localization), the information would be transmitted via the dorsal column-medial lemniscus tract since this sensation is more discriminative.

System: Neuromuscular and Nervous Systems
Content Outline: Foundations for Evaluation, Differential Diagnosis, and Prognosis

 **Level 1** **p. 243, 257**

PTEXAM THREE: QUESTION 98

A physical therapist suspects that a patient's clinical presentation may be associated with cubital tunnel syndrome. Which finding would be the MOST useful when distinguishing this condition from other common conditions affecting the elbow?

1. Visible edema in the posterior elbow
2. Medial-sided elbow pain
3. **Paresthesias in the fourth and fifth fingers**
4. Increased pain with weight bearing on the elbow

Correct Answer: 3 (Brody p. 819)

Cubital tunnel syndrome, also known as ulnar neuropathy, is caused by increased pressure on the ulnar nerve in the cubital tunnel. The cubital tunnel is formed by the medial epicondyle, olecranon, and ulnar collateral ligament of the elbow. Signs and symptoms of the condition can include pain, sensory disturbances, muscle weakness, and muscle wasting. Other conditions with a similar clinical presentation include medial epicondylitis, ulnar collateral ligament sprain, and distal humerus fracture.

1. Visible edema in the posterior elbow would not typically be associated with cubital tunnel syndrome. The finding is more likely associated with olecranon bursitis or a distal humerus fracture.
2. Medial-sided elbow pain may be associated with a variety of conditions such as cubital tunnel syndrome, medial epicondylitis, and ulnar collateral ligament sprain. This finding is not specific enough to distinguish cubital tunnel syndrome from other conditions affecting the elbow.
3. **Cubital tunnel syndrome often produces paresthesias in the ring and little finger since the area is innervated by the ulnar nerve. Temporary paresthesias can be facilitated by sleeping with the hand in a flexed position or repeated leaning on a hard surface.**
4. Increased pain with weight bearing on the elbow may be associated with cubital tunnel syndrome, however, it may also be associated with other conditions such as a distal humerus fracture. This option would be more attractive if the pain corresponded to an area consistent with the ulnar nerve distribution.

System: Neuromuscular and Nervous Systems
Content Outline: Foundations for Evaluation, Differential Diagnosis, and Prognosis

 **Level 2**  **p. 58, 261**

PTEXAM THREE: QUESTION 99

A physical therapist inspects a ramp that conforms to the exact specifications of the minimum requirements for slope by the Americans with Disabilities Act (ADA). The ramp has two 24 foot sections connected by a landing area. How many inches is the MOST likely total height of the ramp?

1. 12
2. 24
3. 36
4. **48**

Correct Answer: 4 (Minor p. 19) 

According to the Americans with Disabilities Act, a ramp must have a minimum of one foot of horizontal run for each inch of rise. In the presented scenario, the total horizontal run of the ramp is 48 feet (two 24 foot sections). The landing area is level and therefore would not be a factor when determining the total height of the ramp.

1. A ramp that is designed to accommodate for 12 inches of total height would be 12 feet in length if the ramp conformed to the exact specifications of the Americans with Disabilities Act.
2. A ramp that is designed to accommodate for 24 inches of total height would be 24 feet in length if the ramp conformed to the exact specifications of the Americans with Disabilities Act. This height would be representative of the height of a single 24 foot section.
3. A ramp that is designed to accommodate for 36 inches of total height would be 36 feet in length if the ramp conformed to the exact specifications of the Americans with Disabilities Act. A ramp with greater than 30 consecutive feet of horizontal run must include a landing area.
4. **A ramp that is designed to accommodate for 48 inches of total height would be 48 feet in length if the ramp conformed to the exact specifications of the Americans with Disabilities Act. Any height greater than 48 inches would require more than 48 feet of horizontal run in order to comply with the Americans with Disabilities Act's minimum specifications.**

System: Non-Systems
Content Outline: Safety and Protection; Professional Responsibilities; Research

 p. 770-771

PTEXAM THREE: QUESTION 100

A physical therapist examines a patient who reports morning stiffness of their hands and visible swelling. The patient indicates that the stiffness seems to diminish with activity. This description would MOST likely be associated with which of the following conditions?

1. Carpal tunnel syndrome
2. Osteoporosis
3. **Rheumatoid arthritis**
4. Osteoarthritis

Correct Answer: 3 (Paz p. 333) 

Rheumatoid arthritis is a chronic systemic autoimmune disorder of unknown etiology characterized by inflammatory changes in joints and related structures. The disease is two to three times more common in women than men.

1. Carpal tunnel syndrome is a medical condition caused by compression of the median nerve resulting in paresthesias, numbness, and muscle weakness in the hand. Symptoms include night pain, muscle atrophy, decreased grip strength, and decreased wrist mobility.
2. Osteoporosis is a metabolic condition that presents with a decrease in bone mass resulting in a greater risk of fracture. Symptoms include compression and other fractures, low thoracic or lumbar pain, loss of lumbar lordosis, kyphosis, decrease in height, Dowager's hump, and postural changes.
3. **Symptoms of rheumatoid arthritis include morning stiffness, limited range of motion, effusion, pain with movement, and low grade fever. Smaller peripheral joints are initially affected, however, symptoms may progress to larger synovial joints.**
4. Osteoarthritis is a chronic disease that is characterized by degeneration of articular cartilage typically in weight bearing joints. Patients with osteoarthritis typically experience an increase in pain and stiffness with activity, rather than a decrease. Subsequent deformity and thickening of subchondral bone results in impaired functional status. The most commonly affected sites include the hands, hips, spine, and knees. Activity tends to exacerbate symptoms in patients with osteoarthritis.

System: Other Systems
Content Outline: Foundations for Evaluation, Differential Diagnosis, and Prognosis

 Level 2

 p. 126, 624-625

PTEXAM THREE: QUESTION 101

A physical therapist performs the Thessaly test to a patient with a suspected meniscal tear. This testing procedure would require the therapist to perform which of the following activities?

1. **Passively medially rotate the patient's tibia and extend the knee**
2. **Cup the patient's heel and allow the knee to extend from a fully flexed position**
3. **Grasp the patient's hands in standing to promote balance**
4. **Passively flex and extend the patient's knee while feeling for "popping"**

Correct Answer: 3 (Magee p. 839)

The Thessaly test for a meniscal tear occurs in single leg stance by having a patient rotate the femur on the tibia medially and laterally three times. A positive test is indicated by joint line discomfort, catching or locking in the knee.

1. The McMurray test is performed with the patient positioned in supine. The therapist grasps the distal leg with one hand and palpates the knee joint line with the other. With the knee fully flexed, the therapist medially rotates the tibia and extends the knee. The therapist repeats the same procedure while laterally rotating the tibia. A positive test is indicated by a click or pronounced crepitation felt over the joint line and may be indicative of a posterior meniscal lesion.
2. The bounce home test is performed with the patient positioned in supine. The therapist grasps the patient's heel and maximally flexes the knee. The patient's knee is then extended passively. A positive test is indicated by incomplete extension or a rubbery end-feel and may be indicative of a meniscal lesion.
3. **The therapist grasps the patient's hands in standing during the Thessaly test to provide additional balance which allows the patient to perform the necessary medial and lateral rotation of the femur on the tibia.**
4. Hughston's plica test is performed with the patient positioned in supine. The therapist flexes the knee and medially rotates the tibia with one hand while the other hand attempts to move the patella medially and palpate the medial femoral condyle. A positive test is indicated by a popping sound over the medial plica while the knee is passively flexed and extended.

System: Musculoskeletal System
Content Outline: Physical Therapy Examination

Level 1  **p. 109**

PTEXAM THREE: QUESTION 102

A physician orders electromyography for a patient who has a brachial plexus injury to objectively determine the extent of the pathology. Which of the following responses is the MOST indicative of a normal muscle at rest?

1. **Electrical silence**
2. **Spontaneous potentials**
3. **Polyphasic potentials**
4. **Occasional motor unit potentials**

Correct Answer: 1 (O'Sullivan p. 172)

Electromyography is a test that assesses the health of the muscles and the nerves controlling the muscles. A needle electrode is inserted through the skin into the muscle. The electrical activity detected by this electrode is displayed on an oscilloscope. The presence, size, and shape of the waveform (i.e., the action potential) produced on the oscilloscope provides information about the ability of the muscle to respond when the nerves are stimulated.

1. **A normally innervated muscle is electrically silent at rest. Once the insertion activity (caused by the trauma of needle insertion) resolves, there should be no action potential on the oscilloscope.**
2. Spontaneous electrical potentials, like fibrillations and positive sharp waves, are seen in an acutely denervated muscle. Fibrillations and positive sharp waves are the result of spontaneous discharge of a single muscle fiber.
3. Polyphasic potentials are the electrical potentials from a denervated motor unit. A motor unit that exhibits five or more phases is referred to as polyphasic.
4. Neurapraxia is likely when occasional motor unit potentials occur during minimal effort muscle contractions two to three weeks after injury.

System: Other Systems
Content Outline: Foundations for Evaluation, Differential Diagnosis, and Prognosis

Level 1  **p. 733-734**

PTEXAM THREE: QUESTION 103

A patient is examined in physical therapy following a mild traumatic brain injury. The physical therapist begins by observing the patient's eyes and notes that the right eye is angled inward so that is rests closer to the midline of the face than the left eye. Which cranial nerve would MOST likely be affected based on the identified abnormality?

1. Cranial nerve II
2. Cranial nerve III
3. Cranial nerve IV
4. **Cranial nerve VI**

Correct Answer: 4 (O'Sullivan p. 151)

There are several different cranial nerves that deal with functioning of the eyes. Cranial nerve II is a purely sensory nerve while cranial nerves III, IV, and VI are motor nerves that supply innervation to the eye muscles to allow for various eye movements.

1. Cranial nerve II, the optic nerve, is an afferent nerve that deals with the sense of vision. A lesion of the optic nerve would result in difficulty with a patient's visual acuity.
2. Cranial nerve III, the oculomotor nerve, is an efferent nerve that supplies innervation to the eye muscles which produce upward, downward, and medial gaze. Since the oculomotor nerve assists with medial gaze, a lesion of this nerve would tend to result in an eyeball that rests in a more lateral position.
3. Cranial nerve IV, the trochlear nerve, is an efferent nerve that supplies innervation to the eye muscles which produce a downward and inward gaze. Since the trochlear nerve assists with inward (medial) gaze, a lesion of this nerve would tend to result in an eyeball that rests in a more lateral position.
4. **Cranial nerve VI, the abducens nerve, is an efferent nerve that supplies innervation to the lateral rectus muscle of the eye, which produces lateral gaze. A lesion of this nerve would tend to result in an eyeball that rests in a more medial position since the medial rectus muscle will have a stronger influence than the lateral rectus muscle.**

System: Neuromuscular and Nervous Systems
Content Outline: Physical Therapy Examination

 **Level 2**  **p. 247-249**

PTEXAM THREE: QUESTION 104

A physical therapist prepares to treat a patient currently undergoing active treatment for an osteosarcoma. Which of the following statements BEST describes this condition?

1. **A malignant growth affecting the long bones**
2. A malignant growth affecting the flat bones
3. A benign growth affecting the long bones
4. A benign growth affecting the flat bones

Correct Answer: 1 (Goodman – Pathology p. 1263)

Osteosarcoma is diagnosed slightly more often in boys and typically presents during periods of rapid bone growth in adolescence. Osteosarcoma may develop insidiously, or secondary to radiation treatment received as part of treatment for other malignancies.

1. **Osteosarcoma is a malignant bone growth (i.e., tumor) affecting the long bones of the body. It is most commonly diagnosed in the distal femur, followed by the proximal tibia, and the proximal humerus.**
2. A malignancy, such as Ewing's sarcoma, may present in both the long bones (e.g., femur) and flat bones (e.g., pelvis, scapula) as well as within soft tissue. Ewing's sarcoma presents most commonly in the spine, pelvis, and long bones of the extremities.
3. Osteochondroma is one of the most commonly occurring types of benign bone tumor. Like osteosarcoma, it is most commonly diagnosed near the ends of long bones.
4. Although more commonly diagnosed in long bones, a small percentage of benign bone tumors (e.g., osteochondroma, osteoblastoma, osteoid osteoma) have been reported in flat bones.

System: Other Systems
Content Outline: Foundations for Evaluation, Differential Diagnosis, and Prognosis

 **Level 1**  **p. 194-195**

PTEXAM THREE: QUESTION 105

A physical therapist treats a patient diagnosed with posterior tibial tendon dysfunction. When observing the posterior aspect of the patient's lower leg and ankle in standing, which of the following findings is the MOST probable for the therapist to observe?

1. Forefoot adduction
2. **Hindfoot valgus**
3. Hypertrophy of the gastrocnemius
4. Swelling in the lateral ankle region

Correct Answer: 2 (Sarwark p. 854)

Posterior tibial tendon dysfunction is the primary cause of medial ankle pain in middle-aged patients. This condition occurs due to the inability of the posterior tibial tendon to support the medial longitudinal arch. As a result, the patient tends to exhibit a flat foot and may feel like the ankle tends to roll inward.

1. The forefoot consists of the tarsometatarsal joints, metatarsophalangeal joints, and interphalangeal joints. Posterior tibial tendon dysfunction is most often characterized by forefoot abduction and hindfoot valgus.
2. **The hindfoot consists of the talus and the calcaneus. Posterior tibial tendon dysfunction is most often characterized by a valgus deformity of the hindfoot due to a flattening of the medial longitudinal arch.**
3. Hypertrophy of the gastrocnemius would not be associated with posterior tibial tendon dysfunction. Hypertrophy of the gastrocnemius may be caused by selected gait deviations such as toe walking or can also be observed in Duchenne muscular dystrophy.
4. General swelling of the ankle can be present with posterior tibial tendon dysfunction, however, the swelling is most often concentrated in the medial aspect of the ankle due to the muscle descending posterior to the medial malleolus and inserting on the navicular and medial cuneiform bone.

System: Musculoskeletal System
Content Outline: Foundations for Evaluation, Differential Diagnosis, and Prognosis

Level 2

PTEXAM THREE: QUESTION 106

A physical therapist is informed that a patient was diagnosed with a Lisfranc injury after returning from a physician visit. The patient was originally diagnosed with a minor lateral ankle sprain, however, returned to the physician after failing to make progress. Which bone would be the LEAST likely to be impacted with this type of injury?

1. **Calcaneus**
2. Cuboid
3. Second cuneiform
4. Navicular

Correct Answer: 1 (Sarwark p. 797)

Lisfranc injuries occur at the midfoot and may include fractures or dislocations often caused by traumatic disruptions of the tarsometatarsal joints. The midfoot includes the cuboid, navicular, and three cuneiforms and their articulations with the bases of the five metatarsal bones. Lisfranc injuries are commonly mistaken for sprains since the clinical presentation is fairly similar and they are often difficult to detect upon x-ray. Undiagnosed Lisfranc injuries can have serious complications such as joint degeneration or even compartment syndrome.

1. **The calcaneus is a quadrangular bone at the back of the tarsus. The bone articulates with the cuboid and the talus. The calcaneus is considered part of the hindfoot.**
2. The cuboid is a lateral bone of the distal row of the tarsus. The bone articulates with the calcaneus, third cuneiform, and fourth and fifth metatarsals. The cuboid is part of the midfoot and could potentially be involved in a Lisfranc injury.
3. The second cuneiform is a wedge-shaped bone positioned between the first and third cuneiforms. The bone articulates with the navicular, second metatarsal, and the first and third cuneiforms. The cuneiforms are part of the midfoot and could potentially be involved in a Lisfranc injury.
4. The navicular bone is located on the medial side of the foot. The bone articulates with the talus, three cuneiform bones, and cuboid. The navicular is part of the midfoot and could potentially be involved in a Lisfranc injury.

System: Musculoskeletal System
Content Outline: Foundations for Evaluation, Differential Diagnosis, and Prognosis

Level 1

PTEXAM THREE: QUESTION 107

A physical therapist completes a sensory assessment on a patient who has multiple sclerosis. As part of the assessment, the therapist examines stereognosis, vibration, and two-point discrimination. What type of receptor is primarily responsible for generating the necessary information?

1. Deep sensory receptors
2. **Mechanoreceptors**
3. Nociceptors
4. Thermoreceptors

Correct Answer: 2 (O'Sullivan p. 83)

Mechanoreceptors generate information related to discriminative sensations. The information is then mediated through the dorsal column-medial lemniscal system. Examples of mechanoreceptors include free nerve endings, Merkel's disks, Ruffini endings, hair follicle endings, Meissner's corpuscles, and Pacinian corpuscles.

1. Deep sensory receptors are sensory receptors that are located in the muscles, tendons, and joints. Muscle and joint receptors are both classified as deep sensory receptors and include Golgi tendon organs, Pacinian corpuscles, muscle spindles, Ruffini endings, free nerve endings, and joint receptors. They evaluate position sense, proprioception, muscle tone, and movement.
2. **Mechanoreceptors are sensory receptors that respond to mechanical deformation of the area surrounding a receptor. They are responsible for sensations of touch, pressure, itch, tickle, vibration, and discriminative touch.**
3. Nociceptors are specialized peripheral free nerve endings that are found throughout different tissues within the body that respond to noxious stimuli and result in the perception of pain. A painful stimulus will ascend through the spinal cord via the lateral spinothalamic tract. Several areas of the brain provide specific responses to the painful stimulus.
4. Thermoreceptors are sensory receptors that respond to changes in temperature. Stimulation of the cold or warm receptors will ascend through the spinal cord via the lateral spinothalamic tract.

System: Neuromuscular and Nervous Systems
Content Outline: Physical Therapy Examination

Level 2

p. 244, 256-259

PTEXAM THREE: QUESTION 108

A physical therapist completes a developmental assessment on an infant. At what age should an infant begin to sit with hand support for an extended period of time?

1. **6-7 months**
2. 8-9 months
3. 10-11 months
4. 12-15 months

Correct Answer: 1 (Ratliffe p. 46)

Infants typically develop the stability to sit with hand support in the sixth to seventh month.

1. **Sitting for a prolonged period of time with upper extremity support usually occurs at 6-7 months of age. The infant will also bring objects to midline, hold a bottle with two hands, and roll to prone.**
2. When an infant is 8-9 months of age, they will typically manipulate toys in sitting, raise themselves from supine to sit, pull to stand with support, and transfer objects with a controlled release.
3. When an infant is 10-11 months of age, they will typically stand briefly without support, transition from supine to sitting or quadruped, pull to stand through half kneel, and use a pincer grasp.
4. When an infant is 12-15 months of age, they will typically stand up through quadruped, use a wide array of sitting positions, walk without support, creep up stairs, throw a ball in sitting, and mark paper with crayons.

System: Neuromuscular and Nervous Systems
Content Outline: Physical Therapy Examination

Level 1

p. 308-310

PTEXAM THREE: QUESTION 109

A physical therapist is examining a patient who has congestive heart failure. During the examination, the patient begins to complain of pain. Which of the following actions is the MOST immediate for the therapist to take?

1. **Notify the nursing staff to administer pain medication**
2. **Contact the referring physician**
3. **Discontinue the treatment session**
4. **Ask the patient to describe the location and severity of the pain**

Correct Answer: 4 (Magee p. 8) 

Congestive heart failure is characterized by the inability of the heart to maintain adequate cardiac output. Before the physical therapist can adequately respond to the patient's report of pain, it is essential to gather additional information.

1. Administering pain medication is premature until more information is known about the pain. Once additional information is collected, the nursing staff will be able to make a more informed decision.
2. Contacting the physician is premature until more information is known about the location and severity of the pain. This type of detailed information is necessary to provide the physician with a better sense of what the patient is currently experiencing.
3. Discontinuing the treatment session based on a subjective report of pain is a viable option particularly given the patient's diagnosis, however, the physical therapist would need to gather additional information about the pain prior to making a definitive decision.
4. **Having the patient describe the location and severity of the pain is the most immediate action the physical therapist should take. The information can be collected in a timely manner and may be useful to determine the relative seriousness of the patient's subjective report of pain.**

System: Cardiovascular and Pulmonary Systems
Content Outline: Physical Therapy Examination

 **Level 3**  **p. 72-73**

PTEXAM THREE: QUESTION 110

A patient demonstrates a significant loss of strength when trying to grasp a cup. However, the patient has much less difficulty when holding onto a pencil. This type of clinical scenario is consistent with pathology affecting which of the following nerves?

1. **Median**
2. **Suprascapular**
3. **Musculocutaneous**
4. **Ulnar**

Correct Answer: 4 (Magee p. 452)

Power grips (e.g., spherical, cylindrical) require use of both the radial and ulnar sides of the hand, typically involving the thumb, to grasp larger objects. Precision grips (e.g., lateral prehension, digital prehension) require use of the radial side of the hand with the thumb to hold onto smaller objects. Grasping a cup would be an example of a power grip while utilizing a pencil would be an example of a precision grip.

1. The median nerve controls flexion of the radial digits and would therefore be involved in both power and precision grips. A patient with pathology of the median nerve would have difficulty grasping both a cup and a pencil.
2. The suprascapular nerve innervates the supraspinatus and infraspinatus muscles. These muscles do not play a direct role in grasping objects.
3. The musculocutaneous nerve innervates the coracobrachialis, biceps brachii, and brachialis muscles. These muscles do not play a direct role in grasping objects.
4. **The ulnar nerve controls flexion of the ulnar digits and would therefore be involved primarily in power grips. The ulnar nerve innervates some muscles of the thumb, therefore it would have a small effect on precision grips, though this effect would be limited in comparison to power grips which rely on the ulnar side of the hand.**

System: Musculoskeletal System
Content Outline: Foundations for Evaluation, Differential Diagnosis, and Prognosis

 **Level 2**  **p. 83, 250, 261**

PTEXAM THREE: QUESTION 111

A patient presents with ape hand deformity due to a peripheral nerve injury. Which of the following findings would MOST likely be noted during examination of the patient?

1. **Decreased strength with thumb opposition**
2. Fixed flexion of the metacarpophalangeal joints
3. Fixed hyperextension of the metacarpophalangeal joints
4. Wasting of the hypothenar eminence

Correct Answer: 1 (Magee p. 436)

It is important for physical therapists to recognize impairments commonly associated with specific wrist and hand deformities. Ape hand deformity is a hand deformity caused by median nerve palsy. The condition, also known as simian hand, is characterized by an individual being unable to move the thumb away from the rest of the hand.

1. **Ape hand deformity is characterized by wasting of the thenar eminence, which results in weakness with thumb flexion and opposition. The patient's thumb may fall back in line with the other digits since the pull of the thumb extensors is stronger than the thumb flexors.**
2. Dupuytren's contracture is a hand deformity that is caused by contracture of the palmar fascia. The shortening of the fascia results in a fixed flexion deformity of the metacarpophalangeal and proximal interphalangeal joints.
3. Claw finger deformity is a hand deformity that is caused by a loss of strength in the hand intrinsics (often secondary to a nerve injury). The loss of intrinsic strength results in a fixed deformity with the metacarpophalangeal joints in hyperextension and the interphalangeal joints in flexion.
4. Wasting of the hypothenar eminence is associated with ulnar nerve pathology. The ulnar nerve supplies the three hypothenar muscles (abductor digiti minimi, flexor digiti minimi brevis, opponens digiti minimi).

System: Musculoskeletal System
Content Outline: Foundations for Evaluation, Differential Diagnosis, and Prognosis

p. 250, 261

PTEXAM THREE: QUESTION 112

A physical therapist reviews a research study that examines knee flexion range of motion two weeks following arthroscopic surgery. Assuming knee flexion range of motion is a normally distributed variable, what percentage of patients in the population would achieve a goniometric measurement value between the mean and one standard deviation above the mean?

1. 14%
2. **34%**
3. 48%
4. 68%

Correct Answer: 2 (Portney p. 399)

Because of the standard properties of the normal distribution, it is possible to determine the proportional areas under the curve represented by the standard deviation. 34.13% of the area under the curve of a normal distribution is bounded by the mean and 1 standard deviation above or below the mean.

1. 14% is the approximate area under the normal curve between 1 and 2 standard deviations above or below the mean.
2. **34% is the approximate area under the normal curve bounded by 1 standard deviation above or below the mean.**
3. 48% is the approximate area under the normal curve bounded by 2 standard deviations above or below the mean.
4. 68% is the approximate area under the normal curve bounded by 1 standard deviation below the mean and 1 standard deviation above the mean.

System: Non-Systems
Content Outline: Safety and Protection; Professional Responsibilities; Research

p. 812-813

PTEXAM THREE: QUESTION 113

An entry in a patient's medical record indicates that the patient has recently received viscosupplementation. This type of procedure is MOST commonly performed to treat which of the following conditions?

1. Arrhythmias
2. Bursitis
3. **Osteoarthritis**
4. Spasticity

Correct Answer: 3 (Ciccone p. 251) 

Viscosupplementation is a technique in which hyaluronan is injected into a patient's joint. Hyaluronan is a polysaccharide that restores the normal viscosity of the synovial fluid and helps to restore the lubricating properties of synovial fluid within that joint.

1. An arrhythmia is a cardiac condition characterized by the cardiac cycle being irregular in either rate or rhythm. Arrhythmias are typically treated with the use of antiarrhythmic agents (e.g., beta blockers, calcium channel blockers).
2. Bursitis is a condition characterized by the inflammation of a bursa, commonly in the hip, knee, shoulder or elbow. Bursitis is typically treated conservatively with rest, ice, physical therapy, and anti-inflammatory drugs. In cases that do not respond to conservative treatment, a steroid injection may be necessary.
3. **Osteoarthritis is a condition characterized by the loss of articular cartilage within a joint secondary to mechanical stresses. Viscosupplementation is commonly used in the treatment of osteoarthritis as the improved lubrication within the joint can help reduce joint stresses and reduce the progression of cartilaginous destruction. The benefits of viscosupplementation are relatively transient.**
4. Spasticity is a symptom characterized by resistance of a muscle to passive stretch and often occurs secondary to damage to the central nervous system. Spasticity is often treated with the use of baclofen, a medication which reduces the effects of spasticity through muscle relaxation.

System: Musculoskeletal System
Content Outline: Interventions

p. 124-125, 168-169

PTEXAM THREE: QUESTION 114

A patient recently visited a podiatrist and was told to purchase a heel lift for one of their shoes. Which of the following conditions would be the LEAST likely to benefit from the use of a heel lift?

1. True leg length discrepancy
2. Achilles tendonitis
3. Achilles tendon repair
4. **Calcaneal bone spur**

Correct Answer: 4 (Tan p. 202) 

A heel lift is a type of shoe orthosis that can be inserted into the heel of the shoe. It is a wedge-shaped piece of material that places the ankle in slightly more plantar flexion. Heel lifts can be used in the management of a variety of orthopedic conditions.

1. A true leg length discrepancy occurs when the bones of one leg are longer than the opposite leg. In standing, a true leg length discrepancy causes an asymmetrical alignment to occur at the pelvis and up the entire spine, which can result in a variety of orthopedic issues. A heel lift can be inserted into the shoe of the shorter leg to ensure that the anatomical alignment remains balanced.
2. Achilles tendonitis occurs when the Achilles tendon becomes inflamed, often secondary to an overuse injury. A heel lift can help promote healing of the tendon by placing the ankle in slight plantar flexion. This position helps reduce traction forces on the tendon that normally occur during the gait cycle.
3. An Achilles tendon repair is performed to repair a torn Achilles tendon. Following surgical repair of the tendon, the patient and therapist must be cautious in placing too much stretch on the healing tendon. A heel lift would place the ankle in slight plantar flexion and reduce traction forces on the tendon.
4. **A calcaneal (heel) bone spur is an area of abnormal bone growth that occurs as a result of excess stress on the bone. Calcaneal spurs can be located on the posterior calcaneus or the inferior calcaneus. A heel lift would not be effective at managing the symptoms of a calcaneal spur. A heel cushion would be more effective at lessening pressure on the spur and thus reducing symptoms.**

System: Musculoskeletal System
Content Outline: Interventions

p. 135

PTEXAM THREE: QUESTION 115

A 45-year-old female with rheumatoid arthritis has complaints of global neck and shoulder pain. She has been on prednisone since she was diagnosed at the age of 30 to help slow the progression of the disease. Which of the following interventions would be unlikely to be included as a component of the patient's care plan?

1. Open chain strengthening with cuff weights
2. Push-ups from a counter top
3. Aquatic therapy
4. **Grade III thoracic spinal mobilizations**

Correct Answer: 4 (Ciccone p. 241)

Prednisone is a glucocorticoid medication that can help to reduce the joint inflammation and pain that is associated with rheumatoid arthritis. Early administration of this medication can help slow the joint destruction that results from this disease. However, administration of glucocorticoids for prolonged periods of time has associated adverse effects, primarily catabolism of bones, muscles, and tendons.

1. Open chain strengthening with cuff weights is a relatively low-level exercise and would not likely pose a significant risk to this patient. Physical therapists should use caution when prescribing therapeutic exercises to patients who have been on prolonged use of glucocorticoid medications to ensure the exercises are not overly aggressive.
2. While more challenging of an exercise than open chain exercises, push-ups from a counter top would still be a relatively low-level exercise for a 45-year-old patient and would not likely pose a significant risk to this patient.
3. Aquatic therapy uses the physical properties of water to achieve therapeutic goals for patients whose pain, lack of muscle strength, and joint deformities are potentially inhibiting factors when exercising on land. Patients with rheumatoid arthritis often benefit from aquatic therapy as a component of their rehabilitation program.
4. **Glucocorticoid medications lead to a weakening of the body's tissues through their catabolic effects. Loss of bone density and strength is one of the most common side effects associated with this medication. Because of this, therapists must take caution when performing interventions that could lead to further structural damage. As a result, grade III thoracic spinal mobilizations would be an inappropriate intervention for this patient.**

System: Other Systems
Content Outline: Foundations for Evaluation, Differential Diagnosis, and Prognosis

Level 3

p. 126, 132-133, 585-588, 624-625

PTEXAM THREE: QUESTION 116

A physical therapist works in the gym of a rehabilitation hospital with a patient who has central cord syndrome. Based on the typical presentation of this condition, which of the following therapeutic activities would the patient have the MOST difficulty performing?

1. **Placing marbles into a cup with the hands**
2. Tandem stance static balance
3. Mini-squats against a wall
4. Ambulation with a single point cane

Correct Answer: 1 (O'Sullivan p. 860)

Central cord syndrome is an incomplete spinal cord lesion that results from compression and damage to the central portion of the spinal cord. The mechanism of injury is usually cervical hyperextension that damages the spinothalamic tract, corticospinal tract, and dorsal columns. The upper extremities present with greater involvement than the lower extremities and greater motor deficits exist as compared to sensory deficits.

1. **A patient with central cord syndrome typically presents with greater motor impairment of the upper extremities compared to the lower extremities. Placing marbles into a cup is a therapeutic activity that requires the patient to be able to manipulate a small object with their hand and fingers and then possess the upper extremity strength and coordination necessary to direct it towards the cup. This activity would be very challenging for a patient with central cord syndrome.**
2. Tandem stance static balance is a therapeutic activity that requires the patient to possess some lower extremity strength and intact balance reactions. Though this activity would be challenging for the patient, it would not be as challenging as Option 1 since the lower extremities are generally less affected with central cord syndrome.
3. Performing mini-squats against a wall is a therapeutic activity that requires the patient to possess some lower extremity strength. Though this activity would be challenging for the patient, it would not be as challenging as Option 1 since the lower extremities are generally less affected with central cord syndrome.
4. Ambulation with a single point cane is a therapeutic activity that requires the patient to possess some lower extremity strength and intact balance. Though this activity would be challenging for the patient, it would not be as challenging as Option 1 since the lower extremities are generally less affected with central cord syndrome.

System: Neuromuscular and Nervous Systems
Content Outline: Foundations for Evaluation, Differential Diagnosis, and Prognosis

Level 2

p. 295, 326-327

PTEXAM THREE: QUESTION 117

A physical therapist is performing gait training with a patient post transtibial amputation. After 15 minutes of training, the patellar tendon-bearing prosthesis is removed and the skin is inspected. Redness is noted on multiple areas of the residual limb. Which area of redness should be the GREATEST concern?

1. Patellar tendon
2. Fibular shaft
3. Gastrocnemius muscle
4. **Distal anterior tibia**

Correct Answer: 4 (May p. 25)

Redness is a normal part of wearing a prosthesis, and depending on a patient's medical history and skin tolerance, various degrees of redness will be noted. The prosthetic socket and supporting components (e.g., socks/liners) are designed to spread the forces throughout the residual limb and focus forces on pressure tolerant areas, such as the patellar tendon. Bony prominences are pressure intolerant and a well-designed socket will minimize pressure in these areas.

1. The patellar tendon is pressure tolerant and redness in this area is not a concern as long as it resolves within 10-20 minutes after doffing.
2. The fibular shaft is a pressure tolerant area and should have resolution of redness within 20 minutes after doffing the prosthesis.
3. The gastrocnemius muscle is pressure tolerant, as it can spread the force of weight bearing across a large area.
4. **The distal anterior tibia is not a pressure tolerant area, as it is covered by a thin layer of skin and has little to no adipose tissue to distribute the transmitted forces. If redness is noted in this area, it is necessary to verify that socks and liners are being worn appropriately prior to contacting a prosthetist.**

System: Musculoskeletal System
Content Outline: Interventions

Level 1 p. 140-142

PTEXAM THREE: QUESTION 118

A physical therapist uses a self-care assessment to examine change over time during rehabilitation programs. The assessment uses a seven-point scale to examine 18 items. The collected information is based on observations of patient performance. This type of assessment MOST closely describes which of the following standardized outcome tools?

1. **Functional Independence Measure**
2. Functional Status Index
3. Physical Self-Maintenance Scale
4. Katz Index of Activities of Daily Living

Correct Answer: 1 (Umphred p. 256)

There are a variety of outcome measures which examine self-care and activities of daily living. Physical therapists should have general knowledge of the more commonly used measures and consider the conceptual and measurement model, reliability, validity, responsiveness, and interpretability inherent to each measure.

1. **The Functional Independence Measure (FIM) tests a subject in multiple areas to determine the overall degree of disability experienced by an adult rehabilitation patient. A seven-point scale is utilized to examine 18 areas, which include self-care, sphincter control, transfers, locomotion, communication, and social cognitive activities. The FIM is commonly used to examine changes in disability status that occur over time.**
2. The Functional Status Index was developed as a comprehensive ADL assessment for adults living in the community. The 18 items include the following domains: gross mobility, personal care, social/role activities, hand activities, and home chores. Scores are generated in three areas: dependence, difficulty, and pain.
3. The Physical Self-Maintenance Scale (PSMS) is a Guttman scale containing six items of self-care. The PSMS was designed as a disability measure for use in planning and evaluating treatment in elderly people living in the community or within institutions.
4. The Katz Index of Activities of Daily Living uses a nominal scale index to identify self-care problems and the level of assistance required within six areas: bathing, dressing, toileting, transfers, continence, and feeding.

System: Neuromuscular and Nervous Systems
Content Outline: Physical Therapy Examination

Level 1

PTEXAM THREE: QUESTION 119

A patient returns from a physician visit and informs a physical therapist that they have decreased their systolic blood pressure by approximately 20 mm Hg over the last two months. Which intervention was MOST likely responsible for the decrease in systolic blood pressure?

1. Dietary changes
2. Limiting alcohol consumption
3. Activity level changes
4. **Pharmacological management**

Correct Answer: 4 (Ciccone p. 318)

Recent revisions in blood pressure guidelines have resulted in more aggressive treatment for hypertension. Treatment often includes lifestyle modifications and pharmacological management.

1. Dietary recommendations include reduced intake of dietary sodium and alcohol and increased consumption of fruits, vegetables, and low-fat dairy products with reduced saturated and total fat content. Following these dietary recommendations would not produce the magnitude of the described blood pressure change.
2. Limiting alcohol intake to two or fewer drinks daily for men and no more than one drink daily for women can assist to reduce blood pressure. Limiting alcohol intake would not produce the magnitude of the described blood pressure change.
3. Activity level recommendations include aerobic physical activity for a minimum of 30 minutes per day most days of the week. An increased activity level would not produce the magnitude of the described blood pressure change.
4. **Pharmacological management for high blood pressure includes medications such as diuretics, beta blockers, calcium channel blockers, ACE inhibitors, angiotensin II receptor blockers, and direct vasodilators. Significant changes such as the described change (i.e., 20 mm Hg decrease in systolic blood pressure) typically occur through pharmacological management.**

System: Cardiovascular and Pulmonary Systems
Content Outline: Foundations for Evaluation, Differential Diagnosis, and Prognosis

 Level 2  p. 403, 414-415, 470

PTEXAM THREE: QUESTION 120

A physical therapist works with a patient who is HIV positive and has been admitted to an acute care hospital for a course of intravenous antibiotics. The patient's medical record states that they have had a persistent cough producing bloody sputum for four weeks and that airborne precautions should be observed. Which of the following rationales is the MOST likely reason for this level of precaution?

1. Decrease the risk of exposing the immunocompromised patient to pneumonia
2. Decrease the risk of exposing the immunocompromised patient to active tuberculosis
3. Decrease the risk of staff and visitor exposure to pneumonia
4. **Decrease the risk of staff and visitor exposure to active tuberculosis**

Correct Answer: 4 (Fairchild p. 34)

Standard precautions should be observed with all patients regardless of their reported medical history. Physical therapists must also be aware of additional precautions which may be associated with more specific forms of infections. Airborne precautions typically include protection of respiratory pathways (e.g., wearing a mask or face shield) in order to prevent the risk of airborne transmission of infectious agents through evaporated droplets in air or dust particles.

1. Although it is important to protect a patient from exposure to potential sources of infection, airborne precautions are typically designated with the intent of preventing transmission of disease from the patient to others. Pneumonia is contracted via droplet transmission.
2. Neutropenic precautions may be instituted in addition to standard precautions for patients who are so immunocompromised that even a mild infection may be lethal. However, the patient's clinical presentation is consistent with active tuberculosis making it much more likely that the precautions have been instituted to protect others.
3. Pneumonia may produce symptoms similar to those described, however, the infection responsible is contracted via droplet transmission of an infectious virus, bacteria or fungi.
4. **Airborne precautions are typically instituted to protect staff and visitors from contracting an infection spread through airborne transmission. There is a significant prevalence of tuberculosis among patients who are HIV positive and the reported persistent cough and bloody sputum are consistent with the clinical presentation of the disease.**

System: Non-Systems
Content Outline: Safety and Protection; Professional Responsibilities; Research

 Level 2  p. 481, 761-762

PTEXAM THREE: QUESTION 121

A physical therapist determines that a patient's cadence is 120 steps per minute. How many seconds would it take the patient to complete 120 full strides?

1. 30
2. 60
3. **120**
4. 240

Correct Answer: 3 (Levangie p. 528) 

Cadence is defined as the number of steps an individual will walk over a period of time and is expressed in steps per minute. The average adult cadence is 110–120 steps per minute. The cadence corresponds to half strides per 60 seconds or full strides per 120 seconds.

1. A period of 30 seconds would allow a patient walking at a cadence of 120 steps per minute to complete 30 strides.
2. A period of 60 seconds would allow a patient walking at a cadence of 120 steps per minute to complete 60 strides.
3. **A period of 120 seconds would be necessary to complete 120 strides since the patient can currently complete 120 steps in 60 seconds. In 120 seconds (two minutes), the patient could complete 120 full strides or 240 half strides based on a cadence of 120 steps per minute.**
4. A period of 240 seconds would allow a patient walking at a cadence of 120 steps per minute to complete 240 strides.

System: Musculoskeletal System
Content Outline: Physical Therapy Examination

 Level 1  p. 87

PTEXAM THREE: QUESTION 122

A physical therapist examines a patient who reports experiencing temporomandibular joint pain. After completing the examination, the therapist suspects that the patient may actually be experiencing referred visceral pain. Which organ is MOST likely involved?

1. **Heart**
2. Liver
3. Diaphragm
4. Pancreas

Correct Answer: 1 (Goodman – Differential Diagnosis p. 124)

Referred pain patterns can be musculoskeletal or visceral in origin. While the presence of temporomandibular joint (TMJ) pain may be caused by pathology of the actual joint, it also could be referred pain from pathology of an organ. It is important that a physical therapist is able to use pain characteristics to differentiate between musculoskeletal and visceral sources of pain.

1. **Pathology of the heart can result in referred pain to the shoulder, neck, upper back or TMJ.**
2. Pathology of the liver can result in referred pain to the shoulder, midthoracic region or low back.
3. Pathology of the diaphragm can result in referred pain to the shoulder or lumbar spine.
4. Pathology of the pancreas can result in referred pain to the shoulder, midthoracic region or low back.

System: Other Systems
Content Outline: Foundations for Evaluation, Differential Diagnosis, and Prognosis

 Level 1  p. 73, 765

PTEXAM THREE: QUESTION 123

A physical therapist reviews risk factors for the development of a pressure injury. Which of the following patients would be the MOST at risk for this type of injury?

1. 55-year-old Caucasian male with diabetes
2. **60-year-old African American female with a C7 spinal cord injury**
3. 80-year-old African American male with chronic obstructive pulmonary disease
4. 65-year-old Caucasian female status post total knee arthroplasty

Correct Answer: 2 (Sussman p. 247) 

Pressure ulcers are areas of local tissue damage, usually developing where soft tissues become compressed between a bony prominence and an external surface for prolonged periods of time. Risk factors for the development of pressure ulcers include female gender, African American race, advanced age, and conditions that cause immobility.

1. A patient with diabetes is at risk for developing an ulcer, though it would more likely be a neuropathic ulcer, not a pressure ulcer. The other patient demographics are not consistent with the risk factors for pressure ulcers.
2. **This patient would be at the greatest risk for the development of a pressure ulcer due to her race (i.e., African American), gender (i.e., female), and medical condition (i.e., spinal cord injury). Patients with spinal cord injuries are often immobile, which places them at high risk for developing pressure ulcers.**
3. While the patient's age and race would place him at increased risk for pressure ulcer development, chronic obstructive pulmonary disease is not a condition that would significantly limit the patient's mobility.
4. While a patient status post total knee arthroplasty may be immobile immediately after surgery, they will not experience the same level of immobility as a patient with a spinal cord injury. The patient is also at less risk due to her race.

System: Other Systems
Content Outline: Foundations for Evaluation, Differential Diagnosis, and Prognosis

 Level 2  p. 297-300, 502

PTEXAM THREE: QUESTION 124

A physical therapist treats a patient wearing a shoe that incorporates a rocker bottom. This type of modification would be the MOST beneficial for a patient diagnosed with which of the following conditions?

1. Achilles tendonitis
2. **Hallux rigidus**
3. Plantar fasciitis
4. Posterior tibial tendonitis

Correct Answer: 2 (Dutton p. 1148)

A rocker bottom shoe has a thicker than normal sole with a rounded heel. This type of shoe serves to reduce the function or replace the lost function of a joint, relieve metatarsal pain, shorten the gait cycle, and assist with dorsiflexion.

1. Achilles tendonitis is a repetitive overuse disorder resulting in microscopic tears of collagen fibers on the surface or in the substance of the Achilles tendon. Management may include a heel lift which places the foot in a relatively plantar flexed position to reduce traction on the Achilles tendon and promote healing. A rocker bottom shoe would offer little clinical benefit to a patient diagnosed with Achilles tendonitis.
2. **Hallux rigidus refers to degenerative arthritis due to bone spurring that affects the first metatarsophalangeal joint. Patients with this condition often experience pain and stiffness with walking, standing or bending. A rocker bottom shoe could be potentially beneficial by reducing extension of the hallux during normal gait. This type of modification may assist the patient to experience decreased pain and allow for an increased activity level.**
3. Plantar fasciitis refers to inflammation of the plantar fascia at the proximal insertion on the medial tubercle of the calcaneus. Management may include a heel cup, medial longitudinal arch taping or orthotics if the condition is caused by excessive pronation. A rocker bottom shoe would offer little clinical benefit to a patient diagnosed with plantar fasciitis.
4. Posterior tibial tendonitis occurs when the posterior tibial tendon becomes inflamed or torn. The tendon functions to maintain the arch and support the foot when walking. Management may include bracing and orthotics designed to support the arch and reduce pressure on the tendon. A rocker bottom shoe would offer little clinical benefit to a patient diagnosed with posterior tibial tendonitis.

System: Musculoskeletal System
Content Outline: Interventions

Level 2  p. 135

PTEXAM THREE: QUESTION 125

A patient post total hip arthroplasty using a posterolateral surgical approach experiences hip instability. Which finding would BEST explain the reason for the hip instability?

1. Trabecular bone erosion
2. Femoral nerve paralysis
3. **Posterior capsule damage**
4. Hip abductor weakness

Correct Answer: 3 (Kisner p. 727)

The specific surgical approach utilized for total hip arthroplasty is determined based on a variety of factors including patient activity level, co-morbidities, life expectancy, anticipated compliance, and surgeon familiarity. Physical therapists must have an awareness of each type of approach including the structures impacted and the associated hip precautions. Surgical procedures utilized when performing total hip arthroplasty include an anterolateral, direct lateral or posterolateral approach.

1. Trabecular bone is synonymous with cancellous or spongy bone. Trabecular bone is typically found at the end of long bones, proximal to joints, and within the interior of vertebrae. Trabecular bone erosion is not typically associated with instability following total hip arthroplasty, rather it is characteristic of conditions such as osteoporosis.
2. A peripheral nerve injury to the femoral nerve can occur during total hip arthroplasty, however, it is unlikely that it would directly result in hip instability. In addition, damage to the femoral nervė is less common with a posterolateral surgical approach than with other surgical procedures used for total hip arthroplasty. Femoral nerve injuries can also occur with a displaced acetabular fracture, anterior dislocation of the femur, hysterectomy, and appendectomy.
3. **A total hip arthroplasty using a posterior surgical approach penetrates the posterior capsule. As a result, it is associated with a high post-surgical dislocation rate. To prevent posterior dislocation of the femoral head component, the patient should avoid excessive hip flexion greater than 90 degrees, hip adduction, and hip medial rotation.**
4. The primary advantage of the posterolateral surgical approach is that the hip abductors remain intact. As a result, it would be unlikely that hip abductor weakness would be associated with instability following total hip arthroplasty using a posterolateral approach.

System: Musculoskeletal System
Content Outline: Foundations for Evaluation, Differential Diagnosis, and Prognosis

 Level 2 p. 127-128, 188-189

PTEXAM THREE: QUESTION 126

A patient is referred to physical therapy with a diagnosis of a grade II syndesmotic ankle sprain. What is the MOST common mechanism of injury for this type of ankle sprain?

1. Excessive plantar flexion with inversion
2. **Forceful external rotation of the foot**
3. Excessive plantar flexion with eversion
4. Vertical compression of the tibia into the talus

Correct Answer: 2 (Dutton p. 1150)

A grade II sprain of one or more of the syndesmotic ligaments is commonly referred to as a "high ankle sprain." The syndesmotic ligaments attach to the tibia and fibula and function to stabilize the ankle mortise. Because they are deep, a great deal of force is required to cause an injury to the syndesmotic ligaments. The primary syndesmotic ligaments include the anterior-inferior tibiofibular ligament, the interosseous ligament, and the posterior-inferior tibiofibular ligament.

1. Excessive plantar flexion with inversion is the most common mechanism of injury for a lateral ankle sprain. The lateral ankle ligament complex resists varus stress and is comprised of the anterior talofibular, calcaneofibular, and posterior talofibular ligaments.
2. **Forceful external rotation of the foot that drives the talus into external rotation within the ankle mortise is one of the most common mechanisms of injury for a syndesmotic (high ankle) sprain. Forceful dorsiflexion or eversion of the talus can also widen the mortise and push the distal fibula away from its articulation with the distal tibia.**
3. Excessive plantar flexion with eversion is an uncommon injury. Eversion is more likely to occur in combination with dorsiflexion and abduction (collectively known as pronation). Injuries to the medial (deltoid) ligament complex due to excessive eversion only account for approximately 5% of ankle sprains. Significant injuries to the deltoid ligament often occur in combination with ankle fractures.
4. Vertical compression of the tibia into the talus is a common mechanism of injury for a distal tibia compression (pilon) fracture. Pilon fractures occur as a result of vertical or axial loads that force or "drive" the tibia into the talus.

System: Musculoskeletal System
Content Outline: Foundations for Evaluation, Differential Diagnosis, and Prognosis

 Level 1  p. 110

PTEXAM THREE: QUESTION 127

A patient with diabetes insipidus is being treated with exogenous administration of antidiuretic hormone (ADH). Which condition would **MOST** likely result from the administration of this medication?

1. **Increased blood pressure**
2. Decreased blood pressure
3. Hypovolemia
4. Constipation

Correct Answer: 1 (Goodman – Pathology p. 482)

Physical therapists must be aware of potential side effects of commonly utilized pharmacological agents. ADH promotes water resorption by the kidneys and assists to control osmotic pressure of extracellular fluid. When ADH production decreases, the kidneys fail to resorb water resulting in large excretions of diluted urine. Patients with diabetes insipidus are often treated with exogenous ADH.

1. **ADH administration can promote increases in blood pressure secondary to stimulation of smooth muscle contraction of the vascular system. ADH may also have an effect on the coronary arteries which can result in angina or myocardial infarction.**
2. Decreased blood pressure is a symptom of diabetes insipidus that results from the excessive excretion of urine. This is not a typical side effect of ADH administration.
3. Hypovolemia is the decreased volume of circulating blood and is a symptom of diabetes insipidus. This is not typically a side effect of ADH administration.
4. Constipation is a symptom of diabetes insipidus. Diarrhea is a potential side effect of ADH administration secondary to stimulation of smooth muscle contraction of the gastrointestinal tract.

System: Other Systems
Content Outline: Foundations for Evaluation, Differential Diagnosis, and Prognosis

 Level 2  p. 525

PTEXAM THREE: QUESTION 128

A physical therapist reviews a patient's medical record and identifies an entry that indicates the patient was recently prescribed an emetic agent. What is the **PRIMARY** purpose of this type of pharmacological agent?

1. Promote defecation
2. **Induce vomiting**
3. Minimize gastrointestinal irritation
4. Reduce diarrhea

Correct Answer: 2 (Ciccone p. 429) 

Physical therapists must possess an awareness of commonly used pharmacological agents, their indications, and potential side effects.

1. Laxative agents are used to promote defecation. Side effects include nausea, abdominal discomfort, and dehydration. Examples of laxative agents include Citrucel and Metamucil.
2. **Emetic agents are used to induce vomiting usually after ingestion of a toxic substance. Side effects include dehydration, electrolyte imbalance, and gastrointestinal erosion with prolonged use. Examples of emetic agents include Apomorphine and Ipecac.**
3. Antacid agents are used to minimize gastrointestinal irritation by chemically neutralizing gastric acid and increasing intragastric pH. Side effects include acid rebound phenomenon and constipation or diarrhea depending on the specific agent. Examples of antacid agents include Tums and Milk of Magnesia.
4. Antidiarrheal agents are used to reduce diarrhea. Side effects include constipation and abdominal discomfort. Examples of antidiarrheal agents include Donnagel and Kapectolin.

System: Other Systems
Content Outline: Foundations for Evaluation, Differential Diagnosis, and Prognosis

 Level 1   p. 539-540

PTEXAM THREE: QUESTION 129

A patient is seen by a physical therapist after being diagnosed with patellofemoral pain syndrome. As part of the session, the patient describes a number of exercises that they were instructed to perform by their personal trainer. Which of the following exercises would be the MOST likely to exacerbate the patient's symptoms?

1. Terminal knee extension in standing
2. Mini-squats from 0-30 degrees of knee flexion
3. **Long arc quads from 0-45 degrees of knee flexion**
4. Quadriceps setting in terminal knee extension in supine

Correct Answer: 3 (Dutton p. 986) 

Patellofemoral pain syndrome is characterized by pain in the region of the patella caused by abnormal contact and/or tracking between the patella and trochlear groove of the femur. Patellofemoral pain typically increases with increasing patellofemoral joint reaction forces. These forces vary depending on whether the activity performed is an open-chain or closed-chain activity.

1. This exercise is a closed-chain activity that occurs near the end range of extension. With closed-chain activities, the patellofemoral joint reaction forces are relatively low from 0-30 degrees of flexion. Exercises performed within this range are unlikely to exacerbate patellofemoral symptoms.
2. This exercise is similar to terminal knee extension in standing, though it uses more knee flexion range of motion. However, the range of motion used (i.e., 0-30 degrees) is still within the acceptable range for avoiding an exacerbation of patellofemoral symptoms.
3. **In contrast to closed-chain activities, the patellofemoral joint reaction forces for open-chain activities are their lowest at 90 degrees of flexion. The joint reaction forces increase as the knee moves closer to full extension. Therefore, open-chain exercises between 0 and 45 degrees of knee flexion are not recommended.**
4. Though quadriceps setting in supine is technically an open-chain exercise performed in terminal knee extension, this exercise is unlikely to exacerbate the patient's condition. Quadriceps setting is a relatively low-level exercise that involves minimal movement of the patella within the trochlear groove.

System: Musculoskeletal System
Content Outline: Interventions

 Level 2  p. 125, 172-173

PTEXAM THREE: QUESTION 130

A patient with a T3 spinal cord injury exercising on a treatment table in the supine position begins to exhibit signs and symptoms of autonomic dysreflexia, including a dramatic increase in blood pressure. Which of the following actions should be the MOST immediate to address the patient's blood pressure response?

1. Elevate the patient's legs
2. Call for assistance
3. **Sit the patient upright**
4. Check the urinary drainage system

Correct Answer: 3 (Fairchild p. 338) 

Autonomic dysreflexia is caused by a noxious stimulus below the level of the lesion that triggers the autonomic nervous system causing a sudden elevation in blood pressure. If untreated, this condition can lead to convulsions, hemorrhage, and death.

1. Elevation of the patient's legs would be contraindicated since the position would serve to increase the return of circulation and further increase blood pressure.
2. Calling for assistance is an acceptable option given the seriousness of autonomic dysreflexia, however, the action would not be the most immediate action to address the patient's blood pressure response.
3. **The physical therapist should immediately position the patient in sitting to address the autonomic nervous system response and reduce the patient's elevated blood pressure. After the patient has been positioned in sitting, the urinary drainage system should be checked since a blocked catheter is a common noxious stimulus that triggers the sympathetic response.**
4. The common causes of autonomic dysreflexia include distended or full bladder, kink or blockage in the catheter, bladder infections, pressure ulcers, extreme temperature changes, tight clothing or an ingrown toenail. A physical therapist should check the urinary drainage system immediately after moving the patient into a sitting position.

System: Neuromuscular and Nervous Systems
Content Outline: Interventions

 Level 3  p. 44, 297, 764

PTEXAM THREE: QUESTION 131

A patient rehabilitating from a traumatic head injury is lethargic since being placed on Phenobarbital. What is the PRIMARY purpose of this medication?

1. Decrease agitation
2. **Prevent seizures**
3. Reduce spasticity
4. Limit arrhythmias

Correct Answer: 2 (Ciccone p. 119)

Physical therapists must possess an awareness of commonly used pharmacological agents, their indications, and potential side effects. Failure to recognize anticipated side effects from a medication may significantly jeopardize patient safety.

1. The most common side effect of Phenobarbital is sedation. As a result, agitation is typically diminished, however, the primary purpose of the medication is to prevent seizures.
2. **Phenobarbital is classified as a barbiturate and is prescribed most often to prevent adult seizures. Side effects include sedation, vitamin deficiencies, nystagmus, and ataxia.**
3. There are many medications that treat spasticity, but the most common include baclofen, diazepam, and dantrolene sodium.
4. Antiarrhythmic drugs are typically classified into four groups: sodium channel blockers, beta-blockers, drugs that prolong repolarization, and calcium channel blockers.

System: Neuromuscular and Nervous Systems
Content Outline: Foundations for Evaluation, Differential Diagnosis, and Prognosis

p. 567

PTEXAM THREE: QUESTION 132

A physical therapist works on gait training with a patient post transtibial amputation. The patient exhibits an extended knee throughout the early stance phase on the prosthetic side. Which of the following changes to the prosthesis is the MOST appropriate to improve the patient's gait deviation?

1. Plantar flex the foot
2. Soften the heel wedge
3. Move the foot anteriorly
4. **Dorsiflex the foot**

Correct Answer: 4 (Lusardi p. 646)

The prosthesis requires slight ankle dorsiflexion to allow for subsequent knee flexion during early stance. A prosthesis with excessive plantar flexion will promote full knee extension during early stance.

1. A prosthetic foot that is plantar flexed will present with an increased extension moment and impede sufficient knee flexion during early stance. The prosthesis must be set into neutral or slight dorsiflexion to allow for knee flexion during stance phase.
2. Softening the heel wedge of a transtibial prosthesis will create an increased extension moment and impede sufficient knee flexion during stance phase.
3. Moving the foot of a transtibial prosthesis anteriorly will create an increased extension moment and impede sufficient knee flexion during stance phase.
4. **A prosthetic foot that is set in slight dorsiflexion will present with an increased flexion moment and assist with knee flexion during stance and when advancing the prosthesis.**

System: Musculoskeletal System
Content Outline: Interventions

PTEXAM THREE: QUESTION 133

A physical therapist examines a patient with carpal tunnel syndrome. As part of the examination, the therapist assesses end-feel. The therapist classifies the end-feel associated with wrist extension as firm. Which of the following provides the MOST logical explanation for this finding?

1. **Tension in the dorsal radiocarpal ligament and the dorsal joint capsule**
2. **Contact between the ulna and the carpal bones**
3. **Contact between the radius and the carpal bones**
4. **Tension in the palmar radiocarpal ligament and the palmar joint capsule**

Correct Answer: 4 (Norkin p. 156)

End-feel is the type of resistance that is felt when passively moving a joint through the end range of motion. Certain tissues and joints have a consistent end-feel and are described as firm, hard or soft. Pathology can be identified through noting the type of abnormal end-feel within a particular joint.

1. A firm end-feel with wrist flexion can result from tension in the dorsal radiocarpal ligament and the dorsal joint capsule.
2. The ulna articulates with the radius at the distal radioulnar joint, however, does not articulate with the carpal bones.
3. Contact between the radius and the carpal bones would result in a hard end-feel and not a firm end-feel.
4. **A firm end-feel with wrist extension can result from tension in the palmar radiocarpal ligament and the palmar joint capsule. Tension in the ulnocarpal ligament can also contribute to the firm end-feel.**

System: Musculoskeletal System
Content Outline: Physical Therapy Examination

 **Level 2**  **p. 79**

PTEXAM THREE: QUESTION 134

A physical therapist identifies the presence of epibole in a pressure injury. With which pressure injury stage is this observation MOST visible?

1. **Stage 1**
2. **Stage 2**
3. **Stage 3**
4. **Unstageable**

Correct Answer: 3 (Sussman p. 234)

Pressure injuries, also referred to as decubitus ulcers, result from sustained or prolonged pressure on tissue at levels greater than that of capillary pressure. Skin covering bony prominences is particularly susceptible to localized ischemia and tissue necrosis due to pressure. Factors contributing to pressure injuries include shearing forces, moisture, heat, friction, medications, muscle atrophy, malnutrition, and debilitating medical conditions. Epibole refers to skin that is rolled or curled under wound edges and may be dry, callused or hyperkeratotic.

1. A stage 1 pressure injury is characterized by intact skin with a localized area of non-blanchable erythema. Epibole is associated with full-thickness skin loss and therefore would not be present in a stage 1 pressure injury.
2. A stage 2 pressure injury is characterized by partial-thickness skin loss with exposed dermis. Epibole is associated with full-thickness skin loss and therefore would not be present in a stage 2 pressure injury.
3. **A stage 3 pressure injury is characterized by full-thickness skin loss, in which adipose tissue is visible in the ulcer. Granulation tissue and epibole are often also present in a stage 3 pressure injury. The depth of tissue damage varies by anatomical location and may include undermining and tunneling.**
4. An unstageable pressure injury is characterized by full-thickness skin and tissue loss in which the extent of tissue damage within the pressure injury cannot be confirmed because it is obscured by slough or eschar. Although epibole may be present in an unstageable pressure injury, the presentation is highly variable making this finding less obvious (i.e., visible) than with a stage 3 pressure injury.

System: Other Systems
Content Outline: Foundations for Evaluation, Differential Diagnosis, and Prognosis

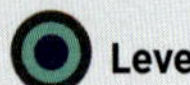 **Level 1**  **p. 502, 504, 622-623**

PTEXAM THREE: QUESTION 135

A physical therapist positions a patient as shown in the image prior to testing for clonus. Which of the following actions is the MOST appropriate to perform to complete this test?

1. **Provide a quick stretch to the plantar flexors**
2. Provide a quick stretch to the dorsiflexors
3. Provide a quick stretch to the plantar flexors while extending the knee
4. Provide a quick stretch to the dorsiflexors while extending the knee

Correct Answer: 1 (O'Sullivan p. 143)

Clonus refers to rhythmic oscillation of a body part resulting from a quick stretch. The test is ideally performed by providing a stretch to the plantar flexors with the gastrocnemius in a relaxed position.

1. **Clonus is evaluated by supporting the knee in a partially flexed position, encouraging the patient to relax, and passively moving the foot. The therapist provides a quick stretch into dorsiflexion and observes any rhythmic oscillations between plantar flexion and dorsiflexion.**
2. When assessing clonus, the therapist provides a quick stretch to the plantar flexor muscle group, not the dorsiflexor muscle group.
3. When assessing clonus, the therapist provides a quick stretch to the plantar flexor muscle group, however, the knee should be partially flexed rather than extended in order to successfully place the gastrocnemius on slack and elicit the response.
4. When assessing clonus, the therapist should provide a quick stretch to the plantar flexor muscle group and maintain the knee in slight flexion. This option is completely opposite (i.e., quick stretch to the dorsiflexors while extending the knee).

System: Neuromuscular and Nervous Systems
Content Outline: Physical Therapy Examination

Level 2

p. 263

PTEXAM THREE: QUESTION 136

A physical therapist examines a patient with multidirectional instability of the shoulder. Which position would be the MOST appropriate when assessing posterior instability of the shoulder?

1. Abduction to 90 degrees with neutral rotation
2. Abduction to 90 degrees with full external rotation
3. **Flexion to 90 degrees with full internal rotation**
4. Arm at the side in neutral rotation

Correct Answer: 3 (Magee p. 307)

There are several special tests that can assess the level of instability in the glenohumeral joint. An examination for shoulder instability often involves an assessment of anterior, posterior, and inferior instabilities. The jerk test is one example of a special test that assesses instability in a posterior direction.

1. Many of the special tests for shoulder instability involve elevation to roughly 90 degrees. Abduction to 90 degrees is more commonly used when testing for anterior shoulder instability. Additionally, these tests usually involve some degree of rotation; external rotation and internal rotation are used to assess for anterior and posterior instability, respectively.
2. Abduction to 90 degrees with full external rotation describes the position used when testing for anterior shoulder instability. One example of this is the apprehension (crank) test. In this test, the therapist passively moves the patient's shoulder into 90 degrees of abduction and then slowly externally rotates the shoulder. The therapist assesses for pain or apprehension as they move the shoulder into more external rotation.
3. **Flexion to 90 degrees with full internal rotation describes the position used when testing for posterior shoulder instability. These motions both move the humeral head posteriorly in the joint and place stress on the posterior capsule. During the jerk test, the patient is placed in this position and the therapist applies an axial load through the elbow in a posterior direction. The therapist can then horizontally adduct the shoulder to place further stress on the posterior capsule.**
4. The arm at the side in neutral rotation describes the position used when testing for inferior shoulder instability. One example of this is the sulcus sign. In this test, the patient stands with their arm relaxed at their side while the therapist pulls the arm inferiorly and looks for the presence of a sulcus between the humeral head and acromion.

System: Musculoskeletal System
Content Outline: Physical Therapy Examination

Level 2

p. 100-101

PTEXAM THREE: QUESTION 137

A physical therapist employed in a busy outpatient orthopedic clinic attempts to determine a schedule for calibration and maintenance of an ultrasound unit. Which of the following factors is the **MOST** important for the therapist to consider when determining an appropriate schedule?

1. Beam nonuniformity ratio
2. **Frequency of use**
3. Cost associated with calibration and maintenance
4. Availability of qualified personnel to inspect the unit

Correct Answer: 2 (Prentice p. 419) 

Electrical equipment must be calibrated and maintained by qualified personnel on a regular schedule consistent with the manufacturer's recommendations. The regular schedule, once established, can be modified based on variables such as increased frequency of use or reports of faulty performance.

1. Beam nonuniformity ratio (BNR) refers to the ratio of intensity of the highest peak to the average intensity of all peaks. The BNR is determined by the intrinsic biophysical properties of the piezoelectric transducer. The BNR of an ultrasound device would not be a factor in determining a calibration and maintenance schedule.
2. **The frequency of use of an ultrasound device is extremely important when determining a schedule for calibration and maintenance. Ultrasound units used frequently may be calibrated several times a year, while a unit used sparingly would likely warrant a longer interval.**
3. The cost associated with calibration and maintenance of the ultrasound unit should not be a factor in establishing a calibration and maintenance schedule. Relying on a variable such as cost implies that when there are ample resources available calibration and maintenance take place and when resources are not available calibration and maintenance can be deferred.
4. The availability of qualified personnel to inspect the ultrasound unit would not be a factor in determining a calibration and maintenance schedule. If appropriate personnel are not available within the health care organization, there are a variety of external companies who can provide the necessary service.

System: Non-Systems
Content Outline: Equipment, Devices, and Technologies; Therapeutic Modalities

PTEXAM THREE: QUESTION 138

A physical therapist positions a patient as shown in the image in order to assess the patient's report of complete paresis of the right lower extremity. The therapist instructs the patient to perform a rapid straight leg raise with the left lower extremity. Which finding would **BEST** dispute the patient's claim of complete paresis of the right lower extremity?

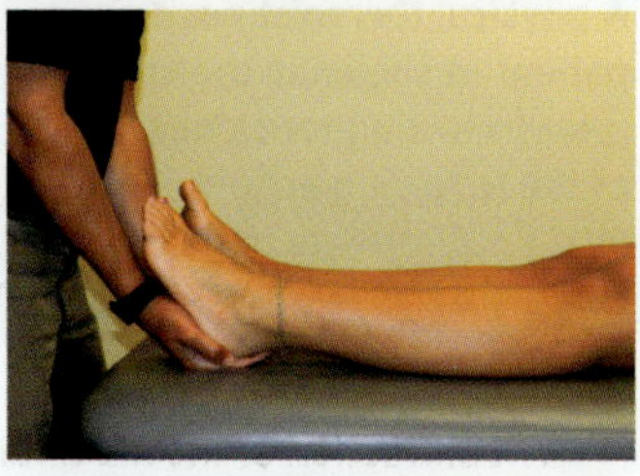

1. Inability to lift the left heel from the therapist's hand
2. Experiencing radiating pain into the right lower extremity
3. **Exerting a downward force into the therapist's hand with the right heel**
4. Reporting severe pain while performing the straight leg raise

Correct Answer: 3 (Magee p. 612)

The Hoover test is often employed as a gross test for malingering. The physical therapist places one hand underneath each calcaneus with the patient lying in supine. The patient is then asked to perform a straight leg raise on the uninvolved extremity while the therapist simultaneously assesses motor output on the involved side.

1. The Hoover test relies on assessing the reaction of the contralateral limb rather than the quality of the straight leg raise.
2. The Hoover test is designed to provide insight on potential malingering rather than serving as a provocative test intended to create radiating pain or other signs or symptoms.
3. **A rapid straight leg raise of the left (uninvolved) lower extremity should result in the patient exerting a downward force into the therapist's hand with the right (involved) heel. This action would be considered a normal response due to the effort associated with performing the straight leg raise, therefore disputing the patient's claim of complete paresis of the right lower extremity.**
4. The Hoover test is not influenced by the presence or absence of pain.

System: Neuromuscular and Nervous Systems
Content Outline: Physical Therapy Examination

PTEXAM THREE: QUESTION 139

A patient who has a grade II lumbar spondylolisthesis experiences symptoms of neurogenic claudication. Which of the following exercises would MOST likely exacerbate the patient's symptoms?

1. **Walking on a treadmill with zero incline**
2. Cycling with varying resistance
3. Abdominal crunches on an exercise ball
4. Contraction of the multifidi in a flexed position

Correct Answer: 1 (Dutton p. 1488) 

Spondylolisthesis is the forward slippage of one vertebra on the vertebra below, most commonly occurring at the L4-L5 level or the L5-S1 level. There are several grades of spondylolisthesis (i.e., grade I-IV) classified by the extent of the forward slippage. Degenerative spondylolisthesis is caused by weakening of the facet joints allowing for the forward slippage due to degenerative changes. These changes include segmental ligamentous instability and subluxation of the hypertrophic facet joints, which can result in stenosis of the spinal canal. This may cause leg pain in a radicular-type pattern or, more commonly, can manifest as neurogenic claudication.

1. **Walking on a treadmill with zero incline will most likely exacerbate the patient's symptoms due to the extension of the spine that occurs when walking upright. Extension decreases the anteroposterior diameter of the canal causing even more compression on the neural tissues and worsening the patient's symptoms. Patients with neurogenic claudication are typically more comfortable leaning forward or sitting, which flexes the spine, thereby widening the anteroposterior diameter of the canal.**
2. Cycling with varying resistance should be easier for the patient since the lumbar spine is in a more flexed position when cycling. Lumbar flexion increases the anteroposterior diameter of the canal, allowing more room for the neural tissues and improving the microcirculation.
3. Abdominal crunches on an exercise ball are appropriate in the management of spondylolisthesis as a means of abdominal strengthening and reduction of the lumbar lordosis. This would be considered part of the progression of abdominal strengthening.
4. Contraction of the multifidi in a flexed position is an appropriate spinal stabilization activity in the management of spondylolisthesis. The required flexed position would also be appropriate to reduce the risk of exacerbating the symptoms of neurogenic claudication.

System: Musculoskeletal System
Content Outline: Interventions

 Level 2  p. 182-183

PTEXAM THREE: QUESTION 140

A physical therapist is treating a patient that has been prescribed levodopa. The patient has been taking the drug as directed for two weeks. Which physical therapy intervention would be MOST affected secondary to the potential negative side effects of the prescribed medication?

1. **Balance activities**
2. Strengthening activities
3. Range of motion activities
4. Endurance activities

Correct Answer: 1 (Ciccone p. 135) 

Dopamine replacement therapy (e.g., levodopa) is the most effective treatment to reduce the symptoms of Parkinson's disease. Symptoms often include bradykinesia, rigidity, tremor, and movement disorders. The medical management of Parkinson's disease relies heavily on pharmacological intervention.

1. **During the initial use of levodopa, patients regularly experience lightheadedness and orthostatic hypotension. Balance activities would pose the greatest challenge for this patient during this period with the newly prescribed medication. The patient should be monitored closely to ensure safety with activities that challenge their balance.**
2. Strengthening activities increase the patient's overall strength and can include isometric, concentric, and eccentric strengthening. Levodopa does not typically negatively influence a patient's strength and therefore strengthening activities should not increase in difficulty due to the prescribed medication.
3. Range of motion activities promote adequate mobility at each joint. Levodopa does not typically negatively influence a patient's range of motion and therefore range of motion activities should not increase in difficulty due to the prescribed medication.
4. Endurance activities improve the aerobic system in order to meet oxygen demands. Levodopa can initially cause orthostatic hypotension which can impact the cardiovascular system, however, the patient should still be able to perform endurance activities. Endurance activities can be performed without significantly challenging the patient's balance.

System: Neuromuscular and Nervous Systems
Content Outline: Foundations for Evaluation, Differential Diagnosis, and Prognosis

 Level 3  p. 273, 586

PTEXAM THREE: QUESTION 141

A patient with ankylosing spondylitis exhibits a forward stooped posture. As part of the patient's care plan, the physical therapist selects a number of active exercises that promote improved posture. Which upper extremity proprioceptive neuromuscular facilitation pattern would be the MOST appropriate to achieve the therapist's objective?

1. D1 extension
2. D1 flexion
3. D2 extension
4. **D2 flexion**

Correct Answer: 4 (Sullivan p. 300)

A proprioceptive neuromuscular facilitation approach utilizes methods that promote or hasten the response of the neuromuscular mechanism through stimulation of the proprioceptors. The two diagonal patterns are commonly referred to as D1 and D2 where "D" stands for diagonal and "1" and "2" refer to specific patterns of movement. To improve the patient's standing posture the therapist should use a pattern that requires the patient to move the arms upward and away from the body (D2 flexion).

1. The command for D1 extension would be to open your hand and push down and away from your body.
2. The command for D1 flexion would be to close your hand and pull up and across your body.
3. The command for D2 extension would be to close your hand and pull down and across your body.
4. **The command for D2 flexion would be to open your hand and pull up and away from your body. The pattern emphasizes shoulder flexion, abduction, and lateral rotation which would facilitate improved standing posture.**

System: Neuromuscular and Nervous Systems
Content Outline: Interventions

 Level 2  p. 288-290

PTEXAM THREE: QUESTION 142

An 80-year-old female patient falls and fractures her femur. Her surgeon performs surgery to fixate the fracture, but warns the patient that she is at risk for delayed union at the fracture site. Which of the following fracture sites would have the GREATEST risk for this complication?

1. **Femoral neck**
2. Intertrochanteric region
3. Subtrochanteric region
4. Femoral shaft

Correct Answer: 1 (Dutton p. 50) 

Femoral fractures can occur in various locations along the femur including the femoral neck, intertrochanteric region, subtrochanteric region, and femoral shaft. The type of fixation used during surgery and the resulting complications following surgery will vary depending on the location of the fracture.

1. **Femoral neck fractures are intracapsular and may lead to a disruption of the blood supply to the femoral head. Because of this, nonunion (or delayed union) and osteonecrosis are more common with these fractures.**
2. Intertrochanteric hip fractures are extracapsular and therefore do not affect the blood supply. Though nonunion is less of an issue, implant failure is more likely with these fractures since the fixation needed to stabilize the break is greater.
3. Subtrochanteric hip fractures occur in the region distal to the trochanters. Because this region is extracapsular, fractures in this area will not affect blood supply and are therefore not at high risk for nonunion or delayed union.
4. Femoral shaft fractures can occur anywhere distal to the subtrochanteric region along the shaft of the femur. Because the femoral shaft is extracapsular, fractures in this area will not affect blood supply and are therefore not at high risk for nonunion or delayed union.

System: Musculoskeletal System
Content Outline: Foundations for Evaluation, Differential Diagnosis, and Prognosis

 Level 1  p. 130, 132

PTEXAM THREE: QUESTION 143

A physical therapist reviews the medical record of a patient diagnosed with peripheral arterial disease prior to initiating treatment. Which of the following objective findings would MOST severely limit the patient's ability to participate in an ambulation exercise program?

1. **Signs of resting claudication**
2. Decreased peripheral pulses
3. Cool skin upon palpation
4. Blood pressure of 165/90 mm Hg

Correct Answer: 1 (Hillegass p. 63) 

Peripheral arterial disease refers to a condition involving the arterial system that results in compromised circulation to the extremities. Resting claudication is typically considered a contraindication to active exercise in patients with peripheral arterial disease.

1. **Claudication pain is a symptom of ischemia of the lower extremity muscles caused by peripheral arterial disease. Resting claudication pain is typically considered a contraindication to exercise with peripheral arterial disease and may be an indication that the disease process is more advanced.**
2. Decreased peripheral pulses are a common sign associated with peripheral arterial disease, but would only severely limit ambulation if blood flow was markedly diminished or absent. Decreased peripheral pulses are a result of plaque buildup in the arteries which decreases blood flow and subsequently oxygen to the extremities.
3. Cool skin may be a sign of peripheral arterial disease, but would only severely limit ambulation if blood flow was markedly diminished or absent. Cool skin results from the diminished circulation, particularly in the extremities.
4. A blood pressure of 165/90 mm Hg can occur during rest or exercise and does not severely limit ambulation.

System: Cardiovascular and Pulmonary Systems
Content Outline: Interventions

 Level 2 p. 404

PTEXAM THREE: QUESTION 144

A seven-year-old child sitting in the physical therapy waiting area suddenly grasps their throat and appears to be in distress. The child slowly stands, but is obviously unable to breathe. Recognizing the signs of an airway obstruction, the physical therapist should administer which of the following procedures FIRST?

1. **Abdominal thrusts**
2. Chest thrusts
3. Rescue breathing
4. Finger sweep

Correct Answer: 1 (Le Baudour p. 150)

An airway obstruction in a child or an adult is best treated by using abdominal thrusts.

1. **Abdominal thrusts (Heimlich maneuver) can be used on a child until the object is expelled or the victim becomes unresponsive. The American Red Cross recommends back blows in combination with abdominal thrusts. Abdominal thrusts are not recommended for infants (less than one year of age) because of an increased risk of injury.**
2. If abdominal thrusts are ineffective, the health care provider may consider using chest thrusts. Research has demonstrated that approximately 50% of the episodes of airway obstruction were not relieved by a single technique. As a result, the likelihood of success may be increased when using combinations of back blows, abdominal thrusts, and chest thrusts.
3. Rescue breathing is recommended for an unresponsive patient who has a palpable pulse, but is not breathing. This would not be an immediate reaction for an airway obstruction since the priority should focus on clearing the airway.
4. A finger sweep is recommended if the health care provider can see solid material obstructing the airway of an unresponsive patient. In the question, the child is conscious.

System: Non-Systems
Content Outline: Safety and Protection; Professional Responsibilities; Research

 Level 1  p. 765-766

PTEXAM THREE: QUESTION 145

A patient reports significant discomfort in the lower extremity during an ultrasound treatment. The physical therapist believes the discomfort is caused by periosteal pain from the ultrasound. Which of the following scenarios would MOST likely be associated with the patient's subjective report of discomfort?

1. **An ultrasound unit with a high beam nonuniformity ratio**
2. An ultrasound unit with a low beam nonuniformity ratio
3. A transducer with a large effective radiating area
4. A transducer with a small effective radiating area

Correct Answer: 1 (Cameron p. 172) 

Beam nonuniformity ratio (BNR) is the ratio between the spatial peak intensity and spatial average intensity. The higher the quality of the crystal, the lower the BNR. The BNR is derived from the intrinsic factors and quality of the piezoelectric crystal.

1. **A high beam nonuniformity ratio produces a less uniform beam and therefore places the patient at greater risk for undesirable side effects such as periosteal pain or hot spots.**
2. A low beam nonuniformity ratio produces a more uniform beam and therefore allows for greater patient comfort and safety.
3. Large ultrasound transducers have relatively large effective radiating areas. Effective radiating area (ERA) refers to the area of the transducer that transmits ultrasound energy. The ERA is more relevant when considering the size of the transducer to utilize and the duration of treatment.
4. Small ultrasound transducers have small ERAs. The ERA is always slightly smaller than the total size of the transducer head. A transducer with a small ERA would be unlikely to produce the described discomfort without additional contributing variables.

System: Non-Systems
Content Outline: Equipment, Devices, and Technologies; Therapeutic Modalities

 Level 2 p. 710-713

PTEXAM THREE: QUESTION 146

A patient with a transtibial amputation displays early knee flexion from midstance through pre-swing. What is a possible cause for this deviation?

1. The foot is set in neutral
2. The socket is set posterior in relation to the foot
3. The prosthesis is too short
4. **The socket is aligned in excessive flexion**

Correct Answer: 4 (Seymour p. 204)

If the socket of a transtibial prosthesis is aligned in excessive flexion, there will be early flexion during stance causing instability of the prosthetic limb. Other contributing factors include excessive posterior displacement of the foot in relation to the socket or excessive dorsiflexion.

1. A neutral foot setting would not cause early knee flexion from midstance through pre-swing.
2. A transtibial socket that is set posteriorly to the foot will create an increased extension moment at the knee and result in insufficient knee flexion during early stance.
3. A prosthesis that is too short would typically create an increased extension moment at the knee and result in insufficient knee flexion during early stance. A prosthesis that is too long may cause excessive flexion during heel strike through midstance.
4. **A socket that is aligned in excessive flexion will create an increased flexion moment at the knee which will result in early flexion through stance phase.**

System: Musculoskeletal System
Content Outline: Physical Therapy Examination

 Level 2  p. 144-145

PTEXAM THREE: QUESTION 147

A physical therapist performing lower extremity range of motion on a patient identifies increased resistance to elongation on both sides of the hip, knee, and ankle joints. The therapist determines that the resistance does not seem to be influenced by speed. Damage to which structure would be MOST consistent with the described clinical scenario?

1. **Basal ganglia**
2. Spinal cord
3. Cerebellum
4. Amygdala

Correct Answer: 1 (Fell p. 156)

Muscle tone can be measured as the amount of resistance to passive stretch within a certain muscle. Spasticity is a component of an upper motor neuron lesion and a secondary effect from central nervous system damage. The degree of increased or decreased tone is dependent on the area of the central nervous system affected by a given pathology.

1. **The basal ganglia are gray matter masses located deep within the white matter of the cerebrum. These structures are responsible for voluntary movement, regulation of autonomic movement, posture, muscle tone, and control of motor responses. Patients with basal ganglia damage present with increased resistance to muscle elongation that does not increase with faster stretch and often persists on both sides of the joint.**
2. The spinal cord is a component of the central nervous system and a direct continuation of the brainstem. The spinal cord functions as a relay for information between peripheral structures and the brain in order to process information. Patients with spinal cord damage present with increased resistance to muscle elongation that increases with the speed at which the stretch is applied (velocity-dependent) on both sides of the joint.
3. The cerebellum is responsible for fine tuning movement as well as assisting with posture and balance by controlling muscle tone and positioning of the extremities in space. Patients with cerebellar lesions will present with decreased resistance to muscle elongation (i.e., hypotonia) and ataxia.
4. The amygdala is a small, almond-shaped nucleus located within the temporal lobes of each hemisphere of the brain. The main function of the amygdala is emotional and social processing. It is also involved with fear and pleasure responses, arousal, processing of memory, and the formation of emotional memories. Patients with damage to the amygdala do not experience tonal abnormalities.

System: Neuromuscular and Nervous Systems
Content Outline: Foundations for Evaluation, Differential Diagnosis, and Prognosis

p. 237, 263

PTEXAM THREE: QUESTION 148

A patient rates the intensity of exercise as a 16/20 using Borg's Rating of Perceived Exertion Scale. This rating BEST corresponds to what percentage of the maximum heart rate range?

1. 40%
2. 60%
3. 70%
4. **85%**

Correct Answer: 4 (ACSM – Resource Manual p. 475)

Borg's Rating of Perceived Exertion Scale (RPE) may be used as an alternative means to monitor the intensity of exercise once the patient becomes familiar with the feeling of exertion associated with exercise at the appropriate target level. The 20-point RPE scale ranges from a minimum value of 6 to a maximum value of 20.

1. A rating of 16 is relatively close to the maximum value and would therefore not correspond to a heart rate percent that is less than 50% of heart rate range.
2. 60% of the heart rate range corresponds to an RPE of 11-12 (fairly light).
3. 70% of the heart rate range corresponds to an RPE of 13-14 (somewhat hard).
4. **A rating of 16 (very hard) on the 20-point RPE scale corresponds to 85% of the heart rate range.**

System: Cardiovascular and Pulmonary Systems
Content Outline: Interventions

p. 432-433

PTEXAM THREE: QUESTION 149

A physical therapist performs a gait analysis on a patient with a lower extremity injury. The therapist begins the session by observing the patient at free speed walking. What is the normal degree of toe-out at this speed?

1. 3 degrees
2. **7 degrees**
3. 14 degrees
4. 21 degrees

Correct Answer: 2 (Levangie p. 528)

The degree of toe-out is measured by determining the angle formed by each foot's line of progression and a line intersecting the center of the heel and the second toe.

1. A measurement of 3 degrees of toe-out may be associated with walking at a relatively fast rate of speed since the normal degree of toe-out decreases as the speed of walking increases.
2. **The degree of toe-out during free speed walking is approximately 7 degrees.**
3. A measurement of 14 degrees is greater than normal and may be associated with a wide range of orthopedic or neurologic abnormalities.
4. A measurement of 21 degrees is excessive and may be associated with more severe orthopedic or neurologic abnormalities.

System: Musculoskeletal System
Content Outline: Physical Therapy Examination

 Level 1  p. 87

PTEXAM THREE: QUESTION 150

A patient with patellofemoral syndrome discusses their past medical history with a physical therapist. The patient reports having anterior cruciate ligament reconstruction surgery on their right knee two years ago, however, the therapist is not able to identify a scar over the anterior surface of the right knee. Assuming the surgeon utilized an autograft for the reconstruction, which of the following tendons would be the MOST likely graft site?

1. Semitendinosus and semimembranosus
2. **Semitendinosus and gracilis**
3. Semimembranosus and gracilis
4. Semitendinosus and biceps femoris

Correct Answer: 2 (Kisner p. 810)

Anterior cruciate ligament (ACL) reconstruction refers to the use of a graft to replace a damaged anterior cruciate ligament. The graft is placed through drilled holes in the femoral and tibial tunnels and then anchored with a fixation device. The most common grafts used are the patellar tendon or the tendons of the semitendinosus and gracilis.

1. The semitendinosus and semimembranosus both function as medial hamstring muscles. The muscles are innervated by the tibial branch of the sciatic nerve (L5-S1). The semimembranosus is not used as a graft for ACL reconstruction.
2. **The semitendinosus and gracilis tendons are commonly used together as a graft for anterior cruciate ligament reconstruction. The grafts result in a decreased incidence of post-operative patellofemoral knee pain, however, provide weaker initial fixation. The gracilis functions as a hip adductor and is innervated by the obturator nerve (L2-L4).**
3. The semimembranosus is not used as a graft for ACL reconstruction.
4. The semitendinosus and biceps femoris are hamstring muscles. The semitendinosus is considered a medial hamstrings muscle and the biceps femoris is a lateral hamstrings muscle. The biceps femoris is not used as a graft for ACL reconstruction.

System: Musculoskeletal System
Content Outline: Foundations for Evaluation, Differential Diagnosis, and Prognosis

Level 2  p. 130-131

PTEXAM THREE: QUESTION 151

A physical therapist examines a patient who reports recent weight gain. Which of the following medical conditions would MOST likely be associated with weight gain?

1. Addison's disease
2. Crohn's disease
3. **Congestive heart failure**
4. Graves' disease

Correct Answer: 3 (Hillegass p. 100)

Weight gain is often associated with a variety of medical conditions such as hypothyroidism, Cushing's syndrome, organ disease, congestive heart failure, essential fatty acid deficiencies, and blood sugar imbalance.

1. Addison's disease is a form of adrenal dysfunction that presents with hypofunction of the adrenal cortex. Subsequently, there is decreased production of both cortisol and aldosterone. Symptoms may include hypotension, weakness, anorexia, and altered pigmentation. Weight loss often results from loss of appetite, chronic diarrhea, and vomiting.
2. Crohn's disease is a form of inflammatory bowel disease that usually affects the intestines. The condition causes inflammation of the lining of the digestive tract. Individuals with Crohn's disease often have a decreased appetite, however, at the same time, the chronic nature of the disease increases an individual's caloric needs. The combination of decreased appetite and increased caloric need often leads to significant weight loss.
3. **Congestive heart failure occurs when the heart can no longer meet the metabolic demands of the body. The heart's inability to pump a sufficient amount of blood occurs when there is insufficient or defective cardiac filling and/or impaired contraction and emptying of the heart. Weight gain primarily results from an increase in the amount of fluid in the body. Pharmacological management, such as diuretics, helps to reduce the amount of fluid in the body.**
4. Graves' disease is caused by an autoimmune disease in which certain antibodies produced by the immune system stimulate the thyroid gland causing it to become overactive. Symptoms are consistent with hyperthyroid presentation including mild enlargement of the thyroid gland (goiter), heat intolerance, nervousness, tremor, and palpitations. Hyperthyroidism increases metabolism which often results in weight loss.

System: Other Systems
Content Outline: Foundations for Evaluation, Differential Diagnosis, and Prognosis

p. 402-403, 454-455

PTEXAM THREE: QUESTION 152

A patient diagnosed with Meniere's disease presents with vertigo. Which of the following signs or symptoms is the LEAST likely to be associated with this medical condition?

1. Hearing loss
2. Tinnitus
3. Vertigo lasting 30 minutes
4. **Head tilt to one side**

Correct Answer: 4 (Goodman – Pathology p. 1648)

Meniere's disease is a disorder characterized by an overaccumulation of endolymph due to a lack of absorption. The excess endolymph backs up into the system and compromises the perilymphatic space. Meniere's disease is one of the possible causes for vertigo.

1. Hearing loss is a common symptom associated with Meniere's disease and is related to the excess endolymph in the perilymphatic space.
2. Tinnitus is an abnormal sound in the ear described as a ringing, buzzing or crackling sound. Tinnitus is a common symptom associated with Meniere's disease and is related to the excess endolymph in the perilymphatic space.
3. Episodes of vertigo can vary in duration depending on the cause of the vertigo. With Meniere's disease, the vertigo may last from 30 minutes to 24 hours. In other conditions, such as benign paroxysmal positional vertigo, the vertigo may only last a few seconds.
4. **Head tilting to one side is not typically associated with Meniere's disease. This sign is more commonly associated with a diagnosis of unilateral vestibular hypofunction. Because the vestibular nerve is affected unilaterally, this condition is characterized by an ocular tilt reaction consisting of head tilt, conjugate eye torsion, skew deviation, and an abnormal weight shift to the side of the lesion.**

System: Other Systems
Content Outline: Foundations for Evaluation, Differential Diagnosis, and Prognosis

PTEXAM THREE: QUESTION 153

A physical therapist reads in the medical chart that a patient is taking digitalis. The patient is MOST likely taking this medication to treat which of the following conditions?

1. Angina
2. **Atrial fibrillation**
3. Hypertension
4. Thrombus formation

Correct Answer: 2 (Hillegass p. 468)

Digitalis is a cardiac glycoside that is generally used in the management of arrhythmias, though it is also commonly used to treat congestive heart failure. Digitalis works by either enhancing parasympathetic activity or depressing sympathetic activity, thus slowing the heart rate and depressing electrical conductivity.

1. Angina is chest pain due to ischemia of the heart musculature, thus it is generally treated with anti-ischemic drugs (e.g., beta blockers, calcium-channel blockers, nitrates). Acute angina attacks are often treated with sublingual nitroglycerin.
2. **Atrial fibrillation is an arrhythmia characterized by erratic electrical conductivity within the atria. By depressing electrical conductivity, digitalis can effectively prevent the conduction of atrial arrhythmias into the ventricles.**
3. Hypertension (i.e., high blood pressure) can be treated by several different classes of medications. Diuretics reduce overall blood volume to decrease blood pressure. Vasodilators decrease peripheral resistance or venous return. Other classes of medications affect the sympathetic nervous system directly to inhibit its activity or act on the kidneys to decrease the production of renin, both of which result in decreases in blood pressure.
4. Thrombi (i.e., blood clots) can form in the lumen of arteries and result in reduced blood flow which may eventually lead to myocardial ischemia or infarction. Thrombi are treated with thrombolytic agents which act to break up the thrombus and maintain normal blood flow. Antiplatelet agents can also be used prophylactically by preventing platelet aggregation and thus thrombus formation.

System: Cardiovascular and Pulmonary Systems
Content Outline: Foundations for Evaluation, Differential Diagnosis, and Prognosis

 **Level 1** **p. 426-427**

PTEXAM THREE: QUESTION 154

A physical therapist works with a patient who has a spinal cord injury that was classified as "B" on the ASIA Impairment Scale. What would be the MOST likely clinical presentation of this patient?

1. Intact anal sensation, normal bowel control
2. **Intact anal sensation, absence of bowel control**
3. Absent anal sensation, normal bowel control
4. Absent anal sensation, absence of bowel control

Correct Answer: 2 (O'Sullivan p. 859)

The American Spinal Injury Association (ASIA) created the ASIA Impairment Scale to differentiate between complete and incomplete spinal cord injuries. A complete injury involves the loss of sensory and motor function below the neurological level of injury, including the sacral segments. Incomplete injuries have some preservation of sensory and/or motor function below the neurological level. An ASIA Impairment Scale classification of B involves intact sensory, but not motor, function below the neurological level including the sacral segments.

1. A patient with intact anal sensation and normal bowel control would have some level of both sensory and motor function preserved below the neurological level of injury and therefore could not be classified as B. A classification of B would include preservation of sensory, but not motor, function. This patient would more likely be classified as C, D or E using the ASIA Impairment Scale.
2. **A patient with intact anal sensation but no bowel control would have some level of sensory function preserved below the neurological level. However, they would not have any motor function preserved below the neurological level. This patient would be classified as B using the ASIA Impairment Scale.**
3. A patient with absent anal sensation and normal bowel control would have some level of motor function preserved below the neurological level. However, they would not have any sensory function preserved below the neurological level and therefore could not be classified as B. They would more likely be classified as C or D using the ASIA Impairment Scale.
4. A patient with absent anal sensation and no bowel control would not have sensory or motor function preserved below the neurological level. Because they do not have sensory function preserved, they could not be classified as B. This patient would more likely be classified as A using the ASIA Impairment Scale.

System: Neuromuscular and Nervous Systems
Content Outline: Physical Therapy Examination

 **Level 2**  **p. 295-296**

PTEXAM THREE: QUESTION 155

A physical therapist discusses the plan of care for a patient who has spinal stenosis with the referring physician. During the discussion, the physician shows the therapist an image of the patient's spine obtained through computed tomography. What color would vertebrae appear when using this imaging technique?

1. Black
2. Light gray
3. Dark gray
4. **White**

Correct Answer: 4 (Magee p. 69)

Computed tomography produces cross-sectional images based on x-ray attenuation. The test is commonly used to diagnose spinal lesions and in diagnostic studies of the brain. The relative color of each item using computed tomography is dependent on the relative density. The greater the density, the less penetration of x-rays and the whiter the image will appear. Specific structures listed in descending degree of density are metal, bone, soft tissue, water, fat, and air.

1. Cerebrospinal fluid would appear as black using computed tomography since it is radiolucent.
2. Soft tissue structures would appear as various shades of gray depending on their relative density.
3. A structure that is darker gray has less relative density than a structure that appears as a lighter shade of gray.
4. **Vertebrae are composed of extremely dense bone and therefore appear to be white.**

System: Musculoskeletal System
Content Outline: Foundations for Evaluation, Differential Diagnosis, and Prognosis

p. 696-700

PTEXAM THREE: QUESTION 156

A physical therapist identifies a number of substances that influence circulation. Which of the following substances is stimulated by decreased arterial pressure and acts as a vasoconstrictor?

1. **Angiotensin**
2. Histamine
3. Epinephrine
4. Norepinephrine

Correct Answer: 1 (Ciccone p. 324)

Physical therapists should possess a general sense of the role of different substances and their influence on normal body processes such as circulation.

1. **Angiotensin is a polypeptide in the blood that causes vasoconstriction, increased blood pressure, and the release of aldosterone from the adrenal cortex. Release of angiotensin is stimulated by decreased arterial pressure.**
2. Histamine is an endogenous chemical that is involved in the normal regulation of a variety of physiologic functions such as gastric secretion as well as various hypersensitivity or allergic reactions.
3. Epinephrine is a naturally occurring hormone released by the adrenal glands. The hormone is released in the fight or flight response. The hormone boosts the supply of oxygen and glucose to the brain and muscles while suppressing other non-emergency body processes such as digestion.
4. Norepinephrine serves dual roles as a hormone and neurotransmitter. Norepinephrine affects parts of the brain where attention and responding actions are controlled and in conjunction with epinephrine underlies the fight or flight response by increasing heart rate, releasing glucose from energy stores, and increasing blood flow to skeletal muscles.

System: Cardiovascular and Pulmonary Systems
Content Outline: Foundations for Evaluation, Differential Diagnosis, and Prognosis

PTEXAM THREE: QUESTION 157

A physical therapist attempts to auscultate over the aortic valve. Which of the following areas is the MOST appropriate site to isolate the desired valve?

1. Second left intercostal space at the left sternal border
2. **Second right intercostal space at the right sternal border**
3. Fourth left intercostal space along the lower left sternal border
4. Fifth left intercostal space at the midclavicular line

Correct Answer: 2 (Roy p. 450)

Auscultation of the heart requires selective listening for each component of the cardiac cycle over the main topographic areas for auscultation.

1. The second left intercostal space at the left sternal border denotes the pulmonary area and is best for auscultating the pulmonary valve.
2. **The second right intercostal space at the right sternal border denotes the aortic area and is best for auscultating the aortic valve.**
3. The fourth left intercostal space along the lower left sternal border denotes the tricuspid area and is best for auscultating the tricuspid valve.
4. The fifth left intercostal space at the midclavicular line denotes the mitral area or apex of the heart and is best for auscultating the mitral valve.

System: Cardiovascular and Pulmonary Systems
Content Outline: Physical Therapy Examination

Level 1

p. 420-421

PTEXAM THREE: QUESTION 158

A physical therapist attempts to estimate the energy expenditure in calories for a patient performing a selected activity for 15 minutes. Assuming the therapist knows the metabolic equivalent value for the activity, which of the following patient variables is necessary in order to obtain an estimate of the patient's energy expenditure?

1. Height
2. **Body weight**
3. Stroke volume
4. Residual volume

Correct Answer: 2 (Roy p. 486)

To estimate the energy expended (calories) of an activity, it is necessary to know the patient's body weight (kg), the metabolic equivalent (MET) value of the activity, and the duration of the activity.

1. Height is not needed to estimate the energy expenditure of an activity. Height and weight are needed to calculate body mass index.
2. **A metabolic equivalent (MET) is a measure of oxygen consumption, 1 MET = 3.5 mL O_2 per kg of body weight per minute. Therefore, the caloric expenditure of any activity can be estimated using the number of METs for the activity, the body weight (kg), and the duration of the activity.**
3. Stroke volume is the volume of blood ejected from the ventricles with each contraction. Stroke volume is not needed to estimate the energy expenditure of an activity. Stroke volume and heart rate are needed to calculate cardiac output.
4. Residual volume is the volume of air that remains in the lungs after a maximum forced exhalation. Residual volume is not needed to estimate the energy expenditure of an activity.

System: Cardiovascular and Pulmonary Systems
Content Outline: Interventions

Level 1

p. 446-447

PTEXAM THREE: QUESTION 159

A physical therapist completes a cranial nerve assessment on a patient with a suspected neurological injury by using a tongue depressor. Which cranial nerves are MOST commonly assessed using this tool?

1. VII, IX
2. **IX, X**
3. X, XI
4. XI, XII

Correct Answer: 2 (O'Sullivan p. 101)

The cranial nerves refer to twelve pairs of nerves that have their origin in the brain. The majority of cranial nerves contain both sensory and motor fibers, however, there are several exceptions including the oculomotor and trochlear nerves.

1. Cranial nerve VII-facial is assessed with sweet and salty substances or testing of selected muscles involved in facial expressions. Cranial nerve IX-glossopharyngeal is assessed by distinguishing objects by taste or by assessing the gag reflex with a tongue depressor.
2. **Cranial nerve IX-glossopharyngeal is assessed by distinguishing objects by taste or by assessing the gag reflex with a tongue depressor. Cranial nerve X-vagus is assessed by assessing the gag reflex with a tongue depressor.**
3. Cranial nerve X-vagus is assessed by assessing the gag reflex with a tongue depressor. Cranial nerve XI-accessory is assessed by applying manual resistance after the patient shrugs the shoulders.
4. Cranial nerve XI-accessory is assessed by applying manual resistance after the patient shrugs the shoulders. Cranial nerve XII-hypoglossal is assessed by asking the patient to protrude the tongue.

System: Neuromuscular and Nervous Systems
Content Outline: Physical Therapy Examination

p. 247-249

PTEXAM THREE: QUESTION 160

A physical therapist critically analyzes the methodology used in a published research study. Which type of probability sample would result in the GREATEST degree of sampling error?

1. Simple random
2. Systematic
3. **Cluster**
4. Stratified random

Correct Answer: 3 (Portney p. 152)

Cluster sampling involves successive random sampling of a series of units in the population. Cluster sampling is often utilized when a researcher is unable to know all elements in the population in advance.

1. A simple random sample is a type of probability sample where every element of the population has an equal chance of being selected for the sample.
2. A systematic sample is a type of probability sample where elements are chosen from lists of population members using specified intervals, such as every 4th element.
3. **A cluster sample is a probability sample in which large subgroups (clusters) are randomly selected first, and then smaller units are selected from the clusters. Because the technique requires two or more samples to be drawn, each sample is subject to sampling error, potentially compounding the accuracy of the final sample.**
4. A stratified random sample is a type of probability sample in which elements of the population are chosen at random from homogenous groups based on some characteristic. Organizing elements into homogenous groups before selection decreases the sampling error.

System: Non-Systems
Content Outline: Safety and Protection; Professional Responsibilities; Research

p. 807

PTEXAM THREE: QUESTION 161

A patient who has cardiac disease experiences angina while exercising on a treadmill. The patient self-administers a nitroglycerin tablet to control the angina. Nitroglycerin helps to control this symptom by which of the following mechanisms?

1. Decreasing heart rate
2. Inhibiting platelet aggregation and thrombus formation
3. **Dilating peripheral arteries and veins**
4. Reducing platelet aggregation

Correct Answer: 3 (Hillegass p. 453)

Beta-blockers, calcium-channel blockers, and nitrates are three different classes of medications that decrease myocardial oxygen demand, which helps to alleviate symptoms during an angina attack. There are other medications, such as antiplatelet agents, thrombolytic agents, and anticoagulants, that help to increase myocardial oxygen supply.

1. Beta-blockers decrease myocardial oxygen demand by inhibiting the binding of epinephrine and norepinephrine to beta receptors. This results in a decrease in heart rate, contractility of the heart, cardiac output, and blood pressure.
2. Anticoagulants increase myocardial oxygen supply by inhibiting platelet aggregation and thrombus formation. They are most commonly used in the acute treatment of venous thrombosis and thromboembolism.
3. **Nitroglycerin acts in three different ways to decrease myocardial oxygen demand: dilation of veins to decrease venous return (i.e., preload), dilation of arteries to decrease afterload, and relaxation of coronary artery smooth muscle to increase coronary blood supply.**
4. Antiplatelet agents increase myocardial oxygen supply and are taken prophylactically to prevent the formation of thrombi. They do so by decreasing the platelet's ability to adhere and aggregate at the site of injury.

System: Cardiovascular and Pulmonary Systems
Content Outline: Foundations for Evaluation, Differential Diagnosis, and Prognosis

 Level 2  p. 399-400, 446, 468

PTEXAM THREE: QUESTION 162

A physical therapist works with a patient who has sustained a lesion to the long thoracic nerve. What objective finding should the therapist expect this patient to MOST likely demonstrate?

1. Decreased sensation on the lateral forearm
2. Atrophy of the deltoid muscle
3. **Difficulty elevating the arm overhead**
4. Fair strength with shoulder extension

Correct Answer: 3 (Dutton p. 75)

The long thoracic nerve is a motor nerve that originates from the C5-C7 nerve roots and innervates the serratus anterior muscle. Due to the nerve's long and superficial course, it is susceptible to injury through entrapment, compression or traction.

1. The long thoracic nerve is purely a motor nerve, therefore, a lesion to this nerve would not result in sensory disturbances. Decreased sensation on the lateral forearm is commonly found with an injury to the musculocutaneous nerve (C5-C6).
2. The deltoid muscle is innervated by the axillary nerve (C5-C6). Atrophy may result when an injury to the axillary nerve occurs.
3. **Injury to the long thoracic nerve results in weakness of the serratus anterior muscle. The serratus anterior works in combination with the trapezius muscle to upwardly rotate the scapula during elevation of the arm. Weakness of the serratus anterior muscle would make it difficult for a patient to elevate their arm overhead.**
4. The serratus anterior does not contribute to the movement of shoulder extension. Weakness in shoulder extension would likely be the result of a thoracodorsal nerve lesion since the latissimus dorsi is the primary shoulder extensor.

System: Neuromuscular and Nervous Systems
Content Outline: Foundations for Evaluation, Differential Diagnosis, and Prognosis

 Level 1  p. 250

PTEXAM THREE: QUESTION 163

A physical therapist reads in the medical record that a patient with suspected cardiovascular disease had a positive graded exercise test. Which type of data would have been the MOST influential when concluding that the test was positive?

1. Anginal symptoms
2. Ventricular dysrhythmias
3. **ST segment changes**
4. Supraventricular dysrhythmias

Correct Answer: 3 (ACSM – Resource Manual p. 388)

Graded exercise testing is used to measure the response of the heart to a graded increase in oxygen demand. Exercise occurs using a systematic protocol that can assess other variables such as evaluation of arrhythmias, functional capacity, and significance of coronary artery disease.

1. Angina is a transient precordial sensation of pressure or discomfort resulting from myocardial ischemia. Changes in anginal symptoms may reflect a change in coronary status. Any increase or change in anginal symptoms should be recorded and receive immediate attention. Although this type of data is critical to assess, it is not independently indicative of a positive graded exercise test.
2. Ventricular dysrhythmias, including premature ventricular contractions, often occur in healthy individuals. Other forms of ventricular dysrhythmias (e.g., multiform premature ventricular contractions, small periods of ventricular tachycardia) are often associated with significant cardiovascular disease and may require a graded exercise test to be terminated. Although this type of data is critical to assess, it is not independently indicative of a positive graded exercise test.
3. **The ST segment is the portion of the electrocardiograph tracing from the end of the S wave to the beginning of the T wave. It represents the initiation of ventricular repolarization and is a sensitive indicator of ischemia of the ventricles. The standard criterion for a positive graded exercise test is greater than or equal to 1 mm of horizontal or downsloping ST segment depression.**
4. Supraventricular dysrhythmias often include isolated atrial ectopic beats or small periods of supraventricular tachycardia. These findings commonly occur during exercise testing and do not have any diagnostic or prognostic significance for cardiovascular disease.

System: Cardiovascular and Pulmonary Systems
Content Outline: Physical Therapy Examination

 Level 2  p. 426-427

PTEXAM THREE: QUESTION 164

A physical therapist observes the gait pattern of a patient with a right hip flexion contracture. Which gait deviation would be MOST likely based on the contracture?

1. **Diminished step length on the left**
2. Diminished step length on the right
3. Steppage gait on the left
4. Steppage gait on the right

Correct Answer: 1 (Dutton p. 313)

A hip flexion contracture is a common cause of gait abnormalities often associated with pathology or immobility. A hip flexion contracture can result in a variety of compensatory findings including reduced contralateral step length, excessive knee flexion, decreased hip extension, increased anterior pelvic tilt, and increased lumbar lordosis. Prone lying is a common positional activity to stretch the shortened hip flexors.

1. **A right hip flexion contracture would decrease hip extension during gait due to diminished muscle length and passive tension of the iliopsoas. Decreased hip extension during terminal stance causes a decrease in single limb support time on the affected limb which results in shorter step length on the unaffected side.**
2. Diminished step length on the right would be more likely to occur if the patient had a left hip flexion contracture.
3. A steppage gait primarily occurs in an attempt to clear the foot in the presence of dorsiflexor weakness. The foot will slap at initial contact with the ground secondary to the decreased control. A hip flexion contracture would not produce a steppage gait.
4. A steppage gait primarily occurs in an attempt to clear the foot in the presence of dorsiflexor weakness. A hip flexion contracture would not produce a steppage gait.

System: Musculoskeletal System
Content Outline: Foundations for Evaluation, Differential Diagnosis, and Prognosis

 Level 2  p. 84-89

PTEXAM THREE: QUESTION 165

A physical therapist intends to use compression therapy as part of a patient's plan of care. The use of compression therapy would be contraindicated for which of the following impairments?

1. **Lower extremity edema due to congestive heart failure**
2. Decreased mobility following total knee arthroplasty
3. Hypertrophic scarring following a burn to the lower extremities
4. Residual limb edema following transfemoral amputation

Correct Answer: 1 (Cameron p. 414)

Compression therapy is the use of external pressure on the body to improve fluid balance and circulation or modify scar tissue formation. Indications for the use of compression include control of edema, prevention of deep venous thrombosis, treatment of venous stasis ulcers, residual limb shaping after amputation, and control of hypertrophic scarring.

1. **Edema of the limbs is an indication for compression therapy. However, in patients with congestive heart failure, compression therapy should not be used since the movement of fluid from the periphery back to the heart may further increase the stress on an already failing heart.**
2. Compression therapy may be used after total knee arthroplasty to decrease the risk for deep venous thrombosis (DVT). The risk for DVT increases when local blood flow is decreased as is seen in immobilized patients who have undergone major surgery. Specifically, compression therapy can help reduce the risk of DVT by increasing circulation.
3. Hypertrophic scarring is a common complication of burn injuries. Compression therapy is the most common treatment used to control hypertrophic scar formation. Compression garments have been shown to decrease the height and increase the pliability of hypertrophic scars.
4. Compression therapy is commonly used after amputation to help shape the residual limb in preparation for proper fit of the prosthesis. Compression helps with residual limb shaping by controlling edema.

System: Cardiovascular and Pulmonary Systems
Content Outline: Interventions

 Level 2 p. 402-403, 454-455, 722-723

PTEXAM THREE: QUESTION 166

A patient who has C5 tetraplegia has made good progress in therapy and is scheduled for discharge from the rehabilitation hospital in one week. During a treatment session, the patient informs the physical therapist that one day in the future they will walk again. Which of the following responses is the MOST appropriate for the therapist to provide?

1. "Walking is an unrealistic goal given your level of injury."
2. **"Future advances in spinal cord research may make your goal a reality."**
3. "You can have a rewarding life even if confined to a wheelchair."
4. "Completing your exercises on a regular basis will help you to walk."

Correct Answer: 2 (Umphred p. 495) 

Physical therapists should encourage patients to reach for their goals even in cases where presently it may be unrealistic. In this scenario, the patient is not asking the therapist directly about their future functional level, rather the patient is simply sharing their optimism about the possibility of one day being able to walk. It would, therefore, be inappropriate for the therapist to do anything to diminish this optimism.

1. The response is accurate, however, it would serve to significantly dampen the patient's current enthusiasm and is not warranted given the described scenario.
2. **Responding in this manner leaves open the possibility that the patient may one day walk, without providing the patient with a sense of false hope.**
3. The response would likely be construed as negative given the patient's proclamation and is made worse by the terminology selected (i.e., "confined to a wheelchair").
4. The response implies that compliance with an exercise program can facilitate walking. This is not accurate based on the patient's level of injury and therefore may provide the patient with a sense of false hope.

System: Neuromuscular and Nervous Systems
Content Outline: Foundations for Evaluation, Differential Diagnosis, and Prognosis

 Level 3

PTEXAM THREE: QUESTION 167

A physical therapist performs several surface palpations on a patient who sustained an acromioclavicular injury. Which anatomical landmark is **MOST** consistent with the location of the therapist's finger as shown in the image?

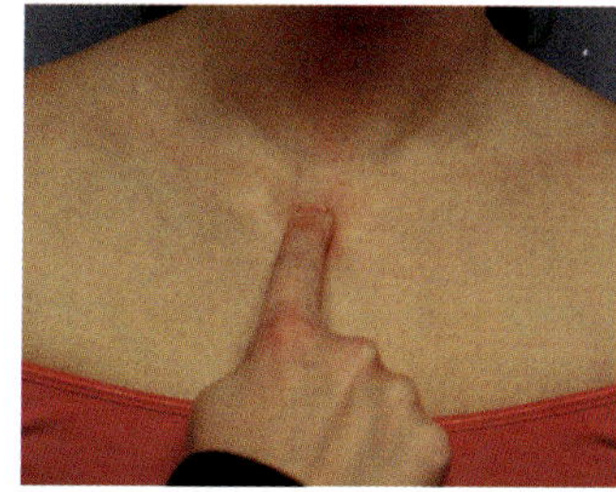

1. Manubrium
2. Sternoclavicular joint
3. **Suprasternal notch**
4. Xiphoid process

Correct Answer: 3 (Dutton p. 1387) 

Physical therapists must possess knowledge of surface anatomy and be able to identify anatomical structures through observation or palpation. It is often important to inspect the integrity of selected structures within a reasonable proximity of the primary injury.

1. The manubrium refers to the broad upper portion of the sternum. The manubrium has a quadrangular shape and articulates with the clavicles and the first two ribs.
2. The sternoclavicular joint consists of the clavicle articulating with the manubrium of the sternum.
3. **The anatomical landmark consistent with the therapist's finger is the suprasternal notch. The suprasternal notch refers to the "V" shaped notch at the top of the sternum.**
4. The xiphoid process refers to the small extension of the lower portion of the sternum. The xiphoid process is cartilaginous at birth and usually ossifies and unites with the body of the sternum by 40 years of age.

System: Musculoskeletal System
Content Outline: Physical Therapy Examination

 Level 1

PTEXAM THREE: QUESTION 168

A physical therapist discusses the plan of care for a patient post total hip arthroplasty using a posterolateral approach with the patient's surgeon. During the discussion, the surgeon indicates that they would like the patient to wear a knee immobilizer in order to help prevent hip dislocation. Which of the following statements would **MOST** likely be the primary rationale for the use of this device?

1. It serves as a constant reminder to the patient that the hip is susceptible to injury
2. **It reduces hip flexion by maintaining knee extension**
3. It facilitates quadriceps contraction during weight bearing activities
4. It limits post-operative edema and as a result, promotes lower extremity stability

Correct Answer: 2 (Paz p. 101)

Hip flexion greater than 90 degrees is often considered a contraindication following total hip arthroplasty surgery using a posterolateral surgical approach. Other contraindications in the early post-operative phase include restricting adduction and medial rotation.

1. A knee immobilizer can serve as an external feedback mechanism to remind the patient that the hip is vulnerable to injury, however, this would not be the primary rationale to use the device.
2. **A knee immobilizer limits hip flexion by maintaining the knee in an extended position. The immobilizer can be particularly helpful in patients who are unable to maintain posterior hip precautions independently.**
3. A knee immobilizer is commonly used following knee surgery to provide stability to the lower extremity. The immobilizer is most often prescribed in the presence of quadriceps weakness to prevent "buckling" or "giving way" of the knee. The knee immobilizer would, however, not improve stability of the hip following total hip arthroplasty.
4. The knee immobilizer offers some compression to the knee, however, would have little impact on the patient's post-operative edema particularly since the surgery involved the hip. In addition, limiting post-operative edema would play a relatively minor role in promoting lower extremity stability.

System: Musculoskeletal System
Content Outline: Interventions

 Level 2  p. 127-128

PTEXAM THREE: QUESTION 169

A patient who sustained a radial head fracture misses their third consecutive treatment session. The physical therapist called the patient after the second missed appointment, but did not receive a return phone call. Which of the following actions is the MOST appropriate for the therapist to implement?

1. Contact the patient's insurance provider
2. Design a home exercise program for the patient
3. Schedule the patient with another physical therapist
4. **Discharge the patient from physical therapy**

Correct Answer: 4 (Shamus – Effective Documentation p. 219)

Patients receiving physical therapy services should demonstrate a commitment to attaining established goals. Failure to attend scheduled therapy sessions, particularly without providing advanced notice, is a strong indication that the patient is not currently exhibiting an appropriate level of commitment.

1. The situation should be formally addressed in the physical therapy clinic prior to contemplating the need to inform the insurance provider.
2. Designing a home exercise program for the patient could be a viable alternative, however, for this to be the correct response there would need to be evidence that suggests the patient has difficulty attending physical therapy sessions due to time constraints or other life activities.
3. The question does not provide any evidence to suggest that there is a conflict between the patient and the therapist or that the patient-therapist relationship is associated with the missed physical therapy sessions.
4. **Multiple missed appointments without a response to a phone call warrants discharging the patient from physical therapy. Failure to act in this manner limits the availability of physical therapy services for other patients.**

System: Non-Systems
Content Outline: Safety and Protection; Professional Responsibilities; Research

 Level 3

PTEXAM THREE: QUESTION 170

A physical therapist treats a patient who has a decubitus ulcer using whirlpool. After treating the wound for ten treatment sessions, the wound still shows little evidence of granulation. Which of the following actions is the MOST appropriate for the therapist to do next?

1. Begin aggressive debridement
2. Recommend a wound culture
3. Apply aseptic ointment to the wound
4. **Discontinue whirlpool treatments**

Correct Answer: 4 (Sussman p. 224) 

The Criteria for Standards of Practice for Physical Therapy published by the American Physical Therapy Association specifies the following: "The physical therapist re-examines the patient/client as necessary during an episode of care to evaluate progress or change in patient/client status and modifies the plan of care accordingly or discontinues physical therapy services."

1. Debridement is typically warranted when there is nonviable tissue present. Debridement can be selective debridement (e.g., sharp, enzymatic, and autolytic) or non-selective debridement (e.g., wet-to-dry dressings, wound irrigation, and hydrotherapy). The question indicates that the wound has not shown evidence of healing after hydrotherapy, however, it does not specify that the wound needs to be debrided.
2. A wound culture is a test in which microorganisms from a wound are grown in a special growth medium. It is performed to identify the microorganism causing an infection in a wound or an abscess. The described scenario does not offer direct evidence suggesting the need for a wound culture and in addition it would be a higher priority to discontinue the ineffective intervention.
3. Aseptic ointment is often used on contaminated or high risk wounds and can be applied to non-contaminated wounds that demonstrate early signs of infection. The question does not provide direct evidence to support aseptic ointment and in addition it would be a higher priority to discontinue the ineffective intervention.
4. **Physical therapists have an obligation to discontinue ineffective interventions. If the selected intervention was beneficial, it is likely that 10 treatment sessions would have been adequate to generate supporting evidence such as signs of healing (e.g., presence of granulation tissue).**

System: Other Systems
Content Outline: Interventions

 Level 3

PTEXAM THREE: QUESTION 171

A physical therapist works with a patient who is in the initial stages of recovery post traumatic brain injury. Based on the typical pattern of spasticity experienced with upper motor neuron disorders, which of the following muscles would MOST likely be affected?

1. **Flexor carpi radialis**
2. Supinator
3. Triceps
4. Extensor digitorum

Correct Answer: 1 (O'Sullivan p. 144)

Spasticity is a hypertonic motor disorder characterized by a velocity-dependent resistance to passive stretch. Spasticity arises when corticospinal pathways become injured. The condition is commonly observed in the presence of upper motor neuron disorders. The typical pattern of spasticity for the upper extremity includes scapula retraction and downward rotation, shoulder adduction and internal rotation, elbow flexion, forearm pronation, wrist flexion and adduction, finger flexion, and thumb adduction.

1. **The pattern of spasticity for the upper extremity includes flexion of the wrist. The flexor carpi radialis is one of the muscles affected by spasticity and serves to maintain the wrist in a flexed position.**
2. The pattern of spasticity for the upper extremity includes pronation of the forearm. The muscles typically affected are the pronator teres and pronator quadratus, not the supinator.
3. The pattern of spasticity for the upper extremity includes flexion of the elbow. The muscles typically affected are the biceps, brachialis, and brachioradialis, not the triceps.
4. The pattern of spasticity for the upper extremity includes flexion of the fingers. The muscle typically affected is the flexor digitorum profundus, not the extensor digitorum.

System: Neuromuscular and Nervous Systems
Content Outline: Foundations for Evaluation, Differential Diagnosis, and Prognosis

Level 2

PTEXAM THREE: QUESTION 172

A physical therapist prepares to administer rescue breathing to a 45-year-old patient who is unresponsive. Which method of ventilation is the MOST appropriate to administer rescue breathing?

1. Mouth to mouth
2. Mouth to nose
3. Mouth to mouth and nose
4. **Mouth to mask**

Correct Answer: 4 (Le Baudour p. 141)

Rescue breathing, also known as positive pressure ventilation, refers to applying external pressure to force air into a patient's lungs. This may be warranted when a patient is not breathing normally or has completely stopped breathing.

1. Mouth to mouth ventilation requires the physical therapist to come in direct contact with the patient's body fluids. When possible, physical therapists should take steps to protect themselves from unnecessary exposure.
2. Mouth to nose ventilation may be warranted in conditions such as injuries to the mouth or jaw, missing teeth or dentures. This method of administration, like mouth to mouth ventilation, exposes the physical therapist to the patient's body fluids.
3. Mouth to mouth and nose ventilation is most often used on infants less than one year old. This method would not be utilized on a 45-year-old male. In addition, this method of administration exposes the physical therapist to the patient's body fluids.
4. **Mouth to mask ventilation allows the physical therapist to provide ventilations without having to experience direct skin to skin contact. Face masks are typically made of durable plastic with a one-way valve and filter. Although several of the other options are appropriate methods to administer rescue breathing, the ability of the mask to serve as a barrier makes this option the most desirable.**

System: Non-Systems
Content Outline: Safety and Protection; Professional Responsibilities; Research

Level 1

p. 767

PTEXAM THREE: QUESTION 173

A physical therapist instructs a patient who sustained a low back injury in a series of five pelvic stabilization exercises. The patient indicates they understand the exercises, however, frequently becomes confused and is unable to perform them correctly. Which of the following actions is the MOST appropriate for the therapist to do next?

1. Repeat the exercise instructions
2. **Reduce the number of exercises in the series**
3. Select a different treatment option
4. Conclude the patient is not a candidate for physical therapy

Correct Answer: 2 (Kisner p. 26) 

A physical therapist should attempt to simplify the exercise session in order to reduce the patient's confusion.

1. Repeating the exercise instructions can be valuable, however, given that the patient "frequently becomes confused" this action is unlikely to resolve the patient's problem.
2. **Reducing the number of exercises in the series serves to simplify the program. Five pelvic stabilization exercises are a significant number for the patient to learn, and as a result, it is reasonable to hypothesize that the number of exercises may be the primary reason for the patient's difficulty.**
3. There is not enough evidence available to suggest that the patient is unable to learn the exercises or that the exercises, if performed appropriately, are not of value. As a result, selecting a different treatment option is not justified.
4. A therapist should attempt to alter the learning environment or the method of providing patient instruction prior to concluding that a patient is not a candidate for physical therapy.

System: Musculoskeletal System
Content Outline: Interventions

  p. 798-799

PTEXAM THREE: QUESTION 174

A physical therapist works on mat activities to improve bed mobility and dressing independence with a patient diagnosed with C7 complete tetraplegia. Preserving tightness of which muscle groups would MOST benefit the patient's functional potential?

1. Finger extensors and hamstrings
2. **Finger flexors and low back**
3. Wrist flexors and hamstrings
4. Wrist extensors and low back

Correct Answer: 2 (Fell p. 866)

A patient with complete C7 tetraplegia may benefit from maintaining tightness in certain muscle groups in order to assist with function. Patients without finger innervation will be able to simulate grasp using shortened long finger flexors to perform a tenodesis grip. Patients without trunk innervation may also be able to derive benefit during transfers and bed mobility through the use of tightness within the low back muscles.

1. Patients should avoid simultaneous wrist and finger extension as it places the flexor muscles on maximum stretch. Finger extensors are not a target muscle group in terms of maintaining a shortened length. Hamstring muscles must have adequate length in order to maintain long sitting and assist with bed mobility and dressing skills. Therefore, stretching these muscles is essential to prevent tightness.
2. **Both finger flexors and low back muscles would benefit from maintaining some tightness of the muscles. When the long finger flexors are tight, the patient can use a tenodesis grasp (wrist extension assists with finger flexion to produce a grasp). Tightness of the low back muscles allows for movement of the head and upper extremities while in long sitting which can assist with functional mobility and activities of daily living.**
3. Patients should avoid tightness of both the wrist flexors and hamstrings muscle groups. The wrist flexors should have adequate length so that the patient can perform wrist extension to use a tenodesis grasp. The hamstrings also require adequate length in order to allow long sitting and functional mobility in bed.
4. While tightness of the wrist extensors will allow the patient to achieve a position of wrist extension, tightness in the long finger flexors would be necessary to perform a strong tenodesis grip. Tightness of the low back muscles allows for movement of the head and upper extremities while still in long sitting.

System: Neuromuscular and Nervous Systems
Content Outline: Foundations for Evaluation, Differential Diagnosis, and Prognosis

  p. 298-301, 350-351

PTEXAM THREE: QUESTION 175

A physical therapist treats a patient diagnosed with chronic arterial disease. The patient is experiencing intermittent claudication with activity. The primary treatment goal is to increase the patient's ambulation distance. Which of the following ambulation parameters are the MOST appropriate to facilitate achievement of the goal?

1. **Short duration, frequent intervals**
2. Short duration, infrequent intervals
3. Long duration, frequent intervals
4. Long duration, infrequent intervals

Correct Answer: 1 (Hillegass p. 593) 

Intermittent claudication occurs as a result of insufficient blood supply and ischemia in active muscles. The condition occurs with activity, subsides during periods of rest, and as a result can limit the duration of exercise activities. Symptoms most commonly include pain and cramping in muscles distal to the occluded vessel.

1. **Treadmill and track walking are the most effective modes of exercise to reduce claudication. The initial workloads are set to elicit claudication symptoms within three to five minutes. This is followed by a period of standing or sitting to allow symptoms to resolve. The exercise-rest-exercise pattern is repeated throughout the exercise session. Due to the short duration of each bout of exercise before the onset of symptoms, more frequent exercise bouts are indicated.**
2. Since the patient can only exercise for shorter durations before the onset of symptoms, exercising at infrequent intervals would not allow the patient to progress toward the goal of increasing ambulation distance.
3. Patients who experience claudication from chronic arterial disease usually can only walk for short periods before the onset of pain limits their ability to continue exercise. Therefore, long duration of exercise with frequent intervals is not a realistic plan to progress toward the goal of increasing ambulation distance.
4. Although the infrequent intervals may provide the patient with less total activity, the long duration of the exercise remains problematic.

System: Other Systems
Content Outline: Interventions

Level 2

PTEXAM THREE: QUESTION 176

A physical therapist instructs a patient who is post bone marrow transplant in an exercise program. The therapist plans to use oxygen saturation measurements to gain additional objective data related to the patient's exercise tolerance. Assuming the patient's oxygen saturation was measured as 95% at rest, which of the following guidelines would be the MOST appropriate to determine when to discontinue exercise?

1. When the patient's oxygen saturation is below 95%
2. **When the patient's oxygen saturation is below 90%**
3. When the patient's oxygen saturation is below 85%
4. When the patient's oxygen saturation is below 80%

Correct Answer: 2 (Fairchild p. 57)

An oxygen saturation at rest greater than 95% is considered to be within normal limits. A rate of 90% or less is often used as a guideline to discontinue exercise activities. Supplemental oxygen may be indicated if oxygen saturation is 90% or less.

1. An oxygen saturation of 95% is within normal limits.
2. **When oxygen saturation falls below 90% exercise should be discontinued and the patient should rest. This corresponds to a partial pressure of oxygen (PaO_2) of approximately 60 mm Hg, which represents a state of arterial hypoxemia. This is the most common indication for supplemental oxygen therapy.**
3. A patient with an oxygen saturation of 85% is in a state of hypoxemia. Exercise should have been terminated before this level of hypoxemia was reached.
4. A patient with an oxygen saturation of 80% is in a severe hypoxemic state. Exercise should have been terminated before this level of hypoxemia was reached.

System: Other Systems
Content Outline: Interventions

Level 2  p. 409, 432

PTEXAM THREE: QUESTION 177

A patient is two days post surgical insertion of a urinary catheter. This procedure is MOST commonly performed with which of the following types of catheters?

1. Condom
2. Foley
3. **Suprapubic**
4. Swan-Ganz

Correct Answer: 3 (Fairchild p. 281) 

An internal or indwelling catheter is inserted through the urethra and into the bladder. Females can utilize internal catheters, while males can use internal or external catheters.

1. An external catheter is applied over the shaft of the penis and is held in place by a padded strap or adhesive tape. The catheter has no practical application for females.
2. A Foley catheter is an indwelling urinary tract catheter that has a balloon attachment at one end. The balloon, which is filled with air or sterile water, must be deflated before the catheter can be removed. The catheter does not require surgical insertion.
3. **A suprapubic catheter is an indwelling urinary catheter that is surgically inserted directly into the patient's bladder. Insertion of a suprapubic catheter is performed under general anesthesia.**
4. A Swan-Ganz catheter is a soft, flexible catheter that is inserted through a vein into the pulmonary artery. The device is used to provide continuous measurements of pulmonary artery pressure.

System: Other Systems
Content Outline: Foundations for Evaluation, Differential Diagnosis, and Prognosis

 Level 1 p. 696

PTEXAM THREE: QUESTION 178

A physical therapist examines an infant in the neonatal intensive care unit. Which of the following data from the medical chart provides the MOST compelling evidence that the child is at high risk for cerebral palsy?

1. Birth weight of 2000 grams
2. Apgar score of 8 at 1 minute
3. **Periventricular leukomalacia**
4. Premature birth at 34 weeks

Correct Answer: 3 (Tecklin p. 187)

Cerebral palsy is characterized by a disturbance or insult to the developing fetal or infant brain. Infections, hemorrhages, brain malformations, and periventricular leukomalacia are common disturbances that may result in cerebral palsy.

1. Birth weight may contribute to conditions in which a hypoxic/ischemic event can occur, but by itself does not place the infant at risk for cerebral palsy. 2000 grams is equivalent to 4.4 pounds.
2. Apgar scores are used to determine if a child requires resuscitation at birth and are not predictive of cerebral palsy or any other developmental condition. Apgar scores range between 0-10. Scores of 7-10 indicate good health and that the infant does not require resuscitation; scores of 4-6 indicate that the infant may need suctioning or oxygen; scores of 0-3 indicate a medical emergency and necessary resuscitation.
3. **Periventricular leukomalacia is an ischemic disturbance around the brain ventricles causing white matter damage. This condition is the most common ischemic pathology resulting in cerebral palsy. Any type of disturbance resulting in brain pathology can be predictive of cerebral palsy.**
4. An infant born at or before 37 weeks is considered premature (full gestation is 40 weeks). Premature birth places the infant at increased risk for cerebral palsy, however, the relative degree of risk is significantly less than the risk associated with periventricular leukomalacia.

System: Neuromuscular and Nervous Systems
Content Outline: Physical Therapy Examination

 Level 2  p. 312, 328-329

PTEXAM THREE: QUESTION 179

A physical therapist reviews the medical record of a patient recently diagnosed with rheumatoid arthritis. Which test would likely have been MOST instrumental in helping establish the diagnosis?

1. Creatine phosphokinase
2. Acid-base (pH)
3. **Erythrocyte sedimentation rate**
4. Fasting lipid panel

Correct Answer: 3 (Goodman – Pathology p. 1317)

Rheumatoid arthritis is a systemic autoimmune disorder of the connective tissue that is characterized by chronic inflammation within synovial membranes, tendon sheaths, and articular cartilage. Blood work assists with the diagnosis of rheumatoid arthritis through evaluation of the rheumatoid factor, white blood cell count, erythrocyte sedimentation rate, hemoglobin, and hematocrit values.

1. Creatine phosphokinase is a cardiac biomarker that is found in the blood following a myocardial infarction. This test would not be useful when diagnosing rheumatoid arthritis.
2. Examination of blood pH can be used to determine acidemia (pH < 7.35) and alkalemia (pH > 7.45). This test would not be useful when diagnosing rheumatoid arthritis.
3. **Erythrocyte sedimentation rate (ESR) is a non-specific test for inflammatory disorders. The test is based on how quickly red blood cells sink to the bottom of a test solution containing anticoagulated blood. An elevated ESR in conjunction with patient history and other objective exam findings may be indicative of rheumatoid arthritis.**
4. A lipid panel measures the amount of cholesterol and triglycerides in the blood in order to determine the risk of atherosclerosis. This test would not be useful when diagnosing rheumatoid arthritis.

System: Musculoskeletal System
Content Outline: Foundations for Evaluation, Differential Diagnosis, and Prognosis

Level 1

p. 123, 126, 614-615, 624-625

PTEXAM THREE: QUESTION 180

A physical therapist performs manual vibration as a means of airway clearance with a patient who has chronic obstructive pulmonary disease. What type of manual contact is the MOST appropriate when performing this technique over the affected lung segment?

1. With a cupped hand
2. **With the entire palmar surface of the hand**
3. With the ulnar border of the hand
4. With the distal phalanx of the middle finger

Correct Answer: 2 (Hillegass p. 544)

Vibration is administered by contracting the muscles of the upper extremities and intentionally causing a vibration to the chest wall with the hands. Vibration should produce a gentle, high frequency force and is a viable alternative to percussion in acutely ill patients with chest wall discomfort or pain.

1. Contact with a cupped hand would be indicated when performing percussion. Percussion refers to a rhythmical clapping applied over an affected lung segment. Percussion is used to loosen retained secretions.
2. **Vibration requires the palmar aspect of the physical therapist's hands to be in full contact with the affected lung segment. The therapist may elect to partially or fully overlap the hands during manual vibration. Vibration is applied at the end of a deep inspiration and is maintained through the end of expiration.**
3. Contact with the ulnar border of the hand can be used as a method to assess tactile fremitus. Tactile fremitus refers to the vibration of spoken words felt through the chest wall. The palmar surface of one or both hands can also be used. Tactile fremitus provides information about the density of the lungs and the thoracic cavity.
4. Mediate percussion is used to evaluate changes in lung density. The technique requires the physical therapist to place the middle finger of one hand flat on the chest wall along the intercostal space between two ribs while the other fingers are lifted off of the chest wall. The opposing hand acts as a fulcrum using the middle finger to strike the middle finger of the opposite hand positioned on the chest wall. The quality of the generated sound provides the therapist with information on lung density.

System: Cardiovascular and Pulmonary Systems
Content Outline: Interventions

Level 1

p. 437, 440

PTEXAM THREE: QUESTION 181

A physical therapist performs gait training with a patient who has right hemiparesis and instructs the patient to side step toward the affected side. The therapist would MOST likely expect the patient to compensate for weak abductors by exhibiting which of the following gait deviations during hip abduction?

1. Hip hiking of the unaffected side
2. Lateral trunk flexion towards the affected side
3. **Lateral trunk flexion towards the unaffected side**
4. Hip extension of the affected side

Correct Answer: 3 (O'Sullivan p. 619)

Gait deviations result from many factors including potential weakness of the affected muscle groups, diminished proprioception, impaired trunk control, decreased awareness of the affected side, and contractures.

1. Hip hiking of the unaffected (left) side would not serve any purpose when side stepping to the right. The left lower extremity can step towards the right without the need to hip hike since motor function on the left is unaffected.
2. Lateral trunk flexion towards the affected (right) side while attempting to side step to the right will only further load the right lower extremity making it more difficult to step toward the right.
3. **Lateral trunk flexion towards the unaffected (left) side can compensate for weak hip abductors while side stepping. This action unweights the right lower extremity and utilizes momentum along with the abductors to perform side stepping.**
4. Hip extension of the affected (right) lower extremity would be important if the person was attempting to step backwards, but would not be a component of side stepping.

System: Neuromuscular and Nervous Systems
Content Outline: Interventions

 Level 2

PTEXAM THREE: QUESTION 182

A patient reports 25 minutes late to an initial physical therapy session for evaluation. The patient was scheduled in a 45 minute block of time for this first visit. The patient referral indicates that the patient is 10 days post arthroscopic medial meniscectomy. Which of the following actions is the MOST appropriate for the therapist to perform?

1. **Begin the examination**
2. Design a home exercise program
3. Consult with the patient's physician
4. Ask the patient to reschedule

Correct Answer: 1 (Criteria for Standards of Practice)

Physical therapists have to possess effective time management skills and adapt their schedule as necessary when warranted. It is important for therapists to attempt to accommodate patients when they happen to be early or late for scheduled appointments, however, they must also be careful that the accommodations do not disadvantage other patients.

1. **The physical therapist should have ample time (i.e., 20 minutes) to begin the examination. This may be particularly important in the described scenario because the patient is 10 days status post arthroscopic surgery.**
2. Although the patient may benefit from a home exercise program, it would be inappropriate to design a home exercise program without first completing a thorough examination.
3. The physician is responsible for the medical management of the patient, however, it is not necessary for a physical therapist to provide the physician with information related to timeliness.
4. Asking the patient to reschedule is a viable option, however, since there is still 20 minutes remaining in the session it is likely that the therapist can effectively use the time.

System: Musculoskeletal System
Content Outline: Physical Therapy Examination

 Level 3

PTEXAM THREE: QUESTION 183

A physical therapist reviews a laboratory report for a 41-year-old male who has chronic obstructive pulmonary disease. Which of the following values would be considered a normal hemoglobin value?

1. 10 gm/dL
2. **15 gm/dL**
3. 20 gm/dL
4. 25 gm/dL

Correct Answer: 2 (Paz p. 170)

Hemoglobin is the protein in red blood cells that carries oxygen. A blood test can determine how much hemoglobin is in the blood. The range of normal values for adult men is approximately 13.3-16.2 gm/dL.

1. 10 gm/dL is well below the normal range for adult men. Lower than normal hemoglobin levels can be due to anemia, acute blood loss, lead poisoning, and nutritional deficiencies of iron, folate, and vitamins B12 and B6.
2. **Although the exact lower and upper values of normal may vary slightly depending on the source, 15 gm/dL is well within the range of normal.**
3. 20 gm/dL is well above the normal range for adult males. Higher than normal hemoglobin levels may be due to cor pulmonale, pulmonary fibrosis, and polycythemia vera (i.e., abnormal increase in blood cells).
4. 25 gm/dL is well above the normal range for adult males.

System: Cardiovascular and Pulmonary Systems
Content Outline: Foundations for Evaluation, Differential Diagnosis, and Prognosis

p. 411

PTEXAM THREE: QUESTION 184

A patient who has an incomplete spinal cord lesion presents with muscle paralysis on the ipsilateral side of the lesion and a loss of pain, temperature, and sensitivity on the contralateral side of the lesion. This presentation BEST describes which of the following syndromes related to spinal cord injury?

1. Posterior cord
2. Central cord
3. Anterior cord
4. **Brown-Sequard's**

Correct Answer: 4 (Umphred p. 462)

Brown-Sequard's syndrome is an incomplete spinal cord lesion resulting in hemisection of the spinal cord. There is paralysis and loss of vibration and position sense on the same side as the lesion (corticospinal tract and dorsal columns) and loss of pain and temperature sense on the opposite side of the lesion (lateral spinothalamic tract).

1. Posterior cord syndrome is a rare incomplete lesion that results from compression of the posterior spinal artery with subsequent loss of stereognosis, proprioception, and two-point discrimination below the level of the lesion. Motor function remains intact.
2. Central cord syndrome is an incomplete lesion resulting from hyperextension. Damage to the spinothalamic tract, corticospinal tract, and dorsal columns produce greater upper extremity involvement than lower extremity; greater motor deficits exist as compared to sensory deficits.
3. Anterior cord syndrome is an incomplete lesion that results from compression to the anterior part of the spinal cord and anterior spinal artery. Presentation consists of a bilateral loss of motor function and pain and temperature sense below the level of the lesion (corticospinal and spinothalamic tracts).
4. **Brown-Sequard's syndrome most commonly occurs from a stab or bullet wound. True hemisection of the cord is rare; most injuries are irregular in nature with a mixture of symptoms.**

System: Neuromuscular and Nervous Systems
Content Outline: Foundations for Evaluation, Differential Diagnosis, and Prognosis

p. 244, 295

PTEXAM THREE: QUESTION 185

A physical therapist discusses modifiable risk factors for developing osteoporosis with a patient diagnosed with osteopenia. Which of the following factors would place the patient at the HIGHEST risk for developing osteoporosis?

1. **Excessive alcohol consumption**
2. Excessive intake of bisphosphonates
3. Inadequate intake of vitamin B12
4. Inadequate intake of zinc

Correct Answer: 1 (Goodman–Pathology p. 1211)

Osteopenia is a condition presenting with low bone mass that is not severe enough to qualify as osteoporosis. Individuals with osteopenia may not have actual bone loss, but have a naturally lower bone density than established norms. Modifiable risk factors associated with the development of low bone mass disorders include inactive lifestyle, smoking, excessive caffeine intake, excessive alcohol consumption, estrogen or testosterone deficiency, insufficient dietary intake of calcium and vitamin D, long-term use of certain medications (e.g., corticosteroids), and low body weight.

1. **Excessive alcohol consumption suppresses osteoblast formation, can impair intestinal absorption, and interferes with the balance of calcium in the body, increasing the risk for low bone mass disorders. It is suggested that alcohol use in excess of two drinks per day can increase a patient's risk for these conditions.**
2. Bisphosphonates are a class of medications that are commonly used to treat patients with osteopenia and osteoporosis since they act to maximize the formation of bone and reduce the rate of bone resorption. Examples of bisphosphonates include alendronate (Fosamax) and ibandronate (Boniva).
3. A vitamin B12 deficiency is not associated with the development of osteoporosis. A vitamin B12 deficiency would be more likely associated with anemia, nerve impairments, and various psychological/cognitive changes.
4. A zinc deficiency is not associated with the development of osteoporosis. A zinc deficiency would be more likely associated with impaired immune function and impaired skeletal growth.

System: Other Systems
Content Outline: Foundations for Evaluation, Differential Diagnosis, and Prognosis

Level 1

p. 521-522, 620-621

PTEXAM THREE: QUESTION 186

A physical therapist performs an examination on a patient diagnosed with iliotibial band syndrome. The patient reports routinely running between 45-60 miles per week before experiencing pain in the knee. When palpating the lower extremity, which structure should the therapist MOST expect to be markedly tender?

1. **Lateral femoral condyle**
2. Lateral joint line
3. Lateral tibial condyle
4. Fibular head

Correct Answer: 1 (Dutton p. 1057)

Iliotibial band syndrome is characterized by localized pain approximately two centimeters above the knee joint line over the lateral femoral condyle. The syndrome can be caused by activities requiring frequent flexion of the knee such as running or cycling which produce an inflammatory reaction.

1. **The iliotibial band is a thickened strip of fascia that extends from the iliac crest to the tibial tubercle. In iliotibial band syndrome there is excessive contact between the iliotibial band and the lateral femoral condyle usually when the knee is in approximately 30 degrees of flexion.**
2. Tenderness along the lateral joint line is more commonly associated with a meniscal injury.
3. The lateral tibial condyle is not typically painful since the irritation tends to be superior in the area of the lateral femoral condyle.
4. The fibular head is located on the lateral side of the knee at the approximate level of the tibial tubercle. The bony structure serves as the insertion for the biceps femoris muscle, but would not typically be involved with iliotibial band syndrome.

System: Musculoskeletal System
Content Outline: Foundations for Evaluation, Differential Diagnosis, and Prognosis

Level 2

PTEXAM THREE: QUESTION 187

The measurement of blood pressure with an aneroid sphygmomanometer is said to have concurrent validity if the pressures measured by the sphygmomanometer are equal to the pressures measured at the same time by which of the following devices?

1. An electrocardiogram
2. **A pressure transducer inserted in the artery**
3. A mercury sphygmomanometer
4. A pulse oximeter

Correct Answer: 2 (Portney p. 103)

Concurrent validity is demonstrated when the measurement to be validated and a "gold standard" are measured at relatively the same time so that they both reflect the same incident or behavior.

1. Since the electrocardiogram does not measure blood pressure, it could not provide evidence of the concurrent validity of a measurement of blood pressure.
2. **For blood pressure measured by an aneroid sphygmomanometer to have concurrent validity, the systolic and diastolic pressures would have to be similar to the pressures measured simultaneously by another instrument considered to be the "gold standard." A pressure transducer inserted in the patient's artery provides a direct and precise measurement of blood pressure.**
3. Like the aneroid sphygmomanometer, a mercury sphygmomanometer provides an indirect measure of blood pressure. The device would not be nearly as accurate as a pressure transducer inserted directly in the artery.
4. Since a pulse oximeter does not measure blood pressure, it could not provide evidence of the concurrent validity of a measurement of blood pressure.

System: Cardiovascular and Pulmonary Systems
Content Outline: Physical Therapy Examination

p. 806-807

PTEXAM THREE: QUESTION 188

A physical therapist reviews the medical chart of a male patient prior to initiating airway clearance techniques. The patient's cell counts are as follows: hematocrit 44%, white blood cells 8,500/mm^3, platelets 30,000/µl, hemoglobin level 15 gm/dL. Which blood test value suggests that chest percussion for airway clearance is contraindicated?

1. Hematocrit
2. White blood cells
3. **Platelets**
4. Hemoglobin

Correct Answer: 3 (Paz p. 170)

Certain blood values may influence the physical therapist's choice of interventions and goals for the treatment session. The platelet value is significantly below the normal value and would therefore result in percussion being contraindicated.

1. The hematocrit is within the normal range for males (39-46%).
2. White blood cell count is within the normal range of 3.5-9.1 x 10^3/mm^3.
3. **The platelet count is well below the normal range of 165,000–415,000/µl. With a platelet count of 50,000/µl or less, the patient is thrombocytopenic and would be placed on thrombocytopenic precautions until the platelet count returns to normal. These precautions include restricting chest percussion due to the increased risk of bleeding. Alternative chest physical therapy techniques may include coughing, deep breathing exercises, and using an incentive spirometer.**
4. The hemoglobin is within the normal range for males (13.3-16.2 gm/dL).

System: Cardiovascular and Pulmonary Systems
Content Outline: Interventions

p. 395, 411

PTEXAM THREE: QUESTION 189

A physical therapist treats a patient post fracture of the left hip. The patient is now weight bearing as tolerated and is ready to progress to a large base quad cane for gait activities. Which of the following descriptions BEST illustrates how the therapist should instruct the patient to use the quad cane?

1. On the left with the longer legs positioned away from the patient
2. **On the right with the longer legs positioned away from the patient**
3. On the left with the longer legs positioned toward the patient
4. On the right with the longer legs positioned toward the patient

Correct Answer: 2 (Minor p. 295)

A quad cane should be utilized in the hand opposite from the affected lower extremity. The device is designed so that the longer legs are positioned away from the patient.

1. The quad cane should be used in the hand opposite the affected lower extremity.
2. **The quad cane, positioned in the right hand with the longer legs pointing away from the patient, will allow for proper distribution of the weight during gait and as a result, the patient will be less likely to trip over the longer legs of the cane.**
3. The quad cane should be used in the hand opposite the affected lower extremity with the longer legs of the quad cane positioned away from the patient.
4. The quad cane should be used with the longer legs positioned away from the patient so that the patient does not trip over them.

System: Musculoskeletal System
Content Outline: Interventions

 Level 2  p. 690-692

PTEXAM THREE: QUESTION 190

A physical therapist inspects a wound that has large quantities of exudate requiring frequent dressing changes. If the therapist applies a dressing that cannot handle the amount of exudate present, which of the following outcomes is the MOST likely?

1. **Maceration**
2. Granulation
3. Epithelialization
4. Infection

Correct Answer: 1 (Sussman p. 376)

Transparent film is an example of a type of dressing that would be unable to handle a significant amount of exudate. Conversely, an alginate dressing would be a better choice for a wound with a significant amount of exudate since the dressing is highly permeable and would therefore tend to absorb the exudate.

1. **Maceration refers to a softening of connective tissue fibers due to excessive moisture. The result is a loss of pigmentation and a wound that is highly susceptible to breakdown or enlargement.**
2. Granulation refers to perfused, fibrous connective tissue that replaces a fibrin clot in a healing wound. The tissue is highly vascular and fills the defects of full-thickness wounds.
3. Epithelialization refers to the process of epidermal resurfacing and appears as pink or red skin.
4. Signs and symptoms of infection include the production of pus, redness, pain, and swelling. More generalized symptoms of infection may include fever, chills, and an increased pulse rate. Laboratory values associated with infection include an increased erythrocyte sedimentation rate and white blood cell count.

System: Other Systems
Content Outline: Interventions

 Level 2  p. 511-512

PTEXAM THREE: QUESTION 191

A physical therapist completes an examination on a patient who has multiple sclerosis. After completing the examination, the therapist should perform which of the following steps FIRST?

1. Develop long-term goals
2. Develop short-term goals
3. **Develop a problem list**
4. Justify the need for physical therapy services

Correct Answer: 3 (Quinn p. 107)

A physical therapist should generate a problem list after completing an examination. The problem list will assist the physical therapist to determine the patient's need for physical therapy services, the frequency of therapy sessions, and the short and long-term goals.

1. The development of long-term goals is vital to the plan of care. The physical therapist will generate long-term goals based on current patient status, typical expected outcome based on diagnosis, patient goals, and the expected timeframe of physical therapy services.
2. Short-term goals are developed to assist in attaining a long-term goal in a step by step manner. The physical therapist will generate short-term goals with a predetermined timeframe based on current patient status and the established long-term goal.
3. **Once an examination has been completed, the physical therapist reviews all of the data and generates a problem list. The problem list assists the therapist to determine if physical therapy services are warranted and to develop an effective and individualized plan of care.**
4. A physical therapist must justify the need for physical therapy services based on the results of the examination, however, the problem list would be developed first to assist the therapist to make an informed decision.

System: Non-Systems
Content Outline: Safety and Protection; Professional Responsibilities; Research

Level 3

PTEXAM THREE: QUESTION 192

A physical therapist observes a patient who sustained an injury to the musculocutaneous nerve complete a number of activities of daily living and functional skills. Which of the following tasks would be the MOST difficult for the patient to perform based on the stated injury?

1. Picking up marbles from the floor
2. Push-ups against a wall
3. **Drinking from a gallon of milk**
4. Holding the arm out to the side

Correct Answer: 3 (Kendall p. 253) 

Peripheral nerves, which supply sensory and motor functions to the entire body, are commonly injured due to compression or shear forces, such as entrapment or sudden stretch. The musculocutaneous nerve innervates the brachialis, biceps brachii, and coracobrachialis muscles. Since the brachialis and biceps are two of the three primary elbow flexors, loss of motor function of these two muscles would dramatically weaken elbow flexion.

1. Picking up marbles from the floor requires a pincer grasp. Since the thenar muscles and muscles that oppose the thumb are innervated by the median nerve, activities that require fine motor skills would be most impacted by an injury to the median nerve rather than the musculocutaneous nerve.
2. Push-ups involve multiple joints and require the contribution of numerous muscles including the pectoralis major, anterior deltoid, and triceps. The muscles primarily involved in a push-up are not innervated by the musculocutaneous nerve.
3. **Drinking a gallon of milk requires elbow flexion range of motion and good strength of the elbow flexors. Since the musculocutaneous nerve supplies both the biceps brachii and brachialis muscles, this action would likely be the most difficult for the patient.**
4. Holding the arm out to the side requires activation of primarily the deltoid and supraspinatus muscles. The deltoid muscle is innervated by the axillary nerve and the supraspinatus is innervated by the suprascapular nerve. Injury to the musculocutaneous nerve would not impact the ability to hold the arm out to the side.

System: Neuromuscular and Nervous Systems
Content Outline: Foundations for Evaluation, Differential Diagnosis, and Prognosis

Level 2

p. 54, 250

PTEXAM THREE: QUESTION 193

A physical therapist examines a patient diagnosed with an anterior cruciate ligament sprain. If the therapist wants to quantitatively measure the anteroposterior translation at the knee, which of the following instruments would provide the MOST accurate measurement?

1. Goniometer
2. **Arthrometer**
3. Tape measure
4. Dynamometer

Correct Answer: 2 (Kisner p. 810)

The anterior cruciate ligament (ACL) extends from the anterior intercondylar region of the tibia to the medial aspect of the lateral femoral condyle in the intercondylar notch. The ACL prevents anterior translation of the tibia on the fixed femur and posterior translation of the femur on the fixed tibia. A grade I sprain involves microscopic tears of the ligament, while a grade III sprain indicates a completely torn ligament.

1. A goniometer is a common instrument used to quantify range of motion at a joint. It measures osteokinematic or angular motion at a joint, such as flexion or extension of the knee. Anteroposterior translatory movement at the knee is a component of arthrokinematic or accessory motion and cannot be measured with a goniometer.
2. **A knee arthrometer, such as the commercially available KT1000, is a non-invasive instrument used to measure the anterior translation of the tibia on a stabilized femur in approximately 30 degrees of knee flexion. It measures the amount of translation in millimeters at a given force, making both intratester and intertester reliability high. Use of a knee arthrometer is considered an objective and accurate method of determining the degree of ACL instability.**
3. A tape measure is a commonly used instrument to quantify circumferential or girth measurements of a body part. Use of circumferential measurements with a tape measure would provide a quantitative assessment of changes in limb size due to edema and joint effusion at the knee. It would not be used to measure translatory movements of the tibia on the femur.
4. A dynamometer is a device used to measure strength through the use of a load cell or spring-loaded gauge. Types of dynamometers used in physical therapy include the handheld dynamometer that measures grip strength, the handheld dynamometer used to measure strength of the extremities through isometric contraction (e.g., manual muscle testing), and the dynamometer used to measure strength through isokinetic contraction.

System: Musculoskeletal System
Content Outline: Physical Therapy Examination

Level 1

PTEXAM THREE: QUESTION 194

A physical therapist prepares to administer iontophoresis over the anterior surface of a patient's knee. The therapist would like to keep the current density low in order to avoid skin irritation. Which of the listed parameters would BEST accomplish the therapist's objective?

1. **Current amplitude of 4 mA; electrode with an area of 12 cm^2**
2. Current amplitude of 4 mA; electrode with an area of 4 cm^2
3. Current amplitude of 3 mA; electrode with an area of 6 cm^2
4. Current amplitude of 3 mA; electrode with an area of 4 cm^2

Correct Answer: 1 (Cameron p. 280) 

The current density may be altered either by increasing or decreasing current intensity or by changing the size of the electrode. Current density with iontophoresis equals current amplitude (mA) divided by electrode size (cm^2). Failure to select appropriate treatment or failure to monitor the patient's response to treatment creates an unnecessary safety risk.

1. **Current density = 4 mA / 12 cm^2 = .33 mA/cm^2**
2. Current density = 4 mA / 4 cm^2 = 1.0 mA/cm^2
3. Current density = 3 mA / 6 cm^2 = .50 mA/cm^2
4. Current density = 3 mA / 4 cm^2 = .75 mA/cm^2

System: Non-Systems
Content Outline: Equipment, Devices, and Technologies; Therapeutic Modalities

Level 2

p. 731-733

PTEXAM THREE: QUESTION 195

A physical therapist examines a patient who has rheumatoid arthritis. During the examination, the therapist observes increased flexion at the proximal interphalangeal joints and hyperextension at the metacarpophalangeal and distal interphalangeal joints. The therapist would **MOST** likely document which of the following deformities in the medical record?

1. **Boutonniere deformity**
2. Mallet finger
3. Swan neck deformity
4. Ulnar drift

Correct Answer: 1 (Magee p. 436)

There are a number of common hand and finger deformities that are often associated with specific medical diagnoses. Physical therapists should be familiar with the clinical presentation of these deformities. Boutonniere deformity, swan neck deformity, and ulnar drift are commonly observed in patients with rheumatoid arthritis.

1. **Boutonniere deformity is characterized by extension of the metacarpophalangeal and distal interphalangeal joints and flexion of the proximal interphalangeal joint. The deformity is caused by a rupture of the central tendinous slip of the extensor hood.**
2. Mallet finger is characterized by the distal phalanx of the finger resting in a flexed position. The deformity is caused by a rupture or avulsion of the extensor tendon.
3. Swan neck deformity is characterized by flexion at the distal interphalangeal joints and hyperextension of the proximal interphalangeal joints. The deformity is caused by a contraction of the intrinsic muscles or tearing of the volar plate.
4. Ulnar drift is characterized by ulnar deviation of the digits due to weakening of the capsuloligamentous structures of the metacarpophalangeal joints and the accompanying effect on the extensor communis tendons.

System: Musculoskeletal System
Content Outline: Foundations for Evaluation, Differential Diagnosis, and Prognosis

 Level 1 p. 126

PTEXAM THREE: QUESTION 196

A physical therapist performs an examination on a patient diagnosed with thoracic outlet syndrome. During the examination, the therapist initiates a special test as shown in the image. Which of the following responses should the therapist consider a positive finding when performing this special test?

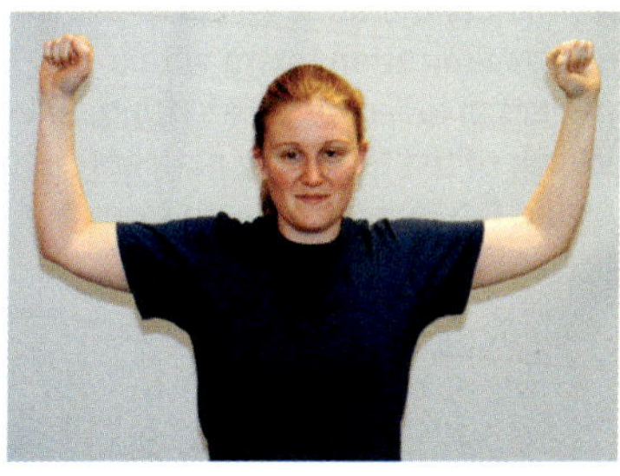

1. **Inability to maintain the test position for three minutes**
2. Subjective report of fatigue in the arms
3. Absence of a radial pulse after one minute
4. Failure of the hands to regain their normal color after 30 seconds

Correct Answer: 1 (Magee p. 345) 

Roos test is a commonly employed special test for patients with thoracic outlet syndrome. The test is performed with the patient positioned in sitting or standing with the arms positioned in 90 degrees of abduction, lateral rotation, and elbow flexion. The patient is asked to open and close their hands for three minutes.

1. **A positive Roos test is indicated by an inability to maintain the test position, weakness of the arms, sensory loss or ischemic pain.**
2. The act of opening and closing the hands for three minutes often produces a subjective report of fatigue in the arms. A subjective report of fatigue would also need to be accompanied by an inability to maintain the test position for three minutes to be considered a positive finding.
3. The absence of a radial pulse after one minute is not considered a positive test when performing Roos test. Unlike other tests for thoracic outlet syndrome (e.g., Adson's test, Halstead maneuver), Roos test does not require the radial pulse to be assessed during the testing procedure.
4. The color of the hands is not typically examined during Roos test. Other special tests such as Allen's test at the wrist or the capillary refill test would be more likely to assess this type of change in appearance.

System: Musculoskeletal System
Content Outline: Physical Therapy Examination

 Level 1  p. 102

PTEXAM THREE: QUESTION 197

A physical therapist elects to use a communication board with a patient in an acute care setting. Which of the following patients would MOST likely benefit from the use of this image?

YES NO
THANK YOU
PLEASE TURN ON
I NEED

1. A 45-year-old male who speaks limited English
2. A 60-year-old female with hemianopsia
3. **A 75-year-old male with Broca's aphasia**
4. An 88-year-old female with end-stage dementia

Correct Answer: 3 (O'Sullivan p. 604) 

Communication boards are often used to communicate with patients that are nonverbal or have impairments in verbal expression. The boards typically use pictures, symbols, and simple words to facilitate communication with individuals who have limited expressive language ability.

1. A 45-year-old male who speaks limited English would most benefit from the use of an interpreter. Although a communication board might provide limited help, the use of an interpreter would be the best choice to maximize communication with the patient.
2. A 60-year-old female with hemianopsia experiences a loss of vision in half of the visual field. Similar to patients with unilateral neglect, patients with hemianopsia may also exhibit a lack of awareness of the side contralateral to the lesion. Use of active visual scanning or tracking movements by turning the head toward the involved side is typically a useful strategy for patients with hemianopsia.
3. **A 75-year-old male with Broca's aphasia would most likely benefit from the use of a communication board. Broca's aphasia is also known as expressive aphasia in which auditory and reading comprehension are intact, but the patient has impaired naming skills and difficulty with language production.**
4. In end-stage dementia, there is typically severe cognitive and physical decline. Individuals lose the ability to communicate or respond to their environment and need constant supervision and assistance with all activities of daily living. A patient in the earlier stages of dementia would be more likely to benefit from the use of a communication board.

System: Neuromuscular and Nervous Systems
Content Outline: Interventions

Level 2  p. 270-271

PTEXAM THREE: QUESTION 198

A physical therapist works with a patient on gait training using bilateral axillary crutches. The right axillary crutch is modified with a platform attachment. Which of the following rationales is the MOST likely reason for this type of modification?

1. **The patient has a radial nerve injury**
2. The patient has a proximal humeral fracture
3. The patient has impaired balance and coordination
4. The patient has a transhumeral amputation

Correct Answer: 1 (Fairchild p. 216) 

A platform attachment can be added to axillary crutches, forearm crutches or a walker. This modification is used for patients who are unable to bear weight through their wrists and hands, who have deformities of the wrists or fingers, who have an amputation distal to the elbow or who are unable to extend the elbow.

1. **A patient with a radial nerve injury would have significant weakness of the triceps muscle and be unable to extend the elbow. The platform modification would be necessary since the patient would be unable to produce elbow extension and would instead need to bear weight through the elbow and forearm.**
2. A platform attachment would not be appropriate for a patient with a proximal humeral fracture. Whether the weight bearing occurs through the patient's hand or the patient's elbow and forearm, the fracture site would still be experiencing increased weight bearing forces.
3. A patient with impaired balance and coordination would not likely be a good candidate for axillary crutches. In the event a patient with impaired balance and coordination was determined to be an appropriate candidate for axillary crutches, the platform attachment would still not offer any additional compensation for the patient's described impairments.
4. A transhumeral amputation occurs at the level of the mid-humerus. Without an elbow joint and forearm, the patient would have nothing to bear their weight through when using a platform attachment.

System: Non-Systems
Content Outline: Equipment, Devices, and Technologies; Therapeutic Modalities

 Level 2  p. 250, 690-691

PTEXAM THREE: QUESTION 199

A physical therapist works with a patient on wheelchair mobility and transfer training. The patient has a history of a CVA with right-sided hemiparesis. Which of the following wheelchair adaptations would be the MOST beneficial for the therapist to recommend to ensure patient safety during stand pivot transfers?

1. Anti-tip tubes
2. **Pull-to wheel lock with brake extensions**
3. Elevating leg rests
4. Removable full-length armrests

Correct Answer: 2 (Tan p. 322) 

Performing transfer training with a patient who has had a cerebrovascular accident is an important component of the physical therapy plan of care to maximize the patient's functional independence. Impairments that are present following a left hemisphere cerebrovascular accident that may affect a patient's ability to safely transfer include weakness, paralysis of the right side, increased frustration, decreased processing, possible motor apraxia, and right hemianopsia.

1. Anti-tip tubes attach to the posterior of the wheelchair to prevent tipping in the event of a posterior loss of balance. Patients who would benefit from anti-tip tubes have impairments in or absence of trunk control. Anti-tip tubes can also be used when mastering wheelchair mobility on steep inclines until the patient gains enough strength and postural control to master the technique.
2. **A pull-to wheel lock allows for closer access to surfaces during transfers. Brake extensions on the right side allow the patient to reach with the uninvolved upper extremity to lock the wheelchair prior to transferring. The patient's ability to use the right hand to lock the brakes is most likely limited due to the right-sided hemiparesis.**
3. Elevating leg rests are indicated for patients who need support of the lower extremity. Elevating leg rests can prevent dependent edema and may assist in redistributing weight bearing forces, however, would not be the most essential wheelchair adaptation to ensure safety during a stand pivot transfer.
4. Removable full-length armrests allow for a squat pivot or sliding board transfer, however, would not be necessary for a stand pivot transfer.

System: Non-Systems
Content Outline: Equipment, Devices, and Technologies; Therapeutic Modalities

 **Level 2** **p. 279-280, 330-331, 684-687**

PTEXAM THREE: QUESTION 200

An athlete sustained a grade III lateral ankle sprain while playing basketball and plans to return to full participation in athletic activities. Which component of the rehabilitation process is MOST important to address the concern of chronic functional instability?

1. Use of ice and compression to rapidly reduce the inflammation and swelling
2. High-voltage pulsed current to promote tissue healing
3. **Single-leg support proprioception exercises with dynamic strengthening**
4. Isometric stabilization exercises and isokinetic ankle strengthening exercises

Correct Answer: 3 (Dutton p. 1154) 

The vast majority of ankle sprains occur due to significant inversion and plantar flexion and involve the lateral ligament complex. A grade III sprain involves complete rupture of the ligament with profound instability and laxity. Functional treatment is often considered the most critical intervention to prevent chronic ankle instability.

1. Use of ice and compression is part of the early intervention of lateral ankle sprains to assist in the reduction of pain and swelling. Since chronic symptoms of weakness, pain, and joint instability may occur after significant inversion sprains, dynamic muscular support, functional closed-chain activities, and proprioception exercises are critical to prevent recurrent ankle sprains and chronic instability.
2. High-voltage pulsed current can be used to help reduce pain and swelling and promote tissue healing. Protecting the torn ligaments from unwanted stress is the cornerstone of the acute phase of healing. Early progression to closed-chain activities and proprioceptive exercises is a vital component of rehabilitation following lateral ankle sprains.
3. **Single-leg support proprioception exercises with dynamic strengthening can be provided with the use of elastic cords or manual perturbations. This provides the dynamic support and balance training needed to stimulate and encourage strength in a weight bearing, closed-chain functional position. Progression to balance board activities and plyometric exercises may also be indicated, depending on patient tolerance, to also address the concern for functional instability.**
4. Isometric stabilization exercises and isometric strengthening can be utilized based on the patient's pain tolerance in the early stages of recovery following a lateral ankle sprain. Isokinetic strengthening exercises may be used in the moderate to minimal protection phases of healing, however, they require specialized equipment and would not be as beneficial as the other presented options.

System: Musculoskeletal System
Content Outline: Interventions

 **Level 2**  **p. 158-159**

Exam References, Exam & Academic Review Indexes, Motivational Moments and Resources

Insight PTEXAM References

American College of Sports Medicine. ***ACSM's Guidelines for Exercise Testing and Prescription***. Tenth Edition. Wolters Kluwer. 2018.

American College of Sports Medicine. ***ACSM's Resource Manual for Guidelines for Exercise Testing and Prescription***. Seventh Edition. Lippincott Williams & Wilkins. 2014.

American Physical Therapy Association. ***Code of Ethics***. HOD S06-09-07-12.

American Physical Therapy Association. ***Criteria for Standards of Practice for Physical Therapy***. BOD S01-14-01-01. Updated: 04/15/14, web site 2017.

American Physical Therapy Association. ***Defensible Documentation Elements***. Updated: 12/08/15, web site 2017.

American Physical Therapy Association. ***Direction and Supervision of the Physical Therapist Assistant***. HOD P06-05-18-26. Updated: 08/07/12, web site 2017.

American Physical Therapy Association. ***Guide for Conduct of the Physical Therapist Assistant***.

American Physical Therapy Association. ***Guide to Physical Therapist Practice***. http://guidetoptpractice.apta.org/ APTA, 2014.

American Physical Therapy Association. ***Guidelines: Physical Therapy Documentation of Patient/Client Management***. BOD G03-05-16-41. Updated: 05/19/2014, web site 2017.

American Physical Therapy Association. ***Standards of Ethical Conduct for the Physical Therapist Assistant***.

Anemaet W, Moffa-Trotter M. ***Home Rehabilitation: Guide to Clinical Practice***. Mosby. 2000.

Avers D, Brown M. ***Daniels and Worthingham's Muscle Testing: Techniques of Manual Examination and Performance Testing***. Tenth Edition. Elsevier. 2019.

Bellew J, Michlovitz S, Nolan T. ***Modalities for Therapeutic Intervention***. Sixth Edition. F.A. Davis Company. 2016.

Bickley L. ***Bates' Guide to Physical Examination and History Taking***. Twelfth Edition. Wolters Kluwer. 2017.

Boissonnault W. ***Primary Care for the Physical Therapist***. Second Edition. Elsevier. 2011.

Brannon F, Foley M, Starr J, Saul L. ***Cardiopulmonary Rehabilitation: Basic Theory and Application***. Third Edition. F.A. Davis Company. 1998.

Brody L, Hall C. ***Therapeutic Exercise: Moving Toward Function***. Fourth Edition. Lippincott Williams & Wilkins. 2018.

Brunnstrom S. ***Movement Therapy in Hemiplegia***. Harper and Row Publishers Inc. 1992.

Cameron M. ***Physical Agents in Rehabilitation: An Evidence-Based Approach to Practice***. Fifth Edition. Elsevier. 2018.

Cameron M, Monroe L. ***Physical Rehabilitation: Evidence Based Examination, Evaluation, and Intervention***. W.B. Saunders Company. 2007.

Carr J, Shepherd R. ***Neurologic Rehabilitation: Optimizing Motor Performance***. Churchill Livingstone. 2010.

Cech D, Martin S. ***Functional Movement Development***. Third Edition. Elsevier. 2012.

Ciccone C. ***Pharmacology for Rehabilitation***. Fifth Edition. F.A. Davis Company. 2016.

Coburn W, Malek K. ***NSCA's Essentials of Personal Training***. Second Edition. Human Kinetics. 2012.

Cohen H. ***Neuroscience for Rehabilitation***. J.B Lippincott Company. 1993.

Davenport T, Kulig K, Sebelski C, Gordon J, Watts H. ***Diagnosis for Physical Therapists: A Symptom-Based Approach***. F.A. Davis Company. 2013.

DeMyer W. ***Technique of the Neurologic Examination***. Fifth Edition. McGraw-Hill Company. 2004.

Dutton M. ***Orthopaedic Examination, Evaluation, and Intervention***. Fourth Edition. McGraw-Hill Inc. 2017.

Dunleavy K, Slowik A. ***Therapeutic Exercise Prescription***. Elsevier. 2019.

Edmond S. ***Joint Mobilization/Manipulation***. Third Edition. Elsevier. 2016.

Ehrman J, Gordon P, Visich P, Keteyian S. ***Clinical Exercise Physiology***. Second Edition. Human Kinetics. 2009.

Fairchild S, O'Shea R, Washington R. ***Pierson and Fairchild's Principles and Techniques of Patient Care***. Sixth Edition. Elsevier. 2018.

Falvo D. ***Effective Patient Education***. Fourth Edition. Jones and Bartlett Publishers. 2011.

Fell D, Lunnen K, Rauk R. ***Lifespan Neurorehabilitation: A Patient-Centered Approach from Examination to Interventions and Outcomes***. F.A. Davis Company. 2018.

Frontera W, Silver J, Rizzor T. ***Essentials of Physical Medicine and Rehabilitation: Musculoskeletal Disorders, Pain, and Rehabilitation***. Third Edition. Elsevier. 2015.

Insight PTEXAM References

Frownfelter D, Dean E. ***Cardiovascular and Pulmonary Physical Therapy: Evidence to Practice***. Fifth Edition. Mosby-Year Book. 2012.

Goodman C, Fuller K. ***Pathology: Implications for the Physical Therapist***. Fourth Edition. Elsevier. 2015.

Goodman C, Heick J, Lazaro R. ***Differential Diagnosis for Physical Therapists – Screening for Referral***. Sixth Edition. Elsevier. 2018.

Guccione A, Wong R, Avers D. ***Geriatric Physical Therapy***. Third Edition. Mosby. 2011.

Gutman S. ***Quick Reference Neuroscience for Rehabilitation Professionals***. Second Edition. Slack Inc. 2008.

Haines D. ***Neuroanatomy in Clinical Context***. Ninth Edition. Wolters Kluwer. 2014.

Hertling D, Kessler R. ***Management of Common Musculoskeletal Disorders***. Fourth Edition. Lippincott Williams & Wilkins. 2006.

Higgins, M. ***Therapeutic Exercise: From Theory to Practice***. F.A. Davis Company. 2011.

Hillegass E, Sadowsky S. ***Essentials of Cardiopulmonary Physical Therapy***. Fourth Edition. Elsevier. 2017.

Hoogenboom B, Voight M, Prentice W. ***Musculoskeletal Interventions***: Techniques for Therapeutic Exercise. Third Edition. McGraw Hill Education. 2014.

Hoppenfeld S, Thomas H, Hutton R. ***Physical Examination of the Spine and Extremities***. Prentice Hall. 1976.

Hurley W, Denegar C. ***Research Methods: A Framework for Evidence-Based Practice***. Lippincott Williams & Wilkins. 2010.

Irwin S, Tecklin J. ***Cardiopulmonary Physical Therapy: A Guide to Practice***. Fourth Edition. Mosby. 2004.

Johansson C, Chinworth S. ***Mobility in Context: Principles of Patient Care Skills***. Second Edition. F.A. Davis Company. 2018.

Kauffman T, Scott R, Barr J, Moran M. ***A Comprehensive Guide to Geriatric Rehabilitation***. Third Edition. Elsevier. 2014.

Kendall F, McCreary E, Provance P. ***Muscles: Testing and Function with Posture and Pain***. Fifth Edition. Lippincott Williams & Wilkins. 2005.

Kisner C, Colby L, Borstad J. ***Therapeutic Exercise Foundations and Techniques***. Seventh Edition. F.A. Davis Company. 2018.

La Baudour C, Bergeron J. ***Emergency Medical Responder: First on Scene***. Tenth Edition. Pearson. 2015.

Levangie P, Norkin C. ***Joint Structure and Function: A Comprehensive Analysis***. Fifth Edition. F.A. Davis Company. 2011.

Lewis C, Bottomley J. ***Geriatric Rehabilitation: A Clinical Approach***. Third Edition. Prentice Hall. 2007.

Long T, Toscano K. ***Handbook of Pediatric Physical Therapy***. Second Edition. Lippincott Williams & Wilkins. 2002.

Lundy-Ekman L. ***Neuroscience: Fundamentals for Rehabilitation***. Fifth Edition. Elsevier. 2018.

Lusardi M, Milagros J, Nielsen C. ***Orthotics and Prosthetics in Rehabilitation***. Third Edition. Elsevier. 2013.

Magee D. ***Orthopedic Physical Assessment***. Sixth Edition. W.B. Saunders Company. 2014.

Martin S, Kessler M. ***Neurologic Interventions for Physical Therapy***. Second Edition. 2007.

May B, Lockard M. ***Prosthetics and Orthotics in Clinical Practice: A Case Study Approach***. F.A. Davis Company, 2011.

McKinnis L. ***Fundamentals of Musculoskeletal Imaging***. Fourth Edition. F.A. Davis Company. 2014.

Means K, Kortebein P. ***Geriatrics***. Demos Medical. 2013.

Minor M, Minor S. ***Patient Care Skills***. Seventh Edition. Pearson Education, Inc. 2014.

Moore K, Dalley A. ***Clinically Oriented Anatomy***. Seventh Edition. Lippincott Williams & Wilkins. 2013.

Myers D. ***Psychology***. Ninth Edition. Worth Publishers. 2009.

Nichols-Larsen, Kegelmeyer D. ***Neurologic Rehabilitation: Neuroscience and Neuroplasticity in Physical Therapy Practice***. McGraw Hill Education. 2016.

Norkin C, White D. ***Measurement of Joint Motion: A Guide to Goniometry***. Fifth Edition. F.A. Davis Company. 2016.

Nosse L, Friberg D. ***Managerial and Supervisory Principles for Physical Therapists***. Third Edition. Lippincott Williams & Wilkins. 2010.

Nyland J. ***Clinical Decisions in Therapeutic Exercise: Planning and Implementation***. Pearson-Prentice Hall. 2006.

Osborne J. ***Documentation for Physical Therapist Practice: A Clinical Decision-Making Approach***. Jones & Bartlett Learning. 2016.

O'Sullivan S, Schmitz T, Fulk G. ***Physical Rehabilitation***. Seventh Edition. F.A. Davis Company. 2019.

Page C. ***Management in Physical Therapy Practices***. Second Edition. F.A. Davis Company. 2015.

Insight PTEXAM References

Palisano R, Orlin M, Shreiber J. ***Campbell's Physical Therapy for Children***. Fifth Edition. Elsevier. 2017.

Paz J, West MP. ***Acute Care Handbook for Physical Therapists***. Fourth Edition. W.B. Saunders Company. 2014.

Perry A, Potter P. ***Clinical Nursing Skills and Techniques***. Eighth Edition. Mosby. 2013.

Plack M, Driscoll M. ***Teaching and Learning in Physical Therapy: From Classroom to Clinic***. Slack Incorporated. 2011.

Porter R. ***The Merck Manual***. Nineteenth Edition. Merck and Company, Inc. 2011.

Portney L, Watkins M. ***Foundations of Clinical Research: Applications to Practice***. Third Edition. Prentice Hall. 2015.

Prentice W. ***Therapeutic Modalities in Rehabilitation***. Fifth Edition. McGraw-Hill Inc. 2018.

Professional Guide to Diseases. Ninth Edition. Lippincott Williams & Wilkins. 2010.

Purtilo R, Haddad A. ***Health Professional and Patient Interaction***. Eighth Edition. Elsevier. 2014.

Quinn L, Gordon J. ***Functional Outcomes: Documentation for Rehabilitation***. Seventh Edition. W.B. Saunders Company. 2010.

Ratliffe KT. ***Clinical Pediatric Physical Therapy: A Guide for the Physical Therapy Team***. Mosby. 1998.

Robnett R, Chop W. ***Gerontology for the Healthcare Practitioner***. Third Edition. Jones & Bartlett Publishing. 2015.

Roy S, Wolf S, Scalzitti D. ***The Rehabilitation Specialist's Handbook***. Fourth Edition. F.A. Davis Company. 2013.

Sadock B, Sadock V. ***Kaplan & Sadock's Comprehensive Textbook of Psychiatry***. Ninth Edition. Lippincott Williams & Wilkins. 2009.

Sahrmann S. ***Diagnosis and Treatment of Movement Impairment Syndromes***. Mosby. 2002

Sarwark J. ***Essentials of Musculoskeletal Care***. American Academy of Orthopaedic Surgeons. Fourth Edition. 2010.

Scott R. ***Promoting Legal and Ethical Awareness***. Mosby. 2009.

Seidel H, Ball J, Dains J, Benedict G. ***Mosby's Guide to Physical Examination***. Fifth Edition. Mosby. 2003.

Seymour R. ***Prosthetics and Orthotics: Lower Limb and Spinal***. Lippincott Williams & Wilkins. 2002.

Shamus E, Stern D. ***Effective Documentation for the Physical Therapy Professional***. Second Edition. McGraw-Hill Inc. 2011.

Shamus E, Van Dujin A. ***Manual Therapy of the Extremities***. Jones & Bartlett Learning. 2017.

Shumway-Cook A, Woollacott M. ***Motor Control: Translating Research into Clinical Practice***. Fourth Edition. Lippincott Williams & Wilkins. 2011.

Smeltzer S, Bare B. Brunnert Suddarth's ***Textbook of Medical-Surgical Nursing***. Wolters Kluwer Health. Twelfth Edition. 2010.

Smith D, Michael J, Bowker J. ***Atlas of Amputations and Limb Deficiencies: Surgical, Prosthetic, and Rehabilitation Principles***. American Academy of Orthopaedic Surgeons. 2004.

Smolin L, Grosvenor M. ***Nutrition: Science and Application***. Third Edition. 2013.

Straus S, Richardson W, Haynes R, Glasziou P. ***Evidence-Based Medicine. How to Practice and Teach EBM***. Fourth Edition. Churchill Livingstone. 2011.

Sullivan P, Markos P. ***Clinical Decision Making in Therapeutic Exercise***. Appleton & Lange. 1995.

Sussman C, Bates-Jensen B. ***Wound Care: A Collaborative Practice Manual for Health Professionals***. Fourth Edition. Wolters Kluwer Health/Lippincott Williams & Wilkins. 2012.

Tan J. ***Practical Manual of Physical Medicine and Rehabilitation***. Second Edition. Elsevier. 2006.

Tecklin J. ***Pediatric Physical Therapy***. Fifth Edition. Lippincott Williams & Wilkins. 2015.

Thomas C. ***Prevention Practice: A Physical Therapist's Guide to Health, Fitness, and Wellness***. Slack Inc. 2007.

Umphred D, Lazaro R, Roller M. ***Neurological Rehabilitation***. Sixth Edition. Mosby. 2013.

Whalen K. ***Pharmacology***. Sixth Edition. Lippincott Williams & Wilkins. 2014.

Wise C. ***Orthopedic Manual Physical Therapy: From Art to Evidence***. F.A. Davis Company. 2015.

Insight Exam Index

Directions for Using the Insight Exams Index

The Insight Exam Index allows candidates to identify specific academic content in each of the three sample examinations. For example, consider the following entry: **Ankylosing spondylitis 1:** 166; **3:** 141. The bold numbers represent the exam number and the non-bold numbers that follow represent the question number within the respective exam. Therefore, questions pertaining to ankylosing spondylitis are located in Exam One: Question 166 and in Exam Three: Question 141. The index provides candidates with an efficient and effective method to review selected academic content after completing each of the sample examinations.

Insight Exam Index

Insight Exam Index

Insight Exam Index

Insight Exam Index

Insight Exam Index

Insight Exam Index

Academic Review Index

Academic Review Index

Academic Review Index

Academic Review Index

Academic Review Index

Academic Review Index

Academic Review Index

Academic Review Index

Academic Review Index

Academic Review Index

Academic Review Index

Academic Review Index

Academic Review Index

Academic Review Index

Academic Review Index

Academic Review Index

Academic Review Index

Academic Review Index

Academic Review Index

Academic Review Index

PTEXAM: The Complete Study Guide

The new edition of **PTEXAM: The Complete Study Guide** is the most comprehensive resource available for the NPTE-PT. The resource is a virtual visual delight with full color and hundreds of images. The detailed academic review section includes chapter essentials and proficiency exercises to ensure student mastery of critical NPTE-PT content.

Students are able to access our eLearning site called **Insight** using a unique registration code located on the inside front cover of the book. **Insight** contains 600 clinically-oriented questions with expansive explanations of the correct and incorrect answers. These questions are thought-provoking, challenging questions designed to be consistent with the specifications and rigor of the NPTE-PT blueprint. A sophisticated performance analysis section allows students to identify their current strengths and weaknesses according to different system and content outline areas.

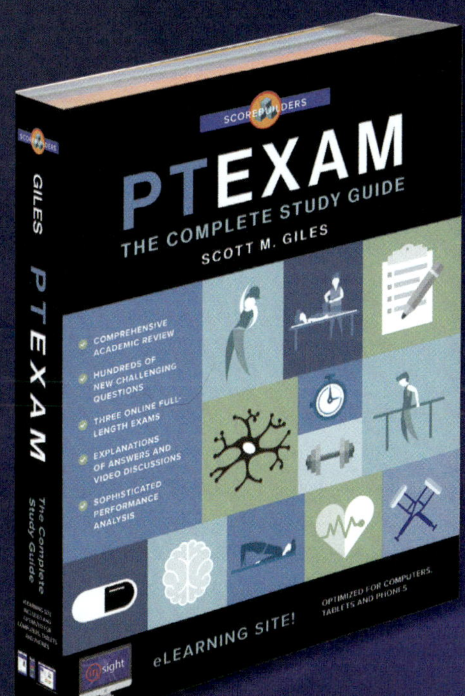

Author: Scott Giles PT, DPT, MBA

ISBN: 978-1-890989-44-6

Price: $90.00

Better Products . . . Better Outcomes!

www.scorebuilders.com

Motivational Moment One

If it was easy, everyone would be a physical therapist. Recognize that you still have some work left to do, but are incredibly close to achieving your goal of being a physical therapist.

PHOTO BY BOB HOYT

Basecamp

Basecamp takes students on a daily journey through five Mountains (Musculoskeletal, Neuromuscular, Cardiopulmonary, Other Systems, Non-Systems) and 140 Trails (e.g., Special Tests, Cardiac - Pathology, Motor Learning, Research Concepts). **Basecamp** collectively includes hundreds of academic assignments, 50 hours of videos, and thousands of multiple-choice questions. Our **Arena** app allows Basecamp users to access 6,000 content-based questions within our competitive games - **King of the Mountain** and **Climb**. Students purchase **Basecamp** for varying periods of time ranging from 30 days (Basecamp - Standard) to Forever (Basecamp - Lifetime).

Price:

Basecamp - Standard: $65.00

Basecamp - Annual: $95.00

Basecamp - Lifetime: $130.00

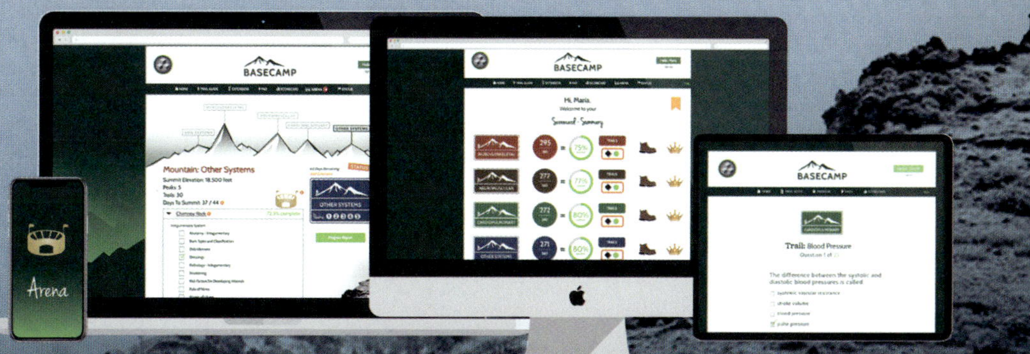

Better Products . . . Better Outcomes!

www.scorebuilders.com

SCOREBUILDERS

Motivational Moment Two

Picture yourself lounging in this hammock in a tropical oasis.
Make a list of other possible celebration activities after you pass the NPTE-PT!

Motivational Moment Three

*Studying for the NPTE-PT is hard work,
but you are only months away from experiencing
something that you have not experienced in a
very long time . . . Positive Cash Flow!*

PT Content Master - Flash Cards

Make reviewing essential academic content enjoyable! **PT Content Master** is designed to assist physical therapists to possess full command of core academic content using flash cards. Vibrant colors and visually pleasing layouts make the flash cards a perfect learning resource to review academic content.

Features

- 200 double-sided flash cards covering only the most essential academic content from our entire physical therapist product line.
- The flash cards provide users with the opportunity to frequently review academic content and in the process, commit the information to long-term memory.

Author: Scott Giles PT, DPT, MBA
ISBN: 978-1-890989-42-2
Price: $45.00

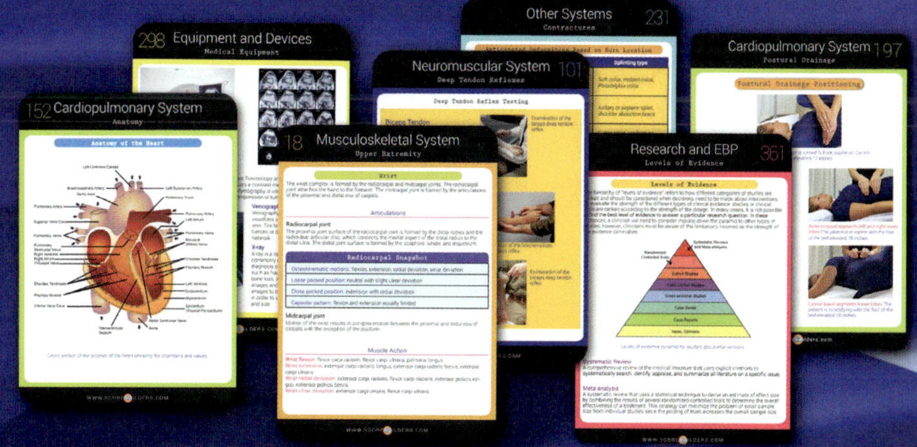

Better Products . . . Better Outcomes!

www.scorebuilders.com

Motivational Moment Four

Imagine the impact you will make on the lives of your patients during a long and distinguished career as a physical therapist!

ACE - A Competitive Edge

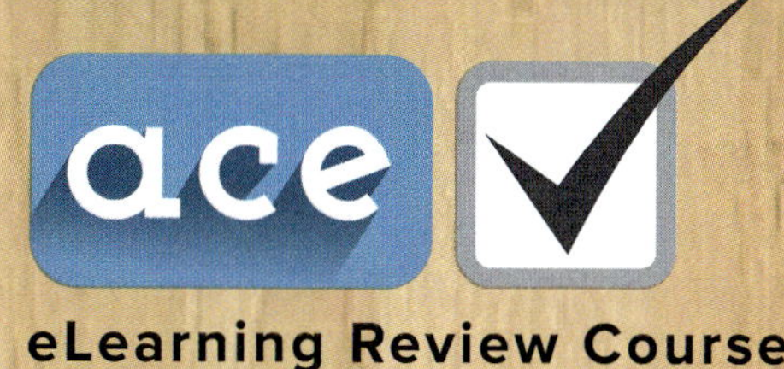

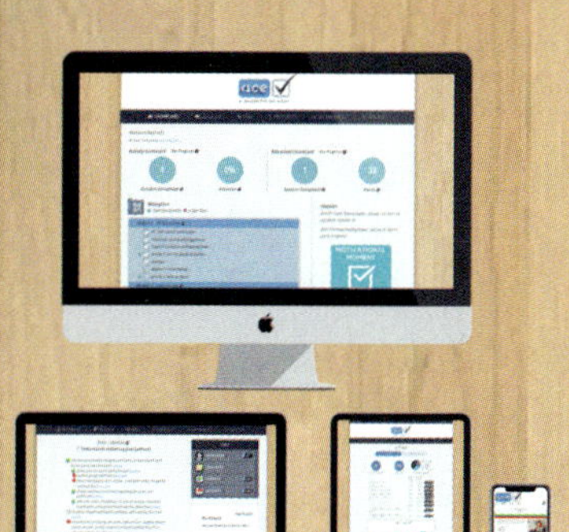

Our eLearning review course provides students with the most personal and effective method to prepare for the NPTE-PT on your own schedule. The course offers all of the same benefits as our traditional review course held annually at over 280 PT and PTA academic programs. The course led by Dr. Scott Giles PT, DPT, MBA utilizes 225 streaming videos, interactive study tools, and challenging multiple-choice questions to assist students to reach their potential on this critically important exam.

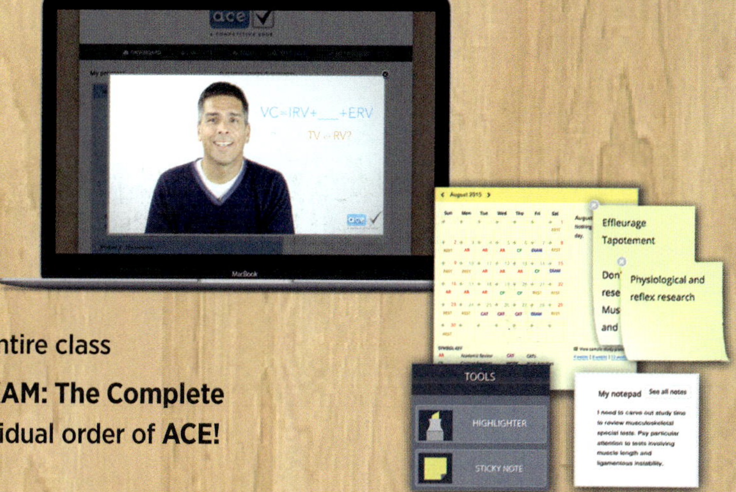

- Active study tools to determine academic mastery level
- Sophisticated performance analysis section
- Decision-making gameplay with Extraction
- Interactive study calendars to track study progress

Access Period: 120 days

Technical Requirements: Internet access

Price: $325.00* for individual orders, $4,000.00 for your entire class

*A coupon located on the inside of the back cover of **PTEXAM: The Complete Study Guide** allows candidates to save $50.00 on an individual order of **ACE!**

ACE includes 120 day **Basecamp** access. **Basecamp** consists of hundreds of academic assignments, 50 hours of videos, and 6,000 multiple-choice questions.

Better Products . . . Better Outcomes!

www.scorebuilders.com

Scorebuilders' Review Courses

Our review course provides students with the most personal, effective, and efficient method to maximize performance on the NPTE-PT. The course introduces students to challenging multiple-choice questions, recent examination trends, a myriad of study tools, and resources designed to increase mastery of essential exam content. Our goal is to maximize the efficiency of a student's study plan by focusing on critical exam content at an appropriate level of breadth and depth.

Scorebuilders offers over 280 review courses annually and is the largest provider of PT and PTA review courses in the United States. Our expert instructors are experienced educators who are superior teachers.

Participants attending our On-Campus Review Course will:

- Improve decision making skills when answering challenging multiple-choice questions.
- Develop a comprehensive study plan to maximize efficiency and performance.
- Identify indicators to determine readiness to take the examination.

All participants attending the course receive a 240 page detailed course manual that includes sample questions, assessment activities, study tools, and other valuable resources to improve performance on the NPTE-PT.

On-Campus Review Course

Our **On-Campus Review Course** is our traditional offering provided by a Scorebuilders' instructor on your campus. This face to face, live offering is ideal when students are collectively on-campus and are able to establish specific course dates.

Webinar Review Course

Our **Webinar Review Course** allows students to experience the equivalent of the On-Campus Review Course with a Scorebuilders' instructor while being away from campus using our remote learning software. This two-day offering is ideal for students that are scattered throughout the United States.

Email info@scorebuilders.com to schedule your review course and move one step closer to licensure

Review Course participants receive free 30 Day **Basecamp - Standard** access ($65 value). **Basecamp** includes hundreds of academic assignments, 50 hours of videos, and 6,000 multiple-choice questions.

Content Master

Content Master

Physical therapists have the option of utilizing flash cards with an app. The app consists of a content review mode covering the same academic content as the traditional flash cards. Users rate their proficiency in selected content areas and create custom Study Stacks to improve academic mastery. This app also includes 750 multiple-choice questions designed to assess a candidate's knowledge of core academic content. Users take the multiple-choice questions in mini exams in unique systems and non-systems categories. A performance analysis section allows users to review questions and examine performance by category and over time. The questions are unique to the app and are not utilized in any other Scorebuilders' product.

Price: $29.99

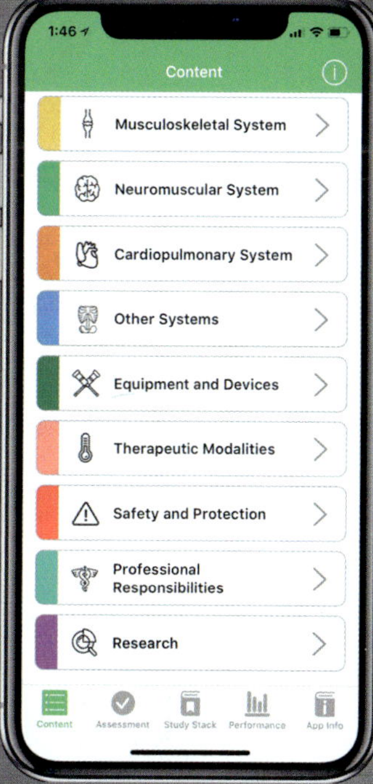

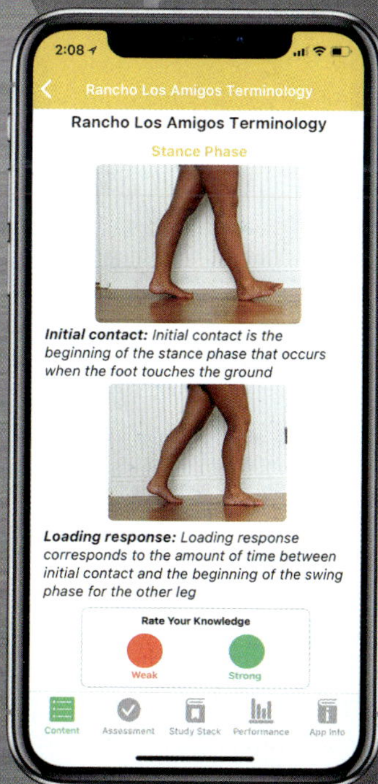

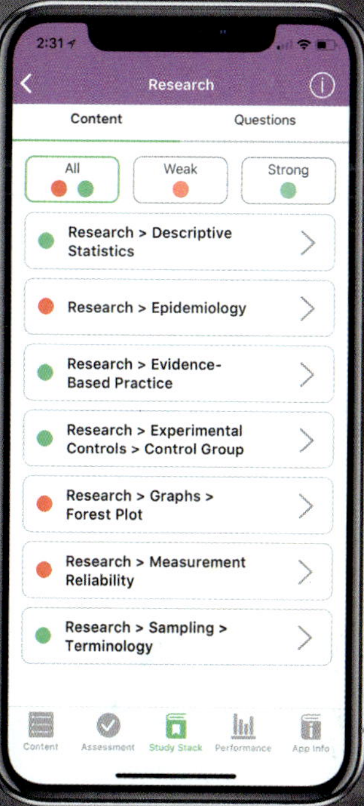

Available through the Apple App and Google Play Stores